Goodheart-Willcox

automotive encyclopedia

fundamental principles, operation, construction, service, repair

WILLIAM K. TOBOLDT

Author of Diesel, Fundamentals, Service, Repair;
Fix Your Ford; Fix Your Chevrolet; Auto Body
Repairing and Repainting. Member, Society of
Automotive Engineers. Associate Member, Auto-
motive Engine Rebuilders Association. Associate
Member, Association of Diesel Specialists.

LARRY JOHNSON

Author of Fix Your Volkswagen. Certified General
Automobile Mechanic by National Institute for
Automotive Service Excellence. Affiliate Member,
Society of Automotive Engineers.

South Holland, Illinois

THE GOODHEART-WILLCOX COMPANY, INC.

Publishers

IMPORTANT SAFETY NOTICE

Proper service and repair is important to the safe, reliable operation of motor vehicles. Procedures recommended and described in this book are effective methods of performing service operations. Some require the, use of tools specially designed for the purpose and should be used as recommended. Note that this book also contains various safety procedures and cautions which should be carefully followed to minimize the risk of personal injury or the possibility that improper service methods may damage the engine or render the vehicle unsafe. It is also important to understand that these notices and cautions are not exhaustive. Those performing a given service procedure or using a particular tool must first satisfy themselves that neither their safety nor engine or vehicle safety will be jeopardized by the service method selected.

This book contains the most complete and accurate imformation that could be obtained from various authoritative sources at the time of publication. Goodheart-Willcox cannot assume responsibility for any changes, errors, or omissions.

Library of Congress Cataloging in Publication Data

Main entry under title:

Goodheart-Willcox automotive encyclopedia.

  Includes index.
  1. Automobiles. 2. Automobiles — Maintenance and repair I. Toboldt, William King,
II. Johnson, Larry, III. Title: Automotive encyclopedia.
TL205.G66   1983   629.2'222   83—5559
ISBN 0—87006—436—3

INTRODUCTION

The automotive service field offers excellent career opportunities for anyone who is mechanically inclined and has the necessary educational background, including extensive training in the fundamentals of service and repair work.

The AUTOMOTIVE ENCYCLOPEDIA is a book of fundamentals. It covers construction details, principles of operation, latest mechanical advances and basic service procedures. This is the foundation on which a sound, thorough knowledge of auto mechanics is based. Once you learn these fundamentals, you can quickly acquire the know-how, through experience, that will enable you to diagnose trouble and perform the service or repair needed on any make of car.

The ENCYCLOPEDIA tells you how each system works. It explains what happens when you turn the ignition key or "step on the gas" or apply the brakes. It shows by clear illustration how the energy in fuel is converted into power, and how that power is transmitted to the driving wheels of the car.

This book helps you explore the sciences involved in vehicle operation: the fundamentals of electricity, hydraulics, pneumatics, internal combustion and exhaust emission control. It also gives basic information on hand tools, fasteners, measuring instruments, service equipment and meters.

The purpose of the AUTOMOTIVE ENCYCLOPEDIA is to provide instruction in auto mechanics as recommended by the Standards for Automotive Service Instruction in Schools, prepared by the Automotive Service Industry - - Vocational Educational Conference. It is intended, too, as a guide for car owners and prospective car owners who want to learn more about the mechanical features of their cars.

William K. Toboldt

Larry Johnson

CONTENTS

Contents

AUTOMOTIVE TOOLS

Tools play an important part in any automotive service operation. Every repair job requires the use of at least one hand tool to remove, disassemble or adjust parts and units.

It follows naturally that anyone studying to be an auto mechanic should be thoroughly familiar with tools he or she will use on the job. In addition, the beginning mechanic must learn the correct methods of using tools, not only to perform the work as quickly as possible, but also to complete the job with maximum accuracy and safety.

Cars have gotten more complex, and a greater variety of hand tools is needed to service them. Without this "kit" of tools, an auto mechanic could not find employment. The kit represents a large investment, but experienced mechanics realize that good quality hand tools help them turn out precision jobs more quickly and safely. And when a mechanic's tool kit is complete, it will include the right tool for every job, Fig. 1-1.

Tool care is important, too. Apprentice mechanics soon learn that time will be saved if they take good care of their hand tools. This includes cleaning after use and returning the tools to their proper place in the kit to avoid future loss of time looking for a particular tool.

WRENCHES

One of the most important and most-used tool in a mechanic's kit is the open-end wrench, Fig. 1-2. These tools are used for loosening or tightening bolts and nuts.

Wrench size is determined by the width of the opening, and both English and metric sizes are available. A standard set of open-end wrenches in the English system usually ranges from 3/8 in. up to and including 1 in., increasing by 1/16 in. steps.

In the metric system, a typical set of open-end wrenches ranges in size from 7 millimetres (mm) to 19 millimetres (mm). Larger and smaller sizes are available in both English and metric wrenches, but usually on an individual wrench basis rather than part of a set.

To permit the open-end wrench to turn a nut in a restricted space, the open end of the wrench is designed at an angle to the center line of the handle. Usually this is 15 deg. By first placing one side of the wrench up, then the other, it is possible

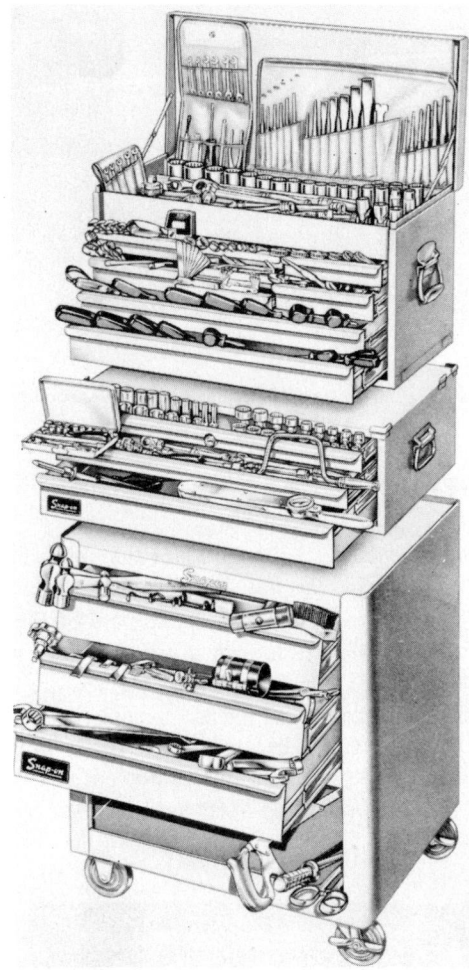

Fig. 1-1. Successful mechanics have a large investment in hand tools.

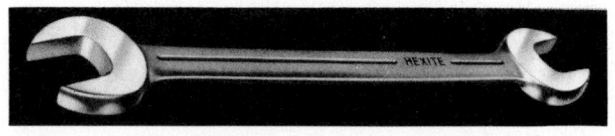

Fig. 1-2. Example of a typical open-end wrench.

7

to turn the nut a few degrees at a time in each position until the nut is removed.

Wrenches are also made with openings at an angle of 22 1/2 deg., 30 deg., 60 deg. and 90 deg. to the handle.

While the smallest opening of a standard wrench set is usually 3/8 in., smaller wrenches known as "miniature," Fig. 1-3, are also available. Such wrenches are needed for work on ignition systems and electrical connections. Openings range in size in 1/32 in. steps from 3/16 in. to 15/32 in.

Special open-end wrenches designed specifically for adjusting valve tappets on L-head engines are also available. These wrenches are thinner and longer than the conventional open-end wrench, and five sizes from 3/8 in. to 5/8 in. are the openings usually provided.

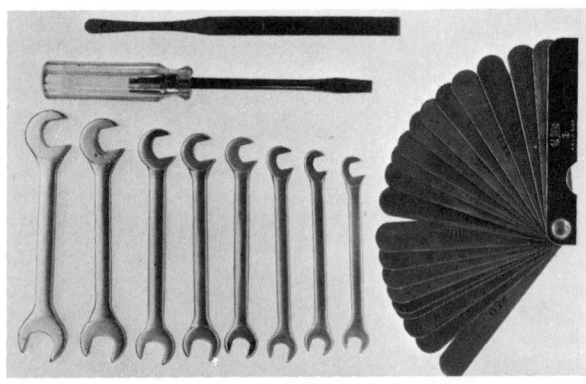

Fig. 1-3. Set of special open-end wrenches with other tools comprising a set for ignition work.

BOX WRENCHES

Box type wrenches, Fig. 1-4, reduce the possibility of the wrench slipping from the nut. Usually, the box is a double hexagon. The 12 grooves engage the corners of the nut and permit moving the wrench through an arc of as little as 30 deg. before repositioning. Also, the walls of the box are relatively thin, so less space surrounding the nut is required.

A box wrench cannot be used on copper tubing fittings. However, a box type wrench with a section cut away, Fig. 1-5, and a foot type wrench, Fig. 1-6, are available.

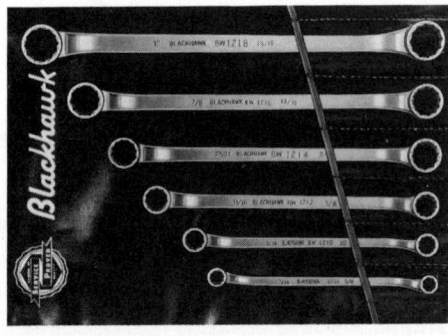

Fig. 1-4. Set of box wrenches.

Fig. 1-5. Special wrench for working on copper tubing fittings.

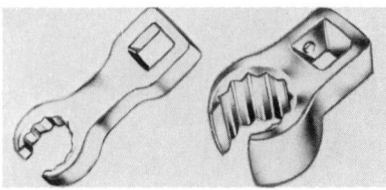

Fig. 1-6. Flare nut wrench for use with extension.

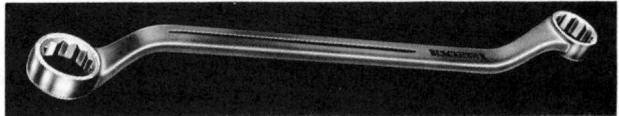

Fig. 1-7. Box type wrench with head at 15 deg. to handle. Offset provides clearance for mechanic's knuckles.

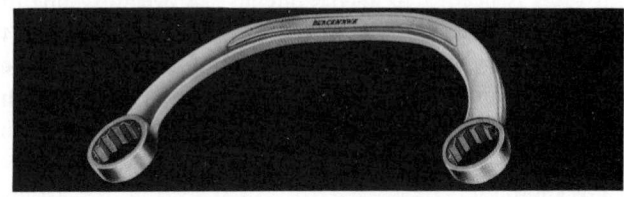

Fig. 1-8. Special wrench for working on exhaust manifolds.

In addition to the regular box wrenches with the straight handles, some have the heads set at angles of 15 deg. to the handle, Fig. 1-7. This tips the end of the wrench which is not on the nut upward, and provides clearance for the mechanic's knuckles. There are also many wrenches designed for specific jobs. Fig. 1-8 shows a special wrench designed especially for manifold work.

A combination box and open-end wrench is shown in Fig. 1-9. Both ends of this wrench are designed to fit the same size nut. This is a general purpose wrench and is preferred by many mechanics.

Fig. 1-9. Combination box and open-end wrench.

Fig. 1-10. Left. Conventional or short sockets. Right. Long sockets. When used for removing spark plugs, long or deep socket is provided with a "soft" insert to grip the spark plug insulator.

SOCKET WRENCHES

Socket wrenches, Fig. 1-10, like the box wrench, completely surround the nut to be tightened or loosened. In that way, there is little chance of the wrench slipping from the nut. With assorted handles they greatly reduce the time for removing nuts.

Usually, the socket wrench used in automotive work has 12 grooves to engage the corners of the nut. Socket wrenches come in sizes from approximately 3/16 in. to 1 5/8 in.

"Sockets" manufactured with six grooves or eight grooves give added protection against slippage. The drive opening of the socket (opening in which wrench handle is placed) is 1/4 in., 3/8 in., 1/2 in. or 3/4 in. square. This is known as the "drive." In addition, one manufacturer has a socket wrench with 7/16 in. drive, which is designed to take the place of both the 3/8 in. and 1/2 in. drive socket sets.

Mechanics usually have a set of 1/4 in., 3/8 in. and 1/2 in. drive socket wrenches in their kits. The 1/4 in. square drive socket set usually includes sockets ranging in size from 3/16 in. to 9/16. The 3/8 in. square drive socket set has sockets from 1/4 in. to 1 in. The 1/2 in. square drive socket set is designed for use on nuts ranging in size from 3/8 in. to 1 1/2 in.

In addition to sockets of standard depth, extra deep sockets are also available. Deep sockets are used primarily for removing spark plugs, sending units, etc.

Socket wrenches used in automotive service work have detachable handles of various types. These handles have various purposes. Some are designed to give increased leverage, others to facilitate reaching areas which are normally obstructed. Still others are designed to speed the removal and installation of nuts.

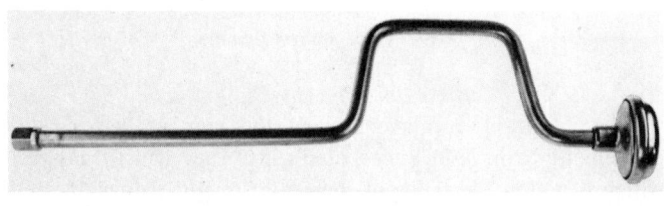

Fig. 1-11. Typical socket speed handle or spinner.

Fig. 1-11 illustrates a socket speed handle which as the name implies is designed to run the nut on or off the bolt more quickly.

Various types of accessory wrench handles are shown in Fig. 1-12. A socket sliding handle, A, makes it possible to slide the handle back and forth without detaching it from the nut. A flex handle, B, provides greater leverage and, in addition, the angle of the handle in relation to the nut can be changed.

A ratchet handle is shown at C in Fig. 1-12. This is a very important tool since the handle can be swung back and forth to tighten or loosen the nut without detaching the handle from the socket or the socket from the nut. A socket and short extension is shown at D, while a longer extension is shown at E. Extensions permit reaching down into enclosed areas where a long handle could not be used.

The ratchet saves time and labor. Inside the head of the ratchet handle is a pawl or dog which engages or fits into one or more of the ratchet teeth. Pulling on the handle in one direction, the dog holds and the socket turns. Moving the handle in the opposite direction, the dog ratchets over the teeth, permitting the handle to be backed up without moving the socket. Since the teeth of the ratchet are relatively fine, the ratchet handle can be swung through a very small angle or arc in order to get a new grip. By using a ratchet handle, it is not necessary to disengage the socket from the nut until it is removed.

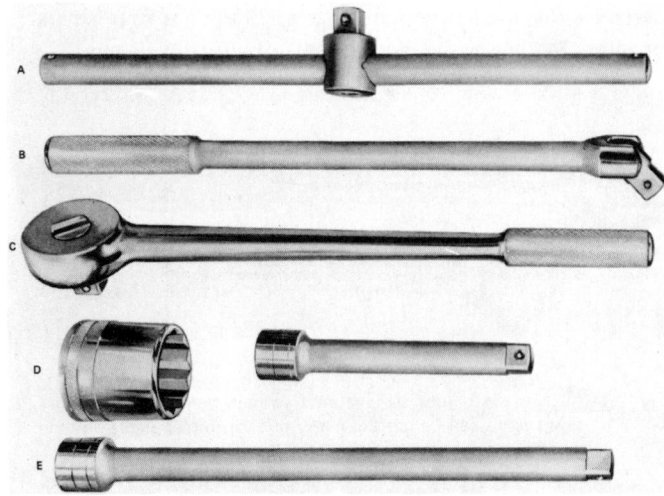

Fig. 1-12. A—Socket sliding handle. B—Flex handle. C—Ratchet wrench handle. D—Socket and extension. E—Extension. (S-K Tools)

A socket spinner wrench, or nut driver, is designed for use on smaller size nuts. This type of wrench is used extensively in ignition and carburetor work.

If it is not possible to get a direct pull when wrenching off a nut, a universal joint is available for use between the handle and the socket. Also available are popular size socket wrenches complete with universal joints. See Fig. 1-13. Note that these are six point sockets. Similar universal sockets also come in eight point and 12 point sets.

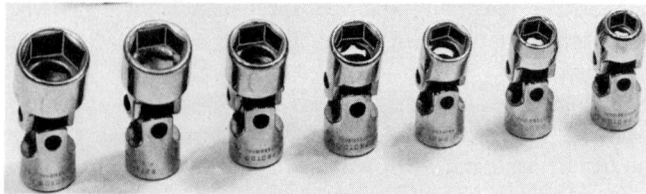

Fig. 1-13. Universal joint adapters and sockets with integral universal joints (shown) are available. A typical, seven piece, 3/8 in. drive set is pictured. A special adaptation of this design is for removing and installing spark plugs.

RATCHET WRENCHES

In many cases, it is impossible to make a complete turn with the wrench handle. To overcome this problem, ratchet wrenches are provided. See Fig. 1-14. With a ratchet wrench, it is possible to swing the handle through a very small arc, then return it to its original position and tighten the nut again.

A ratcheting box wrench is also available. It is preferred for use in continuous operations, such as assembly line jobs.

SPECIAL WRENCHES

Many wrenches are designed to do one specific job. Fig. 1-15 illustrates a wrench used to loosen and tighten bleeder screws on hydraulic brake systems. Another special wrench is designed to loosen wheel nuts. It generally has four separate openings that cover the requirements of virtually all cars.

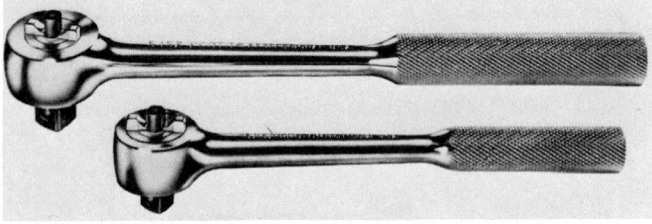

Fig. 1-14. To turn out jobs fast, ratchet wrench handles are a "must." These wrenches can be used in many nut-turning applications.

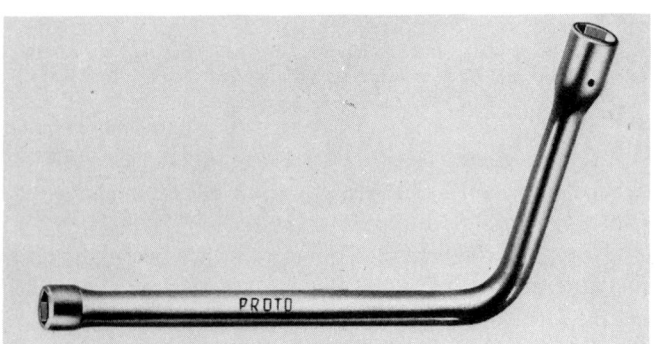

Fig. 1-15. This wrench is designed specifically for use in loosening and tightening brake bleeder screws.

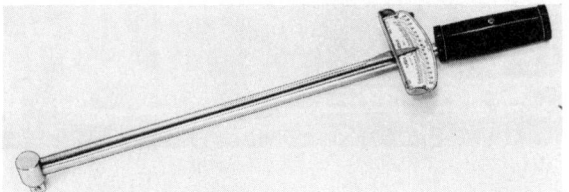

Fig. 1-16. Typical torque wrench calibrated in ft. lb.

TORQUE WRENCHES

Often, a nut must be tightened to a specified amount (torque). If overtightened, the mating parts may be distorted and leakage (oil, coolant, compression, etc.) may occur. Cylinder head bolts and engine bearing nuts and bolts especially need to be "torqued." When tightening these fasteners, a torque wrench is used. See Fig. 1-16.

Torque wrenches indicate torque tightness in foot pounds, inch pounds or newton-metres. To change foot pounds to newton metres, multiply by 1.355. When using a torque wrench, clean and oil the threads of the fasteners so that no additional friction will be present. Torque wrenches are used with special, heavy-duty sockets.

Fig. 1-17. Adjustable-end wrench.

ADJUSTABLE WRENCHES

There are three general types of adjustable wrenches. These include the adjustable-end wrench, Fig. 1-17, the monkey wrench, Fig. 1-18, and the pipe or Stillson wrench, Fig. 1-19.

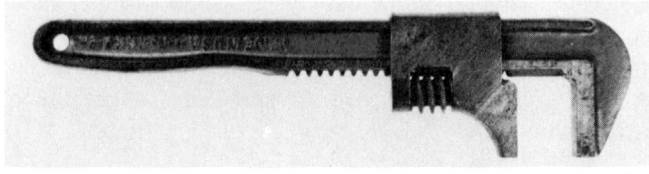

Fig. 1-18. Typical monkey wrench.

The adjustable-end wrench and the monkey wrench are convenient to have in a mechanic's kit. They will fit any nut which is within the range of their adjustment. Adjustable-end wrenches are available in various sizes, and are specified according to their length. The main disadvantage of these two

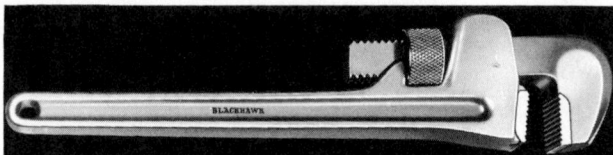

Fig. 1-19. Stillson wrench which is used for pipe work.

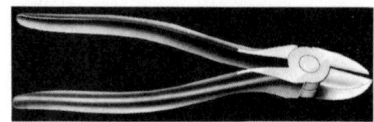

Fig. 1-22. Diagonal cutting pliers are used for cutting wire and for pulling cotter pins.

adjustable wrenches is that they do not hold their adjustment. Consequently they are apt to slip on the nut.

The pipe or Stillson wrench, as the name implies, is designed specifically for tightening and loosening pipes or other circular items.

Pipe wrenches are seldom needed in automotive work, but occasionally they are found necessary on nuts which have been so damaged that conventional wrenches will slip.

Regardless of what type of wrench is being used, be sure that it fits the nut or bolt head, Fig. 1-20. If the wrench

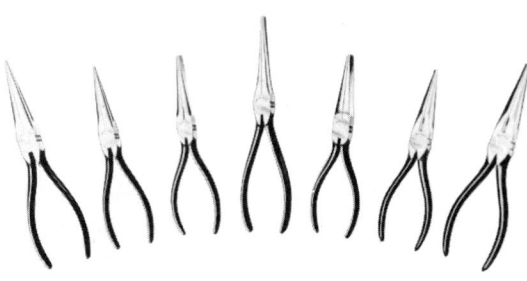

Fig. 1-23. Assorted long nose pliers.

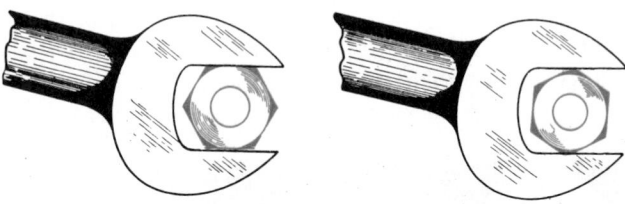

Fig. 1-20. Left. Care must be taken to select wrenches that fit the nut. Right. If wrong size wrench is used, corners of nut will become rounded and correct wrench will no longer fit.

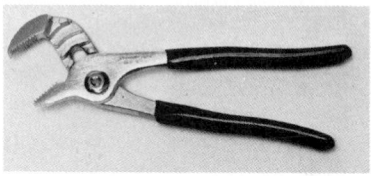

Fig. 1-24. Interlocking joint gripping pliers is adjustable, and holds the adjustment with jaws approximately parallel.

opening is too large for the particular nut, it will slip and round off the corners of the nut. In addition, when the wrench slips, the mechanic may receive a skinned knuckle. Remember, it is always safer to pull on a wrench than to push on it.

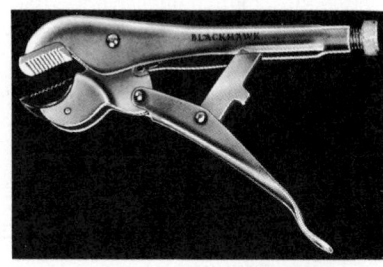

Fig. 1-25. Locking or vise-grip pliers are one of the most important tools in a mechanic's kit.

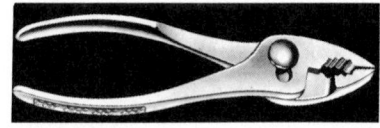

Fig. 1-21. Combination slip-joint pliers.

PLIERS

There are many different types of pliers used in automotive work. One most commonly used is the 6 in. combination slip-joint pliers, Fig. 1-21. The slip-joint permits the jaws to be opened wider at the hinge for gripping larger diameters.

Diagonal cutting pliers, Fig. 1-22, are needed not only for cutting wire but are also used for removing cotter pins.

Long nose pliers, Fig. 1-23, either the flat nose or duck bill type, are needed frequently in recovering a washer or a nut

which has dropped into an inaccessible place. They are also used to aid in positioning small parts.

The interlocking joint gripping pliers, Fig. 1-24, is a variation of the slip-joint pliers in that it is adjustable. The opening of the pliers can be adjusted to several different sizes by means of a dog which engages any one of the circular channels. In that way, the jaws of the pliers remain approximately parallel regardless of the size of the opening.

One of the most versatile tools in the mechanic's kit is the vise-grip, or locking pliers, Fig. 1-25. When locked in position on a part, it will grip it firmly even though the area contacted by the jaws of the pliers is extremely small. It has an infinite number of uses, ranging from holding two parts together while

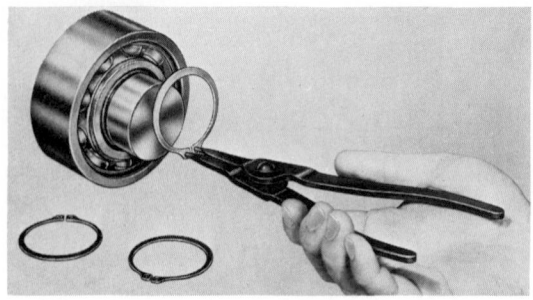

Fig. 1-26. This snap ring pliers is used extensively in transmission work.

STUD REMOVERS

When the threads on studs are stripped, it is necessary to remove and replace the stud. The preferred method is to use a stud remover, Fig. 1-29. These tools are designed with a 3/8 in. or 1/2 in. drive, so they can be used with a flex handle or ratchet wrench.

they are being worked on, to gripping the end of a broken stud and turning it out of its threaded hole.

Snap ring pliers, Fig. 1-26, are important tools in every repair kit. They are used to remove snap rings from various parts, such as hydraulic valve lifters and transmission shafts and bearings.

Fig. 1-29. Wedging-type of stud remover for use with ratchet or other wrench.

SCREWDRIVERS

Many different types and sizes of screwdrivers are needed by the automotive mechanic. The conventional screwdriver, Fig. 1-30, has a flat blade designed to engage a straight groove in the head of the screw.

Fig. 1-27. Special pliers used to disconnect nonmetallic ignition cable from spark plugs.

To avoid breaking nonmetallic conductors in radiation suppression ignition cable, pull should be applied only on the rubber boot covering the spark plug insulator. This can be simplified by using special pliers as shown in Fig. 1-27.

Fig. 1-30. Conventional screwdriver.

Fig. 1-31. Phillips head screwdriver.

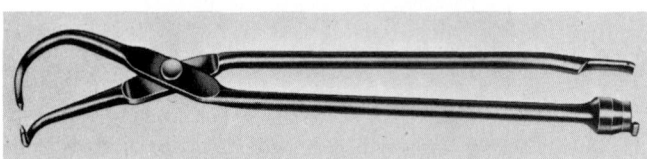

Fig. 1-28. This all-purpose brake pliers aids in the removal and installation of brake shoe retracting springs.

SPECIAL PLIERS

Special pliers designed to assist in the removal and installation of brake shoes and brake shoe springs are also available. See Fig. 1-28.

Another special type of plier is designed to simplify the removal of grease caps, hub caps and wheel covers. The use of this tool also materially reduces the time it takes to complete the job.

NOTE: Pliers and Stillson wrenches should never be used for loosening or tightening nuts.

Fig. 1-32. Clutch-type screwdriver.

The Phillips-type screwdriver, Fig. 1-31, has a pointed end with four grooves which are designed to engage corresponding slots in the head of the Phillips-type screw.

The clutch-type screwdriver, Fig. 1-32, has a fluted end designed to engage a corresponding opening in the head of the screw.

Common lengths of screwdrivers are 3, 4, 6, 8, 10 and 12 inches. A complete set is essential.

Fig. 1-33. Offset-type screwdriver is needed when there is little clearance over screw head.

When the space over the head of a screw is limited, an offset screwdriver, Fig. 1-33, is needed to remove or tighten the screw. These are available in different sizes. They can also be obtained with ratchet heads.

Screwdrivers should only be used on screws. The blade of the screwdriver should fit the slot in the screw, Fig. 1-34, and the blade of the screwdriver should always be held vertical to the screw head. Screwdrivers should fit the screw slot snugly.

Fig. 1-34. Screwdriver blade must always fit slot in screw.

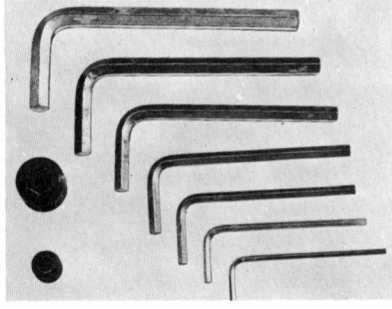

Fig. 1-35. Set of setscrew wrenches, also known as Allen wrenches, with setscrews on left.

SETSCREW WRENCHES

Setscrew wrenches, or Allen wrenches, Fig. 1-35, are used on setscrews with hexagonal recesses in the screw heads. These wrenches are L-shaped bars of steel. A typical set comprises eleven wrenches ranging in size from .050 to 3/8 in., and are designed to fit setscrew sizes No. 4 to 3/4 in.

Spanner wrenches, Fig. 1-36, are used to tighten and loosen round nuts which have a notch or series of notches cut into the outer edge. For the most part, these are special wrenches furnished by the manufacturer to service special parts.

HAMMERS

Automotive mechanics require hammers of various types and sizes. The most important is the ball peen hammer, Fig. 1-37. The flat portion of the head used for most hammering is

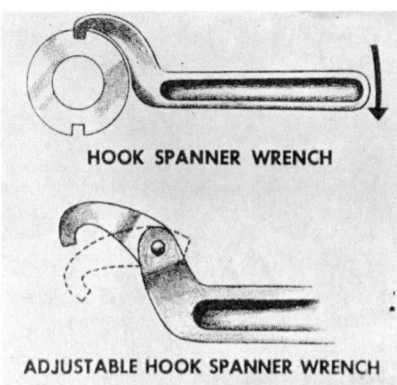

Fig. 1-36. Two types of spanner wrenches used on radial nuts.

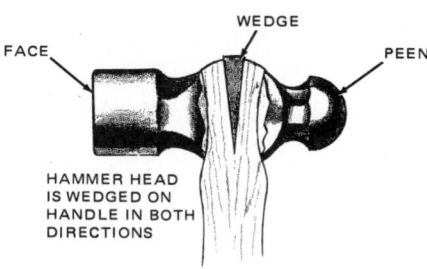

Fig. 1-37. Note double taper in head of hammer and wedge holding head in place.

called the face. The other end is the peen. When the peen is ball-shaped, it is known as a ball peen, which is used primarily for riveting work.

Ball peen hammers usually are classed according to the weight of the head without the handle. A good combination hammer set for automotive work would include 4 oz., 1 lb. and 3 lb. hammers. A small hammer is very handy for light work, especially when cutting gaskets out of sheet stock.

If there is any danger of damaging the surface or work, a "soft" hammer, Fig. 1-38, should be used. These special hammers have faces of rawhide, plastics, brass or lead.

Also available are "dinging" hammers and other peening and shrinking hammers of various sizes and shapes for straightening sheet metal on automobile bodies.

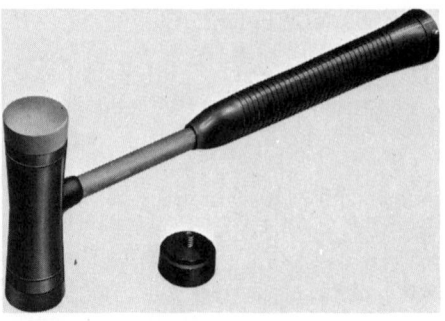

Fig. 1-38. Use a "soft" hammer when there is a possibility of marring the work surface. This hammer has replaceable striking surfaces.

Fig. 1-39. A hammer should be gripped close to end of handle. Full face of hammer should strike work.

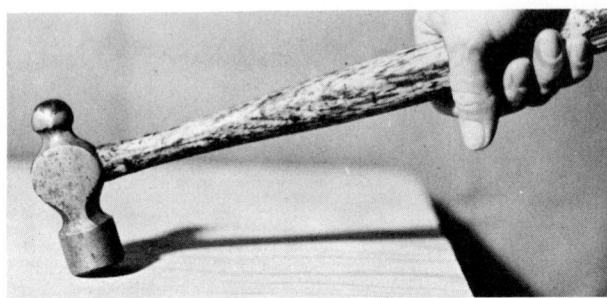

Fig. 1-40. Never strike work with edge of hammer face.

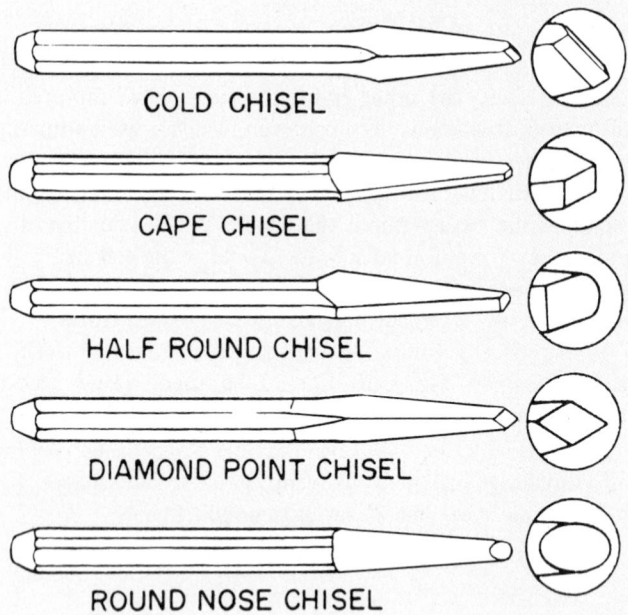

Fig. 1-41. Note cutting edges of these different types of cold chisels.

The hammer should be gripped close to the end of the handle, Fig. 1-39. In this way a heavier blow can be struck with less effort. Be careful not to strike the work with the edge of the hammer face, Fig. 1-40. The full face of the hammer should contact the head of the chisel or other work.

The end of the hammer handle should not be used for bumping purposes, as this will quickly split and ruin the handle. Neither should hammer handles be used as levers.

The hammer handle should always be tight on the head. Never work with a hammer with a loose head. This is dangerous as the head may fly off when the hammer is swung and cause an injury.

The eye or hole in the head of the hammer is made with a slight taper in both directions from the center. After the handle is tapered to fit the eye, it is inserted in the head. A steel wedge is then driven into the end of the handle, Fig. 1-37. This expands the taper in the eye and in that way the handle is wedged in both directions. If the wedge starts to come out, it should be driven in again until it is tight and the handle is secure in the head of the hammer.

CHISELS

Cold chisels, Fig. 1-41, are used for cutting metal, to cut the heads from rivets, chip metal, and to split nuts which have

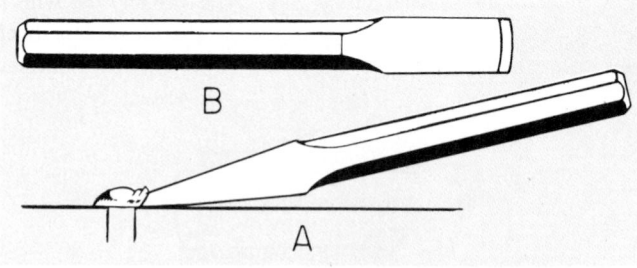

Fig. 1-42. A rivet buster is used to cut the heads from rivets.

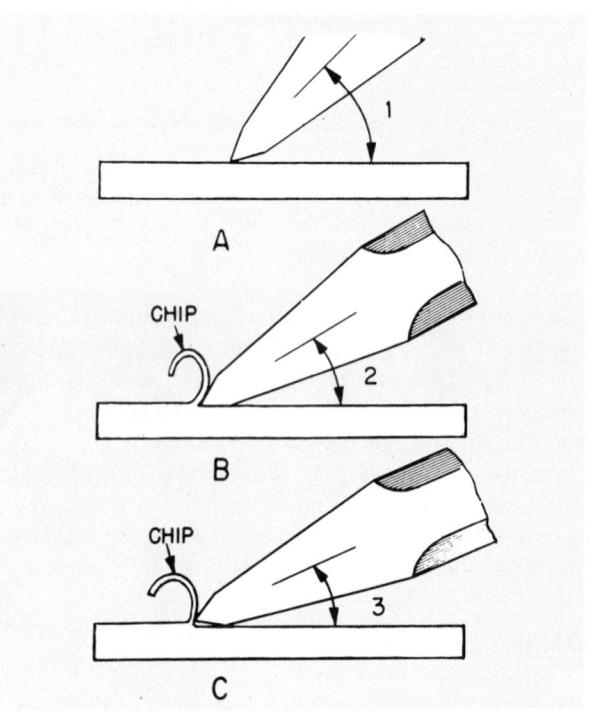

Fig. 1-43. Depth of cut is controlled by angle of chisel.

become rusted and cannot be loosened by means of a wrench.

The cape chisel, Fig. 1-41, has a narrow cutting edge. It is used primarily for cutting keyways and narrow grooves.

In most cases, auto mechanics will use the cold, or flat chisel, and the sizes most frequently used are 3/8 in., 1/2 in. and 3/4 in.

A rivet buster, Fig. 1-42, is a special form of chisel designed specifically for cutting the heads from rivets. It differs from the conventional cold chisel in that only one side of the cutting edge is ground.

When using a chisel, a right-handed person should hold the tool in his left hand and wield the hammer with his right. The chisel should be held rather loosely with fingers curled around the chisel about one inch from the head of the chisel.

When chipping metal, the depth of the cut is controlled by the angle of the chisel, Fig. 1-43. Deeper cuts are taken as the angle of the chisel approaches the vertical. When chipping, the mechanic should keep his eye on the cutting edge, not on the head of the chisel.

Goggles should be worn when chipping and grinding, and take precautions so that chips will not strike anyone who is nearby. Never use a chisel on which the head has been mushroomed, as in Fig. 1-44. When struck with a hammer,

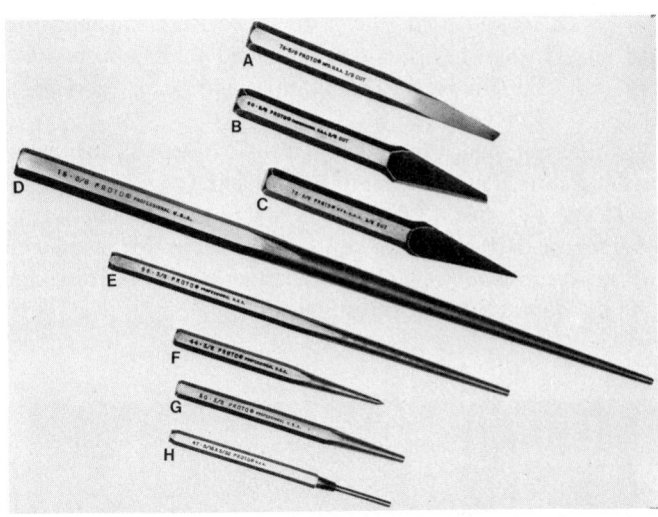

Fig. 1-47. Drifts, punches and chisels are an important addition to a mechanic's toolbox. A—Diamond point chisel. B—Cape chisel. C—Round nose chisel. D—Long aligning punch. E—Aligning punch. F—Center punch. G—Starting punch. H—Drift or pin punch.

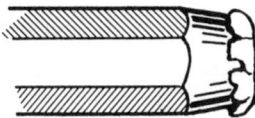

Fig. 1-44. Cold chisels are made to absorb heavy-duty service. Often, however, as a result of heavy hammer blows, the head of the chisel becomes swaged or mushroomed as shown.

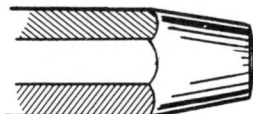

Fig. 1-45. The mushroomed metal should be ground off until the end becomes smooth. This safety measure helps prevent accidents due to flying bits of metal when the chisel is struck with a hammer.

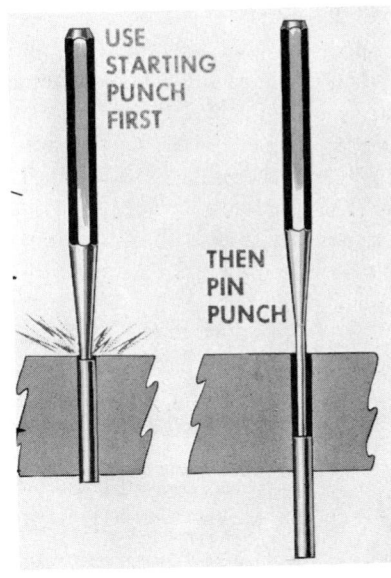

Fig. 1-48. When punching out a pin, use starting punch first and follow through with a pin punch.

portions of the mushroom will fly off at high velocity and cause severe injuries. The battered end of the chisel should be ground off until smooth, as in Fig. 1-45.

When sharpening a cold chisel, Fig. 1-46, the two ground surfaces should form an angle of 60 deg. Rivet busters are ground on one surface only at an angle of approximately 30 deg. See Fig. 1-42.

Many different types of punches, Fig. 1-47, are required in automotive work. The starting punch is designed to punch out rivets after the heads have been cut off. These punches are also used to start driving out straight or tapered pins, Fig. 1-48. After the pin has been driven partly from the hole, the starting punch can no longer be used because of its taper. A

Fig. 1-46. Sharpening chisel on power grinder.

pin punch is then used to complete the job of punching out the pin. Pin punches should not be used to start such work because a hard blow on the punch would bend the slender shank.

A lining-up punch has a long taper. It is used to shift parts to bring corresponding holes into alignment.

The center punch, Fig. 1-49, is ground to a fine point. It is used to mark the location of a hole that is to be drilled. Without such a mark, the drill will wander over the surface and drill the hole at the wrong position.

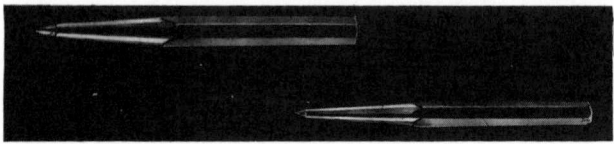

Fig. 1-49. Two types of center punches.

SCREW EXTRACTORS

Screw extractors are used for removing screws and studs which have broken off short and cannot be turned by means of conventional or vise-grip pliers. One type of screw extractor, B in Fig. 1-50, is made with a tapered left-hand thread. After drilling a hole in the broken screw, A in Fig. 1-50, the screw extractor is screwed into the hole. Continued turning of the extractor causes the tapered threads of the extractor to jam in the hole so that the broken screw (right-hand thread) can be screwed out.

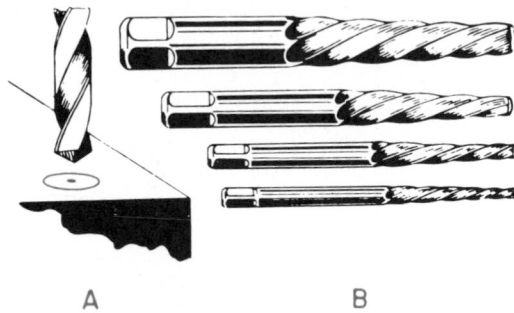

Fig. 1-50. After drilling a hole in broken stud, screw extractor is turned in. This, in turn, will screw out broken stud.

METAL SHEARS

Heavy tin shears, Fig. 1-51, are needed for cutting sheet metal and gasket material. The straight blade shear is the type most usually needed, however the curved blade shear and the scroll pivoter snips are also convenient to have available. The curved blade shears are used for making curved cuts, and the scroll pivoter snips follow an irregular line easily.

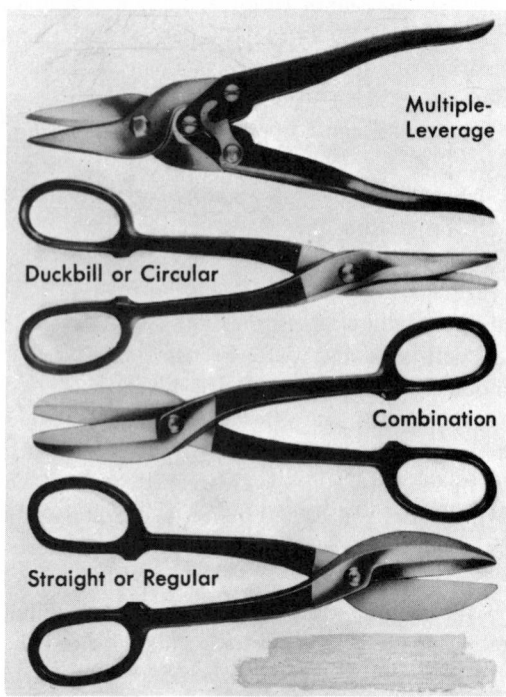

Fig. 1-51. Different types of shears.

ELECTRIC DRILLS

Electric drills, Fig. 1-52, come in several sizes and are a major, labor-saving piece of equipment. They are a must in every mechanic's tool kit, and many mechanics have both a 1/4 in. size and a 1/2 in. size electric drill.

Some drills are provided with special speed controls. This feature is of value because some materials are more easily drilled at slow speeds, while others require a faster speed. For example, soft metals require a faster speed than extremely hard metals.

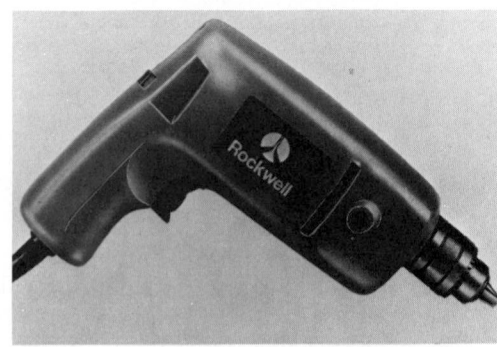

Fig. 1-52. Electric drill is an indispensable tool in automotive mechanic's kit.

POWER WRENCHES

Power wrenches (often called impact tools), Fig. 1-53, are designed for loosening and tightening nuts, quickly. Their use

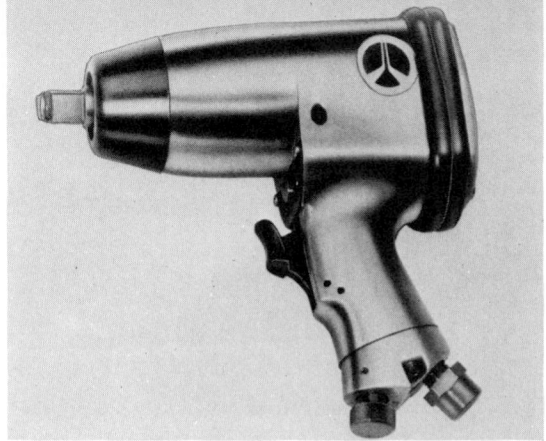

Fig. 1-53. Details of a pneumatic impact tool.

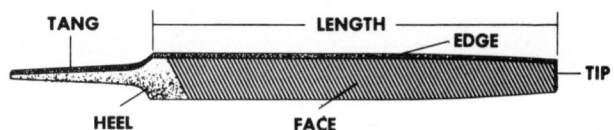

Fig. 1-55. Indicating the different parts of a conventional file.

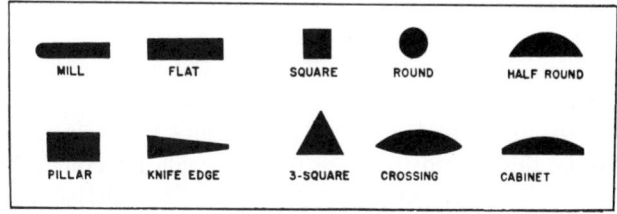

Fig. 1-56. Sectional view of different file shapes.

results not only in a considerable saving of time, but also a noticeable reduction in fatigue on the part of the mechanic. Designed for use with heavy-duty socket wrenches, both electrical and pneumatic types are available.

As an example of the time that can be saved by using a power wrench, a valve job on an automotive engine required 4 hr. 20 min. when conventional hand tools were used. When the same job was done with the aid of a power wrench, only 3 hr. 14 min. were required.

FILES

Files are hardened steel hand tools designed to remove metal. They are also used for smoothing metal surfaces and for polishing.

The cutting edges of a file are diagonal rows of parallel teeth. There are more than 20 different types of files with sizes ranging from 3 to 18 in. A file with a single row of parallel teeth is called a single-cut file, Fig. 1-54. Files which have one row of teeth crossing the other row in a crisscross pattern are known as double-cut, Fig. 1-54.

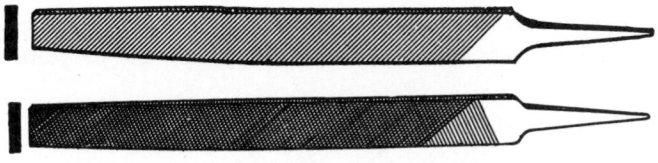

Fig. 1-54. A single-cut or mill file is shown above. A double-cut file is shown below.

Files are graded according to the spacing of the teeth. The terms used to indicate the coarseness or fineness of a file are bastard, second-cut and smooth. The file may also be either a single-cut or double-cut. The terms coarse and dead-smooth are also used in some classifications.

The names of the different parts of a file are shown in Fig. 1-55.

There are many different shapes in which files are available, Fig. 1-56. The mill file is single-cut, tapering in thickness and width for one-third of its length. It is used primarily for fine work and is available with either square or round edges or with

one safe edge (without teeth).

A double-cut file, tapering in thickness and width, is known as a flat file. It is used when a faster cut is desired. The hand file is single-cut and similar in shape to a flat file, with parallel sides and a slight taper in thickness. It has square edges, one of which is a safe edge. For rough filing, the bastard file is used.

The round file is tapered and usually single-cut. In larger sizes, it is also available in double-cut. For enlarging large holes, a round 12 in. bastard file is usually used. If the hole is of small diameter, a round 6 in. file, usually known as a rat-tail is used. Untapered round files are also available. The principal use of round files is to enlarge circular openings and file concave surfaces.

The half-round file is a double-cut file, tapering in thickness and width, with one flat and one oval side. It is used mainly for rough filing on concave surfaces.

The triangular file is useful for filing small notches, square or cornered holes. In addition, it is used for recutting mashed and damaged threads on bolts and other parts.

As previously pointed out, files with coarse teeth are used when it is desired to remove a lot of metal as quickly as possible. Files with fine teeth remove less metal, but produce a smoother surface. In addition, the type of metal must be considered when selecting a file.

When filing cast iron, first use a bastard file, then use a second-cut file for finishing. On soft steel, a second-cut file is used first, and a smooth-cut for finishing. On hard steel, start with a smooth-cut and finish with a dead-smooth file.

For truing ignition breaker points, a point file of the type shown in Fig. 1-57 is used.

Fig. 1-57. Type of file used to true ignition breaker points.

Fig. 1-58. A Vixen-cut file is used by auto body man and for soft metals such as lead and babbitt.

On soft metals, such as brass or bronze, use a bastard-cut first, then a second-cut. On aluminum, babbitt or lead, a Vixen-cut file, Fig. 1-58, similar to those used by automotive body repairmen is preferred. If that type file is not available, a bastard file may be used.

Never use a file without a handle since the pointed tang may be driven into the palm of your hand, inflicting a bad wound. Whenever possible, clamp the work in the jaws of a vise. If the work is soft metal, cover the jaws of the vise with soft caps so that the work will not be marked or otherwise damaged, Fig. 1-59.

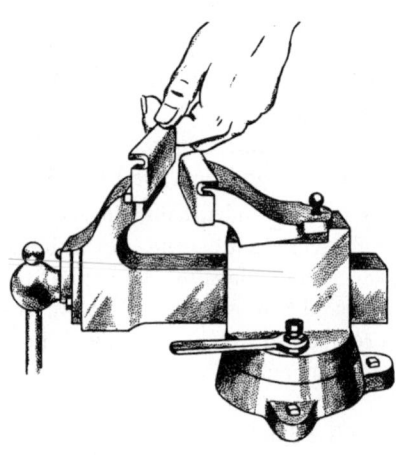

Fig. 1-59. Vises should be fitted with soft caps to hold material that would be easily scored.

Another precaution regarding files is that they should never be used as levers. Files are brittle and will quickly break if hammered on or used as levers.

File teeth are designed to cut only when the tool is pushed forward. So the preferred method of filing is to raise the file from the work before drawing it back to start the next stroke.

Only enough pressure should be applied to the file to keep it cutting. Excessive pressure only results in increased effort being required to move the file forward.

The correct way to hold a file is shown in Fig. 1-60.

If you are a right-handed mechanic, grasp the file handle in your right hand. The other end of the file is held in your left hand with the fingers curled over the end. Your feet should be spread apart and your body should lean slightly forward so that your left shoulder will tend to be over the work. In order that a flat surface is filed, the forward movement of the file must be perfectly horizontal. Any rocking of the file will result in a convex surface.

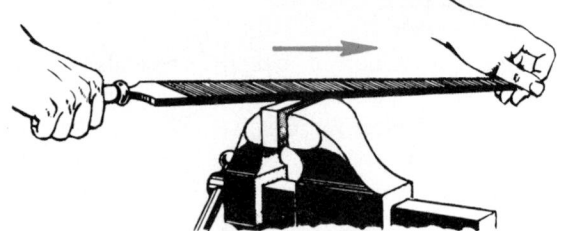

Fig. 1-60. Illustrating the correct method of holding a file.

When filing a round surface, the file should be rocked as shown in Fig. 1-61.

File teeth will tend to become clogged, particularly when soft metals are being filed. As a result such material between the file teeth will tend to scratch the surface being filed. This can be overcome to a degree by first rubbing chalk on the file.

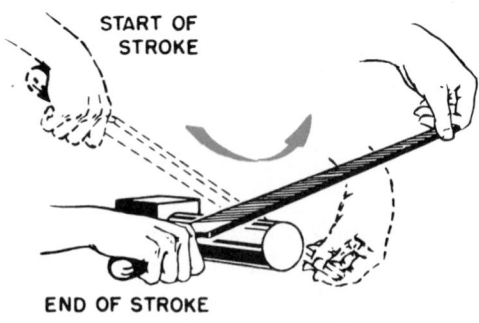

START OF STROKE

END OF STROKE

Fig. 1-61. When filing a round surface, the file should be rocked.

To clean the teeth of a file, the teeth should be brushed with a file card or other wire bristled brush.

Files should be hung on a rack when not in use, as placing them in a drawer with other tools will quickly dull the teeth.

RETRIEVING TOOLS

Special tools have been designed to retrieve objects that have been dropped and are in difficult places to reach. A magnetic tool of this type is shown in Fig. 1-62. The magnet is attached to a handle by means of a universal joint, making the tool more flexible. Gripper-type retrieving tools are designed to grip the object.

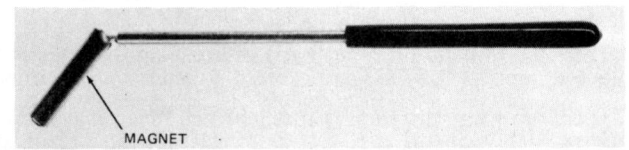

MAGNET

Fig. 1-62. Magnetic-type retrieving tool.

HOW TO SOLDER

Soldering is a method of joining two metals together. On automotive body repair work, solder is used to fill dents to form a smooth surface. Another major use of soldering is in connecting electric wires to instruments and other electrical equipment. This keeps the wires from becoming loose or disconnected as the result of vibration.

Solder is an alloy of varying proportions of lead and tin having a melting point below 800 deg. F. This is known as "soft solder." "Hard solders" (with silver, copper or nickel bases) have melting points above 800 deg. F., but also below that of the base metal.

The process of soldering consists of first cleaning the surfaces to be soldered. Then the joint is heated and a flux is applied. Flux is a chemical that keeps oxides from forming, thereby permitting the solder to adhere to the surfaces. After the flux is applied, the solder is melted into the joint, Fig. 1-63. This can be done by means of a soldering copper or the flame of a torch.

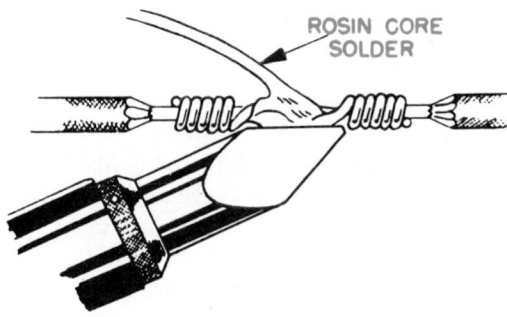

Fig. 1-63. Method of soldering splice in electric wires.

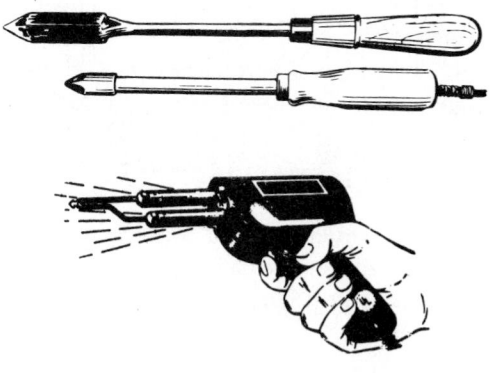

Fig. 1-64. Different sizes of soldering coppers are needed. Electric copper is shown at center, gun type below.

Soldering coppers, Fig. 1-64, often called soldering irons, are used mostly for soldering small pieces and when there is danger of an open flame damaging nearby parts. Made of copper, the tips of these tools must be given a coating of solder before they are used, Fig. 1-65. Known as tinning, the

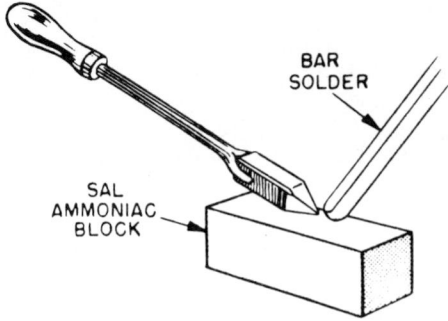

Fig. 1-65. One method of tinning a soldering copper.

process is to first file the tip of the copper so that it is clean and smooth. Then heat it, dip it in flux and apply solder.

Some mechanics prefer to melt the solder on the surface of a building brick, then rub the tip of the copper on the solder. Another method is to use a block of sal ammoniac.

After the iron has been tinned, take care that it is not overheated. That would burn the copper, and it would be necessary to re-tin it.

On some soldering jobs, it is desirable to first tin the surfaces to be joined, then solder them together. That process is usually followed on larger areas where a strong joint is to be made. It is also used when solder is to be applied to sheet iron.

Soldering coppers may be heated in a flame or special oven. Or, soldering irons with electric heating elements may be used, Fig. 1-64.

There are many different types of fluxes available. Select the type best suited for the metals to be joined. For electrical connections, a rosin type flux is recommended. An acid type is used when soldering sheet iron.

HOW TO USE A HACKSAW

Hacksaws are used to cut metal. As shown in Fig. 1-66, the detachable cutting blade is mounted in a metal frame. Different length frames are available, and some frames are made adjustable so that various size blades can be used. The usual lengths of hacksaw blades are 8, 10 and 12 in. The 10 and 12 in. sizes are most frequently used. For power-driven hacksaws, blades of 12, 14, 17, 18, 21 24 and 30 in. lengths are available.

Hacksaw blades are made of high grade tool steel, hardened and tempered. There are two types, the all-hard and the flexible. All-hard blades are hardened throughout, while only the teeth of flexible blades are hardened.

The blades are provided with holes at both ends for installation on the pins on the frame. To adjust the tension of the blade, and also to secure it tightly to the frame, the position of one of the pins is adjustable. This adjustment is made by either a wing nut or by turning the handle.

The "set" in a saw refers to the amount the teeth are pushed out in opposite directions from the sides of the blade. The teeth of all hacksaw blades are set to provide clearance for the blade. The usual types of set are alternate, raker and

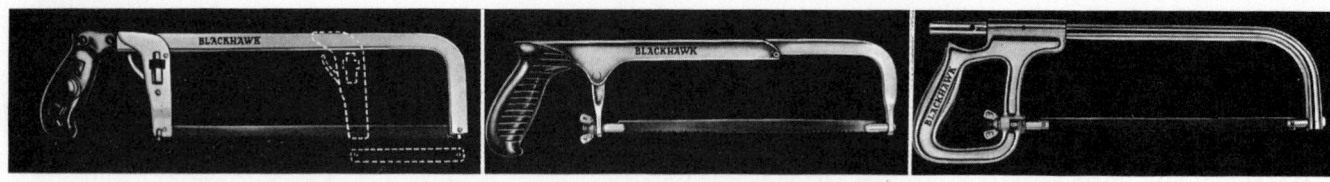

Fig. 1-66. Different types of adjustable hacksaw frames.

undulated. In addition, there is a double alternate set.

Blades for hand-operated hacksaws come with 14, 18, 24 and 32 teeth per inch. It is important that the teeth per inch be considered when selecting a hacksaw blade for a particular job, Fig. 1-67. Also, thought must be given to whether the

14 TEETH PER INCH

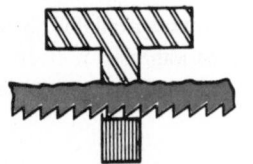

FOR LARGE SECTIONS OF MILD MATERIAL

18 TEETH PER INCH

FOR LARGE SECTIONS OF TOUGH STEEL

24 TEETH PER INCH

FOR ANGLE IRON, HEAVY PIPE, BRASS, COPPER

32 TEETH PER INCH

FOR THIN TUBING

KEEP AT LEAST TWO TEETH CUTTING TO AVOID THIS

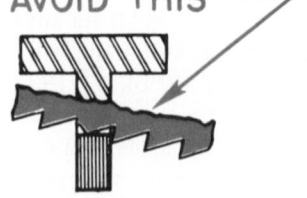

Fig. 1-67. Hacksaw blades must be selected in accordance with type of metal to be cut.

all-hard or flexible blade is more suitable for a particular job.

In general, an all-hard blade is considered best for sawing brass, cast iron, steel and other stock of heavy cross section. For cutting hollow shapes, and metals of light section such as channel iron, tubing tin, copper, aluminum or babbitt, a flexible blade is preferable.

Hacksaw blade manufacturers recommend that 14-tooth saws be used for cutting soft steel, brass, cast iron and stock of heavy cross section. For cutting drill rod, light angles, high speed steel, tool steel and small solids, 18-tooth blades are recommended. Use 24-tooth blades for cutting brass tubing, heavy BX cable, iron pipe, metal conduit and drill rod. For cutting thin tubing, sheet metal, light BX cable, channels, etc., 32-tooth blades are suggested.

After selecting the correct blade for the material, place it on the pins on the hacksaw frame with the teeth pointing toward the front of the frame. The blade is then stretched tightly in the frame.

If an accurate cut is to be made, it is advisable to mark the stock with a scriber, and nick the work with a file. The nick will make it easier for the saw to start cutting and also insure accuracy. Make sure the work is held securely in a vise, with the line to be cut as close to the vise jaws as possible. Use sufficient pressure on the saw when starting the cut, so that the saw teeth immediately begin to bite into the metal. The hacksaw blade should be held vertically and moved forward with a light steady stroke. At the end of the stroke, relieve the pressure and draw the saw straight back. See Fig. 1-68.

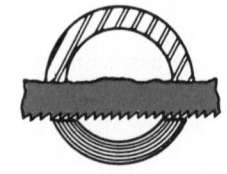

Fig. 1-68. Illustrating correct method of using a hacksaw.

The most effective cutting speed is about one stroke per second. When the material is nearly cut through, the pressure on the blade should be reduced to prevent the teeth from catching. When cutting thin stock, it is advisable to clamp it between two pieces of wood or soft metal, then saw through all three pieces. This will prevent the saw from sticking, and also prevent possible damage to the work.

A hole saw is advisable for cutting round holes in metal. Driven by an electric drill, the hole saw is used for drilling large diameter holes in instrument panels and fire walls for the installation of instruments and other accessories. It is provided with a centering or pilot drill for starting and centering the cut.

DRILLING, REAMING AND TAPPING

The auto mechanic frequently finds it necessary to drill holes in order to install additional accessories and equipment on passenger cars, trucks or tractors. Electric drills, Fig. 1-69, used in most automotive shops are 1/4, 3/8, 1/2 and 3/4 in. The size designations indicate the largest size drill that should be inserted in the chuck. If drills larger than the specified size are used, the electric drill may be overloaded and may overheat. Premature failure can then be expected. It should be pointed out, however, that a well-made electric drill can stand a certain degree of overload for a short period without harm.

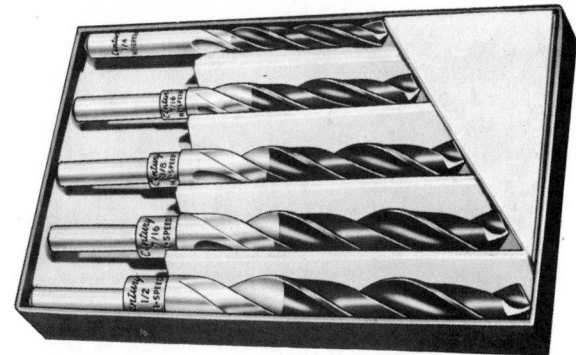

Fig. 1-70. Set of twist drills ranging up to 1/2 in. diameter. All have 1/4 in. shanks for use in a 1/4 in. drill.

Fig. 1-69. Electric drills have many uses and belong in every mechanic's tool kit.

TWIST DRILLS

The tool used to do the actual cutting is known as a twist drill, Fig. 1-70. A twist drill has two cutting edges and is made of either carbon steel or high speed steel. However, the former quickly becomes dull and, if heated excessively, will lose its hardness. High speed steel will retain its temper when red hot, so twist drills of that material are preferred.

There are other types of drills, but the straight shank drill is generally used in automotive maintenance shops.

SHARPENING DRILLS

Before a drill is used, it should be correctly ground and sharpened. Unless the drill is in good condition, it may cut slowly, drill an oversize hole or possible break.

A correctly sharpened drill will have:
1. Equal and correctly sized drill point angles.

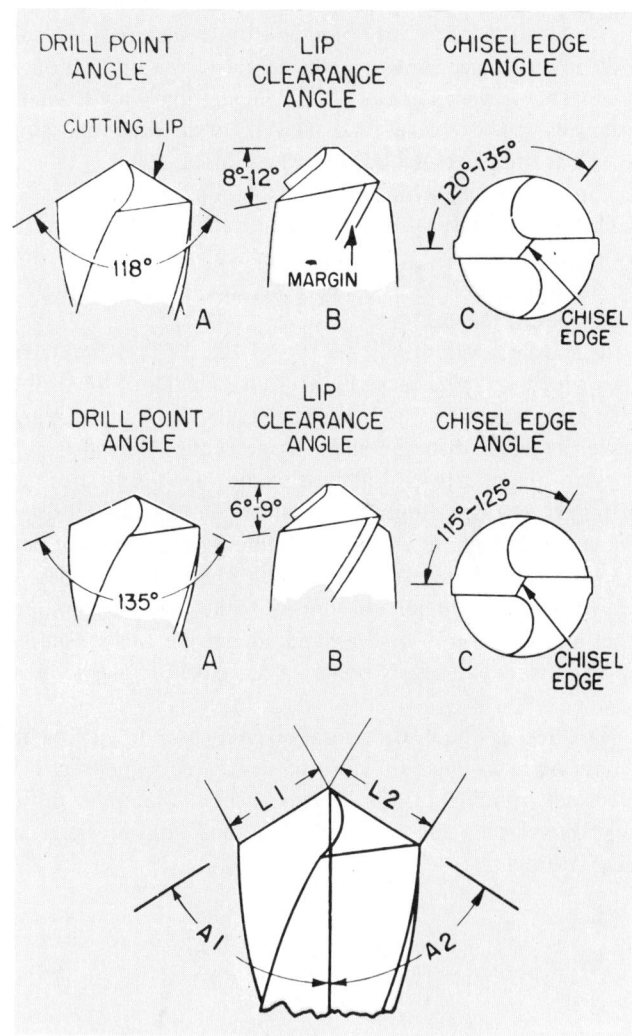

Fig. 1-71. Indicating the various angles on a twist drill.

2. Equal length cutting lips.
3. Correct clearance behind the cutting lips.
4. Correct chisel edge angle.
   All four are equally important, Fig. 1-71.
   For general drilling, the angles shown in the upper part of

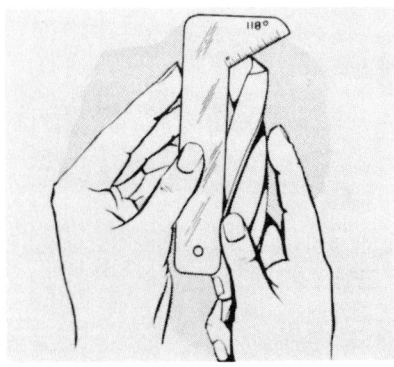

Fig. 1-72. Using a special gauge to measure angle of cutting edge of a drill.

Fig. 1-71 are used. If very hard and tough materials are to be drilled, the angles shown in the center of the illustration are used. The lower portion of the illustration shows what is meant by the two halves (A-1 and A-2) of the drill point angle, as well as the two equal-length cutting lips (L-1 and L-2).

Lip clearance behind the cutting lip of the margin is determined by inspection. The cutting edge, or lip is measured by a gauge, Fig. 1-72. The lip clearance angle may be within certain limits, as shown in Fig. 1-71, but must be the same on both sides of the drill.

The margin, shown at the top of Fig. 1-71, is the narrow strip which extends practically the full diameter of the drill for the entire length of the flutes. The portion back of the margin is slightly less in diameter and is termed body clearance.

Both lips of a twist drill must be the same length. For most materials, the lips should be ground to an angle of 59 deg. If the cutting edges are ground at different angles, and the point is in the center, only one lip will cut. The angle of 59 deg. for the lip is correct when the drill is to be used on aluminum, steel and cast iron. For brass and copper the angle should be 50 deg.; while 45 deg. is preferred for Bakelite, plastic, wood or fiber.

The heel of the drill (surface of point back of cutting lips) should be at an angle of 12 to 15 deg., as shown in Fig. 1-71. Incorrect grinding of the lip clearance will result in drilling holes larger than the diameter of the drill, drill breakage and slow cutting.

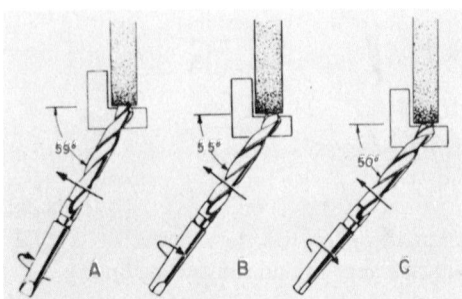

Fig. 1-73. Note how angle of drill is altered as sharpening progresses.

The rake angle of the drill is the angle of the flutes in relation to the axis. A 22 to 30 deg. rake angle is built into the drill by the manufacturer.

Drills should be placed in a grinding jig or attachment for sharpening. This will insure accuracy. When sharpening a drill, it is held as shown in Fig. 1-73. Position "A" is a top view of the first step in grinding the drill. The axis of the drill should make an angle of about 59 deg. (half the drill-point angle) with the face of the grinding wheel. The cutting lip should be horizontal.

The actual grinding of the drill point consists of three definite motions of the shank of the drill while the point is held lightly against the grinding wheel. The three motions are:
1. To the left.
2. Clockwise rotation.
3. Downward.

Fig. 1-73 shows the motion to the left in three views as the angle between the face of the grinding wheel and the drill decreases from about .59 deg. to 50 deg. In Fig. 1-73, clockwise rotation is indicated by the advance of the rotation arrows in A, B and C. Rotation is also illustrated by the change in position of the cutting lip as well as the tang.

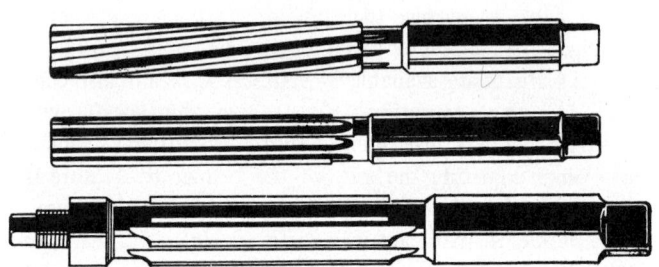

Fig. 1-74. Three types of reamers. Above. Spiral flute reamer. Center. Straight flute reamer. Below. Adjustable reamer.

REAMERS

If you want to finish a hole with a particularly smooth surface or to an exact diameter, a reamer, Fig. 1-74, should be used. The hole is first drilled to a diameter slightly smaller than the desired finished size, then finished with the reamer.

A reamer consists of three parts: body, shank and cutting blades. The reamer can be rotated by means of a suitable wrench or handle; or it can be power driven. When power driven, the speed is approximately 50 rpm.

The blades of a reamer are made of steel, which is hardened to such an extent that it is extremely brittle. Therefore, reamers must be handled carefully and should be stored in a wooden rack with a separate division for each reamer.

When reaming a hole, turn the reamer in the cutting direction only. Remove very little metal at a time since reaming is a finishing operation. Reamers are not designed to make heavy cuts; usually .002 in. is the limit of metal to be removed. Maintain a steady, even rotation of the reamer to reduce "chattering."

Fig. 1-74 shows two solid reamers — a straight flute and a

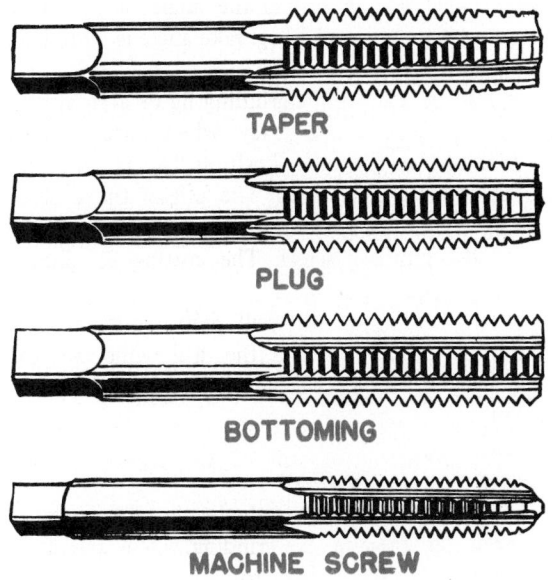

Fig. 1-75. Illustrating four different types of taps.

spiral flute – along with an adjustable reamer. The spiral flute type is more expensive than the straight flute reamer. Its advantage is less tendency toward chattering.

Solid reamers are available in standard sizes and also can be obtained in size variations of .001 in. for special work. Adjustable reamers give more flexibility, but care must be taken when adjusting the size of the reamer to be sure it is correctly set. A micrometer should be used for this purpose.

Adjustable reamers are usually available in standard sizes from 1/4 in. to 1 in. by 32nds. They are designed to allow the blades to expand 1/32 in. For example, a 1/4 in. adjustable reamer will cover hole sizes ranging from 1/4 in. to 9/32 in.

TAPS AND DIES

Taps, Fig. 1-75, and dies, Fig. 1-76, are thread-cutting tools. A tap is used to cut internal threads on parts such as nuts, while a die cuts external threads on bolts and studs.

There is special terminology used when discussing threads,

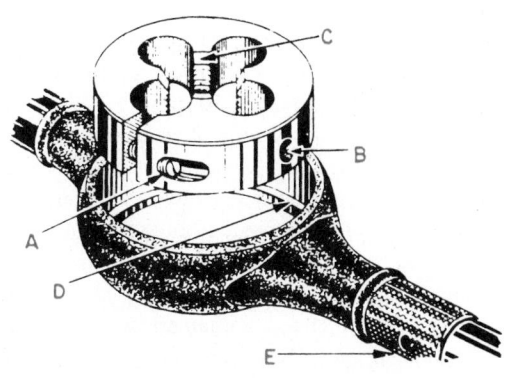

Fig. 1-76. Adjustable round split die for cutting external threads. A—Adjusting screw. B—Drive hole. C—Cutting teeth. D—Shoulder for die. E—Die holder handle.

bolts and nuts, Fig. 1-77. To avoid confusion, it is essential that mechanics know these terms.

The major diameter, formerly known as the outside diameter, is the largest diameter of the thread. The minor diameter is the diameter taken at the base of the thread.

The pitch of the thread is the distance from a point on one screw thread to a corresponding point on the next thread, measured parallel to the axis, Fig. 1-77. You can calculate the pitch (fine threads are hard to measure) by dividing one inch by the number of threads per inch.

If you want to drill and tap a hole, you have to drill the hole to the correct diameter for the particular tap. This is

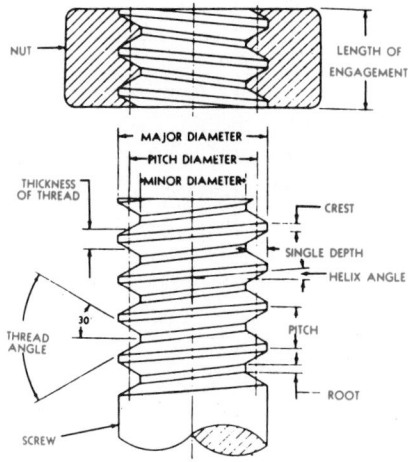

Fig. 1-77. Terms used in describing old American Standard screw threads and current Unified Thread series. See THREADS, page 34.

called a tap drill. Thread size, thread series and tap drill required are given in Fig. 1-78.

If you want to drill a hole through which a bolt is to be inserted, the drill is known as a clearance or body drill.

Taps and dies are marked according to the type and diameter thread they will cut. For example, an 8-32 is designed to cut 32 threads per inch on No. 8 stock.

When tapping a hole with a tap or cutting a thread with a die, considerable care is required. When using a tap or die, reverse the direction the tool is turned to free the tool of chips and also recut the threads. Forcing the tool will result in tool breakage, ruined parts and poor threads.

When threading steel parts, a lubricant such as lard oil should be used. Kerosene is preferred for use with aluminum. No lubricant is required for threading brass or cast iron.

FABRICATING TUBING

Tubing is used extensively in automobiles, trucks and tractors for oil, fuel and brake lines. Great care must be exercised in fitting tubing for specific jobs. Carelessness in fabrication, or in selecting the wrong type of material or fittings, may result in an accident and harm to the occupants of the vehicle.

Soft copper tubing is usually considered satisfactory for

Nominal size	Thr'd series	Major diameter, inches	Root diameter, inches	Tap drill to produce approx. 75% full thread	Decimal equivalent of tap drill
0–80	N. F.	.0600	.0438	3/64	.0469
1–64	N. C.	.0730	.0527	53	.0595
72	N. F.	.0730	.0550	53	.0595
2–56	N. C.	.0860	.0628	50	.0700
64	N. F.	.0860	.0657	50	.0700
3–48	N. C.	.0990	.0719	47	.0785
56	N. F.	.0990	.0758	45	.0820
4–40	N. C.	.1120	.0795	43	.0890
48	N. F.	.1120	.0849	42	.0935
5–40	N. C.	.1250	.0925	38	.1015
44	N. F.	.1250	.0955	37	.1040
6–32	N. C.	.1380	.0974	36	.1065
40	N. F.	.1380	.1055	33	.1130
8–32	N. C.	.1640	.1234	29	.1360
36	N. F.	.1640	.1279	29	.1360
10–24	N. C.	.1900	.1359	25	.1495
32	N. F.	.1900	.1494	21	.1590
12–24	N. C.	.2160	.1619	16	.1770
28	N. F.	.2160	.1696	14	.1820
1/4–20	N. C.	.2500	.1850	7	.2010
28	N. F.	.2500	.2036	3	.2130
5/16–18	N. C.	.3125	.2403	F	.2570
24	N. F.	.3125	.2584	I	.2720
3/8–16	N. C.	.3750	.2938	5/16	.3125
24	N. F.	.3750	.3209	Q	.3320
7/16–14	N. C.	.4375	.3447	U	.3680
20	N. F.	.4375	.3726	25/64	.3906
1/2–13	N. C.	.5000	.4001	27/64	.4219
20	N. F.	.5000	.4351	29/64	.4531
9/16–12	N. C.	.5625	.4542	31/64	.4844
18	N. F.	.5625	.4903	33/64	.5156
5/8–11	N. C.	.6250	.5069	17/32	.5312
18	N. F.	.6250	.5528	37/64	.5781
3/4–10	N. C.	.7500	.6201	21/32	.6562
16	N. F.	.7500	.6688	11/16	.6875
7/8– 9	N. C.	.8750	.7307	49/64	.7656
14	N. F.	.8750	.7822	13/16	.8125
1– 8	N. C.	1.0000	8376	7/8	.8750
14	N. F.	1.0000	9072	15/16	.9375

Fig. 1-78. Table of thread sizes and related information, including tap drill and clearance drill sizes.

gasoline lines. It should never be used for hydraulic brake lines, however, since it is not strong enough to withstand the pressures developed in the brake system. Only special tubing designed for hydraulic brake lines should be used. This tubing is made of seamless steel.

Dimensions of copper and steel tubing are given in the accompanying table. Note that the outside diameter of tubing is used to indicate its size, whereas pipe sizes are determined by their inside diameter.

SIZE OR O.D.	WALL THICKNESS COPPER TUBE	WALL THICKNESS SINGLE WALL STEEL TUBING	WALL THICKNESS DOUBLE WALL STEEL TUBING
1/8	.030	.025	.025
3/16	.030	.025	.025
1/4	.030	.028	.028
5/16	.032	.028	.028
3/8	.032	.028	.028
7/16		.030	.032
1/2	.032	.030	
1/2		.035	
9/16		.030	
5/8	.035	.035	.035

When making a line of tubing, first select the size and material of which the line is to be made. Then unroll the tubing and cut off the desired amount.

The correct way to unroll the tubing is to place the coil of tubing on the workbench in a vertical position. Then hold the end of the tubing against the surface of the bench with one hand and unroll the coil slowly with the other hand. Never try to uncoil tubing by drawing it out sidewise from the coil in a spiral. This will form a twist in the tubing and any attempt to straighten the tubing will work-harden it and create weak spots.

When cutting tubing, only special tubing cutters should be used, Fig. 1-79 It is imperative the tubing must be cut smoothly and at right angles to its center line. Unless the tubing is cut correctly, it will be impossible to make a leakproof joint.

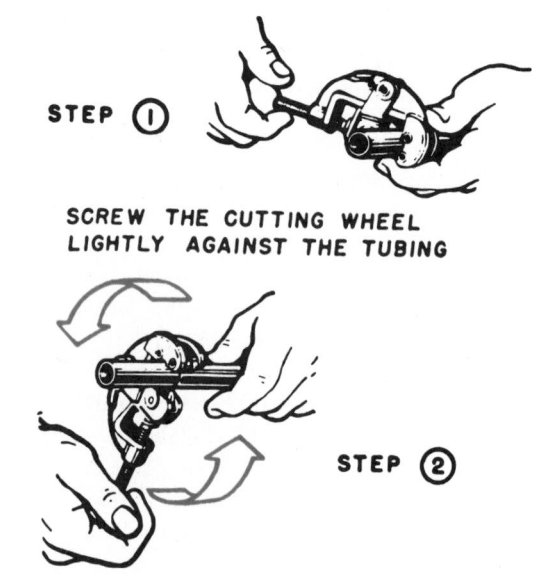

STEP ①

SCREW THE CUTTING WHEEL LIGHTLY AGAINST THE TUBING

STEP ②

ROTATE THE CUTTER KEEPING A SLIGHT PRESSURE AGAINST THE CUTTING WHEEL WITH THE SCREW ADJUSTMENT

Fig. 1-79. Showing procedure for cutting copper tubing with a special cutter.

The tube cutting tool shown in Fig. 1-79 will make a clean cut, square with the sides of the tubing. In addition, there is little possibility of filings getting into the tubing and subsequently causing trouble in the system. To use a tubing cutter, position the cutting wheel until it contacts the surface lightly. Swing the tool completely around the tubing, then readjust the cutting wheel. Repeat this procedure until the cut is completed.

After the tubing has been cut to the desired length, the ends should be reamed or deburred. One method is to use the reamer provided on one end of the tubing cutter. When reaming tubing, hold the end of the tubing pointed down, so metal chips will not drop into the tubing.

One type of reaming tool is an "inner and outer" reamer.

This is a cylindrically shaped tool that reams both the inside and outside edges of the tubing. With the burrs removed, the tubing is ready for one of the several types of flared or flareless fittings available. The type of fitting used is dependent on the type of service and material which the tubing is to carry.

The inverted flare fitting, Fig. 1-80, is widely used as original equipment on motor vehicles. It can be used for tubing of soft copper, aluminum, thin-walled steel and other thin-walled metal tubing.

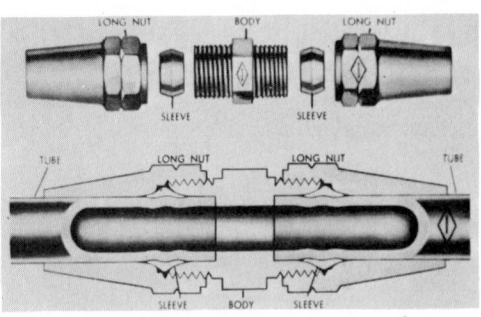

Fig. 1-83. Type of fitting designed for use in air systems of brakes. (Imperial-Eastman)

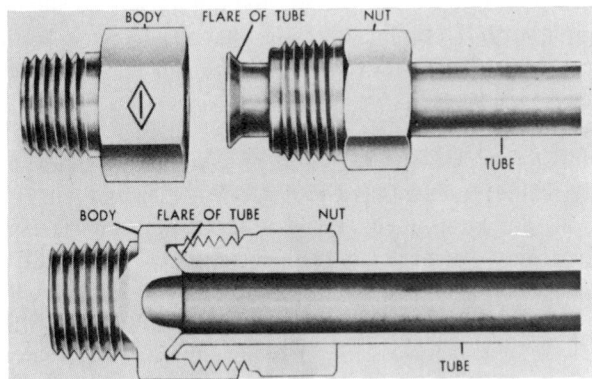

Fig. 1-80. Details of inverted flare fitting. (Imperial-Eastman)

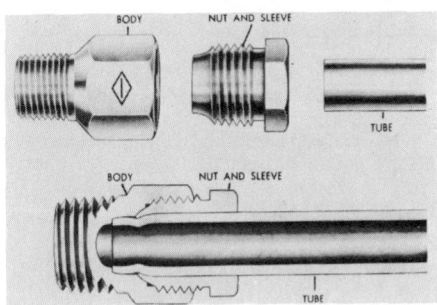

Fig. 1-84. Showing construction of threaded sleeve fitting used for low and medium pressure work. It is not as well adapted for reassembly as other types.

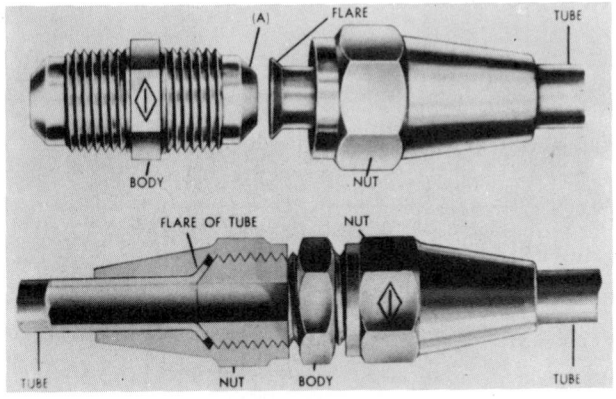

Fig. 1-81. SAE flare fitting used for connecting tubing carrying liquids or gases.

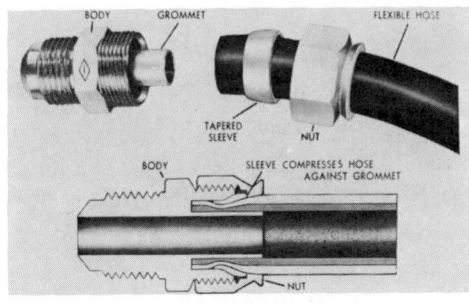

Fig. 1-85. Type of coupling used on flexible hose. (Imperial-Eastman)

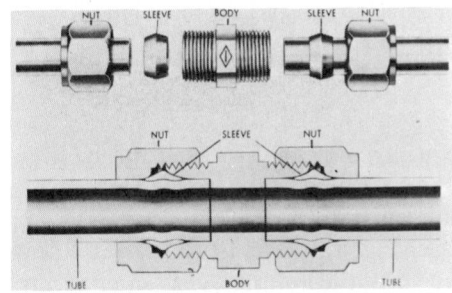

Fig. 1-82. Compression fittings used for connecting gasoline, gas, vacuum and air. (Imperial-Eastman)

When the tubing is to carry liquids or gases, the SAE flare fitting, Fig. 1-81, is used. The tubing can be copper, brass, aluminum or brazed steel (Bundy or GM). The flare fitting also can be used with plastic tubing.

Compression fittings, Fig. 1-82, are used with gasoline, grease, vacuum and air lines. Copper, aluminum, brass and brazed steel tubing can be used with this type of fitting.

Air brake fittings, Fig. 1-83, are used with copper, aluminum and thin-walled steel tubing on Bendix-Westinghouse and other air brake systems.

For low and medium pressure work, the threaded sleeve fitting, Fig. 1-84, is employed. It can be used with almost all types of tubing.

The flexible hose coupling, Fig. 1-85, can be used wherever

flexible hose is installed. It will carry, gasoline, oil, water, cutting oil, diesel oil and many hydraulic fluids.

Where vibration and minor tube movement is encountered, flex fittings are installed. Fig. 1-86 shows the details of this type of fitting.

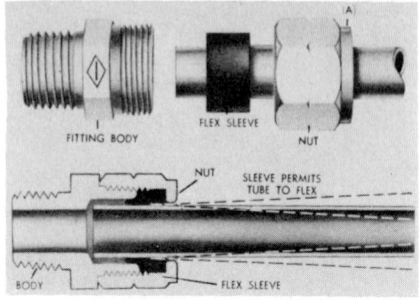

Fig. 1-86. Type of fitting used in systems subject to vibration and minor tube movement.

When lines carry relatively high pressure and are subject to minor vibration, high duty fittings such as illustrated in Fig. 1-87 are used. In addition to brazed steel tubing, these fittings are used with copper, aluminum and steel tubing.

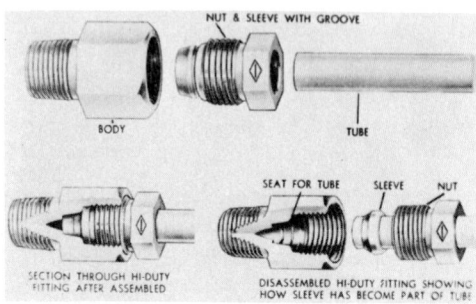

Fig. 1-87. This type of fitting is designed for systems operating under relatively high pressure and minor vibration. (Imperial-Eastman)

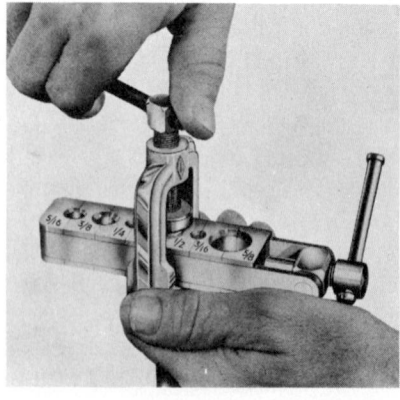

Fig. 1-88. Using a flaring tool on a piece of copper tubing.

FLARING

There are several different types of flaring tools available. One type consists of a flaring bar and screw feed flaring yoke, Fig. 1-88. When making a flare with a tool of this type, place the tubing in the flaring bar with the end protruding slightly above the face of the bar. Firmly clamp the tubing in the bar, so pressure of the flaring cone will not force the tubing through the bar.

Before slipping the yoke over the bar to start flaring, place a little oil on the cone or spreader. Take particular care if the flared connection is to be used on units subject to vibration. Do not work the tubing any more than is necessary. Working will tend to make the metal hard and brittle, so it is more subject to breakage.

On tubes flared too short, the full clamping area of the fitting is not used. Consequently, the joint may leak or suffer early failure. Tubing flared too long will stick and jam on the threads during assembly. Flares that are not straight usually result if the tubing was cut on an angle.

Brazed steel tubing, such as used for hydraulic brake lines, must be double flared. If only single flared, it will invariably crack or split. Double flaring is similar to single flaring except that an additional operation is introduced. To make a double flare with the tool shown in Fig. 1-89, two operations are

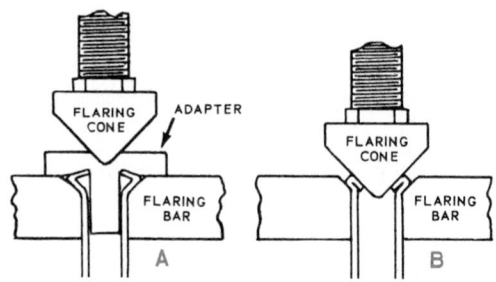

Fig. 1-89. Procedure for making a double flare in tubing.

involved. In the first operation, the tubing is belled through the use of an adapter. In the second operation, the adapter is removed and the flaring cone screwed down. This folds the tubing down on itself and forms on accurate 45 deg. double flare without cracking or splitting the tubing.

BENDING

It is frequently necessary to bend tubing. This should be done only with a special tube bender, and only soft temper tubing should be bent. On smaller size tubing, a simple outside bending coil spring generally is satisfactory. This bender is slipped over the outside of the tubing and prevents the tubing from kinking when it is bent. When using a spring-type tube bender, remember that the tubing must be bent somewhat further than required, then backed up to the desired angle.

This loosens the spring tension in the bender and it can be easily removed.

On larger sizes of tubing, or where precise and uniform bends are required, the use of a lever-type or gear-type bender,

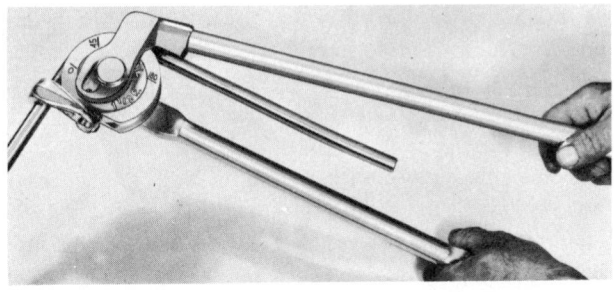

Fig. 1-90. For larger size tubing, a mechanical bender is required.

Fig. 1-90, should be used. These benders can be slipped on the tubing at the exact point the bend is desired. They are particularly advantageous when the tubing has been partly connected, or is located in hard-to-get-at places.

Bulk tubing is sold in coils. When removing a piece of copper tubing from a coil, first place the coil on the bench. Hold down the free end of the tubing, then roll the coil of tubing along the bench until the desired length is obtained. In this way, kinking of the tubing will be avoided.

CLEANING TOOLS

Cleaning parts is a basic requirement of all automotive service work. Having clean parts not only speeds the work, but also aids greatly in locating flaws and wear. A number of essential cleaning tools are illustrated in Figs. 1-91 and 1-92.

Tools such as scrapers and putty knives are hand tools, while certain brushes are designed for hand use and others are power driven. When using power driven wire brushes, goggles should be worn for safety's sake.

PISTON RING COMPRESSOR

A piston ring compressor, Fig. 1-93, is needed to compress the piston rings on a piston so that the assembly may be easily installed in the cylinder. Also, some mechanics are using ring compressors to remove oil filters from engines where, in many cases, there is not enough space to use the conventional strap type tool.

METRIC WRENCH SETS

Since the adoption of the metric system and the growing popularity of foreign built vehicles, there has been increasing interest in metric tools and wrench sets.

Metric socket wrench sets continue to use the 3/8 in. and 1/2 in. drive ratchets, extensions, hinge handles, universal

joints, speed handles, etc. The sockets, however, are built in metric sizes. They range in size from 6 mm to 26 mm, with increments of one millimetre. Similarly, open-end and box wrenches range in size from 7 mm to 26 mm, and also increases in size 1 mm at a time.

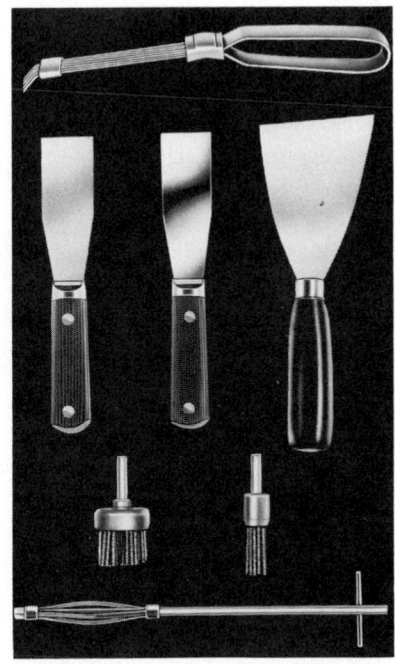

Fig. 1-91. From top to bottom. Carbon scraper. Putty knives used in scraping. Wire cleaning brushes for use with electric drills. Hand-operated cleaner for cleaning valve guides.

Fig. 1-92. Wire brushes designed for use with electric drill.

Fig. 1-93. Piston ring compressor.

REVIEW QUESTIONS – AUTOMOTIVE TOOLS

Write answers on a separate sheet of paper. Do not write in this book.

1. The size of open-end wrenches increases in:
   a. 1/16 in. steps.
   b. 1/32 in. steps.
   c. 1/8 in. steps.
   d. 1/4 in. steps.
2. What is the main reason for using a box type wrench?
3. List the three standard size drives for socket wrenches.
4. Why are torque wrenches needed?
5. A Stillson wrench is used to tighten _____.
6. Interlocking joint gripping pliers are designed to:
   a. Lock channels.
   b. Have adjustable openings of different sizes and, at the same time, the jaws remain parallel.
7. The end of a Phillips-type screwdriver is:
   a. A flat blade.
   b. Pointed end with four grooves.
   c. Fluted end.
8. A setscrew wrench has:
   a. Four sides.
   b. Six sides.
   c. Eight sides.
9. The rounded end of a machinists hammer is known as the _____.
10. A cape chisel is used to cut:
    a. Narrow grooves.
    b. Rivet heads.
    c. Tool steel.
11. When using a chisel, it should be held:
    a. Tightly in the hand.
    b. With a pair of slip-joint pliers.
    c. Loosely in the hand.
12. A screw extractor has:
    a. Tapered right-hand threads.
    b. Tapered left-hand threads.
13. A file with one row of teeth crossing the other is called:
    a. A crisscross file.
    b. A double-cut file.
    c. A Vixen-cut file.
14. A file with a single row of parallel teeth is called a _____.
15. When filing soft steel, which type file should be used first?
    a. A bastard file.
    b. A smooth-cut file.
    c. A second-cut file.
16. Solder is an alloy of:
    a. Lead and tin.
    b. Lead and zinc.
    c. Tin and zinc.
    d. Lead and cadmium.
17. Hacksaw blades are made of:
    a. High grade tool steel.
    b. Chilled cast iron.
    c. Carbaloy.
18. List the usual lengths of blades used in manually operated hacksaws.
19. Which saw blade is recommended to cut soft steel, cast iron and stock of heavy cross section?
    a. 16 tooth.
    b. 32 tooth.
    c. 24 tooth.
    d. 14 tooth.
20. What is the usual cutting lip angle on a twist drill?
21. A tap is used to cut external threads. True or False?
22. After cutting a piece of tubing, why should it be reamed?
    a. To increase its size.
    b. To restore it to its original size.
    c. To remove any burrs from the cut edge.
    d. To true the cut edge.
23. A box-type wrench is used to tighten nuts on brass fittings on tubing. True or False?
24. The SAE flare fitting cannot be used to carry gases. True or False?

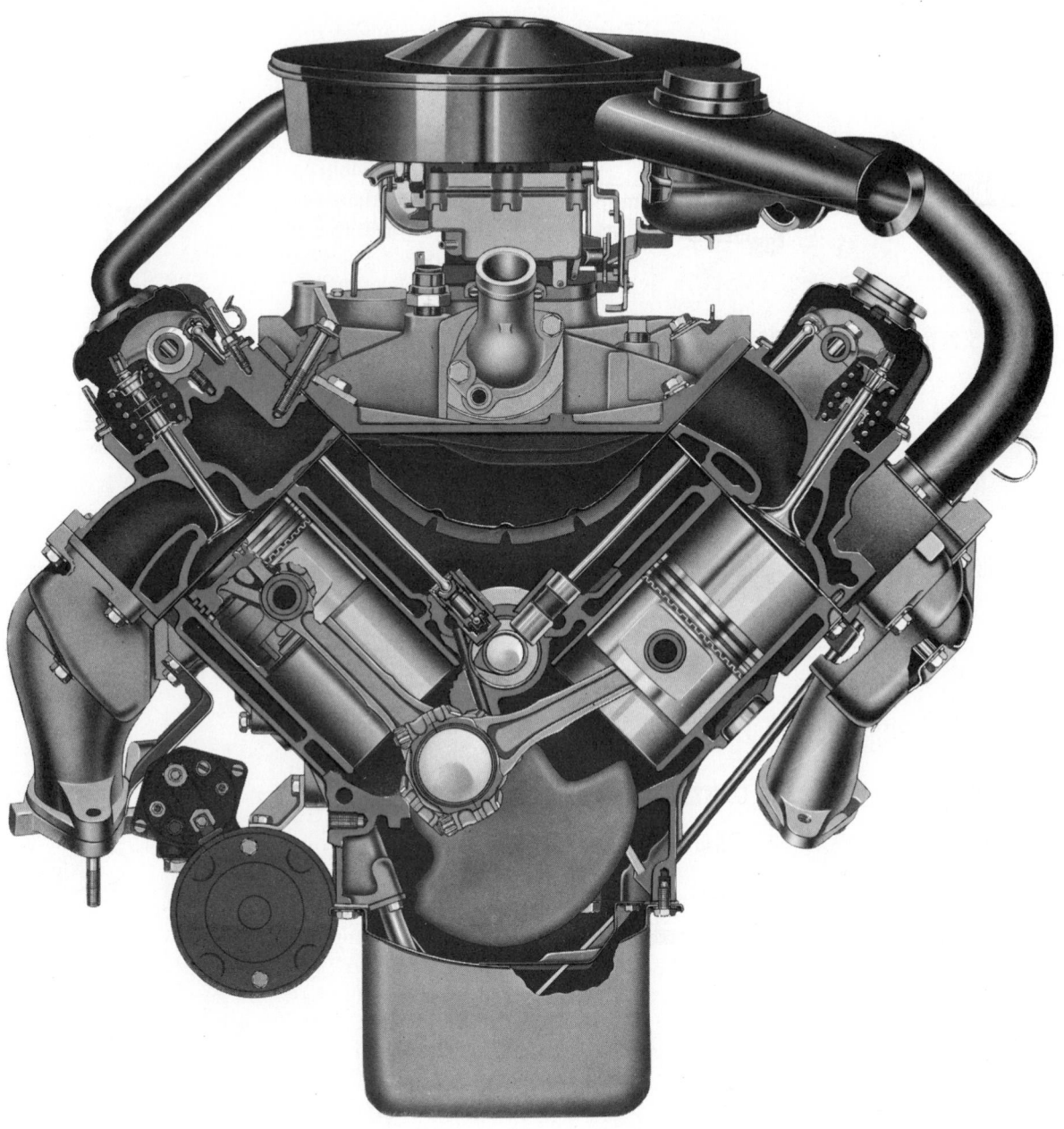

Typical Buick V-8 engine features cast iron crankshaft, five main bearings, tin-plated aluminum alloy pistons, low restriction dual intake manifold. Two barrel carburetor version produces 155 net brake horsepower.

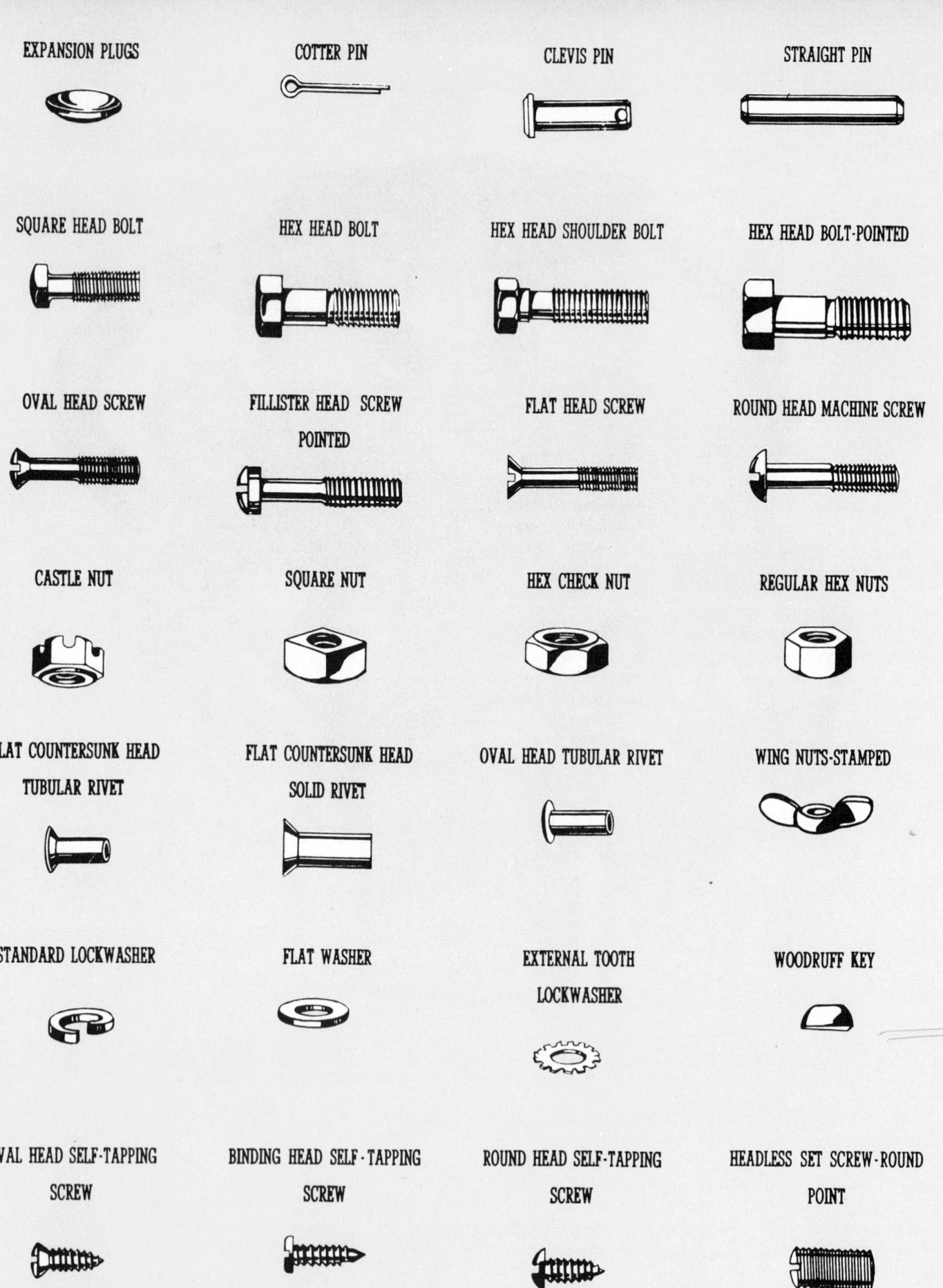

EXPANSION PLUGS

COTTER PIN

CLEVIS PIN

STRAIGHT PIN

SQUARE HEAD BOLT

HEX HEAD BOLT

HEX HEAD SHOULDER BOLT

HEX HEAD BOLT-POINTED

OVAL HEAD SCREW

FILLISTER HEAD SCREW POINTED

FLAT HEAD SCREW

ROUND HEAD MACHINE SCREW

CASTLE NUT

SQUARE NUT

HEX CHECK NUT

REGULAR HEX NUTS

FLAT COUNTERSUNK HEAD TUBULAR RIVET

FLAT COUNTERSUNK HEAD SOLID RIVET

OVAL HEAD TUBULAR RIVET

WING NUTS-STAMPED

STANDARD LOCKWASHER

FLAT WASHER

EXTERNAL TOOTH LOCKWASHER

WOODRUFF KEY

OVAL HEAD SELF-TAPPING SCREW

BINDING HEAD SELF-TAPPING SCREW

ROUND HEAD SELF-TAPPING SCREW

HEADLESS SET SCREW-ROUND POINT

Fig. 2-1. Illustrating fasteners used on automobiles.

FASTENING DEVICES

There are many different devices used for fastening one part to another in the modern automobile. These devices range from the familiar bolt and nut to spring clips and sheet metal screws, Fig. 2-1. You should know the difference between them, and be able to identify the various types of fastening devices.

There are several factors involved in describing bolts, cap screws, machine screws, sheet metal screws and other fasteners. Full information is needed when ordering replacement parts. You need to know the length, type of head, number of threads per unit length, whether measurements are in inches or millimeters, along with type of material and finish.

Basically, a bolt is an externally threaded fastener assembled with a nut when performing its intended service, Fig. 2-2.

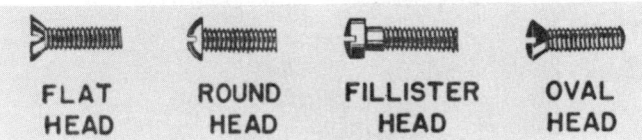

Fig. 2-3. Different types of machine screws.

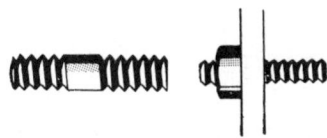

Fig. 2-4. Details of a stud, and an installed stud.

Fig. 2-2. Assorted bolts and nuts.

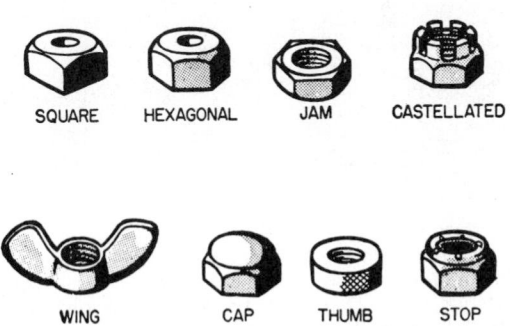

Fig. 2-5. Different types of nuts.

A screw is an externally threaded fastener that must be torqued into a tapped hole to perform its function.

A cap screw is usually torqued with a wrench, while a machine screw is torqued with a screwdriver. The machine screw is smaller in diameter than the cap screw.

The diameter of a cap screw usually is measured in fractions of an inch, while the diameter of a machine screw is given in nominal size by number (such as No. 8, No. 10, etc.) or by a fraction or decimal equivalent. Common types of machine screws are shown in Fig. 2-3.

A stud, Fig. 2-4, has both ends threaded. One end is screwed into a threaded hole of a part, such as a cylinder head. A part to be assembled is placed in position on the stud, then a nut is placed on the exposed end of the stud. When tightened, the parts are held together, Fig. 2-4.

Various types of nuts are illustrated in Fig. 2-5. Square nuts are used primarily in industries other than automotive. The automotive field uses nuts of the hexagonal type. The jam nut keeps an installed nut from coming loose when it is tightened on top of the original nut. The castellated nut is tightened on a bolt or threaded shaft. Then a cotter key is inserted through the castles of the nut and through a hole in the bolt.

A wing nut, Fig. 2-5, is installed finger tight. It is used in places where the nut must be removed frequently, and where tightness is not necessary. Cap nuts are decorative nuts used in such places where the conventional nut would be unsightly. Thumb nuts are used where tightness is not required. They are tightened by thumb and finger. Stop nuts are designed so that they will not come loose readily.

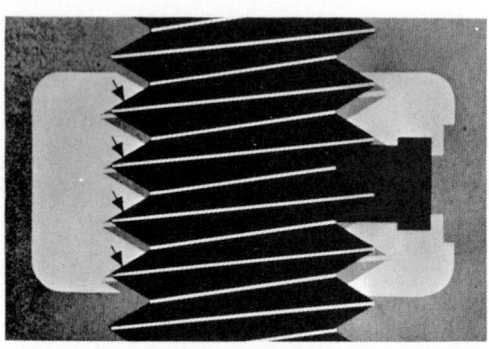

Fig. 2-6. This type of self-locking nut has a composition plug, which is forced against threads to prevent nut from turning.

SELF-LOCKING NUTS

There are several types of self-locking nuts. The type shown in Fig. 2-6 has a composition plug which, when forced against the threads, prevents the nut from turning.

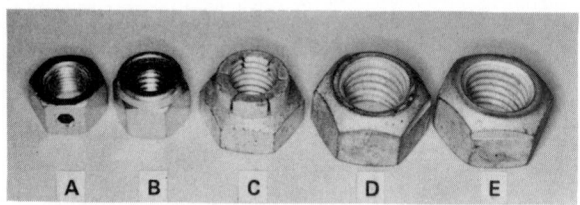

Fig. 2-7. Self-locking nuts: A—Uses an inserted fiber plug to prevent nut from turning. B—Has a fiber washer at outer end that provides locking feature. C—Is a castellated-type with tension provided by castells bent inward. D and E—Provide necessary tension by making outer ends of nuts slightly oval.

Other types of self-locking nuts are shown in Fig. 2-7. The nut at A is similar to the one shown in Fig. 2-6 with the fiber plug in the side. At B, the nut is provided with a fiber or plastic washer in the head of the nut. When this type of nut is threaded into position, threads are cut into the washer to resist loosening of the nut. Shown at C is a form of castellated nut that has been pressed together at the top. At D and E, the threads are slightly deformed at the upper end of the nut so that the hole is slightly oval.

Another type of self-locking nut, not illustrated, is provided with a cut in the side, close to the top. The edge of the nut at that point is pressed down, distorting the threads and providing the necessary locking action.

PALNUTS AND LOCK WASHERS

The palnut is a locking device, Fig. 2-8, stamped from thin sheet steel and designed to bind against the threads of the bolts when installed. The palnut is turned down to make firm

Fig. 2-8. Palnuts of thin gauge metal have inner prongs that engage screw threads to prevent nut from turning.

contact with the regular nut, then it is given an additional one-half turn. The regular nut must be torqued to a specified amount before the palnut is installed.

Lock washers are designed to prevent nuts from coming loose. These washers are provided in several different forms, Fig. 2-9. A conventional flat washer, also shown in Fig. 2-9, is used under the nut to prevent galling of the surface contacted.

FLAT WASHER   SPLIT LOCK WASHER   SHAKE PROOF WASHER

Fig. 2-9. A flat washer with two different types of lock washers.

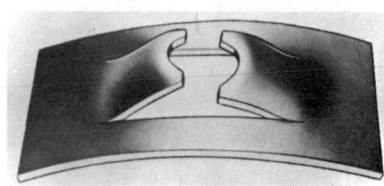

Fig. 2-10. Flat type speed nut, or self-locking nut, takes less time to apply and provides maximum holding power.

SPEED NUTS

In order to reduce the time of assembly of parts, the speed nut was developed. Speed nuts are used extensively in fastening sheet metal body parts and in restricted areas where it is difficult to tighten the nut. A speed nut, Fig. 2-10, is simply pressed onto the bolt or stud and takes the place of the

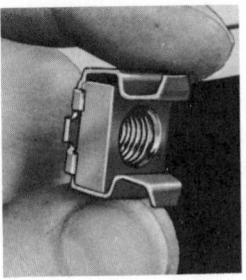

Fig. 2-11. Speed clip nuts are used in blind locations. Self-aligning, they are snapped in place on sheet metal.

conventional threaded nut and lock washer.

Speed clip nuts, Fig. 2-11, are snapped onto the sheet metal. They are self-aligning, primarily, they are used in "blind" locations, such as grilles.

SHEET METAL SCREWS

A special and popular type of fastening device is the familiar sheet metal screw, or self-tapping screw, Fig. 2-12. Because of its fluted or tapered point, it cuts its own threads as it is screwed into the sheet metal. Sheet metal screws are

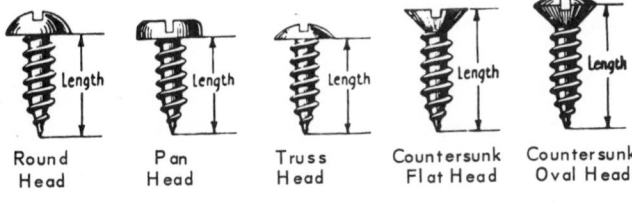

Round Head   Pan Head   Truss Head   Countersunk Flat Head   Countersunk Oval Head

Fig. 2-12. Types of sheet metal screws.

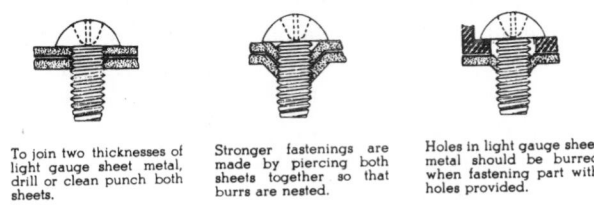

To join two thicknesses of light gauge sheet metal, drill or clean punch both sheets.

Stronger fastenings are made by piercing both sheets together so that burrs are nested.

Holes in light gauge sheet metal should be burred when fastening part with holes provided.

Fig. 2-13. Different methods of using sheet metal screws.

used extensively in holding two metal parts together, Fig. 2-13. First, a hole is punched or drilled into the sheet metal, then the screw is turned into the hole.

KEYS, PINS AND SPLINES

Keys, pins and splines are used to secure gears and pulleys to shafts so they will rotate as a unit. Splines permit the gear to move longitudinally along the shaft; keys and pins do not.

Keys used must frequently in automotive design include the

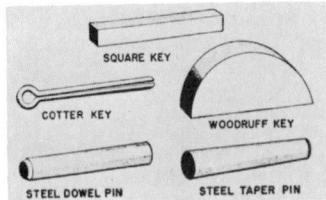

Fig. 2-14. Different types of keys and pins, all designed to prevent parts from working loose.

Woodruff key, square key and gib-head key, Fig. 2-14. The key fits into a slot known as a keyway, which is cut into both the shaft and the mating part, Fig. 2-15. By design, the key extends into both the shaft and the mating part so they will rotate as one.

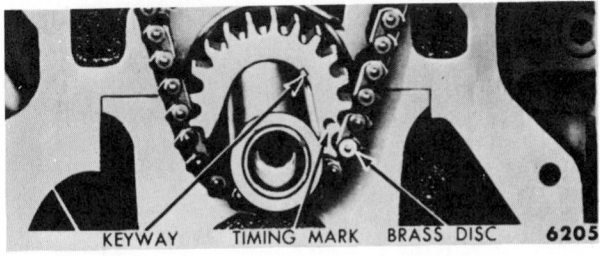

Fig. 2-15. Note keyway on timing gear.

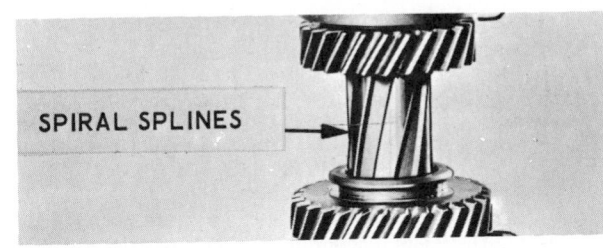

Fig. 2-16. Note spiral splines on this transmission main shaft.

The cotter key, also known as a cotter pin, Fig. 2-14, is used with a castellated nut to prevent it from becoming loose. The cotter key is inserted through the castle of the nut and a hole in the bolt. The ends are then bent back and surplus ends are cut off. In addition to preventing nuts from coming loose, cotter keys are used with clevis pins and in the ends of control rods of the type, for example, used from the accelerator pedal to the carburetor throttle lever.

Dowel pins and taper pins are used to secure one part to another, such as a shaft and a gear. A hole is drilled through the two parts, then the pin is driven into place.

Splines are external teeth cut on a shaft, Fig. 2-16, and corresponding internal teeth on the mating part. In effect, they are mating internal and external gears with a 1 to 1 ratio. Splines are used in the design of transmissions, propeller shafts

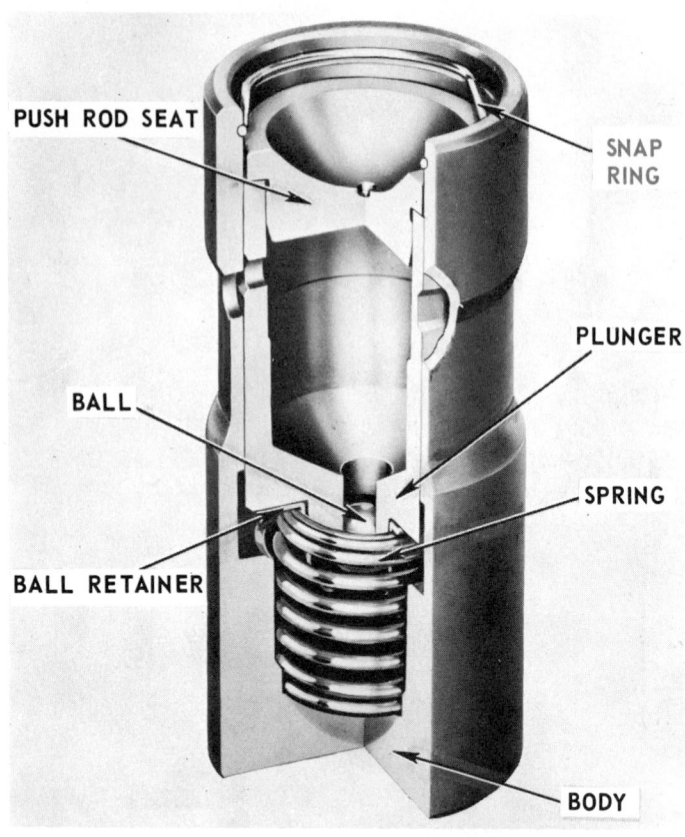

Fig. 2-17. A snap ring is used to hold an assembly together.

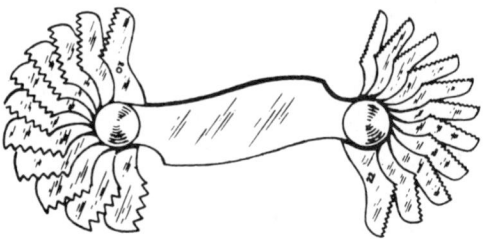

Fig. 2-18. Gauge used for measuring pitch of threads.

and rear axle assemblies. Splines can be cut parallel to the center line of the shaft so that the mating part would move in a straight line back and forth on the shafts. Or, they can be cut in a spiral form, and the mating part will rotate as it moves along the shaft.

SNAP RINGS

Snap rings, Fig. 2-17, are employed to prevent endwise movement of cylindrical parts and shafts. There are both internal and external snap rings. An internal type snap ring is used in a groove cut in a housing. An external snap ring is designed to fit in a groove cut on the outside of a cylindrical space, such as a shaft. They are used extensively in manual shift and automatic transmissions; also in hydraulic valve lifters.

SETSCREWS

Setscrews are designed to lock and position parts. For example, a pulley frequently is secured to a shaft by means of a setscrew. Setscrews are hardened and have different types of heads and ends; flat, pointed or rounded.

In order to prevent the pulley from slipping, the shaft is usually spotted or slightly counterbored to take the point of the setscrew.

THREADS

A thread is a helical or spiral ridge on a bolt or in a nut. Threads on bolts are known as external threads; those in a nut are called internal threads.

The Unified Thread Series is now the basic American standard for fastening types of screw threads. Most commonly used types are Unified Coarse (UNC) and Unified Fine (UNF). In addition, the metric thread is coming into greater use.

Details and terminology of threads were discussed in Chapter 1, and illustrated in Fig. 1-77. In Fig. 1-78, threads of various types and sizes are tabulated. Note that sizes up to 1/4 in. are designated by number; 1/4 in. and larger are given in fractions of an inch.

In order to measure the pitch of a thread, a special gauge, Fig. 2-18, should be used.

REPAIRING THREADS

When internal or external threads are stripped, often they can be repaired by means of the correct size tap or die. Or, in cases of minor damage, a tool known as a thread chaser can be used.

If the threads are severely damaged, other repair techniques can be used. One method is to drill out the thread and tap the hole to the next larger size.

However, in some cases, this presents a problem. If a cylinder head bolt hole in the block was stripped, it would necessitate drilling out the head to accommodate the larger size stud. This could result in breaking through, into the water jacket.

An alternative method provides a patented coil of wire. First, the stripped threads are drilled out of the hole. Next, it is tapped with a special tap. Then, the coil is inserted, Fig. 2-19, restoring the threaded hole to its original condition.

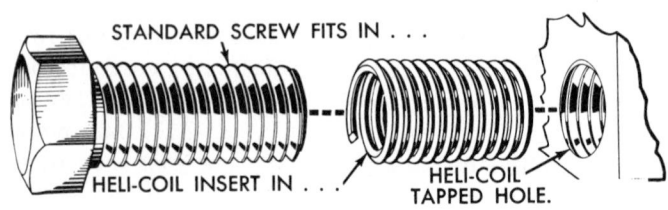

Fig. 2-19. Details of coil-of-wire thread repair device, which is a popular method of repairing damaged screw threads.

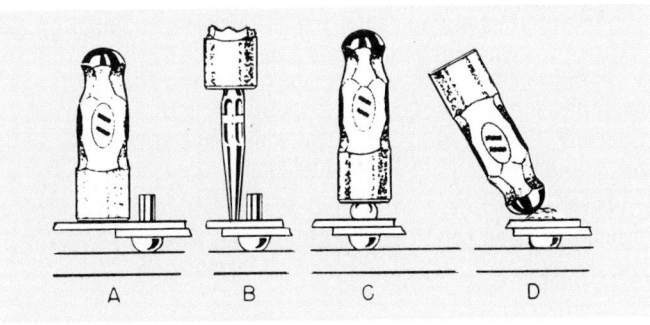

Fig. 2-20. If a rivet set is not available: A and B—Drive two parts down over stem of rivet to its head. C and D—Upset stem of rivet to form another head.

RIVETS

A rivet is a metal pin with a head at one end. It is designed to fasten two parts together. After passing the rivet through the holes in the parts to be joined, the small end of the rivet is formed into a head by means of a rivet set, or by using the peen end of a ball peen hammer, Fig. 2-20.

In addition to riveting pieces of metal together, rivets are used extensively for fastening brake lining to brake shoes.

When a rivet set is available, steps A, B and C, Fig. 2-21 are followed.

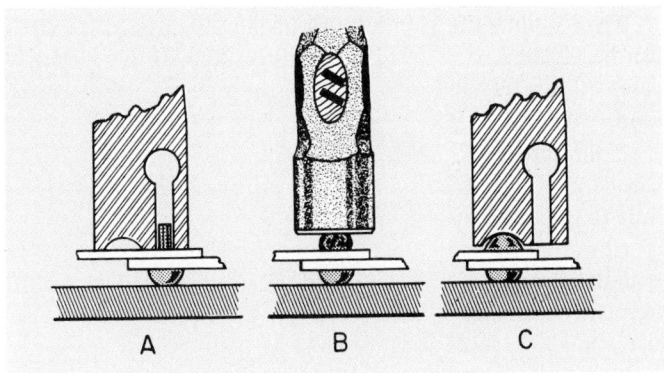

Fig. 2-21. Procedure when using a rivet set.

BLIND RIVETER

A blind riveter is a tool designed to install special rivets when only one side of the parts to be riveted can be reached. These tools are also known as "pop" riveters. They are available in hand-operated types, Fig. 2-22, and power-operated types. Rivets used in a hand-operated blind riveter are shown in Fig. 2-23.

To install a blind rivet, drill a hole through the parts to be joined. Place the long stem of the rivet in the head of the tool, insert the short end in the hole in the parts. Squeeze the handle repeatedly to set the rivet and snap off its end.

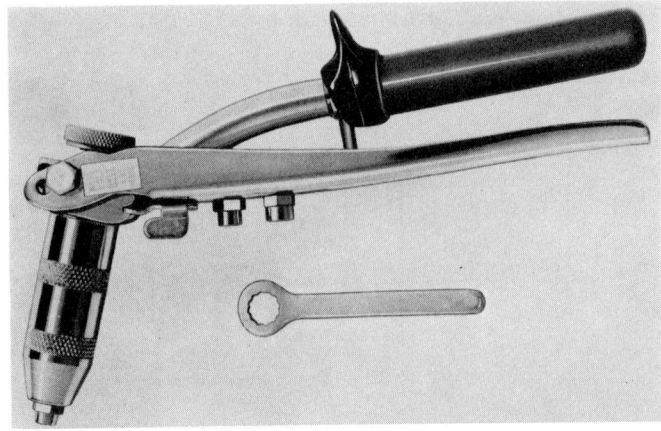

Fig. 2-22. One type of tool designed to install blind rivets.

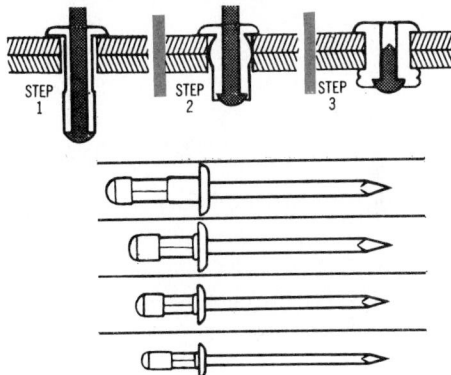

Fig. 2-23. Above. Progressive steps in installation of a blind rivet. Below. Assorted blind rivets.

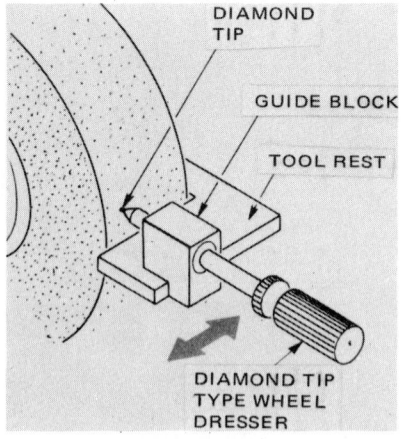

Fig. 2-24. A diamond tip tool is one accepted method of dressing and truing an abrasive wheel.

REPLACING BOLTS AND NUTS

Frequently, it is necessary to replace bolts and nuts when servicing an automobile. When replacing them, be sure the new bolt and nut are equal in strength to the old ones which are being replaced.

The accompanying chart, Fig. 2-25 shows markings on bolt heads and nuts which indicate strength.

S.A.E. GRADE	MARKINGS		STRENGTH IN P.S.I.	
1 or 2			60,000	STANDARD STRENGTH ↑
5			120,000	
7			133,000	↓
8			150,000	HIGH STRENGTH

Fig. 2-25. Markings on bolt heads and nuts serve as a strength code. Replacement bolts and nuts must equal strength of original fasteners.

REVIEW QUESTIONS – FASTENING DEVICES

1. What is the major difference between a machine screw and a bolt?
2. A stud has threads on one end. True or False?
3. The largest diameter on a screw is known as:
   a. Pitch diameter.
   b. Major diameter.
   c. Minor diameter.
4. Most bolts have what shape head?
   a. Square head.
   b. Octagonal head.
   c. Hexagonal head.
   d. Round head.
5. What type of nut is used with a cotter key?
6. Name two methods used to keep nuts from working loose on a bolt.
7. What is the purpose of a spline?
8. A _____ is screwed down on another nut to keep it from getting loose.
9. When using a sheet metal screw, it is first necessary to tap the hole. True or False?

DODGE CHARGER 3, sleek, experimental two-seater, has no doors or windows that open. Jet-aircraft-type canopy swings open, steering wheel-instrument cluster pod moves up and out of way, and seats elevate to admit driver and passenger. Outside air enters driver-passenger area through scoops at base of windshield, circulates in compartment and exhausts through rear bulkhead port.

METRIC CONVERSION TABLES

METRIC TO ENGLISH

Millimetres	X	.0394	=	Inches
Millimetres	=	25.400	X	Inches
Centimetres	X	.394	=	Inches
Centimetres	=	2.54	X	Inches
Metres	X	3.2809	=	Feet
Metres	=	.3048	X	Feet
Kilometres	X	.6214	=	Miles
Kilometres	=	1.6093	X	Miles
Square centimetres	X	.1550	=	Square inches
Square centimetres	=	6.4515	X	Square inches
Square metres	X	10.7641	=	Square feet
Square metres	=	.0929	X	Square feet
Square kilometres	X	247.1098	=	Acres
Square kilometres	=	.0041	X	Acres
Hectares	X	2.471	=	Acres
Hectares	=	.4047	X	Acres
Cubic centimetres	X	.0610	=	Cubic inches
Cubic centimetres	=	16.3866	X	Cubic inches
Cubic metres	X	35.3156	=	Cubic feet
Cubic metres	=	.0283	X	Cubic feet
Cubic metres	X	1.308	=	Cubic yards
Cubic metres	=	.765	X	Cubic yards
Litres	X	61.023	=	Cubic inches
Litres	=	.0164	X	Cubic inches
Litres	X	.2642	=	U. S. Gallons
Litres	=	3.7854	X	U. S. Gallons
Grams	X	15.4324	=	Grains
Grams	=	.0648	X	Grains
Grams	X	.0353	=	Ounces, avoirdupois
Grams	=	28.3495	X	Ounces, avoirdupois
Kilograms	X	2.2046	=	Pounds
Kilograms	=	.4536	X	Pounds
Kilopascals	X	.145	=	Pounds per square inch
Kilopascals	=	6.895	X	Pounds per square inch
Newton-metres	X	.7376	=	Pound feet
Newton-metres	=	1.3558	X	Pound feet
Metric tons (1 000 kilograms)	X	1.1023	=	Tons (2000 pounds)
Metric tons	=	.9072	X	Tons (2000 pounds)
Kilowatts	X	1.3405	=	Horsepower
Kilowatts	=	.746	X	Horsepower
Calories	X	3.9683	=	Btu units
Calories	=	.2520	X	Btu units

MILLIMETRES TO INCHES

mm	in.	mm	in.	mm	in.	mm	in.
.01	.0003937	.11	.00433	.21	.00827	.31	.01221
.02	.00079	.12	.00472	.22	.00866	.32	.01259
.03	.00118	.13	.00512	.23	.00905	.33	.01299
.04	.00157	.14	.00551	.24	.00945	.34	.01338
.05	.00197	.15	.00591	.25	.00984	.35	.01378
.06	.00236	.16	.00630	.26	.01024	.40	.01575
.07	.00276	.17	.00669	.27	.01063	.45	.01772
.08	.00315	.18	.00708	.28	.01102	.50	.01968
.09	.00354	.19	.00748	.29	.01141	1.00	.03937
.10	.00394	.20	.00787	.30	.01181		

METRIC CONVERSION TABLES

CUBIC INCHES TO CUBIC CENTIMETRES

cu. in.	cm^3	cu. in.	cm^3	cu. in.	cm^3
1	16.39	105	1720.95	305	4998.95
2	32.78	110	1802.80	310	5080.90
3	49.17	115	1884.85	315	5162.85
4	65.56	120	1966.80	320	5244.80
5	81.95	125	2049.75	325	5327.75
6	98.34	130	2130.70	330	5408.70
7	114.73	135	2212.65	335	5490.65
8	131.12	140	2294.60	340	5572.60
9	147.51	145	2377.50	345	5655.50
10	165.90	150	2458.50	350	5736.50
11	180.29	155	2540.45	355	5818.45
12	196.68	160	2622.40	360	5900.40
13	213.07	165	2704.35	365	5982.35
14	229.46	170	2786.30	370	6064.30
15	245.85	175	2868.25	375	6146.25
16	262,24	180	2950.20	380	6228.20
17	278.63	185	3032.15	385	6310.15
18	295.22	190	3114.10	390	6392.10
19	311.41	195	3196.05	395	6474.05
20	327.80	200	3278.00	400	6556.00
21	344.19	205	3359.95	405	6637.95
22	360.58	210	3441.90	410	6719.90
23	376.97	215	3523.85	415	6801.85
24	393.36	220	3605.80	420	6883.80
25	409.75	225	3688.75	425	6966.75
30	491.70	230	3769.70	430	7037.70
35	573.65	235	3851.65	435	7129.65
40	655.60	240	3933.60	440	7211.60
45	738.55	245	4016.50	445	7294.50
50	819.50	250	4097.50	450	7375.80
55	903.35	255	4179.45	455	7457.45
60	983.40	260	4261.40	460	7539.40
65	1065.35	265	4343.35	465	7621.35
70	1147.30	270	4425.30	470	7703.30
75	1229.25	275	4507.25	475	7785.25
80	1311.20	280	4589.20	480	7867.20
85	1393.15	285	4671.15	485	7949.15
90	1475.10	290	4753.10	490	8031.10
95	1557.05	295	4835.05	495	8113.05
100	1639.00	300	4917.00	500	8195.00

CUBIC INCHES TO LITRES

cu. in.	Litres	cu. in.	Litres	cu. in.	Litres	cu. in.	Litres
1.0	.0164	10.0	.1639	60.0	.9834	150.0	2.4585
2.0	.0328	20.0	.3278	65.0	1.0653	175.0	2.8682
3.0	.0492	25.0	.4097	70.0	1.1473	200.0	3.2780
4.0	.0655	30.0	.4917	75.0	1.2292	250.0	4.0975
5.0	.0819	35.0	.5736	80.0	1.3112	300.0	4.9170
6.0	.0983	40.0	.6556	85.0	1.3931	350.0	5.7365
7.0	.1147	45.0	.7375	90.0	1.4751	400.0	6.5560
8.0	.1311	50.0	.8195	100.0	1.6390	450.0	7.3755
9.0	.1475	55.0	.9014	125.0	2.0487	500.0	8.1950

MEASURING INSTRUMENTS

A micrometer is an instrument designed for linear measurement with accuracy of .001 in. or better. Micrometers are available to measure in either the metric or English system.

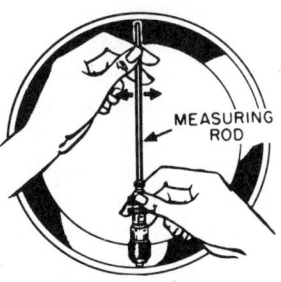

Fig. 3-1. Using an inside micrometer to measure a diameter. Tool can be extended by means of the measuring rod.

The inside micrometer, Fig. 3-1, is used for measuring the distance between two parallel surfaces, and for measuring the inside diameter of cylinders.

The outside micrometer, Fig. 3-2, is designed to measure the outside diameter of cylindrical forms and the thickness of materials. Its spindle is attached to the thimble on the inside, at the point of adjustment. Often, a ratchet stop is provided. The part of the spindle concealed within the sleeve and thimble is threaded to fit a nut in the frame. The frame is stationary.

When the micrometer thimble is revolved by the thumb and finger, the spindle revolves with it and moves through the nut in the frame, moving toward or away from the anvil. The distance or measurement, of the opening between the anvil and the spindle is indicated by the line and figures on the sleeve and the thimble, Fig. 3-3.

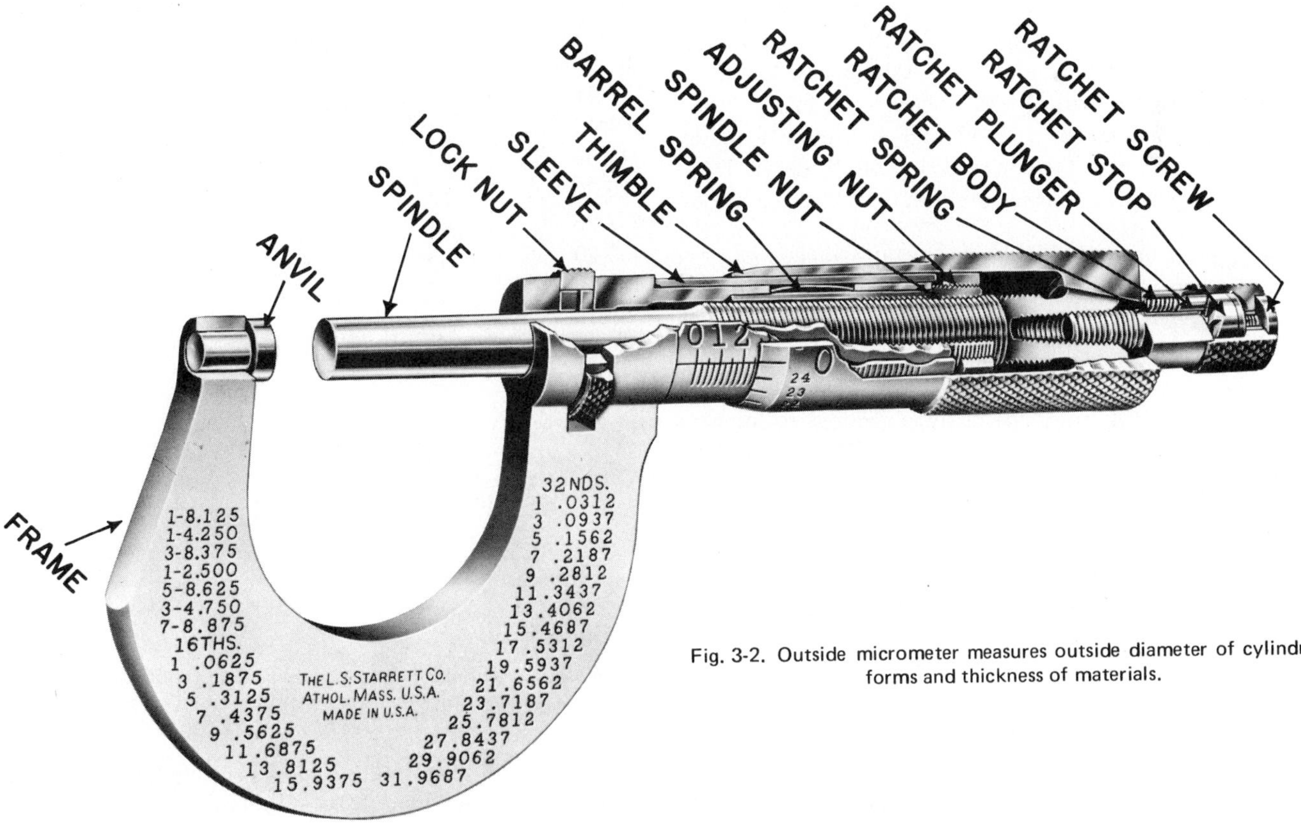

FRAME

ANVIL

SPINDLE

LOCK NUT

SLEEVE

THIMBLE

BARREL SPRING

SPINDLE NUT

ADJUSTING NUT

RATCHET SPRING

RATCHET BODY

RATCHET PLUNGER

RATCHET STOP

RATCHET SCREW

| 1-8.125 |
| 1-4.250 |
| 3-8.375 |
| 1-2.500 |
| 5-8.625 |
| 3-4.750 |
| 7-8.875 |
| 16THS. |
| 1 .0625 |
| 3 .1875 |
| 5 .3125 |
| 7 .4375 |
| 9 .5625 |
| 11 .6875 |
| 13 .8125 |
| 15 .9375 |

32NDS.
1 .0312
3 .0937
5 .1562
7 .2187
9 .2812
11 .3437
13 .4062
15 .4687
17 .5312
19 .5937
21 .6562
23 .7187
25 .7812
27 .8437
29 .9062
31 .9687

THE L. S. STARRETT CO.
ATHOL. MASS. U.S.A.
MADE IN U.S.A.

Fig. 3-2. Outside micrometer measures outside diameter of cylindrical forms and thickness of materials.

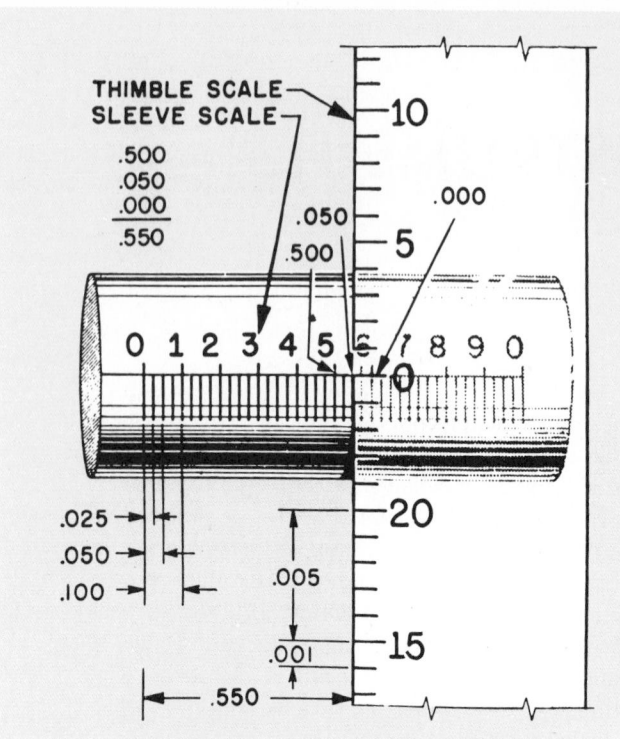

Fig. 3-3. Enlarged micrometer scales. Reading is .550 in.

To overcome this problem of overtightening, some micrometers are provided with a ratchet drive on the thimble. This insures that regardless who uses the micrometer, the same pressure will be exerted on the thimble.

Inside micrometers, Fig. 3-1, are read in the same manner described for outside micrometers. However, the actual use of the inside micrometer is more difficult. To make a measurement with an inside micrometer, the instrument must be held so that it is perpendicular to the two surfaces.

For automotive work, micrometers reading up to 5 in. are needed. Most micrometers have a range of reading of only 1 in. However, other types are available which have interchangeable anvils so that one instrument will have a wide range of reading.

Special micrometers are available for use in special measuring jobs. One is designed for measuring the diameters of crankshaft main bearing journals (after removing bearing cap, but without removing crankshaft).

Another type of micrometer is designed to measure the thickness of engine bearing shells to determine the extent of wear. Its anvil is rounded, so that point contact is made on the inner surface of the bearing while the spindle contacts the outer surface.

When the accuracy of a micrometer is not needed, a conventional caliper, Fig. 3-5, is used. Calipers of both inside and outside types are available. With care, accurate measurements to .01 in. can be attained.

READING A MICROMETER

The pitch of the screw threads on the concealed part of the micrometer spindle is 40 to an inch. Therefore, one complete revolution of the spindle moves it longitudinally 1/40th or .025 in. The sleeve is marked with 40 lines to the inch.

When the micrometer is closed, the bevelled end of the thimble coincides with the line marked 0 on the sleeve. The 0 mark on the thimble also coincides with the horizontal line on the sleeve.

Opening the micrometer by revolving the thimble one full revolution will make the 0 line of the thimble coincide with the horizontal line of the sleeve. The distance between the anvil and spindle is now .025 in.

The bevelled edge of the thimble is marked in 25 divisions. Rotating the thimble from one of these divisions to the next moves the spindle longitudinally 1/25th of .025 in., or .001 in.

To read the micrometer, multiply the number of vertical divisions visual on the sleeve by 25. Then add the number of divisions on the bevel of the thimble from 0 to the line which coincides with the horizontal line on the sleeve. The closeup view of a micrometer's sleeve and thimble, Fig. 3-3, shows a reading of .550 in.

Fig. 3-4 shows the correct method of holding a micrometer. The reading on the micrometer in this illustration is .260 in.

When using a micrometer, take care not to turn the thimble too tight. This will distort the frame and result in inaccuracy of the readings and wear of the screw threads. Only gentle pressure should be used.

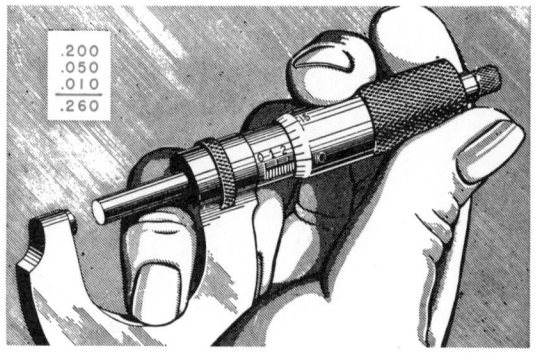

Fig. 3-4. Correct method of holding a micrometer.

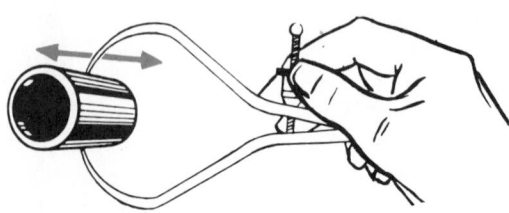

Fig. 3-5. Using a pair of outside calipers for measuring a diameter.

Telescoping gauges, Fig. 3-6, are available for measuring the diameter of small holes. After adjusting the gauge in the hole so that it fits snugly, the gauge is removed and measured with

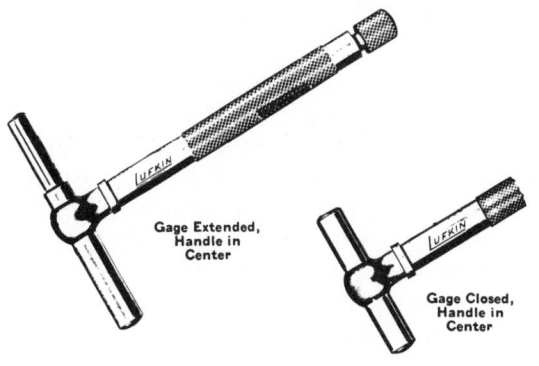

Fig. 3-6. A telescoping gauge is used to measure small internal diameters or width of slots.

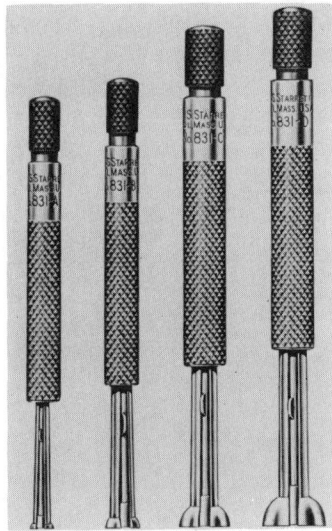

Fig. 3-7. Small hole gauges are adjusted to size by means of knurled knob at top of gauge. Setting of gauge is measured by a conventional outside micrometer.

a conventional micrometer.

The small hole gauge shown in Fig. 3-7 is used in the automotive machine shop for measuring the diameter of valve guide bores. The small hole gauge is inserted in the bore and expanded until it fills the diameter. Then it is withdrawn, and its width is measured with a conventional micrometer.

Metric micrometers are used in the same manner as the English type previously described, except that graduations are in metric units. Readings are obtained as follows:

Since the pitch of the spindle screw in metric micrometers is 0.5 millimeters (mm), one complete revolution of the thimble advances the spindle toward or away from the anvil exactly 0.5 mm.

The longitudinal line on the sleeve is graduated from 0 to 25 mm, and each millimeter is subdivided in 0.5 mm. Therefore, it requires two revolutions of the thimble to advance the spindle a distance equal to 1 mm.

The beveled edge of the thimble is graduated in 50 divisions, every fifth line being numbered from 0 to 50. Since

a complete revolution of the thimble advances the spindle 0.5 mm, each graduation on the thimble is equal to 1/50 of 0.5 mm or 0.01 mm. Two graduations equal 0.02 mm, etc.

To read a metric micrometer, add the total reading in millimeters visible on the sleeve to the reading in hundredths of a millimeter indicated by the graduation on the thimble which coincides with the longitudinal line on the sleeve.

Example: Refer to Fig. 3-8:

The "5" mm graduation is visible, representing . . . . 5 mm
There is one additional 0.5 mm line visible, representing . . . . 0.5 mm
Line "28" on the thimble coincides with the longitudinal line on the sleeve, each line representing .01 mm . . . . . .28 x .01 mm = 0.28 mm
The metric micrometer reading is . . . . 5.78 mm

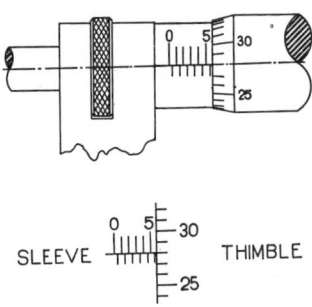

Fig. 3-8. Metric micrometer scales. Reading is 5.78 millimeters. (L. S. Starrett Co.)

VERNIER CALIPER

The Vernier caliper is a measuring device capable of measuring to within one-thousandths of an inch (.001). It can measure both internal and external diameters, and some are provided with both metric and English scales. Fig. 3-9 shows a Vernier caliper being used to measure the inside diameter of tubing.

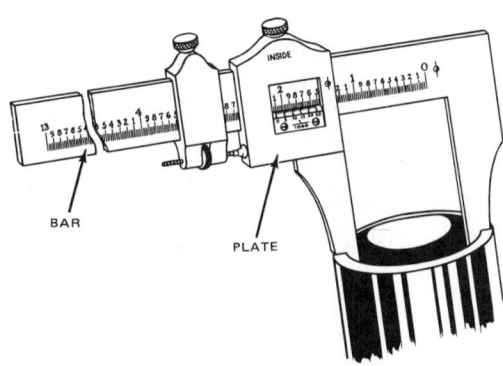

Fig. 3-9. A Vernier caliper can be used to measure inside diameter of tubing.

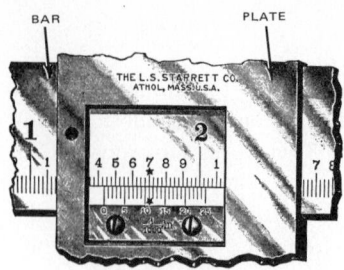

Fig. 3-10. Scale on bar is graduated in .025 in. divisions; scale on bar is in .001 in. increments. Reading is 1.436 in.

The main bar of a Vernier caliper is graduated in fortieths, or .025 in. Every fourth division, which represents one-tenth of an inch, is numbered, Fig. 3-10. The Vernier plate has a space divided into twenty-five divisions, numbered 0, 5, 10, 15, 20 and 25. These twenty-five divisions on the Vernier occupy the same space as the twenty-four divisions on the bar. The difference between the width of one of the twenty-five spaces on the Vernier and one of the twenty-four spaces on the bar is 1/25 of 1/40 or 1/1000 of an inch.

If the caliper is set so that 0 line on Vernier coincides with 0 line on bar, the line to the right of 0 on Vernier will differ from line to the right of 0 on bar by .001 in.; the second line by .002 in., etc. The difference will continue to increase .001 in. for each division until line 25 on Vernier coincides with line 24 on bar.

To read the tool, note how many inches, tenths (.100) and fortieths (.025) the 0 mark on the Vernier is from the 0 mark on the bar. Then note the number of divisions on the Vernier from the 0 to a line which exactly coincides with a line on the bar. For example: In Fig. 3-10, the Vernier has moved to the right one and four-tenths and one-fortieth inches (1.425), as shown on the bar. Also, the eleventh line on the Vernier coincides with a line indicated by the star on the bar. Eleven-thousandths of an inch are added to the reading on the bar, and the total reading is 1.436 in.

DIAL GAUGES

The amount of out-of-round and taper in an engine cylinder can be measured by a dial gauge, Fig. 3-11. The gauge is inserted in the cylinder bore and moved up and down. Movement of the indicating needle of the gauge will show the taper, or variation in measurement. The amount of out-of-round is measured by rotating the gauge in the cylinder. Dial gauges are calibrated to read in .001 in.

By adding a special fixture, dial gauges are used extensively for measuring the backlash of gears. This is particularly important to the adjustment of the rear axle pinion and ring gear.

THICKNESS GAUGE

The thickness gauge, or feeler gauge, is used for measuring the distance between two surfaces that are only a few thousandths of an inch apart. A feeler gauge, Fig. 3-12,

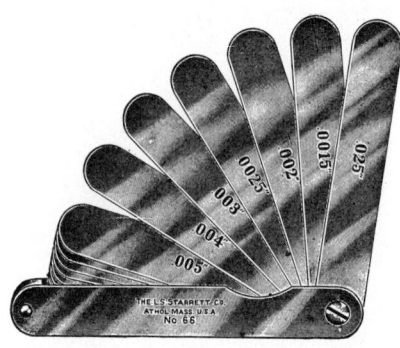

Fig. 3-12. Typical feeler gauge used for measuring width of small gaps and spaces.

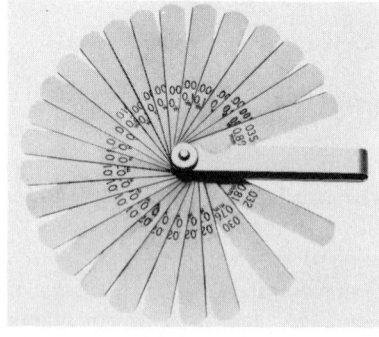

Fig. 3-13. Feeler gauge has thickness of blades marked in both English decimals and metric millimeters. (Auto-Test, Inc.)

consists of an assortment of steel strips of graduated thickness. Each blade of the gauge is marked with its thickness in thousandths of an inch, and/or in millimeters.

Because of the increasing number of imported cars in the U.S. with service specifications given in millimeters, thickness gauges are now available with each blade marked in fractions of an inch and fractions of a millimeter, Fig. 3-13.

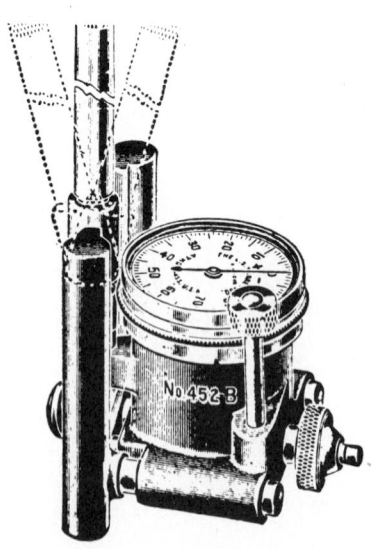

Fig. 3-11. Dial gauges are used extensively to measure diameter and wear of engine cylinders.

Measuring Instruments

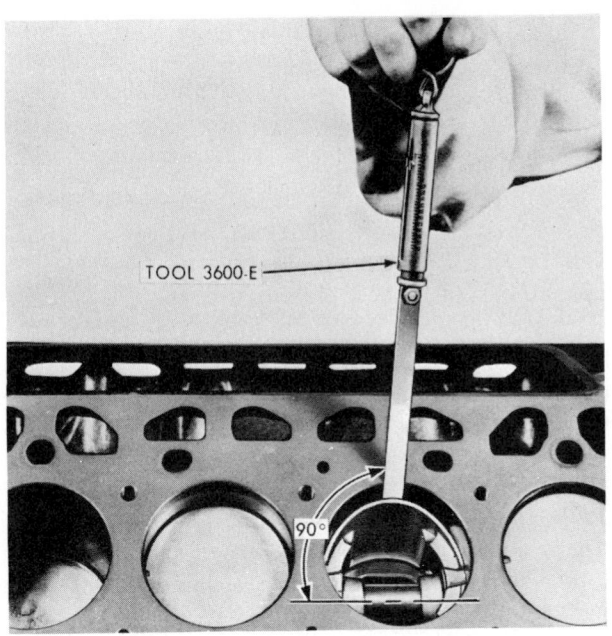

To use a feeler gauge, insert a blade in the space to be measured. If the gauge blade is a snug fit, that space is equal to the blade thickness in thousandths of an inch. Feeler gauges are used extensively for measuring valve clearance, ignition breaker point spacing and the gap of spark plugs.

When a feeler gauge is used to measure the clearance between a piston and cylinder wall, the force required to withdraw it is measured by a spring balance, Fig. 3-14.

In addition to flat blade feeler gauges, thickness gauges having different diameter wire "feelers" are available, Fig. 3-15. Wire gauges are recommended for measuring plug gaps.

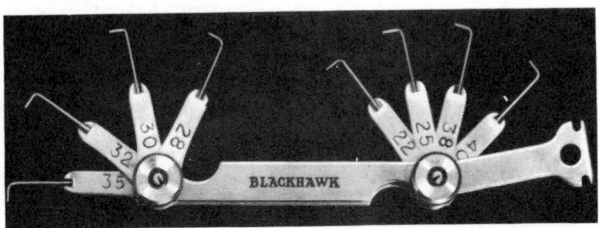

Fig. 3-14. Using a feeler gauge and a spring balance to check clearance between a piston and cylinder wall.

Fig. 3-15. Wire-type thickness gauge is used to measure spark plug gaps. Note bending lever at right.

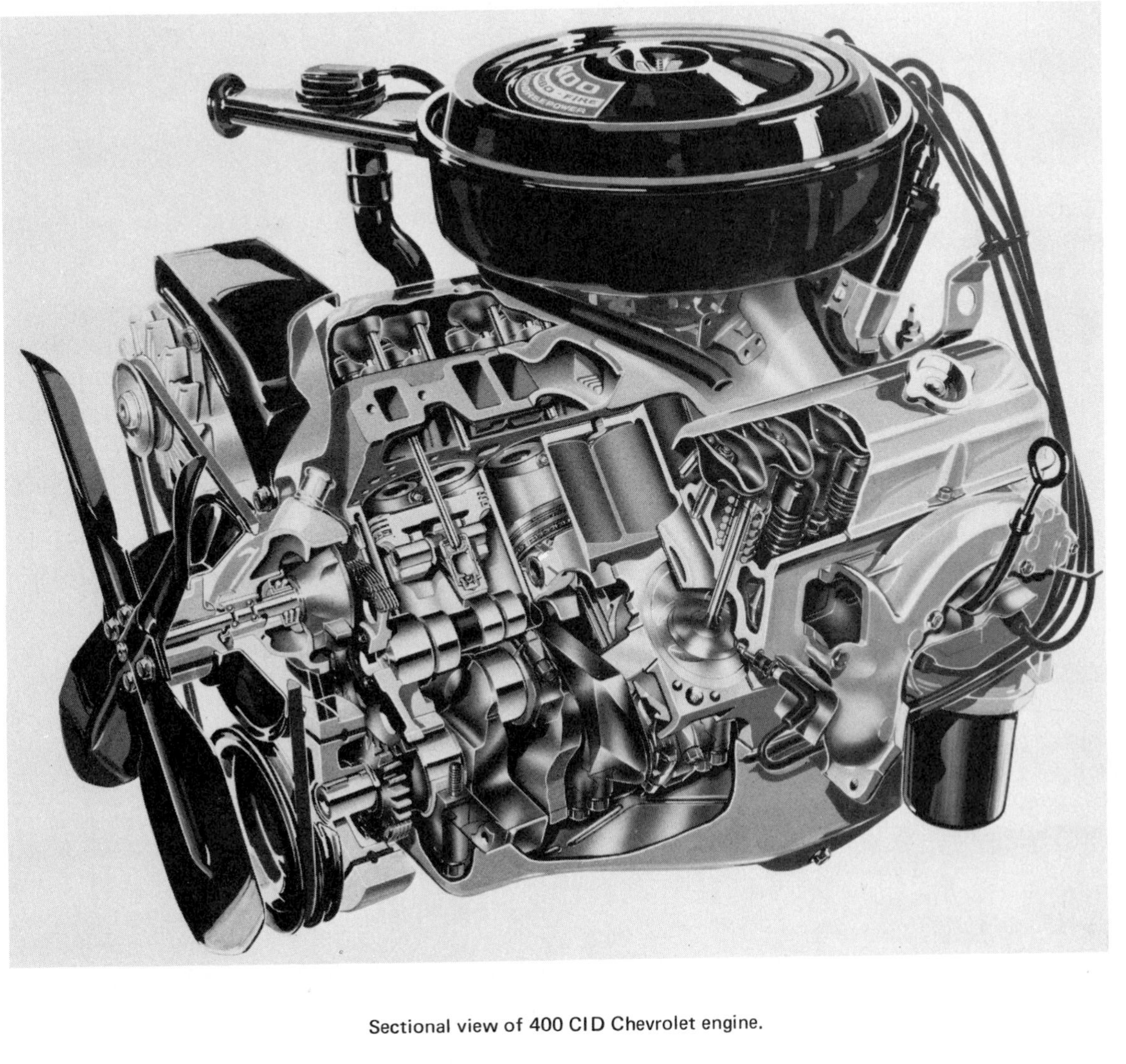

Sectional view of 400 CID Chevrolet engine.

FILLET OR RADIUS GAUGE

When reconditioning crankshafts, it is essential that the correct fillet or radius be ground at the ends of the crankshaft and connecting rod journals. If these fillets are incorrect, bearing life will be reduced and oil consumption increased. Fig. 3-16 shows one of these gauges being used to measure both convex and concave radii.

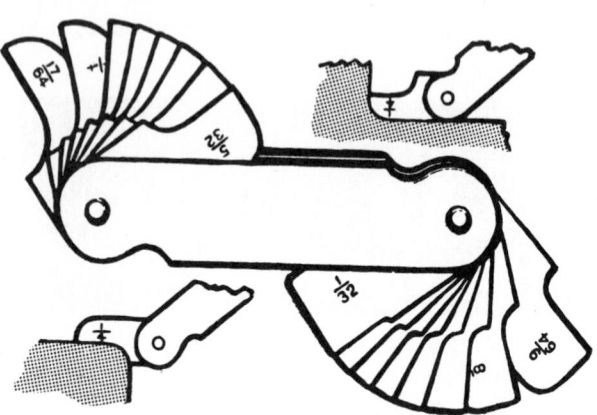

Fig. 3-16. Special dual purpose gauge is shown checking a radius, lower left, and a fillet, upper right.

STRAIGHTEDGE

A straightedge is used frequently to check whether or not a surface is true. Fig. 3-17 illustrates how to check a cylinder head for warpage with a straightedge. The amount of warpage is measured by means of a feeler gauge.

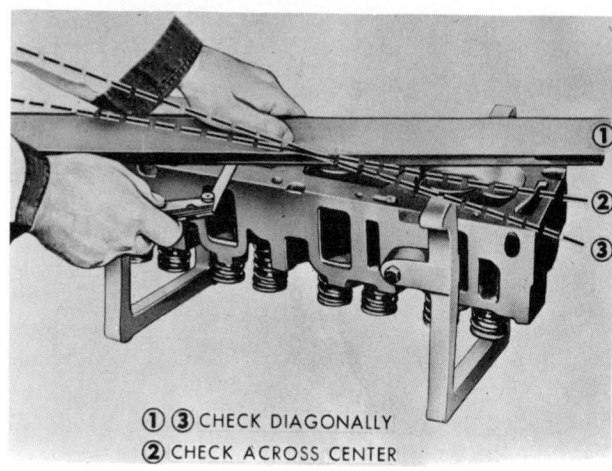

① ③ CHECK DIAGONALLY
② CHECK ACROSS CENTER

Fig. 3-17. Using a straightedge and feeler gauge to measure warpage of a cylinder head.

REVIEW QUESTIONS – MEASURING INSTRUMENTS

1. For what purpose are inside micrometers frequently used in automotive service work?
2. When the thimble of a micrometer is turned one division as indicated by the lines on the beveled edge of the thimble, how far has the spindle moved?
   a. .025 in.   c. .001 in.
   b. .0025 in.   d. .005 in.
3. When the thimble of a metric micrometer is turned one division as indicated by the lines on the beveled edge of the thimble, how far has the spindle moved?
   a. 5.0 mm   c. .05 mm   e. .1 mm
   b. .5 mm   d. .25 mm   f. .01 mm

4. For what two purposes is a dial gauge frequently used in automotive service work?
5. A thickness gauge is used:
   a. To measure the thickness of sheet metal.
   b. To measure the diameter of car engine cylinders.
   c. To measure the space between two surfaces.
6. For what purpose is a straightedge frequently used in an auto shop?
7. What is the small hole gauge used for in the automotive machine shop?
8. A Vernier caliper can measure inside diameters only. True or False?

ENGINE
FUNDAMENTALS

Automobiles have been operated successfully by electric motors, steam engines and internal combustion engines. The internal combustion engine burns fuel within the cylinders, and converts the expanding force of the combustion or "explosion" into rotary mechanical force used to propel the vehicle.

There are several types of internal combustion engines: two and four cycle reciprocating piston engines, gas turbines, free piston and rotary combustion engines. However, the four cycle and, to a lesser degree, the two cycle reciprocating engines have been refined to such a degree that they have almost complete dominance of the automotive field. Engines of other types are described in the chapter on OTHER ENGINES.

ENGINE FUELS

Internal combustion engines can be made to operate on almost anything that can be converted into a gas that will burn: wood, coal, alcohol, vegetable oils, mineral oils, etc. However, because of convenience, a wide variety of petroleum products are used as fuel: gasoline, kerosene, fuel oil, liquefied petroleum gas (LP-Gas), etc. When kerosene, fuel oil, or

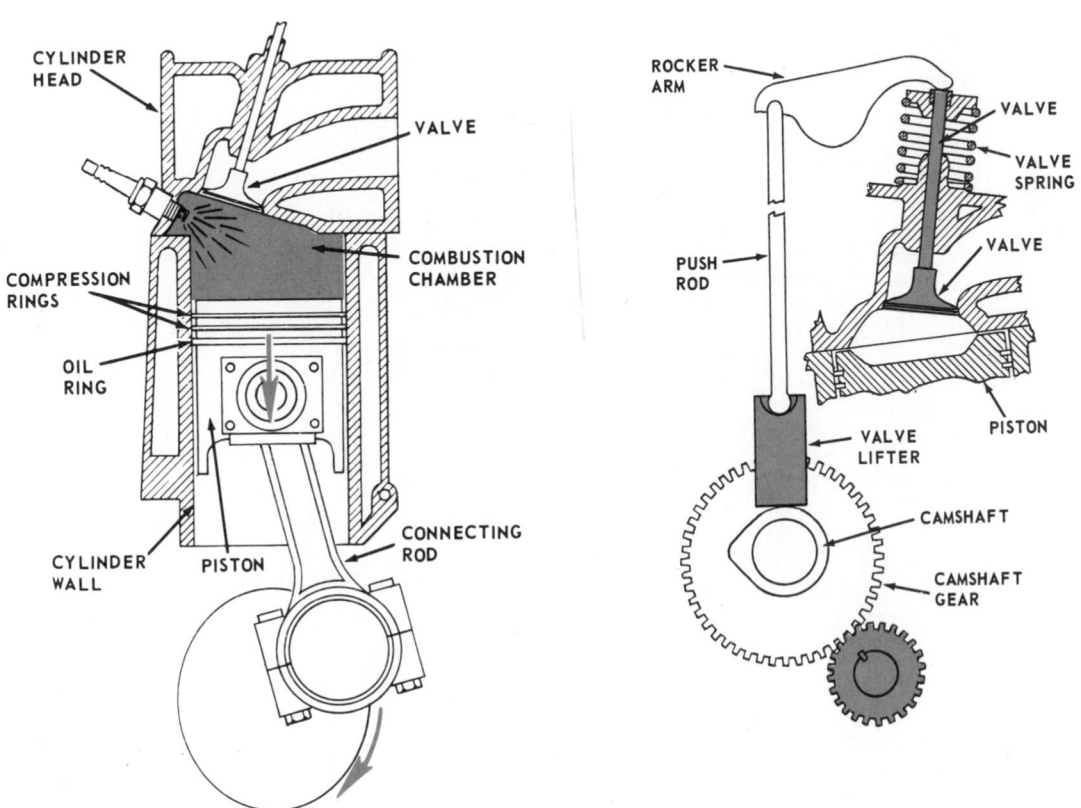

Fig. 4-1. Engine fundamentals. Left. Arrangement of parts in one cylinder. Right. Camshaft drive and valve linkage.

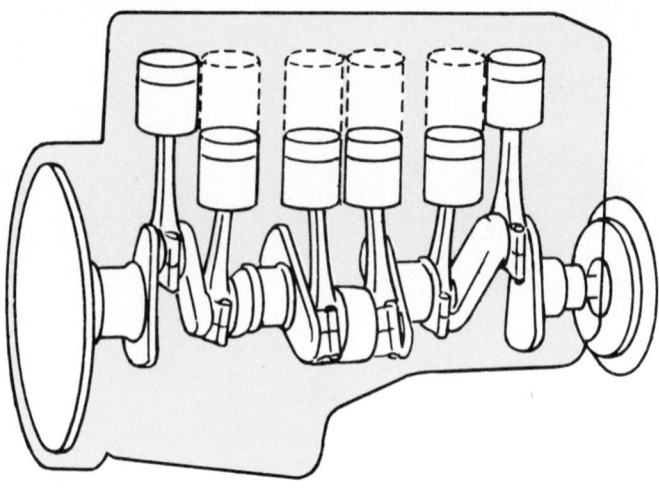

Fig. 4-2. Arrangement of six piston assemblies on crankshaft.

water-cooled or air-cooled. In the United States, four, six and eight cylinder engines are available. In the distant past, twelve and sixteen cylinder engines were available.

The basic automobile engine is the reciprocating piston, four cycle, water-cooled, poppet valve, gasoline engine.

RECIPROCATING ENGINES

Each "cylinder" of the typical automobile engine has a "piston" which reciprocates (moves back and forth) within the cylinder. Each piston is connected to the "crankshaft" by means of a link known as a "connecting rod." See Figs. 4-1, 4-2 and 4-3.

Other types of reciprocating engines substitute an eccentric, an inclined plate or a cam mechanism for the crankshaft. The "free piston" engine has no crankshaft or connecting rods.

ENGINE OPERATING SEQUENCE

In any internal combustion engine, there is a definite series of events that must occur in sequence:

1. Fill cylinder or chamber with an explosive mixture.
2. Compress mixture into a smaller space.
3. Ignite mixture or cause it to explode.
4. Utilize explosive or expansive force for power production.
5. Remove burned mixture from cylinder or chamber.

LP-Gas is used, it is necessary to alter the design or equipment of the engine to other than standard gasoline engine practice.

ENGINE DESIGN

Gasoline engines used in automotive vehicles are of two basic types, four cycle and two cycle. Either may be

Fig. 4-3. Typical Fiat four cylinder, in-line engine. Note arrangement of major parts.

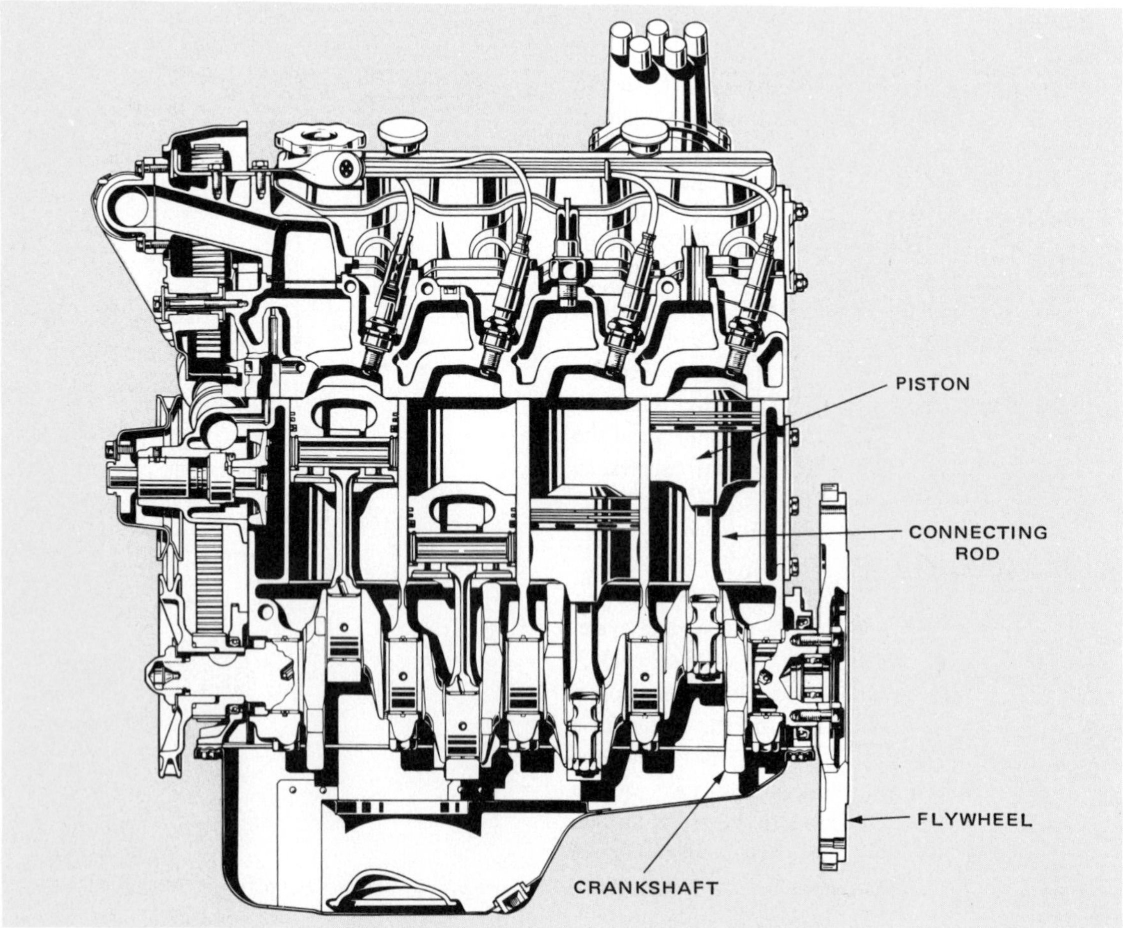

PISTON

CONNECTING ROD

FLYWHEEL

CRANKSHAFT

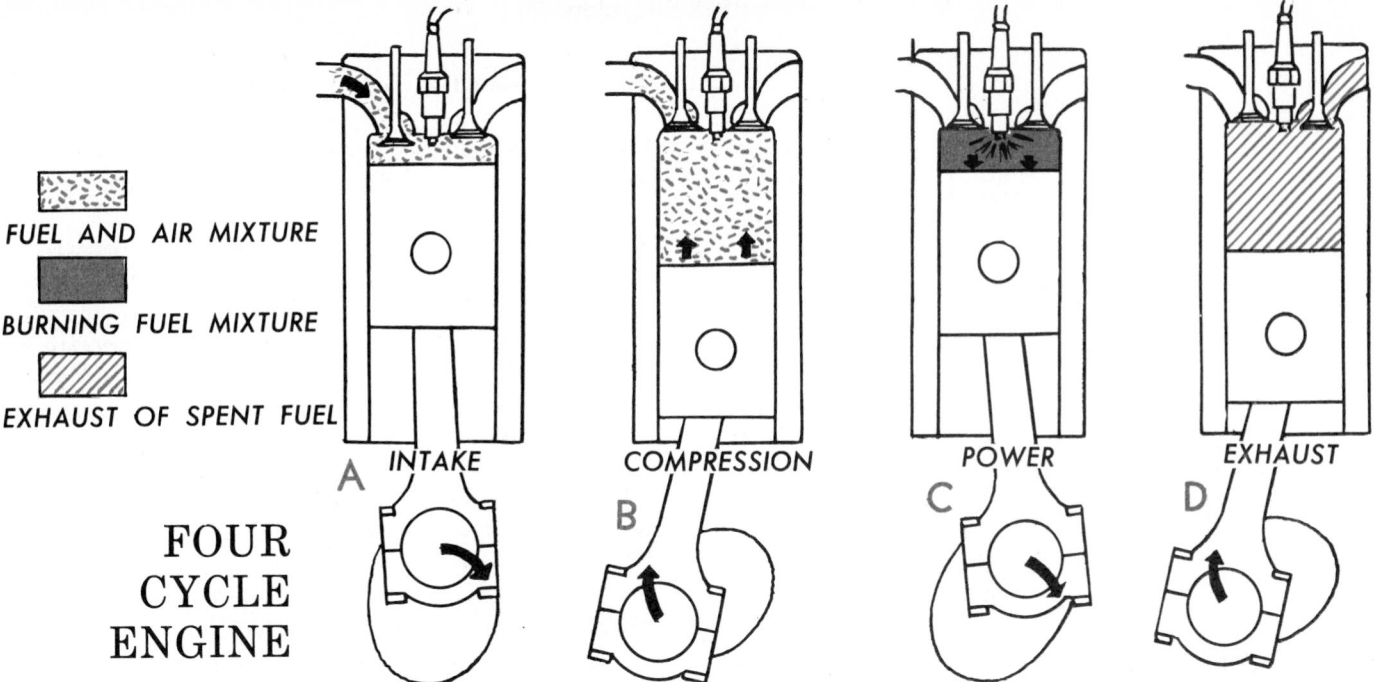

FOUR CYCLE ENGINE

Provides one power impulse for four strokes of piston; each two revolutions of crankshaft.

A. On Intake Stroke, inlet valve opens; piston draws fuel and air mixture into cylinder.

B. On Compression Stroke, both valves are closed. Rising piston compresses mixture.

C. At upper limit of piston movement; both valves closed, mixture is ignited. Explosion forces piston downward on Power Stroke.

D. On Exhaust Stroke, exhaust valve opens, rising piston pushes spent gas from cylinder.

Fig. 4-4. Sequence of operation of four cycle engine.

This series of events must be repeated over and over in the same sequence, automatically in each cylinder, if the engine is to run.

The first need is to fill the cylinder with an explosive mixture. If gasoline is the fuel, it must be mixed with the proper proportion of 10 to 15 parts of air to each part of gasoline to operate in a gasoline engine. This mixture is compounded automatically and continuously by a carburetor. (See chapter on PRINCIPLES OF CARBURETION.)

If the fuel is fuel oil (diesel engine), it is injected into the cylinders under high pressure. (See OTHER ENGINES.) In diesel engines, the heat generated by compressing the air in the cylinder may be used to ignite the fuel. In gasoline engines, an electrical spark is used. (See ENGINE IGNITION.)

FOUR-STROKE CYCLE

Most automobile engines operate on the four-stroke cycle. This type of engine is known as "four cycle" or "Otto cycle," after the name of its inventor, Nikolaus Otto. The power production cycle consists of four strokes of the piston in a reciprocating engine. See Fig. 4-4. The first stroke draws the combustible mixture into the cylinder. The next stroke compresses the mixture. The third stroke is the power stroke, which begins when the mixture is ignited. The final stroke forces burned gases out of the cylinder.

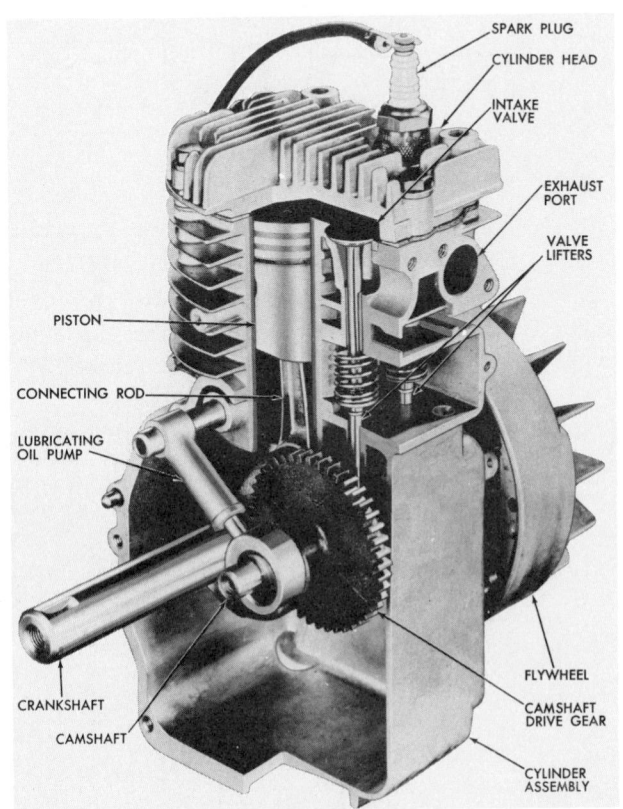

Fig. 4-5. Lauson air-cooled four cycle, single cylinder engine.

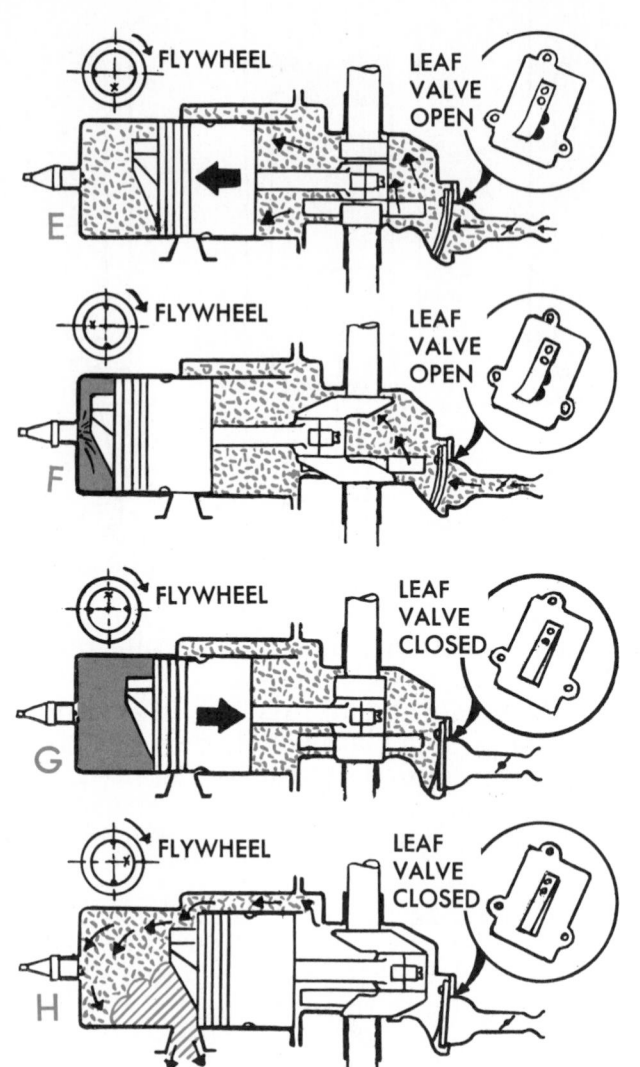

TWO CYCLE ENGINE

Provides power impulse for each two strokes of piston; each revolution of crankshaft.

E. Mixture of fuel and air from carburetor enters engine crankcase through check-valve. When piston is at bottom of cylinder, port is uncovered. As preceding movement of piston has compressed gas in crankcase, mixture flows into cylinder. Further compression in cylinder starts as soon as piston reverses and covers ports.

F. At the same time compression is occurring in cylinder, movement of piston has created vacuum in crankcase which draws fresh charge of mixture from carburetor into crankcase. Charge is fired at limit of piston movement.

G. As expansion of burning charge forces piston downward, check-valve in crankcase closes and mixture in crankcase is compressed.

H. As piston uncovers ports at bottom of stroke, compressed mixture from crankcase enters cylinder and is deflected by baffle on piston head into outer end of cylinder. Incoming fresh mixture assists in pushing spent gas out of cylinder.

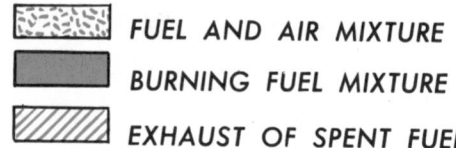

FUEL AND AIR MIXTURE

BURNING FUEL MIXTURE

EXHAUST OF SPENT FUEL

Fig. 4-6. Sequence of operation of two cycle engine.

First, it is necessary to fill the cylinder with an explosive mixture. This is accomplished by atmospheric pressure pushing the mixture into the cylinder to fill the vacuum created by the piston moving toward the crankshaft. The mixture passes from the carburetor through a pipe known as a manifold, and it is regulated by the opening and closing of a valve, Fig. 4-5.

Fig. 4-7. GM's two cycle diesel: A—With piston at bottom of stroke, intake ports are uncovered and blower forces air into cylinder. B—Upward movement of piston closes intake ports and compresses air, thereby raising its temperature. C—At top of piston stroke, fuel is injected and ignited by high temperature of compressed air. D—Expanding gases force piston down on power stroke. Exhaust valve is opened and burned gases are forced out by compressed air.

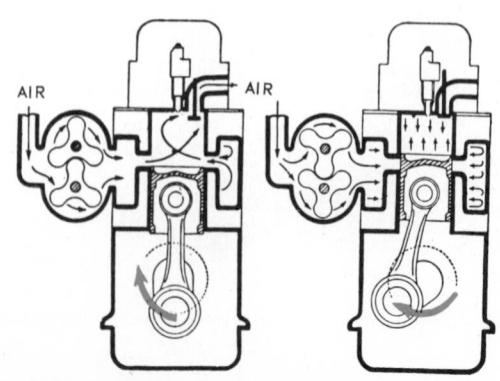
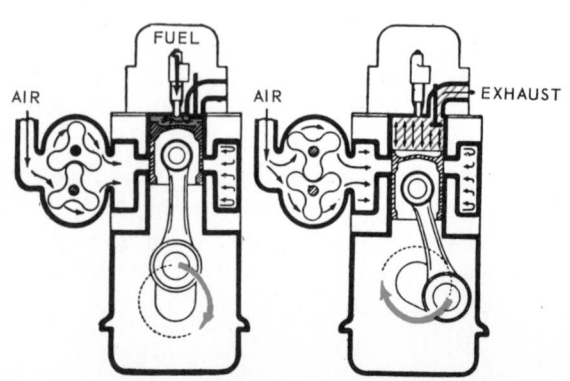

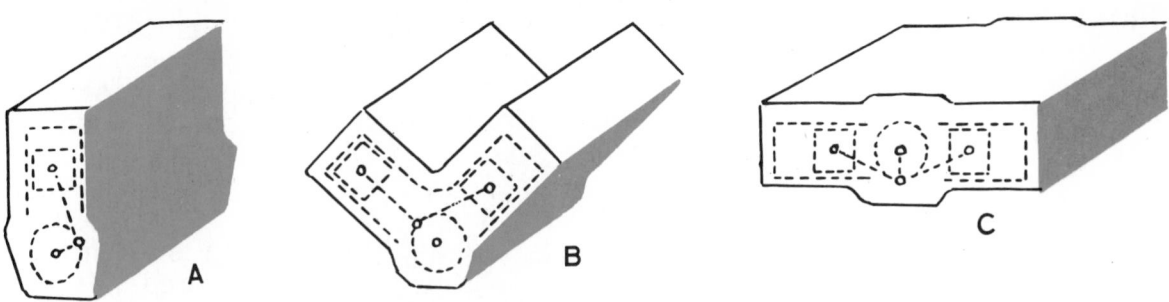

Fig. 4-8. Types of cylinder blocks. A—In-line block. B—V-type block. C—Opposed or "flat" block.

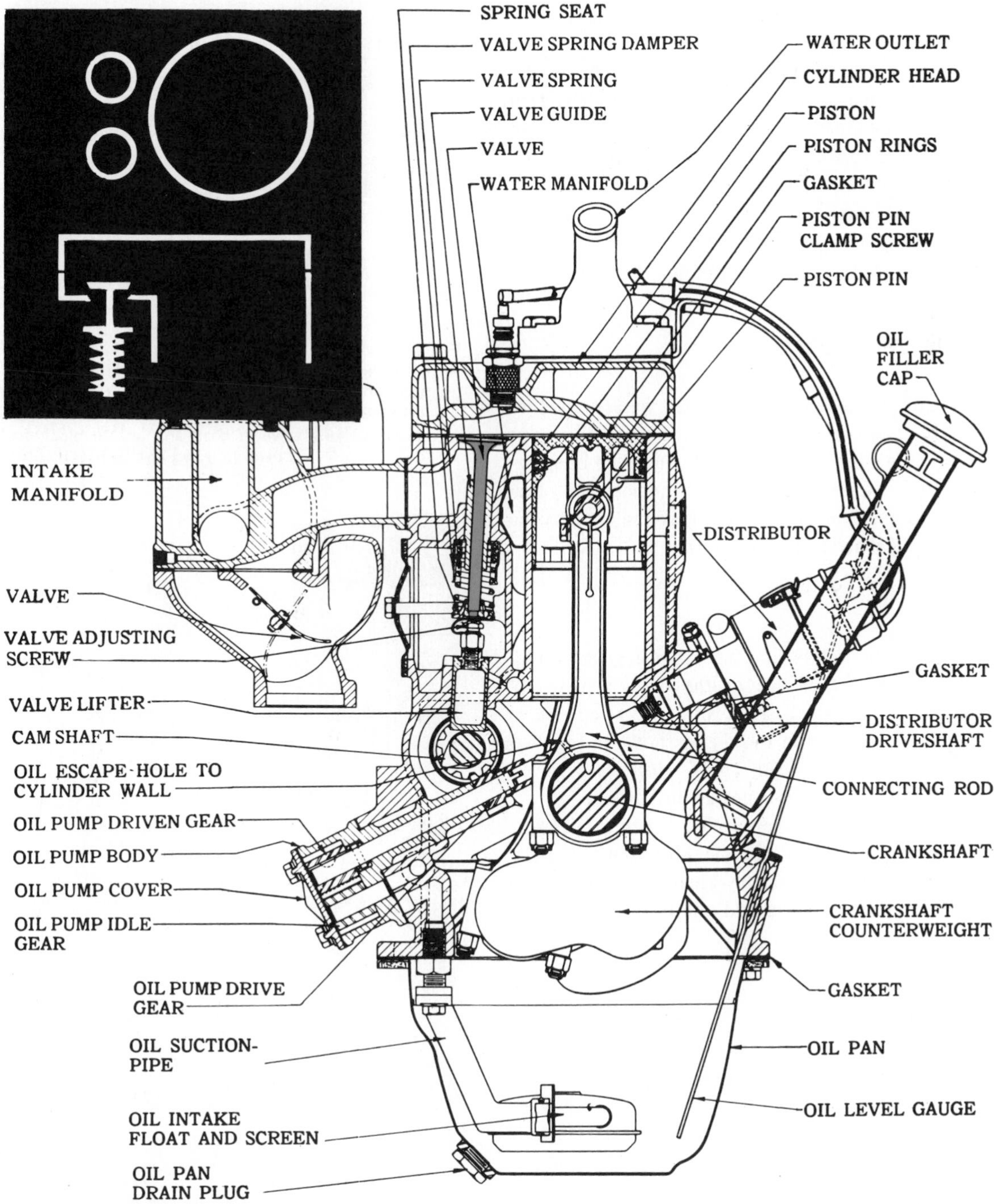

SPRING SEAT

VALVE SPRING DAMPER

VALVE SPRING

VALVE GUIDE

VALVE

WATER MANIFOLD

WATER OUTLET

CYLINDER HEAD

PISTON

PISTON RINGS

GASKET

PISTON PIN CLAMP SCREW

PISTON PIN

OIL FILLER CAP

INTAKE MANIFOLD

DISTRIBUTOR

VALVE

VALVE ADJUSTING SCREW

VALVE LIFTER

CAM SHAFT

OIL ESCAPE-HOLE TO CYLINDER WALL

OIL PUMP DRIVEN GEAR

OIL PUMP BODY

OIL PUMP COVER

OIL PUMP IDLE GEAR

OIL PUMP DRIVE GEAR

OIL SUCTION-PIPE

OIL INTAKE FLOAT AND SCREEN

OIL PAN DRAIN PLUG

GASKET

DISTRIBUTOR DRIVESHAFT

CONNECTING ROD

CRANKSHAFT

CRANKSHAFT COUNTERWEIGHT

GASKET

OIL PAN

OIL LEVEL GAUGE

Fig. 4-9. Cross section of an L-head, or side valve engine. Both valves are on one side of cylinder. See inset. In T-head engine, exhaust valves are on one side of cylinder, intake valves on other side. Engine parts are indicated. Corresponding parts can be identified in Figs. 4-10 and 4-11.

TWO-STROKE CYCLE

In the two-stroke cycle (two cycle) engine, the piston takes over some of the valve function in order to obtain a power stroke each revolution of the crankshaft. Two cycle operation involves the use of ports in the cylinders, Fig. 4-6. These ports are covered and uncovered by the movement of the piston, which acts like a valve in controlling the filling and emptying of the cylinder.

During the two-stroke cycle, both inlet and exhaust ports are covered by the piston, except for a short time at the extreme end of the stroke, H in Fig. 4-6. A deflector is built into the top of the piston on the inlet side, to divert the fresh mixture up into the cylinder, while the exhaust is leaving the cylinder on the opposite side.

Alternate phases of vacuum and compression in the crankcase can be avoided by using a blower or "supercharger" to push air into the cylinder, Fig. 4-7. In this particular design (used in GM diesel), a row of ports around the bottom of the cylinder serves as the inlet. The piston acts as an inlet valve, and cam-operated exhaust valves are placed in the cylinder head. In this design, the blower pumps air into the cylinder and diesel fuel is injected under pressure. (See chapter on OTHER ENGINES.)

MULTI-CYLINDER ENGINES

Almost all automobile engines, whether water-cooled or air-cooled — four cycle or two cycle, have more than one cylinder. These mutliple cylinders are arranged in-line, opposed or in V-form as shown in Fig. 4-8. Engines for other purposes, such as aviation, are arranged as radial, inverted in-line, inverted V, X-shaped and other forms.

CYLINDER TYPES

The location of the valves in four cycle engines, either water-cooled or air-cooled, is one of the basic elements of design. There are four basic designs, three of which are in current use: L-head, I-head, and F-head, as shown in Figs. 4-9 to 4-11, respectively. The T-head, along with sleeve valves, rotary valves and other variations is not in current use.

Note that in L-head design, the valve ports and gas passages are built in the cylinder block. In the I-head engine, these passages are built in the detachable cylinder head. The F-head engine has one valve in the head and one in the block, with necessary passages built into both head and block.

CYLINDER BLOCKS

The engine crankcase and cylinder block, or blocks, are often cast in one piece. Ordinarily, this is the largest and most intricate single piece of metal in the automobile. Even when the cylinders, cylinder heads or cylinder sleeves are separate pieces, the crankcase is still the largest single part in the engine. Practically all of the engine parts are attached to the crankcase, directly or indirectly. See Figs. 4-12 and 4-13.

The crankcase houses the crankshaft and, in most cases, the

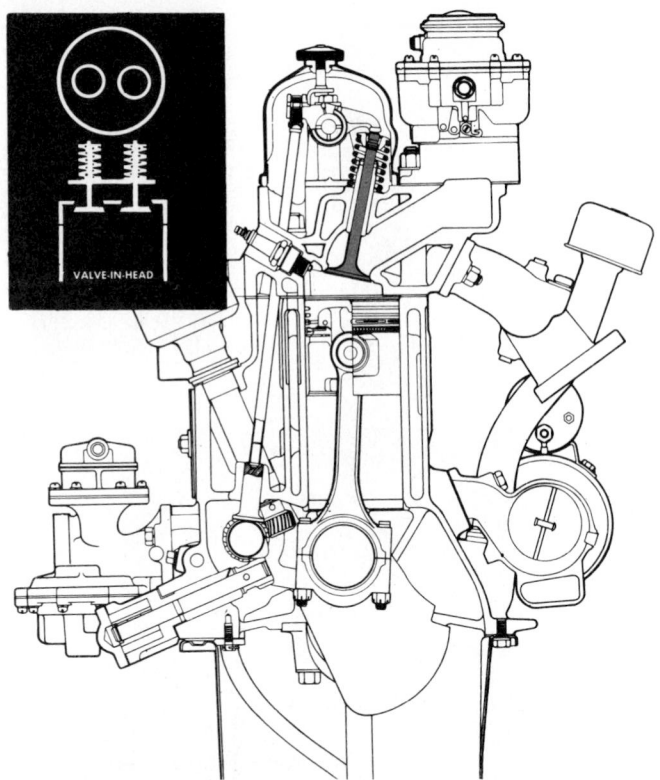

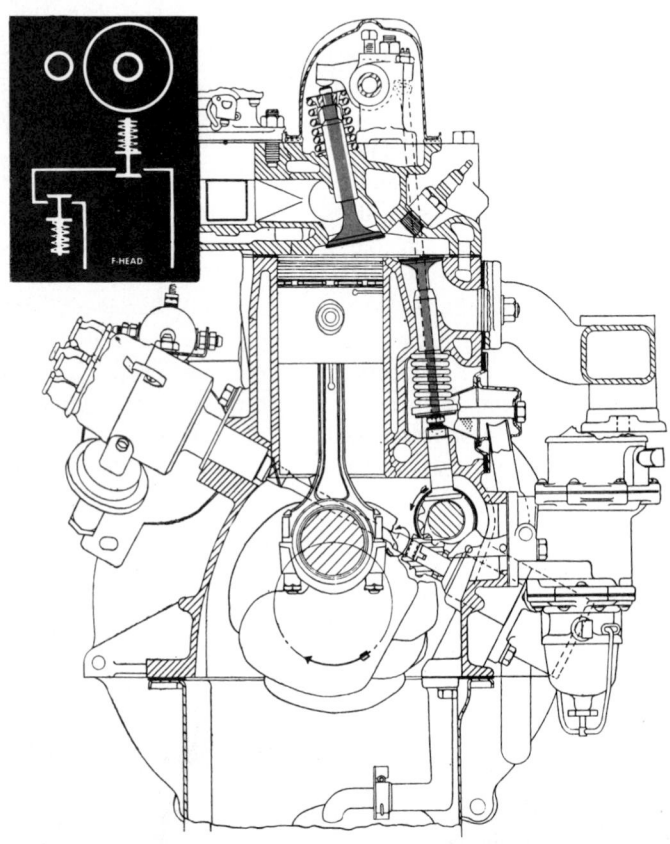

Fig. 4-10. Above. I-head engine is also known as overhead valve or valve-in-head engine with both valves directly over piston. Do not confuse I-head with "overhead camshaft" engines described later. Fig. 4-11. Below. F-head design is a combination of L-head and I-head forms. It has one valve in head and one in block for each cylinder, operated by a single camshaft.

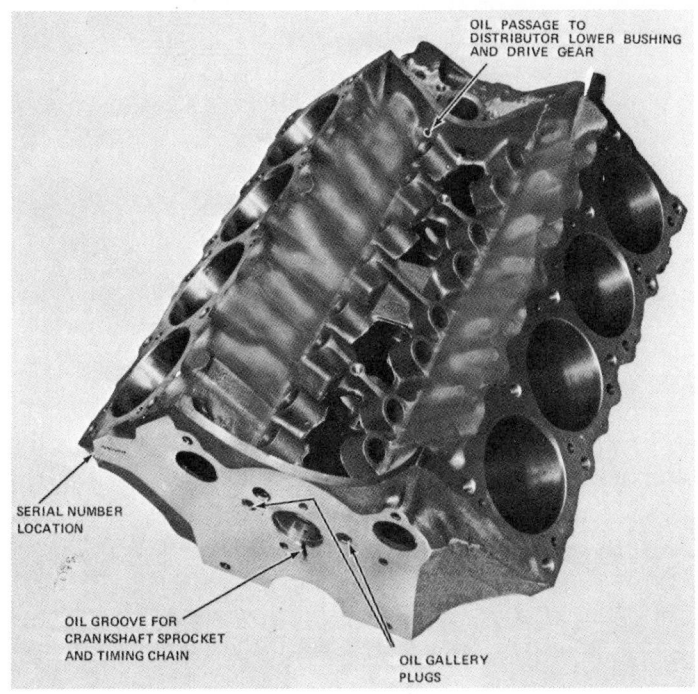

Fig. 4-12. Crankcase and cylinder block casting of Pontiac V-8 engine.

etc.). Distortion can occur in several directions. The cylinder head surface can warp or twist. The cylinder bore may warp longitudinally or become out-of-round. The crankshaft or camshaft bearing bores may be warped out of line, etc.

To stiffen and strengthen engine block and crankcase castings, webs or ribs are often added to the casting at the points of greatest stress. In some cases, the crankcase is extended below the center line of the crankshaft, rather than in the same plane as the crankshaft. See Fig. 4-13.

While the metal used for these castings is ordinarily termed "cast iron" or "aluminum," the terminology is rather loose because these metals usually are alloys. In the case of cast iron, small amounts of chromium, molybdenum or other metals may be added. In the case of aluminum castings, it is customary to add other materials to create an alloy which, along with heat and chemical treatment, increases the strength and wear resisting ability of the metal. In some applications, sleeves are inserted in the cylinder blocks to resist wear, minimize distortion, etc.

camshaft also. With the oil pan, which goes on the lower surface of the crankcase, it forms on oil-tight housing in which the rotating and reciprocating parts operate. The cylinder block contains the pistons which are attached to the crankshaft by means of the connecting rods, Fig. 4-9.

The crankcase and cylinder block are usually made of high grade cast iron with alloys to improve wear characteristics of the cylinders. Obviously, this major unit must be extremely strong and rigid to avoid any bending or distortion.

The crankcase and cylinder block is an intricate casting that varies in thickness and does not always cool uniformly. Internal stresses are created that sometimes cause warpage. However, much has been done in the way of design to minimize the effects of warpage of the cylinder bores.

Distortion may occur from incorrect placing of the metal masses around the cylinders, from expansion and contraction due to the heat of operation, or from excessive mechanical stresses placed upon it (unequal or extreme tightening of bolts,

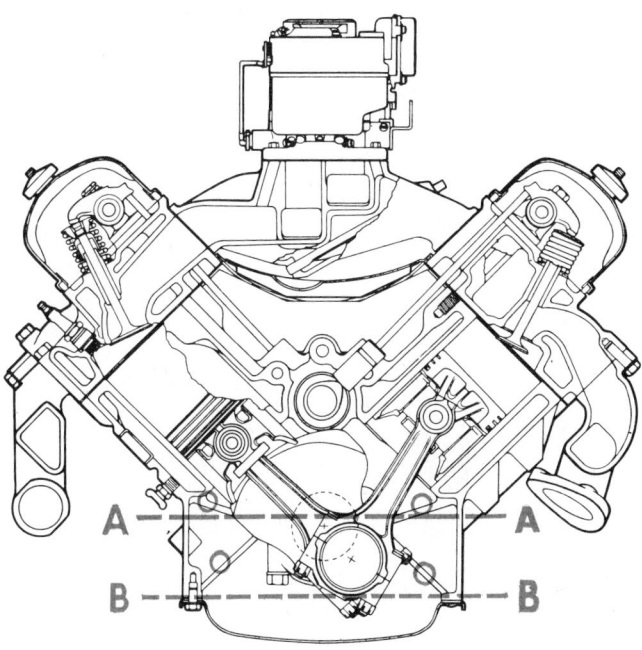

Fig. 4-13. Line A-A is on a plane with center of crankshaft, while crankcase extends to line B-B. Note stiffening webs or ribs at 0-0-0-0 in crankcase.

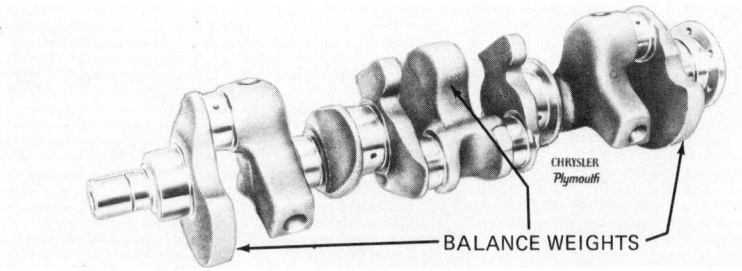

Fig. 4-14. Typical crankshaft illustrated is for a six cylinder engine. It has two throws between main bearing journals.

ENGINE CRANKSHAFTS

The crankshaft is regarded as the "backbone" of the engine. It serves to change the reciprocating motion of the piston into rotary motion, and it handles the entire power output.

The crankshaft revolves in bearings located in the engine crankcase. It must be free to revolve with as little friction as possible, yet have no appreciable looseness in the bearings. Because of the loads imposed, the crankshaft is large in diameter, very accurately machined and the bearings which support it are of generous size and length.

The number of bearings used will depend upon the number of cylinders in the engine, and the design of the engine. By locating a main bearing journal between throws of the crankshaft, Fig. 4-15, it is possible to use a lighter crankshaft than if two throws are placed between main bearing journals. See Fig. 4-14.

Engine crankshafts vary according to design of the engine. A single cylinder engine will have one throw on the crankshaft, Fig. 4-15. A two cylinder engine will have two throws spaced 180 deg. apart. A three cylinder engine will have three throws spaced 120 deg. apart. A four cylinder engine will normally have cylinders 1 and 4 on the same side and cylinders 2 and 3 on the other side, 180 deg. apart, Fig. 4-16.

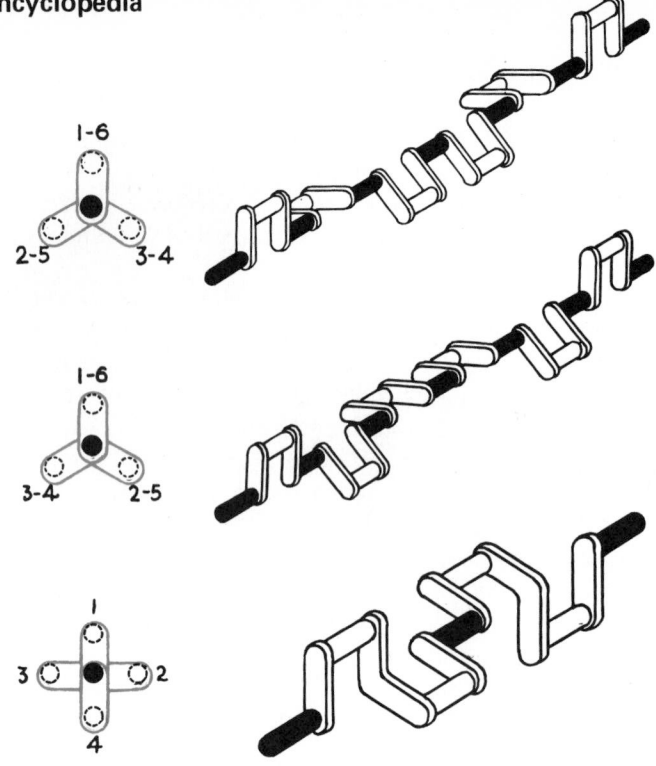

Fig. 4-17. Above. A right-hand crankshaft for a six cylinder engine. Center. A left-hand crankshaft for a six cylinder engine has No. 3 and 4 throws to left of No. 1 and 6. Below. A V-8 crankshaft usually has throws arranged like a four cylinder engine. A possible variation is shown.

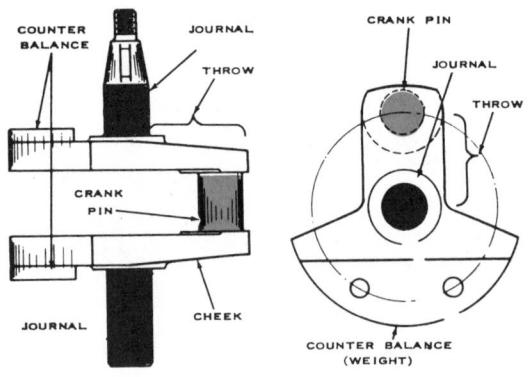

Fig. 4-15. Single throw crankshaft in single cylinder engine has two main bearing journals (solid black) and one connecting rod journal (color).

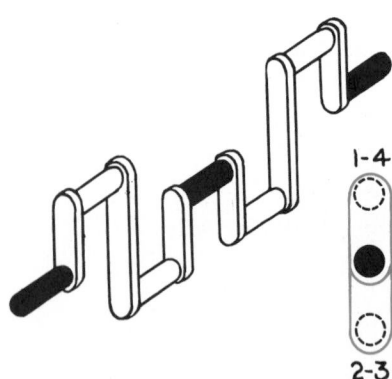

Fig. 4-16. A four cylinder crankshaft normally has throws spaced 180 deg. apart, with cylinders 1 and 4 on same side. Some V-8s use a similar construction.

CRANKSHAFT BALANCE WEIGHTS

Without special balance weights on the crankshaft, severe vibration would result from:
1. Weights of reciprocating parts.
2. Weights of rotating parts.
3. Cyclic variation of inertial force of reciprocating parts.
4. Cyclic variation of gas and combustion pressures.
5. Variation in torque.

To reduce or eliminate such vibration, the crankshaft must be balanced. That is, it must be provided with counterweights that extend radially from the crankshaft centerline in the opposite direction of the crank throws or crank arms, Fig. 4-14. In that way, the forces acting on the crankshaft are balanced and vibration is reduced. In addition, bearing life is increased.

SIX CYLINDER IN-LINE CRANKSHAFTS

An in-line six cylinder engine may have a left-hand crankshaft or a right-hand crankshaft, depending on the firing order of the cylinders (to be covered later). The crank throws are spaced 120 deg. apart in both cases, Fig. 4-17. Cylinders 1 and 6 are on the same side in each case. Likewise, cylinders 2 and 5 are in the same plane, and cylinders 3 and 4 are in the same plane.

V-SIX CRANKSHAFTS

If a 90 deg. V-6 engine has a crankshaft with three throws spaced 120 deg. apart (common crankpin for two connecting rods), it will have uneven firing intervals between cylinders. As a result, there will be varying torque impulses with attendant vibration.

To overcome these problems with its 231 cu. in. (3.8 litre) V-6 engine, Buick "split" each crankpin by an included angle of 30 deg. In doing so, Buick advanced the throws of the crankpins for cylinders 2, 4 and 6 by 15 deg. on the right bank, and delayed the throws of the crankpins for cylinders 1, 3 and 5 a similar amount on the left bank. The firing order of the Buick 3.8 litre V-6 is 1-6-5-4-3-2. The firing interval is 120 deg. for all cylinders.

Chevrolet engineers, meanwhile, also decided to "split" the crankpins on the 3.8 litre V-6, but with an included angle of 18 deg. This crankshaft design results in a firing interval of 132-108-132-108-132-108 deg. The firing order is 1-6-5-4-3-2.

V-8 CRANKSHAFTS

A V-8 engine normally has a four throw crankshaft with two cylinders attached to each throw. However, the location of the crankpins will vary. In one case, all four throws may be in the same plane, two on each side of the crankshaft, Fig. 4-16. Or, the throws may be in two planes, each 90 deg. apart as shown in Fig. 4-17.

REVIEW QUESTIONS — ENGINE FUNDAMENTALS

Write your answers on a separate sheet of paper. DO NOT write in this book.

1. All automobile engines have either six or eight cylinders. True or False?
2. The majority of automobile engines are the _____ cooled type.
3. Is a flat engine the same as an in-line engine? Yes or No?
4. Name the largest single part of the engine.
5. Which engine part changes the reciprocating motion of the pistons to rotary motion?
6. List in proper sequence the events that occur in a four cycle internal combustion engine.
7. A "valve" and a "port" are the same thing. True or False?
8. How does the mixture get into the cylinder?
9. The I-head, valve-in-head and overhead valve engines are identical. True or False?
10. How is the explosive mixture in the cylinder ignited in a gasoline engine?
11. How is the explosive mixture ignited in most diesels?
12. What is the basic difference between a four cycle engine and a two cycle engine?
13. How many "throws" are on the crankshaft of a V-8 engine? Two, four or eight?
14. What causes distortion of engine blocks?
15. All four cylinder crankshafts are alike. True or False?
16. List three causes of crankshaft vibration.

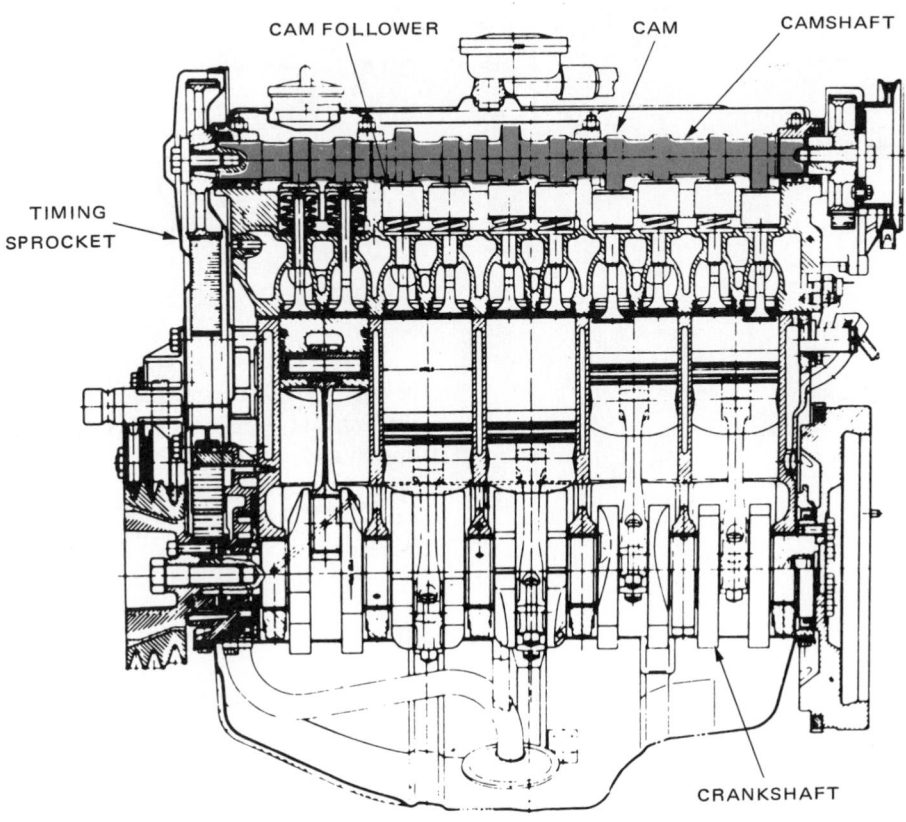

Longitudinal view of five cylinder, in-line Volkswagen engine, showing overhead camshaft arrangement in color.

53

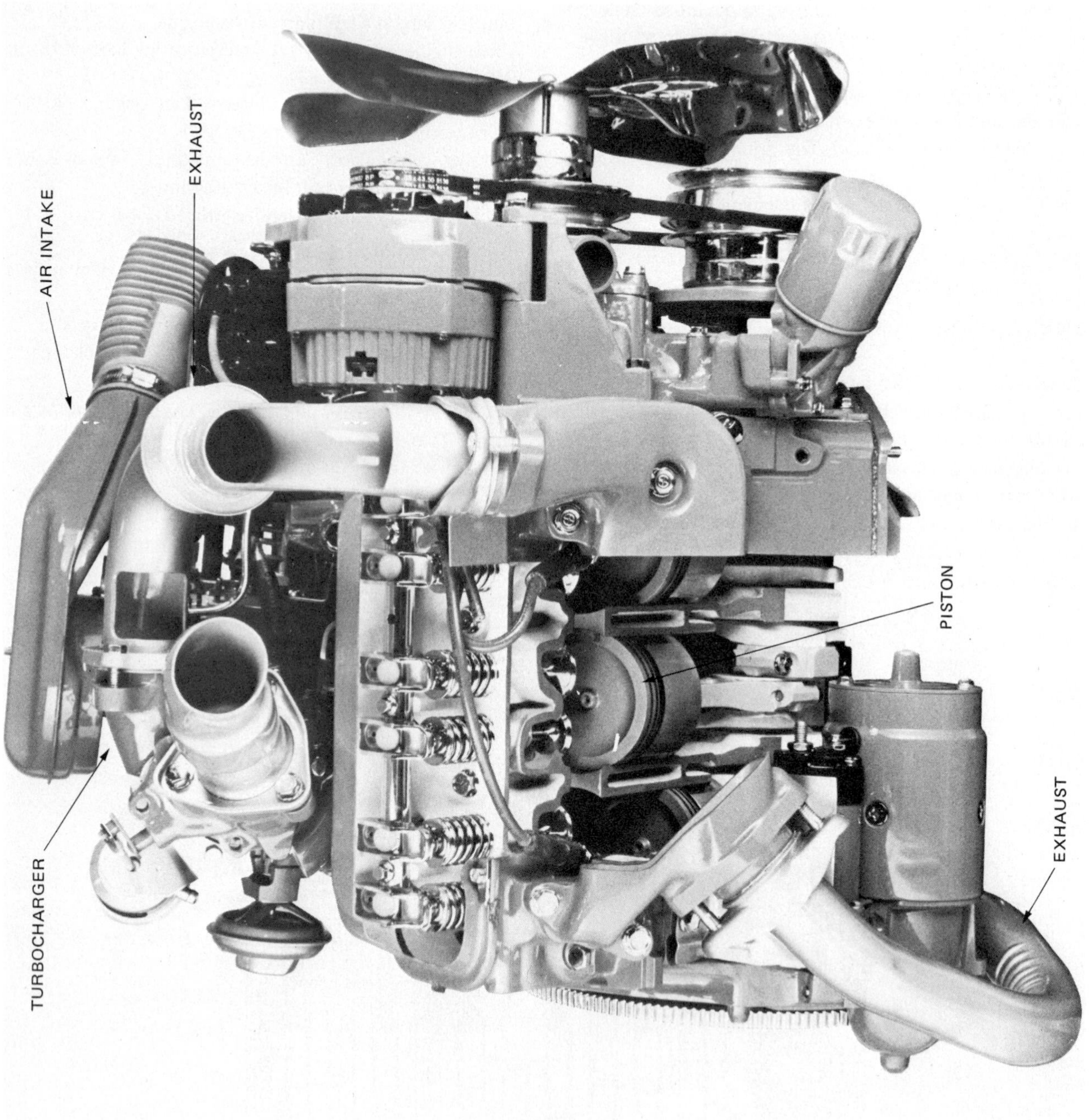

AIR INTAKE

EXHAUST

TURBOCHARGER

PISTON

EXHAUST

The Buick V-6 engine has a 3.8 in. bore, 3.4 in. stroke and a displacement of 231 cu. in. (3.8 L). V-6 shown is turbocharged, boosting horsepower from 115 hp to 170 hp.

ENGINE
CONSTRUCTION

Many things are demanded of an engine used to propel an automobile. Some of the requirements are:

1. Ease of starting regardless of atmospheric temperature.
2. Reliability to go anywhere any time.
3. Power to climb steep grades.
4. Speed to go as fast as desired.
5. Economy in the use of fuel and oil.
6. Flexibility for ease of handling.
7. Quiet operation.
8. Freedom from frequent adjustments.

Some of these factors conflict. For example, a great amount of power can be had from an engine of sufficient size, but a supersize engine is not economical to operate, so all automobile engines are a compromise in several directions in order to obtain the most desirable combination of performance characteristics.

ENGINE SIZE

The size of an engine is determined by its bore, stroke and number of cylinders, Fig. 5-1. Bore is the diameter of the cylinders. Stroke is the length of piston travel. The bore area multiplied by the stroke will give the displacement of one cylinder. Multiply this by the number of cylinders and you will have engine displacement or size.

For example, a Plymouth six cylinder engine has a bore of 3.4 in. and a stroke of 4.12 in. Engine displacement is:

Bore area (πr^2)
3.1416 x 2.9   =   9.1 sq. in.

Bore area x stroke
9.1 x 4.12   =   37.5 cu. in.
One cyl. displacement

One cyl. x No. of cyl.
37.5 x 6   = 225.0 cu. in.
Engine displacement

Size alone, however, is not an exclusive measurement of power developed by the engine. Many other things need to be taken into consideration:

1. Engine rotating speed.
2. Compression ratio.
3. Valve size, lift and timing.
4. Internal engine friction.
5. Mechanical condition of parts.

Each item is subject to alteration by service procedures. Each can be altered and must be understood by the mechanic.

Possibly the most important item is the mechanical condition of the parts and units. Certainly it is the item most directly under the control of the serviceman. If an engine is badly worn or damaged, with little or no compression in the cylinders, the mechanic can do little in any direction until compression has been restored.

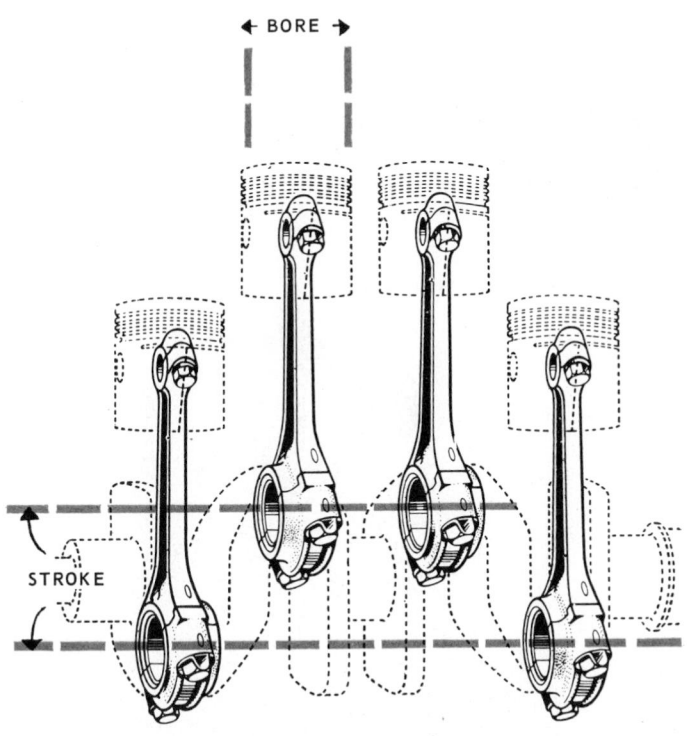

Fig. 5-1. Diameter of cylinder determines bore of an engine, and length of crank arm determines stroke, or distance piston will travel.

Because the cylinders must be round and true, they are machined and finished to an accuracy of a fraction of a thousandth of an inch. This is required so that the piston and rings, which are finished with equal accuracy, will have a true mating surface. Otherwise the compression may leak between the pistons and cylinders on the compression and power strokes, and little power would be developed. Also, the oil might leak through between piston and cylinder wall on the intake stroke, and be burned and wasted.

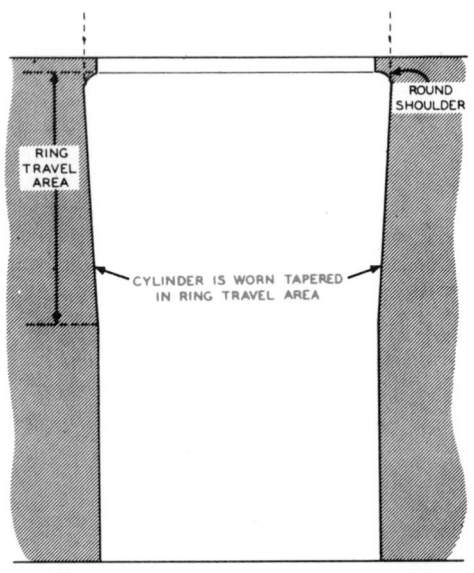

Fig. 5-2. Grit from air plus heat and insufficient lubrication, causes tapered pattern of wear on cylinder walls.

CYLINDER WALL WEAR

Cylinder walls do wear, regardless of kind of material from which they are made and how carefully they are designed and finished. This wear may be caused by:

1. Pressure of piston rings against cylinder walls.
2. Amount of water condensed in cylinder.
3. Temperature of operation.
4. Degree of lubrication.
5. Kind of lubricant.
6. Type of fuel being used.
7. Type of service in which the engine is operated.
8. Amount of abrasive in lubricant and in the combustible fuel drawn into cylinder from carburetor.
9. Length of time since engine was last in operation.

Cylinders wear to a taper, Fig. 5-2, and also out-of-round, as shown in Fig. 5-3.

Taper wear usually is caused by: insufficient lubrication in upper area of cylinder; effects of condensation and consequent corrosion; greater amount of abrasives present; and type of fuel used.

Out-of-round wear results primarily from greater side pressure exerted by the piston on its power stroke than on the other strokes. Design features will also affect cylinder wear. Short stroke engines will tend to wear faster than long stroke

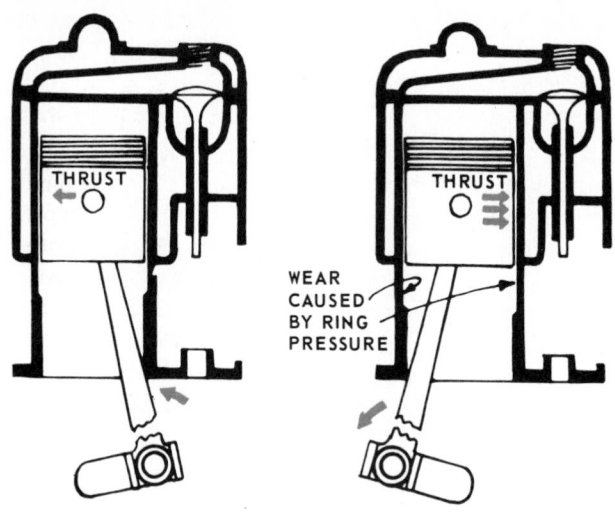

Fig. 5-3. Side thrust on piston is greater on explosion stroke than on compression stroke, because of greater pressures on piston head.

engines. And high speeds will also tend to increase cylinder wear because of increased cylinder wall pressure. The design of the water jackets surrounding the cylinder walls is an important factor, as is the accumulation of rust and other sediment in the water jackets.

Most cylinder wear occurs during the first few miles of operation, before the engine has reached full operating temperature. During that period, there is a maximum amount of condensation in the cylinders (a major factor in causing wear). In addition, there is little oil on the cylinder walls when the engine is first started.

NOTE: Cylinder and ring wear will be given additional consideration later in this text.

In some engines, the cylinders are fitted with sleeves to serve as a bearing surface for the piston rings. These sleeves are of two types, "dry" and "wet." The dry type is simply a sleeve or barrel which is pressed into an oversize bore in the cylinder

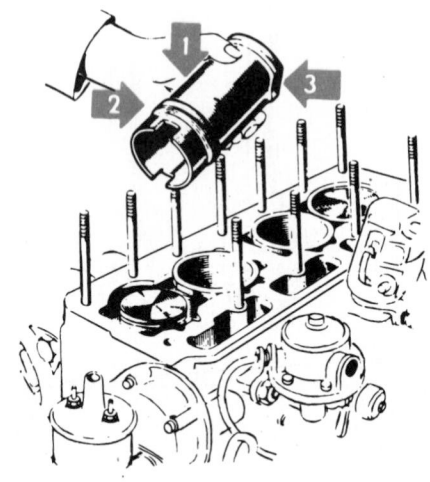

Fig. 5-4. Sleeved engine. 1—Inserted wet sleeve. 2—Bottom sealing gasket. 3—Top sealing surface for head gasket.

block. The wet type is a cylinder sleeve which replaces the cylinder wall. With a wet sleeve, the coolant circulates in contact with the outside surface of the sleeve. In this case, gaskets are required at both ends of the sleeve. See Fig. 5-4.

In some situations, there is a certain service advantage to either the wet or dry type of cylinder sleeve. If one cylinder wall becomes damaged, it may be more economical to replace the sleeve than to rebore the cylinder and fit oversize pistons and rings. Furthermore, if the cylinder had to be oversized very much, the engine would be out of balance. Unless, of course, all the cylinders were oversized the same amount.

Another, seldom used method of reducing wear on the inside of the cylinder, is to chrome plate the surface where the rings bear. It is customary in such cases to provide very small indentations in the plated surface to encourage the retention of an oil film.

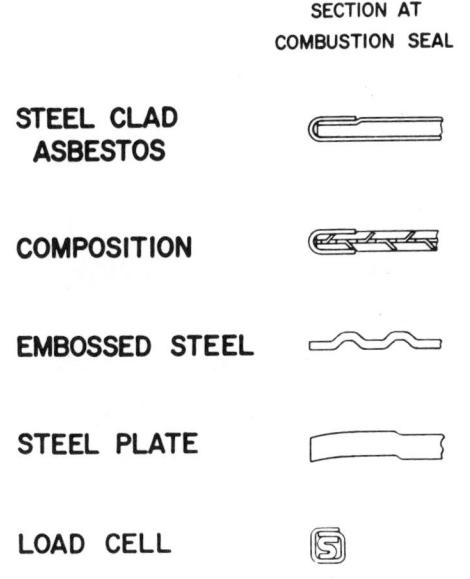

Fig. 5-5. Cross sections of major types of cylinder head gaskets.

CYLINDER HEAD GASKETS

There are several different types of cylinder head gaskets, each with its own advantages. See Fig. 5-5.

The steel or copper clad asbestos cylinder head gasket is the most familiar. Generally, it is made of sheet asbestos about 0.030 in. (0.76 mm) thick and covered on both sides with a sheet of steel or copper about .010 in. (0.254 mm) thick. The entire gasket is coated with a special lacquer or varnish. At gasket openings, the metal ends are flanged over to protect the asbestos.

The composition gasket has a steel core with a soft rubber-asbestos coating on each side, Fig. 5-6. This type gasket has wide application for replacement use and provides a particularly effective seal for the coolant. Condition of the head and cylinder block surfaces is not critical.

The embossed steel gasket has wide acceptance as original equipment on passenger car engines. It is made of cold rolled

steel .015 to .020 in. (.381 to .508 mm) thick with raised sections (embossments) around cylinder openings and water passages. Clamping action provides a sealing pressure of about 10,000 psi. This design provides excellent heat transfer qualities and rigid support for the cylinder head. However, it cannot compensate for irregularities or dirt on the mating surfaces of the head and cylinder block.

The steel plate gasket is used on diesel engines. It is made of sheet steel about .090 in. (2.286 mm) thick, with slight embossments around cylinder bore openings. Rubber grommets are provided for sealing coolant openings.

The load cell is essentially a sealing ring which is fitted one-per-cylinder when the engine is assembled. Rubber O-rings are placed in grooves in both cylinder head and block surfaces at each coolant opening.

GASKET INSTALLATION

When installing gaskets, make sure that the gasket furnished is correct for that particular installation. It must fit all bolt holes and studs, plus any openings for water or oil passages,

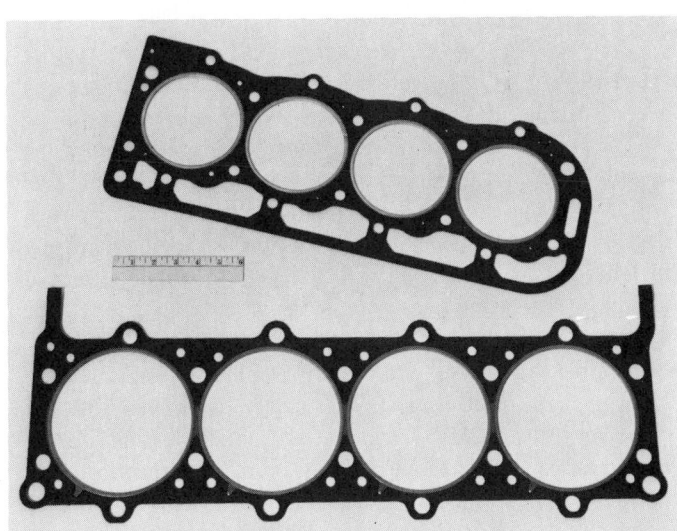

Fig. 5-6. Two examples of diesel engine head gasket having solid steel core with rubber-asbestos coating. Combustion seal around cylinder openings is embossed from steel core and enclosed with steel flange. (McCord Corp.)

cylinders, shafts, push rods, etc. Also inspect gaskets to see that they are not creased from storage or careless handling.

When installing a cylinder head gasket, first flush out all coolant passages of the cylinder head, cylinder block and radiator. Mating surfaces of the head and block must be clean, smooth and true. Use a straight edge to check the block and head for warpage.

Wire brush all head bolts to remove dirt from the threads. Also re-tap and blow out all bolt holes in the block. Otherwise, torque readings will be incorrect and leakage will result. Dirty threads could affect torque readings as much as 20 ft. lb.

If cylinder head bolt lengths vary, be sure to install each bolt in its proper place. If a long bolt is installed in a short hole, it will bottom without holding down the cylinder head. Leakage will result.

Some engines are designed without an exhaust manifold gasket. Occasionally, in these applications, repeated heating and cooling will distort and erode the surfaces. When this occurs, the installation of a gasket is advisable.

Similarly, intake manifold leakage will cause an incorrect air-fuel ratio. Leakage occurs when gaskets are incorrectly installed, or if mating surfaces of the manifold and cylinder head are warped, eroded or dirty. Be sure the intake manifold gasket is properly installed and torqued to manufacturer's specifications.

COMBUSTION CHAMBER

The combustion chamber is the space within the cylinder above the piston where the burning of the air-fuel mixture occurs, Fig. 5-7. Improvements have been made, but research continues on design characteristics of the combustion chamber.

The trend in combustion chamber design has been, and is, to concentrate the expansion force on the head of the piston. This helps to avoid dissipation of the force in directions that do not produce power. Preceding illustrations of cylinder types show that the overhead valve design comes nearer to accomplishing this objective than any of the others.

Another trend in combustion chamber design is toward the creation and control of turbulence (movement of air and fuel within cylinder to create a more uniform mixture). One design developed by an engineer named Ricardo was used extensively in L-head engines, Fig. 5-7. It was very successful in engines of relatively low compression ratio. However, the size of the valves was limited, as was the compression ratio.

As fuels improved and higher compression ratios were sought, the L-head engine was largely superseded by the overhead valve (OHV) engine. OHV design permits larger engine valves and increased compression ratio, permitting more power to be developed by an engine of given size.

The shape of the combustion chamber of the overhead valve engine has gone through many changes. It has ranged from the plain cylindrical form to the wedge type and

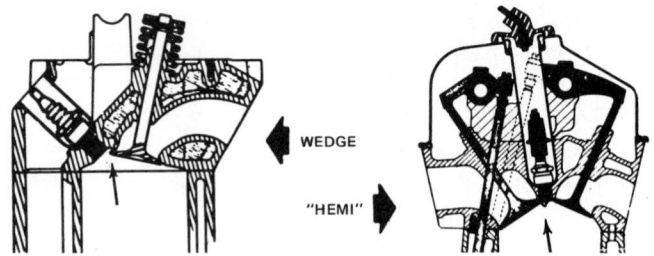

Fig. 5-8. Left. Wedge shaped combustion chamber.
Fig. 5-9. Right. Hemispherical combustion chamber.

hemispherical design shown in Figs. 5-8 and 5-9.

Variations of the wedge type are used in many engines of current design. Fig. 5-10 shows the Toyota engine with wedge shaped combustion chambers. Fig. 5-11 shows the Dodge Colt single overhead camshaft engine and hemispherical combustion chamber.

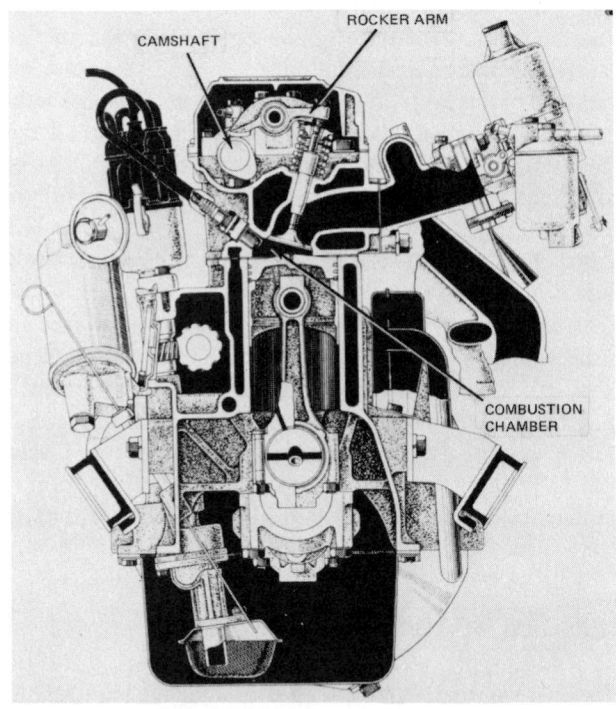

Fig. 5-10. Toyota with wedge shaped combustion chamber.

The wedge shaped combustion chamber is an efficient design used in some engines by General Motors, Ford, Chrysler and American Motors. It is noted for the turbulence produced in the air-fuel charge as the piston moves up on the compression stroke. Stepped-up efficiency is a further result.

The hemispherical design, or "hemi," provides room for larger valves for a given bore. In addition, the "hemi" design permits a centrally located spark plug, which contributes to more efficient combustion, better heat dissipation and higher thermal efficiency.

With increased emphasis being placed on cleaner exhaust, it

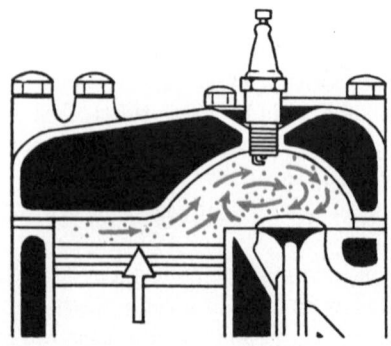

Fig. 5-7. Shape of combustion chamber has much to do with proper mixing of gasoline and air to obtain maximum benefit from combustion.

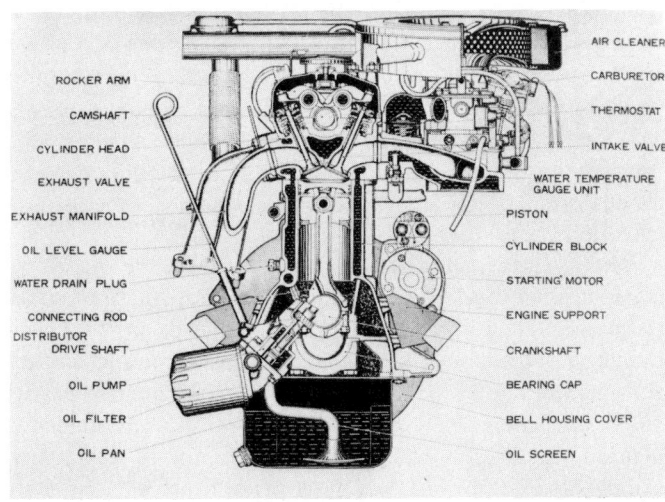

ROCKER ARM
CAMSHAFT
CYLINDER HEAD
EXHAUST VALVE
EXHAUST MANIFOLD
OIL LEVEL GAUGE
WATER DRAIN PLUG
CONNECTING ROD
DISTRIBUTOR
DRIVE SHAFT
OIL PUMP
OIL FILTER
OIL PAN

AIR CLEANER
CARBURETOR
THERMOSTAT
INTAKE VALVE
WATER TEMPERATURE
GAUGE UNIT
PISTON
CYLINDER BLOCK
STARTING MOTOR
ENGINE SUPPORT
CRANKSHAFT
BEARING CAP
BELL HOUSING COVER
OIL SCREEN

Fig. 5-11. Dodge Colt engine with single overhead camshaft. Also see Figs. 8-19, 16-40 and 16-51.

is important to note that the unburned hydrocarbons are proportional to the surface of the combustion chamber. As that area is reduced, the unburned hydrocarbons are also reduced. That area is at a minimum with a hemispherical combustion chamber. Both "wedge" and "hemi" designs feature a reduced tendency toward detonation.

In discussing the Dodge Colt engine, engineers report that "High performance in a wide operational speed range is an essential requirement to keep driving flexible in crowded streets as on expressways."

This flexibility is best attained with minimized surface area for the volume of the combustion chamber; a condition best met by the "hemi" chamber design and "V" arrangement of engine valves. See single overhead camshaft engine in Fig. 5-11.

Other engines use a double overhead camshaft with valves in a "V," Fig. 5-12, to provide still another form of hemispherical combustion chamber. This design permits the

use of larger valves, and a resulting increase in power, than in the same size engine with a single overhead camshaft.

Further in this connection, when the cylinder heads and combustion chambers are made of aluminum, the valves operate at approximately 100 deg. C. lower than in comparable cylinder heads of cast iron. In addition the compression ratio can be increased approximately 1.0 over the cast iron head (11.0:1 over 10.0:1, for example). This is an important plus, since the use of unleaded fuel is on the increase in an effort to produce cleaner exhaust emissions.

The material from which the combustion chamber is made, and the efficiency of the cooling system, also have a distinct bearing on the compression ratio of a given engine. For example, aluminum cylinder heads and aluminum pistons can operate at higher compression ratios than cast iron or steel. This is made possible by the superior heat conducting ability of aluminum. The heat of combustion is dissipated more rapidly to the cooling water or air.

ENGINE PISTONS

Engine pistons serve several purposes:
1. Transmit force of explosion to crankshaft through connecting rod.
2. Act as a guide for upper end of connecting rod.
3. Serve as a carrier for piston rings used to seal piston in cylinder, Fig. 5-13.

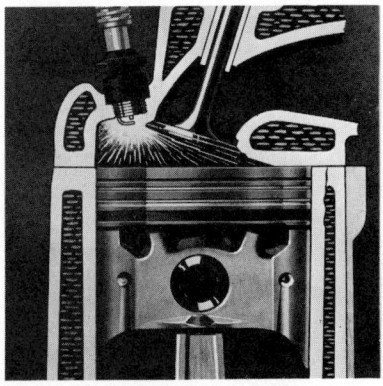

Fig. 5-13. Note wedge type combustion chamber. Piston shown is aluminum "skeleton" type used with an aluminum connecting rod.

4. Aid in the burning of the fuel mixture by introducing a swirling action to the air-fuel mixture. (This is particularly true in the case of diesel engine pistons.) The swirling is accomplished by altering the contour of the piston head. See Figs. 5-22 and 5-27.

Pistons operate under exceedingly difficult mechanical and thermal (heat) conditions, so they must be made and installed with the utmost care. Pistons must be strong enough to stand the force of the explosion, yet light enough to avoid excessive inertia forces when their direction of travel is reversed twice each revolution.

Pistons must be able to withstand the heat from the burning air-fuel mixture, plus the heat generated by friction.

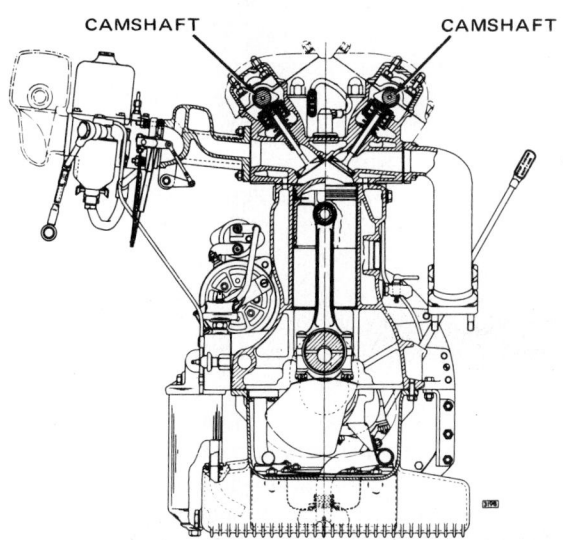

CAMSHAFT   CAMSHAFT

Fig. 5-12. Details of Jaguar XK engine with double overhead camshafts. Note cooling fins on oil pan and hemispherical combustion chamber.

They must slide freely in the cylinder. If fitted too tightly, the engine will overheat and/or seize. If fitted with too much clearance in the cylinder, the pistons will knock and rattle.

VCR PISTONS

High compression for starting and lower compression under load is highly desirable for diesel engines. One method of attaining this goal is the variable compression ratio (VCR) piston, Fig. 5-14.

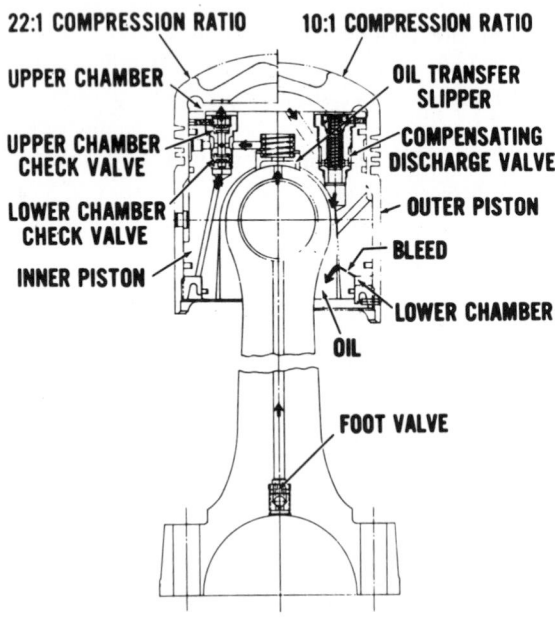

Fig. 5-14. Details of variable compression ratio piston. (Continental Motors Corp.)

The Continental Motors Corp. has developed one form of VCR piston that provides improved starting, better idling and improved output per cubic inch of displacement. Comparisons were made of a VCR piston engine and a conventional engine of the same displacement and same general design. Tests indicated a gross brake horsepower (bhp) for the conventional engine of 550. The engine with VCR pistons produced 1475 bhp.

Other variable compression ratio components include the connecting rod, which is modified to allow engine oil to transfer from the connecting rod bearing through a slipper to the inner piston. The outer piston corresponds to the normal piston in that it contains the combustion chamber and oil rings. The inner piston is an aluminum forging and contains the valves and hydraulic sealing rings. It is connected to its rod by the piston pin in the conventional manner.

The entire assembly of inner and outer pistons is limited in travel by the piston retaining ring, which provides a mechanical stop for upward motion of the piston.

As engine power and combustion pressures are increased, the pressure on the oil in the upper chamber is also increased.

When this pressure exceeds the setting of the spring-loaded discharge valve, a small amount of oil passes to the crankcase, and the outer piston moves downward. This movement results in an increase in clearance volume between the outer piston and the cylinder combustion dome, which reduces the compression ratio. This process continues until the upper piston contacts the inner piston, preventing any further reduction in the compression ratio.

During the exhaust stroke, the outer piston is caused to move upward due to the force of inertia. This motion is restrained by the hydraulic pressure on the oil in the lower chamber. A vent, or orifice, is provided in the lower chamber, allowing the outer piston to move upward approximately 0.005 in. per cycle. If the combustion pressure is suddenly reduced, the piston will immediately return to the higher compression ratio. The piston changes from its lowest to highest compression ratio in 50 to 60 cycles, regardless of engine speed.

Fig. 5-15. Typical piston damage when top of piston becomes overheated.

PISTON MATERIALS

Cast iron or semi-steel has been used extensively as a piston material. It is strong enough to withstand stresses imposed; has a melting point above the cylinder operating temperature; expands at the same rate as cast iron cylinders; and does not generate excessive friction when properly lubricated. The principal objection is excessive weight, a design factor that becomes more important as engine speeds increase.

Aluminum alloy is now preferred as a material for pistons. It is lighter than cast iron. It is readily cast and machined. It does not generate excessive friction in the cylinder.

Aluminum expands more rapidly than cast iron when subjected to the heat of operation, and also has a much lower melting point. In material and design, the aluminum piston has been developed to a point where its advantages apparently outweigh its disadvantages. Because of this, it is used almost universally in automobile engines.

Lighter weight means less inertia for the reciprocating parts and higher speed for the engine along with better acceleration. Less inertia also decreases bearing loads at high speeds and reduces side thrust on the cylinder walls. The piston head runs cooler because of the greater heat conductivity of aluminum and, in general, it is possible to use higher compression ratios.

Early aluminum pistons were noisy because they had to be

fitted in the cylinder with considerably more clearance than cast iron pistons. This resulted in piston slap and rattle when the engine was cold. The difficulty has been largely overcome by designing the piston skirt so it is flexible, by the use of special alloys and by means of steel struts, Fig. 5-21.

Aluminum pistons possess the desirable characteristic of conducting the heat away from the combustion chamber more rapidly than cast iron. But aluminum pistons also melt at a much lower temperature. They seldom melt entirely, but their strength decreases rapidly as the temperature increases. If the rings are stuck or broken, the top edge of the piston or the aluminum lands between the rings may soften and melt or be blown away by the hot gas, as shown in Fig. 5-15.

Severe and continued detonation (too rapid burning or explosion of air-fuel mixture in combustion chamber) is also responsible for broken piston heads. The aluminum becomes soft when overheated, allowing the ring grooves to deform. Aluminum pistons can be strengthened by alloying the aluminum with other metals and also by special heat treatment. Materials added to the aluminum include copper, magnesium, nickel, silicon, etc.

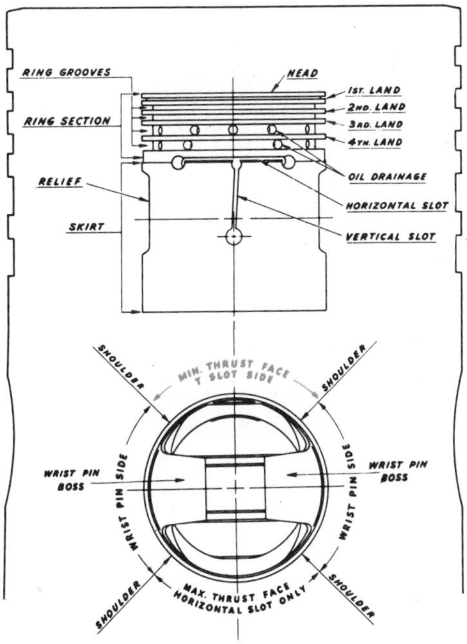

types: "compression" rings and "oil control" rings. Both types are made in a wide variety of designs.

The upper ring or rings are to prevent compression leakage; the lower ring or rings control the amount of oil being deposited on the cylinder wall. The lower groove or grooves often have holes or slots in the bottom of the grooves to permit oil drainage from behind the rings.

The piston ring lands are the parts of the piston between the ring grooves. The lands provide a seating surface for the sides of the piston rings.

The main section of the piston is known as the skirt. It forms a bearing area in contact with the cylinder wall which takes the thrust caused by the crankshaft.

Some thrust is created on both sides of the piston. "Major" thrust is to the side opposite the crank throw as it is driven down on the power stroke. "Minor" thrust is the side opposite the crank throw as the piston moves up on the compression stroke. Pistons are internally braced to make them as strong as possible. See Fig. 5-19.

The piston pin (wrist pin) hole in the piston bosses may

Fig. 5-16. Note that T slot is on minor thrust side. Major thrust side has horizontal slot only.

PISTON CONSTRUCTION

The piston head or "crown," Fig. 5-17, is the top surface against which the explosive force is exerted. It may be flat, concave, convex or any one of a great variety of shapes to promote turbulence or help control combustion, Figs. 5-17 and 5-18. In some applications, a narrow groove is cut into the piston above the top ring to serve as a "heat dam" to reduce the amount of heat reaching the top ring.

Piston rings carried in the ring grooves are of two basic

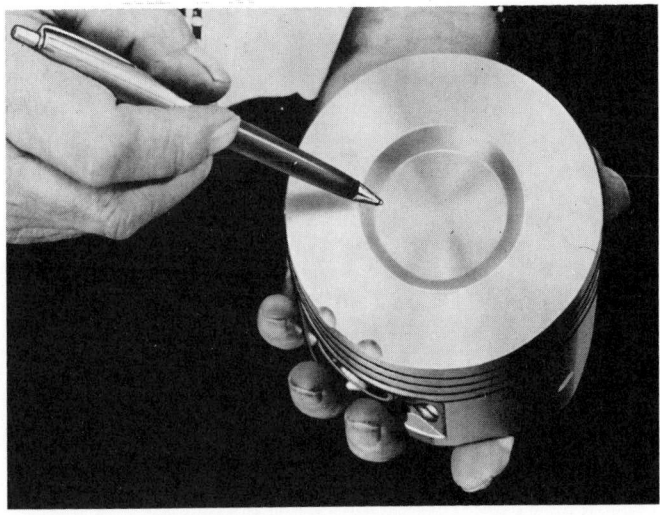

Fig. 5-17. Part of combustion chamber is in this piston head.

Fig. 5-18. Indentations in top of piston provide valve head clearance.

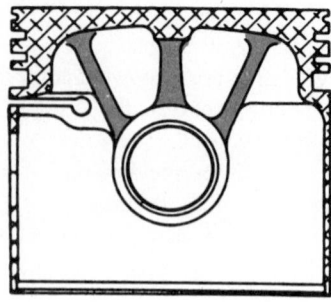

Fig. 5-19. Ribs are cast into inside piston to strengthen area between crown and piston boss.

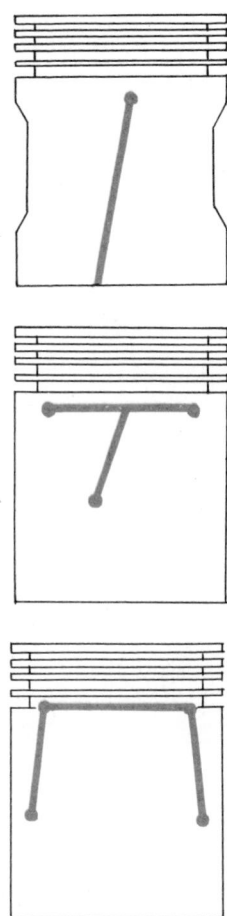

Fig. 5-20. Top. Aluminum pistons may have a diagonal slot cut through skirt on minor thrust side. Center. Some pistons have a slot shaped like a T cut in piston skirt. Bottom. Two slots may be connected by a third slot to form a U-shaped slot design.

also serve as a bearing for the piston pin, and it may not be located exactly in the middle of the piston. It may be placed as much as 1/16 in. to one side to lessen side thrust of the piston on the cylinder wall.

In some designs, the piston skirt is extended downward on the thrust sides to form what is known as a "slipper" piston, Figs. 5-13 and 5-18. This design feature increases the area of piston contact with the cylinder walls at the thrust faces.

Some pistons are also cut away, or partially cut away, around the piston pin holes, Figs. 5-13, 5-16 and 5-17. This "relief" is intended to provide additional clearance to avoid "seizing" if the piston should become overheated and expand excessively.

PISTON DESIGN

Alloy pistons may have the skirts split in a variety of ways, Fig. 5-20. These slots are placed on the thrust sides to provide

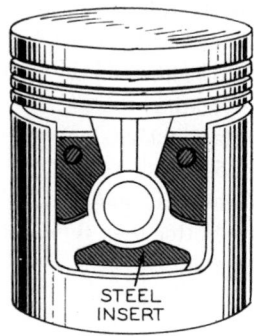

Fig. 5-21. A steel insert may be cast into an aluminum piston to help control expansion rate.

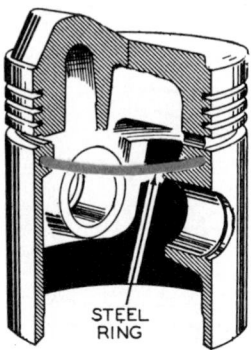

Fig. 5-22. Instead of a vertical insert, a steel ring may be cast into piston to help control expansion.

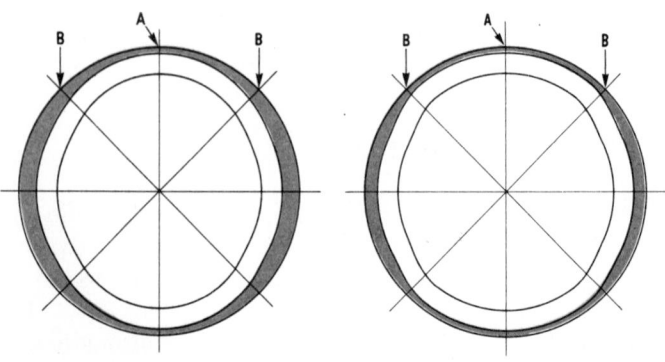

Fig. 5-23. Left. When piston is cold, there is more clearance at shoulders B than at A. Right. As temperature of piston increases, it becomes more nearly round and clearance is more nearly uniform.

flexibility in the piston skirt. By this means, the piston can be fitted more closely when cold, so it can expand when hot, without damage.

Some pistons are of the "strut" type shown in Fig. 5-21. In this case, an alloy steel insert is cast into the aluminum piston to control the expansion of the aluminum and maintain more constant clearance. Pistons are usually "skeleton" type and do not contact the cylinder walls around the piston pin holes.

Still another design is known as the "steel belted" type. It has a steel ring cast into the aluminum piston above the piston pin holes to help control expansion. See Fig. 5-22.

Most aluminum pistons are "cam-ground," or purposely machined with the skirts oval, Fig. 5-23. While the skirts will be out-of-round when cold (thrust faces have greater diameter), the skirt will become more nearly round when the piston expands at operating temperature, Fig. 5-24. In this case, the piston contact surface will be something like the pattern shown in Fig. 5-25.

Pistons are also slightly tapered in many designs. The top of the piston runs much hotter than the bottom, or skirt, so the top is smaller in diameter. This is particularly true in the area above the top ring. Even if the entire piston is not tapered, the top lands are smaller in diameter than the skirt, which needs less clearance.

Pistons in heavy-duty engines have a tendency to get soft from the excess heat at the top. To combat this, the

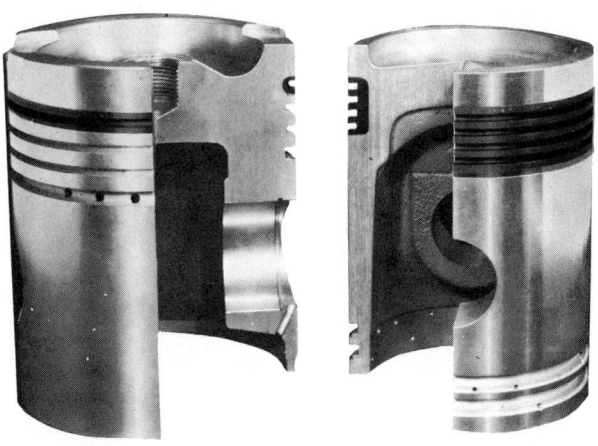
Fig. 5-26. Inserted iron bands are sometimes used in heavy-duty pistons to strengthen ring grooves.

manufacturers insert an iron band for the top ring or rings, Fig. 5-26.

The top surfaces of pistons also vary in designs. They are often contoured to affect turbulent action to the explosive mixture, and thereby providing more efficient combustion. This is particularly true in the case of diesel engines.

A piston known as the Mexican Hat design, Fig. 5-27, is a feature of the Allis Chalmers diesel. In this design, the fuel injector is centrally located over the cylinder and piston, and the fuel is directed downward in a conical spray. The spray will strike the top and rim of the piston, rather than the relatively cool cylinder wall. The manufacturers claim that the fuel will be mixed with a greater percentage of air for improved combustion.

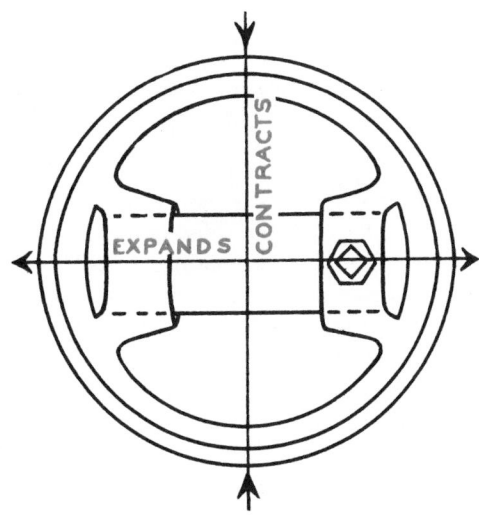
Fig. 5-24. Expansion of piston occurs parallel with piston pin.

Fig. 5-27. Mexican hat type piston for use in diesel engines.

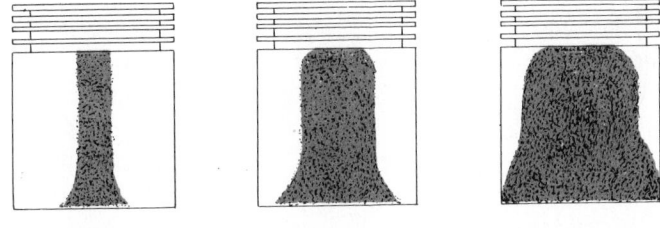
Fig. 5-25. As a cam ground piston expands, pattern of contact with cylinder wall progresses from cold piston at left to warm piston at right.

The piston used in the Mercedes-Benz diesel is shown in Fig. 5-28. It features what is known as an "open" combustion chamber. With this design, turbulence is provided by injecting fuel at an angle.

Another type of piston provides a spherical chamber in which combustion takes place. This piston design is known as

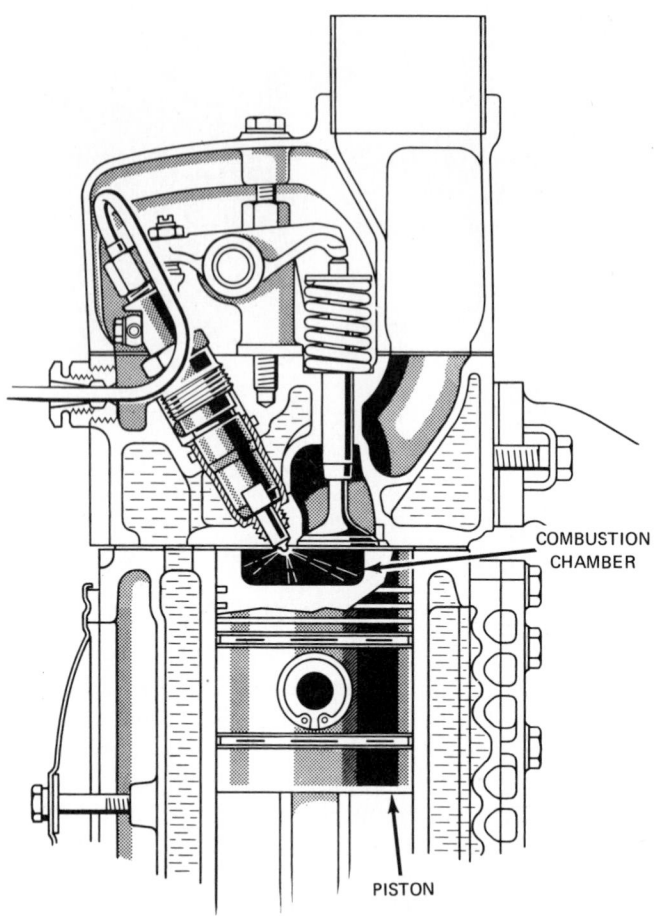

Fig. 5-28. Rim around piston forms "open" combustion chamber on this diesel engine.

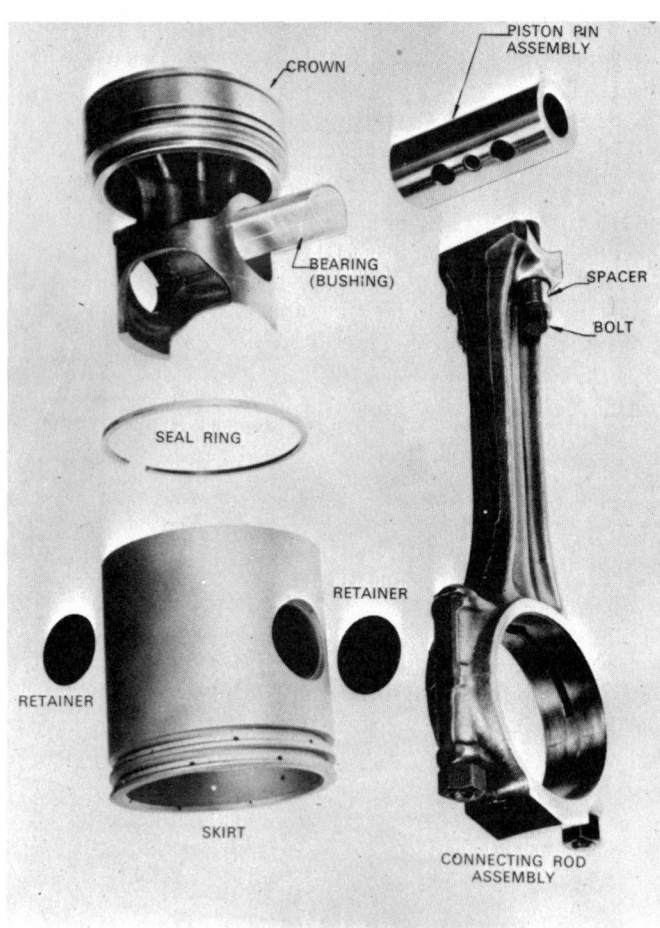

Fig. 5-30. View of crosshead piston.

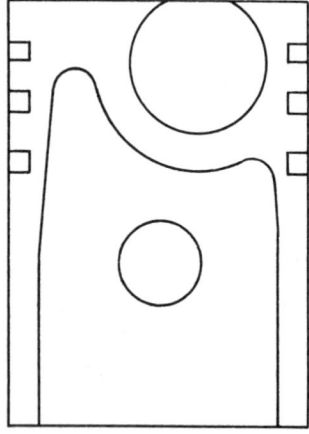

Fig. 5-29. Piston with almost hemispherical cavity that provides M type combustion chamber for diesel engines.

CROSSHEAD PISTON

To increase piston life and provide greater load factor capability, a crosshead piston was developed for diesel engines, Fig. 5-30. This two-piece piston separates the crown of the piston from the skirt. Each part carries out its prescribed function without being forced to react to unnecessary mechanical or thermal loads.

With the crosshead design, the crown and skirt are free to rock on the piston pin axis independently of each other. As a result, the vertical forces of combustion and compression are separated from the side thrust. Side thrust load on the piston caused by various positions of the connecting rod cannot be transmitted to the crown of the piston since it is not solidly connected to the piston pin.

With this construction, wear of the piston rings is reduced and thermal loads are confined to the crown. Pressure lubrication is provided for the piston pin which has a heavy-duty type bearing with a tin-lead overlay. Superior cooling of the piston crown is provided by supplying oil to chambers under the crown. A standpipe in the chamber maintains the oil level at the desired height.

the M-system, Fig. 5-29. Fuel is injected so it strikes the surface of the spherical chamber. In addition to wide commercial application, it is used extensively in multi-fuel engines, particularly military applications.

REVIEW QUESTIONS — ENGINE CONSTRUCTION

1. The power of an automobile engine is determined by the number of cylinders. True or False?
2. The stroke of the engine is determined by:
   a. Length of the cylinder.
   b. Length of the crankshaft throw.
   c. Displacement of the cylinder.
3. How can the displacement of an engine be found?
4. Explain why cylinders wear out-of-round.
5. A wet cylinder sleeve is lubricated, a dry sleeve is not. True or False?
6. Cylinder head gaskets for a V-8 engine are interchangeable and may be used on either side. Yes or No?
7. The combustion chamber is usually:
   a. Above the piston.
   b. Below the piston.
   c. In the crankcase.
8. Name three things required of the piston.
9. Which material is used most for pistons?

10. What is a heat dam in a piston?
11. Which side of the piston is the major thrust side?
12. What is meant by piston relief?
13. Pistons are slotted so that they can be more readily inserted in the cylinders. True or False?
14. The tops of pistons are often contoured to provide turbulence. True or False?
15. Describe a cam-ground piston.
16. How many major types of cylinder head gaskets are there?
    a. Three.
    b. Four.
    c. Five.
    d. Six.
    e. Seven.
17. The "hemi" combustion chamber has greater surface area than other designs. True or False?
18. The wedge shape combustion chamber provides good turbulence. Yes or No?

Cutaway view of General Motors' 200 cu. in. (3.3 litre) V-6 engine. Featured in the Chevrolet Malibu, this engine produces 95 hp @ 3800 rpm.

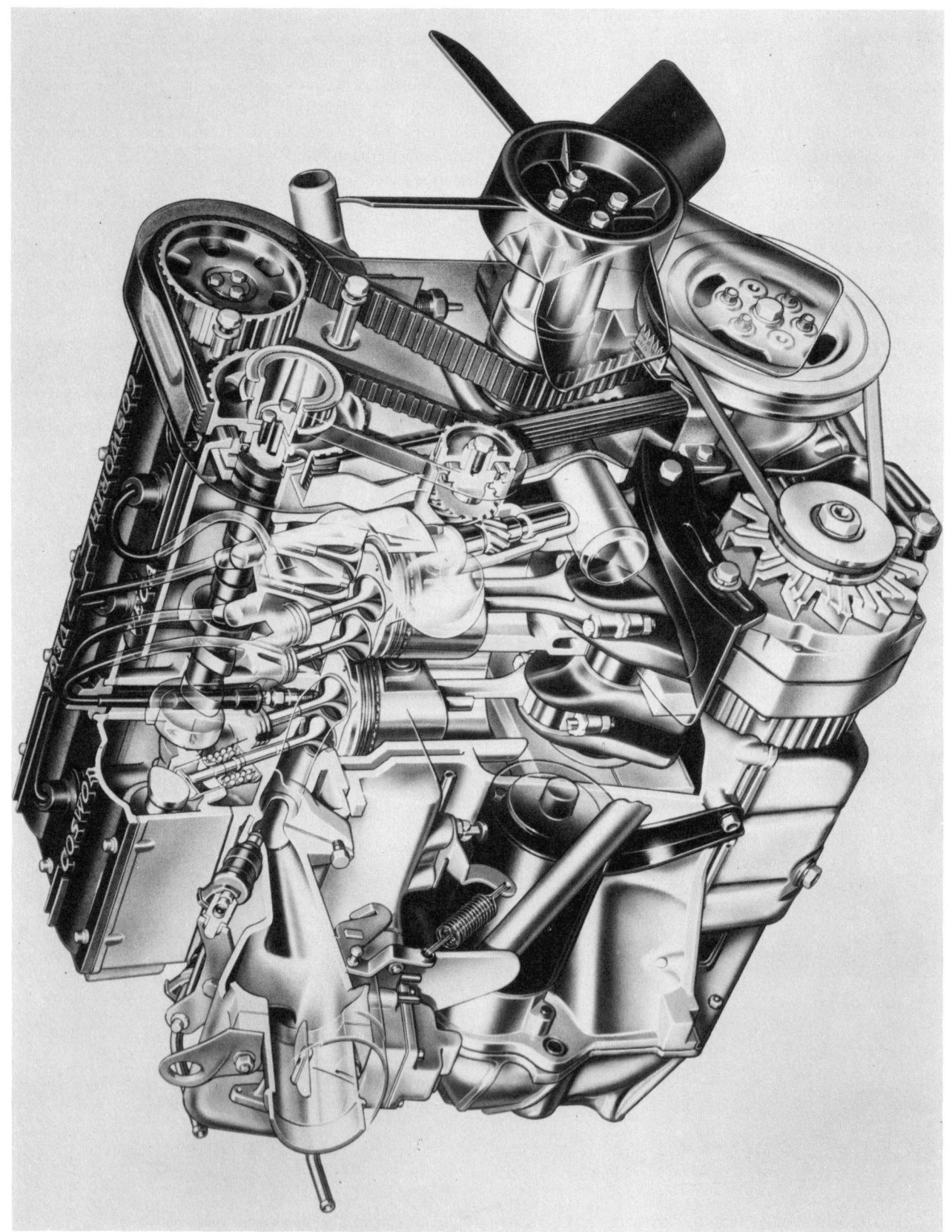

Cosworth Vega engine is unique four cylinder power plant for special production hatchback model by Chevrolet Motor Division. This 122 cu. in., 8.5 to 1 compression ratio engine has double overhead camshafts, four valves per cylinder, electronic fuel injection and magnetic pulse ignition. Front mounted distributor is driven by small cog belt. Large belt is fiber glass cord reinforced neoprene rubber.

ENGINE PISTON
RINGS AND PINS

Piston rings have been designed in an unbelievable multitude of variations. Originally, they were a simple split ring made of cast iron. Since engine power output has constantly increased and oiling requirements have become more complicated, more efficiency and durability has been demanded of piston rings.

Modern piston rings are made of steel, as well as cast iron. Oil control rings often have multiple sections and are quite complicated in design. Different types of rings are heat treated in various ways and plated with other metals. Today's piston rings, however, still fall into two distinct classifications: compression rings and oil control rings. A typical ring installation is shown in Fig. 6-1.

Latest developments in the design of piston rings tend to reduce emissions, together with reducing oil consumption and improving engine durability. According to TRW researchers, improvements in hydrocarbon emissions may be obtained by mounting the top compression ring near the top of the piston. Also, reducing ring friction reduces nitrogen oxide emissions because of lower throttle settings for a given load output.

PISTON RING BLOW-BY

Piston rings would not present much of a problem if cylinders and pistons did not expand, distort out-of-round, and warp when at operating temperatures. But cylinders and pistons DO expand and may also distort and warp, so the rings must be capable of conforming to these changing conditions.

Furthermore, the rings are exposed to high temperatures of combustion and to alternating pressure and vacuum. Rings are expected to prevent the blow-by of pressure in one direction and to control the flow of oil in the other direction.

Compression pressure and explosion pressure can get by the rings in several ways. "Blow-by" can go through the ring gaps which change in width according to the expansion and contraction of the cylinder and rings. If the rings were fitted so precisely that ring ends touched to seal the gap, the cylinder walls would score when the rings expanded from the heat of operation.

Blow-by also can occur if it gets behind the compression rings, as shown in Fig. 6-2. If the rings were fitted too tight in the grooves to avoid possible leakage, there would be danger of sticking when the piston and rings expand.

Blow-by is a serious problem when the cylinder walls distort out-of-round at operating temperature. This condition can be caused by improper engine block or cylinder head

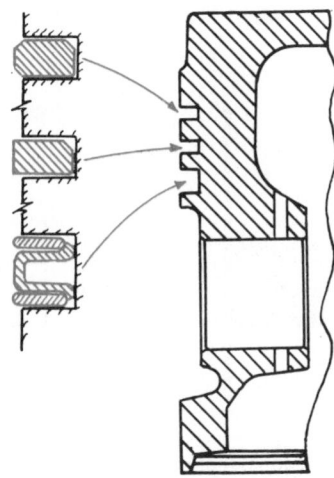

Fig. 6-1. This cross section shows compression rings in two upper grooves; a three-piece oil control ring in lower groove.

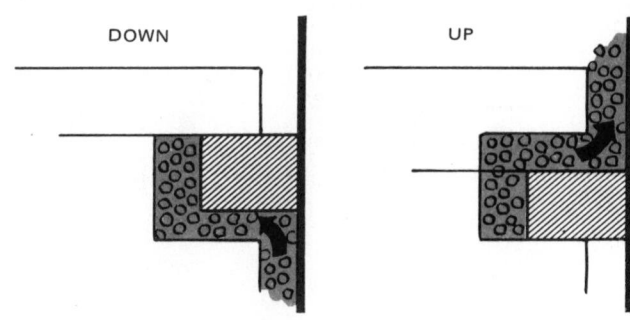

Fig. 6-2. Oil can creep in back of rings to find way into combustion chamber, and gases can creep down into crankcase from combustion chamber in a similar manner, but in opposite direction.

design, improper cooling or unequal tightening of cylinder head bolts adjacent to the cylinders. Distortion may occur in more than one spot on the cylinder wall, and the different spots are often of different size and shape. See Fig. 6-3.

Just as compression can leak down past the rings, oil can also pass upward into the cylinder. The result is known as "oil pumping." This condition causes fouling of the spark plugs, excessive deposits of carbon in the combustion chamber and smoking exhaust as well as loss of oil.

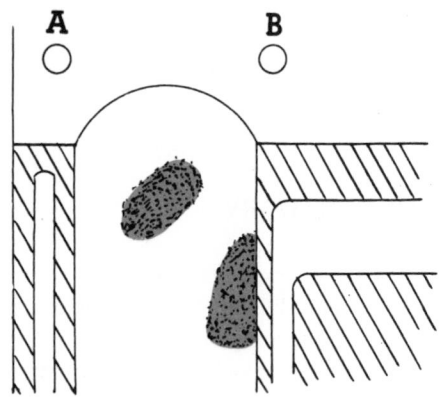

Fig. 6-3. Distortion of cylinder walls can cause cylinders to be out-of-round or to distort in spots.

OIL PUMPING

It is easier for oil to pass upward, in some cases, than it is for compression to leak down past the rings. Therefore, it is possible to have an engine with good compression and power, which is also an oil pumper. The oil may seal excessive side clearance in the ring grooves and prevent leakage of compression. Yet, alternating vacuum and pressure in the cylinder may cause the rings to act as a pump. See Fig. 6-4.

This condition is aggravated if the walls of the ring grooves, and the sides of the rings, are not flat and true. The volume of oil leakage past the back of the ring can be much greater than

through the tiny ring gaps.

From these explanations of blow-by and oil pumping, you can see that great care is required in reconditioning cylinders to make sure they are round and true when new rings are fitted. Equal care is required in selecting the new rings and fitting them to the pistons and cylinders. Many other things which enter into the matter will be considered in this chapter and in Chapter 13.

COMPRESSION RINGS

The top compression ring is usually rectangular in cross section or it has a bevel cut on the inner top corner, Fig. 6-5.

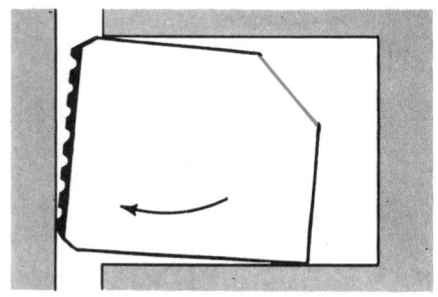

Fig. 6-5. A ring beveled in this manner has a tendency to tilt in ring groove.

Often the ring is chrome plated, Fig. 6-6, or is molybdenum-filled (moly) cast iron to provide better wearing qualities. The second compression ring is often a coated cast iron ring. Some compression rings have a taper on the face, and they may or may not have an inside bevel.

The bevel on the inside upper corner of the ring is to effect a better seal. The bevel causes the ring to twist in the groove so that the outside lower edge presses on the cylinder wall more tightly than the rest of the ring face.

The compression ring with a tapered outer face does the same thing. In both cases, the limited area in contact with the

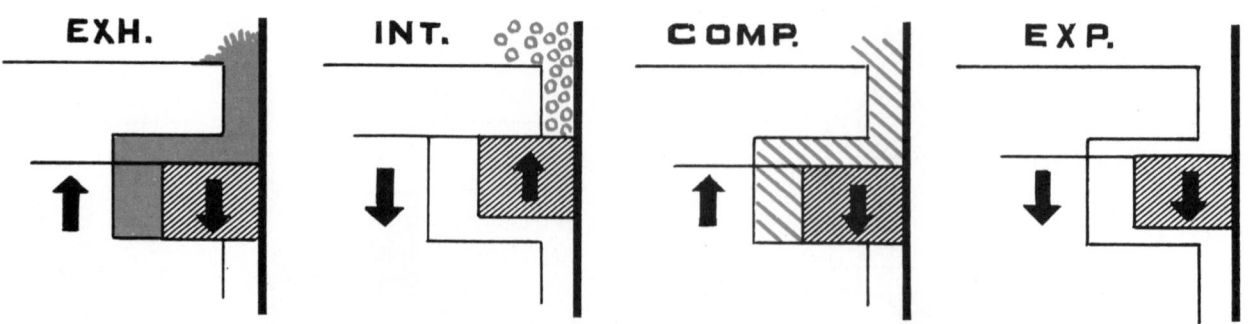

Fig. 6-4. There must be some clearance between ring and bottom of groove, and also on sides of ring. Result is that a ring can act as a pump: On exhaust stroke, exhaust gas tends to hold rings in bottom of groove as piston travels up. On intake stroke, vacuum in combustion chamber tends to hold ring against top of groove while piston goes down. On compression stroke, pressure in combustion chamber again tends to hold ring against bottom of groove. On explosion stroke, expanding gases tend to push both piston and ring in same direction, permitting ring to float in groove.

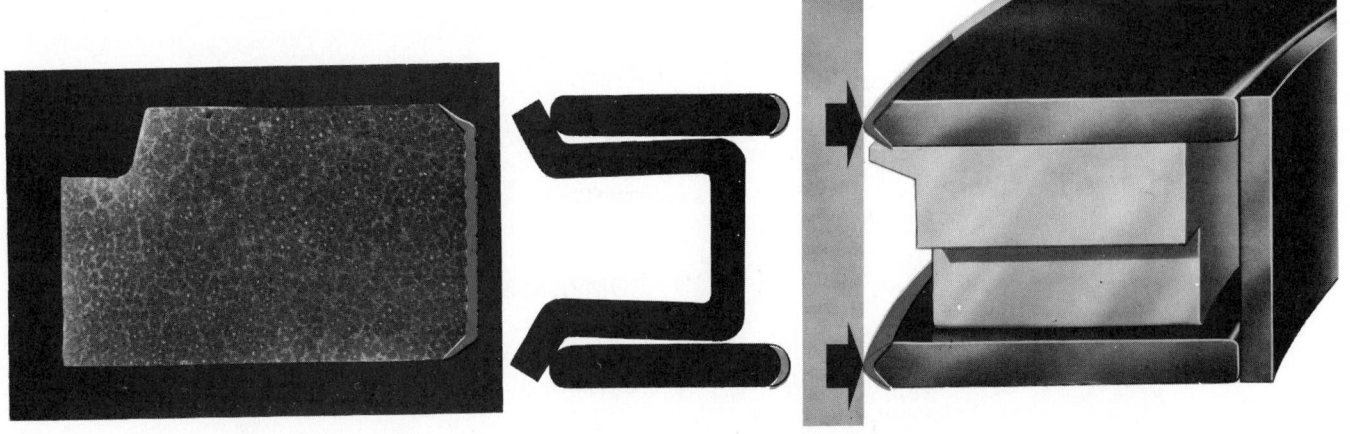

Fig. 6-6. Three different types of chrome plated piston rings.

cylinder wall offers a higher pressure at that point for better sealing. Beveled and/or tapered rings must be installed right side up and are usually stamped "top" on that side of the ring.

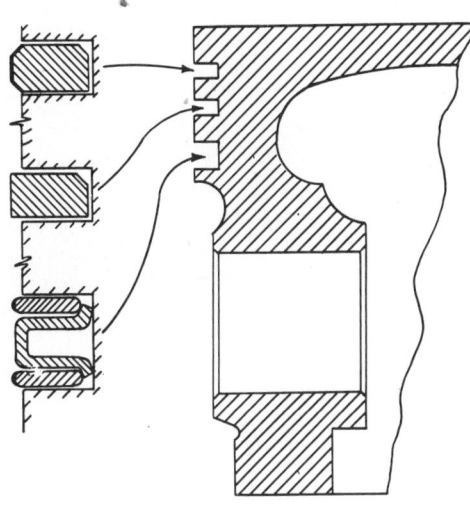

Fig. 6-7. In this installation, top and bottom rings are chrome plated. Second ring is "twist" type.

Usually, the second ring is a compression ring, but it may be slightly different in design since it helps in oil control. This difference might be a bevel cut on the inner or outer corner, Fig. 6-7, which might be combined with a taper on either the inside or outside. These second rings are also known as scraper rings, because one or more edges are designed to aid in scraping the oil from the cylinder walls. Some of these designs are shown in Fig. 6-8, together with details of some oil rings.

OIL CONTROL RINGS

The third ring from the top, and the fourth if four are used, are of the oil-control type. Oil rings vary all the way from simple to extremely complicated types. Several varieties are shown in Fig. 6-9.

Remember that oil scraped from the cylinder wall by the

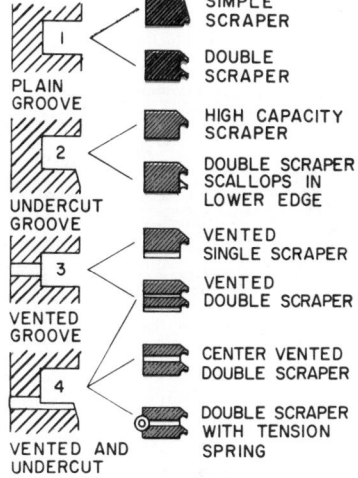

Fig. 6-8. Details of scraper and oil control rings.

oil ring must have a free passage to the inside of the piston. For this reason, holes or slots are cut in the lower ring grooves. When an inner ring or expander is used, these openings must be kept open if the oil ring is to function as intended. See Fig. 6-10.

Another typical piston ring installation is shown in Fig. 6-11. Note that the No. 1 ring has full face contact on the cylinder wall, distributing the ring expansive pressure over a wide area. Ring No. 2 is also a compression ring, but it has a narrower contact surface. Therefore, it exerts a higher pressure on the cylinder wall, because the entire expansive force of the ring is concentrated on the narrow area of the ring. As a result, the top ring will show less tendency to wear the cylinder wall in the driest and hottest part. The second ring will seat more quickly to the cylinder wall even though it has more lubrication than the top ring.

Ring No. 3 is an oil control ring. The design shown in Fig. 6-11 has two narrow edges in contact with the cylinder wall. Slots cut between the two edges permit oil scraped from the

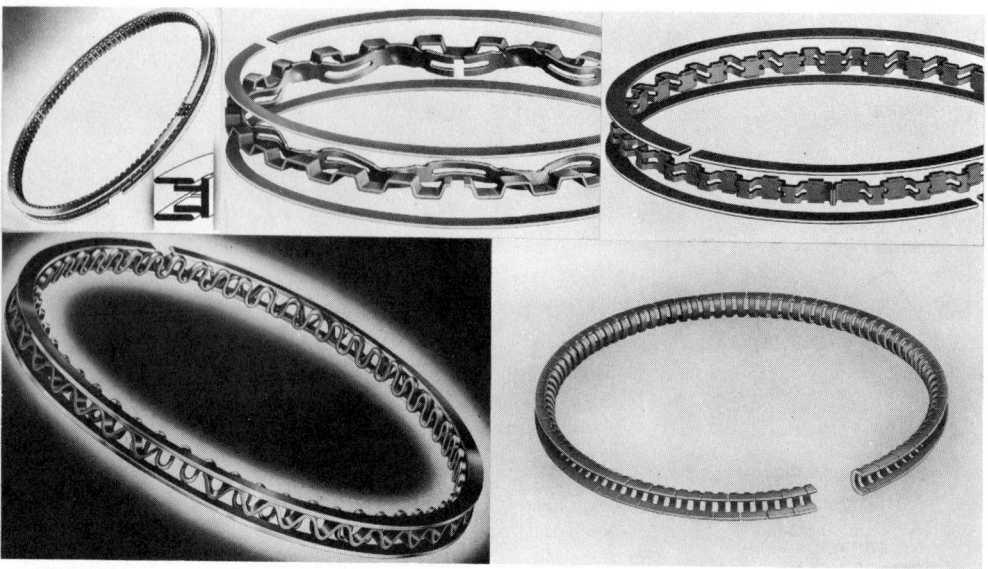

Fig. 6-9. Oil control rings are made in a wide variety of designs.

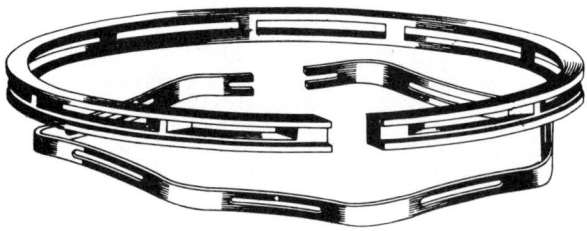

Fig. 6-10. A typical slotted steel expander used with a slotted oil control ring.

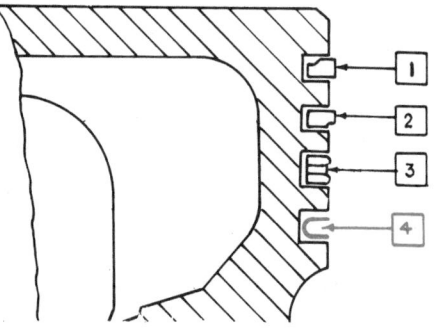

Fig. 6-11. This typical piston ring installation uses an extremely flexible oil control ring in bottom groove.

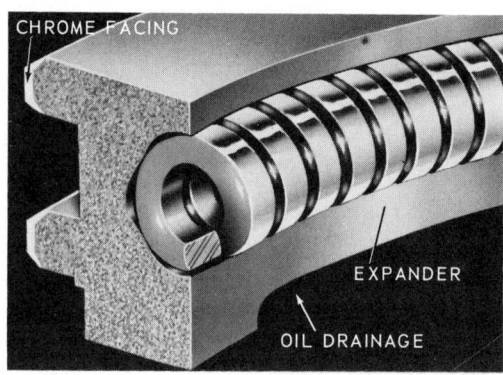

Fig. 6-12. Chrome faced oil ring with stainless steel coiled spring expander. (Sealed Power)

cylinder wall to channel through the slots. Ring No. 4, in this case, is the extremely flexible type which closely follows the contour of the cylinder walls even when they are slightly out-of-round.

In studying piston ring function, remember that the piston ring moves in the groove. Because of the constant reversing of direction of piston travel, and the need for sidewise clearance between ring and groove, piston rings do move up and down in the ring grooves. A film of oil cushions this movement.

Likewise, if the cylinder is worn tapered, the rings will expand and contract as they move up and down in a bore that is larger at one end than the other. Similarly if the cylinder is out-of-round in spots, the rings will be pumping in and out of the grooves as they try to follow the cylinder wall.

Another type of oil control ring is shown in Fig. 6-12. This ring is a cast iron ring with a self expanding stainless steel spring expander. It is designed specifically to prevent oil clogging in heavy duty service. Note that the expander is located above the drainage slots, so oil flow will not be restricted. In addition, drainage slots at the bottom of the ring are curved to eliminate sharp corners. The ring is faced with chrome to reduce wear.

PISTON PINS

Piston pins ("wrist pins") are the connection between the upper end of the connecting rod and the piston, Fig. 6-13. There are three main types:

1. Pins anchored in piston with bushing in upper end of

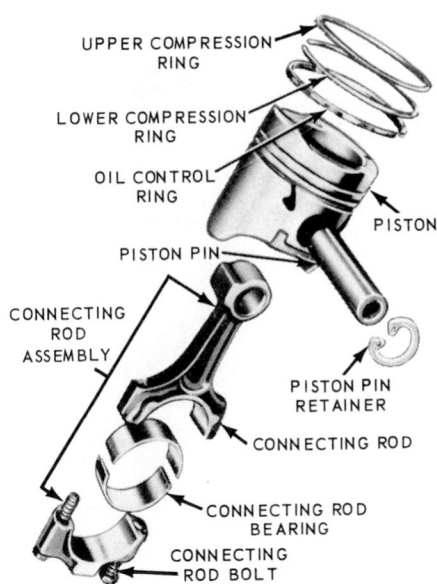

Fig. 6-13. Piston, rod, pin and ring assembly. Note piston pin and retainer. (Ford)

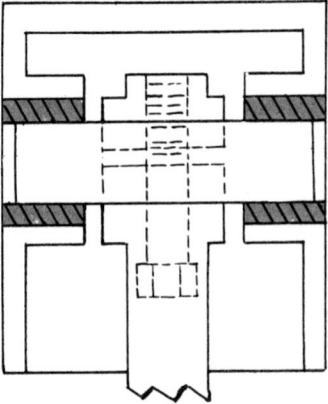

Fig. 6-15. Where piston pin is anchored in connecting rod, a bearing is provided in each piston boss.

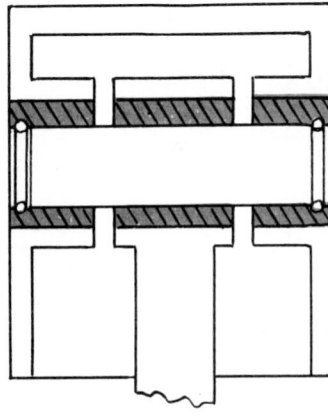

Fig. 6-16. Where piston pin is held in place by snap rings or plugs, pin "floats" and bears in piston bosses and in rod end. This illustration shows principle involved, but actually pin would bear directly in piston bosses of an aluminum piston, and retaining ring grooves would be cut into piston.

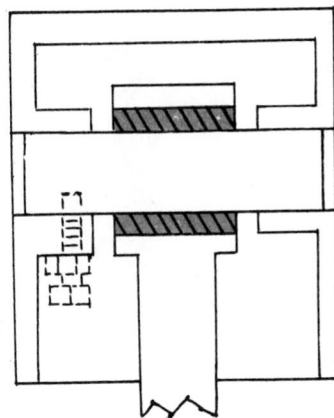

Fig. 6-14. Where pin is anchored in piston, bearing is located in upper end of connecting rod.

connecting rod, oscillating on pin, Fig. 6-14.

2. Pins clamped in rod with pin oscillating in piston, Fig. 6-15.

3. Pins which are full floating in both connecting rod and piston, secured by lock rings or soft metal plugs in both piston bosses to prevent endwise movement of piston pin. See Fig. 6-16.

Other than type of bearing and provision for holding the pins in place, all three types of piston pins are quite similar. Usually, they are hollow steel pins, case-hardened on the outside surface. Piston pins are subjected to extremely heavy loads and are not adjustable for wear. When worn, they must be replaced.

Since piston pins have an oscillating motion in their bearing surface, rather than the high surface speed between the crankshaft and connecting rod bearings, the steel pin can bear directly in the aluminum piston. Or, the pin may be fitted to bronze bushings in either cast iron or aluminum pistons. Or, a bronze bushing may be pressed into the upper end of the connecting rod.

Other variations found in piston pin design include "needle" or roller bearings in hardened bushings, an "interference fit" in the connecting rod (which requires pin be pressed into a hole slightly smaller than pin). In case of an aluminum connecting rod, no bushing may be required.

The proper size for a piston pin presents a design problem. If the pin is large enough in diameter to provide a long wearing bearing surface, the reciprocating weight will be greater and the bearing loads correspondingly increased. If it is as small as permissible to hold down bearing loads, it will be smaller in diameter and have less bearing surface to carry the load.

If the pin is fastened in the piston with a small screw, the assembly will be lighter than if a bolt is used in the connecting rod. However, if it is clamped in the rod, it will have double the bearing surface since there will be a bearing in each piston boss. If it floats in both piston and rod, Fig. 6-16, it will have the greatest bearing surface along with the lightest weight.

One possible drawback with "floating" construction con-

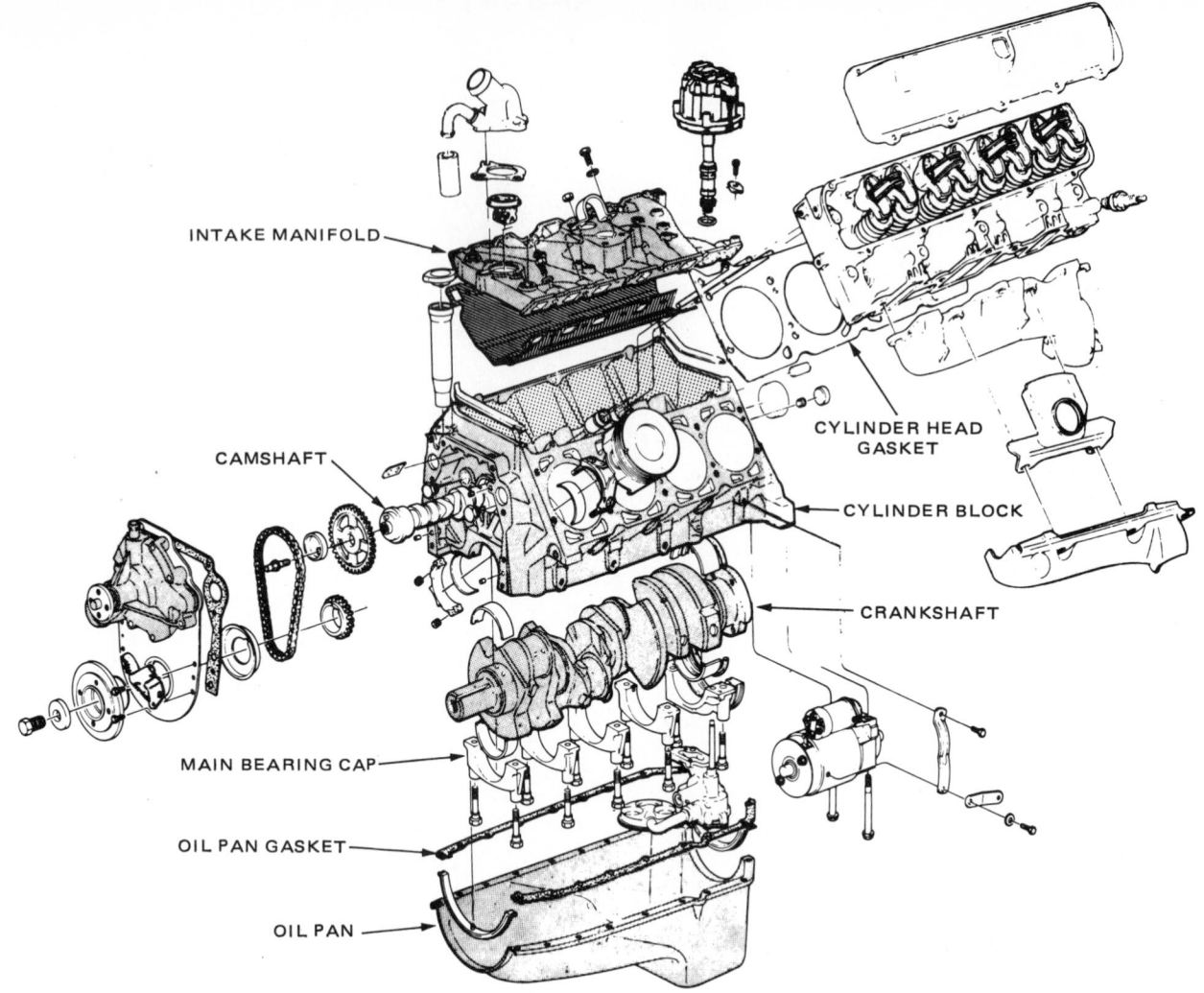

INTAKE MANIFOLD

CYLINDER HEAD GASKET

CAMSHAFT

CYLINDER BLOCK

CRANKSHAFT

MAIN BEARING CAP

OIL PAN GASKET

OIL PAN

Fig. 6-17. Exploded view of a Pontiac 350 cu. in. (5.7 litre) V-8 engine.

cerns the locking ring or retaining plug. If it should fail to stay in place, the pin will score the cylinder wall.

One other complication is the fact that all three metals in contact (steel, bronze and aluminum) have a different rate of heat expansion. Obviously, being attached to the piston, the pins and bushings will run hot. Since heat in any bearing promotes wear, piston pin and bushings could develop excessive clearance and create noise.

While mechanics can do little about the design of engine parts, a thorough understanding of problems involved will motivate them to do the best possible job. (See chapter on PISTON PIN AND RING FITTING.)

REVIEW QUESTIONS – ENGINE PISTON RINGS AND PINS

1. Name two results of oil pumping.
2. Blow-by may be a serious problem after the engine warms up to operating temperature. True or False?
3. Do piston rings move up and down in the grooves? Yes or No?
4. Why must piston rings be flexible?
5. A piston ring may act as a pump. True or False?
6. Give two reasons for cylinder wall distortion.
7. Do piston rings move in and out in the grooves? Yes or No?
8. More oil leakage occurs:
   a.   At the ring gap.
   b.   Around behind the ring.
9. If an engine has good compression it will not pump oil. True or False?

10. Name four ways of holding the piston pin in place.
11. Describe an "interference fit."
12. Bronze bushings can be used with aluminum pistons. True or False?
13. In order to obtain the greatest wearing surface, the piston pin should be clamped in:
   a.   The connecting rod.
   b.   The piston.
   c.   Neither.
   d.   Both.
14. A hardened steel pin can be used in an aluminum piston without any bushings. Yes or No?
15. Aluminum and bronze have about the same rate of heat expansion. True or False?
16. Piston pins are not _____ for wear.

ENGINE CRANKSHAFTS
AND CAMSHAFTS

Automobile engine crankshafts may be forged out of steel, Fig. 7-1, or they may be made out of cast steel by a special process, Fig. 7-2. They are usually in one piece. If they are built up of more than one piece, all pieces must be carefully and rigidly connected.

The bearing journals are all finished in precise alignment with each other. Also, great care is exercised to see that the journals are absolutely round, and not tapered longitudinally. A high degree of accuracy is necessary in any work that is done with an engine crankshaft or any of the bearings.

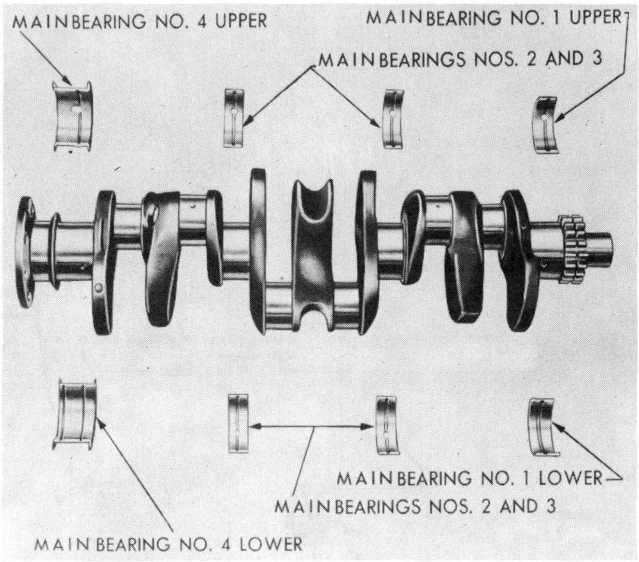

Fig. 7-2. Typical cast steel crankshaft.

Fig. 7-1. Forged steel crankshaft with bearing inserts.

In automobile engines, a gear or sprocket is installed on the end of the crankshaft (opposite the flywheel end) to drive the camshaft either by means of a timing chain or a gear arrangement. Also, a torsional vibration damper usually is attached to the same end of the crankshaft to help smooth out vibrations set up in the crankshaft by power impulses that tend to twist the shaft. See Fig. 7-3.

Fig. 7-3. A counter-balanced crankshaft complete with flywheel and vibration damper.

ENGINE FLYWHEELS

A flywheel ordinarily is mounted near the rear main bearing. This is usually the longest and heaviest of the main bearings, since it must support the weight of the flywheel.

The purpose of the flywheel is to assist the engine to idle smoothly by carrying the pistons through parts of the operating cycle when power is not being produced.

The heavier the engine flywheel, the smoother the engine will idle. However, because of its inertia, an excessively heavy flywheel will cause the engine to accelerate and decelerate slowly. For this reason, heavy-duty or truck engines have large and heavy flywheels, while racing engines or high performance engines have light flywheels.

The rear surface of the flywheel is usually machined flat. This surface is used to mate with one surface of the clutch. With automatic transmissions, where no clutch is used, part of the fluid flywheel or torque converter is attached to and becomes a part of the flywheel.

CRANKSHAFT BALANCE

Because of the forces acting on the flywheel and crankshaft, and the speed at which it revolves, the crankshaft must be balanced with great care. The assembly is first balanced statically, then dynamically. To obtain static balance, the weight must be equal in all directions from the center when the crankshaft is at rest.

Dynamic balance means balance while the crankshaft is turning. It is attained when the centrifugal forces of rotation are equal in all directions at any point. The dynamic balancing operation requires special machinery and involves removal of metal at the heavy points or addition of metal at the light points.

To obtain rotating balance, crankshafts are equipped with counterweights, which are usually forged or cast integrally with the crankshaft, Fig. 7-3. (In some cases, counterweights have been bolted rigidly to crankshaft.) Counterweights are located on the opposite side of the crankshaft from the connecting rod to counter balance the weight of the rod.

In addition to balancing the crankshaft itself, the entire rotating assembly must be balanced dynamically, Fig. 7-4. This

Fig. 7-4. Special equipment is utilized to check running balance of an engine with rotating and reciprocating parts in place.

assembly includes the fan pulley, vibration damper, timing gears, crankshaft, flywheel and the clutch or converter parts attached to it. In addition, the connecting rod assemblies, including piston pins, pistons, bearings, etc., are all carefully balanced one with another so that the rotating mass will have as little vibration as possible.

For a further discussion on crankshaft balancing and methods used to correct unbalance, see Chapter 15.

TORSIONAL VIBRATION

The explosive forces acting on the pistons, and the inertia forces of the reciprocating parts, vary in intensity as the pistons move up and down in the cylinders. This variation in force, or torque, causes the crankshaft to twist or transmit torsional vibration. It is more noticeable at certain speeds than others. The vibration is of greater intensity on long shafts than on short ones.

When the No. 1 cylinder fires, it tends to turn the front end of the crankshaft instantly. This force is transmitted through the length of the crankshaft to the flywheel, which has considerable inertia. At this point, the crankshaft momentarily

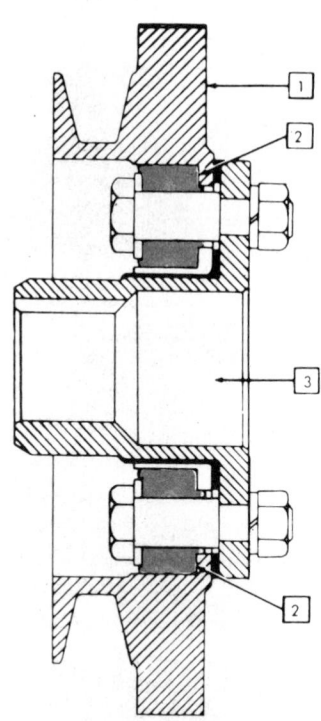

Fig. 7-5. Makeup of a typical vibration damper. 1—Pulley. 2—Rubber blocks. 3—Pulley hub.

"winds up" or twists lengthwise (to a small degree, but enough to create vibration). Any piece of steel, no matter how heavy, can be twisted slightly when enough torque is applied to it.

Twisting of the crankshaft depends upon the forces operating in the engine, so it is more severe at some speeds than others. Vibration dampers are used to help control crankshaft twist, Fig. 7-5.

VIBRATION DAMPERS

Regardless of the type of vibration damper used, they all accomplish the same purpose. They add mass or inertia to the end of the crankshaft opposite the flywheel to minimize crankshaft twist. The simplest vibration dampening device would be a flywheel at each end of the crankshaft. In this case, the weight of both flywheels would be about the same as the weight of a single normal flywheel.

A better way is to use a smaller flywheel on the front end and mount it so that it floats. In one type, Fig. 7-5, rubber is used between the small flywheel and its hub. This permits limited circumferential movement between the crankshaft and small flywheel.

Another type of vibration damper, Fig. 7-6, resembles a miniature clutch. A friction facing, mounted between the hub face and small flywheel face, is regulated and adjusted by means of spring tension.

Still another type of vibration damper has the flywheel floating or suspended in fluid such as heavy oil. In any case, the small flywheel, because of its mass and inertia, resists sudden twisting of the shaft and thereby minimizes torsional vibration.

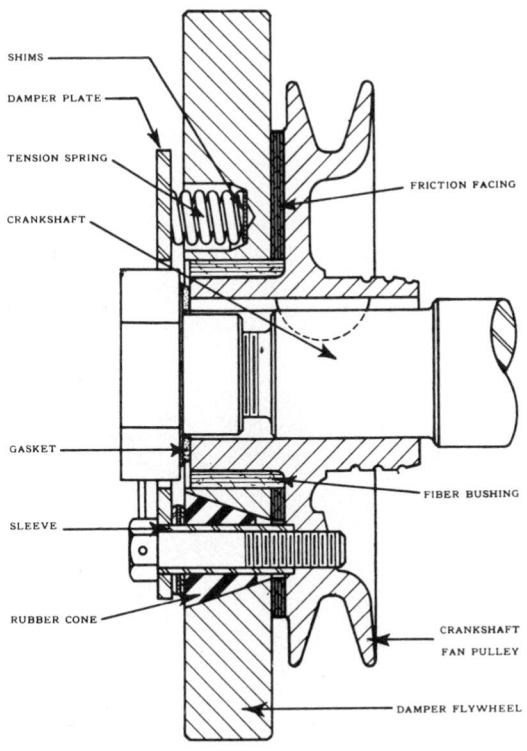

Fig. 7-6. Another design of vibration damper that utilizes friction facings as well as rubber bushings.

CRITICAL SPEEDS

No matter how carefully the crankshaft and parts attached to it are balanced, there will be certain speeds at which some vibration will occur. These are known as critical speeds, where

related other parts also vibrate. By careful design and balancing, these critical periods occur at speeds outside the ordinary working speeds of the engine.

In this connection, it is not too difficult to balance rotating parts. However, when reciprocating parts are attached, the problem becomes much more complicated. Consider that each heavy connecting rod and piston assembly must be started, speeded up, slowed down and stopped twice during each revolution.

OTHER CAUSES OF VIBRATION

Other factors enter into this matter of unbalance. The piston does not accelerate and decelerate uniformly during each quarter of a revolution. During the first quarter revolution from top dead center (TDC), the connecting rod moves down a distance (length of crank throw) and away from the center of the cylinder. Both the downward and outward motions of the rod cause the piston to travel downward.

During the second quarter of a revolution, there is continued downward motion equal to the crank throw. But, the end of the connecting rod is now moving back toward the center line of the cylinder. During the last portion of this movement, the piston is no longer moving downward. As a result, actual movement of the piston during the second quarter revolution is less than during the first quarter, Fig. 7-7.

When you consider all of these forces acting on the crankshaft, it is easy to see why you cannot add or subtract a fraction of an ounce of weight to any of these parts during a repair operation. Furthermore, the crankshaft, bearings, bearing journals, etc. must be in excellent mechanical condition at all times.

ENGINE CAMSHAFTS

A camshaft in its simplest form is a straight shaft with an eccentric lobe or cam on it. Two such camshafts would be used on a one cylinder, T-head, four cycle, poppet valve

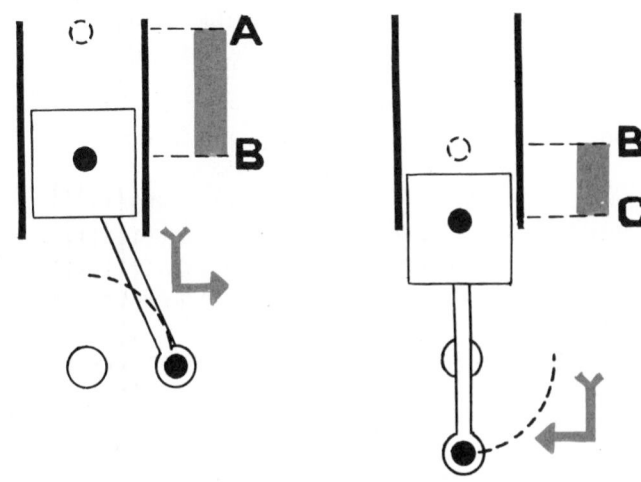

Fig. 7-7. During first quarter revolution of crankshaft from top dead center, piston moves distance from A to B. During second quarter revolution distance moved by piston is less as shown from B to C.

Fig. 7-8. Typical eight cylinder (V-8) camshaft.

engine. One shaft for the inlet valve, another for the exhaust valve. If the engine is of the L-head, I-head or F-head design, both cams would ordinarily be on the same shaft. These cams would be located at different places around the perimeter of the shaft as the valves need to be opened at different times in the operating cycle.

For a multiple cylinder engine, there are ordinarily as many cams as there are valves to be operated. See Fig. 7-8. This is not always the case however as some V-type engines have had one cam so arranged as to operate one valve in each block. This is usually the case in opposed cylinders or "pancake" engines as shown in Fig. 7-9. In four cycle engines, each valve

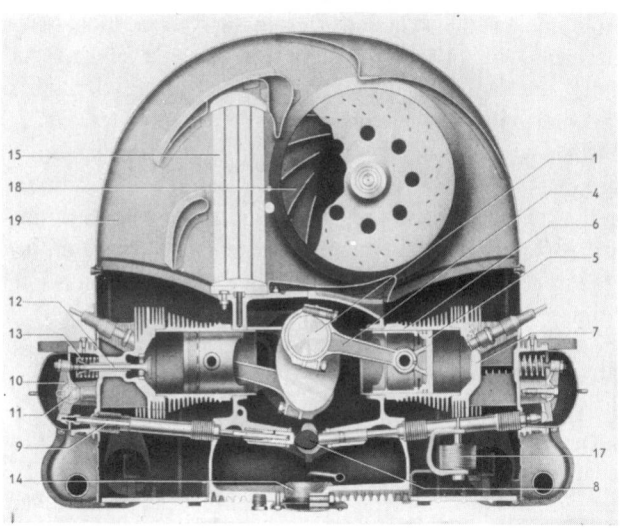

Fig. 7-9. Camshaft (8) is below crankshaft (1) in this Volkswagen pancake engine. Each cam operates two valves, one on each side.

is opened once every other revolution of the engine crankshaft. Therefore, the camshaft is geared to run at half the crankshaft speed. See Fig. 7-11.

Since the camshaft runs at a slower speed than the crankshaft, and it is not subjected to such severe reciprocating forces, it is smaller and has smaller bearings. The camshaft is made of steel. The cams are hardened to avoid rapid surface wear.

These cams appear to have a simple shape, but actually the exact shape of the cam is a meticulous job of design. See Fig. 7-10. The design is worked out after a painstaking and detailed program of mathematical calculation, and checked by lengthy experimentation. If the shape of the cams is altered by wear, the efficiency of the engine deteriorates with great rapidity. There is much more to the matter than just opening and closing a valve.

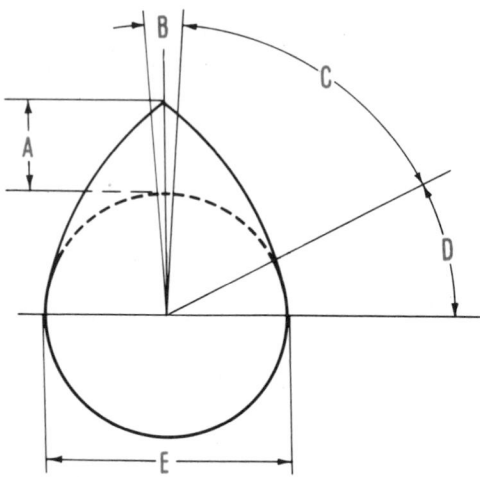

Fig. 7-10. Typical camshaft cam: A—Height of lift. B—Toe section. C—Flank area. D—Ramp. E—Heel diameter of cam.

CAM FUNCTIONS

The cam is designed to lift the valve at precisely the correct instant of piston travel and hold it open long enough to obtain the most efficient filling and emptying of the cylinder. It exerts considerable control over the volumetric efficiency of

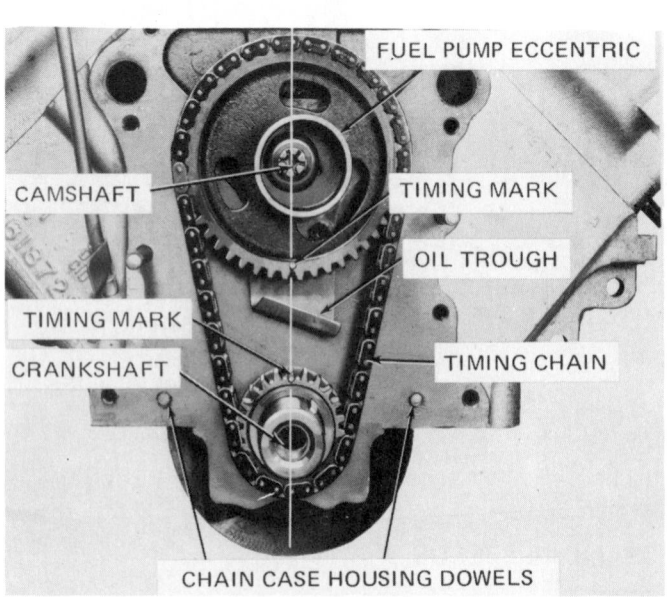

Fig. 7-11. Typical design of chain-driven camshaft in crankcase. Note that camshaft gear is twice the size of crankshaft gear.

the engine. This will be discussed fully later in this text.

In a passenger car engine, ramps on the cams are designed to open the valves smoothly and gradually. This avoids shock to the valves, valve springs, etc., and makes for quietness of operation. The final design is usually a compromise between efficiency and quietness of operation.

On racing engines where noise is not important and utmost efficiency is desired, the cams are often shaped with more abrupt ramps, higher lift, flatter flank and wider toe. The cam is intended to "bat" the valve open quickly, open it wider, hold it open longer and close it rapidly. Such engines are noisy, idle roughly and wear more quickly.

If the camshaft is chain driven, Fig. 7-11, it rotates in the same direction as the crankshaft which is clockwise from the front of the engine. If the camshaft is driven by a gear meshed with a mating gear on the crankshaft, the camshaft rotation is counterclockwise, or opposite from the crankshaft.

CAMSHAFT LOCATION

On an L, F or I-head, in-line engine, the camshaft is usually located to one side and above the crankshaft, Fig. 7-12. On V-type engines, the camshaft is usually located above the crankshaft as shown in Fig. 6-17.

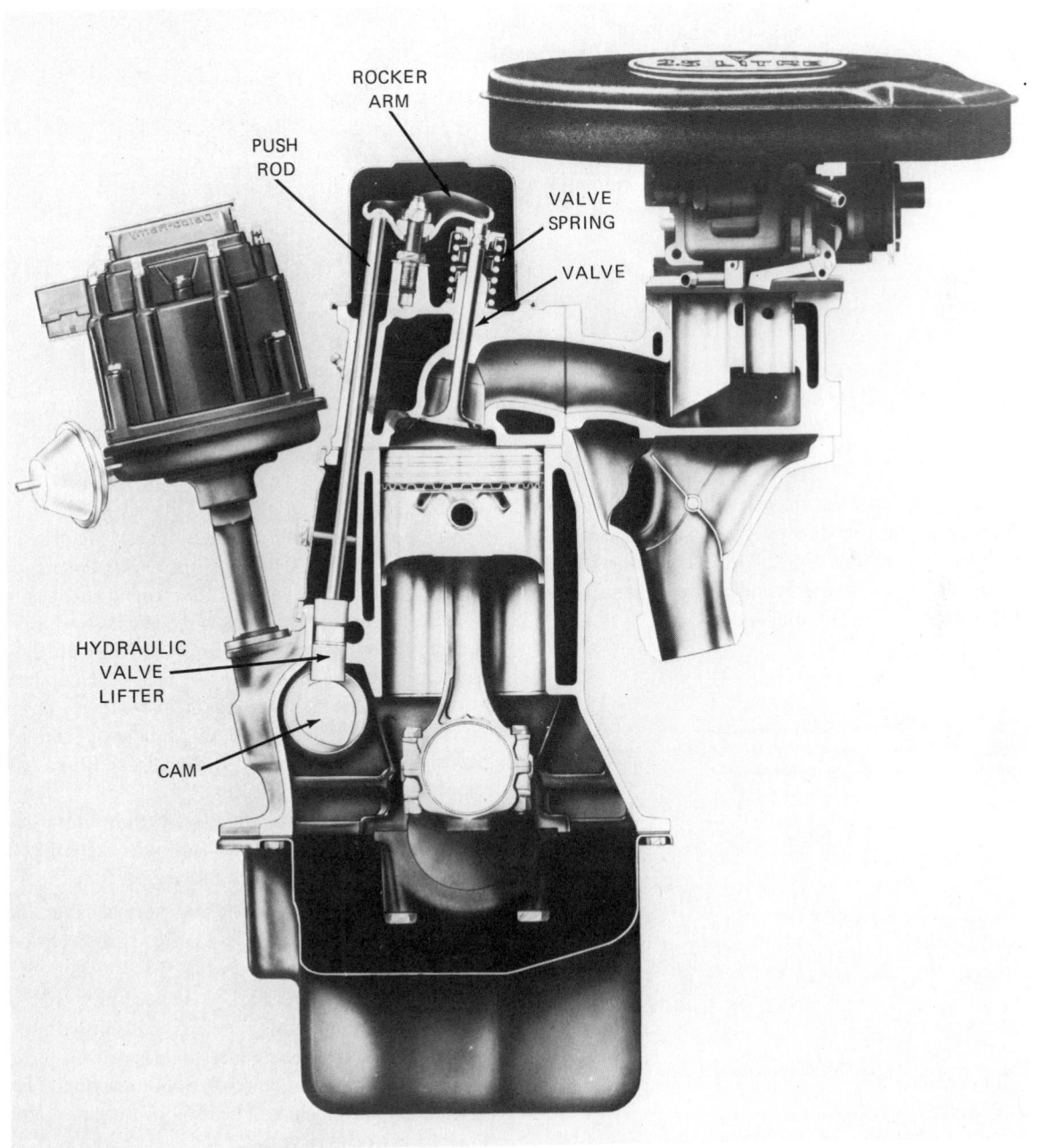

Fig. 7-12. Sectional view showing valve train on Pontiac 2.5 litre engine.

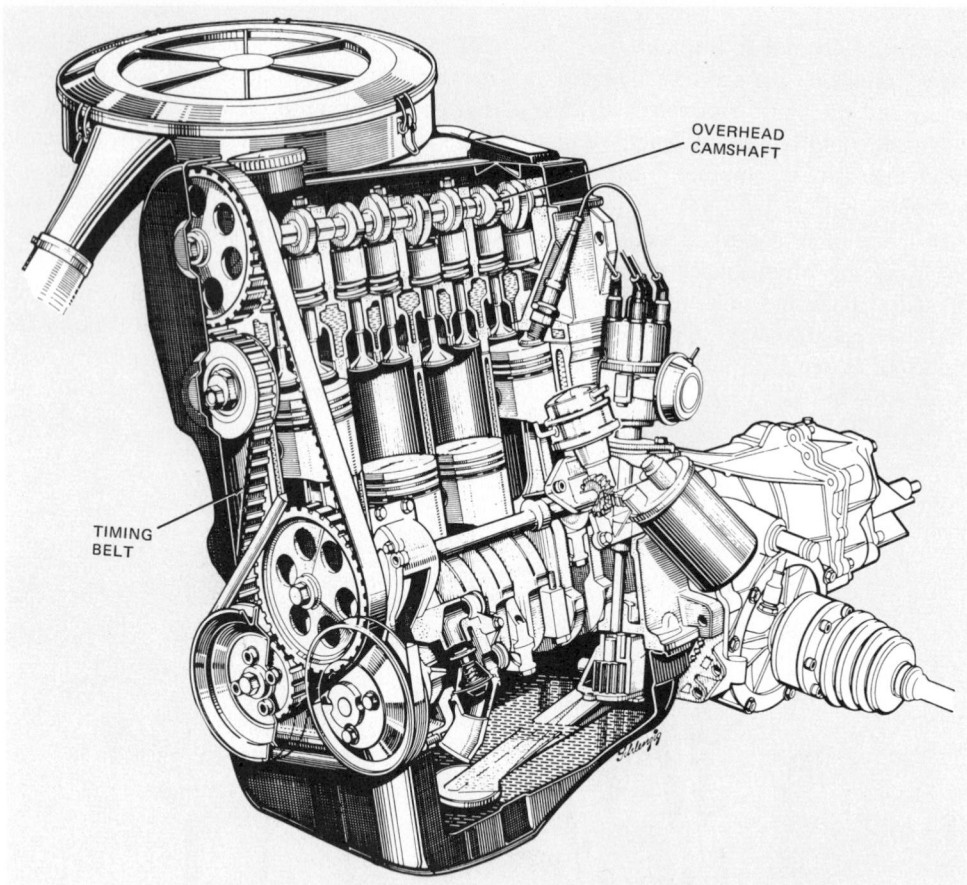

Fig. 7-13. Showing flexible camshaft drive belt and overhead camshaft
on Volkswagen Dasher four cylinder engine.

Camshafts, in most engines, are placed in the crankcase. In this design, they are driven directly from the crankshaft by gears or by silent chain, Fig. 7-13. With the camshaft in the crankcase and the valves in the cylinder head, the valves are operated through push rods and rocker arms.

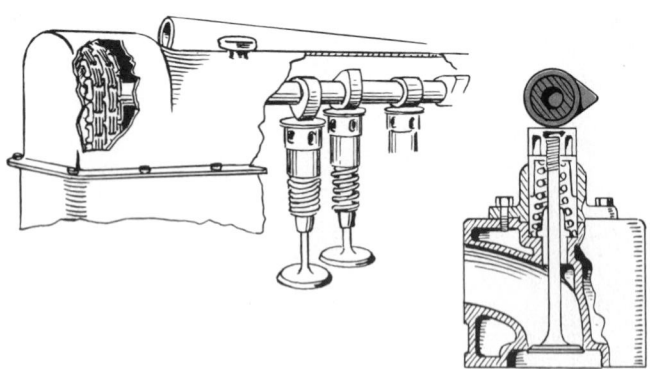

Fig. 7-14. Typical valve layout for overhead camshaft engine.

To avoid the use of this extensive linkage (which wastes power), there is a growing trend to place the camshaft in the cylinder head. With this setup, the camshaft can be driven by a cog belt, Fig. 7-13 and 7-14, or it may be chain driven or gear driven. Some overhead camshaft engines are provided with two camshafts, Fig. 5-12, for each bank of cylinders, one camshaft for the intake valves and the other for the exhaust valves.

Race engines have their overhead camshaft driven either by a shaft or by a series of gears. The cog belt as used on the Pontiac 230 cu. in. engine is made of Neoprene reinforced with fiber glass and among the advantages claimed for this construction are heat and oil resistance, and its ability to absorb shock and constant flexing. In addition, it is inherently quiet and needs no lubrication.

The overhead camshaft construction eliminates the use of push rods and permits excellent valve action at high speeds since there is little inertia of moving parts.

Still another location for the camshaft is at the top and to one side of the cylinders. This design is used on the Renault 16 and permits short push rods, Fig. 7-16.

As with the crankshaft, it is necessary that the camshaft journals be round and true, and the camshaft be straight and true. There should be no measurable wear on the cam surfaces. There must be no appreciable looseness in the bearings, since any radial movement or vibration of the cams would affect the operation of the valves.

The location of the cams around the camshaft along with the design of the crankshaft determines the firing order of the engine.

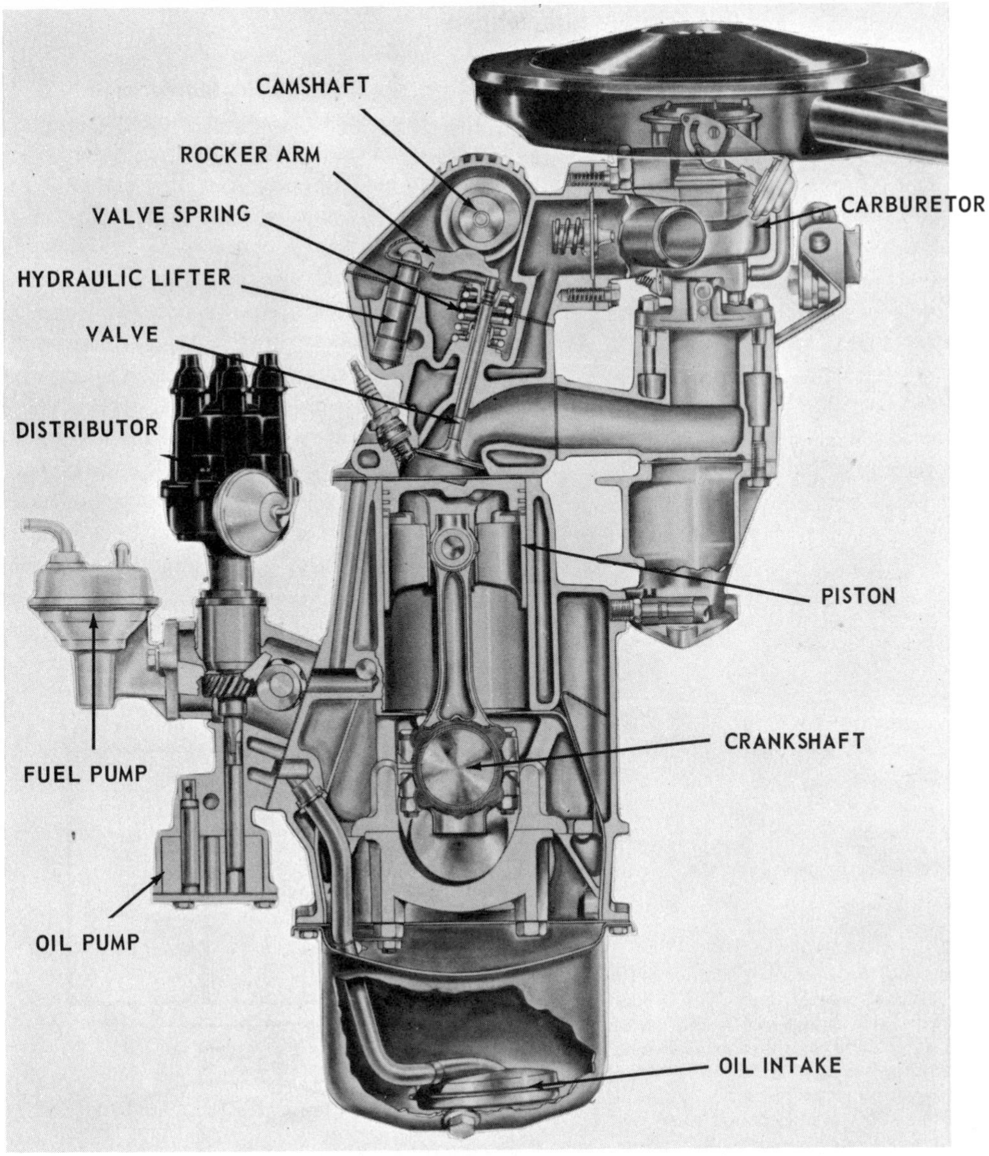

CAMSHAFT

ROCKER ARM

VALVE SPRING

HYDRAULIC LIFTER

VALVE

DISTRIBUTOR

CARBURETOR

PISTON

CRANKSHAFT

FUEL PUMP

OIL PUMP

OIL INTAKE

Fig. 7-15. Sectional view of a Pontiac overhead camshaft six cylinder engine.

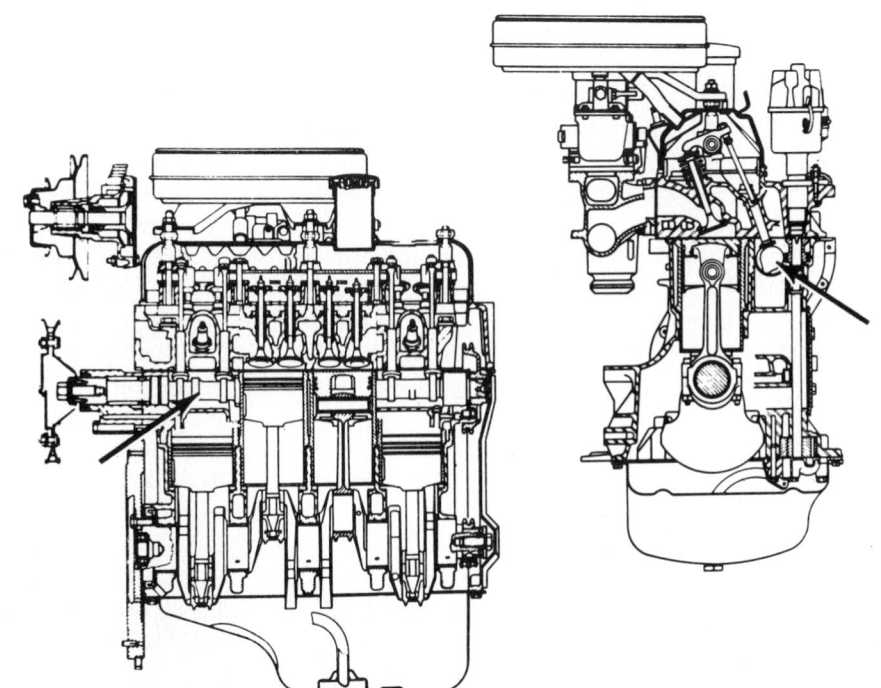

Fig. 7-16. Note location of camshaft on Renault 16 (arrows). This design permits shorter push rods than when shaft is placed in crankcase.

FIRING ORDER

A one cylinder, two cycle engine fires once each revolution. A one cylinder, four cycle engine fires once every other revolution. A two cylinder, two cycle engine fires twice each revolution, while a two cylinder, four cycle engine fires once every revolution so there is no question about firing order.

In a four cylinder, four cycle engine, the No. 1 piston moves downward on the power stroke, while No. 4 is also moving down on the intake stroke. While No. 1 and 4 are going down, 2 and 3 are, of course going up. One is on the exhaust stroke; the other on the compression stroke. There are therefore two possible firing orders, 1, 2, 4, 3 or 1, 3, 4, 2. In either case, one power impulse is obtained every one-half revolution of the crankshaft, giving two power impulses per revolution. See Fig. 7-17.

The six cylinder, four cycle engine (and a three cylinder,

two cycle engine) has the crank throws spaced 120 deg. apart, rather than 180 deg., and gets a power impulse every one-third revolution of the crankshaft. The firing order of a right-hand crankshaft can be 1, 5, 3, 6, 2, 4, or it can be 1, 2, 4, 6, 5, 3. With the left-hand crankshaft, the firing order can be 1, 4, 2, 6, 3, 5, or it can be 1, 3, 5, 6, 4, 2.

With a V-8 engine, the crank throws are spaced 90 deg. apart, and there will be a power impulse every one-quarter revolution of the crankshaft. See diagram at right in Fig. 7-17.

While different firing orders are used, the general idea of an in-line engine firing order is to fire cylinders as nearly as possible at alternate ends of the crankshaft. On a V-8 engine, the objective is to alternate between the ends of the crankshaft and between the left and right banks of cylinders. This tends to distribute the forces throughout the engine and avoid concentrating consecutive power impulses near one point of the crankshaft. This reduces vibration and results in a smoother running engine. A popular cylinder arrangement and typical firing order are shown in Fig. 7-18.

Fig. 7-17. Distribution of forces around the crankshaft of four cycle engines having four, six or eight cylinder engines. Left. With a four cylinder engine, power impulses occur twice during each revolution of the crankshaft. The space between 0 and X indicates time exhaust valve is open during power stroke and no power is obtained. Center. With a six cylinder engine, three power impulses occur per revolution. Power is being exerted at all times, including a slight overlap period when two cylinders are exerting power. Right. With a V-8 engine, four power impulses occur per revolution and there is considerable overlap.

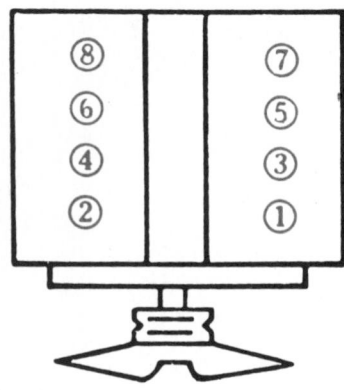

Fig. 7-18. One popular V-8 firing order is 1, 8, 4, 3, 6, 5, 7, 2.

REVIEW QUESTIONS — ENGINE CRANKSHAFTS AND CAMSHAFTS

1. What is the purpose of a flywheel?
2. What is the difference between static and dynamic balance?
3. Give a description of the most simple type of vibration damper.
4. When the crankshaft rotational speed is constant, is the distance traveled by the piston during each quarter revolution the same? Yes or No?
5. How many possible firing orders are there for a four cylinder, four cycle engine? One _____, Two _____, Four _____.
6. A six cylinder, four cycle, in-line engine camshaft has how many lobes on it? Six _____, Twelve _____, Eighteen _____.
7. Is more than one valve ever operated by one cam? Yes or No?
8. A worn cam flank will cause: Noise _____, Loss of power _____, Oil pumping _____.

9. What is the difference between an I-head engine and an overhead camshaft engine?
10. Name one advantage and one disadvantage of overhead camshaft engines.
11. How many power impulses per revolution occur in an eight cylinder, four cycle engine? Four _____, Eight _____, Sixteen _____.
12. How many power impulses per revolution occur in a three cylinder, two cycle engine? Three _____, Six _____, Twelve _____.
13. Why is the firing order of V-type engines arranged differently than on in-line engines?
14. What is the advantage of the overhead camshaft engine as compared to having the camshaft in the crankcase?
    a. Fewer moving parts.
    b. Quieter operation.
    c. Increase height of engine.
    d. Permits larger valves.

Fig. 8-1. General Motors V-6 engine has four main bearings, indicated by arrows.

ENGINE
BEARINGS, VALVES

A one or two cylinder engine usually has two main bearings, Fig. 4-15, one at the front and one at the rear adjacent to the flywheel. A four cylinder engine normally has three main bearings: one at the front; one between cylinders No. 2 and No. 3; and one at the rear. However, some four cylinder engines have five main bearings: front, rear and between crankshaft throws. An in-line six cylinder engine has either three or five mains. A V-6 engine, Fig. 8-1, has four mains. A V-8 engine may have three main bearings, Fig. 4-16, but usually has five.

In a previous chapter, reference was made to cylinder block distortion. This can be serious if the crankcase distorts to

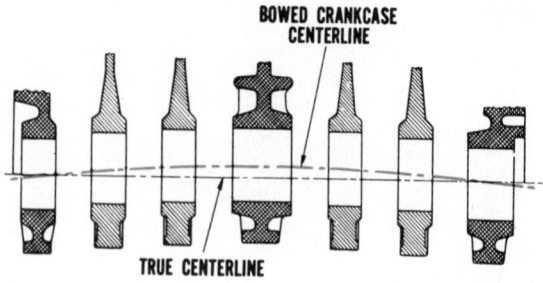

Fig. 8-2. Bearing bores in crankcase can warp out of alignment and cause serious trouble.

throw the engine main bearings out of alignment with each other. An example of this is shown in Fig. 8-2.

On engines having less than eight cylinders, it is customary to provide a throw on the crankshaft for each cylinder. On V-type engines, however, the rods are usually placed side by side, two on each throw, Fig. 8-1.

There are two types of bearings used on automobile engine crankshafts. One is known as the poured, cast-in or integral type. It is now virtually obsolete. The other type is known as the precision insert or slip in type of bearing. The bearing surface is, in all cases, a soft metal with good heat conducting qualities and which will possess a low coefficient of friction in contact with the steel crankshaft journal. The metal must be soft to allow any abrasive material to become imbedded in the bearing, rather than remain between bearing and journal surfaces and damage the journal.

INTEGRAL BEARINGS

Integral or poured bearings are made by pouring molten babbitt or bearing metal into the bearing seats. The seats are first tinned and the bearing metal adheres permanently until melted out, Fig. 8-3. This type of bearing is no longer used in automotive engines.

Fig. 8-3. This connecting rod has an integral type of bearing.

PRECISION BEARINGS

The precision or slip-in type of bearing as shown in Fig. 8-4, has become increasingly popular since engine speeds and loads have been increased so much that a material stronger than babbitt became necessary. It is now used in the majority of automobile engines for both main and connecting rod bearings. The bearing material is an alloy of several metals and may include lead, tin, copper, silver, cadmium, etc. The proportion

of the various metals varies considerably, and the development is the result of much experience and experimentation.

The bearing insert or shell, consists of a hard shell of steel or bronze, perhaps with additional metal linings or laminations, and a thin lining of anti-friction metal or bearing alloy to form the inner surface. These inserts are manufactured to extremely close dimensions and must be handled carefully to avoid damage. When properly installed they are very durable. When they do wear from continued use, they are discarded and replaced with new inserts.

Precision type bearing inserts, being made to such close dimensions, must be used under closely controlled conditions. Fitting and installing them properly involves measurement in fractions of thousandths of an inch. Careless workmanship in installation cannot be tolerated, as they are not adjustable. We will consider fitting them later in this text.

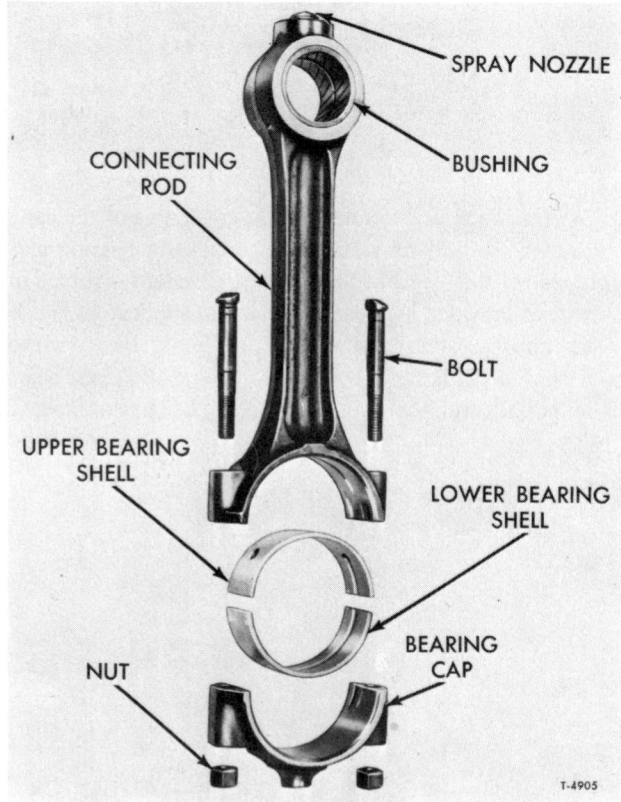

Fig. 8-4. Details of modern connecting rod assembly. Note precision type bearing inserts.

MAIN BEARING CAPS AND SEALS

An exploded view of a typical V-8 crankshaft together with its bearings, caps and seals is shown in Fig. 8-5. Note that there are two bolts for each cap. In larger engines four bolts are often used. The center main bearing in the illustration is designed to take the end thrust as indicated by the flanges on the side. To prevent oil leakage, the rear main bearing is provided with a seal. Seals are either of the wick type or are made of neoprene. In some designs (Chevrolet for example)

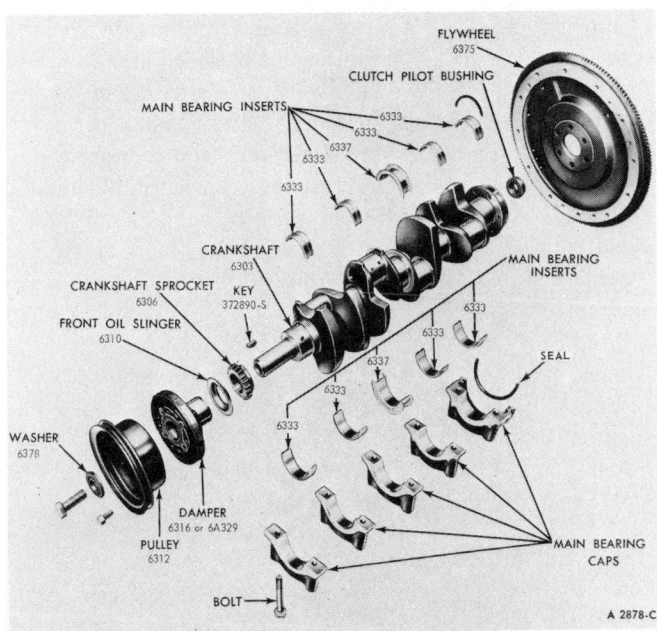

Fig. 8-5. Exploded view of V-8 crankshaft, bearings and seals.

the lower seal will be extended into the bolt area of the cap.

Another method of sealing the rear main bearing cap is employed on the Vega. In this design the sealant is forced into the cavities provided by means of a special applicator, Fig. 8-6.

The upper seal can be removed in most cases, without removing the crankshaft, by first loosening the main bearing cap bolts to lower the crankshaft slightly. Then remove the

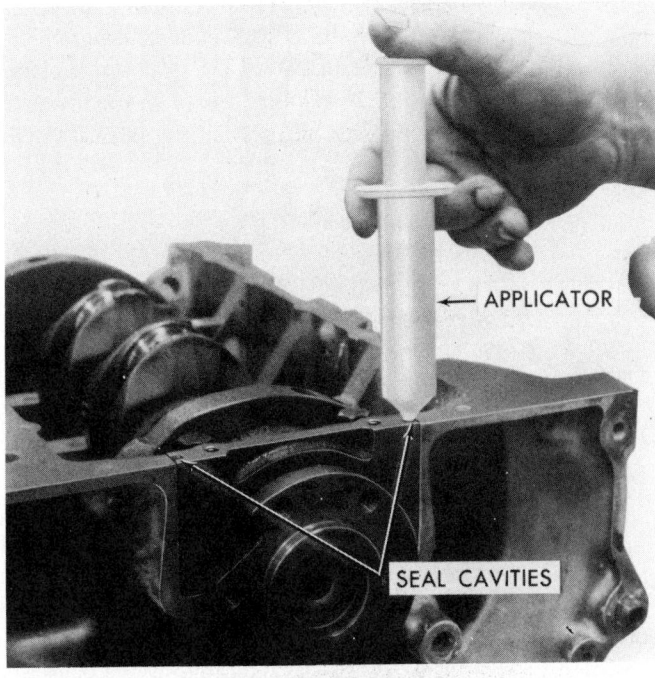

Fig. 8-6. Forcing sealant into cavities with special applicator to seal rear main bearing cap on Vega engine.

rear bearing cap, after which the upper seal can be pushed around the shaft until one end protrudes. The end can then be grasped with pliers and pulled out the rest of the way.

In the case of high performance engines, the main bearing caps are provided with cross bolts, in addition to the usual vertical bolts, Fig. 8-7.

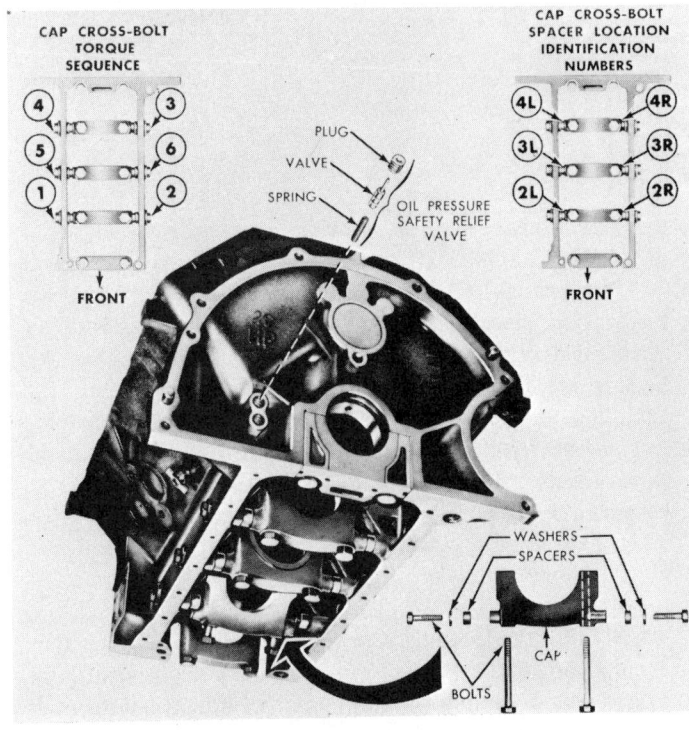

Fig. 8-7. Note side bolts used on this high performance Ford engine.

CAMSHAFT BEARINGS

Camshaft bearings are usually made of bronze, and are bushings rather than in the form of split bearings. See Fig. 8-8. Sometimes the camshaft bears directly in a hole bored in the crankcase without any bushing. Camshaft bushings are not adjustable for wear and are replaced when worn. The degree of wear dictating replacement is more a matter of oil clearance than any tendency toward noise. This will be considered fully in the chapter devoted to lubrication.

ENGINE VALVES

Internal combustion engine valves have a tremendous task to perform and under the very best conditions they are not all that could be desired. The conditions under which the valves operate would seem to impose an impossible task upon them, but they have been developed to a point where they are fairly efficient. A great amount of ingenuity has been expended upon sleeve valves, rotary valves, slide valves and poppet valves. The poppet valve despite all its shortcomings is used almost universally.

Poppet valves are noisy and it is difficult to cool them, but

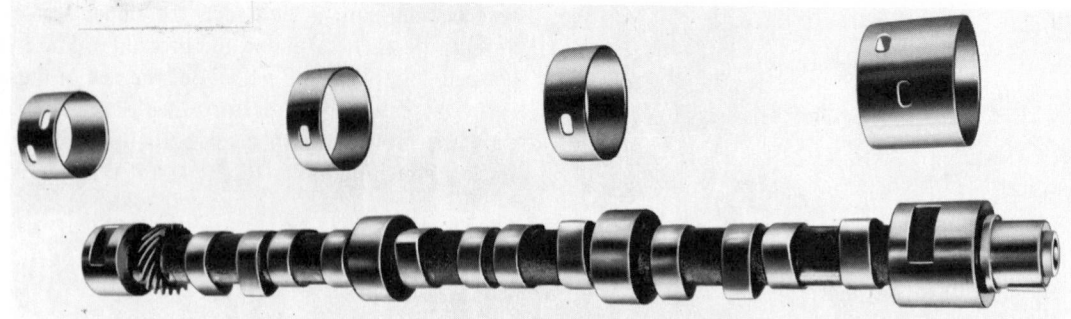

Fig. 8-8. The holes in these camshaft bushings are for lubrication purposes.

they are simple and do provide an effective seal under operating conditions.

These operating conditions are brutal. The valves are in the combustion chamber, exposed to the burning gas but not surrounded with cooling water as is the combustion chamber. Neither are they cooled by the oil as is the piston. The explosion temperature within an engine combustion chamber may momentarily approach 5000 deg. F (2700 C), then the exhaust valve must open and permit these hot gases to go between the valve head and the cylinder block at high velocity.

It may be readily seen that the exhaust valve head may attain a temperature of 1000 deg. F (540 C) or more under these conditions, Fig. 8-9. The valve cannot readily be cooled directly by the cooling water in the engine and the only cooling comes from contact with the valve guides and with the cylinder block during the short space of time it is in contact with the valve seat. How short this space of time is may be realized if thought is given to the speed at which the engine operates.

If the engine is operating at 3000 rpm that means that any one cylinder will fire 1500 times in that minute and that every time the cylinder fires, the exhaust must open to let the burned gas out. In spite of the fact, that the valve is lifted off its seat 1500 times each minute, a large portion of the heat passes from the valve head and into the valve seat and then into the water jacket.

VALVE TEMPERATURES

It is not difficult to understand why exhaust valves are prone to cause trouble. In normal operation, the valve head around the seating surface will operate at a temperature of 1000 to 1200 deg. F (540 to 645 C), Fig. 8-9. The central portion of the valve head will run somewhat hotter, 1200 to 1400 deg. F (645 to 760 C) and the stem adjacent to the head perhaps 800 to 1000 deg. F (425 to 540 C). Running at a red heat under normal conditions, it may be seen that the steel valve may melt under abnormal conditions.

The inlet valve has a somewhat easier task as it is not exposed to the burning as while it is off its seat. The inlet valve is also cooled by the incoming gas mixture which is at below atmospheric temperature.

VALVE AND SEAT MATERIALS

Exhaust valves are usually made of heat resistant alloy steel. Quite often they are partially filled with mineral salts to help them get rid of the heat. See Fig. 8-10. The valve seat is often also made of heat resistant alloy in the form of an insert which is set into the cylinder head or block under the exhaust valve.

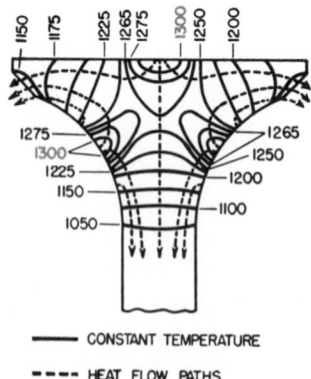

— CONSTANT TEMPERATURE

---- HEAT FLOW PATHS

Fig. 8-9. Temperature measurements made on exhaust valve. Note location of hottest areas.

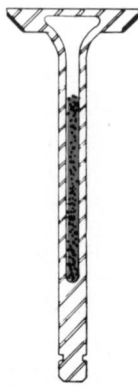

Fig. 8-10. This hollow valve stem is partially filled with sodium, which melts when valve gets hot and bounces back and forth between head and stem to assist heat to flow from head to stem.

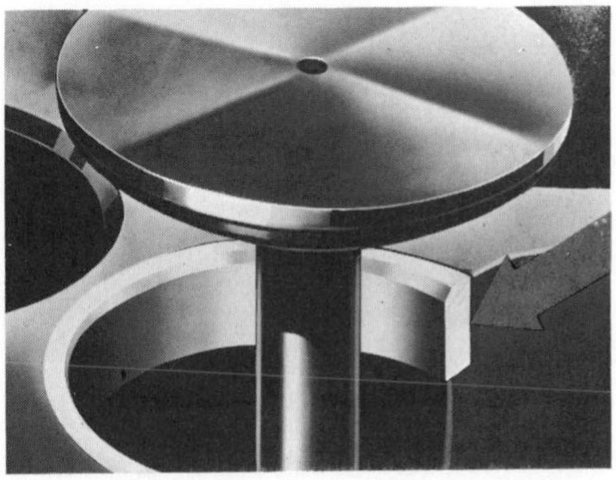

Fig. 8-11. These alloy inserts are often pressed or shrunk in place.

See the alloy inserts in Fig. 8-11. These inserts are used in cast iron blocks or heads as well as aluminum heads or blocks.

The particular construction shown in Fig. 8-12 has a special heat resistant alloy on the valve face and also bears on a heat resistant valve seat insert. Such construction is used in heavy-duty engines.

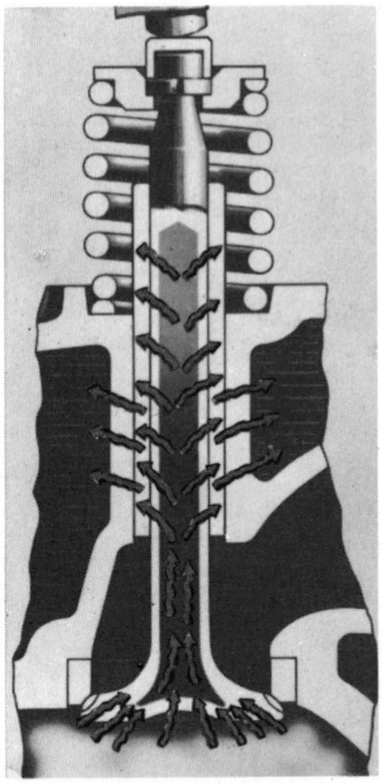

Fig. 8-12. Showing heat path from valve head to mineral salts to valve stem to valve guide and water jacket.

INDUCTION HARDENED SEATS

One of the results of the new low-lead and lead free fuel (not to be confused with the lead free premium fuel which has been available in some areas for years) is higher valve temperatures and attendant valve and seat burning.

In the past the lead in the fuel has acted as a lubricant, at least between the valve face and its seat. When there is no lead in the fuel, the cast iron seats become oxidized by the hot exhaust gases. These oxides abrade the valve face and seat, so there is metal transfer from the seat to the valve. Valve seat wear increases rapidly as valve lash becomes greater. When lash increases from 0.001 to 0.040 in. the impact loads increase up to 30 times which still further valve and seat wear.

To overcome this situation, several methods are available. One method is to use alloys for the valve seats or hard noncorrosive inserts. Instead of ethyl lead in the fuel, boron oxide or iron phosphate can be used, but these materials have an adverse effect on catalytic mufflers which are being installed on some vehicles. Another method is to aluminize the valve face or chrome plate the valve head, which has been adopted by Buick, for example. Valve stems are also being chrome plated in order to reduce wear in that area.

Internally cooled valves such as shown in Fig. 8-10 are also being more widely used and extensive research on water filled valve stems is promising, showing temperature reduction up to 600 deg. F. To further aid in the dissipation of heat, valve stem diameter is being increased in many cases.

Induction hardening of valve seats has been adopted by Dodge, Fig. 8-13. This process heats the valve seats to 1700 deg. and hardens them to a depth of 0.05 to 0.08 in. This gives the seats approximately the same durability as is obtained with leaded fuel.

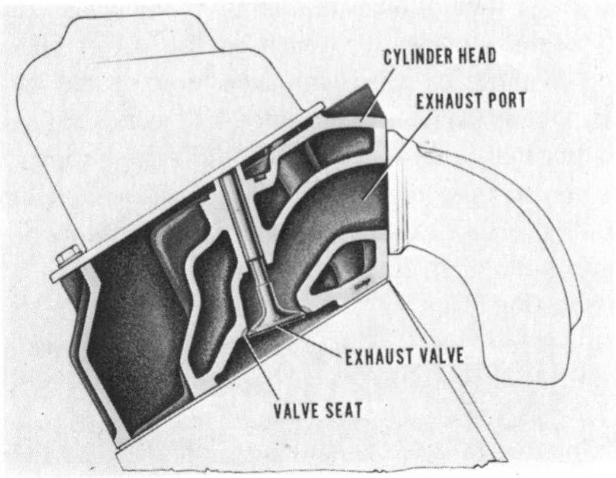

Fig. 8-13. Induction hardened valve seats have been adopted by Dodge to increase durability.

VALVE COOLING

The heat of combustion flows from the valve head to the cooling water. Tests made by Thompson Ramo Wooldridge, Inc., engineers show that the popular conception that solid exhaust valves are cooled primarily by conduction down the stem is not true. Fig. 8-9 shows the temperature measurements made at the cross section of a valve to determine the path of the heat flow. The solid lines are paths of equal temperature and the dotted lines are heat flow paths.

Many of the heat flow paths leave the valve at the face. In fact, the engineers state that over half of the total heat absorbed by the valve leaves through the face.

It will also be noted that the heat flows from the valve stem to the valve guide and from the guide to the head or block,

Fig. 8-12. As heat will flow more readily through one piece of metal than from one piece to another, the separate valve guide on most passenger car engines have been dispensed with and instead the cylinder block or head is reamed and acts as the guide. When that construction is used, replacement valves are provided with oversize stems and the guides are then reamed to the desired size when it becomes necessary to install new valves.

VALVE SEAT CONTACT AREA

From the foregoing, it should be realized that anything that reduces the area of contact between the valve and the cylinder head or block will hamper the escape of heat from the valve. Thus if valve seat is too narrow or valve guide worn excessively, the area of contact will be reduced and valve will overheat.

The area of contact could be increased by widening the valve seat, but it has been found that a wider seat also encourages flakes of carbon to adhere, hold the valve off the seat and cause burning of the valve face. Another method of increasing the contact area would be to increase the diameter of the valve head or the valve stem or both by installing oversize valves, oversize stems or longer guides, etc.

There are of course mechanical limitations to the amount of increase in these dimensions. Of more importance however, would be the increase of weight in the valve. The valve is required to move endwise with such rapidity that it must be kept as light in weight as possible. Any excess weight would add to the inertia and slow down the valve action. So here again a compromise must be made and a reasonable limitation in size imposed. However, the major factor limiting the size of the valve is the diameter of the cylinder bore and the shape of the combustion chamber.

VALVE HEAT DISSIPATION

This matter of valve heat dissipation must be thoroughly understood if automobile engines are to be serviced properly. There are several things to be considered in this connection. Some of them are similar to problems previously discussed in connection with pistons and rings.

For example, the heat of operation causes distortion of cylinder heads, blocks, etc. The same conditions cause distortion of valve and valve seat. Any hot spots in the cylinder head or block near the valves or any unequal tightening of the cylinder head bolts will aggravate distortion and cause valve difficulties. The valve and seat may be round and true when the engine is cold, but may not be round and true when the engine gets to operating temperature.

The valve head is liable to warp due to the difference in temperature at different points. This warpage will be aggravated if the rim of the valve head is thin or uneven. See Fig. 8-14. Furthermore, the temperature may vary around the rim of the valve head in some cases due to the difference in volume and velocity of the gas going between the valve and seat as determined by combustion chamber design and valve port shape.

Fig. 8-14. If valve has a thin edge as shown at the left or if valve head is warped as shown at right, thin edges created will become excessively hot.

In addition to changes in valve and valve seat shape, the diameter of both may change. The valve head runs hotter than the valve seat because the seat is nearer the cooling water. Therefore the valve head may expand more than the seat and as a result the valve may rise on the seat as shown in Fig. 8-15.

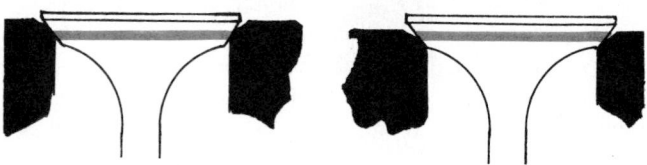

Fig. 8-15. An exhaust valve may be properly seated as at left when cold, but may expand rapidly and climb off seat as shown at the right.

This action results in a change in the valve seat area location.

It will be apparent that the dimension between the valve seat and the valve lifter will be lengthened by such expansion. The length of the valve itself between the seat surface and the end of the stem, will be altered by lengthwise expansion of the valve and valve stem.

One of the most important factors affecting valves temperatures is that of valve lash or tappet clearance. Insufficient clearance will result in the valves contacting the seats for a shorter time and consequently operate at higher temperatures. Excessive clearance will result in noisy operation and loss of power. Great accuracy should therefore be used when adjusting valve lash.

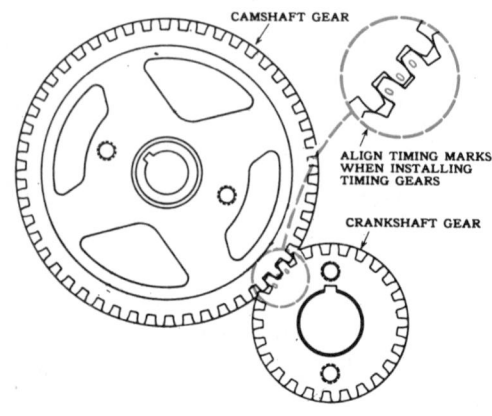

Fig. 8-16. Timing gears are usually marked as shown to insure that valves will be correctly timed.

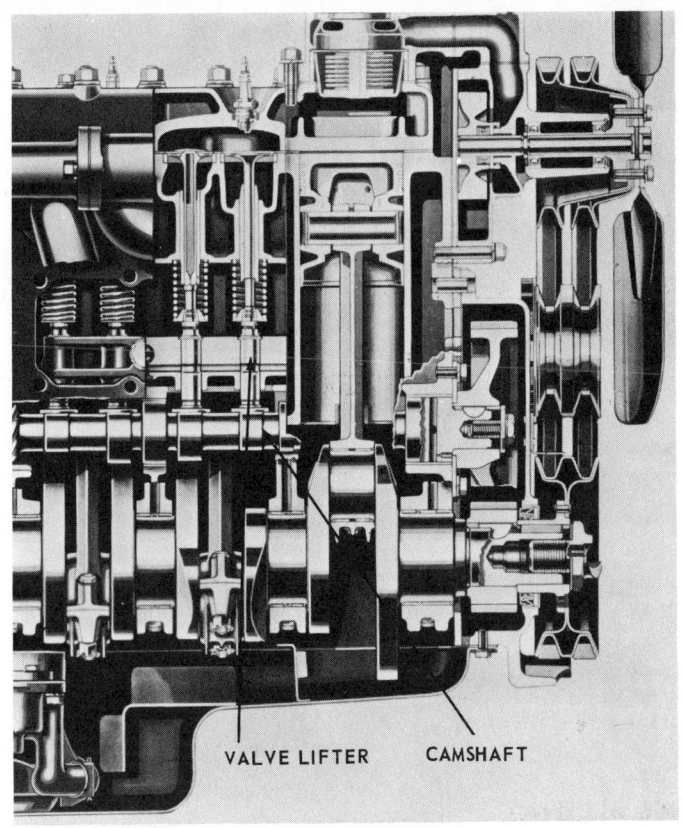

Fig. 8-17. Valves in L-head engines are raised by means of short valve lifters which are usually adjustable as to length.

VALVE OPERATING MECHANISM

The camshaft, Figs. 7-8 and 8-1, is designed to raise the valves from their seats and is rotated by means of gears or chains, meshing with a gear on the crankshaft. In four cycle engines, the camshaft must operate at half the speed of the

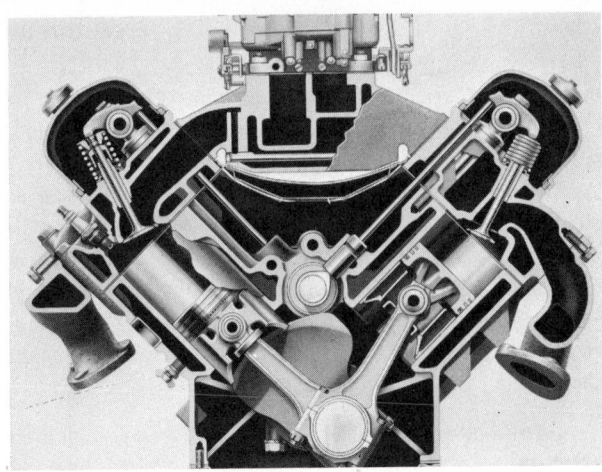

Fig. 8-18. Overhead valves require push rods and rocker arms, mounted individually or on a rocker shaft.

crankshaft and consequently the camshaft gear must be twice the diameter as the gear on the crankshaft, Fig. 8-16.

In the L-head engine, where both valves are on the same side of the cylinder, it is customary to place the camshaft directly under the valves and operate the valves with short valve lifters. See Fig. 8-17.

In the overhead valve engine design, a single camshaft is usual with a cam for each valve. In many designs the camshaft is located in the crankcase and operates the valves by means of long push rods and rocker arms, Fig. 8-18. Because of the weight of the push rod, appreciable power is required to move it. To overcome this problem, some engines are designed with the camshaft placed over the valves, Fig. 8-19. This design eliminates the push rod and power is saved. Still other designs have the cams operating directly on caps on the ends of the valve stems with further saving in power.

On the F-head engine, a single camshaft is ordinarily used,

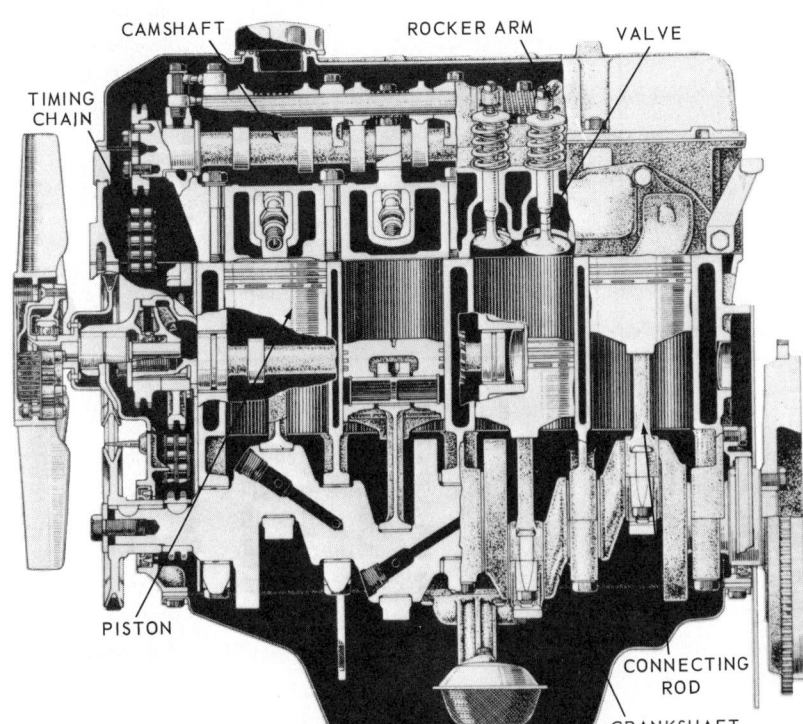

Fig. 8-19. Toyota engine with overhead camshaft with rocker arms.

one valve being operated directly by means of a short push rod, and the other valve being operated by a long push rod and a rocker arm.

As the valves must be precisely opened and closed with relation to the piston travel, any wear in the camshaft driving chain or gear will result in the valve not being opened and closed at the exact instant desired and a loss in engine efficiency will be incurred. For this reason, the engine engineers avoid the use of long chains or multiple gears in designing the camshaft drive arrangement.

WORN CAMS

We have already considered the accuracy with which the cam shape or contour is formed in order to provide the proper operating characteristics for the valves. Ordinarily the surface of the cam is so hard that the exact shape remains substantially unaltered for many thousand miles of operation. There is of course some friction between the cam and the valve lifter that rides on it, and some wear is bound to occur in time. This wear is usually on the highest part of the cam, and will decrease the height or "lift" of the valve. The result is that the valve does not open as wide as it should, and the "breathing" ability of the engine suffers.

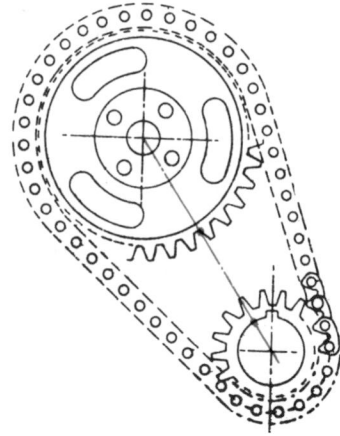

Fig. 8-20. Timing chain sprockets are usually marked so that a line drawn through center of both shafts bisects timing marks, timing is correct. Flywheels are also usually marked to facilitate checking valve timing.

If the wear on the cam is at the sides or on the ramp, the valve action will become noisy, and also the valve will open late or close early, or both. Excessive wear in the valve lifters will have the same results: noise and faulty valve timing.

Usually the wear on cams is so slow and the loss of engine performance so gradual that it goes unnoticed unless the valve lift is checked against factory specifications. In rare cases a defective camshaft has been found, and the loss of engine performance so rapid as to be noticed. In some cases the entire camshaft was not properly hardened, and in other cases it has been one or more individual cams that were soft enough to wear quickly.

TYPES OF CAMSHAFT DRIVES

There are three basic types of drives for camshafts; timing gears, timing chains and the cogged belt. The timing gear method, Fig. 8-16, is used where long life and hard service are expected, as in commercial vehicles and race cars. Timing chains, Fig. 8-20, are used extensively in the passenger car field and, in general, are quieter than timing gears. The cogged belt, Fig. 8-21, is a more recent development and is made of fiber glass reinforced rubber. It eliminates a long series of gears and is used primarily on engines with overhead camshafts. In this case (Chevrolet Vega), adjustment is provided by means of a slotted water pump housing.

Fig. 8-21. Details of cogged type fiberglass-reinforced belt used to drive overhead camshaft on Chevrolet Vega 2300 engine.

In the case of diesel engines it is necessary to provide a drive for the injection pump as well as the camshaft. This involves additional gearing, Figs. 8-22 and 8-23. The former shows the gear train of a two cycle GMC three cylinder diesel engine. Note that in addition to the camshaft and crankshaft gears there is an idler gear, a balance shaft gear, upper and lower blower gears and a governor drive gear. A particularly long gear train is used on the Caterpillar V-12 engine shown in Fig. 8-23. In all there are eleven gears in the train on the double camshaft engine.

Fig. 8-22. Gear train and timing marks on two cycle, three cylinder GMC diesel engine. 1—Balance shaft gear, L. H. Helix. 2—Governor drive. 3—Crankshaft gear. 4—Idler gear. 5—Blower rotor gear. 6—Blower rotor gear upper. 7—Camshaft gear, R. H. Helix.

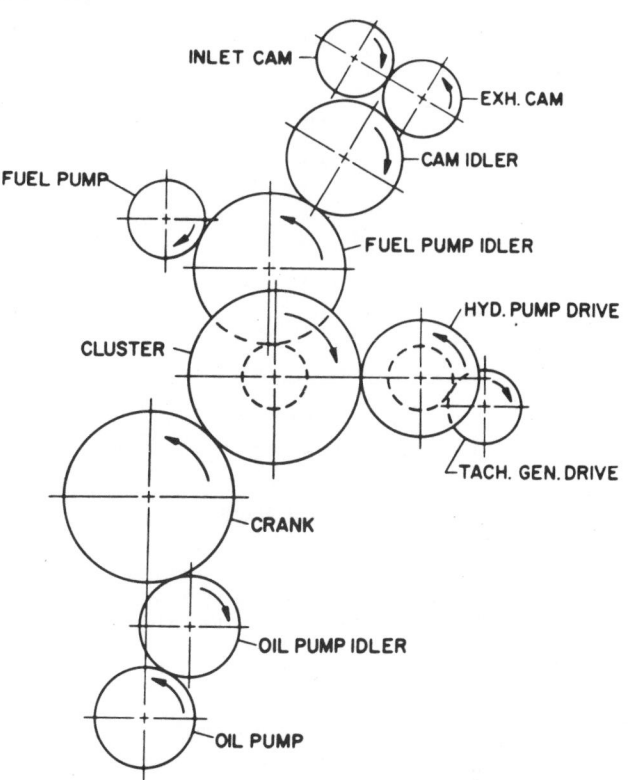

Fig. 8-23. Gear train on Caterpillar vehicular 5.4 bore, V-12 engine.

VALVE TIMING

Anything that occurs to change the time that the valve opens, the duration of the time it is held open, the size of the opening, or the time that it closes, will have a decided affect on engine performance. This fact is seldom fully realized. Many engines run constantly below par because of incorrect valve tappet clearance adjustment.

A full realization of the need for accurate adjustment can come only from a study of valve action and requirements. This study starts with the relation between the crankshaft and camshaft. Due to the difference in the diameter of the circles described by the crank throw and the cam nose, and the difference in the comparative speed of rotation, the crank throw may travel many times as fast as the cam nose. While the cam nose is moving 1/4 in., the crank throw may move 1 1/2 in. If the cam is a few thousandths late in opening the valve, the crank throw and the piston attached to it will move a considerable distance farther than it should before the valve begins to open.

In this manner the motion of the piston is partially lost, and the power output suffers. Obviously therefore, a worn timing chain or gears should be replaced as soon as the wear exceeds the specifications rather than run them until they become noisy or break, which is all too often the case.

In a few cases, adjustment is provided by timing chains such as an eccentric mounting for an accessory shaft, automatic slack adjusters, etc. In most cases it is necessary to install a new chain when the old one becomes worn and stretched. In general, a deflection of 1/2 in. is permitted for timing chains installed on passenger car engines which are used to drive a single camshaft.

In a gear-driven camshaft, the crankshaft gear is usually made of steel but the camshaft gear is often made of nonmetallic composition. This nonmetallic substance is quite durable and also makes for quieter operation. These gears are not adjustable and must be replaced when worn.

The car manufacturers set up specifications as to the amount of wear permissible in the chain or between the gear teeth. They also mark the gears or chains to facilitate correct timing. See Figs. 8-16 and 8-20. In addition, they also furnish timing charts by means of which valve timing can be readily checked.

The extreme accuracy with which it is desired to open and close the valves may be understood when thought is given to the speed at which the valve parts operate. This timing becomes more important as engine speeds are increased. This is the reason for what is known as valve "overlap." Valve overlap means that the intake and exhaust valves may both be open at the same time in any one cylinder. This, however, is to compensate for the time required by the air or gas to flow through the manifolds.

Many things have to be considered when designing the timing of an engine. In order that the engine may operate satisfactorily at high speeds, it is necessary that the exhaust valve open before the end of the power stroke and close after the completion of the exhaust stroke; also that the inlet valve open before the end of the exhaust stroke and close after the completion of the inlet stroke. This involves an overlapping of

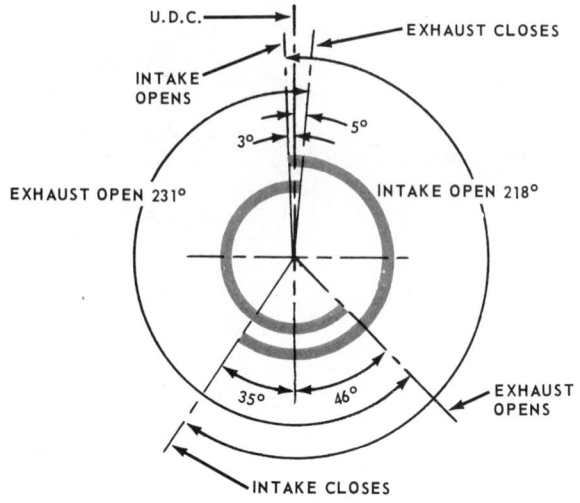

Fig. 8-24. This diagram illustrates overlap or time during which both valves are open in same cylinder. This is necessary in a high speed engine to compensate for inertia of gas moving into and out of cylinders.

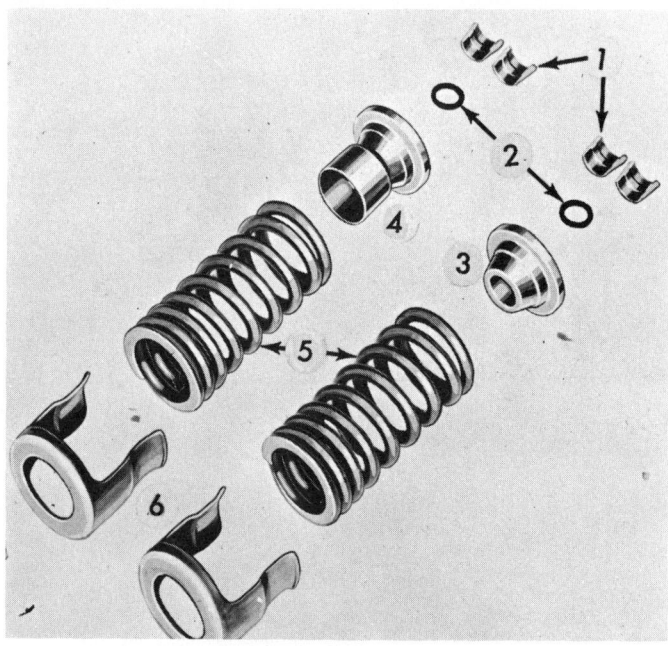

Fig. 8-25. Typical valve springs with accessory parts. 1—Cone type valve spring keepers. 2—O-ring oil seals. 3—Valve spring retainer. 4—Valve spring retainer with oil deflector. 5—Valve springs. 6—Valve spring surge dampers.

the exhaust and inlet periods which is made necessary by the inertia of the gases in the manifold and in part by the slow opening and closing motions of the valves made necessary by the demands for quiet operation. See Fig. 8-24.

VALVE SPRINGS

Valve springs, Fig. 8-25, are required to close the valve after it has been opened by the action of the cam. Valve springs are of the coil type and are made of special high grade steel designed to withstand the high rate of stress applications, temperature and also to keep the valve from bouncing on its seat.

On some engines a single valve spring is used for each valve. On many high performance engines, two valve springs, one within the other, are required in order to obtain the desired pressure characteristics. Usually the end turns of the springs are closer together than the other turns in order to reduce spring surge, Fig. 8-25. Valve springs are also provided with dampers which help to reduce surging, Fig. 8-25.

Valve spring pressure varies with the type of engine. Stronger springs are required on high speed engines and also on engines with heavier push rods, valves, rocker arms, etc.

VALVE LIFTERS

The valve lifter is a device interposed in the valve system and transmits the action of the cam to the valve or push rod as the case may be.

There are two types of valve lifters, mechanical and hydraulic.

The solid or mechanical lifter, Fig. 8-26, is usually of the mushroom type and is provided with an adjusting screw so that the clearance or lash between the valve stem and the lifter is adjustable. This is necessary as engine heat will expand and lengthen the valve stem to such a degree that the valve would

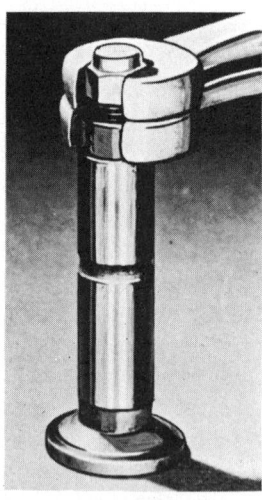

Fig. 8-26. Mechanical valve lifter of the mushroom type.

not close, with the further result that the combustible charge in the cylinder would not be compressed.

Instead of the mushroom type lifter some engines are equipped with roller type lifters. In this design the engine cam strikes a roller mounted on the lower face of the lifter. This has the advantage of reducing friction as compared to the mushroom type lifter.

Hydraulic lifters are designed to automatically take up the clearance that exists between the valve and the lifter, Fig. 8-27. The great advantage of this type of valve lifter is that it is quiet in operation as it has zero valve lash.

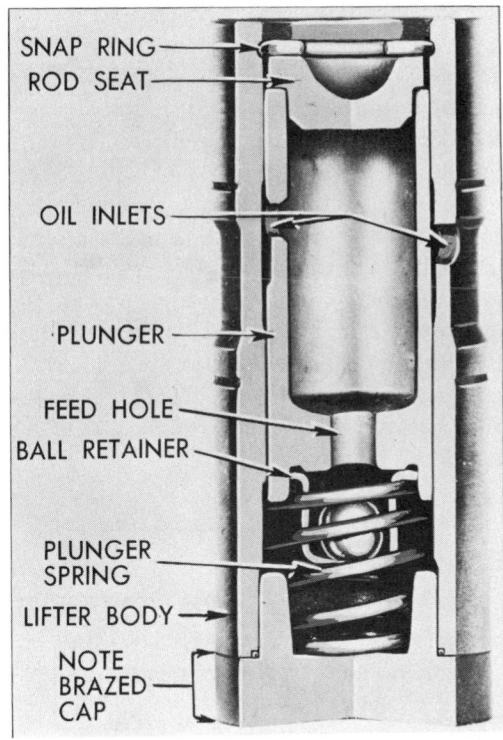

Fig. 8-27. Hydraulic type valve lifter.

oil from the lower chamber. The lifting force is then transmitted through the entrapped oil to the check ball and plunger, so that the plunger and push rod seat move upward with the body to operate the valve linkage which opens the engine valve.

Then as the engine valve seats, the linkage parts and lifter plunger stop, but the plunger spring forces the body of the lifter to follow the cam downward until it again rests on the cam base circle. Oil pressure against the ball check from the lower chamber ceases when the plunger movement stops and allows passage of oil past the ball check into the lower chamber to replace the slight amount of oil lost through "leak down," which is the oil that escapes through the clearance between the plunger and the body.

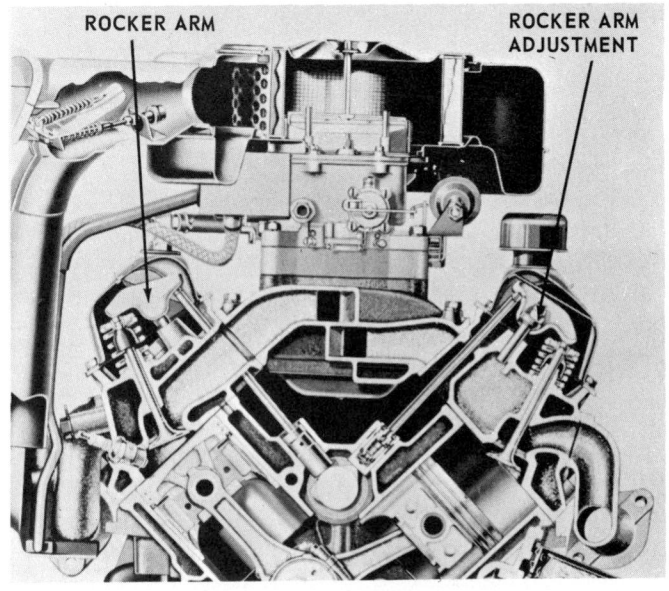

Fig. 8-29. Note semispherical depression in rocker arm and adjusting nut.

Oil enters each lifter through grooves and oil holes in the lifter body and plunger, flows down into the chamber below the plunger through the feed hole and around the ball check. At the start of the cycle the plunger spring holds all lash clearances out of the valve linkage. As the engine cam starts raising the valve lifter body, oil in the lower chamber and the check ball spring firmly seat the check ball to prevent loss of

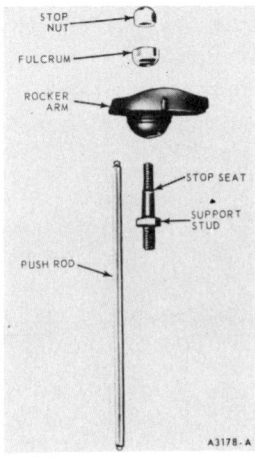

Fig. 8-30. These parts make up spherical rocker arm assembly used on some Ford engines. Individual support studs replace rocker shaft in this design.

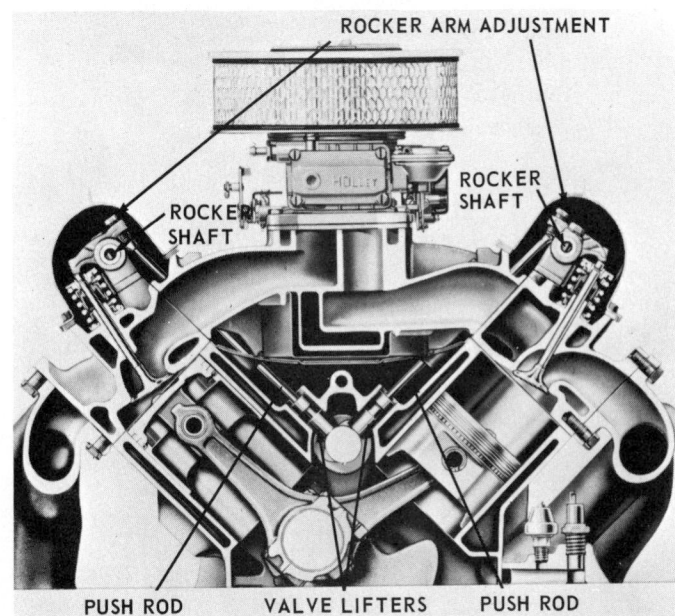

Fig. 8-28. Note rocker arm shaft and rocker arm with adjusting nut.

When valve linkage expands due to engine temperature increases, the plunger must move to a slightly lower position in the lifter body to assure full closing of the engine valve. Similarly, when engine temperature drops, the plunger must move to a slightly higher position. In either case, the capacity of the lower chamber changes, and the volume of oil present is automatically controlled by passage of oil through the plunger feed hole.

To provide for variations in size of parts due to servicing, some systems are provided with adjustable rocker arms, while other manufacturers provide push rods of varying lengths.

ROCKER ARMS

Two methods of adjusting valve lash on overhead valve engines are shown in Figs. 8-28, 8-29 and 8-30.

In Fig. 8-28, the rocker arms are mounted on a rocker shaft and adjustment of the valve lash is made by turning the adjusting screw at the end of the rocker arm and which contacts the upper end of the push rod.

In the design shown in Figs. 8-29 and 8-30, the rocker shaft has been dispensed with. Instead each rocker arm is mounted on an individual stud. The rocker arm has a semispherical depression and a corresponding fulcrum seat rides in the depression and is held down by the adjusting nut. Turning the adjusting screw will move the rocker arm closer to the valve end and push rod end, decreasing the valve lash.

Some engines are provided with nonadjustable rocker arms, so that it is necessary to install new push rods of the desired length in order to adjust valve lash.

REVIEW QUESTIONS — ENGINE BEARINGS, VALVES

1. Is an integral bearing the same thing as a precision bearing? Yes or No?
2. Why is bearing metal comparatively soft?
3. Bushings are always used on all camshaft journals. True or False?
4. Slip-in bearings are not adjustable for wear. Ture or False?
5. Name four metals used in bearing metal alloys.
6. Valve seats can be too wide. True or False?
7. Valves are sometimes hollow to make them lighter in weight. True or False?
8. Excessive heat gets out of valve by flowing to: The valve seat _____. The valve guide _____. Both _____.
9. Why are valves not made larger?
10. An exhaust valve may reach a temperature of: 500 deg. F _____. 1,000 deg. F _____. 3,000 deg. F _____.
11. Valve length is not constant. True or False?
12. At what speed does the camshaft operate? Half crankshaft speed _____ . Same speed _____ . Twice crankshaft speed _____ .
13. What is the objection to a long chain in a camshaft drive?
14. The cam nose on the camshaft travels faster than the crank throw on the crankshaft. True or False?
15. Are timing chains adjustable for wear? Yes _____ . No _____ . Sometimes _____ .
16. What is valve overlap?
17. Are stronger or weaker valve springs used on high performance engines?
18. How many types of valve lifters are there? One _____ . Two _____ . Three _____ . Four _____ .
19. What is the great advantage of a hydraulic valve lifter?
    a. Better valve action.
    b. Closes the valves faster.
    c. Quieter valve action.
    d. More accurate valve timing.
20. The new low-lead fuel increases valve seat temperatures. True or False?
21. Lead in the fuel acts as a lubricant. True or False?
22. The cogged belt is used primarily on what type engine?
    a. L-head engine.
    b. F-head engine.
    c. Overhead valve engine with push rods.
    d. Overhead camshaft engine.

ENGINE PERFORMANCE

The study of engine performance deals with ways in which engines are measured dimensionally and in the power developed. Many factors enter into this study: the basics of inertia, work, power, torque and friction; the affect of barometric pressure, temperature and humidity of the ambient atmosphere; and the engineering decisions that determine engine bore-stroke-displacement, compression ratio, volumetric efficiency, thermal efficiency and mechanical efficiency.

INERTIA

Inertia is defined as the inability of matter to move or stop itself. Another definition is that an object will tend to move in the same direction or speed until acted upon by another force.

WORK

When an object is moved from one position to another, work is said to be performed. Work is measured in units of foot pounds (ft. lbs.). For example: if a three pound weight is lifted 2 ft., the work performed would be 3 lbs. x 2 ft. = 6 ft. lbs. In other words, work equals the force in pounds required to move the object times the distance moved in feet. Work is performed when weights are lifted, springs compressed, shafts rotated.

The ability of capacity to do work is known as energy. A lump of coal or a quart of gasoline has energy stored in it, which when released will perform work. A valve spring can do the work of closing a valve when it is released after having been compressed.

POWER

Power is defined as the rate or speed at which work is performed. One horsepower is defined as the amount doing 33,000 ft. lbs. of work in one minute. The unit of measurement was originated by an engineer by the name of Watt, who found that a strong horse could hoist 366 lbs. of coal up a mine shaft at the rate of one foot per second. In one minute, the horse would have raised the 366 lbs. 60 feet. This would be equivalent to raising 21,960 lbs., one foot in one minute. Arbitrarily, Mr. Watt raised this figure to 33,000 lbs. one foot in one minute.

Expressed as a formula:

$$HP = \frac{\text{ft. lb. per min.}}{33,000} = \frac{DW}{33,000 \, t}$$

where D = the distance the weight is to be moved.
W = Force in pounds required to move the weight through that distance.
t = time in minutes required to move the weight through the distance D.

For example:

Using this formula, how many horsepower would be required to raise a weight of 5000 lbs. a distance of 60 ft. in three minutes?

$$HP = \frac{DW}{33,000 \, t} = \frac{60 \times 5000}{33,000 \times 3} = 3.03 \, hp$$

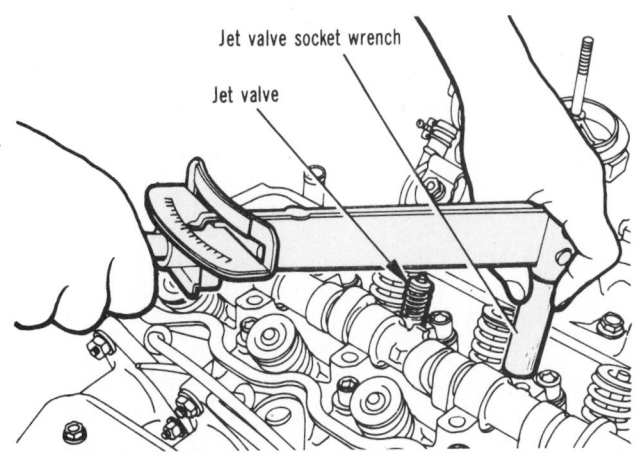

Fig. 9-1. Torque is the effort devoted toward twisting and turning. Here, a torque wrench is pictured in a jet valve torque tightening application. A torque wrench has a built-in indicator to measure applied force — whether the wrench handle moves or not.

Jet valve socket wrench

Jet valve

TORQUE

Torque is defined as turning or twisting effort. While torque is measured in pound feet, it differs from work or power as torque does not necessarily produce motion. For example; if a 50 pound force was applied at the end of a 3 ft. lever, there would be 150 lbs. ft. of torque. Whether the lever moved or not would be beside the point, Fig. 9-1.

In the case of the automotive engine, torque is low at low engine speeds and increases rapidly with the speed. Automotive engineers make every effort to increase the torque at low speeds and to remain as nearly constant as possible. Note the variation in torque and horsepower, as shown in Fig. 9-2.

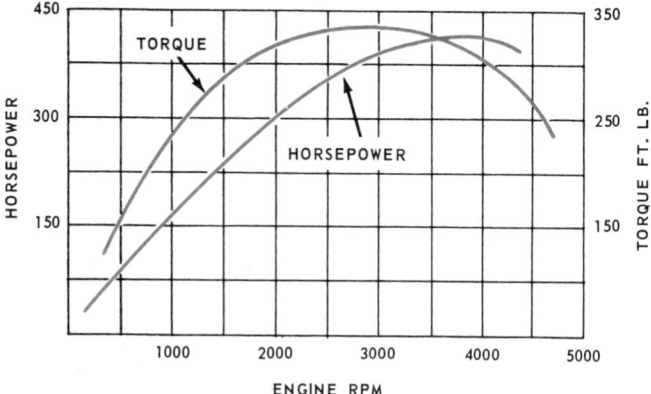

Fig. 9-2. Note variation in torque and horsepower as engine speed changes.

FRICTION

Friction is the resistance to relative motion between two bodies in contact with each other, or separated only by a lubricant.

Friction varies not only with different materials, but also with the surface condition of the materials. Friction was originally attributed to the interlocking of projections and depressions on the surfaces, but present day theory is that molecular attraction is the explanation.

The amount of friction is proportional to the pressure between the two surfaces in contact and is independent of the area of the surfaces in contact, Fig. 9-3. It also depends on the relative velocity of the moving surfaces.

In the case of viscous friction, such as that which occurs when solids move through liquids or gases (an automobile moving through air for example), the force of friction varies directly with the relative velocity and rises very rapidly when the velocity becomes very great.

The friction of lubricated surfaces is much less than that of dry surfaces. It is also greatly reduced when rolling friction (ball and roller bearings) is substituted for sliding friction.

Experiments show that dividing the force required to slide one object over the other at a constant speed, by the pressure

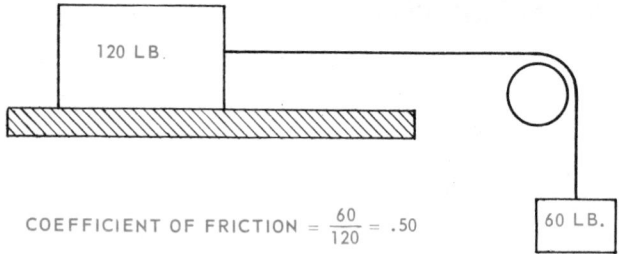

Fig. 9-3. One method of determining coefficient of friction.

holding them together, is a constant which is known as the coefficient of friction. The coefficient of friction is always the same for those materials and surfaces, Fig. 9-3.

For example: If a pull of 60 lbs. is required to keep a weight of 120 lbs. sliding over a surface at a constant speed, the coefficient of sliding friction would be:

$$\frac{60}{120} = 0.5$$

It must be emphasized that more force is required for initial movement than to keep the object moving. Sliding friction is therefore measured after motion has started.

A lubricant is a substance placed or injected between two surfaces to reduce friction. The thin layer of lubricant, adhering to the two surfaces is then sheared by the movement. The friction within the lubricant being less than that between the two surfaces, less force is required to produce movement.

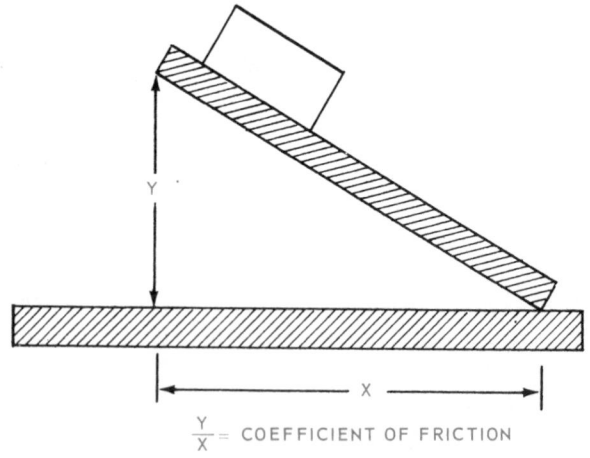

Fig. 9-4. Coefficient of friction equals $\frac{Y}{X}$.

A simple experiment to determine the coefficient of friction can be easily performed by means of a flat board and a weight. The weight is placed on one end of the board and that end is then raised until the weight starts to slide. At that point, the height of the end of the board is measured and also the base of the triangle formed by the tilted board. Dividing the height by the base equals the coefficient of friction, Fig. 9-4.

BORE-STROKE-DISPLACEMENT

The diameter of an engine cylinder is referred to as the bore and the distance the piston moves from bottom dead center to top dead center is called the stroke, Fig. 5-1.

Displacement of an engine is a measurement of its size and is equal to the number of cubic inches the piston displaces as it moves from bottom dead center to top dead center. In other words, it is equal to the area of the piston times the stroke. In the case of a multi-cylinder engine, it is also necessary to multiply by the number of cylinders.

$$Displacement = A \times S \times N$$

Where A is the area of the piston in square inches, S is the length of stroke in inches and N the number of cylinders. Assuming you have a six cylinder engine with a 4 in. bore and a 4 1/4 in. stroke, the procedure is to first calculate the piston area:

$$Area = 4 \times 4 \times .7854 = 12.56 \text{ sq. in.}$$

Then the displacement equals

$$= 12.56 \times 4.25 \times 6 = 320.28 \text{ cu. in.}$$

COMPRESSION RATIO

Compression ratio of an engine is the extent to which the combustible gases are compressed within the cylinder, Fig. 9-5. It is calculated by dividing the volume existing within the cylinder with the piston at BDC, by the volume in the cylinder with the piston at TDC. For example: If the volume with the piston at BDC is 45 cu. in. and at TDC is 5 cu. in., the compression ratio is

$$\frac{45}{5} = 9 \text{ to } 1$$

Therefore, the gases are compressed to one-ninth the original volume.

Up to a certain point, the more the fuel charge is compressed, the more power will be obtained. Experiments made by General Motors engineers, indicate that 17 to 1 compression ratio is the peak efficiency for gasoline engines.

In the service field, the compression ratio of an engine can be increased by planing material from the cylinder head, installing thinner gaskets, by increasing the stroke by regrinding the crankshaft, or by increasing the bore of the engine. However, consideration must be given to the possibility of the valves striking the piston.

In case it is desired to increase the compression ratio of an engine, the following formula may be used:

$$\frac{B}{C - 1} = A$$

Where A equals the volume of the combustion chamber, B is the displacement of the cylinder, and C is the desired compression ratio. For example; if the displacement is 36 cu. in., and the desired compression ratio is 10 to 1, then

$$\frac{36}{10 - 1} = 4 \text{ cu. in.}$$

In that particular engine, the combustion chamber would have to have a volume of 4 cu. in. to obtain a compression ratio of 10 to 1.

VOLUMETRIC EFFICIENCY

No engine is 100 percent efficient. One of the factors affecting the efficiency of a gasoline engine is the difficulty of getting a full charge of combustible mixture into the cylinder. Because of restrictions of the intake manifold, atmospheric temperature, valve timing and similar factors, a theoretically full charge does not reach the cylinder. The ratio of the amount of charge actually taken in per cycle to a complete charge is known as the volumetric efficiency.

After a certain engine speed is reached, the volumetric efficiency drops rapidly. In general, maximum volumetric efficiency is reached at approximately the same point where maximum torque is reached. For example; one engine had maximum efficiency 82 percent at 1500 rpm, but at 2500 rpm it had dropped to 65 percent.

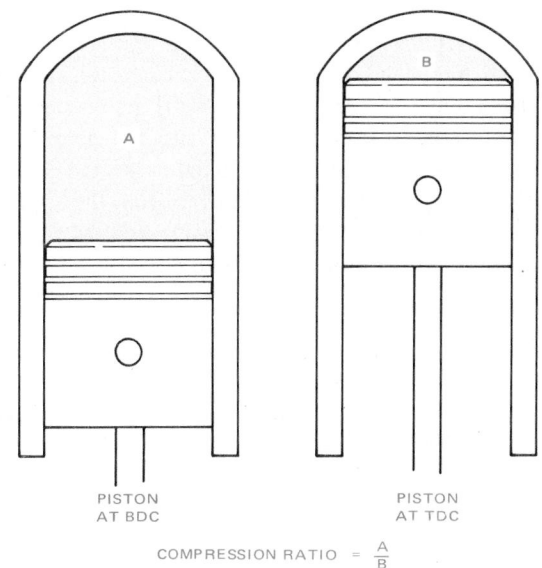

Fig. 9-5. Compression ratio is equal to volume of A divided by the volume of B.

One method of increasing volumetric efficiency is to use a supercharger. See Chapter 26.

As atmospheric pressure drops with increase in altitude, volumetric efficiency will also decrease as it is the difference in pressure between the pressure outside the cylinder and the pressure inside the cylinder that determined the amount of mixture which will enter the cylinder, Fig. 9-6.

THERMAL EFFICIENCY

The performance of various engines is often compared on the basis of their thermal efficiencies. The ratio of the heat equivalent of work done in an engine to the total heat supplied is referred to as its thermal efficiency.

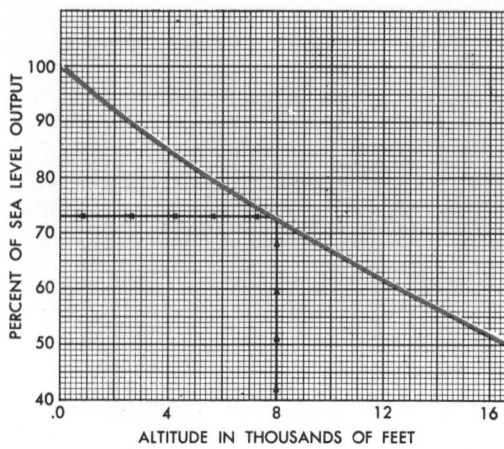

Fig. 9-6. Note how power of an engine drops as altitude increases and atmospheric pressure drops.

BRAKE HORSEPOWER

Brake horsepower may be defined as the power that is available for propelling the vehicle. It is the power developed within the cylinder (indicated horsepower) less the power that remains after the effects of friction and the power that is required to drive the fan, water pump, oil pump and generator.

The term brake horsepower is derived from the equipment first used to determine the power developed by an engine, which is known as the Prony brake, Fig. 9-7.

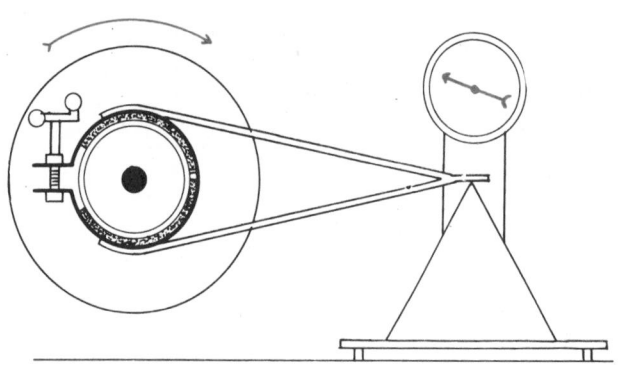

Fig. 9-7. Schematic drawing of a Prony brake used in measuring brake horsepower.

It will be noted that the Prony brake consists of a large drum and a band type brake which operates on the outer surface of the drum. Attached to the brake is a lever, with its free end bearing on a weighing scale.

The drum is directly connected to the engine crankshaft to be tested. As the drum is rotated, the brake is tightened, imposing a load on the engine, which in turn causes the lever to be pressed against the scale.

When making a Prony brake test, the throttle is first set to operate the engine at some specific speed. The brake is then tightened until the speed drops off, and the weight on the scale is noted. This procedure is repeated, each time at 100 rpm higher speed. Then, using 1 hp = 33,000 ft. lb. per min. (see page 93), calculate the brake horsepower developed at each speed, based on the following formula:

$$BHP = \frac{2\pi LRW}{33,000} = \frac{LRW}{5252}$$

Where L = Length of lever arm in feet.
         R = Engine speed in rpm.
        W = Load in pounds on scale.

The data thus produced can then be plotted to scale, as shown in Fig. 9-8, which is typical of the horsepower developed by a gasoline engine.

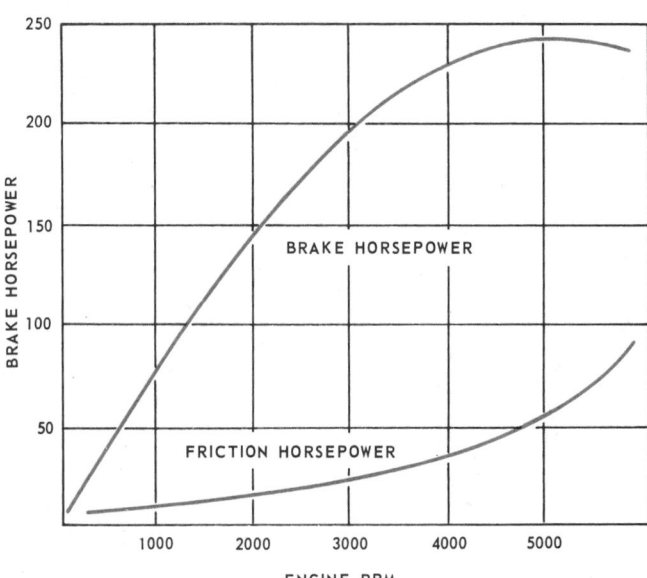

Fig. 9-8. Brake horsepower determined by a prony brake. Friction horsepower calculated from dynamometer tests.

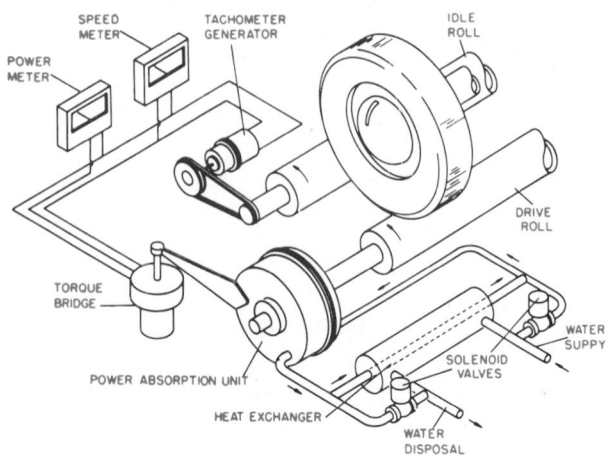

Fig. 9-9. Essential parts of a chassis dynamometer are shown in diagrammatic form.

96

Brake horsepower can also be measured on a dynamometer. Such equipment consists of a resistance creating device, such as an electric generator or a paddle wheel revolving in a fluid, which is so arranged as to absorb and dissipate the power produced by the engine. Suitable gauges are provided to indicate the amount of power absorbed.

In automotive manufacturers' testing laboratories the engines are usually directly connected to the shaft of the dynamometer. When used in service stations, the dynamometer is provided with rollers which are then driven by the wheels of the vehicle, Figs. 9-9 and 9-10.

Fig. 9-10. Type of chassis dynamometer used in service stations and diagnostic centers.

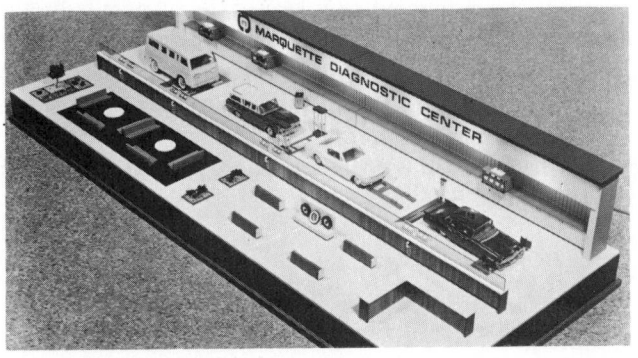

Fig. 9-11. Detailed layout of diagnostic center.

The drive-on type of dynamometer is now used extensively in diagnostic centers to supply factual information of the improvement in performance of the vehicle, Fig. 9-11.

ENGINE TORQUE

As previously described, torque is turning effort. In the case of an automotive engine, the pressure on the piston provides torque. As shown in Fig. 9-12, the torque at idling speed is relatively low, but increases rapidly as the engine speed rises. The torque maintains a high level, but decreases as higher speeds are reached.

In designing the engine, engineers try to have the engine maintain as high a torque as possible throughout the speed range of the engine. Assisting in this are large carburetors, large section manifolds, large valves and exhaust systems with minimum back pressure. However, as engine speed increases, there is less time for the fuel mixture to fill the cylinders due to inertia of the mixture, resistance to its movement offered by the induction system and the valve timing. As a result, volumetric efficiency is reduced and the torque is similarly

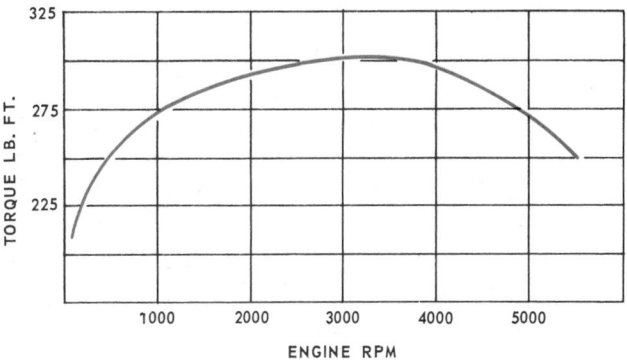

Fig. 9-12. Typical torque curve of automotive engine.

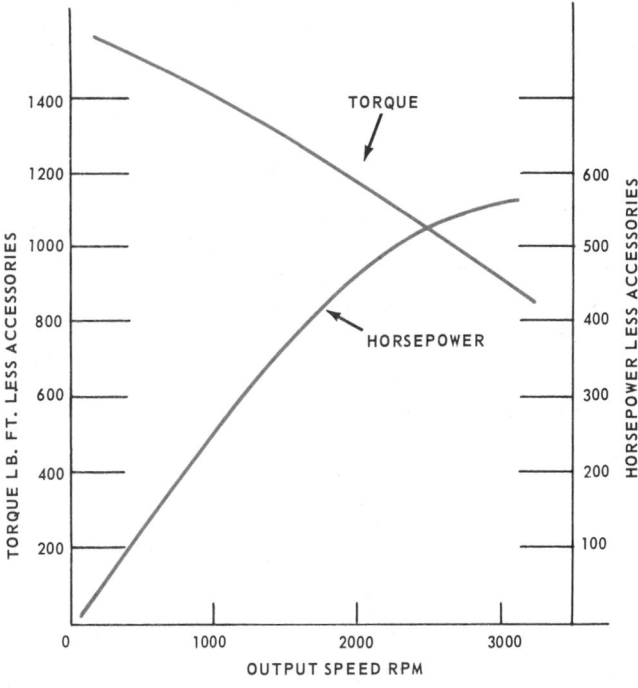

Fig. 9-13. Horsepower and torque curves of experimental Ford turbine developed especially for long distance truck service.

reduced. Compare the general form of the curve, shown in Fig. 9-12, with the curve shown in Fig. 9-13, which is that of a Ford turbine developed especially for long distance truck work. Note the turbine starts with maximum torque, whereas the gasoline engine does not attain maximum torque until it reaches higher rpm.

RATED HORSEPOWER

The rated horsepower of an engine is based on a formula developed in the early days of the industry and is based on the assumption of a brake mean effective pressure of 67.2 psi and a piston speed of a 1000 fpm. Today's engines operate at much higher speeds and pressures and consequently the formula no longer gives any indication of the power output of an engine.

It is often incorrectly referred to as the SAE horsepower, but the correct name is rated or AMA horsepower after an automotive association which is no longer in existence. However, the formula is still used for purposes of licensing automotive vehicles. The formula is as follows:

$$\text{Rated Horsepower} = \frac{NB^2}{2.5}$$

where N is the number of cylinders and B is the diameter of the engine bore in inches. For example; consider a six-cylinder engine with a bore of 4 in. Then:

$$\text{Rated Horsepower} = \frac{6 \times 4 \times 4}{2.5} = 38.4$$

INDICATED HORSEPOWER

Another method of rating an engine is by the indicated horsepower. This is based on the actual power developed in the engine from an indicator diagram, Fig. 9-14. As the indicated horsepower is the power produced within the engine, it includes the power required to overcome the friction within the engine. Subtracting the friction horsepower from the indicated horsepower gives the brake horsepower:

$$BHP = IHP - FHP$$

The indicator diagram is obtained by means of an oscilloscope or a special instrument which makes an actual drawing of the events that are occurring in the cylinder. It records in diagram form, the pressure existing at each instant of a complete cycle of the engine from the time that the combustible mixture is first drawn into the cylinder until the end of the exhaust stroke. The area of the diagram is then proportional to the power developed, i.e., it is the indicated horsepower.

When calculating the indicated horsepower, it is first necessary to determine the mean effective pressure. This is the average pressure during the power stroke, minus the average pressure during the other three strokes of the cycle. The indicated horsepower is then found by the formula:

$$IHP = \frac{PLANK}{33,000}$$

Where P = Mean effective pressure in psi.
    L = Stroke in feet.
    A = Area of cylinder in sq. in.
    N = Number of power strokes per minute.
    K = Number of cylinders.

FRICTION HORSEPOWER

Friction horsepower is the power required to overcome the friction within the engine. The friction results from the pressure of the piston and rings against the cylinder walls, the friction of the crankshaft and camshaft rotating in their bearings and the friction of other moving parts such as the oil pump, fuel pump, the engine valves, timing gear or chain, etc.

Friction horsepower increases with the speed of the engine and also the size of the engine. A typical friction horsepower curve is shown in Fig. 9-8.

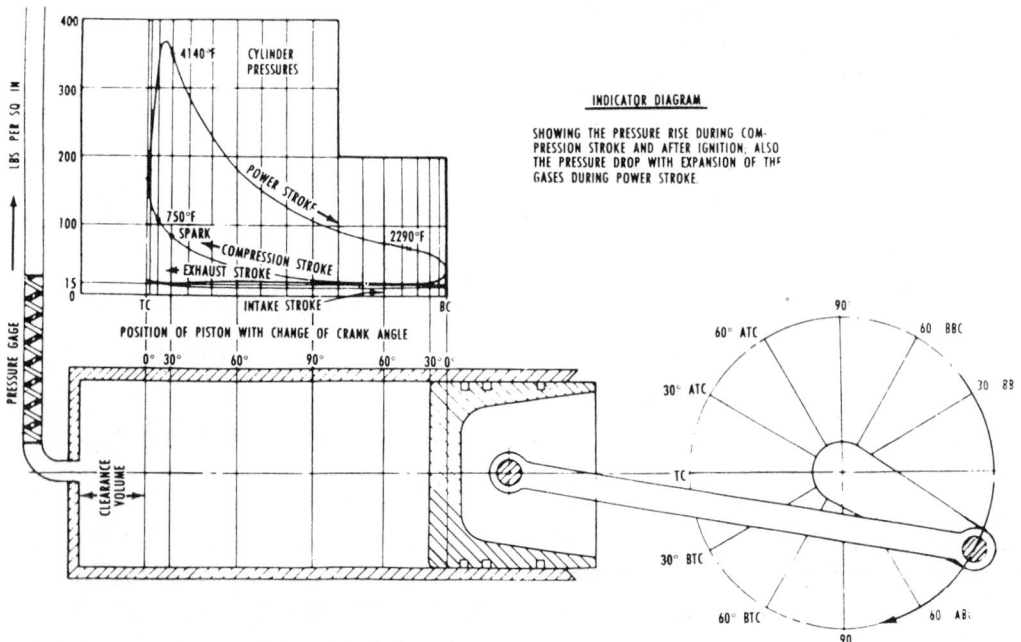

Fig. 9-14. Curve of indicated horsepower of an automotive engine.

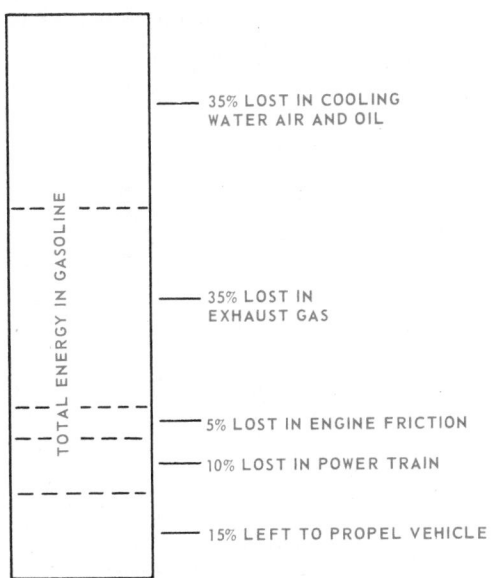

35% LOST IN COOLING
WATER AIR AND OIL

35% LOST IN
EXHAUST GAS

5% LOST IN ENGINE FRICTION

10% LOST IN POWER TRAIN

15% LEFT TO PROPEL VEHICLE

TOTAL ENERGY IN GASOLINE

Fig. 9-15. Graph shows where power goes in a conventional four-stroke cycle engine. If a turbocharger is installed, less power will be lost to the exhaust, and there will be a corresponding gain in power left to propel the vehicle.

ENGINE EFFICIENCY

Engine efficiency is the ratio of power obtained to power supplied. There are many energy losses in gasoline engines. Therefore, in relation to the inherent power in the fuel, only about 15 percent appears as useful power, Fig. 9-15. The rest is lost in the cooling system, exhaust system and friction.

In a turbojet engine, the losses are only about 1 to 2 percent.

The mechanical efficiency of an engine is equal to the relationship of brake horsepower and indicated horsepower.

$$\text{Mechanical efficiency} = \frac{\text{BHP}}{\text{IHP}}$$

This in most cases is approximately 85 percent.

CURRENT HORSEPOWER RATINGS

Comparison of the brake horsepower ratings listed for 1972 and more recent engines shows a marked drop with the listings for similar engines prior to that date.

For example in 1972 the 400 cu. in. Chevrolet V-8 with a two-barrel carburetor was rated at 170 hp @3400 rpm. However, in 1971, this same engine was rated at 255 hp at 4400 rpm. In 1970, the "400" produced 265 hp at 4400 rpm.

Some of this decrease in 1972 results directly from the extra "plumbing" that has been installed to reduce the exhaust emissions of hydrocarbons, carbon monoxide and oxides of nitrogen. But a major reason for the decrease results from quoting NET horsepower instead of GROSS horsepower, which was used in the past.

Engines are now rated in accordance with SAE Test Standard J245, and this rating is obtained with carburetion and ignition set as required by varying operating conditions.

DETONATION – PREIGNITION – RUMBLE

Detonation, preignition and rumble are three conditions that plague both engine designer and service technician alike. Preignition and detonation are often confused as they sound alike, but are two entirely different conditions.

Preignition as the name implies, is ignition that occurs earlier than planned. It results from any heated area or projection in the combustion chamber that has reached a temperature sufficient to ignite the fuel mixture. The result is preignition which has a pinging sound. In severe cases, holes will be burned in the top of the pistons, Fig. 9-16.

Detonation has a similar metallic, ringing sound and results from the use of low octane fuel, the shape of the combustion chamber and excessive compression ratio. The sound of detonation is due to vibration of some portion of the combustion chamber wall caused by almost instantaneous rise of gas pressure.

This rapid rise in gas pressure may start as follows: When the spark ignites the fuel, heat is generated and the pressure within the combustion chamber increases. That portion of the fuel mixture which is still unburned is still further compressed and as a further result the temperature soars. In addition, the charge is further heated by radiation from the burning portion of the charge. As a result, the temperature of the unburned charge is suddenly raised to the ignition point and combustion is then virtually instantaneous.

When detonation does not take place, the combustion proceeds in a controlled and orderly manner across the combustion chamber, Fig. 9-17. See Chapter 20.

In the recent years great progress has been made in the control of detonation by improved fuels which burn more slowly and by advanced design of the combustion chamber.

Rumble is a noise found particularly in high compression engines and is a noise associated with bending vibration of the crankshaft and is caused by abnormally high rates of pressure rise near top dead center.

Surface ignition is a condition which is giving considerable trouble. Research reports indicate that this results largely from the quantity and type of lubricant ash that forms in the combustion chamber.

Results of research indicate that for a given metal type of lubricant additive, high ash lubricants have a greater tendency

Fig. 9-16. In cases of severe preignition, holes will be burned in piston heads.

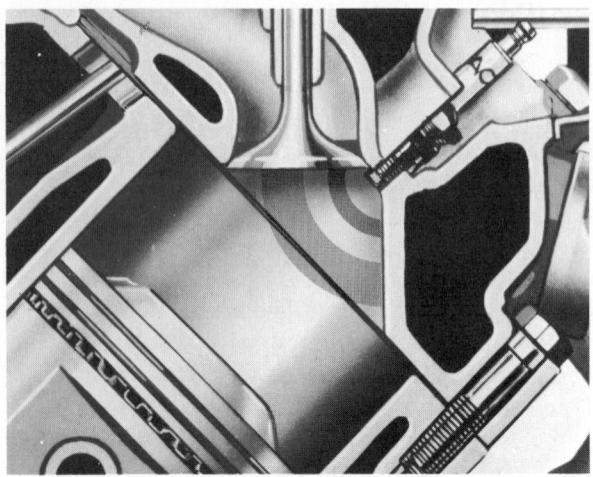

Fig. 9-17. With normal combustion, flame action expanding away from point of ignition.

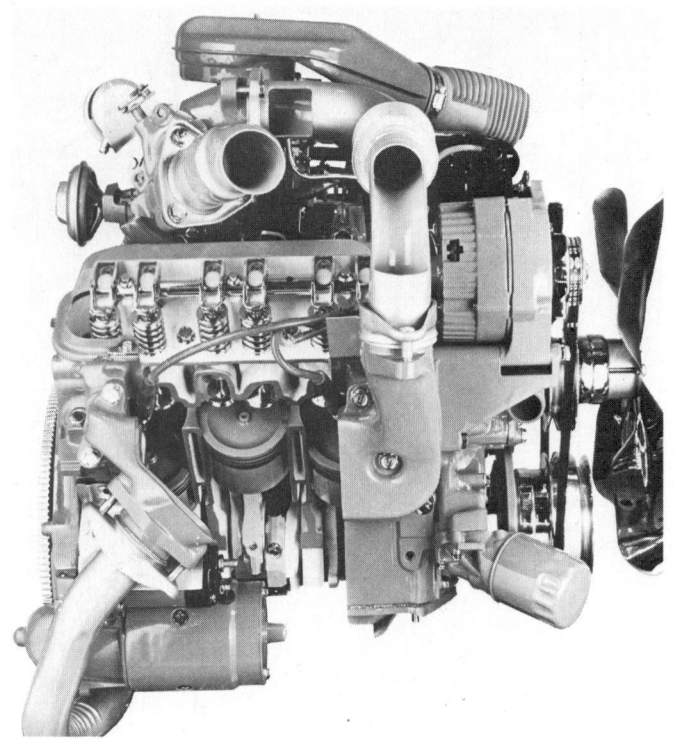

Fig. 9-18. Turbocharged Buick 231 cu. in. (3.8 litre) V-6 engine develops 165 hp or 0.71 hp per cubic inch displacement.

to produce surface ignition than low ash blends. Magnesium based lubricants are less prone to cause surface ignition than barium or calcium lubricants.

After run, or dieseling, is a condition that occurs frequently, particularly on engines fitted with exhaust emission control devices. Precision timing and a reduction in idling speed will reduce such tendencies. Some fuels are more prone to cause this condition than others.

INCREASING HORSEPOWER

Horsepower of an engine can be increased by: raising the compression ratio; reducing back pressure from the exhaust system; increasing the size of the valves and manifolding; using superchargers or turbochargers. Currently, there is strong interest in turbochargers. These devices utilize the force of exhaust gases to drive more air-fuel mixture into the cylinders. (See the chapter on FUEL SUPPLY SYSTEMS.)

Installation of a turbocharger is one of the most effective methods of increasing the output of an engine. In the Buick V-6 engine shown in Fig. 9-18, the conventional engine with a single barrel carburetor develops 105 hp; with the turbocharger, power output is improved to 165 hp.

REVIEW QUESTIONS — ENGINE PERFORMANCE

1. Brake horsepower is a reliable measure of the power developed by an engine. True or False?
2. How is the displacement of an engine determined?
3. Torque is the same as power. True or False?
4. Friction is dependent on the area in contact. True or False?
5. Indicated horsepower does not take into consideration the friction losses within the engine. True or False?
6. Mean effective pressure is another name for: Explosion pressure _____. Compression pressure _____. Average pressure _____.
7. Define the difference between power and torque.
8. Why does torque decrease above a certain speed?
9. A gas is best measured by: Volume _____. Weight _____.
10. Given the bore of the cylinder and the volume of the combustion chamber, it is possible to determine the compression ratio. True or False?
11. Rated horsepower is the same as brake horsepower. Yes or No?
12. The volume within the cylinder of a certain engine is 50 cu. in., and the volume of the combustion chamber is 5 cu. in.; what is the compression ratio?
    a. 10 to 1.
    b. 6 to 1.
    c. One tenth.
13. Current hp ratings are NET figures. Yes or No?
14. The use of a supercharger will increase volumetric efficiency. True or False?
15. Which is correct? Mechanical efficiency of an engine equals: $\dfrac{BHP}{IHP}$ or $\dfrac{Rated\ HP}{IHP}$

ENGINE
LUBRICATION

Without the aid of friction, an automobile could not move itself. Excessive friction in the engine, however, would mean rapid destruction. We cannot eliminate internal friction, but we can reduce it to a controllable degree by the use of friction reducing lubricants.

These lubricants are usually made from the same crude oil from which we obtain gasoline. The petroleum oils are compounded with animal fats, vegetable oils and other ingredients to produce satisfactory oils and greases for automotive use. Lubricating oils and greases are also manufactured from silicones and other materials and have no petroleum products in them.

Lubricating oil in an automobile engine has several tasks to perform:

1. By lubrication, reduce friction between moving parts of engine:
   a. Reduce amount of destructive heat generated by excessive friction.
   b. Conserve power that would otherwise be wasted in overcoming excessive friction.
2. By acting as a seal to prevent leakage between parts such as pistons, rings and cylinders.
3. By flowing between friction-generating parts to carry away heat.
4. By washing away abrasive metal worn from friction surfaces.

Furthermore, the engine oil must function whether the temperature is below zero or above 200 deg. F. This is contrary to the nature of petroleum products since they tend to thicken at low temperatures and thin out at high temperatures. The oil must go through many processes during manufacture to reduce this tendency to change viscosity with changes in temperature.

PROPERTIES OF ENGINE OIL

Engine oil is available in different viscosities. Viscosity is considered to be the internal friction of a fluid. An oil of low viscosity will flow more easily than an oil of high viscosity. Sometimes a low viscosity oil is referred to as a light oil and a high viscosity oil as a heavy oil.

Oils of different viscosities have been assigned numbers by the Society of Automotive Engineers. The lower the viscosity, the lower the assigned number. SAE 10 engine oil, for example, may be recommended for cold weather operation and SAE 30 for warm weather. The SAE number of an oil has nothing to do with its quality.

The added designation of "W" such as 10-W indicates that the W oil has the added ability to remain fluid or flow at a wider range of temperatures. A 10-W oil, therefore, can be used under more severe conditions than an SAE 10 oil.

The viscosity of an oil is determined in the laboratory by means of a viscosimeter under carefully controlled conditions. Engine oils are also designed to form a minimum of carbon, resist oxidation, foaming and the formation of sludge.

Briefly, the American Petroleum Institute (API) rates engine oils according to the following classes of service:

SF oils are available for gasoline engines in passenger cars and some trucks beginning with 1980 models. SF provides increased oxidation stability and improved anti-wear performance over all other API classifications. It also provides protection against engine deposits, rust and corrosion. SF oils may be used where classes SE, SD or SC are recommended.

SE oils are suitable for most severe service of certain 1971 and all 1972 and later gasoline and other spark ignition engines having emission control devices and operating under manufacturers' warranty. SD oils are for service typical of gasoline engines in 1968 through 1970 cars, certain trucks and some 1971 and/or later models.

SC oils are identified for service in gasoline engines in 1964 through 1967 passenger cars and trucks operating under manufacturers' warranty. SB oils are recommended for older cars operating under moderate conditions. Oils marked ONLY for service SB are NOT recommended for engines under manufacturers' warranty. SA oils are for utility and diesel engines operating under such mild conditions that protection afforded by compounded oils is not required.

CD oils are for severe duty diesel engine service. CC oils are for moderate-to-severe duty in diesels and certain heavy-duty gasoline engines. CB oils are for mild-to-moderate diesel service. CA oils are for light, normal conditions such as are typical of most farm tractor and trucking conditions.

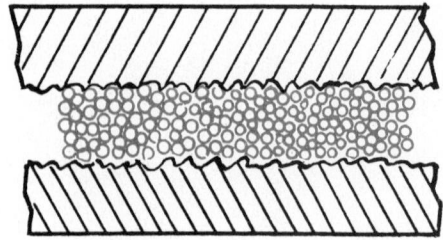

Fig. 10-1. Oil molecules roll one over the other to reduce friction in a manner somewhat similar to ball bearings.

OIL CHANGES

When to change oil is a difficult question to answer since so much depends on the conditions under which the vehicle is being operated and what type of oil is being used.

Most manufacturers have two recommendations: one for normal driving and the other for more severe conditions.

Severe conditions are described as: short trip driving during which the engine does not reach operating temperature for an appreciable time; towing another vehicle; excessive idling conditions; or driving in dusty areas.

Since most cars are operated in cities or towns with a population of 25,000 or greater, it is evident that the cars are used mostly in short trips with much time spent idling. Therefore, most cars are operated under "severe" conditions. Normal driving may be described as: cars driven on individual trips of ten miles or more, do not pull a trailer and operate in an atmosphere that is relatively free of dust.

Car manufacturers' oil change recommendations show a big difference for vehicles used for normal driving and for those being operated under severe conditions. One manufacturer, for example, recommends that the oil and oil filter should be changed: each 3000 miles or three months under severe conditions; each 7500 miles or once a year under normal driving conditions; turbocharged engines each 3000 miles under all conditions. However, oil change intervals are subject to frequent change, so always consult manufacturerers' specifications.

Non-detergent oils and low quality oils are not recommended. Use SE or SF oils and make prescribed oil filter changes.

Oil in the crankcase, while performing its many functions of protecting the engine from wear and corrosion, becomes loaded with acids, dirt and abrasives, not all of which can be trapped by filters. So there is only one way of removing this wear-producing contaminant and that is by changing oil.

Furthermore, many of the additives in the engine oil become depleted from prolonged use and are no longer effective. Unless the oil is changed, wear is accelerated.

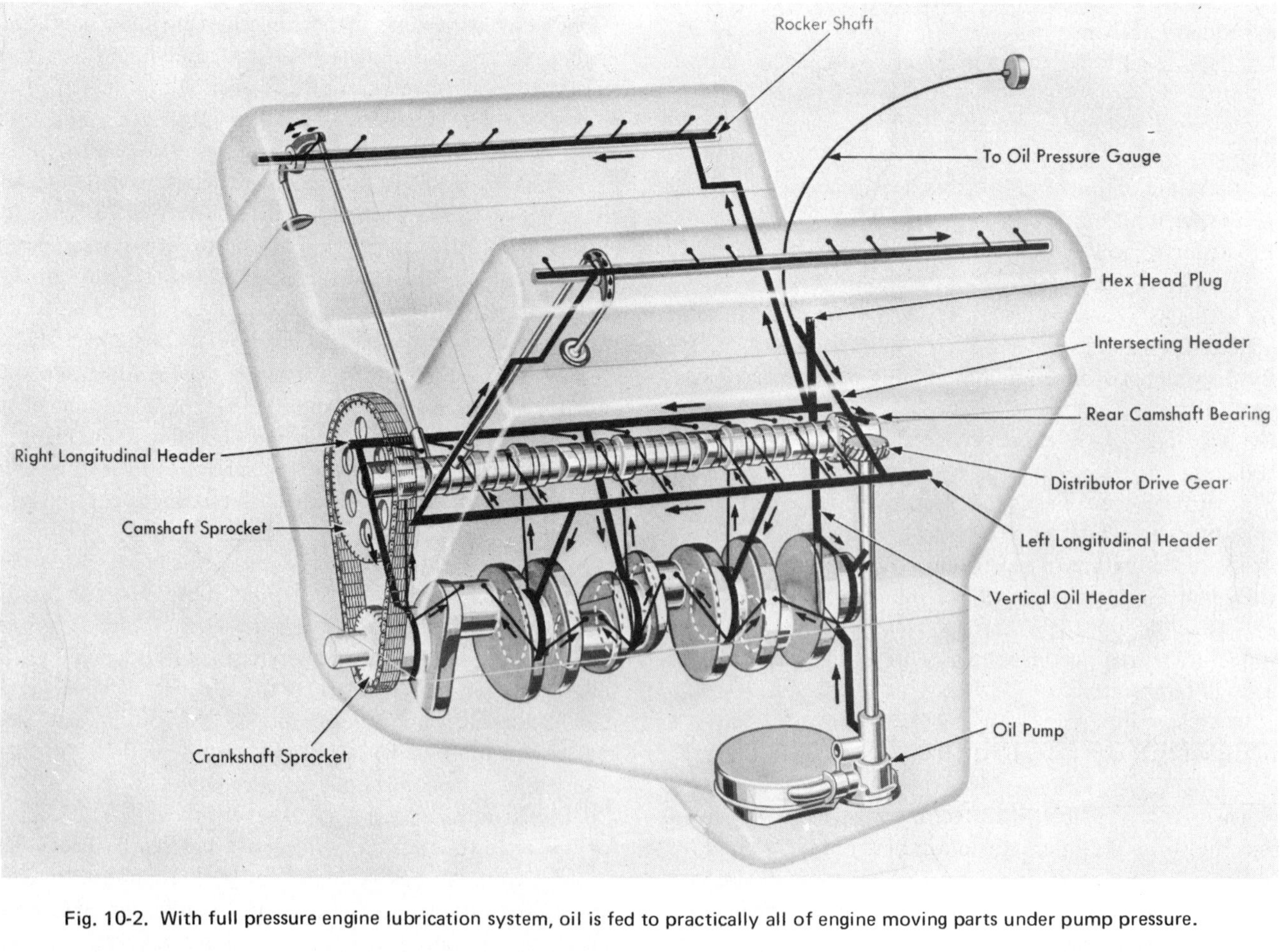

Rocker Shaft

To Oil Pressure Gauge

Hex Head Plug

Intersecting Header

Rear Camshaft Bearing

Distributor Drive Gear

Left Longitudinal Header

Vertical Oil Header

Oil Pump

Right Longitudinal Header

Camshaft Sprocket

Crankshaft Sprocket

Fig. 10-2. With full pressure engine lubrication system, oil is fed to practically all of engine moving parts under pump pressure.

Engine Lubrication

Petroleum-base oils are made more fuel-efficient by adding graphite, molybdenum disulfide or other suspended materials, or by using selected oil soluble compounds.

Extended oil change intervals are claimed for their products by manufacturers of synthetic oils. Synthetics, they state, have certain advantages over petroleum-base oils, mainly in reduced friction between lubricated surfaces.

LUBRICATING METHODS

Oil is supplied to moving parts of the engine by pump pressure or splashing, or by a combination of both. See Fig. 10-2. Splashed oil usually becomes a mist for lubricating parts such as cylinder walls and pistons.

Oil is fed to the majority of engine parts under pressure, especially to main bearings and connecting rod bearings. Leakage or "throw-off" from the rod bearings splashes on other moving parts inside the engine. A typical pressure lubrication system is shown in Fig. 10-2.

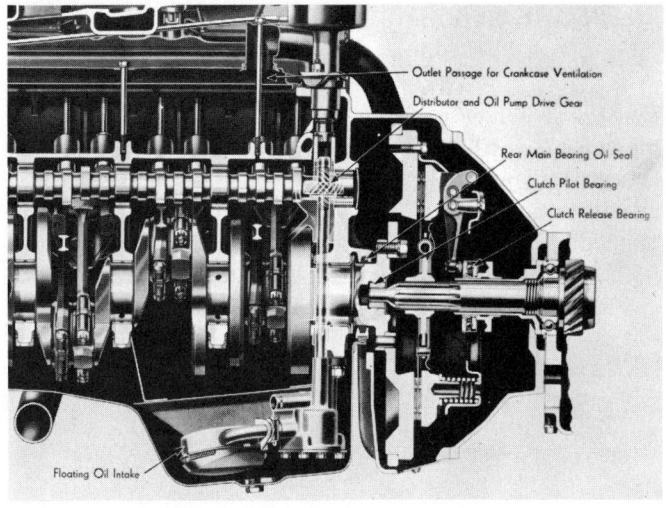

Fig. 10-3. Cadillac sump-located pump is fitted with a floating oil intake screen.

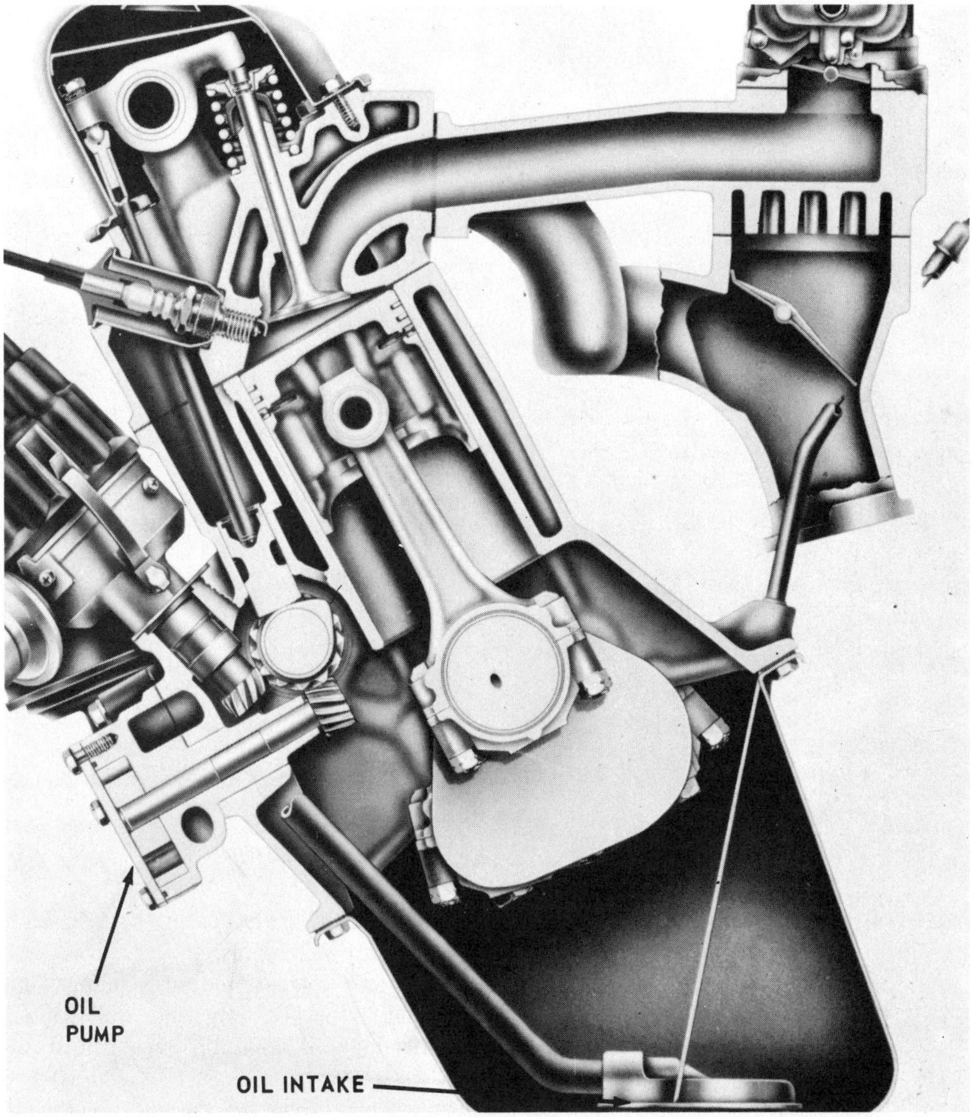

Fig. 10-4. Slant six oil pump is mounted on side of engine and is connected to oil screen by a pipe.

103

PRESSURE SYSTEMS

Fig. 10-3 shows the oil pump located in the sump of the oil pan, and the oil enters the pump through a screen. Sometimes the pump is not located in the sump, and oil is piped from the screen to the pump, Fig. 10-4. Quite often the intake screen is mounted on a hinged float that stays on top of the oil in the sump, Fig. 10-3. The idea is to keep the pump intake away from any dirt that might settle in the bottom of the sump.

Fig. 10-5 shows the path of the oil from the pump to the

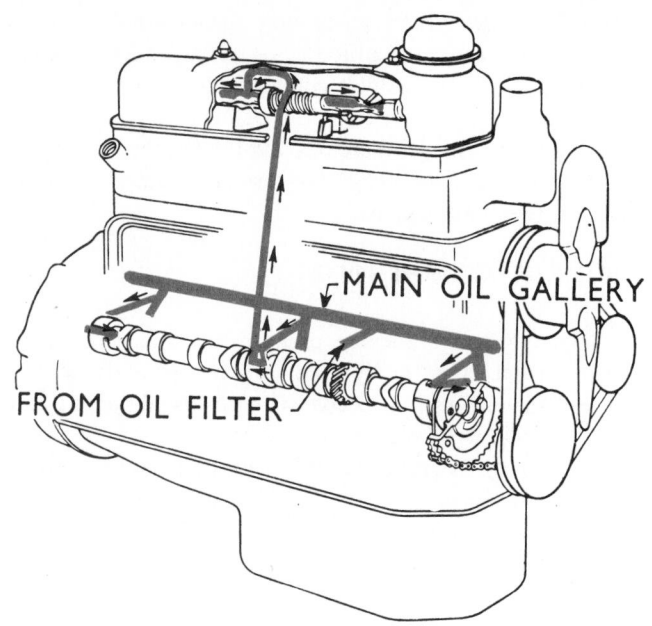

Fig. 10-7. Oil from gallery goes to camshaft bearings, then on to rocker arm shaft.

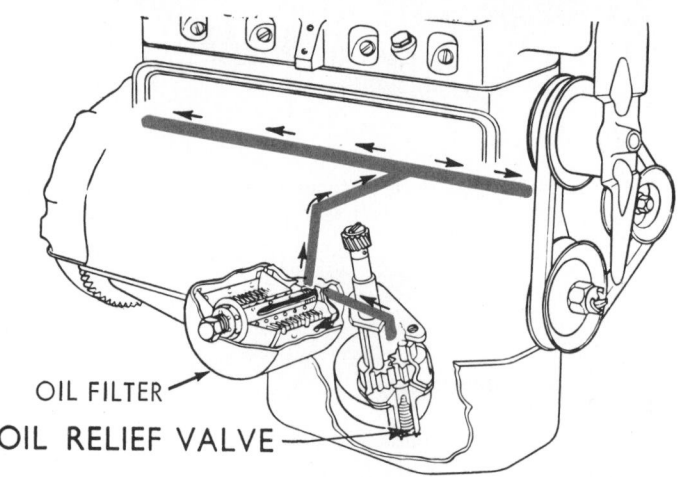

Fig. 10-5. In this engine application, oil goes through a filter placed between oil pump and oil gallery.

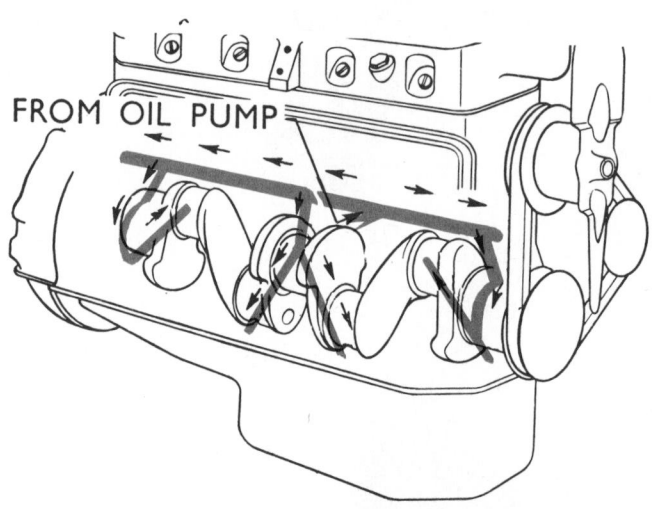

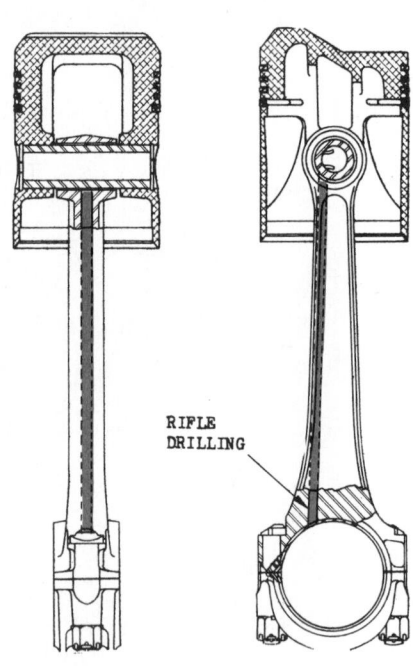

Fig. 10-8. Left. An oil passage is drilled lengthwise in connecting rod.

Fig. 10-9. Right. Passage conducts oil from crankshaft to piston pin.

Fig. 10-6. Oil passages drilled in crankshaft conduct oil from main bearings to connecting rods.

oil gallery or distributing tube in the crankcase. The oil is conducted to the main bearings through drilled passages in the crankcase. Passages are also drilled in the crankshaft to carry the oil from the main bearings to the connecting rod journals, Fig. 10-6. The path of the oil to the overhead valve rocker shaft is shown in Fig. 10-7. So engine oil is carried under

pressure to all parts except the cylinder walls and, in some engines, the piston pins.

In some engines, the oil is pumped into a groove in the cylinder wall for ring and wall lubrication. Also, some connecting rods have oil passages drilled lengthwise to carry oil to the piston pins, Figs. 10-8 and 10-9. Ordinarily, there is enough oil thrown off the main bearings and rod bearings to supply lubrication for the cylinder walls and piston pins, Fig. 10-10. Also, the top of the connecting rod in some engines

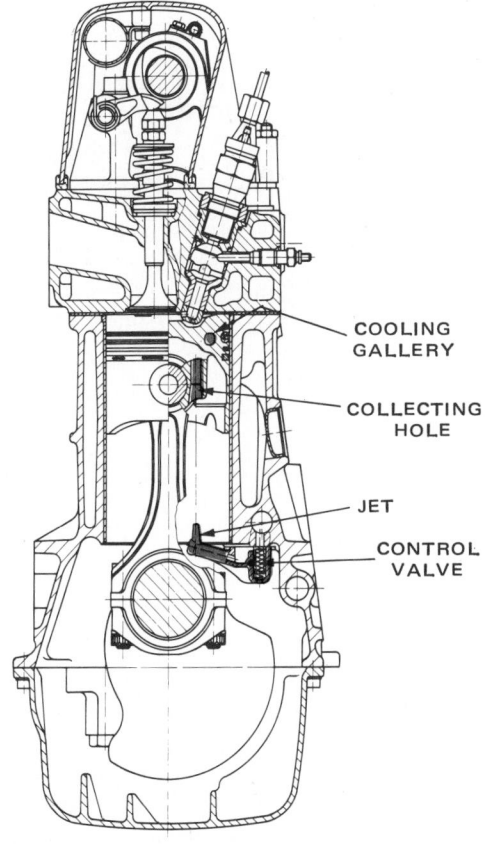

Fig. 10-10. A limited amount of oil leaks out at ends of crankshaft bearings, and connecting rods throw it on cylinder walls.

has a spurt hole drilled in it on one side. A squirt of oil is shot out on the cylinder wall when the hole registers with the oil passage in the crankshaft. See Fig. 10-11.

The pistons are lubricated in various ways. Mercedes, in its turbocharged five cylinder diesel engine, cools the pistons by shooting a stream of oil upward into a collecting hole that carries the lubricating oil into a cooling gallery. See Fig. 10-12.

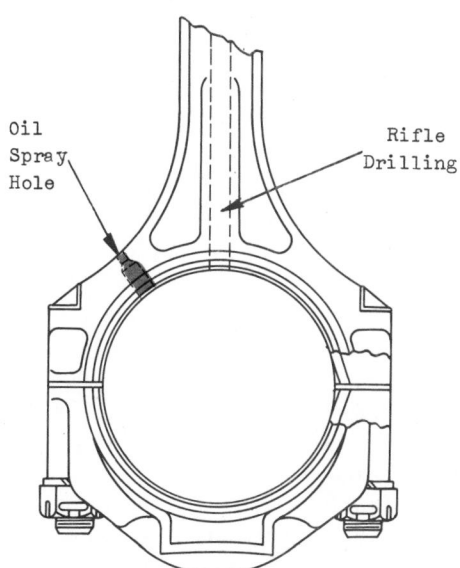

Oil Spray Hole

Rifle Drilling

COOLING GALLERY

COLLECTING HOLE

JET

CONTROL VALVE

Fig. 10-11. An oil spray hole in rod provides lubrication for cylinder walls.

Fig. 10-12. Mercedes five cylinder diesel features an engine lubricating and oil cooling system that shoots oil upward into the piston, which has a specially designed oil collecting hole or tube.

Valves in jets are provided in the Mercedes diesel to shut off the jets of oil when the engine is idling in order to maintain oil pressure when piston cooling is not needed.

A once popular method of lubricating the engine bearings pumped oil through pipes into troughs in the crankcase under each connecting rod. In this system, the pipes are located and aimed so that a jet of oil is directed on the rod bearing as the rod comes around. The rod also splashes into oil in the trough.

OIL PUMPS

The pumps used to circulate the oil are of the positive displacement type in several designs. Vanes, plungers, rotors and gears are all used to build up the necessary pressure. A representative type of gear pump is illustrated in Fig. 10-13.

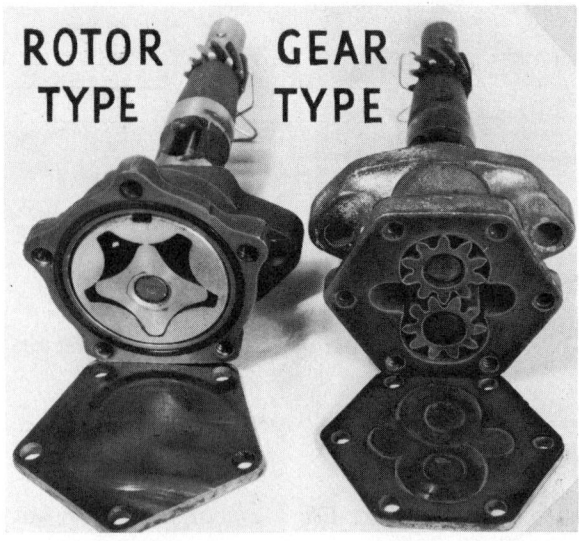

Fig. 10-14. Most automobile engine oil pumps are of either gear type or rotor type.

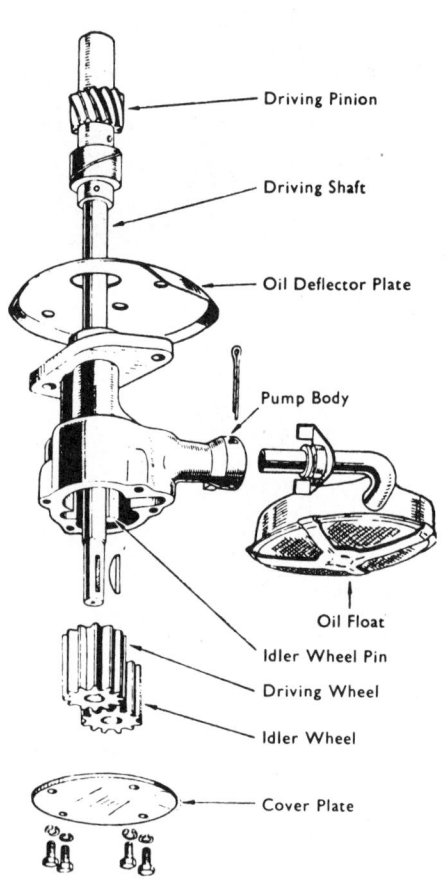

Fig. 10-13. Exploded view of typical gear-type oil pump.

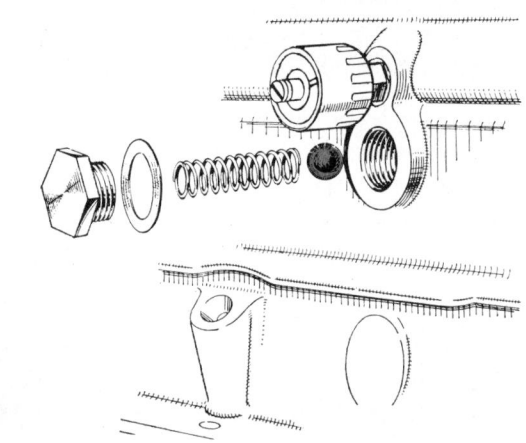

Fig. 10-15. As pressure builds up in line, ball is forced back against spring to uncover a port so that oil can be returned to sump.

OIL PRESSURE

Most cases of lost oil pressure are due to excessive clearance in the bearings of the engine rather than worn oil pumps. Attempts are often made to restore lost oil pressure by adjustment of the oil pressure regulating valve. If the oil pump is in good condition, the pressure regulation valve will REGULATE the pressure of the oil within limits. However, it will not increase the capacity of the oil pump. The regulator is a simple spring-loaded valve which RELIEVES EXCESS PRESSURE in the circulating system by bypassing the excess oil back to the sump. See Fig. 10-15.

Another reason for lack of oil pressure is stoppage in the oil pump supply line or screen. This prevents oil reaching the pump in sufficient volume to maintain pressure. A typical case of "sludge" accumulation in a screen is shown in Fig. 10-16. This sludge stops up the oil passages, with the result that a bearing may "starve" for oil, then friction will melt the metal.

A comparison between the gear and rotor types is shown in Fig. 10-14. These pumps are always positively driven, usually from the camshaft either by means of gears or cams.

Since these pumps handle oil, they are well lubricated at all times and do not suffer from excessive wear. They do, in time, develop an excess of clearance and require replacement of parts. The gear teeth or vane contours may wear, and the gear ends and housings may wear. When excessive wear does occur, the oil pressure will drop.

Fig. 10-16. An accumulation of sludge on screen at left will stop flow of oil and result in burned-out bearings.

OIL SLUDGE

Sludge is a mayonnaise-like mixture of water, oil, dirt and other products of combustion. It is most likely to form in an engine that seldom reaches a satisfactory operating temperature. For example: a light truck used for laundry or milk delivery service in cold weather. Such a vehicle ordinarily runs a short distance at slow speed, stops and then runs another short distance at slow speed.

Slow speed, stop-and-go operation means that the engine seldom gets hot enough to drive the water and vapor out of the crankcase. The water condenses on the cold walls of the crankcase, or in some cases gets into the crankcase through leaking cylinder head gaskets. This water emulsifies with the oil, carbon, dirt, etc., to form sludge. See Fig. 10-17.

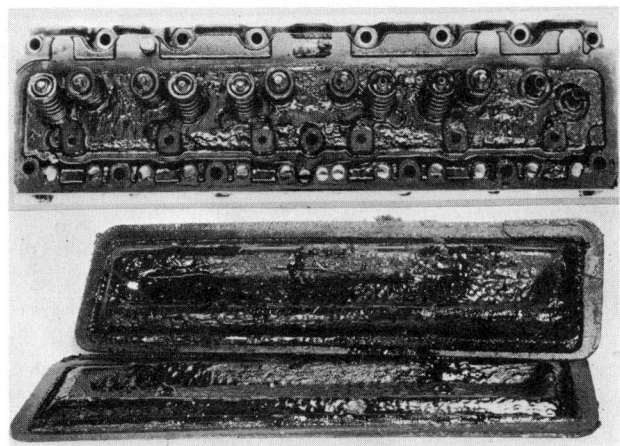

Fig. 10-17. Typical accumulation of sludge on cylinder head and valve cover plates.

Sludge formation can be held to a minimum by using the correct cooling system thermostat to maintain a high engine operating temperature. Using engine oils of high detergency and making frequent changes of oil and filter are necessary. Adequate crankcase ventilation is also important.

Researchers have found that when the cooling system thermostat was removed from the engine water jacket outlet,

temperatures barely exceeded 100 deg. F when the ambient temperature was 60 to 70 deg. F. In general, the engine operated at approximately 20 deg. above the ambient temperature, resulting in sludge build up.

Water jacket outlet temperature usually corresponds to the setting of the cooling system thermostat. It must be emphasized that oil dilution and sludge formation decrease with 195 deg. thermostats as compared to thermostats having a lower opening temperature. Not only is sludge reduced, but production of hydrocarbons and carbon monoxide in the exhaust are also reduced.

Equally important to keeping sludge formation to a minimum is proper crankcase ventilation. Adequate crankcase oil temperature must be maintained to assist in evaporation and purging of volatile blow-by contaminants. Oil temperatures are usually only a problem under conditions involving excessive idling or operation in severely cold weather.

Fuel is a major factor in the formation of sludge. Modern oils with their additives help to control the condition by keeping sludge and other foreign materials in suspension.

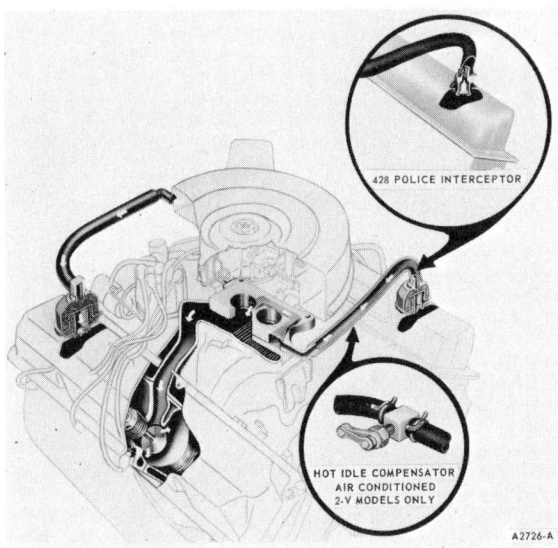

Fig. 10-18. Details of positive closed crankcase ventilating system installed on 390 cu. in. Ford engine.

CRANKCASE VENTILATION

The road draft tube once helped maintain a better climate in the crankcase and reduce a sludge forming tendencies. The crankcase was ventilated by air drawn through the filter in the oil filler cap. After passing through the valve chamber and crankcase, the air and fumes left the engine through a road draft tube. Its opening was below the engine where the movement of the passing air helps exhaust the crankcase fumes. In Figs. 10-19 and 10-20, the fumes are drawn into the intake manifold, then through the engine again.

The effects of passing the fumes into the atmosphere, and the methods used to overcome the conditions, are discussed in the chapter on EMISSION CONTROL.

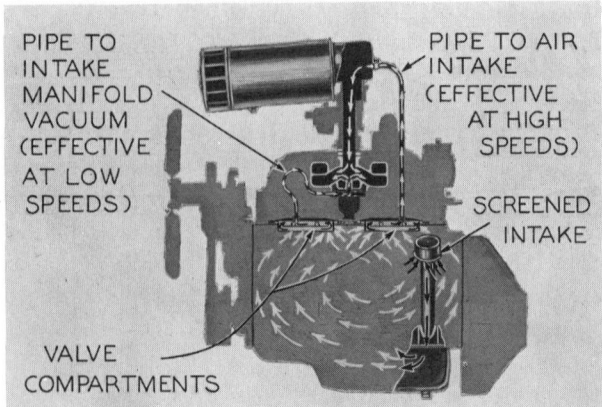

Fig. 10-19. With this "open" system, engine vacuum in inlet manifold is used to draw ventilating air in through a screen on oil filler pipe.

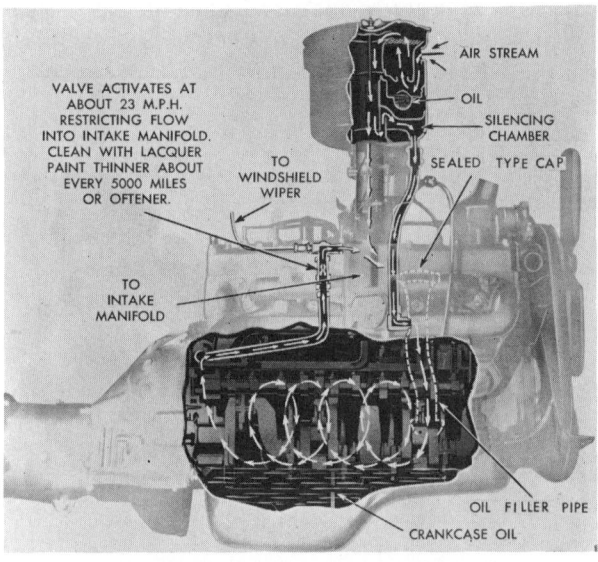

Fig. 10-20. Another method of using intake vacuum is to draw in ventilating air through air cleaner.

ENGINE VARNISH

Another type of engine deposit is known as "varnish" or "lacquer." It is often also called sludge, but it is an entirely different material and forms in a different manner. Varnish or lacquer is formed when an engine is worked hard enough to run hot for extended periods of time. The heat causes the oil to break down, and some of the elements to separate out and deposit as a varnish-like substance on the metal parts.

To avoid such deposits, it is necessary to use the best oil obtainable and change oil regularly. It is also essential to make sure that the cooling system is functioning efficiently.

The importance of regular and frequent oil changes has been emphasized. This is because oil costs less than machinery. Changing oil frequently is merely a form of insurance. It is more economical to throw away a quart of oil costing a few cents than to take a chance on damaging an engine worth several hundred dollars.

OIL FILTERS

Oil filters are placed in the engine oil system to remove dirt and abrasives from the oil. Diluents, such as gasoline and acids, are not removed. However, by removing the solid materials, the possibility of acids forming is reduced, and the rate of wear of engine parts is greatly reduced.

Oil filters installed on modern passenger car engines are full-flow type; all oil passes through the filter before it reaches the bearings. However, in the event the filter becomes clogged or obstructed, a bypass valve is provided so that oil will continue to reach the bearings. The filters in use today are of the "throw-away" type. See Figs. 10-21, 10-22 and 10-23.

ADDITIVES

The requirements of today's automobile engines are far beyond the range of straight mineral oils. All automobile manufacturers now recommend oils which have been improved by additives. The need for improved oil results from higher engine compression, increased bearing loads, stepped-up speeds, greater sensitivity to deposit formation, corrosion and rusting.

There are many different additives in use today. Probably the first one to be used was a pour point depressant, which is designed to overcome the difficulty of pouring oil in cold weather. More important, the oil would not flow to the engine oil pump. At low temperatures, the wax in the oil would crystallize, then form a sort of "honey comb" which in turn would block the flow of oil.

Detergent-dispersant additives are used to prevent sludge and varnish deposits, which otherwise would restrict the free flow of oil and cause valves and lifters to stick.

Foam inhibitors are designed to prevent the formation of foam, which would result from the egg beater action of the rotating engine parts. Unless the foaming is stopped, bearings and other parts would receive only foam instead of oil and would soon fail.

Oxidation inhibitors are used to reduce the possiblility of oil being oxidized. This oxidation usually occurs at higher operating temperatures attained during sustained high speed, full throttle operation. Serious oxidation of the oil and resultant deposit formation will occur unless oxidation is prevented.

Viscosity index improvers, as the words imply, improve the viscosity index. The viscosity index is a measure of the rate of change or variation in the viscosity of a liquid with changing temperature.

A high viscosity index indicates a relatively low rate of viscosity change at two different temperatures. A low index indicates a high rate of viscosity change. Oils designed for automotive engine use have a relatively high viscosity index and are suitable for use in both high and low atmospheric temperatures.

Corrosion and rust inhibitors are designed to help the detergent-dispersant additives in the prevention of rust and corrosion.

Antiwear additives, one of the most important used, have

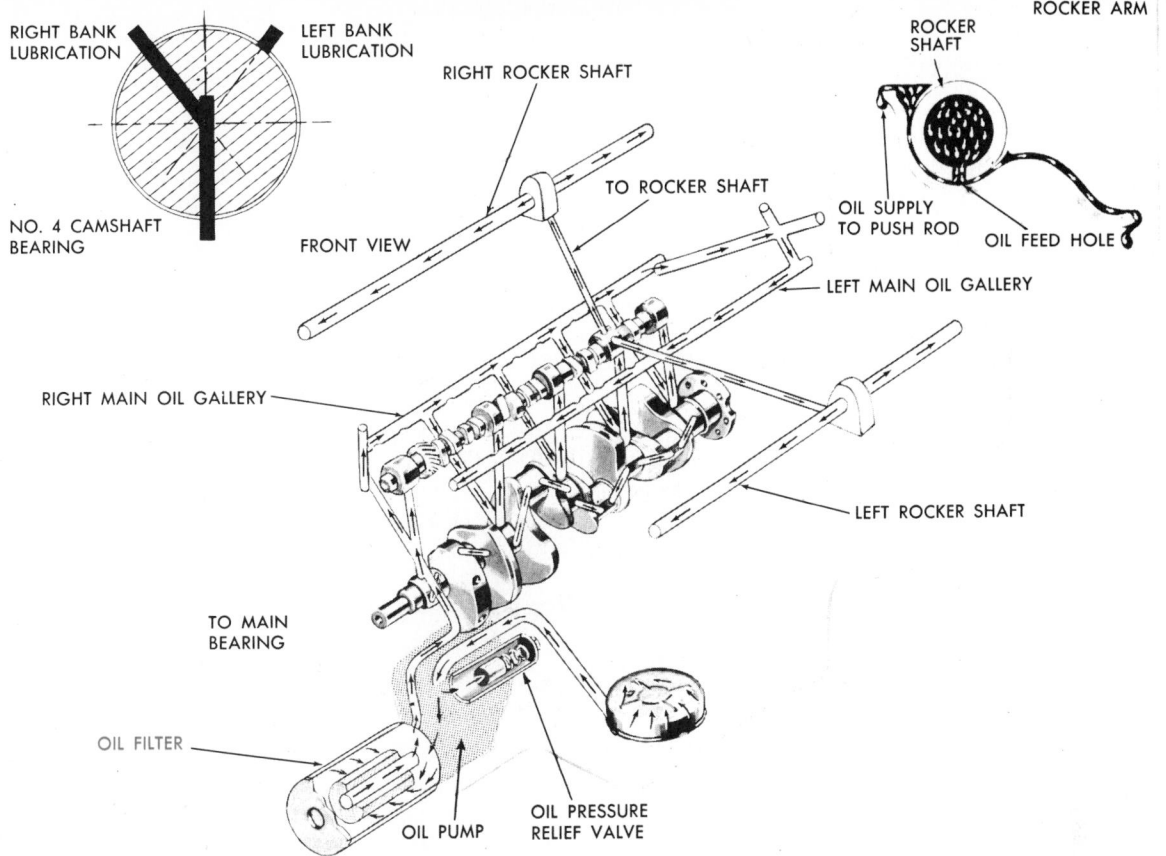

Fig. 10-21. Filters are often connected directly to pressure side of pump to catch any contaminants before they reach small passages in camshaft bearings or rocker arm shaft.

the ability to coat metal surfaces with a strong and slippery film that prevents direct metal-to-metal contact. All modern, top-quality oils contain this additive.

All these additives combine to produce an oil which not only will withstand heavier loads, reduce corrosion, stop foaming, maintain viscosity, stop sludge and varnish formation, but will also keep the interior of the engine cleaner and increase its useful life.

OIL DESIGNATIONS

Until 1971, the following designations were used to classify engine oils:

MS — Motor Severe   DS — Diesel Severe
MM — Motor Moderate   DM — Diesel Moderate
ML — Motor Light   DG — Diesel General

In 1971, and again in 1980, new designations were developed jointly by the American Petroleum Institute (API), the Society of Automotive Engineers (SAE) and the American

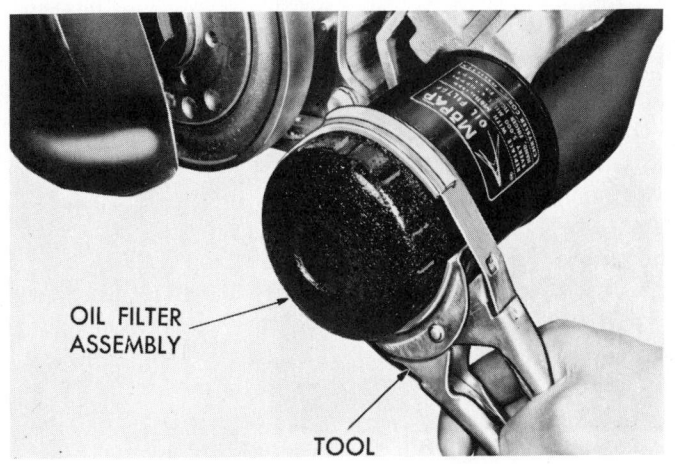

Fig. 10-22. Removing an oil filter.

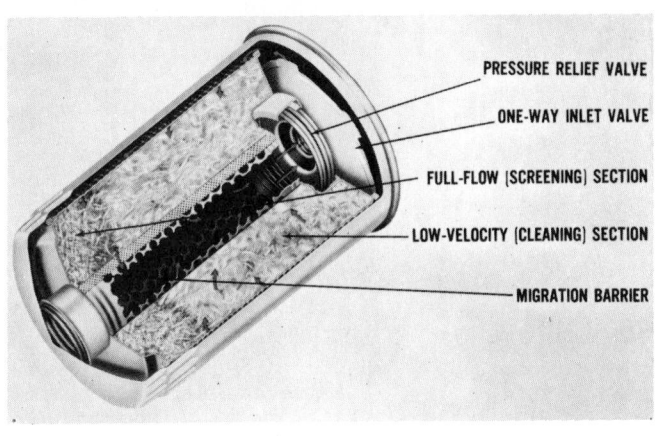

Fig. 10-23. Depth-type, full-flow filter.

Society for Testing Metals (ASTM):

SA — For engines operating under mild conditions. No special protection capabilities.

SB — For light-duty engine operation. Has anti-scuff capabilities, resists oil oxidation, retards bearing corrosion.

SC — Minimum requirements for all 1964 to 1967 passenger cars and light trucks. Controls high and low temperature deposits. Retards rust and corrosion in gasoline engines.

SD — For 1968 and later engines warranty service. Better high and low temperature deposit control than SC. Also rust/corrosion resistant.

SE — For 1972 and later gasoline engine warranty maintenance service. It provides maximum protection against rust, corrosion, wear, oil oxidation and high temperature deposits that can cause oil thickening.

SF — For gasoline engines in passenger cars and some trucks beginning with 1980 model operating under engine manufacturers' recommended maintenance procedures.

CA — For light-duty normally aspirated diesel engines. Provides protection against high temperature deposits and bearing corrosion.

CB — For moderate-duty, normally aspirated diesel engines operating on high sulphur fuel. Protects against bearing corrosion and high temperature deposits.

CC — For moderate-duty, lightly supercharged diesel engines and certain heavy-duty gasoline engines. Protects against rust, corrosion and high/low temperature deposits.

CD — For severe-duty supercharged diesel engines using fuels of a wide quality range. Provides highly effective control of corrosion and deposits.

REVIEW QUESTIONS — LUBRICATION

1. Name four tasks that the lubricating oil in an engine is expected to perform.
2. An SAE 10 oil can be used anywhere that SAE 10-W can be used. True or False?
3. Is a light oil always better than a heavier oil? Yes or No?
4. What is meant by "oil throw-off?"
5. Name two ways of oiling piston rings.
6. Oil pumps are sometimes belt driven. True or False?
7. What is the most frequent cause of low oil pressure?
8. Name three things found in oil sludge.
9. Sludge and lacquer are not the same thing. True or False?
10. All engine oils recommended by the automobile manufacturers have been improved by additives. Name three.
11. Slow speed driving is always desirable in order to maintain the best engine lubrication. Yes or No.?
12. How does engine oil become diluted?
13. Oil classification SA is for engines operating under mild conditions. True or False?
14. Oil classification _____ is for severe-duty supercharged diesel engines.

This General Motors V-6 engine is fitted with an automatic fan clutch that increases or decreases the speed of the fan, depending upon temperature and setting of bimetallic coil. In this way, fan cooling action is tailored to the immediate need.

ENGINE
COOLING SYSTEMS

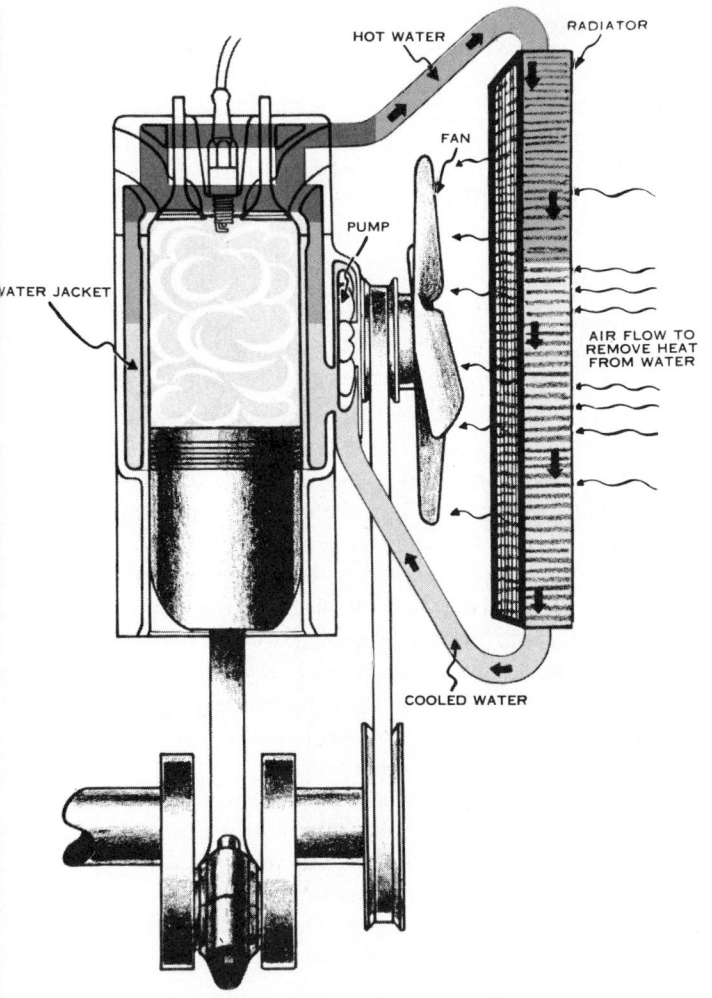

Fig. 11-1. Engine temperatures are regulated by transferring excess heat to surrounding air.

A cooling system of some kind is necessary in any internal combustion engine. If no cooling system were provided, some parts would melt from the heat of the burning fuel, and pistons would expand so much they would seize (could not move in the cylinders).

The pressurized cooling system of a water-cooled engine, Figs. 11-1 and 11-2, consists of the engine water jacket, thermostat, water pump, radiator, radiator cap, fan, fan drive belt and necessary hoses. It must be designed to operate at temperatures ranging up to the boiling point of the coolant under pressure, which in the case of ethylene glycol antifreeze may exceed 250 deg. F.

As fuel is burned in the engine, about one-third of the heat energy in the fuel is converted into power. Another third goes out the exhaust pipe unused, and the remaining third must be handled by the cooling system. This third is often underestimated and even less understood.

Perhaps it will be helpful to describe it in readily understood terms rather than by reference to so many Btu's (British thermal units). The heat removed by the cooling system of an average automobile at normal speed is sufficient to keep a six-room house warm in zero weather.

This means that several thousand gallons of water must be circulated in the cooling system every hour to absorb the heat and carry it to the radiator for disposal. It also means that many thousands of cubic feet of air must flow through the radiator every hour in order to dissipate the heat to the air.

Considering these cooling factors, it is important at this time to distinguish between heat TRANSFER and heat DISSIPATION. The heat generated by the mixture burned in the engine must be TRANSFERRED from the iron or aluminum cylinder to the water in the water jacket. The outside of the water jacket DISSIPATES some of the heat to the air surrounding it, but most of the heat is carried by the cooling water to the radiator for dissipation to the surrounding air. See Fig. 11-1.

HEAT TRANSFER

In an automotive engine, heat flows or transfers from the iron or aluminum cylinder to the cooling water, and from the coolant to the copper or aluminum radiator. Iron, aluminum, copper and water are all good conductors of heat. If they are in good contact with one another, the heat will flow readily from one to another.

If, however, there is a coating of lime or rust between the

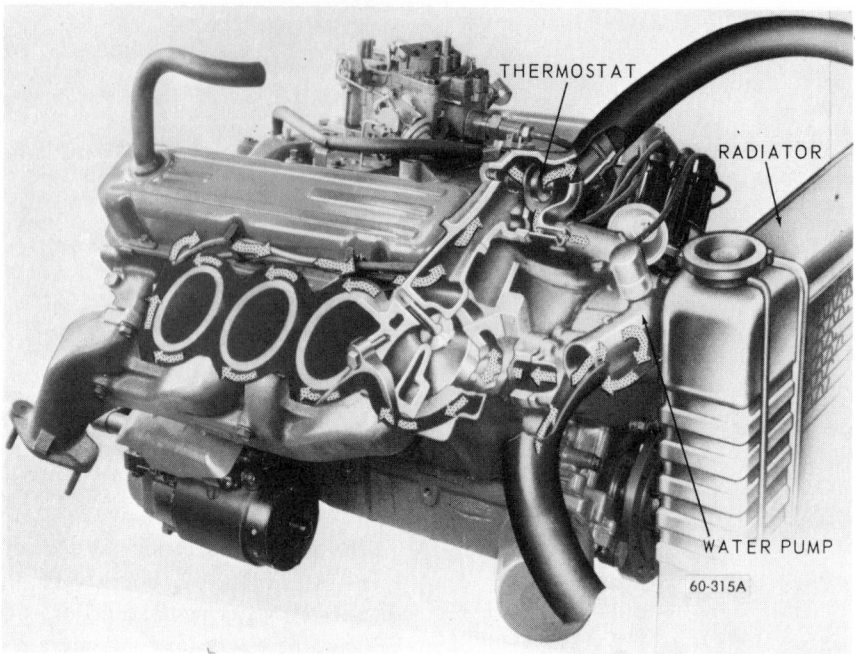

Fig. 11-2. Illustrating passage of coolant through cooling system of modern V-8. (Buick)

water and the bare metal, the flow will be retarded since lime and rust are poor heat conductors. There is a great amount of surface within the water circulation system on which this lime and rust can accumulate as may be seen from Fig. 11-2.

An engine is liable to have rust in the cooling system at any time. Rust is a combination of iron, water and oxygen. We have iron in the engine, water in the engine and some oxygen in the water. Additional oxygen enters by way of the air that finds its way into the cooling system.

Along with rust, lime usually forms in the cooling system. In most parts of the country there is some lime in the water

supply; more in some localities than in others, along with other minerals. Alternate heating and cooling of the engine causes the lime to collect on the inside walls of the water jacket in the same manner that lime collects in a tea kettle.

This accumulation of rust and lime combines with a small amount of grease or oil, which often acts as a binder, and soon a coat of insulation forms on the inside surface of the water jacket. Grease or oil gets into the cooling system from water pump lubricant, leaking cylinder head gaskets, etc.

Scale deposits also collect in corners or pockets of the water jacket where the water circulation is sluggish. This often causes "hot spots" which, in turn, distort cylinders and valve seats. This type of overheating can and does occur without any indication of overheating on the temperature gauge. The gauge is located at one spot in the water jacket, and the overheating condition is localized in another spot.

The scale that collects in corners and narrow passages is also a deposit point for bits of rubber from the inside of hoses, and other foreign matter that finds its way into the cooling system. The result is a mass of insulating sludge and scale which does considerable harm to the engine. These accumulations can be avoided by proper maintenance of the cooling system, the year-round use of ethylene glycol solutions, electrolytic devices and periodic flushing of the cooling system.

COOLING SYSTEM PUMPS

Automobile engine water pumps are of many designs, but most are the centrifugal type. They consist of a rotating fan, or impeller, and seldom are of the positive displacement type that uses gears or plungers. Many are quite efficient, but some are more on the order of agitators or circulators. Sometimes the fan is installed on the water pump shaft, Fig. 11-3.

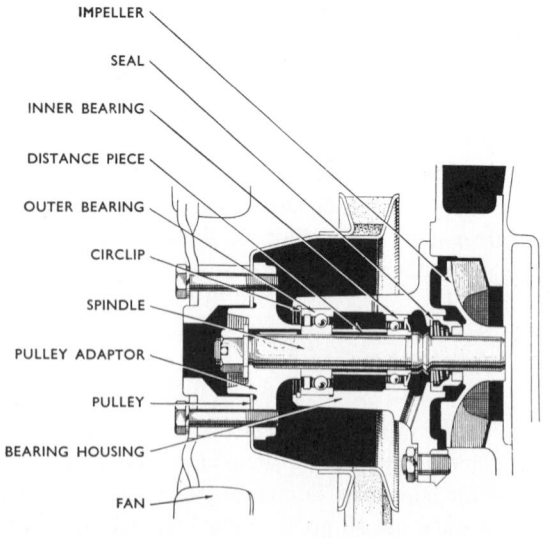

Fig. 11-3. A single belt often is used to drive both fan and water pump by placing both on same shaft (spindle).

Fig. 11-4. Construction of a typical separate water pump. Note curved vanes of impeller.

An exploded view of a typical water pump assembly with all parts in proper relation to each other is shown in Fig. 11-4. Sometimes the vanes on the impeller are straight. In this case, they are curved to accelerate the centrifugal flow of water. These vanes should not touch the housing. But, at the same time, they should not have excessive clearance, Fig. 11-5. For this reason, excessive endwise motion (end play) of the shaft to which the vane is attached is not permissible.

Obviously, impeller type water pumps must turn rapidly to be efficient. Worn or loose belts will permit slippage, which is not readily detected. It is particularly difficult to detect a worn V-belt fan pulley. If the pulley is suspected, the groove can be compared with a new pulley for wear.

Many water pumps have a spring-loaded seal to avoid

leakage of water around the pump shaft, Fig. 11-5. This particular pump is fitted with prepacked ball bearings, which are well sealed at each end to eliminate the need for periodic lubrication.

Late model Chrysler Corporation water pump construction is shown in Fig. 11-6.

Some V-type engines have a water pump on each cylinder block. In other cases, a single pump serves both blocks, Fig. 11-7. While most pumps run on sealed ball bearings and the shaft is sealed from the housing, they do occasionally require attention. Sand and grit in the water will wear the impeller blades and pump housing. Also, the sealing surfaces may be scored enough to leak air if not water. Special reamers are available for resurfacing the seat in the pump housing when the seal is replaced.

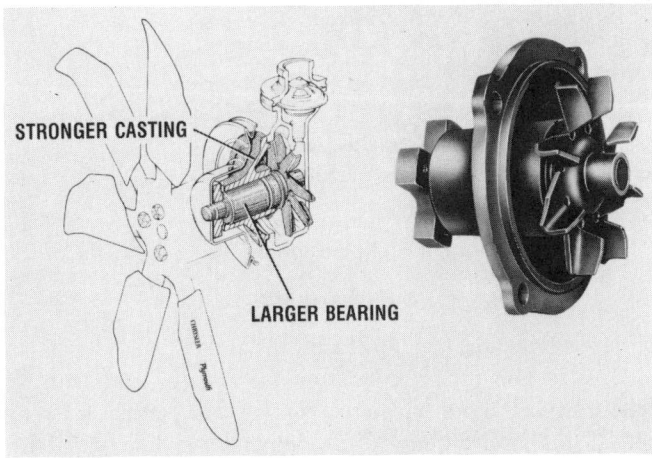

Fig. 11-6. Late model Chrysler-Plymouth 400 and 440 cu. in. engines are equipped with water pumps having high capacity double row ball bearing, heavy-duty cast iron housing and scoop type impeller blades.

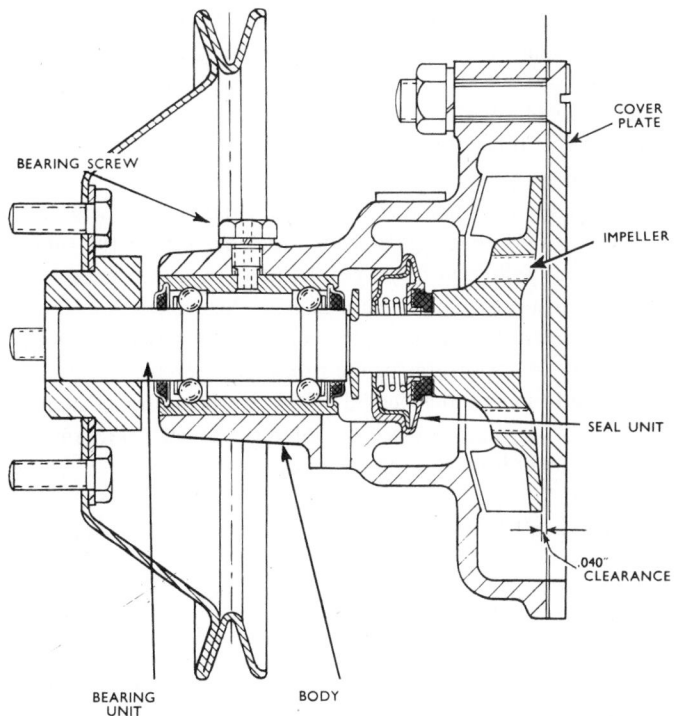

Fig. 11-5. Shaft ball bearings are sealed at each end to keep lubricant in and water out of bearings. A spring-loaded seal (in color) is used to avoid water leakage around pump shaft. Note clearance between impeller and cover plate.

Fig. 11-7. A single water pump serves both blocks of this V-type engine.

RADIATORS

The radiator is a device designed to dissipate the heat which the coolant has absorbed from the engine. It is constructed to hold a large amount of water in tubes or other passages which

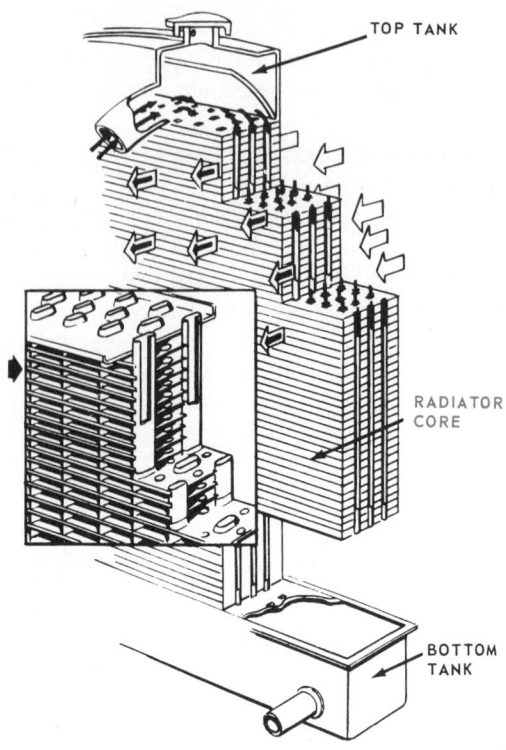

Fig. 11-8. Construction of a typical tube type radiator core.

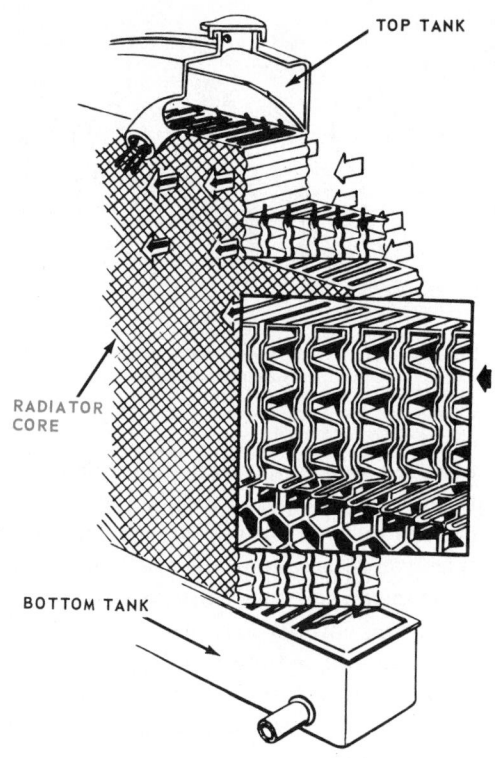

Fig. 11-9. Details of cellular type radiator core.

provide a large area in contact with the atmosphere.

Construction usually consists of the radiator core, with its water-carrying tubes and large cooling area, which are connected to a receiving tank at the top and to a dispensing tank at the bottom, Fig. 11-8.

Radiator cores are of two basic types, the fin and tube type, Fig. 11-8, and the ribbon cellular or honeycomb type, Fig. 11-9.

The popular fin and tube type of radiator core has the advantage of fewer soldered joints and is therefore a stronger construction. It consists of a series of parallel tubes extending

from the upper to the lower tank.

Fins are placed around the tubes to increase the area for radiating the heat.

The honeycomb type core consists of a large number of narrow water passages made by soldering pairs of thin metal ribbons together along their edges. These tubes are crimped and the soldered edges form the front and rear of the vertical tubes. These tubes are separated by fins of metal ribbon which help dissipate the heat.

In operation, water is pumped from the engine to the top (receiving) tank where it spreads over the tops of the tubes. After passing through the tubes, it enters the lower tank, then circulates through the engine again. As the water passes down through the tubes, it loses its heat to the airstream which passes around the outside of the tubes.

To help spread the heated water over the top of all the tubes, a baffle plate is often placed in the upper tank, directly under the inlet hose from the engine.

SPECIAL SYSTEMS

Some cooling systems are supplied with an auxiliary or supply tank, Fig. 11-10. This setup provides additional capacity and also acts as an expansion chamber. The inlet port of the supply tank is connected to the intake manifold coolant passage of the thermostat, thereby permitting coolant circulation through the supply tank and radiator when the thermostat is open.

While the usual construction of a radiator is to have the water circulate from the top to the bottom, crossflow

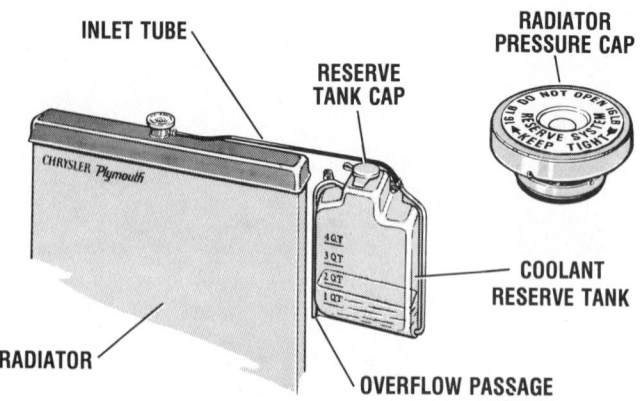

Fig. 11-10. Coolant reserve tank serves as an expansion chamber for cooling system. If level is low, coolant is added to reserve tank, rather than radiator. This Chrysler setup has an overflow passage build into reserve tank, instead of a separate hose.

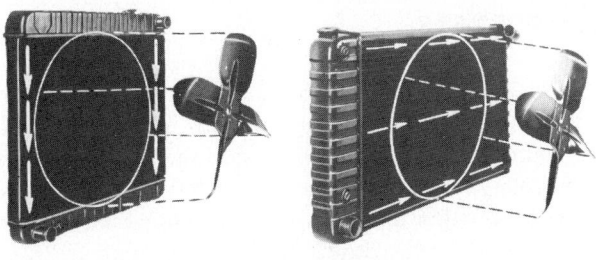

Fig. 11-11. Normally, flow of coolant in radiator is from top to bottom. However, in some installations, side to side flow receives better fan coverage.

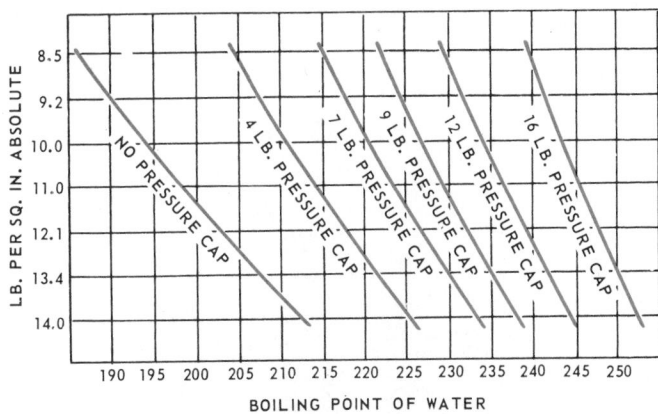

Fig. 11-13. Note how boiling point increases with each rise in pressure. Also boiling point drops as absolute pressure drops with an increase in altitude. An 8.5 psi corresponds to an altitude of about 15,000 ft.

radiators are designed to have the coolant flow from one side to the other, Fig. 11-11. It is claimed there is more efficient fan coverage of the radiator core with this design.

The core capacity of modern radiators is much smaller than in the past for the same size engine. This is possible because systems now operate at pressures ranging up to 17 psi. Pressurization makes the engine more efficient in terms of heat rejection to the coolant per horsepower developed.

Smaller radiators also are the result of improved heat transfer efficiency of the radiator core. For example: the 1954 Chevrolet 235 cu. in. six cylinder engine developed 115 hp, and had a radiator core capacity of 816 cu. in. Now, the Chevrolet 230 cu. in. six delivers 150 hp, and has a radiator core capacity of 406 cu. in.

RADIATOR CAPS

Originally, the radiator cap served only to prevent the coolant from splashing out the filler opening. Today's radiator cap, Fig. 11-12, is designed to seal the system so that it operates under 14 to 17 psi. This improves cooling efficiency and prevents evaporation of the coolant. Losses due to surging are also eliminated.

Since evaporation is reduced or eliminated, it is not necessary to add coolant as often. Consequently, the introduction of rust-forming materials is greatly reduced. Also by operating at higher temperatures, the engine operates more efficiently, as does the car heater.

The higher temperatures result from the higher pressure. Each psi increases the boiling point about 3.25 deg. F. Since current radiator caps maintain a pressure of about 15 psi, the

boiling point would be raised close to 260 deg. F, Fig. 11-13.

The pressure cap fits over the radiator filler opening and seals it tightly. Two spring-loaded valves are provided. The larger valve is designed to relieve pressure at a predetermined value. The smaller valve opens to relieve the vacuum that forms when the steam in the system condenses after the engine is stopped. Otherwise, atmospheric pressure (14.7 psi) on the large, flat surface of the upper tank would cause it to buckle and open the seams.

If you must remove a pressure cap soon after the engine is stopped, PROCEED SLOWLY. Use a large, heavy cloth or a special hand guard to turn the cap counterclockwise to the first stop to let the steam escape. Wait awhile, then cautiously remove the cap. Temperature rises rapidly the first few minutes after the engine is stopped, causing coolant to boil.

COOLING FANS

The fan is designed to draw cooling air through the radiator core, Fig. 11-1. This is necessary at slow speeds or when the engine is idling, since there is not enough air motion under those conditions to provide adequate cooling.

So that none of the force of the fan is dissipated, shrouding is often provided. In that way, the full force of the fan is used to draw air through the radiator core.

The fan is usually mounted on an extension of the water pump shaft, Fig. 11-3, and is driven by a V-belt from a pulley mounted on the front end of the crankshaft. Usually, the same belt drives the alternator, and belt tension is adjusted by swinging the alternator on its mounting.

In order to reduce the noise made by the rotating fan, the fan blades are often placed asymmetrically, and with the tips bent and rounded, Fig. 11-14.

At 3000 rpm, an 18 in. fan will consume over 2 hp, and power requirements increase very rapidly with the speed. Since the fan is required primarily at idling and low vehicle speeds, couplings have been devised to disconnect or reduce the speed of the fan above certain engine speeds.

The fan drive clutch used on Mercury engines is a fluid coupling containing silicone oil. The more silicone oil in the

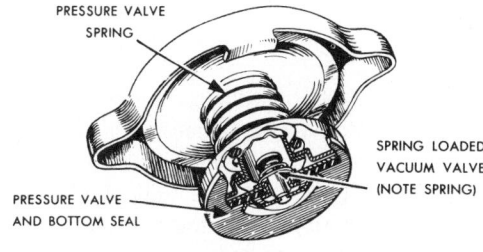

Fig. 11-12. Modern radiator caps are designed to maintain a specified pressure in cooling system.

115

Fig. 11-14. To reduce noise of operation, fan blades are often arranged asymmetrically. In addition, blade ends may be bent and rounded.

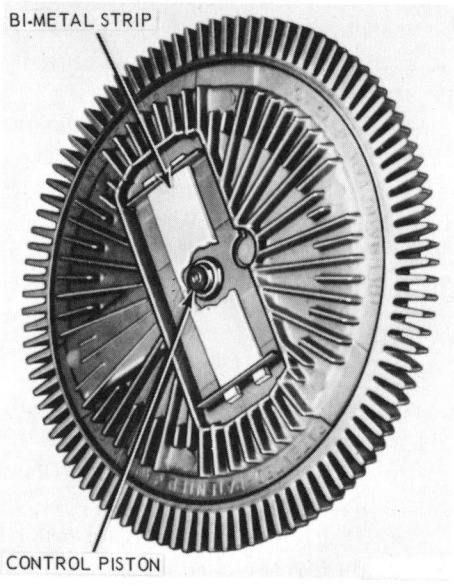

Fig. 11-15. To control fan speed, a bimetallic strip and control piston on fluid coupling regulates amount of silicone oil entering coupling.

THERMOSTATS

Automotive internal combustion engines operate more efficiently when a high temperature is maintained within narrow limits. To attain this objective, a thermostat is inserted in the cooling system. In operation, the thermostat is designed to close off the flow of water from engine to radiator until the engine has reached the desired operating temperature.

Formerly, a bellows type thermostat was used. Currently the thermostat is operated by a bimetallic coil, Fig. 11-17, which expands and contracts with changes in temperature to open and close the valve.

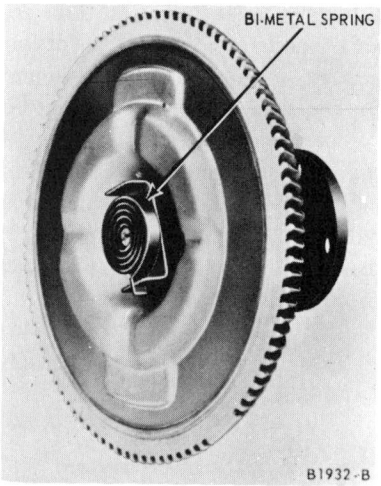

Fig. 11-16. This unit has a heat-sensitive spring connected to an opening plate that controls flow of silicone oil to fluid coupling to govern fan speed.

Fig. 11-17. Two different types of cooling system thermostats in current use.

coupling, the greater the speed. In one construction, Fig. 11-15, a bimetallic strip and control piston on the front of the fluid coupling regulate the amount of silicone oil entering the coupling. The bimetallic strip bows outward when there is an increase in surrounding temperature. This allows the piston-controlled valve to regulate the flow of oil to and from the reservoir. Another design of fan drive clutch, Fig. 11-16, uses a heat-sensitive, bimetallic spring-connected plate, which brings about a similar result. Still another design has flexible fan blades which vary the amount of air drawn through the radiator. The flexible fan automatically decreases (flattens out) the pitch of the fan blades at higher engine speeds.

When the water is cold, the thermostat closes the valve and stops the flow of water to the radiator, Fig. 11-18. Then, as the water becomes hotter, the coil expands to open the valve and permitting the water to reach the radiator, Fig. 11-19.

The opening and closing of the thermostatically controlled valve continues as more or less heat is developed by the engine so that its operating temperature is maintained within narrow limits.

Thermostats are calibrated at the time of manufacture,

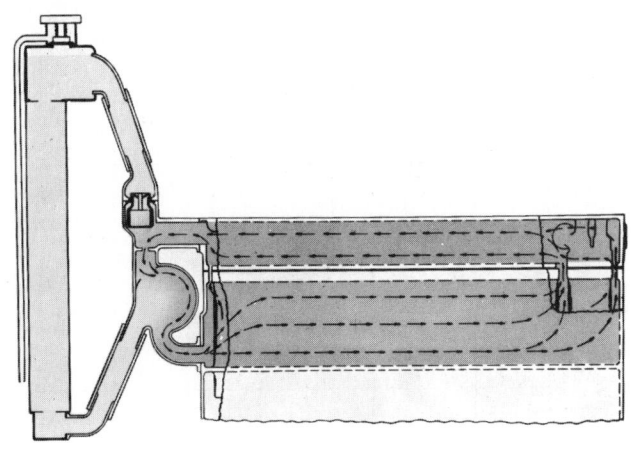

Fig. 11-18. With thermostat closed, water circulates entirely within engine water jacket.

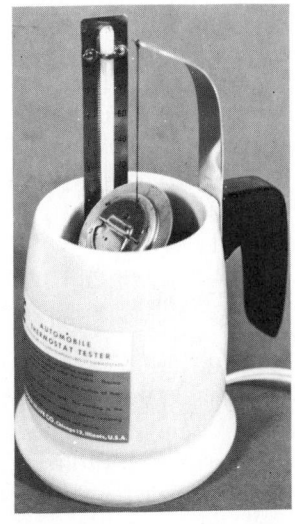

Fig. 11-20. Type of tester used in checking opening and closing temperatures of cooling system thermostats.

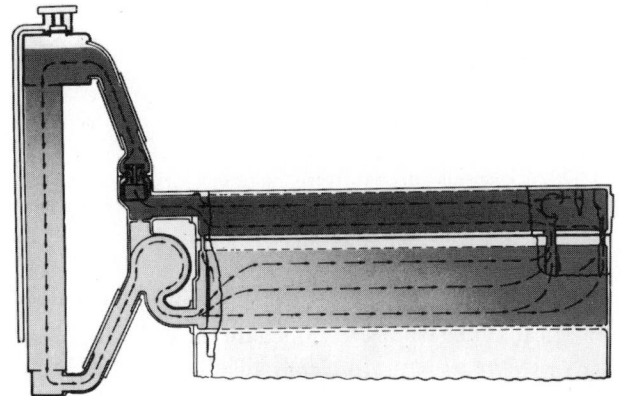

Fig. 11-19. When thermostat opens, water will circulate through radiator, then back to the water jacket.

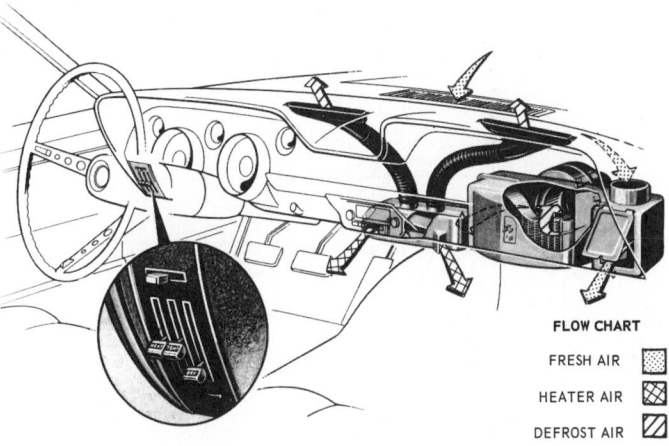

Fig. 11-21. One type of car heater.

when they are stamped with the pressure (psi) at which they are designed to open. A thermostat designed for use with an alcohol type antifreeze usually is calibrated to open at 155 to 160 deg. F (68.3 to 71.1 C), and be fully open at 180 deg. F (82.2 C). Most modern cooling systems are designed to use permanent type antifreeze, and the thermostats are calibrated to open between 188 and 195 deg. F (86.7 and 90.6 C), and be fully open between 210 and 212 deg. F (98.9 and 100 C).

Special thermostat testers are available. See Fig. 11-20.

CAR HEATER

The basic hot water heater core used in automobiles is constructed in the same manner as the radiator. In operation, hot water from the cooling system is circulated through it. The heater fan drives air past the hot heater core tubes and through ducts to the passenger compartment, Fig. 11-21. Therefore, it is important to keep the heater water passages free from rust accumulations. When flushing the system, make sure any valves in the line going to the heater are open. Check the flushing procedure given in ENGINE TROUBLESHOOTING.

The air which passes through the heater is usually supplied from outside the vehicle through openings provided in the top or sides of the cowl. The motion of the car, aided by the action of the fan, serves to force the fresh air through the heater. Vent air valves operated by Bowden wire controls serve to control the amount of air passing through the heater and into the passenger compartment. Warm air from the heater can also be directed to the inside of the windshield to melt any frost which might collect there.

ANTIFREEZE SOLUTIONS

When water freezes, it expands approximately nine percent in volume. Because of this great rate of expansion, it will break or seriously distort the shape of the vessel in which it is contained. Because of this characteristic, it is necessary to use a nonfreezing solution in the cooling system of water-cooled engines operated in climates where the temperature is below the freezing point of water.

Since copper, iron, aluminum, brass, solder, etc. are used in parts of the engine in contact with the coolant, it is important that the antifreeze does not corrode any of these metals. Also, the material should not be harmful to the various types of rubber used in the connecting hoses. Many different materials have been used as antifreeze solutions. Among the more suitable are: methanol (methyl alcohol), ethanol (ethyl alcohol) and ethylene glycol.

FREEZING PROTECTION

The mixing of an antifreeze with water forms a solution that has a lower freezing point than water. The temperature at which an antifreeze will freeze depends on the strength of the solution, and this varies with each antifreeze, Fig. 11-22. Pure ethyl alcohol freezes at -174.6 deg. F; methyl alcohol at -144.2 deg. F; while, a 68 percent solution of ethylene glycol freezes at -92 deg. F. Further concentrations would not further reduce the freezing point of the solution.

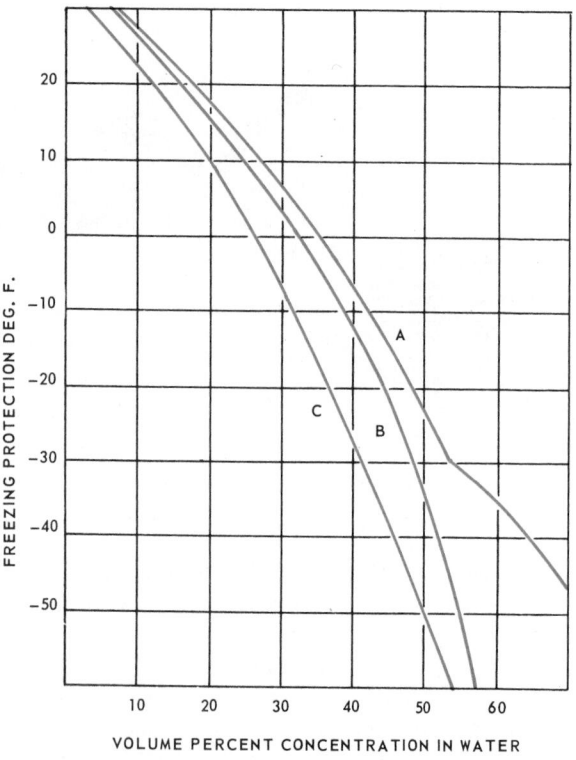

Fig. 11-22. Freezing protection afforded by different concentrations of: A—Ethyl alcohol. B—Ethylene glycol. C—Methyl alcohol.

EXPANSION OF ANTIFREEZE

Antifreeze solutions will expand slightly more than water when heated, Fig. 11-23. When water is heated from 40 deg. F to 180 deg. F, it will expand approximately 1/4 pint per gallon. For the same range of temperature, ethylene glycol will expand 1/3 pint per gallon, methyl alcohol 2/5 pint per gallon and ethyl alcohol 1/2 pint per gallon.

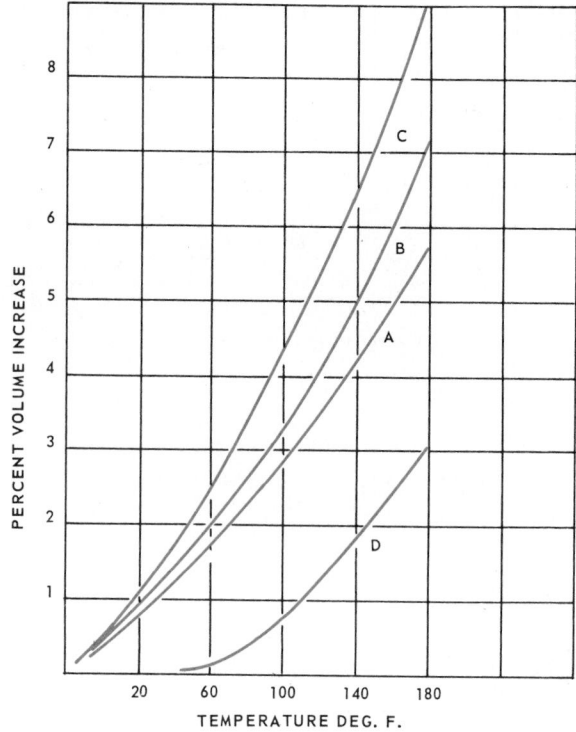

Fig. 11-23. Expansion of antifreeze solutions giving protection to -20 Deg. F: A—Ethylene glycol. B—Methyl alcohol. C—Ethyl alcohol. D—Water.

To avoid loss of antifreeze due to expansion, the cooling system must not be completely filled. In the case of a 20-quart capacity cooling system completely filled at -20 deg. F, there would be a loss of 2 1/3 pints of ethylene glycol; 2 7/8 pints of methyl alcohol; or 3 2/3 pints of ethyl alcohol when the temperature goes up to 180 deg. F.

BOILING POINT

When ethylene glycol is added to water, the boiling point of the solution is raised. When either methyl alcohol or ethyl alcohol is added to water, the boiling point of the solution is lowered. For example, methyl and ethyl alcohol solutions affording protection to -20 deg. F will have boiling points of about 180 deg. F. A similar solution of ethylene glycol will have a boiling point of 223 deg., as compared to 212 deg. for clear water. As the pressure goes up, the temperature at which the solution boils is increased, Fig. 11-24.

The normal boiling point of a coolant solution is important, and so is the change in boiling point brought about by placing the solution under pressure. With pressurized cooling systems used today, a coolant with a higher boiling point than water is necessary. Ethylene glycol fills this requirement, and it is installed as original equipment in all vehicles built in the United States.

The higher boiling point of ethylene glycol makes it a highly satisfactory coolant for use in warm weather as well as cold. In addition to its higher boiling point, glycol is provided with a rust inhibitor. Most manufacturers advise using glycol

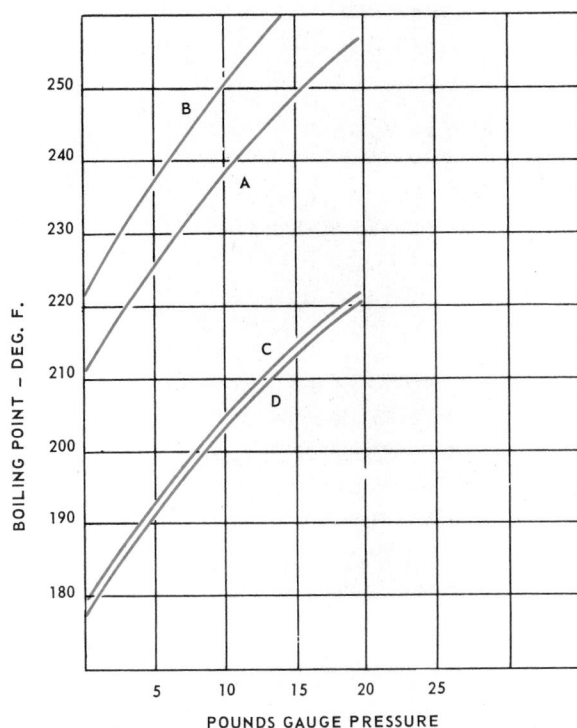

Fig. 11-24. Chart shows how pressure affects boiling point of various antifreeze solutions. A—Water. B—Ethylene glycol. C—Ethyl alcohol. D—Methyl alcohol.

for two years, then draining and refilling with a new solution.

Car manufacturers advise against the use of water as a coolant. If it is used, boiling will result, particularly in hot weather, when towing another vehicle or when the air conditioner is in use.

EVAPORATION

There is virtually no loss of ethylene glycol solution due to evaporation. Any loss of coolant solution that does occur is practically all water. This evaporation loss is greatest under prolonged high speed driving conditions or extended idling periods in heavy traffic. Alcohol based antifreeze solutions have a greater rate of evaporation, so they are seldom used.

REMOVING GLYCOL FROM CRANKCASE

If ethylene glycol leaks into the engine oil, it will clog the oil lines, cause the pistons to seize and result in severe damage to the engine. When it has been determined that ethylene glycol has gotten into the lubricating system, the first step is to locate the cause of the coolant leak (a blown gasket or cracked block), then make the necessary repairs.

Next, remove the engine oil filter and drain the engine oil. Then, fill the crankcase to the full mark on the dipstick with a mixture of 3 qt. SAE 10W engine oil and 2 qt. of Butyl Cellusolve (can be obtained from a chemical supply house).

Run the engine at idling speed for about 30 minutes, paying particular attention to the oil pressure. Then, drain and flush

with 3 qt. SAE 10W oil and 2 qt. kerosene. Idle the engine with this flushing oil for about 10 minutes. Drain, install filter and refill crankcase with correct weight and grade of engine oil.

If difficulty is encountered in cranking the engine, or if there is no oil pressure when the engine starts, run some hot water from a steam cleaner through the cooling system. The heat will soften the glycol on the cylinder walls and in the oil lines, making it easier to crank the engine. This will help clear the oil lines so the cleaning solution can circulate throughout the lubrication system.

RUST INHIBITORS

In order to reduce the formation of rust, commercial antifreeze contains an inhibitor designed to prevent corrosion. Some products also contain antifoaming agents.

The prevention of rust is essential if the cooling system is to be maintained at maximum efficiency. After the cooling system is drained at the end of cold weather, a rust inhibitor should be added if clear water is used as a coolant. Year-round use of antifreeze is a more practical answer, of course.

AIR-COOLED ENGINES

Air-cooled engines were used successfully in the early days of the automobile. Today's best example of an air-cooled engine is Volkswagen's "flat four."

Air cooling of a reciprocating piston engine requires constant circulation of a lot of air. This air should be directed where wanted and the volume of air must be controlled. Forced air circulation is provided by a fan of generous capacity which is usually driven from the engine crankshaft by a belt or by fan blades formed in the flywheel, Fig. 11-25.

Fig. 11-25. Tecumseh single cylinder, air-cooled engine. Note fan blades built into flywheel.

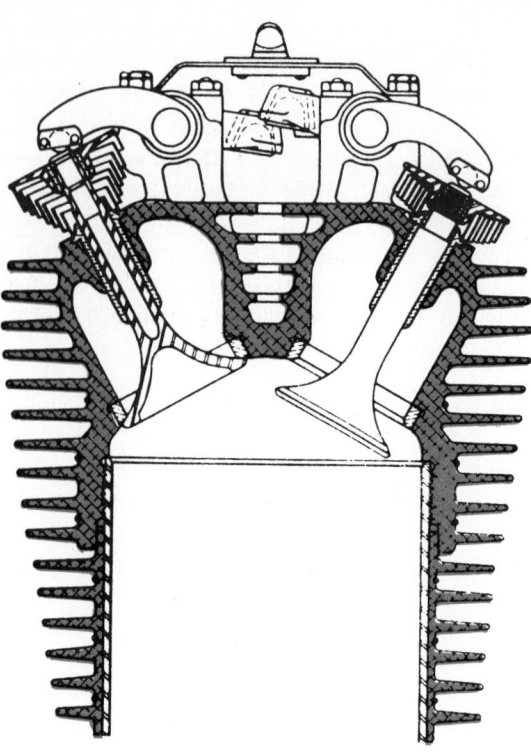

Fig. 11-27. In this V-type, air-cooled diesel (Deutz), cooling fins are larger in diameter on cylinder head and have a much greater mass of metal under fins.

Radiation fins are provided on the cylinders and cylinder heads, Figs. 11-26 to 11-30. In some applications, the crankcase also is "finned," Fig. 11-31.

Air-cooled engines usually are surrounded by a metal housing and baffle plates to direct cooling air where desired.

Fig. 11-26. Note that cooling fins on cylinder head are larger in diameter as well as heavier than those around cylinder.

Fig. 11-28. Instead of solid masses of metal around valves in this Volkswagen engine, metal is finned to increase radiation surface. Also note close fit of sheet metal baffle plates to contour of cooling fins.

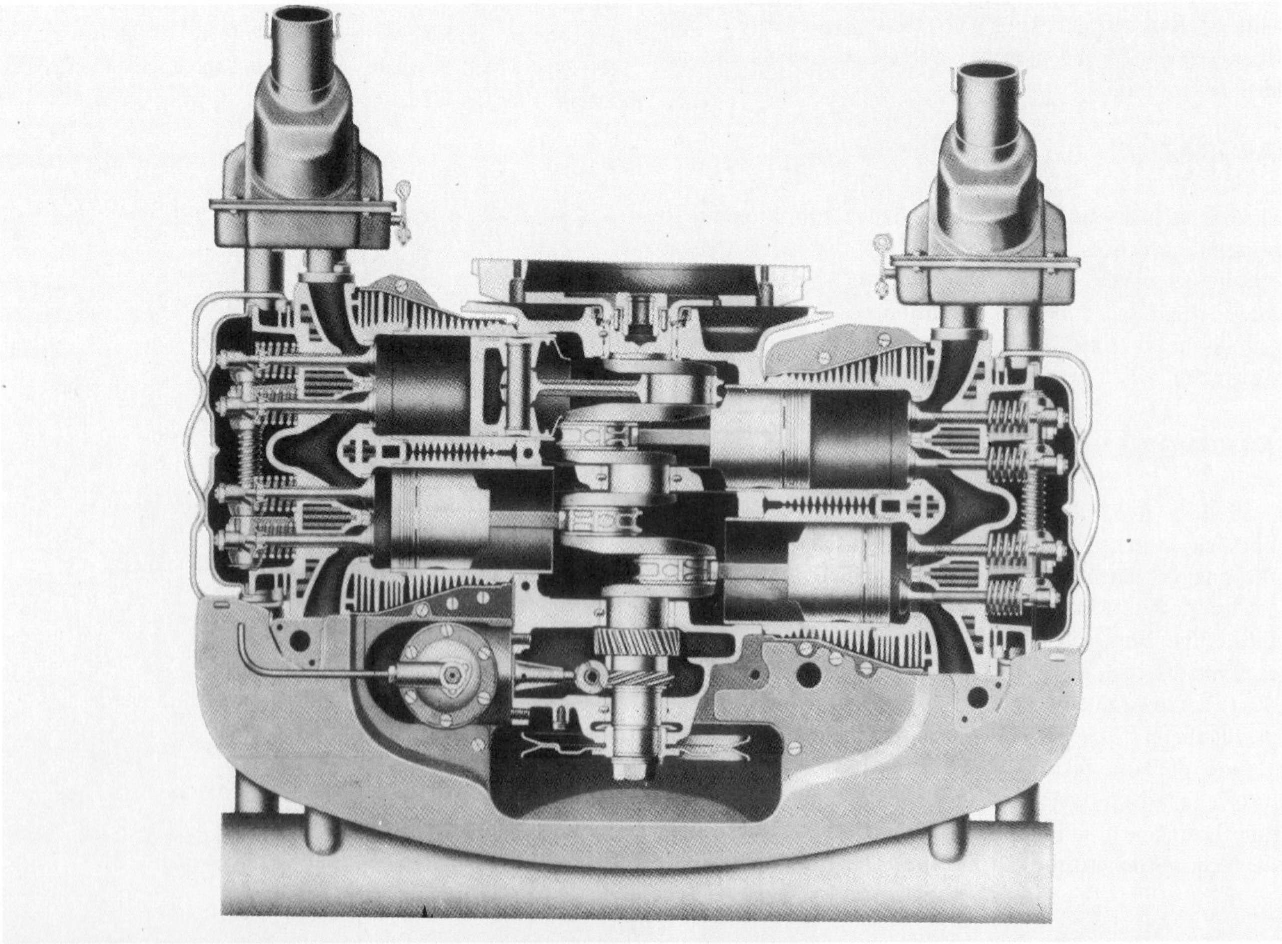

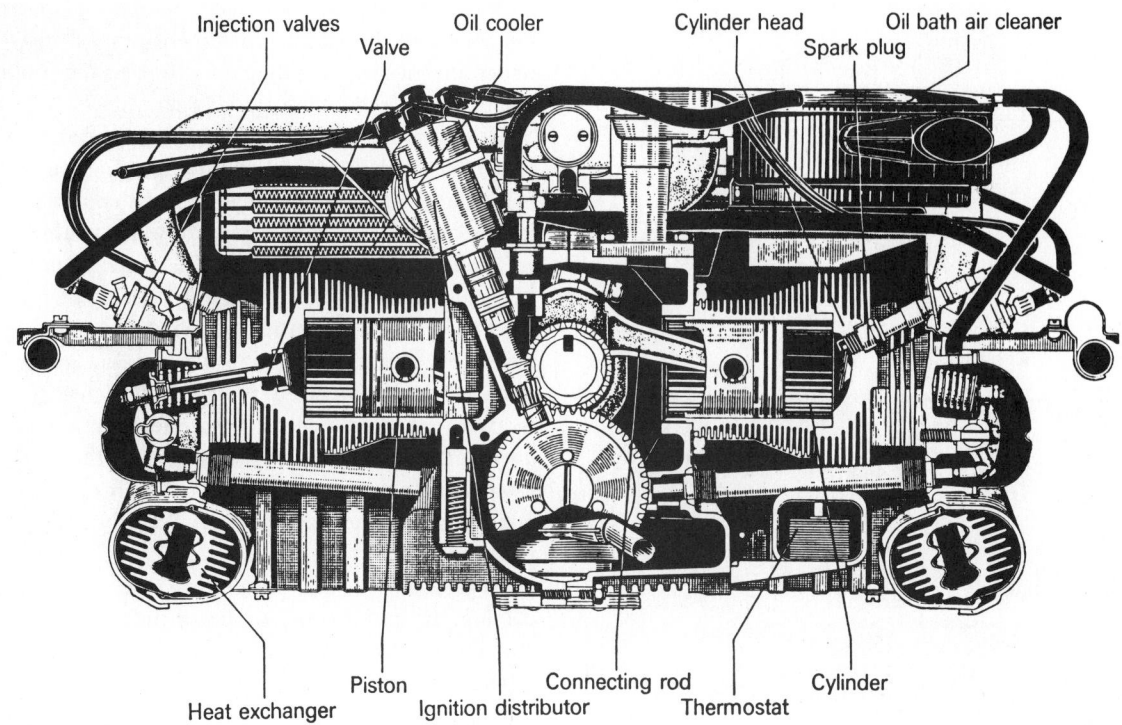

Fig. 11-29. Cross section of Volkswagen fuel injection engine reveals finned cylinders, cylinder head, heat exchanger, thermostat, and oil cooler. About 60° of cooling air flows over cylinder heads; 40° is directed over cylinders. (Volkswagen of America, Inc.)

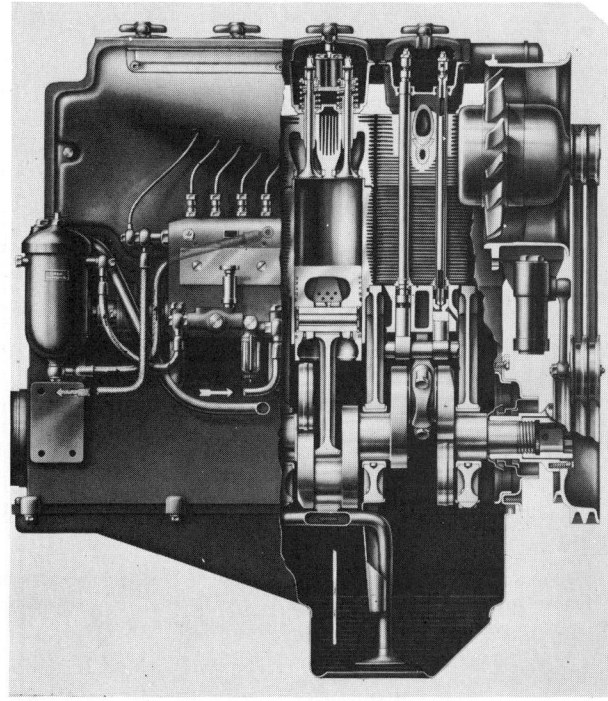

Fig. 11-30. This air-cooled, in-line diesel (Deutz) engine has a cooling fan mounted in one end of engine enclosure. Also note fins between valves.

over and through the fins to dissipate the heat. In order to regulate the engine temperature by controlling the volume of cooling air, a thermostat is installed inside the metal housing which encloses the engine, Fig. 11-29.

The thermostat unit is connected to control flaps, or an air

Fig. 11-31. Three cylinder, air-cooled Teledyne Wisconsin engine. This two cycle engine develops 80 hp. Note cooling fins on cylinder head, cylinders and crankcase.

Examples of this arrangement are shown in the Volkswagen engines in Figs. 11-28 and 11-29, and in the diesel engine in Fig. 11-30. When the engine is running, forced air is directed

Fig. 11-32. Air control ring or valve on Volkswagen engine is mounted within cooling fan and moves in and out as required to control volume of cooling air supplied to fan.

control ring. As the engine becomes hotter the control ring opens wider to admit more air, and closes when the engine is cold. See Figs. 11-32 and 11-33.

With the ring closed, air circulation is restricted, and a cold engine warms up more rapidly. Rapid warm-up is characteristic of air-cooled engines, since they do not have to heat water in cylinder jackets and radiator. This rapid warm-up is helpful in avoiding sludge and crankcase dilution.

Fig. 11-33. Method of controlling Volkswagen air control ring is by swinging it in or out on a cross shaft.

Air-cooled engines normally operate at somewhat higher temperatures than water-cooled engines, but do not overheat under almost any operating conditions if the cooling system is maintained in reasonably good order.

However, air-cooled engines should never be "lugged." If the engine is pulling hard at slow speed, more heat than usual is generated at the same time that less cooling air is supplied. In this case, there is no reservoir of water to absorb excess heat (as on a water-cooled engine). Therefore, engine speed should be maintained by shifting to a lower gear.

Higher engine operating temperatures mean higher engine efficiency, but this characteristic is also accused of causing noise. One reason given for air-cooled engines being noisier than water-cooled engines is that there is no silencing provided by water jackets. Another reason given is the somewhat greater clearances sometimes provided between operating parts. This relates to the fact that higher temperatures require more room for expansion of the metals.

Regardless of the advantages and disadvantages of air cooling, it has proved to be entirely successful for automobiles, trucks, tractors, airplanes, boats and all kinds of small engines.

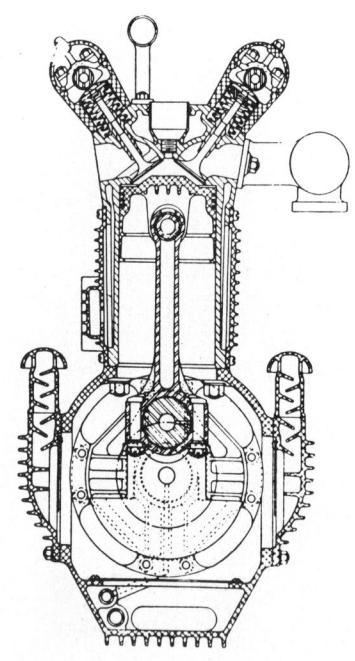

Fig. 11-34. Schematic drawing of Offenhauser race engine shows cooling fins on lower side of oil pan, side of crankcase, side of cylinder water jackets and underside of piston heads.

OIL COOLING

While it is unusual for passenger car engines to provide special cooling for the engine lubricating oil, many race car engines have cooling fins on the oil pan to reduce the temperature of the engine oil. In that way, the viscosity of the oil is also reduced and proper lubrication is maintained.

Fig. 11-34 shows a sectional view of an Offenhauser race

engine provided with cooling fins on the lower outside of the oil pan and on the sides of the crankcase. While this is a water-cooled engine, cooling fins are also provided on the exterior of the water jacket. Note also the cooling fins on the underside of the piston head to help dissipate the heat.

DRAINING COOLING SYSTEM

Draining the cooling system is mostly a matter of opening drain cocks at the bottom of the radiator and in the engine water jacket.

This is true of most models. However, on the 1972 Vega, drain plugs were eliminated from both the radiator lower tank and the engine block.

To drain the cooling system on this engine, it is necessary to use a syphoning procedure:

First fill the system until the water level is even with the top of the filler neck. Insert a length of tubing into the filler neck until the inserted end touches the bottom of the tank. Attach the free end of the tubing to a syphoning device and start the syphoning process by squeezing and releasing the bulb. When the flow begins, pinch the tube and remove the syphoning device. The flow should continue when the pinch is released.

COOLING SYSTEM TROUBLESHOOTING

The most frequent cooling system complaints are leakage of coolant and overheating. Generally, the best troubleshooting approach is test and inspect, followed by the service or parts replacement required.

Since the system is pressurized, it is logical to test the radiator pressure cap for pressure-holding ability and to pressure-test the entire cooling system for coolant leakage.

First, make sure the correct cap for the vehicle is installed on the radiator. The cap must seat properly on the filler neck of the radiator and seal the system so that it operates under 14 to 17 psi (pounds per square inch).

Next, remove the radiator pressure cap and clean it thoroughly. Check the valves and seating surfaces for damage. Wet the rubber seals with water and install the cap on a pressure tester designed for this purpose.

Operate the tester pump and observe the highest pressure gauge reading, Fig. 11-35. The release pressure should be within the manufacturer's specified limits (12 to 15 psi, for example). Allow the maximum pressure reading to remain on the gauge, and watch for a pressure drop. If the cap holds this pressure for 30 seconds or more, reinstall the cap. If the pressure drops quickly, install a new radiator pressure cap.

Pressure-test the cooling system with the engine at normal operating temperature:

1. Carefully remove radiator pressure cap and check coolant level (should be 1 to 1 1/2 in. below base of filler neck).
2. Test freeze protection level of coolant, using an antifreeze hydrometer.
3. Wipe inside of filler neck and inspect inside sealing seat for damage.
4. Inspect overflow tube for dents, kinks or obstruction.
5. Inspect cams on outside of filler neck. Reform cams, if bent.
6. Attach pressure tester to filler neck and operate tester pump to apply specified pressure to system.
7. Observe pressure gauge reading, Fig. 11-36. If system holds this pressure for two minutes, no coolant leakage is indicated. If the pressure drops quickly, examine entire cooling system for external coolant leakage. If no leakage is apparent, check for internal coolant leakage (see troubleshooting list that follows).

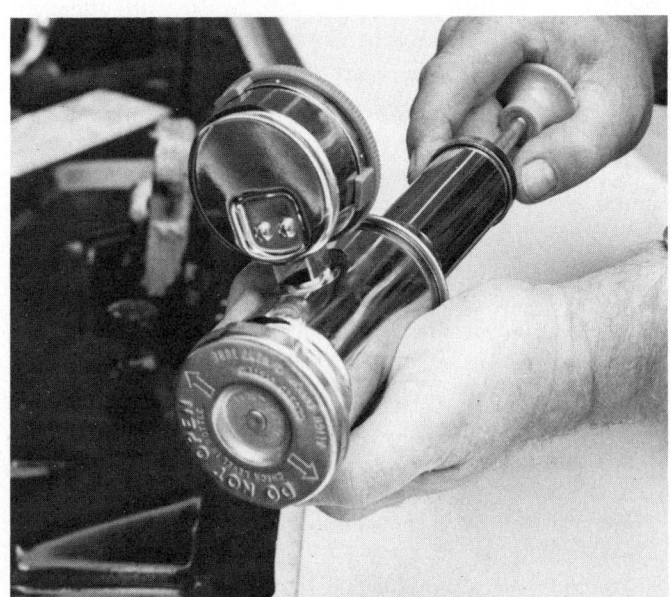

Fig. 11-35. Pressure-testing a radiator cap. Note in troubleshooting list how many areas are affected by a faulty radiator pressure cap. (AC-Delco Div., General Motors Corp.)

Fig. 11-36. Pressure-testing the cooling system. Tester applies pressure to system to psi specified; system should hold pressure for two minutes. (AC-Delco Div., General Motors Corp.)

LEAKAGE OF COOLANT

1. Faulty radiator pressure cap.
2. Defective radiator.
3. Bad thermostat housing gasket.
4. Cracked or deteriorated radiator hose.
5. Cracked or deteriorated heater hose.
6. Defective heater core.
7. Faulty heater water control valve.
8. Defective water pump seal or gasket.
9. Rusted out core hole plugs.
10. Damaged coolant reserve tank.
11. Bad cylinder head gasket.
12. Cracked cylinder head, manifold or block.

OVERHEATING

1. Faulty radiator pressure cap.
2. Defective thermostat.
3. Loose, slipping or broken fan belt.
4. Worn pulleys.
5. Damaged fan.
6. Faulty fan drive clutch.
7. Collapsed lower radiator hose.
8. Obstructed front grille.
9. Clogged radiator fins.
10. Clogged A/C condenser fins.
11. Clogged radiator tubes.
12. Incorrect cooling system components installed.
13. Defective water pump.
14. Low coolant level.
15. Low coolant protection (low boiling point).
16. Water used as coolant (low boiling point).
17. Cooling system capacity inadequate for load being carried or towed.
18. Air trapped in cooling system.
19. Clogged coolant passage in engine block.
20. Excessive use of A/C while vehicle is parked or in stop and go traffic.
21. Retarded ignition timing.
22. Sticking manifold heat control valve.
23. Clogged exhaust system.
24. Low engine oil level.
25. Excessive engine friction.
26. Dragging brakes.

LOW OPERATING TEMPERATURE

1. Wrong cooling fan.
2. Wrong radiator.
3. Wrong thermostat.
4. Defective thermostat.
5. Fan pulley too small.

NO COOLANT FLOW THROUGH HEATER CORE

1. Clogged water pump return pipe.
2. Collapsed or clogged heater hose.

3. Clogged heater core.
4. Plugged outlet in thermostat housing.
5. Obstructed heater bypass hole in cylinder head.

INOPERATIVE COOLANT RECOVERY SYSTEM

1. Faulty radiator pressure cap.
2. Coolant level below add mark.
3. Clogged or leaking overflow tube.
4. Plugged vent in recovery reservoir.
5. Pinched or kinked reservoir hose.

NOISE

1. Fan contacting shroud.
2. Loose water pump impeller.
3. Dry fan belt.
4. Loose fan belt.
5. Rough drive pulley.
6. Worn water pump bearing.

TESTING FOR LEAKS

If frequent additions of coolant are required to maintain the proper level in the system, check all units and connections for leakage. Make the inspection when the system is cold. Small leaks which may show dampness or dripping on cold surfaces can easily escape notice when the engine is hot. This is because of evaporation of the coolant or, in some cases, because the heat will expand the metal and close the cracks. Tell-tale stains of grayish white, rust color or dye stains from the antifreeze are sure signs of coolant leakage.

Exhaust gas or air trapped in the cooling system may cause the level of the coolant in the system to rise, with attendant loss of coolant. Air may be drawn into the system through leakage at the seal in the water pump. Gas may be forced into the system as the result of a defective cylinder head gasket, and extreme overheating can occur.

A piece of rubber tubing and a bottle of clear water can be used to check for air or gas leakage into the cooling system:

1. With cooling system cold, add coolant to bring coolant to proper level.
2. Install a conventional radiator cap (no pressure). Attach a length of rubber tubing to overflow pipe.
3. Operate engine at a safe high speed until it reaches operating temperature.
4. Maintain this speed and insert free end of rubber tubing into bottle of water. A continuous flow of bubbles indicates that air is being drawn into system from water pump seal or being forced into system from blown cylinder head gasket.
5. To determine whether defect is in pump or in head gasket, run a small amount of engine oil through carburetor throat, which will cause smokey bubbles to appear in the bottle if the gasket is defective.

REVIEW QUESTIONS – COOLING SYSTEMS

1. How much of the heat energy in the fuel must be handled by the cooling system?
   a. One fourth.
   b. One third.
   c. One half.
2. What happens to the balance of the heat energy?
3. Several thousand gallons of water are circulated through the cooling system every hour of operation. True or False?
4. The water jackets dissipate most of the heat from the cylinders to the air. Yes or No?
5. What is rust?
6. Name two causes of engine hot spots.
7. Automobile engine water pumps are usually of the positive displacement type. Yes or No?
8. Why are water pump vanes often curved?
9. A water pump seal may leak:
   a. Air?
   b. Water?
   c. Both?
10. Thermostats are installed:
    a. Between the pump inlet and the radiator.
    b. Between the pump outlet and the water jacket.
    c. Between the water jacket outlet and the radiator.
11. Where does the water from the engine usually enter the radiator?
    a. Top.
    b. Bottom.
12. In addition to providing greater capacity, what is the purpose of an auxiliary tank?

a. Provides additional capacity.
b. Acts as an expansion chamber.
c. Connects engine to radiator.
13. Under pressure, does water boil at a higher or lower temperature?
    a. Higher.
    b. Lower.
14. Why is a vacuum valve needed in a radiator pressure cap?
15. When water freezes, it expands approximately:
    a. 4 percent.
    b. 6 percent.
    c. 9 percent.
16. Which protects against freezing to the lowest temperature:
    a. Ethylene glycol.
    b. Methyl alcohol.
    c. Ethyl alcohol.
17. An ethylene glycol solution will boil at a lower temperature than water. True or False?
18. In an air-cooled engine, how much of the total volume of cooling air is usually directed to the cylinder heads?
    a. 40 percent.
    b. 60 percent.
    c. 80 percent.
19. How can air-cooled engine with the cooling system in good working order become overheated?
20. What can be done to avoid such overheating?
21. Name two possible reasons why an air-cooled engine might make more noise than a comparable water-cooled engine.
22. What is one distinct advantage of an air-cooled engine?

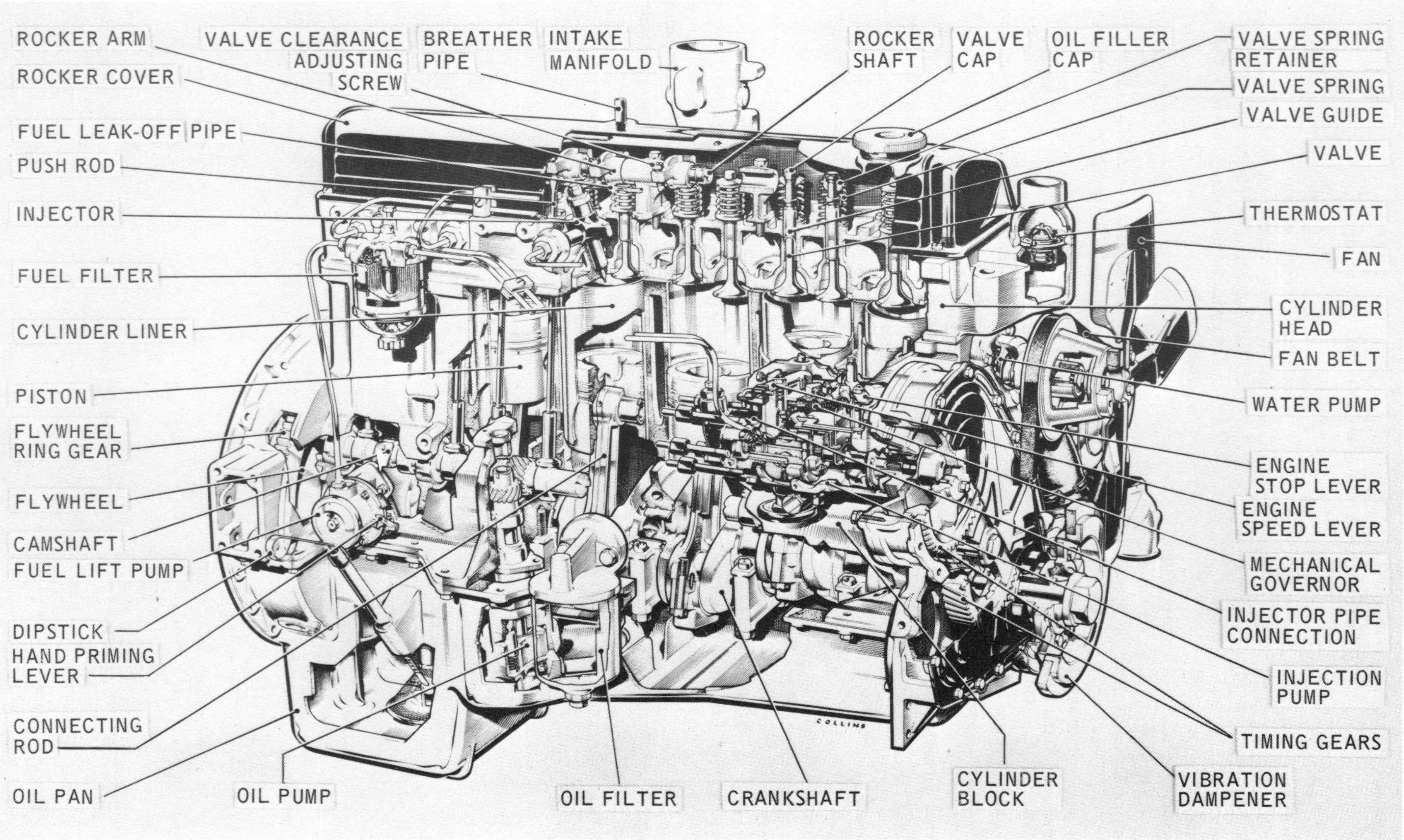

VALVE SPRING RETAINER

VALVE SPRING

VALVE GUIDE

VALVE

THERMOSTAT

FAN

CYLINDER HEAD

FAN BELT

WATER PUMP

ENGINE STOP LEVER

ENGINE SPEED LEVER

MECHANICAL GOVERNOR

INJECTOR PIPE CONNECTION

INJECTION PUMP

TIMING GEARS

VIBRATION DAMPENER

OIL FILLER CAP

ROCKER SHAFT

VALVE CAP

CYLINDER BLOCK

CRANKSHAFT

OIL FILTER

ROCKER ARM

ROCKER COVER

FUEL LEAK-OFF PIPE

PUSH ROD

INJECTOR

FUEL FILTER

CYLINDER LINER

PISTON

FLYWHEEL RING GEAR

FLYWHEEL

CAMSHAFT

FUEL LIFT PUMP

DIPSTICK

HAND PRIMING LEVER

CONNECTING ROD

OIL PAN

VALVE CLEARANCE ADJUSTING SCREW

BREATHER PIPE

INTAKE MANIFOLD

OIL PUMP

Fig. 12-1. Details of Ford diesel engine.

126

OTHER
ENGINES

DIESEL ENGINES

Diesel engines are similar to gasoline engines and are built in both two cycle and four cycle designs. They may be water-cooled or air-cooled. In general, they are heavier in structure than gasoline engines to withstand the higher pressures resulting from the high compression ratios used. In a full diesel engine, the compression ratio may be as high as 18 to 1. What is known as a "semi-diesel" engine usually employs a somewhat lower compression ratio and may use spark plugs for ignition.

Previously, it was established that compressing a gas, such

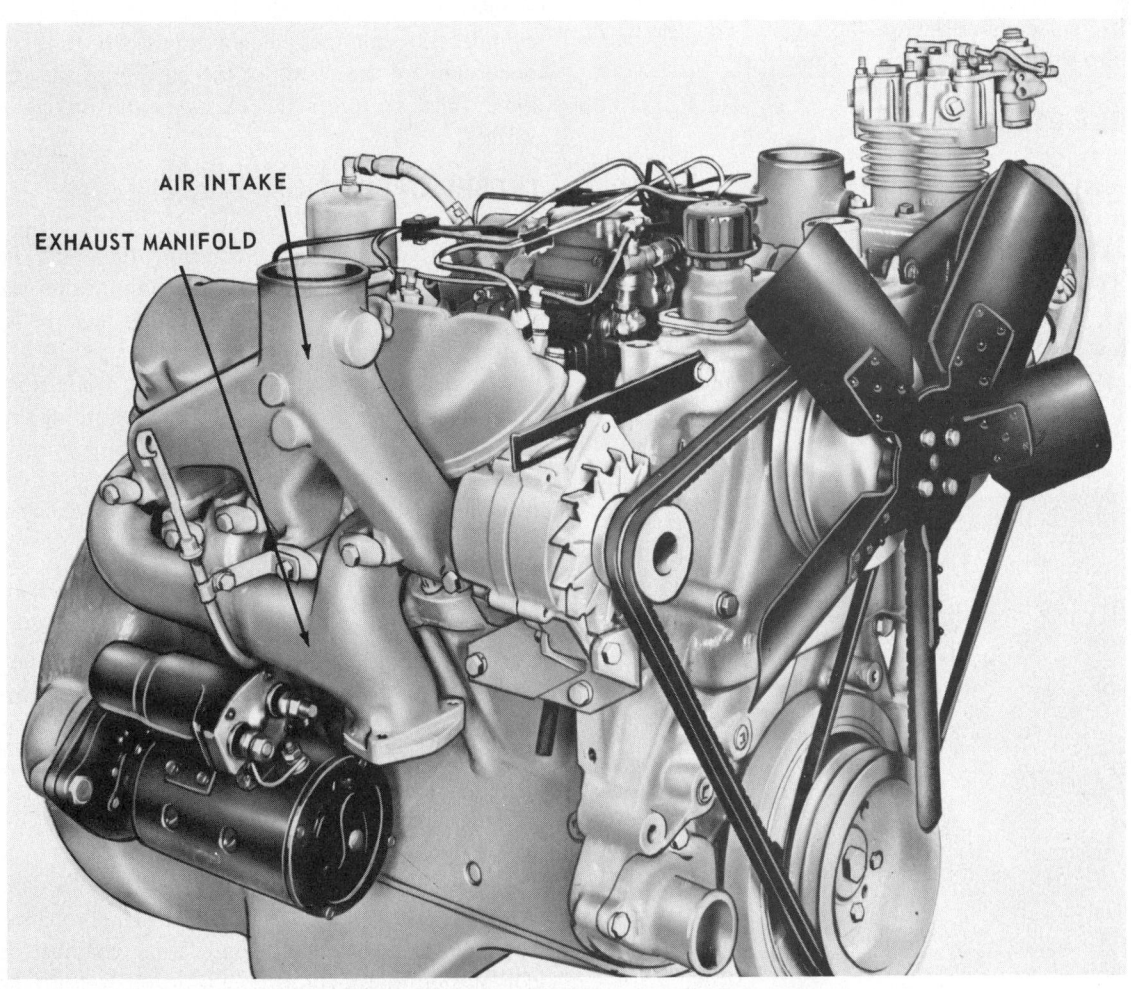

AIR INTAKE

EXHAUST MANIFOLD

Fig. 12-2. Typical GMC Toro-flow V-Six diesel engine.

as air, generates heat. In the diesel engine, air is compressed so much that it becomes hot enough (1000-1200 deg. F) to ignite the fuel. The fuel, in this case, is a petroleum product which is lighter than crude oil, but heavier than gasoline. A gasoline-air fuel mixture cannot be used in a diesel because it would start to burn from the heat generated by the high compression long before the piston reached the top of the stroke.

The diesel has no carburetor. The air is compressed in the cylinder and, at the proper time, fuel is sprayed into the heated air under pressure. The air-fuel mixture then ignites and burns the same as in a gasoline engine to produce power.

Obviously, the entry of the fuel must be "timed" the same as a spark to the spark plug in a gasoline engine.

Generally, the fuel pumping device is driven from the crankshaft and mounted on the side of the engine, Fig. 12-1. A typical GMC Toro-flow V-Six diesel engine is shown in Fig. 12-2. Details of diesel fuel injection are given in Chapter 27.

FUEL VAPORIZATION

As diesel fuel is more on the order of oil than gasoline, it does not vaporize as readily. This means that it must be broken up into fine particles and sprayed into the cylinder in the form of mist. This is accomplished by forcing the fuel through a nozzle or a series of very fine holes. As it enters the cylinder, the fuel combines more thoroughly with the air in the cylinder to form a combustible mixture.

TWO CYCLE DIESELS

As two cycle engines are not efficient as air pumps, it is necessary to force air into the cylinder and to force out the burned gas. One means of doing this is to use a supercharger or "blower." The GM two cycle diesel, Fig. 12-3, uses a positive displacement type supercharger as shown in Fig. 12-4. There are two exhaust valves in each cylinder, and no inlet valves. The fuel injection nozzle, complete with individual pump, is located between the two exhaust valves. It is operated by a

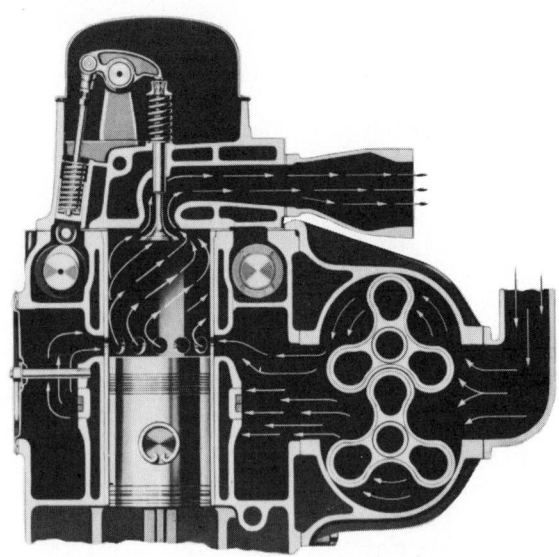

Fig. 12-4. A supercharger or "blower" is used in this design to force air into cylinders.

camshaft, push rod and rocker arm.

Air enters the cylinder through holes in the cylinder liner as shown in Fig. 12-4. The blower forces fresh air into the cylinder through these holes during the time the holes are uncovered by the piston at the bottom of the stroke. At the same time, it forces the exhaust out through the exhaust valves.

DIESEL OPERATION

As the diesel engine depends upon the heat of the compressed air to ignite the fuel, compression pressure must be maintained. Valves and piston rings must be kept in good condition. Leaking cannot be tolerated.

Of equal importance is proper fuel. While it is possible to build a diesel engine to run on almost anything that will burn, the automotive type diesel is designed to operate on a specific type and grade of fuel. Unless it is a multi-fuel engine design, trouble will be experienced if an attempt is made to operate on fuel other than the proper type.

DIESEL COMBUSTION CHAMBERS

A major difference in the design of the various diesel engines is the form or type of combustion chamber. There are four general types:
1. Open combustion chamber.
2. Precombustion chamber.
3. Turbulence chamber.
4. Energy cell.
Each design has certain advantages.

OPEN COMBUSTION CHAMBER: Probably the most common type of diesel combustion chamber is the open combustion design shown in Fig. 12-5. It is also known as the direct injection type. In addition to the form illustrated (known as the Mexican Hat type), there are many variations in

Fig. 12-3. A two cycle diesel engine built by General Motors.

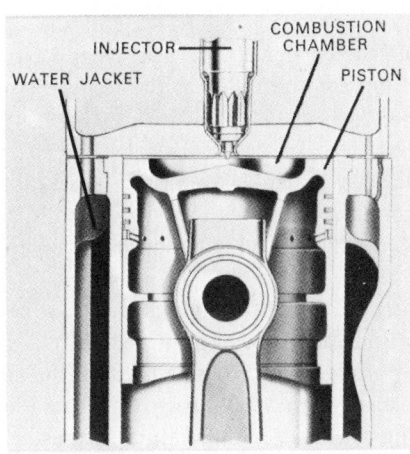

Fig. 12-5. Open combustion chamber of "Mexican Hat" type is also known as direct injection.

the shape of the piston crown and cylinder head. Such variations range from the flat topped piston head through cylindrical forms made by a ridge around the edge of the piston.

However, the basic characteristic of the open combustion chamber is that the fuel is sprayed directly into the combustion chamber. The form of the combustion chamber, together with the manner in which the air enters and the direction of the fuel spray, are designed to give maximum turbulence and improved combustion. The turbulence is of maximum importance if complete combustion of fuel is to be obtained.

An important variation of the open combustion chamber is the M-system, which has a special combustion chamber formed in the piston head, Fig. 12-6. The fuel is directed to the upper

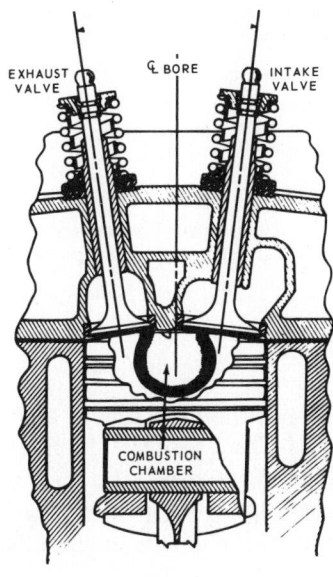

Fig. 12-6. M-type combustion chamber is spherical and located in piston head.

portion of the spherical chamber. High turbulence is created by means of the directional intake port, plus the shape of the chamber and the direction of the injected fuel.

Advantages claimed for the open combustion chamber include a high degree of efficiency, low manufacturing costs and high turbulence. A special advantage of the M-system is the ability to operate on a wide variety of fuels from gasoline to diesel fuel.

PRECOMBUSTION CHAMBER: When a portion of the combustion chamber is contained in the cylinder head or cylinder wall and is connected to the space above the piston with a small passage, the design is known as a precombustion type, Fig. 12-7.

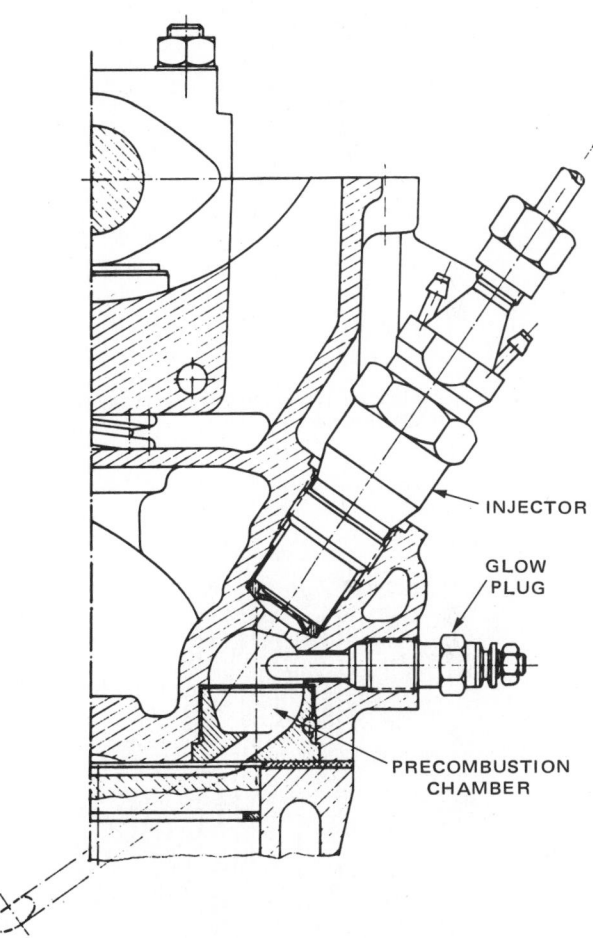

Fig. 12-7. Details of Volkswagen Rabbit diesel engine precombustion chamber, showing locating of injector nozzle and glow plug.

Thermal efficiency of the precombustion chamber engine is slightly lower than the open chamber type due to the greater heat loss from the larger combustion chamber area. The precombustion chamber contains approximately 30 percent of the total volume. However, cylinder pressure is lower and combustion smoother (particularly important when the engine is used in an automotive vehicle). Another important advantage is that the precombustion chamber engine is not as sensitive to the type of fuel used, and it is not necessary to provide such fine atomization.

TURBULENCE CHAMBER: In the turbulence chamber type of construction, up to 80 percent of the clearance volume is contained in the chamber, Fig. 12-8. The passage to the space over the piston is relatively large, and a high degree of turbulence is developed to provide a good mixture of air and fuel. Like the precombustion chamber engine, it is sensitive to the type of fuel provided. Cold weather starting without a glow plug is difficult.

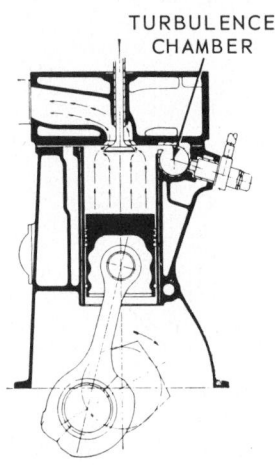

Fig. 12-8. Turbulence type of combustion chamber.
(Hercules Motors)

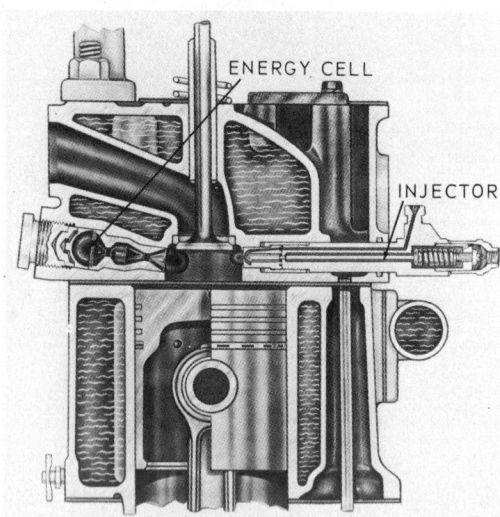

Fig. 12-9. Energy cell type of combustion chamber.

ENERGY CELL: The energy cell (also known as the air cell) type of combustion chamber has the main combustion chamber located in the cylinder head and an anti-chamber placed on the opposite side of the combustion chamber from the injection nozzle, Fig. 12-9. This design is used primarily in high speed diesel engines with a cylinder bore less than 5 in.

High performance approaching that of the open chamber diesel is claimed for the energy cell. High peak pressure and rough operation are controlled as the result of the controlled combustion.

FORD ENGINE: In an effort to develop an engine with a marked reduction in exhaust emission gases, Ford has been doing research on a diesel with spark ignition, Fig. 12-10. This engine combines diesel fuel injection and a compression ratio of 11 to 1.

The reduction in exhaust emissions has been achieved basically by using air throttling and exhaust gas recirculating. Nitric oxide formation is controlled within the engine as well as in the exhaust system. The nitric oxide formation is reduced by controlling peak cycle temperatures, exposure time at high temperatures and availability of oxygen. Recirculation of exhaust gas also plays an important part in reducing nitric oxide.

Hydrogen oxide emission control is effected, primarily by injecting fuel late in the compression stroke with an overall air fuel ratio of 15.5 to 1. The significance of the air-fuel ratio is the fact that it provides sufficient oxygen for secondary oxidation without additional oxygen for the formation of nitric oxide formation.

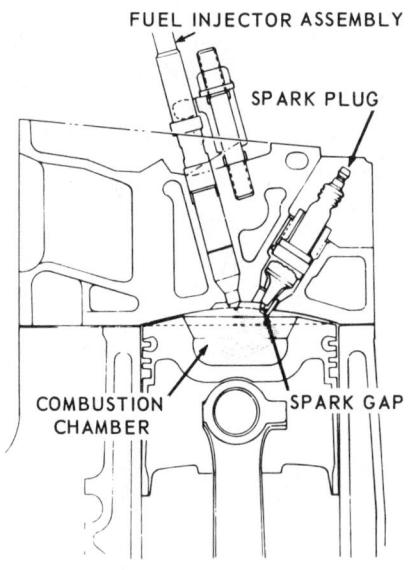

Fig. 12-10. Ford experimental Proco diesel engine with open combustion chamber and spark ignition.

TRUCK ENGINES

Engines used in light-duty trucks are very similar to automobile engines. There are some differences in design and operating conditions, but they are rather minor in nature. Actually, many light trucks use passenger car engines without any change whatever. Heavy-duty trucks usually have special engines.

Any changes that are made in a passenger car engine to adapt it to truck use are intended to compensate for the

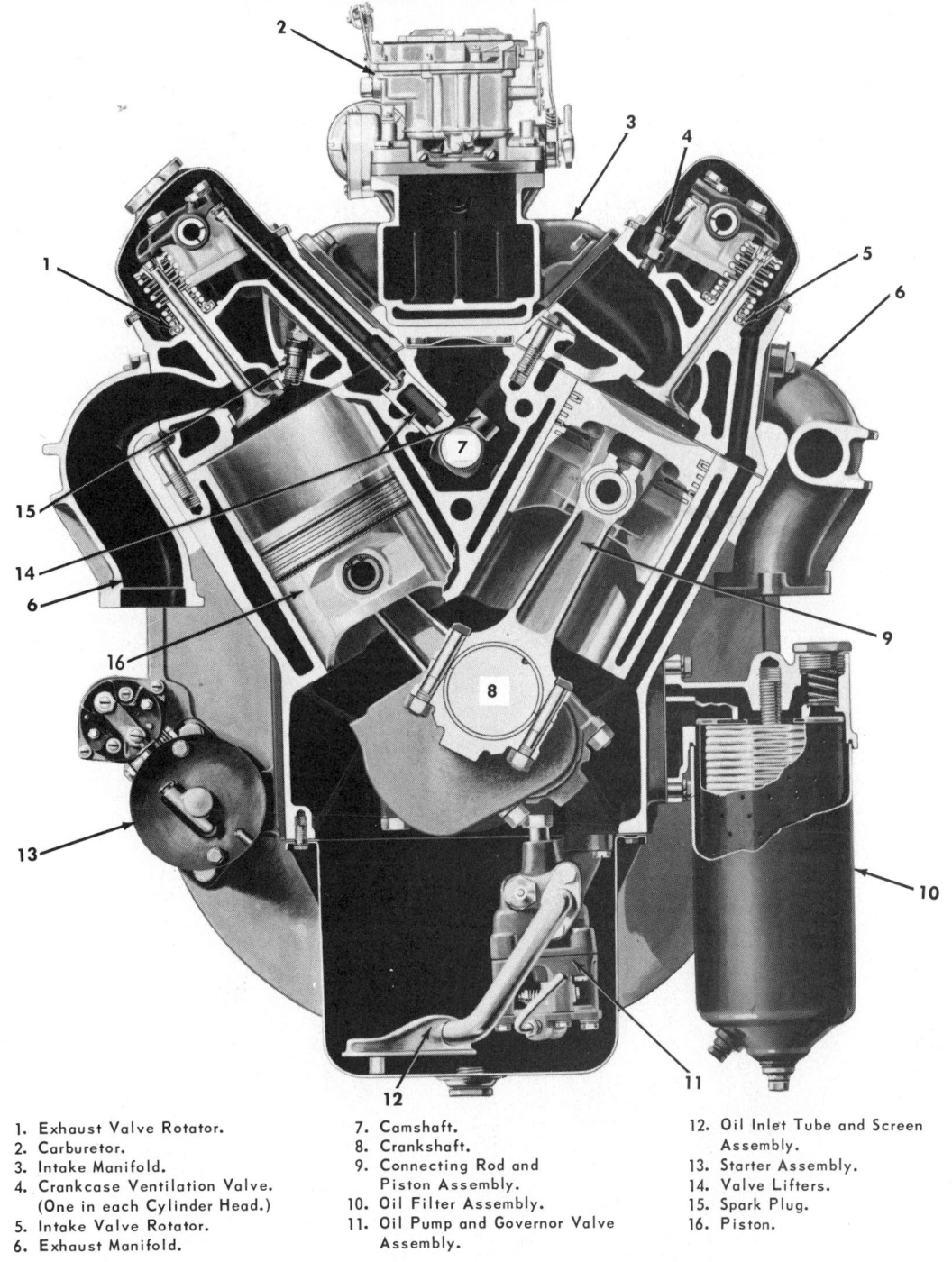

1. Exhaust Valve Rotator.
2. Carburetor.
3. Intake Manifold.
4. Crankcase Ventilation Valve. (One in each Cylinder Head.)
5. Intake Valve Rotator.
6. Exhaust Manifold.
7. Camshaft.
8. Crankshaft.
9. Connecting Rod and Piston Assembly.
10. Oil Filter Assembly.
11. Oil Pump and Governor Valve Assembly.
12. Oil Inlet Tube and Screen Assembly.
13. Starter Assembly.
14. Valve Lifters.
15. Spark Plug.
16. Piston.

Fig. 12-11. Sectional view of GMC V-Six cylinder gasoline engine.

difference in operating conditions. For example, the engine in a truck will be required to move a heavier load, so the axle gearing will be such that the engine can run at higher speed for the same vehicle speed. The result may be that the truck at 60 mph will have a wide-open throttle. Therefore the truck engine will be operating more of the time at full power.

Under these conditions, the exhaust valves will run hotter; may need to be made of heat-resisting steel; and also require special valve seat inserts. The pistons and rings may need slightly greater clearance for heat expansion, etc. The cooling system may require a larger water pump, larger radiator or some increase in capacity. A different bearing material may be

used on the crankshaft to withstand the higher bearing loads, and an oil pan of larger capacity might be installed.

As accelerating ability in a truck is of less importance than in a passenger car, a heavier flywheel may be used in the truck engine. Such changes often serve to adapt the passenger car engine to use in a truck without making any major design changes.

Heavy-duty trucks usually have engines that are designed and built for truck use. They may be of either the two cycle or four cycle type, and may operate on gasoline or diesel oil. Such engines are customarily much heavier in construction than passenger car engines. See Fig. 12-11. Crankshafts are

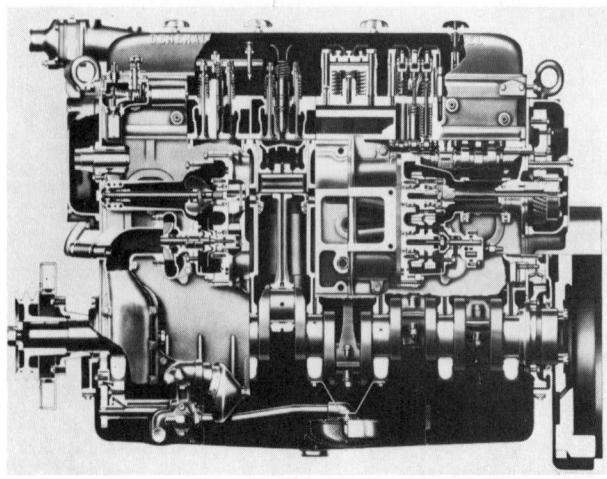

Fig. 12-12. Two cycle GMC series 71 diesel engine is provided with a balance shaft driven from camshaft. Both camshaft and balance shaft have balance weights.

larger in diameter and the bearings are longer. Crankcases are heavier and braced with webs at points of strain. In general, the piston displacement is increased and engine speed decreased for a given amount of power.

The GMC series 71 two cycle engine is shown in Fig. 12-12. The "71" is used extensively in automotive trucks. To reduce vibration, it is provided with a balance shaft driven from the camshaft.

TRACTOR ENGINES

Farm tractors, Fig. 12-13, usually have engines designed for tractor use. However, these engines may be converted from basic automobile engine design with changes as needed to better suit tractor operating conditions. See Fig. 12-14. A passenger car engine is constantly changing speed and seldom operates for any length of time at a steady pace. A tractor engine may operate for hours at a time at a governed speed. In fact, service intervals are based on operating hours.

The farm tractor engine usually is equipped with a governor that holds engine speed at or near peak torque. It can accelerate or decelerate freely up to the governed speed. Some larger tractors have special design engines featuring low speed and large displacement. However, most smaller tractor engines follow automobile engine design. Service procedures are substantially the same.

Some of the larger wheel tractors and most of the larger industrial tractors, particularly of the crawler type, have

Fig. 12-13. This farm tractor is powered by a 127 hp (at drawbar) turbocharged diesel engine. The transmission has 16 speeds forward, 8 in reverse. Fully equipped tractor weighs 11,700 lb. (5 310 kg).
(International Agricultural Equipment, IHC)

Fig. 12-14. This farm tractor engine is a turbocharged, six cylinder diesel with a 436 cu. in. (7.1 L) piston displacement. It has a 27 qt. crankcase capacity and utilizes an 85 gal. fuel tank. International Agriculture Equipment Div., IHC)

Fig. 12-15. Heavy-duty engines of type shown are used to power earth-moving equipment. (Caterpillar Tractor Co.)

MARINE ENGINES

Automobile engines can be adapted for use in boats. However, operating conditions are more like a truck or tractor since boat engines usually run at more constant speed. Changes must be made in the cooling system to avoid overcooling of the engine. Unless closely regulated by suitable thermostats in the cooling system, the engine will operate too cold. The fan and radiator usually are discarded.

It is also necessary in many cases, to use an oil pan of different shape because the engine is often installed with the

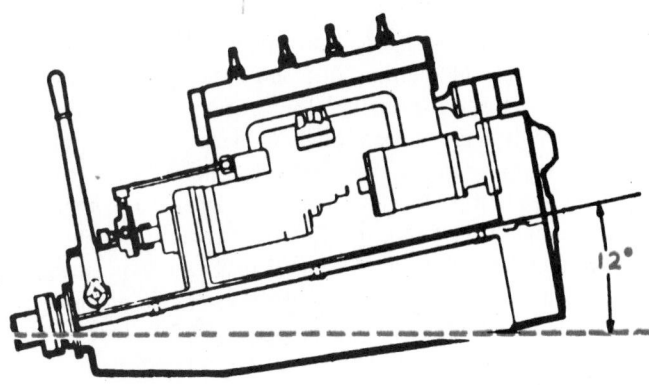

Fig. 12-16. In order to reduce propeller shaft angularity, inboard marine engines are often mounted at a considerable angle in boat.

engines of special design which are as heavy or heavier than truck engines, Fig. 12-15. Huge industrial crawlers often have diesel engines so large that it is impractical for an electrical motor of reasonable size to crank them. In such cases, an auxiliary gasoline engine of smaller size is attached, which serves as a starting engine.

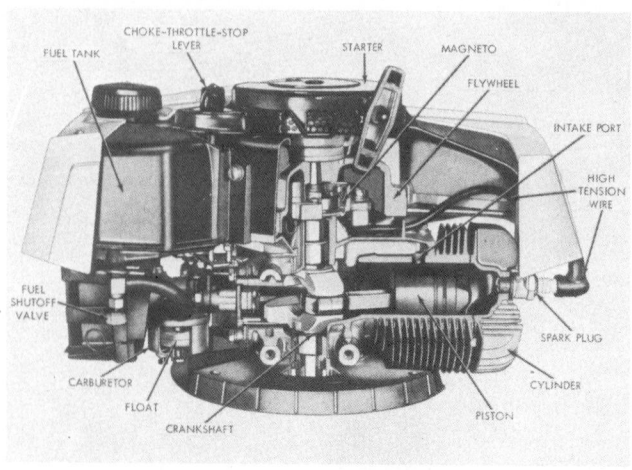

Fig. 12-17. This light-duty, two cycle, single cylinder small gas engine is popular in lawn mower applications. It has a vertical crankshaft, pull cord starter and flywheel type magneto. (Jacobsen Mfg. Co.)

rear end much lower than the front to reduce the angularity of the propeller shaft. See Fig. 12-16. It is desirable to equip the engine with a governor to prevent the engine from racing itself to destruction if the propeller shears a pin, or comes out of the water temporarily in rough water.

Special marine engines of the inboard type are built quite sturdily to withstand the rigors of constant speed operation. At the other extreme, outboard engines are built as light as possible since they usually are portable. Most outboards are two cycle type, so oil for lubricating the engine parts is mixed with the fuel.

The bearings in these two cycle engines are often of the antifriction type, using steel balls or rollers in hardened races. These engines are available in air-cooled or water-cooled types; and in single and multiple cylinder designs to develop almost any amount of power desired.

SMALL ENGINES

Air-cooled engines are used almost exclusively for small machinery such as lawn mowers, chain saws, gardening equipment, etc. Single or multiple-cylinder engines of both two cycle and four cycle types are entirely satisfactory, and operate for long periods of time with little attention and few repairs. See Figs. 12-17 and 12-18.

These small industrial engines are usually self-contained power units having built-in fuel and ignition arrangements similar to an outboard engine. The ignition is often supplied by an in-built high tension magneto which is a part of, or attached to, the engine flywheel. Rotation of the engine generates electricity for ignition. These magnetos are described in the chapter on ENGINE IGNITION.

Snowmobiling is becoming an increasingly popular sport and profitable service market. Most snowmobile engines are two cycle, air-cooled, single or two cylinder design. The McCulloch "twin," for example, has a displacement of 24.3 cu. in. (398 cm^3). This is 1.27 hp per cu. in. displacement, which is approximately twice that of many American passenger car engines.

These "balanced engines" are designed with a balancing cylinder opposite each power cylinder. See Fig. 12-18. The balancing cylinder is about half the size of the power cylinder. Its location increases crankcase capacity and compression ratio of the crankcase, as well as providing dynamic balance. There is no pressure supercharging. The power cylinder has the normal two cycle transfer and exhaust ports, with the exhaust port closing last.

The balance cylinder is primarily used for mechanical balance, but it does control the inlet ports much like a rotary inlet valve. The basic ignition system utilizes a high tension magneto which, on some installations, includes a 70 watt generator.

RACING ENGINES

The most successful racing engines are designed for the purpose and are made of special materials. Passenger car

Fig. 12-18. Cutaway shows details of two cycle, air-cooled two cylinder snowmobile engine. Arrow indicates balancing cylinder, a special design feature that dynamically balances the engine. (McCulloch Corp.)

engines can be adapted for racing purposes, but considerable alteration usually is required. When used for racing, the engine is designed or altered to get the utmost in power and rotational speed regardless of anything else. See Fig. 12-19.

Since noise is a minor consideration, the average race car engine roars and clatters. Actually, however, the clearances are very carefully measured on each working part. Some of this

Fig. 12-19. Ford Indianapolis race engine. Note idler gears to drive camshaft gear. There are two camshafts for each bank of cylinders. Covers over camshaft have been removed.

at high speed. As a result, racing engines seldom idle smoothly. Other reasons, for rough idling are lightweight flywheels for rapid acceleration and the extremely high compression ratios, which approach diesel practice.

In addition to the greater clearances between all moving parts, each rotating part in the engine is balanced to extremely close tolerance. This is done not only to increase the speed of the engine, but to reduce destructive vibration. Every part of the engine is made of the finest material available for the purpose to insure reliability and freedom from mechanical failure.

The race car engine shown in Fig. 12-20 is the Ford-Weslake engine, which develops 455 hp @ 10,500 rpm. It is a 60 deg. V-12 engine with an aluminum cylinder block. Displacement is 182.6 cu. in. (3 liter). Double overhead camshaft operating four valves per cylinder are features. It is scheduled to appear in long distance sport events.

AIRPLANE ENGINES

Liquid-cooled engines have been used in airplanes, but the air-cooled engine dominates the field. Cylinders are arranged in several ways: in-line, pancake, V and radial style. If radial, they may have more than one circle of cylinders around the crankcase. Turbines and jet engines are also used, particularly in military and commercial aircraft.

Aircraft engines of the reciprocating type are made with great precision, but the clearance of most working parts is

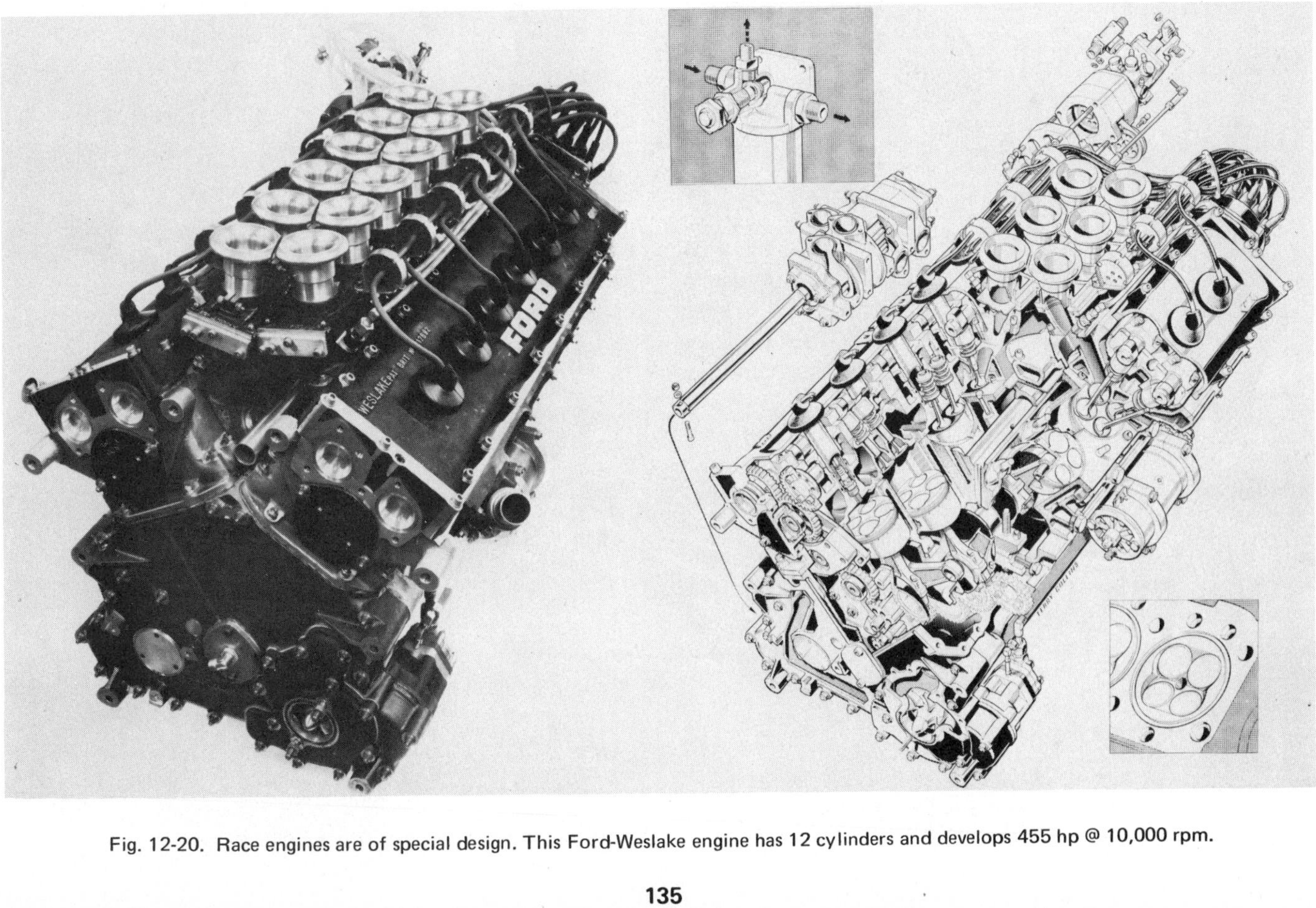

clatter comes from the valve mechanism, which is designed to smack the valves open quickly, raise them high off the seat and close them quickly. Large valves with a high lift will expedite the flow of the gases in and out of the cylinders.

The opening and closing time of the valves, as well as the duration of the valve opening, is designed solely for efficiency

Fig. 12-20. Race engines are of special design. This Ford-Weslake engine has 12 cylinders and develops 455 hp @ 10,000 rpm.

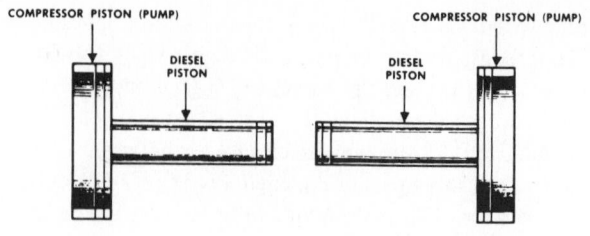

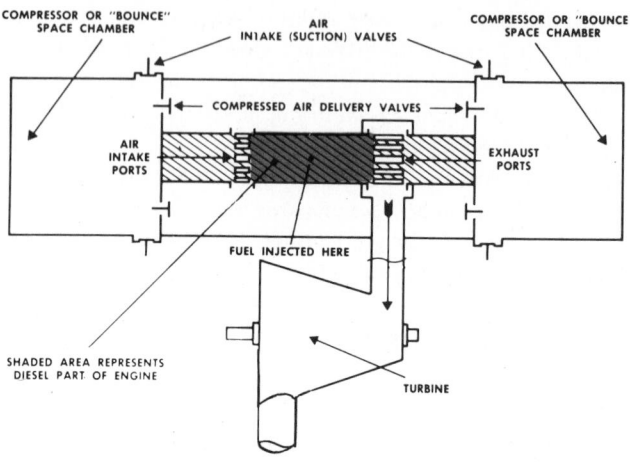

Fig. 12-21. Diagram of free piston type of cylinder and dual pistons with the combustion chamber area in color.

greater than usually provided for water-cooled engines. This excessive clearance is necessary to provide for the great expansion which occurs in operation. Airplane engines operate at or near full power most of the time. The engine is wide open at take-off, and not too far from wide open at so-called cruising speed.

FREE PISTON ENGINES

Free piston engines are closely related to both the diesel and turbine types of power plants. They use the diesel cycle along with a turbine, which is an essential part of the power plant. See Fig. 12-21.

A free piston engine consists of large and small cylinders, each containing a set of two (one large and one small) horizontally opposed pistons. Several of these pairs of cylinders may be assembled into one power plant and coupled to one turbine. An air-fuel mixture is fired between the opposed small pistons — with injectors as in a diesel — which drives the pistons apart, compressing air in the closed chambers at ends of the large pistons.

Air compressed in the large cylinders then bounces the pistons back toward inner center, compressing the mixture in the small cylinders for the next firing stroke. It will be apparent that the compression ratio and piston stroke will vary with the speed of the engine. As the pistons travel inward, the

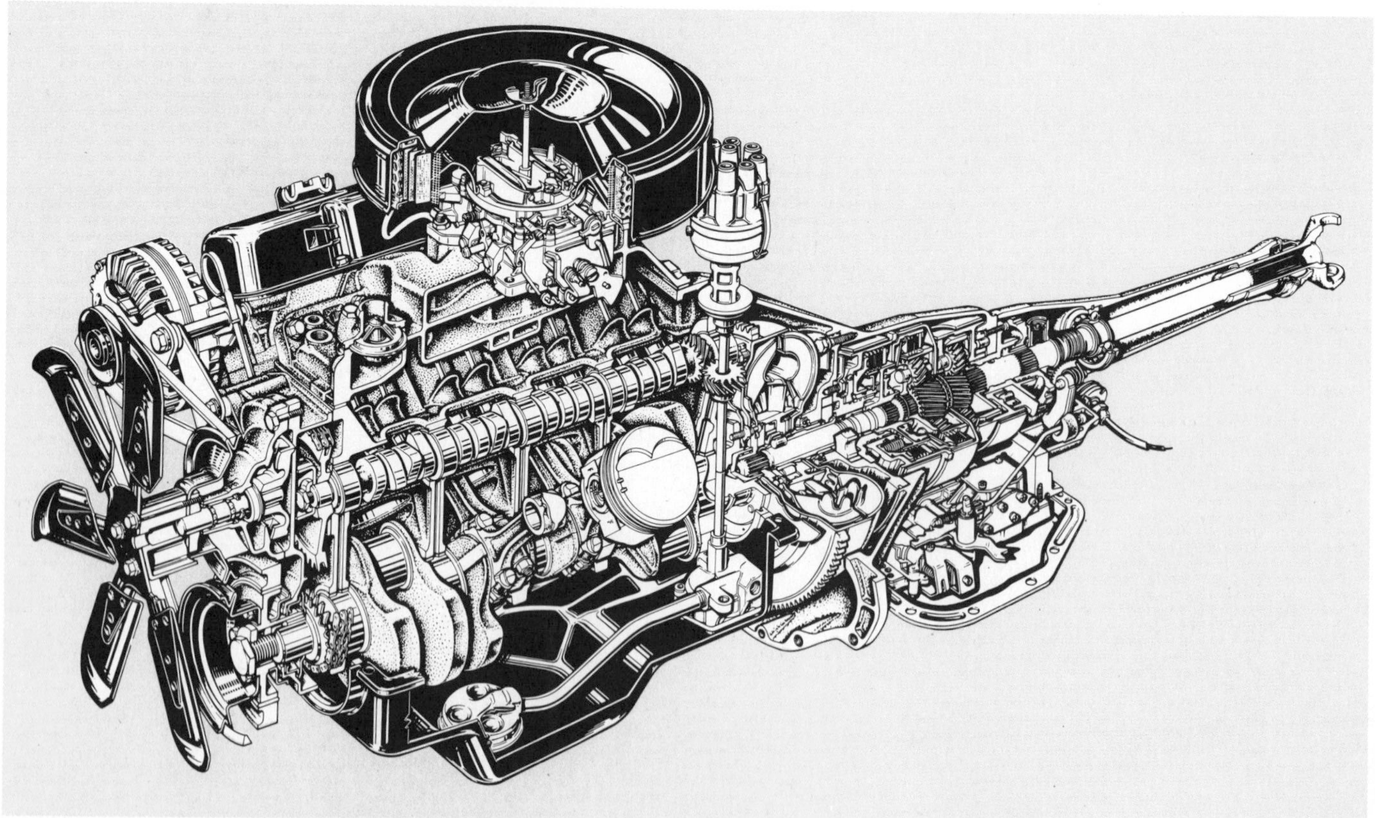

340 cu. in. V-8 power plant used in Plymouth Barracuda. Bore and stroke are 4.04 x 3.31.

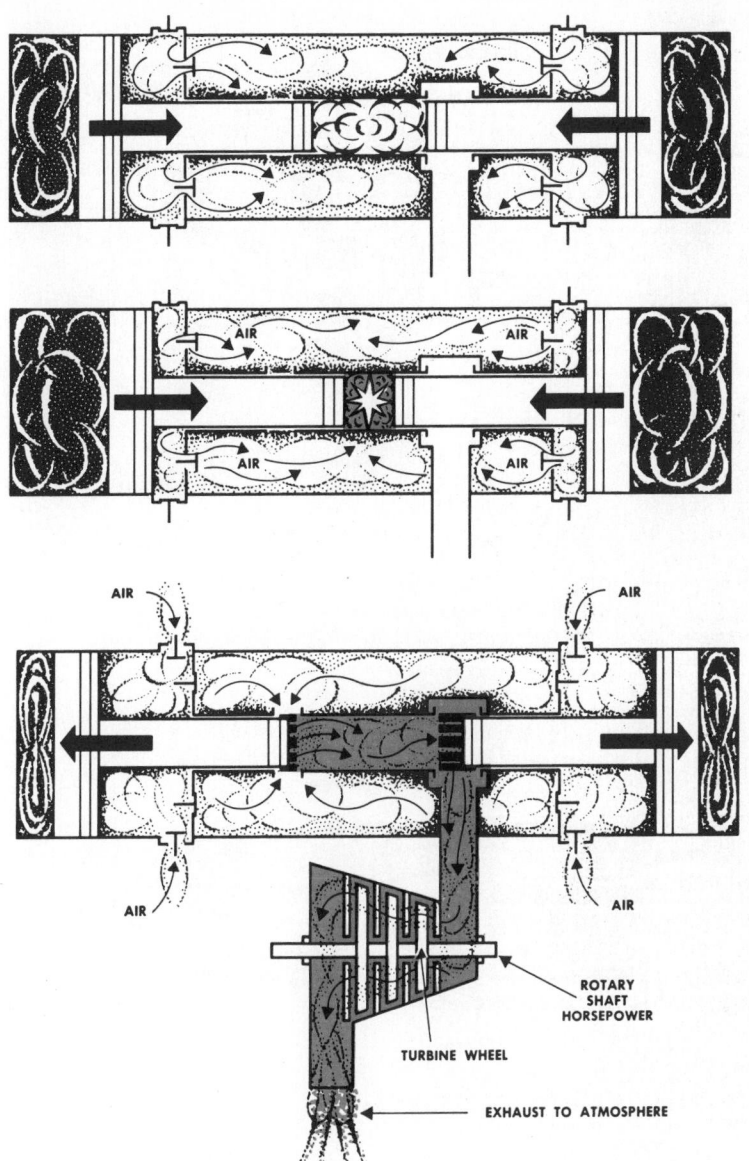

Pistons travel inward pumping air from the compressor cylinder into the air box, trapping air in Diesel combustion space. Intake and exhaust ports are closed-air delivery valves are open.

Pistons are completing inward travel. Fuel is injected into cylinder. This is combustion or the beginning of the power stroke. Intake and exhaust ports are still closed—air delivery valves are open.

End of power stroke compressing air in bounce space to return pistons for next cycle. Exhaust and intake ports are just opening to scavenge Diesel cylinder. Exhaust gases escape to turbine, spinning turbine wheels for usable power. Air is being drawn into compressor cylinder.

ROTARY SHAFT HORSEPOWER

TURBINE WHEEL

EXHAUST TO ATMOSPHERE

Fig. 12-22. Operating cycle of free piston engine.

large pistons also compress air and pump it into the diesel cylinder through the ports uncovered by the small pistons. The cycle of operation is shown in Fig. 12-22.

The expanding hot gas generated goes to the turbine part of the engine to make the power usable. Since there are no connecting rods or crankshaft, the pistons are kept in phase with the aid of connecting linkage.

TURBINES AND JETS

Gas turbines are used to propel automobiles, trucks, boats and airplanes. They also can be designed to serve as stationary power plants. The fundamental principle of a turbine consists of an inclined plane mounted on a rotating shaft, and located in the path of fluid force, Figs. 12-23 and 12-25.

An actual turbine operating with oil as a fluid is found in automatic transmissions of the torque converter type. Several of these are described and illustrated in Chapter 45.

A gas turbine is a heat engine which transforms energy created by the expansion of the burning fuel and air in the combustion chamber to either thrust or shaft power, Fig. 12-26. This power can be utilized directly to push an airplane or vehicle, or it can be turned into shaft power to turn an airplane propeller or an automobile wheel.

The thrust force developed by a turbine can be shown by using a toy balloon for a demonstration. The balloon is inflated with air, then released. As the air rushes out through the neck of the balloon, the balloon will shoot away in the direction opposite the air flow. The force for propulsion is applied against the inside of the balloon, rather than being supplied by a jet of compressed air pushing against free air. This is the same principle of operation employed in a rocket or jet engine. See Fig. 12-24.

The same thrust force can be exerted against a turbine wheel to produce rotary motion, Fig. 12-27. The first stage, or gasifier section, produces the thrust. If shaft power is wanted,

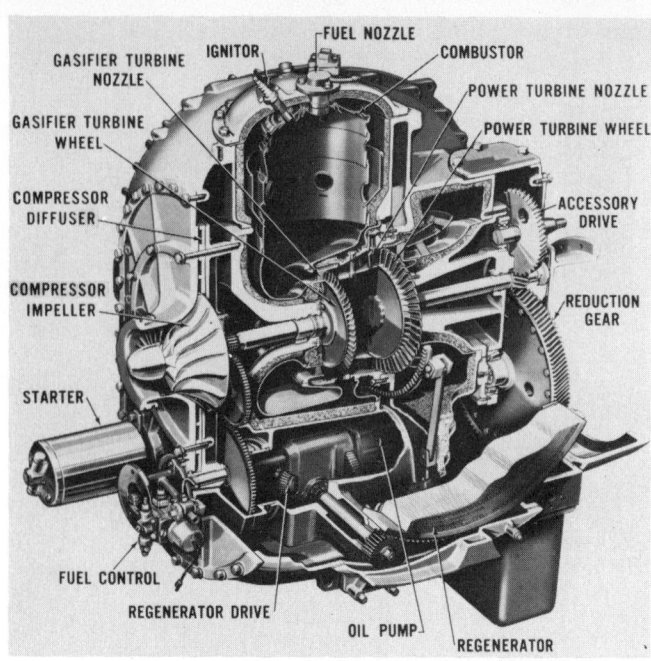

Fig. 12-23. Cutaway view gives details of Ford gas turbine engine.

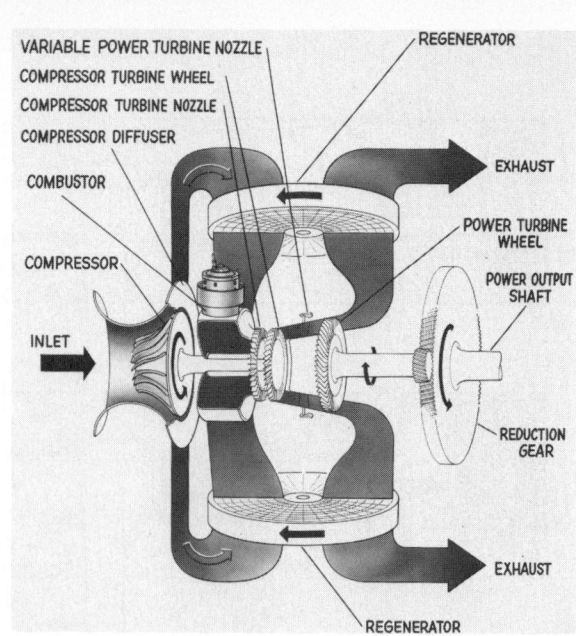

Fig. 12-25. Schematic of Ford turbine shows air flow path and direction of rotation of moving parts.

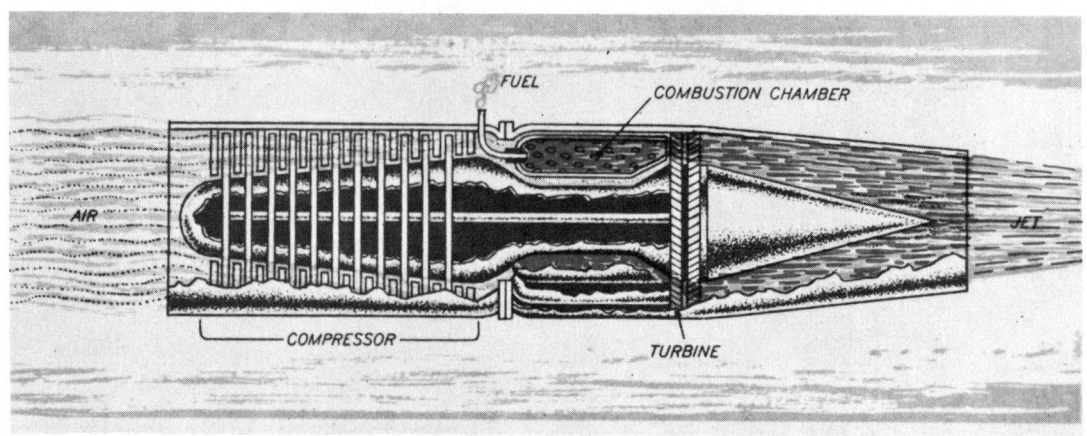

Fig. 12-24. Diagram of jet engine construction.

the section to the right (power section) is added as a second stage. In this particular turbine, Fig. 12-27, the first turbine wheel drives only the compressor. Fuel is sprayed into the two burners receiving compressed air from the compressor. Only a portion of the air is burned in the burners, and the compressor requires only a portion of the energy in the hot gas. The remainder of the air and hot gas is utilized as a thrust force.

If shaft power is wanted instead of thrust, air and hot gas are directed to the second turbine. Basically, then, a gas turbine provides rotary power from the expansion of burning gas without the use of reciprocating pistons and connecting rods operating a crankshaft.

FORD TURBINE

The power turbine of the 470 hp Ford gas turbine engine revolves at 31,650 rpm, while the output shaft turns at 3000 rpm, Fig. 12-26. Torque is 760 ft. lb.

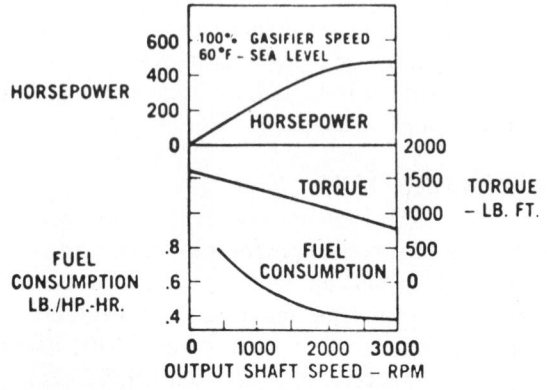

Fig. 12-26. Curves on chart indicate hp, torque and fuel consumption of Ford turbine series 3600.

138

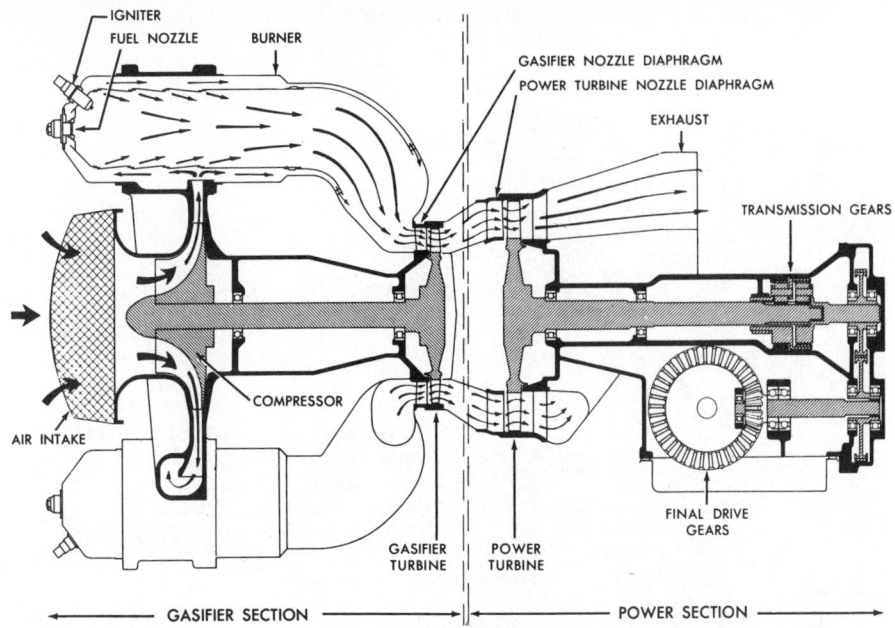

Fig. 12-27. GM turbine arrangement as used to propel a vehicle.

The main housing is the principal structural member of the turbine, to which five subassemblies are attached: gasifier, variable power turbine nozzle, power turbine and reduction gear box, combustor and regenerator, Fig. 12-23. Each is a self-contained unit and, except for the variable power turbine nozzle, can be removed for service without disturbing the remainder of the engine.

Airflow through a turbine engine is shown in Fig. 12-25:

1. Air enters compressor axially after passing through inlet filter and silencer, then it is discharged radially into diffuser.
2. After leaving diffuser, where air flow is split, it passes into forward half of regenerator covers, then inward through regenerator cores and two flows of air rejoin in combustor chamber.
3. Air heated by passing through regenerators is then directed in and about combustor in a flow pattern developed to give good combustion and an even temperature distribution.
4. Combustor then discharges into plenum chamber which conducts hot gases into gasifier turbine nozzle and wheel.
5. High velocity gases leaving gasifier turbine pass through a transition duct into variable nozzle vanes, which direct flow to power turbine wheel.
6. Gases leaving power turbine wheel are diffused and directed outward through rear half of two regenerator cores where heat is recovered for transfer to compressor discharge air.
7. Cooled gases then collect in regenerator covers and are discharged to exhaust.

WANKEL ROTARY ENGINE

The Wankel rotary engine does not have reciprocating parts. Instead, it has a triangular shaped rotor with slightly curved sides that orbits eccentrically around a fixed gear in a housing shaped slightly like a figure eight, Fig. 12-28.

Rotary engines of the Wankel type are being used in virtually all fields, including automotive (Mazda), aircraft,

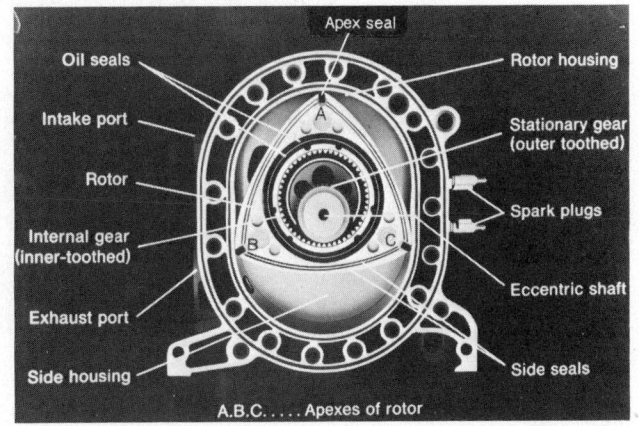

Fig. 12-28. Major parts of a rotary combustion engine. (Mazda)

farm equipment, marine, outboard engines, motorcycles and small electric generators. Air cushion vehicles have also been produced.

The Wankel type rotary engine, Fig. 12-28, is a compact power plant requiring less space than a piston engine of the same horsepower. It is an exceptionally quiet engine with very little vibration, since only rotating parts are used.

There are approximately 630 parts in a Wankel engine compared to about 1050 parts for a piston engine. Ports are used instead of valves, eliminating the need for the complicated valve train of the piston engine.

A Wankel engine weighing 237 lbs. will produce approximately the same power as a conventional V-8 weighing over 600 lbs. The Wankel occupies approximately 5.1 cu. ft. of engine compartment space, while the V-8 requires 23.2 cu. ft. Fuel distribution to the rotor chambers is better than the distribution to the piston engine, consequently volumetric efficiency is higher.

Most of the Wankel type rotary engines in production have

139

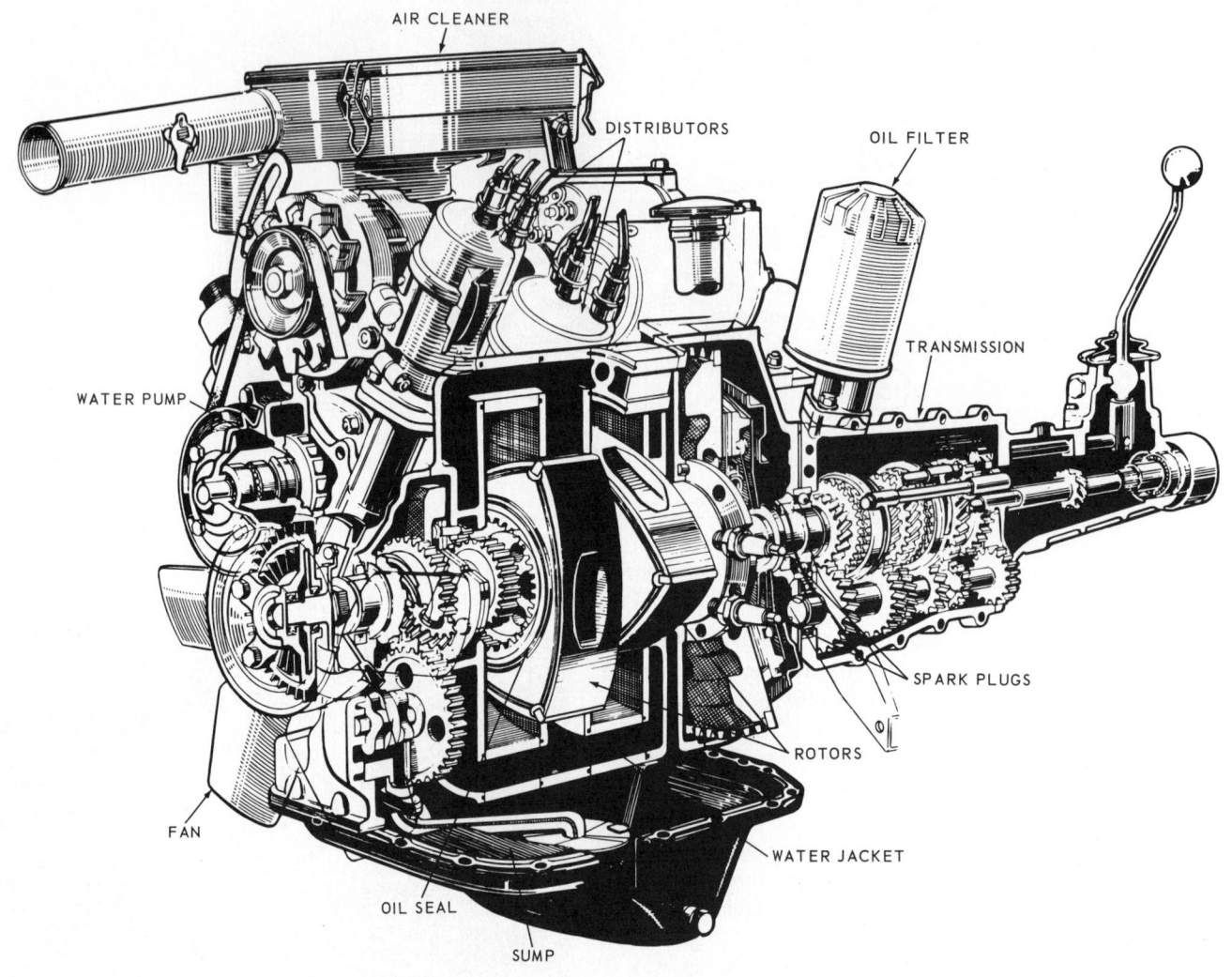

Fig. 12-29. Sectional view of Mazda rotary engine of Wankel type.

two rotors. Fig. 12-29, for example, shows the engine which powers the Japanese Mazda. Some rotary engines have three rotors (Mercedes-Benz CIII) and four-rotor engines have been built. Wankel type engines can be built as small as 18.5 cu. in. per working chamber up to 1920 cu. in. per working chamber.

Fig. 12-30 shows heat balance chart of a typical Wankel rotary engine. The percentages compare favorably with the average piston engine.

WANKEL FUNDAMENTALS

The Wankel rotor is triangular in shape with slightly curved sides. It orbits eccentrically on a fixed gear in a housing shaped slightly like a figure eight, Fig. 12-28. That is, the rotor rotates around its own axis while orbiting around the mainshaft. However, the output shaft makes three turns per rotor revolution. As a result, one operating cycle takes place per output shaft revolution.

As the rotor swings around the fixed gear, the internal gear (rotor gear) transmits the rotary motion to the output shaft. The output shaft is an eccentric shaft and the rotation is such that the tips of the apexes of the rotor, Fig. 12-28, are always

in contact with the side surface of the rotor housing. These tips are provided with seals shown at A, B and C.

All four cycles — intake, compression, power and exhaust — take place in one revolution of the rotor. Since there are three lobes to the rotor, there is a continuous performance of these cycles on every lobe, Fig. 12-31. The crankshaft turns three times for every revolution of the rotor. With one power impulse for each of the rotor sides, there will be three power impulses per rotor revolution, or one power impulse per revolution of the eccentric shaft.

The sequence of the cycles is shown in Fig. 12-31, position A, intake is starting between lobes 1 and 3. Compression is occurring between 1 and 2. Power is being produced between 2 and 3. Exhaust is finishing between 3 and 1.

When the rotor has moved to position B, intake continues between 1 and 3. Compression continues between 1 and 2. Power is finishing between 2 and 3.

In position C, intake is finishing between 1 and 3. Spark has ignited the compressed charge between 1 and 2. Exhaust is occurring between 2 and 3.

In position D, intake of the charge is completed between 1 and 3. Power is produced between 1 and 2. Exhaust is

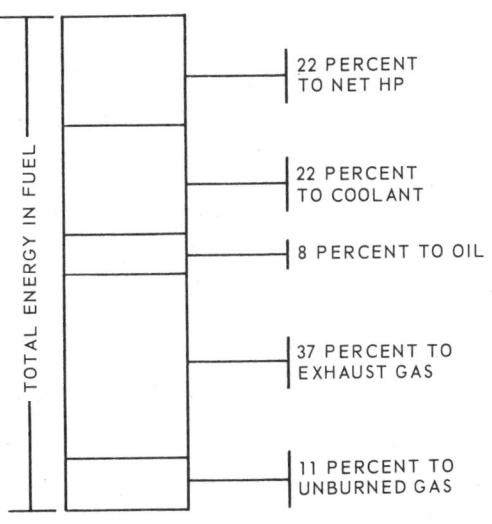

Fig. 12-30. Showing where power goes in a typical Wankel engine.

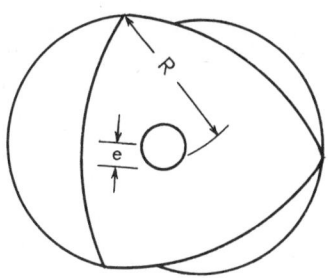

Fig. 12-32. Compression ratio of a Wankel engine equals R/e.

that develops 130 hp @ 5500 rpm. Compression ratio is 9 to 1. The Maxda R100 engine has a displacement of 60 cu. in. and develops 100 hp @ 7000 rpm. Compression ratio is 9.4 to 1.

In a rotary engine, the compression ratio is limited by the rotor radius and the eccentricity. When those two dimensions

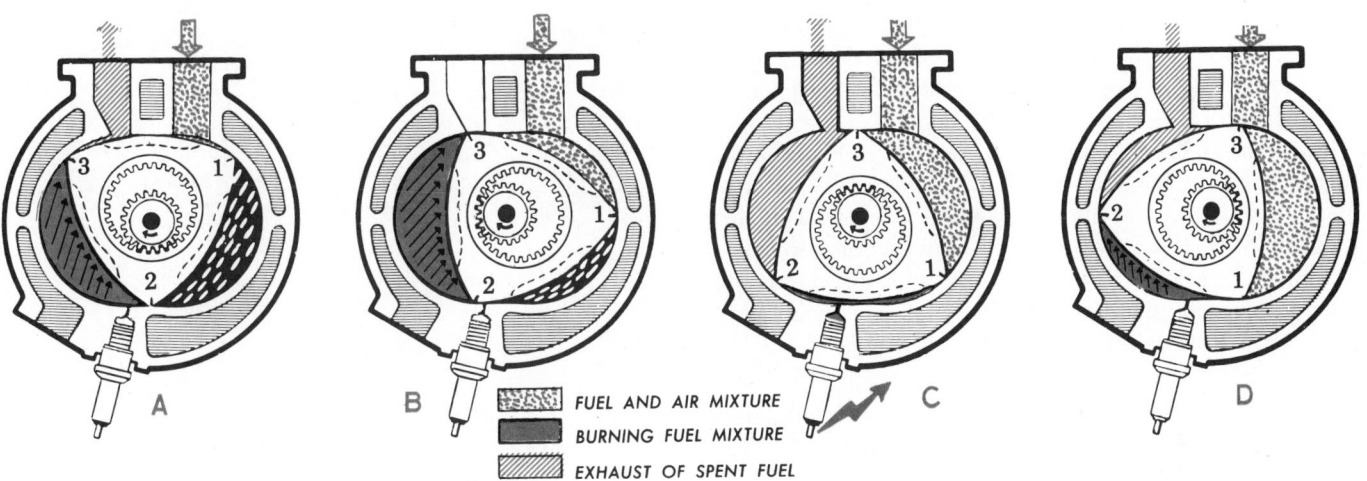

FUEL AND AIR MIXTURE
BURNING FUEL MIXTURE
EXHAUST OF SPENT FUEL

Fig. 12-31. Sequence of events in a Wankel type rotary engine.

continuing between 2 and 3.

From this operational description, it can be seen that when gas pressure on one face turns the rotor, it brings another face into position to produce power.

DISPLACEMENT OF WANKEL ENGINE

There has been considerable discussion as to the method of calculating the displacement of the Wankel engine. The currently accepted method is use twice the combustion volume multiplied by the number of rotors.

POWER DEVELOPED

As is the case with the conventional piston engine, horsepower developed by different makes of the Wankel rotary engine varies considerably.

The Audi-NSU model R080 is a 60.7 cu. in. rotary engine

have been selected, the maximum compression ratio is determined. The compression ratio is then equal to the radius to eccentricity ratio or R/e, Fig. 12-32.

PERFORMANCE

Reports indicate that fuel consumption of about 20 to 25 mpg is not unusual for a two-rotor engine of approximately 60 cu. in. displacement. Carburetors are used on most engines. However, Mercedes-Benz, after preliminary work with carburetors, changed to fuel injection.

Usually carburetors are of the 2 Bbl. type. Weber, Solex, and Hitachi-Stromberg are among the carburetors used on the various engines.

The location of intake and exhaust ports are factors in performance and fuel economy. NSU and Mercedes-Benz are advocates of peripheral ports, while Toyo Kogyo, manufacturer of the Mazda, prefers side location of ports, claiming better idling, low speed performance and light load scavenging. In general, the peripheral ports, Fig. 12-33, provide high speed and power while the side ports, Fig. 12-29, provide performance over a wide range.

The fuel used in the Wankel rotary engine is the same kind used in conventional piston engines. Normal fuel ranges from 87 to 91 octane. Leaded fuel is not required. Tests made on the Mazda showed satisfactory operation with 67 octane fuel. Satisfactory operation has also been obtained on some rotary engines with diesel fuels.

Fuel flow from the carburetor to the Wankel engine is described as being constant. There is no problem of uneven distribution such as encountered in piston engines where some cylinders receive a greater quantity of the air/fuel mixture than others.

IGNITION

The ignition system used on the Wankel rotary engine is of the battery-coil-distributor type. In many cases two distributors are used and two spark plugs per chamber. A transistor system is used on the Mercedes-Benz CIII MK II, together with a direct fuel injection system with a mechanical pump. Note the location of the spark plugs in the Mazda rotary engine shown in Fig. 12-29.

Spark plugs differ greatly from those used in the piston engine. Note the side electrodes shown in Fig. 12-34. Location of the spark plugs is as important in rotary engines as it is in piston engines. Research has shown that by using two spark plugs in each chamber, exhaust emissions are reduced, power is increased, combustion is more complete and duration of combustion is minimized.

Two distributors, Fig. 12-29, are usually provided with both centrifugal and vacuum advance. Researchers have found that a spark advance of approximately five degrees usually is required. This corresponds to an advance of approximately 28 degrees on a piston engine.

In piston engines, the spark plugs receive the benefit of the cooling effects of the incoming fuel charge. This is not the case in a rotary combustion engine. Consequently, spark plug temperatures are materially higher. Therefore, spark plugs used in the engines are an extremely cold type.

Timing the ignition on these rotary engines is in relation to the angle of the shaft. Top center is the same as the top center on a piston engine, but the angle of the shaft is greater than the corresponding angle of the piston engine crankshaft.

EMISSIONS

Currently, Mazda and NSU rotary engines have met Federal requirements for low levels of exhaust emissions. Intense combustion chamber turbulence claimed for the Wankel type engine contributes largely to improved exhaust emissions. In addition, the Wankel engine can give satisfactory operation on relatively lean mixtures, which also contributes to improved exhaust emissions.

In general, the hydrocarbon emission level of the Wankel rotary engine is higher than a piston type engine of the same

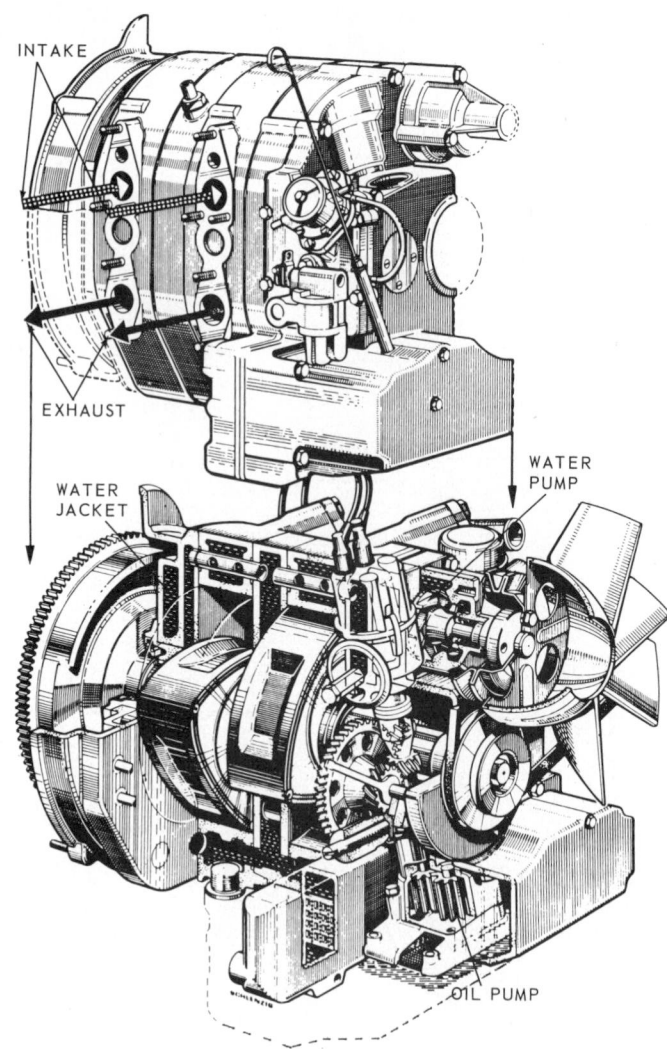

Fig. 12-33. NSU Wankel engine showing peripheral intake and exhaust ports.

general size. However, the carbon monoxide and nitrous oxide levels are lower than that of a reciprocating piston engine.

As is the case of the piston engine, the exact emission quantity and composition of the Wankel exhaust depends on throttle opening and engine speed. With a rich or lean mixture, there is the possibility of incomplete combustion. The problem is worse under light load conditions. However, the Wankel rotary engine operates well under a lean mixture, and has an advantage over the piston engine in that respect.

Thermal reactors have been shown to produce a material reduction in the hydrocarbon emission from the Wankel engine. Tests have shown reductions up to 90 percent when a thermal reactor has been used, Fig. 12-35.

COOLING

While air-cooled Wankel type rotary engines have been produced, the water-cooled type is used most extensively. The water, or coolant, is used primarily for cooling the housing, oil is used to cool the rotor. Typical water-cooled rotary engines are shown in Figs. 12-29 and 12-33.

Fig. 12-34. Type of spark plug used in Wankel rotary engine.

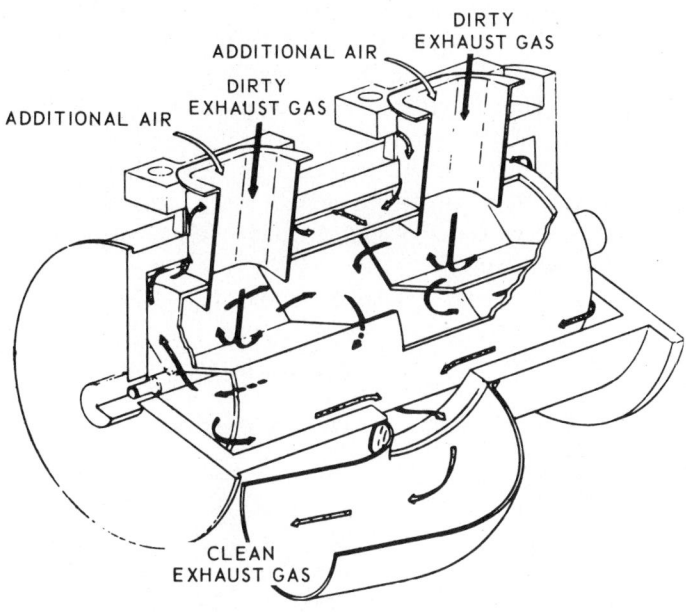

Fig. 12-35. One type of exhaust gas reactor.   (Curtiss-Wright)

Cooling of the Wankel engine is required primarily in the area where combustion and expansion take place (area around spark plugs). The concentration of heat in such a small area tends to cause distortion which, in turn, makes sealing of oil and fuel mixture difficult. Unless adequate cooling is provided, thermal fatigue or shock cracks may form in the spark plug hole area.

To aid in the dissipation of heat and reduce tendency toward distortion, special alloys have been developed for the rotor housing. In the Curtiss-Wright rotary engine, the coolant passages are designed so the coolant passes back and forth through the housing from one end cover to the other. In the area around the spark plug passages, the velocity of the coolant is increased to provide additional cooling needed in that area.

The cooling of the rotor presents a special problem. It is completely enclosed within the housing and does not have the benefit of the cooling provided by the crankcase in a reciprocating engine. In addition, the rotor turns at one third of the mainshaft speed.

While aluminum is lighter than cast iron and also has excellent heat conductivity, most manufacturers prefer cast iron for rotors. For actual cooling, lubricating oil is used. Basically the oil is circulated from the sump, Figs. 12-29 and 12-36, then through the rotor. After cooling the rotor, it passes through a filter and heat exchanger, through the hub of the rotor and returns to the sump. The inside is carefully designed, since it affects not only the cooling of the rotor but also engine balance. Excessive rotor temperatures will result in carbon formation on the interior of the rotor. This could cause an unbalanced condition, as well as further increase engine temperature.

The oil seals on the rotor bearings permit a measured amount of oil leakage to provide lubrication for the sides of the rotor.

Cooling of the engine housing is by water or coolant, which flows through passages in the housing. Water pumps are of the vane type, similar to those used on the piston type engine.

SEALS

Adequate sealing for the various areas of a rotary engine proved to be one of the most difficult problems in the early stages of development. Apex seal and side seals, Fig. 12-28, must be provided to prevent leakage from the working chambers.

The problem of designing effective seals for the apex of the rotor is complicated by the different forces which act on the seal. Forces include positive and negative centrifugal force, gas pressure, and friction against the working surfaces. In addition, the position of the apex seal varies. When at the major and minor axis, it is perpendicular to the working surface. At other positions of the rotor, the seal is at an angle other than 90 deg. to the surface.

Apex seals are straight and inserted in radius slots at each rotor apex. Side seals are curved to conform to the curvature of the rotor and are placed in grooves in the rotor sides. These seals are provided with interlocking ends to reduce leakage.

Various materials have been used for seals. Mazda, for example, originally used carbon for their apex seals, because of its lubricating qualities. Later, a sintered material impregnated with aluminum was adapted. Ceramic seals have also been used in some instances.

LUBRICATION

Since the lubricating oil in a rotary engine is not subject to blow-by and consequent contamination, periodic oil changes have been eliminated in most rotary engine service recommendations. However, additional oil occasionally is needed to replace that metered for lubricating the rotor seals and housing. With fast driving, use of a quart of oil every 1000 miles has been experienced.

Bearings of the output shaft are lubricated with oil from the sump in the normal manner, the oil is supplied under pressure from a gear type pump, Fig. 12-33. The oil supplied to the rotor seals keeps them from sticking. Originally, engine oil was mixed with the fuel, much in the same manner as oil and fuel are mixed for use in two cycle outboard engines. Subsequently, automatic metering of the lubricating oil from the rotor side was adapted. A third method of lubricating the rotor seals consisted of introducing oil into the intake ports in accordance with engine operating conditions.

SERVICING ROTARY ENGINES

While the Wankel type rotary engine is relatively new to the service field, servicing should not present any major problem. First of all, there are no valves to stick or burn. There are no piston rings, but there are seals on the rotor. These, however, should present no problem when replacement is necessary. It can be expected that the life of the seals should approximate that of piston rings.

The carburetor and ignition systems are readily accessible, which greatly simplifies tune-up work. The Weber and Solex carburetors are similar to those used on other imports. Ignition units also follow conventional design.

HONDA CVCC ENGINE

Reports on the Honda (Japan) compound vortex controlled combustion engine (CVCC) indicate that it meets proposed 1975 Federal exhaust gas emission requirements without any exhaust gas treatment device or catalytic converter. Because of these claims. this Honda engine is receiving considerable attention.

The structure of the CVCC engine is similar to a conventional four-stroke cycle engine except for an auxiliary combustion chamber around the spark plug and a small intake valve fitted into the cylinders.

A more complete analysis of the meaning of CVCC reveals that the "C" stands for Compound: stable coexistance of rich and lean mixtures. V is for Vortex: optimum vortex formation of the mixture before ignition. Controlled combustion is control of the burning rate for varying operating loads.

In order to burn the fuel efficiently and produce exhaust emissions which meet Federal requirements, the CVCC engine is designed to lower peak combustion temperatures as much as possible to reduce nitrogen oxides in the exhaust. At the same time, it is necessary to keep the temperature high enough to promote an oxidizing reaction for a long duration, for reducing hydrocarbons. It is also designed to supply an extremely lean mixture. to provide a satisfactory oxidizing atmosphere for reducing carbon monoxide.

The system involves the mixing of air and fuel in different densities in different areas of the combustion chamber:

1. During intake, Fig. 12-36, a large amount of lean mixture and a small amount of rich mixture which makes the overall mixture lean are supplied through the main auxiliary intake valves, respectively.

2. At the end of the compression stroke, Fig. 12-36, there is a

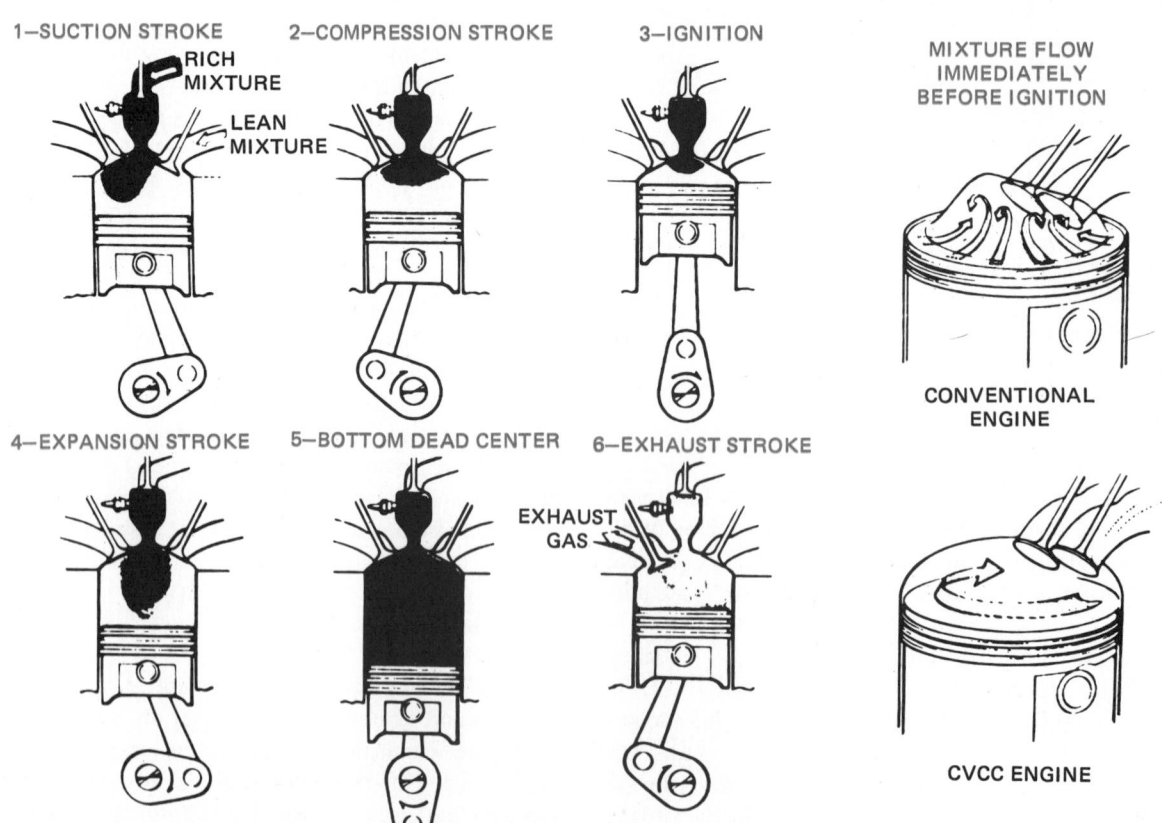

Fig. 12-36. Left. Cycle of events of Honda CVCC engine. Right. Comparison of mixture flow in conventional engine (above) and CVCC engine (below).

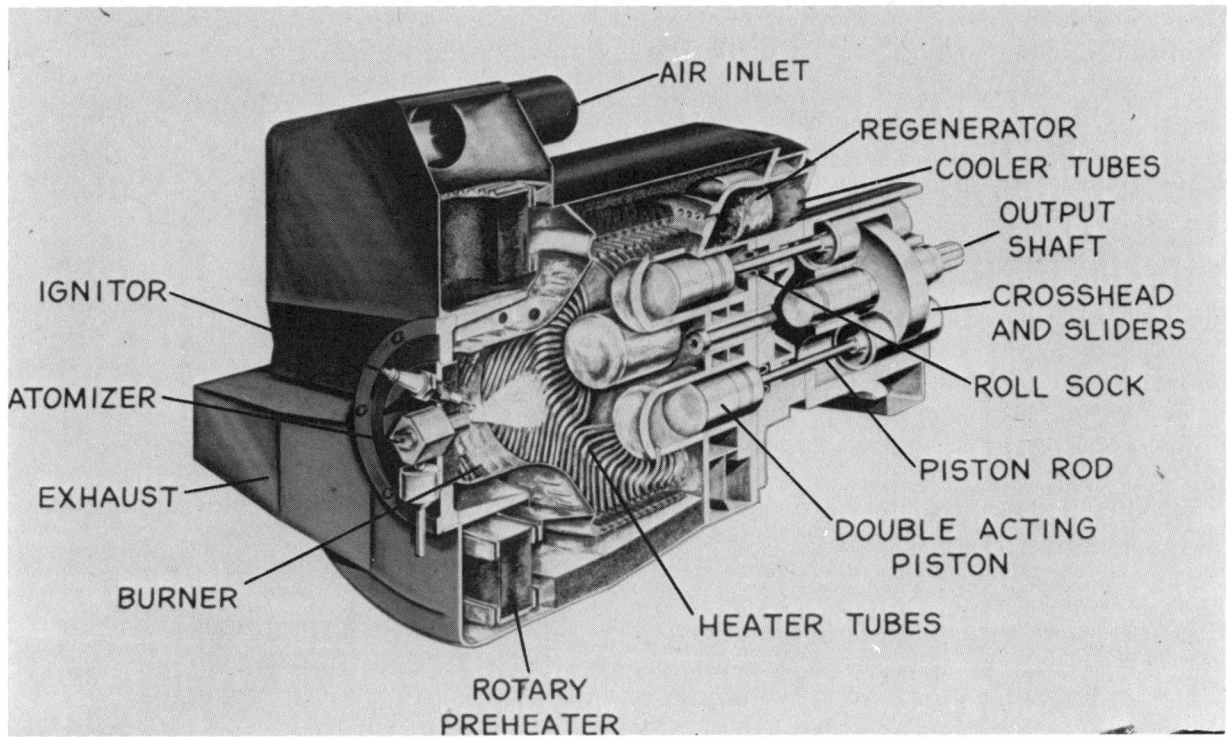

Fig. 12-37. Various parts of Ford's experimental Stirling engine are indicated. This is a continuous combustion engine in which heat expands a fluid to drive pistons and develop power.   (Ford Motor Co.)

rich air-fuel mixture around the spark plug to insure good ignition.

3. At the same time, there is a moderate air-fuel mixture in the vicinity of the outlet of the auxiliary combustion chamber to ensure combustion of the lean mixture in the main combustion chamber. The lean mixture burns relatively slowly, and the temperature of the burned gas is kept relatively high for a long duration.

As the result of rich and lean mixtures throughout the combustion chamber, combustion and temperature are controlled, and exhaust emissions remain within limits specified by the Federal Government.

No mention is made of engine efficiency or fuel economy in reports available on the Honda CVCC engine.

STIRLING ENGINE

Experimental research on the Stirling external continuous combustion engine, Fig. 12-37, by the Ford Motor Company has demonstrated that the engine features low exhaust emissions and gives promise of fuel economy improvements. Water is not used in the Stirling engine. Instead, fluids such as Freon, hydrogen or helium are used.

In the Stirling engine, heat from an external source is transmitted to the working fluid, which is sealed in the engine. The heat expands the fluid to drive the pistons and develop power. There is no combustion within the cylinder. The expansion of the fluid drives the pistons through a "swashplate" (crosshead and slider) mechanism. After driving the pistons, the vapor is cooled.

GENERAL MOTORS STEAM CAR

A passenger car powered by a steam engine is among the many experimental vehicles being developed by General Motors Corporation. The engine is known as the SE-101. The entire steam plant includes the expander (engine), combustion chamber, steam generator and condenser. Quick starting is a feature and only 30 to 45 seconds is required to produce sufficient steam to propel the vehicle.

As soon as the "ignition" key is turned on, the electric pump fills the steam boiler (generator) with water. When the desired level is reached, a sensor engages an electric motor that powers the combustion blower and fuel pump. Fuel is sprayed into the combustion chamber, where it is ignited by a spark plug. Heat from the burner converts the water into high pressure vapor, and expansion of the vapor drives the pistons in the expander. After the steam has driven the pistons it is exhausted into the condenser for recovery of the water.

The expander has four cylinders having 101 cu. in. displacement and developing 160 hp. Valves are poppet type instead of slide valves customarily used in steam engines.

RANKINE ENGINE

The Rankine cycle engine is an external combustion engine. In operation, it transfers heat from the combustion of fuel to a closed system containing a condensable working fluid. The fluid is vaporized by combustion of the fuel, then it is superheated in a boiler and expanded to produce power. Following the power cycle, the vapor is condensed for reuse.

DODGE MCA-JET ENGINE HAS THIRD VALVE

An engine designed for added fuel economy and reduced exhaust emissions has been installed in recent model Dodge Colts and Challengers. This engine is called the "MCA-Jet" engine because it features a third valve in each combustion chamber that adds a high velocity jet of air-fuel mixture to the existing mixture.

In a conventional engine, the air-fuel mixture enters the combustion chamber by way of the intake valve port. See the white arrows in Fig. 12-38. During the burning process, the flame front moves evenly outward from the spark plug and some of the air-fuel mixture farthest from the plug does not burn.

The the MCA-Jet engine, Fig. 12-38, the third valve is designed and timed to provide a swirling action (see black arrow) to the air-fuel mixture in the combustion chamber. This speeds up the combustion process so that more of the air-fuel charge is burned and, in addition, a leaner mixture is permitted. In that way, fuel economy is improved and hydrocarbons, carbon monoxide and oxides of nitrogen are reduced.

The MCA-Jet engine is equipped with an exhaust gas recirculation system. It does not require a catalytic converter.

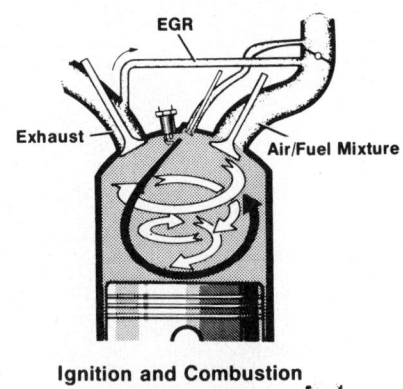

Induction and Compression

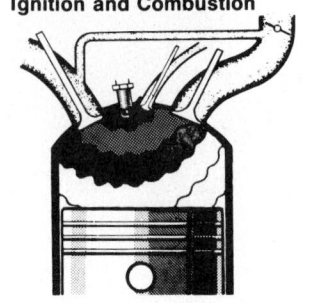

Ignition and Combustion

Fig. 12-38. Third valve in Dodge MCA-Jet engine adds jet of air-fuel mixture to create swirling, more combustible mixture.

REVIEW QUESTIONS – OTHER ENGINES

1. Carburetors are used on diesel engines. True or False?
2. Diesel fuel pumps are usually driven by double or triple V belts. Yes or No?
3. Name two purposes of a supercharger on a two cycle diesel engine.
4. Name five alterations that are often made to passenger car engines to adapt them for use in light trucks.
5. All farm tractor engines are quite similar to automobile engines. True or False?
6. Inboard marine engines are made as light as possible. Yes or No?
7. Outboard engines are cooled by:
   a. Air.
   b. Water.
   c. Either.
8. Small industrial engines are usually air-cooled. True or False?
9. Give three reasons for poor idling of racing engines.
10. Free piston engines are related to:
    a. Diesel engines.
    b. Gasoline engines.
    c. Neither.
11. Do free piston engines have a variable compression ratio?
12. Will a free piston engine produce useful power without the aid of a turbine?
13. Can a turbine engine without gearing be used to propel a vehicle?
14. Describe the operating principle of a jet engine.
15. Name four problems to be overcome in the design of a successful rotary engine.
16. How many general types of combustion chambers are used in diesel engines?
    a. Four.
    b. Five.
    c. Two.
    d. Six.
17. In the M-system, the combustion chamber is formed in what part of the engine?
    a. Cylinder head.
    b. Piston.
    c. Cylinder bore.
18. Is special fuel required for the rotary combustion engine used in the Mazda car?
19. The Wankel engine requires more space than a piston engine of the same power. True or False?
20. The Wankel engine is limited to two rotors. Yes or No?
21. What is the shape of the rotor used in the Wankel engine?
    a. Round.
    b. Triangular.
    c. Square.
    d. Elliptical.
22. There are _____ power impulses in a rotary combustion engine for each revolution of the rotor.
23. Fuel injection cannot be used in a Wankel rotary engine. True or False?
24. In general, the hydrocarbon emission level of the Wankel engine is higher than a piston type engine of the same general size. Yes or No?

ENGINE RECONDITIONING

The first step in any job of reconditioning is to clean the assembly. There are many different methods of cleaning, and the one selected depends on the part and the type of dirt that is to be removed.

When overhauling an engine, many shops will remove the engine from the chassis, then steam clean the entire unit with a steam detergent solution. Steam cleaning can be done with a gun type cleaner or in a tank type cleaner, Fig. 13-1.

Cleaning the engine before disassembly will make subsequent disassembly easier. In addition, cleaning will reveal defects and conditions that will help in diagnosing the cause of the trouble and aid in preventing its early reoccurrence.

Following the removal of the outer dirt and oil, the pan, valve covers and cylinder head are removed. These parts can be cleaned by a gun or one of the other cleaning methods: tank, jet or ultrasonic, to remove accumulations of sludge, carbon and other dirt.

CLEANING PROCESSES

A process used extensively for cleaning automotive parts is called "the hot tank method." Briefly, this method utilizes a tank filled with a detergent solution, which is agitated to hasten the cleaning process. The temperature of the solution varies with the type of detergent and particular metal to be cleaned. In general, parts made of aluminum are cleaned with special detergents designed for that purpose, and at a lower temperature than is used for steel and iron.

Another efficient parts cleaning technique is called the jet method. The cleaning unit has two compartments: the lower chamber holds the solution; the upper chamber provides a revolving platform for the work. A series of jets spray detergent on the slowly revolving part in the upper compartment. Each jet delivers detergent at an extremely high velocity, reaching the work from all sides, top and bottom. Each jet delivers approximately three gallons of hot detergent solution per minute.

Cleaning parts with glass beads is another method used extensively for cleaning automotive parts, Fig. 13-2. Compressed air is the propelling agent which blasts the beads against the part to be cleaned. Both wet and dry blast machines are available. In general, this method is used to clean individual parts rather than complete assemblies.

Glass beads clean the part down to the base metal, leaving no film of detergent. The beads are round in shape and not abrasive. They do not imbed themselves in the surface to be cleaned. Being round, the beads leave a uniform indented surface imparting strength by compressing the metal being cleaned. This method is used extensively in cleaning pistons, valves and connecting rods.

Parts cleaning by use of ultrasonic energy is a more recent advance. Ultrasonic sound differs from normal sound only in that its pitch is above the human hearing range. When high frequency mechanical vibrations are introduced into a liquid, cavitation (extreme agitation) occurs.

Fig. 13-1. Removing a diesel cylinder head from a tank type cleaner.

Fig. 13-2. Cleaning parts in a glass bead type cleaner.
(Van Norman Machine Co.)

Every liquid contains thousands of nuclei in the form of bubbles which range in size from those which are visible to those which are submicroscopic. Under ultrasonic irradiation, these bubbles grow and then collapse. They are said to explode inwardly (implode), at which time pressures up to 15,000 psi and temperatures up to 700 deg. F are created. The thousands

of implosions each second act as countless scrubbing fingers and produce an excellent cleaning action.

The ultrasonic cleaner consists basically of three parts:

1. A generator which is used to convert the line current into high frequency electrical energy.
2. A transducer which converts this electrical energy into mechanical energy of the same frequency.
3. A tank containing a liquid through which the ultrasonic energy is passed, and which produces the cavitation that blasts away any dirt on parts placed in the solution.

Ultrasonic cleaners are used largely in production engine rebuilders, shops servicing diesel engine injectors and pumps and in large jobber machine shops.

Many small auto repair shops use a simple tank with a power sprayer, Fig. 13-3, to clean parts removed from the vehicle to be repaired or replaced. Cleaning parts with a brush and a pan of gasoline is a big fire hazard. In addition, leaded gasoline always carries the threat of lead poisoning if used for cleaning on a regular basis. Instead, use a solvent designed for the cleaning job at hand.

Before cleaning a cylinder block or cylinder head, remove the core hole plugs. This will permit the cleaning solution to flush out any accumulation of rust and scale.

EXAMINATION AND MEASUREMENT

After cleaning, it is possible to make a careful examination of the individual parts, along with accurate measurement, to spot defects, determine the extent and type of wear and pinpoint what caused the worn condition.

The starting point for actual engine reconditioning is the cylinder block, because practically all other parts are fitted to it. If the block is damaged in any way, it must be repaired or replaced. There are many things to be inspected and checked.

The engine block or head may be cracked, warped, worn or otherwise damaged. The damage may affect the operation of the crankshaft, pistons, rings, bearings, camshaft, cooling, lubrication, etc. The extent of the damage will determine whether or not the block is repairable. There are many methods of changing the condition or dimensions of metal parts. Several different methods may be used to restore an engine to good condition.

METAL PARTS RESTORATION

If you want to reduce the size of a part, you can cut, grind or etch the metal away. Or, in some cases, you can shrink it with freezing, or pressure.

If you want to increase the size of a part, you can add metal by soldering, brazing, welding, plating or spraying. In some cases, you can expand it by heat and pressure.

In many cases, then, you can compensate for wear by expanding or shrinking the metal. Or, you can add metal to the worn surface to restore it to usefulness. In adding metal, you have a wide choice of materials, each of which possesses certain characteristics which may be desired for the particular purpose.

If you want a soft surface, use tin or bronze. If you want a

Fig. 13-3. Cleaning small parts in a tank with a power spray unit.

hard surface add steel of any desired degree of hardness by welding. Another method of adding a hard surface is by the electroplating process, such as the chrome surface on a piston ring.

In engine repair work, there is a way to add material to, or increase the size of, one part without disturbing the mating part. An example of this is to spray molten metal on a worn crankshaft journal to avoid installation of undersize bearings. Or, you may expand a piston with heat or pressure, or both, and reinstall it in the mating cylinder.

In other cases, remove metal from one part, and install an oversize or undersize mating part, in order to obtain the proper clearance. Examples of this are rebored cylinders and oversize pistons or a reground crankshaft and an undersize bearing.

In still other cases, metal is removed for the sole purpose of obtaining better surface fit of two mating parts. An example of this is the correction of a warped cylinder head by surface grinding to restore a flat and true surface.

For practically all of these operations, special tools and equipment are available. These tools will do a satisfactory job if they are properly handled. Obviously, it will be essential to measure accurately, adjust carefully and operate in accordance with the manufacturers' instructions.

Fig. 13-5. Special Helicoil thread insert restores damaged threads in holes.

welding, brazing, iron welding, Fig. 13-6, or by one of the patented processes such as the Seal Lock process. Many mechanics prefer electric welding to gas welding. Working with lower temperatures in the area of repair is not so apt to produce warpage of the cylinder block.

Fig. 13-6. Typical repair to cracked water jacket.

Fig. 13-4. Leaking plugs are punched or cut out, and new expanding plugs installed.

CRACKED CYLINDER BLOCKS

When the cylinder block and head are clean, make a visual inspection for cracks or serious damage. Include a close look at the condition of the core hole of water freeze plugs, Fig. 13-4. If signs of leakage or corrosion are found, replace the plugs.

Threads on studs and in stud holes must be checked for condition. Install new studs if needed. If a stud hole in the casting has worn or damaged threads, they can be repaired by means of special inserts, Fig. 13-5. This thread check is particularly important in the case of aluminum blocks, or heads, as careless tightening often overstresses the metal and the threads are deformed or stripped.

If the block was cracked by water freezing in the water jacket, the crack can usually be closed satisfactorily by copper

Fig. 13-7. Peening over special keys which tie sides of crack together. (Seal Lock Co.)

In the case of the Seal Lock process the sides of the crack are tied together by driving special keys or locking pins into previously drilled holes, Fig. 13-7. Then the surface is carefully peened and further sealed.

In cases where a panel or section of the water jacket is broken out, it is sometimes possible to shape a metal plate into a patch corresponding to and slightly larger than the opening. The patch is then attached to the block by means of multiple screws around the edge of the patch. Holes are drilled and tapped in the block for the screws.

In the case of small cracks (depending upon location), iron cement can be used for a quick repair. If the crack is in a thin, large section which is readily accessible, it may be possible to tin the cast iron and solder the crack. It is very difficult to solder aluminum.

The choice of the repair method will depend upon the size of the damaged area, the location of the crack, the cost of a new block as well as the value of the automobile.

INTERNAL CRACKS

At times, the cylinder wall will crack through to the valve port as shown in Fig. 13-8. Or, the crack may be in the cylinder head of overhead valve engines. Usually, a cracked cylinder head is replaced, rather than repaired.

Fig. 13-8. A cracked valve seat may extend into the cylinder bore or water jacket of block or head.

Fig. 13-9. Cylinder block cracks between valve port and cylinder wall may be closed with a peening hammer. In more serious cases, welding or plugging may need to be employed.

If the crack is between the cylinder wall and the valve seat, the repair will need to be made with extra care. One method is welding. If the crack is small, it may be possible to peen it shut with a power peening hammer, Fig. 13-9.

Still another method of crack repair consists of drilling holes at the ends of the crack, threading the holes and inserting threaded plugs or screws. Another hole is then drilled partly in the block and partly in the plug or screw. A second plug or screw is then inserted and this process continued to the other end of the crack.

After the screws are all installed and the crack sealed, the surface is machined smooth. Then the cylinder bore and valve seat are resurfaced. If the valve seat is badly damaged, the block can be counterbored and a new valve seat inserted. Sometimes these seats are screwed into place. In other cases, they are pressed in place and the edge of the metal block peened over slightly to hold them in place.

In either case, they must be a tight fit, so that metal-to-metal contact will offer a full and free flow of heat from the insert to the block and cooling water.

The same need for care is true in the case of serious cylinder damage, where the repair consists of reboring the cylinder and inserting a sleeve. The contact between sleeve and cylinder must be full and complete.

In repairs of this nature, keep in mind that the heat and pressure in the cylinder will cause expansion, contraction and possibly warpage of the cylinder wall, valve seat and cylinder block surface as soon as the engine is operated. Therefore, the work must be done as carefully and accurately as possible, with no great amount of excess metal added at any point to aggravate distortion.

LOCATING CRACKS

Cracks in cylinder heads and blocks are often so fine that they are difficult to see with the naked eye. Many shops use a strong magnifying glass to aid in locating such cracks. A better procedure is to use special dyes or chemicals which, when painted on the surface of the metal, will quickly make the cracks visible. There also are several magnetic and electrical methods specifically designed to reveal the location of the cracks. See Fig. 13-10.

CORROSION

In the case of aluminum engine blocks or heads, the visual inspection should be particularly thorough to detect any possible corrosion of the metal. Sometimes, corrosion of the metal around the water circulation openings will occur from chemicals in the cooling water, particularly in localities where the water supply contains more than the usual amount of chloride.

Corrosion from electrolytic action also may occur, because of the dissimilar metals found in the engine cooling system. If corrosion is serious enough, it may interfere with the seal of the gasket between head and block. This would permit coolant to enter the combustion chamber, or allow compression pressure to escape to the water jacket.

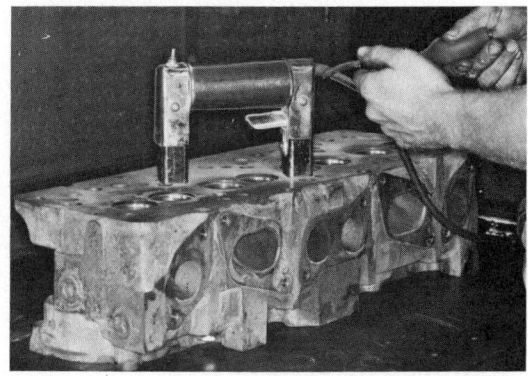

Fig. 13-10. Checking for cracks in a cylinder head with special equipment.

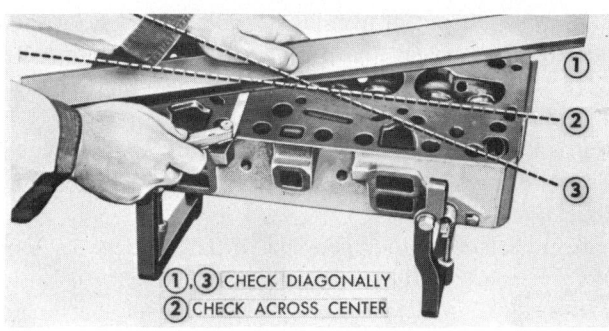

① ③ CHECK DIAGONALLY
② CHECK ACROSS CENTER

Fig. 13-11. Cylinder head and cylinder block surfaces may be checked for distortion in same manner.

Fig. 13-12. Equipment used to resurface blocks and cylinder heads.

CYLINDER HEAD WARPAGE

Cylinder heads often become warped. Sometimes the cylinder block mating surface also warps. These surfaces should be true within .003 in. in any 6 in., or within .006 in.

overall. Measurement is made by means of a steel straightedge and feeler gauge strips as shown in Fig. 13-11. If the surfaces are warped or otherwise damaged, they can be reconditioned on special equipment, as shown in Fig. 13-12.

CYLINDER RECONDITIONING

Cylinder wall wear and the reasons for it were described previously in this text. They wear in tapered form, and also out-of-round. When wear exceeds specifications, the cylinders require machining to restore the wall surface. Maximum wear limitations are .005 in. out-of-round and .010 in. taper.

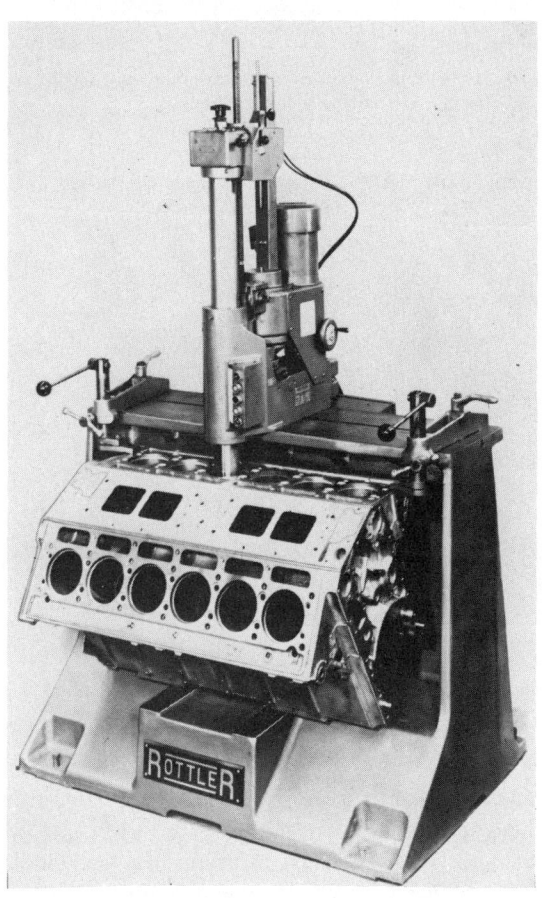

Fig. 13-13. Cylinder bore reconditioning equipment is shown set up for reboring a V-12 engine block.

Either boring bars, Fig. 13-13, or hones, Fig. 13-14, may be used to recondition the cylinder walls. In many shops, the preferred method is to first use a boring bar, Fig. 13-13, and then finish with a hone, Fig. 13-18. Another method is to first use a hone with coarse stones and then finish with stones of about No. 180-220 grit, making sure the stones are clean and sharp.

Bear in mind that many manufacturers of piston rings claim their rings give satisfactory service in cylinders up to .005 in. out-of-round and .010 in. taper.

Before any cylinder is refinished, all main bearing caps must be in place and tightened to the specified torque. Otherwise

Fig. 13-14. Hone type cylinder reconditioning equipment used in engine rebuilding shop.

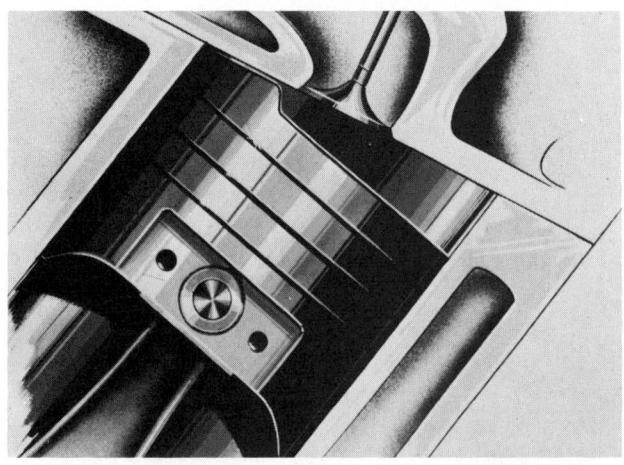

Fig. 13-15. Here a flat head is used with an angle block, and combustion chamber is mostly in piston head.

the crankshaft bearing bores may become distorted from the refinishing operation.

Precautions must be taken to insure that the cylinders be refinished parallel to each other and at right angles to the crankshaft. Special care must be taken when setting up the reconditioning equipment, particularly when the top of the cylinder block is not at right angles to the cylinder bore, Fig. 13-15.

When the cylinder block is formed with an angular surface, special adapters must be used with the cylinder boring bar so that the cylinder will be reconditioned parallel to its original center line.

When dry honing, a vacuum cleaning device is provided. However, regardless of the method used in reconditioning the cylinders, the block must be thoroughly cleaned to remove all cutting and abrasives. Some machinists advise scrubbing with soap and water. Others advise first wiping down the walls with fine crocus cloth.

The job of cleaning a cylinder block after reconditioning is not easy. Many jobs which were mechanically correct have been ruined because some abrasives and dirt remained in the cylinders. All oil holes in the block must be cleaned. Core plugs should be removed so the water jacket can be cleaned. The final cleaning is usually done on specialized cleaning equipment, Fig. 13-16.

When reconditioning cylinders, it is best to find out what sizes are available in oversize pistons before starting the operation. Otherwise, the cylinders may be bored to a size for which stock pistons are not available. Then the pistons would have to be reground to the desired size.

CYLINDER WALL REPAIRS

Occasionally, a cylinder wall will be badly damaged, so much metal must be removed in the reconditioning process that the cylinder walls would be severely weakened. Because of variations in engine construction, it is impossible to give any figure on the amount of metal that could be removed without weakening the cylinder wall. However, you can govern this by the size of the replacement pistons that are available.

If damage is so deep that reboring to fit the largest oversize piston is not sufficient to remove the score marks, it is still possible to recondition the cylinder by installation of a cylinder sleeve.

The procedure is to rebore the cylinder until the score marks are removed. Then a sleeve is prepared with an outside diameter .0001 in. larger than the diameter of the rebored cylinder, and with an inside diameter slightly smaller than required for the available piston. The sleeve is shrunk in dry ice to reduce its diameter, then it is pressed into the cylinder with an hydraulic press. Finally, the cylinder is finish honed, remove any wrinkles that may have formed when the sleeve was pressed in position.

Another method of reconditioning a cylinder which has been badly scored, and which is used occasionally on industrial engines or when it is impossible to obtain a replacement cylinder block, is to cut a deep groove in the cylinder wall to remove the score. This can be done on a milling machine. A strip of metal (same as cylinder) is then machined to fit the prepared groove. After being packed in dry ice, it is pressed in place in the groove.

Fig. 13-16. One type of internal engine cleaning equipment is demonstrated.

CYLINDER WALL SURFACE

After reconditioning, check the cylinder walls with a dial type cylinder gauge to make sure of roundness and straightness. Then hone cylinder sleeves after installation to remove any wrinkles that may have been formed during installation process.

When new rings are installed in cylinders which have not been reconditioned, the hone should be run through the cylinder a few times to break the glaze formed on the cylinder wall through normal operation.

The desired cylinder wall finish is not a mirror surface. Since this type surface does not produce the best lubricating conditions for the piston rings. The proper finish should have a pattern of diagonal crosshatch scratches, but no longitudinal scratches, Fig. 13-17. This pattern can be obtained with a few strokes of the hone, pulling it up and down in the bore while the hone is rotating. If a hone is not available, the pattern can be made by using abrasive cloth or paper of the proper grit.

Fine scratches in surface of cylinder wall permit more rapid seating of rings. This is highly desirable since the fine scratches retain a film of oil to provide lubrication for ring surface and prevent scoring.

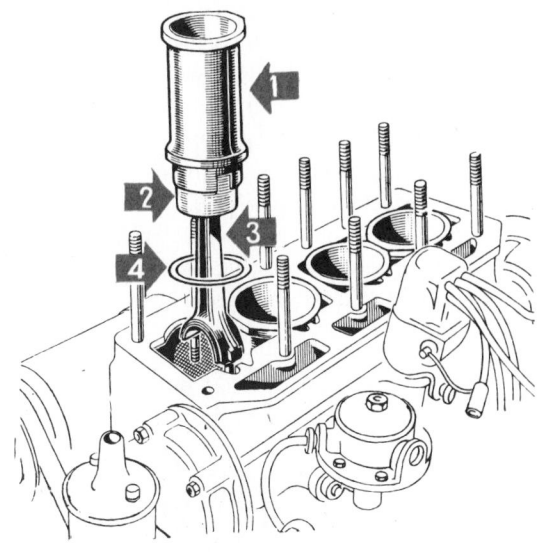

Fig. 13-19. Wet-type sleeve used by Renault: 1—Sleeve. 2—Piston. 3—Connecting rod. 4—Copper sealing ring.

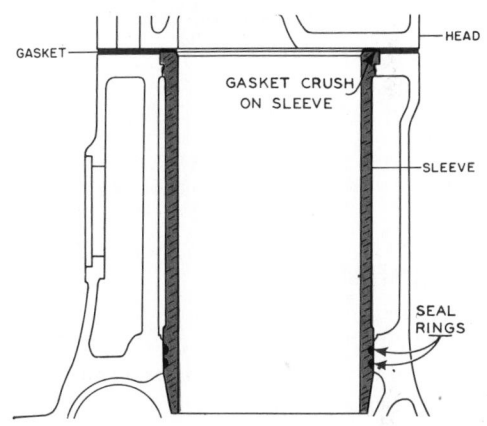

Fig. 13-20. Rubber seals are used at bottom of sleeves in Oliver tractor engine.

Fig. 13-17. Note pattern of cutting marks left by refinishing hone.

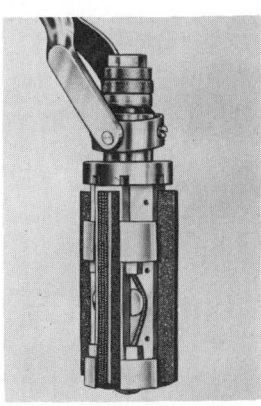

Fig. 13-18. Typical cylinder hone.

WET TYPE CYLINDER SLEEVES

Passenger car engines built in the U.S.A. usually have the cylinders bored directly in the engine block. Some truck, tractor and industrial engines use the wet type of cylinder sleeve. A wet sleeve is in the form of a barrel or sleeve which is inserted in the block in contact with the cooling water. Several European passenger car engines have liners or inserted sleeves, Fig. 13-19.

In the wet-sleeve type of construction, each cylinder barrel is a separate sleeve inserted in the block. Each sleeve is sealed at the bottom of the water compartment by means of a copper or rubber gasket, Fig. 13-20. The cylinder head gasket, of course, provides a seal at the top end of the sleeve.

In construction, the engine coolant circulates directly around and in contact with the sleeve. Since the thickness of the sleeve or cylinder wall is uniform, cylinder wall distortion is minimized.

Another advantage of cylinder sleeves is the ease and comparative low cost of replacing a damaged cylinder bore. These sleeves quickly pull out, Fig. 13-21, and a new sleeve is slipped in place.

The advantages of wet-sleeve construction apply to most air-cooled automobile engines, since the cylinders are usually in the form of sleeves or barrels. The Volkswagen is a good example of this type of construction. Each cylinder is simply a tube with cooling fins on the outside. One end of this tube fits into a recess in the crankcase; the other end fits into a recess in the cylinder head.

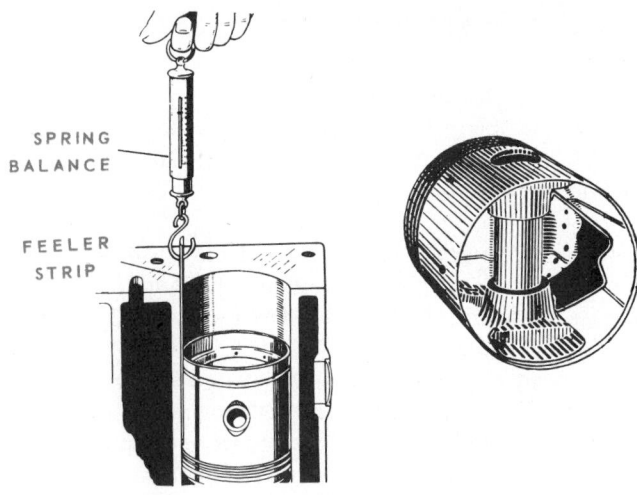

Fig. 13-22. Left. Checking piston clearance in cylinder. Pull required should be 4 to 5 lb. Right. Piston expander installed inside piston pushes outward on piston pin bosses.

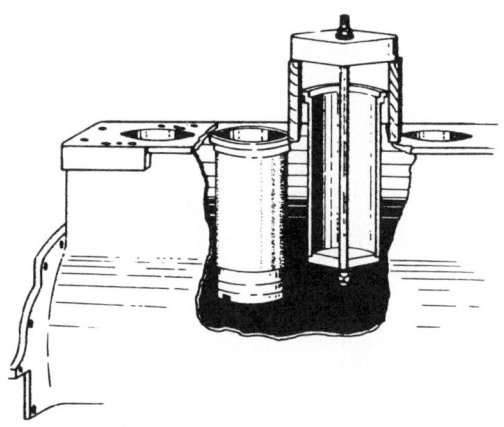

Fig. 13-21. Method of removing wet-type sleeves..

PISTON CLEARANCE

There is no set rule on the amount of clearance to be provided between the piston and cylinder. Much depends upon the design of the engine cylinders and the cooling system, the piston design and material and, to a certain extent on the service conditions under which the engine operates.

For example, if a passenger car engine will be driven mostly at slow speeds in city traffic, the pistons can be fitted with a minimum of clearance. If the engine is in a fire department pumper, it may be required to stand in one spot and run at full power for hours at a time. Such service would generate a great amount of heat in the cylinders and cause the pistons to expand considerably. Therefore, the internal engine parts would be fitted with maximum clearances.

In general, it is customary to fit solid skirt cast iron pistons to about .00075 to .001 in. per inch of piston diameter. A four inch piston would be .003 to .004 in. smaller than the cylinder. Some aluminum pistons can be fitted more closely, but much depends upon the design of the piston. Instructions given by the manufacturer should be obtained and followed.

Surface treatment will also have a bearing on the piston clearance. Some pistons are tin plated, others have an oxide coating or some other surface treatment. Sometimes the surface is serrated or interrupted to provide minute pockets for the retention of oil. These treatments are intended to lessen the tendency of the piston to stick or score, particularly during the time it is seating to the wall.

CLEARANCE MEASUREMENT

The clearance between cylinder and piston is measured in most cases by means of a feeler gauge inserted between piston and cylinder. See Fig. 13-22. The strip of feeler gauge should be about 1/2 in. wide and long enough to extend the full length of the cylinder. This strip with a thickness equal to the desired clearance should be placed on the thrust side of the skirt. Four to five pounds pull as measured on a spring scale should be required to remove the feeler.

The clearance can also be measured by subtracting the maximum diameter of the piston from the minimum diameter of the cylinder, as measured with inside and outside micrometers. In this case, measurement must be made at several points in the cylinder and on the piston. All piston clearance recommendations are made for use with the temperature at approximately 70 deg. F.

As pistons wear, or if they become overheated, the skirt is liable to collapse, or become smaller in diameter. When this happens the piston will "slap" in the cylinder. Also, it will allow an excessive amount of oil to pass up to the rings. This, of course, places an undue load on the oil control rings and may result in oil pumping.

CYLINDER WEAR

The greatest amount of wear in a cylinder occurs at the top of the travel of the piston rings. The difference between the diameter at that point and the diameter of the cylinder at the lower end is known as the taper. Cylinders also wear most in the area where the greatest thrust of the piston occurs. The difference between that diameter and the fore-and-aft diameter is known as out-of-round. See Fig. 13-23.

In passenger car engines, maximum taper, or wear limit is usually specified as 0.010 in. and the out-of-round as 0.005 in. Both of these measurements can be made with the aid of

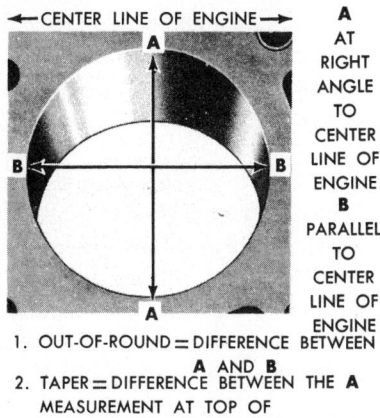

← CENTER LINE OF ENGINE →

A AT RIGHT ANGLE TO CENTER LINE OF ENGINE

B PARALLEL TO CENTER LINE OF ENGINE

1. OUT-OF-ROUND = DIFFERENCE BETWEEN **A** AND **B**
2. TAPER = DIFFERENCE BETWEEN THE **A** MEASUREMENT AT TOP OF CYLINDER BORE AND THE **A** MEASUREMENT AT BOTTOM OF CYLINDER BORE

Fig. 13-23. Measurements to be taken when checking cylinder taper and out-of-round.

inside and outside micrometers. Or, if preferred, a dial gauge can be used. Using a dial gauge requires less skill than using a micrometer.

PISTON RESIZING

There are several ways to expand or resize the pistons. One method consists of heating the piston, and expanding it with special equipment made for the purpose. Another method requires special equipment for "peening" the inside of the piston with steel shot. This procedure compacts the metal on the inside, and causes it to expand on the outside. Electric and pneumatic peening hammers are made for the purpose.

Various types of equipment, or tools, are available for "knurling" the piston skirt. This method raises the surface of the metal in ridges or patterns along the path of the knurling, increasing the diameter of the piston. An additional claim made for this method is that it creates "pockets" on the piston surface, which gather and retain a film of oil to assist in sealing and lubricating.

PISTON EXPANDERS

Another procedure is to install piston expanders inside the pistons. There are a number of these devices on the market. They vary in design, but usually consist of a steel spring strut that is compressed and installed in a way that exerts internal pressure on the split piston skirt. See Fig. 13-22.

Piston expanders are often effective for collapsed pistons, but they should not be installed in only one of the cylinders. If used, they should be installed in all pistons of a reconditioned engine because of balance requirements. The expanders are made as light in weight as possible, but most automobile engines have pistons matched in weight at the factory to a few hundredths of an ounce. Any replacement pistons should also be carefully matched for weight with the other pistons; otherwise engine vibration may occur.

Buick 231 cu. in. (3.8 litre) V-6 engine produces 105 hp at 3400 rpm.

GASKET INSTALLATION

Gaskets should never be used the second time. This applies to all types of gaskets. Having been compressed between two surfaces, the old gasket conforms to all the microscopic irregularities and, if reinstalled, would invariably leak.

Before installing a gasket, the mating surfaces of the parts, such as the cylinder head and cylinder block must be carefully cleaned and checked for warpage.

Bolt holes should be chamfered, and the area around stud and bolt holes should be smoothed with a file. Often, the metal has been pulled up by the force of tightening the bolts or nuts. Always be sure the correct gasket is being used for the particular installation. See Figs. 13-24 and 13-25.

CAUTION: Gaskets should always be stored flat and in their original carton. They should never be hung on hooks.

All threads must be clean and undamaged. The nuts must spin on easily. A thread compound should be used, particularly on aluminum heads and cylinder blocks. This will prevent leakage in those cases where the bolt holes enter the water jacket.

Be sure to install the specified bolt in the correct hole as bolt holes frequently vary in depth. A torque wrench should be used to tighten bolts and nuts to specified torque, Fig. 13-26. They should be tightened in the correct sequence to prevent distortion of parts. If the manufacturer's diagram of the tightening sequence is not available, start tightening at the center of the head and work progressively from side to side and toward the ends of the head, Fig. 13-19.

The usual procedure is to tighten the bolts in three successive steps. For example, tighten first to 25 ft. lb., then 50 ft. lb. and, finally, 95 ft. lb.

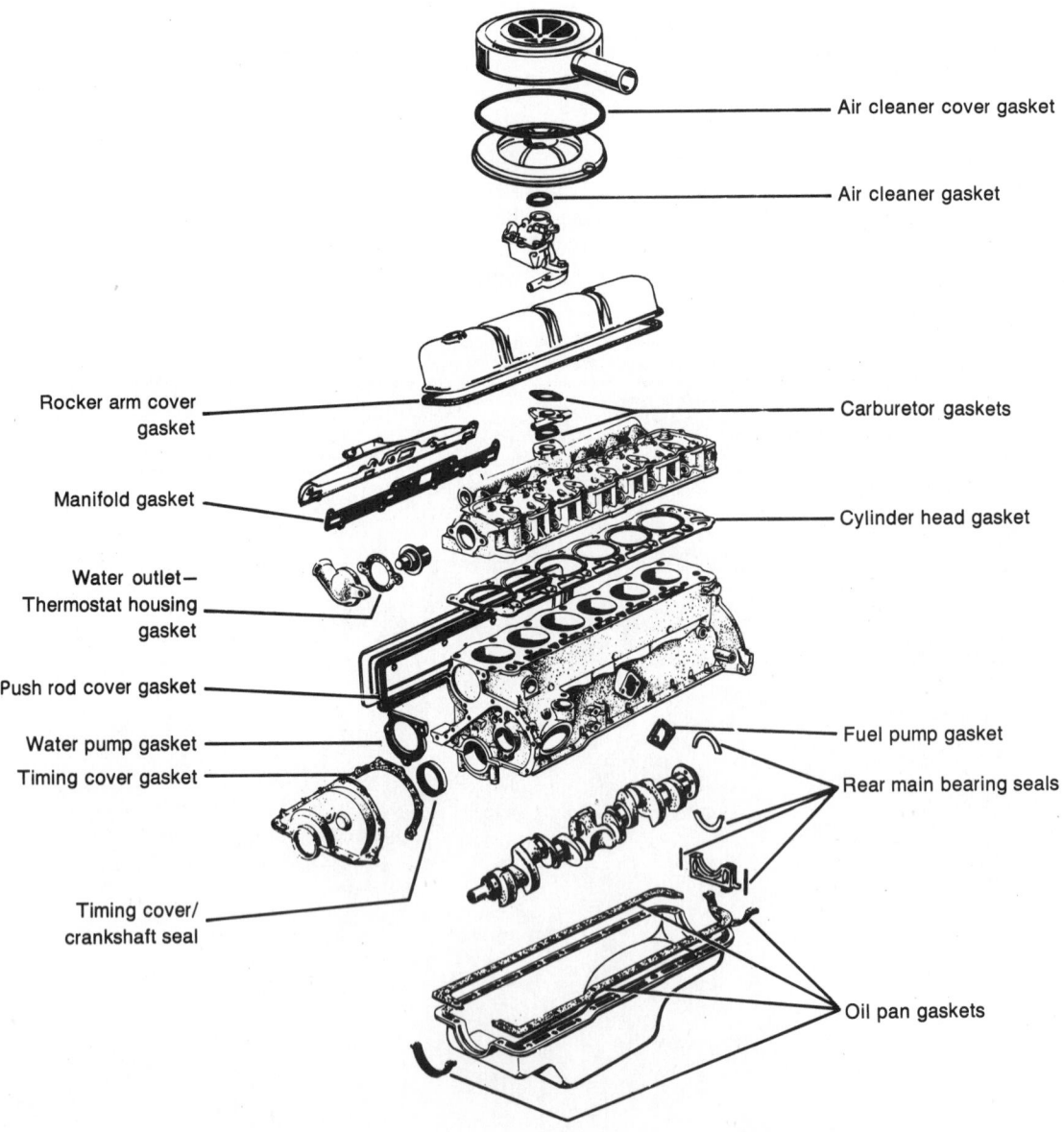

Air cleaner cover gasket

Air cleaner gasket

Rocker arm cover gasket

Carburetor gaskets

Manifold gasket

Cylinder head gasket

Water outlet— Thermostat housing gasket

Push rod cover gasket

Water pump gasket

Fuel pump gasket

Timing cover gasket

Rear main bearing seals

Timing cover/ crankshaft seal

Oil pan gaskets

Fig. 13-24. Gasket and seal locations on a typical six cylinder engine. (McCord Corp.)

BALANCING ENGINES

With the increase in engine speeds, it becomes increasingly important that all rotating and reciprocating parts of the engine are precision balanced. Unless this is done, wear is accelerated and engine life materially reduced. In addition, operating costs increase.

Unbalance causes increased bearing loads and greater vibration, both of which absorb power and cause wear and fatigue of parts. In addition, the vibration will cause alternator brackets and other accessory brackets to crack. Driver fatigue also increases.

With precision balancing of engine parts, bearing life has been increased in excess of 200 percent, and horsepower and acceleration have been improved nearly 15 percent. While increased top speed is what interests the speed enthusiast, it is

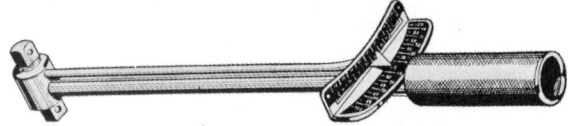

Fig. 13-26. Typical torque wrench. All bolts and nuts must be tightened to the specified torque.

the longer engine life and reduce maintenance cost which interest the truck and fleet operator.

Manufacturers producing parts for their engines specify certain tolerances for the various parts. For example, the weight specification for a piston may be given as 25 oz. plus or minus 1/4 oz. (1/4 oz. is equal to 7.09 grams). Connecting

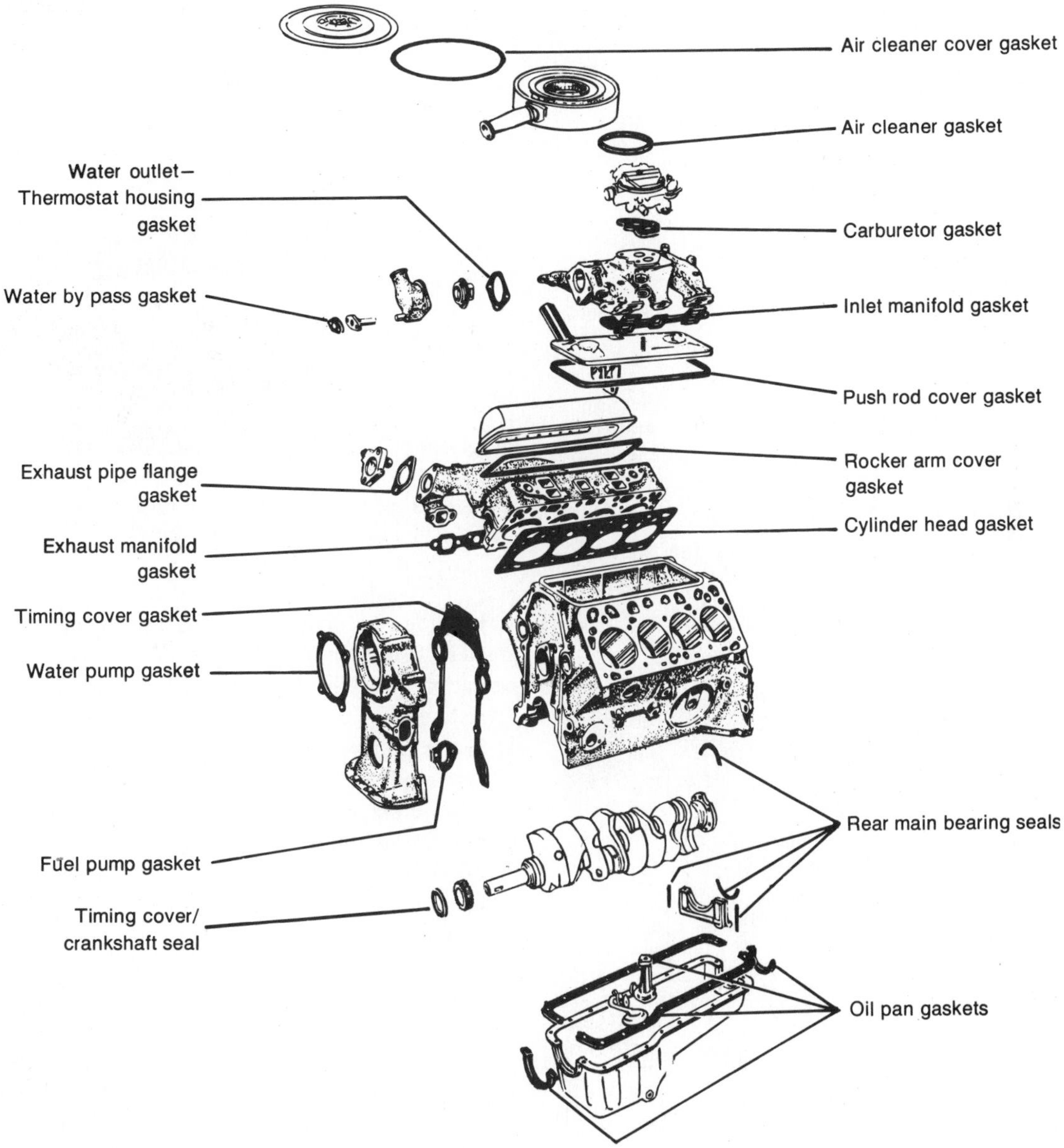

Water outlet—
Thermostat housing gasket

Water by pass gasket

Exhaust pipe flange gasket

Exhaust manifold gasket

Timing cover gasket

Water pump gasket

Fuel pump gasket

Timing cover/ crankshaft seal

Air cleaner cover gasket

Air cleaner gasket

Carburetor gasket

Inlet manifold gasket

Push rod cover gasket

Rocker arm cover gasket

Cylinder head gasket

Rear main bearing seals

Oil pan gaskets

Fig. 13-25. Gasket and seal locations on a typical V-8 engine.
(McCord Corp.)

Fig. 13-27. Numbers indicate sequence in which cylinder head bolts should be tightened. (Typical)

rods may have a similar weight specification and, in addition, the center-to-center length of the rod is held to a close tolerance.

It is therefore possible to have a V-8 engine with eight pistons of different weights, but all within the specified tolerance of 1/4 oz. As an extreme case, one of the pistons may weigh 25 1/4 oz. and another piston 24 3/4 oz.

Fig. 13-28. Preparing to balance a crankshaft on an electronic balancing machine.

Obviously, a set of pistons of varied weights will result in considerable vibration, plus higher loads on the bearings. If similar variations are found in the connecting rods, volume of the combustion chambers and misalignment of the intake and exhaust manifolds with their respective ports in the cylinder head, a very rough engine will result. As pointed out, not only will top speed be affected, but extreme wear of parts also will result.

Precision balancing will help to eliminate the possibility of wear due to vibration. It also will step up performance and boost economy of operation. With modern balancing equipment, Fig. 13-28, the weight of rotating and reciprocating parts can be brought within 1/2 gram of each other, Fig. 13-29.

Fig. 13-29. Special scales are available for weighing pistons and connecting rods.

In order to achieve the highest output of the engine, greatest fuel economy, longest life of parts and smoothest operation, the following parts must be precision balanced.
1. Pistons.
2. Piston rings.
3. Piston pins.
4. Connecting rods.
5. Connecting rod bearings.
6. Crankshaft.
7. Front pulley or vibration damper.
8. Clutch and disc.

UNBALANCE

Unbalance is simply the uneven distribution of weight. When a part is rotated, the unbalance becomes power, which wastes power output. Even a small amount of unbalance is harmful. Just one ounce placed one inch away from the center of rotation will be multiplied 40 times at a speed of 1200 rpm. At 5000 rpm, the force will reach 45 lbs. 10 oz., Fig. 13-30.

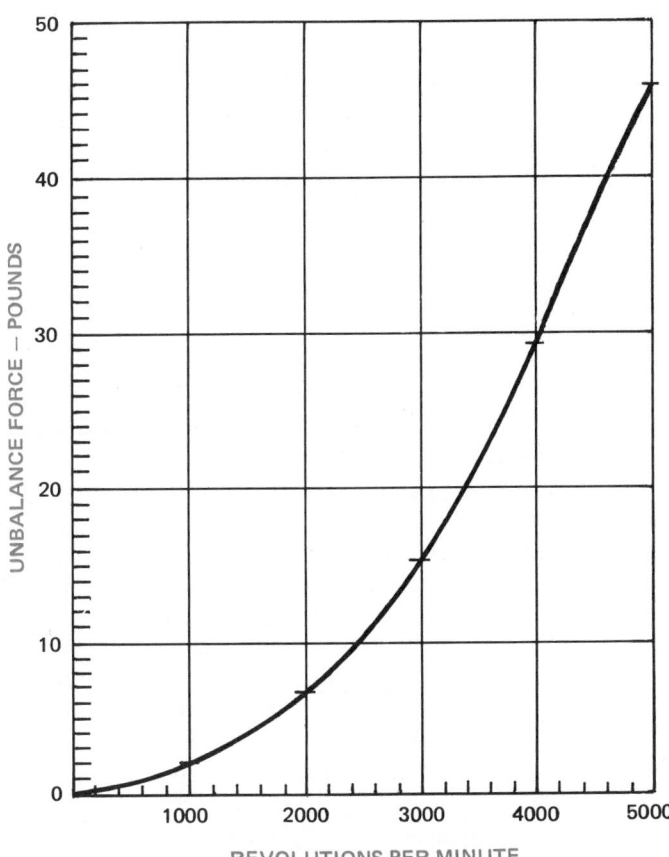

Fig. 13-30. Chart shows a sharp increase in unbalanced force as rpm goes up.

(weight times distance from axis of rotation). Therefore, if the first weight is 8 oz. at a distance of 2 in. from the center, the other weight could be 4 oz. at a distance of 4 in. from the center. Both weights would provide the same turning effort of 16 oz. in.

DYNAMIC BALANCING

A shaft or rotor may be in perfect static balance but, when rotated, will vibrate considerably because it was not in dynamic balance. When the center line of the weight mass of a revolving rotor is in the same plane as the center line of the rotor, it is in dynamic balance.

If there is excess weight on one side of the shaft at one end, which is balanced statically by an equivalent weight on the other side, but at the opposite end, the shaft would not be balanced dynamically, Fig. 13-32. When the shaft with this condition is rotated, a centrifugal couple is formed, resulting in an unbalanced condition with attendant vibration.

In Fig. 13-33, a heavy section W, weighing 9 oz., is located

Fig. 13-32. Weights at opposite ends of rotor cause a twisting motion, and rotor is not dynamically balanced.

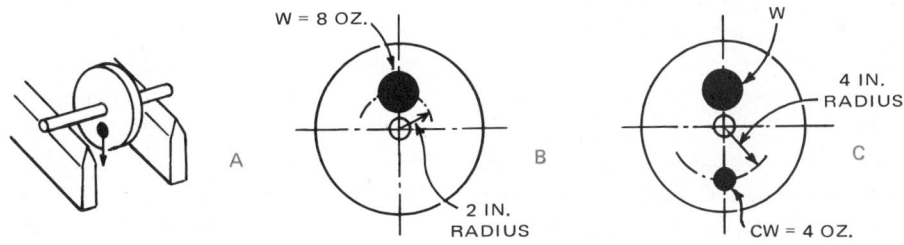

Fig. 13-31. To test balance: A—Place rotor on knife edge blocks. B—Unbalance totals 8 oz., 2 in. from center. C—Correction calls for counterbalancing with 4 oz. weight, 4 in. from center.

STATIC BALANCE

When a rotor has an absolutely even distribution of weight mass around its axis, it will be in static balance. That is there will be no tendency toward rotation about its axis.

View A in Fig. 13-31 shows a rotor and a shaft on two knife edges. A heavy area, indicated by a dot, will turn the rotor until it reaches its lowest point. In view B, this weight is 8 oz. located 2 in. from the center.

To make the rotor in Fig. 13-31 stop in any position, it will be necessary to add a counterweight directly opposite the heavy area, as shown in view C. This would put the rotor in static balance, if the two weights provided the same torque

2 in. from the axis of the cylinder. A counterweight of 6 oz. is located 3 in. from the axis, but at the other end of the cylinder. Both are equal to 18 oz. in., so the cylinder is in static balance. However, because the weights are at opposite ends of the cylinder, a centrifugal couple or twisting action is formed and a dynamic unbalanced condition exists. By adding compensating weights of 9 oz. and 6 oz., as indicated in Fig. 13-33, the cylinder is in static and dynamic balance.

BALANCING IN-LINE AND V-TYPE ENGINES

In V-8 and V-12 engines, the crankshaft basically is in an unbalanced condition. To balance a V-type engine, it is

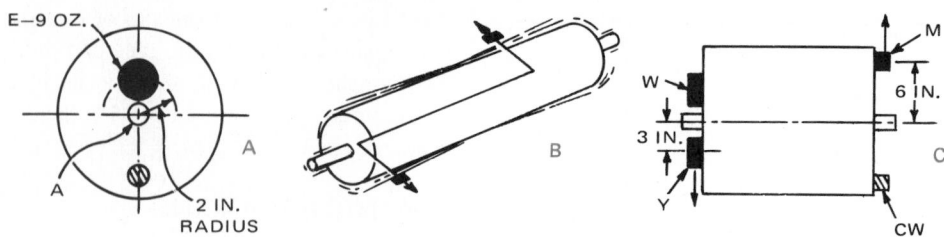

Fig. 13-33. A—9 oz. and 6 oz. weights at opposite ends of cylinder create dynamic unbalance. B—Twisting action causes vibration. C—Cylinder is balanced by adding compensating weights of 9 oz. and 6 oz.

Fig. 13-34. Crankshaft has bob weights attached, ready for balancing on machine. (Bear Mfg. Corp.)

necessary to attach weights to each of the crank throws as substitutes for the weights of the connecting rods and piston assemblies. Such weights are known as "bob" weights, Fig. 13-34.

When balancing in-line engines, such as the four and six, "bob" weights are not needed because the crankshaft throws are symmetrically arranged.

In the case of two cycle engines, the GMC series 71 diesel requires special consideration. These engines are counterbalanced by a combination of balance weights on the camshafts (on in-line engine, one camshaft and a balance shaft are used), Fig. 13-35. Connected to the crankshaft through a small gear are a pair of shafts driven by gears the same size as

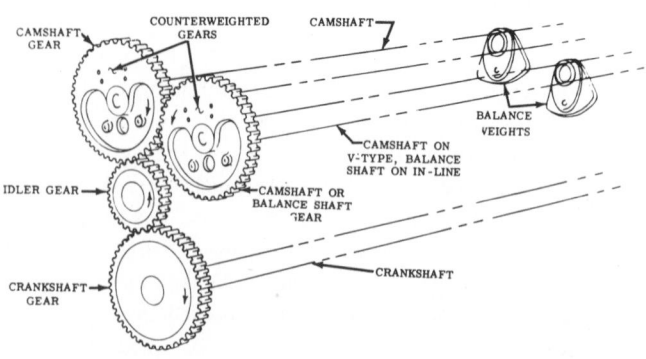

Fig. 13-35. Balancing two cycle GMC 71 series diesel engine involves counterweighted gears, a balance shaft and balance weights on far end of each shaft to counterbalance counterweighted gears.

that on the crankshaft. On in-line engines the first shaft is the camshaft, the second is the balance shaft.

On V-type engines, both shafts are camshafts, with counterweighted gears. Also, on the far end of each shaft, a counterweight is located diametrically opposed to the counterweight on the gear. The amount of counterweight on one end should counterbalance the counterweight on the other end.

Theoretically, all four ends, gears and balance weights should have identical oz.-in. amounts of unbalance. Because these parts (gears and balance weights) are diametrically opposed, the shaft when assembled should have no force (kinetic) unbalance, but a desired high couple (dynamic) unbalance.

Therefore, in order to properly balance a GMC 71 series engine, bob weights must be used on the crankshaft, and the counterweighted gears and the counterbalance weights must be balanced on a special fixture.

BALANCING SINGLE CYLINDER ENGINES

Single cylinder engines, and other inherently unbalanced engines such as outboard, motorcycle, go-cart etc., require special balancing procedures because of their relatively high speeds. These small engines will not be as vibrationless as multi-cylinder engines, but they are precision balanced for smoothest operation.

When determining the bob weight for a single cylinder engine, use 100 percent of the rotating weight (same as for a V-8 engine), but use a higher percentage of the reciprocating weight. V-8 engines usually use 50 percent of the reciprocating weight.

For the single cylinder engine, the weight should range from 55 percent up to 65 percent according to the engine speed.

BOB WEIGHTS

As previously pointed out, bob weights are temporarily attached to the crankshaft while it is being balanced to compensate for the weights of the pistons and connecting rod assemblies.

Part of the piston and connecting rod assembly is a rotating weight and part is a reciprocating weight. The weight of the piston with its pin and rings, along with a portion of the upper end of the connecting rod, is considered as reciprocating weight. The weight of the big end of the connecting rods is considered as rotating weight.

To obtain the actual weight of these parts, first weigh all of the pistons with their rings and pins. Then, using the weight of the lightest piston assembly, reduce the weight of the other pistons to conform to the weight of the lightest one.

To reduce the weight of a piston, chuck it in a lathe and remove metal from the inside of the piston skirt. In some piston designs, pads have been provided on the inner surface of the skirt from which the necessary metal can be removed.

Take care not to weaken the strength of the piston. To insure that the exterior of the piston is not scored by the jaws of the lathe chuck, first cover the piston with thin sheet steel or copper.

Special weighing scales are used to measure the weights of the pistons. These scales must have an accuracy of less than 1/2 gram, Fig. 13-29.

Special weighing scales are also used to weigh the connecting rods. While one end of the rod rests on the scales, the other end is supported. When the weight of the crank ends has been found, the heavier crank ends should be balanced by removing metal so they are equal in weight with the rod with the lightest crank end. Similarly, the weights of the pin ends of the rods must be made to conform to the weight of the rod with the lightest pin end. A grinder or belt sander is usually used to remove metal from the connecting rods. NOTE: The weight of the individual rods and pistons should be carefully recorded.

On V-type engines which carry two rod and piston assemblies on each crank throw, the bob weight for each throw will include:
1. The weight of two crank ends of rods with bearing inserts, lock nuts and oil in crank throw.
2. The weight of one piston, pin, pin lock, one set of rings, weight of one piston end of rod.
3. The total of weights in 1 and 2 will be the weight of the bob weight to be attached to each crank throw when balancing the crankshaft.

On V-type engines which carry one rod and piston assembly on each throw, the bob weight for each throw will include:
1. The weight of crank end of one rod with its bearing inserts, lock nuts and weight of oil in crank throw. This is the rotating weight.
2. The reciprocating weight to be included in the bob weight includes 50 percent of the pin end of the rod, piston, piston pin, pin locks set of rings.
3. The sum of the rotating and the reciprocating weight in 1 and 2 is the bob weight which must be attached to each crankpin when balancing the crankshaft.

As pointed out, in-line four and six cylinder engines do not require bob weights when balancing the engine crankshaft. However, the weights of the piston and rod assemblies must be made equal within a tolerance of 1/2 oz.

CRANKSHAFT BALANCING PROCEDURE

The degree of unbalance of the crankshaft is determined by placing the shaft (V-8 with its bob weights or in-line shaft without bob weights) in the balancing machine. As the shaft is rotated, the degree of unbalance and its location will be indicated.

In general, the unbalanced condition can be corrected by removing metal from the counterweight. In those cases where the throws are light, then it is necessary to tack weld thin steel sheets to the sides of the counterweights.

Normal weight removal is accomplished by using a 1/2 in. drill. Special fixtures allow the drilling to be performed with the shaft in balancer. If, inadvertently, too much metal is removed, the 1/2 in. drilled hole can be plugged with 1/2 in. rod, then redrilled the desired amount.

REVIEW QUESTIONS – ENGINE RECONDITIONING

1. Name five ways of increasing the size of a metal part.
2. An oversize bearing is required on a reground crankshaft journal. True or False?
3. Name five ways of repairing a water jacket cracked by freezing.
4. How much warpage, overall, usually can be tolerated in a cylinder head?
   a. .001 in.   b. .003 in.   c. .006 in.
5. When installing a new dry sleeve in a cylinder, should the sleeve be smaller or larger in diameter than the cylinder?
6. Why do pistons sometimes seize in cylinders?
7. Name two ways of repairing badly scored cylinders.
8. Why must dry cylinder sleeves fit tightly in the block?
9. If a newly installed dry sleeve is round, straight, smooth and free from wrinkles, is it ready for servce? Yes or No?
10. A cylinder sleeve should be _____ after installation.
11. The limitation for cylinder wear is .010 in. out-of-round and .005 in. taper. True or False?
12. How can a proper cylinder wall finish be described?
13. In general, how much clearance, per inch of diameter, should cast iron pistons have in cylinders?
    a. .0075 to .01 in.
    b. .00075 to .001 in.
    c. .00005 to .00015 in.
14. Name three ways of expanding pistons.
15. Piston expanders should always be used in sets. True or False?
16. The greatest amount of wear in the cylinder takes place at the _____ of the travel of the piston rings.
17. What is the maximum amount of taper usually specified for cylinder wear in passenger car engines?
    a. 0.010 in.   b. 0.005 in.   c. 0.075 in.
18. Only static balance of engine parts is required. True or False?
19. Unbalance of engine parts _____ bearing loads.
20. The affect of engine unbalance increases with engine speed. Yes or No?
21. To balance a GMC series 71 diesel, follow the same procedure used for a _____ engine.

Chevrolet 307 cu. in. V-8 engine with 2-barrel carburetor develops 115 hp
@3600 rpm, fitted with Controlled Combustion System.

PISTON RING
AND PIN FITTING

Piston ring design and purpose was covered in a previous chapter in this text. It included a reference to the fact that a ridge is formed at the top of the cylinder wall as the cylinder wears. To avoid damage to pistons and rings, this ridge must be cut away before an attempt is made to remove the pistons from the cylinders. Special tools are made for this purpose, Fig. 14-1.

Cylinder wall reconditioning and piston fitting have been discussed. Now, some consideration should be given to proper fitting of the rings to the piston and cylinder, and also to fitting piston pins in the pistons.

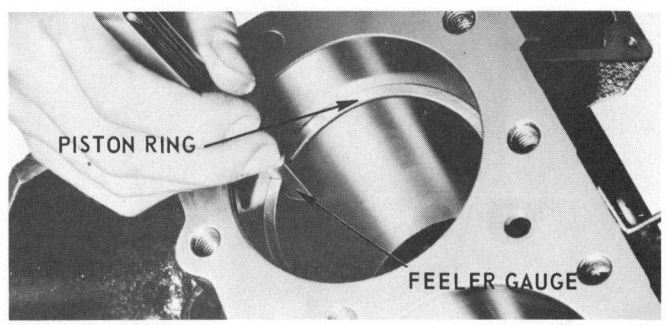

Fig. 14-2. Measure piston ring gap with rings seated squarely in smallest diameter of cylinder.

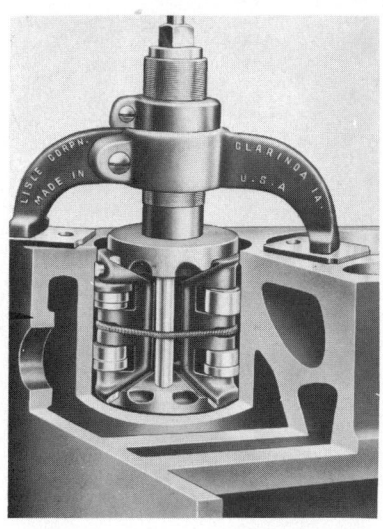

Fig. 14-1. Cutaway engine block shows one type of special tool for removing ridge at top of cylinder.

The ring is pushed into the smallest diameter of the cylinder bore, which is usually below the travel of the bottom ring. A piston without rings is used to push the ring in place since this method locates the ring squarely in the bore. Piston rings of the correct size for the application should be purchased to avoid fitting. If necessary, minor increases in gap clearance can be made by filing the ends of the ring.

In case specific clearance dimensions are not available, it is customary to allow .004 in. gap clearance per inch of piston diameter for the top ring, and .003 in. per inch diameter for the other rings. For example, a 3 in. in diameter cylinder

PISTON RING GAP

It is obvious that the top piston ring runs hotter than the lower rings. Therefore, the top ring will expand the most. This means that the top ring will need more gap clearance at the ends, and more sidewise clearance in the piston grooves than the other rings. The piston ring manufacturer specifies the clearance needed. His instructions should be followed.

Piston ring gap clearance is measured as shown in Fig. 14-2.

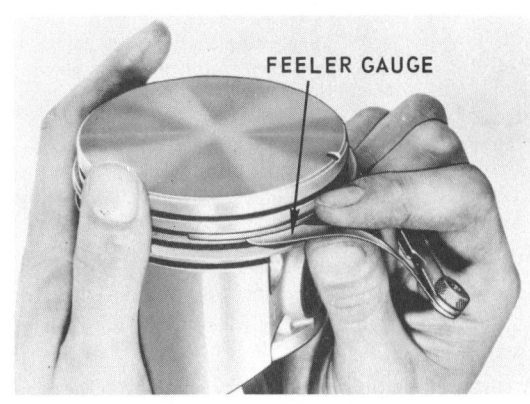

Fig. 14-3. Measuring sidewise clearance of piston ring in groove.

would require .012 in. gap in the top ring and .009 in. in the other rings. The exception is the "U" type oil ring, which is extremely flexible. These rings require no gap clearance.

RING GROOVE CLEARANCE

The sidewise clearance of the ring in the groove is measured as shown in Fig. 14-3, using a feeler (thickness) gauge. In the absence of specific instructions, it is customary to allow at least .003 in. side clearance on the top ring and at least .002 in. on the other rings. More than .005 in. side clearance on any ring calls for new rings.

Remember that new rings should never be installed in worn ring grooves. Invariably, this practice results in poor oil economy and increased blow-by, Fig. 14-4. In addition, ring

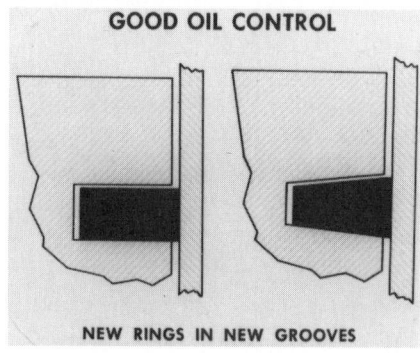

GOOD OIL CONTROL

NEW RINGS IN NEW GROOVES

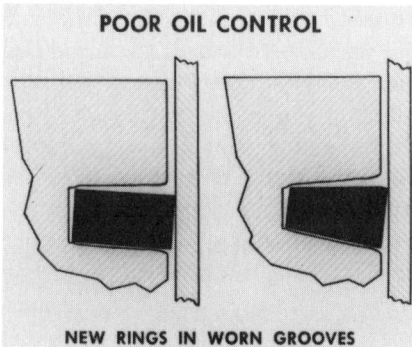

POOR OIL CONTROL

NEW RINGS IN WORN GROOVES

Fig. 14-4. Above. New rings in new grooves provide good oil and blow-by control. Below. When grooves are worn, oil will blow-by and ring life will be shortened.

life will be materially shortened. No matter how accurately a piston ring is made, it cannot form an effective oil and blow-by seal against worn or uneven sides of the piston ring groove. The importance of checking ring grooves for wear cannot be overemphasized. Groove wear gauges greatly simplify wear checks.

New rings can be purchased in any standard size, oversize or overwidth as desired. Overwidth rings may be used if the sides of the ring grooves are flat, smooth and square.

If the grooves are worn excessively, Fig. 14-5, or in tapered fashion, Fig. 14-6, they can be repaired in two ways. One way is to machine the grooves wider and install overwidth rings. The other way is to install spacers with standard width rings, as shown in Fig. 14-7. In either case the ring grooves in the piston will need to be trued up. Special equipment is available for this purpose. See Fig. 14-8.

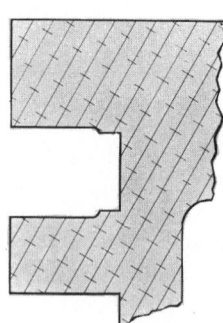

Fig. 14-5. Shoulders formed in bottom of groove might not leave clearance for new rings.

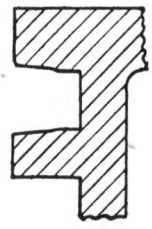

Fig. 14-6. Usual groove wear pattern is tapered in form.

Fig. 14-7. Standard width rings may be used with a spacer in remachined grooves.

The depth of the ring groove also must be checked when replacing rings. Sometimes shallow grooves are used with thin rings, and a replacement with normal thickness rings will cause them to "bottom." The groove must be deep enough to allow the ring to enter the groove below the surface of the ring land, Fig. 14-9. If the grooves are too shallow, they can be machined out deeper.

Rings tend to turn slightly in the grooves. When installing

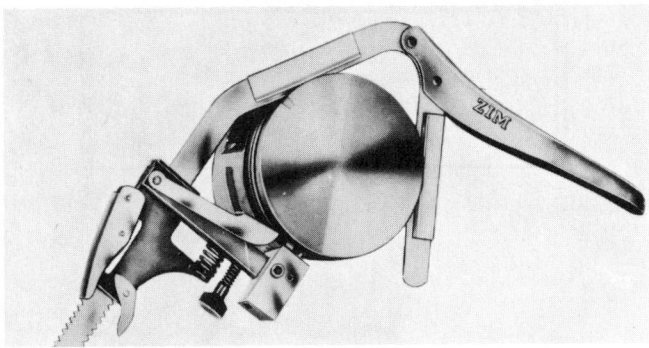

Fig. 14-8. One type of special ring groove tool shown in operation.

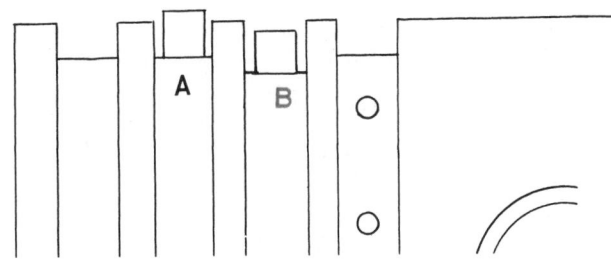

Fig. 14-9. Ring should fit freely in ring groove, below surface of lands as shown at B.

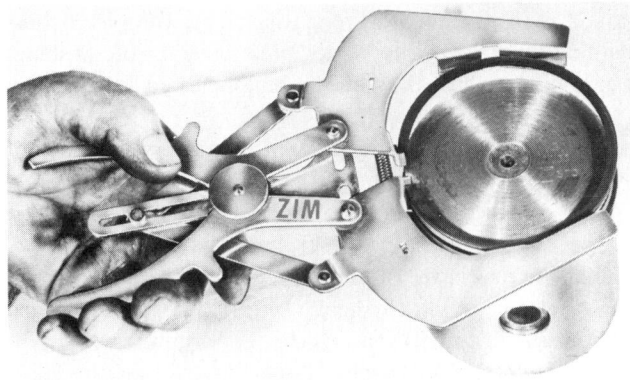

Fig. 14-10. Illustrated is one type of piston ring expander used to place rings on pistons.

Fig. 14-11. Electric powered hydraulic press is used for assembly and disassembly of press fit piston pins. (Sunnen Products Co.)

rings, space the gaps around the pistons to avoid any possibility that gaps will align one above the other, and encourage blow-by.

The manufacturers' instructions should always be followed when installing new rings. They know how their own products should be fitted, and they have studied the peculiarities of the different engines.

Piston ring grooves must be thoroughly cleaned before installing new rings. Special tools are available for scraping the carbon from the grooves, Fig. 14-8. In an emergency, a broken segment of a piston ring can be used for this purpose.

Piston rings are fragile and must be handled carefully. They should be placed in the piston ring grooves with the aid of a ring expander, Fig. 14-10, and not by stretching them by hand over the piston. Even if they do not break, they may become distorted by careless handling.

It is also important to use a ring compressor when inserting the piston with rings into the cylinder. Otherwise the sharp edge of the ring may be deformed, and the ring rendered useless.

If there is any doubt about proper clearances for rings and pistons, it is safer to err on the side of too much clearance rather than too little. In this connection, it is often assumed that an engine pumps oil because of worn rings. This is not always the case. Sometimes, new rings are installed, only to have the engine pump oil worse than ever.

If the bearings are worn in a pressure-lubricated engine, excess oil will be thrown upon the cylinders. The engine will pump oil, regardless of how good the rings are, or how well

they are fitted. The oil is supplied in such quantities that it is beyond the ability of any ring to control it.

PISTON PIN REPLACEMENT

Usually, you will find wear in both pin and bearings when piston pins become loose. If the bushing is in the connecting rod only, it can be pressed out. Then, a new standard size bushing can be pressed in and reamed or honed to fit a new standard size pin. Never remove the old bushing with a hammer and drift, because there is danger of bending the connecting rod.

If the pin is clamped in the rod, and the bushings are in the piston bosses, the same pressing method can be used. When replacing bushings in the piston avoid hammering, since the

165

piston can be distorted by rough handling. The piston boss should be supported firmly in the press while the old bushings are pressed out and the new bushings pressed in. See Fig. 14-11.

Many piston pins are an interference fit in the upper end of the rod. That is, the diameter of the piston pin is slightly larger than the diameter of bearing in upper end of the connecting rod. Special equipment, Fig. 14-11, is needed for removing and installing the pins in the piston and rod assembly.

In addition to an hydraulic press, equipment needed includes special anvils on which the piston assembly is mounted, pilots and, in some cases, a spring for the anvil. These differ for each piston design.

The pressing procedure is to mount the piston assembly on the anvil. Then, by means of a pilot and hydraulic press or an electro-hydraulic pin press, Fig. 14-11, the pin is pressed from the assembly. A similar procedure is followed when assembling the piston pin to the rod and piston.

OVERSIZE PISTON PINS

If oversize new pins are to be installed, and the old bushings in the piston are to be reamed or honed to fit the oversize pin, the connecting rod clamp hole will need to be enlarged accordingly. This condition also arises where the pistons are not bushed, and the pin bearing is directly in the piston bosses.

If difficulty is experienced in reaming the rod end due to the split for clamping, a shim may be placed in the slot, and the clamp bolt drawn down tight. The shim must be the same thickness as the opening in the slot when the rod is clamped on the standard size pin. The inner edge of the shim should be flush with the hole so that the reamer will cut both shim and rod.

In the full floating type, the installation of new oversize pins will require reaming or honing of the piston bushings or bosses, along with the bushing or rod (in the case of aluminum rods without bushings).

In every case where reaming or honing is done on either piston or connecting rod, it is of utmost importance to have the finished hole at precisely a right angle to the connecting rod. Also, both piston boss bearings must be in precise alignment. The hole must be straight through both bosses. Equipment used for reconditioning piston pin holes is shown in Figs. 14-12 and 14-15.

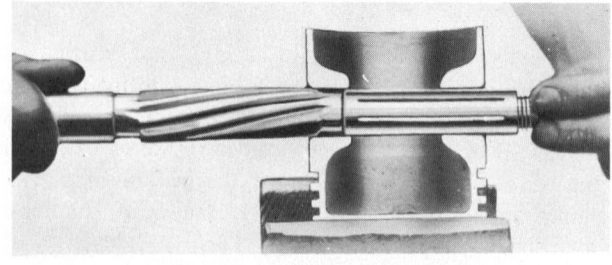

Fig. 14-12. Aligning type of reamer used to insure straight holes in both piston bosses.

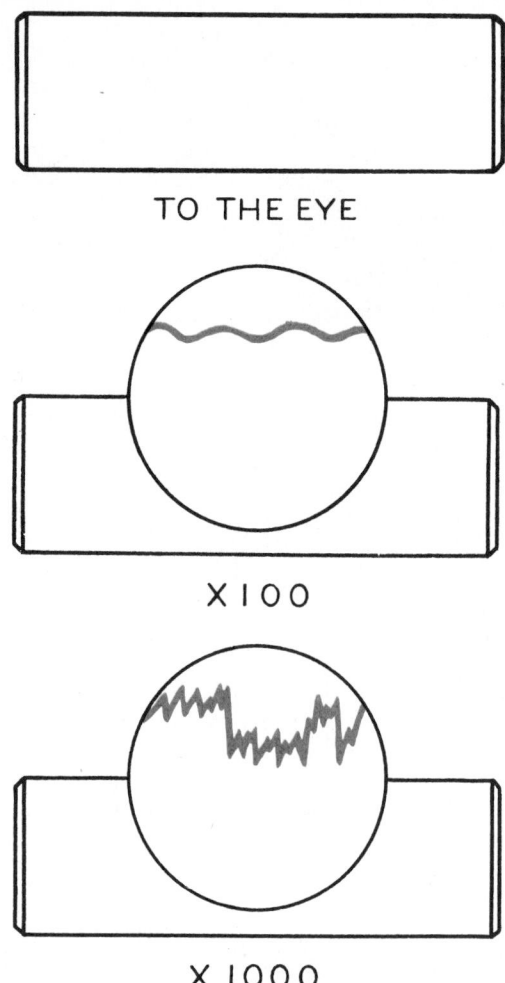

TO THE EYE

X 100

X 1000

Fig. 14-13. An apparently smooth pin may be rough indeed when magnified on the surface.

PISTON PIN FITTING

Fitting piston pins is one of the most delicate operations to be found in automobile repair work. Suitable equipment for fitting piston pins properly is available.

Accuracy measurements in thousandths and tenths of thousandths is fairly common in automobile repair work. However, in dealing with piston pins, you have to split the tenths, and deal with microinches or millionths.

In fact, it is useless to use the term microinch without specifying the temperature at which the measurement is made. A few degrees rise or fall in the temperature will expand or contract the metal enough to change the measurement given in microinches.

Furthermore, we are dealing with steel, bronze and aluminum, each of which has a different rate of heat expansion. We fit the piston pins at room temperature (assumed to be 70 deg. F) then put them in an engine which quickly attains a temperature of at least 140 deg. F. This temperature expands the pin, the bushings (if used) and the piston. If working with a cam ground piston, it also changes shape from oval when cold to round when hot.

This change in shape of the piston may also disturb the alignment of the two holes in the piston bosses. If the hole is round and straight through the two bosses (which would stay round and straight when hot) and a round and straight pin to fit with suitable clearance for the oil film.

There must be room for a film of oil around the piston pin. Otherwise, metal-to-metal contact will occur, and the friction generated will score the pin or bushing or both.

Standards of manufacture have improved, and most piston pins are round and straight within one tenth of a thousandth of an inch. A pin so finished looks perfect and appears to be glass-smooth. When the surface is magnified 100 times it does not look so smooth. When magnified 1000 times, it looks rough indeed. See Fig. 14-13.

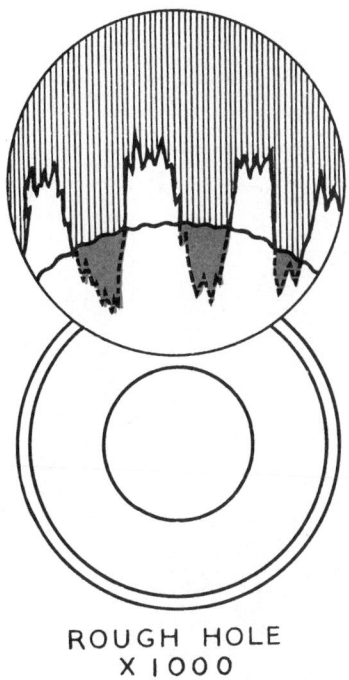

ROUGH HOLE
X 1000

Fig. 14-14. Forcing a smooth pin into a rough hole will cause high points of peaks to be sheared off, resulting in metal-to-metal contact between pin and parts of bushing.

Reaming, grinding and honing equipment is now available which will produce a hole which appears to be dead smooth. It is, like the pins, accurate to one tenth of a thousandth. When magnified, however, it looks much like the bearing surface on the pins.

With the use of good equipment, it is possible to produce a hole that enables a good working fit to be made. Obviously, when working with such close dimensions, the clearance will be determined by the surface finish.

Unless the hole finish is practically perfect, the "peaks" will be sheared off when the pin is forced into the hole, Fig. 14-14. The result of such a condition is rapid wear of the peak base, and the pin and bushing are worn OUT before they wear IN to a working fit.

Piston pins must not be fitted too tight, Fig. 14-14.

If the hole is finished to the correct size, there will be room for a film of oil to prevent metal-to-metal contact. When such a fit is obtained, the pin will enter the hole readily without force being applied. It will have sufficient bearing surface to

Fig. 14-15. Honing machine is used in reconditioning connecting rods and pin fitting in pistons and rods. (Sunnen Products Co.)

wear satisfactorily. This precision fit can be obtained by a skillful operator using modern equipment in accordance with the manufacturers' instructions. Fig. 14-15 shows a precision honing machine designed for manual operation. Fig. 14-16 pictures a connecting rod heater for use in press-fit rod work.

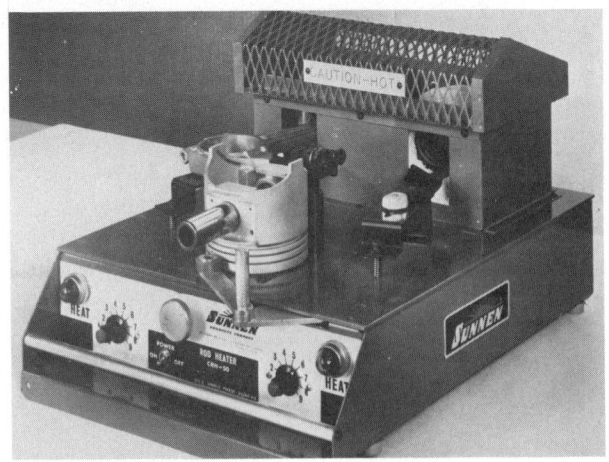

Fig. 14-16. Connecting rod heater heats rod eye to give exact expansion required to permit pin to be hand-pushed in place.

REVIEW QUESTIONS — PISTON RING AND PIN FITTING

1. How much end gap should the top ring have in a four inch diameter cylinder?
   - a. .009 in.
   - b. .012 in.
   - c. .016 in.
2. How much gap should the oil ring have in a cylinder three and one half inches in diameter?
   - a. .009 in.
   - b. .012 in.
   - c. .015 in.
3. The top ring should have at least .005 in. side clearance in the ring groove. True or False?
4. How deep should the ring groove be?
5. Piston pins are case-hardened, so do not wear. True or False?
6. Can oversize pins be installed when the pin floats in both piston and connecting rod?
7. What is meant by "room temperature?"
8. New piston pins can be expected to be round within:
   - a. .002 in.
   - b. .0001 in.
   - c. .00005 in.

Experimental electric vehicle engineered by Ford of Great Britian, for short range urban use. This vehicle. has four 12V, lead-acid batteries, and uses two series-wound 24V electric motors to drive the rear wheels.

CRANKSHAFT, CAMSHAFT AND CONNECTING ROD SERVICE

In studying the forces applied to a journal of the crankshaft, it will be found that the load is much heavier at some points of rotation than at others. For example, the force of the explosion is several times as strong as the force of the compression stroke. Also, the explosion stroke always applies the force at the same spot on the journal.

Finally, an additional load is imposed by the action of centrifugal force resulting from the rotation of the crankshaft with its connecting rods and pistons. The result is out-of-round crankshaft journals and crankpins.

If a connecting rod is bent, or is out of alignment, it will tend to wear the crankpin journal in a tapered fashion. That is, it will wear more at one end of the bearing surface than the other end. Also any twisting of the engine crankcase or any excessive vibration of the crankshaft will cause the main crankshaft journals to wear in tapered form.

Furthermore, if abrasive material gets into the engine oil, wear may be unequal. It will wear more at one bearing or more on one spot of the bearing, depending on where the abrasive enters in greatest quantity.

Bearings seldom wear equally. One bearing may operate with a smaller volume of oil than another. Likewise, one bearing, because of location in the engine, may operate at a higher temperature than the others. All of these things cause or contribute to unequal wear on the crankshaft journals.

If a connecting rod journal has taper or a flat spot, it simply cannot be used. Either condition would ordinarily cause such an increase in oil consumption that it would be essential to recondition the crank throw.

Because of close clearances in the bearings, a sprung crankshaft cannot be tolerated. The main bearings must fit the crankshaft journals all around the circumference with only enough clearance for a film of lubricating oil. If the bearing journal is scored or other than absolutely round, it cannot be used until it is reconditioned or replaced.

DAMAGED CRANKSHAFTS

Engine crankshafts usually are large and expensive parts, so it is desirable to repair damage rather than replace the shaft. Before any extensive work is started, however, it is well to have the shaft checked by a specialist with proper special

Fig. 15-1. With "Magnaflux" method, part is sprayed with a material that will show any fracture by glowing under hood which shuts out some of light.

magnetic or chemical equipment to make sure there are no invisible cracks in it. See Fig. 15-1.

If damage has occurred to one or more crankpin journals,

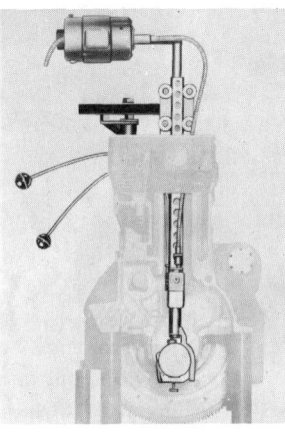

Fig. 15-2. One type of special equipment for machining connecting rod journals with engine in car.

and the crankshaft has not been removed from the engine, it is possible to recondition the crankpin with the aid of special equipment made for this specific purpose. See Fig. 15-2.

An engine crankshaft is subjected to terrific vibration and stress. It may develop tiny cracks, particularly at or near the ends of the connecting rod throws or at the ends of the main bearing journals. Occasionally, an invisible crack may develop near the oil feed holes in the shaft.

If the crankshaft is sound, journals worn slightly tapered or out-of-round, can be reground and undersize bearings fitted. See Fig. 15-3. Here again, as in the case of reboring cylinders,

Fig. 15-4. In some cases, metal worn away can be replaced by spraying on new metal with special equipment. Part is then refinished to size.

Fig. 15-3. Special equipment is available for reconditioning crankshafts.

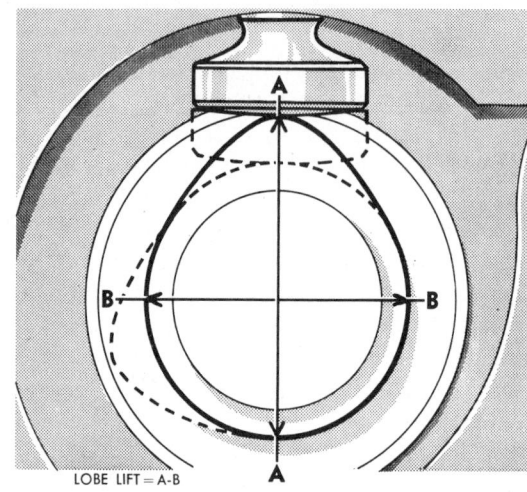

LOBE LIFT = A-B

Fig. 15-5. Difference between measurements AA and BB equals actual cam lift. Comparison should then be made with specified lift to determine extent of wear.

it is desirable to check out available sizes of bearing inserts, then have the shaft journals ground to an undersize for which inserts are carried in stock.

If the shaft is badly damaged, it may be possible to restore the journal by spraying metal on it. The shaft is built up oversize, then reground to the desired size. This type of work usually is done by specialists. See Fig. 15-4.

WORN CAMSHAFTS

Some wear does occur on camshafts, as on any other engine part. Since the camshaft operates at slower speed than the crankshaft, wear usually is less pronounced. The entire shaft is hardened, so wear ordinarily occurs in the bushings rather than on the shaft journals. However, because of the weight of push rods and rocker arms, plus the stronger valve springs and today's higher engine speeds, the load on the cams is greater. Consequently, there is an increased tendency toward wear.

The lift of the cam is the difference in measurements, AA and BB, Fig. 15-5. The amount of wear is then obtained by comparison with specified lift. Cam lift also can be measured by mounting a dial gauge on the cylinder head with its button contacting the upper end of the valve push rod. Then, as the

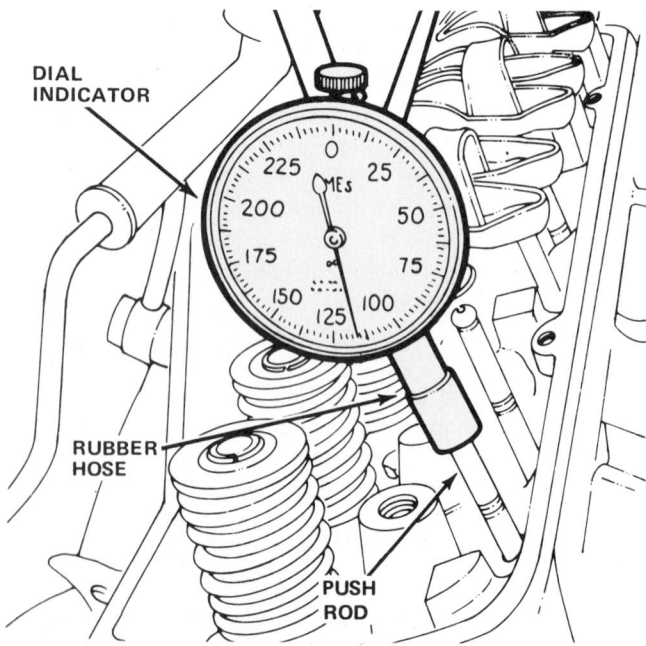

DIAL INDICATOR

RUBBER HOSE

PUSH ROD

Fig. 15-6. Using a dial gauge to measure cam lift. Check gauge reading against factory specification to see whether wear is excessive.

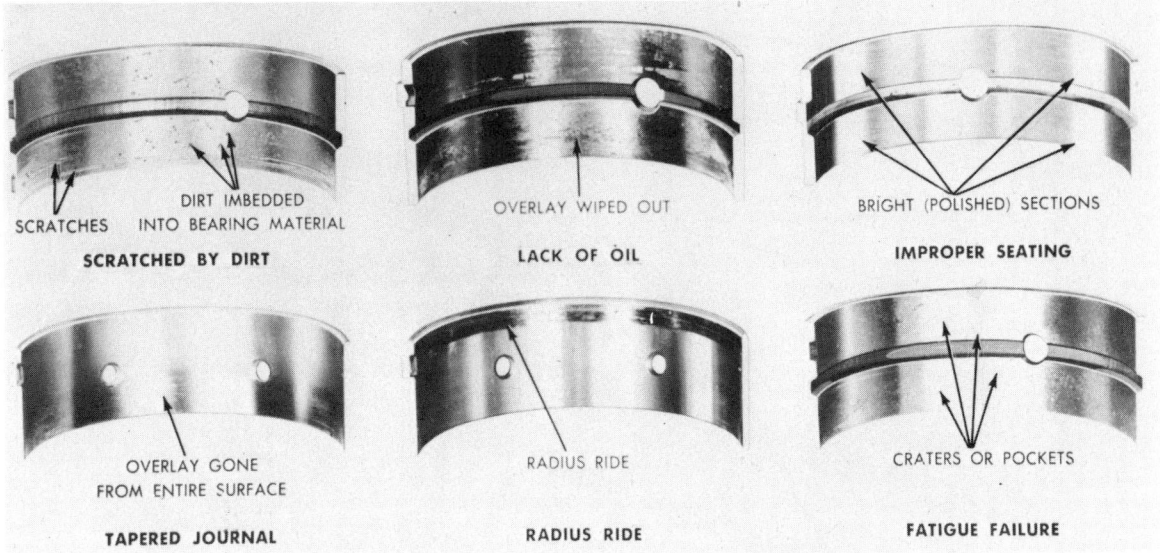

Fig. 15-7. Illustrating major causes of engine bearing failures.

engine is slowly cranked, the distance from the lowest point to the highest will be the lift of the cam, Fig. 15-6.

It is important to measure the lift of all cams in the engine to determine if any are worn, since the cams do not all wear at the same rate.

Worn cams occasionally are the cause of lost power or misfiring, which is often overlooked when troubleshooting. If a check on valve lift shows that it is less than it should be, the cams can be reground on special machinery. In most cases, however, the camshaft is replaced.

BEARING CLEARANCES

A previous study of engine lubrication revealed that oil is pumped under pressure to the various bearings in the engine. However, to get this oil into the bearing and lubricate it, clearance for an oil film must exist.

The one most important thing to keep in mind in this connection is that the steel crankshaft journal MUST be separated from the bearing metal when the engine is running or the bearing will melt. The heat generated by friction when steel moves rapidly on soft, dry metal WILL melt the soft metal. Therefore, an automobile engine uses a film of oil between the journal and the bearing. SPACE MUST BE PROVIDED FOR THAT FILM.

The oil film serves to hold the two metals apart and also circulates to carry away the heat generated by friction. The space is not great (measured in thousandths), but those thousandths are all important. See Fig. 15-7.

This film thickness will vary with the design of the engine and the type of lubrication system used. In general, a splash lubrication system is less critical of oil clearances than a pressure lubrication system. In the splash system, the oil is churned up by internal parts of the engine into a combination of liquid and mist, which is sprayed over the entire interior of the engine.

In the pressure lubricated engine, the oil is pumped under pressure to the bearings, Fig. 15-8. In this case, the flow of oil must be controlled by maintaining limited clearance all around a ROUND bearing and a ROUND shaft. If there are unequal clearances in the circulation system, too much oil will collect in one place, and not enough in other places. This is because oil under pressure will go through the largest clearance space in the greatest quantity.

CLEARANCE MEASUREMENT

One method of measuring oil clearance is to measure the diameter of the journal with a micrometer caliper. See page 39. The diameter of the shaft is measured at several points around the circumference to determine the size and to check for roundness. See Fig. 15-9. Measuring each end of the bearing surface will determine the amount of taper, if any.

The inside of the bearing is measured with the cap bolted in place, using a telescoping gauge or an inside micrometer, Fig. 15-10. The difference in these two measurements represents the clearance between the journal and the bearing.

An alternate method is the use of a plastic material called "Plastigage," which flattens between the journal and bearing when the cap is drawn down to proper tightness. The amount of increase in the width of the plastic material, as it flattens out, is then measured with a furnished gauge to determine the clearance between journal and bearing. See Fig. 15-11.

The oil pressure test (page 201) will also disclose if there is excessive clearance between the crankpins and inserts.

The amount of diametral clearance on crankshaft bearings is specified by the car manufacturer. In the absence of specifications, use a minimum of .0005 to .001 in. (0.0127 to 0.0254 mm) for small shafts and up to .0015 to .002 in. (0.381 to 0.0508 mm) for large shafts. Clearance in excess of .005 in. (0.1270 mm) on either main bearings or rod bearings usually calls for the installation of new undersize bearings.

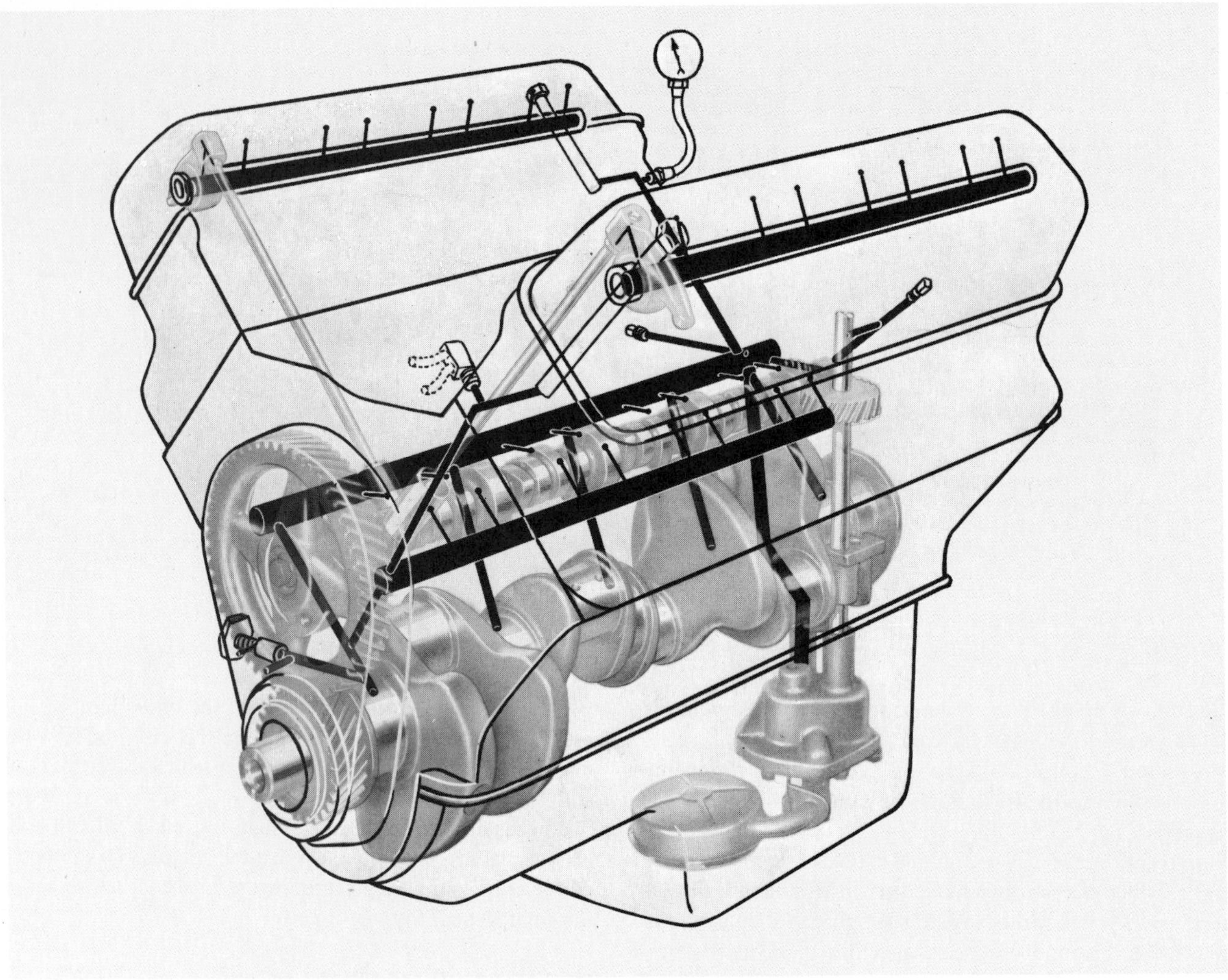

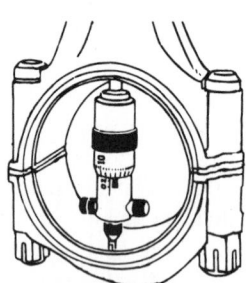

Fig. 15-8. A typical full pressure oil circulation system carries oil to practically all working parts.

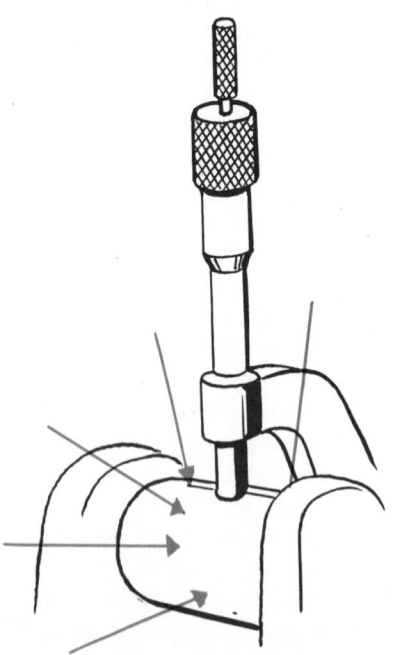

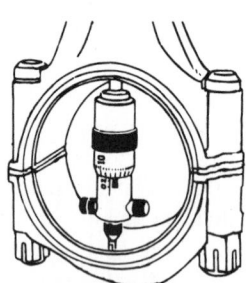

Fig. 15-10. The inside bore of the bearing is measured for size and roundness with an inside micrometer or a special dial gauge.

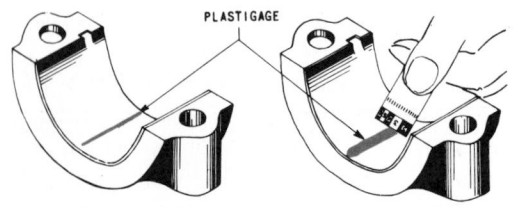

Fig. 15-9. Bearing journals should be measured at several points around diameter and also along length of bearing surface.

Fig. 15-11. Using Plastigage to check bearing clearance.

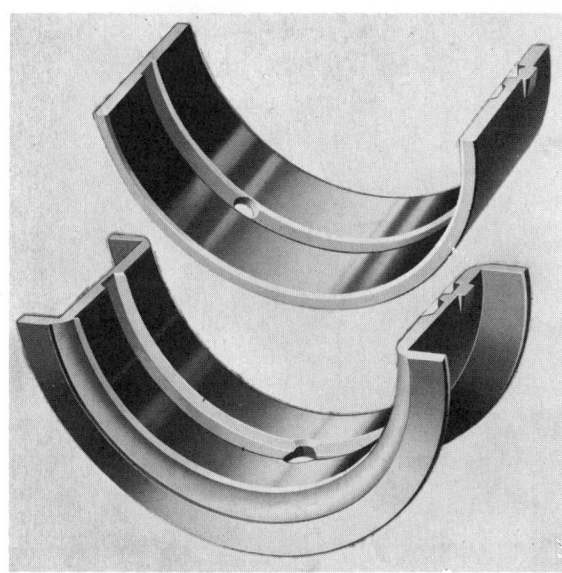

Fig. 15-12. Plain and flanged types of shell bearing inserts.

ENDWISE CLEARANCE

Obviously, the crankshaft must not move endwise to any great extent; so one of the main bearings usually is provided with cheeks or flanges that bear against a machined flange on the crankshaft. See Fig. 15-12. In older engines, bronze washers were installed to absorb the end thrust. See Fig. 15-13. There is always some end thrust on the crankshaft. This may originate in the clutch pushing against the end of the shaft, or the thrust of the helical timing gears, or both.

Just as in the case of diametral clearance, there must be

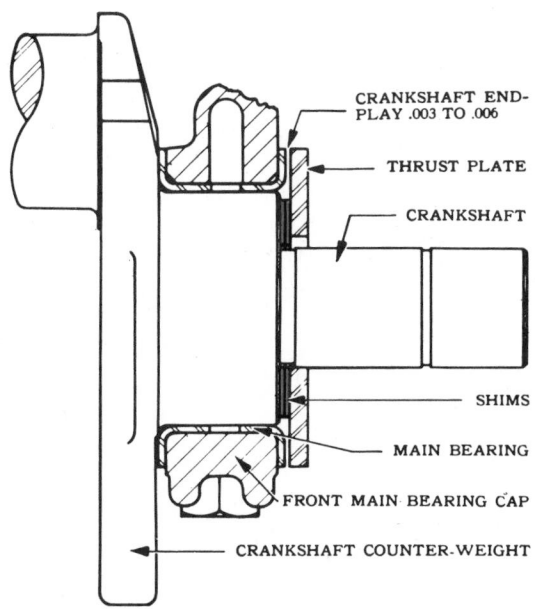

Fig. 15-13. Bronze washers are sometimes used as shims to regulate endwise motion of crankshaft.

some clearance on the thrust faces. Otherwise, expansion of the shaft and bearings from the normal heat of operation would cause metal-to-metal contact and burning of the thrust bearing. Here again the car manufacturers' instructions should be followed. It is customary to provide a minimum of .004 in. and a maximum of .008 in. clearance. End thrust can be measured with a feeler gauge, as shown in Fig. 15-14.

Fig. 15-14. Use of feeler gauge is usual method of checking endwise clearance of crankshaft. A suitably mounted dial gauge also can be used.

CONNECTING ROD REMOVAL

It is quite a chore to get the connecting rods out of some engines. On many small bore European engines, the big end of the connecting rod is too large to go through the cylinder bore. In some cases, the engine has removable cylinder sleeves which, when removed, will allow the rod to come through the block opening. In many engines the rod is split at an angle, Fig. 15-15, to facilitate removal. Note that cap screws with lock washers, rather than studs or bolts, are used to hold the rod bearing cap in place with this type of construction.

An unusual situation is found in one English engine. The connecting rod will not come out through the cylinder bore, and the piston will not clear the crankshaft. The solution in this case, however, is to remove the connecting rod cap and push the piston up out of the bore on top. The floating piston pin is then removed to free the piston, and the rod is removed from below.

The opposed, or pancake, engine usually has a barrel crankcase split longitudinally, and it is necessary to dismantle the engine to get the rods out. Sometimes it may be possible, with the engine out of the car, to get one rod out by removal of the cylinder barrel on the opposite side.

Generally, on U.S. engines, the first step is ridge reaming to remove the unworn portion of the cylinder wall above piston ring travel. Then the rod caps are removed, and the entire piston and rod assembly is pushed up and out of the cylinder. Rods and their respective caps must be kept together and marked for cylinder location.

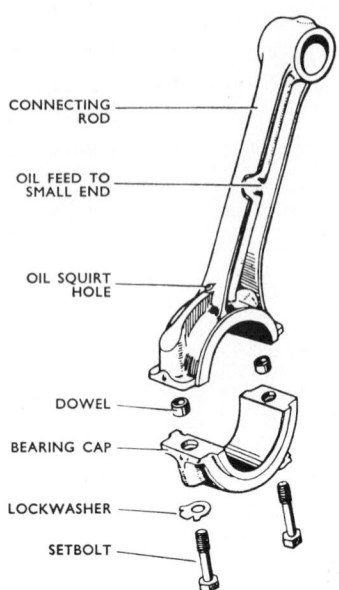

Fig. 15-15. Some connecting rod big ends are split at an angle for easier removal from cylinder.

REPLACEMENT OF INSERTS

With the insert, or shell type of bearing, it is usually possible to replace all main and all connecting rod bearings without removing the crankshaft or cylinder head. See Fig.

Fig. 15-16. Proper size of main bearing insert needed can be determined with crankshaft in place by means of this special tool.

15-16. These bearing inserts require no fitting by hand, since they are made to extremely close limits of accuracy. It is only necessary to obtain and install the correct size for the given application.

Even in the case of bushing or sleeve type bearings used in old Volkswagen engines, Fig. 15-17, replacement bearings are available in an assortment of sizes to meet almost any requirement.

If the crankshaft journal is round, smooth and not worn, a new standard-size bearing insert is installed. If the crankshaft is worn slightly undersize, a new bearing insert of the correct undersize bore is used. If the crankshaft has been damaged,

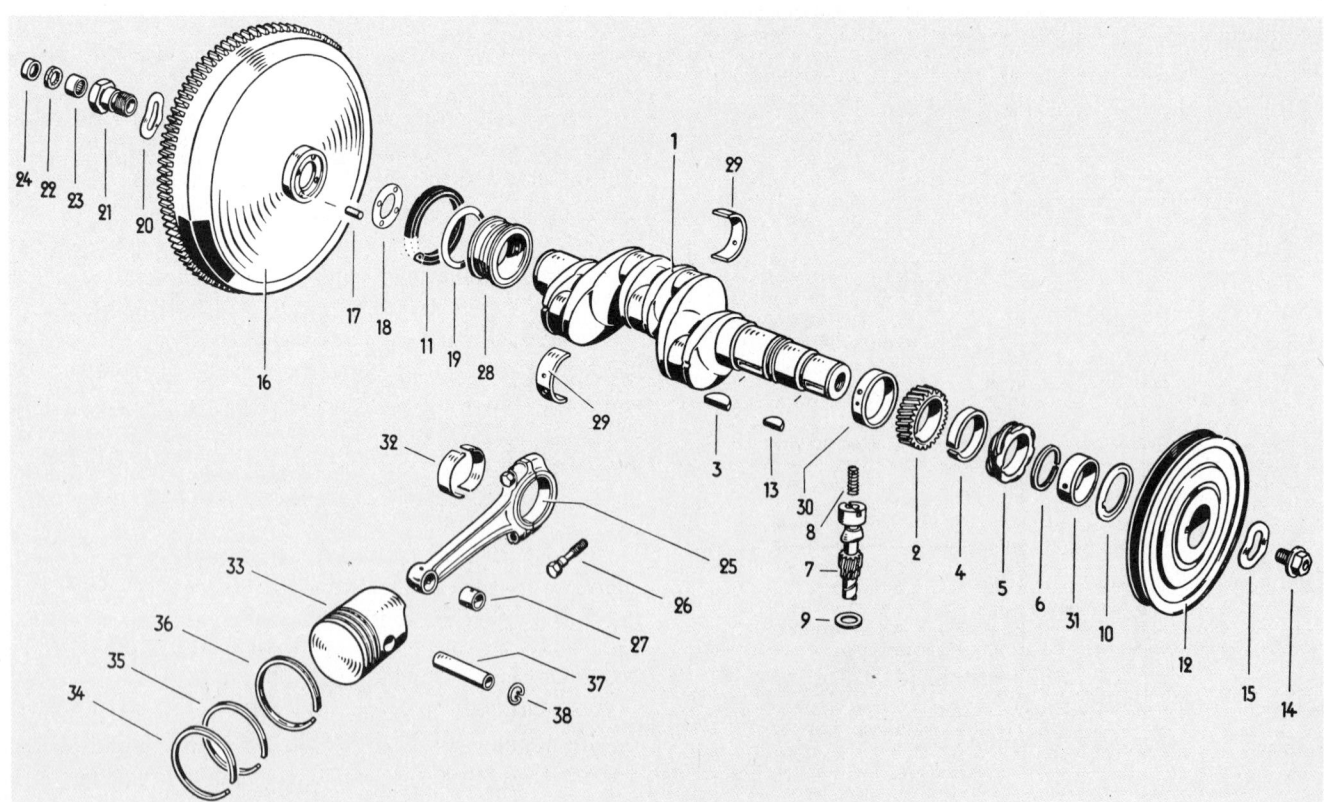

Fig. 15-17. Rear main bearing (28), two front main bearings (30 and 31) on Volkswagen engine are of sleeve type. Center main (29) is split.

and the journal is reconditioned to a standard undersize dimension, a still smaller undersize insert is used.

If the crankshaft journal has been reduced in diameter so much that a standard undersize insert will not fit, inserts are available with excess bearing metal that can be bored out to the size desired.

If the bearing bore and journal are round, these new inserts require no fitting or adjustment. If the journal is out-of-round more than .0015 in., it should be trued up or machined until it is round. The same applies to the bearing bore in which the insert seats. Any errors in the bore will distort the bearing shell when the bolts are drawn down to the proper specification. In general, when a connecting rod bearing has worn sufficiently to require replacement, the bore of the connecting rod will have worn to such an extent that reconditioning of the rod is also required.

It is, of course, impractical to measure the bore of the main bearing seats with the crankshaft in place to make sure they are round. However, the main bearing caps are heavier and less liable to distort than the connecting rod caps.

The connecting rod cap can be installed and bolted down without the bearing shell in it, and measured for roundness or taper with an inside micrometer, Fig. 15-10, or gauges made for the purpose. If slightly distorted, they can be machined true. If seriously distorted, the rod and cap should be discarded. It is not advisable to remove any appreciable amount of metal which might weaken the connecting rod.

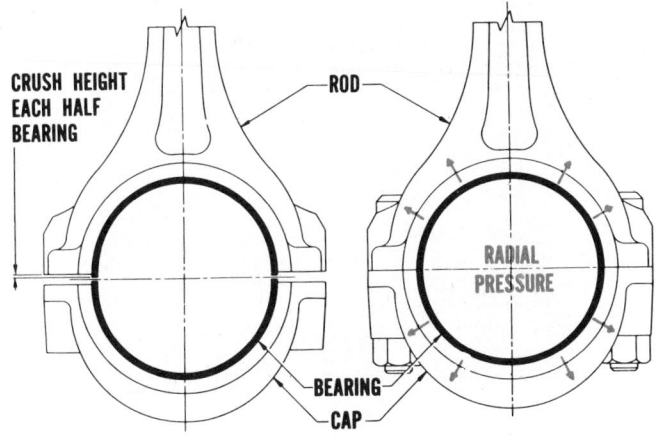

Fig. 15-18. Edges of bearing inserts should extend slightly beyond bearing seat so they will be forced into intimate contact with seat when cap is drawn up tight.

BEARING INSERT SEATING

The bearing seat and bearing insert MUST be round and true, as there MUST be intimate contact between the inside of the bearing seat bore and the outside of the bearing insert. If true and intimate contact does not exist, the heat will not flow from the insert to the crankcase or connecting rod, and the bearing may melt. It may be seen that no shims of any sort should be used between the insert crank seat in an effort to correct for wear or distortion.

This matter of heat dissipation is one reason for bearing "crush." Crush means that the two halves of the bearing shell extend a few thousandths beyond the bearing seat bore, as shown in exaggerated form in Fig. 15-18. When the bearing cap nuts are drawn down to specified tightness, the insert is forced to seat solidly and intimately in the bearing seats.

Another reason for crush is to make sure the bearing remains round. If it were not tightly held on the edge it might distort as shown in exaggerated form in Fig. 15-19, enough to allow the edges to touch the journal.

Still another reason for crush is to avoid any possible movement of the insert in the seat. If the shell should become slightly loose, it might oscillate in the seat and wear on the outside. This would interfere with both oil control and heat transfer. Any dirt between the shell and the bore will have the same effect. See Fig. 15-20.

Bearing crush must always be there, so the edges of the

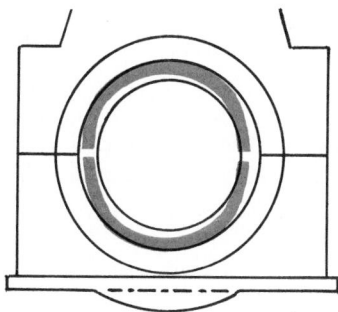

Fig. 15-19. Lack of proper crush in bearing insert installation may permit edges of insert to curl in toward shaft.

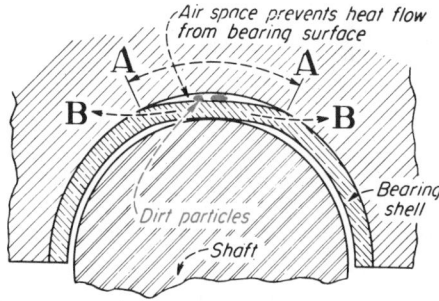

Fig. 15-20. Dirt between bearing insert and bore creates a dry spot on the bearing surface as well as hindering heat flow.

insert should not be dressed down flush with the bearing seats. Of course, the amount of crush must not be excessive. If it were, the insert would be distorted when the cap is drawn down and the bearing would be deformed, Fig. 15-21.

The amount of crush is only .001 or .002 in., and is finished to dimension the same as the bore and outside diameter. These inserts are extremely accurate and must be handled with care. They should be purchased to the precise size required, and inserted with no alteration or fitting.

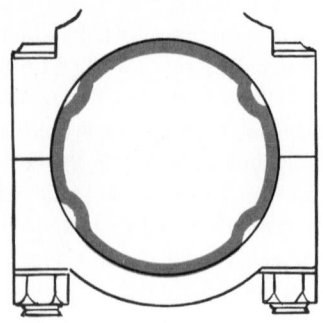

Fig. 15-21. An excessive crush will cause insert to buckle when cap is drawn down tight.

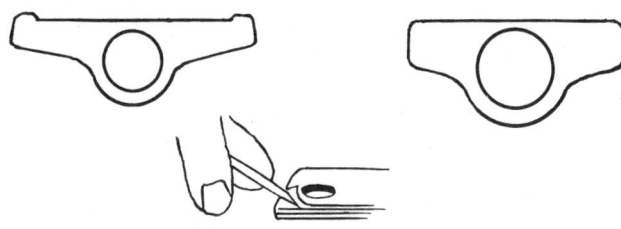

Fig. 15-23. Laminated shims may be of any shape desired. If equipped with a babbitt edge, babbitt will need to be dressed down as laminations are peeled off.

INTEGRAL BEARING ADJUSTMENT

When bearings of the integral type require adjustment, it can be done at the bearing cap. The result will probably be a bearing that is out-of-round, but a small engine lubricated by the splash method can operate satisfactorily with a slightly oval bearing on a round shaft. A pressure-fed bearing uses a controlled volume of oil and must be round.

An adjustable bearing is usually provided with thin shims on each side. See Fig. 15-22. These shims are placed between

the cap face on the abrasive. Care must be exercised to avoid lapping the cap crooked when this method is used. A skilled machinist can dress the cap down by draw-filing, but an amateur will ruin the cap by filing it crooked.

When all main bearings are adjusted properly, and the caps drawn up tight, there should be little resistance toward rotation of the shaft. If there is resistance: one or more bearings are fitted too tightly; there is insufficient end clearance on the thrust bearing; the crankshaft is sprung; or the bearings are not in correct alignment.

If the engine is stiff after a bearing job, it should not be started until the cause of the stiffness is located and eliminated.

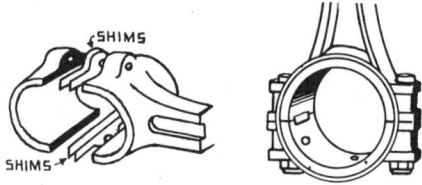

Fig. 15-22. An adjustable connecting rod bearing provided with shims for adjusting clearance.

the crankcase or rod when the bearing is poured, so we start out with a round bearing. Each time the bearing is adjusted for wear by the removal of these shims, it becomes more oval.

These shims are usually installed in several thicknesses; that is, .0005, .001, .002 in. etc., and the same quantity of each on both sides. Also the shims may be in laminated form; that is, a stack of shims each .0005 in. thick are soldered together at the edge to form a block. By peeling off as many layers as desired, the shim block is reduced in thickness. See Fig. 15-23.

The usual adjustment procedure for main bearings, is to loosen all of the bearing caps and adjust one bearing at a time. Shims are removed in equal numbers of the same thickness from each side until a slight resistance to rotation of the shaft is felt. Shims of proper thickness to provide the clearance desired are then reinserted, and shaft rotation again checked.

If the bearing cap is warped so that the faces are not flat and level, or if the bearing is not provided with shims, the cap is dressed down. Usually, this is done by placing a sheet of emery paper on a face plate or piece of plate glass and rubbing

Fig. 15-24. A feeler gauge can be used to check side clearance of connecting rod bearing.

SIDE CLEARANCE

The connecting rod must have some side clearance at the crankpin. If it has too much, the bearing may move sidewise and cause a knock. The clearance is measured by inserting a feeler gauge between the side of the cap and cheek of the crankshaft throw, as shown in Fig. 15-24. Manufacturers' specifications vary somewhat, but the usual side clearance is .005 to .010 in. Since there is no adjustment of the side clearance, excessive clearance requires replacement of the bearing inserts.

CONNECTING ROD MAINTENANCE

In addition to the proper fit of the large end of the connecting rod on the crankshaft, and the proper condition of the piston pin at the other end of the rod, consider the alignment of the rod itself, and the condition of the bearing bore in the big end of the rod.

Most V-type and opposed cylinder type engines have the cylinder blocks slightly offset from each other, endwise, to facilitate placement of the rod bearings on the crankshaft. It is also customary to offset the connecting rods, Fig. 15-25, to

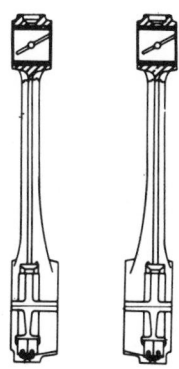

Fig. 15-25. Connecting rods are often off-set with regard to bearing surface. With short side of off-set usually being nearest main bearing.

place the power load as near to the main bearings as possible. This tends to reduce vibration of the crankshaft. On most engines, the connecting rods are marked on the same side. It is something that should be watched during engine assembly. If unmarked, align prick-punch marks on the same side of each rod end and cap, using one mark for cylinder No. 1, two marks for cylinder No. 2, etc.

Obviously, the piston pin and crankshaft journal must be precisely parallel. If the piston pin is not parallel with the crankshaft, every force on the piston will cause it to try to slide endwise on the piston pin. This will cause the piston to "slap" in the cylinder and create a knock or noise. The large end of the connecting rod will also have a tendency to knock.

Special equipment of suitable accuracy is available for checking the connecting rods, Fig. 15-26. This type of equipment checks the rods for twist as well as bends. EVERY connecting rod should be checked for proper alignment, just before it is installed in the engine. Many hard-to-locate noises in an engine originate in misalignment of the connecting rods.

Each rod should be checked again for location after it is installed in the engine. The rod might have a double bend in it, which would not be noticed on the alignment tester. Such a double bend might leave the piston pin parallel with the crankshaft, yet the upper end of the rod might be close enough to one of the piston bosses to cause a knock.

ROD BORE RECONDITIONING

Connecting rods are subjected to a lot of forces. The explosive pressure may reach as much as five tons on each rod. Forces of inertia which, at engine speeds in excess of 4000 rpm, reach huge values. Variation in temperature from below freezing to over 200 deg. F also contribute to operating stress.

These conditions tend to stretch the rod and distort the bore. Unless the bore of the connecting rod is true, without variation in diameter and without taper, the installed bearing insert will be distorted. Rapid wear will occur and excessive oil consumption will result. To be sure that the new inserts will fit properly in the rod bore, it is necessary to restore the bore diameter to its original size.

To recondition the rod bore, it must be reduced slightly below the original dimensions, then restored to the desired diameter. To accomplish this, material is removed from the parting surfaces of the rod end and cap. See Fig. 15-27. This is a precision operation and great accuracy is required. After the parting surfaces are precision ground, the cap is installed and accurately torqued.

Resurfacing will leave the rod bore slightly smaller than standard size, primarily in the vertical position. Next, the bore is honed to standard diameter, so that it meets the

Fig. 15-26. Typical connecting rod alignment fixture.

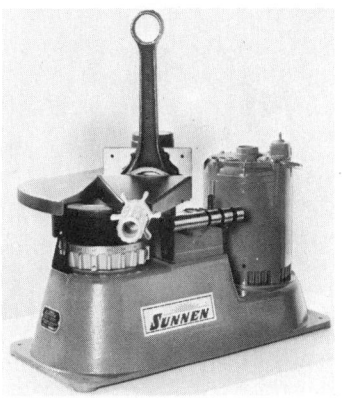

Fig. 15-27. Connecting rod cap and rod grinding equipment. (Sunnen Products Co.)

manufacturer's specificiaties for roundness, straightness and surface finish. Particular care must be taken to make certain that the center line of the rod bore is at right angles to the center line of the rod, and also parallel to the center line of the piston pin.

CAMSHAFT BEARINGS

Some camshafts bear directly in the metal of the crankcase, but most run in bearings in the form of bronze bushings pressed into the crankcase. These bushings are not adjustable for wear and must be replaced when worn. The degree of wear dictating replacement is more a matter of oil clearance than any tendency toward noise. If seriously worn, they may create noise and vibration in the timing gears and valve train.

The camshaft must be removed to replace the camshaft bearings. This involves removal of the valves and operating mechanism, or raising and holding the valve lifters up off the camshaft against the tension of the valve springs. Actually, it is seldom necessary to replace a camshaft bearing or bearings until the engine is dismantled for other work.

After the camshaft is removed, the bearings are pressed out of their bores with a special tool made for the purpose. The bushings can be driven out with a hammer and drift. However, the special tool will be needed for inserting the new bushings, so it should be used to remove the old ones, Fig. 15-28.

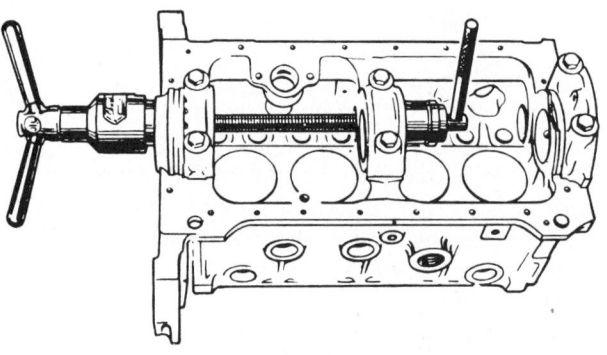

Fig. 15-28. One type of special tool for removing and inserting camshaft bushings.

New bushings are available in the proper outside diameter and standard, as well as undersize, inside diameter. If the camshaft has been undersized by regrinding worn journals, the bearings can be align reamed to any size desired by use of the proper equipment. See Fig. 15-29.

Before the new bushings are pressed into place, they are coated lightly on the outside with white lead. The white lead facilitates insertion by acting as a lubricant, and it helps avoid distortion of the bushing. The oil holes in the bushings are lined up with the oil holes in the crankcase before pressure is applied, since the bushing cannot be turned after it starts in the bore.

It is essential to start the bushing squarely in the bore and apply pressure steadily and evenly. If the bushing cocks in the

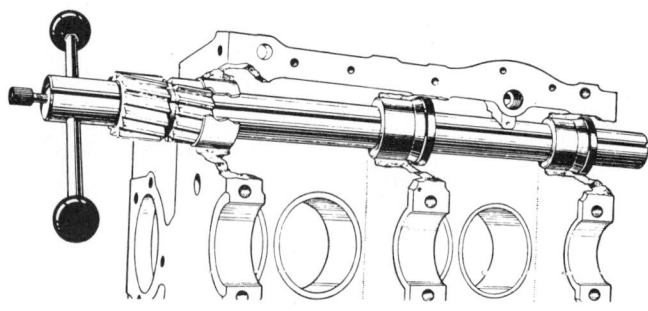

Fig. 15-29. Special boring bar for align reaming camshaft bearings.

bore, it will be distorted and the inside diameter decreased.

The bushings should be pushed fully into the bore. If one end extends, the valve lifter may strike it. It is good policy to check the installation after the valve operating parts are installed to make sure there is sufficient clearance for the lifters. Also, end-play of the camshaft should be checked and corrected if it exceeds the manufacturers' specifications (usually about the same as for crankshafts).

Usually, the camshaft is provided with a thrust plate under which shims are placed for adjustment of clearance. In other cases, there is a spring and button at the end of the shaft that holds the camshaft against a flange on one of the bearings to eliminate excessive end-wise movement.

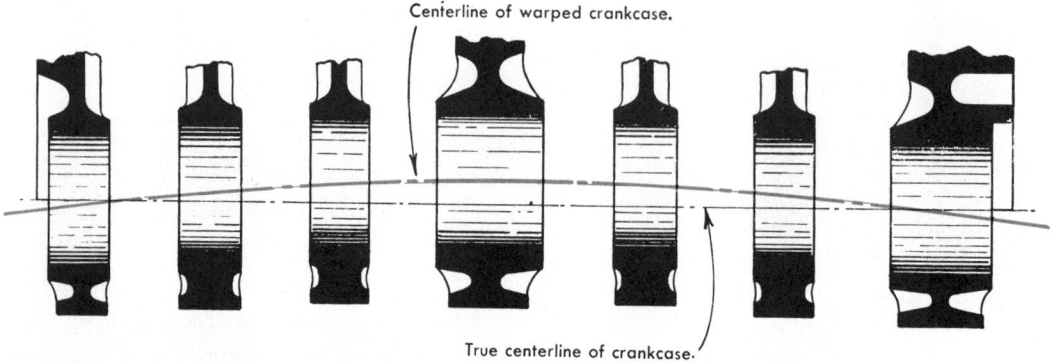

Fig. 15-30. When a crankcase becomes warped, centerline of bearing bores will form an arc. Condition is remedied by align boring.

Fig. 15-31. Special equipment used to align hone main and camshaft bearing bores. (Sunnen Products Co.)

MAIN BEARING INSTALLATION

The replacement of main bearings of the insert type present a problem only when the cylinder block has become warped, Fig. 15-30, and/or when the crankshaft is scored or badly worn. If the cylinder block is not warped and the shaft is in good condition, all that is necessary is to remove the old bearing inserts and slip in new ones of the correct size.

Main bearing inserts are replaced on one journal at a time. The procedure is to remove the bearing cap and slip out the bearing insert. To remove the upper half of the bearing insert, a "roll-out-pin" is inserted into the oil hole of the crankshaft. The end of this pin protrudes slightly from the surface of the crankpin. When the crankshaft is rotated, the pin will force out the upper insert. A tool for this purpose can be fashioned from a cotter pin. See Fig. 15-32.

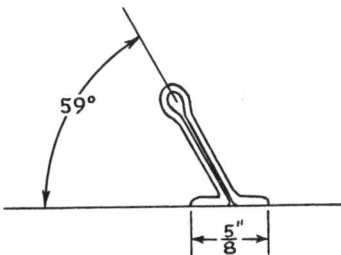

Fig. 15-32. Method of bending cotter pin, which is then placed in oil hole to remove upper main bearing insert.

The new bearing insert is slipped into position by hand. In some cases it may be necessary to use the "roll-out-pin" to complete the installation. After installing the bearing cap and insert, the same procedure is followed with the other bearings.

Bearing cap bolts are not tightened completely until all the bearing inserts are in position. Then the bolts are tightened to the specified torque.

If the crankshaft is scored and the crankcase warped, the engine must be removed to do a complete reconditioning job. This includes regrinding the crankshaft, Fig. 15-3, and align boring or honing the bearing bores, Fig. 15-31.

If the crankcase is not warped, the crankshaft is reground to a standard undersize for which bearing inserts are available. If the crankcase is warped, semifinished bearings are installed in the crankcase. The bearings are align bored or align honed, then the crankshaft is reground to the correct size to fit bearings.

Before align boring or honing the semifinished bearings, make sure caps are properly assembled and bolts tightened to the specified torque. Also, all oil ways should be plugged with substantial pieces of clean cloth to prevent chips and bearings from getting into the lubrication system.

When locating the boring bar or honing unit, great care must be exercised to insure that the center line of the finished bearings will be the correct distance from the top of the cylinder block, parallel with it and at right angles to the cylinder bores.

In an engine built with a gear to drive the camshaft, the distance between the center line of the camshaft and the bore of the main bearings must be very accurately maintained. Otherwise, the crankshaft and the camshaft gears will not mesh properly. A little more tolerance is permitted if the camshaft is driven by a chain or a cog belt.

After all boring or honing and thrust bearing facing operations are completed, all plugs must be removed from the oilways and all chips cleaned from the interior of the crankcase. All inside edges of each bored or honed surface should be hand chamfered with a scraper about 1/64th in.

In all bearing work, extreme accuracy and cleanliness are required. Particular attention must be paid to the areas contacting the backs of the bearing inserts, the bearing surfaces and also the interior of all oil lines and oil passages.

In case of a leaking rear main bearing, it is often possible to replace the bearing seal and bearing without removing the crankshaft.

To do this, loosen all the main bearing caps slightly to lower the crankshaft. Then, remove the rear main bearing cap. With a small pin punch, start to drive out the seal. Grasp it with a pair of pliers and pull it out. To replace the upper part of the seal, first lubricate it with engine oil. Start it into the groove by hand and have the crankshaft turned until the seal slides in place.

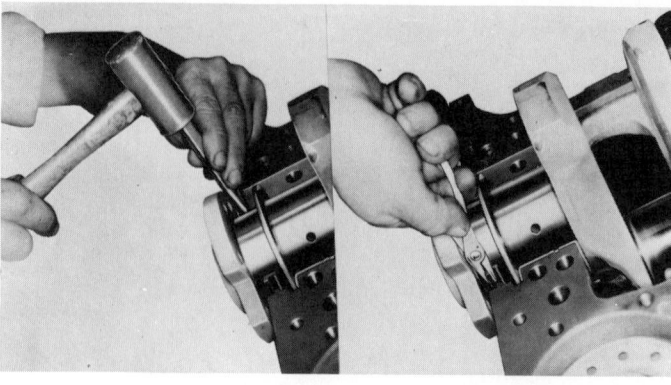

Fig. 15-33. Removing seal from rear main bearing.

The upper insert can be removed by first inserting a special tool or a bent cotter pin, Fig. 15-32, into the oil hole of the crankshaft. Then, as the crankshaft is turned, the pin will push out the bearing half. Start removing the seal with a punch, Fig. 15-33, then pull it out with a pair of pliers.

CARE OF GRINDING WHEELS

Grinding wheels are an important piece of automotive maintenance equipment. They are used in a large variety of grinding operations: refacing valves, grinding crankshafts and camshafts, resurfacing cylinder heads, grinding brake drums and discs. These are all precision operations, and if the precise results are to be attained, it is essential that the grinding wheels are properly stored, serviced and used.

First of all, when using a grinding wheel, see that the machine is properly equipped with safety guards; also that the operator wears appropriate goggles and gloves. Equally important, the operator should avoid standing in front of the rotating grinding wheel, in case the wheel should break.

Remember that a rotating grinding wheel is an extremely dangerous piece of equipment. Should the wheel break, the flying pieces would cause severe injury or death to anyone who would be struck.

Before installing a grinding wheel, there are additional safety precautions that should be taken. The wheel should be tapped with a light, nonmetallic implement (such as the handle of a screwdriver), for lighter wheels, and a "soft" hammer for heavier wheels. If the resultant sound is dull, the wheel should be discarded as unsafe to use. A good wheel when tapped will give a resonant sound. When making this test, the wheel should be dry and free of any foreign matter. Incidentally, organic-bonded wheels do not emit the clear metallic ring as do vitrified and silicate wheels. The wheels should be tapped about 45 deg. each side of the vertical center line and about 1 to 2 in. from the outer edge.

Wheels should be stored in a dry area, away from steam, exhaust and spray. Store straight wheels vertically.

When mounting new wheels, first be sure to match the wheel speed with the spindle, and be sure the maximum speed is not exceeded. Also, the hole in the wheel must match the spindle diameter accurately, and the flange should be at least one-third of the wheel diameter. Be sure to use the "blotter" furnished by the manufacturer and tighten carefully, using the crisscross pattern. Follow torque specifications, if available. Avoid heavy cuts and excessive cutting speeds.

When the work is completed, shut off the coolant and let the wheel run long enough to throw off surplus coolant. If the coolant is left on, it can throw the wheel out of balance.

When dressing a wheel to uncover sharp new teeth, support the dresser on a work rest adjusted away from the wheel so it will not jam. Guide it evenly across the work.

Examine the machine bearings to be sure there is no excess wear; also check for loose mountings or loose floor anchorage.

REVIEW QUESTIONS — CRANKSHAFT, CAMSHAFT AND CONNECTING ROD SERVICE

1. Give three reasons for crankshaft wear.
2. Invisible cracks in steel parts may be found by means of:
   a. Chemical equipment.
   b. Magnetic equipment.
   c. Either.
3. An undersize crankshaft journal can be altered to become oversize. True or False?
4. Camshafts are hardened all over. True or False?
5. Clearance between crankshaft and bearing in a splash lubricated engine may be _____ than in a pressure lubricated engine.
   a. More. b. The same. c. Less.
6. What happens if oil clearances are unequal in a pressure oiling system?
7. Name two ways of measuring bearing clearance.
8. In general, the diametral clearance in a small engine main bearing should be:
   a. .0005 to .001 in.
   b. .001 to .0015 in.
   c. .0015 to .002 in.
9. In general, endwise clearance for crankshafts should not exceed:
   a. .004 in.   b. .006 in.   c. .008 in.
10. What provision is made for removing connecting rods from top of engine where rod end is too large to pass through cylinder bore?
11. A bearing bore should be trued up if it is out-of-round more than:
    a. .0015 in.   b. .0025 in.   c. .005 in.
12. Name two reasons for bearing crush.
13. The short side of the offset on the No. 1 connecting rod should be toward the _____ of the engine.
14. A piston pin can be properly fitted and parallel with the crankshaft and still cause a knock. True or False?
15. If a camshaft bushing is pressed in crooked, the inside diameter will be _____.
16. Should coolant be left running after grinding operation is completed?

VALVE SERVICE

The condition of the valves has much to do with engine efficiency. Poppet valves lead a hard life, so it is not surprising that valve service is a frequently performed operation in automotive service shops.

Valve service was once a hand lapping procedure using an abrasive paste between the valve face and valve seat. This procedure was assumed to provide a gas-tight valve, and little attention or thought was given to valve seat width, heat dissipation, concentricity of valve with seat, strength of valve springs, wear in valve guides and all the other things that

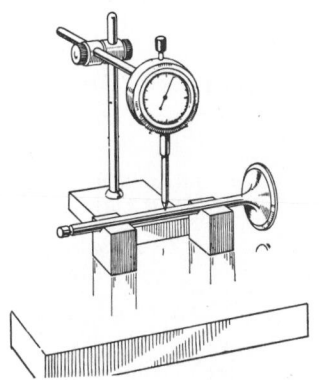

Fig. 16-1. Method of mounting dial gauge to check valve stem for straightness.

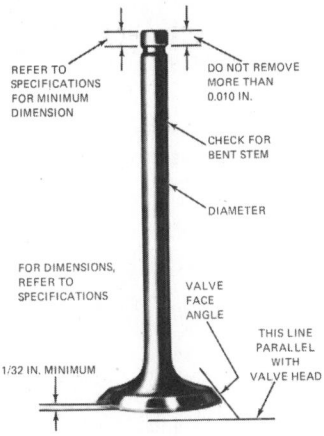

Fig. 16-2. Some key points to check when inspecting an engine valve.

require attention on the modern high speed engine.

Modern "valve grinding" is a true grinding process. Every part of the operation is governed by careful measurement with accurate test equipment. The first step after the valves are removed and cleaned, is to determine whether the valve can be reconditioned or whether it must be replaced. If the stem is scored, pitted, bent or worn more than .002 in., it should be discarded.

A dial gauge and V-blocks can be used to check the stem for straightness, Fig. 16-1. For other visual checkpoints, see Figs. 16-2 and 16-3. The stem diameter can be checked for wear with a micrometer, Fig. 16-4.

Visual inspection, for example, may disclose a seriously warped valve head, split valve face or lack of margin. If the face is burned, badly warped or worn to a thin margin, the

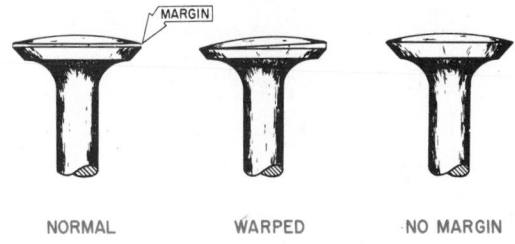

Fig. 16-3. Visual inspection may disclose serious defects.

valve is discarded. See Fig. 16-3. If the valve appears to be in good condition, it is placed in a special grinding machine known as a valve refacer, and a new surface is ground on the face at the proper angle with and concentric (having same center) with the stem. See Fig. 16-5.

Most valve faces are cut at an angle of 45 deg. with the stem. An angle of 30 deg. is also used. In either case, a slight interference angle, about 1/2 to 1 deg., may be cut on either the valve face or valve seat, to improve the seating ability, Fig. 16-6. However it is invariably cut on the valve face as valve refacers can be adjusted to any desired angle.

VALVE SEAT RECONDITIONING

The seat in the block or head is also resurfaced with the aid of special reamers or grinders, Fig. 16-7. First of all, it is

Fig. 16-4. Measuring valve stem for wear.

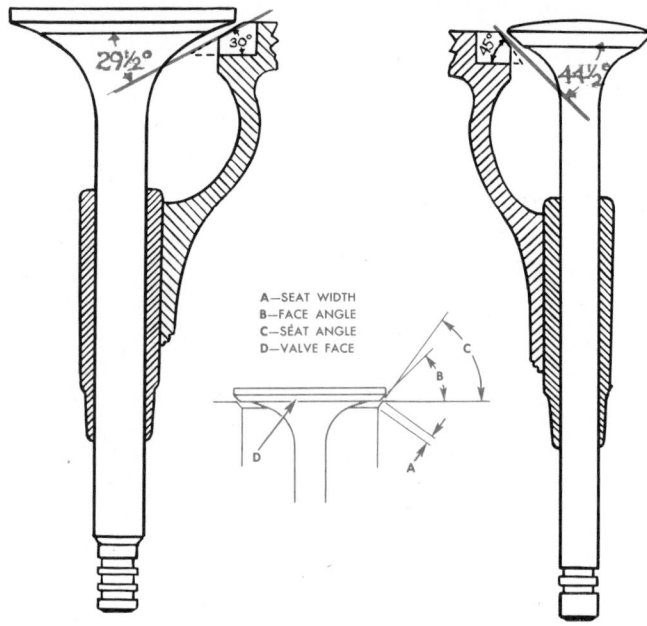

A—SEAT WIDTH
B—FACE ANGLE
C—SEAT ANGLE
D—VALVE FACE

Fig. 16-6. In many cases, a slight interference angle is cut on valve face.

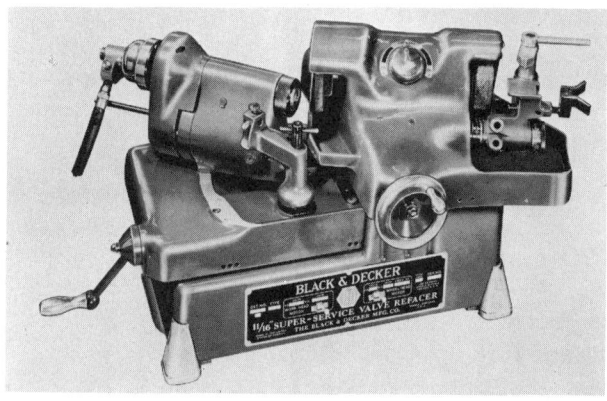

Fig. 16-5. A special valve refacing machine designed for grinding valves accurately.

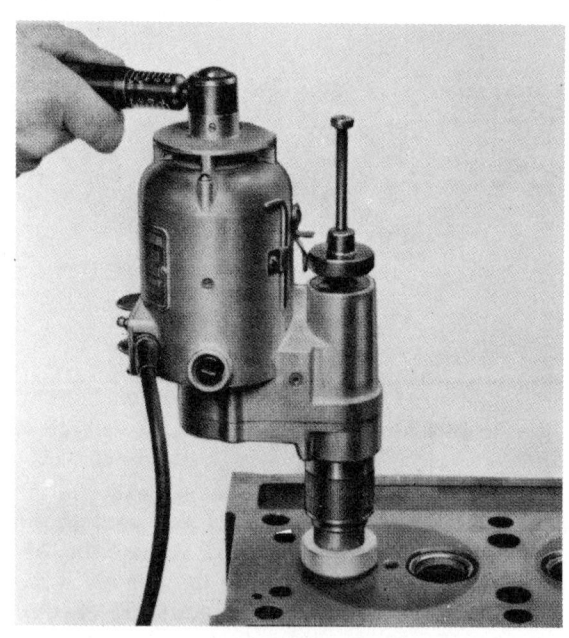

Fig. 16-7. Special equipment used for grinding valve seats. This equipment is essential where hardened seats are used.

necessary to position the tool so it will be located to cut the seat concentric with the valve stem guide and at the proper angle. This is difficult to do if the guide is worn. Guides should be replaced if worn out-of-round, bell-mouthed, or worn to an excessive degree at any point.

Valve seats that are too narrow will not dissipate the heat properly and, if too wide, will encourage carbon to adhere to them. In the absence of factory specifications, a seat 1/16 in. wide is usually satisfactory. If the seat is wider than this, the first operation will be to narrow the seat by cutting an acute angle under the seat, and an·obtuse angle above the seat. This is done with special reamers or grinders made for the purpose. See Fig. 16-8.

After the seat is sufficiently narrowed, the seat surface is cut or ground to the proper angle. This cutting or grinding must result in a smooth true surface if the valve is to be gas-tight. It cannot be true, if the seat is not concentric with the valve stem. A method of testing with a dial gauge is shown

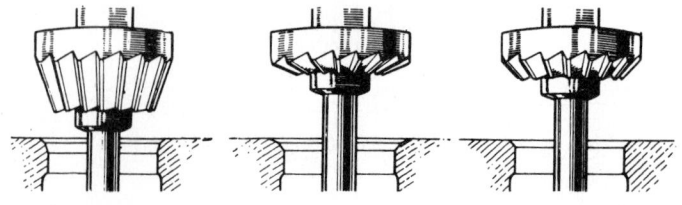

Fig. 16-8. A set of special reamers is used to narrow valve seats.

Valve Service

Fig. 16-9. A specially mounted dial gauge is used to check concentricity of valve seat with valve guide.

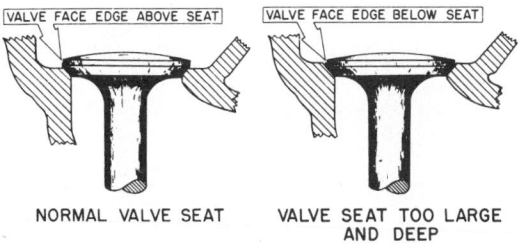

NORMAL VALVE SEAT — VALVE SEAT TOO LARGE AND DEEP

Fig. 16-10. Oversize valves can be used in cases where block or head cannot be bored out for inserted valve seats.

in Fig. 16-9. The seat should be concentric with the guide within .001 in.

Sometimes the valve seat becomes so enlarged that the valve head sinks into the seat. See Fig. 16-10. In this case, the remedy is to install oversize valves or install valve seat inserts.

VALVE SEAT INSERTS

Hardened valve seat inserts are ordinarily used in air-cooled automobile engines having aluminum cylinder heads. Induction hardened valve seats are also used in many late model engines having cast iron heads, Fig. 16-11.

If the insert is badly worn or burned, it may be easier to replace the insert than to try to recondition it. These seats are made of hard, heat-resisting metal, refaced by grinding with special grinders.

If the seat is the old screw-in type, it is a simple matter to unscrew the old seat and screw in the new one. The seating surface is ground after the insert is in place. The pressed-in, or shrunk-in, inserts are usually held tightly in place by rolling or peening the metal around the edge of the insert, after it is in place.

Since it is sometimes difficult to clean up the peening enough to allow the insert to be pulled, the inserts are usually broken for removal. Whether the old insert is pulled or broken out, it is essential that the hole for the insert be round and true. If the insert does not bottom fully in the hole, or if it does not fit tightly all around the hole, there will be poor heat transfer from the insert to the head or block. Then of course, the insert will run hotter than it should.

For this reason, the inserts are usually sized to provide an "interference fit." That is, the insert is one or two thousandths larger in diameter than the hole into which it is to be installed. In this case, to avoid the stresses imposed in pressing them in

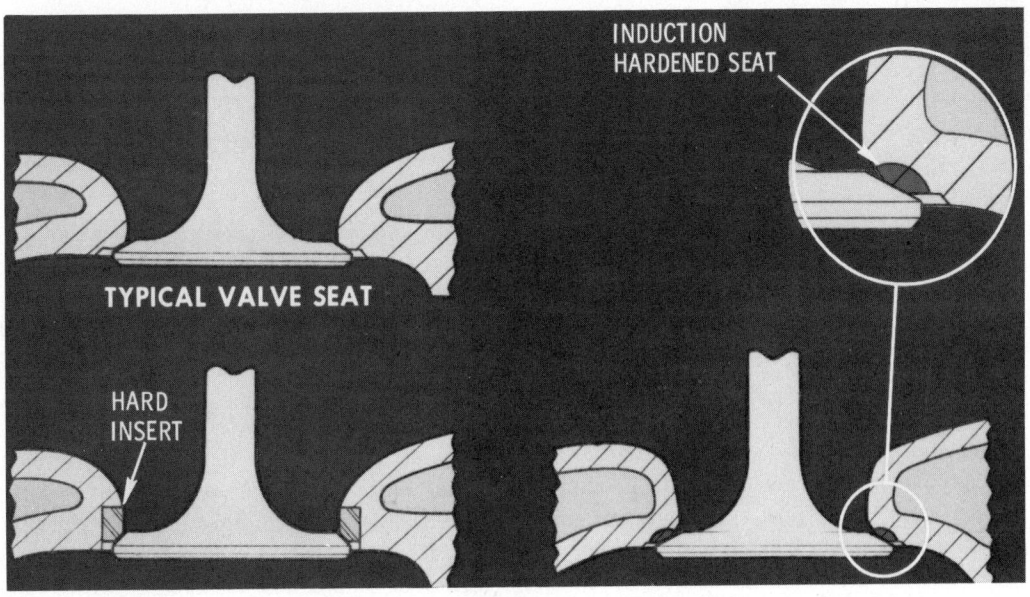

Fig. 16-11. Typical valve seat and valve seat of hardened insert design are shown at left. The induction hardened seat is at the right.

place, the inserts are often shrunk for insertion.

For service installation, the inserts may be placed in a deep freeze for a few hours, or packed in dry ice for a few minutes. Either of these procedures will shrink them sufficiently for easy insertion. When frozen, the inserts must be handled carefully and quickly, since they are quite brittle and will crack or split easily.

After insertion, the metal around the insert may be lightly rolled or peened over the top outside edge of the insert, to help hold it firmly in place. The final step is to grind the valve seat true with the valve guide.

VALVE STEM GUIDES

Older engines have separate pressed-in valve guides. Now, they are built with the valve stem in direct contact with a hole bored in the cylinder head. Heat dissipation is better where pressed-in guides are not used, but wear in the guides means honing the holes out larger, and fitting new valves with oversize stems. Separate guides are made of cast iron. Bronze is also used because of the superior wearing characteristics and more rapid heat dissipating ability.

Press-in guides are often identical for the exhaust and inlet valves, but are sometimes installed differently. In other cases, the exhaust and inlet guides are not interchangeable. See Fig. 16-12. In still another case, the guides are identical, but the

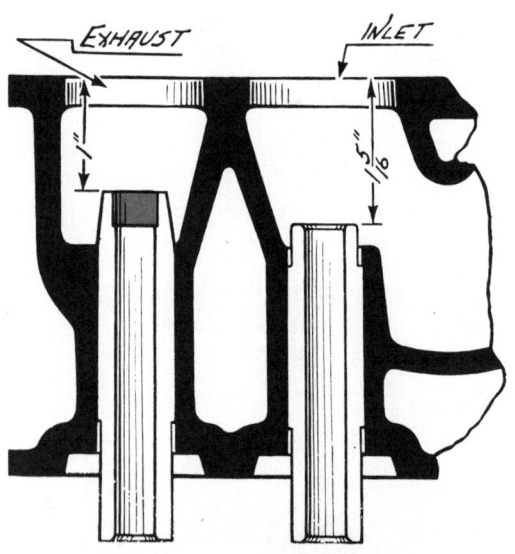

Fig. 16-12. These valve guides are not identical. Exhaust guide extends farther into port than inlet. Note counterbore in exhaust guide.

inlet guides are installed upside down from the exhaust guides. Some exhaust guides are cut off shorter in the port opening, and others are counterbored in the port end, to reduce the tendency for carbon to accumulate in the guide.

Carbon does accumulate in the guide bore and on the stem of exhaust valves. This causes them to stick partly open or to slow down in action. The tendency for carbon to accumulate increases as the exhaust valve stem and guide wear, because

more hot gas blows by between the stem and guide. Wear on the intake stem and guide is equally undesirable, because it permits air to be drawn in through the clearance to dilute the air and gasoline mixture. Under such conditions, it is impossible to obtain a satisfactory carburetor adjustment.

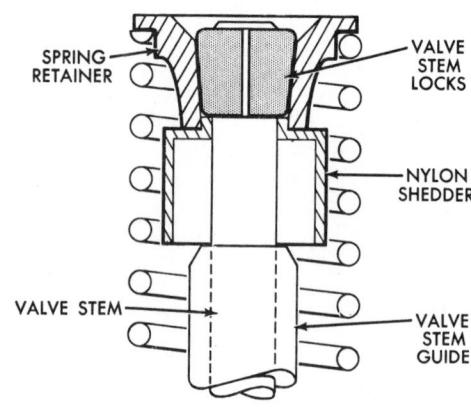

Fig. 16-13. Special oil shedder of nylon used on Cadillac engine valves. While not an oil seal, it greatly reduces amount of oil reaching valve stems.

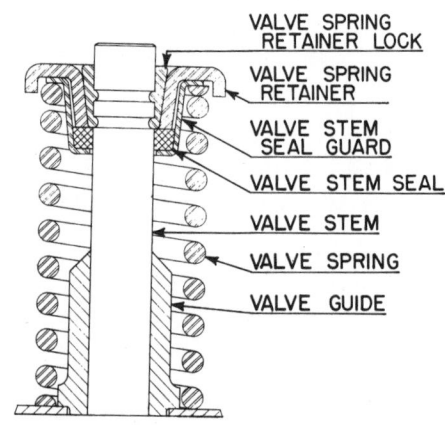

Fig. 16-14. Here a retainer or guard is used to hold a seal near end of overhead valve stem.

Also, oil from the valve chamber may be sucked in between valve and guide to increase oil consumption and carbon up the engine. This oil leakage is sometimes pronounced on overhead valve engines, as oil is pumped up on the valve operating rocker arms. To discourage this tendency, a special cutter is available to cut a bevel on the end of untapered valve guides.

It is customary to place seals either on the valve stem or in the guide on overhead valve engines to exclude excess oil. Several types are shown in Figs. 16-13 through 16-16. One manufacturer vents the valve guide to the atmosphere to break up this suction, as shown in Fig. 16-17.

Another undesirable result of excessive valve guide wear is to permit the valve to wobble enough to cause it to ride to one side of the valve seat as shown in Fig. 16-18. Quite naturally, this interferes with proper seating and sealing of the valve and

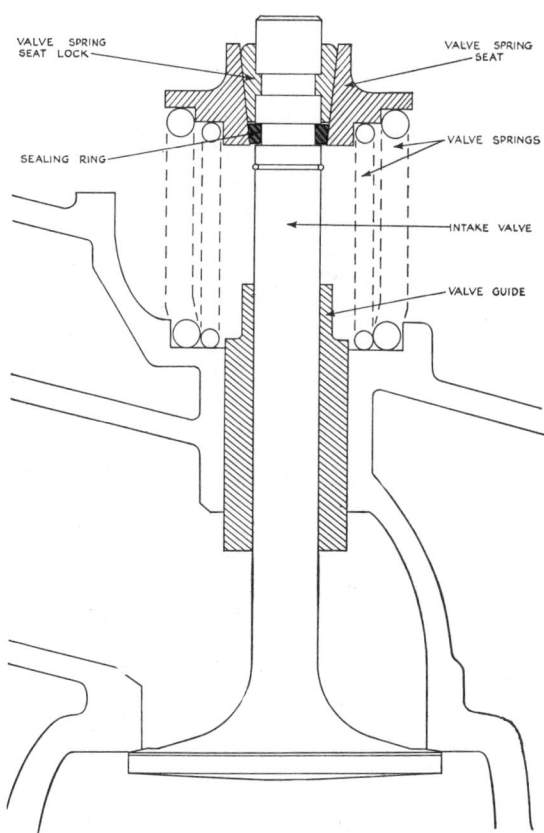

Fig. 16-15. In this case, a seal is placed in a groove in overhead valve stem.

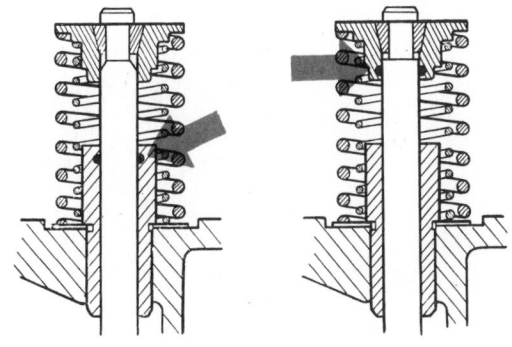

Fig. 16-16. Two methods of using O-ring seals on overhead valves.

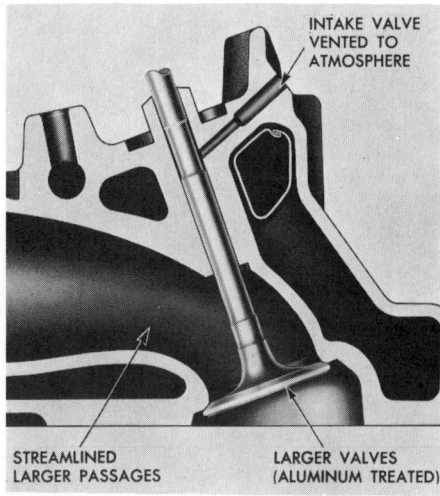

Fig. 16-17. Note reduction in part of valve stem diameter at vent opening on this Pontiac inlet valve design.

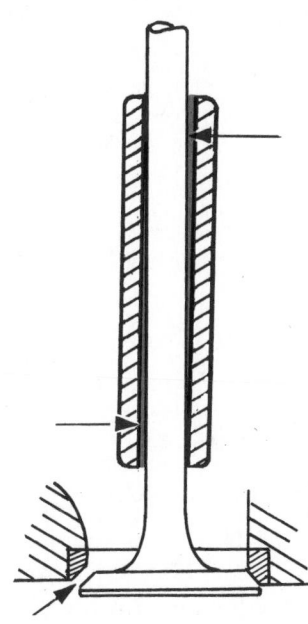

Fig. 16-18. Looseness in valve guide permits valve to wobble and cause undue wear of valve and seat.

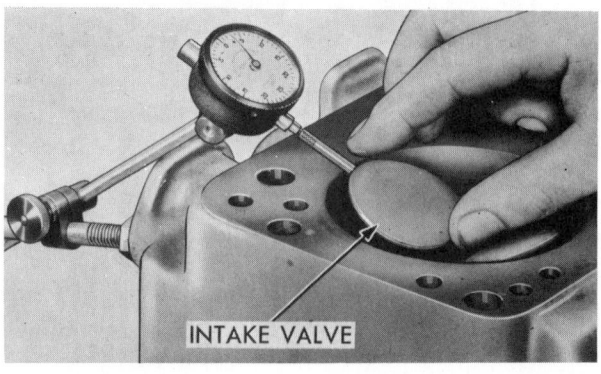

Fig. 16-19. When measuring clearance between valve and guide, valve must be off seat.

also promotes wear. It is customary to replace the valve guides or valves, or both, whenever more than .005 in. clearance for small valves or .006 in. for large valves exists between valve stem and guide. One method of measuring clearance is shown in Fig. 16-19.

Before any measurement is made, the valve stem must be cleaned and polished, and the valve stem guide thoroughly cleaned of carbon deposits. Special tools are made for cleaning carbon out of valve guides, Fig. 16-20. The measurement for clearance should be made with the valve slightly off the seat as shown in Fig. 16-19. The valve spring must also be removed while making the measurement.

Fig. 16-20. Method of cleaning carbon out of valve guides with special tool.

Fig. 16-21. Valve guide partially cut away to show spiral groove made by special tool.

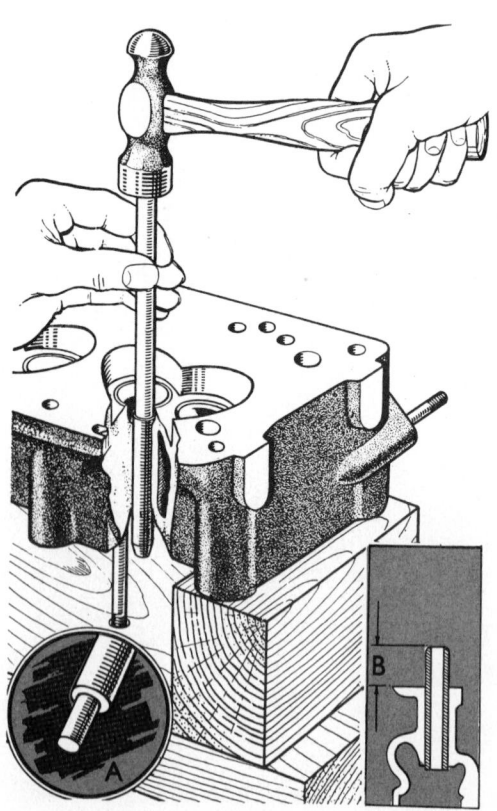

Fig. 16-22. A is end of pilot driver used in removing and replacing valve guide. B is dimension specified by manufacturer.

One repair method for valve guide troubles, that does not involve replacement of the guides, is to upset the metal inside the valve guide bore by rolling a spiral groove through it. See Fig. 16-21. The idea here is to decrease the inside diameter slightly and, at the same time, form a continuous pocket for oil to gather and act as a seal. A special tool is made for this purpose. The guide is then reamed to the desired diameter.

When valve guides of the press-in type are replaced, it is important to have them positioned properly in the block or head. See Fig. 16-22. The car manufacturer specifies the proper position with regard to some accessible surface, from which measurement can be made. An example of this is shown in Fig. 16-23.

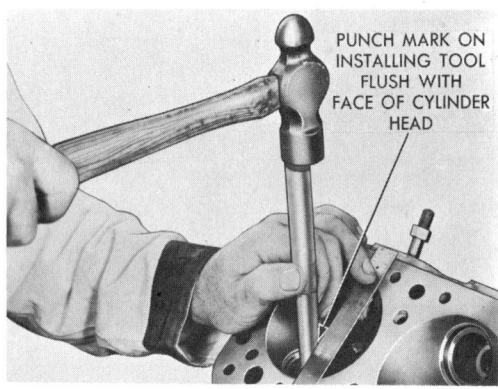

Fig. 16-23. Valve guides must be accurately positioned in head in accordance with manufacturers' specifications.

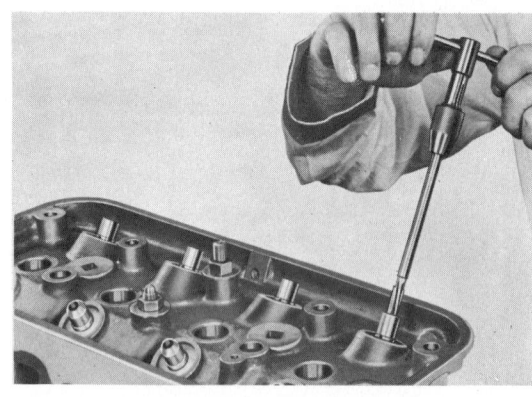

Fig. 16-24. Special reamers make it possible to ream valve guides to accurate dimensions required.

In cases where an unusual amount of trouble is experienced with exhaust valves sticking because of rapid accumulation of carbon, it has been found helpful to cut off the end of the exhaust guide. This is often done with a drill ground to a flat angle on the end. The guide is cut down even with the opening in the port in which the guide is located.

After the guides are pressed in place, it is usually necessary to ream them to proper size, and provide clearance for heat expansion of the valve stem. Special reamers are made for this purpose, Fig. 16-24. This operation must be performed carefully so that the hole will be straight and true with a good surface. Exhaust valve stems require more clearance in the guides than intake valves. Fit intake valves with .001-.003 in. clearance, and exhaust valves with .002-.004 in. clearance, depending on the size of the valve stem. To reduce cylinder head reconditioning time, special equipment has been designed to recondition valve guides and seats, Fig. 16-25.

VALVE SPRINGS

Valve springs seldom receive the attention they deserve. They are an exceedingly important part of the engine, and have much to do with the engine performance. They are seldom replaced unless broken, yet they should be replaced when not up to specifications. They work hard, being subjected to millions of cycles of high speed operation, and all of it under shock conditions.

The valves are opened with lightning-like speed by the action of the cam, and the spring is expected to close the valve just as fast as it is opened. If the spring is weak and does not hold the lifter in contact with the cam, noise will be created and the valve, spring, lifter and cam will be subjected to hammer-like blows that cause metal fatigue. Many broken valves result from shock caused by sticking stems, weak valve springs or excessive tappet clearance.

The car manufacturer provides specifications on the free length of the spring, and the pressure in pounds that the spring should exert when it is compressed to a measured length. Special tools are available for measuring the length and strength of the spring. Valve springs are simple coil wire springs. They should not be expected to last forever.

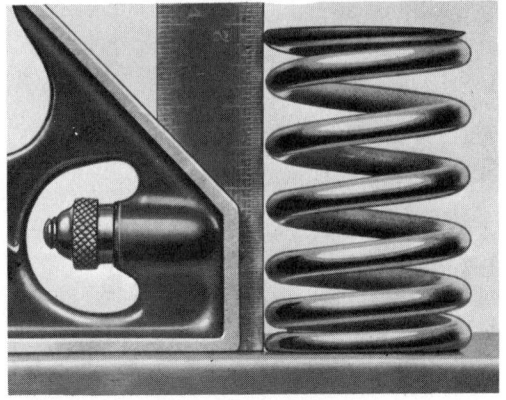

Fig. 16-26. Valve springs should be square on each end and of proper length.

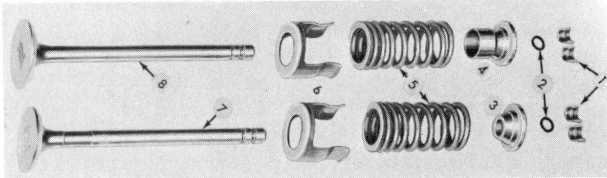

Fig. 16-27. Typical valve with accessory parts. 1—Split cone type valve spring keepers. 2—"O" type oil seals. 3—Valve spring retainer. 4—Valve spring retainer and oil sheddar. 5—Valve springs. 6—Surge dampers. 7—Exhaust valve. 8—Intake valve.

Fig. 16-28. Dual coil spring at left, tapered spring at right.

Valve springs should be square on each end. Otherwise, they will have a tendency to pull the valve stem to one side and cause undue wear on the valve stem and guide. They can be checked for squareness and free length as shown in Fig. 16-26. When the coils of the spring are wound closer together at one end than at the other, the close coils are to be placed next to the engine block or head. See Fig. 16-27. This uneven coiling is done to lessen the tendency of the spring to vibrate or "flutter" at high speeds.

Another method of reducing flutter is to install dampers, as shown in Fig. 16-27. Still another method is to taper the spring or to use two lighter springs, one within the other, instead of one heavy spring. See Fig. 16-28. The two springs

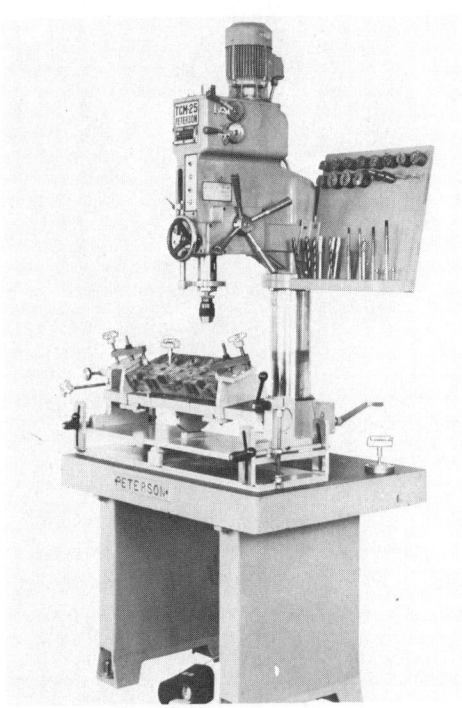

Fig. 16-25. Valve guide and seat reconditioning machine.

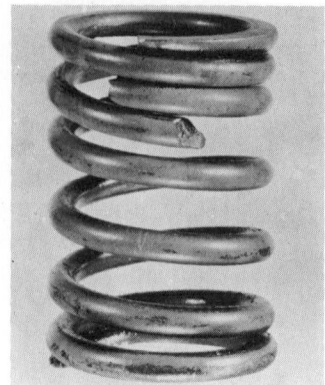

Fig. 16-29. Although not heavily etched, spring broke in service.

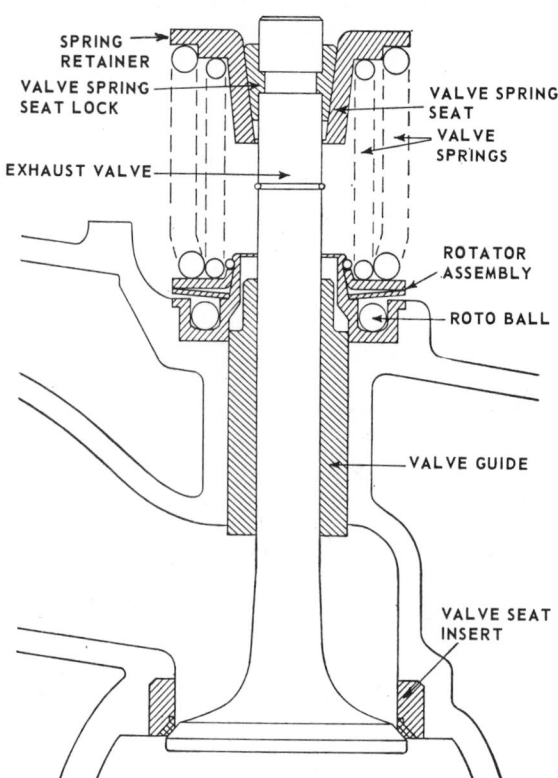

Fig. 16-30. Typical tapered C valve spring seat lock as installed on valve assembly. Note valve rotator.

are usually wound in opposite directions. Whatever the construction used, it is important to check the springs whenever they are out, and replace them whenever they are not up to specifications.

Periodic replacement is also good to avoid unexpected failure. Valve springs often become "etched" when the valve chamber is subject to corrosive vapors. Some valve chambers are not well ventilated and steam or moisture containing acids formed from combustion will collect and cause flecks of rust to form on the valve springs. This etching is likely to cause the spring to break. See Fig. 16-29.

This corrosive action is similar to the corrosion that causes pits and rust to eat into valve stems. On the valve stems it means wear. A broken valve spring on an overhead valve engine may permit the valve to drop into the cylinder and damage or ruin a piston, or cylinder head.

VALVE SPRING RETAINERS

Valve spring locks, or keepers, are usually of the split cone, horseshoe or flat rectangular key type. They fit into an appropriate slot in the end of the valve stem. Fig. 16-30 shows the split cone type in position. A cupped washer called the spring retainer fits over these keepers, Fig. 16-27, and the tension of the spring bearing on the retainers holds the locks in place. Other methods are also used: slots cut near the end of the stem, and a key or pin pushed through the slot; threads cut on the end of the stem for a nut and locknut; etc.

Removal is accomplished by holding the valve stationary while the spring is compressed enough to allow the retainer to be raised from the locks. See Fig. 16-31. The locks are removed and the valve spring released. This allows the valve to be removed first, then the spring and retainer can be removed. Valves should never be mixed up when removed, unless it is known that new valves or guides are to be installed. The valves should always be replaced in the same guide from which they were removed.

VALVE ROTATORS

Some retainers are more complicated and are intended to permit or encourage the valve to rotate slightly with regard to

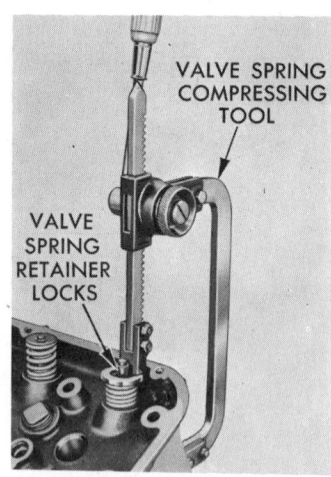

Fig. 16-31. Compressing valve spring allows retainer locks to be removed which frees valve and spring for removal.

the seat. Some of these are called "free valves" and the purpose is to provide a longer lasting seal between valve and valve seat. Rotation of the valve will discourage the formation of carbon deposits, and help prevent valve warpage.

Some of these free valve devices release the valve from the valve spring tension at one point in the cycle of operation, so that it is free to rotate slightly. One type is illustrated in Fig. 16-32. With this type it is important to maintain the clearances

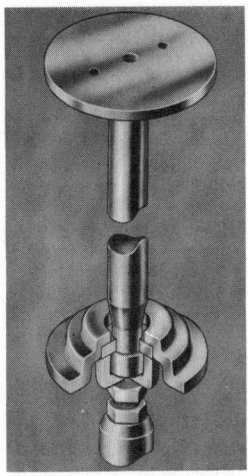

Fig. 16-32. Construction of free valve device.

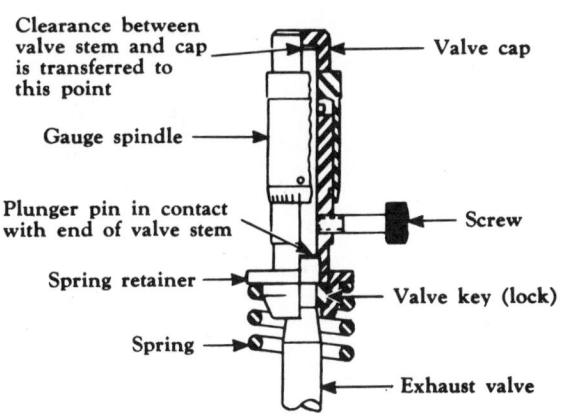

Fig. 16-34. Special gauge for measuring free valve clearance.

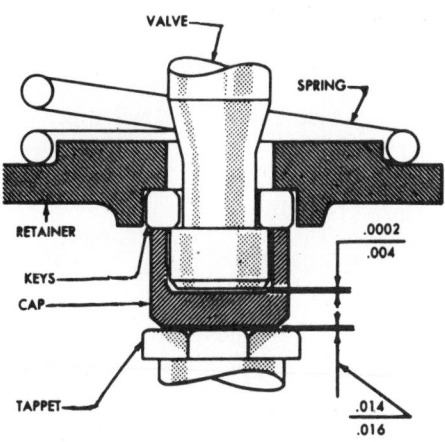

Fig. 16-33. With this free valve device, it is important to maintain clearance between end of valve and cap.

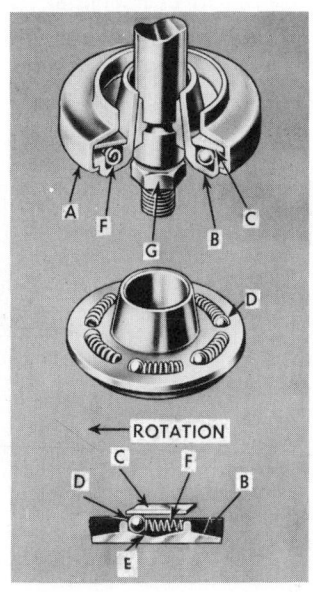

Fig. 16-35. In this case, positive rotation of valve is caused by inclines down which balls roll when pressure is applied. A—Housing. B—Retainer. C—Cupped washer. D—Balls. E—Ramp. F—Spring. G—Valve lifter.

between stem and cup and between cup and retainer within specified limits. See Fig. 16-33. If the clearance between stem end and cap is too little, the end of the valve stem is ground off as needed. If the clearance is too great, the skirt of the cap is ground off as required. A special tool is available for measuring the clearance accurately. See Fig. 16-34.

Other devices are known as valve rotators, and impart a positive rotational effort to the valve once during each cycle of operation. One such device is illustrated in Fig. 16-35. Also see Fig. 16-30.

Regardless of type of device used to provide or permit rotation of the valves, there appears to be no question about their ability to assist in maintaining a satisfactory seal between valve and seat.

Valve rotators keep the seat and valve face clean and, in that regard, help maintain emission control.

Valve rotators also minimize sticking and wear between guide and stem. Other than cost and complication, the only apparent objection to them is the slightly increased weight of the reciprocating assembly, which might encourage a tendency

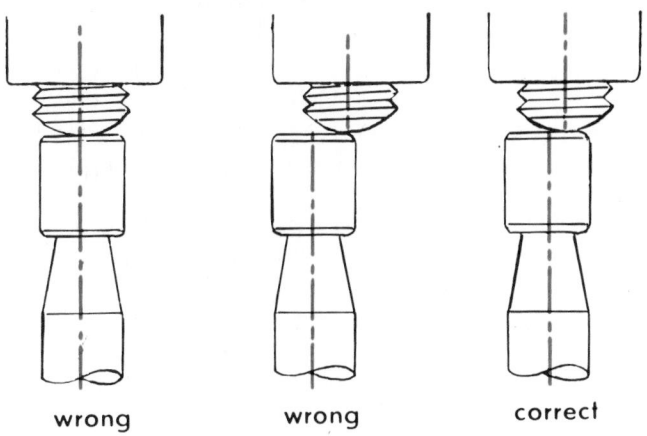

Fig. 16-36. Method of obtaining valve rotation on a Volkswagen engine.

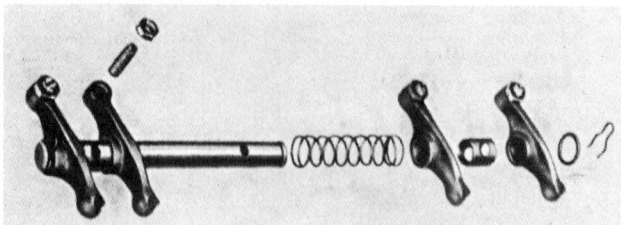

Fig. 16-37. Spacers are placed on the valve rocker shaft on either side of the rocker arms to obtain proper offset.

toward flutter in an extremely high speed engine.

The Volkswagen engine design contemplates slight rotation of the valves without adding any extra parts. This is done by adjusting the valve rocker arms to contact the valve stems slightly off center. The correct amount of offset is indicated in Fig. 16-36. This adjustment is accomplished by adding or removing spacers on either side of the rocker arms, as required to move the rocker arm lengthwise as needed. See Fig. 16-37.

Fig. 16-38. Typical timing gear installation.

VALVE ACTUATING MECHANISMS

It is customary in U.S. built engines to mesh the camshaft drive gear directly with the crankshaft gear or, in the case of chain drive, to locate the sprockets near each other. See Figs. 16-38 and 16-39. In the case of an overhead cam engine, such as the Chevrolet Monza, a cog belt is used. On the AMC Jeep 230, Fig. 16-40, and Opel, Fig. 16-41, the camshaft is chain driven.

The cog belt used on the overhead camshaft Chevrolet is made of reinforced fiber glass. While this is a relatively long drive, no difficulties have resulted from stretching. Adjustment of the cog belt tension is made by positioning the water pump housing. The material of which the belt is made is described as being heat resistant as well as oil resistant. It is inherently silent in operation, requires no lubrication and absorbs the shock of opening and closing the valves.

Where long chains are used to operate camshafts, the

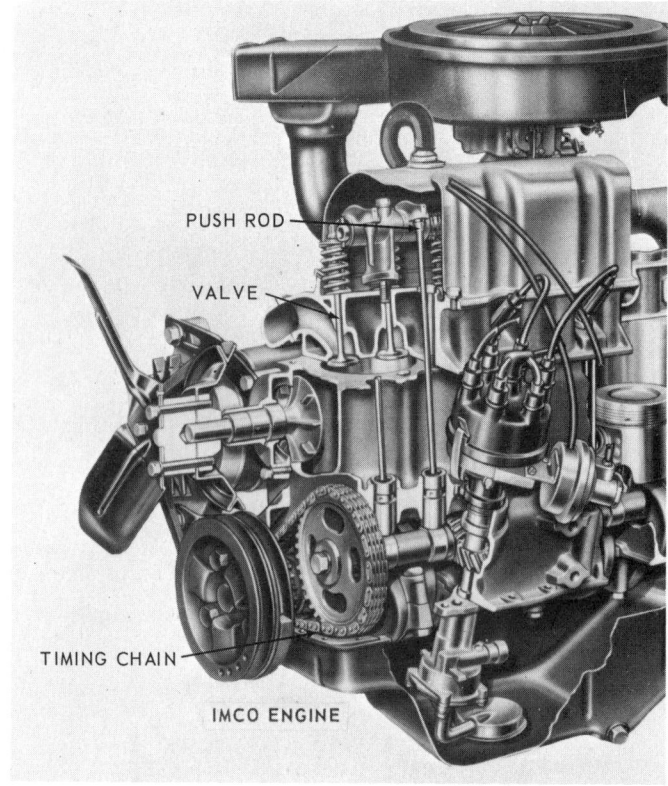

Fig. 16-39. Location of timing chain on six cylinder overhead valve engine. V-8 is similar.

problem of slack or lost motion presents intself. Valve timing must be precise. Sloppy motion cannot be tolerated. Several devices have been tried to control this. One of the most interesting is an automatic hydraulic chain tightener, as used on the English Rover. This design is shown in Fig. 16-42. Engine oil pressure is used in the hydraulic cylinder.

WORN VALVE MECHANISM

The camshaft and camshaft drive are only part of the mechanism used to operate the valves. To continue the study of valve action and timing, consider the operation of parts such as lifters, push rods, rocker arms, etc. Each has something to do with valve timing. Consider, too, that many minor faults may equal a major fault. A little wear at many points in the valve train may be equal, in effect, to considerable wear at one point.

For example, suppose there is .005 in. excess wear between the gear teeth. This will allow the valves to open late and close early. Add to this another .005 in. excess wear in the camshaft bearings. This will reduce valve lift, as well as increase late opening and early closing of the valves. Add another .005 in. worn from the cam contour, which also changes the valve lift or timing, or both.

On an overhead valve engine, additional wearing parts include both ends of the rocker arm operating rod, the rocker arm, rocker arm bushing and shaft. See Fig. 16-41. Now, on top of all this, add another .005 in. excess wear between the

EXHAUST ROCKERS
INTAKE ROCKERS
CAMSHAFT
TIMING CHAIN

Fig. 16-40. Details of AMC Jeep six cylinder single overhead camshaft engine.

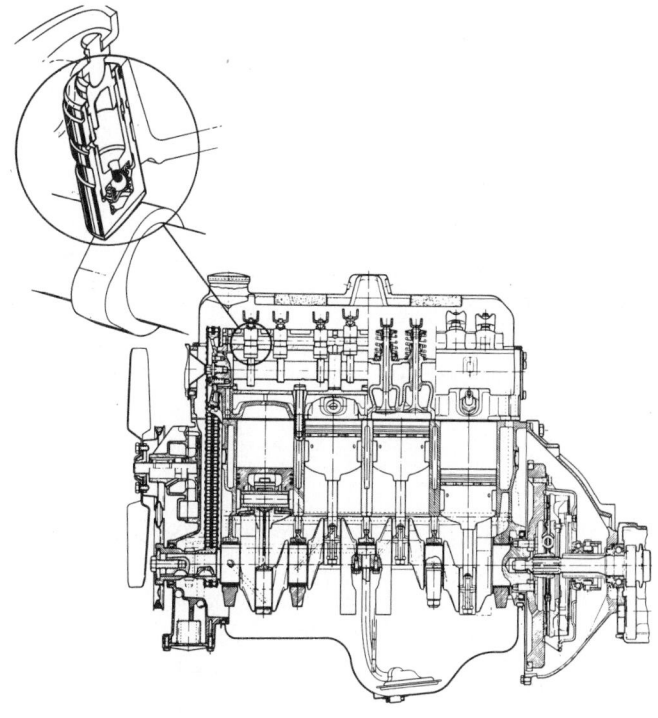

Fig. 16-41. Note timing chain driving overhead camshaft on Opel four cylinder engine. Hydraulic lifters are a feature.

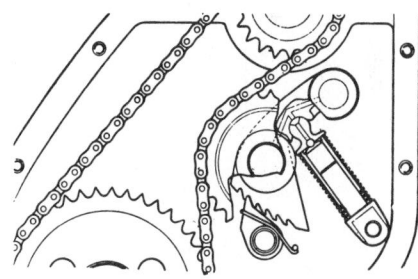

Fig. 16-42. Automatic hydraulic timing chain tensioner, or adjuster used on Rover engine.

lifter and guide. This results in the lifter moving sidewise in the guide before it starts to lift the valve.

Obviously, all this cumulative wear will interfere with efficient operation of the engine. On engines having solid valve lifters, such conditions are often further aggravated by careless adjustment of the valve tappets. Many mechanics who do not understand valve action, adjust the tappets with too much clearance to make sure there is no possibility of the valve holding open. They do not realize that they are restricting the ability of the engine to draw in a full charge of mixture, and to dispose of the exhaust gas properly.

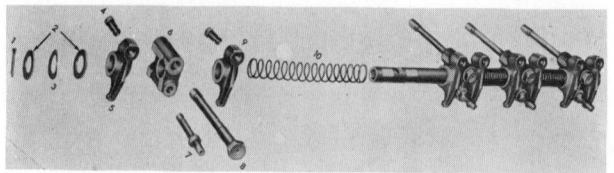

Fig. 16-43. Rocker shaft assembly consists of multiple parts.

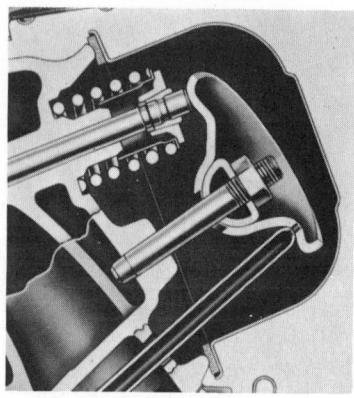

Fig. 16-45. Instead of a rocker arm shaft, many cars now have rocker arms mounted on individual studs.

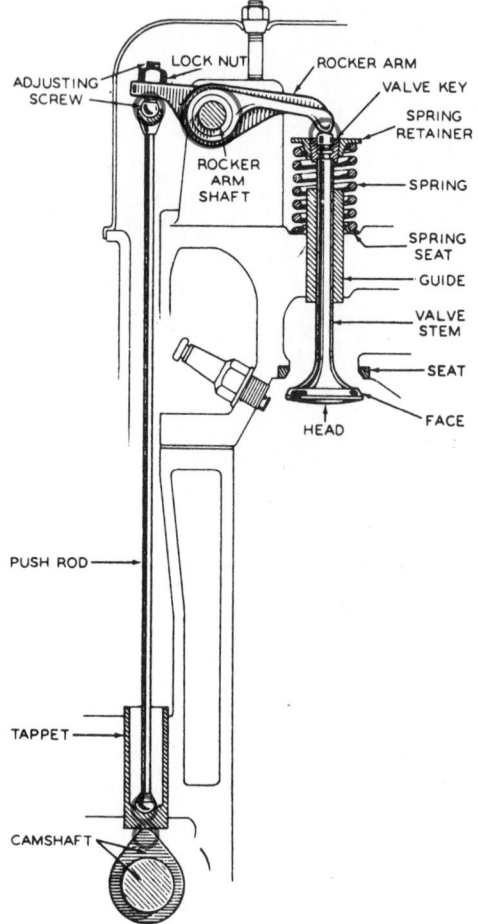

Fig. 16-44. There are many points of wear (circled areas) in valve operating train. A little wear at each point adds up to a lot of wear in train.

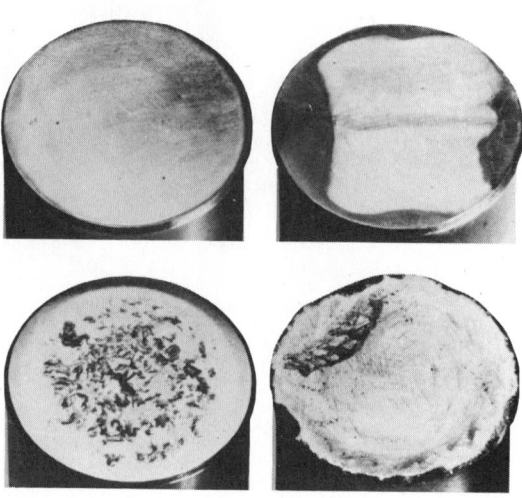

Fig. 16-46. Above. Normal wear on base of valve lifter. Below. Abnormal conditions include galling and excessive wear beyond case hardening.

If excess wear exists at all of those points, it becomes a serious matter indeed. For these reasons, the valve tappet clearance on overhead valve engines must be more carefully adjusted.

The engine manufacturer furnishes precise valve tappet clearance specifications in all cases, and these should be followed explicitly. Otherwise, the efforts of the design engineer to build efficiency into the engine are partially wasted. These specifications are so precise that they state whether the engine should be hot or cold when the adjustment is made. Furthermore, some manufacturers provide a different specification for checking the valve timing.

It should be evident that accurate adjustment is impossible if the various contacting surfaces are worn to untrue dimen-

sions. See Figs. 16-44 and 16-45. If such parts are not too seriously worn, they can be restored by grinding with equipment made for the purpose. If they are worn enough to be through the case-hardened shell, they should be discarded and replaced with new parts.

When checking valve lifters, it is essential that the surface contacted by the cam be examined for wear. Fig. 16-46 shows a lifter with normal wear, and others with varying degrees of wear. A method of checking the cam for wear is illustrated in Fig. 15-6.

VALVE SPRING INSTALLED HEIGHT

As the result of valve and seat reconditioning, the valve will be recessed further into the cylinder head, with the result the valve spring will not be compressed as much as it normally would be. In other words, the installed height of the spring would be increased. The effect is just the same as weak valve springs.

The installed height is measured from the surface of the

Fig. 16-47. Measuring the installed valve spring height.

Fig. 16-49. Use of special gauge to adjust valve tappets on overhead valve engine.

spring pad to the underside of the spring retainer, Fig. 16-47.

This condition can be remedied by the installation of new valves and seats. Another method is to install spacing washers between the spring and the cylinder head. These spacers should be of such thickness that the installed height of the spring is in accordance with the specified height.

VALVE TAPPET ADJUSTMENT

Adjustment of the tappet clearance is made by means of a feeler gauge as shown in Fig. 16-48, or with the aid of a special dial gauge as shown in Fig. 16-49. In these cases, the adjustment is readily accessible on an overhead valve engine.

Several European engines are of the flat or pancake type with opposed cylinders. In these cases, the overhead valves are on the outside of the engine. On the German Volkswagen for example, the engine is a flat four in the rear of the car. Adjustment of the valve clearance is made from under the rear fender on each side. See Fig. 16-50.

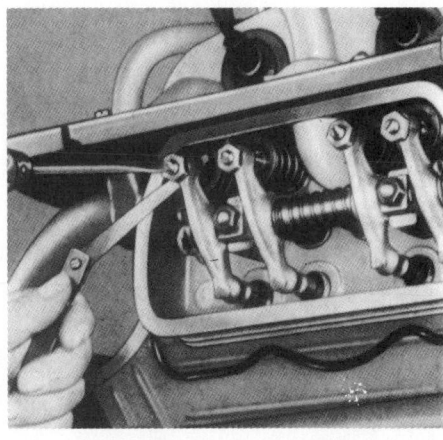

Fig. 16-50. Volkswagen valves can be adjusted from under the rear fenders on each side.

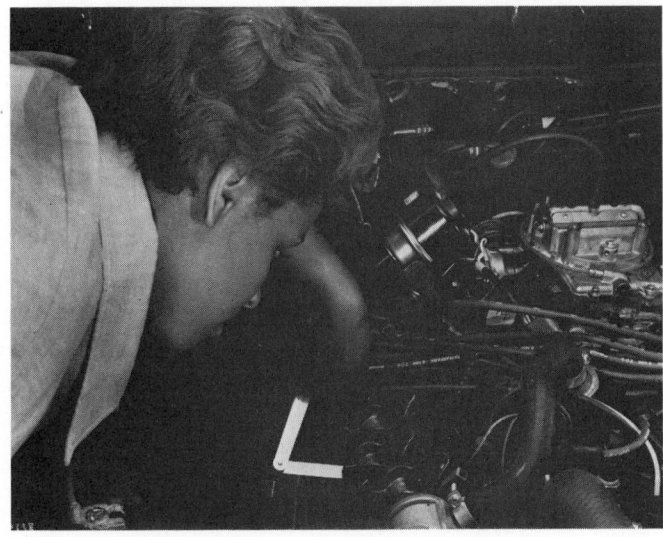

Fig. 16-48. Method of using a feeler gauge to adjust valve clearance on an overhead valve engine.

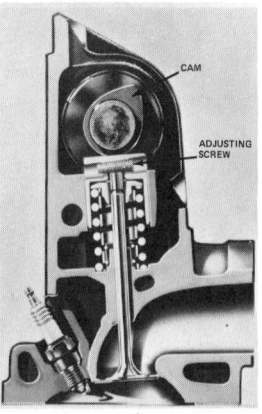

Fig. 16-51. Vega engine valve clearance is adjusted by rotating adjustment screw one full turn at a time to keep flat surface on screw against end of valve stem.

ADJUSTING VEGA VALVE LASH

Valve lash on the overhead camshaft Vega is adjusted by an unusual method. The valve adjusting screw, Fig. 16-51, is threaded in all areas except the valve contact surface. This makes it necessary to turn the adjusting screw a complete revolution to maintain correct valve stem-to-adjusting screw relationship. A special tool is inserted in the hole in the adjusting screw, and a leaf type feeler gauge is used to measure the clearance as the screw is turned.

HYDRAULIC VALVE LIFTERS

Many engines have self-adjusting valve lifters of the hydraulic type which operate at zero clearance at all times. See Fig. 16-52. In this case, the engine oil circulation system supplies a constant flow of oil under pressure to the lifters. Operating at zero clearance, these lifters compensate for changes in engine temperature, adapt automatically for minor wear at various points, and provide ideal valve timing as well as freedom from noise.

Fig. 16-52. On this overhead valve installation, oil supply holes are drilled directly into oil galleries on each side.

Another type of hydraulic lifter is shown in Fig. 16-53. In this illustration, 1 is the tube that carries the oil coming in at 2 from the engine supply to the ball check 3, which rests on seat 8. The supply chamber inside body 9 is kept full of oil at all times, when the engine is running, since port 2 is connected into the engine oil pressure system. Similarly, the oil, being under pressure, can raise ball 3 and keep the pressure chamber below 6 full at all times, by going through port 4.

When the lifter body 9 rests on the heel of the cam, spring 5 pushes the plunger 6 into contact with the end of the valve stem. This spring is not strong enough to lift the engine valve off its seat. This gives zero tappet clearance. As the plunger lifts, it creates a slight vacuum in the pressure chamber, oil is drawn through port 4, through tube 1 and seat 8, past the ball check 3.

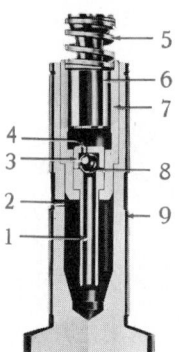

Fig. 16-53. Cutaway section of hydraulic valve lifter shows how oil from engine oiling system enters lifter assembly through port hole 2 located in an external groove.

As the cam rotates and lifts body 9, it carries cylinder 7 with it. This tends to push plunger 6 down into cylinder 7. The pressure generated causes the ball check valve to seat and hold the oil in the pressure chamber under plunger 6. As oil, for all practical purposes is incompressible, the valve is lifted on a column of oil and supported while the valve is open. When the valve seats, the operating cycle is repeated.

There are several types of hydraulic valve lifters in use. They vary somewhat in design, Fig. 16-54, but all work on the same general principle.

There is a small amount of oil leakage between the lifter plunger and the cylinder while the engine valve is off its seat. This is desirable in order that the valve clearance will be adjusted to zero each time the valve is opened. This clearance must be controlled closely as excess leakage at this point would reduce the valve lift. The leakage rate is specified by the

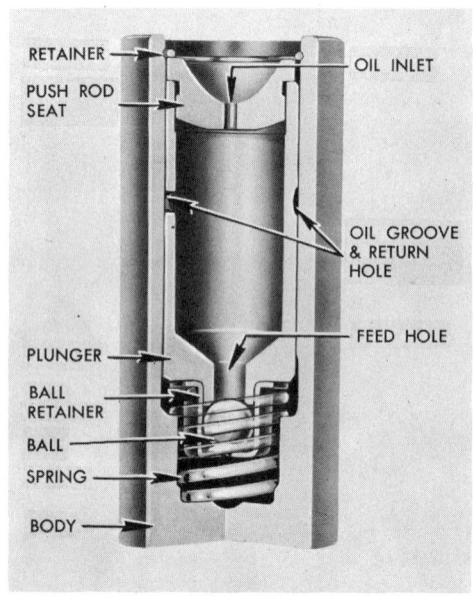

Fig. 16-54. Another typical hydraulic valve lifter, which differs in design, but operates on same principle as example described.

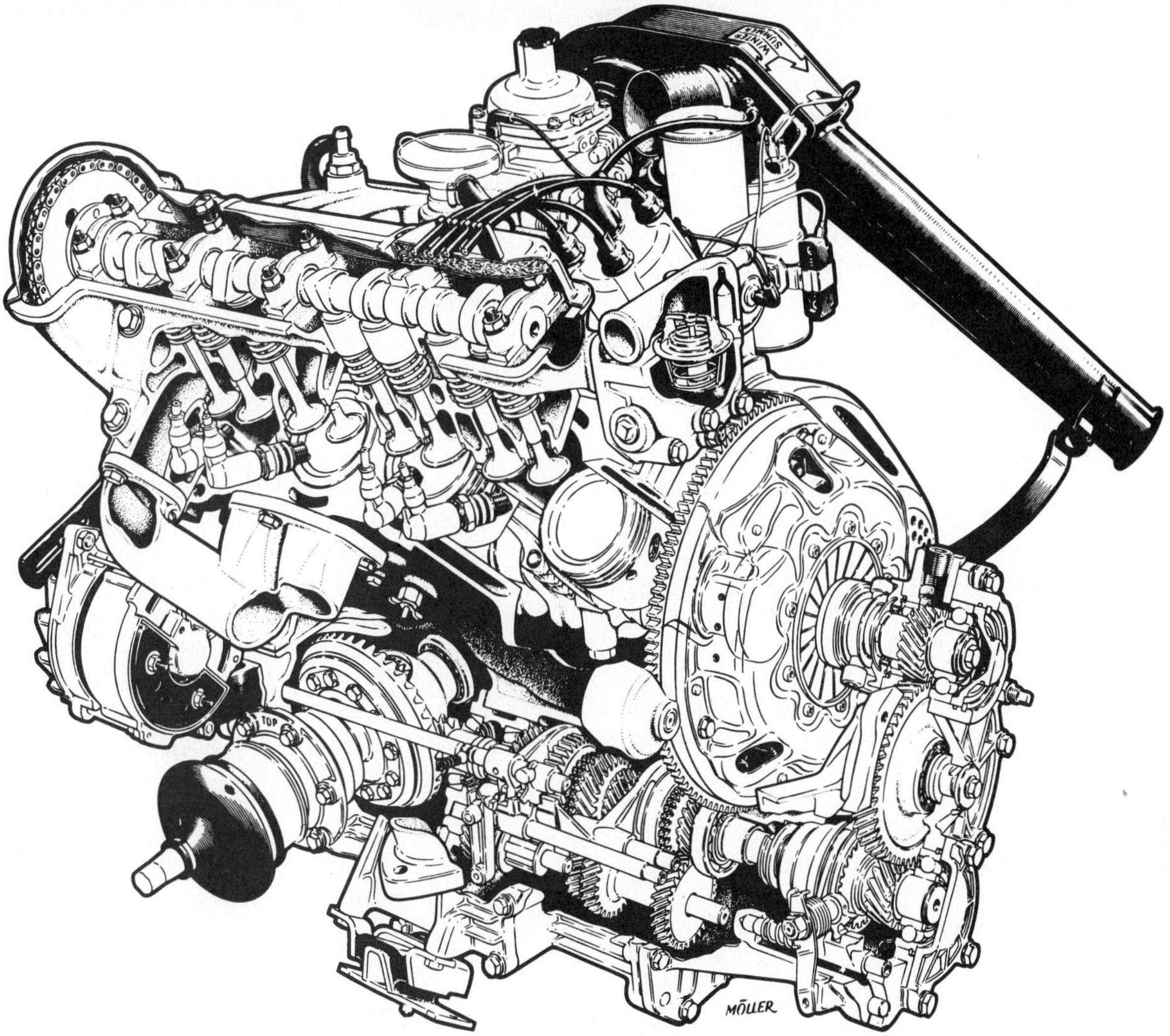

Sweden's Saab 99 is powered by a 105 cu. in., 87 hp, 4-cylinder engine which mounts over transaxle of front wheel drive car. Engine and transaxle have separate lubricating systems. Engine block is set at 45 deg. angle to right; overhead camshaft is driven by a single track chain.

manufacturer, who also supplies tools for checking the leakage rate. See Figs. 16-55 and 16-56.

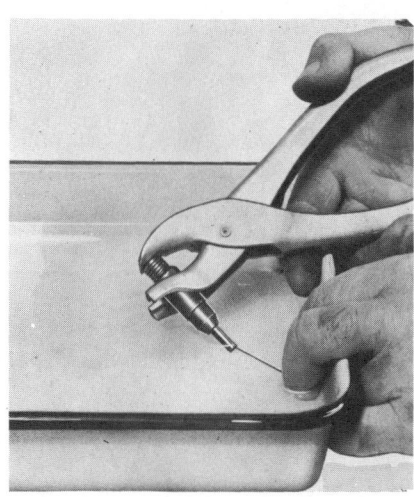

Fig. 16-55. Special tools are available for checking the leak-down rate of hydraulic valve lifters.

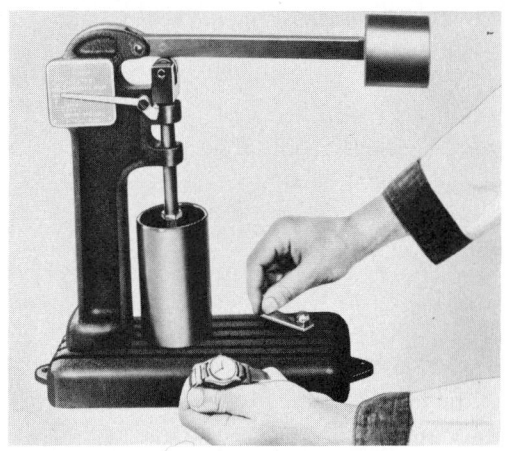

Fig. 16-56. Measuring leak-down rate of hydraulic valve lifter.

HYDRAULIC LIFTER PROBLEMS

While hydraulic valve lifters do provide ideal valve operation, they are subject to certain difficulties and require some attention. Obviously, clearances between the moving parts must be controlled closely. This has caused some difficulty because of dirt or varnish, causing the lifters to stick.

The plunger and cylinder are held to dimensional tolerances of one-tenth of a thousandth of an inch or less in manufacture, then are selectively assembled. That is, different plungers are tried in different cylinders until a pair is found that fits closely enough without being too tight. For this reason, lifters should not be mixed up when they are removed for service. Each plunger should be kept with the cylinder in which it operates.

With clearances so small, the tiniest fleck of carbon, a fine thread of lint from a wiping cloth, a speck of dust, or any foreign matter whatever could wedge between the plunger and cylinder, and cause them to stick. Anything as large as an eyelash or hair will put it completely out of order.

For this reason, it is necessary to keep the engine oil CLEAN when hydraulic lifters are used. The very best grade of oil must be used in the engine and the oil MUST be changed frequently. Oil filters must be replaced regularly.

Another reason for using the best possible oil in the engine, and changing it frequently, comes about from a general increase in driving speeds for long continued periods. Highways and cars are so constructed that car owners do not hesitate to drive at high speeds for hours at a time. This type of operation is certain to generate heat, and the inside of the engine and the engine oil reach temperatures that are destructive to the oil.

The engine oil often becomes hot enough to "crack" some of the petroleum fractions (just as in an oil refinery). In decomposing, these elements form a "varnish" or "lacquer," which collects on the plunger and in the cylinder, and causes sticking. In many cases this varnish is so thin and clear as to be invisible to the naked eye.

These deposits can be removed mechanically by brushing or friction, but there is a danger of harming the surface of the plunger or cylinder. The safest method of removal appears to be the use of chemical solvents. After cleaning, the units should be dried by air and kept covered to avoid dust until they are installed in the engine. They should not be wiped with a cloth for fear that a thread of lint will adhere to them.

Of course, these parts must be handled with extreme care when out of the engine. If dropped on the floor, or dropped one on another, a nick or scratch could result that would cause them to stick. When clean and dry, the plunger should fall into or drop out of the cylinder of its own weight.

When reinstalled, the clearance should be checked to make sure it is adequate. The tappet clearance dimension is much greater than with mechanical linkage, and it varies considerably among the different makes. The manufacturers' recommendations should be obtained and followed.

As in the case of any other valve tappet adjustment, the lifter must be on the heel of the cam when measured. The usual procedure is to turn the engine until the ignition distributor rotor is in the firing position for the cylinder to be checked. This assures that the piston is on top center and both valves completely closed.

REVIEW QUESTIONS — VALVE SERVICE

1. A valve should be discarded if the stem is bent more than:
   a. .002 in.
   b. .004 in.
   c. .006 in.
2. A valve interference angle should be cut on the:
   a. Combustion chamber side.
   b. Port side.
   c. Both sides.
3. A narrow valve seat will dissipate the heat better than a wide one. True or False?
4. The valve seat should be concentric with the guide within:
   a. .001 in.
   b. .002 in.
   c. .003 in.
5. Valve seat inserts are not used in cast iron cylinder blocks or heads. True or False?
6. Describe an interference fit for a valve seat insert.
7. Name two ways of shrinking inserts.
8. Heat dissipation is better when valve guides are not used. True or False?
9. Leaking intake valve guides:
   a. Cause excessive oil consumption.
   b. Upset carburetor adjustment.
   c. Both.
10. Valve stem seals are placed:
    a. In the valve stem.
    b. In the valve guide.
    c. Either.
11. Valve stem to guide clearance should not exceed:
    a. .003-.004 in.
    b. .004-.005 in.
    c. .005-.006 in.
    d. .006-.007 in.
12. Why must valve springs be square on each end?
13. What causes valve stem and valve spring etching?
14. What is the difference between a free valve device and a valve rotator?
15. Worn camshaft bearings will cause a valve to open early. True or False?
16. No leakage is permissible between the plunger and cylinder of hydraulic valve lifters. True or False?
17. What is meant by a selective fit?
18. Clean cloths must be used to wipe parts of hydraulic valve lifters. True or False?

ENGINE
TROUBLESHOOTING

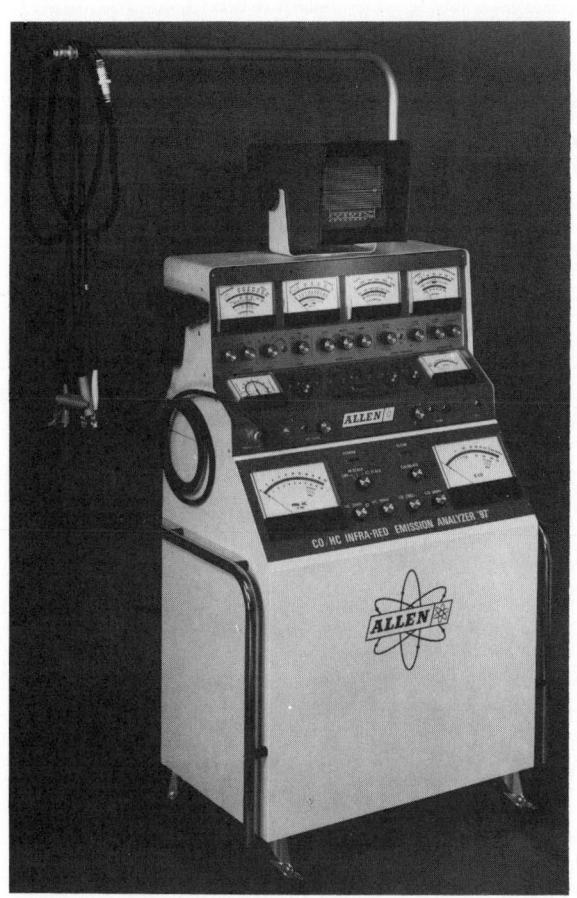

Fig. 17-1. In addition to oscilloscope tests, this engine analyzer checks spark advance, dynamic compression, rpm, carburetor adjustment, current, distributor dwell, ignition timing, carbon monoxide and hydrocarbon emissions, vacuum and ohms resistance.

Troubleshooting is a process of reasoning supported by deduction and elimination. As a defect in one part may have a definite relation to trouble in another spot, the troubleshooter must of necessity have the ability to keep the entire automobile in mind at all times. This requires mental alertness as well as specific knowledge.

Troubleshooting in its most elementary form consists of "shorting out" a spark plug with a screwdriver to locate a

misfiring cylinder. In its most advanced form it involves the use of elaborate testing equipment. In addition, many late model cars are now being equipped with plug-in connections so that specialized equipment can be plugged into the circuits and more quickly locate existing trouble.

TEST EQUIPMENT

In many cases, trouble areas can be located by visual inspection, which usually requires considerable disassembly. With instruments, the source of trouble can be pinpointed more quickly and with greater accuracy.

Until recently, engine testing equipment consisted principally of voltmeters, ammeters, tachometers, distributor testers, dwell meters, oscilloscopes, exhaust gas analyzers, compression gauges, vacuum gauges and timing lights. In addition, special equipment is available for checking generators, alternators, starting motors and the wiring system; and apparatus for aiming headlights.

Typical modern test stands are shown in Figs. 17-1 and 17-2. These console models are provided with voltmeters, ammeters, and other gauges for accurately testing the condi-

Fig. 17-2. A late type diagnostic computer which incorporates a microprocessor that diagnoses seven area tests such as cranking, alternator output, idle, low cruise, power cylinder balance, snap acceleration and high cruise, in addition to pinpoint tests displayed on a screen. The scope features all standard wave forms. A paper printout of the diagnosis is provided.

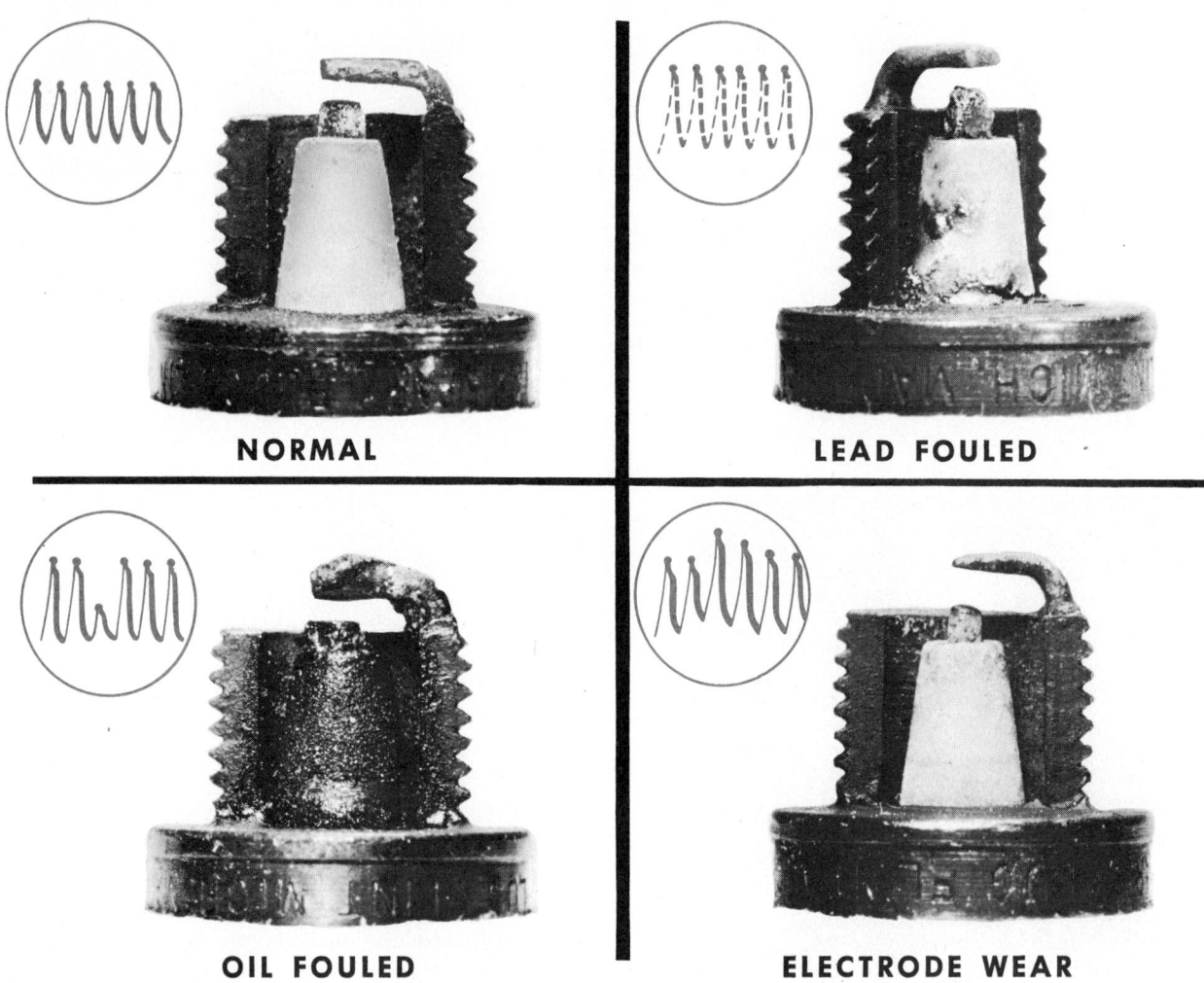

NORMAL   **LEAD FOULED**

OIL FOULED   **ELECTRODE WEAR**

Fig. 17-3. Spark plug conditions as portrayed by wavy lines on the oscilloscope screen.

tion of various systems and components of the engine. With this equipment, it is possible to: locate shorts and opens in the electrical wiring; measure the resistance of electrical circuits; test compression of the engine, manifold vacuum and degrees of advance of the distributor; analyze the exhaust gas; test spark intensity; check timing of the engine and condition of the spark plugs, Fig. 17-3.

Test equipment also facilitates precision adjustment of the carburetor, ignition and engine operation in general, as well as setting of the voltage regulator. Specialized equipment is covered in detail in other chapters of this text.

Troubleshooting has become more difficult since the introduction of exhaust emission control equipment on engines. Alterations and additions are designed to control the amount of hydrocarbon, carbon monoxide and nitrogen oxides in the exhaust. Limits have been set by the U.S. Government on the amount of such pollutants permitted in the exhaust, so the engine must be tuned and adjusted to conform to such limits.

So modern troubleshooting techniques must be adjusted to not only determine the cause of poor performance and economy, but also why the limits set for hydrocarbon, carbon monoxide and nitrogen oxides are exceeded.

For example, adjustments that affect the air-fuel ratio will also affect the amounts of hydrocarbon and carbon monoxide in the exhaust. If adjustments are made to make the air-fuel ratio richer, the carbon monoxide level in the exhaust will also increase. If the mixture is made leaner, the carbon monoxide will decrease. If adjustments are made so lean that misfiring occurs, the hydrocarbon level in the exhaust will increase.

Latest testing equipment includes necessary instruments for checking chemical elements in the exhaust, Fig. 17-4; power developed by the engine, Figs. 17-5 and 17-7; efficiency of the transmission, Fig. 17-8.

The basic instrument for checking the condition of the distributor is the distributor tester, Fig. 17-6. With this tester, wear on the distributor cam and shaft bearings is quickly disclosed, as well as point dwell, vacuum advance and distributor rpm.

PLUG-IN DIAGNOSIS

Equipment being studied will make it possible to plug diagnostic equipment into an outlet on the vehicle. In that way, the condition of the various units on the car can be ascertained.

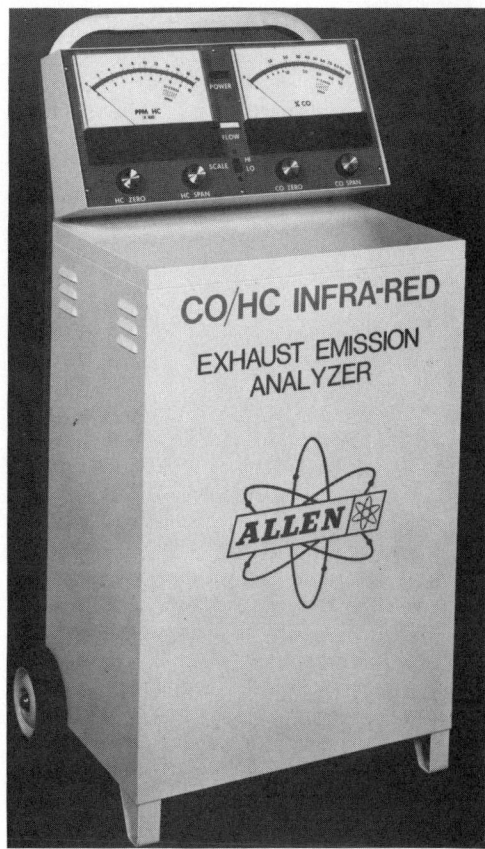

Fig. 17-4. Modern exhaust gas analyzer of infra-red type is used to determine amount of hydrocarbon and carbon monoxide in exhaust.

Fig. 17-5. This type of equipment is called a "total vehicle evaluator." It indicates developed horsepower, checks brake performance, makes vibration tests and engine performance tests according to a pre-programmed diagnosis.

The computer compares the readings taken from the control plug and makes a print out of the results of the test. The computer gets its instructions from the program card which contains the manufacturer's specifications for comparison with the readings taken from the test vehicle. There are different cards for each model of the car.

Fig. 17-6. Distributor test bench has drive mechanism and full complement of meters and gauges to perform all required distributor tests.

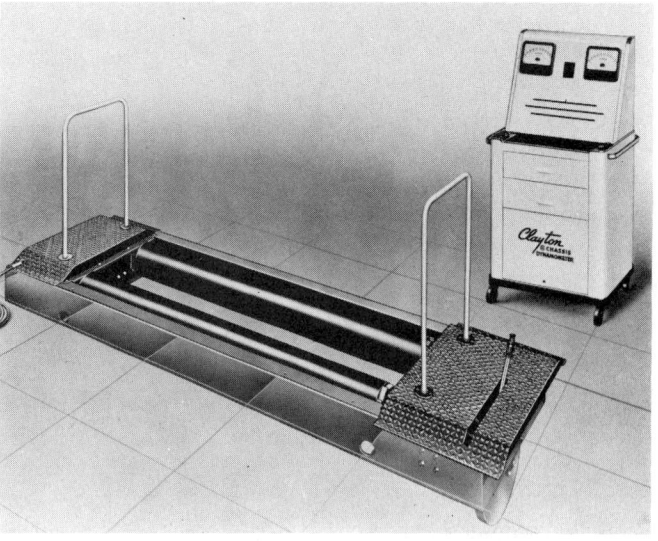

Fig. 17-7. This is a floor type dynamometer. The car is driven into position with the drive wheels on the rollers. The recording instruments are shown in the stand.

One of the pioneers of this method of diagnosis is the Volkswagen, which has developed a complete diagnostic system now being utilized by many VW dealers. The system consists of a computer, a card reader, a hand control unit, an umbilical cord for connecting the equipment to the vehicle, a tachometer and a timing light.

Fig. 17-8. Typical automatic transmission test stand.

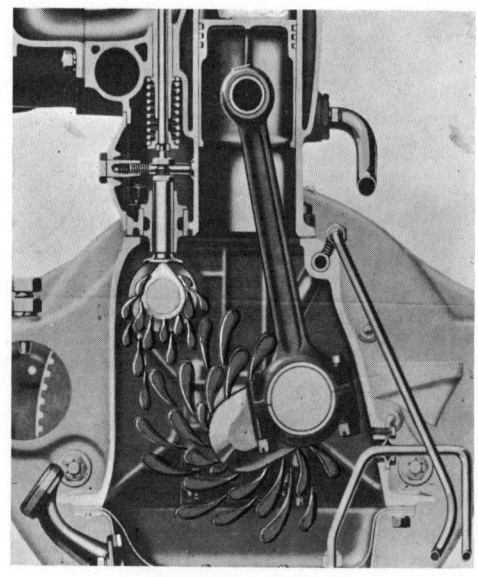

Fig. 17-9. Loose bearings can cause a flood of oil to be thrown up on cylinder walls so no piston ring can control oil consumption.

The card reader in the main console reads the program electronically and relays the card's instructions to the computer. Small switches, triggered by holes in the card, start the test procedure. The diagnostician uses the hand control unit to perform the tests not done automatically by the computer.

Somewhat similar systems are being used on a limited number of U.S. cars. Some of the major problems that preclude more widespread use of "plug-in diagnosis" are multiplicity of models, cost of the equipment and cost of necessary installation and wiring on the vehicle.

HIGH OIL CONSUMPTION

Quite often high oil consumption is blamed on the piston rings. The engine is disassembled, the cylinders reconditioned and the new piston rings carefully fitted. Upon reassembly, the engine may use more oil than before. The mechanic hopes the new rings will "wear in" to a better fit in the cylinders, and advises the car owner to drive the car a few hundred miles.

The driving seldom does any good, so the engine is again disassembled to find the trouble. While worn piston rings and cylinder walls do cause increased oil consumption, there are a great number of other things that could be at fault, either singly or in combination. In most cases, the oil is leaking out of one or more of the pressure lubricated bearings, and is being splashed or thrown up into the cylinders under the pistons in such large quantities that no piston ring can control the excess. See Fig. 17-9. This is covered under piston rings elsewhere in this text.

High oil consumption can result from external leakage of the oil or as the result of oil passing through the engine. In the case of some older engines equipped with a combination vacuum and fuel pump, a broken diaphragm will permit oil to be drawn directly from the crankcase into the intake manifold, and from there into the combustion chambers. Worn valve guides are also a frequent cause of high oil consumption.

If high oil consumption is the complaint, it will be necessary to determine the exact source of the oil, whether it is leaking from the engine or passing through the combustion chambers. The exterior of the engine will be covered with oil, particularly in the immediate area of the source of the leakage. So the usual procedure of locating the source is to first carefully clean the exterior of the engine, then take the vehicle for a short drive. Stop the vehicle over a clean area and examine the exterior for evidence of oil leakage. Also, if oil has dripped on the ground; it will aid in locating the source.

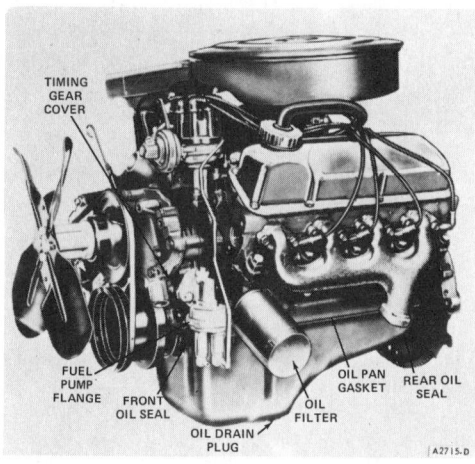

Fig. 17-10. Called out on this left-front view of a late model V-8 engine are some areas from which oil can leak.

It is not unusual to confuse an oil leak at the rear main bearing seal with oil leakage from some other point, Fig. 17-10. To determine the exact source of the leakage, carefully wipe all road dirt and oil from the sides of the engine, valve covers, oil pan, push rod covers and clutch housing.

Then, plug the breather pipe and oil filler pipe with rags. With the engine idling, blow compressed air into the dipstick pipe or opening. Watch for oil leakage, and trace it to its source. Determine whether the leak is at the pan gasket, pan gasket end seal, line fittings, rocker cover gaskets, push rod cover gaskets, timing case cover gasket, front crankshaft seal or rear main bearing seal.

When oil is being consumed by passing through the engine, it usually will cause heavy blue smoke to come from the exhaust, particularly after the engine has idled for several

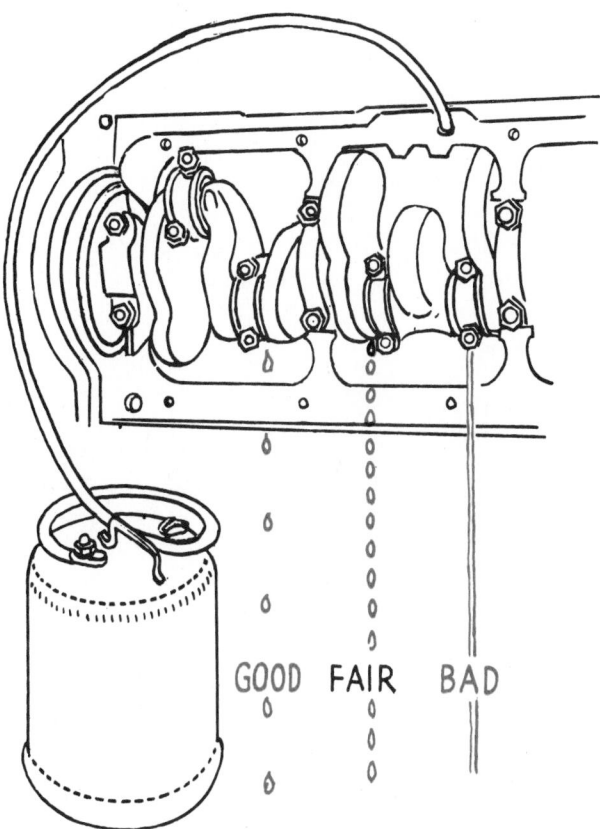

Fig. 17-11. Note how clearance in engine bearings is judged by amount of oil under pressure flowing from sides of bearings.

The testing equipment can be used with the engine in or out of the car, since it is a special pressure tank connected into the oil line. The oil pan is removed so that each of the bearings can be observed. The pipe from the test tank is connected to the engine oil line. It is customary to use SAE 20 oil in the pressure tank. The oil and the engine should be at room temperature when the test is made. If the shop is cold, allowance will have to be made for the lessened flow.

The engine crankshaft is rotated slowly by hand after the air pressure is applied to the oil so that the various passages may register. The amount of oil coming from each bearing is an indication of the amount of clearance between the shaft and the bearing. Fig. 17-11 graphically shows how this clearance is judged.

This type of oil pressure test is of no value on a splash lubricated bearing, or in a few cases where the bearings of a pressure system are beveled at the parting halves. It is, on all other pressure-feed engines, the one best method of checking for the cause of oil pumping.

Many first class shops make this test on an engine before it is dismantled for repair. By this, they know where to look for trouble when the engine is apart. Shops also use this test after the repair work is completed to make sure the job is satisfactory to that point.

Fig. 17-12. This bearing insert might not cause a knock, but it certainly would leak oil.

minutes. After the idling period, the engine should be raced briefly and smoke should appear. Points where oil can enter the combustion chambers are listed in subsequent paragraphs.

If the oil consumption is the result of a defective diaphragm in a combination vacuum and fuel pump, check by disconnecting the vacuum line. If oil drips from the line, the diaphragm is defective and should be replaced.

OIL PRESSURE TEST

An oil pressure test is made before the engine is disassembled with the aid of special equipment made for the purpose. See Fig. 17-11. Such a test will ordinarily disclose the following defects:

1. Worn connecting rod bearings.
2. Loose connecting rod bearings.
3. Excess side clearance in connecting rod bearings.
4. Worn main bearings.
5. Loose main bearings. See Fig. 17-12.
6. Excessive crankshaft end play.
7. Worn camshaft bearings.
8. Worn camshaft journals.
9. Worn crankshaft journals. See Fig. 17-13.
10. Oil leaking past front and rear main bearings.
11. Defective crankshaft seals.
12. Leaking seal plug at rear camshaft bearing.
13. Broken oil line.

Fig. 17-13. Note scored condition of crankshaft journal.

ENGINE DIAGNOSIS

Condition and Possible Cause

Engine Will Not Start
1. Weak battery.
2. Corroded or loose battery connections.
3. Loose ground connections for battery and/or engine.
4. Faulty starter or solenoid.
5. Moisture on ignition cables and distributor cap.
6. Faulty ignition cables.
7. Faulty coil.
8. Incorrect spark plug gap.
9. Incorrect ignition timing.
10. Dirt or water in fuel line or carburetor.
11. Carburetor flooded.
12. Incorrect carburetor float setting.
13. Faulty fuel pump.
14. Carburetor percolating (vapor lock).
15. Sticking choke.
16. Defective neutral starting switch.
17. Defective ignition switch.
18. Air cleaner obstructed.
19. Faulty emission control units.
20. Faulty ignition distributor.

Engine Stalls
1. Idle speed set too low.
2. Incorrect choke adjustment.
3. Idle mixture too lean or too rich.
4. Incorrect carburetor float setting.
5. Intake manifold leak.
6. Worn distributor rotor.
7. Incorrect ignition wiring.
8. Faulty coil.
9. Incorrect valve lash (mechanical lifters).
10. Carburetor float needle valve inoperative.
11. Float level incorrect.
12. Choke defective or incorrectly set.
13. Moisture on ignition cables and plugs.
14. Loose engine and battery grounds.

Loss of Power
1. Incorrect ignition timing.
2. Defective or maladjusted emission control system.
3. Worn or burned distributor rotor.
4. Dirty or incorrectly gapped spark plugs.
5. Dirt or water in fuel line.
6. Clogged air cleaner.
7. Incorrect carburetor float setting.
8. Faulty fuel pump.
9. Incorrect valve timing.
10. Blown cylinder head gasket.
11. Leaking engine valves.
12. Restricted exhaust system.
13. Faulty ignition cables.
14. Faulty coil.
15. Weak valve springs.
16. Low float level.
17. Incorrect valve lash (mechanical lifters).
18. Lean air-fuel mixture.

Engine Misses on Acceleration
1. Dirty spark plugs or gaps too wide.
2. Incorrect ignition timing.
3. Dirt in carburetor.
4. Defective accelerator pump in carburetor.
5. Leaking engine valves.
6. Faulty coil.
7. Weak valve springs.
8. Sticking engine valves.
9. Lean air-fuel mixture.

Engine Misses at High Speed
1. Dirty spark plugs or gaps too wide.
2. Worn distributor shaft.
3. Faulty coil.
4. Worn or burned distributor rotor.
5. Faulty condenser.
6. Incorrect ignition timing.
7. Clogged carburetor jets.
8. Dirt in fuel line.
9. Leaking engine valves.
10. Sticking engine valves.
11. Incorrect valve lash.
12. Worn valve lifters.
13. Worn engine cams.
14. Worn valve guides.

Noisy Valves
1. High or low oil level in crankcase.
2. Thin or diluted oil.
3. Low oil pressure.
4. Dirt in hydraulic lifters.
5. Bent push rods.
6. Worn rocker arms and/or shafts.
7. Worn rocker arms.
8. Worn valve lifters.
9. Excessive runout of valves or seats.
10. Excessive valve lash (mechanical lifters).

Connecting Rod Noise
1. Insufficient oil in crankcase.
2. Defective oil pump.
3. Low oil pressure.
4. Thin or diluted oil.
5. Excessive connecting rod bearing clearance.
6. Rod bearing journals out-of-round.
7. Bent connecting rods.
8. Dirt behind bearing inserts.

Main Bearing Noise
1. Insufficient oil supply.
2. Low oil pressure.
3. Excessive end play of crankshaft.
4. Crankshaft out-of-round.

5. Loose flywheel.
6. Dirt behind bearing inserts.
7. Dirt in oil supply lines.

Noisy Piston Rings

1. Rings striking ridge at top of cylinder wall.
2. Excessive clearance between ring and piston groove.
3. Broken piston ring.
4. Incorrect ring gap.

Noisy Pistons

1. Excessive piston clearance.
2. Collapsed piston skirt.
3. Piston pin incorrectly fitted.
4. Connecting rods incorrectly aligned.
5. Loose piston strut.

Excessive Oil Consumption

1. Worn piston rings.
2. Clogged drain holes in piston rings.
3. Incorrect ring gap.
4. Ring gap incorrectly spaced.
5. Rings installed up-side-down.
6. Excessive oil throw-off from engine bearings.
7. Rings too tight in grooves.
8. Oil level too high.
9. Excessive bearing clearance.
10. Wrong size rings installed.
11. Worn pistons and cylinder walls. See Figs. 17-14 and 17-15.
12. Valve seals damaged or missing.
13. Worn valve stems and guides.
14. Plugged drainback in cylinder head.
15. Worn crankshaft journals.
16. Overheated engine.

External Oil Leakage

1. Defective fuel pump gasket.
2. Defective push rod cover gasket.
3. Defective valve cover gasket.
4. Defective oil filter gasket.
5. Defective oil pan gasket.
6. Defective timing chain cover gasket.
7. Worn timing chain oil seal.
8. Worn rear main bearing oil seal.
9. Loose oil line plugs.
10. Engine oil pan plug improperly seated.
11. Clogged oil drain from rocker area to oil pan.

Low Oil Pressure

1. Low oil level.
2. Faulty oil pressure sending unit.
3. Clogged oil filter.
4. Worn oil pump.
5. Diluted oil.
6. Excessive bearing clearance.
7. Oil pump relief valve stuck.
8. Oil pump suction tube loose, bent or cracked.

Dieseling

1. Check exhaust emission system.
2. Wrong type spark plugs.
3. Excessive carbon in combustion chamber.
4. Poor quality fuel.
5. High engine idle speed.

Burned Valves and Seats

1. Lean air-fuel mixture.
2. Use of lead-free gasoline.
3. Insufficient valve lash.
4. Valve seat too narrow.
5. Valve face too thin.
6. Warped valve head.
7. Worn valve stems and guides.
8. Loose valve seats.

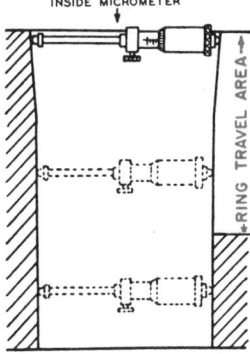

Fig. 17-14. Wear is greatest in ring travel area, causing customary taper at top of cylinder.

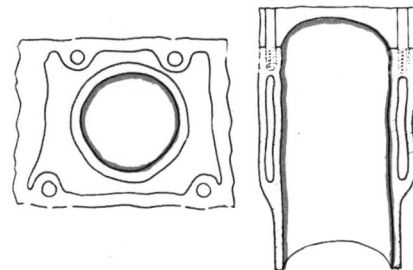

Fig. 17-15. Exaggerated illustration of cylinder distortion caused by unequal or excessive tightening of cylinder head bolts.

ENGINE OVERHEATING

There are many conditions of the automobile that result in overheating, and the degree of overheating is indicated by the temperature gauge on the instrument panel. Or, some models use only a signal lamp on the dash, which lights as a warning when a prescribed high temperature is reached.

Some conditions will cause only a slight change in the recorded temperature, other causes will result in a rapid rise in temperature and violent boiling of the coolant. Still others,

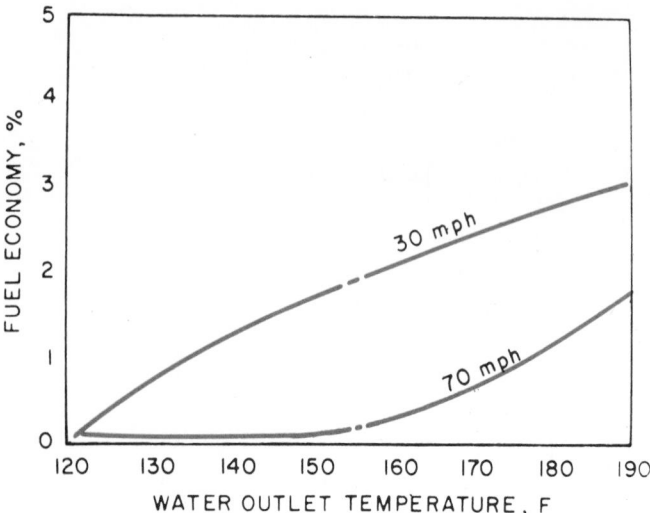

Fig. 17-16. Note how fuel economy improves as water outlet temperature is raised.

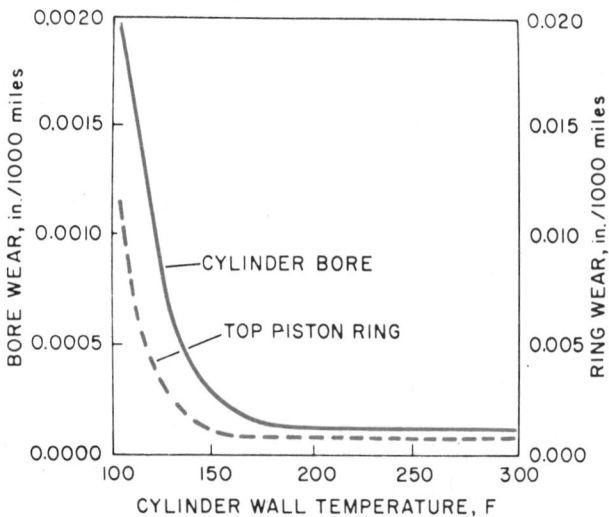

Fig. 17-17. Both cylinder wall wear and top piston ring wear decrease as cylinder wall temperature increases.

The higher the temperature, the more effective the cooling system will be in dissipating heat. Heat dissipation from the radiator results from the difference in temperature between that in the cooling system and the air flowing through the radiator. Increased operating temperature within limits also improves economy, Fig. 17-16, and reduces wear, Fig. 17-17.

Modern automobiles, because of cost and styling limitations, have had radiator sizes reduced. As a result, more heat is being dissipated from smaller radiators.

To produce the desired pressure in the cooling system, the radiator is provided with a pressure type cap, Fig. 17-18. This

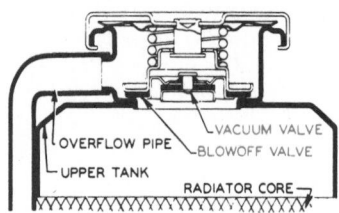

Fig. 17-18. Details of typical pressure type radiator cap. Note vacuum valve and blow-off valves.

is basically a safety valve, designed to release the pressure at some specified amount, usually 14 to 17 psi, Fig. 17-19. This pressure relief valve seals the cooling system off from the overflow tube and the atmosphere. So the cooling system automatically pressurizes as the coolant is heated.

The pressure cap also has a vacuum valve, which opens as the temperature drops and the steam condenses. The condensation of the steam produces a vacuum, and the atmospheric pressure of 14.7 psi acting on the broad surfaces of the radiator tank would cause them to collapse.

When troubleshooting the cause for overheating and consequent loss of coolant, Fig. 17-20, the first step is to make a

while causing only a slight increase in recorded temperature, will be more noticeable in engine performance.

Before discussing the many causes of overheating, it is important to emphasize that when the engine is hot and the coolant boiling, water should not be added unless the engine is running. When the system is hot and the water level low, cold water will go directly to the cylinder head and the rapid chilling could cause the cast iron to crack.

Water has the physical characteristic of changing its boiling point with every change in pressure. For example, under a vacuum of 22 in., water will boil at 150 deg. F. At atmospheric pressure 14.7 psi, it boils at 212 deg. F. At 15 psi above atmospheric pressure it will boil at 250 deg. F and most cooling systems on recent model automobiles operate at from 14 to 17 psi.

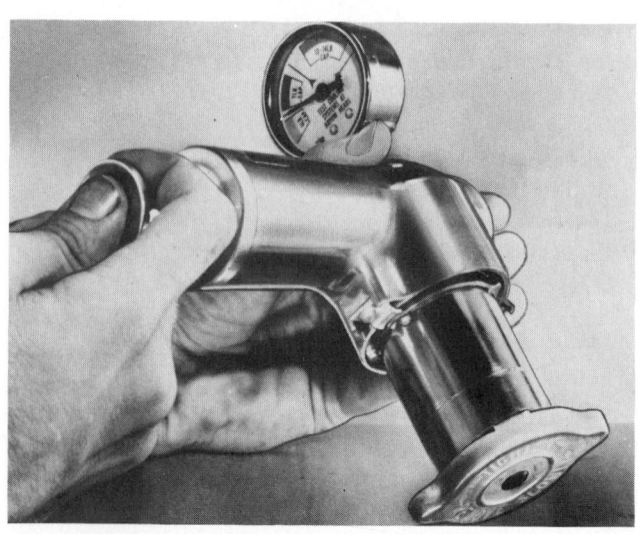

Fig. 17-19. Pressure type radiator cap being tested on specialized equipment.

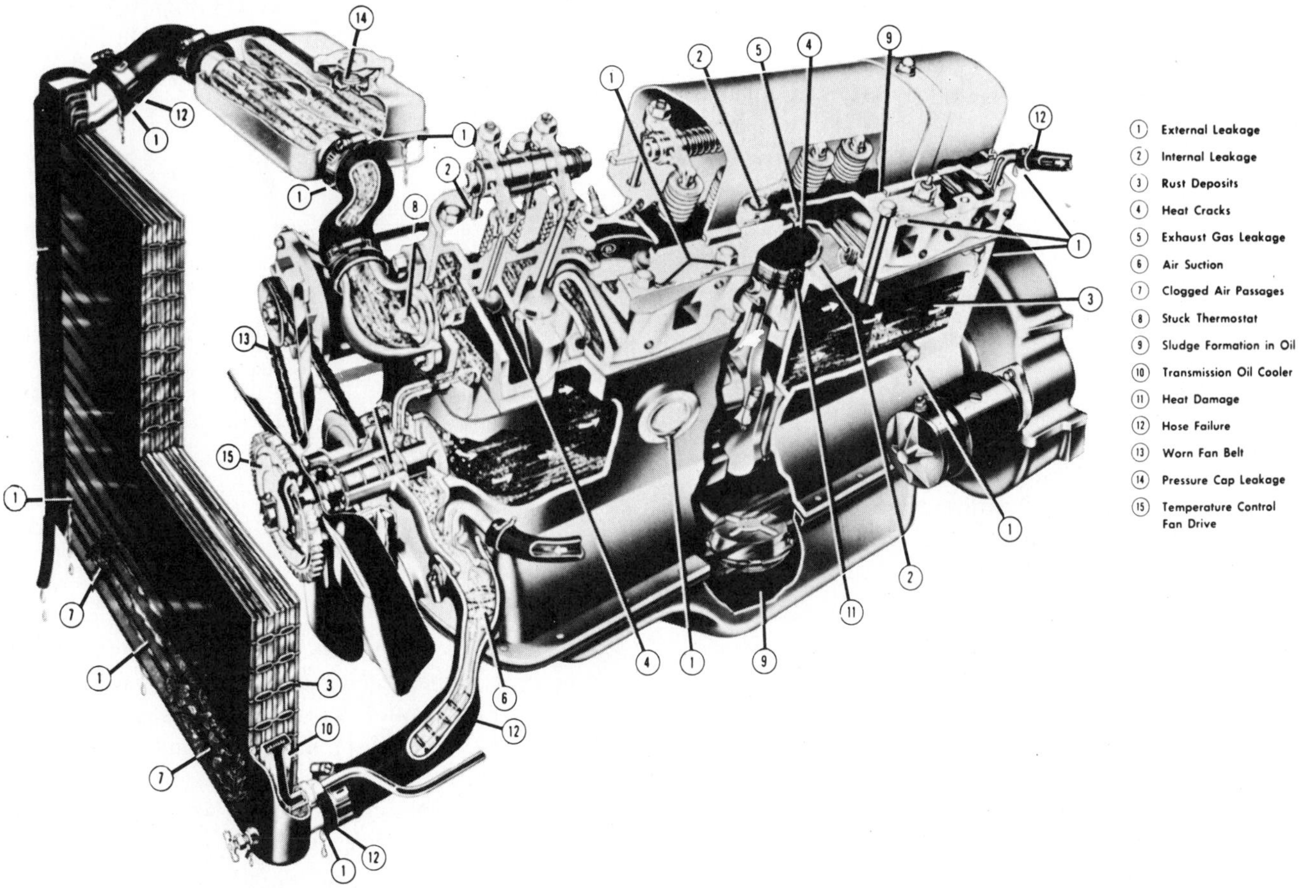

Fig. 17-20. Points to check when looking for causes of overheating and loss of coolant.

(1) External Leakage
(2) Internal Leakage
(3) Rust Deposits
(4) Heat Cracks
(5) Exhaust Gas Leakage
(6) Air Suction
(7) Clogged Air Passages
(8) Stuck Thermostat
(9) Sludge Formation in Oil
(10) Transmission Oil Cooler
(11) Heat Damage
(12) Hose Failure
(13) Worn Fan Belt
(14) Pressure Cap Leakage
(15) Temperature Control Fan Drive

careful visual inspection to see if there is any evidence of external leakage. All surfaces of the radiator and its hose connections should be carefully inspected. Leaks generally cause corrosion, which is easily seen.

The engine also needs careful inspection, paying particular attention to the core plugs and edges of the cylinder gasket. Do not overlook the rear face of the engine. Since there is little clearance between the rear face of the engine and the fire wall, a mirror will sometimes be of assistance. The water pump must be checked for evidence of leakage; also the car heater and its hose connections.

The visual inspection also must include the cooling fan and its drive belt. The blades should not be bent. The belt must be in good condition and adjusted to the proper tension. It should not have any ridges, nor should it be frayed.

Not all coolant leakage is external. Severe cases of overheating and coolant loss result from leaks into the combustion chamber. When the cylinder head is cracked, or there is a blown cylinder head gasket, the hot gases of combustion can enter the cooling system. Since combustion chamber temperature could be in excess of 5000 deg. F, coolant temperature rises rapidly and boiling takes place.

If the crack in the head or the opening in the gasket is large, coolant will flow into the combustion chamber. Then, on the compression stroke, the incompressible coolant will break either the cylinder head or the top of the piston.

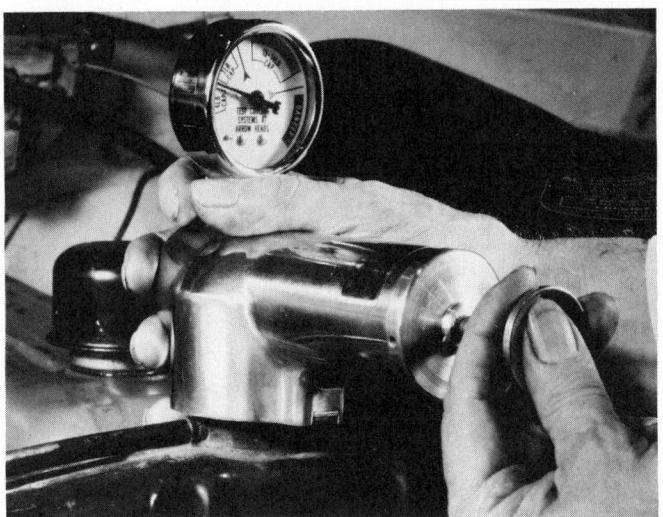

Fig. 17-21. Testing cooling system for leaks by placing coolant, under pressure. Same equipment is used for checking radiator caps.

Applying pressure to the system will help disclose any leaks, but not their location. To make the test, pressure is applied to the system. A system free from leaks should maintain pressure for at least two minutes, Fig. 17-21.

Another test, known as the combustion pressure test,

should be made. This test involves operating the engine under load to detect high-pressure leaks into the combustion chamber.

To perform this test, remove the fan belt, drain coolant and remove thermostat. Add coolant until the level is just below the water outlet opening of the cylinder head and all trapped air is removed. To load the engine, raise the rear wheels and run the engine in high gear, or "D," while simultaneously opening the throttle and applying the brakes. While applying engine load, watch coolant for the appearance of bubbles or a sudden rise of level which would indicate leakage from the combustion chamber into the cooling system.

The preceding test should be made before boiling starts to avoid confusion with any steam bubbles that might be formed.

A faster method is to use a combustion leakage tester. This is a chemical test, and the tester is applied to the filler neck of the radiator, Fig. 17-22. Then, with the engine running, any gas from the combustion chamber which enters the coolant will be drawn into the tester and cause the chemical to change its color.

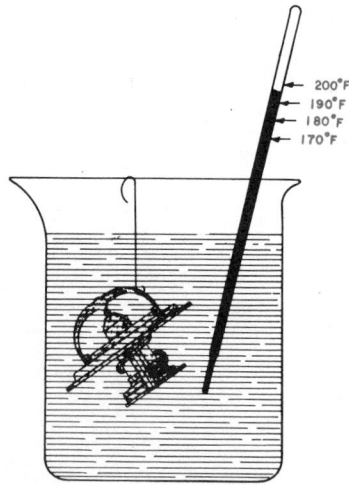

Fig. 17-23. Using a thermometer to check opening and closing points of a cooling system thermostat while water is being heated.

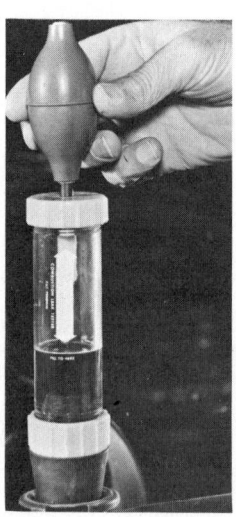

Fig. 17-22. Using a special tester to check for combustion leakage. Leakage of combustion gases will cause color of chemical in tester to change.

Making a compression test of the system will also be helpful in checking for internal leaks, particularly in the case of a blown head gasket. (Low readings on adjacent cylinders indicates blown gasket.) Similarly the spark plugs should be examined for evidence of moisture.

A thermostat "frozen" in the closed position will also cause extreme overheating. So it is important to check each thermostat in a tester, Fig. 17-23, to be sure it is opening and closing at the correct temperatures.

FLUSHING THE COOLING SYSTEM

It is important to flush the cooling system, preferably once each year. This is usually done in fall to put the cooling system in proper order for the cold months ahead.

Most authorities agree that permanent type antifreeze should be kept in the system throughout the year. Ethylene glycol with various additives serves as a good summer coolant as well as offering freezing protection in winter. Remember, however, that water should not be added to certain other types of permanent antifreeze, since that would form a heavy, mud-like substance which effectively clogs the system.

When flushing the system, the car heater control must be in the "ON" position, so it too will be drained and flushed. Also, see that the engine drain plugs be opened, as well as the drain plug at the bottom of the radiator.

Before flushing, the thermostat should be removed and the water outlet housing installed. Disconnect the radiator upper hose at the engine and direct it away from the engine and toward the floor. Also disconnect the radiator lower hose. With a "reverse flush" gun, Fig. 17-24, air and water are then applied to the lower hose, forcing water in a reverse flush through the radiator.

With the radiator disconnected, the engine is reverse flushed in the same manner by applying the air and water to the upper outlet.

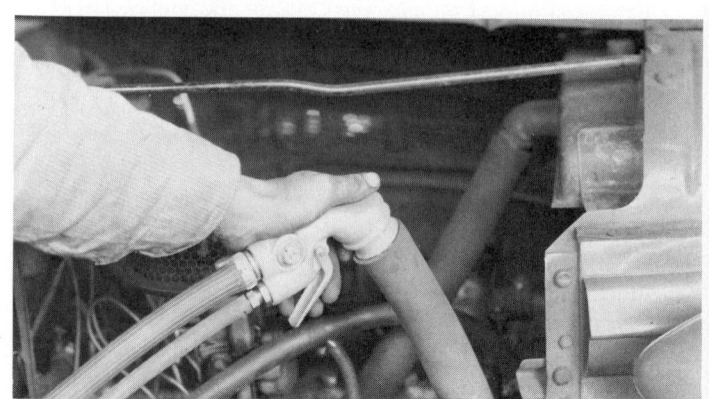

Fig. 17-24. Using a power flushing gun to reverse flush cooling system.

The reverse flush gun is so designed that water and compressed air are delivered to the nozzle, and the quantity of water and the amount of air pressure can both be controlled with suitable valves. This method is effective in flushing out all soft mud and sludge that may have collected in the system.

To determine whether a radiator is clean, first plug the lower outlet and fill the radiator to the top with water. Then remove the plug from the lower outlet, and the water should spurt out with a vigorous stream to a height of approximately 6 in., Fig. 17-25.

Fig. 17-25. One method of checking a radiator for free flow.

COOLING SYSTEM CHECKS

To test for restrictions in the radiator, first bring the system up to operating temperature. Then shut off the engine and feel the front surface of the radiator. On cross flow radiators, the radiator should feel hot along the left side and warm along the right side with an even temperature rise from right to left bottom to top. On vertical flow radiators, the radiator should feel warmer at the top than at the bottom. Any cold spots would indicate clogged sections.

Water pump operation can be checked by running the engine while squeezing the radiator upper hose. A pressure surge should be felt. Check for a plugged vent hole in pump.

Note: A defective head gasket may allow exhaust gases to leak into the cooling system. This is particularly damaging to the system since the gases combine with the water to form acids which tend to corrode radiator and engine parts. This is also a cause of excessive temperature.

LOCATING CRACKS

It is not too unusual for cracks to form in the engine water jacket. When cracks occur, the condition is usually indicated by extreme overheating. The crack is often difficult to locate, because it is not always visible to the naked eye. The condition is also complicated by the fact that the crack usually will close when the engine is cold, and open only when the engine is at operating temperature.

When cracks are suspected as the result of excessive water loss or extreme overheating, the procedure is to remove the cylinder head and close the openings of the water jacket with suitable plugs or with special equipment, Fig. 17-26. Air is

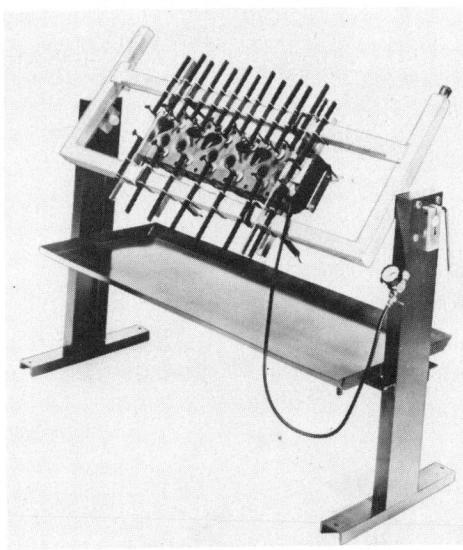

Fig. 17-26. Shown is one method of locating cracks in an engine block by clamping all valves closed and introducing compressed air into block.

then applied to the water jacket, and the head is immersed in water. Air bubbles will quickly reveal the location of the crack. Using hot water will warm the head and tend to open the crack.

This method of locating cracks is particularly helpful when the crack is located in a valve port and cannot be reached with other methods. The same method is used to locate cracks located in the cylinder block, and also for retesting after repairs have been made. Also see Fig. 13-10.

CLEANING THE COOLING SYSTEM

Unless very severely clogged with rust and hard scale, cooling systems can be cleaned with special chemicals designed for the purpose. The procedure is to fill the system with water, then put in the chemical. Then the engine is operated for a designated length of time. The chemical, after dissolving the rust and scale, is flushed from the system.

Care must be taken not to leave the chemical in the system

longer than the designated length of time, since it may attack the metal core of the radiator and cause leaks.

In severe cases of clogged radiators, it is necessary to remove them and have them cleaned by specialized equipment, Fig. 17-27. In some cases, the entire radiator is immersed in a cleaning solution. In other cases, the upper and lower tanks are removed. After softening the rust by placing the radiator in a chemical bath, thin rods are forced through the radiator tubes to clean out the softened rust (rodding).

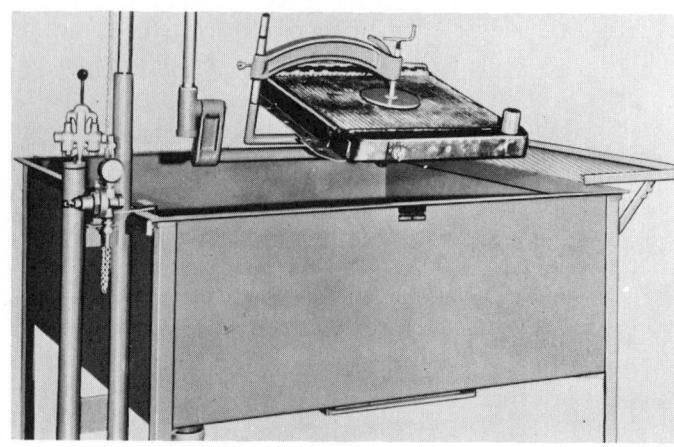

Fig. 17-27. Specialized equipment used in cleaning, testing and repair of radiators.

RUST INHIBITORS

Whenever a cooling system has been cleaned and flushed, it is necessary to use a rust inhibitor when refilling the system with water. Antifreeze coolant includes several inhibitors, so it is not necessary to use an additional rust inhibitor.

CAUSES OF OVERHEATING

A slight amount of overheating may result in little or no coolant loss. However, when the condition causing the overheating becomes more extreme, coolant loss will result. The list of causes follows:

1. Manifold heat control valve sticking.
2. Fan belt slipping.
3. Thermostat stuck.
4. Radiator fins obstructed.
5. External leak at cylinder head gasket.
6. Internal leak at cylinder head gasket.
7. Internal leak into combustion chamber.
8. Radiator cap valve leaks.
9. Radiator cap valve stuck.
10. Faulty fan drive clutch.
11. Worn pulleys.
12. Defective water pump.
13. Radiator hose collapsing.
14. Blocked or restricted water manifold.
15. Cooling system clogged with rust and scale.
16. Radiator frontal area obstructed.
17. Air pocket in cooling system.
18. Leaking radiator.
19. Leaking cooling system hoses.
20. Leaking engine water jacket.
21. Leaking car heater.
22. Leaking radiator supply tank.
23. Cylinder core hole plugs leaking.
24. Excessive engine friction.
25. Thermostat defective.
26. Ignition timing retarded.
27. Brakes dragging.
28. Cooling system capacity inadequate for load being carried or towed.
29. Excessive use of air conditioner while vehicle is parked.

AIR COOLING PROBLEMS

Remember, air-cooled engines should never be overloaded or "lugged." The cooling system is dependent on fan speed which, in turn, is dependent on engine speed. Transmission gears should be shifted as needed to maintain engine speed at a good level.

Air-cooled automobile engines are usually enclosed entirely in a sheet metal housing or shroud. The cooling air volume entering this shroud is controlled by an automatic, thermostatically operated valve. Obviously, air flow cannot be controlled and directed if there are any air leaks in the shroud. Even the spark plugs are sealed to the shroud, as shown in Fig. 17-28. These seals must be in good condition and properly installed.

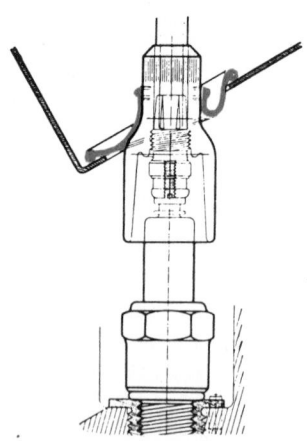

Fig. 17-28. Location of seals on Volkswagen spark plugs.

The Volkswagen has an unusual method of adjusting the fan belt tension by fitting more or less spacer washers between the two pulley halves. See Fig. 17-29. Removal of washers increases the effective diameter of the driven pulley. When all washers have been removed, a new belt is installed. The correct relationship is shown in Fig. 17-30. When washers are removed from between the pulley halves, they are placed between outer

Fig. 17-29. Method of transferring spacing washers to tighten Volkswagen fan belt.

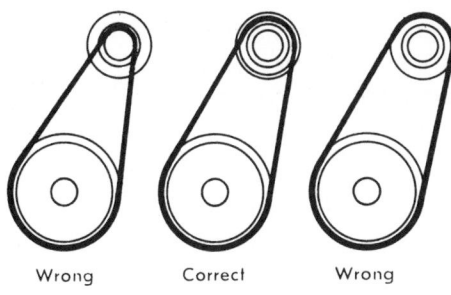

Wrong   Correct   Wrong

Fig. 17-30. Proper and improper pulley relations on Volkswagen engine.

pulley half and pulley nut, and left there until needed. DO NOT attempt to remove or replace this belt by stretching it over either of the pulley flanges.

Basic causes for overheating of air-cooled engines are:
1. Dirt on cooling fins.
2. Oil cooler dirty.
3. Air leaks in shroud or seals.
4. Loose spark plug boots.
5. Thermostat stuck in closed position.
6. Improper adjustment of air control ring.
7. Worn fan belt.
8. Slipping fan belt.

RELATED TROUBLES

It is obvious that many engine defects are common to both high oil consumption and overheating. There is a definite relationship between the two. Searching for the cause of either trouble will often disclose the need for correction in either or both the oil and water circulation systems.

LOW OIL PRESSURE

In most cases of low oil pressure, the pressure is satisfactory when the engine is first started up, then it drops as the engine warms up. This condition is almost positive proof that excessive clearance exists at some point, or points, such as connecting rod bearings, main bearings, camshaft bearings, etc.

When cold, the oil has thickened and does not flow as readily through the clearance. When the oil heats up and thins out, it flows through the worn bearings so fast that the pump cannot maintain sufficient pressure.

EXHAUST BACK PRESSURE

If the exhaust pipe, muffler or tailpipe should be partially restricted, the heat is unable to escape readily with the result the combustible charge will be severely diluted and full power will not be developed. In addition, temperature of the exhaust valves will rise to such an extent that the valves will burn and have to be replaced. In extreme cases, the engine will start readily, quickly lose speed and power, then stop.

CHASSIS AND ENGINE VIBRATION

A process of elimination is often the only way to discover where vibration trouble lies. Consider the case where there is a pronounced vibration in the car at a certain speed range. First of all it is necessary to determine whether the unbalance is in the engine or the chassis, or both.

If it is in the engine, or the parts that rotate with the engine, the vibration should occur at the critical engine speed when the car is not in motion. If it is in the chassis, it will occur only when the car is operated at the critical speed. It is most likely to be found in the chassis, because the engine assembly is carefully balanced at the factory. Out-of-balance tires and propeller shafts are the most common causes of chassis vibration.

UNBALANCE CORRECTION

Wheel unbalance may be in the wheel itself. However, it is often found in the tire or brake drum assembly. Each wheel can be checked easily with a wheel spinning device, and the correction made by the addition of weights, as described in Chapter 40.

Another frequent cause of chassis vibration is unbalance in the driveshaft or universal joints. Methods of location and correction are described in Chapter 47.

If the chassis is eliminated as a source of the trouble, and the vibration is in the engine or related parts, you can carry the process of elimination further. If the vibration can be altered or eliminated by holding the clutch out of engagement, the trouble could be in the clutch or transmission shaft.

If the trouble is suspected to be in the fan, water pump or generator, the drive belts can be removed. Then the engine is checked with these units inoperable. If the vibration continues, it is possible that repair work on the engine or clutch has destroyed the original balance of the engine. For example, the installation of one or more new pistons or connecting rods of unmatched weight, reinstallation of the clutch cover plate in incorrect position, etc. Even an accumulation of dust from wear of the clutch facing lodging in one place in the clutch housing can cause trouble. With automatic transmission-equipped cars, a low fluid level in the transmission may cause unbalance.

Often, it is possible to compensate for minor unbalance in the engine and clutch assembly by installing flat washers under the heads of the cap screws holding the clutch to the flywheel. This is a tedious procedure of trying the washers at different spots around the bolt circle, and checking each time for any improvement or worsening of the vibration. The same procedure is possible where an automatic transmission torque converter or fluid flywheel needs correction for unbalance.

ENGINE NOISE

One of the most difficult of all troubleshooting jobs is to locate the source of noise or "knocks" in an engine. Actually, every rotating or reciprocating part in the engine is a potential source of noise. In many cases, however, certain noises possess characteristics which help identify their origin.

These characteristics vary somewhat between different engines. In most cases, it will be helpful to utilize an instrument of the stethoscope type to localize the noise at some definite section of the engine. See Fig. 17-31. These instruments magnify the intensity of the noise, and the sound becomes louder as the tip of the instrument nears the origin of the noise.

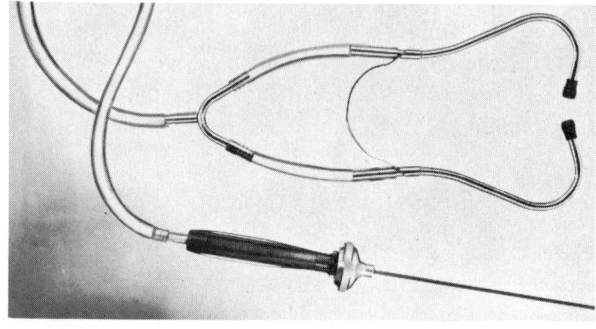

Fig. 17-31. Stethoscope type of instrument for locating noise in engine parts.

LOOSE CONNECTING RODS

The conditions of operation under which the noise is heard, and the "timing" of the noise, are also useful in determining the source. Some noises are louder as the engine speed is increased, or while the engine is under load. For example, a connecting rod bearing that is slightly loose will usually knock loudest around an engine speed of about 40 mph and, of greatest intensity, just as the engine goes from a pull to a coast (just as driver releases the accelerator).

A rod in very bad condition will be heard at all speeds and under both idle and load conditions. One rod will make a distinct noise. If all rods are loose, the noise becomes a rattle or clatter. A pressure-lubricated engine seldom becomes this bad, because excessive oil throw-off would cause oil consumption to become so high that the rods would need to be replaced long before they become noisy.

In many cases, slightly loose rods are confused with piston slap or loose piston pins. This is particularly true when all rods are loose, and experience will be helpful in deciding which part is at fault. It is not of too much importance to decide definitely, because the remedy for either fault involves removal of the rod or rods in practically all cases. Measurement and inspection of the parts will then disclose where the trouble lies.

LOOSE PISTON PINS

Using a stethoscope is sometimes helpful, since piston or pin may sound loudest when the instrument prod is placed on the cylinder head or block. The rod knock is often loudest with the prod on the crankcase. Shorting out the spark plug on one cylinder may change the intensity of the knock, but it will not always eliminate it entirely.

Shorting out one or more spark plugs will help to locate which cylinder or rod is at fault, in cases where the noise is not due to looseness in all cylinders or rods.

PISTON SLAP

There is much confusion between the noise caused by a piston with excessive clearance in the cylinder and a loose piston pin. Either defect produces a click which is quite distinct. If noisy in all cylinders, it becomes a rattle. One indication of piston slap is a decrease in the noise as the engine warms up. A piston slap is always louder when the engine is cold.

A piston slap may occur in an engine when new piston pins are installed in old pistons. This is particularly true if the pins are fitted too tight. This noise may disappear entirely after the engine is operated a few hundred miles, and the pins have loosened up a bit.

Loose piston pins usually, but not always, produce a double rap each revolution of the crankshaft. They rap once at the top of the stroke and again at the bottom. On most engines, the knock is loudest at idling speed. And it will become even louder if the spark is advanced. Often, the knock will be louder if the spark plug is shorted out in cases where not all pins are loose.

PISTON RING NOISE

The installation of new piston rings will almost surely cause a knock if the ridge at the top of the cylinder bore is not removed completely before the new rings are installed. Somewhat similar is the condition where the cylinders have been rebored oversize, and the standard cylinder head gasket extends into the combustion chamber. The piston strikes the gasket and makes a distinct knock, Fig. 17-32.

Piston rings that are loose in the grooves will not ordinarily make any noise, since the oil tends to cushion them. If they are excessively loose, particularly the top ring, they may cause a clicking noise similar to a loose valve lifter. There is a difference in the timing of the click. The piston rings will click twice each revolution of the crankshaft, while the valve click will be heard once every other revolution.

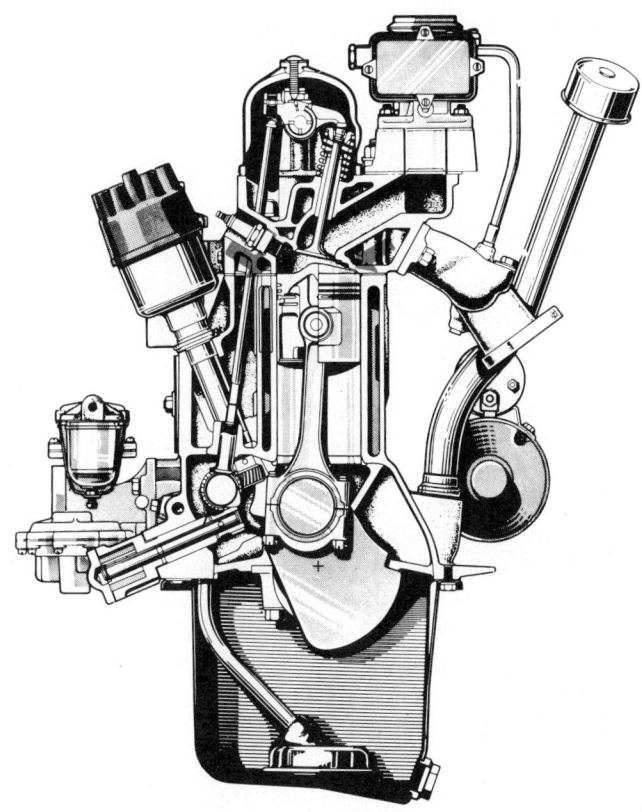

Fig. 17-32. In a rebuilt engine, a piston may strike edge of head gasket when engine is first started.

VALVE NOISES

Valves are a common source of noise for two reasons. There are two valves for each cylinder, and there are several points in each unit of the valve train that can create noise. Usually, it is easy to determine which valve or valves are causing the noise by inserting a feeler gauge of suitable thickness between the end of the valve and the rocker arm with the engine running.

Clicking caused by wear between the valve lifter and lifter guide, or by damage on the end of the lifter next to the camshaft, is not readily located. Here, the timing of the click is

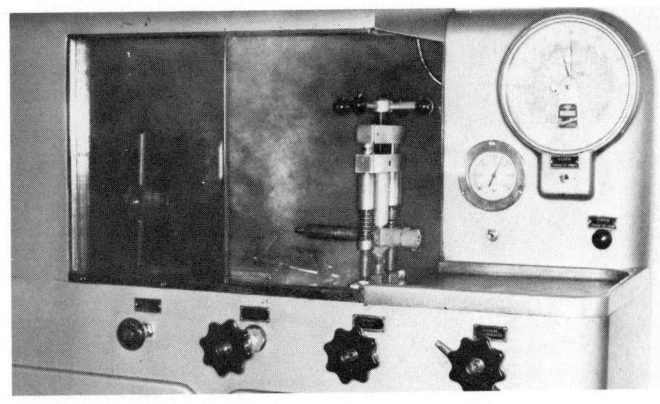

Fig. 17-33. Analyzer and tester used for testing spray pattern of multiple and pintle injector nozzles.

helpful, as well as the use of a stethoscope.

Hydraulic valve lifters often will be noisy when the engine is first started, because oil has leaked from the unit. The noise should disappear after a few minutes operation, during which the lifter will be filled with oil. If the noise does not disappear, the defective lifter can be located by means of a stethoscope.

WORN TIMING GEARS

Another knock that is difficult to diagnose is caused by worn timing gears. Shorting out the spark plugs has no effect on the noise, and it is about the same intensity whether the engine is idling or pulling. A stethoscope is useful in this case to determine where the noise originates.

LOOSE MAIN BEARINGS

A main bearing knock is more of a bump than a knock, and it can be located by shorting out the plugs near it. The noise is loudest when the engine is "lugging" (pulling hard at slow speed). The sound is heavier and more dull than a connecting rod knock.

CRANKSHAFT END PLAY

Excessive end play in the crankshaft will produce an intermittent rap or knock that is sharper than a loose main bearing. The noise usually will be affected by applying or releasing the clutch. If the car is equipped with an automatic transmission, the noise is more difficult to diagnose. It will rap once, loudly, on sudden acceleration.

LOOSE FLYWHEEL

If the flywheel is loose on the crankshaft flange, the noise will be similar to a main bearing knock. Ordinarily, it will not change when the plugs are shorted out. Furthermore, the noise may come and go rather than being constant. One sure test is to turn off the ignition, then turn it on again just as the engine is about to stop. The sudden twist applied to the crankshaft will produce the knock in noticeable form.

NOISY ENGINE MOUNTINGS

If the rubber engine mountings are drawn down too tightly, or, if the rubber had deteriorated enough to allow the metal parts of the mounting to contact each other, a knock may occur. This particular knock appears under high torque conditions during rapid acceleration.

MISCELLANEOUS NOISES

At times, a knock will occur in an engine when all parts have been checked for wear; or even a rebuilt engine may knock. These knocks are usually due to misalignment or excessive endwise motion. Examples include: Too much side clearance in a connecting rod bearing. Excessive endwise motion of the crankshaft or camshaft. A loose manifold heat

211

control valve. Endwise movement of an oil pump or ignition distributor shaft.

Improper alignment of connecting rods is a common source of engine knocks. Fan and accessory drive belts often cause noise, but the defect is readily detected. Squeaking belts can be made quiet by the application of special products, or a small amount of soap or talcum powder.

Noise in belt-driven units, such as water pumps, fans and alternators, can be isolated by removing the drive belts, then operating the engine.

Since the diesel engine does not have an ignition distributor or a carburetor, troubleshooting procedure is simplified. Basically, it includes checking compression pressure and fuel injector performance.

Checking compression requires the removal of the injectors and testing compression pressure at each cylinder with a compression gauge. Because the compression ratio of a diesel may range as high as 23 to 1, a gauge which will check pressures up to and exceeding 650 psi (4 500 kPa) is needed.

Special equipment is necessary to check the injectors and the pattern of spray. One type of service equipment is illustrated in Fig. 17-33.

TROUBLESHOOTING ELECTRONIC SYSTEMS

For details covering troubleshooting electronic ingition and fuel systems, see the chapters on CARBURETOR ADJUST-MENT AND SERVICE, FUEL SUPPLY SYSTEMS, FUEL INJECTION and ENGINE IGNITION.

REVIEW QUESTIONS
ENGINE TROUBLESHOOTING

1. What is the principal cause of high oil consumption?
2. Name two defects, other than worn journals and bearings, that can be found by an oil pressure test.
3. Why must the crankshaft be rotated while an oil pressure test is being made?
4. An oil pressure test should be made:
   a. Before an engine is disassembled.
   b. After it has been rebuilt.
   c. Neither of above.
   d. Both of above.
5. List five causes for engine overheating.
6. Water under 25 psi pressure has a higher boiling point than water under atmospheric pressure. Yes or No?
7. What is the pressure in a modern automotive cooling system?
   a. 10 psi.
   b. 15 psi.
   c. 25 psi.
8. When flushing a cooling system, the thermostat should be removed. Yes or No?
9. What procedure should be followed when most of the coolant has boiled from the cooling system?
   a. Add water immediately.
   b. Stop the engine and add water.
   c. Keep the engine running and add water.
10. Water coming from the tailpipe is a sure indication that a cylinder head gasket is blown. True or False?
11. Spark plugs on an air-cooled engine are sealed in the shroud. True or False?
12. When flushing the cooling system, should the hot water heater control be in the "on" or "off" position?
13. What is the function of a pressure type radiator cap?
    a. Control pressure in a cooling system.
    b. Control vacuum in a cooling system.
    c. Control vacuum and pressure in a cooling system.
14. What is the principal cause of low oil pressure?
15. A kink in the tailpipe may cause engine overheating. True or False?
16. Name two common causes of chassis vibration.
17. How can vibration in an alternator be detected?
18. Insufficient fluid in an automatic transmission may cause engine vibration. True or False?
19. A slightly loose connecting rod bearing will usually knock loudest at:
    a. High speed.
    b. Medium speed.
    c. Low speed.
20. Shorting out a spark plug will help locate a loose piston pin. Yes or No?
21. Shorting out a spark plug will help locate a loose flywheel. True or False?
22. A loose main bearing and end play in a crankshaft sound about the same. Yes or No?
23. What is a common source of knocks in a rebuilt engine?
24. With pressurized cooling systems, can alcohol be used as an antifreeze?
25. Better fuel economy is obtained with a cool engine. True or False?

ENGINE TUNE-UP

An engine tune-up is a service operation designed to restore the engine's best level of performance, while maintaining good fuel economy and minimum exhaust emissions. It consists of a series of tests and corrections made according to a prescribed tune-up test procedure.

In the past, peak performance was the only goal sought by the tune-up mechanic. Today, the mechanic must try to meet two new objectives:
1. Fulfill the obligation to tune the engine to meet Federal and state emission standards.
2. Satisfy the car owner's demand for performance AND economy of operation.

Consequently, the auto mechanic, or tune-up specialist, must understand the close relationship between conventional tune-up factors (compression, ignition, carburetion), engine performance, emission controls and fuel mileage.

TUNE-UP AND THE POLLUTION PROBLEM

The automobile is said to be the major source of air pollution in the U.S. Combustion of the air/fuel mixture gives off hydrocarbons (HC), carbon monoxide (CO), oxides of nitrogen (NOx) and other unburned gases that pollute the atmosphere. (See chapter on EMISSION CONTROL.)

Even a well-tuned, clean-burning engine emits some pollutants. If it operates inefficiently because of maladjustments (incorrect settings) or malfunctions (improper operation), it will discharge excessive exhaust emissions. According to the results of research conducted by the Champion Spark Plug Company, a tuned engine (on the average) produces 57 percent less carbon monoxide at idle and 48 percent less hydrocarbons than an untuned engine, Fig. 18-1. Corresponding reductions are realized at higher steady driving speeds.

To help solve the problem of air pollution from automobile exhaust emissions, the car manufacturers are trying to design a near-zero emissions engine. They have been and still are involved in costly emission control research and development programs. In one direction they have made extensive internal engine modifications (changes in design and construction). In another, they have upgraded emission control systems each new model year. All of which have had an adverse (bad) affect on engine performance, fuel economy and operating expenses.

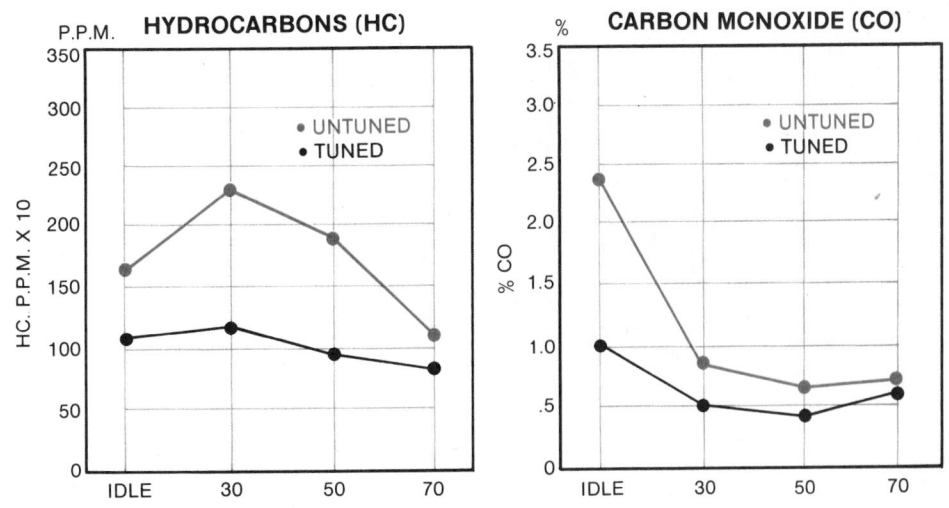

Fig. 18-1. Cars driven over 10,000 mi. (16 093 km) since last engine tune-up were tested on chassis dynamometer, first untuned, then tuned. Graphs show how tune-up reduced emission. (Champion Spark Plug Co.)

As a result, car maintenance services, including engine tune-up, are more complex and costly. In some applications, even spark plug replacement has become a tune-up specialist's chore. On the positive side, the more difficult-to-service emission control engines have taken tune-up from the hands of the do-it-yourselfer and given it back to the trained auto mechanic or tune-up specialist.

Today's professional mechanic must be able to test and correct problems that exist in compression, ignition and carburetion; see that the various emission control systems are operable (working as designed); and maintain all related systems (induction, exhaust, temperature control, etc.) in good working order.

As it stands, today's piston engine cannot be tuned to provide maximums in all of these areas at the same time. Instead, the mechanic must work toward obtaining the best possible performance, fewest emissions and most fuel mileage possible by tuning the engine exactly as prescribed by the manufacturer's specifications.

INSTRUMENTATION NEEDED

An engine tune-up requires the use of certain types of gauges, testers and test equipment. With this instrumentation, you can perform tests that will reveal weak or defective components that should be replaced. Or, on the other hand, test results will verify the satisfactory condition of good used units that need not be replaced.

In still another valuable application, you can connect these testers to a given system or circuit to see if a particular setting is as specified, Fig. 18-2. If it is not, the reading on the tester will serve as a means of guiding you in making adjustments to obtain the correct setting.

Tune-up test equipment in the list that follows will permit you to perform all of the checks and tests described later in the TUNE-UP TEST PROCEDURE. They will assist you in making precise settings to manufacturer's specifications.

Compression tester
Vacuum-pressure gauge
Voltmeter (or volt-amp tester)
Ammeter (see above)
Ohmmeter
Tachometer (or tach-dwell meter)
Dwell meter (see above)
Battery-starter tester
Alternator-regulator tester
Emissions tester (exhaust gas analyzer reading in HC and CO)
Engine analyzer with oscilloscope
Distributor tester
Stroboscopic timing light
Hydrometer
PCV (positive crankcase ventilation) system tester
Cooling system pressure tester
Spark plug cleaner and tester
Fuel injection test bench
Solid state circuit testers
Vacuum systems tester

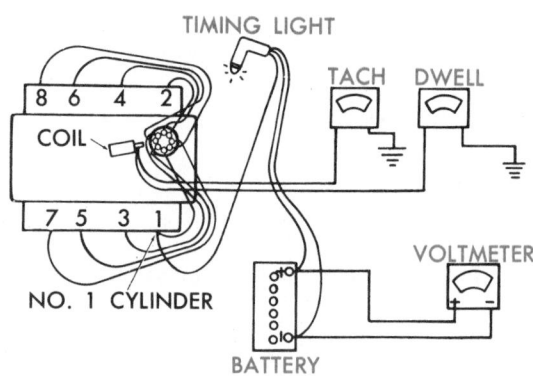

Fig. 18-3. Hookups are shown for tachometer, voltmeter, dwell meter and timing light.

Fig. 18-3 illustrates basic testers needed to perform an engine tune-up. Connect tester test leads as follows:
1. Voltmeter
   Positive lead to positive battery post.
   Negative lead to ground.
2. Tachometer and Dwell Meter
   Positive lead to distributor side of coil.
   Negative lead to ground.
3. Timing Light
   Positive lead to positive battery post.
   Negative lead to ground.
   Trigger lead to No. 1 spark plug cable at plug terminal (connect to short adapter placed between cable end and plug terminal).

In addition, other sophisticated instrumentation is available, Fig. 18-2, that will speed the process and, in some cases, provide more precise readings of a unit's capacity, output,

Fig. 18-2. This distributor tester combines most popular meters in one mobile unit. Included are: tachometer, dwell meter, condenser meter and vacuum gauge. (Sun Electric Corp.)

range or level of performance.

Check test results against engine tune-up specifications in the back of this text.

TUNE—UP TEST PROCEDURE

Most of the work involved in an engine tune-up job is concerned with tests of the battery, starter, alternator, distributor, carburetor and emission controls. Each is a complete subject in itself, and each is covered in detail in separate chapters of this text.

To illustrate the broad scope of an engine tune-up, the procedure that follows gives brief descriptions of the key steps, arranged in the most logical sequence of operations for doing an effective job. Tests requiring a more in-depth explanation are spelled out in detail after the basic steps have been covered.

1. Preliminary Tests and Inspection
   A. Check engine oil, coolant and automatic transmission fluid levels.
   B. Note where hoses attach to air cleaner. Disconnect hoses and remove air cleaner. Make a general visual inspection of engine and accessories, including battery condition and possible need for carburetor cleaning. If levels were low in Step A, look for evidence of oil, fuel or coolant leaks.
   C. Use an oscilloscope, if available, to make area checks of ignition system operation. Or, use an ignition tester to test ignition system efficiency.
2. Internal Engine Condition
   A. Use a voltmeter to test battery voltage while cranking engine. (Should be 9V or more.) Also listen to sound of cranking engine. (Should be strong and steady.)
   B. Remove spark plugs. Use a compression gauge and remote starter switch to test compression pressure of individual cylinders, with choke and throttle valves wide open. If remote cranking will damage ignition switch in LOCK or OFF position, turn key ON. Also, GM cautions: On HEI systems, disconnect ignition switch connector from distributor (or coil on some engines) when cranking engine for compression testing.

   C. Or, use a cylinder leakage tester to test for leakage of air under pressure into intake or exhaust manifold, crankcase or cooling system.
   D. Use a vacuum gauge to check for vacuum leaks, Fig. 18-4. Start with manifold vacuum test, with throttle valve closed and vacuum gauge connected directly to intake manifold. (Should hold steady reading.)
3. Inspect and Test Spark Plugs
   A. Examine spark plug insulator and electrodes for wear or breakage.
   B. Analyze deposits to pinpoint source of problem.
   C. Use spark plug cleaner and tester to test efficiency of plugs under pressure.
   D. Clean electrodes, then file and regap good used plugs. Or, replace defective plugs with a new set of specified type and proper heat range. (Use new gaskets unless plugs have a tapered seat.)
   E. Install new plugs to correct torque tightness. Average torque values for various sizes are: 18 mm, 25 to 30 ft. lb.; 14 mm, 25 ft. lb.; 10 mm, 10 to 12 ft. lb.
   F. Connect spark plug cable terminals securely to plugs in correct firing order. See Fig. 18-5, which applies to American Motors' engines. In addition, there are several other firing orders for V-8, V-6 and 4 cylinder engines. Consult the TUNE-UP AND MECHANICAL SPECIFICATIONS charts in the back of this text.
4. Test and Service Battery
   A. Clean posts, cable clamps and top of battery.
   B. Check level of electrolyte in cells, and use a hydrometer to check specific gravity of each cell. (Should be at least 1.250, corrected to 80 deg. F (26.6 C), with no more than 25 points of gravity difference between high and low cells.)
   C. Load test battery at three times its amphere hour rating, noting voltmeter after 15 sec. discharge. (Should be 9.5 volts or more.)
   D. Recharge weak battery. Replace defective battery.
5. Check Starting System
   A. Inspect condition of cables and wires, mounting of components.

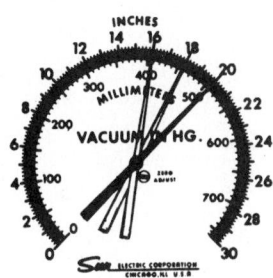

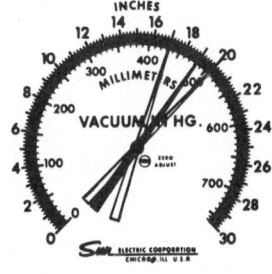

WITH MOTOR AT IDLING SPEED VAC-CUUM POINTER SHOULD HOLD STEADY.

WITH MOTOR AT IDLING SPEED DROP-PING BACK OF VACUUM POINTER IN-DICATES STICKY VALVES.

WITH MOTOR AT IDLING SPEED FLOAT-ING MOTION RIGHT AND LEFT OF VAC-UUM POINTER INDICATES CARBURETOR TOO RICH OR TOO LEAN.

WITH MOTOR AT IDLING SPEED LOW READING OF VACUUM POINTER INDI-CATES LATE TIMING OR INTAKE MANI-FOLD AIR LEAK.

Fig. 18-4. Diagrams show typical action of vacuum gauge needle when various abnormal conditions exist in engine under test.

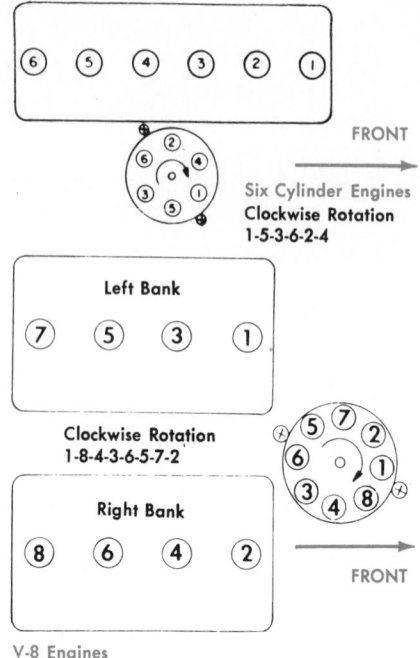

Fig. 18-5. Manufacturers furnish charts that indicate cylinder arrangement, firing order, distributor wiring sequence and rotor rotation. (American Motors Corp.)

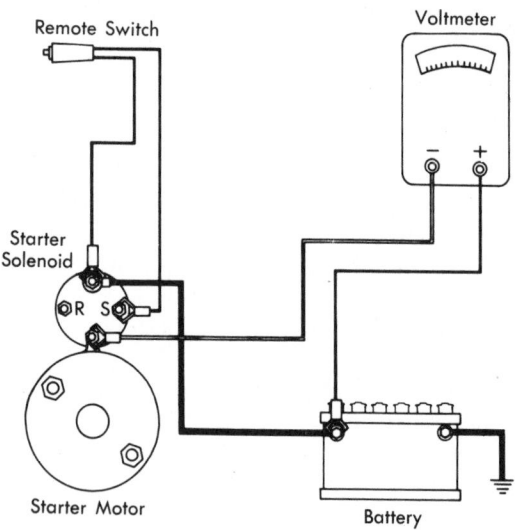

INSULATED CIRCUIT TEST

Fig. 18-6. Voltage drop tests aid in pinpointing excessive resistance in starting circuit. This voltmeter hookup tests drop in insulated circuit. Voltmeter should show .6V or less while engine is cranked.

B. Test for voltage drop in battery cables, connections, switch, solenoid and starting motor. See Fig. 18-6.

C. Test for amperage draw of starting motor. Remove high tension coil wire from distributor cap tower. Ground coil wire to metal part of engine. Connect leads of battery-starter tester to battery terminals. Crank engine for 15 seconds and note voltmeter

reading. Stop cranking and adjust resistance unit on tester to obtain voltage previously noted, then read amperage draw on ammeter. (Check reading against manufacturer's specifications.)

6. Test Ignition Coil

A. Use a voltmeter to check primary ignition voltage at battery side of igniton coil. (Voltage should be equal to battery voltage while starting motor is operating, since resistor is bypassed.)

B. Perform same test with engine running. (8-10V.)

C. If an oscilloscope is available, check required and available high tension voltage and high tension polarity. (Should be negative.)

D. Test high tension cables with ohmmeter. (Readings should not exceed 5,000 ohms per foot, and not more than 20,000 ohms maximum per cable.)

7. Service Ignition Distributor (breaker point type)

A. Check condition of distributor cap (inside and out) and rotor.

B. Note position of rotor and remove distributor from engine.

C. Clean distributor and check condition of lead wires, plate, cam, bushings and advance mechanism.

D. Replace breaker points and condenser. Align points, if necessary, and adjust gap to manufacturer's recommended setting.

E. Test breaker arm spring tension.

F. Lubricate wick in center of cam assembly with two drops of engine oil. Lubricate cam lobes with light coating of high melting point grease. Or replace cam lubricator.

G. Check operation of mechancial and vacuum advance units. Free or replace inoperative units. Check emission controls that effect timing advance. (See chapter on ENGINE IGNITION.)

H. Test distributor point dwell (cam angle) and readjust point gap, if necessary. Test dwell variation. (Generally, variation should not exceed 3 deg. from 250 rpm to 2,000 rpm.)

I. Install distributor in engine with rotor in original position.

J. Leave spark advance vacuum line(s) disconnected, but plug open end(s), Fig. 18-7.

8. Service GM High Energy Ignition (HEI) distributor. (Magnetic pickup assembly replaces breaker points. Distributor shaft rotates timer core to accurately signal electronic module which, in turn, controls on and off flow of current through coil primary circuit.)

A. To test system operation in nonstart situations, disconnect a spark plug wire and use an insulated pliers to hold the wire 1/4 in. (6.35 mm) from a grounded surface. Crank engine. A heavy blue spark should jump the gap.

B. Check for loose or corroded connections and/or poor ground.

C. Check routing of high tension wires through brackets. See Fig. 18-8. Note that coil is built into distributor

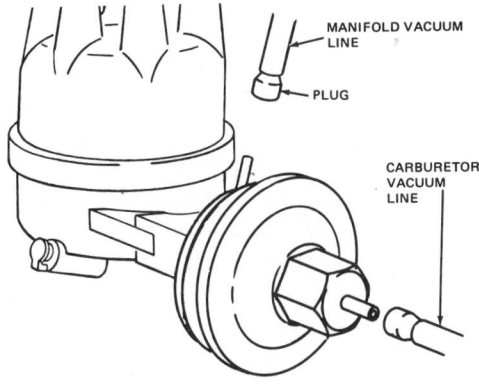

Fig. 18-7. To set initial ignition timing, disconnect and plug vacuum advance line. On Ford's dual diaphragm distributor, plug both lines.

cap and spark plug cable boots fit between cap and cover.

D. Disconnect ignition switch feed wire at distributor (V-6 and V-8) or coil (4 and L6). Connect voltmeter leads to wire and ground. With ignition switch ON, test voltage in the START and RUN positions. Both readings should be battery voltage.

E. Remove distributor cap.

F. Wiggle distributor shaft to check for bushing wear. Reluctor and pickup coil must not touch. HEI distributor shaft bushings do not need periodic lubrication.

G. Apply vacuum to vacuum advance unit to test diaphragm operation. Leave vacuum hose disconnected and plugged for ignition timing check.

H. Connect leads of low reading ammeter: one to disconnected switch wire: other to distribuor (V-6 and V-8) or coil (4 and L6) terminal. Turn on ignition switch: ammeter should read 0.1 to 0.2 amp. (Crank engine: ammeter should read 0.5 to 1.5 amps. If not, test pickup, module and coil primary current.)

I. Use proper dielectric compound on primary wire connections. Also use this compound on underside of module and on distributor base where module seats.

J. Use prescribed instruments to test electronic ignition components. Note, too, that some HEI systems have diagnostic plug-in connectors.

K. On engine speed tests, use a tachometer that is compatible with system. Do not connect tachometer lead to ground, nor allow tach terminal on distributor to touch ground. Damage to module or ignition coil could result.

L. Ignition timing specifications are listed on engine tune-up decal attached to or near radiator support. When connecting timing light leads, use an adapter between No. 1 spark plug and No. 1 spark plug wire, or use an inductive pickup. Also, on certain engines, a magnetic timing probe hole permits the use of special electronic timing equipment.

M. NOTE: When making tests that call for a spark plug to be shorted out, do not run engine longer than necessary. Otherwise, catalyst in catalytic converter will be damaged.

N. See chapter on ENGINE IGNITION for more information on HEI and other electronic ignition systems.

9. Service Ford Dura Spark ignition systems. (An electronic control module, a "spoked" armature and a magnetic pickup assembly are used in place of breaker points.)

A. Use an oscilloscope to test ignition system performance. No adjustments are to be made to Dura Spark systems except initial ignition timing and spark plug gap.

B. To test system operation in no-start situations, remove a spark plug cable and insert a modified spark plug, Fig. 18-9, into cable. Ground plug shell and crank engine to check for spark.

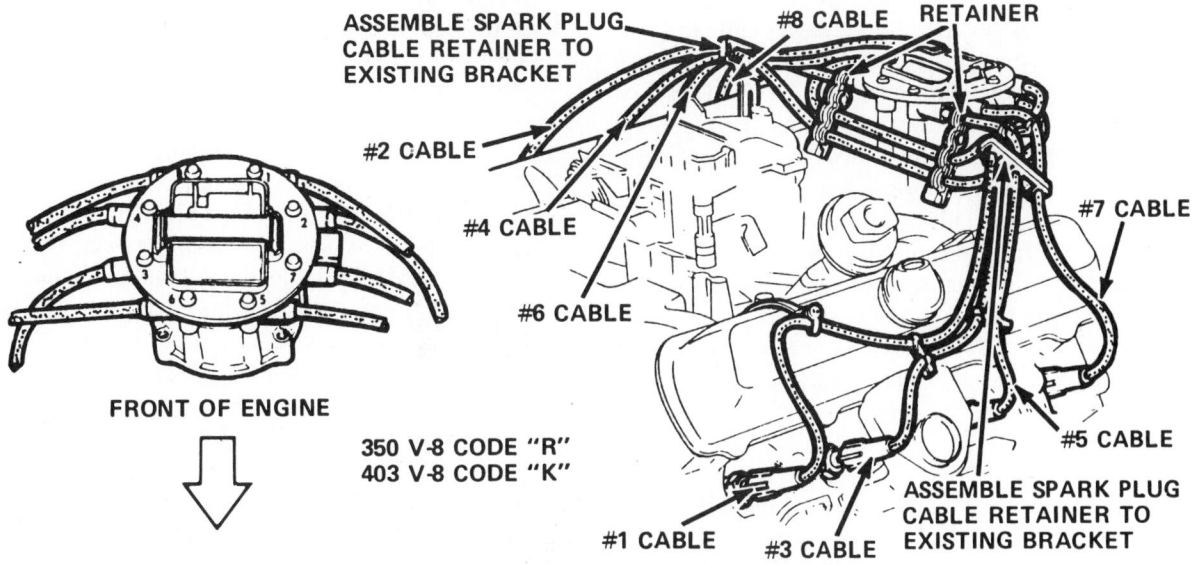

ASSEMBLE SPARK PLUG CABLE RETAINER TO EXISTING BRACKET

#8 CABLE   RETAINER

#2 CABLE

#4 CABLE

#6 CABLE

#7 CABLE

#5 CABLE

ASSEMBLE SPARK PLUG CABLE RETAINER TO EXISTING BRACKET

#1 CABLE   #3 CABLE

FRONT OF ENGINE

350 V-8 CODE "R"
403 V-8 CODE "K"

Fig. 18-8. Spark plug routing is shown for V-8 engine in GM cars equipped with High Energy Ignition (HEI) system.

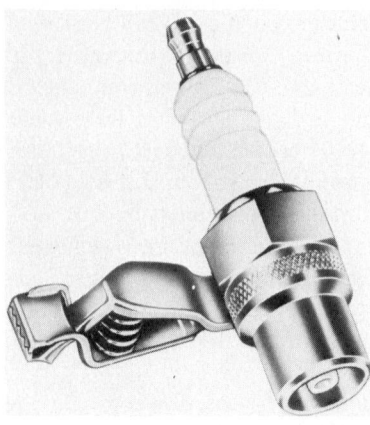

Fig. 18-9. A modified test plug is available that simulates conditions under which regular spark plugs operate. Plug terminal is connected to spark plug wire and clipped to engine block. Engine is cranked. If a spark jumps across test plug, Dura Spark system is satisfactory.

C. Check for loose or corroded connections and/or poor ground. Clean and tighten connections.

D. Remove and inspect distributor cap for cracks, burned contacts, broken carbon button, carbon tracking or corroded tower contacts. NOTE: On Dura Spark II systems, when ignition switch is ON, so are the control module and coil. Therefore, before removing distributor cap, be sure that ignition switch is OFF. This will prevent inadvertent engine rotation due to firing of ignition system.

E. Inspect rotor for breaks, carbon tracking or burns.

F. When installing a new distributor cap and rotor, coat (about 1/16 in. or 1.6 mm thick) brass electrode surfaces on all sides (away from plastic and including outer edge) with silicone grease. Also, do not remove silicone from new distributor cap electrodes.

G. Inspect distributor components. See that all snap rings are in place. Test pickup assembly for free movement on fixed base plate. Use compressed air to blow out dirt, filings or metal chips.

H. Apply vacuum to vacuum advance unit to test diaphragm operation. Leave vacuum hose disconnected for ignition timing operation. NOTE: On some air conditioned cars, a fast idle compensator applies intake manifold vacuum to primary side of diaphragm during hot engine conditions. This causes an increase in engine idle speed, which aids cooling.

I. Also check centrifugal advance unit located below distributor base plate. Inspect condition of springs. Weights should freely pivot outward and inward.

J. On Dura Spark II systems, a vacuum switch is used (at module) to sense intake manifold vacuum and provide an automatic spark retard signal to the distributor under heavy engine load.

K. Dura Spark I systems automatically shut down in one second after control module senses no distributor rotation. To reestablish the module cycle, turn ignition key to START or OFF, then ON again.

L. When servicing Dura Spark system, maintain at least 3/4 in. (19.0 mm) clearance between high tension wires and wire connections. NOTE: Wires are positioned in brackets on valve rocker arm covers in special order from front to rear to prevent cylinder crossfire. Be sure to reinstall wires in that special order.

M. Ignition coil connector on Dura Spark II systems allows hookup of tachometer test lead to DEC (distributor electronic control) terminal without removing connector. See Fig. 18-10.

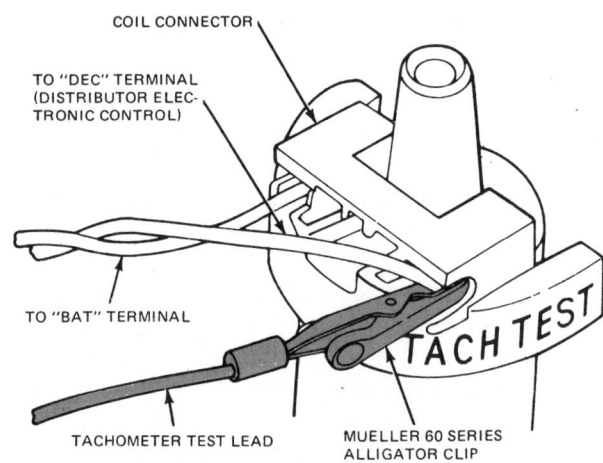

Fig. 18-10. Coil connector serves to distinguish Dura Spark II system from Dura Spark I. To install a tachometer on a Ford engine equipped with a Dura Spark II system: connect one lead to tach test terminal of coil connector; ground other lead.

N. Ignition timing specifications are listed on tune-up decal on or near engine. Use an inductance pickup type timing light clamped to No. 1 cylinder spark plug wire. Plug disconnected vacuum lines and set initial ignition timing. Reconnect vacuum lines and visually verify that advance vacuum line is routed to spark port of carburetor. Retard vacuum line should be routed to manifold vacuum connection.

10. Service Chrysler Electronic Ignition system distributor. (System uses electronic control unit, reluctor and pickup coil to replace braker points. Rotating reluctor produces voltage pulse in magnetic pickup. Pulse is transmitted to switching transistor in control unit, which interrupts flow of current through coil primary circuit. See Fig. 18-11.)

A. Inspect condition of wiring harness and connections, secondary cables and ballast resistor. With ignition switch OFF, remove multiwiring connector from control unit. NOTE: Some Chrysler cars are equipped with diagnostic plug-in connectors.

B. With ignition switch ON, hook up a voltmeter with a 20,000 ohm/volt rating: negative lead to ground: positive lead to wiring harness connector cavity No. 1. See Fig. 18-12. Available voltage should be at least 11 volts with all accessories OFF.

C. Repeat primary system test at connector cavities No. 2 and No. 3.

D. Use an ohmmeter with 1 1/2 volt battery to test pickup coil. Connect leads of ohmmeter to wiring

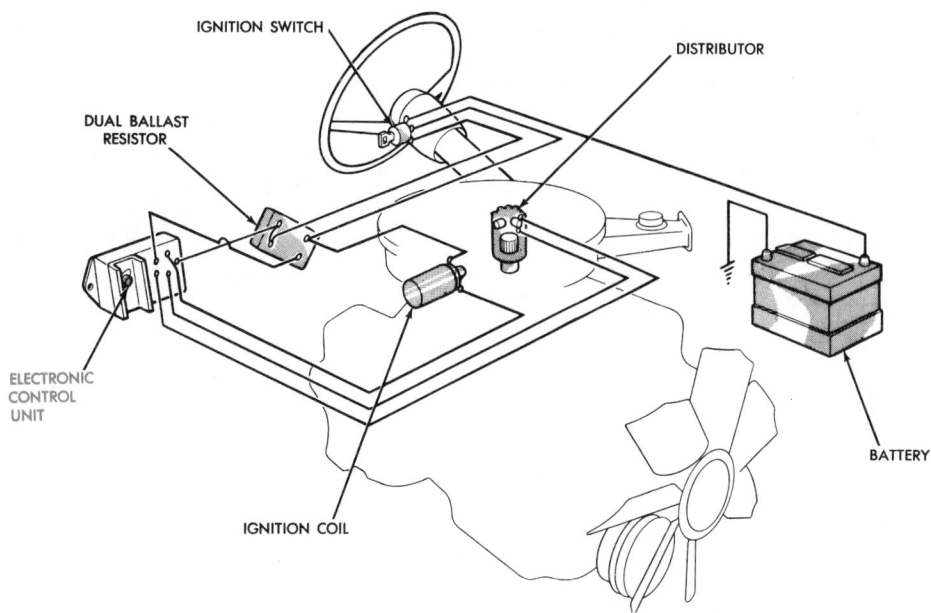

Fig. 18-11. Chrysler's electronic ignition system. For identification, note two primary wires to distributor.

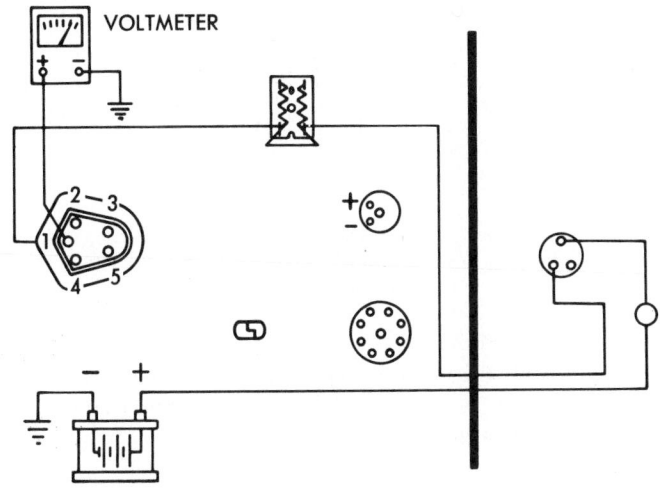

Fig. 18-12. On Chrysler electronic ignition system, test available voltage at wiring harness connector cavity No. 1 as shown.

harness connector cavity No. 4, then No. 5. Resistance should be between 150 and 900 ohms.

E. If resistance is out of limits, disconnect dual lead connector from distributor. Using ohmmeter, test resistance at dual lead connector. If resistance is still out of limits, replace pickup coil.

F. Connect one ohmmeter lead to ground, other lead to either connector of distributor. Ohmmeter should show open circuit (infinity). If not, replace pickup coil.

G. Check electronic control unit: Connect one ohmmeter lead to ground; other lead to control unit connector pin No. 5. Ohmmeter must show continuity. If not, tighten control unit mounting bolts and retest. If no continuity, replace control unit.

H. With ignition switch OFF, reconnect wiring harness at control unit and distributor.

I. Remove distributor cap. Inspect cap for cracks, burns, flashover, worn or grooved terminals. Clean or replace cap.

J. Inspect rotor for cracks, burns and tension of spring terminal. Clean or replace rotor.

K. Check centrifugal advance unit for free operation.

L. Apply vacuum to vacuum advance unit to test diaphragm operation. Leave vacuum hose disconnected and plugged for ignition timing operation.

M. Check air gap between reluctor tooth and pickup coil. Adjust gap to .006 in. (.15 mm), if necessary.

N. Reinstall distributor rotor and cap.

O. Check ignition secondary circuit. Remove high voltage cable from center tower of distributor cap. Hold cable approximately 3/16 in. (4.76 mm) from grounded surface of engine. Crank engine. If arcing does not occur, replace control unit.

P. Crank engine again. If arcing does not occur, replace ignition coil.

Q. Connect a power timing light to No. 1 spark plug wire and No. 1 spark plug, using an adapter. Check ignition timing at hot idle speed.

11. Service AMC Solid State Ignition distributor. (Electronic control unit, trigger wheel and sensor replace breaker points. SSI system can be distingushed from earlier Breakerless Inductive Discharge system by its unusual coil connector, Fig. 18-13. BID system tests are similar, but specifications differ.)

A. To test system operation in nonstart situation, disconnect oil wire from center tower of distributor cap. (Do not remove No. 3 or No. 4 plug wire of of a six cylinder engine or No. 3 or No. 4 plug wire of a V-8 engine when performing this test.) Disconnect 4-wire connector at control unit. Use an insulated pliers to hold coil wire 1/2 in. (12.7 mm) from a grounded surface. See Fig. 18-13. Crank engine. A spark should occur.

B. If no spark occurs, use an ohmmeter to test coil wire resistance. It should not exceed 10,000 ohms.

C. Connect ohmmeter leads to cavities D2 and D3 or 4-wire connector. Ohmmeter should indicate 400 to 800 ohms.

D. Connect DC voltmeter leads to cavities D2 and D3 of 4-wire connector. Crank engine. Voltmeter needle should fluctuate if trigger wheel and sensor are operating properly.

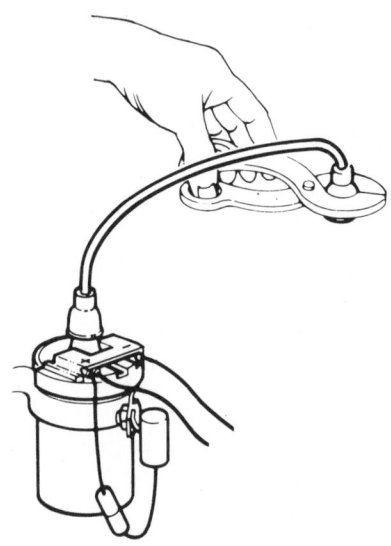

Fig. 18-13. On AMC electronic ignition system, hold disconnected end of coil high tension wire 1/2 in. from a grounded surface. Crank engine and observe intensity of spark.

E. Inspect primary ignition system for loose or corroded terminals, poor ground connections or defective wiring.

F. Check routing of spark plug wires from distributor cap towers to spark plugs.

G. Remove distributor cap. Check cap for corrosion, cracks and/or carbon tracks.

H. Check rotor for wear or deterioration of firing tip.

I. Wiggle distributor shaft. Trigger wheel and sensor must not touch.

J. Apply vacuum to vacuum advance unit to test condition of diaphragm. Leave vacuum hose disconnected for ignition timing check.

K. Reinstall distributor rotor and cap. Recheck routing of high tension cables.

L. Apply silicone dielectric compound to connector blades and cavities. Connect distributor-to-control unit primary wiring connector.

M. Connect timing light to No. 1 spark plug wire and No. 1 spark plug, using an adapter. Also, timing case cover on late models has a hole for using a magnetic timing probe.

N. Test centrifugal advance operation after initial ignition timing is set. With vacuum hose disconnected

and plugged, accelerate engine from 500 rpm. Timing should advance smoothly to 2,000 rpm.

12. Check Cooling System

A. Inspect condition of radiator, hoses and clamps, including transmission oil cooler lines and fittings.

B. Test radiator cap for pressure release point and pressure-holding ability.

C. Check level of coolant in radiator or in coolant reserve tank and degree of antifreeze protection.

D. Use pressure tester to test cooling system for leaks. Pressurize system to pressure release point of cap and observe reading for at least two mintues. (Drop in pressure indicates leak in system.)

E. Check condition and tension of V-belts, Fig. 18-14.

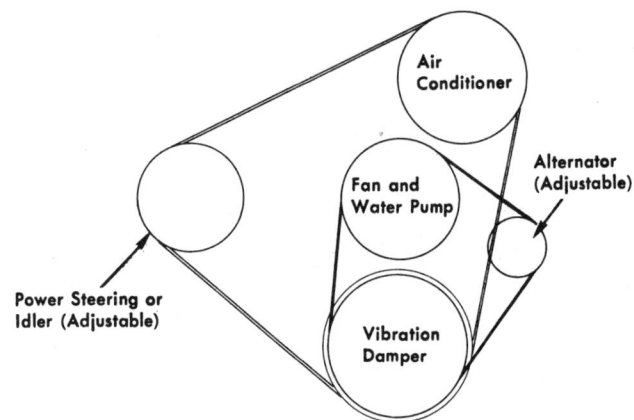

Fig. 18-14. Diagram shows V-belt arrangement on American Motors 232 or 258 cu. in. Six with air conditioning and with or without (idler) power steering.

13. Inspect Fuel System

A. Torque-tighten intake manifold attaching bolts.

B. Check freedom of operation of manifold heat control valve, if so equipped, Fig. 18-15.

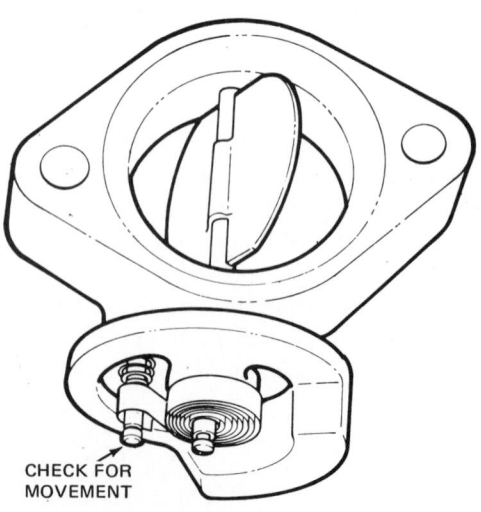

CHECK FOR MOVEMENT

Fig. 18-15. Exhaust manifold heat control valve provides quick warm-up of induction system. Manually check movement of valve counterweight for freedom of operation.

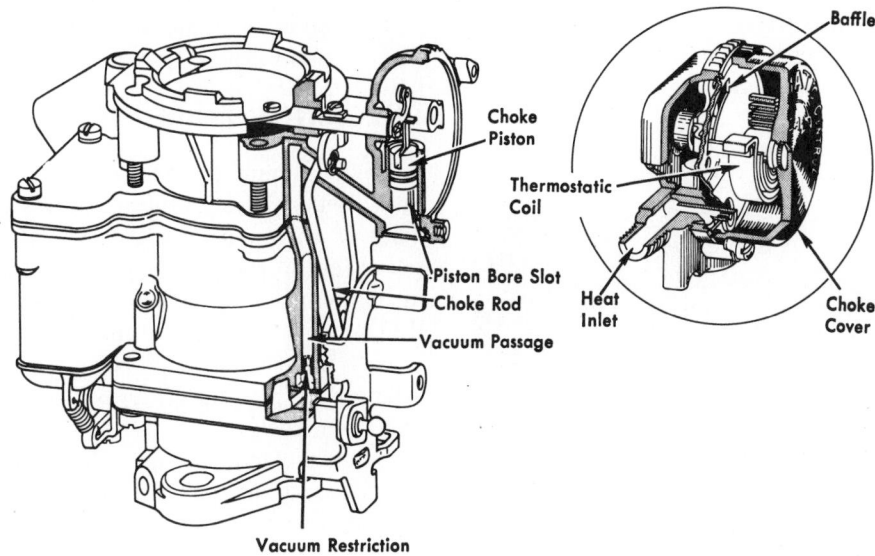

Fig. 18-16. To check choke valve operation, open throttle valve and manually work choke valve through full travel. Shaft, choke piston and linkage must move freely.

C. Check carburetor base heating units on engines so equipped.

D. Service all air filters and fuel filters; clean or replace elements as required.

E. Tighten carburetor attaching nuts or bolts and cover screws.

F. Clean automatic choke mechanism and test choke valve and linkage for freedom of operation, Fig. 18-16.

G. Check adjustment of choke, unloader and kickdown. Tighten heat tube fittings, if so equipped. Test continuity (current flow) of circuit on electric choke applications.

H. Inspect fuel lines, hoses and connections for fuel leaks, kinks, restriction or deterioration.

I. Check operation of accelerator linkage. Clean and adjust as required, Fig. 18-17.

J. Check for proper fuel tank venting on older cars. Check evaporative emissions control system hoses and filter on later models.

K. Test fuel pump pressure, capacity (volume) and vacuum.

L. Service positive crankcase ventilation (PCV) system. Replace PCV valve, if required by manufacturer's recommendation.

M. Service all emissions control systems on later engines.

14. Start Engine and Make Preliminary Adjustments

A. Run engine, check choking action and fast idle operation.

B. Connect timing light to ignition system, Fig. 18-18, and check initial timing. Reconnect vacuum line(s) and recheck advance with timing light.

C. Examine entire exhaust system for leaks.

D. Run engine to operating temperature and check thermostat operation.

E. Install tachometer and vacuum gauge; adjust air-fuel mixture and engine idle speed. Adjust throttle stop solenoid on engines so equipped, Fig. 18-17.

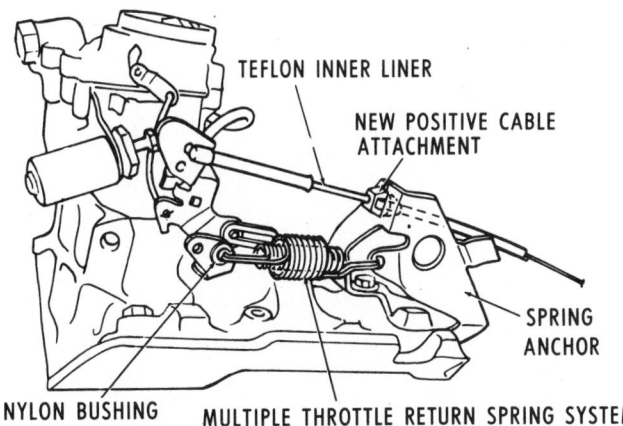

Fig. 18-17. Accelerator linkage check is important to idle speed adjustment and throttle return on deceleration. New Chevrolet multiple throttle return spring system is shown.

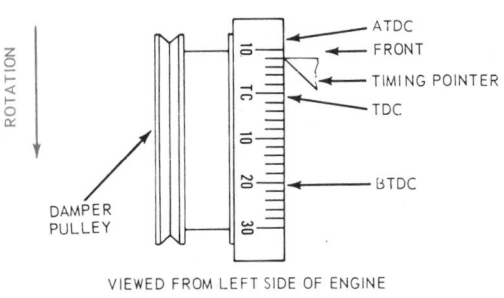

Fig. 18-18. Most engines have timing marks on crankshaft vibration damper with timing pointer attached to timing cover. Mark degree line as specified and rotate distributor to align pointer and mark.

F. Connect an emissions tester (exhaust gas analyzer) to engine and tailpipe of car. Test HC and CO emission levels at speeds ranging from 500 to 1750 rpm, Fig. 18-19.

G. Adjust valve lash, if engine has solid lifters.

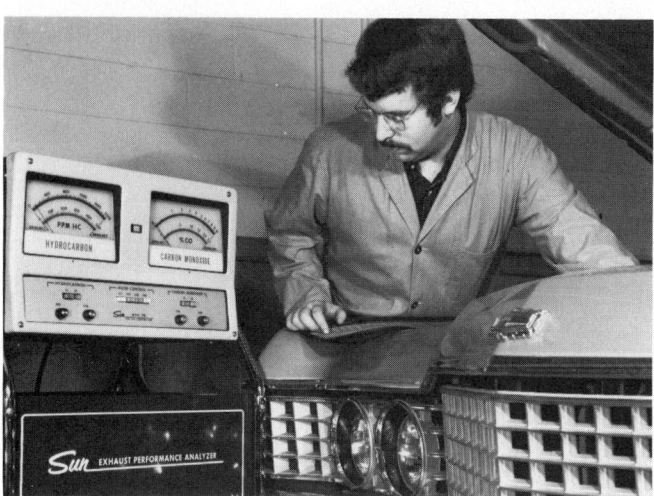

Fig. 18-19. Exhaust emissions tester samples exhaust gas and reads out in levels of hydrocarbon (HC) and carbon monoxide (CO).

15. Test Charging System
A. Use an alternator tester to test voltage and current output of alternator.
B. Check operation of voltage regulator.

16. Road Test Car
A. Check starting and idle; test engine performance at all speeds.
B. Check automatic transmission shift points and kick-down operation.

C. Make final adjustments to obtain best possible engine performance, fewest emissions and most fuel mileage.

CHECKING COMPRESSION PRESSURE

Never attempt to tune-up an engine having worn piston rings, faulty valves, incorrect valve timing, worn camshaft lobes or an internal coolant leak. If internal parts are not sound (not in good working order), poor engine performance usually results. This performance problem, however, is beyond the corrective powers of an engine tune-up.

Most internal engine problems can be detected by making a compression pressure test, which is one of the first and most important steps of an engine tune-up. Twenty years ago, engine manufacturers specified "minimum compression allowed," such as 100 psi. Then they added a maximum variation specification, such as 20 psi.

More recently, manufacturers provided minimum/maximum compression pressure charts, Fig. 18-20. Today, most manufacturers specify that the lowest compression reading must be 70 to 75 percent of the highest.

To use the chart, first record compression pressures for each engine cylinder. Use a special compression gauge to make the test. The engine should be at normal operating temperature. The engine oil should be of the proper grade and not seriously diluted.

Make the test with all spark plugs removed and with choke and throttle valves of the carburetor wide open. Use a remote starter switch to crank over the engine while holding the tip of the compression gauge in each spark plug port in turn. Crank the engine for at least four revolutions, recording the highest reading on the gauge for each cylinder. Compare the high and low figures on your list with the satisfactory ranges shown on the manufacturer's specification chart, Fig. 18-20. If one or more cylinders is "out-of-specification," there is no use tuning

Maximum PSI	Minimum PSI	Maximum PSI	Minimum PSI	Maximum PSI	Minimum PSI
134	101	174	131	214	160
136	102	176	132	216	162
138	104	178	133	218	163
140	105	180	135	220	165
142	107	182	136	222	166
144	108	184	138	224	168
146	110	186	140	226	169
148	111	188	141	228	171
150	113	190	142	230	172
152	114	192	144	232	174
154	115	194	145	234	175
156	117	196	147	236	177
158	118	198	148	238	178
160	120	200	150	240	180
162	121	202	151	242	181
164	123	204	153	244	183
166	124	206	154	246	184
168	126	208	156	248	186
170	127	210	157	250	187
172	129	212	158		

Fig. 18-20. This chart gives generally acceptable compression pressures. The values are based on an engine manufacturer's typical compression specification, "Lowest cylinder must be at least 75 percent of highest."

up the engine until the cause has been determined and corrected.

Diesel engines have much higher compression pressures than gasoline engines. Diesel compression is in the area of 650 psi (4482 kPa). Therefore, the conventional pressure gauge used for checking compression of a spark ignition engine cannot be used when checking compression of a diesel engine.

If the compression pressure varies more than the prescribed range between cylinders, it can be assumed that the cylinders, rings or valves are defective. To check, introduce a tablespoonful of engine oil into the low-reading cylinder. Then recheck compression. If there is a definite improvement, the piston rings are probably at fault. If there is no improvement, one or both valves in the low cylinder may be burnt or not seating.

If two weak cylinders are adjacent, it could indicate a "blown" cylinder head gasket. In any case, the cylinder head will probably have to be removed to remedy the defect. It is good practice, however, to check further with a vacuum gauge before removing the head.

USING A VACUUM GAUGE

In the hands of an experienced operator, a vacuum gauge can provide considerable useful information about the condition of the internal parts of an engine. However, it is easy to misinterpret the readings of the instrument and reach false conclusions. In using the gauge on an engine, it is much more important to note the action of the needle (floating or vibrating, for example) rather than the numbers on the dial.

When properly used and understood, a vacuum gauge will indicate: incorrect carburetor adjustment; ignition timing errors; ignition defects; improper valve action; restricted exhaust system; cylinder leakage; intake system leakage.

If an engine is in good internal condition and running in good adjustment, the vacuum gauge needle will hold steady at a reading between 17 and 21 at idling speed. There will be some variation with changes in altitude and atmospheric conditions. For example, each 1,000 (304.8 m) above sea level will lower the reading about one point (or one inch of mercury). Vacuum gauges are manufactured with dials marked in inches of mercury (Hg) to correspond to "U" tube laboratory instruments that serve as a standard.

INTERPRETING THE READINGS

With the engine warmed up to operating temperature and running slightly higher than at low idling speed, attach a vacuum gauge to the intake manifold. Attach it directly to the manifold, in order to avoid any leaks that might exist in vacuum-operated systems or connections. Then make the following analysis of the various readings.

NORMAL: Needle will be steady between 15 and 21 while idling. When the throttle is suddenly opened and closed, the needle will drop to below 5, then bounce up to around 25.

LEAKING RINGS: Needle may be fairly steady, but will read 3 to 4 points lower than normal. When throttle is suddenly opened and closed, needle may sink to zero, then bounce back to around 22. A compression pressure test,

following introduction of oil in the cylinder, may be necessary as a final check.

SLOW TIMING: If compression is good and needle reads low, ignition timing may be slow, Fig. 18-4. If reading is considerably lower than it should be, valve timing may be slow. If adjusting carburetor will not increase vacuum to normal, make a check to see if either or both, ignition or valve timing, should be advanced.

LEAKING INTAKE: If needle is steady but from 3 to 9 points low, throttle valve is not closing, or an air leak probably exists in carburetor, intake manifold or gaskets.

LEAKING CYLINDER HEAD GASKET: If needle floats regularly between a low and a high reading, the cylinder head gasket probably is "blown" between two adjacent cylinders.

CARBURETOR OUT OF ADJUSTMENT: Needle floats slowly over a range of 4 to 5 points.

SPARK PLUG GAPS: If needle floats slowly over a narrower range, perhaps 2 points, the spark plug gaps may be spaced too close, or else the ignition points are not operating properly.

RESTRICTED EXHAUST: If needle reads in normal range when engine is first started, sinks to zero, then rises slowly to below normal, the muffler may be clogged or the tailpipe kinked or plugged.

DEFECTIVE VALVE ACTION: Experience will help you to distinguish between valve troubles such as leaking, burned, sticking valves, weak valve springs or worn valve guides. Action of the needle and range of motion are indications of which is at fault, Fig. 18-4. Since the valve must be removed in most cases to remedy the defect, correctness of diagnosis can be determined.

ENGINE MECHANICAL CONDITION: If vacuum gauge indicates loss of compression or improper valve action, do not proceed with tune-up until all faults are corrected. If, however, tests indicate timing errors, intake leaks, carburetor out of adjustment or a restricted exhaust system, correct these defects as the next step.

HIGH SPEED TUNING

An engine tune-up can be carried to extremes if you want to get maximum speed and power from a given engine. A high performance tune-up procedure often involves extensive mechanical alteration of the engine. Modifications include: enlarging the valves and seats; porting and relieving the cylinder heads; altering the bore and stroke of the engine; increasing the compression ratio; installing a custom camshaft.

Additional changes are: revising valve timing and ignition timing; enlarging and streamlining intake and exhaust manifolds; installing multiple carburetors or fuel injection. High performance tuning is a separate and complicated subject, not within the scope of this text.

TUNING EMISSION CONTROLS

Great care, methodical checks and precise adjustments are required when tuning engines equipped with emission controls. Failure to follow factory instructions and specifications may result in rough idle, surging, loss of power, increased emissions and dieseling (run-on after ignition key is turned off).

Systems and controls installed to reduce emissions are covered in the chapter on EMISSION CONTROL. Some industry-wide applications include:

1. Positive crankcase ventilation.
2. Heated carburetor air intake.
3. Injection of air into exhaust ports.
4. Catalytic converters.
5. Electronic engine controls.
6. Carburetor throttle stop solenoids.
7. Altitude compensation.
8. Vacuum throttle modulating system.
9. Closed loop feedback carburetors.
10. Distributor advance controls, such as dual diaphragm distributor and transmission controlled spark advance.
11. Evaporative emissions control system.
12. Limiters on idle air-fuel mixture adjustment.
13. Exhaust gas recirculation system.
14. Thermal vacuum switch.
15. Choke control systems.
16. Spark delay systems.
17. Electronic spark control.
18. Internal engine modifications that permit engine to run on lead-free or low-lead gasolines.

These devices must be in good working order and properly adjusted to function as designed — as emission controls. The emission standards are being lowered each year, making emission control tuning more important than ever.

Also worth noting, government regulations forbid removing, disconnecting, disengaging, or otherwise rendering emission controls inoperative. Set them up as specified by the manufacturer to maintain the controls at maximum operating efficiency to help fight air pollution.

REVIEW QUESTIONS — ENGINE TUNE-UP

1. What is the purpose of an engine tune-up?
2. What is one of the first and most important steps of a tune-up?
3. Name three different types of exhaust emissions that pollute the atmosphere.
4. Engine manufacturers have worked in two directions to reduce exhaust emissions. What are they?
5. To hook up tachometer test leads, connect the positive lead to the No. 1 spark plug cable terminal; ground the negative lead. True or False?
6. Most of the work involved in an engine tune-up job is concerned with tests of the battery, starter, alternator, distributor, carburetor and _____ _____.
7. As part of tune-up procedure, examine spark plug insulators and electrodes for _____ or _____.

8. Which tester is used to test amperage draw of the starting motor?
   a. Battery-starter tester.
   b. Voltmeter.
   c. Ohmmeter.
9. What is the maximum time of high rate discharge during a battery load test?
   a. 5 seconds.
   b. 15 seconds.
   c. 25 seconds.
10. Which tester is used to test the resistance of the high tension cables?
    a. Battery-starter tester.
    b. Voltmeter.
    c. Ohmmeter.
    d. Ammeter.
11. In testing the resistance of the high tension cables, the readings should not exceed _____ per foot.
12. When pressure testing the cooling system, the tester shows a drop in pressure. What does this indicate?
13. What check is required on manifold heat control valve?
    a. Valve lash.
    b. Torque tightness.
    c. Freedom of operation.
14. What three tests are required on the fuel pump?
15. You must adjust valve lash on engines with solid lifters. True or False?
16. Which meters are used to help set the carburetor air-fuel mixture adjustment and engine idle speed?
17. Car manufacturers now specify a "minimum compression allowed" of 100 psi. True or False?
18. What would the vacuum gauge indicate on an engine in good condition at an altitude of 5,000 ft. (1 524 m) above sea level?
    a. 12-17.
    b. 17-21.
    c. 21-26.
19. If the vacuum gauge needle is steady, but extremely low, what trouble is indicated?
    a. Narrow spark plug gap.
    b. Leaking piston rings.
    c. Air leak in intake system.
20. When the vacuum gauge needle floats slowly over a range of 4 or 5 points, what is the probable cause?
    a. Ignition timing is retarded.
    b. Carburetor is out of adjustment.
    c. Exhaust system is restricted.
21. How can you identify an electronic ignition system on a Chrysler engine by one quick visual check?
22. How can you identify a Dura Spark II ignition system on a Ford engine?
23. How can you identify a High Energy Ignition (HEI) system on a General Motors' engine?
24. Never remove, disconnect or disengage an emission control device or system. True or False?

AUTO
SHOP SAFETY

Safety is everyone's responsibility, and it is concerned with all areas where people live and work. Even the U.S. Government is in the act with far-reaching safety regulations for the business world.

All of which makes your school shop the ideal place to:

1. Study safety regulations.
2. Learn to set up a safe shop.
3. Establish safe working conditions.
4. Make safety a part of every service procedure.

To be specific, the Occupational Safety and Health Administration (OSHA), which is a branch of the Department of LABOR, was formed to lay down guidelines for all types of businesses to insure they are operated under conditions of maximum safety and health. Now, every auto repair shop and service station is under the watchful eyes of OSHA to be sure the shop or station is operated under specific safe working conditions prescribed by the Government.

Most of the safety regulations set forth have already been put into practice by the careful shop or station owner. But, under the conditions of the act which went into effect in April, 1971, inspections will be made to be sure that its edicts are being followed.

Before discussing any of the provisions of the act, it is important to know that it provides that any employee (or representative thereof) who believes that a violation of job safety or health standard exists may request an inspection by sending a signed statement to the Department of Labor. While the employer may receive a copy of the complaint, the names of the complainants need not be furnished.

The safety inspectors may enter, without delay and at any reasonable time, any establishment covered by the act to inspect the premises and all pertinent conditions, structures, machines, apparatus, devices, equipment and materials therein, and to question privately any employer, owner, operator, agent or employee.

Where an investigation reveals a violation, the employer is issued a written citation describing the nature of the violation. All citations shall fix a reasonable time for abatement of the violation.

Willful or repeated violations of the act's requirements by employers may incur very substantial fines for each particular violation. Citations issued for serious violations incur manda-

tory penalties. Any employer who fails to correct a violation for which a citation has been issued within the prescribed time period may be penalized by a substantial fine for each day that the violation persists.

A willful violation by an employer which results in the death of an employee is punishable by a very large fine or imprisonment up to six months. A second conviction doubles these penalties.

Every employer must keep occupational injury and illness records of employees in the establishment at which the employees usually report for work. The records must be kept up to date and available to governmental representatives. And, the employer must post a summary of all occupational injuries and illnesses at the conclusion of the calendar year.

The law also requires that employees must be informed of job safety and health provisions. A poster is provided which must be posted in a prominent place in the establishment to which the employees must report for work.

Some of the safety and health items set forth in the act include basic points, such as clean floors free of grease, oil and dirt. Washrooms must be kept clean and sanitary. Paint spray booths must be ventilated and meet specific requirements. Buildings must be designed with a sufficient number of exits, and aisles must not be obstructed.

Personal protective equipment for eyes, face, head and extremities as well as protective respiratory devices, shields and barriers must be provided, Fig. 19-1. And, the employer is responsible for employee-owned equipment.

Equipment must be in good condition and provided with any safety guards, Fig. 19-2, and safety devices that may be necessary. And, management is responsible for the safe operation of welding and cutting equipment. Electric wiring and equipment must meet underwriters' specifications and be in good conditions, Fig. 19-3. No smoking signs must be prominently displayed, Fig. 19-4, and all combustible liquids must be kept in specified containers and limited as to the quantity that is permissible within the building.

These are some of the major points set forth in the OSHA act. However, auto shop and service station operators should not limit their safety and health program to the regulations of the OSHA. There are many conditions not covered by the act that should be followed and enforced by every owner.

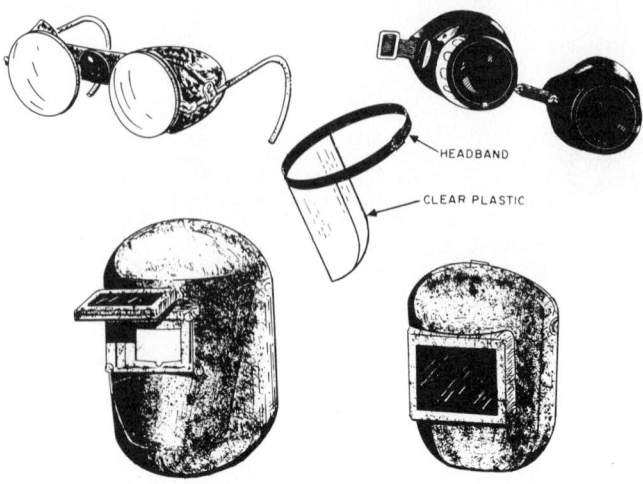

Fig. 19-1. Various types of eye protection devices.

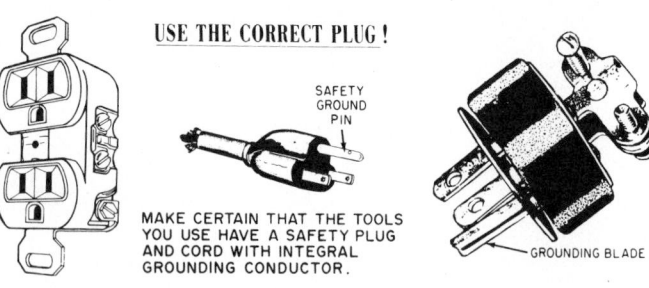

Fig. 19-3. Electrical underwriters' rules must be followed.

help prevent fire, but also help prevent evaporation of the chemicals with attendant loss of profits.

Painting should be done in paint spray booths provided with exhaust fans and conforming to underwriters' requirements. Smoking and unshielded flames should never be permitted. No Smoking signs, Fig. 19-4, should be prominently displayed.

Fig. 19-2. Guards on grinding wheels must always be kept in place. (Van Norman Machine Co.)

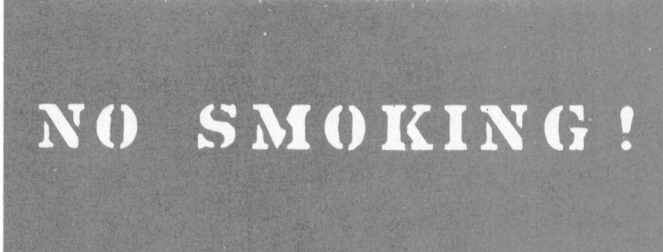

Fig. 19-4. No Smoking signs must be prominently displayed and strictly enforced.

Special care, for example, must be taken — and goggles worn — when adding the hardener (catalyst) to fiber glass resin. If one drop of the hardener gets in your eye, it will progressively destroy eye tissue and result in blindness.

Immediate remedial action must be taken. The hardener must be washed from the eye within four seconds after the accident to avoid destruction of the eye.

Also important, there can be no running, no practical jokes nor horseplay in the shop. Such conduct invariably results in accidents, as well as distracting others in the shop from the work they are supposed to do.

Because the many combustibles, such as gasoline, lacquer thinner and certain cleaning fluids used in automobile repair shops, special precautions are needed to prevent fire. Fuel, thinner and other combustibles should always be kept in closed containers designed for the purpose. This will not only

All shops should be provided with an ample number of fire extinguishers. Everyone should be familiar with their location and use. Remember, water cannot be used to extinguish a gasoline or grease fire. Use carbon tetrachloride, foam or, if nothing else is available, sand will help smother it.

As a further protection against fire, oil and paint rags should be kept in suitable containers. Care must be exercised so that spontaneous combustion does not occur.

Painters should always use masks when spraying as a guard against respiratory illnesses resulting from the inhalation of paint fumes. Mechanics using grinding wheels or sanders, or when chipping metal, should wear goggles as protection for the eyes, Fig. 19-5. Goggles also should be worn when using compressed air to blow dirt from parts.

Special safety precautions are necessary when working on automotive electrical circuits. Unless the starting battery is needed for making tests of the circuit, it should be disconnected. This precaution will eliminate the possibility of any short circuits and attendant possibility of fire or damage to the circuit and tools.

Most important, a naked flame should not be used to

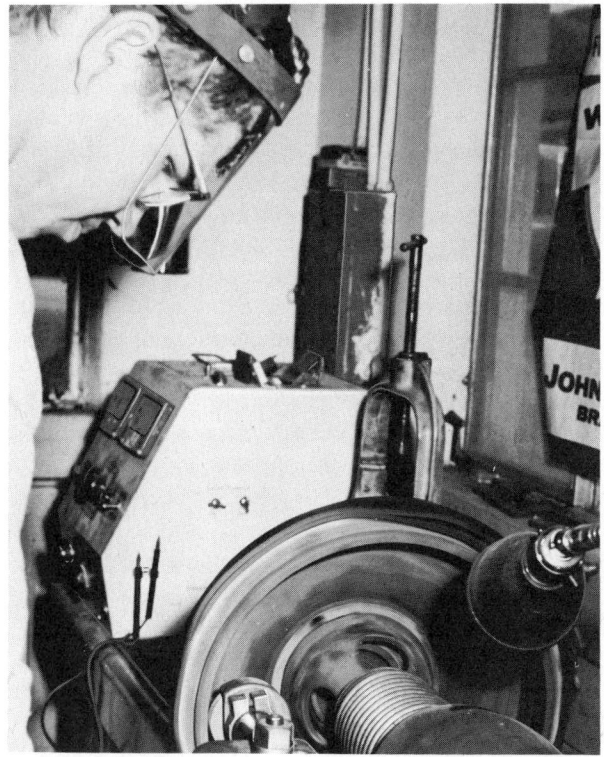

Fig. 19-5. Protective goggles or eye shield should be worn during grinding operations or other jobs when there is a possibility of injury to eyes.

Fig. 19-6. The fumes from starting batteries are highly explosive. Use a flashlight when checking the level of the electrolyte.

observe the level of the electrolyte in the starting battery. Acid fumes are highly explosive, and acid would be splashed into the mechanics eyes. When it becomes necessary to note the electrolyte level, a flashlight should be used, Fig. 19-6.

Special care must be observed when removing the pressure cap from a radiator. The cooling system is under 14 to 17 lb. pressure, and the sudden removal of the radiator cap will cause the superheated steam and water to be forced out. This could cause severe burns. When removing a radiator cap, cover it with a cloth and give it a half turn. Then, after the steam has escaped and the pressure is reduced, remove the cap completely.

VENTILATION IS IMPORTANT

One of the most important safety precautions to be followed in an auto shop is proper ventilation. If it is necessary to operate an engine for more than a few seconds, the car should be driven outside. A large portion of exhaust fumes consist of carbon monoxide, which is a deadly poison. In small quantities, it produces drowsiness and headaches. In large quantities, death results.

Many shops are provided with special conduits which are connected to the tailpipe of the automobile. These conduits conduct the exhaust gases out-of-doors, eliminating the danger from carbon monoxide poisoning.

Care must be exercised to keep the shop floor clean and free from grease and oil. These spots are slippery and frequently result in accidents to mechanics and other persons walking through the shop. Whenever any oil or grease is spilled or drips on the floor, it should be wiped up immediately. Special preparations are available for absorbing oil, and cleaning the spots.

Equally important, is the need for keeping the floor clear of tools and parts. When laid in the aisle, there is always the possibility of someone tripping over them. A similar condition results from a jack handle sticking out into the aisle where it may trip someone. If lifts are not available, and it is necessary to keep the car raised for a protracted period, the car should be placed on stands. In that way, there will be no chance of the car falling as the result of a faulty jack. In addition, such practice frees the jack for work on other vehicles.

USING TOOLS SAFELY

There are many safety precautions related to the use of tools:

Files should never be used without a handle, since there is always the danger of running the pointed tang into the palm of the hand. Neither should files be used as pry bars, nor should they be hammered. Files are made with hard temper. Consequently, they are quite brittle. When hammered, small pieces may fly off and cause severe wounds or loss of eyesight.

Hardened surfaces, such as the face of an anvil, should not be struck with a hammer as bits of steel may fly off and cause damage. Further, in connection with hammers and sledges, care must always be exercised that the head is always securely attached to the handle. Loose hammer and sledge heads may fly off when the tool is used. Anyone standing in the way will be struck and severely injured.

When the head of a chisel becomes swaged over, it should be discarded, or reground to remove the swaged edges. This will prevent bits of steel from flying off and causing damage.

Whenever grinding is done, the mechanic should wear goggles to protect the eyes, Fig. 19-5. The grinding wheel should always be provided with a protecting guard, Fig. 19-2.

When using a wrench, pull on the handle rather than push on it. Should the wrench slip, there will be less danger of skinning your knuckles. When the jaws of a wrench become worn or sprung, discard the wrench.

Compressed air is an important "tool" in every shop. The air gun should not be pointed at anyone. The high pressure of the air can blow dirt particles at such high speed that they will puncture the skin and/or get into the eyes.

When changing large size truck tires with a detachable ring, do not lean over the tire while it is being inflated. These rings have been blown off the rim by the force of the compressed air and severely injured the mechanic.

Never stand in the same plane as a rotating part, such as the fan belt on an automobile, drive belts of lathes and other machinery, flywheels and grinding wheels. Should a belt break, or part of the rotating unit be thrown off by centrifugal force, severe injuries could result.

Use care when working around any machinery, engine or motor that there is a chance of loose clothing being caught and entangled in rotating parts. For that reason, it is advisable to tuck neckties within the shirt. If long sleeves are being worn, these should be buttoned at the cuff. Caps without brims are considered safer than those with brims, because of the possiblity of the protruding brim being caught in some rotating part.

In regard to safety precautions when using oxygen and acetylene for welding, there are many points to observe. Never allow oil or grease to contact oxygen under pressure. Do not lubricate welding and cutting apparatus. Never use oxygen as a substitute for compressed air, as a source of pressure, or for ventilation. Before starting to weld or cut, make sure that flame, sparks, hot slag or hot metal will not be likely to start a fire. Always wear goggles when working with a lighted torch.

Be sure to keep a clear space between the cylinders and the work, because you may find it necessary to reach and adjust the regulators quickly. Do not risk hand burns by lighting the torch with a match. Use a friction type lighter; it is safer and easier. Never use acetylene pressure higher than 15 psi. Never release acetylene where it might cause a fire or an explosion. Always check equipment before starting to work. Never braze, weld or use acetylene flame on gasoline or other fuel tanks.

Oxygen and acetylene tanks should always be in a special carrier or chained to a post to prevent falling.

GRINDING PRECAUTIONS

Grinding operations are an important part of an automotive mechanics job, and several safety precautions must be followed when using grinders of any type:

Before mounting a grinding wheel, make sure it is the type recommended for that particular operation. Also check the soundness of the wheel by tapping it with the handle of a screwdriver or similar tool. A ringing sound should be heard when the wheel is tapped in this manner. If not, the wheel is defective and should not be used. It is probably cracked and would burst when rotated at grinding speed.

The wheel should fit the spindle snugly, and the compressible washers (known as blotters) should be large enough to extend beyond the wheel flanges. After mounting, bring the grinding wheel up to speed slowly, if possible, and do not stand in the rotational plane of the wheel. In case of failure, the flying parts will cause severe injury. Always be sure that the wheel is provided with a proper guard as protection against breakage.

After completing the grinding operation, let the wheel rotate for several minutes in order to throw off excess coolant. If this is not done, coolant will remain in the lower portion of the wheel where it could cause a severe unbalance condition and consequent danger of bursting when put into operation.

Remember:
1. Always wear goggles when doing a grinding operation.
2. Keep the tool rest as close to the wheel as possible.
3. When doing precision grinding, such as crankshaft journals, use a light feed.
4. Do not strike a grinding wheel while it is rotating.

REVIEW QUESTIONS – AUTO SHOP SAFETY

1. Why study OSHA (Occupational Safety and Health Administration) safety regulations?
   a. Regulations affect all businesses.
   b. Regulations give employee a voice in maintaining safe working conditions.
   c. All of above.
   d. None of above.
2. Under OSHA, employers are responsible for employee-owned equipment. True or False?
3. Why are running and practical jokes prohibited in shops?
4. Why should a mask be worn while spraying paint?
5. Starting batteries should always remain connected in the circuit while working on the electrical system. True or False?
6. What happens when a file is used as a pry bar?
   a. It bends.
   b. It breaks.
   c. It will mar the surfaces.
7. Which of the following is correct?
   a. Carbon monoxide is used in welding.
   b. Carbon monoxide is a deadly poison.
   c. Carbon monoxide is used to inflate tires on race cars.
8. Why is it dangerous to stand in the plane of a rotating part?
9. Oxygen fittings on welding equipment should be well lubricated with mineral oil. True or False?
10. When using a grinding wheel, position the tool rest 1 in. from the wheel. Yes or No?

AUTOMOTIVE
FUELS

The fuel used in most automobiles and internal combustion engines is gasoline. Other fuels include methanol, benzol, alcohol, alcohol-gasoline blends and liquid petroleum gas (LP-Gas).

Gasoline is a colorless liquid obtained from crude petroleum as a result of a complicated distillation and cracking process. Two important characteristics of gasoline used for fuel in automotive engines are volatility and antiknock characteristics.

The volatility of any liquid is its vaporizing ability. In the case of a simple substance, it is usually determined by its boiling point. For example, the boiling point of water is 212 deg. F. Gasoline is a mixture of hydrocarbon compounds, each having its own boiling point. Gasoline used for fuel in automobiles has a range of boiling points extending from approximately 100 deg. F up to 400 deg. F, Fig. 20-1.

The fuel must remain a liquid until it enters the air stream in the carburetor throat. At this time, it must quickly vaporize and mix uniformly in the correct proportions with the intake air.

The volatility of gasoline affects ease of starting, length of warm-up period and engine performance during normal operation. For easy starting with a cold engine, the fuel must be highly volatile. In other words, it must vaporize easily. Therefore, when cold weather approaches, fuel refiners increase the percentage of highly volatile fuel contained in gasoline, to insure easier starting under the cold weather operating conditions.

If the percentage of volatile fuel is too high, a condition known as vapor lock occurs. Vapor lock is created by fuel vaporization, which causes the engine to be starved for fuel and stop running. This is not an unusual occurrence, particularly in spring before the refiners have reduced the percentage of highly volatile fuel in the gasoline.

In addition to the highly volatile fuel needed for easy starting, fuel not quite so volatile is required for quick warm-up.

A portion of the fuel must be sufficiently volatile to insure proper vaporization during periods of acceleration. If fuel sprayed from the accelerating pump jet does not vaporize readily, it could result in a lean mixture that would exist only for a moment, but which is known as a "flat-spot."

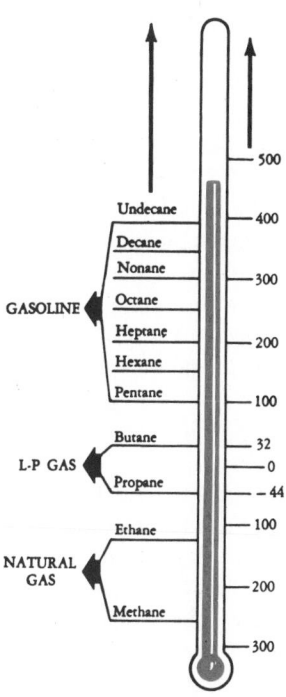

Fig. 20-1. Range of boiling points of hydrocarbons such as gasoline, LP-Gas and natural gas.

For maximum power and economy of operation, fuel with a lower volatility but high heat content is required.

When weather conditions, or overchoking, or a over-rich mixture leaves an excessive amount of fuel unvaporized, the raw fuel seeps by the piston and piston rings into the crankcase. This dilutes the lubricating oil, reduces its lubricating qualities and tends to form sludge and deposit varnish on the pistons and rings.

Petroleum contains many impurities that must be removed during the refining process before gasoline suitable for automotive use is produced. At one time, considerable corrosion was caused by the sulfur contained in petroleum products. However, modern refining procedure has greatly eliminated that problem.

Another difficulty was the tendency for the hydrocarbons in gasoline to oxidize into a sticky gum when exposed to air.

This resulted in clogged carburetor passages, stuck engine valves and excessive deposits in the combustion chamber. Chemicals that control the gumming tendency are now added to gasoline.

ANTIKNOCK QUALITIES

One of the most important qualities of modern fuel is the ability to burn without causing detonation or knocking. The tendency toward detonation is overcome by the addition to the fuel of such compounds as tetraethyl lead. In addition, refining processes also aid materially in producing knock-free gasoline.

To understand what is meant by antiknock quality, consider the process of combustion. When substance burns, it is actually uniting in rapid chemical reaction with oxygen (one constituent of air). During the burning process, the molecules of the substance and oxygen are set into very rapid motion and heat is produced.

In the combustion chamber of an engine cylinder, the gasoline vapor and oxygen in the air are united and burned. They combine, and the molecules begin to move about very rapidly as the high temperatures of combustion are reached. The molecules bombard the combustion chamber walls and the head of the piston with a rain of fast-moving molecules. It is this bombardment that causes the heavy push on the piston, forcing it downward on the power stroke.

NORMAL COMBUSTION

The normal combustion process in the combustion chamber, Fig. 20-2, goes through three stages sometimes termed formation (nucleus of flame), hatching out and propagation.

As soon as the ignition spark jumps the gap of the spark plug, a small ball of blue flame develops in the gap. This ball is the first stage or nucleus of the flame. It enlarges with relative slowness and, during its growth, there is no measureable pressure created by the heat.

As the nucleus enlarges, it develops into the hatching-out

stage. The nucleus is torn apart, so that it sends fingers of flame into the mixture in the combustion chamber. This causes enough heat to give a slight rise in temperature and pressure in the entire air-fuel mixture. Consequently a lag still exists in the attempt to raise pressure in the entire cylinder.

It is during the third stage, or propagation, that the effective burning of the fuel takes place. The flame burns in a front which sweeps across the combustion chamber, burning rapidly and causing great heat with its accompanying rise in pressure. It is this pressure which causes the piston to move downward.

During normal combustion, the burning is progressive. It increases gradually during the first two stages. But, during the third stage, the flame is extremely strong as it sweeps through the combustion chamber. However, there is no violent or explosive action such as when detonation (ordinarily responsible for pinging or knocking) occurs.

DETONATION

. If detonation takes place, it occurs during the third stage of combustion, Fig. 20-3. In the propagation stage, flame sweeps from the area around the spark plug toward the walls of the combustion chamber. Parts of the chamber the flame has passed may contain inert, nonburnable gases, but the section not yet touched by flame contains highly compressed, heated, combustible gases.

As the flame races through the combustion chamber, the unburned gases ahead of it are still further compressed and are heated to higher temperatures. Under certain conditions, the extreme heating of the unburned part of the mixture may cause it to ignite spontaneously and explode.

It is this rapid, uncontrolled burning in the final stage of combustion that is called detonation. It is caused by the rapidly burning flame front compressing the unburned part of the mixture to the point of self-ignition. This secondary wave front collides with the normal flame front and makes an audible knock or pinging sound.

Detonation may harm an engine or hinder its performance

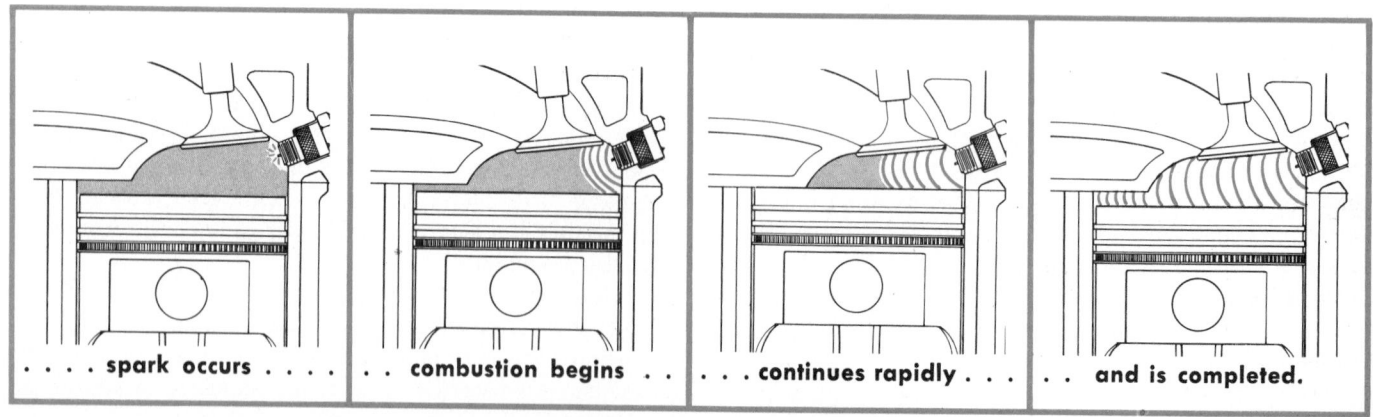

Fig. 20-2. Under conditions of normal combustion, air-fuel mixture does not burn all at once. Flame front moves rapidly, but with controlled speed from igniting spark to outer edges of combustion chamber.
(Perfect Circle Div., Dana Corp.)

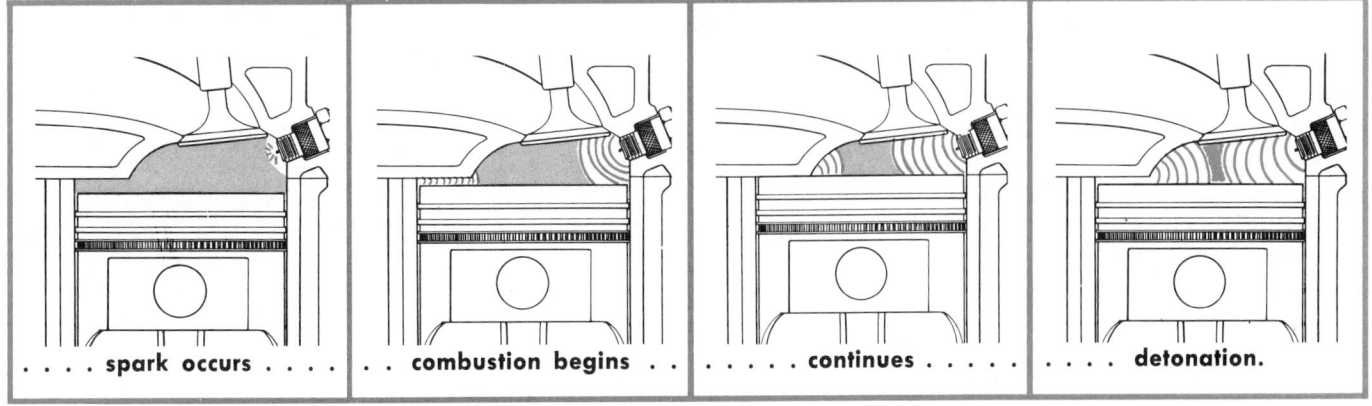

Fig. 20-3. Detonation is burning of a portion of air-fuel charge before spark-originated flame front reaches it.

Fig. 20-4. Preignition is igniting of air-fuel charge before regular ignition occurs.
(Perfect Circle Div., Dana Corp.)

in several ways. In extreme cases, pistons may shatter, cylinders burst or cylinder heads crack. At times, these temperatures resulting from detonation may reach the point where the piston actually melts. Other effects of detonation may be: overheating of the engine, broken spark plugs, overloaded bearings, high fuel consumption, loss of power.

The causes of detonation include:
1. Lean air-fuel mixtures.
2. Fuel of too low an octane rating.
3. Ignition timing overadvanced.
4. Lugging the engine (further depressing of accelerator does not produce any further increase in speed).
5. Excessive carbon accumulations in the combustion chamber.

PREIGNITION

Preignition is the igniting of the fuel charge before the regular ignition spark. If the premature combustion is completed before the occurrence of the regular spark, there may be no identifying noise. However, if the regular ignition spark follows shortly after the preignition occurs, there will be a pinging noise when the two flame fronts collide, Fig. 20-4.

Also, preignition can lead to detonation. These two types of abnormal combustion are closely linked and often it is difficult to distinguish between them.

The main causes of preignition include:
1. Carbon deposits that remain incandescent.
2. Valves operating at higher than normal temperature.
3. Hot spots caused by defects in cooling system.
4. Spark plugs that run too hot.
5. Sharp edges in the combustion chamber.
6. Detonation.

OCTANE RATING

The ability of a fuel to resist detonation is measured by its octane rating. The octane rating of a fuel is determined by matching it against mixtures of normal heptane and iso-octane in a test engine under specified test conditions. The test continues until a mixture of these pure hydrocarbons is found which gives the same degree of knocking in the engine as the gasoline being tested.

The octane number of the fuel, then, is the percent of the iso-octane in the matching iso-octane normal-heptane mixture. For example, a gasoline rating of 90 octane is equivalent in its knocking characteristics to a mixture of 90 percent iso-octane and 10 percent normal heptane.

The tendency of a fuel to detonate varies in different engines. It also varies in the same engine under different operating conditions. The shape of the combustion chamber is important but, most important of all is the compression ratio.

It should be emphasized that octane number of a fuel has nothing to do with its starting qualities, power, volatility or other major characteristics. If an engine operates satisfactorily with a fuel of a certain octane rating, its performance will not be improved by using fuel of a still higher octane rating.

FUEL ADDITIVES

Tetraethyl lead is the most popular compound added to fuel to suppress knocking. In addition to additives used to suppress detonation, some fuels also contain additives designed to reduce the accumulation of deposits in the combustion chamber, and to absorb any moisture which may condense in the fuel. Still another additive is provided to lubricate the valve stems and the upper area of the cylinder wall.

Detonation is not to be confused with preignition. Detonation takes place late in the burning process after the spark has occurred. Preignition, Fig. 20-4, however, is an igniting of the air-fuel mixture during compression, before the spark has occurred, as caused by some form of hot spots within the cylinder.

DIESEL FUELS

The type of fuel available for use in diesel engines varies from highly volatile jet fuels and kerosene, to the heavier furnace oil. Automotive diesel engines are capable of burning a wide range of fuel between these two extremes. How well a diesel engine can operate with different types of fuel is dependent upon engine operating conditions, as well as fuel characteristics.

A large variety of fuel oils are marketed by the petroleum industry for diesel engine use. Their properties depend on the refining practices employed, and the nature of the crude oil from which they are produced. Fuel oils, for example, may be produced within the boiling range of 300 to 750 deg. F and have many possible combinations of other properties.

The classification of commercially available fuel oils that has been set up by the American Society for Testing Materials is shown in Fig. 20-5. Grade 1D fuels range from kerosene to what is called intermediate distillates. Grades 2D and 4D each have progressively higher boiling points and contain more impurities.

The fuels commonly known as high-grade fuels, kerosene and 1D fuels, contribute a minimum amount to the formation of harmful engine deposits and corrosion. There are less impurities present in those fuels. Therefore the tendency to form deposits is kept to a minimum.

While refining removes the impurities, it also lowers the heat value of the fuel. As a result, the higher grade fuels develop slightly less power than the same quantity of low-grade fuel. Often, however, this is more than offset by

ASTM DIESEL FUEL CLASSIFICATION D075-49T

Grade of Diesel Fuel Oil	Cetane Number (Min.)	Sulfur % by Wt. (Max.)	Distillation Temperatures, °F		Viscosity at 100° F Kinematic Centistokes (or SUS)	
			90% Boiling Point (Max.)	100% Boiling Point (Max.)	(Min.)	(Max.)
No. 1-D	40	0.50		625	1.4 1.8 (32.0)	5.8 (45)
No. 2-D	40	1.0	675		5.8 (45)	26.4 (125)
No. 4-D	30	2.0				

Fig. 20-5. Excerpt from American Society of Testing Materials specifications for diesel fuels.

other maintenance advantages. Some diesel fuel systems undergo modification to form what are classified as jet fuels.

CETANE RATING

The delay between the time the fuel is injected into the cylinder and ignition by the hot air is expressed as a cetane number. Usually, this is between 30 and 60. Fuels that ignite rapidly have high cetane ratings, while slow-to-ignite fuels have low cetane ratings.

A fuel with better ignition quality would assist combustion more than a lower cetane fuel during starting and idling conditions when compression temperatures are cooler. For that reason, ether with a very high cetane rating of 85-96 is often used for starting diesel engines in cold weather. The lower the temperature of the surrounding air, the greater the need for fuel that will ignite rapidly.

When the cetane number of the fuel is too low, it may result in difficult starting, engine knock and puffs of white exhaust smoke, particularly during engine warm-up and light load operation. If these conditions continue, harmful engine deposits will accumulate in the combustion chamber.

BOILING RANGE

The boiling temperature of fuel is also the temperature at which it is completely vaporized. Furthermore, fuel can be completely burned in an engine only in vaporized form. Because of this, the boiling range of fuel oil should be low enough to permit complete vaporization of the existing engine temperature.

For engines operating at reduced speed and load, or in cold weather, lower boiling point fuels will give more satisfactory performance. Fuels that cannot be completely vaporized and burned will accumulate and form sludge and other harmful deposits in the engine.

SULFUR CONTENT

Sulfur content in fuel oil should be as low as possible in order to keep the amount of corrosion and deposit formation at a minimum. Tests have shown that increasing sulfur content from .25 to 1.25 percent increases deposits and wear 135 percent.

LIQUEFIED PETROLEUM GAS

A mixture of gaseous petroleum compounds, principally butane and propane, together with smaller quantities of similar gases, is known as liquefied petroleum gas (LP-Gas).

LP-Gas is used as fuel for internal combustion engines, principally in the truck and farm tractor fields.

Chemically, LP-Gas is similar to gasoline since it consists of a mixture of compounds of hydrogen and carbon. However, it is a great deal more volatile. At usual atmospheric temperatures, it is a vapor. For that reason, when LP-Gas is used as a fuel for internal combustion engines, a special type of carburetor is required.

For storing and transporting LP-Gas, it is compressed and cooled so that it is a liquid. Depending upon conditions, it takes approximately 250 gallons of LP-Gas to be compressed into one gallon of liquid. Because of the pressure it is under, it must be stored in strong tanks. The boiling point of propane is approximately 44 deg. F below zero.

At temperatures below their boiling points, butane and propane exert no pressure. But as the temperature increases, the pressure increases rapidly. At 40 deg. F, liquid propane will have a pressure of 65 lbs.; while butane will have a pressure of about 3 lbs. At 65 deg. F, the pressure of propane will have increased to 100 lbs. and butane to 15 lbs.

LP-Gas is made of surplus material in the oil fields, and it is becoming more widely distributed as an increasing number of trucks and tractors are being fitted with the equipment required to make use of it.

In addition to its low cost, LP-Gas has the advantage of having a high octane value. Pure butane has a rating of 93 octane, while propane is approximately 100. The octane rating of LP-Gas will range between these two values, depending upon the proportion of each gas used.

Since it is a dry gas, LP-Gas does not create carbon in an engine, and does not cause dilution of the engine oil. As a result, maintenance and internal parts replacement on engines is reduced. In addition, oil changes for the engine can be made at less frequent intervals because LP-Gas is such a clean-burning fuel.

Other advantages claimed for LP-Gas are easy cold weather starting, lack of objectionable exhaust odor and elimination of evaporation.

ALCOHOL

Alcohol is sometimes used as fuel for automotive internal combustion engines. It is a distillate of wood or grain and has a relatively high octane rating.

Alcohol is frequently used as an additive to commercial gasoline. In that way, it will absorb any condensed moisture which may collect in the fuel system.

Water will not pass through the filters in the fuel line. Consequently, when any water collects, it will prevent the free passage of fuel. In addition, water will tend to attack or corrode the zinc die castings of which many carburetors and fuel pumps are made. This corrosion will not only destroy parts, but also clog the system and prevent the flow of fuel. By using alcohol in gasoline, any water present will be absorbed and pass through the fuel filters and carburetor jets into the combustion chamber.

Alcohol is frequently used in combination with benzol as a fuel for race engines.

BENZOL

Benzol is a volatile liquid hydrocarbon obtained in the refinement of coal tar. It has a high octane value, and it is used occasionally to blend with gasoline to increase its octane value. It is also used in combination with alcohol for race car engines.

HEAT VALUE

The power obtained from any fuel is determined by its heat value, which is measured by burning a unit amount of fuel in an excess of air or oxygen. It is measured in British thermal units per pound of fuel. One British thermal unit (Btu) is the amount of heat required to raise one pound of water from 39 deg. to 40 deg. F. One Btu is equal to 778.6 foot-pounds.

Some of the higher heat values of hydrocarbon found in gasoline are as follows:

1. Hexane   20700
2. Heptane   20600
3. Octane   20500
4. Monane   20450
5. Dicane   20420
6. Undecane   20375
7. Dodecane   20350

COMBUSTION OF GASOLINE

Rapidly combining fuel with oxygen produces heat. This is known as combustion. In the case of gasoline, combustion is the rapid oxidation of the carbon and the hydrogen constituting the fuel. The heat produced is the result of the chemical change.

The chemical equation of combustion for octane is:

$$C_8H_{18} + 12.5\ O_2 = 8\ CO_2 + 9\ H_2O$$

In this equation, C_8H_{18} represents the chemical formula for gasoline. The 12.5 O_2 is the oxygen required to burn one part of gasoline. This produces eight parts of carbon dioxide (CO_2) and nine parts of water (H_2O).

However, air is used in actual operation of an engine, instead of pure oxygen. Air consists of a mixture of 1/5 oxygen and 4/5 nitrogen, by volume. From the standpoint of weight, it consists of one part oxygen, and 3 1/2 parts of nitrogen or, more exactly, 23 parts of oxygen and 77 parts of nitrogen.

The atomic weights for the different elements entering into the combustion of octane and air are as follows:

1. Carbon   = 12
2. Nitrogen = 14
3. Oxygen   = 16
4. Hydrogen = 1

On a weight basis, the chemical formula of combustion is:

$$114 \ C_8H_{18} + 400 \ O_2 = 352 \ CO_2 + 162 \ H_2O$$

Since air is a mixture of oxygen and nitrogen in a ratio of 23 to 77, the nitrogen must also be considered in writing the combustion equation for octane and air. The amount of nitrogen present with 400 weight units of oxygen is:

$$400 \times \frac{77}{23} = 1339$$

This nitrogen is present in the combustible mixture and also in the products of combustion. So it must be added to both sides of the equation:

$$114 \ C_8H_{18} + 400 \ O_2 + 1339 \ N_2 = 352 \ CO_2 + 162 \ H_2O + 1339 \ N_2$$

For one pound of octane the formula becomes:

$$3.09 \ lb. \ CO_2 + 1.42 \ lb. \ H_2O + 11.76 \ lb. \ N_2$$

or

1 lb. of fuel + 15.27 lb. air = 16.27 of exhaust gas.

The amount of power developed in an internal combustion engine is dependent on the heat that can be obtained from burning the fuel. This, in the case of gasoline or any of the hydrocarbons, is equal to the total of the heats due to the combustion of the carbon and hydrogen. From that must be subtracted the heat required to break up the hydrocarbon molecules.

When carbon becomes carbon dioxide, due to combustion, 14,542 Btu are liberated for each pound of carbon burned. In the combustion of hydrogen to steam, 62,032 Btu are liberated for each pound of hydrogen. To break up the octane into carbon and hydrogen, 1523 Btu are required for each pound of octane.

In octane (C_8H_{18}), the carbon is 84.2 percent, while the hydrogen is 15.8 percent. The heat produced by combustion is:

84.2 percent of 14,542 Btu = 12,244
15.8 percent of 62,032 Btu = 9,801

This makes a total of 22,045 Btu. From this, subtract 1523 Btu required to break up the fuel into carbon and hydrogen. The difference, 20,522 Btu, is the total heat from burning one pound of octane.

COMBUSTION CHAMBER TEMPERATURE

During combustion, temperatures vary through a relatively wide range. Temperatures are affected by compression ratio, combustion chamber contour, cooling system effectiveness, richness of air-fuel mixture and amount of burned gases remaining in the cylinder from the previous cycle.

At the end of the compression stroke (but before ignition), temperatures of approximately 985 deg. F may be considered average for an engine with a compression ratio of 9 to 1.

Immediately after ignition, the temperature increases very rapidly and will reach a value of approximately 5500 deg. F.

LEAD-FREE GASOLINE

Lead-free gasoline is motor fuel without tetra-ethyl lead. Formerly, lead was added to gasoline to improve its octane rating. Now, lead-free gasoline is required because leaded fuel would quickly destroy the chemicals in the catalytic converter. These converters (page 331) are designed to reduce the amount of carbon monoxide and hydrocarbons in the exhaust.

Both leaded and lead-free gasolines have certain advantages. In addition to the higher octane rating, leaded gasoline has a good effect on valves and valve seats. With lead in the fuel, valve and valve seat life are materially extended, particularly at high speeds. The lead in the fuel is deposited on the valve seats where it acts as a lubricant.

Valve seat wear has been shown to result from the adhesion of hard abrasive oxide particles from the valve seat onto the valve face. This is followed by the failure of the valve and seat. Tests made by TRW Inc. engineers show a ten to twenty times greater valve recession rate when lead-free gasoline is used. In recent years, several car manufacturers have improved the valve seats in their engines to better withstand the affect of lead-free gasoline.

ALCOHOL AS A FUEL

The increasing cost and scarcity of gasoline has turned the attention of car and truck designers, and the motoring public, to various substitutes. Chief among the alternate fuels is alcohol.

Considerable research has been done and is being carried on for alcohol is spark ignition engines. In Germany, during World War II, alcohol fuels were used extensively. Currently, alcohol and alcohol blends are used in many vehicles in Brazil. In the U.S., alcohol blends are readily available in some areas.

Methanol and ethanol are two forms of alcohol receiving the most attention. Both are made from non-petroleum products. Methanol can be produced from coal. Ethanol can be made from farm products such as sugar cane, corn and potatoes. Characteristics are compared below.

PROPERTY	METHANOL	ETHANOL	GASOLINE
Heat of vaporization	265	216	70-100
Calorific heat value	4200	6400	10,500
Air required	6.4	9.0	14.9
Air-fuel ratio	2.15 to 15.5	3.5 to 17.0	6.0 to 22.0
Self-ignition temperature	478 deg. F	420 deg. F	300-450 deg. F
Research octane number	110	100	92-98
Motor octane	92	89	84-88

Both alcohols have a higher octane number than gasoline. The high heat of vaporization indicates that the use of alcohol could give hard starting problems. The calorific heat values of the alcohols are higher than gasoline, which translates into the need for a larger fuel tank and larger jet sizes in the carburetor. However, the alcohols require less air for combustion, which compensates for their high calorific values. Proportionately, this could result in practically the same air-fuel ratio for all three fuels. In fact, experimental tests have shown that alcohol-fueled spark ignition engines can produce as much or slightly higher power than gasoline.

Alcohol fuels have a higher self-ignition temperature than gasoline, which rates them better from a safety standpoint. However, this same quality bars them from use in a diesel engine that depends on the heat of compression to ignite the fuel.

Either methanol or ethanol can be used straight or blended in small concentrations (10 percent) with gasoline. Because of the high octane rating, alcohols can be used with relatively high compression ratios ranging from 8.4:1 to 11:1. Experiments also indicate that emissions from alcohol-fueled engines would not require the use of exhaust gas recirculation controls.

NATURAL GAS AS A FUEL

Experiments have also been made on the use of natural gas for operation of automobiles. These experiments, as reported in the SAE Journal, show that exhaust emissions from dual-fuel cars burning natural gas are below the levels set by California and are substantially below those from the same engine using gasoline. Both carbon monoxide and reactive hydrocarbons are well within the prescribed limits which equal or surpass the proposed standard set for 1975 by California.

Natural gas is rated as 130 octane without any lead additive and, consequently, there is no lead in the exhaust. Also, there are virtually no combustion chamber deposits. However, power with natural gas is reduced approximately 10 percent from power with gasoline.

REVIEW QUESTIONS – AUTOMOTIVE FUELS

1. Name three different fuels used in internal combustion engines.
2. The volatility of gasoline is equivalent to its:
   a. Octane rating.
   b. Boiling point.
   c. Cetane rating.
   d. Distillation.
3. What characteristic of fuel affects easy starting?
4. Name the three stages of normal fuel combustion in an internal combustion engine.
5. Describe detonation.
6. Describe preignition.
7. Iso-octane and what other material are used to determine the octane rating of a fuel?
   a. Cetane.
   b. Propane.
   c. Heptane.
   d. Benzol.
8. Alcohol is added to gasoline primarily to:
   a. Provide easier starting.
   b. Absorb any moisture that may be present.
   c. Increase the volatility of the fuel.
9. Automobile diesel engines are capable of burning a wide range of fuels. True or False?
10. Cetane number of a diesel fuel is a measure of:
    a. volatility.
    b. Viscosity.
    c. Time between fuel injection and ignition.
11. Sulfur content of a fuel should be:
    a. High as possible.
    b. Low as possible.
    c. Does not matter.
12. LP-Gas is a mixture of:
    a. Benzol and heptane.
    b. Butane and propane.
    c. Butane and heptane.
    d. Heptane and cetane.
13. The power of any fuel is determined by its:
    a. Molecular weight.
    b. Heat value.
    c. The amount of carbon it contains.
14. Immediately after ignition, combustion chamber temperatures may reach a value of:
    a. 1500 deg.
    b. 2500 deg.
    c. 5500 deg.
    d. 7500 deg.
15. Carbon deposits in the combustion chamber are responsible for increased levels of hydrocarbon emissions. Yes or No?
16. Lead-free gasoline promotes longer valve and valve seat life. True or False?

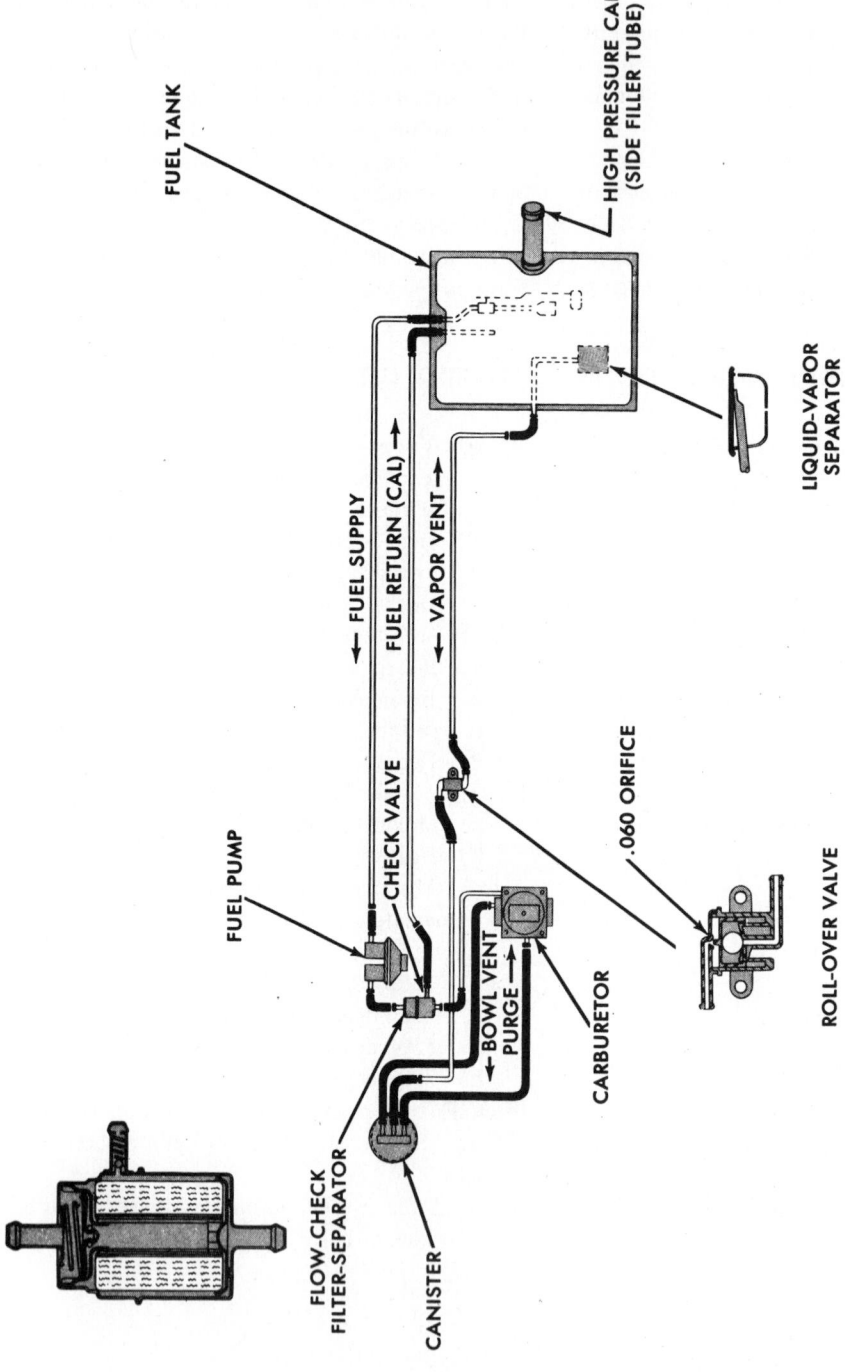

FUEL TANK

HIGH PRESSURE CAP
(SIDE FILLER TUBE)

LIQUID-VAPOR
SEPARATOR

FUEL SUPPLY

FUEL RETURN (CAL)

VAPOR VENT

CHECK VALVE

FUEL PUMP

.060 ORIFICE

BOWL VENT
PURGE

CARBURETOR

ROLL-OVER VALVE

FLOW-CHECK
FILTER-SEPARATOR

CANISTER

Fig. 21-1. Because of the need to conform to governmental emission standards, modern fuel systems have become more complicated. The Chrysler fuel system is shown. Note the roll-over valve, which shuts off the supply of fuel if the vehicle turns over.

PRINCIPLES OF CARBURETION

The purpose of the fuel supply system, Fig. 21-1, is to provide a combustible mixture of fuel and air to the engine cylinders. The ratio of fuel to air must always be in the correct proportion regardless of the speed and load on the engine.

Major elements of the fuel supply system include: fuel tank and cap, fuel system emission controls, fuel lines, fuel pump, fuel filter, carburetor, air cleaner and manifold. In addition, there is the fuel gauge, which indicates the amount of fuel in the tank.

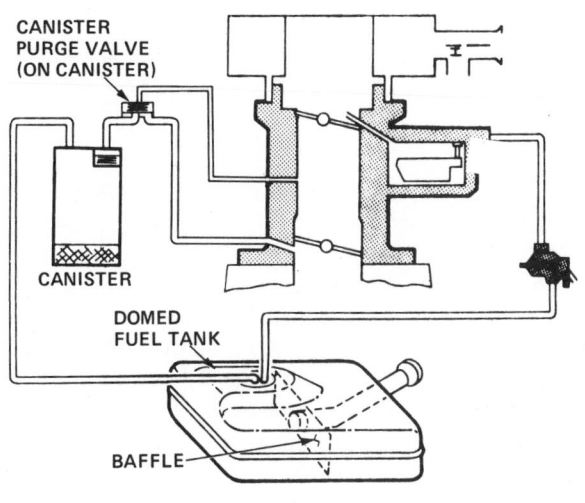

Fig. 21-1. Details of fuel system on late model car.

CANISTER
PURGE VALVE
(ON CANISTER)

CANISTER

DOMED
FUEL TANK

BAFFLE

PURPOSE OF CARBURETOR

The purpose of the carburetor is to prepare and supply a mixture of fuel vapor and air, in proper proportion for efficient combustion, to the engine cylinders.

Because of varying conditions of temperature, engine speed and load on the engine, perfect carburetion is difficult to attain. When an internal combustion engine is started, it is cold and an air-fuel mixture containing a larger proportion of fuel is required. When the engine reaches operating temperatures,

better vaporization of the fuel is attained and, as a result, the initial mixture of fuel and air is too "rich." This mixture contains more fuel than is normally required. It is not efficient and the engine will not operate satisfactorily, particularly at idling speed.

Still another difficulty must be overcome by the carburetor. When the engine is idling or operating at low speed, a richer mixture is required than when operating at medium speed and power. Then, when maximum power is required, the amount of fuel in relation to air must be increased. Similarly, during periods of acceleration, a richer mixture is needed.

A problem encountered in designing carburetors results from the fact that the rate of air flow through the carburetor changes in a ratio of more than 100 to 1. This is a direct result of the changes of engine speed. At low speed, the flow of air through the carburetor is at a minimum. At maximum engine speed, it will be at least 100 as great.

Variations in types and characteristics of fuels also complicate the carburetor design operation. Gasoline is a blend of various parts or fractions of crude petroleum. As a result, some fractions contained in commercial gasoline will boil or vaporize at 100 deg. F, others have boiling points ranging up to 400 deg. F.

Depending on the temperature of various parts of the intake manifold, some cylinders may receive a mixture with some portions of the fuel completely vaporized, while other portions of the fuel may be in liquid form. In addition, some cylinders will receive fuel having greater antiknock qualities than others. Consider, too, that when the engine and manifold are cold, the problem is still more difficult.

AIR-FUEL RATIO

For normal operating conditions, the best economy is obtained by a mixture of 1 part by weight of gasoline to between 16 to 17 parts of air. For quick acceleration and maximum power, a richer mixture of about 1 part of gasoline to 12 to 13 parts of air is needed. For idling, a somewhat richer-than-normal mixture is required. When starting a cold engine, an extremely rich mixture is needed. (See the chapter on MANUAL AND AUTOMATIC CHOKES.)

EVAPORATION

All substances, whether solid, liquid or gas, are made of molecules. In solids such as steel and copper, the particles are so close together they seem to have no motion. In liquids, the molecules are not held together so tightly. They can move with respect to each other and, as a result, liquids flow. In gases, such as air, there is even less tendency for the molecules to hold together, so they move quite freely.

When molecules of a liquid move from the liquid into the air, the liquid is said to evaporate. As this continues, the liquid disappears from its container and forms vapor in the air.

Rapidity of evaporation varies with a number of factors. These factors, include temperature, the pressure above the liquid, the amount of liquid that has already evaporated into the air and the volatility of the liquid.

The term volatility refers to the ease with which a liquid vaporizes. For example, alcohol and benzene are more volatile than water because they evaporate more easily. A highly volatile liquid evaporates rapidly. A liquid of low volatility evaporates slowly.

At higher temperatures, molecules move faster. As a result, the rate of vaporization is increased. Furthermore, when there is little pressure above the liquid, the molecules can escape from the liquid more easily. If evaporation takes place in a closed chamber, the evaporation of the liquid will soon stop because the closed space above the liquid becomes filled with escaped molecules of the liquid. When this occurs, the space above the liquid is said to be saturated.

If a liquid is broken up into tiny particles or globules, it will vaporize more easily. Breaking a liquid into tiny particles is known as vaporization. Spray guns of the type used for spraying insecticides or paint will vaporize a liquid. For example, if gasoline is placed in an ordinary spray gun, Fig. 21-2, the fuel will be broken into a fine mist that will change into vapor almost instantly.

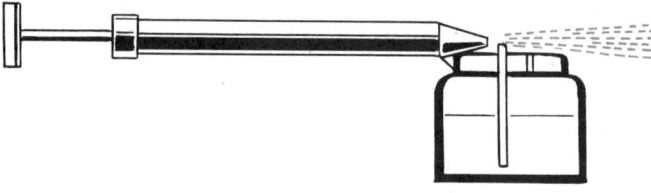

Fig. 21-2. Fuel leaving jet in a carburetor is vaporized like a spray from a conventional spray gun.

PRINCIPLES OF CARBURETOR OPERATION

Both air and gasoline are drawn through a carburetor and into the engine combustion chambers by suction created by the pistons moving downward in the cylinders. As the piston moves down, a partial vacuum is created in the cylinder and combustion chamber. The difference between this low pressure within the cylinder and the atmospheric pressure outside of the carburetor causes air and fuel to flow into the cylinder from the carburetor.

Directly related to this air flow into the carburetor is the principle or method whereby the moving air draws fuel from the carburetor jet and fuel supply. It is called the venturi principle, a means by which the suction within the carburetor is increased. Actually, a venturi is an hour-glass shaped constriction placed in a carburetor, so that incoming air must pass through it on its way to the intake manifold and engine cylinders, Fig. 21-3.

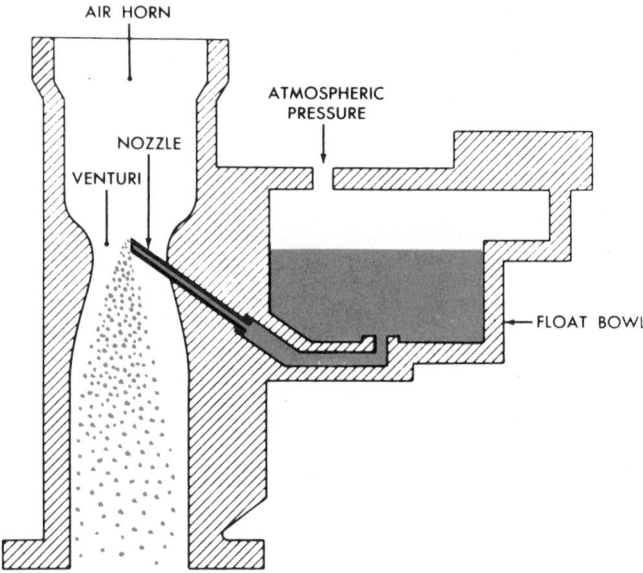

Fig. 21-3. Simplified carburetor consisting only of air horn, venturi, float bowl and nozzle.

A venturi is simply a specially designed section of a pipe line or tube where the area of the tube is reduced. This reduction in area increases the speed of the air that is passing through the tube. The same volume of air or fluid flows through all sections of the tube. Therefore, if the area of the tube is decreased, the velocity of the air or fluid must increase as it passes through the restricted area.

The venturi not only increases the velocity of the flow of air which passes through it, but it also produces a vacuum at its point of maximum restriction, Fig. 21-4. The outlet of a fuel jet is placed at that point, so that fuel is drawn from the jet and immediately mixes with the passing air.

This mixing of the fuel with air is known as vaporization, and it closely resembles the action of the familiar spray gun used for spraying insecticides, Fig. 21-2.

Some carburetors have as many as three ventures, Fig. 21-15 and Fig. 21-37. This design permits a more accurate metering of the flow of air and fuel for different conditions of engine operation. It improves the efficiency of combustion, which has become increasingly important in reducing exhaust emissions.

Remember that the difference between the pressure at the open carburetor jet at the venturi and surface pressure on the fuel in the float bowl, Fig. 21-3, causes the fuel to flow.

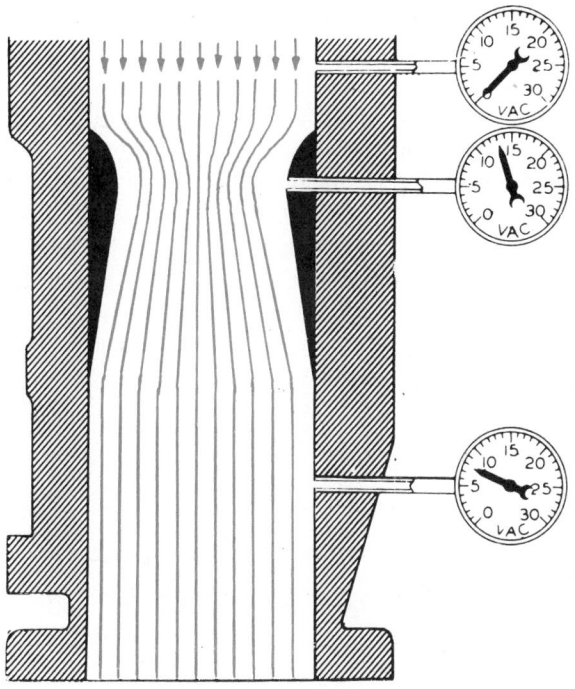

Fig. 21-4. Note how vacuum varies through different sections of carburetor.

CARBURETOR CIRCUITS

In order to supply an air-fuel mixture suitable for all the different operating conditions of low to high speeds, and light loads to full loads, a carburetor must be provided with additional circuits and controls. These circuits include: float system, idle system, main metering system, accelerating system and high speed system. Under controls, there are: the throttle, anti-percolator, fast idle, unloader, anti-icing, hot idle compensator and anti-stall dashpot.

THROTTLE

One of the important controls on a carburetor is the throttle valve, or valves. The throttle valve is a device for varying the amount of air-fuel mixture that enters the intake manifold. This control is necessary so the speed of the vehicle can be changed.

The throttle valve, Fig. 21-5, is simply a round disk mounted on a shaft, so that it can be tilted at various angles in the carburetor throttle valve body. It is connected by means of suitable linkage to the accelerator pedal in the driving compartment of the vehicle. Depressing the pedal opens the throttle valve, permitting an increased amount of air-fuel mixture to reach the manifold.

FLOAT CIRCUIT

Fuel in the carburetor must be maintained at a specified level for correct fuel metering under all operating conditions. This is the function of the float circuit, Fig. 21-6. Maintenance of the desired fuel level is accomplished by the float or

pontoon when its attached lever forces the needle valve closed and shuts off the flow of fuel.

Then, as soon as fuel is withdrawn from the float bowl, the float drops, the needle valve opens and fuel again flows into the bowl. In that way the fuel level is maintained at the opening of the main discharge nozzle.

The float level must be set with a high degree of accuracy. If the level is too low, insufficient fuel will be supplied to the system and engine performance will suffer. On the other hand, if the level is too high, excessive fuel will flow from the nozzle.

Under conditions of a high fuel level in the float bowl, excessive fuel consumption results and carbon will accumulate in the combustion chambers of the engine. In actual operation, the float and needle valve maintain a position that permits the fuel coming into the float bowl to balance the fuel issuing from the carburetor jets.

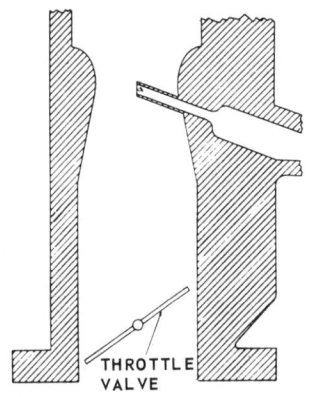

Fig. 21-5. Illustrating position of throttle valve or plate.

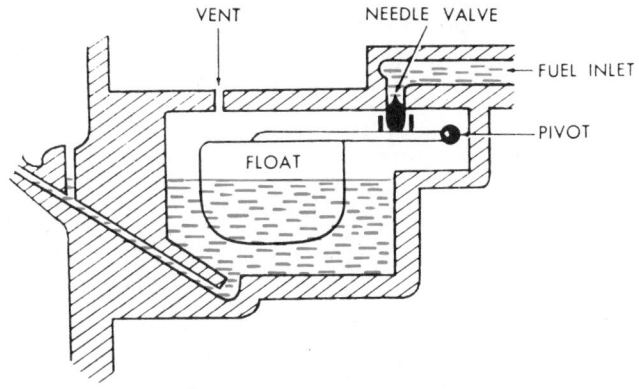

Fig. 21-6. Typical carburetor float system.

LOW-SPEED CIRCUIT

The idle system or low-speed circuit, Fig. 21-7, is designed to supply the proper amount of mixture for the engine at idle and extremely low speeds. It operates from idle speed to approximately 25 mph. Above that speed, the idle system gradually passes out of operation and fuel is supplied by the main metering system.

When the throttle valve is almost closed, there will be very little air passing through the venturi. Consequently, there will be very little vacuum to draw fuel from the fuel nozzle.

However, on the manifold side of the throttle valve, the vacuum will be at a maximum as long as the throttle is in the closed position. A fuel discharge port is located immediately below the closed position of the throttle, Fig. 21-7. It is supplied by fuel from the float bowl. Atmospheric pressure in the float bowl will force fuel from the idle discharge port as long as there is some degree of vacuum of the port.

When the throttle valve is opened, vacuum at the discharge port decreases. It continues to decrease as the valve opens further until there is no flow of fuel from that port. An adjustable needle valve is provided, so that the amount of fuel discharged from the idle port can be governed.

Immediately above the venturi is another port, Fig. 21-7, which is designed to permit air to bleed into the idle circuit as long as the idle circuit is operating. The air mixes with fuel to help atomize it before the fuel leaves the idle discharge port.

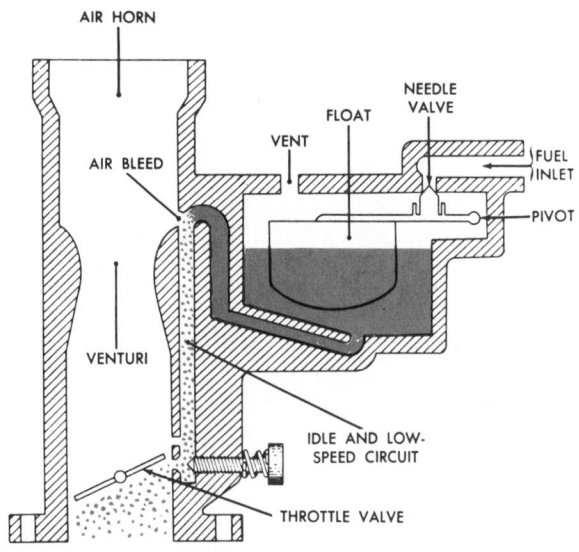

Fig. 21-7. Details of carburetor idle system.

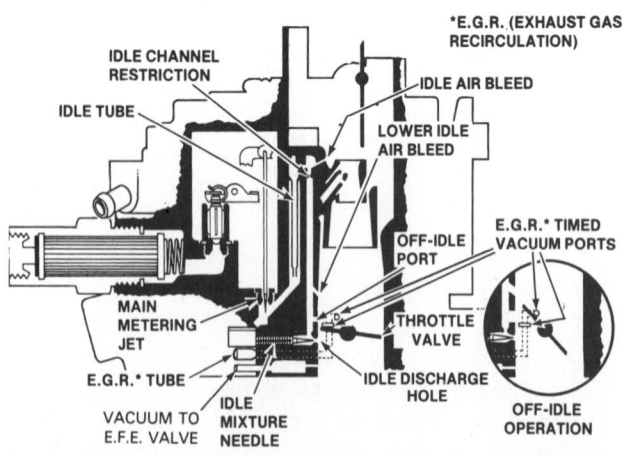

Fig. 21-8. Note location of idle discharge ports on this Rochester M2ME carburetor.

OFF IDLE OPERATION

In addition to the basic idle system, some carburetors (Rochester 2GC and M2ME) are provided with an off idle system. As the throttle valves are opened during acceleration, more fuel is supplied by the off idle discharge port, Fig. 21-8.

The off idle port gradually is exposed to manifold vacuum and supplies the additional fuel needed for the increase in engine speed. Improved fuel control is achieved by an adjustable off idle air bleed screw. The adjustment screw, which regulates air passing from a separate channel into the idle channel, is factory adjusted.

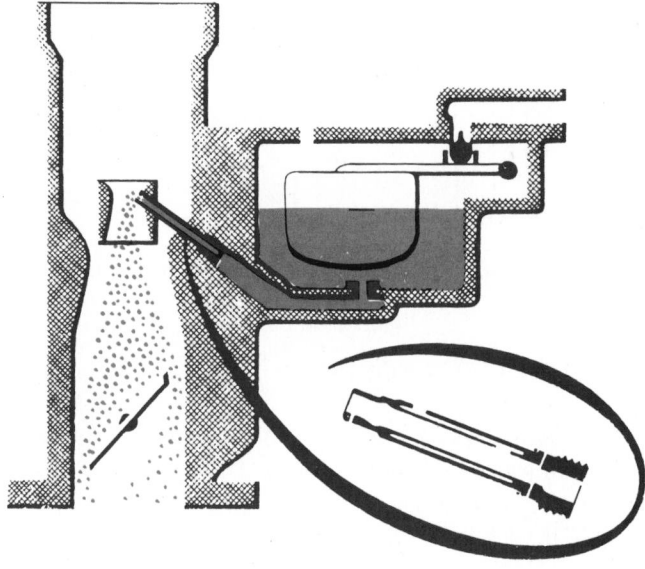

Fig. 21-9. Main or high-speed system.

AIR FLOW IS RESTRICTED

When the throttle is opened a little, the flow of air is still too restricted for the venturi to discharge fuel from the main jet or nozzle, Fig. 21-5. However, with the increased movement of air through the carburetor, more fuel must be supplied in order to maintain the correct proportions of air and fuel.

To supply additional fuel during this stage of low-speed operation, another port is included in the idle circuit. This hole is positioned slightly above the closed position of the throttle valve, Fig. 21-7. As soon as the valve is opened a small amount, the port will be uncovered, intake manifold vacuum will act on it and the additional fuel needed will be obtained.

Another type of idling system is used on Zenith carburetors on many industrial engines. In this system, air mixes with the fuel in proportions determined by the position of an idle-adjusting needle valve. The tube of the idling jet projects down into a well filled with fuel when the engine is at rest. As more air is admitted by means of the needle valve adjustment, less fuel will flow.

MAIN CIRCUIT

As the throttle is opened, the flow of fuel from the idle ports gradually decreases in volume. However, vacuum at the venturi gradually increases, so fuel starts to flow from the main or high-speed system. The main system consists essentially of the main nozzle or jet, which is centered in the venturi, Fig. 21-9, and supplies fuel from partly open to fully open throttle positions.

Remember, as the rate of flow of the air through the carburetor increases, the flow of the fuel also increases at a much faster rate. This results from the fact that the density of the fuel does not change, while that of the air does. So the mixture in a simple carburetor will be much too rich under wide-open throttle valve conditions. In fact, with a simple carburetor, the correct mixture of air and fuel would be provided at only one position of the throttle valve. So provision must be made to supply the correct ratio of air to fuel for all positions of the throttle valve.

POWER ENRICHMENT SYSTEM

To supplement the main metering system, some carburetors are provided with a power enrichment system, Fig. 21-10. Power enrichment is designed to provide proper mixtures

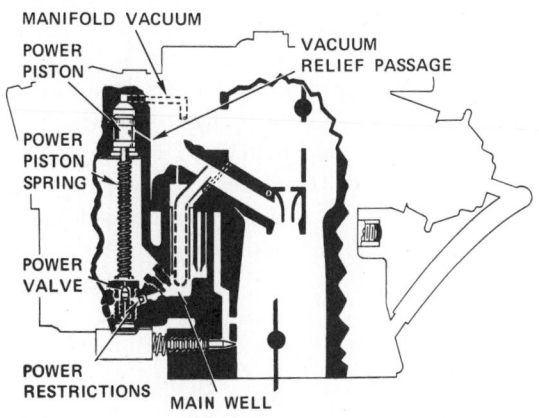

Fig. 21-10. Details of a Rochester power enrichment system.

when more power is desired, or for extreme high-speed driving. The system consists of a vacuum-operated power piston in the air horn and a power valve located in the bottom of the float bowl. The power piston cylinder is exposed to engine manifold vacuum at all times through a connecting vacuum passage from the base of the carburetor.

During idle and part throttle operation, the relatively high vacuum holds the power piston against spring pressure, and the power valve remains closed. The increase in engine load lowers the manifold vacuum. When it has dropped sufficiently, the power piston spring overcomes the upward pull of vacuum. Under spring pressure, the power piston moves downward. This opens the power valve to allow additional fuel to flow through calibrated restrictions into the main well.

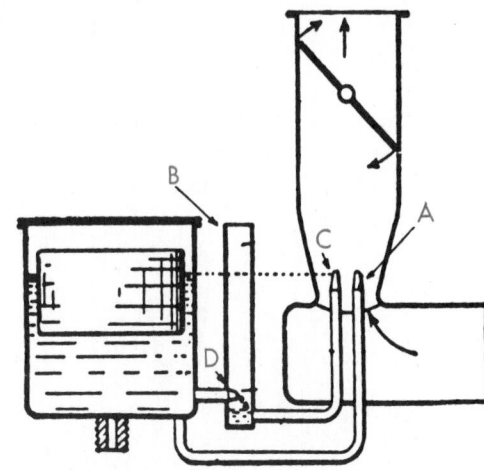

Fig. 21-11. Main nozzle A secures fuel directly from float chamber. Compensating nozzle C receives fuel from standpipe B. Fuel supplied by nozzle C depends on size of metering orifice D which delivers fuel to standpipe B.

COMPENSATION OR DOUBLE NOZZLE PRINCIPLE

One method of controlling the mixture of fuel and air is to provide, in addition to the main nozzle, another nozzle with a constant rate of discharge. In combination, the two nozzles give a substantially constant mixture.

In Fig. 21-11, the main nozzle is supplied with fuel directly from the float chamber. The compensating nozzle, which has a constant rate of discharge, is supplied from a standpipe that receives its fuel from the float chamber. The upper end of the standpipe is open to the atmosphere.

Fuel enters the standpipe through a metered opening. Since the fuel in the float chamber is at a constant level, the flow to the standpipe will be constant. In addition, the rate at which fuel can be drawn from the compensating nozzle also will be constant. At high engine speed, the compensating nozzle delivers less fuel than at low engine speed. In this way, it compensates for the natural tendency of the main nozzle to deliver a mixture that is too rich at high speed.

Also at high engine speed, and when the compensating nozzle is delivering smaller amounts of fuel (due to reduced vacuum), the level of the fuel in the standpipe will rise until its level is equal to that in the float chamber. Then, as suction on the compensating nozzle draws fuel from it, the fuel level in the standpipe will be lowered. If the throttle valve is maintained at the same opening for a sufficient length of time, all the fuel will be drawn from the standpipe. Then the compensating nozzle will be supplied directly from the compensating jet or submerged metering orifice.

AIR BLEED PRINCIPLE

The use of air bleeds is another method of compensating for the increased richness of the mixture caused by increased air velocity through the carburetor throat. Fig. 21-12 shows

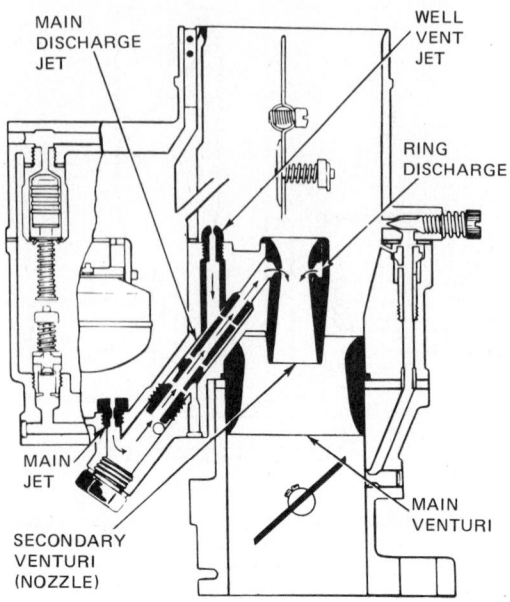

Fig. 21-12. Illustrating air bleed principle used on Model 228 Zenith carburetor.

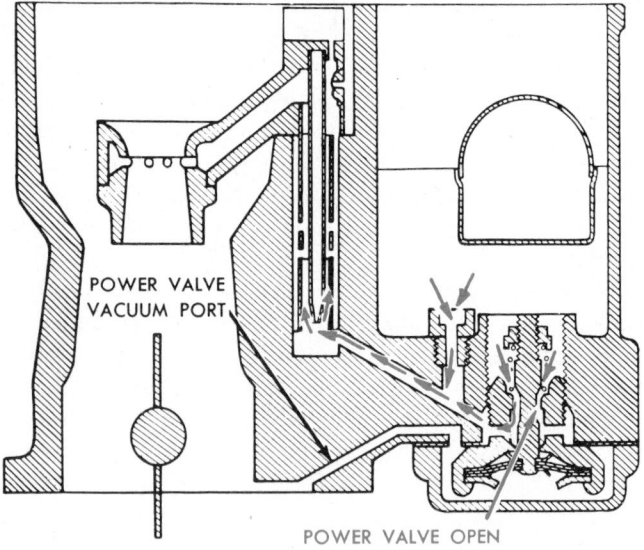

Fig. 21-13. Motorcraft 2150 carburetor power valve, or economizer valve, which supplies additional fuel needed for wide open throttle.

the air bleed system used on a Zenith carburetor. In this case, the high-speed system of the carburetor consists of a primary venturi, a secondary venturi, a main jet, a well jet and a discharge jet.

The main jet controls the fuel mixture from about one-fourth to about three-fourths throttle valve opening. The mixture is controlled by a small amount of air admitted through the well vent or high speed bleeder. The air bleed holes are located in the upper section of the discharge jet at a point below the level of the fuel in the jet.

Introduction of air at that point reduces the surface tension of the fuel and helps fuel flow at low pressures. This bleed also restricts fuel flow through the main jets under high vacuum conditions. In combination, these two factors control the air-fuel ratio and offset the tendency toward increased richness of mixture that occurs when a plain nozzle is subjected to increased air velocity.

FULL POWER CIRCUIT

With its air bleed maintaining the air-fuel ratio at a constant rate, the main circuit provides economical operation for all speeds, from low speed up to but not including wide-open throttle. However, for maximum speed and power, additional fuel must be supplied. There are several ways that this additional fuel is provided for maximum power. These methods include the economizer valve or power jet, and the metering rod.

POWER VALVE

The power valve, or economizer valve, depends upon manifold vacuum for its operation. It is connected to a vacuum port on the engine side of the throttle valve, Fig.

21-13. By design, when full throttle operation is approached, engine vacuum acting on the diaphragm or plunger of the power valve will permit the required amount of fuel to pass through the main nozzle.

Another type of power valve is shown in Fig. 21-14. In this design, the power jet valve is controlled by a vacuum-actuated piston assembly, operating in accordance with throttle valve opening. With the throttle closed (high manifold vacuum), atmospheric pressure in the float chamber moves the vacuum-controlled piston assembly to the top of its cylinder against the tension of a spring. This closes the power valve. When the throttle valve is opened to a point where additional fuel is required, manifold vacuum has decreased sufficiently so that

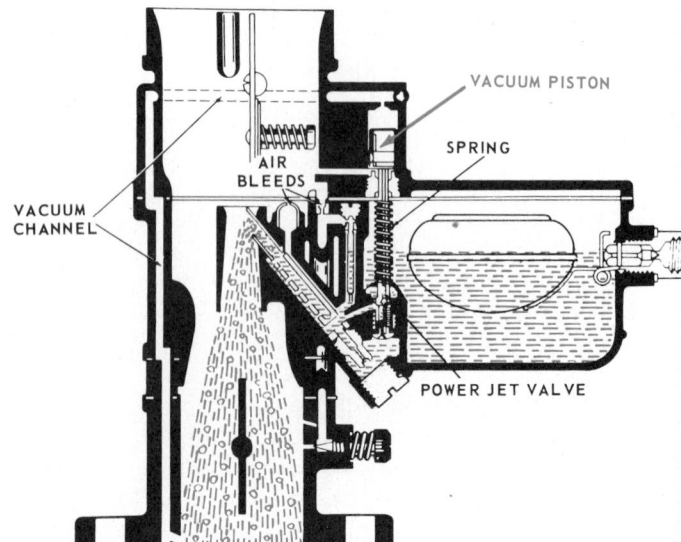

Fig. 21-14. Another type of power jet valve is controlled by vacuum piston.

the spring moves the piston down, opening the power jet to feed additional fuel into the high-speed circuit.

Mechanical means are also used on some carburetors for supplying the additional fuel needed for high-speed operation. In this design, the power jet is opened by the accelerator pump when the pump is at the bottom, or end, of its stroke.

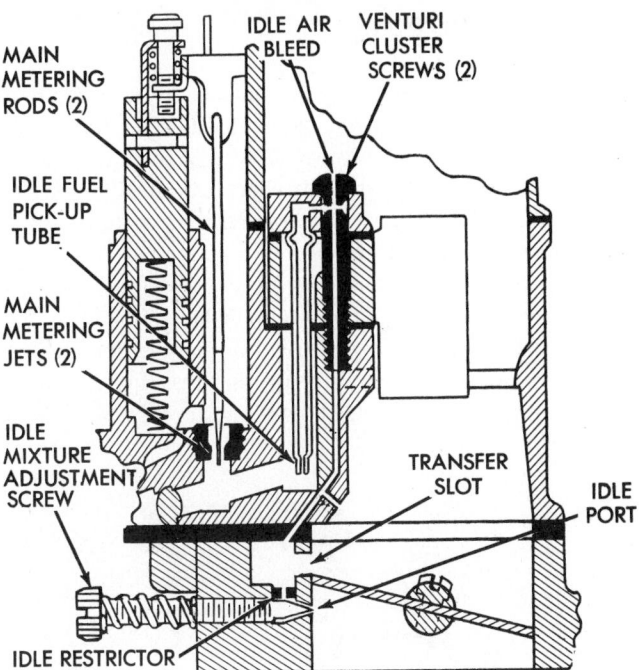

Fig. 21-16. Metering rods (2) are operated by a vacuum piston on a Carter BBD carburetor.

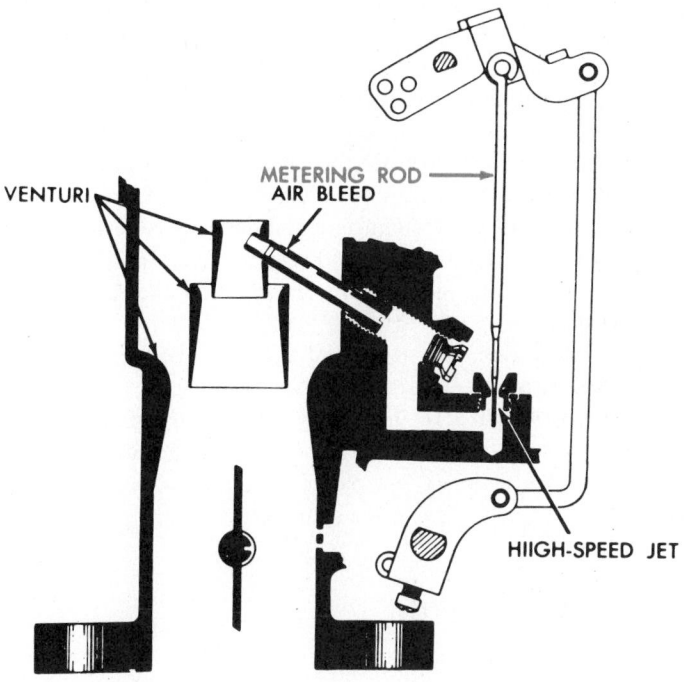

Fig. 21-15. Metering rod varies amount of fuel flowing from a jet.

METERING ROD

Instead of using a power jet, some carburetors accomplish the same results by employing a metering rod that varies the size of the high-speed jet openings. In this design, Fig. 21-15, fuel from the float bowl is metered to the high-speed circuit through the calibrated orifice provided by the high-speed jet and the metering rod within it. From this point, the fuel is conducted to the nozzle extending into the venturi.

As the throttle valve is opened, its linkage raises the metering rod in the jet. The rod has several steps, or tapers, on the lower end. As it is raised in the jet, it makes the effective size of the fuel orifice greater, permitting more fuel to flow through the circuit. Obviously, metering rod position must be carefully synchronized with every throttle position so that the correct air-fuel ratio is maintained throughout all engine speeds.

Metering rods are also operated by means of a vacuum controlled piston as shown in Fig. 21-16.

VACUUM STEP-UP

The vacuum step-up circuit, Fig. 21-17, operates much like the power jet. It consists of a step-up piston fastened to a step-up rod. When high vacuum develops in the intake

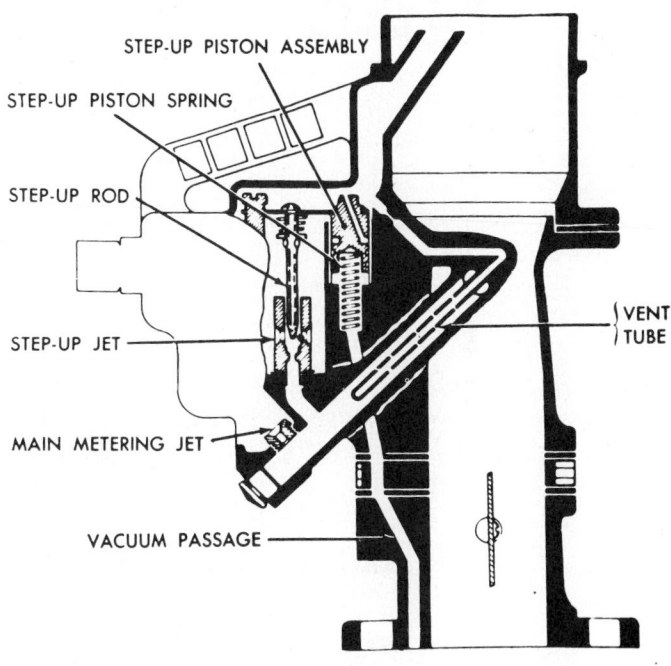

Fig. 21-17. Details of vacuum step-up circuit designed to supply additional fuel needed for full power operation.

manifold (part throttle operation), atmospheric pressure holds the step-up piston down against spring pressure. This, in turn, holds the step-up rod down in the step-up jet, closing the jet.

With low vacuum in the intake manifold (wide-open throttle), the difference in pressure above and below the piston is small. Consequently, the piston is moved up by spring pressure and the rod is raised out of its jet. In this way, additional fuel is supplied for maximum power.

ACCELERATING PUMP

When a throttle valve is opened quickly to produce rapid acceleration of the engine, the carburetor fuel mixture tends to become too lean and a "flat spot" occurs. This results from the fact that the fuel is of greater weight than air. Consequently, when the accelerator is opened suddenly the flow of fuel will lag behind the flow of the air.

To supply the additional fuel needed to overcome this condition, a small accelerating pump is incorporated in the design of the carburetor, Fig. 21-18. This pump is operated by the throttle linkage. In some designs, the strokes of the pump can be adjusted to any one of three positions. The longest

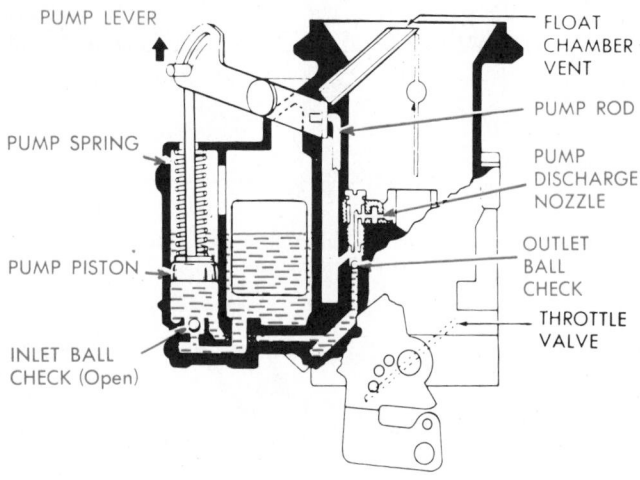

Fig. 21-18. Accelerator pump supplies additional fuel for rapid acceleration.

stroke provides the maximum amount of fuel, so this is the setting usually used during cold weather.

The accelerating pump circuit generally consists of:
1. A pump cylinder.
2. A plunger, mechanically actuated by a lever mounted on throttle shaft, or vacuum-operated by intake manifold vacuum.
3. An intake check valve located in bottom of pump cylinder to control passage of fuel from bowl to pump cylinder.
4. A discharge or outlet check valve.
5. An accelerating jet to meter fuel used.

When the throttle is opened, the pump plunger moves downward in its cylinder. In the mechanically-operated design, the downward movement is obtained by direct linkage with the throttle. In the vacuum-actuated design, a sudden throttle opening will cause the manifold vacuum to drop, allowing the accelerating pump spring to force the pump plunger down in the cylinder.

In either case, the downward travel of the plunger forces the fuel past the discharge check valve of the acelerating jet.

Fuel is supplied to the pump cylinder through the intake check valve at the bottom. This valve permits a supply of fuel to reach the cylinder, but closes on the down stroke of the plunger to prevent fuel in the cylinder from being pushed back into the float bowl.

ANTI-PERCOLATOR

During extremely hot weather, there is a tendency for the fuel to vaporize in the fuel line, the fuel pump or within the carburetor. When this condition occurs in the carburetor, it is known as "percolation."

To overcome percolation when it occurs, special provisions

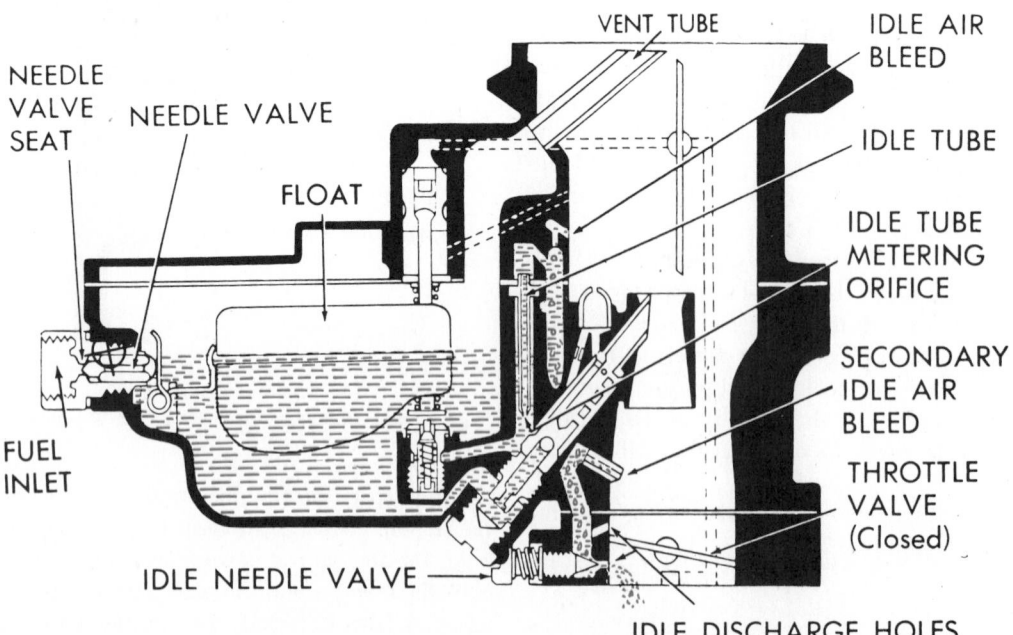

Fig. 21-19. Vent tube from float bowl to air horn prevents vapor lock and equalizes effect of a clogged air filter. This illustration also shows a typical idling system.

are made. One method is to provide a passageway or vent tube between the top of the float bowl chamber and the upper part of the air horn, Fig. 21-19. By this means, any vapor developing in the float bowl chamber will be drawn into the air stream in the air horn. From there, it will pass through the carburetor and into the intake manifold.

Venting the float bowl in this manner has the added advantage that it will equalize the effect of a clogged air filter. A clogged filter will cause a somewhat greater vacuum at the venturi and consequent increased flow of fuel. Venting the float bowl into the carburetor air horn relieves this condition.

Another method vents the float bowl chamber directly into the atmosphere, Fig. 21-16. In this carburetor design, the vent is provided with a cap to prevent dust and dirt from entering the float bowl chamber.

Still another design incorporates a special valve that vents the main discharge nozzle to the atmosphere. Linkage is arranged so that closing of the throttle valve will open an anti-percolator valve. Another method designed to accomplish the same thing provides a vent for the passages to the discharge nozzle without the use of a valve.

With the coming of evaporative emission controls, venting of fuel vapors to the atmosphere was discontinued. See Chapter 29.

FAST IDLE

To prevent an engine from stalling before it reaches operating temperature, it must be operated at a faster-than-normal speed. This is done by preventing engine speed from dropping below a predetermined rpm. To accomplish this, the choke shaft is linked to a cam on the outside of the carburetor, Fig. 21-20. The linkage is arranged so that as long as the choke is in a partially closed position, the high spot on

the cam comes under the fast idle speed adjusting screw. In this way, the throttle valve will be held open a sufficient amount to prevent stalling.

After the engine reaches operating temperature, opening of the choke valve will move the cam from under the fast idle speed adjusting screw, and the engine will idle at normal speed.

CARBURETOR UNLOADER

When an engine does not start immediately, prolonged cranking will result in a flooded condition. The air-fuel mixture in the manifold and engine is so rich that it is no longer a vapor. Consequently, the spark plugs cannot fire it. To overcome this condition, linkage is provided on the carburetor which will hold the choke valve open when the accelerator is pushed to the floor, Fig. 21-21. Then, as the engine is cranked again, air will enter the manifold and cylinders to clear excessive gasoline from the system. This is accomplished by special linkage between the throttle and choke levers, Fig. 21-21.

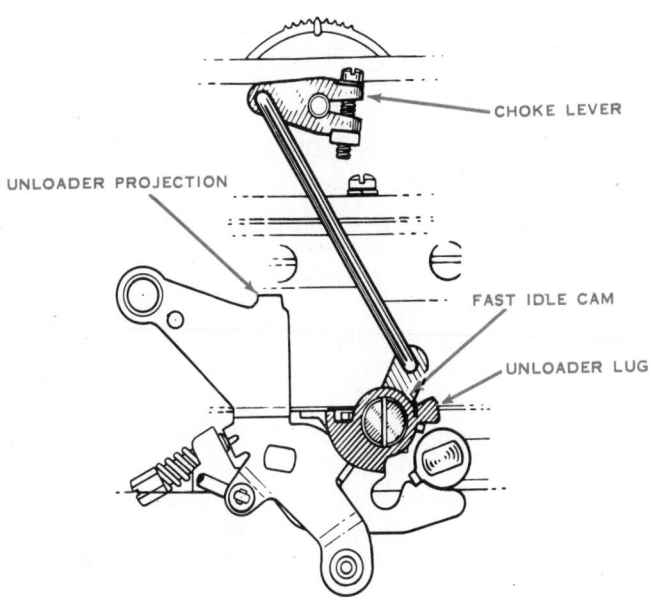

Fig. 21-21. Showing relationship of unloader lug or cam, unloader projection, choke lever and fast idle cam.

ANTI-ICING

When fuel is evaporated, it absorbs heat from the surrounding air and metal parts of the carburetor. When the humidity of the air is high and temperatures are at approximately the freezing point, the evaporation of fuel in the carburetor often causes "icing." The ice forms around the closed position of the throttle plate, and the idle port becomes closed with ice. This, in turn, will cause the engine to stall at low speeds.

To overcome this icing condition, some carburetors are provided with special passages that carry hot exhaust gases around the carburetor, heating the area surrounding the

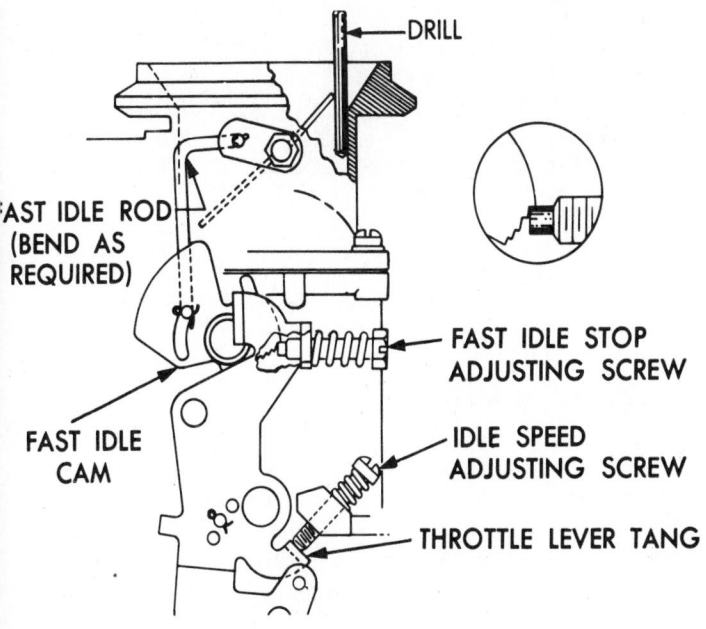

Fig. 21-20. Showing fast idle and choke linkage, together with fast idle adjustment and idle speed adjustment.

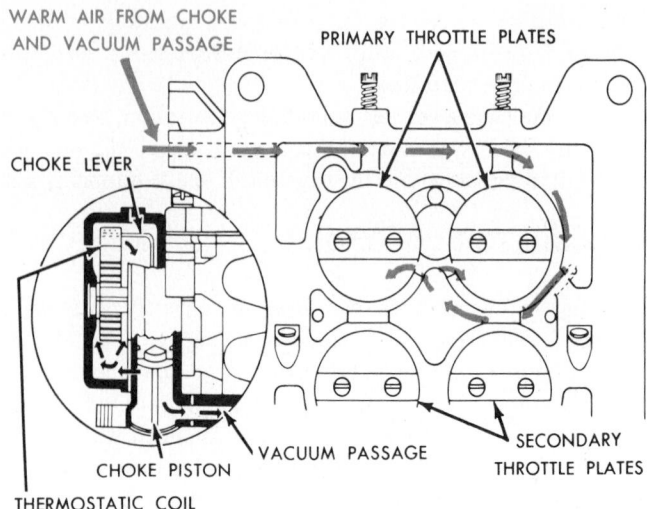

Fig. 21-22. Showing path of warm air from choke passing around throttle valves to prevent formation of ice.

throttle plate, Fig. 21-22.

Another method of overcoming this difficulty is to provide a water jacket for the carburetor. This water jacket, of course, is connected to the cooling system of the vehicle.

HOT IDLE COMPENSATOR

During long periods of idling with an extremely hot engine, the fuel in the carburetor bowl becomes hot enough to form vapors. These vapors enter the carburetor bores by way of the inside bowl vents, mixing with the idle air and causing an extremely rich mixture. This will result in loss of engine rpm and, eventually, in stalling. To overcome this condition (on Carter AFB carburetors, for example), a hot idle compensator valve is placed in the secondary side of the carburetor. This is calibrated to permit additional air to enter the manifold below the secondary throttle valve, where it mixes with the fuel vapors to provide a more combustible mixture.

On Rochester 4GC carburetors, the hot idle compensator is placed on the secondary side of the float bowl and permits additional air to enter the primary bores under extreme hot idle conditions, Fig. 21-23.

ANTI-STALL DASHPOT

Most older cars with automatic transmissions have an anti-stall dashpot connected to the carburetor linkage, Fig. 21-24. The purpose of this dashpot is to prevent the throttle valve from closing too fast. Too rapid closing often causes the engine to stall. Installation of the dashpot prevents the throttle from being closed too quickly, thereby avoiding stalls.

This condition would not occur with a manual transmission since the momentum of the vehicle would continue to drive the engine through the stall period.

Also, to insure easy starting, some engines have special carburetor linkage designed to automatically hold the throttle valve slightly open during cranking.

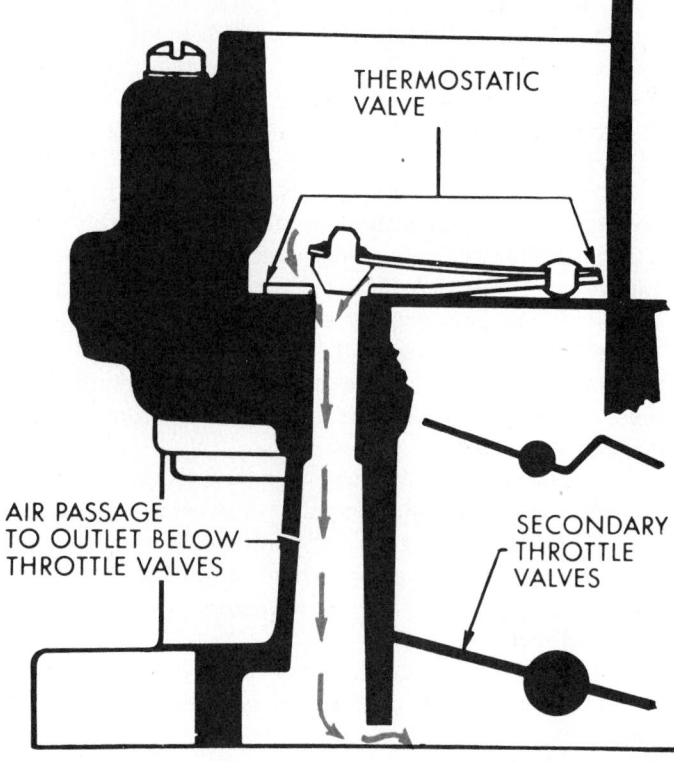

Fig. 21-23. Hot idle compensator permits additional air to enter primary bores of carburetor under extreme hot idle conditions.

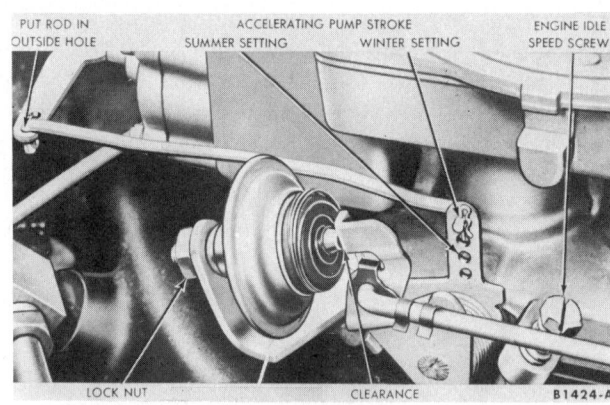

Fig. 21-24. Showing anti-stall dashpot mounted on side of Ford carburetor. Some carburetors have anti-stall dashpot built into carburetor. Note provision for adjustment of accelerator pump.

VACUUM ADVANCE

Vacuum from the carburetor is used to control the spark advance on the Ford Loadomatic distributor. By design, vacuum is transmitted to the distributor diaphragm from three interconnected passages in the carburetor, Fig. 21-25. All manifold vacuum to the distributor passes through the spark control valve.

Under normal load conditions, the spark valve is held open against spring pressure by a combination of atmospheric

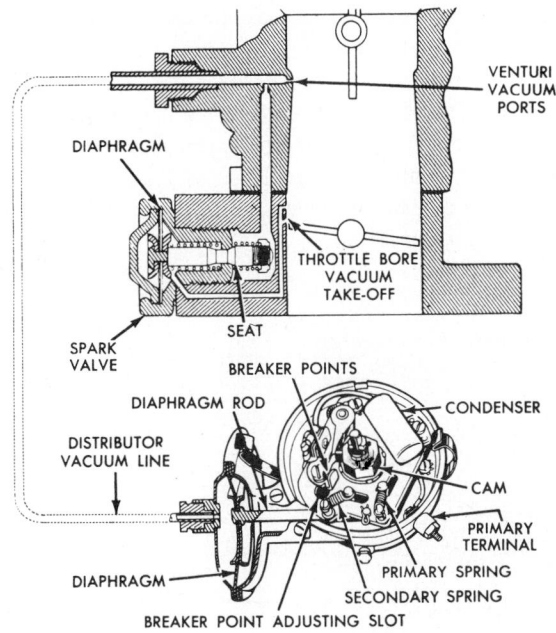

Fig. 21-25. Method of using vacuum at venturi and at throttle valve to control spark advance.

governor diaphragm. The differential is provided by vacuum below the governor throttle plates and atmospheric pressure above the plates.

At low engine rpm, the governor control valve weight is held away from its seat by the tension of the valve weight spring. During this period, the valve is wide open to allow outside air to flow to the governor so that no governing action occurs. As engine speed increases, the differential between atmospheric pressure and engine vacuum decreases, causing the governor diaphragm to exert a pull on the governor lever. This turns the throttle shaft and partly closes the throttle.

Another method of limiting the speed of an engine is by means of a velocity type governor. In this design, the unit is inserted adjacent to the throttle. As the gas goes through the manifold, its velocity acts on a spring-loaded floating obstruction in the form of a ball or disk attached to the throttle. As engine speed increases, the gas flowing through the manifold tends to carry the obstruction along with it. Since this disk or ball is attached to the throttle plate of the carburetor, its movement closes the throttle against the tension of a spring. In this way, the speed of the engine is controlled.

pressure and manifold vacuum. When accelerating, manifold vacuum drops and spring pressure closes the spark valve which shuts off the vacuum and prevents excessive spark advance. Venturi vacuum prevents full retard. When manifold vacuum increases, the spark valve will again allow a higher vacuum to advance the distributor.

GOVERNORS

Governors are used principally on industrial engines and commercial vehicles so that economical and safe speeds are not exceeded. One type of Holley unit, Fig. 21-26, is inserted between the carburetor and the intake manifold, where it is actuated by the pressure differential acting against the

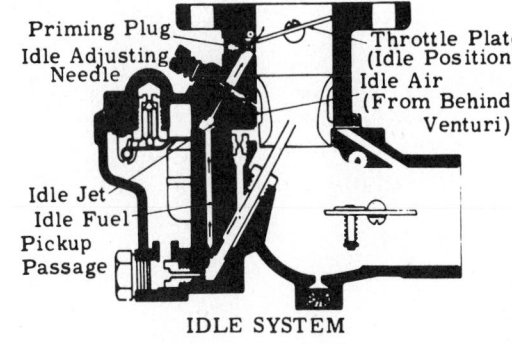

Fig. 21-27. Sectional view of updraft carburetor. Air enters at right and passes upward through venturi and past throttle plate.

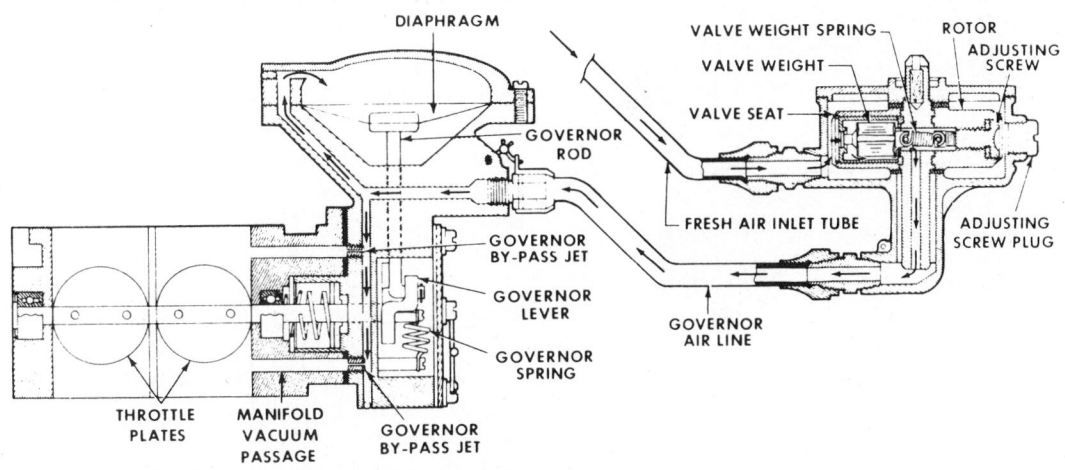

Fig. 21-26. This Holley governor uses vacuum below governor throttle plates and atmosphere above to control speed of vehicle.

TYPES OF CARBURETORS

While there are many variations in the design and construction of carburetors, there are three basic types:
1. Updraft.
2. Downdraft.
3. Sidedraft.

The direction of the air flow at the carburetor outlet to the manifold determines the classification.

The updraft carburetor, Fig. 21-27, is placed low on the side of the engine. It is supplied with fuel by gravity feed. However, the fuel mixture must be lifted from the carburetor, through the manifold and into the engine. Air velocities must be high; a requirement that can be attained only by using carburetors and manifold passages of small diameter. As a result, power output is limited.

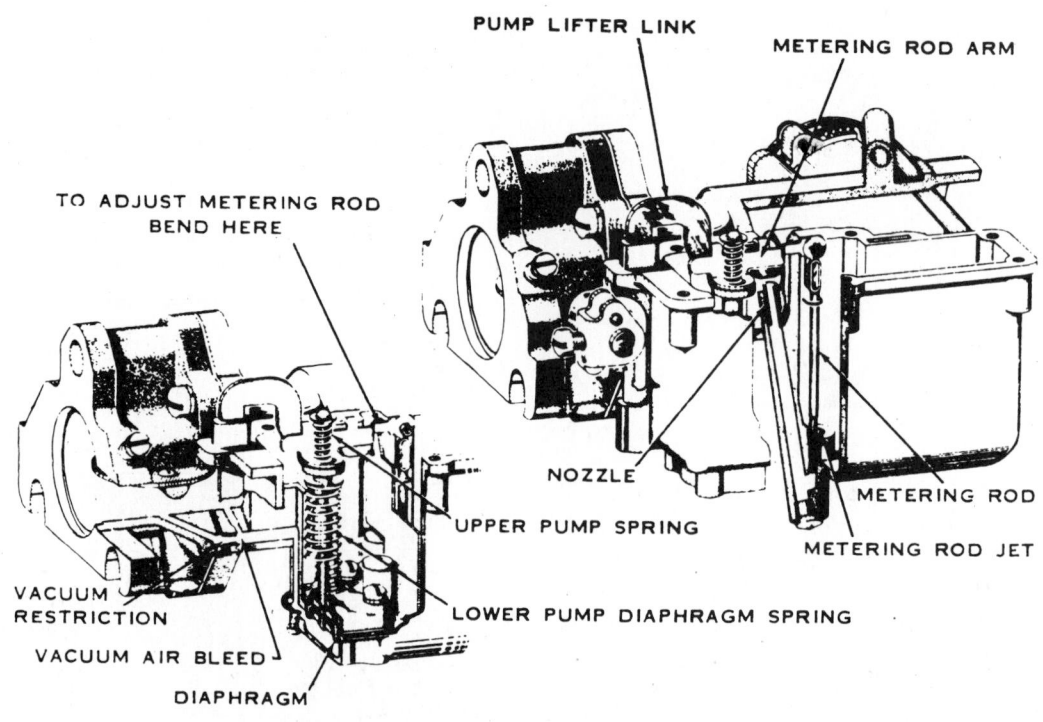

Fig. 21-28. Typical sidedraft, or crossdraft, carburetor.

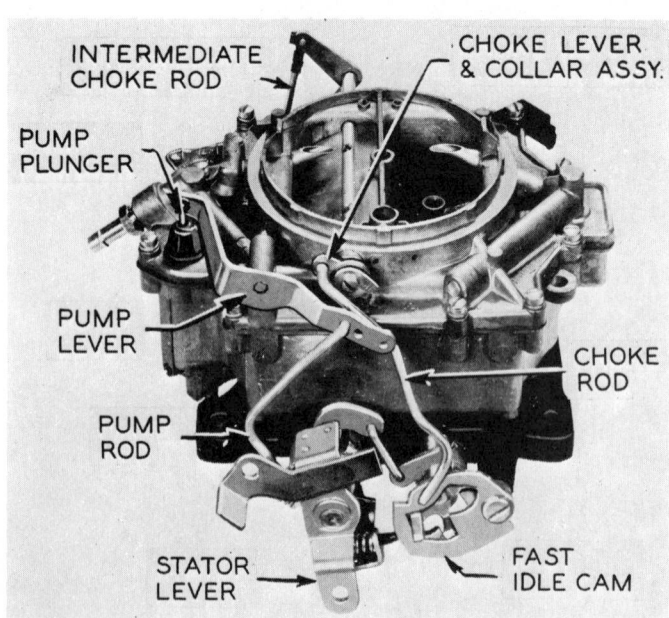

Fig. 21-29. Typical single-barrel, downdraft carburetor.

The sidedraft, or crossdraft, carburetor shown in Fig. 21-28 is used where there is little space over the engine. The air cleaner naturally is positioned lower in a sidedraft carburetor installation. Another application of this carburetor is where the vaporized mixture is heated by water in the engine water jacket.

U.S. passenger car engines are equipped almost exclusively with the downdraft carburetor, Figs. 21-14 and 21-29. In this design, the air-fuel mixture will reach the engine even though the air velocity is low. The carburetor throat and manifold can be made larger, by design. This, in turn, increases the size of the air-fuel intake system, making high speeds and high specific output possible.

SINGLE-BARREL CARBURETOR

While there are three basic types of carburetors, they also may be classed by number of throats, or barrels. A single-barrel carburetor, Fig. 21-29, has one outlet to the intake manifold. It is designed to take care of all the requirements of the engine for all operating conditions. Such carburetors are used extensively on engines having six cylinders or less.

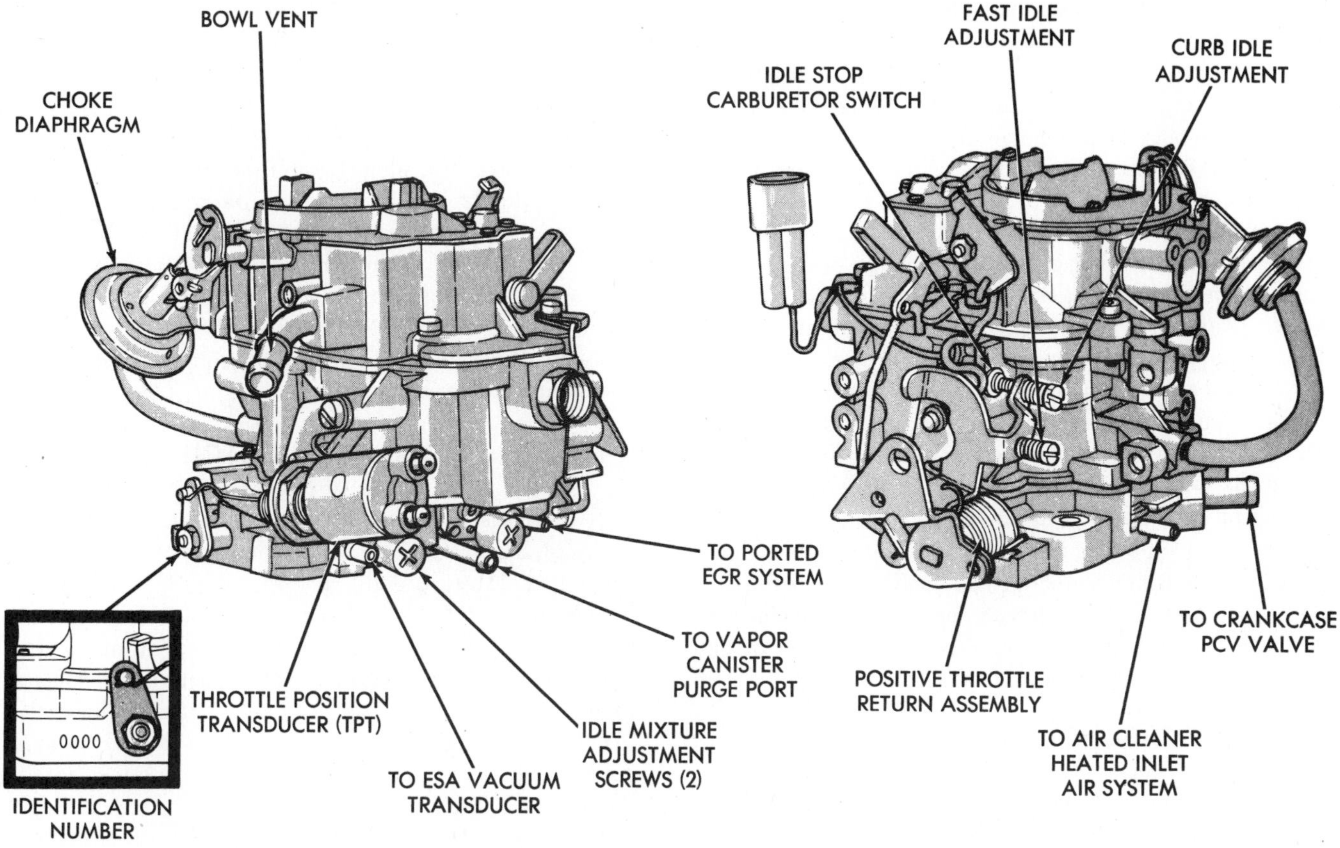

CHOKE
DIAPHRAGM

BOWL VENT

FAST IDLE
ADJUSTMENT

IDLE STOP
CARBURETOR SWITCH

CURB IDLE
ADJUSTMENT

TO PORTED
EGR SYSTEM

TO VAPOR
CANISTER
PURGE PORT

IDENTIFICATION
NUMBER

THROTTLE POSITION
TRANSDUCER (TPT)

TO ESA VACUUM
TRANSDUCER

IDLE MIXTURE
ADJUSTMENT
SCREWS (2)

POSITIVE THROTTLE
RETURN ASSEMBLY

TO AIR CLEANER
HEATED INLET
AIR SYSTEM

TO CRANKCASE
PCV VALVE

Fig. 21-30. Two views of Holley 2280 dual venturi carburetor as installed on Chrysler 318 cu. in. (5.2 litre) V-8 engine. This carburetor has four basic metering systems: idle system provides mixture for idle and low speed; accelerator pump system pumps additional fuel for acceleration; main metering system meters an economical mixture for normal cruising conditions; power enrichment system which combines a mechanical and vacuum operated power valve to provide additional fuel for maximum power.

TWO-BARREL CARBURETOR

Carburetors with two outlets to the intake manifold are known as two-barrel or two-throat carburetors, Fig. 21-30. Basically, these units are two carburetors in one, with two complete idling systems, two high-speed systems, two power systems, two accelerating systems, two throttle valves, two choke valves, but only one float system.

With a two-barrel carburetor, each barrel or mixing tube supplies alternate cylinders in the firing order. In a conventional six cylinder engine, one barrel supplies cylinders 1, 3 and 2, while the other barrel supplies cylinders 5, 6 and 4.

FOUR-BARREL CARBURETOR

In the four-barrel carburetor, Fig. 21-31, generally used on V-8 engines, there are four openings to the intake manifold within the single unit. Some systems, such as the float system, may be common to all four barrels. In some four-barrel carburetor designs, half of the carburetor operates as a two-barrel unit during light load and cruising speeds, while the other half of the carburetor is supplemental for top speed and full-throttle operation. The two barrels supplying fuel for light load operation are known as the primary side, while the supplementary two barrels are known as the secondary side.

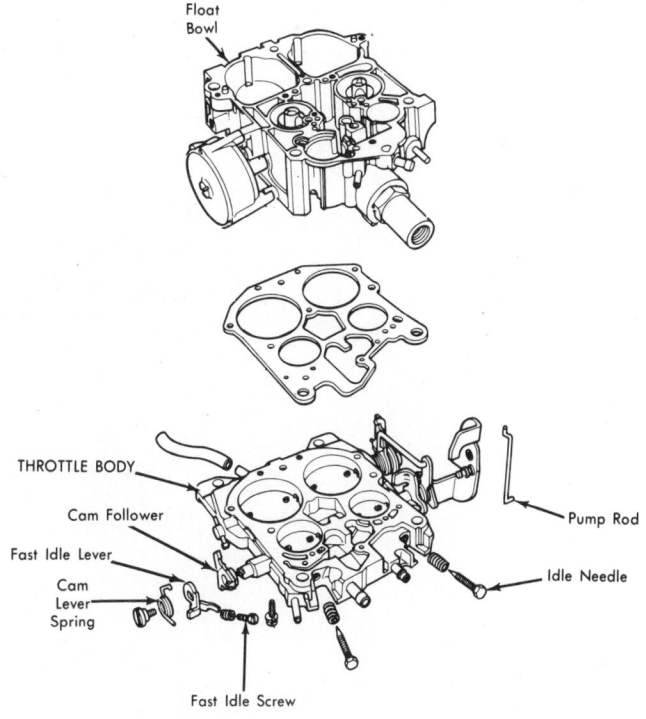

Float
Bowl

THROTTLE BODY

Cam Follower

Fast Idle Lever

Cam
Lever
Spring

Pump Rod

Idle Needle

Fast Idle Screw

Fig. 21-31. Four-barrel carburetor. Note four openings to manifold.

When two barrels of a four-barrel carburetor supply fuel to the engine throughout the entire speed range, a portion of the idle system fuel is routed to the secondary barrels for satisfactory fuel distribution. Also in this design, the secondary throttle plates remain closed at lower engine speeds. As engine speed increases, the throttle plates of the secondary barrels are opened.

In some designs, the secondary throttle plates are operated mechanically through linkage. On other models, the secondary throttle plates are controlled automatically by a vacuum-operated diaphragm. In general, the secondary throttle plates will start to open when the primary plates are open 50 deg.

In a four-barrel carburetor on a V-8 engine, primary and secondary barrels form a pair to supply cylinders 1-7-4-6, while the other primary and secondary barrels will supply fuel to cylinders 3-5-2-8. However, this applies only to an engine having a firing order of 1-8-4-3-6-5-7-2.

In general, manifolding for both two-barrel and four-barrel carburetors is designed as follows: One half of the carburetor supplies fuel to the end cylinders on one side of the engine and two center cylinders on the other side. The other half of the carburetor supplies fuel to the remaining cylinders.

MULTIPLE CARBURETORS

Maximum engine performance requires perfect distribution of large quantities of the air-fuel mixture. One way to attain this is by using several carburetors. One installation on a V-8 engine uses three two-barrel carburetors.

In this installation (Chevrolet), the center carburetor is known as the primary, Fig. 21-32. It takes care of all engine

requirements up to 60 deg. opening of the throttle. Above that, the secondary carburetors come into operation to supply the additional fuel required for maximum performance.

The primary carburetor is a complete unit, containing all the usual carburetor systems (float, idle, choke, port throttle, power and accelerator pump). The front and rear carburetors do not include idle, part throttle or choke systems.

A combined mechanical and vacuum linkage is used to operate the throttle valves. The primary carburetor throttle valves are operated mechanically. When they are opened 60 deg., a vacuum slider valve causes vacuum to act on a diaphragm which, in turn, operates the throttle valves on the secondary carburetors.

MOTORCRAFT 4300 CARBURETOR

The Motorcraft model 4300 4-V carburetor, Fig. 21-33, is a three-piece, separately cast design consisting of the air horn, main body and throttle body.

A cast-in center fuel inlet has provision for a supplementary fuel inlet system. The fuel bowl is vented by an internal balance vent; and a mechanical atmospheric vent operates during idle.

The idle bypass system is designed to provide a more consistent idle, and a hot idle compensator, Fig. 21-33, is used to help idle stability.

These adjustments for idle air and idle fuel must be made at the same time. Opening the idle air screw to increase engine rpm leans the air-fuel mixture. Consequently, the idle fuel mixture must also be adjusted to provide the correct air-fuel mixture for smooth engine idle.

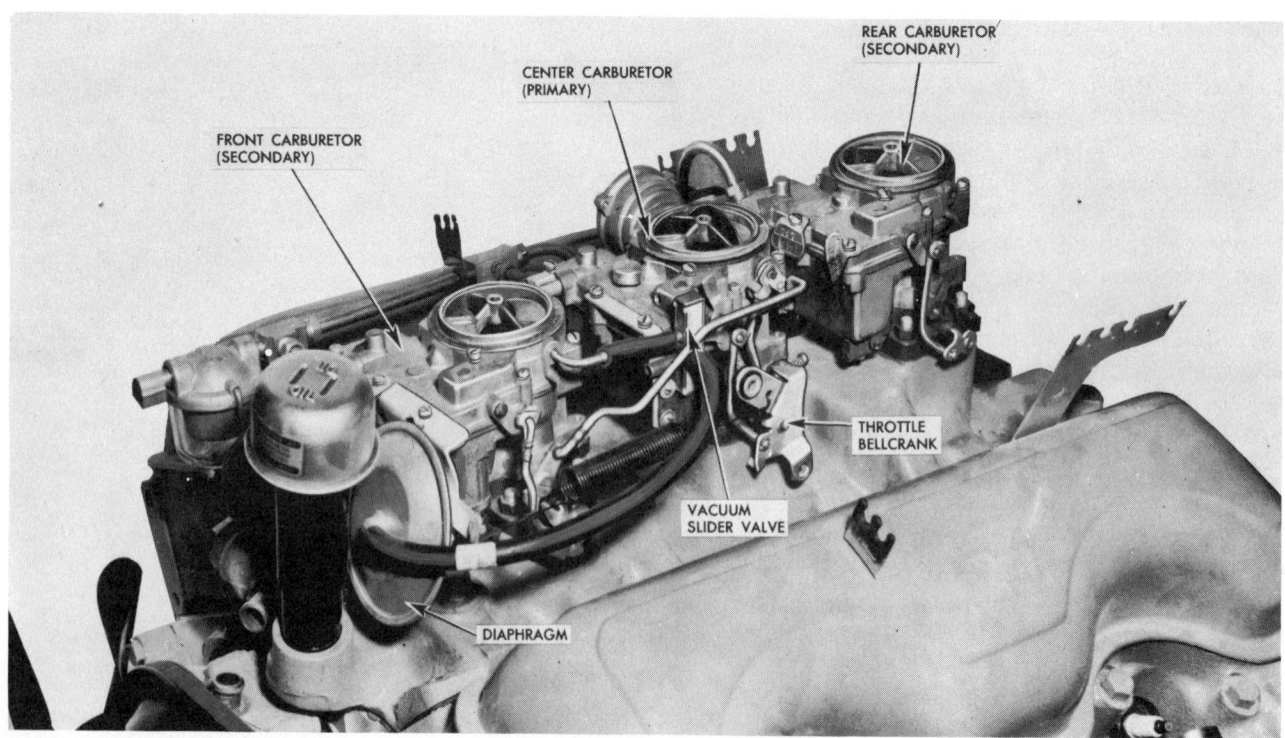

Fig. 21-32. Showing installation of three two-barrel carburetors on a Chevrolet V-8 engine.

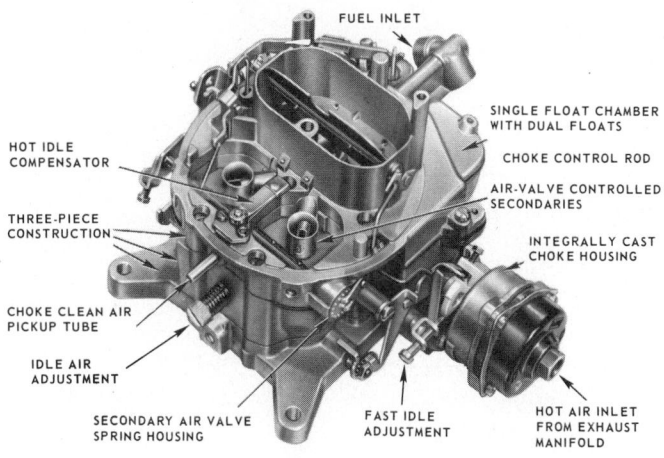

Fig. 21-33. Details of Motorcraft 4300 4-V carburetor. Note idle air adjustment.

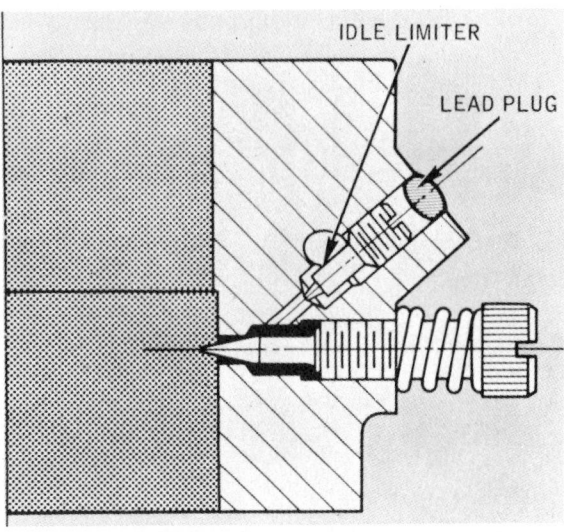

Fig. 21-35. Details of idle fuel limiter on Carter model YF carburetor.

AIR-FUEL MIXTURE ADJUSTMENTS

Starting with 1968 models, most carburetors have been modified or recalibrated to provide leaner air-fuel mixtures to conform to the Federal regulations governing exhaust emissions.

These leaner mixtures result primarily from better control of the idle mixture, and from better combustion during periods of deceleration. In some cases the idle mixture screws have a finer pitch, making for more accurate control of the air-fuel ratio.

On Motorcraft carburetors, idle mixture adjustments are provided with an idler limiter device, Fig. 21-34, which sets a limit on enrichment of the idle mixture. Holley and single-venturi Carter carburetors contain a preset fixed mixture restriction in idle fuel passages that accomplishes the same thing, Fig. 21-35.

In the case of the Monojet carburetor used on six cylinder

Chevrolet, Buick, Pontiac and Oldsmobile engines with automatic transmissions, an idle stop solenoid is used to stop engine "dieseling" after the ignition is turned off.

Idle rpm with exhaust emission control carburetors is slightly higher than normal and, in every case, must be accurately set to specified value. On the Monojet, Fig. 21-36, the idle speed is adjusted with the transmission in "drive"

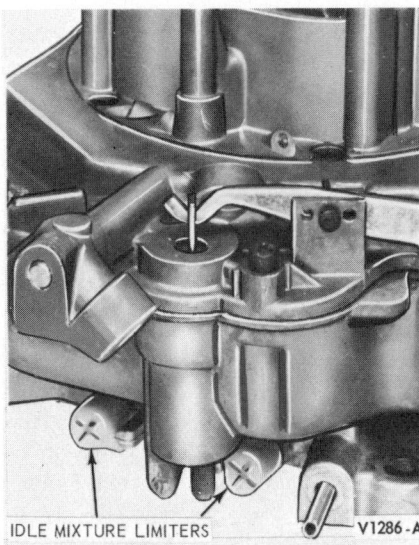

Fig. 21-34. Note idle mixture limiters on Motorcraft carburetor.

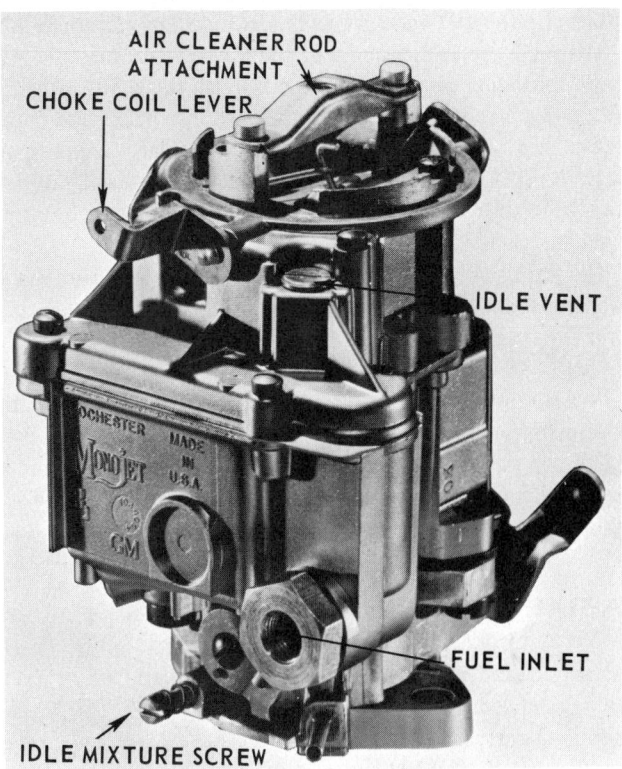

Fig. 21-36. Rochester Monojet carburetor is used on six cylinder Buick, Chevrolet, Oldsmobile and Pontiac engines.

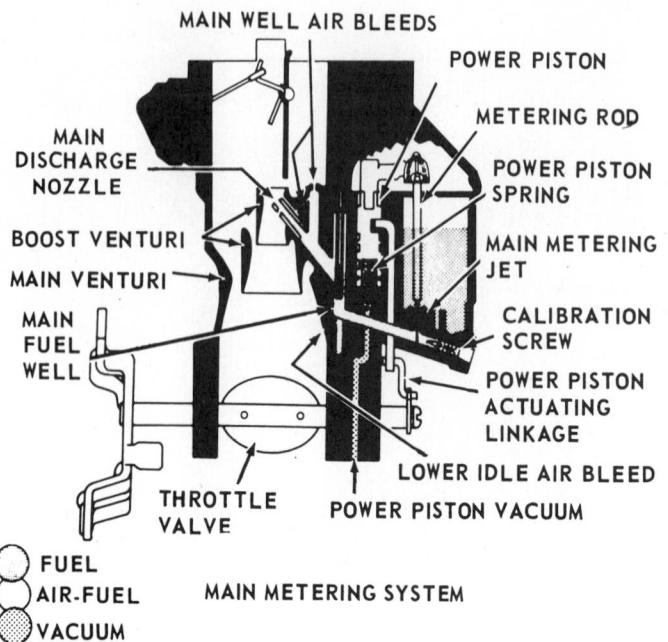

Fig. 21-37. Details of main metering system on Monojet carburetor.

Fig. 21-38. Float bowl of this Carter Thermo-Quad carburetor is made of molded phenolic resin to reduce heat transfer.

position. When the owner is about to turn off the ignition, he places the transmission in "park" or "neutral." With the load off the engine, idle speed will rise to the 700 rpm range. With the engine running at that speed, plus higher operating temperatures and slightly retarded spark, "dieseling" may occur. The idle stop solenoid eliminates the possibility by closing the throttle valve when the ignition key is turned off.

The main metering system of the Monojet carburetor, Fig. 21-37, feeds fuel whenever air flow through the venturi is great enough to maintain fuel flow through the main discharge nozzle. The triple venturi stack-up is particularly sensitive to air flow. This means finer and more stable metering control from light to heavy loads, an important factor in the control of exhaust emissions.

The main metering system consists of the metering jet, a mechanical and vacuum-operated metering rod, main fuel well, main well air bleeds, fuel discharge nozzle and the triple venturi.

Power enrichment in the Monojet is obtained by the movement of a spring-loaded vacuum piston that senses changes in manifold vacuum. The amount of enrichment is controlled by the clearance between the groove in the power piston and the diameter of the power piston drive rod.

CARTER THERMO-QUAD CARBURETOR

One method of controlling hydrocarbon end carbon monoxide is to reduce the heat transfer to the fuel. The Carter Thermo-Quad carburetor installed on some Chrysler, Dodge and Plymouth engines has a float bowl made of molded phenolic resin which acts as an effective heat insulator, Fig. 21-38. A reduction of 20 deg. F over all-metal carburetors is claimed. The Thermo-Quad carburetor and others of the

Chrysler line form a part of the proportional exhaust gas recirculation (EGR) system, Fig. 21-39. The system includes a recirculation control valve and a vacuum sensor to insure proper flow of exhaust gas is proportional to vacuum sensed in the carburetor.

In this EGR system, a slot type port in the carburetor throttle body is exposed to an increasing percentage of manifold vacuum as the throttle valve opens. This throttle bore port is connected through an external nipple direct to the EGR valve. The flow rate is dependent on the manifold vacuum, throttle position and exhaust back pressure.

Recycling of exhaust gases is eliminated at wide-open throttle. This is done by calibrating the valve opening point above manifold vacuum available when the throttle valves are wide open, since port vacuum cannot exceed manifold vacuum. Elimination of wide-open throttle recycle provides maximum performance.

ROCHESTER 2GV CARBURETOR

The current Rochester 2GV carburetor has many features designed to reduce exhaust gas emissions. This carburetor uses calibrated cluster design that places the main well tubes, idle tubes, mixture passages, air bleeds and pump jets in a compact assembly. The cluster is removable for cleaning and inspection purposes.

The venturi cluster fits on a flat portion of the carburetor bowl in front of the main venturi with a gasket underneath. The idle and main well tubes are permanently installed in the cluster body by means of a precision press fit.

The main nozzles and idle tubes are suspended in the main wells of the float bowl. Removable plastic main well inserts surround the main fuel nozzles to insulate the nozzles and prevent percolation. The plastic inserts also provide smooth fuel flow through the main metering system during hot engine operation.

Rochester 2GC-2GE carburetors have similar construction. A sectional drawing in Fig. 21-40 shows the major parts of these carburetors.

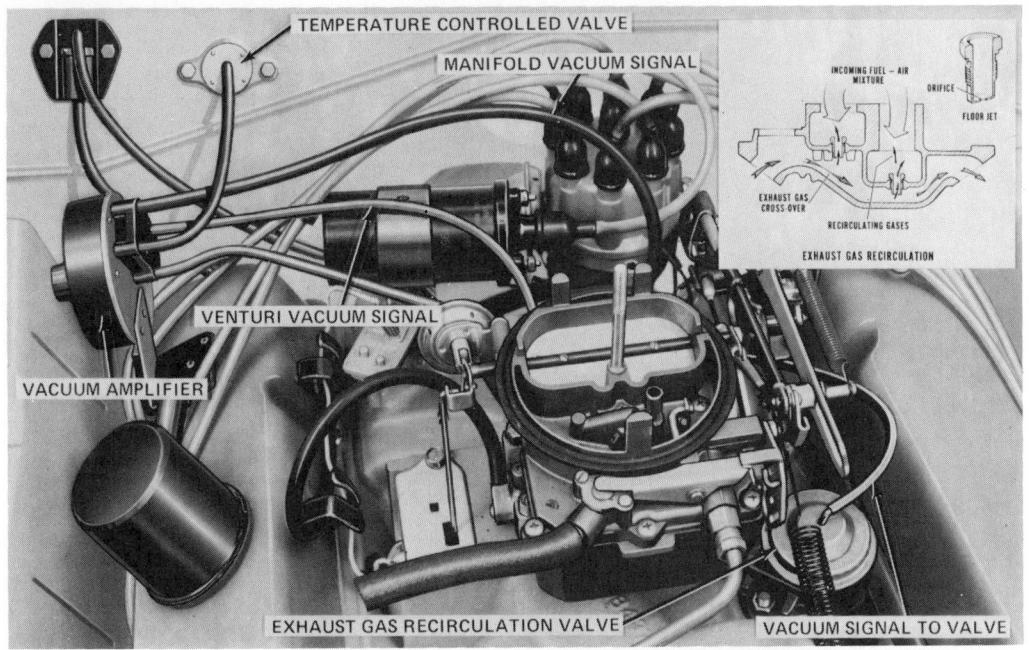

Fig. 21-39. Note details of proportional exhaust gas recirculation system installed on late model Chrysler Corp. engines.

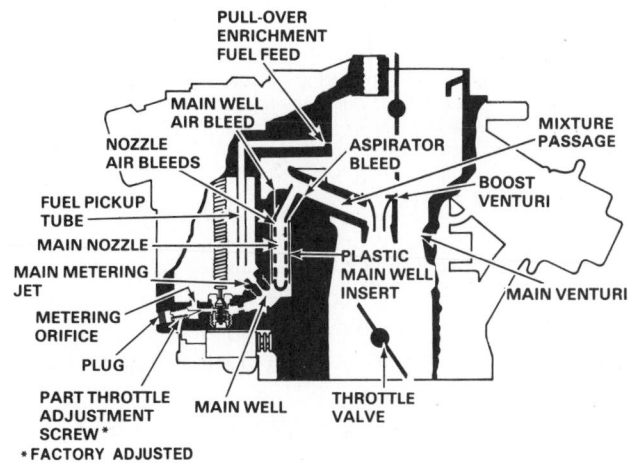

Fig. 21-40. Details of major parts of Rochester 2GC-2GE carburetors.

Fig. 21-41. Thermostatically controlled heated air intake is provided on modern carburetors. Ford 302 cu. in. V-8 is shown.

HOT AIR INTAKE — RAM AIR

Many of the carburetors designed for exhaust emission control have thermostatically controlled air intake systems. Hot air intake provides advantages ranging from improved cold start-up through warm-up and, more particularly, in more complete combustion and reduced exhaust by-products. The warm air is obtained from a heat stove on the exhaust manifold. See Ford design in Fig. 21-41. (Also see the chapters on AIR CLEANERS and EMISSION CONTROL.)

The Ford carburetor heated air intake system is equipped with a vacuum override control that opens the upper valve for direct air intake of unheated air for maximum air volume at full throttle opening. The override operates only when maximum air volume is needed for rapid acceleration. When high air volume is no longer needed, the override releases and the selector valve returns to the position indicated by underhood temperatures.

By placing carburetor intake air scoops at the front of the vehicle, full advantage is taken of air motion due to the speed of the car. This provides a ramming effect to the air entering the carburetor, and a degree of supercharging is obtained. Some Oldsmobiles with 400 cu. in. (6.6 litre), 10.5 to 1 compression ratio V-8 engines have scoops with 13 in. x 2 in. openings to feed ram air to the twin snorkels of the air cleaner.

FORD'S VARIABLE VENTURI CARBURETOR

Ford's Motorcraft model 2700 variable venturi carburetor, Figs. 21-42 and 21-43, varies the area of the venturi as a function of speed and load. Most other carburetors have

253

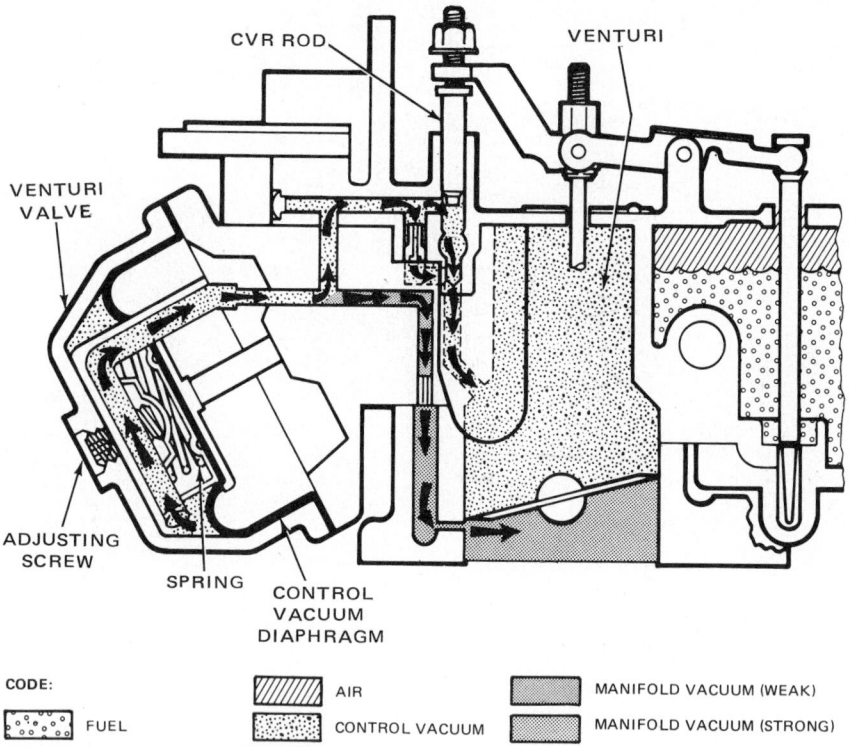

CODE:

FUEL	AIR	MANIFOLD VACUUM (WEAK)
	CONTROL VACUUM	MANIFOLD VACUUM (STRONG)

Fig. 21-42. In Ford's variable venturi carburetor, the venturi valve position is controlled by spring pressure and control vacuum. The spring pressure tends to close the valve. Control vacuum acts through a rubber diaphragm to open the valve. Control vacuum is vacuum below the venturi valve and above the throttle valves. See arrows in diagram.

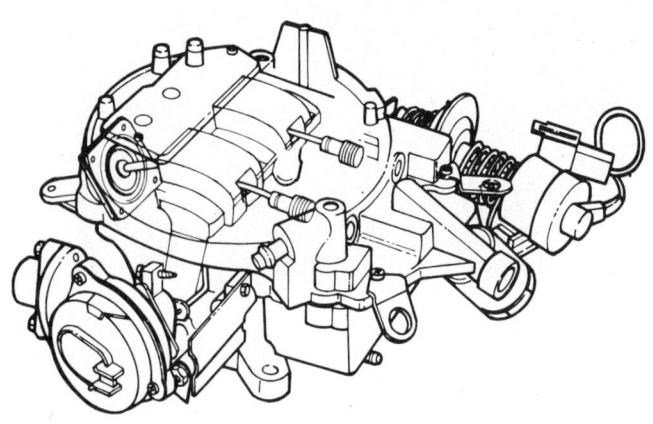

Fig. 21-43. Ford's Motorcraft variable venturi carburetor.

venturis that are fixed. In this design, changing the size of the venturi maintains sufficient air velocity and pressure drop to the main metering system. This is accomplished by means of tapered metering rods attached to the venturi valve, which changes the area of the venturi.

There is one rod and one jet for each bore of the carburetor. The rod moves back and forth in the jet when the air valve moves. When the venturi valve is closed, the largest diameter of the rod is in the jet. When the valve is wide open, the smallest diameter of the rod is in the jet. In that way, effective metering of the fuel is controlled by the position of the rod, Fig. 21-42.

SPECIAL FEATURES

Float spring: A requirement of fuel metering systems is that the fuel level in the float bowl be maintained at as near a constant level as possible. In the Holley 4150C carburetor, a float spring is incorporated under the float to keep the float in a stable position, Fig. 21-44.

Float needle valves: Instead of using steel for float needle valves, most carburetors are now using nylon or a similar material for their construction. A better seal is obtained and, in addition, the material has better wearing qualities. Also it is not readily affected by small foreign particles.

Secondary throttles: Four-barrel carburetors have two primary bores supplying air-fuel mixtures throughout the entire engine operation, while the two secondary bores function only when speed and load require them. At lower speeds, the secondary throttle plates remain closed.

When engine speed increases to a point where additional breathing capacity is required, vacuum is used to open the secondary throttle plates. Vacuum taken from one of the primary barrels, and the secondary barrels, acts on a diaphragm which controls the secondary throttle plates, Fig. 21-45.

CARBURETOR DEGASSER

The degasser, Fig. 21-46, is an auxiliary device built into the carburetor. It is used to correct the over-rich mixture condition that occurs when the throttle is closed suddenly.

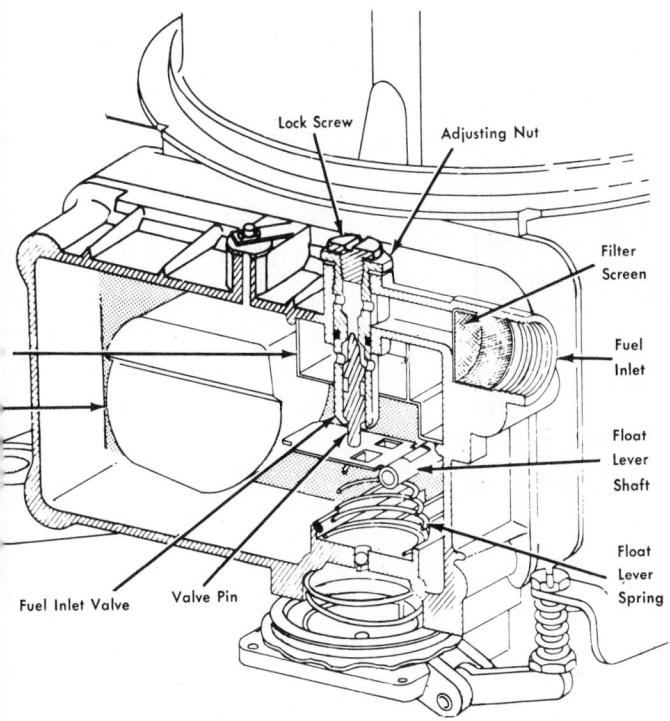

Fig. 21-44. Float lever spring helps steady action of float in maintaining a constant fuel level in float bowl.

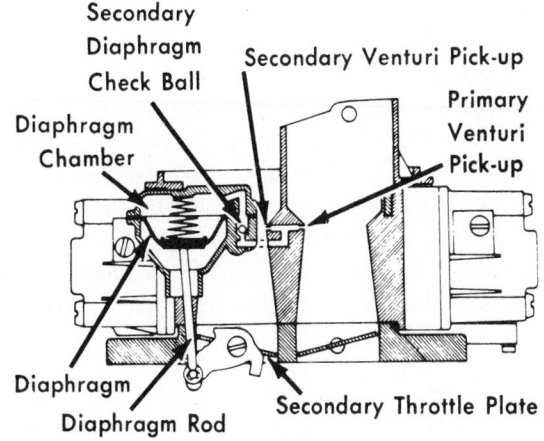

Fig. 21-45. Showing connections for operation of secondary throttle plate in a Holley carburetor.

Under this condition, abnormally high vacuum builds up above the throttle valve, resulting in too much fuel being drawn into the engine through the idle system.

The degasser consists of two die-cast housings clamped together with a diaphragm sandwiched between them. The diaphragm is attached to a plunger which actuates a walking beam, the end of which bears against a needle valve. Normally the valve is held off its seat by the spring. The upper diaphragm chamber is connected, by a bypass line, to an opening into the intake manifold above the throttle.

With the throttle in the idle position and the engine turning

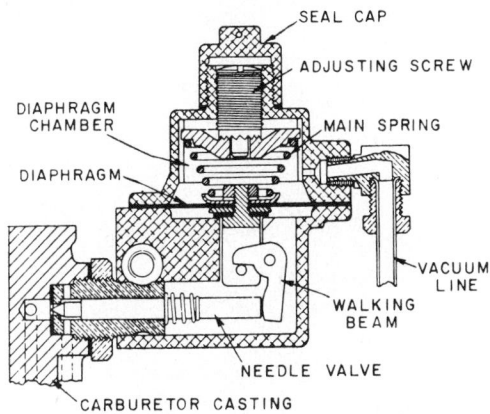

Fig. 21-46. Details of Bendix degasser.

over at idle speed, the proper amount of fuel is drawn through the idle jet. During periods of deceleration, the engine rpm will be much higher than normal idle rpm, causing the vacuum in the passages above the throttle plate to rise much higher than at normal idle speeds.

With the degasser in operation, the abnormally high vacuum during deceleration is transferred to the chamber above the diaphragm, raising the plunger and compressing the diaphragm spring. This movement actuates the walking beam to force the needle valve against its seat to shut off the flow of fuel through the idle hole.

As engine speed approaches idle, and intake manifold vacuum decreases to normal, the diaphragm is forced down by the spring. This backs off the walking beam, which unseats the needle valve and restores the flow of fuel to the idle hole.

DECEL VALVE

Some recent model cars, such as the Ford Pinto, are equipped with a decel valve which is designed to meter to the engine an additional amount of fuel and air during engine deceleration. This additional amount of fuel and air together with engine modification, permits more complete combustion with resultant lower levels of exhaust emissions.

During periods of engine deceleration, manifold vacuum forces the diaphragm assembly against the spring, Fig. 21-47, which, in turn, raises the decel valve. With the valve open, existing manifold vacuum pulls a metered amount of air and fuel from the carburetor through the valve body assembly into the intake manifold. The decel valve remains open and continues to feed additional air and fuel for a specified time.

THROTTLE SOLENOID

The Motorcraft-Weber model 5200 carburetor installed on the Ford Pinto 2000 cc engine is equipped with a throttle solenoid adjustment designed to control idling speed on automatic transmission-equipped cars. The curb idle is adjusted by turning the throttle solenoid plunger. First, disconnect the throttle solenoid wire, then, set the lower curb idle speed screw. Connect the throttle solenoid wire, open the throttle

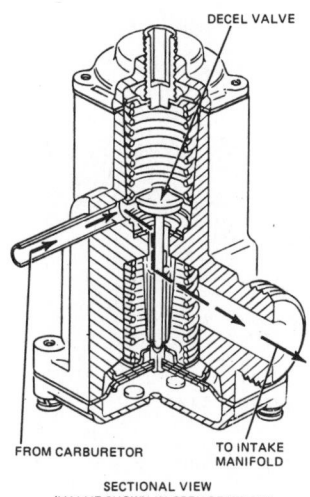

Fig. 21-47. Sectional view of decel valve showing valve in open position.

Fig. 21-48. Throttle solenoid adjustment on Motorcraft-Weber model 5200 carburetor.

slightly by hand to allow the plunger to extend, then, set the higher curb idle speed by turning the solenoid plunger, Fig. 21-48.

SMALL ENGINE CARBURETORS

Many of the basic principles found in large carburetors are also incorporated in carburetors used on small engines. This is particularly true in the case of engines used on many lawn mowers, Fig. 21-49. Carburetors using the float system of controlling fuel flow are good examples of this similarity.

Two cycle engines designed to operate at varying angles (chain saws) are often equipped with a floatless carburetor. On these installations, a diaphragm type carburetor is used

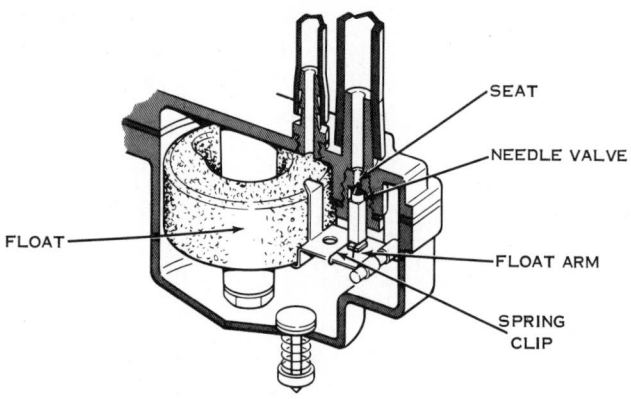

Fig. 21-49. Some small engines use float type carburetors. Note similarity of float bowl parts to large automotive carburetor parts.

because it will function at a steep angle or even in an inverted position for a short time.

Diaphragm type carburetors use the upper part of the unit for carburetion, while the lower part houses a fuel pump. The two parts are bolted together to form a single assembly.

The pump utilizes the positive and negative pressure pulsations in the crankcase for its operation. Fuel is delivered to the inlet supply channel either by the integral fuel tank or by gravity.

When the engine is idling at nearly closed throttle, fuel is drawn through an idle tube or, for inverted operation, past the idle adjusting screw and into the engine via the primary idle discharge port.

As the throttle is opened progressively, the vacuum at idle position is nearly eliminated, but the increase in air velocity through the venturi puts increased vacuum on the nozzle to unseat a nylon ball. The nozzle then delivers the power mixture metered in relation to the demands of the engine.

In the case of the suction feed carburetor fuel system, the fuel tank is mounted below the carburetor, Fig. 21-50.

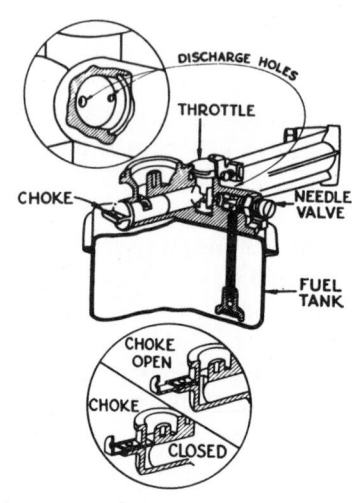

Fig. 21-50. Sectional view of suction feed carburetor used on lawn mowers and similar small engines.

Atmospheric pressure is utilized as the force to move the fuel. The fuel tank cap is vented to allow pressure in the tank to remain constant. As the piston goes down on the intake stroke with the throttle open, a low pressure is created in the carburetor throat. A slight restriction is placed between the air horn and the carburetor throat and the choke. This helps maintain the low pressure.

Therefore, the difference in pressure in the tank and in the carburetor throat forces the fuel up the fuel pipe, past the needle valve, through the two discharge holes. The throttle is relatively thick on this type of carburetor, so there is in effect a venturi at this point to aid vaporization. A spiral is placed in the throat to help acceleration and also to help keep the engine from dying when the throttle is opened suddenly.

The amount of fuel flowing at operating speed is metered by the needle valve and seat. Because of its compact design, the suction feed carburetor fuel system is used primarily on lawn mower engines.

REVIEW QUESTIONS — PRINCIPLES OF CARBURETION

1. What is the purpose of the fuel system in an internal combustion engine?
2. List the main parts of a fuel system.
3. The rate of flow through a carburetor is the same under all operating conditions. True or False?
4. When starting an internal combustion engine, the fuel mixture should be:
   a. Rich.
   b. Lean.
   c. Average.
5. Which speed requires a richer mixture?
   a. Idling.
   b. 30 mph.
6. Will all cylinders of a multi-cylinder engine receive an air-fuel mixture having the same octane rating?
7. For normal operating conditions, what air-fuel ratio will give the best economy?
   a. 16 to 1.
   b. 20 to 1.
   c. 25 to 1.
8. For quick acceleration, what is the best air-fuel ratio?
   a. 5 to 1.
   b. 10 to 1.
   c. 12 to 1.
   d. 20 to 1.
9. Are the molecules forming a gas held more tightly together than those of a metal?
10. Name two factors affecting the rapidity of evaporation.
11. What causes the air-fuel mixture to be drawn into the combustion chamber of an internal combustion engine?
12. The purpose of a venturi in a carburetor is to:
    a. Increase speed of air passing through carburetor.
    b. Maintain correct air-fuel ratio.
    c. Provide extra fuel for acceleration.
13. There are five main circuits in a modern carburetor. Name four of them.
14. In a carburetor venturi, which point has the highest vacuum?
    a. Entrance to the venturi.
    b. Narrowest point of the venturi.
    c. Point one inch beyond the venturi.
15. The idle system of a carburetor supplies fuel at what speeds?
    a. Idle speed only.
    b. Speeds up to 40 mph.
    c. Speeds up to 25 mph.
16. How many fuel discharge ports does the conventional idle system have?
    a. One.
    b. Two.
    c. Three.
    d. Four.
17. When the idle system is no longer supplying fuel to the engine, which system then supplies fuel?
    a. Air bleed system.
    b. Main system.
    c. Vaporizing system.
18. The purpose of an economizer valve is to supply more fuel, or less fuel?
19. The metering rod is designed to vary the size of which jets?
    a. Idle jets.
    b. Accelerating jets.
    c. High speed jets.
    d. Float level jets.
20. Under what conditions is ice most likely to form in a carburetor?
    a. 20 deg. below zero and high humidity.
    b. 32 deg. above zero and high humidity
    c. Zero deg. and low humidity.
21. On what type of car are you most likely to find an anti-stall dashpot?
    a. Cars with automatic transmission.
    b. Cars with conventional transmission.
    c. Cars fitted with 1 Bbl. carburetors.
    d. Cars fitted with 4 Bbl. carburetors.
22. In addition to updraft and downdraft carburetors, what other basic type is there?
23. The calibrated cluster in the Rochester 2GV carburetor cannot be removed from the carburetor. True or False?

However, on some engines, the intake manifold is built into the cylinder block where it is wholly or partly surrounded by water in the cooling system. In this way, the temperature of the manifold throughout its length is maintained at substantially the same temperature, regardless of weather. Carburetion and distribution are improved and essentially, the same economy is obtained regardless of air temperatures.

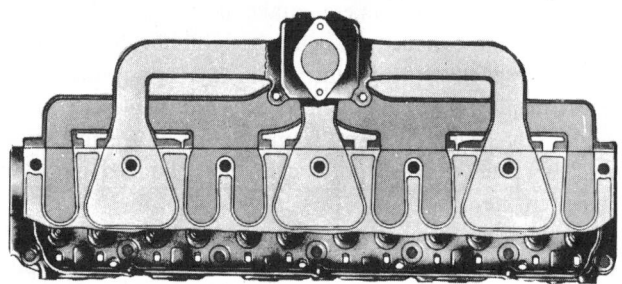

Fig. 23-9. Relative position of intake and exhaust manifolds permits hot exhaust gases to heat incoming air-fuel mixture.

A radical departure from conventional manifold design is shown in Fig. 23-10. In this design, the arms of the manifold make long sweeping curves from the carburetor to the cylinder block. The purpose of the design is to provide more equal

Fig. 23-10. Note unusual manifolds on this Plymouth engine.

distribution of fuel to the individual cylinders, and reduce the variation in octane rating and air fuel ratio of the fuel reaching the various cylinders.

With the coming of emission controls, the intake manifold took on added importance. First, the positive crankcase ventilation system was connected to it, metering crankcase fumes and vapors into the incoming air-fuel mixture for re-burning in the combustion chambers. Then, various emission control devices were developed that rely on intake manifold vacuum. These include vacuum-controlled spark timing devices, vacuum-operated motors for heated air cleaners and intake manifold-based exhaust gas recirculation systems. See chapter on EMISSION CONTROL for details.

MANIFOLD HEAT CONTROL

The purpose of a carburetor is to deliver a metered amount of atomized fuel mixed with air, to the manifold. However, regardless of how well mixed and vaporized the fuel mixture is as it leaves the carburetor, its characteristics are changed as it passes through the manifold. Cold surfaces in the manifold will cause some of the vaporized fuel to condense, and changes in direction of flow will, through inertia, cause some portions of the mixture to settle out. These conditions have been observed by using glass manifolds.

The problem is further complicated by the characteristics of the fuel itself. Formerly, when the fuel was highly volatile, the problem was not so difficult. With today's fuels, which are relatively nonvolatile, it is necessary to supply heat to obtain better vaporization and more equal distribution of the fuel to each cylinder.

Heat to the intake manifold is most needed when the manifold is cold, and also when the engine is idling. When idling, suction on the carburetor is low, and the fuel is not sprayed very finely. It is important that a minimum of heat reach the carburetor as excess heat would tend to vaporize the fuel before it reaches the carburetor jets, causing flooding.

In order to supply heat to, and also regulate, the amount of heat reaching the intake manifold, a thermostatic manifold heat control valve is installed. Details are shown in Figs. 23-11 and 23-12.

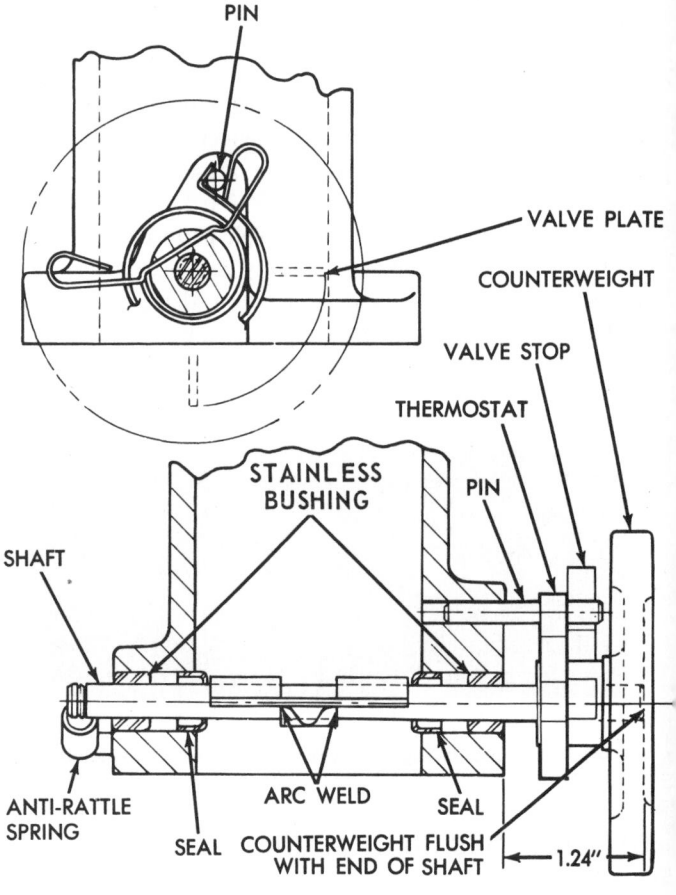

Fig. 23-11. Details of manifold heat control valve. Note stainless steel bushings and counterweight.

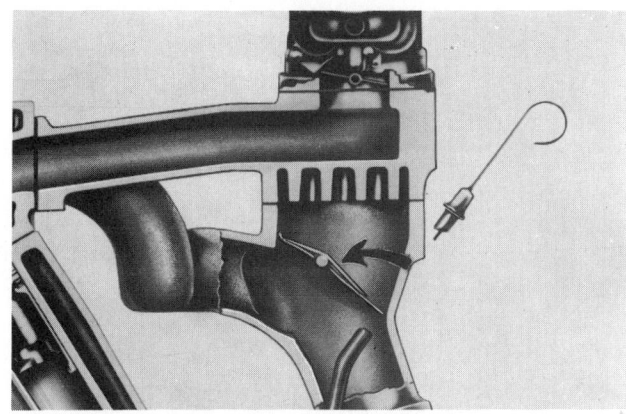

Fig. 23-12. Manifold heat control valve is indicated by arrow. Valve is shown in position it assumes when engine is hot.

The manifold heat control valve is built into the exhaust manifold, Fig. 23-13, or sandwiched between the manifold and exhaust pipe. When the engine is cold, a maximum amount of heat is directed against an area of the intake manifold. As the engine reaches operating temperature, the thermostat changes the position of the valve. When the valve opens, exhaust gases flow directly into the exhaust pipe.

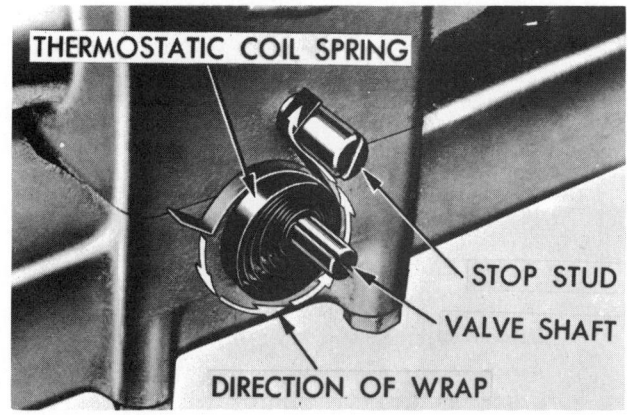

Fig. 23-13. Typical thermostatic spring used to control position of manifold heat control valve.

Fig. 23-12, shows the location of a manifold heat control valve on an in-line six cylinder engine. In this case, the valve is in the position it assumes when the engine has reached operating temperature. Then, exhaust gases are not directed to the intake manifold, but into the exhaust pipe. With a cold engine, the valve will have rotated in a clockwise direction, directing the gases against the lower surface of the intake manifold. This surface is finned to increase the area exposed to hot gases.

A typical thermostatic coil spring used on a manifold heat control valve is shown in Fig. 23-13. The thermostat is mounted on the outside of the exhaust pipe or manifold, and

it is provided with a counterbalance weight, Fig. 23-11. Often, the valve shaft is mounted on stainless steel bushings. This is important because of the high temperatures and acids of the exhaust, there is a strong tendency for these valves to become rusted in position.

In order to supply heat to the intake manifold of a V-8 engine, an exhaust crossover passage is provided. It carries exhaust gases from one side of the intake manifold to the other. See Fig. 23-14. The heat control valve, located in one of

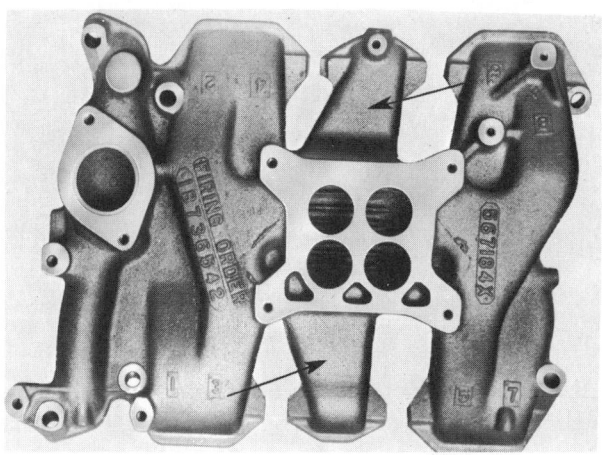

Fig. 23-14. Arrows point to exhaust crossover passage of this V-8 in-take manifold.

the exhaust manifolds, directs the exhaust gases through this crossover passage during the warm-up period.

It is particularly important that the manifold heat control valve be kept free and not rusted in position. If it becomes "frozen," so that no heat is directed to the intake manifold, fuel will not be properly vaporized and fuel economy will drop. If the manifold heat control valve is "frozen" so that heat is directed to the intake manifold at all times, too rapid vaporization will result, and maximum power will not be developed.

To insure free operation of the manifold heat control valve, special oils, usually containing graphite, should be applied to the ends of the valve shaft and bushings at regular intervals. To free a stuck valve, penetrating oil should be applied when the manifold is cold. After allowing the oil to penetrate, tap the valve shaft back and forth with a light hammer.

Air entering the carburetor on recent model engines is heated either electrically or by heat from the exhaust manifold. This greatly improves combustion and reduces the amount of objectionable exhaust gases. For more information on hot and cold air intake, see the chapters on AIR CLEANERS and EMISSION CONTROL.

EXHAUST MANIFOLDS

As indicated, exhaust manifolds take many forms. Recent design trends lean strongly toward increased internal dimensions to reduce resistance to the flow of exhaust gases.

Fig. 23-15. Details of Pontiac 2.5 litre, four cylinder engine.

Fig. 23-16. Turbocharged Buick V-6. Note manifolding.

By reducing back pressure, engine performance is improved. Note the manifolding on the Pontiac 2.5 litre, four cylinder engine in Fig. 23-15, and in the turbocharged Buick V-6 in Fig. 23-16.

Exhaust manifolds have been modified and supplemented over the years to aid in exhaust emission control. Primarily, they have been shrouded, or furnished with a "heat stove," to trap heat otherwise being dissipated. The heated air is routed to the air cleaner, where it serves to preheat carburetor intake air.

Another exhaust manifold application in the area of emission controls is the increasingly popular air injection system. An "air injection engine" has specially designed exhaust manifolds that incorporate air passages to each exhaust port. Through these ports, the system adds a controlled amount of pressurized air to the exhaust gases, causing oxidation of the gases for a considerable reduction of carbon monoxide and hydrocarbons in the exhaust emissions.

Also related to emission control are thermal reactors. These units, in effect, replace the exhaust manifolds on an engine. Thermal reactors, by design, will withstand extreme heat. By using the reactors in place of exhaust manifolds, most of the noxious carbon monoxide and hydrocarbons are reduced to harmless carbon dioxide and water.

REVIEW QUESTIONS — ENGINE MANIFOLDS

1. What is the purpose of the intake manifold?
2. Why is heat applied to the intake manifold?
3. Where is the intake manifold on a V-type engine located?
   a. Between the two banks of cylinders.
   b. On each side of the engine, on the outside.
   c. On the front of the cylinder block.
4. On an in-line engine, where is heat usually applied to the intake manifold?
   a. At the center.
   b. At the rear.
   c. At the front.
5. What causes unequal distribution of fuel?
6. All cylinders receive fuel of the same octane rating. Yes or No?
7. Which cylinders of a V-8 engine do the barrels of a 2 Bbl. carburetor supply?
   a. Both barrels supply all cylinders.
   b. Left barrel supplies cylinders on left side of engine, and right barrel supplies cylinders on right.
   c. Right barrel will supply center cylinders on right bank of cylinders and end cylinders on left bank. Left barrel will supply center cylinders of left bank of cylinders and end cylinders on right bank.
8. The manifold heat control valve is designed for what purpose?
9. Why are carburetors of more than one barrel used on some multi-cylinder engines?
10. The intake manifold serves as part of the positive crankcase ventilation system. True or False?
11. The intake manifold is incorporated in which of the following emission control systems?
    a. Exhaust gas recirculation.
    b. Air injection.
    c. Thermal reactor.
12. Which emission control system replaces the exhaust manifolds?
    a. Exhaust gas recirculation.
    b. Air injection.
    c. Thermal reactor.
    d. Catalytic converter.

AIR CLEANERS

Air drawn into a carburetor and mixed with fuel must be as clean as possible. If dust or other foreign matter enters the intake system of the engine, it acts as an abrasive that wears machined parts to a rough or undersized finish. Under extreme conditions, it results in the need for a complete engine reconditioning job.

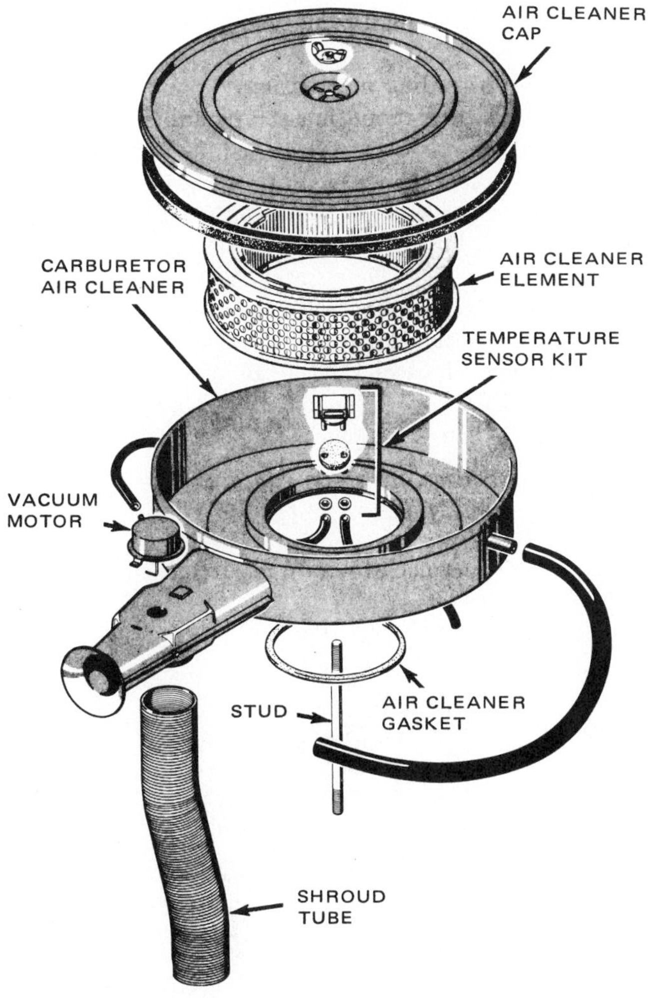

Fig. 24-1. Paper element, dry type air cleaner is used to filter intake air to carburetor in most modern engines.
(American Motors Corp.)

To reduce the amount of dust entering the carburetor, an air cleaner is installed at the air intake (air horn) of the carburetor. The air cleaner houses an element that filters all incoming air. It also acts as a silencer to reduce the noise of air rushing into the carburetor.

There are several types of air cleaners in use. These include:
1. Oil wetted mesh cleaner.
2. Oil bath cleaner.
3. Polyurethane cleaner.
4. Paper element cleaner.

Today, U.S. passenger car engines are fitted almost exclusively with air cleaners having the paper element filter, Fig. 24-1. The typically accordian-pleated, treated paper element was found to be considerably more efficient than any other type, and it is compatible with emission control devices.

OIL WETTED MESH CLEANER

From the automotive standpoint, the oil wetted mesh air cleaner is one of the older type cleaners. It does, however, have some current application in the small gas engine field, and in some tractors and stationary engines.

In the oil wetted mesh design, air passes through a copper mesh filter ring, which has been "wetted" with engine oil to help trap airborne particles. This type of air filter has the disadvantage of lack of efficiency in removing extremely fine dust particles from the airstream.

The oil wetted mesh element must be washed in kerosene or other solvent, squeezed dry, then dipped in engine oil. After excess oil has drained off, the element is reinstalled in the two-part air cleaner housing.

The oil wetted mesh air cleaner must be serviced at frequent intervals depending on dust conditions in the area of operation. In garden tractor applications, for example, the manufacturer recommends air cleaner service after every use.

OIL BATH CLEANER

The oil bath type air cleaner also utilizes a copper mesh element, but it is built into the upper housing of the air cleaner. The lower housing contains the "oil bath," which is an oil sump maintained at a specific level.

When the engine is in operation, incoming air enters through a snorkel or at the full-circumference opening between the housings. The airstream is immediately deflected downward across the surface of the oil sump, causing dust particles to be retained in the oil. The air then passes through the oil wetted copper mesh element and into the carburetor.

The usual recommendation for servicing the oil bath air cleaner is to clean it every 5000 miles. However, time and dust conditions put this particular service on an individual car basis.

The copper mesh portion of the unit is cleaned in the same manner as the oil wetted mesh cleaner previously described. However, since it cannot be removed from the housing, a "soak-and-swish" cleaning technique is recommended.

The oil bath portion of the cleaner is serviced by emptying the oil and scraping the dirt from the bottom of the reservoir. Then, the entire housing is washed in solvent, and the reservoir is refilled with SAE 40 engine oil.

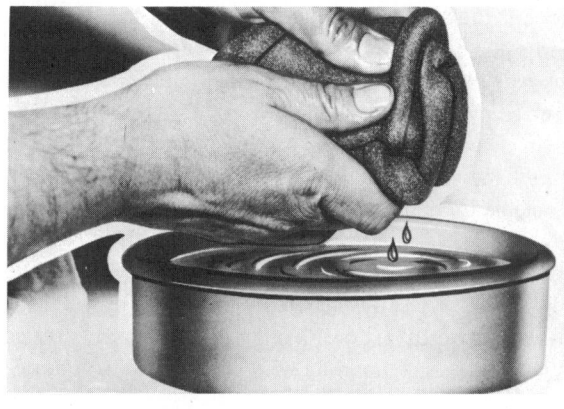

Fig. 24-2. Wash polyurethane filter in kerosene and squeeze dry. Do not "wring" dry; that would damage polyurethane.

POLYURETHANE CLEANER

Air cleaners with a polyurethane filtering element, Fig. 24-2, were introduced in the early 1960s. Today, some small displacement passenger car engines still use this very efficient and serviceable unit.

Generally, the polyurethane element is supported by a perforated metal ring. When a ring is used, the element is flanged top and bottom to provide a seal between the ring and the air cleaner housings.

When servicing the polyurethane element:
1. Take care to avoid damage when removing element from metal ring.
2. Wash element in kerosene or mineral spirits. Hot degreasers should not be used.
3. Squeeze out excess solvent, Fig. 24-2. Element is soft and will tear if abused. Manufacturers say, "Never shake, swing or wring element to remove excess solvent or oil."
4. Dip element in engine oil and allow it to drain.
5. Wash two-part air cleaner housing in solvent.
6. Squeeze element, then install it around one side, top and bottom of metal ring.
7. Reinstall filter/ring assembly in air cleaner housing.

PAPER ELEMENT CLEANER

The paper element, or dry type, air cleaner is most efficient and, in most servicing situations, simple replacement of the element is required. The element consists of special paper formed into an accordian pleated ring and sealed top and bottom by plastic rings, Fig. 24-3.

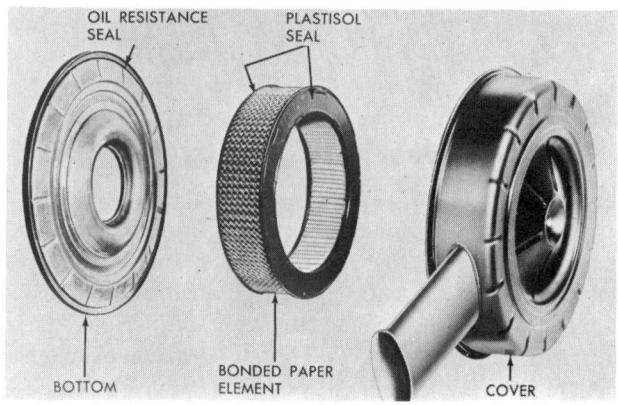

Fig. 24-3. Paper element, dry type air cleaner features plastic sealing surfaces.

The element can be cleaned, if necessary, by removing it from the housing and tapping it against some hard, flat surface to shake off accumulated dirt. Or, Chrysler recommends removing the element and gently blowing out accumulated dirt with an air hose. Direct the air from inside out and keep the nozzle 2 in. away from the element. Paper elements should never be immersed in solvent. Special equipment is available for testing the element, before and after cleaning, Fig. 24-4.

Another type of paper element air cleaner, known as a heavy-duty, dual-stage cleaner, consists of a replaceable oil wetted paper inner filter surrounded by a glycol wetted

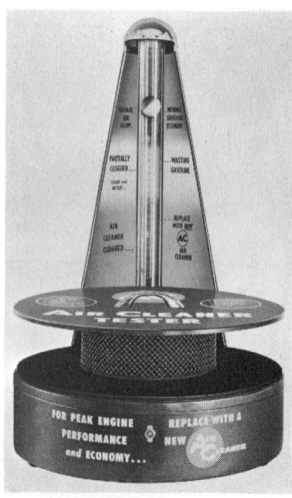

Fig. 24-4. One form of tester for checking condition of dry type air cleaner. Air is forced through cleaner, and amount of restriction is indicated by height of ball in tube.

polyurethane foam outer filter. Wash the polyurethane element in solvent and reoil it with SAE 30 engine oil.

A special type of paper element used on some high performance engines is shown in Fig. 24-5. Note that a single air cleaner is provided for three carburetors. Although it offers some resistance to the free flow of air, it is preferred to the "open stack" because it provides some protection against dust entering the engine through the carburetor.

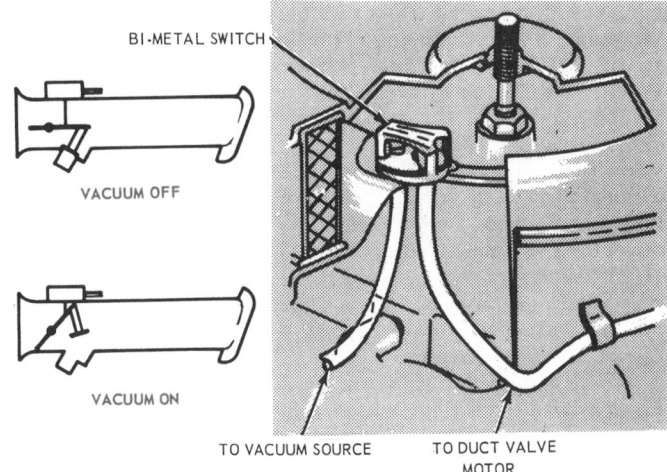

Fig. 24-6. Details of vacuum-operated duct and valve assembly installed in air cleaner of some late model Ford cars.

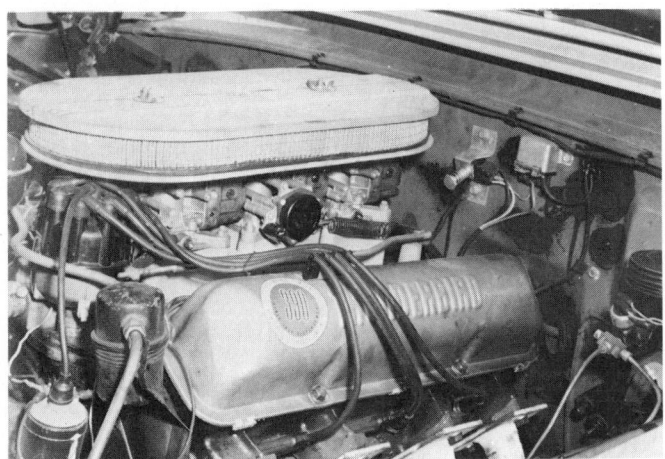

Fig. 24-5. A single paper element air cleaner for three carburetors on high performance engines.

HOT AND COLD AIR INTAKE

Most late model carburetors are equipped with a thermostatically controlled air inlet temperature device. Air from the engine compartment, or heated air from a shroud around the exhaust manifold, is routed to the air cleaner.

The temperature of the air entering the air cleaner is thermostatically controlled by the carburetor air duct assembly. A thermostatic bulb in the duct is exposed to incoming air, and a spring-loaded valve is connected to the bulb through linkage. The valve plate spring holds the valve in the closed ("heat on") position until reaction of the thermostatic bulb overcomes valve tension.

During the engine warmup period, when air entering the air duct is less than 75 deg. F, the thermostat is in the retracted position and the valve plate is held in the "heat on" position, shutting off the air from the engine compartment.

As the air temperature passing the thermostatic bulb approaches 85 deg. F, the thermostat starts to pull the valve down and allows cooler air from the engine compartment to enter the air cleaner. When air temperature reaches 105 deg. F, the valve will be in the "heat off" position so that only engine compartment air will enter the air cleaner.

VACUUM-OPERATED DUCT AND VALVE ASSEMBLY

A vacuum-operated duct and valve assembly, Fig. 24-6, currently is used on all Ford cars except Pinto. The duct valve should be open when the engine is not operating. When the

engine is started, the valve should close while the engine is idling unless the engine has reached operating temperature.

If the engine is cold and the duct valve does not close during idle, check for disconnected or leaking vacuum lines to the vacuum motor and bimetal switch.

Check the bimetal switch to see that the bleed valve is seated. Open and close the throttle rapidly. The bleed valve should open when the throttle valve opens. If the valve does not function properly, check for a binding condition.

The bimetal switch can be checked for operation by subjecting the switch to heated air or by removing and immersing the switch in water heated to 80 deg. F. Only slight movement of the bimetal will unseat the bleed valve.

TEMPERATURE-OPERATED DUCT AND VALVE ASSEMBLY

The hot and cold air intake system used on many Ford cars forms part of the carburetor air cleaner, Fig. 24-7. It is an essential part of the exhaust emission control system.

A thermostatic vacuum-controlled unit is attached to the air cleaner. In operation, it controls the temperature of air entering the air cleaner for improved combustion. The assembly takes the air from the engine compartment, or heated air from a shroud around the exhaust manifold. This tempered air is then passed through the air cleaner and into the carburetor.

A thermostat, Fig. 24-7, in the air duct is exposed to the heated air, and the action of the thermostat controls the position of the valve so that the hot and cold air are blended to maintain a temperature of approximately 100 deg. F. The valve should be in the "heat on" position when the temperature is 100 deg. F or less and in the "heat off" position, Fig. 24-7, when the temperature exceeds 135 deg. F.

Vacuum at the vacuum motor should be 15 in. To check the vacuum motor, remove it from the assembly and connect it to a vacuum source of 15 in. The motor should move the motor rod one-half inch. If not, the motor should be replaced.

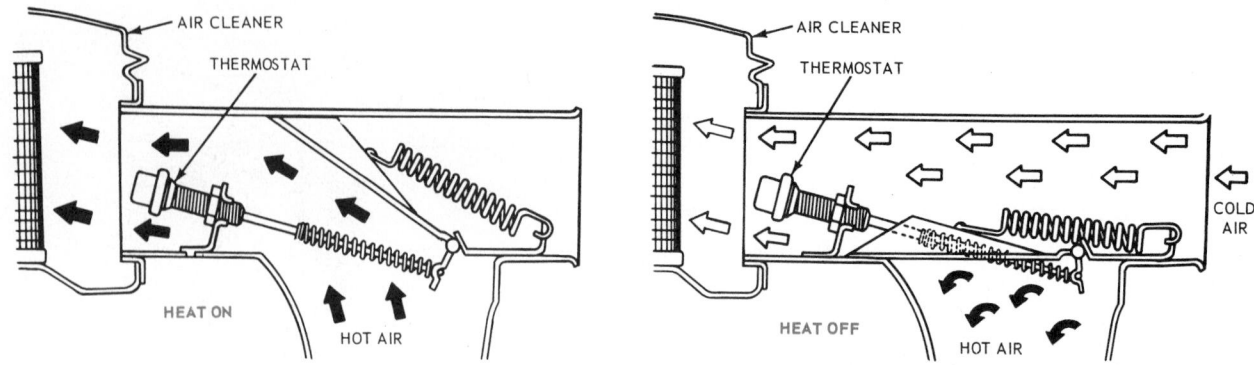

Fig. 24-7. Ford's temperature-operated duct and valve assembly is shown in "heat on" and "heat off" positions.

When the engine is cold and the ambient temperature in the engine compartment is less than 100 deg. F, the duct valve should be in the "heat on" position. If not, check for interference of valve and duct. The operation of the duct assembly can be checked by immersing the thermostat in water of specified temperature.

CHEVROLET AIR CLEANER SYSTEM

The thermostatically controlled air cleaner system installed on Chevrolet cars and other General Motors vehicles is designed to improve carburetion and engine warmup characteristics. This is done by keeping the air entering the carburetor at a temperature of at least 100 deg. F.

The thermostatic air cleaner assembly, Fig. 24-8, includes: a temperature sensor, vacuum motor, vacuum control hoses, manifold heat stove and connecting pipes. The vacuum motor is controlled by the temperature sensor.

The vacuum motor operates the air control damper assembly to regulate the flow of hot air and/or underhood air to the carburetor. The hot air is obtained from the heat stove on the exhaust manifold.

Visual inspection is made by checking for secure connections at heat pipe and hose connections; also for kinked or deteriorated hoses.

An operational inspection is made as follows:

1. Remove air cleaner cover and install a thermometer close to sensor. If engine is warm, allow it to cool to below 85 deg. F.
2. Replace air cleaner cover without wing nut.
3. Start and idle engine.

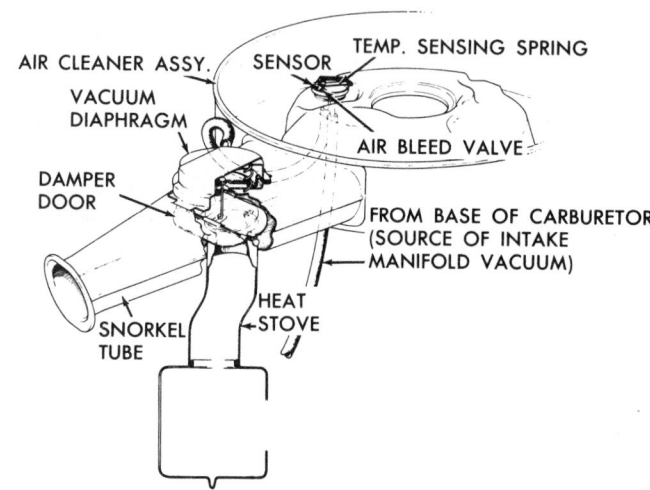

Fig. 24-8. Thermostatically controlled air cleaner system is used on Chevrolet and other GM engines.

4. When control damper assembly starts to open, remove air cleaner cover and observe temperature.
5. Damper should open at 85 to 115 deg. F. If not, check vacuum motor and sensor.

With engine off, check the position of the control damper assembly. It should be in cold air delivery position. To determine if the vacuum motor is operable, apply at least 9 in. of vacuum to the fitting on the vacuum motor. The control damper should close the cold air passage as long as vacuum is applied. Also check the vacuum motor linkage.

REVIEW QUESTIONS — AIR CLEANERS

1. Name four types of air cleaners.
2. Where is the air cleaner installed?
   a. Between the carburetor and the manifold.
   b. At the air intake of the carburetor.
   c. On the carburetor air bleed.
3. Which type of air cleaner is most efficient?
4. What precautions should be taken when cleaning a polyurethane type filter element?
5. Generally, how should a paper element air filter be cleaned?
   a. Washed in cleaning solvent.
   b. Cleaned by blowing out the dirt with compressed air.
   c. Tapping against some hard flat surface.
6. The duct valve in the vacuum-operated air cleaner system installed on some Ford cars should be open when the engine is not operating. True or False?
7. The damper on the thermostatically controlled air cleaner used on some Chevrolet cars should open when incoming air temperature reaches 85 to 115 deg. F. True or False?

CARBURETOR
ADJUSTMENT, SERVICE

Modern carburetors are accurately calibrated to work efficiently with the individual engines for which they are designed. For this reason, points of adjustment have been reduced to a minimum. Today, adjustments are provided for idle speed, fast idle and in most cases, "limited" adjustment of air-fuel mixture.

Formerly carburetors were provided with two and three adjustments so that the amount of fuel could be controlled throughout the complete range of engine speeds and conditions. Obviously, these carburetors required considerable time and skill to adjust, and only a fair degree of accuracy could be attained after prolonged road testing under all speeds and conditions.

PRELIMINARY ADJUSTMENTS

Before making carburetor adjustments, see that the ignition system is in good condition, and that compression pressure is approximately equal in all the cylinders. There must be no leaks in the intake manifold. The carburetor must be clean internally. It must be in good mechanical condition, and the float level must be correctly set. Finally, the engine must be at normal operating temperature.

Before attempting to adjust the air-fuel mixture, it is necessary to adjust engine idling speed. This is particularly necessary on a vehicle fitted with an automatic transmission, for if idling speed is too fast, the car will tend to "creep" when the engine is idling, and the transmission is in "drive."

To adjust the idling speed, first bring the engine up to operating temperature, then make sure the fast idle cam is not holding the throttle valve open. In addition, the choke valve must be wide open.

With manual shift cars in "neutral," and automatic transmission cars in "drive," adjust the idle speed adjustment screw, or throttle stop screw, Fig. 25-1, to obtain the desired speed. This will vary slightly with different engines. In general, the

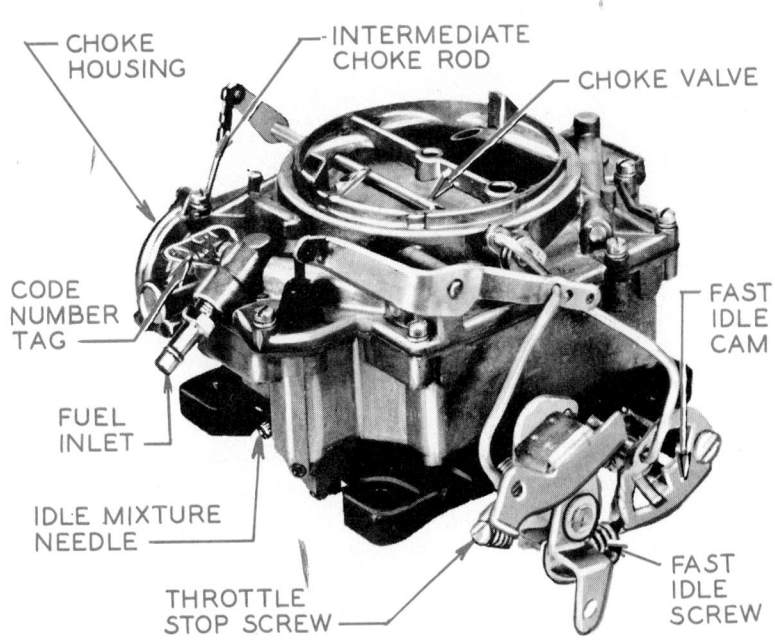

Fig. 25-1. Showing some of the points that require adjustment on a carburetor. Note particularly the throttle stop screw, fast idle cam and screw, choke rod and idle mixture needle.

idling speed for a late model car fitted with a manual transmission is specified at 600-650 rpm and automatic transmission at 700-750 rpm.

ONE-BARREL CARBURETORS

Today, virtually all carburetors have limited idle mixture adjustment, Fig. 25-2. On older 1 Bbl. carburetors, the adjustment is made by turning the adjusting screw to the position which gives maximum idling speed.

Obviously, the idle speed or throttle valve position must not be altered until after the idle mixture has been correctly set. The usual method of making the idle mixture adjustment on older carburetors is to first set it approximately one turn open. Then, with the engine running normal at operating temperature, gradually open the adjusting screw until the engine falters. Then, turn the screw in until the engine operates smoothly.

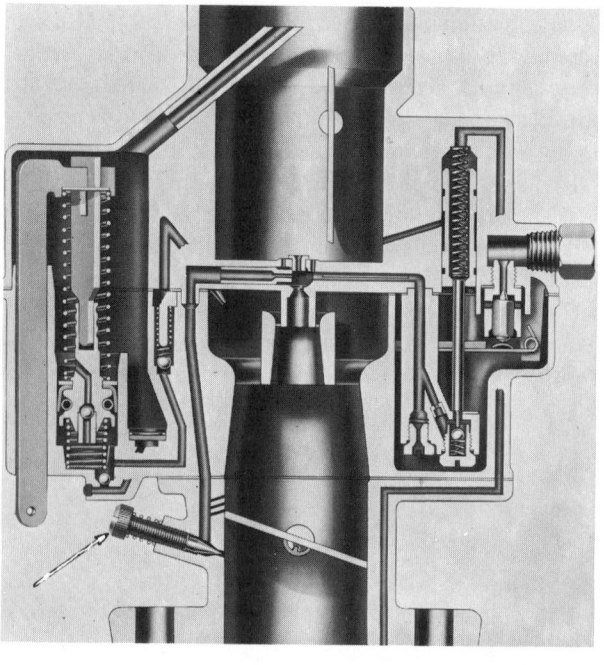

Fig. 25-2. Arrow points to idle mixture adjustment on this Rochester carburetor.

A more accurate method of carburetor adjustment is to attach a vacuum gauge, Fig. 25-3, to the intake manifold, then adjust the idle mixture screw to obtain the maximum steady reading on the vacuum gauge. A tachometer (to determine speed of engine) may also be used for this purpose.

Many factors, in addition to the condition of the engine, will affect the reading of the vacuum gauge. Compression ratio, carburetor and valve restrictions, and the speed at which the test is made, will all influence the reading. Vacuum readings for tune-up purposes are always made at idling speed.

In connection with engine vacuum readings, note that the vacuum decreases with an increase in altitude. Approximate

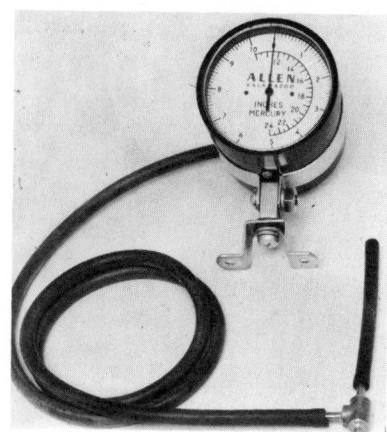

Fig. 25-3. Vacuum gauge with hose for connecting to intake manifold.

vacuum readings for engines of different numbers of cylinders are given in the following table:

Elevation in Feet	Number of Engine Cylinders		
	Four	Six	Eight
Zero to 1000	18 to 20	19 to 21	21 to 22
1000 to 2000	17 to 19	18 to 20	19 to 21
2000 to 3000	16 to 18	17 to 19	18 to 20
3000 to 4000	15 to 17	16 to 18	17 to 19
4000 to 5000	14 to 16	15 to 17	16 to 18
5000 to 6000	13 to 15	14 to 16	15 to 17

MULTI-BARREL CARBURETORS

Adjusting 2 Bbl. or 4 Bbl. carburetors is slightly more difficult, since these carburetors are provided with two idle mixture adjustments. On multi-barrel carburetors, it is advisable to use the vacuum gauge or tachometer when adjusting the carburetor. A more accurate adjustment can be obtained.

Before making the idle mixture adjustment on a 2 Bbl. or 4 Bbl. carburetor, Fig. 25-4, turn in both idle adjustments until they seat. Then back them out on equal amount, usually one turn. Then, after starting the engine and running it to operating temperature, turn out the two adjustments equal amounts until the maximum reading on the vacuum gauge is attained.

On most engines, the best adjustment will be secured when both idle mixture screws are turned out equal amounts. However, in some instances, slightly smoother idling will be secured by turning one adjustment a bit more than the other. Normally, there should never be more than one quarter turn difference between the position of the two adjustments.

The procedure for adjusting 4 Bbl. carburetors is given with the detailed description of individual makes. The procedure for 4 Bbl. units is similar since two idle mixture adjusting screws are provided on each.

The result of carburetor adjustment can be checked by an analysis of the exhaust gases by means of proper equipment.

OTHER ADJUSTMENTS

Other basic carburetor adjustments are in the area of throttle linkage, fast idle cam, automatic choke setting, choke

Fig. 25-4. Arrows indicate two idle mixture screws on this 4 Bbl. carburetor. Adjustments on a 2 Bbl. carburetor are similar.

unloader and accelerating pump. Some of these adjustments are made only in connection with a carburetor overhaul, and adjustments vary considerably in different applications.

In this connection, throttle linkage adjustment is relatively critical on cars equipped with automatic transmissions. Procedure and specifications vary with different makes and models. Unless all linkage (throttle accelerator pedal and transmission) is correctly adjusted, trouble may be experienced in the shift points of automatic transmissions.

The fast idle cam, Fig. 25-1, must be adjusted in correct relationship to the automatic choke. At start-up, the choke valve will be closed and the fast idle adjusting screw will be adjusted to provide specified rpm while bearing against the high step (or second step, in some cases) of the cam.

During engine warmup, the choke valve will be partially open and the adjusting screw will bear at approximately the halfway point on the cam. When the choke valve is wide open, the fast idle adjusting screw will be on the low step of the cam and not holding the throttle lever away from the slow idle adjusting screw.

Unloaders are adjusted by means of special gauges on some cars; on others, simple measurements are used.

A change has been made on some General Motors carburetors to limit the range of idle mixture adjustment on the rich side. Backing out the idle mixture screws will not provide an appreciable richer mixture. A new idle mixture adjustment procedure requiring artificial enrichment by the addition of propane is necessary for checking and resetting idle mixture on these carburetors.

Idle mixture screws have been preset at the factory and capped. Do not remove the caps during normal engine maintenance. Idle mixture should be adjusted only in case of major carburetor overhaul, throttle body replacement or high

idle CO as determined by state or local inspections. Adjusting the mixture by other than the following method may violate Federal and/or California or other state or Provincial laws:

1. Set parking brake and block drive wheels.
2. Disconnect and plug hoses as directed on emission control information label under hood.
3. Engine must be at normal operating temperature, choke open and air conditioning off.
4. Connect accurate tachometer to engine.
5. Disconnect vacuum advance and set timing to specification shown on emission label. Reconnect vacuum advance. On Oldsmobile Toronados equipped with electronic spark

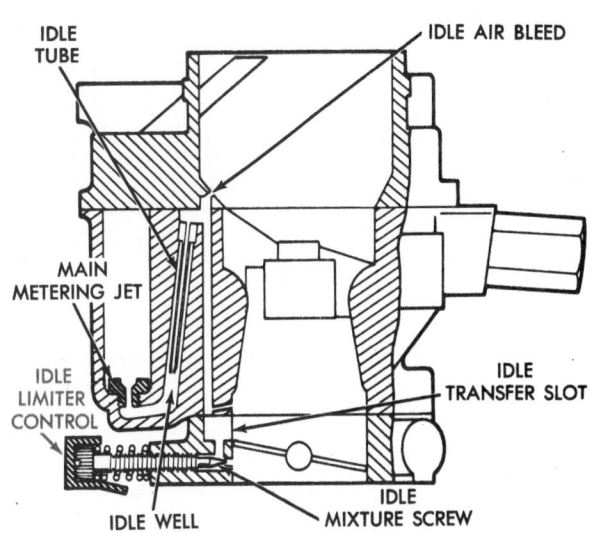

Fig. 25-5. Idle mixture screws on late model carburetors have limiter controls installed to prevent over-rich adjustment.

timing, check timing as directed on emission label.

6. Disconnect crankcase ventilation tube from air cleaner.

7. Insert hose with rubber stopper from propane enrichment device into crankcase ventilation tube opening in the air cleaner.

8. Propane cartridge must be in vertical position.

9. Slowly open propane control valve until maximum engine speed is reached with the transmission in drive. (Neutral for manual shift.) Note: Too much propane will cause engine speed to drop.

10. Observe propane flow meter to insure propane cartridge is adequately full.

11. With propane flowing, adjust idle speed screw (special tool will be required on some models). Adjust to specified enriched rpm (starting point for lean drop setting as given in specifications). Readjust propane flow to be certain of maximum engine speed. Adjust idle speed again, if necessary.

12. Turn off propane. Place transmission in PARK. Run engine at approximately 2,000 rpm for 30 second. Then, reduce to slow idle. Put transmission in Drive, or in Neutral for manual shift.

13. Check idle speed against rpm shown on emission control label. If it does, the idle mixture is correct. In this case, proceed to step 17.

14. If speed is too low, carefully remove caps from mixture screws and back out screws 1/8 turn at a time until speed

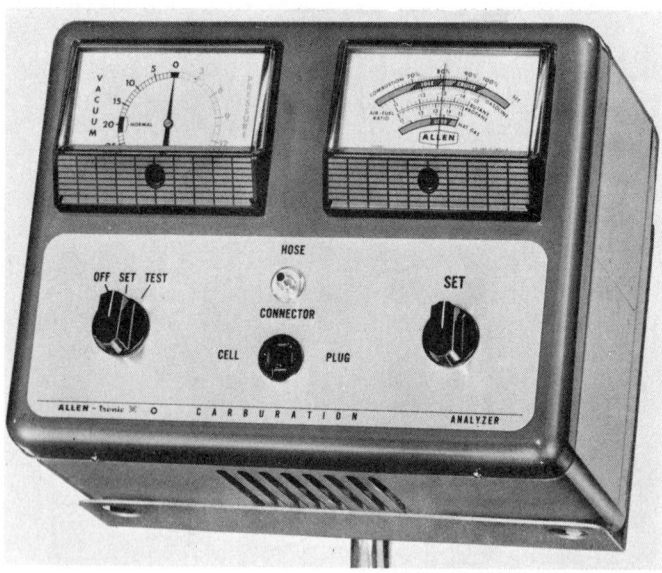

Fig. 25-6. Equipment used for analyzing exhaust gases. (Allen Test Products)

on emission label is reached. If speed is too high, carefully remove mixture screws and turn in screws equally 1/8 turn at a time until speed on emission label is reached.

15. Turn on propane to check maximum engine idle speed. If speed differs from specification (enriched rpm starting point for lean drop setting), readjust idle speed screw to

enrich rpm with propane flowing.

16. Turn off propane. Place transmission in PARK and run engine at approximately 2,000 rpm for 30 seconds. Reduce to slow idle. Then, put transmission in Drive, or in Neutral for manual shift. Check idle speed against idle speed shown on emission control label. If it does not agree, repeat the adjustment procedure given in step 14.

17. If rough idle persists, turn in mixture screws until lightly seated. Back them out equally to the average previous

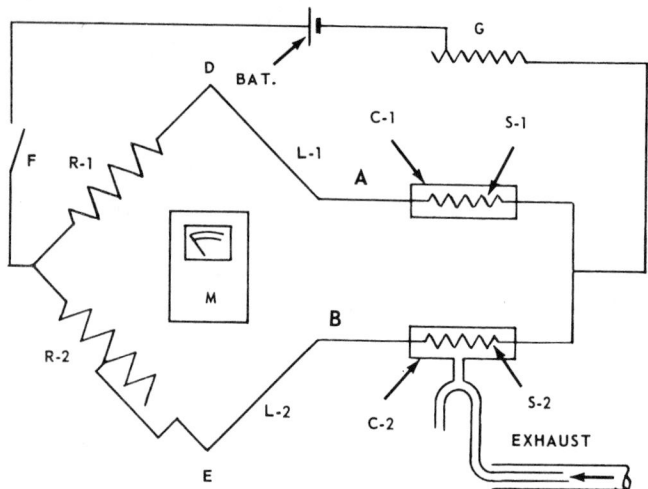

Fig. 25-7. Electrical circuit of exhaust gas analyzer.

position and rerun propane idle test starting with step 9.

18. Turn off engine and remove propane equipment. Reconnect crankcase ventilation hose to air cleaner.

EXHAUST EMISSION CONTROL IDLE ADJUSTMENTS

Accurate adjustment of idle mixture and idle speed is particularly important on engines equipped with exhaust emission control systems. The instructions vary with different engines and different manufacturers. However: the engine must be at normal operating temperature, with the choke open; with the air cleaner thermostatic valve open on engines so equipped; with the hot idle compensator closed on carburetors so equipped; and with the air cleaner installed. In the case of automatic transmission-equipped cars, the selector lever should be Drive position.

The importance of accurately adjusting idle mixture and speed is shown by the fact that all late model cars have detailed instructions covering idle adjustments on a decal affixed to the radiator shroud.

As mentioned, most carburetors on engines with exhaust emission control equipment are fitted with devices which limit the range through which the idle mixture can be adjusted, Fig. 25-5. Limiters must not be removed or otherwise made ineffective.

EXHAUST GAS ANALYZERS

In the chapter devoted to fuels and combustion, it was pointed out that for perfect combustion of one pound of fuel, 15.27 lb. of air is required. This is the theoretical relationship. However, to obtain maximum power in an internal combustion engine, a definite air-fuel ratio is required which is different from the ratio that will give maximum economy.

If an engine is being operated with a lean mixture, (excessive amount of air), obviously the power developed will increase if more fuel is supplied. This increase in power with an increase in fuel will continue until all of the oxygen in the air being supplied to the cylinder is consumed in the combustion of the fuel.

However, the fuel and air reaching the cylinders are imperfectly mixed. The mixture is diluted by exhaust gases that have remained in the cylinder, and fuel reaching the cylinder ranges from a vapor to wet particles. Therefore, it is necessary to supply more fuel than is called for theoretically perfect combustion. In general, maximum power is secured from air-fuel ratios of 14 to 1. The maximum economy ratio is approximately 16 1/2 to 1.

Measuring the quantities of air and fuel entering an engine is a complicated process. The same results can be obtained with relatively simple equipment that analyzes the exhaust gases. See Figs. 25-6 and 25-7.

VAPOR LOCK

Just as water turns to steam when it is heated, gasoline turns to vapor when sufficient heat is applied. Early vaporization of the fuel can cause complete or partial interruption of fuel flow. Since the vapor of motor fuel occupies a greater volume than in liquid form, the amount of fuel flow will be reduced. Loss in power and missing will occur and, under extreme conditions, the engine will stop. This condition may occur anywhere in the fuel line, the fuel pump, or in the carburetor itself.

Whether or not vapor is likely to form depends on vapor pressure, or ease with which the fuel will vaporize. The standardized method of measuring or determining vapor pressure in the laboratory is known as the Reid Method. U.S. Government specifications for motor gasoline require that the Reid vapor pressure at 100 deg. F should not exceed 12 psi.

Carburetors are now vented to a charcoal canister as part of the evaporative emission control system. This also aids in relieving the problem of vapor blocking the flow of liquid fuel.

In another design technique, the Thermo-Quad carburetor has a molded phenolic resin fuel bowl. It keeps the fuel about 20 deg. F cooler than in an all-metal fuel bowl.

Also in the area of insulation, some manufacturers place an asbestos gasket approximately 1/2 in. thick between the carburetor and manifold. This reduces the transmission of heat to the carburetor.

In addition, fuel pumps are placed where they will be cooled by air blasts and shielded from the heat of the exhaust manifold. Also to reduce the possibility of vapor lock, fuel lines are routed away from the exhaust pipe and muffler.

Low pressure on the fuel will also promote vaporization. A pusher type pump, located in the fuel tank, would avoid this problem with conventional, suction type fuel pumps.

In addition to design of carburetor, fuel pump and lines, vaporization is also controlled by gasoline refineries by changing the vapor pressure. During winter months, a fuel that is easily vaporized is supplied to facilitate starting. During summer months, when temperatures are high, a fuel that is not so easily vaporized is provided. However, during unseasonably warm weather in the spring, and before refiners have supplied their summer grade fuel, it is not unusual to encounter early vaporization difficulties.

CARBURETOR ICING

The formation of ice in carburetors is a problem which will occur under certain weather conditions. It is most likely to occur when the atmospheric temperature is between 28 and 55 deg. F, with the relative humidity between 65 and 100 percent. It usually occurs after the engine is started, and before it has reached operating temperature. As a result, the engine will stop or stall when operated at idling speed. Each time the engine stops, it can be restarted, but when the engine speed is reduced to idling it will stop again.

The ice is formed at the edge of the throttle valve, Fig. 25-8. When this occurs, it will restrict the flow of the air-fuel

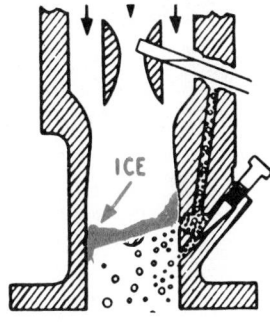

Fig. 25-8. Ice and frost will collect on throttle valve restricting flow of fuel from idling jets, when air temperature ranges from 28 to 55 deg. F, and relative humidity ranges from 65 to 100 percent.

mixture when the throttle valve is at or near the idle position, causing the engine to stop. The engine will start again, without difficulty, since it is necessary to open the throttle to permit the air-fuel mixture to flow to the engine.

The formation of ice results from rapid vaporization of the fuel. This may lower the temperature as much as 25 deg. F, which causes the moisture in the air to freeze, resulting in ice forming on the edge of the throttle valve, where the air speed is greatest.

As soon as the engine reaches operating temperature, the carburetor will be warm enough so that it will be impossible for ice to form.

Fuel refiners also use special additives that aid materially in overcoming rapid vaporization. A faster than normal idling speed is of help in minimizing the trouble, but adjustment of the carburetor fast idle linkage should be made with care.

Many carburetors are now provided with a passage that conducts exhaust heated air around the area of the idle mixture ports. In this way the possibility of carburetor icing is greatly reduced.

CARBURETOR SERVICING

Because of the great number of different makes and types of carburetors in use, space limitations will not permit complete descriptive coverage of service and repair techniques. However, there are certain basic points that should be observed when overhauling all carburetors.

First of all, manufacturers provide kits of repair parts and gaskets for overhauling their carburetors. See Fig. 25-9. Most

Fig. 25-10. Using a straightedge to check gasket surface of carburetor for warpage.

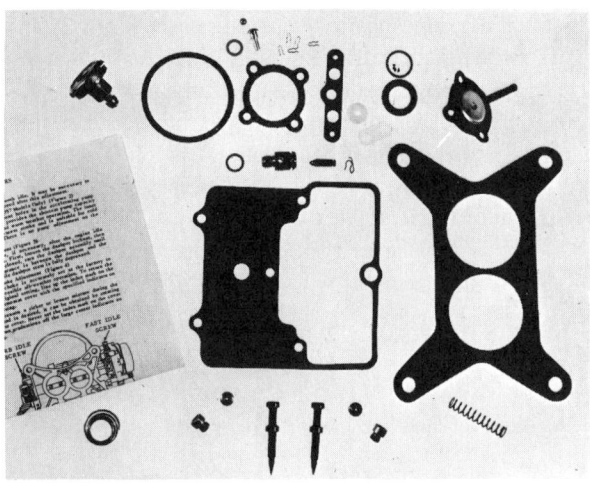

Fig. 25-9. Parts supplied in a typical carburetor repair kit. Note sheet from illustrated repair instruction folder on left.

of the manufacturers include illustrated instructions for replacing the parts.

When the carburetor is disassembled, all parts should be placed in a convenient tray so they can be washed in clean commercial carburetor cleaning fluid. Wash parts except the accelerator pump diaphragm or plunger, power valve diaphragm, and anti-stall dashpot assembly. Do not wash parts made of fabric or rubber, which would be injured by the cleaning solution.

After cleaning, wash away all traces of the cleaning solution with a stream of water. Then, blow the parts dry with compressed air. Force compressed air through all passages of the carburetor to be sure they are thoroughly clean. Do not use a wire brush. Do not run a fine wire through any jets. This may damage the ports.

Check the choke shaft for grooves, wear and excessive looseness or binding. Inspect the choke valve for nicked edges. Test the choke piston for ease of operation. Check for wear in the throttle shaft and its bearings. Replace worn parts.

Inspect all parts such as the air horn, main body, throttle body, choke housing, etc., for cracks and other defects. Check

all gasket surfaces for warpage, Fig. 25-10. This is particularly important on die castings.

Check the floats for leaks by holding them under water that has been heated to about 200 deg. F. Bubbles will appear if a leak is present.

Inspect all gasket surfaces for nicks. Replace any parts that have been damaged. Install all parts contained in the repair kit. Set the float level with the gauge provided, Fig. 25-11.

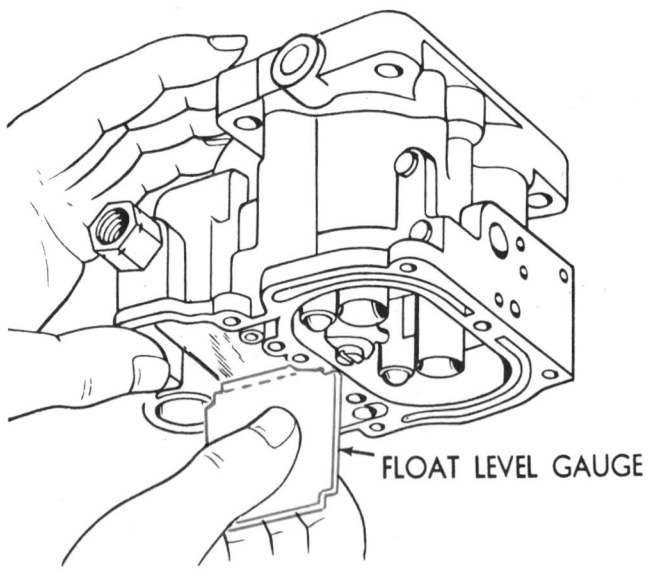

FLOAT LEVEL GAUGE

Fig. 25-11. Using a gauge to check float level setting.

TROUBLESHOOTING CARBURETORS/FUEL SYSTEMS

While defective or poorly adjusted carburetors will seriously affect the economy and performance of the vehicle, complete failure of the engine to operate seldom originates in the carburetor. Therefore, when the engine fails to start or operate efficiently, it is advisable to first check ignition, compression and supply of fuel to the carburetor before disassembling the carburetor.

If ignition and compression are good, the next step is to check choke operation. Make sure that when the engine is cold, the choke is closed. If the engine is hot, the choke should be open. To make these checks remove the air cleaner and observe the position of the choke valve.

If the operation of the choke and choke linkage proves to be satisfactory check to make sure that fuel is reaching the carburetor. To check, operate the carburetor linkage by hand. The fuel should spurt from the accelerator pump jets, which can be noted by looking into the carburetor air intake.

If no fuel is observed squirting from the accelerator pump jets, there is no fuel in the carburetor float bowl. This indicates that the fuel pump is inoperative or the fuel filter is clogged. To check this condition, disconnect the fuel line at the carburetor and direct the line into a small receptacle. Crank the engine with the starter. Fuel should flow in heavy spurts from the fuel line into the receptacle. Damaged or defective parts in the fuel supply system, including lines with air leaks, will prevent fuel from reaching the carburetor.

To make sure the line connecting the fuel pump to the fuel supply tank is not clogged or leaking, disconnect it from the fuel pump and force compressed air through it. If the line is clear, air will be heard bubbling through fuel in the tank. Visually inspect every inch of fuel line for leaks.

AIR LEAKS

Air leaks in the fuel line are difficult to find. The usual method is to locate the trouble by the process of elimination. First make sure the line is not obstructed, and that the fuel pump is in good condition. If no fuel is pumped from the supply tank, it is reasonable to assume that air leaks are present. Check carefully where line attaches to frame.

The flexible fuel line leading from the end of the main fuel line to the fuel pump is a frequent source of trouble. It may crack or deteriorate on the inside and cause stoppage of fuel flow. Test vacuum at pump inlet, then with hose attached.

Also make sure that the nuts holding the carburetor to the manifold are tight. Torque-tighten the nuts holding the manifold to the cylinder block. If the carburetor or manifold are loose, air leaks will result. Carburetion will be affected since air drawn in will dilute the air-fuel mixture.

Troubles with the carburetor may be caused by worn linkage, dirt, residue left by stale fuel, incorrect fuel level, worn parts or maladjustment.

Some carburetors are fitted with sight plugs in the side of the float bowl, so the fuel level can be determined without disassembling the carburetor. On these carburetors, the fuel should be level with the bottom edge of the plug hole. Worn external carburetor linkage can be determined by examination.

Carburetors are usually cleaned by first disassembling and washing the individual parts in special carburetor cleaning solutions. This provides the opportunity for inspection and replacement of worn parts. It also is when internal adjustments should be made, such as resetting the float level.

Special solutions are available that will clean the interior of the carburetor while the engine is operating. These solutions are used by disconnecting the fuel line at the carburetor and connecting a can of the cleaning solution to the carburetor inlet. The engine is started and operated until the can (usually one pint) of the cleaning solution has been used.

Carburetor cleaning solutions are designed to dissolve the gum that accumulates with varnish-like consistency both on the inside and outside of carburetors. This gum is formed by heat acting on the fuel.

CARBURETOR TROUBLESHOOTING

While the basic causes of carburetor trouble will vary somewhat with different makes and designs of carburetors, the usual conditions or difficulties and their respective causes are outlined below.

POOR ENGINE PERFORMANCE

1. Air leak at carburetor or manifold.
2. Air leak in fuel line.
3. Clogged carburetor air filter.
4. Clogged fuel lines or fuel filter.
5. Defective fuel pump.
6. Incorrect fuel level in fuel bowl.
7. Automatic choke incorrectly set.
8. Dirt in carburetor jets and passages.
9. Worn or inoperative accelerating pump.
10. Wrong or incorrectly set metering rod (Carter carburetor).
11. Inoperative power valve, economizer or jet.
12. Damaged or wrong size main metering jet.
13. Worn idle needle valve and seat.
14. Loose jets in carburetor.
15. Defective gaskets in carburetor.
16. Worn throttle valve shaft.
17. Clogged exhaust system.
18. Defective manifold heat control valve.
19. Leaking vacuum lines to accessory equipment.

POOR IDLING

1. Incorrect adjustment of idle needle valve.
2. Incorrect float level.
3. Sticking float needle valve.
4. Defective gasket between carburetor and manifold.
5. Defective gaskets in carburetor.
6. Loose carburetor-to-manifold nuts.
7. Loose intake manifold attaching bolts.
8. Idle discharge holes partly clogged.
9. Defective automatic choke.
10. Loose jets in carburetor.
11. Leaking vacuum lines to accessory equipment.
12. Vacuum leaks which are partly compensated for by a rich idle adjustment.
13. Worn main metering jet.
14. Restricted or clogged air cleaner.
15. High float level.

HARD STARTING

1. Incorrect choke adjustment.
2. Defective choke.
3. Incorrect float level.
4. Incorrect fuel pump pressure.
5. Sticking fuel inlet needle.
6. Improper starting procedure.

POOR ACCELERATION

1. Accelerator pump incorrectly adjusted.
2. Accelerator pump inoperative.
3. Corroded or bad seat on accelerator bypass jet.
4. Accelerator pump leather hard or worn.
5. Clogged accelerator jets or passages.
6. Defective ball checks in accelerator system.
7. Incorrect fuel level.

CARBURETOR FLOODS

1. Fuel level too high.
2. Stuck float needle valve.
3. Defective gaskets in carburetor.
4. Cracked carburetor body.
5. Excessive fuel pump pressure.

EXCESSIVE FUEL CONSUMPTION

There are many causes of excessive fuel consumption other than defective carburetion. Consider: Poor engine compression. Excessive engine friction. Dragging brakes. Misaligned wheels. Clogged muffler. Defective ignition. Quick starts. High speed driving.

1. Adjustment of idle mixture.
2. Fuel leaks in carburetor or lines.
3. Clogged air cleaner.
4. High fuel level.
5. Defective fuel economizer.
6. Defective manifold heat control valve.
7. Defective carburetor gaskets.
8. Defective manifold gaskets.
9. Excessive fuel pressure.
10. Sticking fuel inlet needle.

REVIEW QUESTIONS – CARBURETOR ADJUSTMENT, SERVICE

1. Which should be adjusted first?
   a. Ignition.
   b. Carburetor.
2. How is a vacuum gauge used when adjusting a carburetor?
3. Describe briefly the procedure for adjusting a single throat carburetor.
4. Describe briefly the procedure for adjusting a 2 Bbl. carburetor.
5. With other conditions remaining the same, where would you have the highest manifold vacuum?
   a. In a valley.
   b. At the top of a high mountain.
6. In general, which engine has the highest intake manifold vacuum?
   a. Four cylinder.
   b. Six cylinder.
   c. V-8.
7. For perfect combustion, how many pounds of air are required to burn one pound of gasoline?
   a. 27.15 lb.
   b. 13.50 lb.
   c. 15.27 lb.
   d. 12.75 lb.
8. What is the advantage of analyzing the exhaust gas?
9. A new idle mixture adjusting procedure requiring artificial enrichment by the addition of _____ is necessary for checking and resetting idle mixture on some GM carburetors.
10. On engines with emission controls, accurate adjustment of _____ and _____ is important.
11. Ice forms at what point in the fuel system when the engine is first started?
    a. Fuel pump.
    b. At the air inlet to the carburetor.
    c. At the edge of the throttle valve.
    d. In the fuel filter.
12. Which of the following parts should not be washed in carburetor cleaning solution?
    a. Carburetor float.
    b. Anti-stall dashpot.
    c. Idle needle valve.
    d. Accelerator pump diaphragm.
    e. Accelerator pump plunger.
    f. Main jets.
    g. Throttle valve.
13. How can a float be checked for leaks?
    a. By inflating with air.
    b. Immersing in water at 120 deg.
    c. Immersing in water at 200 deg.
    d. Immersing in gasoline.
14. If engine fails to start, and ignition, compression and fuel in tank are satisfactory, what should be checked next?
    a. The position of the choke valve.
    b. The idle mixture adjustment.
    c. The float level.
15. List three causes for carburetor flooding.
16. List three causes for hard starting that originate in the fuel system.
17. List five causes of excessive fuel consumption originating in the fuel system.

FUEL
SUPPLY SYSTEMS

On small gas engines and many industrial engines, fuel is supplied to the carburetor by gravity feed. On automobiles, either mechanical or electric fuel pumps are used.

Mechanical pumps are operated by means of a cam or an eccentric on the camshaft of the engine. Older mechanical pumps are serviceable. The upper and lower housings are held together by machine screws, and rebuilding is possible. Later mechanical pumps are permanently sealed. Service is limited to replacement.

In the past, some mechanical fuel pumps were combined with a vacuum pump used to operate the windshield wipers.

Electric fuel pumps are energized by a built-in electric motor. Some are designed to be submerged in the fuel in the tank; others are installed in the fuel line between the tank and carburetor.

FUEL PUMP OPERATION

A typical, single-action, "sealed" mechanical fuel pump is shown in Fig. 26-1. Working parts include an actuating lever, diaphragm and spring, inlet valve and outlet valve.

In operation, an eccentric on the engine camshaft actuates

Fig. 26-2. External view of mechanical fuel pump that can be disassembled and rebuilt.

the pump lever, which is linked to the diaphragm. The lever movement extends the diaphragm, creating suction that draws fuel through the inlet valve. Next, the lever retracts as the eccentric rotates and spring pressure pushes the diaphragm toward its relaxed position. This action forces fuel through the outlet valve to the carburetor.

When the carburetor float needle valve closes, fuel pump output is limited to the small amount that bleeds back through the fuel return line to the fuel tank. The lever keeps working, maintaining fuel pressure in the fuel pump chamber to keep the diaphragm extended and inoperative. Fuel flow to the carburetor is halted until excess fuel under pressure bleeds through the return line or the carburetor needle valve opens. This cycle of operation continues as long as the engine is in operation.

Typical "rebuildable" fuel pumps are illustrated in Figs. 26-2 and 26-3. Fuel pumps of this type have a built-in air dome with a diaphragm to dampen pulsations in the fuel stream. The main diaphragm is actuated by a rocker arm (through a link and pull rod) riding a cam on the camshaft.

A rocker arm spring holds the rocker arm in constant contact with the cam, causing the rocker arm to move up and down as the camshaft rotates. As the arm swings downward, it bears against the shoulder on a link that is pivoted on the rocker arm pin. The link swings upward, pulling up the diaphragm by means of the connecting pull rod. Upward

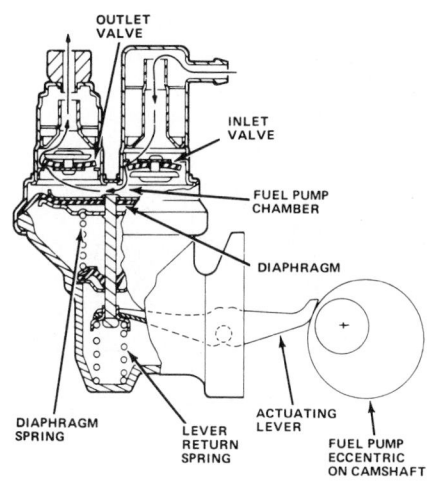

Fig. 26-1. "Sealed" diaphragm type mechanical fuel pump. (American Motors)

movement of the fuel diaphragm compresses the diaphragm spring, creating a vacuum in the fuel chamber under the diaphragm. Vacuum causes the outlet valve to close, and fuel from the tank enters the fuel chamber through the inlet valve.

As the rotating eccentric on the camshaft permits the rocker arm to swing upward, the arm releases the fuel link (but cannot move it downward). The compressed diaphragm spring exerts pressure on the diaphragm and on the fuel in the fuel chamber. This pressure closes the inlet valve and forces fuel through the outlet valve to the carburetor.

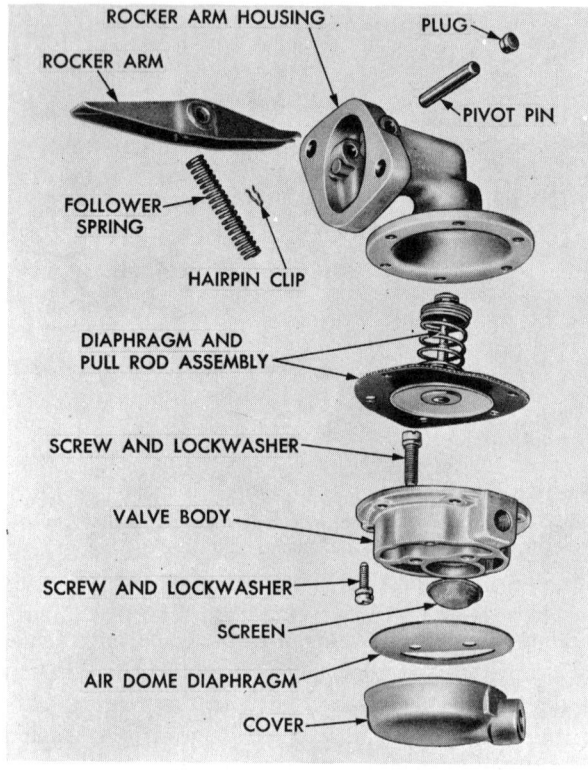

Fig. 26-3. Exploded view of mechanically operated take-apart fuel pump.

FUEL AND VACUUM PUMP

A combination fuel and vacuum pump is used on older engines and some truck engines.

The vacuum booster portion of the pump, Fig. 26-4, operates as follows:
1. Rocker arm forces diaphragm up against spring pressure.
2. Outlet valve opens, forcing air in upper chamber out through exhaust port.
3. Vacuum created in lower chamber causes air to be drawn from windshield wiper motor through inlet port on booster, into upper inlet chamber, then through lower inlet valve into lower chamber.
4. On return stroke, spring pressure forces diaphragm downward, expelling air in lower outlet valve.
5. This creates a vacuum in upper chamber, which again draws air from wiper motor into inlet chamber, and through upper chamber inlet valve into upper chamber.
6. This type of vacuum booster makes it possible to supply vacuum to windshield wiper motor on both up and down strokes of diaphragm.

PERMANENTLY SEALED FUEL PUMP

A typical permanently sealed fuel pump is shown in Fig. 26-5. This is a mechanically operated pump, actuated by means of the fuel pump rocker arm and an eccentric on the camshaft.

To remove the rocker arm:
1. Scrape away staking mark and remove rocker arm retaining plug.
2. Release tension on rocker arm pin by pressing arm downward against diaphragm and rocker arm spring pressure, or remove rocker arm spring and allow rocker arm pin to fall out.
3. Remove rocker arm.

A Chrysler Corporation mechanical fuel pump is shown in Fig. 26-6. It too, is permanently sealed. In case of failure, the entire pump must be replaced.

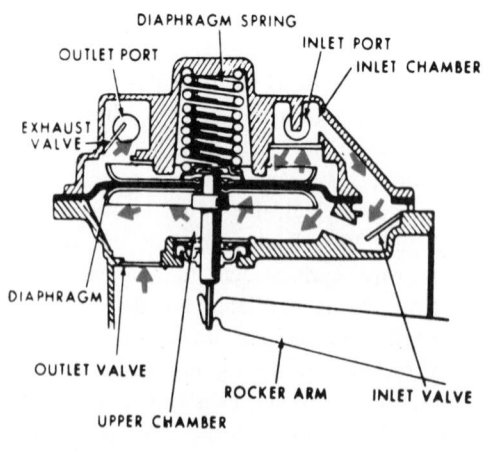

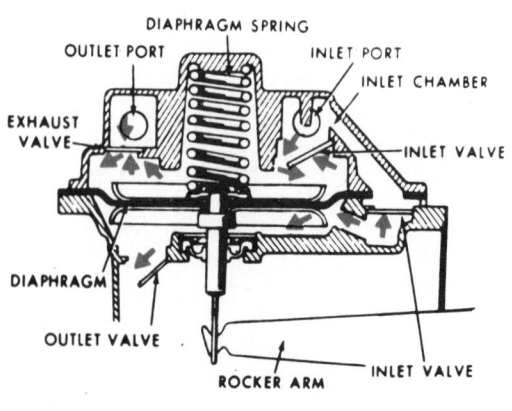

PRESSURE CYCLE

RETURN CYCLE

Fig. 26-4. Showing details of operation of vacuum portion of fuel and vacuum pump.

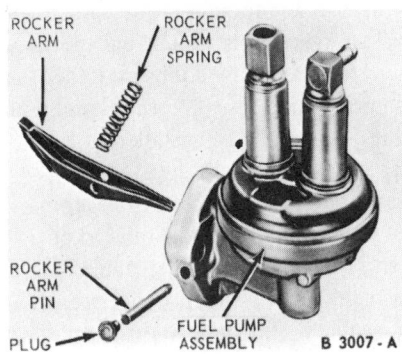

Fig. 26-5. Mechanically operated and permanently sealed fuel pump. (Carter)

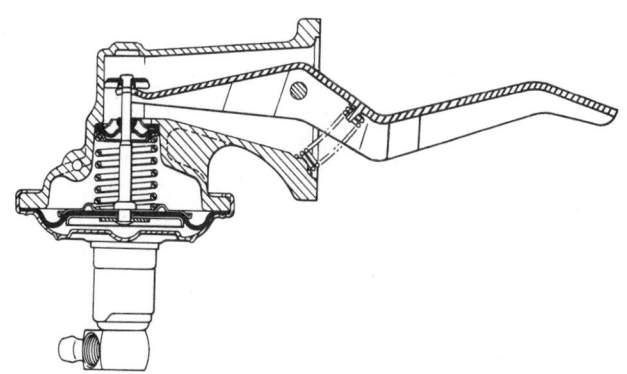

Fig. 26-6. Typical mechanical fuel pump with rocker arm operated by an eccentric on engine camshaft. (Chrysler-Plymouth Div.)

The 318 and 360 cu. in. V-8 engines, for example, use this diaphragm type pump operated from an eccentric on the engine camshaft. NOTE: On 400 and 440 cu. in. V-8 engines, a push rod is used between the camshaft eccentric and the fuel pump rocker arm.

In operation, the eccentric presses down on the pump rocker arm, lifting the pull rod and diaphragm against the tension of the main spring of the pump. This creates a vacuum in the valve housing, opens the inlet valve and fuel is drawn into the valve housing chamber.

On the return stroke, the main spring forces the diaphragm down, closing the inlet valve and fuel is pumped from the chamber through the outlet valve to the fuel filter and carburetor. Each revolution of the camshaft repeats this cycle.

Most mechanical fuel pumps are designed to prevent an oversupply of fuel when the carburetor float rises and fuel flow is shut off by the needle and seat assembly. At this point, the fuel pump diaphragm spring is held in a compressed position and the rocker arm "idles" on the camshaft eccentric. Diaphragm action is reduced to a slight movement, just enough to provide a reduced flow of fuel to replace fuel which enters the carburetor between pump strokes.

In effect, this idling action produces a constant pressure on the fuel in the line to the carburetor. This pressure is proportional to the force exerted by the diaphragm spring.

DIAGNOSING FUEL PUMP TROUBLES

Modern fuel pumps give many thousands of miles of trouble-free service without the need for maintenance. When a pump no longer supplies fuel in sufficient volume, it should be replaced with a new or rebuilt unit.

To determine if the fuel pump is at fault, first make sure the supply tank has a sufficient quantity of fuel. If satisfactory, disconnect the fuel supply line at the carburetor and direct the fuel line into a small container. Then, with the distributor primary wire to the ignition coil grounded, crank the engine by means of the starter. If the fuel pump is in good condition, strong spurts of fuel will come from the supply line.

If no fuel is pumped, or only a small quantity, the pump is probably defective and should be replaced. Of course, it must be verified that the fuel line between the pump and supply tank is not clogged, or have an air leak. Also, check the condition of the fuel filter and the flexible fuel line connecting the pump with the end of the rigid fuel line leading to the supply tank. These flexible lines, may develop air-leaks, or the interior may swell and obstruct the flow of fuel.

An infrequent trouble is when the fuel pump supplies too much fuel. Excessive pressures result in flooding of the carburetor. Fuel pump pressure may be tested with a suitable pressure gauge.

To make the test: Connect the gauge to the outlet side of the pump. When the engine is cranked by the starter, the gauge should register 3 to 5 lbs. pressure. The length of the hose connecting the gauge to the fuel pump should not exceed 6 in., otherwise inaccurate readings may result.

Another fuel pump test can be made by directing fuel flow from the pump into a pint or quart measure. With the engine operating at idling speed, a pint of fuel should be pumped in approximately 45 seconds. The fuel in the float bowl will keep the engine operating long enough to make the test.

The vacuum side of the fuel pump can be checked by connecting a vacuum gauge to the intake connection. With the engine operating at idle speed, the vacuum should be a minimum of 10 in.

When the vacuum diaphragm is punctured, there will be a "open line" from the engine crankcase, through the vacuum pump to the intake manifold. Engine vacuum, then, will draw oil from the crankcase to the engine and excessive oil consumption will result.

A rough check for a punctured diaphragm can be made by disconnecting the vacuum line leading from the pump to the intake manifold. Disconnect this line at the lower end after the engine has been running for a short period. If oil drips from the line, the vacuum diaphragm is punctured.

It has been established that there are four points where wear or damage will affect the performance of a fuel pump. These points are: worn linkage, worn valves or seats, worn pull rod and punctured diaphragm.

ELECTRIC FUEL PUMPS

Electrically operated fuel pumps are of two basic types:
1. Suction type draws fuel from tank in a manner similar to

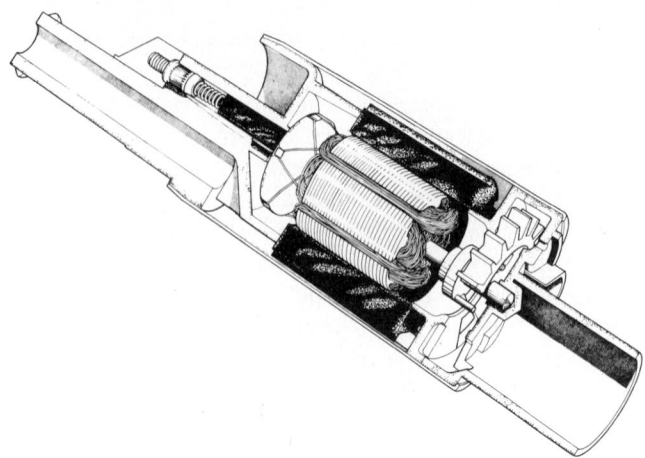

Fig. 26-7. Tank-mounted electric fuel pump specially designed for installation inside fuel tank of Buick Riviera. (AC Spark Plug Div., GMC)

mechanically operated pumps.

2. Pusher type placed in bottom of fuel supply tank "pushes" fuel to carburetor.

An in-tank, pusher type fuel pump by AC Spark Plug Div., GMC, is illustrated in Fig. 26-7. Autopulse and Bendix electric fuel pumps are shown in Figs. 26-8 and 26-9, respectively. Both of these pumps are of the suction type.

An advantage of the externally mounted electric pump is that several pumps can be installed. Then, larger quantities of fuel can be supplied to the carburetor and, if one pump should fail, the others would continue to supply fuel.

An important advantage of an electric fuel pump is that

there is a considerable reduction in the tendency toward vapor lock. The reason for this is that it can be mounted on the firewall or any other relatively cool spot under the hood.

The mechanical pump, on the other hand, is driven by the engine camshaft and must be installed in a location where it will operate at a higher temperature.

Another advantage of the electric pump is that it will supply fuel as soon as the ignition is turned on.

The pusher type of electric fuel pump has the advantage that the fuel in the supply line is under pressure. Consequently, there is a reduced tendency toward vapor lock. There are no valves between the pump and the carburetor. Therefore, the fuel drains back into the tank when the engine is stopped. This eliminates pressure buildup and consequent hard starting of a hot engine. The delivery of the fuel is steady and nonpulsating.

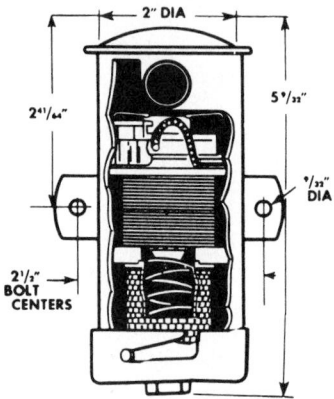

Fig. 26-9. Construction of Bendix electric fuel pump.

IN-TANK ELECTRIC FUEL PUMPS

The AC electric fuel pump, Fig. 26-7, is located in the fuel tank as part of the electric fuel pump and fuel gauge tank unit assembly. The assembly is installed through the fuel tank access hole in the trunk floor. Electrical connections are by means of two wires to the fuel pump terminals, an outside ground wire and a two-way connector.

The pump is a turbine type hydraulic unit directly coupled to a permanent magnet motor, Fig. 26-7. Fuel is drawn into the pump through a woven plastic filter, then "pushed" through the fuel line to the carburetor.

Buick fuel systems using the electric pump have a paper filter element in the inlet fitting of the carburetor. A control switch located near the oil filter is hydraulically connected to the engine oil system, so that oil pressure actuates the diaphragm of the switch.

During cranking of the engine, current for the electric fuel pump control switch is taken from the starter solenoid, as long as engine oil pressure is below 3 psi. Once the engine starts and oil pressure is normal, the pump is energized through the ignition switch, gauge fuse, control switch and in-line pump fuse. Turning off the ignition switch de-energizes the pump.

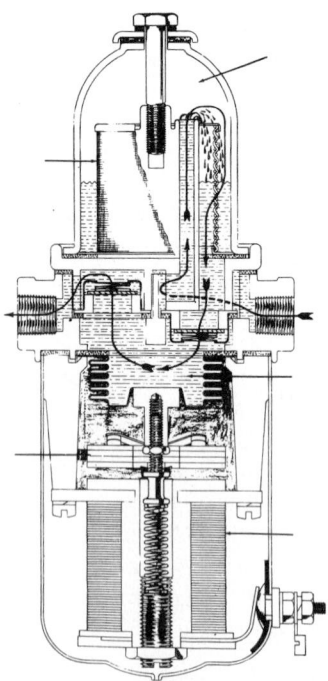

Fig. 26-8. Sectional view of Autopulse electric fuel pump. Arrows show path of fuel.

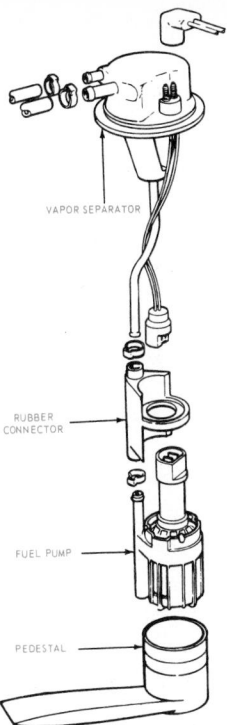

Fig. 26-10. Details of an in-tank electric fuel pump.
(Carter Carburetor Div., ACF Industries, Inc.)

operation, the pump will be de-energized, and the engine will stop running as soon as fuel from the fuel bowl is burned.

The in-tank electric fuel pump, Fig. 26-10, delivers fuel to the carburetor through the vapor separator, which includes an additional outlet for the fuel line. When the engine is cranked, current is delivered through a special by-pass circuit. Current passes through the oil pressure switch to the pump, delivering the full 12V. When the engine starts, the current will pass through a resistor, cutting voltage to 8 1/2 to 10V. This Carter pump is serviced as an assembly.

SERVICING THE AUTOPULSE

When Autopulse fuel pump trouble is suspected, disconnect the fuel line at the carburetor and direct the fuel line from the pump into a small container. Turn on the ignition switch, then place a finger over the open end of the fuel line. If the pump stops or clicks very infrequently, pump and fuel line connections are satisfactory.

Next, remove your finger from the open end of the fuel line. If ample fuel flows, the pump is operating satisfactorily. Always be sure that electrical connections are in good condition, and that the correct voltage is reaching the unit.

STEWART-WARNER ELECTRIC PUMPS

Stewart-Warner electric fuel pumps, Fig. 26-11, are of the bellows type, operated by the action of an electromagnet

If the engine stops running, oil pressure will drop below 3 psi, and the oil pressure switch contacts will return to normal position. If oil pressure drops below 3 psi during engine

Fig. 26-11. In-line electric fuel pumps. Left. Maximum performance pump delivers 42 gph (gallons per hour) and has an adjustable pressure regulator (1 to 8 psi). Right. Replacement pump for all cars should be mounted as close as possible to fuel tank. It starts at turn of ignition key.
(Stewart-Warner Corp.)

and rocker arm and pin. Electric current to the armature is opened and closed by means of tungsten and platinum breaker points. While the points open and close, the rocker arm causes the bellows to move up and down to produce the necessary vacuum to draw the fuel from the supply tank.

SUPERCHARGERS

The power developed by an internal combustion engine is largely dependent on the amount of combustible mixture reaching the cylinders. The design of manifolds, carburetors and the size of valves and valve ports are all important factors in determining the amount of this mixture. Therefore, to overcome friction losses in the intake system and to aid in scavenging the cylinders of burnt gases, superchargers can be used to blow the combustible mixture into the cylinders of spark ignition engines, Fig. 26-12.

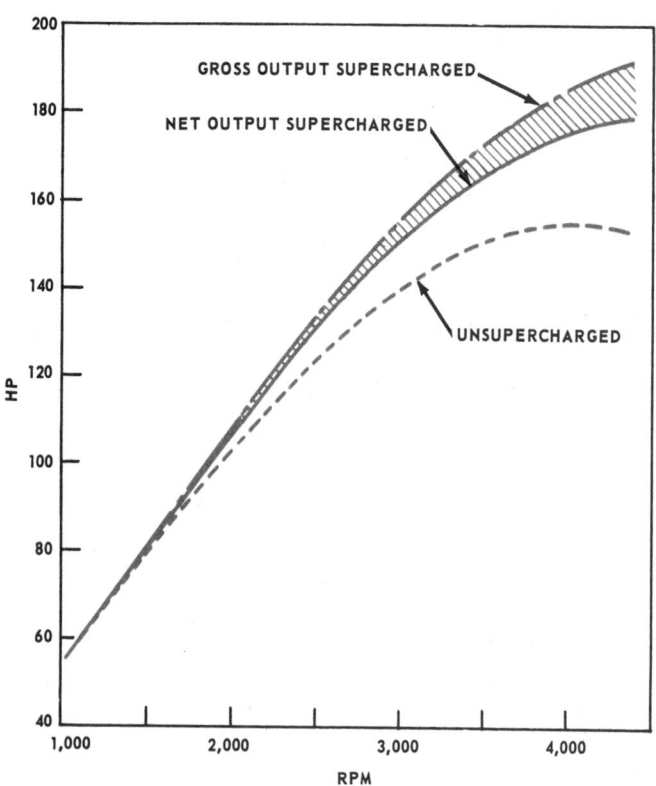

Fig. 26-12. Comparison of power developed by a nonsupercharged engine and an engine equipped with a mechanically driven supercharger.

Superchargers were first developed for racing cars and other high performance engines. Later, they found wide application on aircraft. In this application, the power of an engine falls rapidly as the airplane attains higher altitudes. As air density decreases, smaller amounts of air will be drawn into the cylinders. Finally, at an altitude of 18,000 feet, only one half the normal charge will reach the cylinder, and only one half the power will be developed. Superchargers, then are used on aircraft to help maintain power at high altitudes.

Basically, a supercharger is a compressor. Therefore, a supercharged engine will have higher overall compression than a nonsupercharged engine having the same combustion chamber volume and piston displacement.

However this higher overall compression will increase the tendency toward detonation of spark ignition engines. So, when a supercharger is used, fuel of higher-than-standard octane rating is required to avoid detonation.

When a supercharger is installed on a diesel engine, only air is blown into the cylinders, and the tendency toward detonation is reduced.

Superchargers are designed to develop from 4 to 20 lb. pressure. Obviously, the greater the pressure developed, the more air-fuel mixture or air that will be carried to the cylinders. The power required to drive the supercharger increases rapidly. It may be as much as 50 hp per lb. of air per second.

Basically, a supercharged engine will burn more fuel than when it is nonsupercharged. However, the increase in power is not proportional to the increase in fuel consumed.

Fig. 26-13. Rootes type supercharger.

TYPES OF SUPERCHARGERS

There are two general types of superchargers, the Rootes type and the centrifugal type. The Rootes "blower" has two rotors, Fig. 26-13. The centrifugal supercharger utilizes an impeller rotating at high speed inside a housing.

In most designs of the Rootes supercharger, each of the two rotors has two lobes. In shape, they resemble a figure 8. However, some Rootes units are fitted with rotors of three or more lobes. Fig. 26-13. The shafts of the two Rootes rotors are interconnected through gearing and operate at the same speed. With action similar to the gear type oil pump. The rotors do not quite touch each other. There is also a slight clearance between the rotors and the surrounding housing.

In operation, then, air enters the housing by the action of the rotors. It passes between the lobes of the rotors and the housing, then is forced through the outlet of the unit.

With the Rootes blower, the rate of delivery varies slightly faster than the speed of rotation, because the leakage decreases as the speed increases. Above a certain minimum speed, the amount of supercharging is almost constant. Rootes blowers are driven at speeds from one to two times engine speed.

The centrifugal type supercharger, used in many racing applications, consists of an impeller rotating at a high speed inside a housing. Clearance between the blades and the housing must be kept at a minimum. Since the speed of rotation is approximately five times engine speed, it can easily attain a speed of 25,000 rpm.

Therefore, it is essential that the rotor is accurately balanced, both statically and dynamically. Furthermore, the rotor blades must be made strong enough so that the centrifugal force at high speeds will not cause them to stretch and strike the housing.

On racing car installations, the air from the impeller first passes to a diffuser, where the force of the moving air is converted to static energy. The diffuser consists of a ring-shaped housing containing blades or vanes.

Coolers are used in conjunction with centrifugal superchargers to reduce the temperature of the air. This is important because the act of compressing the air will increase its temperature. The warm air entering would reduce the efficiency of the engine. The coolers consist of several lengths of finned tubing.

The rate of delivery of the centrifugal supercharger increases as the square of the speed of rotation. As a result, very little supercharging is obtained at lower speeds, and the variation between different speeds is large. Carburetion is more difficult with a centrifugal supercharger than with a Rootes type unit.

LOCATION OF SUPERCHARGER

Superchargers can be placed either between the carburetor and the manifold or at the air inlet of the carburetor. Racing cars usually have the supercharger between the carburetor and the manifold.

The carburetor/manifold design has the advantage that the fuel can be supplied to the carburetor by the same system as is used in conventional carburetion. If the supercharger is placed ahead of the carburetor, the fuel must be supplied under sufficient pressure to overcome the added air pressure at the carburetor fuel nozzles.

When the carburetor is placed between the supercharger and the engine, it is necessary to connect the carburetor float chamber and the outlet side of the supercharger with a pressure equalizing tube.

TURBOCHARGER

Most superchargers in the past have been driven mechanically by means of gearing to the crankshaft. Another method is to have the supercharger driven by the force of the exhaust gases, Fig. 26-14. In this way, the power needed to drive the unit mechanically is saved.

A turbocharged 215 cu. in. Oldsmobile engine is shown in Fig. 26-15. This experimental aluminum V-8 engine with

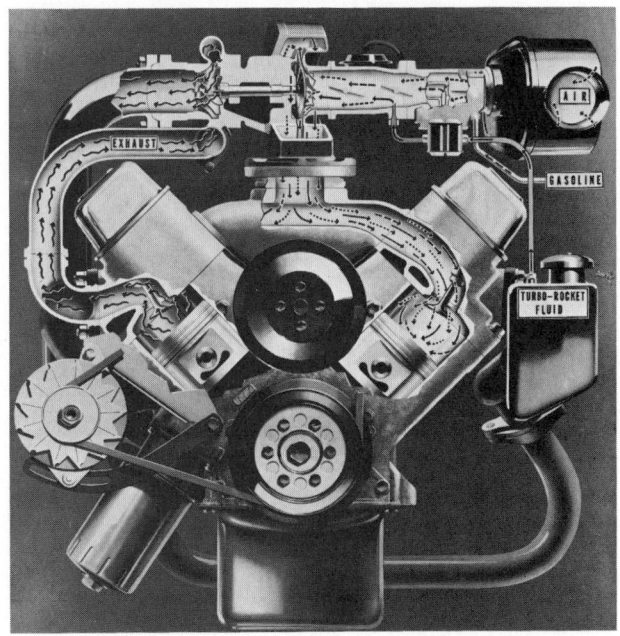

Fig. 26-15. Details of turbocharger as installed on 215 cu. in. aluminum V-8 Oldsmobile engine.

conventional 4 Bbl. carburetor developed 185 hp @ 4800 rpm. When equipped with the turbocharger, horsepower was increased to 215.

In addition to the turbocharger, the design includes the injection of special Turbo-rocket fluid in proportion to the octane requirements of the engine. During sudden acceleration and under full throttle conditions, this fluid is injected to increase the octane value of the air-fuel mixture reaching the engine. Fluid injection makes it possible to operate the engine with its 10.25 to 1 compression ratio with ordinary premium grade gasoline.

By studying Fig. 26-15, it will be noted that after the exhaust gases (curved arrows) leave the cylinder, they are directed against the vanes of the turbine, causing it to rotate. The supercharger is mounted on the other end of the

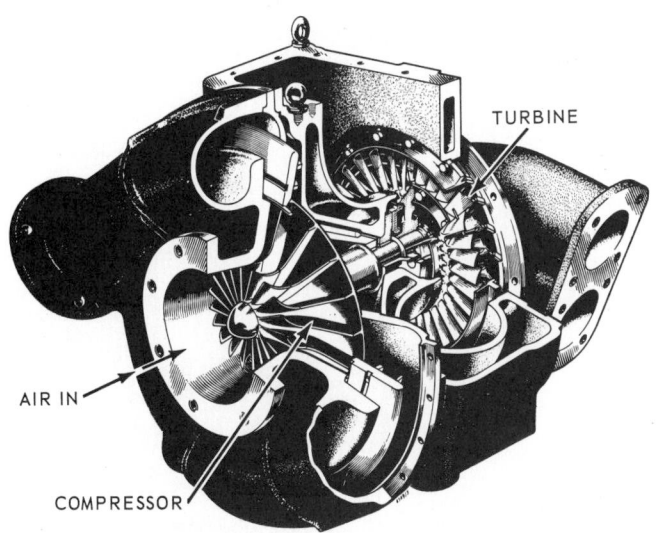

Fig. 26-14. A turbocharger with an axial flow type turbine driving a centrifugal blower. The turbine is on the right and the blower on the left.

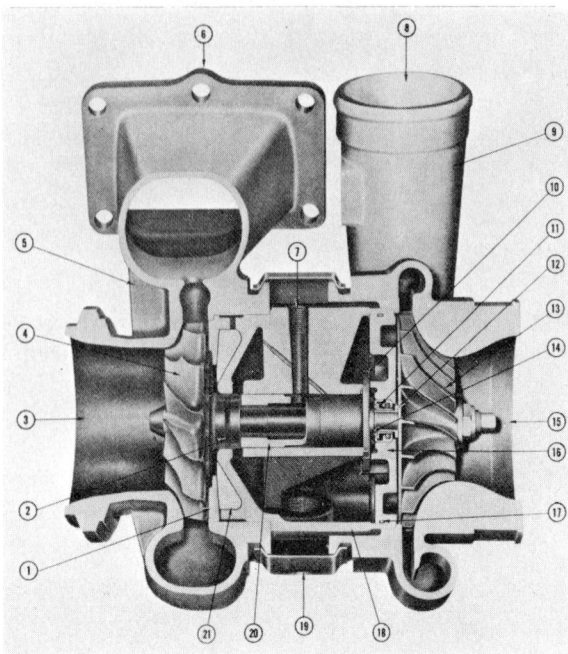

Fig. 26-16. Details of Cummins turbocharger used on diesel engines. 1—Heat shield. 2—Piston ring seal. 3—Exhaust out. 4—Turbine wheel. 5—Turbine casing. 6—Exhaust in. 7—Oil in. 8—Air to engine. 9—Compressor casing. 10—Bearing insert. 11—Oil seal. 12—Sleeve. 13—Compressor wheel. 14—Thrust washer. 15—Air in. 16—Seal plate. 17—Seal ring. 18—Bearing housing. 19—Oil out. 20—Bearing. 21—Insulation pad.

turbo-shaft and forces the air-fuel mixture (dotted arrows) into the intake manifold, then into the combustion chamber. The Turbo-rocket fuel (solid arrows) is injected into the intake manifold under low vacuum conditions.

The turbocharger, as installed on some Cummins diesel engines, is shown in Fig. 26-16. The Cummins turbocharger consists of a turbine wheel and a compressor wheel separately incased but mounted on, and rotating with, a common shaft. The turbine side of the turbocharger mounts to the exhaust manifold outlet flange, and the compressor wheel side connects with the air intake manifold. Lubrication and cooling is obtained from filtered engine oil through flexible lines of tubing.

Power to drive the turbine wheel which, in turn, drives the compressor wheel, is obtained from energy of exhaust gases. The rotating speed of the turbine wheel changes as the energy level of exhaust gases change, so the engine is supplied with enough air to burn fuel for its load requirements.

FORD TURBOCHARGED FOUR

The 140 cu. in. (2.3 litre) Ford engine with the turbocharger, Fig. 26-17A, has increased its output over the unturbocharged model by more than 35 percent. The unturbocharged engine turned out approximately .62 hp per cu. in., while the same engine with turbocharger turned out .92 hp per cu. in.

The power system is shown in Fig. 26-17B. As a safety measure, a wastegate or exhaust valve is provided which permits exhaust gases to escape. In that way, excessive turbine speeds are prevented.

The turbine speed approaches 100,000 rpm. Should excessive pressure be produced, a safety red light on the instrument panel would indicate the condition. Normally, a green light indicates satisfactory operation. These warning lights and other details of the turbocharged engine are shown in Fig. 26-17C.

BUICK TURBOCHARGED V-6

Buick's 231 cu. in. (3.8 litre) turbocharged V-6 engine, Fig. 26-17D, is an even firing engine. See page 53. It develops 165 hp at 4000 rpm or .72 hp per cu. in. of displacement, and the turbine speed exceeds 100,000 rpm. The unturbocharged engine turns out 115 hp or .50 hp per cu. in. Further details of Buick's turbocharged engine are pictured in Fig. 23-16.

Fig. 26-17A. Ford's turbocharged four cylinder engine.

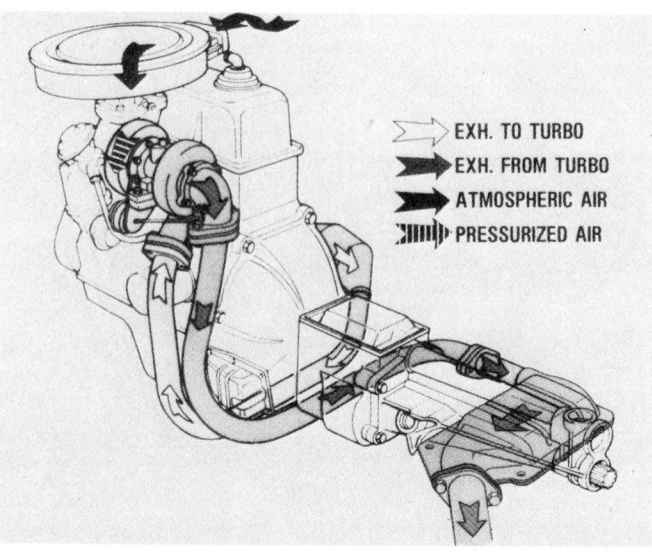

EXH. TO TURBO
EXH. FROM TURBO
ATMOSPHERIC AIR
PRESSURIZED AIR

Fig. 26-17B. Power system of Ford's turbocharged engine.

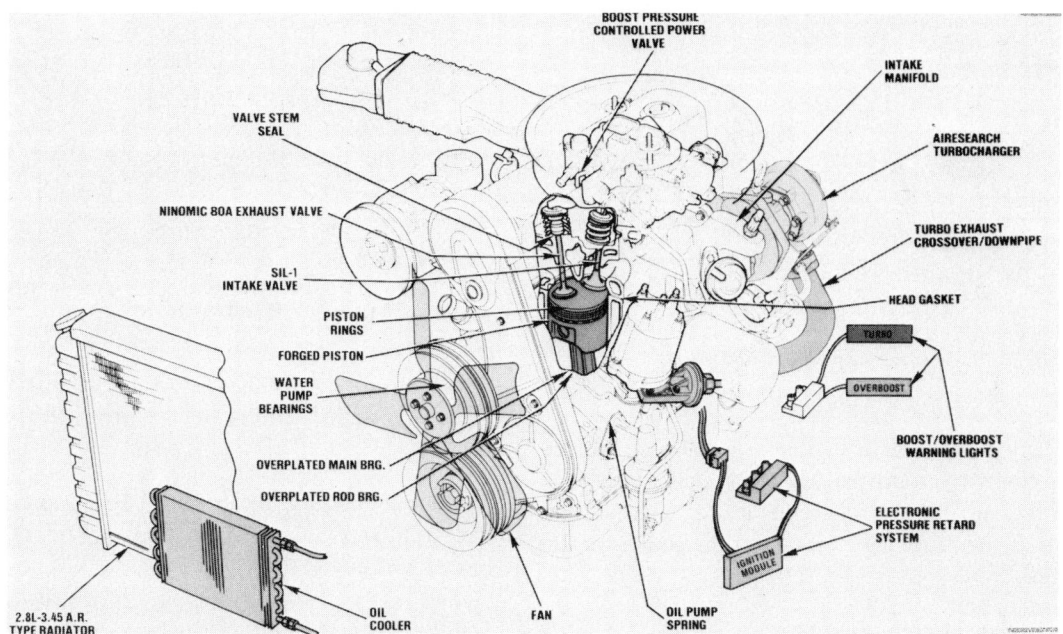

Fig. 26-17C. Various parts of Ford's turbocharged engine are indicated.

Fig. 26-17D. Details of Buick's turbocharged V-6 engine.

FUEL GAUGES

There are two basic types of fuel gauges in use, the thermostatic type and the balancing coil type.

THERMOSTATIC GAUGE

The thermostatic type of fuel gauge consists of a sending unit located in the fuel tank and gauge (registering unit) located on the instrument panel. In addition, there is a voltage regulator unit, which is designed to maintain an average value of 5.0 volts at the gauge terminals. It is compensated for temperature variations and is provided with an adjustment which controls the rate at which the contacts make and break. It controls the voltage supplied to the gauge system.

The gauge pointer is controlled by a bimetallic arm and heating coil, Fig. 26-18. The sending unit in the fuel tank has a rheostat that varies its resistance depending on the amount of fuel in the tank.

When the fuel tank is empty, the grounded sliding contact, Fig. 26-18, is at the end of the resistance wire of the rheostat. With all of the resistance in the circuit, only a small amount of current will flow through the heating coil of the gauge unit, and the gauge will register zero.

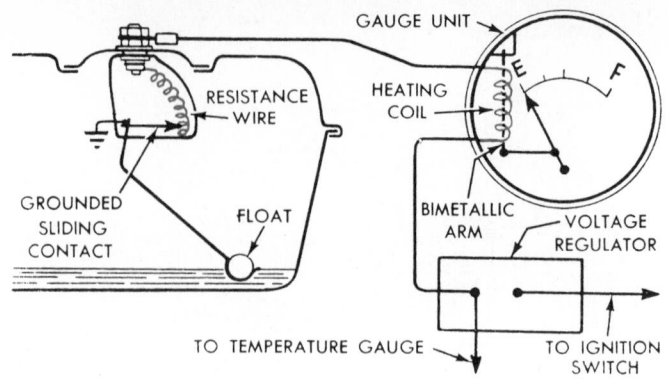

Fig. 26-18. Thermostatic type of fuel gauge.

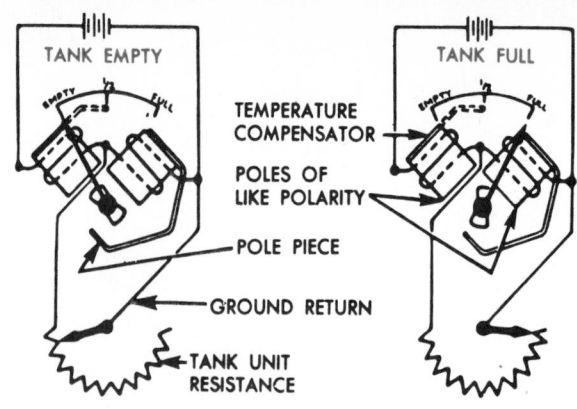

Fig. 26-19. Circuits of AC fuel gauge. Left. Conditions for tank empty. Right. Full position.   (AC Spark Plug Div., GMC)

When the tank is full, the float rises with the fuel, moving the grounded contact toward the beginning of the resistance coil. More current will flow through the heating coil, and the bimetallic arm of the gauge unit will deflect the pointer to the "Full" position.

BALANCED COIL FUEL GAUGE

The AC fuel gauge used by General Motors cars and trucks, as well as some independent manufacturers, is of the electrically operated balanced coil type. It consists of a dash unit and a tank unit, Fig. 26-19.

The dash unit is made of two coils placed at 90 deg. to each other. An armature and pointer assembly is mounted at the intersection of the center line of the two coils. To prevent vibration of the pointer, the armature is provided with a dampening device.

The tank unit consists of a rheostat with a movable contact arm. Position of the contact arm is controlled by a float that rests on the surface of the fuel. To prevent splashing of the fuel from seriously affecting the movement of the float, a torque washer and spring are used.

The tank unit is grounded out of the gauge circuit when the fuel tank is empty, and the float is in its lowest position. Then, current passes through the coil on the empty side of the dash unit ("full coil" is of higher resistance), and the pointer is pulled to indicate zero.

As fuel is added to the supply tank, there is corresponding rise of the float. Movement of the rheostat arm places resistance in the circuit, and current will flow through the "full" coil. As a result, the pointer will be attracted to indicate the quantity of fuel in the tank.

Since an increase or decrease of battery voltage will affect both coils equally, the accuracy of the gauge will not be affected. Compensation for temperature variation is also provided.

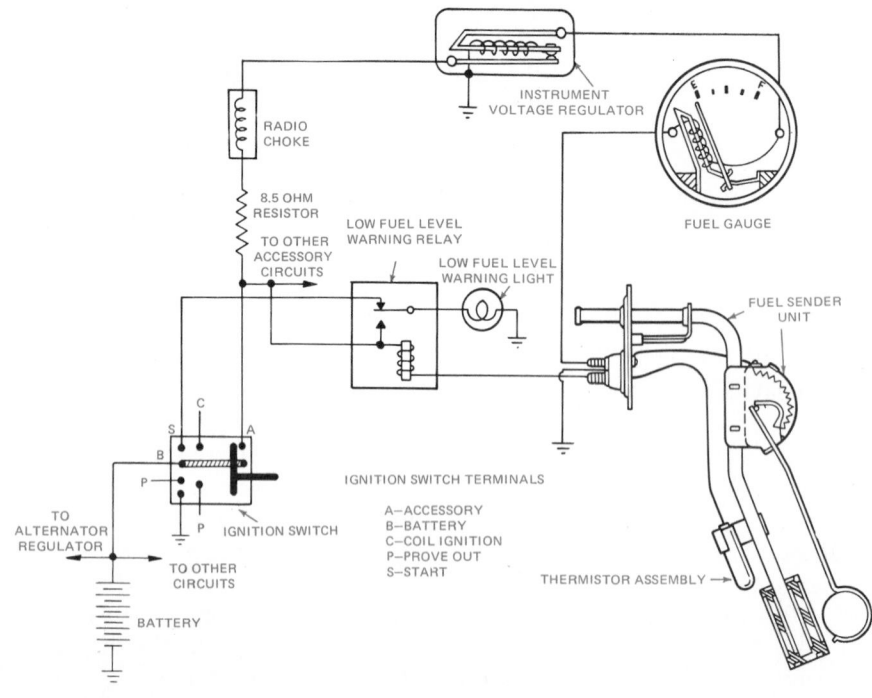

Fig. 26-20. Diagram of low fuel indicating system installed on some Ford cars.

LOW FUEL INDICATOR

In recent model years, some cars are equipped with a device that indicates when the quantity of fuel in the supply tank is nearly exhausted. The system installed on some Ford cars is shown in Fig. 26-20.

The Ford low fuel warning system makes use of a thermistor assembly attached to the fuel sender outlet tube located in the fuel tank. Also utilized is a low fuel relay and a low fuel light located on the instrument panel. The low fuel light will glow just before the fuel gauge pointer indicates empty and/or when there is approximately 4 1/2 gal. of fuel in the tank.

The thermistor assembly is kept cool as long as it is covered with gasoline. When the fuel level drops low enough, the thermistor is exposed to air. This causes it to heat up, its resistance decreases and allows current to flow through the low fuel signal relay. The relay contacts then close the circuit to the low fuel indicator light on the instrument panel, as shown in Fig. 26-20.

FUEL FILTERS

Clean fuel is essential, because of the many small jets and apertures in the carburetor. To insure this cleanliness, fuel filters are installed in the fuel line between the fuel pump and carburetor, or before the fuel pump on some engines.

Fuel filters of various types and construction are used, all designed to filter out all foreign matter. Some remove any water that may be present.

Most fuel filters are disposable. Some are designed so that they can be quickly disassembled and easily cleaned.

A strainer of copper mesh usually is incorporated in the design of the fuel pump. In addition, some fuel pumps have effective filters built into the units.

In many cases, the filter is built into the carburetor. A ceramic type filter is shown in Fig. 26-21 and a paper element type filter in Fig. 26-22.

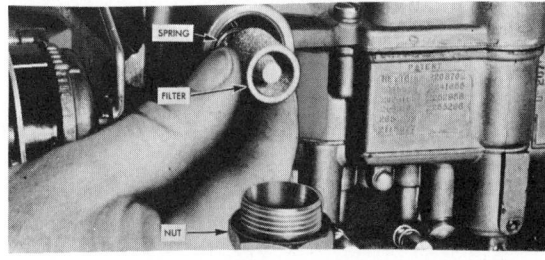

Fig. 26-21. Ceramic type fuel filter may be cleaned and reinstalled in carburetor inlet.

Many different materials are used to filter the fuel. Ceramic, Fig. 26-23, a series of copper disks, copper screening, and impregnated fiber disks are used. Since the fuel pump delivers a pulsating flow of fuel, some fuel filter designs include an air dome which smooths out the pulsations.

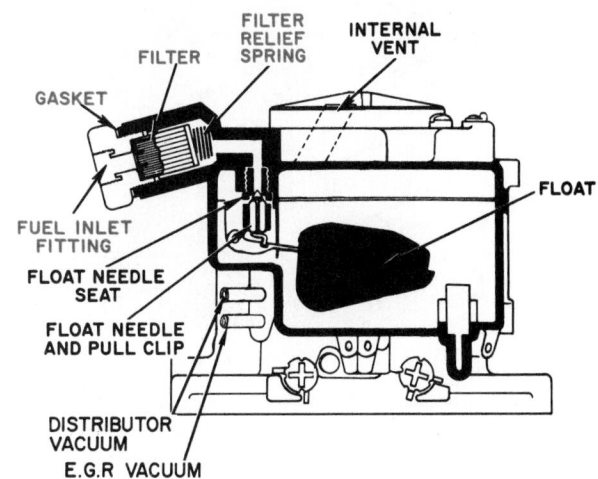

Fig. 26-22. Paper type fuel filter may be found at carburetor inlet or clamped in fuel line on either side of fuel pump.

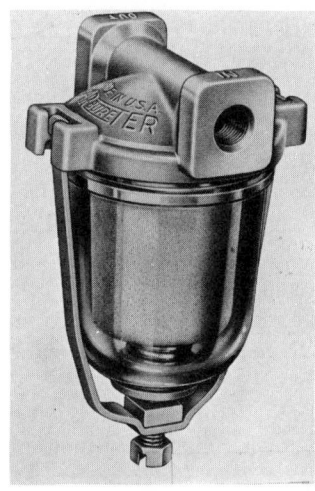

Fig. 26-23. A ceramic element is used in the Carter fuel filter. (Carter Carburetor Div., ACF Industries, Inc.)

Since accumulations of dirt and water in the filter tend to restrict the flow of fuel, it is essential that the unit is disassembled and cleaned periodically. Usually, this is done twice a year, in spring and in fall.

Examination of the filter will quickly show how it is disassembled. Frequently, on trucks, the filter bowl is held in place by a bale wire or strap and screw, Fig. 26-23. Loosening the screw will permit slipping aside the bale wire, after which the filter bowl and filter element can be removed.

The filter element should be washed in a good carburetor cleaning solution. Filter elements of the copper disk type should be blown dry with compressed air. Replacement elements are available in case the original element is damaged.

When reassembling a filter, use a new gasket between the bowl and the body of the unit to insure against leakage. If the top of the filter is a die casting, it should be checked for warpage. If found to be warped, a new unit should be installed.

Fig. 26-24. Throwaway fuel filter. Replace every 30,000 miles or sooner, depending on operating conditions.

A can type throwaway fuel filter with vapor drain is used in certain systems. The vapors are returned to the fuel tank through a separate line. A replaceable in-line filter, Fig. 26-24, is used in many applications.

LIQUEFIED PETROLEUM GAS

A mixture of gaseous petroleum compounds principally butane and propane, together with small quantities of other similar gases, is known as liquefied petroleum gas (LP-Gas).

LP-Gas is a by-product of the manufacture of gasoline, Crude oil yields 2 percent propane and 2 percent butane. LP-Gas can also be obtained from natural gas. It is used for cooking, heating and as fuel for internal combustion engines. In this case, it is found principally in large trucks, tractors and fork lift trucks. Some installations are shown in Figs. 26-25 and 26-26.

Currently, more attention is being given to the use of LP-Gas as a fuel for internal combustion engines in general, because of reduced exhaust emissions and the increased scarcity of gasoline. Likewise, interest in LP-Gas by high performance enthusiasts is growing.

Chemically, LP-Gas is similar to gasoline, since it consists of a mixture of compounds of hydrogen and carbon. However, it is a great deal more volatile and, at usual atmospheric

Fig. 26-26. Zenith LP-Gas system installed on a tractor.

temperatures, it is a vapor. For this reason, a special type of carburetor is required on internal combustion engines.

Because LP-Gas must be stored and transported, it is compressed and cooled so that it is a liquid. Depending on conditions, approximately 250 gal. of LP-Gas from 1 gal. of liquid, Because of the pressure involved, it must be stored in strong tanks. The boiling point of propane is approximately 44 deg. F below zero.

At temperatures below their boiling points, butane and propane exert no pressure. As their temperature increases, pressure rises rapidly. For example, at 40 deg. F, liquid propane will have a pressure of 65 lb., while butane will have a pressure of about 3 lb. Then, at 65 deg. F, the pressure of propane will have increased to 100 lb. and butane to 15 lb., Fig. 26-27.

Fig. 26-25. LP-Gas installation on a truck.

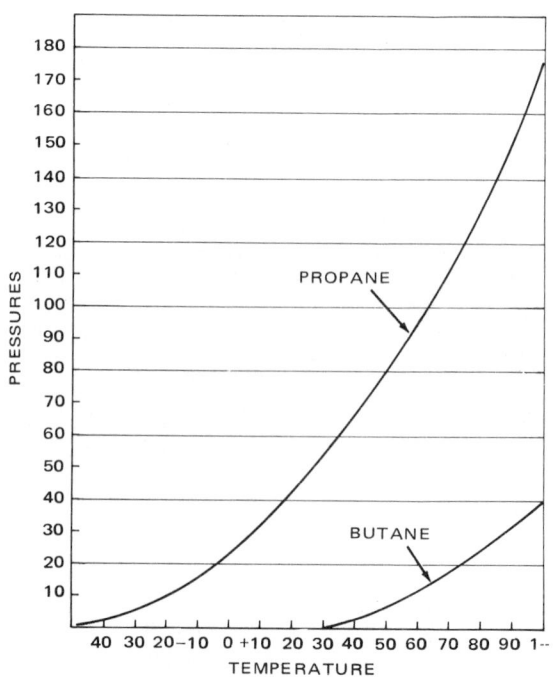

Fig. 26-27. Chart shows how pressure increases with rise in temperature of propane and butane.

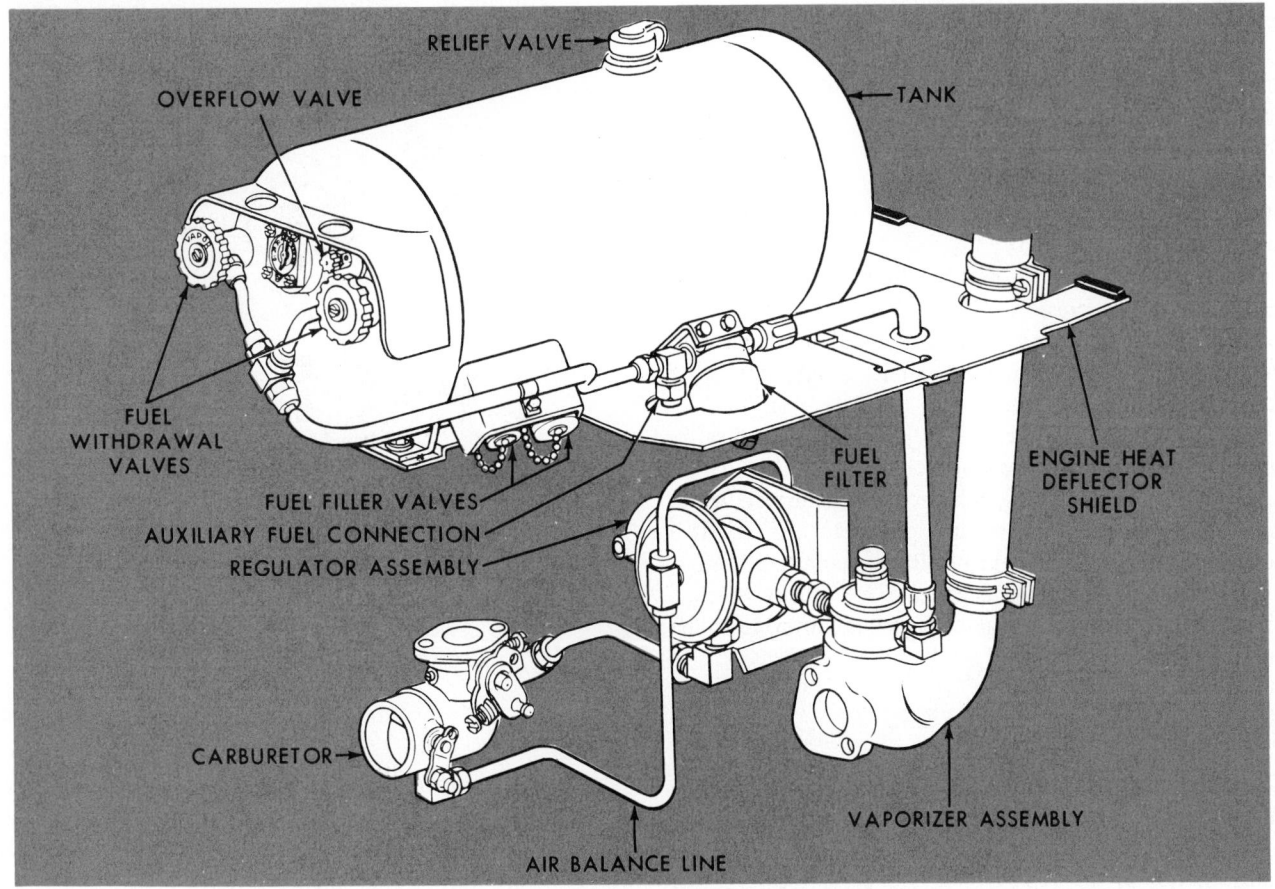

Fig. 26-28. Layout of Zenith LP-Gas system.

LP-Gas is becoming more widely distributed as an increasing number of trucks and tractors are being fitted with the necessary equipment. In addition to its lower cost, LP-Gas has the advantage of having a high octane value. Pure butane has a rating of 93, while propane is approximately 100. Therefore, the octane rating of LP-Gas will range between these two values, depending on the proportion of each gas used.

Since it is a dry gas, LP-Gas does not create carbon in the engine and does not cause dilution of the engine oil. Therefore, its use reduces valve grinding, cylinder and ring wear, and other engine maintenance. The oil changes for the engine can be made at less frequent intervals because it is such a clean burning fuel.

In order to get maximum power and other advantages from the use of LP-Gas, it is generally advisable to have the engine designed especially for its use. However, many satisfactory conversions of conventional gasoline engines have been made. Such conversions are usually made with an engine designed for use with premium fuel (a compression ratio of 10 to 1 or higher).

Other advantages claimed for LP-Gas are easy cold weather starting, lack of objectionable exhaust odor and elimination of evaporation and spillage losses. A pressure tank must be used and the entire fuel system must be kept sealed to avoid loss.

Marvel-Schebler/Tillotson, Div. of Borg-Warner Corp. point out the following advantages:

1. LP-Gas engines last 3 to 4 times as long.
2. LP-Gas greatly reduces cost of maintenance.
3. Very few operators using LP-Gas as a fuel change their engine oil sooner than 500 hours or 15,000 miles of operation.
4. Spark plug life is greatly increased.
5. LP-Gas costs less than gasoline, greatly reduces "down" time and permits a smaller service staff.

Another primary advantage of LP-Gas as an automotive fuel is the low level of exhaust emissions. Compared to gasoline-fueled engines, far less emission control equipment is required.

Disadvantages of LP-Gas as an automotive fuel are:

1. Research Octane number can range from 105 to 112, yet fuel exhibits poor anti-knock quality.
2. Fuel's sensitivity can range as high as 16 to 17 units. Sensitivity is defined as numerical difference between Research and Motor Octane numbers of fuel measured in laboratory. NOTE: Higher the number, the more likely engine will knock under part throttle operation. Compression ratios of LP-Gas engines are limited to some extent by this sensitivity.
3. LP-Gas is a hot burning fuel, which results in premature exhaust valve and seat failure (unless special materials are used).
4. LP-Gas fuel tanks are heavy, because they must withstand high pressure under which fuel is stored.

OPERATION OF LP-GAS SYSTEM

Briefly, the operation of an LP-Gas system on an internal combustion engine is as follows:

1. Gas leaves supply tank, Fig. 26-28, as a liquid at high pressure.
2. Fuel passes through fuel filter and contaminants are removed.
3. Next, vaporizer and/or regulator allows liquid to expand into a gas at low pressure. NOTE: Vaporizers usually are mounted near engine and, if water-jacketed, are connected to engine water circulation system to avoid frosting of internal parts in cold weather.
4. Then, dry gas at low pressure is piped to mixing valve, which is used in place of a carburetor.
5. Engine starts and operates under control of throttle valve, same as when gasoline is used in a carburetor. NOTE: It is desirable to have a cold intake manifold when using LP-Gas, so the manifold heating arrangements are usually blocked off when a conventional gasoline engine is converted to the use of LP-Gas.

LP-GAS CARBURETOR SYSTEMS

The differences between the LP-Gas and gasoline carburetion systems are basically mechanical and arise from the different characteristics of the two fuels.

Since LP-Gas in the supply tank is under pressure, a fuel pump is not required. Being under relatively high pressure, the fuel first passes through a pressure reducing regulator which operates from a coil spring working against a diaphragm. This regulator reduces the pressure to between 10 and 3 psi.

From the primary regulator, the LP-Gas passes to the secondary regulator (also a diaphragm type). Because of reduced pressure, the fuel reaching the secondary regulator is a vapor. The secondary regulator reduces the pressure to atmospheric pressure, and the fuel is delivered to the carburetor where it is mixed with the correct proportion of air.

There are two main types of LP-Gas carburetion systems.

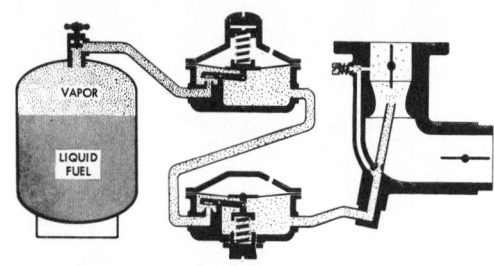
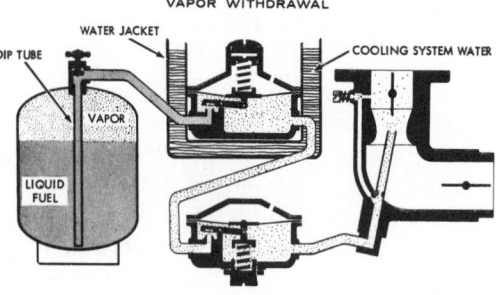

Fig. 26-29. Illustrating two types of LP-Gas fuel and carbureting systems.

One system, known as the vapor withdrawal system, takes the vapor from the top of the supply tank. The other type called liquid withdrawal, draws liquid fuel from the bottom of the supply tank, Fig. 26-29.

In the vapor system, all regulators operate on gas. In the liquid system, the first regulator works on liquid, with the second on gas. Liquid systems include a positive action vaporizer, supplied with heat from the engine. Fig. 26-30.

Some gasoline engines converted to LP-Gas use the original carburetor. The carburetor body is drilled, and a tube is inserted into the verturi. The location of the opening of the tube corresponds to the opening of the main discharge. A similar arrangement is used on installations that can be switched to operate on either gasoline or LP-Gas.

Another design, known as the adapter type carburetor,

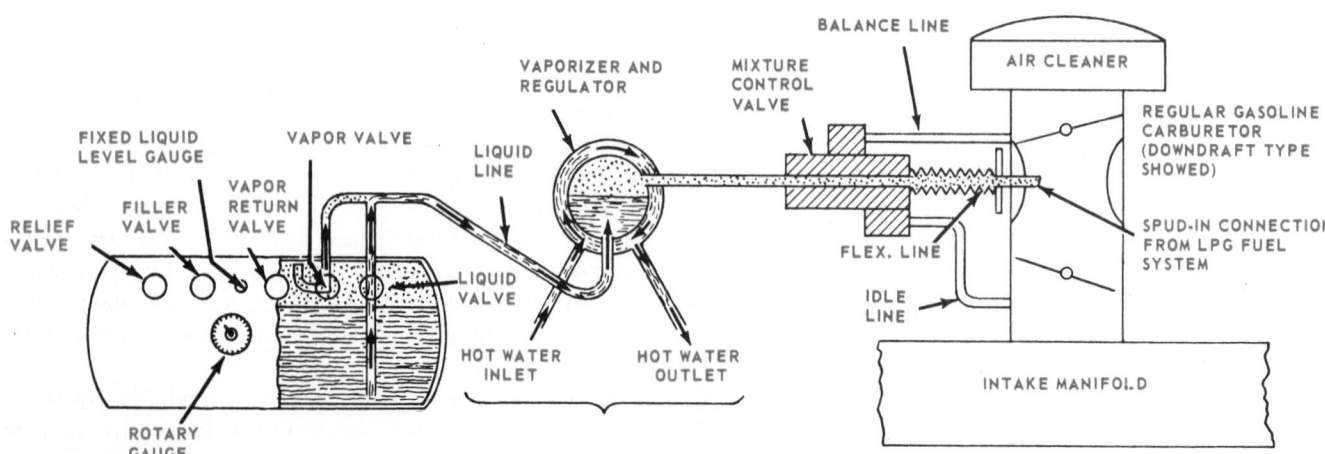

Fig. 26-30. Diagram of Century Gas Equipment liquid withdrawal system. (Marvel-Schebler/Tillotson Div., Borg-Warner Corp.)

consists of an air-fuel mixing unit. This is installed between the gasoline carburetor and the air cleaner. No throttle plate is provided in the adapter carburetor; the throttle of the gasoline carburetor is used.

Obviously, when a conversion installation is made which permits operating on either gasoline or LP-Gas, special shut-off valves are installed. This avoids the possibility of feeding both fuels simultaneously. These valves may be controlled either manually or electrically. In addition, there is a main hand-operated shut-off valve at the LP-Gas tank. It is needed when the supply tank is filled.

In still another design, a combined vaporizer and pressure reducing device is used on some engines. This device takes the liquid butane-propane under tank pressure, and converts it into a dry gaseous fuel at slightly below atmospheric pressure. It regulates the flow of gas through the carburetor in the correct volume and pressure to meet the demands of the engine at all speeds and loads.

controlled by a fuel metering cone which is linked directly to the throttle doors. There is a simple adjustment to permit proper setting of fuel flow in proportion to air flow. The adjustment is made by setting the correct idle fuel mixture, after which the metering cone contour will provide correct fuel flow for other engine speeds and loads.

A full-power adjustment and an automatic fuel enrichment system are also provided for maximum performance, acceleration and wide open throttle operation.

The automatic fuel enrichment device is diaphragm operated and preadjusted to enrich the fuel mixture when engine manifold drops to 6 in. (15.2 cm) of mercury or less. This system also provides fuel enrichment for starting.

IMPCO CARBURETOR

Details of an Impco carburetor of the air valve type are shown in Fig. 26-33. This carburetor is designed to use natural

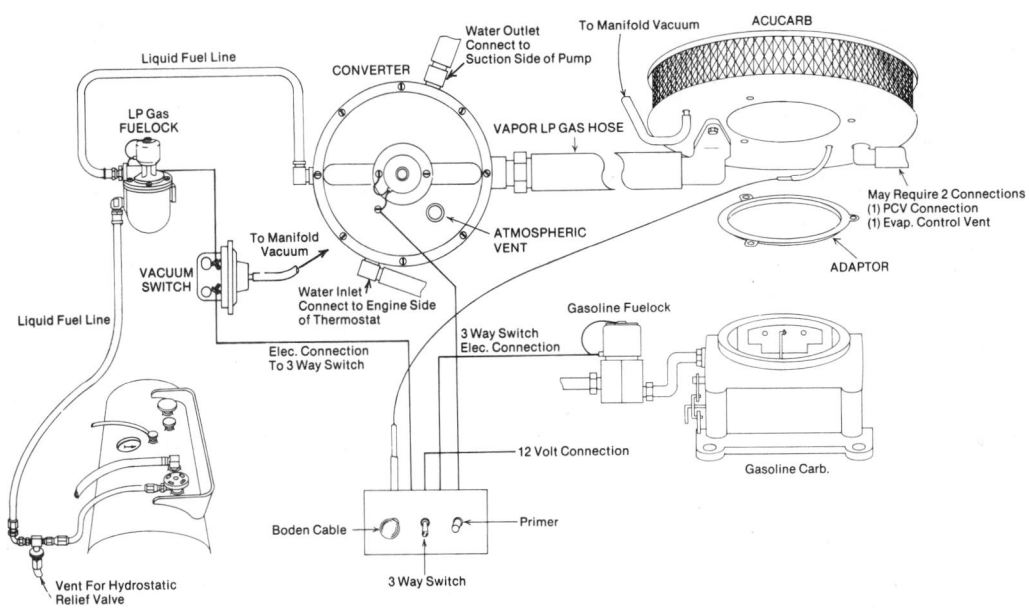

Fig. 26-31. Typical installation of Century AcuCarb carburetion system.   (Marvel, Schebler/Tillotson Div., Borg-Warner Corp.)

ACUCARB DUAL FUEL OPERATION

The Century AcuCarb carburetion system is designed to permit operation on either gasoline or propane fuel with nearly equal power. It is available for installation on all U.S. V-8 or six cylinder engines having a displacement of 300 cu. in. (4.9 litre) or more.

This system provides throttle doors that communicate directly with fuel vapor passages in the base of the unit. See Figs. 26-31 and 26-32. In that way, engine vacuum is transmitted to the secondary side of the converter, providing uninterrupted fuel flow into the AcuCarb. The fuel vapor is thoroughly mixed with the incoming air at the top edge of the throttle doors, providing correct air-fuel mixtures for all engine operating conditions.

The amount of fuel metered through the AcuCarb is

gas under pressure. However, it may be used with LP-Gas by using a final stage of regulation at atmospheric pressure.

Airflow through the Impco is controlled by a butterfly valve in the carburetor throat. The amount of airflow is sensed by a measuring valve in the bowl of the carburetor. The greater the airflow, the higher the airflow measuring valve rises.

The gas metering valve is connected directly to the air valve, to insure that they rise exactly the same amount. The gas valve is shaped to admit the correct amount of gas at any height to which the airflow measuring valve rises.

The airflow measuring valve sets up a pressure drop of 0.5 in. Hg., which gives a very high metering force to the fuel entering the carburetor at low engine speeds. This allows easy starting without priming.

At full engine speed, with the airflow measuring valve at the top of its travel, it becomes a venturi and will allow passage of

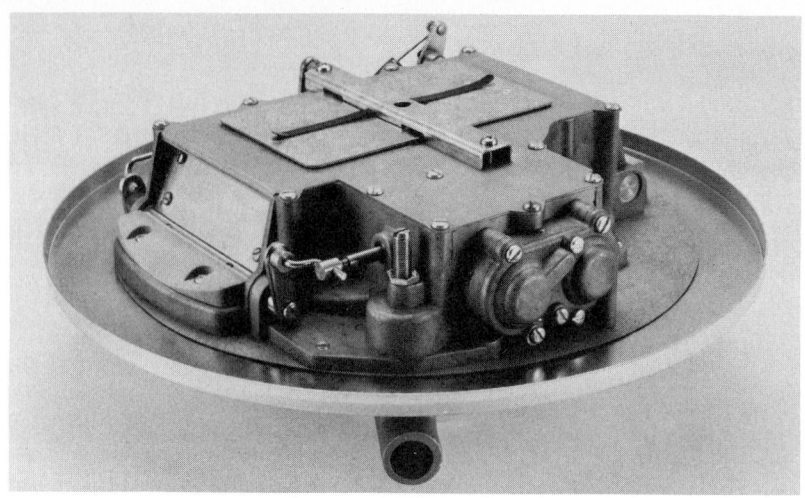

Fig. 26-32. View of dual fuel carburetion unit used in AcuCarb system.

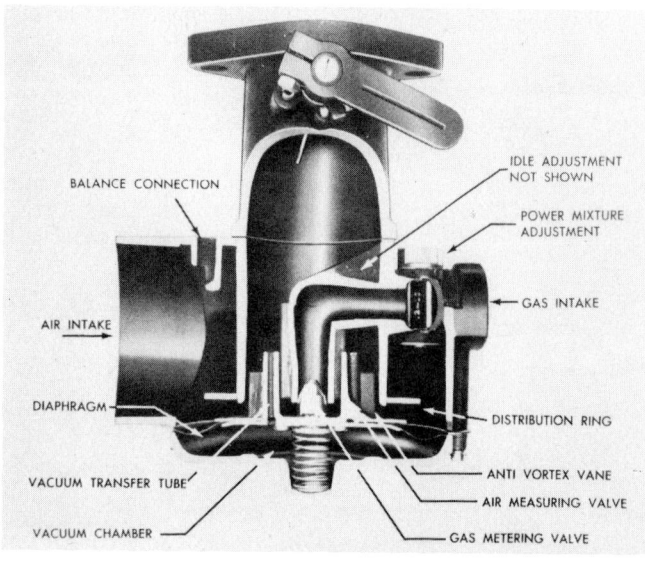

Fig. 26-33. Call outs give details of Impco diaphragm-operated, air-gas valve carburetor.

a great amount of air beyond that point. Impco carburetors have a built-in shut-off valve to stop the flow of gas when the engine is stopped.

All mixtures are controlled by pressure in these air valve carburetors. LP-Gas contains more Btu value than natural gas. Consequently, the inlet pressure to the carburetor must be lower on a fuel with more Btu value and higher pressure with natural gas or with manufactured gas.

VARIABLE VENTURI CARBURETOR

A variable venturi Impco LP-Gas carburetor has broad application. It has a reciprocating, piston-like motion inside the cylindrical cavity of the throttle body assembly, Fig. 26-34. The carburetor is designed for use of any size LP-Gas engine from a small lift truck to heavy-duty engines of maximum power.

When the engine is not running, the venturi or air valve assembly is held in a closed position by a metering spring. The gas passage in the throttle body is completely closed off by

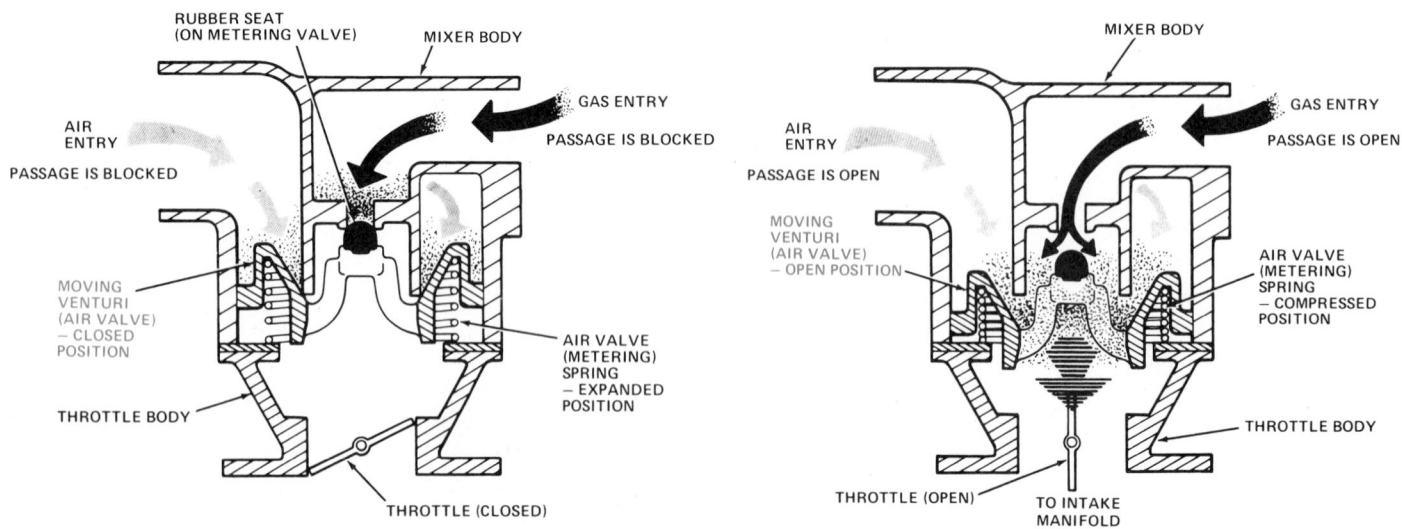

Fig. 26-34. Sectional drawing shows operation of Impco variable venturi LP-Gas carburetor.

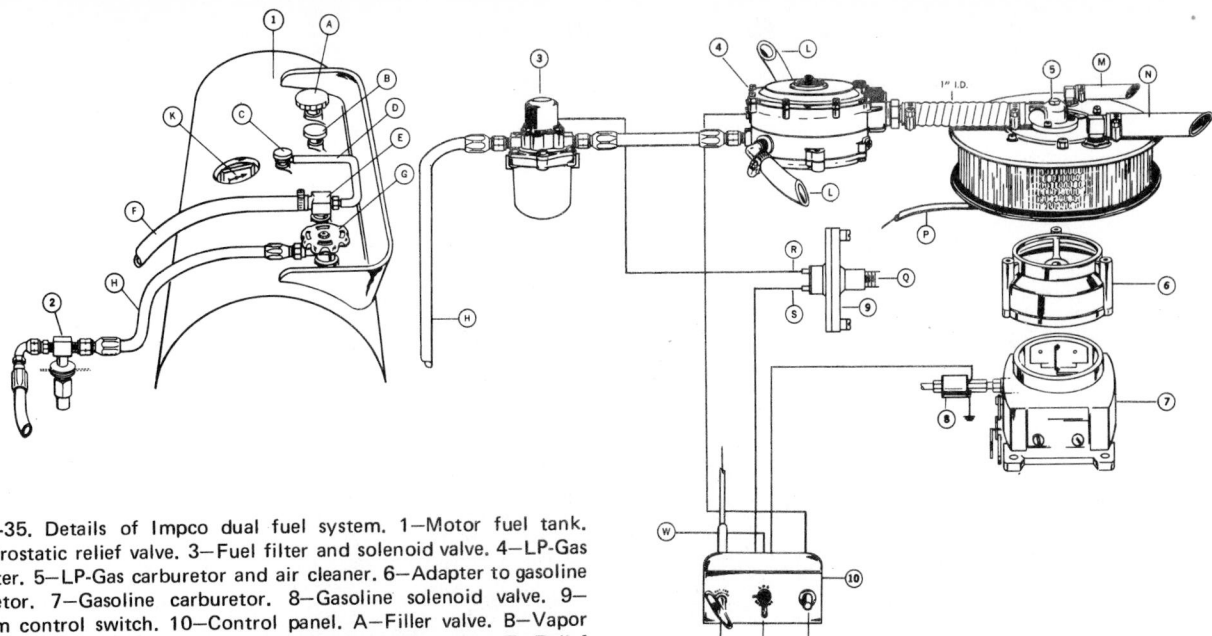

Fig. 26-35. Details of Impco dual fuel system. 1—Motor fuel tank. 2—Hydrostatic relief valve. 3—Fuel filter and solenoid valve. 4—LP-Gas converter. 5—LP-Gas carburetor and air cleaner. 6—Adapter to gasoline carburetor. 7—Gasoline carburetor. 8—Gasoline solenoid valve. 9—Vacuum control switch. 10—Control panel. A—Filler valve. B—Vapor return valve. C—10 percent outage valve. D—Vapor vent. E—Relief valve. F—Vent line. G—LP-Gas valve. H—Gas high pressure hose line. K—Fuel gauge. L—Water inlet and outlet. M-N—Water inlet and outlet. P—Bowden wire cable, which opens air valve when engine is run on gasoline. Q—Connects to intake manifold. R—Connects to LP-Gas solenoid hot line. S—Connects to toggle switch hot line. T—Toggle switch, which activates valves for fuel control. U—Electric primer switch for converter. W—Connects to 12V battery.

means of a synthetic rubber seat on the metering valve.

When the engine is started, the air valve venturi moves upward off the gas passage inlet. This allows entry of the gas into the venturi throat, where it mixes with high velocity inlet air. The air valve opens in direct proportion to the breathing requirements of the engine; the higher the load demand, the greater the opening.

DUAL FUEL OPERATION

In many operations, it is desirable to be able to operate the engine on either LP-Gas or gasoline. This "dual" Impco system, Fig. 26-35, is similar to the usual LP-Gas system, except for the following:
1. LP-Gas carburetor and air cleaner, mounted on an adapter so gasoline carburetor can be used.
2. Generator solenoid valve.
3. Vacuum control switch, which prevents flow of fuel when engine stops and ignition switch is on.
4. Control panel.
The complete dual fuel system is shown in Fig. 26-35.

REVIEW QUESTIONS — FUEL SUPPLY SYSTEMS

1. On lawn mower engines, how is fuel usually supplied to the carburetor?
2. On modern passenger cars, what two methods are used to drive the fuel pumps?
3. How much pressure should the conventional mechanical type fuel pump develop?
   a. 5 lb.
   b. 10 lb.
   c. 15 lb.
4. In 45 seconds, how much fuel should be pumped by the average mechanical type fuel pump?
   a. 1 pint.   c. 3 pints.
   b. 2 pints.   d. 32 ounces.
5. What is the average vacuum developed by a vacuum pump that is built into a fuel pump?
   a. 5 in.   c. 10 in.
   b. 7 1/2 in.   d. 18 in.
6. What is a major advantage of using an externally mounted, electrically operated fuel pump?
7. Name two main types of mechanically driven superchargers.

8. Which type of internal combustion engine will tend to detonate more?
   a. Supercharged.   b. Nonsupercharged.
9. What is a major advantage of the turbosupercharger over the mechanically driven type?
   a. Little or no power required to drive it.
   b. Develops more pressure.
10. Name the two general types of fuel gauges.
11. Name two types of materials used in fuel filters.
12. Liquefied petroleum gas is a mixture of:
    a. Butane and propane.
    b. Propane and heptune.
    c. Methane and octane.
    d. Butane and methane.
13. Is the boiling point of propane higher or lower than zero degrees Fahrenheit.
14. Does LP-Gas produce more or less carbon in an engine than gasoline?
15. Name the two types of LP-Gas withdrawal systems.
16. All mixtures are controlled by pressure in an Impco air valve carburetor. Yes or No?

Sectional view of "Fuel Pincher" diesel V-8 engine. Note open type combustion chamber and unit type fuel injectors. The turbocharger is mounted at top of engine between banks of cylinders. (Detroit Diesel Allison Div., GM)

FUEL INJECTION

A diesel engine compresses air and, at the point of maximum compression, fuel is injected into the combustion chamber. Ignition takes place as a result of the high temperature created.

The fuel is forced into the combustion chamber of a diesel engine by means of a pump and injector. Since high pressures exist in the combustion chamber at the time of injection, the injection system must develop pressures well in excess of combustion chamber pressure.

In delivering the fuel to the combustion chamber, a diesel fuel injection system must fulfill five main requirements:
1. Meter or measure correct quantity of fuel injected.
2. Time fuel injection.
3. Control rate of fuel injection.
4. Atomize fuel into fine particles.
5. Properly distribute fuel in combustion chamber.

DIESEL FUEL INJECTION

There are two different methods of fuel injection: air injection and mechanical injection.

In the air injection system, a blast of air from an external source forces a measured amount of fuel into the cylinder.

In the mechanical injection system (now used almost exclusively), fuel is forced into the cylinder by hydraulic pressure on the fuel.

In the automotive field, there are four basic types of mechanical fuel injection systems:
1. Common rail system.
2. Pump controlled (or jerk pump) system.
3. Unit injection system.
4. Distributor system.

COMMON RAIL SYSTEM: The common rail system consists of a high-pressure pump which distributes fuel to a common rail or header to which each injector is connected by tubing, Fig. 27-1.

PUMP CONTROLLED SYSTEM: This is also known as the jerk pump system and provides a single pump for each injector. The pump is separately mounted and is driven by an accessory shaft. Connection to the injectors is made by suitable tubing.

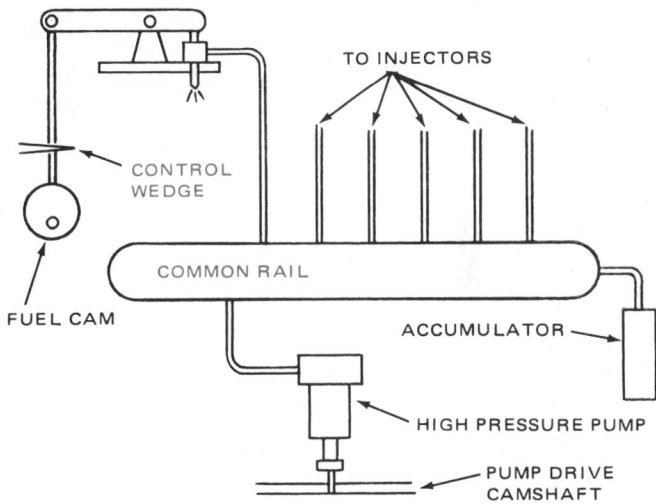

Fig. 27-1. Diagram shows simplified layout of common rail system of mechanical fuel injection.

UNIT INJECTOR SYSTEM: This system combines the pump and the injector into a single unit. High-pressure fuel lines are eliminated. Operation of the unit injector is usually by means of push rods and rocker arms.

DISTRIBUTOR SYSTEM: There are several types of distributor systems. One type provides a high-pressure metering pump with a distributor which delivers fuel to the individual cylinders. Another design provides a low-pressure metering and distribution. High pressure needed for injection is provided by the injection nozzles which are cam operated.

MECHANICAL INJECTION PUMPS

The mechanical fuel injection pump performs many functions. It times, meters and forces the fuel at high pressure through the spray nozzle.

Most designs are of the plunger type and are cam operated, but there is considerable variation in the method used to control the quantity of fuel delivered. Among the methods of controlling the quantity of fuel are:

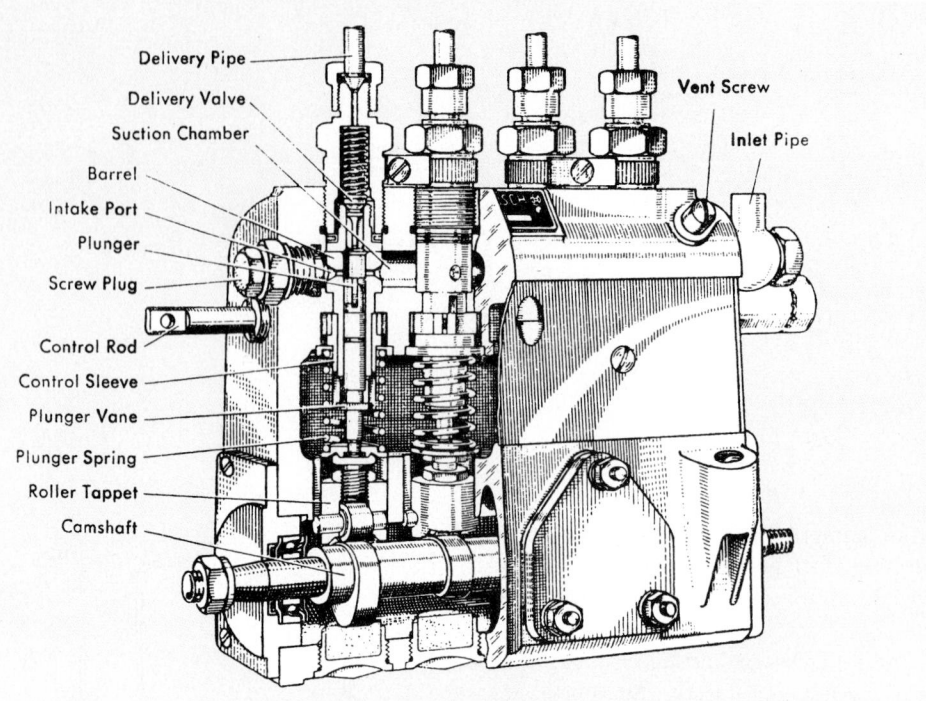

Fig. 27-2. American Bosch type APE diesel injection pump for four cylinder engine.

1. Variable stroke.
2. Throttle inlet.
3. Throttle bypass.
4. Timed bypass.
5. Control of port opening.

Current design favors the port opening type of control.

VARIABLE STROKE DESIGN: The stroke in the variable stroke design is changed by sliding a cam plate in or out of its slot in the hollow camshaft. Axial movement of the camshaft is governor controlled which in turn produces radial displacement of the cam plate.

THROTTLE INLET DESIGN: In the throttle inlet design, the flow of fuel into the pumping cylinder is throttled. This is done by rotation of a metering valve, which varies the port opening into the plunger bore.

THROTTLE BYPASS DESIGN: In the throttle bypass method of controlling fuel, metered fuel in the plunger chamber is discharged to the nozzle and at the same time is bypassed through a throttle valve back to the inlet. The size of the bypass port opening is varied by governor action controlling a needle valve.

TIMED BYPASS DESIGN: Metering the fuel in the timed bypass method is controlled by spilling excess fuel to a mechanically operated bypass valve. The quantity of fuel discharged is controlled by rotation of an eccentric shaft on which a rocking lever pivots. Fuel delivery starts on the upstroke of the plunger, and ceases when the bypass valve is lifted by contact with the rocking lever.

PORT CONTROL DESIGN: In the port control method of metering fuel, a portion of the plunger functions as a valve to cover and uncover ports in the plunger barrel. A groove on the plunger is designed to rotate so that the plunger stroke can be varied, thus controlling the quantity of fuel delivered on each stroke.

AMERICAN BOSCH DIESEL SYSTEMS

The American Bosch Arma Corporation produces fuel injection pumps for single and multi-cylinder engines. The pumps for single cylinder engines are of the constant stroke, lapped plunger, port controlled type. For multi-cylinder engines, American Bosch produces the constant stroke type and also the single plunger distributor type pump.

Typical of the port controlled type are the APE and APF series. A pump of the APE series is shown in Fig. 27-2. Each pump element is so accurately fitted in the barrel that it provides a seal without any packing, even at high pressures and low speeds. The plunger jacket is milled out along a helical line to provide for the control helix on the plunger. The plunger has two opposing radial holes through which the fuel oil reaches the delivery chamber of the barrel. See Fig. 27-3.

The pump plunger is actuated by a cam on the compression stroke; by the plunger spring on the suction stroke. The valve is closed by a spring-loaded delivery valve, connected with the delivery pipe to the respective nozzles in the engine cylinder.

To vary pump output, the pump valve has a control sleeve with a toothed quandrant clamped on the upper end. A control rod meshes with the toothed quandrant so that the pump plunger can be rotated during operation.

Various positions of the plunger are shown in Fig. 27-4. In its upward movement, the plunger closes the intake port, shown at 2 in Fig. 27-4. This forces the fuel through the

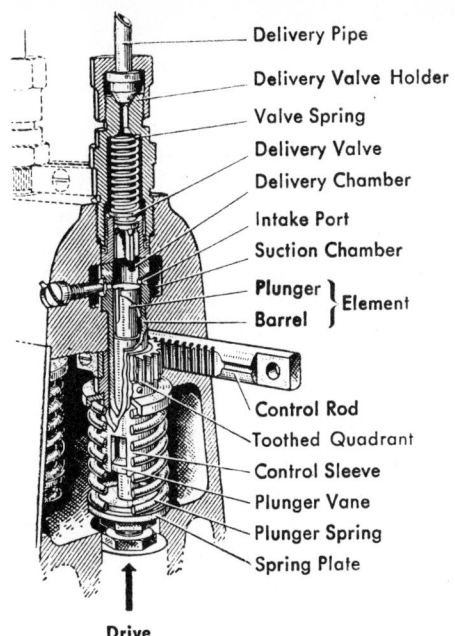

Fig. 27-3. Sectional view of American Bosch pump element.

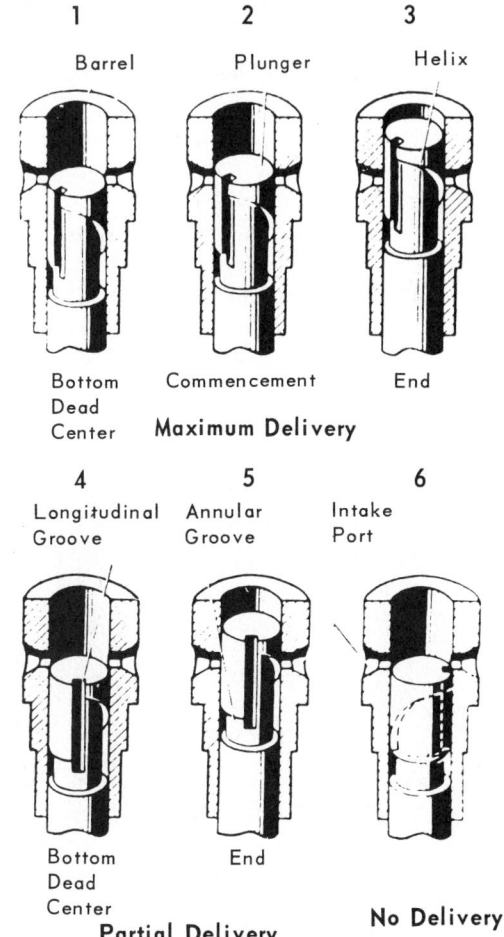

Fig. 27-4. Rotation of plunger controls quantity of fuel delivered.

delivery valve to the delivery pipe. Fuel delivery stops as soon as helix and inlet port coincide, since the delivery chamber of the barrel is (from that moment) connected to the suction chamber through the longitudinal and annular grooves. The fuel is forced back into the suction chamber. If the plunger is turned far enough for the longitudinal groove and inlet port to meet, as at 6 in Fig. 27-4, the fuel in the delivery chamber is not subjected to pressure, and no fuel will be delivered.

The injection nozzle used in the diesel system made by American Bosch is designed to control the mixture formation in the combustion chamber. American Bosch nozzles are either of the pintle type or hole type, Figs. 27-5 and 27-6.

In the case of the pintle type, the nozzle valve carries an extension on the lower end in the form on a pin called a "pintle," which protrudes through the closely fitting hole in

Fig. 27-5. Details of Bosch nozzle holder with pintle type nozzle. (Inset)

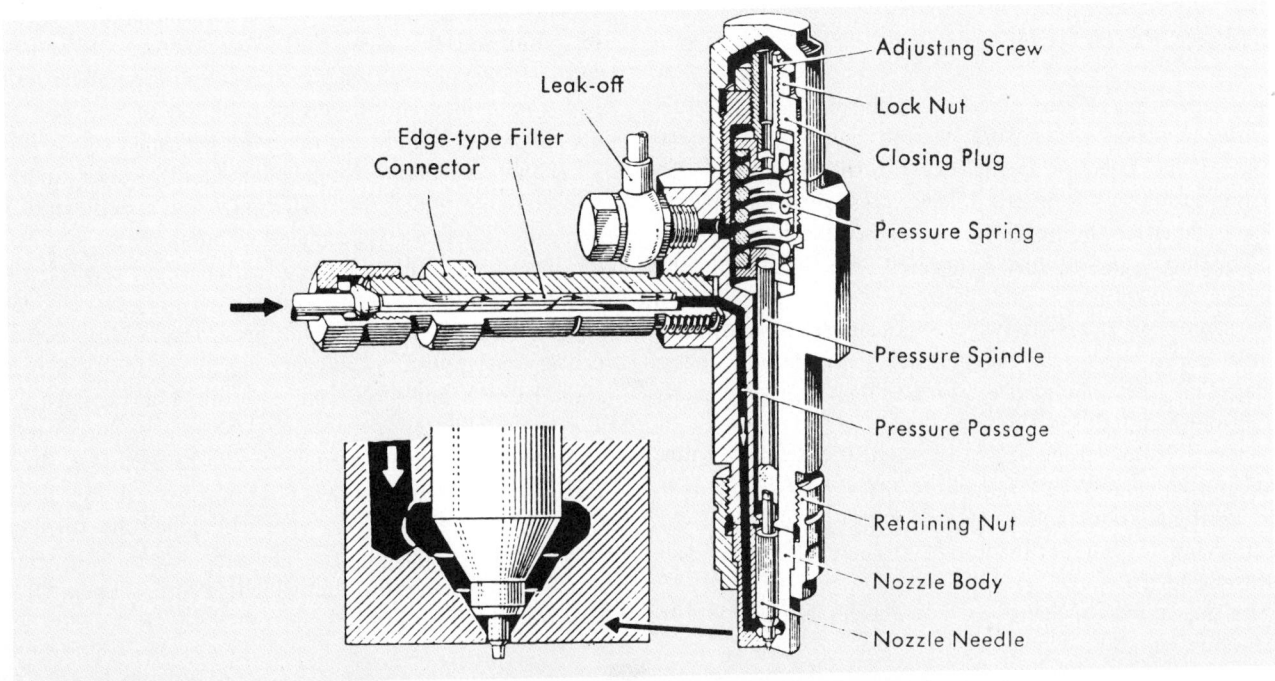

the nozzle bottom. This requires the injected fuel to pass through a round orifice to produce a hollow-cone shaped spray. The projection of the pintle through the nozzle induces a self cleaning effect thereby reducing the accumulation of carbon at that point.

The hole type nozzle has no pintle, but is basically similar in construction to the pintle type. The hole type nozzle has one or more spray orifices which are straight round holes through the tip of the nozzle body beneath the valve seat, Fig. 27-6. Spray from each individual orifice is relatively dense and

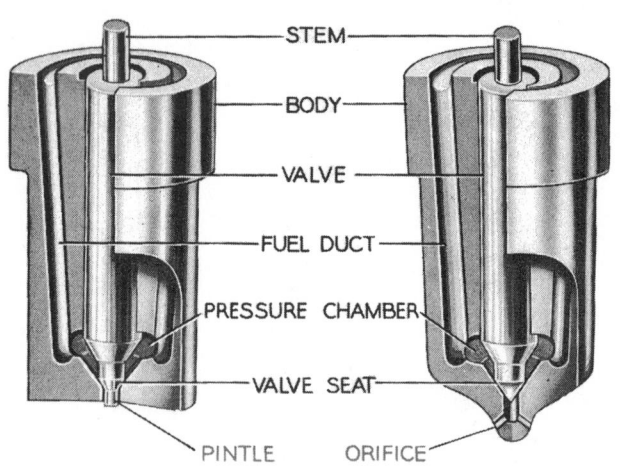

Fig. 27-6. Details of construction are called out for pintle and hole type fuel injectors.

compact. The general spray pattern is determined by the number and arrangement of the holes. As many as 18 holes can be provided in the larger nozzles. The diameter of the individual orifices may be as small as .006 in. The spray pattern may or may not be symmetrical (regular in shape), depending on the contours of the combustion chamber and fuel distribution requirements.

NOZZLE OPERATION

The operation of the nozzle is controlled by the fuel pressure. As soon as pressure exerted during the delivery stroke of the injection pump exceeds the tension of the pressure spring in the nozzle holder, pressure acting on the pressure taper of the nozzle needle causes the needle to be lifted off its seat and fuel is injected into the combustion chamber.

Nozzle opening pressure (which is adjustable) is determined by the initial tension of the pressure spring in the nozzle holder, Fig. 27-5. The needle stroke is limited by the plane surface on the nozzle holder.

When injected, fuel flows through the delivery pipe, connector and pressure passage of the nozzle holder, Fig. 27-5, then through groove and passage of nozzle, and out of the injection hole or holes of the nozzle into combustion chamber of the engine.

The importance of delivering only absolutely clean fuel to

the nozzles cannot be overemphasized. Because of the closely fitted parts, even microscopic size foreign matter can cause malfunctioning and wear of the parts. Consequently, two or more filters usually are installed, Fig. 27-7. The first, or primary, filter is designed to remove the larger and heavier particles. Often, it is the cleanable metal edge type. The final filter should be capable of removing particles down to 3 to 5 microns (0.00012 to 0.00020 in.).

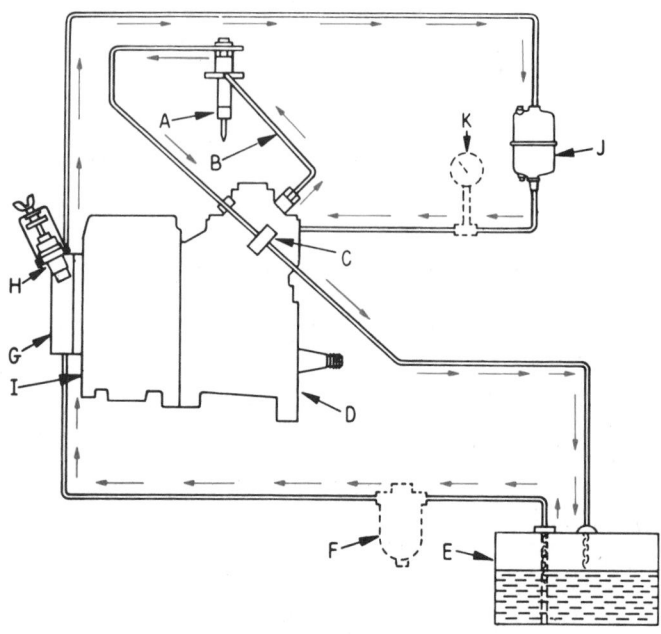

Fig. 27-7. Schematic diagram of American Bosch PSJ fuel system. A—Injection nozzle. B—High-pressure fuel line. C—Overflow valve. D—Injection pump. E—Fuel tank. F—Primary filter. G—Supply pump. H—Operational hand priming pump. I—Governor housing. J—Final filter. K—Fuel oil pressure gauge, if used.

AMERICAN BOSCH DISTRIBUTOR TYPE PUMPS

There are two American Bosch distributor type pumps, the PS series and the series 100. These pumps utilize a single, hardened steel plunger that reciprocates for pumping action. It also rotates for continuous distribution of the fuel to the discharge outlets and from there to the engine.

The model 100 is a flange mounted, high speed (up to 3200 rpm) variable timing, governor controlled, high-pressure, single plunger, distributor type injection pump. See Fig. 27-8. It is designed for over-the-road and off-highway vehicles, and for marine and industrial applications.

The replaceable hydraulic head, Fig. 27-9, contains a delivery valve and a plunger which, in addition to being actuated by a multi-lobe cam, is continuously rotated to serve as a fuel distributor.

Fuel distribution does not need to be adjusted. Therefore, the only adjustments necessary are for average fuel deliveries. Changes in fuel delivery are controlled by the vertical movement of the plunger metering sleeve. This sleeve is actuated by the control unit which, in turn, is operated by the control rod.

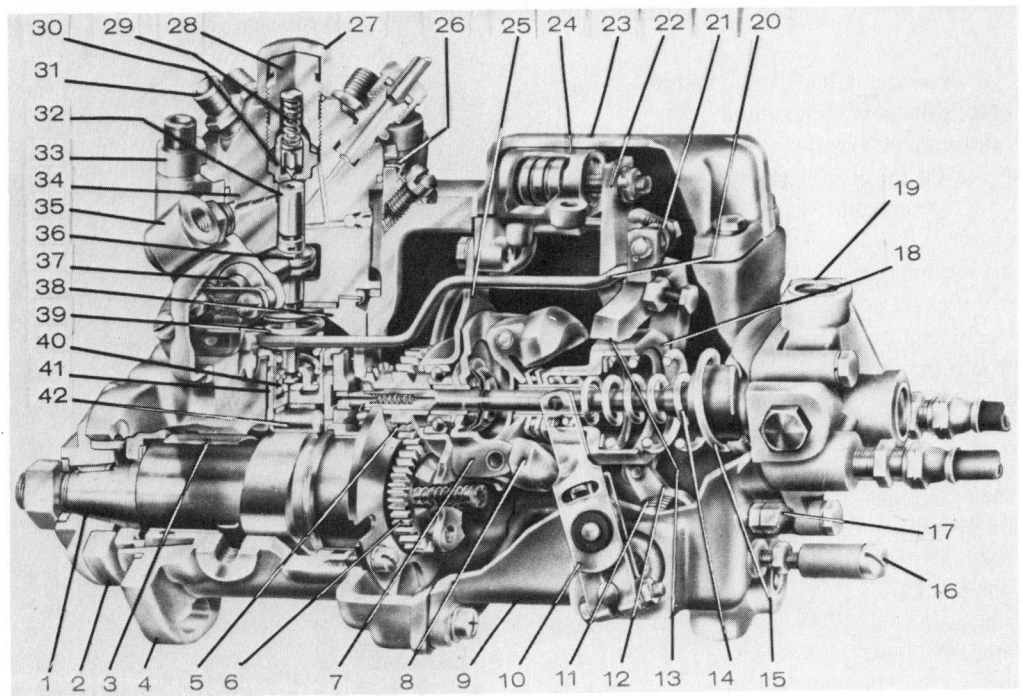

Fig. 27-8. Details of American Bosch series 100 fuel injection pump: 1—Camshaft. 2—Drive plate. 3—Camshaft bearing. 4—Pump mounting flange. 5—Governor and hydraulic drive gear. 6—Camshaft gear. 7—Governor weight spider. 8—Governor weights. 9—Governor housing. 10—Operating lever. 11—Operating shaft spring. 12—Fulcrum lever bracket. 13—Fulcrum lever. 14—Inner governor spring. 15—Outer governor spring. 16—Low idle screw (spring loaded). 17—High idle screw. 18—Governor sliding sleeve. 19—Fuel supply pump. 20—Control rod. 21—Torque cam. 22—Stop plate. 23—Governor top cover. 24—Excess fuel starting device. 25—Ball bearing support plate. 26—Head indexing plate. 27—Delivery valve cap nut and gasket. 28—Delivery valve holder. 29—Delivery valve spring. 30—Delivery valve and spring guide. 31—Fuel discharge outlet. 32—Hydraulic plunger. 33—Hydraulic head clamping screw and holder. 34—Hydraulic head assembly. 35—Overflow valve. 36—Fuel metering sleeve. 37—Control unit assembly. 38—Face gear. 39—Plunger return spring. 40—Plunger button and spring seat. 41—Tappet guide. 42—Tappet roller.

A centrifugal, mechanical type governor actuates the control rod. The governor controls idle speed, maximum no-load speed and fuel delivery throughout the operating speed range for any given throttle position.

The fuel supply pump draws fuel from the supply tank, through a primary filter, then supplies the fuel through a final filter stage to the hydraulic head sump area, Fig. 27-8. Fuel pressure in the sump area is controlled by the overflow valve assembly. The fuel supply pump contains an integral pressure relief valve which prevents fuel system damage in the event of downstream restriction.

An internal timing device, known as the Intravance[R] automatically advances or retards the beginning of fuel injection as engine speed requires. In addition, there is an internal, excess fuel starting device which provides increased fuel at cranking speeds.

GM DIESEL INJECTION SYSTEM FOR COMMERCIAL VEHICLES

This General Motors diesel engine operates on the two cycle principle and has a unit injector fuel system. In this system, a single unit measures the amount of fuel to be injected under varying conditions of speed and load. Next, it builds up the high pressure needed to inject the fuel into the combustion chamber, which is filled with air at an approximate pressure of 1000 lbs. per sq. in. Then, it atomizes the fuel. There is no

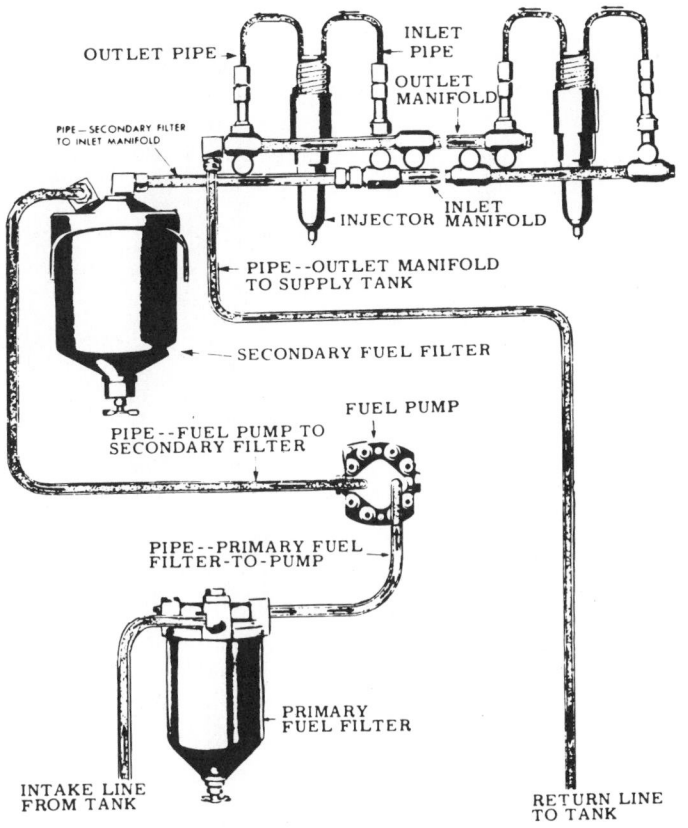

Fig. 27-9. Complete fuel system for General Motors two-cycle diesel engine.

central metering or pressure pump and, therefore, high-pressure fuel distributing lines are eliminated.

In the General Motors unit injection system, high pressures exist only at the tip of the injector. Each injector is complete. After repair work, or having run dry, it is not necessary to prime the GM injector.

The complete fuel system, Fig. 27-9, consists of the fuel supply tank, fuel line, fuel filters, fuel pump, fuel line manifold and the fuel injector. A separate injector is provided for each cylinder. From the supply tank, fuel is drawn through the first fuel strainer or filter by the fuel pump. Then, the fuel is forced through the second filter to the fuel intake manifold that supplies fuel to the individual injectors. The surplus fuel is returned through the outlet manifold to the supply tank.

The cross-sectional view of the engine, Fig. 27-10, shows the injector mounted in the cylinder head, and Fig. 27-11 shows details of the injector.

In the GM unit injector, Fig. 27-11, fuel is supplied to the injector at approximately 20 psi (pounds per square inch), and enters the body through the filter cap. The fuel passes through the filter and fills the chamber between the bushing and the spill deflector. The plunger operates up and down by means of the engine camshaft, push rods and rocker arms. It operates in

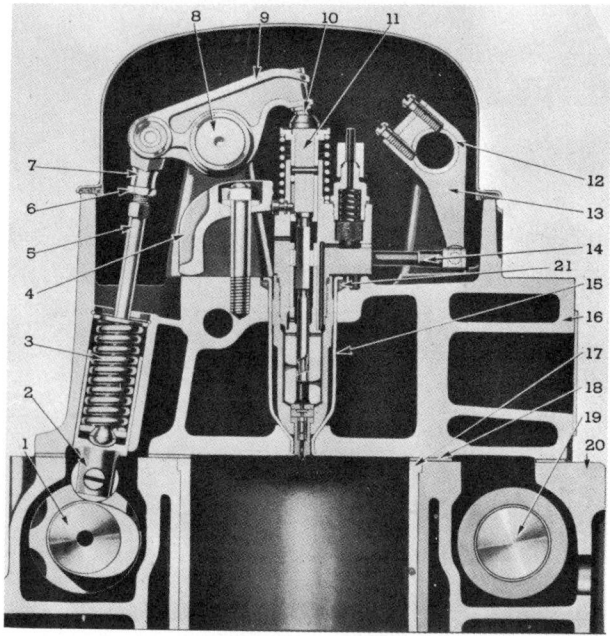

Fig. 27-10. Cross section of General Motors diesel cylinder head and fuel injector.

1. FOLLOWER.
2. FOLLOWER GUIDE.
3. PLUNGER SPRING.
4. FOLLOWER PIN.
5. STOP PIN.
6. GEAR.
7. RACK.
8. SEAL RING.
9. GEAR RETAINER.
10. UPPER HELIX.
11. METERING RECESS.
12. UPPER PORT.
13. BUSHING.
14. SPILL DEFLECTOR.
15. SPACER.
16. CHECK VALVE.
17. VALVE SEAT.
18. VALVE.
19. VALVE SPRING.
20. VALVE STOP.
21. FILTER CAP.
21A. GASKET-FILTER CAP.
22. FILTER SPRING.
23. FILTER ASSEMBLY.
24. INJECTOR BODY.
25. INJECTOR NUT.
26. INJECTOR PLUNGER.
27. FUEL CHAMBER.
28. LOWER HELIX.
29. LOWER PORT.
30. SPRAY TIP.

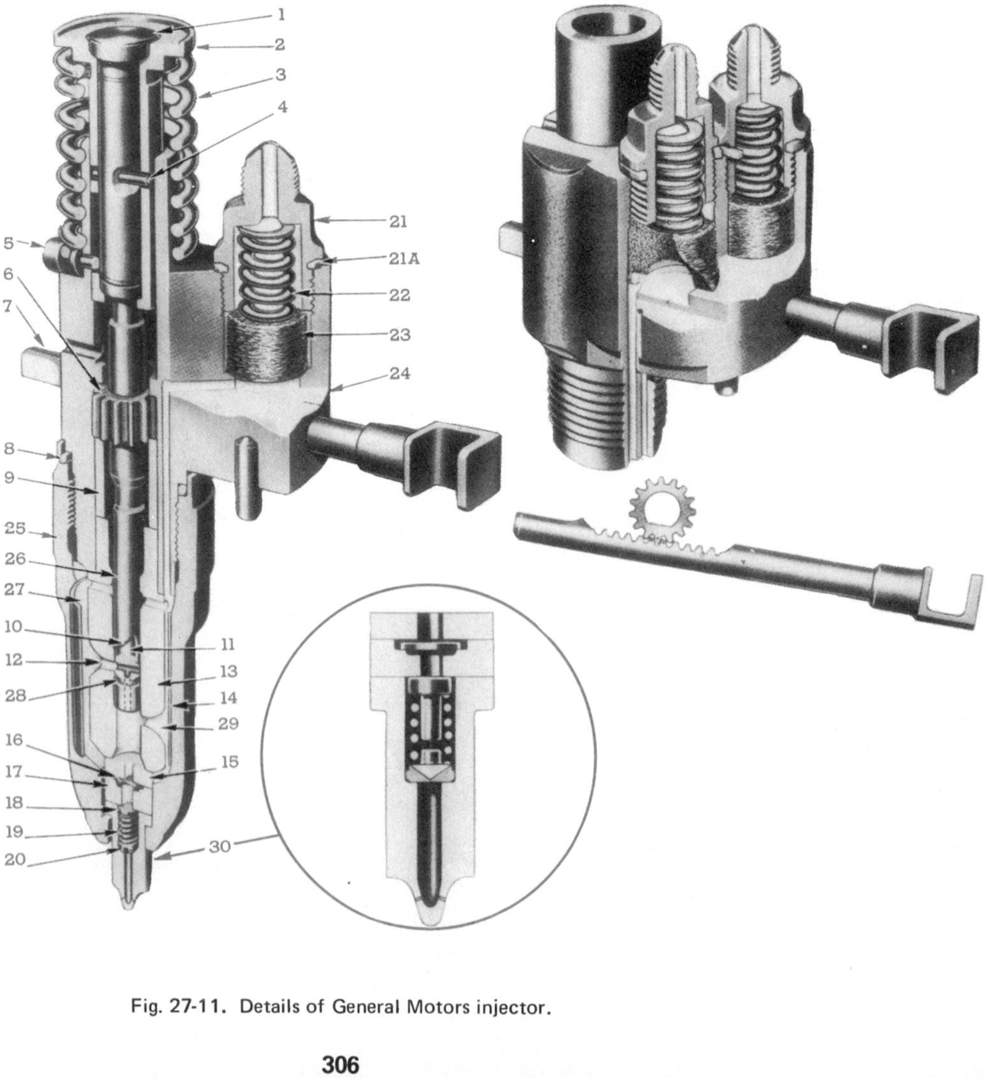

Fig. 27-11. Details of General Motors injector.

a bushing connected by means of ports to the fuel supply in the annular chamber.

The motion of the injector rocker arm is transmitted to the plunger by means of the follower that bears against the return spring. By means of the gear and rack, the plunger can be rotated. An upper and lower helix are machined into the lower end of the plunger for the purpose of metering fuel. As the plunger is rotated, the relation of the two helices with the plunger ports is changed.

As the plunger moves downward, fuel in the injector high-pressure cylinder is displaced through two ports, back into the supply chamber until the lower edge of the plunger closes the port. The remainder of the oil is then forced upward through the central passage in the plunger into the recess between the two helices. From there, it can still flow back into the supply chamber of the injector until the upper helix closes the upper port.

At this point, both upper and lower ports are closed. The fuel remaining under the plunger is then forced through the spray tip and into the combustion chamber of the engine. Changing the position of the helices by rotating the plunger retards or advances the closing of the ports. It also signals the beginning and ending of the injection period while, at the same time, controlling the desired amount of fuel that remains under the plunger for injection into the combustion chamber.

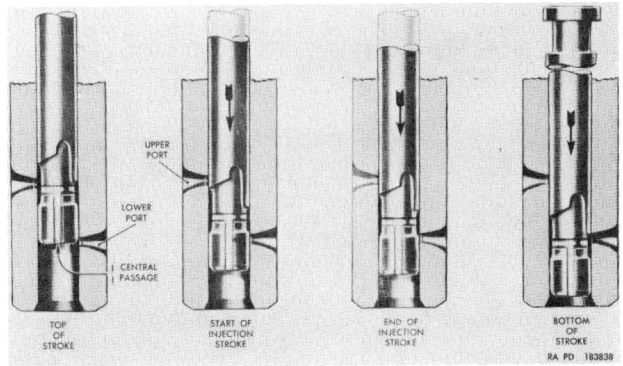

Fig. 27-13. Four positions for downward travel of General Motors injector.

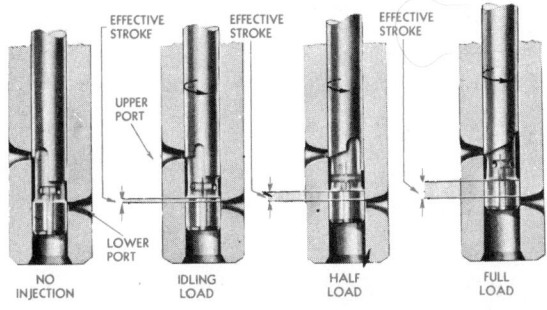

Fig. 27-12. Four positions of General Motors injector plunger from no injection to full injection.

The various positions of the plunger from no injection to full injection are shown in Fig. 27-12. Full injection is obtained with the control rack pushed in. In this position, the upper port is closed shortly after the lower port has been covered. In this way, a full effective stroke and maximum injection is produced. When the control rack is pulled out completely, the upper port is not closed by the helix until after the lower port is uncovered. As a result, all of the fuel charge is forced back into the supply chamber and no injection of fuel occurs.

The four positions for the downward travel of the plunger are shown in Fig. 27-13. On downward travel, the plunger forces the metered amount of fuel through the valve assembly, through the check valve, Fig. 27-11, and against the spray tip valve (see inset).

When sufficient pressure has been built up on the fuel, the spray tip valve is lifted from its seat and fuel is forced through the small orifices in the spray tip into the combustion chamber. The check valve prevents air leakage from the engine combustion chamber into the injector. If the valve is accidentally held open by a particle or carbon or dirt, the check valve permits the injector to continue to operate until the foreign matter works through the valve.

On the upward return movement of the plunger, the high-pressure cylinder is again filled with fuel through the ports. The constant circulation of fresh fuel oil in the fuel supply chamber helps maintain even operating temperatures. In addition, all traces of air are eliminated.

Each injector control rack is operated by a lever on a common control shaft. This shaft, in turn, is linked to the governor and the throttle. These levers can be rotated independently on the control shaft by the adjustment of two screws, which permit a uniform setting of the injector racks.

CUMMINS PRESSURE TIME SYSTEM

The Cummins PT system for diesel engines operates on the pressure time principle. This principle is based on the fact that by changing the pressure of a liquid flowing through a pipe, the amount of liquid coming out the open end is changed. Raising the pressure increases the amount of liquid delivered. The Cummins PT system consists of the fuel pump (with governor), the supply and drain lines and the injectors, Fig. 27-14.

The fuel pump, Fig. 27-15, is made of three main units:
1. Gear pump that draws fuel from the supply tank and delivers it under pressure through pump and supply lines to each injector.
2. Pressure regulator that limits the pressure of fuel to injectors.
3. Governor and throttle that act independently of pressure regulator to control fuel pressure to regulators. Fuel pump is driven at crankshaft speed.

The gear pump is located at the rear of the fuel pump, Fig. 27-15, and consists of a single set of gears which pick-up and deliver fuel throughout the system, Fig. 27-14.

The pressure regulator is a bypass valve to regulate the fuel under pressure to the injectors.

Fuel for the engine flows past the pressure regulator to

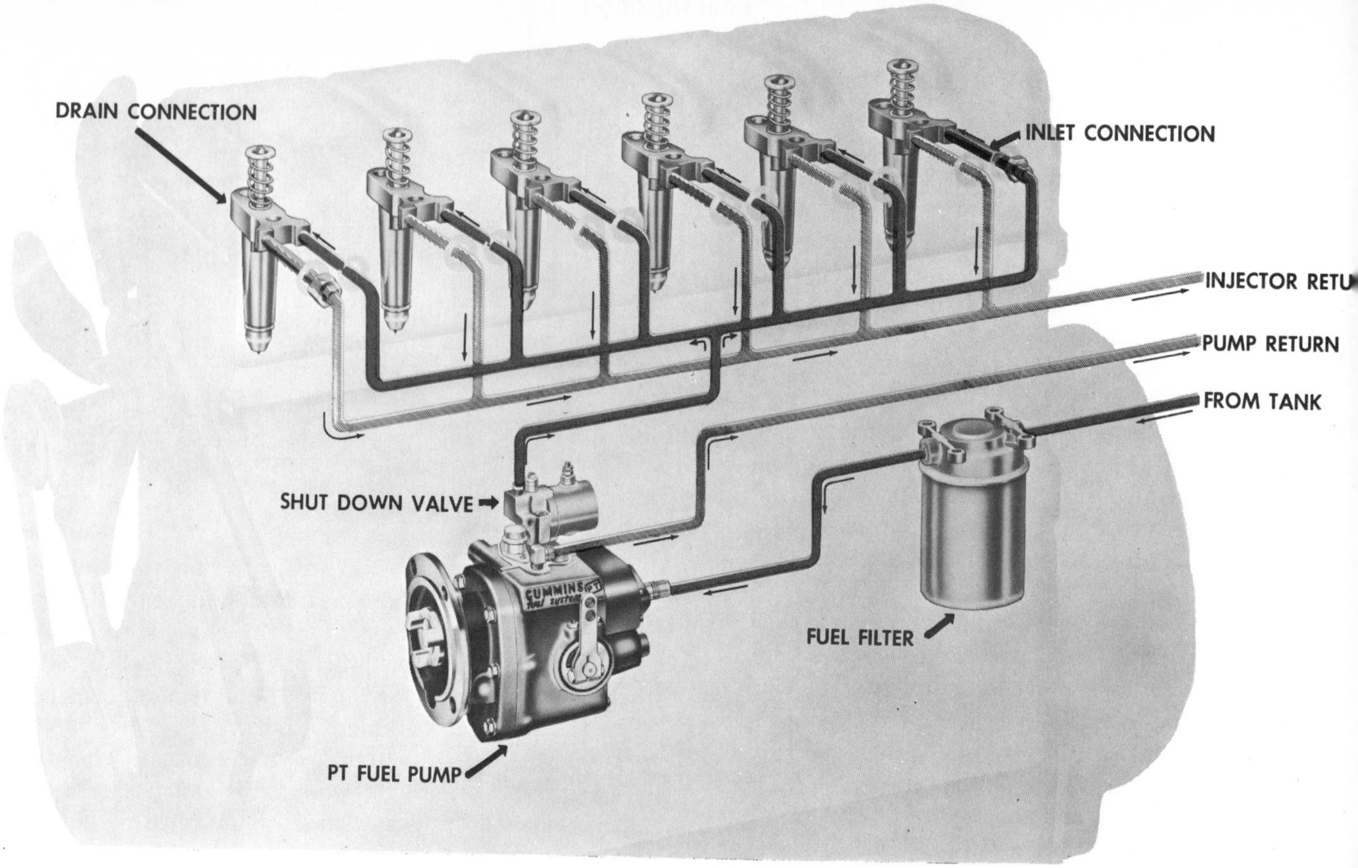

DRAIN CONNECTION

INLET CONNECTION

INJECTOR RETU[RN]

PUMP RETURN

FROM TANK

SHUT DOWN VALVE

FUEL FILTER

PT FUEL PUMP

Fig. 27-14. Fuel flow diagram of the Cummins PT (Pressure Time) system.

Fig. 27-15. Cross section of Cummins PT pump with idling and high speed mechanical governor.

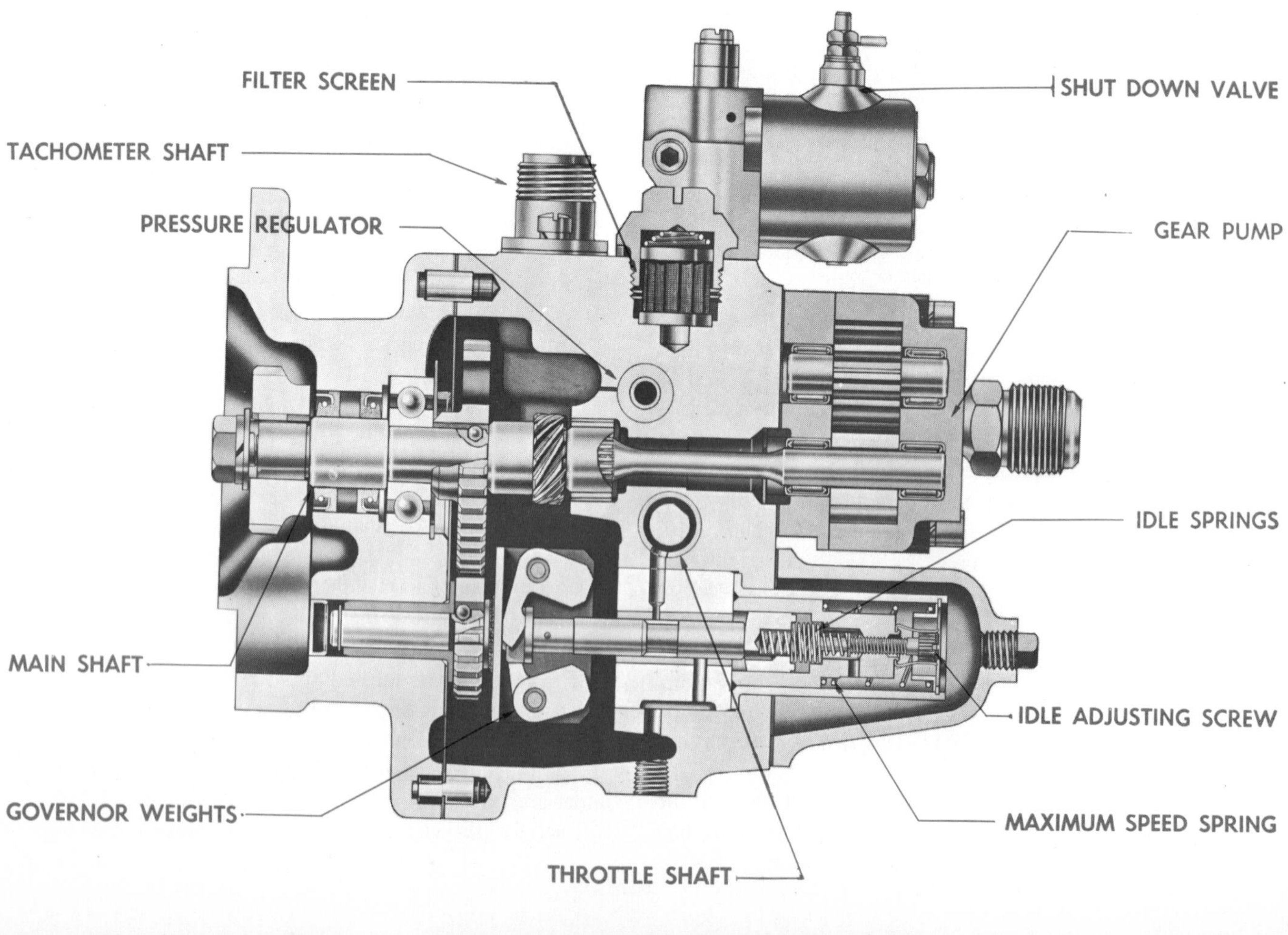

FILTER SCREEN

SHUT DOWN VALVE

TACHOMETER SHAFT

PRESSURE REGULATOR

GEAR PUMP

IDLE SPRINGS

MAIN SHAFT

IDLE ADJUSTING SCREW

GOVERNOR WEIGHTS

MAXIMUM SPEED SPRING

THROTTLE SHAFT

Fuel Injection

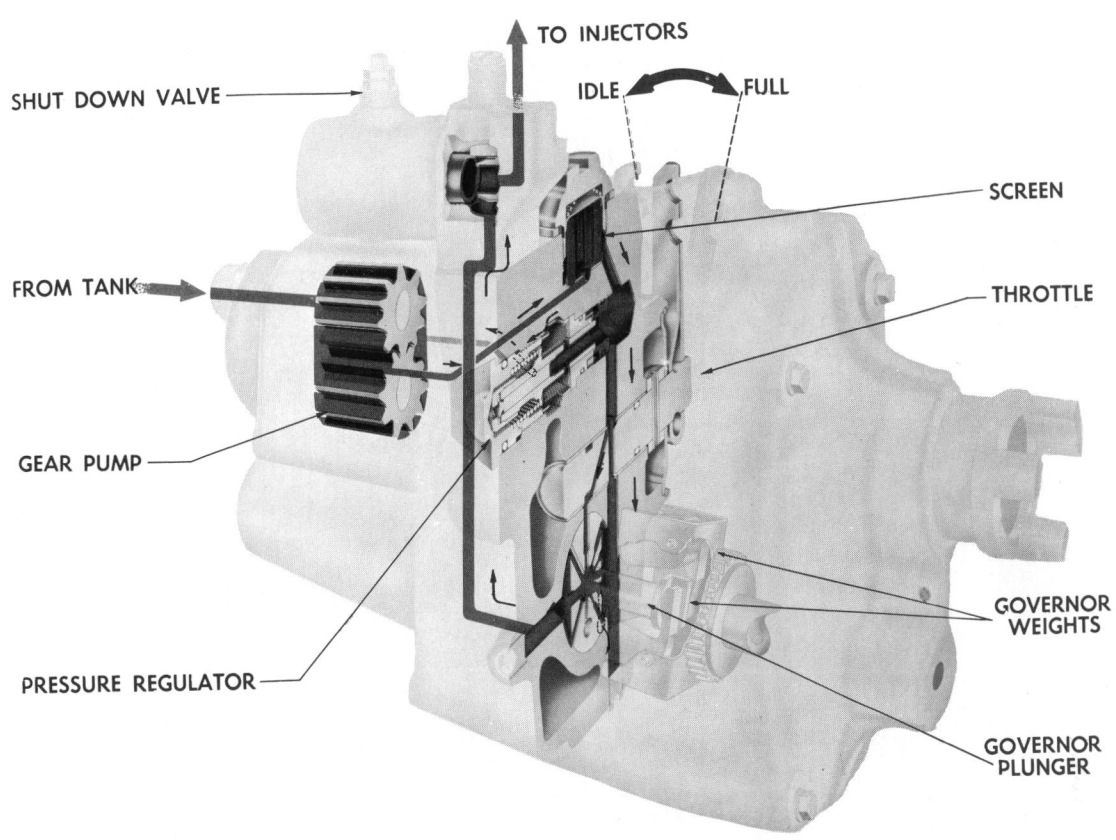

Fig. 27-16. Fuel flow through fuel pump.

throttle shaft, Fig. 27-16. The fuel passes around the shaft to the idle jet in the governor. For operation above idle, fuel passes through the throttling hole in the shaft and enters the governor through the primary jets.

Mechanical governor action is provided by a system of springs and weights, Fig. 27-16. The governor maintains sufficient fuel for idling and cuts it off above rated rpm. Governors vary according to engine requirements.

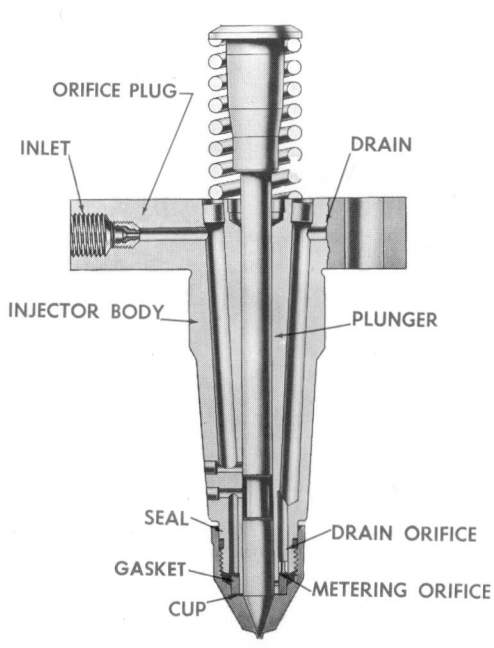

Fig. 27-17. Cross section of Cummins injector.

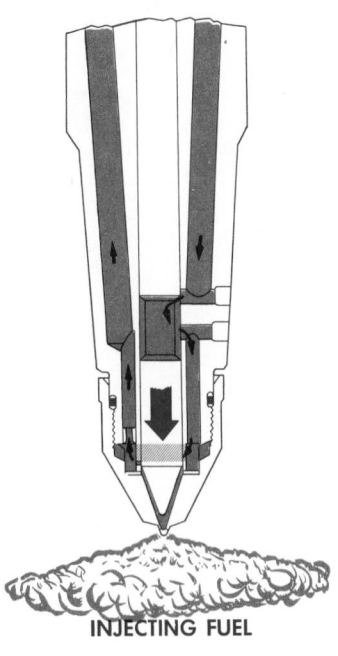

Fig. 27-18. Fuel flow through injector while injecting fuel.

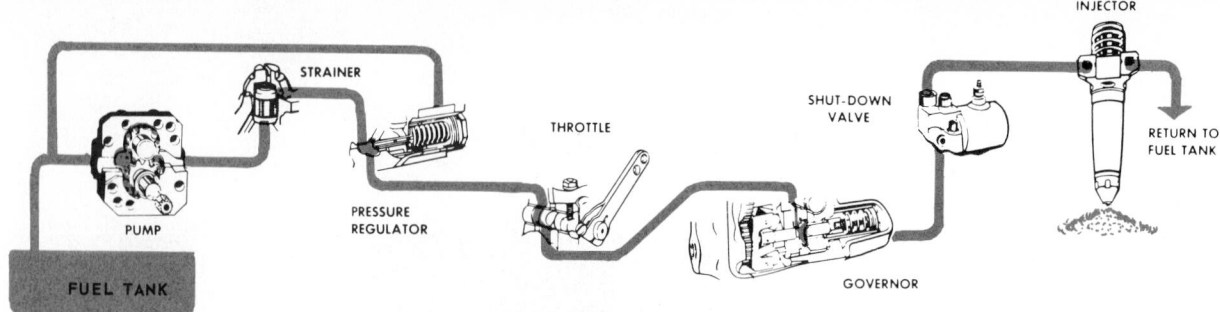

Fig. 27-19. Pressure flow diagram of Cummins PT System.

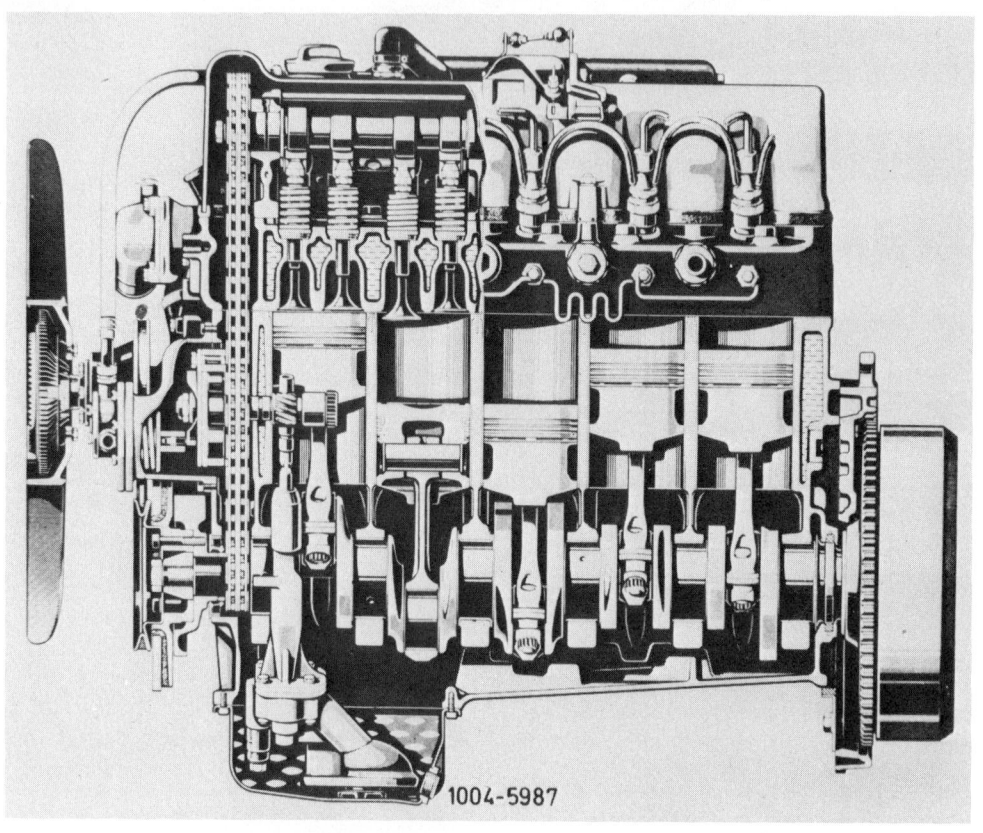

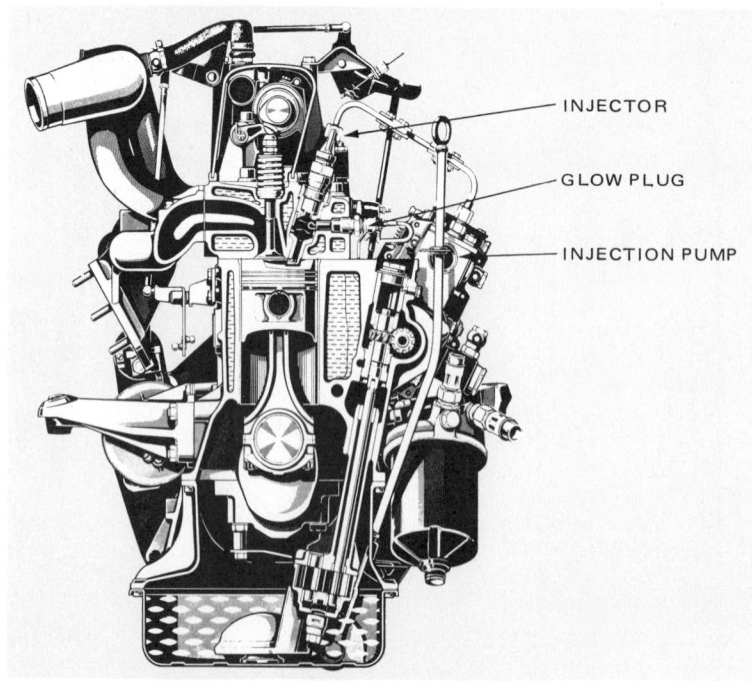

Fig. 27-20. Sectional views of Mercedes—Benz five cylinder diesel engine, showing location of injectors, glow plugs and pump.

CUMMINS INJECTORS

The injector used with Cummins PT system is shown in Fig. 27-17. Fuel constantly circulates through the injector, except during a short period following injection into the combustion chamber. From the inlet connection, fuel flows down the inlet passage of the injector, around the injector plunger, between the body end and cup, up the drain passage to the drain connections and manifold and back to the supply tank.

As the plunger comes up, the injector feed passage is opened and fuel flows through the metering orifice into the cup. At the same time, fuel flows past the cup and out the drain orifice. The amount of fuel entering the cup is controlled by the fuel pressure against the metering orifice. Fuel pressure is controlled by the fuel pump.

During injection, Fig. 27-18, the plunger comes down until the orifice is closed, and the fuel in the cup is injected into the cylinder. While the plunger is seated in the cup, all fuel flow in the injector is stopped.

The flow diagram of the Cummins Pressure Time System is shown in Fig. 27-19.

CUMMINS METERING PUMP INJECTION SYSTEM

Another Cummins system, classified as the distributor type, employs a metering pump to measure each charge of fuel delivered at low pressure to the injectors.

The injectors build up pressure of the fuel and inject it into the engine combustion chamber.

The Cummins diesel fuel pump, as used in the distributor system, performs four functions:
1. Draws fuel from supply tank.
2. Measures or meters fuel in equal charges for each cylinder.
3. Distributes and delivers metered fuel at correct instant to individual injectors in engine.
4. Provides a governor for control of idling and maximum engine speeds.

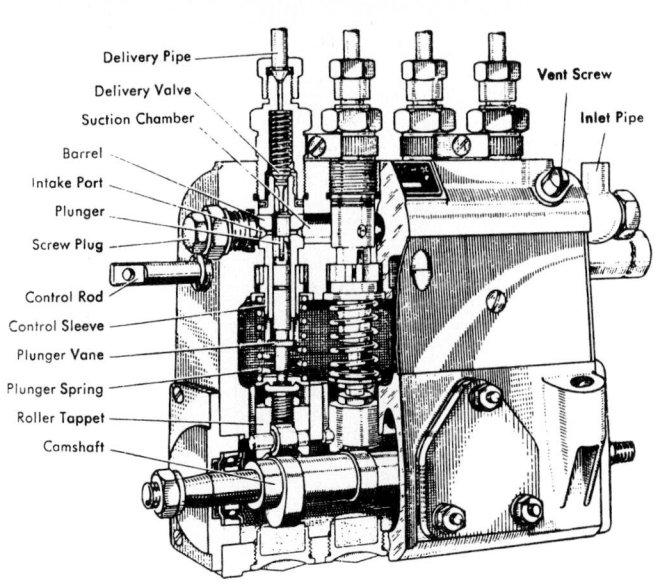

Fig. 27-21. Typical Robert Bosch Model PE diesel injection pump.

ROBERT BOSCH INJECTION SYSTEM

The diesel fuel injection pump installed on many engines, including the Mercedes-Benz five cylinder diesel, Fig. 27-20, is a PE series type. Also see Figs. 27-21, 27-22 and 27-23. The PE pump contains one pump element, consisting of a cylinder and plunger for each engine cylinder. The plunger is lapped in the cylinder and has a clearance of two to three thousandths of a millimetre (.0001 in.). This small clearance serves to emphasize the importance of extreme cleanliness when working on injectors.

Plungers and cylinders are interchangeable only in complete sets. An injection timing device is incorporated in the drive assembly of the pump, so fuel injection is timed in relation to engine speed. The control rod, 11 in Fig. 27-23, is geared to the pinion, 12. The pump plunger, 9, can be turned with the

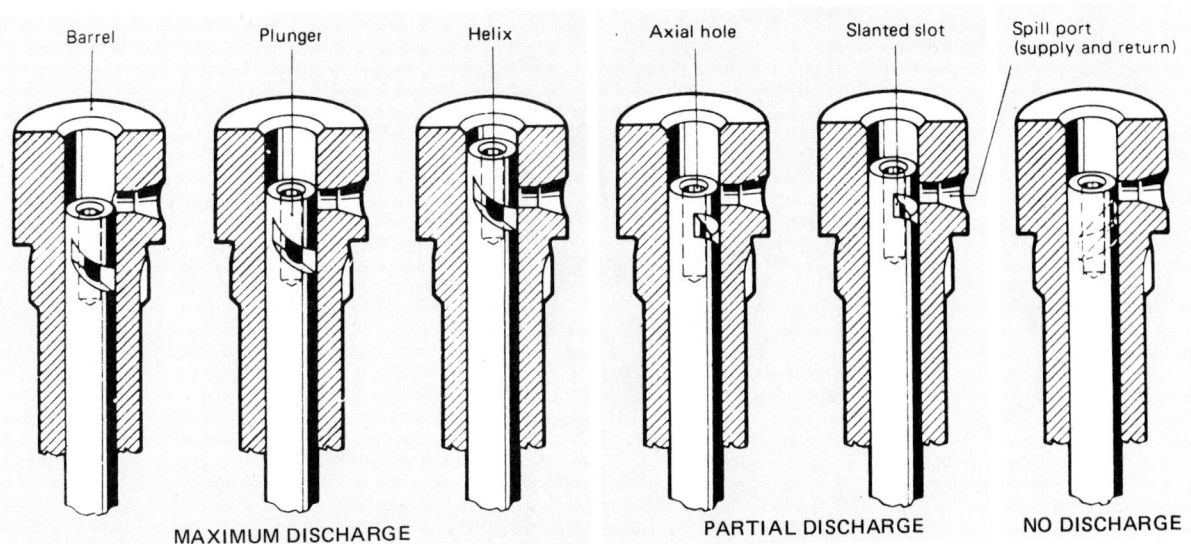

Fig. 27-22. Sequence of plunger position in Robert Bosch diesel injection pump.

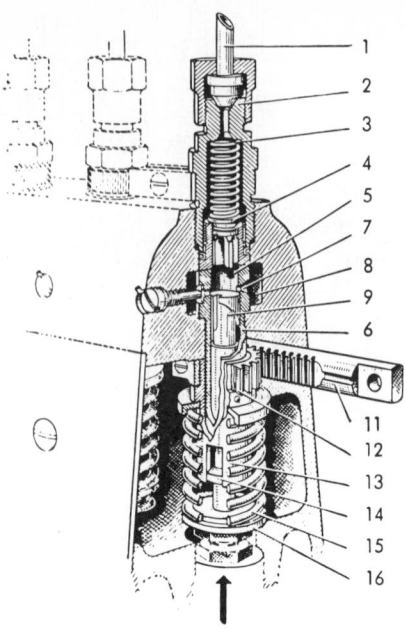

Fig. 27-23. Drive mechanism of Robert Bosch PE fuel injection pump.
1—Pressure line. 2—Pipe connection. 3—Valve spring. 4—Pressure valve.
5—Pressure space. 6—Pump cylinder. 7—Control port. 8—Suction space.
9—Plunger. 11—Control rod. 12—Pinion. 13—Control rod. 14—Plunger
lug. 15—Plunger spring. 16—Spring retainer.

control rod, and the discharge rate of the pump can be infinitely varied from zero to maximum.

During the pressure stroke, the plunger is lifted by the cam. During the suction stroke, the plunger is forced down again by the plunger spring, 15 in Fig. 27-23. The stroke of the pump plunger cannot be varied. The suction space, 8, is constantly filled with fuel and is kept under pressure by the feed pump. If the pump plunger is at bottom dead center, the control port, 7, is opened and the pressure space, 5, is filled with fuel.

During the upward motion, the plunger closes the control port and pushes fuel through the pressure valve, 4 in Fig. 27-23, into the pressure line, 1. The delivery ends as soon as the upper control edge has reached the control port, since the pressure space is connected with the suction space by the compensating hole in the plunger. The discharge rate is varied by turning the plunger, Fig. 27-23. The plunger opens the control port sooner or later, depending on the amount the plunger is rotated.

Glow plugs, Fig. 12-7, are necessary in diesel engines because compression temperatures are not sufficient to ignite the fuel in very cold weather. The current is turned on briefly to provide heat in the combustion chambers or intake manifold, which insures combustion of the fuel.

Fig. 27-24. Sectional view of Roosa Master fuel injection pump. 1—Inlet strainer. 2—Fuel transfer pump. 3—Regulating valve.
4—Axial passage. 5—Head. 6—Annular groove. 7—Metering valve. 8—Charging port. 9—Fuel passage. 10—Axial passage. 11—Plunger.
12—Leaf spring. 13—Roller. 14—Cam. 15—Rotor discharge port. 16—Outlet port.

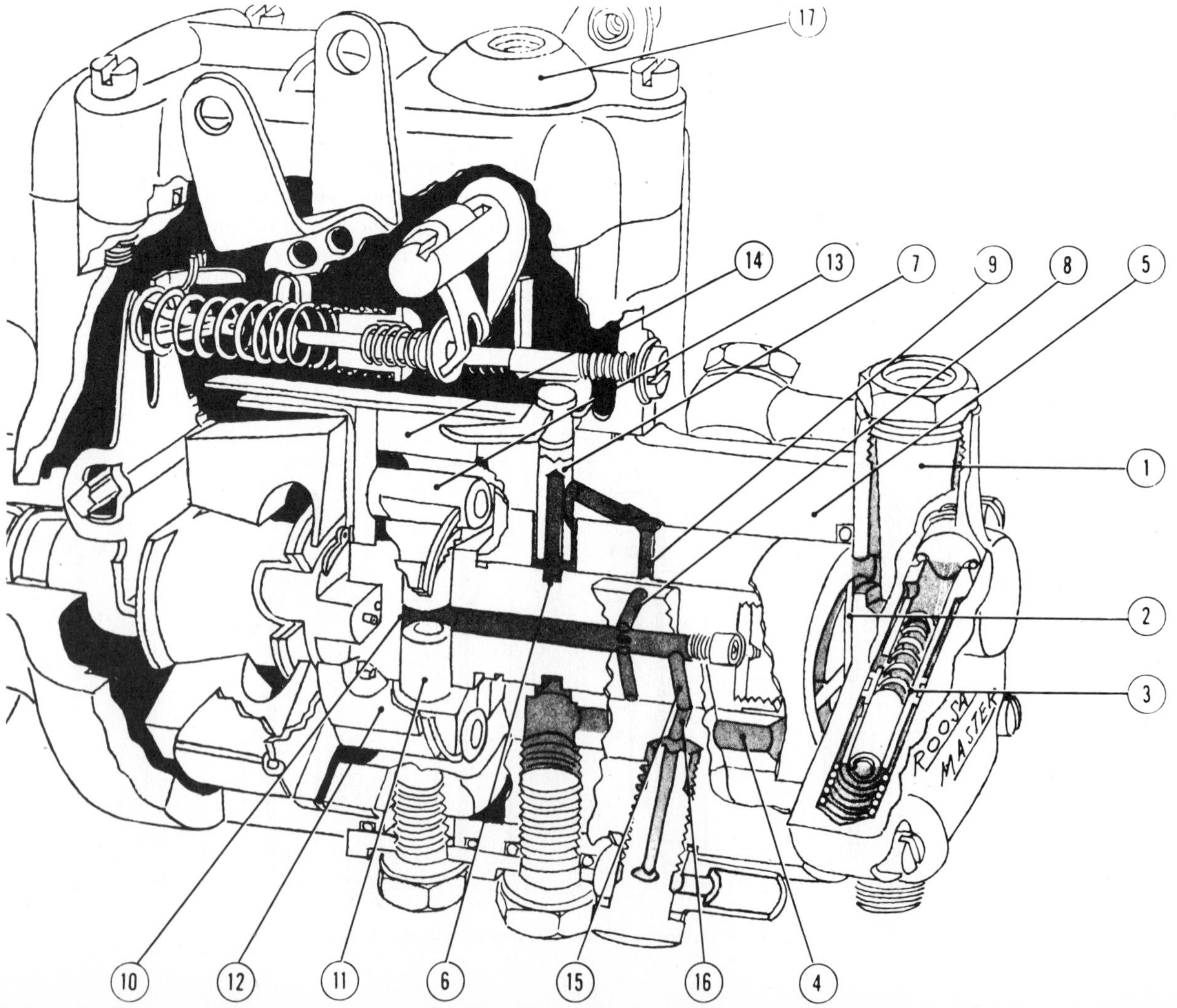

ROOSA MASTER FUEL INJECTION PUMP

The Roosa Master fuel injection pump is a single cylinder, opposed plunger, inlet metering, distributor type unit, Fig. 27-24. It is used largely in high speed diesel engines. The main components are: drive shaft, distributor rotor, transfer pump, pumping plunger, internal cam ring, hydraulic ring, end plate and governor.

The Roosa Master fuel injection pump is a self-lubricated unit, with the filtered fuel it pumps. There are no spring-loaded lapped surfaces, no ball bearings, no gears and most accessories are built in.

The rotating members revolve on a common axis. These are the drive shaft, distributor rotor (containing plungers and mounting governor) and the transfer pump.

Fuel is drawn from the supply pump into the inlet strainer, Fig. 27-24, by the vane type fuel transfer pump. Excess fuel is bypassed through the regulating valve back to the inlet side. The amount of flow bypassed increases in proportion to the speed, and the regulating valve is designed so that transfer pressure also increases with speed.

Fuel, under transfer pump pressure, is forced through an axial passage to the head and into an annular groove milled around the rotor shank. The fuel flows around the groove and through the metering valve in a quantity determined by engine demands.

As the rotor revolves, one of its charging ports comes into register with a passage (see 9 in Fig. 27-24), permitting the fuel to enter the axial passage. Inflowing fuel forces the plungers outward for a distance that is proportionate to the quantity of fuel to be injected on the following stroke.

If only a small amount of fuel is admitted into the pumping cylinder, as at idling, the plungers move out very little. As additional fuel is admitted, the plunger stroke increases to the maximum quantity permitted by a leaf spring arrangement. See Fig. 27-24.

At this point (charging) of the cycle, the rollers are in the "valley," or relieved part of the cam, between lobes. The fuel is trapped in the cylinder for a short interval after charging is complete. The charging port has passed out of registry with the passage, and the rotor discharge port has not yet come into registry with an outlet port in the hydraulic head.

Further rotation of the rotor brings its discharge port into registry with an outlet port, while the rollers simultaneously contact the opposing cam lobes and the plungers are forced toward each other. Fuel trapped between the plungers is forced from the pump through one of the outlet ports into an injection line.

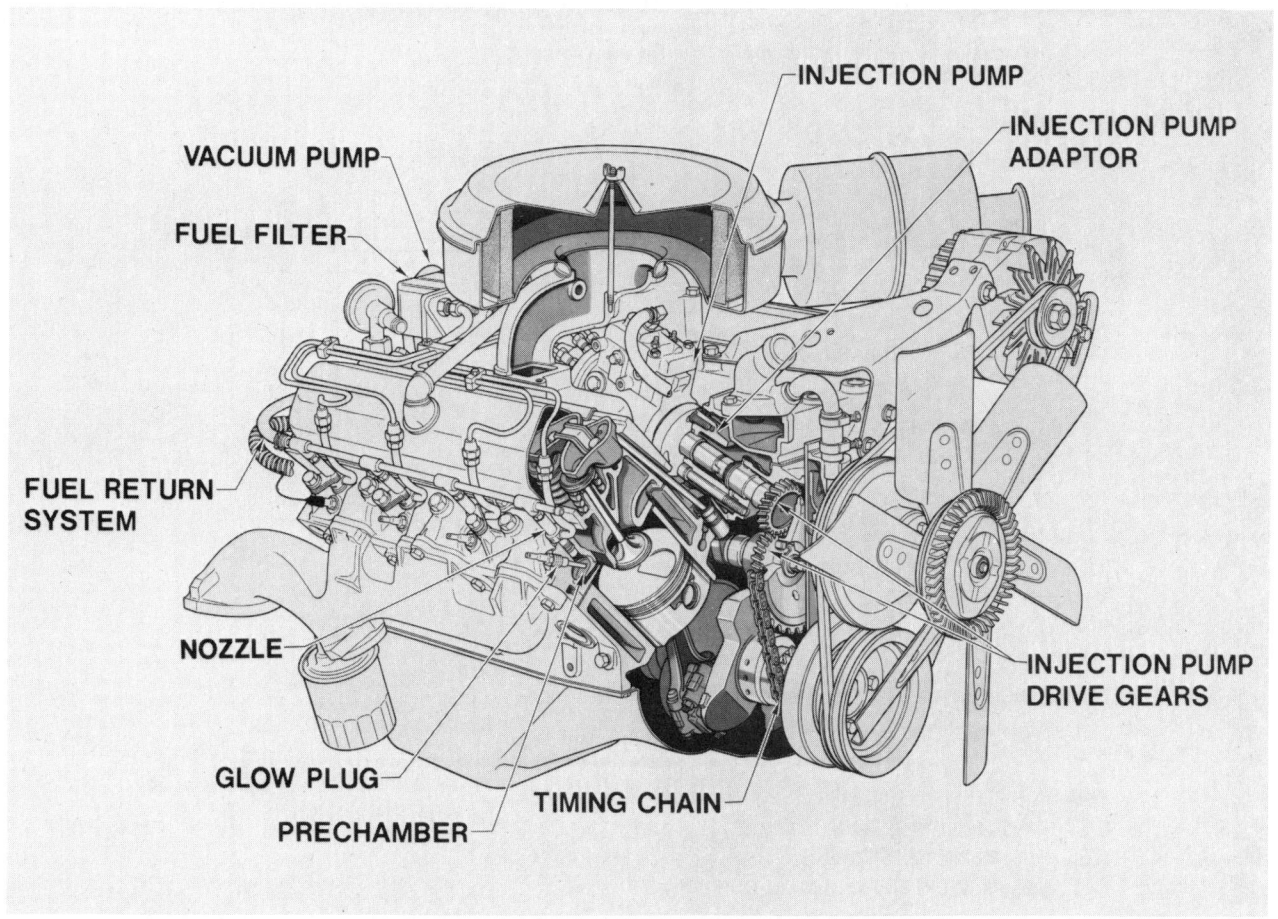

Fig. 27-25. General Motors 350 cu. in. (5.7 litre) V-8 diesel engine.

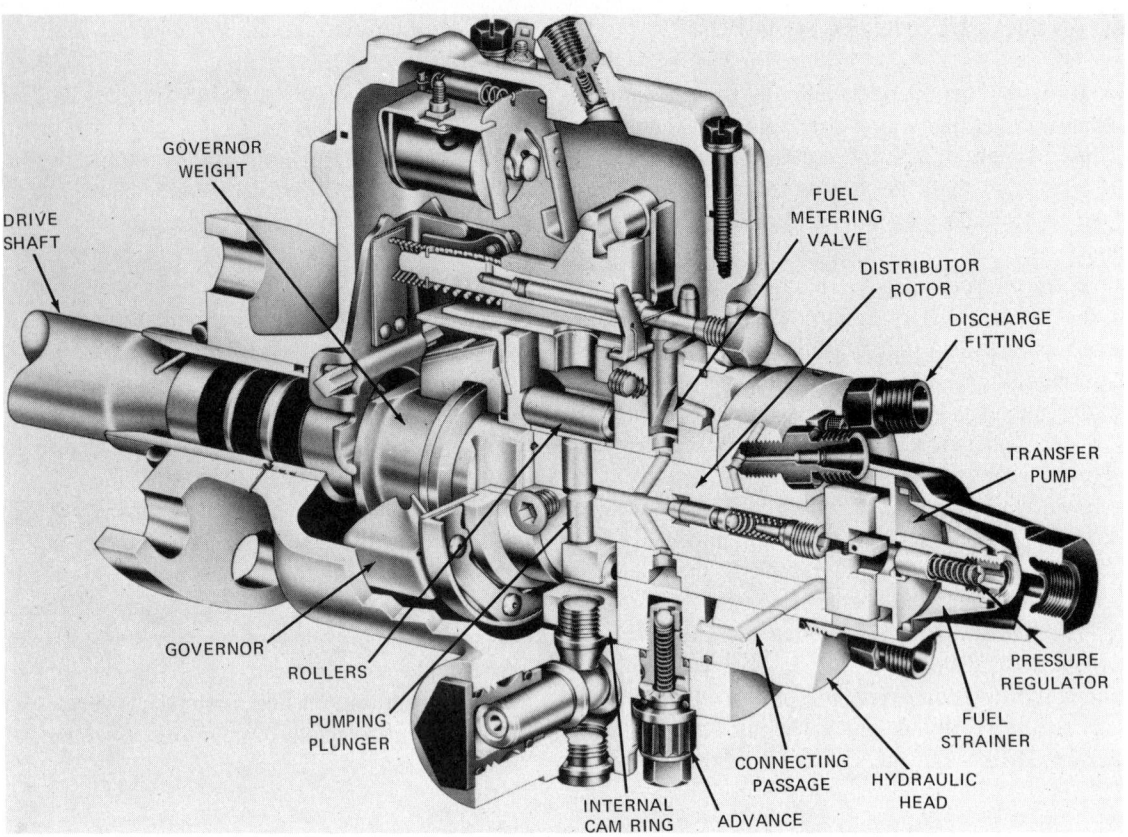

Fig. 27-26. Sectional view of fuel injector pump as installed in GM diesel.
(Oldsmobile Div., General Motors Corp.)

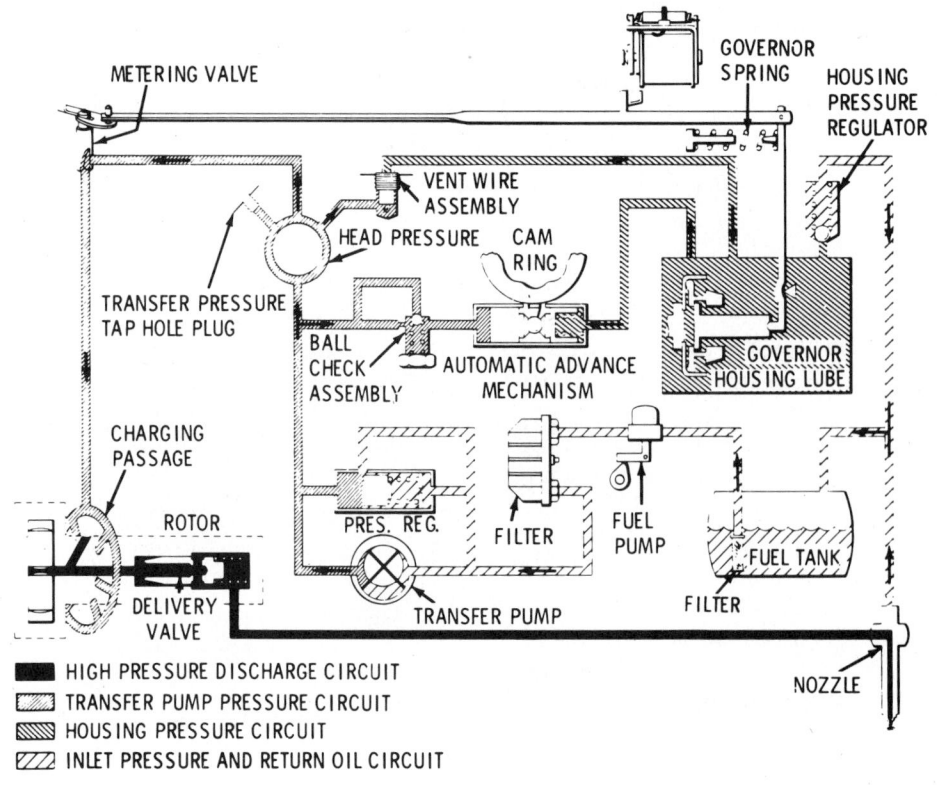

Fig. 27-27. The various fuel circuits used in General Motors 350 cu. in. (5.7 litre) diesel engine.

GENERAL MOTORS DIESEL ENGINE

The General Motors (Oldsmobile) diesel engine used in late model GM vehicles is a 350 cu. in. (5.7 litre) engine that is basically similar to the gasoline powered V-8 of the same displacement. See Fig. 27-25. The diesel engine is of the precombustion chamber type. Compression ratio is 22 to 1.

The major differences between this diesel and the 350 cu. in. gasoline engine are in the cylinder head with its precombustion chambers and in the fuel distribution system and air intake manifold. Also, basic diesel engine parts are of heavier construction because of the higher compression and the higher temperatures created by compression ignition.

COMPRESSION IGNITION

Ignition takes place in the precombustion chamber, which is made of stainless steel and located in the cylinder head. The precombustion chamber can be serviced separately from the cylinder head. After the head is removed, the glow plug and injection nozzle can be unscrewed. Then, the precombustion chamber can be pushed out.

INJECTION PUMP

The injection pump is Roosa Master construction of the distributor type with inlet metering. Working parts of the pump are shown in Fig. 27-26. The flow plan is given in Fig. 27-27. Note that the engine driven fuel pump draws fuel from the fuel supply tank. The fuel then passes through a filter.

The diesel injection pump, Fig. 27-26, is mounted on top of the engine. It is gear driven off the camshaft, turning at camshaft speed. The eight high pressure delivery pipes from the pump to the injection nozzles are all of the same length to prevent a difference in timing. The injection pump provides the required timing advance under all operating conditions.

Engine speed is controlled by a rotary fuel metering valve. See Fig. 27-27. Note that excess fuel is returned to the supply tank.

As is the case with all diesel engines, the importance of supplying only clean fuel to the injectors cannot be over-emphasized. The fuel filter (located at top rear of engine) should be changed at the designated interval, or more frequently if clogged.

Oldsmobile also warns that the exterior of the engine should not be cleaned until it has cooled to ambient temperature. Spraying water or engine cleaning fluid on a hot or warm engine will damage the injector pump.

GASOLINE INJECTION

A system of gasoline injection is somewhat different from a diesel injection system. The gasoline engine is a good vacuum pump. So it is customary to inject the gasoline into the intake manifold near the intake valve, and allow vacuum to suck fuel into the cylinder. Because gasoline is not injected into the cylinder against compression pressure, a low-pressure pump system is used.

Fuel injection is of two types:
1. The constant, or "dribble," system where a very small stream of fuel runs constantly into the intake manifold while the engine is running.
2. The timed or intermittent system where a shot of fuel is supplied on the suction stroke of each cylinder.

The constant supply system does not need to be timed. The intermittent system, on the other hand, is timed with the crankshaft in the same manner as the ignition distributor.

One of the first gasoline injection systems was developed in Germany for Mercedes racing cars. The fuel was timed for injection near the inlet valves. A number of American racing cars use fuel injection of the constant type and find it satisfactory. Some passenger car engines produced by both Mercedes-Benz and Volkswagen are equipped with gasoline fuel injection systems.

Advantages of fuel injection include:
1. Increased power.
2. Higher torque.
3. Improved fuel economy.
4. Quicker cold starting.
5. Faster warmup.
6. No need for manifold heat.
7. Lower intake temperatures.

MERCEDES-BENZ GASOLINE INJECTION

Manifold fuel (gasoline) injection and port fuel injection are both used on certain Mercedes-Benz cars.

As the names imply, fuel is injected directly into the

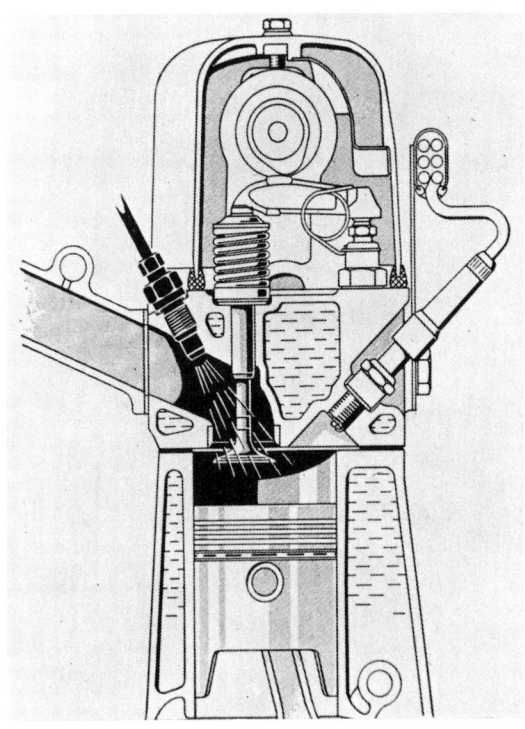

Fig. 27-28. Sectional view of Mercedes-Benz gasoline injection system. Note location of spray nozzle.

manifold with the one type of gasoline injection. In the other, it is injected into the valve port directly under the intake valve head, Fig. 27-28.

The injection valve used in the manifold type of injection system is shown in Fig. 27-29. The injection pump and

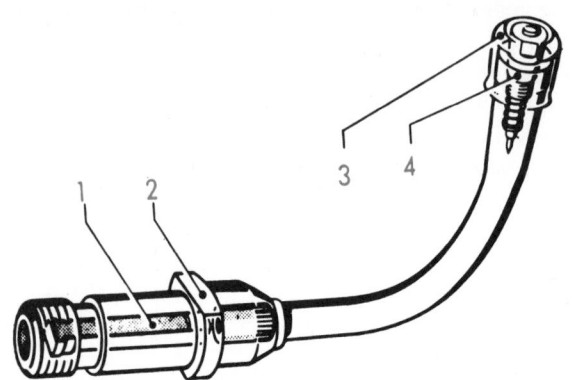

Fig. 27-29. Detail of injection valve used in Mercedes-Benz gasoline injection system. 1—Filter. 2—Retainer. 3—Locking cap. 4—Valve insert.

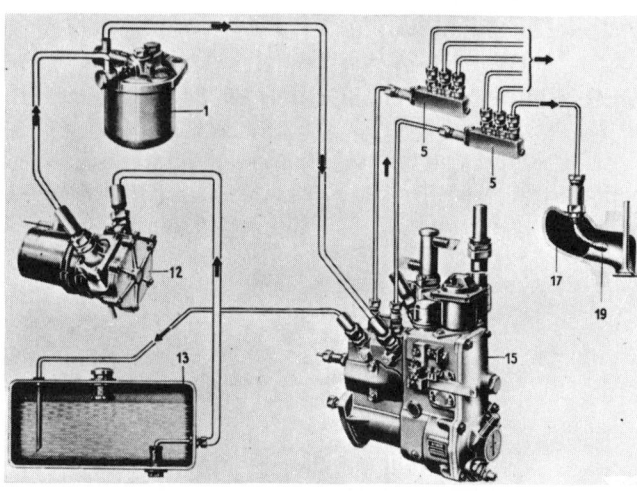

Fig. 27-30. Fuel flow system of Mercedes-Benz gasoline injection system. 1—Fine fuel filter. 5—Fuel distributor fittings. 12—Fuel feed pump. 13—Fuel tank. 15—Injection pump. 17—Intake manifold. 19—Injection valves.

complete system is shown at Fig. 27-30. With manifold injection, the pump injects finely atomized fuel into the intake manifold for three cylinders at one time. As a result, fuel may not always be injected during the intake stroke with the intake valve open. But injection takes place at various times, although the time does not vary for any one cylinder.

Since the camshaft of the injection pump turns at half crankshaft speed, but has double cams, fuel is injected at every turn of the crankshaft. As a result, the fuel quantity for any one cylinder is injected in two equal parts.

In the port injection system, Fig. 27-28, the principal of "jerk" injection has been retained. However, the nozzles inject fuel into the port of the intake valve.

During the injection process (which coincides with suction stroke of piston), part of the atomized fuel is injected into the combustion chamber past the opened valve, taking up heat from the cylinder. The electric starting valve is arranged in the middle of the intake manifold so that the fuel jets are directed toward the individual intake ports.

VW ELECTRONIC FUEL INJECTION SYSTEM

The electronic fuel injection system installed on some Volkswagen cars was devised to help meet the need for exhaust emission control. The system provides accuracy both in fuel metering and in mixture distribution to the individual cylinders.

Each cylinder is provided with a solenoid-operated injector valve through which the fuel is injected intermittently to the intake ports. The firing order of the VW engine is 1-4-3-2. The injector valves of each two cylinders which follow one another

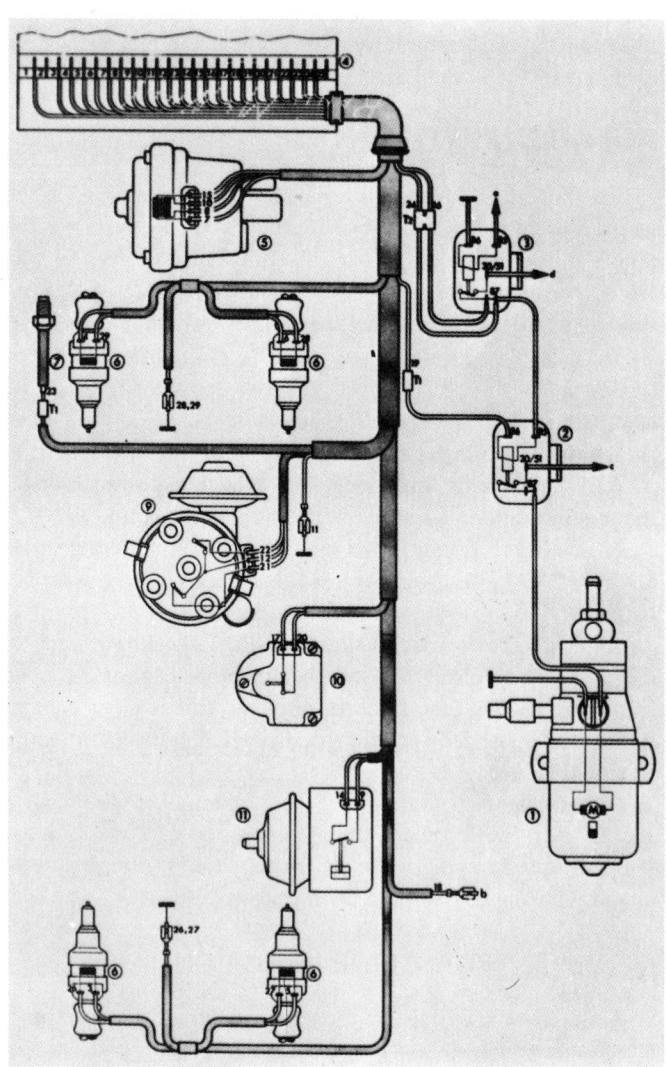

Fig. 27-31. Main components of the VW electronic fuel injection system. 1—Electric fuel pump. 2—Pump relay. 3—Main relay. 4—Electronic control unit. 5—Pressure sensor. 6—Injectors. 7—Temperature sensor. 9—Distributor with trigger contacts. 10—Throttle switch. 11—Pressure switch.

in this firing order are operated simultaneously. That is, the injector valves of cylinders 1 and 4 and those of cylinders 3 and 2 operate together.

In operation, Fig. 27-31, current is supplied to a control unit via a main relay and to the electric fuel pump via a pump relay. A time switch in the control unit activates the fuel pump for 1 to 1 1/2 seconds after ignition is turned on to permit build up of fuel pressure. Fuel injectors are kept under constant pressure of 28 psi, so the amount of fuel injected depends on length of time injectors are kept open and is metered according to engine requirements.

Engine speed and intake manifold pressure are used primarily as the input signals to the electronic control system. The ignition distributor houses trigger contacts that signal the control unit when more fuel is to be injected. The throttle switch (see 10 in Fig. 27-31), cuts off the supply of fuel during deceleration.

The electric fuel pump forces fuel into the pressure line, through a filter to the ring main. The pressure regulator, connected to the ring main, maintains pressure at approximately 28 psi. Surplus fuel returns to the supply tank through a special line. The ring main feeds fuel to the electromagnetic injectors by way of fuel distributor pipes.

The intake air distributor, Fig. 27-32, keys the air supply to four intake manifolds and to the four cylinders of the engine. The amount of air required by the fuel injection system is controlled during engine operation by the throttle valve in the intake air distributor. Since the throttle valve is connected to the accelerator pedal, it is completely closed during idle. At this time, intake air must pass through an idling circuit in which an adjusting screw controls engine idling speed.

The idling circuit supplies sufficient air at normal operating temperatures. However, at lower temperatures, more air is required and an auxiliary air regulator supplies it. This regulator is a rotary valve in an auxiliary air line from the air cleaner. (See 8 in Fig. 27-32.) On-off positions are controlled by an oil temperature sensor.

Variations in barometric pressure have no influence on the mixture richness of the VW system. The pulse generator in the distributor supplies information about the angular position of the crankshaft. This determines injection timing, which is constant at 15 deg. crank angle after top center under all operating conditions. There are no adjustments to be made on this system, nor is matching to the individual engine necessary.

Specialized equipment is available for checking the VW system. However, the fuel system should be checked for leaks and pinched lines, especially at the tank, pump, filter and pressure regulator. The fuel filter should be replaced every 6,000 miles: Use a clamp to pinch fuel hose between filter and tank with a clamp. Also clamp hose between Y connector and pump. Remove old filter. Install new filter, with arrow facing pump. Remove clamps. The air filter should be cleaned and refilled with new SAE 30 oil every 6000 miles.

Trigger contacts of the distributor are nonadjustable. Make sure all electrical connections are clean and tight. Set engine idle speed. Adjust idle air screw to obtain 850 rpm with engine at operating temperature. (See 7, Fig. 27-32.)

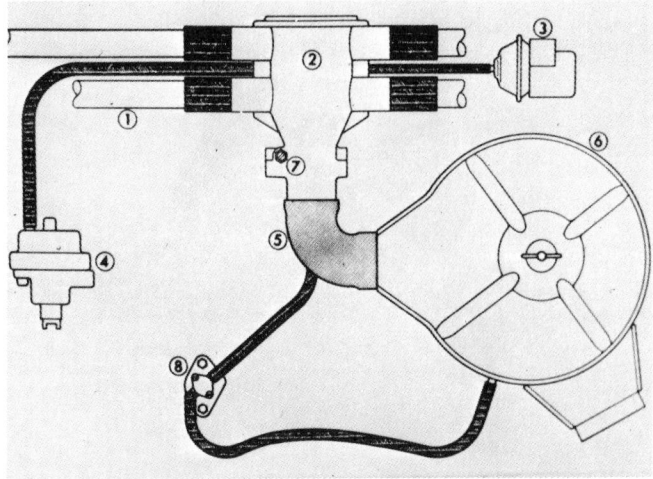

Fig. 27-32. Air system of VW electronic fuel injection system. 1—Intake pipes. 2—Intake air distributor. 3—Pressure switch. 4—Pressure sensor. 5—Elbow. 6—Air cleaner. 7—Idle air screw. 8—Auxiliary air regulator.

ELECTRONIC FUEL INJECTION

In the chapter on carburetors and intake manifolds, mention was made of the difficulty of providing the same air-fuel mixture to all cylinders. Uneven distribution boosts fuel consumption and exhaust emission of hydrocarbons, carbon monoxide and oxides of nitrogen are at unacceptable levels. These conditions are greatly minimized by the use of fuel injection.

In a fuel injection system, each cylinder receives the same amount of fuel. As a result, fuel economy is improved and each cylinder produces an equal amount of power. In addition, exhaust emissions are reduced.

In the electronic fuel injection system, these gains are accomplished by monitoring selected engine operating conditions and electronically metering the fuel requirements to meet these conditions.

In the General Motors system, Electronic Fuel Injection (EFI) basically involves electrically actuated fuel metering valves which, when actuated, spray a predetermined quantity of fuel into the engine. These valves, or injectors, Fig. 27-33, are mounted in the intake manifold with the metering tip pointed toward the head of the intake valve. This is known as "port injection," which is used extensively in race car engines. There is another method which injects the fuel directly into the combustion chamber.

The injection timing is in accordance with the engine frequency so that the fuel charge is in place prior to the intake stroke of the piston.

Gasoline is supplied to the injectors through the fuel rail, Fig. 27-34. It is pumped at a pressure designed to obtain good atomization of the fuel, and to prevent vapor formation in the fuel system during extended operation at high temperature.

When the solenoid operated valves are energized, the injector metering valve moves to the full open position. Since the pressure differential across the valve is constant, the fuel quantity is changed by varying the time the injector is held open.

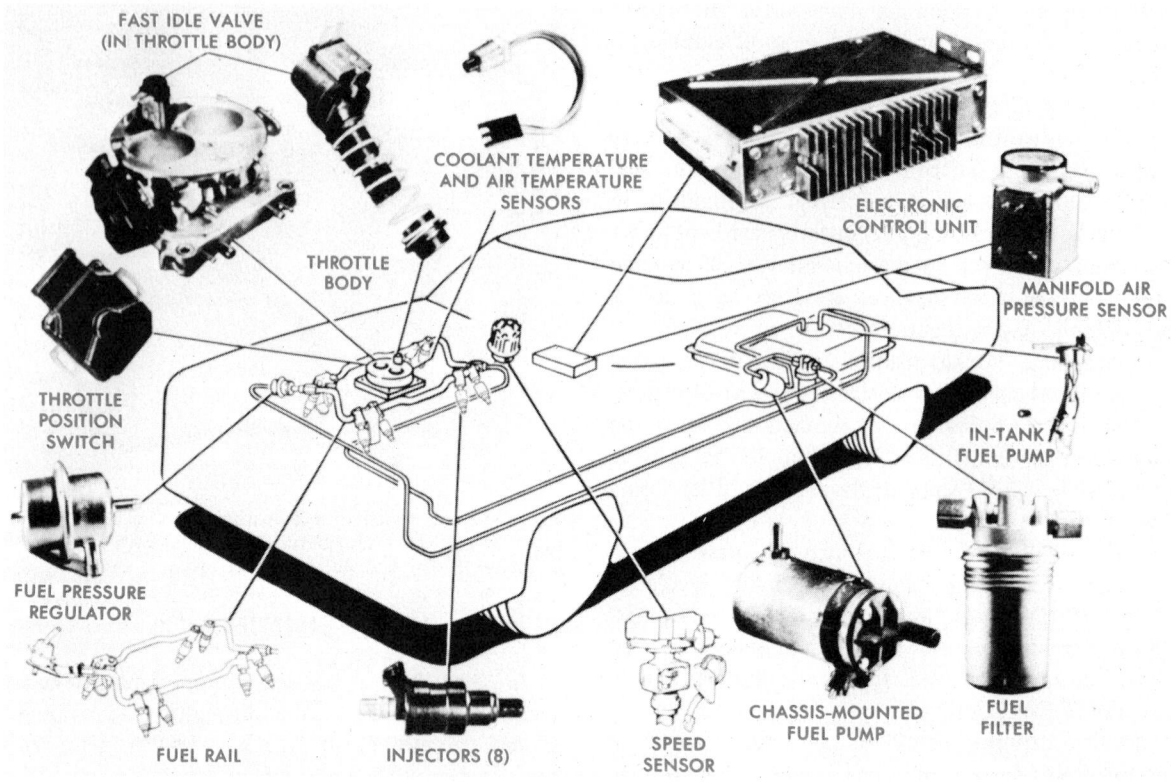

Fig. 27-33. Cadillac's electronic fuel injection system features an electronic control unit, plus fuel delivery, air induction and engine sensing systems.

The injectors could be energized all at the same time, which is called continuous injection. Or, they could be energized one after the other in phase with the opening of each intake valve, which is known as sequential injection. Or, the intake valves can be energized in groups.

In the fuel injection system used on Cadillac engines, the intake valves are operated in two groups of four valves each. Cylinders 1, 2, 7 and 8 form one group. Group two consists of cylinders 3, 4, 5 and 6. All four injectors in a group are opened and closed simultaneously, while the groups operate alternately.

The amount of air entering the cylinder is measured and controlled by monitoring the intake manifold absolute pressure, the inlet air temperature and engine speed in rpm.

This information allows the electronic control unit to compute the flow rate of air being inducted into the engine. As a result, the flow rate of fuel is controlled to achieve the desired air-fuel ratio for the particular engine operating condition.

As shown in Fig. 27-35, the prevailing engine conditions are monitored with sensors and provide the necessary information to the electronic control unit, Fig. 27-34. The ECU converts all of this information into an injector pulse which opens the injectors for the proper duration and at the proper time with respect to the engine firing order.

The entire Electronic Fuel Injection system includes four major subsystems:

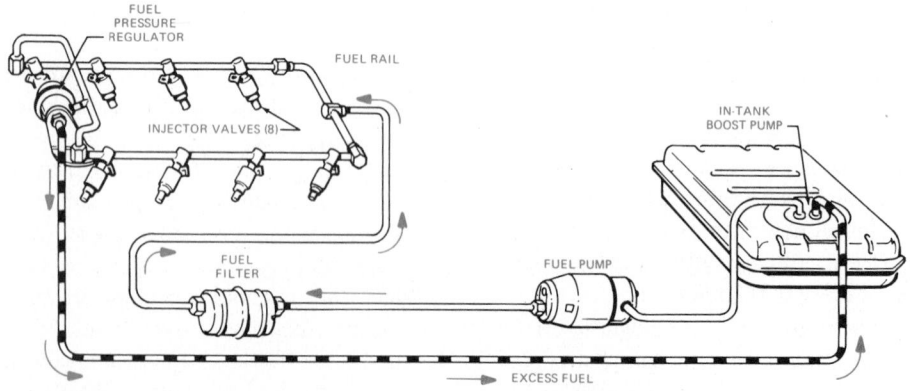

Fig. 27-34. The fuel delivery system for Cadillac's EFI system is shown in simplified form. Note key location of fuel pressure regulator.

1. Fuel delivery.
2. Air induction.
3. Sensors.
4. Electronic control unit.

The fuel delivery system, Fig. 27-34, includes an in-tank boost pump, a chassis constant displacement pump, a fuel filter, the fuel rails, one injector for each engine cylinder, a fuel pressure regulator and supply and return fuel lines.

Both pumps are electrically operated and start as soon as the ignition switch is turned on.

The fuel tank has a reservoir directly below the in-tank pump which insures a constant supply of fuel for the pump even at a low fuel level. The chassis-mounted fuel pump is electrically operated and is of the roller-vane type.

The fuel filter is of the disposable, paper element type. It should be replaced every 15,000 mi.

The fuel pressure regulator is mounted on the fuel rail toward the front of the engine. It maintains a constant 39 psi across the injectors.

The injector valve is a solenoid operated pintle valve that meters fuel to each cylinder and is controlled by the electronic control unit. When energized, the valve sprays the fuel in fine droplets.

The air induction system consists of the throttle body assembly, fast idle valve assembly and intake manifold. Air for combustion enters the throttle body and is distributed to each

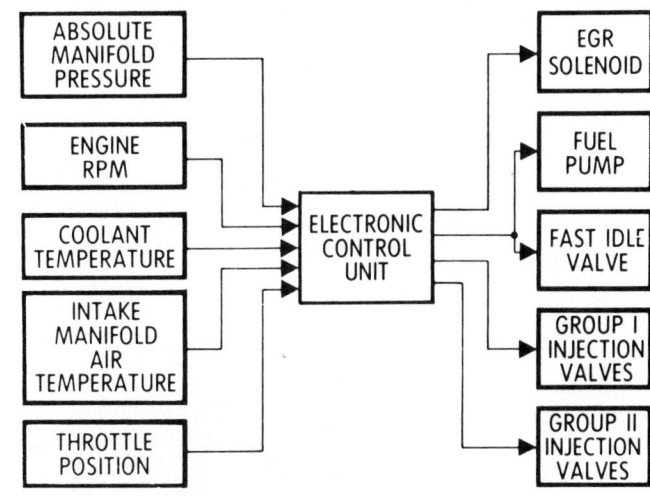

Fig. 27-35. Block diagram of an electronic fuel injection system.

cylinder through the intake manifold. The primary air flow rate is controlled by the throttle valves, which are connected to the accelerator pedal. An adjustable idle by-pass air passage in the throttle body allows a regulated amount of air to by-pass the throttle valves. Additional air for cold starts and warm-up is provided through an electrically controlled fast idle valve mounted in the top of the throttle body.

REVIEW QUESTIONS – FUEL INJECTION

1. On the compression stroke, what does a diesel engine compress?
   a. Air.
   b. Air-fuel mixture.
   c. Diesel fuel.
2. What are the four basic types of diesel fuel injection used on automotive engines?
3. What five requirements must a diesel fuel injection system fulfill?
4. In the Bosch system, what does the rotation of the pump plunger control?
   a. The quantity of fuel delivered.
   b. Timing of injection.
   c. Compression.
5. What type engines are the General Motors diesel?
   a. Four cycle.
   b. Two cycle.
   c. Sleeve valve.
6. What type of injector system is used on the General Motors diesel engine?
7. How many high pressure distributing lines are used on a four cylinder General Motors diesel engine?
   a. Four.
   b. Eight.
   c. None.
8. After repair work, or having run dry, is it necessary to prime a General Motors injector?
9. In the General Motors system, fuel is supplied to the injector at what pressure?
   a. 5 lb.
   b. 10 lb.
   c. 15 lb.
   d. 20 lb.
10. In the Cummins PT diesel system what method is used to increase the flow of fuel?
    a. Increased pressure.
    b. Increased size of jet.
    c. Rotation of plunger.
11. Fuel flows at all times in the Cummins injector. True or False?
12. In a gasoline injection system, are the injection pressures higher or lower than in a diesel system?
13. Name two types of gasoline injection systems.
14. The injection pump on an American Bosch gasoline injection system is driven at what speed?
    a. Engine speed.
    b. Half engine speed.
    c. Twice engine speed.
15. In the Volkswagen fuel injection system, fuel is injected into the combustion chamber. True or False?
16. Injector valve for cylinders one and two operate together in the Volkswagen injection system. True or False?

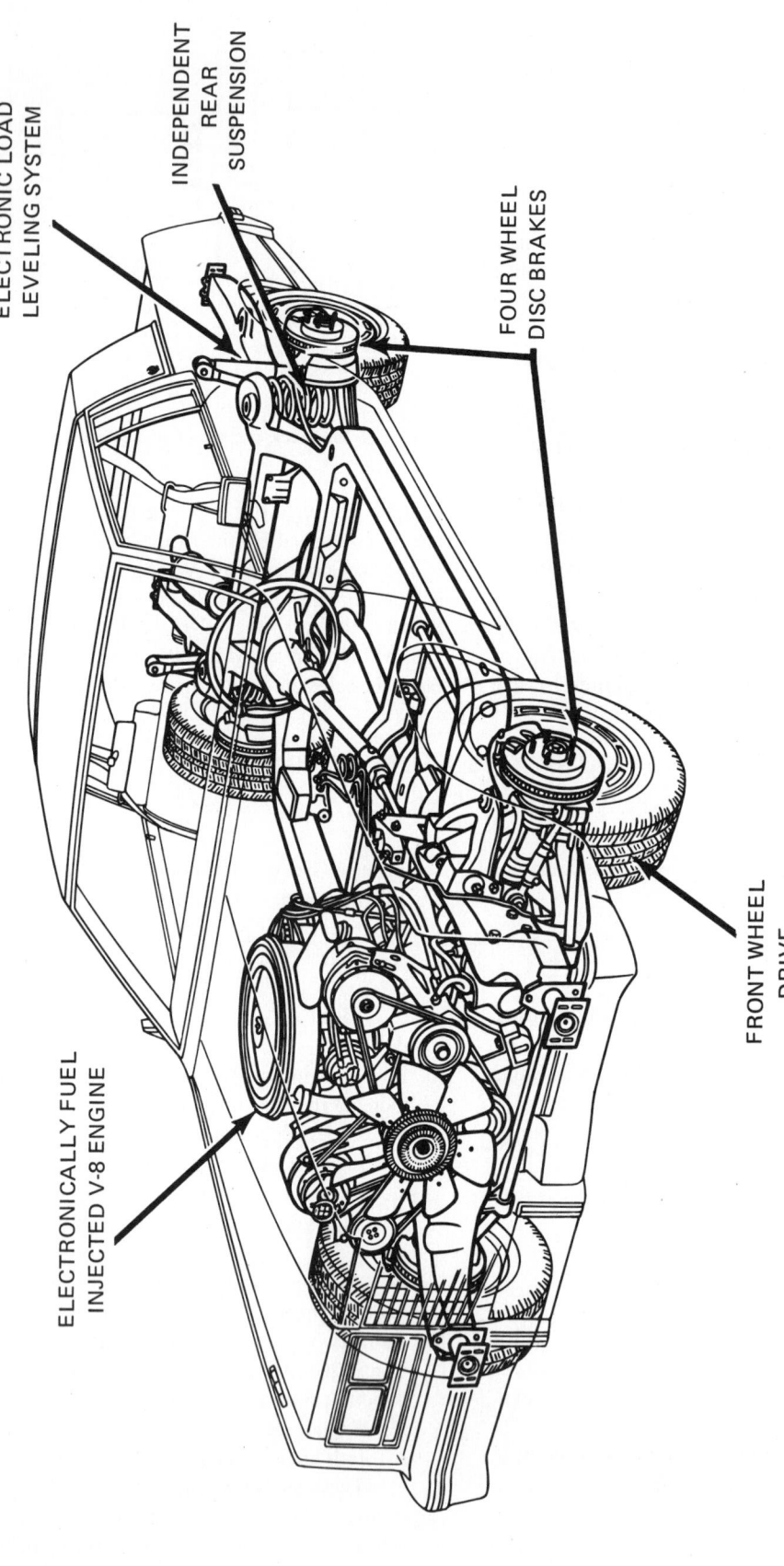

ELECTRONIC LOAD
LEVELING SYSTEM

INDEPENDENT
REAR
SUSPENSION

FOUR WHEEL
DISC BRAKES

ELECTRONICALLY FUEL
INJECTED V-8 ENGINE

FRONT WHEEL
DRIVE

Cadillac's front wheel drive Eldorado has an electronically fuel injected V-8 engine. Displacement is 350 cu. in. (5.7 litres). Net brake horsepower is 170 @ 4200 rpm.

EXHAUST
SYSTEMS

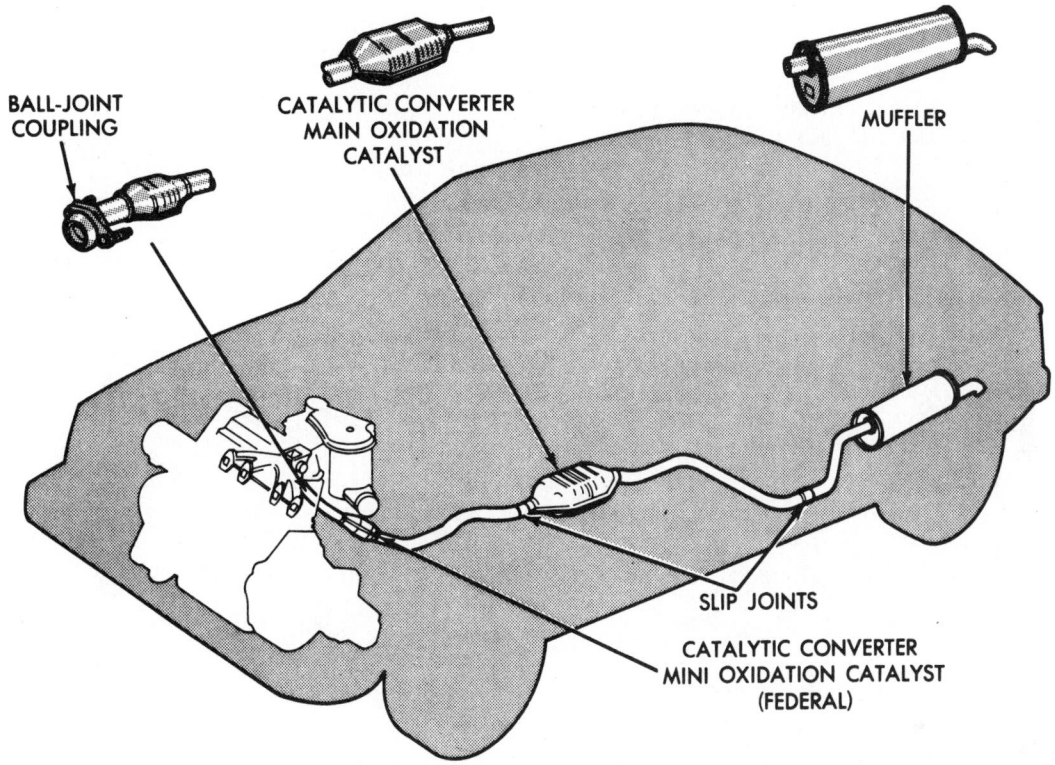

BALL-JOINT COUPLING

CATALYTIC CONVERTER MAIN OXIDATION CATALYST

MUFFLER

SLIP JOINTS

CATALYTIC CONVERTER MINI OXIDATION CATALYST (FEDERAL)

Fig. 28-1. Phantom view shows complete exhaust system installed on typical late model car equipped with a four cylinder in-line engine mounted crosswise in the engine compartment. (Chrysler Corp.)

The exhaust system of an automotive engine, Figs. 28-1 and 28-2, is designed to conduct the burned gases (exhaust) from the engine to the rear of the vehicle and into the atmosphere. This system also serves to silence the sounds of combustion and emission of the gases.

Major parts of the exhaust system include the exhaust manifold, exhaust pipe, catalytic converters (on late model cars), muffler and tailpipe. In addition, some cars have a crossover pipe (connecting two manifolds on V-type engines) and/or an intermediate pipe (connecting exhaust pipe to muffler). Older models occasionally were fitted with a resonator, a secondary silencing device.

Catalytic converters have been incorporated in the exhaust systems of most U.S. cars since 1975. Basically, they are emission control devices that contain chemically treated substances that convert noxious emissions into harmless carbon dioxide and water vapor. See the chapter on Emission Controls.

EXHAUST MANIFOLD

Exhaust manifolds are of many different types. On an in-line engine, the manifold is usually bolted to the side of engine, Fig. 28-3. On V-8 engines, separate manifolds are provided for each side of the "V," Fig. 28-4.

In V-8 applications, a completely separate exhaust system may be provided for each side of the engine. Or, the two sides may be joined together by means of a "crossover pipe."

Regardless of the individual design, the passageways forming the manifold are made as large in size as practical in order to reduce the resistance to the flow of the burned gases. Included in the design of the exhaust manifold on some engines is the manifold heat valve, which together with special passageways, conducts heat to the intake manifold to improve the vaporization of the fuel. Chrysler used a vacuum-controlled "power heat control valve" to reduce emissions during engine warm-up.

321

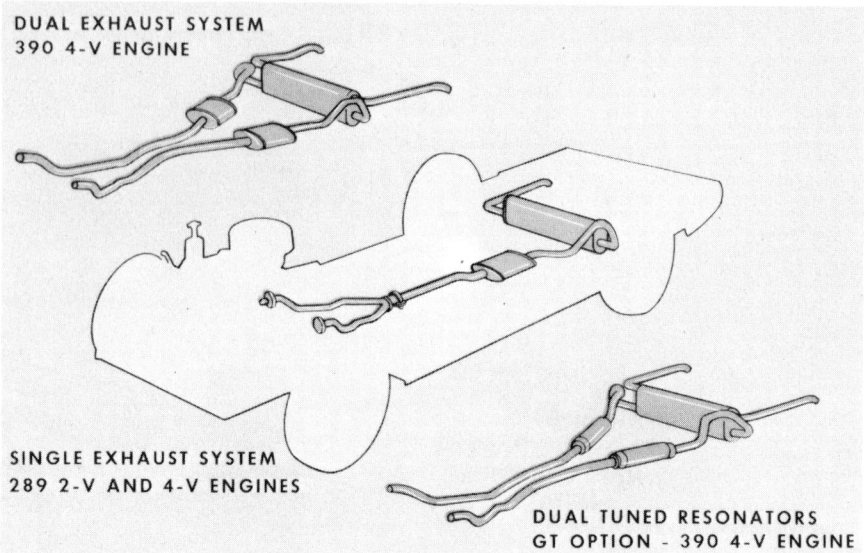

Fig. 28-2. Three different types of V-8 engine exhaust systems.
(Lincoln-Mercury Div.)

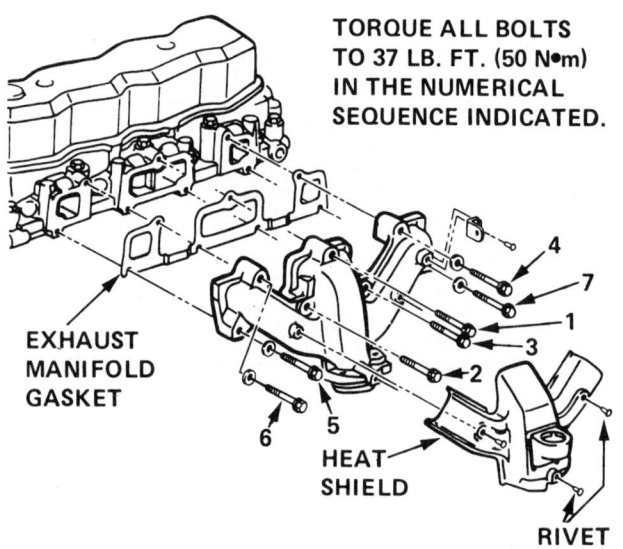

Fig. 28-3. Typical exhaust manifold installation on an in-line four
cylinder engine. Manifold on in-line six cylinder engine also bolts on
side of engine. (Chevrolet Motor Div., GM)

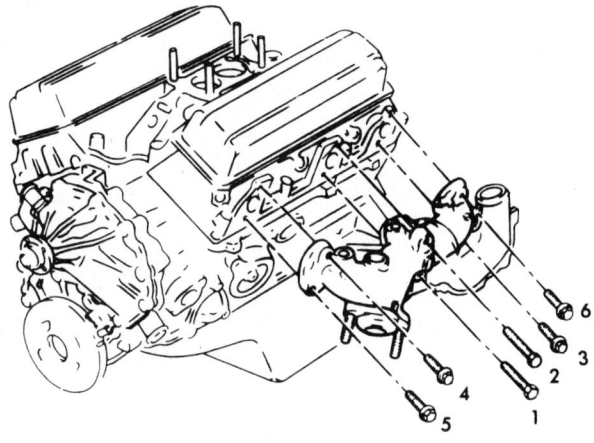

Fig. 28-4. Typical exhaust manifold installation on a V-6 engine. V-8
installation is similar. (Chevrolet Motor Div., GM)

MUFFLERS

In order to reduce the noise of the combustion and exhaust of an internal combustion engine, exhaust gases from the engine are passed through a muffler, Fig. 28-5. The muffler is designed so that the gases are expanded slowly, and are also cooled before they are discharged through the tailpipe to the atmosphere.

In addition, muffler design must be such that there is a minimum of back pressure developed. Back pressure prevents free flow of the exhaust gases from the engine and, as a result, not all of the burned gases will be exhausted from the cylinders. Such unexpelled gases dilute the incoming combustible gases and engine power is reduced.

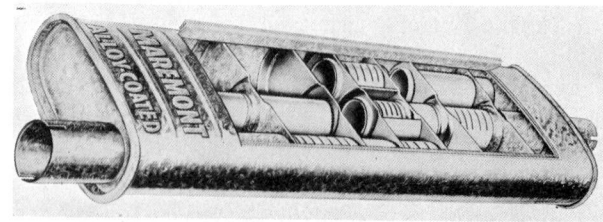

Fig. 28-5. Special layers of aluminum, cadmium, lead and zinc alloy coatings are used to protect this muffler against corrosion.

In the exhaust train of an automotive vehicle, the engine first exhausts into the exhaust manifold, Figs. 28-3 and 28-4. Then, the gas passes through the exhaust pipe into the muffler. From the muffler, it passes into the tailpipe and from there into the atmosphere at the rear of the vehicle.

In addition, some cars utilize resonators in the system, Fig.

28-2. Also, latest models are equipped with catalytic converters to reduce noxious emissions in the exhaust gases. See Fig. 28-6.

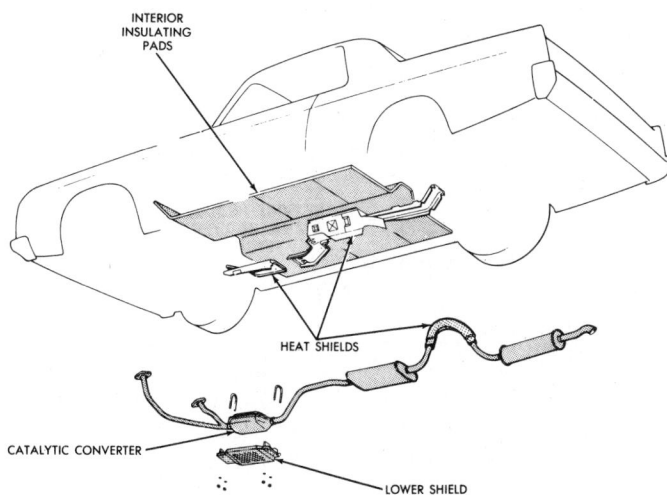

Fig. 28-6. Because of the high temperatures in a catalytic converter, it is necessary to install heat shields to protect the body of the car.

Since temperatures in excess of 1,000 deg. F. (537 C) may be generated in a catalytic converter, heat shields are installed, Fig. 28-6. These high temperatures result when engine misfiring occurs or if the engine is operating below peak efficiency. Therefore, do not disconnect spark plug wires or short out plugs when checking an engine equipped with a catalytic converter. Also, do not undercoat or paint heat shields. This would destroy converter effectiveness.

A certain amount of expansion and cooling of the exhaust gas is provided for in the design of the exhaust manifold and exhaust pipe. Usually these are designed to provide from two to four times the volume of a single cylinder of the engine. Additional expansion is provided for in the muffler, Fig. 28-7.

MUFFLER DESIGN

The design of the muffler varies with different manufacturers. One type is known as the straight through type. See B in Fig. 28-7. In this design, a straight path for the gases extends from the front to the rear of the unit.

With the straight through muffler, centrally located pipe with perforations is provided. Surrounding this pipe is a sheet metal shell, approximately three times the diameter of the pipe. In some instances, the space between the outer shell and inner pipe is open. In other cases, it is filled with steel wool or some other heat-resistant sound deadener and porous material.

Another type of muffler reverses the flow of the exhaust gases, Fig. 28-7, and has the advantage of conserving space. The double shell and two shell designs are still other forms of modern mufflers.

In order to reduce the noise of the exhaust below that attained by a single muffler, many systems are equipped with two mufflers in each line, Fig. 28-2. This type of construction is particularly necessary on cars with a long wheelbase and powered with a high output engine. The additional unit is usually called a resonator.

The design of a muffler is a precision operation as the size and shape of the different chambers will affect it acoustical properties and back pressure. In Fig. 28-8, chambers marked 1 are known as Helmholtz tuning chambers. These areas within the muffler are precisely tuned, taking into account chamber volume, tuning tube size and temperature of the gases in the chamber.

If the exhaust pipe is the right length and diameter, the frequency of the explosions can cause a resonance in that pipe, much the same as blowing across the neck of a bottle. These Helmholtz tuning chambers can be designed to absorb resonance and reduce the noise level of the exhaust system.

The high frequency tuning chamber, marked 2 in Fig. 28-8, reduce the sound level of the high frequencies present in the

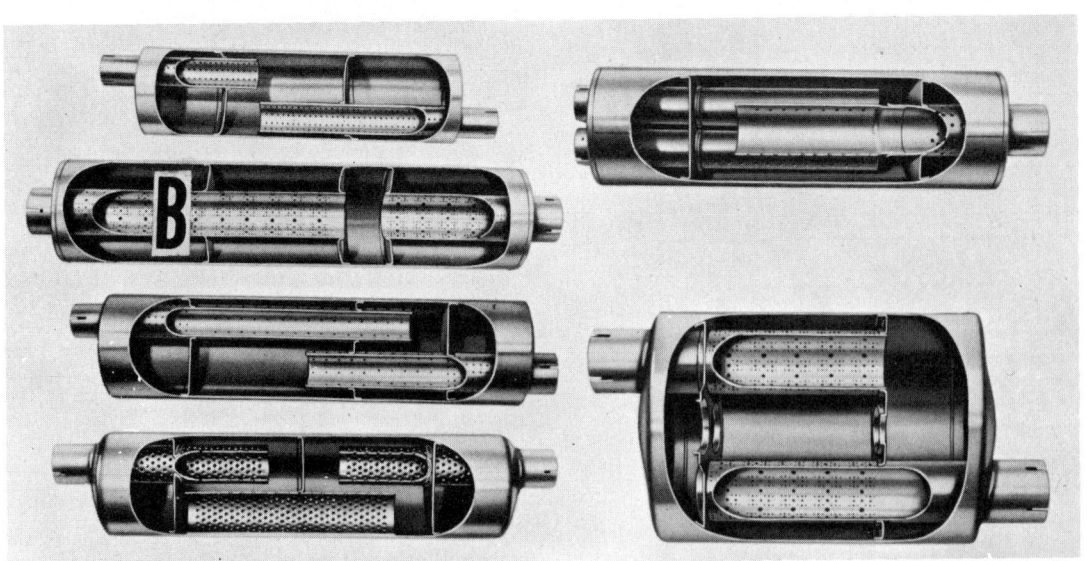

Fig. 28-7. Different types of muffler construction. Muffler B is a straight-through design, while the others are variations of the reverse flow type of construction.

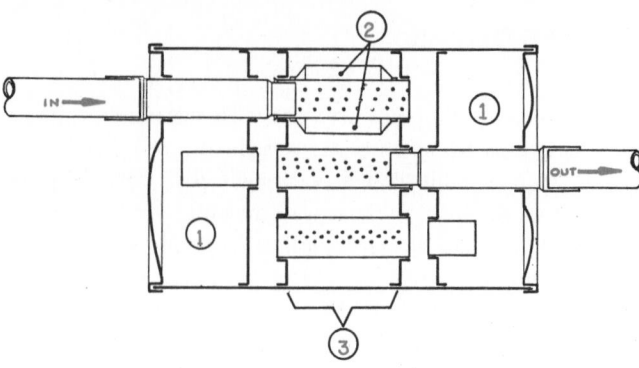

Fig. 28-8. Acoustical features of a typical muffler include: 1—Helmholtz tuning chambers. 2—High frequency tuning chamber. 3—Reversing unit crossover passages. (Maremont Corp., Automotive Group)

exhaust system. (Helmholtz chambers primarily affect low frequency sounds.) The high frequencies can be generated by exhaust flow past a sharp edge in the exhaust train, venturi noise in the carburetor and friction between the forceful exhaust flow and the pipes.

Generally, high frequencies show up as a whistling noise. So each perforation in the inner tube of the high frequency tuning chamber acts as a small tuning tube, Fig. 28-8.

The reversing unit crossover shown at 3 in Fig. 28-8 is most effective in removing or reducing the mid-range of frequencies missed by the high and the low frequency chambers. The amount of crossover is determined by the size and amount of holes in the adjacent tubes.

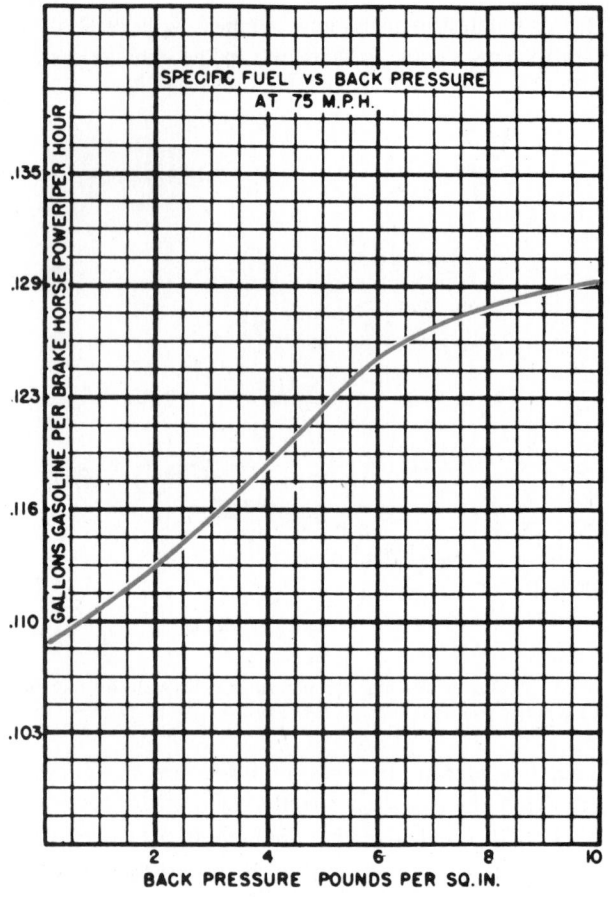

Fig. 28-10. Fuel consumption increases rapidly with increased back pressure.

BACK PRESSURE

In Fig. 28-9, the loss in engine power due to back pressure from the exhaust system is charted. Note that as the speed of the vehicle increases, back pressure increases. For a given car speed, the loss in power increases very rapidly with the increase in back pressure. For example, with 2 lb. back pressure at 70 mph, the power loss is 4 hp. When the back pressure is 4 lb., power loss has increased 8 hp.

Similarly, fuel consumption is increased as muffler back pressure increases. This is shown graphically in Fig. 28-10.

Care must be exercised that there are no kinks or flattened areas in the exhaust system that would tend to obstruct the free flow of the exhaust gases. Any obstruction caused by restricted passages or internal blockage, will reduce power and fuel economy.

CORROSION OF EXHAUST SYSTEM

Mufflers, tailpipes and exhaust pipes wear out due to corrosion, which occurs both inside and outside. External rusting is due to rain, snow and humidity. In some northern metropolitan sections, this external rusting is accelerated by the use of salt on icy road surfaces.

By far the greatest amount of corrosion occurs inside the

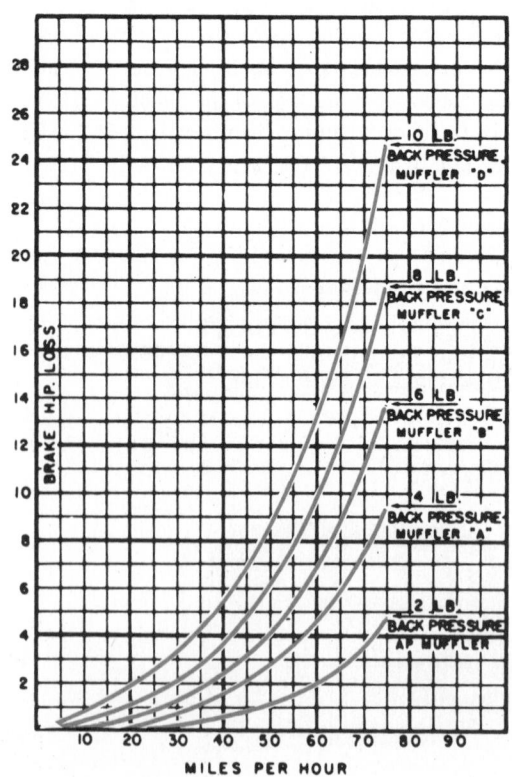

Fig. 28-9. Showing loss in horsepower due to exhaust back pressure.

exhaust system, particularly in the muffler. This is because approximately a gallon of water is formed for every gallon of fuel burned. The water is produced by combustion of the air-fuel mixture, which passes through the exhaust system. Acids are also formed in the combustion process, so the combination of acids and water quickly rusts the interior of the exhaust system.

Until the exhaust system has reached operating temperature, much of the moisture will condense on the cool surfaces and collect in the muffler. Then, as the muffler becomes hot, the collected moisture will evaporate and be forced out of the tailpipe.

Engineers have found that condensate boils at 202 to 210 deg. F. Therefore, mufflers must be operated at or above that temperature to expel the condensate. On short drives, the muffler will not reach that temperature and corrosion will occur.

In addition to the affect of corrosion, mufflers and the rest of the exhaust system will wear out or become less effective due to the accumulation of carbon, hot exhaust gas leaks, loose parts causing vibration, etc.

In order to reduce the tendency toward corrosion, most manufacturers are using some form of rust-resisting coatings and/or special alloys in the construction of their mufflers and pipes. In addition, stainless steel is being used, or a ceramic coating is applied to the interior of mufflers and pipes.

EXHAUST GAS IS DEADLY

It is imperative that no leaks occur in the muffler and exhaust system, because exhaust gases contain carbon monoxide (CO). Carbon monoxide is a deadly poison. When CO finds its way into the interior of the vehicle, it causes headache, drowsiness and nausea. As the quantity of CO is increased, unconsciousness and finally death results.

Surveys show that approximately 5 percent of the cars on the road contain sufficient carbon monoxide to cause drowsiness and seriously impair driver judgment and reflexes.

Any exhaust leaks that occur in the exhaust system, anywhere from the exhaust manifold back to the tailpipe, should be repaired immediately by tightening connections, installing gaskets or new parts.

Not only is exhaust gas dangerous to the occupants of a vehicle, it is also dangerous to mechanics working in a repair shop. Engines should never be operated in a closed garage, unless adequate ventilation is provided. In large shops, special ventilating ducts are provided. These ducts are connected to the tailpipe of the vehicle so the exhaust is conducted outdoors.

SERVICING EXHAUST SYSTEMS

Because of the rusting that occurs in exhaust systems, it is often necessary to replace the various parts. The muffler and tailpipe are the parts replaced most frequently. Their life is largely dependent on the type of service in which the vehicle is used. If the car or truck is used mostly for short trips, it is not unusual for the muffler to require replacement in less than 20,000 miles. This is particularly true in dual exhaust systems on V-8 engines, if the exhaust is divided into two separate lines. Generally, one pipe does not attain as high a temperature as the other. Operating at a lower temperature, less moisture is evaporated and, consequently, more rusting occurs.

Fig. 28-1 shows an exhaust system consisting of exhaust manifold, exhaust pipe, muffler and tailpipe. The joint between the manifold and the exhaust pipe is usually of the flange-and-gasket type. Brass nuts on steel bolts are usually used to hold the flanges together, since the brass will not rust on the steel and is more easily dismantled.

The usual construction simplifies parts replacement.

PARTS REPLACEMENT

Replacement exhaust system parts are readily available, either by picking up specific system parts from a supplier or by maintaining a sizable inventory of parts in the shop. However, stocking an adequate supply of exhaust pipes, mufflers and tailpipes takes a lot of space and involves a large financial investment.

To help overcome this stocking problem, tube bending equipment is available. With this equipment in the shop, it is only necessary to stock straight tubing in various diameters. Then, based on immediate need, the tube bender can be used to bend the straight lengths to the desired shape.

The tube bender shown in Fig. 28-11, for example, is a fully automatic unit with forward and reverse foot pedal control. This equipment is designed to produce bends through 3 in. outside diameter tubing. Therefore, truck tubing and passenger car tubing of all sizes can be bent to shape.

A heavy-duty swager/expander can be used on the ends of the cut and shaped tubing to form slip connections and produce flare and ball joint tubing connections.

The usual construction of the exhaust pipe is to make the

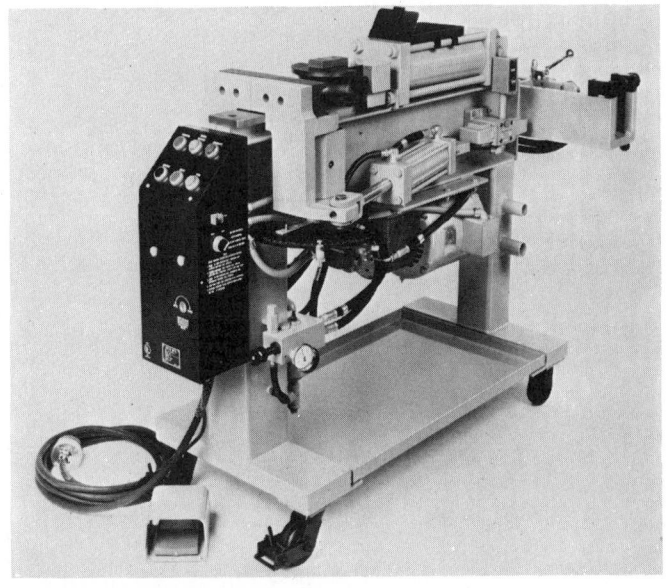

Fig. 28-11. This electro-hydraulic equipment is designed for bending exhaust system tubing. (Huth Manufacturing Co.)

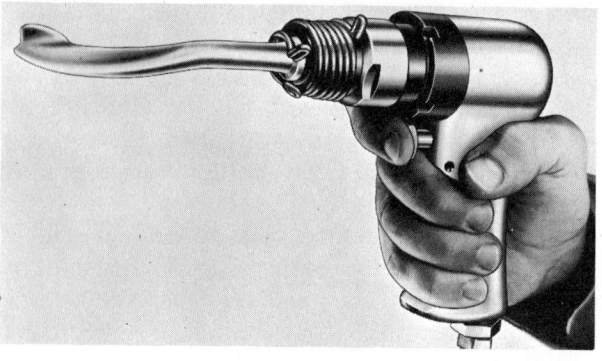

Fig. 28-12. One type of pneumatic muffler gun with special chisel designed for muffler and pipe removal work.

it difficult to separate then at the joint. If any of the parts are to be used again, penetrating oil should be liberally applied to the joints before attempting to pull them apart.

In most cases, exhaust system parts are not to be used again and, consequently, they can be cut apart.

Hacksaws can be used for muffler removal, but power-driven tools, Fig. 28-12, will do the job much more quickly. To speed the job of installation, it is frequently necessary to expand the end of a muffler pipe, tailpipe or exhaust pipe, so that the pipes can be more easily assembled. A special tool for this purpose is shown in Fig. 28-13.

lower end slightly larger in diameter than the opening in the muffler. The muffler opening can then be slipped into the end of the exhaust pipe. A clamp is placed around the end of the exhaust pipe, when tightened, the two parts are held together securely.

The connection between the tailpipe and muffler is of similar construction. Metal or combination metal-and-fabric straps are used to hold the muffler and pipes in proper alignment and with leak-proof connections.

To replace a muffler and tailpipe, remove the clamps and supporting straps holding the tailpipe in place.

Next, remove the front of the tailpipe from the back of the muffler. The tailpipe usually rusts to the muffler, which makes

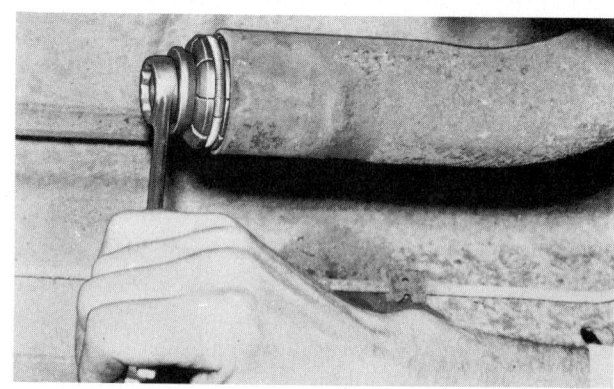

Fig. 28-13. Special tool being used to expand end of pipe to facilitate installation of new muffler.

REVIEW QUESTIONS – EXHAUST SYSTEMS

1. What four major parts form the exhaust system on an automobile?
2. On an in-line engine, where is the exhaust manifold usually attached?
3. What affect does back pressure have on the operation of an engine?
   a. Reduces power.
   b. Increases power.
   c. Increases the amount of carbon monoxide.
4. What affect does back pressure have on fuel economy?
   a. None.
   b. Reduces it.
   c. Increases it.
5. What is a major factor in the rusting of a muffler?
   a. Short distance driving.
   b. Long distance driving.
   c. High speed.
   d. Idling for extended periods.
6. What material is used in making the nuts used to bolt together the flange between the manifold and exhaust pipe?
   a. Cast iron.
   b. Steel.
   c. Castellated.
   d. Brass.

EMISSION CONTROL

Many factors, natural and otherwise, contribute to pollution of the air we breathe. Our atmosphere is being polluted daily by the growing and decaying processes of nature, by emissions from motor vehicles and by smoke from factories, power plants and the heating of homes, commercial buildings, industrial plants and institutions.

Industry contributes the largest share of air contaminants, mostly in the form of sulfur compounds and particulates (solid matter). Motor vehicle emissions, on the other hand, are carbon monoxide (CO), hydrocarbons (HC) and oxides of nitrogen (NOx).

THE AUTOMOBILE AND ITS EMISSIONS

The fight for clean air began in Los Angeles County in 1947. The air was heavy with what they called "smog," a condition that not only reduced visability on otherwise clear days, but also irritated the eyes, nose and throat. They took tests of the polluted air and found that it contained hydrocarbons and oxides of nitrogen from motor vehicle emissions. These contaminants reacted in the presence of sunlight to form a yellow smoke, or smog. The motor vehicle was at fault, they said, and something had to be done about it.

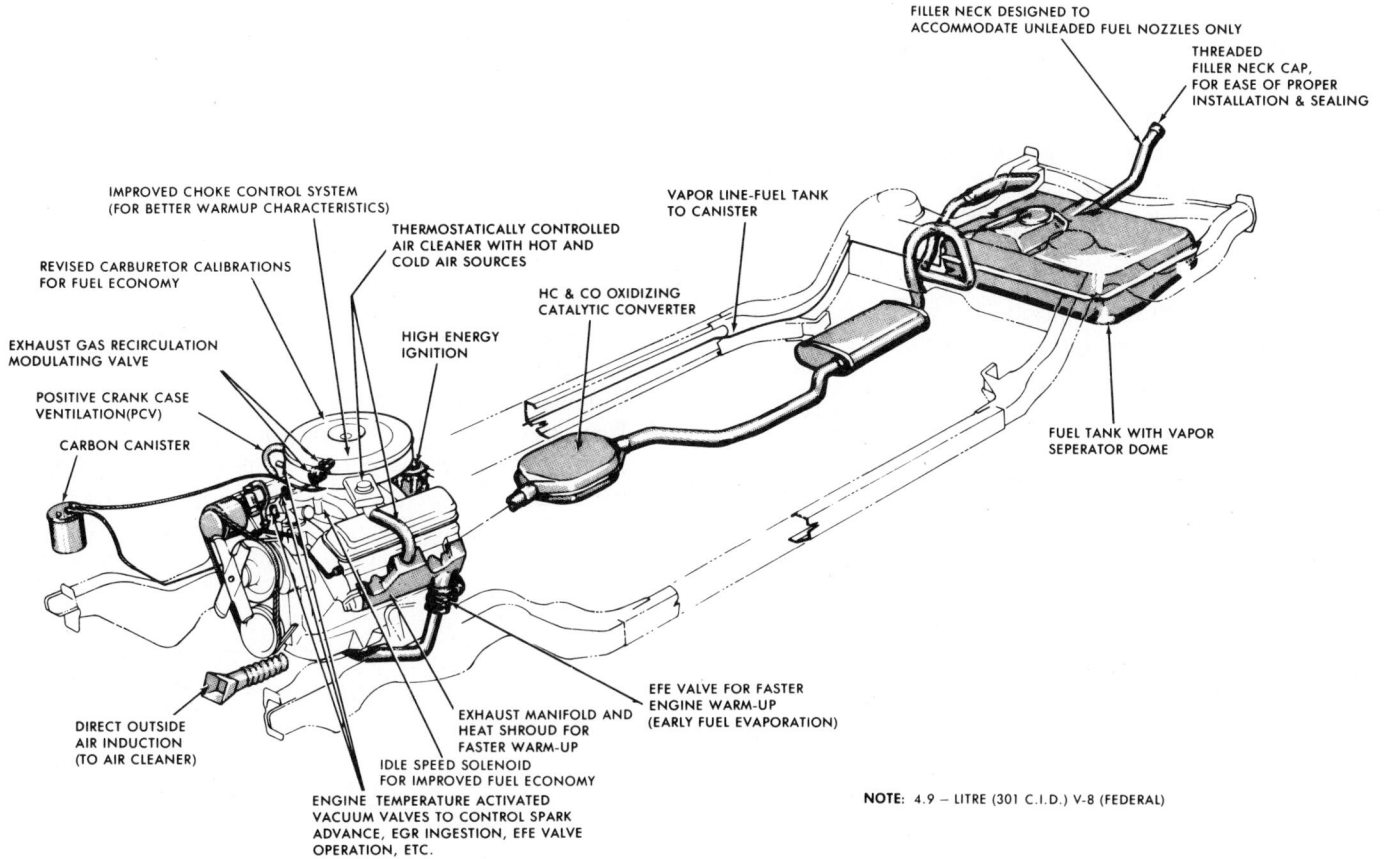

FILLER NECK DESIGNED TO ACCOMMODATE UNLEADED FUEL NOZZLES ONLY

THREADED FILLER NECK CAP, FOR EASE OF PROPER INSTALLATION & SEALING

IMPROVED CHOKE CONTROL SYSTEM (FOR BETTER WARMUP CHARACTERISTICS)

REVISED CARBURETOR CALIBRATIONS FOR FUEL ECONOMY

THERMOSTATICALLY CONTROLLED AIR CLEANER WITH HOT AND COLD AIR SOURCES

VAPOR LINE-FUEL TANK TO CANISTER

HC & CO OXIDIZING CATALYTIC CONVERTER

EXHAUST GAS RECIRCULATION MODULATING VALVE

HIGH ENERGY IGNITION

POSITIVE CRANK CASE VENTILATION(PCV)

CARBON CANISTER

FUEL TANK WITH VAPOR SEPERATOR DOME

DIRECT OUTSIDE AIR INDUCTION (TO AIR CLEANER)

EXHAUST MANIFOLD AND HEAT SHROUD FOR FASTER WARM-UP

IDLE SPEED SOLENOID FOR IMPROVED FUEL ECONOMY

ENGINE TEMPERATURE ACTIVATED VACUUM VALVES TO CONTROL SPARK ADVANCE, EGR INGESTION, EFE VALVE OPERATION, ETC.

EFE VALVE FOR FASTER ENGINE WARM-UP (EARLY FUEL EVAPORATION)

NOTE: 4.9 – LITRE (301 C.I.D.) V-8 (FEDERAL)

Fig. 29-1. Typical emission control setup on late model General Motors cars is pictured. Some engines also require air injection and additional exhaust gas catalysts. (Pontiac Motor Div., General Motors Corp.)

The Californians went to work on the problem. By 1959, seven air control districts had been created around the state, the first air pollution agency was organized and the first standards for air quality and motor vehicle emissions were established. During the next ten years, both state and Federal pollution control programs were set up, expanded and strengthened. Each year, emission levels were lowered.

Now, with the Federal Clean Air Act being implemented by the U.S. Environmental Protection Agency (EPA), the car manufacturers have responded with great strides in engine engineering and in the development of emission control systems and devices, as shown in Fig. 29-1. Today's stringent emissions standards are being met. Motor vehicle emissions are definitely on the decline.

POSITIVE CRANKCASE VENTILATION

First of the emission controls adopted by the automotive industry was a crankcase ventilation system that routed blow-by gases, condensation vapors and crankcase fumes to the combustion chambers of the engine. It was introduced nationwide on the 1963 models.

Called the positive crankcase ventilation (PCV) system, the early version is classified as the "open" type, because it uses an oil filler cap that is open to the atmosphere. Fresh air enters the oil filler cap in the normal manner. It passes through the crankcase, picks up blow-by gases, enters the valve rocker cover chamber, flows through the hose and PCV valve and into the intake manifold. Blending with the air-fuel mixture, the fresh air and crankcase gases are distributed to the cylinder combustion chambers and burned again.

With this system, the connecting tubing and PCV valve must be kept clean. A quick check on the condition of the system can be made by removing the valve and breather cap from the rocker cover. If the valve is working properly, a hissing noise will be heard as the air passes through the valve. Also, strong vacuum should be felt when a finger is placed over the valve inlet. Also, a light suction should be felt at the oil filler pipe.

The open type of PCV system was satisfactory — to a point. As long as the PCV valve was working, and the tubing and ports were open, blow-by gases were recycled to the combustion chambers. However, lack of maintenance or a stuck valve would cause pressure to build in the crankcase. With no other place to go, the blow-by gases would be forced through the "open" oil filler cap, polluting the atmosphere.

Recognizing the problem, the emission control engineers came up with the "closed" type of crankcase ventilation system. It first appeared on California cars, then nationwide. It still is in use today, Fig. 29-2, removing approximately one-third of the total vehicle emissions.

In the closed PCV system, incoming air first passes through the carburetor air filter before entering the oil filler cap, which is closed, or the valve rocker arm cover. Usually a separate air filter is incorporated in the air cleaner for this system. See Fig. 29-3. From that point on, the closed PCV system is similar to the open type.

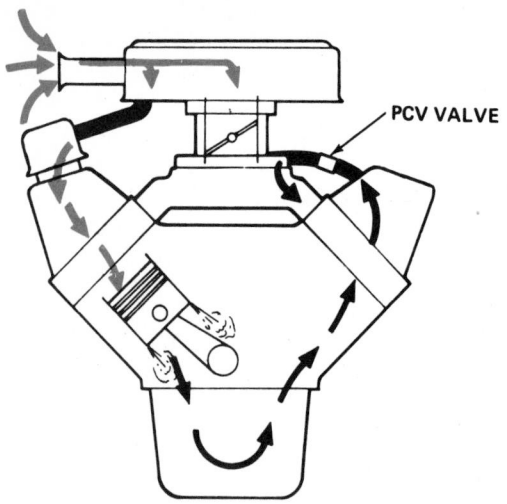

Fig. 29-2. Closed type of positive crankcase ventilation. Note that airflow is from air cleaner to valve rocker cover to crankcase, through other rocker cover, hose and PCV valve to intake manifold.

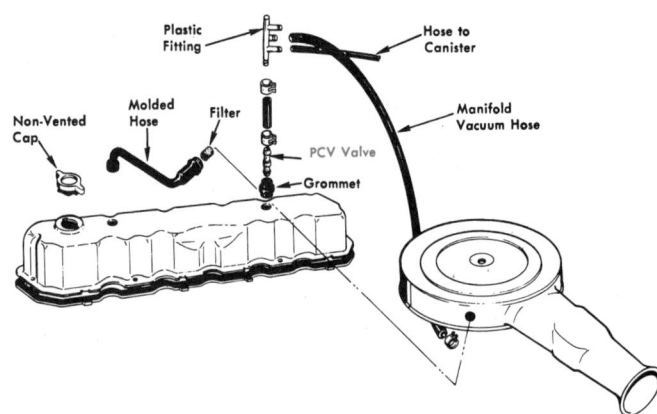

Fig. 29-3. Exploded view of positive crankcase ventilation system reveals convenient location of valve for service.

Service is similar in that connecting tubing and parts must be kept clean, and the valve must be operable (in working order). In addition, the air filters must be cleaned or replaced.

The purpose of the valve, located between the valve cover and the manifold, Fig. 29-3, is to prevent excess airflow during idling. At idle speed, intake manifold vacuum is high. The

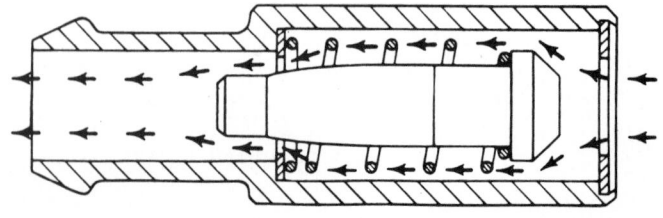

Fig. 29-4. PCV valve opens under relatively high manifold vacuum to permit crankcase fumes and vapors to be sucked into intake manifold, then into combustion chambers for burning.

strong vacuum overcomes the tension of the spring, Fig. 29-4, and moves the valve to the low flow position. With the valve in this position, all the ventilating air passes through a restricted passage and there is minimum ventilation. As engine speed increases and manifold vacuum decreases, the spring forces the valve out of the passage to full-open position, thereby increasing airflow and great amounts of blow-by gases are recycled.

A plugged PCV system can cause condensation of the blow-by gases in the crankcase, resulting in the formation of acids, sludge and oil dilution. A plugged PCV valve can also cause oil to be forced into the air filter.

EXHAUST EMISSION CONTROLS

With crankcase emissions eliminated by PCV, engine engineers concentrated their efforts on exhaust emissions from the tailpipe and gasoline vapors from the fuel tank and carburetor. The vapor problem has been solved by evaporative emission controls (EEC — to be covered later), but the struggle to reach near-zero exhaust emissions goes on.

Since 1970, a substantial improvement in exhaust emission levels has been realized through changes and modifications in internal engine design and by the use of a wide array of emission control systems and devices. At that time, the Clean Air Act Amendment was passed, proposing standards that called for a 90 percent reduction from emission levels then (1970) in force.

Interim standards for emission levels through 1974 were met by means of various control devices and systems. But standards set for 1975-1976 were so low-level, meeting them with most engines required the installation of catalytic converters, which chemically transform noxious emissions into harmless carbon dioxide and water vapor.

A look at the standards through 1981 in gpm (grams per mile) reveals the sharp lowering of emission levels for 1975 and again for 1981.

	1973	1975	1978	1981
CO	39.0 gpm	15.0 gpm	15.0 gpm	3.40 gpm
HC	3.4 gpm	1.5 gpm	1.5 gpm	0.41 gpm
NOx	3.1 gpm	3.1 gpm	2.0 gpm	1.00 gpm

Current exhaust emission controls and other prospective devices are explained in the rest of this chapter.

SYSTEMS AND DEVICES

There are several different methods of precombustion control of exhaust emissions. Attempts have been made to eliminate the problem at its source by modification of engine design, carburetion and ignition.

To comply with federal regulations for the control of exhaust emissions, the car manufacturers and their suppliers have developed and installed many different devices and systems. These "controls" can be grouped into two broad classes:

1. Those designed to reduce or eliminate the formation of harmful pollutants in the engine (precombustion controls).
2. Those designed to destroy or otherwise alter the pollutants after they have been formed (post-combustion controls).

The difficulties to overcome in solving the overall problem can be appreciated by considering the many different conditions that help produce these pollutants:

1. Combustion chamber design.
2. Quantity of combustion chamber deposits.
3. Displacement of the cylinder.
4. Temperature.
5. Air-fuel ratio.
6. Engine speed.
7. Manifold vacuum.
8. Spark advance.
9. Valve timing.
10. Exhaust back pressure.
11. Type of transmission (automatic's easier to control).
12. Maintenance.

Engine modifications made with exhaust emission control in mind have brought about many new advances in internal engine design. Areas affected by these engineering changes include:

1. Compression ratios have been lowered for compatability with no-lead and low-lead fuels.
2. Combustion chamber configuration has been redesigned for better surface-to-volume ratio (area of combustion chamber surface compared with its volume with piston at top dead center). Also, combustion chamber modifications have been made for more efficient flow rate and burning time of the air-fuel charge.
3. Pistons and piston rings have been redesigned in piston crown contour, smaller upper ring lands and top ring has been moved closer to top of piston.
4. Intake manifolds have better air-fuel flow and balanced distribution of charge to each combustion chamber.
5. Valve ports have been given soft curves and smooth surfaces.
6. Exhaust gas recirculation has been incorporated in manifolds to provide a metered amount of exhaust gas for recirculation with air-fuel mixture to slow combustion and reduce combustion chamber temperatures.
7. Camshafts have been redesigned to modify valve timing and to increase valve overlap periods.
8. Cylinder heads have been modified to accept air injection system tubes near each exhaust valve.
9. Cylinder head gaskets have been redesigned for an improved "fit."
10. Spark plug location has been changed.

Also incorporated in most late model engines are the following conditions, modes of operation or "controls" designed to help provide more complete combustion and fewer exhaust emissions:

1. Higher engine operating temperatures.
2. Ignition distributor recalibrations with modified ignition advance and better correlation with speed and load.
3. Leaner carburetor recalibrations with higher curb idle speeds, idle stop solenoids and "limiter" caps on idle mixture screws.

4. Electric assist automatic chokes with more sensitive action and faster release.
5. Thermostatically controlled heated air cleaners (to be covered later).
6. Fuel evaporation control systems (to be covered later).

ENGINE MODIFICATION SYSTEMS

At first, the car manufacturers made an all-out effort to meet emissions standards by means of engine modifications. Ford named their system IMCO (Improved Combustion). Chrysler named theirs CAS (Cleaner Air System). General Motors had CCS (Controlled Combustion System). American Motors had Engine-Mod. Since 1970, the car makers have relied on emission control systems and devices, Fig. 29-5.

more complete combustion of the air-fuel mixture. Changes include: alteration of the camshaft, reduced compression ratio, revised intake manifold, changes in the carburetor and ignition system. Carburetor idle screws are equipped with limiters or limiting caps that prevent over-rich air-fuel mixture adjustment, Figs. 29-6 and 29-7. Carburetors are calibrated at the factory to obtain the desired lean ratio, then the limiter caps are installed.

The Motorcraft distributor, Fig. 29-8 is dual advance type, and has two diaphragms. The spark is at the normal position for starting. When engine speed drops to idling, the spark is automatically retarded. The outer (advance) diaphragm contols the spark advance as a single diaphragm does on conventional distributors. The inner diaphragm works in the opposite direction to retard the spark at idling and during

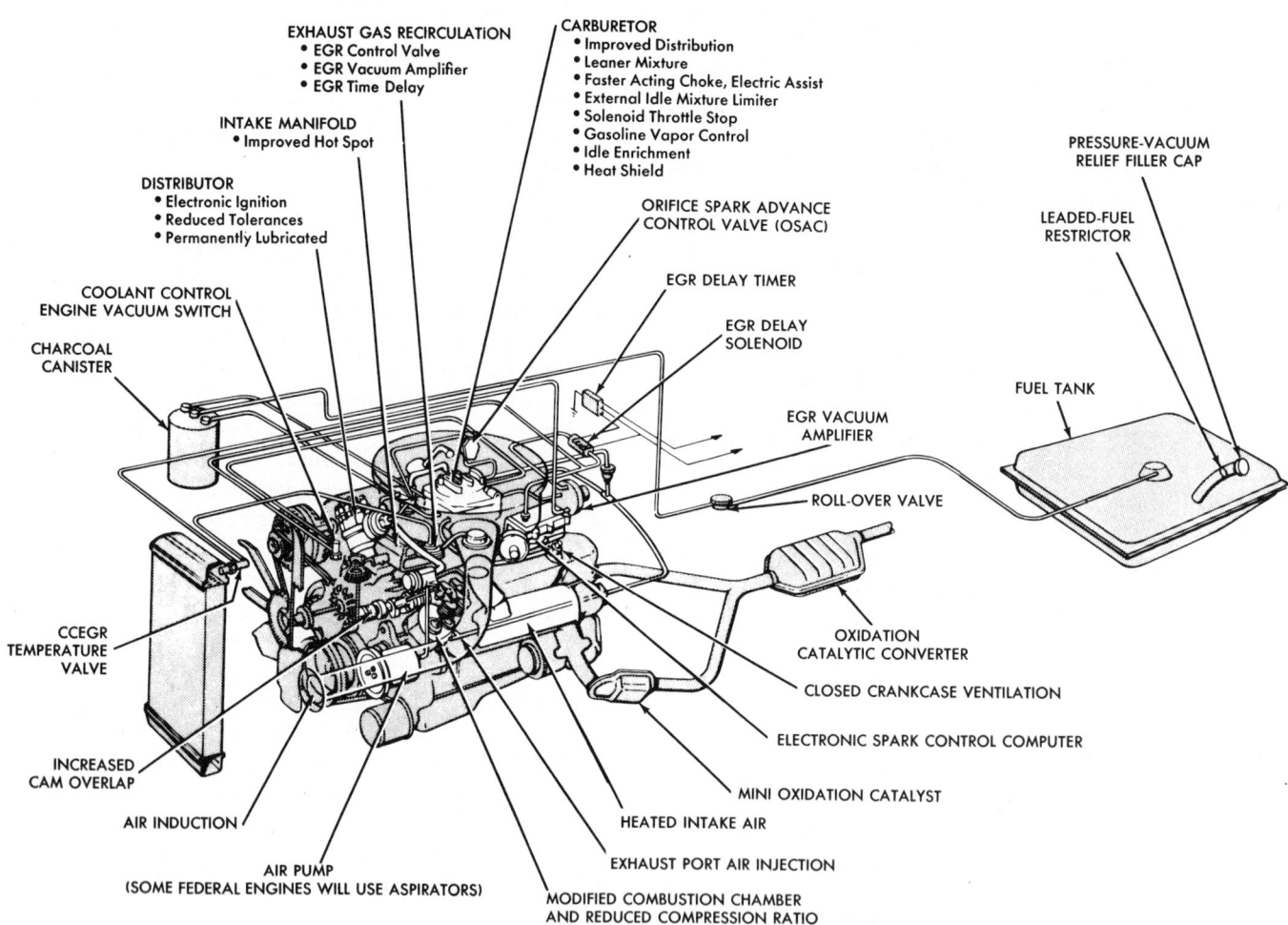

Fig. 29-5. Emission control systems and devices used on late model Chrysler Corporation V-8 engines.

FORD IMCO SYSTEM

The Ford IMCO exhaust emission control system is designed to reduce the amount of carbon monoxide, hydrocarbons and oxides of nitrogen formed in the combustion chambers. Design modifications are tailored to the requirements of each vehicle and its power train.

Internal engine modifications have been made that promote

periods of deceleration.

Calibrated coil springs, Fig. 29-8 bear on the vacuum sides of both diaphragms to supply resistance to the actual force of the vacuum. A link connects the outer diaphragm to the distributor breaker plate, passing through the center of the inner diaphragm. The inner diaphragm serves to position a return stop for the outer diaphragm to govern the amount of spark retard when spark advance vacuum is reduced.

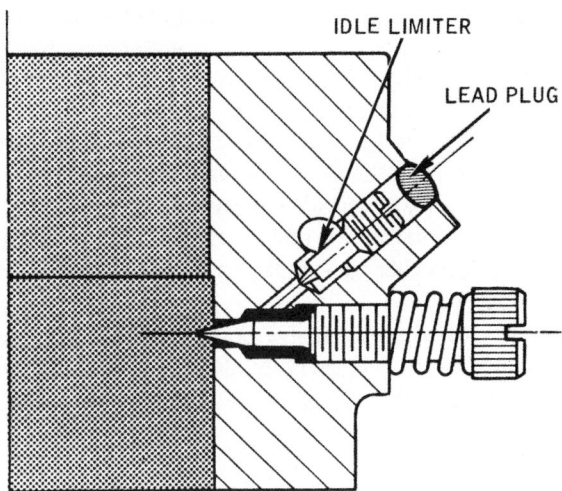

Fig. 29-6. One method of limiting idle mixture adjustment in order to prevent excessively rich mixtures. (Ford)

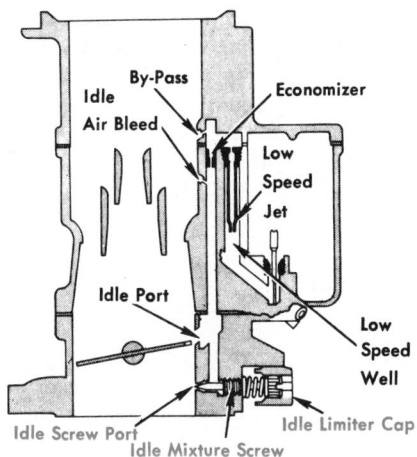

Fig. 29-7. Idle limiter caps are designed to regulate adjustment range of idle mixture adjusting screws to effectively avoid over-richness and comply with Federal emissions standards.

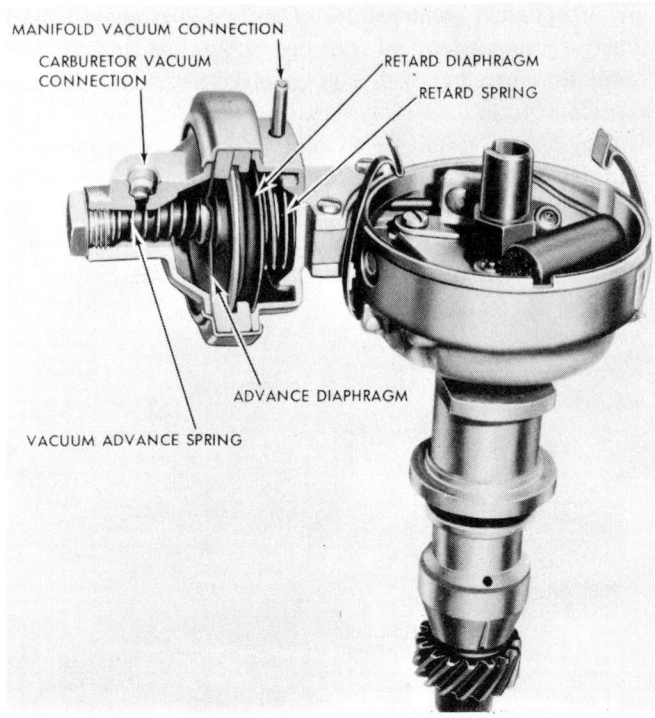

Fig. 29-8. Dual diaphragm ignition distributor design provide special retardation of spark at idle speeds and during deceleration.

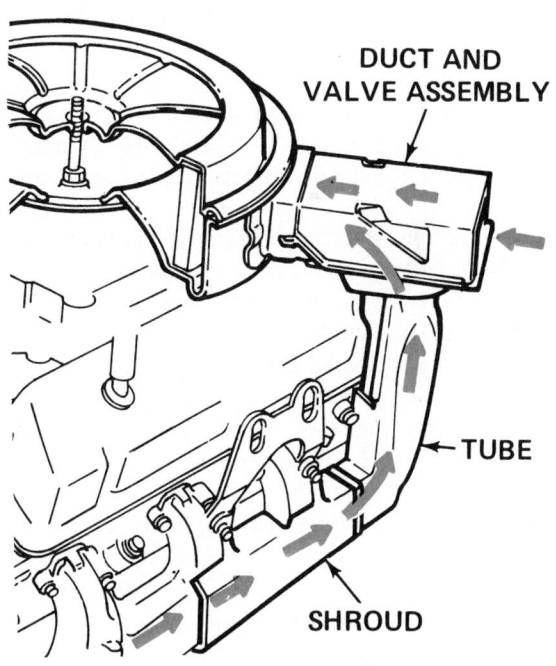

Fig. 29-9. Ford's inlet air regulator in air cleaner snorkel utilizes a duct and valve assembly in conjunction with a connecting tube and exhaust manifold shroud. Heated air from manifold enters carburetor during warmup. Thermostatically controlled valve maintains inlet air at approximately 100 deg. F (38 C).

Retarding the spark at idle and controlling the air-fuel ratio significantly reduces the emission of noxious fumes from the exhaust, keeping them within the desired limits.

The IMCO system also depends on an inlet air temperature regulator, which consists of a duct and valve assembly attached to the air cleaner, Fig. 29-9. Ford uses two methods of heating inlet air. One is a temperature controlled unit in which the valve is operated by a thermostat. The other is a vacuum-operated unit equipped with a vacuum motor and bimetallic switch. See chapter on AIR CLEANERS.

CHRYSLER CLEANER AIR SYSTEM

The method developed by Chrysler Corp. engineers to limit the emission of carbon monoxide, hydrocarbons and oxides of nitrogen from the engine includes improvements in the engine, carburetion and ignition systems. At first, Chrysler called this system the "Cleaner Air Package." Starting in 1972, it became the "Cleaner Air System."

The "Cleaner Air Package" reduces emission levels by the

use of optimum combinations of air-fuel mixture and spark timing. Modifications of existing carburetors and ignition distributor, together with a new distributor vacuum control valve constitutes the CAP system.

Chrysler's Cleaner Air System incorporates many more emission controls, coupled with further internal engine modifications. An evaporative emission control system, for example, features a domed fuel tank, vapor-liquid separator, a charcoal canister and an overfill limiting valve, Fig. 29-10.

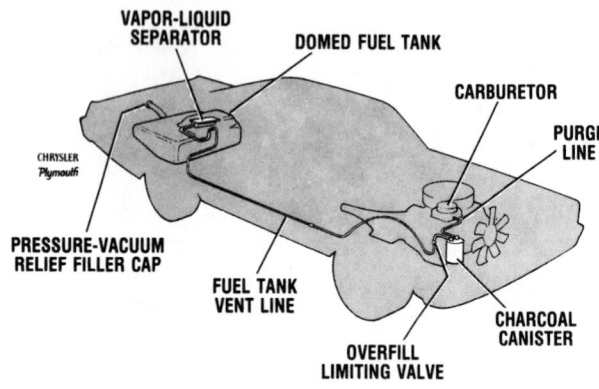

Fig. 29-10. Chrysler Corporation's evaporative emission control system has expansion space and fuel vapor separator integrated into dome in fuel tank. Carburetor is vented internally on older models. Later models include a roll-over valve combined with the separator or mounted on the frame, and carburetor is vented to the canister.

With CAS, exhaust and evaporative emissions are controlled (depending upon application) by orifice spark advance control valve, air injection, exhaust gas recirculation and evaporative control systems.

Chrysler also incorporates a heated air inlet system on all engines. Basic parts include a stove over the exhaust manifold, a flexible connector to the air cleaner snorkel, a vacuum diaphragm and air control valve in the snorkel and a thermostat in the bottom of the air cleaner housing.

The colder the underhood air, the greater the flow of heated air through the stove. The warmer the underhood air, the greater the flow of ambient (surrounding) air through the air cleaner snorkel. The air control valve is positioned by the movement of the vacuum diaphragm which, in turn, is actuated by the thermostat and manifold vacuum. As a result, a temperature of about 100 deg. F (38 C) is maintained inside the air cleaner housing to permit leaner carburetor calibration, fewer emissions and improved engine warmup.

GM CONTROLLED COMBUSTION SYSTEM

In essence, the Controlled Combustion System increases combustion efficiency through different carburetor and distributor calibration and higher engine operating temperatures. Complete effectiveness of the system, as well as full power and performance, depends on idle speed, idle mixture and ignition timing being set according to specifications.

CCS features a thermostically controlled air cleaner assem-

bly. In general, the carburetors are calibrated leaner, and the timing is retarded during low speed and deceleration. However, the system is designed specifically for each engine-trans-mission-rear axle combination.

The thermostatically controlled air cleaner is designed to keep the air entering the carburetor at approximately 115 deg. F (46 C). It is composed of a special air cleaner and a heat stove. The heat stove is a sheet metal case surrounding the exhaust manifold that uses trapped heat to warm the air going to the carburetor.

The air cleaner consists of a body, filter element, sensor unit, vacuum diaphragm assembly, damper door and connecting hoses and links, Fig. 29-11.

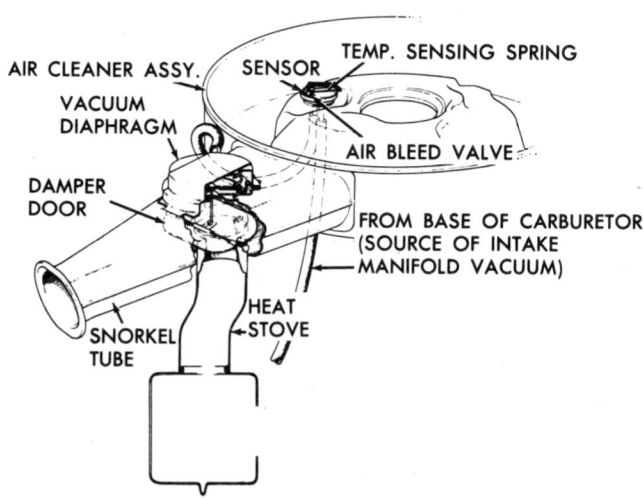

Fig. 29-11. General Motors thermostatically controlled air cleaner, as installed on some Chevrolet engines.

The sensor unit is mounted in the body of the air cleaner on the clean air side of the filter. The sensor unit regulates (depending on temperature of air passing it) the amount of vacuum supplied to the vacuum diaphragm. The vacuum diaphragm (depending on amount of vacuum supplied to it by sensing unit) opens the damper door, allowing heated air from the heat stove to enter the cleaner and shuts off the passage for ambient air. The damper door is fully open (all warm air) at 8 in. Hg. and fully closed at 6 in. Hg. or less.

The vacuum signal measured at the diaphragm assembly will not be the same as actual engine vacuum, since the thermostatic control valve in the sensor unit provides a controlled vacuum leak for regulation of the supply signal. A bimetal strip accomplishes the temperature-sensitive controlled vacuum leak.

To attain the desired retarded spark during idle, the Controlled Combustion System uses "ported" spark advance, with the vacuum take-off just above the throttle valve. With this setup, there is no vacuum advance at closed throttle. However, there is vacuum advance as soon as the throttle is opened slightly.

Because of the greater heat rejection to the coolant during idle with no spark advance, some engines are likely to overheat if allowed to idle for an extended period. For this reason, some engines are provided with a thermo-vacuum switch located in the coolant passage. There are three connections to this vacuum switch. One connection is to the intake manifold, another to the "ported" vacuum source and the third connection is to the distributor vacuum advance unit.

When the engine coolant is at normal temperature, the thermo-vacuum switch supplies "ported" vacuum to the distributor. However, should the coolant temperature rise above 220 deg. F (104 C) full intake manifold vacuum will be supplied to the distributor even at closed throttle, thereby advancing the spark, increasing engine rpm, and causing the temperature to drop.

Servicing the CCS system is basically a precision tune-up job, with special care being taken in adjusting the idle mixture and idle speed. The sensor unit requires no adjustment. The cooling system thermostat must be 195 deg. F (91 C).

AMC ENGINE MOD

At American Motors, the initial emission control effort was in the direction of internal engine modifications, so it was named "Engine Mod." Advances include induction system improvements, leaner carburetor calibration, complete vaporization of fuel in the air-fuel mixture, complete homogenization of the mixture, improved mixture distribution and increased curb idle speed.

Changes were made in combustion chamber quench areas and surface-to-volume ratio has been reduced. Controls were developed to tailor spark timing and timing advance to given engine applications. Later, AMC engineering added a thermostatically controlled air cleaner, transmission controlled spark, fuel evaporation control, exhaust gas recirculation and installed an air injection system on engines that required it.

EVAPORATIVE EMISSION CONTROLS

Evaporative Emission Controls (EEC) prevent the escape of gasoline vapors from the fuel tank and carburetor, whether or not the engine is running, Fig. 29-12. Most vehicles built during and since the 1971 model year use an activated charcoal canister to trap the vapors when the engine is shut off. On restarting, a flow of filtered air through the canister purges the vapors from the charcoal. The mixture goes through one or more tubes feeding into the carburetor and/or carburetor air cleaner, and it is burned in the engine.

The fuel tank cap has a pressure-vacuum relief valve which permits air to enter the tank as the fuel level goes down. The vented gas cap cannot be used on cars equipped with EEC.

OTHER PRE-COMBUSTION DEVICES

The two areas in which car manufacturers have concentrated their emission control efforts are ignition timing and timing advance. Since timing in all modes of engine operation has a strong influence on combustion efficiency, a wide variety of timing control devices has been introduced.

Transmission Controlled Spark (TCS) is a timing control device on AMC cars that permits spark advance only during high gear operation or after 36 mph (automatic transmission). See Fig. 29-13. Heart of the system is the solenoid switch that permits vacuum to be applied to the distributor vacuum advance unit in relation to car speed or gear range.

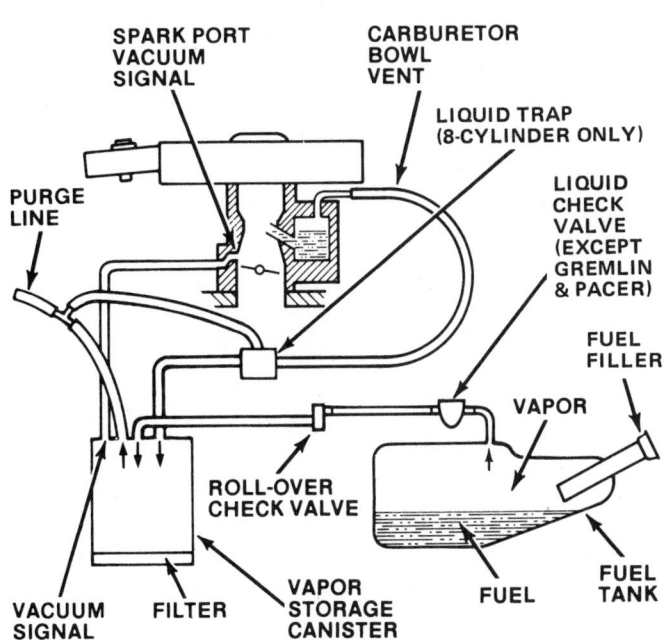

Fig. 29-12. Typical fuel vapor control system used on late model American Motors vehicles prevents evaporative emissions.

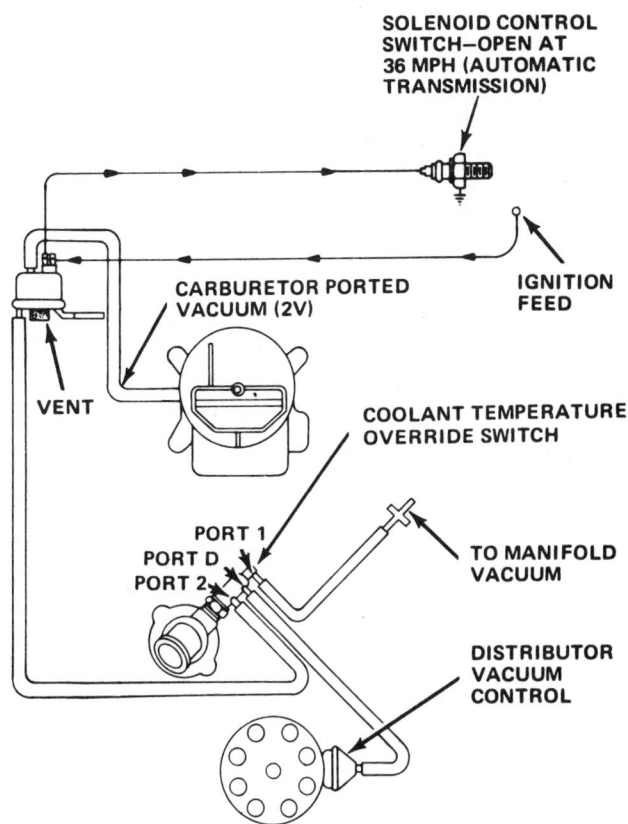

Fig. 29-13. Transmission controlled spark (TCS) system used on automatic transmission equipped American Motors cars reduces NOx.

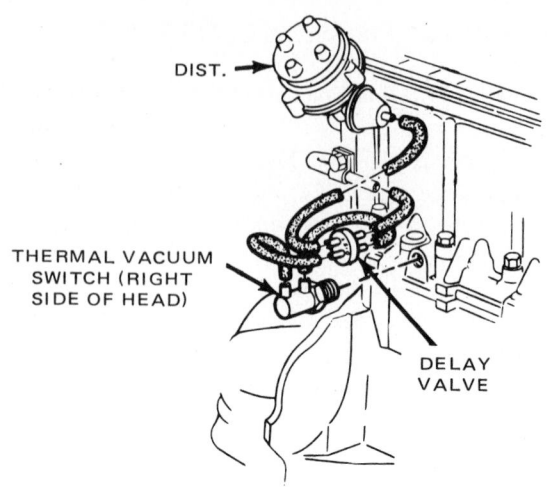

DIST.

THERMAL VACUUM
SWITCH (RIGHT
SIDE OF HEAD)

DELAY
VALVE

Fig. 29-14. On some four cylinder engines, General Motors uses a Trapped Vacuum Spark Advance system to control vacuum level to the distributor vacuum advance unit. This improves engine warmup and reduces emissions.

SPARK CONTROL DEVICES

The Combination Emission Control (CEC) is GM device that also limits vacuum spark advance to high gear operation only. Key element is an electromagnetic valve (solenoid) mounted on the carburetor. This solenoid controls vacuum applied to the distributor vacuum advance unit, opening or closing a vacuum port, depending upon transmission gear selection. A temperature override switch is provided.

A Distributor Vacuum Delay Valve is located in the vacuum advance circuit on some General Motors V-8 engines. Distributor ported vacuum is metered through a .005 in. (.13 mm) orifice in the valve, requiring up to 30 sec. for full advance.

Another GM device called a Spark Advance Vacuum Modulator is a dual diaphragm regulating valve with ports to the distributor, manifold vacuum and ported vacuum. The device balances output to the vacuum advance unit at approximately 7 in. It is responsive only to engine load.

A Trapped Vacuum Spark Advance system is used on some GM four cylinder engines. See Fig. 29-14. The system utilizes a delay valve and a thermal vacuum switch. The delay valve keeps vacuum to the distributor at a high vacuum level during acceleration. The TVS bypasses the delay valve at temperatures above 115 deg. F (46 C).

A Speed Control Switch (SCS) is fitted on some General Motors cars. SCS functions in conjunction with a sensor in the transmission that is integrated with the speedometer driven gear. The switch remains closed at speeds under 31 mph, shutting off the carburetor vacuum supply. It opens 31 to 35 mph, restoring vacuum spark advance to the distributor.

A Distributor Vacuum Control switch is mounted on some GM engines and tapped into the cooling system. This switch serves a dual function, much like the CEC valve. It applies distributor vacuum spark advance only when the transmission is in high gear. Or, if engine temperature goes above 220 deg. F (104 C), the distributor vacuum control switch applies full manifold vacuum to the distributor vacuum advance unit.

Other spark control devices include the following:

1. Ford's Electronic Distributor Modulator or Electronic Spark Control (ESC) that prevents vacuum spark advance at speeds below 23 mph.
2. Ported Spark Advance provides a degree of spark retard during closed throttle operation and during deceleration. To accomplish this, the distributor vacuum advance unit is connected to a vacuum port above the throttle plates.
3. A Spark Delay Valve is used on some Ford engines to delay vacuum spark advance during rapid acceleration. It also cuts off vacuum advance during deceleration.
4. A Distributor Advance Solenoid is installed on some Chrysler Corporation cars. Mounted in the distributor vacuum advance unit, it gives the engine the benefit of a 7 1/2 deg. spark advance during the cranking period.
5. A distributor Retard Solenoid was fitted on older Chrysler cars. This solenoid provides spark timing retard during closed throttle operation while idling or decelerating.
6. A Deceleration Vacuum Advance Valve is found on some Ford and Chrysler cars. On deceleration, this valve applies high intake manifold vacuum, momentarily, to distributor vaccum advance unit to help reduce exhaust emissions.
7. A Decel Valve provides an enriched air-fuel mixture to the engine on deceleration. This vacuum-operated valve is mounted on the intake manifold next to the carburetor. During deceleration, high vacuum lifts the valve for 3 to 5 sec. to permit additional air-fuel flow.
8. An Orifice Spark Advance Control (OSAC) valve is used on all late model Chrysler engines. It is attached to the outside of the air cleaner housing and is connected to a port just above the throttle plates of the carburetor. The valve has a small orifice, which serves to delay the change in ported vacuum from 17 to 27 sec. while going from idle to part throttle, Fig. 29-15.

NOTE: From these descriptions of vacuum spark control systems, it can be seen that all types are designed to vary ignition spark timing to suit existing conditions by applying, or not applying, vacuum to distributor vacuum control unit.

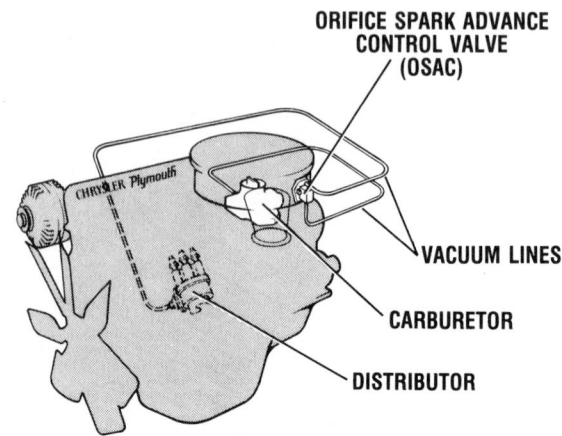

ORIFICE SPARK ADVANCE
CONTROL VALVE
(OSAC)

VACUUM LINES

CARBURETOR

DISTRIBUTOR

Fig. 29-15. Chrysler's Orifice Spark Advance Control (OSAC) aids in control of oxides of nitrogen by delaying vacuum buildup in distributor vacuum advance chamber during vehicle acceleration.

Devices used to supplement those covered include the following:

1. The Thermostatic Vacuum Switch (TVS) is used to sense high coolant temperatures and switch to the most suitable vacuum source for the distributor vacuum advance unit.
2. The Idle Stop Solenoid is an anti-dieseling device. It prevents engine run-on by holding the throttle lever at a higher idle speed when energized, then allowing the lever to drop back to the slow idle cam when de-energized.

POST—COMBUSTION DEVICES

Emission controls that are designed to reduce carbon monoxide, hydrocarbons and oxides of nitrogen AFTER the combustion process can be termed "post-combustion devices." These include:

1. Air injection system.
2. Exhaust gas recirculation.
3. Catalytic converter.
4. Thermal reactor.
5. Lead particulate trap.

FORD'S THERMACTOR SYSTEM

Ford's Thermactor Exhaust Control System reduces HC and CO emissions by injecting fresh air into the hot exhaust gases. In operation, a belt-driven pump forces air under pressure into the exhaust valve ports. Routing is by way of an external air manifold or internal drilled passages in the cylinder head or exhaust manifold. On later models equipped with a Three-Way Catalyst, the Thermactor system also pumps air into the catalytic converter (see Ford's EEC system). Oxygen in the injected air reacts to the heat of the exhaust gases, causing further oxidation (burning) which converts these gases to carbon dioxide and water.

System components generally include: air supply pump; pump muffler (some engines); air bypass valve; vacuum differential valve; (some engines); external or internal air supply system; cylinder heads drilled with air passages to exhaust ports; air supply check valves; vacuum reservoir (some engines); vacuum vent valve (with 2700 carburetor).

GENERAL MOTORS AIR SYSTEM

The General Motors Air Injector Reactor system (AIR) reduces the amount of hydrocarbons and carbon monoxide in the exhaust gases by injecting air directly into the exhaust port of each cylinder. The air, added to the hot gases, causes further oxidation of the gases before they enter the exhaust pipe.

The equipment usually incorporated in this system consists of a belt driven pump (located with front accessory group), a rubber formed air hose, a metal tubing manifold between the cylinder heads and specially designed heads that incorporate air passages to the rear of each exhaust valve.

There is a diverter valve and silencer on the AIR pump to control pressures within the system, and a check valve to

protect hoses and pump from hot gases. Manufacturers say: Do not operate engine with drive belt disconnected.

Failure of the air supply may be caused by loose or broken drive belt, leaks in hoses or connections, diverter valve failure, check valve malfunction or pump failure. Noises may result from leaks, loose parts or failure of the diverter valve, check valve or pump.

CHRYSLER AIR INJECTION SYSTEM

Chrysler air injection adds a controlled amount of air to exhaust gases in the exhaust ports, causing oxidation of the gases. The Chrysler system consists of a belt-driven air pump, rubber hose, check valves, switching valve, injection tubes and a combination diverter and pressure relief valve assembly. The exhaust manifolds incorporate air passages to each exhaust port. See Fig. 29-16.

The belt-driven air pump pumps air through the diverter valve and rubber hose to the air injection manifold. The diverter valve prevents backfire in the system during sudden deceleration. It senses the increase in manifold vacuum when the throttle valve closes. This causes the diverter valve to open, allowing air from the air pump to pass through the valve and silencer to the atmosphere.

The check valve has a one-way diaphragm that prevents hot exhaust gases from backing up into the hose and pump. The pressure relief valve controls pressure in the system by releasing excessive pump output to the atmosphere at higher engine speeds.

The switching valve permits air injection to the exhaust ports during engine warmup. This assists oxidation in the mini-catalysts. Then, after warmup, the system airflow is "switched" to a point just ahead of the power heat control valve (V-8) or just beyond the mini-converter (six), where it assists oxidation in the main catalyst.

EXHAUST GAS RECIRCULATION

Among the more recent developments in emission control is the Exhaust Gas Recirculating (EGR) system. It is designed to

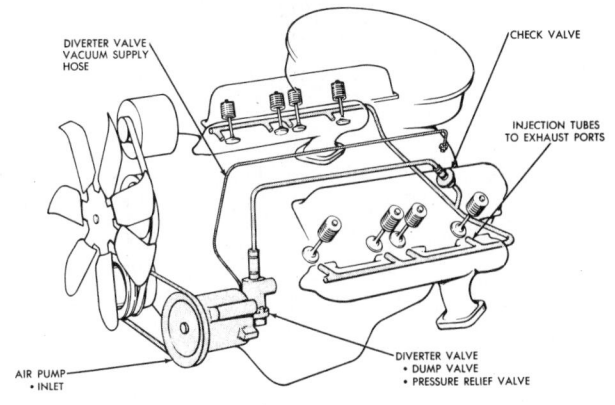

Fig. 29-16. Chrysler's air injection system has specially designed exhaust manifolds with air passages to each exhaust port, where controlled amounts of compressed air are fed into exhaust gases for more complete burning.

control nitrogen oxide (NOx) emissions. Basically, the EGR system recirculates a metered amount of exhaust gas into the air-fuel mixture in the combustion chambers where it slows down the combustion process and absorbs heat. Since NOx is produced by high temperatures, the EGR system serves to reduce temperatures and NOx emissions.

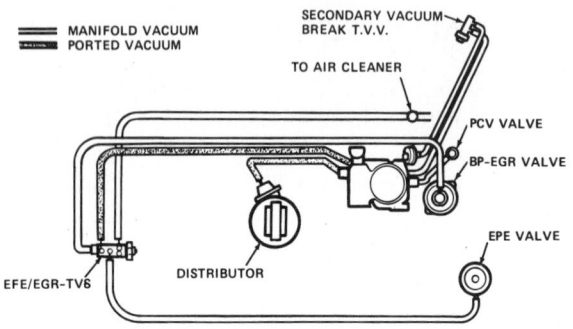

Fig. 29-17. Vacuum hose routings are shown for EGR and EFE systems on Pontiac 231 cu. in. V-6 engine with automatic transmission.

Pontiac, for example, uses two types of EGR systems, ported and exhaust back pressure modulated. The ported system uses a timed vacuum port in the carburetor to regulate the amount of EGR. The back-pressure modulated system, Fig. 29-17, regulates the timed vacuum according to the exhaust back-pressure level. An exhaust manifold heat control valve and a Thermal Vacuum Switch (TVS) constitute the Early Fuel Evaporation (EFE) system, Fig. 29-17.

American Motors uses two types of EGR valves on late model engines. The "four" is equipped with a simple, single diaphragm valve mounted on the side of the intake manifold. The valve assembly uses carburetor ported vacuum to open the valve and allow a metered amount of exhaust gas to enter the intake manifold and mix with the air-fuel charge. This reduces combustion temperatures which, in turn, reduces NOx.

All "six" and V-8 engines use an EGR valve that is combined with a back-pressure sensor. See Fig. 29-18. This double diaphragm valve is located on the side of the intake manifold on sixes; in a machined surface at the rear or the intake manifold on V-8s. Within the valve, the pintle is connected to the control diaphragm. Recirculation of the exhaust gases is controlled by the movable pintle.

American Motors uses a coolant temperature override (CTO) switch in the EGR system to cut off EGR until coolant temperature reaches 115 deg. F (46.1 C) or 160 deg. F (71.1 C). The CTO switch has two ports. The inner port (marked S) is connected by a hose to the EGR port at the carburetor. The outer port (marked E) is connected by a hose to the exhaust back-pressure sensor.

Some Ford engines use a vacuum-operated EGR flow control valve attached to a spacer between the intake manifold and the carburetor. See Fig. 29-19. A venturi vacuum amplifier converts a weak venturi vacuum signal into a strong intake manifold vacuum signal to operate the EGR valve. The amplifier is connected to a vacuum reservoir, and a check valve

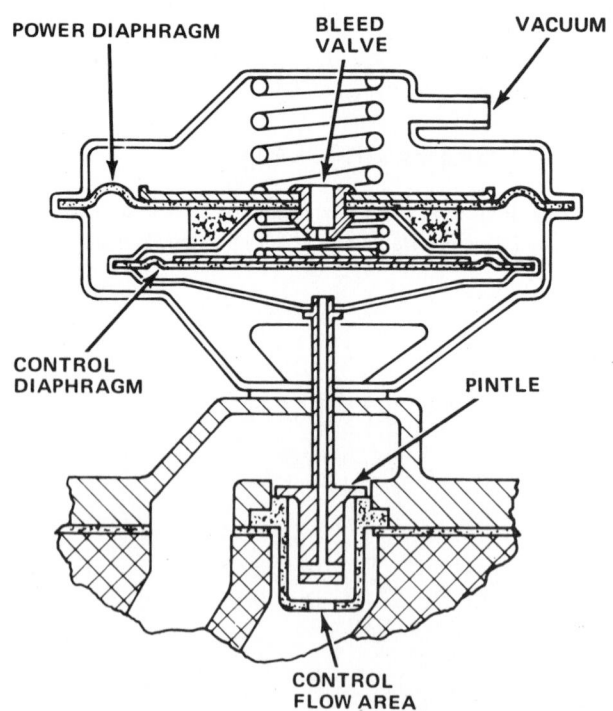

Fig. 29-18. American Motors exhaust gas recirculation valve is combined with a back-pressure sensor unit on late model V-8s and six cylinder engines. Double diaphragm and bleed valve control EGR.

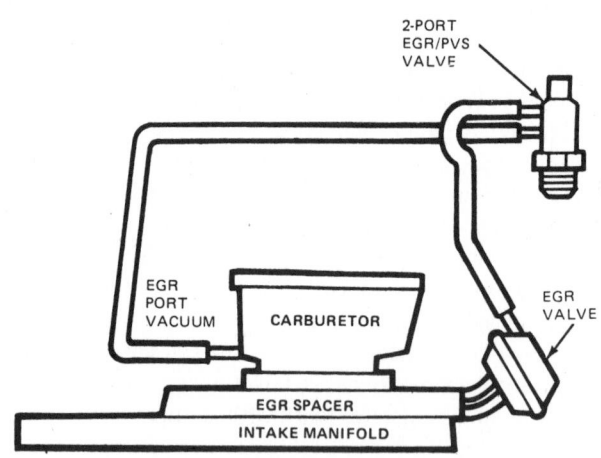

Fig. 29-19. One of Ford's EGR setups uses a spacer under the carburetor, a ported vacuum switch and an EGR valve.

helps maintain an adequate vacuum supply regardless of engine manifold conditions. Ford EGR systems also include a Ported Vacuum Switch (PVS) that restricts EGR until the engine warms up.

Chrysler uses two different EGR systems. One is a venturi vacuum control system that operates by means of a vacuum tap at the throat of the carburetor venturi. The other system is the ported vacuum control type, utilizing a slotted port in the carburetor throttle body that is exposed to greater amounts of manifold vacuum as the throttle valve opens.

The venturi vacuum control EGR system requires the use of a vacuum amplifier, Fig. 29-20, to increase vacuum to the level needed to operate the poppet type EGR valve. Both Chrysler systems include a thermal valve mounted in the top tank of the radiator to control the vacuum signal to the EGR valve.

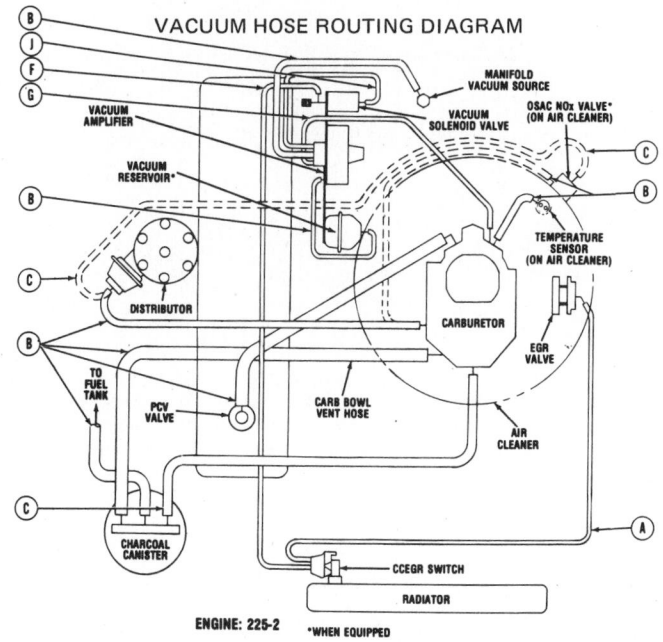

VACUUM HOSE ROUTING DIAGRAM

ENGINE: 225-2   *WHEN EQUIPPED

Fig. 29-20. Chrysler Corporation emission control vacuum hose routing on a 225 cu. in. six with 2 Bbl. carburetor (with manual or automatic transmission). The color code is: A—White. B—Black. C—Red (solid). F—Blue. G—Yellow. J—Orange.

Chrysler has equipped certain engines with an "Electronic Lean Burn" system, starting in 1976. The system consists of a "spark control computer," various engine sensors and a specially calibrated carburetor. In 1979, the system was renamed "Electronic Spark Control." Some changes were made, including replacement of the coolant temperature sensor with a time-and-temperature switch in the vacuum control circuitry to delay EGR until incoming air-fuel temperature reaches 68 deg. F (20 C).

CATALYTIC CONVERTERS

Beginning in 1975, car manufacturers added catalytic converters to most engine/drive train applications. See Figs. 29-21 and 29-22. Basically, a catalytic converter is a container of chemically treated pellets, Fig. 29-23, or a chemically treated honeycomb, that is incorporated in the exhaust system. It operates at approximately 1,500 deg. F (815.6 C) to transform noxious emissions into harmless carbon dioxide and water vapor.

General Motors catalytic converters utilize beads coated with platinum and palladium to reduce HC and CO. Some GM engines require a Phase II catalytic converter, Fig. 29-24, containing beads coated with platinum and rhodium to reduce HC, CO and NOx. The containers are stainless steel.

Chrysler Corporation installs catalytic converters with one or two ceramic honeycomb elements coated with platinum and palladium, or with platinum only. The monolithic (single block) catalytic elements are wrapped in a stainless steel mesh and encased in a stainless steel container. See Fig. 29-25.

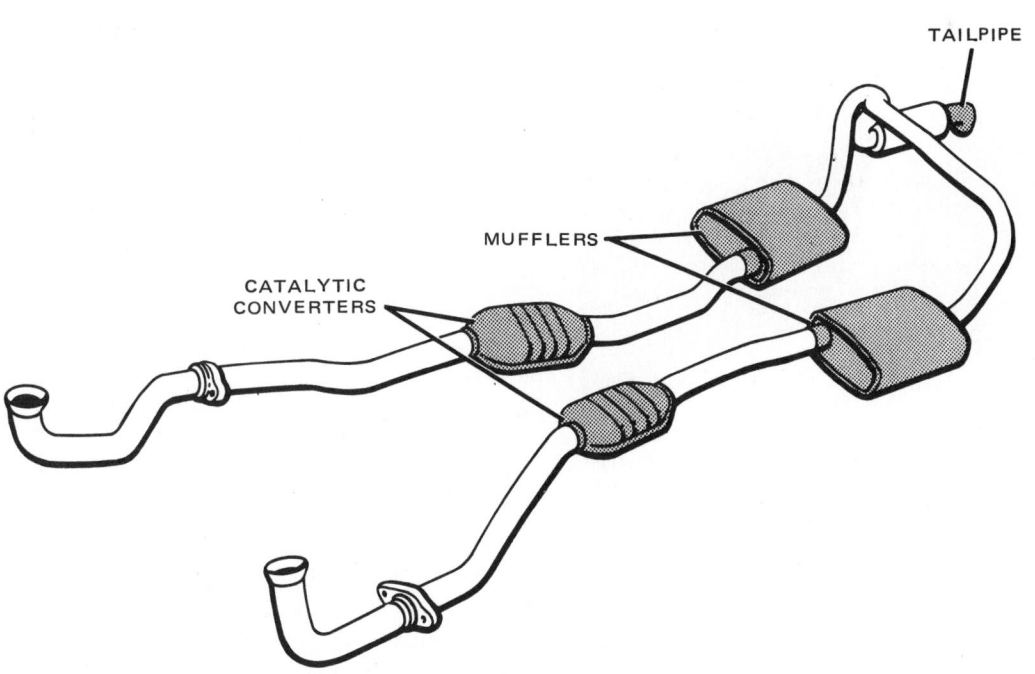

Fig. 29-21. Late model Chrysler Corporation dual exhaust system. Main catalytic converters contain honeycomb elements coated with platinum. Catalyst is stimulated by internal converter heat and reacts with exhaust gases to oxidize unburned HC and CO into CO_2 and H_2O.

337

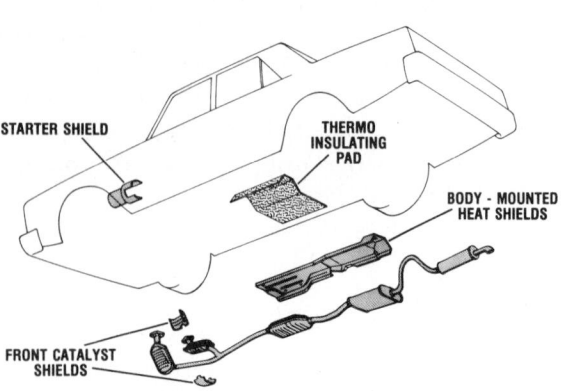

HEAT SHIELDING FOR EXHAUST SYSTEM

Fig. 29-22. Heat shields protect car from high temperatures developed by catalytic converter. Avoid application of rustproofing compounds or undercoating materials to exhaust system floor pan heat shields. (Chrysler Corporation)

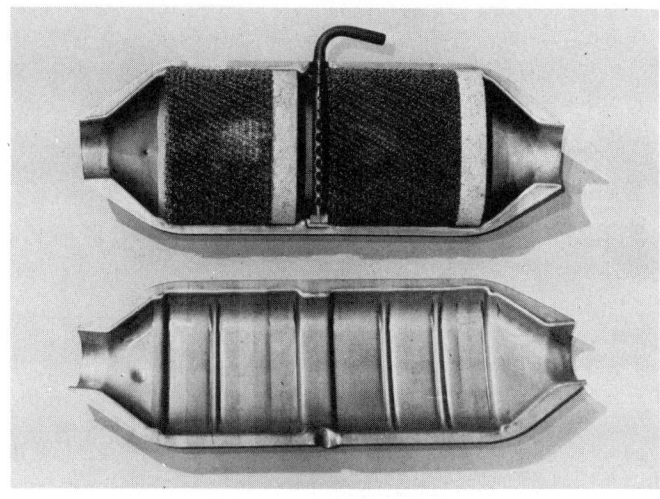

Fig. 29-24. Dual bed, three-way monolith catalytic converter used on some GM cars is designed to reduce emissions of hydrocarbons, carbon monoxide and oxides of nitrogen. The monolith is coated with a material that contains platinum, palladium and rhodium.

Fig. 29-23. Catalysts used in catalytic converters may be pellet type illustrated or a honeycomb monolith (single block). Sphere-shaped pellets provide high surface area for treatment of exhaust gases passing through converter. (Universal Oil Products Company)

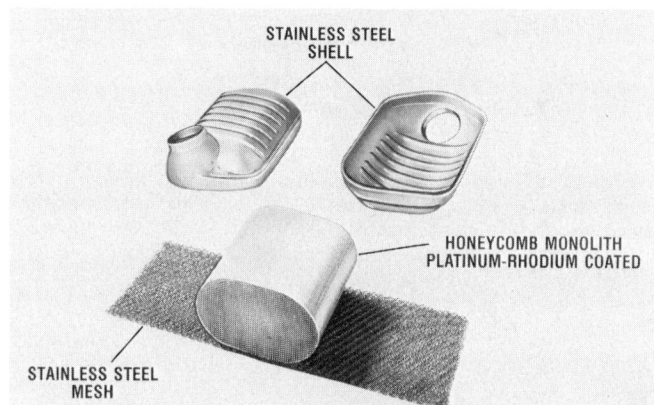

Fig. 29-25. Breakdown of Chrysler Corporation three-way catalytic converter reveals two stainless steel shells, two coated honeycomb monoliths and stainless steel mesh. Cars equipped with catalytic converters must use unleaded fuel.

Chrysler's catalytic system operates at 1,600 deg. F (871.2 C) under normal conditions. This intense heat permits the catalyst to function. To protect the underbody from excessive heat, upper and lower heat shields are used, Fig. 29-22. If removed, all heat shields and insulation materials must be reinstalled according to specifications.

As with all other U.S. car manufacturers, Chrysler's catalytic converter equipped cars must use unleaded gasoline (to avoid "lead poisoning" catalytic elements). With this development, an unleaded gas fuel filler tube became standard equipment, beginning with 1975 models. See Fig. 29-26. This tube accomodates the proportionately smaller fuel nozzle made mandatory on all unleaded gasoline pumps.

As further warning to the car owner, and the service station attendants, a label on the instrument panel reads "Unleaded Gasoline." A label near the fuel filler reads "Use Unleaded Gasoline Only."

Starting in 1978, two mini-oxidation catalytic converters are used in conjunction with the main converter. Each "mini-ox" unit has a single ceramic biscuit wrapped in a stainless steel mesh blanket. The primary job of the "mini-ox" units is to start the exhaust gas oxidation before the exhaust gases reach the main catalytic converter.

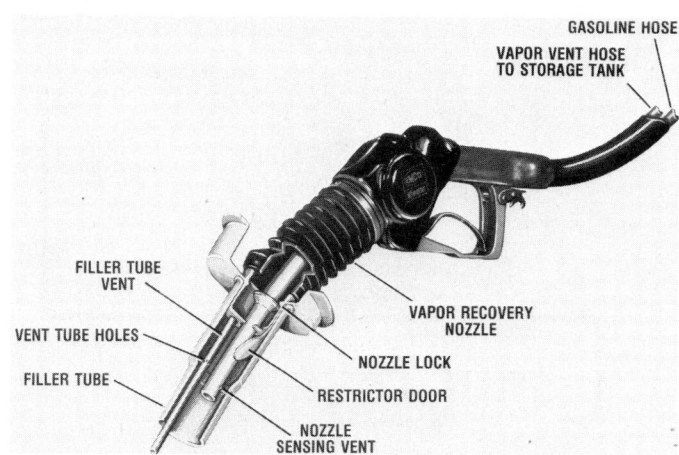

Fig. 29-26. All cars equipped with a catalytic converter have a filler tube designed to accomodate small, unleaded gasoline nozzle.

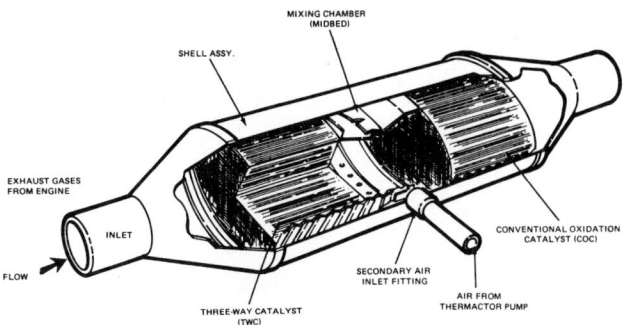

Fig. 29-27. Ford's dual catalytic converter has a three-way catalyst in front and a conventional oxidation catalyst at rear.

Ford introduced Electronic Engine Control (EEC-I) on some 1978 engines. The system utilizes a dual catalytic converter, Fig. 29-27, Thermactor air control and electronic feedback carburetion. These subsystems work together to improve fuel economy, engine performance and emission control.

An improved EEC-II system, Fig. 29-28, replaced EEC-I in expanded engine applications for 1979. EEC-II controls: carburetor air-fuel mixture; secondary air to the catalytic converter; purging of the evaporative emission storage canister; engine speed at idle; engine ignition timing; EGR flow. When all components of the subsystems are functioning together, the system is said to be "under closed loop control."

The "closed loop" circuit is formed by the EEC-II computer module, an oxygen sensor and feedback carburetor. Its purpose is to maintain as near-ideal air-fuel mixture as possible for best efficiency of the three-way catalyst system.

The manifold oxygen sensor monitors oxygen content in the exhaust gases. It indicates whether the mixture is too rich or too lean by sending a voltage signal to the EEC-II computer. The computer, in turn, signals the closed loop carburetor to readjust the air-fuel mixture.

As a result, exhaust gases entering the forward section of the catalytic converter, Fig. 29-27, must pass through a ceramic substrate coated with platinum and rhodium. This catalyst reduces NOx, HC and CO. Next, the treated gases pass through the mixing chamber where secondary air is injected by the Thermactor pump. The oxidized gases then pass through the rear section of the converter where a substrate coated with platinum and palladium further decreases HC and CO.

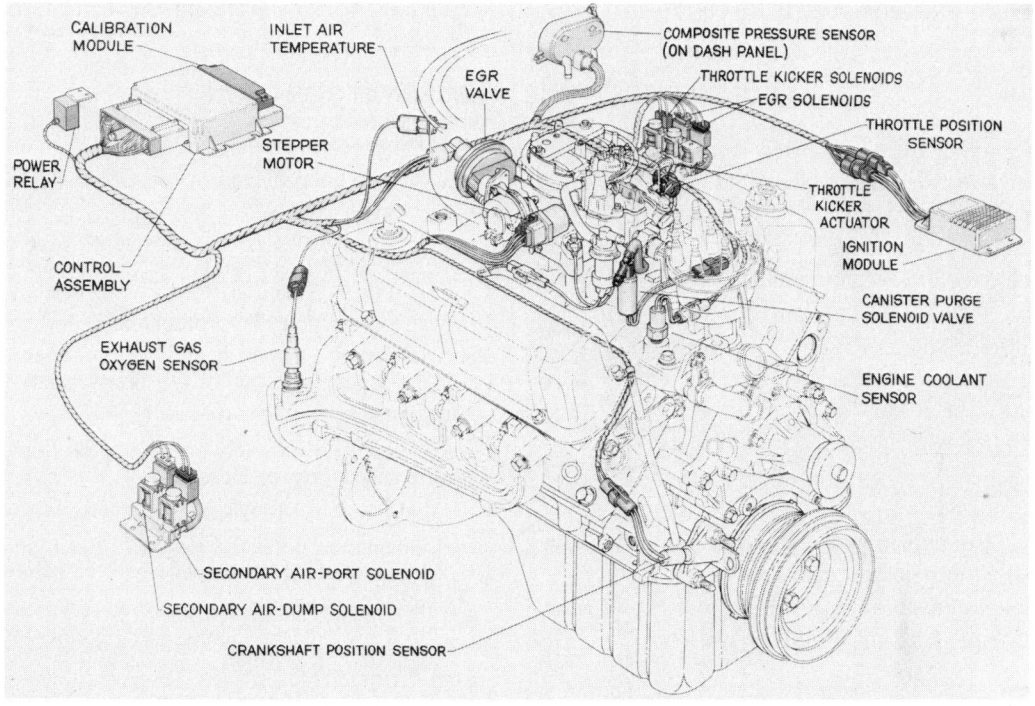

Fig. 29-28. Ford's Electronic Engine Control (EEC-II) system uses sensors and a control module to send commands to various engine controls.

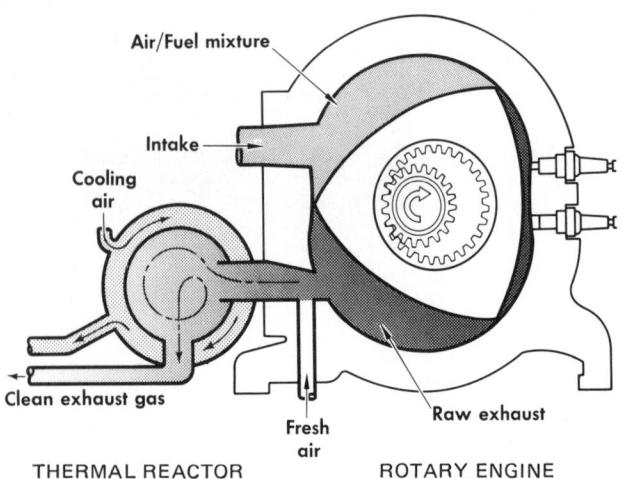

Fig. 29-29. Thermal reactors are emission control devices that accept raw exhaust gases from engine and subject them to extremely high temperatures to oxidize emissions. Mazda engines have been fitted with thermal reactors for several model years.

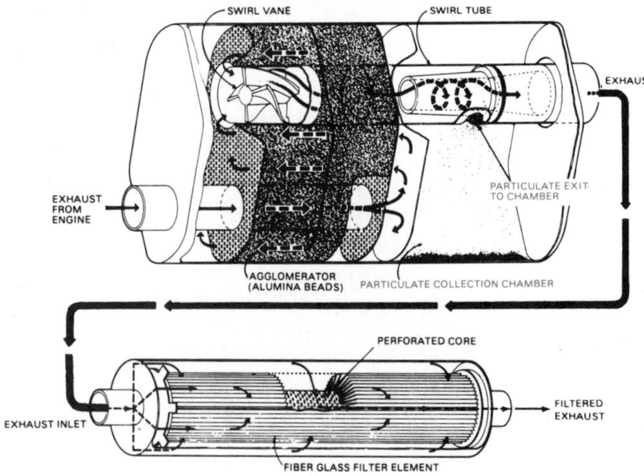

Fig. 29-30. Particulate emission control system. After agglomerator forms small particles into large ones, cyclone unit spins off large particles into collection chamber. Small particles remaining are trapped in the fiberglass final filter. (PPG Industries, Inc.)

THERMAL REACTORS

Thermal reactors are emission control devices generally installed in place of the exhaust manifolds. Basically, a fresh air injection system is used to mix oxygen with a rich air-fuel mixture, or a lean air-fuel mixture is used without a pump. Reacting in a 2,000 deg. F (1 094 C) zone within the thermal reactor, the exhaust gas components are oxidized (burned) more completely and become carbon dioxide and water.

U.S. car manufacturers are experimenting with various forms of thermal reactor, but their use is limited to test vehicles. Mazda rotary engines, on the other hand, have been equipped with a thermal reactor since 1970, Fig. 29-29.

PARTICULATE TRAPS

Although particulate emission standards have not been set, this type of emission logically is next in line for restrictive control. While the use of unleaded gasoline will help reduce particulate emission levels, a number of companies are researching means of trapping exhaust particulate lead.

One company has devised a control system, Fig. 29-30, that makes use of a device called an agglomerator, which mechanically collects small particles to form larger particles that are easier to trap. An inertial separator, or cyclone, spins the exhaust flow to remove the large particles and deposit them in a reservoir. A fiber glass final filter removes small particles.

REVIEW QUESTIONS — EMISSION CONTROL

1. What is the purpose of the PCV flow control valve placed between the valve cover and the manifold in the crankcase ventilating system?
   a. Provide extra air for idling.
   b. Prevent excess airflow during idling.
2. The Chrysler Cleaner Air System injects air into the exhaust manifold. True or False?
3. Retarding the spark at idle increases the emission of hydrocarbons. True or False?
4. On cars equipped with automatic transmissions, it is more difficult to control the emission of exhaust gases. True or False?
5. The amount of unburned hydrocarbons is proportional to combustion chamber surface area. True or False?
6. In the Autolite emission control distributor, how many diaphragms are provided to control the spark?
   a. One.
   b. Two.
   c. Three.
7. Ford uses two methods of heating inlet air to the carburetor. Name them.
8. Is heated air provided in the GM Controlled Combustion System? Yes or No?
9. Basically, what is the function of the Transmission Controlled Spark (TCS) system?
10. In GM's Air Injector Reactor (AIR) system, where is the air injected?
11. What is the purpose of the diverter valve in air injection systems?
12. American Motors uses a pintle type exhaust gas recirculation valve. True or False?
13. What is the principle of the catalytic converter used to reduce exhaust emissions?
14. Why must unleaded gasoline be used in cars equipped with catalytic converters?
15. Chrysler's catalytic converter operates at approximately 1,600 deg. F. (871.2 C). Yes or No?
16. What is operating temperature of a thermal reactor?
    a. 1,000 deg. F. (547 C). b. 2,000 deg. F. (1 093 C). c. 3,000 deg. F. (1 648 C).

FUNDAMENTALS OF ELECTRICITY, MAGNETISM

Electricity plays a vital role in the operation of modern automotive vehicles. The 12 volt (12V) system is used almost universally in passenger cars. Recently, however, there has been some experimentation with 24V systems as car manufacturers try to find a means of meeting increased electrical demands.

These demands include: starting, lighting and ignition systems; horns, turn signals and emergency 4-way flashers; control circuits for automatic transmissions and overdrive units; windshield wipers and washers; fuel gauge, cigarette lighters and multiple instrument panel convenience and warning lamps; radio, heater, clock and many other electrically operated accessories such as power windows, power seats, speed control unit and stereo tape player.

It follows logically that anyone who expects to successfully maintain, repair and troubleshoot today's vehicles must have a thorough knowledge of the fundamentals of electricity.

STATIC ELECTRICITY

The ancient Greeks had a word for it. "Electric" is derived from a Greek word meaning amber, because they found that by rubbing a piece of amber with a piece of silk, bits of paper, straw and dry leaves were attracted to it. Later experiments showed that the same effect can be produced by rubbing a rod of glass or hard rubber with a handkerchief. In fact, many other nonmetallic materials are found to have this property, which is called "static electricity."

For example, if you rub a rod of hard rubber with a piece of fur, then hold it close to a pith ball suspended on a thread, the pith ball will be attracted to the rod. But if you allow the rod to touch the ball, the ball will bounce away. You can get the same effect by rubbing a glass rod with a piece of silk.

ATTRACTION AND REPULSION

Further experiments show that all electrified materials behave either as glass or rubber. Glass is said to have a POSITIVE charge; hard rubber has a NEGATIVE charge. If you electrify two strips of hard rubber by rubbing them with fur, they will repel each other. Two glass rods will behave in a similar manner. However, if you electrify a rod of rubber and suspend it near an electrified rod of glass, they will attract each other.

This simple experiment demonstrates one of the most important laws of electricity: Bodies with similar charges repel each other; bodies with opposite charges attract each other. This law also applies to magnets (to be covered later).

ELECTRON THEORY OF ELECTRICITY

In spite of the fact that people have experimented with and controlled the use of electricity for scores of years, no one can explain just what electricity is. Many different theories have been advanced regarding the nature of electricity. Today, the ELECTRON THEORY is generally accepted.

In essence, the electron theory proposes that all matter (the earth, rocks, minerals, chemicals, elements, etc.) consists of tiny particles called molecules. These molecules, in turn, are made of two or more smaller particles called atoms. These atoms are further divided into even smaller particles called protons, neutrons and electrons.

These particles, protons, neutrons and electrons are the same in all matter, regardless of whether it is a gas, a liquid or a solid. The different properties or characteristics of the matter take form according to the arrangement and number of protons, neutrons and electrons that make up the atoms.

The PROTON has a natural positive charge of electricity. The ELECTRON has a negative charge. The NEUTRON has no charge at all, but adds weight to the matter.

CENTRAL CORE OF ATOM

Protons and neutrons form the central core of the atoms about which the electrons rotate, Fig. 30-1. Electrons carry

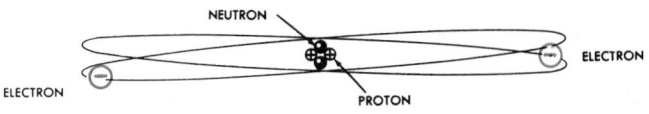

Fig. 30-1. Electrons rotate about central core of atoms, much as earth and other planets rotate about sun.

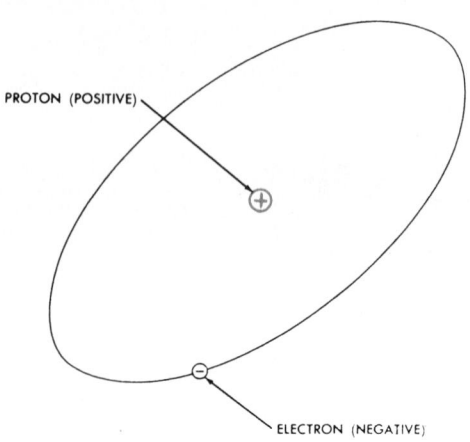

Fig. 30-2. Simple hydrogen atom consists of one positively charged proton and one negatively charged electron.

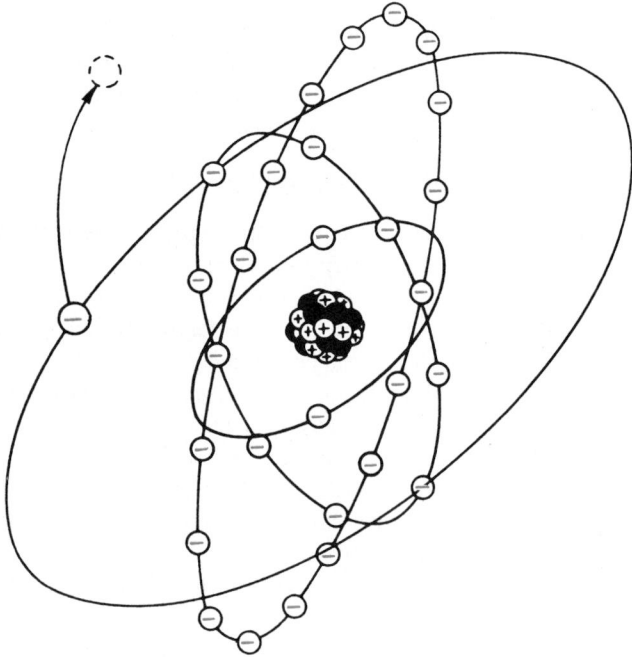

Fig. 30-3. Copper atom consists of 29 electrons circling about its nucleus of neutrons and protons in 4 different orbits.

small negative charges of electricity, which neutralize the positive charges of the protons.

The simplest atom of all is the hydrogen atom. It consists of one positively charged proton and one negatively charged electron, Fig. 30-2. Other atoms, such as those forming copper, iron or silicon, are much more complicated. Copper, for example, has 29 electrons circling about its nucleus in four different orbits, Fig. 30-3.

SIZE OF ATOM

It is difficult to conceive the size of the atom. Research by physicists has established that the mass of one electron is

about .000,000,000,000,000,000,000,000,000,911 of a gram. If you assume that the size of a proton in a hydrogen atom is the size of a baseball, located in Kansas City, then its orbit would reach from the Atlantic coast to the Pacific.

So, along with the extremely small size of electrons and protons, they are separated by relatively vast distances. An appreciation of the distance between the proton and electron is necessary to understand the electron flow.

INSULATORS

In most elements, the nucleus is composed of protons and neutrons, which are surrounded by closely held electrons that never leave the atom. These are called "bound" electrons. When bound electrons are in the majority in an element or compounded material, the material is called an INSULATOR or a NONCONDUCTOR of electricity.

CONDUCTORS

In other types of material, the nucleus is surrounded by another group of electrons which can be freed to move from one atom to the other when electricity is applied, Fig. 30-3. Electrons of this kind are known as "free" electrons, and the materials made up of these atoms are called CONDUCTORS of electricity.

SPEED OF ELECTRICITY

The speed of electricity is 186,000 miles per second. However, the electrons do not travel at this tremendous speed. Free electrons, which are available because electron orbits overlap in conducting materials, are pulled from one atom to another. As they move, the free electrons temporarily rotate about each new center. Since an electron carries a negative charge of electricity, electron flow (current flow) is assumed to be from negative to positive.

ELECTRON DRIFT

The rate at which the free electrons drift from atom to atom determines the amount of CURRENT. In order to create a drift of electrons through a circuit, it is necessary to have an electrical pressure, or VOLTAGE.

Electric current, then, is the flow of electrons. The more electrons in motion, the stronger the current. In terms of automotive applications, the greater the concentration of electrons at a battery or generator terminal, the higher the pressure between the electrons. The greater this pressure is, the greater the flow of electrons.

VOLTS, AMPERES, OHMS

The pressure between the electrons is measured in VOLTS. The flow of electrons (current) is measured in AMPERES. Opposing the flow of electrons is the resistance of the conductors, which is measured in OHMS.

Some materials offer greater resistance to electron flow

than others: iron more than copper; copper more than silver. The length of the connecting wiring also contributes to the amount of resistance in a circuit. And, finally, the size of the wiring is also a resistance factor. A conductor of small diameter will offer greater resistance to the flow of electrons than will a conductor of large diameter.

OHM'S LAW

There is a definite relationship between voltage, resistance and the amount of current in an electrical circuit. Each affects the other, and this relationship is known as OHM'S LAW.

Ohm's Law states that the voltage impressed on a circuit is equal to the product of the current in amperes multiplied by the resistance in ohms. Mathematically, this law reads:

$$E = IR$$

E is the voltage. I is the current in amperes. R is the resistance in ohms. Also, by transposing the factors:

$$R = \frac{E}{I} \quad \text{or} \quad I = \frac{E}{R}$$

As a memory aid in learning to make good use of Ohm's Law, try writing the basic equation as follows:

$$\frac{E}{IR}$$

Then cover the unknown factor with a fingertip, and you will have the formula you need to get your answer. For example:

If you cover the E, the formula is I x R.
If you cover the I, the formula is E ÷ R.
If you cover the R, the formula is E ÷ I.

Ohm's Law is used extensively in checking and trouble-shooting electrical circuits and parts in automobiles. For example: the current flowing through the coils of a 12V alternator is 3.0 amperes. What is the resistance of the coils? Answer: 4 ohms.

Studying Ohm's Law reveals exactly how a change in one factor affects the others. If the resistance of a circuit increases and the voltage remains constant, current will decrease.

To cite a practical example: If the connections of a starting battery are loose or corroded, a high resistance will be caused. The result will be insufficient current reaching the starting motor, lights or other units to provide proper operation.

TYPES OF CIRCUITS

There are three general types of electrical circuits: Series, Fig. 30-4. Parallel, Fig. 30-5. Series-Parallel, Fig. 30-6.

All circuits, regardless of type, consist of a source of electricity (battery or alternator), pieces of electrical equipment or devices, and electrical conductors that connect the equipment or devices to the source.

In a series circuit, Fig. 30-4, the current passes from the

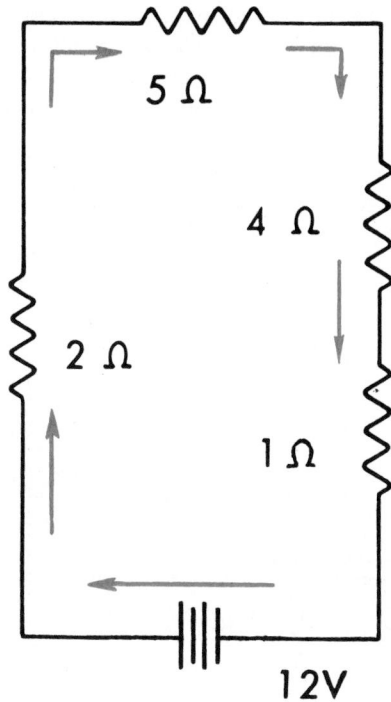

Fig. 30-4. In a series circuit, total resistance is sum of individual resistances shown by Greek letter Omega.

power source (battery, in these examples) to each device in turn, then back to the other terminal of the battery. The current has only one path to flow, and the amount of current (amperage) will be the same in all parts of the circuit.

In parallel electrical circuits, Fig. 30-5, there will be more

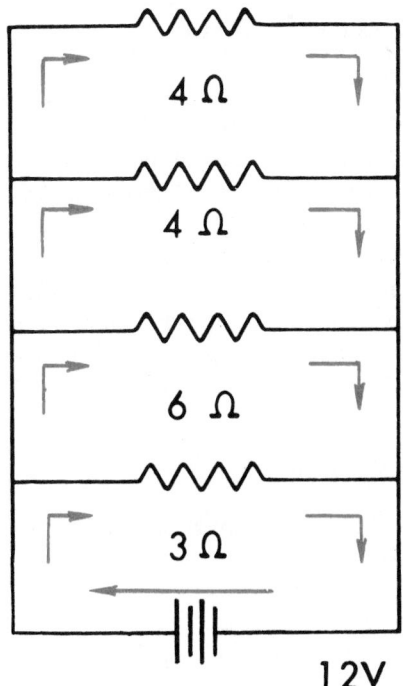

Fig. 30-5. Note how current divides through different branches of this parallel circuit.

than one path for the current to flow. In this type of circuit, one terminal of each device is connected to a common conductor, which leads to one terminal of the battery. The remaining terminals of each device are connected to another common conductor which, in turn, is connected to the other terminal of the battery.

Series-parallel circuits, Fig. 30-6, are those which have some electrical devices connected in series and others in parallel.

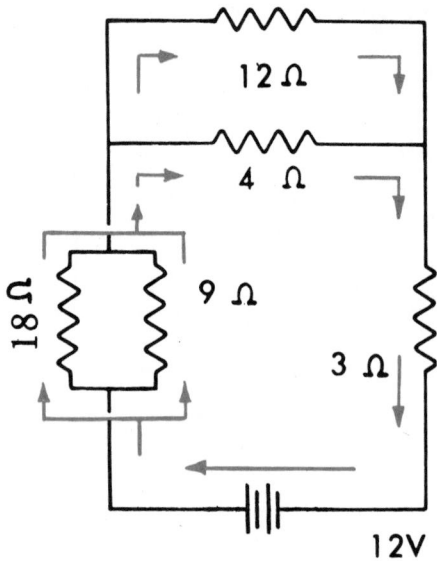

Fig. 30-6. A series-parallel circuit has some electrical devices connected in series, others in parallel.

MEASURING RESISTANCE

To find the total resistance of a series circuit, add the resistance of each device. In Fig. 30-4, the total resistance would be 12 ohms. The current flowing can be found by applying Ohm's Law. The current would be 12 ÷ 12 ohms = 1 ampere.

In parallel electrical circuits, there are several paths for the current to take. Consequently, the total resistance of all the devices will be less than the resistance of any single device. To find the total resistance of a parallel circuit, use the following formula:

$$R = \frac{1}{\frac{1}{R_1} + \frac{1}{R_2} + \frac{1}{R_3} + \frac{1}{R_4}} \text{ etc.}$$

Substitute the values shown in Fig. 30-5 for R factors in the above formula:

$$R = \frac{1}{\frac{1}{4} + \frac{1}{4} + \frac{1}{6} + \frac{1}{3}}$$

$$R = \qquad 1 \text{ ohm}$$

The total current flowing through the circuit will be 12V ÷ 1 ohm = 12 amperes.

The current flowing through any single branch of a parallel circuit is found by dividing the voltage by the resistance of that particular branch. In Fig. 30-5, the current flowing in the upper branch would be 12V ÷ 4 = 3 amperes. The other branches would be 3, 2 and 4 amperes. Adding these gives 12 amperes, which checks with the value found for the total circuit.

To make the calculations for a series-parallel circuit, treat each portion separately. Then, having calculated the resistance of each parallel portion, add those resistances as you would in a simple series circuit.

In Fig. 30-6, the resistance of the upper parallel circuit is 3 ohms. The parallel circuit on the left of the diagram is 6 ohms. Adding these values to 3 ohms of the series circuit on the right side of the diagram makes a total of 12 ohms.

VOLTAGE DROP

The decrease in voltage as current passes through a resistance is known as voltage drop. The sum of the individual drops in voltage is equal to the total voltage impressed on the circuit.

Ohm's Law can be used to calculate voltage drop in different parts of a circuit. In Fig. 30-4, assume, that 1 ampere of current is flowing.

Since voltage drop is equal to E = IR, the voltage drop across each of the resistances would be 1 x 2 = 2, 1 x 5 = 5, 1 x 4 = 4 and 1 x 1 = 1. Adding these drops in voltage, you have 2 + 5 + 4 + 1 = 12 volts, which checks with the voltage impressed in the circuit.

ELECTRICAL WORK AND POWER

The electrical unit for measuring work is called the joule. One joule is equal to one ampere flowing for one second under the pressure of one volt.

First bear in mind that work is done when energy is expended. Work is the product of force multiplied by the distance through which it acts in overcoming resistance.

An electrical force may exist without work being done. This is the condition that exists between the terminals of a battery when no equipment is connected to them. When a piece of equipment is connected to the terminals of the battery, current will flow and work will be done.

Power is the rate of doing work:

$$\text{Power} = \frac{\text{work}}{\text{time}}$$

$$\text{Electrical power} = \frac{\text{electrical work}}{\text{time}}$$

The watt is the electrical unit of power and is equal to one joule of electrical work per second.

$$\text{Watt} = \frac{\text{Joules}}{\text{Seconds}} = \frac{\text{Volts x Amperes x Seconds}}{\text{Seconds}}$$

$$\text{Watts} = \text{Volts x Amperes}$$

For example: In an automotive lighting circuit, the current is 8 amperes and the voltage is 12. The number of watts is 8 x 12 = 96 watts.

The unit for measuring mechanical power is horsepower (hp). Experimentally, it has been found that one horsepower is equal to 746 watts.

MAGNETISM

Magnetism, like electricity, is still a mystery. We know many laws governing its behavior and have applied it in the automotive field to starting motors, electric generators and alternators, ignition coils, voltage regulators, etc. However, no one knows just what magnetism is.

The effects of magnetism were first discovered when it was found that pieces of iron ore from certain parts of the world would attract each other and also other pieces of iron. In addition, it was found that fragments of this ore, when suspended in air, would always point toward the North Star. The end of the ore that pointed toward the north was called the "north pole," the other end became the "south pole."

MAGNETIC FIELDS

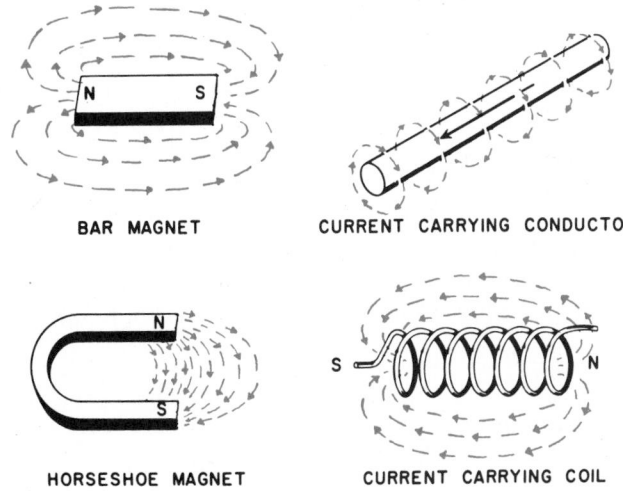

BAR MAGNET   CURRENT CARRYING CONDUCTOR

HORSESHOE MAGNET   CURRENT CARRYING COIL

Fig. 30-7. Note that lines of force leave magnet or loop of wire at north pole, reenter at south pole.

All magnets have a magnetic field, which is evidence by lines of force, or magnetic flux, around the magnet, Fig. 30-7. The strength of the magnetic field varies. It is strongest close to the magnet and gets progressively weaker away from it.

The area or extent of the magnetic field can be determined by means of a compass, which also shows the direction of the lines of force. In Fig. 30-7, note how the lines of force leave the north pole of the magnets (and coil), and reenter at the south pole. Also note that the lines of force exerted by the horseshoe magnet are more concentrated between the two poles of the magnet.

THEORY OF PERMANENT MAGNETS

The effects, direction and extent of magnetic fields can be studied. However, there is no actual knowledge as to why certain materials have magnetic properties and others do not. The electron theory generally is accepted as the best explanation of magnetism.

According to the theory, an electron moving in a fixed circular orbit around the proton creates a magnetic field with the north pole on one side of the orbit and a south pole on the other side, Fig. 30-8. It is assumed that the orbiting electron

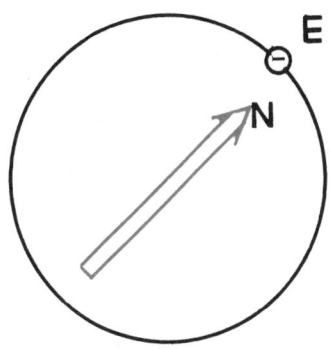

Fig. 30-8. An electron, moving in a fixed circular orbit, creates a magnetic field.

carries a negative charge of electricity, which is the same as electrical current flowing through a conductor. Current flow, then, is from negative to positive.

In magnetic substances (iron, cobalt and nickel), the electron orbits align themselves in parallel planes, and in the same direction when placed in a magnetic field, Fig. 30-9. This arrangement of the electron-created magnets produces a strong magnetic effect.

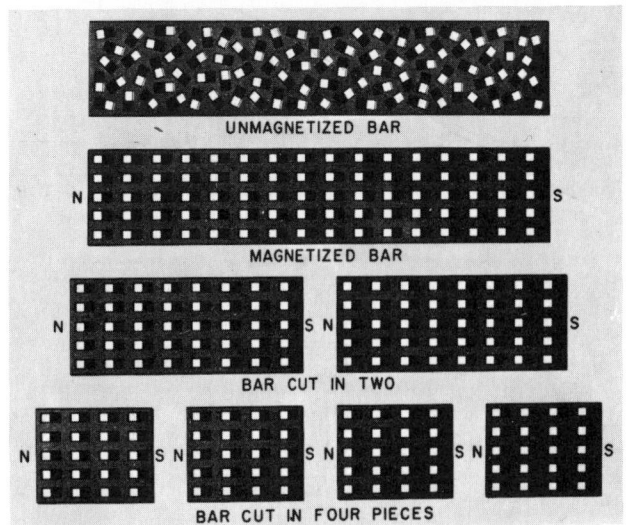

UNMAGNETIZED BAR

MAGNETIZED BAR

BAR CUT IN TWO

BAR CUT IN FOUR PIECES

Fig. 30-9. In magnetic substances, electron orbits align themselves in parallel planes and in same direction when placed in a magnetic field.

In non-magnetic substances, the orbits of the various electrons are arranged so that the magnetic fields cancel each other.

It is also interesting to note that soft iron will lose virtually all of its magnetic effect as soon as it is removed from the magnetic field. Hard steel will retain its magnetic characteristics for an indefinite period. Special alloys of tungsten, chromium and cobalt produce magnetic fields of considerably greater strength than other materials and retain their magnetism for a longer period. These alloys are used to form the magnets used in specialized electrical equipment where a strong magnetic field is required.

Magnetic lines of force seem to penetrate all substances, and they are deflected only by magnetic materials or by another magnetic field. There is no insulator for magnetism or lines of force.

Another interesting property of magnets is illustrated by the following experiment. A magnet is cut in two and the individual pieces were checked for north and south poles. It was found that each piece had north and south poles, situated as in the original magnet, Fig. 30-9.

ATTRACTION AND REPULSION

When two permanent magnets are placed so that the north pole of one is close to the south pole of the other, the magnets attract each other. Also, if the magnets are placed with similar poles close together, they repel each other, Fig. 30-10. This attraction and repulsion of magnets forms a fundamental law of magnetism: Like poles of magnets repel each other; unlike poles attract each other.

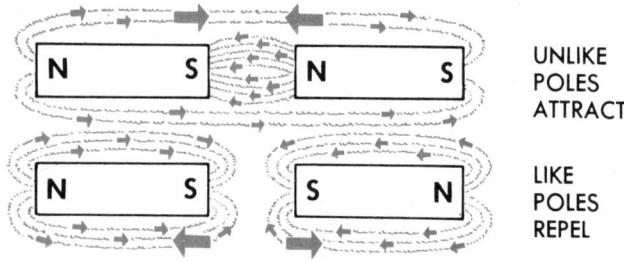

UNLIKE POLES ATTRACT

LIKE POLES REPEL

Fig. 30-10. Lines of force leaving north pole of one magnet will enter south pole of an adjacent magnet since all lines are in same direction. Lines leaving similar poles are repelled as they have opposite direction.

PRODUCING MAGNETS, MAGNETIC FIELDS

By stroking a piece of hardened steel with a natural magnet, it will be found that the piece of steel will become a magnet. (Steel railroad tracks laid in a north-to-south direction become magnetized because they lie parallel to the magnetic field of the earth.) Much stronger magnets and magnetic fields can be produced by electrical means. Placing a piece of steel in any strong magnetic field will cause it to become magnetized.

A magnetic field surrounds any conductor carrying an electrical current. The discovery of that fact resulted in the

development of much of our electrical equipment. The field of force is always at right angles to the conductor. This can be shown by placing a magnetic compass close to a conductor of electricity, Fig. 30-11.

Since a magnetic force is the only force known to attract a compass needle, it is obvious that a flow of electric current produces a magnetic field similar to that produced by a permanent magnet. When making this experiment, pass direct current through the conductor. Alternating current will cause the magnetic field to change with each alternation of the current.

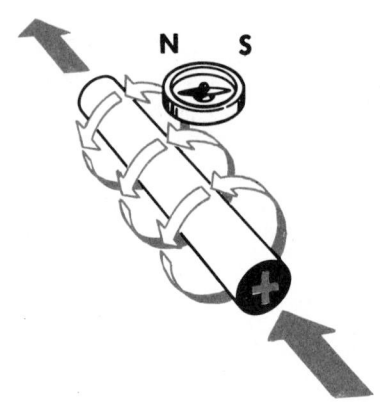

Fig. 30-11. A magnetic field surrounds any conductor carrying an electrical current, and field is at right angles to conductor.

Not only is the field of force at right angles to the conductor, but the field of force also forms concentric circles about the conductor, Fig. 30-12. Also, when the current in the conductor increases, the field of force is increased. Doubling the current will double the strength of the field of force.

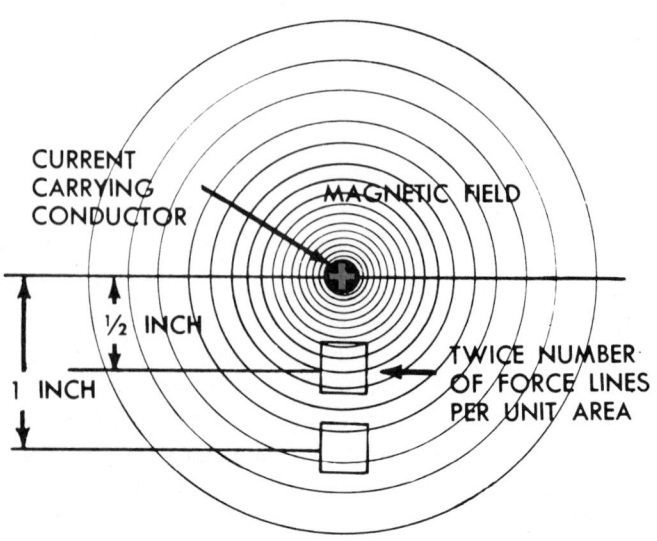

CURRENT CARRYING CONDUCTOR

MAGNETIC FIELD

½ INCH

1 INCH

TWICE NUMBER OF FORCE LINES PER UNIT AREA

Fig. 30-12. A magnetic field forms concentric circles around a conductor carrying an electric current.

LEFT HAND RULE

In many cases, it is helpful to know the direction of the lines of force that surround a conductor. Their direction is dependent on the direction the current is traveling in the conductor.

To determine the direction of the lines of force, grasp the conductor with the left hand with the thumb extended in the direction the current is flowing. The fingers will then indicate the direction in which the lines of force surround the conductor, Fig. 30-13. This left hand rule can be used to determine the direction the current is flowing after having first determined the direction of the magnetic field by means of a compass.

Fig. 30-13. Fingers of left hand around conductor show direction of lines of force, and extended thumb shows direction of current in conductor.

MAGNETIC FIELD AROUND A LOOP

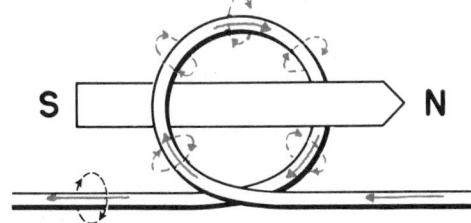

MAGNETIC FIELD AROUND A COIL

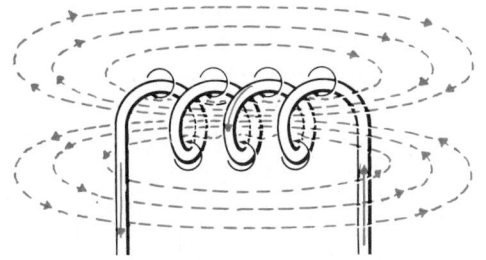

Fig. 30-14. Illustrating magnetic field surrounding a single loop carrying current, and field surrounding a coil of wire.

STRENGTHENING THE FIELD

As mentioned, the magnetic field surrounds the conductor, which is carrying an electric current. If this conductor is formed into a loop, Fig. 30-14, the lines of force on the outside of the loops spread out into space; lines on the inside of the loop are confined and crowded together. This increases the density of lines of force in that area, and a much greater magnetic effect is produced with the same amount of current flowing.

In this setup, one side of the loop will be a north pole and the other side will be a south pole. By increasing the number of loops, the magnetic field will be greatly increased. By winding the loops or coils on a core of soft iron, the field is further intensified.

COMBINING MAGNETIC FIELDS

Another interesting experiment with magnetism is combining magnetic fields. Figs. 30-7 and 30-10 show the fields of horseshoe magnets and the fields resulting from similar and unlike poles. Fig. 30-15 shows magnetic fields surrounding adjacent conductors. In accompanying drawings, the + mark on the end of the conductor simulates the butt end of an arrow. It indicates that the current is moving away from you. The dot on the other end is the point of the arrow. The current is coming toward you.

MAGNETIC EFFECT OF PARALLEL CONDUCTORS

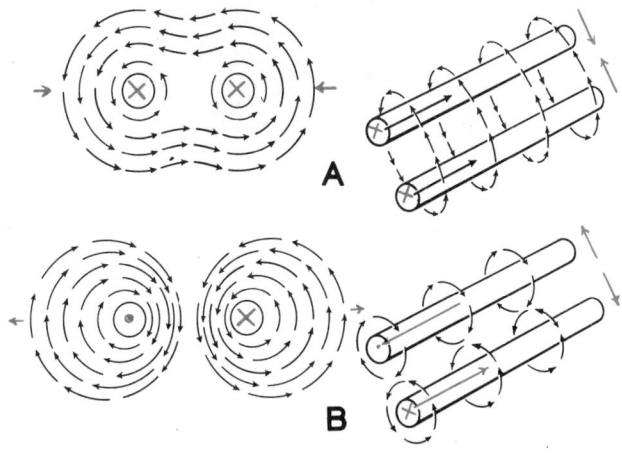

Fig. 30-15. A—With current flowing in same direction in adjacent conductors, resultant magnetic field tends to draw conductors together. B—If current is flowing in opposite direction, magnetic field will force conductors apart.

Current flowing in the same direction, and in opposite directions, in two adjacent and parallel conductors are shown in Fig. 30-15. A field of force surrounds each conductor, and the direction of the field can be determined by applying the left hand rule. The field will be clockwise around one conductor and counterclockwise around the other. However, in the area between conductors, the lines of force move in the same direction.

Since the amount of current is the same in both conductors, the number of lines of force between the conductors is the same as the number of lines outside the conductors. And since the distance between the conductors is limited, the lines of force will be more dense in that area than beyond the conductors. This condition is known as unbalanced density, which will cause forces to act on the conductors.

When current is moving in the same direction in two parallel conductors, the unbalanced density will tend to draw the conductors together, as in A in Fig. 30-15. If the current is moving in opposite directions in two parallel conductors, the unbalanced density will tend to force the conductors apart, as shown in B.

As illustrated in A in Fig. 30-15, two parallel conductors carrying current in the same direction will tend to move closer together. The two conductors act basically like a single conductor carrying a current equal to the sum of the two currents. As a result, twice as many lines of force are created than would be produced by either conductor with its original current. When several more current-carrying conductors are placed side by side, Fig. 30-16, the lines of force join and

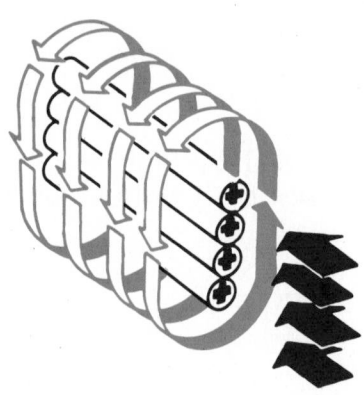

Fig. 30-16. When several current-carrying conductors are placed side by side, magnetic lines of force join and surround all conductors.

surround all of the conductors. This kind of magnetic pattern is obtained in coils of a generator, alternator, starter solenoid or an ignition coil.

The strength of the magnetic field surrounding the coil of wire is directly proportional to the number of turns of wire in the coil and the strength of the current. To calculate the magnetizing force created, multiply the amperes flowing by the number of turns of wire. This force is known as ampere-turns.

DETERMINING POLARITY

To determine the magnetic polarity of any coil or electromagnet when the direction of current flow is known, use the left hand rule for coils. Grasp the coil with your left hand so

that your fingers extend in the direction the coil is wound and in the direction of current flow, Fig. 30-17. The thumb will then point toward the north pole created by the current flow through the coil. Remember that both the direction of current flow and the direction of coil winding determine the polarity of a coil.

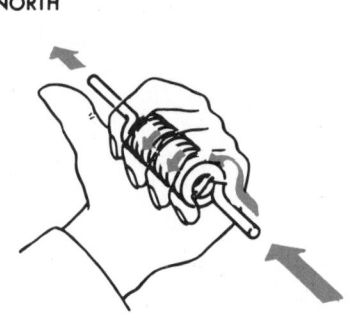

Fig. 30-17. Left-hand rule for coils may be used to determine polarity of a current-carrying coil.

MAGNETIC CONDUCTIVITY

The conductivity of air for lines of force has been adopted as a standard, so air is rated as having a permeability of one. "Permeability of a substance," as defined by Kelvin, "is the ease with which lines of force may be established in any medium as compard with a vacuum." Basically, permeability is the magnetic conductivity of a substance.

When a soft iron core is inserted in a coil to form a true electromagnet, Fig. 30-18, the lines of force, or magnetic flux, will be increased several hundred times. By means of the better conductor (iron core), more lines of force are created. Field coils in generators and starters, regulator windings on iron cores and ignition coils all use this same principle.

SOLENOIDS

A solenoid is a tubular coil of wire with an air core. It is designed to produce a magnetic field. In most cases, the solenoid also includes an iron core that is free to move in and out of the tubular coil, Fig. 30-19. The movement of the iron core is used to operate some mechanism or switch. Its major application in the automotive field is to shift a starting motor drive into engagement with the flywheel ring gear. When a solenoid is used to close the contacts of an electrical switch, it is called a magnetic switch.

In Fig. 30-19, note that the south pole of the iron core is adjacent to the north pole of the coil. The polarity of the movable iron core is induced by the lines of force from the coil. Because the adjacent poles of the coil and the core are of opposite polarity, there is an attraction which draws the movable core into the center of the coil whenever current flows through the coil.

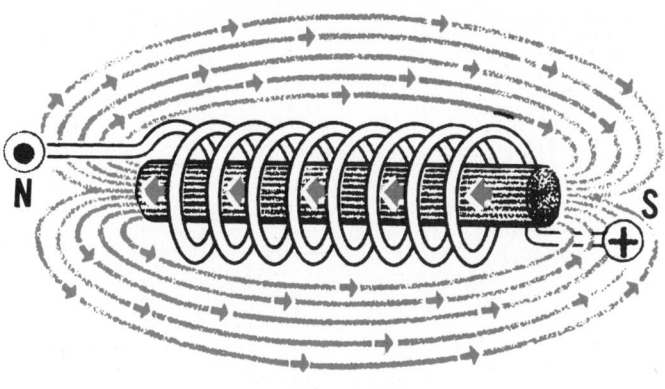

Fig. 30-18. Magnetic field of a coil can be strengthened by winding coil on a core of soft iron to form an electromagnet.

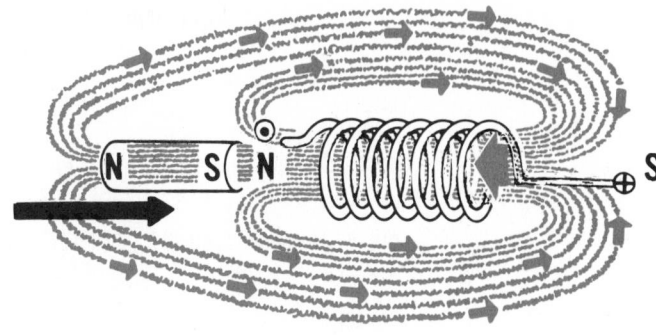

Fig. 30-19. A solenoid usually consists of a tubular coil of wire and an iron core which is free to move into coil when current is applied.

REVIEW QUESTIONS – ELECTRICITY, MAGNETISM

1. How will an electrified piece of rubber react when placed close to an electrified piece of glass?
   a. Attract. b. Repel.
2. Similarly charged electrified bodies attract each other? True or False?
3. What tiny particles form an atom?
4. Electrons have a _____ electrical charge.
5. The nucleus of an element consists of:
   a. Protons and neutrons.
   b. Atoms and electrons.
   c. Neutrons and electrons.
6. Electrons in a conductor are:
   a. Bound. b. Free.
7. State Ohm's Law.
8. What is the total resistance in a series circuit having four individual resistances of four ohms, ten ohms, five ohms and two ohms?
9. Write the formula for determining the total resistance of a number of resistances in a parallel circuit.
10. In an automotive circuit, there is a current of 6 amperes and the voltage is 12. How many watts are there?
11. How many watts are there in one electrical horsepower?
    a. 764. c. 746.
    b. 464. d. 674.
12. What is the name of the area surrounding a magnet?
13. Which of the following are magnetic substances?
    a. Iron. c. Nickel.
    b. Brass. d. Lead.
14. The magnetic field of force surrounding an electrical conductor is in what direction?
    a. Parallel to the conductor.
    b. At right angles to the conductor.
15. When you place the fingers of your left hand around a current-carrying conductor, with extended thumb showing direction of current, what does direction of the fingers indicate?
16. If you insert an iron core in a coil of wire carrying current, the field will be _____.
17. Will the magnetic force tend to separate or attract two parallel conductors carrying current in the same direction.
    a. Separate.
    b. Attract.
18. How much will the field be strengthened if you insert a magnetic core in a coil of wire carrying current?
    a. Twice.
    b. Reduce it.
    c. Several hundred times.
    d. Fifty times.
19. When using the left-hand rule as applied to a current-carrying coil, what does the direction of the thumb indicate?
    a. The direction of current flow.
    b. The direction of electron flow.
    c. The North pole.
    d. The South pole.
20. Where is a solenoid used in a modern automobile?

AUTOMOTIVE ELECTRICAL SYMBOLS

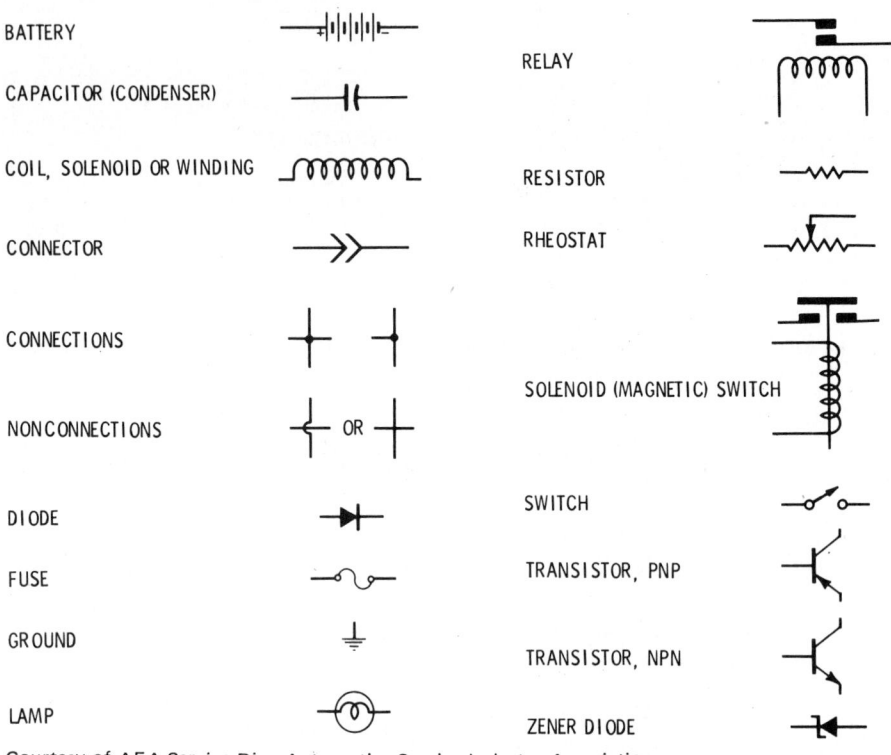

BATTERY

CAPACITOR (CONDENSER)

COIL, SOLENOID OR WINDING

CONNECTOR

CONNECTIONS

NONCONNECTIONS   OR

DIODE

FUSE

GROUND

LAMP

RELAY

RESISTOR

RHEOSTAT

SOLENOID (MAGNETIC) SWITCH

SWITCH

TRANSISTOR, PNP

TRANSISTOR, NPN

ZENER DIODE

Courtesy of AEA Service Div., Automotive Service Industry Association.

STANDARD ABBREVIATIONS

ac	alternating current	I	current	mW	milliwatt
AWG	American Wire Gauge	kHz	kilohertz	min	minimum
amp	ampere	k	kilohm	mmf	magnetomotive force
C	capacitance	kV	kilovolt	pF	picofarad
CEMF	counter electromotive force	kWh	kilowatt hour	Q	transistor
dB	decibel	L	inductance	R	resistance
dc	direct current	max	maximum	rpm	revolutions per minute
DPDT	double pole, double throw	meg	megohm	SPDT	single pole, double throw
DPST	double pole, single throw	μ	micro	SPST	single pole, single throw
E	voltage, EMF	μA	microampere	sw	switch
EMF	electromotive force	μF	microfarad	uhf	ultra high frequency
F	farad	μH	microhenry	vhf	very high frequency
gnd	ground	μV	microvolt	V	volts
H	henrys	mH	millihenry	W	watts
Hz	hertz	mA	milliampere	X	reactance
hp	horsepower	mV	millivolt		

ELECTRIC GENERATORS AND ALTERNATORS

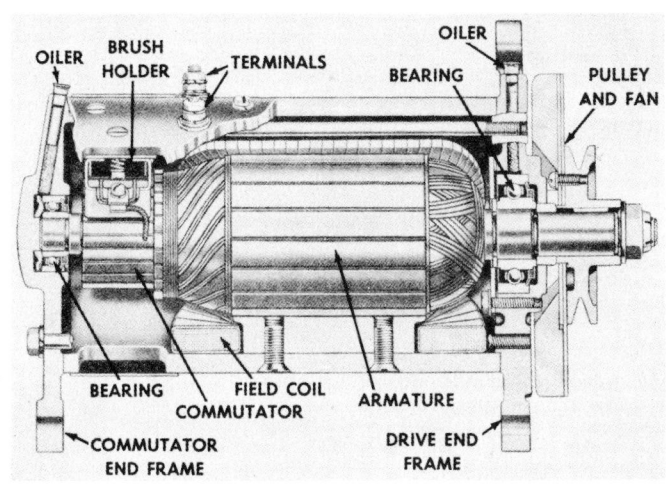

Fig. 31-1. The cutaway view shows major parts of direct current shunt wound generator.

No. 1. The DC unit generates voltage in coils of wire as the assembly (armature) rotates in a stationary magnetic field (field coils), Fig. 31-1.

The AC generator (popularly called "alternator") in current use operates on generating principle No. 2. The magnetic field (rotor) is rotated and voltage is generated in the stationary coils (stator), Fig. 31-2.

In general, then, voltage is induced in a coil whenever there is a change in the lines of force passing through the coil. Fig. 31-3 illustrates what happens when lines of force are cut by rotating coil.

When the coil is in a vertical position, as shown at A in Fig. 31-3, the lines of force surrounding the conductor are balanced. For that instant, no lines of force are being cut. Therefore, no voltage will be induced in the coil.

An automotive generator of electricity, Figs. 31-1 and 31-2, is an electromagnetic device that converts mechanical energy supplied by the engine into electrical energy. In operation, it maintains the storage battery in fully charged condition and supplies electrical power for the ignition system and accessory equipment.

ELECTROMAGNETIC INDUCTION

The operation of automotive electric generators is based on the principle that when a coil of wire is moved through a magnetic field, a voltage will be induced or generated in the coil. This principle can be demonstrated by connecting the ends of a loop of wire to a sensitive electrical measuring instrument and moving the loop through a magnetic field.

Actually, voltage can be produced in either of two ways:
1. By moving the coil of wire through a stationary field.
2. By keeping the coil stationary and moving the magnetic field.

The old DC (direct current) generator, which was used on most U.S. cars until 1962, operated on generating principle

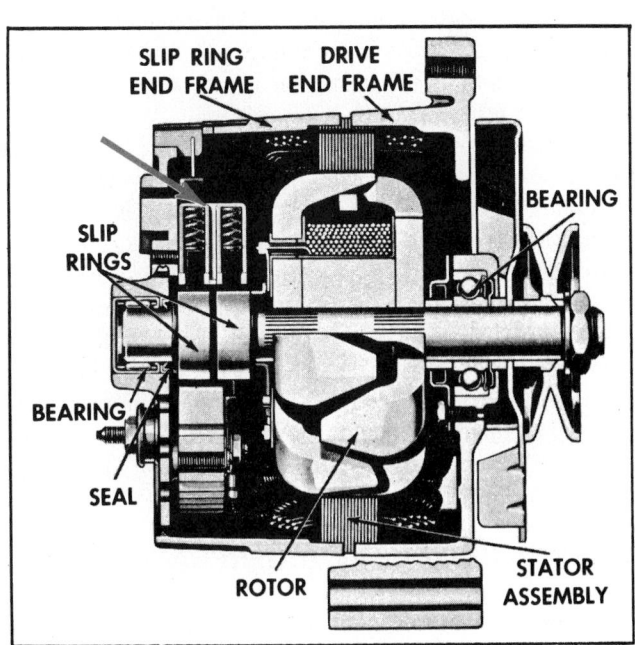

Fig. 31-2. Late model Oldsmobile alternator has conventional arrangement of rotor, stator, slip rings, diodes and brushes; also an internal transistorized regulator to control output (colored arrow).

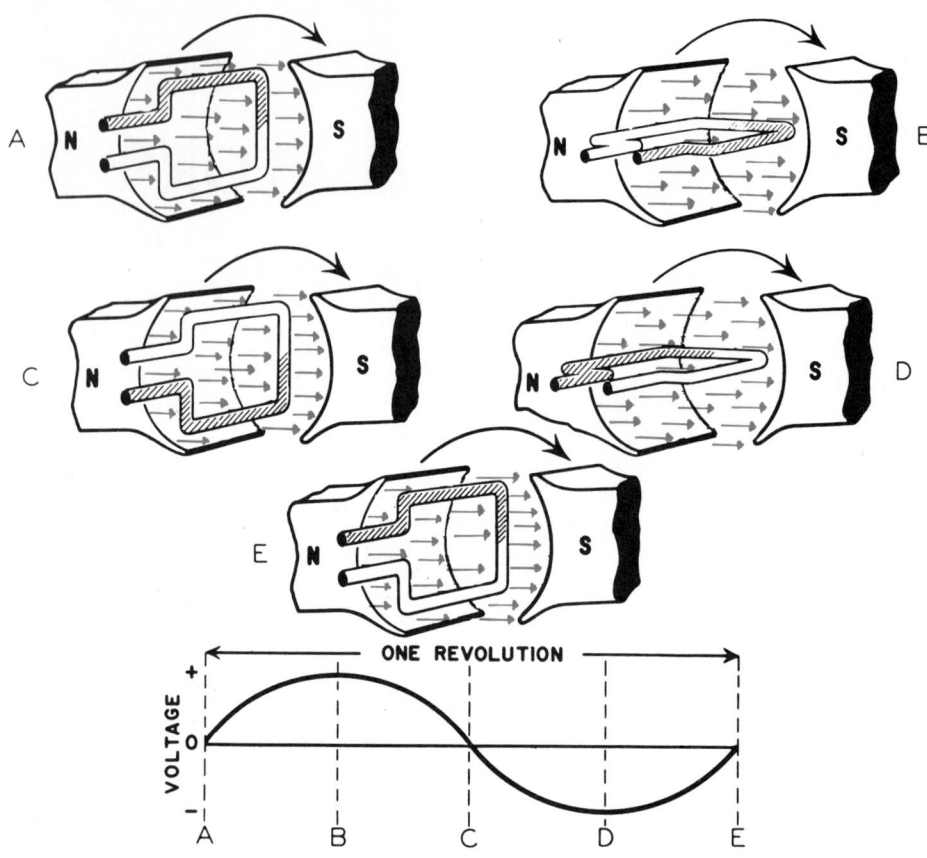

Fig. 31-3. Illustrating how voltage is induced in a coil that is revolved in a magnetic field. Curve at bottom shows variation in voltage for each position of revolving coil.

As the coil approaches position B in Fig. 31-3, an increasing number of lines of force will be cut. The generated voltage will continue to increase until it reaches a maximum of position B.

After passing position B, the voltage will start to decrease as fewer lines of force are being cut. It will become zero when position C is reached.

As rotation continues, another maximum will be reached at position D. However, the lines of force are now being cut in the opposite direction to that of position B. Therefore, the current generated will flow in the opposite direction.

Since the current keeps changing its direction as the loop of wire is rotated, it is called an alternating current. The variations in the value and direction of the generated voltage are shown in the lower portion of Fig. 31-3.

To make use of the electrical energy that is being generated, each end of the coil is connected to a ring which rotates with the coil of wire. Contact with these rotating rings is made by brushes which bear against the rings.

ALTERNATING CURRENT GENERATOR

All automotive generators produce alternating current (AC) which, in turn, must be rectified (converted) to direct current (DC) to satisfy the needs of the storage battery and the various DC electrical systems and accessories.

In an alternating current generator, or alternator, Fig. 31-2,

the magnetic field is rotated and voltage is generated in the stationary coils. Rectifiers, or diodes are built into the alternator to limit current flow to one direction only to provide direct current at the output terminal.

Alternators and matched or integral voltage regulators are used on all U.S. passenger car engines since 1961 or 1962. Some foreign cars have retained DC generators much longer. Volkswagen, for example, just switched to alternators across the line in 1974 models.

DIRECT CURRENT GENERATOR

A DC generator, Fig. 31-1, operates basically in the same manner as an alternator in that it produces alternating current. However, the DC generator works on the principle that voltage is generated in a coil, or coils, of wire (armature) as it is rotated in a stationary magnetic field. Instead of using a rectifier to convert the AC to DC, a mechanical switch (brushes and commutator) is provided.

The commutator is a segmented portion of the armature which, in turn, is composed of many coils, each connected to a bar or segment of the commutator, Fig. 31-1. The field poles are secured to the frame with heavy screws, and the armature is carried in bearings mounted in the end plates. Commutator brush holders, brushes and brush springs complete the assembly. Long bolts are used to hold the end plates securely against the main frame.

Most DC generators incorporate a cooling fan, which usually forms part of the driving pulley. On some generators, the field frame is engineered with openings so the brushes and commutator can be inspected.

OPERATING PRINCIPLES

In operation, the armature rotates between pole shoes wound with field coils. The spinning armature builds voltage in the field coils, and the field coils, in turn, produce more voltage and current in the armature.

The commutator is attached to the armature shaft and rotates with it. Coils of the armature are connected to bars or segments of the commutator. Each segment of the commutator is insulated from the other, and spring-loaded brushes ride on the commutator and transmit the voltage and current to the generator terminals then to the battery and other electrical accessories.

Two important points tell the story about DC generators:
1. The commutator changes the alternating current generated within the armature to direct current as it leaves the brushes.
2. The strength of the voltage induced in the armature coil is proportionate to the strength of the magnetic field, the speed with which the conductor or coil is moved through the field, and the number of turns of wire used to form the coil.

One of the shortcomings of DC generators is that low speed output is limited. This is serious because the starting battery does not receive a charge at idling and low speed operation. In addition, there is insufficient current for the operation of other electrical equipment. This is the main reason why the DC generator was replaced by the alternator.

Another major advantage of the alternator is that the magnetic field (which is rotating) carries only 2 to 3 amperes of current, and voltage is generated in the stationary coils. This field current is supplied through slip rings and, since it is low current output, no arcing will occur at the brushes. The DC generator, on the other hand, passes 25 to 45 amperes through the brushes from the commutator. With this relatively high current output, arcing is difficult to overcome, and rapid commutator and brush wear results.

OTHER GENERATORS

The "shunt type" generator described earlier serves as the basic design for most DC generators used in the automotive field. It has two pole pieces with field coil, an armature, commutator and two brushes. The field coil is connected in parallel with the armature, thereby shunting off some armature output.

Two variations of shunt generators are used: the "A" circuit, Fig. 31-4, on Delco-Remy generator equipped passenger cars (GM); the "B" circuit, Fig. 31-5, used on Ford built passenger cars. Today, the "A" circuit generator is used primarily on farm and industrial equipment.

"Third brush" generators have three brushes instead of two.

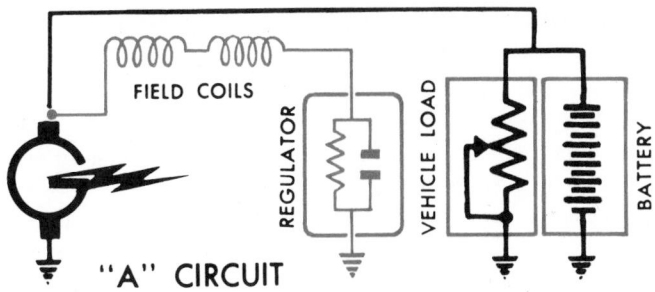

Fig. 31-4. In "A" type generator circuit, regulator resistance is inserted between field and ground when regulator points are open.

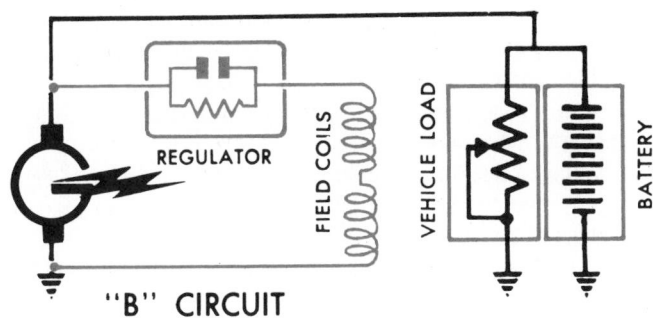

Fig. 31-5. In "B" type generator circuit, regulator inserts resistance between insulated side of circuit and field coil.

The third brush is adjustable, and its position controls voltage applied to the circuit and generator output. Currently, the use of third brush generators is limited to slow speed equipment.

In certain truck and bus applications with heavy electrical loads, special generator circuits are necessary. As loads increase, three things happen: strengthening of the magnetic field; greater distortion and shifting of the field; arcing between the brushes and commutator.

An "interpole" generator solves these problems by means of a narrow, additional pole piece mounted on the generator frame between the two regular pole pieces. This interpole coil is connected in series with the armature. It is wound in the opposite direction of the regular field winding to counteract the magnetic field created by current flowing through the armature.

A "bucking field" generator solves the problem of obtaining adequate current output at low generator speeds, yet avoids over-charging at high speeds. This type of DC generator is controlled by means of a bucking field coil of high resistance. It is wound on one field pole in the opposite direction of the regular coil, and it is connected directly across the armature.

A "split field" generator has two field circuits, each controlled by its own voltage and current regulator. By almost doubling magnetic field strength, voltage necessary to provide current for the load circuit can be reached at a much lower speed. City buses are a common application for split field generators.

GENERATOR REGULATORS

Some external means of controlling DC generator output must be provided to prevent current and voltage from exceeding predetermined values. The generator regulator was found to be the answer, Figs. 31-4 and 31-5.

Regulators consist basically of spring-loaded contact points and a resistance. The contact points are opened electromagnetically by means of a winding. When the points are open, the resistance is automatically connected to the field coils of the generator, thereby reducing the amount of current flowing in that circuit. This in turn reduces the strength of the magnetic field and lowers the output of the generator. When the points are closed, the resistance is shorted out of the circuit so the field current is increased and the generator output rises.

Most regulators used in conjunction with DC generators have three units:

1. A cutout relay to prevent battery from discharging through generator when engine is stopped or idling.
2. A voltage regulator to prevent circuit voltage from exceeding a predetermined safe value; also to maintain a constant voltage in system.
3. A current regulator to protect generator from overload by limiting current output to a safe value. See Fig. 31-6.

THE ALTERNATOR

An alternator (AC generator), Fig. 31-2, consists of three major units:
1. A rotor which provides the magnetic field.
2. A stator in which voltage and current is produced.
3. A diode (rectifier) assembly which changes AC to DC.

The rotor assembly incorporates an iron core on a shaft with a wire coil wound around it. The coil is enclosed between two iron pole pieces with interspaced sections, or fingers. The ends of the coil are connected to two slip rings mounted on one end of the rotor shaft.

Small brushes ride on the slip rings. One brush is grounded, the other is insulated and connects to the alternator field terminal. This terminal, in turn, is connected through the alternator regulator and ignition switch to the battery.

The stator has three sets of windings assembled around the inside circumference of a laminated core, Fig. 31-2. This core forms part of the exterior frame in most alternators, and it provides a path for the flow of magnetic flux between two adjacent poles of the rotor.

Each winding of the stator generates a separate voltage, Fig. 31-7. One end of each winding is connected to a positive and negative diode. The other ends of the stator windings are connected to form a "Y" arrangement. See Fig. 31-8. On heavy-duty applications, the windings are connected to form a triangle (delta-connected stator). See Fig. 31-9.

The diode assembly basically consists of six diodes mounted at the slip ring end of the alternator housing. On negative ground systems, three negative diodes are mounted in the end frame or in a heat sink bolted to the end frame. Three positive diodes are mounted in a heat sink insulated from the end frame. Some alternators use "diode trio" assemblies.

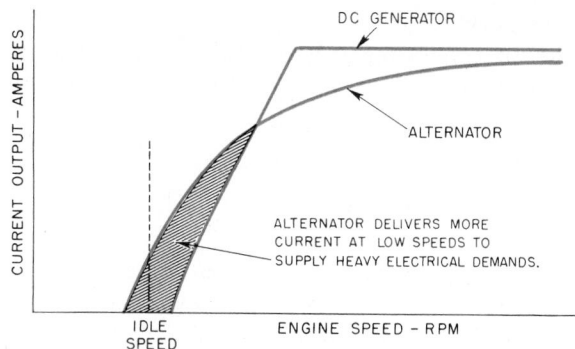

Fig. 31-6. Output of DC generator and alternator is compared from idle to high speed operation.

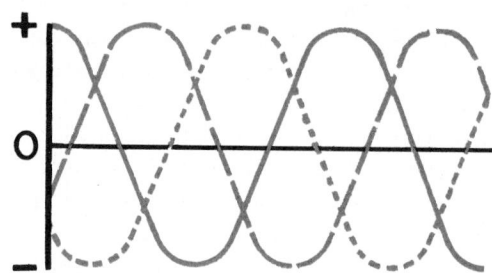

Fig. 31-7. Each winding of stator generates a separate voltage to make alternator a three-phase unit.

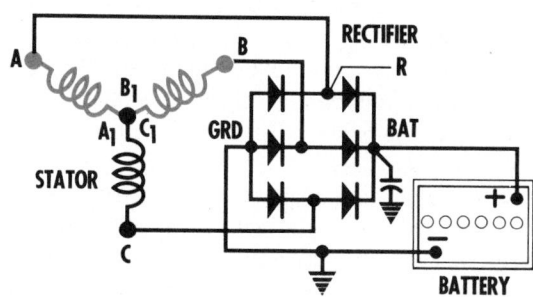

Fig. 31-8. When stator leads A, B and C are connected together at A_1, B_1 and C_1, a three phase "Y" circuit stator is formed.

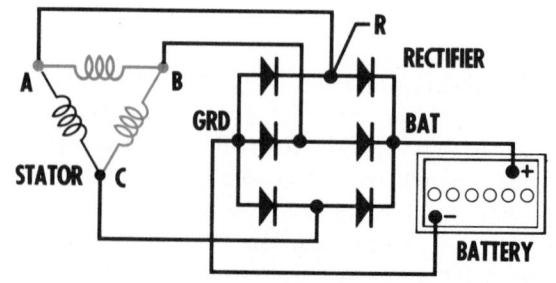

Fig. 31-9. When stator lead A is connected to B, B to C and C to A, a triangular, three phase "delta-connected" stator is formed.

The diodes are connected to the stator leads and serve as one-way valves that permit current to flow through in one direction only. Each phase of the three-phase output of the alternator ranges from positive to negative and back to positive again. The diodes convert this alternating current to direct current at the alternator output terminal.

Note in Fig. 31-11 that while the voltage of each phase ranges from zero to maximum, the effective voltage of all phases maintains a reasonably even current output.

The front and rear cases, or shields, of the alternator generally are held together by "through bolts." A fan mounted on the front of the rotor shaft draws air through the cases for cooling. The cases support the bearings; usually a sealed thrust ball bearing at the front and an axial roller bearing at the rear.

ALTERNATOR OPERATION

The DC generator and alternator produce direct current at their output terminals, but they do it in different ways. The principle of operation of the DC generator, Fig. 31-3, involves moving a conductor (armature) through a stationary magnetic field (field poles and coils). The alternator reverses this procedure by moving the magnetic field (rotor) across a stationary conductor (stator).

The alternator, like the DC generator, produces alternating current within, then converts it to direct current at the output terminal. But before an alternator will begin to charge, direct current must flow through the rotor field coil to magnetize the pole pieces, Fig. 31-10. That is, the rotor (alternator field) must be externally excited before it will deliver voltage and current.

To help provide field excitation, some alternators utilize an isolation diode and a charge indicator light hooked up in parallel. This extra diode acts as an automatic switch between the battery and alternator to block current flow back to the alternator and regulator when the alternator is not operating.

When the ignition switch is turned "ON," voltage is supplied to one side of the indicator lamp on the dash. This causes a small amount of current to pass through the regulator to the insulated brush. It flows through the slip ring, field coil, other slip ring and other brush to ground. This direct current passing through the coil creates a magnetic field in each section of the rotor and lights the charge indicator lamp.

Then, as the rotor turns, its magnetic field induces voltage in the stator windings. Because the rotor sections have alternate north and south poles, and because current direction is reversed each half revolution of the rotor, alternating current is produced. See Fig. 31-7.

The stator sends this three phase alternating current to the diode assembly, which permits current to pass through in one direction only to provide direct current at the alternator output terminal. See Fig. 31-11.

OTHER ALTERNATORS

Alternators vary according to application. Most modern passenger car units have a rated output from 35 to 55 amp. Some special applications, such as fleet operations or police cars, have alternators that put out from 70 to 90 amp. Heavy-duty trucks are equipped with 105 to 160 amp. alternators, Fig. 31-12.

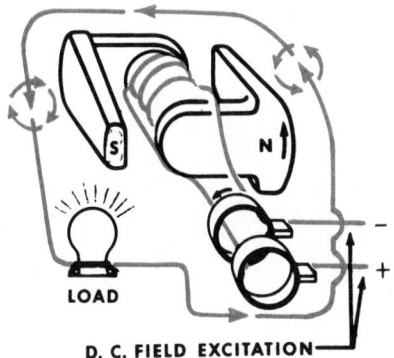

Fig. 31-10. Current for the field excitation of an alternator is supplied through brushes and slip rings from battery.

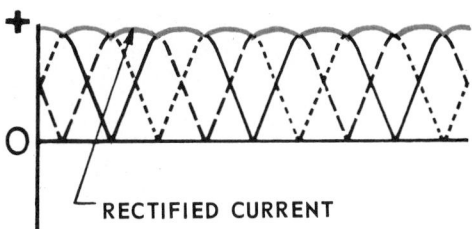

Fig. 31-11. Rectifier (diode assembly) permits current to pass through in one direction only. Rectified three-phase current is shown.

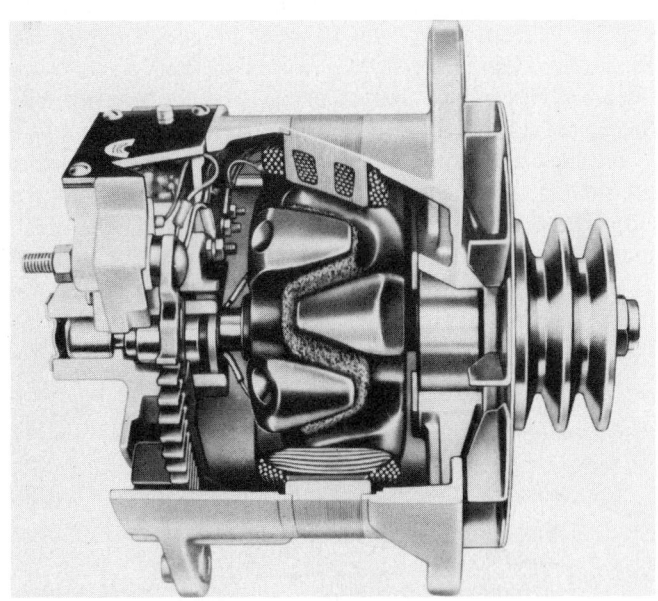

Fig. 31-12. Heavy-duty, 105 amp. truck alternator has removable plate at top rear, permitting inspection of brushes, diode trio and regulator without removing alternator from truck. (Leece-Neville Co.)

In addition to higher output, design differences affect internal make-up, size, shape and mounting configuration of the alternator. Open frame (vented) alternators are used in passenger cars operated under normal driving conditions. Closed units are used in marine or off-the-road applications. Some models feature enclosed brushes and slip rings for use

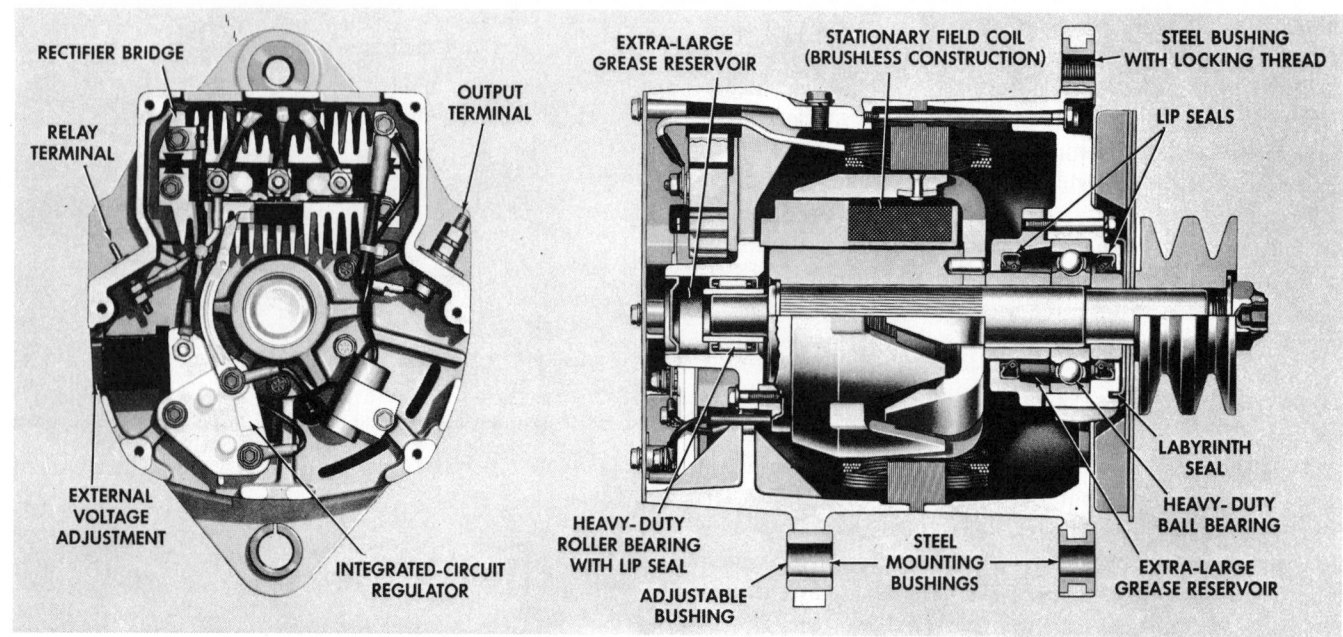

Fig. 31-13. Both stator and field in this brushless alternator are stationary, eliminating shorts and grounds more likely to occur when field winding must rotate. (Delco-Remy Div., GM)

where explosive mixtures may be present. Oil cooled, totally enclosed units with stationary conductors are available for use on motor coaches.

Some alternators have dual brush sets; others are brushless, Fig. 31-13. Rotors vary with 12 poles, 14 poles, 16 poles, etc. Diodes may be pressed-in, screwed-in or come as a "trio" assembly. Heavy-duty alternators may have dual internal fans. Some have side terminals; others have rear terminals.

Brushless alternators are different enough to require further explanation. Generally, they produce direct current at the output terminal because of a special rotor having the north and south poles connected by a non-magnetic ring, Fig. 31-14.

With this construction, the rotor pole pieces fit closely over the STATIONARY field coil winding, which is mounted on the end frame. The non-magnetic ring supports the rotor

segment opposite the drive end, and it serves to make the magnetic lines of force more dense, going from the north poles to the south poles.

As the rotor turns between the stationary field coil and stationary stator, the magnetic field cuts across the stator windings and three phase alternating current and voltage are generated. AC is rectified to DC by six large threaded diodes.

These design differences only serve to emphasize that whatever the design, diodes change alternating current from the stator windings to a flow of direct current at the output terminal of the alternator. The rotor (magnetic field), stator (conductors) and diodes (rectifiers) act as a team to produce the direct current electricity to keep the battery fully charged and to supply electrical energy to the vehicle's current-consuming devices.

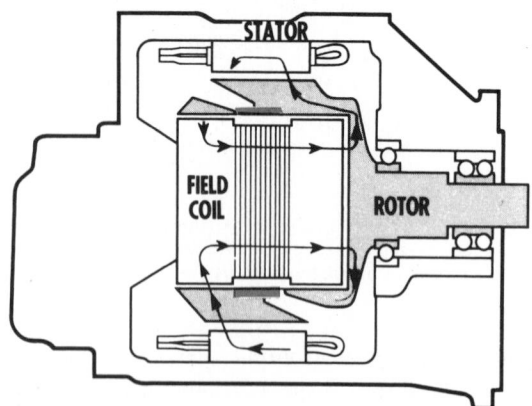

Fig. 31-14. Arrows show flow of voltage and current in one design of brushless alternator. Note how non-magnetic ring, in color, separates rotor poles.

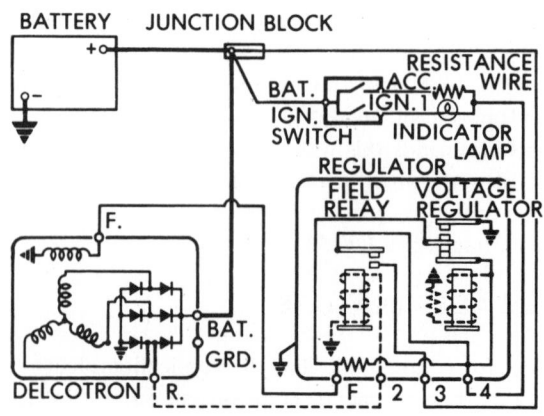

Fig. 31-15. This AC charging system wiring diagram illustrates how two unit electromagnetic regulator is connected to battery, indicator lamp, ignition switch and alternator field coil.

ALTERNATOR REGULATORS

Regulators used with alternators often have only one element, a voltage regulator. No current regulator is needed because the alternator sets up its own opposing field during operation to limit output. In most applications, the function of the cutout relay is performed by diodes.

Regulators most commonly used with alternators are one and two unit electromagnetic, transistorized and integral types. A wiring diagram for a two unit electromagnetic regulator and "Y" stator alternator are shown in Fig. 31-15.

A typical transistorized regulator has transistors (current flow control switches), diodes, resistors, a capacitor and a thermistor (temperature-compensated resistor). Integral regulators usually are sealed, solid state units mounted inside the alternator slip ring end frame.

REVIEW QUESTIONS – ELECTRIC GENERATORS

1. For what purpose is the automotive generator used?
2. What happens when a coil of wire is moved through a magnetic field?
3. When rotating a coil of wire through a horizontal magnetic field, maximum voltage will be produced in what position of the coil?
   a. Horizontal.
   b. Vertical.
4. Why are cooling fans incorporated in the design of modern automotive alternators?
5. In a direct current generator, voltage is generated in which unit?
   a. Armature.
   b. Field.
   c. Stator.
   d. Regulator.
6. In a direct current generator, what device is used to change alternating current to direct?
   a. Commutator.
   b. Rectifier.
   c. Transistor.
7. What three methods can be used to increase the strength of the generated voltage?
8. Which type of generator has a built-in output adjustment.
   a. Shunt.
   b. Third brush.
9. In the A-type generator circuit, where is the regulator resistance inserted?
   a. Between the field and ground.
   b. Between the insulated side of the circuit and the field coil.
   c. Shunted across the armature.
10. In the B-type generator circuit where does the regulator insert the resistance?
    a. Between the insulated side of the circuit and the field coil.
    b. Shunted across the armature.
    c. Shunted across the field.
11. What is the purpose of an interpole in a generator?
    a. Increase output.
    b. Decrease arcing at the brushes.
    c. Maintain constant voltage.
12. What is the purpose of a bucking field generator?
    a. Control the voltage.
    b. Increase the output.
    c. Strengthen the magnetic field.
13. What is a major advantage of an alternator over a direct current generator for automotive service?
14. In most alternators, the voltage is generated in which part of the unit?
    a. Rotor.
    b. Stator.
15. In most alternators, what is the name of the part which supplies the field?
16. In an alternator, what is the name of the part which changes the current from alternating to direct?
    a. Converter.
    b. Commutator.
    c. Rectifier.
17. What kind of current is supplied to the field of an alternator?
    a. Direct.
    b. Alternating.
18. For what purpose is a diode used in a modern automotive alternator?
19. How many windings are there in a Y-type stator?
    a. One.
    b. Two.
    c. Three.
    d. Five.
20. Some alternators are rated at over 100 amp. output. True or False?
21. A brushless alternator makes use of a _____ ring to connect the north and south poles of a special rotor.
22. A brushless alternator has a stationary stator and a _____ field coil.

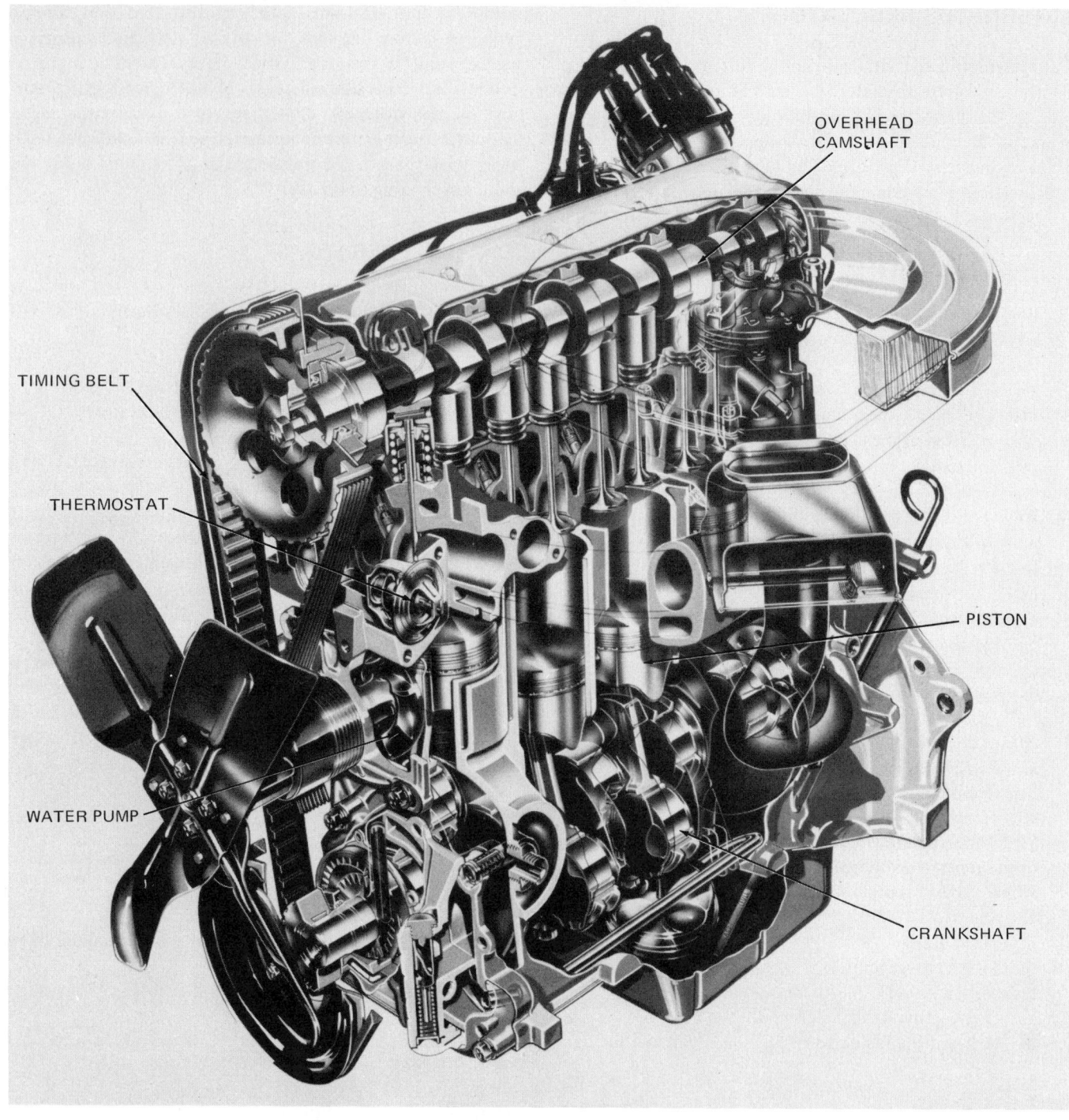

OVERHEAD
CAMSHAFT

TIMING BELT

THERMOSTAT

PISTON

WATER PUMP

CRANKSHAFT

Chevrolet Monza four cylinder engine has an overhead camshaft with cog type timing belt fitted to crankshaft sprocket and camshaft sprocket. Note that back of belt is positioned in water pump track.

GENERATOR AND ALTERNATOR TESTING AND SERVICING

Whenever an engine operates, the generator or alternator is performing its task of producing enough voltage and amperage to meet the needs of the vehicle. It follows, then, that regular inspection and occasional maintenance is necessary.

A DC generator requires periodic lubrication, inspection of brushes and commutator, and testing of brush spring tension. In addition, check electrical connections for clean, metal-to-metal contact and tightness.

When generators have hinged cap oilers, observe these procedures:
1. On generators containing bushing-type bearings, lubricate bushings at every lubrication period with a few drops of medium viscosity engine oil.
2. Lubricate ball bearing-equipped generators with 8 to 10 drops of medium viscosity engine oil. Do not over oil.

Visually and manually inspect condition of all starting and charging system cables, clamps, wires and terminal connections. See that generator drive pulley is tight on shaft, and that drive belt is in good condition and adjusted to proper tension. Also make sure that starter, generator and voltage regulator are securely mounted to insure good ground circuits.

Remove cover band, if generator is so equipped, and inspect commutator, brushes and electrical connections. If commutator is dirty or slightly rough, sand it with number 00 sandpaper or by means of a special sanding tool. Never use emery cloth on a commutator.

To sand commutator, wrap end of a flat piece of soft wood with a strip of number 00 sandpaper. Then, with generator in operation, hold sandpaper against commutator and move it back and forth so that entire surface of commutator is sanded.

NOTE: If commutator is rough and pitted, or inaccessible for on-car service, generator must be removed, disassembled and serviced on bench, Fig. 32-1.

Blow interior of generator clean with compressed air. If brushes are worn down to one-half their original length, replace them. Lift brushes in brush holder to see that they are

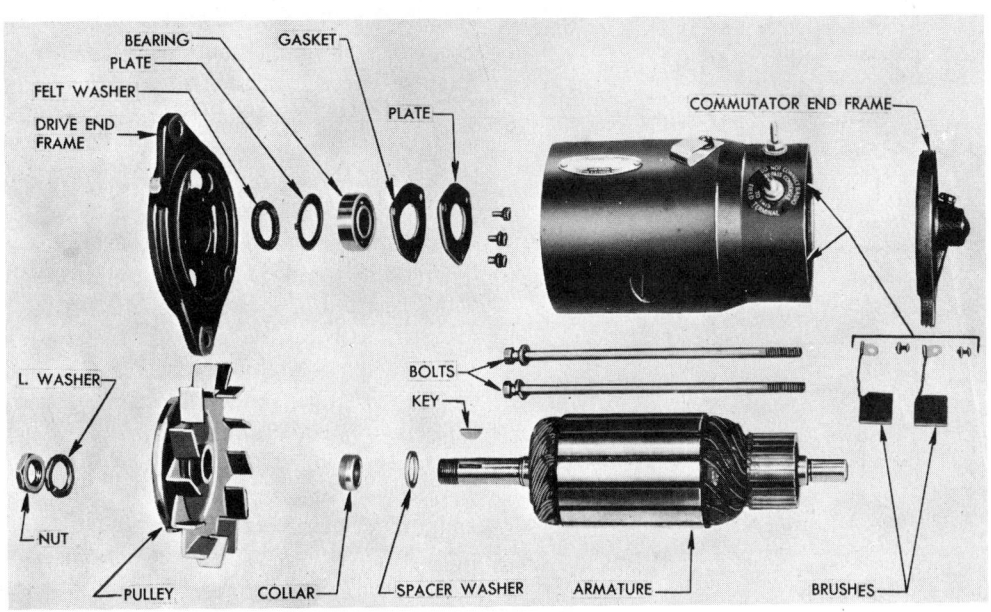

Fig. 32-1. Exploded view of DC generator reveals two long through bolts which hold end frames to main frame.

free to operate and test tension of brush springs.

Inspect the inner surface of the generator cover band for tiny globules of solder. If any solder is found, the generator is producing excessive current and has melted the solder used in connecting armature wires to commutator bars. Replace armature or resolder connections.

IDENTIFYING "A" AND "B" GENERATORS

Identification of the generator is important. The "A" circuit generator has the field grounded through the regulator, while the "B" circuit has the field grounded within the generator.

A sure method of identifying whether you have an "A" or "B" unit is to disconnect the field wire from the generator field terminal, taking care not to let this wire "ground." Connect a voltmeter from the generator field terminal to the ground, then, with the engine operating at a fast idle, a voltage reading indicates that the generator is the "A" circuit type. If no reading is indicated, the generator is a "B" circuit.

Another method of determining the type of generator is to note the connection between the field and the brushes (on generators which have a removable cover band). If the generator field coil lead is connected to the insulated brush inside the generator, the generator has an "A" circuit. If the generator field coil is connected to the grounded brush or the generator field frame, the generator has a "B" circuit.

CAUTION: On cars with double contact regulators, never ground generator field with the regulator connected to generator. This will burn upper set of contact points in regulator. Double contact regulators are usually found on cars equipped with air conditioning and other electrical equipment which imposes a heavy load on generator.

TESTING "A" CIRCUIT GENERATOR

To test voltage output of an "A" circuit shunt-type generator, connect a voltmeter as shown in Fig. 32-2. Make

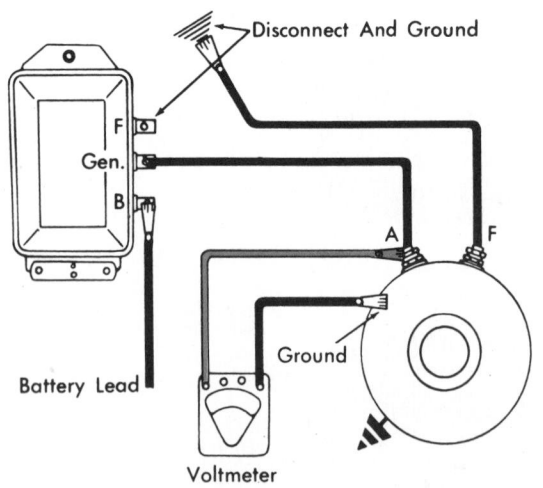

Fig. 32-2. Install a voltmeter in charging system as indicated to test voltage output of "A" circuit generators.

sure all lights and accessories on vehicle are turned off. Speed up engine until voltmeter indicates in excess of 16V. Do not operate engine at this speed for more than a second or two as it will damage generator. If this voltage is not reached, disconnect wire from regulator to generator armature terminal. If correct voltage is then attained, starting battery is defective. If correct voltage is not attained with battery out of circuit, overhaul generator.

TESTING "B" CIRCUIT GENERATOR

To test current output on a "B" circuit generator, disconnect regulator armature and field wires of generator. Connect a jumper wire from generator armature terminal to generator field terminal. Also connect positive lead of a 0-50 ampere ammeter to generator armature terminal, Fig. 32-3.

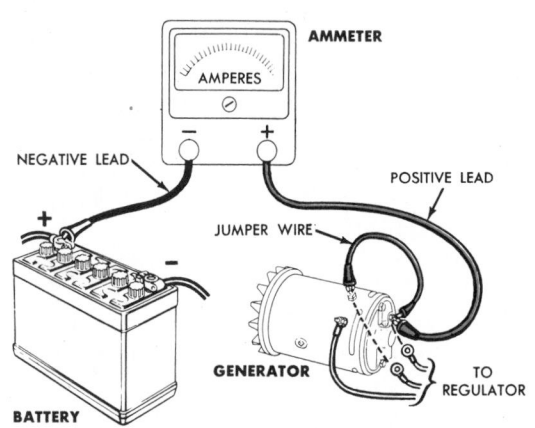

Fig. 32-3. Connect an ammeter and a jumper wire as shown to check output of "B" circuit generators.

Start engine and, while it is idling, connect ammeter negative lead to positive lead of battery. Run engine at 1500 rpm and read current output on ammeter. Generator should reach or exceed its specified output. Disconnect test leads as soon as test is completed to prevent overheating of generator.

POLARIZING THE GENERATOR

After a generator has been disconnected, tested or repaired, it should be polarized to make sure it has the correct polarity with respect to the battery in the circuit. If the generator is operated with reverse polarity, it may be damaged and, in addition, the regulator contacts may be burned. The method of polarizing a generator will depend on whether the generator field is grounded through the regulator ("A" circuit) or is internally grounded ("B" circuit).

On "A" circuit generators, Fig. 30-4, after reconnecting leads, momentarily connect a jumper wire between "GEN" and "BAT" terminals of the regulator. This permits a momentary surge of current to pass through the generator to polarize it correctly.

To polarize "B" circuit generators, Fig. 30-5, disconnect

the lead from the field terminal of the regulator and momentarily touch that lead to the regulator battery terminal. The resulting surge of current will correctly polarize the generator.

On cars with double contact regulators, disconnect field lead from regulator and ground it. Then momentarily place jumper lead from battery to the generator armature terminal.

AC CHARGING SYSTEM INSPECTION

Alternator-equipped charging systems also require regular inspection and maintenance. The frequency of inspection depends on operating conditions. High-speed operation, high temperatures, dust and dirt all tend to increase wear on alternator components.

Inspect alternator systems visually and manually at approximately 5,000-mile intervals to make sure that brushes, slip rings and bearings are in good operating condition. Also test the battery's state of charge and the condition of starting and charging system cables, wires and connections.

Check for tightness of alternator and regulator mounting bolts to insure good ground circuits. Look over the alternator drive belt for signs of wear or slippage. See that the tension adjustment is correct. The belt should deflect 1/2 in. in the center of a long span. Alternator drive belt tension is more critical because the inertia created by the rotor is greater than that produced by the armature of a DC generator, Fig. 32-4.

could burn out alternator diodes (silicon rectifiers) and damage vehicle wiring.

2. Do not purposely or accidently "short" or "ground" system when disconnecting wires or connecting test leads to terminals of alternator or regulator. For example, grounding of field terminal at either alternator or regulator will damage regulator. Grounding of alternator output terminal will damage alternator and/or charging circuit.

3. Never operate an alternator on an open circuit. With no battery or electric load in circuit, alternators are capable of building high voltage (50 to over 110 volts) which may damage diodes and could be dangerous to anyone who might touch the alternator output terminal.

4. Do not try to polarize an alternator. Polarity of alternator system cannot be lost or changed, so attempts to polarize system serve no purpose and may cause damage to diodes, wiring harness, or other system components.

Maintenance is minimized by the use of prelubricated rotor bearings and long brushes in most modern alternators. If a problem exists, such as low output or overcharging, check for a complete field circuit (rotor) by placing a large screwdriver on the alternator rear bearing surface. If the field circuit is complete, there will be a strong magnetic pull on the blade of the screwdriver which indicates that the field is energized. If there is no field circuit, a modern alternator will not charge because it is excited by battery voltage.

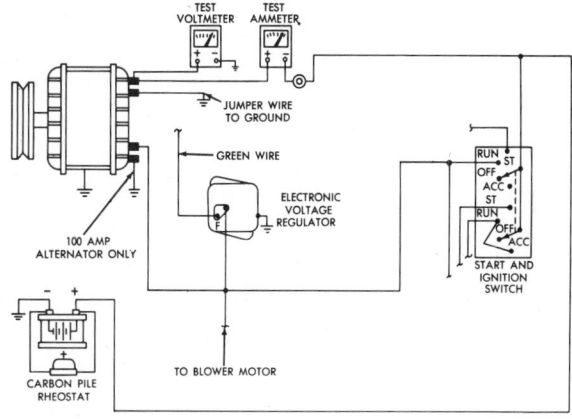

Fig. 32-5. Make test connections as shown to check current output of alternator at specified speed and voltage.

Fig. 32-4. Adjust alternator drive belt tension to manufacturer's specifications. Good operating condition and correct tension must be maintained.

ON—CAR TESTING

Alternator testing and service call for special precautions since the alternator output terminal is connected to the battery at all times:

1. Use care to avoid reverse polarity when performing battery service of any kind. A surge of current in opposite direction

CURRENT OUTPUT TEST

Make test connections shown in Fig. 32-5 to measure a Chrysler alternator's ability to produce its rated output at specified speed and voltage at normal operating temperature:

1. Disconnect battery ground cable.
2. Disconnect BAT lead wire at alternator output terminal.
3. Connect a 0-100 amp. (minimum) ammeter in series between disconnected wire and terminal.
4. Connect positive lead of a 0-15 volt (minimum) voltmeter to BAT terminal of alternator.

5. Connect negative lead of voltmeter to ground.

6. Disconnect regulator (green) field wire from alternator.

7. Connect "jumper" from alternator field terminal to ground.

8. Connect a tachometer to engine, then reconnect battery ground cable.

9. Install a variable pile rheostat (with carbon pile OFF) between battery terminals.

10. Start engine and operate at idle.

11. Gradually adjust carbon pile and engine speed until a speed of 1,250 rpm (900 rpm on 100 amp. alternator) and voltmeter reading of 15 volts (13 volts on 100 amp. alternator) is obtained. NOTE: Do not exceed 16 volts.

12. Ammeter reading must be within limits given for alternator being tested:

41 amp. alternator — 40 amp. minimum
50 amp. alternator — 47 amp. minimum
60 amp. alternator — 57 amp. minimum
65 amp. alternator — 62 amp. minimum
100 amp. alternator — 72 amp. minimum

CHARGING CIRCUIT RESISTANCE TEST

If current output test indicates a malfunction in the charging system, make the circuit resistance test shown in Fig. 32-6. This will determine whether the trouble is in the insulated circuit, ground circuit or alternator:

1. Disconnect battery ground cable.

2. Disconnect BAT lead wire at alternator output terminal.

3. Connect a 0-100 amp. (minimum) ammeter in series between disconnected wire and terminal.

4. Connect positive lead of low range voltmeter to disconnected BAT lead wire.

5. Connect negative lead of voltmeter to battery positive post.

6. Disconnect green field wire (to voltage regulator) at alternator.

7. Connect a jumper wire from alternator field terminal to ground.

8. Connect a tachometer to engine, then reconnect battery ground cable.

9. Install a variable pile rheostat (with carbon pile OFF) between battery terminals.

10. Start engine and operate at idle.

11. Adjust carbon pile and engine speed to maintain 20 amp. current flow in circuit.

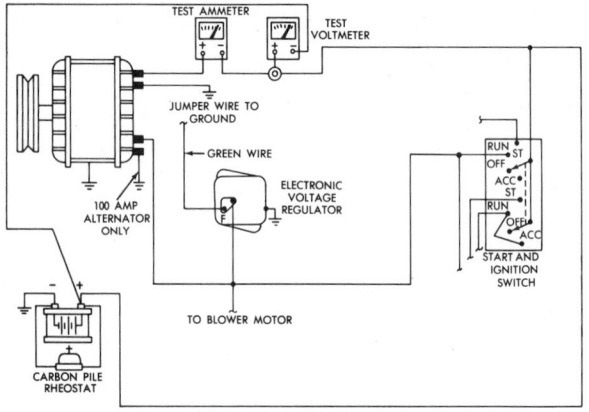

Fig. 32-6. If current output is low, make circuit resistance tests of alternator to pinpoint cause.

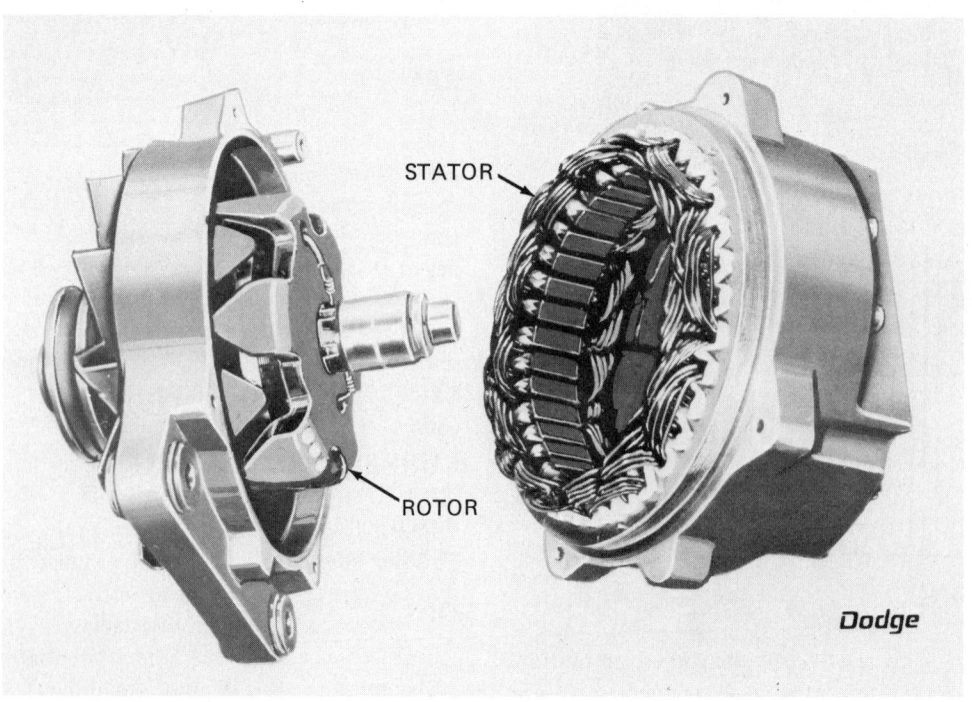

Fig. 32-7. First step of disassembly of Chrysler alternator shows relationship of components, and how stator and rotor are sandwiched between end shields.

12. Observe voltmeter reading. It should not exceed .7 volts (voltage drop).

If higher voltage drop is indicated, clean and tighten all connections in the charging circuit. If necessary, make voltage drop tests at each connection in circuit.

ALTERNATOR REMOVAL AND DISASSEMBLY

If the alternator system fails to meet current output specifications, yet passes the circuit resistance tests, remove the alternator from the vehicle for disassembly and bench tests, Fig. 32-7.

Remove ground cable from negative post of battery. Disconnect leads from alternator output terminal (BAT.) and from field terminal (FLD.). Disconnect ground lead. Unscrew mounting bolts and adjusting arm bolts. Slip off drive belt, or belts, and remove alternator from engine.

To disassemble unit: Scribe marks on front and rear housings to aid reassembly. On Chrysler and Motorola and Leece-Neville alternators, remove brushes before separating housings, Fig. 32-8. Also remove isolation diode from Motorola units at this time.

Remove through bolts and separate housings by lightly

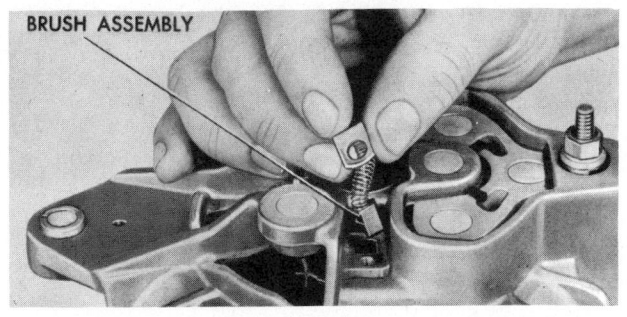

Fig. 32-8. Remove brushes from Chrysler Corp. alternator as shown before separating shields, or housings.

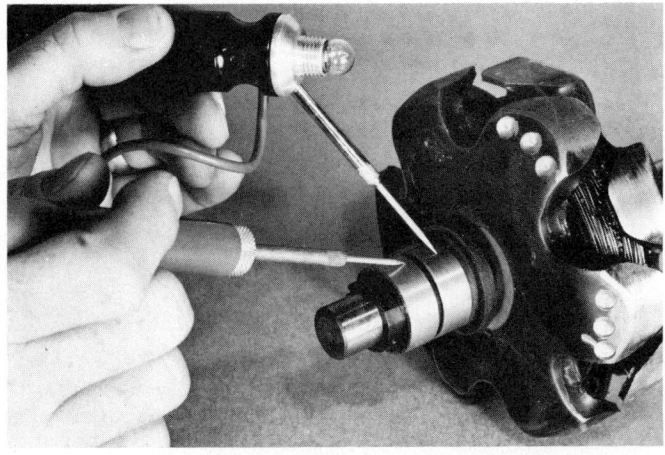

Fig. 32-9. Test rotor for open circuit by using test lamp and touching test prods to each slip ring.

tapping front case, or by prying gently between front case and stator (stator should remain with rear housing). When housings come apart, remove brush assemblies from Ford and Delcotron alternators.

Use a puller to remove pulley from rotor shaft on Chrysler units. Other alternator rotors can be supported in a vise for removal of drive end shaft nut, pulley and fan.

On Chrysler alternators, pry drive end bearing retainer spring from shield, then support shield and tap rotor shaft through bearing.

On Motorola units, remove split ring washer, and separate rotor and bearing from drive end housing. On other alternators, support rotor in a vise, attach a suitable tool to drive end housing, pull housing and bearing from rotor shaft. Special tools are available to pull or press bearings from rotor shaft or housing.

ROTOR TESTS

To review: The rotor consists of a field coil wound around a shaft and enclosed between two multipoled end pieces. The field winding is insulated from the shaft and connects to two slip rings at the rear of the shaft. One ring is contacted by the insulated brush; the other by the ground brush. Current passes through the insulated brush, through the field winding and back to ground through the ground brush.

To test the rotor for an "open circuit": Connect test lamp leads to each slip ring. If lamp lights, circuit is complete, or closed, Fig. 32-9.

To test for a "short circuit": Connect one test lamp lead to rotor shaft, other to one slip ring. Lamp should not light, showing that there is no connection or "short" between windings or slip rings and rotor shaft.

If the rotor fails either test, replace it.

STATOR TESTS

To review: The stator consists of three windings wound around the inside of a circular laminated core and connected to each other at one end. The other end of each winding is connected to a set of two diodes, one positive and one negative, all insulated from the core. Tests for "opens" are made between the windings and ground to the core.

To test for an open circuit: Connect one test lamp lead to stator core and, with other lead, prod each of three stator leads. Lamp should not light, showing no connection, or completed circuit, between the core and windings.

To test the stator windings for continuity: Contact each of three stator leads in turn, two at a time, Fig. 32-10. Lamp should light, showing a complete circuit, or good continuity.

Replace the stator if it fails either of these two tests.

DIODE TESTS

To review: A diode is a silicon rectifier connected to a terminal and mounted in a heat sink. It will allow current to pass through in one direction only, within its capabilities. As long as the current passes through the system in the proper

Automotive Encyclopedia

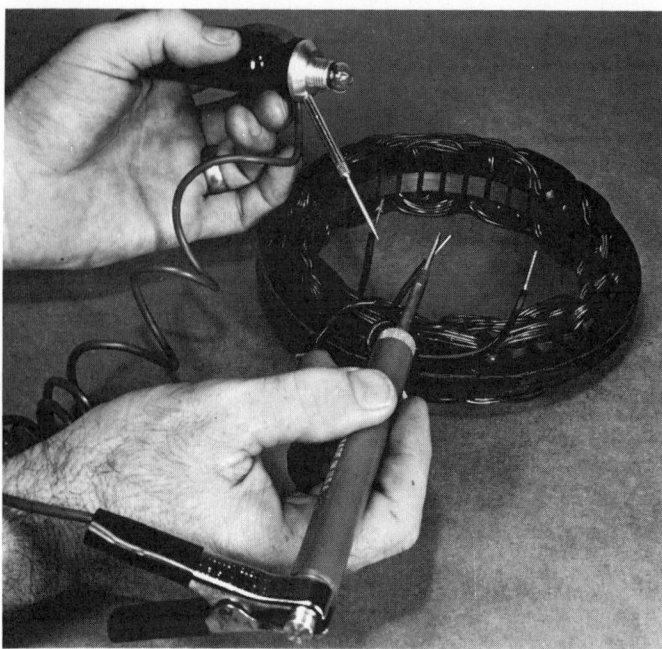

Fig. 32-10. Check stator windings for continuity by touching test lamp prods to two stator leads at same time.

direction and within the limitations set by the manufacturer, a diode will function properly. In doing its job, it prevents a battery from draining its current back through the alternator.

A diode will fail if the current passing through exceeds its limitations. And it will fail if a surge of current is applied to its reverse side. It will also fail if it is subjected to excessive heat due to a poor solder joint, a loose crimp connection at the lead or a loose fit in the heat sink.

Several testers permit diode testing without removing the stator leads; others require that the leads be disconnected.

To make positive diode test: Clip one test lead to output terminal of alternator and other to each of positive diodes in turn. Meter readings should fall in "good" band and in relatively same area.

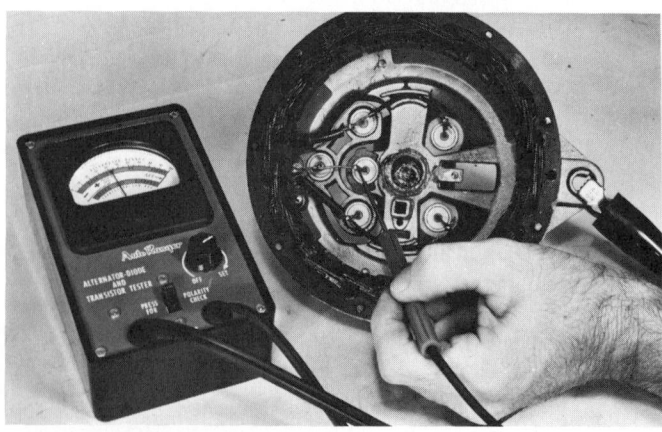

Fig. 32-11. Test negative diodes as shown; change test lead to output terminal of alternator to check positive diodes.

To test negative diodes: Move test lead from output terminal to ground on housing and touch other test lead to each negative diode in turn. Again, meter readings should be in "good" zone and relatively close, Fig. 32-11.

To test individual diodes: Connect one test lamp clip to diode base and one to diode lead. Then reverse connections: Lamp should light only once, Fig. 32-12. If lamp lights both times, diode is shorted. If it does not light at all, diode is open.

An isolation diode is used in Motorola alternators to provide a solid state switch to control the charge-discharge light on the dash, and to automatically connect the voltage regulator to the alternator and battery terminal when the alternator is operating. It also is designed to eliminate electrical leakage over the alternator insulators. Testing procedures are the same as for the rectifying diodes in the alternator end housing and heat sinks.

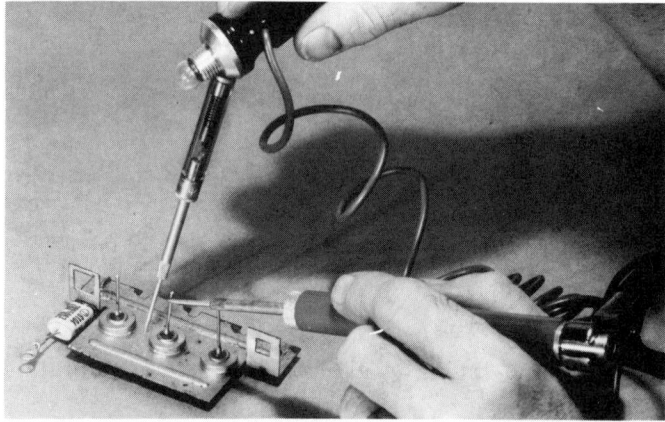

Fig. 32-12. Check condition of individual diodes by using test lamp and touching prods to diode base and its lead.

MAKING NECESSARY REPAIRS

Occasionally, the slip rings on the rotor shaft require service. Slip rings that merely need cleaning can be polished with 00 sandpaper or a 400 grain polishing cloth. Slightly scored rings can be turned true on an armature lathe, but only enough stock should be removed to clean up the marks.

Diode replacement can be handled by disconnecting, cutting or unsoldering the lead, then pressing out the defective unit. Use special diode removing tools and support the housing from the inside, Fig. 32-13. Some diodes in heat sinks can be replaced as an assembly; others mounted in the end housing must be replaced on an individual basis.

REASSEMBLY AND REINSTALLATION

After all bench tests have been completed, defective parts replaced and diodes connected to stator leads, the parts can be reassembled in reverse order of disassembly, Fig. 32-14.

Make sure that replacement bearings are fully seated in housings. Position front housing on rotor shaft and press it in place. On Chrysler alternators, press pulley on rotor shaft until

364

Generator and Alternator Testing and Servicing

Fig. 32-13. Usually, defective diodes must be pressed out of rear case while supporting it to avoid distortion.

hub just touches inner race of front bearing, Fig. 32-15. Assemble fan, pulley and drive end shaft nut on other alternators, tightening nut approximately 50 ft. lbs.

Install brushes before assembling two housings, using a straight stiff wire or thin welding rod pushed through end housing to retain brushes in holder until reassembly of housings is completed.

Align scribe marks made on housings and carefully install rear housing on front housing. See that brushes are not damaged by slip rings, then slip out stiff wire or welding rod and allow brushes to seat on slip rings.

Install through bolts, tightening them evenly. Check rotor rotation for freedom of movement and seating of brushes on slip rings. Output tests of reconditioned alternator can be made on a special generator-alternator test bench before reinstallation on engine (or on-car output tests covered earlier can be repeated after reinstallation).

Reinstall alternator on engine. Adjust drive belt tension,

but do not pry against stator section of alternator. Connect lead wires to field terminal, battery terminal and ground. Reconnect ground cable to negative post of battery. Alternator will be polarized when ignition switch is turned on.

Fig. 32-15. Install drive pulley on Chrysler Corp. alternator by means of a press, while rotor is properly supported.

LATE MODEL CHANGES

Chrysler alternators have incorporated changes that make the units more durable and serviceable. Late models have "built out" rear end shields (frames) to house the diode and

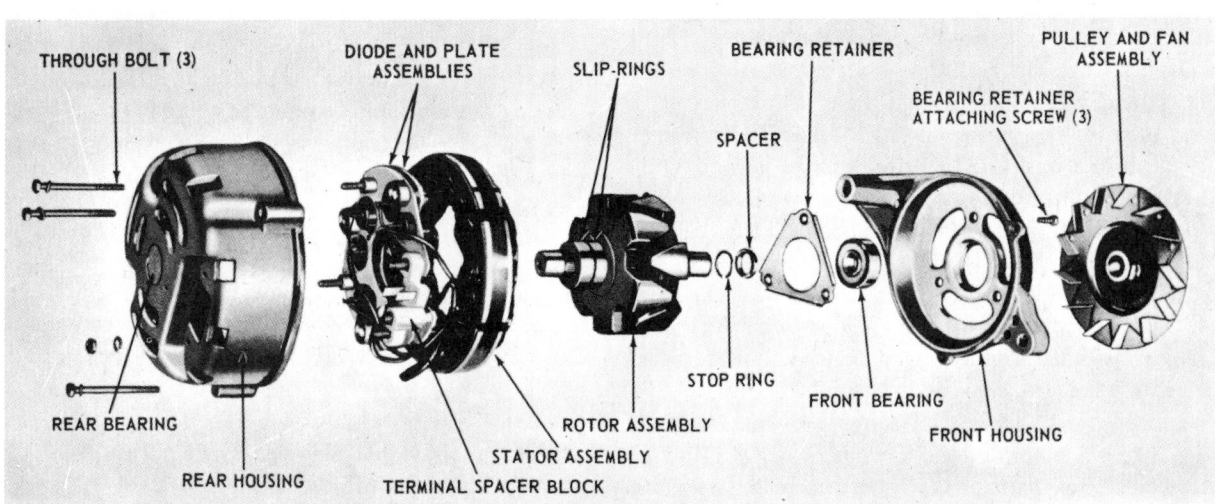

Fig. 32-14. Exploded view of Ford alternator gives details needed for performing correct disassembly and reassembly.

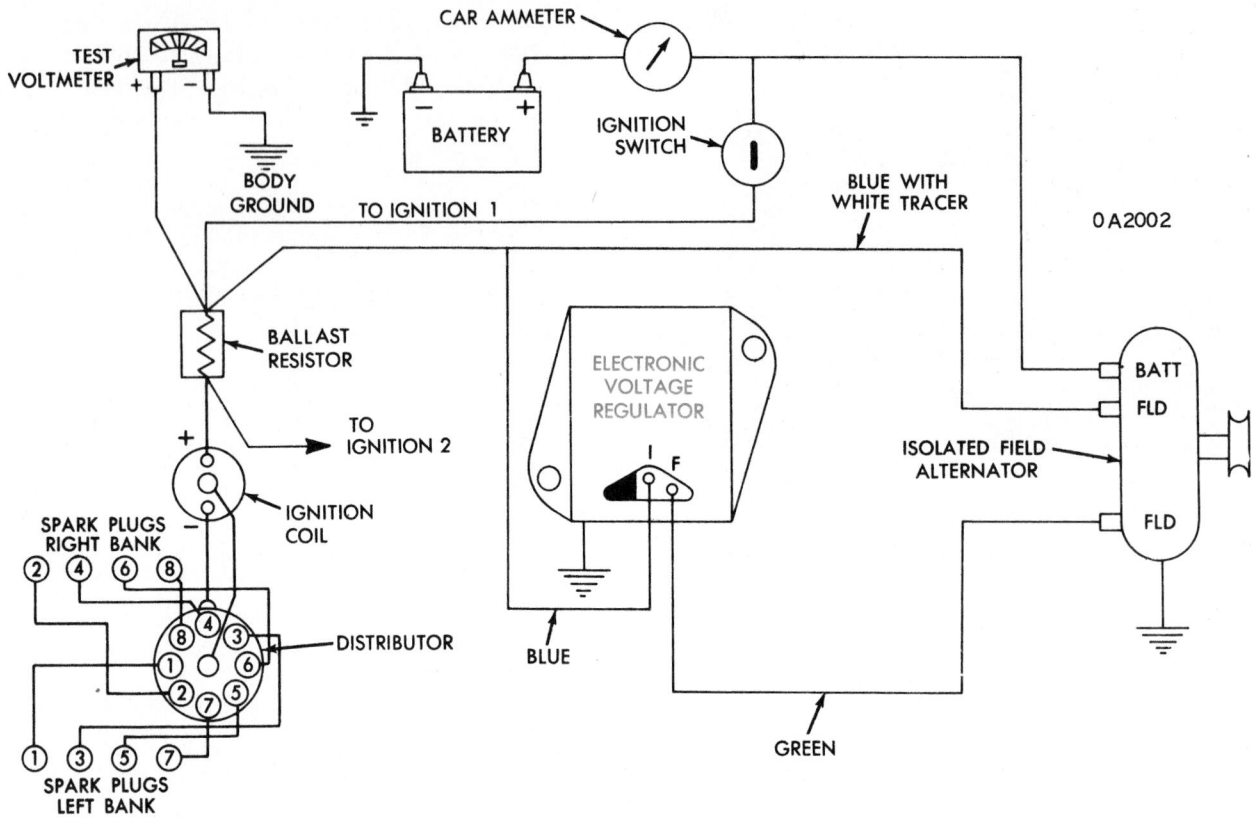

Fig. 32-16. Chrysler introduced an electronic voltage regulator in the charging system. Voltmeter hookup shown is for voltage regulator test. Also see Fig. 33-43 for arrangement used on later models.

heat sink assemblies. Field brushes are mounted in this end shield (one horizontally, other vertically) where they can be removed from plastic holders before separating the end shields.

In addition, Chrysler alternators now have replaceable slip rings. Damaged slip rings can be chiseled off; new ones pressed on the rotor shaft and field coil wires soldered in place.

CAUTION: When using probes to test diodes for continuity in one direction, avoid contact with the plastic insulators around the diodes. If a diode is shorted or open, replace the entire diode and heat sink assembly.

Chrysler also uses an electronic voltage regulator in the charging system, Fig. 32-16. To test the regulator, connect a voltmeter across the system: positive lead to Ignition 1 terminal of ballast resistor; negative lead to a good body ground. Operate the engine at 1250 rpm with lights and accessories turned off. The voltmeter should read from 13.8 to 14.4V at 80 deg. F.

Cadillac has several new alternators suited to the individual need: 42 amp. unit for cars without air conditioning; 63 amp. unit for cars with air conditioning; 80 amp. unit for cars equipped with a trailer towing package.

Also optional for Cadillacs with commercial chassis only is a heavy-duty, 145 amp. Integral Charging System. The AC generator contains all parts of the system, including a voltage adjustment cap, Fig. 32-17. If adjustment is necessary, remove the cap, rotate it 90 deg., then reinsert it in the connector body. Setting desired is aligned with an arrow on the

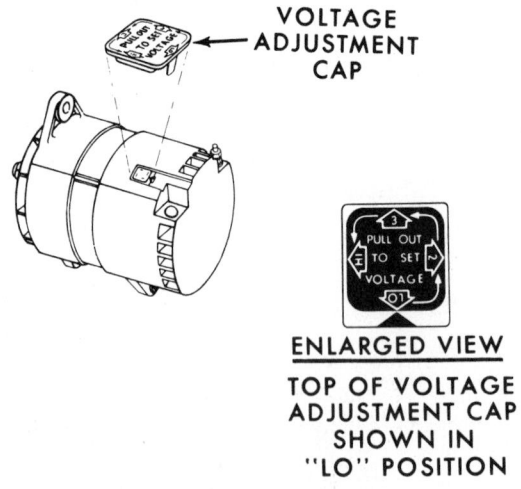

Fig. 32-17. Voltage adjustment on Cadillac's heavy-duty Integral Charging System is accomplished by removing and reinserting voltage adjustment cap in a new position.

connector body: LO is lowest setting; 2 is medium low; 3 is medium high; HI is highest setting.

Ford's side terminal alternator calls for extra care when disconnecting and hooking up leads and push-on connectors when alternator must be removed from the engine.

Generator and Alternator Testing and Servicing

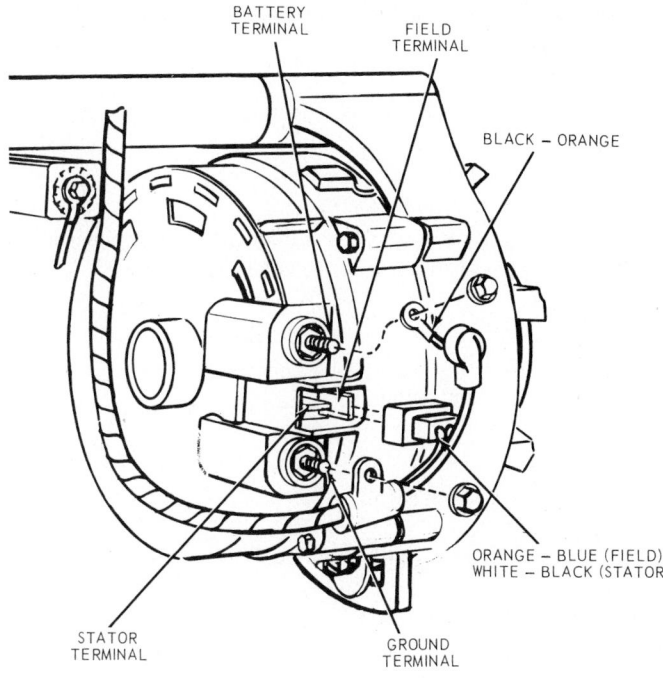

Fig. 32-18. Rear view of Ford's side terminal alternator reveals terminal and terminal identification; also color code for leads and connector.

REMOVAL:

1. Disconnect battery ground cable.
2. Loosen alternator attaching bolt and remove bolt holding adjustment arm to alternator.
3. Disengage drive belt from alternator pulley.

4. Remove electrical connectors from alternator, Fig. 32-18. To release push-on stator and field connectors, depress lock tab and pull straight off terminals.
5. Remove alternator attaching bolt and lift alternator from engine.

INSTALLATION:

1. Position alternator on engine, install spacer (if so equipped) and tighten alternator attaching bolt finger tight.
2. Install bolt that holds adjustment arm to alternator.
3. Position drive belt on alternator pulley and adjust belt tension to specification. NOTE: Apply pressure on alternator front housing adjusting ear when tightening belt.
4. Tighten adjustment arm bolts and alternator mounting bolt.
5. Clean all electrical connections and terminals. Securely connect all leads to alternator.
6. Connect battery ground cable.

American Motors has a charging system diagnosis guide that can be generalized to fit trouble shooting procedures for most late model charging systems:

Ignition On – Engine Running – Indicator Light Dim
1. Defective diode trio.
2. High resistance in wire connections: at alternator output terminal; at starter relay main harness connector; at 4 amp. fuse for gauges; or at ignition feed terminal or printed circuit, Fig. 32-19.

Ignition Switch On – Engine Running
– Indicator Light Flashes On and Off
1. Defective feed wire to printed circuit.

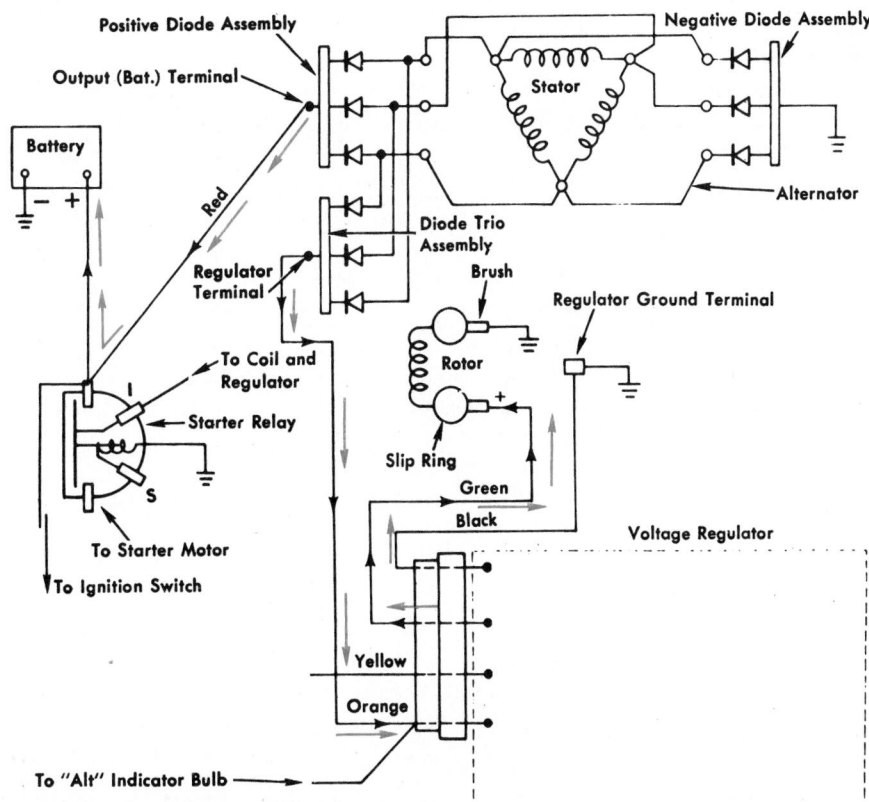

Fig. 32-19. American Motors uses "delta-connected" stator, positive and negative diode assemblies plus diode trio. Diagram also shows regulator hookup and wiring color code.

Ignition On — Engine Running
— Indicator Light Bright
1. Defective seat belt warning relay or buzzer.
2. Defective diode trio.
3. Defective negative or positive diodes.
4. Open printed circuit.
5. Defective voltage regulator.
6. Grounded circuit from printed circuit to main harness connector or from main harness connector to voltage regulator.
7. Open circuit from alternator to starter relay, from starter relay to main harness connector, from main harness connector to 4 amp. fuse, or from 4 amp. fuse to printed circuit.
8. Broken drive belt.
9. Loose drive belt.
10. Defective brush assembly.
11. Open circuit in rotor or stator.

12. Open circuit between regulator terminal on alternator and voltage regulator.

Ignition Switch On — Engine Not Running
— Indicator Light Out
1. Bulb burned out.
2. Open in printed circuit.
3. Open from printed circuit to main harness connector or from main harness connector to voltage regulator.

Ignition Switch Off — Indicator Light Bright
1. Defective positive diode.
2. Defective ignition switch.

Noise In Alternator
1. Loose or misaligned pulley.
2. Worn bearings.
3. Shorted diode (high pitched whine).

REVIEW QUESTIONS
GENERATOR AND ALTERNATOR TESTING, SERVICING

1. What material should be used when cleaning a DC generator commutator?
   a. No. 80 sandpaper.
   b. Very fine emery paper.
   c. No. 00 sandpaper.
2. If the inner surface of a generator cover band is covered with globules of solder, what is indicated?
   a. Generator has been operating at excessive speed.
   b. Generator was producing excessive current.
   c. Generator was not polarized.
3. Where is the field circuit of a "B" type generator grounded?
   a. Within the generator.
   b. Outside the generator.
4. How would you polarize an "A" type generator?
5. How would you polarize a "B" type generator?
6. How would you polarize an alternator?
   a. Connect a jumper lead between output and field terminals of alternator.
   b. Disconnect wire from field terminal of alternator and touch that wire to output terminal.
   c. An alternator does not need to be polarized.
7. The first step in removing an alternator from an engine is to disconnect the ground cable from the negative post of

the battery. True or False?
8. To test a rotor for an "open" circuit, connect test lamp leads to each slip ring. If the lamp lights, the circuit is _____.
9. To test a stator for an "open" circuit, connect one test lamp lead to the stator core and, with the other lead, prod each of the three stator leads. If the lamp lights, the circuit is _____.
10. A diode prevents the alternator from draining current back to the battery. True or False?
11. When adjusting drive belt tension, be sure to pry against the stator section of the alternator. Yes or No?
12. If a voltage adjustment is necessary on Cadillac's 145 amp. Integral Charging System, remove the voltage adjustment cap, turn it _____ deg. and reinsert it in the connector body.
13. When removing an electrical connector from Ford's side terminal alternator, depress the _____ _____ and pull connector straight off terminal.
14. If the charge indicator light on a late model American Motors' car flashes on and off, check for a defective feed wire to the _____ _____.
15. A high pitched whine in an American Motors' alternator could be caused by a shorted _____.

GENERATOR AND ALTERNATOR
REGULATORS AND RELAYS

The generator or alternator produces the electricity needed to charge the battery and to operate electrical equipment. But, by design, its output continues to rise as its speed increases. So, in order to control the output of the generator or alternator, the charging system is provided with a regulator.

Basically, a regulator is an automatic switch which controls charging system output so that excessively high voltage and current will not damage the battery, generator or other units of the system. Regulation is needed on both direct current (DC) generators and on alternating current (AC) generators or alternators to maintain voltage output at a constant rate.

DC GENERATOR REGULATOR OPERATION

The DC generator regulator, Figs. 33-1 and 33-2, controls the voltage and the current by automatically cutting additional resistance in or out of the field circuit of the generator. Varying the resistance will alter the amount of current passing through the fields. This, in turn, changes the strength of the magnetic field and generator output is regulated.

To review: Generator-regulator circuitry uses one of two

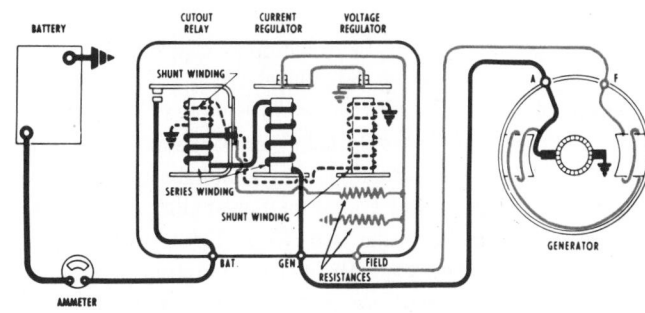

Fig. 33-2. Diagram of Delco-Remy three unit "A" circuit regulator shows: series windings in cutout relay and current regulator in solid black; shunt windings in cutout relay and voltage regulator in dashed black; field circuit and resistors in red.

methods of connecting the additional resistance in the field circuit. In one circuit, the resistance is inserted between the field windings and the ground, Fig. 33-3. This is known as the "A" or standard-duty circuit. In the other setup, additional resistance is connected into the field circuit between the

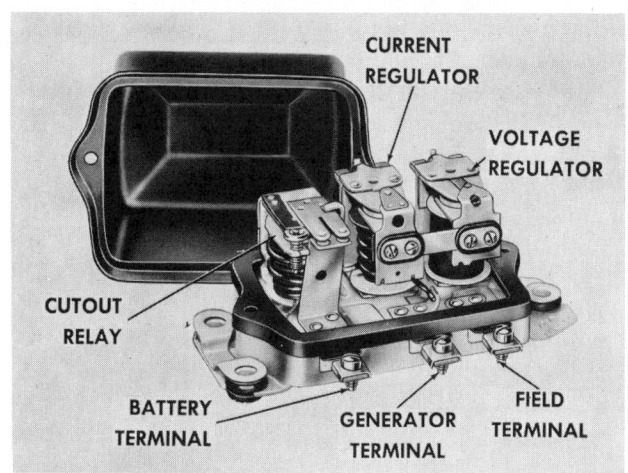

Fig. 33-1. This three unit, single-contact regulator is a typical Delco-Remy assembly used on many "A" circuit DC charging systems.

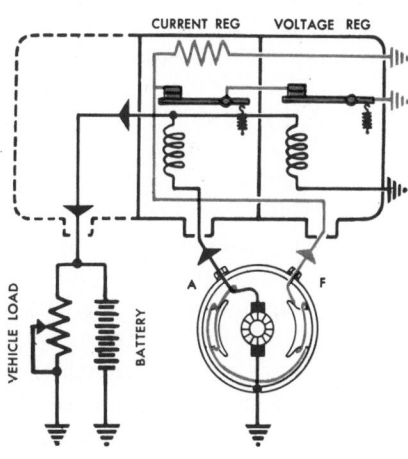

Fig. 33-3. On standard-duty "A" circuit generators, field coil is connected to insulated brush and is grounded through regulator.

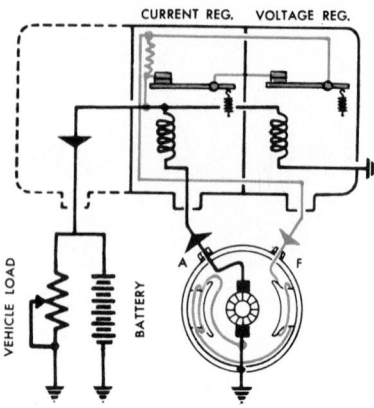

Fig. 33-4. On heavy-duty "B" circuit generators, field coil is connected to insulated brush outside generator. In this setup, field circuit grounds through generator.

insulated brush and the field windings, Fig. 33-4. This is known as the "B" or heavy-duty circuit.

When DC generators were standard equipment, "A" circuit generator regulators were installed on General Motors and Chrysler Corporation passenger cars and light trucks, while "B" circuit regulators were used on Ford-built passenger cars and light trucks, and on American Motors cars.

Regulators used on most DC generator-equipped passenger cars consist of three elements: cutout relay, voltage regulator, and current regulator, Figs. 33-1 and 33-2. However, in some applications using a third brush generator (off-road equipment, for example), only a cutout relay is used. Others utilize a cutout relay and step-voltage control unit. Later installations incorporate a cutout relay and vibrating voltage regulator, or a cutout relay and combined current-voltage unit.

CUTOUT RELAY

The purpose of the cutout relay, Fig. 33-4, is to prevent the battery from discharging through the generator when the engine is stopped or is turning at slow speed. In operation, this relay closes the circuit between the generator and the battery when generator speed is high enough to develop sufficient voltage to charge the battery. It opens the circuit when generator speed is too low to develop charging voltage.

VOLTAGE REGULATOR

The purpose of the voltage regulator, Fig. 33-4, is to prevent charging circuit voltage from exceeding a predetermined safe value, and to maintain a constant voltage in the system. When the battery needs charging, the voltage regulator automatically cuts resistance out of the field circuit, which increases the flow of current and boosts output. When the battery becomes fully charged, the resistance is cut into the field circuit and the charging rate is decreased.

The battery will actually regulate its own charge, within certain temperature limits, if the voltage in the circuit is kept at a constant value. This occurs because opposing or counter voltage of the battery increases as the battery comes up to

charge. A constant-system voltage becomes less and less able to overcome this increasing counter voltage, so that the charge rate to the battery automatically tapers off.

CURRENT REGULATOR

The current regulator is a magnetic switch in the charging circuit designed to protect the generator from overload by limiting current output to a safe value. Usually, the current regulator is the center unit mounted on the base of a three unit regulator, Figs. 33-1 and 33-2.

The current regulator has a series winding of a few turns of heavy wire, and the entire output of the generator passes through this winding. When the current regulator is not working, the spiral spring holds the armature away from the core so the points are in contact. In this position, the generator field circuit is completed to ground through the regulator contact points in series with the voltage regulator contact points.

When generator current output reaches a set value, magnetic pull draws the armature down, opening the contact points. This inserts a resistance into the generator field circuit, reducing its output and relaxing the pull on the armature. With that, the spiral spring pulls the armature up and closes the contact points. This grounds the generator field circuit, causing generator output to increase. This cycle is repeated from 30 to 50 times per second, limiting generator output so it does not exceed its rated maximum.

RESISTANCES

The current and voltage regulator units use one or two common resistances, Fig. 33-5. One is inserted in the field circuit when either the current or voltage regulator unit operates. The second resistance is connected between the regulator field terminal and the cutout relay frame, which places it in parallel with the generator field coils.

The sudden reduction in field current, occurring when either the current or voltage regulator contact points open, is accompanied by a surge of induced voltage in the field coils as the magnetic field changes in strength. These surges are partly dissipated by the two resistors and reduce the arcing at the contact points.

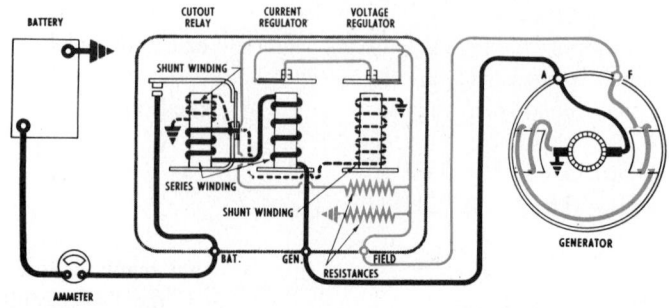

Fig. 33-5. Diagram of three unit "B" circuit Delco-Remy regulator shows: series windings in cutout relay and current regulator in solid black; shunt windings in cutout relay and voltage regulator in dashed black; field circuit and resistors in red.

TEMPERATURE COMPENSATION

Cutout relays, voltage regulators and current regulators are usually wound with copper wire. The resistance of these windings increases as they become warm, so it is necessary to compensate for the change to avoid variation in voltage and current settings.

In most designs, the necessary temperature correction is provided by means of a bimetallic hinge on the armature of the relay or regulator. This bimetallic hinge is made of two thin layers of different metals which are fused together. These metals have different rates of expansion caused by heat.

Thermostatic action takes place as the hinge gets hot. One side expands more than the other, causing the hinge to bend. The hinge acts on the regulator or relay armature to reduce the tension of the spring.

The change of spring tension compensates for the increased resistance of the copper windings as the temperature goes up. Now, the regulator will operate at the same or slightly lower voltage.

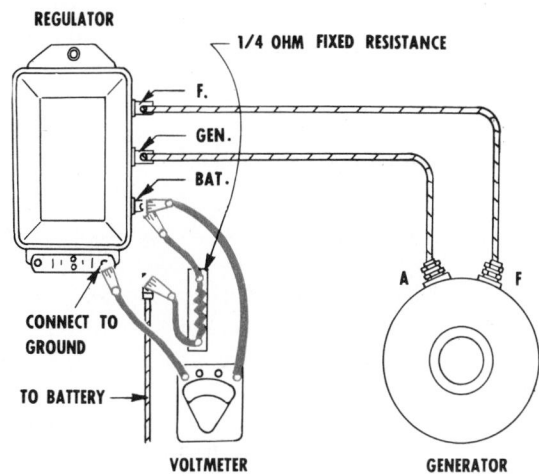

Fig. 33-7. Connect fixed resistance and voltmeter leads, as illustrated, to check voltage regulator settings of "A" circuit Delco-Remy charging system. Note disconnected battery wire.

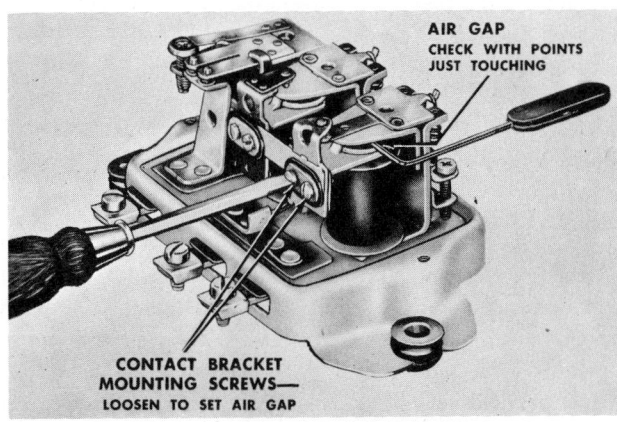

Fig. 33-6. Follow procedure illustrated here to adjust air gap on Delco-Remy single contact voltage regulator.

VOLTAGE REGULATOR ADJUSTMENT

To make the voltage regulator air gap adjustment, push down on armature until contact points are just touching. Measure the air gap between the armature and winding core, Fig. 33-6. Adjust by loosening contact mounting screws and moving mounting bracket as required. Consult manufacturer's specifications.

To test the voltage regulator setting, use what is known as the "fixed 1/4 ohm resistance method." Make connections as shown in Fig. 33-7. Bring regulator up to operating temperature by operating generator at 3500 rpm (generator) for 15 minutes. Regulator cover must be in place.

It is not necessary to measure the current while test is being made, but it is important that no load other than ignition be on the generator. Cycle the generator by reducing its speed until the contacts of the cutout relay open. Then bring generator back to 3500 rpm. (Engine about 1500 rpm.) Note

REGULATOR POLARITY

Most regulators are designed for use with systems having the negative terminal of the battery grounded. Using the wrong polarity regulator on a system will cause the regulator contacts to pit badly and shorten its life.

The polarity of regulators is clearly marked on their base.

DELCO–REMY THREE UNIT REGULATORS

The Delco-Remy three unit single contact regulator, used mostly on General Motors passenger cars, is the "A" circuit type and grounds the field circuit in the regulator. This type regulator has only a single winding on the voltage regulator unit as compared to the two windings used on the two unit regulator and some three unit regulators.

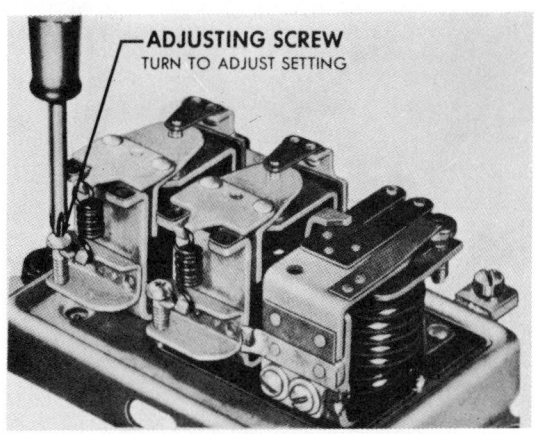

Fig. 33-8. Adjust Delco-Remy single contact voltage regulator by turning adjusting screw clockwise to increase voltage, counterclockwise to reduce voltage.

reading on voltmeter.

Adjust voltage setting by turning adjusting screw, Fig. 33-8. To increase voltage, turn screw clockwise. After each setting, recycle generator.

CUTOUT RELAY ADJUSTMENT

The cutout relay requires three checks and adjustments. These are air gap, point opening, and voltage required to close the contacts. When adjusting the air gap and the point opening, it is necessary to disconnect the battery.

The air gap is measured when the armature is held down so that the contact points are closed. To adjust, loosen the adjusting screws and raise or lower the armature until the desired gap is obtained, Fig. 33-9. Be sure the points are in

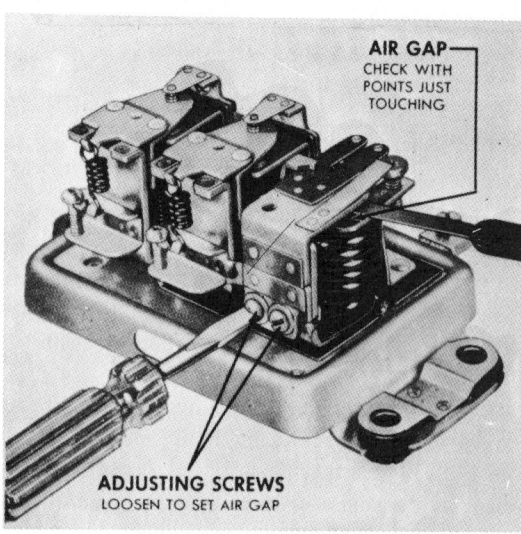

Fig. 33-9. To set air gap of cutout relay in Delco-Remy regulators, raise or lower armature, with battery disconnected.

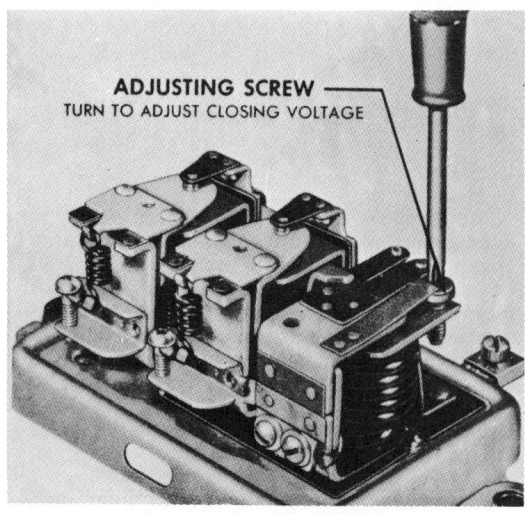

Fig. 33-10. Adjust closing voltage of cutout relay by turning screw clockwise to increase voltage, counterclockwise to lower voltage.

alignment and the adjusting screws are tightened when the adjustment is completed.

The point opening or gap between contacts is adjusted by bending the upper armature stop.

To check the voltage at which the points of the cutout relay close, connect a voltmeter from the "GEN" terminal of the regulator to ground. When making the test, increase generator speed slowly until sufficient voltage is produced to close the relay contact.

To adjust the closing voltage, turn the adjusting screw clockwise to increase the closing voltage and counterclockwise to lower the closing voltage, Fig. 33-10. After each adjustment, the generator should be stopped and then its speed increased slowly to check the closing voltage. Follow manufacturer's specifications.

CURRENT REGULATOR ADJUSTMENT

It is necessary to check the air gap and the current setting of single contact current regulators. Make the air gap check and adjustment in the same manner described for the voltage regulator.

To check the current regulator setting, the voltage regulator must be prevented from operating. One method is shown in Fig. 33-11. Insert a screwdriver through the hole in the

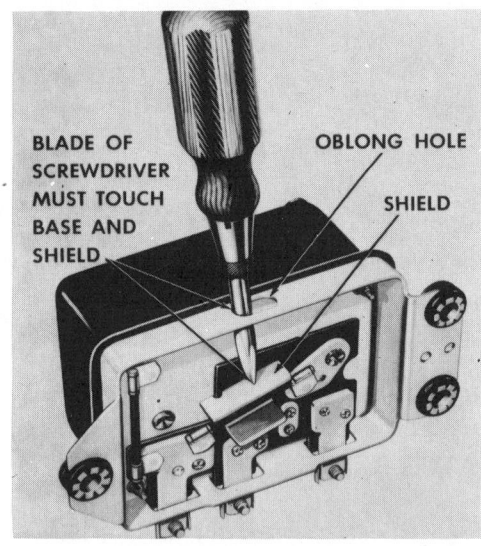

Fig. 33-11. To keep Delco-Remy voltage regulator from operating while checking current regulator setting, insert screwdriver through hole in regulator base.

regulator base, with the screwdriver firmly contacting the regulator base and the shield at the same time.

When making the current setting, connect an ammeter in series with the regulator battery terminal and the wire disconnected from that terminal. Turn on all lights and accessories and operate the generator at specified speed for 15 minutes with the cover in place. Short the voltage regulator by inserting the screwdriver through the base. Cycle generator and note current setting. Adjustment is made by turning the screw controlling spring tension of current regulator.

CHECK FOR OXIDIZED REGULATOR POINTS

Regulator contact points will not operate indefinitely without some attention and the great majority of regulator trouble can be overcome by simple cleaning, plus occasional adjustment. On some negative grounded regulators which have the flat contact point on the regulator armature, loosen the upper contact bracket mounting screws so that the bracket can be tilted to one side, Fig. 33-12.

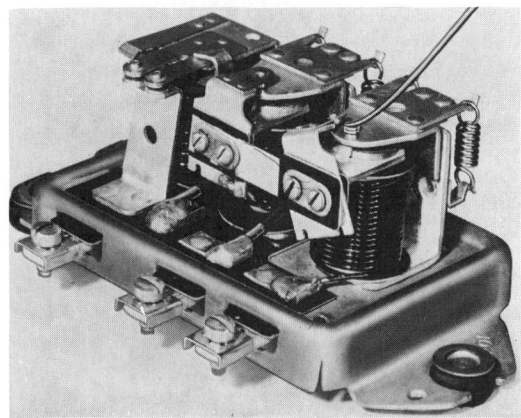

Fig. 33-12. Clean large, flat voltage regulator points on Delco-Remy regulators with a spoon or riffler file. Use crocus cloth on cutout relay points.

The large flat points should be cleaned with a spoon or riffler file. A flat file will not touch the center where wear is most apt to occur. Emery cloth or sandpaper must never be used. Remove all oxides; it is not necessary to remove pitting or cavities.

Cutout relay contact points are of soft material and should not be cleaned with a riffler file. Use crocus cloth or fine abrasive material, followed by cleaning with fresh commercial solvent to remove any foreign material.

DELCO-REMY DOUBLE CONTACT REGULATOR

Because of increased electrical load, many older cars are provided with DC regulators of the double contact type, Fig. 33-13.

CAUTION: On all cars with double contact regulators, NEVER GROUND generator field with regulator connected to generator. This will instantly burn upper set of contact points of regulator. Also, before polarizing the generator of a system fitted with a double contact regulator, always insulate the brushes from the commutator. The instruction given previously for checking current output, voltage output, testing for ground in generator, generator circuit resistance test, and generator ground circuit test are also applicable to double contact regulator systems.

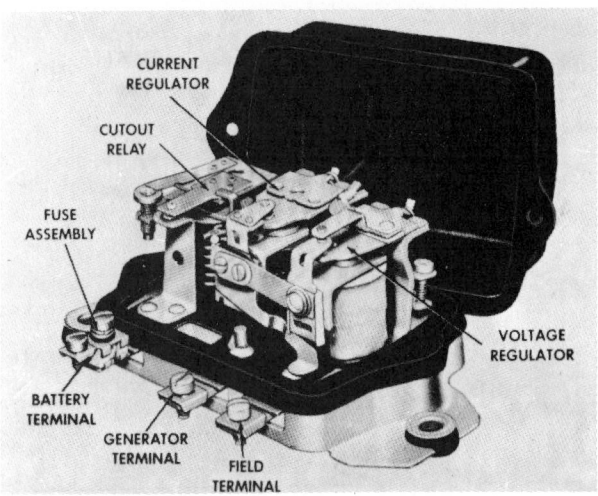

Fig. 33-13. Double contact regulators by Delco-Remy are so-called because voltage regulator unit has two sets of contact points.

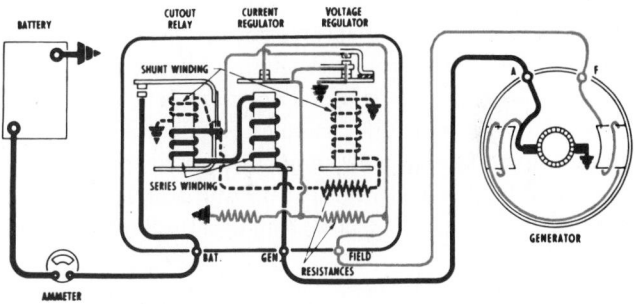

Fig. 33-14. Lower set of voltage regulator points controls voltage at low speeds, upper set of points provides control at high speeds.

Regulators of the double contact type are similar to the single contact unit. However, the voltage regulator unit of a double contact type generator regulator is provided with two sets of points instead of one to accommodate the high field current used in the generator, Fig. 33-14.

The lower set of contacts limits the generator voltage of low speeds as vibration of the contacts intermittently inserts resistance in the generator field circuit. When the speed is increased, the lower set of points can no longer control the voltage and the armature closes the upper set of points. A vibrating action takes place on the upper contacts to regulate the voltage at high speeds. The upper set of contacts alternately places a short circuit across the generator field circuit, or inserts resistance in the circuit, thus limiting the voltage to a predetermined value.

VOLTAGE REGULATOR TESTS

Never ground generator field with regulator connected to generator. This will instantly burn up the upper set of contact points when the system is operated.

To check voltage regulator, make connections shown in Fig.

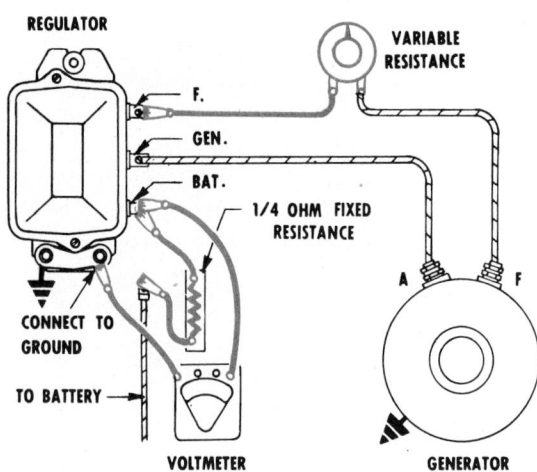

Fig. 33-15. To check the setting of a double voltage regulator, connect voltmeter test leads, 1/4 ohm fixed resistance and variable resistance as indicated in schematic.

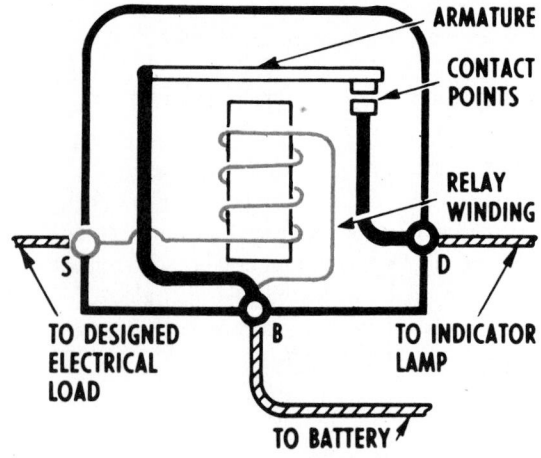

Fig. 33-16. Telltale relays are designed to make and break current flow to an indicator light on dash when a malfunction occurs in circuit.

33-15. Then, with the variable resistance turned to position of minimum resistance, operate generator at a medium or higher speed, so that regulator is operating on upper set of contacts. Operate at that speed for 15 minutes. Regulator cover must be in place. Cycle generator by turning the variable resistance to open position momentarily, then slowly decrease resistance. Regulator should be operating on upper contacts between specified voltages.

Increase generator field control slowly until regulator begins to operate on lower set of contact points. The lower set should operate at specified voltage below the upper set of contacts.

To adjust the voltage setting while operating on the upper set of points, turn the adjusting screw on regulator clockwise to increase voltage setting, Fig. 33-8. Final setting should always be made when increasing the tension on spring.

The difference in voltage between operation of the upper set of contacts and the lower contacts can be increased by slightly increasing air gap, and decreased by slightly decreasing the air gap. This adjustment can be made while the regulator is operating, Fig. 33-9. If it is found necessary to make this air gap adjustment, the voltage setting of both sets of contacts must be rechecked. Air gap should be measured with contact points just touching.

SINGLE WINDING RELAYS

Other relays include:
1. Solenoid relays used in conjunction with starter solenoids to prevent starting motor from operating when engine is running.
2. Horn relays used to close circuit between horns and battery when horn ring or button is depressed.
3. Teltale relays used in connection with indicator lights on dash to warn of a malfunction in a particular electrical circuit, Fig. 33-16.
4. Buzzers in which contact points "buzz" to signal that an

abnormal condition exists in circuit (for example, a preset speed has been exceeded).

These relays utilize a single core with single winding and an armature arrangement which controls the operation of a set of contact points to open and close the circuit being controlled.

FORD REGULATORS

With the exception of a double contact Delco-Remy regulator used on some Ford cars equipped with air conditioning, all Ford regulators are of the "B" circuit type which ground the field inside the generator. The double contact regulator made by Delco-Remy grounds the field in the regulator. Other regulators used on Ford-built automobiles are made by Ford, Bosch or Autolite.

Ford DC generator regulators consist of the familiar three units: cutout relay, current regulator and voltage regulator. The units operate in a manner similar to units previously described.

Temperature compensation in Ford regulators is by means of an armature hinge of bimetal construction. The temperature sensitivity of the bimetal causes the voltage regulator setting to change according to temperature. Therefore, it is necessary to establish a normal or stabilized regulator operating temperature to coincide with the specified setting. The temperature of the surrounding air for this setting is 70 to 80 deg. F. The regulator temperature for this or any other setting is the temperature of the regulator after one-half hour of operation on the car, or after the regulator has been heated until it becomes stabilized.

REGULATORS FOR ALTERNATORS

Regulators most commonly used in AC charging systems are the electromagnetic, transistorized and integral types. Carbon pile regulators are also used, but mainly in heavy-duty, high-output applications.

In electromagnetic regulators, Fig. 33-17, the voltage regulator unit limits voltage output by controlling the amount

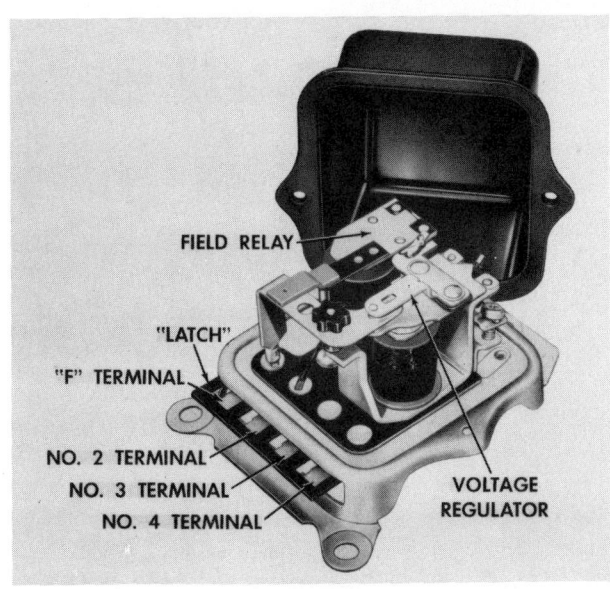

Fig. 33-17. Some General Motors cars utilize a Delcotron AC generator in conjunction with a two unit, double contact regulator.

of current applied to the rotating field (alternator rotor). The field relay, on regulators so equipped, connects the alternator field windings and voltage regulator windings directly to the battery. In some cases, it also serves as an indicator lamp relay.

The conventional cutout relay is eliminated by the diodes in the alternator. The current limiter (regulator) is eliminated by the current-limiting characteristic of alternator design.

Transistorized regulators have no moving parts. Consequently, they have a long life. These regulators usually consist of transistors, diodes, resistors and a capacitor, all working together to regulate alternator field current and thereby limit output voltage to a safe value.

Integral regulators, as the name implies, are built into the alternator. In most applications, the integral regulator is small, flat, transistorized and attached to the inside of slip ring end frame.

DELCO—REMY ALTERNATOR REGULATORS

Delco-Remy electromagnetic regulators utilize a voltage regulator unit to limit voltage output of "Delcotron" AC generators to a preset value. This unit is incorporated in single, two or three unit regulators in many standard equipment applications. The single unit regulator is used only in circuits with an ammeter. The two unit, double contact regulator is suitable for use in circuits containing either an ammeter or indicator lamp. The three unit, double contact regulator contains a voltage regulator, field relay and indicator lamp relay.

Regulator terminals are of the slip-connection type. Slots in the regulator base are keyed to mating surfaces of a connector on the wiring harness to insure correct connections. Since the regulator terminals are the slip-on type, a special adapter must be used during testing so that test connections can be made.

TWO UNIT, DOUBLE CONTACT REGULATORS

Many General Motors cars are equipped with a Delco-Remy two unit regulator, Fig. 33-17. A double contact voltage regulator unit and a field relay unit make up the regulator assembly. If an indicator lamp is used in the charging circuit, it lights when the ignition switch is turned on, goes out when the Delcotron begins to produce charging voltage. If the indicator lamp lights when the Delcotron is in operation, trouble exists in the charging system.

The voltage regulator actually has many stages of operation. A typical two unit, double contact regulator, Fig. 33-18, will operate as follows:

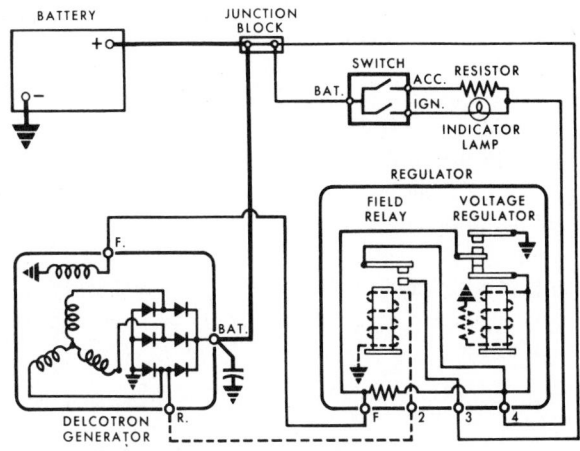

Fig. 33-18. Most alternator equipped cars use an electromagnetic regulator assembly having a double contact voltage regulator unit.

1. Field relay points close when engine starts and Delcotron stator windings put out voltage. As soon as points close, field current is supplied directly from battery instead of through ignition switch and resistance wire, Fig. 33-18.
2. When engine speed is low and battery or accessories need a lot of current, lower contacts of voltage regulator unit remain closed to allow full field current (approximately 2 amps.) to flow.
3. As engine speed increases, or load lessens, lower contacts vibrate between open and closed position to reduce field current to between 2 amps. and 3/4 amp.
4. When speed and load requirement reach a point where exactly 3/4 amp. field current provides needed output, voltage regulator armature will "float" between upper and lower contacts. In this situation, entire field current passes through a resistor that limits current to 3/4 amp.
5. When engine speed is high and load is low, increased voltage in charging circuit will cause voltage regulator armature to be drawn down, closing upper set of contacts to ground circuit and no field current will flow.
6. As engine speed is reduced and load again calls for a small charge, upper contacts will vibrate and field current will flow at from 0 to 3/4 amp., depending on rate of vibration. Erratic operation of any alternator regulator could be

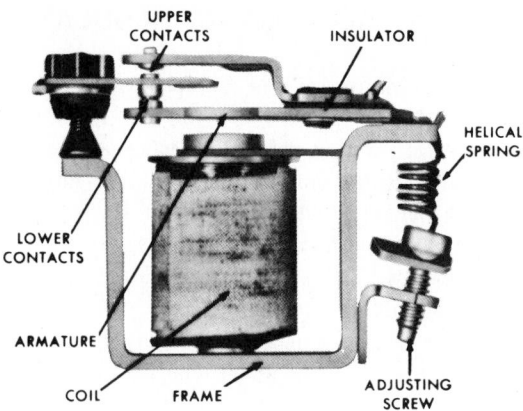

Fig. 33-19. Double contact regulators have upper and lower contacts on a movable armature with stationary contacts mounted on a contact arm in between.

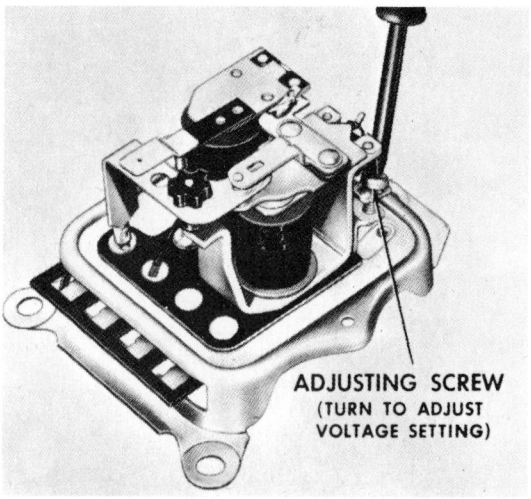

Fig. 33-21. To adjust voltage setting of voltage regulator unit, turn adjusting screw clockwise to increase voltage, counterclockwise to decrease voltage.

caused by dirty or pitted contact points. To clean the contacts, fold over a sheet of very fine silicon carbide abrasive paper and rub it against another piece of abrasive paper to wear off the sharp edges. Then pull it between the contacts to clean them.

Maintain this cleanliness during tests. When checking point gaps, for example, be sure that blade of feeler gauge is absolutely clean.

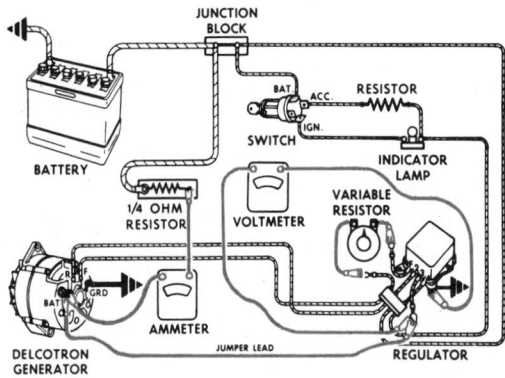

Fig. 33-20. To check voltage of Delco-Remy two unit regulators, connect a test adapter, ammeter, voltmeter, 1/4 ohm resistor, 25 watt variable resistor and jumper lead as indicated.

TWO UNIT REGULATOR TESTS AND ADJUSTMENTS

To test and adjust the voltage regulator setting, make the test connections as shown in Fig. 33-20. Turn the variable resistor to the "no resistance" position and operate the Delcotron for approximately 15 minutes at 1500 rpm with the regulator cover in place. Turn off all accessories and lights, then proceed as follows:

1. Cycle Delcotron: turn variable resistance to "full resistance" position; disconnect leads at No. 2 and No. 4 terminals of wiring harness connector; reconnect both of

these leads; return variable resistance to "no resistance" position.

2. Accelerate engine to approximately 2500 rpm; check voltmeter reading, and compare with manufacturer's specifications. (Typical setting is 13.8 to 14.6 at 85 deg. F.)

3. To adjust voltage setting, turn adjusting screw, Fig. 33-21. Always turn screw clockwise to make final setting to be sure spring holder is seated against head of screw.

4. If specified voltage setting cannot be made, check point opening between upper contacts with lower contacts touching, Fig. 33-22. Check specifications. If adjustment is necessary, bend upper contact arm to obtain correct setting.

5. Cycle Delcotron and recheck voltage setting with cover in place. (When removing and installing cover, remove No. 4 lead at harness connector and jumper wire from Delcotron

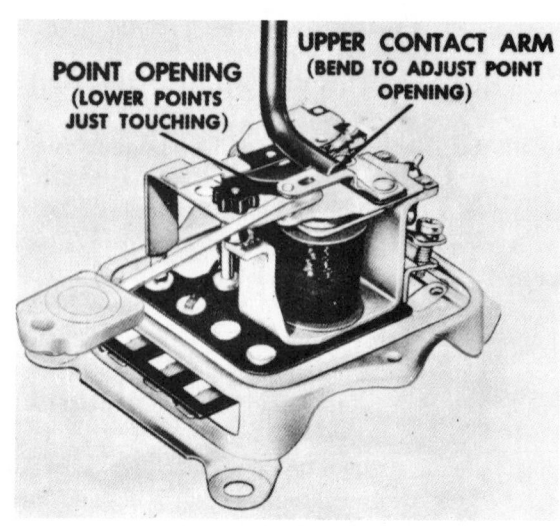

Fig. 33-22. If voltage cannot be set by turning adjusting screw, readjust point gap to specifications by bending upper contact arm.

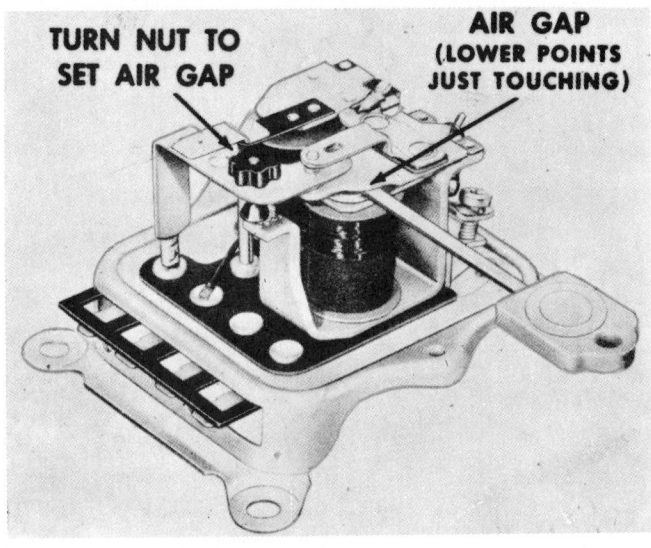

Fig. 33-23. If voltage setting is still out of specification, reset air gap by turning nylon nut on contact support.

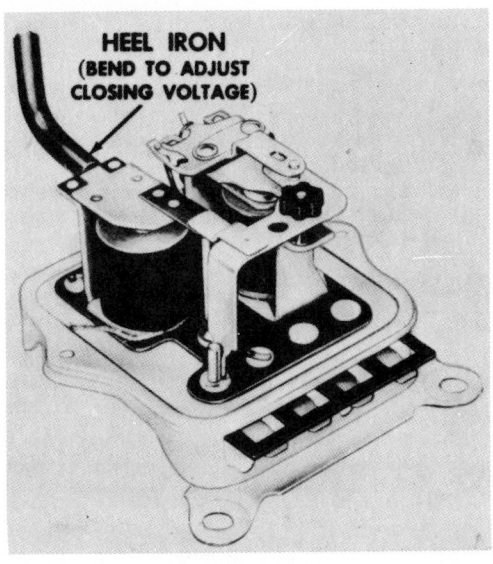

Fig. 33-25. To adjust field relay closing voltage, bend heel iron, then turn variable resistor to "no resistance" position and recheck voltage.

battery terminal.)

6. Slowly increase resistance with engine operating at 2500 rpm until regulator begins to operate on lower set of contacts.

7. Take voltage reading and compare with specifications.

8. To adjust voltage setting while operating on lower set of contacts, increase voltage by turning nylon nut to enlarge air gap between armature and core; decrease voltage setting by turning nut to reduce air gap, Fig. 33-23.

9. If air gap adjustment is necessary, be sure to recheck voltage setting while regulator is operating on upper contacts.

To check closing voltage of the field relay, make test connections shown in Fig. 33-24. Turn the variable resistor to

"full resistance" position with the ignition switch "off," then slowly decrease resistance and watch voltmeter for closing voltage of relay. If necessary, adjust closing voltage setting by bending heel iron of field relay unit, Fig. 33-25.

SINGLE AND THREE UNIT REGULATOR ADJUSTMENTS

Test connections for checking the voltage settings on single unit, double contact regulators are shown in Fig. 33-20, except that leads No. 2 and No. 4 are left disconnected. Compare tests results with specifications. Adjustments are made as indicated in Figs. 33-21 and 33-23.

Test connections for checking the voltage settings on three unit, double contact regulators are shown in Fig. 33-26. Test procedures and adjusting methods are similar to those used on two unit voltage regulators. However, on some models, air gap adjustment is made by sliding the contact support bracket up or down.

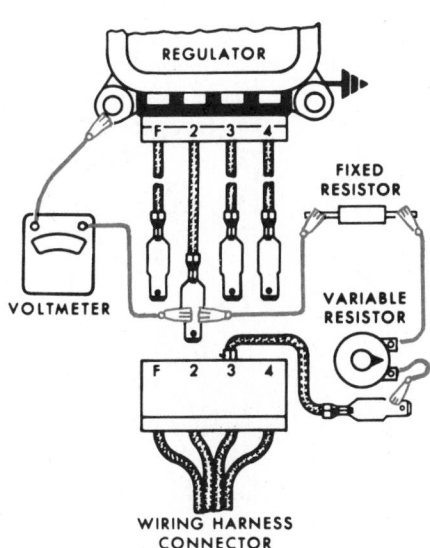

Fig. 33-24. To test field relay closing voltage, connect a 100 ohm variable resistor, a 60 ohm fixed resistor and voltmeter test leads to test adapter.

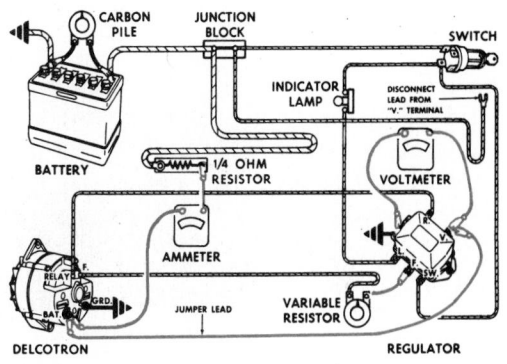

Fig. 33-26. Make these test lead connections to check voltage setting of Delco-Remy three unit regulator used on some General Motors cars.

Three unit regulators are fitted with an indicator lamp relay unit. If the lamp and relay are good, the lamp will light when the ignition switch is turned on, go out when the engine starts. However, if the lamp stays lit after the engine starts, the relay may be defective or the system may have a malfunction.

To check, make connections shown in Fig. 33-27. Operate the engine and check voltage reading. If it is more than 5 volts,

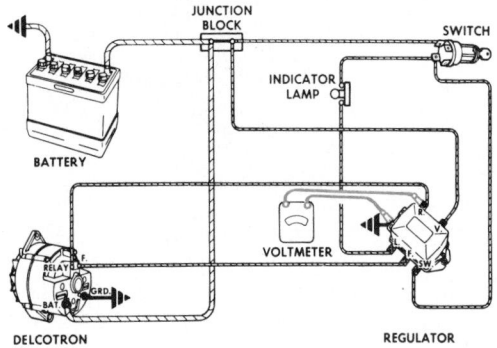

Fig. 33-27. To test indicator lamp circuit of three unit regulators connect voltage leads to regulator (R) terminal and ground.

the indicator lamp relay is defective. If it is less than 5 volts, the trouble is elsewhere in the system. The air gap of the relay can be adjusted by bending the upper contact support; the opening voltage can be adjusted by bending the heel iron as in field relay adjustment, Fig. 33-25.

DELCO—REMY TRANSISTOR REGULATOR

Each of the various models of Delco-Remy transistor is matched to the generator field circuit it must control and to the vehicle application. Inner construction is similar, but the various models are not interchangeable, Fig. 33-28. Basically, the transistor is "switched" on and off to control generator field current. The frequency of switching depends on generator speed and accessory load, with the possibility that the "on-off cycle" may be repeated as often as 7,000 times per second.

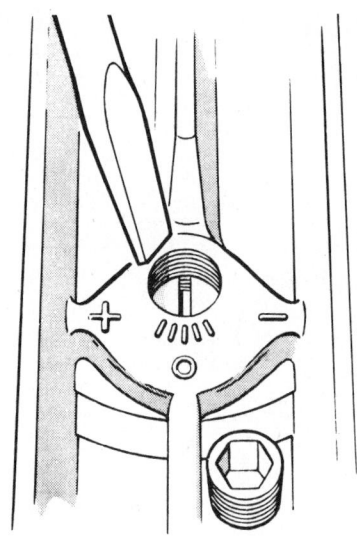

Fig. 33-29. With pipe plug removed from transistor regulator, turn adjusting screw carefully to obtain higher or lower voltage setting as required. Movement of one notch changes setting 0.3V.

To test the voltage regulator setting, operate the engine at approximately 1500 rpm for 15 minutes with the low beam headlights "on." Place a thermometer 1/4 in. from the regulator cover. Connect voltmeter test leads to regulator terminal No. 3 and to ground, and compare the voltmeter reading with the manufacturer's specification for the normal voltage setting at indicated ambient temperature. (Typical setting is 13.9 to 14.7 volts at 85 deg. F.) Adjust voltage regulator as required.

An external adjustment is provided on some models, Fig. 33-28, to permit tailoring generator output to individual driving needs. If adjustment is necessary, remove the access plug from the regulator cover. Note the position of the adjusting screw slot with regard to lines cast on the regulator cover, Fig. 33-29.

For an undercharged battery, turn the adjusting screw one notch clockwise to increase regulator voltage 0.3 volt. For an

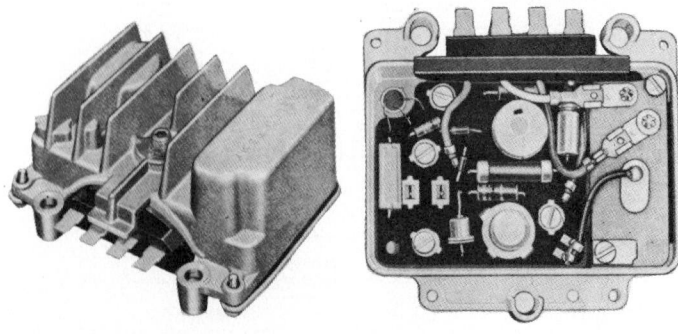

Fig. 33-28. Late model Delco-Remy transistor regulators are similar, but internal construction differs. They are not interchangeable.

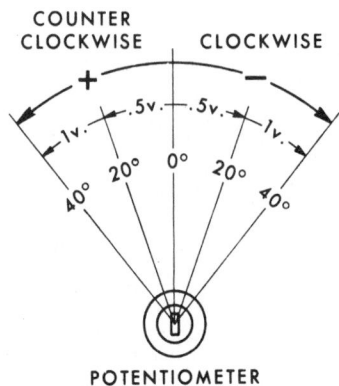

Fig. 33-30. Some Delco-Remy transistor regulators have an internal adjustment to raise or lower voltage. With bottom cover plate removed, turn adjusting screw as marking dictates.

overcharged battery, turn the screw one notch counterclockwise to reduce regulator voltage 0.3 volt. Check for improved battery condition over a reasonable length of time, then repeat the one-notch adjustment if necessary.

On transistor regulators with an internal adjustment, remove the regulator from its mounting with all wiring and voltmeter leads attached to No. 3 terminal and ground. Take off the bottom cover and turn the adjusting screw clockwise to lower regulator voltage, counterclockwise to raise it, Fig. 33-30. (Adjusting screw is very sensitive, should be turned only a few degrees.) Then reinstall the cover, remount the regulator on the vehicle, and retest the voltage regulator setting.

MOTORCRAFT ALTERNATOR REGULATORS

Many Ford Motor Company cars utilize an electromagnetic, two unit alternator regulator consisting of a field relay and a double contact voltage limiter (regulator), Fig. 33-31. As is

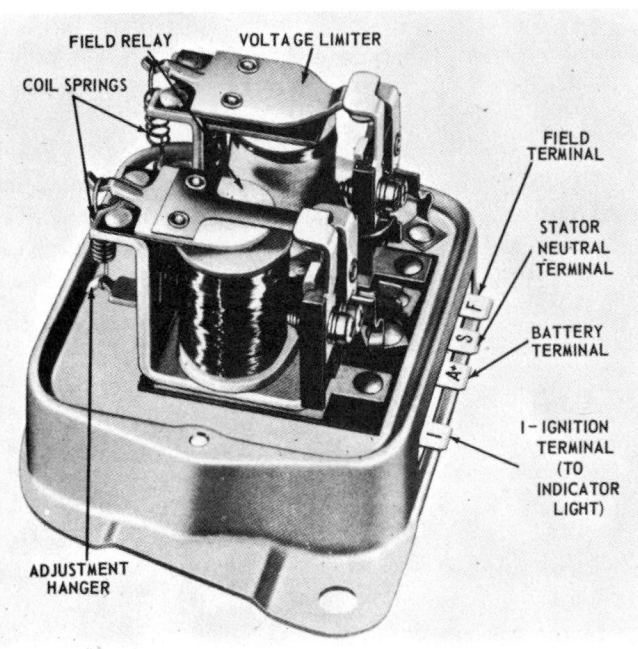

Fig. 33-31. Ford Motorcraft electromagnetic alternator regulators have two control units and four slip-on terminals coded as shown.

generally the case with alternator-equipped charging systems, a cutout relay and a current regulator are not needed.

The field relay connects the battery and alternator output to the field circuit when the engine is running. The double contact voltage limiter controls the amount of current supplied to the rotating field.

At low engine speed and with a load applied, the upper contacts of the voltage limiter are closed, full system voltage is applied to the field and maximum field current will flow. At high engine speed and with little or no load, the lower contacts are closed and no current flows to the field. A resistor is connected from the field terminal to ground to absorb

electrical surges when the voltage limiter armature vibrates on the contacts or floats between them.

On Ford cars with charge indicator lights on the dash, battery current flows through the indicator light and a parallel resistor, and through the voltage limiter contacts to the field coil. When the ignition switch is turned "on," this small current permits the alternator to start charging. On cars with ammeters, closing of the field relay contacts connects battery and alternator output to the field through the voltage limiter contacts.

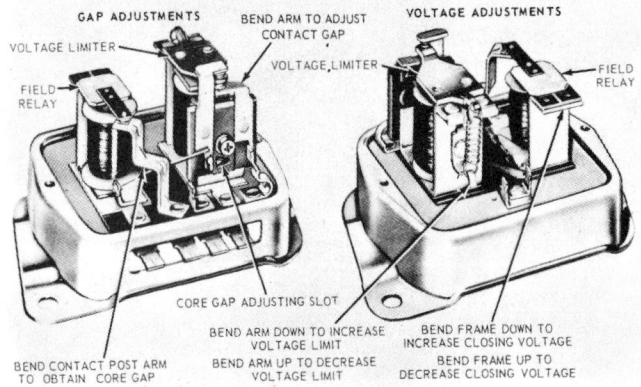

Fig. 33-32. Gap and voltage adjustments are pointed out in front and rear views of typical Motorcraft regulator.

MOTORCRAFT ALTERNATOR REGULATOR ADJUSTMENTS

Certain gap adjustments may be checked before electrical tests are performed. If an adjustment is required, it should be made with the regulator removed from the car.

With the upper contacts of the voltage limiter closed, bend the lower contact bracket to obtain a .017 to .022 in. gap at the lower contacts, Fig. 33-32.

Adjust the core gap with the upper contacts closed. Loosen the lock screw 1/4 turn; insert a screwdriver in the adjustment slot and adjust the core gap to a .049 to .056 in. clearance between the armature and the edge of the core closest to the contacts. Tighten the lock screw and recheck the core gap.

To adjust the field relay, place a .010 to .018 in. feeler gauge on top of core close to the contacts and hold the armature down on the gauge. Then bend the contact post arm until the bottom contact just touches the upper contact.

VOLTAGE TESTS AND ADJUSTMENTS

Make the voltage limiter test with the regulator cover in place and with regulator at normal operating temperature (run engine 20 minutes with hood down). Connect test leads as shown in Fig. 33-33, then proceed as follows:

1. Close battery switch, start engine, then open switch.
2. Operate engine for 5 minutes at 2,000 rpm.
3. With no resistance in circuit, ammeter should indicate less

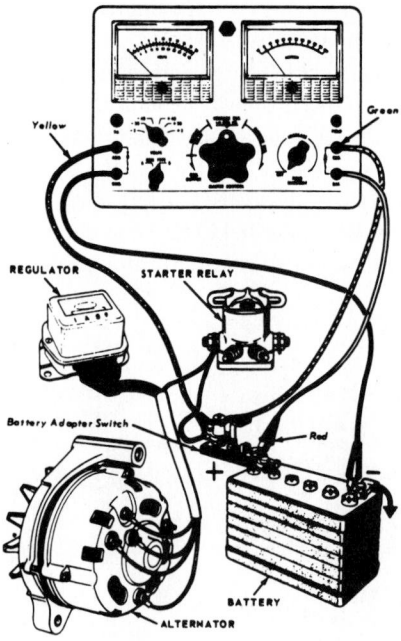

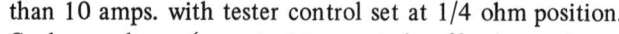

Fig. 33-33. To make a voltage limiter test on a Motorcraft regulator, install a battery adapter switch and connect volt-amp test leads as illustrated.

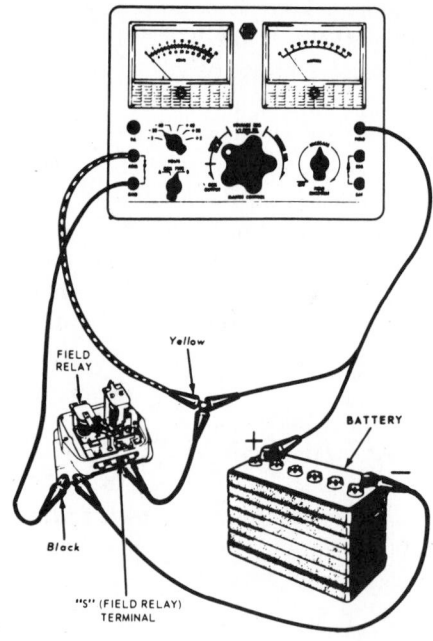

Fig. 33-34. To make a field relay test on a Motorcraft regulator, disconnect regulator terminal plug, install jumper wire and connect volt-amp test leads as shown.

than 10 amps. with tester control set at 1/4 ohm position.

4. Cycle regulator (turn ignition switch off, close adapter switch, start engine, open adapter switch).

5. Check voltmeter reading and reading on thermometer mounted on regulator. Compare readings with these specifications:

    50 deg. — 14.3 to 15.0 volts.
    75 deg. — 14.1 to 14.9 volts.
    100 deg. — 13.9 to 14.7 volts.
    125 deg. — 13.8 to 14.6 volts.

6. Make following voltage limiter adjustments as necessary: Bend spring arm "down" to increase voltage setting, "up" to decrease voltage, Fig. 33-32.

To test the field relay, connect test leads as shown in Fig. 33-34. With the engine at normal operating temperature, proceed as follows:

1. Slowly rotate field resistance control from off position while observing relay contacts and noting voltmeter reading as contacts closed.

2. Make following field relay closing voltage adjustment if necessary: Bend relay frame "down" to increase closing voltage, "up" to decrease closing voltage, Fig. 33-32.

The Motorcraft transistorized voltage regulator, Fig. 33-35, controls alternator voltage output electronically with the use of transistors and diodes. The voltage sensing element is a zener diode which changes its resistance to suit voltage requirements. The field relay unit is mounted separately.

The only adjustment is the voltage limiter setting. With the regulator at normal operating temperature, remove the mounting screws and take off the bottom cover of the regulator. Adjust the 40 ohm adjustable resistor to obtain the correct voltage setting. See Fig. 33-35.

A Leece-Neville regulator, Fig. 33-36, is used on some Ford cars. The unit used in conjunction with an ammeter charge indicator has three terminals. The unit used with a charge indicating light has four terminals.

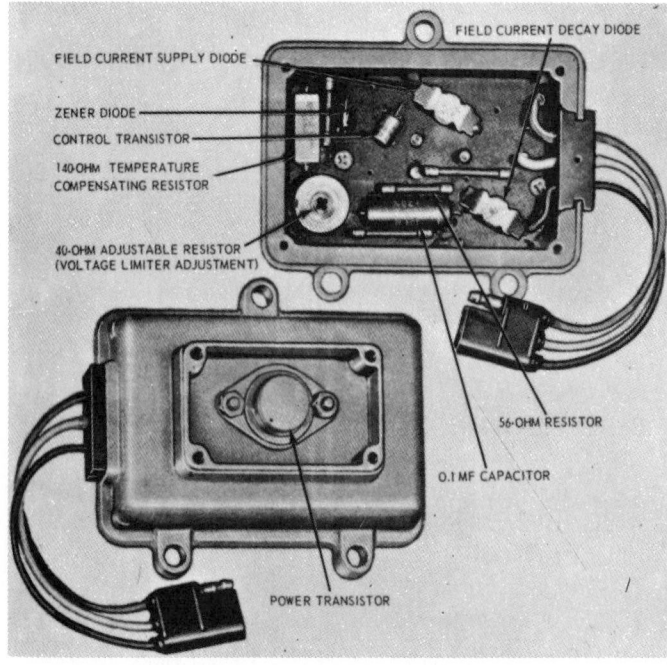

Fig. 33-35. Certain late model Ford-built cars are equipped with Motorcraft transistorized voltage regulators. Bottom cover must be removed for access to 40 ohm adjustable resistor.

AMERICAN MOTORS REGULATORS

Voltage regulators used on late model AMC cars equipped with V-8 engines are electromechanical and nonadjustable. The regulator is mounted on the wheelhouse near the battery.

Regulators used on four and six cylinder engines utilize an integrated circuit to regulate current applied to the alternator field. These nonadjustable, electronic units and the brush holder assembly are attached inside the rear housing of the alternator.

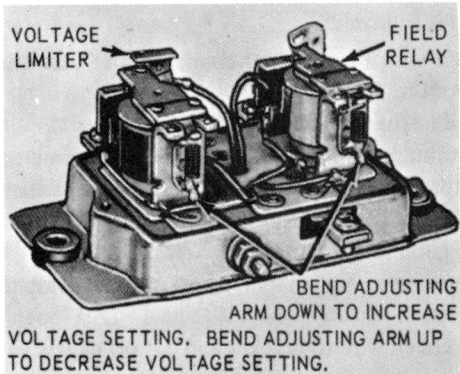

Fig. 33-36. Some Ford models are produced with Leece-Neville alternator regulators as standard equipment. Test procedures and adjustments are similar to Autolite except as noted here.

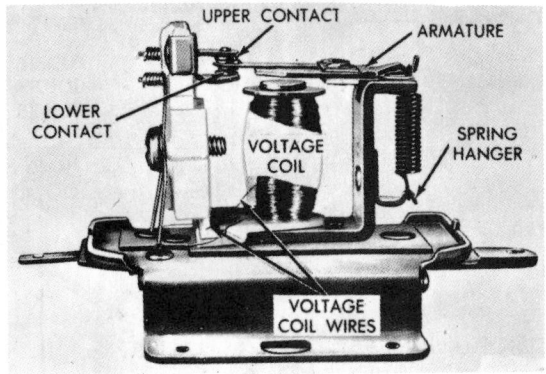

Fig. 33-37. Chrysler cars are equipped with a single unit alternator regulator. Later units have plastic bracket arrangement with upper and lower stationary contacts attached.

CHRYSLER REGULATOR ADJUSTMENT

To test Chrysler's single unit, double contact voltage regulator, Figs. 33-37 and 33-38, operate regulator under a 10 amp. load for 15 minutes. Make connections shown in Fig. 33-39, then:

1. Close battery post adapter bypass switch and start engine.
2. Open bypass switch while making tests.
3. Operate engine at 1250 rpm and rotate tester control knob until ammeter reads 15 amps.
4. Cycle system: rotate field control knob from "direct" to "open," then back to "direct."

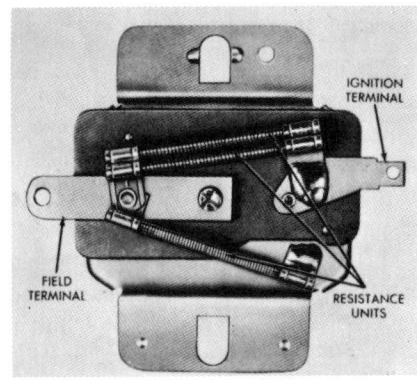

Fig. 33-38. Bottom view of late-type Chrysler alternator regulator reveals three resistance units, two of which are connected in series with field circuit.

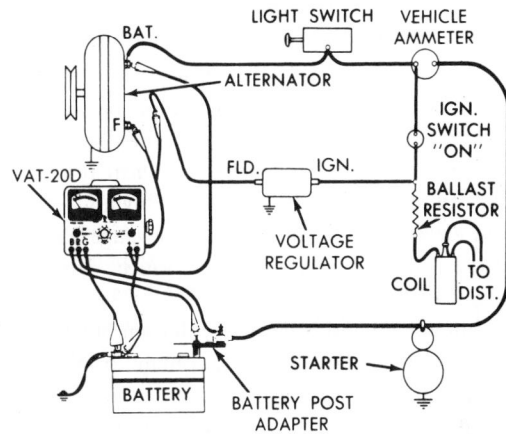

Fig. 33-39. Voltage regulator test on Chrysler regulators calls for installation of a battery post adapter switch to simplify "cycling system" and a volt-amp. tester having a field control unit.

5. Take voltmeter reading and compare with specifications.

If upper contact voltage setting is not within specifications, remove regulator and its mounting, take off regulator cover and adjust setting:

1. Use an insulated bending tool, Fig. 33-40, to bend regulator lower spring hanger "down" to increase voltage setting, "up" to decrease voltage setting.
2. Reinstall, connect and retest regulator after each adjustment of lower spring hanger.
3. If this adjustment fails to bring voltage setting within specifications, measure lower contact gap. It should be .014 in. Bend lower stationary contact bracket if necessary.

To test lower contacts:

1. Increase engine speed 2200 rpm.
2. If test ammeter reads over 5 amps., rotate tester knob to 1/4 ohm position.
3. Cycle system.
4. Read voltmeter for voltage setting of lower contacts and compare with manufacturer's specifications.
5. Voltage should increase not less than 0.2 volt or more than 0.7 volt above the voltage setting of upper contacts.
6. If voltage is still out of specifications, check air gap, Fig.

6. If voltage is out of limits, turn off ignition key and disconnect voltage regulator connector.

7. Remove regulator. Scrape and clean regulator cover, mounting surface, mounting screws and thread holes.

8. Remount regulator and reconnect connector. Retest. If voltage is still out of limits, replace regulator.

FORD ALTERNATOR REGULATORS

Ford uses three different regulators in late models: an electromechanical regulator, a transistorized regulator and an electronic regulator. All operate on the principle of controlling alternator voltage by regulating the alternator field current. The transistorized unit has a voltage limiter adjustment; the electromechanical and electronic units are factory calibrated, sealed and nonadjustable.

To test regulator operation with a voltmeter:

1. Battery must be charged to at least 1.200 specific gravity. Turn off all lights and electrical components. Connect tachometer.

2. Connect voltmeter negative lead to negative battery cable clamp.

3. Connect voltmeter positive lead to positive battery cable clamp.

4. Read voltmeter and record battery voltage.

5. Start engine and operate at approximately 1500 rpm. With no other electrical load, voltmeter reading should increase 1V and not exceed 2V above first recorded battery voltage. NOTE: Take reading when voltmeter needle stops moving.

6. With engine running, turn on heater or air conditioner blower (HIGH) and turn on headlights (high beam).

7. Increase engine speed to 2000 rpm. Voltmeter should indicate a minimum of 0.5V above first recorded battery voltage.

8. If test results are satisfactory, charging system is in good working order.

9. If voltmeter indicates excessive voltage, stop engine and check ground connections between regulator and alternator and/or regulator and engine. Clean and tighten connections securely and repeat Steps 5, 6 and 7.

10. If excessive voltage condition still exists, disconnect regulator wiring plug from regulator and repeat Steps 5, 6 and 7.

11. If excessive voltage condition is eliminated, replace electromechanical regulator with a new unit, or adjust voltage limiter on transistorized unit, Fig. 33-44. Repeat test procedure.

12. If excessive voltage condition still exists with regulator wiring plug disconnected, look for a short in wiring harness between alternator and regulator.

13. If, after Steps 5, 6 and 7 of original test procedure, voltmeter reading does not increase as it should, check for presence of battery voltage at alternator "BAT" terminal and regulator plug "A" terminal. Repair wiring if no voltage is present. Repeat test procedure.

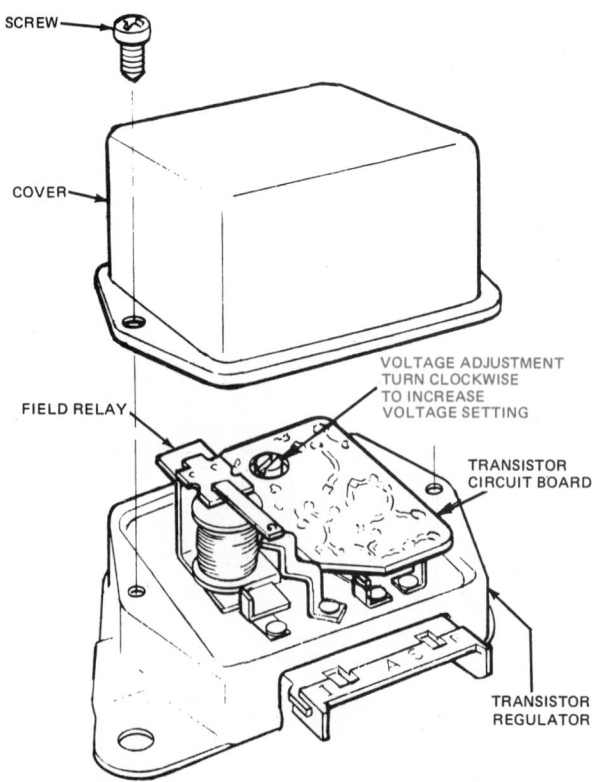

Fig. 33-44. Ford uses an adjustable transistor regulator in charging system of some late model cars. Note removable cover and adjustment screw.

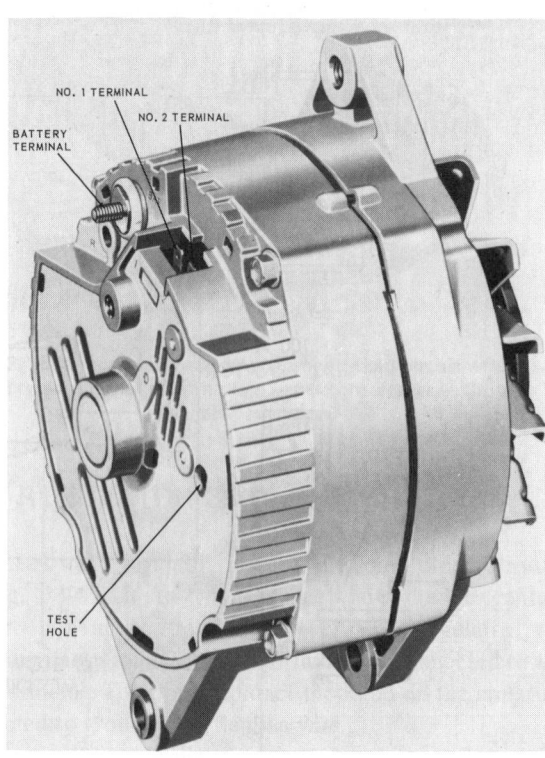

Fig. 33-45. This AC generator is typical of integral regulator type used extensively in GM cars. Note test hole through which screwdriver is inserted to ground winding while testing output.

GM INTEGRAL REGULATOR

The AC generator in most late model General Motors' cars has an integral regulator. With this setup, an output test also serves as a regulator test. Oldsmobile's test procedure is typical of those recommended by other GM divisions.

To test current output and regulator operation:

1. Disconnect battery ground cable.
2. Disconnect wire from AC generator "BAT" terminal.
3. Connect ammeter negative lead (black) to disconnected wire. Connect ammeter positive lead (red) to "BAT" terminal on AC generator.
4. Connect battery ground cable.
5. Turn on all accessories (windshield wipers, rear window defogger, hazard warning lamps, headlights on high beam and blower on high speed). NOTE: If battery is fully charged, use starter to partially discharge battery, or connect a carbon pile resistor across battery and adjust it to obtain maximum current output while running engine.
6. Run engine just fast enough to obtain maximum current reading on ammeter.
7. If ammeter reading is within 10 amp. of rated output, charging system is normal. Turn off all accessories and check for drain on battery or question owner whether or not lights have been left on.
8. If current is not within 10 amp. of rated output, insert a screwdriver in test hole of AC generator end frame, Fig. 33-45. Screwdriver should touch tab in test hole and ground against side of hole.
9. If current is still below 10 amp. of rated output, remove AC generator and disassemble for further testing.
10. If current is within 10 amp of rated output, remove AC generator, disassemble and replace regulator. Reassemble AC generator, reinstall on engine and retest.

REVIEW QUESTIONS
GENERATOR AND ALTERNATOR, REGULATORS AND RELAYS

1. When the battery is low in charge, what does the regulator do?
   a. Cuts resistance out of the generator field circuit.
   b. Cuts resistance into the generator field circuit.
   c. Cuts resistance into the armature circuit.
2. In an "A" circuit generator, the voltage regulator inserts resistance of what point in the circuit?
   a. Between the field windings and ground.
   b. Between the insulated brush and field.
   c. Between the armature and ground.
3. In a "B" circuit generator, the voltage regulator inserts resistance at what point in the circuit?
   a. Between the field windings and ground.
   b. Between the insulated brush and field.
   c. Between the field and ground.
4. What is the purpose of the cutout relay?
   a. Prevent battery from discharging through the generator.
   b. Cut the battery out of the circuit.
   c. Cut resistance out of the field circuit.
5 What is the purpose of the voltage regulator?
   a. Maintain a constant charging rate.
   b. Prevent the circuit voltage from exceeding a predetermined value.
   c. Prevent battery from discharging through the generator.
6. What is the purpose of the current regulator?
   a. Protect the generator from overload.
   b. Maintain a constant charging rate.
   c. Prevent battery from discharging through the generator.
7. In a current regulator, how much of the current passes through the winding?
   a. All the current.
   b. 75 percent.
   c. 50 percent.

8. Why is temperature compensation needed on a voltage regulator?
9. It is necessary to consider the polarity of the electrical system when selecting a voltage regulator. Yes or No?
10. When checking the voltage setting of a voltage regulator, where is the voltmeter connected?
   a. To battery terminal of regulator and to ground.
   b. To ground and armature terminals.
   c. To field and battery terminals.
11. What three adjustments should be made on a cutout relay?
12. When checking the voltage at which cutout relay points close, where should the voltmeter be connected?
   a. To battery and ground connections.
   b. To generator terminal of regulator and ground connections.
   c. To generator and battery connections.
13. When checking the setting of a current regulator, the voltage regulator should be operating. Yes or No?
14. Why are double contact regulators used on some installations?
15. Why are two sets of points used on some voltage regulators?
   a. Because of higher field current.
   b. Because of higher armature current.
   c. Because of heavy-duty battery.
16. What type generator-regulator circuit is used on most Ford cars?
   a. "A" circuit.
   b. "B" circuit.
17. How do Delco-Remy electromagnetic AC generator regulators limit voltage output?
18. What method of adjustment is used on voltage regulator unit of Delco-Remy two unit alternator regulator?
   a. Adjust spring tension.
   b. Bend heel iron.

19. How do you adjust closing voltage of the field relay unit of a Delco-Remy two unit alternator regulator?
    a. Adjust spring tension.
    b. Bend heel iron.
    c. Raise or lower mounting bracket.

20. What job does the transistor do in a Delco-Remy transistor regulator?

21. What is the "makeup" of a Ford Motorcraft alternator regulator?
    a. Voltage regulator and current regulator.
    b. Voltage regulator and field relay.
    c. Current regulator and field relay.

22. What two important requirements must be met before you can adjust any Motorcraft regulator?

23. What is the name of the voltage sensing element used in an Autolite transistorized regulator?

24. How do you adjust the voltage setting of a Leece-Neville regulator used on Ford cars?
    a. Adjust spring tension.
    b. Raise or lower mounting bracket.
    c. Bend adjusting arms.

25. What type alternator regulator is used on most late model Chrysler-built cars?
    a. Electromagnatic.
    b. Electronic.

26. Do older Chrysler alternator regulators use a double contact voltage regulator unit?

27. What is the purpose of using a battery post adapter switch when testing Chrysler alternator regulators?
    a. It sells more switches.
    b. It simplifies "cycling" the system.
    c. It makes it easier to connect test leads.

28. What is the best way to replace a fusible wire in Chrysler regulators?
    a. Unsolder "blown" wire, resolder new one in place.
    b. Snip off "blown" wire, resolder new one in place.
    c. Replace entire regulator.

29. Do Essex regulators used on Chrysler cars call for exactly the same test procedures as Chrysler regulators?

30. When testing charging circuit resistance on a Chrysler Corporation car with an electronic voltage regulator, where do you connect the "jumper" lead?

31. With 20 amp. flow in Chrysler charging system during a circuit resistance test, the voltmeter reading should not exceed _____.

32. Ford uses three different regulators in late model cars. What are they?

33. Late model GM cars have an AC generator with _____ _____.

34. In performing an output test on a late model Oldsmobile AC generator, the ammeter should read within _____ amp of rated output.

35. What is the purpose of the test hole in Oldsmobile's AC generator?

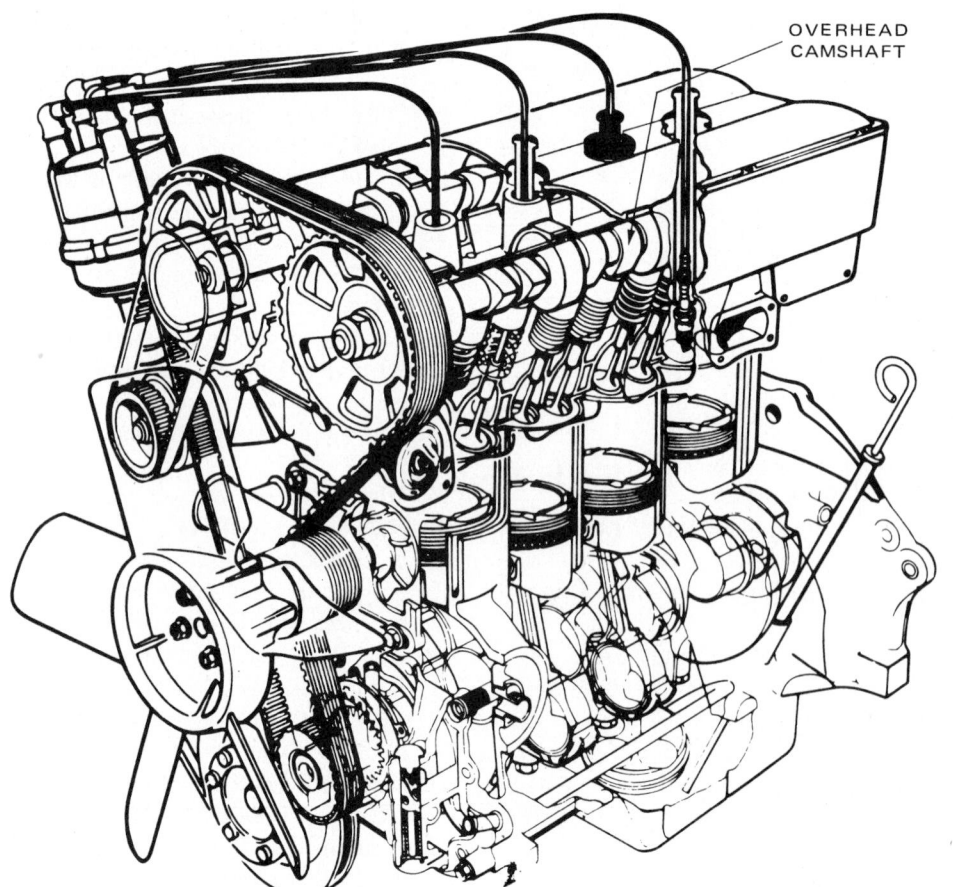

OVERHEAD CAMSHAFT

Industry illustration. Cosworth Vega engine with twin overhead camshafts.   (Chevrolet)

STARTING MOTOR FUNDAMENTALS

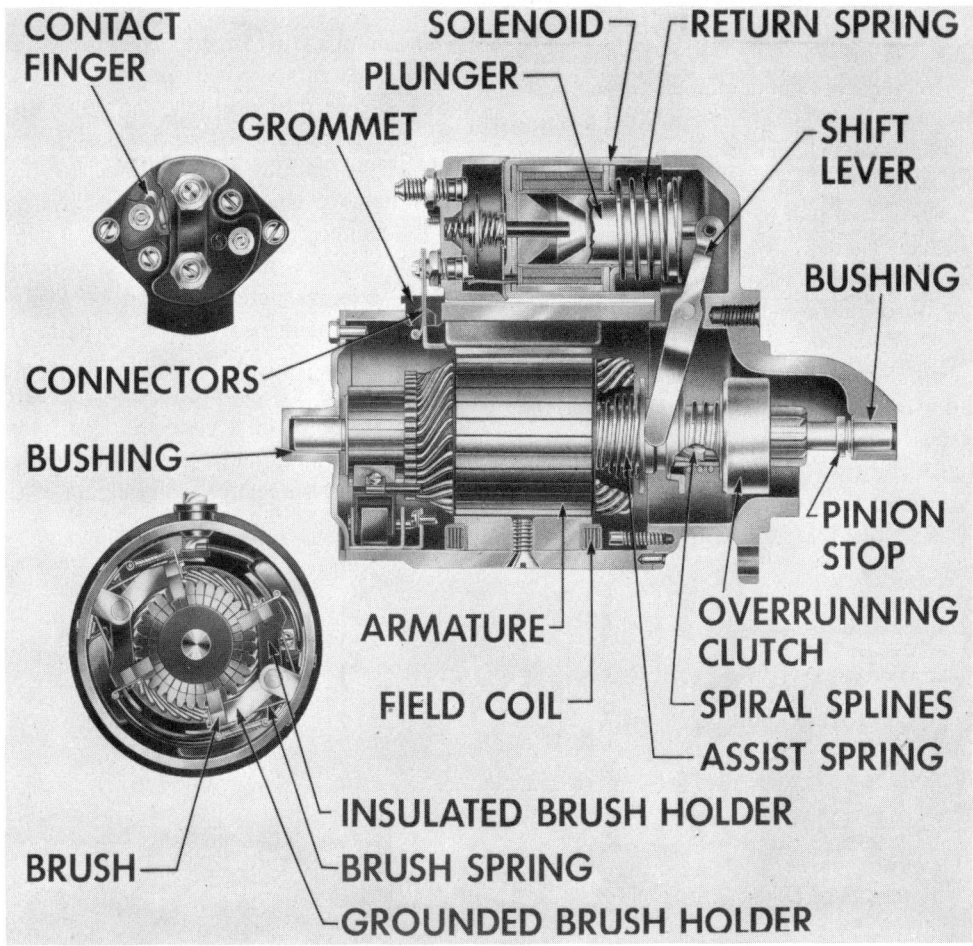

Fig. 34-1. Sectional and end views of starting motor with solenoid and overrunning clutch drive unit.

The starting motor, Fig. 34-1, is an electric motor designed specifically for cranking internal combustion engines at speeds which will permit starting.

Electric motors of this type operate on the principle that a current-carrying conductor will tend to move from a strong magnetic field to a weak magnetic field. To illustrate, if a single current-carrying conductor is placed in a magnetic field created by a permanent magnet, as in Fig. 34-2, the flow of current in the conductor will cause a magnetic field to encircle the conductor in a clockwise direction (left-hand rule applies).

This circular magnetic field will tend to cancel out and weaken those lines of force between the poles of the permanent magnet BELOW the conductor. At the same time, both fields will combine ABOVE the conductor to create a strong magnetic field. In effect, there is more magnetism above the conductor and less below it. Then, as the distorted lines of force tend to straighten out, they exert a downward thrust on the conductor.

Fig. 34-2. When a current-carrying conductor is placed in a magnetic field, conductor will tend to move in direction indicated.

ROTARY MOTION

To see how downward thrust is converted into rotary motion, the conductor is bent into a loop as shown in Fig. 34-3. The rotating part is known as the armature. It will be noted that the ends of the loop are connected to two semicircular brass bars called the commutator. The magnetic field of the two magnetic poles is created by two electromagnets. Current for the electromagnets, which in this case are called field coils, is provided by a battery. Tracing the circuit from the battery, it will be seen that the armature coil and the field coils are connected in series. In other words, when the circuit is completed, current flows from the battery, through the armature winding, through the field coils and back to the battery.

The current flowing through the field coils produces a strong magnetic field which flows from the north pole (on the left) to the south pole (on the right). At the same time, current flowing through the armature coil produces a circular magnetic field to surround the conductor as shown by the arrows, Fig. 34-3. This circular magnetic field is in a clockwise

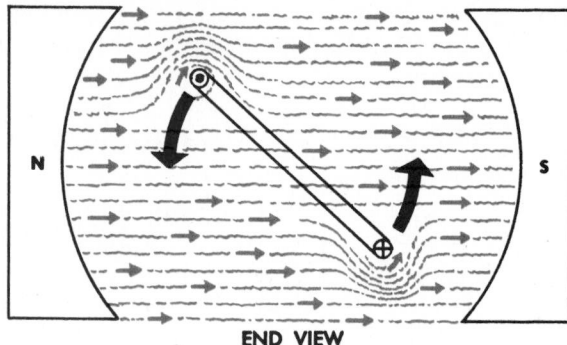

END VIEW

Fig. 34-4. Lines of force react to distortion of magnetic field to create a downward thrust at left and upward thrust at right, causing armature coil to rotate.

The combination of the two thrusts causes the armature to rotate. This rotation will continue, for as the armature coil passes the vertical position, the commutator, which rotates with the armature, will automatically connect the armature coil so the current will continue to flow away from the commutator in the right hand, and toward the commutator in the left-hand coil.

The tendency for a current-carrying coil to move when placed in a magnetic field can be easily demonstrated by means of a permanent magnet, a battery and some wire as shown in Fig. 34-5. After connecting the battery to points A and B, reverse the connections of the battery, and the wire bent in the form of a yoke will then swing in the opposite direction. Turning the horseshoe magnet over from its original position will also change the direction of thrust on the yoke.

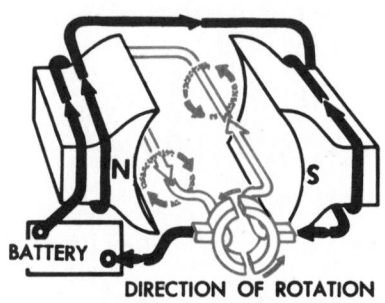

BATTERY

DIRECTION OF ROTATION

Fig. 34-3. Drawing depicts simple electric motor, using single loop of wire for an armature. Note direction of current flow (outlined arrows) and field around conductor (solid arrows).

direction on the left-hand conductor of the armature, and counterclockwise around the right conductor. Note that the current in the left-hand side of the armature coil is flowing toward the commutator, which is the same direction as shown in Fig. 34-2. This results in a downward thrust on the conductor. As the current is flowing in the opposite direction in the right-hand side of the armature coil, the thrust will be in the opposite direction, or upward, Fig. 34-4.

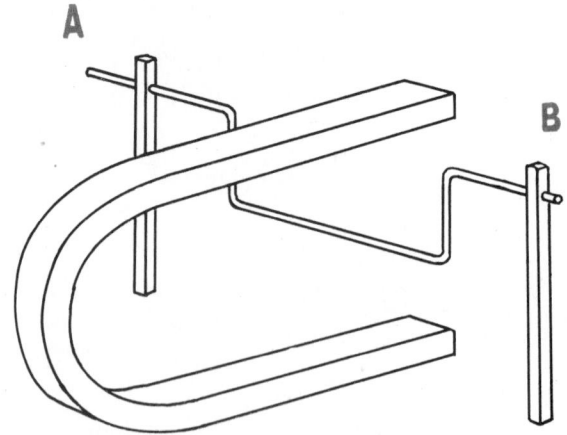

Fig. 34-5. Simple equipment shown will demonstrate basic principle of electric motor. Connecting battery to end of loop of wire, at A and B, will cause loop to swing.

COUNTER VOLTAGE

As was pointed out in the unit on the Fundamentals of Electricity, when any conductor is moved through a magnetic field, a voltage will be induced in the conductor. This condition also occurs in a motor, when the conductor is being supplied with current. However, the voltage induced in the conductor (by virtue of the fact that it is cutting magnetic lines of force) will be in the opposite direction to the voltage that is being supplied to the motor. Such voltage is known as a back voltage, or counter electromotive force, (EMF).

EFFECT OF COUNTER EMF

The effect of the counter EMF is to limit the current in the armature, and as the speed of the armature increases, the counter EMF also increases. As it is opposed to the voltage applied to the motor, it has the effect of decreasing the effective voltage. As a result, the voltage that is forcing current through the armature is the difference between the applied voltage, and the counter EMF. Actually this counter EMF is the same voltage the armature would develop, if it were operated as a generator.

ARMATURE REACTION

Armature reaction in motors is similar to armature reaction in generators. However, the current in a motor armature is opposite to that of a generator rotating in the same direction, Fig. 34-6. As a result, the armature reaction in a motor is

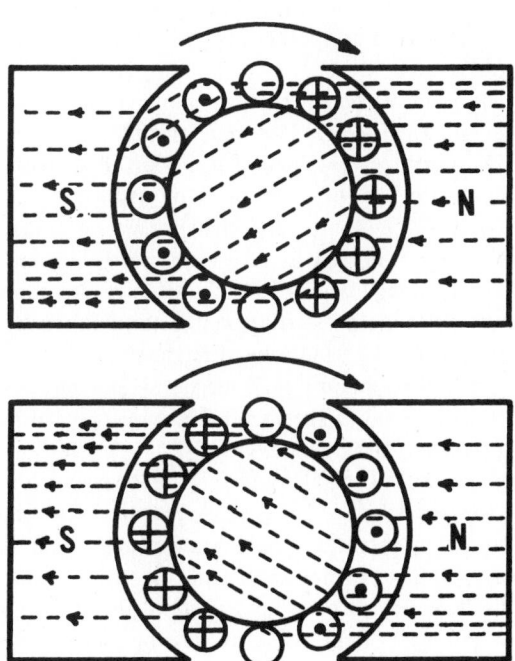

Fig. 34-6. Field distortion caused by armature reaction in a motor is shown in top drawing. Reaction in a generator is diagrammed below.

similar in principle to that of a generator, which is explained in detail in the unit dealing with the fundamentals of generators. The difference lies in the fact that the current in the armature, moving in the opposite direction, will magnetize the armature core in the opposite direction. Since the direction of the field current is the same in both machines, the reaction of the two

magnetic fields in each case, will be in opposite directions. A comparison of the armature reactions of a motor and a generator is shown in Fig. 34-6.

SPEED AND TORQUE CHARACTERISTICS

A reason for using a series-wound motor for cranking internal combustion engines is that it has extremely high torque. Torque varies with the strength of the magnetic field and the current in the armature. With the armature and field coils in series, any increase in current will produce an increase in the strength of the field. As the load on the motor increases, the current through the fields and armature will also increase. As a result, the torque will keep increasing as the load increases. This is shown in Fig. 34-7.

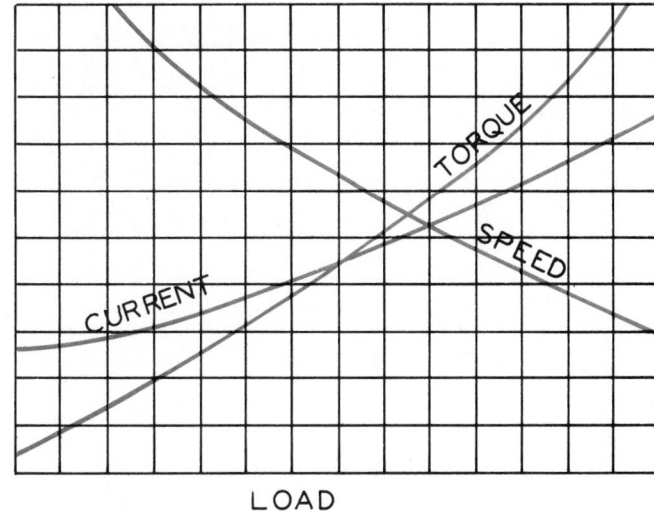

Fig. 34-7. Chart curves illustrate that increased load on a series motor will cause its speed to drop, while current and torque will rise.

The speed of a series-wound motor will vary with the load. For any given load which a certain series motor is driving, there will be a certain definite speed. With heavy loads, series-wound motors will operate at a relatively slow speed. With a light load, such motors will operate at very high speeds. The explanation is as follows:

Any armature always tends to operate at such a speed that the voltage used in overcoming its resistance, plus the counter EMF, will be equal to the voltage being applied to the motor. At heavy loads the current, and the voltage consumed in overcoming the internal resistance, will be large. Consequently, the armature will not have to rotate at very high speed to produce the required counter EMF to equal the applied voltage, However, under light loads, the motor speeds up, inducing a higher counter EMF and decreasing the current through the field and armature coils. This weakens the strength of the field, causing a further increase in armature speed, which again decreases the counter EMF.

With no load, the speed of a series-wound motor will continue to increase to such an extent that centrifugal force will destroy the armature. Series-wound motors used for cranking internal combustion engines should never be operated without a load except under controlled conditions.

In addition to using series-wound motors for cranking purposes, they are also used to operate convertible top mechanisms.

CRANKING MOTOR INTERNAL CIRCUITS

While the basic characteristics of the series-wound motor is used in all cranking motors, there are many modifications of the method of connecting the field coils to each other and to the armature. Some variations in the internal circuits of cranking motors are shown in Figs. 34-8, 34-9 and 34-10.

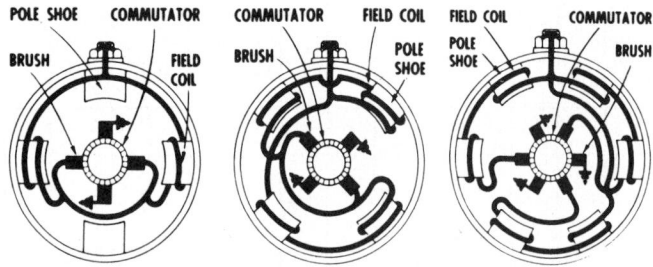

Fig. 34-8. Three typical starting motor circuits include: Left. Four-pole, two-field coil design. Center. Four-pole, four-field coil design. Right. Six-pole, six-field coil design.

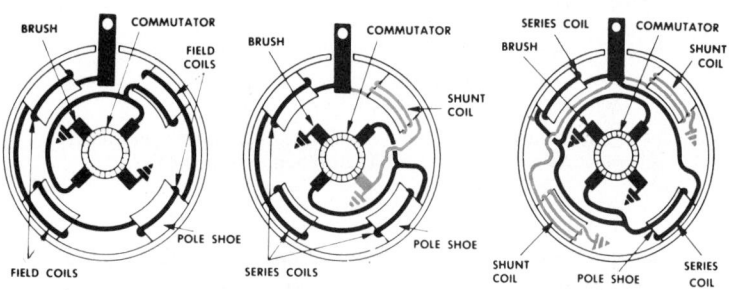

Fig. 34-9. Four-pole starting motor circuits also in use are: Left. Four field coils all in series. Center. Three series field coils and one shunt field coil. Right. Two series field coils and two shunt field coils.

Fig. 34-8 (left) shows a four-pole, two-field coil design which is used on many motors. The two windings are connected in parallel to each other, and in series with the armature, permitting the high current to divide in equal amounts and pass through each field winding. All of the current then passes through the armature, with the result that high cranking torque is produced. The two poles which have no windings serve to complete the magnetic circuits.

The starting motor in Fig. 34-8 (center) has four field coils on four poles. With this setup, one half of the current flows through one pair of windings to one of the insulated brushes, and the other half flows through another pair of windings to the other insulated brush. The current then combines at the commutator and goes through the armature. Four field coil

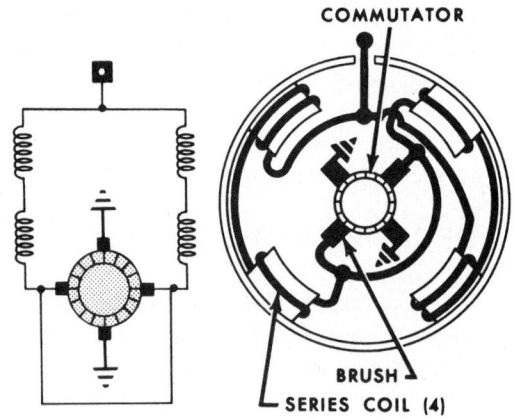

Fig. 34-10. Oldsmobile uses a starting motor with four field coils on Toronado engines. Wiring arrangement is termed a series compound winding. Note separate lead between insulated brushes.

windings of low resistance create stronger magnetic fields and produce starting motors with greater torque and cranking ability.

A variation of this principle of dividing the current is found in starting motors having six poles and six field windings paired off three ways, Fig. 34-8 (right). In this motor, one-third of the current flows through each of three pairs of field windings to one of three insulated brushes. Increasing the number of circuits through the starting motor keeps resistance low, so that high horsepower can be developed for use in heavy-duty service.

As mentioned earlier, a starting motor with all field coils connected in series, Fig. 34-9 (left), would crank up to an extremely high top free speed if not controlled. With this in mind, shunt connections are used on many 12V starting systems, Fig. 34-9 (center and right). Two, or three, heavy field coils are connected in series and carry current to the armature. The remaining field coil, or coils, are shunt coils connected between the starting motor terminal and ground. The shunt coil has two purposes, first to assist the series coils to build up and maintain a high magnetic field, and second to prevent excessive motor speed and noise, when the armature is not subjected to cranking load.

When the motor is cranking the engine, heavy current flows through the series windings to form the magnetic field. The ampere turns in the shunt field provide additional strength under this condition. When the engine starts, the load on the starter immediately drops. Less current flows through the armature and series field, which makes this field weaker, and would result in high rotational speed if the shunt field was not used. The shunt field continues to produce its maximum field strength so that the motor is held to a safe speed.

Oldsmobile has a variation of the internal circuit with four field coils in series between the terminal and armature. Late model Toronado engines are equipped with a modification of this pure series starting motor. Note in Fig. 34-10 that, in addition to windings connecting the four poles of the motor, a separate lead connects the insulated brush leads. Therefore, this winding is not a straight series circuit, and it is not a straight shunt hookup. Oldsmobile calls it a "series compound winding."

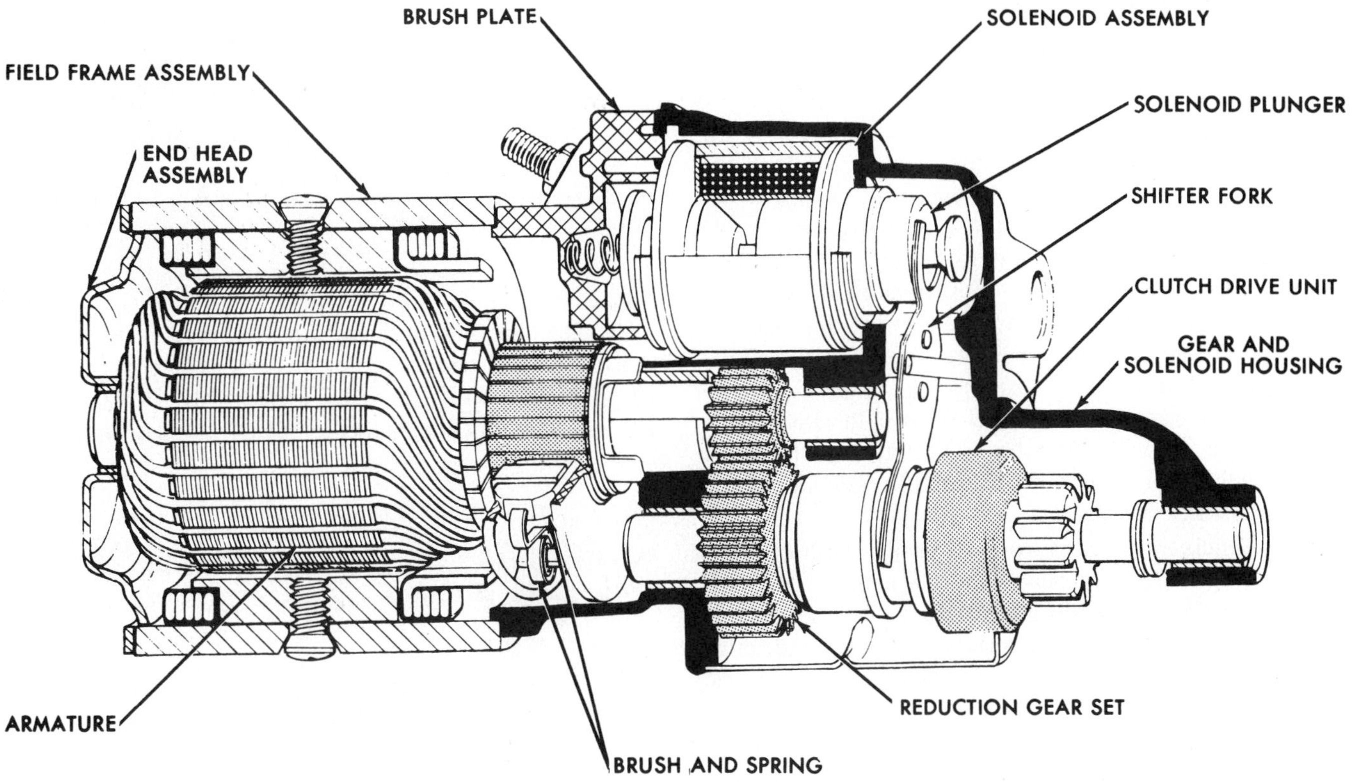

FIELD FRAME ASSEMBLY

BRUSH PLATE

SOLENOID ASSEMBLY

SOLENOID PLUNGER

END HEAD ASSEMBLY

SHIFTER FORK

CLUTCH DRIVE UNIT

GEAR AND SOLENOID HOUSING

ARMATURE

BRUSH AND SPRING

REDUCTION GEAR SET

Fig. 34-11. Chrysler starters use a 2.0 to 1 or a 3.5 to 1 reduction gear set.

STARTER DRIVE CONTROL CIRCUITS

The starting motor armature must revolve at a fairly high speed to produce sufficient torque to rotate the engine. In order to accomplish this, the starter is fitted with a small drive pinion which meshes with gear teeth on the engine flywheel. The gear reduction is approximately 15 to 1. That is, the starter armature revolves 15 times for each revolution of the flywheel, except when special reduction gear motors are used, Fig. 34-11.

As soon as the engine starts, its speed is much greater than the cranking speed, and if the starter drive pinion remained engaged with the flywheel, the starter speed would be excessive. For example, if the engine speed was 1000 rpm, the starter speed would be 15 times as great or 15,000 rpm. Such a speed would ruin the armature and to prevent this, various mechanisms have been developed which permit the gears to mesh during the cranking period but which demesh the gears as soon as the engine is started.

For many years, Bendix drives were used almost exclusively to engage the flywheel. Now, most starters use a positive engagement or pre-engagement drive, Fig. 34-20, a moving pole shoe, Fig. 34-18, or a reduction mechanism, Fig. 34-11.

STARTER DRIVES

A basic starting motor Bendix drive unit is shown in Fig. 34-12. The Bendix drive provides an automatic means of engaging the drive pinion with the flywheel ring gear for

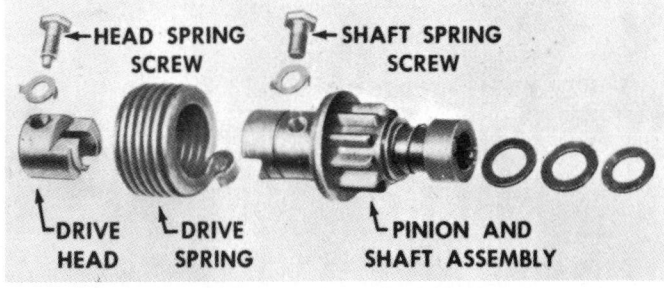

Fig. 34-12. Exploded view of standard Bendix drive shows features of construction and location of head spring screw, which is key to disassembly of starter drive.

cranking the engine and for automatic disengagement of the starter pinion after the engine starts.

The drive pinion is mounted on a threaded sleeve or hollow shaft which has spiral threads that match the internal threads in the drive pinion. The sleeve is a loose fit on the starter motor armature shaft. One end of the sleeve is bolted to the Bendix drive spring, while the other end of the drive spring is keyed and bolted to the armature shaft through the drive head to anchor the assembly in place.

When the starter is not in operation, the pinion is not meshed with the flywheel ring gear. As soon as the circuit is completed to the starter, the starter armature begins to revolve. Being a series-wound motor, its speed increases very rapidly. The threaded drive sleeve picks up speed with the armature as it is driven through the drive spring. However, the drive pinion being a loose fit on the sleeve, does not pick up speed instantly.

The result is that the sleeve turns within the pinion, forcing the pinion along the shaft and into engagement with the flywheel ring gear. The action is similar to holding a nut stationary and turning a screw into it so that the nut would move from one end of the screw to the other. As the drive pinion reaches the stop on the end of the sleeve, it must then rotate with the sleeve and the armature so that the engine is cranked. The drive spring compresses slightly to absorb the shock of engagement.

As the engine starts, the flywheel will spin the drive pinion more rapidly than the armature and threaded sleeve are turning, with the result that the pinion is backed out of mesh with the flywheel ring gear.

Some Bendix drive units are provided with a small anti-drift spring between the drive pinion and the pinion stop which prevents the pinion from drifting into mesh when the engine is running. Another design uses a small anti-drift pin and spring inside the pinion which provides sufficient friction to keep the pinion from drifting into mesh.

The Bendix "Folo-Thru" drive, Fig. 34-13, is designed to hold the drive pinion in mesh with the flywheel ring gear until a predetermined engine speed is reached. In operation, a spring-loaded detent pin locks the pinion in the engaged position. When the engine starts and reaches a given rpm, centrifugal action will force the detent pin out of the notch and allow the pinion to demesh from the flywheel.

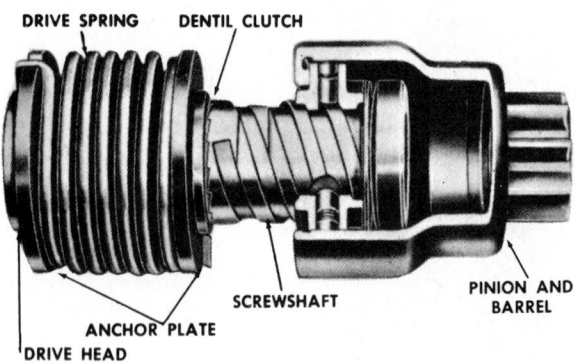

Fig. 34-13. Folo-Thru Bendix Drive must not be disassembled. Remove faulty unit by screwing pinion out to drive position, then force pin from shaft and slide unit from armature shaft. Install new assembly.

BARREL TYPE DRIVE

Starting motors are sometimes equipped with barrel type drive units as shown in Fig. 34-14. In this design the drive pinion, as it meshes, moves toward the starting motor and for that reason is referred to as an inboard drive. The barrel which is integral with the drive pinion is assembled on the spiral sleeve of the shaft assembly. The end of the spiral sleeve is attached to the inner end of the drive spring by an anchor

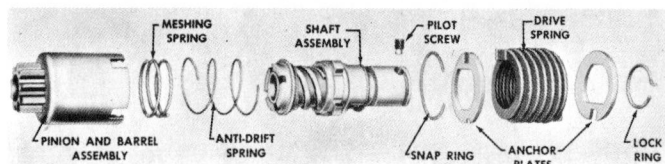

Fig. 34-14. Barrel-type Bendix drive mounts on an extra long armature shaft to facilitate inboard meshing of drive pinion with engine flywheel ring gear.

plate. The other end of the spring is attached to the armature shaft through the end of the drive shaft assembly. The action of the barrel type Bendix unit is similar to that of the standard unit. As the armature begins to rotate, the drive spring and

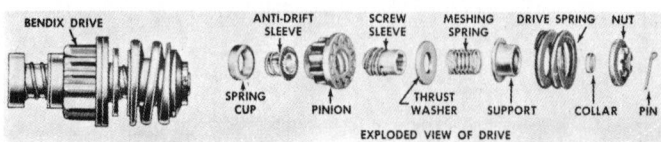

Fig. 34-15. Compression-spring Bendix drive is also designed for inboard meshing. In operation, pinion forces screw sleeve back against drive spring to absorb shock of engagement.

sleeve pick up speed with the armature. The barrel and drive pinion assembly do not pick up speed instantly, with the result that the pinion moves into mesh with the flywheel ring gear. After the engine starts, the pinion is spun out of mesh.

Starting motors on some older Ford engines utilize barrel type drive units, Fig. 34-16. Another type of drive used by

Fig. 34-16. Popular starter drives include: Left. Ratchet barrel spring type. Center. Ratchet barrel rubber base type. Right. Screw type.

Ford is called "Positive Action Drive." This mechanism features a movable pole which is connected to a fork that slides the drive gear into engagement with the flywheel, Fig. 34-17. American Motors' integral positive engagement drive starter is shown in Fig. 34-18.

COMPRESSION SPRING TYPE BENDIX DRIVE

The operation of a compression spring type inboard Bendix drive is somewhat different from the standard and barrel types. In the compression spring type, Fig. 34-15, meshing of the drive pinion forces the screw sleeve back against the drive spring through the thrust-washer and support so that the drive spring is compressed to absorb the shock of engagement.

For heavy-duty cranking, a friction clutch type Bendix drive is used. This type of drive operates in much the same

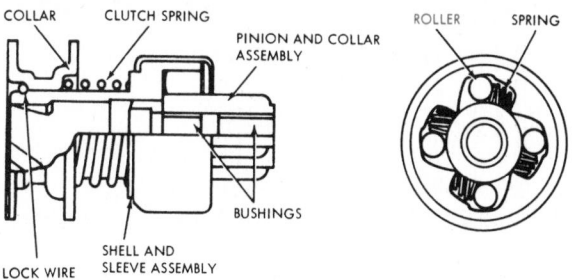

Fig. 34-19. Sectional view of overrunning clutch reveals details of construction and location of rollers in clutch. (Pontiac Motor Div., GM)

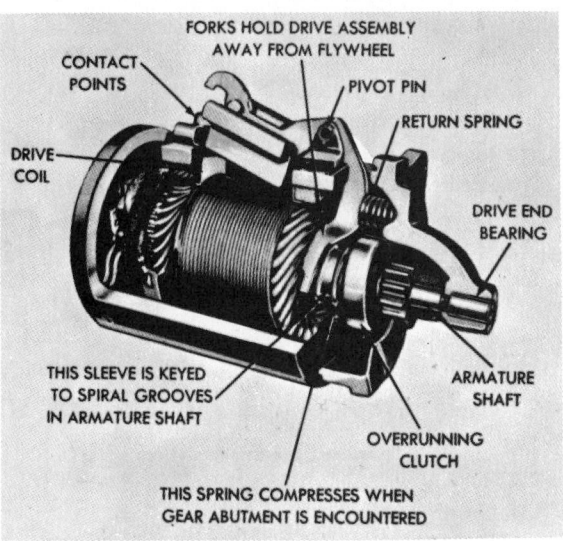

Fig. 34-17. Starting motor on Lincoln Continentals features positive action drive via a starter drive actuating lever.

manner as other Bendix drives, except that it uses a series of spring-loaded clutch plates which slip momentarily under shock of engagement.

OVERRUNNING CLUTCH

The overrunning clutch is designed to provide positive meshing and demeshing of the starter drive pinion and the flywheel ring gear, Fig. 34-19. A solenoid operated unit is illustrated in Figs. 34-20 and 34-21.

The overrunning clutch starter uses a shift lever which slides the clutch and drive pinion assembly along the starter armature shaft so that it can be engaged and disengaged with the flywheel ring gear. The clutch transmits cranking torque from the starter to the flywheel gear, but permits the pinion to overrun (run faster) the armature once the engine has started. This protects the starter armature from excessive speed during the brief interval that the drive pinion remains enmeshed and the engine has started.

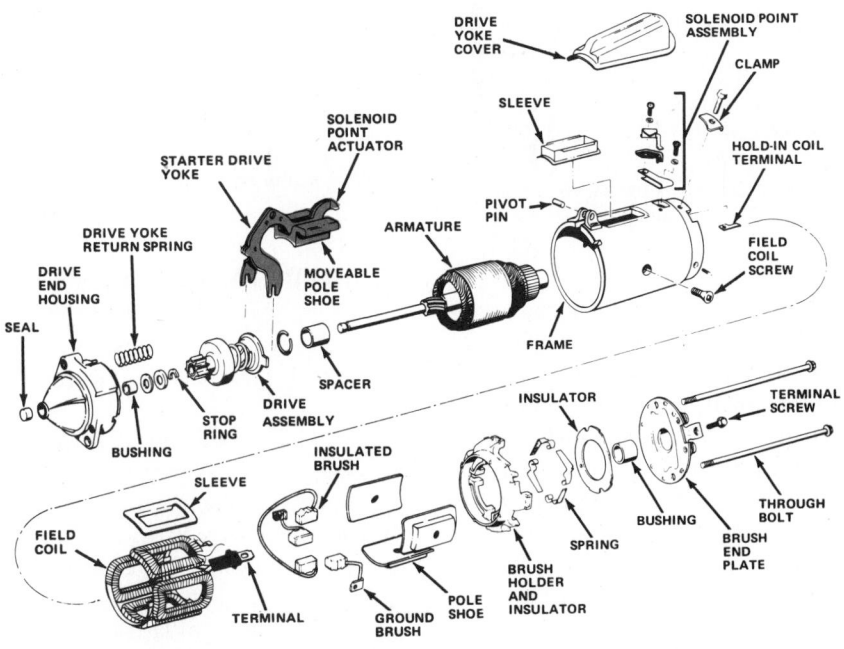

Fig. 34-18. American Motors' starter has a movable pole shoe attached to starter drive yoke (see call out). When heavy current passes through a grounded field coil, pole shoe moves and yoke pushes starter drive into mesh with flywheel.

393

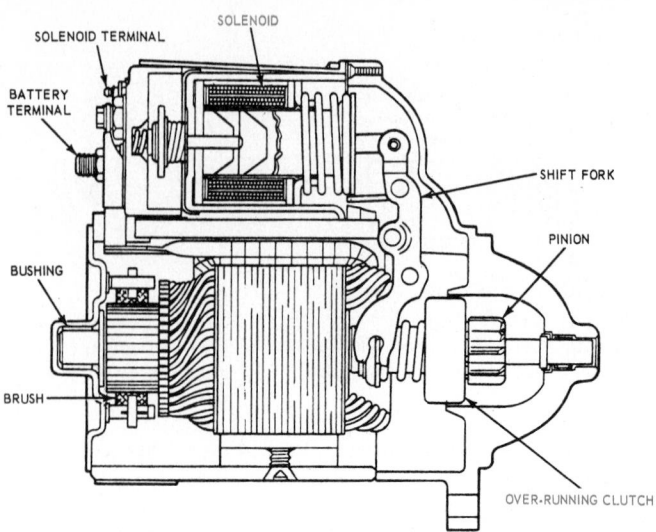

Fig. 34-20. Cutaway view of a Ford starter gives details of solenoid actuated overrunning clutch.

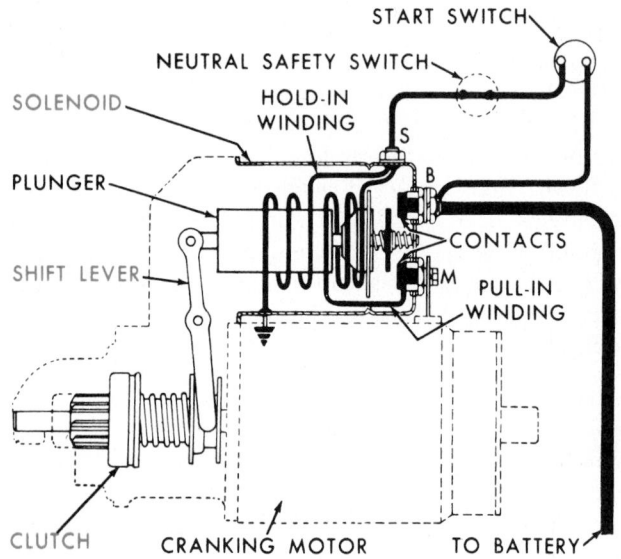

Fig. 34-21. Schematic of Chevrolet starting motor shows windings of solenoid circuit and details of shift lever and clutch-type starter drive

spring-loaded against the ring gear teeth. Then as the armature starts to rotate, the gears are forced into engagement.

As movement of the shift lever is completed, the starter switch is closed so that the starter armature begins to rotate. This rotates the shell and sleeve assembly, causing the rollers to jam tightly in the smaller sections of the shell rotator. The rollers will then jam between the pinion collar and the shell so that the pinion is forced to rotate with the armature and crank the engine.

When the engine starts to operate, it tries to drive the starter armature through the pinion. This causes the pinion to rotate with respect to the shell so that it overruns the shell and armature. The rollers are turned back toward the larger section of the shell notches where they are free and the pinion is therefore permitted to overrun.

This protects armature for the instant that car operator leaves starter switch closed or until automatic controls take over so that shift lever is released. The shift lever spring then pulls the overrunning clutch drive pinion out of mesh with the ring gear. Movement of the shift lever also opens the starting motor switch.

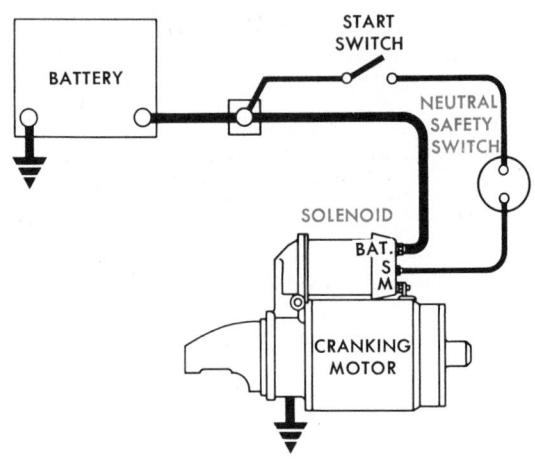

Fig. 34-22. Diagram of simplified starting system circuitry includes neutral safety switch and solenoid hookup. (Delco-Remy Div., GM)

STARTING MOTOR CONTROL CIRCUITS

There are various types of controls used with starting motors. Typical circuits are shown in Figs. 34-20 through 34-24.

On most installations, a magnetic switch or solenoid is connected in series with the ignition switch. When the switch is turned to the "start" position, the magnetic winding becomes connected to the battery so that the magnetic switches are operated and the circuit between the battery and starter is completed, Fig. 34-22.

The solenoid switch on a starting motor also shifts the starter pinion into engagement with the flywheel ring gear. This is accomplished by means of linkage between the solenoid plunger, and the shift lever on the starter. When the circuit is completed to the solenoid, current from the battery passes

The overrunning clutch, consists of a shell and sleeve assembly which is splined internally to match the splines on the starter armature shaft. In that way, both the shell and sleeve assembly and armature shaft must turn together. A pinion and collar assembly fits loosely into the shell, and the collar is in contact with four hardened steel rollers which are assembled into notches cut in the inner face of the shell. The notches taper inward slightly so that there is less room in the end away from the rollers than in the end where the rollers are shown in Fig. 34-19. The rollers are spring-loaded by small springs and plungers.

When the shift lever is operated, the clutch assembly is moved along the armature shaft until the pinion meshes with the flywheel ring gear. If the teeth should butt instead of mesh, the clutch spring compresses so that the pinion is

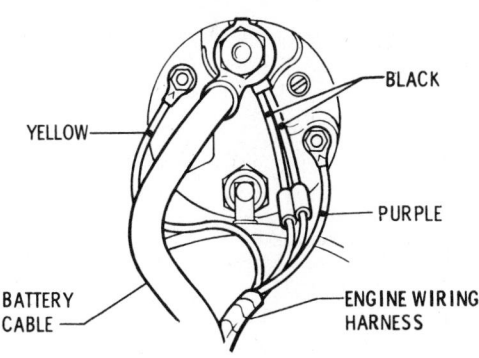

Fig. 34-23. Sketch of connections on a Buick solenoid gives wiring color code. Black leads go to battery terminal of solenoid; yellow lead to "R" terminal; purple lead to "S" terminal.

through two separate windings, known as the "pull-in" and "hold-in" windings. The combined magnetic field of these windings pull in the plunger so the drive pinion is shifted into mesh, and the main contacts of the solenoid switch are closed, Fig. 34-21.

Different size wires are used on the two windings, but approximately the same number of turns. The heavy pull-in winding is used to complete the plunger movement, but when the air gap is decreased, the hold-in winding is sufficient to retain the plunger. The closing of the main switch contacts closes the circuit between the battery and the starter and at the same time shorts out the pull-in winding.

When the control circuit is opened, after the engine is started, current no longer reaches the hold-in winding.

However, current flows from the battery through the main switch contacts, through the pull-in winding (in reverse direction) and then through the hold-in winding to the ground. With the same number of turns of winding in both coils and the same current, the magnetic forces are equal but opposed and counteract each other. Tension of the return spring then causes the plunger to return to the "at rest" position and break the circuit.

Should cranking continue after the control circuit is broken, it would probably be caused by shorted turns in the pull-in circuit or a misalignment of the solenoid resulting in binding of the plunger. Low voltage or an open circuit in the hold-in winding will cause an oscillating action of the plunger. Check for a complete circuit of the hold-in winding as well as the condition of the battery whenever chattering of the switch occurs.

Whenever a solenoid is replaced, it is necessary to adjust the pinion travel. The clearance should be 1/8 to 3/16 in. The exact clearance will vary slightly with different starter designs.

NEUTRAL SAFETY SWITCH: All cars equipped with an automatic transmission are provided with a neutral safety switch, Fig. 34-22. This switch eliminates the possibility of starting the engine while the transmission selector lever is in position to drive the car. Fig. 34-25 shows the neutral safety switch connected in series between the ignition switch and the solenoid.

On some applications, the transmission selector lever may be placed either in PARK or NEUTRAL position before the circuit to the starter is completed. In other installations, it must be placed in PARK position.

STARTER SERVICE

Checking the condition of the starting motor periodically helps reduce roadside failures. The frequency of the inspection is dependent on type of operation. In normal passenger car service, the starting system should be inspected and have an operational test every 10,000 miles. In door-to-door delivery service vehicles, and similar extended duty operations, a more frequent check is desirable.

Modern starters generally do not permit thorough inspection unless disassembled. A visual inspection for clean, tight electrical connections Fig. 34-21, and secure mounting at the flywheel housing is about the extent of a maintenance check. Then operate the starter and observe the speed of rotation and steadiness of operation. To prevent the motor from overheating, do not operate the starter for more than 15 seconds at a time.

If necessary, remove the starter, disassemble it and examine the commutator and brushes. If the commutator is dirty, clean it with a strip of No. 00 sandpaper. If the commutator is rough, pitted or out of round, or if the mica is high (insulation between commutator bars), chuck the armature in lathe and recondition the commutator. Also undercut the mica 1/32 in.

Brushes should be at least half of full length. If not, replace them. The brushes should have free movement in the brush holders. They should have the specified spring tension and make good clean contact with the commutator.

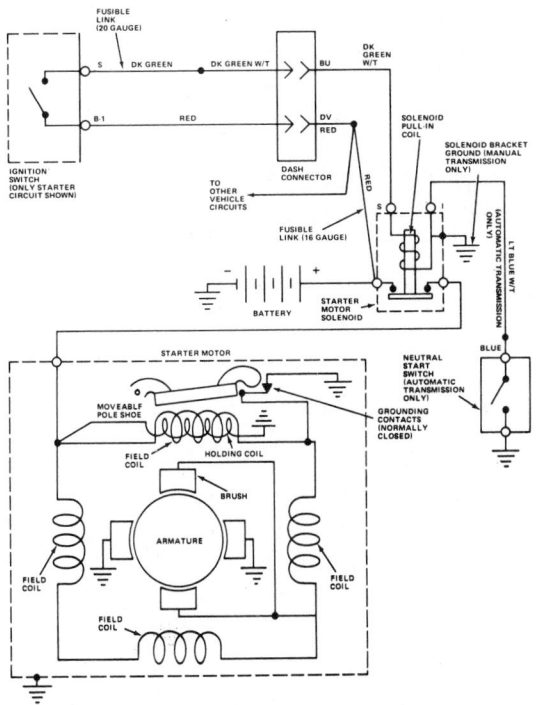

Fig. 34-24. Starting system on American Motors' cars includes battery, starter, relay, ignition switch, cables and wiring.

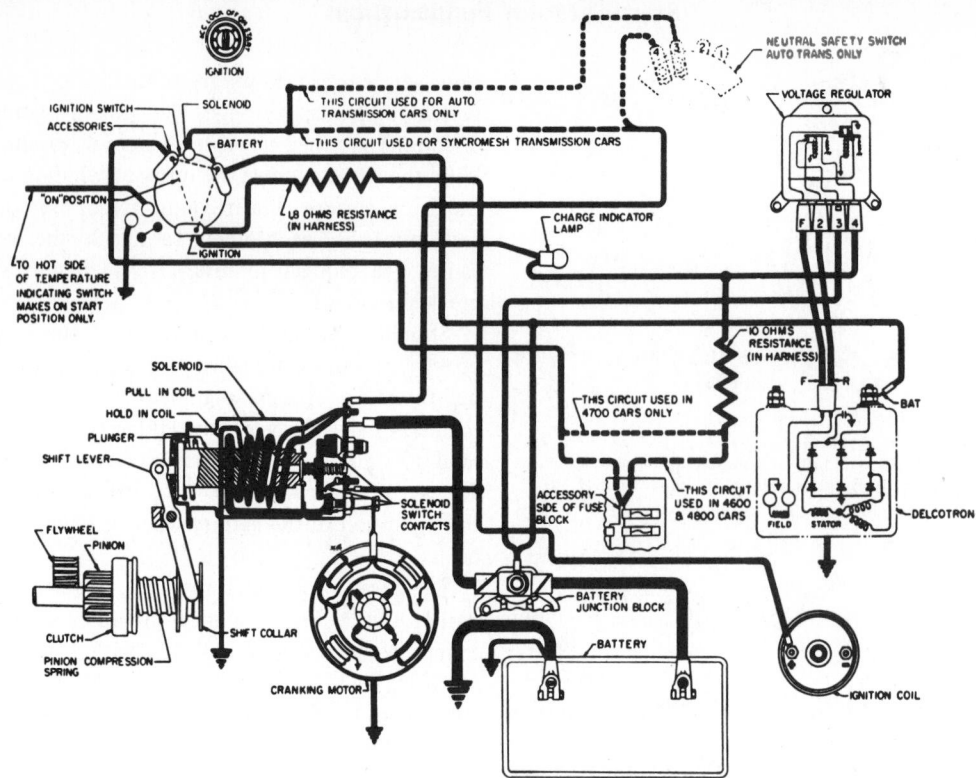

Fig. 34-25. Starting system, used on older Buick engines with automatic transmission, incorporates neutral safety switch connected in control circuit between ignition switch and solenoid.

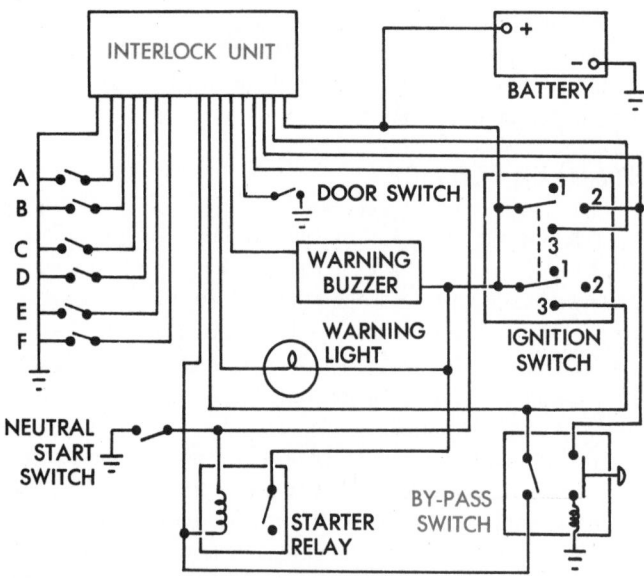

NOTE:
SCHEMATIC IS SHOWN WITH IGNITION SWITCH OFF AS IN POSITION 1. RUN IS POSITION 2. START IS POSITION 3.

Fig. 34-26. Wiring diagram details Chrysler's starter interlock and seat belt warning system. Note bypass switch, located under hood, which permits engine to be cranked without seat belt usage.

Do not use a grease-dissolving or high temperature cleaning solution on armature and field windings. It could damage the insulation. The same caution goes for overrunning clutch drive units, Figs. 34-11 and 34-19.

Test the operation of the drive pinion on the overrunning clutch drive unit. It should turn freely in the overrunning direction, and it should not slip in the driving direction. If the starter is equipped with a basic Bendix drive, Fig. 34-12, clean it with kerosene and lubricate the spiral sleeve lightly with engine oil.

Reassemble the starter, seating the brushes carefully. Align the housings and install the through bolts securely. Install the starter in the opening in the flywheel housing and tighten the attaching bolts to specified torque. Connect the cables and wire leads firmly to clean terminals. See Fig. 34-23.

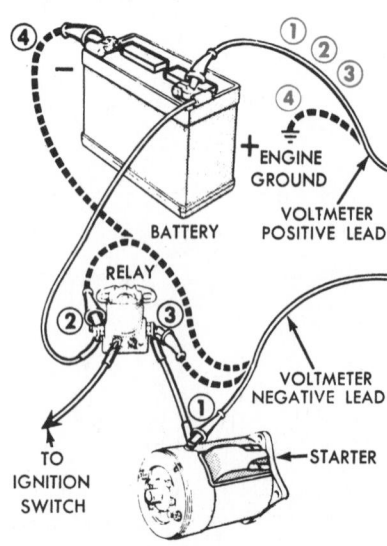

Fig. 34-27. To test for high resistance in vehicle's starting system, use low-reading voltmeter (0.1V calibrations) to test voltage drop between four sets of points indicated.

PASSENGER RESTRAINT SYSTEMS WITH STARTER INTERLOCK

Federal regulations for 1974 models only decreed that shoulder and lap belts must be fastened in both driver and occupied front seat passenger positions before the car can be started. Suitable warning signals in the designs signal the driver and occupants if the belts are not properly fastened.

The car manufacturers met these requirements by installing seat belt/starter interlock systems. The wiring diagram for Chrysler's interlock system is shown in Fig. 34-26. For further information, see chapter on BUILT-IN SAFETY SYSTEMS.

TROUBLESHOOTING: STARTING SYSTEM

TROUBLE: STARTER CRANKS ENGINE SLOWLY

Possible Cause

1. Discharged battery or defective cell.
2. Excessive resistance in starter.
3. Excessive resistance in cranking circuit.
4. Engine oil too heavy for prevailing temperature.
5. Excessive engine friction.

Correction

1. Make specific gravity and load tests. Recharge or replace battery.
2. Disassemble and check for bent armature, or armature dragging on field poles. Straighten or replace armature.
3. Make voltmeter or ohmmeter checks at cable connections, solenoid or relay, and at ground connections. Repair or replace units as required.
4. Change oil to suit conditions.
5. Check the tight-fitting engine bearings, pistons, rings, etc.

TROUBLE: STARTER INOPERATIVE

Possible Cause

1. Loose or corroded battery terminals.
2. Discharged battery.
3. Dead battery.
4. Open starting circuit.
5. Inoperative solenoid or relay.
6. Faulty ignition switch.
7. Defective starter.
8. Inoperative neutral safety switch (cars with automatic transmission).

Correction

1. Clean battery posts and cable clamps. Tighten clamps securely.
2. Recharge battery.
3. Replace battery.
4. Check cable connections, ignition switch, solenoid or relay and wiring. Repair as required.
5. Use heavy jumper cable to bypass unit. Replace faulty solenoid or relay.

6. Replace switch.
7. Disassemble starter and inspect parts. Repair or replace starter.
8. Check operation of switch. Adjust or replace switch.

TROUBLE: STARTER TURNS BUT DRIVE DOES NOT ENGAGE

Possible Cause

1. Broken teeth in flywheel ring gear.
2. Rusted starter drive shaft.
3. Defective starter drive.

Correction

1. Replace ring gear.
2. Clean, lubricate shaft.
3. Replace drive unit.

TROUBLE: STARTER DOES NOT DISENGAGE

Possible Cause

1. Faulty ignition switch.
2. Short circuit in solenoid.
3. Stuck solenoid contact switch plunger.
4. Broken solenoid plunger spring.
5. Faulty starter relay.

Correction

1. Replace switch.
2. Replace solenoid.
3. Repair solenoid.
4. Replace spring or solenoid.
5. Replace relay.

STARTING MOTOR TESTS

There are many ways of testing a starting motor to determine its operating condition. Begin by making on-car tests, follow up with stall and no-load tests, then pinpoint the cause of the problem with bench tests.

ON—CAR STARTING MOTOR TESTS

The following tests will help determine whether or not the starting motor must be removed for stall and no-load tests:

STARTING CIRCUIT TESTS: Excessive resistance in the starting circuit can be located by using an expanded-scale voltmeter to test voltage drop across the various points shown in Fig. 34-27. Remove the primary lead from the ignition coil and crank the engine.

Maximum allowable voltage drop is as follows:

1. With voltmeter connected to positive post of battery and to starter terminal — 0.2V.
2. With voltmeter connected to positive post of battery and to battery terminal of starter relay — 0.1V.
3. With voltmeter connected to positive post of battery and to starter terminal of starter relay — 0.3V.

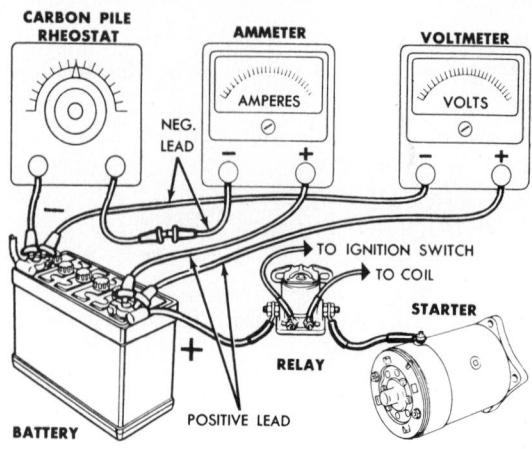

Fig. 34-28. To test starter on-car under load (amperage draw), make test lead connections as shown and crank engine.

4. With voltmeter connected to negative terminal of battery and to ground – 0.1V.

AMPERAGE DRAW TEST: To test starting motor on the car under load:

1. Engine must be at normal operating temperature.
2. Connect test equipment to starting circuit. See Fig. 34-28.
3. Remove primary lead from ignition coil and adjust variable resistance to its maximum resistance to keep current from flowing through ammeter.
4. Then crank the engine for no more than 15 seconds and note the exact reading on the voltmeter.
5. Stop cranking and adjust variable resistance until voltmeter indicates same voltage as obtained while the starter cranked the engine.
6. The ammeter reading will then indicate amperage draw of starting motor under load.
7. Compare this reading with manufacturer's specifications (usually 150 to 200 amps.).

STALL AND NO–LOAD TESTS

The stall test is made to determine resistance of starting motor by testing current draw at a specified voltage with armature locked. The no-load test will determine:
1. How fast the armature will revolve.

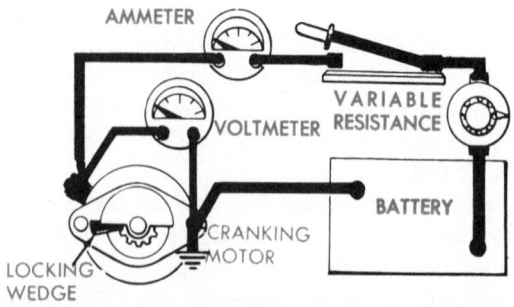

Fig. 34-29. To test starter under stalled conditions, make connections as indicated and install a locking wedge at drive pinion.

2. The amount of current draw at a specified voltage.

STALL TEST: Clamp the starting motor in a vise and proceed as follows:

1. Install a locking wedge between starter drive housing and drive pinion. See Fig. 34-29.
2. Connect high current-carrying variable resistance and an ammeter in series with starter and a battery.
3. Adjust the variable resistance unit to full-resistance position.
4. See that battery is charged to above-normal battery voltage so it can supply proper test voltage as controlled by variable resistance unit.
5. With voltmeter connected across starter terminals, close circuit and adjust resistance until given voltage is obtained at starter.
6. Note amount of current draw on ammeter. It should fall within manufacturer's specified limits.

For example, if specifications call for testing at 4.0, adjust the variable resistance control to obtain this value and take an ammeter reading. A typical current draw specification for this test might be: minimum, 400 amps.; maximum, 450 amps.

NO-LOAD TEST: Connect the test equipment as shown in Fig. 34-30, using a tachometer attached to the end of armature shaft and omitting the locking wedge for this test:

1. Adjust variable resistance control to obtain given voltage value.
2. Starter will run at no-load speed.
3. Read ammeter and tachometer and compare these readings with specifications. Typical test specifications might read: voltage, 11; amperage draw, 90; rpm 1925 to 2400.

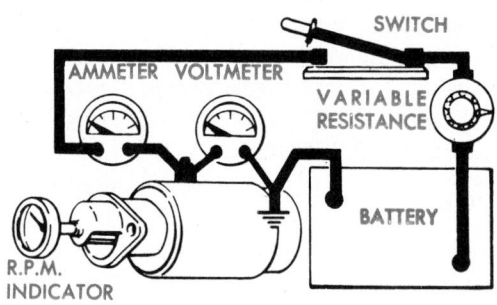

Fig. 34-30. To make no-load test on starter, connect test leads as shown and attach tachometer to armature shaft to provide a means of controlling engine rpm.

BENCH TESTS

When stall or no-load tests indicate that trouble exists in the starting motor, the following bench tests should be performed to pinpoint the cause:

ARMATURE AND FIELD OPEN CIRCUIT TEST: An open circuit armature may sometimes be detected by examining the commutator for evidence of burning. The spot burned on the commutator, is caused by an arc formed every time the commutator segment connected to the open circuited winding passes under a brush.

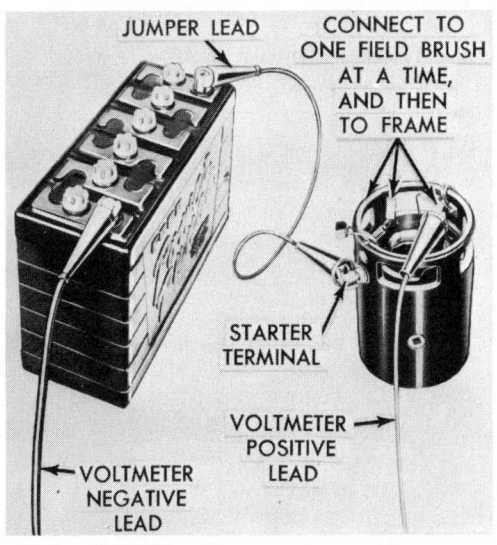

Fig. 34-31. To make open circuit test of field windings of starting motor, connect voltmeter leads and jumper lead to points indicated.

An open circuit test of the field can be made by means of a 110V test lamp, or by connecting a voltmeter and battery as shown in Fig. 34-31. As starters have several windings, it will be necessary to check each winding separately. If the lamp fails to light, or if no reading is obtained on the voltmeter, the field winding is open and will have to be repaired or replaced.

ARMATURE AND FIELD GROUNDED CIRCUIT TEST: This test will determine if the winding insulation has failed, which would permit a conductor to touch the starter frame or armature core. It can be made with a 110V test lamp, or by using a voltmeter.

To test the armature by means of a test lamp, touch one test prod to the armature shaft and touch the other prod to each commutator bar in turn. If the lamp lights, the armature windings are grounded.

To make the test with a voltmeter, connect a jumper lead from the positive post of the battery to the armature shaft. Connect the voltmeter leads to the negative post of the battery and to each commutator bar in turn. See Fig. 34-32. If any voltage is indicated, the windings are grounded.

To test for grounded field circuit windings, connect a jumper lead from one terminal of the starter to one post of the battery. Contact the other post of the battery with a test prod and see that the brushes are away from the frame of the starting motor. Then touch the other test prod to the field

frame of the starting motor. If the lamp lights, or if any voltage is indicated on the meter, the field windings are grounded.

ANALYZING TEST RESULTS

If the starting motor produces a correct amperage draw at specified voltage under the stall test — and if, under no-load conditions, it rotates at normal rpm at specified voltage and amperage draw — the starting motor is in good condition.

However, if trouble is indicated, consider the following:

1. If starting motor fails to rotate under no-load tests and shows high amperage draw, there may be direct ground in armature or field windings or "frozen" armature shaft bearings.

2. Low no-load speed and a high amperage draw indicate a dragging armature, worn bearings, tight or dirty bearings.

3. Low no-load speed and a low current draw, point to high resistance in starting motor. One of the field windings may be "open," or other causes could be broken brush springs, badly worn brushes, high insulation between the commutator bars, extremely dirty or oily commutator.

4. High no-load speed and high current draw is a sign of "shorted" field windings.

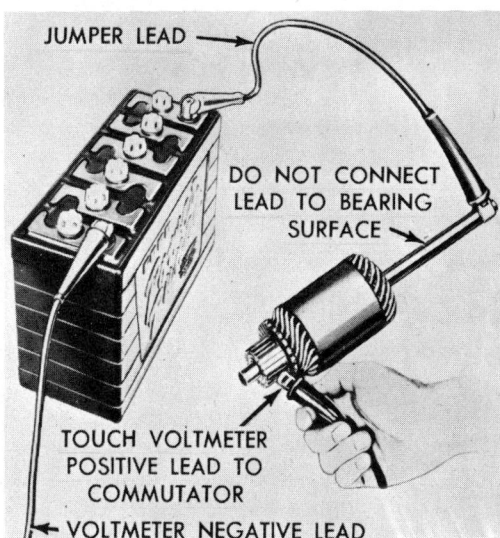

Fig. 34-32. To test for grounded circuit in armature, make above connections and use voltmeter positive lead to probe each commutator bar in turn.

REVIEW QUESTIONS — STARTING MOTOR FUNDAMENTALS

1. In which direction does a current-carrying conductor tend to move when placed in a magnetic field?
   a. From strong magnetic field to weak one.
   b. From weak magnetic field to strong one.
2. Describe the reaction between the field formed around a current-carrying conductor and the field of a permanent magnet.

3. To what are the ends of an armature coil connected?
4. Describe the operation of a starting motor.
5. In an electric motor, the rotating coils are cutting magnetic lines of force, thereby generating voltage. In which direction does the current flow?
   a. In the same as the applied voltage.
   b. Opposed to the applied voltage.

6. Why is a series-wound motor used for cranking an internal combustion engine?
   a. Higher speed.
   b. Higher torque.
   c. Constant speed.
7. On a light load, a series-wound motor will rotate at what speed?
   a. Low speed.
   b. High speed.
   c. Normal speed.
8. As the load on a series motor increases, will the current through the armature and fields increase or decrease?
   a. Increase.
   b. Decrease.
   c. Remain the same.
9. What is the purpose of the shunt field coil used in conjunction with series coils on some cranking motors?
10. What is the approximate gear ratio between the cranking motor pinion and the engine flywheel ring gear?
11. Why is it necessary for the starter pinion to disengage from the flywheel as soon as the engine starts?
12. What is the purpose of the Bendix drive?
13. Describe the operation of an overrunning clutch as used on a starter.
14. For what purpose is a solenoid used in a starting circuit?
15. On what type chassis is a neutral safety switch found and what is its purpose?
16. Give four reasons why a starting motor may fail to crank an engine.
17. There are six tests described for use with cranking motors. Name four of them.
18. Under load, approximately what current will be flowing through a 12 volt starting motor?
    a. 50 amps.
    b. 150 amps.
    c. 300 amps.
19. A burned commutator is usually an indication of what condition?

DIESEL   **GASOLINE**

Oldsmobile compares the sizes of two starting motors available for use on 260 cu. in. (4.3 litre) engines for 1979. Note that the heavy-duty starter at left is used on the "4.3 litre diesel."

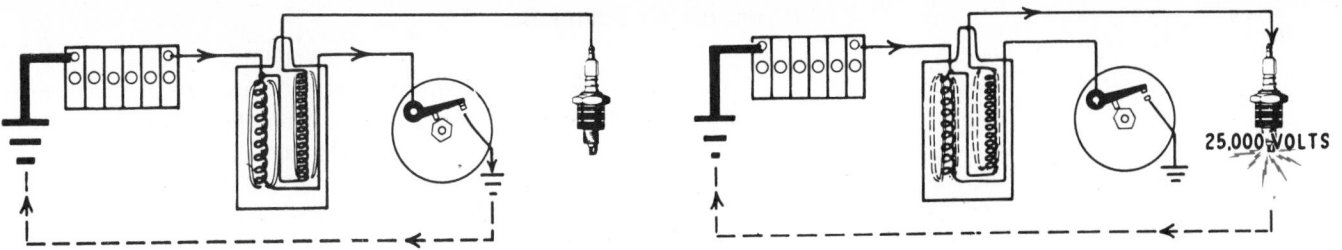

Fig. 35-1. Diagram of typical automotive ignition system in operation. Left. With breaker points closed, coil magnetic field is energized by current flowing in primary circuit. Right. When points break, coil magnetic field collapses and induces high voltage in secondary circuit.

ENGINE
IGNITION

The ignition system on an internal combustion engine provides the spark that ignites the combustible air-fuel mixture in the combustion chamber.

Modern ignition systems operate from a battery. Conventional systems consist of the battery, ignition coil, distributor, condenser, ignition switch, spark plugs, resistor and the necessary low and high tension wiring. Fig. 35-1 shows a wiring diagram of a typical 12V ignition system having these components. Electronic ignition systems will be covered later in this chapter.

FUNCTION OF COMPONENTS

The purpose of the ignition coil, Fig. 35-2, is to transform or step up the 12V from the battery to the high tension voltage of approximately 20,000V required to jump the spark plug gap in the combustion chamber.

The ignition distributor, Fig. 35-3, has several functions. It

Fig. 35-2. Sectional view of a 12V ignition coil.
(AC Spark Plug Division)

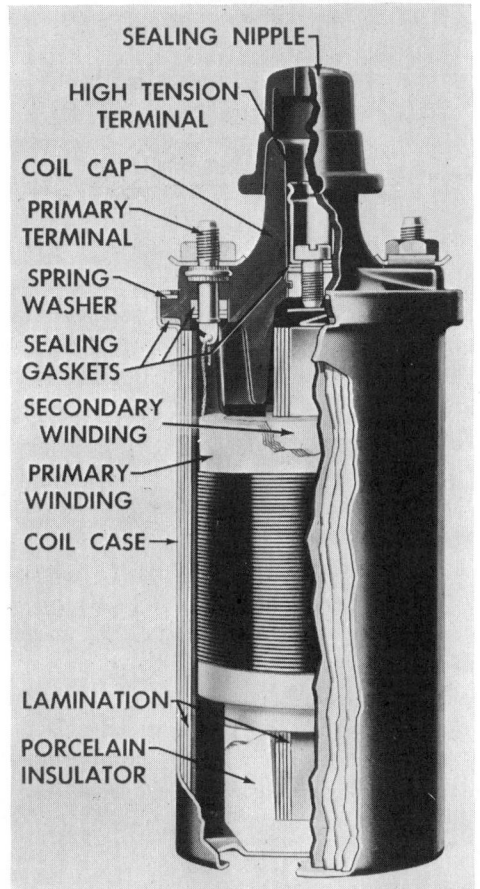

SEALING NIPPLE

HIGH TENSION
TERMINAL

COIL CAP

PRIMARY
TERMINAL

SPRING
WASHER

SEALING
GASKETS

SECONDARY
WINDING

PRIMARY
WINDING

COIL CASE

LAMINATION

PORCELAIN
INSULATOR

Fig. 35-3. Sectional view of an ignition distributor for a V-8 engine.

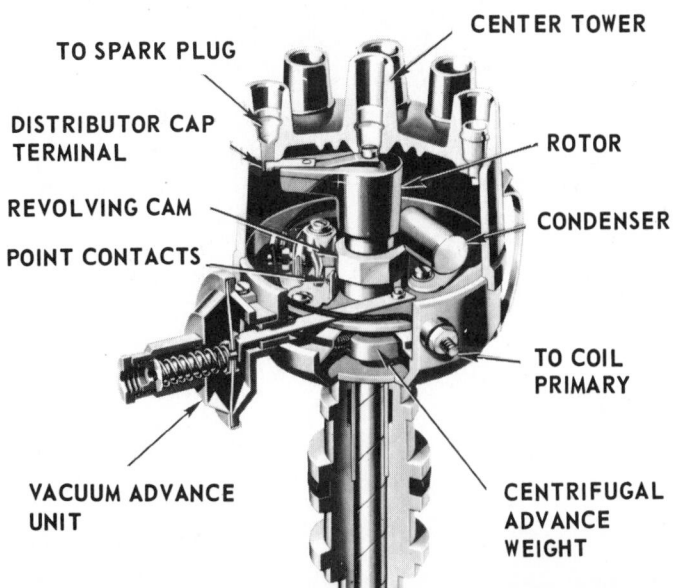

TO SPARK PLUG

CENTER TOWER

DISTRIBUTOR CAP
TERMINAL

ROTOR

REVOLVING CAM

POINT CONTACTS

CONDENSER

VACUUM ADVANCE
UNIT

TO COIL
PRIMARY

CENTRIFUGAL
ADVANCE
WEIGHT

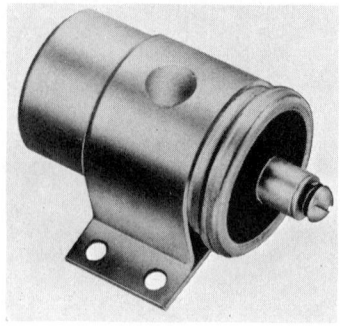

Fig. 35-4. Ignition condenser with mounting bracket.

opens and closes the primary ignition circuit. It distributes the high tension current to the respective cylinders of the engine. It also has a mechanism that controls the point at which the breaker points open, thereby advancing or retarding the spark in accordance with engine requirements.

The purpose of the ignition condenser, Fig. 35-4, is to reduce arcing at the breaker points, and prolong their life.

The spark plug, Fig. 35-5, provides the gap in the combustion chamber across which the high tension electrical spark jumps to ignite the combustible charge.

The purpose of the ignition switch is to connect and disconnect the ignition system from the battery, so the engine can be started and stopped as desired.

With the ignition switch ON, Fig. 35-1, and ignition distributor contacts closed; current will flow from the battery, through the primary winding of the ignition coil, to the distributor contact (breaker) points, to the ground connection and back to the battery.

The current flowing through the primary winding of the ignition coil produces a magnetic field in the coil. When the distributor contact points open (break), the magnetic field collapses and the movement of the magnetic field induces current in the secondary winding of the coil. Since there are many more turns of wire in the secondary winding than there are in the primary winding, the voltage is increased up to 20,000V.

The distributor then directs this high voltage to the proper spark plug, where it jumps the gap. The heat of this spark ignites the air-fuel mixture in the combustion chamber. The burning fuel expands and forces the piston down. Downward motion of the piston, in turn, rotates the crankshaft.

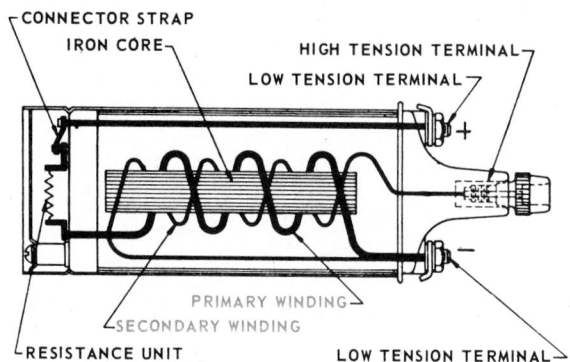

Fig. 35-6. Details of ignition coil, showing primary and secondary windings and terminals.

IGNITION COILS

The ignition coil, Figs. 35-2 and 35-6, is a pulse transformer designed to step up primary voltage (received from battery and generator) of 12V to approximately 20,000V. It is composed of a primary winding, secondary winding and core of soft iron.

The primary winding is made up of approximately 200 turns of relatively heavy wire (approximately No. 18 gauge). The secondary winding may have as many as 22,000 turns of fine wire, (approximately No. 38 gauge). The usual construction is to have the secondary winding wound around the soft iron core, and the primary winding surrounds the secondary. The purpose of the core is to concentrate the magnetic field.

This coil assembly usually is placed in a steel case with a cap of molded insulating materials that carries the terminals. Some ignition coils have their windings immersed in oil or paraffin-like material. This is done to improve insulation and reduce the effects of moisture. In addition, oil-filled coils can better withstand corona (faint glow) and heat. Oil has the

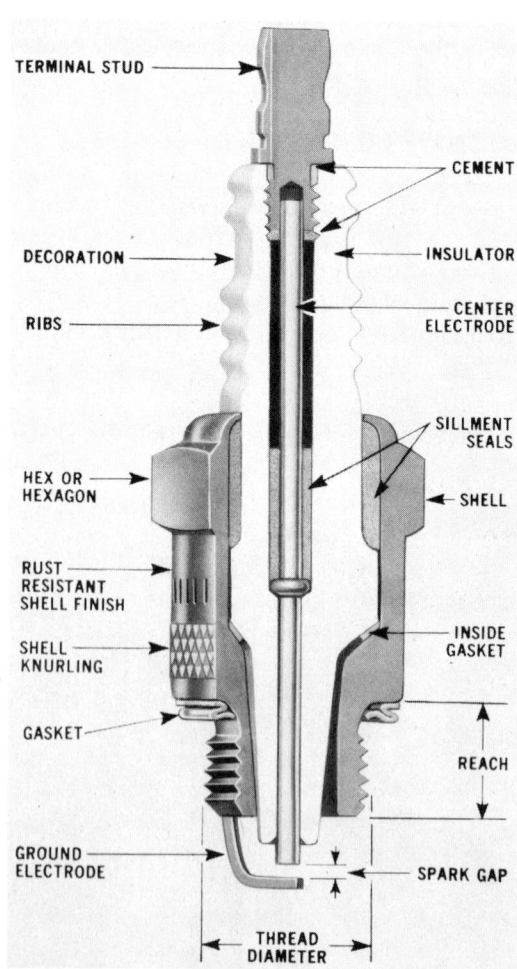

Fig. 35-5. Sectional view of a non-resistor spark plug.

advantage of automatically healing itself if any breakdown in insulation occurs.

To prevent coils from absorbing moisture, they are hermetically sealed. On some coils, the outer housing is finned for increased cooling. Heavy-duty coils are built with larger cores and provided with greater insulation. The higher inductance of these coils limits top speed performance, but their life expectancy is materially lengthened.

IGNITION CONDENSER

As mentioned, primary current produces a magnetic field around the coil windings. However, this does not occur instantly, since it takes time for the current and, consequently, the magnetic field to reach its maximum value.

This time element is determined by either the resistance of the coil winding or the length of time the distributor contacts are closed. In general, the current does not reach the maximum because the contacts remain closed for such a short time, particularly at higher engine speeds.

When the breaker points begin to open, the primary current will tend to continue flowing. This natural condition in a winding is increased by means of the iron core. Without an ignition condenser, the induced voltage causing this flow of current would establish an arc across the contact points and the magnetic energy would be consumed in this arc. As a result the contact points would be burned and normal ignition would be impossible.

The condenser prevents this arc by providing a place for the current to flow. As a result of condenser action, the magnetic field produced and sustained by the current flow will quickly collapse. It is this rapid cutting out of the magnetic field, that, induces high voltage in both the primary and secondary windings.

VOLTAGE VARIATIONS AND REQUIREMENTS

Engine speed, compression pressures, carburetor air-fuel mixture ratios, spark plug temperatures and width and shape of plug gap all affect the voltage required to produce a spark at the plug gap.

As mentioned, the length of time the ignition points are closed (which, in turn, is dependent on engine speed) will affect the voltage produced by the coil. However, there is a wide range between maximum and minimum voltages produced at low engine speeds, Fig. 35-7.

The variation in voltage produced is caused by increased tendency toward arcing under unusual conditions. Whenever an arc occurs at the breaker points, the voltage induced in the secondary winding is reduced. Obviously, if the amount of voltage induced reaches the minimum required to jump the gap at the plug, missing will occur.

New distributor contact points, correctly installed, make possible the maximum voltage from the coil secondary. New spark plugs have the lowest firing requirements. After use, however, the electrodes of the plugs become worn and eroded, and a higher voltage is required to jump the gap.

After approximately 10,000 miles of operation, the breaker

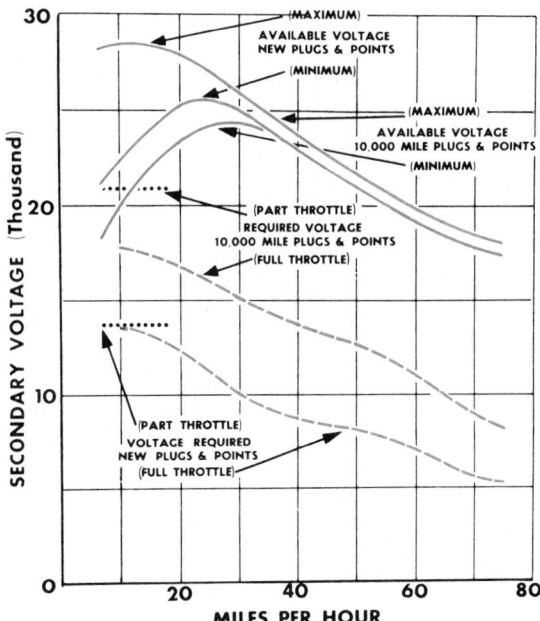

Fig. 35-7. Variation of ignition voltage under different conditions.

points usually are covered with oxide that will lower voltage available at low speeds. In addition, plug gaps often increase as much as .015 in. (approximately 50 percent). Therefore, it is necessary to provide a margin of voltage available over and above that required to fire a plug under ideal conditions.

To improve ignition system efficiency, the ignition coil is placed close to the distributor, and the distributor is located centrally to keep spark plug leads as short as possible.

When carburetor mixtures are lean, voltage required may be as much as 40 percent higher than normal. The highest voltage requirements exist at low engine speed under very light acceleration. Missing under such conditions indicates that there is insufficient voltage available to fire the plug.

NEGATIVE HIGH TENSION POLARITY

Most ignition manufacturers consider negative polarity of the high tension outlet of the ignition coil as a means of conserving electrical energy. This is because the center electrode is the hottest part of the spark plug.

When the center electrode is connected to the negative high tension voltage, the spark gap becomes ionized more readily and forms a lower resistance path for the spark. Therefore, a lower voltage is required to fire the same plug gap.

A simple means of testing coil polarity on a car can be made with a voltmeter. The positive lead is connected to a good ground and the negative lead is connected to the spark plug terminal of No. 1 cylinder. With this connection, the voltmeter is connected across the coil high tension windings. Run the engine at idling speed. If the voltmeter indicates "up" scale, the coil has a negative polarity.

Also, an ordinary lead pencil can be used to check polarity. Insert the pencil point in the gap between the end of disconnected spark plug cable and the spark plug terminal. If the flare appears on the plug side, the polarity is correct.

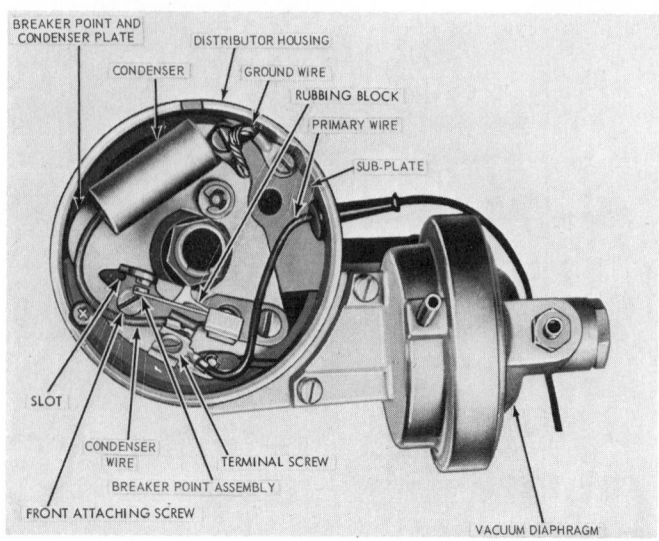

Fig. 35-8. Typical breaker point type ignition distributor. Note location of condenser. In some ignition systems, the condenser is mounted outside of the distributor.

IGNITION CONDENSERS

Ignition condensers, or capacitors, Figs. 35-4 and 35-8, prevent an arc at the distributor contact points when the points first open. The condenser provides a place where current can flow until the contact points are fully open.

Condensers are made of alternate sheets of metal foil and insulation. The sheets are in the form of long narrow strips, which are rolled to form a compact cylinder. Then, to eliminate the possibility of moisture entering the condenser, they are hermetically sealed.

Alternate sheets of foil are connected to one terminal of the condenser, while the remaining sheets of foil are connected together to provide the other terminal. The condenser is connected directly across the distributor contact points.

The capacity of a condenser is measured in microfarads and is proportional to the total area of the foil and inversely proportional to the thickness of the insulating sheets, which are called the dielectric. So, the thinner the dielectric, the greater the capacity of the condenser. Ignition condensers usually vary in capacity from .15 to .25 microfarad.

Loosened or corroded connections will increase the series resistance of a condenser, causing it to be slow in taking a charge. This, in turn, causes high voltage and arcing at the distributor contact points. In general, a resistance up to .5 ohm does not seriously affect ignition performance.

Arcing at the breaker points causes transfer of tungsten from one contact to the other. As a result, a tip builds up on one contact while a pit forms on the other. The direction in which the tungsten transfers can be used as basis for troubleshooting the cause of the pitting. If the material transfers from the negative to the positive point, Fig. 35-9, make one or more of these corrections: Increase condenser capacity. Shorten condenser lead. Separate distributor-to-coil low and high tension leads. Move these leads closer to ground.

If the tungsten transfers from the positive to the negative

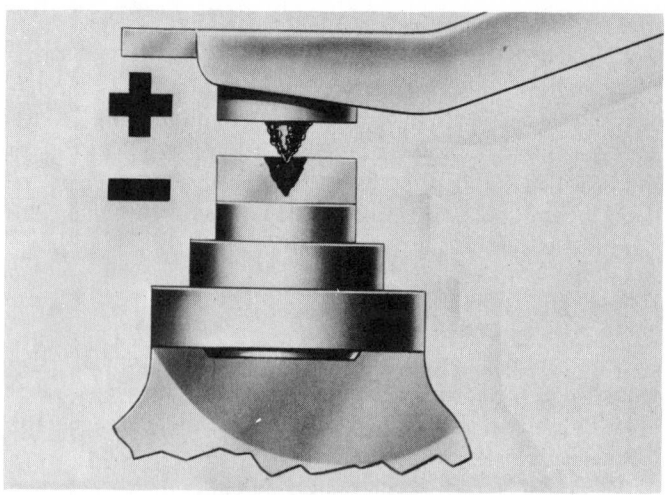

Fig. 35-9. Low condenser capacity will cause transfer of metal from negative to positive breaker point.

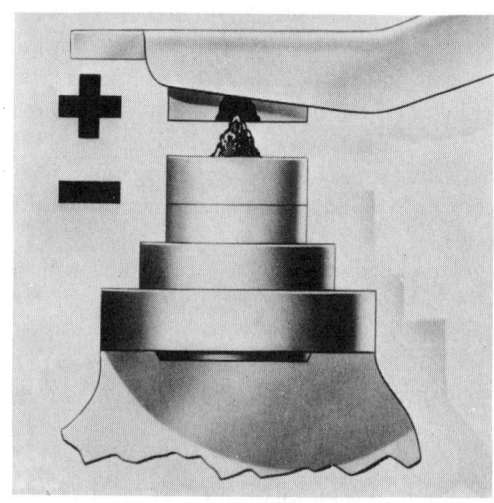

Fig. 35-10. High condenser capacity will cause transfer of metal from positive to negative breaker point.

point, Fig. 35-10: Reduce condenser capacity. Move distributor-to-coil leads closer together. Move these leads away from ground or lengthen condenser lead.

IGNITION DISTRIBUTORS

The ignition distributor, Figs. 35-8 and 35-11, makes and breaks the primary ignition circuit. It also distributes high tension current to the proper spark plug at the correct time.

The distributor is driven at one half crankshaft speed on four cycle engines. Usually, it is driven by the camshaft. Although in some cases, an accessory shaft is used. While it is desirable to have the distributor centrally located on the engine, many designs have it mounted at the front or rear of the engine.

Detailed construction of the ignition distributor varies considerably with different manufacturers. Basically, it consists of a housing into which the distributor shaft and centrifugal weight base assembly are fitted with suitable bearings. In most cases, these bearings are of the bronze bushing type. Heavy duty distributors frequently employ ball bearings. In low-priced distributors, the shaft turns directly in the cast iron housing.

Details of a Delco-Remy distributor are shown in Fig. 35-11. A window in the cap is provided for adjustment of the breaker point gap, while the cap is in position. The circuit breaker plate located below the centrifugal advance mechanism uses the outer diameter of the main shaft bushing for its bearing surface. A retainer clip in the upper shaft bushing holds the movable plate in position. In this distributor, Fig. 35-11, the contact set is attached to the movable breaker

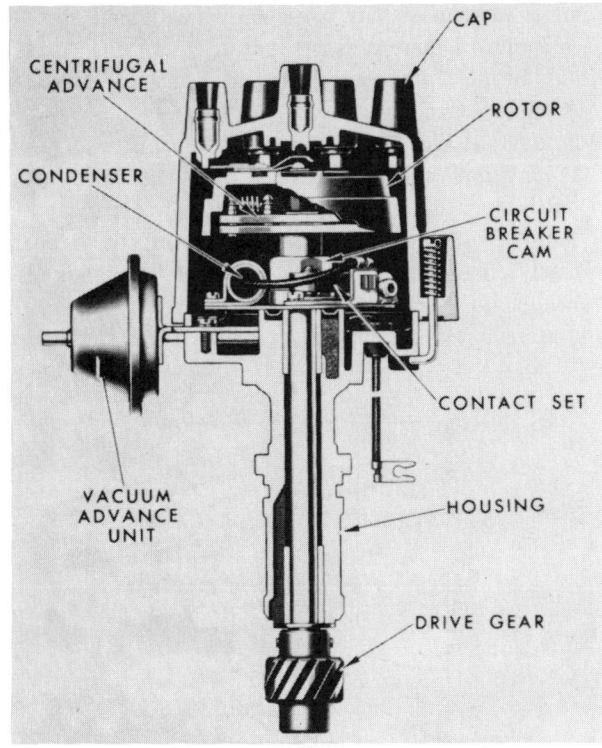

Fig. 35-11. Details of typical Delco-Remy distributor.

plate. A vacuum advance unit attached to the distributor housing is mounted under the breaker plate. The rotor covers the centrifugal advance mechanism, which consists of a cam actuated by two centrifugal weights.

As the breaker cam rotates, each lobe passes under the breaker lever rubbing block, causing the breaker points to separate. Since the points are in series with the primary winding of the ignition coil, current will pass through that circuit when the points close. When the points open, the magnetic field collapses and a high tension voltage is induced in the secondary winding of the coil by the movement of the magnetic field through the coil windings.

The usual design is to provide one lobe on the breaker cam for each cylinder of the engine. A six cylinder engine will have a six lobe cam in the distributor, and a V-8 will have an eight

lobe cam. As a result, every revolution of the breaker cam will produce one spark for each cylinder of the engine.

On a four cycle engine, each cylinder fires every other revolution. Therefore, the distributor shaft must revolve at one half crankshaft speed. On a two cycle engine, the distributor shaft would revolve at the same speed as the crankshaft.

After the high tension surge is produced in the ignition coil by the opening of the breaker points, the current passes from the coil to the center terminal of the distributor cap. From that point, it passes down to the rotor mounted on the distributor shaft and revolves with it. The current passes along the rotor, then jumps the minute gap to the cap electrode under which the rotor is positioned at that instant. This cap electrode, in turn, is connected by high tension wiring to the spark plug designated by the firing order of the engine. As the rotor continues to rotate, it distributes current to each of the cap terminals in turn, Fig. 35-11.

SPARK ADVANCE

For efficient engine operation throughout the range of speed and operating conditions, it is essential that the spark occur at the correct instant. That instant will vary according to engine load and speed. Therefore, a mechanism is provided to automatically advance and retard the spark as conditions require. On automotive engines, two methods usually are employed to actuate that mechanism, centrifugal force and engine vacuum.

CENTRIFUGAL ADVANCE

When the engine is idling, the spark generally is timed to occur just before the piston reaches the top of the compression stroke. Under idling conditions or when driving at a sustained speed under part throttle conditions, cylinders take in only part of the full charge. As a result, compression pressures are relatively low and combustion is slow.

At higher engine speeds, there is a shorter interval of time for the mixture to ignite and expand. Therefore, in order to obtain maximum power at higher speeds, it is necessary to have the spark occur slightly earlier in the engine cycle.

This spark advance is accomplished by means of the centrifugal advance mechanism. In Fig. 35-11, the advance mechanism is above the contact set assembly. In Fig. 35-12, it is below the ignition breaker plate.

The centrifugal advance mechanism consists of two weights, which the centrifugal force developed by the rotating shaft tends to throw outward against the tension of springs. The faster the distributor shaft rotates, the greater the centrifugal force, and the greater the movement of the advance weights.

In older distributor designs, movement of the weights was transmitted to the breaker cam, so that the cam rotated to an advanced position in respect to the distributor drive shaft. In modern designs, the cam is integral with the distributor shaft, and the movement of the centrifugal weights will rotate the breaker plate around the axis of the distributor shaft. The amount of centrifugal advance required varies considerably for each make and model of engine. The optimum setting in each

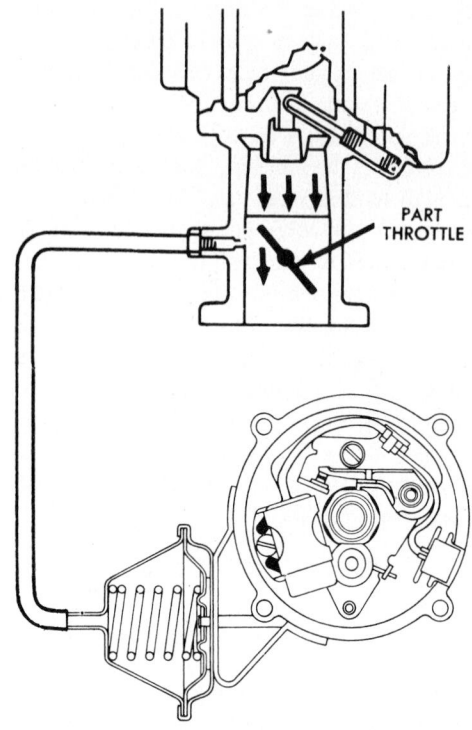

Fig. 35-12. Diagram showing details vacuum advance mechanism. (Chevrolet Motor Div., GMC)

case is determined experimentally on a dynamometer.

However, still another advance mechanism is necessary at part throttle operation, intake manifold vacuum is high and, therefore, a smaller amount of mixture is sucked into the engine and compression pressure is low. With lower pressures, the mixture does not burn as rapidly. To obtain maximum efficiency under such conditions, the spark should be advanced more than that obtained by the centrifugal mechanism. This additional advance is obtained by means of the vacuum advance unit.

VACUUM ADVANCE

The vacuum advance unit, Figs. 35-8 and 35-12, utilizes the vacuum in the intake manifold to provide the additional

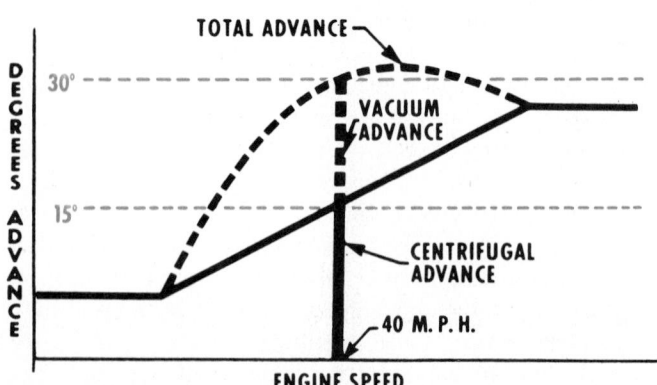

Fig. 35-13. Typical centrifugal and vacuum advance curves.

spark advance required under part throttle operation. It has a spring-loaded diaphragm connected by linkage to the ignition distributor. The spring-loaded side of the diaphragm is airtight and is connected by tubing to a point on the atmospheric side of the carburetor throttle valve (when valve is in idling position).

With the throttle valve in idling position, there is virtually zero vacuum at the point where the vacuum spark control connection is made. However, as soon as the throttle valve is opened, it swings past the opening of the vacuum passage and vacuum can then act on the diaphragm of the spark advance mechanism. Suction created causes the diaphragm to deflect. This motion is transmitted by linkage to the distributor and the breaker plate is rotated.

The amount of movement, of course is proportional to the amount of vacuum. At any particular engine speed, there will be a definite amount of spark advance resulting from the operation of the centrifugal advance mechanism, and also from the vacuum advance unit.

For example, Fig. 35-13 shows that the centrifugal advance at 40 mph supplies 15 deg. spark advance. If the throttle is only partly opened, an additional vacuum advance of up to 15 deg. may be obtained. However, if the throttle is opened completely, manifold vacuum will approach zero. As a result, there will be no vacuum spark advance provided.

Another chart of advance curves is shown in Fig. 35-14.

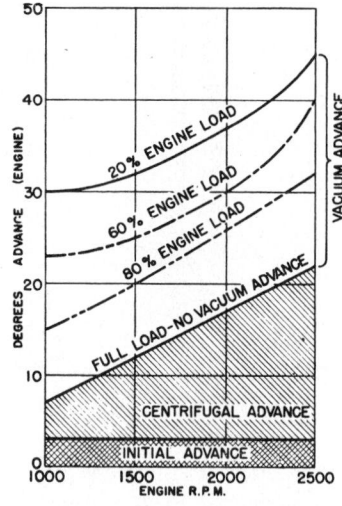

Fig. 35-14. Chart of spark advance on a typical V-8, showing rapid decrease in vacuum advance between 20 percent engine load and full engine load.

FACTORS GOVERNING SPARK ADVANCE

Many variables affect spark advance in an engine and ignition system. Consider these factors:
ENGINE LOAD
Less Load: Combustion is slower and more spark advance required.
More Load: Combustion is faster and less spark advance required.

ENGINE SPEED

Low Speed and Load: Combustion slower and more spark advance required.

Low Speed and Full Load: Combustion faster and less spark advance required.

High Speed and Full Load: Combustion slower and more spark advance required.

ENGINE TEMPERATURE

Cold Engine: Combustion slower and more spark advance required.

Hot Engine: Combustion faster and less spark advance required.

CYLINDER BORE

Larger Bore: Combustion slower and more spark advance required.

Smaller Bore: Combustion faster and less spark advance required.

COMPRESSION RATIO

Low Compression Ratio: Combustion slower and more spark advance required.

High Compression Ratio: Combustion faster and less spark advance required.

CHARACTER OF FUEL

Low Volatile Fuel: Combustion slower and more spark advance required.

High Volatile Fuel: Combustion faster and less spark advance required.

AIR-FUEL MIXTURE

Lean Mixture: Combustion faster and less spark advance required.

Rich Mixture: Combustion slower and more spark advance required.

KNOCK RATING OF FUEL

High Octane Fuel: Combustion slower and more spark advance required.

Low Octane Fuel: Combustion faster and less spark advance required.

In addition to the above factors that affect spark timing, others includes the shape of the combustion chamber; location of the spark plug; amount of carbon in the combustion chamber; equality of fuel and distribution to the individual cylinders.

CAM ANGLE

Cam angle or dwell angle is the number of degrees through which the distributor cam rotates while the breaker points are closed. It is directly related to the breaker point gap. Decreasing the breaker point gap will increase the cam angle.

In a six cylinder engine, the average cam angle is 36 deg. Since there are 60 deg. of cam rotation involved in firing each cylinder of a six cylinder engine, the points are open for 24 deg. and closed for 36 deg. The cam angle of a V-8 engine is approximately 31 deg., while on a four cylinder engine the cam angle would be about 41 deg.

The breaker point gap and/or cam angle must be set accurately. If the cam angle is too small, the current will have insufficient time to pass through the primary winding of the ignition coil. A weak spark will result.

If the cam angle is too great, the breaker points will not open far enough. They will tend to stick together and misfiring will result. The best method of adjusting breaker points, is by means of a dwell meter. Cadillac, for example, specifies cam angle only in tune-up specifications.

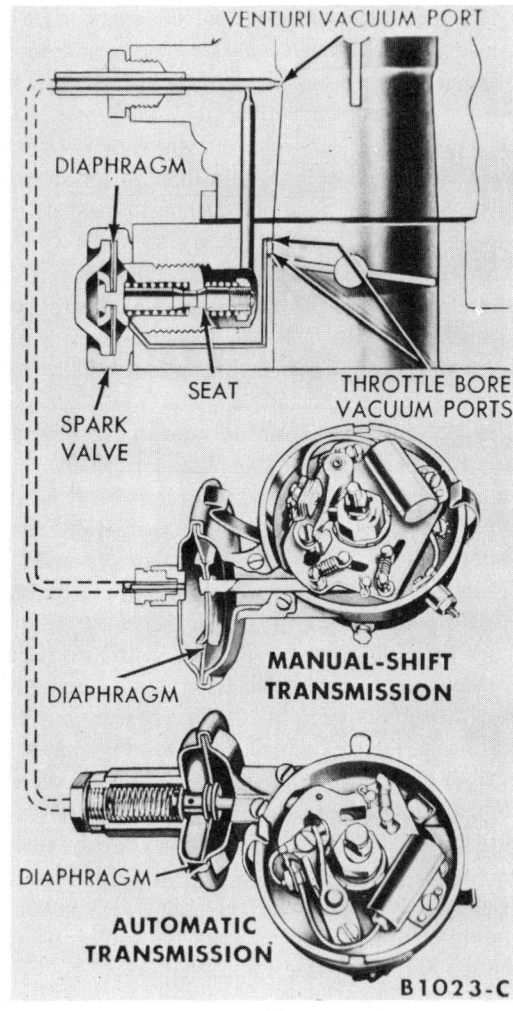

Fig. 35-15. Ford Loadomatic distributor used on some older cars with manual shift transmission and with automatic transmission.

FORD LOADOMATIC ADVANCE

Spark advance on the Ford Loadomatic distributor, Fig. 35-15, is controlled entirely by vacuum. The demands of the engine are satisfied by the action of the breaker plate. The breaker plate is controlled by a vacuum actuated diaphragm working against the action of two calibrated breaker plate springs.

The breaker plate is free to rotate on the shaft upper bushing. The diaphragm moves the breaker plate in a counterclockwise direction to advance the spark. The springs move the plate in a clockwise direction to retard the spark. The degree of spark advance is determined by the strength of the vacuum acting on the diaphragm.

Vacuum is transmitted to the distributor diaphragm from three interconnected passages in the carburetor, Fig. 35-15. Older designs used only two passages in the carburetor and did not have a spark valve. The opening of one passage is in the throat of the venturi. The openings of the other two passages are in the throttle bore, just above the closed throttle plate.

All manifold vacuum passes through a spark control valve located in the carburetor throttle body, Fig. 35-15. Under steady, part-open throttle operation, the spark valve is held open against the pressure of a calibrated spring. A combination of atmospheric pressure outside of the spark valve diaphragm, and manifold vacuum from within, holds the spark valve open.

When accelerating, manifold vacuum momentarily drops below a predetermined point. The calibrated spring closes the spark valve, shutting off manifold vacuum to the distributor to prevent excessive spark advance.

Vacuum from the venturi prevents full spark retard. As engine speed approaches the throttle setting, manifold vacuum increases sufficiently to open the spark valve. This allows a higher vacuum to operate the diaphragm in the distributor.

At high engine speed, manifold vacuum falls and the valve closes. This prevents loss of venturi vacuum due to bleed back and assures full spark advance at high engine speeds.

The spark valve operates in a similar manner. It provides an intermediate spark retard when engine load is increased to a degree where normal road load spark advance would be too great, and wide open throttle retard would reduce the efficiency of the engine.

On Ford cars using the Loadomatic distributor and automatic transmission, the operation is different. Vacuum to the distributor is transmitted in the same manner, but the distributor has three spark advance systems, Fig. 35-15:
1. At port throttle operation, there is a rapid spark advance which is controlled by the breaker plate spring.
2. A stop in the vacuum chamber allows steady advance at steady part throttle operation.
3. Additional advance at higher speeds is controlled by calibration shims, located between the spring and vacuum connection in the diaphragm housing.

Fig. 35-16. Distributor tester affords full range of distributor checks.

DISTRIBUTOR SERVICE

Complete distributor service calls for replacement of the breaker points. Also, testing and replacement, when necessary, of the condenser, rotor, distributor cap, distributor cam, centrifugal and vacuum advance mechanisms, and distributor shaft bearings.

Various tests should be made on distributor operation to be sure all parts are functioning properly. Distributor testing equipment, Fig. 35-16, is required. Check dwell of the breaker points, degree of spark advance at various speeds, wear of the distributor cam as indicated by the regularity and spacing of the sparks on the stroboscope.

DISTRIBUTOR CAP

The distributor cap should be carefully checked to see that sparks have not been arcing from point to point within the cap. Both the interior and exterior must be clean. The firing points should not be eroded, Fig. 35-17, and the interior of

Fig. 35-17. Part of distributor cap cut away to show eroded condition of firing points.

the towers must be clean and free from corrosion.

If necessary, the interior of the distributor cap towers can be cleaned by means of a round wire bristle brush. When cleaning distributor caps, care must be exercised not to use any cleaning solution that would injure the cap, which usually is made of some form of Phenol-resin.

There are two principal methods of holding the distributor cap in place on the distributor housing. One is by means of external clips or cap springs, Fig. 35-18, and the other is by means of a latch, Fig. 35-19. The clips can be pulled back, permitting the cap to be lifted from the distributor housing. To release the latch, a screwdriver is inserted in upper slotted end of cap retainer, pressed down and turned until the latch is disengaged.

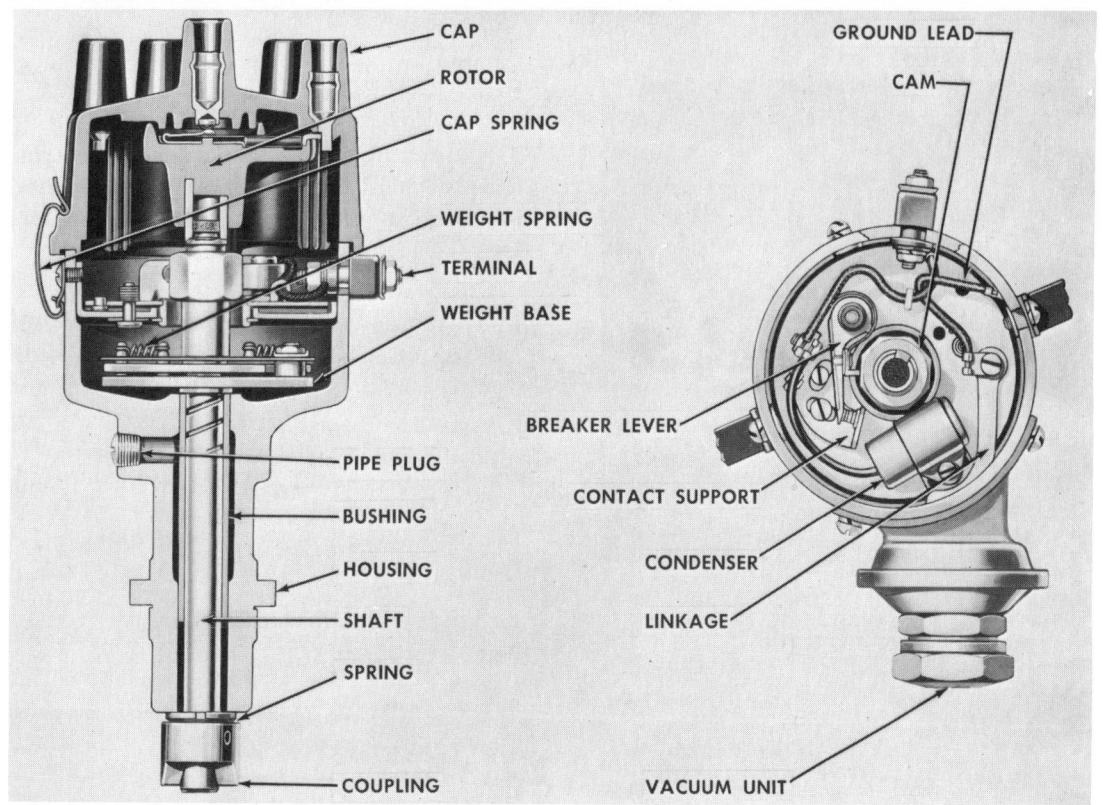

Fig. 35-18. Illustrating parts of an ignition distributor. (Delco-Remy)

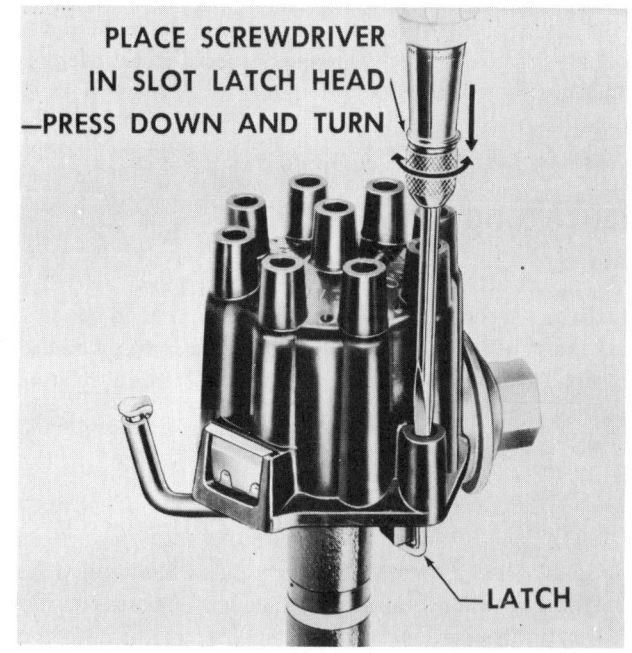

Fig. 35-19. Method of removing distributor cap from one type of Delco-Remy distributor.

ROTOR

A distributor rotor is a conductor designed to rotate and distribute the high tension current to the towers of the distributor cap. They are provided with some sort of spring connection to the center tower or terminal of the distributor cap. This spring must have ample tension to provide good electrical contact.

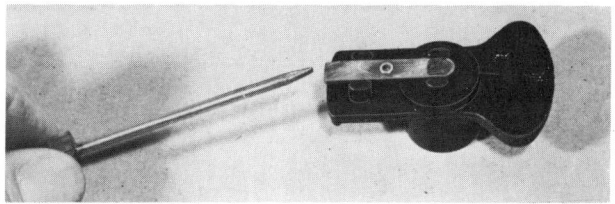

Fig. 35-20. Firing end of rotor must not be worn.

The firing end of the rotor, Fig. 35-20, from which the high tension spark jumps to each of the cap terminals in turn should not be worn. Any wear or irregularity will result in excessive resistance to the high tension spark. Most rotors simply carry the high tension current. However, some are designed to include a resistor for the suspression of radio and TV interference.

Rotors are mounted on the upper end of the distributor shaft, Fig. 35-18. In most cases, all that is necessary to remove them is to pull them off. In this connection, the rotor must have a snug fit on the end of the shaft. On another popular design, two screws are used to attach the rotor, Fig. 35-21, to a plate on the top of the distributor shaft. Built-in locators on the rotor, and holes in the plate, insure correct reassembly. One locator is round; the other is square.

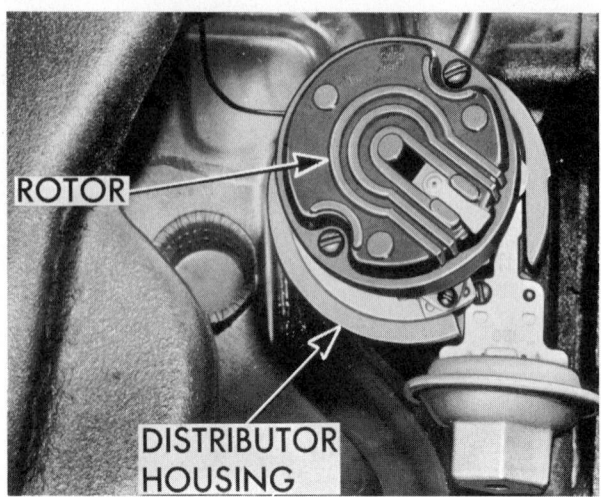

Fig. 35-21. This type rotor is attached to a plate on top of distributor shaft by means of two screws.

DISTRIBUTOR SHAFT

There should not be more than .002 in. side clearance between the distributor shaft and its bearings. The gear and its coupling, or drive, must be tight on the end of the shaft. It must not be worn.

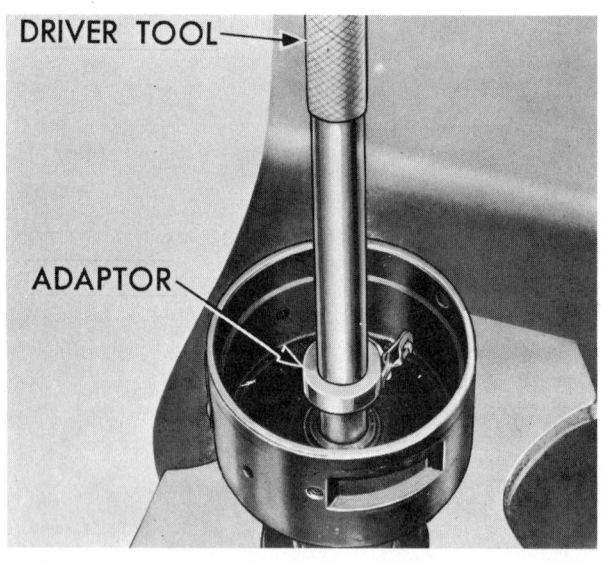

Fig. 35-22. Pressing out bushings from distributor housing.

When replacing bushings in the distributor housing, a special puller or press, Fig. 35-22, should be used. Most manufacturers recommend burnishing the bushings after installation. However, the porous bushings used in many Delco-Remy units are manufactured to exact size and should not be reamed, scraped or filed. Some bushings should be soaked in engine oil prior to installation. Check manufacturer's recommendations.

BREAKER PLATE

The bearings of the breaker plate must not be worn, and the plate must operate smoothly. In the case of the Delco-Remy center bearing breaker plate, Fig. 35-23, by means of a spring balance, the spring tension can be measured.

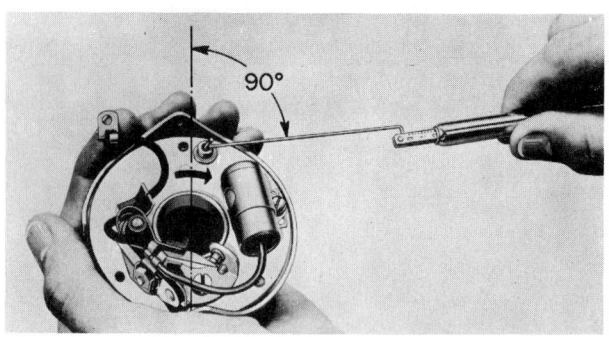

Fig. 35-23. Measuring tension on movable plate.

BREAKER CAM

The breaker cam must be smooth and not worn. Any inaccuracies will be revealed when the assembled distributor is tested on the distributor tester, Fig. 35-16, by an examination of the spark pattern on the stroboscope. On assembly, the cam should be given a very light coating of special grease. Many late model distributors incorporate special lubrication wicks that should be "turned around" or replaced when the distributor is serviced.

INSULATORS

Insulators at the primary lead connection, Fig. 35-26, should be checked to make sure they are in good condition. There must be no possibility of grounds. In some distributors, the sequence of assembly of wire terminals and insulators is specifically given.

BREAKER POINTS

Breaker points must be centered and in accurate alignment, Fig. 35-24. Misalignment of breaker points will severely reduce their life and result in misfiring. When aligning breaker points, bend only the stationary point bracket, Fig. 35-25. Never attempt to bend the movable breaker arm. Breaker points are fastened to the breaker plate by means of a lock screw, Fig. 35-26, or by two attaching screws, Fig. 35-27.

To remove the breaker point assembly shown in Fig. 35-26: After removing distributor cap and rotor, remove screw holding condenser to breaker plate. Disconnect condenser lead, together with breaker arm spring. Remove lock screw, permitting point assembly to be lifted from pivot post. Some Delco-Remy breaker points have the condenser attached directly to the breaker plate.

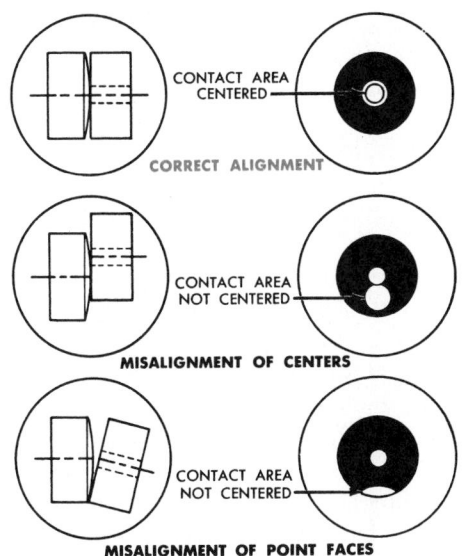

Fig. 35-24. Ignition breaker points must be accurately aligned for efficient operation and long life.

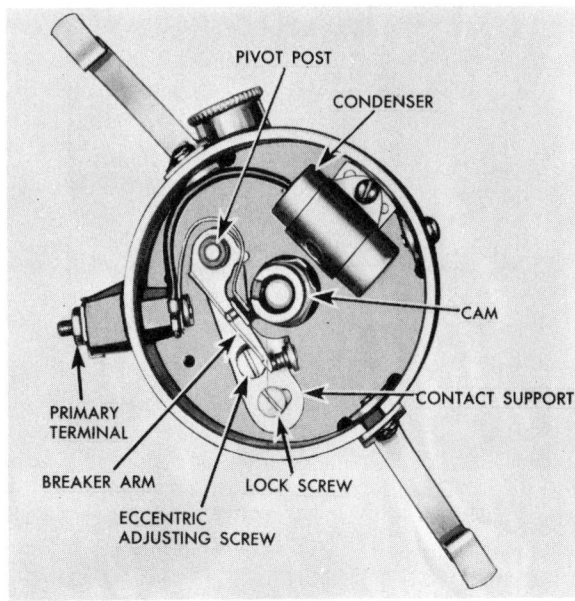

Fig. 35-26. Note eccentric adjustment for setting breaker point gap.

Fig. 35-25. To align ignition breaker points, bend only the stationary point bracket. Special bending tools are available for the purpose.

When setting the point gap, a blade of a feeler gauge of specified thickness is placed between the points. The gap is adjusted by turning the eccentric screw. Instead of an eccentric screw, some distributors have a notched hole in the breaker plate in which a screwdriver is inserted.

In the case of the distributor shown in Fig. 35-27, the point gap is adjusted by means of a horizontal screw, which moves the stationary point backward or forward as required. In this way, alignment of the points is not altered.

The point adjustment is controlled by inserting an Allen wrench into the hexagon hole in the screw head. This adjustment can be made without removing the distributor cap. A cap is provided with a window, Fig. 35-28, through which

For the distributor shown in Fig. 35-27, the procedure is similar, except the contact assembly is held in position by two screws. Note in this design, breaker points form a single assembly and, according to the manufacturer, there is no need to align the points. The only adjustment required is that of point dwell (point gap adjustment).

The installation of breaker points, or contact point assemblies, is accomplished in the reverse order. To adjust the breaker point gap, or dwell setting, an eccentric adjustment screw usually is provided, Fig. 35-26. This moves the position of the stationary point in relation to the movable point, thereby altering the gap between the two. When setting the gap, the rubbing block on the movable arm must be on a high point of the distributor cam, then the gap is adjusted to a specified width.

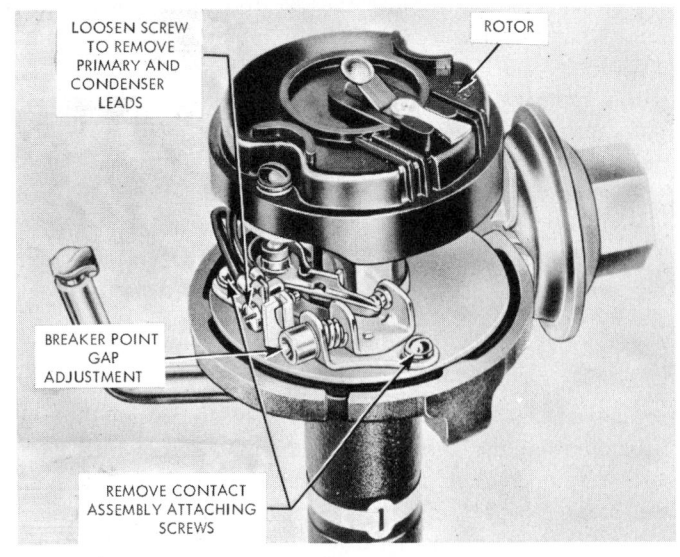

Fig. 35-27. External adjustment type distributor with cap removed.

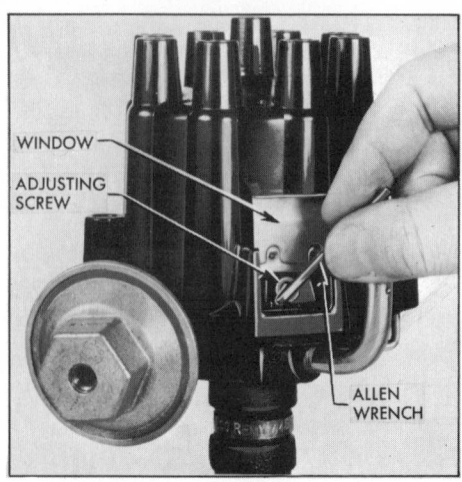

Fig. 35-28. Adjusting breaker point gap which affects cam angle, on external adjustment type distributor.

the adjustment can be reached with the Allen wrench. This permits making the adjustment while the engine is running to the specified dwell angle.

Another method can be used if a dwell meter is not available. Connect a test lamp in series in the primary lead. Rotate the distributor shaft until the rubbing block is on the high point of one of the cams. Then turn the adjusting screw, Fig. 35-28, until lamp lights. Then back off on the adjustment one-half turn.

Dirty and slightly pitted ignition breaker points can be dressed with a few strokes of a fine-cut contact point file. The file must be free of dirt and oil. Care must be taken to keep the surfaces of the points parallel. Except in emergencies, it is advisable to install a new set of breaker points.

BREAKER ARM SPRING TENSION

Breaker arm spring pressure must fall between specified limits (usually 19-23 oz.). Weak spring tension will result in chatter and missing at high speeds. Too much tension will cause excessive wear of the points, rubbing block and distributor cam. Contact point pressure should be checked with a spring gauge hooked to the end of the breaker lever and pull exerted at 90 deg. The reading should be taken just as the points separate.

The pressure should be adjusted by bending the breaker lever spring. To decrease pressure, pinch the spring carefully. To increase pressure, the breaker points must be removed from the distributor, so the spring can be bent away from the lever.

CAM ANGLE

Cam angle, or dwell, is the number of degrees of cam rotation from the instant the ignition breaker points close until they open again. It is controlled entirely by the width of the breaker point gap. Decreasing the width of the breaker point gap, increases the cam angle.

Special equipment is required to measure the cam angle. A dwell meter is included in the design of the distributor tester

shown in Fig. 35-16. When checking the cam angle, instructions accompanying the equipment specifications for the individual ignition system should be followed.

IGNITION RESISTORS

In most 12V systems, a resistor is connected in series with the primary circuit of the ignition coil, Fig. 35-6, during normal operation. However, during the cranking period, the resistor is cut out of the circuit so that full voltage is applied to the coil. This insures a strong spark during the cranking period, and in that way quicker starting is provided.

Contacts on the cranking motor solenoid are used to cut the resistor out of the primary circuit during the cranking period. The ignition coil and its windings are designed to operate efficiently at a voltage lower than full battery voltage. So, when full battery voltage is applied, a hotter than normal spark is provided.

Remember that during the cranking period, the excessive load applied on the battery will reduce the voltage reaching the ignition system. If full battery voltage was used continually for normal operation, the coil would burn out.

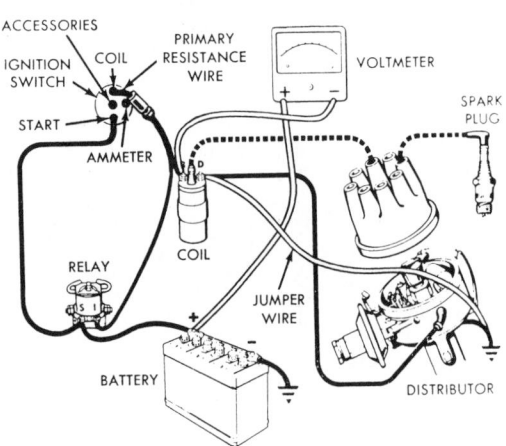

Fig. 35-29. Ford ignition system showing primary resistance wire. Voltmeter is connected to check voltage at coil. Dashed line indicates secondary circuit.

On older systems, the resistor was of the block type. Recently, a wire type resistance is being used to connect the coil to the battery, Fig. 35-29.

There are two types of wire used for this resistance. Prestolite and Chrysler use a wire that is sensitive to heat. As the temperature of the wire increases, so does its resistance. As a result, when the engine reaches operating temperature, its resistance is six volts applied to the coil.

The resistance of the Delco-Remy and Ford resistance wire is not affected by heat. However, the starting circuit is designed so as long as the starting motor is operating, full battery voltage is applied to the coil. When the starter is not cranking the engine, the resistance wire is cut into the circuit to reduce the voltage applied to the coil.

If the engine starts when the ignition switch is turned on,

but stops when the switch is released to running position, it usually indicates that the resistor is defective and should be replaced. At no time should the resistor be shorted out of the circuit, since that would supply continuous full voltage to the coil and burn it out.

Resistors and resistor wires should be checked whenever the breaker points are burned or when the ignition coil is burned out. With the ignition switch turned on, the voltage reading from the resistor side of the coil to the ground should be approximately 5 to 7V, unless other specifications are available. Resistance of resistor as used on 12V systems is approximately 1.5 ohms.

IGNITION TIMING

The ignition system must be timed accurately so that the spark occurs in the combustion chamber at the correct instant. Incorrect timing results in loss of efficiency and power. If the spark "fires" too early, preignition and attendant "pinging" occurs. If continued, the engine will be damaged. If the spark "fires" too late, both fuel economy and power will be sacrificed.

Timing of the spark varies considerably in different engines. For this reason, factory specifications must be carefully observed. The spark is timed in relation to the position of the No. 1 piston in most engines (small number use No. 8). Usually, timing is specified as so many degrees before top center (BTC). The top center referred to is at the end of the compression stroke.

Timing marks are placed on the flywheel, vibration damper at the front of the crankshaft or on the fan pulley. A typical timing mark setup is shown in Fig. 35-30.

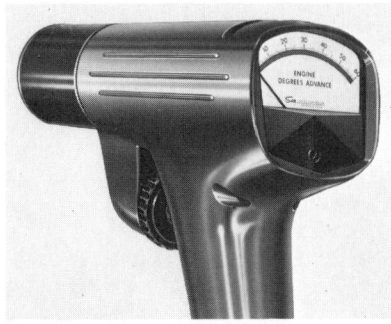

Fig. 35-31. Ignition timing light with special advance control. Note meter for indicating amount of advance.

spark plug. The beam is then directed to the timing marks and, with the engine running, the light will flash each time the spark occurs. The timing marks will have the appearance of standing still, so that the time the spark occurs is easily noted.

The specified timing mark should coincide with the index mark. If not, the clamp screw of the distributor is loosened and the distributor is rotated to the correct position. Moving the distributor housing against shaft rotation advances the timing. Moving it with shaft rotation retards timing.

Some special timing setups do exist. The 1974 Oldsmobile engine, for example, is equipped with a timing notch on the vibration damper. The notch, Fig. 35-32, is designed to receive a magnetic probe when timing the engine. With the aid of this device, precision timing is assured for the maintenance of lowest emission levels.

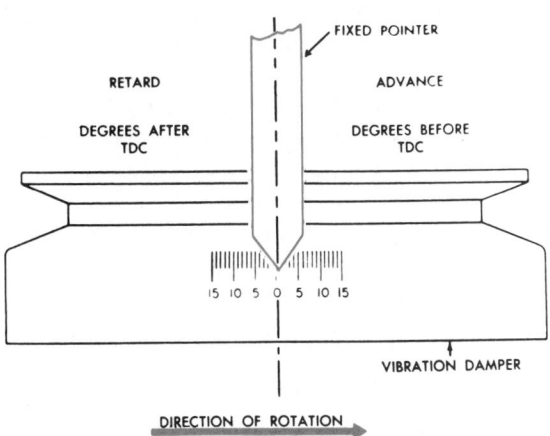

Fig. 35-30. Typical of timing marks on vibration damper.

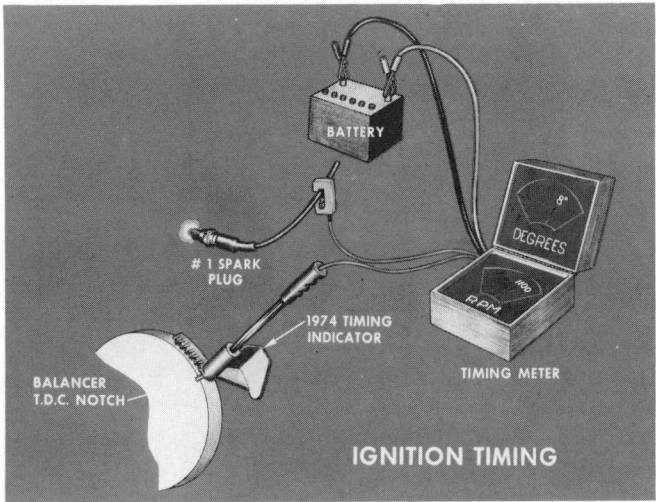

Fig. 35-32. Top-dead-center notch in vibration damper is used in conjunction with magnetic probe placed in timing indicator to time ignition of 1974 Oldsmobile engines.

To time the ignition of an engine, the ignition breaker points should just start to open as the piston of No. 1 cylinder approaches top dead center on its compression stroke. The most accurate method, and the one most frequently used, is to use a stroboscopic type of timing light, Fig. 35-31.

The timing light is connected to the battery and to No. 1

DISTRIBUTOR TYPES

In addition to the distributors previously illustrated and discussed, there are several other types of distributors used on vehicles. Fig. 35-33 shows the dual advance distributor used on

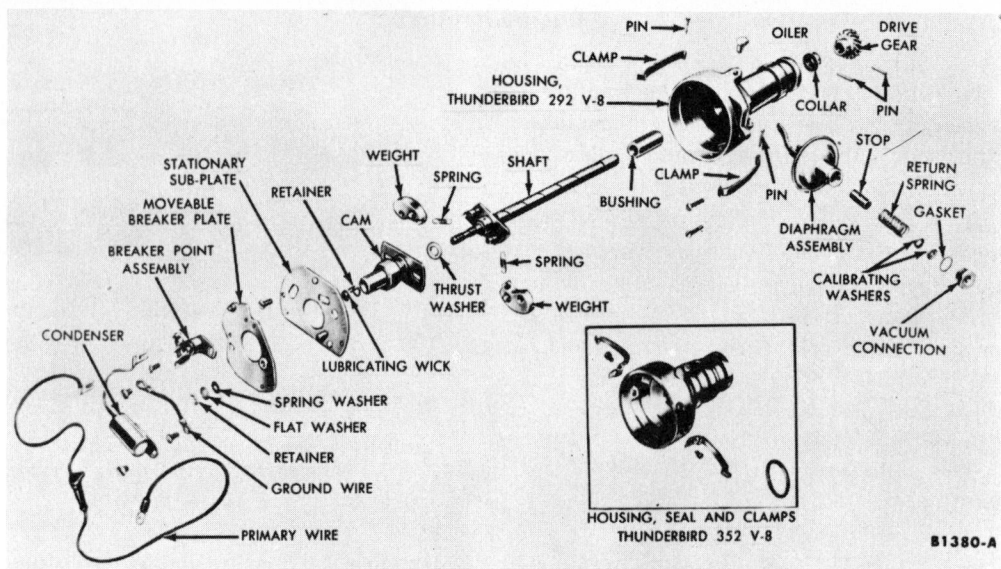

Fig. 35-33. Details of dual advance distributor used on some Ford engines. This design includes both centrifugal and vacuum advance.

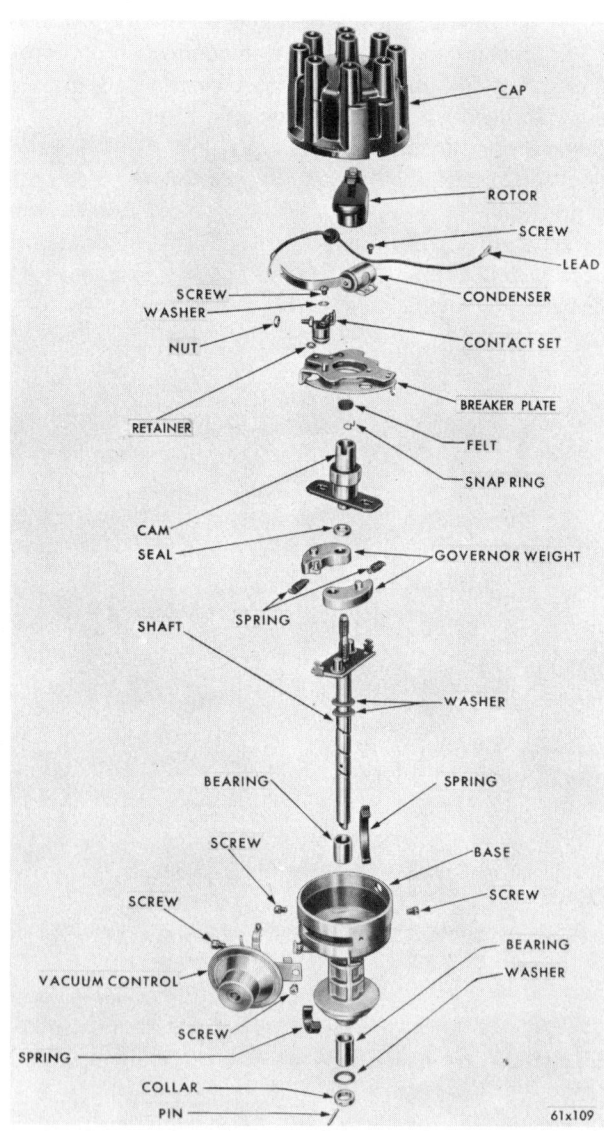

Fig. 35-34. Exploded view of distributor used on Plymouth V-8.

some Ford engines. On this distributor, centrifugal advance is decreased by bending a spring post (located below breaker plate) away from the distributor shaft. Vacuum advance on this distributor is controlled by shims placed behind the vacuum diaphragm spring. Adding washers will decrease the advance.

In the Plymouth V-8 distributor shown in Fig. 15-34, note that the distributor cam is not integral with the shaft, but is a separate unit. A felt wick is provided in the top of the distributor cam for lubrication.

SPECIAL DISTRIBUTORS

Ignition distributors used on most cars have a single set of breaker points and a cam lobe for each cylinder of the engine. At higher engine speeds, breaker points remain closed a very short time. As a result, there is very little time for the coil to build up. This difficulty can be overcome to a degree by means of twin ignition distributors or double alternate distributors.

Twin ignition distributors, Fig. 35-35, are built as if two complete distributors are combined into a single unit. This type has two complete and independent ignition systems: two ignition coils and two sets of breaker points plus two spark plugs for each cylinder. Usually the two systems operate simultaneously, so the spark at both plugs in the cylinder occurs at the same instant. However, they can be designed so that one set of breaker points opens slightly before the other to offset a lag in combustion.

Double alternate distributors, Fig. 35-36, have two breaker arms that operate alternately. This permits a cam to be used that has half as many lobes as there are cylinders. In some installations the two sets of breaker arms are connected to a single ignition coil. In other cases, two coils and a special cap and rotor are used. In this way, each set of contacts remains closed for a longer interval and, with separate coils, there is greater time for the coil to be saturated.

Before attempting to synchronize the breaker points of

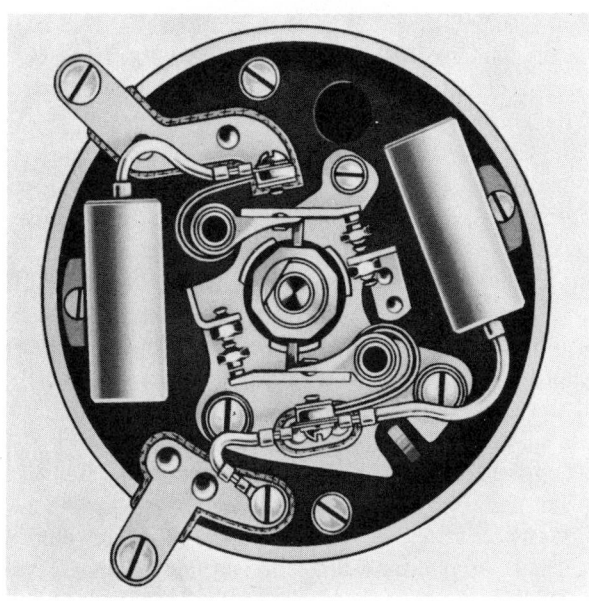

Fig. 35-35. Breaker plate for twin ignition distributor.

35-36, has one set of points on the breaker plate and another set of points on the subplate. The first step in synchronizing the breaker points is to set the gaps exactly the same. The assembly is then mounted on a test fixture.

When operated, there should be a 45 deg. interval between the opening of one set of points and the opening of the other. Adjustment can be made by adjusting the position of the subplate, which is controlled by an eccentric.

The distributor shown in Fig. 35-37 is similar to that shown in Fig. 35-36, except that two coils are used and the breaker contacts are not 45 deg. apart. The interval between the contacts varies with the angle of the V of the engine cylinders.

A test fixture is required when synchronizing the breaker points of a double alternate distributor. As in the other types of distributors, both sets of contact points are adjusted to the same specified gap. Then with the distributor mounted in a testing fixture, the subplate is adjusted to obtain the firing interval specified for that particular distributor.

twin ignition distributors, Fig. 35-35, it is important that each set of points has the same gap. The fixed point assembly is mounted on the breaker plate, while the adjustable point assembly is mounted on the subplate.

To test and adjust, the distributor is mounted on a test stand, and an indicator light lead is connected to each primary terminal. Operate the distributor in the correct direction and observe if the two sets of lights are synchronized. If not, loosen the screws holding the subplate and rotate the subplate until the two lights are exactly synchronized.

The double alternate distributor with 45 deg. spark, Fig.

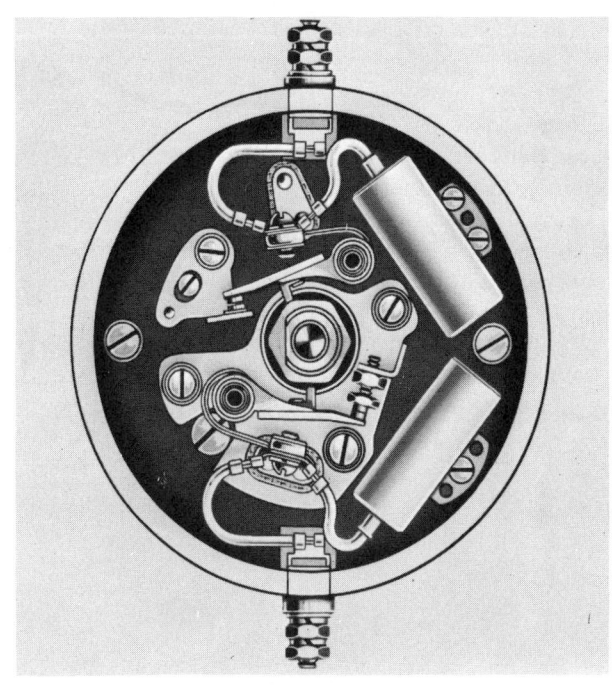

Fig. 35-37. Breaker plate for double alternate distributor using two ignition coils. (Motorcraft)

EXHAUST EMISSION CONTROL DISTRIBUTORS

As explained in the chapter on EMISSION CONTROL, Ford uses a special distributor with two diaphragms, Fig. 35-38, as one means of controlling exhaust emissions. This distributor permits the spark to be retarded the correct amount while idling. Yet, during deceleration it also provides the correct advance for acceleration and other types of driving.

The outer, or advance diaphragm, Fig. 35-38, controls the spark in the same manner as the conventional distributor. The inner, or retard, diaphragm works in the opposite direction to retard the spark at slow engine speeds and during deceleration.

Calibrated coil springs bear on the vacuum sides of both

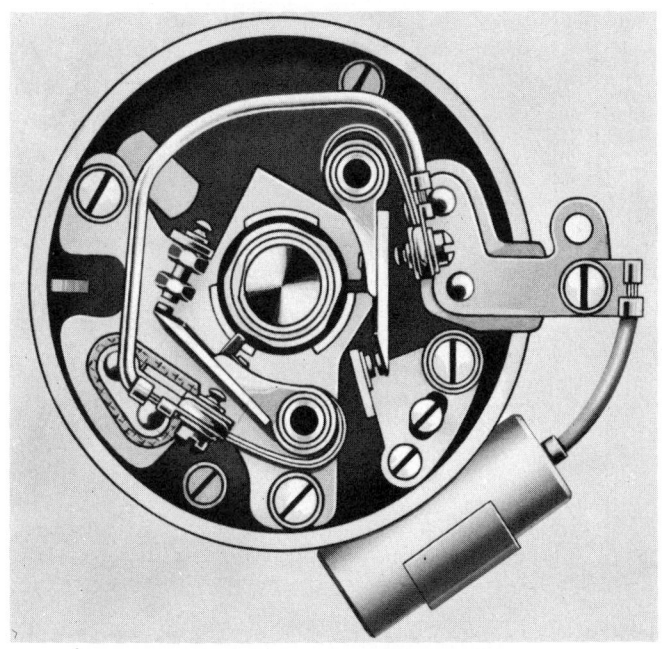

Fig. 35-36. Breaker plate for double alternate distributor using a single coil. (Motorcraft)

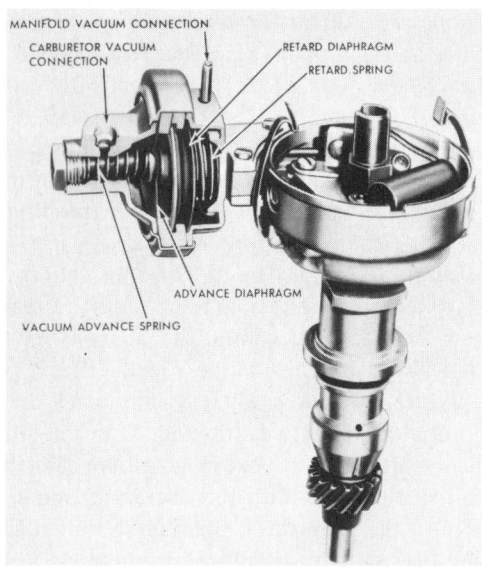

Fig. 35-38. Motorcraft distributor designed especially to limit production of noxious exhaust gases. Note the two diaphragms.

diaphragms to supply resistance to the actuating force of the vacuum. Only the outer diaphragm, Fig. 35-39, is linked to the distributor breaker plate. The link passes through the center of the retard diaphragm without touching it. The inner diaphragm serves to position a return stop for the outer diaphragm to govern the amount of spark retard when spark advance vacuum is reduced.

The dual diaphragm assembly is designed to provide the distributor with two distinct spark retard stops: a normal setting of 6 deg. BTC, and an additional 12 deg. retard, ATC.

The normal retard gives the desired spark time for starting, while the additional retard position provides a setting suitable for more complete combustion and minimum emission of contaminants after starting.

The vacuum sides of the two diaphragms are at either extreme of the diaphragm housing, so they provide opposing operating forces. Carburetor vacuum from a port above the throttle plate is supplied to the outer diaphragm. Vacuum from the intake manifold, or below the throttle plate, is supplied to the inner or retard diaphragm.

During cranking, there is no vacuum. Consequently, both diaphragms are at rest, Fig. 35-39, and the diaphragm link holds the breaker plate in the normal retard position until the engine starts.

When the engine runs at idle or fast idle, carburetor vacuum is weak. Manifold vacuum is strong, so it moves the diaphragm against the resistance of the retard spring until the retard stop is reached. At the same time, the vacuum advance spring is stronger than carburetor vacuum, so the advance diaphragm is moved against the retard diaphragm plate. In this position, the diaphragm plate turns the breaker plate to retard ignition timing another 12 deg.

As the carburetor throttle valve is opened, carburetor vacuum increases. This causes the advance diaphragm to move away from the retard diaphragm against the tension of the advance spring. Movement of the advance diaphragm pulls the link and breaker plate with it to advance the spark. At speeds above 1400 to 1600 rpm, the advance diaphragm functions like a conventional diaphragm.

The centrifugal advance in the dual diaphragm distributor controls the position of the cam in relation to the distributor shaft to provide basic full power setting. The diaphragm assembly functions to increase the degree of advance for better

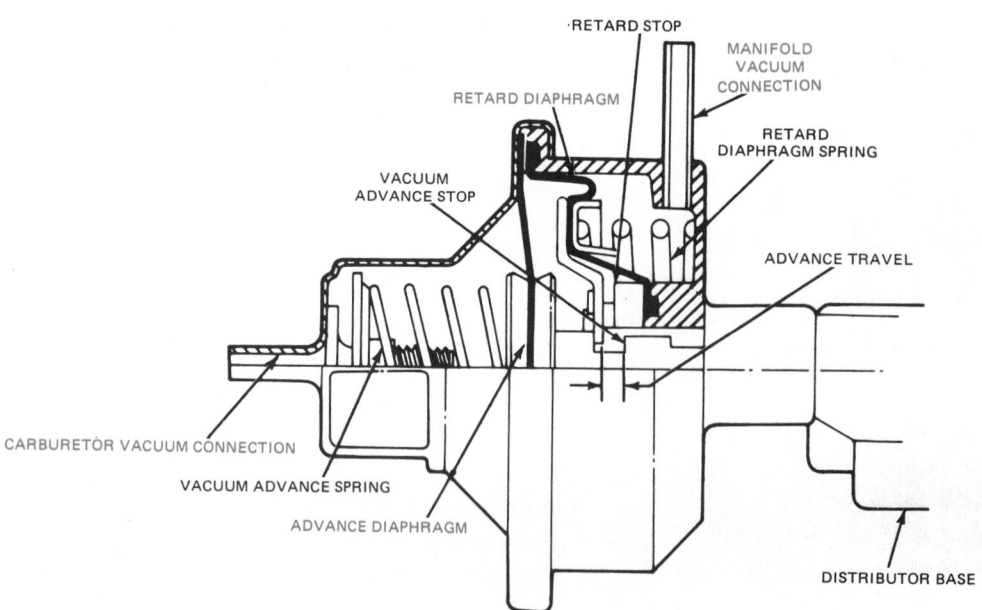

VACUUM ADVANCE AND RETARD DIAPHRAGMS AT REST

Fig. 35-39. Schematic drawing of Motorcraft dual diaphragm vacuum advance unit. Note connections for manifold and carburetor vacuums.

engine efficiency under normal loads at steady speeds.

When timing an engine equipped with an Autolite distributor with dual diaphragms, remove both vacuum lines from the distributor and plug the manifold vacuum line. Attach the timing light and, with the engine idling at 550 to 600 rpm, check the initial timing. Make any needed adjustments.

Quick checks on the centrifugal advance mechanism can be made in the usual manner by "reving" up the engine. Then, with the vacuum hose reconnected, there should be further advance if the vacuum advance is functioning.

To check the vacuum retard, return the engine speed to 550 to 600 rpm and reconnect manifold vacuum to the distributor. If the retard diaphragm is working, the spark timing should retard after the manifold vacuum hose is reconnected.

DELCO UNITIZED IGNITION

A unitized ignition system is available on some General Motors vehicles. It has only one component and 9 connections, compared to 12 components and 21 connections on the conventional unit. The unitized system incorporates coil, distributor, electronic amplifier, wiring and spark plug wires.

A magnetic pickup assembly located over the shaft, Fig. 35-40, contains a permanent magnet, a pole piece with internal teeth and a pickup coil. When the teeth of the timer core are rotating inside, and the pole piece lines up with the teeth, an induced voltage in the pickup coil sends a signal to the all electronic module. On signal, the module opens the ignition coil primary circuit. Primary current immediately decreases and a high voltage is induced in the ignition coil secondary

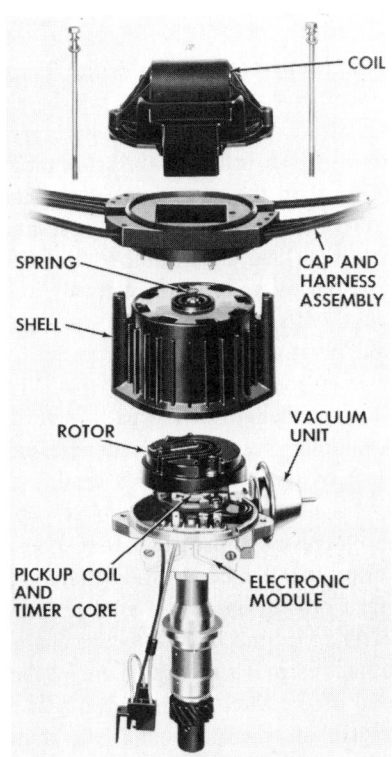

Fig. 35-40. Details of the GM unitized ignition system installed on some Pontiac engines.

winding. Then, as with conventional ignition the high voltage is directed through the rotor and high voltage leads to fire the spark plugs.

The magnetic pickup assembly is mounted over the main bearing on the distributor housing. It is made to rotate by the vacuum control unit and thereby provides vacuum advance. The timer core is made to rotate about the shaft by conventional advance weights, to provide centrifugal advance.

When making compression checks on an engine equipped with unitized ignition, disconnect the ignition switch connector from the system. No periodic lubrication is required. Engine oil lubricates the lower bushing and an oil-filled reservoir provides lubrication for the upper bushing.

FIRING ORDER

In order to reduce engine vibration and secure an even flow of power, the cylinders of internal combustion engines must fire in the correct sequence. When describing the firing order of different engines, the cylinders are numbered. On in-line engines, the No. 1 cylinder is the one immediately behind the timing gears. The remaining cylinders are in numerical order. On V-8 engines, the usual practice is to call the first cylinder on the left bank No. 1. The first cylinder on the right bank would be No. 5. In a twelve cylinder engine, it would be No. 7.

The firing order of in-line six cylinder engines in the United States is 1-5-3-6-2-4. The most popular firing order of a V-8 is 1-8-4-3-6-5-7-2. Other firing orders used on V-8 engines are: 1-5-6-3-4-2-7-8, 1-5-4-2-6-3-7-8 and 1-3-7-2-6-5-4-8.

The firing order of four cylinder in-line engines can be either 1-3-4-2 or 1-2-4-3. Firing order on the four cylinder, horizontal opposed, Volkswagen engine is 1-4-3-2, with No. 1 cylinder being marked by a notch on the rim of the distributor.

SPARK PLUGS

The spark plug in a spark ignition engine provides the gap across which the high tension voltage jumps, to create the spark that ignites the compressed air-fuel mixture.

The spark plug, Fig. 35-41, consists of a center electrode, which is connected to the ignition coil secondary through the distributor. The center electrode is insulated from the spark plug shell by means of a molded insulator resembling porcelain. The side electrode protrudes from the bottom edge of the spark plug shell. It is positioned so that there is a gap between it and the center electrode.

The spark plug gap is adjusted by bending the side electrode. Fig. 35-42 shows a combined spark plug gauge and tool for adjusting the gap by bending the side electrode.

Spark plug gaps (U.S. engines) range from approximately .020 to .080 in. (0.501 to 2.032 mm). The gap must be carefully set in accordance with the manufacturer's specification. The size of the gap is dependent on the compression ratio of the engine, and on characteristics of the combustion chambers and ignition system. The trend toward wider spark plug gaps was made possible by improved ignition systems.

Once, a .025 in. (0.635 mm) gap was virtually standard on all

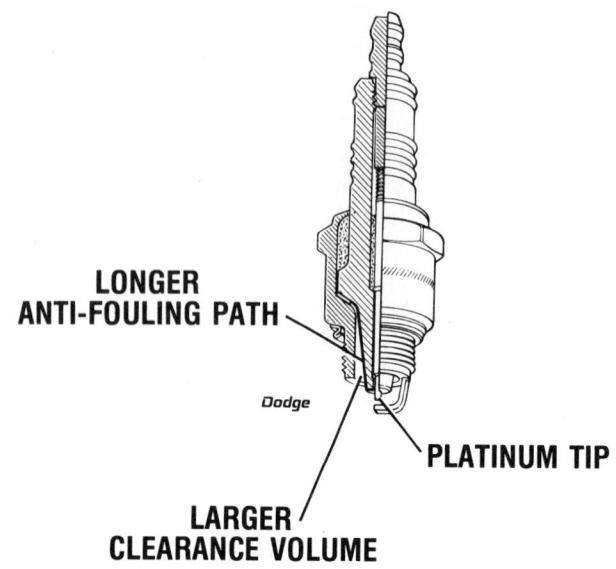

LONGER ANTI-FOULING PATH

Dodge

PLATINUM TIP

LARGER CLEARANCE VOLUME

Fig. 35-41. Long life spark plug introduced on 1975 Dodge cars equipped with 440 cu. in. engine has chrome-plated platinum center electrode to minimize erosion.

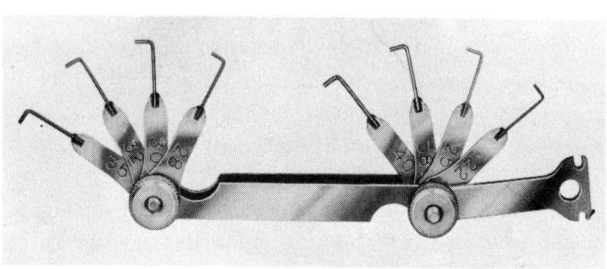

Fig. 35-42. Spark plug gap gauge, with gap adjuster at right end. Various gauges are of wire type for more accurate measurement of gap.

engines. Today, however, manufacturers specify gaps of .030, .035, .060 and .080 in. (0.762, 0.890, 1.52 and 2.03 mm). A wider gap includes more air-fuel mixture than a narrow gap, so there is more opportunity to ignite it.

The shell of the spark plug is threaded, so it can be removed and reinstalled with ease. All but tapered seat plugs require a gasket. The following thread sizes are used: 10 mm., 14 mm. and 18 mm.

In addition to having the correct size thread, the spark plug must extend into the combustion chamber the correct amount (reach). The correct point for the spark plug electrodes in the combustion chamber is determined by the engine engineer.

Installing plugs with a longer reach than specified may result in the valves or piston striking the spark plug. If a plug with a short reach is installed, the electrodes become partly sheltered by the spark plug hole in the cylinder head. In this case, engine roughness and missing probably will result.

HEAT RANGE

Spark plugs must be designed so the temperature of the firing end of the plug is high enough to burn off any carbon or

other combustion deposits. Yet, the plug must not get too hot or it will cause preignition or deterioration of the insulator or electrodes. This is a difficult situation since the temperature of the spark plug tip varies greatly with different engines and with different operating conditions. Engineers of the AC Spark Plug Division of General Motors Corp., point out that in conventional automotive service, the center wire temperatures range from a low of 200 deg. C at 10 mph to a high of 800 deg. C at 80 mph.

The temperature of the spark plug insulator is dependent on the characteristics of the spark plug and on the burning fuel in the combustion chamber. The latter temperature will, of course, vary with the design of the engine, compression ratio, cooling system and air-fuel ratio.

As the tip of the spark plug absorbs heat from the burning air-fuel mixture, the heat travels up the insulator to the spark plug shell, then to the cylinder head and to the water jacket. The path the heat travels is shown in Fig. 35-43. The heat

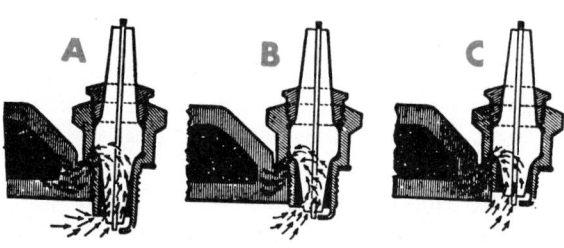

Fig. 35-43. Illustrating path that heat must take from tip of spark plug to reach water jacket of engine. Longer path, hotter plug. Spark plug A is a hotter plug than plugs B or C.

absorbed by the insulator increases as the temperature in the combustion chamber rises. More heat will be absorbed as the area of the insulator exposed to the hot gases is increased.

More heat will be absorbed by the spark plug shown on the left in Fig. 35-43 than the one on the right, since the area of its tip exposed to the combustion chamber is greater.

If the path the heat must follow to reach the cooling system is short, the tip will have a relatively low temperature. Therefore, plugs with short paths for the heat to travel are known as cold plugs. Plugs with long paths for the heat to travel are known as hot plugs.

In addition to the length of the path traversed by the heat in reaching the cooling system, insulator material and insulator shape will affect its temperature. As a result, some spark plug insulators have a narrow neck just above the tip. Another design will have recessed tip sections that more readily follow temperature changes in the combustion chamber.

Other designs provide increased volume between the shell and the insulator to permit more effective charge cooling, Fig. 35-44. Still other design has the tip of the insulator protruding beyond the end of the shell for improved heat characteristics.

The heat range of any spark plug is its ability to transfer heat from the firing end up through the insulator, gasket and shell to the cylinder head and water jacket. Heat range is also known as the "Thermal Characteristic."

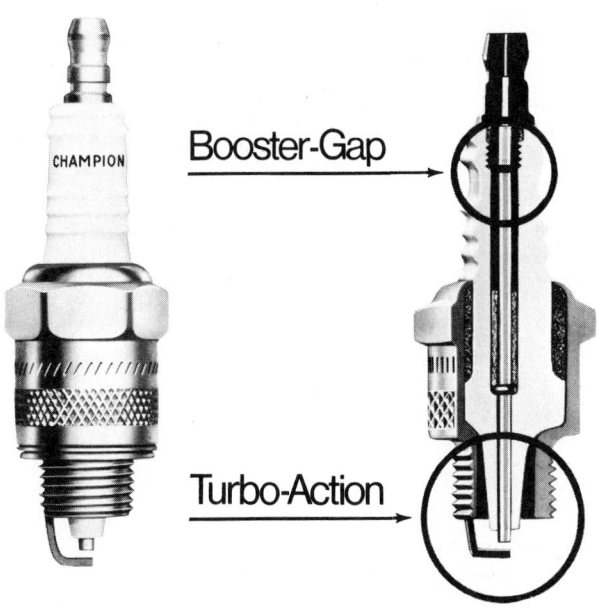

Fig. 35-44. Special spark plug with booster or series gap which affords protection against low temperature fouling so plug continues to fire under severe fouling conditions.

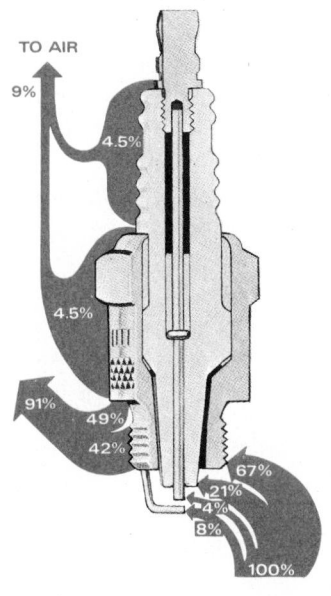

Fig. 35-45. Illustrating the heat flow from a spark plug.

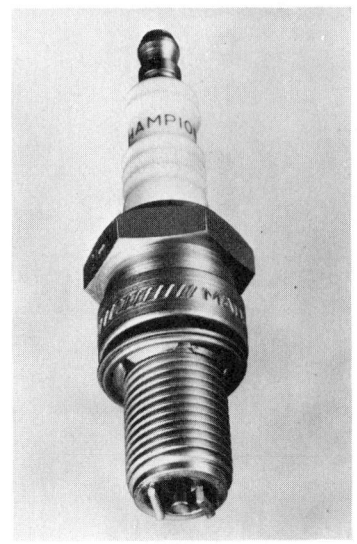

Fig. 35-46. Note twin firing points on the spark plug designed for a Mazda rotary engine.

Fig. 35-45 shows typical heat flow in an automotive spark plug. A spark plug designed for the Mazda rotary engine is shown in Fig. 35-46. Note the unusual dual firing points.

Engine designers select spark plugs that will give good performance for average driving conditions. However, if the engine is operated for long periods under approximately full load conditions, the standard equipment plug will operate at too high a temperature, and preignition will result. Therefore, it is necessary to install a colder plug that will carry off the greater heat more rapidly.

On the other hand, if the engine is operated for long periods of slow speed at part throttle opening, the standard equipment plug will tend to foul. The insulator tip will become covered with carbon and other products of combustion. As a result, high tension voltage will leak across the accumulations (because of their lower resistance) rather than jump the gap at the electrodes. In this situation, a hotter plug (one with a longer heat path) should be used.

SPARK PLUG FOULING

As mentioned, there is a tendency for products of combustion to accumulate on the portion of the insulator of the spark plug within the combustion chamber. As a result, there are three types of spark plug fouling:

1. Carbon fouling.
2. High speed or lead fouling.
3. Oil and carbon fouling.

Carbon fouling, Fig. 35-47, results primarily from extended low speed operation and when the carburetor mixture is

Fig. 35-47. Example of carbon fouled spark plug which results from prolonged low speed operation and excessively rich carburetor mixture.

Fig. 35-48. High speed or lead fouling results from fuel additives and prolonged high speed driving.

Fig. 35-49. Example of oil and carbon fouling which results from excess oil reaching combustion chamber.

Fig. 35-50. Abnormal electrode erosion results from extreme temperatures. Plug must be correct heat range.

excessively rich. Carbon fouling, which causes missing or roughness, usually is relatively soft black soot that is easy to remove from the spark plug.

Lead fouling, Fig. 35-48, results from the tetraethyl lead used in the fuel to improve its antidetonating characteristics. Lead fouling is caused by extended high speed operation.

Spark plugs with lead fouling frequently will operate satisfactorily at low and medium loads. When full load is applied, however, missing will occur. This results from the higher temperatures melting the lead salts, which increases their electrical conductivity, and the plug will short out.

Lead compounds added to gasoline have a particularly bad effect on some spark plug insulators. They react with the silica in the insulator to form lead silicate glass, which has a low melting point. At high temperatures, it is a relatively good conductor of electricity. For this reason, a spark plug may give satisfactory operation under light loads, but fail when full loads and high combustion chamber temperatures are reached.

In some cases of lead fouling, it is possible to operate the engine at a speed just below the point where missing will occur. Then, by gradually increasing the speed (always keeping below "missing" speed), it will be possible to burn off the lead fouling and full throttle operation attained.

Lead fouling will sometimes appear as a heavy crusty formation, or as tiny globules. The form it takes will depend on fuel, operating conditions and time.

The third type of fouling, Fig. 35-49, is found on engines that are so badly worn that excess oil reaches the combustion chamber, either past the piston rings or past the valve guides.

Another condition that affects spark plug operation is the condition of the gap across which the spark jumps. Fig. 35-50 shows a spark plug with extreme electrode erosion, resulting from high temperatures and prolonged use of the plug. High capacity of the system also affects electrode life.

VOLTAGE REQUIRED TO JUMP GAP

There are many factors which will affect the voltage required to jump a certain gap. These factors include the shape of the electrodes forming the gap, the conductivity of the gases in the gap, temperature, pressure and the air-fuel ratio existing within the gap. AC Spark Plug Division of General Motors Corp. gives data shown in Fig. 35-51. Note that voltage required to jump a gap increases rapidly until 12,000V is needed to jump a gap of .060 in. The measurements were made in a conventional automotive engine at road load.

As mentioned earlier in this chapter, the current delivered to the plugs is dependent on the current flowing in the primary, and the amount of current decreases as the engine speed increases. The voltage at the plug is also dependent on the cleanliness of the spark plug electrode. For example, an ignition system that is capable of delivering 20,000V to a clean plug may be able to deliver only one half that amount to a plug that is partly fouled.

The reason why plug fouling cuts down on peak voltage is because it takes appreciable time for the voltage to build up to a value where it can jump the plug gap. When the ignition breaker points are closed, energy is stored in the ignition coil in the form of the magnetic field. Then, when the breaker points open, the magnetic field collapses, causing high voltage. However, this high voltage is not reached instantaneously. It is built up to a maximum and then drops to zero, which requires an appreciable length of time (electrically speaking), or about 1/20,000 sec.

The secondary voltage increases until it reaches a value that is capable of jumping the gap at the spark plug. However, if the plug is partly fouled, some current will flow across the coating on the insulator, which acts as a shunt across the gap. This loss of current reduces peak voltage to the point that it will not jump the gap of a badly fouled plug.

A paper presented before the Society of Automotive Engineers reports that the faster the high tension voltage is built up, the less effect fouling will have. One method of attaining fast electrical buildup condition is by means of high frequency ignition systems. Another method is by means of a series gap.

SPARK PLUG GAPS

Spark plug gaps do not remain constant, but increase in size. The amount of increase is dependent on mileage, chemical characteristics of the fuel, combustion chamber temperatures and, particularly, the action of the electrical spark which tears off portions of the electrode.

The electrical characteristics of the ignition system also affect the rate of wear of the spark plug electrodes. In this connection, the electrical capacity of the ignition coil and the wiring is an important factor. Systems with high capacity will cause more rapid gap wear than systems with low capacity. Inserting a resistor in or near the spark plugs will tend to counteract this condition. Resistors reduce the peak current which passes through the electrodes when the capacity of the system is being discharged.

The standard spark plug gap varies with different engines. For example, the recommended gap on many American cars is .035 in., while it is often less than .025 in. on European cars.

Experimentally, it has been determined that the combustion process in an engine is independent of the spark. If a spark is obtained at the plug gap, it will ignite the mixture, and the minimum amount of energy required in the spark to start combustion is only a small part of the total energy available.

However, in actual practice, some engines operate better with wider spark plug gaps than others. Many engineers are in agreement that the explanation is in the characteristics of the air-fuel mixture in the vicinity of the plug gap. The mixture varies in different parts of the combustion chamber of different engines. This is due to the design form of the combustion chamber, the turbulence imported to the mixture, and the amount of burned gases remaining in the combustion chamber from the previous cycle of operation.

should be filed until the end of the center electrode is flat and smooth, and the surface of the side electrode is parallel to the end of the center electrode.

Higher voltages are required to fire a spark plug with worn electrodes. As shown in Fig. 35-52, considerably higher voltage is needed to fire a used spark plug than a new plug. This is particularly true at low speeds where the difference may be as much as 4000V.

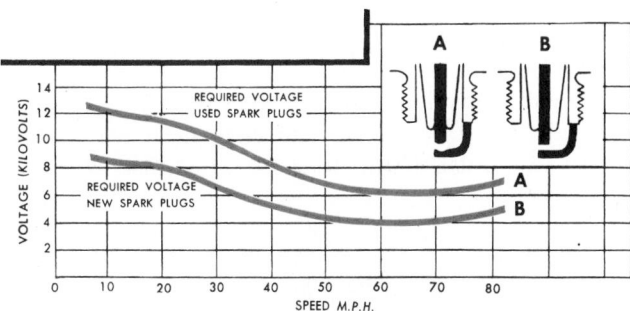

Fig. 35-52. Comparison of voltage required to fire new and old plugs.

CLEANING AND TESTING SPARK PLUGS

Fig. 35-53 shows a combined spark plug cleaner and tester. In this unit, the plug is cleaned by blasting the firing end with an abrasive compound. The ability of the plug to fire is tested under compression. However, when the electrodes become worn, the plugs should be replaced. It takes higher voltage to jump the spark across worn electrodes even though the gap has been adjusted to the correct size.

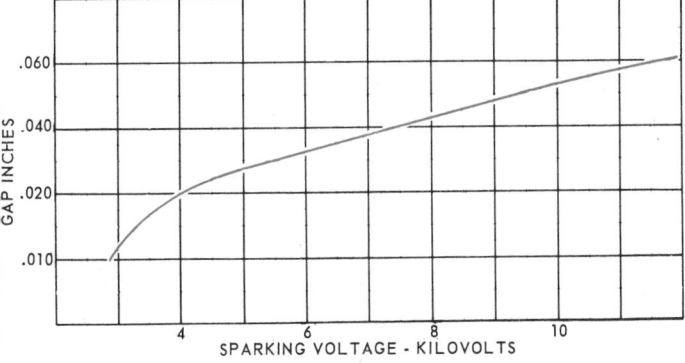

Fig. 35-51. Voltage required to jump different size gaps.

SPARK PLUG LIFE

Under favorable operating conditions, the life of a spark plug ranges from 10,000 to 15,000 miles. Beyond that mileage, they lose efficiency and should be replaced. Plug condition is especially important in the maintenance of low emission levels.

Higher engine temperatures, added emission controls and greater accessory loads have made the conditions under which the spark plug operates increasingly severe.

Spark plug life can be materially extended by frequent cleaning and regapping. As the electrodes become worn, they

Fig. 35-53. Combined spark plug cleaner and tester.

INSTALLATION OF SPARK PLUGS

Before installing a spark plug, it must be clean (if a used plug is being installed) and the gap must be adjusted in accordance with manufacturer's specifications. When adjusting the gap, bend the side electrode only. Never bend the center electrode. This will crack the insulator.

After adjusting the gap, make sure the threads of both the spark plug and the threads in the engine cylinder head are clean. Also clean the surface of the port in the cylinder head against which the spark plug gasket seats. If dirt is present, compression leaks may occur. Dirt also acts as a heat insulator so the spark plug will run hot, and faulty operation will result.

In addition, it is important to clean the threads in the cylinder head with a thread chaser, Fig. 35-54. Only with clean

Fig. 35-54. Special thread chaser for cleaning threads in spark plug holes. (AC Spark Plug Div., GMC)

threads can accurate torque readings be obtained.

A torque wrench should be used when tightening spark plugs. While most spark plugs should be tightened to 25 to 30 ft. lbs. torque, there are many exceptions. Manufacturer's specifications should be consulted. Spark plugs should be tightened to the degree that the gasket (if used) is just crushed. When spark plugs are replaced, new gaskets should be used (except tapered seat plugs).

The external portion of the spark plug insulator, together with the terminal, should always be covered with a rubber

boot made for that purpose, Fig. 35-55. This prevents accumulation of dust and moisture on the insulator, which would permit high tension voltage to leak across from the terminal to the shell of the plug. Without boots, secondary voltage is greatly reduced.

MAGNETOS

A magneto is a self-contained device which generates and distributes electricity for igniting the combustible mixture in the combustion chamber of the internal combustion engine. The magneto not only generates the electricity, but it also steps up the low voltage to a high tension voltage and distributes it to the various cylinders at the correct instant. It does this without the aid of a battery.

Some magnetos are of the low tension type, generating and stepping up a low voltage to a high voltage by means of a separate coil. High tension magnetos produce voltage of sufficient value to jump the spark plug gap without any external coil.

MAGNETO IGNITION ADVANTAGES

Magneto ignition systems have several advantages. First of all, they do not require any battery or other source of current. Secondly, the intensity of the generated voltage does not decrease with the engine speed, but increases.

Magnetos were used extensively on automobiles during the early years of the industry, but they have been superseded by battery ignition. Now, magnetos are found on trucks, tractors and small engines used on lawn mowers, garden fillers, etc. They are also used on internal combustion engines for industrial power.

Magnetos are particularly popular for internal combustion engines that do not require a battery for starting or lighting. Recent developments in permanent magnets of increased strength has materially improved magneto performance.

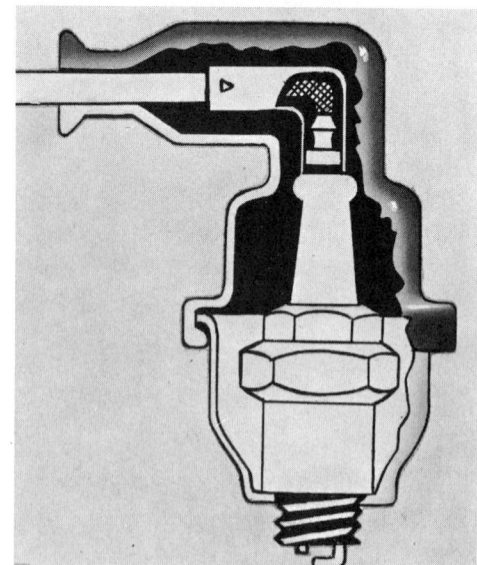

Fig. 35-55. Spark plug insulator, plug terminal and cable terminal are protected by a special rubber boot.

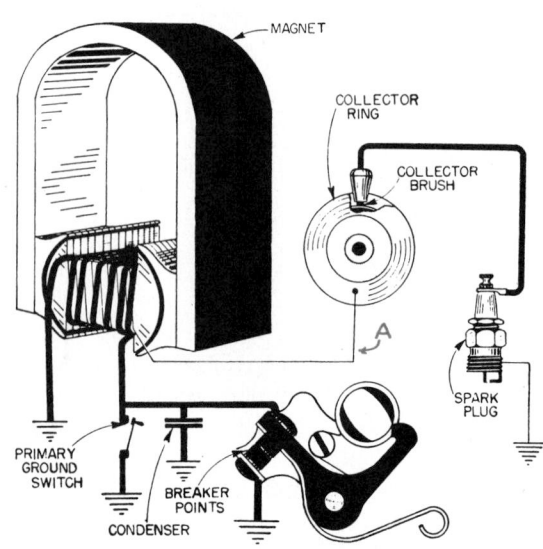

Fig. 35-56. Diagram of shuttle wound high tension magneto. Lead to high tension winding on rotor is shown at A.

PRINCIPLES OF OPERATION

As explained in Chapter 30, electricity can be generated by revolving a coil of wire in a magnetic field. In the conventional generator, the magnetic field is produced by passing some of the generated current through coils of wire (field coils) which, in turn, produce the magnetic field. The magnetic field, then, is produced electrically.

In the case of the magneto, the magnetic field is produced by means of permanent magnets. At first, these magnets were made of high quality carbon steel. Then, special alloy steels with greatly improved magnetic characteristics were developed. Magnets made of special alloys are stronger for the same size, and then retain their magnetism for much longer periods. Alloys used on modern magnets are usually tungsten, chromium and cobalt.

TYPES OF MAGNETOS

There are two ways in which magnetos may be classified. Originally, they were classified as to the type of current they produced, low tension or high tension. The low tension magneto developed a low voltage and required an external coil to step up the voltage. The high tension magneto incorporated the coil in the magneto itself.

The other method of classifying magnetos takes into consideration the portion of the magneto which is revolved. Magnetos are "shuttle wound" if they have the windings on an armature that is revolved in a magnetic field. See Fig. 35-56. Magnetos are the "inductor type" if both the coil and magnet are mounted in stationary positions and movement of the magnetic field is obtained by breaking and reestablishing the magnetic field, Fig. 35-57.

Magnetos known as the "revolving magnet" design have been made possible by the new magnetic steels. In this design, the coil (together with a short magnetic circuit) is mounted in a stationary position, and one or more magnets are revolved

between the pole pieces of the magnetic circuit. Some manufacturers classify this construction as "induction type."

LOW TENSION MAGNETOS

The low tension magneto was the first type of magneto put to use. It is still used extensively on industrial engines. In this construction the permanent magnets are U-shaped, with the armature (carrying a single primary winding) revolving between the pole pieces.

As explained in Chapter 30, revolving a coil of wire in a magnetic field will cause current to flow in the coil. This current is the alternating type.

In the magneto, the armature winding is connected to the primary winding of an ignition coil. Breaker points, which revolve with the armature, are timed to open the circuit at peak voltage. This interruption of the primary current produces a high tension current in the secondary winding of the coil, which is carried back to the distributor rotor on the magneto, where it is directed to the proper spark plug.

Breaker points on a low tension magneto can be connected either in series with the armature winding, or in parallel. In the series connection, the magneto serves simply as a current source. The value of the current is relatively low, because the resistance of the primary winding of the coil is included in the circuit. However, when the breaker points are in parallel with the armature winding, a heavier current flows through the armature as the resistance of the primary winding of the coil is no longer included in the circuit. Then when the breaker points open, this heavy current surges through the primary winding of the coil with a strong inductive effect. The result is that the magnetic field of the coil is built up very rapidly.

ROTARY INDUCTOR MAGNETOS

In the rotary inductor type magneto, Fig. 35-57, both the magnet and coil are stationary, and current is induced in the primary winding by rotating one or both legs of the magnetic circuit. When only one leg of the magnetic circuit is broken, the magnetic flux in the coil alternates from maximum to minimum. However, it does not undergo complete reversal when both legs of the magnetic circuit are interrupted.

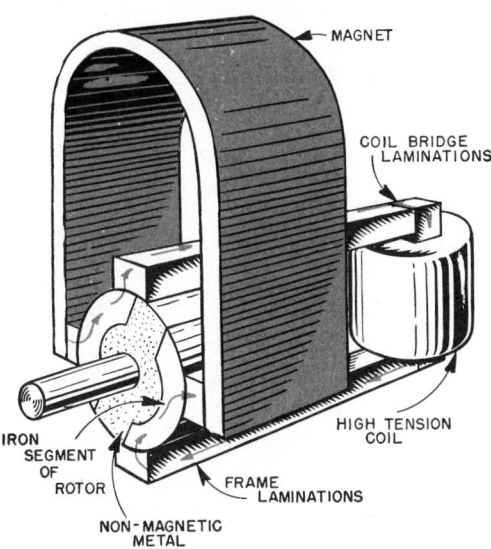

Fig. 35-57. Rotary inductor type magneto.

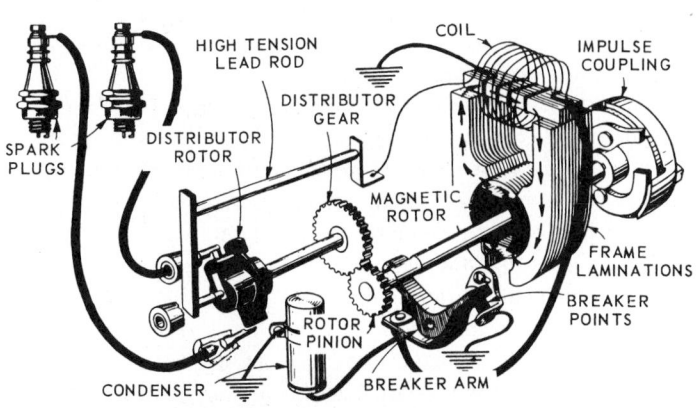

Fig. 35-58. Schematic diagram of rotating magnet magneto.

ROTATING MAGNET MAGNETOS

The introduction of the more powerful permanent magnets of special alloy steel made possible the design of magnetos in which the magnet was revolved. Known as rotating magnet magnetos, they have virtually replaced the original design with stationary U-shaped magnets.

In the rotating magnet design, the coil condenser and breaker points are stationary. Advantages include: simplified design; more sturdy construction; moving connections are eliminated; tests and repairs are more easily made; smaller and more compact units are possible.

A schematic drawing of a rotating magnet magneto is shown in Fig. 35-58. Rotation of the magnetic rotor produces an alternating magnetic flux or field which cuts the stationary primary winding each time it increases and decreases. As a result, alternating electric current induced in the primary circuit during the period the circuit is completed through the closed breaker points. As the density of the magnetic field varies, the strength of the current induced in the primary circuit also varies. It reaches a maximum value each time a complete magnetic flux reversal occurs in the magnetic circuit.

The current induced in the primary winding produces a magnetic field that surrounds the secondary winding. This field reaches its maximum when the current in the primary winding reaches its maximum. At this instant, the breaker points are opened by the action of the breaker cam. This stops the flow of current in the primary circuit and causes the collapse of the magnetic field. The collapsing field then induces a current in the secondary circuit. Since the ratio of turns in secondary winding is high compared to those in the primary, a high tension voltage is produced.

The self-induced voltage produced in the primary winding, resulting from the collapsing magnetic field, is absorbed by the condenser, which is shunted across the breaker points. In effect, this action promotes a more rapid collapse of the primary field and, at the same time, reduces arcing at the breaker points.

FLYWHEEL MAGNETOS

Flywheel magnetos, Fig. 35-59, are revolving magnet type used extensively for ignition on small gasoline engines used on lawn mowers, garden tractors, outboard motors, etc. Flywheel magnetos are used on single cylinder engines and, occasionally, on two and four cylinder engines.

The theory of operation is similar to that of the rotary magneto. The magnet is mounted on the outer rim of the flywheel, which revolves around the stationary ignition coil, condenser and breaker point assembly. As the ends of the magnet pass by the pole pieces, an alternating magnetic flux is established through the ignition coils, and current is generated in the primary circuit during the period that the breaker points are closed. A cam located on the crankshaft opens the breaker points when the primary current is at a maximum. This interruption of the current causes the magnetic field to collapse which, in turn, induces a high tension voltage in the secondary winding.

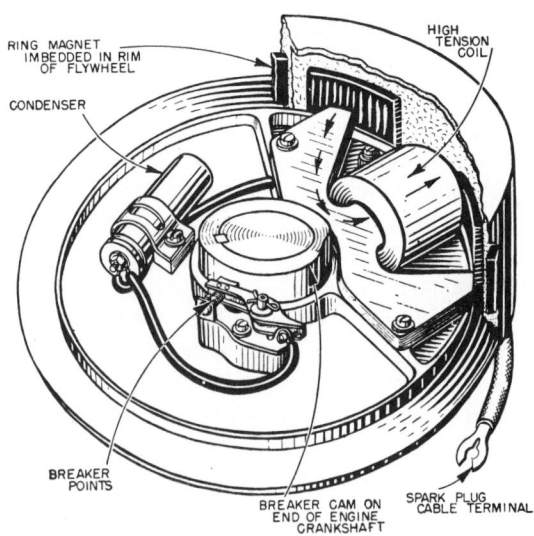

Fig. 35-59. Flywheel magneto of type used on small gas engines.

TRANSISTOR IGNITION SYSTEM

The output of a conventional ignition system is limited by the amount of current in the primary circuit. This, in turn, is limited by the amount of current that can be interrupted by the "breaking" of the contact points (approximately 5 amp.).

Another factor limiting output of a conventional system is the period of time the breaker points remain closed (dwell). As engine speed increases, dwell time becomes increasingly short.

To overcome these problems, the transistor ignition system has been developed.

The transistor is a solid metallic device with the ability to switch large currents through the action of a very small control or relay current. Basically there are four types of transistor ignition systems:

1. The contact controlled transistor system, in which a transistor makes and breaks the ignition primary circuit. However, the transistor control circuit is triggered by the

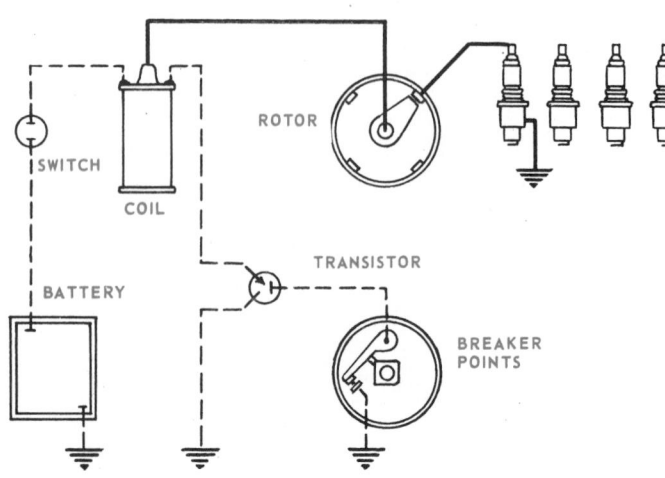

Fig. 35-60. Schematic of a contact controlled transistor ignition system.

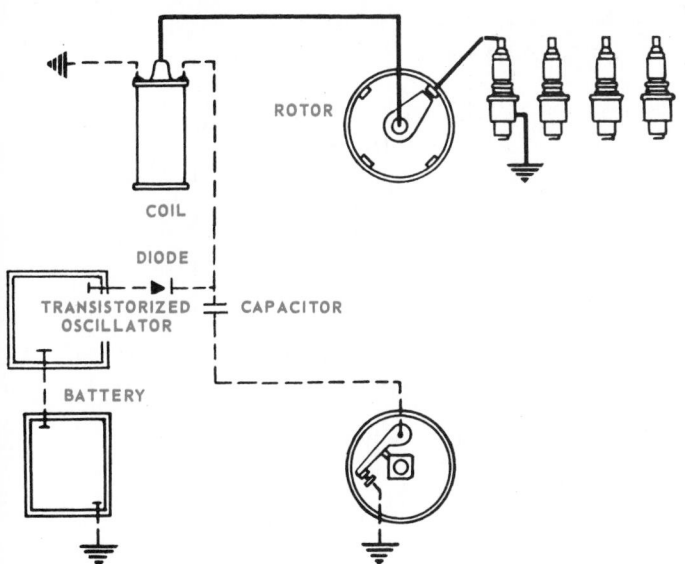

Fig. 35-61. Contact controlled capacitor discharge circuit.

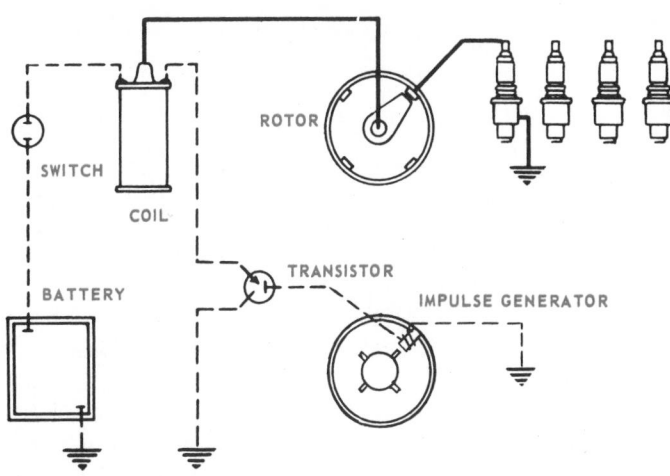

Fig. 35-63. Magnetic controlled capacitor discharge system.

conventional distributor breaker points. See Fig. 35-60.

2. The contact controlled capacitor discharge system, in which the spark discharge is triggered by conventional distributor breaker points. See Fig. 35-61.

3. The magnetic controlled transistor system (full transistor system), in which a pulse generator is used to trigger the transistor, eliminating the breaker points. See Fig. 35-62.

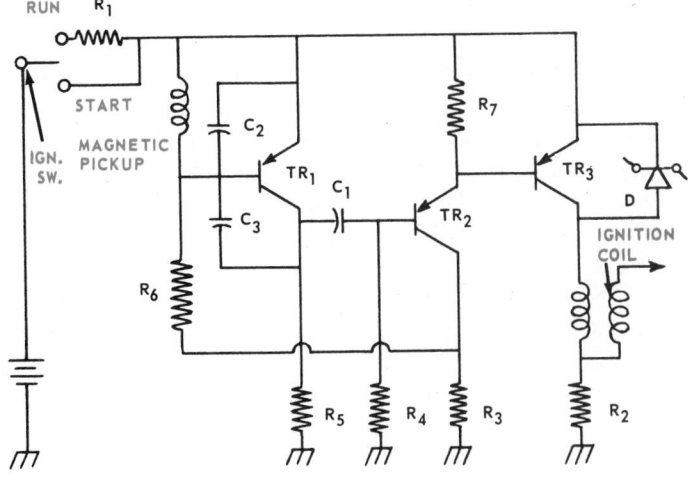

Fig. 35-62. Circuit diagram of a magnetic controlled transistor ignition system.

4. The magnetic controlled capacitor discharge system, in which a pulse generator triggers the spark discharge, eliminating the distributor breaker points. See Fig. 35-63.

As mentioned, a transistor has the ability to switch large currents through the action of a small current. The switching action of the transistor involves no moving parts, and it can be made instantaneous through proper circuit design. In transistors

of the PNP type (positive-negative-positive), current goes to the emitter, Fig. 35-64, then it flows to and through the collector under the control of the base circuit.

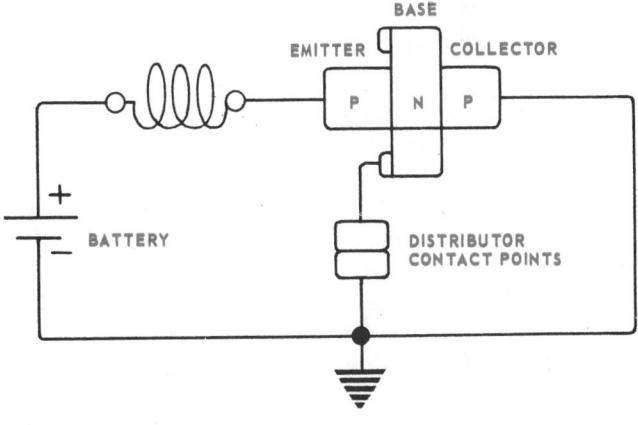

Fig. 35-64. Diagram of simple transistor ignition system using conventional breaker points.

The base circuit of the transistor has a negative bias. When the contact points in the circuit-to-ground are closed, current flows. But, when the contact points interrupt the base circuit, this also interrupts the flow of current from the emitter to the collector.

The current flow through the emitter and the collector is interrupted entirely by electronic means. There is no motion of any kind in a transistor, with no switch contacts or moving blades. It is this action which makes the transistor well suited for ignition systems since it breaks the circuit so rapidly no condenser is required, and there is no arcing.

The transistor may be compared to a horn relay in that a small current is used to control a heavy current. In the case of the transistor there are no moving parts, and it acts with virtually no time lag.

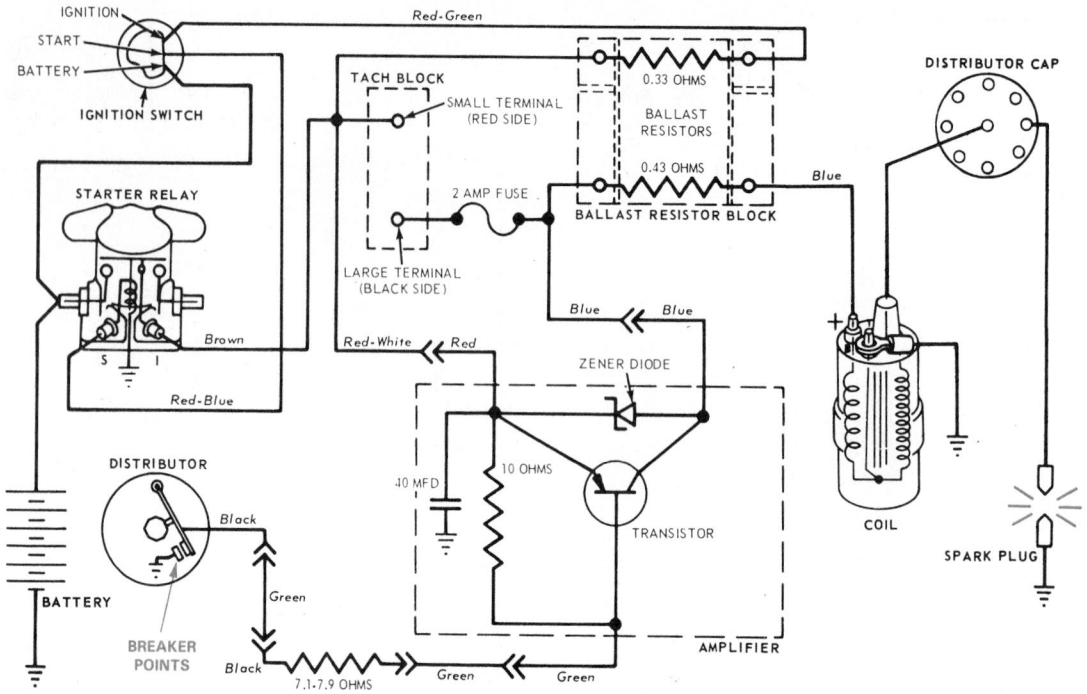

Fig. 35-65.· Transistor ignition system circuit as installed on older Ford vehicles. Note breaker points.

CONTACT CONTROLLED TRANSISTOR SYSTEM

Transistor ignition used by Ford in the early '70s is an example of the contact controlled system, Fig. 35-65. The ignition coil primary in the transistor system is designed to draw 12 amp. peak current, or approximately 5.5 amp. average current. With this design, the system will provide high spark plug voltage at higher engine speeds.

The transistor is connected between the battery and the coil. It is used to make and break the coil primary circuit. The distributor breaker points are used to control the transistor.

A 7.1 to 7.9 ohm resistor is connected between the distributor and the transistor is located in the wiring harness and limits the transistor control current to 0.5 amp. This low current greatly reduces pitting and wear of the distributor points.

The amplifier assembly is mounted under the instrument panel to protect the parts from engine heat. A ceramic ballast resistor block and a tachometer connector block are mounted in the engine compartment. A 2 amp. fuse between the large black terminal of the tach block and the coil primary circuit prevents the transistor from being damaged by the application of external devices (other than testing equipment).

The tachometer block is used to connect a tachometer or dwell meter into the circuit. Do not connect either of these instruments into the circuit in any other manner.

Most of the contact controlled transistor ignition systems on the market include one or two ballast resistors, which must be in balance with the rest of the circuit. Therefore, the original ballast resistor must be bypassed. This can be done by running a new lead from the ignition switch if the ballast resistor is in the wiring harness. Or, if the resistor is readily accessible, a jumper wire bypassing the unit can be used.

MAGNETIC PULSE TRANSISTOR

An example of the magnetic pulse transistor ignition system is produced by Delco-Remy and used by Pontiac, Fig. 35-66. It features a specially designed magnetic pulse distributor, an ignition pulse amplifier and a special coil. The other units of the system are of standard design and include resistors or resistance wire, switch and battery.

The internal construction of the distributor differs greatly from conventional design. An inner timer core replaces the conventional breaker cam. The timer core has the same number of equally spaced projections or vanes as there are engine cylinders. The timer core rotates inside a magnetic pickup assembly, which replaces the conventional breaker plate, contact point set and condenser.

The magnetic pickup assembly consists of a ceramic permanent magnet, a pole piece and a pickup coil. The pole piece is a steel plate having equally spaced internal teeth with one tooth for each engine cylinder.

In operation, the steel plate rotates inside a stationary pole piece. The pickup coil (mounted under pole piece) picks up variations in the magnetic flux as the teeth on the rotor and stationary piece alternately have their teeth in and out of alignment. This varying magnetic flux, causes a tiny current impulse to operate the transistor. The distributor rotor and cap are the same as parts used in a conventional system.

The magnetic pickup assembly is made to rotate by the vacuum control unit. In this way, vacuum advance is provided. The timer core is made to rotate about the shaft by conventional advance weights to provide centrifugal advance. The ignition pulse amplifier consists primarily of transistors, resistors, diodes and capacitors with a printed circuit.

A wiring diagram for a typical magnetic pulse transistor

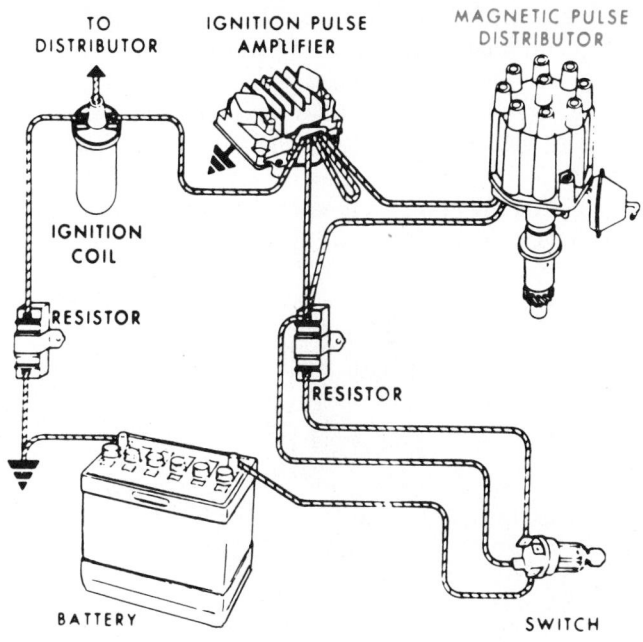

Fig. 35-66. Note magnetic pulse distributor used on this Delco-Remy transistor ignition system.

ignition system is shown in Fig. 35-66. There are two resistors used in this circuit. The resistor connected directly to the switch is bypassed during cranking. The other resistor is always in the circuit.

When the engine is not running and the switch is closed, the current flows through a part of the circuit shown in color, Fig. 35-67. The current flows from the battery through the switch and resistor R-7 to the amplifier. From there, it flows through transistors TR-1 and TR-2, resistors R-1, R-2 and R-3, the coil

primary and resistor R-8 to ground. The condenser, C-1, is charged with positive voltage toward transistor TR-2.

When the engine is running, the induced voltage in the pickup coil causes transistor TR-3 to conduct, resulting in current flow in the circuit shown in color, Fig. 35-67. This condition exists until the charge on the condenser C-1 is dissipated through resistor R-2. When that occurs, the circuit reverts to the conditions shown in Fig. 35-67.

Resistor R-4 is known as a feedback resistor. Its function is to turn TR-3 off when TR-2 returns to the "on" condition. Resistor R-1 is a biasing resistor, which allows transistor TR-1 to operate. The Zener diode D-1 protects transistor TR-1 from high voltages that may be induced in the primary winding. Condensers C-2 and C-3 protect transistor TR-3 from high voltages that appear in the system.

CHRYSLER ELECTRONIC IGNITION

The basic circuits of the Chrysler Electronic Ignition system introduced in 1972 are shown in Fig. 35-68. The primary circuit consists of the battery, ignition switch, compensating side of the dual ballast resistor, primary winding of the ignition coil, the power switching transistor of the control unit and the vehicle frame acting as a ground.

The secondary circuit consists of the ignition coil secondary winding, distributor cap and rotor, spark plugs and vehicle frame.

The compensating resistance serves the same purpose as in the contact ignition system. It maintains constant primary current with variation in engine speed. While starting, this resistance is bypassed, applying full battery voltage to the ignition coil. The compensating resistance is in series with both the control unit feed and the auxiliary ballast circuits, Figs. 35-69 and 35-70.

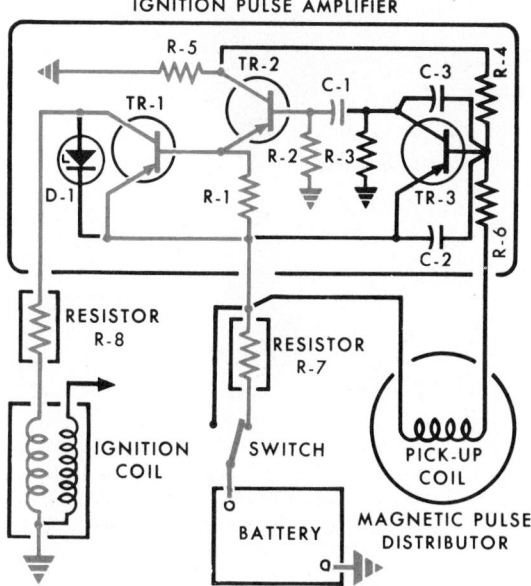
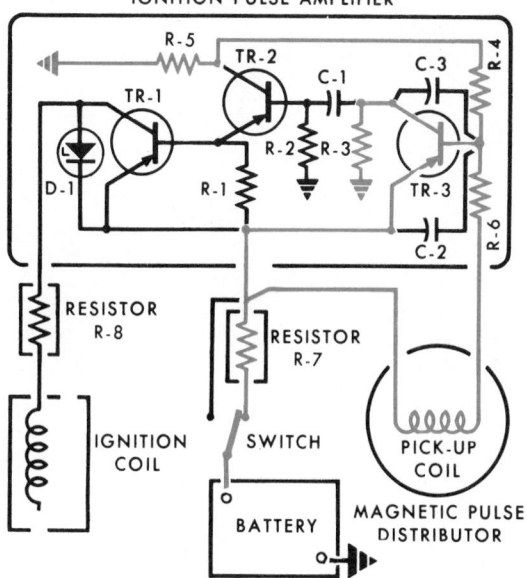

Fig. 35-67. Delco-Remy magnetic pulse transistor ignition system. Left. Internal wiring diagram of ignition pulse amplifier, showing current flow in color with switch on and engine not running. Right. Internal wiring diagram of ignition pulse amplifier, showing current flow in color when spark plug fires.

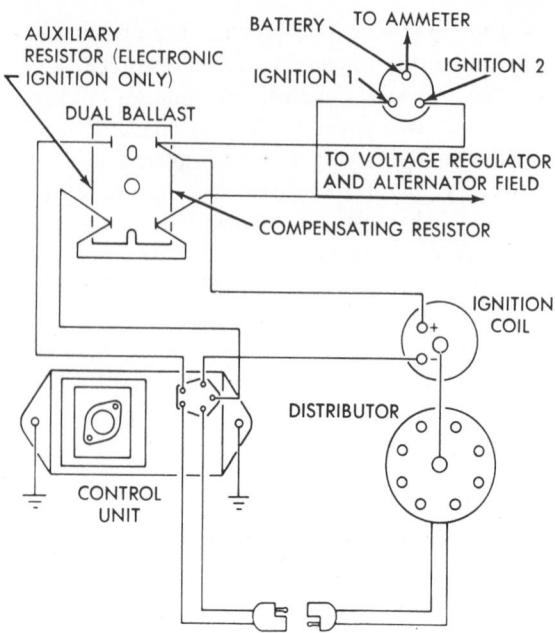

Fig. 35-68. Wiring diagram of Chrysler electronic ignition.

In addition to the two basic circuits, there are the pickup circuit, control unit feed circuit and auxiliary ballast circuits. Two circuits are used to operate the circuitry of the control unit. These are the auxiliary ballast circuit (which uses 5 ohm section of dual ballast resistor) and the control unit feed circuit.

The pickup circuit is used to sense the proper timing for the control unit switching transistor, Figs. 35-70 and 35-71. The

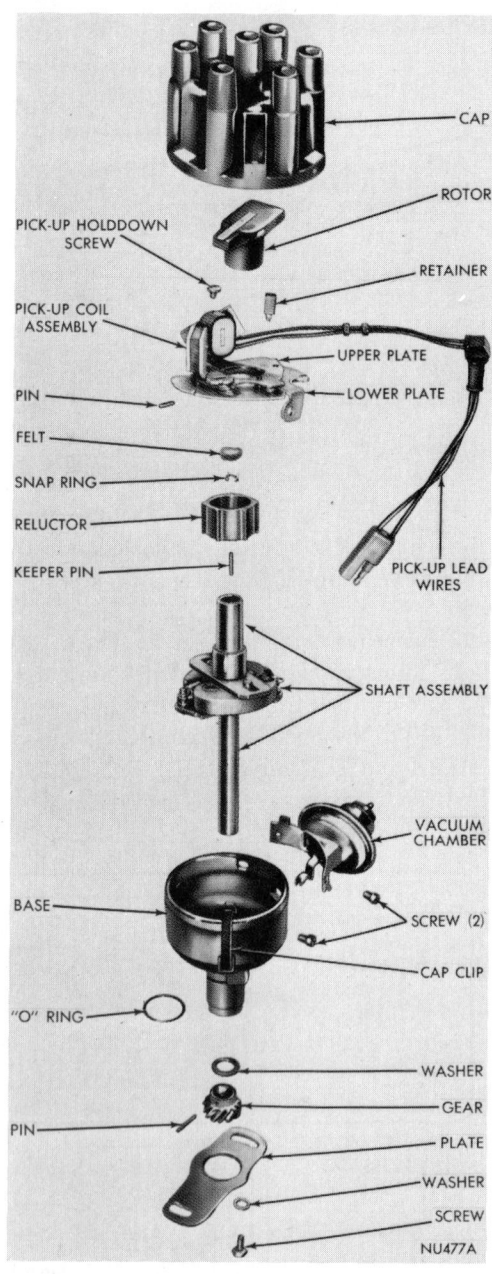

Fig. 35-71. Exploded view of Chrysler electronic ignition distributor shows use of reluctor in place of cam. When checking air gap between reluctor and pickup magnet, a non-magnetic feeler gauge is required.

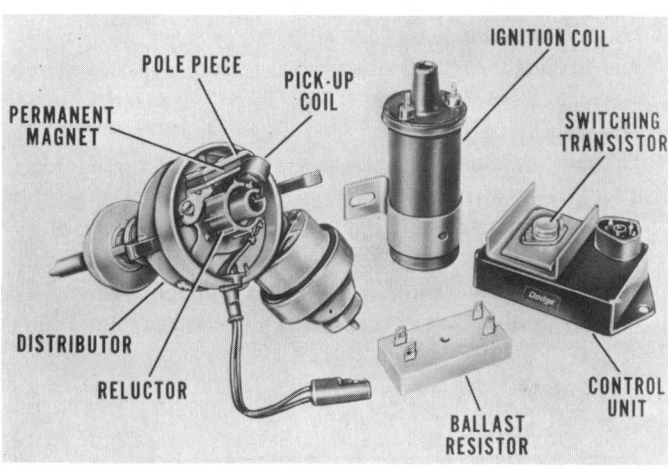

Fig. 35-69. Chrysler electronic ignition system components.

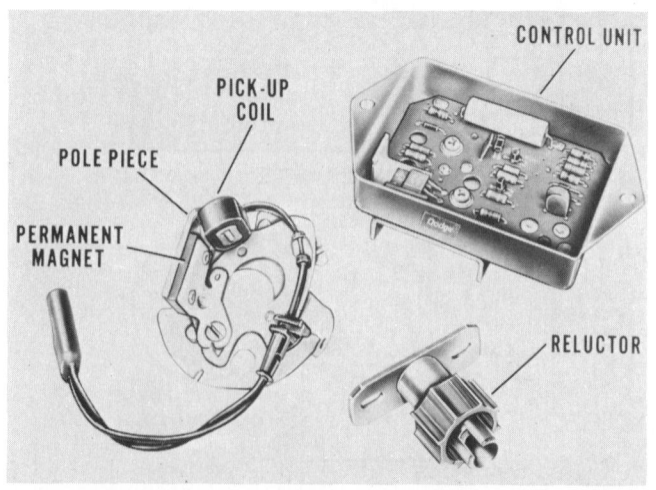

Fig. 35-70. Magnetic pickup components and control unit of Chrysler electronic ignition system.

reluctor, rotating with the distributor shaft, produces a voltage pulse in the magnetic pickup each time a spark plug is to be fired. This pulse is transmitted through the pickup coil in the power switching transistor in the control unit, causing the transistor to interrupt current flow through the primary circuit. This break in the primary circuit induces high voltage in the secondary coil and fires a spark plug.

The length of time that the switching transistor blocks the flow of current to the primary circuit (dwell) is determined by the electronic circuitry in the control unit. Even though dwell may be read with a dwell meter, there is no means provided to change it.

The magnetic pickup and the control unit have replaced the function of the breaker points and, unlike the breaker points, show no signs of wear. Therefore, periodic checks of timing and dwell are not necessary. Ignition maintenance is reduced to inspection of wiring, and cleaning and changing of spark plugs as needed.

DELCO HIGH ENERGY IGNITION

Recent models of General Motors engines are equipped with the Delco-Remy High Energy Ignition (HEI) system, Fig. 35-72. It is an electronic system that eliminates the ignition breaker points and condenser.

All HEI components are mounted in or on the distributor. The coil is built into the distributor. This reduces the length of the high tension lead, which results in increased energy at the spark plugs. Also contributing to the high efficiency of this ignition system is the use of improved silicone leads and boots.

With conventional ignition systems, less than 30 kilovolts with a duration of 1.5 milliseconds is available at the plug points. With HEI, the kilovoltage is increased to nearly 40, with a duration in excess of 2.0 milliseconds, Fig. 35-74.

This system includes a magnetic pulse distributor with integrated electronics and a high energy ignition coil. These elements form a single unit, Fig. 35-72, except on the in-line six cylinder engine application in which the coil is mounted separately.

The basic HEI distributor contains a pickup coil, permanent magnet and a pole piece with internal teeth. In the case of V-8 models, there are eight equally spaced teeth. The in-line six has six equally spaced teeth. The V-6 has three banks of teeth with two teeth per bank. These teeth are located and retained on the distributor shaft upper bushing. See Fig. 35-73. The distributor also contains an electronic module, a condenser for noise suppression and a vacuum advance unit.

Attached to the lower part of the centrifugal advance weight base is a timer core. External teeth on the timer core are spaced in the same manner as those on the pole piece.

When the distributor shaft rotates, the teeth of the timer core align with the teeth of the pole piece to induce voltage in the pickup coil. This signals the all-electronic module to open the ignition coil primary circuit. Maximum inductance occurs at the instant the timer core teeth are aligned with the teeth on the pole piece. At the instant the timer core teeth start to pass the teeth on the pole piece, the primary current decreases. This results in a collapse of the magnetic field, which induces a current in the primary coil winding. This, in turn, induces a high voltage in the secondary winding of the coil. The rotor then carries the current to spark plugs in correct firing order.

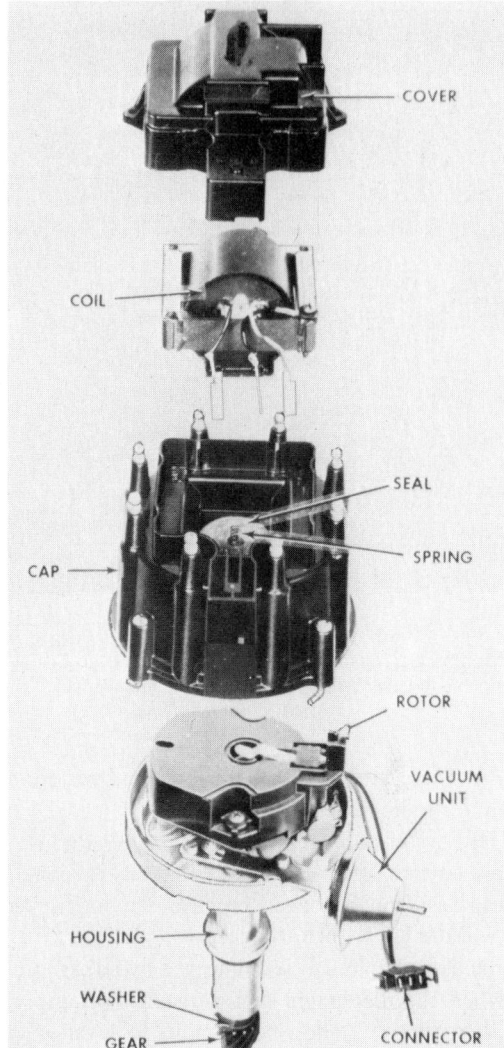

Fig. 35-72. Individual parts of HEI ignition unit.

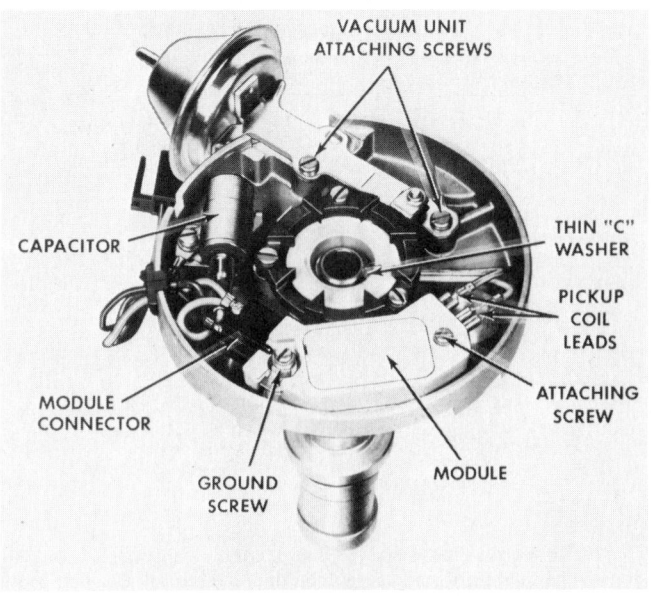

Fig. 35-73. Distributor housing with coil removed.

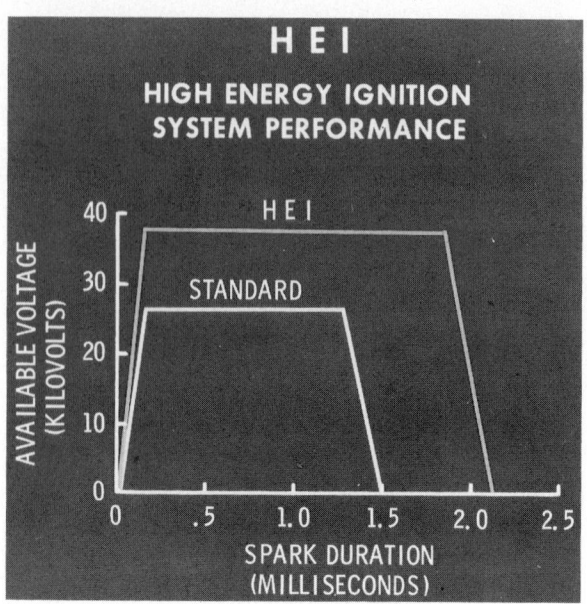

Fig. 35-74. Chart compares performance of GM's High Energy Ignition with standard (breaker point type) ignition for available voltage and spark duration.

NOTE: There are no breaker points, and the condenser is used only for radio noise suppression.

The HEI system operates for many miles without requiring any replacements since there are no breaker points. Spark plugs also last much longer because the higher secondary voltage will fire larger than normal spark plug gaps.

The vacuum diaphragm is connected by linkage to the pole piece. When the diaphragm moves against spring pressure, it rotates the pole piece, allowing the poles to advance relative to the timer core. The timer core is rotated about the shaft by conventional advance weights, which provide centrifugal advance.

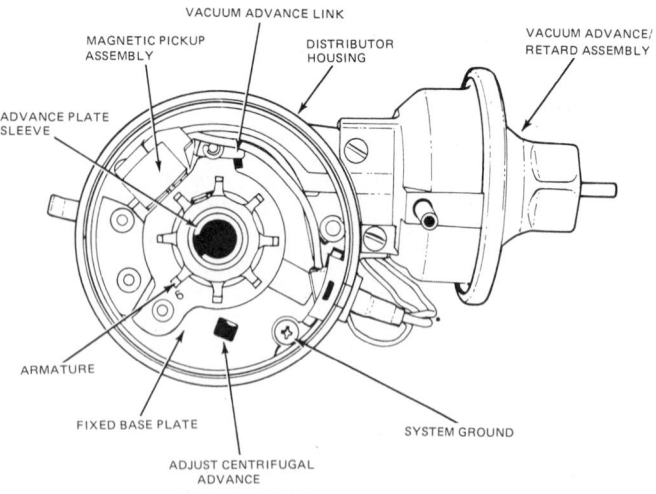

Fig. 35-75. Ford's breakerless ignition distributor operates in conjunction with a solid state module. Ignition timing is critical. One-half tooth misalignment between armature and pickup magnet will result in a 7 3/4 deg. static timing error.

FORD SOLID STATE IGNITION

Beginning in 1974, the Ford solid state ignition system is installed on all 400 cu. in. V-8 engines with 2 Bbl. carburetor, and on all 460 cu. in. V-8 engines with 4 Bbl. carburetor. It also appears on some 200 cu. in. six cylinder engines equipped with California emission controls.

Ford's new solid state system has a coil, high tension wiring, spark plugs and a permanent magnet, low-voltage generator, plus the solid state unit, Fig. 35-75.

The generator consists of an armature with six or eight gear-like teeth (one for each cylinder) mounted on top of the distributor shaft, and a permanent magnet located inside a small coil. The coil is riveted in place to provide a preset air gap with the armature. The distributor base, cap, rotor and the vacuum and centrifugal spark advance mechanisms are essentially the same as in the conventional system.

The distributor is connected to the solid state module, which is located in the engine compartment. The module is approximately 4 in. square and 2 in. deep. Its aluminum housing is provided with cooling fins. Inside are the necessary resistors, capacitors, transistors and diodes, totaling 35 units.

The module performs two functions that are done mechanically in the conventional system. The module senses a signal from the magnetic generator to perform the "switching function" of the conventional breaker points, and it also controls "dwell."

Some of the module components are used as protective devices, so the module will not be damaged from high voltage or reversed polarity.

In operation, the permanent magnet generator sends alternating current to the module, with the current changing from positive to negative each time one of the gear teeth on the armature passes the permanent magnet in the coil.

When a gear tooth is exactly opposite the coil, there is zero voltage. The electronic module senses this and cuts off current to the coil. This causes the magnetic field surrounding the coil to collapse, and high tension current generated is directed to the cylinders by a conventional rotor.

Performance characteristics of Ford's solid state ignition compared to its conventional ignition system:

	SPARK PLUG VOLTAGE	
	Start	Run
	10V @	14V @
	200 rpm	800 rpm
Solid State	32,000	26,000
Conventional	26,000	25,000

In addition to providing improved starting, Ford's solid state ignition system has no breaker points that wear and require replacement. Consequently, spark timing does not change.

FORD ELECTRONIC ENGINE CONTROL

Electronic Engine Control II (EEC II), Fig. 35-76, was introduced on 1979 Fords (sold in California and on Mercury models in all 50 states) equipped with the 5.8 litre (351 W CID)

V-8 engine. The system is composed of seven sensors, an electronic control assembly, several control solenoids and a vacuum-operated thermactor air system. EEC II also features a carburetor equipped with a controllable air/fuel mixture and an exhaust gas oxygen sensor that provides a rich/lean signal to the electronic control assembly.

EEC II also has a four-lobe pulse ring integral with the crankshaft damper and a crankshaft position (CP) sensor attached to the timing bracket pointer. The distributor has no advance or retard mechanism as the spark timing is controlled entirely by the electronic control assembly. This is done according to engine operating conditions and individual vehicle calibration. Calibration is controlled by the calibrating assembly attached to the electronic control assembly.

Power for the EEC II system is provided by the power relay attached to the same bracket as the electronic control assembly.

There are a total of seven sensors in the EEC II system:

1. Barometric pressure.
2. Manifold absolute pressure sensors contained in a single housing.
3. Engine coolant sensor.
4. Crankshaft position sensor.
5. Throttle position sensor.
6. EGR valve position sensor.
7. Exhaust gas oxygen sensor.

During engine starting and operation, the electronic control assembly constantly monitors these sensors to determine the

ELECTRONIC ENGINE CONTROL II (EEC II) SYSTEM

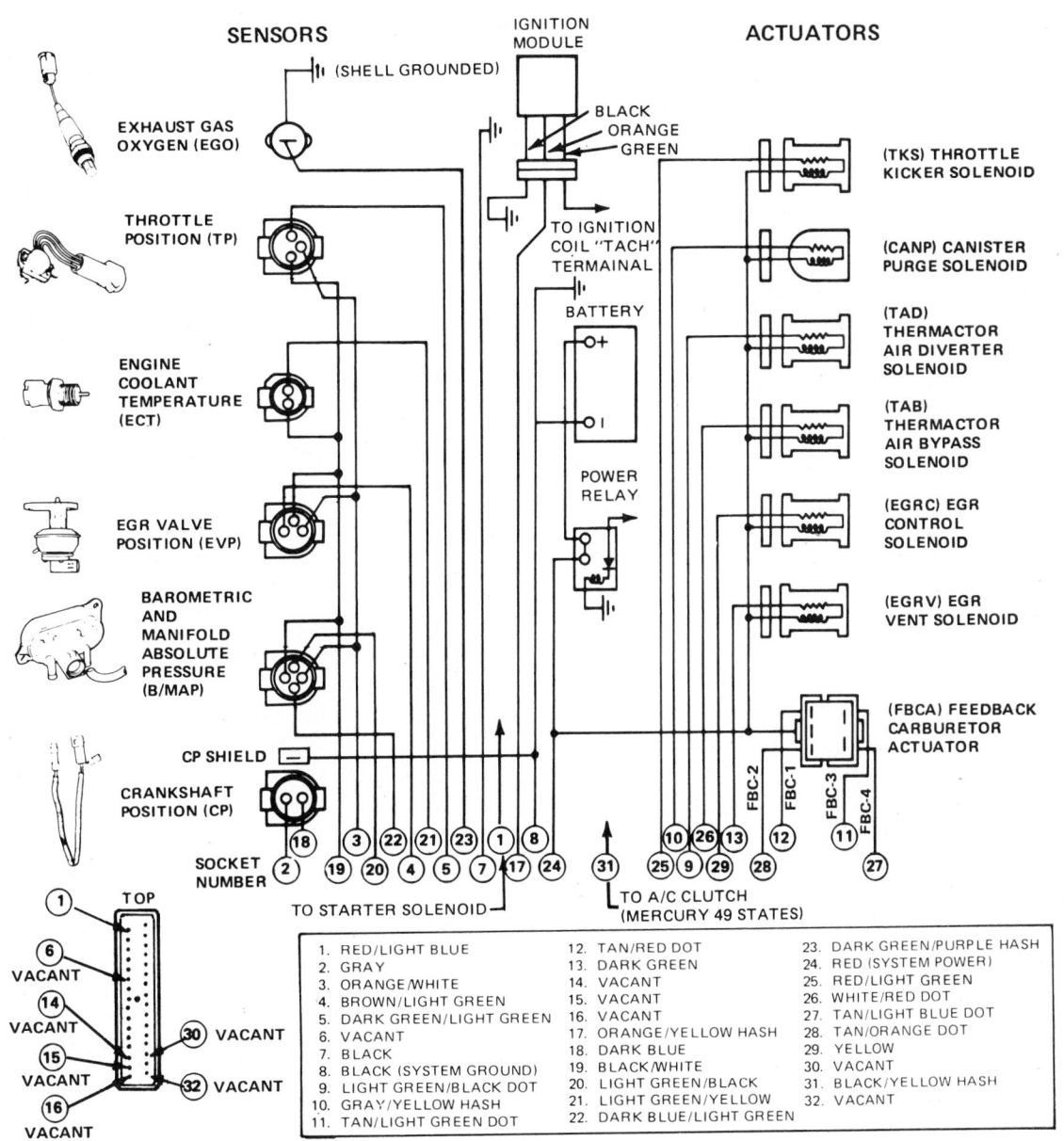

Fig. 35-76. The 1979 Ford Electronic Engine Control II system.

required timing advance, EGR flow rate, thermactor air mode and air/fuel ratio for any given instant of vehicle operating conditions. The electronic control assembly then sends output commands: to the ignition module for spark timing; to the EGR control solenoids to direct thermactor airflow; to the canister purge solenoids; to the feedback carburetor actuator to adjust air/fuel mixture; to the termactor solenoids.

The continuous control and adjustment of ignition timing, EGR flow rate and air/fuel ratio results in optimum performance under all operating conditions.

If for some reason there is a failure in the electronic engine control assembly, the system goes back into what is called the "limited operational strategy" mode. In this mode, the electronic control assembly output commands are cut off. At this time, the engine operates with initial spark advance only, regardless of sensor input signals. The engine will operate in this manner until repairs are made, but with poor performance.

IGNITION CIRCUIT TESTS

If the checks indicated under Troubleshooting show that the ignition system is at fault, the following checks may help locate the trouble. All tests are to be made in the order shown with the lights and accessories off.

If the engine starts, but immediately stops when the starting switch is turned off, steps one to four may be omitted. Voltmeter connections are shown in Fig. 35-77, in which meter connections are shown by dotted lines in color.

1. Check all connections in primary and secondary circuit.
2. Remove secondary coil lead from distributor cap. Hold 1/4 in. from engine while cranking. If spark occurs, check distributor cap, rotor and spark plug wiring.
3. Connect voltmeter as shown at V-1, Fig. 35-77. Reading should be 1V maximum, while cranking engine. If no reading is obtained, trouble may be:
   a. Open ignition circuit used during cranking.
   b. Ignition switch not closing ignition circuit during cranking.
   c. Ground in circuit from coil terminal to ignition switch.
   d. Ground in coil.
4. Connect voltmeter as shown at V-2 with ignition switch on, breaker points open. Meter should show normal battery voltage. If not, trouble may be:
   a. Low battery.
   b. Breaker points not open.
   c. Ground in circuit from coil to distributor.
   d. Ground in distributor.
   e. Ground in coil.
   f. Ground in ignition circuit used during cranking, or in lead connecting coil to resistor.
5. Connect voltmeter as shown at V-2, ignition switch on, points closed. Meter reading should be 5 to 7V. If higher than 7V:
   a. Contacts may not be closed.
   b. A loose connection in distributor.
   c. Distributor not grounded to engine.
   d. Faulty breaker points.

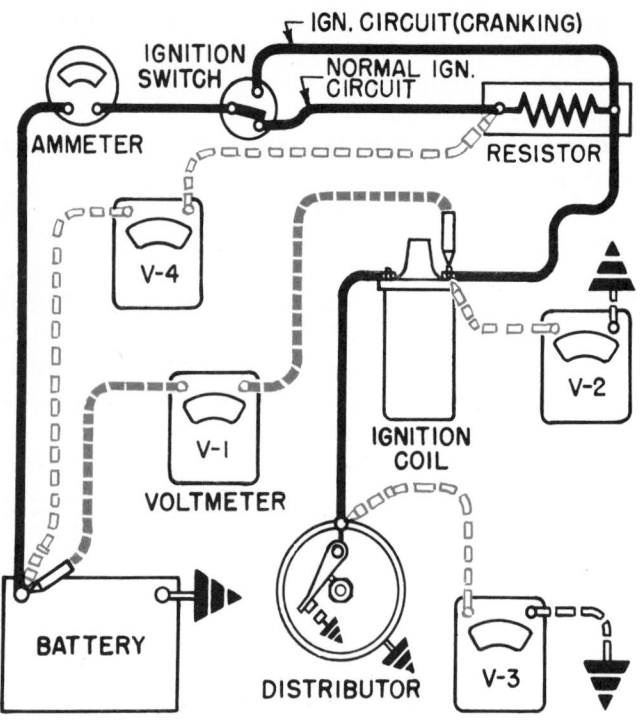

Fig. 35-77. Checking voltage drop in ignition circuit.

   e. Loose connection between coil and distributor.
   f. Resistor out of circuit due to shorted or incorrect wiring.
   g. Starting contacts of ignition switch may stay closed.
   h. Resistor has too little resistance.
   If meter reading is less than 5V, trouble may be:
   a. Loose connection from resistor through ignition switch to battery.
   b. Loose connection between resistor and coil.
   c. Resistance is open, or too much resistance.
6. Connect voltmeter as shown at V-3, ignition switch on and points closed. Reading should be 0.2 maximum. If not:
   a. Contacts are not closed.
   b. Loose connection in distributor.
   c. Distributor not grounded to engine.
   d. Defective breaker points.
   e. Voltage drop across ignition breaker points should not exceed 0.125V.
7. Connect voltmeter as shown at V-4. Ignition switch on and points closed. Meter reading should not exceed 0.7V. If greater check for loose connection from resistor through ignition switch circuit to battery.
8. If these checks fail to find cause of trouble, remove coil, distributor and resistor. Check separately for all functions. Also check wiring harness.

IGNITION TROUBLESHOOTING

ENGINE WILL NOT START

1. Weak battery.
2. Excessive moisture on high tension wiring and spark plugs.

3. Cracked distributor cap.
4. Faulty coil.
5. Faulty condenser.
6. Coil to distributor high tension lead not in place.
7. Loose connections or broken wire in low tension circuit.
8. Faulty ignition breaker points.

HARD STARTING

1. Faulty or improperly gapped spark plugs.
2. Faulty or improperly adjusted breaker points.
3. Loose connections in primary circuit.
4. Defective high tension cables.

5. Low capacity condenser.
6. Faulty distributor cap or rotor.

ENGINE MISFIRES

1. Dirty or worn spark plugs.
2. Damaged insulation on high tension wires.
3. High tension wires disconnected.
4. High tension wires incorrectly routed to plugs.
5. Defective distributor cap.
6. Poor cylinder compression.
7. Breaker points incorrectly adjusted.
8. Weak breaker point spring.

REVIEW QUESTIONS — ENGINE IGNITION

1. List the major elements of a conventional ignition system.
2. What is the purpose of the ignition coil?
3. What is the voltage at the secondary terminal of the ignition coil?
   a. 5,000 volts.
   b. 12 volts.
   c. 110 volts.
   d. 20,000 volts.
   e. 100,000 volts.
4. In addition to opening and closing the primary ignition circuit, what else does an ignition distributor do?
5. What is the purpose of the ignition condenser?
6. What is the purpose of the spark plug?
7. With the closing of the ignition switch, describe what happens in an ignition system.
8. Is ignition voltage higher at low speed or high speed?
9. Is there any advantage in keeping the high tension leads as short as possible?
10. What advantage is there in having the high tension outlet of the ignition coil negative?
11. Describe the lead pencil test for determining the polarity of the ignition system.
12. The capacity of an ignition condenser is measured in what units?
    a. Volts.
    b. Farads.
    c. Joules.
    d. Microfarads.
13. If metal is transferred to the positive point of ignition breaker points, is condenser capacity too large or too small?
    a. Too small.
    b. Too large.
14. On a four-cycle engine, at what speed is the distributor driven?
    a. Engine speed.
    b. Half engine speed.
    c. Twice engine speed.
15. On a two-cycle engine, at what speed is the distributor driven?
    a. Engine speed.

    b. Half engine speed.
    c. Twice engine speed.
16. On a typical distributor, how many lobes are there on the breaker cam for a six cylinder engine?
    a. Three. b. Six. c. Twelve.
17. The rotor in a distributor distributes the current to the various spark plugs. Where does it get the current?
18. What engine conditions will affect the time that ignition should occur?
19. When the engine is idling, when is the spark usually timed to occur?
    a. Before top center.
    b. After top center.
    c. Before bottom center.
20. At higher engine speeds, why is it necessary to have the spark occur earlier?
21. At what point in the intake system is the vacuum advance connected?
    a. Atmospheric side of the carburetor throttle.
    b. Engine side of the carburetor throttle.
    c. Vacuum side of the fuel pump.
22. As load on an engine is increased, is more or less spark advance required?
    a. More spark advance.
    b. Less spark advance.
23. What is cam angle?
24. When cam angle is small, will there be more or less time for current to pass through the primary circuit?
    a. More time.   b. Less time.
25. In the Ford Loadomatic distributor, how is the spark advance controlled?
    a. By centrifugal force only.
    b. By vacuum only.
    c. By a combination of vacuum and centrifugal force.
26. What items can be checked with a modern distributor testing equipment?
27. When aligning breaker points, which part of the assembly should be bent?
    a. The stationary point.
    b. The movable point.
28. Why is a resistor used in the primary ignition circuit?

29. There are two general types of resistors used in the primary ignition circuit. One is a single unit or block type and is mounted on the fire wall of the engine. What is the other type?

30. What is the approximate resistance of the resistors used in the primary circuit?
    a. 18 ohms.
    b. 25 ohms.
    c. 1.5 ohms.
    d. 15 ohms.

31. List two places where timing marks are placed on an engine.

32. Give the firing order of an in-line six cylinder engine.

33. Give a firing order of a V-8 engine.

34. What is meant by the heat range of spark plugs?

35. At high speeds, what is the approximate temperature of the center wire of a spark plug?
    a. 212 deg. C.
    b. 400 deg. C.
    c. 800 deg. C.
    d. 3,200 deg. C.

36. Which plug is termed the hotter: a plug with a long path for the heat to travel, or a plug with a short path?
    a. Long path.
    b. Short path.

37. What three types of fouling are spark plugs subject to?

38. An ignition system that is capable of delivering 20,000 volts to a clean spark plug, may be able to deliver only half that amount to a fouled plug. Why?

39. Why are wider spark plug gaps favored over narrow gaps?

40. Give two reasons why the surface of the cylinder head against which the spark plug seats must be clean.

41. What are some advantages of magneto ignition?

42. What method is used to produce the magnetic field in a magneto?

43. When reconditioning a spark plug, what should be done to the center electrode?

44. Give two classifications of magnetos.

45. In the inductor-type magneto, where are the coil and magnet mounted?
    a. Both in stationary positions.
    b. The magnet rotates and the coil is stationary.

46. In a rotating magnet magneto, which of the following parts rotate and which are stationary? Coil. Condenser. Breaker points.

47. Describe the operation of a flywheel-type magneto.

48. What is the purpose of an impulse coupling?

49. In a transistor ignition system, what does the transistor do?
    a. Transforms the battery voltage to high voltage.
    b. "Switches" primary current on and off.
    c. Distributes the high tension current.

50. Give five causes, originating in the ignition system, why an engine will not start.

51. Give five causes, originating in the ignition system, why an engine will be hard to start.

52. Give five causes, originating in the ignition system, why an engine misfires.

53. What type is the Delco transistor ignition system?
    a. Pulse type.
    b. Capacitor discharge system.
    c. Magnetic controlled system.
    d. Contact controlled system.

54. What type is the Ford transistor ignition system?
    a. Pulse type.
    b. Capacitor discharge system.
    c. Magnetic controlled type.
    d. Contact controlled type.

55. In the Autolite double diaphragm distributor, carburetor vacuum is connected to which diaphragm?
    a. Advance diaphragm.
    b. Retard diaphragm.

56. The ignition primary resistance wire used by Chrysler is sensitive to heat. True or False?

57. How many connections are there to the Delco Unitized Ignition system?
    a. Four.
    b. Five.
    c. Nine.
    d. Twenty one.

58. Full battery voltage is applied to the coil during cranking in the Chrysler electronic ignition system. Yes or No?

59. Delco-Remy's High Energy Ignition system features:
    a. Low-voltage generator.
    b. Coil built into distributor.
    c. Solid state module.

60. How many sensors are used in the Ford Electronic Engine Control II system?

LIGHTS, LIGHTING CIRCUITS, WIRING, AND HORNS

Fig. 36-1. Typical rectangular sealed beam head lamp.

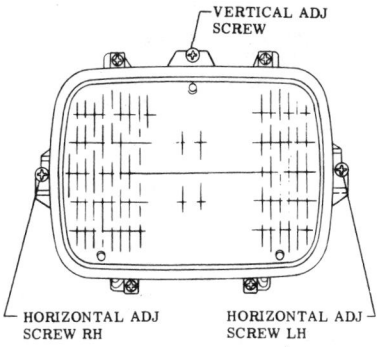

Fig. 36-3. Location of head lamp adjusting screws.

Most modern cars have more than 70 lights, ranging from a miniature indicator lamp drawing approximately .27 amp. to a sealed beam head lamp drawing over 5 amps.

SEALED BEAM HEAD LAMPS

A typical sealed beam head lamp, Fig. 36-1, incorporates the filament, reflector and lens to form a single, sealed unit. The filament is correctly focused in relation to the reflector and to the lens at the time of manufacture, so there is no need

Fig. 36-2. Unhooking spring from retainer ring of head lamp.

to focus these lamps.

On cars having dual head lamps, Fig. 36-2 a number "1" is embossed in one head lamp and a number "2" in the other. These numbers identify the lamps: number "1" for inboard mounting; number "2" for outboard mounting. The outboard lamps ("2") have two filaments each, one for the low beam and one for the high beam. The inboard lamps ("1") have only one filament. Cars not having dual lamps are equipped with two number "2" lamps.

When the headlight switch completes the circuit to the head lamps, the low beam of the outboard lamps lights the way for city driving and for use when meeting oncoming traffic on the highway. When the dimmer switch is activated, the inboard head lamps go on, along with the high beam of the outboard lamps. The next actuation of the dimmer switch returns the headlighting system to low beams only on the outboard lamps.

Occasionally, head lamp replacement is required, Fig. 36-2. Also, it is necessary to aim the headlights correctly, Fig. 36-3, to provide maximum illumination on the road and to avoid "blinding" approaching drivers.

REMOVING SEALED BEAM UNITS

Removing a sealed beam unit from a car is simple:
1. Remove the screws that secure the head lamp door (bezel), then remove door. See Fig. 36-4.
2. On some older models, unhook the springs that hold the retaining ring, Fig. 36-2.

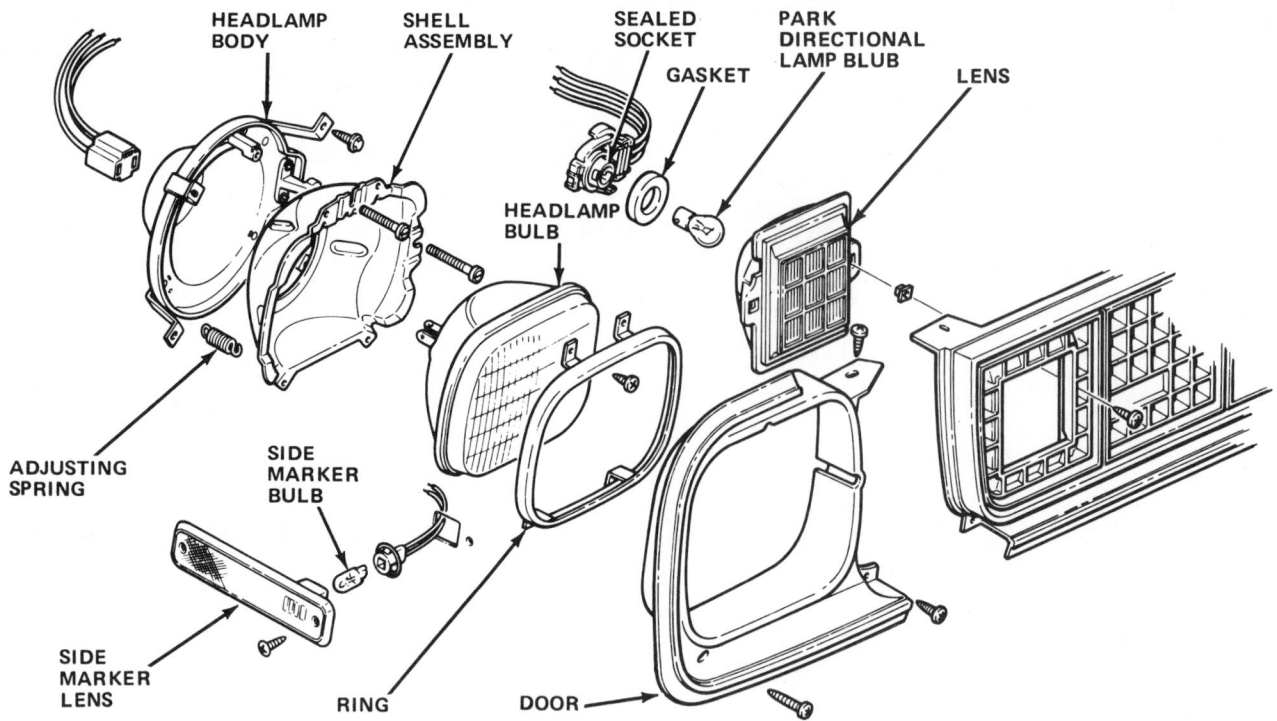

Fig. 36-4. Exploded view of a typical single head lamp setup on an American Motors' car.

3. Remove the screws that hold the retaining ring to the shell assembly (mounting ring). Do not turn adjusting screws, Fig. 36-3.
4. Remove the retaining ring.
5. Pull lamp forward and remove electrical connector.
6. Remove lamp.

AIMING HEADLIGHTS

To facilitate aiming the headlights, adjusting screws are provided. In most cases, the screws for vertical aiming are at the top of the unit, Fig. 36-3, and the horizontal aim adjusting screws are at the side, Fig. 36-3. In some instances, however, the vertical adjusting screw is placed at the bottom. The aim adjusting screws should not be turned unless it is necessary to aim the headlights.

The three guide points formed in the front of the lens glass on sealed beam units are used with mechanical aimers, Figs. 36-5 and 36-6. With some mechanical aimers, aiming may be done in daylight without turning on the lights. The equipment is provided with an accurate level, so it is not necessary for the vehicle to be on a level floor.

AIMING BY WALL LAYOUT

Headlights also may be aimed by using a wall layout, as shown in Figs. 36-7 and 36-8. In using this setup, the floor

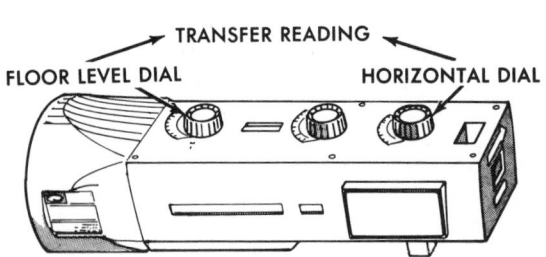

Fig. 36-5. Equipment is available for aiming headlights mechanically. This unit features floor level compensation and optical contrast bubble.

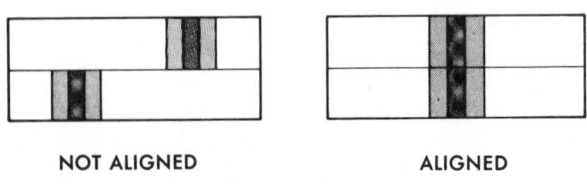

NOT ALIGNED   ALIGNED

Fig. 36-6. After aimers are calibrated and installed on head lamps, horizontal knob on each unit is turned until split image aligns.

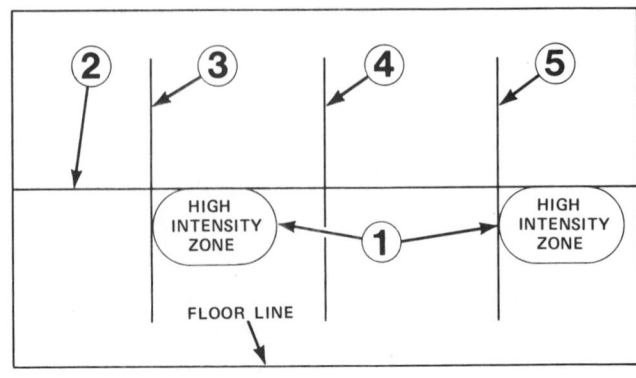

Fig. 36-7. Text tells how to draw a wall layout for aiming headlights. Number 1 indicates zone of high intensity for low beam.

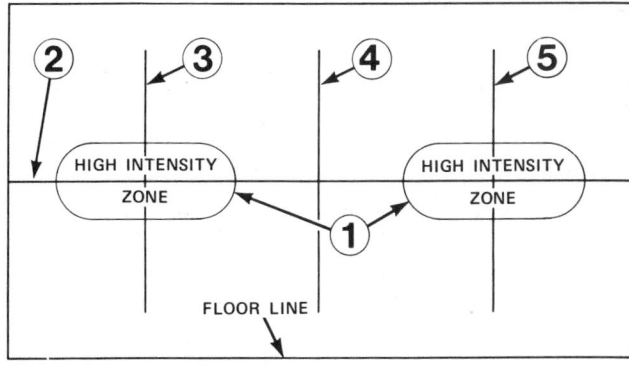

Fig. 36-8. Using same wall layout to check aim of high beam, note that high intensity zone is centered on vertical and horizontal center lines.

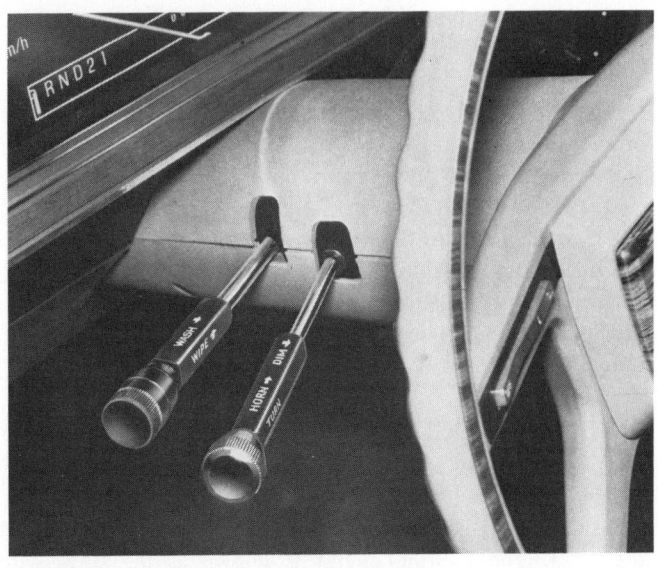

Fig. 36-10. Multi-function controls are popular. This Ford turn signal lever also controls the horn and dimmer switch. A matching windshield wiper/washer control lever is also featured.

must be level and the tires correctly inflated. Draw a line on the floor parallel to the wall and exactly 25 ft. from it. Position the car at right angles to the wall with the head lamps right over the line marked on the floor. Then, referring to Figs. 36-7 and 36-8, proceed as follows:

1. Measure height of center of head lamps from floor.
2. Transfer this measurement to wall and draw line 2.
3. Measure width of windshield and rear window. Find center and mark with tape.
4. Sight through rear window, aligning tapes and establishing line 4 as vertical center line of wall layout.
5. Add line 3 to wall layout in line with vertical center line of left head lamp.
6. Add line 5 to wall layout in line with vertical center line of right head lamp.
7. Turn on headlights and check high intensity zones against those shown at 1 in Fig. 36-7 (low beam) and Fig. 36-8 (high beam).
8. Generally, a 2 in. tolerance is permitted below line 2 and to right of lines 3 and 5. Check local and state requirements.

When adjusting the aim of a sealed beam head lamp, the adjusting screw at the top, Fig. 36-9, will raise or lower the light beam, while the adjustment at the side will swing the beam to the right or the left. These screws are reached on older cars after the outer door has been removed. On many late models, it is not necessary to remove the door, Fig. 36-9.

HEAD LAMP DIMMING

Sealed beam head lamps provide the choice of driving with the help of low beams or high beams. A dimmer switch, Fig. 36-10, permits selection of the required illumination.

Some vehicles are equipped with a device that automatically dims the headlights. In the case of Ford-built vehicles, a driver-operated electronic device automatically switches the headlights from high to low beam in response to light from an approaching vehicle or light from the taillights of a vehicle being overtaken. Major components of the system are: sensor-amplifier unit, power relay, driver sensitivity control and an interconnecting wire harness. See Fig. 36-11.

The sensor-amplifier combines a light-sensing optical device and a transistorized amplifier into a single unit with sufficient power to operate a power relay for switching the headlight

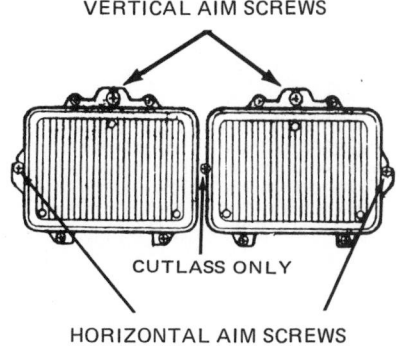

Fig. 36-9. Head lamp adjusting screws permit vertical and horizontal adjustment of headlights, usually without removing head lamp door.

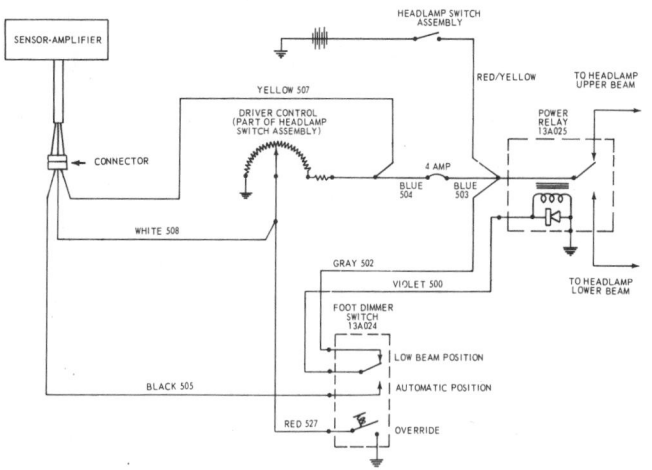

Fig. 36-11. Wiring diagram of automatic headlight dimmer.

beams. A pre-calibrated level assembly is attached as a part of the sensor-amplifier unit for setting the correct vertical aim. The unit is adjusted and completely sealed at the factory.

The power relay contains a diode for damping purposes to protect the sensor-amplifier. Be sure to observe proper polarity when connecting to prevent burn-out of diode.

The foot switch is a special dimmer override type that replaces the standard dimmer switch. With the foot switch in the automatic position, a slight downward pressure on the switch provides upper beam regardless of amount of light on the sensor-amplifier lens. A wiring diagram of the system is shown in Fig. 36-11.

LIGHTING CIRCUIT

The modern lighting circuit, Fig. 36-12, includes the battery, frame, all the lights and various switches that control their use. The lighting circuit is known as the single-wire system since it uses the car frame for the return.

The complete lighting circuit of the modern passenger car can be broken down into individual circuits, each having one or more lights and switches. In each separate circuit, the lights are connected in parallel, and the controlling switch is in series between the group of lights and the battery.

The parking lights, for example, are connected in parallel and controlled by a single switch. In some installations, one switch controls the connection to the battery while a selector switch determines which of two circuits is energized. The headlights, with their upper and lower beams, are an example of this type of circuit.

In some instances, such as the courtesy lights, several switches may be connected in parallel so that any switch may be used to turn on the light.

When studying the wiring diagram, all light circuits can be traced from the battery, through the ammeter to the switch (or switches) to the individual light.

HEAD LAMP DOORS

Head lamp doors, or hidden head lamps, are a feature of several cars. There are two types of head lamp doors: one is electrically operated by a series wound motor; the other is opened and closed by a vacuum powered motor.

Chrysler-built cars with this feature are provided with electrically operated doors using a series wound motor with two field coils. This is mounted behind the center of the grille and has a worm gear drive and internal limit switches. A relay and circuit breaker assembly is mounted to the instrument panel lower reinforcement, left of the steering column.

To open the head lamp doors in the event of an electric failure, first disconnect the motor electric leads. Then, rotate the hand wheel located at the lower end of the motor clockwise as indicated by the decal on the radiator yoke until the head lamp doors are completely open.

Electrical causes of operational failure include faulty motor, defective wiring or connections, malfunctioning of motor limit switch and circuit breaker failure, and faulty head lamp switch or relay. See Fig. 36-12.

Mechanical troubles include: torsion bar disconnected; crank screws missing; torsion bar twisted; stripped drive gear; rubber bumpers worn or missing; door pivot bushings worn, missing or dry; door rubbing against grille; torsion spring missing.

A head lamp door system powered by intake manifold vacuum is used on some General Motors cars. The head lamps are in a barrel housing that is pivoted into position by a linkage system actuated by the power cylinder push rod.

The headlight switch controls the electrical circuit and the vacuum circuit that controls head lamp door operation. A large reserve tank supplies vacuum for operation of the doors when the engine is stopped. As a safety measure, its capacity is sufficient to operate the doors through one up-and-down cycle without the engine operating.

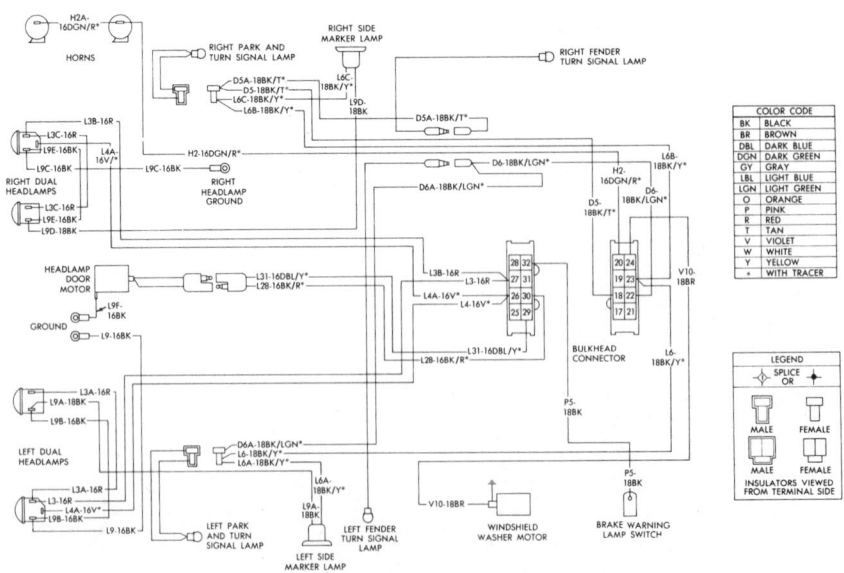

Fig. 36-12. Example of a modern lighting wiring diagram.

There is one power cylinder for each headlight door and a relay valve controls the vacuum to the power cylinders. A manual valve is provided so the doors can be opened to replace bulbs and for aiming. The manual switch must be pushed in before the doors can be operated by the headlight switch. The head lamp door can be opened from the front of the car by pushing on the housing directly under the doors until the housing locks in the open position. The headlights should be aimed only when there is 20 in. Hg. in the system.

HEAD LAMP SERVICE KINKS

Short life or frequent burning out of head lamps results from excessive voltage. This in turn, may result from loose or corroded electrical connections in the battery circuit or the charging rate may be excessive. The setting of the voltage regulator should be checked.

Dim lights result from low voltage, which may be caused by loose or corroded terminals in the lamp circuit. Or, the charging rate may be too low or the battery may be defective.

The wiring in lighting circuits should be inspected periodically for loose or corroded connections, or chafed insulation. The connections at junction blocks and plug-in connectors should be carefully checked. Switches, bulb sockets, lamp shells, reflectors and lenses should be inspected for loose mounting and corrosion.

In order to overcome the effects of rust on old cars, it is frequently necessary to solder a lead to a lamp socket case and ground the other end of the lead on the frame.

The voltage drop between the various lamp sockets (not the holder, reflector or shell) and ground should be measured with a low-reading voltmeter. Each light should be turned on when making this test for high resistance at ground connections. If any reading is obtained on the voltmeter, it is an indication that there is resistance present. The shell and socket must be thoroughly cleaned to obtain a good electrical connection.

Another test that should be made is checking voltage drop between the battery and each individual lamp. To make this test, connect a long positive lead of a voltmeter to the positive battery terminal. Attach a test probe to the other lead of the voltmeter. Turn on the lights and touch the voltmeter probe to the insulated terminal of each lamp. The voltage drop should be less than 0.6V.

If voltage drop is greater than 0.6V, follow the circuit back through the switch and ammeter to locate the part of the circuit in which the loss occurs. If the loss in voltage is due to a defective ammeter or switch, the part should be replaced. Usually, the loss will be found at a terminal or plug-in connector. In such cases, cleaning and tightening will overcome the trouble.

FUSES AND CIRCUIT BREAKERS

A fuse block, Fig. 36-13, usually is connected between the battery and the main lighting switch. Usually, the fuse block is mounted on driver's side of the firewall.

When a short circuit or overload occurs in a circuit, the fuse burns out and opens the circuit so that no further damage will result. The excess current will open the circuit breaker terminals, indicating there is something wrong in the circuit. The circuit breaker will remain open until the trouble is corrected.

LIGHTING WIRE SIZES

In order to conserve current, lighting wire must be of adequate size. The voltage loss in a length of wire is equal to the product of the current flowing and the resistance of the wire. The resistance of a length of wire decreases as its diameter increases. Therefore, it is advisable to use wire of relatively large cross section. In general, nothing smaller than No. 16 gauge wire should be used for lights of low candle power; for headlights, and other lights of high candle power, wire of still larger gauge is required. See Fig. 36-14.

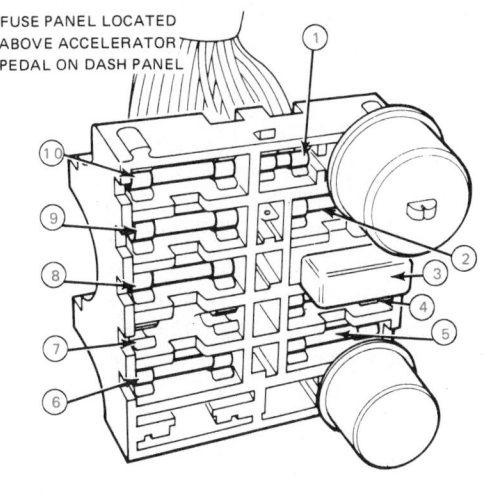

FUSE PANEL LOCATED ABOVE ACCELERATOR PEDAL ON DASH PANEL

① (4 AMP. FUSE)   CLUSTER, HEATER OR AIR CONDITIONER CONTROL, RADIO, ASH TRAY, AND CLOCK ILLUMINATION LAMPS.

② (7.5 AMP. FUSE)   OIL, BRAKES, BELTS INDICATOR LAMPS, SEAT BELTS MODULE, BUZZER, THROTTLE SOLENOID POSITIONER.

③ (6.0 AMP. CIR-CUIT BREAKER)   WINDSHIELD WIPER MOTOR

④ (15 AMP. FUSE)   WINDSHIELD WASHER PUMP, DOOR AJAR, PARK BRAKE, HEAD-LAMP INDICATOR LAMPS, HEATER BACKLITE CONTROL INDICATOR LAMP AND ANTI-THEFT MODULE.

⑤ (7.5 AMP. FUSE)   RADIO/TAPE PLAYER

⑥ (20 AMP. FUSE)   HORN AND CIGAR LIGHTER

⑦ (15 AMP. FUSE)   DOME LIGHT, GLOVE BOX, MAP, TRUNK, DOOR, INSTRUMENT PANEL, COURTESY, HEADLAMPS INDICATOR LIGHTS. KEY, HEAD-LAMP WARNING BUZZER, CLOCK FEED, ANTI-THEFT TRIGGER, HORN FEED AND SEAT BELT MODULE STOP AND EMERGENCY WARNING LAMPS

⑧ (15 AMP. FUSE)   HEATER

⑨ (30 AMP. FUSE)   AIR CONDITIONER

⑩ (15 AMP. FUSE)   BACK-UP LAMPS

Fig. 36-13. Fuse panel is readily accessible in most cars. Individual fuse and circuit breaker capacities are shown, along with circuits protected by each.

WIRE SIZE FOR LIGHTING CIRCUITS

Total Candle Power	Wire Gauge (for length in feet)							
12V	3 Ft.	5 Ft.	7 Ft.	10 Ft.	15 Ft.	20 Ft.	35 Ft.	50 Ft.
6	18	18	18	18	18	18	18	18
16	18	18	18	18	18	18	18	18
30	18	18	18	18	18	18	16	16
60	18	18	18	18	18	16	14	14
80	18	18	18	18	16	16	14	12
100	18	18	18	18	16	14	12	12
120	18	18	18	18	14	14	12	10
160	18	18	16	16	14	12	10	10
200	18	18	16	16	12	12	10	8

Fig. 36-14. Chart shows gauge of wire required for circuits having lights of specific candle power value with connecting wire of a given length in feet.

The chart shows specifically what gauge of wire is required for a lighting circuit of a given candle power. Note that the length of the connecting wire affects the wire gauge required. The longer the wire: the larger the gauge (the smaller the number).

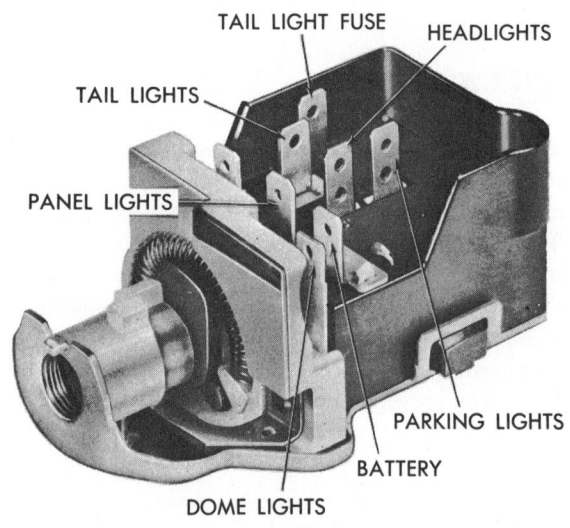

Fig. 36-15. Main lighting switch with contacts exposed and identified.

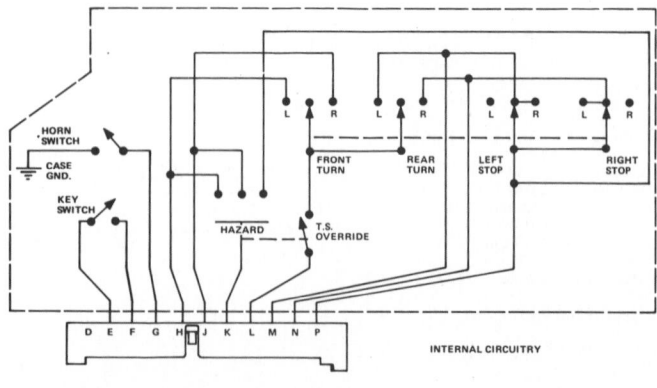

Fig. 36-16. Wiring diagram of typical directional signal system.

MAIN LIGHTING SWITCH

The main lighting switch is the heart of the lighting system. It controls the headlights, parking lights, side marker lights, taillights, license plate light, instrument panel lights and interior lights. See Fig. 36-15. Individual switches are provided for special purpose lights such as directional signals, hazard warning flasher, backup lights and courtesy lights.

The main lighting switch may be of either the "push-pull" or "push-pull with rotary contact" type. A typical switch will have three positions: "off," "parking" and "bright." Some switches also contain a rheostat to control the brightness of the instrument panel lights. The rheostat is operated by rotating the control knob, separating it from the push-pull action of the main lighting switch.

DIRECTION SIGNAL SWITCH

The direction signal switch, Fig. 36-16, is installed just below the hub of the steering wheel. A manually controlled lever projecting from the switch permits the driver to signal the direction of the turn he is about to make, Fig. 36-10. Moving the switch handle down will light the turn signal bulbs on the left front and left rear of the car, signaling a left turn. Moving the switch upward will light the turn signal lights on the right (front and rear), signaling a right turn. With the switch in a position to indicate a turn, the lights are alternately turned off and on by a flasher in the circuit.

Incorporated in this switch on late model cars is the lane-change directional signal, Fig. 36-17. This feature provides the opportunity for the driver to signal a lane change by holding the lever against a detent, then releasing it to cancel the signal immediately. Also related is the hazard warning flasher shown in Fig. 36-17.

STOPLIGHT SWITCH

In order to signal a stop, a brake pedal operated switch is provided to operate the stoplights. In older installations, the stoplight switch is located at the end of the brake master

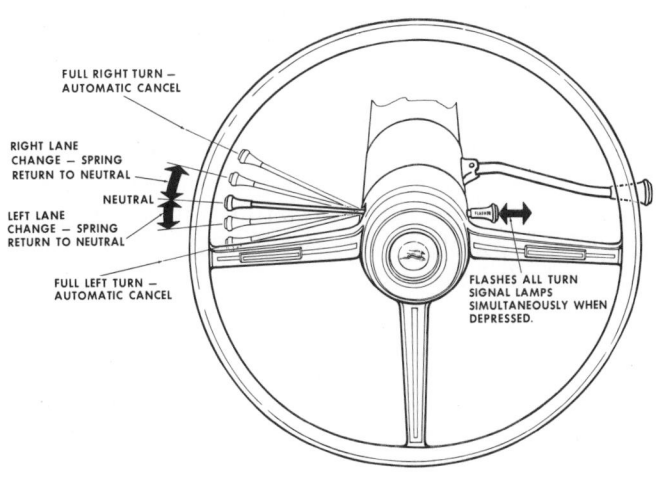

Fig. 36-17. When turn signal lever is held in lane change position, directional lights signal intent to change lanes. When lever is released, signal is immediately cancelled.

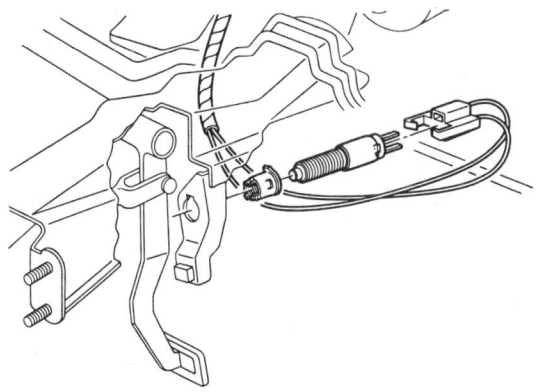

Fig. 36-18. Details of stoplight switch mounted on brake pedal.

cylinder, so that the contacts are closed by increasing brake fluid pressure. In later installations, Fig. 36-18, it is operated directly by movement of the brake pedal. Another type of mechanical switch is shown in Fig. 36-19.

ELECTRIC WIRES AND CABLES

Wires and cables, usually made of copper, are used to carry electricity to the various electrical devices and equipment on passenger cars and trucks. These wires and cables must be the correct size and have proper insulation.

If the diameter of the wire or cable is too small, its resistance will be too great, and valuable voltage will be lost in overcoming the increased resistance. This, in turn, will result in poor operation of the particular electrical unit. In the case of lights, they will not provide maximum illumination. In the case of starting motors, lower cranking speeds will result.

Cable size and length determines its resistance. The smaller the diameter of the wire or cable, the greater its resistance. Also, the longer the cable or wire, the greater its resistance.

Wire and cable sizes are expressed by a gauge number, which indicates the cross-sectional area (not diameter) of the conductor. Note in the wire gauge table in Fig. 36-20 that the cross-sectional area of wires is given in circular mils.

A circular mil is a unit of area equal to the area of a circle one mil in diameter. A mil is a unit of length equal to .001 in. Therefore, a wire 10 mils in diameter has a cross-sectional area of 100 circular mils (or 78.54 sq. mils).

Again consulting the chart in Fig. 36-20, you will find that the wire being checked is 30 gauge. Cables are made up of a number of strands of wire. Therefore, the cross-sectional area of a cable is equal to the circular mil area of a single strand times the number of strands.

Special gauges, Fig. 36-21, are available for measuring the

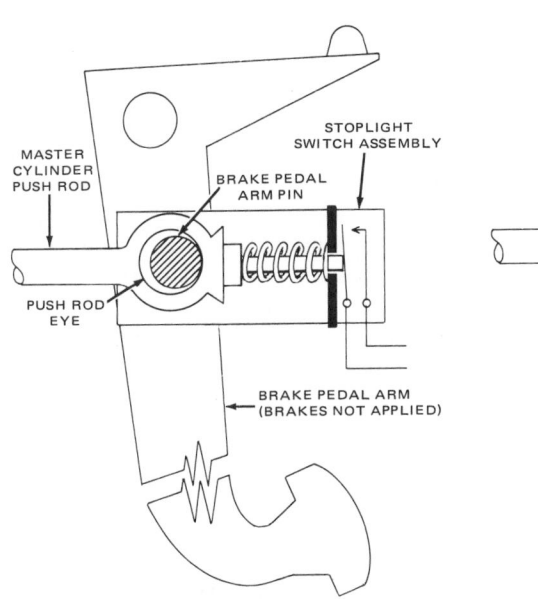

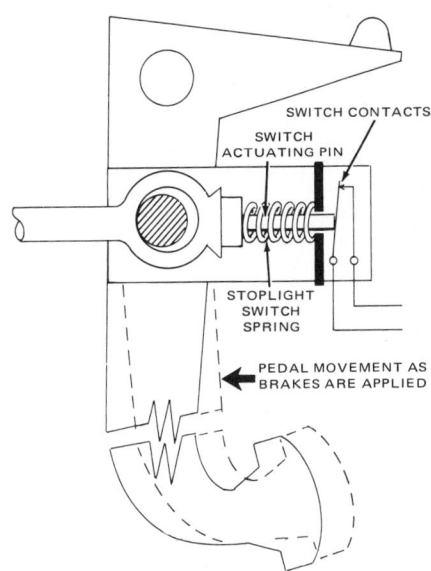

Fig. 36-19. Ford's mechanical stoplight switch assembly is installed on pin of brake pedal arm, straddling master cylinder push rod. When pedal is depressed, switch contacts close to complete stoplight circuit. When pedal is released, contacts open and circuit is broken.

Wire Diameter Inches	American Wire Gauge	Circular Mil Area
.4600	0000	211600
.4096	000	167800
.3648	00	133100
.3249	0	105500
.2893	1	83690
.2576	2	66370
.2294	3	52640
.2043	4	41740
.1620	6	26250
.1285	8	16510
.1019	10	10380
.0808	12	6530
.0640	14	4107
.0508	16	2583
.0403	18	1624
.0319	20	1022
.0284	21	810.1
.0253	22	642.4
.0225	23	509.5
.0201	24	404.0
.0179	25	320.4
.0159	26	254.1
.0142	27	201.5
.0126	28	159.8
.0112	29	126.7
.0100	30	100.5
.0089	31	79.7
.0079	32	63.2
.0070	33	50.1
.0063	34	39.7
.0056	35	31.5
.0050	36	25.0

Fig. 36-20. Wire gauge table.

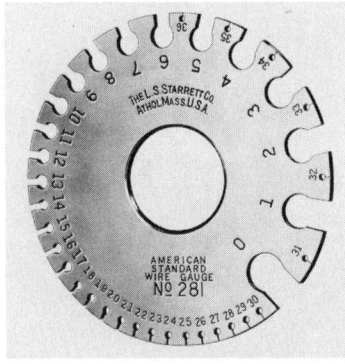

Fig. 36-21. Typical gauge used for measuring size of wire.

gauge size of wires. If a wire gauge is not available, the diameter can be measured by means of a micrometer. Then, by checking the diameter obtained with the wire table in Fig. 36-20, its gauge size can be determined.

To determine the gauge size of a cable, first count the number of strands. Next, measure the diameter of a single strand with a micrometer. Consulting the wire table, determine the area in circular mils for that diameter wire. Then, multiply the area of the single wire in circular mils by the number of strands in the cable. Finally, locate in the wire table the area in

circular mils that is closest to that value. The gauge size corresponding to the total area in circular mils will be the gauge size of the cable.

When comparing cables, remember that the external diameter of a wire or cable has nothing to do with its current-carrying capacity. Thick insulation will make a small gauge wire look much larger. So it is important that only the size of the metal conductors is compared. The way to do that is by means of a wire gauge or micrometer.

BATTERY CABLES

Because a starting motor cranking an engine will draw approximately 150 amp., it is imperative that the cable connecting the battery to the starter is of sufficient gauge to carry such heavy current. For that reason, it is usually made of No. 1 or No. 2 gauge cable.

The cable connecting the battery to ground also must carry the same current. However, since it is grounded, there is less need to have the strands insulated. On some older cars, in fact, the ground cable is a flat woven wire strap.

Because the cables are close to the battery and could corrode, it is important that the cables make good electrical contact with the cable clamps. Likewise, clamps must make good electrical contact with the battery posts. Any looseness or corrosion between the cable and its clamp, or between the cable clamp and the battery, will result in high resistance and consequent voltage drop.

High resistance between cables and terminals can be checked easily by means of a voltmeter. With a current of approximately 20 amp. flowing, connect one lead of a voltmeter to the cable, connect the other lead to the other cable terminal. The voltage drop should be approximately 0.1V. Voltage drop in the starter-to-ground circuit should not be more than 0.1V.

HIGH TENSION CABLE

In order to carry the high voltage to the spark plugs with minimum loss, it is essential that the high tension cables are of the correct gauge. In addition, they must be covered with ample insulation that will withstand heat, cold, moisture, oil, grease, chafing and corona.

Corona is an electrical phenomenon not readily visible, but it rapidly deteriorates rubber. The passage of high tension electricity through a cable builds up a surrounding electrical field. The electrical field liberates oxygen in the surrounding air to form ozone, which will attack the rubber insulation if it is not properly protected. Ozone causes the rubber to deteriorate and lose its insulating qualities. Electrical losses result which, in turn, will seriously weaken the spark at the plug gap.

High quality ignition cable is designed to withstand corona, heat, cold, oil, grease and moisture. In recent years, great improvements have been made in the insulation of high tension cables.

High tension cable is available in cut lengths designed for installation on the different makes and models of engines.

However, the mechanic can make up the cable set, using the original cable as a guide in cutting the desired lengths. When installing new cable, the individual pieces should be cut as short as possible, yet sufficient length should be provided so that sharp bends are avoided.

In addition, it is advisable to separate the individual cables as much as possible. Short cables, well spaced, reduce the electrical capacity of the system and thereby improve ignition.

Insulating boots should always be used at both ends of the ignition cable to reduce leakage and losses due to moisture. Dried out or cracked boots should be replaced.

When checking high tension copper cables, both the insulation and the terminals should be carefully examined. If the insulation is hard or brittle, the set of cables should be replaced. The usual method of checking the insulation is to bend the cable to form a small circle, then note if any cracks appear in the insulation. If the end of the copper cable has receded so the insulation extends beyond, it is probably not making good contact with the terminal. In such cases, it is probable that the entire cable has deteriorated and should be replaced.

The spark plug cables should be removed from the distributor cap sockets, and each socket should be thoroughly cleaned. These sockets frequently become corroded, and all corrosion must be removed. Otherwise, engine performance will be seriously affected. When replacing the cables, be sure they are pushed to the bottom of the towers of the distributor cap. If this is not done, the spark will jump the air gap and cause corrosion and burned contacts. Press boots firmly in place over the towers of the cap.

RESISTOR IGNITION CABLE

To reduce interference with radio and TV reception, automotive ignition systems are provided with resistance in the secondary circuit. This may be in the form of a resistance unit built into the rotor or in the distributor cap. Resistor spark plugs or special resistor-type ignition cable may be used. All U.S. manufacturers currently use resistor cable.

Some resistor cable is made of parallel strands of linen thread covered with braided rayon thread. This core is then impregnated with graphite to make it a conductor for the high tension current. For insulation, a rubber-like substance that is virtually impervious to oil and heat is used.

However, cable constructed this way has very little tensile strength and could easily be broken if pulled. When the conductor is broken, a spark will jump across the gap and the conductor will disintegrate. Misfiring would result.

So it is imperative not to pull on the cable when disconnecting a spark plug. Instead, the rubber boot covering the end of the cable and the spark plug insulator should be grasped, twisted and firmly lifted when disconnecting a spark plug. Also, the insulation should not be punctured when making a connection for timing an engine. This puncture would probably sever the conductor, and eventual failure would result.

Resistor cable formerly had a resistance of approximately 4000 ohms per foot. Currently, SAE specifications for ignition

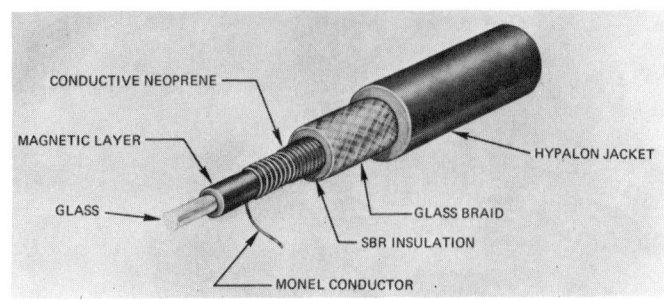

Fig. 36-22. An ignition cable of wire wound magnetic core type.

resistance cable call for 3000 to 7000 ohms per foot for low resistance (LR) cable and 6000 to 12,000 ohms per foot for high resistance cable (HR) cable.

High resistance cables are now available with conductors made of monel metal which is wound around a magnetic core, Fig. 36-22. This cable has a resistance of 4000 to 7000 ohms per foot.

Another type of high resistance cable is hypalon jacketed, Fig. 36-23, and it uses a metallic conductor that terminates in a high resistance of alloy wire wound on a ceramic core. The end of the cable is provided with a spark plug protector.

Chrysler has adopted a special silicone jacketed cable for their electronic ignition system. It has a nonmetallic conductor of the distributed resistance type. The jacketing may withstand 350 deg. F for 192 hours without cracking.

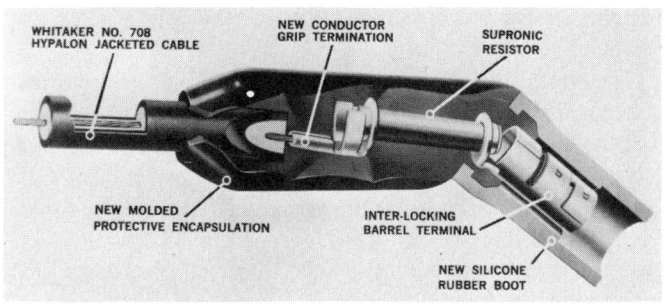

Fig. 36-23. Metallic conductor type cable with the resistor element built into terminal end.

POSITIONING IGNITION CABLE

Care must be taken when replacing high tension ignition cables to install them in their original position. Not only must they be connected to the correct spark plug, but they must also be placed in the correct point in their respective brackets. If this is not done, cross firing will result and maximum power will not be attained.

Basically the wires should be so located in their brackets that the cables for cylinders next in firing order are as for apart as possible. For example: if the firing order is 1-5-4-2-6-3-7-8, the cables for cylinders four and two should be separated as much as possible since cylinder No. 2 fires immediately after cylinder No. 4.

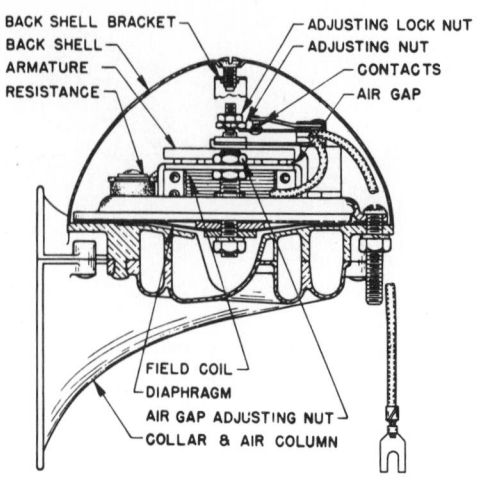

Fig. 36-24. Sectional view of typical horn. (Delco-Remy)

HORNS AND WARNING SIGNALS

Most modern horns consist of a diaphragm, which is vibrated by means of an electromagnet. See Fig. 36-24. When the electromagnet is energized, it pulls on an armature that is attached to the diaphragm. Movement of the armature flexes the diaphragm and opens a set of electrical contacts. Since the contacts are in series with the circuit, the current will be turned off and on at a high rate.

The tone and character of the horn signal is largely dependent on the manner in which the movement of the diaphragm is utilized and also on the stiffness of the diaphragm.

The horn should be inspected periodically. Dust and other foreign matter should be wiped from the outside of the horn and projector. If it is rusted or corroded, it should be replaced. Naturally all mounting bolts and electrical connections should be tight. If the horn is not operating, the relay, fuse or fusible link and wiring should be inspected. The fusible link is a protective device that consists of a wire of smaller gauge that will "blow" if the circuit is overloaded. New links come with connectors or must be soldered in place.

To test whether a horn is inoperative, connect a jumper wire from the battery to the horn terminal. If the horn still does not operate, provide a good ground for the horn. If the horn then operates, it indicates that the ground connection is at fault. To help prevent this, cadmium plated mounting screws are used on some cars.

Two-wire horns will not operate with only the battery jumper wire in place, but require a second jumper wire connecting the other horn terminal to the ground. If horns operate with these tests, trouble will be found in the relay, wiring or horn ring.

The usual cause for continuous operation of the horn is a ground in the wiring leading from the horn ring to the horn relay or horn.

Because of the relatively heavy current required to operate a horn, a replacement wire selected for horn circuits must be as large as the original.

Horns that are inoperative or do not have the correct tone, should be removed for inspection after making sure the difficulty is not in the wiring relay or connections. Horns on late models are not serviceable. If adjustment will not correct the malfunction, the horn must be replaced. However, first check the horn switch, relay and all connections.

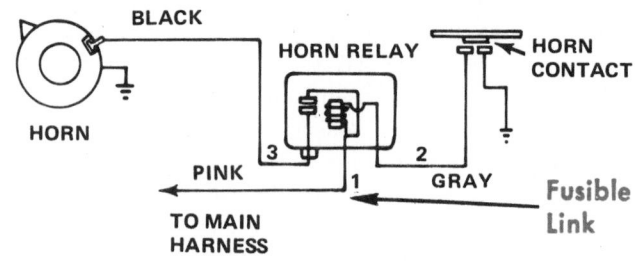

Fig. 36-25. A typical horn and horn relay circuit. Note location of fusible link in wire to main harness. Link will "blow" if current exceeds basic design requirement.

HORN RELAYS

The horn relay is connected into the horn and battery circuit, Fig. 36-25, to make a more direct connection between the horn and the battery. In that way, the voltage drop in the wiring from the horn to battery is eliminated and higher voltage is available for operating.

The horn relay consists of a winding on a core above which an armature is placed. The armature is provided with a contact point which meets a stationary contact point.

A typical horn circuit is shown in Fig. 36-25. When the horn button is depressed, the circuit from the battery to the horn relay is completed and the relay contact points are closed. As shown in the diagram, when the contacts are closed,

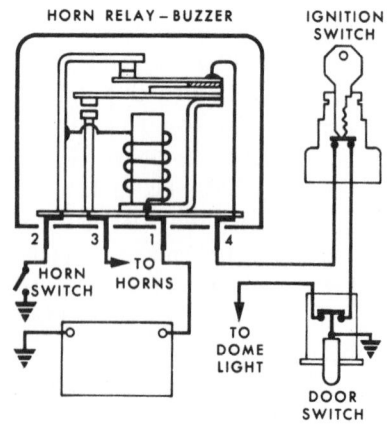

1. Red – "Bat."
2. Black
3. Black – Green Tracer
4. Pink – Black Tracer

Fig. 36-26. Oldsmobile's horn relay-buzzer unit relays battery voltage to horn terminals to sound horns. Second set of contacts buzzes when driver's door is left open with key in ignition switch.

current direct from the battery is supplied to the horns.

In late model cars, the horn relay usually is modified to include a warning buzzer that sounds off when the driver's door is opened while the ignition key is still in the switch. A wiring diagram of the horn relay-buzzer used on most Oldsmobile cars is shown in Fig. 36-26.

MULTIPLE CONNECTORS

The car manufacturers have worked toward improving the serviceability of the chassis electrical system. They have designed and produced modular instrument panels or instrument clusters. They have devised multiple connectors at the bulkhead, Fig. 36-27, that divide the main chassis harness into two separate sections: instrument panel harness and engine compartment harness.

Each circuit routed through the bulkhead connector is numbered, or it is coded with two letters. See Fig. 36-27. These letters identify the terminal location of a wire. To locate the correct terminal, sight along both lettered columns. The terminals at which the two lines of sight intersect is the proper terminal for that wire.

If the connector is removed from the dash panel, note that the center of the connector is filled with a nonconductive grease. Do not remove this grease. Also, if any wires are replaced on the engine compartment side of the connector, the

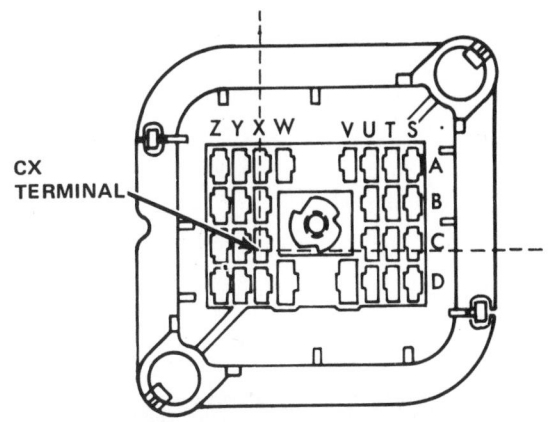

Fig. 36-27. Typically, the bulkhead connector is coded with two letters. Note how wire terminal CX is located by aligning the C and X columns.

terminal opening must be resealed with a waterproof sealer.

Other improvements in the chassis electrical system include: more weather-resistant wire and cable insulation; more durable sockets; greater use of plastics to avoid rusting; long life bulbs; higher intensity head lamps, and halogen head lamps for 25-50 percent more sealed beam output; simpler adjustment of head lamps for headlight aiming.

REVIEW QUESTIONS — LIGHTS, LIGHTING CIRCUITS, WIRING, HORNS

1. How much current does a sealed beam lamp on a 12 volt circuit draw?
   a. 8 amps.
   b. 4 amps.
   c. 12 amps.
2. How are the wires connected to a sealed beam head lamp?
   a. Pull apart, bayonet type connector.
   b. Soldered connections.
   c. Screw type connectors.
3. What provision is made on modern sealed beam head lamps to assist in aiming the unit?
4. When aiming a sealed beam head lamp, what does the adjustment at the top of the retaining ring control?
   a. Vertical control of beam.
   b. Swing beam from side to side.
5. In the single wire system of automotive lighting, what is used for the return of the current to the battery?
6. Give two causes of excessive voltage in the lighting circuit.
7. What is the permissible voltage drop between the battery and the lamp?
   a. 12 volts.
   b. 0.6 volts.
   c. 1.0 volts.
8. What is the purpose of the fuse or circuit breaker in the lighting circuit?
9. Which size wire can carry greatest amount of current? No. 16 gauge or No. 4 gauge?

10. What is the purpose of the rheostat used on some main lighting switches?
11. Define the term circular mil.
12. What is the diameter of No. 16 gauge wire?
    a. .0508 in.
    b. .0805 in.
    c. .0160 in.
13. What size cable is used to connect the starting motor?
    a. No. 1 or No. 2.
    b. No. 000.
    c. No. 36.
14. High tension ignition cables should be placed as close together as possible. True or False?
15. What is the purpose of ignition resistor cable?
    a. Improve the spark at the spark plugs.
    b. Reduce interference with radio and TV sets.
16. What is the purpose of the horn relay?
17. How are the automatic headlight doors on Chrysler cars operated?
    a. Vacuum motor.
    b. Electrically.
18. Oldsmobiles horn relay-buzzer buzzes when:
    a. Driver's door is opened and lights are left on.
    b. Driver's door is opened and key is left in ignition switch.
    c. Driver's door is opened and transmission selector lever is not in PARK position.

STORAGE
BATTERIES

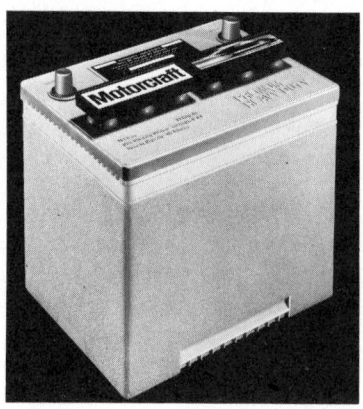

Fig. 36-27. Typical starting battery for use in starting and lighting passenger cars.

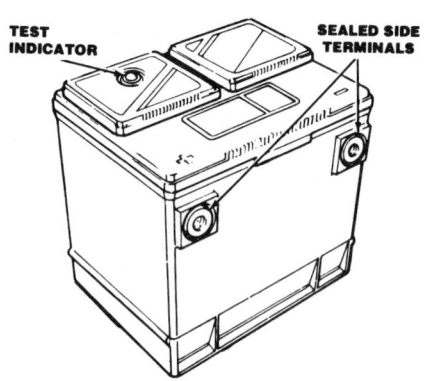

Fig. 36-28. General Motors "Freedom" battery has a sealed-in lifetime supply of electrolyte. Test indicator shows whether or not battery needs to be tested for state of charge.

A lead-acid storage battery, Fig. 36-27, serves as a source of power for cranking the internal combustion engine. At the same time, it provides electrical energy for the ignition system and acts as a stabilizer of voltage for the entire automotive electrical system. In addition, the battery will furnish current for a limited time whenever electrical demands of the vehicle exceed alternator output. See Fig. 36-28.

The lead-acid storage battery is not a storage tank for electricity. It is an electrochemical device for converting chemical energy into electrical energy. The amount of electrical power in the storage battery is determined by the amount of chemical substances in the battery. When these substances have been used up, they are restored to their original chemical condition by passing recharging current through the battery in the opposite direction to discharging current.

Each cell of a lead-acid storage battery will produce approximately 2V. Therefore, a 12V battery has six cells, Fig. 36-29, connected in series.

Each cell contains an element composed of a negative plate group and a positive plate group. The plate is formed of lattice-like grids of an alloy of lead an antimony (calcium alloy on maintenance-free batteries). The grids are filled with special lead-oxide pastes. These pastes, after processing to make them solid but porous, become the active materials of the battery after it has been charged.

The amount of current that can be produced by a storage battery is determined by the active area and weight of the

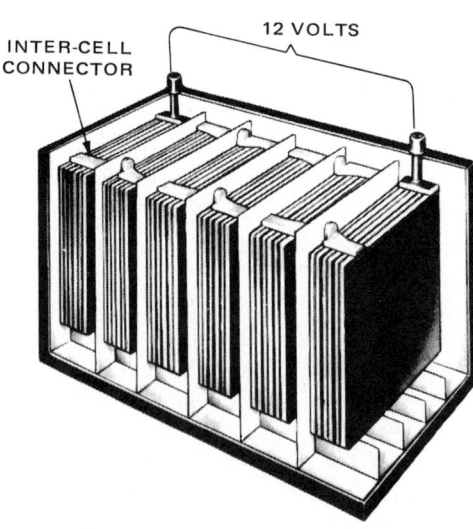

Fig. 36-29. Typical arrangement of cells and straight-through cell connectors in a 12 volt battery.

materials in the plates, and by the quantity of sulphuric acid in the electrolyte. After most of the available active materials have been activated, little or no current can be produced, and the battery is said to be discharged.

Before the battery can provide current again, it is necessary to restore the plates to their original chemical condition. This "recharging" is accomplished by passing an electric current, from an external source, through the battery. The charging current must flow through the battery in a direction opposite to the current flow from the battery.

Recharging of the battery, then, results in a reversal of the discharge chemical reactions in the storage battery, and the chemicals are restored to their original active condition.

The construction of an automotive type lead-acid storage battery, Fig. 36-29, is relatively simple. The positive and negative plates, Fig. 36-30, generally consist of special active materials contained in cast grids of lead-antimony alloy. These grids usually are rectangular, flat, lattice-like castings with relatively heavy frames and a mesh of vertical and horizontal wires. The positive plates contain lead peroxide, which is chocolate brown color. The negative plates contain sponge lead, which is gray in color.

Each cell of a storage battery is made of alternate positive and negative plates. A plate group is made by welding (lead burning) a number of plates of the same polarity to a plate strap. During assembly, plate groups of opposite polarity are interlaced; negative and positive plates alternate, Fig. 36-30.

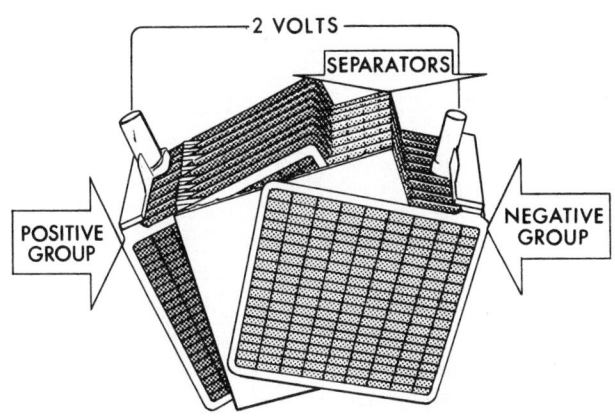

Fig. 36-30. One element of battery consists of a group of positive plates, and a group of negative plates, plus separators.

Usually, negative plate groups contain one more plate than the positive plate group within the same cell. As a result, there will be a negative plate on both sides of the interlaced plate groups. The reason for this is that the chemicals forming the negative plates are not as active as those forming the positive plates. By providing the additional negative plate area, the chemical activity of the plate groups is more nearly equalized.

With this setup, each battery cell will have an uneven number of plates. The larger the number of plates, or plate area, the greater the capacity of the cell, and the more current that will be available. Passenger car 12V batteries generally have 9, 11, or 13 plates per cell for a total of 54, 66, or 78 plates per battery.

To insure against adjacent plates touching each other, separators are placed between them. See Fig. 36-30. This assembly of positive and negative plates and separators is called an element.

The separators are made of sheets of porous, nonconducting material such as chemically treated wood, porous rubber, resin-impregnated fiber and glass fiber. Separators usually have ribs on one side, facing the positive plate to provide a greater volume of acid next to this most active plate. It also improves efficiency by increasing acid circulation. In addition, some separators are designed to aid in the reduction of loss of active material from the positive plate.

Battery separators must be chemically resistant to sulphuric acid and, at the same time, mechanically strong. They must be porous enough to permit free passage of the electrolyte, yet prevent the active chemicals in the plates from touching each other through expansion.

The elements of positive and negative plates and separators are placed in each cell of the battery case, between partitions built into the case. The lower edge of each element rests on ribs, or element rests, Fig. 36-29. The spaces between the rests are known as sediment chambers, where loosened material from the plates may accumulate without causing a short circuit.

The battery case usually is a one-piece, molded type, made of hard rubber or bituminous composition. The case, too, must withstand the action of sulphuric acid. It must be mechanically strong and not affected by wide variations in temperature.

With the elements in place in the battery case, inter-cell connectors are inserted through holes in the partitions, and sealed. Then the connectors are welded to the plate straps to connect all of the elements of the battery. A one-piece cover is bonded to the case with sealing compound, and the terminals are sealed at the cover.

Vents are provided in the covers to permit the cells to be filled with electrolyte and, periodically, with water that has been lost through evaporation. In addition, the vents allow gases to escape.

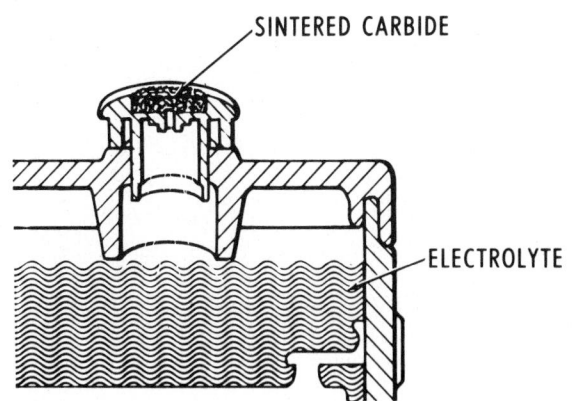

Fig. 36-31. Battery vent caps have been improved. This Chevrolet cap has a flame arrestor of sintered carbide that disperses fumes and protects battery from flame entry.

There are many different types of vent caps, Fig. 36-31. Recent designs have materially reduced evaporation of water, so replenishment is seldom necessary.

Fig. 36-32. Battery hydrometer with temperature correction.

ELECTROLYTE

After the battery is completely assembled, it is filled with electrolyte. Lead-acid storage batteries use a fairly concen-

trated solution of sulphuric acid and water, having a specific gravity of 1.290 at 80 deg. F. Specific gravity is the weight of a given volume of a liquid, divided by the weight of an equal volume of water at a temperature of 39.1 deg. F. When an electrolyte has a specific gravity of 1.290, it is 1.290 times as heavy as an equal volume of water, when both liquids are at the same temperature.

The specific gravity of a solution is measured by using a test instrument called a hydrometer, Fig. 36-32. It consists of a glass tube with a bulb syringe for sucking up samples of the electrolyte. Within the glass tube, a calibrated float sinks to a depth which is a measure of the specific gravity of the solution when read at surface level. The float sinks further in solutions having a low specific gravity than it does in solutions having a high specific gravity.

The float is made of glass, and its scale is precisely calibrated to indicate the specific gravity of the solution. Its weight is accurately determined by the manufacturer to insure correct readings.

Since temperature affects the specific gravity of a solution, it is necessary to take the temperature at the same time the

Sulphuric Acid %	10	20	30	40	50	60	70	80	90	100	110	120	130
COMPLETELY DISCHARGED													
10.2			1.076	1.074	1.072	1.070	1.068	1.066	1.063	1.060	1.057	1.055	1.052
11.7			1.086	1.084	1.082	1.080	1.078	1.075	1.072	1.070	1.067	1.064	1.061
13.1			1.096	1.094	1.092	1.090	1.088	1.085	1.082	1.079	1.076	1.073	1.070
14.4		1.109	1.107	1.105	1.103	1.100	1.097	1.095	1.092	1.089	1.086	1.083	1.080
15.7		1.120	1.118	1.115	1.113	1.110	1.107	1.104	1.101	1.098	1.096	1.092	1.089
17.1		1.131	1.129	1.126	1.123	1.120	1.117	1.114	1.111	1.108	1.105	1.102	1.099
18.4		1.142	1.139	1.136	1.133	1.130	1.127	1.124	1.120	1.118	1.114	1.111	1.108
19.7	1.156	1.153	1.149	1.146	1.143	1.140	1.137	1.134	1.130	1.127	1.124	1.120	1.117
BARELY OPERATIVE													
21.0	1.166	1.163	1.160	1.156	1.153	1.150	1.147	1.143	1.140	1.137	1.133	1.130	1.127
22.3	1.177	1.173	1.170	1.167	1.163	1.160	1.157	1.153	1.150	1.146	1.143	1.140	1.136
23.5	1.187	1.183	1.180	1.177	1.173	1.170	1.167	1.163	1.159	1.156	1.152	1.148	1.145
ONE FOURTH CHARGED													
24.7	1.198	1.194	1.190	1.187	1.184	1.180	1.176	1.173	1.169	1.165	1.162	1.158	1.154
26.0	1.208	1.204	1.200	1.197	1.194	1.190	1.186	1.183	1.179	1.175	1.171	1.168	1.164
27.2	1.218	1.214	1.211	1.207	1.204	1.200	1.196	1.193	1.189	1.185	1.181	1.177	1.174
28.5	1.228	1.224	1.221	1.217	1.214	1.210	1.206	1.203	1.199	1.195	1.191	1.187	1.183
ONE HALF CHARGED													
29.7	1.238	1.234	1.231	1.227	1.224	1.220	1.216	1.212	1.208	1.204	1.200	1.196	1.193
31.0	1.249	1.246	1.242	1.238	1.234	1.230	1.226	1.222	1.218	1.214	1.210	1.206	1.202
32.2	1.259	1.256	1.252	1.248	1.244	1.240	1.236	1.232	1.228	1.224	1.220	1.216	1.212
THREE FOURTHS CHARGED													
33.3	1.270	1.266	1.262	1.258	1.254	1.250	1.246	1.242	1.238	1.234	1.230	1.226	1.222
34.5	1.280	1.276	1.272	1.268	1.264	1.260	1.256	1.252	1.248	1.244	1.240	1.236	1.232
35.8	1.290	1.286	1.282	1.278	1.274	1.270	1.266	1.262	1.258	1.254	1.250	1.246	1.242
FULLY CHARGED													
37.0	1.300	1.296	1.292	1.288	1.284	1.280	1.276	1.272	1.268	1.264	1.260	1.256	1.252
38.1	1.310	1.306	1.302	1.298	1.294	1.290	1.286	1.282	1.278	1.274	1.270	1.266	1.262
39.2	1.320	1.316	1.312	1.308	1.304	1.300	1.296	1.292	1.288	1.284	1.280	1.276	1.272

Fig. 36-33. Specific gravities of various percentages of sulphuric acid at given temperatures.

specific gravity is taken. Better quality hydrometers have a built-in thermometer, so the temperature can be measured and the necessary correction made.

Temperature correction amounts to about .004 specific gravity for every 10 deg. F change in temperature. The specific gravity of various percentages of sulphuric acid at given temperatures is shown in Fig. 36-33.

Basically for every 10 deg. F of electrolyte temperature above 80 deg., four gravity points (.004) must be added to the gravity reading. This compensates for the loss of gravity caused by the expansion of the solution as its temperature increases.

For every 10 deg. of electrolyte temperature below 80 deg., four gravity points must be subtracted from the gravity reading. This compensates for the gain in gravity due to the contraction of the liquid, as its temperature decreases.

CHEMICAL ACTION

The chemical actions that take place during charging and discharging of a lead-acid storage battery are shown in Fig. 36-34. In a charged condition, the positive plate material is essentially pure lead peroxide, PbO_2. The active material of the negative plate is spongy lead, Pb. The electrolyte is a solution of sulphuric acid, H_2SO_4, and water. The voltage of the cell depends upon the chemical difference between the active materials. The concentration of the electrolyte also has a slight affect on voltage.

DISCHARGE

When an electric load is connected to the battery, current will flow. This current is produced by the chemical reactions

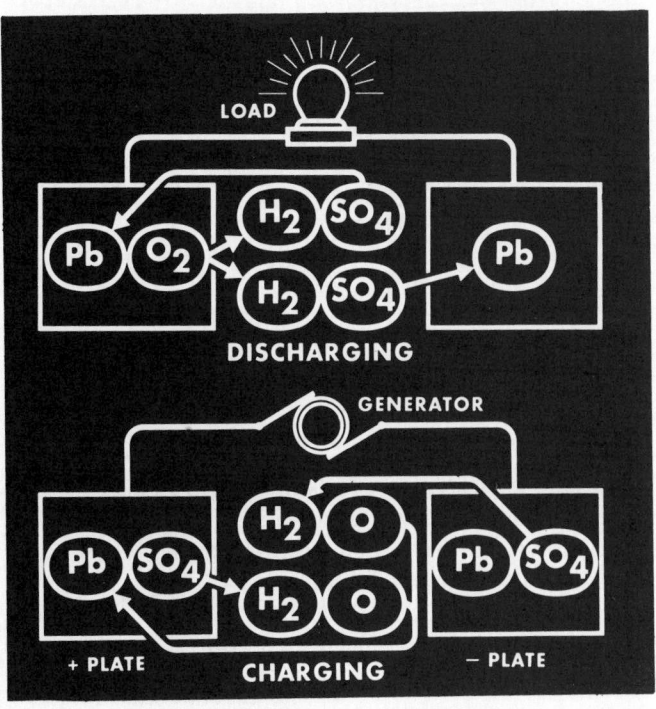

Fig. 36-34. Chemical action in a lead-acid storage battery.

between the active materials of the two kinds of battery plates and the sulphuric acid. As shown in Fig. 36-34, the oxygen in the PbO_2 combines with the hydrogen, H_2, from the sulphuric acid to form water, H_2O. At the same time, the lead, Pb, in the lead peroxide combines with the SO_4 portion of the sulphuric acid to form lead sulphate, $PbSO_4$.

A similar action takes place at the negative plate, where the lead, Pb, of the negative active material combines with the SO_4 of the sulphuric acid to form $PbSO_4$, lead sulphate.

While there is an electric load on the battery, lead sulphate is formed on both positive and negative plates in the battery, and the electrolyte becomes diluted with water. As the discharge continues, the accumulation of lead sulphate on the plates, and the dilution of the electrolyte, brings the chemical reactions to a halt. At low rates of discharge (small current), the reactions are more complete than at high rates, since more time is available for the materials to come into contact. When the chemical action can no longer take place, the battery is said to be discharged.

CHARGE

During charge, the chemical reactions are basically the reverse of those which occur during discharge. The $PbSO_4$, lead sulphate, on both plates is split up into Pb and SO_4, Fig. 36-34, while the H_2O, water, split into hydrogen, H, and oxygen, O_2. The passage of the charging current, which is in the reverse direction to the discharging current, forces the SO_4 from the plates and combines with the H_2 to form H_2SO_4, sulphuric acid. At the same time, the oxygen, O_2, enters into chemical combination with the lead at the positive plate to form PbO_2.

The specific gravity of the electrolyte decreases during discharge for two reasons. Not only is the sulphuric acid used up, but new water is formed. Since the water is formed at the positive plates and diffuses slowly through the electrolyte, the positive plates are more likely to be damaged during freezing weather. When the battery is fully charged, the specific gravity of the solution increases, sulphuric acid is formed, and water is used up. As a result, there is little danger of a fully charged battery freezing.

Specific gravity of the electrolyte may continue to rise for some time after a battery has been quick charged, as the newly formed acid requires time to diffuse from the plates to the electrolyte. Specific gravity readings taken while a battery is gassing will be erroneously low.

VOLTAGE VARIATIONS

Battery voltage and specific gravity vary while the battery is being charged, so it is important to check these factors. Starting batteries are designed to maintain a definite relationship between charging voltage and charging rate. As the specific gravity increases, charging voltage must be increased if the same charging current is to be maintained.

Charging voltage is determined entirely by the battery, until the charging voltage reaches the limit established by the setting of the voltage regulator. When charging voltage reaches that limit, the regulator operates to limit the voltage to that value.

But, as the battery comes up to charge, increased voltage is required to maintain the charging current at the same value. Since additional voltage is no longer available, the charging current decreases and, in this way, adjusts itself to the gradual change in the state of charge.

A battery in normal use tends to operate at lower and lower voltages for a given charging current. On the other hand, a battery that has not been used for a long period tends to operate at higher voltages for a given charging rate. A battery in this condition usually becomes discharged very quickly when placed in service. The maximum allowable setting of the regulator can be ineffective because the battery will tend to heat excessively when charged at higher rates. So it is advisable to charge batteries that have been stored at a very low rate until there is no further increase in specific gravity readings.

BATTERY VOLTAGE AND CAPACITY

The open circuit voltage of a fully charged storage battery cell is 2.1 volt for acid of approximately 1.280. This is true, regardless of the number of plates in the cell, or their area. The voltage is determined only by the character of the chemicals in the plates and the specific gravity of the electrolyte. A 6V battery will be made up of three cells, connected in series, and a 12V battery will consist of six cells, Fig. 36-29.

The capacity of a battery (amount of current it will deliver) depends on the number and area of the plates in the cell and also on the amount of acid present. Cells having a large number of plates will deliver more current than cells having a smaller number. Automotive batteries are built with thin plates to provide maximum plate area so the electrolyte will have quick access to as much active plate area as possible.

Battery capacity drops rapidly as the temperature is reduced. This is because the battery is an electrochemical device and, like virtually all chemical actions, it is aided by heat. For example, if the capacity of cranking power of a battery at 80 deg. is given as 100 percent, at 32 deg., the capacity will be only 65 percent and at 0 deg., only 40 percent. See Fig. 36-35.

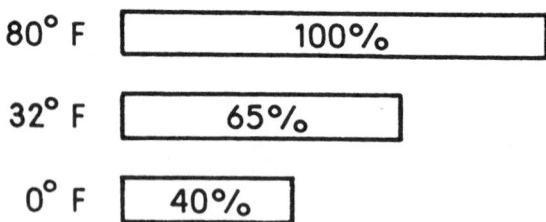

80° F	100%
32° F	65%
0° F	40%

Fig. 36-35. Chart compares cranking power of a fully charged battery at different temperatures.

BATTERY RATINGS

Two methods of rating SLI (Starting-Lighting-Ignition) lead-acid storage batteries have been developed jointly by the Society of Automotive Engineers (SAE) and the Battery Council International (BCI). The new standards are designed to indicate a battery's power-delivering capability. They are: a Cold Cranking Test and a Reserve Capacity rating.

The Cold Cranking Test determines the amount of current (amps.) a battery can deliver for 30 seconds at 0 deg. F and still maintain a terminal voltage of 7.2V, or 1.2V per cell. The rating is given as amps. @ 0 deg. F. The Cold Cranking Test provides a means of determining whether a battery will crank a given engine (based on amperage draw of starter) over a wide range of ambient (surrounding air) temperatures.

The Reserve Capacity rating is the time required to reduce a fully charged battery's terminal voltage below 10.2V (1.7V per cell) at a continuous discharge rate of 25 amps. at approximately 80 deg. F. This test is a straight draw on the battery, without any charging system input. The Reserve Capacity rating appears on the battery as a time interval. For example, a rating of 100 min. means that, once the indicating lamp comes on, the driver has 1 hr. and 40 min. of driving time under minimum electrical load to get to a service facility.

BATTERY TESTING

There are several methods used to test the condition of a storage battery. In general, these include: measurement of specific gravity by means of a hydrometer, Figs. 36-32 and 36-36; test of open circuit voltage; light load test; heavy load test, Fig. 36-38; "cad-tip" test, Fig. 36-40; "421" test.

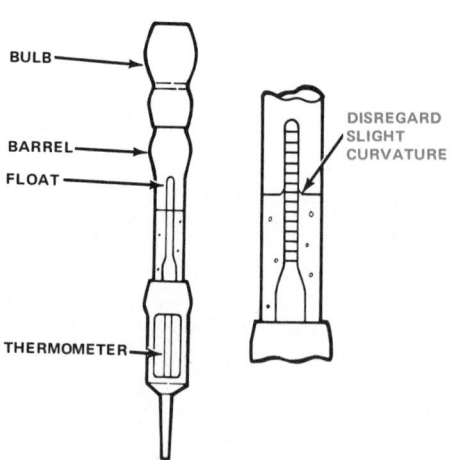

BULB

BARREL

FLOAT

THERMOMETER

DISREGARD SLIGHT CURVATURE

Fig. 36-36. To read hydrometer, float must not touch tube and reading is taken at surface level of electrolyte, then corrected according to temperature. See Fig. 36-37.

Checking the condition of a battery by hydrometer should not be done immediately after water has been added to bring the electrolyte to the desired level. Measurement should be made before the water is added in order to obtain a representative sample. If the level is too low to obtain a sample, water should be added as needed. Then, after the battery has been operated long enough to thoroughly mix the water with the electrolyte, the sample may be taken with the hydrometer.

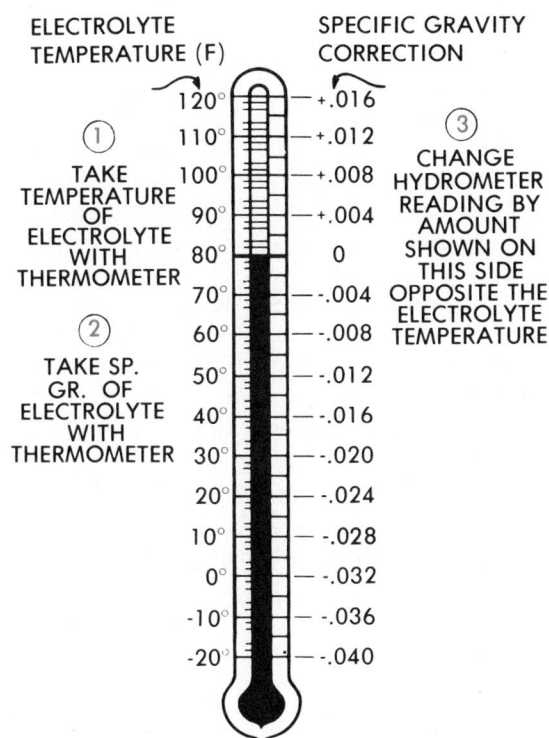

ELECTROLYTE
TEMPERATURE (F)

SPECIFIC GRAVITY
CORRECTION

① TAKE TEMPERATURE OF ELECTROLYTE WITH THERMOMETER

② TAKE SP. GR. OF ELECTROLYTE WITH THERMOMETER

③ CHANGE HYDROMETER READING BY AMOUNT SHOWN ON THIS SIDE OPPOSITE THE ELECTROLYTE TEMPERATURE

120°	+.016
110°	+.012
100°	+.008
90°	+.004
80°	0
70°	-.004
60°	-.008
50°	-.012
40°	-.016
30°	-.020
20°	-.024
10°	-.028
0°	-.032
-10°	-.036
-20°	-.040

Fig. 36-37. Temperature correction of hydrometer reading involves changing reading .004 points of specific gravity for each 10 deg. that electrolyte temperature is above or below 80 deg. F.

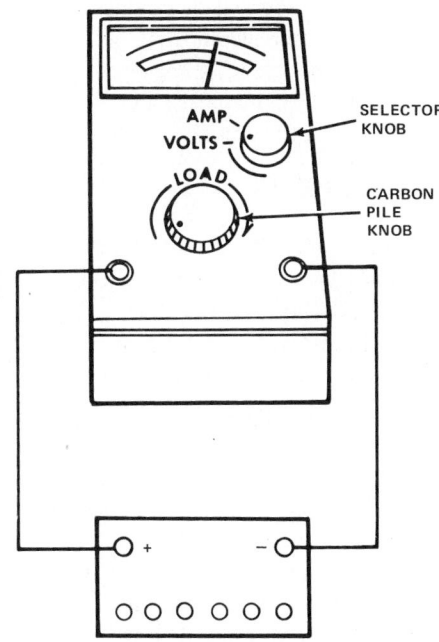

SELECTOR KNOB

AMP
VOLTS
LOAD

CARBON PILE KNOB

Fig. 36-38. Battery load tester has carbon pile to impose heavy load of three times ampere hour rating of battery. Voltage reading after 15 sec. under load determines battery condition. See Fig. 36-39.

Note, too, that hydrometer readings should not be taken while the battery is gassing. This condition would affect the accuracy of the reading.

Remember, when checking the specific gravity of a cell, it is necessary to check the temperature of the electrolyte and make the necessary correction. Fill, empty and refill the hydrometer tube with samples of electrolyte to get a sample of the proper temperature. See Fig. 36-37.

There are many different types of equipment available for making an open circuit voltage test. In general, such equipment operates on the principle of connecting the positive post of the battery to the negative post and measuring the voltage. A battery in good condition should show approximately 12V.

The light load battery test is claimed to be simpler and more conclusive than the hydrometer test. A voltmeter having 0.01V divisions is needed. The procedure is:

1. Place a load on battery for 3 seconds by closing starter switch.
2. If engine starts, turn off ignition.
3. Turn head lamps on (low beam). Connect voltmeter and measure voltage of each cell.
4. If any cell reads 1.95 volts or more, and difference between highest and lowest cell is less than .05 volts, battery is good.
5. If any cell reads 1.95 volts, but there is a difference of 0.05 volts or more between highest and lowest cell, battery should be replaced.
6. If all cells read less than 1.95 volts, battery is too low to test. Recharge battery and repeat test.

Temperature °F	Minimum Voltage
70° or greater	9.6
60° to 69°	9.5
50° to 59°	9.4
40° to 49°	9.3
30° to 39°	9.1
20° to 29°	8.9
10° to 19°	8.7
0° to 9°	8.5

Fig. 36-39. Chart shows minimum acceptable voltage at given temperature when battery is subjected to specified load for 15 sec. and is at least 1.200 specific gravity at 80 deg. F.

HEAVY LOAD TEST

The heavy load test (also called high rate discharge or capacity test) is a good test of the battery's ability to perform under load. In this test, a good battery will produce current equal to three times its ampere hour rating for 15 seconds and still provide minimum voltage to start the engine, Fig. 36-39.

To make the heavy load test:

1. Charge battery, if necessary, until all cells are at least 1200 specific gravity. Remove vent caps and install a thermometer in electrolyte.
2. Connect a battery load tester, Fig. 36-38, or a battery-starter tester directly to battery posts.
3. Turn carbon pile knob to apply a load equal to three times ampere hour rating of battery being tested.
4. Read voltmeter while load is applied for 15 seconds. Turn carbon pile knob to off position.
5. Read thermometer and check temperature and voltage against chart in Fig. 36-39.

451

6. Replace battery if minimum voltage is below specification.
7. If reading is same or greater than voltage shown on chart, clean, fully charge and return battery to vehicle.

CADMIUM TEST OR "CAD—TIP"

Batteries with one-piece hard covers cannot be checked by testing the voltage of the individual cells, since the cover cannot be pierced by the test prods. However, the individual cells of these batteries can be tested by means of a hydrometer or the cadmium, or "cad-tip," tester, Fig. 36-40.

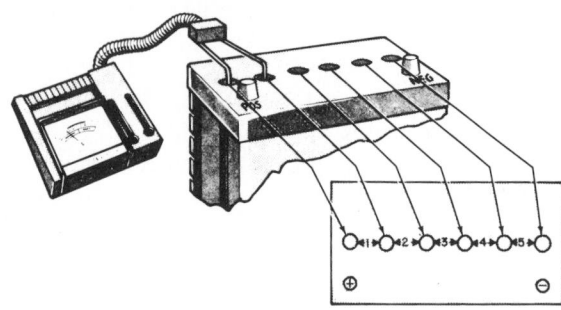

Fig. 36-40. Checking a battery with a cadmium tester.

The principle on which this tester operates is simple. The prod tips are one inch long cadmium tubes that contain an absorbent material which serves to keep the cadmium moist. When inserted into adjacent filler holes in the battery, the prods contact the electrolyte and carry electrical impulses to the voltmeter. The meter face, of course, is graduated to show the efficiency of the cell being tested.

If the readings of any two cells vary five scale divisions or more, the battery is at or near the point of failure.

421 TEST

Some car manufacturers recommend testing solid top batteries with a 421 tester. Several brands of 421 testers are on the market, with approved units carrying a "421" seal, signifying that the equipment has been produced to rigid test standards. Although printed instructions may vary from one tester to another, all are constructed to perform the identical electrical test sequence.

The 421 test is a programmed procedure based on a comparison of two open circuit voltage readings. One is taken after the battery plates have been conditioned by a specific discharge; the second after the plates have been conditioned by a specific charge. These timed discharge and charge events take from two to three minutes.

The 421 testers have a simple good/bad band. If the battery tests "bad," it must be replaced. If it tests "good," but past performance has been unsatisfactory, a specific gravity test should be taken. If there is a difference of 50 points of specific gravity between highest and lowest readings, the battery should be replaced. If the difference is less than 50 points, clean, fully charge and return battery to vehicle.

BATTERY WATER

Water for use in automotive batteries may be a good grade of drinking water, excluding mineral water. It is advisable to use distilled water, or other water that is free from impurities.

Check batteries that require excessive water. This problem is usually an indication that the charging rate is too high. Test output and make the necessary corrections.

CHECKING CABLE RESISTANCE

Battery cable and terminal connections may be tested with a battery-starter tester and a remote starter switch. Connections are shown in Figs. 36-41 and 36-42. The battery must be fully charged.

To make the voltage drop test of insulated circuit, Fig. 36-41:
1. Disconnect primary lead of distributor from coil so engine will not start.
2. Turn voltmeter selector switch on battery-starter tester to 16V scale.
3. Operate remote starter switch and turn voltmeter selector switch to 4V scale while cranking. Observe reading and immediately turn selector switch to 16V scale.
4. Voltmeter should show .6V or less while engine is being cranked. If more, cables or connections are corroded or dirty, solenoid switch is defective, starter is drawing too much current or engine is tight.

To make a voltage drop test of ground circuit, Fig. 36-42:
1. Turn voltmeter selector switch to 4V scale.
2. With starting motor cranking engine, voltage drop should not exceed .3V. If more, resistance is indicated due to loose, corroded or dirty connections.

BATTERY CHARGING

Only direct current can be used for charging batteries, and some method must be provided for controlling the amount of charging current. Before placing a battery on charge, the exterior of the battery and the terminals must be cleaned. In addition, electrolyte must be brought up to desired level.

When charging batteries, the positive lead from the charger is connected to the positive terminal of the battery, and the negative lead from the charger is connected to the negative terminal of the battery. Do not reverse polarity. The battery will be ruined.

If several batteries are to be charged at the same time and connected in series, the positive terminal of one battery should be connected to the negative terminal of the next battery. The positive terminal of the end battery of the series is connected to the positive terminal of the charger. The negative terminal of first battery of the series is connected to the negative terminal of the charger.

The terminals of storage batteries are marked so they can be easily distinguished. The positive terminal is usually marked with a P, Pos or +. Negative terminals are marked N, Neg or — In addition, the positive terminal of the battery is larger in diameter than the negative terminal.

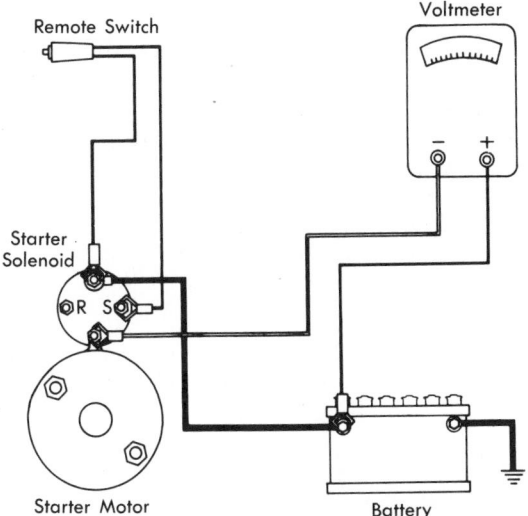

INSULATED CIRCUIT TEST

Fig. 36-41. Proper hookup is shown for making voltage drop test of battery cables, connections and components of insulated side of battery/starting circuit.

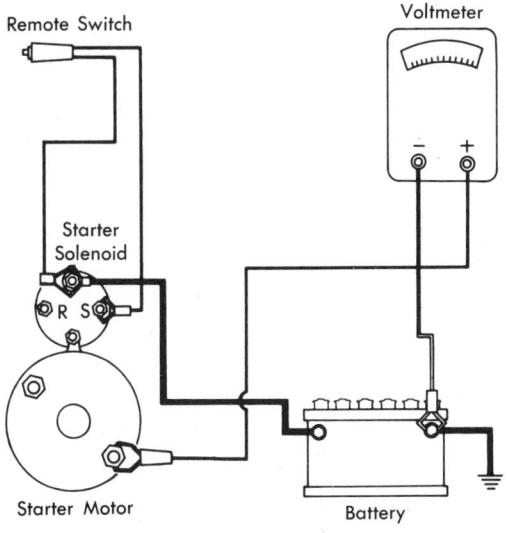

GROUND CIRCUIT TEST

Fig. 36-42. Hookup is shown for testing voltage drop on ground side of battery/starting circuit, including starter to flywheel housing, battery to engine ground cable and connections.

Commercial electricity usually is of the alternating type, so it is necessary to convert the AC to DC before it can be used for battery charging purposes. Methods used to convert AC to DC are motor-generators, tungar bulb rectifiers, and dry disk-type rectifiers.

The Constant Current method of charging batteries is used extensively. This method is particularly advantageous when the condition of the battery is not known, because the charging rate varies with different conditions. However, a safe rate of charge would be equal to the number of positive plates per cell. For example, the charging current in amperes for a 9 plate cell would be 4 amps.

When several batteries of different sizes are connected in series for charging, the charging current is determined by the size of the smallest battery in the series. During charge, the temperature of the batteries should be watched carefully. If the temperature approaches 125 deg. F, the charging rate should be reduced.

To check the progress of the charge, hydrometer readings should be taken every hour. The battery is fully charged when the cells are gassing freely, and there is no increase in hydrometer reading for three successive hourly readings.

Excessive charging will damage the battery, particularly the positive plates. Depending on the charging rate, most batteries can be charged in 12 to 16 hours. Batteries with sulphated plates will require a longer period.

Constant Potential chargers, as the name implies, maintain the same voltage on the batteries throughout the period of the charge. As a result, the current is automatically reduced as the battery approaches full charge. Batteries in good condition will not be damaged by this method of charging.

However, a badly sulphated battery may not come up to charge when the Constant Potential method is used. Also, with this method of charging, battery temperature may rise rapidly. So it is important that frequent temperature checks are made.

High Rate Battery charging is a relatively new method. Prior to 1945 only low charging rates were advocated as it was believed that high rates would damage the battery plates. However, by using a high rate charger, batteries can be charged in approximately 30 minutes. As a result, the method has become popular since it permits charging the battery while the customer waits. In addition, it has reduced or eliminated the necessity for a shop to have a number of batteries on hand which may be loaned to the car owner, while his original battery is being charged.

High charging rates can be used, provided the temperature

Fig. 36-43. This battery charger provides six different charging rates and can be used for either 6V or 12V batteries.

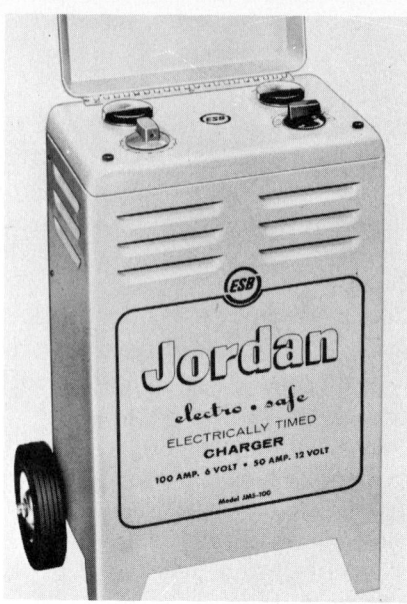

Fig. 36-44. This charger can be moved to car. It is electrically timed to turn off charge at proper moment.

Fig. 36-45. One type of trickle charger designed particularly for the car owner. Other types are available for maintaining stocks of batteries in good condition.

of the electrolyte does not exceed 125 deg. F, and does not cause excessive gassing and loss of electrolyte.

Most high rate battery chargers, Figs. 36-43 and 36-44, are of the Constant Potential type. They are designed to provide an initial charging rate of 40 to 50 amps. Some types of high rate chargers are equipped with a time cut-off or temperature limiting device, so that electrolyte temperature cannot exceed

125 deg. F. Should the temperature reach 125 deg. F, the charger is shut off automatically.

Trickle chargers, Fig. 36-45, are designed to charge batteries at a rate of approximately 1 amp. They are used primarily for maintaining display and stocks of batteries in fully charged condition. While the charging rate is extremely low, batteries can be damaged if left on a trickle charge for long periods. Common practice is to leave the batteries on a trickle charge during the day and take them off charge during the night. In that way, danger of severe overcharging is eliminated.

STORAGE BATTERY TESTING CHART

HYDROMETER TEST, 80 DEG. F	CONDITION	REMEDY
More than 1300	Specific gravity too high	Adjust specific gravity
1.250 to 1.295	Probably good	If variation among cells is less than 0.015 specific gravity, no correction is required. If greater than that amount, give heavy load test. If cells test O.K., recharge and adjust specific gravity of cells.
1.225 to 1.250	Fair	Battery should be recharged. Test charging system output. Also, check electrical system for loose connections, shorts, grounds or corroded terminals.
Less than 1.225	Poor	Recharge battery. Test charging system output. Also, check electrical system for loose connections, shorts, grounds or corroded terminals.
Cells show more than .025 variation in specific gravity	1. Short in low cell 2. Loss of electrolyte 3. Cracked cell partition	Recharge battery at approximately 7 amp. until gravity readings show no increase in three successive readings taken 1 hour apart. Adjust specific gravity of cell. Make a heavy load test 12 hours after charging. If more than 0.15V difference is shown between cells, battery is no longer serviceable.

Fig. 36-46. This dry charged battery is of unusual three piece design (top, bottom and sleeve), which protects against vibration damage. Also, inter-cell connectors are built into sleeve and partitions.

Fig. 36-47. Filling a dry charged battery with electrolyte.

DRY CHARGED BATTERIES

A dry charged starting battery contains no electrolyte until it is placed in service, Fig. 36-46. The cell elements are given an initial charge on special equipment at the factory. Then, they are thoroughly washed, dried and assembled into battery cases, and shipped in the dry state.

A dry charged battery will retain its full charge indefinitely, if moisture does not enter the cells. When ready for service, the electrolyte (shipped in individual plastic containers) is poured into each cell and the battery is ready for use.

When filling a dry charged battery with electrolyte, the manufacturers advise that protective glasses be worn. Then follow this procedure:

1. Remove vent plugs and discard white restrictors found in vent openings.
2. With electrolyte container right side up, remove lid, then unfold top of plastic bag which contains electrolyte. Do not attempt to remove plastic bag from carton. It is sealed to container and may rupture.
3. Cut a small opening in a corner of double-walled bag; a large opening will cause acid to spatter.
4. Using a glass or acid-proof funnel, fill each battery cell with electrolyte as shown in Fig. 36-47.
5. Cell is correctly filled when electrolyte reaches split ring at bottom of vent well.
6. After filling cells, wait five minutes. If level has fallen, add electrolyte to bring to proper level.
7. Place battery on "charge" for a brief period to make sure it is fully charged.

WATER ACTIVATION

After a dry charged battery has been activated with acid, it often requires a boost charge to meet industry standards. To combat this, several manufacturing techniques have been employed, and several temporary sealing methods have been used to keep moisture from entering the dry charged battery

plates while the battery is in storage.

A sealed, dry charged, lead-acid battery has been developed that stores concentrated sulphuric acid in phenolic foam blocks apart from the battery plates. When the seals are broken and clear water is added, the battery can be placed in service immediately after activation. The need for a boost charge is minimized.

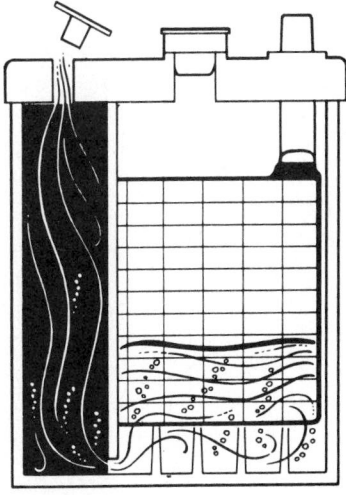

Fig. 36-48. Water-activated battery. Left. Water passes through acid-treated foam blocks. Right, Water becomes electrolyte and activates plates. (Prestolite)

The water-activated battery, Fig. 36-48, has six cells with higher plates that are closer together than those in conventional batteries. However, since the water-activated battery has a series of foam blocks alongside of, but separated from, the plates in each cell, the plates necessarily are narrower. Note Fig. 36-48.

The foam blocks are treated with concentrated sulphuric acid and have vertical holes to aid in water distribution when the battery is activated. The water percolates through the foam blocks, diluting and mixing with the concentrated acid as it flows. The mixture enters the plate area through slots in the partition at the base of the battery. The electrolyte formed rises over the plates, causing their activation.

The container and cover of the water-activated battery are made of fiberglass reinforced polyethylene, said to have high resistance to impact and vibration, particularly at low temperatures. The sealing feature of this battery involves sealing discs manufactured into both the vent and initial fill openings. When the battery is to be activated, the installer breaks the seals, activates all cells with water, then he permanently installs the initial fill caps. Future service is by way of the vent caps and openings.

THREE—PIECE CONSTRUCTION

Another breakthrough in battery manufacturing techniques is a three-piece battery design that contrasts sharply with conventional, two-piece box and top construction. This battery features through-the-partition inter-cell connectors and heat-sealing of the elements (plates, separators and partitions) to the bottom of the sleeve and element rests of the reservoir to withstand vibration.

The battery is assembled in three basic pieces. The sleeve is injection molded with the inter-cell connectors as an integral part. Plates are automatically stacked into cells and loaded into the sleeve from the bottom as a single unit. The cell unit is then heat-sealed into the reservoir, keeping the plates, separators and partitions in register and imbedded into the bottom of the sleeve and element rests in 300 places.

Next the inter-cell connectors, plate straps and plates are welded together simultaneously and the top is heat-sealed on. Finally, post-burning torches automatically fuse the posts to the stub posts to a specific height. Throughout assembly, several vacuum and pressure leakage tests are made to guarantee against inter-cell leakage.

The three-piece battery has a polypropylene casing, and a polypropylene element protector is built in the sleeve mold to protect the plates from accidental damage by probes of testing instruments. In comparing the impact resistance of polypropylene against hard rubber, tests by the manufacturer at 0 deg. F showed that the polypropylene casing is three times stronger. At 75 deg. F, polypropylene is said to be about 100 times as strong as hard rubber.

SODIUM BATTERY

With further development, the new Ford sodium-sulphur battery may play an important part in transportation of the future. This new battery can produce 15 times as much power as the familiar lead-acid battery of the same weight.

In the Ford unit, positive sodium ions, No. 1 in Fig. 36-49, pass through the electrolyte to form sodium sulphide, 2. Sodium electrons, which cannot get through, are channeled into the circuit, becoming the current, 3. The electrons pass from the negative terminal through the motor (or other load) to the positive terminal, then into sodium sulphide, 4, where they attract more positive sodium ions through the electrode.

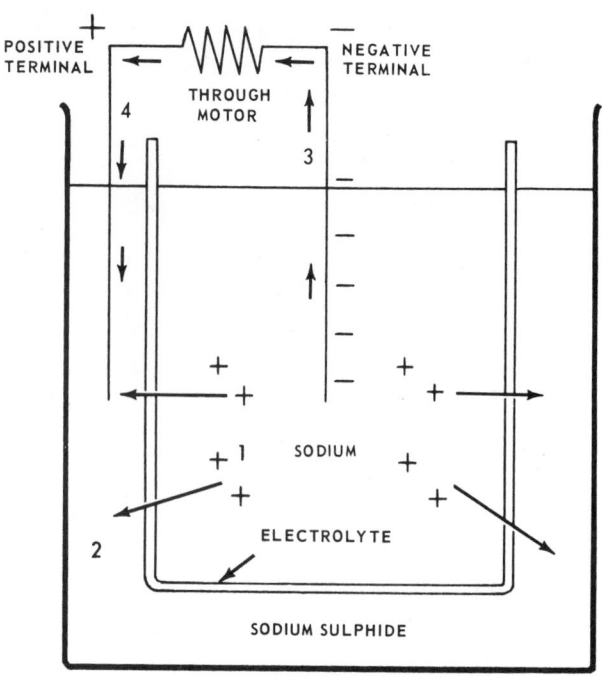

Fig. 36-49. Ford's sodium-sulphur battery.

To charge the battery, the current is reversed. Actually the chemical process to charge and discharge the sodium battery is actually less complicated than that of the lead-acid battery, described earlier in this chapter.

A comparison between lead-acid batteries and sodium batteries can be set up to estimate the performance that can be expected from the sodium battery. A 36 volt, 600 amp. lead-acid battery, of the type used in industrial trucks weighs 1500 lb. A sodium-sulphur battery of the same capacity would weigh one-fifteenth as much or 100 lb.

From a power standpoint, the lead-acid battery has available 21,600 watts, or 29.0 hp. If a sodium battery of the same weight can provide 15 times as much power, it will put out 435 hp. That is a lot of power, but it must be remembered that an internal combustion engine of the same power weighs only about 500 lb.

While the major advantages of the new battery are high energy output and relatively inexpensive construction materials, there are severe disadvantages, including high operating temperature. This means that while the car is in the garage, the battery would have to be heated to 800 deg. F. This results from the ceramic electrolyte which permits only sodium ions to flow through it and nothing else, but only as long as it is heated to 800 deg. F.

In that connection, remember that many chemicals and fuels with ignition temperatures less than that amount are stored in the average garage. For example, the ignition temperature of acetylene is 760 to 820 deg. F. Fire insurance underwriters would probably view the new battery as a fire hazard, and rates would be high.

Other batteries in the development stage include a General Motors' unit using silver and zinc as reactants, and another using zinc and air which is being developed by General Dynamics Corporation.

A lithium-chlorine fuel cell, designed to convert chemical energy into electric energy, is also under development by a General Motors' division. At present, electrical propulsion by fuel cells is technically feasible, but size, weight and cost must be radically improved to make it practical for vehicles, according to a General Motors' spokesman.

Meanwhile, maintenance-free batteries are the primary electrical power source in most modern passenger cars. A "Freedom" battery, Fig. 36-28, is said to be free of scheduled periodic maintenance. This battery has wrought lead-calcium grids, centered plate straps, separator envelopes and small gas vents with built-in flame arresters. A special liquid-gas separator returns any liquid to the reservoir. The cover is heat-sealed to the polypropylene case.

Chrysler, too, has a maintenance-free battery that eliminates the need to add water during its normal life of 30 to 40 months. It has a battery test indicator that tells whether the battery needs to be recharged or replaced.

REVIEW QUESTIONS – STORAGE BATTERIES

1. What is a lead-acid storage battery?
   a. A storage place for electricity.
   b. A converter of chemical energy to electrical energy.
2. How much voltage can be obtained from a single cell of a storage battery?
   a. About 2V.
   b. About 6V.
   c. About 12V.
   d. Varies with size of plates.
3. What factors control the amount of current that can be produced by a single cell of a storage battery?
4. What is used to fill the positive plate grids of a storage battery?
   a. Lead peroxide.
   b. Sponge lead.
   c. Antimony oxide.
   d. Sulphuric acid.
5. Name three materials used to make plate separators in a storage battery.
6. What is the specific gravity of the electrolyte used to fill lead storage batteries?
   a. 1.290.
   b. 1.920.
   c. 1.450.
7. What instrument is used to measure the specific gravity of a liquid?
   a. Hygrometer.
   b. Barometer.
   c. Hydrometer.
   d. Gravometer.
8. The specific gravity reading of a storage battery is 1.290 at 90 deg. F. What is the correct specific gravity?
9. While a storage battery is discharging, what chemicals are formed from the lead peroxide and the sulphuric acid?
10. How many cells in a 12 volt storage battery?
11. As the temperature drops, does a storage battery have more or less cranking power?
12. When making a heavy load test on a storage battery, what is the minimum acceptable voltage at 80 deg. F?
    a. 4.9V.
    b. 6.8V.
    c. 9.6V.
    d. 11.2V.
13. When making a light load battery test, what is the permissible voltage variation between cells?
    a. 0.05V.
    b. 0.15V.
    c. 0.20V.
14. When charging a battery, to which terminal of the battery is the positive lead of the charger connected?
    a. Positive terminal.
    b. Negative terminal.
    c. Either terminal.
15. If the positive terminal of a battery is not otherwise marked, how can it be recognized?
16. What would be the normal safe rate for charging an 11 plate battery?
    a. 5 1/2 amps.
    b. 11 amps.
    c. 22 amps.
17. When charging a battery by the high rate method, what is considered as being a safe temperature which should not be exceeded?
    a. 212 deg. F.
    b. 125 deg. F.
    c. 80 deg. F.
18. When are trickle chargers used?
19. What is meant by a dry charged battery?
20. If the acid-treated foam blocks in a water-activated battery are separated from the plates, how does the electrolyte enter the plate area during activation?
21. During assembly of the new three-piece construction battery, the plates are loaded into the sleeve from the bottom so that all of the elements remain in register while the bottom of the sleeve is heat-sealed on. True or False?
22. Ford's experimental sodium-sulphur battery can produce 50 times as much power as the familiar lead-acid battery of the same weight. Yes or No?

SPEEDOMETERS

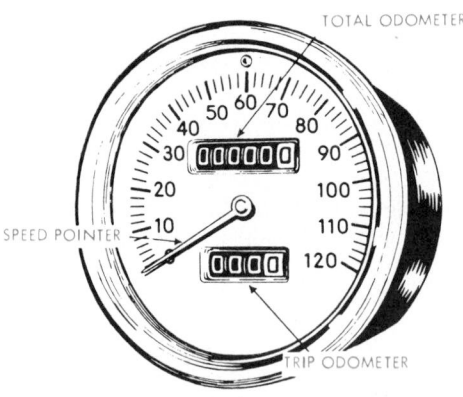

Fig. 36-50. Typical speedometer with total and trip odometer.

Fig. 36-52. Method of driving speedometer from front wheel.

The speedometer used on automotive vehicles indicates speed of the vehicle and records distance traveled, Fig. 36-50.

A speedometer is driven by a flexible shaft, Fig. 36-51, connected with gearing within the transmission, or occasionally from the front wheel, Fig. 36-52.

Speedometers are calibrated in miles per hour or in kilometers. When the instrument also records the distance traveled, this will be recorded in either miles or kilometers. That portion of the instrument is known as the odometer, Figs. 36-50 and 36-53. Most odometers record the total

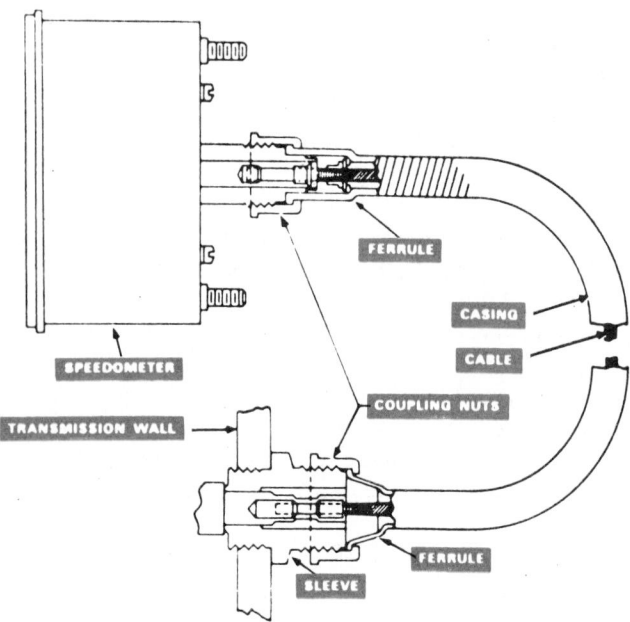

Fig. 36-51. Details of speedometer drive from transmission.

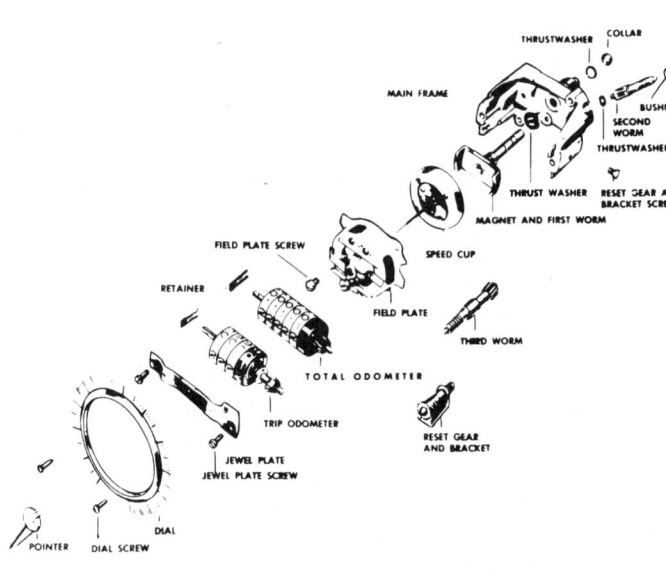

Fig. 36-53. Exploded view of typical speedometer.
(AC Spark Plug Div., GMC)

distance traveled, while some also record the distance of individual trips. These can be reset to zero, Fig. 36-50.

To measure the speed of the vehicle and register the distance traveled requires a separate series of parts. Internal components of different makes and types of speedometers vary in appearance. The parts of a typical speedometer are shown in Fig. 36-53.

OPERATION OF A SPEEDOMETER

The speedometer and odometer are driven by a cable housed in a casing, Fig. 36-51. The cable is connected to a take-off gear at the transmission or front wheel. This gear is designed for the particular vehicle model and takes into consideration the tire size and rear axle ratio.

In most cases of transmission take-off, the speedometer is designed to convert 1,001 revolutions of the drive cable into a registration of one mile on the odometer. In other words, 1,001 cable revolutions in a minute, will result in a speed indication of 60 mph.

SPEED INDICATION

The speed indication of a typical speedometer or tachometer operates on the magnetic principle. It includes a revolving permanent magnet driven by the cable connected to the transmission. Around this permanent magnet is a stationary field plate. Between the magnet and field plate is a nonmagnetic movable speed cup on a spindle. The magnet revolves within the speed cup, Fig. 36-54.

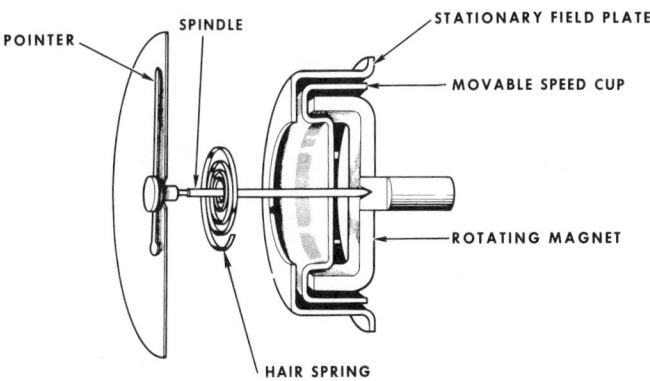

Fig. 36-54. Schematic drawing of speedometer showing speed cup, magnet, field plate, hairspring and pointer with dial.

The revolving magnet sets up a rotating magnetic field which exerts a pull on the speed cup, making it revolve in the same direction. The movement of the speed cup is retarded and held steady by a hairspring attached to the speed cup spindle. The speed cup comes to rest at a point where the magnetic drag is just balanced by the retarding force created by the hairspring. An additional function of the hairspring is to pull the pointer of the instrument back to zero when the magnet stops rotating.

There is no mechanical connection between the revolving

magnet and the speed cup. As the speed of the magnet increases, due to the movement of the vehicle, the magnet drag on the speed cup also increases and pulls the speed cup further around. In that way, a faster speed is indicated by the pointer on the face of the dial.

The magnetic field is constant, and the amount of movement of the speed cup is (at all times) directly proportional to the speed at which the magnet is being rotated. Temperature affect on the magnet is compensated for by a special alloy attached to the magnet.

This operating description applies to all magnetically driven speedometers, including disk and indicating cylinder types.

ODOMETER OPERATION

Both trip and total odometers are driven through a series of gears originating from a special gear on the end of the first gear and magnet shaft, Fig. 36-55. The total odometer usually has

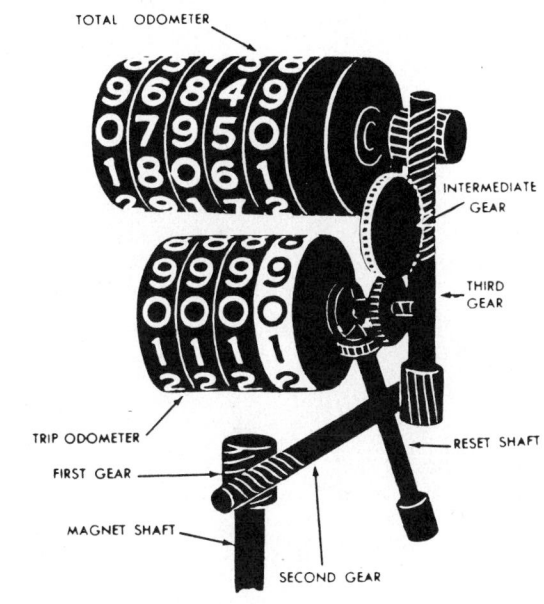

Fig. 36-55. Gear train of typical speedometer from magnet shaft to odometers.

five figure wheels and a dummy wheel. The trip odometer has three figure wheels and a decimal wheel.

Both odometers are constructed so that any wheel completing one revolution will turn the wheel on its left 1/10 of a revolution.

The trip odometer mileage can be set as desired by means of a reset mechanism and a special trip drive sleeve.

RESETTING THE ODOMETER

To reset the odometer, note and record indicated mileage on the odometer. Note position and alignment of projecting ears of pinion carriers. Remove the odometer.

Hold the first odometer wheel on the right (dummy or tenth wheel) between right-hand thumb and index finger.

With the left-hand index finger, rotate counterclockwise the first (to left of dummy or tenth wheel) metal separator with slotted projection (pinion carriers).

Continue rotating the first carrier counterclockwise (looking at dummy wheel side of odometer assembly) until the second figure wheel indicates the desired figure when in the odometer window opening.

Shift right-hand thumb and index finger to hold and keep in alignment the first figure wheel, the first pinion carrier and the second figure wheel.

With the left-hand index finger, rotate the second pinion counterclockwise until the third figure wheel indicates the desired figure when in the odometer window.

Proceed working from right to left until each figure wheel is in its desired position. Then reinstall the odometer in the instrument.

INSPECTION AND LUBRICATION

To test the speedometer for a tight mechanism, insert a test cable and turn, Fig. 36-56. No binding or tightness should be felt. The test cable is the drive end of a short length of

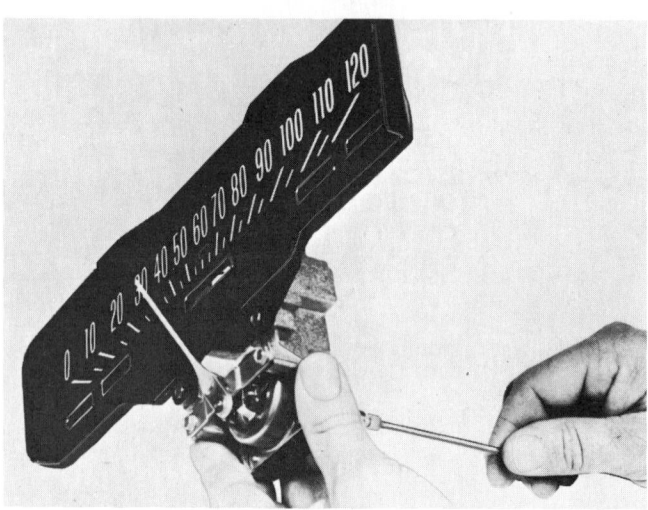

Fig. 36-56. Test for tightness of operation is made by inserting short length of cable in meter to spin mechanism.

conventional speedometer cable. An initial fast spin of the test cable should swing the pointer of the instrument from zero to about half scale. From half scale, the pointer should quickly return to zero. This indicates that the hairspring and magnet are in good working order.

The same basic test also applies to the drum or indicator cylinder type of speedometer. The indicator cylinder should advance to at least 30 mph, then quickly return to zero.

To test the speedometer for calibration, proceed as follows. Providing the instrument mechanism turns freely, place unit in test stand and run at various speeds. Compare readings of speedometer and test stand pointer movement.

Operate the speedometer in test stand and note the amount of noise. The noise level should be low enough not to be

objectionable. Operate speedometer long enough to record several miles. All figure wheels should be lined up evenly, except those wheels which may be operating. If excessive grease is present in the speedometer head, the cable and casing should be cleaned.

Some speedometers are provided with a lubrication felt or wick. However, lubrication is not necessary on modern speedometers except when the cable is being serviced for some other reason. When lubricating a speedometer cable, the special lubricant should be applied lightly. Excessive lubrication may result in the lubricant working up the cable and into the speedometer head.

SPEEDOMETER ACCURACY

The accuracy of a speedometer and odometer is affected by the size of the tires, the rear axle pinion ratio and the gears used to drive the speedometer. Changing to a different size tire or a different rear axle ratio will alter the accuracy of the speedometer and odometer.

In order to provide maximum accuracy of the instrument, vehicle manufacturers provide a variety of drive pinions for their speedometers. This availability of replacement pinions will give you the correct ratio needed for a given tire size and rear axle ratio on that particular vehicle.

In the case of Dodge and other Chrysler-built vehicles, the margin of error of their speedometers has been reduced from 0 to 5 percent to 0 to 3 percent. This was done by increasing the number of teeth on both the worm gear machined on the transmission output shaft and on the speedometer drive pinion. In that way, a large number of different ratios are made available, and a greater number of different tire sizes and rear axle ratios can be accomodated.

All speedometer drive pinions may be interchanged because of the pinion adapter, Fig. 36-57. The bearing hole in the adapter is off center and any of the three families of drive pinions may be installed to provide the desired gearing.

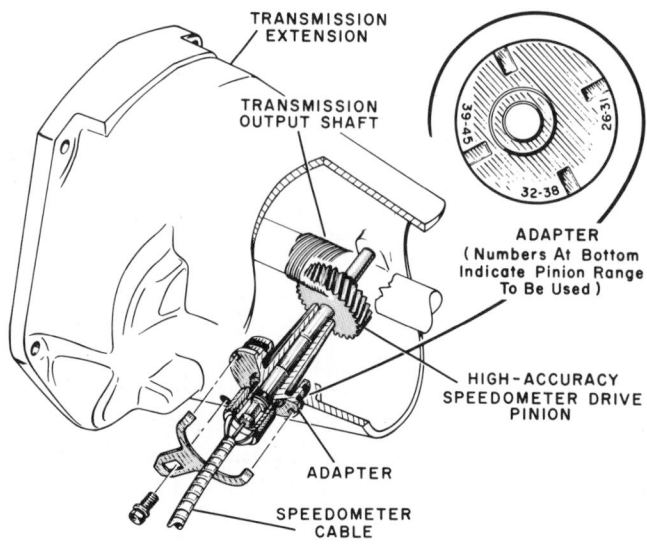

Fig. 36-57. Speedometer drive pinion and adapter installed on Dodge cars provides a greater number of gear ratios.

CALIBRATING THE SPEEDOMETER

Calibration of a speedometer is the operation of mechanically balancing the torque of the magnet with the hairspring so that it checks with a test stand at no less than three points on its dial scale, Fig. 36-58.

Fig. 36-59. Equipment used to magnetize the magnets of speedometer.

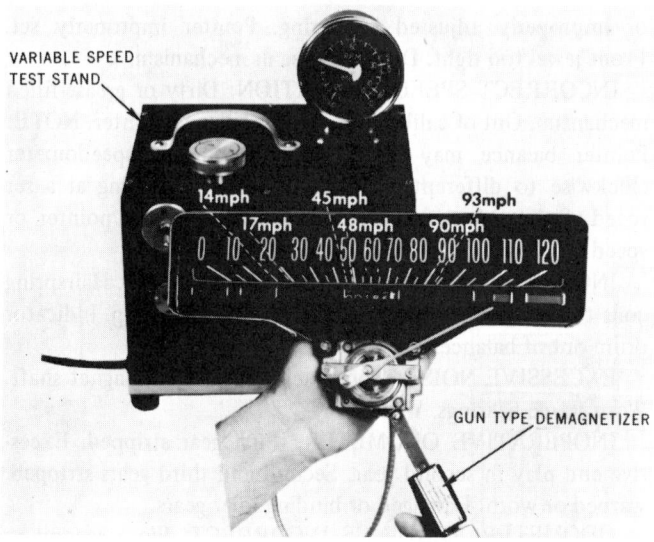

Fig. 36-58. Speedometer test stand with gun type demagnetizer.

A speedometer test stand includes a method of rotating the speedometer at specified rates of speed. Also included, is a method of recharging the magnets and a demagnetizer, Fig. 36-59. Follow the equipment manufacturers' instructions.

SPEEDOMETER CABLE REPLACEMENT

Speedometer cables break as the result of age, lack of lubrication or because the cable casing has sharp bends.

To correct the problem of sharp bends, the clamps holding the casing must be relocated to straighten the casing.

When the bends have damaged the interior of the casing, it will be necessary to replace the assembly, because the rough spots would tend to cause binding, friction and rapid wear of the cable.

Another cause of frequent breakage of the speedometer cable is excessive friction in the speedometer head. The test for this condition has been described.

Replacement cables can be secured as a complete assembly with both end tips in place or in kit form. In the latter case, it is necessary to cut the cable to the desired length and attach the tip.

If a "tailor-made" cable is to be installed, the casing should be disconnected from the speedometer head, then the old cable is withdrawn from the casing. If the old cable is broken, it will also be necessary to disconnect the casing at the transmission end so that the other section of the broken cable can be removed.

After withdrawing the old cable, spread a thin coat of speedometer cable grease evenly over the lower two-thirds of the new cable. Do not apply grease to the entire cable as that would result in the lubricant working up the cable and into the speedometer head and causing damage.

After applying the lubricant to the cable, insert the cable into the upper end of the casing, lower end first. This will spread the grease evenly over the entire length of the cable.

Connect the upper end of the casing to the speedometer case, making sure that the cable tip engages correctly in the speedometer drive member. Tighten the ferrule nut, finger tight. Then twist the lower end of the cable with your fingers to make sure it turns freely. A sharp twist of the cable should cause the speedometer needle to register. Finally, connect the lower end of the casing to the transmission fitting, making sure that the cable engages in the speedometer driven gear.

When a cable kit is being used as a replacement, the procedure is as follows:

First cut the new cable the same length as the old cable. Be sure to include the length of the tip which is to be staked on the cut end of the cable. Fit the new tip of correct shape to the cut end of the cable. Place the tip in the staking tool and squeeze the tool in the jaws of a vise or strike it a sharp blow with a hammer, Fig. 36-60. Finally, check the new cable against the original cable to be sure overall length is the same.

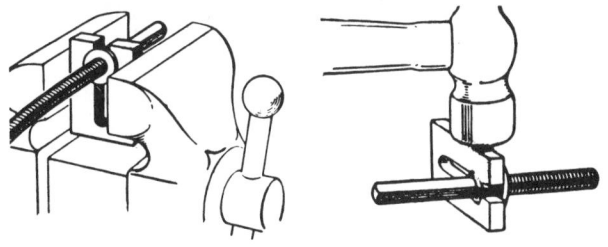

Fig. 36-60. Flexible speedometer cable can be staked to tip by using staking tool by either method shown.

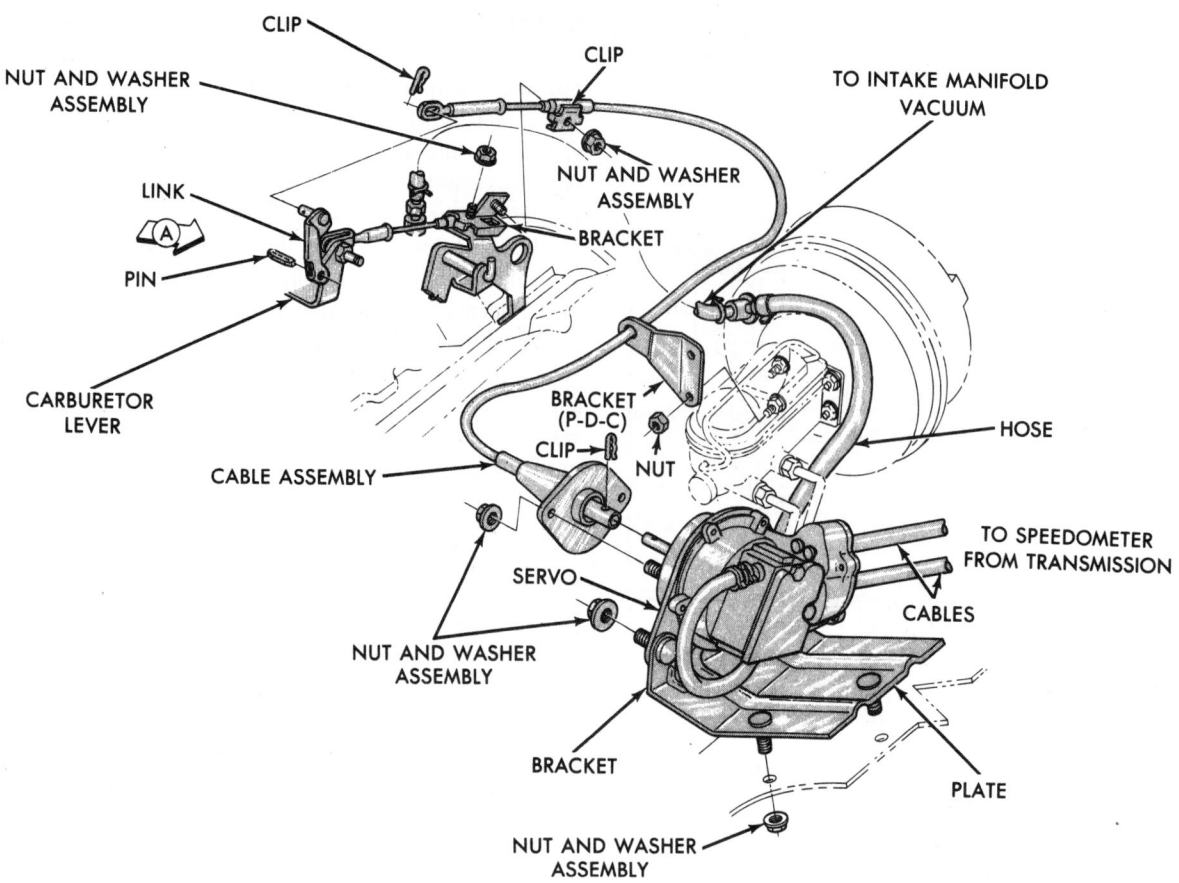

Fig. 36-69. Chrysler system utilizes a servo unit and throttle cable assembly in engine compartment.

AMERICAN MOTORS CRUISE COMMAND

AMC's speed control system called Cruise Command senses car speed through the speedometer cable, much like the General Motors unit. It also uses intake manifold vacuum to regulate the accelerator and to maintain any preset cruising speed between 30 and 85 mph. The control switches are built into the turn signal lever. They include the OFF-ON and RES (resume) slide switch, located on the side of the lever, and the push button system engagement switch at the end of the lever.

In operation, the slide switch is moved to ON, and the vehicle is accelerated to designated speed. Then, the driver presses the engagement button on the end of the lever, releases it and the control system will maintain the selected speed.

The system can be disengaged by depressing the accelerator pedal. It can be re-engaged by accelerating to at least 30 mph, and moving the slide switch to the RES position, then releasing the switch. The vehicle will automatically return to the previously selected speed.

The system can be reset to higher or lower speeds by either accelerating or braking to attain the new designated speed. Then the engagement push button is pressed and released to activate the system at the new rate of speed.

Key elements of the Cruise Command system are:
1. Regulator, which senses speed through speedometer cable located between transmission and regulator. A flyweight

governor reacts to cable speed and engages low speed switch at approximately 30 mph.
2. Vacuum servo, which receives modulator vacuum to actuate a neoprene bellows that, in turn, moves throttle to control vehicle speed.
3. Control switch, which is an integral part of turn signal lever. When actuated, switch energizes either solenoid valve or coupling coil, or both, thereby controlling speed.
4. Release switch, which de-energizes solenoid valve when brake pedal is depressed slightly to disengage speed control.

The electrical parts of the Cruise Command system are energized from the fuse panel, Fig. 36-70, through the slide switch, push button, low speed switch, solenoid valve and coupling coil. The coupling coil is grounded through the regulator case. The solenoid valve is grounded through the brake release switch.

PERFECT CIRCLE (DANA) SPEED CONTROL

The Speedostat electronic speed control, Fig. 36-71, has five major components:
1. Engagement switch.
2. Servo.
3. Regulator.
4. Road speed pick-up coil.
5. Disengage switch.

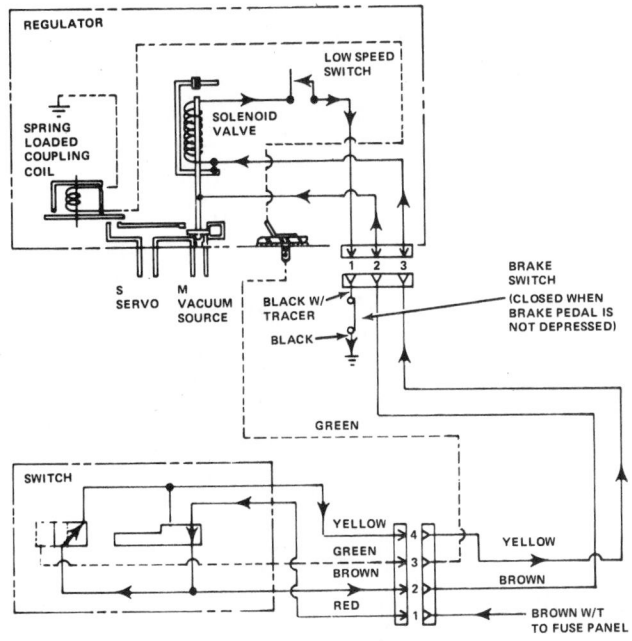

Fig. 36-70. American Motors speed control system diagram shows system being actuated by push button control switch.

When the vehicle speed is about 30 mph (48 km) or above, and the engagement switch is activated, the road pick-up coil will send a signal to the regulator which electronically senses any difference between actual vehicle speed and the desired speed. The regulator then signals the servo unit to either open or close the throttle, bring the vehicle to the desired speed and hold it there.

The disengage switch on the brake pedal is a combination electrical disconnect and vacuum vent valve. When the brake is applied, the switch cuts the electrical power to the unit and also, as a safety measure, vents the servo.

The Speedostat does not operate below 40 mph. Above that speed, the driver turns on the master switch, brings the vehicle up to the desired speed, pushes the engagement switch and removes his foot from the accelerator pedal. The vehicle then maintains the speed at which the control is set.

The speed can be further increased by depressing the accelerator and activating the engagement switch. By depressing the brake pedal, the master switch is turned off and the vehicle returns to normal operation.

GM

The servo (1) is mounted in the engine compartment, while the road speed pick-up (2) is under the car near the drive shaft. The electronic regulator (3) and the disengagement switch (4) are mounted under the instrument panel. The engagement switch (5) is attached to the turn signal lever on the steering column. The servo should be mounted in line with the carburetor linkage and within 20 deg. of the linkage center line.

The servo is vacuum operated and controls the throttle by responding to signals from the solid state regulator. The magnets of the road speed pick-up coil are mounted on each side of the propeller shaft and rotate with it. The speed pick-up coil is mounted close to the magnets, on a level with them, and in the magnetic field of the rotating magnets.

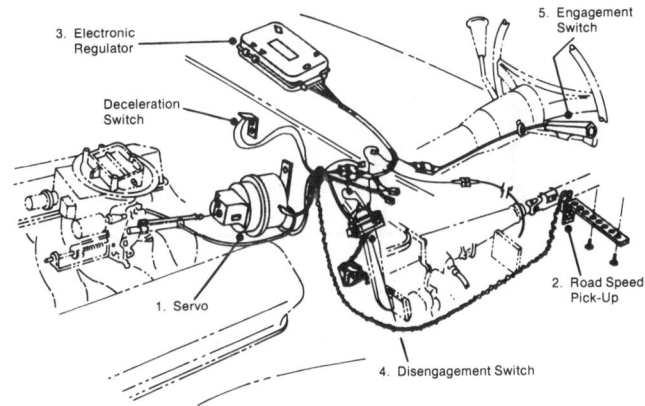

Fig. 36-71. Location of various parts of late type Perfect Circle Electronic Speed Control System.

REVIEW QUESTIONS – SPEED CONTROL SYSTEMS

1. In the Ford speed control system, where is the amplifier located?
2. To engage the Ford speed control system, at what speed must the vehicle be traveling with the engine running?
3. What free play should the bead chain have in the Ford speed control system?
   a. 1/2 in.
   b. 1/4 to 1/2 in.
   c. No more than 1/4 in.
4. What is the function of the transducer, or regulator, in the GM speed control system?
5. GM utilizes a brake release switch that disengages the system electrically when the brake pedal is depressed. True or False?
6. GM's brake release valve is actuated when the brake pedal is depressed. In operation, it does the following:

a. Dumps vacuum from servo unit.
b. Releases the engagement switch.
c. Deactivates the transducer.
7. How can the driver override the GM speed control system?
8. How can the driver disengage the Chrysler speed control system without erasing the speed memory?
9. American Motors speed control system senses car speed through the speedometer. Yes or No?
10. The electrical parts of the AMC speed control system are energized from the fuse panel. True or False?
11. AMC's system incorporates a slide switch:
   a. On dash panel.   c. On steering column.
   b. On turn signal lever.   d. On transmission.
12. How many parts form the Perfect Circle Electronic Speed Control System?

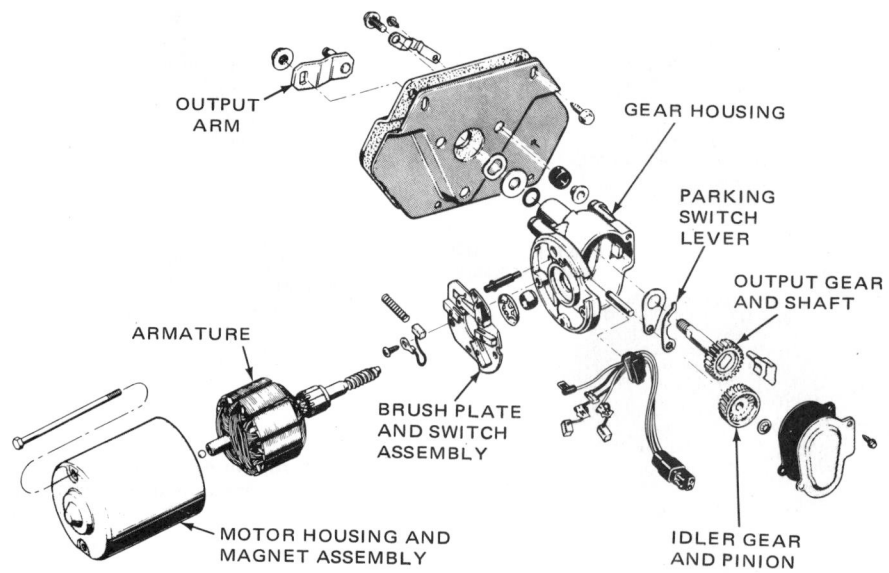

OUTPUT ARM

GEAR HOUSING

PARKING SWITCH LEVER

OUTPUT GEAR AND SHAFT

ARMATURE

BRUSH PLATE AND SWITCH ASSEMBLY

IDLER GEAR AND PINION

MOTOR HOUSING AND MAGNET ASSEMBLY

Fig. 36-78. Exploded view shows elements of typical Ford or American Motors two speed wiper motor.

With the relay coil energized, the relay contacts close, completing the 12 volt circuit to the motor relay windings. Current then flows through the series field coil and divides. Part of the current passes through the armature to ground via circuit breaker. The other part of the current passes through the shunt field coils to ground at the wiper switch.

The windshield washer pump is attached to the wiper motor. Washer pump operation is described later.

FORD AND AMERICAN MOTORS WIPERS

Late model Ford and American Motors cars are equipped with windshield wiper motors of similar design. Two types of motors are used, the depressed park type and the non-depressed park type. An exploded view of the motor used in non-depressed park applications is shown in Fig. 36-78. It is a permanent magnet, two speed, rotary type.

Ford and AMC also make an intermittent wiper available. When the wiper switch is turned to the right, the wiper arm and blade assemblies operate at low or high speed as desired. When the switch is turned to the left, a variable resistor built into the switch works in conjunction with an electronic governor, Fig. 36-79, to regulate the time interval between sweeps of the wiper blades.

CHRYSLER WIPERS

Chrysler cars generally have a two speed wiper system used with either an electric washer pump or a foot-operated pump. On cars with the non-depressed park system, the wiper blades park in the lowest portion of the wipe pattern. On cars with the depressed park system, the blades automatically park in the depressed position when the wiper switch is turned off.

The two speed wiper motor has a permanent magnet field, controlled by feeding current to different brushes for low and

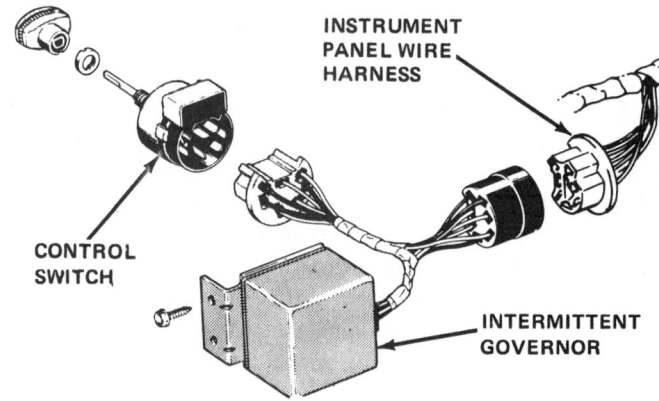

INSTRUMENT PANEL WIRE HARNESS

CONTROL SWITCH

INTERMITTENT GOVERNOR

Fig. 36-79. Electronic governor is used, along with a variable resistor in wiper switch, to provide proper delay interval for intermittent sweeps of wiper blades.

high speed operation. The low speed circuit incorporates a torque limiting resistor, Fig. 36-80.

Chrysler's three speed wiper motors all have the depressed park feature. It is accomplished by means of an eccentric motor shaft and by reversing the direction of motor rotation. When the switch is turned off, the inner shaft of the motor stops, while the outer shaft rotates 180 deg. This changes the length of the drive link/crank to park the wiper blades in the depressed position.

All Chrysler windshield wiper systems incorporate a circuit breaker with the wiper switch to protect the circuitry of the wiper system and the vehicle.

HIDDEN WINDSHIELD WIPERS

Some cars have the windshield wipers hidden under an access door that is vacuum operated. The door is linked to a

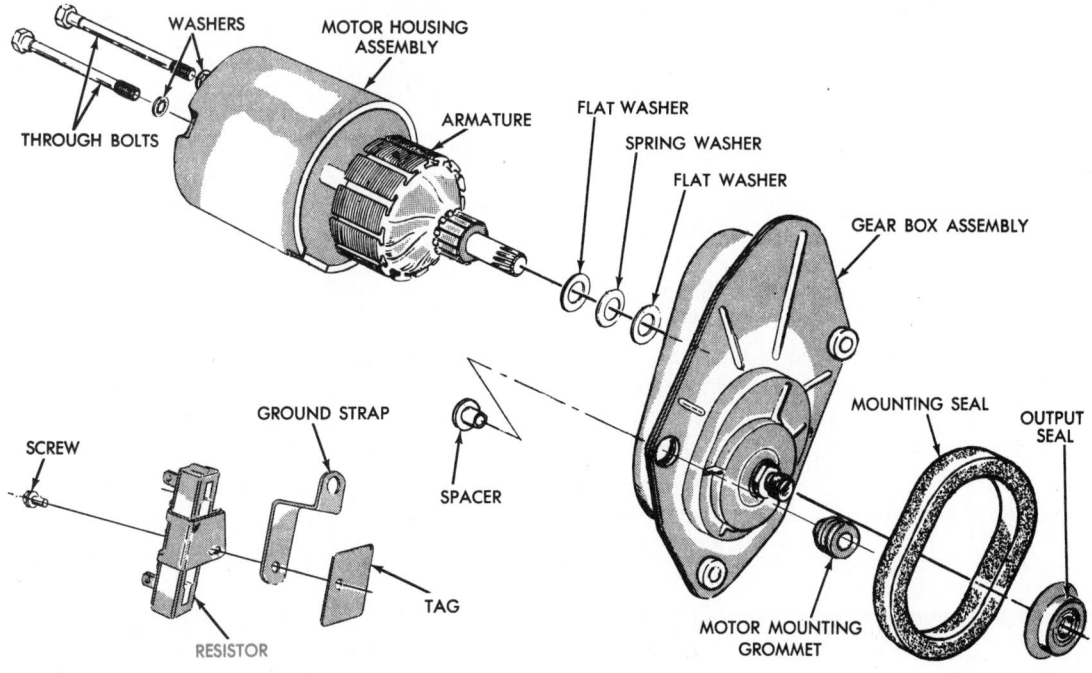

Fig. 36-80. Chrysler's two speed wiper motor can be disassembled for service. Note resistor for low speed circuit.

torsion bar housed in the plenum chamber. When the wiper system is actuated, the door swings up and forward. Manifold vacuum is used to operate the system. A diagram is shown in Fig. 36-81.

Vacuum from the manifold is supplied to the vacuum reserve tank, then to the center terminal of the relay valve. When the wiper switch is in the "OFF" position, the solenoid valve is deactivated. However, vacuum is allowed to pass through the valve to the manual valve, which allows passage of the vacuum to the diaphragm portion of the relay valve.

Vacuum on the relay valve diaphragm pulls the internal

valve to the right and opens a path for vacuum at the center terminal (yellow) to pass into the red terminal circuit. From there, it is routed to the left side of the wiper door actuator piston which pulls the rod in and holds the access door closed.

When the wiper switch is turned on, the solenoid is actuated and the control vacuum is stopped at the solenoid valve. The diaphragm spring then forces the internal valve to the left, completing the vacuum circuit to the opposite side of the windshield wiper access door actuator piston. The actuator rod then moves forward, opening the door through the connecting linkage.

For manual operation of the door, the manual valve cuts off the vacuum to the relay valve. The manual valve must be in the "IN" position in order to close the door or return the system to automatic.

TROUBLESHOOTING

For any electric windshield wiper to operate satisfactorily, it is essential that the motor, linkage and drive pivots operate freely. Otherwise, the wiper system may be noisy, slow, balky or inoperative.

Noisy operation of electric wipers is sometimes caused by excessive end play of the motor armature. The amount of end play varies with different makes and types of installations. Noise will also be caused by incorrect relation between the motor and the linkage and pivot shaft assemblies. Elimination of excessive friction in the driving mechanism should reduce noise and binding that produces slow or balky operation.

Failure to operate can be caused by a blown fuse, open circuit, wiring harness connector loose, wiper motor not grounded properly, defective wiper switch or motor.

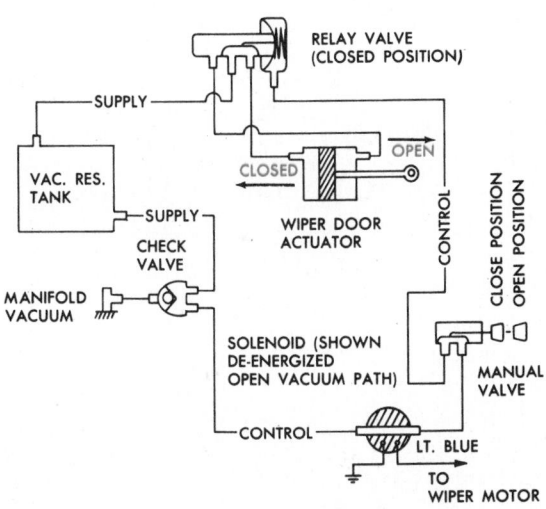

Fig. 36-81. Vacuum circuit for operation of access door to hidden windshield wiper.

Most windshield wiper motors are fitted with oilless type bushings and do not require any lubrication. The gear box should be filled three-quarters full of special lubricant, before assembly, and all crank arm shafts should be greased their entire length. Before final hook up and test, make sure that the linkage pivots freely.

REVIEW QUESTIONS — WINDSHIELD WIPERS

1. Electric motors for windshield wipers usually are shunt wound or _____ wound.
2. What is a "pulse" or "intermittent" wiper system?
3. What is a depressed park system?
4. With most combination wiper/washer units, the motor section, gear box section and washer section may be serviced independently. True or False?
5. Ford and American Motors wiper motors are similar in design. True or False?
6. Late model Ford and American Motors cars have a _____ resistor in the wiper switch to provide intermittent wiper operation.
7. Chrysler cars use _____ speed and _____ speed wiper motors.
8. All Chrysler windshield wiper systems incorporate a _____ _____ in the wiper switch.
9. Give four reasons why a wiper motor would fail to operate.
10. What is the source of vacuum for operating the access door to uncover hidden windshield wipers?

This instrument panel was designed to offer improved serviceability with removable major components.   (Oldsmobile)

WINDSHIELD WASHERS

Windshield washers are installed in different ways in different vehicles. As mentioned, Chrysler uses both foot-operated and electric pump-operated windshield washers. Ford and American Motors incorporate an electric pump with the washer reservoir. General Motors continues to combine the washer pump with the wiper assembly.

A positive displacement washer pump is used on all windshield wiper/washer systems on General Motors cars. The pump is driven by a four lobe nylon cam assembled on the output shaft of the wiper motor. (A typical setup is shown in Fig. 36-74.)

When the pump is attached to the rectangular wiper motor, the four lobe cam actuates a spring-loaded cam-follower arm and pin assembly. However, no pumping action occurs because the pumping mechanism is "locked out."

Although pump design varies among vehicles produced by different GM divisions depressing the control switch completes the pump solenoid circuit to ground at the switch, on all applications. This mechanically actuates the wiper switch to turn on the wiper motor.

In GM designs designated "F" and "X," Fig. 36-82, the solenoid plunger is pulled toward the coil, allowing the ratchet pawl to engage the ratchet wheel and the wheel starts to rotate, one tooth at a time.

As each lobe of the four lobe cam actuates the cam follower, the follower, in turn, moves the piston actuator plate and piston away from the valve assembly and compresses the piston spring. This creates a vacuum in the pump cylinder through the intake valve, Fig. 36-83.

As the high point of each cam lobe passes the cam-follower pin, the piston spring expands. This forces the piston toward the valves, pressuring the wash solution out the two exhaust valves to the spray nozzles.

Intake and exhaust strokes occur four times for each revolution of the wiper motor output gear. The pumping operation is completed automatically when the ratchet wheel has been rotated through 360 deg., Fig. 36-82. Then the spring-loaded plunger pushes through an opening in the rim of the ratchet wheel, pushing the ratchet pawl away from the

ratchet teeth. At this point, the ratchet wheel has moved to a position where it is holding the piston actuator plate in a "lock-out" position until the washer switch is again depressed.

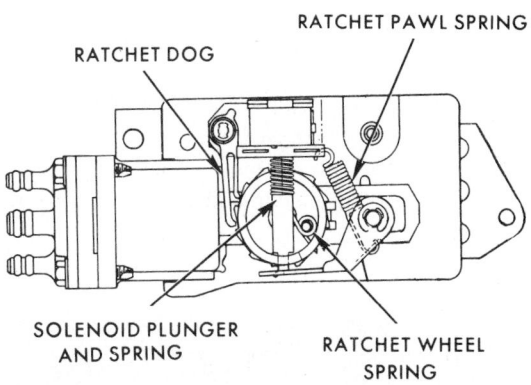

Fig. 36-82. Details of control section of General Motors washer pump used with rectangular wiper motor.

TROUBLESHOOTING WASHERS

When troubleshooting General Motors "F" or "X" washer pumps, consider these suggestions:

Washer Inoperative

1. Insufficient washer solution.
2. Hoses damaged, loose or kinked.
3. Plugged screen at end of reservoir cover hose.
4. Defective wiper switch.
5. Defective pump valve.
6. Plugged washer nozzles.
7. Loose electrical connection to washer pump or wiper switch.
8. Open circuit in feed wire to pump solenoid coil.
9. Pump solenoid coil defective.
10. Missing ratchet wheel tooth.
11. Missing ratchet pawl spring.

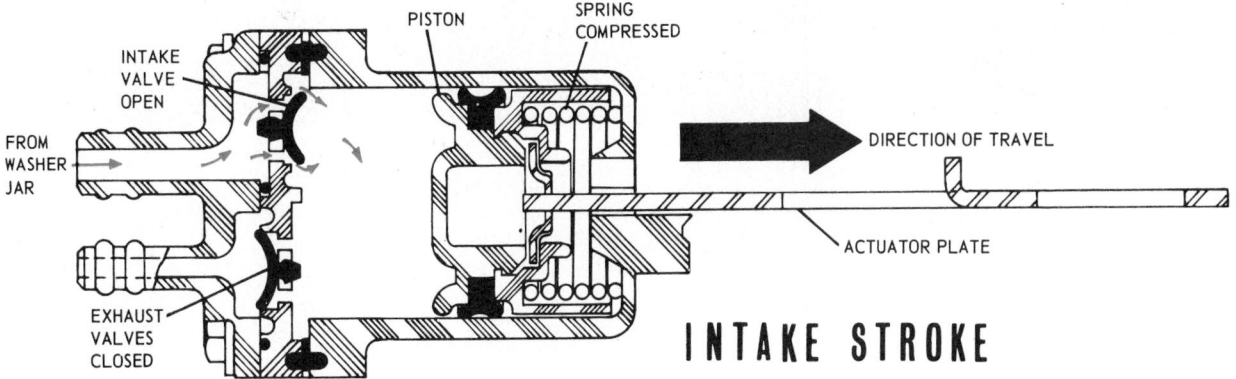

Fig. 36-83. Sectional view of piston and pump cylinder of type "F" or "X" GM wiper motor shows flow of wash solution on intake stroke.

Washer Pumps Continuously While Wiper Is Operating

1. Defective wiper switch.
2. Grounded wire from pump solenoid to switch.

3. Missing ratchet wheel tooth.
4. Ratchet wheel pawl or dog not contracting ratchet wheel teeth.
5. Lock-out tang broken or bent on piston actuator plate.

REVIEW QUESTIONS — WINDSHIELD WASHERS

1. The washer pump is attached to the wiper motor in General Motors applications. Yes or No?
2. Chrysler continues to offer both a _____ _____ washer pump and an electric motor-operated washer pump.

3. What type of washer pump is used on all GM cars?
4. A GM washer pump is driven by an eight lobe nylon cam. True or False?
5. What is the No. 1 problem when a windshield washer is inoperative?

Mechanic checks wheel alignment settings on computer aligner. Electronic system performs necessary calculations, including automatic runout compensation before standard alignment checking procedure is accomplished. (FMC Corporation)

METERS, TESTERS
AND ANALYZERS

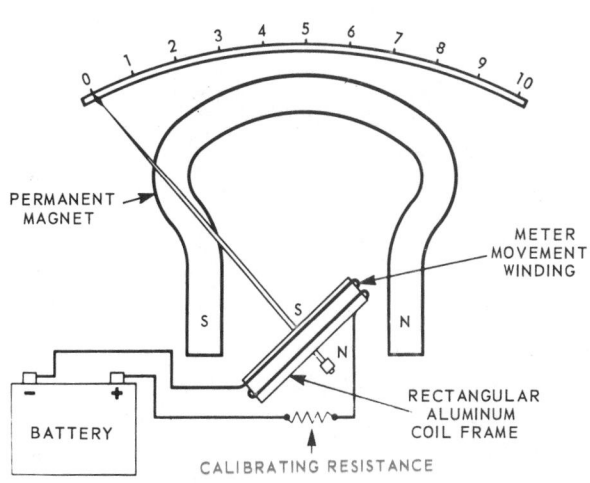

Fig. 37-1. Schematic drawing of makeup of a typical voltmeter. Note calibrating resistance in series with moving coil.

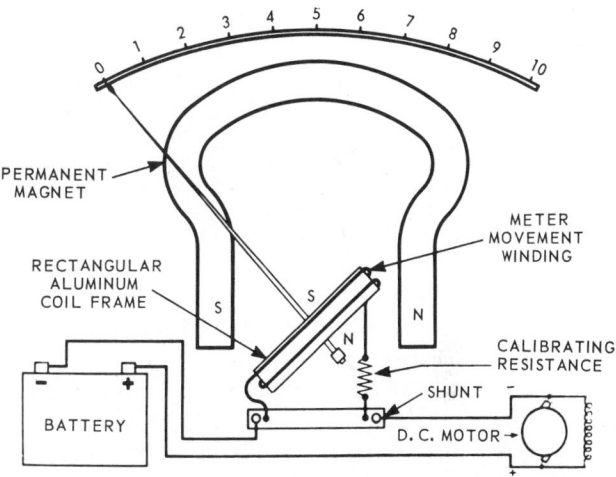

Fig. 37-2. Note that ammeter has a heavy resistance connected across moving coil and another resistance connected in series with moving coil.

There is one particular demonstration of know-how that makes an engine mechanic stand out as an expert. It is the ability to systematically test, evaluate and correct performance problems in all five engine systems: starting, charging, compression, ignition and fuel.

The expert mechanic, however, does require the help of a full range of reliably accurate meters, testers and analyzers. For electrical testing, basic instruments include the ammeter for measuring the current in amperes, and the voltmeter for measuring the voltage or pressure. The mechanic also makes regular use of an ohmmeter, battery/starter tester, alternator/regulator tester, tachometer, dwell meter, distributor tester, timing light, engine analyzer and oscilloscope.

METER DESIGN

Most modern ammeters and voltmeters used in the automotive service field are of the moving coil type, Fig. 37-1 and Fig. 37-2. These instruments consist of a permanent horseshoe, or hoop-shaped magnet, and a movable coil. The pole pieces on the ends of the magnet are shaped to provide a uniform magnetic field.

Current flowing through the movable coil reacts with the magnetic field, causing the coil to rotate against the tension of a light spring that is similar to the hairspring of a watch.

Relative movement of the coil is directly proportional to

the current flowing through it. A pointer attached to the coil moves across a calibrated scale to indicate the amount of current flowing through the coil.

The basic design of ammeters and voltmeters is the same. However, a study of Figs. 37-1 and 37-2 will reveal that the ammeter is provided with a heavy shunt of low resistance connected across the movable coil. In addition, there is another resistance connected in series with one end of the shunt and the coil. This resistance is used for calibrating the instrument.

The voltmeter, Fig. 37-1, does not have a resistance shunted across the coil. Instead, it has only the calibrating resistance in series with the coil.

Ammeters are always connected in series with the circuit. Voltmeters are always connected in parallel to, or across, the terminals of the device or circuit. See Fig. 37-3.

A single voltmeter can be designed to cover several different ranges of voltage. This is accomplished by varying the resistance in series with the movable coil. When this is done, a separate resistance is provided for each range of the instrument. The resistance is changed by means of a switch located on the instrument.

Ammeters also can be designed to cover several different ranges of current, by providing several different shunts.

When working with ammeters, it is important to use the leads provided by the manufacturer. Leads having a different

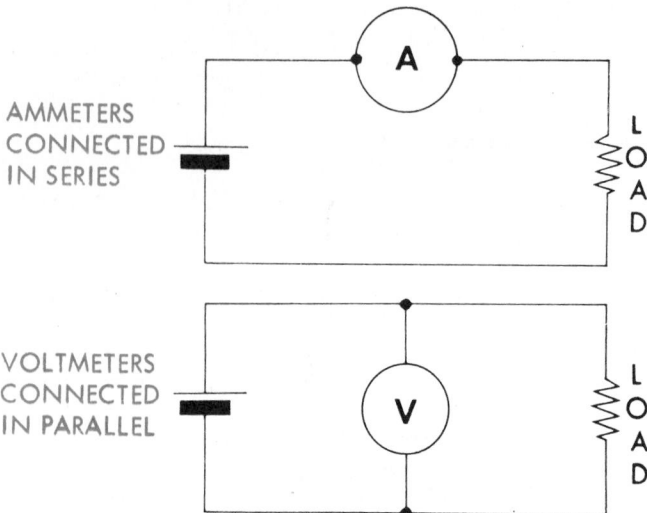

AMMETERS CONNECTED IN SERIES

VOLTMETERS CONNECTED IN PARALLEL

Fig. 37-3. Ammeters are always connected in series with circuit to measure current in amperes. Voltmeter is always connected in shunt or across circuit to measure voltage.

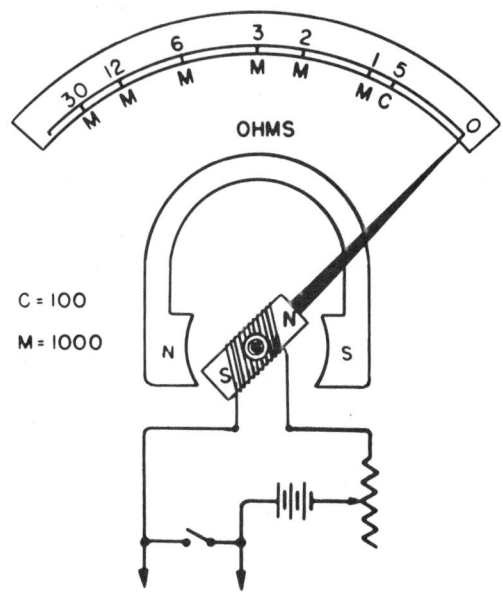

OHMS

C = 100
M = 1000

Fig. 37-4. Details of ohmmeter. Note battery and adjustable resistance.

resistance will seriously affect the accuracy of the instrument. This will be particularly noticeable when checking and adjusting voltage regulators.

A generally accepted standard for the maximum resistance of an ammeter is 0.1V drop across the ammeter terminals of the connected ammeter leads with 10 amp. flowing in the circuit. Therefore, the resistance would be .01 ohms.

The resistance of a good voltmeter is 100 ohms per volt.

In general, ammeters and voltmeters used for automotive service work should have an accuracy of one percent of full scale deflection. In addition, they should be compensated for changes in temperature.

OHMMETER

The ohmmeter is an instrument designed to measure the resistance of an electric circuit or unit in ohms. In automotive service work, it is used particularly to measure the resistance of resistors and resistance type high tension wiring.

Generally, the ohmmeter consists of a conventional D'Arsonval galvanometer, as used in a voltmeter or ammeter. In the ohmmeter, Fig. 37-4, in addition to the D'Arsonval unit, there is a calibrated resistance, a variable resistance and a self-contained battery. The leads used to connect the ohmmeter to the unit to be tested are of special low resistance. Since they are used when calibrating the instrument, these same leads must be used when measuring the resistance of the circuit or unit, Fig. 37-5.

Before using the ohmmeter, it is necessary to standardize the battery voltage. This is done by joining the two instrument leads together to establish zero resistance. Then, the variable resistance is adjusted to bring the indicating needle to the zero mark on the dial.

When measuring the resistance of a circuit or piece of equipment, no current should flow through it other than from the battery within the ohmmeter. To measure resistance,

simply connect the leads from the ohmmeter to its terminals of the unit to be tested. Then read the resistance in ohms on the dial.

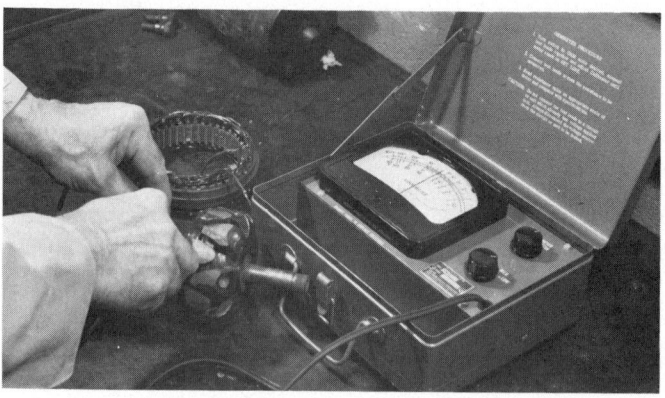

Fig. 37-5. Ohmmeter is a resistance tester especially useful in checking alternator circuits and condition of spark plug cables.

TACHOMETER

The tachometer is designed to indicate the speed of a rotating part in revolutions per minute. In automotive service work, it is a specially designed instrument since it is used exclusively to measure the speed of the engine.

The tachometer used in automotive service work usually consists of a D'Arsonval galvanometer, a condenser, a single-pole double-throw relay and provision for calibrating the instrument for variation in voltage of the instrument battery cell. Resistances also included can be selected to allow for four, six or eight lobe distributor cams.

Basically, the tachometer operates by charging a condenser

by means of a self-contained flashlight battery or mercury cell, then discharging the condenser through a D'Arsonval galvanometer. This is accomplished by the action of a single-pole double-throw relay, and the meter reading depends on the frequency of interruption. The higher the engine speed, the higher the rate of condenser discharge and recharge.

One lead of the instrument is connected to primary connection on the distributor and the other to the ground. Then, (engine running), when the breaker points open, battery voltage from the vehicle ignition system is applied to the relay. The relay armature then contacts the lower relay point, and the meter battery cell will charge the condenser. When the breaker points are closed, practically no current is applied to the relay windings, and the relay points will separate. This allows the condenser to discharge through the meter, an action that is repeated each time the points open and close.

A combination tester featuring a tachometer is shown in Fig. 37-6.

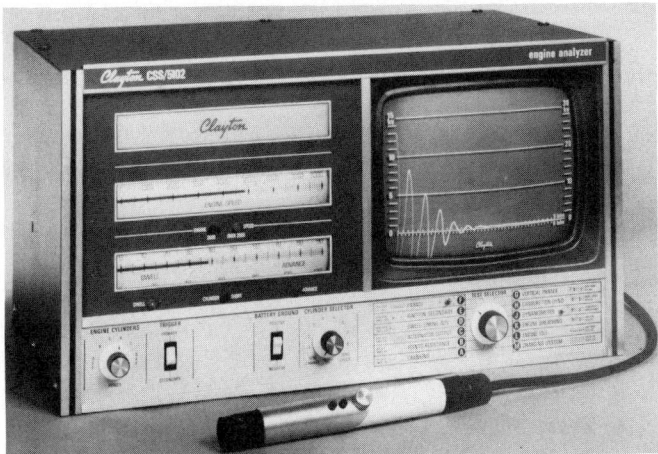

Fig. 37-6. Tachometer, dwell meter and oscilloscope are combined in a single case.

DWELL METER

The dwell meter is designed to measure the angle through which the distributor shaft turns while the distributor breaker points are closed. This is known as point dwell or cam angle. The dwell meter is often contained in the same case as the tachometer. However, it does not operate from the charge and discharge of a condenser.

The dwell meter is operated by the voltage which is present across the breaker points. With the meter leads connected with proper polarity to the distributor primary terminal and to ground, open breaker points will impose full battery voltage on the meter. Under this condition the meter will indicate zero percent of dwell.

With the breaker points closed, practically no voltage will be applied to the meter, so it will indicate 100 percent of dwell. In terms of degrees, 100 percent of dwell depends on the number of lobes on the distributor cam. For a four lobe cam, 100 percent dwell would be 90 deg. For a six lobe cam, it would be 60 deg. For an eight lobe cam, it would be 45 deg.

Therefore, when the breaker points are closed, the meter attempts to indicate 90, 60, or 45 deg., depending on the position of the lobe selector switch.

As the distributor rotates, the points will alternately open and close and the meter will then attempt to indicate alternately zero and 100 percent dwell. The inertia of the meter movement and the high capacity damping condenser connected across the meter will prevent rapid fluctuation of the indicating needle.

As a result, the meter will indicate an average value. If the points remain closed longer than they remain open, this average value will be closer to 100 percent. If they are open longer than they are closed, the average value will be closer to zero. Vehicle manufacturers specify what the angle of dwell should be.

THE OSCILLOSCOPE

The oscilloscope, Figs. 37-6 and 37-7, is an electronic device used to visually observe and measure the instantaneous voltage in an electric circuit. Basically, aside from operational circuitry, the oscilloscope consists of a cathode-ray tube. So it operates in much the same manner as a television set.

The oscilloscope produces a graph-like picture showing voltage values with respect to time. This picture is generally referred to as the pattern or waveform, Figs. 37-6 and 37-7.

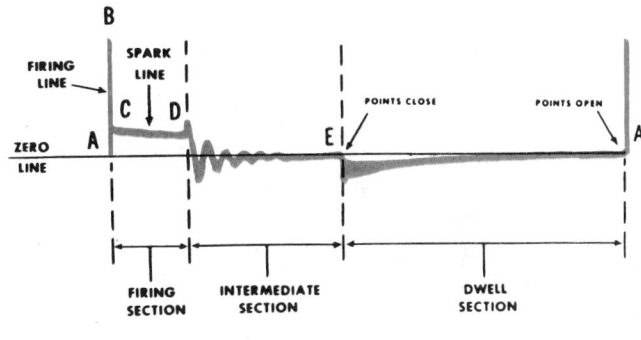

Fig. 37-7. Basic pattern, or wave form, of ignition system.

The pattern is produced by the cathode ray, or stream of electrons, striking the face or screen of the tube, which is coated with a phosphorescent material. When the electrons strike this material, it gives off a brilliant glow, making it possible to see or trace the path of the ray as it moves across the screen.

In addition to being able to measure voltage in an electrical circuit, the oscilloscope can be used to determine the polarity of the voltage, which is indicated by the vertical movement of the ray. When the oscilloscope test leads are connected to the secondary circuit of an ignition system, the voltage (normally negative) will appear ABOVE the zero reference.

The oscilloscope pattern is controlled by the voltage in the electrical system to which it is connected. Oscilloscopes can also be connected to non-electrical components by means of special pickups known as transducers. These devices, which convert other forms of energy to electrical impulses, are used to observe engine compression and valve action, and to locate noises and vibrations.

As an ignition system analyzer, the oscilloscope can be used to detect the following:

1. Spark plug firing voltage.
2. Coil action.
3. Condenser action.
4. Breaker point action.
5. Coil available voltage.
6. Reversed coil polarity.
7. Low voltage available.
8. Insulation leakage.
9. Worn spark plug electrodes.
10. Lean air-fuel mixtures.
11. Excessive rotor gaps.
12. Breaks in high tension wiring.
13. Excessive primary circuit resistance.
14. Excessive secondary circuit resistance.
15. Poor rotor-to-cap clearance.
16. Fouled spark plugs.
17. Grounded high tension wires.
18. Shorted coils.
19. Shorted condensers.
20. Defective breaker points.
21. Engine load on spark plug voltage.
22. Distributor point dwell.

OSCILLOSCOPE WAVE FORM

When studying the oscilloscope pattern, Fig. 37-7, consider it to be graphs of voltage with respect to time. The vertical displacement from the horizontal zero line (either up or down, depending on polarity) represents voltage at any instant along the zero line. As oscilloscopes are used mostly in connection with the secondary circuit the screen is laid out in kilovolts to permit accurate voltage measurements of secondary circuit patterns.

Each part of the pattern represents a specific phase of ignition system operation. Usually, it is divided into three sections: firing section, intermediate section and dwell section.

The firing section, Fig. 37-7, is so called because it is during this period that the actual firing of the spark plug takes place. This section of the pattern is composed of only two lines. The firing line is the vertical line indicating the voltage required to overcome the rotor and spark plug gaps. The spark line is a horizontal line indicating the voltage required to maintain the spark and its duration.

Point A in Fig. 37-7 represents the instant at which the breaker points have opened. The resulting high voltage is indicated by the vertical rise from A to B in the pattern. The height of point B shows the voltage required to fire the plug and rotor gaps. This is often known as ionization voltage.

After the spark plug fires, there is a noticeable drop in secondary voltage to point C in Fig. 37-7. As the spark continues to bridge the gap, the spark voltage remains at a fairly constant low value until the spark stops at point D.

The intermediate section, which immediately follows the firing section, is seen as a series of gradually diminishing oscillations, which just about disappear by the time the dwell section begins. Beginning at point D in Fig. 37-7, the remaining coil energy dissipates itself as an oscillating current, which gradually dies out as it approaches point E. The oscillation results from the combined effects of the coil and the condenser in dissipating this energy.

The dwell section represents the period of time during the ignition cycle in which the breaker points are closed. The dwell section begins at point E in Fig. 37-7 when the breaker points close. Closing of the points causes a short downward line, followed by a series of small rapidly diminishing oscillations. The dwell section continues until the points open at the beginning of the next pattern at point A.

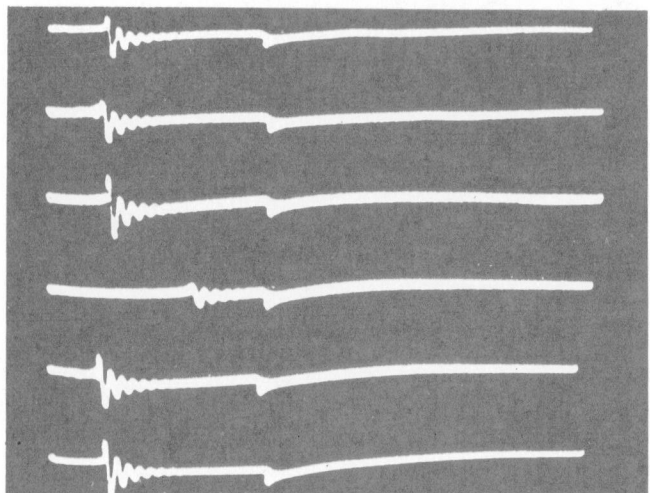

Fig. 37-8. This oscilloscope pattern places one cylinder above another in firing order for easy comparison. Note that No. 3 (bottom to top) does not conform with others, indicating a shorted spark plug.

Some oscilloscopes will show the pattern of each cylinder, one above the other, Fig. 37-8. Others will show the pattern of each cylinder, one after the other, Fig. 37-9.

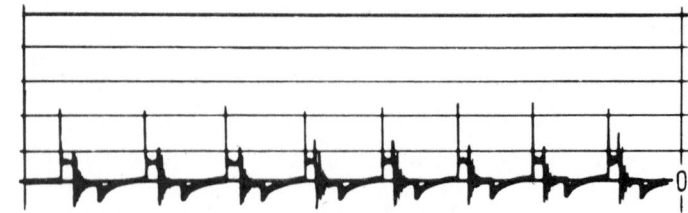

Fig. 37-9. Many oscilloscopes have a pattern where cylinders are placed one after another.

In Fig. 37-8, all cylinders except No. 3 are firing correctly. That cylinder has a shorted spark plug as indicated by the fact that the firing voltage (AB in Fig. 37-7) has not built up. Excessive spark plug gaps would be indicated when the firing line is longer than usual. When breaker points are defective or incorrectly gapped, the pattern of the dwell section will not be normal. Each difficulty in the ignition circuit will show up in the pattern of the oscilloscope.

The oscilloscope does not replace existing equipment. It is used as an additional aid to troubleshooting. It will show in what area of the ignition system the trouble is occurring; then, regular metered equipment is used to pinpoint the trouble. For this reason, oscilloscopes usually are incorporated in an engine analyzer, Figs. 37-10 and 37-11, along with multi-range

Fig. 37-11. Suspended engine performance tester offers infra-red exhaust performance analyzer in conjunction with oscilloscope, meters, gauges, timing light and timing advance tester.

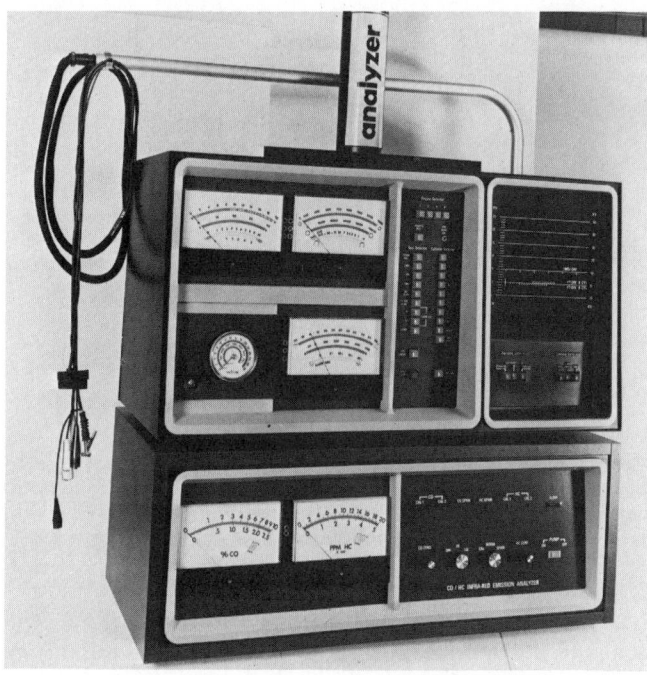

Fig. 37-10. Scope engine analyzer has an infrared system for testing percent of carbon monoxide and parts per million of hydrocarbons. (Allen Group, Testproducts Div.)

voltmeter, ammeter, tachometer, dwell meter, ohmmeter, vacuum gauge, emissions analyzer, timing light and timing advance tester.

EXHAUST ANALYSIS

With so much emphasis on exhaust emission control, an auto mechanic must have suitable test equipment to verify through various modes of engine operation, whether or not the engine is emitting excessive amounts of air pollutants. (See the chapter on EXHAUST EMISSION.)

Most equipment designed to detect amounts of carbon monoxide (CO) and hydrocarbon (HC) in exhaust gas is infra-red type, Fig. 37-11. This unit utilizes nondispersive infra-red optical benches as sensing devices. The meter readouts of hydrocarbons and carbon monoxide result from the amount of energy these gases absorb, or block off, as they pass through a beam of infra-red light in each optical bench. The higher the concentration of either HC or CO, the higher the readout.

The tester is easy to operate. A probe is placed in the tailpipe of the test vehicle, and an exhaust gas sample is drawn through the tester by means of a positive displacement pump.

On its way to the infra-red optical benches, the gas sample is dried and filtered. The same sample then passes through the infra-red light sources in both benches before being expelled. Output signals from both benches are fed to their respective meters by solid state amplifiers. The two-scale HC meter reads from 0 to 500 and 0 to 2000 in parts per million (PPM). The two-scale CO meter reads from 0 to 10 percent and 0 to 25 percent.

Two other meters are included in the tester instrument panel, the tachometer and the exhaust flow indicator. These instruments monitor engine speed and the passage of the exhaust gas sample through the unit.

The infra-red exhaust emission tester is more accurate than the combustion efficiency tester that operates with a thermal conductivity cell designed to measure the heat of the exhaust gases. This arrangement works fine, until the exhaust gas is too thin to heat the TC filament. Then the lean mixture cools the filament, and the meter starts going the wrong way.

With the infra-red tester, the HC scale will back up the CO reading. The operator sets the carburetor air-fuel mixture and engine idle speed to bring the CO reading within the carbon monoxide limits allowed. Then he reads the HC meter. If it is lower than the established maximum, the engine is operating within emission standards. If the HC reading is high, further work or parts replacement is necessary.

A portable engine exhaust analyzer is shown in Fig. 37-12. It operates on the infra-red system, with a range of 0 to 100 PPM (parts per million) hydrocarbon and 0 to 8 percent carbon monoxide.

COMBINATIONS AND CONSOLES

In recent years, combination testers have become extremely popular. Volt-amp testers and tach-dwell meters lead the way. Latest electrical system testers will test transistorized, capacitor discharge or conventional ignition systems, Fig. 37-10.

Console units incorporating engine analyzing instrumenta-

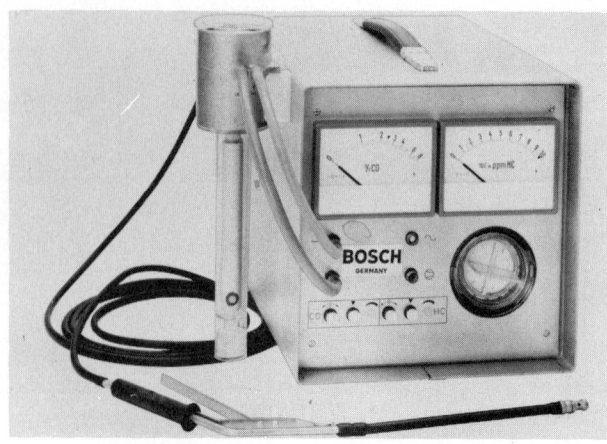

Fig. 37-12. Portable engine exhaust analyzer utilizes built-in suction pump, flow monitor and infra-red system to test CO and HC.

Fig. 37-13. Computerized tester and hand-controlled unit is combined with dynamometer to provide a fully instrumented road test facility and diagnostic lane.

tion come in many "packages." Some are built up by adding individual or combination testers to the basic test stand. Others are unitized and put on wheels to provide mobility. Still others are suspended from overhead and are used in conjunction with a dynamometer. See Fig. 37-13.

Fig. 37-14. Computerized testing system uses sensors attached to engine to measure vehicle's operating performance. Computer compares tested conditions with performance specifications, then furnishes print out of results.

Most sophisticated of all is the master analyzer with computerized operation. Factory-approved specifications are fed into the unit for comparison with test results of the vehicle being diagnosed. Upon completion of a programmed series of tests, a readout is printed for the mechanic and the car owner. It contains both "specified" and "actual" readings for each test. See Fig. 37-14.

REVIEW QUESTIONS – METERS, TESTERS AND ANALYZERS

1. What type magnet is used in a conventional voltmeter?
   a. Electromagnet.
   b. Permanent magnet.
2. In a voltmeter, is the calibrating resistance in series or in shunt with the movable coil?
   a. Series.
   b. Shunt.
3. What is the major difference between a voltmeter and an ammeter?
4. When using an ammeter, how should it be connected in the circuit?
   a. In series.
   b. In parallel.
5. When using a voltmeter, how should it be connected in the circuit?
   a. In series.
   b. In parallel.
6. When using an ammeter, why is it important to always use the leads provided by the manufacturer?
7. What is an oscilloscope used for?
8. What can the pattern shown on an oscilloscope screen tell about the ignition system of an automobile? Give five possibilities.
9. Name the three sections of the pattern shown by an oscilloscope.
10. If the pattern shown on an oscilloscope screen rises very little above the horizontal zero line, what is indicated?
11. Why is an oscilloscope usually incorporated in an engine analyzer?
12. The infra-red tester detects and measures the level of two emissions for which maximum allowable standards have been established. What are they?

SPRING SUSPENSION AND STEERING

The modern automobile has come a long way since the days when "just being self-propelled" was enough to satisfy the car owner. Improvements in suspension and steering, increased strength and durability of components, and advances in tire design and construction have made large contributions to riding comfort and driving safety.

SUSPENSION SYSTEMS

Basically, suspension refers to the use of front and rear springs to suspend a vehicle's frame, body, engine and power train above the wheels. These relatively heavy assemblies constitute what is known as "sprung" weight. "Unsprung" weight, on the other hand, includes wheels and tires, brake assemblies, the rear axle assembly and other structural members not supported by the springs.

The springs used in today's cars and trucks are engineered in a wide variety of types, shapes, sizes, rates and capacities. Types include leaf springs, coil springs, air springs and torsion bars. These are used in sets of four per vehicle, or they are paired off in various combinations and are attached to the vehicle by a number of different mounting techniques.

FRONT SUSPENSION TYPES

There are two types of front suspension in general use: the independent system, Fig. 38-1, and the solid axle system, Fig.

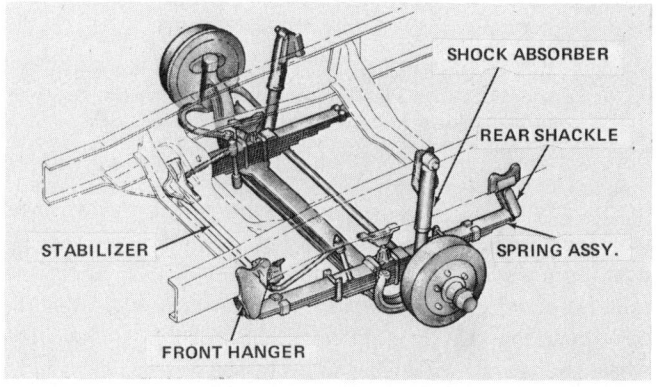

Fig. 38-2. A solid front axle beam and leaf springs are used on most medium and heavy-duty trucks.

38-2. Independent suspension usually operates through heavy-duty coil springs or torsion bars and direct, double-acting shock absorbers. In solid axle construction, the axle beam and wheel assemblies are connected to the car by leaf springs and direct or indirect-acting shock absorbers.

With the solid axle setup, the steering knuckle and wheel spindle assemblies are connected to the axle beam by

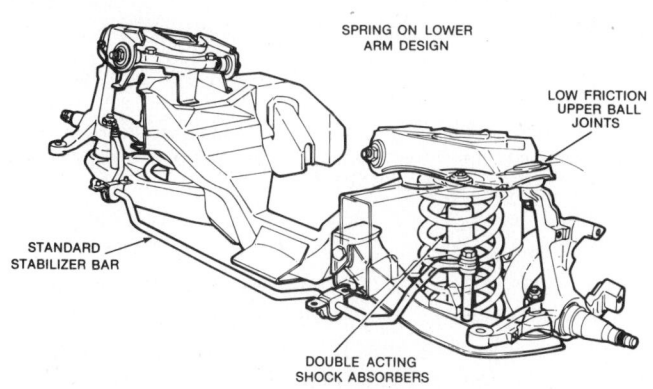

Fig. 38-1. Independent front suspension with coil springs, control arms and ball joints are used on most passenger cars and light-duty trucks.

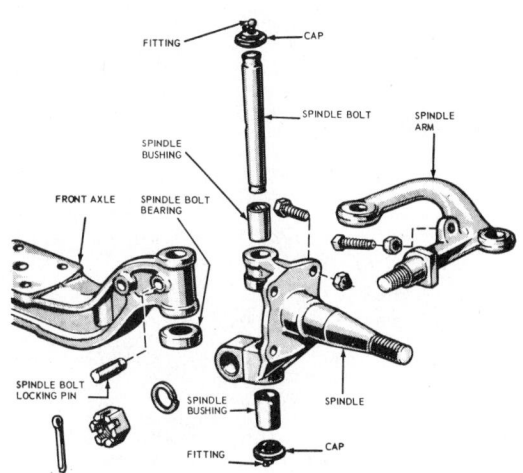

Fig. 38-3. In solid axle front suspension, axle beam is connected to front wheel spindle by means of kingpins, or spindle bolts.

483

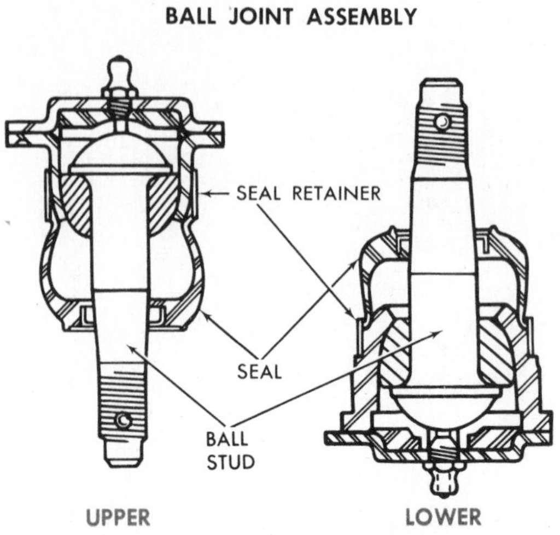

BALL JOINT ASSEMBLY

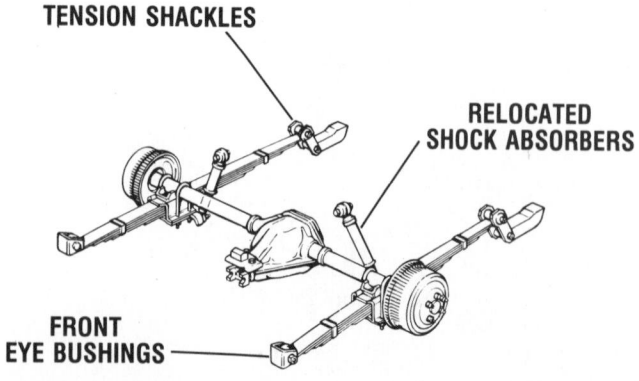

Fig. 38-4. Ball joints provide key pivot points in front suspension set-up. Some late models have lubrication fittings, others have plugs that must be replaced with fittings at lubrication intervals.

bronze-bushed kingpins, or spindle bolts, which provide pivot points for each front wheel. See Fig. 38-3. Modern independent front wheel suspension systems use ball joints, or spherical joints, to accomplish this purpose, Fig. 38-4. In operation, the swiveling action of the ball joints allows the wheel and spindle assemblies to be turned left or right and to move up and down with changes in road surface.

LEAF SPRINGS

Front leaf, or plate, springs are used in conjunction with solid axle beams in most truck applications. Rear leaf springs are used on trucks and some passenger cars. Single leaf or multi-leaf springs are usually mounted longitudinally over the front axle beam or under the rear axle housing. See Fig. 38-2.

The spring center bolt fastens the leaves together, and its head locates the spring in the front axle beam or saddle on the rear axle housing. U-bolts clamp the spring firmly in place and keep it from shifting. Eyebolts, brackets and shackles attach it to the frame at each end.

In many cases, leaf springs are used at the rear of the

TENSION SHACKLES

RELOCATED SHOCK ABSORBERS

FRONT EYE BUSHINGS

Fig. 38-5. Chrysler cars use leaf springs at rear, torsion bars in front. Latest improvements in rear suspension are called out.

vehicle in combination with another type spring in front. Chrysler, for example, uses leaf springs at the rear, Fig. 38-5, torsion bars in front. The larger models have longitudinal torsion bars between the body cross member and an anchor in the lower control arm. Smaller cars have transverse bars between the front cross member and lower control arm.

For many years, Ford used leaf springs at rear, coil springs in front. Now, full-size cars have coil spring suspension, front and rear. Ford's small cars have coil springs in front; leaf springs at rear, Fig. 38-6. Buick still uses coil springs all

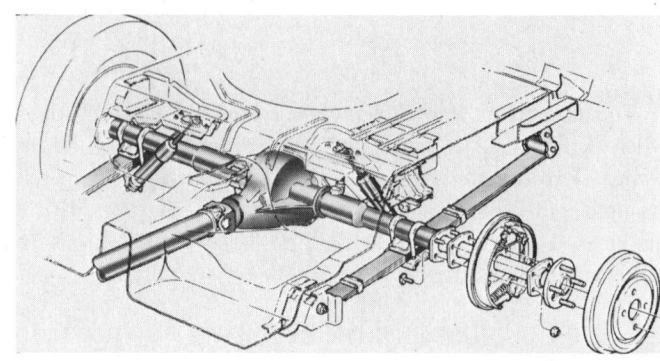

Fig. 38-6. Currently, Ford installs leaf springs at rear in small cars. Rear coil springs and control arms are used on intermediate and full-size cars.

around. See Fig. 38-7. In some foreign cars, torsion bars are used front and rear; in others, leaf springs are mounted crosswise for use with independently suspended wheels.

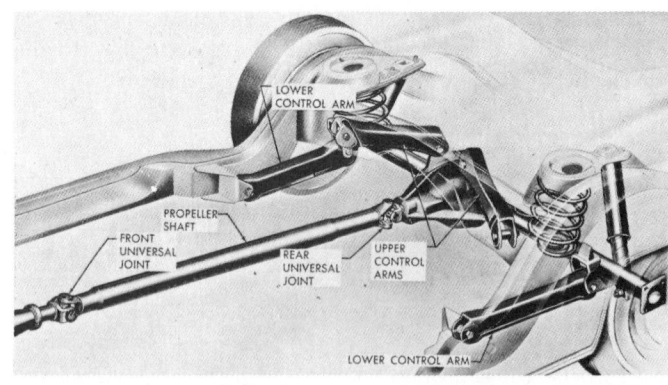

Fig. 38-7. Full-size Buicks have front springs mounted between lower control arms and frame (see Fig. 38-1). Rear springs are between axle housing and pockets in frame.

Rear leaf springs in U.S. vehicles generally are placed parallel to the frame to absorb the torque of the driving wheels. See Figs. 38-5 and 38-6. The front half of each rear leaf spring acts like a radius rod or control arm to transmit the driving force from the rear wheels to the frame (Hotchkiss drive). With this suspension setup, the leaf springs also serve as stabilizers to control side sway of the chassis.

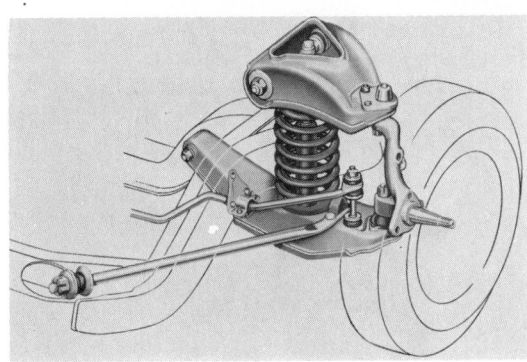

Fig. 38-8. Most front coil springs are located between seat formed in lower control arm and spring housing in frame. Shock absorbers mount inside springs.

COIL SPRINGS

Many independent front suspension systems incorporate compression-type coil springs mounted between the lower control arms and spring housing in the frame. See Figs. 38-1 and 38-8. Others have the coil springs mounted above the upper control arms, compressed between a pivoting spring seat bolted to the control arm and a spring tower formed in the front end sheet metal, Fig. 38-9.

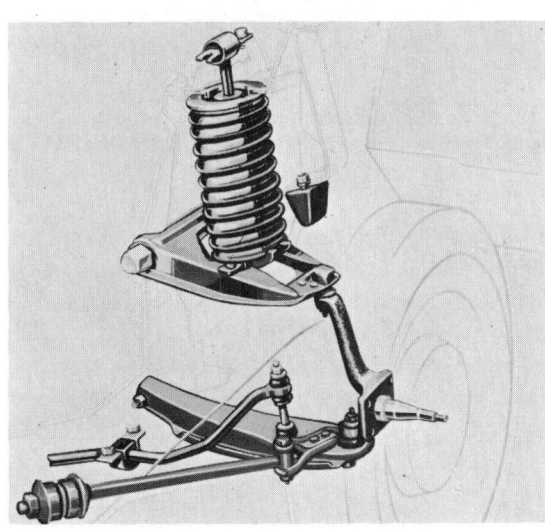

Fig. 38-9. Smaller cars often have front coil springs installed above upper control arms. Shock absorbers mount inside between spring seats and brackets in engine compartment.

Generally, the upper control arm pivots on a bushing and shaft assembly which is bolted to the frame. The lower arm pivots on a bushing and shaft assembly or on a bolt in the frame cross member. When the lower control arm is not the A-frame type, it is supported by a strut which runs diagonally from the lower control arm to a bracket attached to the frame. See Figs. 38-8 and 38-9. On some models, this strut serves as a support; on others, it provides a means of adjusting caster.

Stabilizers or sway bars are used in conjunction with front

suspension on many cars to dampen road shocks and minimize road sway. These bars are bracketed to the frame front cross member and extend from one lower control arm to the other. See Fig. 38-10.

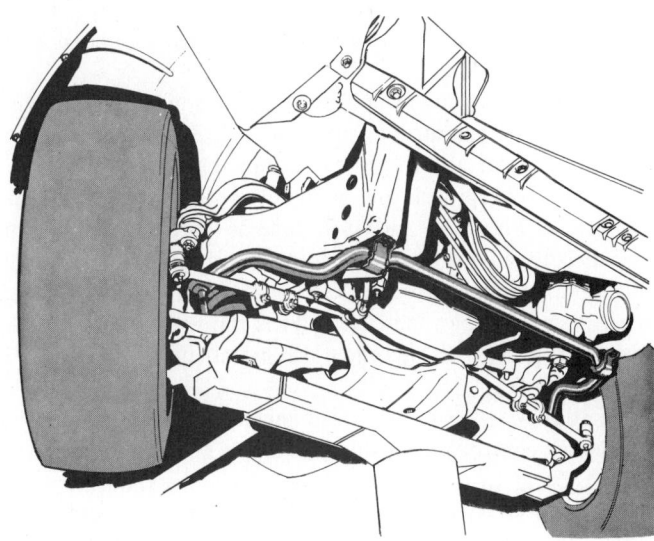

Fig. 38-10. Stabilizers provide added support for front suspension members. This 1 1/8 in. stabilizer is part of Pontiac's optional "handling package" for intermediates.

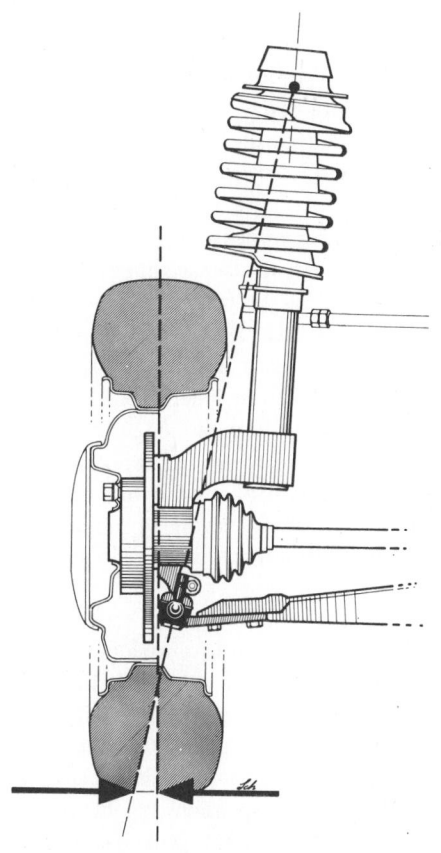

Fig. 38-11. MacPherson strut front suspension is used in many small foreign cars, including Audi Fox and VW Dasher. Strut assembly consists of coil spring, shock absorber and strut.

Actually, the S.L.A. (short-long arm) system of front suspension has been adopted almost universally for passenger cars. The proportionate lengths of the upper and lower control arms (and their engineered placement) are designed to keep the rise and fall of each front wheel in a vertical plane. With this arrangement, changes in wheel angularity, weight balance and tire-scuffing tendencies are negligible when compared with solid axle suspension.

Another coil spring setup that is gaining application in small cars is MacPherson strut suspension, Fig. 38-11. It combines coil spring, shock absorber and strut in a single assembly.

When coil springs are used in both front and rear suspension, Figs. 38-1 and 38-7, three or four control arms are placed between the rear axle housing and the frame to carry driving and braking torque. The lower control arms pivot in the frame members and sometimes support the rear coil springs to provide for up and down movement of the axle and wheel assembly.

In addition, a sway bar (track bar) is usually attached from the upper control arm to the frame side rail to hold the rear axle housing in proper alignment with the frame and to prevent side sway of the body. However, if the rear coil springs are mounted between the frame and a swinging half axle, the independently suspended rear wheels have a sturdy axle housing attached to the differential housing which, in turn, is bolted to the frame.

TORSION BARS

Although torsion bars were and are used extensively on European cars, this type of suspension system received only token attention from the U.S. manufacturers until Chrysler developed their system in the early 1950s. Before that, only a few buses, trailers and race cars were equipped with torsion bar suspension.

Basically, torsion bar suspension is a method of utilizing the flexibility of a steel bar or tube twisting lengthwise to provide spring action. Instead of the flexing action of a leaf spring, or the compressing-and-extending action of a coil spring, the torsion bar twists to exert resistance against up-and-down movement. For example, an independently suspended front system with torsion bars mounted lengthwise would have one end of the bars anchored to the car frame and the other end attached to the lower control arms. With each rise and fall of a front wheel, the control arm pivots up and down, twisting the torsion bar along its length to absorb road shock and cushion the ride.

Chrysler cars are equipped with left and right, non-interchangeable, front torsion bars with hex-shaped ends, Fig. 38-12. In position, the bars extend from hex-shaped rear anchors in the frame cross member to hex-shaped holes in the front lower control arm. Adjusting bolts are provided at the front mounting to increase or decrease torsion bar twist and thereby control front suspension height. Over the years, Chrysler has made many improvements in the system, including lengthening the torsion bars to lower the spring rate; adding a removable rear anchor cross member that is rubber-isolated from the frame; devising a plastic plug and a balloon

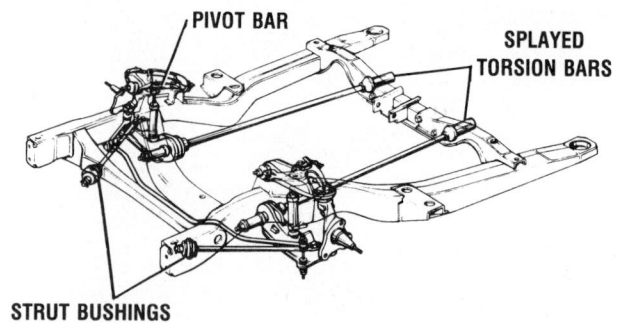

Fig. 38-12. Torsion bars on Chrysler cars are not interchangeable side for side. Bars are marked either right or left by an R or L stamped on end of bar. Note recent improvements.

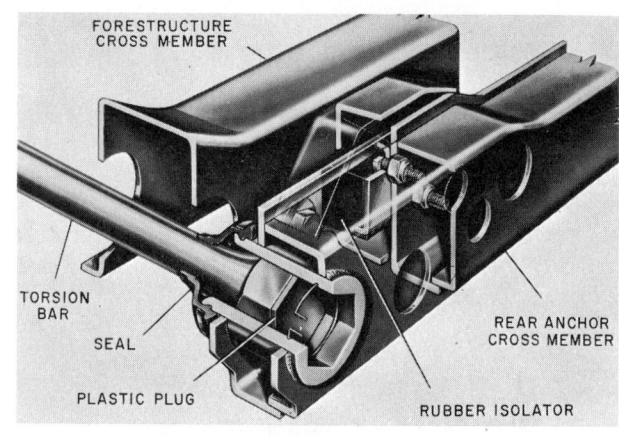

Fig. 38-13. Some Chrysler Corporation cars are fitted with a removable cross member with rubber-isolated mounts at torsion bar rear anchors.

seal for the rear anchor. See Fig. 38-13. Oldsmobile Toronado and Cadillac Eldorado front wheel drive cars also use lengthwise mounted torsion bars to support the front end and to provide for height adjustment, Fig. 38-14.

Torsion bars can also be used laterally to provide spring action for front and/or rear wheel independent suspension

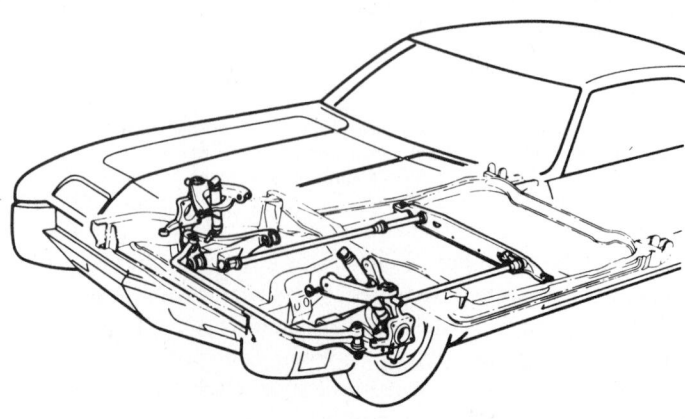

Fig. 38-14. Drawing highlights Oldsmobile Toronado torsion bar front suspension. Adjusting mechanism is located at rear of torsion bars, which are not interchangeable.

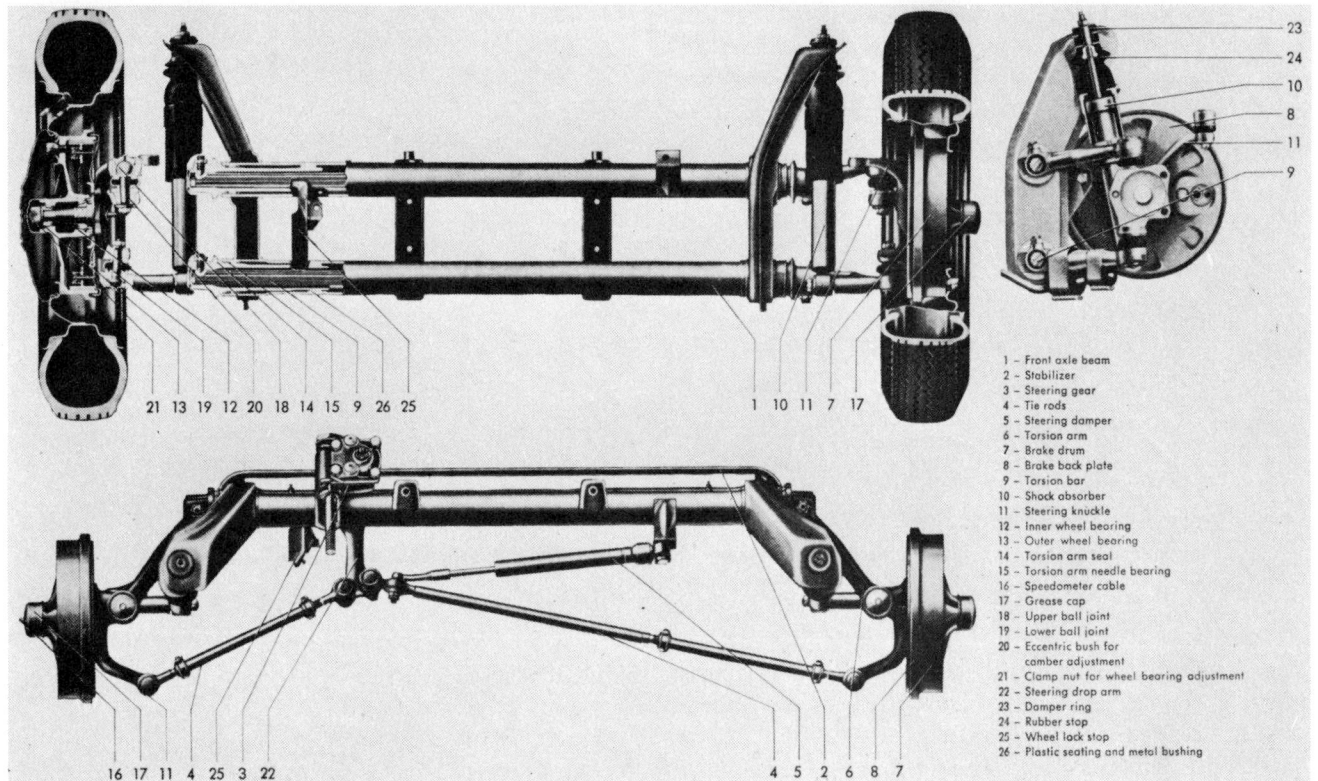

Fig. 38-15. Volkswagen used dual torsion bars in front. Wheels are attached to swinging lever arms that trail behind torsion bars.

systems. Older Volkswagen cars offer a unique torsion bar arrangement with all four wheels independently suspended, but with two different torsion bar setups in use. At the front, two laminated square torsion bars housed in separate axle tubes are anchored at the center to counteract twisting and lateral movement, Fig. 38-15. Each bar has a lever or torsion arm attached to its outer end. Ball joints connect the torsion arms to the steering knuckle. The wheel spindle trails behind the axle and tends to swing in an arc when moved up and down by road irregularities.

At the rear, Volkswagen utilized one short, round torsion bar on each side. These bars are splined at both ends and anchored in the center of the frame cross member. The outer ends of the torsion bars carry the spring plates to which the wheels are attached. Here, too, the wheels follow behind the torsion bars on "trailing arms."

AIR SUSPENSION

Air suspension systems are designed to cushion the ride and keep the car, bus or truck level fore and aft and at a constant height regardless of load. Air suspension was introduced on many luxury cars in the late 1950s, but it was dropped after one or two model years. Recently, however, new leveling systems have been researched and developed for passenger car use, including air-adjustable rear shock absorbers.

A typical air suspension system consists of an engine-driven air compressor, supply tank, filter or condenser, valves, piping, controls and air springs or bellows. In operation, the air compressor maintains a constant pressure in the supply tank. Air is piped to the control valves, which feed air to each spring as needed. Pressure is automatically increased on either side or at front or rear as required to keep the car level and at any desired height from the road (within limits of system).

MANUAL, AUTOMATIC LEVEL CONTROL

Air springs are not used in Cadillac's Automatic Level Control (ALC) system. Rather, the rear shock absorbers extend or compress to bring the rear of the car to the same level as the front. This automatic system utilizes an air compressor, reservoir tank assembly, pressure regulator, hoses, flexible air lines, height control valve and special shock absorbers. See Fig. 38-16.

Since 1978, Cadillacs use Electronic Level Control (ELC). Components include a compressor assembly, air dryer, exhaust solenoid, compressor relay, height sensor, air adjustable shock absorbers, wiring and air tubing. When weight is added to the rear suspension, an arm on the height sensor signals the compressor relay to turn on the compressor and pump air to the air chambers of the shock absorbers. The shocks extend, raising the rear of the car. Then, at the proper level, the arm signals the relay to turn off the compressor.

Older Ford cars used one of two leveling systems that utilize air bags in conjunction with rear coil springs. The automatic system consists of air reservoir and pump, leveling valve, air bags, nylon tubing and metal fittings and connectors, Fig. 38-17. The manual system has similar air bags connected

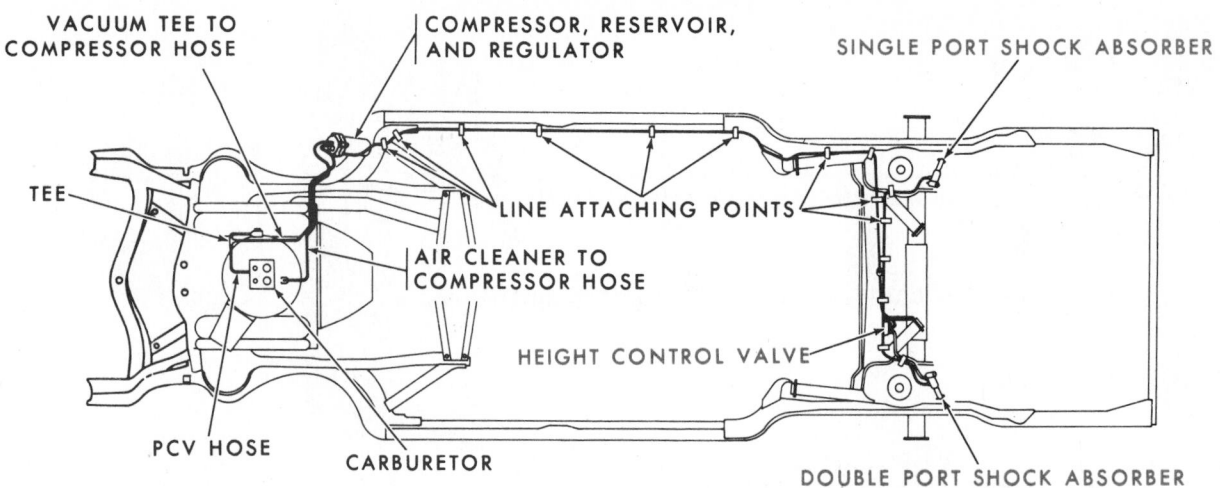

VACUUM TEE TO
COMPRESSOR HOSE

COMPRESSOR, RESERVOIR,
AND REGULATOR

SINGLE PORT SHOCK ABSORBER

TEE

LINE ATTACHING POINTS

AIR CLEANER TO
COMPRESSOR HOSE

HEIGHT CONTROL VALVE

PCV HOSE

CARBURETOR

DOUBLE PORT SHOCK ABSORBER

Fig. 38-16. Cadillac automatic level control arrangement utilizes air-adjustable rear shock absorbers to provide automatic leveling when needed. Note that line from compressor leads to height control valve, then to left shock absorber with double port, and finally to right shock absorber.

to lines leading to the trunk of the car where an air valve connection permits leveling by application of air under pressure from an outside compressed air source.

Late model Ford cars carry an option for a rear suspension automatic load-leveling system that functions only after a load (approximately 400 lbs.) is added to the vehicle. When the load lowers the vehicle to a specific level, air sleeve rear shock absorbers inflate and extend, raising the vehicle to design height. When the load is removed, the air sleeve shock absorbers deflate and lower the vehicle to design height.

Beginning with 1976 models, Ford offered only the manual fill load leveler system, also featuring the same type of air sleeve rear shock absorbers used earlier, Fig. 38-18.

Chrysler cars use an automatic height control system consisting of a vacuum powered air pump, a leveling valve assembly and air chambered rear shock absorbers.

SHOCK ABSORBERS

A wide variety of shock absorbing devices have been used to control spring action. Today, however, direct double-acting, "telescoping" hydraulic shock absorbers have almost universal application, Fig. 38-19.

At the front, each shock absorber often extends through the coil spring from the lower control arm to a bracket attached to the frame, Fig. 38-8. On Chrysler cars with torsion bar suspension, the front shock absorbers attach to the lower control arm and mount to a bracket on the frame.

In the case of high-mounted coil springs, Fig. 38-9, each front shock absorber extends from the upper control arm to a platform mounted in the spring tower or to a bracket on the wheel housing in the engine compartment.

At the rear, the lower end of the shock absorber usually is

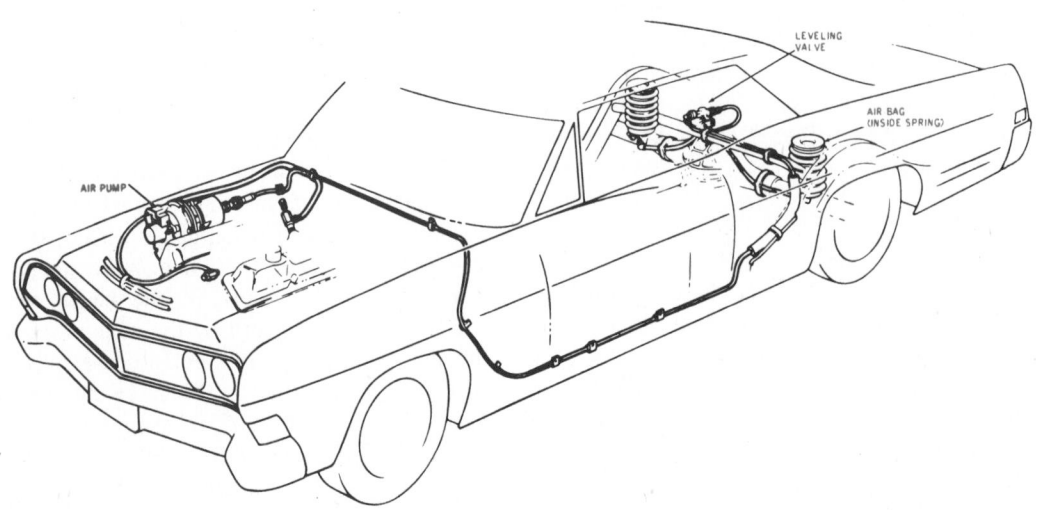

LEVELING
VALVE

AIR BAG
(INSIDE SPRING)

AIR PUMP

Fig. 38-17. Older Fords had an optional air spring stabilizing system in which minimum clearance is maintained between body frame and rear axle under loaded conditions.

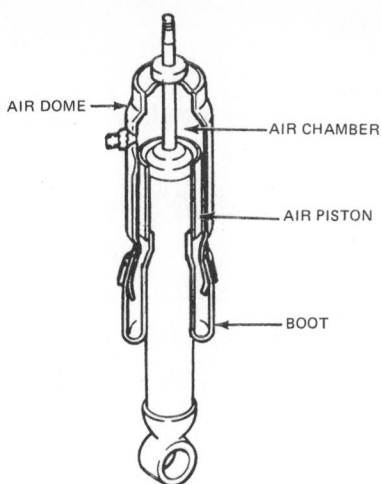

Fig. 38-18. Late model Ford cars with load-leveling option utilize two air sleeve rear shock absorbers to change vehicle height as required by load.

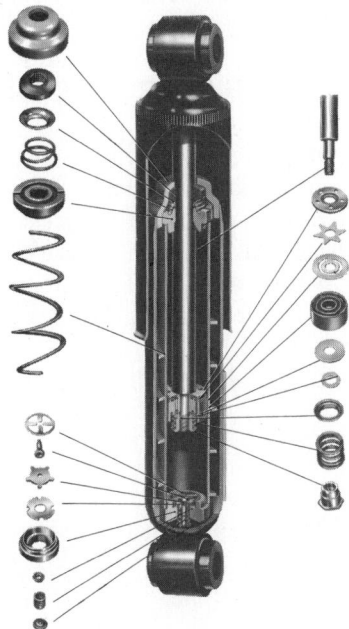

Fig. 38-19. Parts are arranged alongside cutaway view of a double-acting shock absorber.   (Monroe Auto Equipment Co.)

attached to a bracket welded to the axle housing. The upper end is fastened to the frame or to the coil spring upper seat, which is integral with the frame or body.

On cars with rear leaf springs, the rear shock absorbers generally extend from a stud attached to the spring U-bolt mounting bracket to the frame cross member. Quite often the rear shock absorbers are mounted at an angle to assist in restricting lateral movement as well as vertical movement.

Some Oldsmobile Toronado and Cadillac Eldorado cars use four rear shock absorbers to give better ride control. And, for this same reason, some Chevrolet cars have "bias-mounted" rear shock absorbers. The curb-side unit is mounted in front of the axle housing; the street-side unit is mounted in back of the housing. See Fig. 38-20. Some Ford cars feature this arrangement, too, Fig. 38-6.

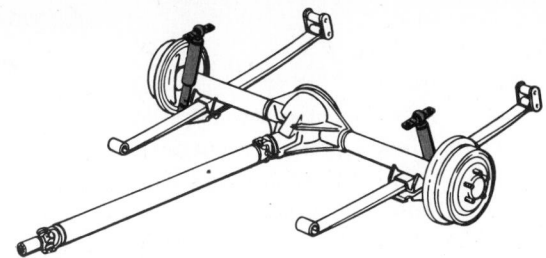

Fig. 38-20. Certain Chevrolet models have "bias-mounted" rear shock absorbers. Curb-side units are mounted in front of axle housing, street-side units in back.

The operating principle of direct-acting hydraulic shock absorbers consists of forcing fluid through restricting orifices in the valves. The restricted flow serves to slow down and control the rapid movement of the car springs as they react to road irregularities. Generally, fluid flow through the piston is controlled by spring-loaded valves, Fig. 38-19.

The hydraulic shock absorber automatically adapts itself to the severity of the shock. If the axle moves slowly, resistance to the flow of fluid will be light. If axle movement is rapid or forceful, the resistance is much stronger since more time is required to force fluid through the orifices.

By these hydraulic actions and reactions, the shock absorbers permit a soft ride over small bumps and provide firm control over spring action for cushioning large bumps. The double-acting units operate efficiently in both directions. Spring rebound can be almost as violent as the original action that compressed the shock absorber.

STEERING SYSTEMS

Basically, there are two general types of steering systems: manual and power. In the manual system, the driver's effort to turn the steering wheel is the primary force that causes the front wheels to swivel to left or right on the steering knuckles. With power steering, the driver's turning efforts are multiplied

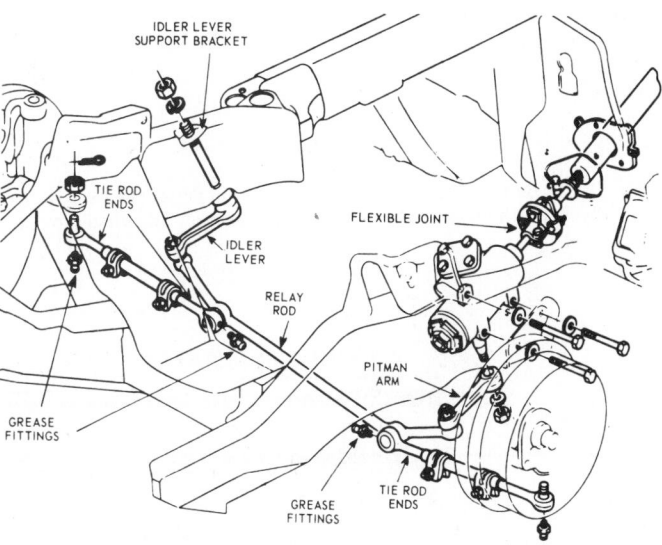

Fig. 38-21. Drawing of a typical manual steering system details end of shaft through gearbox, rods and arms.

by a hydraulic assist.

The manual system incorporates a steering wheel and shaft, manual gearbox, linkage, steering knuckles and wheel spindle assemblies, Fig. 38-21. Power steering adds a hydraulic pump, fluid reservoir, hoses, lines and either a steering assist unit mounted on the linkage or a power steering gear assembly. See Fig. 38-22.

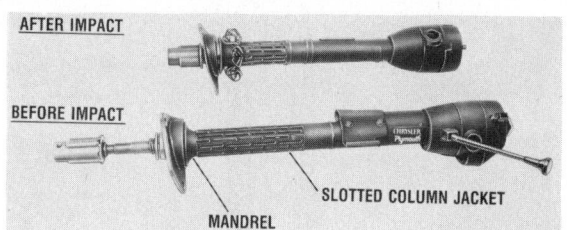

Fig. 38-24. Energy-absorbing steering column reduces chance of serious injury in a collision. Upon impact, multiplier slot mesh jacket compresses, steering shaft and shift tube telescope. (Chrysler—Plymouth)

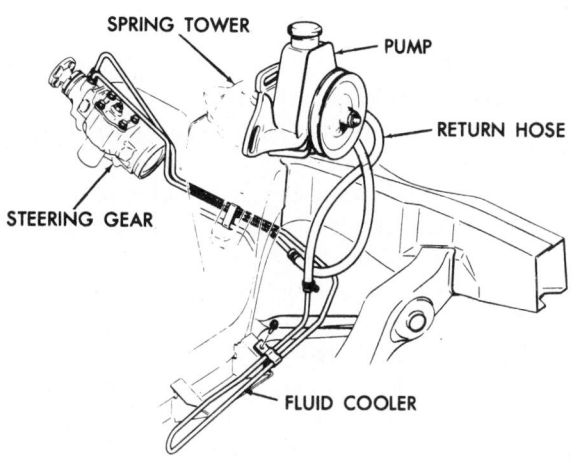

Fig. 38-22. Typical power steering system involves use of an integral steering gear mounted in line with steering column, an engine-driven pump and connecting lines and hoses.

Generally, round steering wheels are splined to the top end of the steering shaft. Tilting steering wheel assemblies, Fig. 38-23, offer the advantage of angular adjustment to suit the individual driver and the particular situation. Collapsible steering columns, Fig. 38-24, are used in late model cars as a safety item. Looking ahead, lever-type steering arrangements are being researched and developed.

MANUAL STEERING GEARS AND LINKAGE

There are several different manual steering gears in current use. The rack and pinion type, Fig. 38-25, is featured on various foreign cars. Worm and sector gears, Fig. 38-26, are popular in England and have been installed on some smaller U.S. makes. Most U.S. cars with manual steering, however, are fitted with worm and recirculating ball systems, Figs. 38-27 and 38-28.

The worm and recirculating ball steering gear works on the

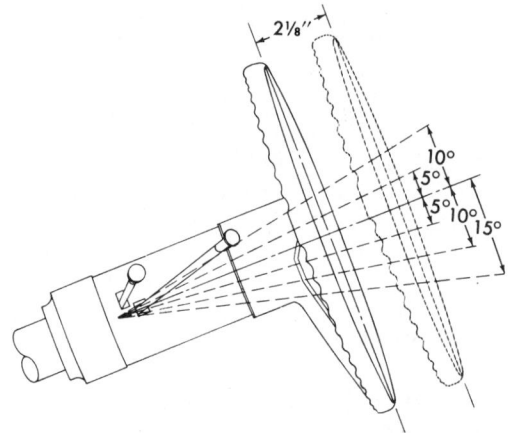

Fig. 38-23. Cadillac's tilt and telescope steering wheel has six different driving positions, selected while lifting a lever on side of column.

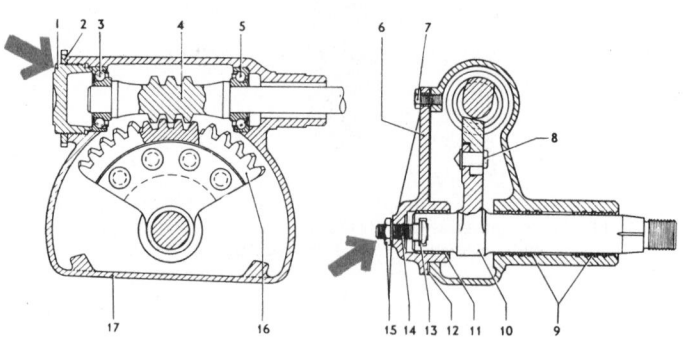

Fig. 38-26. Worm and sector steering gear used on some English cars features: 1—Worm bearings adjuster. 14—Gear mesh adjuster screw.

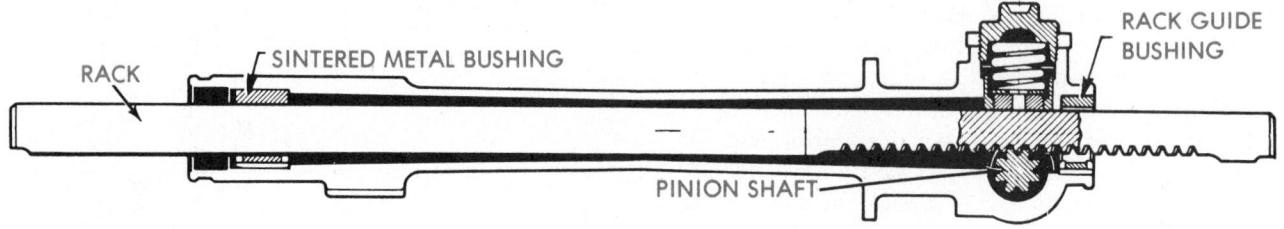

Fig. 38-25. Rack and pinion type of manual steering gear used on Opel 1900 models.

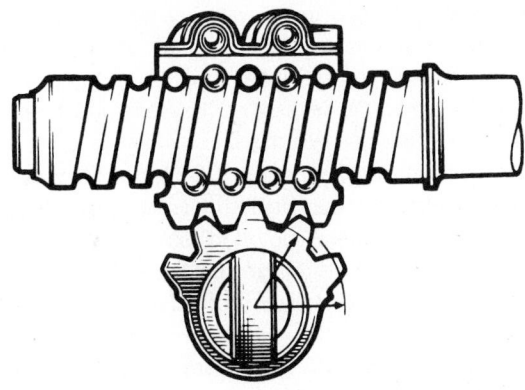

Fig. 38-27. Steering gear on Dodge Colt utilizes a 5-tooth sector and ball nut that travels on a worm shaft, while riding on recirculating ball bearings.

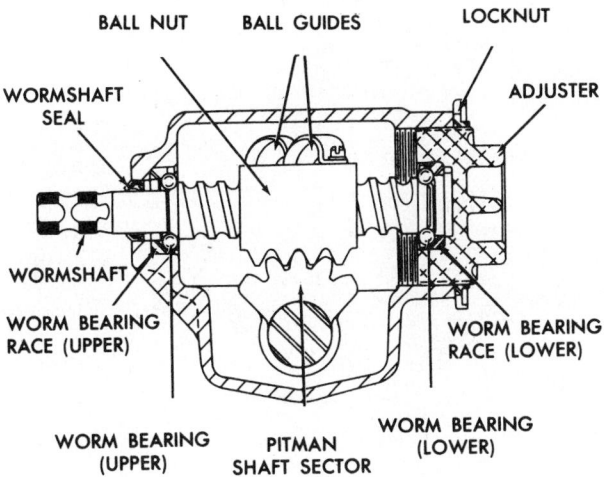

Fig. 38-28. Principle of worm and recirculating ball steering gear is revealed by this cutaway. Note ball return guides that permit balls to recirculate.

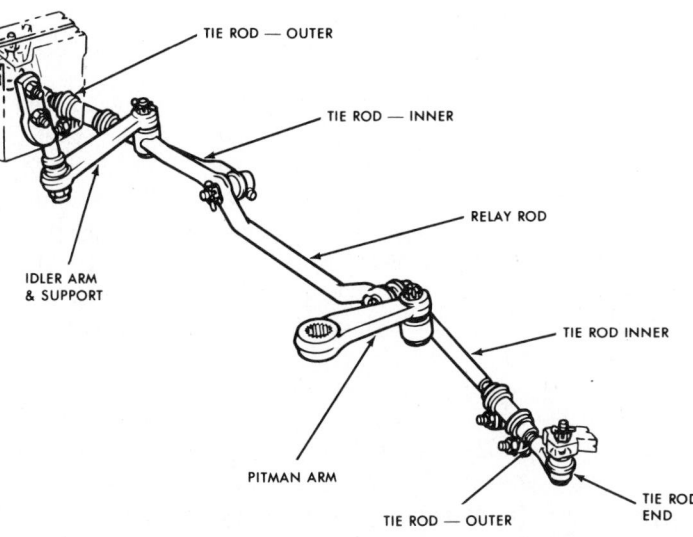

Fig. 38-29. Basic arrangement of parallelogram steering linkage is illustrated. Ball studs on tie rod ends connect to steering arms.

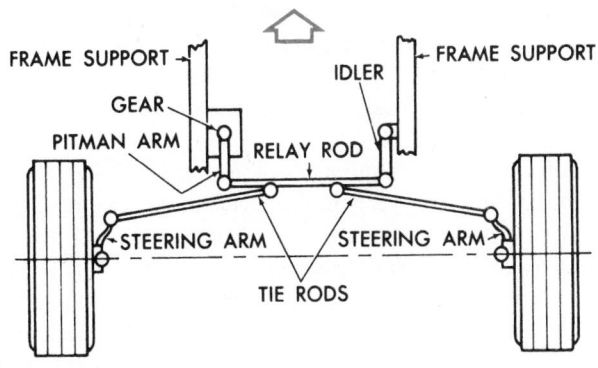

Fig. 38-30. Some steering linkage systems are placed in front of wheel spindle center line, with steering arms extending forward.

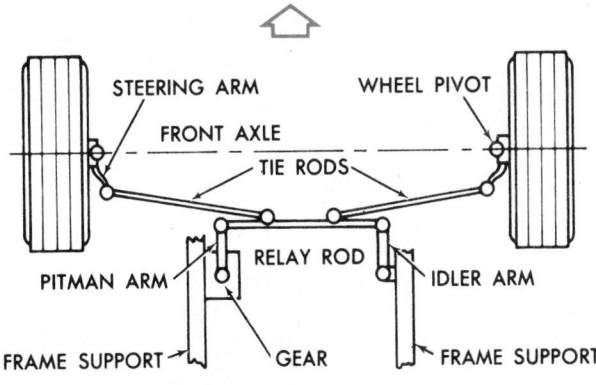

Fig. 38-31. More conventional placement of steering linkage is to rear of wheel spindles, with steering arms extending rearward.

principle of having turning forces transmitted through ball bearings from a worm gear on the steering shaft to a sector gear on the pitman arm shaft. In operation, a ball nut assembly is filled with ball bearings which "roll" along grooves between the worm teeth and grooves inside the ball nut.

When the steering wheel is turned, the worm gear on the end of the steering shaft rotates, and movement of the recirculating balls causes the ball nut to move up and down along the worm. Movement of the ball nut is carried to the sector gear by teeth on the side of ball nut. The sector gear, in turn, moves with the ball nut to rotate the pitman arm shaft and activate the steering linkage. The balls recirculate from one end of the ball nut to the other through a pair of ball return guides, Fig. 38-28.

A steering gearbox houses the manual steering gear assembly, Fig. 38-21. It is securely attached to the frame side rail and is filled with a water-resistant, extreme pressure lubricant. The pitman arm shaft projects downward from the gearbox. It is splined to the pitman arm, which converts rotary motion of the shaft to lateral movement of the arm. See Fig. 38-29.

The pitman arm, generally, is connected to a relay rod which reaches across to an idler arm attached to the frame side rail on the opposite side. The relay rod is connected to two adjustable tie rods that transmit lateral movement of the relay rod to the steering arms, Figs. 38-30 and 38-31.

The various rods and arms roughly form a parallelogram during a turn, so the arrangement is called "parallelogram" linkage. In some cars, the linkage is in front of the front wheel spindles, Fig. 38-30. In others, the linkage is to the rear of the spindles, Fig. 38-31.

Manual steering is considered to be entirely adequate for smaller cars and for cars with the engine in the rear. It is light, fast and accurate in maintaining steering control. However, larger and heavier engines, greater front overhang on U.S. cars, and the trend toward wide tread tires have increased the steering effort required. Gearboxes with higher gear ratios were tried, bu. dependable power steering systems were found to be the best answer.

POWER STEERING

Advanced power steering got its start during World War II in military vehicles of all kinds. With the development of heavier and faster cars in the early 1950s, modified versions of the wartime gears were installed by the car manufacturers. As popularity increased, new power steering setups were devised until a lightweight, compact, self-lubricating, in-line power steering gear was developed in the late 1950s.

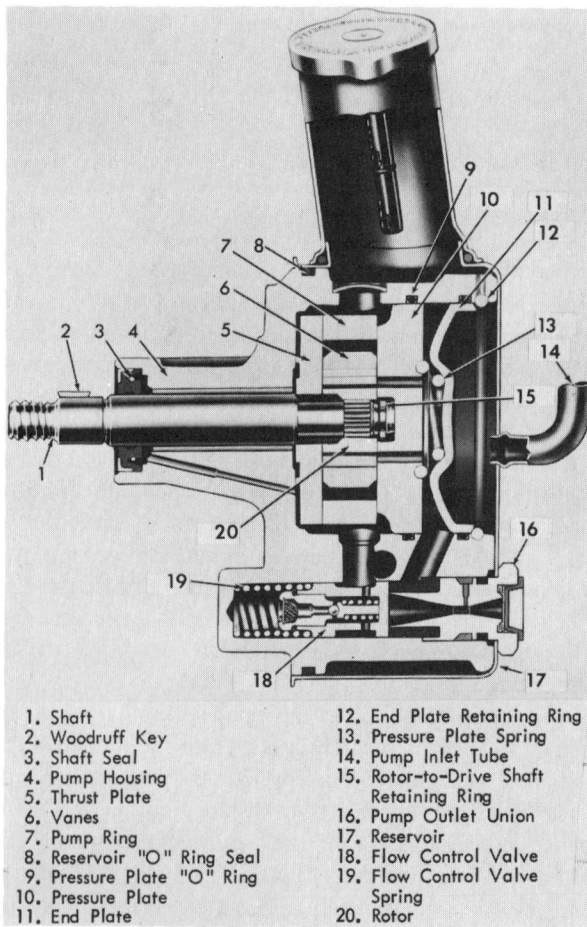

1. Shaft	12. End Plate Retaining Ring
2. Woodruff Key	13. Pressure Plate Spring
3. Shaft Seal	14. Pump Inlet Tube
4. Pump Housing	15. Rotor-to-Drive Shaft
5. Thrust Plate	Retaining Ring
6. Vanes	16. Pump Outlet Union
7. Pump Ring	17. Reservoir
8. Reservoir "O" Ring Seal	18. Flow Control Valve
9. Pressure Plate "O" Ring	19. Flow Control Valve
10. Pressure Plate	Spring
11. End Plate	20. Rotor

Fig. 38-32. Vane-type power steering pump is encased in reservoir of fluid. Pressure relief valve limits pressures; flow control system allows external pump flow to drop off at higher speeds.

Now, an integral-type rotary valve system is used on most factory-installed, power steering-equipped cars. Other systems include the linkage-booster type which is "applied" to the steering linkage and the semi-integral system which combines features of the other two systems.

The power steering pump, Fig. 38-32, is belted, geared or otherwise attached to the engine or some driven accessory. (Some earlier units were mounted on generator armature shaft.) The pump is connected to the power unit by lines and hoses, and it incorporates a control valve somewhere in the hydraulic circuit.

Automobile power steering is actually "power assisted steering." All automotive systems are constructed so that the car can be steered manually when the engine is not running or if any failure occurs at the power source.

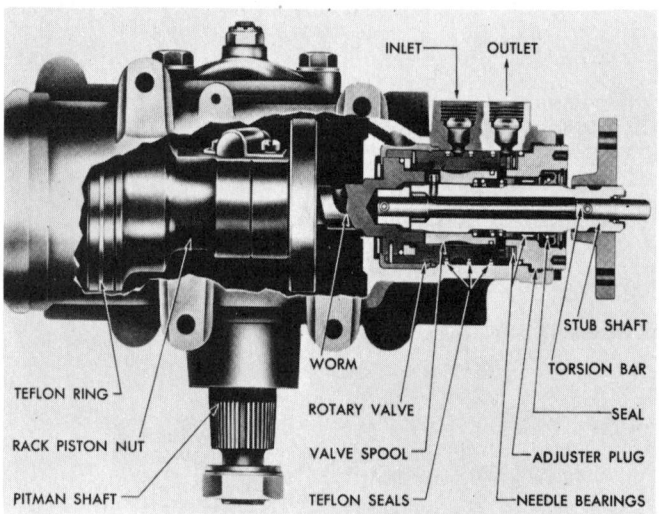

Fig. 38-33. Rotary valve power steering gear displaces fluid to provide hydraulic fluid pressure assists when turning. Mechanical element of gear is a recirculating ball system.

INTEGRAL TYPE POWER UNIT

The integral type of power steering gear is constructed with the power cylinder and control valve built into the steering gear unit. One model of Saginaw gear, Figs. 38-33 and 38-34, is shown to illustrate system operation.

Note that in the straight ahead position, the hydraulic fluid is circulating through the "open" position of the valve assembly and back into the pump reservoir. It is not circulating in the power cylinder in which the rack piston is located. See Fig. 38-34.

When the steering wheel is turned to the right, resistance between the front tires and road causes the torsion bar to be deflected. This changes the register of the valve grooves and valve body grooves, Fig. 38-34. The right turn grooves are closed off from the return grooves and opened to the pressure grooves. The left turn grooves are closed off from the pressure grooves and opened to the return grooves. This causes the oil to flow under pressure into one half of the power cylinder,

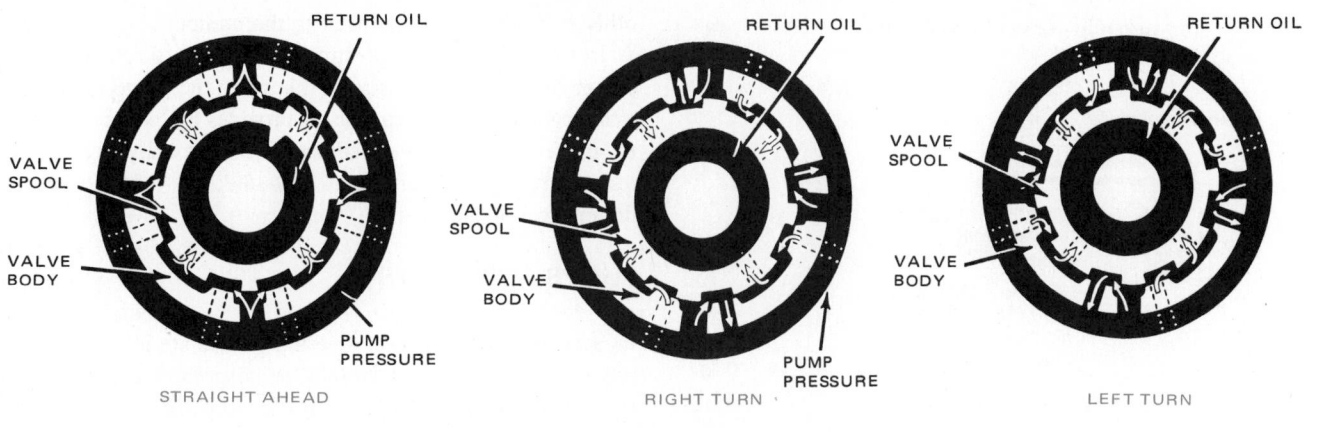

RETURN OIL

VALVE SPOOL

VALVE BODY

PUMP PRESSURE

STRAIGHT AHEAD

RETURN OIL

VALVE SPOOL

VALVE BODY

PUMP PRESSURE

RIGHT TURN

RETURN OIL

VALVE SPOOL

VALVE BODY

LEFT TURN

ROTARY VALVE OIL FLOW

Fig. 38-34. Rotary valve operation in integral power steering gear is illustrated in straight ahead, right turn and left turn positions. Lower gear assembly is always full of oil.

moving the rack piston and pitman shaft gear to overcome tire friction in that direction. Fluid in the other end of the power cylinder is forced out through the valve and back to the pump.

When the driver stops turning the steering wheel, the valve returns to its neutral position, and pressures on both sides of the power piston are equalized. Steering geometry causes the front wheels to return to the straight ahead position.

When the steering wheel is turned to the left, reverse operation occurs within the power steering unit. The valve grooves register for left turn operation, and the rack piston moves in the opposite direction, Fig. 38-34, to give the driver a power-assisted left turn.

Chrysler's integral power steering gear is illustrated and described in Fig. 38-35.

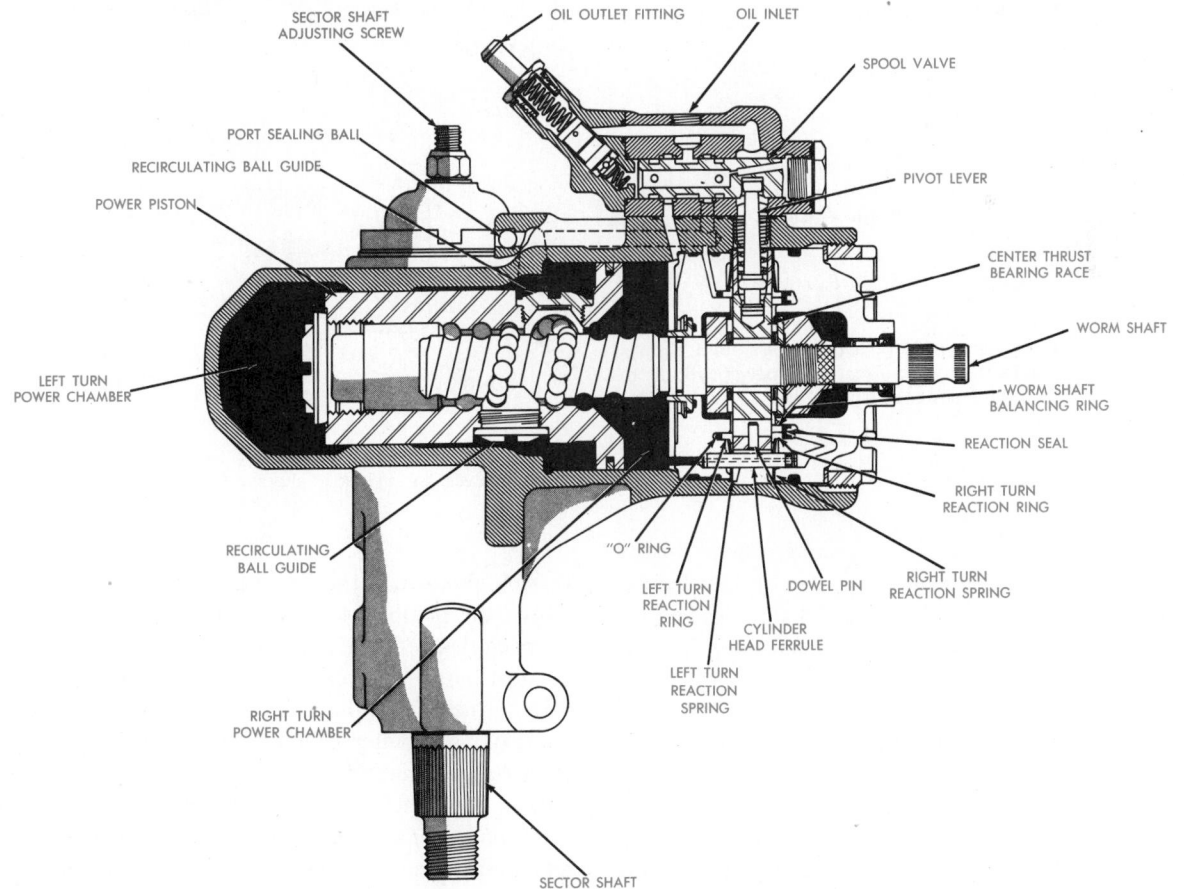

SECTOR SHAFT ADJUSTING SCREW

OIL OUTLET FITTING

OIL INLET

SPOOL VALVE

PORT SEALING BALL

RECIRCULATING BALL GUIDE

POWER PISTON

PIVOT LEVER

CENTER THRUST BEARING RACE

WORM SHAFT

LEFT TURN POWER CHAMBER

WORM SHAFT BALANCING RING

REACTION SEAL

RIGHT TURN REACTION RING

RECIRCULATING BALL GUIDE

"O" RING

LEFT TURN REACTION RING

DOWEL PIN

RIGHT TURN REACTION SPRING

CYLINDER HEAD FERRULE

LEFT TURN REACTION SPRING

RIGHT TURN POWER CHAMBER

SECTOR SHAFT

Fig. 38-35. Chrysler's integral power steering gear has gear teeth broached in side of power piston, which is geared to worm shaft through recirculating balls. Steering valve is mounted on top.

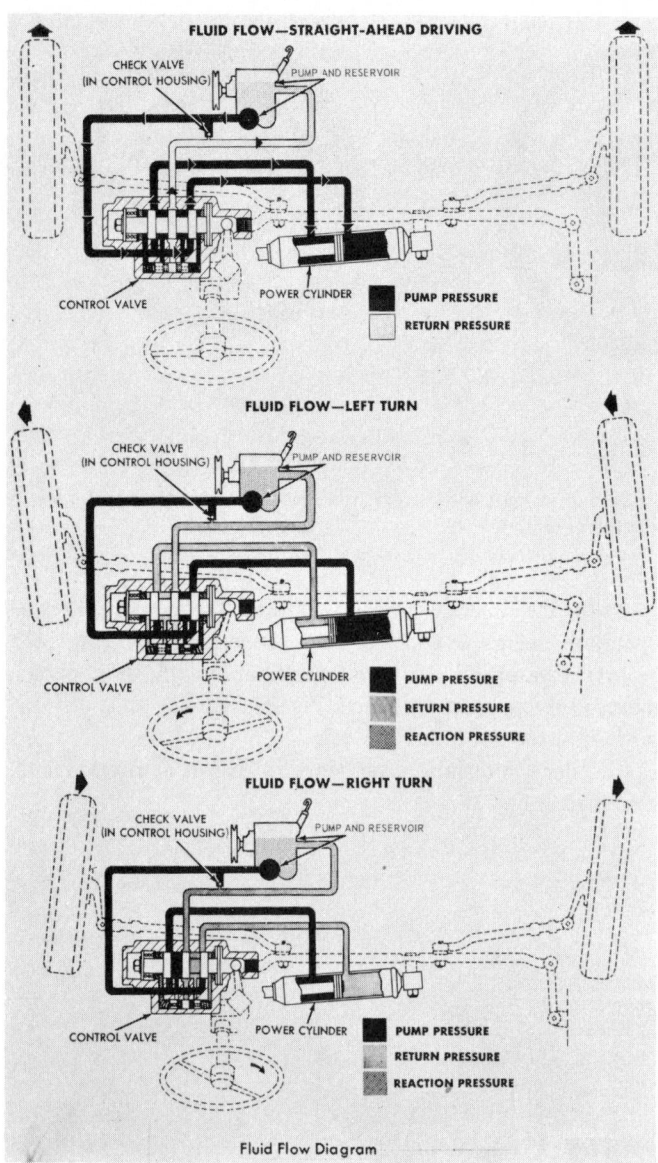

FLUID FLOW—STRAIGHT-AHEAD DRIVING

CHECK VALVE
(IN CONTROL HOUSING)
PUMP AND RESERVOIR

CONTROL VALVE
POWER CYLINDER
■ PUMP PRESSURE
□ RETURN PRESSURE

FLUID FLOW—LEFT TURN

CHECK VALVE
(IN CONTROL HOUSING)
PUMP AND RESERVOIR

CONTROL VALVE
POWER CYLINDER
■ PUMP PRESSURE
▨ RETURN PRESSURE
▨ REACTION PRESSURE

FLUID FLOW—RIGHT TURN

CHECK VALVE
(IN CONTROL HOUSING)
PUMP AND RESERVOIR

CONTROL VALVE
POWER CYLINDER
■ PUMP PRESSURE
▨ RETURN PRESSURE
▨ REACTION PRESSURE

Fluid Flow Diagram

Fig. 38-36. With linkage-booster type of power steering system, control valve directs fluid under pressure to proper section of power cylinder to provide power assist.

LINKAGE-BOOSTER TYPE

The linkage-booster type of power steering system consists of a power cylinder, a control valve mounted on the steering linkage and a pulley-driven pump, Fig. 38-36. The control valve is mounted between the pitman arm and the relay rod. Two flexible hoses connect the control valve to the booster cylinder, which is also attached to the relay rod.

The power cylinder is double acting. By proper routing of fluid under pressure, the booster can be made to apply force to the steering linkage in either direction. When the steering wheel is turned, movement of the pitman arm actuates a valve, and fluid is directed to one side of the booster cylinder. This hydraulic action moves the valve in one direction or the other and thereby imparts power assistance directly to the relay rod. The control valve also directs fluid being forced out of the

other side of the cylinder back to the pump.

In the straight ahead position, fluid passes through the open center of the valve and is routed back to the pump reservoir. A small piston in the control valve provides hydraulic "reaction" to movement of the valve spool in the valve body. This resistance opposes turning of the steering wheel to give the driver "feel-of-the-road."

PUMPS AND HOSES

Several types of power steering pumps are in use. The vane type hydraulic pump, Fig. 38-32, incorporates a rotor with six to ten vanes which rotate in an elliptical housing. Fluid trapped between the vanes is forced out under pressure as the vanes move from the long diameter of the housing to the short diameter. Some vane type pumps are capable of 1450 psi output.

A roll type pump operates much like the vane type. Instead of vanes, six rollers on a toothed carrier unit rotate inside of a cam insert to build up fluid pressure.

A slipper type pump produces pressure by rotating four to ten spring-loaded slippers around a cam insert within the pump body, Fig. 38-37. The internal gear pump has a six-tooth

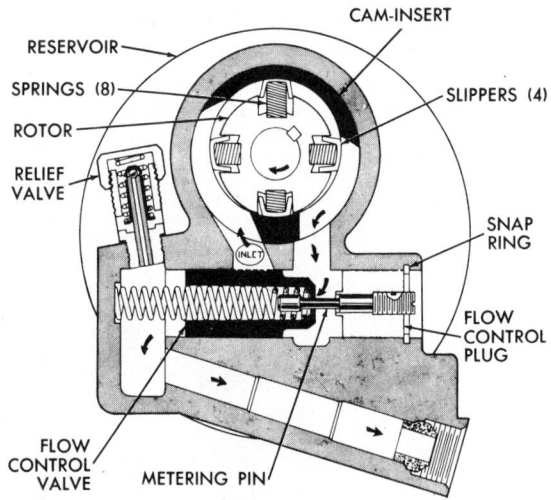

RESERVOIR
CAM-INSERT
SPRINGS (8)
SLIPPERS (4)
ROTOR
RELIEF VALVE
SNAP RING
INLET
FLOW CONTROL PLUG
FLOW CONTROL VALVE
METERING PIN

Fig. 38-37. This slipper-type power steering pump is belt-driven. As rotor revolves, spring-loaded slippers face fluid from inlet side of pump to flow control valve.

gear mounted eccentrically with the internal gear that rotates within the pump housing. As the gear turns, fluid is trapped between the teeth and is emitted under pressure.

Most modern power steering pumps contain a flow control valve, which limits fluid flow to the power cylinder to about two gallons per minute, and a relief valve which limits pressure according to system demands.

The power steering hoses serve as a means of transmitting the fluid under pressure from the pump to the power cylinder and return. In addition, the hoses must provide the proper amount of expansion to absorb any shock surge and offer enough restriction to the fluid flow to keep the pump cavity full of fluid at all times.

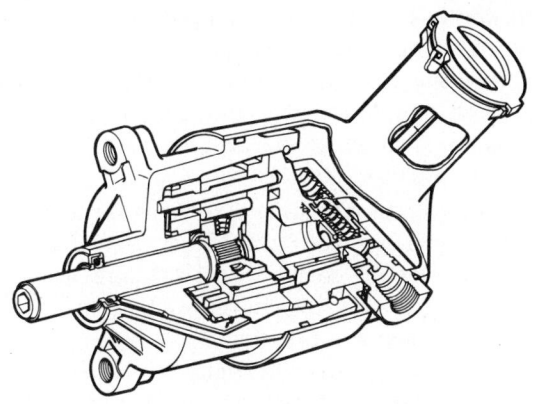

Fig. 38-38. Ford's belt-driven power steering pump.

Ford introduced a ten slipper type pump with an integral fiberglass nylon reservoir, Fig. 38-38. The reservoir is attached to the rear of the aluminum pump housing. The pump body is encased within the housing and reservoir. On this design, the pump pressure fitting allows the pump pressure line to swivel.

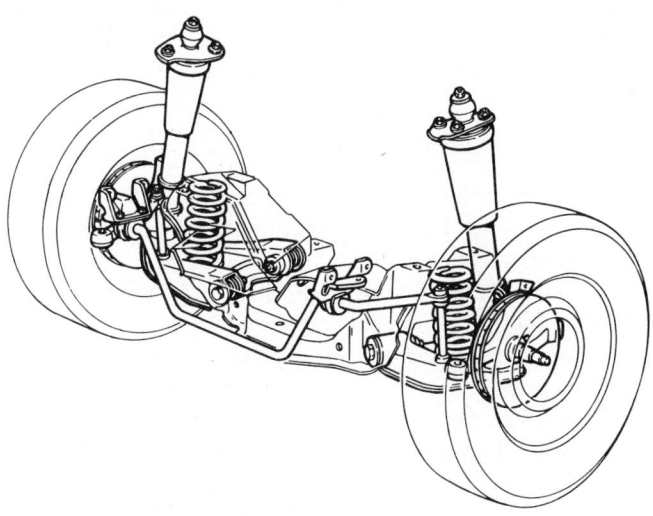

Fig. 38-39. Hydraulic shock strut front suspension. (Ford)

STRUT TYPE FRONT SUSPENSION

Ford Mustang and Mercury Capri models use a hydraulic shock strut to replace the conventional upper control arm. See Fig. 38-39. This strut design differs from MacPherson struts, Fig. 38-40, in that the coil spring is located between the lower control arm and the body structure instead of being mounted directly on the strut.

Long-life components are used in this shock strut. However, if the strut needed to be replaced, no special tools (such as a spring compressor) would be required.

Chrysler installed MacPherson struts on its late model Plymouth Champ and Dodge Colt models. See Fig. 38-40. This type of front suspension is gaining in popularity on U.S. compact and subcompact cars.

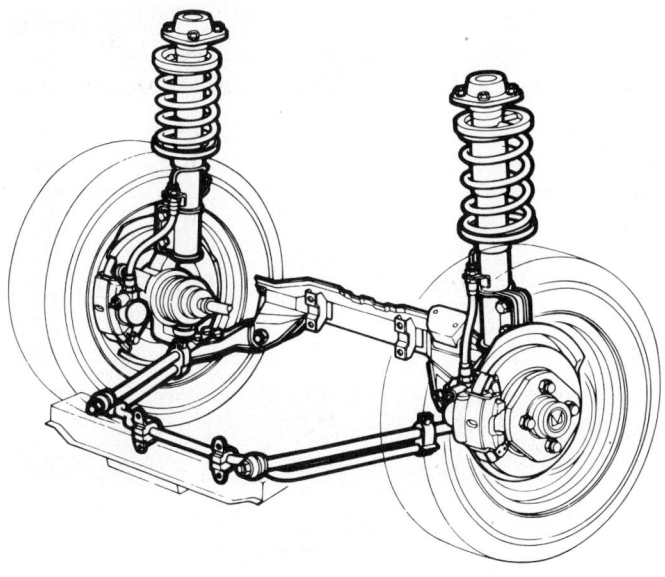

Fig. 38-40. MacPherson strut front suspension. (Chrysler)

"MacPherson" front suspension features vertical shock absorbing struts housed within the front springs.

REAR SUSPENSION

Oldsmobile designed and developed an independent rear suspension system, Fig. 38-41, for use on Toronado models. The system features lower control arms much like the front suspension arms. In operation, they also perform the same basic tasks as independent front suspension control arms.

Pontiac installed torque arm rear suspension on Astre and Sunbird models. The principal components are the long torque arm, two rubber-bushed lower control arms, one track rod between axle housing and underbody, coil springs and shock absorbers. The torque arm serves as the upper control arm. It extends from a rigid mounting at the differential housing to the side of the extension housing on the transmission through a rubber bushing.

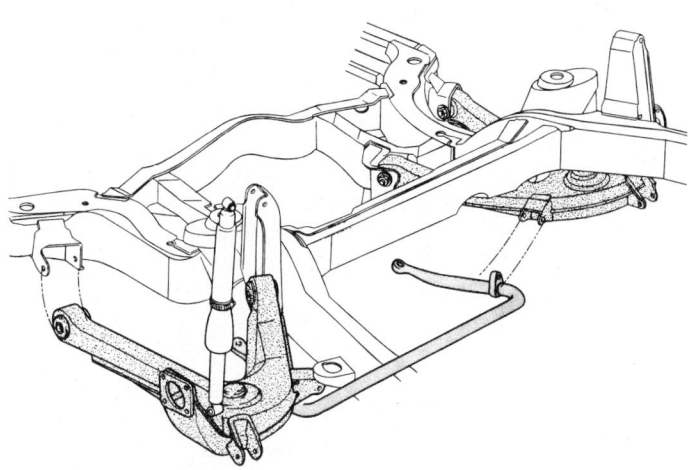

Fig. 38-41. Toronado independent rear suspension. (Oldsmobile)

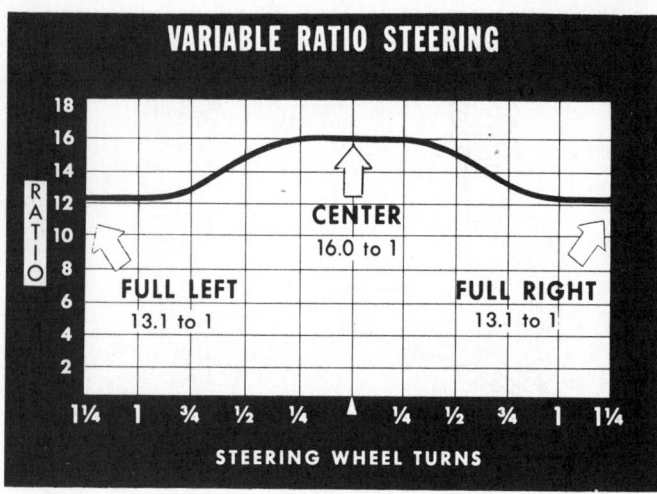

Fig. 38-42. Advantage of variable ratio steering is that front wheels respond more quickly to steering wheel movement as the degree of turn increases.

VARIABLE RATIO STEERING

A major step forward in steering gear design was accomplished with the introduction of variable ratio steering. In conventional (constant ratio) steering, the degree of turn of the front wheels is always in direct proportion to the degree of turn of the steering wheel. In variable ratio steering, the ratio remains constant for approximately the first 40 deg. of steering wheel movement. Then the ratio decreases and the response of the front wheels quickens for every degree of turn of the steering wheel, Fig. 38-42.

The "variable" effect is made possible by the design of the steering gear. With constant ratio gears of the sector and rack type, the teeth of the sector are all the same length. This causes the sector to swing the pitman arm the same number of degrees with each tooth of the sector.

With variable ratio gears, the center tooth of the sector is longer than the other teeth, which produces a slower response of the pitman arm in shallow turn situations and faster response near the extremes of steering wheel travel for sharp turns. In some applications, Fig. 38-27, a specially contoured worm gear alters the ratio.

Typically, a variable ratio steering gear will provide a ratio of about 16:1 for straight ahead driving, and about a 13:1 ratio in full turns. In relation to steering wheel movement with variable ratio steering, the first quarter-turn in either direction will produce a relatively "slow" response from the front wheels. Then the response "speeds up" as the steering wheel is turned from one-half to full turn. After that, the lowest ratio comes into effect when it is needed for parking or backing up.

REVIEW QUESTIONS — SPRING SUSPENSION AND STEERING

1. What are the two basic types of front suspension?
2. What is "unsprung" weight?
3. What type of spring is used with solid axle beams?
   a. Coil springs.
   b. Leaf springs.
   c. Torsion bars.
4. Front coil springs are always placed between the lower control arm and the frame. Yes or No?
5. What keeps the rise and fall of the front wheels in a vertical plane in independent suspension systems?
   a. Proportionate lengths of control arms.
   b. Front suspension height specification.
   c. Correct caster setting.
6. When coil springs are used at the rear, what carries driving and braking torque?
   a. Control arms.
   b. Shock absorbers.
   c. Torsion bars.
7. Torsion bars usually can be adjusted. True or False?
8. How is tension increased on a torsion bar?
   a. By flexing.
   b. By compressing.
   c. By twisting.

9. What is the main purpose of a shock absorber?
10. Are cars always equipped with four shock absorbers, two in front and two at rear?
11. What is the operating principle of a shock absorber?
12. What are the two general types of steering systems?
13. Which manual steering gear type is most popular on late model cars?
14. Name three components of manual steering linkage.
15. What are the three basic power steering systems?
16. Give two types of power steering pumps.
17. MacPherson strut suspension is a specific design that:
    a. Connects front lower control arm to frame and provides point of adjustment for caster.
    b. Connects rear axle housing to frame by means of three or four control arms.
    c. Combines front coil spring, shock absorber and strut in a single assembly.
18. Hydraulic shock strut front suspension and MacPherson strut suspension are alike. True or False?
19. Cadillac's level control systems make use of rear air adjustable _____.
20. Older Ford cars utilize _____ in conjunction with rear coil springs in the leveling systems.

WHEEL ALIGNMENT

Aligning the front wheels is the task of balancing the steering angles with the physical forces being exerted. The steering angles are caster, camber, toe-in, steering axle inclination and toe-out on turns. The physical forces are gravity, momentum, friction and centrifugal force.

Since so many factors are involved in front wheel alignment, it is also called front end alignment, steering alignment, steering balance or steering geometry. Alignment, then, is more than adjusting the angularity of the front wheels. You also must consider and correct if necessary:
1. Suspension, steering and tire condition.
2. Wheel bearing adjustment and wheel balance.
3. Car weight balance.
4. Wheelbase and tread width.
5. Rear wheel track.
6. Suspension height.
7. Shock absorber action.

STEERING BALANCE

The entire matter of steering control relies on whether or not the tires maintain close contact with the road surface. Tire-to-road contact is influenced by the condition of the tire tread, tire inflation, wheel balance, weight on the wheels, shock absorber action, spring action and wheel angularity. A balanced condition between these elements will establish a perfect pivot point from which the wheels can rotate with the least friction. This point on the tread of each front tire is the target of all steering angle adjustments, Fig. 39-1.

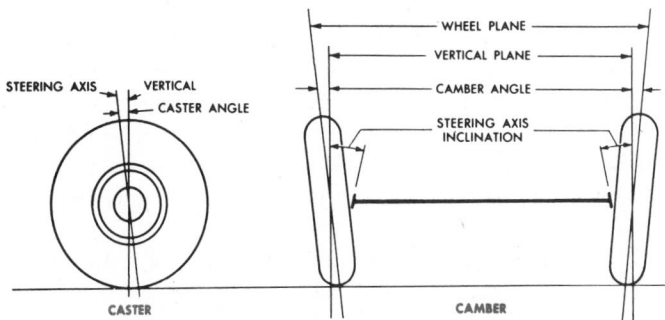

Fig. 39-1. Exaggerated alignment angles show various settings of front wheels which work together to provide smooth rolling and easy steering that extends tire life.

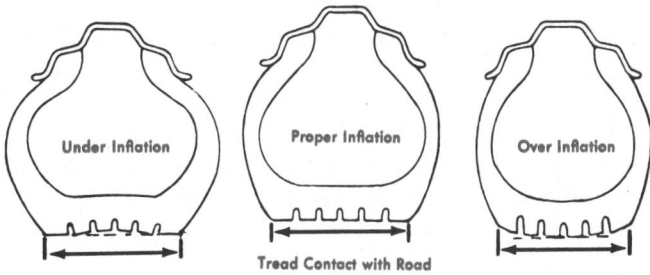

Fig. 39-2. Tire wear is goverened by tread contact with road surface. Note area of contact under conditions of underinflation, proper inflation and overinflation.

The area of tire-to-tread contact varies with tire inflation pressure and load, Fig. 39-2. Underinflation or overinflation affects the rolling characteristics of the wheels by changing the degree of friction between the tires and the road surface. If one tire is underinflated, or has a worn tread, it will have a tendency to hold back, and the car will steer toward the side holding back. Anything that tends to increase the area of tire tread contact with the road will increase the rolling resistance, and the car will steer to that side.

For satisfactory wheel alignment, certain conditions must be met. Ideally, both front tires will be the same brand, size and type. Each will have the same degree of tread wear, and be inflated to the same pressure. Each will be carrying the same weight. Then, if each front wheel is properly and equally adjusted for angularity, each tire will maintain the same contact on a smooth road surface.

Obviously, though, it is impossible to maintain constant contact. The wheels bounce up and down at different times, at different rates of speed and to varied heights. Here, the effects of momentum and inertia change the area of tread contact. Deflection of the car springs constantly changes the angles at which the steering system operates. Centrifugal force on the wheels emphasizes any lack of balance, and the extremely flexible characteristic of tires defeats the possibility of true and uniform steering geometry.

It follows, that a tire must be almost perfectly round if it is to maintain constant contact with the road (or, as constant contact as road conditions will allow). Also, each of the four wheels acts as a flywheel, storing energy as it acquires momentum. The tire, wheel and brake drum rotate as a unit. Anything added to this rotating mass (such as tires with excessively heavy treads) will increase the flywheel effect.

WHEEL BALANCE AND UNBALANCE

Basically, static balance is the equal distribution of weight around the wheel and tire assembly. Dynamic balance is the equal distribution of weight on each side of the vertical center line of the wheel and tire assembly. It follows, then, that unbalance exists when there is an unequal distribution of weight around the horizontal axis of the wheel and tire assembly.

Another important matter to be considered before alignment angles are set is the possibility that the wheels and tires are unbalanced. The tires may be round and true when rotated slowly, yet give trouble on the road when they turn fast enough to get into the realm of centrifugal force. This unbalance can exist in the tire, wheel, brake drum or hub. Or, it may occur in any combination of the four.

When an unbalanced wheel revolves, centrifugal force acts on the heaviest portion and tends to lift the wheel off the road, then slam it down during each revolution. This results in flat spots on the tire tread and worn out ball joints, tie rod ends, steering gears and shock absorbers.

If the unbalance lies in the plane of wheel rotation, it is known as static (or kinetic) unbalance, Fig. 39-3. If it lies on

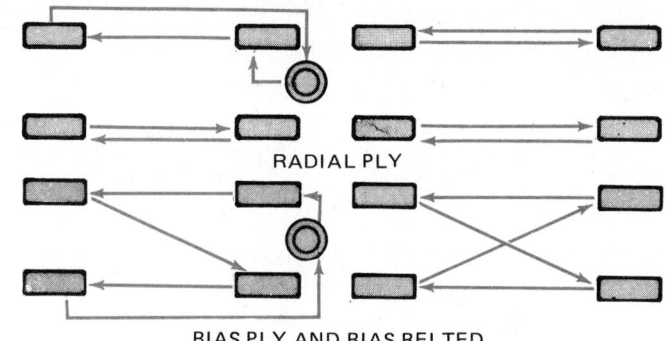

RADIAL PLY

BIAS PLY AND BIAS BELTED

Fig. 39-4. Planned tire rotation extends tire life.

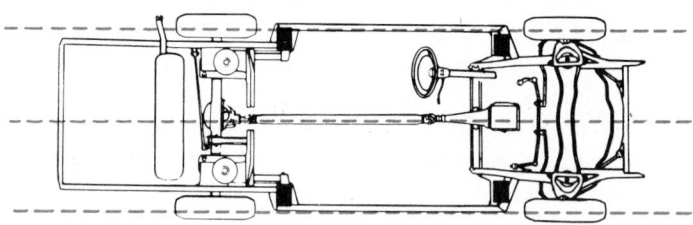

Fig. 39-5. Before making alignment checks, see that frame is straight, square and level. Side rails must be parallel to center line.

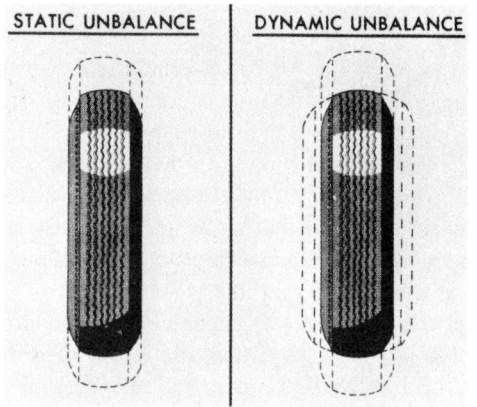

STATIC UNBALANCE   DYNAMIC UNBALANCE

Fig. 39-3. Static (kinetic) unbalance is uneven distribution of weight in tire assembly in plane of rotation. Dynamic unbalance is uneven distribution of weight to right and left of plane of rotation.

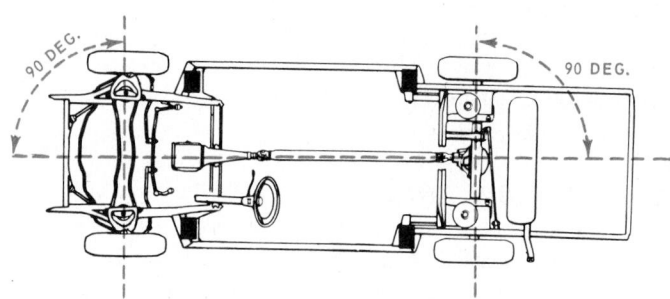

90 DEG.   90 DEG.

Fig. 39-6. Straight lines drawn through centers of both rear axle and front spindle locations must be parallel and form right angles with center line of frame.

either or both sides of the plane of rotation, it is dynamic unbalance. Either condition will cause the wheels to bounce. Dynamic unbalance in the front wheels will cause them to wobble as well. Rear wheels should be kept in balance to avoid a bouncing action, which could set up a heavy vibration in the chassis and affect steering balance.

Unbalance can be detected with the aid of special equipment, which usually indicates the proper location for weights to restore balance. In spite of regular maintenance, however, uneven tire wear can result from drivers' habits as their modern automobiles accelerate faster, take curves at a higher rate of speed and stop more quickly. To counteract uneven wear that leads to unbalance, most manufacturers recommend that tires should be rotated every five or six thousand miles. See Fig. 39-4.

CAR WEIGHT BALANCE

The next step in balancing wheel alignment is to check the accuracy of attachment of the wheels to the load being carried. The frame must be checked to see that it is square and level, and the axles and wheels must be located properly in relation to the frame. This involves making a series of measurements to establish the parallel and right angle relationships between the frame and wheels. This must be done, of course, before attempting to make any angular adjustments of the front wheels.

The essential part of this relationship is a straight, undistorted frame, Fig. 39-5. First, an accurate center line must be established. Then, if straight lines are drawn through the centers of both rear and both front spindle locations, they must be parallel to each other and form right angles with the center line of the frame, Fig. 39-6.

Then, when the wheels are attached to the front spindles and rear axles, the rear wheels should be parallel to the center line of the frame. Likewise, the front wheels in their straight ahead position should be parallel to this line (except for slight toe-in or toe-out). This is necessary so that each wheel will roll straight and true in relation to the frame center line.

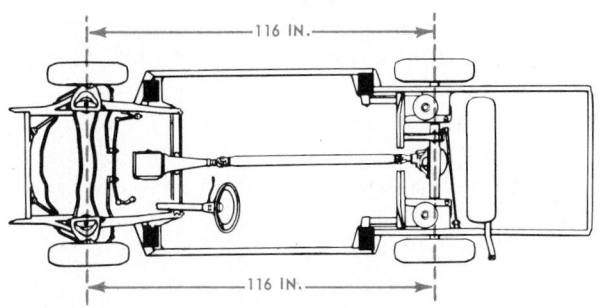

Fig. 39-7. Wheelbase, or distance between centers of front and rear wheels, must measure as specified and be exactly equal on each side.

WHEELBASE — TREAD WIDTH

Another point of importance when locating axles and spindles is the wheelbase measurement. Wheelbase is the distance between the center of the front wheel and the center of the rear wheel, Fig. 39-7. This distance (left front to left rear, right front to right rear with front wheels in "straight ahead" position) must be exactly the same on each side for proper weight balance and the ability of the car's rear wheels to track correctly.

Tread width is also a key measurement with respect to weight balance and rear wheel track. Tread width is the distance between the center points of the left tire tread and the right tire tread as they come in contact with the road. See Fig. 39-8. While the front and rear wheels may have different

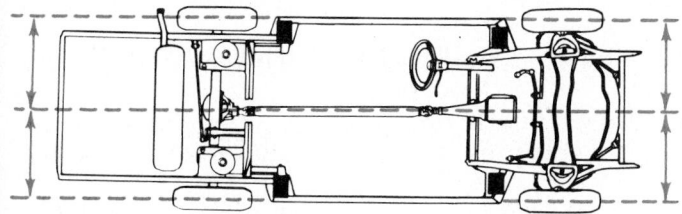

Fig. 39-8. Tread width is distance between center points of left tire tread and right tire tread. Note that measurements are taken from frame center line to center of tire in each case to establish correct frame-to-wheels relationship, left to right.

tread widths, each front wheel must be the same distance from the center line of the frame, and each rear wheel must be the same distance from this center line.

This parallel relationship between the frame center line and wheels establishes a balance between front and rear, and between right and left. While this balance may not mean equal

weight at these points, it does mean that a balanced distribution of weight and stress has been acquired for the proper setting of front wheel angles.

However, if the car has been damaged in an accident, the impact may have shifted the frame side rails, forcing the frame into a diamond shape and changing the relationship between the axle and spindle locations and the frame center line.

REAR WHEEL TRACK

An out-of-line condition not caused by an accident usually can be traced to a mechanical defect or sag due to stress in the middle, or at one corner, of the frame. In any case, a frame that is out of line must be straightened before it is possible to obtain correct steering alignment. The frame rails must be the same height from the floor on each side at the spring seats, along with the essential parallel and right angle relationships.

Also vital in this matter of weight balance is the condition of the car springs. They control the up-and-down motion of the car and, therefore, the height of the car above the road. If one or more of the springs is collapsed or broken, it causes an unbalanced distribution of weight. This unbalance creates a lopsided appearance, puts an added strain on related parts and changes the angularity of the front wheels.

This condition also may occur when the load is distributed unequally. In fact, anything that changes the ratio of weight on the springs will have a definite bearing on the alignment angles and on the area of tire-to-road contact.

SUSPENSION HEIGHT

The height of the car above the road must be checked (front and rear, right and left) before any steering angles are adjusted, Fig. 39-9. Although the method of checking varies with type of suspension, the measurements should be made with the car parked on a level floor (or on an alignment machine) with the tires equally inflated, fuel tank full, no passenger load and no excess weight on either side.

SHOCK ABSORBER ACTION

Still another factor involved in controlling the up-and-down motion of a moving vehicle is efficient shock absorber action.

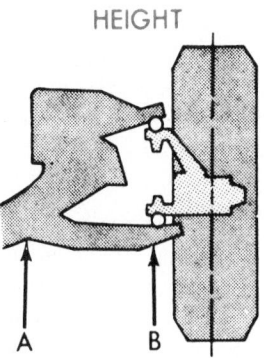

Fig. 39-9. Front suspension height must be correct if wheel alignment angles are to be maintained. Proper height helps provide trim appearance and satisfactory ride.

The shock absorbers serve as an aid to wheel alignment by furnishing a dampening affect that protects the springs from sudden overloading or unloading action. Obviously, if the shock absorbers are not operating properly, the car will bounce excessively and steering angles will change oftener and to a greater extent.

Occasionally, steering angles will check out correctly on the alignment equipment, yet the car will not handle satisfactorily on the road. This situation could be caused by defective springs or shock absorbers, worn parts in the steering gear or front system, driving conditions, or habits of the driver.

One other chassis control feature that merits consideration is the use of stabilizers or "sway bars." Some cars require these bars to steady the chassis against front end roll and sway on turns. Stabilizers are designed to control this centrifugal tendency that forces a rising action on the side toward the inside of the turn.

With all of these weight balance factors to be checked out and corrected, it is obvious that wheel alignment is more than just an adjustment of the steering angles. It involves many essential preliminary steps ranging from tire inflation to weight on the wheels, and it concerns everything from habits of the driver to the wide range of physical forces exerted.

The whole theory of wheel alignment revolves around balanced weight distribution on the wheels and proper tire tread contact with the road surface while the vehicle is in motion.

FRONT WHEEL ANGULARITY

The angles involved in front wheel alignment are caster, camber, toe-in, steering axis inclination and toe-out on turns. They refer to the tilt of the wheels and steering axis, Figs. 39-10 through 39-15. These angles govern the way the front

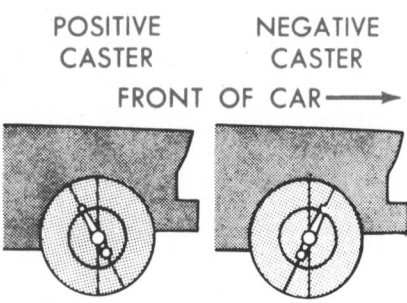

Fig. 39-10. Caster is degree of tilt of steering axis forward or backward from vertical center line of wheel.

wheels behave while the vehicle is in motion.

Actually, the alignment angles are so closely related that changing one will often change the others. In order to check and adjust them properly, it is necessary to use special equipment capable of a high degree of accuracy. In many cases, caster and camber specifications are given in minutes (fractions of a degree).

Here again, balance enters the picture. The adjustment goal

becomes a balanced relationship of the steering angles, with due regard for road and load factors involved in each individual case.

CASTER

Caster is the steering angle that utilizes the weight and momentum of the car's chassis to lead the front wheels in a straight path. See Figs. 39-1 and 39-10. Caster is the backward or forward tilt of the steering axis that tends to stabilize steering in a straight direction by placing the weight of the vehicle either ahead or behind the area of tire-to-road contact.

It would be easier to visualize the effect of the caster angle by projecting an imaginary line lengthwise through the center of the ball joints and downward to the road surface. This line, called the "steering axis," would be found to intersect the road at a point ahead of or in back of the center point of tire-to-road contact. Considering this, if the front wheels were given a generous amount of caster, they would be subjected to a leading or trailing action like a furniture caster that tends to line up and drag its wheel in the direction of movement.

"Positive" caster is the angular amount that the upper ball joint is farther back than the lower joint. "Negative" caster is the condition when the upper ball joint is farther ahead than the lower one. See Fig. 39-10. The caster angle, then, is the number of degrees (or fraction of one degree) that the steering axis is tilted backward or forward from the vertical axis of the front wheels.

Specifications for solid front axle systems call for as much as 8 or 9 degrees of positive caster as compared with the fractional-degree requirements of independent suspension. This reduction was possible because of the relatively smaller changes in the caster angle during the up-and-down movement of independently suspended wheels in relation to the frame.

This up-and-down movement will affect the other steering angles to a great extent regardless of the type of suspension involved. Camber and steering axis inclination, for example, vary considerably during fast stop and extreme bounce conditions.

CAMBER — STEERING AXIS INCLINATION

Camber is the inward or outward tilt of the wheel at the top, Fig. 39-11. It is built into the wheel spindle by forming

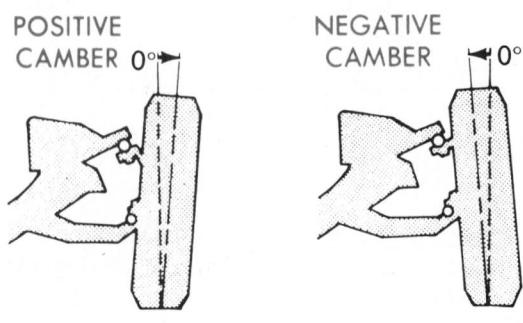

Fig. 39-11. Camber is amount wheel tilts in or out at top from its vertical center line.

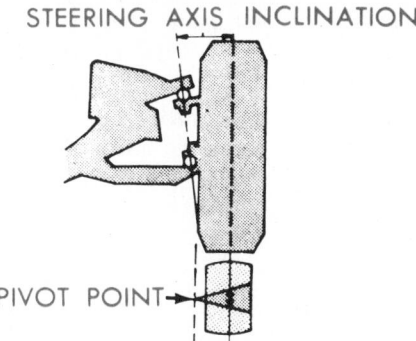

Fig. 39-12. Steering axis inclination is inward tilt of steering knuckle from vertical center line of wheel.

the spindle with a downward tilt to provide positive camber. Steering axis inclination is the inward tilt of the steering knuckle, Fig. 39-12. It is so interrelated with camber that they share a common side (vertical axis of wheel). The combination of these two angles forms what is known as the included angle.

The purpose of this two-angle team is to place the turning point of the wheel at the center of the tire tread contact area. To clarify this, remember that, originally, the front wheels were pivoted to swing in a vertical position. This created a difference between the pivoting center line and the wheel center line which caused the wheels to pull or scuff on rough roads.

The car manufacturers recognized this fact and went about solving it by tilting the pivoting center line in at the top (steering axis inclination) and tilting the wheel out at the top (camber). This created an included angle that intersected close to the center of tire tread contact and reduced the scuff area to a minimum. See Fig. 39-1.

When camber and steering axis inclination are correct, they contribute to steering ease and tire life. Also, by placing the tread contact area more nearly under the point of load, a "straightening up" tendency is provided that serves to minimize the need for a large caster angle.

To illustrate this, consider the movement of the front wheel spindle with the weight off the wheels. First, the downward tilt of the spindle provides camber. Then, with a vertical steering axis, the spindle would pivot at right angles and its tip would move in a horizontal plane when turning from one extreme to the other.

However, with the steering axis tilted inward (steering axis inclination), the end of the spindle will describe an arc that is noticeably lower in the extreme turn position than in the center or straight ahead position. In normal operation, the weight of the car prevents the spindle from moving up and down. Therefore, the car is forced upward when the front wheels are turned, and the force of gravity tends to straighten the wheels.

In this way, the weight of the car helps to provide an automatic steering effect brought about by accurate adjustment of the steering angles. Additional alignment benefits become apparent when some of the troubles caused by misalignment are noted. These include hard steering, wander, pull to one side and unequal or excessive tire wear.

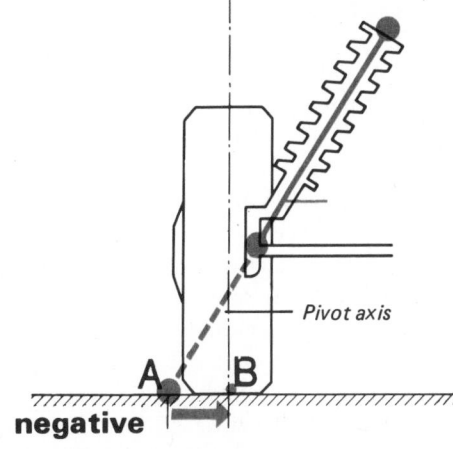

Fig. 39-13. Negative kingpin offset is advance by Volkswagen that gives small car steering a self-centering effect. Any added resistance to one front tire will cause that wheel to seek straight ahead path.

Also in the area of steering axis inclination, Volkswagen has come up with "Negative Kingpin Offset," a modification of MacPherson strut design. This term refers to the fact that the steering axis of each front wheel is offset so that an imaginary line drawn along the axis would strike the ground outside the center line of the tire, Fig. 39-13.

Most cars have a front end setup in which the steering axis is closer to vertical. In conventional design, a line drawn along the steering axis would strike the ground inside the center line of the tire. Both designs, conventional and VW, provide easy steering.

However, the side benefit of negative kingpin offset is a self-centering effect. Under uneven braking or rough road conditions, or if one front tire goes flat, a car with conventional geometry would pull toward the side with more resistance. With VW geometry, the wheel encountering more resistance automatically turns toward the straight ahead path.

TOE—IN

Equally important with respect to steering ease is the correct setting of toe-in. Toe-in is the term used to specify the amount (in fractions of an inch) that the front wheels are closer together in front than at the rear, when measured at hub

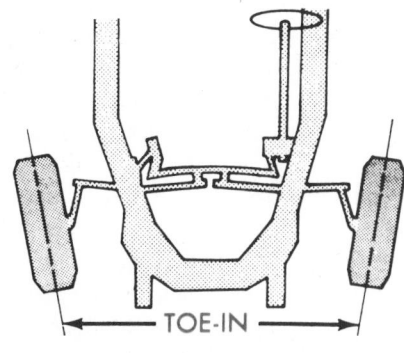

Fig. 39-14. Toe-in is amount front wheels are closer together in front than at rear at hub height.

height, Fig. 39-14. Toe-in specifications, for example, generally call for a setting of 1/16 in. to 3/16 in. Here again, precision testing equipment and careful measurement and correction will prevent any slipping or scuffing action between the tires and road.

Actually, the slight amount of toe-in that is specified serves to keep the front wheels running parallel on the road by offsetting other forces which tend to spread the wheels apart. The major force is the backward thrust of the road against the tire tread while the car is moving forward. Other factors include compensation for unavoidable play in the tie rod assembly and allowance for angular changes caused by wheel bounce or variations in road conditions.

If toe-in is incorrect, the tires will be dragged along the road, scuffing and featheredging the tread ribs. Changes in road or load conditions will affect more than one steering angle, and uneven tread wear patterns will result. Also in this respect, toe-in will change when other angular adjustments are made. For this reason, toe-in should be measured first and corrected last on all wheel alignment jobs.

From the mechanical standpoint, the parallel relationship between the front wheels is controlled by the tie rod and the angularity of the steering arms, Fig. 39-15. Since these

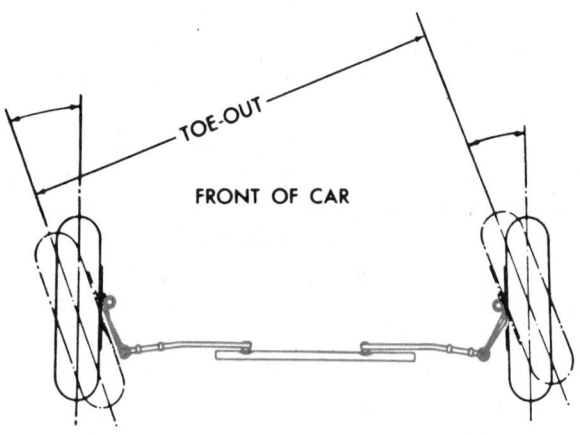

Fig. 39-15. Tie rods and steering arms control parallel relationship between front wheels, both in straight ahead driving and on turns.

connecting links are relatively rigid, it might be assumed that toe-in would remain constant. This could be the case when a single tie rod is used. But when a car is equipped with independent suspension and has more than one tie rod, toe-in will vary under excessive load or bounce conditions.

TOE—OUT ON TURNS

It is obvious that driving conditions make it impossible to keep the front wheels parallel at all times. Regardless of how accurately the front wheels are positioned for straight ahead driving, they could be out of their correct relative position on turns.

Considering that the outside wheel is approximately five

feet farther away from the point about which the car is turning, it must turn at a lesser angle and travel in a greater circle than the inside wheel. This condition is called "toe-out on turns," which means that each front wheel requires a separate turning radius to keep the inside tire from slipping and scuffing on turns, Fig. 39-16.

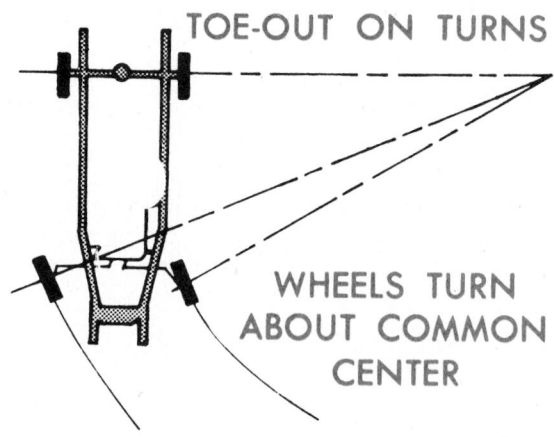

Fig. 39-16. Toe-out on turns is angular relationship between front wheels when turned to right or left.

Toe-out on turns, then, is the relationship between the front wheels which allows them to turn about a common center. To accomplish this, the steering arms are designed to angle several degrees inside of the parallel position, Fig. 39-17.

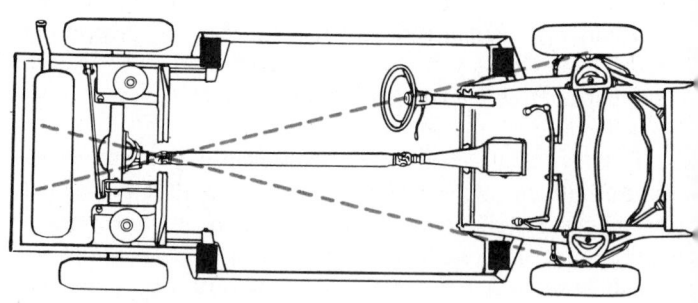

Fig. 39-17. Steering arms are angled inward to provide a separate turning radius for each front wheel.

The exact amount depends on the tread and wheelbase of the car and on the arrangement of the steering control linkage.

The theory of this design is that an imaginary line drawn through each steering arm will intersect near the differential. In practice, this serves to speed the action of steering arm on the inside of the turn as it moves toward the center line of the wheel spindle. The effect on the outside steering arm is to slow it down as it moves away from the center of the wheel spindle. Therefore, the outside wheel turns at a lesser angle, and its turning circle is greater. True rolling contact is obtained.

Consider that a turning car must pivot about some theoretical point along the extended center line of the rear axle. Then recall that the front wheels must turn about a common center. Put these facts together, and it becomes clear that the turning radius lines for both front wheels must intersect at some point along the rear axle center line, regardless of degree of turn. The sharper the turn, the nearer this point is to the car itself.

A typical specification for toe-out on turns calls for 23 deg. angularity on the inside wheel, while the outside wheel is turning 20 deg. If a bent steering arm is indicated, it must be replaced. However, all other possibilities should be eliminated:
1. All other steering angles must be correct.
2. Steering control linkage must be aligned properly.

REVIEW QUESTIONS – WHEEL ALIGNMENT

1. Name five things that influence tire tread contact with the road surface.
2. Name the five steering angles.
3. Does dynamic unbalance of the assembly lie in the plane of wheel rotation?
4. What is the correct terminology for the distance between the center points of the left tire tread and the right tire tread as they come in contact with the road?
   a. Wheelbase.
   b. Tread width.
   c. Toe-in.
5. Name three things beside improperly adjusted steering angles that could cause car handling complaints.
6. If the upper ball joint is farther back than the lower ball joint, what angularity is the wheel said to have?
   a. Positive caster.
   b. Positive camber.
   c. Positive steering axis inclination.
   d. Negative steering axis inclination.
7. Which two steering angles make up the included angle?
8. What is the purpose of the included angle?
9. When a car is turning, should the front wheels toe-in or toe-out?
10. Why are the steering arms angled several degrees inside the parallel position?
11. What is "Negative Kingpin Offset?"

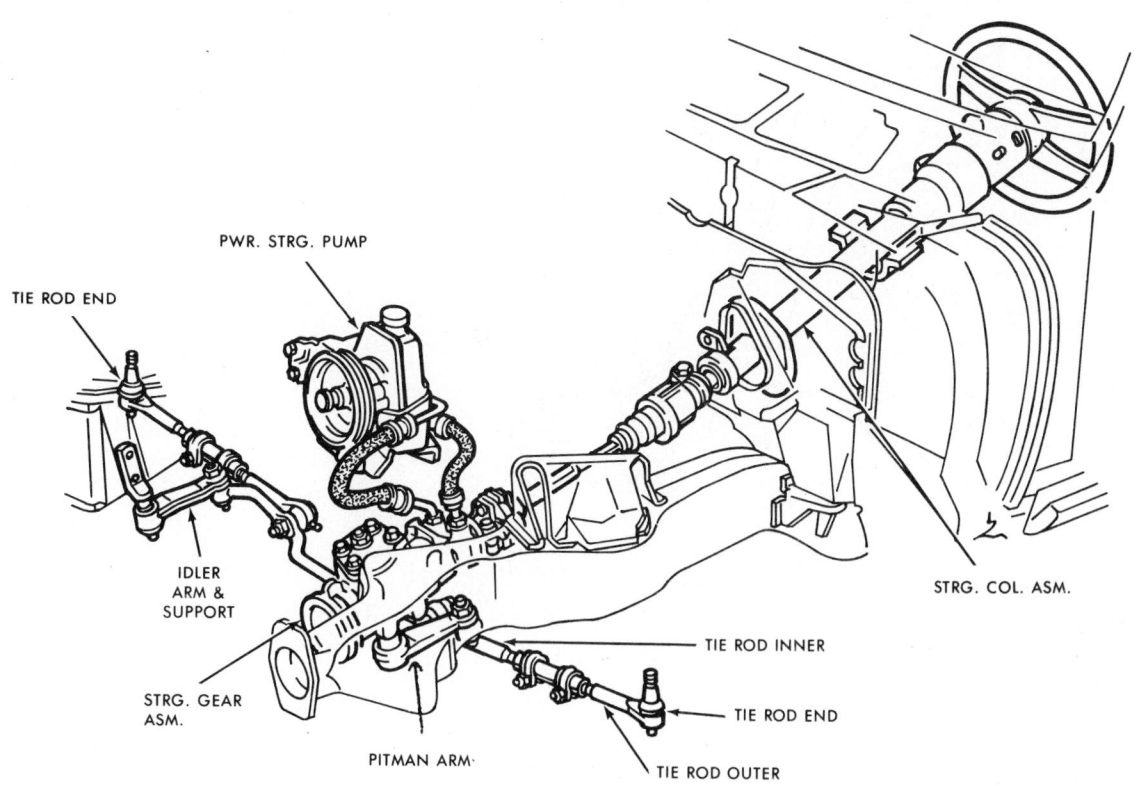

One most important wheel alignment factor is front wheel toe-in, which involves adjustment of the tie rods to center the steering wheel and to keep the front wheels running parallel on the road. (Pontiac Motor Div., General Motors Corp.)

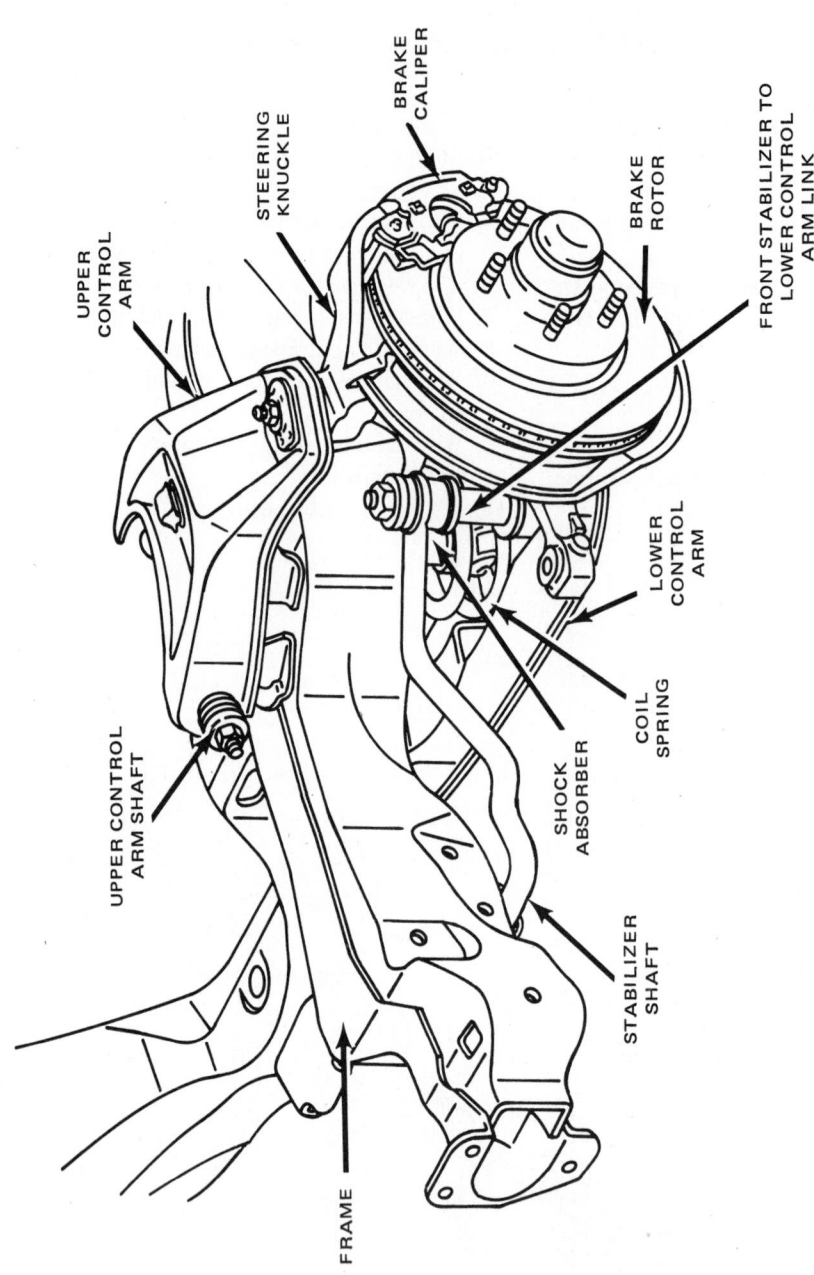

UPPER CONTROL ARM

STEERING KNUCKLE

BRAKE CALIPER

BRAKE ROTOR

FRONT STABILIZER TO LOWER CONTROL ARM LINK

UPPER CONTROL ARM SHAFT

FRAME

STABILIZER SHAFT

SHOCK ABSORBER

COIL SPRING

LOWER CONTROL ARM

Front suspension is the wheel support system that is vital to wheel alignment correction. Points of adjustment for both caster and camber are contained within these support members. (Pontiac Motor Div., General Motors Corp.)

WHEEL ALIGNMENT CORRECTION

Wheel alignment correction calls for a careful determination of whether or not the problem lies in misalignment, steering, suspension or in the wheel and tire assemblies. A good alignment specialist must be able to visualize the behavior of a loaded vehicle going 70 mph on a superhighway, while making corrective adjustments on an empty car standing on an alignment rack.

A thorough understanding of the principles involved and enough imagination to picture actual operating conditions are absolutely essential in this specialized field. In addition, the service technician must have and know how to use equipment of outstanding accuracy.

As for the vehicles themselves, the need for frequent and regular wheel alignment checks has increased with technological advances. Power steering, softer springing, rubber-bushed suspension parts, improved soundproofing, the use of wide tread tires and lower inflation pressures allow constant abuse of car suspension without forewarning the driver.

You can add to this: more moving parts in modern suspension systems; more miles driven per car per year. With this set of circumstances in mind, most manufacturers recommend wheel alignment checks at least once a year. Or, for another rule-of-thumb, wheel alignment should be checked at the first sign of uneven tread wear.

CONSIDER INTERRELATED ANGLES

Remember, alignment correction includes adjustment of all interrelated factors affecting the running and steering of the front wheels of the vehicle. Changing one angle will often change others, Fig. 40-1, so it is necessary to recheck all angles when one is changed.

The method of wheel alignment inspection and detection varies with type of equipment but, generally, the angles should be checked in the following order:
1. Front suspension height.
2. Caster.
3. Camber.
4. Toe-in
5. Steering axis inclination.
6. Toe-out on turns.

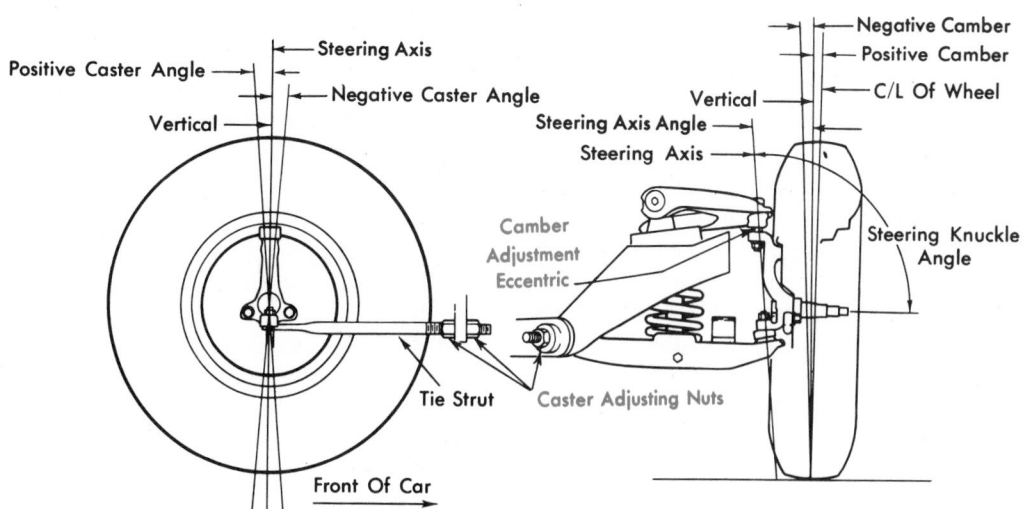

Fig. 40-1. Interrelation of alignment angles is shown in these views of a front wheel with coil-spring, ball-joint front suspension. Note typical points of adjustment for caster and camber.

However, certain preliminary checks should be made to eliminate obvious problems and to set up the vehicle for the alignment tests.

PRELIMINARY CHECKS

Ordinarily, cars should be checked for alignment at "curb height" and "curb weight." (Certain car manufacturers specify use of alignment spacers to insure proper suspension heights.) "Curb weight" means the basic automobile, less passengers, with a full fuel tank and proper amounts of coolant and lubricants. The spare tire and wheel, jack and jack handle must be in design position, and the front seats should be in their rear-most position.

Then proceed as follows:

Check front tires to see that tread wear is approximately the same, and not abnormal, Fig. 40-2. Test for recommended

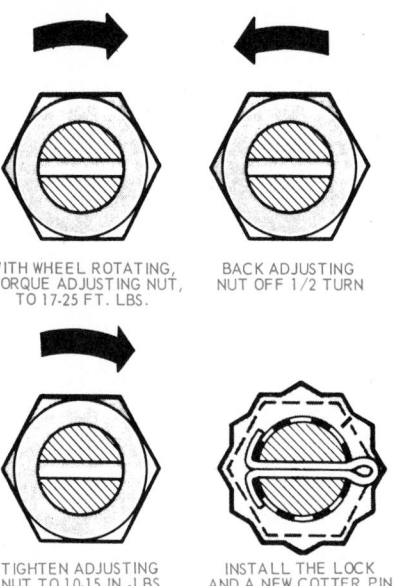

WITH WHEEL ROTATING, TORQUE ADJUSTING NUT, TO 17-25 FT. LBS.

BACK ADJUSTING NUT OFF 1/2 TURN

TIGHTEN ADJUSTING NUT TO 10-15 IN.-LBS.

INSTALL THE LOCK AND A NEW COTTER PIN

Fig. 40-3. Front wheel tapered roller bearings should not be preloaded Using a dial indicator, end play should be from 0 to .005 in. on most cars. Ford recommendation is shown.

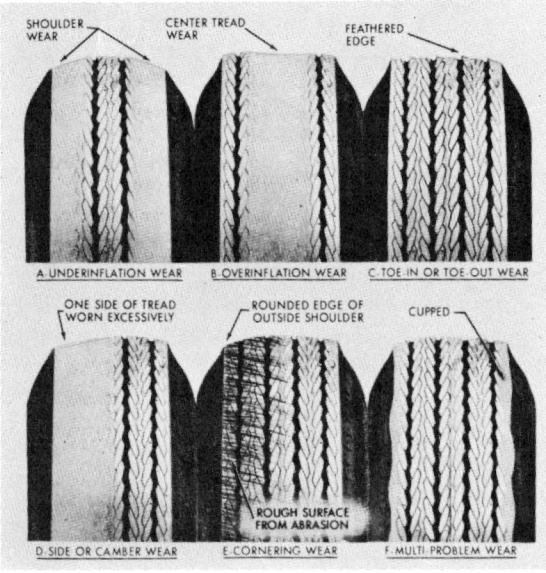

SHOULDER WEAR

CENTER TREAD WEAR

FEATHERED EDGE

A. UNDERINFLATION WEAR

B. OVERINFLATION WEAR

C. TOE-IN OR TOE-OUT WEAR

ONE SIDE OF TREAD WORN EXCESSIVELY

ROUNDED EDGE OF OUTSIDE SHOULDER

CUPPED

ROUGH SURFACE FROM ABRASION

D. SIDE OR CAMBER WEAR

E. CORNERING WEAR

F. MULTI-PROBLEM WEAR

Fig. 40-2. Comparison of worn tire treads depicts pattern of wear and what caused it. If alignment is correct, life of tires depends on car operating conditions and driving habits.

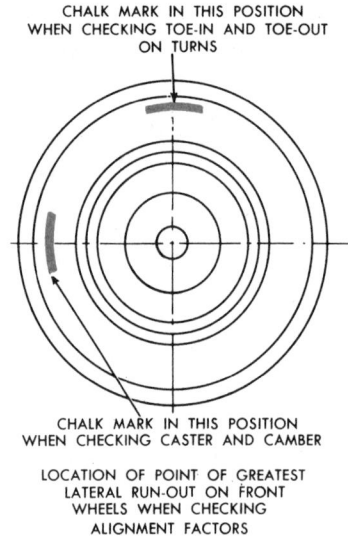

CHALK MARK IN THIS POSITION WHEN CHECKING TOE-IN AND TOE-OUT ON TURNS

CHALK MARK IN THIS POSITION WHEN CHECKING CASTER AND CAMBER

LOCATION OF POINT OF GREATEST LATERAL RUN-OUT ON FRONT WHEELS WHEN CHECKING ALIGNMENT FACTORS

air pressure in all four tires and remove stones and caked mud from wheels and tires.

Check wheel lugs for looseness and/or improper installation. Test action and rebound of all shock absorbers by jouncing all four corners of car. Car should rebound slowly, not bounce.

Test steering effort and steering wheel return from both directions. Check for inconsistent effort, harshness, noise, binding or excessive free play. Check steering gear for excessive backlash and for "high point," with reference to steering wheel position and straight ahead position of front wheels. Adjust steering gear, if required.

Raise the vehicle and test front wheel bearings for looseness. Grasp tire at top and bottom and try to rock assembly on its spindle. Adjust bearings, if necessary, Fig. 40-3. Use a dial indicator to check each front wheel and tire

Fig. 40-4. Point of maximum lateral runout should be marked on front tire sidewall. Place mark to front or rear for caster/camber checks, at top for toe-in.

assembly for runout, making sure that wheel is not damaged and tire beads are seated in rim of wheel. Mark point of maximum runout on tire sidewall, Fig. 40-4, then spin each front wheel and balance as required.

Manually check front end parts for looseness of wear. Inspect control arm pivot shafts or bolts, suspension ball joints, struts, stabilizer and all mounting bolts and nuts. Visually check condition of suspension ball joints and seals. Inspect all springs for sagging or breakage. Check for looseness of brake caliper attaching bolts on vehicles so equipped.

Test for looseness of steering gear attaching bolts at frame. Manually check for looseness or wear at all steering pivot

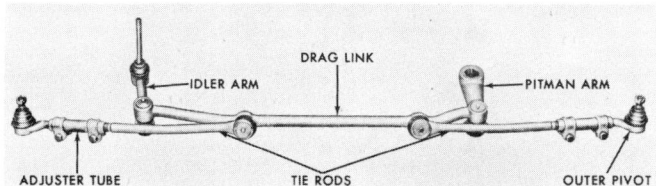

Fig. 40-5. Typical steering linkage arrangement as viewed from above. Points of greatest wear include tie rod ends, idler arm bushings and relay rod-to-tie rod connections.

points: pitman arm, relay rod, tie rod ends and idler arm, Fig. 40-5. Inspect for bent steering arms.

SETTING UP THE CAR

Lower the car and drive it far enough in a straight line to establish the straight ahead position of the front wheels. Then, mark the steering wheel hub and steering column collar for use as a reference point during the alignment procedure, Fig. 40-6.

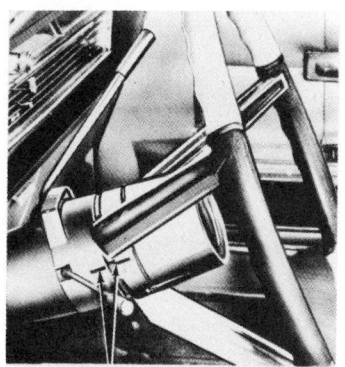

Fig. 40-6. Mark straight ahead position of front wheels on steering wheel hub and steering column collar for future reference in making alignment checks.

At this time, rear wheel track can be checked by running the car in and out of a wet area and examining the tread marks left by the front and rear tires. Since front and rear tread widths are seldom the same, the marks may not coincide. However, there should be equal spacing between marks left by the left front tire and left rear, and also between the right front tire and right rear.

If the accuracy of the car's tracking ability is questionable, make more precise measurements of the frame-to-wheels relationship. See Figs. 39-5 to 39-8.

MEASURING SUSPENSION HEIGHT

To prepare the car for a suspension height check, jounce it lightly front and rear, until suspension parts equalize. If excessive friction in the suspension system is suspected, make two quick checks of bumper height and compare the difference. First lift the car manually by the bumper and let it settle

slowly to normal standing height. Measure from the center of the bumper to the floor. Then push down on the bumper and release it slowly. Take this measurement and compare it with the first. If the two height measurements are not within one inch of each other, excessive suspension friction exists.

If the above checks are within the limit, jounce the car lightly and measure front suspension height at the points specified by the car manufacturer. Then, compare the measurements with specifications, Fig. 40-7. If the suspension

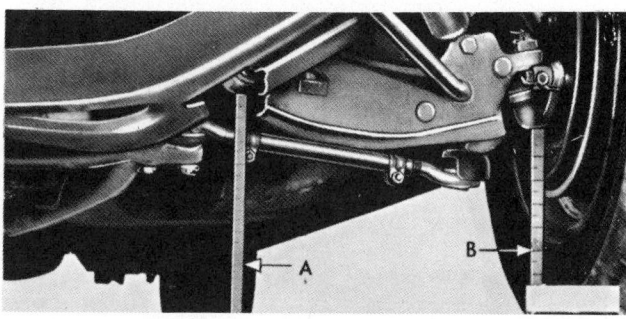

Fig. 40-7. Suspension height is measured, left and right, to help guarantee accuracy of angular checks which follow.

height is below minimum requirements on cars with coil springs, replace both springs. If one side is within specifications and the other side is not, replace the weak spring. In cars equipped with torsion bars, make the necessary adjustments to obtain correct front suspension height, Figs. 40-8 and 40-9.

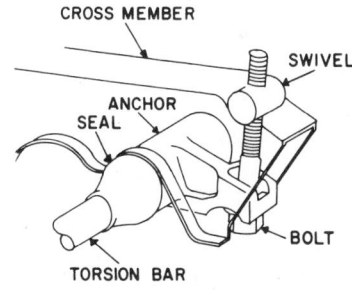

Fig. 40-8. Older Chrysler Corporation cars with torsion bars have adjusting device located at rear anchors in frame center cross member.

If alignment spacers are required for making certain angular checks: place car on floating turntables; raise car body and install spacers front and rear; lower car body. Generally, spacers in front are placed between suspension lower control arms and frame spring pockets, Fig. 40-10. At rear, install spacers between rear axle housing and frame, Fig. 40-11.

CHECKING AND SETTING CASTER

Caster is the angle measured between a true vertical line through the center of the wheel and the center line through the upper and lower ball joints. See Fig. 40-1. To increase

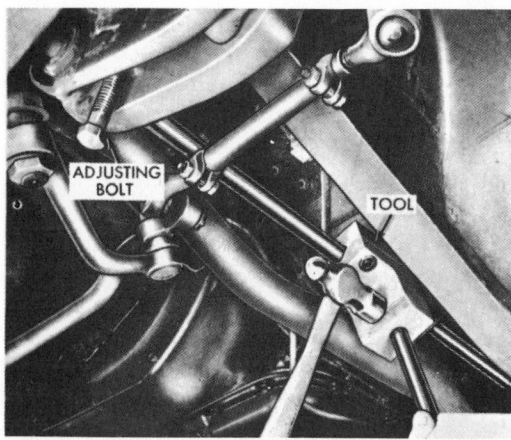

Fig. 40-9. Later Chrysler cars, except Imperial models, utilize torsion bar adjustment at front suspension lower control arm. A special torsion bar removing tool is shown.

Fig. 40-10. Correct suspension height is such a critical preliminary alignment step that some manufacturers recommend using alignment height spacers during camber and caster checks.

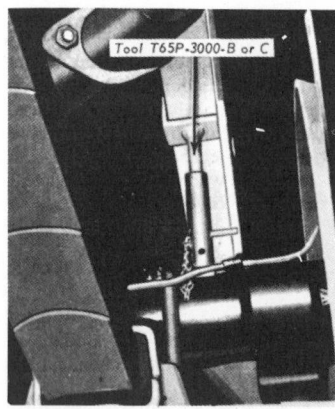

Fig. 40-11. Alignment spacers, front or rear, serve to support car body at specified height above wheels, so alignment checks are valid.

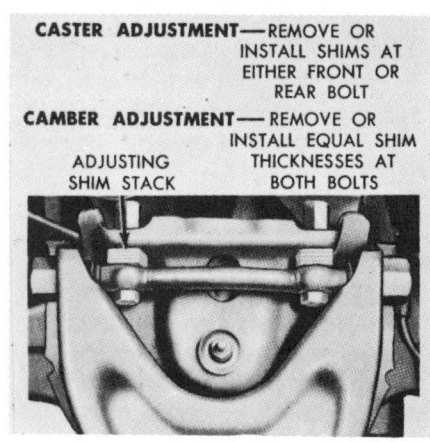

Fig. 40-12. Shim adjustment of caster and camber provides simple expedient for positioning suspension control arms.

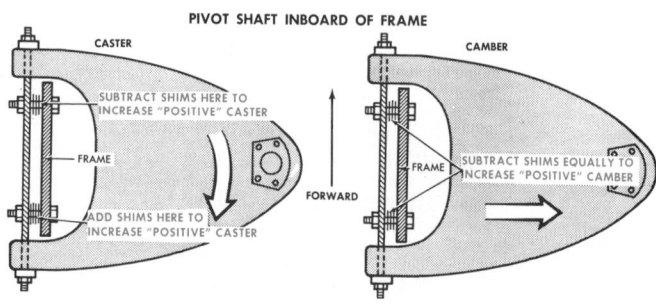

Fig. 40-13. This shim adjustment moves pivot shaft farther inboard when shims are added, in contrast to outboard movement in Fig. 40-12.

However, if the control arm pivot shaft is located inboard of the frame bracket, then the entire shimming procedure is reversed. See Fig. 40-13.

Either of these caster adjustments affect camber, so caster and camber adjustments should be made simultaneously. Detailed charts are available that give exact shim changes for each misalignment situation.

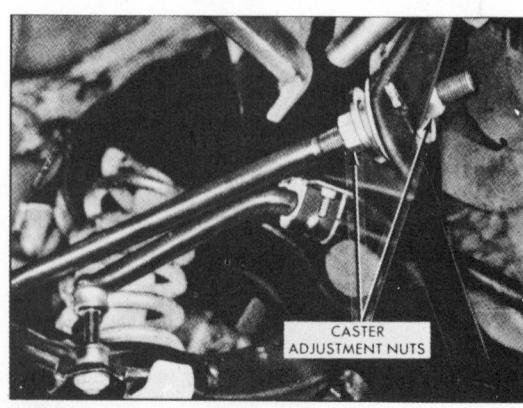

Fig. 40-14. Some late model cars use diagonal strut rods, or tie-struts, as a means of caster adjustment. Struts also lend support to lower control arms.

positive caster, move the upper ball joint to the rear or the lower ball joint to the front.

Many cars are provided with shims under the upper control arm mounting bolts, Fig. 40-12. In this design, transferring shims from under the rear bolt to the front bolt increases caster. Reversing this transfer of shims decreases caster.

Another popular caster adjustment design is the strut rod type. With this arrangement, adjustable strut rods run diagonally from the lower control arms to the frame front cross member, Fig. 40-14. To make an adjustment, loosen the locknuts at the forward end of the struts, then shorten the rod to increase caster (this moves lower ball joint forward). Lengthening the rod by locknut adjustment decreases caster.

Ford cars have used still another means of caster adjustment, Fig. 40-15. Elongated bolt holes are provided in the

Fig. 40-15. Caster and camber is adjusted on some Chrysler and Ford cars by moving pivot shaft of upper control arm in or out by means of elongated bolt holes. Special tools aid in moving and holding pivot shaft.

chassis frame where the upper control arm pivot shaft attaches. To make an adjustment, loosen the attaching bolts and slide the shaft in or out at the front or rear to tilt the steering axis forward or backward as required by the prescribed caster setting. Here again the same adjustment point is used for obtaining correct camber, so both angular adjustments should be made simultaneously.

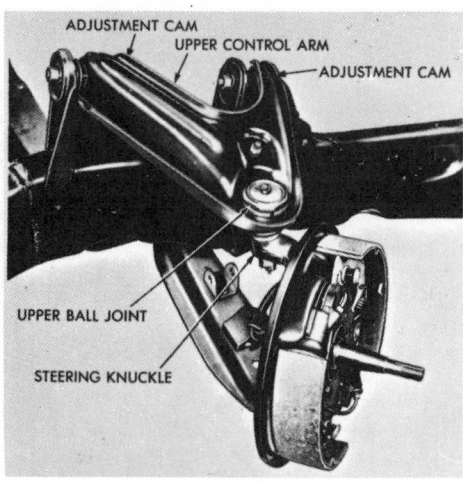

Fig. 40-16. Cam-bolt adjustment at inner ends of upper control arm on Chrysler cars, offers convenient way of positioning arm and setting correct camber.

Some cars have cam-bolt adjustments located at the inner ends of the upper control arms, Fig. 40-16, or at the lower control arms, Fig. 40-17. After loosening the locknut, turn

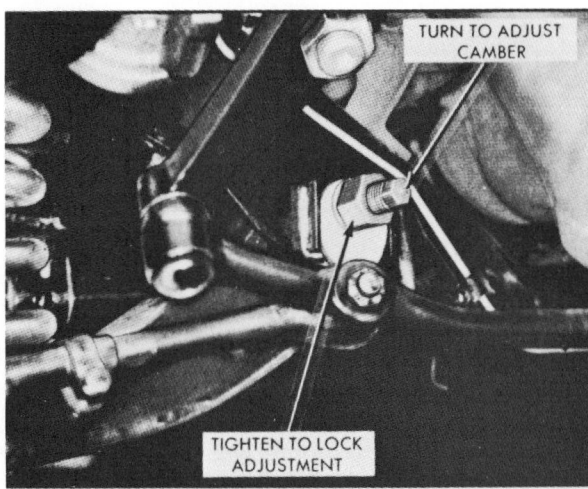

Fig. 40-17. Cam-bolt adjustment on lower control arm of Chevrolet cars is accessible and close to strut bar adjustment of caster, making it easier to balance angles.

each cam bolt to reposition the control arm and obtain correct caster and camber settings. For least effect on camber, the correct caster setting can be obtained by turning the cams an equal amount in opposite directions.

Some older models with kingpins incorporate caster-camber adjusting pins at the outboard end of the upper control arms. To make an adjustment, remove the grease fitting and loosen the clamp bolt. Then turn the adjusting pin to tilt the kingpin fore and aft to get the correct caster setting.

ADJUSTING CAMBER

Camber is the angle formed by the true vertical center line and the vertical center line of the tire. See Fig. 40-1. Increase positive camber by moving the upper ball joint outward or lower ball joint inward. On cars with shims under the upper control arm pivot shaft bolts, add an equal number of shims under front and rear bolts to increase positive camber, remove an equal number of shims to decrease camber, Fig. 40-12. This adjustment must be made in conjunction with the caster adjustment to relate the angles to each other.

If the control arm pivot shaft is located inboard of the frame bracket, reverse the shimming procedure. Naturally, if the shims are located under the lower control arm pivot shaft, the opposite effects are obtained, so opposite shimming procedure must be followed.

Other types of camber adjustments that are integrated with caster settings (elongated bolt holes in chassis frame, cam bolts, and upper control arm adjusting pins) must be adjusted with both caster and camber settings in mind. This means many trial-and-error settings are necessary. although several car manufacturers and equipment manufacturers provide detailed charts giving the number of shims or amount of cam-bolt rotation necessary to obtain a given degree of correction.

The other relatively new camber adjustment design has a camber eccentric located in the steering knuckle upper support, Fig. 40-18. To make an adjustment, loosen locknut

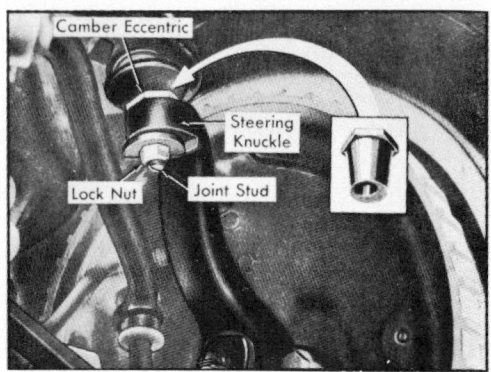

Fig. 40-18. Many Cadillac cars are fitted with camber eccentrics at base of upper ball joints. This setup is used in conjunction with strut-rod type caster adjustment.

one turn, tap bottom of stud with a soft mallet to free the eccentric in the knuckle. Turn the eccentric to obtain the specified camber angle, then tighten the locknut and recheck camber. This type of camber adjustment is usually used in conjunction with strut rods for caster adjustment.

In all cases, follow the manufacturer's recommendation for the camber setting. If, however, the vehicle is equipped with radial tires, set camber as close to zero as specifications will allow. This also holds true for the toe-in setting.

CORRECTING TOE—IN

Toe-in is the amount in fractions of an inch that the front wheels are closer together in front than at the rear. It is measured at hub height with the wheels in the straight ahead position. Most cars utilize two adjustable tie rods to facilitate the adjustment, Fig. 40-5.

To make the toe-in adjustment, loosen the clamp bolts on the tie rod sleeves and turn the sleeves to adjust tie rod length, Fig. 40-19. A tie rod behind the front wheels must be lengthened to increase toe-in; a tie rod ahead of the front wheels must be shortened.

However, tie rod adjustment also controls the position of the steering wheel. So the following "centering" adjustment

should be made after correct toe-in has been established. By turning each tie rod adjusting sleeve, shorten or lengthen each tie rod an equal amount to center the steering wheel without disturbing the toe-in adjustment.

In some cases, alignment spacers are specified to be in place during the toe-in adjustment. In others, the spacers are removed and the car must be correct curb weight before the adjustment can be made.

CHECKING STEERING AXIS INCLINATION

Steering axis inclination is the angle formed by the true vertical center line and the center line of the upper and lower ball joints. See Fig. 40-1. It is created by the inward tilt of the steering knuckle and is not adjustable. If steering axis inclination is out of specifications, replace the steering knuckle and check all alignment factors.

TOE—OUT ON TURNS

Toe-out on turns is the variation in the respective turning angles of the front wheels to avoid side slip on turns. It is built into the steering arms and is not adjustable. To get comparative readings, place the car on floating turntables, with weight of car on wheels. Set the inside wheel to a 20 deg. turn, then check the reading of the outside wheel against specifications.

Repeat this check with the wheels turned in the opposite direction. If all other angles are correct and toe-out on turns is not, replace the steering arm on the side that is out of specifications.

Straightening or welding of parts should not be attempted. Bending of parts when cold may cause stresses and cracks. Straightening by heat will destroy the original heat treatment. Welding will change the grain structure of the metal.

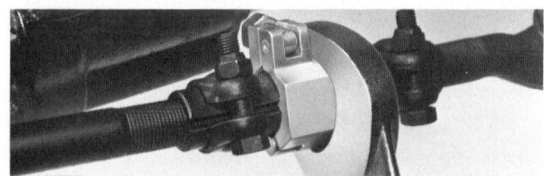

Fig. 40-19. Tie rod sleeves permit adjustment of toe-in. When tightening clamp, open side should be down and within 45 deg. of vertical to avoid interference with frame.

Fig. 40-20. Checks for toe-in and toe-out on turns are an important part of wheel alignment troubleshooting. (Ammco Tools, Inc.)

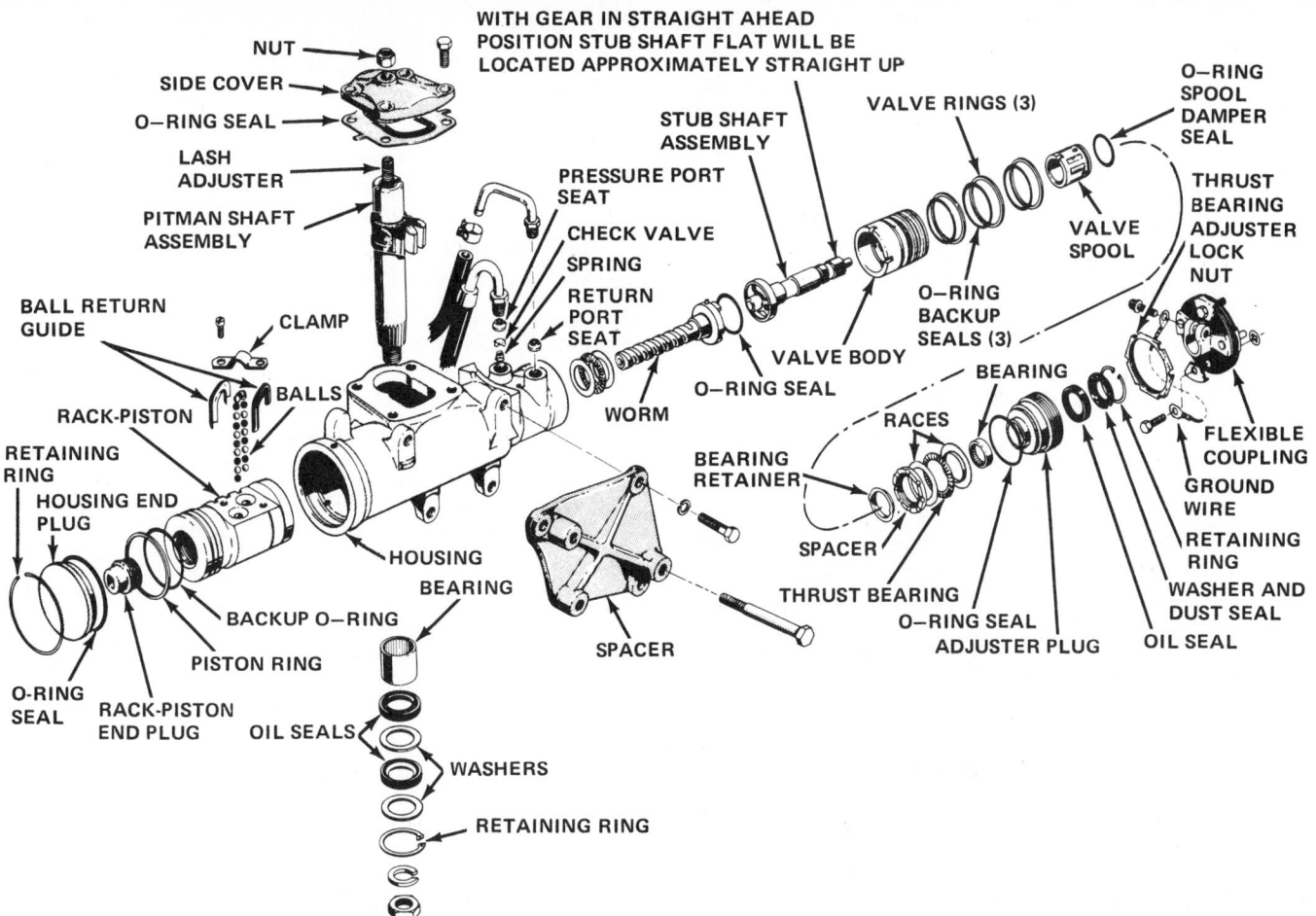

Fig. 40-21. Increased number of parts used in power steering integral unit complicates service procedures, although control valve adjustment is common correction. Rotary valve system displaces fluid to provide hydraulic pressure assists only when turning. (American Motors Corp.)

ALIGNMENT TROUBLESHOOTING

Proper steering control depends on more than just the steering system. Suspension and wheel alignment contribute so much to steering that all three must be considered when troubleshooting car handling complaints. See Figs. 40-20 through 40-24.

Bear in mind that the car, load and passengers must be balanced above the tires and springs while the vehicle is being subjected to many and varied driving conditions. This weight on the wheels moves up and down with road irregularities, tends to go sideways from the action of centrifugal force and wind pressures, and alternately shifts forward and backward under acceleration and braking. Or, there may be an unequal distribution of load because of:

1. Engine torque reaction on the frame.
2. Uneven passenger loading.
3. Uneven cargo loading.

Usually there is no quick easy remedy for a given handling problem. A series of causes and effects must be analyzed with due regard for the alignment theories involved. Often a combination of minor defects add up to more serious trouble.

The following alignment troubleshooting check list gives some of the more common causes of car handling problems:

Shimmy or Wheel Tramp

1. Incorrect or unequal tire pressures.
2. Cupped, eccentric or bulged tires.
3. Unbalanced wheels.
4. Out-of-round wheel or brake drum.
5. Weak or inoperative shock absorbers.
6. Loose wheel bearing adjustment.
7. Incorrect front wheel alignment, particularly caster.
8. Loose or worn control arm bushings.
9. Loose or worn suspension ball joints.
10. Loose or worn steering linkage.
11. Loose steering gear on frame.
12. Loose steering gear adjustment.
13. Inoperative stabilizer.
14. Loose or worn strut bushings.

Hard or Rough Ride

1. High air pressure in tires.
2. Wrong type or size of tire.
3. Tight steering gear adjustment.
4. Incorrect wheel alignment, particularly caster.
5. Inoperative shock absorbers.
6. Overloaded or unevenly loaded vehicle.
7. Sagging or broken spring.
8. Lack of lubrication, front suspension steering linkage.
9. Binding front suspension parts.

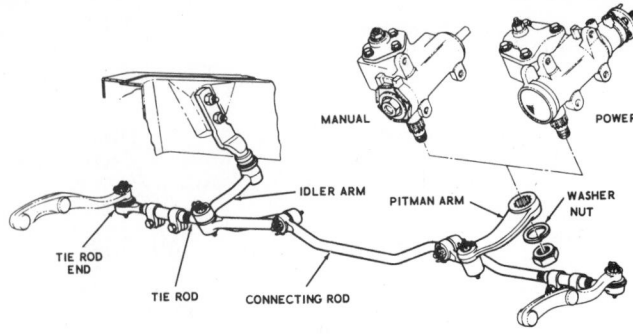

Fig. 40-22. Exploded view shows how manual and power steering gears use basically same steering linkage to turn front wheels.

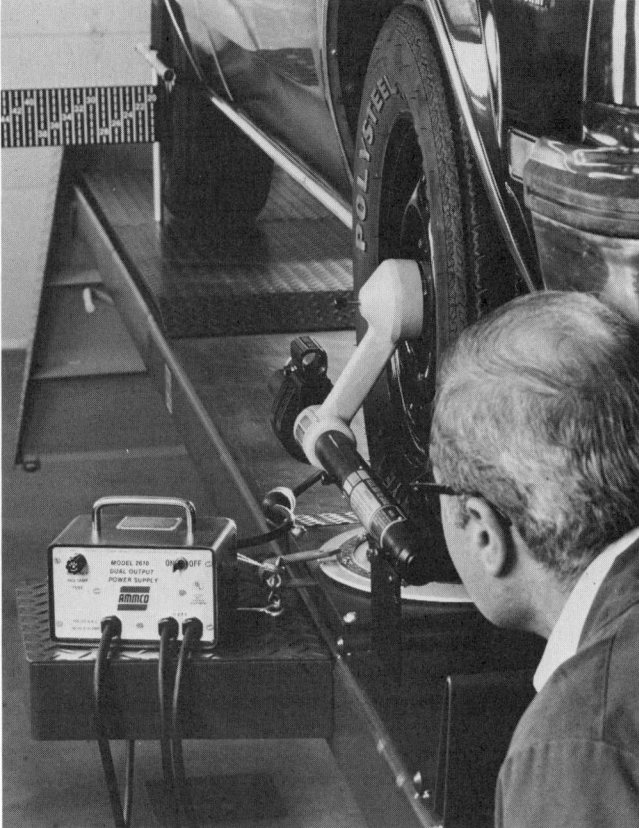

Fig. 40-23. All four wheels must be centered and tracking before wheel alignment correction. To check, mechanic is sighting through scope of a wheel tracking and toe gauge at a flag mounted on rear tire. A bright red dot rests on a numbered line. That reading is compared with a left side reading. If numbers agree, all four wheels are centered and tracking. If not, adjustments are made at front tie rods.
(Ammco Tools, Inc.)

Car Leads to One Side

1. Unequal tire pressures.
2. Varied tire sizes.
3. Unevenly loaded vehicle.
4. Dragging front brakes.
5. Tight front wheel bearings.
6. Bent spindle, spindle arm or steering knuckle.
7. Incorrect or uneven front wheel alignment.

8. Loose strut bushings.
9. Sagging or broken front spring.
10. Inoperative shock absorber.
11. Broken rear spring center bolt.
12. Off-center rear spring center bolt.
13. Bent rear axle housing.
14. Out-of-line frame or underbody.

Wander to Either Side

1. Incorrect or uneven tire pressures.
2. Varied tire sizes or excessive wear.
3. Unmatched tire construction.
4. Overloaded or unevenly loaded vehicle.
5. Tight front wheel bearing adjustment.
6. Bent spindle, spindle arm or steering knuckle.
7. Incorrect front wheel alignment.
8. Tight suspension ball joints.
9. Binding control arm shafts.
10. Tight idler arm bushing.
11. Loose, worn or damaged steering linkage.
12. Loose steering gear on frame.
13. Incorrect steering gear adjustment.
14. Inoperative shock absorbers.
15. Broken rear spring center bolt.

Rear Suspension Out of Line

1. Broken rear spring center bolt.
2. Off-center rear spring center bolt.
3. Broken rear spring main leaf.
4. Mislocated rear spring front hanger.
5. Bent rear axle housing.
6. Out-of-line frame or underbody.

Uneven Tire Tread Wear

1. Incorrect tire pressures.
2. Failure to rotate tires.
3. Incorrect front wheel alignment, particularly camber and toe-in.
4. Excessive wheel runout.
5. Bent spindle, spindle arm or steering knuckle.
6. Grabbing brakes.
7. Loose, worn or damaged suspension parts.
8. Excessive speed on turns.

Tire Squeal on Turns

1. Low air pressure in tires.
2. Varied tire sizes.
3. Bent spindle, spindle arm or steering knuckle.
4. Incorrect front wheel alignment, particularly toe-in.
5. Loose or weak shock absorbers.

Noise in System

1. Loose front wheel bearing adjustment.
2. Loose shock absorber mountings.
3. Loose steering gear adjustment.
4. Loose steering gear on frame.
5. Worn steering linkage.
6. Worn control arm bushings.

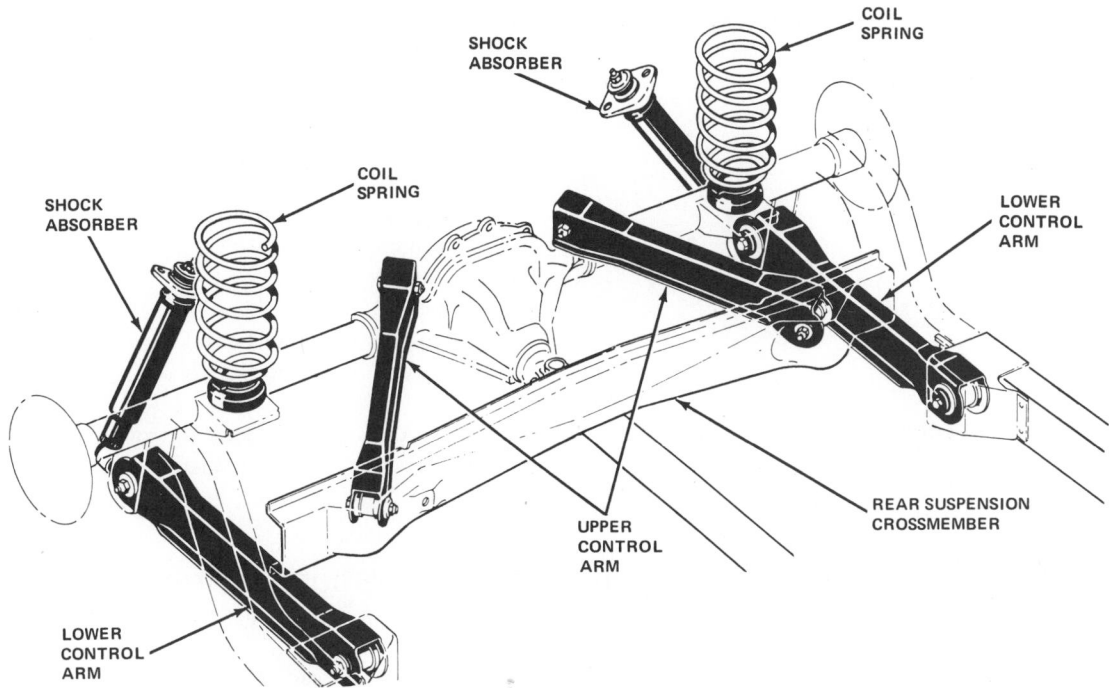

Fig. 40-24. Typical rear suspension system utilizes coil springs, shock absorbers and three or four control arms, or links, to connect rear axle housing to frame.

7. Loose suspension strut bushings.
8. Insufficient suspension ball joint lubrication.
9. Worn idler arm bushings.
10. Loose or worn spring shackles.
11. Loose or worn stabilizer bushings.

POWER STEERING TROUBLESHOOTING

When a car is equipped with power steering, it is important to make sure that the wheels are in correct alignment, that tires are properly inflated, and all parts of the steering linkage are adequately lubricated and in good operating condition.

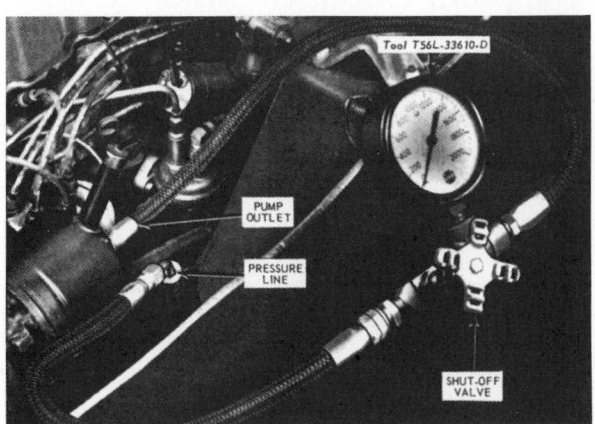

Fig. 40-25. Pressure gauge for testing power steering system is connected in series between pump outlet and pressure line hose. Test setup calls for shutoff valve so that tests can be made with unrestricted flow or under load.

Power steering may prevent the driver from realizing that binding or looseness exists, so he may ignore it until serious damage is done.

Use a suitably calibrated pressure gauge to check hydraulic pressures that may approach 1450 psi, Fig. 40-25. Power steering pressure lines are usually marked for high or low pressure. In any case, different fittings are used for attachment to the pump and steering gear power cylinder.

When checking fluid pressure, the engine and the power steering fluid should be at normal operating temperatures. Maximum pressure will be generated with the steering wheel held in the extreme turn position.

NOTE: Do not hold wheel in extreme turn position for more than a few seconds or it may cause undue wear or damage to pump parts.

Check the Alignment Troubleshooting check list for causes common to both manual and power systems. Then, follow this check list to pinpoint the cause of problems in the power steering system:

Hard Steering
1. Loose pump V-belt.
2. Low fluid level.
3. Insufficient pump pressure.
4. Tight or frozen steering shaft bushings.
5. Binding steering wheel.
6. Low front suspension height.
7. Incorrect steering gear adjustment.
8. Sticking pressure control valve.
9. External oil leaks.
10. Internal oil leaks.
11. Air in fluid.

Excessive Steering Looseness

1. Incorrect steering gear adjustment.
2. Maladjusted pressure control valve.
3. Air in fluid.

Poor Return from Turns

1. Tight steering shaft bushings.
2. Misaligned steering gear.
3. Binding steering wheel.
4. Sticking pressure control valve.
5. Internal fluid leakage.
6. Air in fluid.

Temporary Loss of Power Assist

1. Loose pump V-belt.
2. Low fluid level.

3. Internal fluid leakage.
4. Too slow engine idle speed.
5. Air in fluid.
6. Binding steering linkage.

Noise in System

1. Sticking pressure control valve.
2. Loose pump V-belt.
3. Low fluid level.
4. Air in fluid.
5. Scored pump vanes or body.
6. Improperly routed pressure hoses.

NOTE: A hissing or squealing sound may occur in any power steering system when steering wheel is held in extreme turn position. This is normal, unless it is especially loud.

REVIEW QUESTIONS – WHEEL ALIGNMENT CORRECTION

1. Are alignment angles independent of each other or interrelated?
2. Generally, does the adjustment of front wheel roller bearings call for end play or preload?
3. Each front wheel and tire assembly should be checked for runout and balance before checking alignment angles. Yes or No?
4. Can front suspension height be adjusted on Chrysler cars with torsion bars?
5. How are alignment spacers used?
   a. As a means of adjusting position of control arms to set caster and camber.
   b. As a means of supporting car body above wheels for alignment checks.
6. Name two common caster adjusting points.
7. How is toe-in adjusted?
   a. Shortening or lengthening tie rods.
   b. Shortening or lengthening relay rod.
   c. Shimming control arms.

8. Where is toe-in reading taken?
   a. At vertical center lines of front tires at top.
   b. At point of tread-to-road contact of left and right front tires.
   c. At hub height of left and right front wheels.
9. Why is correct toe-out on turns important?
10. How is toe-out on turns checked?
    a. With weight of car on wheels.
    b. With alignment spacers in place.
    c. With front wheels in straight ahead position.
11. If toe-out on turns is out of specifications, what correction is usually required?
12. If steering axis inclination is out of specification, what correction is usually required?
13. Which steering angle, if incorrect, causes shimmy or wheel tramp?
14. Which steering angles, if incorrect, cause uneven tire wear?
15. What type of tester is used to check for malfunctions in power steering system operation?

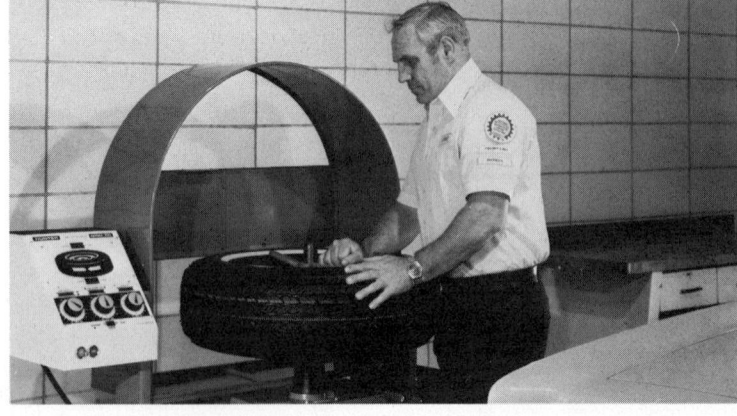

This computerized wheel balancer has digital display showing amount of imbalance to 1/10 oz. (2.8 gr) on upper and lower planes. (Hunter Engineering Co.)

AUTOMOTIVE BRAKES

WARNING: BREATHING DUST CONTAINING ASBESTOS FIBERS CAN CAUSE SERIOUS BODILY HARM. ASBESTOS IS A KNOWN CARCINOGEN — A SUBSTANCE WHICH TENDS TO CAUSE CANCER. SINCE BRAKE AND CLUTCH FRICTION MATERIALS CONTAIN ASBESTOS, DO NOT CREATE AIRBORNE DUST BY GRINDING, SANDING OR BY CLEANING THESE PARTS WITH A DRY BRUSH OR WITH COMPRESSED AIR. INSTEAD, WEAR A MASK WITH AN APPROVED FILTER AND FLUSH BRAKE AND CLUTCH PARTS WITH WATER OR USE A VACUUM SOURCE.

An automotive brake is a friction device designed to change power into heat. When the brakes are applied, they convert the power of momentum of the moving vehicle (kinetic energy) into heat by means of friction.

In an equally fitting description, "Brakes are a balanced set of mechanical devices used to retard the motion of the vehicle by means of friction."

FRICTION

Friction is the resistance to relative motion between two bodies in contact. Friction varies with different materials and with the condition of the materials. For example, friction is less between polished surfaces than between rough. It is less between surfaces of different material than between those of the same material. It is less when one surface rolls over the other, than when it slides.

Friction is caused by the interlocking of the projections and depressions of the two surfaces in contact. Rolling friction is supposed to be caused by the fact that the wheel indents (more or less) the surface over which it rolls. So, in effect, the wheel is always climbing a little hill. If the surface is very hard: the indentation is less, so that the friction will be less.

The amount of friction is proportional to the pressure between the two surfaces in contact. It is independent of the area of surface contact.

The amount of friction developed by any two bodies in contact is said to be their coefficient of friction. C.O.F. is found by dividing the force required to slide the weight over the surface, by the weight of the object.

For example, Fig. 41-1, if it requires a 60 lb. pull to slide a 100 lb. weight, then the coefficient of friction would be 60 divided by 100, or .60. If only 35 lb. is required to slide the 100 lb. weight, then the coefficient of friction is .35.

It has been established that the coefficient of friction will change with any variation of the condition of the surfaces. Any lubricant, of course, will greatly reduce the coefficient of friction. This is why it is so important to keep any oil or grease from brake lining. Even an extremely damp day will cause some variation in the coefficient of friction.

BRAKING FORCES

Tremendous forces are involved when braking a vehicle, because the vehicle must be brought to a stop in a much shorter time than is required to bring it up to speed. To better visualize this, make a comparison between the horsepower required to accelerate a vehicle, and the horsepower required to stop it.

A vehicle with a 100 hp engine requires about 60 seconds to accelerate to 60 mph. However, the same vehicle is expected to be able to stop from 60 mph in not more than 6 seconds. In other words, the brakes must do the same amount of work as the engine, but in one-tenth the time. This means they must develop approximately 1000 hp to stop the vehicle.

EFFECT OF WEIGHT AND SPEED

The effect of weight and speed of the vehicle on braking is important for both passenger cars and trucks. If the weight of the vehicle is doubled: the energy of motion to be changed into heat energy is doubled; and the amount of heat to be dissipated and absorbed also will be doubled. For this reason, it is important that vehicles not be overloaded.

The effect of higher speeds on braking is much more serious. If the speed is doubled, four times as much stopping power must be developed. At the same time, the brakes must absorb or dissipate four times as much heat.

It naturally follows that if both weight and speed of a

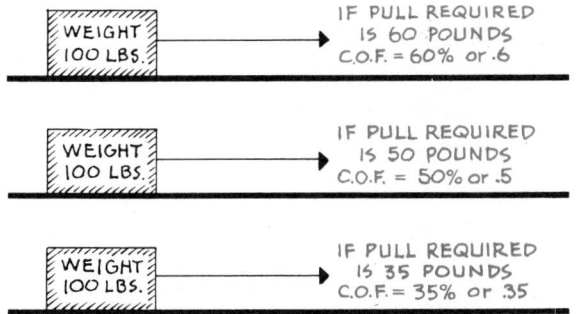

Fig. 41-1. Coefficient of friction is equal to the force required to slide a body across a surface divided by weight of the body.

Fig. 41-2. Effect of weight and speed on braking.

vehicle are doubled, the stopping power must be increased eight times and the brakes must absorb or dissipate eight times as much heat, Fig. 41-2.

STOPPING DISTANCE

Average stopping distance is an important consideration that is directly related to vehicle speed. As charted in Fig. 41-3, a vehicle that can be stopped in 38 ft. from 20 mph will

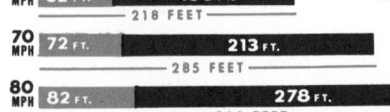

Fig. 41-3. Average stopping distances when traveling at various speeds.

require 111 ft. to stop from 40 mph. At 70 mph, the vehicle will require 285 ft. to stop; almost the length of a football field. These figures are based on use of the vehicle on smooth, dry pavement.

To calculate the distance required to stop a vehicle, consider the time you require to note the need for making a sudden stop, and the time you need to move your foot and apply the brakes. This is known as reaction "time."

Note in Fig. 41-3, the car will travel 21 ft. before the brakes are actually applied when travelling at 20 mph. When travelling at 90 mph, the car will travel 92 ft. before the brakes are applied, and the total distance needed to bring the vehicle to a stop is 452 ft.

BRAKE TEMPERATURES

As mentioned, brakes are devices which convert the energy of the moving vehicle into heat whenever the brakes are applied. This heat must be absorbed, then dissipated by the brake parts. Unless the heat is carried away as fast as it is produced, brake part temperatures will rise.

Since the heat generated by brake applications usually is greater than the rate of heat dissipation, high brake temperatures result. Ordinarily, the time interval between brake applications avoids a heat buildup. If, however, repeated panic stops are made, temperatures may become high enough to damage the brake lining, brake drums, brake fluid and, in extreme cases, the tires have been set on fire.

Factors that tend to increase brake temperatures include:
1. Load on vehicle.
2. Driver abuse.
3. Speed of vehicle.
4. Maladjustment of brakes.
5. Incorrect installation of brake parts.
6. Unbalanced braking.

The amount of heat developed in stopping a vehicle can be calculated. Assume that a car weighing 4000 lb. is travelling at a speed of 60 mph (88 ft. per second). The heat developed in stopping this car can be computed as follows:

$$\text{Kinetic energy in ft. lb.} = \frac{W\,V^2}{64.4}$$

W is the weight of the car in pounds, and V is the velocity in feet per second.

$$\text{Kinetic energy} = \frac{4000 \times 88^2}{64.4} = 480,994 \text{ ft. lb.}$$

Heat energy is measured in British thermal units (Btu), and one Btu = 778 ft. lb. Therefore, the heat energy developed in stopping the car is:

$$\text{Btu} = \frac{480,994}{778} = 618 \text{ Btu}$$

If the car is stopped, the 618 Btu will go into the braking system. First, assume that: all of this heat goes into the brake drums (about 90 percent usually does); each brake drum weighs 10 lb. or a total of 40 lb.; and specific heat of the brake drum is .110. Then, compute the drum temperature rise as follows:

$$\frac{618}{40 \times .110} = 140 \text{ deg. F.}$$

Finally, assume that the atmospheric temperature is 80 deg. F. Then, the final drum temperature will be:

$$80 + 140 = 220 \text{ deg. F.}$$

If road speeds are increased and/or more weight is placed in the vehicle, brake temperatures will soar. In fact, under extreme conditions of unbalanced brakes on a heavy truck making an emergency stop from high speed, enough heat will be generated to melt a cube of iron weighing 11.2 lb.

Other factors enter into the buildup of brake temperatures. If the brake lining surface does not conform to the surface of the brake drum, all the work of stopping the vehicle will be done by a small area of brake lining. The same amount of work will be done but, being concentrated on a small area, the temperature will be much higher. If the area of braking is one fourth the normal area, braking temperatures will be four times higher than normal. If the full area of contact is 40 sq. in., and normal braking temperature is 150 deg., the temperatures will soar to 600 deg. if only one fourth of the braking area is used.

BRAKE AND TIRE FRICTION

When brakes are applied on a vehicle, the brake shoes are forced into contact with the brake drums to slow the rotation of the wheel. Then, the friction between the tires and the road surface slows the speed of the vehicle.

However, friction between the brake shoes and brake drum does not remain constant. Rather, it tends to increase with temperature. From tests, the coefficient of friction of brake lining has been found to range from 0.35 to 0.50. Still other variables are the materials of which the brake lining is made, and also the material of the brake drum.

The friction of the tire on the road is approximately .02, but this also varies with the road surface. Surface contact is the determining factor. The fastest stops are obtained with the wheels rotating. As soon as the wheels become locked, there is less friction and the car will not stop as quickly or as evenly.

While the coefficient of friction of many linings tends to increase with higher temperatures, this is not always the case. In Fig. 41-4, for example, note how the coefficient of friction

of one lining increased with higher temperatures, resulting in grabbing brakes. Another remained practically constant. On a third lining type the coefficient dropped rapidly and fading brakes resulted.

HYDRAULIC BRAKES

As covered in the chapter on hydraulics, liquids are virtually incompressible, and pressure throughout a closed system will be the same in all directions. This principle is used to operate the service brakes on most passenger cars.

A schematic drawing of a hydraulic brake system is shown in Fig. 41-5. In this system, the foot pedal is attached to a

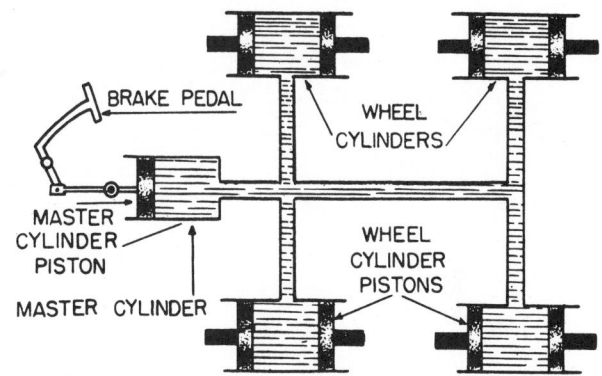

Fig. 41-5. Schematic drawing of hydraulic brake system.

master cylinder. As the pedal is depressed, it moves a piston within the master cylinder, forcing hydraulic fluid throughout the system and into cylinders at each wheel. Here, it causes the wheel cylinder pistons to move which, in turn, forces the brake shoes against the brake drums to retard their movement.

Fig. 41-6 shows how the force applied to the brake pedal is multiplied. In this instance, 800 lbs. is applied to a piston area of 0.8 sq. in., resulting in a pressure in the system of 1000 psi.

At the front wheel cylinders, which have a piston area of 0.9 sq. in., a force of 900 lbs. is produced for each piston.

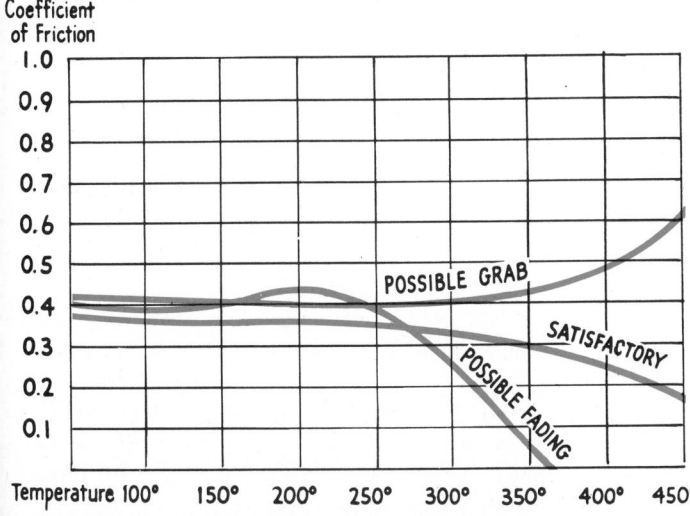

EFFECT OF TEMPERATURE ON COEFFICIENT OF FRICTION OF BRAKE LININGS

Three types of linings on cast iron drums
Same friction at low temperatures. Different at higher temperatures.

Fig. 41-4. Note how temperature affected coefficient of friction of three different brake linings.

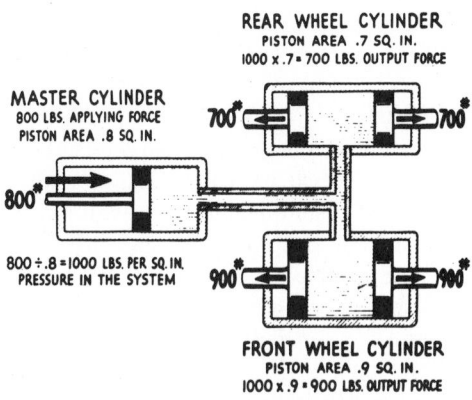

Fig. 41-6. Sketch shows how force applied to brake pedal is multiplied hydraulically at wheel cylinders.

Since each wheel cylinder has two pistons, a total force of 1800 lbs. per cylinder is produced. Each rear wheel cylinder, with a piston area of 0.7 sq. in., have a combined force of 1400 lbs.

WEIGHT TRANSFER

In Fig. 41-6, the wheel cylinders on the front wheels are larger than those on the rear wheels. This compensates for weight transfer to the front of the vehicle when the brakes are applied for a rapid stop. Because of this natural weight transfer, the front brakes are required to do more work than the rear brakes.

This weight transfer effect comes about because the center of gravity of the automobile is located above the center of the car wheels. See Fig. 41-7. The result of this action is noticeable by a "sinking" of the front of the car, and simultaneous "rising" of the rear of the car whenever a severe brake application is made.

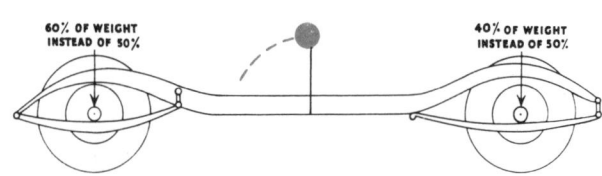

Fig. 41-7. Center of gravity is above wheel centers, so a sudden stop will remove some weight from rear wheels and place it on front wheels.

BRAKE EFFECTIVENESS

There are several factors that contribute to the effectiveness of brakes. These include:
1. Area of brake lining.
2. Amount of pressure applied to brake shoes.
3. Radius of brake drum.
4. Radius of car wheel.
5. Coefficient of friction of braking surfaces.
6. Coefficient of friction between tire and road surface.

Points 3 and 4 are simply a matter of leverage. It is obvious that a brake drum of small diameter applied to a wheel of large diameter will require more frictional surface, or higher pressures on the surface, than a large brake drum on a small wheel.

If the road surface is covered with ice, or is in a condition where there is little friction between the tires and road surface, braking effectiveness will be reduced. Also, a worn tread on one tire and a new tread on another tire will provide unequal braking. As pointed out earlier in this chapter, maximum braking action is obtained as long as the wheel is rotating. But once the brake has become locked and the wheel does not rotate, braking effectiveness is reduced.

Point 2 is among the more important points to be considered in the effectiveness of brakes. The pressure of the brake shoes against the brake drums starts with the force applied to the brake pedal. Then, it is multiplied by leverage

(and frequently assisted by a power brake unit) and further increased hydraulically by the size of the master cylinder and wheel cylinders. In addition, there are the important factors of self-energization and servo action that greatly multiply the force pressing the brake shoes against the drums.

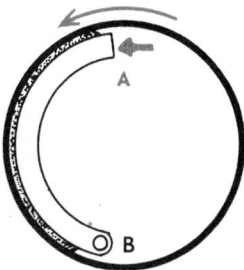

Fig. 41-8. Typical brake shoe installation and application. A—Force is applied. B—Shoe pivots, trying to turn shoe around anchor pin.

Self-energization is created by the tendency of the rotating drum to drag the lining along with it. Fig. 41-8 shows that the frictional force between the brake drum and lining tries to turn the shoe around the anchor pin. Since the drum itself prevents this, the shoe is self-energized, or forced even more strongly against the drum than the applying force is pushing it.

Servo action is obtained by the location of the anchor pin. The nearer the center of rotation the anchor pin is located, the more powerful the wedging action will be. This wedging action starts at the toe of the shoe and keeps increasing as it nears the anchor pin, Fig. 41-9. If the drum is revolved in the opposite

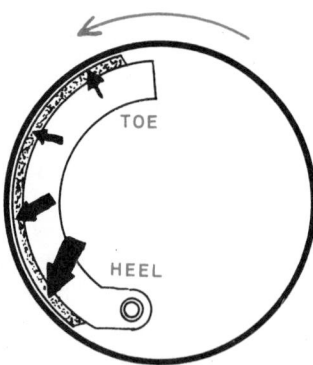

Fig. 41-9. Relative size of arrows indicates increase of pressure from toe to heel with pivot point set toward center.

direction, there will be no self-energization. However, since there are two brake shoes, one or the other is effective either way the drum turns.

Self-energization can be amplified to include both shoes by letting one shoe push the other, Fig. 41-10. This amplification of forces is known as servo-action. To accomplish it, the shoes are linked together at the bottom, and clearance is provided between the ends of the shoes and the anchor pin. In this way, the shoes can be rotated slightly in relation to the axle shaft or

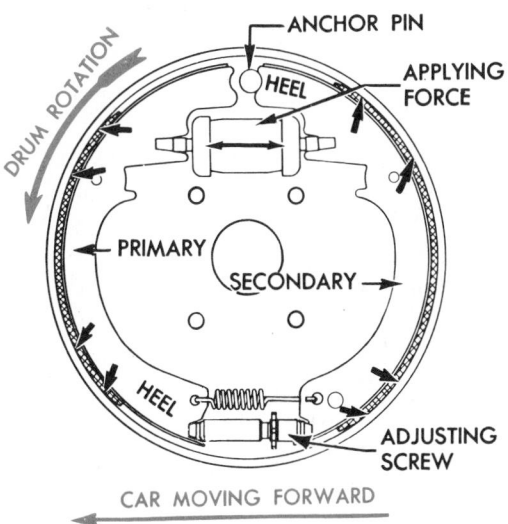

Fig. 41-10. Showing how thrust of brake shoes against brake drum is multiplied by servo-action.

wheel spindle.

When the brakes are applied, both shoes will move with the rotation of the drum until the rearward shoe is stopped by the anchor pin. The forward shoe also stops, since it is linked to the rearward shoe through the connecting link or adjusting screw. The shoe that generates the servo-action is known as the primary shoe; the one being actuated is the secondary shoe.

BRAKE LINING MATERIALS

There are two basic types of brake linings, organic and metallic. Organic lining consists of a gray-white compound of asbestos, filler materials and powdered resins. These are thoroughly mixed, formed into shape and placed under heat and pressure until a hard, slate-like board is formed. The material is cut and bent into individual segments and attached to brake shoes. This is known as "molded lining."

Some organic lining is woven from strands of asbestos and threads of other materials, and impregnated with a rubber compound. Sometimes, fine metal wires are included.

WARNING: WHEN SERVICING WHEEL BRAKE PARTS, BREATHING DUST CONTAINING ASBESTOS FIBERS MAY CAUSE SERIOUS BODILY HARM.

Metallic brake lining is made of sintered metal. It is composed of finely powdered iron or copper, graphite and lesser amounts of inorganic fillers and friction modifiers. After thorough mixing, a lubricating oil is added to prevent segregation of different materials. Mixture is then put through a briquetting process and compressed into desired form.

The organic type brake lining is used almost exclusively for ordinary brake service. Under extreme braking conditions (police cars, ambulance and sports cars), the metallic type lining is being used extensively. Under severe usage, the frictional characteristics of the metallic lining are more constant than that of the organic lining. However, metallic brake lining has low initial friction and resultant hard pedal.

BRAKE DRUM MATERIALS

The use of cast iron for the braking surface of brake drums is practically universal. In the past, some steel brake drums were used. However, the coefficient of friction of steel is less than cast iron, and there is a greater tendency for such material to gall.

Although cast iron has proved to be ideal material for the braking surface, it conducts heat more slowly than aluminum. As a result, some drums are now made of aluminum with a cast iron liner for the braking surface, Fig. 41-11. Because of

Fig. 41-11. Cutaway brake drum reveals special construction. Basic drum is finned aluminum. Hub and liner are cast iron.

its higher conductivity of heat, a brake drum of such construction will operate at much lower temperatures. To determine which material was most suitable, tests were made with 50 mph fade stops of 0.2 mile intervals. It was found that the conventional cast iron drum reached a temperature of 700 deg., while the aluminum drum with cast iron liner was slightly less than 500 deg. Obviously, brake lining life is greatly improved under such conditions, and safer conditions are established.

Many brake drums are made of steel with inner linings of cast iron. In this way, the assembly has the strength of steel and the frictional properties of cast iron. In addition, there is no difficulty in getting the cast iron to bond with the steel. This was found to be the case when aluminum was used with cast iron.

Brake drums usually are provided with cooling fins, regardless of the material used in the construction. Fig. 41-12 a finned aluminum brake drum.

OPERATION OF HYDRAULIC BRAKES

The conventional hydraulic brake system applies the brakes at all four wheels with equalized pressure. It is pedal operated.

Fig. 41-12. Fins are·used on brake drums to increase dissipation of heat. (Oldsmobile Div., General Motors Corp.)

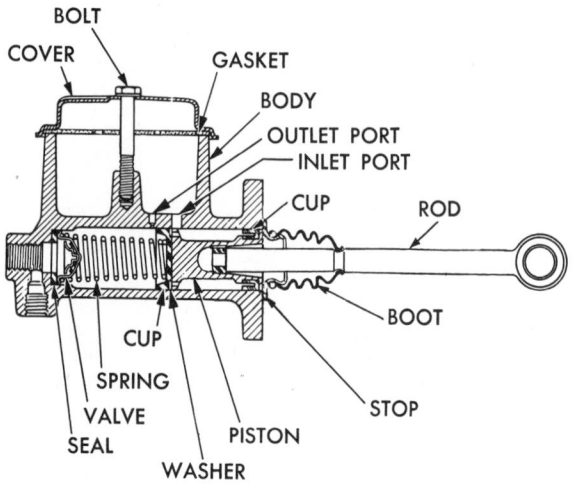

Fig. 41-13. Single piston master cylinder was used in all U.S. cars until mid-'60s when dual master cylinder and split hydraulic system became standard equipment.

The hydraulic system consists of one master cylinder, Fig. 41-13, connected by pipes and flexible tubing, to the wheel cylinders, Fig. 41-14, which control the movement of the brake shoes at each wheel.

The master cylinder, connecting lines and wheel cylinders

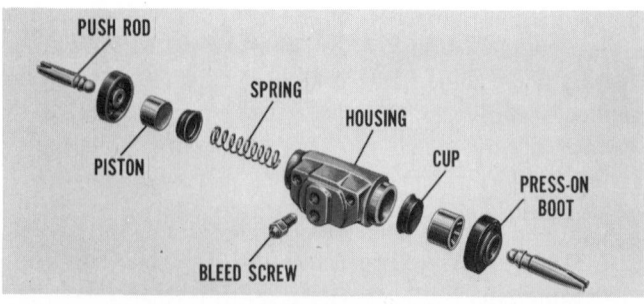

Fig. 41-14. Exploded view of typical wheel cylinder.

are filled with special hydraulic fluid, which is forced through the system by the movement of the master cylinder piston.

SINGLE—PISTON MASTER CYLINDER

A single-piston master cylinder was used until the mid-1960s. Fig. 41-15 illustrates how it works in views A, B, C, D.

View A: When brakes are fully released, master cylinder piston is held against stop plate. Primary cup is held just clear of compensating port by master cylinder spring, which also holds check valve against its seat on head nut.

Pressure chamber is filled with fluid at atmospheric pressure due to open compensating port and reservoir vent. All lines and cylinders are filled with fluid under a static pressure of 8 - 16 psi, which helps to hold lips of wheel cylinder cups in firm contact with cylinder walls to prevent loss of fluid or entrance of air into system.

View B: When brake pedal is applied, push rod forces master cylinder piston and primary cup forward. As movement starts, lip of primary cup covers compensating port to prevent escape of fluid back to reservoir.

Continued movement of piston builds pressure in pressure chamber, and fluid is then forced through holes in check valve and out into lines leading to each of wheel cylinders. Fluid forced into wheel cylinders between pistons and cups causes pistons and connecting links to move outward, forcing brake shoes into contact with brake drums.

When brake pedal is released, master cylinder spring forces pedal back until push rod contacts stop plate in master cylinder. This spring also forces piston and primary cup to follow push rod, and pushes check valve firmly against its seat.

View C: At start of a fast release, piston moves faster than fluid can follow it in returning from wheel cylinders and lines, momentarily creating a partial vacuum in pressure chamber. Fluid supplied through breather port is then drawn through bleeder holes in piston head, and past primary cup, to keep pressure chamber filled.

As pressure drops in master cylinder, shoe return springs retract all brake shoes, and connecting links push wheel cylinder pistons inward, forcing fluid back to master cylinder.

View D: Pressure of returning fluid causes a rubber disk to close holes in check valve, and forces check valve off its seat against tension of master cylinder spring. Fluid then flows around check valve into pressure chamber. With piston bearing against stop plate, and lip of primary cup just clear of compensating port, excess fluid which entered through bleeder holes, or was created by expansion due to increased temperature, now returns to reservoir through uncovered compensating port. When pressure in wheel cylinders and lines becomes slightly less than tension of master cylinder spring, check valve returns to its seat on head nut to hold 8 to 16 psi static pressure in lines and cylinders.

DUAL MASTER CYLINDER

The dual master cylinder, also known as the split system or tandem master cylinder, Figs. 41-16 and 41-17, is designed to give the front and rear brakes separate hydraulic systems.

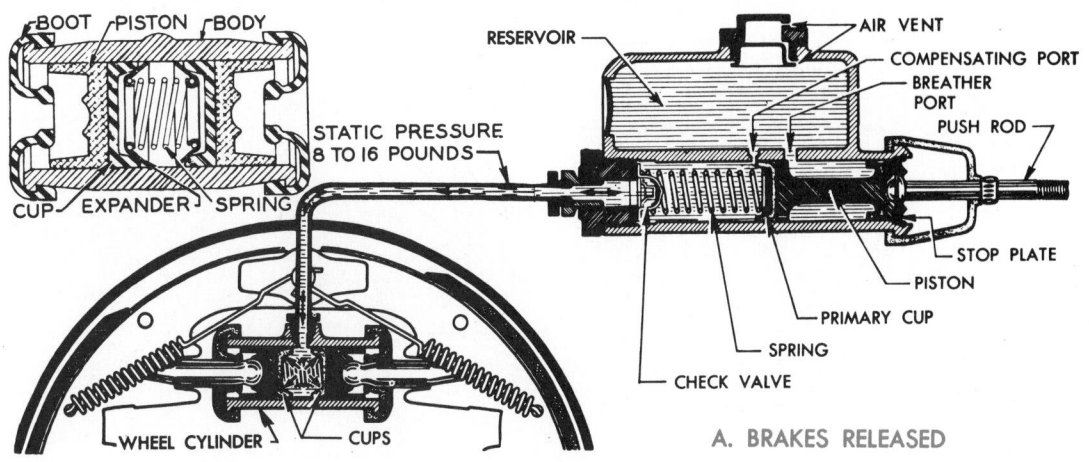

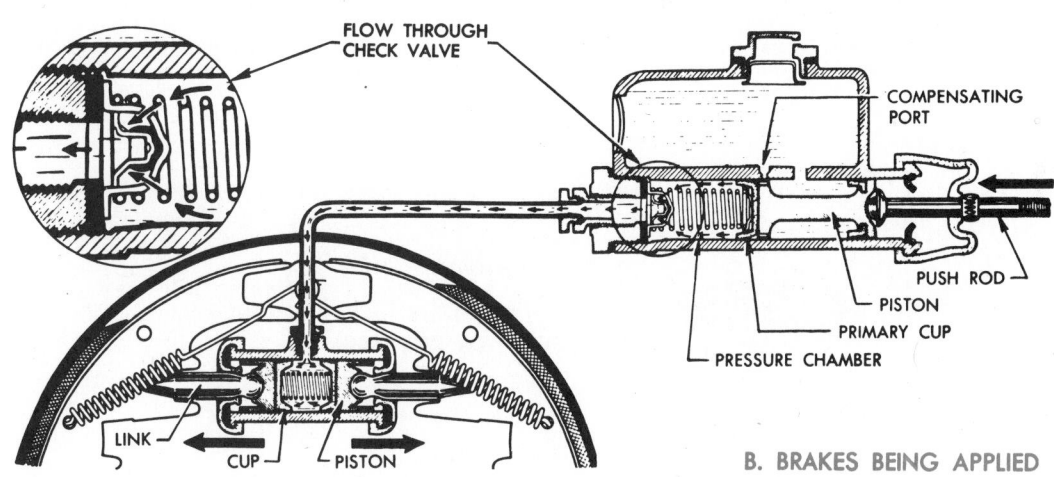

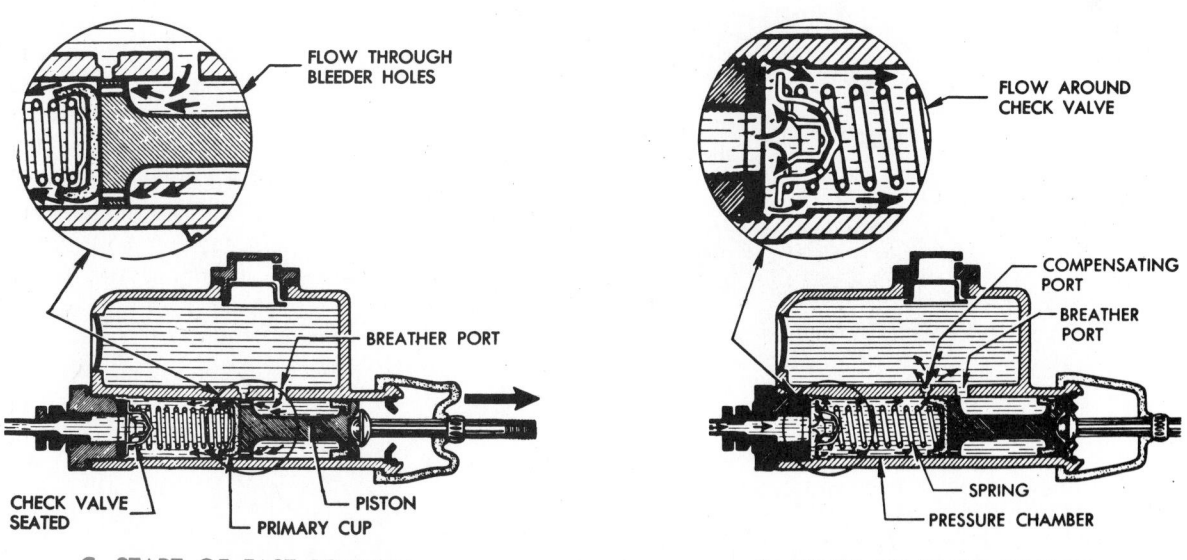

Fig. 41-15. Operation of typical hydraulic brake system, having a single-piston master cylinder.

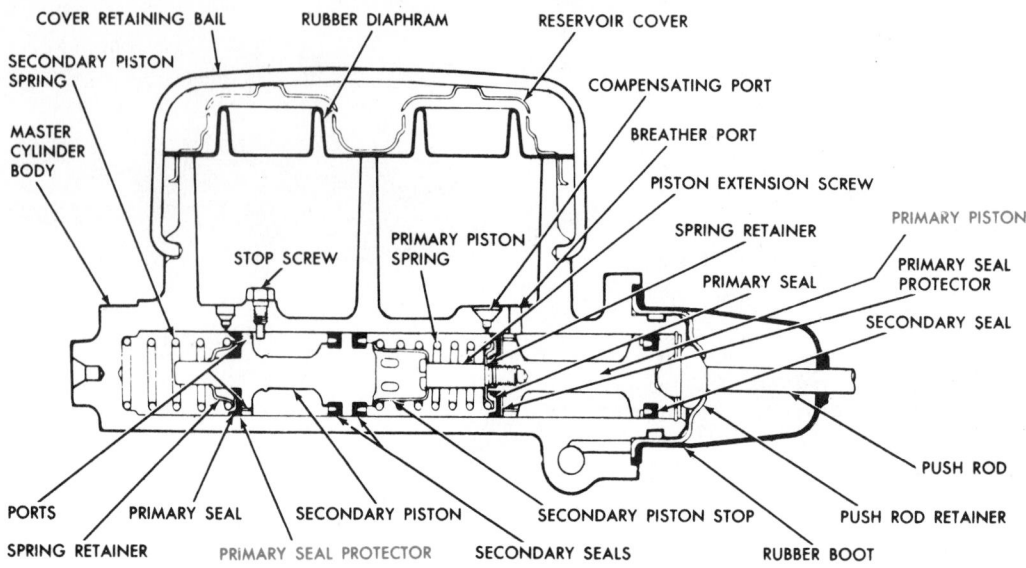

COVER RETAINING BAIL
RUBBER DIAPHRAM
RESERVOIR COVER
SECONDARY PISTON SPRING
COMPENSATING PORT
BREATHER PORT
MASTER CYLINDER BODY
PISTON EXTENSION SCREW
SPRING RETAINER
PRIMARY PISTON
STOP SCREW
PRIMARY PISTON SPRING
PRIMARY SEAL
PRIMARY SEAL PROTECTOR
SECONDARY SEAL
PORTS
PRIMARY SEAL
SECONDARY PISTON
SECONDARY PISTON STOP
PUSH ROD
SPRING RETAINER
PRIMARY SEAL PROTECTOR
SECONDARY SEALS
PUSH ROD RETAINER
RUBBER BOOT

Fig. 41-16. Typical dual master cylinder. When primary and secondary pistons move forward, their primary seals cover both compensating ports. Hydraulic pressure builds up and is transmitted to front and rear wheel brakes.

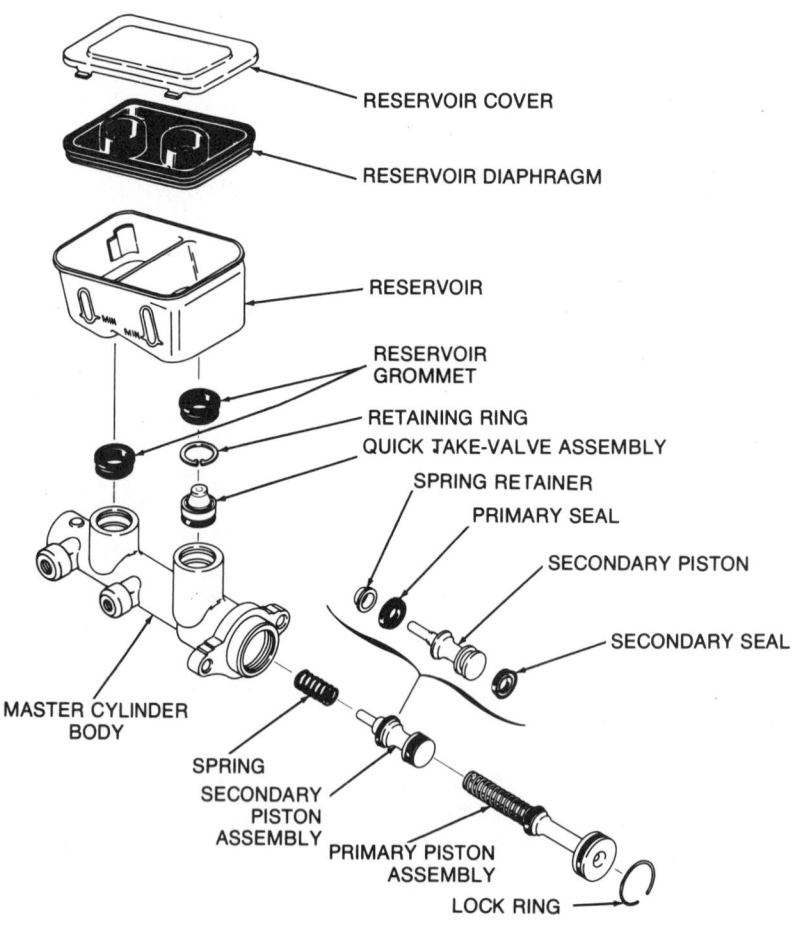

RESERVOIR COVER
RESERVOIR DIAPHRAGM
RESERVOIR
RESERVOIR GROMMET
RETAINING RING
QUICK TAKE-VALVE ASSEMBLY
SPRING RETAINER
PRIMARY SEAL
SECONDARY PISTON
SECONDARY SEAL
MASTER CYLINDER BODY
SPRING
SECONDARY PISTON ASSEMBLY
PRIMARY PISTON ASSEMBLY
LOCK RING

A "quick take-up" master cylinder is used on some late model General Motors passenger cars. This dual reservoir unit is designed to function with a system that incorporates low drag front brake calipers. The quick take-up feature provides a large volume of brake fluid to wheel brakes at low pressure with initial brake application. Low pressure fluid quickly provides for displacement requirements created by seal-retracting pistons in front calipers and spring retraction of rear drum brake shoes. (Cadillac Motor Car Div., GM)

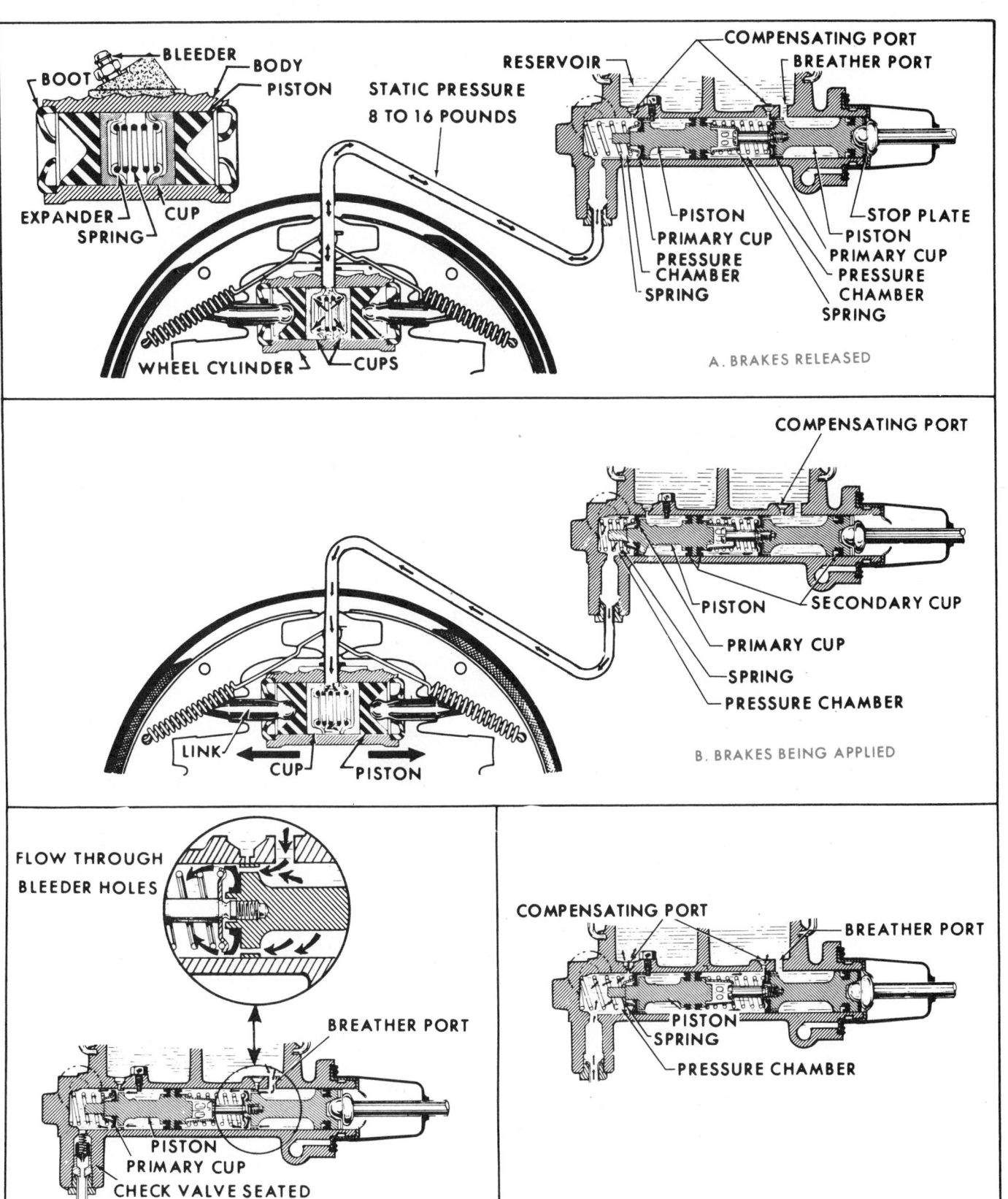

Fig. 41-17. Operation of a typical dual hydraulic system. A—When fully released, pistons are held against retaining ring and primary cups clear compensating port. Fluid in pressure chambers is under atmospheric pressure. B—In applied position, pistons move forward and primary cups cover bypass holes, causing hydraulic pressure to be transmitted to front and rear wheel cylinders. C—On fast release, pistons move faster than returning fluid and a partial vacuum is created. Fluid enters pressure chamber via breather and bleeder holes in piston heads. (Check valve is not used with disc brakes.) D—At finish of release, piston returns against retaining ring and fluid returns to reservoirs by way of compensating ports.

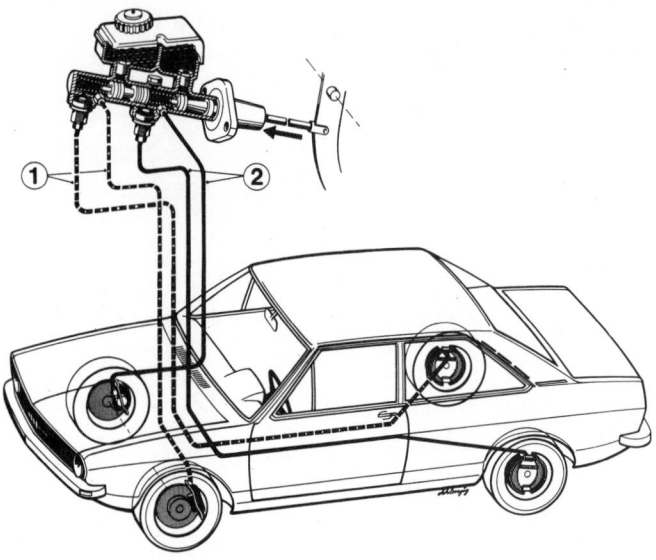

Fig. 41-18. Split hydraulic system has separate circuits in front and at rear. This Audi Fox split system pairs diagonally opposite wheel brakes: left front and right rear, right front and left rear. (Volkswagen of America, Inc.)

split hydraulic system.

As shown in Fig. 41-19, the dual master cylinder is provided with two separate reservoirs, one primary piston and one secondary piston. The reservoirs are completely separate (earlier dual master cylinders had reservoirs joined at top).

Dual brake system operation is described in views A, B, C and D in Fig. 41-17. Note that basic principles are the same as in single-piston master cylinder operation, except for double reservoir, double-piston setup, double compensating port, etc., and no check valve in disc brake circuit. See Fig. 41-19.

ALUMINUM MASTER CYLINDERS

A variety of dual master cylinder designs have been used on U.S. cars. Most of the differences are contained in the size and shape of the main body and cover. Recently, in keeping with efforts being made to reduce overall vehicle weight, aluminum master cylinders have been introduced.

Chrysler, for example, makes use of a two-piece master cylinder mounted either on the firewall or on the brake booster. The main body of the master cylinder is aluminum,

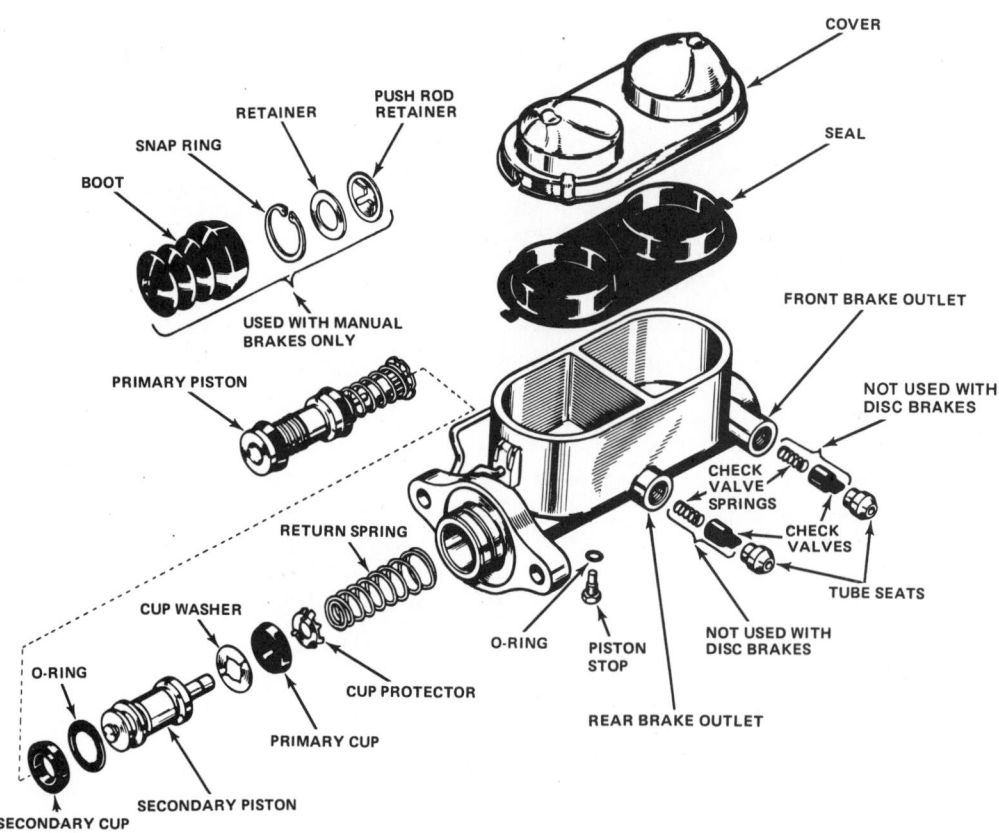

Fig. 41-19. Exploded view of dual master cylinder shows internal parts in assembly sequence. Note that check valves are not used with disc brakes.

Should a leak occur in one system, the other system will still be in operation, making it possible to stop the car.

Some manufacturers are installing "diagonal" split systems, instead of front and rear. Fig. 41-18 illustrates this type of

Fig. 41-19A. The fluid reservoir is made of molded plastic. It is fastened to the aluminum body by means of two rubber grommets. Separation of the two major parts is accomplished by rocking the reservoir from side to side and lifting it free.

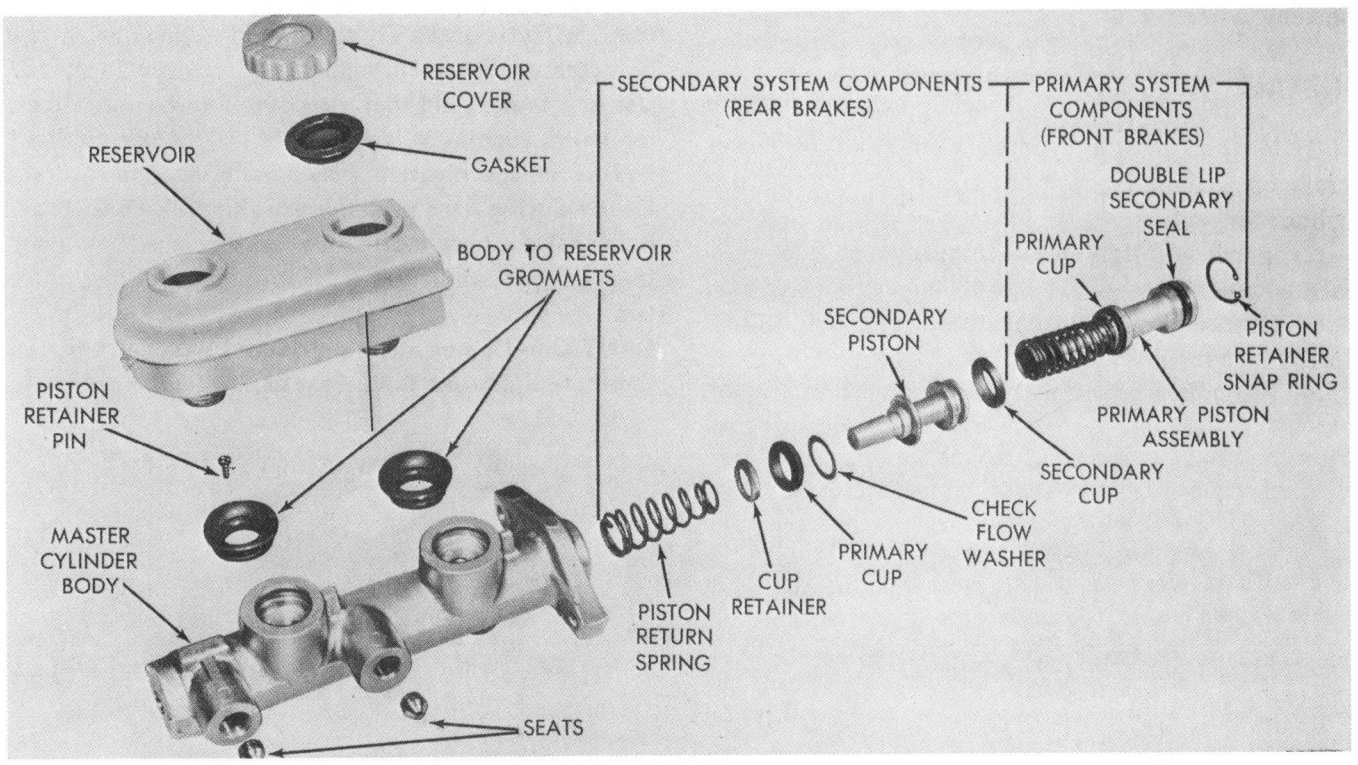

Fig. 41-19A. Chrysler's aluminum master cylinder with plastic reservoir.

To reassemble, lubricate the grommets with brake fluid and press the reservoir in place on the cylinder.

Chrysler's aluminum master cylinder has several advantages over its cast iron counterpart:
1. It is 6 lb. lighter.
2. It incorporates a two-stud mounting flange.
3. The see-through plastic reservoir permits checking the fluid level without removing the two caps. (The reservoirs are marked "FULL" and use a V to indicate correct fluid level.)
4. The caps feature a simple quarter turn release-and-seal locking motion for retention to the reservoir.

The main disadvantage of the aluminum master cylinder is

Fig. 41-19B. General Motors' aluminum master cylinder.

the softness of the metal, and that it is subject to corrosion. To combat this, Chrysler has anodized the bore to make it wear resistant and corrosion resistant.

Note, however, that if the bore becomes scratched during use, or while being serviced, it should NOT be honed. A scratched, scored or pitted bore of an aluminum master cylinder signals the positive need for replacement by a complete master cylinder assembly.

General Motors also makes use of an aluminum master cylinder on some Chevrolets and certain other model lines. The General Motors' aluminum master cylinder is a two-piece unit, using a plastic fluid reservoir set in grommets in the aluminum main body. See Fig. 41-19B. Chevrolet says: "Polishing the bore of the master cylinder with the cast aluminum body with anything abrasive is prohibited."

HYDRAULIC BRAKE FLUID

To provide positive braking action under all conditions, brake fluid must meet a lot of requirements. First of all, hydraulic brake fluid must not swell or soften the rubber parts used throughout the system. Failure to meet this requirement results in brakes locking up, leaks or short life of rubber parts.

Brake fluid must be compatible with the different metals used in the system. If rusting occurs, the result will be "frozen" brakes, pulling brakes or loss of brakes due to leaks.

Brake fluid must not vaporize at the highest temperature encountered in actual service. Failure to meet this requirement results in complete loss of brakes without warning. It must remain fluid at low temperatures, even when a small amount of water is added.

Brake fluid must act as a lubricant to the moving parts of the system. It must retain all its characteristics over a long period of time. It must mix satisfactorily with other makes of hydraulic brake fluid.

As mentioned, stopping a 4000 lb. car from 60 mph will result in raising the temperature of the brakes to 250 deg. F. If repeated stops are made every 0.2 miles from 50 mph, 700 deg. F will be reached. With high temperatures possible, care must be exercised in selecting brake fluid. Only brake fluid meeting the Society of Automotive Engineers specification J1703 (and DOT-3) should be used.

When the brake fluid in the system becomes hot enough to vaporize, it emits gas, and a drop of fluid changed into vapor forms a gas bubble many times the volume of the liquid drop. This gas formation forces some of the brake fluid back through the lines, through the master cylinder check valve, and through the small by-pass hole into the reservoir.

The check valve holds a static pressure in the line, which tends to keep the fluid from boiling. Once the brake fluid reaches the boiling point, it may continue to change into gas until a large bubble is formed. If this bubble has pushed more brake fluid back into the reservoir than one stroke of the pedal can pump into the system, complete loss of brakes will occur.

Small quantities of bubbles produce what is known as a "spongy pedal," with partial loss of braking.

In addition to vapor lock occurring in the wheel cylinders, it may also occur in the master cylinder. In these cases, brakes will fail without warning. Pumping the pedal will not remove the vapor lock.

Mountain driving puts increased duty on brakes and brake fluid. With every 2000 ft. increase in altitude, the atmospheric pressure drops approximately one pound, and the boiling point of the brake fluid drops 2 deg. to 3 deg. This naturally increases the tendency toward vapor lock.

BRAKE TYPES

Brake systems have varied among manufacturers over the years. Today, self-adjusting brakes are standard equipment on rear wheels. Front wheel brakes are either self-adjusting drum type or disc type, mostly of the single-piston, floating or sliding caliper type.

BENDIX SINGLE ANCHOR

Forerunner of today's most popular drum type brake is the Bendix single anchor brake shown in Fig. 41-20. In some installations, the anchor is fixed. In other designs, it is adjustable. There are two types of adjustable anchors. In one design, the anchor is eccentric and can be turned to move the anchor pin. In the other design, the anchor pin is mounted in an elongated hole, so the pin can be moved up or down as desired.

A single wheel cylinder is used in this Bendix brake, and the shoes are held in the released position by means of individual retracting springs from the anchor pin to each shoe. Each shoe is also provided with a hold-down spring and clip to hold the

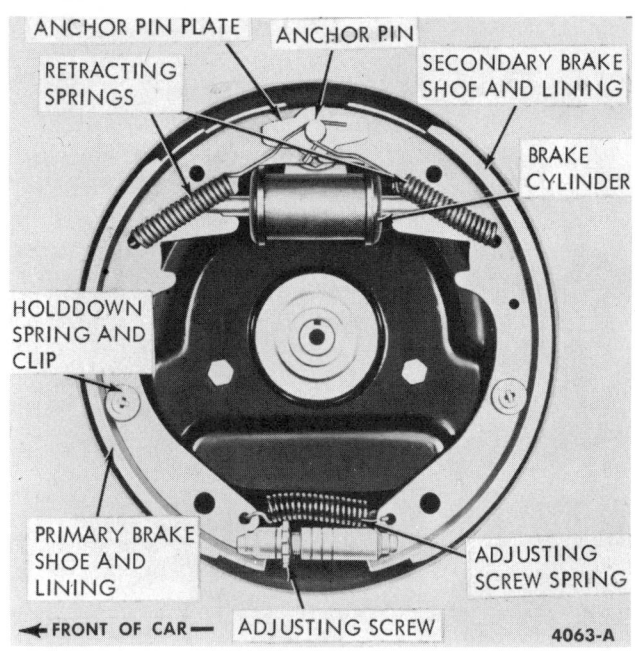

Fig. 41-20. Details of Bendix duo-servo, single anchor pin brake.

Fig. 41-21. Method of making adjustment on Bendix duo-servo brake.

shoes in place against the backing plate.

A single adjustment is provided, which is reached through a port in the backing plate, Fig. 41-21. Working the handle of the tool up or down will spread or reduce the length of the star wheel to obtain correct brake shoe-to-drum clearance.

BENDIX SELF—ADJUSTING BRAKE

The Bendix self-adjusting brake, which replaced the single anchor brake, is illustrated in Fig. 41-22. The two brake shoes rest on the single anchor pin, until the wheel cylinder expands the upper ends of the shoes against the brake drums. As the drum rotates, one shoe is pulled away from the anchor pin by this rotation, and the shoe is moved slightly in the direction of drum rotation. The floating link connecting the two shoes at the bottom forces the second shoe to contact the drum at the bottom, and both shoes are energized.

The action of the brake is similar to that of the conventional single anchor brake. When applying the brakes in reverse, the opposite shoe becomes the lead shoe. As it pulls away from the anchor pin, it pulls on the cable of the self-adjusting mechanism, Fig. 41-22, which raises the adjust-

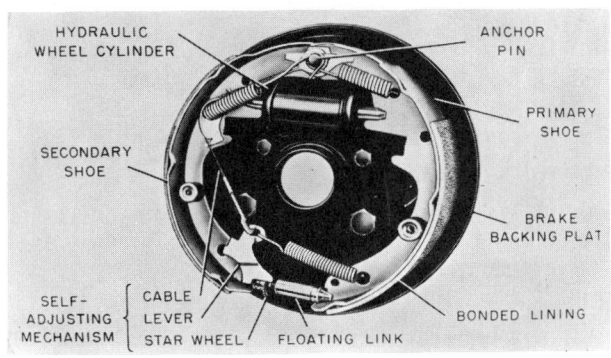

Fig. 41-22. Bendix self-adjusting brake.

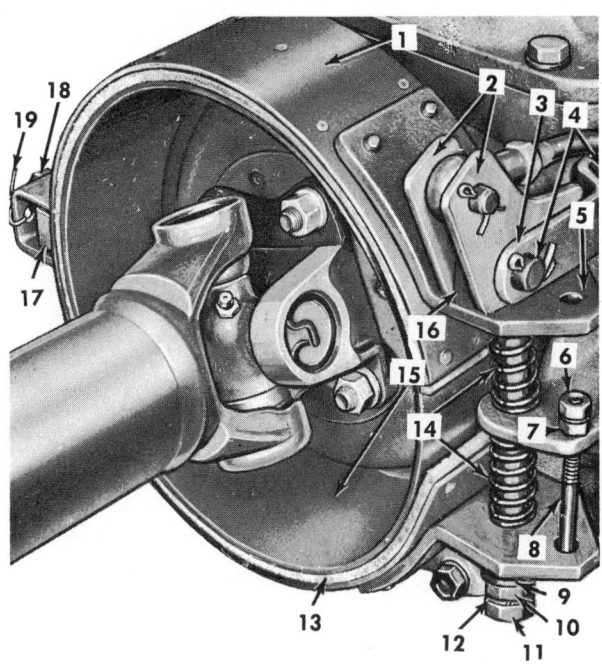

Fig. 41-23. Parking brake on medium-duty Chevrolet trucks includes: 1—Brake band. 2—Cams. 3—Links. 4—Clevis pins. 5—Cam shoe. 6—Lock nut. 7—Adjusting nut. 8—Locating bolt. 9—Washer. 10—Adjusting nut. 11—Lock nut. 12—Lock washer. 13—Brake linings. 14—Release springs. 15—Brake drum. 16—Adjusting bolt. 17—Anchor bar. 18—Anchor screw. 19—Lock wire.

ing lever. When sufficient lining wear has occurred (and not before), the lever can engage the next notch in the star adjusting wheel. A spring on the lever pulls it down, and this increases the length of the floating link 0.0005 in. to expand the shoes.

The self-adjusting feature operates only when the car is moving backward and the brakes are applied. When the driver desires, he can back up and stop abruptly. Then drive forward for approximately 25 ft. and stop again. He can repeat this pattern of stops until brake pedal height is satisfactory.

PARKING BRAKES

When the parking brake is mounted on the drive shaft, it is operated by a cable within a conduit, leading to a lever in the passenger compartment. Multiplication of leverage at the brake band is obtained by the design of the band operating cams and the length of the parking brake hand lever or pedal lever.

An external contracting type of parking brake is shown in Fig. 41-23. The external band is anchored at the center, and its two ends are tightened around the drum by means of a locating bolt, adjusting bolt and lock nuts.

An internal expanding type of parking brake mounted on the drive shaft is also available. It has the shoes anchored at the top, with the adjusting star wheel at the bottom.

However, these drive shaft brake assemblies are limited to use on trucks. Most automobiles use the rear wheel brakes for both service and parking. To do this, mechanical linkage is provided, Fig. 41-24.

When the parking brake lever is pulled, or the pedal is depressed, the cables connected to the rear brake shoes are pulled taut. Each rear brake cable is attached to an actuating lever that is connected to the secondary shoe web. When the

cable pulls the lever forward, it engages a strut that forces the primary shoe against the brake drum. As the primary shoe is applied, the secondary shoe is forced against the drum.

Automatic or manual adjustment of rear brake shoe-to-drum clearance also adjusts the parking brake. There is an additional adjustment possible by shortening or lengthening the lever-to-equalizer cable, Fig. 41-24. A double nut locking arrangement is provided at the threaded end of the cable where it connects to the equalizer.

DISC BRAKES

With the demands for increased safety in the operation of automotive vehicles, many cars are now equipped with disc brakes, Fig. 41-25. The major advantage of the disc brake is a great reduction in tendency toward brake fade and consequent marked reduction in the distance required to stop the vehicle.

Braking with disc brakes is accomplished by forcing friction pads, Fig. 41-26, against both sides of a rotating metal disc, or rotor. The rotor turns with the wheel of the vehicle and is straddled by a housing called the caliper assembly, Fig. 41-27. The caliper contains pistons, somewhat similar to those used in conventional drum type hydraulic brakes.

When the brake pedal is depressed, hydraulic fluid forces the pistons and the friction pads (lining) against the machined surfaces of the rotor. The pinching action of the lined pads, Fig. 41-27, quickly creates friction and heat to slow down and stop the vehicle.

Disc brakes do not have servo or multiplying action.

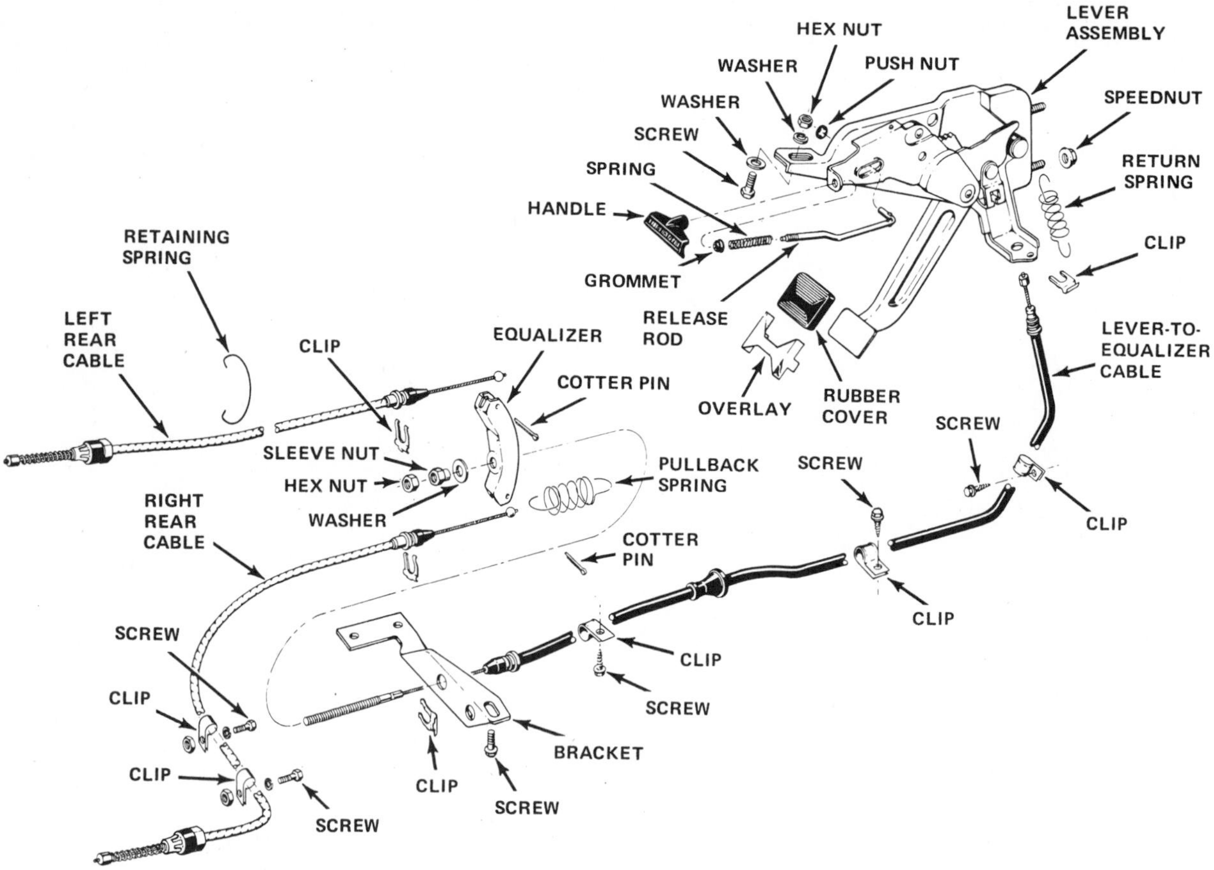

Fig. 41-24. One method of hooking mechanical leverage to the hydraulic shoes for a pedal operated parking brake. (American Motors Corp.)

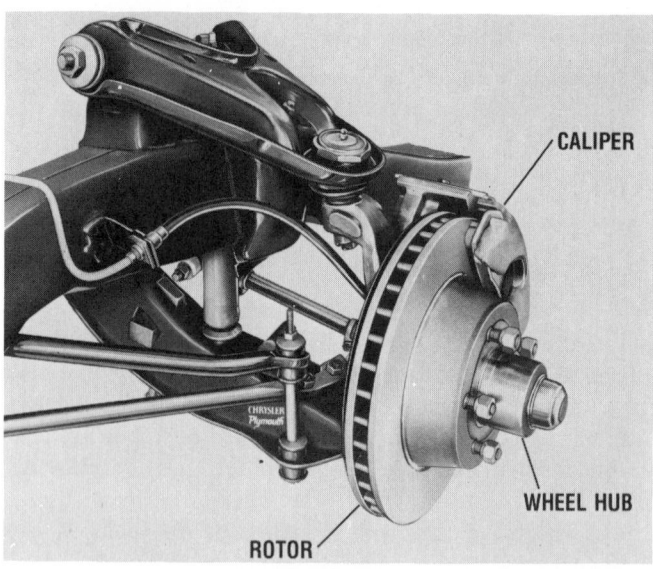

Fig. 41-25. Ventilated rotor disc brakes feature fade resistance and maximum stopping ability. Latest full size Chrysler Corporation cars have "slider" and "pin slider" types of front disc brake calipers.

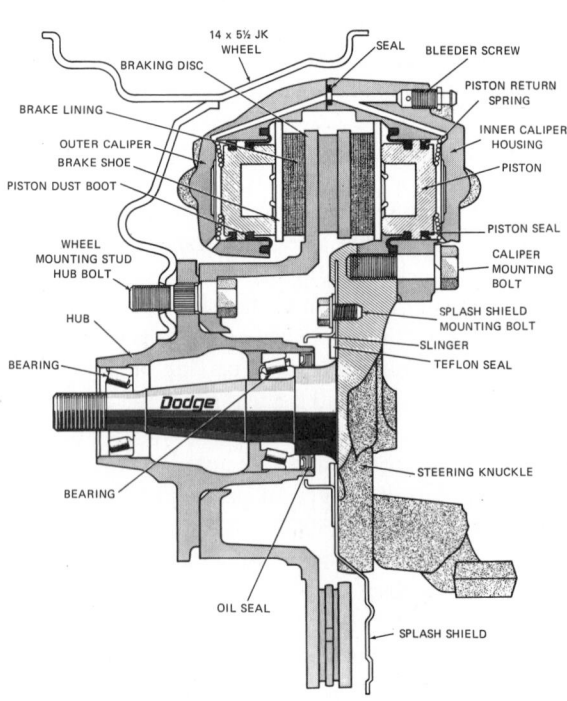

Fig. 41-26. Older Chrysler Corporation cars are equipped with four piston, fixed caliper disc brakes. Caliper fits across rotor like a C-clamp. In operation, pistons force shoe and lining assemblies against machined faces of rotor to stop rotor and vehicle.

Therefore, the applying force on the brake pedal must be very great in order to obtain a brake force comparable to that obtained with the conventional drum brake. Consequently,

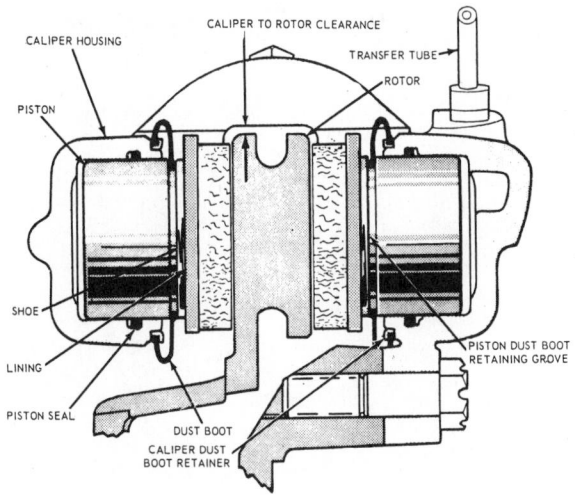

Fig. 41-27. Sectional view of fixed caliper assembly on Ford disc brake.

disc brakes are usually provided with a power or booster unit and a conventional master hydraulic cylinder.

In many installations, disc brakes are used only on the front wheels, while the familiar drum brake is continued on the rear. In other applications, disc brakes are used on all four wheels.

FORD, LINCOLN, MUSTANG BRAKES

The disc brake design, Figs. 41-27 and 41-28, used on older Lincoln, Thunderbird, Mustang and other makes is described as a fixed caliper, opposed piston, non-energized, ventilated disc type unit, energized by the hydraulic system.

There is no lateral movement of the rotor. The Ford caliper assembly consists of two caliper housings, Fig. 41-28, bolted together. Each half contains two cylinders and each cylinder contains a piston with attached molded rubber dust boot to

seal the cylinder bore from contamination. Square-sectioned rubber piston seals are positioned in the grooves in the cylinder bores, Fig. 41-27. The piston seals perform three important tasks:

1. Provide a seal between cylinders and pistons.
2. Return pistons to released position when hydraulic pressure is released.
3. Maintain friction pads in correct alignment at all times, by action that is comparable to automatic adjusters on drum brakes.

The cylinders of the Ford fixed caliper are connected hydraulically by means of internal passages in the caliper housings and an external transfer tube between the two halves of the caliper assembly, Fig. 41-28. One bleeder screw and fluid inlet fitting is provided on each caliper assembly.

The shoe and lining assemblies are located between parallel machined abutments within the caliper. They are supported radially by tabs on the outer ends of the shoe assemblies. The shoes slide axially in the caliper abutments by means of tabs which ride on machined ledges (bridges) when hydraulic pressure is applied to the piston, Fig. 41-28.

A shoe and lining assembly consists of friction material

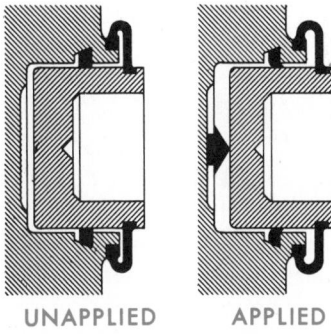

Fig. 41-29. Square cut seal fitted in groove in caliper cylinder wall serves to seal in fluid, seal out dirt and return piston to unapplied position when brake pedal is released.

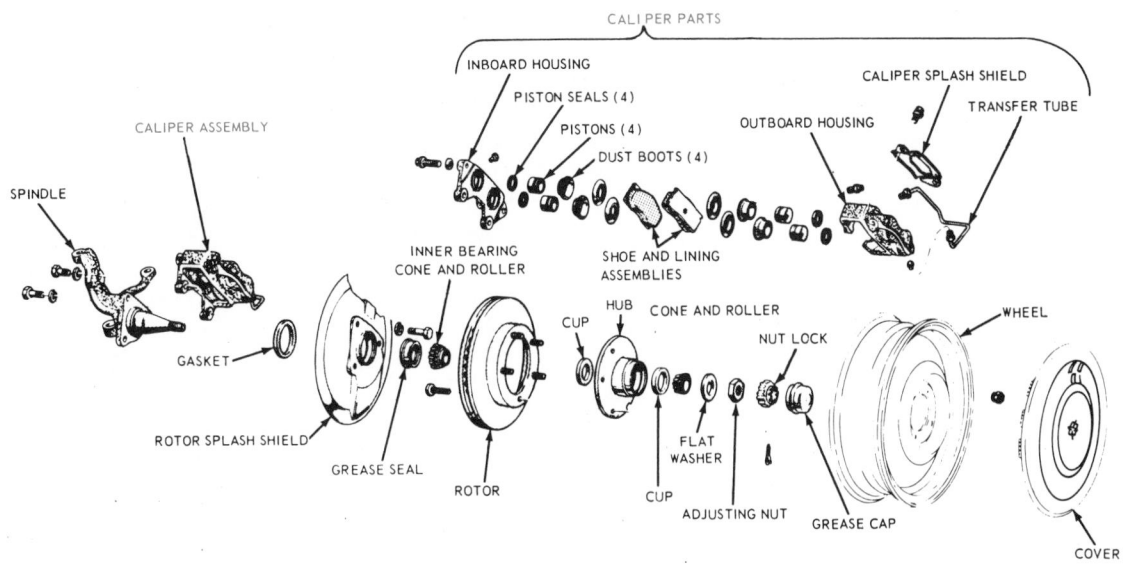

Fig. 41-28. Exploded view of Ford fixed caliper disc brake.

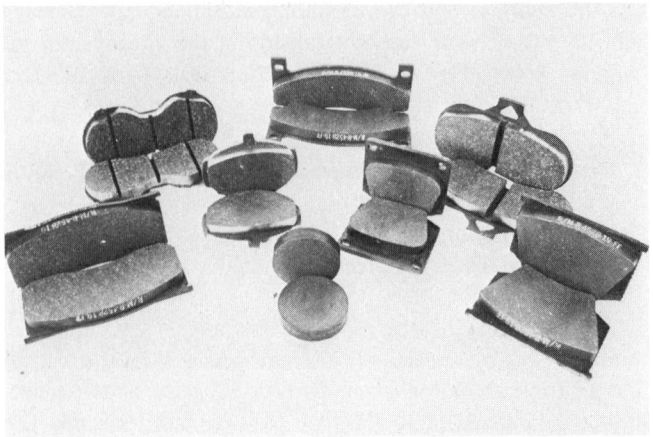

Fig. 41-30. Disc brake shoe and lining assemblies vary with vehicle application. In many cases, inboard and outboard shoes on a given vehicle are not interchangeable. Manufacturers of replacement assemblies make pads for most U.S. and foreign cars and race vehicles. (Grey-Rock Div., Raybestos-Manhattan)

Fig. 41-31. Disc brake used on rear wheels of Corvette. Method of adjusting shoe-to-drum clearance in parking brake drum is shown. (Chevrolet Div., General Motors Corp.)

riveted to a metal plate called the shoe. It is replaced as a unit. See Fig. 41-30. The rotor is ventilated, permitting circulation of air and resulting in more rapid cooling and reduction in brake fade.

SYSTEM OPERATION

As the brake pedal is depressed, hydraulic pressure from the master cylinder forces the pistons out of the caliper bores against their respective shoe and lining assemblies. The force of the pistons against the shoes moves the linings against both sides of the revolving rotor to effect braking action.

During braking application, the rubber seal on each piston stretches as the piston moves against the shoe, Fig. 41-29. When the hydraulic pressure is released, the seal relaxes, returns to its normal position and pulls the piston away from the shoe approximately .005 in. In this way, the force of the lining against the rotor is relieved and permits the needed running clearance.

A proportioning valve is located between the master cylinder and the rear brake wheel cylinders. It provides balanced braking action between the front and the rear brakes under a wide range of braking conditions. In addition, the unit includes a warning light system which indicates when one portion of the brake systems fails.

CORVETTE DISC BRAKE

In the Corvette disc brake system, Figs. 41-31 and 41-32, the caliper assembly has no external transfer tube to conduct the fluid from one side of the caliper to the other. Fluid delivered to one piston area is routed to the piston area on the opposite side of the caliper by a drilled internal passage that is sealed by an "0" ring where the two castings join. Each half of the caliper assembly contains two pistons, making four pistons per wheel.

A deep groove in the center of the pads indicates when pad

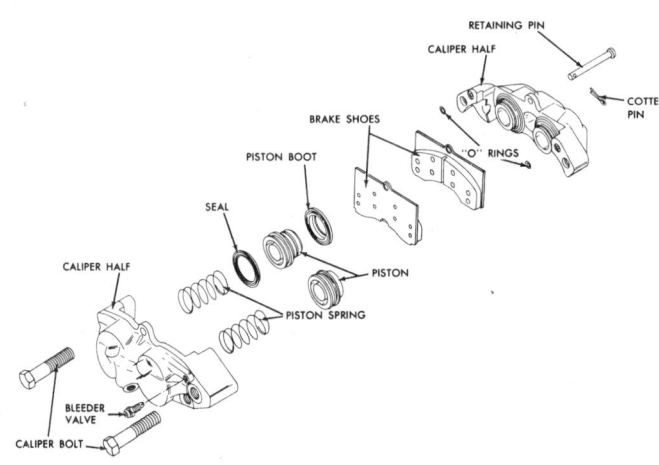

Fig. 41-32. Exploded view of Corvette disc brake caliper gives relative position of working parts. Note that four pistons actuate brake shoe assemblies, while caliper remains "fixed" in place.

replacement is necessary. When the groove is worn to the point where it is almost unnoticeable, new pads should be installed. An arrow printed on the back of all new shoes indicates the direction of forward wheel and disc rotation.

The shoes, Fig. 41-32, are held in position in the caliper by a clevis type shoe guide pin, retained by a spring clip or cotter pin. Removing the wheel and guide pin permits the pads to be lifted out of the caliper. However, a special set of thin spring steel clamps are required to hold the pistons in the bores when the pads are being removed and replaced.

On the Corvette, disc brakes are installed on the rear as well as the front wheels.

An opening in the upper surface of the caliper permits a check on lining thickness. Lining worn past the center groove on older applications, or bonded lining worn to approximately 1/16 in. thick, should be replaced with new shoe and lining assemblies (pads). Riveted lining should be replaced when the old lining is worn to approximately 1/32 in. over the rivet heads. See replacement "pads" in Fig. 41-30.

Fig. 41-32. On four wheel disc brakes, a lever-operated mechanism is used to actuate the parking brake.

FOUR WHEEL DISC BRAKES

Corvettes have been equipped with four wheel disc brakes for many years. In designing the rear wheel parking brakes, Chevrolet engineers have stayed with the supplemental brake drum and internal expanding brake shoes, Fig. 41-31, operated by a cable. With this disc and drum brake setup at each rear wheel, the Corvette parking brake is, in effect, a separate system.

More recently, several car manufacturers have introduced four wheel disc brakes with a parking brake that mechanically applies the rear calipers through foot-operated linkage. See Fig. 42-32.

Cadillac utilizes a semi-automatic parking brake arrangement in which a lever-actuated mechanism causes the rear brake shoes to engage the disc with the engine running and the transmission in Neutral or Park.

When the lever is moved automatically or manually; a screw within the mechanism turns and forces a tapered nut against a cone. The cone, in turn, forces the piston outward in the cylinder and the shoes are applied to the rotor.

The Cadillac parking brake is released automatically by means of a vacuum controlled diaphragm when the transmission sector lever is moved to any Drive position with the engine running. A foot pedal provides manual engagement or release of the parking brake, as desired.

Larger Ford, Mercury and Lincoln vehicles also make use of a lever-operated mechanism, Fig. 41-32A, to apply the rear parking brake on four wheel disc brake applications. The mechanism incorporates three steel balls, located in pockets on opposing heads of the operating shaft and the thrust screw. On application, the balls roll between ramps in the ball pockets and force the thrust screw away from the operating shaft. Movement of the thrust screw drives the shoe lining against the rotor to create braking force.

Automatic release of the parking brake is available on some models. A vacuum motor is actuated to release the parking brake whenever the engine is running and the transmission is in either reverse or forward driving gear. The lower end of the release leaver extends for alternate manual release in case of vacuum power failure or for optional manual release.

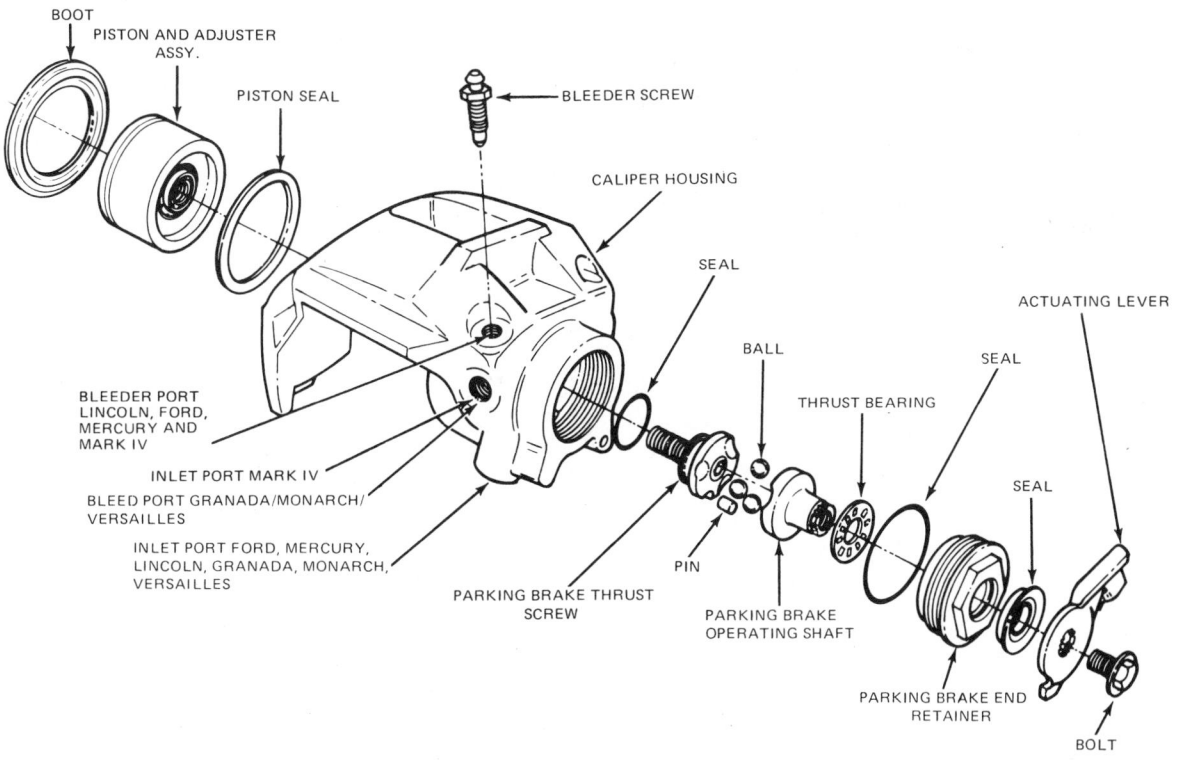

Fig. 41-32A. Exploded view of a rear brake caliper on some Fords with four wheel disc brakes.

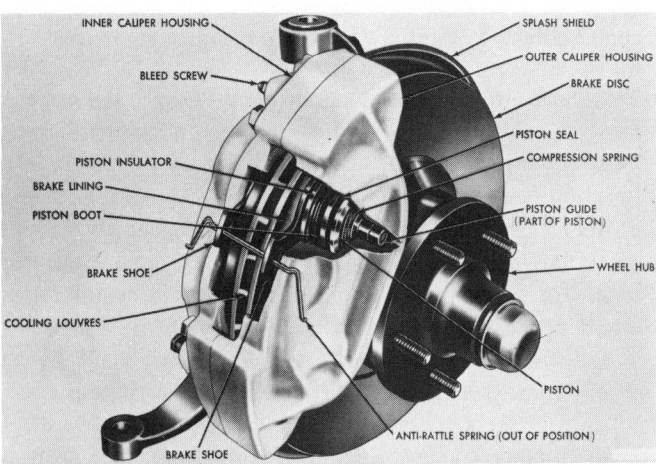

Fig. 41-33. Disc brake installation on some Plymouth, Dodge and Chrysler cars.

PLYMOUTH, DODGE, CHRYSLER DISC BRAKES

Chrysler introduced disc brakes in the late 1960s. Disc brakes found on the older Plymouth Fury, Dodge Polara and Monaco, and Chrysler cars consist of a fixed caliper, two friction pads bonded to steel shoes, four pistons, piston return springs, piston seals, dust boots and retainers. See Fig. 41-33, which presents a typical Chrysler disc brake assembly mounted on the brake disc (rotor). Fig. 41-34 shows an exploded view of the four-piston caliper assembly. The single piston caliper design was adopted because of fewer parts and simpler service.

The Chrysler brake disc is mounted on the front wheel hub and is straddled by the caliper, Fig. 41-33. The caliper is attached to the steering knuckle and steering knuckle arm. It is composed of two housings, each having two cylinder bores containing a piston, piston seal, piston return spring. These internal parts are protected by a dust boot and retainer.

Attached to the outer end of the piston is a heat-resistant pad, which contacts the shoe and acts as a heat insulator. Inserted between the pistons and the disc is the segmented lining and shoe assembly held in position by the shoe anti-rattle spring, Fig. 41-34.

As the brake pedal is depressed, the hydraulic pressure forces the pistons against the brake shoe pads. When the pedal is released, the piston return springs position the brake shoes lightly against the disc, ready for the next application. As a result, the design automatically compensates for lining wear. Shoe and lining assemblies should be replaced when the groove is no longer visible on the lining pad.

To replace the brake lining and shoe assembly:
1. Raise car and remove wheel and tire assembly.
2. Remove anti-rattle spring.
3. Remove bolts that attach caliper assembly to steering knuckle and steering arm.
4. Remove caliper from disc by sliding caliper assembly up and away from brake disc.
5. Remove each brake shoe and lining assembly one at a time through top opening.
6. Insert a piston compressing tool between piston insulator pads to keep pistons compressed.

GENERAL MOTORS DISC BRAKES

The disc brake installed on Pontiac, Oldsmobile and Cadillac Eldorado in the late 1960s is illustrated in Figs. 41-35 and 41-36. In this four-piston system, hydraulic pressure applied to the pistons forces the lining against the rotor,

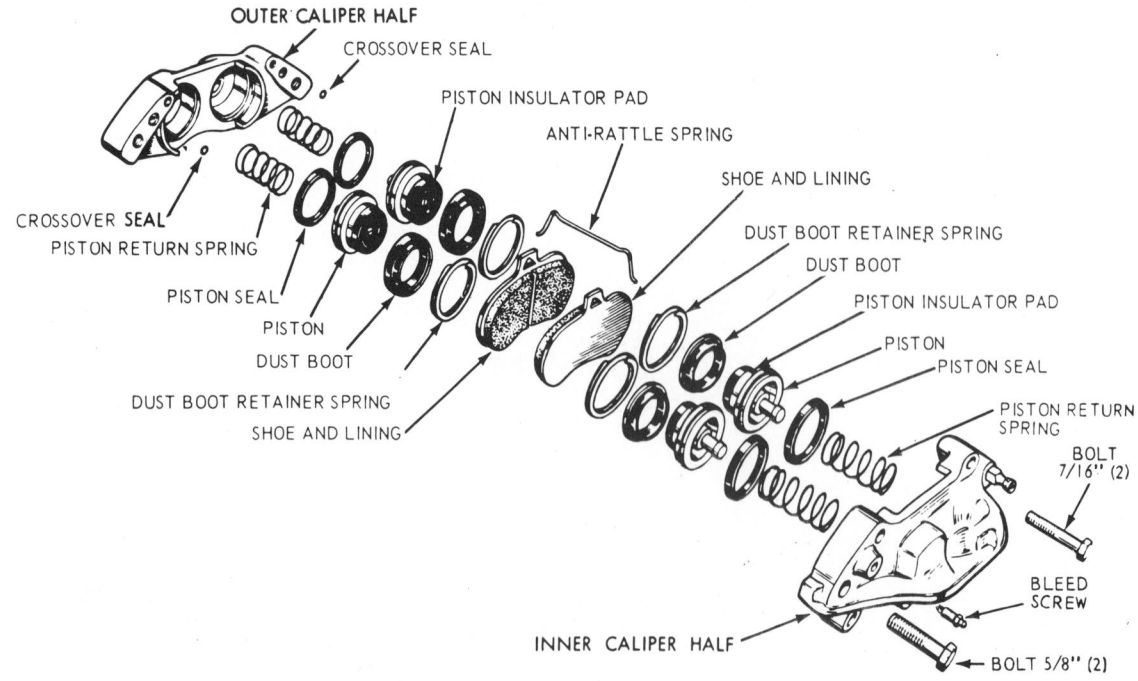

Fig. 41-34. Exploded view of caliper as installed on older Plymouth, Dodge and Chrysler cars.

clamping it between the pads with equal and opposite force.

When the brake pedal is released, the pressure decreases and the compressed piston springs in the cylinder bores position the linings lightly against the rotor, ready for the next brake application.

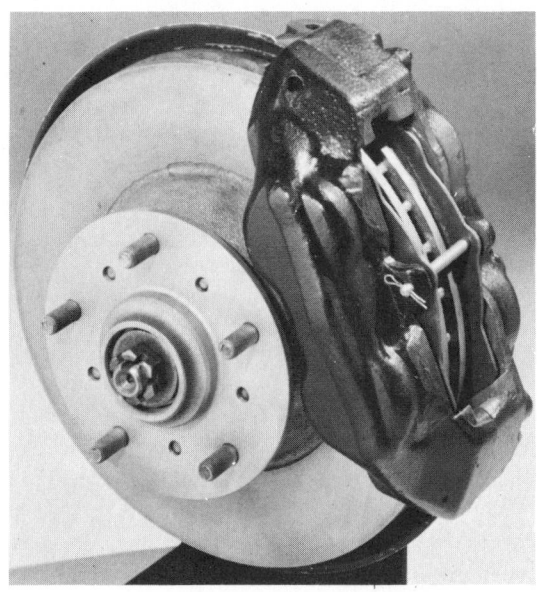

Fig. 41-35. Oldsmobile and other GM cars used 4-piston fixed caliper disc brake in late 1960's.

Since the brake linings brush lightly against the rotor when the brakes are released disc brakes automatically compensate for lining wear. Therefore, no adjustment is required. As lining wears, the pistons move further out of the caliper cylinder bores. The large diameter of the cylinder bores requires considerable volume of brake fluid. Consequently, the master cylinder fluid level should be checked at regular intervals.

Shoe and lining assemblies should be changed if the lining is less than .020 in. thick over the rivet heads.

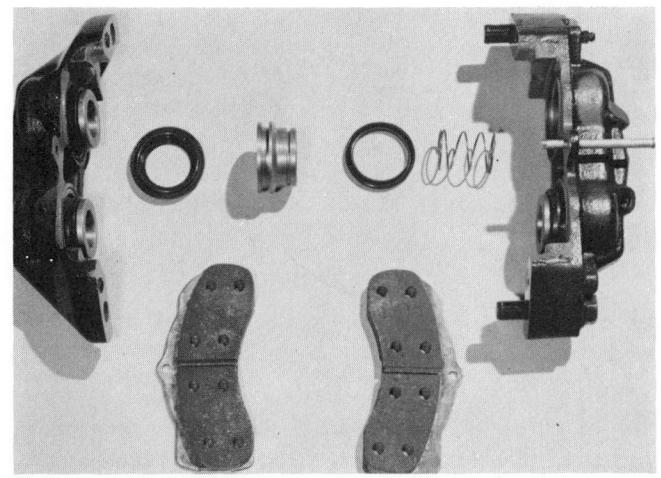

Fig. 41-36. Details of disc brake caliper installed on some Oldsmobiles.

Fig. 41-37. Beginning in 1969, most GM cars featured single-piston, floating caliper disc brake. Cadillac brake is shown.

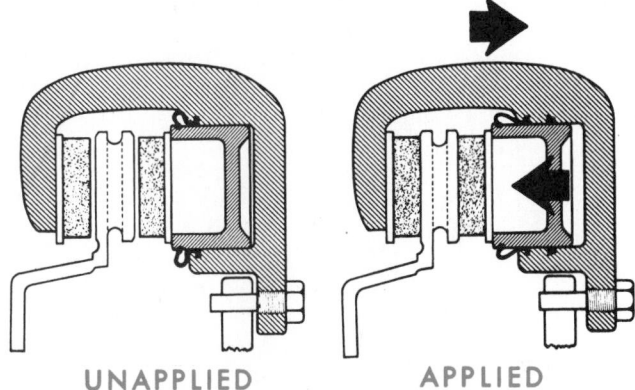

UNAPPLIED   APPLIED

Fig. 41-38. Key to floating caliper operation is when hydraulic pressure on bottom of cylinder bore causes caliper to float sideways and apply brake shoes to rotor surfaces.

BRAKE SHOE INSTALLATION

When replacing brake shoes: First attach a drain hose to caliper bleed screw and submerge other end in a container partly filled with clean brake fluid. While bottoming pistons, open bleed screw to allow excess fluid to drain. Then, tighten bleed screw before relieving pressure on the pistons. This is necessary because insertion of full thickness lining will force the pistons back into the caliper, displacing the brake fluid.

After bleeding the brakes as indicated, remove and discard cotter pin from inboard end of shoe retaining pin. Then slide out retaining pin.

Starting with the pad assembly closest to the car, push it back from the rotor as far as it will go. Use a special tool or screwdriver to press pistons to bottom of cylinder bores. Piston springs will not permit pistons to remain completely bottomed. Remove worn shoes.

Insert replacement shoes by rotating either end into caliper, Fig. 41-33. Shoes must be replaced in axle sets only.

FLOATING CALIPER DISC BRAKES

The four piston, fixed caliper disc brake was dropped from most U.S. passenger car lines in 1968 or 1969 in favor of the single piston, floating caliper assembly. Cadillac, for example, adopted the single piston setup in 1968, then modified it still further in 1972 with the introduction of an integral front wheel hub/disc brake rotor/front wheel spindle, Fig. 41-37.

The principle of operation of the floating caliper disc brake is to allow the fluid pressure to build up between the bottom of the piston and bottom of the cylinder bore. Pressure on the piston forces the inboard shoe and lining against the inboard rotor surface. Pressure against the bottom of the bore causes the caliper to float or slide on mounting bolts or sleeves, Fig. 41-38, forcing the outboard shoe and lining against outboard rotor surface. Then, as line pressure continues to build up, the clamping action of the friction surfaces stops the rotor and the vehicle.

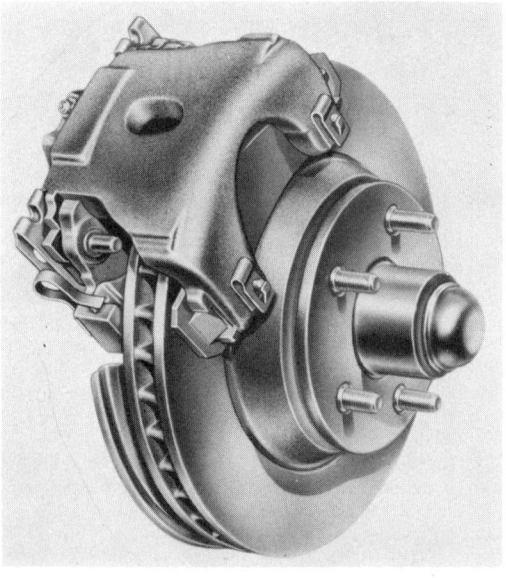

Fig. 41-39. Caliper on late model Ford disc brake has a one-piece housing that moves inward and outward as brakes are applied.

FORD SINGLE PISTON DISC BRAKE

Disc brakes installed on some late model Ford cars are similar to those used in the preceding years, but the caliper is a one-piece housing instead of two, Fig. 41-39. It is not held in a fixed position, but is free to move inboard and outboard as the brakes are applied and released. Only one piston is used in each caliper. This double acting piston applies braking pressure

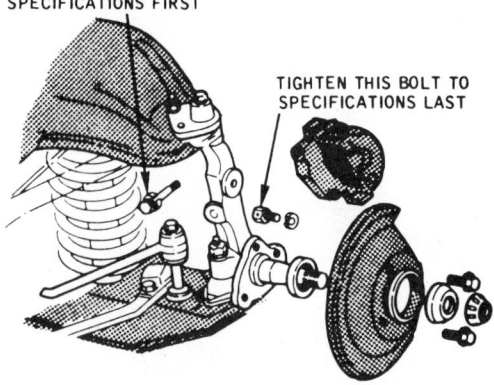

INSTALL BOTH CALIPER ATTACHING BOLTS FINGER-TIGHT, THEN TIGHTEN THIS BOLT TO SPECIFICATIONS FIRST

TIGHTEN THIS BOLT TO SPECIFICATIONS LAST

Fig. 41-40. Showing installation procedure on Ford single piston, floating caliper disc brake.

directly to the outboard shoe through the movable caliper.

The caliper over the anchor plate is bolted to the wheel spindle. On brake application, braking thrust is transferred from the caliper and brake shoes to the anchor plate, preventing rotation of the entire assembly. The caliper is held on the anchor plate by flexible steel stabilizers, Fig. 41-40.

When the brakes are applied, hydraulic pressure moves the piston outward, bringing the lining of the inboard brake shoe against the inner face of the rotor. However, no appreciable braking takes place until more fluid enters the brake cylinder and slides the entire caliper inward. This movement brings the lining of the outboard shoe (attached to caliper) into contact with the outer face of the caliper. Then, any further increase in hydraulic pressure is transmitted equally to both shoes and faces of the rotor. Brake shoes are retracted by the action of the square cross section of the piston seal, Fig. 41-29.

The caliper is removed by unscrewing two attaching bolts. Care must be taken on reassembling, however, to obtain correct alignment of the anchor plate.

Reassembling procedure is as follows:
1. Place caliper and anchor plate in position on rotor and spindle, Fig. 41-40.
2. Install lower bolt that holds anchor plate to spindle, then run it up finger tight.
3. Install upper bolt and torque it to specifications.
4. Torque lower bolt and wire two bolts together, being sure to twist ends of wire at least five times. Then position ends of wires away from the brake hose.

Unlike previous disc brakes, worn shoe and lining assemblies can be replaced only by removing the caliper and anchor plate from the spindle. Inboard and outboard shoe and lining assemblies are not interchangeable.

FORD SLIDING CALIPER BRAKE

More recently, Ford engineers developed a "sliding caliper," then a "pin slider caliper," disc brake. Both of these designs are variations of the floating caliper, utilizing a single piston and operating on the same principle whereby the piston applies one brake shoe and the movable caliper applies the other.

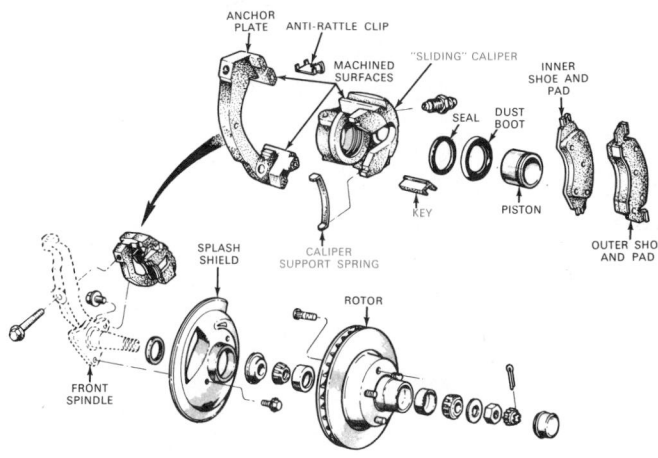

Fig. 41-41. Ford "sliding" caliper disc brake uses machined surfaces on caliper and anchor plate for sliding action during brake application. Key and support spring hold caliper against anchor plate.

This design has two major sections, the sliding caliper and an anchor plate, Fig. 41-41. Each has two angular machined surfaces, and this is where the sliding contact comes into play. The machined surfaces on the upper end of the caliper housing slide on mating machined surfaces on the anchor plate, when the brakes are applied.

A steel plated key and a caliper support spring fit between the machined surfaces of the caliper and anchor plate. The key is locked in place by an Allen head retaining screw. The spring is designed to hold the caliper in place against the anchor plate. The anchor plate is bolted to the wheel spindle arm with two bolts, Fig. 41-41.

CHRYSLER SINGLE PISTON BRAKES

Chrysler engineering has moved disc brake design through fixed four piston to single piston calipers, first "floating," now "sliding caliper" design, Figs. 41-42 and 41-43.

The floating caliper disc brake appeared for several model years on Dodge and Plymouth cars, while the Chrysler Imperial retained the four piston stationary caliper brake. Latest models use only the single piston caliper; full size models using the sliding caliper and compacts using the floating caliper. Imperials have sliding caliper disc brakes, front and rear, Fig. 41-44.

The floating caliper assemblies, Fig. 41-42, float through four rubber bushings on two steel guide pins threaded into an adapter having four machined abutments that position and align the caliper. The guide pins also locate and hold both brake shoe assemblies. In operation, all braking force is taken by the caliper from the outboard shoe, and by the machined lugs on the adapter from the inboard shoe.

The sliding caliper assemblies, Fig. 41-43, have two machined abutments on the adapter to position and align the caliper. Two retainer clips are used to keep the caliper in the machined "ways" of the adapter, yet allow lateral movement of the caliper.

The outboard brake shoe has retention flanges to help

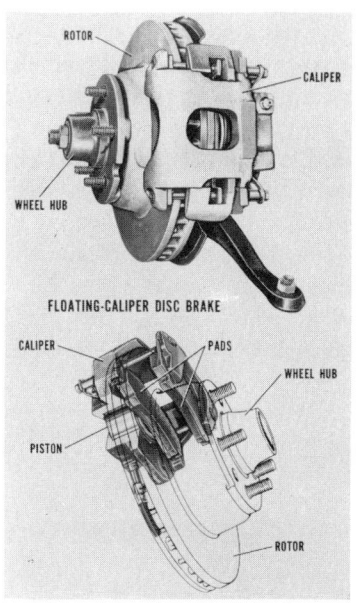

Fig. 41-42. Chrysler's floating caliper brake.

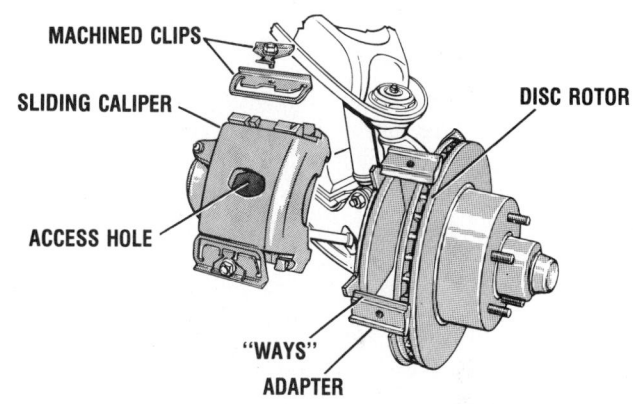

Fig. 41-43. Chrysler Corporation "slider type" disc brake has caliper positioned and aligned so that machined base of casting slides on two machined abutments or "ways" on adapter.

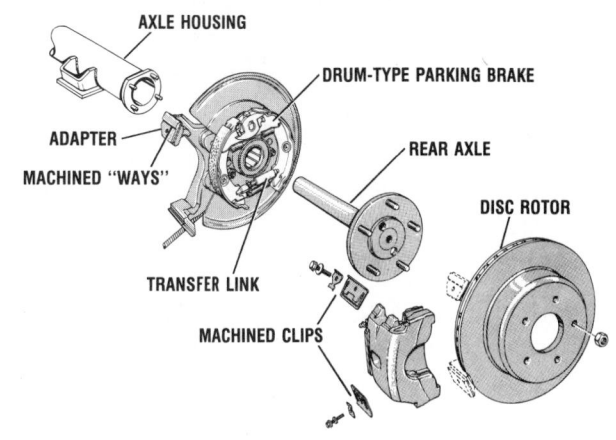

IMPERIAL – REAR DISC BRAKE

Fig. 41-44. Late model Chrysler Imperial cars are equipped with four wheel disc brake system. "Slider type" caliper is used all around.

locate and position the shoe on the caliper. All braking force from this shoe is taken by the caliper. The inboard shoe is held in place by the adapter, and it reacts directly on the adapter when the brakes are applied.

As mentioned, Chrysler Imperial models also have sliding calipers at the rear wheels, Fig. 41-44. The caliper assembly is mounted on the end of the rear axle housing by means of an intermediate adapter. The disc brake adapter is attached to the intermediate adapter.

The rotor at the rear is slipped over the lug bolts that protrude through the axle flange, Fig. 41-44. Then the wheel and tire assembly is installed over the lug bolts to hold the rotor in place. The inside surface of the rotor hub is machined to act as a "drum" for the parking brake. The parking brake is cable operated.

GENERAL MOTORS DISC BRAKE

Late model General Motors cars are equipped with single piston, floating caliper disc brakes on the front wheels (except Corvette). Cadillac changed from the four piston stationary caliper brake to the single piston, floating caliper brake in 1968, Fig. 41-37. Major components are the hub and rotor assembly, caliper assembly, splash shield and shoe and lining assemblies.

The single piston caliper is constructed from a single casting, with one large piston bore in the inboard section. The caliper housing is mounted to the support plate by two housing retainer bolts, two sleeves and four rubber bushings, Fig. 41-45.

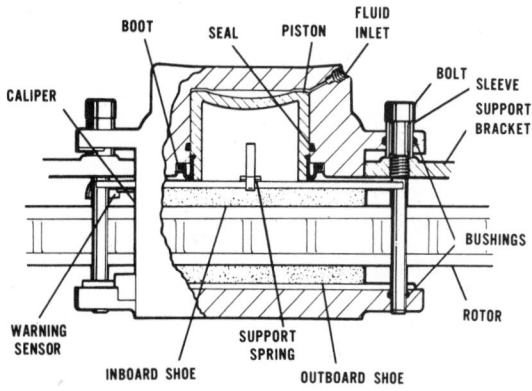

Fig. 41-45. Most General Motors cars are equipped with single piston, floating caliper disc brakes at front (except Corvette).

The shoe and lining assemblies differ. The outboard shoe has thinner metal and slightly thinner lining. It has ears near the outer edge bent over at right angles to the shoe. The top ends have holes to accept the caliper retaining bolts. A large tab is bent over at the bottom of the outboard shoe to fit a cutout in the caliper.

The inboard shoe has ears on the top ends which fit over the caliper retaining bolts. A spring inside the hollow piston supports the bottom edge of the shoe. Also, a lining wear

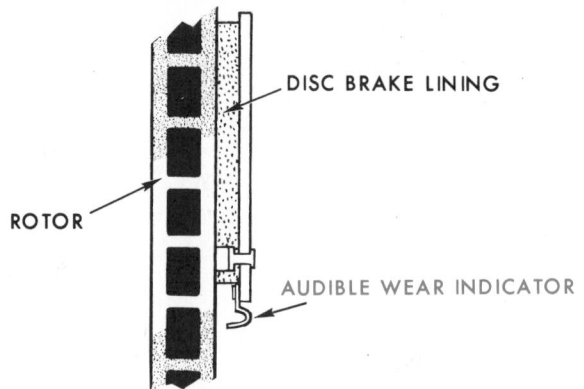

Fig. 41-46. Late model General Motors cars with disc brakes have an audible wear indicator that signals by "squealing" that brake lining is worn almost to rivets.

sensor is incorporated on each inboard brake shoe, Fig. 41-46.

General Motors cars, and others, use a combination valve when equipped with disc brakes, Fig. 41-47. This valve acts as a metering valve, failure warning switch and proportioning valve. The metering valve "holds off" front disc braking until the rear drum brakes make contact with the drums. The failure warning switch lights a dash warning lamp if either front or rear brake systems fail. The proportioning valve improves front to rear brake balance at high deceleration by reducing rear brake pressure to delay a rear wheel skid.

AMERICAN MOTORS DISC BRAKE

American Motors cars also have single piston, floating caliper disc brakes at the front. AMC uses a ventilated cast iron hub and rotor assembly. The braking surfaces are protected from road splash by a splash shield.

The caliper floats in four rubber bushings supported by two steel guide pins threaded into an adapter, Fig. 41-48. Two bushings are located on the outboard side of the caliper, two are on the inboard side.

Machined abutments on the caliper and adapter position and align the caliper fore and aft. Two positioners installed over the guide pins hold the inner bushings in position and, along with the piston seal, maintain proper shoe clearance.

The caliper is a one-piece casting containing a piston, piston seal and dust boot. The cylinder is machined to hold the piston seal. The piston seal fits around the piston to provide a fluid seal between the piston and cylinder. The dust boot fits into a recess in the cylinder and groove in the piston.

POWER BRAKES

Power brake units used on passenger cars are of two general types: vacuum suspended and air suspended. In addition, a new power braking system called the Hydro-Boost uses hydraulic pressure from the vehicle's power steering pump as a power source.

VACUUM SUSPENDED OPERATION: In the released position, both sides of the power piston and diaphragm are

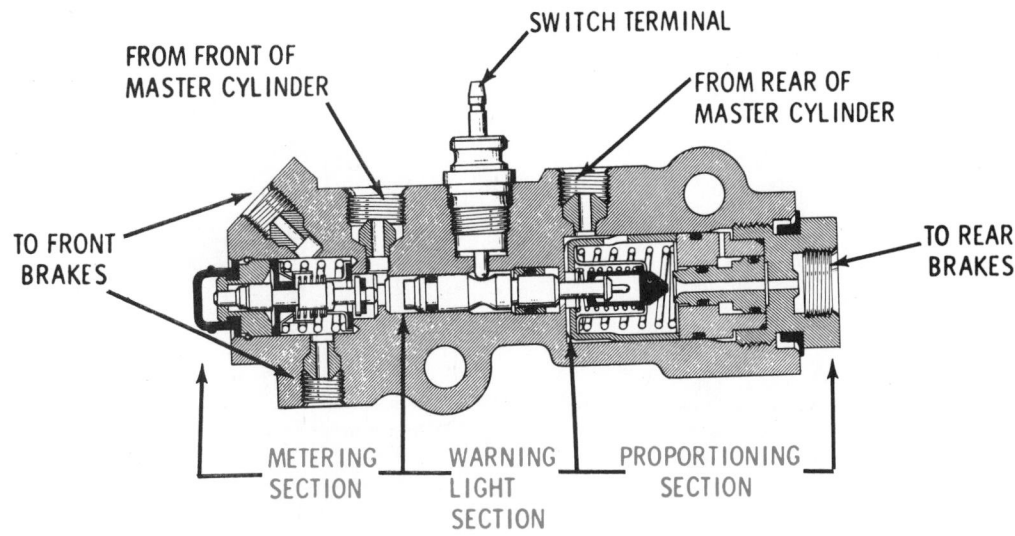

FROM FRONT OF
MASTER CYLINDER

SWITCH TERMINAL

FROM REAR OF
MASTER CYLINDER

TO FRONT
BRAKES

TO REAR
BRAKES

METERING
SECTION

WARNING
LIGHT
SECTION

PROPORTIONING
SECTION

Fig. 41-47. Combination valves combine several valve functions in a single assembly. This one used in GM cars has metering, warning light and proportioning sections.

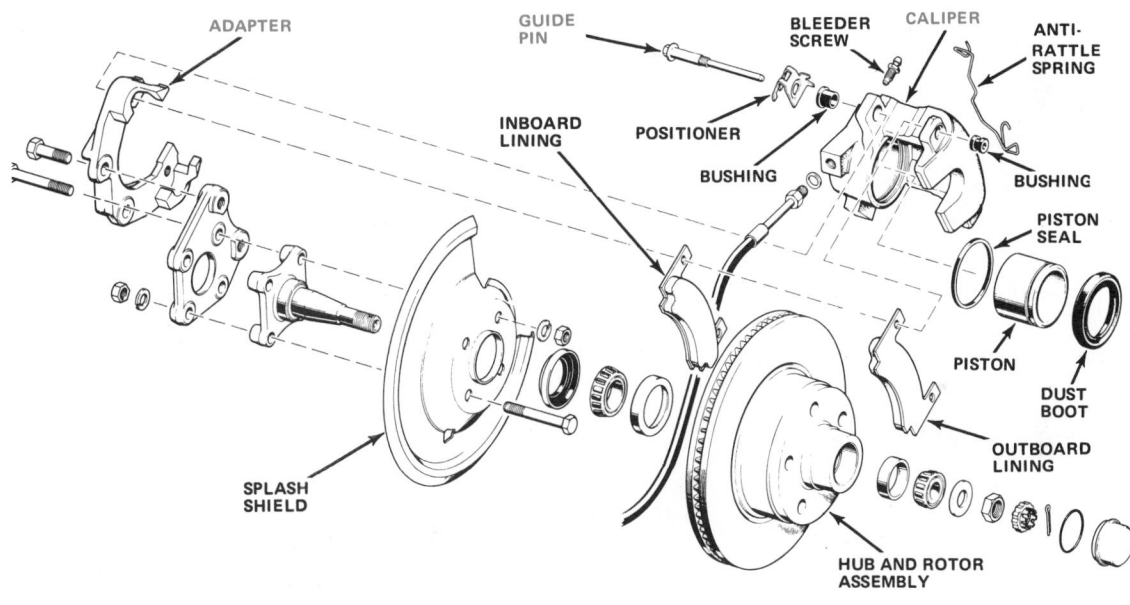

ADAPTER

GUIDE
PIN

BLEEDER
SCREW

CALIPER

ANTI-
RATTLE
SPRING

INBOARD
LINING

POSITIONER

BUSHING

BUSHING

PISTON
SEAL

PISTON

DUST
BOOT

OUTBOARD
LINING

SPLASH
SHIELD

HUB AND ROTOR
ASSEMBLY

Fig. 41-48. Exploded view of American Motors disc brake reveals use of guide pins that screw into adapter, permitting pin portion to guide floating caliper assembly in and out of application.

open to intake manifold vacuum. As the brakes are applied, Fig. 41-49, air is admitted through the control valve to one side of the piston and diaphragm. Immediately, atmospheric pressure causes the diaphragm and power piston to move forward, causing the push rod to actuate the master cylinder pistons and apply the brakes.

AIR SUSPENDED OPERATION: In the released position, both sides of the power piston are under atmospheric pressure. When the brakes are applied, manifold vacuum is admitted through the control valve to one side of the piston. Immediately, atmospheric pressure on the other side causes the piston to move, forcing the push rod forward and actuating the

master cylinder pistons to apply the brakes.

HYDRO-BOOST OPERATION: In the release position, fluid flows from the power steering pump through the open center valve in the power booster, then to the power steering gear and back to the pump reservoir. When the brakes are applied, the center valve closes and fluid under pressure actuates the booster which, in turn, actuates the master cylinder pistons to apply the brakes. In the event of a loss of power steering fluid pressure, foot pressure on the brake pedal opens the accumulator valve, Fig. 41-50, which furnishes a reserve power supply of fluid to the booster. When this supply is depleted, the system reverts to manual operation.

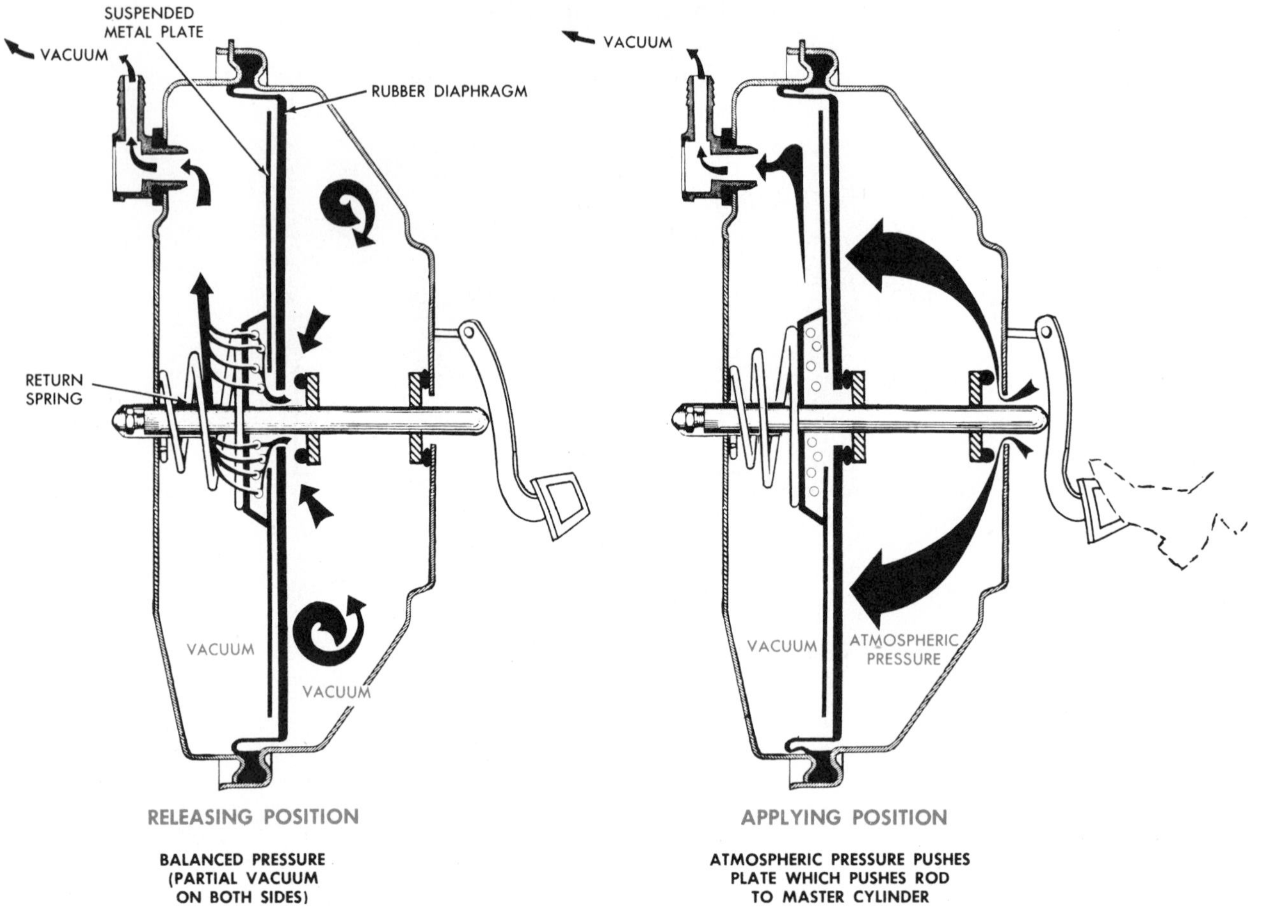

RELEASING POSITION

BALANCED PRESSURE
(PARTIAL VACUUM
ON BOTH SIDES)

APPLYING POSITION

ATMOSPHERIC PRESSURE PUSHES
PLATE WHICH PUSHES ROD
TO MASTER CYLINDER

Fig. 41-49. Principle of operation of vacuum suspended power brake unit is illustrated. Left. Vacuum exists in both chambers. Right. Atmospheric pressure in rear chamber forces diaphragm and plate forward to afford power assist to fluid pressure in system.

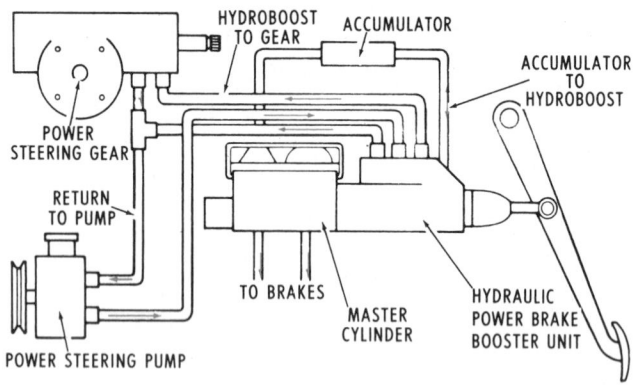

Fig. 41-50. Hydro-Boost power assist is used on light trucks and some cars. Schematic shows fluid flow from power steering pump to booster unit, with some fluid going to power steering gear and some to accumulator. (Bendix Automotive Control Systems Group)

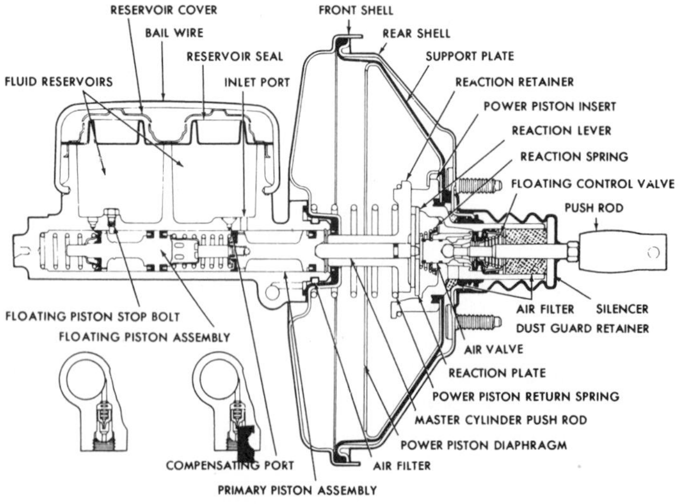

Fig. 41-51. Details of Delco Moraine vacuum suspended type of power brake unit.

DELCO MORAINE UNIT

The Delco Moraine power brake unit, shown in Fig. 41-51, is the vacuum suspended type. The line from the intake manifold is connected to the vacuum check valve in the front housing of the power brake.

In the released position, the air valve is seated on the floating control valve. Air at atmospheric pressure entering through the air filter, is shut off at the floating control valve. Vacuum is at both sides of the power piston, and any air at the right side of the piston is drawn off by the vacuum over the floating control valve seat and through two small holes in the power piston.

As the brake pedal is depressed, the valve operating rod carries the air valve away from the floating control valve. The control valve will follow the air valve until it is in contact with the raised seat in the power piston. This shuts off vacuum to the right of the piston, allowing air at atmospheric pressure to travel past the air valve and through two passages into the housing on the right side of the power piston. This causes the power piston to move to the left, carrying the master cylinder push rod with it, to operate the master cylinder.

When the desired pedal pressure is reached, the power piston moves to the left until the floating control valves (still seated on power piston) again seats on the air valve. At this point of operation, the power brake will remain stationary until pressure on the brake pedal is altered.

When pedal pressure is released, the air valve spring forces the air valve back until its snap ring rests against the power piston. As it returns, the air valve pushes the floating control valve off its seat on the power piston, opening the space to the right of the power piston to vacuum. When both sides of the piston are under vacuum, the power piston return spring will return the piston to the released position.

BENDIX TANDEM DIAPHRAGM UNIT

Another vacuum suspended type of power brake is the Bendix tandem diaphragm unit, Fig. 41-52. It has three basic elements:

1. A vacuum power chamber that consists of a front shell, rear shell, center plate, front diaphragm, rear diaphragm, hydraulic push rod and vacuum diaphragm and plate return spring.

2. A mechanically actuated control valve (integral with vacuum power diaphragms) that controls degree of power brake application or release in accordance with foot pressure applied to valve operating rod through brake pedal linkage. Control valve consists of a single poppet with an atmospheric port. Vacuum port seat is a part of valve body attached to diaphragm assembly. Atmospheric port seat is a part of valve plunger that moves within valve housing hub of diaphragm plates.

3. A hydraulic cylinder that contains all elements of conventional master cylinder, except for hydraulic push rod which has a self-locking adjustment screw at one end with a piston head at other.

With the brakes in the released position, Fig. 41-52, and the engine running, vacuum from the intake manifold is admitted through the vacuum check valve to the front (left) vacuum chamber and to the vacuum chamber to the front (left) of the rear diaphragm, Fig. 41-52. The valve operating rod and valve plunger are held to the right in the valve housing by the valve return spring to close the atmospheric port and open the vacuum port.

With the valve in this position, the chambers to the rear of

both the front and the rear diaphragms are open to vacuum through the portings around the edge of the center plate and through the hub of the valve housing. The vacuum power diaphragms are now balanced, since the same degree of vacuum is on each side. The vacuum power diaphragm return spring is then free to return the diaphragm and plate assembly with the hydraulic push rod to the released position.

As the brakes are applied, the valve operating rod and valve plunger move to the left in the power diaphragm and plate assembly. This compresses the valve return spring and brings the poppet valve into contact with the vacuum valve seat in the valve housing to close the vacuum port, Fig. 41-53. Any

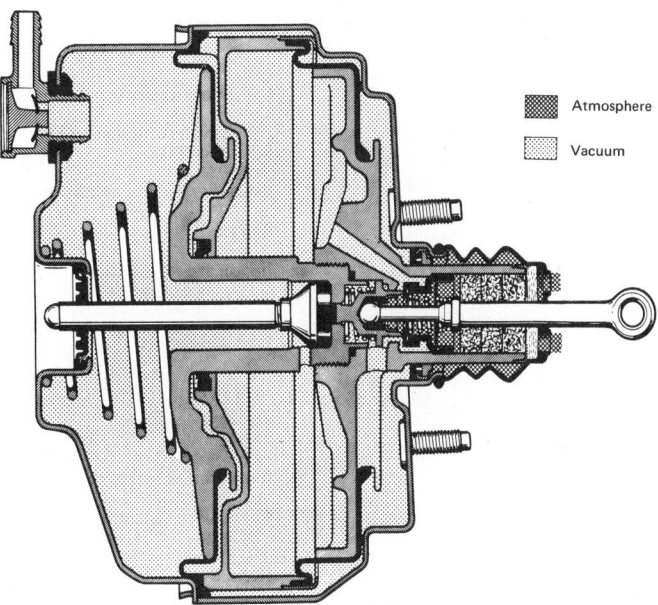

Fig. 41-52. Bendix tandem diaphragm power brake in released position.

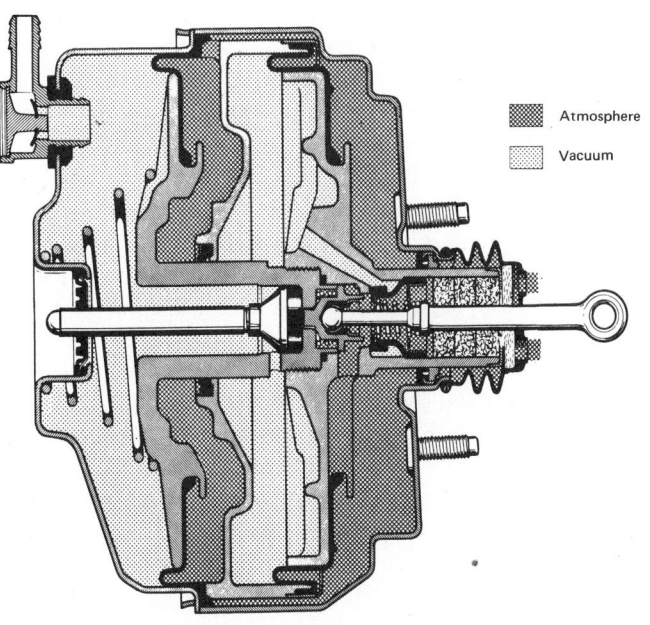

Fig. 41-53. Tandem diaphragm power brake unit in applied position.

additional movement of the valve operating rod in the applied direction moves the valve plunger away from the poppet valve. This opens the atmospheric port and admits atmosphere through the filter to the chambers on the right side of both the front and the rear vacuum power diaphragms.

With vacuum on the left side of the front and rear diaphragms, and atmospheric pressure on the right side of the front and rear diaphragms, a force is developed to move the vacuum power diaphragm and plate assembly and hydraulic push rod to operate the master cylinder in the usual manner.

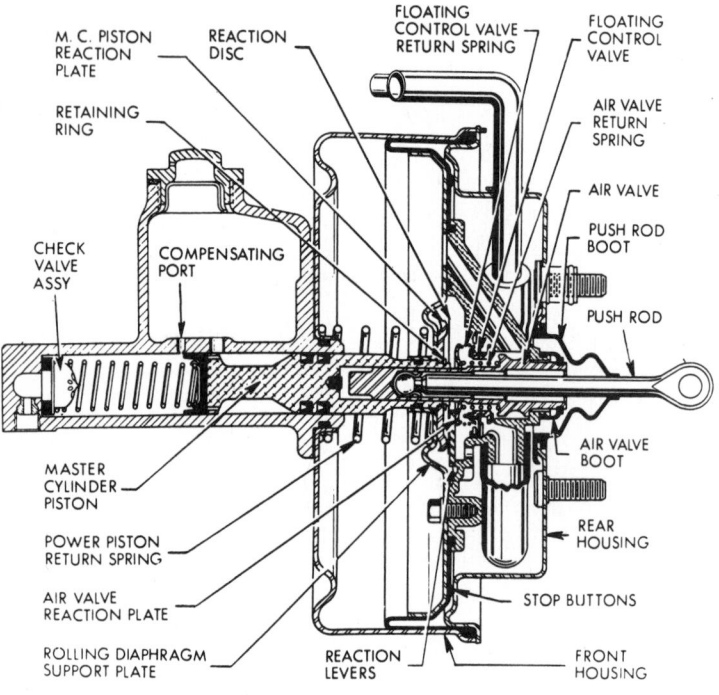

Fig. 41-54. Air suspended type of power brake unit in released position.

OPERATION OF AIR SUSPENDED UNIT

The released position of a typical air suspended power brake unit is illustrated in Fig. 41-54. The air valve return spring holds the air valve, push rod and brake pedal rearward, so the air valve is clear of the floating control valve. Although vacuum is present at the floating control valve through the flexible hose, the control valve return spring holds the rubber face of the valve against its annular seat in the power piston, closing off manifold vacuum.

Atmospheric air enters through the air filter into the air chamber, and flows through holes in the power piston into the reaction lever area. From here, it flows past the open annular seat on the air valve, through a passage in the power piston into the vacuum chamber. With the vacuum passage closed, and the vacuum chamber open to outside air, the power piston is balanced by atmospheric pressure on both sides, and is held against the rear housing by the return spring.

The air valve return spring and the floating control valve return spring are holding the air valve reaction plate against the

inner ends of the reaction levers. Since the outer ends of these levers are against their pivot points in the power piston, the levers are pushing forward against the reaction discs. The disc, in turn, is holding the master cylinder piston and reaction plate assembly forward so that the reaction plate is against its stop. In the released position of the power cylinder, the reaction mechanism is fully forward, and the two valves are fully rearward.

When the brakes are applied, the push rod moves the air valve forward until its annular seat contacts the floating control valve. At this point, atmospheric pressure is sealed off from the vacuum chamber. Further movement of the air valve pushes the floating control valve away from its annular seat in the power piston, connecting the vacuum chamber to the vacuum source. As air is exhausted out of the vacuum chamber, atmospheric pressure in the air chamber starts moving the power piston forward, Fig. 41-55.

As the power piston moves forward, it forces the master cylinder piston into the master cylinder to build pressure in the hydraulic system and apply the brakes. At the same time, a reaction pressure is transmitted back to the brake pedal to give the driver an indication of the power being applied to the brakes.

As soon as pressure builds in the hydraulic system, pressure on the end of the master cylinder piston causes the master cylinder reaction plate to move away from its stop and press against the reaction discs and reaction levers. The levers, in turn, swing around their pivots in the power piston and push the air valve reaction plate back against the floating control valve snubbers, Fig. 41-55.

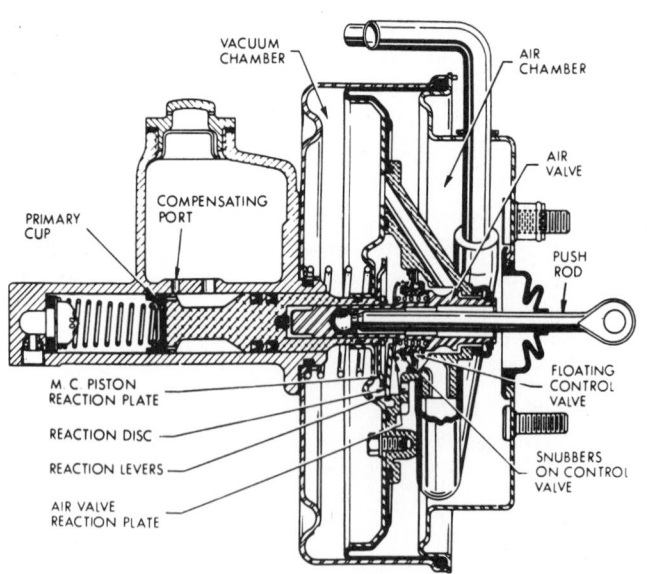

Fig. 41-55. Air suspended type of power brake unit in applied position.

When the brake pedal is released, the air valve return spring forces the air valve away from the floating control valve. This allows the floating control valve return spring to seat the control valve against the power piston, closing the vacuum passage. Since both sides of the piston are now open to atmospheric pressure, the piston return spring forces the power piston and related parts rearward to the unapplied position, Fig. 41-54.

ELECTRIC BRAKES

Several electrically operated braking systems have been developed. To date they have not been used as extensively as vacuum and air operation. There are several different ways of using electrical energy to operate brakes. It is customary to control the severity of the brake operation, by the amount of current flowing through a magnet.

In one popular electric brake, the armature is attached to the wheel and the magnet attached to the axle. The magnet has a lug and cam levers on it which press the brake shoe lining against the drum when current flows in the magnet. The amount of pressure applied to the lining is regulated by a foot pedal or hand lever, which operates a rheostat connected to the battery.

Various anti-skid braking devices that include electrical components have been developed. Ford's "Sure-Track," for example, is a system of sensors, valves, an actuator and a small computer that help keep the rear end of the vehicle tracking the front by controlling rear wheel brake locking.

Rear wheel skid is undesirable in panic stops. The ideal situation is to have maximum braking of the rear wheels just short of skidding or "locking up." Sure-Track accomplishes this by automatically "pumping" the brakes in cycles, as rapid as four times per second when the rear wheels begin to lock up under heavy braking. By this rapid cycling of brake application and release, the locking point is never reached.

The Sure-Track system includes:
1. Hydraulic pressure system.
2. Electrical controls system.

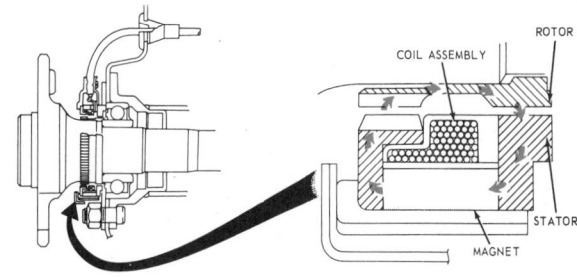

Fig. 41-56. In Sure-Track anti-skid brake system by Ford, a mechanically driven electronic sensor located at each rear wheel transmits wheel speed to a control module, which signals an actuator solenoid to release or apply rear brakes. Result is automatic "pumping" of rear brakes to avoid lock-up.

3. Vacuum and air control systems.

In operation, sensors located at each rear wheel, Fig. 41-56, detect the velocity of the rear wheels and transmit it to the computer, or control module. The control module, located under the glove compartment, determines the optimum braking cycle and signals the vacuum-powered brake actuator in the engine compartment. The actuator valves regulate brake fluid pressure to the rear wheels.

The cycling, or rapid pumping of the brakes, takes place only when the driver's foot applies full pressure to the system, and the rear wheel brakes tend to lock up.

AIR BRAKES

Air-operated brakes should not be confused with vacuum boosters. Air brakes are used on trucks and heavy-duty vehicles, but are not necessary on passenger cars. An air braking system is expensive and complicated, but it does prove effective for heavy-duty operation. See Fig. 41-57.

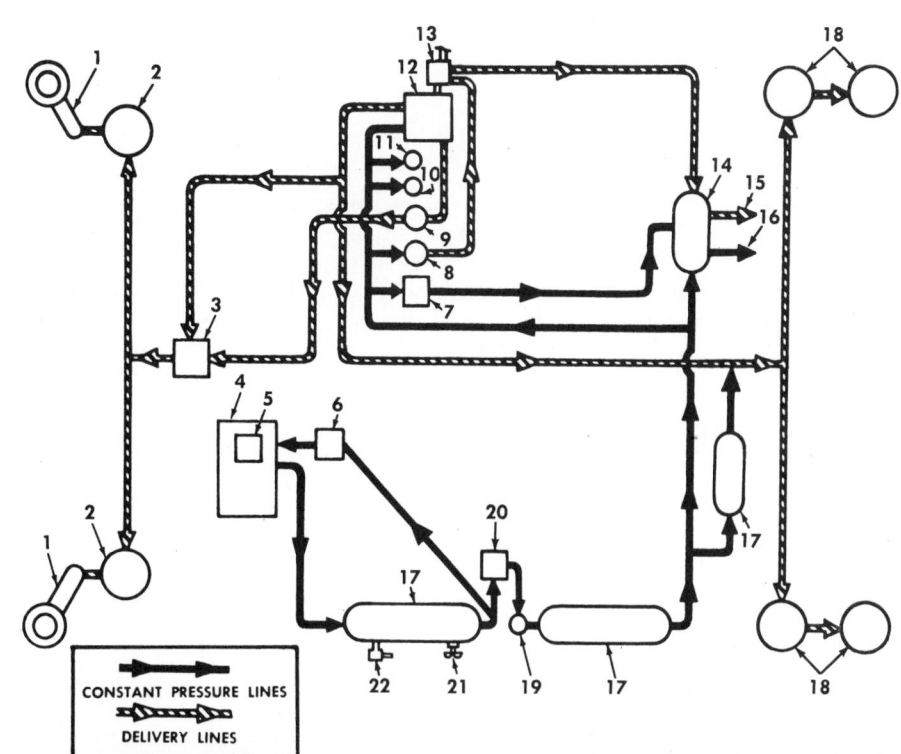

Fig. 41-57. Typical air brake system includes: 1—Slack adjuster. 2—Standard brake chamber. 3—Limiting and quick release valve. 4—Air compressor. 5—Air intake. 6—Governor. 7—Tractor protection control valve. 8—Trailer brake hand control valve. 9—Two-way valve. 10—Low air buzzer switch. 11—Air gauge. 12—Application valve. 13—Double check valve. 14—Tractor protection valve. 15—Trailer brake service line. 16—Trailer brake emergency line. 17—Air tanks. 18—Stop-master brake chambers. 19—Check valve. 20—Moisture ejector valve. 21—Drain valve. 22—Safety valve.

The system consists of an air compressor attached to the engine, storage tanks to hold the compressed air, a governor, pressure cylinders or diaphragm chambers at each wheel, suitable control valves and necessary piping and connections. The air also may be piped to a trailer equipped with air brakes. Therefore, the truck driver can control the trailer as well as the truck-tractor. See Fig. 41-58. A typical brake application cylinder is shown in Fig. 41-59.

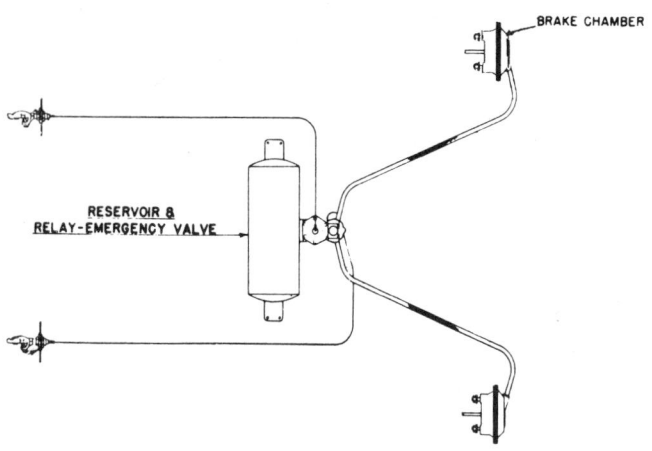

Fig. 41-58. Braking system used on a two wheel trailer. This air brake is connected to truck-tractor system.

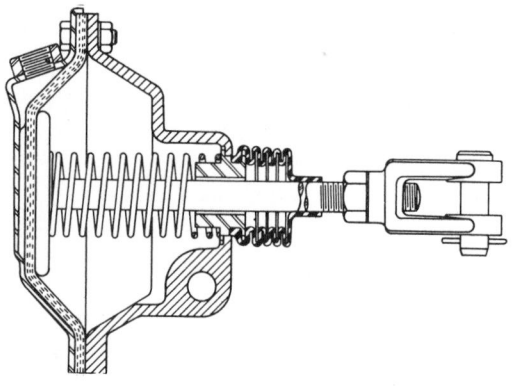

Fig. 41-59. Cross section shows construction of a typical power brake application cylinder.

COMBINATION OF UNITS

Now it becomes apparent that a vehicle can have various combinations of units to fit different conditions. There are passenger cars with hydraulic brakes, with or without vacuum boosters.

There are trucks with electric brakes or hydraulic brakes that use vacuum boosters, vacuum power operation or air power operation.

There are trailers with electric brakes or with hydraulic brakes operated by either air power or vacuum power.

Also all sorts of combinations of these different units are

possible. For example, a diesel truck (which has no intake manifold vacuum) may be equipped with air-operated hydraulic brakes. Perhaps it is desired to pull a trailer that is equipped with vacuum-operated hydraulic brakes. In this case, the truck must be provided with a vacuum pump to operate the trailer brakes.

There are dozens of combinations of different units in this fashion. Furthermore, air cylinders or diaphragms are combined with hydraulic cylinders in one unit, etc. For this reason the brake serviceman must understand all of the different units and know how each should function separately and in combination with the other units.

For convenience, several automatic accessories are added to the hydraulic system and become a part of it. For example, the stoplight switch is often hydraulically operated and mounted on the master cylinder. Or, a mechanically actuated switch is actuated by brake pedal application.

Standard equipment on late model cars is a brake line pressure differential warning system. A warning lamp on the instrument panel is incorporated in the hydraulic system to indicate when a difference in brake fluid pressure exists between the front and rear hydraulic braking systems. Generally, a pressure differential of 80 to 150 psi is required to operate the switch that controls the warning lamp.

A parking brake warning lamp on the instrument panel appears on most late model cars. If the parking brake is in the applied position when the engine is started, the warning lamp lights to signal the driver to release the parking brake.

BRAKE SERVICE

WARNING: WHEN SERVICING WHEEL BRAKE PARTS, BREATHING DUST CONTAINING ASBESTOS FIBERS MAY CAUSE SERIOUS BODILY HARM. (See page 515.)

There are two general methods of attaching brake lining to brake shoes: by using rivets and by bonding. With riveting, there reportedly is less possibility of the lining coming loose. With bonding, the full surface of the lining is used, since none is sacrificed for rivet holes.

When molded lining is to be installed on internal expanding brake shoes, it is advisable to use a special brake lining clamp to force the lining down tightly against the brake shoe at all points. If a clamp is not available, the next best method is to rivet in the middle, and work out to the ends, Fig. 41-60.

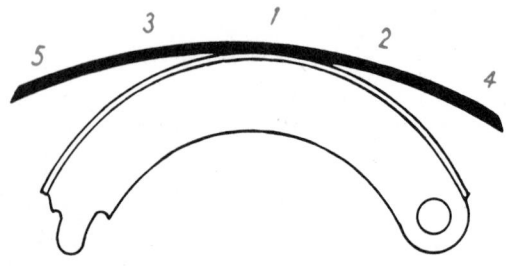

Fig. 41-60. Rivets should be placed first in middle, then at 2, 3, 4 and 5 when riveting lining to a shoe, unless a suitable clamp is available.

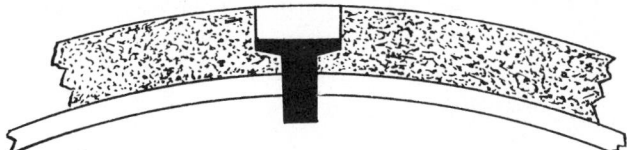

Fig. 41-61. Countersink hole in lining should be accurate to size and shape of rivet.

Rivets used in fastening brake lining to brake shoes usually are brass, copper or aluminum. If the head of the rivet touches the brake drum, scoring will result. Therefore, the rivets must be countersunk below the surface of the lining, Fig. 41-61. It is customary to countersink the rivet hole about two thirds of the way through the lining and exactly the same size as the rivet head for greatest strength. Also, the rivet hole in the lining should be the same size as the hole in the brake shoe.

It is essential that the rivet is a snug fit in the rivet hole and of the right length to "upset" easily. A good rule for rivet length is to have the rivet extend through the hole about two thirds of the rivet diameter. A 3/16 in. rivet should have a 1/8 in. shank sticking out for riveting over, Fig. 41-62.

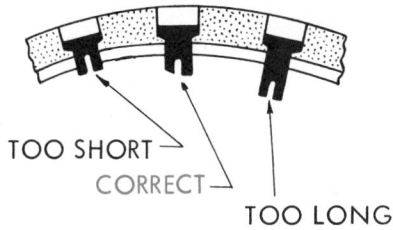

TOO SHORT
CORRECT
TOO LONG

Fig. 41-62. Rivets should be set with a roll punch instead of a star punch. Select correct rivet length.

In bonding brake lining to the shoes, a cement is used between the shoes and the lining. Then, the lining is clamped tightly and placed in a special oven for curing. The cement can be applied to the lining in the form of a paste. Or, a tape may be interposed between the lining and the shoe.

Before applying new lining to a shoe, the surface of the shoe must be perfectly clean. Cleanliness is essential, whether the new lining is to be riveted in place or bonded. Special sanders are available for cleaning the shoes. The new lining must adhere tightly to the shoe, yet with minimum resistance to the transmission of the heat of braking.

PREPARATION OF SHOES

Before relining brakes, make sure that the diameter of the brake drum is standard, Fig. 41-63. If the brake drum has been reconditioned, it will be larger in diameter. If the diameter has been increased more than .030 in., lining of oversize thickness should be installed.

The surface of the brake lining of newly relined shoes does not conform accurately to the surface of the brake drum. New lining has slight high and low spots. In addition, the brake

Fig. 41-63. Using a special gauge to check the diameter of a brake drum. (Ammco Tools, Inc.)

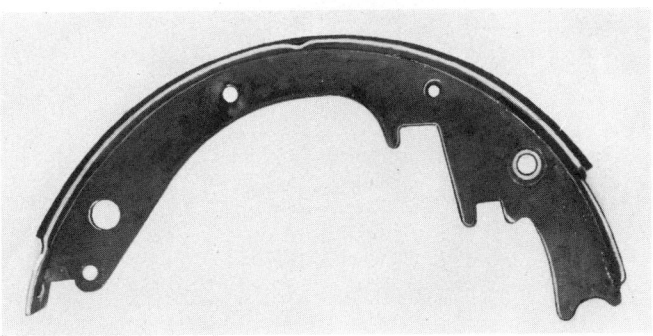

Fig. 41-64. Note that most wear is at center of brake shoe, indicating shoe was used in over-size drums or brake shoe is warped.

shoes may be bent or warped, Fig. 41-64. Or, if the drum has been reconditioned, it will be slightly larger in diameter and will not conform to the arc of the brake shoes.

Brake shoes should be ground with special brake shoe-grinding equipment, Fig. 41-65, not only to smooth the surface, but to conform to curvature of the brake drum.

If the brake shoes are used without grinding, the high spots of the lining will do all the braking, and much higher than

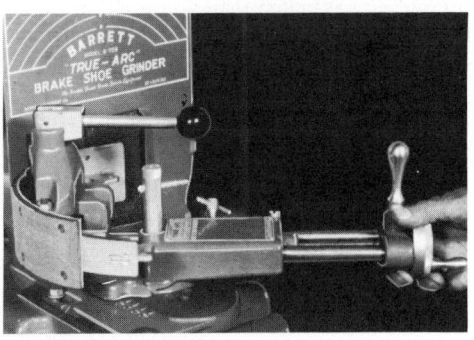

Fig. 41-65. Grinding surface of a brake shoe.

normal temperatures will result. High heat will quickly heat check or completely ruin new lining.

Care must be exercised so that no grease, oil or brake fluid reaches the brake lining. Any fluid contamination will affect the coefficient of friction and grabbing brakes will result. In this connection, always replace the grease seals when new brake lining is installed. Also, wheel cylinders should be examined to make sure they are not leaking. When handling brake shoes, care must be taken that the hands are not greasy.

When lubricating the front wheel bearings, use only grease specified for that purpose, and only enough to lubricate the bearing. Excess lubricant may get on the brake lining and ruin it. Or, a low melting point grease may thin out and enter the brake shoe/drum area.

Fig. 41-67. Reconditioning a brake drum by turning on a brake drum lathe. Feed and speed can be adjusted.

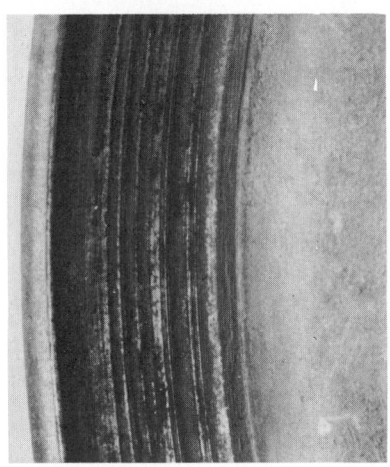

Fig. 41-66. Badly scored brake drum.

SERVICING THE DRUMS

The surface of the brake drum must be smooth and free from galling, ridges and heat checks, Fig. 41-66. In addition, the drum must not be bell-mouthed or out-of-round. The ridges, galling and check marks are easily visible, but a drum gauge should be used to check for other conditions, Fig. 41-63. The manner in which the brake lining is worn on the shoe will also indicate the condition of the drum. A drum that is bell-mouthed, for example, will cause the lining to wear more on one side of the shoe than on the other.

Another important reason for measuring the diameter of the drum is to note whether there is enough metal to permit reconditioning. Passenger car brake drums should not be reconditioned more than 0.060 in. oversize. If more than 0.060 in. is removed (0.030 in. per side) it will severely weaken the drum. The drum will become oval when the brakes are applied and, because of less metal, it will operate at much higher temperatures, with attendant brake fade and short lining life.

Brake drums can be reconditioned either by turning on a lathe, Fig. 41-67, or by grinding, Fig. 41-68. Both methods are used extensively. The regrinding method is used particularly in

Fig. 41-68. Grinding a brake drum.

cases where the drum has hard spots.

When preparing to turn a drum on a lathe, care must be exercised that the lathe tool is sharpened correctly. Also, tool feed must be correct. If too fast, it would produce in a "screw thread" surface which would cause rapid wear of the brake lining.

ANCHOR PINS

Centralization of the brake shoes within the drum is largely dependent on the position of the anchor pin. If the anchor pin is not correctly placed, braking effectiveness will be reduced. Fig. 41-69, shows how the effective force is reduced when the anchor pin is too low. Fig. 41-70, shows the results of having it too high, with a strong possibility of a grabbing condition.

Fig. 41-71, shows how the servo action of the brake is built up smoothly and rapidly when the anchor pin is correctly located. On brakes with adjustable anchor pins, careful adjustment of the anchor pin is one of the first steps of reassembly.

HYDRAULIC SYSTEM SERVICE

No hydraulic brake system can operate satisfactorily unless the various parts are in good mechanical condition and the system is full of clean fluid of the approved type. Mineral oil of any kind will swell and ruin the rubber cups and other parts of the system. Furthermore, it does not have the proper

Brake shoes low on anchor
(Arrow shows effective force)

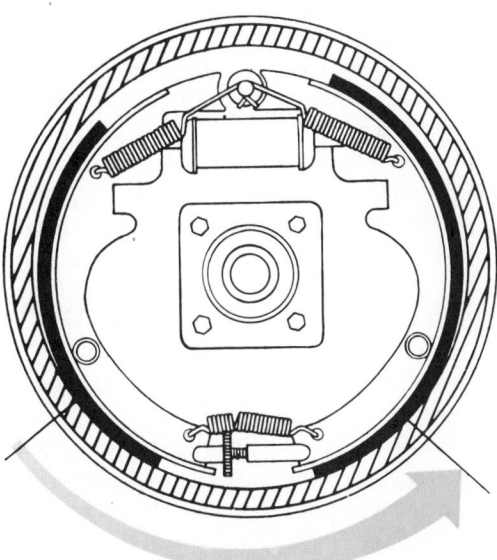

Fig. 41-69. Unless anchor pins are correctly located, full braking will not be attained. Anchor pin is adjusted too low.

Brake shoes high on anchor
(Arrow shows effective force)

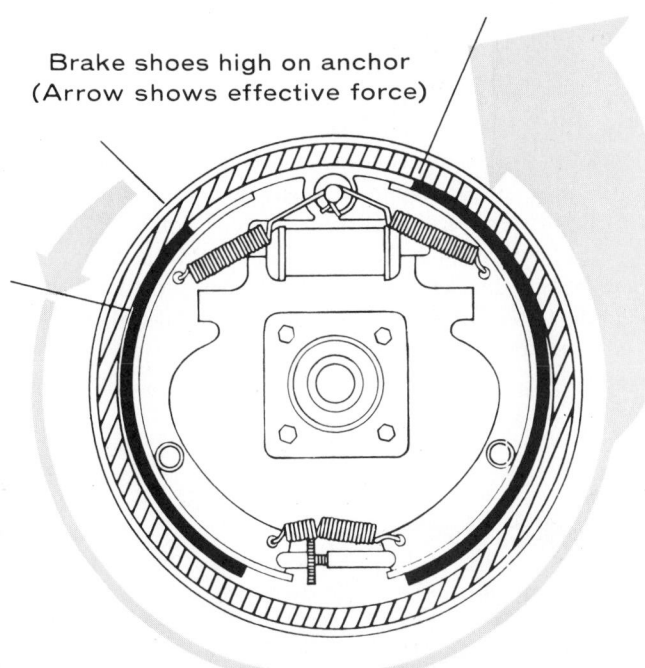

Fig. 41-70. Grabbing brakes result when anchor pins are too high.

Brake shoes properly centered in drum
(Arrow shows effective force)

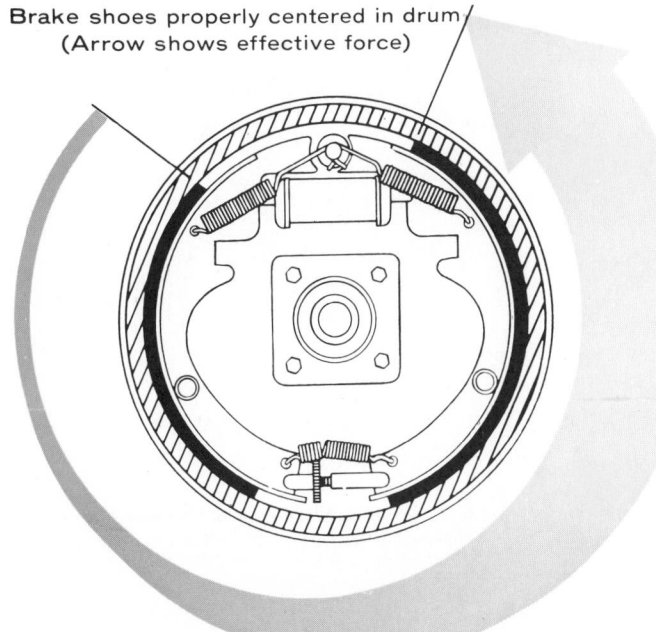

Fig. 41-71. Smooth, even braking results when anchor pins are set so that brake shoes are centralized.

viscosity characteristics for use in an automobile.

The fluid MUST BE CLEAN. Any dirt is liable to get in the valves and cause them to leak. If there is any doubt about dirt being in the system, it should be drained out and flushed. Equipment and material are available for flushing out hydraulic systems. Flushing will avoid clogging of ports, sticking valves, leaking and scored cylinders and erratic brake action. In addition, periodic flushing (once a year is usual recommenda-tion) will remove any gum from the old fluid, condensed moisture, bits of scale and rubber, etc.

Before adding new fluid to the brake system of an old car, inspect the flexible lines or hoses to make sure that they are not weakened, frayed or swollen. All connections and fittings should be checked for leaks and to make sure that lines are securely fastened to the frame to avoid vibration and eventual breakage. Sometimes lines get kinked, dented or worn thin from rubbing against sheet metal. If defective in any way brake lines should be replaced.

If the master cylinder and wheel cylinders are known to be in good condition, fresh fluid can then be added and the system "bled" to remove all air. If there is any air in the system, the pedal will have a "spongy" feel since hydraulic pressure is compressing the air in the system. When the brakes are applied, the pedal should be solid.

BLEEDING BRAKES

There are two general methods used to bleed hydraulic brake systems. The manual method requires two men. Pressure bleeding is faster and only requires the services of one service-man. However, it involves the use of special equipment. This equipment usually consists of a closed, airtight container of brake fluid to which air pressure is applied. See Fig. 41-72.

The fill plug opening and area around it must be thoroughly cleaned before the plug is removed and the hose connected, so no dirt can fall into the master cylinder. Then, the container of fluid is connected to the master cylinder fill opening by suitable fittings and flexible hose. The bleeder forces fluid under pressure to each wheel cylinder. Each cylinder is bled, in turn, by opening the bleeder valve and closing it when the fluid is clear and bubbles no longer appear.

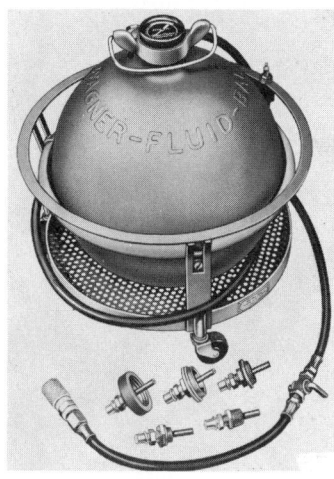

Fig. 41-72. One type of pressure flushing and bleeding equipment complete with necessary fittings.

This equipment can be used for flushing the system, when desired, by using a flushing fluid instead of brake fluid.

When the manual brake bleeding method is employed, one man "pumps" the pedal to force the fluid through the lines, while the other man bleeds the brakes. The first wheel bled is the one farthest from the master cylinder. In most cases, this is the right rear; next, left rear; then right front; and front left.

With either power or manual bleeding, a hose is attached to the bleeder valve and the other end immersed in a glass jar containing brake fluid. This enables bubbles to be seen and also avoids waste of fluid, Fig. 41-73.

When bleeding brakes by the manual method, it is necessary to watch the level of the fluid in the master cylinder. If it gets too low, air will be drawn into the cylinder. Air also may get into the system by being drawn in around a master cylinder

secondary cup. Any repair to a cylinder, hose or tubing means an "open" system that must be bled.

Sometimes brake fluid may boil and gas in the lines in hot weather, especially if the master cylinder or brake lines are located too near the muffler or an exhaust pipe. Also, if one brake would drag long enough to overheat the wheel cylinder, air might form in the line.

After bleeding, the master cylinder reservoir should be checked for fluid level, approximately one-half inch from the top of the reservoir. Also, it is wise to check the breather ports in filler plugs so equipped to make sure they are not plugged.

BLEEDING SPLIT—SYSTEM MASTER CYLINDER

When pressure bleeding a tandem piston (split system) master cylinder with a rectangular cover, the procedure is to fill both reservoirs and attach a special pressure bleeder cover to the master cylinder (in place of regular cover). Then, as fluid under pressure is applied to the system, bleed rear, then front brakes in the usual manner.

In the tandem piston master cylinder with two filler caps, a different procedure is necessary. Attach the pressure bleeding hose to the front filler opening. As pressure is applied, bleed the rear wheel cylinders in the usual manner. Then attach the pressure bleeding hose to the rear opening of the master cylinder and repeat the bleeding operation on front wheel cylinders. In the case of the Corvette, however, the front reservoir to the rear wheels.

Due to the extra components inside the dual master cylinder, it is more difficult to remove the air bubbles than from a single piston cylinder. Therefore, it is advisable to purge the master cylinder of air before connecting the brake lines. This can be done in the car or on the workbench.

The best method of purging is to connect short lengths of brake tube to the outlet port of the master cylinder, then bend up and immerse the other ends in the master cylinder reservoirs, Fig. 41-74. Then, apply the master cylinder push

Fig. 41-73. A plastic container permits observation of bubbles in brake fluid during bleeding process.

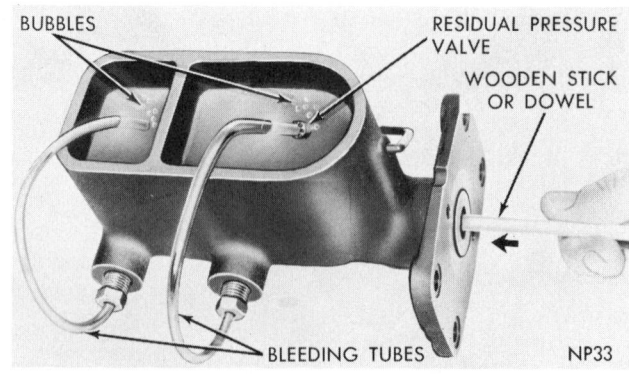

Fig. 41-74. Bench bleeding a dual master cylinder.

rod a full stroke, and repeat until all air bubbles have been eliminated. Then reconnect the brake lines to the master cylinder and bleed each of the wheel cylinders, in turn.

SERVICING HYDRAULIC CYLINDERS

When any work must be done on either the master cylinder or wheel cylinders, absolute cleanliness is of utmost importance. Of course, solvents or gasoline should NOT be used to clean the boots, cups, check valve assembly or any rubber parts. Alcohol is the proper cleaning fluid. The metal parts may be cleaned in solvent, if they are rinsed in alcohol.

The compensating port in the master cylinder must be open. This can be checked by pushing a very small gauge wire through it. The cylinders must be free of scratches, grooves or pits and should be measured to make sure that they have not been honed oversize. If the cylinder is oversize, it will be necessary to replace it or use an oversize piston.

If a cast iron master cylinder is not oversize, but rough, it can be polished with a special hone made for the purpose. (NOTE: DO NOT hone aluminum master cylinders.) After honing the cast iron cylinder, ream the by-pass port with a special burr removing tool. The honing operation may have formed a sharp edge around the hole that might scratch the primary cup as it moves back and forth in the cylinder.

Before reassembling the master cylinder, all parts should be washed in clean alcohol and dipped in brake fluid. Gasoline, kerosene, solvents and cleaning fluids should not be used.

When installing the master cylinder, the piston push rod must be adjusted so that the edge of the piston cup does not cover the compensating port. Check by inserting a small diameter wire through the fill cap opening with the brake pedal in the released position. If the adjustment is correct, the wire will go through.

If this port is covered when the pedal is in the released position, the fluid cannot return from the lines to the reservoir. This will cause the brakes to drag.

The rubber boot that fits around the push rod should be firm and fit snug at both ends to prevent the entry of dust or dirt which would score the piston.

The wheel cylinders also have rubber boots to keep dirt out. These, too, must be in good condition. If the boots are wet inside, Fig. 41-75, brake fluid might get on the lining and cause the brakes to grab. Put clamps on the wheel cylinders before removing the retracting springs from the shoes. Other-

wise, the wheel cylinder cups may move outward and cause air to enter the system. This would necessitate brake bleeding.

DISC BRAKE SERVICE

All disc brake services begin with sight, sound and stopping tests. The feel of the brake pedal adds a check on the condition of the hydraulic brake system.

Stopping the car will indicate whether the brakes pull in one direction, stop straight or require excessive effort to stop. Listening while stopping permits fair diagnosis of braking noises such as rattles, groans, squeals or chatter. Take a wheel off and visually inspect the outer shoe and lining assembly at the end of the caliper. Check the inner lining through the hole on top of the caliper, Fig. 41-76.

Fig. 41-76. After wheel and tire assembly have been removed, visual inspection of inner shoe and lining assembly can be made through hole in top of caliper. Outer shoe can be viewed from end of caliper. (Buick Motor Div., GMC)

A good rule of thumb guide to the need for lining replacement is to compare lining thickness to the thickness of the metal shoe. If the lining is not as thick as the metal shoe, it should be replaced. If the thickness of the lining is marginal, remove the caliper, carefully check the condition of the lining and measure its thickness. Compare this measurement with manufacturer's specification. NOTE: If lining requires replacement, always replace both front wheel sets to assure equal braking action.

To remove the caliper:

1. Siphon half of brake fluid from master cylinder reservoir

Fig. 41-75. A wet boot signals trouble in wheel cylinder. Cylinder must be reconditioned or replaced.

that feeds disc brake system. This prevents fluid overflow when piston is pushed back.

2. Remove two caliper guide pins that hold caliper to adapter. Positioners and bushings will come off with pins. (In typical application.)

3. Lift caliper off adapter and away from rotor, taking care not to let caliper hang by brake hose. Hook or tie caliper to suspension member, so rotor can be rotated for test and inspection.

4. If inner brake shoe remains in adapter, remove this shoe.

5. Slide outer brake shoe out of caliper.

6. Remove outer bushings from caliper ears by forcing them out with a blunt tool.

7. Slide inner flanged bushings and positioner from guide pins. If bushings did not come off with guide pins, remove them from caliper ears.

8. Check for fluid leaks around piston area. Inspect boot for cracks or damage. Recondition caliper if necessary.

9. If no defects are found, clean caliper thoroughly, especially holes in all four ears of caliper. Check all mating surfaces of abutments on adapter and caliper.
To replace brake shoes:

1. Force piston into caliper bore until it bottoms.

2. Install two new inner guide pin bushings into inner ears of caliper, making sure that flanged end of each bushing is against inboard side of ears.

3. Compress bushings and work them into holes of outer ears of caliper.

4. Place a new inner brake shoe into adapter.

5. Slide a new outer brake shoe into caliper with anti-rattle spring resting on back of shoe.

6. Hold outer shoe in position in caliper and slowly slide caliper down over rotor until holes in both shoes line up with holes in adapter.

7. Place two new positioners over guide pins with open ends facing outside.

8. Slide guide pins through bushings in caliper, through adapter, inner and outer brake shoes and into bushings in outer ears of caliper.

9. Screw guide pins into adapter, being careful not to crossthread. Tabs on positioners should be over top of machined surfaces of calipers, with arrows pointing up.

10. Refill master cylinder reservoir with brake fluid. Test pedal reserve. If pedal is spongy, bleed system.

11. Install tire and wheel assembly, lower car to floor and torque wheel lugs or nuts to specification.
To overhaul caliper:

1. Remove caliper as outlined in steps 1 through 3 to caliper removal procedure.

2. Disconnect and remove brake hose from caliper. Disconnect hydraulic line and plug end of line.

3. Place caliper assembly on clean work bench and remove outer brake shoe, anti-rattle spring, guide pin bushings, loosen bleeder screw and drain OUT remaining fluid. Retighten bleeder valve.

4. Place caliper on bench, piston side up. Put block of wood opposite piston and feed compressed air through inlet port until piston is forced out against block of wood.

5. Remove dust boot from its groove in caliper.

6. Using a thin-bladed tool, remove square cut seal from bore.

7. Remove bleeder valve from caliper.
Cleaning and inspection:

1. Clean and inspect piston for scoring, pitting, corrosion or worn spots in plating. Replace piston, if necessary. Do not use abrasives to clean piston.

2. Blow air through passageways in caliper. Inspect caliper bore for scoring, pitting, scratches or corrosion. Use crocus cloth to clean bore, then clean bore with denatured alcohol and blow dry.

3. Use crocus cloth to clean all metal-to-metal contacts.

4. Check condition of bleeder valve and guide pins. Replace damaged parts.

REASSEMBLY

1. Coat cylinder bore and a new square cut seal with assembly fluid. Place seal in cylinder bore groove, making sure it is not twisted.

2. Fit small diameter of a new dust boot over piston with large diameter facing bottom of piston. Place large diameter of boot into upper groove with small screwdriver. Or, use a special dust boot installer, Fig. 41-77. Apply even pressure

Fig. 41-77. Use of disc brake dust boot installer insures against boot damage during installation. Disc brakes are relatively exposed and must be well "sealed." (Gibson Products Div., Rolero, Inc.)

downward on piston until it bottoms in bore. Boot will automatically position itself into piston groove.

3. Install bleeder screw.

4. Place two new outer guide pin bushings into outer ears of caliper.

5. Install anti-rattle spring over outboard section of caliper.

6. Slide a new outer brake shoe into position in caliper with anti-rattle spring against metal back of shoe.

7. Install new inner guide pin bushings into inner ears of caliper, making sure that flanged end of each bushing is against inboard side of ears.

8. Install brake hose on caliper, using copper washer.

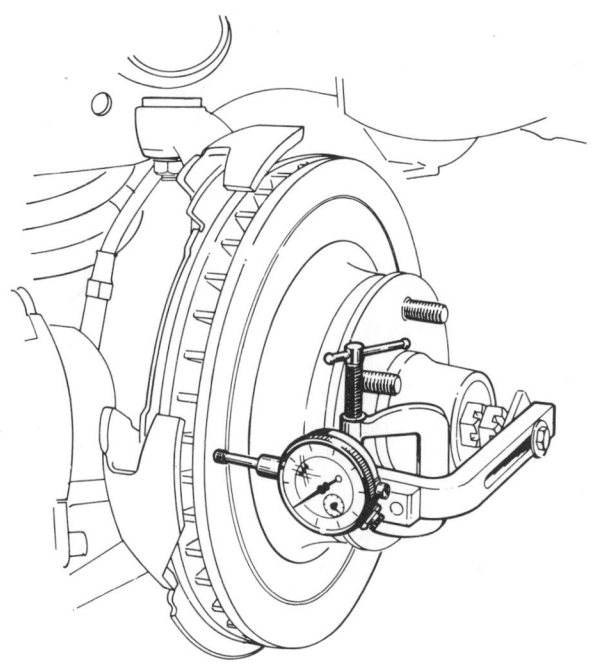

Fig. 41-78. Lateral runout check with dial indicator gives good check of flatness of rotor face. Typical runout limit is .005 in.

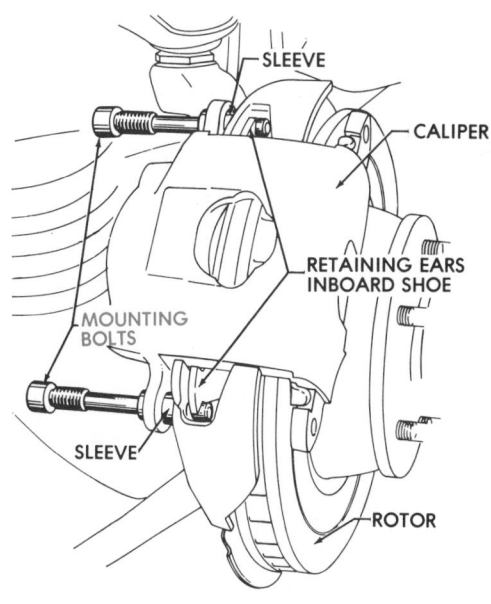

Fig. 41-79. Mounting bolts serve a double purpose on a floating caliper. 1—Bolts attach caliper to adapter. 2—Pin portion of bolts permit caliper to float in and out of application. (Buick Motor Div., GMC)

INSTALLATION

1. Before installing caliper on rotor, check lateral runout of rotor. Tighten spindle nut to remove play from wheel bearings. Fasten a dial indicator to spindle, Fig. 41-78, or steering linkage so that point of stylus contacts rotor face approximately 1 in. from rotor edge. Check rotor runout for one revolution and compare reading with manufacturer's specification (ranges from .002 to .005 in.).
2. Also check rotor for parallelism. Use a micrometer to measure rotor thickness and thickness variation at five equidistant points from outer edge of rotor. (Thickness variation calls for maximum of .0005 to .0007 in.)
3. Service rotor as required (clean, resurface or replace).
4. Clean adapter, especially metal-to-metal contacts, and place a new inner brake shoe in adapter.

5. Hold outer brake shoe in position in caliper, and slowly slide caliper down over rotor until holes in both shoes line up with holes in adapter.
6. Remove old positioners and bushings for guide pins, and install new positioners with open ends facing toward outside.
7. Slide guide pins through inner bushings in caliper, through adapter, inner and outer brake shoes and into bushings in outer ears, Fig. 41-79.
8. Screw guide pins into adapter. Do not crossthread. Tabs on positioners should be over top of machined surfaces of caliper with arrows pointing up.
9. Connect brake hose to hydraulic line and install lock washer.
10. Bleed system.
11. Install tire and wheel assembly and lower car to floor. Torque wheel lugs or nuts to specification.

Brake Troubleshooting

Symptom Or Probable Cause	Probable Remedy

Pedal Spongy

1. Air in brake lines.	1. Bleed brakes.

All Brakes Drag

1. Mineral oil in brake system.	1. Flush entire system and replace all rubber parts.
2. Improper push rod to master cylinder piston clearance.	2. Adjust push rod, or recondition master cylinder.
3. Faulty metering valve.	3. Replace metering valve.
4. Faulty proportioning valve.	4. Replace proportioning valve.

One Brake Drags

1. Loose or damaged wheel bearing.	1. Adjust or replace bearing.

2. Weak, broken or unhooked brake shoe retracting spring.
3. Incorrect parking brake adjustment.
4. Damaged or frozen parking brake cable.
5. Defective self-adjusting mechanism.
6. Caliper piston sticking, frozen or seized.

2. Replace spring.
3. Readjust parking brake at equalizer.
4. Free-up or replace parking brake cable assembly.
5. Replace worn or defective parts.
6. Recondition caliper assembly.

Excessive Pedal Travel

1. Normal lining wear or improper shoe adjustment.
2. Fluid low in master cylinder.
3. Excessive rotor runout.
4. Incorrect wheel bearing adjustment.

1. Adjust brakes.
2. Fill master cylinder to correct level.
3. Resurface or replace rotor.
4. Adjust wheel bearing as specified.

Pedal Gradually Goes To Floor When Brakes Are Applied

1. External fluid leaks.
2. Master cylinder leaks fluid past primary cup.
3. Caliper cylinder seals worn or damaged.
4. Air in hydraulic system.

1. Check master cylinder, wheel cylinders and lines for leaks.
2. Overhaul master cylinder.
3. Recondition caliper assembly.
4. Bleed system.

Brakes Uneven

1. Grease on lining.
2. Tires improperly inflated.
3. Front suspension faulty.
4. Rough turned brake drum.
5. Caliper piston sticking, frozen or seized.
6. Restricted hose or line.
7. Loose or misaligned caliper.
8. Loose wheel bearings.

1. Replace brake shoes and correct cause of grease leak.
2. Inflate tires.
3. Correct alignment.
4. Have drum finish turned.
5. Recondition caliper assembly.
6. Correct as required.
7. Torque mounting bolts to specification.
8. Adjust wheel bearings as specified.

Excessive Pedal Pressure

1. Grease or water on lining.
2. Full area of lining not contacting drums.
3. Scored brake drums.
4. Disc brake lining worn or shoe distorted.
5. Loose or misaligned caliper.
6. Heat-spotted or scored rotor.

1. Clean or replace lining.
2. Adjust anchor pin. Replace shoes.
3. Turn drums and install new shoes.
4. Install new shoe and lining assemblies.
5. Torque mounting bolts to specification.
6. Resurface or replace rotor.

Pedal Pulsation

1. Drums out of round.
2. Excessive rotor runout.
3. Excessive out-of-parallel rotor faces.

1. Replace drums.
2. Resurface or replace rotor.
3. Resurface or replace rotor.

Brake Fade

1. Defective master cylinder.
2. External fluid leaks.
3. Vapor lock.
4. Thin brake drums.
5. Overheated rotor.
6. Crystallized lining.

1. Overhaul master cylinder.
2. Locate and repair source of leak.
3. Flush and refill hydraulic system with quality fluid.
4. Install new brake drums.
5. Inspect rotor and correct as required.
6. Install new shoe and lining assemblies.

Diving

1. Shoes not centralized.
2. Primary and secondary shoes reversed.

1. Adjust anchor pins.
2. Transpose shoes.

3. Distorted disc brake shoes.
4. Restricted hose or line.

3. Install new shoe and lining assemblies.
4. Correct as required.

Brake Chatter

1. Loose brake lining.
2. Shoes not centralized.
3. Rough turned brake drum.
4. Excessive rotor runout.
5. Excessive out-of-parallel rotor faces.
6. Loose or misaligned caliper.
7. Heat-spotted or scored rotor.
8. Loose wheel bearings.

1. Install new shoe and lining assemblies.
2. Adjust anchor pins.
3. Finish turn brake drum.
4. Resurface or replace rotor.
5. Resurface or replace rotor.
6. Torque mounting bolts to specification.
7. Resurface or replace rotor.
8. Adjust wheel bearings as specified.

Troubleshooting Power Brakes

1. Test for power brake operation as follows: With engine stopped, depress brake pedal several times to eliminate all vacuum from system. Apply brakes and, while holding foot pressure on brake pedal, start engine. If power cylinder is operating, pedal will move slightly forward when vacuum power reaches system.

2. If test shows power system is not working, check following: Check all vacuum lines (including those to other vacuum operated units) to be sure there is no fluid leakage at any point. Check condition of air cleaner. Check for badly dented vacuum cylinder. Check for defects within power brake unit, requiring removal and overhaul.

REVIEW QUESTIONS – BRAKES

1. What is friction?
2. Friction is the same for all materials. True or False?
3. If area between two contacting surfaces increases, what happens to the coefficient of friction?
   a. It increases.
   b. It decreases.
   c. Remains the same.
4. How is the coefficient of friction calculated?
5. If the weight of a vehicle is doubled, will the amount of heat developed in braking be twice as much, or four times as much?
6. If the speed of a car is increased from 30 mph to 60 mph, will the heat developed in stopping, be twice as much or four times as much?
7. Define reaction time as applied to applying brakes.
8. Give the formula used in calculating the kinetic energy developed in stopping a car.
9. List five factors that tend to increase brake temperatures.
10. When will the fastest stops be made? With the wheels rotating or with the wheels locked.
11. Is the hydraulic pressure in a brake system the same through the entire system or does it vary?
12. How is the force in a hydraulic brake system multiplied?
13. If the pressure provided by the master cylinder is 500 psi, what is the total force at a wheel cylinder if each piston is 2 sq. in. in area?
    a. 500 lb.
    b. 1000 lb.
    c. 2000 lb.
14. What is meant by the term weight transfer?
15. List five factors that contribute to brake effectiveness.
16. Describe self-energization.

17. Which brake will have the greater self-energization? One with the anchor pin nearer the center of rotation or one with the anchor pin far from the center of rotation.
18. List the two main types of brake lining materials.
19. What material is used mostly for the braking surface of brake drums?
    a. Cast iron.
    b. Wrought iron.
    c. Steel.
20. What is the advantage of using aluminum in a brake drum?
21. Describe the operation of a hydraulic brake system.
22. What is meant by the term split system master cylinder?
23. List five qualities that a good hydraulic brake fluid must meet.
24. What is the purpose of the check valve in the master cylinder?
25. Under extreme conditions, what temperature may be expected in the brakes?
    a. 700 deg. F.
    b. 100 deg. F.
    c. 2000 deg. F.
    d. 950 deg. F.
26. What causes vapor lock in a brake system?
27. Where is there the greater tendency toward vapor lock?
    a. On top of a mountain.
    b. At sea level.
28. What is meant by the vacuum suspended type of power brake unit?
29. What is meant by the air suspended type of power brake unit?
30. When riveting brake lining to a brake shoe, how far should the hole be countersunk into the lining?

a. 1/3.
b. 1/2.
c. 2/3.

31. Give one advantage of bonded lining over riveted lining.
32. When should oversize lining be installed on brake shoes?
33. What is the limit in oversize when reconditioning brake drums?
    a. .060 in.
    b. .125 in.
    c. .030 in.
34. Why must care be exercised when setting the adjustable type of anchor pin?
35. What results will happen if mineral oil is used in an hydraulic brake system?
36. Describe the procedure for bleeding brakes.
37. When cleaning hydraulic brake parts, what type cleaning fluid should be used?
    a. Alcohol.
    b. Good grade of cleaning solvent.
    c. Kerosene.
38. What is the basic major advantage of a split, or dual, hydraulic brake system?

39. In disc brake design, how many pistons are incorporated in a fixed caliper?
    a. One.
    b. Two.
    c. Four.
40. How many pistons in a floating caliper?
    a. One.
    b. Two.
    c. Four.
41. How does a floating caliper work?
42. Wheel bearing adjustment has no affect on disc brake operation. True or False?
43. Give three advantages of an aluminum master cylinder over a cast iron master cylinder.
44. The main disadvantage of aluminum master cylinders is the _____ of the metal.
45. If an aluminum master cylinder bore becomes scratched, scored or pitted, the cylinder should be _____.
46. Corvettes use internal expanding brake shoes and drums for the parking brake. True or False?
47. Cadillac and Ford vehicles use a _____ mechanism to apply the parking brake on four wheel disc brake applications.
48. Cadillac and Ford rear brake calipers are released automatically by means of a _____.
    a. Vacuum-actuated diaphragm.
    b. Pressure switch.

ASBESTOS WARNING

It has been found that dust containing asbestos, if inhaled, can cause serious bodily injury. As a result, all car manufacturers include repeated warnings to service personnel in their Shop Manuals:

WARNING: WHEN SERVICING WHEEL BRAKE PARTS, DO NOT CREATE DUST BY GRINDING OR SANDING BRAKE LININGS OR BY CLEANING WHEEL BRAKE PARTS WITH A DRY BRUSH OR WITH COMPRESSED AIR. MANY WHEEL BRAKE PARTS CONTAIN ASBESTOS FIBERS WHICH CAN BECOME AIRBORNE IF DUST IS CREATED DURING SERVICING. BREATHING DUST CONTAINING ASBESTOS FIBERS MAY CAUSE SERIOUS BODILY HARM.

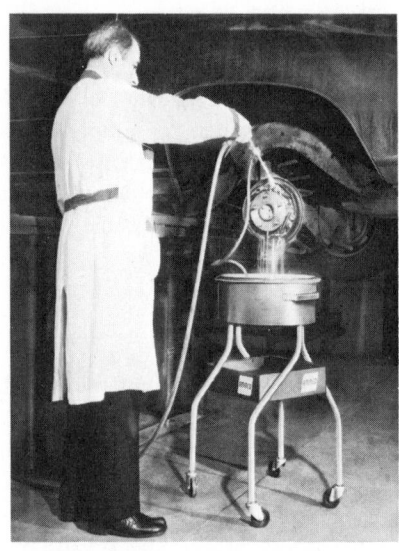

A brake washer greatly reduces asbestos dust problem. A breathing mask should be worn during this operation.

CLUTCHES

A clutch is a friction device used to connect and disconnect a driving force from a driven member. In automotive applications, it is used in conjunction with an engine flywheel to provide smooth engagement and disengagement of the engine and manual transmission.

Since an internal combustion engine develops little power or torque at low rpm, it must gain speed before it will move the vehicle. However, if a rapidly rotating engine is suddenly connected to the drive line of a stationary vehicle, a violent shock will result.

So gradual application of load, along with some slowing of engine speed, is needed to provide reasonable and comfortable starts. In vehicles equipped with a manual transmission, this is accomplished by means of a mechanical clutch.

DESIGN AND CONSTRUCTION

Most cars with manual transmissions use a single plate, dry disc clutch. The disc has friction material facing on each side

and is operated by a pressure plate, Fig. 42-1, and release bearing. Some heavy-duty trucks use two discs in conjunction with a pressure plate and an intermediate pressure plate, Fig. 42-2. In either case, the disc or discs are positioned between the engine flywheel and the pressure plate.

Engagement and disengagement of the clutch assembly is controlled by a foot pedal and linkage that must be properly adjusted and relatively easy to apply. The machined surfaces of the flywheel and pressure plate against which the clutch facings bear must be flat, true and free from cracks or score marks. The transmission, pressure plate, flywheel housing, clutch disc, flywheel and crankshaft must be properly aligned to prevent slippage, vibration and noise.

OPERATION

When the clutch pedal is depressed, this movement is transmitted to the clutch fork by way of rods or a cable, a cross shaft and fork push rod, Fig. 42-3. The fork, in turn,

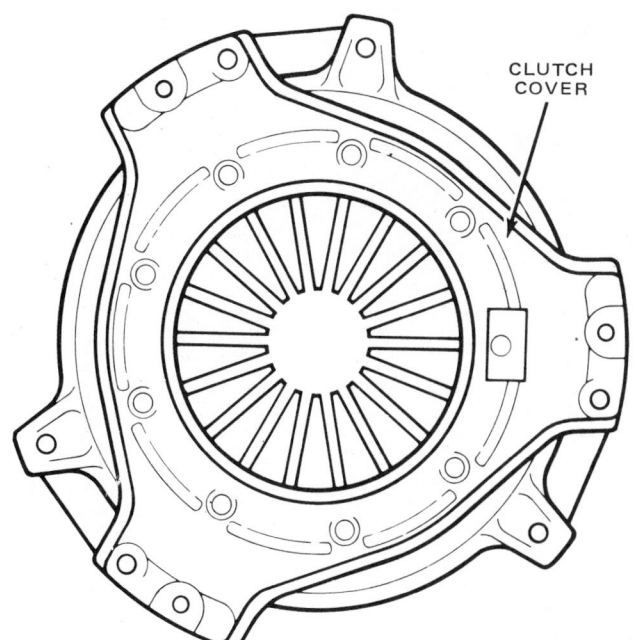

CLUTCH COVER

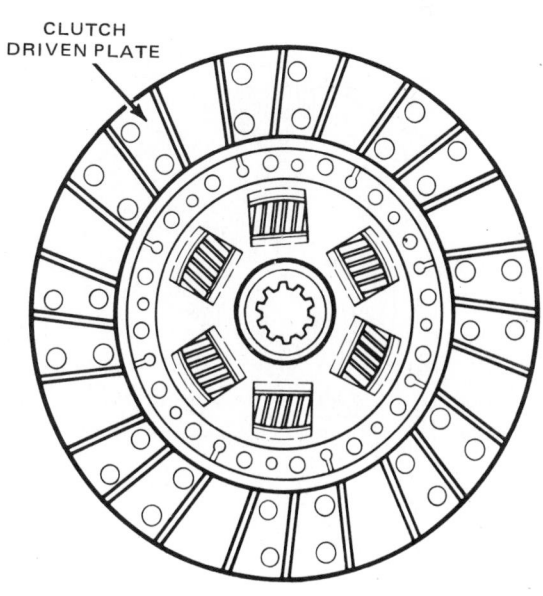

CLUTCH DRIVEN PLATE

Fig. 42-1. Typical clutch assembly in cars equipped with a manual transmission consists of a diaphragm type clutch cover and a single, dry-disc driven plate. (American Motors Corp.)

Fig. 42-2. Trucks and some cars use two-plate clutches in which front and rear discs and an intermediate pressure plate are sandwiched between the pressure plate and flywheel.

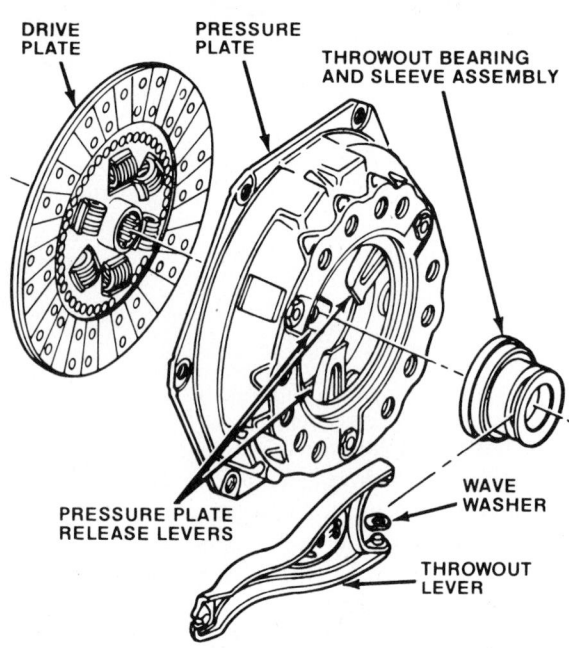

Fig. 42-4. Callouts identify parts in sectional view of single disc clutch assembly and lever type pressure plate. (American Motors Corp.)

moves the clutch release bearing (throw-out bearing) against the release levers of the pressure plate, relieving the spring pressure on the plate and releasing the clutch disc from the engine flywheel, Fig. 42-4.

When the driver releases the clutch pedal, a return spring pulls the linkage into driving position and returns the pedal against a pedal stop. This also lets the clutch fork and release bearing back away from the pressure plate release levers, permitting the pressure plate springs to compress the clutch disc between the plate and engine flywheel, Fig. 42-5.

CLUTCH DISCS AND FACINGS

The clutch disc is made up of a circular metal plate attached to a reinforced, splined hub. Often, the disc hub is mounted on coil springs to provide cushioned engagement. The outer half of the disc is covered over with friction facings on both sides. Generally, the clutch facings are made of molded or woven asbestos riveted or bonded to the clutch disc, Fig. 42-5. The thickness of the disc assembly must be

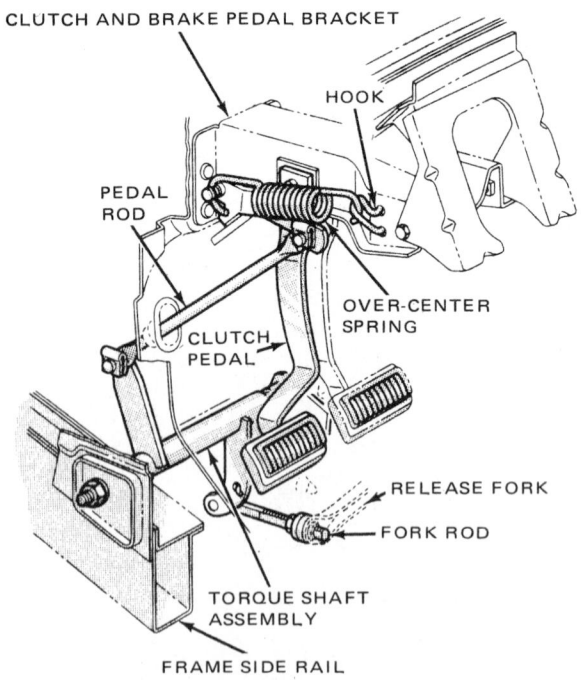

Fig. 42-3. Clutch linkage arrangement on typical suspended pedal setup features pedal and rod and over-center spring. Pedal free play adjustment is at end of fork rod. (Dodge Div., Chrysler Corp.)

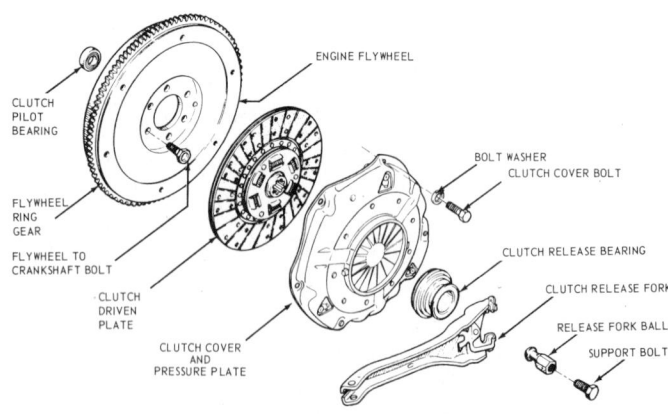

Fig. 42-5. Basic components of clutch assembly are shown: diaphragm type pressure plate; clutch disc; flywheel; clutch release bearing and clutch release fork. (Pontiac Motor Div., GMC)

uniform and its friction facings must be smooth.

WARNING: WHEN SERVICING CLUTCH ASSEMBLIES, BREATHING DUST CONTAINING ASBESTOS FIBERS MAY CAUSE SERIOUS BODILY HARM. SEE PAGE 515.

When clutch is fully engaged, pressure plate springs press the disc and facings flat between flywheel and pressure plate.

When two clutch discs are used, they are located on either side of the intermediate pressure plate, Fig. 42-2. The flywheel, intermediate plate and pressure plate are made to rotate together, but are mounted so that the pressure plate and intermediate plate can move in or out of engagement.

PRESSURE PLATES

The pressure plate assembly basically consists of the heavy plate, coil springs or a diaphragm, release levers or fingers and a cover, Figs. 42-4 and 42-5. The cover is bolted to the engine flywheel, and spring pressure is exerted between the pressure plate and cover. Most clutches use many small coil springs for this purpose, although diaphragm springs are equally popular. See Figs. 42-5 through 42-8.

In multiple spring pressure plates, Fig. 42-9, the springs are spaced around the pressure plate inside the cover so that uniform pressure will be placed on the clutch disc when it is engaged. The diaphragm spring is shaped like a dished plate, Fig. 42-8. It utilizes pivot rings to give it an over-center action in applying and releasing pressure on the pressure plate and clutch disc.

To disengage the clutch, the spring pressure must be released. In the diaphragm spring type of pressure plate, this is accomplished when the clutch release bearing bears against and

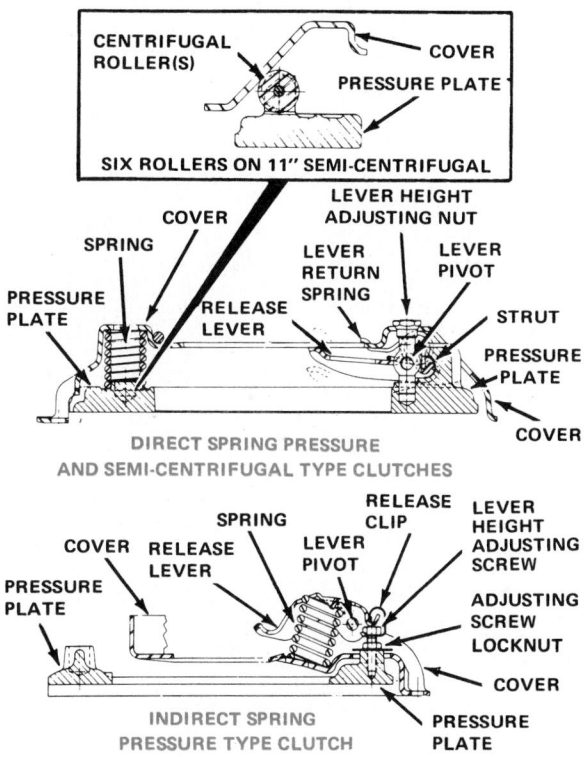

Fig. 42-6. American Motors' pressure plate assemblies consist of pressure plate, release levers and springs. Three different types are used, including semi-centrifugal roller arrangement detailed in inset at top.

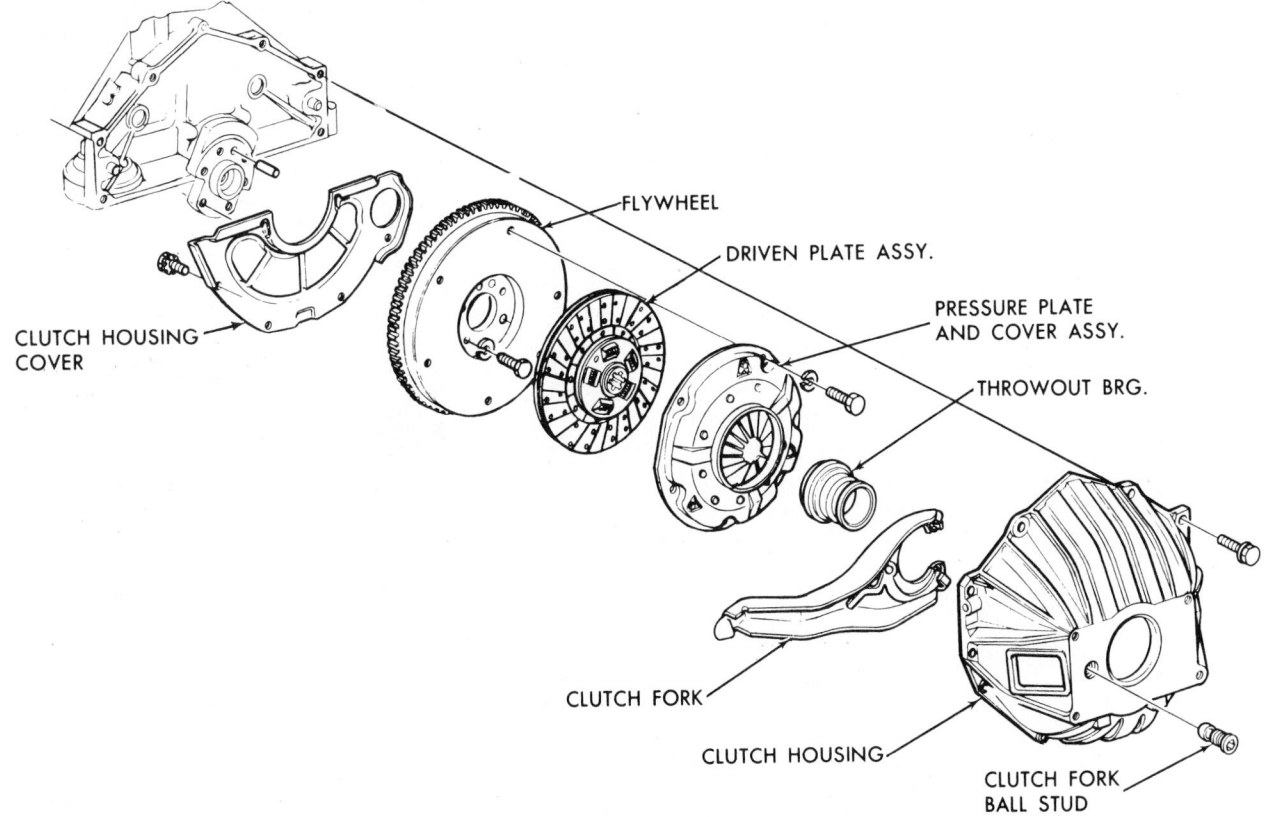

Fig. 42-7. Diaphragm spring type of pressure plate is used in many General Motors' applications. Exploded view of Chevrolet Division setup illustrates clutch and flywheel assembly sequence.

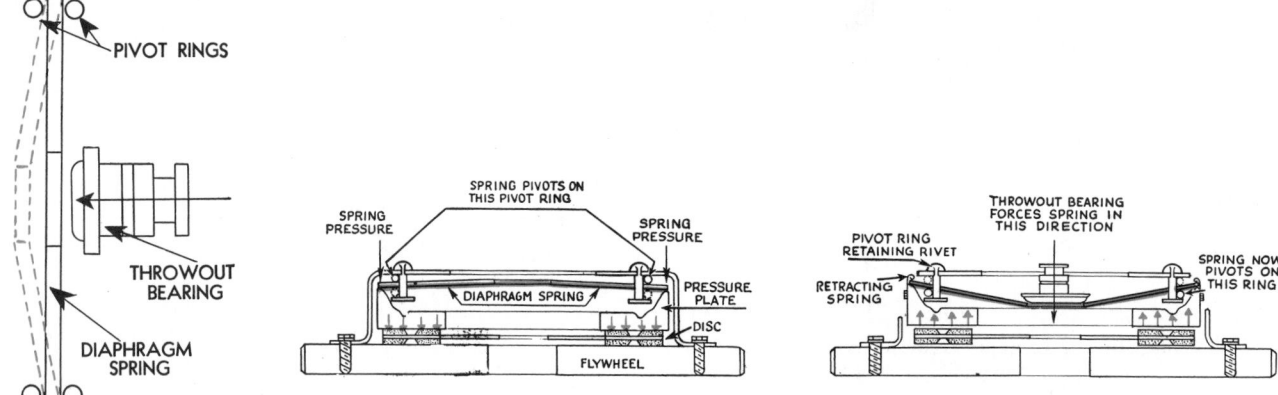

Fig. 42-8. Three diagrammatic views illustrate how pivot rings give diaphragm spring on over-center action when clutch release bearing forces spring toward engine flywheel.

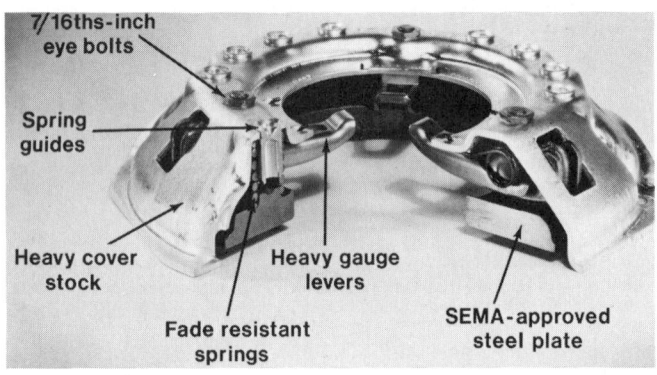

Fig. 42-9. Cutaway of typical replacement pressure plate assembly reveals thickness of pressure plate, positioning of three release levers and design configuration of clutch cover.

Fig. 42-10. Various clutch release bearings are pictured, along with ball bearing cage and ball bearing assembly featured in this particular line of replacement clutch release bearings.

compresses the spring, Fig. 42-1. In the multiple spring type, spring pressure is released by three levers, or fingers, spaced at equal intervals around the clutch cover and activated by a clutch release bearing, Fig. 42-10. In most cases a ball bearing assembly is used, although some clutch arrangements use a bearing made of a composition such as carbon or graphite.

The clutch cover serves to contain the pressure plate assembly. Most covers are vented to allow heat to escape and cooling air to enter. Some are designed to provide a fan action for forced circulation of air to help cool them. Even proper use of a clutch generates some heat because of normal slippage while it is being engaged.

SEMI—CENTRIFUGAL CLUTCH

A more-or-less unusual clutch pressure plate set-up is used on late model Chrysler and American Motors cars, Figs. 42-6 and 42-11. Called a semi-centrifugal clutch, the pressure plate has six cylindrical rollers which move outward under centrifugal force until they contact the cover. As engine speed increases, the rollers wedge themselves between the pressure plate and cover so that the faster the clutch rotates, the greater the pressure exerted on the pressure plate and disc, Fig. 42-6.

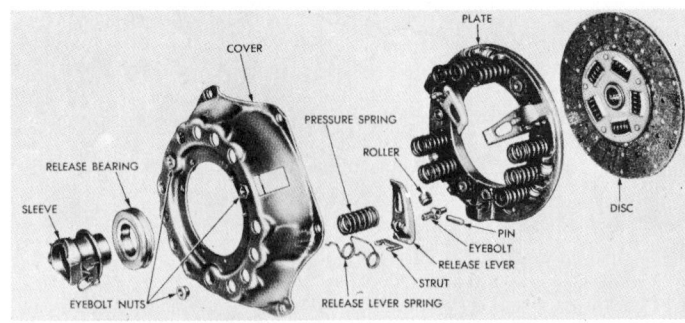

Fig. 42-11. Semi-centrifugal clutch in Chrysler cars has cylindrical rollers which are forced outward by centrifugal action to apply extra pressure on pressure plate.

CLUTCH LINKAGE

Clutch linkage connects the clutch pedal to the fork mounted in the clutch housing at the rear of the engine, Fig.

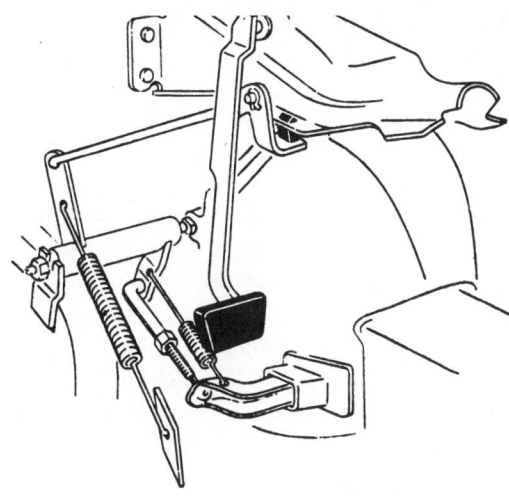

Fig. 42-12. Chevrolet clutch linkage arrangement affords positive transfer of pedal movement by way of pedal rod, cross shaft and clutch fork push rod.

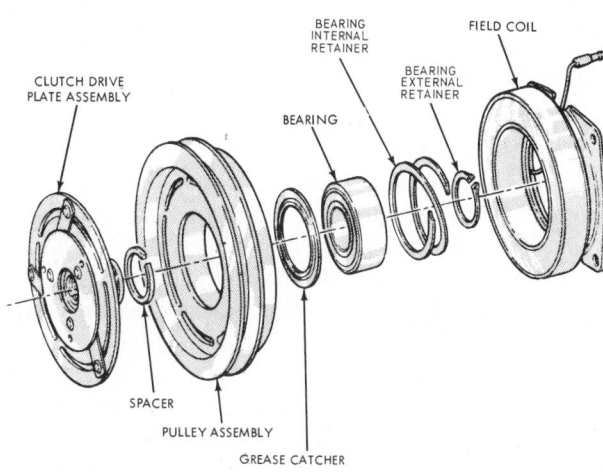

Fig. 42-14. This magnetic clutch is used on Ford air conditioner compressor. When field coil is energized, clutch drive plate assembly (hub not shown) is drawn against face of pulley, engaging pulley to compressor shaft.

42-3 and 42-12. The linkage usually consists of a pedal rod or cable, a cross shaft assembly to provide pivoting action, an adjustable fork push rod and a return spring, Fig. 42-13.

Linkage varies on practically every make and model, but its basic goal is to relay clutch pedal movement to the clutch fork and afford a means of adjustment to compensate for normal clutch facing wear. At the same time, correct adjustment of clutch pedal free play positions the clutch release bearing far enough from the release levers of the pressure plate to prevent the bearing from running continually until failure.

Frame design and location of clutch units in several European cars sometimes cause complications in the clutch linkage. In these cases, hydraulic operation of the clutch is utilized. A master cylinder, very similar to a brake master cylinder, is attached to the clutch pedal. A slave cylinder, somewhat similar to a brake wheel cylinder, is attached to the clutch release shaft.

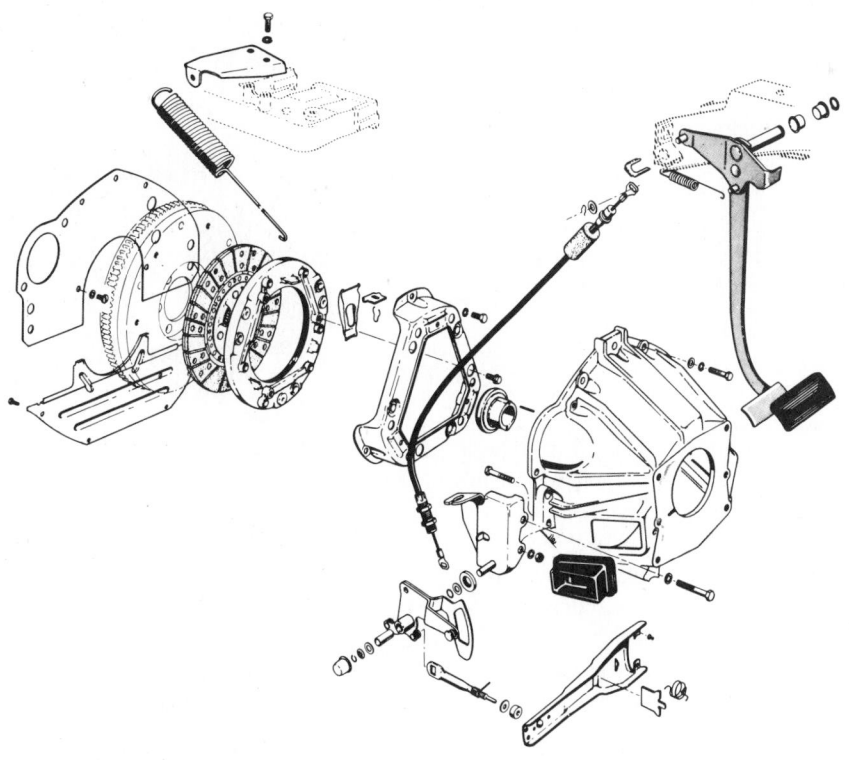

Fig. 42-13. Exploded view of entire clutch system includes cable-operated clutch release mechanism and self-adjusting feature. Pedal movement causes wire extension on end of fork rod to extend threaded portion of self-adjuster.

AUTOMATIC CLUTCHES

Automatic clutches were used in certain U.S. and European cars. American Motors' "E-Stick" clutch eliminated the need for physical operation of the clutch pedal. A German car maker engineered an automatic clutch system called "Hydrak," which consisted of a fluid flywheel connected to a single, dry disc clutch.

In the "E-Stick" setup, the pressure plate levers "engage" the clutch disc rather than "release" them. Also, the clutch remains disengaged until a servo unit is applied by oil pressure when the shift lever is placed "in gear" with the engine running.

The "Hydrak" unit also begins operation when the lever is "in gear." This activates a booster unit, which disengages the clutch disc. The hydraulic clutch parts are bridged over by a free-wheel unit, which goes into action when the speed of the rear wheels is higher than the speed of the engine. A special device controls engagement of the mechanical clutch, depending on whether the rear axle is in traction or is pushed by car momentum.

Automatic adjustment was another American Motors' innovation. As the clutch disc facings wear, the stroke of the clutch pedal actuates the spring steel wire extension on the self-adjuster and automatically extends the threaded portion, Fig. 42-13.

MAGNETIC CLUTCHES

A different type of clutch is used on air conditioning compressors. Known as a magnetic clutch, the assembly generally consists of a stationary electromagnetic coil, a pulley, bearing and clutch plate and hub, Fig. 42-14.

When voltage is applied to the clutch coil, the clutch plate and hub assembly (solidly coupled to compressor shaft) is drawn back against the pulley, forcing the compressor shaft to turn with the pulley. When voltage is removed from the clutch coil, springs in the clutch plate and hub move the clutch plate away from the pulley and the compressor shaft stops turning. In this way, the clutch serves to engage and disengage the compressor to suit the need for more or less cooling action by the air conditioning system.

CLUTCH SERVICE

Perhaps the most common cause of clutch trouble is misalignment. The transmission input shaft upon which the clutch disc is mounted should be in perfect alignment with the engine crankshaft and at right angles to the flywheel face.

Imperfect alignment can be caused in many ways: bent crankshaft flange; bent flywheel web; burr on a bolt or a chip between the crankshaft flange and flywheel web; warped clutch housing; warped transmission housing; incorrectly centered transmission housing; chips between the clutch housing and transmission housing.

In addition to misalignment of the housings, there is always a possibility of misalignment of the transmission input shaft. A worn front bearing in the transmission or excessive wear in the

pilot bearing or bushing will permit the input shaft to run untrue. Another frequent cause of misalignment is a sprung input shaft.

A bent or sprung input shaft or clutch disc is usually caused by carelessness in removing or replacing the transmission. If the transmission is unsupported while being removed or installed, the weight of the unit is liable to spring the shaft or disc. For this reason, a transmission lift or hoist should always be used to aid in moving the transmission in or out of place.

To check clutch housing alignment, use a dial indicator attached to a special tool installed in the pilot bearing or bushing, Figs. 42-15 and 42-16. Then check the flywheel for proper alignment by mounting the dial indicator on the clutch housing.

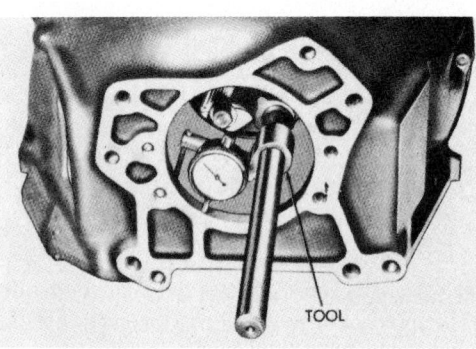

Fig. 42-15. To check clutch housing bore for runout, dial indicator is installed and flywheel is rotated.

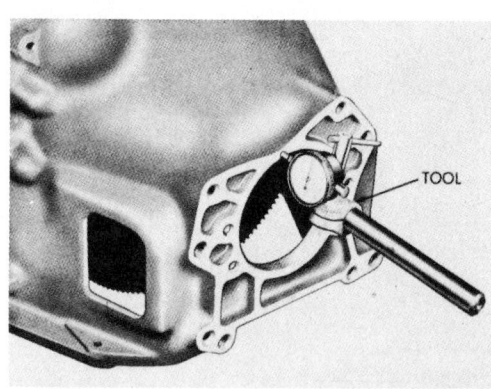

Fig. 42-16. To check clutch housing face alignment, dial indicator is mounted as shown, and flywheel is turned one revolution.

In most applications, the misalignment limit is .010 in. To correct alignment of the clutch housing, install shims between the housing and the rear face of the engine block. Late model Chrysler engines have offset dowel pins on the rear face, permitting adjustment to compensate for runout of the clutch housing bore. Fig. 42-17.

Distortion of the clutch cover will also cause misalignment. Such distortion or warpage is caused by carelessness in removing or replacing the cover. The retaining bolts must be

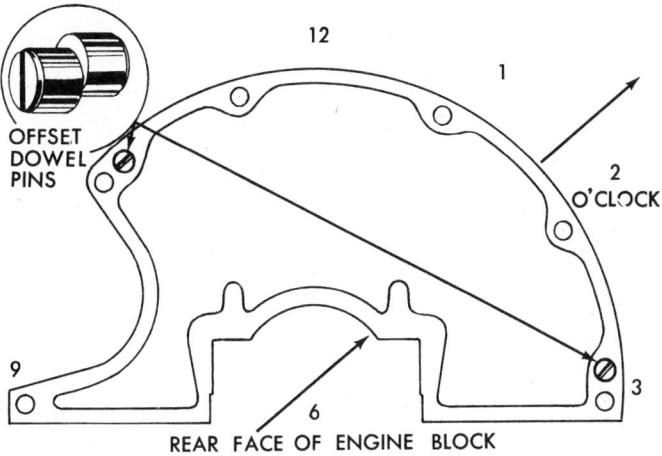

Fig. 42-17. Chrysler-Plymouth engines utilize offset dowel pins in rear face of engine block as point of adjustment to align clutch housing and eliminate bore runout.

loosened and tightened evenly, or the cover may be sprung or distorted by spring pressure. The safest method is to insert wood blocks between the release levers and the cover before the bolts are loosened. These blocks keep the spring tension off of the bolts and facilitate removal and replacement of the bolts. After reinstallation, remove the wedges.

Another thing to be kept in mind is that the engine is usually balanced with the clutch assembly installed. Before removing the clutch cover, mark the cover and flywheel and reinstall the cover in the same relative position, Fig. 42-18. Otherwise, the rotating balance of the engine assembly may be disturbed and vibration will occur.

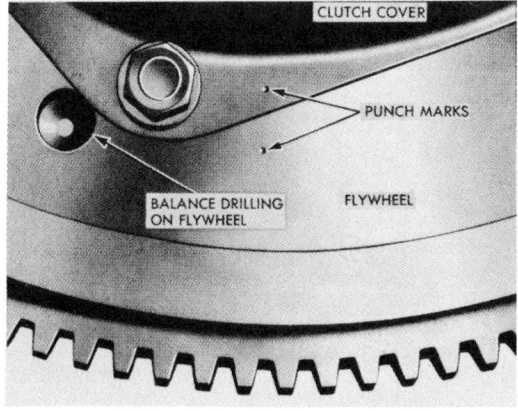

Fig. 42-18. Flywheel and clutch cover should be punch marked to maintain balance if original pressure plate is reinstalled.

CLUTCH ADJUSTMENT

The principle cause of a damaged clutch release bearing is neglect of clutch adjustment to compensate for wear. As the lining is gradually worn from the disc in normal use, the pressure plate moves closer to the flywheel and the release levers move outward. This forces the release bearing backward

and the clutch pedal with it. If the pedal is forced against the pedal stop, the bearing will contact the release levers and turn at all times. This continuous pressure on the clutch release bearing will tend to partially disengage the clutch, causing the clutch disc friction facings to slip and wear rapidly.

So it pays to check clutch pedal free play occasionally and adjust when necessary to restore proper clearance. Clearance should be about 1 in. of free play. Usually, this adjustment can be made at the clutch fork push rod, Fig. 42-19, or outer end of the clutch pedal rod.

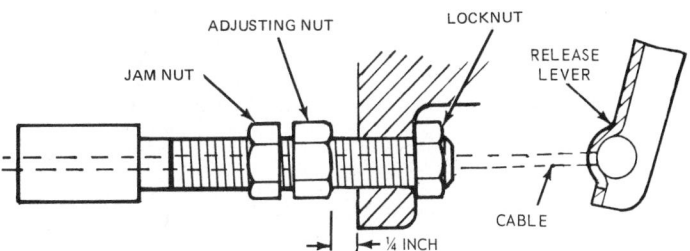

Fig. 42-19. To adjust cable-operated clutch release mechanism for correct clutch pedal free play on Pinto cars: Place 1/4 in. spacer between adjusting nut and housing. Turn adjusting nut against spacer and lock it with jam nut. Tighten locknut and remove spacer.

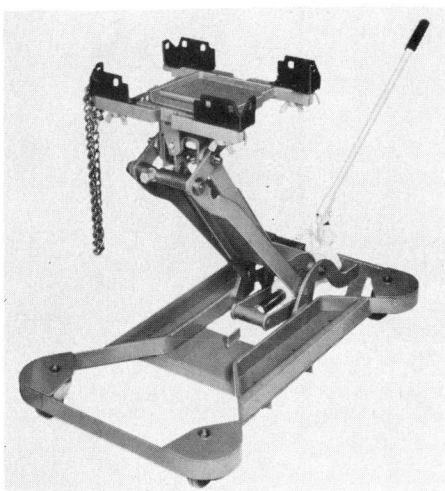

Fig. 42-20. With misalignment considered to be major cause of clutch trouble, a transmission jack provides best means of moving transmission in and out of place.

CLUTCH OVERHAUL

Corrective service usually consists of repair, adjustment or replacement of the faulty part or assembly. To inspect and correct major troubles in clutch operation, proceed as follows:
1. Remove drive shaft and transmission, Fig. 42-20.
2. Remove flywheel cover or clutch bell housing, if so equipped.
3. Locate X marks on flywheel and clutch cover, or prick-punch these units to insure proper installation if old clutch is to be reused.

4. Unhook clutch return spring, back off clutch adjustment if necessary and remove release bearing assembly.

5. Install wooden wedges between release levers and cover, then loosen clutch-to-flywheel bolts evenly, one turn at a time, until spring pressure is released.

6. Remove bolts and clutch assembly.

7. Clean flywheel and inspect pilot bearing or bushing for wear or score marks. Replace if necessary, using a special installing tool.

8. Pack bearing with lubricant, or wipe lubricant on bushing and install small quantity of lubricant in crankshaft depression in front of bushing.

9. Check clutch housing alignment, Figs. 42-15 and 42-16. Correct as required by shimming or dowel replacement.

10. Check flywheel alignment. Correct as required.

11. Check fit of new clutch disc on transmission input shaft spline.

12. Lubricate pressure plate between driving lugs and edge of plate openings.

13. Install clutch disc and pressure plate, using an aligning tool or old transmission input shaft, Fig. 42-21.

Fig. 42-21. Aligning arbor inserted through hub of clutch disc and into pilot bushing centers disc on flywheel while pressure plate is bolted in place.

14. Tighten clutch-to-flywheel bolts evenly, then remove aligning tool or input shaft.

15. Install new clutch release bearing on bearing retainer, using care to insure proper seating and to avoid damage to bearing. Then check free sliding fit of bearing assembly on transmission input shaft bearing retainer.

16. Wipe light coating of lubricant on face of release bearing, using care to avoid getting lubricant on clutch disc. Also wipe film of lubricant on arms of clutch fork and lubricate fork ball and socket.

17. Place release bearing assembly on arms of clutch fork and center assembly over wheel hub hole in clutch disc.

18. Install clutch bell housing, if so equipped.

19. Apply light coat of lubricant on transmission input shaft bearing retainer, then install transmission and drive shaft, torquing attaching bolts to specified values.

20. Adjust fork push rod to obtain specified amount of free play at clutch pedal, Figs. 42-3 and 42-19. If equipped with over-center assist spring, make this adjustment first.

21. Install flywheel cover, if so equipped.

22. Test clutch operation.

CLUTCH TROUBLESHOOTING

Chattering

1. Oil or grease on clutch disc facing.
2. Glazed or worn facing.
3. Warped clutch disc.
4. Worn or loose splines in hub or on transmission input shaft.
5. Splined hub sticking on splined shaft.
6. Warped pressure plate.
7. Cracked or scored pressure plate or flywheel face.
8. Sticking or binding release levers.
9. Unequally adjusted release levers.
10. Unequal length or strength of clutch springs.
11. Bent transmission input shaft.
12. Worn, loose or spongy engine mounts.
13. Worn or loose universal joint, differential, drive axle, torque tube or torque rod mounting.
14. Misalignment of clutch housing, clutch assembly, etc.

Dragging

1. Oil or grease on clutch disc facing.
2. Warped clutch disc.
3. Broken disc facing.
4. Splined hub sticking on splined shaft.
5. Accumulation of dust in clutch.
6. Warped pressure plate or clutch cover.
7. Excessive clutch pedal free play.
8. Sticking pilot bearing or bushing.
9. Sticking release bearing retainer.
10. Engine idling too fast.
11. Misalignment of clutch housing, clutch assembly, etc.

Squeaks

1. Clutch release bearing needs lubrication.
2. Pilot bearing needs lubrication.
3. Release bearing retainer needs lubrication.
4. Pressure plate release lever driving lugs and pins need lubrication.
5. Misalignment of clutch housing, clutch assembly, etc.

Rattles

1. Loose hub in clutch disc.
2. Broken or loose coil springs in clutch disc.
3. Worn splines in hub or on shaft.
4. Worn driving lugs or pins in pressure plate.
5. Unequal adjustment of release levers.
6. Worn release bearing.
7. Worn release parts.
8. Worn pilot bearing or bushing.
9. Bent transmission input shaft.
10. Worn transmission bearings.

11. Wear in transmission or drive line.
12. Misalignment of clutch housing, clutch assembly, etc.

Grabbing

1. Oil or grease on clutch disc facing.
2. Glazed or worn facing.
3. Splined hub sticking or binding on splined shaft.
4. Sticking driving lugs or pins in pressure plate.
5. Sticking or binding release levers.
6. Sticking or binding clutch pedal or linkage.
7. Misalignment of clutch housing, clutch assembly, etc.

Slipping

1. Worn clutch disc facing.
2. Oil or grease on disc facing.
3. Warped disc.
4. Weak or broken pressure plate springs.
5. Warped pressure plate.
6. Sticking release levers.
7. Pressure plate sticking or binding at driving lugs and pins.

8. Insufficient clutch pedal free play.
9. Misalignment of clutch housing, clutch assembly, etc.

Failure

1. Disc hub torn out.
2. Friction facing torn off or worn off.
3. Splined hub stuck on splined shaft.
4. Broken springs in pressure plate.
5. Incorrect adjustment of pressure plate.
6. Insufficient clutch pedal free play.

Vibration

1. Defective clutch disc.
2. Dust in clutch.
3. Use of rigid disc instead of flexible type.
4. Improper installation of clutch on flywheel.
5. Bent transmission input shaft.
6. Unmatched pressure plate springs.
7. Misalignment of clutch housing, clutch assembly, etc.
8. Loose engine mountings.

REVIEW QUESTIONS – CLUTCHES

1. What is the function of a clutch mounted on the engine flywheel?
2. Do the clutch springs, or diaphragm spring, hold the clutch disc against the flywheel or the pressure plate?
   a. Flywheel.
   b. Pressure plate.
   c. Both.
3. Describe the action of a diaphragm spring in a clutch cover.
4. Should all clutch springs in a multi-spring clutch be of the same length and strength?
5. How many clutch release levers are customarily used on a clutch having six springs?
   a. One.
   b. Three.
   c. Six.
6. What is the most common application of a single magnetic clutch in an automobile?
7. What added components afford centrifugal action to a semi-centrifugal clutch?
   a. Cylindrical rollers.
   b. Heavier driving lugs.
   c. Stronger pressure plate springs.
8. What is the function of the clutch release bearing?
9. Where is the clutch adjustment usually located?
   a. At clutch cross shaft.
   b. At clutch pedal stop.
   c. At clutch fork push rod.

10. Where should dial indicator be mounted to check runout of flywheel?
11. Where should dial indicator be mounted to check alignment of clutch housing?
12. Rule-of-thumb figure for clutch pedal free play is:
    a. 1/2 in.
    b. 1 in.
    c. 1 1/2 in.
13. Name six causes for misalignment of a clutch.
14. Generally, what is the maximum allowable runout on the machined face of the flywheel housing?
    a. .001 in.
    b. .005 in.
    c. .010 in.
15. How is misalignment of the clutch housing corrected?
16. Why should you put aligned prick-punch marks on the flywheel and pressure plate before removing the old clutch?
17. The clutch release bearing and clutch release fork do not require lubrication. True or False?
18. Usually, what is the first major step in the replacement of a clutch assembly?
19. When installing a clutch disc and pressure plate, use an aligning tool or old transmission input shaft to center the clutch disc while the pressure plate is bolted in place. True or False?
20. A worn clutch release bearing can cause the clutch to slip. Yes or No?

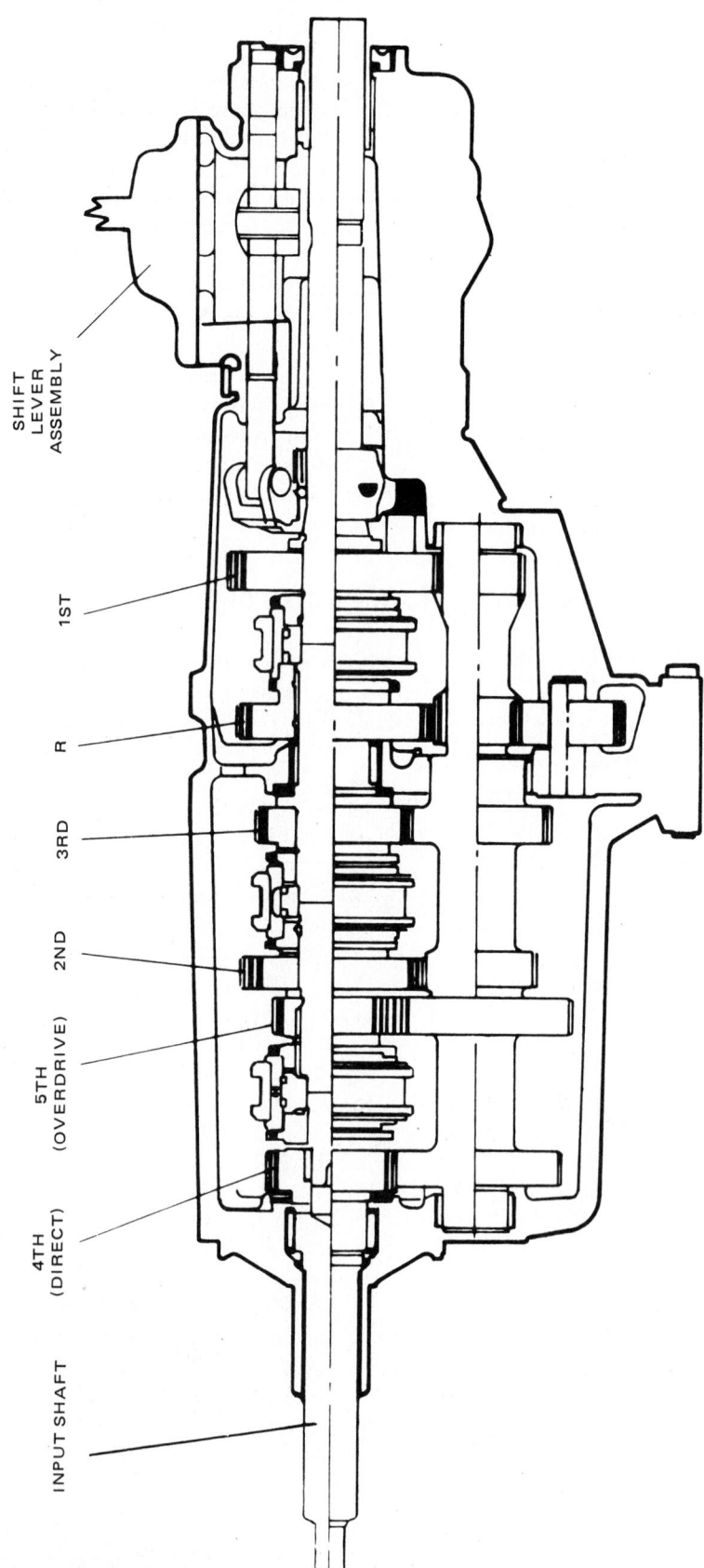

SHIFT
LEVER
ASSEMBLY

1ST

R

3RD

2ND

5TH
(OVERDRIVE)

4TH
(DIRECT)

INPUT SHAFT

Five speed manual transmission used on some late model Buicks. This floor shift transmission is fully synchronized in all forward gears. Fifth gear is an overdrive. This means that the output shaft turns faster than the input shaft; the engine turns fewer rpm; fuel economy is improved.

TRANSMISSION FUNDAMENTALS

A transmission is a speed and power changing device installed at some point between the engine and driving wheels of the vehicle. It provides a means for changing the ratio between engine rpm (revolutions per minute) and driving wheel rpm to best meet each particular driving situation.

Given a level road, an automobile without a transmission could be made to move by accelerating the engine and engaging the clutch. However, a start under these conditions would be slow, noisy and uncomfortable. In addition, it would place a tremendous strain on the engine and driving parts of the automobile.

So in order to get smooth starts and have power to pass and climb hills, a power ratio must be provided to multiply the torque and turning effort of the engine. Also required is a speed ratio to avoid the need for extremely high engine rpm at high road speeds. The transmission is geared to perform these functions.

APPLICATION OF TORQUE

Power is the rate or speed at which work is performed. (See Chapter 9.) Torque is turning or twisting effort.

Torque is derived from power but because of operating characteristics, a gasoline engine does not attain maximum torque, or turning effort at the peak of power output. The engine section of this text makes it clear that the amount of torque obtainable from a source of power is proportional to the distance from the center of rotation at which it is applied.

It follows, then, that if we have a shaft (engine crankshaft) rotating at any given speed, we can put gears of different sizes on the shaft and obtain different results. If we put a large gear on the shaft, we will get more speed and less power at the rim than with a small gear.

If we place another shaft parallel to our driving shaft and install gears or pulleys on it in line with those on the driving shaft, we can obtain almost any desired combination of speed or power within the limits of the engine's ability. That is exactly what an automobile transmission does by means of gears, devices and, in automatic transmissions, by the routing of oil under pressure.

GEAR USAGE

Gears are simply a means of applying leverage to rotating parts. An ordinary lever, for example, has more power as the fulcrum gets closer to the object of power application, Fig. 43-1. The closer the fulcrum approaches the object, the longer the distance the lever end has to be moved. The same principle applies to gears and pulleys. The smaller the number of teeth on the driving gear, the slower the driven gear rotates, but with multiplied power.

A modern transmission provides both speed and power. The engineer who designed it selected the gear sizes that would give the best all around performance. It is geared to a power ratio that puts the car in motion, then it shifts, or is shifted, to one or more speed ratios that keep it rolling.

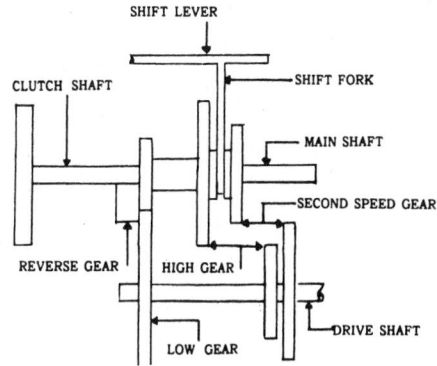

Fig. 43-2. In diagrammatic form: A small gear on main shaft is meshed with a large low gear for maximum power. Second speed gears are nearly same size for more speed on drive shaft. High speed gear on main shaft is larger than high gear on drive shaft, so higher speed on driven shaft would result.

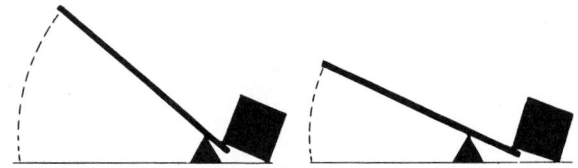

Fig. 43-1. Distance between fulcrum and object is comparable to distance between center and rim of a pulley or gear. Therefore, a small gear will drive a large gear slowly, but with great power.

A Frenchman named Levassor is generally credited with developing the first sliding gear transmission. It consisted of two shafts mounted parallel to each other and fitted with slideable spur gears of different sizes. The gears were arranged to mesh with each other to provide a change in the relative speed of the driving and driven shafts, Fig. 43-2. Levassor's transmission had a low, intermediate and high gear, as well as reverse. It was an ingenious "first."

GEAR RATIOS

Gear ratios in transmissions are not standardized, but are engineered to fit changes in the engine, car weight, etc., in order to obtain maximum performance.

A typical automobile sliding gear transmission has ratios as follows:

Reverse gear	3.8 to 1
Low gear	2.8 to 1
Second gear	1.7 to 1
High gear	1.0 to 1
Overdrive	0.7 to 1

To compute the gear ratio at the output shaft, see Fig. 43-8. Note that high gear output is direct drive or a 1:1 ratio. To figure other ratios, each meshing of gears in a given speed must be computed as a separate ratio. Then, the overall transmission gear ratio for that speed would be a mathematical computation of all of these values.

The gear ratio can be determined by counting the teeth on a pair of gears. If the driving gear has 20 teeth and the driven gear 40 teeth, the ratio would be 2 to 1. If the driving gear had 40 teeth and driven gear 20 teeth, the ratio would be 1 to 2.

Transmission gear ratios should not be confused with the final drive ratio or car gear ratio which refers to the overall ratio between the engine revolutions and the rear axle shaft

revolutions. This, of course, includes the gear reduction in the rear axle or differential.

In high gear, for example (1 to 1 ratio), the output shaft of the transmission turns at the same speed as the engine crankshaft. In overdrive, the output shaft turns faster. In all other gear combinations, the output shaft turns more slowly, but provides greater power.

To illustrate gear arrangement, a conventional, spur gear, three-speed transmission is shown in Fig. 43-3. The housing is split in two in a vertical plane and an end view of the reverse gearing appears at the right. Installed in the vehicle, the clutch attaches to the pinion shaft at the left; the drive shaft attaches to the splined main shaft at the right.

The forward end of the main shaft is not splined but runs in the main shaft bushing within the pinion gear. As illustrated in Fig. 43-3, the transmission gears are in the neutral position.

NEUTRAL POSITION

In neutral position: The clutch turns the pinion shaft, which rotates the countershaft gear, second speed, low and reverse gears. The main shaft does not revolve. See Fig. 43-4.

REVERSE GEAR

In order to engage reverse gear: Low and reverse sliding gear A on the main shaft is moved backward to engage reverse gear B, which is driven by gear C on the countershaft. Interposing idler gear B between gears A and C reverses the rotation of the main shaft. See Figs. 43-3 and 43-5.

LOW GEAR

To engage low gear: The low and reverse sliding gear on the main shaft is moved forward into mesh with the low gear. With

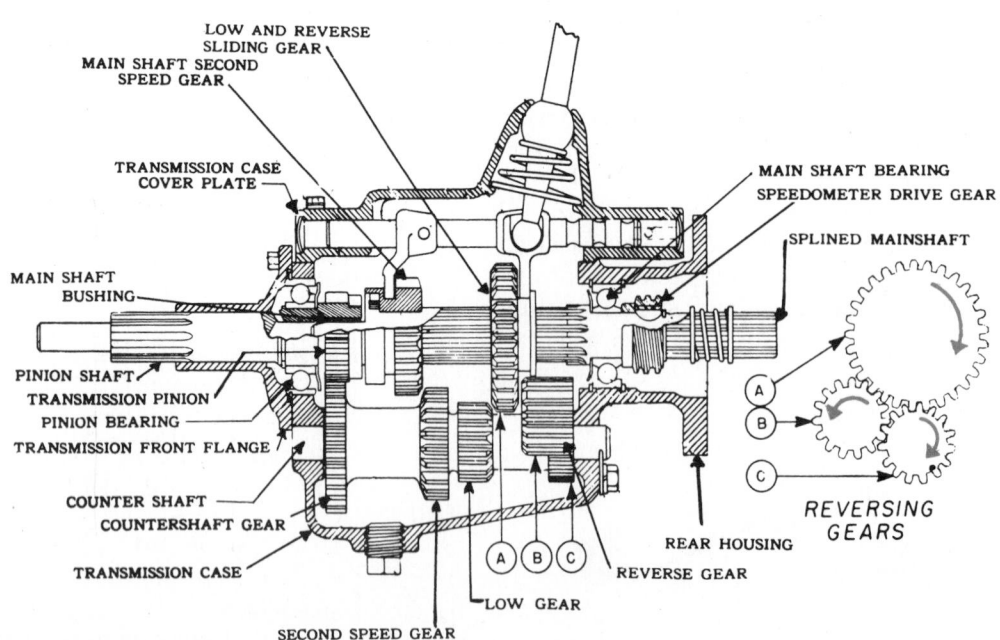

Fig. 43-3. Typical spur gear three-speed transmission is shown with reverse gearing inset at right: A—Low and reverse sliding gear. B—Reverse idler gear. C—Countershaft gear.

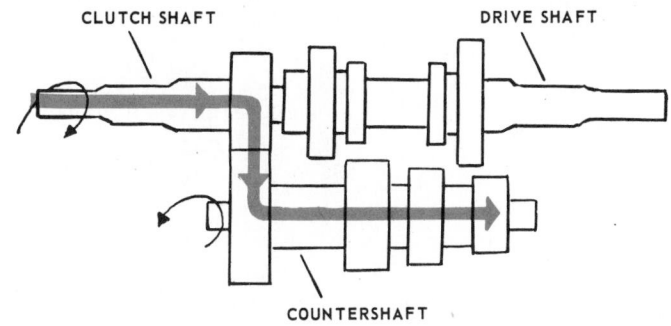

Fig. 43-4. With engine running and three-speed manual transmission in neutral position, clutch shaft turns countershaft, but no power is applied to drive shaft of transmission.

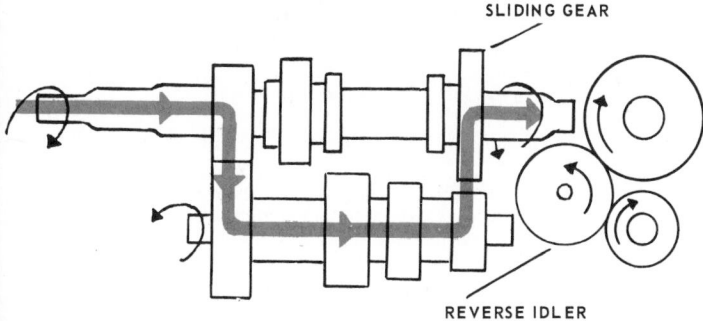

Fig. 43-5. When shift lever is moved to reverse position, an idler gear is interposed between main shaft and countershaft to reverse direction of rotation of drive shaft.

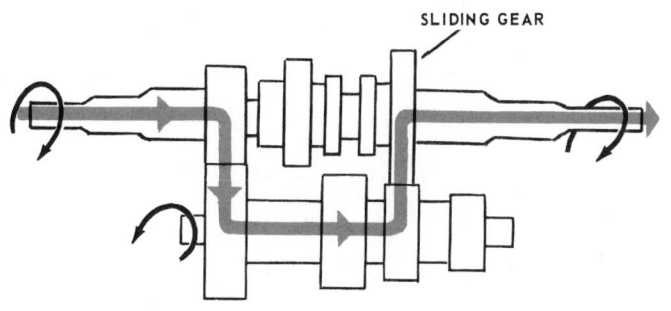

Fig. 43-6. When shift lever is placed in low gear, power is transmitted through countershaft to low and reverse sliding gear to main shaft.

this move, the pinion shaft turns the countershaft gear (attached to lower gear), which turns the low and reverse gear. The low gear on the countershaft, being smaller than the mating gear on the main shaft, provides a gear reduction. Therefore, it turns the main shaft at slower speed with greater power. See Fig. 43-6.

SECOND GEAR

To shift into second gear: The low and reverse sliding gear is returned to neutral, Fig. 43-4, and the main shaft second speed gear is moved backward into mesh with the second speed gear on the countershaft. Since there is less difference in

the size of these gears, the main shaft will turn at a higher rate of speed than in low gear. The principal gear reduction is now between the pinion shaft gear and the countershaft gear. See Fig. 43-7.

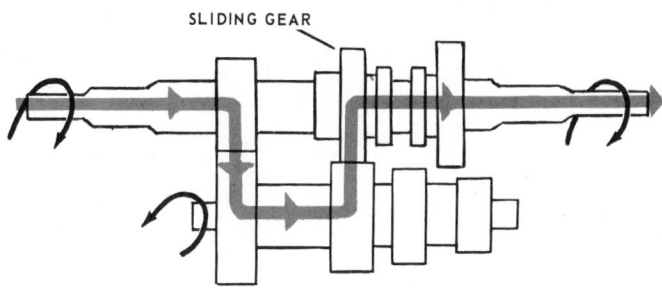

Fig. 43-7. With shift lever in second gear, power flow is through countershaft to second speed sliding gear to main shaft.

HIGH GEAR

For high gear: The main shaft second speed gear is disengaged from the second speed gear on the countershaft and moved forward until projections on the rear face of the pinion shaft gear engage with matching indentations or notches in the forward face of the main shaft second speed gear. This locks the pinion shaft and main shaft together, and they turn at the same speed. The gears on the countershaft continue to rotate, but do not carry power since they are not coupled to any of the gears on the main shaft. See Fig. 43-8.

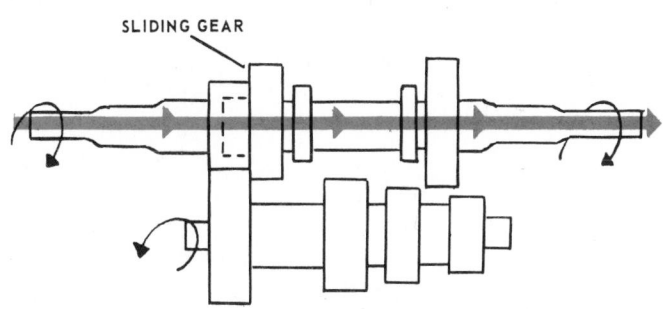

Fig. 43-8. In high gear position, power does not go through gears but is transmitted directly from input shaft to main shaft.

All shift operations on the main shaft are controlled by collars or forks. The forks are attached to two parallel shafts, and the gear shift lever can be moved to the side, forward or backward to engage either shifting shaft as desired. An interlocking device is placed between the shafts so that only one shaft can be moved at a time to avoid engaging more than one pair of gears at a time.

HELICAL GEARS

Helical gear synchromesh transmissions, Fig. 43-9, are somewhat similar to the spur gear type. The principal

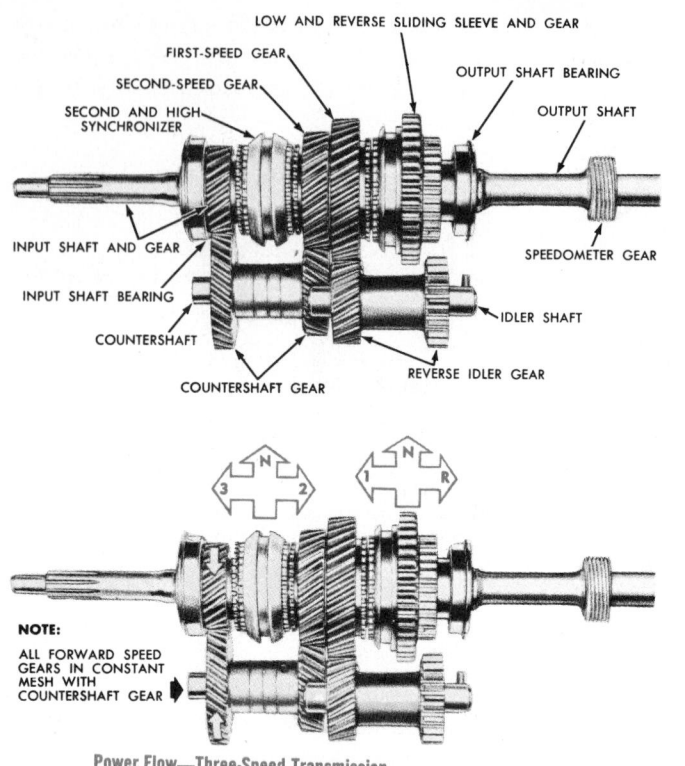

Power Flow—Three-Speed Transmission

NOTE:
ALL FORWARD SPEED GEARS IN CONSTANT MESH WITH COUNTERSHAFT GEAR

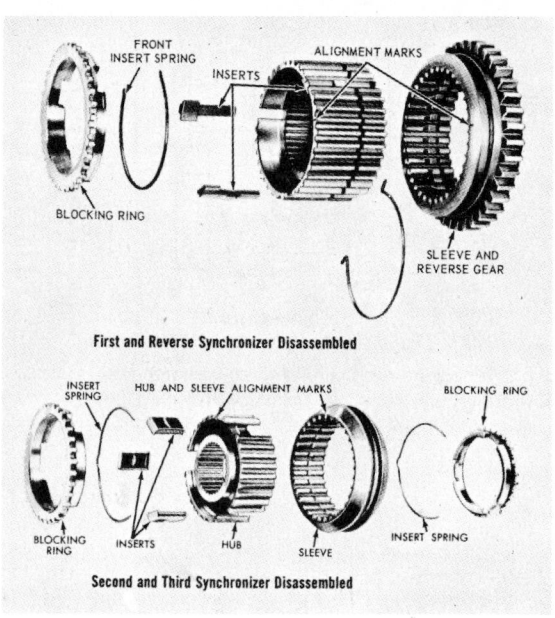

First and Reverse Synchronizer Disassembled

Second and Third Synchronizer Disassembled

Fig. 43-10. Exploded views of synchronizer assemblies show relative positions of internal and external splined hub, sleeve inserts, insert springs and blocking rings.

Fig. 43-9. Above. Gear setup in a typical helical gear synchromesh three-speed transmission features constant mesh gears with synchronized shifts. Below. Position of shift forks is indicated for neutral, first, second, third and reverse.

differences are:
1. The shape of the gear teeth.
2. The addition of synchronizing clutches to the second and high speed gears (first gear too, in many cases).

Fig. 43-11. Exploded view shows assembly sequence of typical three-speed manual transmission: 1—Second and third clutch assembly. 2—Second gear. 3—Main shaft. 4—First gear. 5—First and reverse clutch assembly. 6—Reverse gear. 7—Shifter forks. 8—Countershaft gear. 9—Reverse idler gear. 10—Pinion gear. 11—Case. 12—Countershaft. 13—Speedometer drive gear. 14—Extension housing.

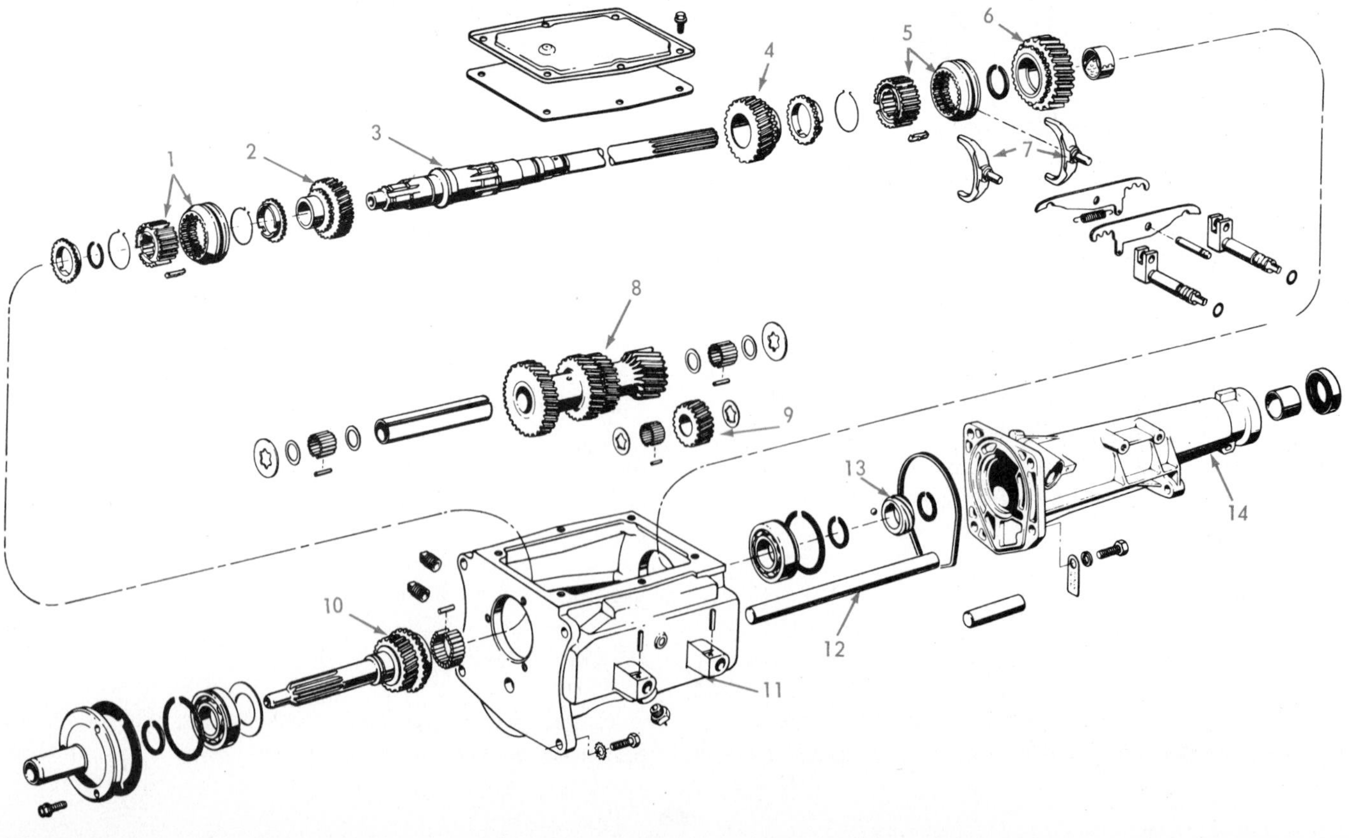

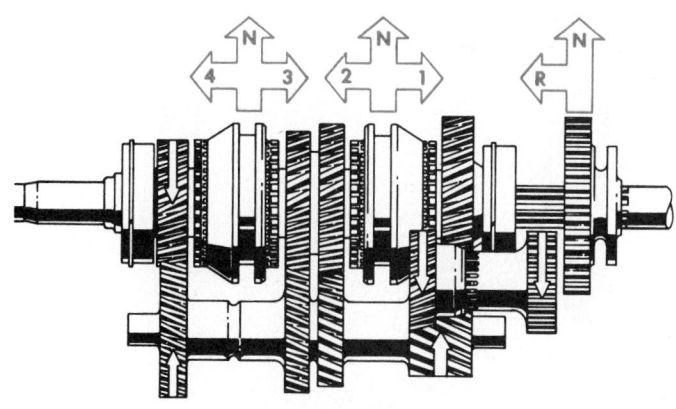

4-Speed Transmission

Fig. 43-12. Four-speed transmission is a favorite of sports car enthusiasts. Fully synchronized, all upshifts and down shifts can be made while car is in motion.

3. The fact that some of the main shaft gears are free to turn on bearings until engaged.

Ordinarily, the low and reverse sliding gear does not need a synchronizing clutch, because the car usually is standing still when the transmission is shifted into low or reverse.

SYNCHRONIZING CLUTCH

The synchronizing clutch is a drum or sleeve that slides back and forth on the splined main shaft by means of the shifting fork. Generally, it has a bronze cone on each side that engages with a tapered mating cone on the second and high speed gears. When this drum is moved along the main shaft, the cones act as a clutch. Upon touching the gear which is to

be engaged, the main shaft is speeded up or slowed down as required until the speeds of the main shaft and gear are synchronized.

This action occurs during partial movement of the shift lever. Completion of lever movement than slides the drum and gear into complete engagement. This action can be readily understood by remembering that the hub of the drum slides on the splines of the main shaft to engage the cones, then the drum slides on the hub to engage the gears. See Fig. 43-10. Fig. 43-9 shows the synchronizers and all other parts in their assembled positions. Fig. 43-11 shows an exploded view of a typical three speed manual transmission.

FOUR—ON—THE—FLOOR

Four-speed manual transmissions are popular combinations with high performance engines. Generally, all four forward speeds are synchronized and engineered with closely spaced gear ratios to provide minimum loss of engine speed at shift points. All gears are in constant mesh with the exception of the reverse sliding gear, Fig. 43-12. With four-speed transmissions, manual gear shifting is usually accomplished with a floor-type shift lever mounted on a console.

When a four-speed manual transmission is in neutral, with clutch engaged, the input shaft drives the countershaft. However, with all synchronizers neutrally positioned and the reverse sliding gear out of mesh, power does not flow to the main shaft. See Fig. 43-12.

In all forward speeds, power is transmitted from the input shaft to the countershaft gear and to first gear, then to second, third or fourth speed gears, in turn, each locked with a synchronizer assembly to drive the main shaft. See Fig. 43-13.

POWER FLOW

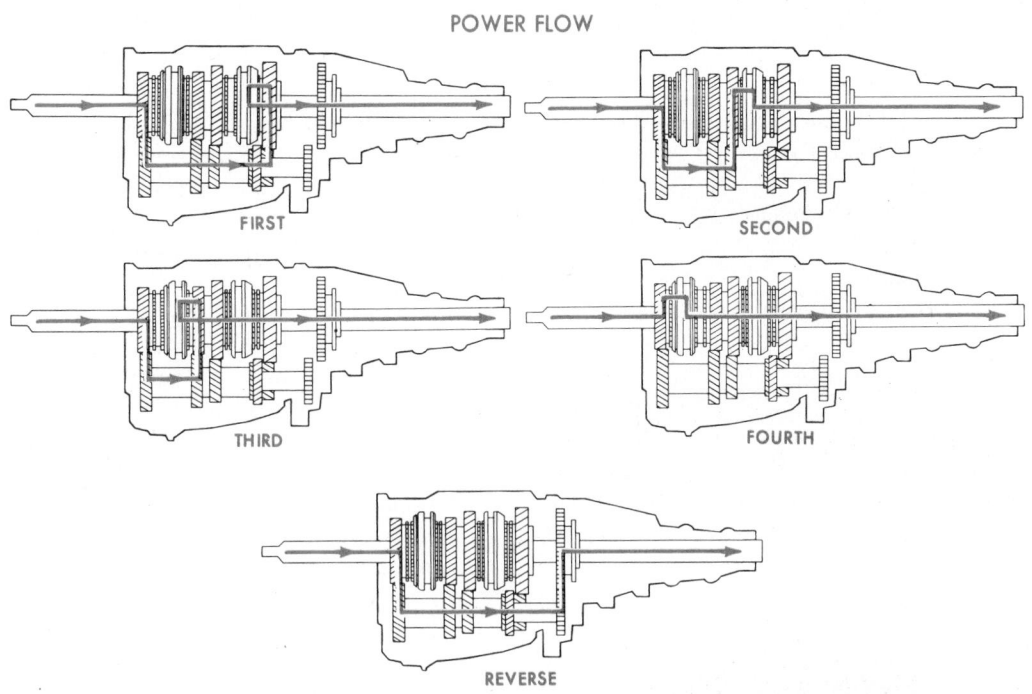

Fig. 43-13. Power flow of four-speed transmission is illustrated in each drive position forward, and also in reverse.

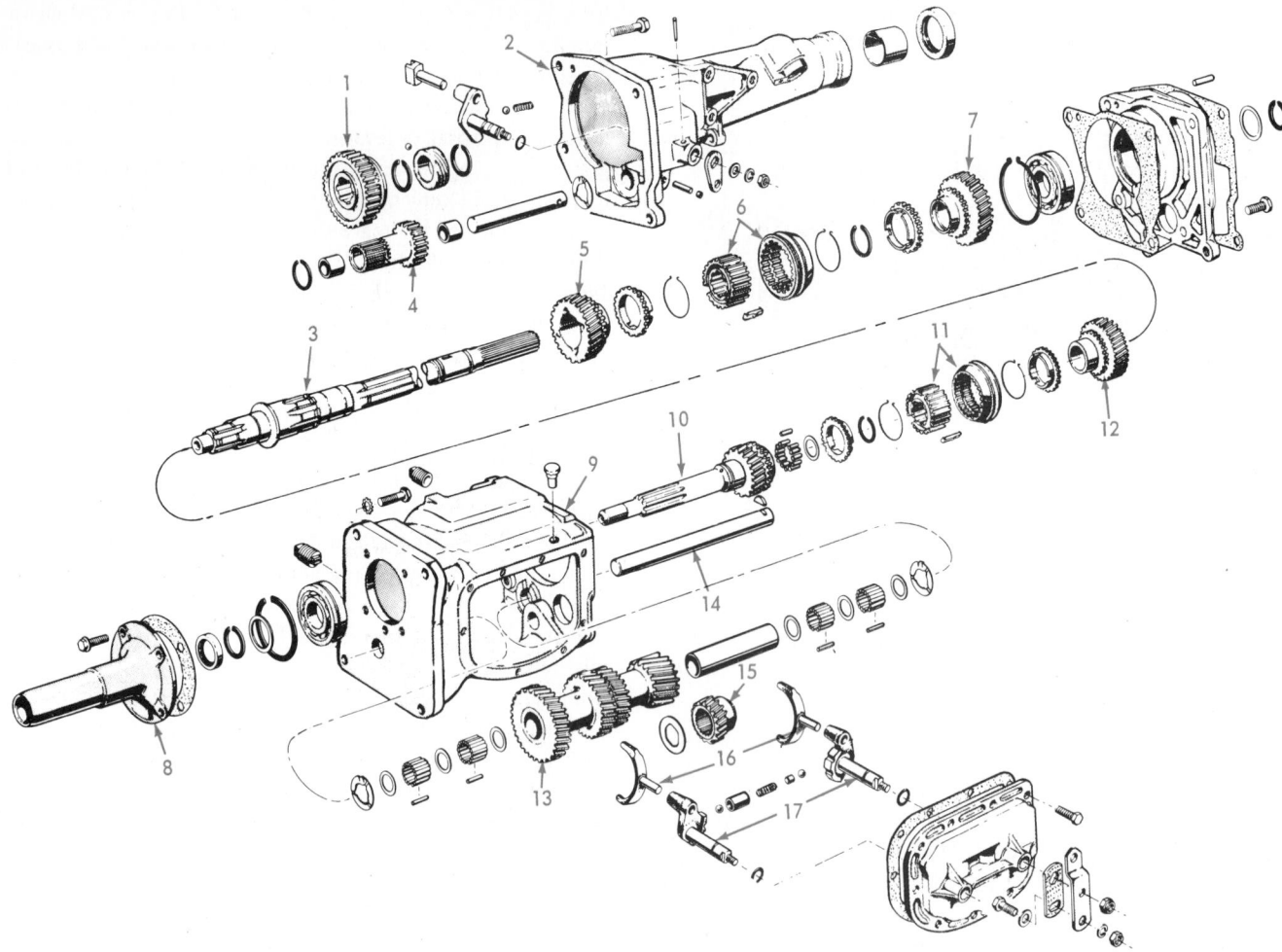

Fig. 43-14. Major elements of typical four-speed manual transmission include: 1—Reverse gear. 2—Reverse gear housing. 3—Main shaft. 4—Reverse idler gear. 5—Second gear. 6—First and second clutch assembly. 7—First gear. 8—Front bearing retainer. 9—Case. 10—Pinion gear. 11—Third and fourth clutch assembly. 12—Third gear. 13—Countershaft gear. 14—Countershaft. 15—Reverse idler gear. 16—Shifter forks. 17—Shifter fork shafts.

In reverse, the reverse sliding gear is moved into mesh with the reverse rear idler gear. Power is transmitted from the input shaft to the countershaft gear, then to the constant mesh reverse front idler gear and through splines and reverse gearing to the main shaft, Fig. 43-13.

To illustrate all components of a four speed manual transmission, an exploded view is shown in Fig. 43-14.

PLANETARY GEAR SYSTEMS

Planetary gears are used in one form or another to a great extent in automatic transmissions and overdrives. (See the chapter on TORQUE CONVERTER AUTOMATIC TRANS-MISSIONS.) The name is derived from their similarity to our solar system, since the pinions or planet gears each turn on their own axis while rotating around the central or sun gear. These gears are surrounded by a ring gear, Fig. 43-15.

Planetary gears are used in one form as a reduction gear and in another form as an overgear. They are used for reverse and are used in multiple sets where more than two forward speeds are wanted. Earlier designs were operated by levers or pedals.

Now, planetary gear sets usually are controlled by hydraulic pressure in combination with automatic mechanical governors, electrical solenoids and vacuum diaphragms.

METHODS OF CONNECTING PARTS

In a planetary gear set, the gears are in mesh at all times and are never shifted in and out of engagement. The gears are attached to different drums which, in turn, are attached to other operating parts of the system. This enables the gears to function in different ways as the various drums are held from rotation by brake bands.

A simple form of planetary gear set, Fig. 43-15, has three pinions mounted between, and meshed with, both the sun gear and ring gear at all times. The pinions revolve on pins or axles which are a part of the planet carrier drum. The pinions are held in spaced relationship with one another, yet can turn freely on their own pins and also can rotate around the sun gear and within the ring gear.

Basically, we have three units:
1. The sun gear.

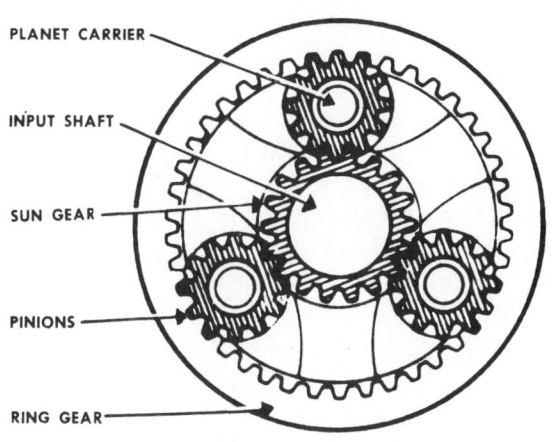

Fig. 43-15. This planetary gear set utilizes a typical three-pinion arrangement. Two and four-pinion types also have been used.

2. The planet carrier, drum and pinions.
3. The ring gear and drum.

The gears can be arranged so that they will function as driving elements or driven elements to provide different results by connecting them in different ways.

For example, if the engine is connected to the sun gear and the planet or pinion carrier is connected to the drive shaft, the entire assembly will rotate as a unit (pinions do not turn on their pins). In this case, there will be no gear reduction; the drive shaft (driven shaft in this case) will rotate at the same speed as the engine shaft (driving shaft).

If, however, a brake band is placed around the ring gear to hold it from turning, the pinions will be forced to travel around inside the ring gear carrying the pinion carrier along at reduced speed. In this case, the pinion gears turn on their pins in the opposite direction of rotation of the sun gear, while the pinion carrier turns in the same direction as the sun gear but at reduced speed.

With these few gears and a band to hold the drum, we have a basic transmission of the planetary type with a gear reduction for low gear and a direct drive for high gear. In addition, a clutch is needed between the engine and transmission to allow the car to stand still while the engine runs.

Also required is some means of reversing the transmission. These additions to the basic setup are shown in Fig. 43-16.

METHOD OF OPERATION

The operation of a two forward speed and reverse planetary transmission is shown in Figs. 43-17 through 43-20. In each

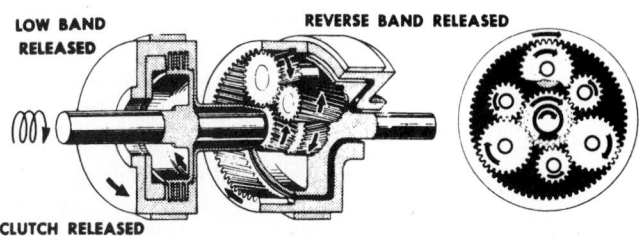

Fig. 43-17. In neutral, planet carrier which is attached to drive shaft is standing still while all gears rotate around it.

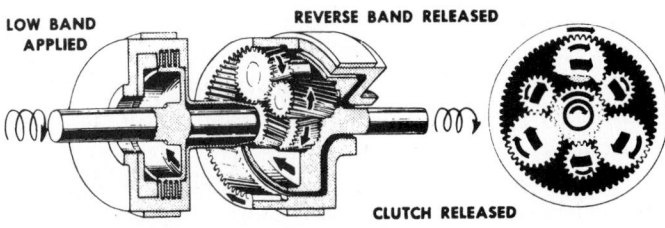

Fig. 43-18. In low speed position, planet carrier and gears all revolve, but at different relative speeds.

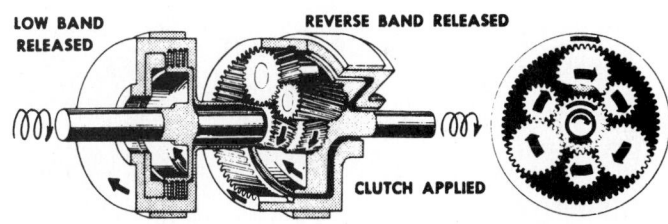

Fig. 43-19. In high gear (direct drive), everything turns and speed of rotation of output shaft is same as speed of input shaft.

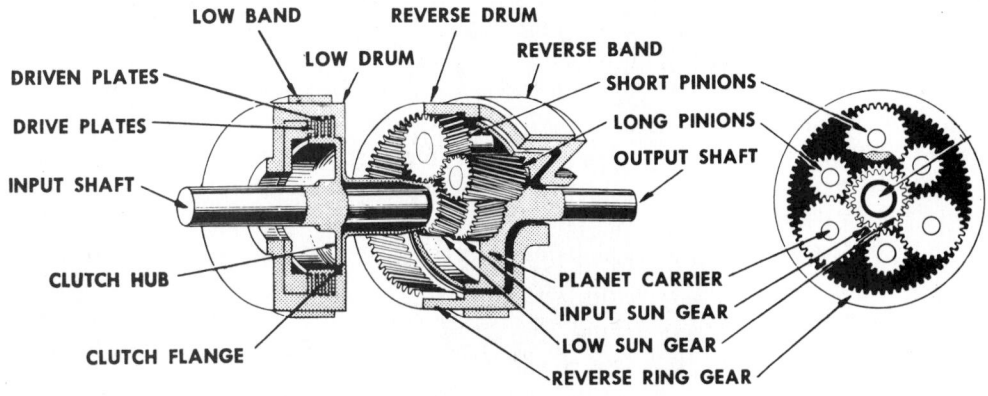

Fig. 43-16. Addition of three more pinions and a clutch to basic three-pinion planetary gear setup provides transmission with neutral and reverse.

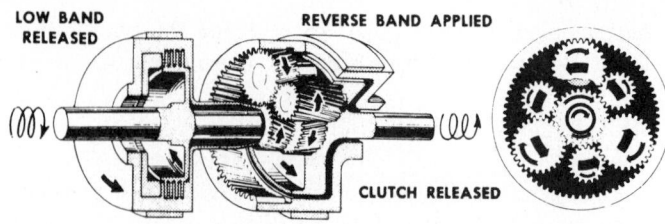

Fig. 43-20. In reverse position, ring gear stands still and planet carrier rotates in opposite direction.

case, the rotation of each gear is shown by light arrows, while the rotation of the gear assembly is shown by heavy arrows. A thorough study of all these gear actions is absolutely necessary in order to be able to understand the operation of the more complicated automatic transmissions.

TRANSMISSION OVERDRIVES

Utilizing the same fundamental gears used in planetary transmissions, we can change the hookup to get an overdrive. If we attach the engine to the planet carrier instead of the sun gear and attach the drive shaft (or driven shaft) to the ring gear instead of the planet carrier, we would change the entire operation.

By holding the sun gear, we can reverse the action of the gearing and get an increase in gear ratio instead of a reduction. See View J in Fig. 43-21. That is, the drive shaft will turn

faster than the engine shaft. The engine will not work as hard to produce high road speeds and there will be some improvement in gasoline mileage.

Of course, the gear ratio could be changed either in the transmission or the rear axle. The two-speed rear axle was used for a time in certain passenger cars. Then someone worked out the answer to the overdrive problem: combining the planetary gears with a free-wheel unit (overrunning clutch).

This combination was light in weight, not too expensive to build and could be attached to the transmission where it would be carried by the car springs as part of the sprung

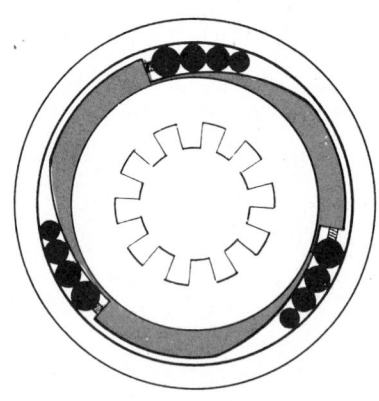

Fig. 43-22. On an overrunning clutch: If outer rim turns clockwise, rollers will roll up on cams and hub will turn at same speed as rim. If rim turns counterclockwise, rollers roll down cams against springs and hub will "free wheel" (cease to rotate).

Fig. 43-21. Any one of three units in a planetary gear set, sun gear, ring gear or planet carrier, can be held from rotating to obtain different results.

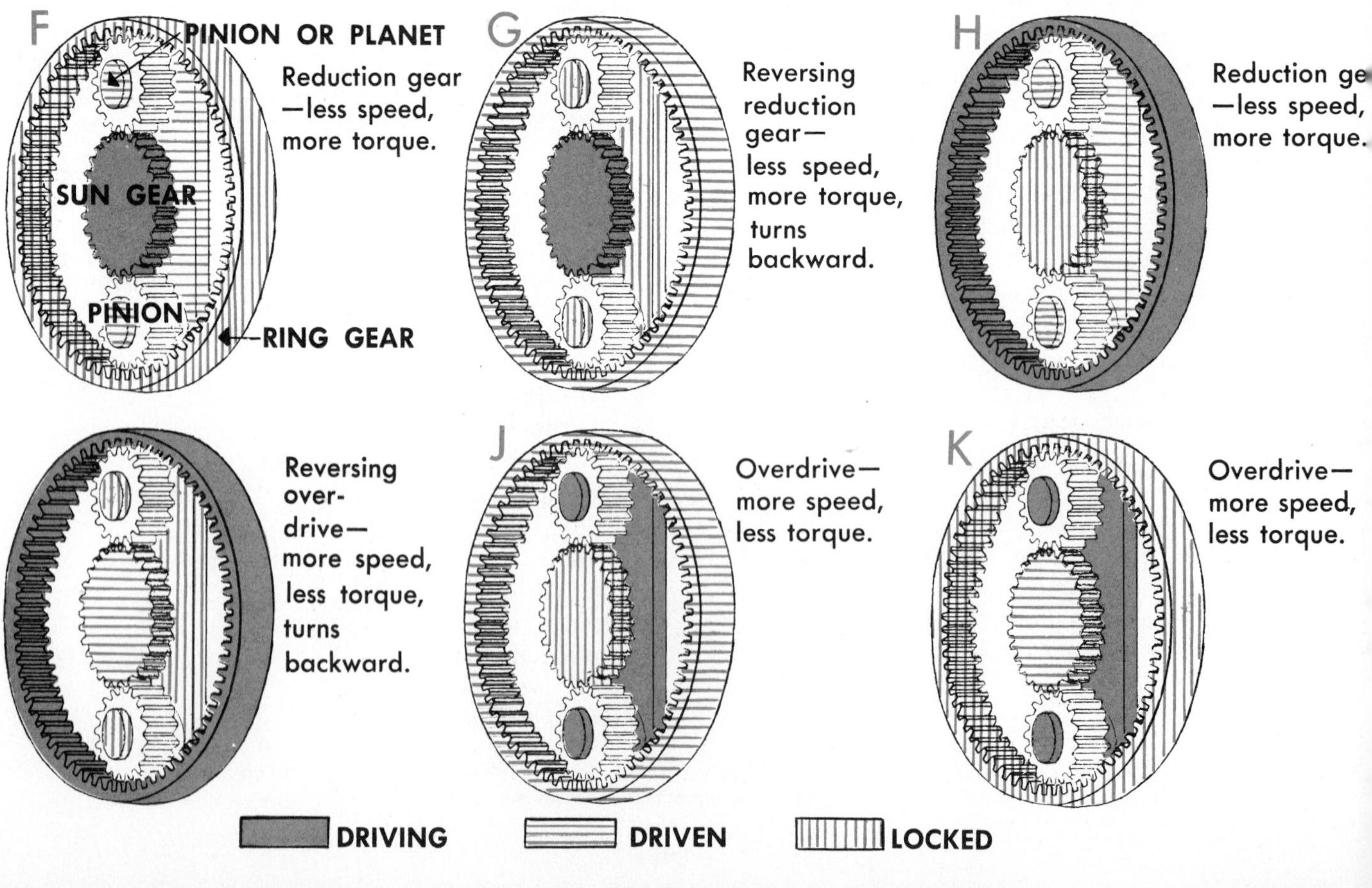

F — PINION OR PLANET — Reduction gear —less speed, more torque. SUN GEAR, PINION, RING GEAR

G — Reversing reduction gear— less speed, more torque, turns backward.

H — Reduction gear —less speed, more torque.

Reversing over-drive— more speed, less torque, turns backward.

J — Overdrive— more speed, less torque.

K — Overdrive— more speed, less torque.

DRIVING   DRIVEN   LOCKED

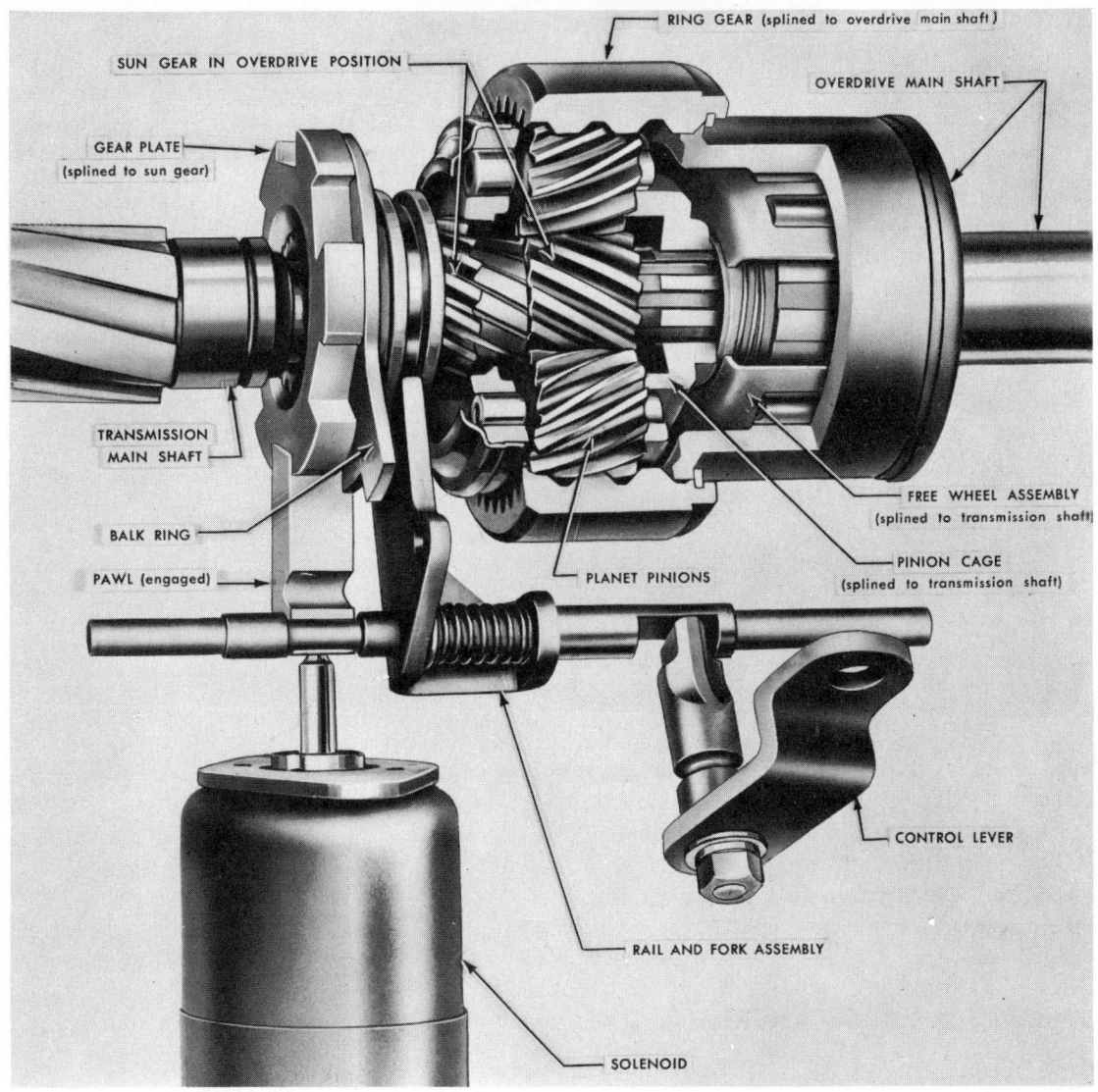

Fig. 43-23. Overdrive transmission in overdrive: Sun gear is locked in place by pawl in balk ring. Planet gears drive internal ring gear. Ring gear drives overdrive main shaft.

weight. Furthermore, it could be controlled by the driver and could be made automatic in operation.

ARRANGING OVERDRIVE

There are several ways of hooking up planetary gearing to accomplish different results. One method is to increase gear ratio by attaching the driven shaft to the ring gear, while holding the sun gear from rotating. However, when the sun gear is released, the pinions will simply chase around between the sun gear and ring gear in the opposite direction and no power will be transmitted.

This problem was solved by installing a free-wheel unit on the transmission main shaft. Then, when drive shaft speed exceeds engine speed (coasting), the rollers release. When accelerating the engine, the rollers are wedged on the cam and power is transmitted, Fig. 43-22.

METHODS OF CONTROL

Control of an overdrive transmission must be in the hands of the driver. Free-wheeling can be dangerous, unless it is

locked out when braking effect of the engine is needed.

With the control handle pushed in, a solenoid switch is energized at speeds above 25-30 mph. Then, if the accelerator pedal is momentarily released, a locking pawl engages the sun gear hub and balk ring assembly. When the accelerator is again depressed, overdrive is in operation and free-wheeling becomes inoperative. See Fig. 43-23.

With the control handle pulled out, overdrive is locked out. A cable from the handle is connected to a transmission lever that operates a shifting fork. The fork mates with a shifting collar on the sun gear which is shifted into engagement with lock-up teeth on the planet carrier. The entire overdrive and free-wheel unit is locked together, and the car will operate as if it is equipped with a three-speed manual transmission.

SOLENOID MAGNET OPERATION

Solenoids are used extensively as control devices for vacuum and power units which do the actual shifting. The solenoid, in an overdrive transmission, consists of an iron plunger within coils of wire through which electricity flows,

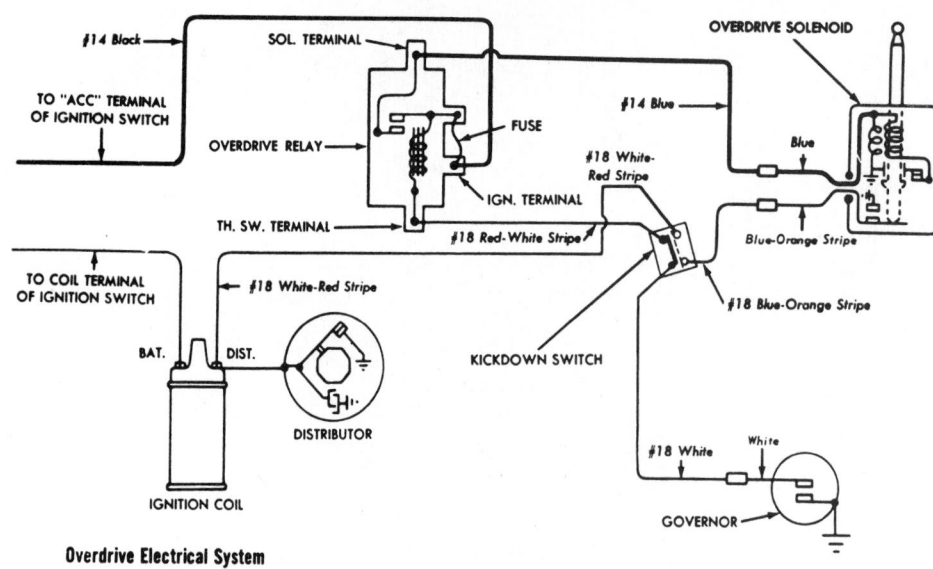

Overdrive Electrical System

Fig. 43-24. Overdrive electrical system consists of: Governor circuit, which opens and closes relay. Solenoid circuit, which supplies current to energize solenoid. Ignition interrupter circuit.

Fig. 43-24. When the current is turned on, the iron core moves into the magnetic field and pushes the pawl into engagement. In this case, there are two coils of wire: a heavy winding to move the plunger; and a lighter winding to hold it in place after it is moved. Both coils are used to move the plunger, which opens the contacts for the closing coil and leaves the holding coil in operation.

MECHANICAL GOVERNOR OPERATION

Since it is desirable to have the overdrive function above a car speed of about 25 mph and undesirable to have it in use below that speed, some automatic device is needed to connect it and disconnect it. This is accomplished by a mechanical centrifugal governor which operates an electrical switch to control the flow of electricity to the solenoid.

The overdrive governor is geared to, and driven by, the drive shaft, Fig. 43-25. Centrifugal force causes the weights to fly outward and raise a floating shaft which closes the contact points in the cover. The governor is designed and adjusted to close at a somewhat higher speed than it opens.

KICKDOWN SWITCH NEEDED

It is desirable to be able to change from overdrive to direct drive when climbing a hill or accelerating to pass another car. For this purpose, an electrical switch is located under the accelerator pedal or in a position where it can be operated by the accelerator linkage.

Pushing the accelerator pedal down will close contacts in the switch and cut out the overdrive. This action momentarily "shorts out" the ignition distributor to permit the locking pawl to be released. As soon as it releases (one or two turns of the crankshaft), ignition is restored.

USE OF BALK RING

The balk ring is intended to avoid harsh and sudden locking of the sun gear. Under kickdown conditions, the car will stay in direct drive until the accelerator is eased up again. If engine speed is above cut-in speed (25-30 mph), the solenoid is energized, allowing the locking pawl to engage the sun gear hub and balk ring assembly. See Fig. 43-23.

OPERATION OF VACUUM CYLINDERS

Since an internal combustion engine is also a vacuum pump, there is always vacuum power available while the engine is

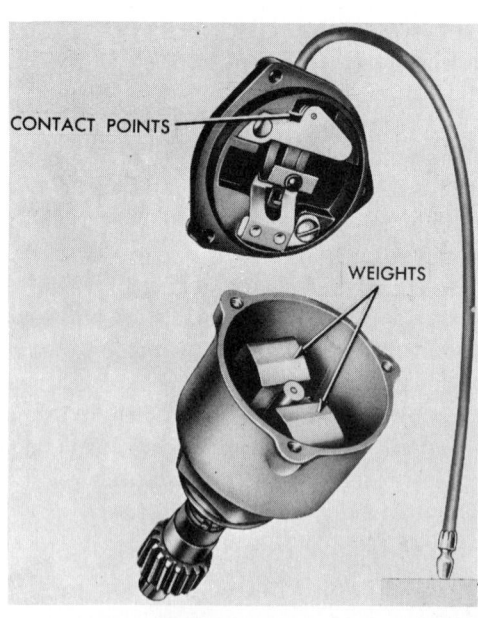

Fig. 43-25. At approximately 25-30 mph, governor weights raise floating shaft to close contact points and permit current to flow from battery through relay to solenoid.

running. Designers have taken advantage of this fact to build a multitude of vacuum-operated accessories such as windshield wipers, brake boosters, gear shifters, etc. A small pipe connection is made to the intake manifold, and vacuum is piped to wherever it is needed.

However, suction derived from the engine through a small pipe is not powerful enough to apply brakes and shift gears. Instead, it is used to allow air power to do the actual work. The amount of power created in this fashion is directly dependent upon the size of the diaphragm in the vacuum cylinder upon which atmospheric pressure acts.

Obviously, then, a vacuum cylinder can be attached to the brake pedal to operate the brakes, or to the clutch pedal to operate the clutch, or to the gear shift lever to shift the gears.

OVERDRIVE REVIVAL

After a lengthy lull, overdrive units (either planetary type or with built-in or built-on gears and synchronizers) are popular again. The emphasis on fuel economy has stimulated the availability of overdrive from almost every U.S. car manufacturer and manufacturing division.

American Motors offered an overdrive planetary gearbox made by Laycock in England. See Fig. 43-26.

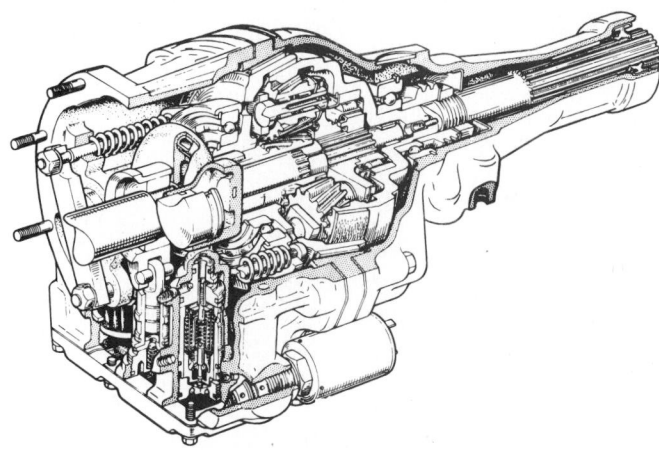

Fig. 43-26. Cutaway view of the AMC-Laycock four-speed overdrive planetary gearbox. (American Motors Corp.)

The AMC-Laycock overdrive is considered an auxiliary unit because it attaches to the rear of a three speed manual transmission. This overdrive is a hydraulically operated unit with engagement controlled by a solenoid valve, which is activated by a switch in the turn signal lever. Overdrive can be engaged only in third gear at speeds above 38 mph. Cut-in and cut-out speeds are controlled by a governor speed switch on the speedometer cable. A kickdown switch is provided for use when sudden acceleration is desired.

Chrysler came up with an Overdrive-4 transmission as an option on certain models, Fig. 43-27. It provides a 0.73:1 fourth speed ratio for highway cruising above 30 mph. The overdrive gear is installed on the transmission mainshaft immediately in back of the third speed-overdrive synchronizer. It is controlled by an external shift lever on the transmission case. See Fig. 43-27.

The gear shifting in the Overdrive-4 transmission is manually operated through shift control rods to the transmission. Any forward gear can be engaged while the vehicle is in motion through the use of synchronizers. The synchronizers also permit downshifting without gear clashing as an aid to deceleration.

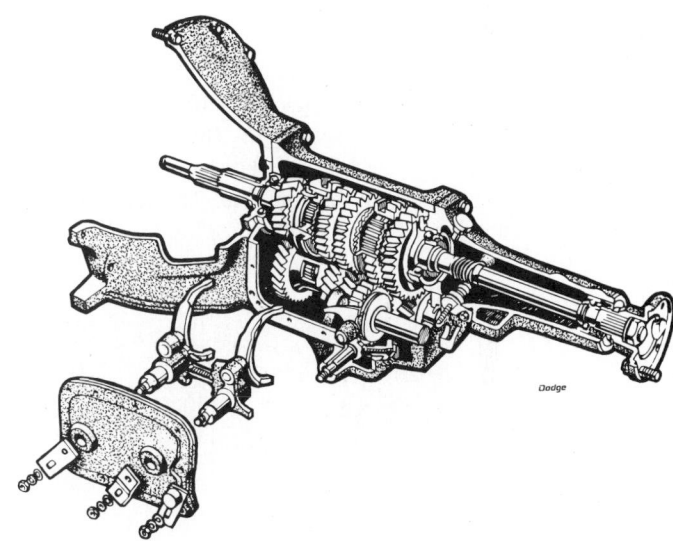

Fig. 43-27. Chrysler's optional Overdrive-4 manual transmission is designed for use on sixes and V-8s.

Ford used a four speed, fully synchronized overdrive transmission in smaller vehicles through 1978. All gears except the reverse sliding gear are in constant mesh in this overdrive design. All forward speed changes are accomplished with synchronizer sleeves.

Helical gears are used with the exception of the reverse sliding gear and the external teeth of the first speed-second speed synchronizer sleeve. These are spur type gears (teeth are parallel to bore of gear).

The shift control unit on this older Ford overdrive unit is not to be disassembled. Only the shift lever, knob, backup light switch retainer and switch may be removed.

FORD SINGLE-RAIL OVERDRIVE TRANSMISSION

Ford replaced its older overdrive transmission with a new single-rail shift, four-speed overdrive transmission for use in

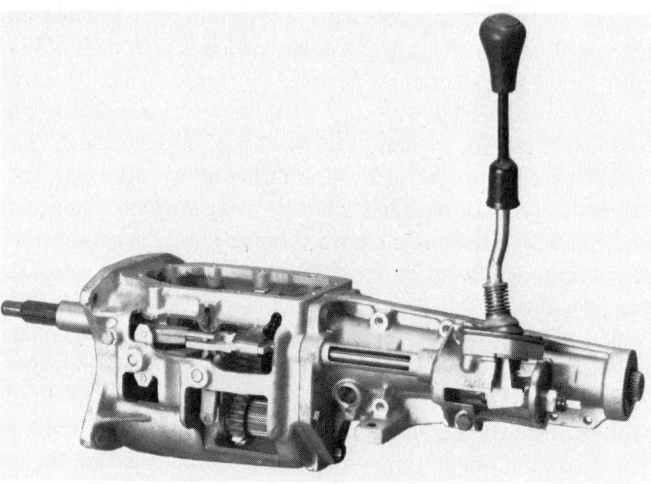

Fig. 43-28. Ford's single-rail shift, four-speed overdrive transmission was introduced in 1979.

certain 1979 models. See Fig. 43-28.

Major change is the use of a single-rail shift mechanism that replaces the old external linkage system. The new mechanism is enclosed within a special rear housing, a connecting extension tube and the transmission case. The mechanism is totally enclosed and needs no adjustment or lubrication.

The standard "H" shift pattern remains unchanged except that reverse is obtained by pushing down (instead of lifting up) on the shift lever.

The aluminum case, extension housing, bearing retainer and shift housings result in a 30 lb. weight savings over the older four-speed overdrive transmission.

Two sets of gear ratios are available for Ford's single-rail overdrive transmission. One set is for all six cylinder engine applications. It features an overdrive ratio of 0.81:1. The other offering has lower numerical ratios to match the higher horsepower output of the 302 cu. in. (5.0 litre) V-8. This overdrive ratio is 0.70:1.

FIVE-SPEED SYNCHROMESH TRANSMISSION

A five-speed manual transmission is used in certain General Motors cars. Fifth gear is built-in overdrive. It is obtained by means of an overdrive gear on the output shaft and one of the gears on the countergear inside the transmission, instead of a bolt-on overdrive.

The five-speed unit is fully synchronized in all forward gears. The transmission has a single shift rail with the shifting mechanism totally enclosed within the transmission. All gears are in constant mesh with the countergear, including reverse through the reverse idler. When shifting gears, the chosen gear is locked to the output shaft through the synchronizer clutch hub.

Oldsmobile's five-speed synchromesh transmission is shown in Fig. 43-29. It was made available for use in the 260 cu. in. (4.3 litre) diesel engine.

The Fiat five-speed, all synchronized transmission pictured in Fig. 43-30 is designed for use in the Fiat 124 Sport model.

Fig. 43-29. Oldsmobile's five-speed, synchromesh transmission for use with 260 cu. in. (4.3 litre) diesel.

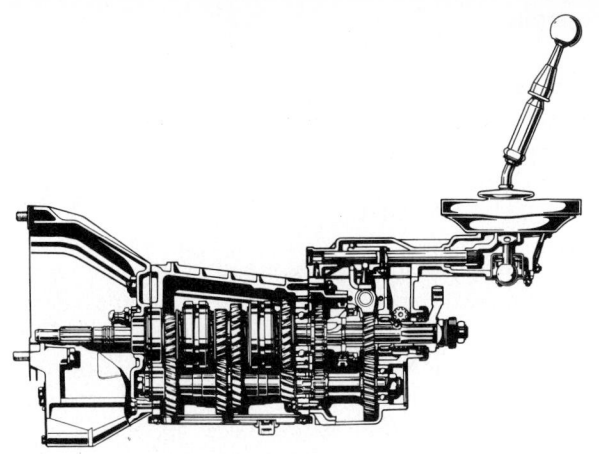
Fig. 43-30. Fiat's five-speed overdrive transmission.

AUTOMATIC TRANSMISSION

Hydraulic pressure, too, can be utilized for shifting gears and in the control of automatic transmissions. By using an oil pump driven by the engine, we can obtain almost any amount of hydraulic pressure or power we need. This power can be piped or channeled to any point where required.

The amount of pressure in an automatic transmission can be controlled by spring-loaded valves. Since a fluid under pressure expands equally in all directions, engineers can control the power exerted by changing the size of the passages and the pressure on the fluid.

It is a fact, then, that there are several ways to approach automatic transmission operation:

1. Use electricity, air pressure or hydraulic pressure for either or both clutch and transmission. We can also combine each of three sources of power with others.
   A. To shift a sliding gear transmission.
   B. To operate the clutch.
   C. To operate a planetary transmission.
2. Use a fluid coupling instead of a power-operated clutch.
3. Combine various elements to obtain automatic operation.
4. Use a hydraulic torque converter instead of some gearing, or in combination with gearing, and with or without a clutch.

TRANSMISSION LUBRICATION

Lubrication is required for the gear teeth, bearings upon which the shafts turn, splines upon which the gears slide and other working parts. Therefore, the gear case is made oil tight by placing gaskets between the case and cover and any other parts that are bolted to the case. Oil seals are also placed at each of the bearings on the main shaft.

The oil used in manual transmissions is heavier than engine oil, in most cases, and is known as SAE 80 or 90 Gear Oil. The case is filled to the level of the bottom of the fill plug opening, which is usually slightly below the center of the countershaft.

In automatic transmissions, light oil is a satisfactory lubricant for the gears, bearings and bands of the planetary set. Late model Ford Motor Company cars use Ford Specification M2C33F, or "Type F" automatic transmission fluid (ATF). All GM cars, Chrysler Corporation cars and American Motors'

cars with automatic transmissions use "Dexron" ATF.

When planetary gears are used in an overdrive, no bands are required and the gear oil used in the transmission housing is satisfactory in most cases. The tooth pressures in planetary gearing are low and an extreme pressure lubricant is not required. Engine oil SAE 60 or transmission oil SAE 80 are ideal lubricants for overdrives.

TRANSMISSION TROUBLESHOOTING SPUR AND HELICAL GEARS

Transmission Noisy in Neutral

This may be a growl or hum that can be stopped by depressing clutch pedal. In some cases a bump or thud also will be present, indicating a broken gear or bearing. Defects in main shaft, other than pilot bearing, are not included in this group because main shaft does not rotate when transmission is in neutral.

1. Insufficient lubricant in transmission.
2. Abnormal end play in countershaft gears, reverse idler gear or pinion shaft.
3. Pinion gear badly worn or broken.
4. Pinion shaft bearing badly worn or broken.
5. Misalignment between engine and transmission.
6. Wear in countershaft drive gear.
7. Wear in reverse and/or reverse idler gear.
8. Countershaft bearings badly worn.
9. Reverse idler shaft bearings badly worn.
10. Countershaft sprung or bent.
11. Pilot shaft bearing worn or broken.

NOTE: If replacement of a gear is required, mating gear should be replaced too.

Transmission Noisy in Gear

Most causes of noises in neutral will also appear when transmission is in gear. Some parts are still in operation, plus main shaft which adds following:

1. Main shaft rear bearing worn or broken.
2. Sliding gears badly worn or broken.
3. Excessive end play of main shaft.
4. Badly worn speedometer gears.

Transmission Slips Out of High Gear

Principal cause is misalignment between transmission and engine. Front end of pinion shaft runs in a bearing in crankshaft, and rear end in transmission case. If this shaft is not in a straight line with engine crankshaft and transmission main shaft, it will create an angular contact. Other less frequent causes are:

1. Pinion gear teeth worn or tapered.
2. Pinion gear bearing badly worn.
3. Improper adjustment of shift linkage.
4. Worn shift detent parts.
5. Damaged main shaft pilot bearing.
6. Pilot bearing loose in crankshaft.

Transmission Slips Out of Second Gear

1. Badly worn or broken gear.
2. Badly worn transmission bearings.

3. Improper adjustment of shift linkage.
4. Worn shift detent parts.
5. Excessive end play of main or countershaft.

Transmission Slips Out of First or Reverse Gear

1. Badly worn or broken gears.
2. Badly worn transmission bearings.
3. Main shaft splines worn or distorted.
4. Excessive end play of main, countershaft or reverse idler shaft.
5. Worn shift detent parts.
6. Improper adjustment of shift linkage.

Transmission Difficult to Shift

1. Engine clutch not releasing.
2. Distorted or burred main shaft splines.
3. Improper adjustment of shift linkage.
4. Misalignment of column control levers.

Transmission Oil Leaks

1. Damaged oil seals.
2. Damaged oil throw rings.
3. Damaged or missing gaskets.
4. Case or cover bolts loose or missing.
5. Case plugs loose or threads stripped.
6. Oil level too high.
7. Vent stopped up.
8. Use of a lubricant that foams excessively.
9. Loose or broken pinion gear retainer.
10. Shift lever seals leak.

PLANETARY TROUBLESHOOTING

Growling or Humming Noises

1. Insufficient lubricant in housing.
2. Dragging bands.
3. Excessive wear in gear teeth.
4. Excessive wear in gear bushings or shafts.

Rough or Harsh Engagement

1. Glazed or burned band linings.
2. Lubricant excessively thin.
3. Scored drums.
4. Improper adjustment of band operating device.
5. Burned or gummed clutch plates.

Grinding or Clicking Noises

1. Excessive wear in gears.
2. Damaged gear teeth.
3. Worn bushings or broken needle bearings.
4. Insufficient lubricant.
5. Excessive wear in clutch hub or drum driving pins or slots.

Slipping or Slow Engagement

1. Bands too loose.
2. Improper adjustment of band operating device.
3. Scored or burned drums.

4. Scored or burned band linings.
5. Warped, scored or burned clutch plates.
6. Clutch plates sticking on hub or in drum.

OVERDRIVE TROUBLESHOOTING

When attempting to diagnose trouble with an overdrive, bear in mind that trouble can be caused by electrical defects, mechanical defects or a combination of both. Since electrical troubles are more likely to occur, check electrical system first and eliminate any defects before going on to mechanical difficulties. Electrical troubles can occur in relay, solenoid, governor, kickdown switch or in any wires connecting these units. Most common trouble is loose or dirty connections on wiring terminals. Any wire or connection can be tested with electrical meters or by temporary substitution of a "jumper," or test wire.

Overdrive Does Not Engage

1. Fuse blown on relay.
2. Defective connecting wires, loose or corroded terminals.
3. Defective relay unit.
4. Defective solenoid.
5. Defective governor contacts.
6. Defective kickdown switch.
7. Dash control improperly adjusted.
8. Governor gear drive pin sheared.
9. Damaged gears, bearings or shifting parts within overdrive unit.

Overdrive Does Not Release

1. Defective relay unit.
2. Defective connecting wires, loose or corroded terminals.
3. Sticking, bent or damaged pawl.
4. Defective kickdown switch.
5. Damaged gears, shafts or shifting parts within the overdrive unit.

Kickdown Does Not Operate

1. Kickdown switch improperly adjusted.
2. Loose or corroded terminals or defective connecting wires.
3. Defective operation of contacts in solenoids.
4. Defective kickdown switch.

Engine Stops When Kickdown Is Used

1. Defective kickdown switch.
2. Ground in wiring or solenoid.

Car Will Not Reverse

1. Shift rail operation defective.

Harsh Overdrive Engagement

1. Defective balk ring action.

All splines, shafts and bushings should operate smoothly and be free from nicks or excessive wear. All gear teeth should be smooth, free from nicks and excessive wear. Free-wheel rollers, cam and shell surfaces should be smooth and free from nicks or pronounced indentations. All ball, roller and needle bearings should be free and smooth in operation and have no perceptible wear or noise. Balk ring friction fit should be checked with a spring scale and replaced if not within friction limits specified by manufacturer.

REVIEW QUESTIONS — TRANSMISSION FUNDAMENTALS

1. What function does a transmission perform?
2. Are power and torque the same? Yes or No?
3. A larger gear on the driving shaft will increase the speed of rotation of the driven shaft. True or False?
4. How can the ratio of mating gears be determined?
5. What is the gear ratio of a setup where the driving gear has 20 teeth and the driven gear has 50?
   a.   2.5 to 1.
   b.   1 to 2.5.
   c.   5 to 2.0.
6. Which two manual transmission shafts turn in neutral?
   a.   Input shaft and main shaft.
   b.   Input shaft and countershaft.
   c.   Main shaft and countershaft.
7. When a manual transmission is shifted into reverse, what extra gear is interposed to reverse the direction of the main shaft?
   a.   Low and reverse sliding gear.
   b.   Reverse idler gear.
   c.   Reverse synchromesh ring.
8. Name the three major units in a planetary gear set.
9. In an overdrive planetary transmission: If the sun gear is held and the ring gear is driven by the pinions, will this increase or decrease the speed of the driveshaft?
10. What is the function of an overrunning clutch in an overdrive transmission?
    a.   Eliminates the clutch.
    b.   Disengages the overdrive unit.
    c.   Restricts drive to one direction only.
11. Which control device on an overdrive transmission operates the locking pawl?
    a.   -Solenoid.
    b.   Governor.
    c.   Relay.
12. Which control device connects and disconnects the overdrive unit?
    a.   Solenoid.
    b.   Governor.
    c.   Relay.
13. What is the purpose of the balk ring in an overdrive?
14. Generally, what grade or weight of oil is used in a manual transmission?
15. Name three possible causes for a manual transmission slipping out of high gear.
16. Name three possible causes for slippage in a planetary transmission.
17. Name four possible causes for a transmission overdrive not engaging.

Manual transmission manufacturer provides replacement gearsets for installation in 4-speed transmission during rebuilding operation. Set includes pinion gear, countershaft gear, synchronized gears, synchronizing rings and varied width spacers and snap rings to provide correct end play in assemblies.

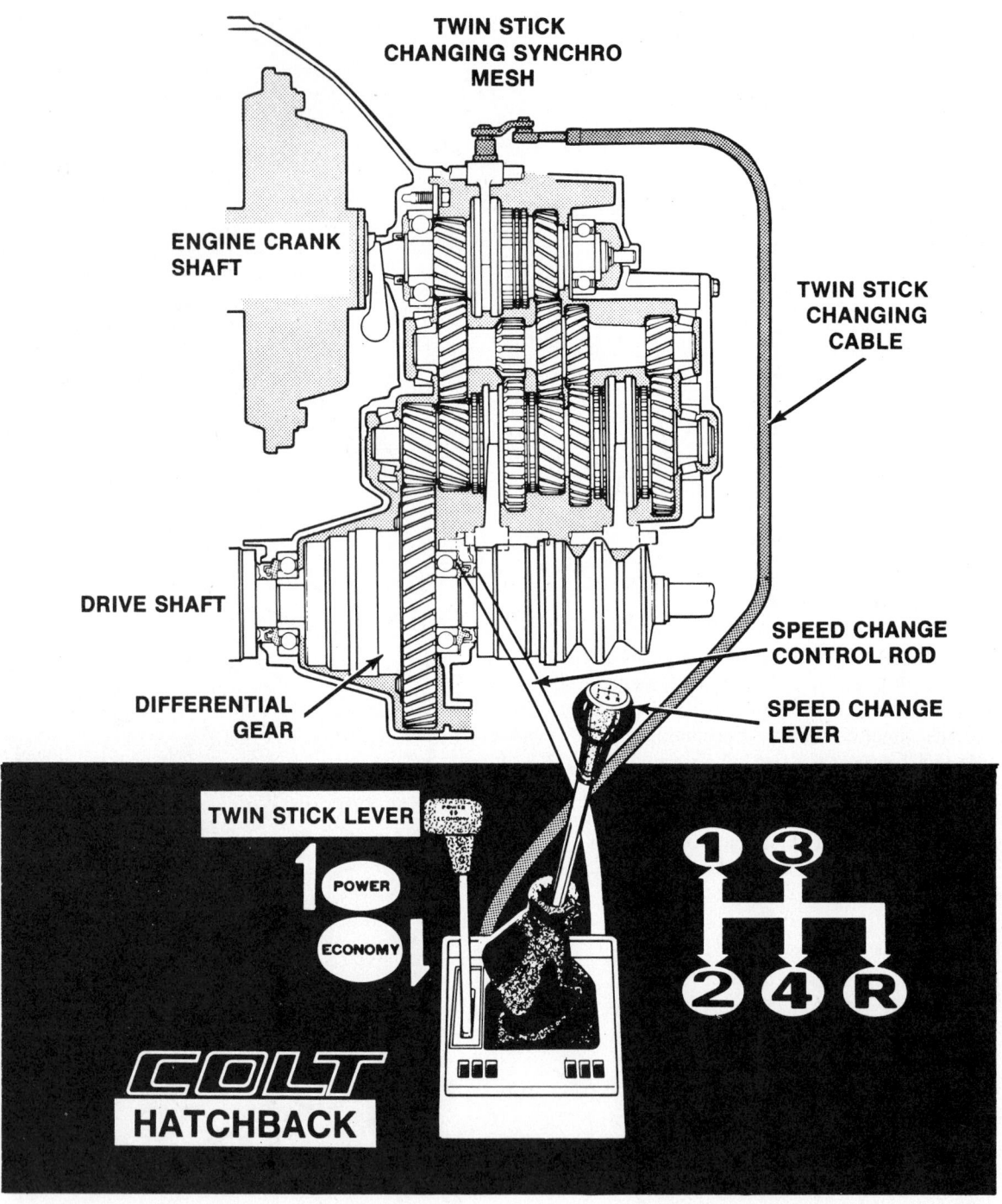

TWIN STICK
CHANGING SYNCHRO
MESH

ENGINE CRANK
SHAFT

TWIN STICK
CHANGING
CABLE

DRIVE SHAFT

SPEED CHANGE
CONTROL ROD

DIFFERENTIAL
GEAR

SPEED CHANGE
LEVER

TWIN STICK LEVER

1 POWER

ECONOMY

COLT
HATCHBACK

Chrysler's "Twin Stick" manual transmission is a basic four-speed gearbox combined with a countershaft and two extra gears to provide a dual range transmission. The transmission has four gear positions. Each position has two modes, economy and power. Result is eight available forward speeds. (Dodge Div., Chrysler Corp.)

FLUID COUPLING AUTOMATIC TRANSMISSIONS

Automatic transmissions are installed in over 90 percent of the U.S. cars coming off assembly lines. Car buyers want the comfort and convenience afforded by these labor-saving, automatically controlled, power transfer devices.

Design and construction differs between makes, but all modern automatic transmissions incorporate the following elements:

1. One or more fluid couplings or a torque converter.
2. One or more planetary gearsets.
3. Suitable valves to direct the flow of automatic transmission fluid (ATF).
4. Various valve controls or combinations of valve controls.

FLUID COUPLINGS

Fluid couplings, or flywheels, were widely used with early automatic and semiautomatic transmissions, Fig. 44-1.

In operation, a fluid coupling acts like an automatic clutch: it slips at idling speed; holds to transmit power as engine speed increased. Power is transmitted through oil. There is no mechanical connection between the engine and drive shaft.

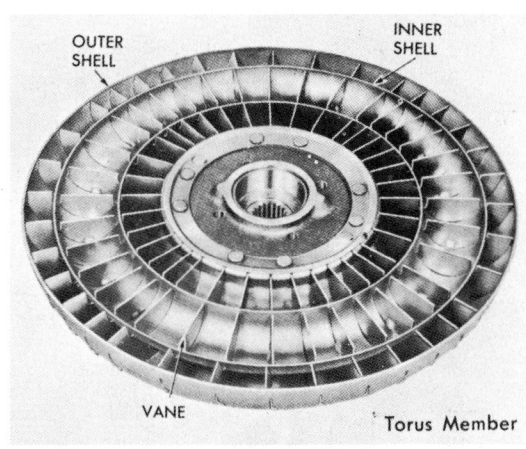

Fig. 44-2. Each torus member of fluid coupling is divided into many sections by designed arrangement of inner and outer shells and vanes.

One side of the unit is attached to the engine, the other side to the drive shaft. Each side is made up of vaned sections facing each other, Fig. 44-2. A fluid coupling used with a sliding gear transmission is partially filled with oil and is a sealed unit, Fig. 44-3. In automatic transmissions, the oil is

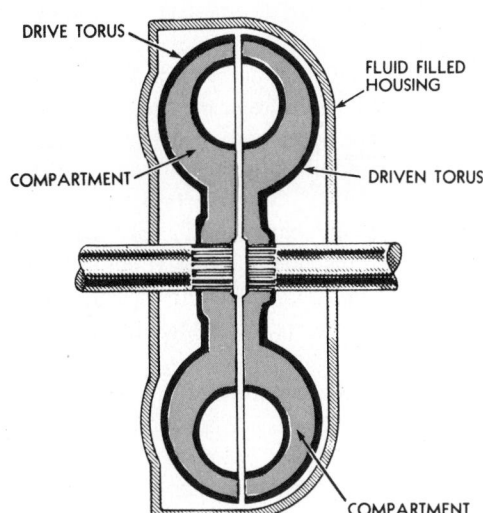

Fig. 44-1. Typical fluid coupling has two facing halves called "torus members" which are splined to separate shafts and operate in a fluid-filled housing.

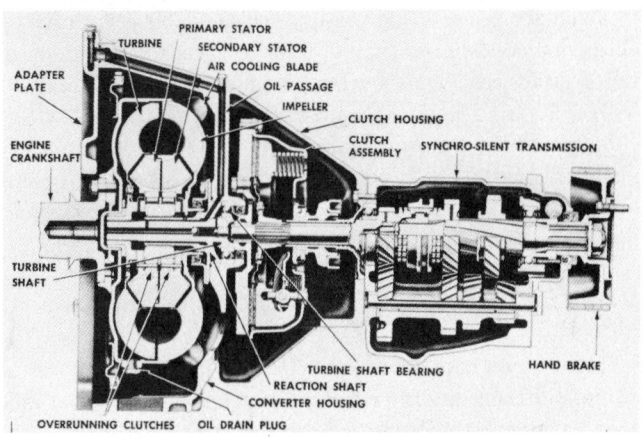

Fig. 44-3. A fluid coupling used in connection with a dry-disc clutch serves to reduce slippage and wear of clutch disc and eases gear shifting in sliding gear transmissions.

circulated by pump pressure to the fluid coupling as well as to other parts of the transmission. When the engine operates fast enough, oil is thrown from the "impeller" side to the "runner" side, causing it to turn in the same direction.

A fluid coupling is not a hydraulic torque converter. (See the chapter on TORQUE CONVERTER AUTOMATIC TRANSMISSIONS.) The fluid coupling transmits little power at slow speed; but when the "impeller" (driving torus) speeds up, it forces oil against the vanes of the "runner" (driven torus) with increasing force, and vehicle movement results.

AUTOMATIC TRANSMISSION OPERATION

When used in conjunction with an automatic transmission, a fluid coupling serves as a hydraulic clutch that transmits engine torque to the transmission and "cushions" the flow of power. A torque converter performs similar duties but, in addition, steps up or multiplies engine torque when operating conditions demand it.

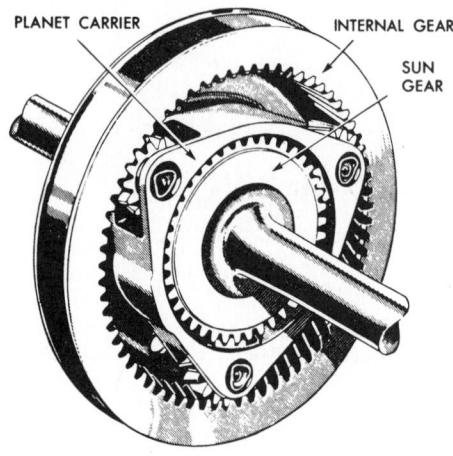

Fig. 44-4. In operation, planetary gearsets provide automatic transmission with various gear ratios as one element is "held" while power is applied to another.

Planetary gearsets, Fig. 44-4, provide suitable gear ratios for all driving conditions. They operate by means of pinion gears turning on their own axis, while rotating around a sun gear and within a ring gear having internal teeth. When used with a combination of clutches, brake bands and valves, a number of planetary gearsets will automatically provide all of the forward and reverse gear ratios needed for efficient operation under normal operating conditions.

VALVES AND VALVE CONTROLS

There are numerous valves and valve controls in an automatic transmission, ranging from simple mechanical linkage to a complicated valve body assembly. See Fig. 44-5.

One means of mechanical control of an automatic transmission is by connecting a valve to a hand lever operated by the driver. Another is by connecting a valve to the accelerator

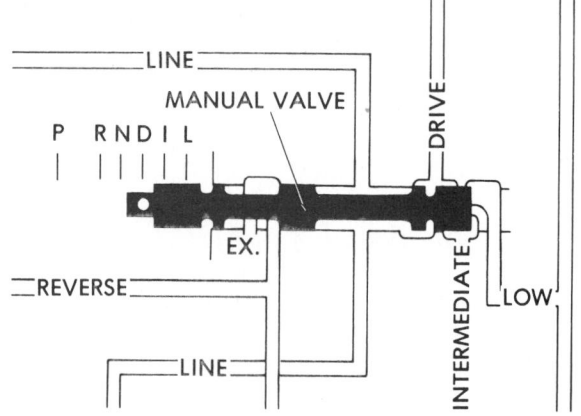

Fig. 44-5. Automatic transmissions are fitted with many different types of valves and valve controls that provide means for application and release of various clutches and bands.

pedal so that driver demands (pressure on pedal) will automatically operate the valve.

In addition, action of a control valve may be regulated automatically as required by load on the engine. This is done by connecting the valve to the intake manifold (vacuum in manifold decreases as load increases). Also, a valve may be operated hydraulically by oil pressure generated in the transmission by an oil pump or pumps.

Engine speed may be used to operate control valves by connecting them to speed-sensitive governors mounted on the engine. In like manner, car speed will control a valve if the governor is attached to the drive shaft of the automobile. Any of these valves may be opened or closed entirely or partially, slowly or rapidly.

Along with mechanical, hydraulic and vacuum operation, almost any type of electrically operated device can be incorporated in the control system of an automatic transmission. Several of these devices can be combined to provide almost any kind or degree of control desired.

For example, it is possible to attach more than one control to a single valve in order to balance the action. One control might be connected to the accelerator pedal and another to the intake manifold. In this case, the system could be set up so that pressure on the accelerator pedal would open the valve under light load conditions (high vacuum). But if the engine is put under heavy load, valve action is delayed by the interconnected vacuum control until engine load decreases.

In any case, by connecting different controls to the valves in the transmission, adjustment to speed, load, and the demands of the driver are automatically made in the transmission ratios.

To provide specific examples of how an automatic transmission operates, and how it is controlled, various typical units will be described and illustrated in this chapter and the next. However, the extreme variety of makes and models precludes the possibility of giving detailed and explicit repair and trouble shooting procedures in this text. Complete repair manuals are available from the car manufacturers and gear manufacturers if a transmission overhaul or extensive repairs are contemplated.

HYDRA–MATIC TRANSMISSIONS

The old Hydra-Matic transmission provides an outstanding example of an automatic transmission since it was used for many years on a number of different makes of automobiles. It was introduced as a fluid coupling unit, then gradually evolved through several major revisions to become a well-accepted torque converter automatic transmission in most General Motors' cars.

Early Hydra-Matics employ a fluid coupling to connect the engine to the transmission. Inside the case, front and rear planetary gearsets, one behind the other, are connected in series, Fig. 44-6. A reverse planetary set is used in conjunction with a reverse "cone" clutch.

The fluid coupling operates full of fluid which circulates through it from the transmission. An inner shell and outer vanes are incorporated in the driving torus and driven torus (oil-filled members) to better control the action of centrifugal force on the oil.

This action can be compared to a shallow, round bowl placed on a spinning turntable, Fig. 44-7. If water is poured into the center of the bowl, it will fly up and out due to the action of centrifugal force. If an identical bowl is inverted over the first one, the water will enter the upper bowl, be guided toward the center and drop back in the lower bowl. A system of circulation of the fluid is established, and this is the action that takes place in the Hydra-Matic fluid coupling, Fig. 44-8.

At high speed, the fluid coupling is very effective as loss of speed between the two torus members is probably not over one or two percent. At low speeds, there is considerable slippage. At idling speed, almost 100 percent slippage. However, some energy is transmitted and the car may have a tendency to creep. To overcome this, Hydra-Matic transmissions utilize gear reduction of the front planetary unit to turn the driving torus slower than the idle speed of the engine.

PLANETARY GEAR CONTROLS

The planetary gear bands operate hydraulically, so an oil pump is required to furnish the pressure. Earlier Hydra-Matics

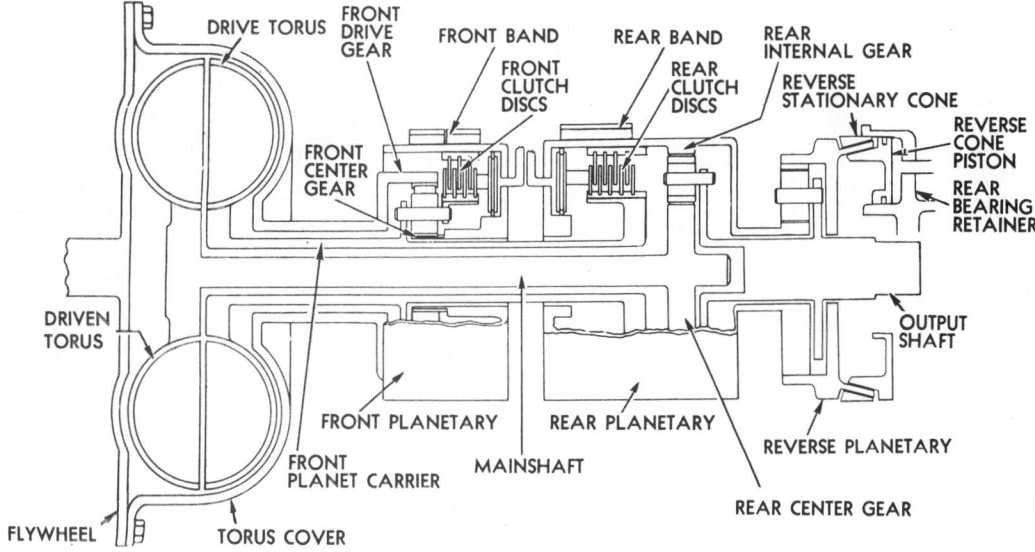

Fig. 44-6. Early Hydra-Matic fluid coupling automatic transmissions used major elements called out in this diagram.

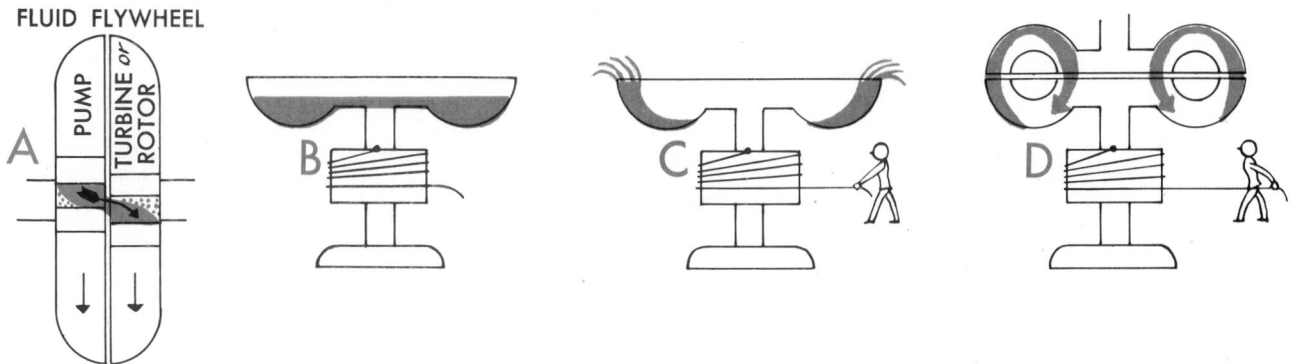

Fig. 44-7. A—In theory, fluid from pump half of fluid coupling crosses over to make turbine or rotor rotate in same direction. This principle of centrifugal force is shown in B, C and D as lower bowl revolves rapidly, causing fluid to climb into upper bowl, then drop back again.

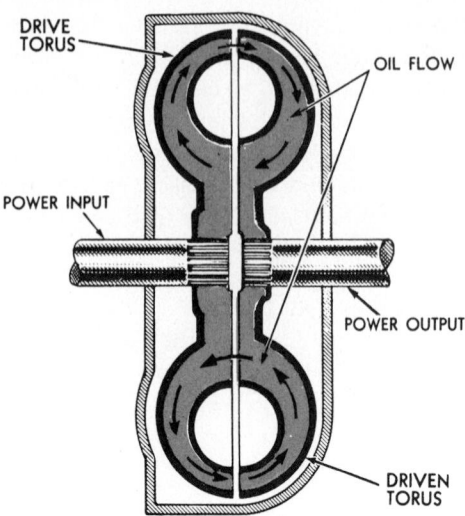

Fig. 44-8. In actual operation, driving torus of fluid coupling causes oil within it to be forced radially outward against vanes of driven member.

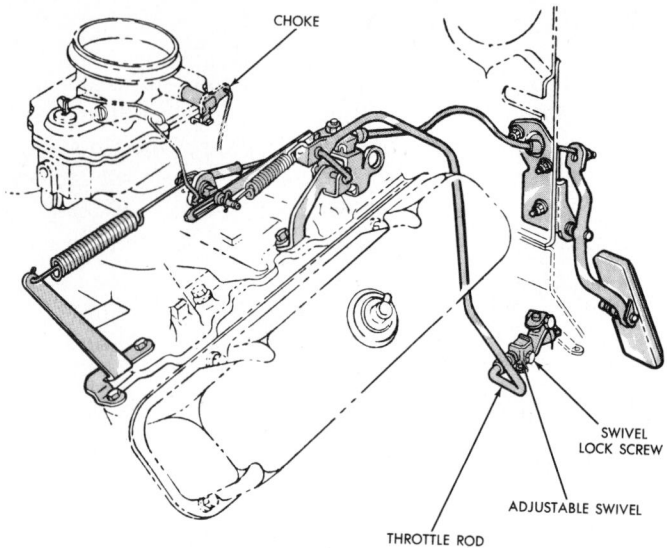

Fig. 44-10. Throttle control linkage provides driver with firm control over automatic action of transmission through degree of pressure exerted on accelerator pedal.

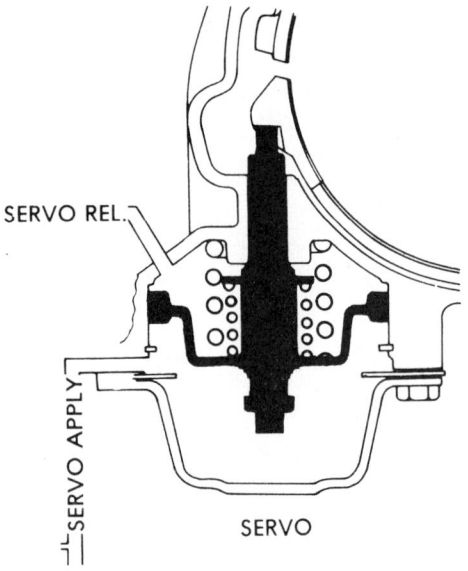

Fig. 44-9. A servo is a hydraulically operated piston and cylinder assembly used to control brake bands in automatic transmissions.

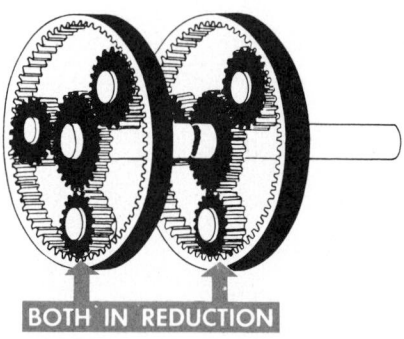

Fig. 44-11. Hydra-Matic utilizes two planetary gearsets in series to obtain four forward speeds. In first speed, both planetary units are in reduction.

have two pumps: one driven by the engine and another driven by the vehicle drive shaft. These pumps circulate oil under pressure through the fluid coupling and to the hydraulic operating pistons known as "servos." See Fig. 44-9. Control valves are needed to direct the flow of oil, to turn the flow off and on, to regulate pressure, etc. This built-in control system is a combination of balanced pressures depending on car speed, engine speed and the demands of the driver.

DRIVER CONTROL

Obviously, the matter of gear selection and shifting cannot remain entirely automatic, but must be under the control of the driver, Fig. 44-10. Because of varied traffic conditions, car speed is not always the most desirable method of choosing

gear reduction. The driver expresses his desires through the accelerator pedal, which is linked to a throttle valve in the transmission. This valve is regulated so that throttle valve pressure varies with throttle opening. If the throttle is opened slightly, oil pressure on the shift valves will be low, oil pressure from the governor will open the shift valves and the shift will occur at low speed. If the throttle is opened wide, greater car speed will be required to build up governor pressure and the transmission will shift at higher car speed.

An automatic transmission control system operates on a balanced pressure plan. Spring action and varying pressures and speeds are balanced one against the other until sensitive and responsive control is obtained over the transmission mechanism. These varying pressures are obtained with springs of different size, length and strength and can be further varied by screw adjustments.

BALANCING THE FORCES

Different amounts of power can be obtained from a hydraulic cylinder by altering the size of the cylinder or by varying the amount of pressure. For example, if a spring is placed on one end of a piston in a hydraulic cylinder, pressure can be regulated by means of a screw adjustment. Then if oil under pressure is placed on the other side of the piston, at less than spring pressure, the piston will go in one direction.

However, if the speed of the pump is increased, higher oil pressure starts the piston moving the other way. See Fig. 45-34. Since spring pressure increases with the amount the spring is compressed, and hydraulic pressure varies with the speed of the oil pump, almost any series of control variations can be obtained.

AUTOMATIC GEAR SHIFTING

A planetary gearset provides only one reduction and one direct drive in the same direction of rotation, so it is necessary to use two planetary units connected together in series to obtain four forward speeds, Figs. 44-11 through 44-14. Front and rear planetary units in the Hydra-Matic are similar, but the rear unit is larger and provides a greater gear reduction.

In first speed, the front unit supplies 40 percent gear reduction and the rear unit 60 percent, Fig. 44-15. In second speed, only the rear unit is in reduction (60 percent). In third speed, only the front unit is in reduction (40 percent). In fourth speed, neither unit is in reduction (direct drive).

LATER HYDRA–MATIC TRANSMISSIONS

Certain changes were made in later Hydra-Matic transmissions in order to provide a dual range in the drive position, but necessary alterations did not change the transmission. The selector dial was changed to provide "Dual Range" markings.

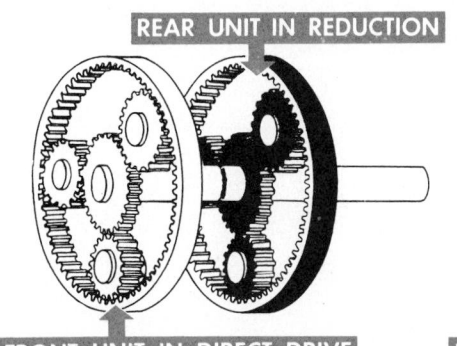

Fig. 44-12. In second speed, front planetary unit is in direct drive, rear unit in reduction.

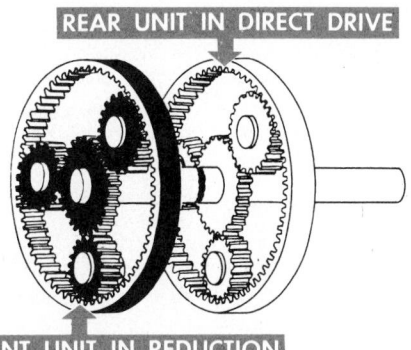

Fig. 44-13. In third speed, front planetary unit is in reduction, rear unit in direct drive.

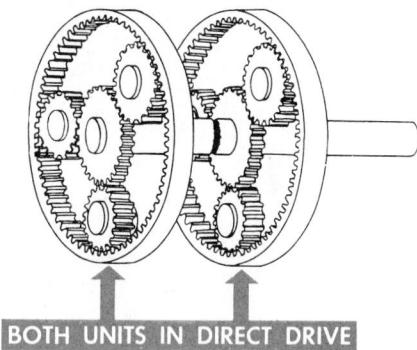

Fig. 44-14. In fourth speed, both planetary units are in direct drive.

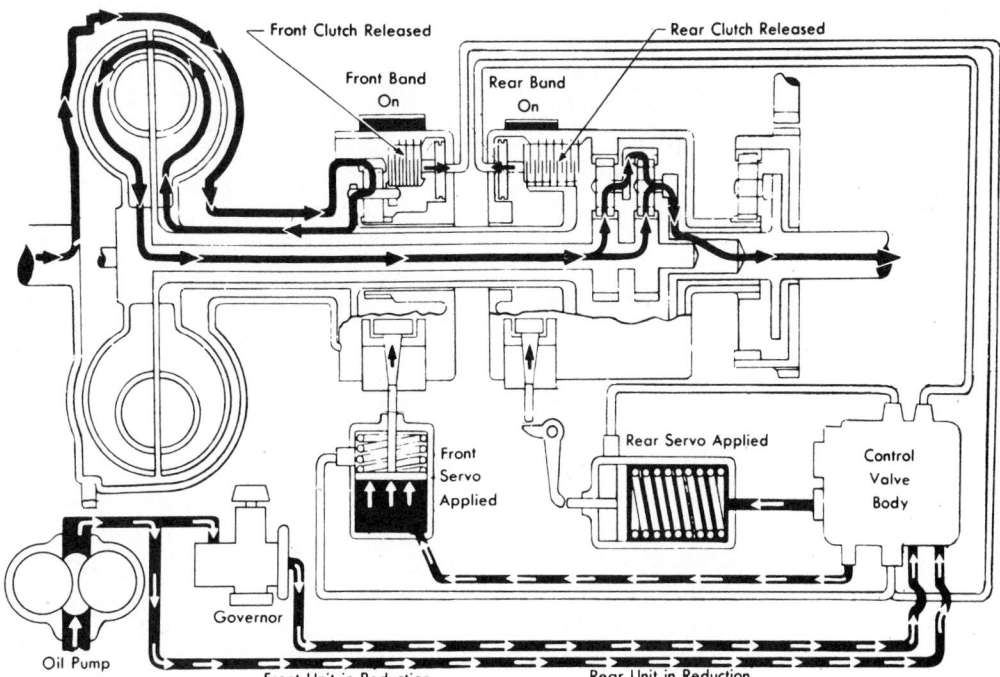

Fig. 44-15. Flow of power from engine through transmission in first gear is traced by black arrows. Oil flow under pressure is shown in white arrows.

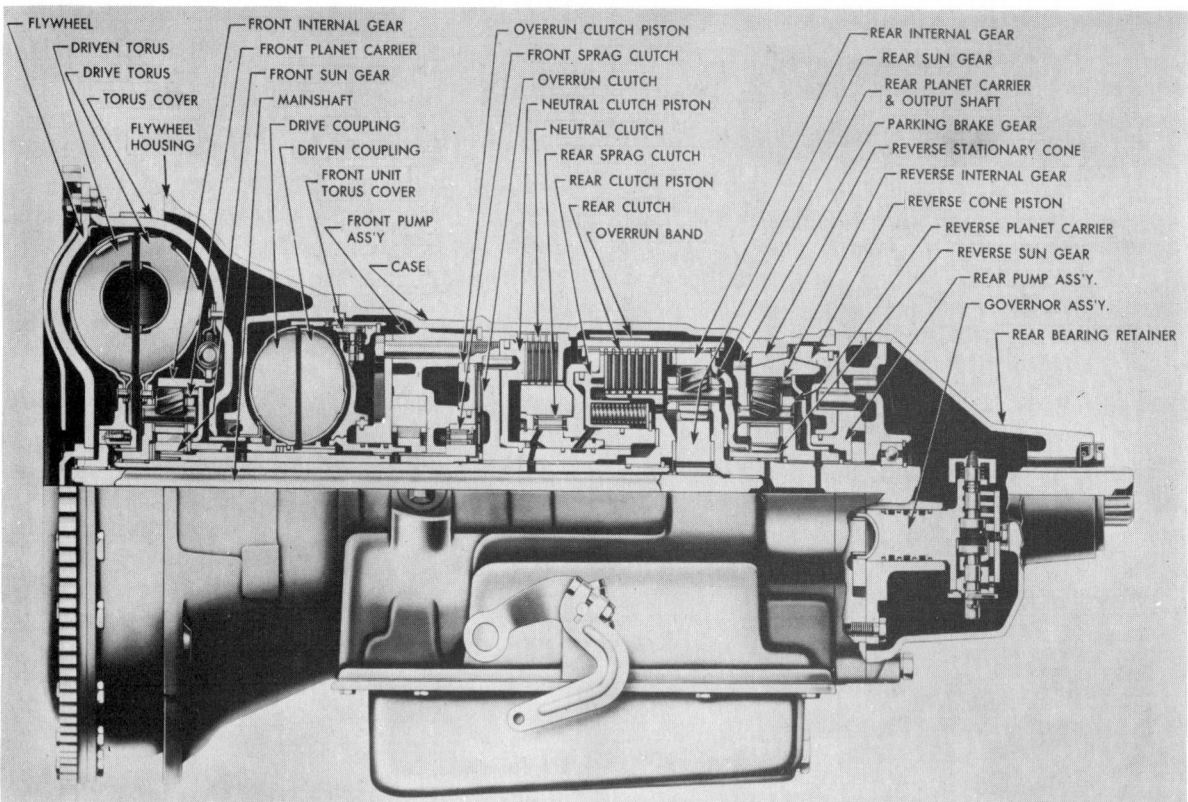

Fig. 44-16. Construction details of Controlled Coupling Hydra-Matic transmission are called out. Note smaller controlled coupling in back of primary fluid coupling.

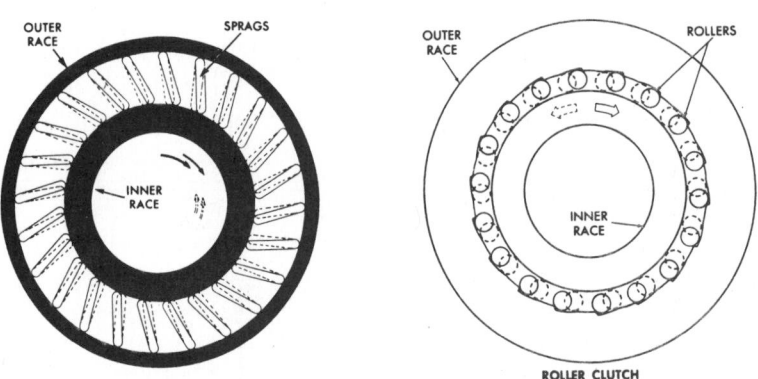

Fig. 44-17. Principle of sprag clutch is illustrated by operation of individual sprag segment. Action allows rotation in one direction but not in other.

New parts included an improved front pump of the vane type with a moving slide that determined pump output. Minor changes were made in hydraulic valves and controls to adapt them to the needs of the dual range construction.

The next new Hydra-Matic to be offered was a complete redesign, Fig. 44-16. This Controlled Coupling Hydra-Matic became the first to offer a positive-shift automatic transmission with no band adjustments, greater manual control and smoother operation. Principal changes in this second generation Hydra-Matic include:

1. Multiple disc type front clutch eliminated and replaced by a controlled coupling (fluid clutch).

2. Front band eliminated and replaced by a sprag type clutch, Fig. 44-17.

3. Rear band eliminated and replaced by a sprag clutch.

The controlled coupling is located to the rear of the larger fluid coupling, Fig. 44-16. By providing a rapid method of filling and emptying this controlled coupling, it is possible to have a complete release of power application or a positive connection.

The sprag clutch, Fig. 44-17, operates in much the same manner as the roller and ramp type of free-wheel device, but uses special-shape sprag segments instead of rollers to lock inner and outer races together in one direction only.

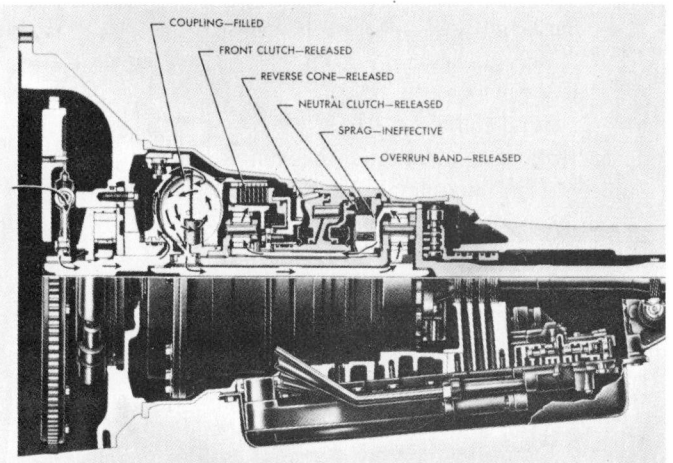

Fig. 44-18. Roto Hydra-Matic, last of Hydra-Matic transmissions using a fluid coupling, is shown in neutral. Both front and rear unit internal gears spin freely, so no torque is transferred to carriers or output shaft.

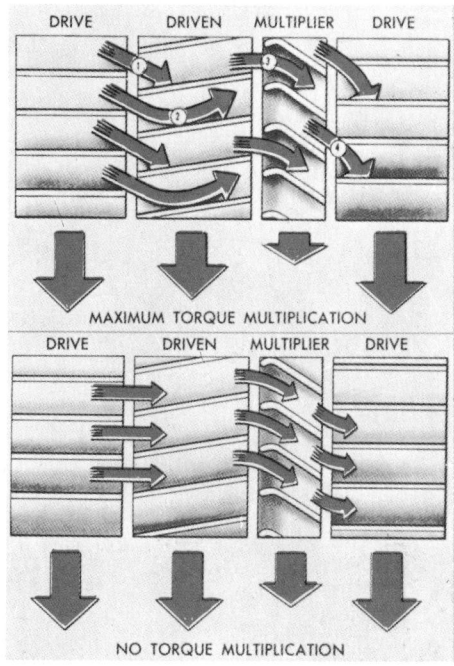

Fig. 44-19. Torque multiplier featured in Roto Hydra-Matic transmission operates on principle shown. Multiplier directs fluid to back side of drive member vanes.

ROTO HYDRA—MATIC

The third generation Hydra-Matic transmission is known as Roto Hydra-Matic or Accel-A-Rotor Hydra-Matic, Fig. 44-18. This transmission is unusual in that it does not have the conventional fluid coupling between the engine and the transmission case.

The Roto Hydra-Matic, however, does use a small "fill and dump" coupling similar to the one used in the Controlled Coupling unit, but with the addition of fixed stator blades between the two coupling halves. In effect, it is a small torque converter, although, Oldsmobile and Pontiac prefer to call it a "torque multiplier." See Fig. 44-19.

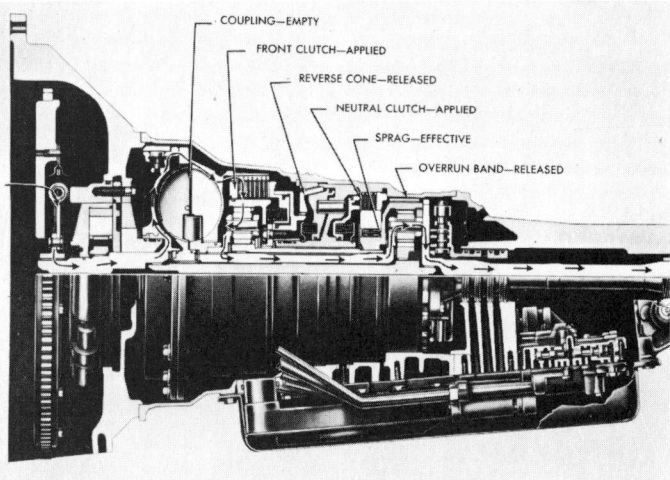

Fig. 44-20. In third drive range, coupling is empty so engine torque is mechanically applied to front planetary unit internal gear. Torque multiplication is due to front unit gear ratio.

This four speed transmission retains the cone clutch for reverse operation, the overrun band, the two multiple disc clutch packs, but eliminates one of the sprag clutches and one planetary gearset, Fig. 44-18. The most interesting feature of this unit is that in third speed range, the multiplier "empties" and power flow between the engine and output shaft becomes a pure mechanical lockup. See Fig. 44-20.

From this point, the fourth generation Turbo Hydra-Matic became a torque converter automatic transmission.

REVIEW QUESTIONS — FLUID COUPLING AUTOMATIC TRANSMISSIONS

1. Name the four elements generally found in automatic transmissions.
2. What purpose does a fluid coupling accomplish in an automatic transmission?
   a. Serves as hydraulic clutch.
   b. Multiplies engine torque.
   c. Builds up hydraulic pressure to operate valves.
3. What is the primary function of a planetary gearset in an automatic transmission?
   a. Connects engine to fluid coupling.
   b. Cushions effect of gear changes in transmission.
   c. Provides suitable gear ratios.
4. Which of these three factors is used to control automatic transmission operation?
   a. Engine speed.
   b. Engine weight.
   c. Engine compression.
5. Which of these three factors is NOT used to control automatic transmission operation?
   a. Hand levers.
   b. Foot pedals.
   c. Car weight.

6. Is the hydraulic fluid sealed in the fluid coupling of a Hydra-Matic transmission?

7. When is a fluid coupling most effective?
   a. High speed.
   b. Low speed.
   c. Idling speed.

8. Can hydraulic pressure and spring action be combined on a single valve to provide a balance of forces?

9. Can more than one fluid coupling be used in an automatic transmission?

10. Can more than one free-wheel clutch be used in an automatic transmission?

11. A sprag clutch and a free-wheel clutch operate in the same manner. True or False?

12. What replaced bands in Controlled Coupling Hydra-Matic transmissions?

   a. Servo units.
   b. Sprag clutches.
   c. Overrun clutches.
   d. Neutral clutch.

13. The Roto Hydra-Matic transmission uses a "torque multiplier" fluid coupling. What element provides torque multiplication?
   a. Drive torus.
   b. Driven torus.
   c. Fixed stator blades.

14. In which speed does power flow between the engine and output shaft become a pure mechanical lockup?
   a. First.
   b. Second.
   c. Third.
   d. Fourth.

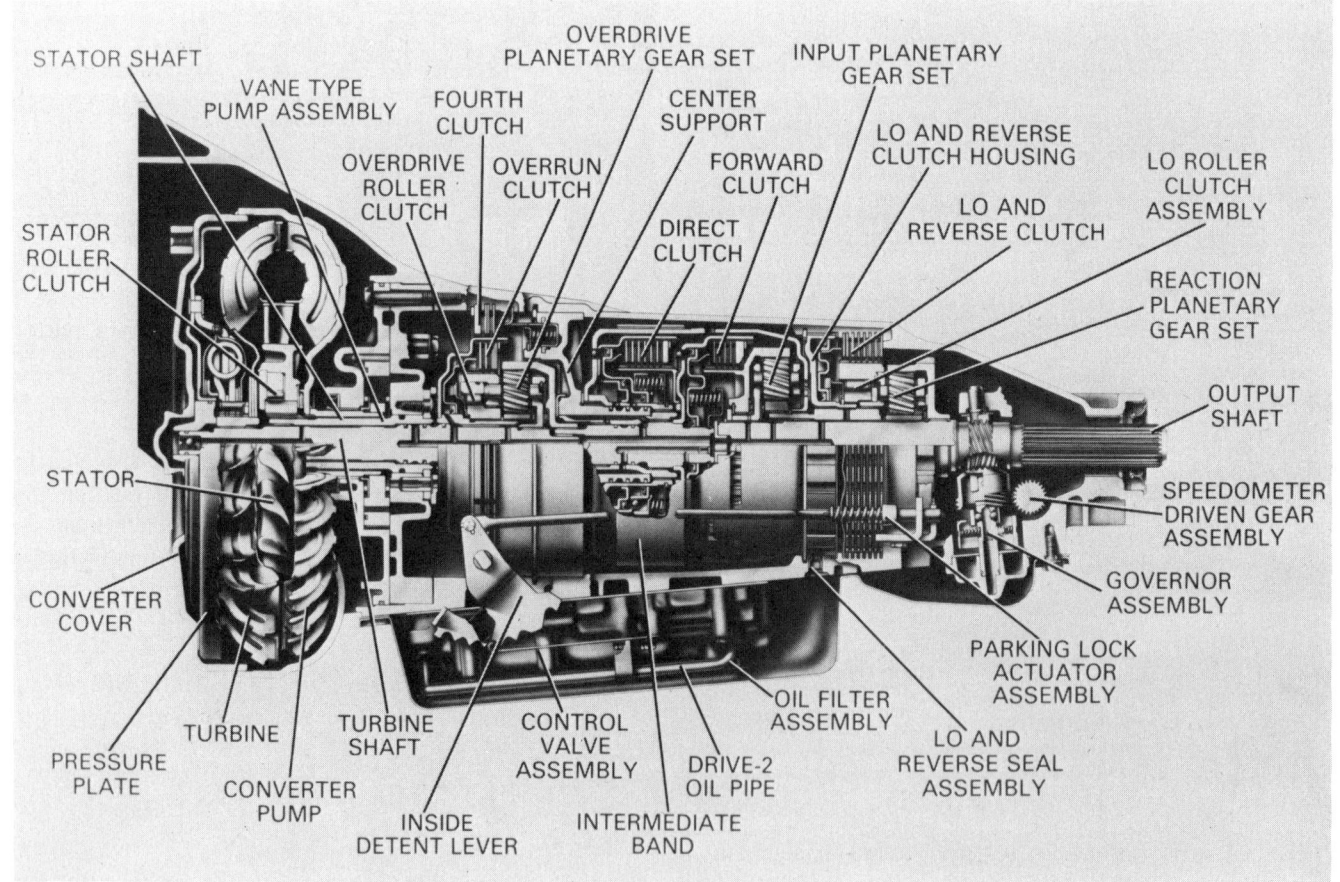

General Motors Model 200-4R is a fully automatic overdrive transmission with three-element hydraulic torque converter and converter clutch. Five multiple disc clutches, two roller clutches and a band are friction elements needed to operate the compound planetary gearset and 0.67 ratio overdrive (fourth gear) unit.   (Pontiac Motor Div., GM)

TORQUE CONVERTER
AUTOMATIC TRANSMISSIONS

Automatic transmissions are powered by the engine through one or more fluid couplings or a torque converter. As established in the chapter on Fluid Coupling Automatic Transmissions, a fluid coupling merely transmits engine torque applied to it, while a torque converter multiplies it.

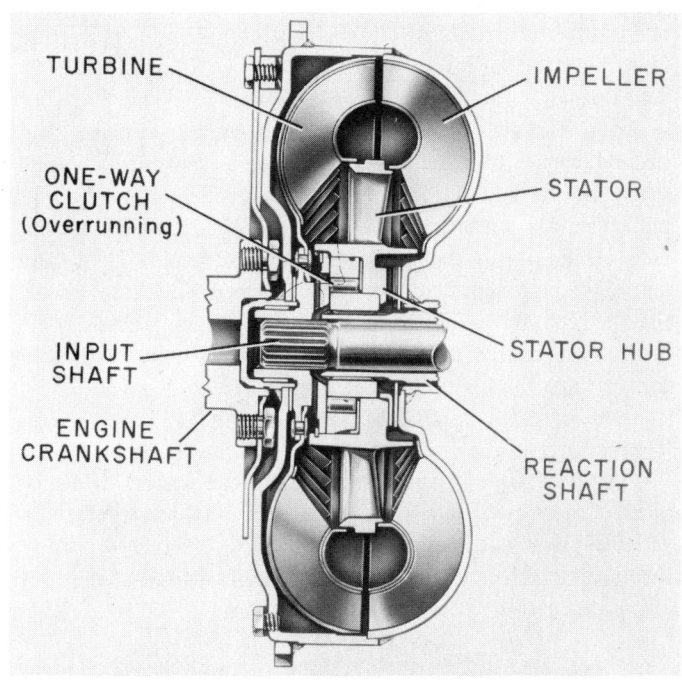

Fig. 45-1. Cross-sectional view of a typical torque converter shows attachment of unit to engine crankshaft and relationship of three major elements: impeller, turbine and stator.

Modern torque converters, Fig. 45-1, utilize three major rotating elements to multiply engine torque:

1. An engine-driven pump or impeller.
2. A fluid-driven turbine.
3. A stator.

Some older automatic transmissions, Buick Dynaflow, for example, have four or five-element torque converters (which include first turbine and second turbine, primary and secondary stators, etc.). However, the three-element unit has proved to be efficient and remarkably troublefree.

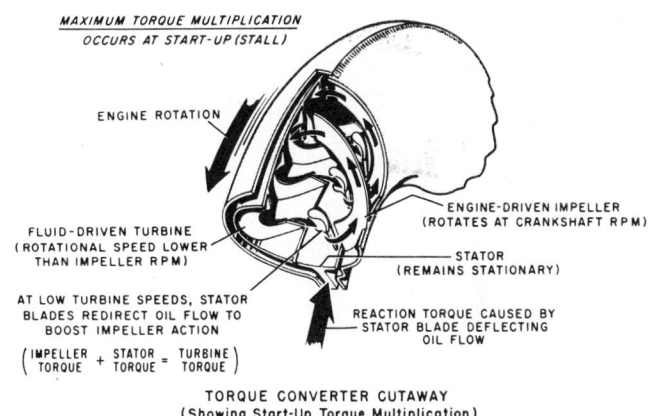

Fig. 45-2. Three elements are pictured in operation at point of start-up stall with stator stationary and torque multiplication at maximum.

METHOD OF OPERATION

All hydraulic torque converters are based on the same principle of operation, Fig. 45-2. All use the engine to drive the impeller which, in turn, impels fluid against the vanes of a turbine connected through transmission gears to the drive shaft of the automobile. The third (middle) element, the

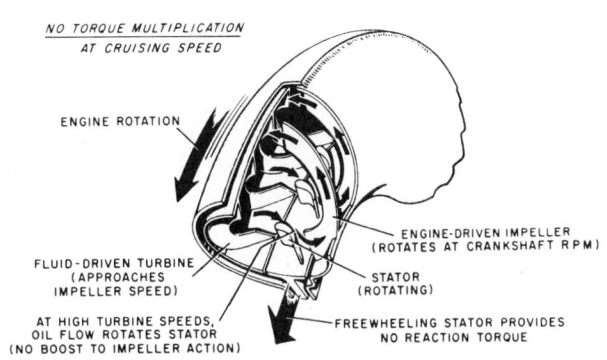

Fig. 45-3. In this position, car is at cruising speed and one-way clutch permits stator to free-wheel and rotate with impeller and turbine.

587

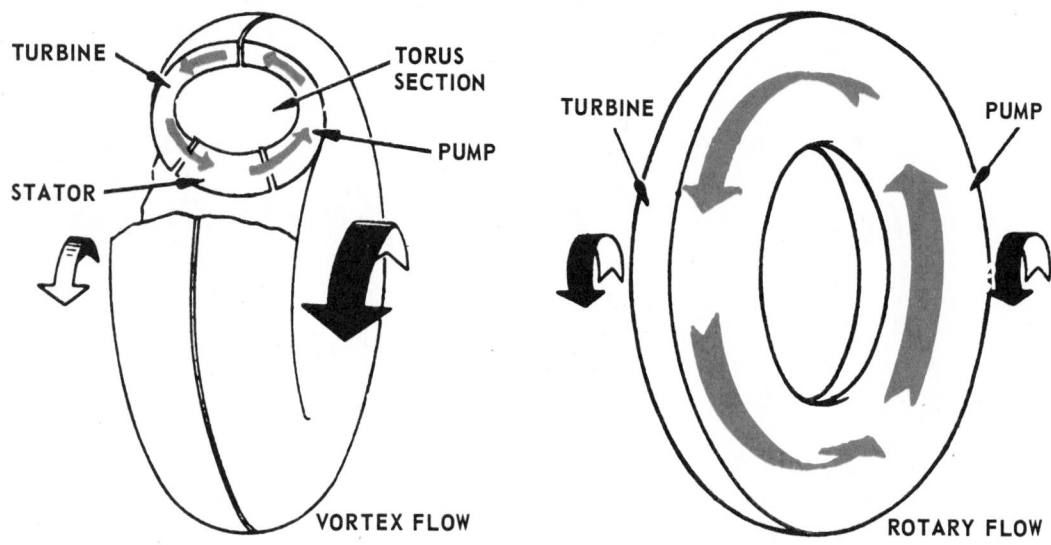

Fig. 45-4. When torque converter is in operation, there are two types of oil circulation within unit: vortex and rotary flow.

stator, serves to redirect oil flow from the turbine to boost impeller action and multiply engine torque.

These three elements work together in a fluid-filled housing to provide the desired torque multiplication at low speed and perform as an efficient fluid coupling at high speed, Fig. 45-3.

When the engine is running, the fluid in the torque converter is pumped from the impeller vanes across to the turbine vanes, then back to the impeller through the stator, Fig. 45-4. The action of centrifugal force sets up a vortex flow of oil within the torque converter, while the angle of the vanes tends to set up a rotary flow. The combined flow results in a corkscrew action, which sets up a pattern something like a coil spring with the ends connected, Fig. 45-5.

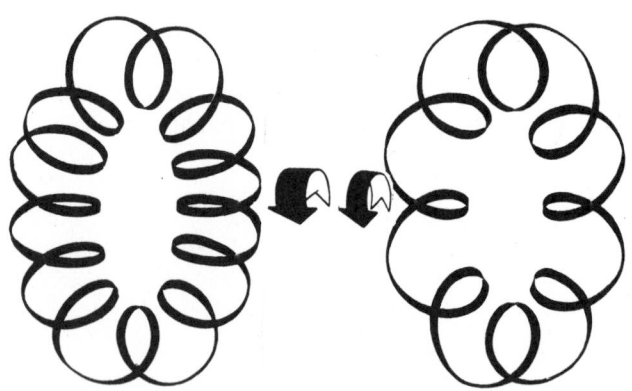

Fig. 45-5. Two types of oil flow in torque converter combine to produce a spiral action or coil spring effect.

This whirling ring of oil emerges from the twisting passages of the turbine, in a direction opposite to pump rotation. If directed into the pump at this time, it would cause a loss of power. Instead, it is directed against the curved face of the stator blades. See Fig. 45-2. The impact of the oil flow creates

reaction torque since the stator is held stationary by a one-way, or overrunning, clutch. This multiplies engine torque at variable ratios up to at least 2:1 when the turbine is in start-up stall.

When enough torque is developed by the impeller, the turbine begins to rotate, along with the transmission input shaft. As turbine speed approaches impeller speed, torque multiplication lessens, since the angle of fluid flow against the face of the stator blades becomes less efficient. Then, just before turbine speed equals impeller speed, the fluid strikes the back face of the stator blades, which releases the overrunning clutch and permits the three elements to rotate together as a fluid coupling. See Fig. 45-3.

In most cases, including special designs like the Chrysler TorqueFlite torque converter illustrated, the stator blades are "fixed" at a predetermined angle. In special designs, Oldsmobile Jetaway and Buick Super Turbine 300, for example, a variable pitch stator assembly is used, Fig. 45-6. For normal operation in drive range, the stator blades are automatically set

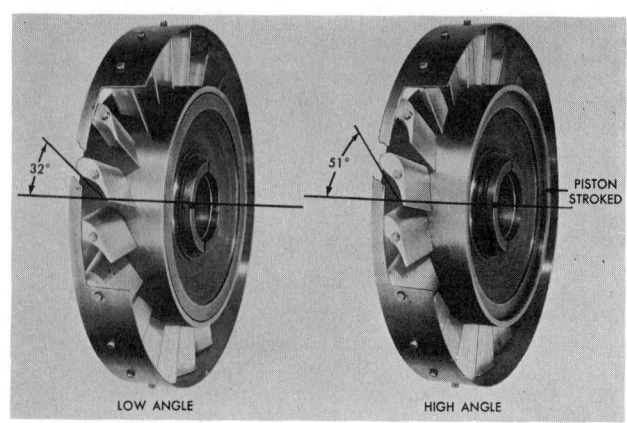

Fig. 45-6. Variable pitch stator affords automatic adjustment of stator blade angle to provide greater torque when needed.

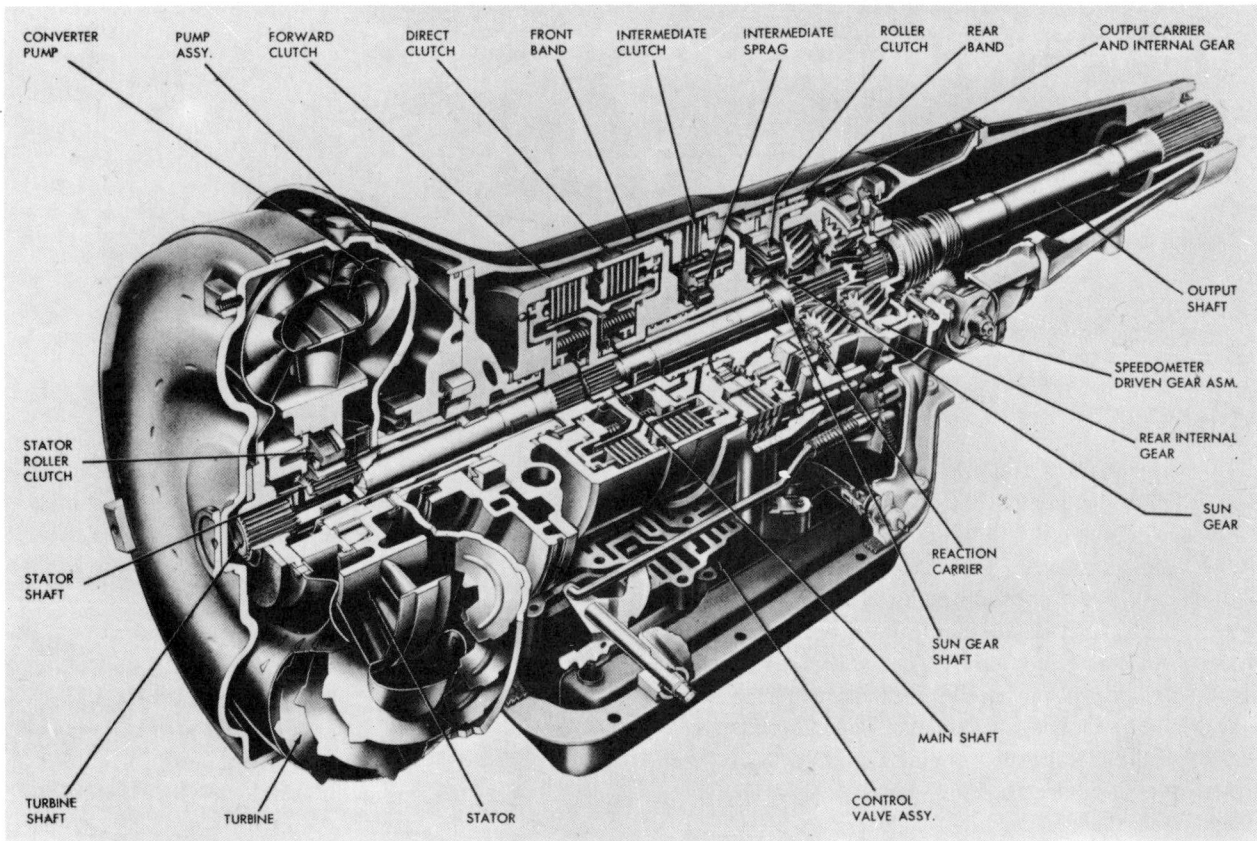

Fig. 45-7. Turbo Hydra-Matic construction differs slightly among various applications, but basic assemblies indicated are used in all automatic transmissions of this type.

at a low angle. For increased acceleration, greater torque is obtained by setting the stator blades at a high angle.

TURBO HYDRA–MATIC

The Turbo Hydra-Matic is a torque converter automatic transmission used in broad application in late model General Motors cars. The typical THM three-speed transmission incorporates a torque converter, at least one planetary gearset, three multiple-disc clutches, two bands and two roller clutches. Modifications in this arrangement occur across the various General Motors lines but, basically, these are the major elements. See Fig. 45-7.

The torque converter is a three-element unit consisting of

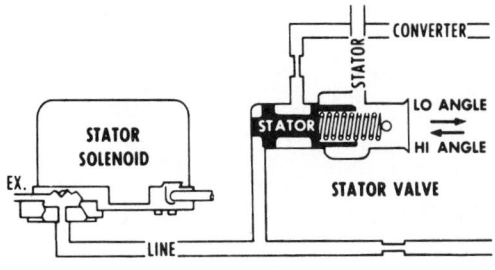

Fig. 45-8. Stator valve piston shifts in its housing according to throttle position to change angle of stator blades to high or low pitch.

impeller, turbine and stator assembly. The stator is mounted on an overrunning clutch and provides torque multiplication on acceleration. Some older Turbo Hydra-Matic torque converters are equipped with variable pitch stator blades, Fig. 45-6. The high stator blade angle means increased engine speed and torque multiplication. The low angle results in more efficient converter operation as a fluid coupling at cruising speed and above.

VARIABLE PITCH STATOR

The angle of the variable pitch stator blades usually is controlled by a switch mounted on the throttle linkage, a stator solenoid and a stator valve, Fig. 45-8. At engine idle speed, the switch activates the solenoid, which exhausts line pressure and the stator valve shifts the blade angle from low to high. At light or medium throttle, the solenoid is not activated and line pressure on the stator valve puts the blades at a low angle. At about 3/4 throttle opening, or under heavy acceleration, the solenoid again exhausts line pressure, and the stator valve moves the stator blades to the high angle for maximum performance.

TRANSMISSION CONTROLS

The automatic transmission fluid (ATF) is pressurized by a gear-type pump, which provides working oil pressure needed

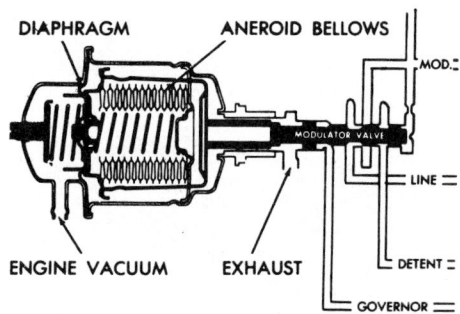

Fig. 45-9. Vacuum modulator operates in conjunction with modulator valve, to control line pressure to various units, including torque converter, according to engine vacuum.

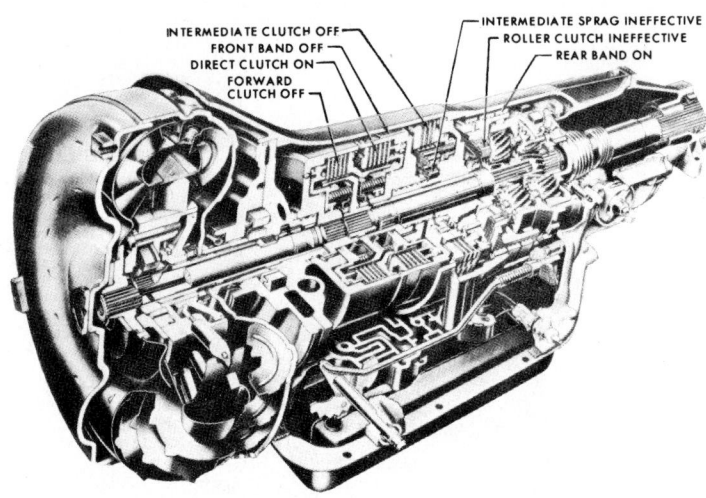

Fig. 45-10. In reverse, power flow is through turbine sun gear shaft, sun gear, front planetary pinions, front internal gear to output shaft.

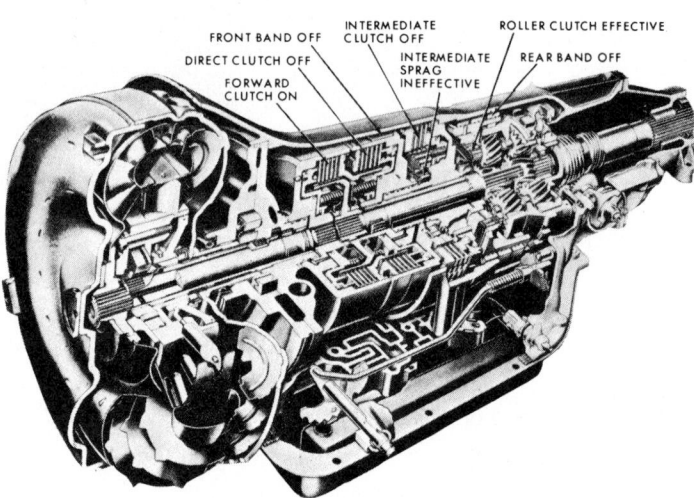

Fig. 45-11. In first gear, power flow is through turbine main shaft, rear planetary internal gear, rear pinions, sun gear, front planetary pinions, front internal gear, output carrier to output shaft.

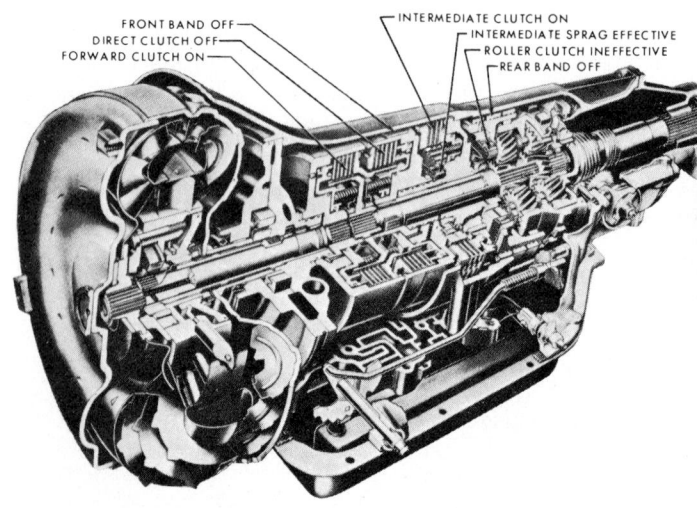

Fig. 45-12. In second gear, power flow is through turbine, forward clutch, main shaft, rear planetary internal gear, rear pinions, output carrier to output shaft.

to operate valve controls and friction elements. A pressure regulator valve in the pump controls main line pressure, as directed by the modulator valve, Fig. 45-9, and it also controls the flow of oil that charges the torque converter.

The modulator valve, in turn, is controlled by the vacuum modulator, which is attached to the outside of the transmission case. It is connected to the engine intake manifold and basically changes line oil pressure in the transmission to meet engine needs. For example, the vacuum modulator increases line pressure at full throttle, or under heavy load (low vacuum), to provide more "holding" power for the clutches. Under light load (high vacuum), it reduces line pressure to promote smooth shifts.

Other controls include: a governor which increases or decreases oil pressure according to car speed; a manual valve which establishes the particular range of transmission operation selected by the driver; a shift valve which permits 1-2 or 2-1 shifts; another shift valve for shifts from 2-3 or 3-2; a detent valve which provides a downshift when the throttle is opened wide; an accumulator which permits smooth clutch and band engagements; regulator valves that regulate modulator pressure and detent pressure to help control shift valves; and front and rear servos which apply and release front and rear bands.

TURBO HYDRA–MATIC OPERATION

The selector quadrant for a Turbo Hydra-Matic has six positions: P,R,N,D,L2,L1 or P,R,N,D,S,L.

Park position locks the transmission output shaft to the case to prevent the car from moving forward or backward.

In Neutral, all clutches and bands are released, permitting the engine to run but not drive the vehicle.

In Reverse, the direct clutch is engaged and rear band is applied, permitting the car to move backwards, Fig. 45-10.

In Drive range, the forward clutch is engaged when the transmission is in first gear; forward and intermediate clutches are engaged in second gear; forward, intermediate and direct clutches are engaged in third gear (direct drive). See Figs. 45-11 to 45-13.

In L2 or S position, forward and intermediate clutches and front band are engaged, Fig. 45-14.

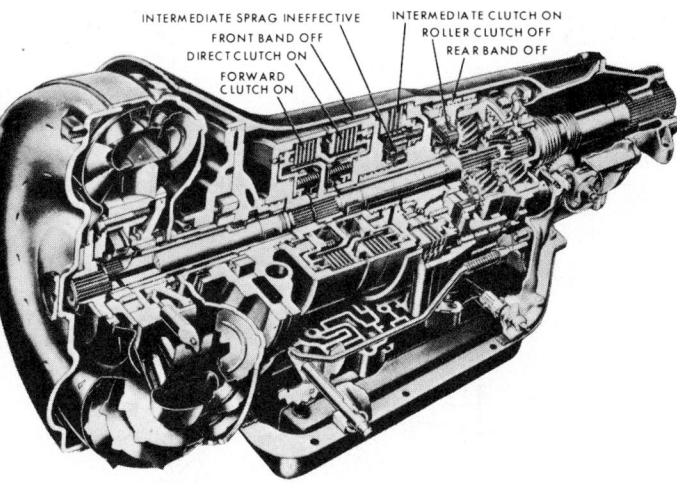

Fig. 45-13. In third gear (direct drive), power flow is through turbine, forward clutch, main shaft, rear planetary internal gear, sun gear shaft to sun gear. Planetary gearset turns as a unit to drive output shaft.

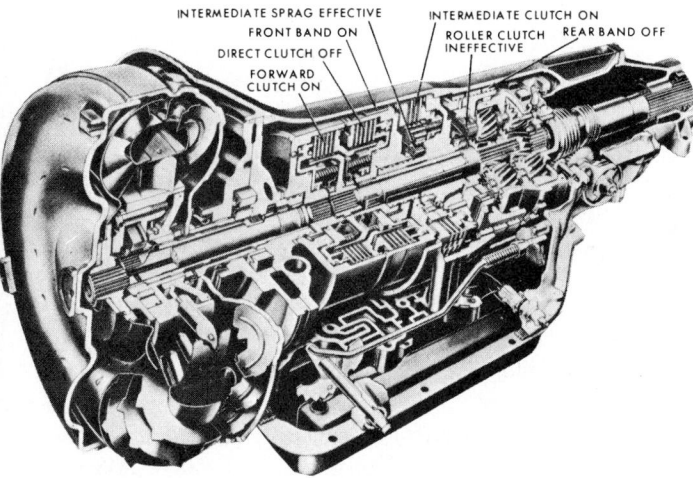

Fig. 45-14. In L2 or S position, power flow is through turbine, forward clutch, main shaft, rear planetary internal gear, rear pinions, output carrier and output shaft.

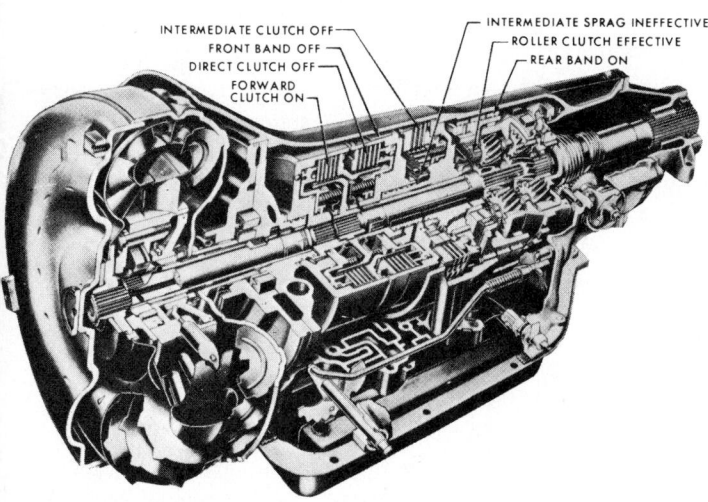

Fig. 45-15. In L1 to L position, power flow is through turbine, forward clutch, main shaft, rear planetary internal gear, rear pinions, front internal gear, output carrier and output shaft.

In L1 or L position, forward clutch is engaged and rear band is applied. The transmission cannot upshift regardless of car speed or engine speed, Fig. 45-15.

JETAWAY OR SUPER TURBINE 300

The Oldsmobile Jetaway, Buick Super Turbine 300 and Pontiac Automatic are similar torque converter transmissions having only minor differences in internal construction. This basic two-speed automatic transmission has a three-element torque converter, compound planetary gearset, two multiple disc clutches and low band.

The torque converter consists of a pump, turbine and either fixed or variable-pitch stator assembly in which the stator blades operate at high angle or low angle, much like the Turbo Hydra-Matic converter of this type.

A positive-displacement, gear-type pump is used to supply oil to the converter and provide oil under pressure for the engagement of forward and reverse clutches and for the application and release of the low band. It also circulates oil for lubrication and heat transfer.

The planetary gearset consists of input sun gear, low sun gear, short and long pinions, a reverse ring gear and planet carrier. See Fig. 45-16. The input sun gear is splined to the

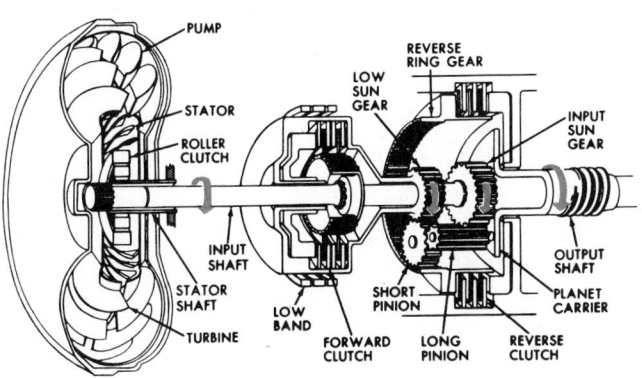

Fig. 45-16. In direct drive, power flow in two-speed transmission is through turbine, forward clutch, low sun gear, short pinions, long pinions, input sun gear to output shaft.

input shaft and is in mesh with the three long pinions. These long pinions are in mesh with the three short pinions which, in turn, are in mesh with the low sun gear and reverse ring gear.

The forward clutch assembly consists of a drum, piston, springs, seals and a clutch pack. When oil pressure is applied to the piston, the clutch plates are pressed together, connecting the clutch drum to the input shaft in direct drive.

The low band surrounds the forward clutch drum. It is hydraulically applied by the low servo piston and released by spring pressure. When the low band is applied, the transmission operates in low range.

The reverse clutch consists of a piston, seals, springs, clutch pack and reaction plate. When oil pressure is applied to the piston, the clutch plates are engaged, "holding" the reverse ring gear and causing reverse rotation of the output shaft.

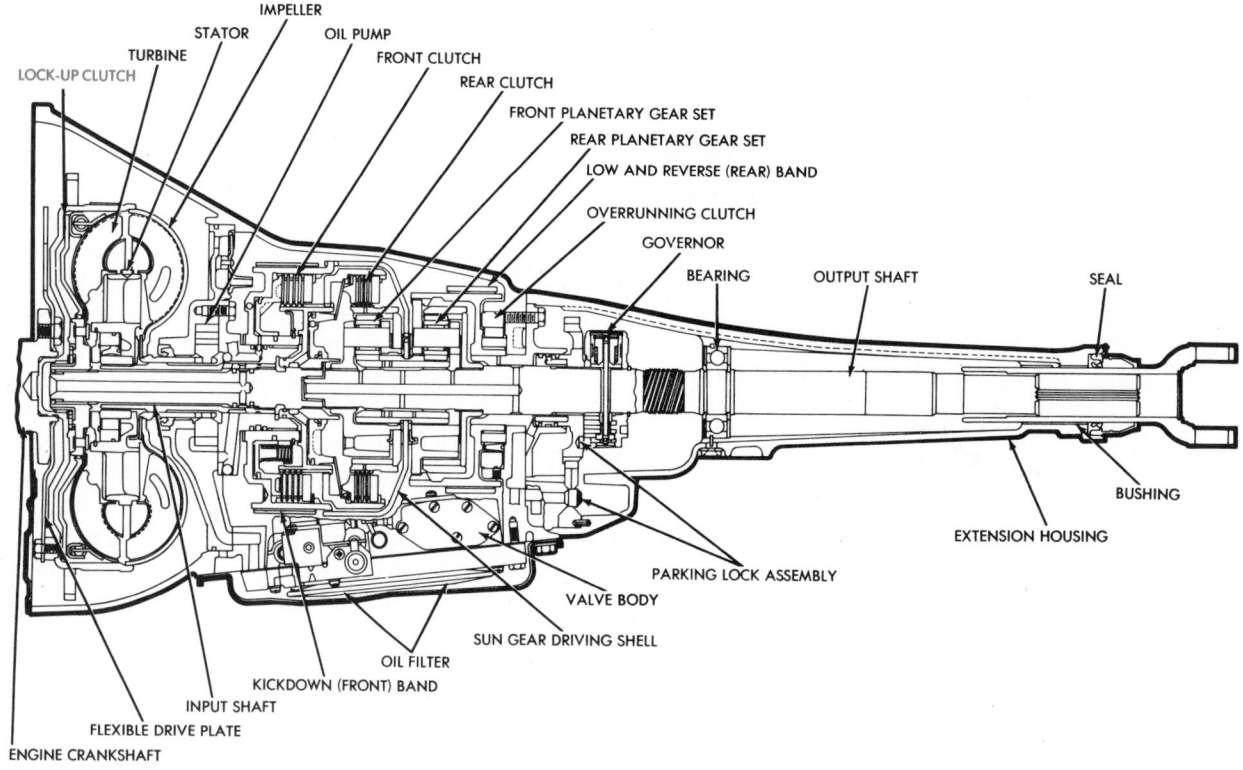

Fig. 45-17. Since 1978, Chrysler's TorqueFlite automatic transmission has been coupled to a "lockup torque converter." Basically, the lockup unit locks the turbine to the front of the converter housing with a friction clutch operated by hydraulic pressure. The lockup torque converter is designed to improve fuel mileage by eliminating normal slippage during high gear cruising.

TORQUEFLITE

The Chrysler Corporation's TorqueFlite automatic transmission evolved from the three-speed torque converter-type unit introduced on some 1956 Imperials. Over the years, many of the basic concepts of this introductory model have been retained and improved upon, Fig. 45-17.

Some of these improvements include: a one-piece aluminum housing; higher capacity elements developed to transmit the higher torque of larger V-8 engines; internal oil filters;

harder clutch discs, reaction shaft and impeller hubs; larger input shaft; sliding-spline output shaft; higher helix angle on planetary gear teeth; internally actuated parking sprag; high accuracy speedometer pinion; new clutch disc lining materials; lockup torque converter, Fig. 45-17; also, elimination of the rear oil pump and drain plug.

TORQUE CONVERTER CONSTRUCTION

The modern TorqueFlite has a three-element torque converter that transmits power from the engine through the transmission shafts to the drive shaft, Fig. 45-17. The converter utilizes an impeller, turbine and fixed-blade stator to more than double engine torque at start-up stall. See Fig. 45-2. Cooling of the converter is accomplished by circulating the transmission fluid through an oil-to-water type cooler built into the lower radiator tank.

HYDRAULIC SYSTEM MAKEUP

The hydraulic system involves four basic control groups:
1. The pressure supply system which consists of the single front oil pump which furnishes oil under pressure for all hydraulic and lubrication requirements.
2. The pressure regulating valves which include the regulator valve, torque converter control valve, governor valve and throttle valve.
3. The flow control valves which consist of 1-2 shift valve, 2-3 shift valve, manual, kickdown and shuttle valves.

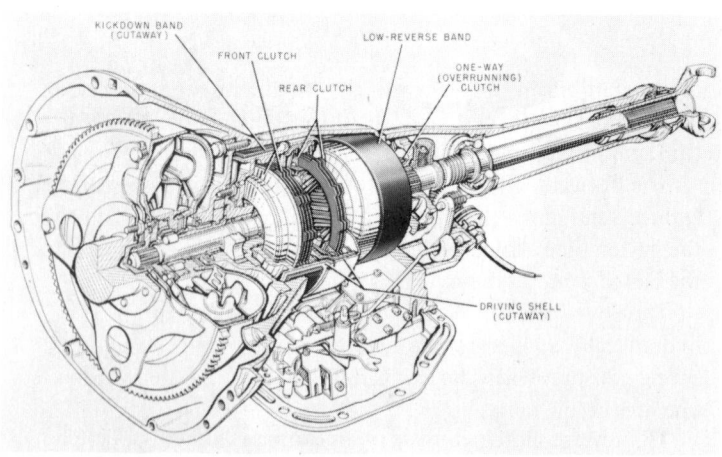

Fig. 45-18. Clutches and bands applied by hydraulic controls called servos, transmit engine torque through planetary gearsets.

4. The clutch and band servos and accumulator. See Fig. 45-18.

The TorqueFlite gear selection is controlled by a push-button system on older models, by a lever-type gearshift on the steering column, or in a floor console on later models. The control has six positions: P,R,N,D,2,1.

PLANETARY SYSTEM OPERATION

The planetary gear system consists of two planetary gearsets which operate individually or together to produce three forward ratios and one reverse ratio, Fig. 45-19. In drive,

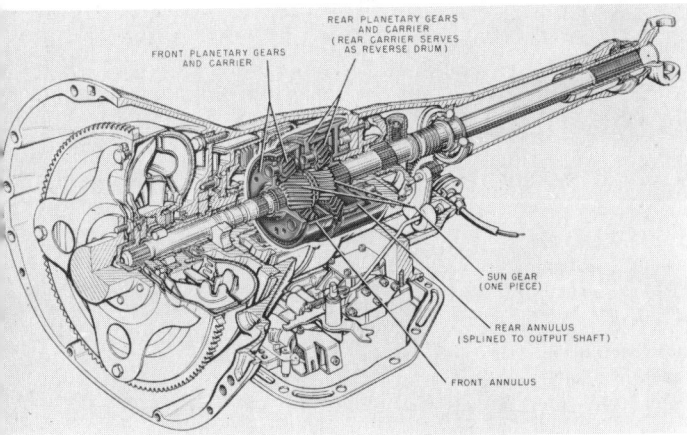

Fig. 45-19. Planetary gear train provides various gear ratios, including three in forward speeds and one in reverse.

for example, the front and rear clutches are applied and all planetary gears are locked together and rotate as a unit, Fig. 45-20. Power flow is direct, from input shaft to output shaft.

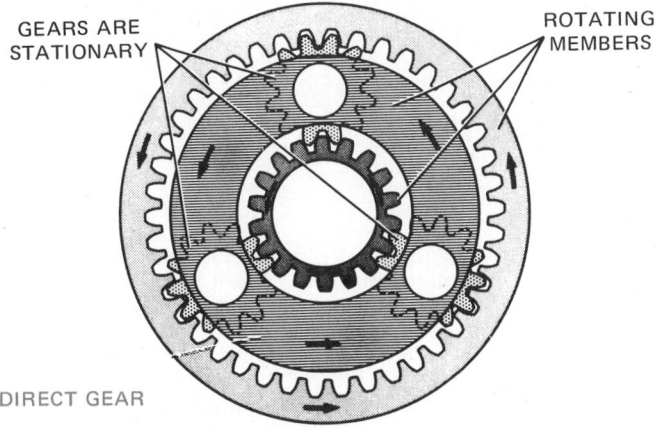

Fig. 45-20. TorqueFlite planetary gearset in direct drive is locked together and rotates as a unit.

In reverse, Fig. 45-21, the front clutch and rear band are applied. This setup holds the planet carrier stationary. Torque is applied to the sun gear and the planet pinions rotate, causing

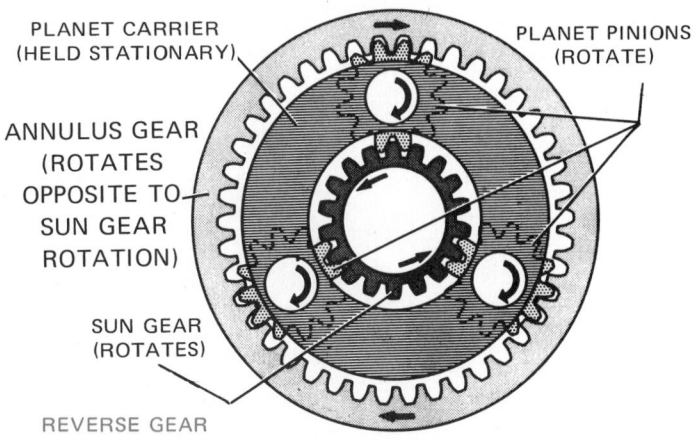

Fig. 45-21. In reverse, planet carrier is stationary and pinions rotate, driving internal gear in opposite direction.

the annulus gear to turn in the opposite direction.

In operation then, the four principle elements of each planetary gearset are driven or held as directed by the hydraulic control system, Fig. 45-22, to produce the ratios built into the TorqueFlite transmission.

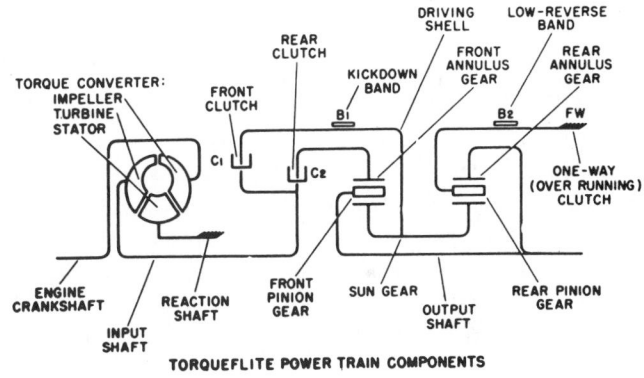

Fig. 45-22. Schematic of TorqueFlite power train components spells out basic assemblies and shows their relationship to each other.

POWERFLITE

Chrysler's PowerFlite transmission was a running mate of the TorqueFlite for about ten years. The major difference between the two is in the number of forward speeds: PowerFlite, two; TorqueFlite, three.

Early PowerFlites used a four-element torque converter. Later, the three-element converter was adopted. It has two planetary gearsets, two bands and a multiple disc clutch.

With the selector placed in neutral position, no units are applied. In low gear, only the kickdown band is applied. In high — or direct drive — the kickdown band is released and the multiple disc clutch is engaged. In reverse, both the kickdown band and the clutch are released and the reverse band is applied. The bands and clutch are automatically controlled by the hydraulic system which consists of two oil pumps, several regulating valves and a valve body.

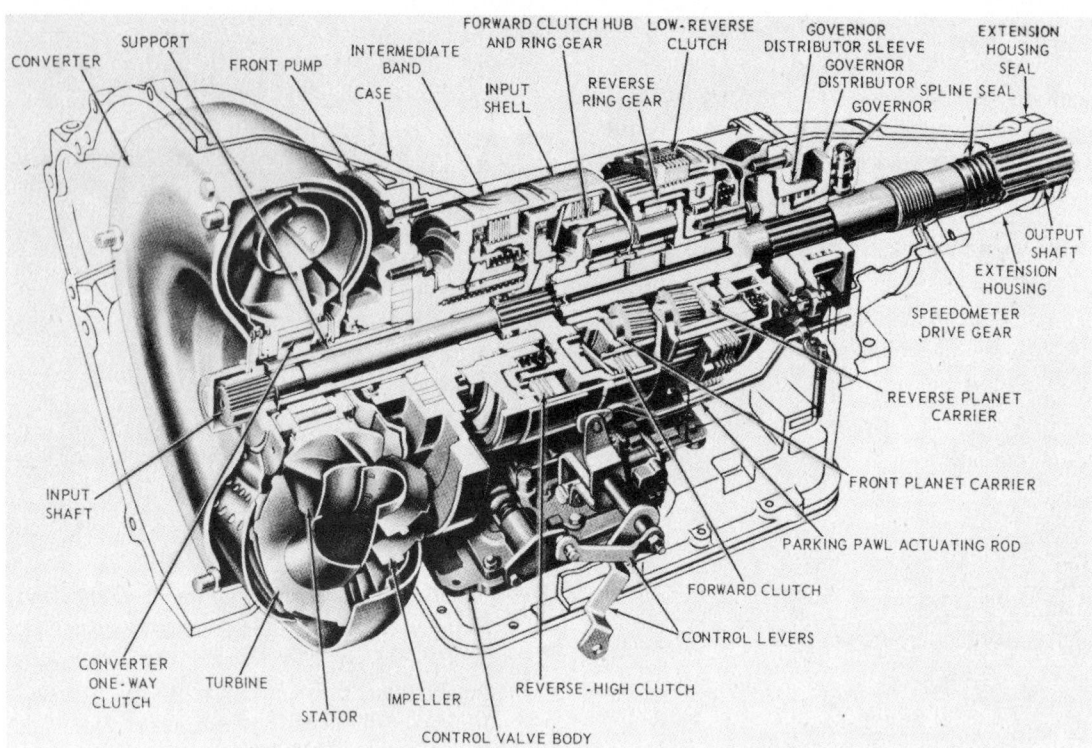

Fig. 45-23. Ford Select Shift Cruise-O-Matic transmissions incorporate select shift feature, permitting driver option of selecting gears manually.

SELECT SHIFT CRUISE—O-MATIC

The Ford Select Shift Cruise-O-Matic transmissions (labeled C6 in earlier models) are built in three versions, each tailored to a particular engine, axle ratio and load capacity, Fig. 45-23. Variations in construction exist, but all incorporate the "Select Shift" feature, which provides either automatic upshifts and downshifts or manual selection of first and second gears.

Major assemblies consist of a three-element torque converter, planetary gear train, forward clutch, low-reverse clutch, reverse-high clutch, intermediate servo and band. Hydraulic system components include: gear-type pump, main oil pressure regulator valves; manual valves; primary throttle valve and altitude compensating diaphragm assembly; main oil pressure booster; governor and various other valves.

The planetary gear train consists of an input shaft splined to the turbine of the converter and to the forward clutch cylinder, Fig. 45-24.

When the reverse-high clutch is engaged, its hub drives the input shell and rotates the sun gear. When the forward clutch is engaged, its hub and ring gear drives the forward planet gears. When the intermediate band is applied, it "holds" the reverse-high clutch drum, input shell and sun gear from rotating.

The sun gear, driven by the input shell, is meshed with the forward and reverse planet gears. The reverse planet carrier is splined to the low-reverse clutch hub which can be held from rotating by a one-way clutch. The forward planet carrier, reverse ring gear hub, park gear and governor distributor are all

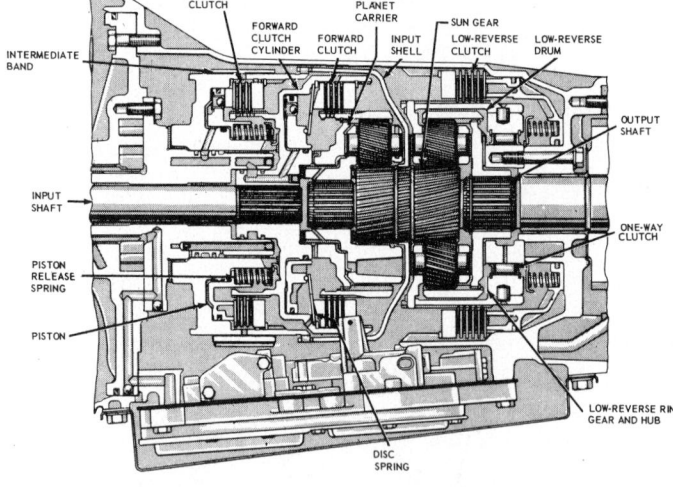

Fig. 45-24. Cruise-O-Matic planetary gear train has input shaft splined to turbine of torque converter and forward clutch cylinder.

splined to the output shaft, Fig. 45-24.

In neutral, no clutches or bands are applied, Fig. 45-25.

In low gear, Fig. 45-26, the forward clutch is engaged and the planet one-way clutch or low-reverse clutch is holding the low-reverse clutch hub and reverse planet carrier from rotating.

In intermediate gear, the forward clutch is engaged and the intermediate band is holding the reverse-high clutch drum, input shell and sun gear from turning, Fig. 45-27.

In high gear, Fig. 45-28, the forward and reverse-high clutches are engaged.

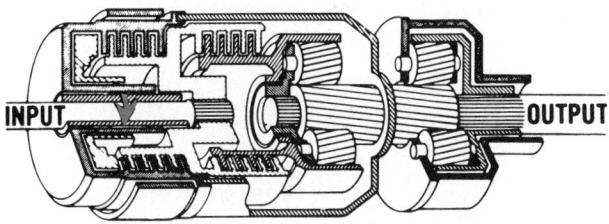

CLUTCHES AND THE BAND ARE RELEASED

NEUTRAL

Fig. 45-25. In neutral, input shaft turns with torque converter turbine; output shaft remains stationary.

THE FORWARD CLUTCH IS APPLIED. THE FRONT PLANETARY UNIT RING GEAR IS LOCKED TO THE INPUT SHAFT.

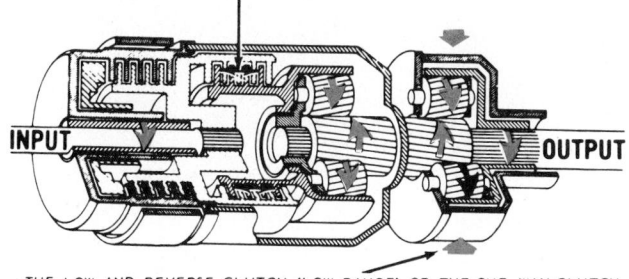

THE LOW AND REVERSE CLUTCH (LOW RANGE) OR THE ONE-WAY CLUTCH (D1 RANGE) IS HOLDING THE REVERSE UNIT PLANET CARRIER STATIONARY.

FIRST GEAR

Fig. 45-26. In first gear, power flow is through: input shaft, forward clutch, clutch cylinder and hub and ring gear, reverse planet gears, reverse ring gear and hub to output shaft.

THE INTERMEDIATE BAND IS APPLIED. THE REVERSE AND HIGH CLUTCH DRUM, THE INPUT SHELL AND THE SUN GEAR ARE HELD STATIONARY.

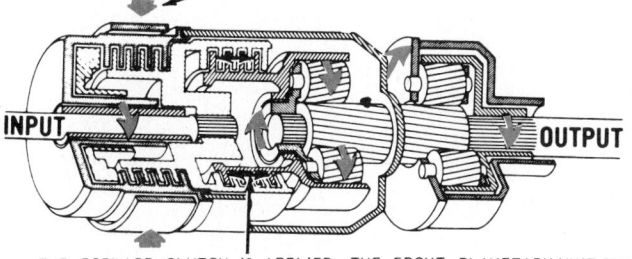

THE FORWARD CLUTCH IS APPLIED. THE FRONT PLANETARY UNIT RING GEAR IS LOCKED TO THE INPUT SHAFT.

SECOND GEAR

Fig. 45-27. In second gear, power flow is through: input shaft; forward clutch; forward planet assembly ring gear and pinions, forward planet carrier to output shaft.

In reverse gear, the reverse-high clutch and low-reverse clutch are engaged, Fig. 45-29.

FORD C4 AUTOMATIC TRANSMISSION

Major components of the C4 transmission include: a three-element torque converter; planetary gear train; forward clutch; reverse-high clutch; intermediate servo and bands; low-reverse servo and band, Fig. 45-30. The torque converter is

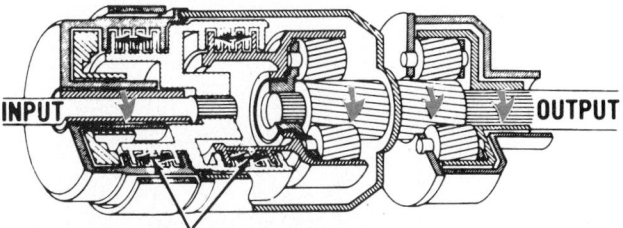

BOTH THE FORWARD AND THE REVERSE AND HIGH CLUTCH ARE APPLIED. ALL PLANETARY GEAR MEMBERS ARE LOCKED TO EACH OTHER AND ARE LOCKED TO THE OUTPUT SHAFT.

HIGH GEAR

Fig. 45-28. In third gear, power flow is through: input shaft, forward clutch; hub and ring gear; forward planet carrier. Reverse-high clutch directs power flow through: input shell through sun gear; front planet assembly to output shaft.

THE REVERSE AND HIGH CLUTCH IS APPLIED. THE INPUT SHAFT IS LOCKED TO THE REVERSE AND HIGH CLUTCH DRUM, THE INPUT SHELL AND THE SUN GEAR.

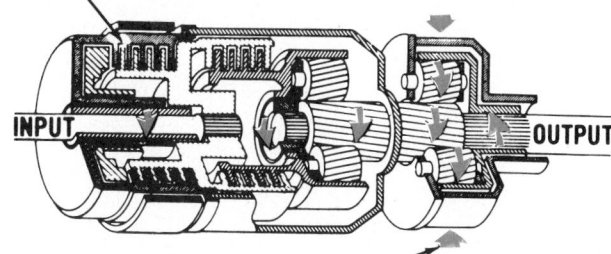

THE LOW AND REVERSE CLUTCH IS APPLIED. THE REVERSE UNIT PLANET CARRIER IS HELD STATIONARY.

REVERSE

Fig. 45-29. In reverse, power flow is through input shaft; reverse-high clutch; input shell; sun gear; reverse planet gears to output shaft.

the fixed-stator type. Front and reverse planetary gearsets provide the ratios needed for the three speeds forward and one in reverse.

A gear-type pump supplies fluid for the operation of the hydraulic control systems. A constant flow of fluid to the converter is maintained. Fluid from the converter is forced through a cooler located in the radiator tank.

Pressure to the various valves is controlled by the main pressure regulator valve. The manual valve is positioned by the manual linkage according to the desires of the driver. Positions are P,R,N,D1,D2,L.

In Neutral, the clutches and bands are not applied. In Low gear (L and D1), the forward clutch is engaged and the one-way clutch or low-reverse band is "holding" the low-reverse drum and reverse planet carrier from rotating. In Intermediate gear (D1 and D2), the forward clutch is engaged and the intermediate band is "holding" the reverse-high clutch drum, input shell and sun gear. In High gear (D1 and D2), the forward and reverse-high clutches are engaged. In Reverse, the reverse-high clutch is engaged and the low-reverse band is applied.

To go one step further, with the C4 transmission in low and selector lever in D position, Fig. 45-31, the front clutch is applied and the primary sun gear is coupled to the input shaft.

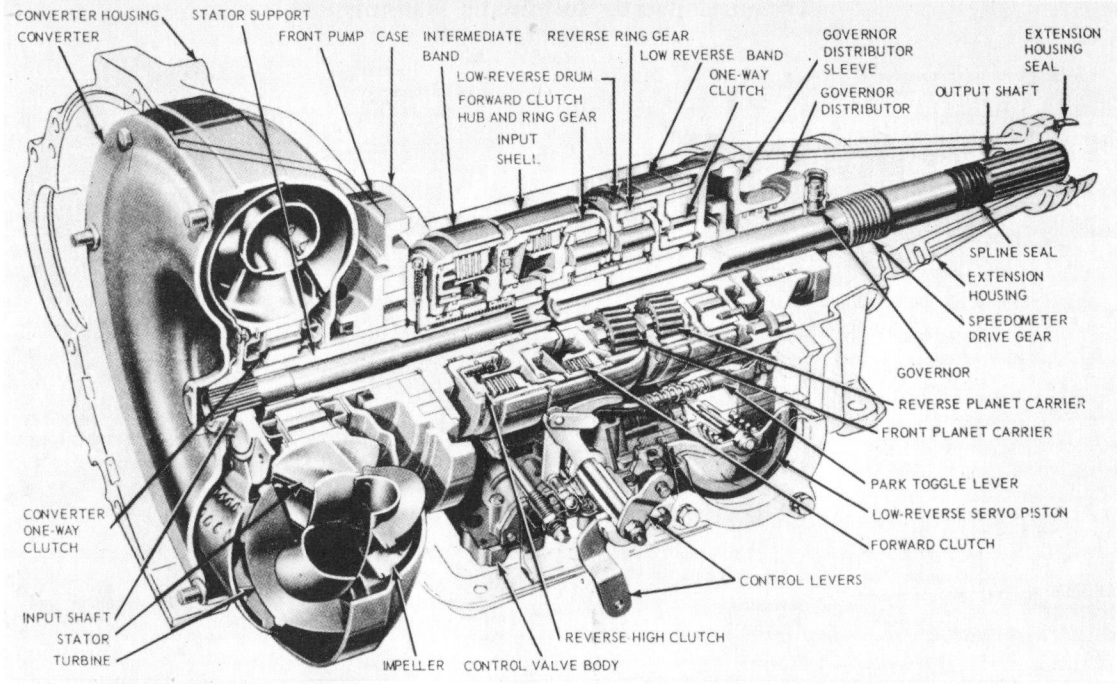

Fig. 45-30. Major assemblies that make up Ford C4 automatic transmission. In unusual arrangement, when reverse-high clutch is engaged, clutch drives input shell to rotate sun gear.

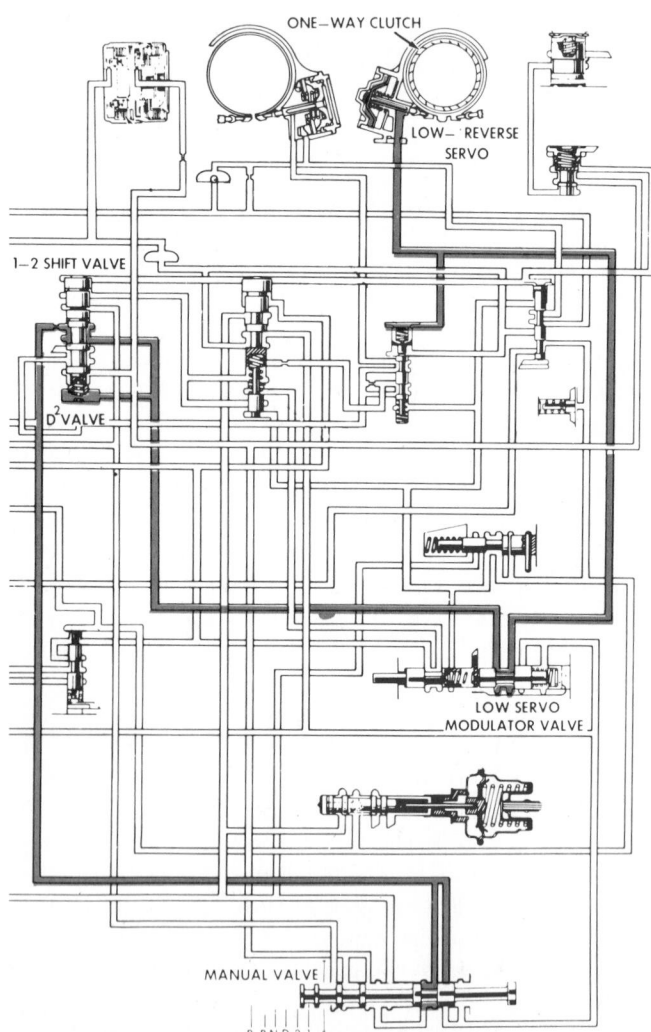

Torque reaction in the planetary gearset engages a one-way clutch and holds the planet pinion carrier from turning. The primary sun gear drives the pinions, which transfer engine torque to the internal gear on the output shaft.

In intermediate with the selector lever in D position, Fig. 45-32, the front clutch couples the primary sun gear to the input shaft. The front band holds the secondary sun gear from turning, while engine torque rotates the primary sun gear

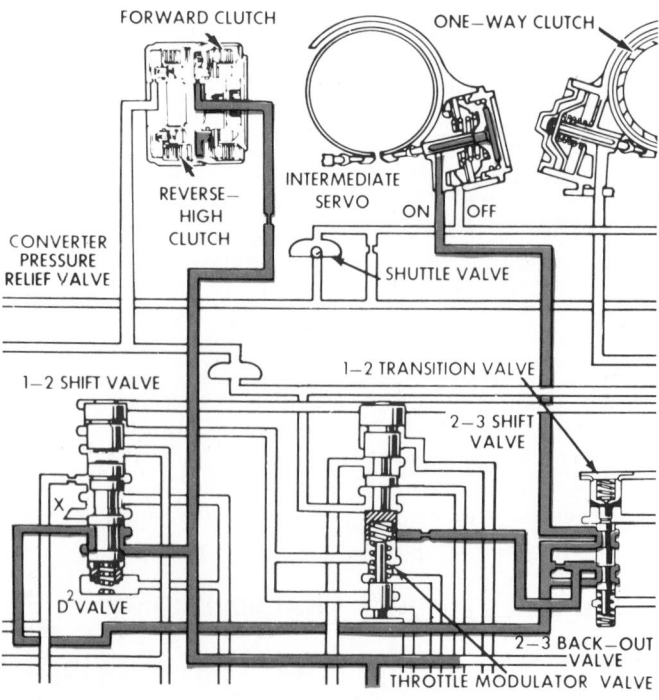

Fig. 45-31. With Ford C4 in D, low gear, fluid under pressure is transmitted to low-reverse servo through 1-2 shift valve, and one-way clutch is applied.

Fig. 45-32. With Ford C4 in D, intermediate, fluid under pressure flows through 2-3 back-out valve to apply side of intermediate servo, and reverse-high clutch is applied.

which drives the planetary pinions. Since the secondary sun gear is locked in place, the planetary pinions are forced to "walk" around the secondary sun gear, driving the internal gear at intermediate speed.

In high with the selector lever in D position, the front and rear clutches couple both sun gears to the input shaft. All units lock together and turn in direct ratio to the input shaft.

FORDOMATIC

The Fordomatic transmission is a torque converter type using three elements: the usual impeller, turbine and stator units connected to a planetary gear transmission. Ford terms the torque converter a combination hydraulic torque multiplier and fluid coupling. The planetary gear system is a compound gearset. On later models, one multiple disc clutch and two bands provide two forward speeds and one speed in reverse.

Two pumps are used to supply oil under pressure to operate the control band and clutch, lubricate the entire transmission and keep the converter filled. One pump is driven by the converter impeller, the other by the transmission output shaft.

The selector lever has five positions: P (Park), R (Reverse), N (Neutral), D (Drive) and L (Low).

In Neutral and Park positions, the clutch and both bands are released by spring pressure, and drive through the transmission is impossible. In Drive position – first gear – in Low position and also in kickdown, the low band is applied. In Drive position – high gear – the low band is released and the high clutch is engaged. In Reverse position, the reverse band is applied.

FLASH–O–MATIC

The Flash-O-Matic consists of a torque converter coupled to a three-speed dual driving range automatic transmission, Fig. 45-33. The converter incorporates an impeller connected to

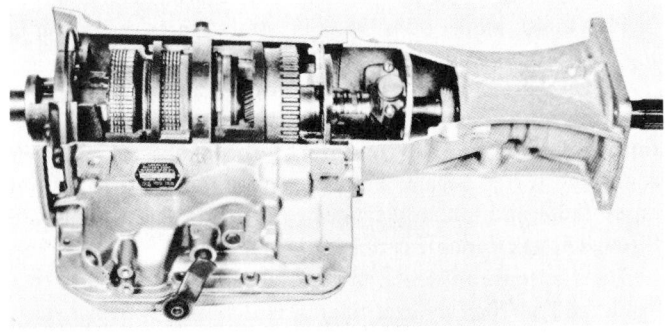

Fig. 45-33. Flash-O-Matic features three-element torque converter and dual driving range transmission that may be manually controlled.

the engine crankshaft, a turbine splined to the transmission input shaft, and a stator connected to and controlled by a free-wheel unit.

Front and rear oil pumps, Fig. 45-34, are used to supply fluid to the converter, lubricate the parts and build pressure in

HYDRAULIC SYSTEM

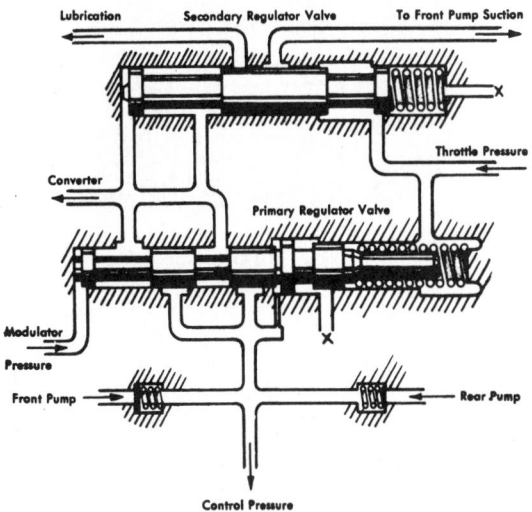

Fig. 45-34. Hydraulic system utilizes two oil pumps which provide working oil pressure needed to operate various control units and valves.

the various oil circuits. A primary regulator valve regulates control pressure to meet all driving requirements. A manual valve, controlled by the transmission selector lever, opens combinations of oil passages to the valve and units which are required for the drive range selected.

A compound planetary gear train supplies the necessary gear combinations to provide neutral, low, intermediate, high and reverse gear ratios. Major elements include a primary sun gear, secondary sun gear, primary and secondary pinions held in a common pinion carrier, and an internal gear attached to the transmission output shaft, Fig. 45-33. The selector lever has six positions: P,R,N,D2,D1 and L. In D2, the transmission starts in intermediate and automatically upshifts to direct drive. In D1, it starts in low and automatically upshifts to intermediate, then direct. In L, the transmission stays in low gear. The selector lever may be moved from D2 to D1 to L or from L to D1 to D2 at any car speed.

The various gear ratios are dependent on which gears are being held and which are driving. This phase of automatic transmission control is accomplished by clutches, bands and servos. Front and rear multiple disc clutches are used. Actuation of the front servo applies the front band to the rear clutch drum and locks the secondary sun gear to the transmission case. Actuation of the rear servo applies the rear band to the pinion carrier, locking it to the transmission case.

In Neutral position, none of the gear train members are held or driving, so there is no transfer of power. In Park, the parking pawl is engaged with external teeth on the output shaft internal gear, locking the output shaft to the transmission case.

In Drive range, D1, the front clutch couples the primary sun gear to the input shaft, Fig. 45-35. The sprag clutch is engaged and holds the planetary pinion carrier. The primary sun gear drives the planetary pinion which, in turn, drives the internal gear and output shaft.

In Intermediate position (second speed), the front clutch

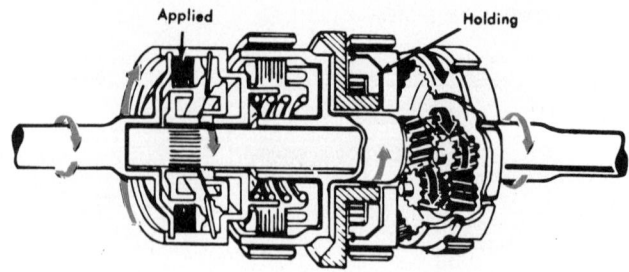

Power Flow in Low (First Gear Range Shown)

Fig. 45-35. In first gear, front clutch is engaged.

connects the primary sun gear to the input shaft, while the front band "holds" the secondary sun gear stationary. Power flow is through the primary sun gear, planet pinions and carrier to the internal gear and output shaft, Fig. 45-36.

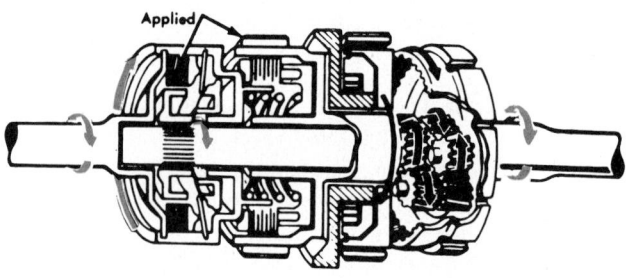

Power Flow in Intermediate (Second Gear)

Fig. 45-36. In second gear, front clutch is engaged and front band is applied to drive through primary sun gear.

In High position (direct drive), the front clutch connects the primary sun gear to the input shaft, while the rear clutch connects the secondary sun gear to the input shaft. This locks the pinions together and all units turned in direct ratio to the input shaft, Fig. 45-37.

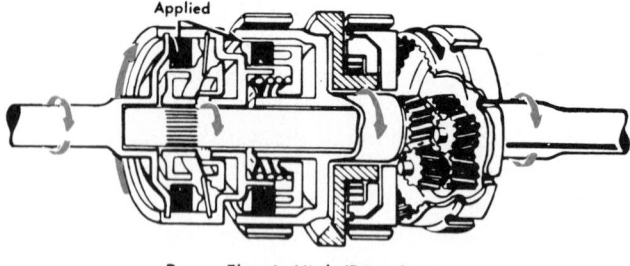

Power Flow in High (Direct)

Fig. 45-37. In high, front and rear clutches are engaged.

In Low range (L), Fig. 45-38, the front clutch connects the primary sun gear to the input shaft, while the rear band "holds" the pinion carrier stationary.

In Reverse, Fig. 45-39, the rear clutch connects the

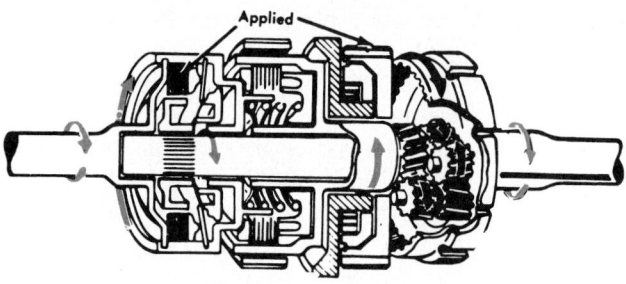

Power Flow in Low (L-Range)

Fig. 45-38. In low range (L), front clutch is engaged and rear band is applied to hold pinion carrier.

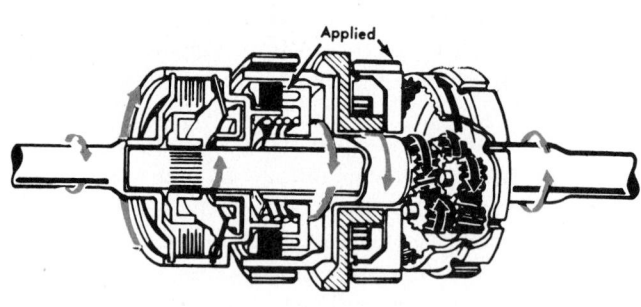

Power Flow in Reverse

Fig. 45-39. In reverse, rear clutch is engaged and rear bands applied.

secondary sun gear to the input shaft, while the rear band "holds" the pinion carrier stationary. Power flow is through the secondary sun gear, secondary pinions to the internal gear and output shaft.

TORQUE—COMMAND TRANSMISSION

Currently, American Motors' cars use three-speed automatic transmissions much like Chrysler's TorqueFlite. Three different models are used, and they are similar in size, appearance and operation. AMC's Torque-Command transmission is shown in Fig. 45-40. Model 904/998 is illustrated in cross section in Fig. 45-41.

All models combine a torque converter and planetary gear system, giving three forward gear ratios and one reverse. The three element torque converter incorporates an impeller connected to the engine, a turbine splined to the transmission input shaft and a stator connected to the transmission case through an overrunning clutch.

The transmission contains two multiple disc clutches, two bands and servos, an overrunning clutch and two planetary gearsets with a common sun gear. The two gearsets are connected to the two clutches through a driving shell, Fig. 45-41, which is splined to the sun gear and front clutch retainer.

The hydraulic system of the AMC units includes a single oil pump, a valve body containing the pressure regulating and shift control valves, the governor valve assembly, two band-actuating servos and the accumulator.

Dexron transmission fluid is cooled by circulation through

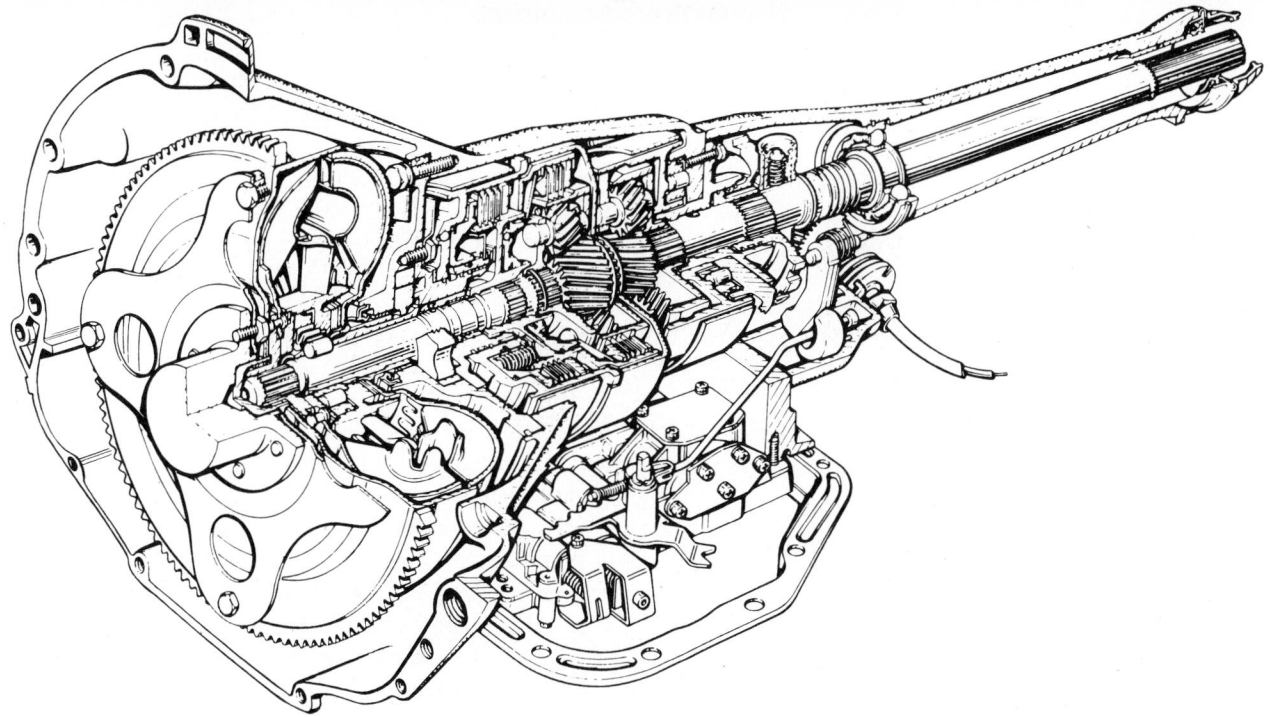

Fig. 45-40. American Motors' Torque-Command automatic transmission basically is a three-speed, hydraulically controlled gearbox with 500 parts housed in an aluminum casting. It does not require band adjustment and, under normal conditions, oil changes are not required.

Fig. 45-41. American Motors' 904 and 998 automatic transmissions are similar three-speed units. Power flow is through converter, input shaft, multiple disc clutches, compound planetary gear system and output shaft.

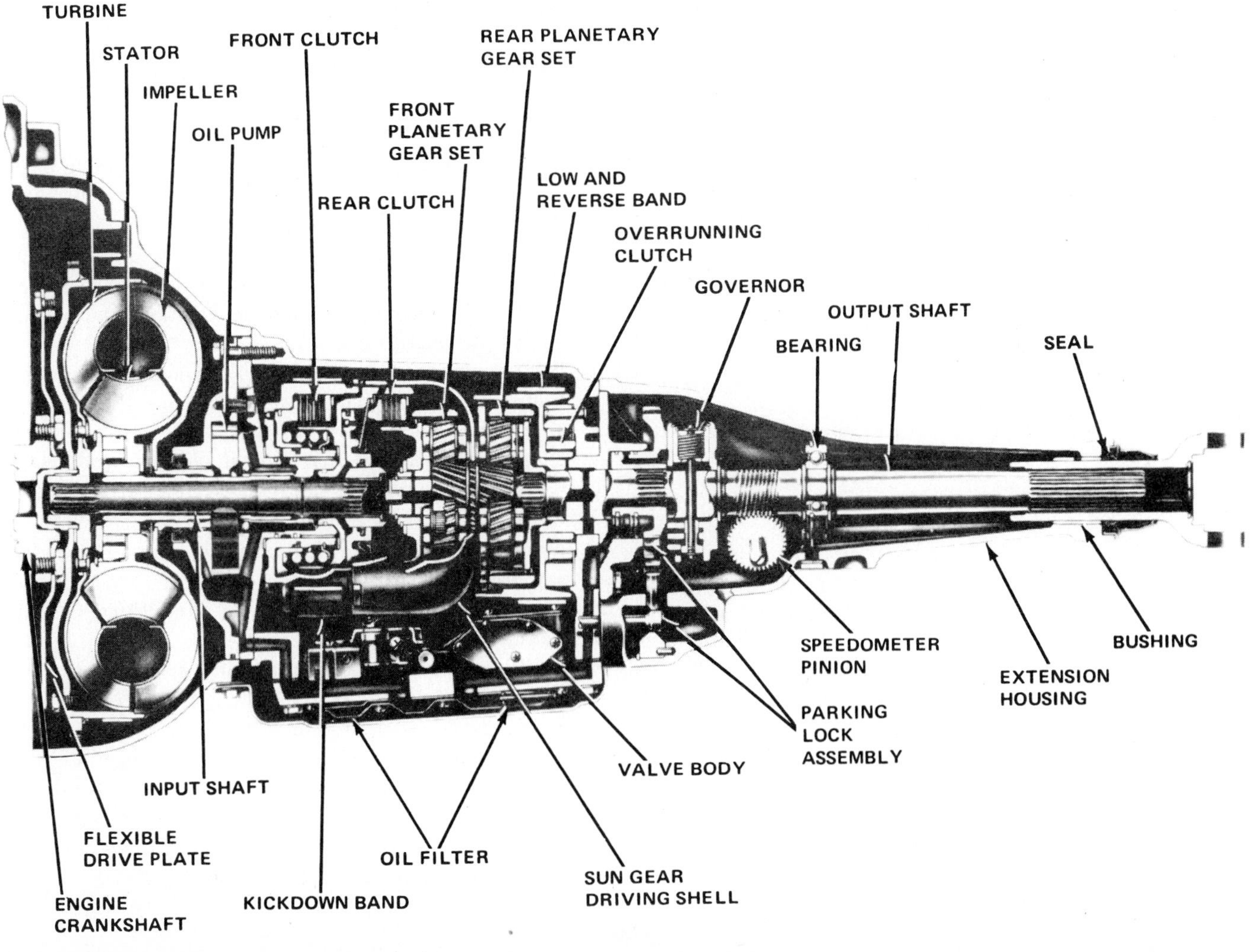

TURBINE

STATOR

IMPELLER

OIL PUMP

FRONT CLUTCH

REAR CLUTCH

FRONT PLANETARY GEAR SET

REAR PLANETARY GEAR SET

LOW AND REVERSE BAND

OVERRUNNING CLUTCH

GOVERNOR

BEARING

OUTPUT SHAFT

SEAL

SPEEDOMETER PINION

PARKING LOCK ASSEMBLY

BUSHING

EXTENSION HOUSING

VALVE BODY

SUN GEAR DRIVING SHELL

OIL FILTER

KICKDOWN BAND

INPUT SHAFT

FLEXIBLE DRIVE PLATE

ENGINE CRANKSHAFT

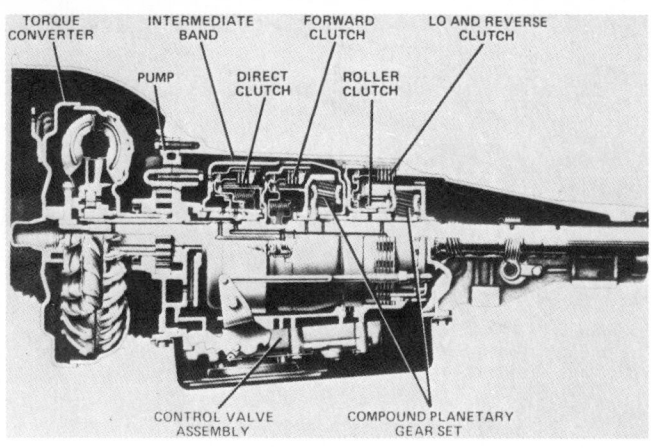

Fig. 45-42. Pontiac, and other General Motors divisions, are achieving significant weight savings by the use of the THM 200 automatic transmission. Smaller size, simpler design and the use of stamped metal instead of cast iron parts have reduced weight of the 200 by 50 to 60 lb. under other GM automatics.

gear the front band and rear clutch are applied. In D, third gear, both the front and rear clutches are applied.

In the 2 range, first gear, the rear and overrunning clutches are applied. In the 2 range, second gear, the front band and rear clutch are applied. In the 1 range, the rear clutch and rear band are applied. In reverse, the front clutch and rear band are applied.

TROUBLESHOOTING TIPS

This information is helpful in diagnosing an automatic transmission problem by road testing. If slippage occurs, for example, the clutch or band that is slipping can be determined by noting transmission operation in all selector positions and which internal units are applied in those positions.

Note that the front and rear clutches are applied in third gear. By shifting to reverse, the unit slipping can be determined. If the slippage also occurs in reverse, the front clutch is slipping. If the transmission does not slip in reverse, the rear clutch is slipping. It is diagnosis by the process of elimination, and it does pinpoint the malfunctioning unit. However, hydraulic pressure tests must be performed to find the cause.

All automatic transmissions have pressure testing ports to which a pressure gauge may be attached. Then, with fluid level and condition and control linkage adjustments checked and found to be correct, pressure test procedures are followed and diagnosis guides consulted to determine the cause of problems within the transmission. The car manufacturers' service manuals carry this information, along with full details on transmission disassembly, parts replacement and reassembly.

an external oil cooler located in the radiator lower tank. The fluid is filtered by a Dacron element filter that is attached to the valve body.

Basic power flow in the three AMC transmissions is from the engine through the torque converter, to the input shaft of the transmission, then to the multiple disc clutches, through the compound planetary gearset to the output shaft.

In the park and neutral positions of the PRND21 selector lever, none of the bands or clutches is applied. In D, first gear, the rear and overrunning clutches are applied. In D, second

REVIEW QUESTIONS – TORQUE CONVERTER AUTOMATIC TRANSMISSIONS

1. What is the difference between a fluid coupling and a torque converter?
2. What are the three major rotating elements in most torque converters?
3. Which element creates reaction torque in a torque converter?
   a. Impeller.
   b. Turbine.
   c. Stator.
4. Torque multiplication in a torque converter is greater at what speed?
   a. Low speed.
   b. Cruising speed.
   c. High speed.
5. Are stator blades always "fixed?"
6. What are the main advantages of a variable pitch stator?
7. What is the purpose of the vacuum modulator and modulator valve in a Turbo Hydra-Matic transmission?
   a. Permits smooth clutch and band engagements.
   b. Establishes range of transmission selected by driver.
   c. Changes line oil pressure in transmission to meet engine needs.
8. What is the purpose of a manual valve?
   a. Permits smooth clutch and band engagements.
   b. Establishes range of transmission selected by driver.

   c. Changes line oil pressure in transmission to meet engine needs.
9. What is the purpose of an accumulator?
   a. Permits smooth clutch and band engagements.
   b. Establishes range of transmission selected by driver.
   c. Changes line oil pressure in transmission to meet engine needs.
10. What is the primary function of TorqueFlite automatic transmission clutches and bands?
    a. Smooth transmission shifts.
    b. Transmit engine torque through planetary gearsets.
    c. Provide various gear ratios selected by driver.
11. Name four principle elements of a planetary gearset?
12. What is the purpose of a planetary gear train in an automatic transmission?
13. What is "Select Shift" feature of Ford Cruise-O-Matic transmission?
    a. Permits driver to shift gears manually.
    b. Provides extra forward speed range.
    c. Gives driver option of "kickdown" from high to second gear.
14. Do Fordomatic and Flash-O-Matic transmissions use two oil pumps?
15. The Torque-Command transmission uses Dexron automatic transmission fluid. True or False?

DRIVE LINE, UNIVERSAL JOINTS, DIFFERENTIALS

In basic passenger car design, the drive line connects the transmission with the driving axles. In effect, it transmits engine power to the driving wheels.

Ordinarily, the engine is mounted on the frame, and the driving wheels are free to move up and down in relation to the frame. In between, the angularity of the line of drive is constantly changing. This means flexibility is needed in the drive system and, usually, it is provided by universal joints. See Figs. 46-1 and 46-2.

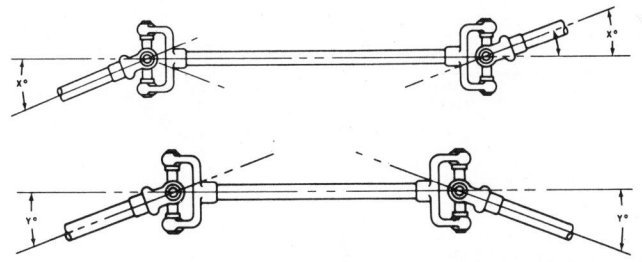

Fig. 46-1. Universal joints at both ends of drive shaft compensate for changes in angularity of drive.

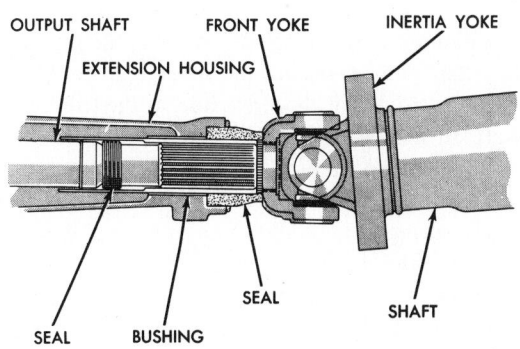

Fig. 46-2. A cross and roller universal joint with sliding spline is front joint arrangement on late model Chrysler-built cars that are equipped with TorqueFlite transmission.

UNIVERSAL JOINTS

Although it would be desirable to have the drive shaft in line with the engine crankshaft, this design is not practical. In

the first place, the wheels move up and down because of road irregularities. Second, the frame moves up and down in relation to the wheels. How much it moves depends on the amount of weight in the automobile body and the limits of the suspension springs and linkage. So a compromise is made, and the "workable" design is intended to provide a line of drive as straight as possible under average conditions.

The universal joints, Fig. 46-2, serve to compensate for changes in the line of drive by transmitting power from a driving shaft through an angle to a driven shaft. Most cars use two or three universal joints in the drive line between the transmission and differential, Fig. 46-3.

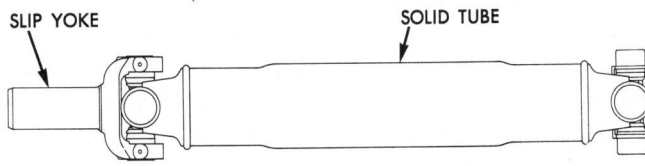

Fig. 46-3. A typical drive shaft assembly on compact and intermediate cars generally utilizes a single cross universal joint at both ends.

DIFFERENTIALS

The differential is a gear system that transfers power from the drive shaft to the driving axles, Fig. 46-4. It also permits

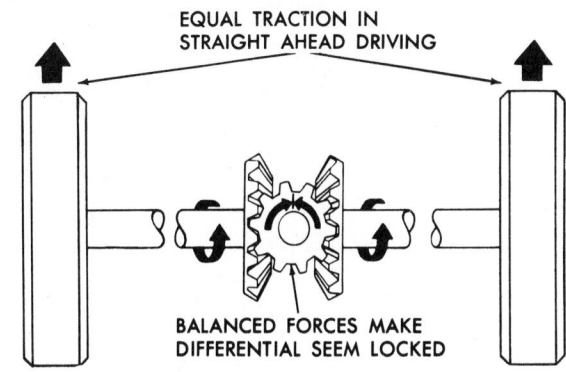

Fig. 46-4. In straight ahead driving, entire differential assembly rotates as a unit with side gears and pinion gears locked together.

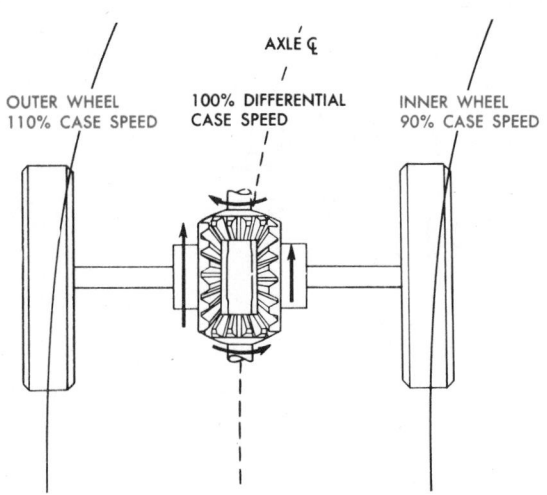

Fig. 46-5. On turns, pinion gears turn on their axis and roll around side gears to permit driving wheels to rotate at unequal speeds.

one driving wheel to turn faster than the other to prevent skidding and scuffing of tires on turns, Fig. 46-5.

In tracing the drive train to this point, power is relayed:
1. From drive shaft to pinion gear.
2. From pinion gear to ring gear.
3. From ring gear to attached differential case, pinion gears and side gears.
4. From side gears to driving axles.

TORQUE CHANGES

However, when engine power is applied to the drive train, torque is developed in the driving wheels. This action creates further changes in the angularity of the drive line, Fig. 46-6.

When power is transmitted by the drive shaft, the pinion gear tries to turn the ring gear. Since the ring gear must turn the axle shafts (and the wheels, indirectly), it resists being

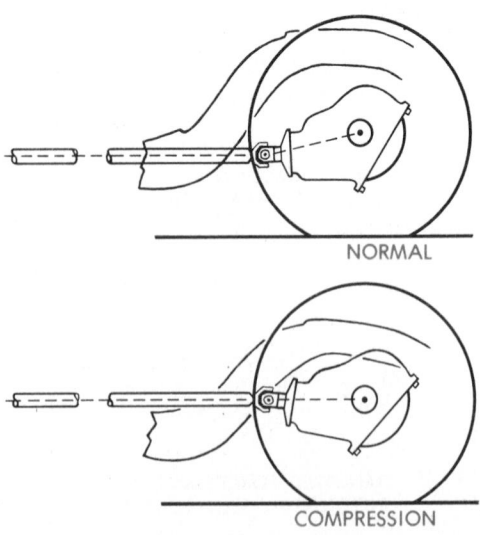

Fig. 46-6. Differential housing will tilt upward when engine torque is relayed from drive shaft to drive pinion to rear axle housing.

moved. The pinion gear attempts to "roll around" the ring gear. Since it cannot, the pinion instead transfers the turning effort, or torque, to the axle housing. The magnitude of this torque is indicated by the tendency of the back end of the car to dip when power is suddenly applied to the driving wheels.

TORQUE TRANSFER

This powerful torque force is transferred from the pinion shaft to the axle housing and from the axle housing to the springs, torque tube or control arms. In the Hotchkiss type of drive, it results in flexing and distortion of the spring. This distortion or "wind-up" of the springs will raise the pinion shaft at the front end, thereby decreasing the angle between the pinion shaft and the drive shaft.

HOTCHKISS DRIVE

Two universal joints are used in the Hotchkiss type of drive to compensate for variations in road surfaces, load conditions and power application which cause changes in alignment between the transmission output shaft and drive pinion shaft. When the Hotchkiss type of drive is used, the vehicle is moved forward by the front end of the rear springs pushing against the frame, Fig. 46-7.

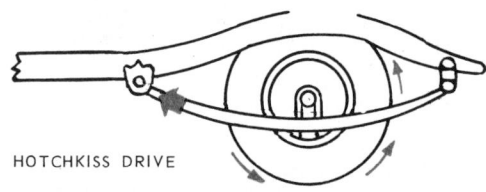

Fig. 46-7. In Hotchkiss drive setup, driving force is transmitted from rear wheels to front of rear springs.

TORQUE TUBE DRIVE

In cars equipped with torque tube drive, the pushing action is at the front end of the torque tube, Fig. 46-8. Only one universal joint is used in the drive line, at the front end of the drive shaft. In this case, the drive shaft is within a stout tube which is anchored to the axle housing. This torque tube does not permit the axle housing to twist when engine power is applied. The springs do not absorb any torque and are required only to cushion the ride.

With torque tube drive, the engine is usually mounted as low as possible in the frame or at an angle with the rear end lower than the front. The object is to obtain a line of drive as straight as possible for power transmission, because power is always lost by any angularity in the drive line.

An unusual development in torque drive was engineered into early Pontiac Tempest cars. A comparatively slender drive shaft was used within a torque tube, fastened rigidly to the engine at one end and to a transaxle (combination transmission and axle) at the other end. The drive shaft bends or flexes as required to compensate for relative movement between

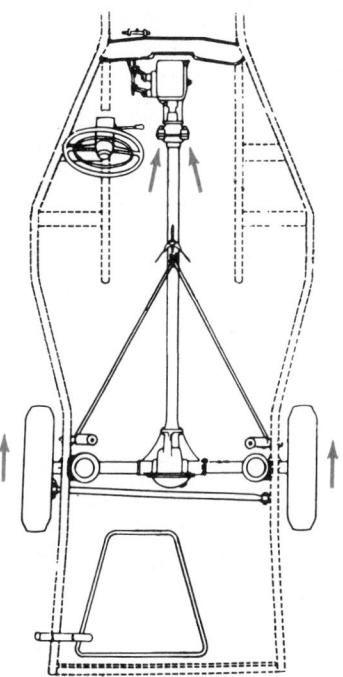

Fig. 46-8. In torque tube drive, driving force is transmitted from rear wheels to front of torque tube.

engine and axle. Vibration and whipping is minimized by a rubber mounted ball bearing near the middle of the shaft.

CONTROL ARM DRIVE

In control arm drive, driving and braking forces are transferred to the front end of heavy-duty control arms, Fig. 46-9. The torque transfer effect is similar to Hotchkiss drive, but coil springs are used at the rear rather than leaf type springs. Some cars use three control arms, most use four.

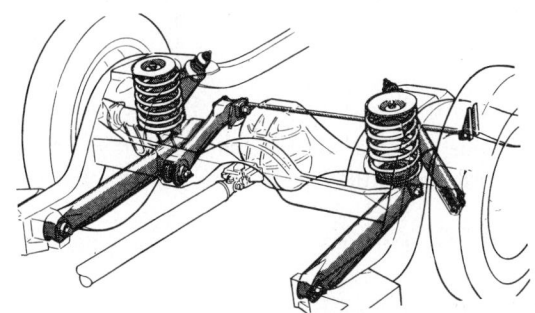

Fig. 46-9. Ford-Mercury rear suspension features control arm drive. Two parallel lower arms extend forward to rubber-bushed anchors for transfer of driving force.

DRIVE SHAFT LENGTH

In addition to line of drive problems caused by angularity of the drive shaft, the distance between the transmission output shaft and the drive pinion shaft is subject to change.

This creates the need for some flexibility in the length of the drive shaft.

In referring to the Hotchkiss drive in Fig. 46-10, the front end of the drive shaft is attached to the transmission shaft at B. The rear end is attached to the drive pinion shaft at C. As the wheels move up and down, the drive shaft swings up and down in arc A-A around pivot B. At the same time, the pinion shaft C — being attached to the rear axle — swings in an arc D-D around the pivot where the spring is anchored to the frame at E. Therefore, as the arcs A-A and D-D do not coincide, it will be necessary for the drive shaft to alternately lengthen and shorten as the wheels move up and down in relation to the frame.

SLIP JOINTS

One method of lengthening or shortening the drive shaft is by means of a splined shaft coupling or "slip joint," Fig., 46-11. This movement is less pronounced on a torque tube drive, but a slip joint is used at the one universal joint.

When the type of slip joint shown in Fig. 46-11 is used, it is possible to assemble it incorrectly. This results in annoying vibration. Such joints are usually marked for correct assembly. If they are not marked, make sure both yokes are in the same plane, or "in phase."

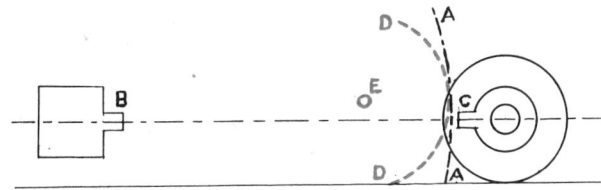

Fig. 46-10. In Hotchkiss drive, length of drive shaft varies because of changes in wheelbase as rear wheels move up and down with road surface irregularities.

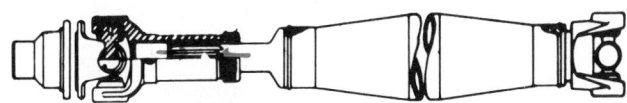

Fig. 46-11. Arrows must align when splined end of drive shaft is installed in universal joint yoke. On unmarked shafts, front and rear yokes must be "in phase."

EFFECT OF VARYING SHAFT SPEEDS

When the two yokes of the drive shaft are "in phase," the speed of the transmission output shaft and the pinion shaft will be constant and the same if the line of drive of both shafts is uniform. The velocity of the drive shaft will not be constant, but this is unimportant as long as the velocity of the driving and driven shafts is uniform.

When the two yokes are "out of phase," the rotational speed of the shafts will be uniform only if the shafts are operated in a straight line. When operating at an angle with the yokes "out of phase," a conventional universal joint will cause the driven shaft to speed up and slow down each revolution. The number of turns per shaft will be the same, but the velocity of the driven shaft will fluctuate.

In an attempt to absorb some of the natural vibration created by the drive line, Ford introduced a "tuned dynamic absorber" as standard equipment on lighter vehicles. This absorber consisted of a 7 lb. weight suspended by a beam below the front universal joint. The beam was attached to the rear of the transmission extension housing and is engineered to an exact length so that the weight oscillates at the natural frequency of the drive line.

More recently, Chrysler took a different design approach, building into the drive shaft an "internal vibration absorber," Fig. 46-12. This unit obtains the same basic effect as the Ford

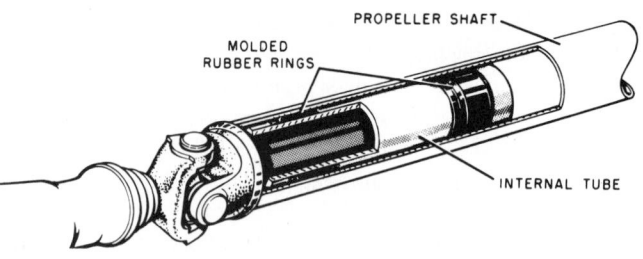

Fig. 46-12. Drive shaft on late model Chrysler-built cars, has an internal vibration absorber designed to absorb vibrations created by normal fluctuating speeds of universal joints.

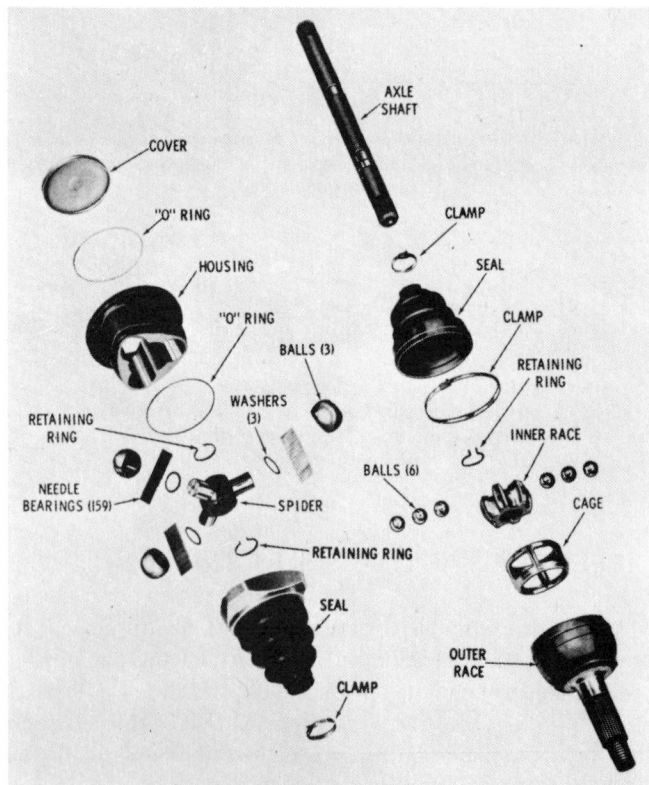

Fig. 46-13. Exploded view details left drive axle assembly used on Oldsmobile Toronado front wheel drive cars. Cadillac Eldorado setup is similar in this and most engine-related assemblies.

"absorber." It absorbs the natural vibrations created by the fluctuation in speed of the drive shaft.

This fluctuation of speed is further emphasized in the design of driving axles. In the case of front wheel drive vehicles, the universal joint, or joints, used in the driving axle assemblies must transfer driving power to the front wheels and, at the same time, compensate for steering action on turns.

CONSTANT VELOCITY JOINTS

To solve this problem, special universal joints known as "constant velocity" types were developed, Fig. 46-13. In the example shown, rolling balls in curved grooves are utilized to obtain uniform motion. The balls, which are the driving contact, move laterally as the joint rotates. This permits the point of driving contact between the two halves of the coupling to remain in a plane which bisects the angle between the two shafts. By this means, the fluctuation in speed is avoided.

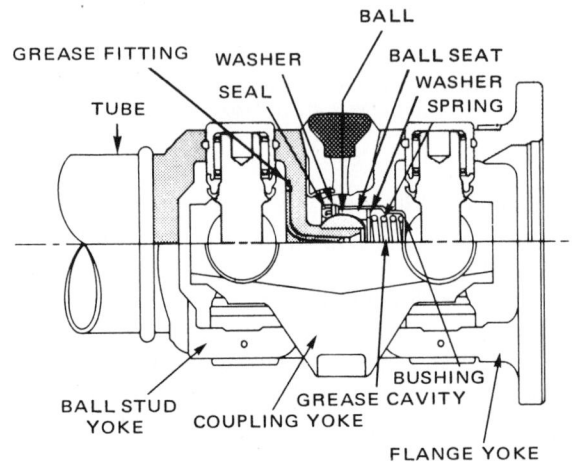

Fig. 46-14. This constant velocity universal joint consists of two single joints connected by a link yoke and maintained in relative position by a center ball and socket.

In a parallel development, Fig. 46-14, for use in propeller shafts, Fig. 46-15, two yoke and cross universal joints are placed adjacent and connected to achieve the desired results.

TRANSFER CASES

When a vehicle is driven by both front and rear wheels, it is necessary to provide a sort of power takeoff to drive both axles. This auxiliary device is known as a transfer case, Fig. 46-16. It is customary to provide a shifting device on such units so that the front drive can be disconnected if desired.

As the angularity of the drive shafts between front and rear wheels changes constantly, the transfer case is positioned in the best possible compromise to serve both axles. Each drive shaft is fitted with a slip joint to accommodate changes in distance between axles and transfer case as the wheels move up and down. See Fig. 46-16.

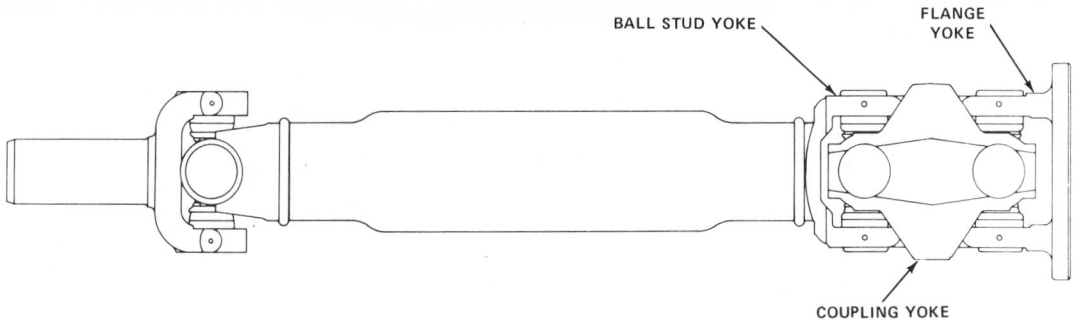

BALL STUD YOKE

FLANGE YOKE

COUPLING YOKE

Fig. 46-15. Constant velocity universal joint (at right) cancels out vibration that could occur from speed fluctuation with single joint setup.

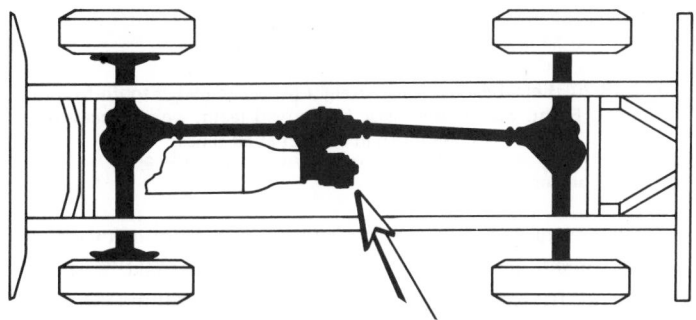

Fig. 46-16. Engine torque goes from transmission to transfer case where it is applied to drive shafts extending to each driving axle.

CENTER BEARINGS

In the case of long trucks and some passenger automobiles, the drive shaft is divided into two lengths and a supporting "center bearing" is utilized, Fig. 46-17.

This type of bearing is used to stabilize the shaft and reduce vibration and "whip." The whip comes from centrifugal force aided by an unbalance that may exist in the shaft. For this reason, drive shafts are carefully balanced.

DIFFERENTIALS AND AXLES

Early automobiles were driven by means of belts or ropes around pulleys mounted on the driving wheels and engine shaft or transmission shaft. Because there always was some slippage of the belts, one wheel could rotate faster then the other when turning a corner.

When belts proved unsatisfactory, the builders borrowed an idea from bicycle design and applied sprockets and chains. This was a positive driving arrangement, so it was necessary to provide differential gearing to permit one driving wheel to turn faster than the other, Figs. 46-5 and 46-18.

DIFFERENTIAL GEARS

In a typical differential gear arrangement, Fig. 46-19, the pinion gear turns the ring gear and the differential case

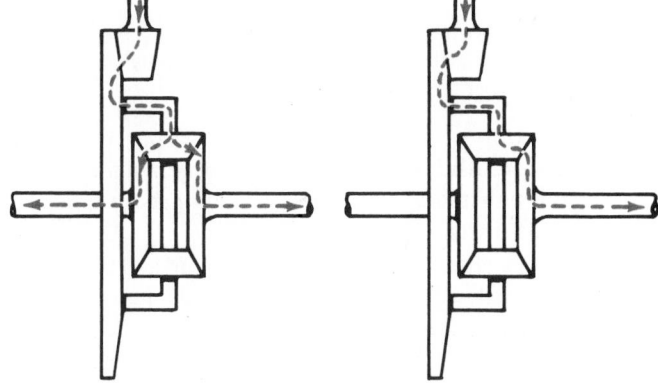

Fig. 46-18. Differential gearing shown in diagrammatical view indicates flow of power: (left) straight ahead; (right) during left turn.

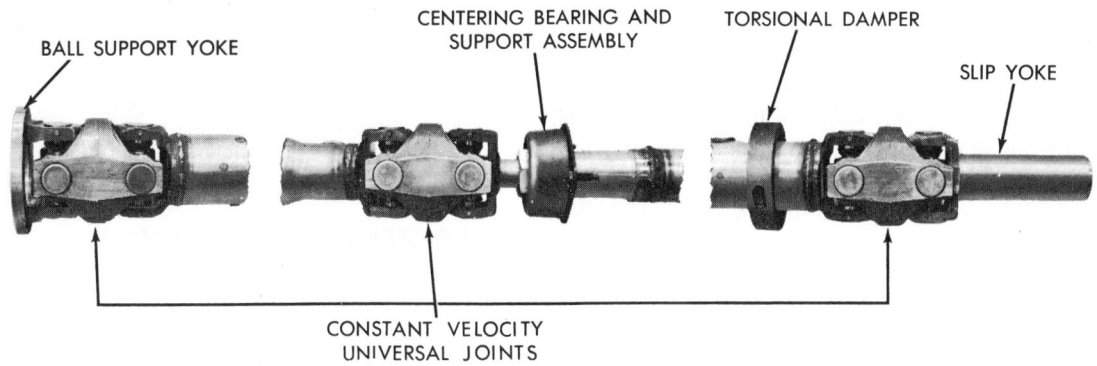

CENTERING BEARING AND SUPPORT ASSEMBLY

TORSIONAL DAMPER

BALL SUPPORT YOKE

SLIP YOKE

CONSTANT VELOCITY UNIVERSAL JOINTS

Fig. 46-17. On applications having two drive shafts, a center bearing usually supports front drive shaft. Bearing is mounted in rubber to insulate it from frame.

Fig. 46-25. Bearing adjusters are secured by heavy saddles (arrows), which are tightened in place after adjustment is completed. Special locks keep adjusters from turning.

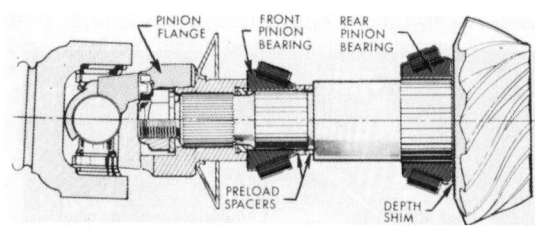

Fig. 46-26. Most drive pinion assemblies have two opposed, tapered roller bearings, which are preloaded to a light rotating torque by applying a heavy torque to the pinion nut.

Fig. 46-27. Pinion shaft and bearing assembly is arranged in proper sequence of assembly. Note special preload bushing at center.

BEARING PRELOAD

Many car manufacturers specify "preloading" of drive pinion bearings. In some cases, this is done by slight overtightening of the bearing adjustments. In other cases, it is accomplished by the use of a special bearing spacer or sleeve, Fig. 46-27. The sleeve between the two bearings is made with a weakened section. After installation, the bearings are pulled together until the sleeve distorts, Fig. 46-28.

Equally important, there should be no radial movement of

Fig. 46-28. A new bearing spacer sleeve is compared with a distorted one. Obviously, a new sleeve must be installed each time assembly is taken apart and reassembled.

the pinion. In heavy-duty units, the pinion is often "straddle mounted." That is, there is a bearing on each side of the pinion, Fig. 46-29.

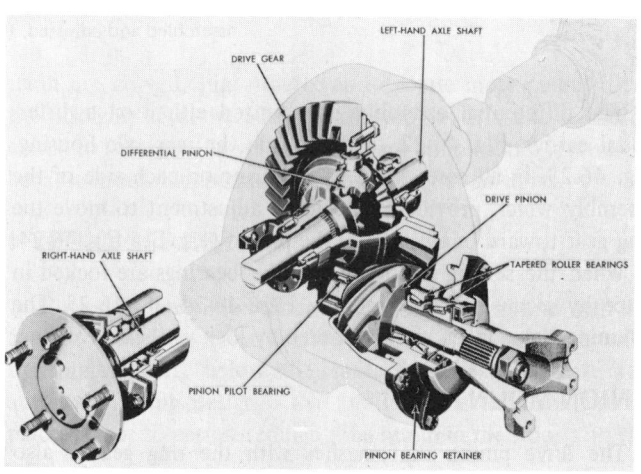

Fig. 46-29. Drive pinion on heavy-duty applications is supported by bearings on both sides of pinion gear.

LIMITED SLIP DIFFERENTIALS

Limited slip differentials are a popular option on a number of different makes of automobiles under a number of different names. Some use cone clutches, and others use disc clutches to direct power flow to the axle of the wheel having the best traction. At the same time, less power is applied to the wheel that tends to slip so better traction is obtained for both driving wheels. See Figs. 46-30 and 46-31.

One commonly used limited slip design has beveled ends on the differential pinion shafts and corresponding "ramps" cut in the shaft openings of the differential case, Figs. 46-32 and 46-33. With this construction, the differential pinions and pinion shafts float between the differential side gears and the case. When power is applied, the ramps tend to force the side gears apart and apply pressure to the clutch assembly having the best traction.

Another popular limited slip differential utilizes cone clutches that are preloaded with six springs. The frictional surface of the cones contain a coarse spiral thread that provides passages for the flow of lubricant, Fig. 46-34. In

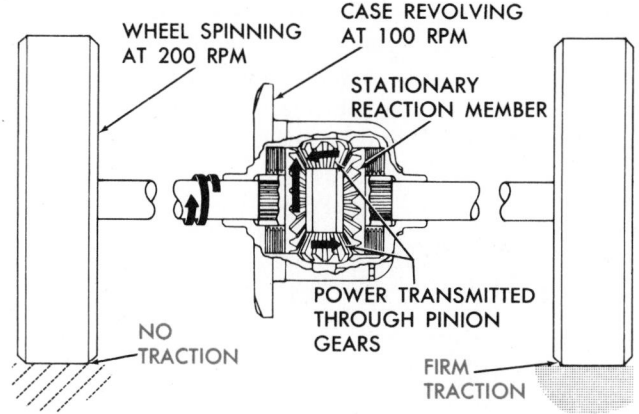

Fig. 46-30. Limited slip differential eliminates problem of conventional differentials where power flow is directed to driving wheel that is slipping.

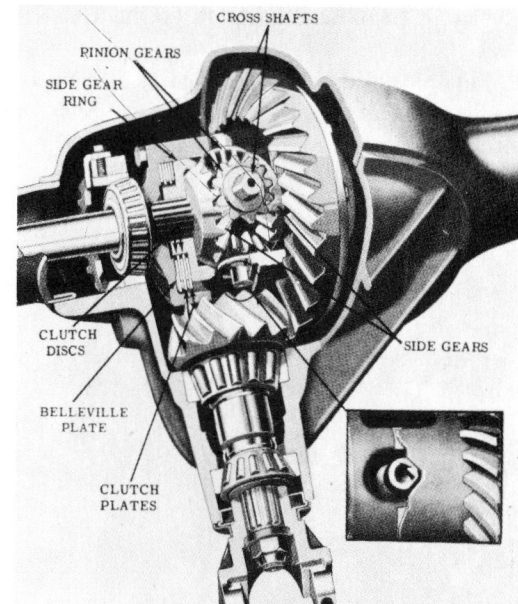

Fig. 46-32. Typical limited slip differential utilizes disc clutches and notched case for differential pinion cross shafts, which are shaped to fit notches in case.

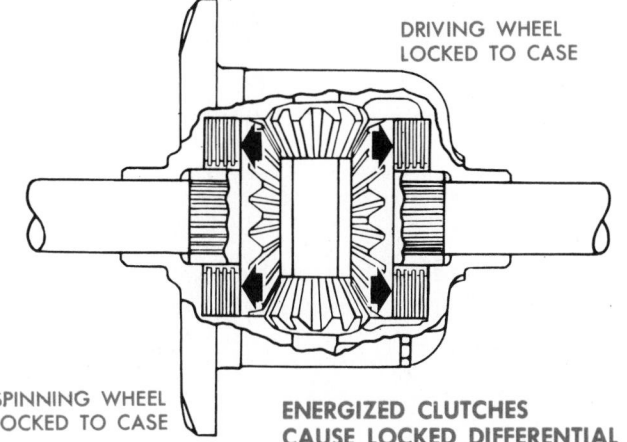

Fig. 46-31. In wheel spinning situations with a limited slip differential, power is transmitted through pinion gears and energized clutches to driving wheel having best traction.

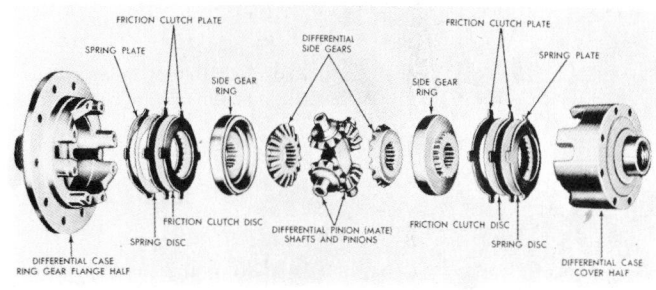

Fig. 46-33. Exploded view of limited slip differential illustrates location and arrangement of friction clutch plates.

straight ahead operation, the pressure of the springs and separating force created between the pinion gears and side gears forces the clutch cones against the case. On turns, the axles are automatically unlocked by differential action, overcoming the spring load on the clutch cones and permitting them to overrun.

Another disc clutch type of limited slip differential is shown in Fig. 46-35. In this unit, an S-shaped spring is used to preload the differential side gears.

PLANETARY DIFFERENTIALS

A planetary differential is used on certain front wheel drive cars to provide an axle gear package of minimum width alongside the engine. Early models of the Oldsmobile Toronado, for example, coupled a spiral bevel ring gear with a spiral bevel drive pinion gear that is straddle mounted by two tapered roller bearings, Fig. 46-36. During straight ahead driving, the ring gear, planet pinions and sun gear rotate as a unit. On turns, the planet gears and sun gear rotate within the

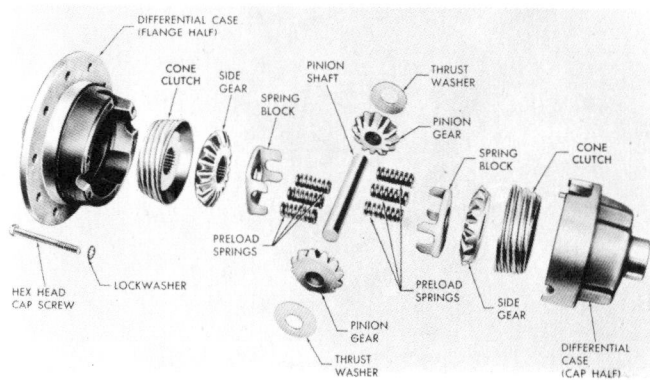

Fig. 46-34. Exploded view of another type of limited slip unit shows cone clutches and preload spring construction.

ring gear, and allow the drive axles to rotate at different speeds. In Fig. 46-36, sun gear drives the right output shaft, carrier drives left output shaft.

TWO—SPEED, DOUBLE REDUCTION AXLES

Other variations in differential design include "two-speed" and "double reduction." These units have been made in various arrangements and types.

A double reduction differential, Fig. 46-37, uses a hypoid pinion meshed with a comparatively small gear for primary reduction. The ring gear shaft is fitted with two helical gears, which mesh with a like pair attached to the axle shafts to accomplish the secondary reduction.

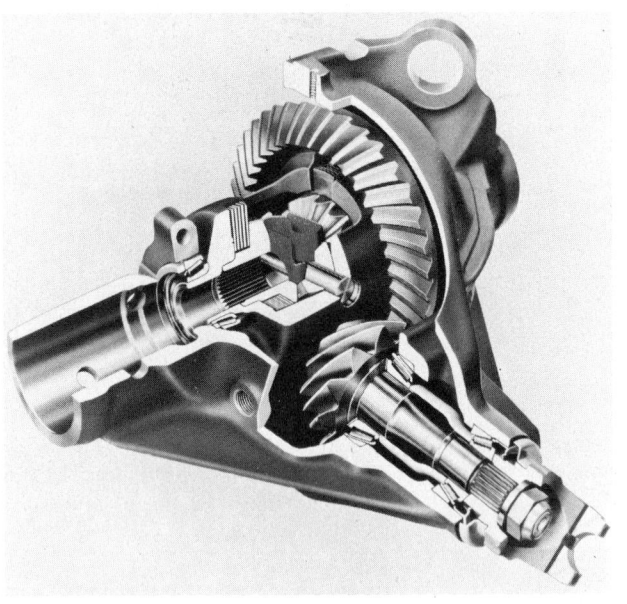

Fig. 46-35. Later developments in limited slip differentials permit use of fewer parts. In this unit, S-shaped spring preloads disc clutches.

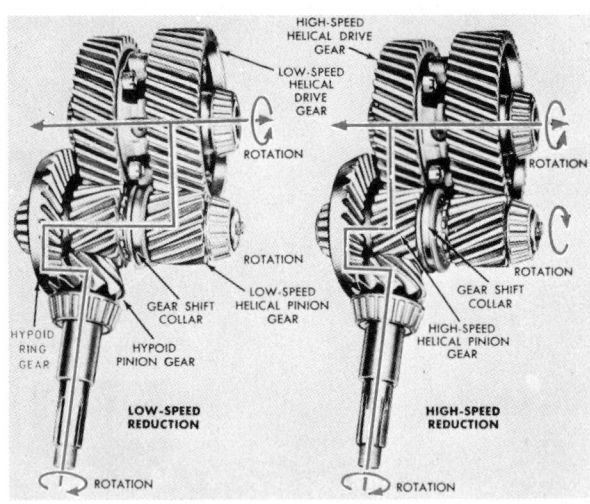

Fig. 46-37. Power flow is traced in a two-speed, double-reduction rear axle, first in low-speed then in high.

One two-speed design uses planetary gearing. (For a full explanation of planetary gearing, see the transmission section

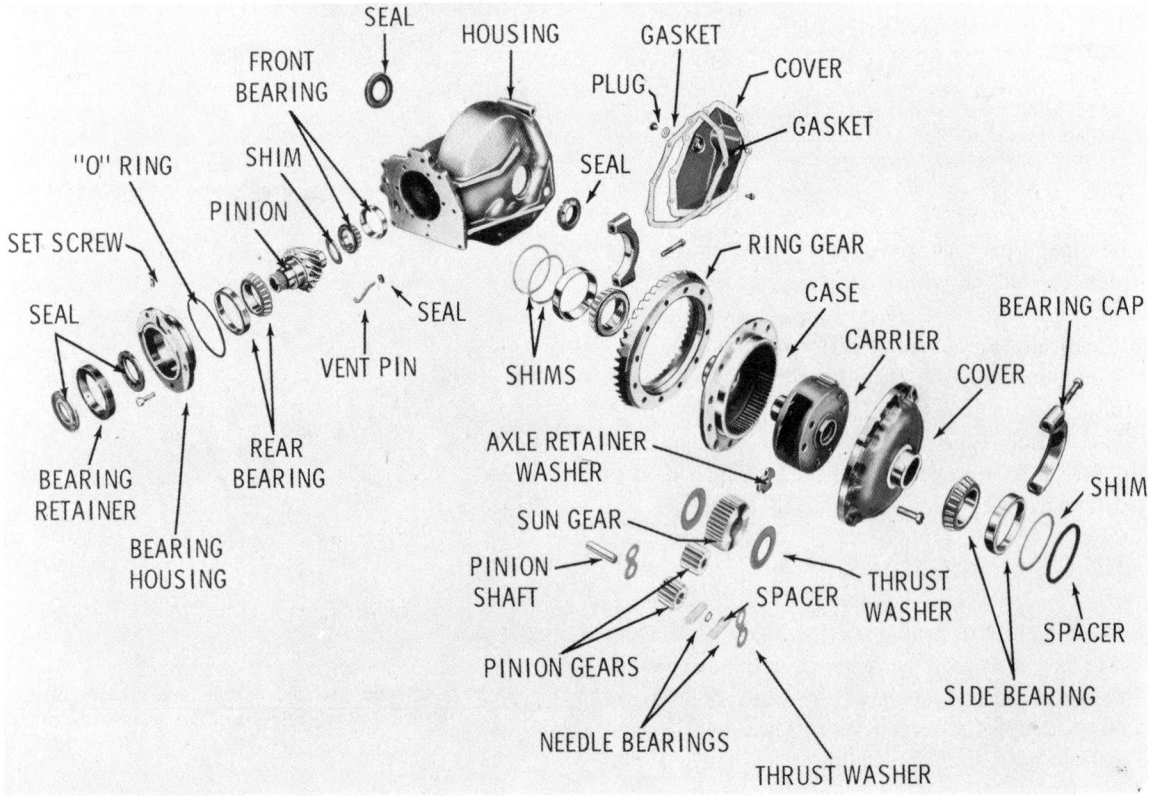

Fig. 46-36. Early Oldsmobile Toronado front wheel drive cars had a specially designed planetary differential mounted along left side of engine.

of this text.) A means of shifting these axles usually is provided by an electrically operated shift unit controlled by the operator of the vehicle. In some cases, both types are combined and called "two-speed, double-reduction" axles.

FULL—FLOATING AXLES

In addition to different types of gearing, axles used for driving vehicles are known as "full-floating," and "semi-floating." These designations have to do with the duties imposed on the axle shaft. In the full-floating type, the axle shaft does not carry any of the car weight. Its sole duty is to propel the vehicle.

A typical full-floating axle construction is shown in Fig. 46-38. Note that the axle housing is fitted with two roller bearings which carry the weight of the vehicle. The axle shaft is upset or flanged on the outer end and bolted to the hub. A full-floating axle can be removed without disturbing the wheel.

SEMI—FLOATING AXLES

In a semi-floating axle, a bearing is placed between the axle shaft and axle housing, Fig. 46-39. The axle supports the weight of the vehicle in addition to being the means of propulsion. In some cases, a semi-floating axle shaft is tapered at the outer end to fit into a tapered hub. It is also keyed in place and held by a nut on the threaded end of the axle shaft. To remove the hub from this type of axle, it is necessary to use a wheel puller.

Other semi-floating designs are shown in Figs. 46-40 and

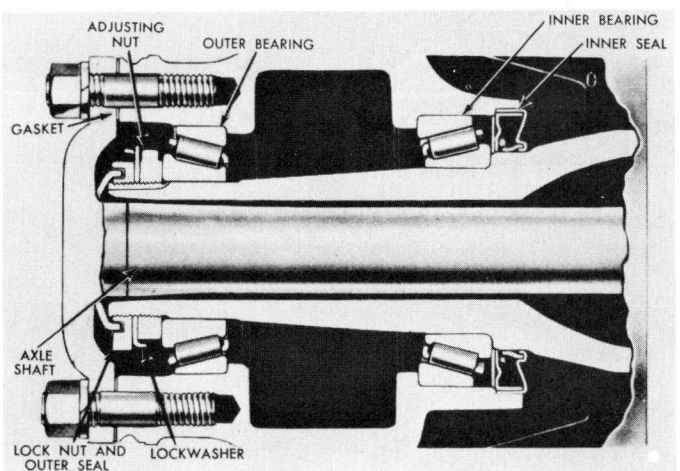

Fig. 46-38. Full-floating rear axle and hub is used in truck applications. Weight of vehicle rests on roller bearings mounted on axle housing.

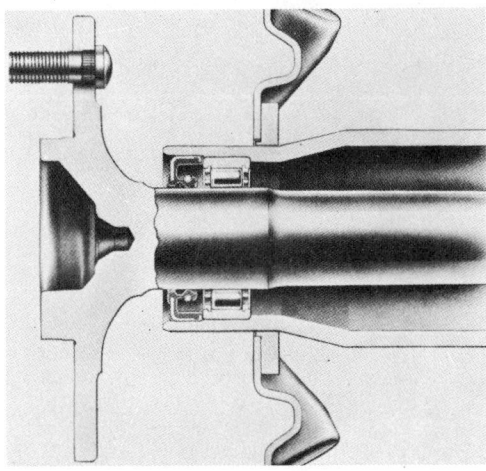

Fig. 46-40. Another semi-floating axle design, featured on most cars produced by General Motors divisions, has flanged outer end to which brake drum and wheel are attached by lug nuts or bolts.

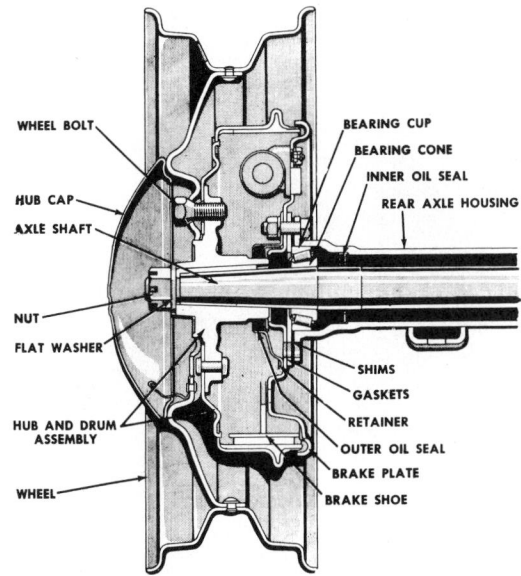

Fig. 46-39. This semi-floating rear axle design is used on Chrysler-built cars earlier than 1965. With this principle, weight of car rests on axle shafts and wheel bearings.

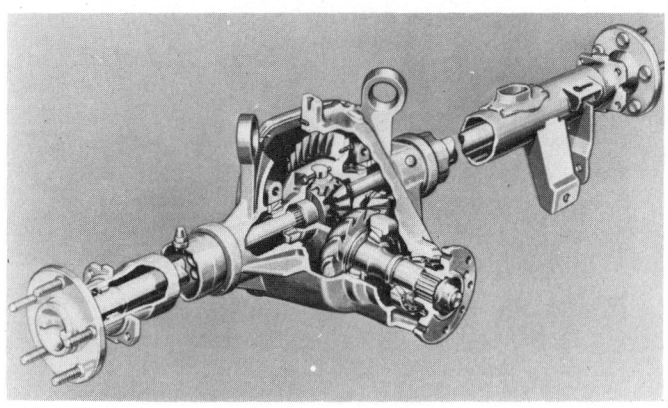

Fig. 46-41. Late model Ford LTDs also have flanged type semi-floating rear axles utilizing straight, roller-on-shaft bearings.

46-41. In these cars, the brake drum is bolted to the flanged end of the axle shaft instead of being keyed. A straight, roller-on-shaft bearing is used. The LTD axle uses solid adjuster shims in place of threaded adjusters.

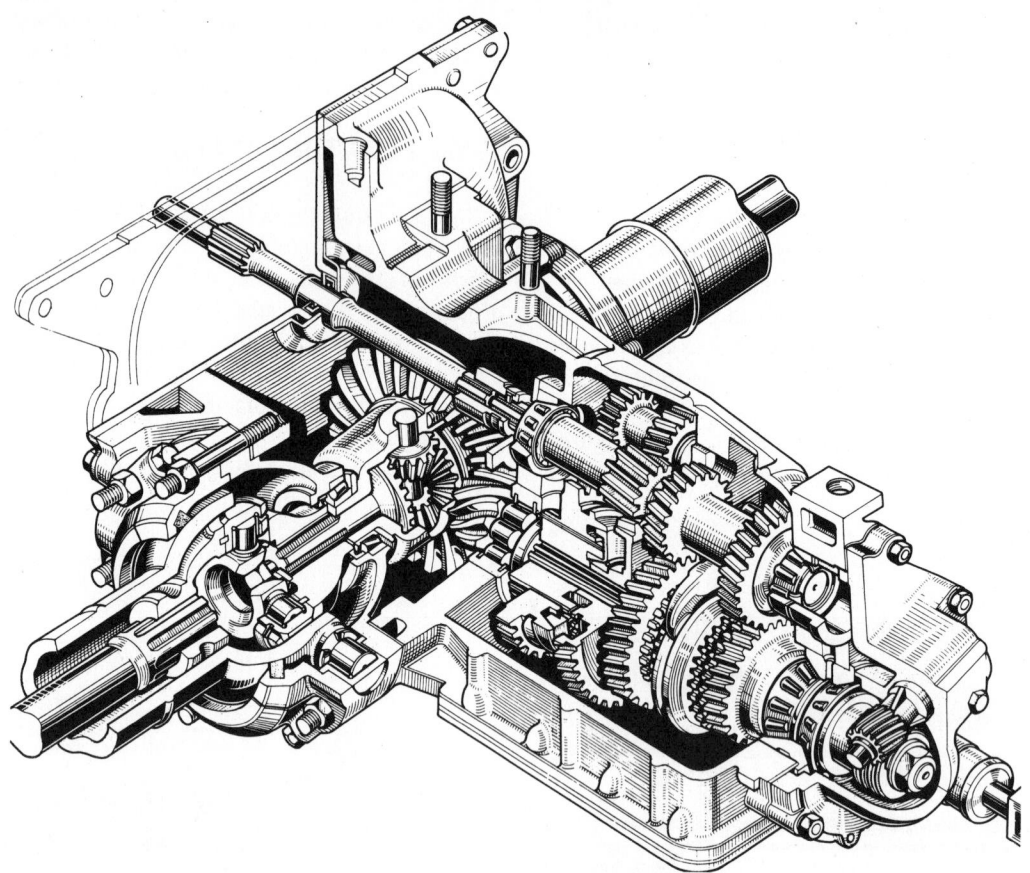

Fig. 46-42. Swing-type rear axles are used on Renault cars. In this design, inner end of each drive axle is fitted with a universal joint, outer end is not.

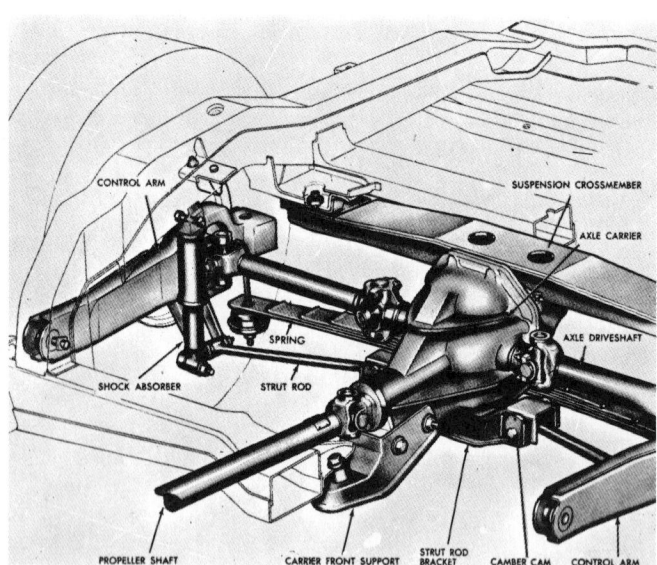

Fig. 46-43. Corvette rear suspension and drive line components show De Dion drive axle setup. In this concept, two universal joints are used on each drive axle.

joints (De Dion system), Fig. 46-43. One advantage of De Dion construction is that the weight of the differential is carried on the springs. On cars with swing axles — unlike De Dion suspension — the tread of the rear wheels varies as the wheels

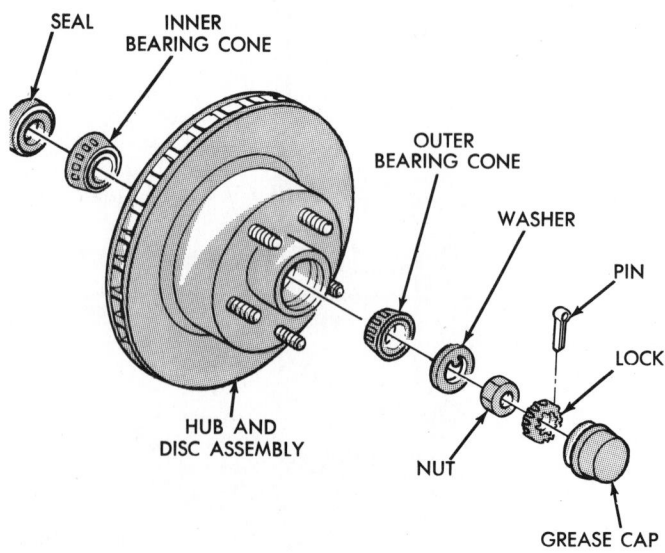

Fig. 46-44. Generally, passenger car front wheel assemblies have tapered roller bearings mated to races installed in both sides of hub and disc assembly and adjusted by a spindle nut.

INDEPENDENTLY SUSPENDED WHEELS

Independently suspended rear wheels may be hung on swing axles, Fig. 46-42, or on axle shafts using two universal

rise and fall. In some cases, the rear wheels may be toed-in or toed-out slightly, depending upon the angles of the axle supporting members.

Independent rear wheel suspension is popular in European-built automobiles, notably Volkswagen and Renault. U.S.-built Corvette also has independent rear wheel suspension.

The Oldsmobile Toronado and Cadillac Eldorado front wheel drive cars suspend the front wheels on drive shafts utilizing inner and outer universal joints on each side. See Fig. 46-13. Note that joint construction differs.

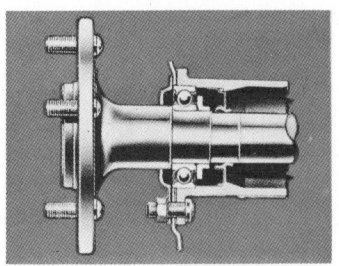

Fig. 46-45. Lighter vehicles sometimes have ball bearing assemblies installed on rear axle shafts and seated against a shoulder in axle housing.

WHEEL BEARINGS

Each front wheel hub ordinarily uses a pair of roller bearings, Fig. 46-44. The front wheels on some older cars, Chevrolet and Buick for example, are fitted with ball bearings. Straight and tapered roller bearings are used in the rear wheel assemblies of medium weight and heavier passenger cars, Figs. 46-40 and 46-41. Ball bearings are used in the rear wheels of lighter vehicles, Fig. 46-45.

Wheel bearing lubrication, service and adjustment are covered in the chapter on DRIVE LINE SERVICE.

INTEGRAL WHEEL BEARINGS

General Motors introduced integral wheel bearings on Oldsmobile Toronado, Buick Riviera and Cadillac Eldorado vehicles in 1979. Both front and rear ends of these cars feature integrated ball bearing assemblies, Fig. 46-46. The inner bearing races are combined with a conventional spindle. The outer bearing races are part of the hub/flange.

The spindle is bolted to a brake drum or disc brake rotor. The hub is bolted to the front steering knuckle or rear suspension arm.

The integral wheel bearings are lubricated for life. They are not adjustable. Failure calls for unit replacement.

FARM TRACTOR WHEEL BEARINGS

The wheel bearings, axle assemblies, differentials and gearing of wheel type farm and industrial tractors are quite similar to those used in automobiles and trucks. Service procedures and lubrication also are similar.

TRANSAXLES

When the transmission and rear axle differential are combined in one unit, it is called a "transaxle." Examples of this gear arrangement are shown in Fig. 46-47. In rear engine cars, it is customary to bolt the transaxle directly to the engine.

This method of construction has the advantage of providing an extremely rigid unit of engine and drive components. Misalignment is generally avoided and compactness is achieved. By mounting the differential to the frame in this manner, the weight of the differential assembly is above and supported by the car springs, and better riding qualities are obtained.

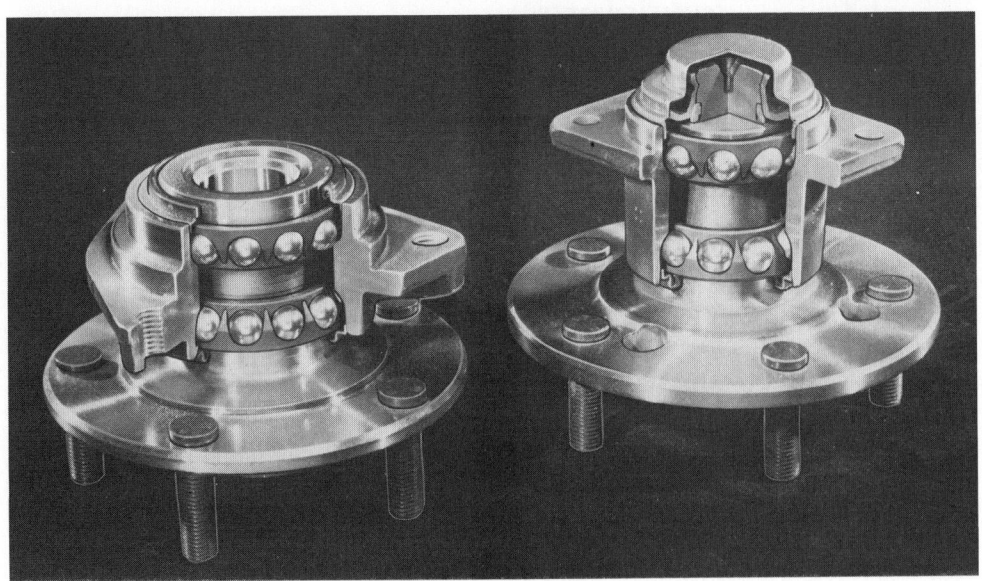

Fig. 46-46. General Motors eliminated another point of periodic maintenance when integral wheels bearings were introduced on several model lines.

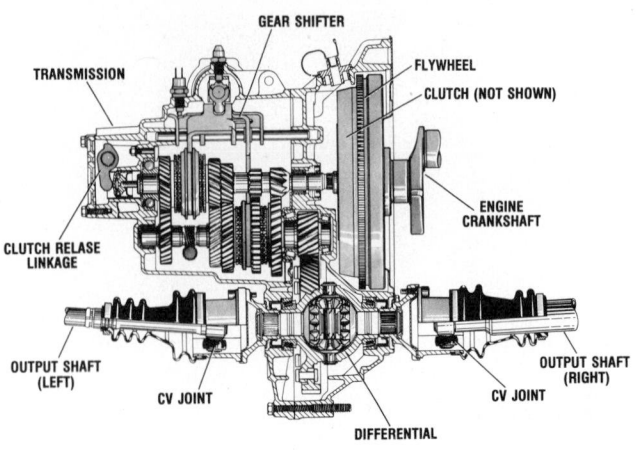

Fig. 46-47. Chrysler's four speed manual transaxle.

On front wheel drive cars, the transaxle is bolted to the rear of the crosswise engine and geared to the output shafts through an integral differential unit.

FOUR WHEEL DRIVE SYSTEMS

As the name implies, four wheel drive systems provide power to all four wheels. Usually, a shift lever is used to manually engage the four wheel drive unit for off-highway use,

then it is disengaged for road travel in rear wheel drive only. See Fig. 46-48.

These manually controlled four wheel drive systems have been around for a long time. They have been used extensively in military vehicles and trucks, giving exceptional mobility under adverse surface conditions. With many four wheel drive systems, however, power is not distributed through a differential. Both drive shafts operate at the same speed. As a result, the vehicle cannot be turned without sliding and scuffing the tires.

To overcome these handling and tire wear problems, some four wheel drive transfer cases incorporate a differential that is similar in operation to rear axle differentials. It compensates for different speeds of the front and rear axles. In this way, front and rear axles rotate at varying speeds while turning or operating over different terrains. It also permits four wheel drive on dry, hard surfaced highways.

AUTOMATIC FOUR WHEEL DRIVE

Automatic four wheel drive units are used on the AMC Eagle, Figs. 46-49 and 46-51, and on certain Jeep vehicles, Figs. 46-50 and 46-51. The Quadra-Trac system used on Jeeps is available in single range and dual range setups. A controlled type of limited slip differential in the drive system has a cone clutch biasing unit that allows each driving wheel to operate at its own speed.

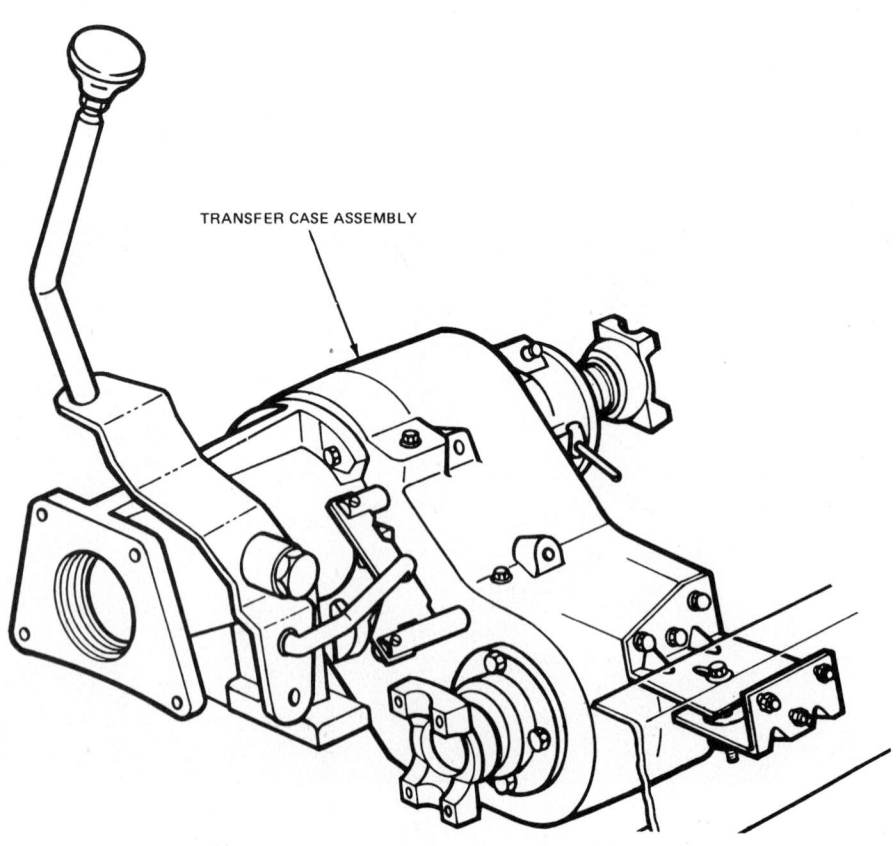

Fig. 46-48. Ford's basic four wheel drive unit.

The AMC Eagle automatic four wheel drive system, Model NP 119, has a single speed transfer case, Fig. 46-49. The transfer case utilizes a viscous coupling which acts as a limited slip differential, transmitting available torque to the axle with the best traction. A phantom elevated view of the AMC Eagle is shown in Fig. 46-51.

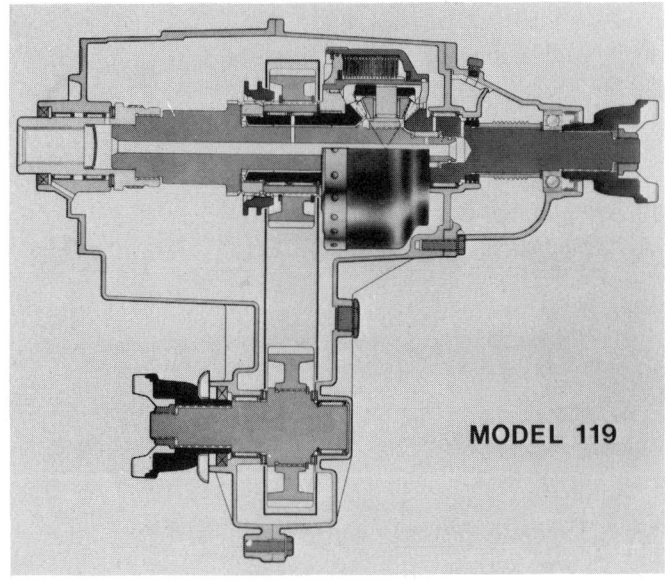

Fig. 46-49. The American Motors Eagle automatic four wheel drive transfer case uses a liquid silicone to act as a limited slip differential between the drives. The liquid silicone has a viscosity nearly the consistency of honey.

Fig. 46-50. Differential and chain drive are part of transfer case. (Warner Gear/ Warner Motive Div., Borg-Warner Corp.)

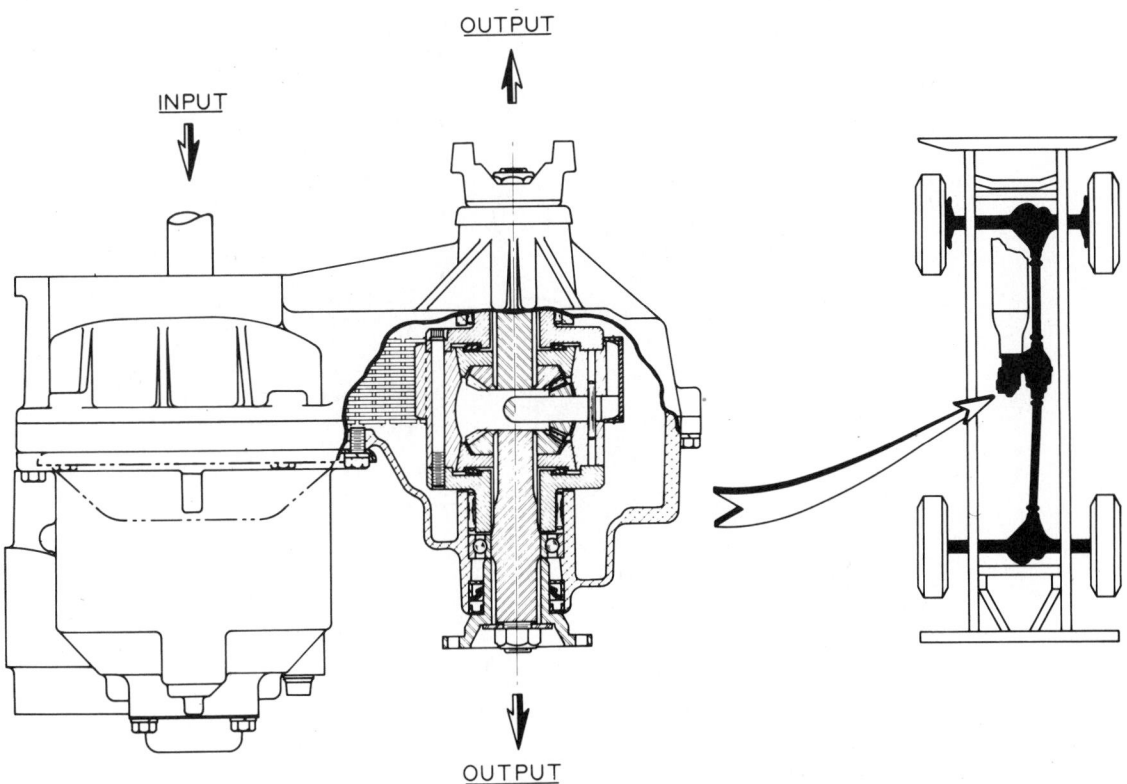

Fig. 46-51. Schematic of Quadra-Trac transfer case and its location on the vehicle.

REVIEW QUESTIONS — DRIVE LINE, UNIVERSAL JOINTS, DIFFERENTIAL

1. On acceleration, engine torque will cause the drive pinion shaft to:
   a. Dip.
   b. Raise.
2. Driving force is transmitted to the front of the rear springs on cars equipped with:
   a. Hotchkiss drive.
   b. Torque tube drive.
   c. Control arm drive.
3. Does the length of the drive shaft change while the car is being driven?
4. What is the purpose of a slip joint in the drive line?
5. Why are center bearings used on two-piece drive shafts?
   a. To support the front shaft.
   b. To support the rear shaft.
   c. To support the drive pinion.
6. With a conventional differential, does the wheel having better traction tend to turn faster than the wheel having poor traction?
7. Does a spiral bevel gear or a hypoid gear have the drive pinion shaft below the center of the ring gear?
8. Can the differential ring gear be moved toward and away from the drive pinion gear?
9. Can the drive pinion gear be raised or lowered vertically with regard to the ring gear?

10. What is meant by the term "preloading" a bearing?
11. A limited slip differential directs the power flow to the axle of the driving wheel having better traction. Yes or No?
12. With full-floating rear axles, the weight of the car is carried by:
    a. Axles.
    b. Control arms.
    c. Bearings and axle housing.
13. With semi-floating rear axles, the weight of the car is carried by:
    a. Axles and bearings.
    b. Control arms.
    c. Axle housing.
14. What is a "swing axle?"
15. How does a De Dion axle differ from a swing axle?
    a. Has no univeral joints.
    b. Has one universal joint.
    c. Has two universal joints.
16. Are rear wheels ever toed-in or toed-out?
17. What is meant by "straddle mounting?"
18. Why are constant velocity joints necessary?
19. Describe the difference between a two-speed differential and a double-reduction differential?
20. Does rear wheel tread ever vary on an automobile?

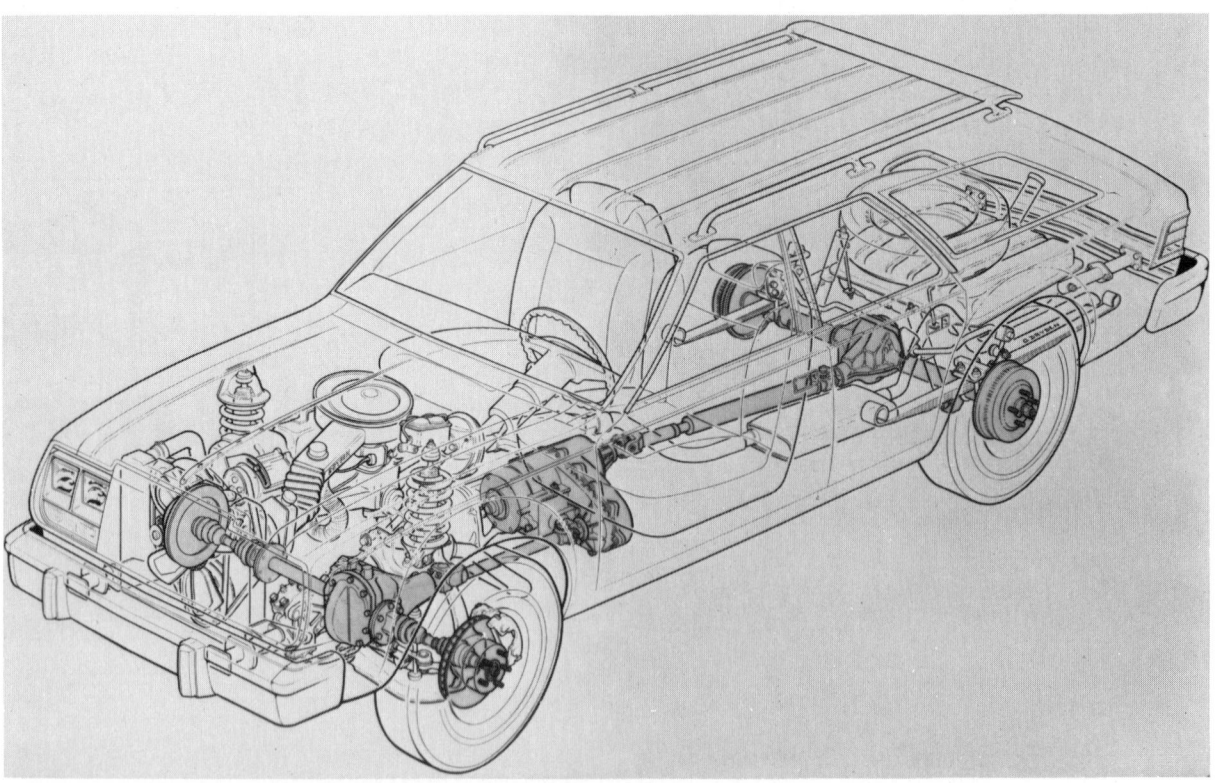

Fig. 46-51. Phantom view of Eagle shows automatic four wheel drive elements in shaded relief, including transfer case, drive shafts and drive axle assemblies. (American Motors)

DRIVE LINE
SERVICE

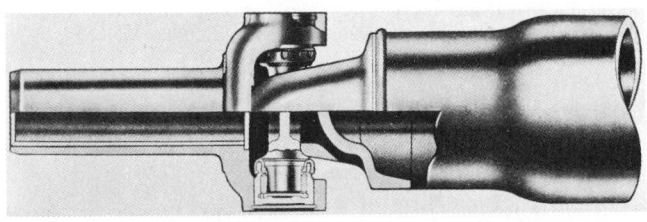

Fig. 47-1. Cross section of cross and roller universal joint, shows precise positioning of cross in bearing cups to maintain balance.

The drive shaft is a long part rotating at fluctuating speeds and operating at constantly changing angles. Therefore, it is susceptible to vibration. Add to this any lack of rotating balance and the result is a serious vibration that will shake the entire vehicle.

For example, a 1 oz. weight placed on a drive shaft 2 in. from the center of rotation will exert a force of 50 lb. at 3750 rpm. At that speed, this force will be exerted in opposite directions 62 1/2 times per second, causing a heavy vibration.

From this example, it is easy to see why all drive shafts must be balanced, properly mounted assemblies with all working parts lubricated by a special, high melting point lubricant. Even when the drive shaft is balanced, the flanges to which the universal joints are bolted must be machined true, and the spline machining must be accurate.

Also, on cross and roller joints, the cross must be centered within the bearing cups, Fig. 47-1. Some bearing assemblies are held in place by snap rings, others by trunnion straps. Recent GM joints have trunnions retained by a nylon material injected into a groove in the yoke, Fig. 47-2.

In any case, all parts must be "opposed identical pairs" to help maintain drive shaft balance. In addition, all bolts, washers, nuts, seals and retainers used to assemble the joints and flanges must be the same weight.

DRIVE SHAFT REQUIREMENTS

It follows, then, that drive shafts must be:
1. Carefully and accurately manufactured.
2. Correctly assembled.
3. Straight.

4. Balanced.
5. Properly mounted in the automobile.
6. Frequently checked.

Even when all these things are done, the shaft still can get out of balance when in use. Journal cross bearings can wear. Splines wear. Bolts and keys get loose. The drive shaft can become bent. Balance weights can fall off. Lubricant becomes misplaced or leaks out. Sometimes a drive shaft is thrown out of balance by careless spraying of undercoating.

New developments in universal joint design, Fig. 47-2, and

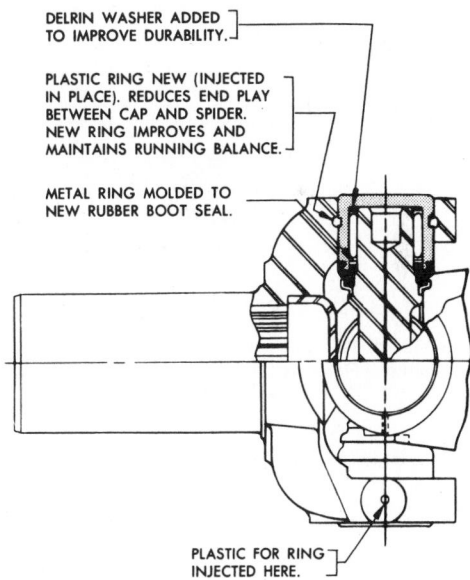

DELRIN WASHER ADDED TO IMPROVE DURABILITY.

PLASTIC RING NEW (INJECTED IN PLACE). REDUCES END PLAY BETWEEN CAP AND SPIDER. NEW RING IMPROVES AND MAINTAINS RUNNING BALANCE.

METAL RING MOLDED TO NEW RUBBER BOOT SEAL.

PLASTIC FOR RING INJECTED HERE.

Fig. 47-2. Improvements in universal joint design include tapered needle bearings for better load distribution.

the use of constant velocity joints, Fig. 47-3, have eliminated the need for regular maintenance service. The joints are prelubricated and sealed at the time of manufacture. However, the manufacturer does specify frequent inspections for universal joint wear or lubricant leakage.

If a universal joint becomes worn or noisy, a service kit must be installed. The kit consists of a cross with bearing cup assemblies and bearing retainer, Fig. 47-4.

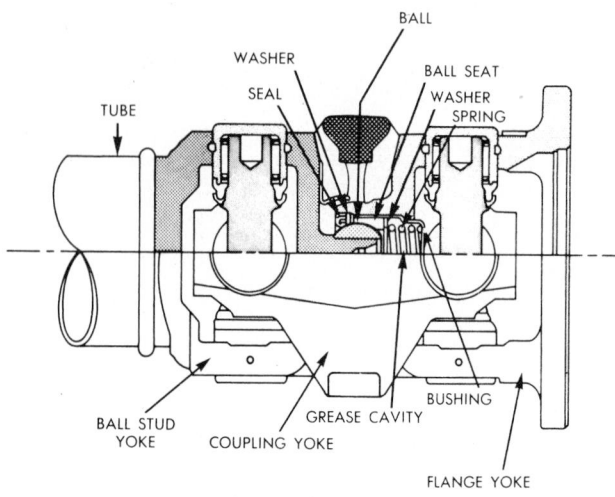

Fig. 47-3. Constant velocity joint is a double universal joint separated by a centering ball and phased to harmonize individual joint speed changes when rotating at an angle.

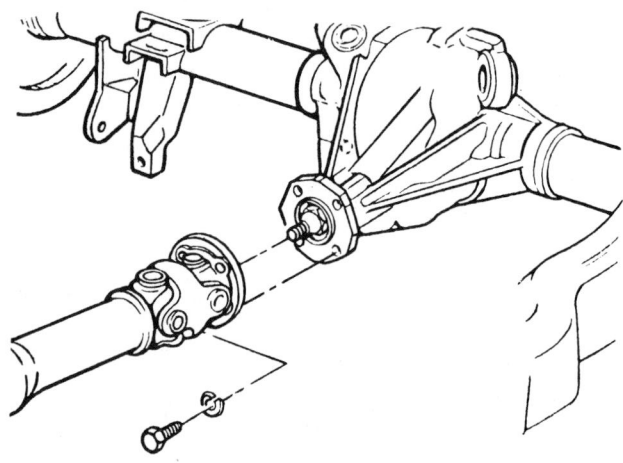

Fig. 47-5. Before removing drive shaft, mark companion flange and drive shaft to insure proper reinstallation.

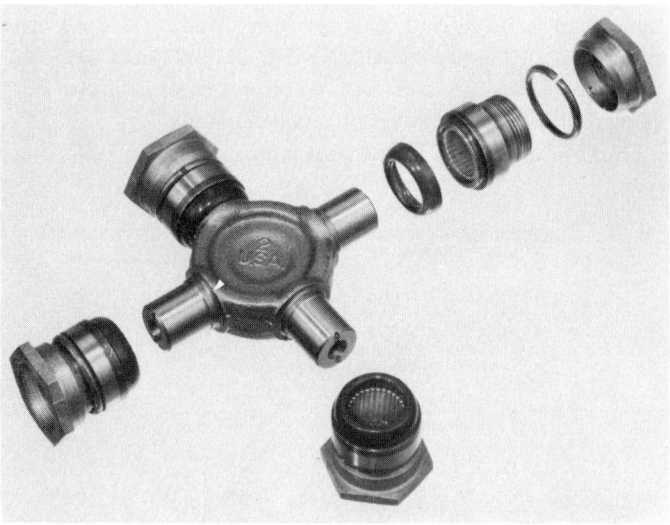

Fig. 47-4. This kit replaces GM's universal joints with injected nylon bearing retainers. Retainer clips hold new bearings in place.

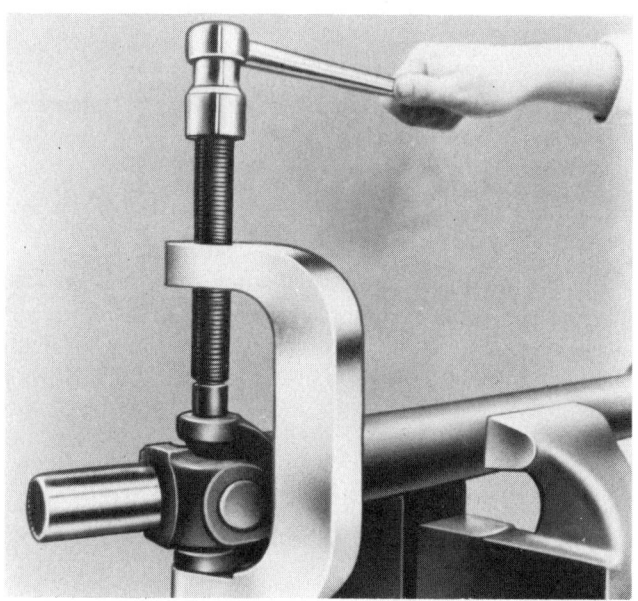

Fig. 47-6. Special universal joint pressing tools simplify bearing removal and installation of a new kit.

UNIVERSAL JOINT SERVICE

The drive shaft must be removed from the car to service or repair the universal joints. Mark the relationship of the yoke or companion flange to the drive shaft. Disconnect the rear universal joint by removing bearing straps or unscrewing bolts from the companion flange, Fig. 47-5. Then tape bearing caps, if necessary, and remove the drive shaft.

If a double drive shaft is used, handle it with care to avoid jamming the joints, and keep it in a relatively straight line. Clamp the drive shaft in a vise by the universal joint yoke.

Disassemble the universal joints by means of a special tool set or press, Fig. 47-6. Constant velocity joints, in particular, require special service equipment to do the job right. Inspect the bearing cups for wear, roughness, pitting or brinnelling (ripples). If wear or damage is evident, install a complete service kit.

Reassemble the drive shaft carefully, Fig. 47-7, to maintain balance. See that the newly installed joints operate freely in all directions. Tighten the attaching bolts to the proper torque value. Check the angularity of the drive shaft against the manufacturer's specifications, Fig. 47-18.

Angularity can be checked with a protractor or cable-and-bracket setup. With this gauge, a spring-loaded steel cable is stretched between the front of the chassis and the differential carrier. If the angle is correct, this cable will clear the underside of the pinion flange by a given amount. If not, shims or wedges must be added to the rear springs, Fig. 47-9.

CENTER BEARING SERVICE

The center bearing is usually attached to a cross member mounted between the left and right side rails of the frame.

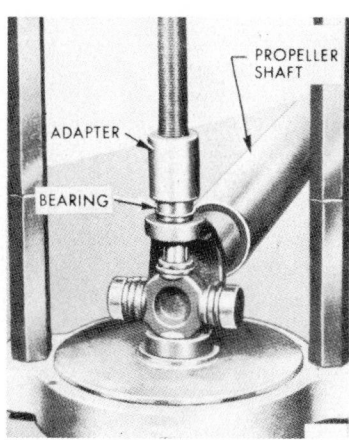

Fig. 47-7. A bench vise or press can be used to install kit parts in drive shaft. Bearing cups must be locked in place on cross.

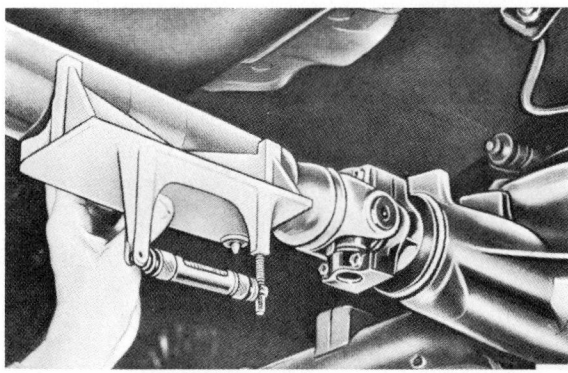

Fig. 47-8. A protractor will reveal rear universal joint angle, which is difference between drive shaft angle and tilt of differential housing.

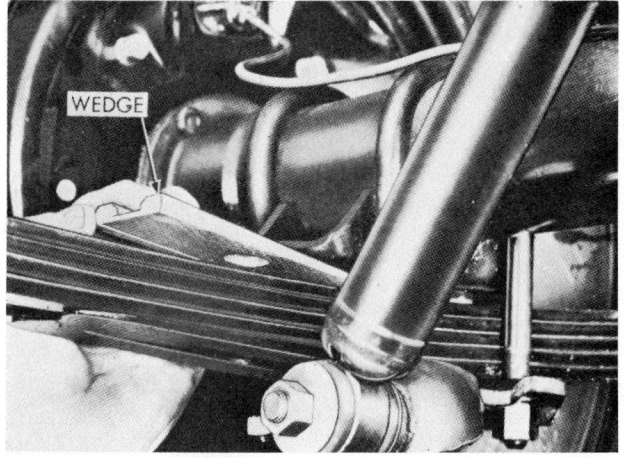

Fig. 47-9. If an adjustment of rear universal joint angle is necessary, add wedges or shims to rear spring to tilt differential housing.

Center bearings on older models are equipped with lubrication fittings. Most late models have prepacked bearings that do not require maintenance. If service is required, the center support can be disassembled by use of a special puller, Fig. 47-10.

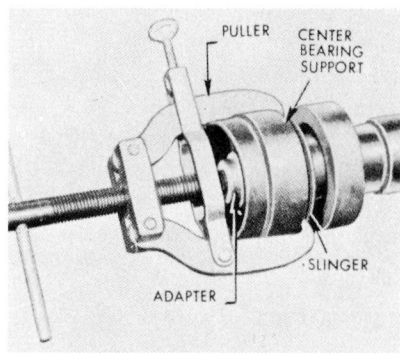

Fig. 47-10. With drive shaft held in vise, remove retaining nut and pull bearing from machined surface of shaft.

Fig. 47-11. Differential drive pinion and ring gear are mated to each other by lapping process to obtain proper contact of gear teeth.

DIFFERENTIAL REQUIREMENTS

Differentials are heavy-duty, precision-produced, mated-gear assemblies that generally do not require maintenance other than occasional lubricant. Because of the tremendous power transmitted through the differential assembly, the pressures involved are exceptionally high. The pressures are so high that considerable distortion of the heavy and, in most cases, hardened parts is bound to occur, Fig. 47-11. Because of the high standards of quietness demanded, adjustments must

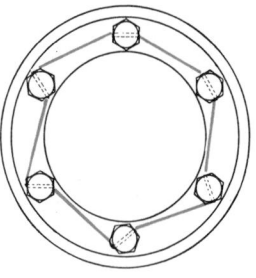

Fig. 47-12. Note that ring of cap screws is wired so that tension of lock wire is exerted in direction of tightening.

be made to extremely close dimensions and distortion under stress held to a minimum.

The differential housing, or case, is attached to the ring gear, and the entire propelling force is transmitted through this attachment. This calls for a tight union of parts, and several methods of assembly are used: cold riveting, hot riveting, bolts or cap screws. In any case, it is essential that the size of the holes is accurate, and that the rivets or bolts are a tight fit in the holes.

BOLT ATTACHMENT

If the ring gear is bolted to the case, the bolts are machined to an accurate diameter and the holes are drilled and reamed to correct size for a tight fit. The nuts on the bolts are then drawn up to specified torque tightness and securely locked, Fig. 47-12.

If cap screws are used, the holes in the ring gear are threaded before the gear is hardened. The threads on the cap screw do not extend into the holes in the differential case, and the cap screw often has a shoulder between the threads and the head. This shoulder is finished to a size that fits tightly in the holes in the differential case.

TROUBLES AND REMEDIES

Service problems are usually limited to lubricant leakage at the drive pinion oil seal or noisy operation of the differential.

To replace the drive pinion oil seal:

1. Disconnect rear universal joint.
2. Remove drive pinion flange nut, washer and flange.
3. Use a special seal puller to remove pinion oil seal.

Reassemble in reverse order, but observe the following precautions:

1. Install oil seal with sealing lip facing lubricant.
2. Coat OD of seal body with nonhardening sealing compound.
3. Use correct driving tool to bottom seal against shoulder in rear axle housing.
4. Make sure machined bearing surface of pinion flange is not worn, scored or nicked in area where it rotates against seal.
5. Tighten drive pinion nut to original position, plus 1/8 turn to preload pinion bearings (typical).
6. Refill rear axle housing to correct level with recommended lubricant, Fig. 47-13.

Noisy operation of a differential unit is usually caused by worn or damaged gears or bearings. However, a thorough test should be made to pinpoint where the noise is coming from: rear axle assembly; rough road surface; under-inflated tires, or tires with unevenly worn tread; front or rear wheel bearings; engine or transmission. Noises telegraph to other parts of the car, so establishing the source of the noise is of first importance.

If the differential assembly is noisy, check for: low level of lubricant in rear axle housing; excessive backlash between teeth of the drive pinion gear and ring gear; looseness of pinion bearings. Removal and complete disassembly of the differential unit probably is required.

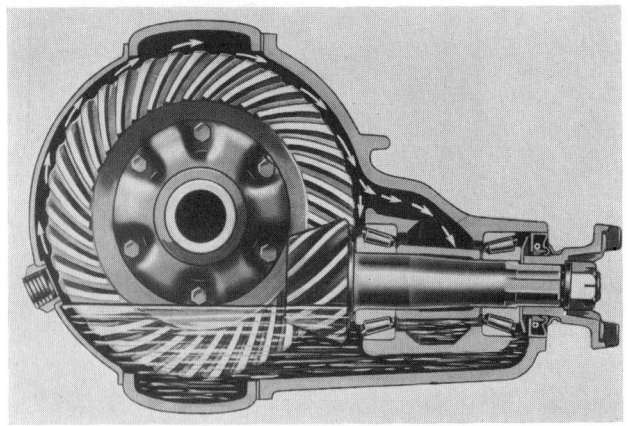

Fig. 47-13. Rotation of ring gear distributes lubricant to all gears and bearings, if lubricant level is maintained at lower edge of filler hole.

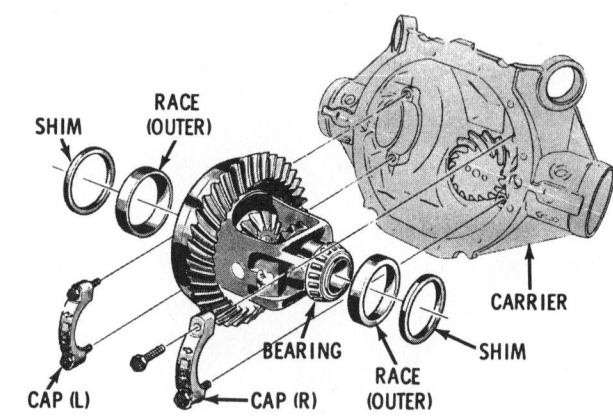

Fig. 47-14. Partially exploded view of Oldsmobile differential case and bearings. Note importance of marking caps before disassembly.

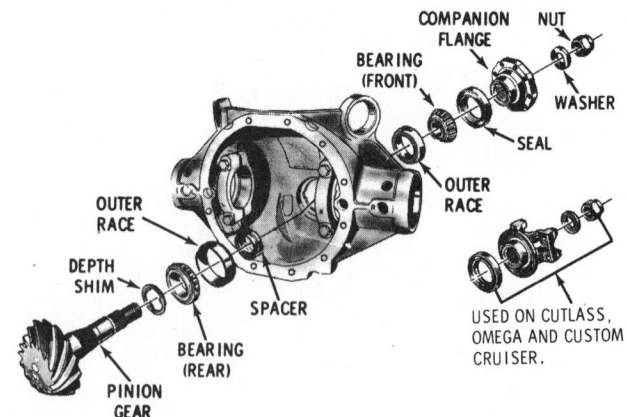

Fig. 47-15. Oldsmobile pinion gear and bearings are shown in sequence of assembly. Note two different types of universal joint attachment.

INSPECTION

When disassembling the differential, Figs. 47-14 and 47-15, be sure to mark mating parts so that they can be reassembled on the correct side and in the proper position. For example, mark the two halves of the differential case, the two bearing adjusters, etc. Since the gears and bearings are a press fit, in many cases, avoid the use of hammers and drifts. Use a suitable press or puller to prevent chipping of hardened parts and distortion of other parts.

After the parts have been disassembled and thoroughly cleaned, carefully inspect them for scuffed surfaces, cracks, warpage or any other visible defects. If the surfaces of the gear teeth are scratched or scuffed, the gears must be replaced. If there are any cracks visible in the differential case, the case should be replaced. If the differential pinion bushings or shaft are worn or loose, new parts are required.

Pay particular attention to the pinion shaft and differential side bearings. Check the shaft or housings on which, and in which, the bearings seat. The inside cone of the bearings must be a tight fit on the shaft or housing upon which they are mounted. The outer race or cone must be a snug fit in the housing in which it seats. No looseness can be tolerated. The bearings must not show any indication of wear. The races and rollers or balls and cups must be absolutely smooth and polished on the contact surfaces.

Hardened antifriction bearings are used. No other type of bearing could stand the speeds and pressures and continue to maintain correct alignment of the gears. Such high standards of manufacture deserve equally high standards of careful work and adjustment when repairs are made.

REASSEMBLY AND ADJUSTMENT

When reassembling, use new shims, spacers, washers, gaskets and oil seals. Lock all cap screws in place, either by locking strips or soft steel wire, Fig. 47-12. Thoroughly clean the inside of the housing of all grease and oil to make sure that no metal chips or abrasive material is left inside to be circulated by the lubricant.

The manufacturer's instructions concerning whether or not the bearings are to be preloaded, and how much, are needed for proper assembly. Also required is the method of adjusting gear contact by measurement with special gauges or micrometers. Necessary, too, are specifications on the amount of torque to be applied to all the bolts and nuts. When ball bearings are used, make sure that the thrust side of the bearing is correctly placed to handle endwise thrust in the proper direction.

Two adjustments can be made which will affect tooth contact pattern: backlash and the position of the drive pinion in relation to the ring gear.

Backlash is adjusted by means of side bearing adjusters, Fig. 47-16, or bearing adjusting shims, Fig. 47-17, which move the entire case and ring gear assembly closer to, or farther from, the drive pinion. To increase backlash, remove shims from ring gear side and install them on pinion side. To reduce backlash, reverse this procedure.

The position of the drive pinion is adjusted by increasing or decreasing the shim thickness between the pinion head and the inner face of the rear pinion bearing, Fig. 47-17. Adding shims will move it closer to the center line of the ring gear; removing shims will move the pinion farther away, Fig. 47-18.

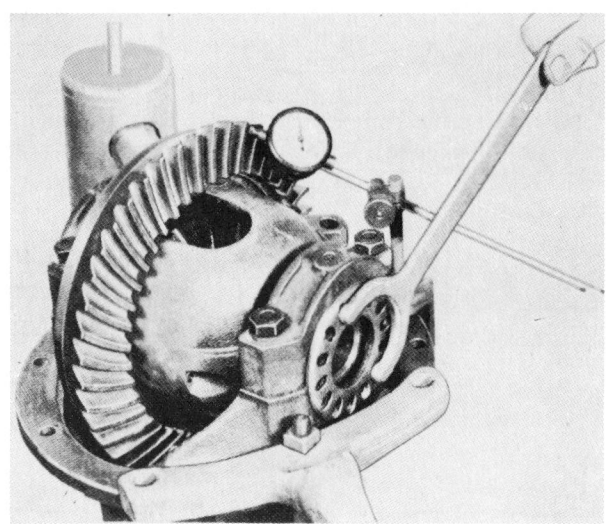

Fig. 47-16. Special adjusting tools are provided to set correct position of ring gear and preload of differential side bearings.

While specifications for these adjustments are usually available, in an emergency adjust the bearings so that there is no perceptible movement of the shaft, yet no bind in the bearing. Check the tooth contact with red lead and oil, and move the pinion gear and ring gear experimentally until the proper contact is obtained, Fig. 47-18. Tighten all bolts and nuts gradually and equally to reasonable tightness if torque specifications are not available.

Correct adjustment of hypoid gears is of paramount

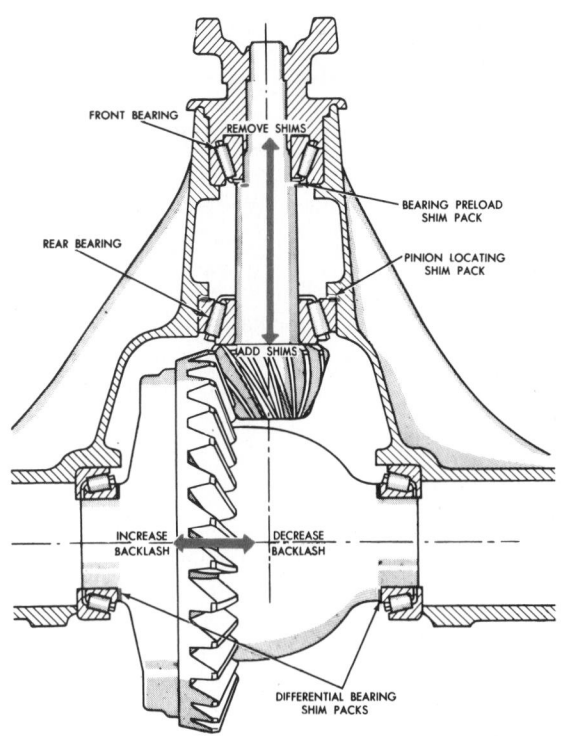

Fig. 47-17. Some differential designs demand placement of shims under side bearings to position ring gear for correct tooth contact.

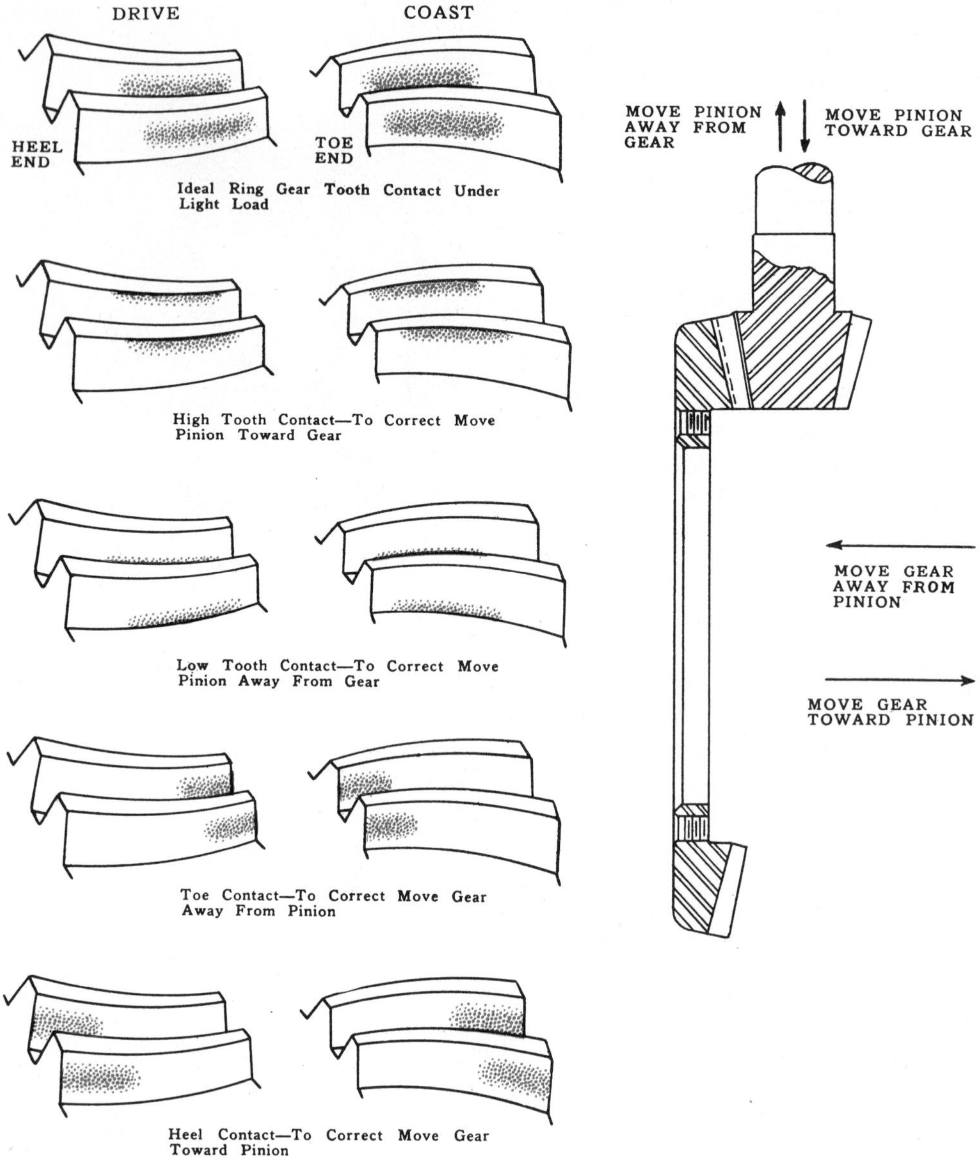

DRIVE   COAST

MOVE PINION   MOVE PINION
AWAY FROM   TOWARD GEAR
GEAR

HEEL   TOE
END   END

Ideal Ring Gear Tooth Contact Under
Light Load

High Tooth Contact—To Correct Move
Pinion Toward Gear

Low Tooth Contact—To Correct Move
Pinion Away From Gear

MOVE GEAR
AWAY FROM
PINION

MOVE GEAR
TOWARD PINION

Toe Contact—To Correct Move Gear
Away From Pinion

Heel Contact—To Correct Move Gear
Toward Pinion

Fig. 47-18. Pattern of ring gear tooth contact is shown along with corrective steps required to provide ideal contact.

importance because they will often wear excessively without making any noise. There is such a pronounced wiping action between the gear teeth, they can overheat and gall very quickly unless correctly adjusted and lubricated by a special hypoid lubricant.

GEAR LUBRICATION

Proper lubrication is of utmost importance. The straight bevel and spur gears were successfully lubricated with a heavy mineral gear oil. When spiral bevel gears were adopted, it was found necessary to add some ingredients to the oil to enable it to withstand the high pressure sliding or wiping action of the gear teeth.

With the adoption of hypoid gears, the sliding action was greatly increased, and previously used straight gear oils and extreme pressure gear oils were found inadequate. Special

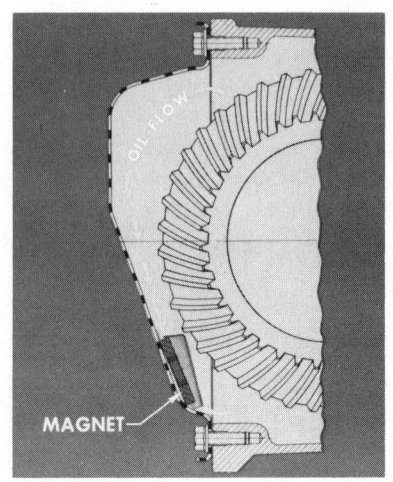

Fig. 47-19. Built-in magnet in differential is innovation by General Motors to attract and remove metal chips from gear lubricant.

622

hypoid lubricants were developed and must be used with these gears. The vehicle manufacturer furnishes specific recommendations for type of lubricant, proper level and frequency of change.

Note from Fig. 47-13 that the ring gear acts as a circulating pump to distribute the lubricant over the gear teeth and to the bearings. Since the oil is in constant circulation when the vehicle is in motion, any abrasive material or metal chips will be promptly carried to the working surfaces. If abrasive, undue wear of gear teeth and bearings will occur. If a metal chip goes through the gears, it will probably break gear teeth, spring parts out of alignment, or both. Care must be exercised to keep the oil clean before and during refilling. Some late model GM cars utilize a magnet to attract chips, Fig. 47-19.

TRANSAXLE LUBRICATION

In transaxles, the differential unit is combined with either a manual or automatic transmission. While some types of gearing require an extreme pressure type of lubricant, this lubricant is unsuited to other types of gears. Whether or not the transmission and differential are interconnected, there is always the possibility that lubricant will seep or leak from one unit to the other.

For these reasons, it is absolutely essential to follow the manufacturer's instructions when adding to or replacing lubricant in a transaxle.

WHEEL BEARING LUBRICATION

While some rear wheel bearings are automatically lubricated by oil creeping along the axle shaft from the differential, others are sealed off and require separate lubrication. The manufacturer supplies lubrication charts which should be followed both as to type of lubricant and frequency of lubrication.

Front wheel bearings call for the use of a special wheel bearing grease. This is a short fiber grease with a high melting point. The high melting point is essential because the brake drums surrounding the wheel bearings get hot, sometimes approaching 700 deg. F. Not all this heat is applied to the wheel bearings, but a considerable amount is absorbed by the hubs. If the grease melts, it may get by the oil seal and ruin the brake linings.

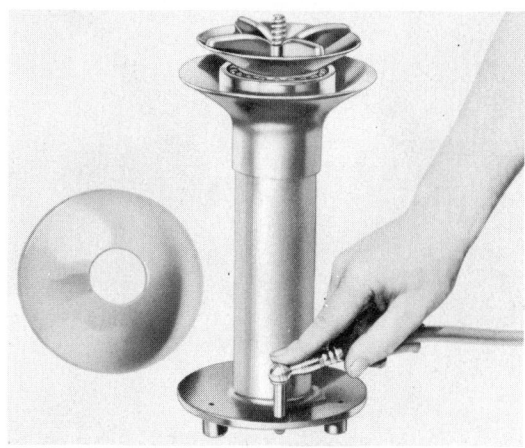

Fig. 47-21. Bearing packers do a thorough job of forcing grease under pressure through and around rollers.

In this connection, front wheel bearings are often overfilled. The hubs and hubcaps should not be packed full of grease. Fig. 47-20 shows a properly packed front wheel hub. The bearings are packed by hand or by use of a bearing packer, Fig. 47-21. A reserve is placed in the hub. When the proper type of grease is used, this method provides adequate lubrication.

WHEEL BEARING SERVICE

A defective rear wheel bearing can be replaced by removal of the rear axle on the side affected. Pull the old bearing from the machined surface of the axle shaft and press on the replacement bearing until it bottoms against a shoulder on the shaft, Fig. 47-22. Always install a new oil seal when an axle shaft is removed.

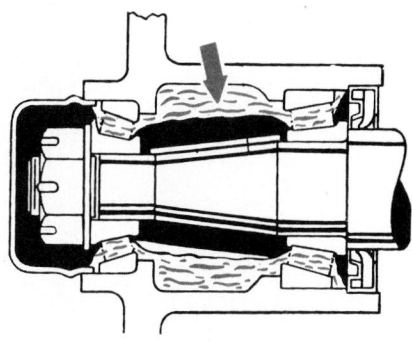

Fig. 47-20. Front wheel bearings should be packed with special short fiber lubricant. Note small reserve supply packed in hub.

Fig. 47-22. A press must be used to force old bearing from rear axle shaft. New bearing should be "bottomed" against shoulder on shaft.

Constant velocity joint used on late model GM cars has recessed fitting for lubricating centering ball.

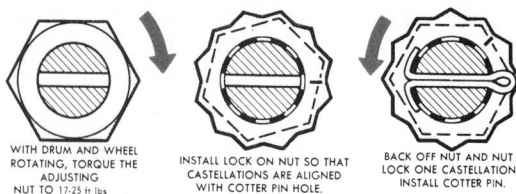

Fig. 47-23. Spindle nut torque seats wheel bearings, then nut is backed off to hole in spindle. Ford specifications are shown.

Front wheel bearings require occasional repacking with grease. Remove the old bearings from the hub and inspect them carefully for wear, score marks, pits, nicks and discolor-

ation from overheating.

Replace a faulty bearing and race as an assembly: Press old race from hub. Clean hub and spindle thoroughly (never add grease, some wheel bearing greases are not compatible). Install a new race. Apply a light coating of wheel bearing grease to wheel spindle and inside of wheel hub, Fig. 47-20. Make certain bearing assemblies are free to creep on spindle of steering knuckle. Pack roller bearings with wheel bearing grease, by hand or by special packer, Fig. 47-21. Install a new oil seal and place wheel on spindle. Adjust spindle nut to provide zero preload or end play according to manufacturer's specifications, Fig. 47-23.

REVIEW QUESTIONS – DRIVE LINE SERVICE

1. The drive shaft must be removed from the car to service or repair universal joints. True or False?
2. Angularity of the drive shaft is usually checked with a:
   a. Pinion setting gauge.
   b. Universal joint tester.
   c. Protractor.
3. What is the best way to "hold" a drive shaft for servicing?
   a. Clamp drive shaft tube in vise.
   b. Clamp universal joint yoke in vise.
   c. Clamp end of drive shaft in vise.
4. Give three noises that could be incorrectly diagnosed as differential noise.
5. Noisy operation of a differential is usually caused by:
   a. Worn or loose drive pinion bearings.
   b. Rough or maladjusted differential side bearings.
   c. Damaged differential pinion gears.
6. What is the correct level of lubricant in a differential housing?
7. Why do hypoid gears require a special type of lubricant?
8. How can the ring gear and pinion be checked for proper tooth contact?
9. What two methods are used to adjust backlash between the ring gear and pinion?
10. What type of grease is used to lubricate most front wheel bearings?
    a. Long fiber.
    b. Short fiber.
    c. Extreme pressure.
11. Always replace a faulty front wheel bearing and race as an assembly. True or False?
12. Why is a permanent magnet built into some General Motors differentials?
13. The differential housing, or case, is attached to the ring gear by one of several methods. Name three.
14. The drive shaft is a long part rotating at fluctuating speeds and operating at constantly changing _____.
15. Before removing a drive shaft for service, mark the relationship of the _____ or _____ to the drive shaft.
16. A _____ joint is, in effect, a double universal joint.

AUTOMOBILE
AIR CONDITIONING

The history of automotive air conditioning, in terms of cooling by refrigeration, dates back to a few buses in the late 1930s and a few thousand Packards in the early 1940s. Now, about three-fourths of the cars ordered each new model year are equipped with factory-installed air conditioning, and over a half-million "hang-on" units per year are installed in the field.

Air conditioning system service is no longer a mysterious, infrequent service operation. It has become a regular maintenance, service and/or repair assignment in most garages, service stations and specialty shops.

FUNDAMENTALS OF REFRIGERATION

Air conditioning is the process by which surrounding air is cooled and dehumidified. In an automobile, this process is performed by a closed refrigeration system that circulates

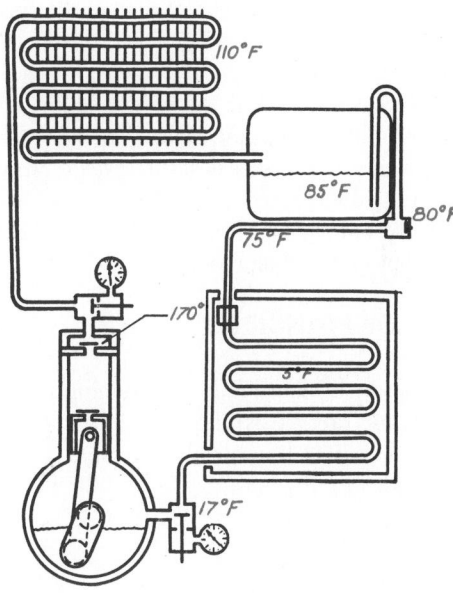

Fig. 48-2. Refrigeration process is based on thermal law that fluids absorb heat while changing from a liquid to a gas, and give up heat in changing from a gas to a liquid. Note variation in refrigerant temperature throughout each refrigeration cycle.

refrigerant under pressure. See Fig. 48-1. While making its rounds, the refrigerant cycles from gas to liquid to gas, absorbing heat from the warm air inside the passenger compartment and discharging it to outside air, Fig. 48-2.

Changes from a liquid to a gas are often accomplished by means of heat and evaporation. Heat, for example, causes water to boil and sends vapor (gas) into the air.

This same vapor can be returned to liquid form (water) by cooling and condensation. If a glass of cold water is placed in a warm room, the warm air collects on the outside of the glass, becomes cooler and condenses into water.

This transformation of liquid into gas and gas into liquid occurs at atmospheric pressure. Higher pressures can also be used to reduce a gas to liquid form. "Bottled gas" for the home and liquefied petroleum gas (LP Gas) for engines are examples of pressure used for this purpose.

Basically, automotive air conditioning systems operate on these principles of evaporation and condensation. In the

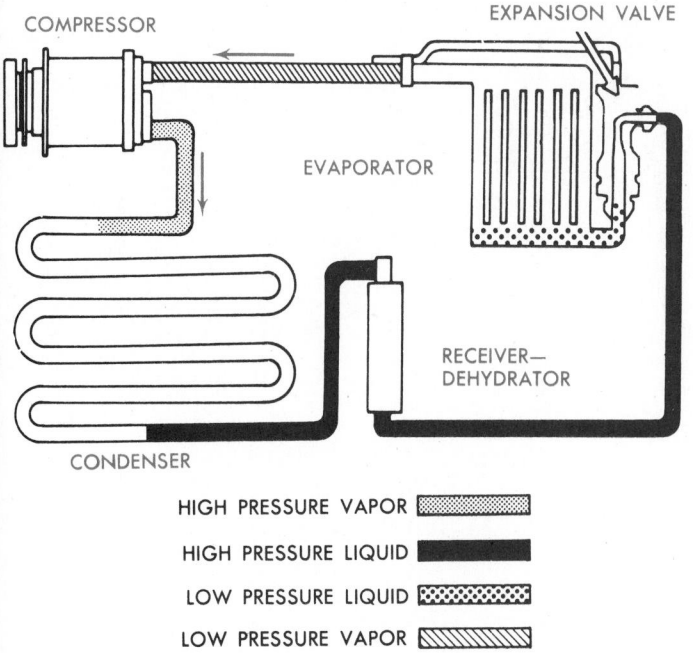

HIGH PRESSURE VAPOR

HIGH PRESSURE LIQUID

LOW PRESSURE LIQUID

LOW PRESSURE VAPOR

Fig. 48-1. Schematic depicits typical refrigerant circuit in automobile air conditioning system. Refrigerant is a liquid in black high pressure area, then becomes a vapor in lighter low pressure area.

passenger-compartment end of the system, the liquid refrigerant is sprayed into an evaporator where it vaporizes. At the other end, refrigerant gas is pumped into the condenser where it condenses into a liquid.

These two key steps directly relate to principles stated in this two-part thermal law:

1. A fluid will absorb heat when it changes from a liquid to a gas. This process occurs in the evaporator, which is placed in the passenger compartment specifically for the purpose of removing heat.
2. A fluid will give off heat when it changes from a gas to a liquid. This principle is put to use in the condenser, which generally is positioned in the airstream in front of the engine cooling system radiator.

Each of these principles is utilized in automotive air conditioning by a series of major components, connected by tubing and hoses, and actuated by a belt-driven compressor that pressurizes the refrigerant.

Five major elements do the job of circulating, condensing and vaporizing the refrigerant. These include compressor, condenser, receiver-drier, thermostatic expansion valve and evaporator, Fig. 48-3. Each is equally important. A malfunction of any one element will interrupt the heat transfer cycle and disrupt system operation.

A MATTER OF PRINCIPLE

Here is how an automotive air conditioning system works:
1. Hot refrigerant vapor (gas) is drawn into the compressor, where the gas is placed under high pressure and is pumped into the condenser, Fig. 48-1.

2. In the condenser, a change occurs as intake air passing through the core removes heat from the refrigerant vapor as it changes to its liquid state.
3. The refrigerant, having done its job of discharging the heat, then flows into the receiver-drier where it is filtered, demoisturized and stored for use as required to meet cooling needs. Also, see CCOT PRINCIPLES.
4. As the compressor continues to draw refrigerant vapor from the outlet side of the evaporator, liquid refrigerant under high pressure is circulated from the receiver-drier to the thermostatic expansion valve.
5. The expansion valve then meters the refrigerant into the inlet side of the evaporator.
6. Pressure drops at this point in the system as the refrigerant, suddenly released to the broad area of the evaporator coils, vaporizes and absorbs heat from the air in the passenger compartment.
7. This heat-laden refrigerant vapor is then drawn into the compressor to start another refrigeration cycle.

In operation, the refrigerant constantly recycles in the sealed system from a gas to a liquid to a gas. Meanwhile, heat in the passenger compartment is constantly being absorbed by the refrigerant and carried away under pressure to be given off to the atmosphere. So, in effect, the automotive air conditioning system is a heat transfer unit, cooling the air by removing the heat.

However, to better understand how an air conditioner works, you need to know the nature of heat, the affect of heat and pressure on the state of matter, how heat is transferred from one object to another, and how cooling action is accomplished.

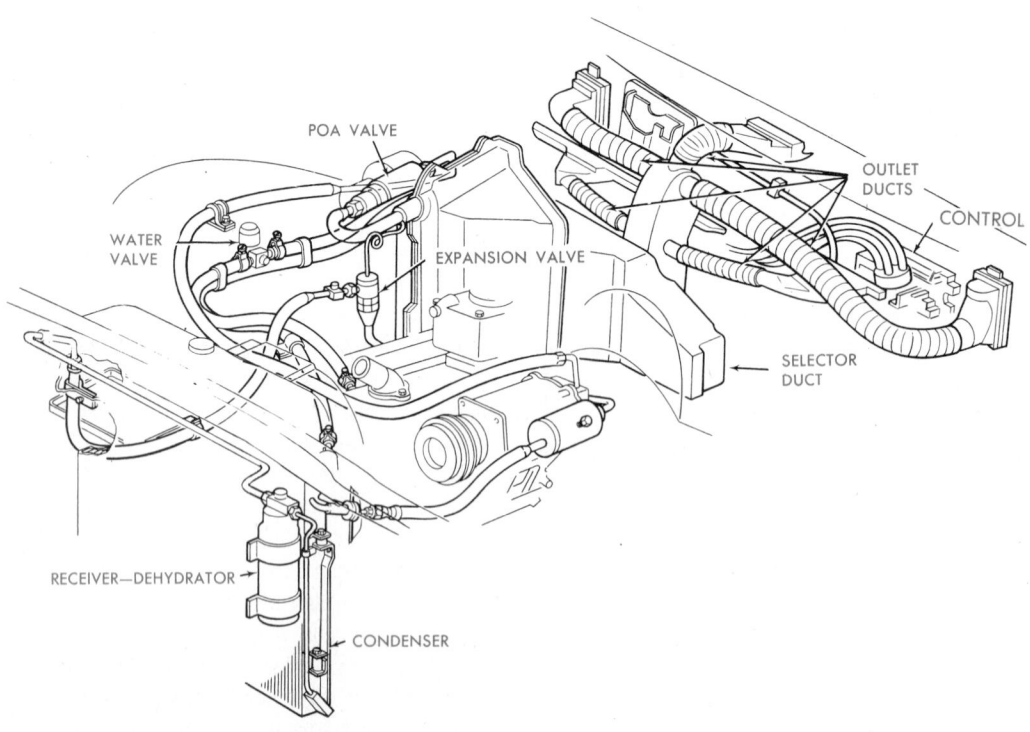

Fig. 48-3. Layout of typical Chevrolet air conditioning system includes identification of major components, connecting hoses and metal lines, controls, ducts and related heater water valve.

NATURE OF HEAT

Specifically, the words hot and cold are relative terms that refer to the degree of heat that is present. An object or thing is considered to be hot or cold only when it is related to something else.

If an exhaust manifold is "hot to the touch," it merely is hotter than the hand of the person touching it. If an auto shop is said to be "cold," the air within it simply contains less heat than does the air in a comfortably warm room. All these terms relate to the presence of heat. Cold refers only to the degree that heat is absent.

Actually, heat is a form of energy that has no substance. It is contained in all matter to some degree of intensity or concentration. Because of this characteristic, it is termed "sensible heat" or "temperature," which can be measured on a thermometer.

Based on the fact that heat stimulates matter, it logically follows that heat can be used to change the state of matter. Whether it is in a solid state, a liquid state or a gaseous state, matter will change if some outside source is used to add or remove enough heat.

How fast matter will change its state, and the temperature at which it changes, depends on the makeup and movement of its molecules. Ice, for example, is matter in a solid state. It will melt at 33 deg. F and become water, a liquid state. Water will boil at 212 deg. F and become steam, a gaseous state.

HEAT TRANSFER

An unusual characteristic of heat is that it always flows (transfers) from hotter to cooler objects by one or more of three methods: conduction, convection or radiation.

Conduction of heat is the condition when a solid object gradually heats up particle-by-particle. Metal objects heat by conduction and are considered to be good thermal conductors. Copper, for example, is used in air conditioner condensers so that the heat will readily transfer from the refrigerant, to the copper coils and fins, to the air.

Convection of heat occurs in liquids and gases as heated portions rise and are displaced by cooler portions, creating a convection current. Convection of heat takes place, for example, when a furnace circulates heated air within a room.

Radiation is the transfer of heat by waves through space, such as rays of the sun. Actually, anything heated gives off radiated energy. It may be reflected (by a car painted a light color); or, it may be absorbed (by a car painted a dark color).

COMFORT CONSIDERATIONS

In dealing with human comfort, other things besides actual temperature must be considered:
1. Humidity control.
2. Air movement and circulation.
3. Air filtering, cleaning and purification.

The amount of humidity in the air affects the rate of evaporation of perspiration. If the air contains much moisture, one may feel uncomfortable even if the air is relatively cool.

Air circulation is also important because if cool, dry air is moved past a warm body, radiation of heat from the body will increase.

Air filtering, cleaning and purification is also necessary to keep out dust, eliminate smoke and odors, and add to comfort. For these reasons, it is necessary to consider factors other than the actual temperature attained if an air conditioning system can be expected to operate efficiently and satisfactorily.

REQUIREMENTS OF THE REFRIGERANT

The ability to absorb and discharge heat is the prime requirement of any refrigerant. With its high boiling point, water is not suitable for use as a refrigerant. Refrigerant—12 (R—12), on the other hand, boils at -22 deg. F and absorbs heat readily. How readily can be shown in terms of how much heat is required to cause a substance to change from one state to another without changing its temperature.

Consider that the amount of heat being applied to or being given off by any object is measured in British thermal units (Btu). As established, one Btu is the amount of heat required to raise the temperature of a pound of water one degree Fahrenheit at sea level pressure.

The basic Btu measurement can be used to illustrate how well R—12 serves as a refrigerant:
1. In order to change water to steam at 212 deg. F, each pound of water must absorb 970 Btu.
2. To change R-12 to a vapor at 5 deg. F, only 69.5 Btu per pound are needed.

The ability to change its state easily and repeatedly, yet maintain good stability in either state, is what makes R—12 especially well suited for repeated recycling within the air conditioning system, Fig. 48-2.

Another point in R—12's favor is its instantaneous reaction to pressure. An increase in pressure will raise the boiling point of a liquid, while a drop in pressure will lower the boiling point. Water at atmospheric pressure will boil at 212 deg. F. Under 20 psi pressure, water will boil at 258 deg. F. R—12 at atmospheric pressure will boil at -22 deg. F. Under 20 psi pressure, it will boil at +19 deg. F.

This pressure-temperature relationship works well with R—12 in the system, Fig. 48-4. By changing the pressure on the refrigerant, its temperature can be controlled. This, in turn, controls how much heat the refrigerant can absorb, and how readily it rids itself of the heat when the tubing carrying the refrigerant is exposed to outside air.

The value of this pressure-temperature relationship lies in the fact that pressure tests made on the "low side" will reveal the refrigerant temperature at this point in the system. For example, if the pressure reading on the low side is 30 psi, the temperature of the evaporator coils and fins will be down near the 32 deg. F mark. So you immediately know that the air conditioning system is running efficiently enough to cool the passenger compartment.

As a rule of thumb, the temperature goes up about one degree for each pound of increased pressure on the low side of the system. See Fig. 48-4. The objective of automotive air

PRESSURE-TEMPERATURE CHART
NORMAL OPERATING RANGES

LOW-SIDE GAUGE READING	EVAPORATOR TEMPERATURE
14	10
16	14
18	18
20	20
22	22
24	24
26	27
28	29
30	32

HIGH-SIDE GAUGE READING	AMBIENT TEMPERATURE DEG. F
150—170	80
165—185	85
175—195	90
185—205	95
210—230	100
230—250	105
250—270	110

Fig. 48-4. Temperature-pressure relationship of Refrigerant—12 is charted. If low-side reading is 30 psi, evaporating temperature is 32 deg. F; which is effectively low enough to absorb heat from a 72 deg. F passenger compartment.

conditioning, then, is to get the refrigerant temperature low enough so the evaporator will reach its coldest point without icing up. See Fig. 48-2.

THE WORKING PARTS, AND HOW THEY FUNCTION

A typical automotive air conditioning system consists of five major components: compressor, condenser, receiver-drier, thermostatic expansion valve and evaporator, Figs. 48-3 and 48-5. Other parts are used (POA suction throttling valve, for example) but only to control and increase the efficiency of the system. High pressure hoses and metal lines connect the various parts and form the continuous circuit for recirculation of the refrigerant.

Each of the major components is equally important to the system. A malfunction of any one of these units will interrupt the heat transfer cycle, Fig. 48-2, and disrupt operation of the whole system.

COMPRESSOR

The compressor is the power unit of the system, pumping out refrigerant gas under high pressure and high heat on the discharge side (high side of system) and sucking in low pressure gas on the intake side (low side). See Fig. 48-6.

Pressure builds because of a restriction in the high side of the system in the form of the thermostatic expansion valve or an orifice tube (see CCOT SYSTEM). The small valve or metered orifice offers resistance to the flow of pressurized refrigerant to build pressure. See Fig. 48-15.

The heat buildup is obtained when heat molecules in the low pressure refrigerant (returning from the evaporator) are

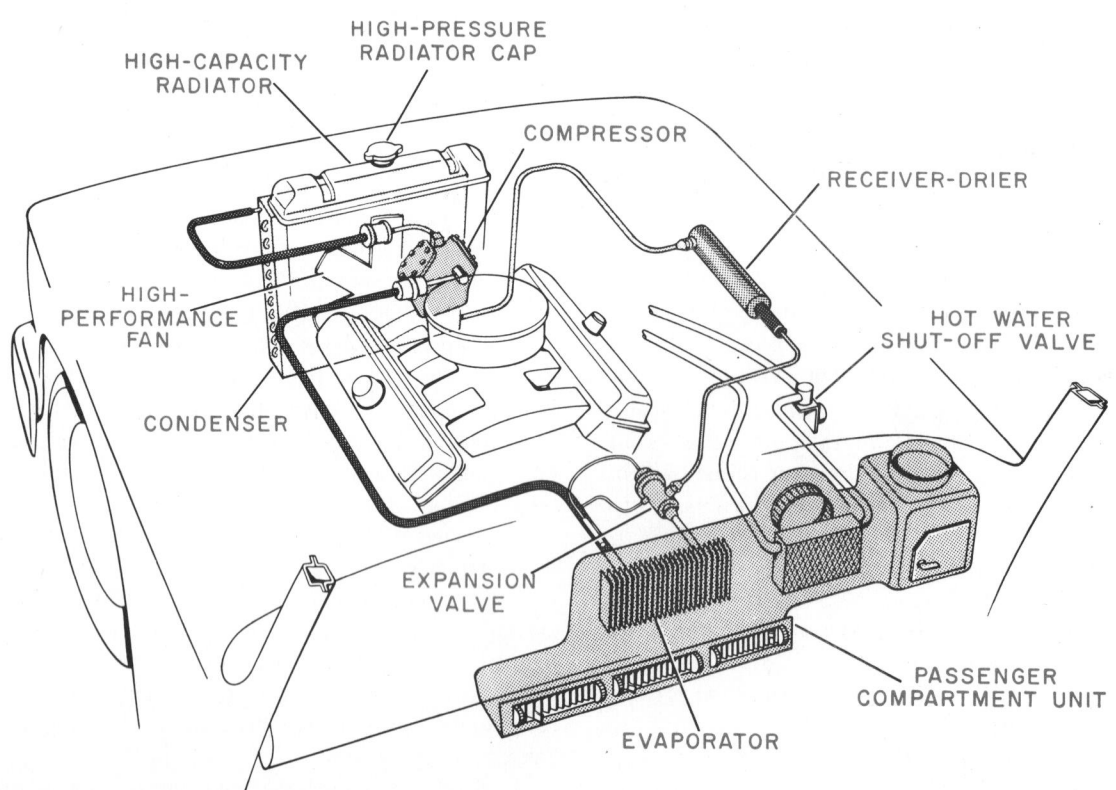

Fig. 48-5. Basic units contained in typical automobile air conditioning system are shown in relative locations. In this installation, car heater is "packaged" with evaporator and one blower assembly is used.

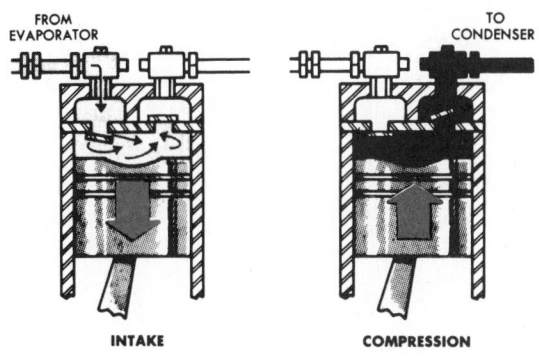

Fig. 48-6. Engine-driven compressor draws in low pressure refrigerant gas on downstroke of piston, compresses it on upstroke to increase its temperature and pressurize the system.

concentrated by the pressurizing effect of compressor operation. This action serves to raise the temperature of the refrigerant gas flowing to the condenser, stimulating rapid heat flow from the hot refrigerant to cooler outside air, Fig. 48-2.

Remember, heat always flows from hotter objects to cooler objects.

COMPRESSOR MAKEUP

Several types of air conditioning compressors are in use in automotive applications. Belt-driven, reciprocating piston-type compressors are found on many engines. Not all A/C compressors have crankshafts. General Motors factory-installs, a Frigidaire six cylinder, axial piston unit, Fig. 48-7.

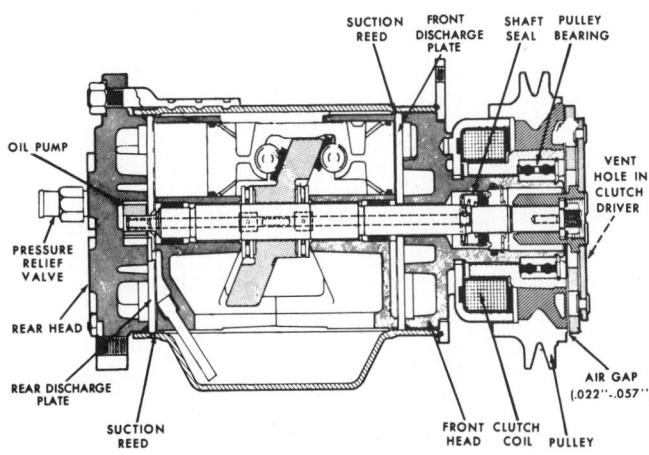

Fig. 48-7. GM compressor is six cylinder, axial piston type with clutch coil and clutch plate and hub. Also note oil sump and oil pick-up tube.

The six cylinder GM compressor has, in effect, three cylinders at each end of its inner assembly. A swash plate of diagonal design is mounted on the compressor shaft. It actuates the pistons, forcing them to move back and forth in the cylinders as the shaft is rotated, Fig. 48-7. Reed valves control suction and discharge; crossover passages feed refrigerant to both high and low service fittings at the rear end of the

GM compressor. A gear-type oil pump located in the rear head provides for compressor lubrication.

Chrysler Corporation uses Air-Temp compressors of the two cylinder, "Vee," reciprocating piston type, Fig. 48-5. Beginning in 1979, some Chrysler, Dodge and Plymouth cars used a lightweight, six cylinder, swashplate type compressor. Ford Motor Company and American Motors use compressors of the two cylinder, "in-line" type. Late model Fords are equipped with a six cylinder axial piston unit. Most independent (hang-on type) air conditioning systems make use of compressors of the reciprocating piston design. See Fig. 48-6.

The more conventional, crankshaft-type compressors are two cycle, two cylinder units. Reed valves generally are used to control the intake and exhausting of the refrigerant gas during the pumping operation. Older models were lubricated by an oil pump fitted into the rear head. Later models made use of a positive pressure lubrication system which utilizes the difference in pressure at the suction intake and pressure in the crankcase, plus centrifugal force.

Chrysler Air-Temp units also use the familiar reciprocating piston arrangement, and incorporate a rotor-type oil pump in the rear cover plate. These compressors also contain a control valve under the low-side fitting to regulate refrigerant flow through the evaporator to prevent icing of the evaporator core.

During operation of a typical reciprocating piston com-

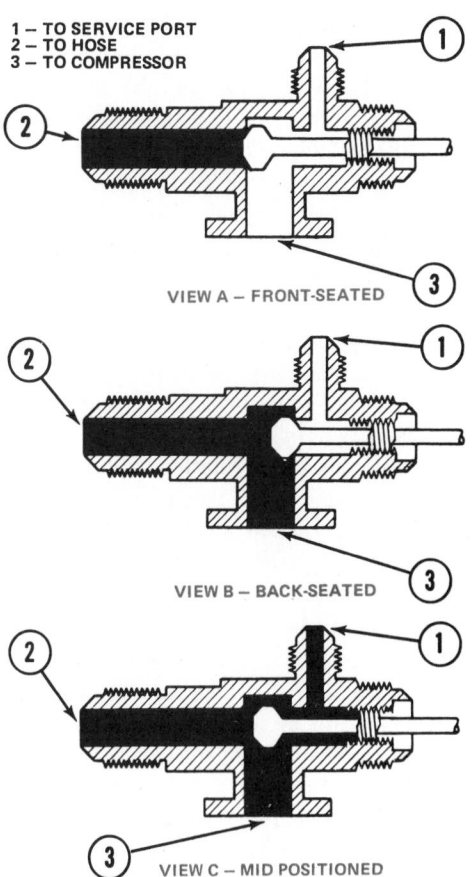

Fig. 48-8. Service valve operating positions. A—For isolating compressor. B—For normal operation of air conditioning system. C—For testing, evacuating and charging system.

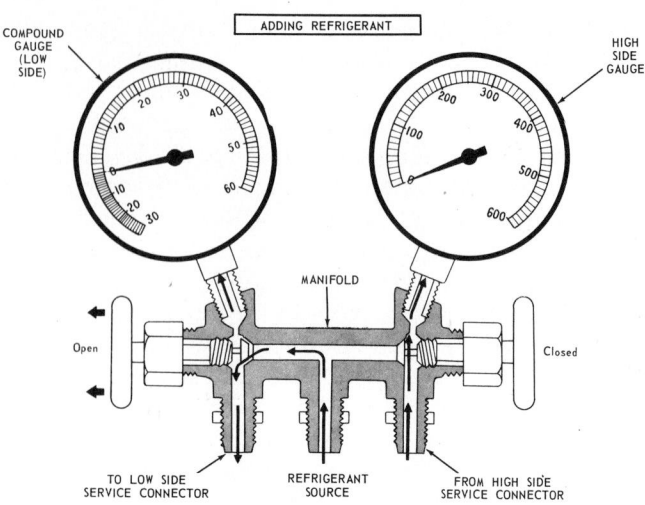

Fig. 48-9. Manifold gauge set, with either two or three test gauges, can be attached to compressor service valves or connectors to test, discharge, evacuate and charge system.

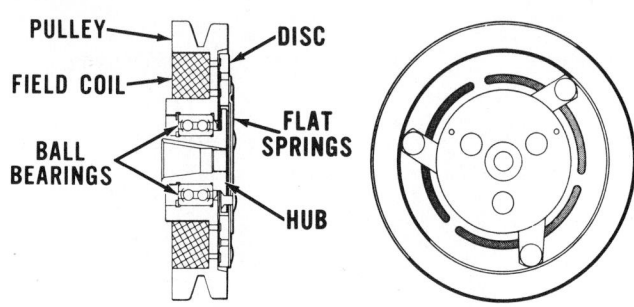

Fig. 48-10. Ford pulley assembly has electrically controlled magnetic clutch, which cuts compressor in and out of operation, depending on ambient temperature.

pressor, Fig. 48-6, the piston creates a suction on the downstroke (intake). This draws the intake reed valve open and sucks refrigerant gas into the cylinder. On the upstroke (compression), the piston pressurizes the refrigerant, forcing it past the exhaust reed valve and into the hoses and metal lines to the condenser. The hot refrigerant gas leaves the compressor at 175 to 195 psi to trigger system operation.

Compressor service valves are built into some systems. They serve as a point of attachment for test gauges or servicing hoses. The service valves are three-position controls: front-seated, mid-position, and back-seated, Fig. 48-8.

Position of this double-faced valve is controlled by rotating the valve stem with a service valve wrench. Clockwise rotation will seat the front face of the valve and shut off all refrigerant flow in the system. This position will isolate the compressor from the rest of the system.

Counterclockwise rotation will unseat the valve and open the system to refrigerant flow (mid-position). Systematic checks are performed with a manifold gauge set, Fig. 48-9, with the service valve in mid-position.

Further counterclockwise rotation of the valve stem will seat the rear face of the valve. This position opens the system to the flow of refrigerant but shuts off refrigerant to the test connector. The service valves are used for testing pressure; for isolating the compressor for repair or replacement; and for discharging, evacuating and charging the system.

Instead of service valves, many modern compressors have "Schrader" or "Dill" service connectors or gauge port fittings. Special test hoses are available to fit these connectors, or adapters can be used with standard test hoses. The refrigerant is sealed in the system until the special hose or adapter is attached. Removal of the hose or adapter closes the system.

Compressors used in automotive air conditioning systems generally are equipped with an electromagnetic clutch which energizes and de-energizes to engage and disengage the compressor, Fig. 48-10. Two types of clutches are in general use: the once-popular rotating coil type and the stationary coil

type, which is now used almost universally.

1. The rotating coil clutch has a magnetic coil mounted in the pulley, and it rotates with the pulley. It operates electrically through connections to a stationary brush assembly and rotating slip rings. When signalled by an automatic thermostatic switch, the clutch permits the compressor to engage or disengaged as required for adequate air conditioning.

2. The stationary coil clutch has the magnetic coil mounted on the end of the compressor. Electrical connections are made directly to the coil leads.

On air conditioning systems in which the compressor operates continuously when the system is "on." compressor clutch operation is controlled by an on-off switch. On systems in which the compressor is "cycled" to monitor system output, the clutch is controlled by an automatic thermostatic switch.

The clutch, in effect, is the connecting link between the compressor pulley and the compressor. The belt-driven pulley is always in rotation while the engine is running. The compressor is in rotation, and operation, only when the clutch engages it to the pulley.

CONDENSER

The condenser's job in the air conditioning system is to change high pressure refrigerant gas to a liquid. See Fig. 48-11. It does this by providing a means for emitting heat from the hot refrigerant to the cooler atmosphere.

The means by which the condenser performs its function is a design factor: place the hot refrigerant in contact with the inner walls of as many feet of tubing as possible. Place this tubing in the airstream to bring about a heat transfer situation. When the refrigerant gas reaches the pressure and temperature that causes condensation, a large quantity of heat will be given off and the hot refrigerant gas will change to a warm liquid.

In an automobile, the condenser consists of a crisscross arrangement of tubing through thin, supporting, cooling fins. In construction, it resembles an engine radiator and usually is mounted directly in front of the radiator. This places it in the best position to receive the benefits of ram air flowing into the engine compartment while the vehicle is in motion.

When the vehicle is at rest or moving slowly, the engine fan draws outside air across the condenser coils and fins. In some engines in air conditioned cars, clutch-type cooling fans engage

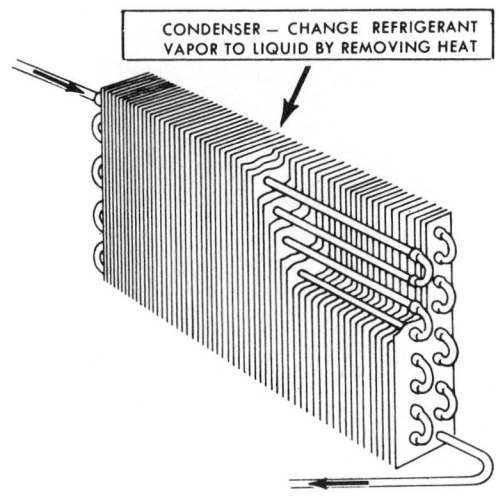

CONDENSER — CHANGE REFRIGERANT VAPOR TO LIQUID BY REMOVING HEAT

Fig. 48-11. Condenser used in air conditioning systems is a heat exchanger. Hot refrigerant vapor enters top of condenser, cools as it passes through coils, gives up heat to surrounding air, then condenses back to a liquid.

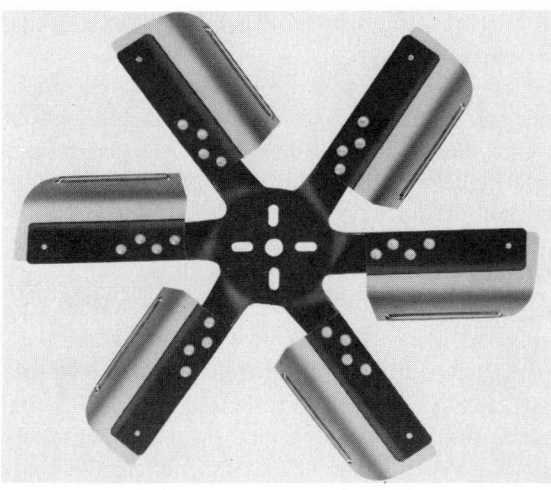

Fig. 48-12. Flexible blade fan provides full ram air cooling at low engine rpm, because blades are at maximum pitch. At higher rpm, pitch is reduced, yet strong airflow is maintained with less load on engine than with conventional cooling fan.

to permit full rpm at low vehicle speeds and "slip" at high speed when ram air cooling takes over.

Designed to achieve a similar effect is the flexible blade fan found in some air conditioned applications, Fig. 48-12. The blades of this unit have a high pitch at rest and at low rotational speeds to create a strong airflow. At high speeds, the flexible blades flatten out. As the pitch of the blades decreases, so does the airflow the fan creates. Again, ram air at high speed furnishes the necessary airflow for efficient condenser operation.

In operation, refrigerant gas under high pressure enters the condenser through an inlet at the top, Fig. 48-1. Under an average heat load, the upper half or 2/3 of the condenser coils contain hot refrigerant gas changing into a hot liquid. The lower half or 1/3 will carry the warm liquid refrigerant. This

liquid, still under high pressure, flows from an outlet at the bottom of the condenser through a refrigerant line to the receiver-drier.

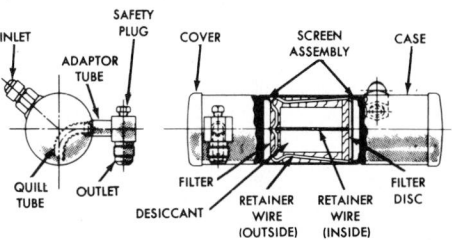

INLET — SAFETY PLUG — ADAPTOR TUBE — COVER — SCREEN ASSEMBLY — CASE — QUILL TUBE — OUTLET — DESICCANT — FILTER — RETAINER WIRE (OUTSIDE) — RETAINER WIRE (INSIDE) — FILTER DISC

Fig. 48-13. Receiver-drier stores liquid refrigerant and removes moisture that could cause freezing in system. Most units incorporate filters, screens and a drying agent; some mount horizontally, others vertically.

RECEIVER-DRIER

Next in line in the series of five major components that make up an automotive air conditioning system is the receiver-drier, Fig. 48-13. This is the storage tank for liquid refrigerant, and it also contains a filter and a desiccant to remove foreign particles and moisture from the circulating refrigerant.

It's necessary to have a point to store the refrigerant because the demands of the evaporator vary under different operating conditions. The filter and drying agent are required to keep harmful contaminants from circulating through the system.

A sight glass provided for viewing the condition of the refrigerant charge usually is built-into or adjacent to the top of the receiver-drier assembly, Fig. 48-14. It reveals the interior

SIGHT GLASS

Fig. 48-14. Sight glass in system provides means of checking refrigerant level. When normalized and operating under heavy load, no bubbles or foam should appear in sight glass if system is charged.

of the system at a point where the charge of liquid refrigerant passing it reveals whether or not the system is fully charged.

A "clear" glass, for example, indicates that the system has a full charge of refrigerant. If bubbles appear, it is apparent that air has entered the system. A milky white cloudiness signals that the desiccant is escaping from the receiver-drier and is circulating through the system with the refrigerant.

In operation, the receiver-drier receives the high pressure liquid refrigerant from the condenser and delivers it through tubing to the thermostatic expansion valve.

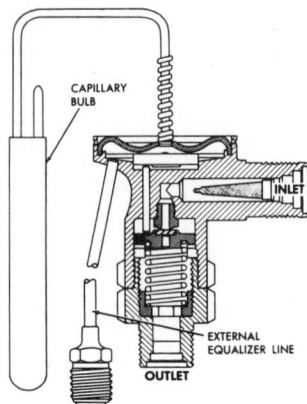

Fig. 48-15. Thermostatic expansion valve meters liquid refrigerant under high pressure into low pressure area of evaporator, as directed by a temperature sensing bulb located at evaporator outlet.

THERMOSTATIC EXPANSION VALVE

The expansion valve, Fig. 48-15, is a metering device that removes pressure from the liquid refrigerant so that it can expand and become refrigerant gas in the evaporator. The metering action is performed by an orifice (the restriction that permits the compressor to build up pressure on the high side of the system) within the valve body. The refrigerant enters the expansion valve as a warm, high pressure liquid. It passes through the orifice and is released from the valve as a cold, low pressure, atomized liquid.

Actually, the thermostatic expansion valve has three functions: metering, modulating and controlling. Its metered orifice, Fig. 48-15, releases the pressure on the liquid refrigerant to change it from high to low and provide a starting point for the "low side" of the air conditioning system.

Its thermostatically controlled valve opens and closes on signal from a thermal bulb connected to the tailpipe of the evaporator. This creates a modulating effect as the valve varies the flow of liquid refrigerant to the orifice. If the tailpipe gets warm, the bulb signals the thermostatic valve to open and allow greater refrigerant flow. When the tailpipe cools, the bulbs triggers the valve to close and restrict flow.

The control feature of the thermostatic expansion valve ties in with the modulating function. When the valve opens or closes, it must respond quickly to changes in heat load at the tailpipe of the evaporator. No liquid refrigerant must leave the evaporator and enter the compressor or damage to internal parts will result. Therefore, the thermostatic expansion valve must respond immediately to the signals sent by the thermal bulb to insure that vaporization of the R—12 is completed by the time it reaches the tailpipe of the evaporator. (Also see CCOT PRINCIPLES.)

THE EVAPORATOR

The evaporator is another heat exchanger in the air conditioning system, Fig. 48-16. In contrast to the condenser, however, its coils carry cold refrigerant, which picks up heat from the passenger compartment to cool the interior.

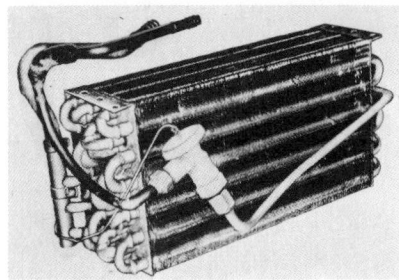

Fig. 48-16. Evaporator has coil and fins like condenser but functions in reverse. It allows refrigerant vapor to expand into gas and absorb heat from surrounding area (passenger compartment of automobile).

The evaporator is similar to the condenser in construction. It, too consists of a lengthy coil mounted in a series of thin cooling fins. Generally, the evaporator is mounted in a housing under the cowl where warm air from the passenger compartment is blown by a fan across its coils and fins.

The evaporator receives the cold, low pressure, atomized liquid refrigerant from the thermostatic expansion valve. As this cold liquid passes through the coils of the evaporator, heat naturally moves from the warm air through the cool coils and into the cold refrigerant.

When the liquid refrigerant reaches a pressure and temperature that will cause evaporation, a large quantity of heat will move from the air into the refrigerant and the low pressure atomized liquid will change to a low pressure refrigerant gas. This gas returns to the inlet, or low side, of the compressor, where the whole refrigeration cycle begins again.

SAFE WAY TO HANDLE REFRIGERANTS

Labels on R—12 containers usually include a safe handling warning. R—12 is available in drums and cans, with a 15 oz. disposable can most widely used to recharge automotive air conditioning systems. Since the refrigerant in the container, regardless of size, is under considerable pressure at ordinary temperatures, you must observe certain precautions to prevent accidents or damage to the air conditioning system:

1. Always wear goggles when working with a refrigerant. Do not allow liquid refrigerant to strike the eyes (could cause blindness) or the body (could cause frostbite). If an accident does occur, immediately wash your eyes with dilute boric acid or another suitable eyewash solution.
2. Open sealed air conditioning systems in a well-ventilated area having good circulation. Do not let the refrigerant contact an open flame or heated metal. Inhaling the phosgene gas which forms could cause violent illness.
3. Always discharge refrigerant slowly. Fast discharge could bleed refrigerant oil from the system along with the refrigerant.
4. Do not add anything except pure R—12 and refrigerant oil to the air conditioning system. Anything else may contaminate the refrigerant or cause it to become chemically unstable.
5. Handle refrigerant containers with care. Do not drop or strike the containers.

6. Wear gloves when handling a damp refrigerant container; bare hands may freeze to the container. If this does happen, wet the container with water to thaw and free your hand from the can.

7. To warm a refrigerant container, use hot water, or rags saturated with hot water, at a temperature of not more than 125 deg. F. Never use a direct flame or heater.

8. When preparing to dispense refrigerant from a can, use a can valve that punctures the can only after the valve is installed. Also, a "safety can valve," Fig. 48-17, is avail-

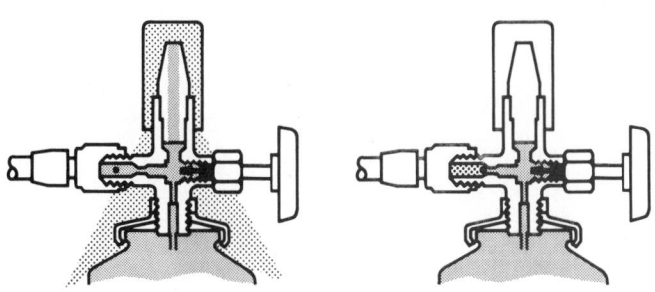

Fig. 48-17. Safety can valve protects serviceman two ways. Left. If heat is applied to can of refrigerant, relief valve releases refrigerant to relieve pressure. Right. If high side manifold hand valve is accidentally opened, ball check seats to keep high pressure from bursting can. (Imperial-Eastman)

able that prevents the refrigerant from flowing back into the can from the air conditioning system (which could cause an explosion).

9. Store your refrigerant containers in a cool, dry place. Never store them in direct sunlight or near a heater. If the refrigerant is stored in a drum, keep the drum in upright position and install a metal cap over the outlet connection.

10. Use care when transporting refrigerant drums or cans. Do not carry refrigerant containers in the passenger compartment of your car. If hauling containers in an open truck, use a cover to protect the refrigerant from the radiant heat of the sun.

HOW MOISTURE AFFECTS REFRIGERANT

All top quality refrigerants recommended for use in automotive air conditioning systems are formulated to high standards of chemical purity. They are sealed in suitable containers for safe shipment and delivery.

The quality of R—12 is manufactured-in, and regardless of brand name, its purity is assured by use of the designation "12." However, if moisture, air, dirt or some other contaminant enters the air conditioning system, the refrigerant will lose its effectiveness as a cooling agent.

Moisture, especially, is a serious refrigerant contaminant because it also causes damage to internal parts. The unwanted water reacts with R—12 to form hydrochloric acid. The more water in the refrigerant, the more concentrated the hydrochloric acid becomes. The strong acid eats holes in the evaporator and condenser coils, damages aluminum parts of

the compressor and corrodes valves and fittings. All the while the hydrochloric acid is reacting with metal parts, oxides are being given off to further contaminate the refrigerant and affect its ability to absorb and discharge heat.

Moisture usually enters the system through a break in a refrigerant line or by way of an improperly sealed connection. To combat this threat of contamination by moisture, all automotive air conditioning systems are fitted with a container of desiccant (receiver-drier). This drying agent will absorb all moisture in the system, up to its saturation point.

If an air conditioning system is contaminated by moisture, the best way to remove it is by using a vacuum pump, Fig. 48-18, to evacuate all traces of refrigerant, air and moisture. Once repairs are made and a new receiver-drier is installed, the system can be evacuated and recharged with pure R—12.

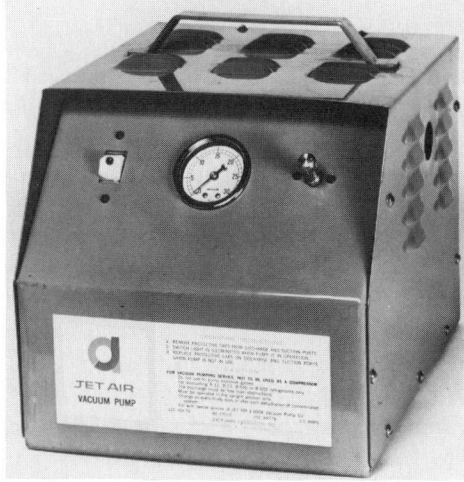

Fig. 48-18. Typical vacuum pump illustrated serves to evacuate air and moisture from contaminated air conditioning systems.

THE NEED FOR REFRIGERATION OIL

All automotive air conditioning systems require internal lubrication of seals, gaskets, the thermostatic expansion valve and the moving parts of the compressor. To accomplish this, a moisture-free refrigeration oil is circulated through the system with the refrigerant.

Use non-foaming oil formulated specifically for use in each air conditioning system. This highly refined oil comes in several grades or viscosities for use in automotive air conditioning systems. Oils of 300, 325 and 1000 viscosity are most commonly used.

Generally, compressors have an oil sump and an oil dipstick. The oil level of a reciprocating piston type compressor should be checked every time the air conditioner is serviced, Figs. 48-19 and 48-20. Six cylinder axial piston compressors must be removed from the vehicle for an oil check and refill, Fig. 48-7.

Precautions in handling refrigeration oil include:

1. Replace used refrigeration oil if there is any doubt about its condition.

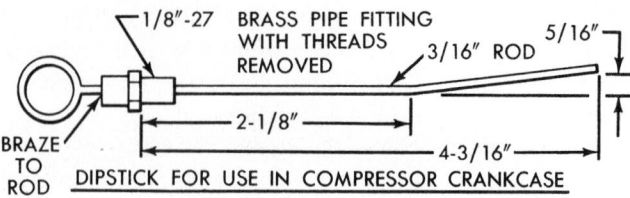

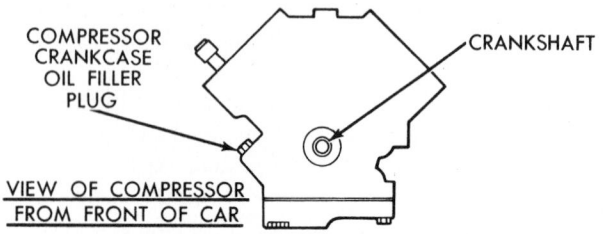

Fig. 48-19. Chrysler Vee type compressor has oil sump. Level of oil can be checked by means of dipstick made to specifications shown.

2. Discard used oil.
3. Use only approved refrigeration oil in air conditioning systems.
4. Buy refrigeration oil in smallest size containers consistent with immediate needs.
5. Do not transfer refrigeration oil from one container to another.
6. Make sure cap is tight on refrigeration oil container when its not in use.
7. When installing refrigeration oil, make sure it is proper type and viscosity for system being serviced.

Refrigeration oils have been dewaxed, dried and otherwise processed to keep pace with rapid advances in compressor design. These special oils are shipped in tightly capped containers to prevent contamination before use.

The key cautions, then, in handling any refrigerant or refrigeration oil are: provide adequate ventilation; handle with care; avoid contamination in any form.

	DIPSTICK READING	
	INCHES @ 6 OUNCES MINIMUM	INCHES @ 8 OUNCES MINIMUM
ENGINE		
ALL 6 CYLINDER ENGINES	1 3/4	2 3/8
ALL 8 CYLINDER ENGINES	1 5/8	2 3/8
COMPRESSOR SET VERTICALLY ON BENCH	1 5/8	2 3/8

Fig. 48-20. After dipstick check of Chrysler compressor oil level, add wax-free refrigeration oil to bring level up to 6 oz., or remove oil to bring level down to 8 oz.

SERVICE TOOLS AND EQUIPMENT

Mechanic's hand and specialty tools are needed to install and service automobile air conditioners. In addition, a manifold gauge set, refrigerant leak detector, vacuum pump, thermometer, tachometer and goggles are needed to test and

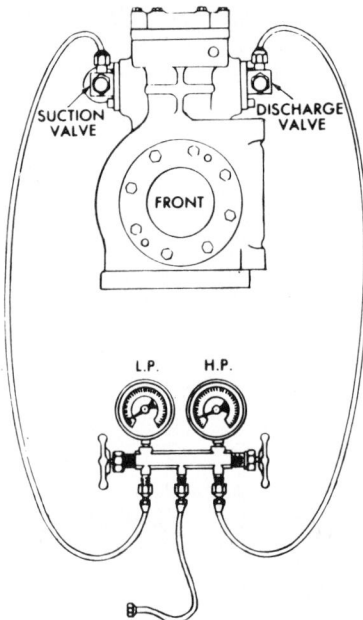

Fig. 48-21. In attaching manifold gauge set for testing pressure in system. Low pressure gauge is connected to suction service valve. High pressure gauge is connected to discharge service valve.

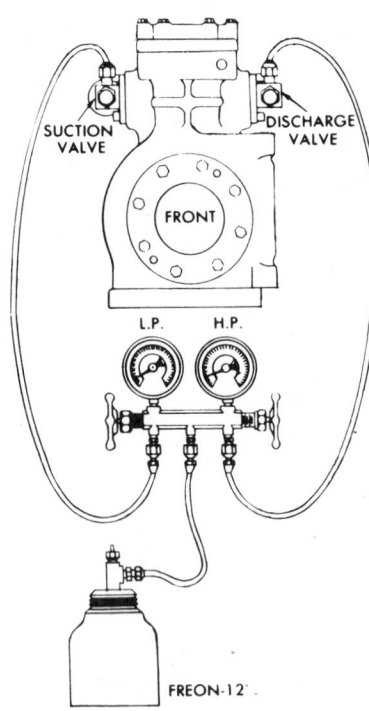

Fig. 48-22. In using manifold gauge set to charge system, hose from center port of manifold is connected to refrigerant supply. Refrigerant is drawn into system on low pressure side.

service the system.

More elaborate equipment includes charging stations on two-wheel carts and mobile air conditioning system service centers, Fig. 48-24. Automatic temperature control system analyzers are also available.

The manifold gauge set, Fig. 48-21, is used to test pressure on the high and low sides of the compressor. There are usually two gauges in the set (Chrysler cars require three gauges). The gauges are mounted on a manifold assembly, complete with shutoff valves.

Connections to the compressor are made at the suction and discharge service valves, or to connectors on the compressor fitted with "Schrader" or "Dill" valves. The suction (low pressure) side of the compressor is where the hose from the evaporator attaches. The discharge (high pressure) side is where the hose to the condenser attaches.

The manifold gauge set also has a center port to which a hose can be attached to bleed excess refrigerant from the system. In addition, it can be used to discharge (purge) refrigerant from the system, evacuate air and moisture, and charge the system with Refrigerant–12, Fig. 48-22.

The leak detector may be anything from a colored dye additive for the refrigerant, a Halide detector, or a sophisticated electronic unit that provides maximum sensitivity and accuracy when used according to the manufacturer's operating instructions.

The colored dye leak detector is added to the refrigerant. Then, with the air conditioning system in operation, any discoloration at a hose connection, etc., will reveal the point of leakage.

The Halide detector, or propane torch, is a commonly used refrigerant leak detector, Fig. 48-23. In operation, the unit's

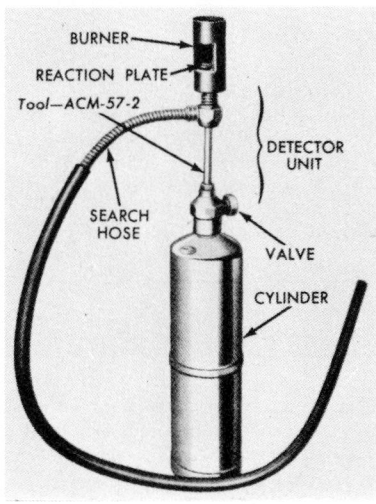

Fig. 48-23. Halide type refrigerant leak detector utilizes a small flame and a search hose to "sniff" for leaks in air conditioning system. Flame changes color if leak is detected.

sampling hose is moved under all parts and connections of the air conditioning system. Throughout the test, the color of the flame is observed. A blue flame is normal; yellow indicates a slight leak; purple signals a high-quantity leak of R–12 gas. This test should be made in a well ventilated area, because R–12 passing over an open flame will give off a toxic phosgene gas.

The vacuum pump, Fig. 48-18, is a device used to evacuate (remove air and moisture to create a vacuum) the air conditioning system. The pump hoses are connected to the

suction and discharge ports of the compressor, then the unit is plugged into a 120V AC receptacle and turned on. In operation, the pump draws out air and moisture until a vacuum of 25 to 30 in. Hg. is created.

Some manufacturers place the vacuum pump in a mobile air conditioning service center, along with pressure gauges, compound (vacuum/pressure) gauges, automatic timers, test hoses and connectors, switches, controls and a stock of R–12, leak detector and compressor oil. See Fig. 48-24.

Fig. 48-24. Auto air conditioning tester gives simple hose hookup for all functions: testing, discharging, evacuating, recharging. An automatic charging pump accurately measures and injects liquid R–12.

SERVICING THE SYSTEM

When an automotive air conditioner is not cooling properly, check the condition of engine cooling system components. Experts say, "The cooling system must function properly for the air conditioning system to work right."

Check the condition of the V-belts, Fig. 48-25, and hoses. Inspect the fan shroud, Figs. 48-12 and 48-26, radiator and pressure cap. Look for signs of coolant leakage and/or refrigerant leakage. Also check the air conditioning system for loose or broken compressor mounting brackets, improper hose routing, condition of the condenser (clogged with bugs, leaves, etc.) and receiver-drier (age and appearance).

CAUTION: When performing air conditioning diagnosis on vehicles equipped with a catalytic converter, warm the engine to normal operating temperature before attempting to idle the engine for periods greater than five (5) minutes. Once the choke is open and fast idle speed drops to normal idle, diagnosis and adjustments can be made.

Then, clean or uncap the sight glass and run the engine at

Fig. 48-25. Compressor drive belt tension check assures proper "drive" to compressor pulley. Tester also permits check on fan belt and/or water pump belt tension.

Fig. 48-27. Thermometer installed in air discharge duct gives close check on evaporator temperature. Discharge air should be from 35 to 45 deg. F.

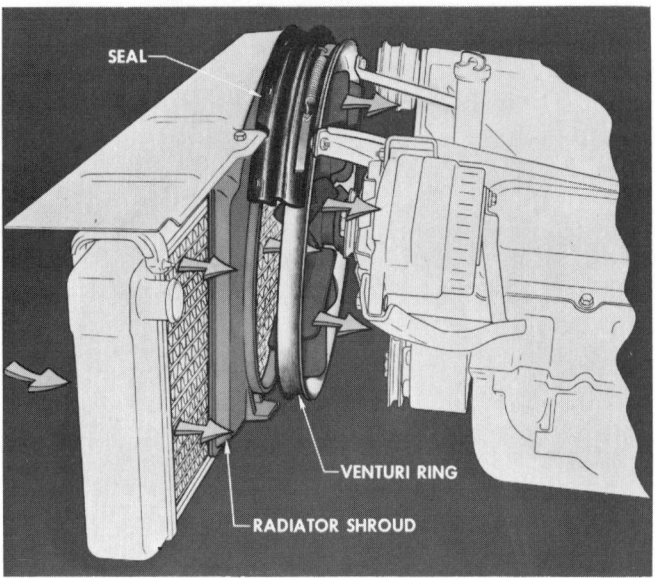

Fig. 48-26. Radiator shroud and venturi on Oldsmobile engine fan directs airflow back over and around engine, cooling system components and air conditioning compressor, lines and related parts.

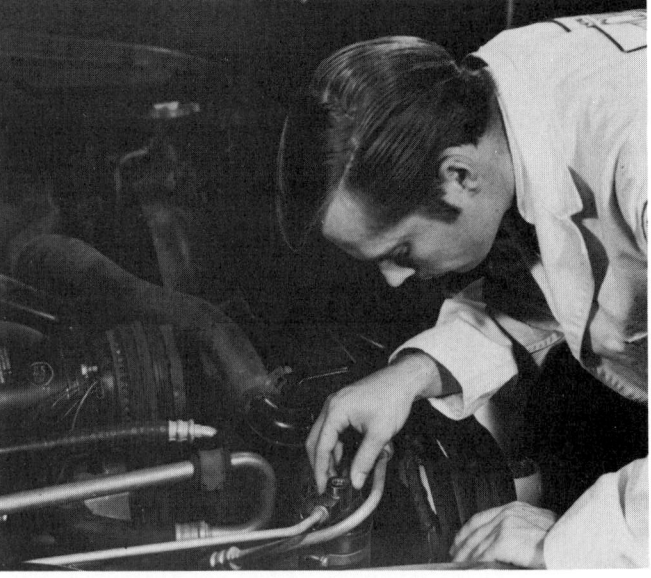

Fig. 48-28. Sight glass indicates whether or not air conditioning system has full charge of refrigerant. Bubbles in refrigerant passing through unit signals need for a recharge.

1700 to 2000 rpm. Make an operational test of the air conditioner with the hood up and the doors open (unless otherwise specified by the manufacturer). Adjust the air conditioning controls for maximum cooling with the blower at high speed.

Place a large fan in front of the vehicle to substitute fan airflow for ram airflow through the condenser. Run the engine for approximately 15 minutes to stabilize all parts of the system.

Place a thermometer in an air conditioning discharge duct, Fig. 48-27, place another thermometer in the engine compartment. Drop blower speed to "low" and close doors and hood.

Check the sight glass, Fig. 48-28. A clear glass indicates that the system is fully charged (or empty if system fails to blow cold air). Bubbles in the glass point to a low refrigerant level.

Check the thermometer reading at the air discharge duct; it should be 35 to 45 deg. F. If not, shut off engine and prepare to discharge the air conditioning system.

DISCHARGING SYSTEM

Discharging (purging) the air conditioning system is the act of releasing refrigerant from the high and low sides of the system until no pressure exists.

To discharge the system:

1. Protect your eyes with goggles. Car engine should be off and air conditioner not operating.
2. Remove compressor port caps and install manifold gauge set, Fig. 48-9.

3. Attach test hose to center connection of manifold assembly. Wrap large shop towel around other end of center manifold hose.

4. Set both manifold gauge valves at maximum open position.

5. Crack open high pressure service valve, Fig. 48-8, and discharge refrigerant vapor from system. Check shop towel to make sure no oil is discharged. If it is, cut down on service valve opening.

6. When high pressure gauge reading falls below 50 psi, crack open low pressure service valve to obtain maximum discharge of refrigerant without loss of oil.

7. On compressors with Schrader valves, disregard steps 4, 5 and 6. Instead, crack open high pressure manifold hand valve, discharge slowly, then crack open low pressure manifold hand valve and complete discharge operation (zero on gauges).

8. Repair cause of refrigerant leak or other problem. Also replace receiver-drier unit with a new one of good quality.

EVACUATING SYSTEM

Evacuation is the process by which all air and moisture is removed from the air conditioning system. Using a heavy-duty vacuum pump, Fig. 48-18, it takes at least 30 minutes to "pull down" the system to the 28 or 29 in. Hg. required before recharging.

To evacuate the system:

1. Connect vacuum pump to center manifold hose.

2. Open exhaust port on vacuum pump.

3. Set both compressor service valves at mid-position, Fig. 48-8.

4. Open both manifold hand valves.

5. Plug vacuum pump power cord into 120V AC electrical receptacle and turn on pump.

6. Operate pump and watch vacuum reading on low side gauge. Once gauge reading reaches 25 in. Hg., allow pump to run for an additional 30 minutes.

7. Then close both high and low side manifold hand valves. Close pump valve and shut off pump. Vacuum should hold at point of shut-down for 3 to 5 minutes if system is free of leaks.

8. Resume pump-down for an additional 30 minutes.

9. Turn off vacuum pump. Close both high and low side manifold hand valves.

CHARGING SYSTEM

Before disconnecting center manifold hose from vacuum pump, have sufficient cans, or a refrigerant tank of R–12, Fig. 48-22, available to charge system. Also, make use of a safety can valve to prevent high pressure from causing a backflow of refrigerant into can and exploding it.

To charge system:

1. Install safety can valve in can of refrigerant, Fig. 48-17.

2. Disconnect center manifold hose from vacuum pump and attach hose to can valve.

3. Now system is under vacuum, but hose contains trapped air. Open can valve and purge air from hose by cracking hose connector loose at manifold. Allow all air to escape, then retighten connector.

4. Hold refrigerant can upright and open low side manifold hand valve, allowing refrigerant vapor to enter system while observing gauges. NOTE: Occasionally tap refrigerant can. When it sounds empty, shut off low side manifold hand valve and can valve. Remove used can and install new can of R–12 on can valve. Resume charging.

5. As soon as both gauge needles stop rising, close low side manifold hand valve and can valve.

6. Start engine and run at fast idle (2000 rpm on GM cars; 1700 rpm on others). Turn air conditioner controls for maximum cooling with blower at high speed.

7. Open can valve and low side manifold hand valve to draw additional refrigerant through low side. Check system capacity chart for amount of full charge. NOTE: Never open high side manifold hand valve when engine is running. If system does not accept enough R–12, rock can from side to side, or place refrigerant can in container of water heated to 125 deg. F to increase flow of refrigerant.

8. Observe high side gauge reading and thermometer reading in engine compartment to avoid overcharging system. High side pressure should not exceed 240 psi. Observe low side gauge reading; it should not exceed 60 psi.

9. When high and low side gauge pressures reach normal (15 to 30 psi, low side; 175 to 195 psi, high side), and bubbles disappear in sight glass, close low side manifold hand valve and can valve.

10. Check thermometer reading at air discharge duct nearest evaporator. Normal reading should be 35 to 45 deg. F on low blower speed.

11. Stop engine. Set both compressor service valves at maximum counterclockwise position (backseat), remove manifold gauge hoses from compressor ports and install service port caps. On compressors with Schrader valves, simply remove hoses and install port seal caps.

12. Remove refrigerant can from center manifold hose. Store can and can valve assembly for future use, or open safety can valve and purge remainder of refrigerant before removing can valve and disposing of refrigerant can.

GENERAL MOTORS ADVANCES

General Motors has developed an air conditioning system in which a Valves-In-Receiver (VIR) unit performs the functions of the receiver-drier, thermostatic expansion valve, sight glass and POA (pilot operated absolute) suction throttling valve. See Figs. 48-29 through 48-31.

The VIR assembly is mounted next to the evaporator, which eliminates the need for an external equalizer line between the thermostatic expansion valve and the outlet of the POA suction throttling valve. The equalizer function is accomplished by a drilled hole (equalizer port) between the two valve cavities in the VIR housing. See Fig. 48-30.

Also eliminated are the thermobulb and capillary line for the thermostatic expansion valve. The diaphragm of the VIR expansion valve is exposed to the refrigerant vapor entering

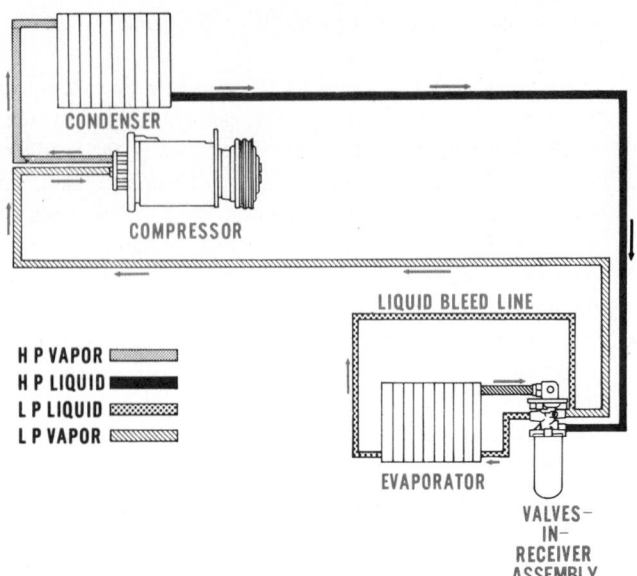

HP VAPOR

HP LIQUID

LP LIQUID

LP VAPOR

Fig. 48-29. GM'S Valves-In-Receiver (VIR) air conditioning system has been adopted by all divisions. It is more compact than previous systems and it uses fewer connecting lines and control devices.

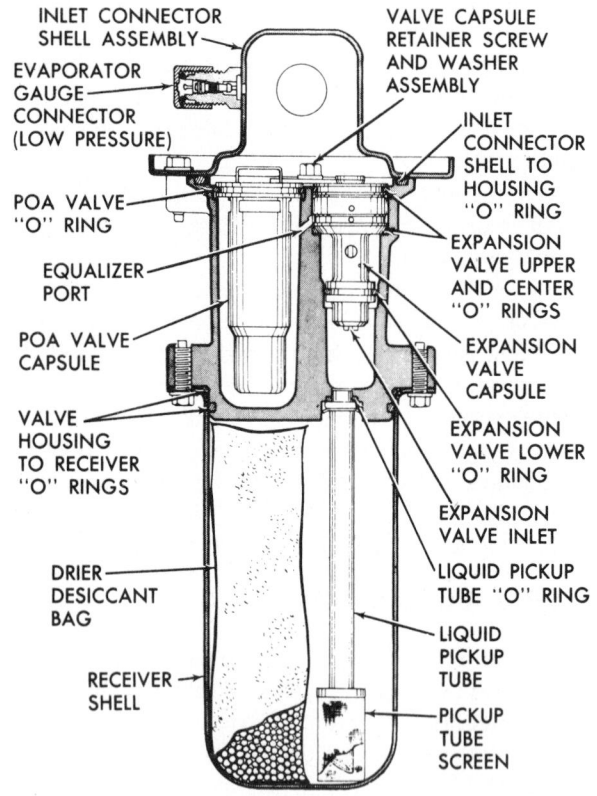

Fig. 48-30. VIR unit combines two major valves, receiver-drier and sight glass in a single assembly to control evaporator pressure and regulate amount of refrigerant being metered into evaporator.

The VIR thermostatic expansion valve controls the flow of refrigerant to the evaporator by sensing the temperature and pressure of the refrigerant gas as it passes through the VIR unit on its way to the compressor. The POA suction throttling valve controls the flow of refrigerant from the evaporator to maintain a constant evaporator pressure of 30 psi. These are capsule type valves. When found to be defective, the complete valve capsule must be replaced.

The drier desiccant is contained in a bag in the receiver shell, Fig. 48-30. It is replaceable by removing the shell and removing the old bag and installing a new bag of desiccant.

Another GM advance incorporated in the VIR system is a

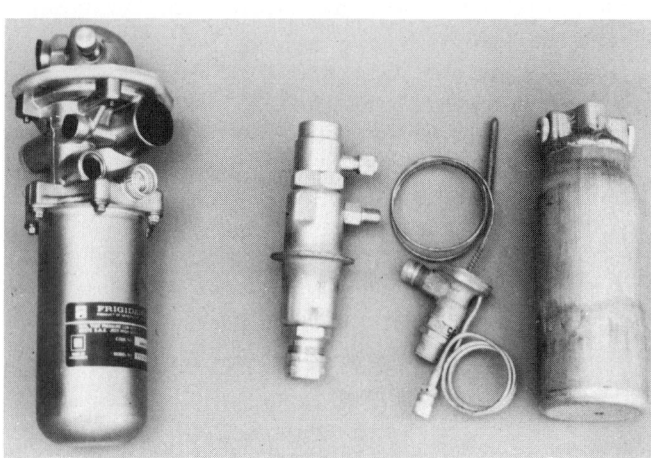

Fig. 48-31. VIR assembly, at left, replaces three individual assemblies previously used, at right. These include POA suction throttling valve, thermostatic expansion valve and receiver-drier.

superheat switch in the compressor rear head, Fig. 48-32. The superheat switch serves to shut off the air conditioning system if it senses a partial or total loss of refrigerant in the system.

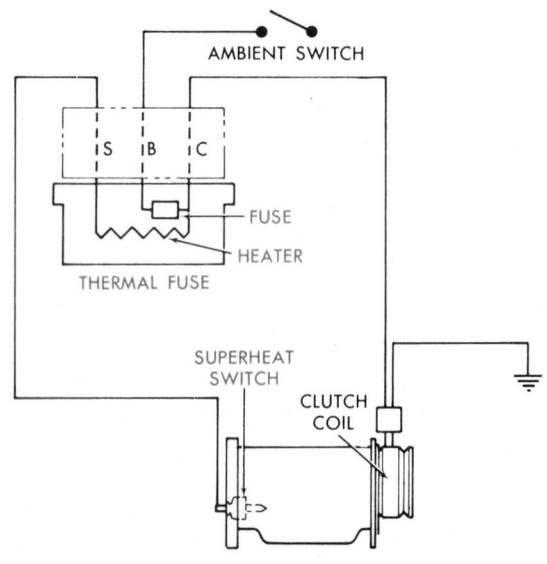

Fig. 48-32. Superheat shut-off switch turns on heater, which melts fuse and shuts off system if low refrigerant charge results in low system pressure and high suction gas temperature.

the VIR unit from the outlet of the evaporator. The sight glass is located in the valve housing at the inlet end of the thermostatic valve cavity, where it gives a liquid indication of the refrigerant level.

The superheat switch works in conjunction with a thermal fuse link in the circuit to the compressor clutch coil. See Fig. 48-32. If the superheat switch detects low system pressure and high suction gas temperature, its contacts close and energize a resistance type heater in the thermal fuse. The fuse melts, opening the circuit to the clutch coil and preventing compressor damage due to loss of refrigerant.

Service procedures for the VIR system differ in some respects from services performed on conventional automotive

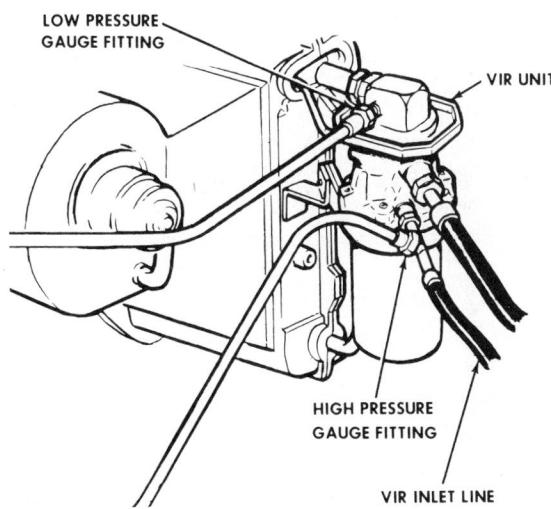

Fig. 48-33. Manifold gauge hose connections to VIR system differ from conventional compressor port hookup. Note location of high and low pressure service fittings.

air conditioning systems. Because of space limitations, for example, it is recommended that the complete VIR unit should be removed when parts replacement is necessary. GM also recommends that the desiccant bag be replaced any time the VIR unit is removed for valve service.

Discharging, evacuating and charging procedures for the VIR system are similar to those used when servicing conventional air conditioning systems. However, the hookup of the manifold gauge set is to the VIR unit. The high pressure fitting is located in the VIR inlet line. The low pressure fitting is in the VIR unit, Fig. 48-33.

CCOT SYSTEM

Many late model General Motors cars equipped with manual and automatic air conditioning use a cycling clutch orifice tube (CCOT) system. See Fig. 48-33A.

The CCOT air conditioning refrigerant control system incorporates the following major components:
1. Conventional evaporator.
2. Conventional four or six cylinder compressor.
3. Conventional condenser.
4. Thermostatic switch.
5. Accumulator with desiccant.
6. Orifice tube.
7. Pressure cut-off switch.
8. High-pressure line.
9. Low-pressure line.

The CCOT system mainly differs from conventional A/C systems in that the orifice tube replaces the thermostatic expansion valve. Also, the accumulator with desiccant replaces the receiver-drier. Note, too, in Fig. 48-33A, that the accumulator is located at the evaporator outlet, while the receiver-drier generally is mounted between the condenser and thermostatic expansion valve.

CCOT PRINCIPLES

The CCOT cycle starts at the compressor. The R–12 leaves the compressor as a high-pressure, high-temperature vapor. As the R–12 vapor flows through the condenser tubes, it gives up heat to the air passing through the condenser and changes from a high-pressure vapor to a high-pressure liquid.

The high-pressure liquid R–12 then passes through a fine screen and enters the orifice tube, where it becomes a low-pressure liquid that is fed into the evaporator. As the passenger compartment air passes through the evaporator (and since the air is much warmer than the liquid R–12), the warm air is absorbed by the refrigerant.

When the low-pressure liquid in the evaporator absorbs heat, it again turns into low-pressure vapor. The vapor passes out of the evaporator, along with some liquid R–12 that is separated from the vapor in the accumulator. From the accumulator, the low-pressure vapor enters the compressor, and the cycle starts again.

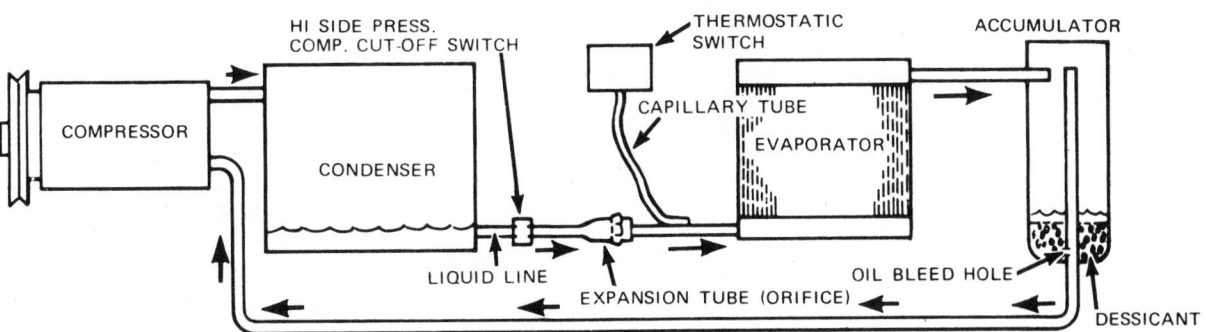

Fig. 48-33A. Components and refrigerant flow in GM's cycling clutch orifice tube (CCOT) refrigerant control system.

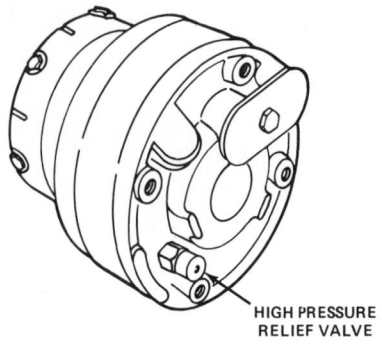

HIGH PRESSURE
RELIEF VALVE

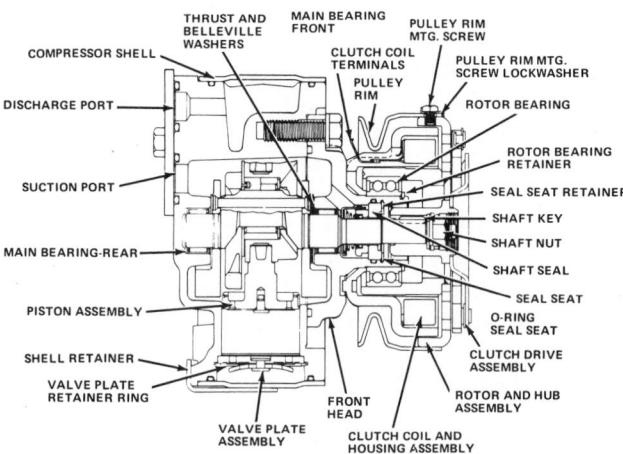

THRUST AND
BELLEVILLE
WASHERS

MAIN BEARING
FRONT

PULLEY RIM
MTG. SCREW

COMPRESSOR SHELL

CLUTCH COIL
TERMINALS

PULLEY RIM MTG.
SCREW LOCKWASHER

PULLEY
RIM

DISCHARGE PORT

ROTOR BEARING

ROTOR BEARING
RETAINER

SUCTION PORT

SEAL SEAT RETAINER

SHAFT KEY

MAIN BEARING-REAR

SHAFT NUT

SHAFT SEAL

PISTON ASSEMBLY

SEAL SEAT

O-RING
SEAL SEAT

SHELL RETAINER

CLUTCH DRIVE
ASSEMBLY

VALVE PLATE
RETAINER RING

FRONT
HEAD

ROTOR AND HUB
ASSEMBLY

VALVE PLATE
ASSEMBLY

CLUTCH COIL AND
HOUSING ASSEMBLY

Fig. 48-38B. General Motors radial, four cylinder, belt-driven compressor is used on many late model, air conditioned GM cars and on AMC four cylinder engines. (American Motors Corp.)

HVAC SYSTEM MODULES

Late model, full-size General Motors cars use preassembled modules for the heating, ventilating and air conditioning (HVAC) systems. All outside air for the system enters the car through a module that is assembled, tested and installed in the vehicle as a unit.

This modular concept makes the HVAC system more serviceable because it allows for rapid removal of the heater and evaporator cores and the blower motor.

CHRYSLER SYSTEM

Late model Chrysler Corporation cars use an evaporator heater assembly in conjunction with the Vee type, two cylinder, reciprocating piston compressor to condition the air in the passenger compartment. The evaporator heater housing is located beneath the instrument panel. Air conditioner controls are built into the instrument panel.

Chrysler's air conditioning system operates on the reheat principle, Fig. 48-34. All incoming air first passes through the evaporator coil, then it flows through or around the heater core. A blend air door proportions the amount of air permitted to pass through the heater core as a means of a controlling the temperature of the outlet air.

The temperature lever on the control panel positions the blend air door through a flexible cable. This lever also controls the shut-off water valve through a vacuum switch. Operation of this lever controls the temperature of the discharge air in all mode lever positions.

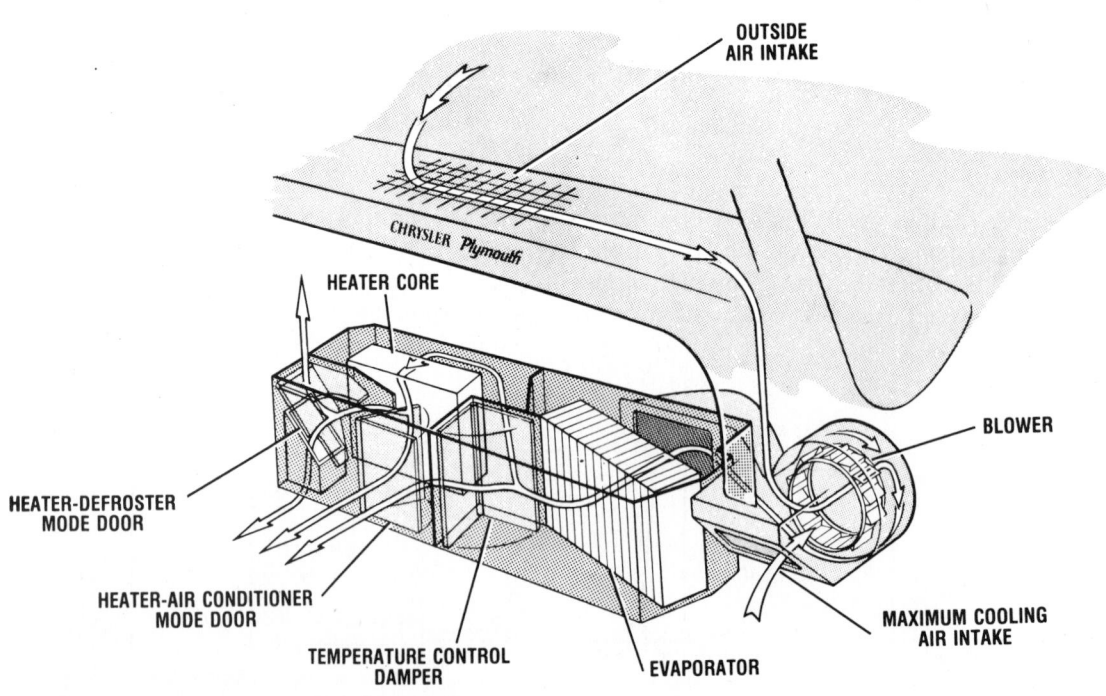

OUTSIDE
AIR INTAKE

HEATER CORE

CHRYSLER Plymouth

BLOWER

HEATER-DEFROSTER
MODE DOOR

HEATER-AIR CONDITIONER
MODE DOOR

TEMPERATURE CONTROL
DAMPER

EVAPORATOR

MAXIMUM COOLING
AIR INTAKE

Fig. 48-34. Late model Chrysler, Plymouth and Dodge air conditioners employ reheat principle for controlling air temperature and humidity. Airflow is through evaporator for cooling, then all or part of cooled air is routed through heater core for outlet temperature control.

The mode lever operates a six-position, vacuum-electric switch to permit selection of the following modes: OFF, MAX A/C (using inside air); A/C (using outside air); VENT (same as A/C except compressor is off), HEAT and DEF (windshield defrosting).

CHRYSLER COMPRESSOR, CONDENSER

Beginning in 1979, certain Chrysler Corporation lines feature a six cylinder air conditioning compressor. See Fig. 48-34A. Also introduced is an aluminum A/C condenser, Fig. 48-34B, that is designed to provide maximum heat dissipation.

The compressor is the swashplate type. It is more compact and weighs 13.3 lb. less than the previously used Vee type compressor. Broader use is anticipated.

The aluminum condenser has "rectangular-section" tubes and newly designed fins which create a larger surface area for greater cooling capacity. It is used in conjunction with the swashplate type compressor on V-8 engines and some six cylinder engines with air conditioning.

COMPACT A/C SYSTEM

Chrylser compact and intermediate cars feature a "packaged" air conditioning system. See Fig. 48-34C. The evaporator is rubber mounted, and the blower is encased in a sound absorbing housing.

Vehicles equipped with this compact air conditioning system include the Plymouth Volaré, Dodge Aspen and Diplomat, and Chrysler Le Baron models.

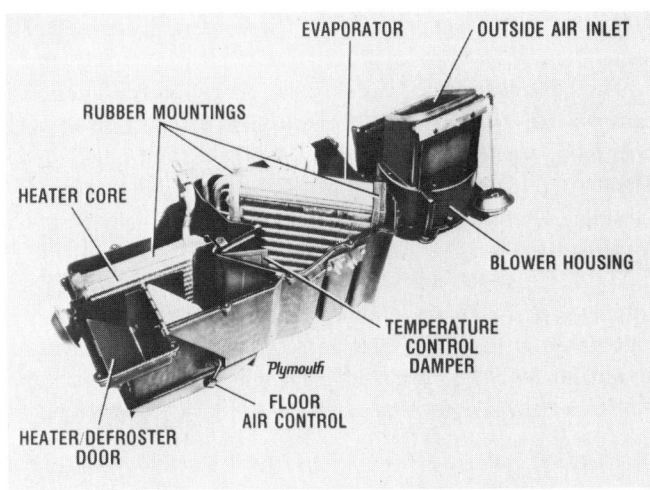

Fig. 48-34C. Major components of Chrysler's compact air conditioning system are identified.

Fig. 48-34A. A lightweight, swashplate type air conditioning compressor is used on certain late model Chrysler cars.

Fig. 48-34B. Chrysler's aluminum condenser has rectangular-section tubes and new design fins.

AUTOMATIC TEMPERATURE CONTROL

Automatic temperature control is the general term for the various types of automatic air conditioning systems. Specific names include: Automatic Climate Control (Buick); Tempmatic (Oldsmobile); Auto-Temp II (Chrysler); Automatic Air Conditioning (Cadillac, Chevrolet, AMC); Automatic Temperature Control (Pontiac, Ford).

Automatic temperature control (ATC) has become increasingly popular, especially in the luxury car field. ATC systems, generally, use the same "freon system" as the manually controlled model by the same manufacturer. In addition, ATC features completely automatic control of discharge air temperature.

To the driver, the only apparent difference in the two systems is in the control panel. With ATC, he selects the temperature he desires, Fig. 48-35, and the ATC system will control the heating and air conditioning functions to maintain that temperature, regardless of outside temperature changes. ATC also controls the circulation and humidity of the air inside the car.

The control head for the ATC system includes a functional control lever with which the driver may select modes of operation, such as HIGH, LOW, VENT, DEFOG, DEF, etc. The desired temperature is set by sliding the TEMP lever, or by turning a wheel, to any position on the scale, usually from 65 to 85 deg. F.

If ATC is not working properly, first visually inspect cooling system and air conditioning system components to see that all are in good condition and correctly adjusted. Examine and manually check hose and line connections. Check vacuum hoses, electrical connections, fuses, control lever operation and

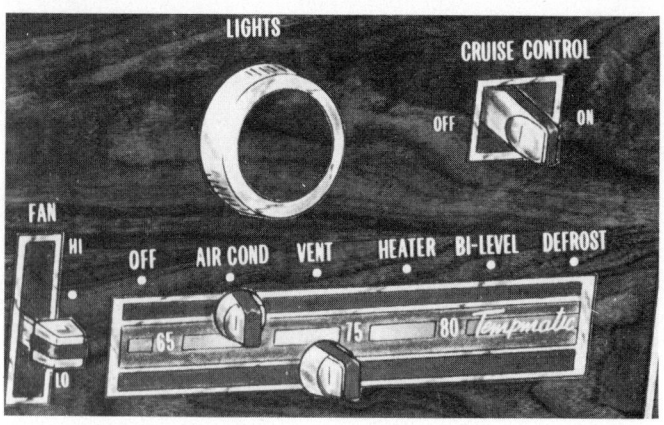

Fig. 48-35. Automatic temperature control permits driver to select temperature of incoming air by positioning lower lever on control panel. Upper lever provides air outlet selection. Fan switch varies blower speed.

blower operation.

Clean debris from the condenser fins. Check the condition of drive belts, cooling system hoses, radiator, pressure cap, coolant level and cooling fan. Make an operational test of the air conditioning system. Check the sight glass for bubbles (low on refrigerant). Test high and low side pressures with a manifold gauge set, as described earlier in this chapter. Make necessary corrections.

Further tests of the more complicated controls, such as the programmer or amplifier or servo assembly, call for special test equipment and extensive test procedures that are beyond the scope of this text.

AIR CONDITIONING TROUBLESHOOTING CHART

COMPLAINT	CAUSE	CORRECTION
System does not produce cool air; no refrigeration action at all.	1. Drive belt loose or broken.	1. Replace belt or tighten to correct tension.
	2. Compressor inoperative. Belt slips on pulley, or pulley will not turn when clutch is engaged.	2. Remove compressor for service or replacement.
	3. Compressor valves inoperative. High and low gauge readings show only slight variation at different engine speeds.	3. Service or replace compressor valves.
	4. Expansion valve stuck open. Low gauge reading "high," evaporator flooding.	4. Replace expansion valve.
	5. Fuse blown; wire disconnected or broken; switch or blower motor inoperative.	5. Replace fuse; repair or replace wire, switch or blower motor.
	6. Refrigerant line broken or leak in system. High or low gauge reads zero.	6. Replace line; leak-test system and repair as required. Replace receiver-drier.
	7. Clogged screen in receiver-drier or expansion valve; plugged hose or coil. Low gauge shows vacuum. Frosting usually occurs at point of restriction.	7. Repair as required. Replace receiver-drier.

AIR CONDITIONING TROUBLESHOOTING CHART
(continued)

COMPLAINT	CAUSE	CORRECTION
System does not produce sufficient amount of cool air at discharge side of blower.	1. Compressor clutch slipping.	1. Remove clutch assembly for service or replacement.
	2. Insufficient air comes from discharge passage.	2. Clean or replace air filter; remove obstruction from passage or kinks from flexible ducts.
	3. Blower motor sluggish.	3. Replace motor.
	4. Outside air vents open.	4. Close vents.
	5. Insufficient air circulation over condenser coils. High gauge reading excessively high.	5. Clean engine radiator and condenser. Install heavy-duty fan, fan shroud or reposition radiator and condenser.
	6. Evaporator clogged with lint, dust or residue.	6. Clean evaporator coils and fins.
	7. Evaporator control valves defective or improperly adjusted. Low gauge usually reads high.	7. Replace or adjust valves as required.
	8. Insufficient refrigerant. Bubbles appear in sight glass; high gauge reads low.	8. Recharge system until bubbles disappear and gauge readings stabilize.
	9. Expansion valve not operating properly. High and low gauge readings excessively high or low.	9. Purge system; clean screen or replace expansion valve.
	10. Receiver-drier screen clogged. High and low gauges higher or lower than normal.	10. Purge system; replace receiver-drier.
	11. Moisture in system. Excessive high side gauge reading.	11. Purge system; replace receiver-drier.
	12. Air in system. High gauge reads excessively high; sight glass is cloudy or shows bubbles.	12. Purge, evacuate and charge system.
	13. Service valves improperly set.	13. Turn valves to maximum counterclockwise position.
System runs too cold.	1. Faulty thermostatic control.	1. Replace control.
	2. Poor air distribution.	2. Adjust linkage to control panel switch.
System cools intermittently.	1. Compressor clutch slipping; high gauge reading builds up.	1. Remove compressor for service or replacement.
	2. Defective circuit breaker, blower motor or blower motor switch.	2. Replace defective part.
	3. Compressor clutch coil or solenoid has loose connection or poor ground.	3. Remove clutch coil or solenoid for service or replacement.
	4. Moisture in system, causing unit to ice up intermittently.	4. Replace expansion valve and receiver-drier.
	5. Thermostatic control defective. Low gauge reads low or excessively high.	5. Replace control.
	6. Evaporator control valve stuck.	6. Purge and evacuate system; replace receiver-drier and free or replace stuck valves. Charge system.

AIR CONDITIONING TROUBLESHOOTING CHART
(continued)

COMPLAINT	CAUSE	CORRECTION
Noise in air conditioning system.	1. V-belt loose or excessively worn.	1. Tighten to correct tension, or replace belt.
	2. Compressor parts worn or mounting bracket loose.	2. Remove compressor for service or replacement; tighten bracket.
	3. Compressor oil level low.	3. Fill to correct level.
	4. Clutch slips or makes noise.	4. Remove clutch for service or replacement.
	5. Blower motor loose or worn.	5. Tighten motor mounting or remove motor for service or replacement.
	6. Excessive charge in system, causing rumbling or thumping noise, excessive high and low gauge readings, bubbles in sight glass.	6. Discharge excess refrigerant until pressure gauge readings drop to specifications and bubbles disappear from sight glass.
	7. Low charge in system, causing hissing at expansion valve; bubbles and cloudiness in sight glass; low gauge reading excessively low.	7. Locate leak in system, purge system and repair. Evacuate system and replace receiver-drier; charge system.
	8. Moisture in system, causing noise at expansion valve.	8. Purge and evacuate system; replace receiver-drier; charge system.
	9. High pressure service valve closed, causing compressor to knock and high gauge to read excessively high.	9. Open valve immediately.

REVIEW QUESTIONS – AUTOMOBILE AIR CONDITIONING

1. Fluids give up heat when changing from a liquid to a gas. True or False?
2. Can pressure be used to reduce a gas to a liquid?
3. What is a Btu?
4. Heat flows always from a warmer body to a cooler one. Yes or No?
5. What refrigerant is used in automobile air conditioning systems?
6. What is the state of the refrigerant when it is pumped by the compressor to the condenser?
   a. Liquid.
   b. Gas.
   c. Liquid and gas.
7. The expansion valve raises the pressure of the refrigerant flowing to the evaporator. True or False?
8. What is the function of the evaporator?
   a. Removes heat from refrigerant.
   b. Absorbs heat from passenger compartment.
   c. Absorbs moisture from refrigerant.
9. What is indicated if bubbles appear in sight glass?
   a. System is fully charged with refrigerant.
   b. System is low on refrigerant.
   c. Refrigerant is fully discharged from system.
10. What is the primary usage of a manifold gauge set?
11. Give five safety precautions to observe when working on an air conditioning system.
12. How can the need for recharging be determined, visually?
13. How can the need for recharging be determined by test?
14. General Motors Valves-In-Receiver assembly replaces three individual assemblies used in previous systems. What are they?
15. In General Motors CCOT A/C refrigerant control system, the _____ replaces the conventional thermostatic expansion valve.
16. In the CCOT system, the _____ replaces the receiver-drier.
17. Chrysler's six cylinder compressor is the _____ _____ type.

TIRES, TIRE SERVICE

Modern pneumatic tires provide traction for moving the vehicle and to assist the brakes in stopping it. Properly inflated, today's tires will absorb irregularities of the road surface, give a safe and comfortable ride while providing a reassuring grip on the road at all speeds.

TIRE TYPES AND BASIC STRUCTURE

There are two basic tire types: tubeless tires for passenger cars and light-duty trucks; and those requiring inner tubes for medium and heavy-duty trucks.

The tubeless tire is designed so that the air is sealed within the rim of the wheel and the tire casing, Fig. 49-1. When an inner tube is used in the tire casing, the air is contained within the tube, while the casing serves mainly to protect the tube and provide traction.

A tubeless tire is composed of a carcass, sidewall and tread, Fig. 49-1. The carcass is the entire tire structure except

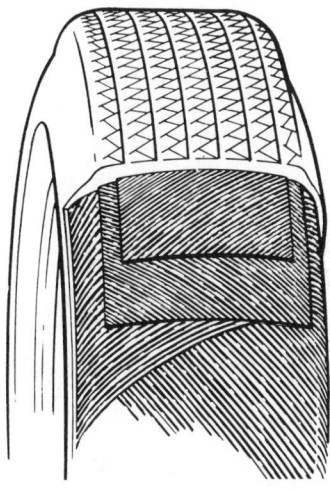

Fig. 49-2. Carcass of belted bias tire consists of plies laid diagonally and belts laid around circumference of tire.

strands. The cords are laid parallel in layers and impregnated with rubber to form plies.

The plies are arranged at various angles and in different combinations of layers and belts (plies laid circumferentially around tire). See Fig. 49-2. Then the sidewall and tread material is applied and vulcanized in place, Fig. 49-3.

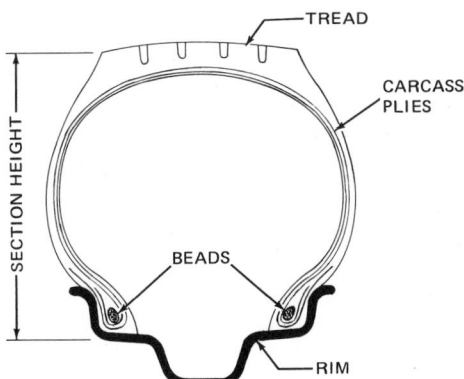

Fig. 49-1. Cross section of tubeless tire shows basic structure and air-tight fit of tire beads in bead seats of wheel rim.

sidewall and tread. The sidewall is that portion of the tire between the bead and tread. The tread is the portion that comes in contact with the road.

The carcass of a tire is made up of layers of cord materials such as rayon, nylon, polyester, fiber glass or steel wire

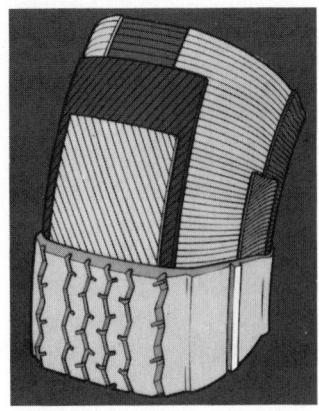

Fig. 49-3. In radial construction: carcass plies are laid radially and steel belts circle tire; sidewall and tread material is vulcanized in place.

TIRE SIZES

The acceptance of tubeless tires throughout the passenger car tire field triggered research and development in the tire manufacturers' laboratories and at the proving grounds and test tracks. In fact, advances made in tire design and construction soon outmoded existing tire size designations.

Before 1966, all tire manufacturers specified tire sizes in terms of section width and rim diameter. Then "wide oval" tires were introduced, and the need for new tire size designations became clear. The simple, two-dimension system for specifying tire size was no longer valid because it did not take section height into consideration. See Fig. 49-1.

Section height is the height of an inflated tire from the bottom of the bead to the top of the tread. It is an important size factor since modern tires generally are low profile in contrast to the almost round cross section of older tire designs. Section height also governs aspect ratio, and aspect ratio is a key area of identification of tires by size, Fig. 49-4.

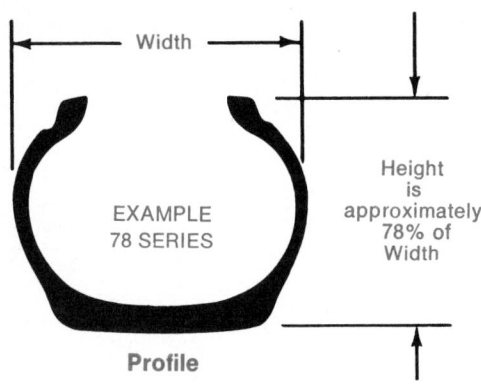

Fig. 49-5. Aspect ratio, or profile, is figured by dividing section height by section width. In this example, aspect ratio is 78.

.78, .70 AND .60 ASPECT RATIO TIRES

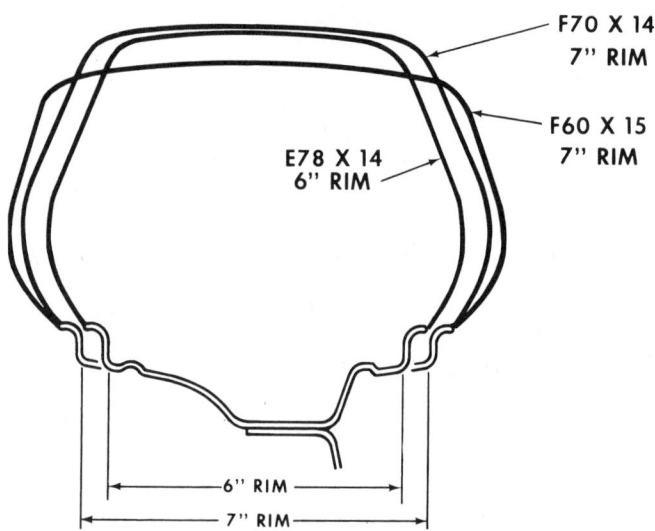

Fig. 49-4. Profile of modern tires is low and wide, resulting in aspect ratios of 78, 70 and 60. Latest low profile tire has a 50 aspect ratio (section height is 50 percent of section width).

ASPECT RATIO

The aspect ratio of a tire is the ratio of tire section height to section width. It is height divided by width. A "78 Series" tire, for example, has a section height that is 78 percent of the section width. See Fig. 49-5.

Under the old tire size system, a tire bearing the size designation 8.25-14 will measure 8 1/4 in. from outside sidewall to outside sidewall. The 14 stands for rim diameter. The new tire size designations provide all information previously contained in the size code, plus the aspect ratio.

Under the new tire size designation system, an F78-14 size, for example, tells three things about the tire:

1. The first letter, F, is the load carrying capacity.

2. The first set of numbers, 78, is the aspect ratio, meaning that the section height of the tire is 78 percent of the section width. The lower the ratio, the wider the tire.

3. The second set of numbers, 14, is the rim diameter. Some car manufacturers refer to this designation as the inner diameter of the tire.

Obviously, the variety of aspect ratios available has broadened tire applications for any given vehicle, Fig. 49-4. In addition, other elements of tire construction have affected tire designations and applications. The Size Comparison Chart in Fig. 49-6, indicates tire availability by size and type.

Other areas in which tire manufacturers have made advances include cord materials and ply layout, ply rating, load range and tread patterns.

CORD MATERIALS AND PLY LAYOUT

As mentioned, the cords of the tire make up the plies, and the plies are arranged to form the carcass of the tire. It is this arrangement of plies that determines the basic construction of the tire.

There are two general methods of arranging or laying down tire plies, radially and on the bias, Fig. 49-7. On "belted" tires, an additional belt of cord (tread ply) is laid directly under the tread. Often, the belt is made of a different cord material than the carcass plies. For example, the belt may be fiber glass or steel, while the carcass plies may be rayon or polyester.

The conventional tire for many years, and still popular, is the bias-ply tire. The term "bias" means that the plies are laid in criss-cross fashion from bead to bead, giving strength to the tire carcass.

The bias tire may have two, four or more carcass plies that cross at an angle of approximately 35 deg. with the center line of the tire. Alternate plies extend in opposite directions. See Fig. 49-7.

Belted bias tires have a carcass construction similar to bias tires, plus two or more belts circle the tire under the tread, Figs. 49-2 and 49-7.

The belts serve to keep the tread more firmly on the road and virtually eliminate "tread squirm." Belted tires reportedly give longer mileage and make the tire much more resistant to punctures, cuts and bruises.

Size Comparison Chart

Interchangeability is **NOT** implied.

Interchangeability between corresponding sizes of different construction tires is not always possible due to differences in load ratings, tire dimensions, fender clearances and rim sizes, or vehicle manufacturers' recommendations.

DIAGONAL (BIAS) PLY	DIAGONAL (BIAS) AND BELTED BIAS PLY				RADIAL PLY				
	'78 Series	'70 Series	'60 Series	'50 Series	Metric	'78 Series	'70 Series	'60 Series	'50 Series
					155R13				
6.00-13					165R13				
	A78-13	A70-13	A60-13			AR78-13	AR70-13	AR60-13	
6.50-13	B78-13	B70-13	B60-13	B50-13	175R13	BR78-13	BR70-13	BR60-13	BR50-13
7.00-13	C78-13	C70-13	C60-13	C50-13	185R13	CR78-13	CR70-13		CR50-13
	D78-13	D70-13	D60-13	D50-13		DR78-13	DR70-13		
					195R13	ER78-13		ER60-13	
					155R14				
	A78-14					AR78-14		AR60-14	
6.45-14	B78-14		B60-14		165R14	BR78-14			
6.95-14	C78-14	C70-14	C60-14		175R14	CR78-14	CR70-14		
	D78-14	D70-14	D60-14			DR78-14	DR70-14		
7.35-14	E78-14	E70-14	E60-14		185R14	ER78-14	ER70-14	ER60-14	
7.75-14	F78-14	F70-14	F60-14	F50-14	195R14	FR78-14	FR70-14	FR60-14	
8.25-14	G78-14	G70-14	G60-14	G50-14	205R14	GR78-14	GR70-14	GR60-14	GR50-14
8.55-14	H78-14	H70-14	H60-14	H50-14	215R14	HR78-14	HR70-14	HR60-14	
8.85-14	J78-14	J70-14	J60-14		225R14	JR78-14	JR70-14	JR60-14	JR50-14
		L70-14	L60-14				LR70-14	LR60-14	
				M50-14					
				N50-14					
	A78-15	A70-15				AR78-15			
	B78-15		B60-15	B50-15	165R15	BR78-15	BR70-15		
6.85-15	C78-15	C70-15	C60-15		175R15	CR78-15	CR70-15		
	D78-15	D70-15				DR78-15	DR70-15		
7.35-15	E78-15	E70-15	E60-15	E50-15	185R15	ER78-15	ER70-15	ER60-15	
7.75-15	F78-15	F70-15	F60-15		195R15	FR78-15	FR70-15	FR60-15	
8.25-15	G78-15	G70-15	G60-15	G50-15	205R15	GR78-15	GR70-15	GR60-15	GR50-15
8.55-15	H78-15	H70-15	H60-15	H50-15	215R15	HR78-15	HR70-15	HR60-15	HR50-15
8.85-15	J78-15	J70-15	J60-15		225R15	JR78-15	JR70-15	JR60-15	JR50-15
9.00-15		K70-15				KR78-15	KR70-15		
9.15-15	L78-15	L70-15	L60-15	L50-15	235R15	LR78-15	LR70-15	LR60-15	LR50-15
	M78-15					MR78-15	MR70-15		
8.90-15	N78-15			N50-15		NR78-15			

Fig. 49-6. This chart compares old and new tire size designations, but interchangeability is not implied. (Rubber Manufacturers Assoc.)

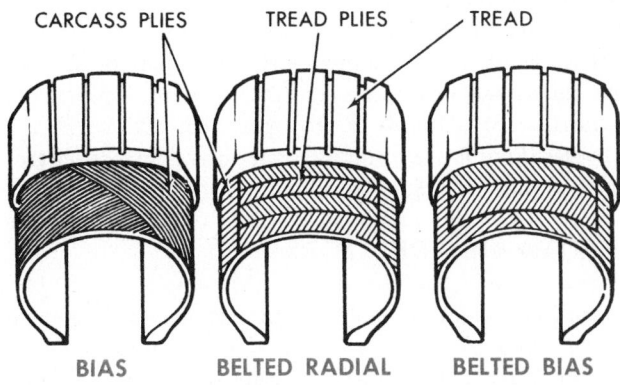

Fig. 49-7. Three basic types of tire construction can be identified by direction plies are laid to form carcass of tire. Bias and belted bias plies are diagonal; radial plies cross tire from bead to bead.

Radial tires have the carcass plies laid across the circumference of the tire from bead to bead, plus two or more belts are laid under the tread. This construction gives greater strength to the tread and flexibility to the sidewall.

Radial tires are said to give longer tread life, better handling and a softer ride at medium and high speeds than either the bias or belted bias tire. However, radial tires give a more firm, almost rough, ride at low speeds (especially on cars with suspension systems not designed for use with radials).

Other special cautions when installing radial tires:

1. Radials should not be mixed with other types of tires on the car, especially not on the same axle.
2. Radials require a special tire rotation plan, which keeps them on the same side of the vehicle. See Fig. 49-8.
3. Radials appear to be underinflated, in comparison with

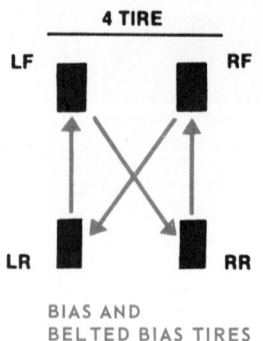 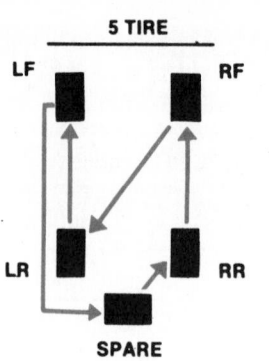 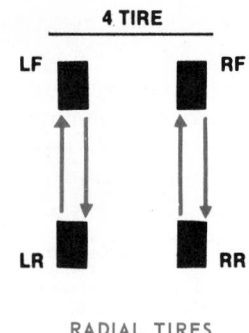 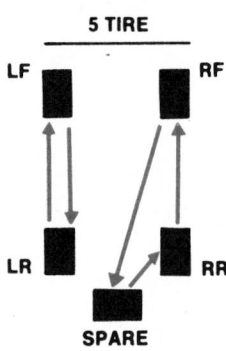

Fig. 49-8. Tire rotation patterns are shown for 5000 to 6000 mile intervals. Left. Bias and belted bias tires. Right. Radial ply tires.

bias-ply tires at the same inflation pressure. Follow manufacturer's pressure recommendation.

PLY RATING

The ply rating of a tire is its index of tire strength. The rating does not necessarily represent the actual number of plies in the tire. Rather, ply rating is used to relate a given size tire with its load and inflation limits.

In use, a passenger car tire marked "4-ply rating/2-ply" has the same load-carrying capacity as a current 4-ply tire of the same size at the same inflation pressure. When the 2-ply tire was introduced, some objections were raised with regard to cutting the conventional number of plies in half. However, cord break strength for the two plies totaled 142 lb., while it totaled only 104 lb. for the four plies.

The ply rating system is being phased out in favor of the load range system. For the present, both designations may be used on tire sidewalls. Load range B tires may be marked 4-ply rating/2-ply, or 4-ply; load range C tires, 6-ply rating/4-ply, or 6—ply; load range D tires, 8-ply rating/4-ply, 8-ply rating/6-ply, or 8-ply.

LOAD RANGE

The term "Load Range" is used in conjunction with a letter (B, C, D, etc.) to identify a given size tire with its load and inflation limits when used in a specific type of service. As load range increases, letters progress in the alphabet. (See previous paragraph.)

A tire's load range and proper inflation pressure determine how much of a load the tire can safely carry. These important figures are marked on the sidewall of the tire, along with the new and old size designations, tire ply composition, manufacturer's name and the letters DOT, which signify that the tire complies with Department of Transportation safety standards. In addition, tire sidewalls must be marked either "tubeless" or "tube-type" and, if a radial tire, the word "radial" must appear.

"Proper inflation," according to the Rubber Manufacturers Association (RMA), "is the most important rule in tire safety and tire mileage." Correct tire inflation provides better traction and braking, easier steering, better cornering and

longer, safer tire life.

The U.S. Department of Transportation (DOT) has established Uniform Tire Quality Grading (UTQG) for passenger car tires. The grades are molded on the sidewall of the tire. All tires are graded in accordance with DOT test procedures in the areas of treadwear, traction and temperature resistance.

The treadwear grading system uses comparative ratings by the number (100, 110, 120, etc.) with regard to tests performed under controlled conditions. A tire graded 150, for example, can be expected to give 50 percent more treadlife than a tire graded 100.

The traction grade uses the symbols A, B and C with A being the top grade based on the tire's ability to stop on wet pavement in tests made on concrete and asphalt surfaces.

The temperature resistance grading system also rates tires as A, B or C, with A the highest grade. Grade C corresponds to the level of Federal Motor Vehicle Safety Standard No. 109.

TREAD PATTERNS

Tire treads are grooved traction surfaces around the circumference of the tire. The grooves and ribs formed during the tire manufacturing process are carefully engineered to provide good traction on wet or dry roads, control when cornering, minimum distortion at high speeds, reduced rolling resistance and increased wear resistance. The tread and tire are designed to place the full width of the tread on the road when the tire is properly inflated.

The variety of tread patterns is very broad. Consider the fact that one publisher has produced a tread pattern identification guide that illustrates over 3000 patterns. Apparently, the number of patterns is so great because of design improvements and the manufacturers' desire for distinctive patterns of their own. See Fig. 49-9.

TREAD WEAR INDICATORS

Tread wear indicators molded into most modern tires serve as visual proof that the tire tread is approaching worn-out condition. These 1/2 in. wide indicators are located in several positions around the circumference of the tire.

As long as the tread grooves are at least 1/16 in. deep, the grooves are unbroken. When tread depth reaches that point, the

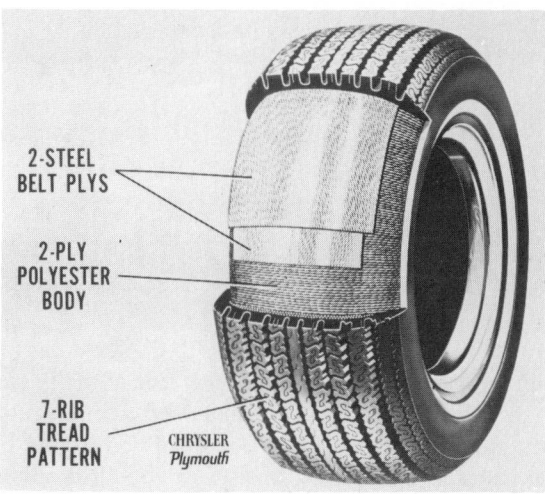

Fig. 49-9. The tread patterns vary with manufacturer and tire type. One recent model year, Chrysler's original equipment steel belted radial ply tires featured a wide, seven rib tread pattern.

tread wear indicators will appear as solid strips across the tire, Fig. 49-10. These strips interrupt tread continuity and are clearly visible on inspection. The tire should be replaced when this condition occurs.

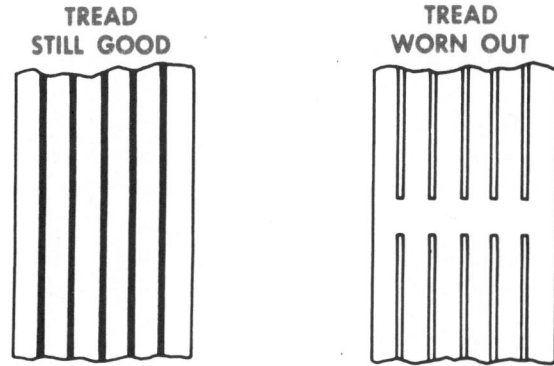

Fig. 49-10. Tire tread wear indicator appears as solid strip in the tread when tread depth is reduced to 1/16 in.

TIRE SERVICE

Excessive or uneven tread wear results from underinflation, rapid stops, fast acceleration, misalignment and unbalanced conditions. Road surface condition also affects tire life. Gravel roads and rough-finished concrete will wear tires quickly. Smooth concrete and asphalt surfaces aid in promoting maximum tire life.

Normal wear causes the tire tread to be reduced evenly and smoothly. Types of abnormal tread wear include:
1. Spotty wear.
2. Overinflation wear.
3. Underinflation wear.
4. Toe-in wear.
5. Toe-out wear.
6. Camber wear.
7. Cornering wear.

Fig. 49-11. Spotty wear results from a combination of causes, including underinflation and misalignment.

Fig. 49-11 shows a condition of spotty wear. This wear pattern usually results from a combination of conditions, including the design of the particular tire tread. Underinflation and incorrect camber are the main factors, along with excessive toe-in or toe-out.

Overinflation causes tires to wear excessively at the center of the tread surface, Fig. 49-12. In addition, there is usually a little wear on the outer edges of the tire. This causes early failure at the center ribs and also breaks in the tire wall.

Fig. 49-12. Overinflation causes wear in center of tread.

Fig. 49-13. Underinflation wear occurs at both shoulders of tread.

Wear due to underinflation is shown in Fig. 49-13. This is characterized by excessive wear on the two tread ribs adjacent to the inner and outer shoulder ribs. In many cases, underinflation also causes spotty wear, Fig. 49-11. The chart shown in Fig. 49-14 reveals percent of tire service lost due to incorrect inflation pressure.

The amount of front wheel toe-in or toe-out is one of the most important factors governing tire wear. Unless toe-in is

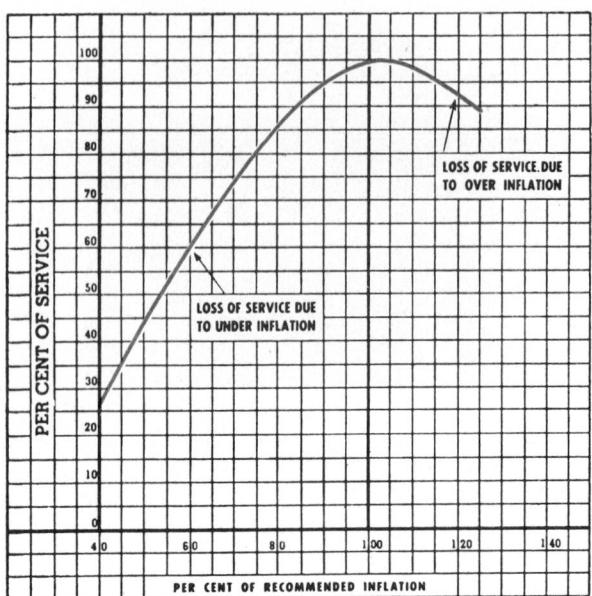

Fig. 49-14. Percent of tire service lost by excessive tire wear is charted according to inflation pressure.

Fig. 49-15. Excessive toe-in will cause featheredging of inner edges of tread ribs. NOTE: Left front tire viewed from front.

correct, the tires will have a scrubbing action on the road surface, and excessive wear will result. Fig. 49-15 shows typical tread wear due to excessive toe-in. It produces a featheredge on the inner edges of the tread ribs, which can be felt by rubbing the hand across the face of the tire.

Wear resulting from toe-out is just the reverse. The featheredge is produced on the outer edges of the tread ribs. See Fig. 49-16.

Fig. 49-16. Excessive toe-out will cause featheredging of outer edges of tread ribs. NOTE: Left front tire viewed from front.

Excessive camber will produce wear on one side of tire tread, as illustrated in Fig. 49-17. If there is too much positive camber, the tread wear will be on the outer ribs. If camber is

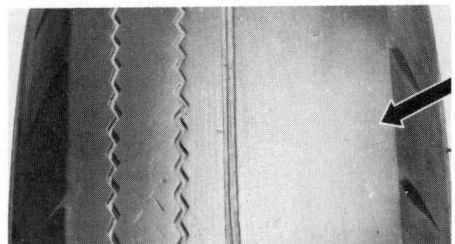

Fig. 49-17. Excessive side-of-tread wear results from incorrect camber.

negative, the wear will occur on the inner side of the tire tread. If there is excessive wear on both inner and outer areas of the tread, it probably was caused by excessive skidding on turns.

When considering any tire tread wear condition and what caused it, remember that excessive or uneven wear usually results from a combination of conditions. Tires wear at a different rate on all four wheels due to driving conditions, weight of the vehicle, power on the driving wheels, crown of the road, alignment of wheels, overloading the vehicle, tire inflation and probably most important of all, driving habits of the person behind the steering wheel.

Fast starts, quick stops, high speeds and fast turns, all take their toll of tire life. Conservative driving habits promote maximum tire life and economy.

TIRE ROTATION

In order to distribute wear evenly and to help obtain maximum tire life, manufacturers recommend that tires should be rotated from one wheel to another every 5000 to 6000 miles. The generally accepted plan for rotating tires is shown in Fig. 49-8. Up to 20 percent more tire life can be obtained if the tires are rotated at regular intervals.

WHEEL AND TIRE RUNOUT

Precision balanced wheel and tire assemblies are essential for a smooth, comfortable ride and for maximum tire life. (See the chapter on WHEEL ALIGNMENT). When checking wheel balance, remember that unbalance and out-of-round are two separate conditions. A perfectly round wheel and tire assembly can be out of balance, and an annoying thump or vibration will be evident when the car is driven. An out-of-round assembly can be in balance, yet a tire thump on a smooth road will be heard and felt.

One of the major difficulties in trying to obtain smooth, vibration-free rotation of the wheel and tire assemblies is eccentricity. They are not round, so the first step is to determine whether the runout problem is in the wheel or tire. To make the check, the wheel bearings must be properly adjusted and the tires inflated to recommended pressure. An accurate dial indicator should be used.

The correct procedure is to first check radial runout of the entire assembly as it slowly rotates through one revolution. Place the tip of the stylus of the dial indicator against the tread, rotate the assembly and see if it is running true. If radial

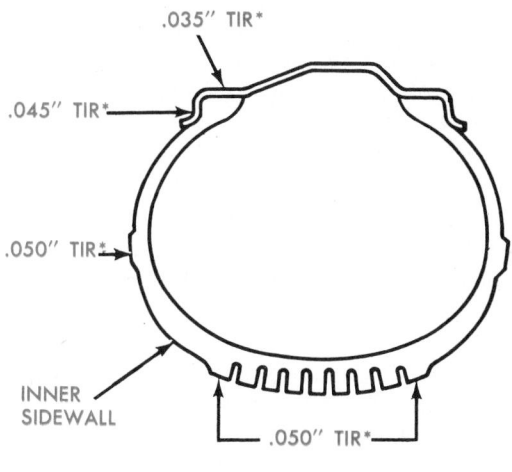

Fig. 49-18. Wheel and tire runout guide furnished by Cadillac Motor Car Division gives maximum limits for radial and lateral runout of wheel alone, and of wheel and tire assembly.

runout of the assembly exceeds .050 in., the tire should be removed from the wheel and the wheel checked separately for radial runout. See Fig. 49-18. Likewise, if lateral runout (wobble or waddle) exceeds .050 in., the wheel must be checked separately.

When checking a wheel for runout, it should be mounted on a hub that is free to rotate, but without end play that would give a false indicator reading. Generally, radial runout of the wheel should not exceed .035 in. Lateral runout should not exceed .045 in. See Fig. 49-18.

If the wheel checks out satisfactorily, the tire can be reinstalled in a different position (180 deg.). Of course, dust and dirt must be removed from the bead seats of the wheel, and the seats must be free of nicks or burrs. The tire beads must be clean and lubricated with a light film of rubber lubricant before it is reinstalled on the wheel.

With the tire on the wheel, properly inflated, and the wheel carefully installed on the drum or axle flange, the wheel nuts are tightened in an alternating sequence with uniform snugness. See Fig. 49-19. Then, using the same alternating sequence, the wheel nuts are tightened firmly, and runout of

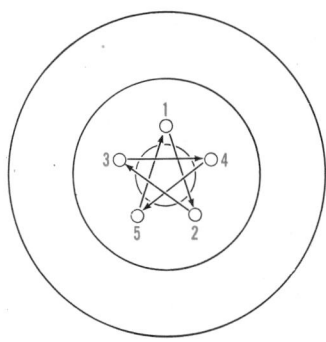

Fig. 49-19. Correct wheel nut installation involves tightening nuts in an alternating sequence to uniform snugness, then final tightening in same sequence.

the wheel and tire assembly is rechecked.

If moving the tire to different positions on the wheel does not bring lateral runout within limits, a new tire must be installed. If radial runout is excessive, the tire tread can be "trued" so that it will be concentric with the center of rotation.

It would seem that removing rubber from the tire tread would shorten the life of the tire. Actually, its life is extended by truing since the tire will roll smoothly without thumping. The amount of runout usually is less than .125 in. Truing is not recommended if the high spots exceed 7/16 in.

Tire truing is accomplished by placing the out-of-round tire in a machine that shaves off only the high spots (excess rubber) to the level of the tread, rounding the tire and lengthening its life.

TIRE DEMOUNTING AND MOUNTING

With today's low profile tubeless tires and safety wheel rims, manual demounting and mounting of tires is not recommended. In an emergency, the job can be done with smooth tire irons to avoid scoring the beads or nicking the bead seats. After breaking the bead loose from the bead seats, the tire is worked off of the wheel by taking "small bites" with the two tire irons while the beads on the opposite side are pressed into the wheel well.

To mount the tire on the wheel, a light film of rubber lubricant is applied to the beads and the tire is "started" on the wheel, then worked into place with the two tire irons. Again, care must be exercised to avoid damaging the beads or bead seats.

Once the tire is in place on the wheel, the tire is lifted to place the outer bead against the outer bead seat and a sudden rush of compressed air is introduced to seat the bead. Air pressure up to 40 psi may be used to seat the bead, with the valve core removed. Once the beads are seated, the valve core is reinstalled and the tire is inflated to recommended pressure.

Before installing the assembly on the car, check the position of the tire in relation to the rim, making sure that it is concentric. To assist in this check, tires have a ring molded on the tire sidewall. The ring should be concentric with the edge of the wheel rim. If it is not concentric, the tire and wheel assembly can be jounced on the floor until the tire is correctly mounted. Then inflate the tire to the recommended pressure.

The recommended means of demounting and mounting tubeless tires is by the use of a power operated tire changer, Fig. 49-20. Many different changers are available and most get the job done in minutes. Generally, the wheel and tire assembly is placed on the bed of the tire changer and locked in place. Shoes of the power bead breaker are dropped in place at the point where bead and rim meet and pressure is applied.

After loosening both beads from the rim flanges, the inside of the wheel and both beads are lubricated. A special tool is used to manually, or with power assistance, remove the beads from the rims of the wheel, using the tire changer center post as a fulcrum.

This procedure is reversed to reinstall the tire on the wheel. Again, a film of lubricant is applied. If the beads will not seat,

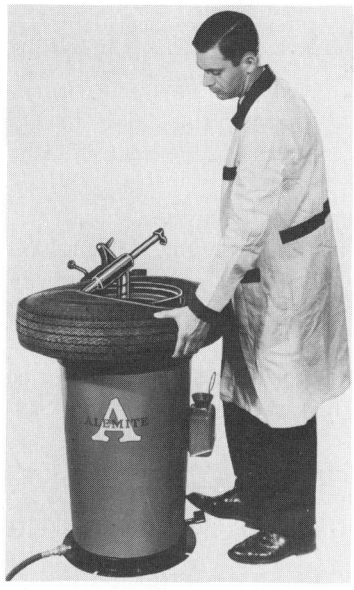

Fig. 49-20. Power operated tire changer speeds tire removal and reinstallation with no damage to tire beads or wheel rim.

a bead expander can be installed around the circumference of the tire. Tightening it, or inflating it, will force the tread inward and the beads outward to aid the bead-seating process.

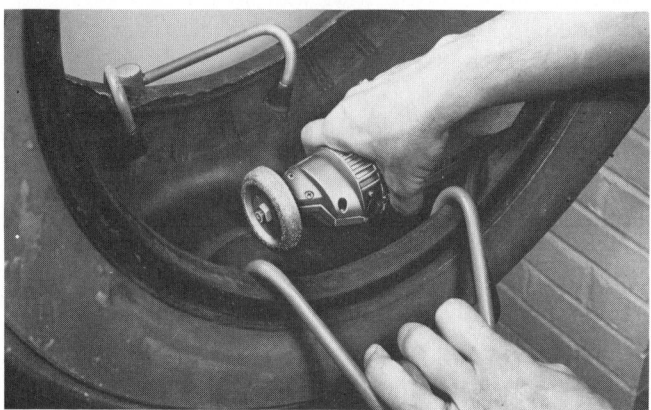

Fig. 49-21. One recommended tubeless tire puncture repair is by installing a plug from inside-out, then covering it with a cold patch or self-vulcanizing patch.

TIRE REPAIRS

Tire repairs can be made in many different ways. Puncture holes up to 1/4 in. in diameter can be plugged and patched from the inside of the tire. Small nail hole type punctures can be repaired quickly from outside-in by inserting a plug, shooting a rubber rivet or sealing the hole with several plies of cord type material saturated with vulcanizing cement. However, these are emergency only methods. A permanent inside-out repair must be made as soon as possible.

Permanent repair methods include head type plug, cold patch, hot patch and chemically or electrically vulcanized

patch. Plugs and rivets are designed to stretch for easy installation into the puncture hole, then return to full molded size to seal in air and seal out dirt and moisture. Plugs and rivets can be installed by using an inserting needle, guide-and-plunger tool or a gun. When installed, the plug top or rivet tail is cut off flush with the tire tread.

Patches are cemented in place over the puncture hole by creating a bond between the underside of the patch and the inner wall of the tire. Installing filler rubber or tire repair dough in the puncture hole before the patch is installed is recommended by some repair kit manufacturers. Others have a soft, laminated patch having a layer of soft rubber that flows into the puncture hole while the car is being driven.

The cold patch and the self-vulcanizing patch are installed in the same way: The puncture hole is probed with a tool dipped in vulcanizing cement. An area twice the size of the patch is buffed and cleaned with solvent. Filler rubber is installed. A uniform coat of vulcanizing cement is applied to the buffed area and allowed to dry. The patch is installed over the puncture hole and stitched in place, Fig. 49-21.

The electric vulcanizing patch is snapped in place in the heating element. This assembly is centered over the puncture hole and a U-clamp is locked in place over it, Fig. 49-22. Secondary and ground wires are attached to a transformer, patch heating element and the U-clamp. The transformer power lead is plugged into a 120V AC receptacle and electric vulcanization takes place automatically.

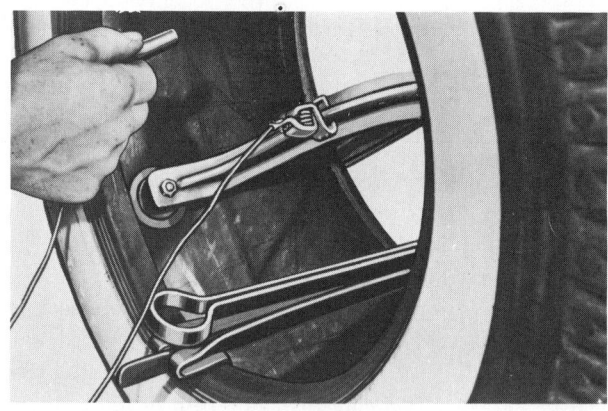

Fig. 49-22. Tire spread apart for repair by electric vulcanization.

TIRE VALVES

Basically, tire valves are air checks that open under air pressure and close when pressure is removed. Details of a tire valve used in a tubeless tire are shown in Fig. 49-23. The inner valve or core acts as a check valve for the air. Positive sealing is provided by the valve cap, which contains a soft rubber washer or gasket. It is this gasket, pressed against the end of the valve stem which seals the air in the tire. The careless practice of operating tires without the valve cap should not be followed. Without the valve cap in place, there usually is a slow seepage of air from the tire, with the result that the tire will be operated in an underinflated condition.

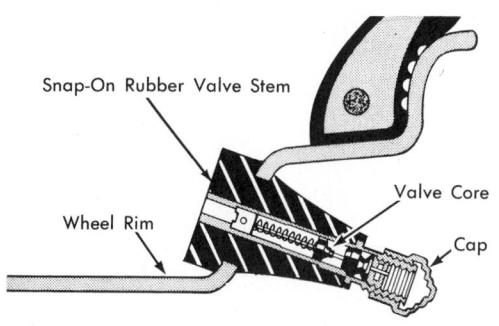

Fig. 49-23. Cross section shows location and details of tire valve in rim of tubeless tire.

Should air leaks occur around the valve base, it is necessary to install a new tire valve assembly. This is easily accomplished by means of a special lever type tool shown in Fig. 49-24.

RETREADING AND RECAPPING

The life of a tire can be materially extended by either recapping or retreading. Recapping means adding a top strip (called camelback) of synthetic or reclaimed rubber to the buffed and roughened surface of a worn tire. Retreading means adding full width new rubber to the worn tire. The terms are used rather loosely and interchangeably in the tire

Fig. 49-24. Lever type tools are available for pushing or pulling a tire valve assembly into a wheel rim.

industry, but a retread is ordinarily a better and more thorough job since new rubber is bonded from one tire shoulder to the other.

The experience of truck fleet operators shows that by retreading tire life is increased from 75 to 100 percent. In general, truck tires are in need of retreading after 35,000 to 70,000 miles of service, depending on road conditions, climate and type of service. Radial tires are said to add 12 percent more mileage to these figures.

Tires with weak spots should not be retreaded. Most operators retread before the tread design is worn off.

METRIC MARKINGS

The tire industry is going metric. Some of the major manufacturers are stamping their tire size designations in metrics. See Fig. 49-25. The industry objective is to have uniform tire size markings worldwide.

Fig. 49-25. Passenger car tire size designations are being stamped in metric markings. Note P215/75R15.

An example of a popular size in metric is P215/75R15, which replaces the former "alpha-numeric" size GR78-15. Each letter and number has a meaning:

P — Indicates passenger tire.

215 — Width of tire cross section in millimetres.

75 — Means the tire cross section is 75 percent as high as it is wide (aspect ratio).

R — Denotes radial construction.

15 — Rim diameter in inches.

If the tire is bias-belted construction, the letter before the rim diameter would be "B." If the body construction is bias-ply, the letter would be "D" (for diagonal). To help simplify the changeover, many tires have both metric and the old alpha-numeric size designations molded in the sidewalls.

Another unfamiliar marking on new tires is maximum air pressure, which is marked in both the familiar psi and in metric kilopascals (kPa). A typical air pressure would be 26 psi in the old system and 180 kPa in the metric system. (Multiply psi by 6.9 to get kPa.)

Maximum load is also given in metric and English measures. Note in Fig. 49-25 that MAX LOAD is 790 kilograms or 1,742 pounds.

Air pressure gauges that measure pressure in kilopascals are available.

REVIEW QUESTIONS — TIRES, TIRE SERVICE

1. What are the three major parts of a tubeless tire?
2. Tire cords are laid parallel in layers and impregnated with rubber to form _____.
3. What is section height of a tire?
4. What is aspect ratio of a tire?
   a. Ratio of section height to section width.
   b. Ratio of section width to section height.
5. In the new tire size designations, what does the first letter stand for in size F78-14?
   a. Ply rating.
   b. Aspect ratio.
   c. Load range.
6. How does a belted bias tire differ from a bias-ply tire?
7. Radial tires have carcass plies laid circumferentially around the tire. True or False?
8. Radial tires give a softer ride than bias-ply or belted bias tires at medium and high speeds. Yes or No?
9. Ply rating is a tire designation that is being dropped in favor of _____ _____.
10. Does tire inflation pressure increase or decrease as its temperature rises?
11. Tire wear _____ molded into the tread of most modern tires serve as visual proof that the tread is approaching worn-out condition.
12. Name five types of abnormal tread wear.
13. Taking turns too fast (cornering) will wear:
    a. Center of tread.
    b. Outer edges of tread.
14. Describe wear of tire treads resulting from excessive toe-in.
15. How much radial runout is permitted on a wheel rim?
16. What is the purpose of the ring molded in the sidewall of the tire?
17. Outside-in plug repairs of punctures in tubeless tires are not recommended. True or False?
18. Which provides positive sealing for a tire:
    a. Valve cap.
    b. Valve core.
19. Recapping and retreading are two good methods of extending tire life. Which is considered better?

Inspector at Firestone tire plant examines tire tread, beads and interior of tire, three of more than 1000 checks made during tire production.

Driver uses a pressure gauge to make monthly check of radial tire inflation to assure maximum life of tire tread, beads and interior of tire.

BODY REPAIRING, REFINISHING

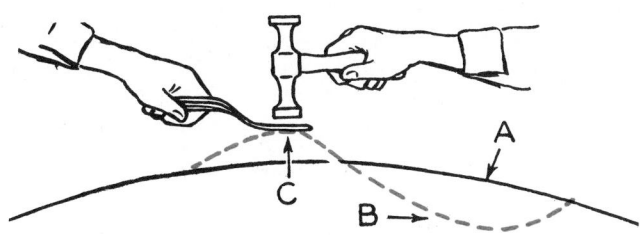

Fig. 50-1. To remove a dent, apply pressure first at the ridge farthest from where the panel was struck.

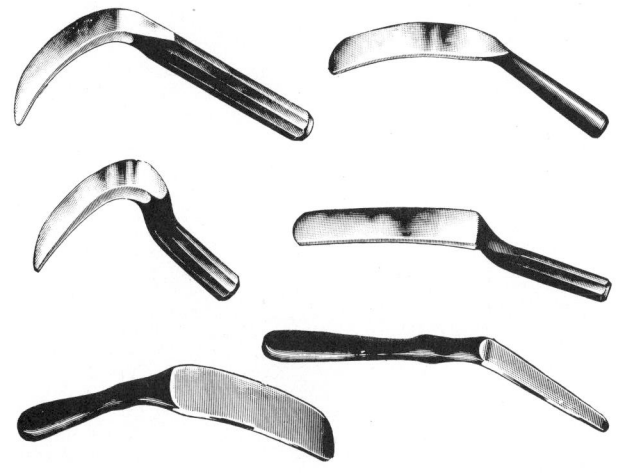

Fig. 50-2. Various types of spoons. Above. Short elbow and curved spoons. Center. Offset straight and long elbow spoons. Below. Curved flat and flat long spoons. (Duro Metal Products Co.)

Regardless of how badly a body panel or fender has been damaged, it can be straightened. Special tools and equipment are necessary, plus the required skill on the mechanic's part. However, in cases of severe damage, it may be quicker and more economical to replace the part than to repair it.

Straightening sheet metal is much easier than it appears to be. With modern equipment and tools, the work proceeds rapidly. The necessary skill can be attained in a relatively short time by practicing on junked fenders, doors or panels.

The ease and speed with which sheet metal can be straightened is largely dependent on starting the repair work in the right way. When done correctly, the amount of "dinging" is reduced, Fig. 50-1. Also, stretching of the sheet metal will be kept to a minimum, and the amount of hand filing and sanding will be materially reduced.

When straightening a wrinkled panel, the damage should be removed in the reverse order in which it was made. When a collision occurs, there will be a major depression in the panel, followed by a buckled area and then by a series of ridges.

Without proper instruction, a mechanic will usually apply pressure at the spot where the panel was struck first and where it is depressed the most. The correct method is to apply pressure at the ridge farthest from the point where the body was struck first. Occasionally when this is done, the entire damage will spring back into its original position.

To make the procedure clear, assume that the orginal form of the panel is shown at A in Fig. 50-1. Point B is where it was struck, and C is a ridge formed last. As indicated, start at point C. Place a spoon, Fig. 50-2, on top of the ridge and strike it

with a mallet or hammer. Follow the ridge with the spoon and mallet, and you will find that as the ridge is removed, the major depression at B will also spring back and conform very closely with the original contour of the panel.

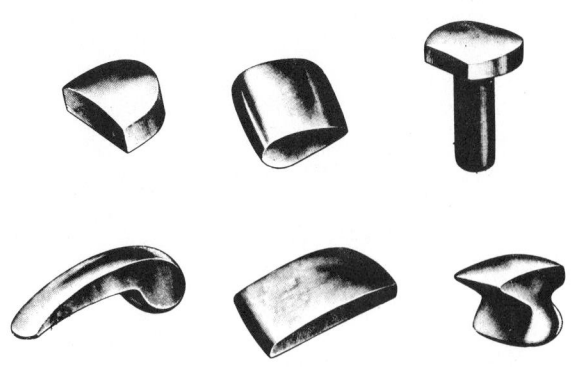

Fig. 50-3. Assortment of dolly blocks. Above. Heel, utility and mushroom dollies. Below. Wedge, toe and general purpose dollies.

The few remaining dents are then removed with a dolly block, Fig. 50-3, and hammer. Select a dolly block with a face of the same general curvature as the panel. Hold it under the panel and strike the high point of the dents with a dinging hammer. In this way, the dolly block acts as an anvil. The blows tend to stretch the metal by making it thinner.

TOOLS REQUIRED IN BODY REPAIR WORK

Hand fender-straightening tools
Bench for straightening panels and doors
Bolt cutters
Car stands
C-clamps
Center punches and drifts
Cold chisels
Air compressor
Creepers
Drill sets
Bolt extractors
Fender covers
Fire extinguishers
Bench grinder
Hammers
Chain hoist
Garage jack
Hand jacks
Lift
Metal shears
Pliers
Pry bars
Hacksaws
Hole saws
Power saws
Screwdrivers
Power sheet metal saw
Seat covers
Soldering iron
Steel rule
Stepladder
Tap-and-die sets
Headlight testers
Radiator repair equipment
Thread chasers
Tire service and repair equipment
Towing and wrecking equipment
Complete wrench sets, pull rods
Electric drills (1/4, 1/2 and 3/4 in.)
Trouble light and extension cords
Paint sprayer, striping brushes
Spray booth, drying lamps
Welding equipment and accessories
Sander and polisher, glass cutting and grinding outfit
Panel-clamping repair units
Frame straightener, body straightening jacks
Wheel alignment equipment, wheel balancer
Wheel pullers, wheel straightener
Workbench, bench vise, arbor press
Ventilating fan and exhaust conduits

HAMMERS AND DOLLY BLOCKS

All that is required of the hammer is to press the sheet metal back into position. Therefore, a lot of light hammer blows should be used rather than a few heavy ones. If the metal is stretched, a large bulge will result which will require shrinking.

The hammer blows should be at the rate of approximately 60 per minute, and try to "pull" the hammer so it strikes the surface of the sheet metal with a sliding or glancing blow.

Note, too, that when the dent rises above the surface of the dolly block, the hammer should strike the center of the dent. But if the dent is below the surface of the metal and toward the dolly, place the dolly against the head of the dent and direct the hammer blows against the edge of the dent. Hold the hammer loosely with the thumb along the top of the handle for better control of the bounce.

There are many different designs of hammers, Figs. 50-4 to 50-6. They come in different size faces (square faces, round faces, serrated faces) and varying length shanks (pointed shanks, roughing hammers, etc.), each designed for a specific type of work.

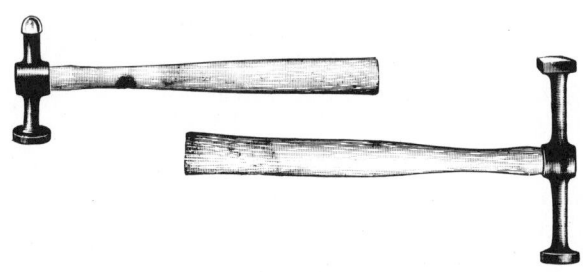

Fig. 50-4. Two types of dinging hammers.

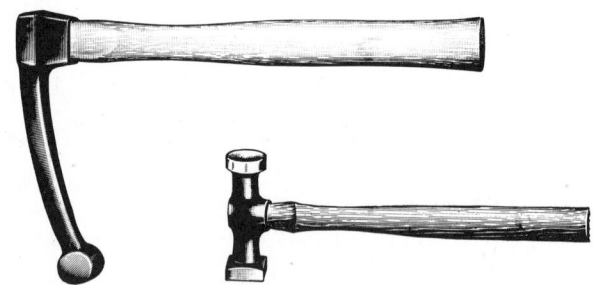

Fig. 50-5. Two roughing hammers.

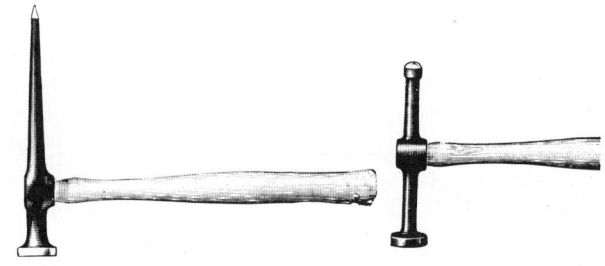

Fig. 50-6. Left. Pick hammer. Right. Another dinging hammer.

These hammers are not to be used to strike against other hardened objects. They are to be used only for striking automotive type sheet metal.

A short shank hammer is needed where there is limited space to work. The long shank type is needed when working in a deep contour. The serrated face hammer is for shrinking metal; the tapered shank type is for working on molding, etc. All should be included in a body worker's kit.

Similarly, there are a large variety of spoons, Fig. 50-2, and dolly blocks, Fig. 50-3, each shaped and sized to make certain tough jobs easy. The spoons are used primarily on polished surfaces. That is, the spoon is placed against the finished surface of a panel and is struck with the hammer. Spoons occasionally are used as a dolly, if space limitations prevent the use of a regular dolly. They are also used for prying a bulge in a door or trunk lid back into place.

Dollies vary in weight, shape and contour so that they will conform to the curve of the panel and can be used in cramped quarters. Some provide grooves for working beads and molding. Skill is using these tools can be quickly attained by working on junk panels and fenders. The important point is to have a wide selection of spoons, dollies and hammers so that all types of body work can be handled.

As the dents in the body panel are gradually removed, occasionally rub your hand over the surface. This will help determine those spots which require further straightening. Then when that method fails to show any high or low spots, use the body file, Figs. 50-7 and 50-8. Only light cuts should

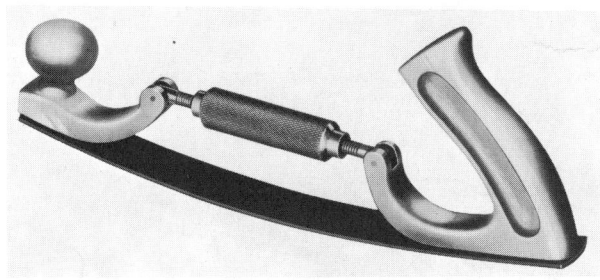

Fig. 50-7. Flexible type body file holder.

Fig. 50-8. Flexible milled tooth body file for use in holder shown in Fig. 50-7.

be made. Remember that the purpose is not to remove metal, but to show the areas that require further attention with the dolly and hammer.

Finally, use a sander to locate the few remaining irregularities, and to remove any slight roughness that cannot be removed with the dolly.

Fig. 50-9. To prepare for use of pull rods, drill series of 9/64 in. (3.6 mm) holes in deepest part of crease.

USING PULL RODS

When removing dents and creases from auto body panels, considerable time is often required to first remove interior trim. Also, the work is complicated when the damage is located in doors and rear trunk lids. In these areas, metal braces and other structural members make it difficult to use the conventional dolly and hammer method.

On many such jobs, the use of pull rods makes it unnecessary to remove upholstery or interior trim since the work is done entirely from the outside of the damaged panel.

The procedure is to drill a series of 9/64 in. (3.6 mm) holes in the deepest part of the creases. These holes should be about 1/4 in. (6.4 mm) apart, Fig. 50-9. The crease is then worked up gradually by inserting the hooked ends of the pull rods in the holes and pulling on the handles, Fig. 50-10. Two in each hand may be used.

In Fig. 50-9, the repair is started at the front edge of the door. Work to the rear, then start at the front again. Pull on the rods should be at right angle to the surface of the panel. Be sure to pull and not pry. In this method, light reflection is a big help in locating high and low spots.

After the dents have been removed, fill the holes with solder, Fig. 50-11.

In cases of severe damage, a slide hammer can be used in a similar manner to pull out the dents in the panel. If necessary, a reinforcing plate can be placed on the inside of the panel to prevent the slide hammer from pulling through the sheet metal of the panel.

POWER STRAIGHTENING

While the hand dolly and dinging hammer are used extensively, there is a growing trend toward the use of power dinging equipment. Power tools of this type are available from a number of different manufacturers. Both electric and pneumatic types are available. On accessible panels where they can be used, considerable time can be saved. In addition,

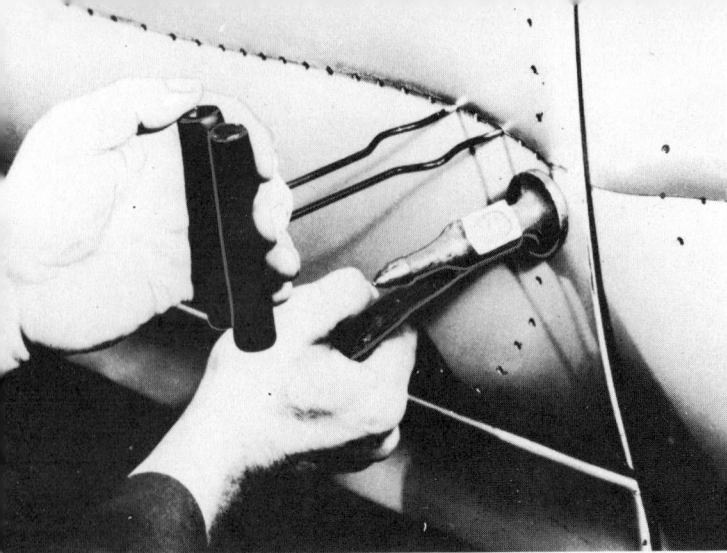

Fig. 50-10. Metal is pulled out by means of pull rods until it coincides with original contour.

Fig. 50-11. After straightening sheet metal, holes are filled with solder.

Fig. 50-12. Using a belt sander with vacuum attachment.

Fig. 50-13. Using a disk sander.

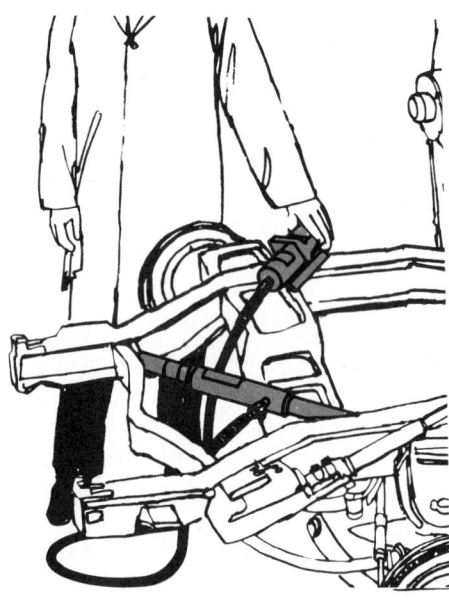

Fig. 50-14. Using hydraulic power equipment to straighten a frame. (Blackhawk, Applied Power, Inc.)

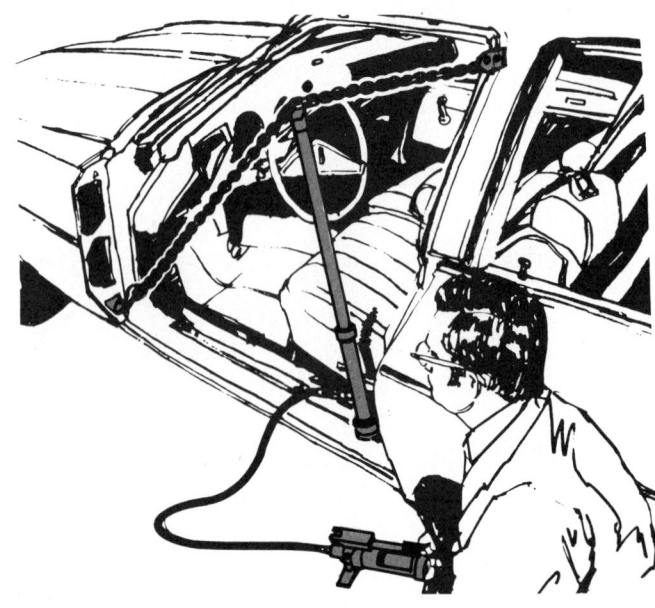

Fig. 50-15. Using a hydraulic pump, ram, extension tube and chain to pull a door post into alignment. (Blackhawk, Applied Power, Inc.)

power tools will not stretch the metal as much as conventional dolly and hammer work. The amount of filing or sanding required to finish the fender or panel usually is less than required with hand methods. See Figs. 50-12 and 50-13.

Occasionally, it is awkward to use power operated dinging hammers on car tops and other large areas where damage is more than 18 or 20 in. from the edge of the panel. However, power equipment works well where damage is close to the edge.

Another important piece of equipment for straightening bodies is the specialized hydraulic jack or pump and ram. This type of repair kit has fittings and accessories designed to remove dents and to push or pull damaged panels and parts back into position, Figs. 50-14 to 50-17.

In addition to rough straightening of panels, hydraulic rams and accessories have many other uses. Applications include: straightening diamond-shaped door and window frames; squaring bodies; correcting door curvature; assisting in frame and bumper work. See Figs. 50-21 to 50-26.

Fig. 50-17. In another application, pump, ram, base plate and extension tube are used to push door opening into alignment.

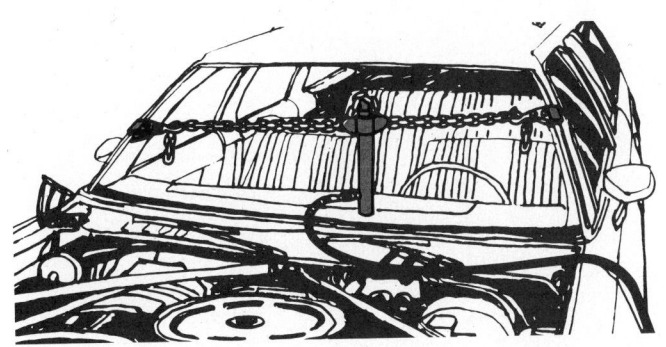

Fig. 50-16. Setup used to straighten window opening. (Blackhawk, Applied Power, Inc.)

When using hydraulic equipment to take a dent out of a panel, the same principle used with hand dollies should be followed. Apply pressure first at the outer edge of the dent, then proceed to work around the dent. Gradually approach the center. Complete the work on the panel with a hand dolly.

Before starting to straighten a panel, clean all the dirt from both sides. This can be done by scraping or by heating it lightly with a torch. Similarly, remove any undercoating material from the fenders and panels. Mud and grit adhering to panels will mar the surface of the straightening tools. Undercoating will make the job more difficult.

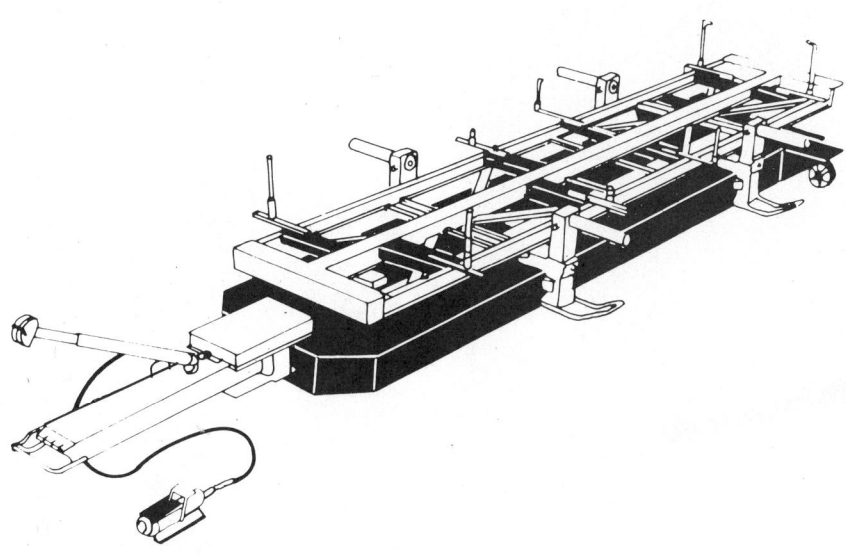

Fig. 50-18. This universal measuring and correction system measures in three directions at the same time. Vehicle is secured to "bench" for power straightening of damaged areas. (Blackhawk, Applied Power, Inc.)

Another piece of equipment that is of value in straightening doors and other panels is the straightening table, Fig. 50-19. The damaged part is clamped rigidly to the table and in position to be straightened with hand or power tools.

STRAIGHTENING UNITIZED BODIES

Heat and the use of heavy-duty jacks must be carefully controlled when straightening unitized bodies. Care must be taken because of the difference in the gauge of the metal in the subframe of the body and at the stress points. Ford Motor Company, on the other hand, says it is possible to pull

Fig. 50-21. Spreading engine compartment sheet metal with hydraulic straightening equipment. (Hein-Werner Corp.)

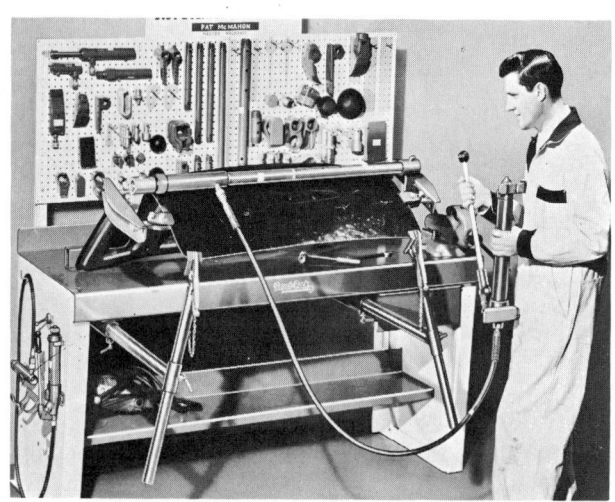

Fig. 50-19. Special straightening table is designed to "hold" damaged panel while being straightened.

Fig. 50-20. With this power straightening equipment, unitized body is secured to steel members set in floor, then pressure is applied at several different places at the same time. (Blackhawk, Applied Power, Inc.)

Fig. 50-22. Making direct push with special equipment to straighten front end damage. (Hein-Werner Corp.)

Fig. 50-23. Spreading front fenders of a van to align hood opening. (Hein-Werner Corp.)

damaged areas back into place and in alignment by means of lightweight jacks and hydraulic equipment without the use of heat.

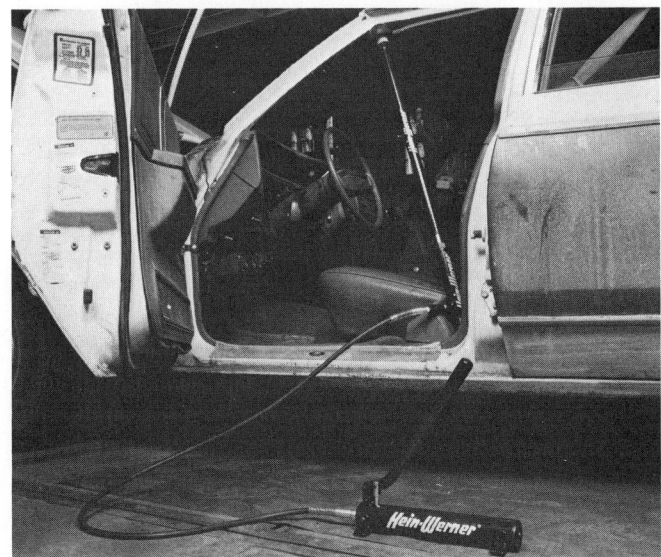

Fig. 50-24. Using hydraulic ram and extension tube to push windshield pillar into alignment with door. (Hein-Werner Corp.)

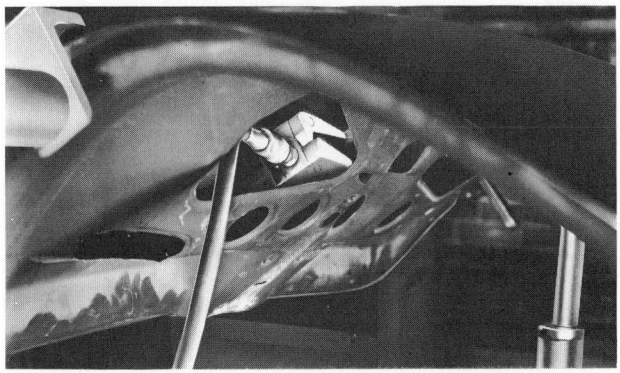

Fig. 50-25. Popping out dent in deck lid with hydraulic spreader. (Blackhawk Mfg. Co.)

Fig. 50-26. Using hydraulic pump, ram and extension tube to realign trunk opening with trunk lid. (Hein-Werner Corp.)

However, many body shops find that repairs can be made more quickly if specialized equipment is used. With certain types of equipment, the damaged vehicle is first secured to a "bench" (floor or rack type), Figs. 50-18 and 50-20. Then, corrective pulls and/or pushes are made at several points at the same time.

Dimensional drawings of the vehicle are needed when working on a unitized body. Wheel alignment settings of caster and camber are built into the body in most cases.

When checking a unitized body for misalignment, it is necessary to check measurements taken between reference points on the vehicle against those indicated on the drawings. These measurements are indicated not only in the horizontal plane, but also vertically from the floor or from the bench to which the vehicle has been secured. These dimensions are held to 1/16 in. (1.6 mm) limits.

In general, damaged areas should be roughed out before taking any measurements for squaring up the body. In severe cases, reinforcement brackets and other inner construction may have to be removed before restoration of the outer shell and pillars. This will avoid excessive strain on the parts. Always straighten, install and secure such parts in place before attempting to align the unitized body.

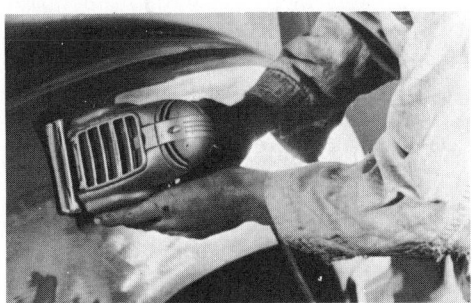

Fig. 50-27. Featheredging with a block-type sander. Disk-type sanders are also used for this purpose.

BODY FILES, SANDING EQUIPMENT

After the sheet metal has been made as smooth as possible by means of a hammer and dolly, the next step is to file or sand the surface to remove any tool marks or other dents that are too small to remove by the hammer and dolly. In addition, it is necessary to sand back (feather) the paint, Fig. 50-27, surrounding the edges of the straightened area of sheet metal. This is important because a smooth surface must be provided for the filler, primer and other coats of refinishing material.

Special files, sanding materials and equipment designed especially for automotive body work are available.

A body file is flexible and made to fit a special holder, Fig. 50-7. The holder can be adjusted to arch the file to conform to the curvature of the body panel. The teeth of the file are curved and designed to cut fast and not load up when used on the sheet iron of the body or a solder-filled dent.

The surface is filed first in one direction, then in the other at approximately a right angle. On the return stroke, the file should be lifted from the surface being filed. This will not only produce a smoother surface but will also prolong the life of the file. Dragging the file along the surface of the metal on the return stroke will tend to dull the teeth. It is important to note, however, that special body files can be resharpened.

POWER SANDING

Because a sanding disk is flexible, it will follow the larger indentations in a body. For that reason, a power sander is used to locate the high and low spots when the straightening process has been nearly completed. Of course, its primary function is for the final finishing of the metal surface. In addition, a sander can be used to remove the paint or other refinishing material surrounding the damaged area. This is known as featheredging.

Before sanding a panel, it is important to select the disk having the correct abrasive for that particular surface. In this connection, many shops use three different grits to prepare the surface for repainting. They first use a 16 grit disk to remove rust and loose paint and for cutting down solder spots. This is followed with a 24 grit disk for surfacing the metal, restoring contours, and for cutting down welds. Then, for an excellent final finish, a 50 grit disk is used.

Instead of three different grits, some body workers prefer to use a 24 grit disk as an all-purpose sander. However, one manufacturer of sanding disks claims that on a comparable job the three-disk method will take 11.7 minutes to complete the work while 15 to 18 minutes will be required for the single abrasive method.

For sharply curved surfaces, which cannot be reached by conventional sanders, special cone-type sanders are available. These sanders will reach curved surfaces around headlights, fender joints, back deck panels, etc.

After the surface of the panel has been thoroughly sanded, it is necessary to sand the edges of the paint surrounding the area of the straightened panel. Some body workers use a disk-type sander, others prefer an oscillating or block-type sander, Fig. 50-27.

In disk featheredging, a 100 grit disk is usually recommended. An 80 grit disk is used in the oscillating sander and for hand sanding too, with 220 grit being used for finished featheredging.

When disk sanding, hold the disk grinding machine at an angle of approximately 20 degrees to work, Fig. 50-28. Apply sufficient pressure so that about 1 inch of the disk is bent and is in contact with the surface being sanded. The disk sander should never be operated so the entire area of the disk is flat against the surface of the work, nor at an extreme angle.

Also worth noting, the disk grinder should not be swung in an arc. It should always be moved so that it is perpendicular to the scratch lines. By sanding in this fashion, less conditioning is required to prepare the metal for priming.

An oscillating sander should be operated so that the scratch lines will be approximately parallel. Hand sanding should produce the same effect.

There are many different types and grits of sanding disks available. Follow the manufacturers' instructions for their use.

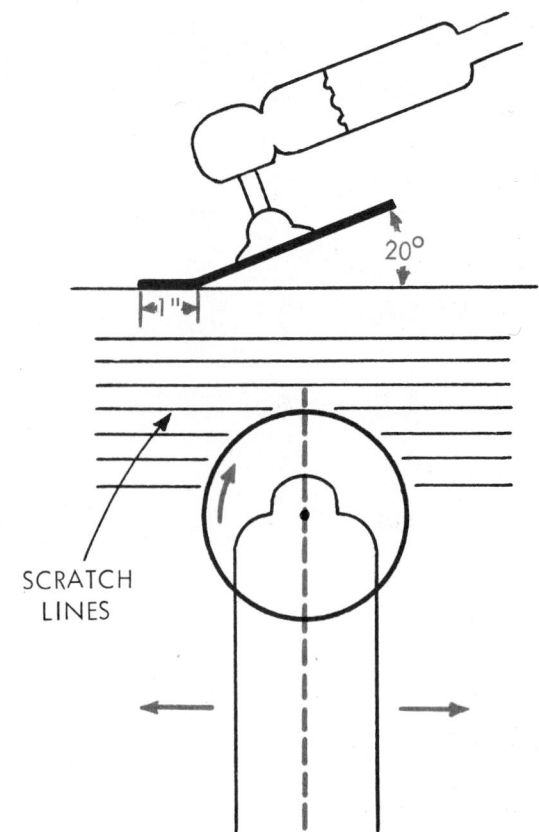

Fig. 50-28. When using a disk sander, hold it at approximately 20 deg. to surface of panel.

PATCHING RUSTED AREAS

When body panels have become rusted through or badly dented many body workers repair the damage by one of the commercial methods developed for this purpose. One popular method consists of using sheets of special "fabric" such as fiber glass. The fiber glass method of repair is used extensively on doors and other panels where heat and solder cannot be used without first removing interior upholstery and trim.

For example, the dent in the door shown in Fig. 50-29, could not be filled with solder. Heat used in the operation would destroy the interior trim, so it had to be removed first.

With the fabric plastic method, such additional work is not necessary. First thoroughly sand the surface of the dent to remove all traces of rust, paint and other foreign material. Then fill it with resin-soaked fiber glass patches, cutting the final patch large enough to lap over the surrounding undamaged surfaces, Fig. 50-30. Next, apply epoxy metal solder, Fig. 50-31, over the last patch to build area to final contour and to fill pits and indentations. When thoroughly dry, sand the surface of the epoxy solder, Fig. 50-32, and the job is ready for painting.

WARNING: Use special care — and goggles — when adding hardener (catalyst) to fiber glass resin. If one drop of hardener gets in your eye, it will progressively destroy eye tissue and result in blindness. The hardener MUST be washed from the eye within four seconds after the accident.

Fig. 50-29. Dents like this can be repaired with special body compounds or fiber glass, without removing interior trim.

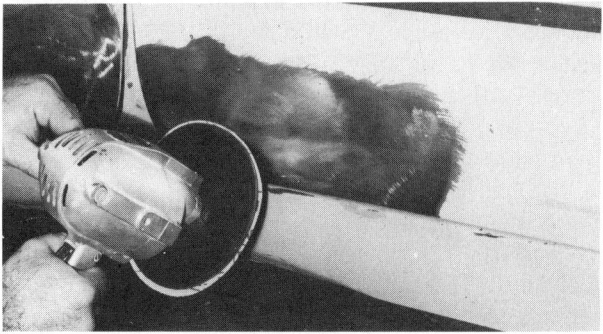

Fig. 50-32. After thorough drying, surface is sanded and made ready for painting.

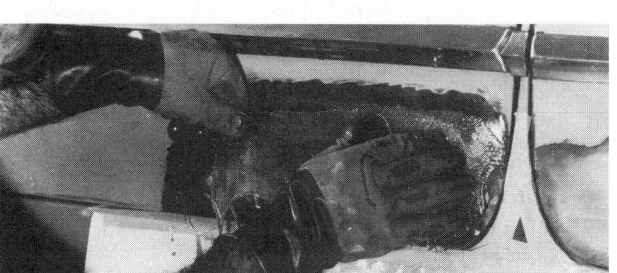

Fig. 50-30. After sanding dented surface, sheet of fiber glass soaked in special solutions is used to fill area.

Fig. 50-33. Applying a special body cement of plastic solder to fill dents in a fender.

Fig. 50-31. Epoxy metal solder is then applied with a putty knife.

all that is needed. Usually, you can apply it with a putty knife or spatula. If the dents are deep, allow ample time for drying.

BODY SOLDER

An early, and still occasionally used, method of filling dents in automobile bodies is by means of solder. With this method, solder is used extensively for filling small dents and smoothing rough surfaces which are difficult to straighten completely with dolly block and hammer.

Another use for solder is to form crushed drip moldings and other contours which are difficult to restore to their normal shape. Also, solder can be used for filling large dents, but most bodymen prefer to at least "rough out" the damaged surface. In that way, the amount of solder used is materially reduced.

Manufacturers provide solder of special formulas designed especially for automotive body repairing. This solder is correctly proportioned so that it can be applied to vertical surfaces, can be sanded, and refinishing materials will adhere to it.

Before attempting to fill a dent with body solder, thorough-

Another method of repair is to use a body cement or plastic solder. The material is first mixed according to the manufacturer's directions, then applied as shown in Fig. 50-33. It is then sanded in the usual manner.

Naturally, details for making body repairs of this kind will differ somewhat with the various manufacturers' products. However, in all cases, the surface of the metal must be thoroughly cleaned and sanded before making the repair. This is necessary in order to obtain proper adherence between the repair material and the sheet metal of the body.

This type of repair material (epoxy metal solder, body cement, plastic solder, etc.) sands well, is readily featheredged, and the sanded surface is well adapted for all forms and types of paint. When properly applied and prepared, the final finish cannot be distinguished from the original body finish.

If the area to be repaired is small, the special body metal is

ly clean the surface to remove all paint, rust and grease. This is important because it is impossible to tin a dirty surface. Most bodymen use a No. 16 grit open coat paper and follow that up with a No. 24 grit closed coat. When the surface is clean, give it a coat of flux, then tin it.

Since the body metal is sheet steel, a flux designed for use on that metal should be used. Always follow the manufacturer's instructions if a commercial flux is used. Many shops, however, use a solution made from zinc dissolved in hydrochloric acid. The body panel surface is heated slightly, then it is given a coating of flux.

There are several different methods used by bodymen in tinning. Some use a conventional soldering iron. Others use a torch. The solder is pressed against the body panel with the hot iron or torch, until it melts. Then the solder is distributed over the desired area by means of the soldering iron or torch. On large areas, it will be necessary to apply additional quantities of solder until the entire surface is tinned.

Another method of tinning is to use steel wool or a piece of cloth to distribute the solder over the surface of the panel, Fig. 50-34. With this technique, a few drops of solder are melted

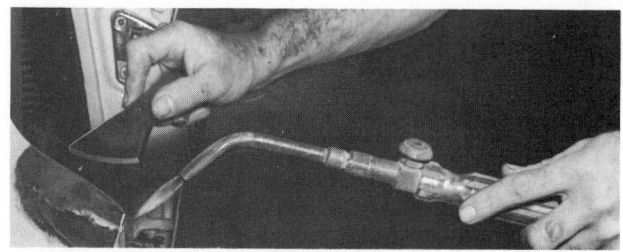
Fig. 50-35. While keeping solder soft with torch, it is spread with a wooden paddle.

After the dent has been filled and the surface made as smooth as possible with the paddle, dress it with a body file, Fig. 50-36, and then sanded with a power sander. Painting is done in the usual manner.

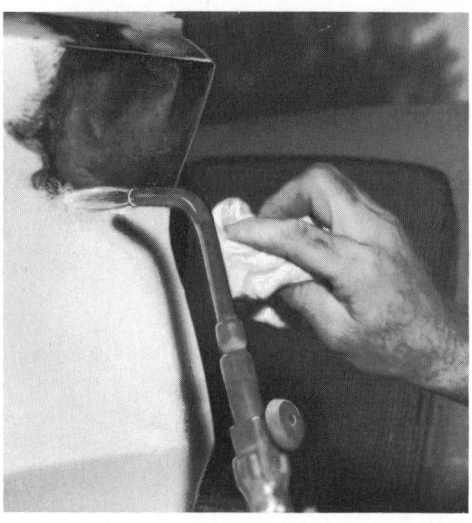
Fig. 50-34. Melting solder with a torch, preparatory to tinning surface.

by the torch so that they adhere to the panel. Then, as more heat is applied, the solder becomes liquified and can be spread over the surface by using the steel wool. The advantage of the steel wool method is that the solder can be brushed down into crevices, cracks and depressions.

Once the surface has been tinned, body solder can be applied. As heat is applied, the body solder, becomes plastic, but not liquid, so that it can be spread with a paddle, Fig. 50-35. After some lead has been applied to the panel, keep the torch in motion over the area being worked.

The distance you should hold the torch from the panel varies with the size of the flame. A little experimenting will enable you to judge the distance the flame must be held from the work, and the speed at which it should be moved back and forth across the work surface.

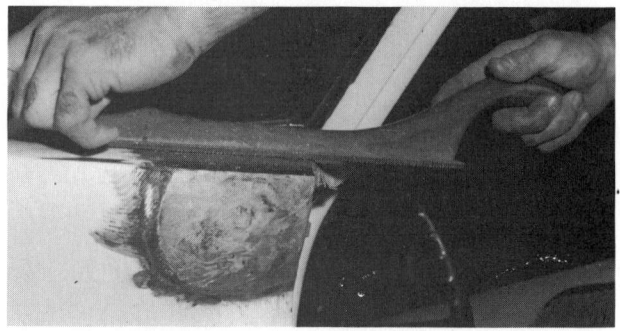
Fig. 50-36. Smoothing solder-covered surface with a body file.

Lead solder is also used to cover welds, Fig. 50-37. First, the welded seam is driven below the surface of the surrounding metal. Use a blunt-edged dolly and a hammer or power tool to make a groove a little wider than the weld. Make it about 3/16 in. deep. Then sand the groove and tin and fill it with solder. Use a body file to rough down the surface of the solder. Use a power sander for final finishing.

Rain gutters and beading on car bodies are difficult to straighten. A lot of time can be saved by forming them with body solder. After tinning, apply the solder in the usual manner and rough form it with the paddle while still soft. Then use files, scrapers and sanders to finish form the gutter or beading to the desired shape.

REPLACING PANELS

Instead of straightening a badly damaged area, time can be saved by installing a new panel or part (complete door or trunk lid).

In case of a damaged body panel, cut out the damaged area and weld in a section of a new panel. Replacement panels are available. Either the entire panel can be replaced, or only a portion, depending on the size of the damaged area.

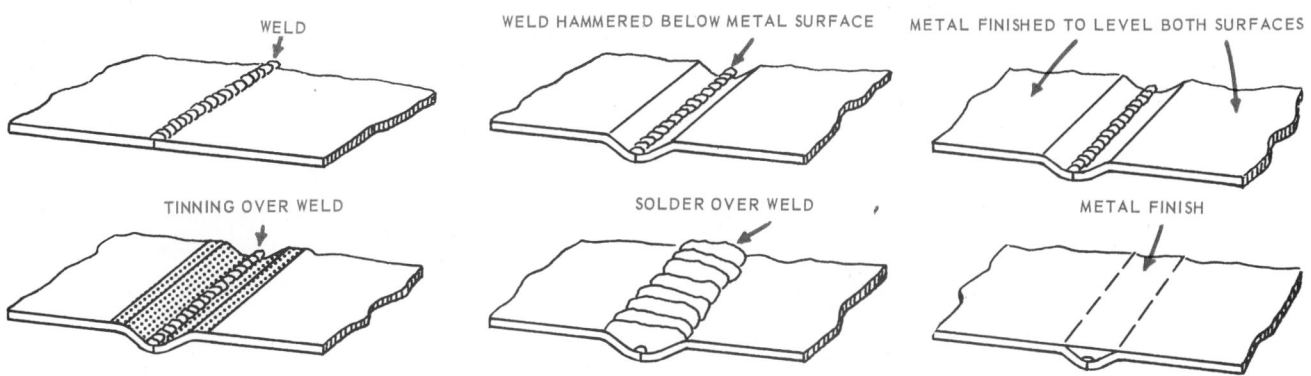

Fig. 50-37. Steps in covering welded joint with solder.

In replacing the panel, proceed as follows:

Rough out and shape the damaged area, making sure that the undamaged portion is in correct contour and not sprung out of alignment. Carefully measure the piece of metal to be replaced, Fig. 50-38. Take these measurements from the edge

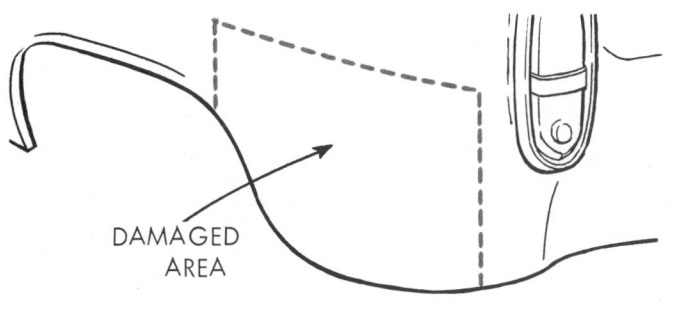

Fig. 50-38. Outline damaged area of fender as shown.

of the panel, the molding or beading. This is important since these points are to be transferred to the replacement.

Next scribe a line around the area to be cut from the service panel, then cut along the scribed line. The method of cutting will vary with the type of equipment available: electric arc, gas or mechanical cutters can be used.

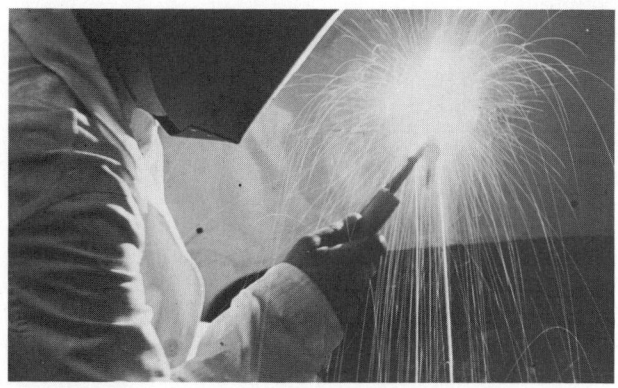

Fig. 50-39. Cutting damaged area from fender with electric torch.

Straighten the edges of this portion of new panel and position the new section over the damaged area. Scribe a line around its outer edge, and use this line as a guide in cutting out the damaged area, Fig. 50-39.

After straightening the cut edge of the fender on the car, fit the new section in position and hold it by means of C-clamps, Fig. 50-40. Tack weld the section in place, starting the welds

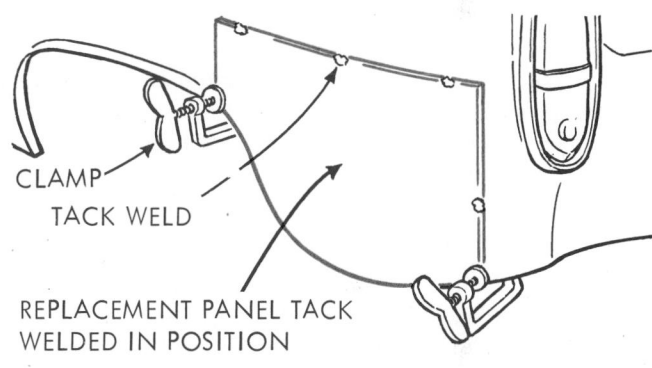

Fig. 50-40. Secure section of new fender in place with C-clamps, then weld in place.

at the top center. Work out to the sides, then down the sides. Make a continuous weld, doing a length about six inches long at a time. To reduce distortion, stagger the welds.

With a grooved dolly, hammer the weld so it is about 1/16 in. below the surface of the surrounding panel, Fig. 50-37. Sand the area around the weld with a power sander or file the surface to produce the correct contour. Next, fill the groove with hot or cold solder, then sand the surface to prepare it for painting.

If the damaged area to be replaced is at a pillar post or at a spot-welded seam, split the seam by driving a thin sharp chisel between the two pieces.

MASKING

In order to protect surfaces and panels while adjacent areas are being painted, the car should be covered with paper secured in position with tape. The paper is called masking paper, and the tape is known as masking tape.

Manufacturers of masking tape and paper have devoted much time and expense to improving their products. Their research in this field has produced special tape and paper dispensers, Fig. 50-41, as well as shortcut methods of masking.

Fig. 50-41. Dispenser for masking paper and tape.

Quality masking paper will not permit paint to penetrate or seep through to the panel it is protecting. It should be tough, but flexible enough not to scratch the paint.

The tape must adhere easily to painted and unpainted surfaces, chrome and other materials. It must have a strong texture so that it will not tear readily while being applied. The masking tape must also retain its adhering qualities when it is drenched during wet sanding operations. Flexibility or stretch is another desirable characteristic. This is important when applying the tape to curves and circles.

One timesaving method automatically applies the tape along the edge of the masking paper so that half of the width of tape extends beyond the edge of the paper. When the paper is placed in the desired position on the car, the exposed area of the tape is pressed against the panel or trim to hold the masking paper in place.

Fig. 50-42. After taping masking paper around the headlamps, overlap it with second piece of paper to form a cone.
(3M Co., Automotive Trades Div.)

MASKING HEADLIGHTS

Headlights vary in shape and size. Some are rectangular; others are round. Whatever the shape, the same basic masking procedure is used for all styles. Usually masking paper 6 to 8 in. wide is satisfactory.

First cut a piece of masking paper that will go about three-quarters of the distance around the light, or lights. Start at one side and continue until the first sheet of paper is in place. Next, apply a second piece of masking paper so that a "funnel" of paper surrounds the light, Fig. 50-42. Then fold the paper over the front of the light and hold it down with strips of masking tape, Fig. 50-43.

FRONT END MASKING

Masking a car with large areas of chrome on the front end can be most quickly accomplished by using wide paper. Each car presents a different problem and slightly different treatment. The masking procedure for a sports car is shown in Fig. 50-44. The operation is started on one side of the vehicle and the tape on the side of the masking paper is applied to the edge of the chrome trim. At the inner edge of the headlamp, the paper is folded as shown in Fig. 50-44. The masking is then carried to the other headlamp by way of the grille. Or, the headlamps, grille and bumper may be masked separately.

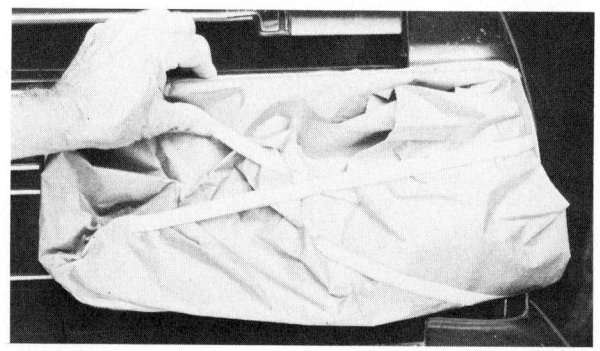

Fig. 50-43. Complete masking of headlamp by folding paper over headlamps and taping in place. (3M Co., Automotive Trades Div.)

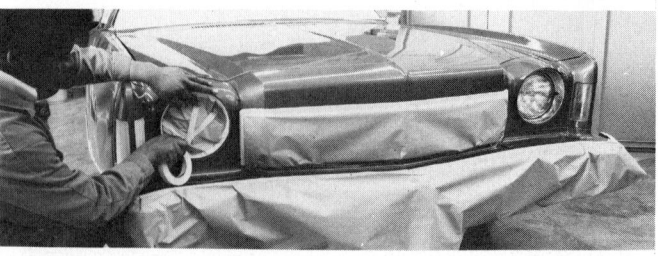

Fig. 50-44. Masking the front end of a vehicle includes bumper, grille and headlamps. (3M Co., Automotive Trades Div.)

There are many different methods of masking a window. One method is shown in Figs. 50-45 to 50-47. The first piece of taped paper is applied along the upper edge. The second goes along the right side and on a portion of the bottom edge.

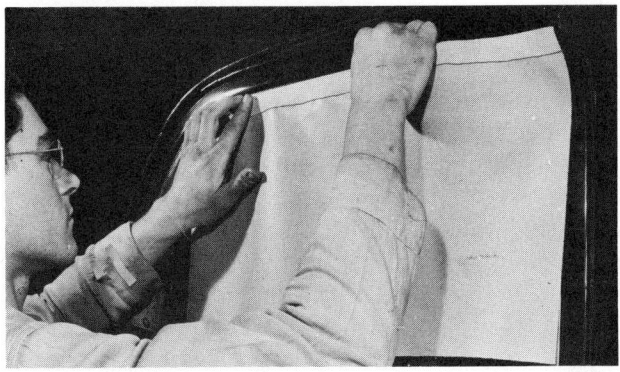

Fig. 50-45. When masking a window, first piece of paper is placed along upper edge.

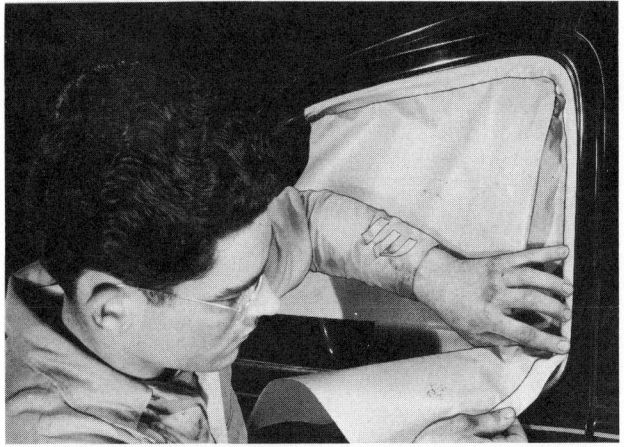

Fig. 50-46. Next step is to place masking paper along right side of window.

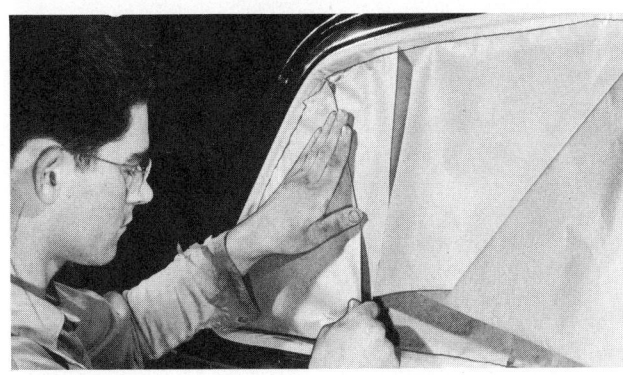

Fig. 50-47. Install third piece of masking paper over forward portion of window, using short pieces of tape to hold edges down.

The third piece covers the wind deflector and remaining portion of the lower edge.

Use short pieces of tape to hold folds down, with lower sheets underneath the upper sheet. This will keep water from wet sanding from running underneath the paper.

When you have to apply a masking apron around an inside curved surface, first pleat the apron, Fig. 50-48. This will make it easier to follow the curved contour, and it will prevent the

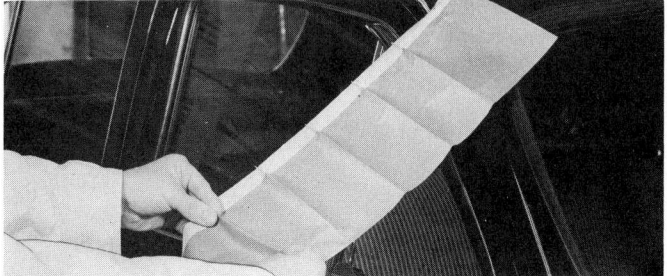

Fig. 50-48. When applying masking paper to a curved edge, first step is to pleat paper.

apron from bunching and wrinkling. Here's how it is done:
1. Cut desired length of masking paper.
2. Make a pleat about 1/4 in. deep by crimping both edges. Pleat should extend full width of apron.
3. Continue making a pleat every two to four inches.
4. Apply apron to surface. Then, after pleated apron is in place, fold untaped edge so it will catch overspray.

The "pleating" method of installing masking tape can be used to good advantage on wheels, Fig. 50-49, and also on the curved edge of doors as shown in Fig. 50-50.

The pleating method of masking a wheel saves the time of removing the wheel and tire. The procedure is to simply apply

Fig. 50-49. Taping pleated masking paper to a wheel.

a pleated, 6 in. wide mask around the entire circumference of the rim, securing the tape to the surface of the tire. Then, after removing the hubcap, the wheel and hub can be sprayed.

If the wheel is not being painted, hang masking paper from the top of the tire. This protects wheel and tire from overspray.

When masking a windshield, one method is to use 3/4 in. tape on 12 in. wide masking paper for the initial step, Fig. 50-51. Next, lay the paper on the windshield from bottom to top, securing the tape to the window's bottom edge. Curve the overlapping ends of the mask up the two side edges.

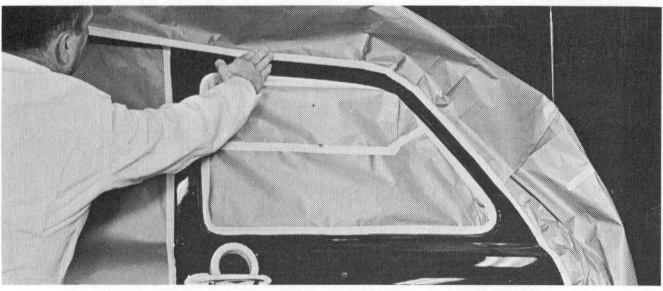

Fig. 50-50. Applying masking paper to curved edge of a door. Note pleats in paper.

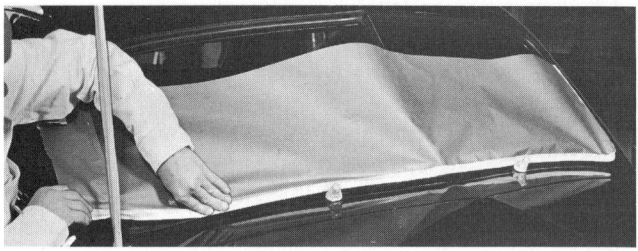

Fig. 50-51. To mask a windshield, use 3/4-in. tape on 12-in. masking paper, covering lower section of windshield first.

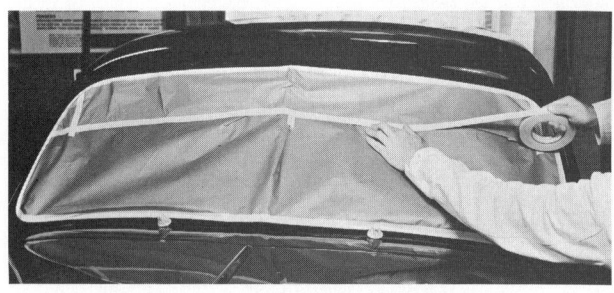

Fig. 50-52. Next, apply masking paper to top of windshield. Cover overlapping edge with a strip of tape.

running a partially pleated 12 in. mask along the door's forward and top edges (pleating permits paper to conform to door's curved edges). This protects the fender and roof from overspray while painting.

Some manufacturers emphasize that masking tape should never be pulled or stretched during application. The proper method, they say, is to lay it down easily as it comes from the roll. In this way, the possibility of it pulling back during the painting operation is eliminated. By not stretching the tape's crepe backing, it is permitted to expand and contract without pulling away when the solvents are applied.

For inside curves, narrow moldings and tabbing, 1/4 in. or 1/2 in. tapes are used. For wider moldings, 3/4 in. and 1 in. are more satisfactory.

When masking fender emblems, Fig. 50-53, 3/4 in. tape will do an excellent job. First apply the tape along the edges of the emblem to form a sharp separation line. At sharp outside curves, lay the tape over the sharpest point of the curve and draw the loose ends back along the edge of the emblem. After all the edges have been masked, finish by filling the open areas with short strips.

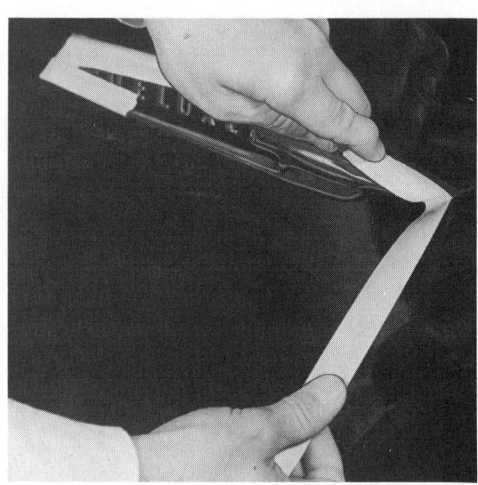

Fig. 50-53. Masking emblems can be done quickly with wide tape.

After the 12 in. mask is in place, lay a 6 in. mask along the windshield's top edge, allowing the paper to overlap the surface of the first covering, Fig. 50-52. When both the 6 in. and 12 in. masks are in place, finish the job by applying a 3/4 in. strip of tape over the seam formed by the overhanging mask. For very large windshields, it may be necessary to use 12 in. masks on both the lower portion and upper portion of the window.

Before masking a front door, first mask off all chrome fittings and moldings. Secondly, apply a 12 in. wide length of masking paper over the lower portion of the window, and place a 6 in. wide mask over the upper portion. For the third step, apply a 12 in. wide mask from the door's rear edge, back over the rear window and side panel area.

Next, install a 6 in. wide mask from the front fender to the rear fender along the door's bottom edge. Finish the job by

WELDING BODY PANELS

The importance of welding in an auto repair shop can best be appreciated from the fact that over 85 percent of shops have welding equipment. Skill in using the equipment is not difficult to develop. In gas welding, practice and a thorough understanding of the adjustment of the flame and in the selection of the correct tip for a given job are the main requisites. When welding or cutting with electricity, correct current is the most important consideration.

Before starting any gas welding or cutting job, the oxygen and acetylene cylinders must be chained either to a post or placed in a special cylinder truck, Fig. 50-54. This prevents them from being tipped over. Before attaching the regulators, Fig. 50-55, to the cylinders, each valve should be opened slightly to blow any dirt from the valve seat.

Fig. 50-54. Oxygen and acetylene cylinders should be mounted in a truck or chained to a post or workbench.

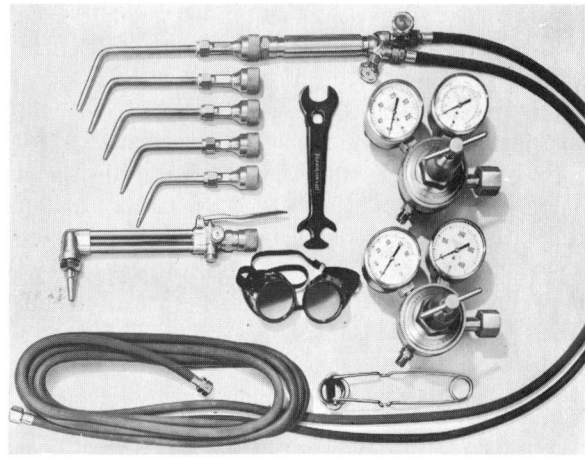

Fig. 50-56. Welding and cutting torch, together with gauges, wrench and igniter. Note assorted tips for welding.

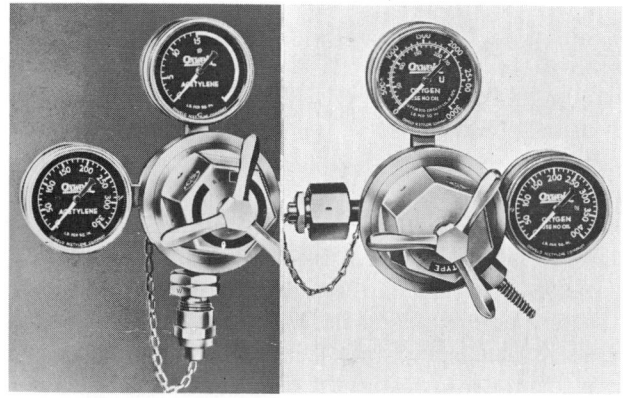

Fig. 50-55. An acetylene regulator is shown at left. An oxygen regulator is at right.

To avoid danger of fire, be sure there is no flame (or sparks) close to the acetylene cylinder. And always be certain that fire extinguishers are nearby. Remember too, that acetylene connections have left-hand threads, and they are painted red. Oxygen connections are green.

Install the oxygen regulator and open the regulator handwheel. The lower gauge will register the pressure in the tank. Attach the acetylene regulator and open the acetylene valve about 1 1/2 turns.

Connect the welding hoses to their respective regulators, welding head (tip) and torch, Fig. 50-56, to the other end of the hoses. The size tip selected will depend on the type of welding or cutting to be done. The size designation varies with different manufacturers. Usually, the smallest tip is used when welding body sheet metal. Similarly, if body sheet metal is to be cut, a small tip is preferred. Larger size tips are needed to weld or cut heavy sections, such as frames. Still larger tips are

used to heat axles preparatory to straightening, etc.

Different pressures are needed for welding and cutting different thicknesses of metal. For welding sheet metal: acetylene pressure should be 5 psi, oxygen pressure should be 10 psi. For cutting sheet metal: the pressure of the oxygen should be 10–25 psi, and acetylene 3–5 psi.

To light the flame, first open the oxygen valve 1/4 turn.

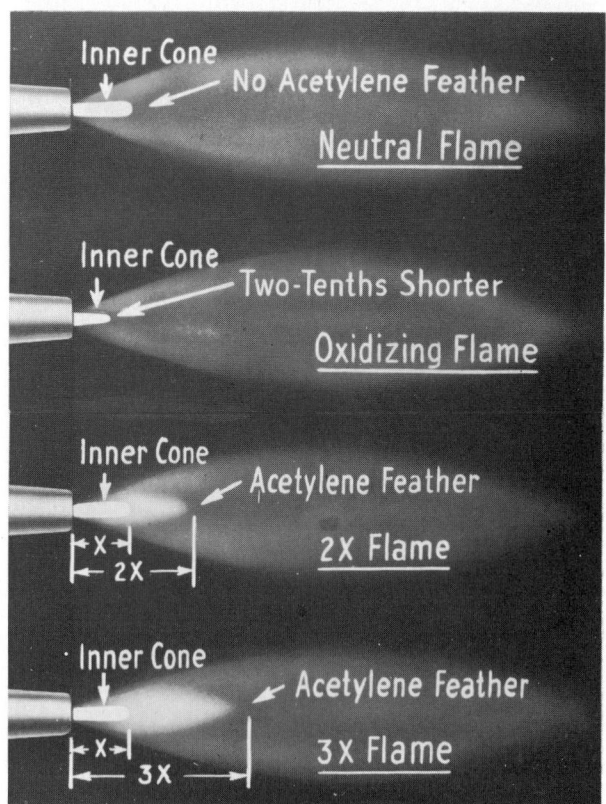

Fig. 50-57. Illustrating method for indicating amount of excess acetylene to be used. Adjust flame to neutral, open torch acetylene valve, or close oxygen valve, until desired acetylene feather is obtained.

Then open the acetylene valve one full turn, and light the gas at the tip with a friction-type lighter. Never use matches. When lighting the gas, have the tip of the torch turned down and away from any person standing nearby.

Adjusting the flame is accomplished by opening the oxygen valve slowly. The flame will change from a yellow acetylene flame to a blue flame, which is called a reducing flame. Start with an excess acetylene flame, then adjust to get a neutral flame by closing the acetylene valve until the acetylene "feather" around the tip of the inner cone of the flame disappears, Fig. 50-57.

To obtain an oxidizing flame, either increase the oxygen or decrease the acetylene until the inner cone of the flame is about 2/10 shorter.

If the flame is yellow or backfires, readjust the acetylene to 10 psi, and open the torch needle valve more. If this does not correct the condition, the torch probably needs cleaning.

To weld sheet metal, a neutral flame should be used. Skill can be attained by practicing on strips of sheet metal. At first, do not attempt to weld two pieces of sheet steel together, but move the flame across the surface of the sheet metal, carrying the "puddle" along the surface, Fig. 50-58. Do not use any welding rod.

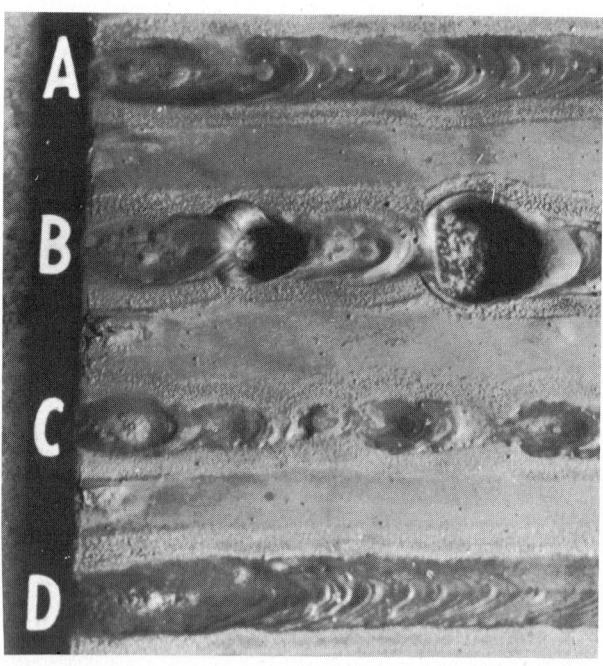

Fig. 50-58. A practice piece shows good results at (A) and (D). Excess heat caused holes to be burned at (B), while too little heat was used at (C). No welding rod was used. (Linde Div., Union Carbide Corp.)

The purpose of this exercise is to obtain skill in carrying a puddle across the surface of the sheet. The torch should be held so that the flame points in the same direction that the weld will be made, and at an angle of about 45 deg. The inner cone of the flame should be about 1/8 in. away from the surface of the sheet.

Hold the torch in this position until a pool of molten metal

about 3/16 to 1/4 in. in diameter is formed. Then move the torch slowly to move the puddle in the desired direction to obtain an even ripple effect. To do this, swing the torch from side to side in a small arc. If you move the torch too slowly, holes may be burned through the sheet metal. If you move it too quickly, the desired degree of melting and overlapping of the puddles will not be obtained.

After the desired skill is attained without using a welding rod, repeat the preceding exercise, using a welding rod, Fig. 50-59. The addition of the welding rod will produce a slight

Fig. 50-59. Examples of good and poor welds: A—Satisfactory. B—Shows effects of too much heat. C—Insufficient heat, little fusion and improper melting of welding rod. D—Satisfactory. (Linde Div., Union Carbide Corp.)

ridge of metal above the surface of the sheet.

When using welding rod, hold the rod in about the same position as the welding torch. Hold it in the left hand and at an angle of slightly more than 45 deg. Try to bring the spot on the sheet and the tip of the welding rod to the melting temperature at the same time. The best position for the end of the welding rod is just inside the outer end of the flame, while the flame is being concentrated on the spot at the start of the weld.

After having practiced with welding rod, place the edges of two pieces of sheet metal 1/16 in. apart and weld them together. In this case, make sure that the welding action penetrates completely through to the underside of the sheet so that the weld will have sufficient strength.

During the welding action, control the welding puddle so it will not fall through the gap. However, the metal added from the rod must be thoroughly fused with the base metal on both sides of the joint for the entire thickness of the sheet.

Once sufficient skill has been attained in welding small pieces of sheet metal together, try welding an actual fender or body panel.

BODY PANEL CUTTING METHODS

With the type of car body construction used today, many shops have adopted the policy of replacing sections of panels rather than attempting any straightening operations. In cases of severe damage, this procedure saves time and enables the shop to turn out more jobs per day. Replacement panels are

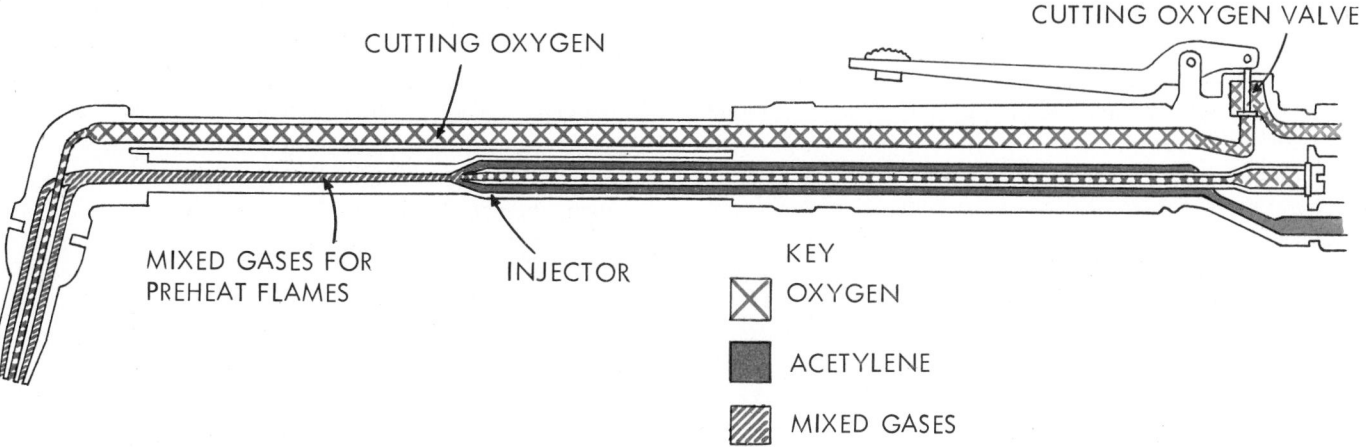

Fig. 50-60. Sectional view of oxyacetylene cutting torch.

available from car dealers and independent parts jobbers.

Cutting out panels for replacement is relatively simple with modern equipment: the oxyacetylene cutting torch, Fig. 50-60; the electric torch, Fig. 50-61; and various types of power-driven cutters, Fig. 50-62.

A special torch is needed to cut sheet metal with oxyacetylene, Fig. 50-60. It differs marterially from the one used for welding. A cutting torch provides a stream of pure oxygen which does the actual cutting after the starting point of the cut has been heated to a red temperature by small oxyacetylene flames.

In the cutting torch, the oxyacetylene flames are produced at a series of openings in the tip. These openings surround the central opening or jet from which the oxygen passes. Details of construction vary with different manufacturers.

Cutting is accomplished when the sheet metal is heated red hot, then exposed to the oxygen. An intense reaction takes place, and much heat is liberated. Not only is the oxide that is formed melted, but some of the unoxidized steel or iron is heated sufficiently so that it, too, is melted.

The direction of the cut can be changed because the cutting nozzles are made with a ring of openings, usually four or more, which surround the oxygen orifice. In this way, several smaller flames of oxyacetylene are supplied, permitting the change in direction of the cut.

The cutting torch has three valves: two to regulate the quantities of oxygen and acetylene that are mixed for the preheat flame; a third valve, usually operated by a lever, to control the stream of oxygen.

When using a cutting torch, follow the same safety precautions specified for welding. Fire extinguishers should be readily available. Remember, it is unsafe to feed oxygen into a confined space, since it will cause oil, wood, clothing or sound deadening material to burn with great intensity, once it ignites.

When cutting out a body panel, mark the line with chalk where the cut is to be made. Make allowance for the width of the metal that will be melted, keeping the chalk mark approximately 1/2 in. from the desired line. Remove any upholstery or other material from the opposite side of the body panel.

Use both hands when cutting metal with a torch, one to control the flow of oxygen and the other to steady the torch. Hold the torch nozzle perpendicular to the surface of the work and in the same spot until the metal is bright red. Open the oxygen valve. As soon as the flame starts cutting, there will be a shower of sparks from the opposite side of the metal. Then move the torch slowly, but steadily, in the desired directions.

If you move the torch too slowly, heat from the preheating flames will tend to melt the edges of the cut and produce a ragged appearance. If you move it too fast, the cutting jet will fail to go through the metal. Should this occur, close the oxygen valve and reheat the point where the cut stopped.

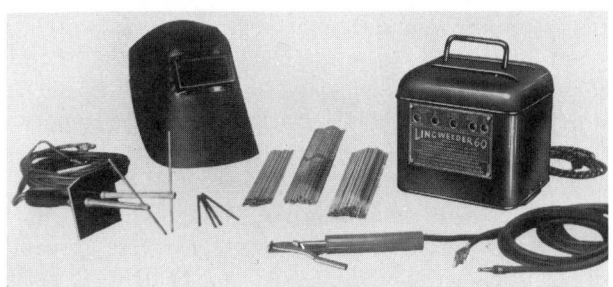

Fig. 50-61. Electric equipment for welding and cutting.

Fig. 50-62. One type of mechanical cutter for use on body panels.

Then reopen the oxygen valve to start the cut again.

Cutting is also done with an electric arc, Fig. 50-61. While any electric arc welder can be used for cutting, the use of large, high-capacity units results in too wide a cut and considerable wastage of metal. Smaller, low-amperage units are preferred for cutting and also welding body sheet metal.

Hand shears can be used, but most bodymen prefer special cutters driven by electric or pneumatic drills, Fig. 50-62. These cutters can cut curves with radii as small as 1 in., and they will cut sheet metal up to .040 in. They have the advantage of not bending or stretching the metal, and no burrs are produced.

PREPARING THE SURFACE FOR PAINTING

The following procedure is a popular one for preparing a surface for touch-up and for refinishing individual panels. It is also used for the entire vehicle if the original paint is in poor condition.

Before actual painting begins, it is essential that you prepare the surface for the paint by removing all traces of wax, grease, oil and dirt. If the paint on the car or truck is of poor quality or seriously deteriorated, remove it.

In this final preparation of the body before applying paint, you have several methods to choose from. The method you select depends on the conditions of the existing paint, the equipment available and quality of the finished job desired.

If the paint on the car is in good condition (good adherence and without surface defects), go over the surface with a disk sander. An open coated disk of No. 16 to 24 grit is recommended. Hold the disk at a slight angle to the surface and work it forward and backward. This will remove most of the old finish down to the metal. Follow this with a No. 50 close coated disk to remove scratches.

If the paint is being removed from only a portion of the panel, taper the sanded area into the old paint to produce a featheredge, Fig. 50-11. Follow up with a 150 grit paper in a block sander, and complete the featheredge by water sanding with wet or dry paper of 280 or 320 grit. Some manufacturers of abrasive paper advise different grits with variations of the above procedure. Follow the instructions of the manufacturer.

For removing paint from the entire vehicle, many shops prefer sandblasting, hot caustic strippers or paint removers.

When using paint removers, follow the manufacturer's instructions. The usual procedure is to apply the remover to the surface with either a paintbrush or sponge. Then, after the proper time interval, scrape the paint from the surface with a putty knife or flush it from the surface with a strong stream of water or steam. Because of fumes created by the paint remover, the room should be well ventilated.

Removing paint by sandblasting is favored by many shops. In metropolitan areas, specialists limit their work to removing paint by this method. Their shops are patronized by car dealers, independent repair shops and paint shops. Among the advantages claimed for the sandblasting method are: speed and low cost, and the surface that results has good paint adherence.

After removing the old paint, prepare the surface for repainting by using special cleaners to remove any rust, wax or oil film. This is necessary to obtain good paint adherence.

Apply the primer coats as soon as possible after the paint is removed. This is particularly important when the surface has been sandblasted, because the metal surface is practically in the raw state and quickly starts rusting.

Steam cleaning of a chassis and engine forms part of any good paint job. In addition, steam cleaning alone is a profitable shop operation.

AIR REQUIREMENTS FOR PAINTING

Too often when a shop owner decides to start a paint department, he simply runs an air line to the compressor, connects a spray gun and thinks he is ready for business. True, this setup will spray paint, but it will also spray a lot of oil, dust and condensed moisture from the compressor. In addition, pressure variation will cause an inconsistent spray pattern. The net result is poor paint jobs.

One of the first steps in setting up a paint department is to make sure there is adequate air to handle the spray guns and other air operated equipment. In addition, the shop air compressor must be in good mechanical condition and delivering its rated capacity. Many shops install a separate compressor for paint work. This avoids overloading the shop air compressor, the additional equipment can be cut into the shop line in case of emergency.

To estimate the compressed air requirements of the shop and the load on the compressor, it is necessary to know the amount of air used by the pneumatic equipment in the shop. The method of calculating the total requirements is given in Fig. 50-63.

Referring to Fig. 50-63, note columns A,B,C,D,E and F. Column D is for equipment in average intermittent repair shop use. Column E is for use where specialized departments are maintained. For example, a paint department where several different air operated tools may be used by one man. Column F is for the use by large shops where there may be several hammers, paint guns or other equipment requiring a relatively steady supply of air.

In using this form, obtain the actual air consumption of the tools in your shop. When column C is completely filled out, multiply each figure in the column by the factor given in column D, E, or F, whichever applies to your shop conditions. Place the answer in that column.

When these figures have all been totaled, you will have the minimum cfm required of the compressor. However, to have a safe working margin for unusually busy periods and to handle additional tools or equipment, add 25 percent to the total.

Simply totaling the cfm demands of the various pieces of equipment in the shop does not furnish the capacity of the air compressor required. Some tools and equipment are used for only a short period and at irregular intervals; others are used almost constantly. To obtain the capacity of the compressor required to operate the shop's equipment, follow the instructions in the table, Fig. 50-63.

To get the best performance and long life from any air compressor, it must be serviced and inspected at regular intervals. A compressor and its separator or transformer used for paint spraying require more special care if clean air is to be supplied. Daily maintenance is required.

AIR OPERATED EQUIPMENT	ESTIMATED AVERAGE C.F.M. AIR CONSUMPTION	A NO. OF UNITS OF EACH TYPE	B C.F.M. PER UNIT	C TOTAL C.F.M.	D TOTAL C.F.M. TIMES 100	E TOTAL C.F.M. TIMES 300	F TOTAL C.F.M. TIMES 500
Air filter cleaner							
Dusting gun							
Car lift							
Drill							
Engine cleaner							
Fender hammer							
Garage door opener							
Grease gun							
Spray gun (touch-up)							
Spray gun (production)							
Sander							
Spark plug cleaner							
Tire inflator							
Tire changer							
Undercoat gun							
Vacuum cleaner							
Wrench							
					Total D	Total E	Total F

1. Add D, E, F together. Place a decimal point before the last three figures. This will give the minimum C.F.M. required of the compressor.
2. Add on 1/4 of the above as a safety factor.
3. Add the above two for recommended minimum rating of the compressor required.

Transfer Total → Here

Transfer Above Total → Here

Fig. 50-63. Estimating compressed air requirements of shop.

Follow the manufacturer's service instructions. If instructions are not available, change the oil in the compressor every 60 to 90 days. Clean the air filter each month. Drain the air tank or receiver every morning. Another daily job is draining the air transformer. In fact, in extremely humid weather, this should be done several times each day.

If the equipment is provided with a separate receiver with a pop valve, check it occasionally to make sure that it is operating properly. Otherwise, check the pressure gauges and switches, noting the time required to cut-in and cut-out. This time interval, compared to the specified time, will serve as a warning for many air supply system troubles.

Check all lines for leaks. When installing a new system, be sure to select pipe of sufficient size to carry the necessary amount of air. Also, when installing the piping see that it drains back to the receiver, rather than forward to the air hose.

Air hose, too must be of adequate size to keep air pressure drop at a minimum, Fig. 50-64. Common sizes of spray gun air hose are 1/4 in., 5/16 in. and 3/8 in. Naturally, the smaller the diameter, the greater loss in pressure. The 3/8 in. diameter hose is preferred.

CARE OF A SPRAY GUN

The condition of the spray gun and the way in which it is used often determines the quality of the paint job. It is impossible to do a good job of spray painting with a gun that has not been cleaned or is otherwise defective.

Furthermore, the compressed air used for spraying must be free of moisture, oil and dirt. In addition, pressures must be accurately regulated. Basically, then, the compressor must be equipped with an extractor or transformer, Fig. 50-65, which

Size of Air Hose	AIR PRESSURE DROP AT SPRAY GUN				
	5 ft. length	10 ft. length	15 ft. length	20 ft. length	25 ft. length
¼ in.					
at 40 lbs. pres.	6.0 lbs.	8.0 lbs.	9.5 lbs.	11.0 lbs.	12.7 lbs.
at 50 lbs. pres.	7.5 lbs.	10.0 lbs.	12.0 lbs.	14.0 lbs.	16.0 lbs.
at 60 lbs. pres.	9.0 lbs.	12.5 lbs.	14.5 lbs.	16.7 lbs.	19.0 lbs.
5/16 in.					
at 40 lbs. pres.	2.2 lbs.	2.7 lbs.	3.2 lbs.	3.5 lbs.	4.0 lbs.
at 50 lbs. pres.	3.0 lbs.	3.5 lbs.	4.0 lbs.	4.5 lbs.	5.0 lbs.
at 60 lbs. pres.	3.7 lbs.	4.5 lbs.	5.0 lbs.	5.5 lbs.	6.0 lbs.

Fig. 50-64. Air pressure drop at spray gun.

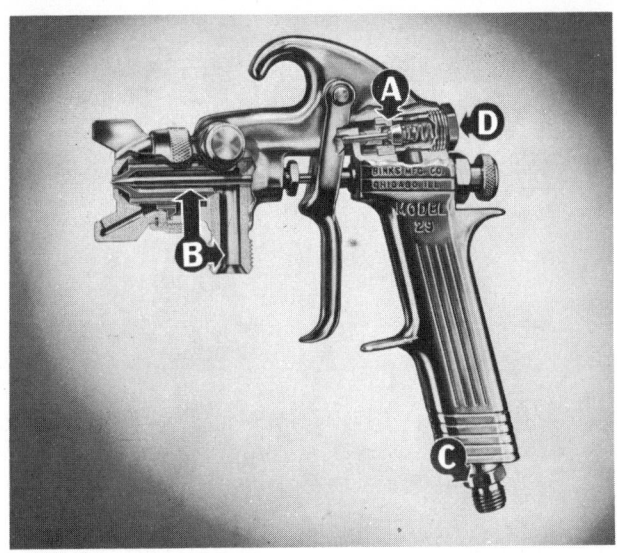

Fig. 50-66. Sectional view of a paint spray gun. A—Cartridge type air valve. B—Passage for paint, lacquer or enamel. C—Air entrance. D—Alternate air entrance.   (Binks Mfg. Co.)

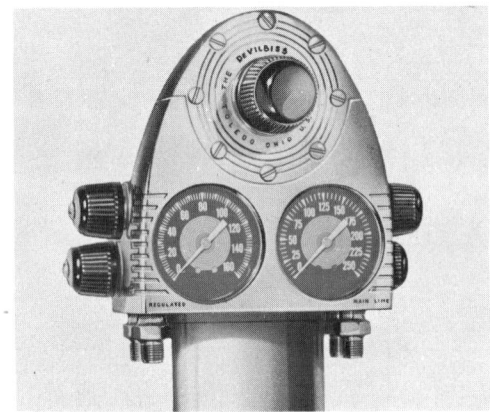

Fig. 50-65. Air transformer with regulator provides clean air and regulates air pressure.   (DeVilbiss Co.)

Fig. 50-67. Air compressor designed specifically for spray painting.

not only regulates the pressure but also provides clean, filtered air for painting.

Be sure to follow the manufacturer's instructions when taking care of a spray gun. In general, they recommend thorough cleaning each time the gun is used, and lubrication of bearing surfaces and packing at regular intervals. A typical spray gun is shown in Fig. 50-66.

Use thinner to clean the gun, but never immerse the gun in the solution, since thinner will destroy the lubricant in the packing. Never use caustic acid solutions for cleaning. They will corrode aluminum alloy portions of the gun.

The gun and cup should be cleaned as soon as spraying is completed. Empty all remaining lacquer or enamel from the cup. Rinse the cup throughly with some thinner, then put a small quantity of thinner in the cup and spray through the gun in the usual manner. This will clean all the passages in the gun. Then dry the parts with air. The gun and cup are ready for the next job.

Lubricate the air valve stem daily with a few drops of light oil. All packing should be kept soft and pliant by occasional oiling.

To insure that the compressed air used for spray painting is clean and free from oil or moisture, the air compressor must be provided with an air transformer, or oil and water extractor. These units are designed not only to trap oil and water vapor and prevent them from reaching the gun, but also to supply air to specified pressures suitable for different types of spray paint.

Transformers or extractors, Fig. 60-65, are available in different sizes so that one or more spray guns can be operated from a single unit. For large departments, pressure feed paint tanks are available. These are designed for conveyance of large quantities of finishing material to the spray guns, under constant and accurate control.

When setting up a paint spray department, sufficient air must be available. Many shops, therefore, find it advisable to use a separate compressor, Fig. 50-67. The size required will depend on the type and quantity of paint spray guns, and the

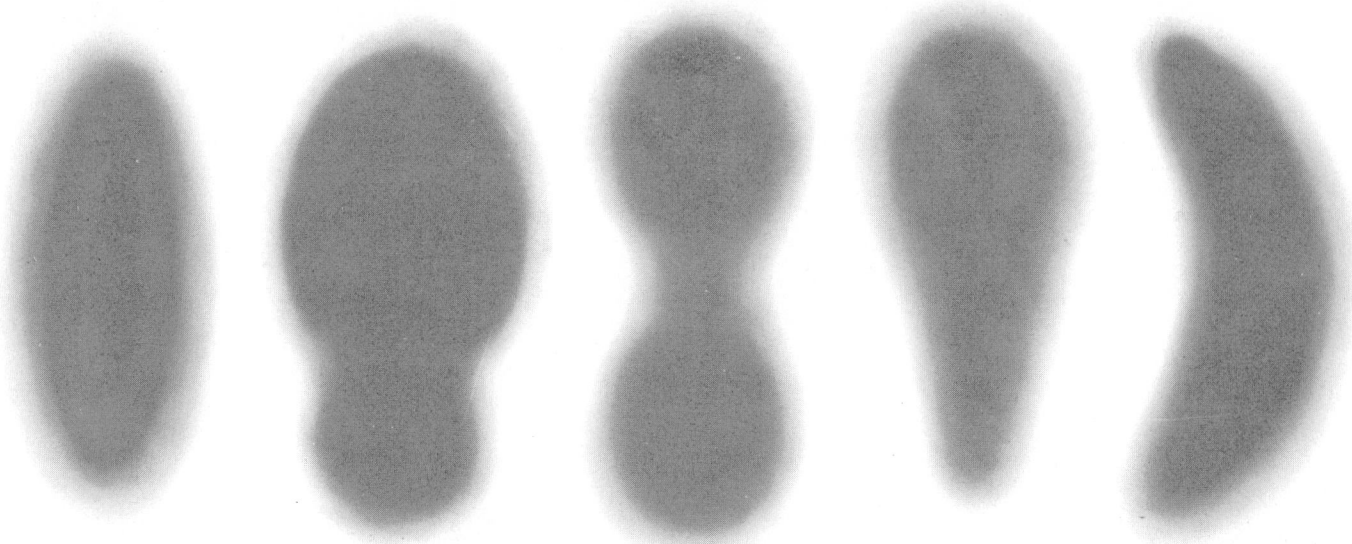

Left to Right: Fig. 50-68. A clean and properly adjusted spray gun, held at correct distance from work, should give a symmetrical pattern as shown. Fig. 50-69. Insufficient atomizing pressure will give a pattern heavy in center or heavy at one end and light at other. Fig. 50-70. If spray pattern is light in center and heavy at each end, it indicates that atomizing air pressure is too high. This problem can be corrected by increasing width of spray pattern or reducing fluid pressure. Fig. 50-71. Dried fluid around outside of fluid nozzle tip will restrict atomizing air and cause pattern to be heavy and wider at either top or bottom. Fig. 50-72. A crescent-shaped pattern is caused by a wing port being clogged by dry material.

refinishing material to be sprayed. Compressor units capable of handling any number of guns are available.

Spray guns are provided with two adjustments: one controls the amount of fluid being sprayed; the other governs spray shape, so that either a round or fan-shaped spray can be obtained. The various patterns obtained from a spray gun are shown in Figs. 50-68 through 50-72.

TIPS ON SPRAYING

Anyone can spray paint. But to do a job that will dry smooth with maximum lustre (no sag or ripple) takes know-how that can be acquired with a little practice.

The gun used for refinishing cars is usually of the syphon cup type, Fig. 50-73. With this gun, the trigger controls both the air and the paint. All spray guns suitable for the first-class work have an assortment of tips, needles and spray cups which will adapt the gun for use with any type material and any size job. Most shops have several guns, one each for primer, lacquer, synthetic enamel and acrylic enamel. In this way, there is no danger of mixing different types of paints, which results in poor paint jobs.

One of the "musts" in spray painting is that the paint should have the correct viscosity. This can be determined by following the instructions on the paint can. Too many painters determine the viscosity by the rate at which the paint runs from the stirring rod. This can lead to plenty of trouble, since only a slight change in viscosity can spoil an otherwise good job. This happens because the amount of thinner only determines the thickness of the coat, but it also influences the evaporation rate between the time the material leaves the gun and the time it contacts the body panel.

High viscosities usually result in sag and orange peel, while low viscosities produce improper flow-out and waste of thinner. To avoid these problems, take great care to measure the proportions of thinner and lacquer or enamel accurately in a graduated measuring cup.

The temperature at which the spraying is done is also an important factor in turning out a good job. This applies not only to the temperature of the shop, but to the temperature of the car or truck as well.

Shop temperatures should be maintained at 70 deg. F. Try to bring the vehicle into the shop well in advance of spraying time so that it becomes the same temperature as the shop.

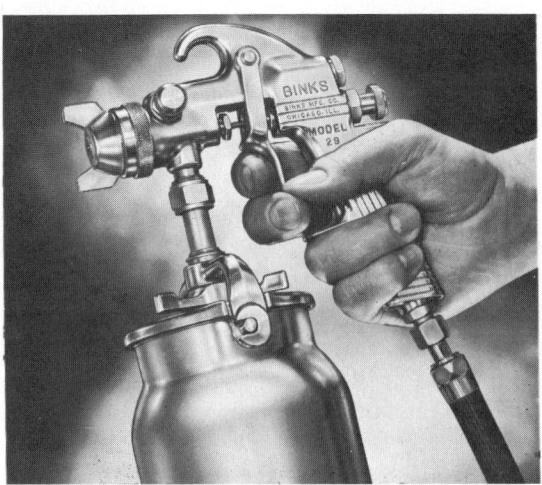

Fig. 50-73. For refinishing automobiles, spray guns of syphon cup gun type are used.

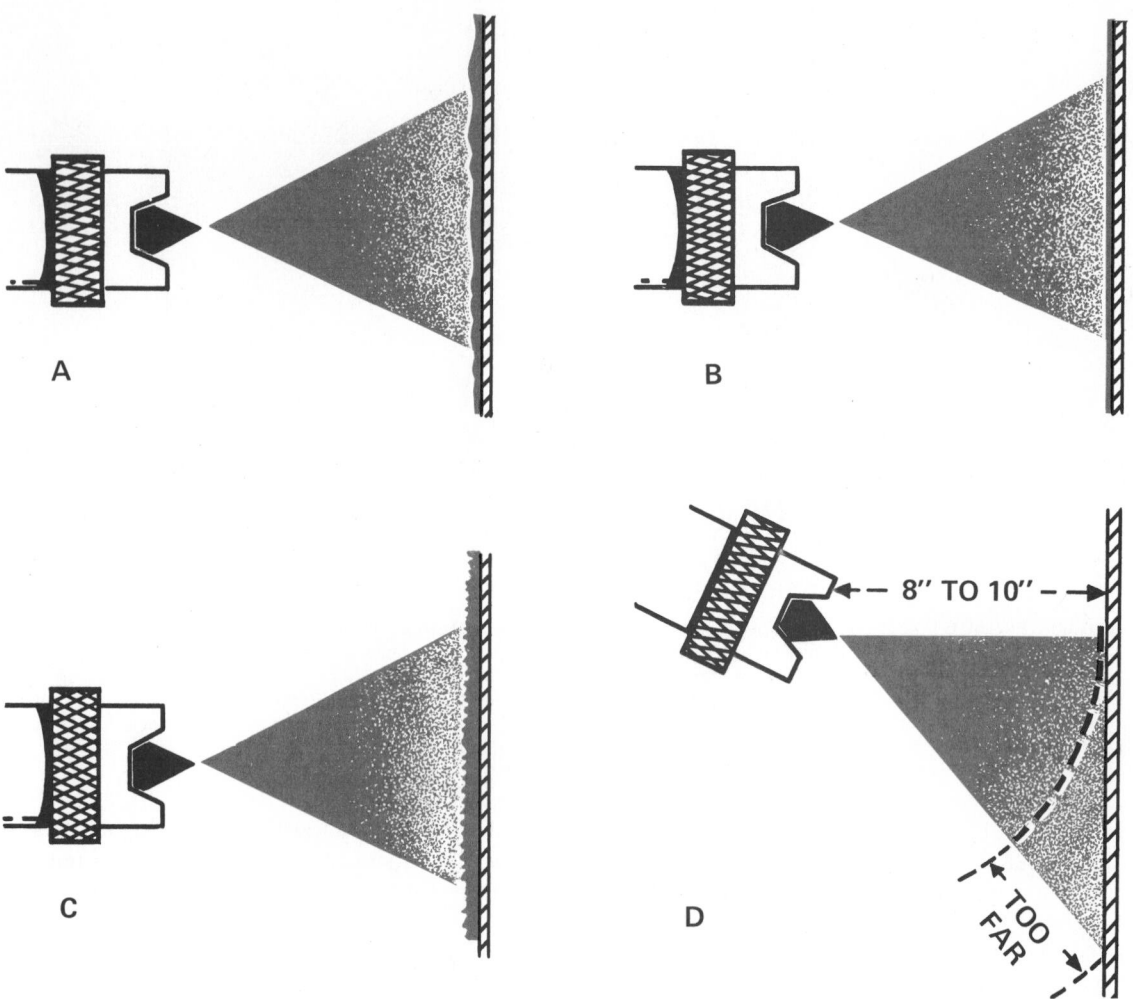

Fig. 50-74. A—Heavy coat of paint with sags, ripples or orange peel may be caused by a dirty air nozzle, gun too close to work, paint too thin, low air pressure, gun movement too slow or too much overlap. B—Good flow-out and no orange peel can be obtained with a clean, properly adjusted gun held at correct distance from work; paint must be correctly thinned, air pressure must be right and gun must be stroked at correct speed and with 50 percent overlap. C—Thin coats which are rough, dry and without lustre are caused by using wrong type air nozzle, holding spray gun too far from work, incorrect air adjustment, stroking too fast or with insufficient overlap. D—A gun with a separate cup must be used. Thickness of coat will taper if gun is fanned or held at an angle to work.

Spraying lacquer on a surface that is too cold, or too hot from being in the sun, will upset the flowing time of the material and will cause orange peel and poor adherence to the surface.

Another important factor in doing a good paint job is the thickness of the paint film on the surface. Obviously, a thick film takes longer to dry than a thin one. As a result, the paint will sag, ripple or orange peel. If enamels are used, blistering may result.

Ideally, you should produce a coat that will remain wet long enough for proper flow-out, but no longer. The amount of material you spray on a surface with one stroke of a gun will depend on the width of the fan, the distance of the gun from the sprayed surface, the air pressure and the amount of thinner used.

In addition, the speed of the spray stroke will also affect the thickness of the coat. The best procedure is to adjust the gun to obtain a wet film which will remain wet only long enough for good flow-out. Get the final finish thickness by spraying an additional coat after the first one has dried.

Nearly all standard spray guns are designed to give best performance when held at a distance of 8 to 12 in. from the surface to be sprayed. When the gun is held too close, the air pressure tends to ripple the wet film, especially if the film is too thick. If the distance is too great, a large percentage of the thinner will be evaporated in the spraying operation. Orange peel or a dry film will result, because the spray droplets will not have an opportunity to flow together.

It is imperative, then, to hold the spray gun at the specified distance from the work. In addition, do not tilt it or hold it at an angle. Also, never swing the gun in an arc, but move it parallel to the work. The only time, it is permissible to fan the gun is when you want the paint to thin out over the edges of a small spot.

The effects of incorrect handling of the spray gun are shown in Fig. 50-74.

For most painting, the conventional spray gun with

attached cup is satisfactory. However, many modern bodies have undercut surfaces where it is necessary to hold the gun at such an angle that a gun with attached cup cannot be used. A gun with a remote or separate cup is necessary.

CLEAN SURFACE REQUIRED

The life and appearance of a repaint job is largely dependent on the condition of the surface to which the finish coats are applied. So it is important to do a good job of straightening the sheet metal, and to make sure that the rest of the surface of the vehicle is in good condition. The surface must be clean, free from rust, dirt, wax, oil or other foreign matter. In addition, the old paint must have good adherence to the base metal.

So, before starting a refinish job, there are two points which have to be checked before any spraying is done. First, see that any original paint has good adhesion. Second, make sure the surface is clean.

To check for adhesion, sand a small spot through to the base metal and feather the edges. If the thin edge does not break or crumble, it is safe to assume that there is good adhesion.

The other point in preparing a surface for paint is that the surface must be clean. Old wax, rust, oil film and other foreign material must be removed. The best method is to use one of the special cleaners that are available. Gasoline is not satisfactory, since it will not dissolve wax.

Use the special cleaner before and after the final sanding. Directions accompanying the cleaner should be carefully followed. When wiping the surface, do not use the ordinary shop cloths, because they usually retain a certain amount of grease or other chemicals as received from the laundry. If air is used to blow off dust, the compressor supplying the air must be fitted with a transformer so the air is free of oil and moisture.

Another important point to remember is not to touch the clean surface with your hands. Natural oil from the skin will cause poor adhesion and the finish will tend to peel. Examples of paint that has been applied to various types of poorly

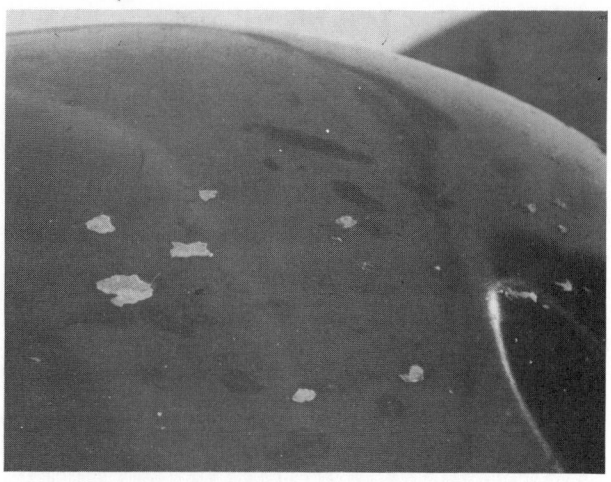

Fig. 50-76. Bruises and Chipping—Not due to finish, but caused by stones, etc., striking surface. REMEDY: Sand and refinish.

Fig. 50-77. Peeling Over Solder Spot—Usually noticeable a few weeks after refinishing. Typified by loss of luster, spot gets progressively worse until paint peels from surface. REMEDY: After soldering, wash surface with a solution of equal parts of ammonia, alcohol and water. Be sure surface is thoroughly dry before refinishing.

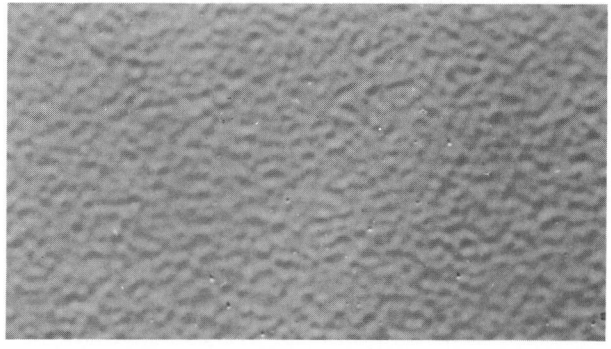

Fig. 50-78. Orange Peel—This condition may result from improper air pressure at gun, insufficient reduction and poor selection of solvent, use of a thinner that dries too quickly or lacquer sprayed on a hot surface. REMEDY: Check thinner, air pressure and make sure surface temperature is 70 deg.

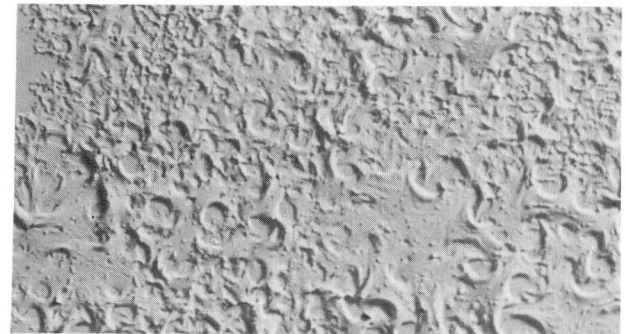

Fig. 50-75. Lifting—A puckering and wrinkled effect, usually resulting from application of material carrying strong solvents over a partially oxidized surface. It also could be caused by lack of cleanliness, wax, etc. REMEDY: Sand and refinish.

prepared surfaces are shown in Figs. 50-75 through 50-88.

You also must determine whether the original finish is lacquer or enamel. To make a quick check, moisten a finger with lacquer thinner and rub a small area. If the finish is lacquer, it will dissolve.

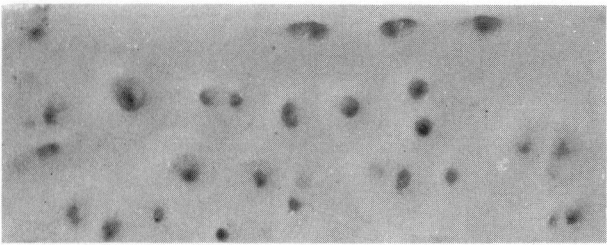

Fig. 50-79. Fish-eyes—A problem usually caused by failure to remove silicone polish. REMEDY: Sand, thoroughly clean surface, then refinish.

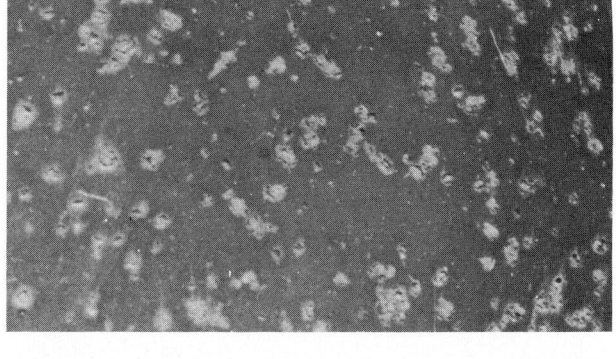

Fig. 50-82. Rust—Spots under finish usually appear as raised sections, or blistering. Problem is caused by poor penetration and cleaning of surface. REMEDY: Sand off surface, treat surface with rust remover and refinish.

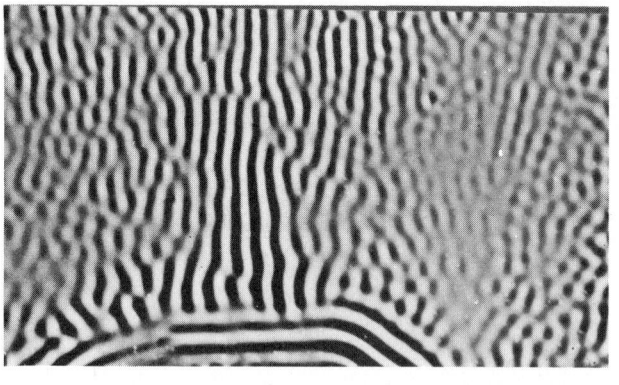

Fig. 50-80. Wrinkling—Usually found only in synthetic enamel finish. Results from application of a heavy coat, aggravated by high temperatures. REMEDY: Apply thinner coats.

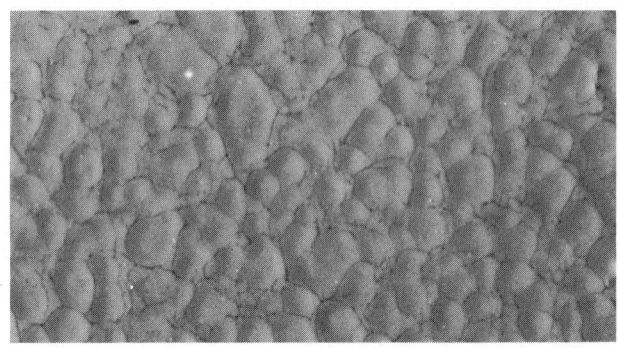

Fig. 50-83. Pitting—Usually caused by oil or moisture escaping through air line. REMEDY: Sand down to smooth surface and refinish. Also overhaul compressor and separator.

Fig. 50-81. Water Spotting—Caused by washing car in bright sunlight. REMEDY: Use paste cleaner and refinish.

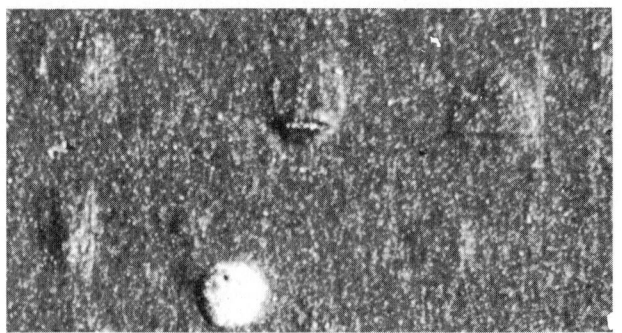

Fig. 50-84. Blistering—This condition is caused by rust, moisture, oil, grease or other foreign material working in between coats and causing them to separate. Oil or water in air lines will cause blistering, as will high temperatures and high humidity. REMEDY: Remove finish to bare metal and refinish.

On lacquer jobs which are to be refinished with lacquer, you have to prevent swelling of the old coat. Swelling usually occurs when sanding has been done, and unless you can keep the new solvents from reaching the old finish, no amount of care will prevent the old scratches from showing.

Swelling of the old coat does not occur on the unmarred or scratched surface of the lacquer, which is covered with an insoluble outer layer. It does occur when the new lacquer contacts freshly exposed surfaces in the scratches. After all the solvents have evaporated, and the new finish shrinks, small

furrows following the scratches will result.

So it is necessary to use a "sealer" on lacquer repaint jobs where much of the old refinishing material remains. Apply the sealer after sanding and treating the bare metal. Sealer has good adhesion to the old finish and will prevent penetration of the new lacquer and prevent swelling. If it is necessary to use any primer surfacer for filling rough spots, apply this first. Then, after sanding, apply the sealer.

Enamel finishes must be sanded carefully. Make sure that the abrasive is not too coarse, and sand the old finish to produce a good surface for the new finish. It is not necessary to use a surfacer if the enamel is in good condition. However,

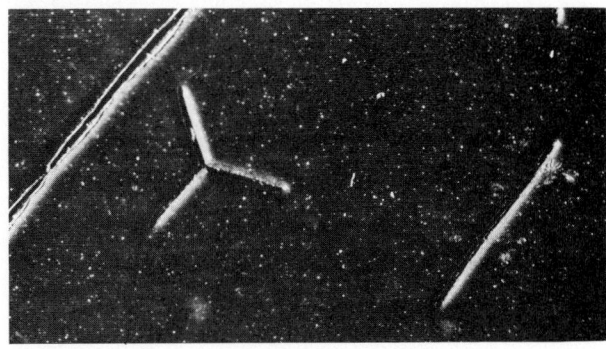

Fig. 50-87. Cracking and Checking—Flaws may extend to the metal. Or, it may go only as far as undercoating. Depressions in film caused by cracks in undercoat also are typical. Simple line cracks are caused by temperature stresses, flexing of body panels, second-coat application before first is dry or poor paint mixing. REMEDY: Remove finish to bare metal and refinish.

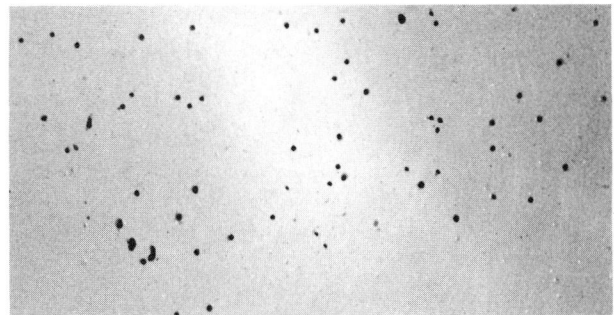

Fig. 50-85. Pinpoint Blistering—Often confused with pitting because small broken blisters have appearance of pits. Pinpoint blisters range in size from a pinhead to a point. REMEDY: Sand down to metal and refinish.

STEPS IN REFINISHING

Lacquer Over Old Finishes

1. Remove old wax or silicone polish with special remover. Water sand old finish, using No. 320 paper.
2. Using clean air, blow out all cracks.
3. Clean surface with special grease, rust and wax remover.
4. Spray surfacer on bare metal spots. If necessary, use spot putty or equivalent.
5. Water sand undercoats with No. 320 paper. If any spots are sanded through to base metal, spray again with surfacer and water sand.
6. Seal scratches with special sealer if car was previously finished with lacquer.
7. Blow out cracks with clean air.
8. Again clean surface with special cleaner.
9. Apply lacquer color coats. Three double coats are recommended.
10. Water sand with No. 400 paper.
11. Polish.

if the old enamel is badly worn and pitted use a surfacer or primer for better adhesion and better appearance.

Modern primers, glazing putties, fabric patches, cold solder and hot solder will fill almost any rough surface. However, the surface should be as smooth as possible before any of these materials are applied.

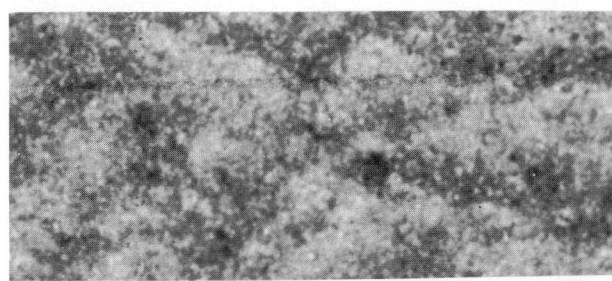

Fig. 50-86. Mottled Appearance—Usually occurs if paint is applied on surface which had been polished with silicone polish. REMEDY: All traces of polish must be removed from the surface before refinishing.

After the primer and/or other surfacing material is applied, thorough sanding is essential. Many painters recommend three or four grades of paper, ranging from coarse to fine. For example, use a No. 16 open coated paper first, followed by No. 50 close coated, and final sanded with No. 150 paper.

Modern surfacing and refinishing materials have greatly simplified automobile painting. However, good appearance and long life of the finish is still dependent on the care taken in preparing the surface for the final finish coats.

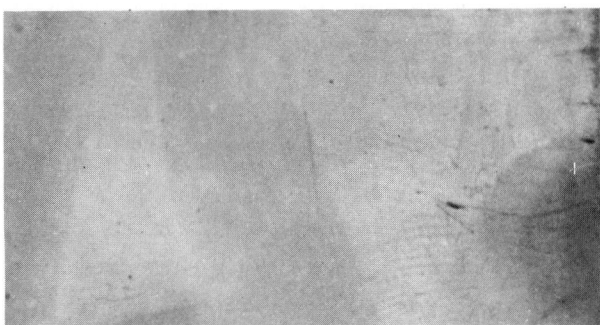

Fig. 50-88. Chalking—This is surface disintegration. Primarily, it is due to weathering and sunlight. It is characterized by dulling and powdering of surface. REMEDY: Apply paste cleaner, followed by polish. In extreme cases, refinishing is necessary.

Enamel Over Old Finishes

1. Remove all wax and silicone polish with special cleaner.
2. Wet sand old finish with No. 320 paper.
3. Clean surface with a special wax, grease and rust remover.
4. Spray on undercoats.
5. Sand undercoats with No. 280 paper.
6. Respray undercoats if sanding has gone through to base metal.
7. Resand undercoat.
8. Blow out all cracks with clean air.
9. Clean surface with special cleaner to remove hand marks.
10. Wipe surface with tack rag to remove lint and dust.
11. Spray a light coat of enamel over all cracks.
12. Apply a tack coat and follow immediately with a full coat of enamel. If drying lights or oven are not available, allow to dry at least 12 hours in dust-free room.

REMOVING SAND SCRATCHES

Sand scratches have spoiled many jobs which otherwise would have been perfect. Unfortunately, the scratches do not show up until after the finish coat has been sprayed.

The basis of any good paint job is smooth metal. Unless the bodymen finishing the metal does a good job, it will be virtually impossible for the painter to fill the scratches so that they will not show. Careless filing or bearing too hard on a coarse disk leaves scratches, gouges and furrows that are hard to fill.

Many experienced body workers use a coarse disk for roughing and cutting down weld spots and high areas only. Then the major part of the sanding is done with a No. 24 disk and final finishing of the metal with a disk of No. 50 or 80 grit. Even with such care, some sand scratches may occur, because of small burrs or fins of torn metal along the edges of the sand scratches. It pays to follow up the heavy power sanding with a little hand sanding, using No. 150 paper.

While primers have been vastly improved in their ability to fill and cover a surface, they cannot be depended on to do a job with a single coat. Apply several coats of primer and allow ample time for the individual coats to dry. This is a better practice than applying a single heavy coat, since it is difficult to tell when the heavy coat has dried all the way through.

Use fine paper when sanding priming coats. No. 220 or 240 paper will produce scratches that usually show through the first coats. In some instances, this paper can be used for the initial sanding of primers, but experienced bodymen advise the use of No. 320 or 360, then final finish sanding with No. 400 paper.

When lacquer is used to finish a car, the lacquer thinner penetrates the undercoat and causes swelling where the undercoat is heaviest. The swelling will be greater if the lacquer is sanded and polished before all the thinner has evaporated. A good practice is to first spray a light fog coat of lacquer. This will reduce the possibility of sand scratch swelling, which spoils the appearance of the finished job.

Scratches can also be caused in the final polishing of the finish coat if care is not exercised in the selection of the rubbing compound. The finer the abrasive in the rubbing coat, the less chance there is of producing any scratches.

When doing spot painting, featheredge the spot carefully. Give the area and edge a careful final sanding with No. 360 or No. 400 paper to eliminate any scratches. If rubbing compound is used, clean the area with a good wax and grease remover. Many rubbing compounds contain a lubricant.

In general, exercise the same care with synthetic enamel. While there are no strong solvents to cause difficulty, the high lustre of the enamel will tend to magnify any scratches that may be present.

MATCHING COLORS

Even though paint manufacturers make ready-mixed paints for standard production colors of automobiles, the number is so great that virtually no jobber carries the complete line. Consequently, the painter is often faced with the problem of mixing his own colors.

Matching colors is not easy. Since automobiles are being turned out with ever increasing varieties of shades and tones, paint men are finding their work more difficult. The problem of fading further complicates the situation. Fortunately, various paint manufacturers provide instructions, specialized equipment and basic colors that help solve the color matching problem. One type of equipment designed to prepare paint of a desired color is shown in Fig. 50-89.

Fig. 50-89. One type of equipment designed to prepare a desired shade of color.

Probably the most important requirement in color mixing is that the painter must have good color perception. Many color mixing aids are available, including thirty basic colors, mixing containers, stirring paddles, test panels and color mixing equipment.

Another important point related to color matching is that every color has what is known as a "mass-tone" and a "tint-tone." The mass-tone can be judged from the color as it appears on the painted panel or in the can. The tint-tone of a

enamel at 35 to 45 lb. pr
surface being sprayed and s

Shops using hot sprayir
money. Less thinner is r
lacquer is reduced from 1
that the solids comprise o
lacquer work, the materia
50 percent. Adding heat
matter at the spray noz:
about one and a half tin
surface than with cold spra

As a result, refinishers I
done on a medium size ca
use only 2 to 2 1/2 qts.
same size car requires only
double or cross coat of hot
coats of lacquer sprayed in

Hot spraying has the
Lacquer applied by hot sp
minutes, and out of tack in

Hot lacquer provides a
apparent in cold applicatic
lacquer can be compounde

Hot lacquer dries wit
synthetic enamel. If comp
effort is required.

As for thinner, the an
conditions and the charac
conditions, some manufac
thinner to one part of lacqu

Before spraying the surf
and grease with a cleaner d
the surface dry with a clear

Cut the edges of the
abrasive paper. Then feath
paper. On new metal, use
water and dry.

The surface is now r
surfacer. Follow the instr
manufacturer. Do not app
three medium coats, allow
dry for at least 30 minutes

The next step is sandin;
If wet sanding is preferr
imperfections in the surf
drying time, sand the surf
coat of primer surfacer.

In spot area repairs, rut
compound to remove overs

Then spray on three o
finish. Allow each coat tc
coat. In spot repair, exten
previous coat to blend int
ties advise application of
improve leveling and gloss.

If possible, allow the s
However, in an emergency

color is the shade resulting from mixing a small quantity of the color with a large quantity of white.

A dark green masstone, for example, usually will have a blue tint-tone, and most maroons have a violet or purple tint-tone. Usually it is impossible to add white to a dark green to get a light green, or add white to a maroon to get a light red. Small additions of color will tint according to its tint-tone. Large amounts will influence others according to mass-tone.

Black, of course, darkens a color and white lightens it. Black tends to dull a shade. Addition of white dilutes the tint.

Clean equipment is a must when matching colors. Dust, old paint or other material will spoil the desired effect.

Thoroughly stir each basic color or mixture. Do your color matching in sunlight or northern exposure. Artificial light changes tints and tones. Tightly close cans of paint not in use to reduce evaporation of the solvents and because light affects color.

Since almost all shades darken on drying, wait until the color is dry before making comparisons. When matching a color on a car, remove all waxes and polish because they tend to change the color. Also, when making comparisons, remember that the larger the surface, the lighter the color will appear because of light reflection. Always compare areas of equal size.

You can save a lot of material by mixing small amounts and using predominating colors first. If a formula is being followed, start with the major shade, adding the minor quantities according to volume.

Usually the larger proportion of the formula will provide the desired depth of color. Further toning will be needed to produce the particular shade being matched. Ordinarily, only a very small amount of color is required for toning. For example, a touch of red may mean a small quantity on the tip of a spatula added to a quart batch. Add this touch last.

Mix colors full strength for matching, then dilute them to spraying consistency.

Generally, white or opalescent is the base of almost all colors. Exceptions are reds, maroons, dark greens, dark browns and dark blues. Red, blue, yellow and green will impart brightness to a mixture.

PAINTING MATERIALS

Acrylic lacquer, acrylic enamel, urethane enamel and synthetic enamel are now being used in the refinishing of automobiles. In addition, thinners, primers, surfacers, reducers, solvents, sealers and metal conditioners are required. Also used for exterior finish are wood grained overlay and vinyl.

ACRYLIC LACQUER: This material dries by evaporation of volatile solvents. Since it remains more or less soluble, the new coat of acrylic lacquer will bond or unite with the original coat.

ACRYLIC ENAMEL: A solvent blend of binder and pigment materials, acrylic enamel dries in two stages. The first stage is oxidation of the solvent. The second is oxidation of the binder. No polishing is necessary.

URETHANE ENAMEL: Used in the refinishing of auto-

motive vehicles, urethane provides a hard, tile-like finish. It has high gloss, improved flow and appearance, good adhesion and flexibility. Urethane enamel dries more slowly than acrylic enamel.

SYNTHETIC ENAMEL: Not soluble in ordinary solvents, synthetic enamel is currently used for refinishing commercial vehicles. In general, refinishing shops prefer either acrylic enamel or acrylic lacquer.

COMPARISON OF COSTS: Acrylic lacquer is more easily applied than acrylic enamel. However, the lacquer requires several coats and, therefore, more time is needed for application. This is an important cost consideration.

PRIMER SURFACERS: These are designed to improve adhesion to the metal and to fill slight surface imperfections. After drying, the primer surfacer is sanded to a fine, smooth surface. Two types are available. One is used under acrylic enamels. Another is used under acrylic lacquers.

PRIMERS: For adhesion to special surfaces, manufacturers provide primers. These are different from primer surfacers. Primers are widely used when painting aluminum or galvanized surfaces. If the surface also needs filling, a primer surfacer is applied over the primer.

SEALERS: These are used for sealing sanding scratches made when preparing to paint over an acrylic surface. Special bleeder sealer is used over a red or maroon surface.

METALLICS: When metallic flakes (usually aluminum) are added to lacquers and enamels, a luminous quality is given to the surface. This is a popular finishing material, but presents a problem in matching colors.

THINNERS AND REDUCERS: These are solvents used to thin or reduce paints to the desired viscosity (thickness). Thinners are used for acrylic products. Reducers are used for synthetic base materials.

PUTTY: Usually made of the same material as the primer surfacer, putty is used for filling deep nicks and scratches.

WAX AND POLISH REMOVERS: Traces of wax, polish or grease must be removed from the surface before applying paint. Removers are used to do this job. Otherwise, flaking will result.

METAL CONDITIONERS: These compounds are applied to metal after all paint has been removed. They prevent rusting.

TACK RAG: This is a specially treated cheese cloth. It has been dipped in a thin nondrying varnish. Used to wipe the surface of the car before painting, it removes all traces of dust.

RUBBING COMPOUNDS: Mildly abrasive, these pastes or liquids are used to polish acrylic lacquer surfaces. They bring a higher polish to the surface.

SELECTING PAINT

When refinishing a vehicle, use of proper materials is important. In general, fewer troubles arise if the same material is used for refinishing as was originally used.

Today, most cars are refinished in either acrylic enamel or acrylic lacquer. Nitrocellulose lacquer is used only when there is little drying time. This material may also be used occasionally for retouching small scratches.

Acrylic lacquer i
finished in nitrocellul
enamel, a sealer sh
Complete panels, ne
trouble in matching c

When spraying acr
need not be sanded b
the surface must be tl

If acrylic lacquer
surface must be sande

When repairing c
surface must be tho
both good adhesion a

Synthetic enamels
inally finished with en
ed when enamel is us
paint a small area wit

Some painters pre
is not required. Othe
lower costs. When an
many shops prefer th

Desireable qualiti
include durability, gl

DETERMINING T

Before applying an
to determine whethe
enamel, alkyd enamel

There are several d
tion. The easiest me
refinished, is to consu

Another method i
produced for that pu
compound. Lacquer
lacquer will require

Fig. 50-90. With this sp
sprayed

---

distribute forces applied at the foot pedal and transmitted by the master input cylinder.

In drum brake applications, the cylinder in which the master input piston moves is connected by tubing to a cylinder at each wheel, Fig. 51-7. Generally, each of these cylinders contains two opposed pistons, and each piston operates a brake shoe. When force is applied at the brake pedal, pressure

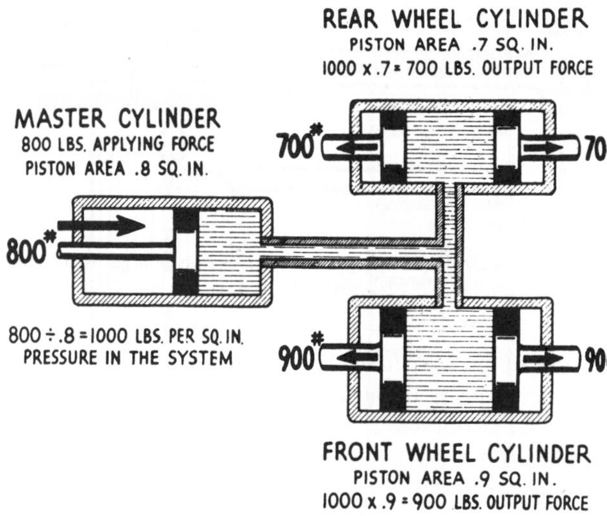

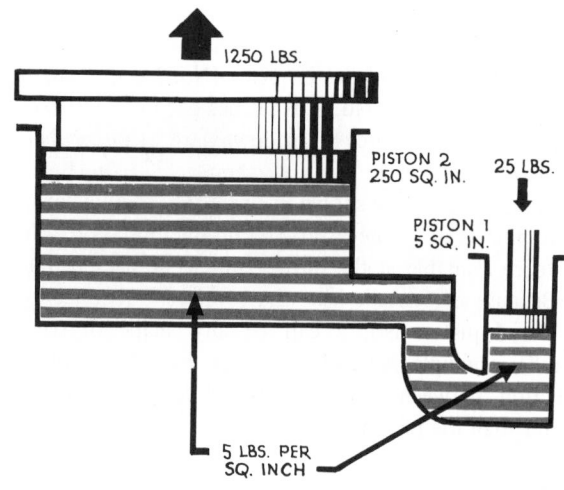

Fig. 51-7. Automobile hydraulic brake system illustrates how motion and force is transmitted, and how amount of force is changed.

is transmitted equally throughout the fluid to each of the wheel cylinders. As a result, all of the wheel cylinders are forced outward, forcing the brake shoes against the brake drums.

When the pressure is removed from the brake pedal, springs on the brake shoes force the shoes back to their normal released position. This movement of the shoes, in turn, forces the pistons inward, returning the fluid to the master cylinder and its reservoir.

This description covers the operation of a simple hydraulic brake with all wheel cylinders of the same diameter. In actual practice, smaller pistons are often used to operate the rear wheel brakes, and some designs provide individual cylinders for each shoe. In some instances, the wheel cylinders have stepped diameters with a large piston operating the forward shoe and a smaller piston operating the rear shoe of a single brake. This type of construction is discussed in the chapter on brakes.

HYDRAULIC JACKS

A schematic drawing of the principle used in the operation of hydraulic jacks is shown in Fig. 51-8. In the illustration, the small piston (where force is applied) has an area of 5 sq. in. Its cylinder is connected to a large cylinder with a piston having an area of 250 sq. in. This large piston supports the platform used to raise the load.

If a force of 25 lbs. is applied to the small piston, a pressure

---

of 5 psi will be produced in the hydraulic fluid. This 5 psi will act over the entire area of the large piston with its 250 sq. in. surface. The resulting force will be 250 x 5 psi = 1250 lbs. lifting force. The initial force of 25 lbs. has been multiplied into a force capable of lifting more than one half ton.

Remember, however, that while the original force has been multiplied 50 times, the distance traveled is just the opposite. The large piston will travel only 1/50 as much as the small piston.

By way of explanation: If the small piston is moved 5 in., then 25 cu. in. of liquid will be displaced. Distributing this amount over 250 sq. in. of the larger piston, it will be raised 25 divided by 250 or 0.1 in. (1/50 of 5 in.)

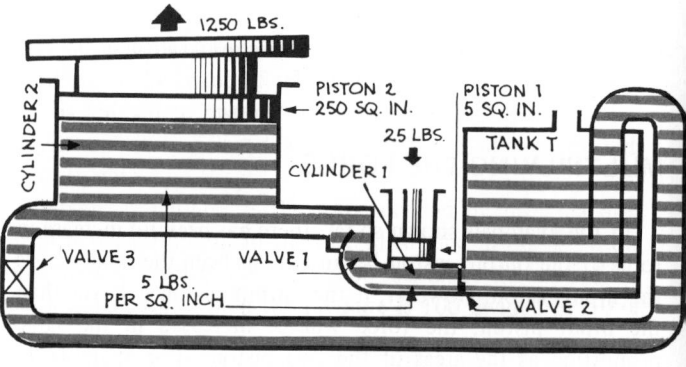

Fig. 51-8. Principle of hydraulic jack is based on multiplication of force applied at small piston.

To prevent the weight of the load on the platform from forcing the fluid back through the system, and to provide a means of lowering the load, it is necessary to include various valves in the hydraulic system, Fig. 51-9.

Fig. 51-9. Schematic drawing of hydraulic jack showing valving necessary to maintain load at desired height and also to permit load to be lowered when desired.

REVIEW QUESTIONS – HYDRAULICS

1. Give three examples of the use of hydraulics in the automotive field.
2. Define hydraulics.
3. Name four major advantages of a hydraulic system.
4. State Pascal's law.
5. What is meant by hydraulic head?
6. On what two factors does hydraulic head depend?
7. What is the weight of a cu. in. of water?
8. What is the weight of a cu. in. of hydraulic fluid?
9. Define density of a fluid.
10. Define specific gravity.
11. What automotive assembly depends on specific gravity for its operation?
12. Define pressure as applied to a hydraulic system.
13. If a force of 50 lbs. is applied to a piston of 2 sq. in. in area on a hydraulic cylinder, what is the pressure?
14. In a hydraulic jack, the input piston has an area of 3 sq. in. and the output piston has an area of 300 sq. in. If 30 lbs. is applied at the input piston, what is the lifting force at the output piston?

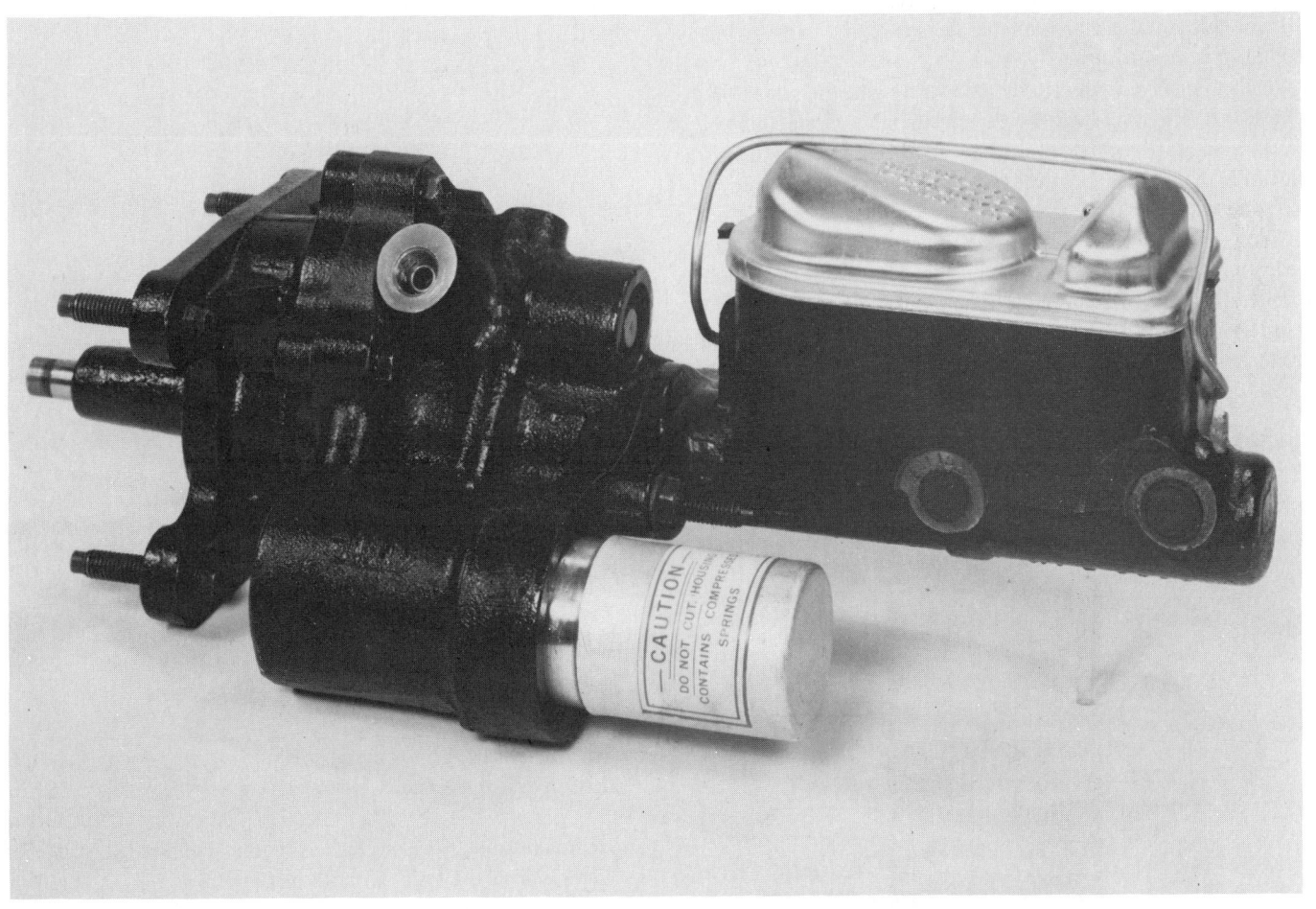

Hydro-Boost unit, with attached master cylinder, is designed for use in a crowded engine compartment. Operated by power steering fluid under pressure, this unit replaces larger vacuum operated power brake units.
(Bendix Automotive Control Systems Group)

PNEUMATICS

Pneumatics is the study of the mechanical properties of air and other gases. It has many automotive applications, particularly in the study of carburetion and pneumatic or air brakes.

Technically, air and other gases are considered fluids. They have many of the same characteristics as liquids, but differ mainly in that they are highly compressible and completely fill any containing vessel. Gases are the same as liquids in two ways: they conform to the shape of their containers; and pressure in a gas acts equally in all directions.

Air and any gas has weight. Therefore, pressure is exerted by virtue of its head; that is, the depth from its upper surfaces to its lower surface. Although any small volume of any gas weighs very little, the pressure of air at sea level under normal conditions amounts to 14.7 psi. The pressure, or the head, is the weight of the air from the surface of the earth to many miles upward into space.

Since air is compressed by its own weight, the same volume of air at sea level will weigh considerably more than on a mountain top. In other words, air becomes less dense as altitude or distance from the earth increases.

This natural factor is particularly important because of its affect on carburetion. As altitude increases, less air enters the carburetor. Consequently, the mixture of fuel and air becomes richer. Instruments designed to measure the pressure of the atmosphere are known as barometers. In most applications, they are used for forecasting weather and in measuring altitudes.

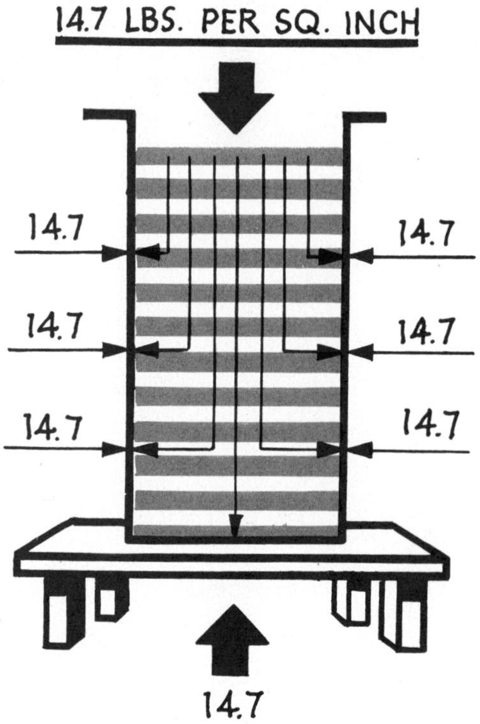

As pointed out, gases are compressed by their own weight. Therefore, the same volume of air will weigh considerably more at sea level than on top of a mountain. In addition, gases expand as their temperature increases, making a volume of gas at high temperature weigh less than the same volume of gas at low temperature. This particular property of gases is why the efficiency of an automobile decreases as the temperature of the air entering the carburetor increases.

Atmospheric pressures obey Pascal's law in the same manner as liquids, Fig. 51-10. Atmospheric pressure acting on the surface of the gas is transmitted equally to the inner walls of the container, but it is balanced by the pressure on the outer walls.

In another example, the thinnest paper suspended in the atmosphere will not be torn, in spite of the fact that air pressure of 14.7 psi is pressing on it, Fig. 51-11. It is not torn because atmospheric pressure is exerted on both sides of the sheet and the pressures are balanced.

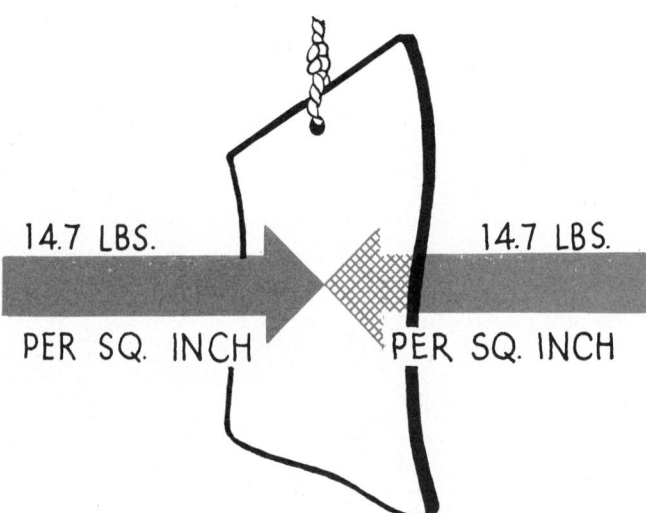

Fig. 51-11. Thin paper suspended in the atmosphere will not be torn because pressure of 14.7 psi is pressing on both sides.

In Fig. 51-12, atmospheric pressure acting on one piston is balanced by the same pressure acting on the surface of the other piston. The fact that the two pistons are of different areas makes no difference since the unit pressure (pressure per square inch) is the same on both pistons.

EFFECT OF VACUUM

Note, too, in Fig. 51-12, with equal atmospheric pressure acting on the two surfaces, the liquid will be at the same height in both sides of the U-shape tube. If the pressure on one side of the tube is reduced, there will be a movement of liquid to the side of reduced pressure.

This can be illustrated by the familiar situation of drinking liquid through a straw, Fig. 51-13. Sucking on the straw disturbs the balance of pressures acting on the liquid. Pressure within the straw is reduced, as the result of suction, and

Fig. 51-10. Atmospheric pressure acting on surface of gas or liquid is transmitted equally throughout.

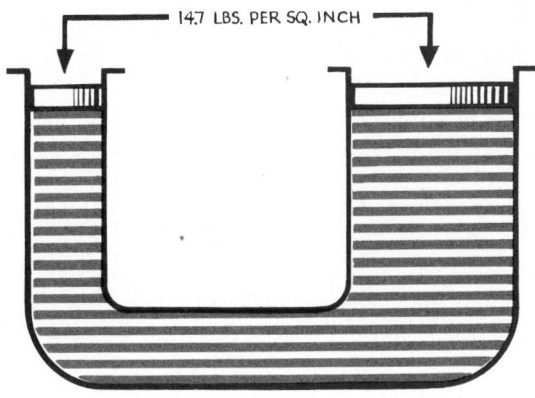

Fig. 51-12. Atmospheric pressure acting on one piston is balanced by same pressure acting on other piston.

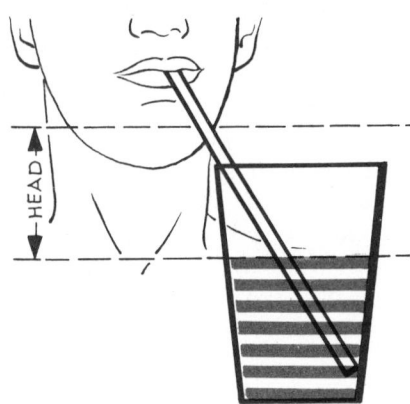

Fig. 51-13. When air pressure within straw falls below pressure of atmosphere, liquid is forced through straw.

atmospheric pressure (14.7 psi) acting on the surface of the liquid in the glass forces the liquid into the straw.

The liquid can be held at any desired level in the straw. This level will always be at a point where the pressure of the head of the liquid, Fig. 51-13, equals the difference between the pressure in the straw and that on the surface of the liquid.

Sucking on the straw has produced a partial vacuum on the surface of the liquid within the straw. A partial vacuum is actually a pressure less than prevailing atmospheric pressure. Theoretically, the limit of this process would be a condition of zero pressure, or a complete vacuum. In actual practice, this condition is never attained.

This simple principle, illustrated by sucking liquid through a straw, is identical with that which is used in the operation of a conventional power brake, Fig. 51-14. Vacuum from the intake manifold is connected to one side of a cylinder.

Atmospheric pressure on the other side causes a piston to move toward the vacuum side. This motion is used to apply the brakes.

COMPRESSED AIR

Compressed air is air which has been forced into a smaller space than which it would ordinarily occupy in its free or atmospheric state. In the automotive field, compressed air has many uses. In addition to inflating tires, it is used for such purposes as spraying paint, blowing dirt and other foreign matter from parts, operating brakes on heavy trucks, and in powering impact tools and wrenches.

As mentioned, normal air (due to the weight of air above it) has a pressure of 14.7 psi. However, when speaking of compressed air, its initial pressure of 14.7 psi is ignored, and

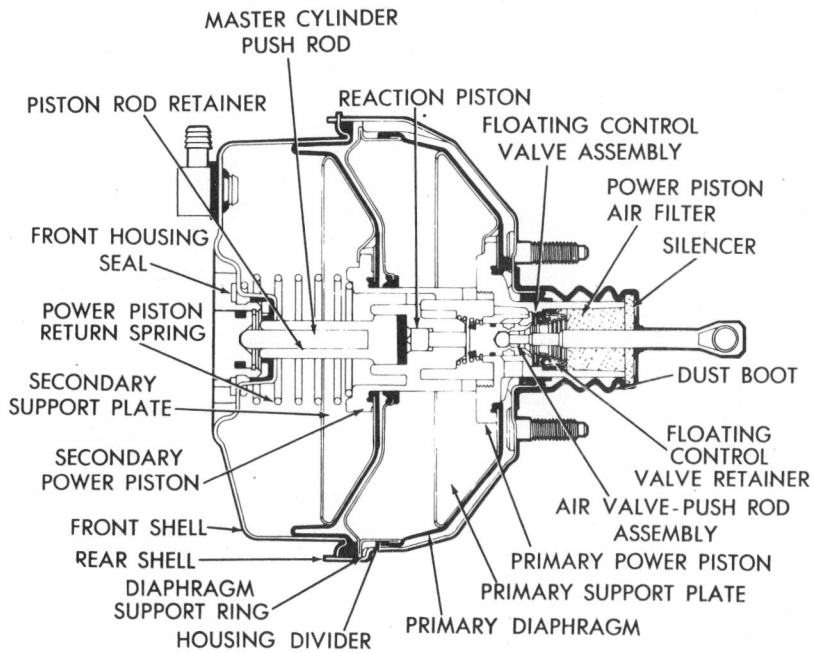

Fig. 51-14. In this power brake booster, two diaphragm and plate assemblies utilize difference in pressure between intake manifold vacuum and atmospheric pressure to operate master cylinder push rod and apply brakes.

the pressure of the compressed air is given as the amount of pressure above atmospheric. In other words, a gauge for measuring the pressure of compressed air registers zero when connected only to the atmosphere.

By providing suitable piping, compressed air will "flow" in much the same manner as liquids flow through connecting pipes. For example, if one reservoir contains air under pressure, and another one contains air at atmospheric pressure, air will flow from the reservoir of higher pressure to that of lower pressure. This flow will continue until both reservoirs are at the same pressure.

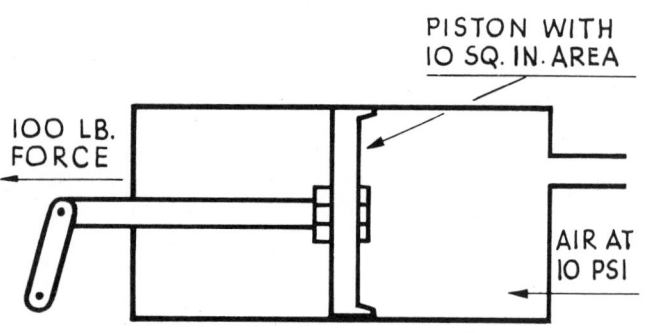

Fig. 51-15. Illustrating principle of a simple air brake.

AIR BRAKES

The application of compressed air in the operation of automotive air brakes is relatively simple. In Fig. 51-15, compressed air is admitted into a cylinder which encloses a piston. The force of the compressed air will cause the piston to move until it encounters a resistance equal to the force developed by the compressed air. For example, the piston in Fig. 51-15 has an area of 10 sq. in., while the compressed air has a pressure of 10 psi. The total force developed will be 10 x 10 or 100 psi. This is similar to the effect of hydraulic power illustrated in Figs. 51-4 and 51-6.

Remember that the quantity of air acting on the piston does not affect the force developed. The only factors involved are the air pressure and the area of the piston on which the air pressure is acting.

PRINCIPLE OF THE SYPHON

Normal air pressure (atmospheric pressure) is used to do many kinds of work. For example, a syphon drains tanks by means of atmospheric pressure. In a syphon, a tube or pipe is connected to two tanks, one higher than the other, Fig. 51-16. Once the connecting tube has been filled with liquid, it will continue to flow to the lower tank until the level of the liquid is the same in both tanks or until the upper tank is empty.

The force that causes the liquid to flow is the pressure of the atmosphere. This pressure forces the liquid up the short arm of the syphon (AB). (Theoretically, water can be raised a height of 34 ft.) At higher altitudes, where air pressure is less

than at sea level, the liquid would be raised a shorter distance.

The action of the syphon is interesting. The force of the atmosphere tending to push the liquid up the short arm of the syphon is opposed by downward pressure of the weight of the liquid. See AB in Fig. 51-16. Similarly, atmospheric pressure tends to drive the liquid up the long arm, CD. However, it is resisted by the weight of the liquid in CD, which is greater than in AB. So the atmospheric pressure meets greater resistance in pushing the liquid up CD than in pushing it in the opposite direction. The liquid will therefore flow up the arm, AB, and continue until it reaches the lower reservoir.

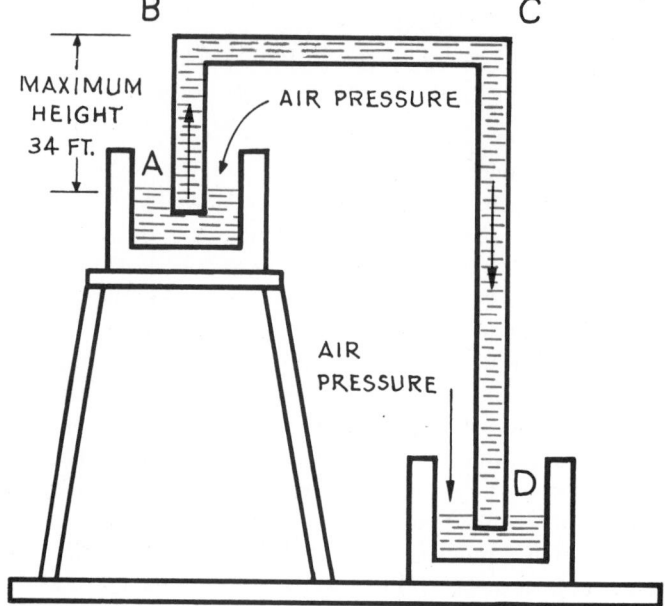

Fig. 51-16. Atmospheric pressure causes liquid in a syphon to flow from upper tank to lower tank.

VENTURI TUBE

The venturi tube is important in carburetion. A venturi is a tube with a restricted section, Fig. 51-17. When a liquid or air is passed through a venturi tube, the speed of flow is increased at the area of restriction, and fluid pressure is decreased. The same amount or volume of air flows through all sections of the carburetor throat. Obviously, if the throat area decreases, the velocity must increase in order to maintain the same rate of flow. Then, when the area increases, the velocity will decrease.

This is clearly illustrated in Fig. 51-17, which shows how venturi action vacuum varies in different sections of the carburetor. Vacuum is measured in inches of mercury and designated as inches Hg, (initials used in chemical symbol representing mercury). Note that vacuum and velocity of airflow are at a maximum at the point of maximum restriction. Also worth noting, vacuum is zero at the air inlet to the carburetor where air pressure is normal.

Venturi action is used in carburetors to maintain the correct air-fuel ratio throughout the range of speeds and loads of the engine.

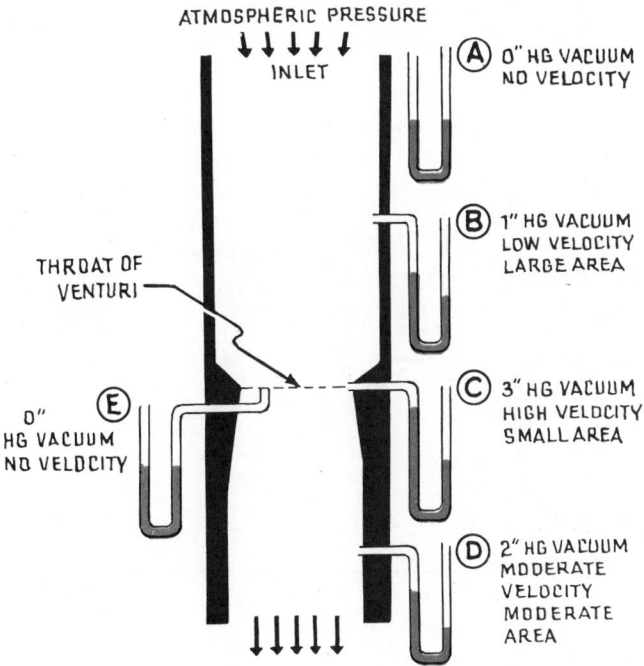

ATMOSPHERIC PRESSURE

INLET

THROAT OF VENTURI

(A) 0" HG VACUUM NO VELOCITY

(B) 1" HG VACUUM LOW VELOCITY LARGE AREA

(C) 3" HG VACUUM HIGH VELOCITY SMALL AREA

(D) 2" HG VACUUM MODERATE VELOCITY MODERATE AREA

(E) 0" HG VACUUM NO VELOCITY

Fig. 51-17. Air moving in throat of venturi will have greatest velocity and maximum vacuum will exist, as shown at C. However, if airflow is stopped, vacuum becomes zero.

BOYLE'S LAW

An important characteristic of air and other gases is explained in Boyle's law. It states that if the pressure on a gas in a confined space is doubled, the gas will be compressed to half its original volume, provided the temperature remains the same.

Boyle's law is normally given as follows: If the temperature of a confined gas is kept constant, its volume will vary inversely with its pressure.

This may be expressed as follows:

$$P'V' = PV$$

P and V represent the pressure and volume of a gas before compression; P' and V' are the pressure and volume after compression. For example, the pressure of a quantity of gas is 50 psi, and it occupies 10 cu. ft. This air is compressed until it exerts a pressure of 75 psi while the temperature remains constant. What is the volume of the gas after compression?

$$\frac{V}{V'} = \frac{P'}{P}$$

$$\frac{75}{50} = \frac{10}{P}$$

$$75P = 500$$

$$P = 6.66 \text{ cu. ft.}$$

CHARLES' LAW

Another important law relating to the behavior of gases under different conditions is known as Charles' law. It states that under constant pressure, the volume of a gas varies directly with its absolute temperature. The absolute temperature is the temperature in C. degrees plus 273. This law is expressed as follows:

$$\frac{V'}{V_2} = \frac{T'}{T_2}$$

V' is the volume of a gas when its absolute temperature is T' and V_2 is the volume of the same gas when its absolute temperature is T_2.

Example: To what volume will 110 cu. ft. of gas at 15 deg. C. expand if heated at a constant pressure to 55 deg. C.?

$$T' = 15° + 273 = 288° \text{ absolute}$$
$$T_2 = 55° + 273 = 328° \text{ absolute}$$

$$\frac{110}{V_2} = \frac{288}{328}$$

$$36080 = 288V_2$$

$$V_2 = 125.3 \text{ cu. ft.}$$

An understanding of the principles of pneumatics is more important than ever to auto mechanics. Today's energy absorbing bumpers, passenger restraint systems, vacuum door locks and temperature control systems utilize those principles. See chapter on BUILT-IN SAFETY SYSTEMS.

REVIEW QUESTIONS — PNEUMATICS

1. What is the normal pressure of the atmosphere?
2. What is the major difference between a liquid and a gas?
3. What causes the liquid to rise in a straw?
4. In the conventional power or booster brake used on a passenger car, what power is used to assist the driver to apply the brakes?
5. What will a conventional gauge on a tank of compressed air register when the tank is open to the atmosphere?
6. Draw an illustration and explain the principle of a syphon.
7. What is a venturi tube?
8. In what area of a carburetor is airflow the fastest?
9. For what purpose is the venturi used in a carburetor?
10. State Boyle's Law.
11. State Charles' Law.

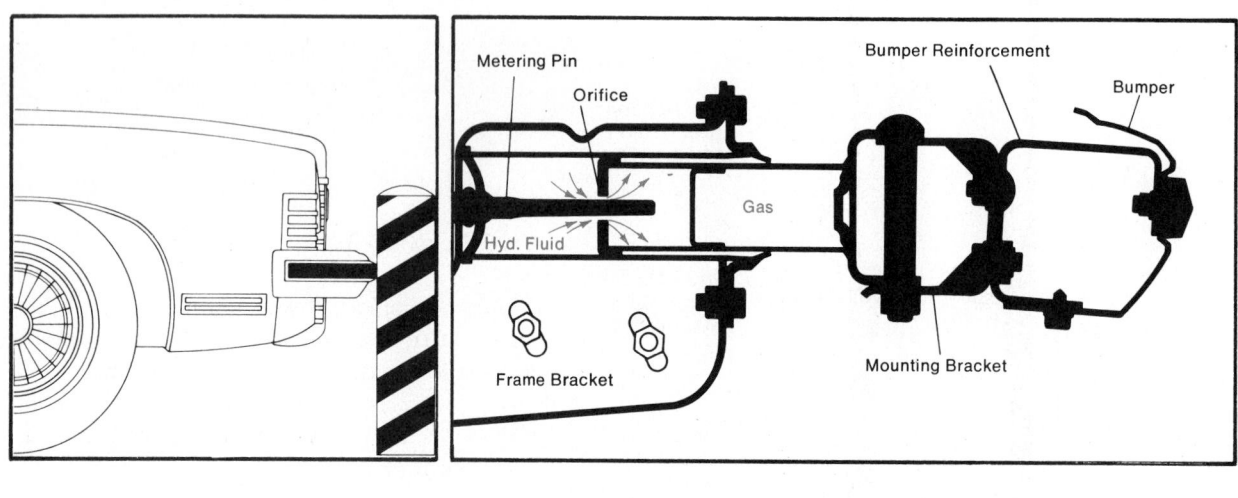

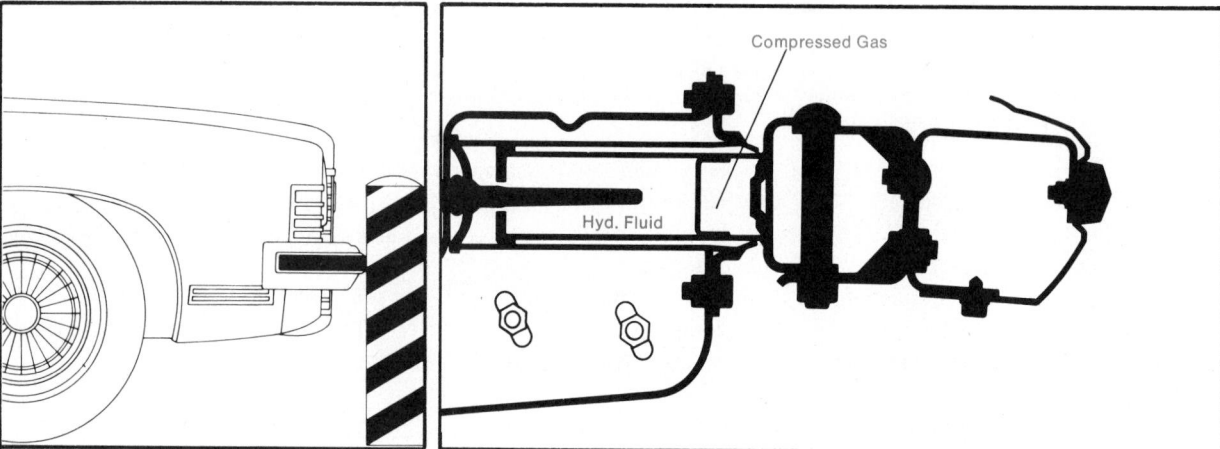

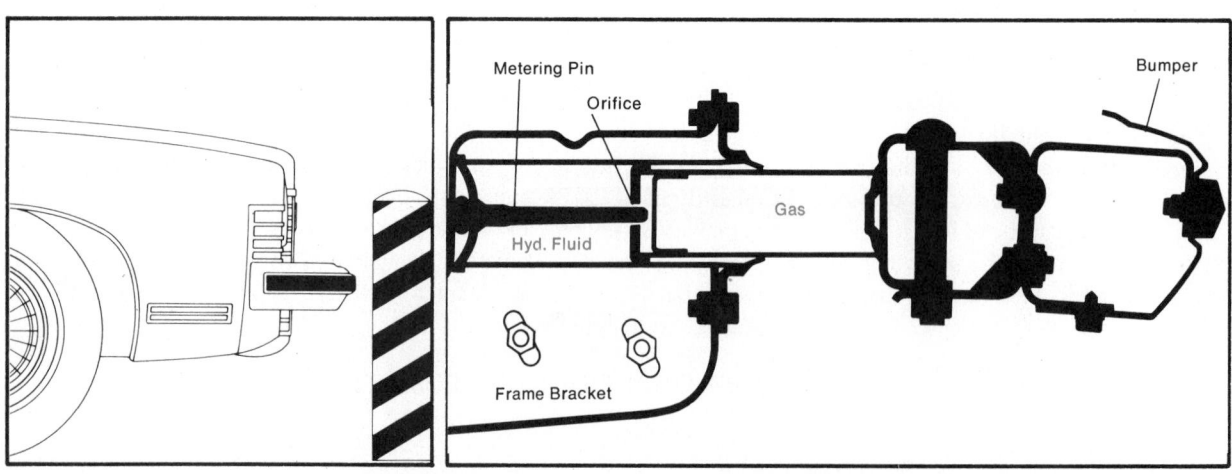

Fig. 52-1. Above. Impact triggers hydraulic action in energy absorbing unit. Center. Unit is compressed and fluid has moved from rear chamber to front chamber, while absorbing impact. Compressed gas forces fluid back to its original chamber and bumper returns to normal position.

BUILT-IN
SAFETY SYSTEMS

Safety has always been a key word in automotive engineering, but more so in the last decade. The split hydraulic brake system was introduced; steering shafts were made collapsible; cross beams were installed in doors for side impact protection; the crash (cushioned) dash and non-protruding control knobs became part of interior styling.

Now, tires, suspension and brakes are vastly improved; signal lights, warning buzzers, neutral safety switches and steering wheel locks are mandatory. Front, side and rear lighting is better than ever, and color-coded.

Seat belts, shoulder harnesses and head rests have become standard equipment, as have starter interlocks that prevent the engine from starting until front seat occupants have "buckled up." Also, to afford greater protection to the car and its occupants, and to better withstand a 5 mph barrier impact, frames and bumpers have been strengthened. In most cases, energy absorbing units have been added.

GM BUMPERS

The latest bumper system installed on some 1973 General Motors cars is shown in Fig. 52-1. In the upper view, the bumper has made contact with a barrier (simulating a collision) and hydraulic fluid is flowing past the tapered metering pin.

In the center view, the bumper has stopped moving and the energy of impact has been absorbed by forcing the fluid from the rear chamber of the energy absorber to the front chamber. Entry of the hydraulic fluid has forced the floating piston, Fig. 52-2, forward compressing the gas in the front chamber in preparation for bumper recovery.

The lower view, Fig. 52-1, shows the compressed gas forcing the fluid back to the rear chamber while the telescoping tube moves forward, restoring the bumper to its original position.

SERVICE TIPS

Several precautions must be observed when servicing energy absorbing bumper units. First, no heat should be applied to these units. Likewise, they should not be welded. In case of faulty operation, each energy absorbing bumper unit must be tested separately.

If a unit is to be scrapped, relieve pressure by breaking the

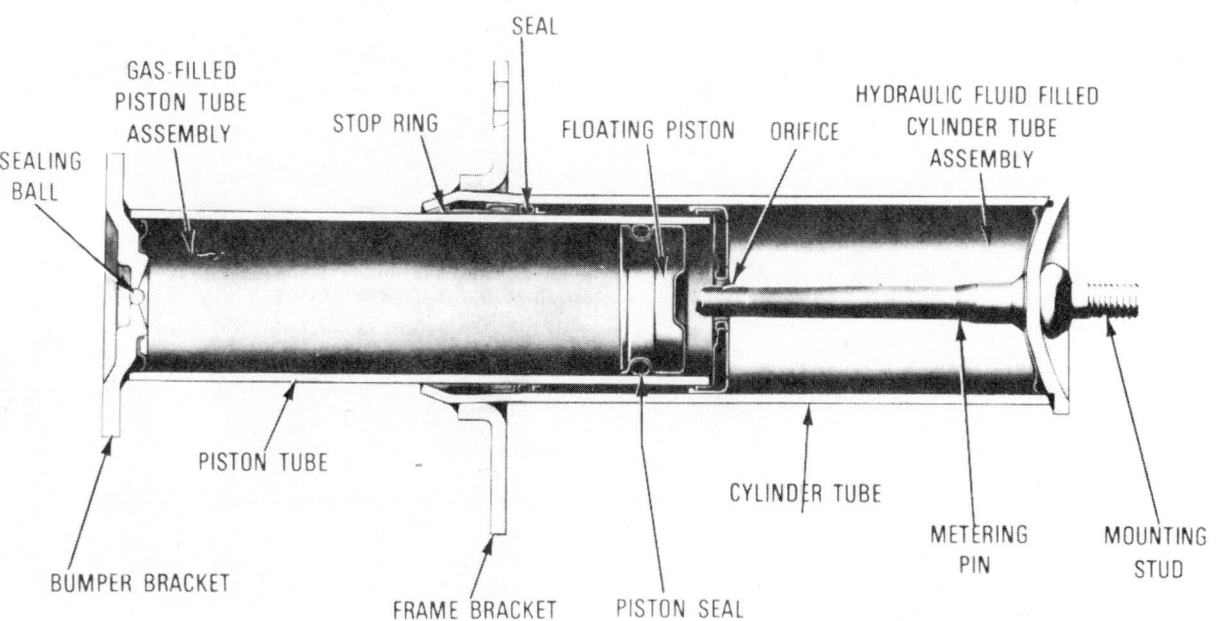

Fig. 52-2. Sectional view of General Motors' energy absorber in extended position.

699

weld at the sealing ball end of the piston tube with a punch and hammer.

If the unit will not extend, provide a positive restraint such as a chain or cable and stand clear of the bumper. Relieve the gas pressure by drilling a small hole in the piston tube near the bumper bracket. Remove the unit only after the pressure has been released.

When removing a unit from a vehicle, it may be necessary to support the bumper to prevent rotation of the other unit.

A further precaution is not to immerse the unit in a solvent.

If oil is continuously dripping from the crimp or stud end of the energy absorbing unit, replace the unit. However, some oil wetting may be due to grease packed in crimp area.

The energy absorbing unit should not be tested by driving the vehicle into a barrier. However, it can be tested by the following procedure:

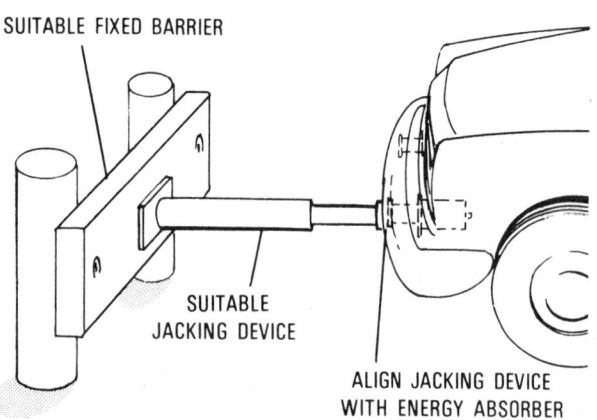

Fig. 52-3. One method of testing General Motors' energy absorbing unit.

1. Park the vehicle about 18 in. from a strongly constructed wall or pillar. Place the transmission selector lever in "Park" position, apply the hand brake and turn off the ignition switch.
2. Place a hydraulic jack between the bumper and the wall, taking care to align it with the energy absorbing device, Fig. 52-3. Apply pressure to compress the unit at least 3/8 in. (Place a six inch rule on the ram of the hydraulic jack to make this measurement.)
3. Release the pressure, and the bumper should return to its normal position. If the unit does not return, it should be replaced.

NOTE: If the energy absorbing unit is not mounted on a car, it can be tested in a similar manner by placing it in an arbor press and compressing it 3/8 in.

In addition to the energy absorbing bumper described, some 1972 Pontiacs have an energy absorbing bumper which uses blocks of urethane to absorb impact, Fig. 52-4. This was the first step away from conventional bumpers.

Another method of protecting the front of the vehicle is shown in Fig. 52-5. This is an Oldsmobile design on certain 1973 models which permits the upper part of the hinged grille to swing back, lessening the extent of the damage.

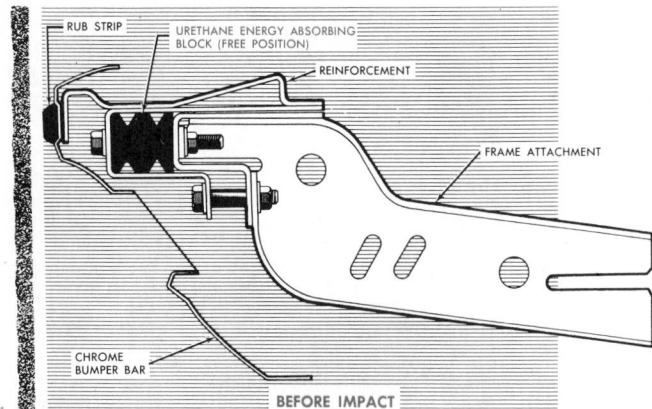

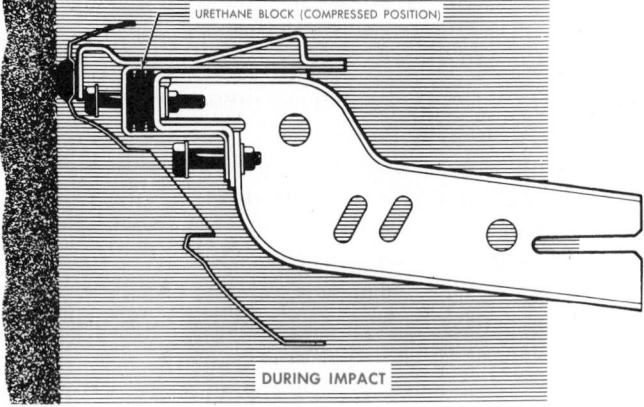

Fig. 52-4. Details of another GM bumper which uses urethane blocks to absorb energy of impact.

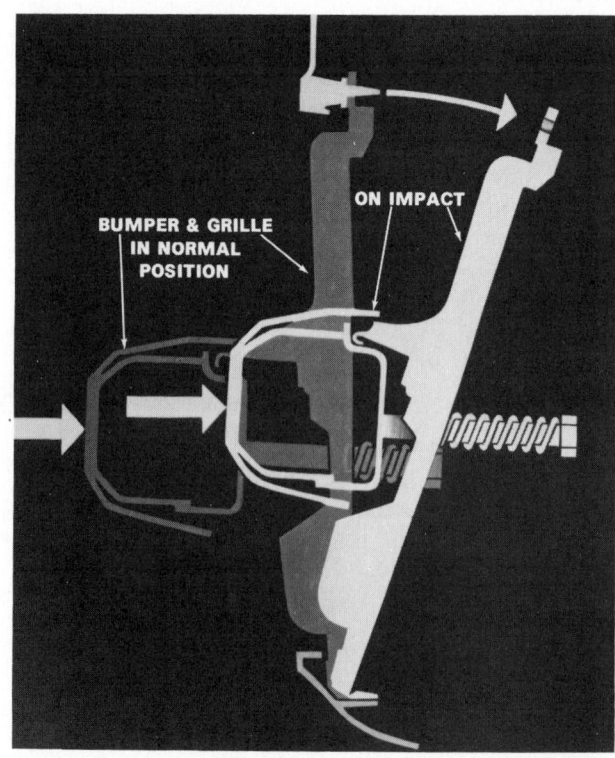

Fig. 52-5. Oldsmobile's hinged grille that tilts back with bumper on impact.

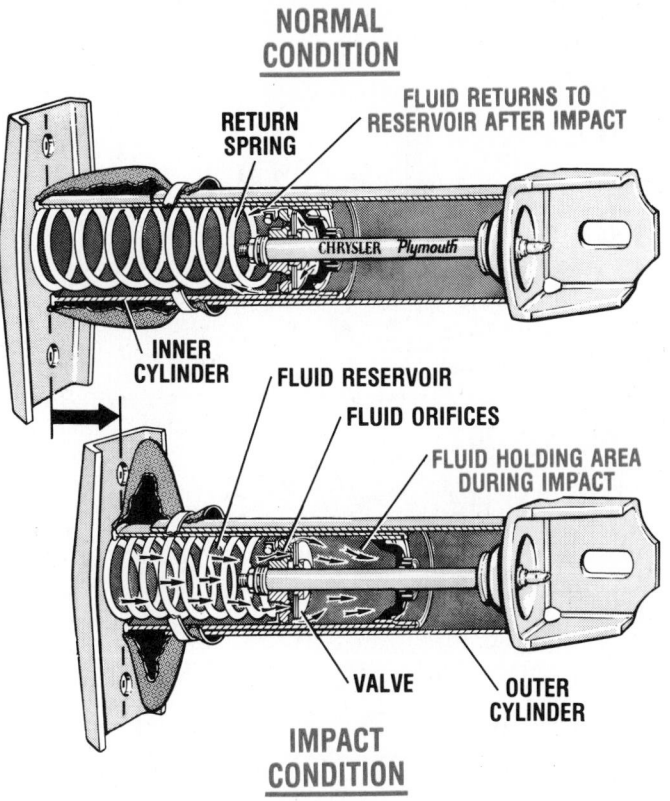

<figure>NORMAL CONDITION</figure>

Fig. 52-6. Chrysler's hydraulic bumper system uses hydraulic action on impact-absorbing stroke, spring action on return stroke.

CHRYSLER'S BUMPER SYSTEM

Late model Chrysler-Plymouth and Dodge cars have bumpers equipped with hydraulic units similar to a suspension system shock absorber, Fig. 52-6. These units are designed to absorb an impact, then return to the original position.

The outer cylinder of the hydraulic unit attaches to the frame or underbody of the vehicle; the inner cylinder is attached to the bumper. When an impact load reaches approximately 10,000 lb., a valve in the hydraulic unit opens and fluid is forced through a set of orifices (small openings). This produces a shock-absorbing reaction, until the impact load is removed. Then a spring inside the unit returns the bumper to its original position.

Chrysler engineers have matched the stroke of the hydraulic unit to the weight of the car. Units have a 2 in. stroke on small cars; a 2 1/2 in. stroke on intermediates; a 2 3/4 in. stroke on full size cars.

PASSENGER RESTRAINT SYSTEMS

Seat belts and shoulder belts of various types have been used in passenger cars for many years. See Fig. 52-7. Typically, the lap belt and shoulder belt are fixed to a connector. The lap belt has an automatic locking retractor, while the shoulder belt has an inertial-locking retractor that locks only when the vehicle stops abruptly. Suitable warning signals alert the driver to buckle up upon starting the engine.

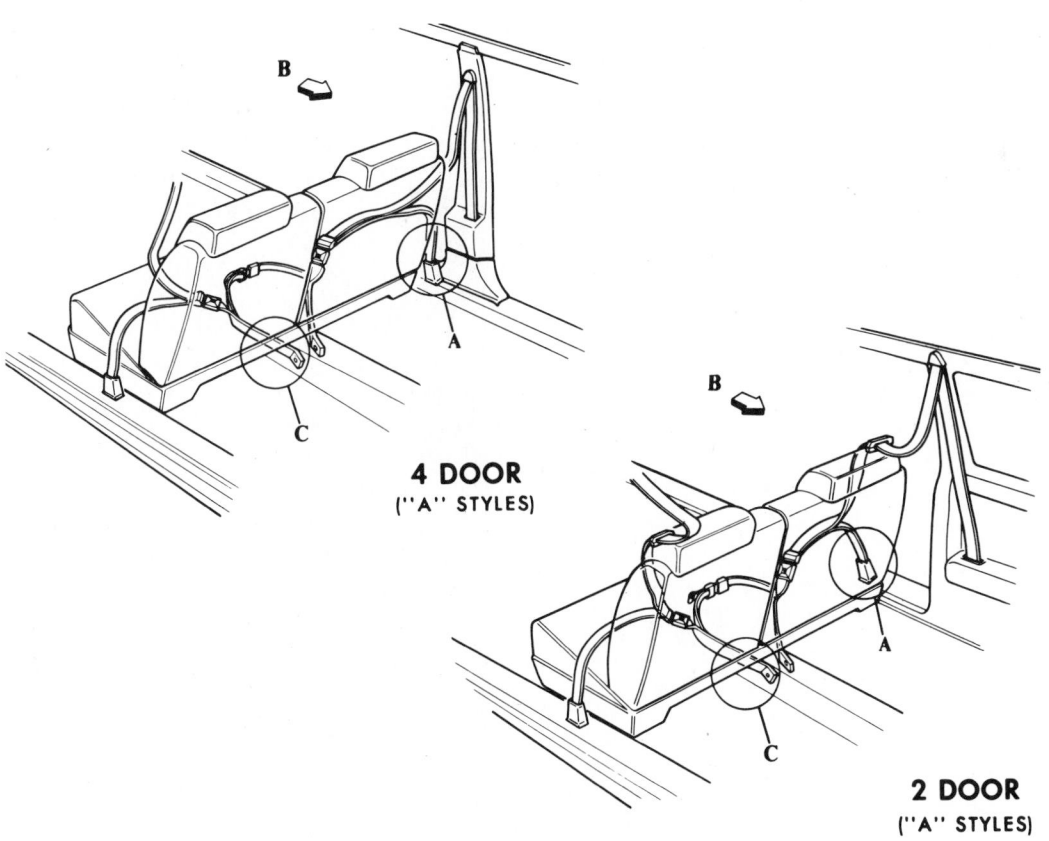

4 DOOR ("A" STYLES)

2 DOOR ("A" STYLES)

Fig. 52-7. Front seat lap belt and shoulder belt attaching locations. (Fisher Body Div., GM)

SHOULDER BELT ATTACHMENT
2 DOOR STYLES

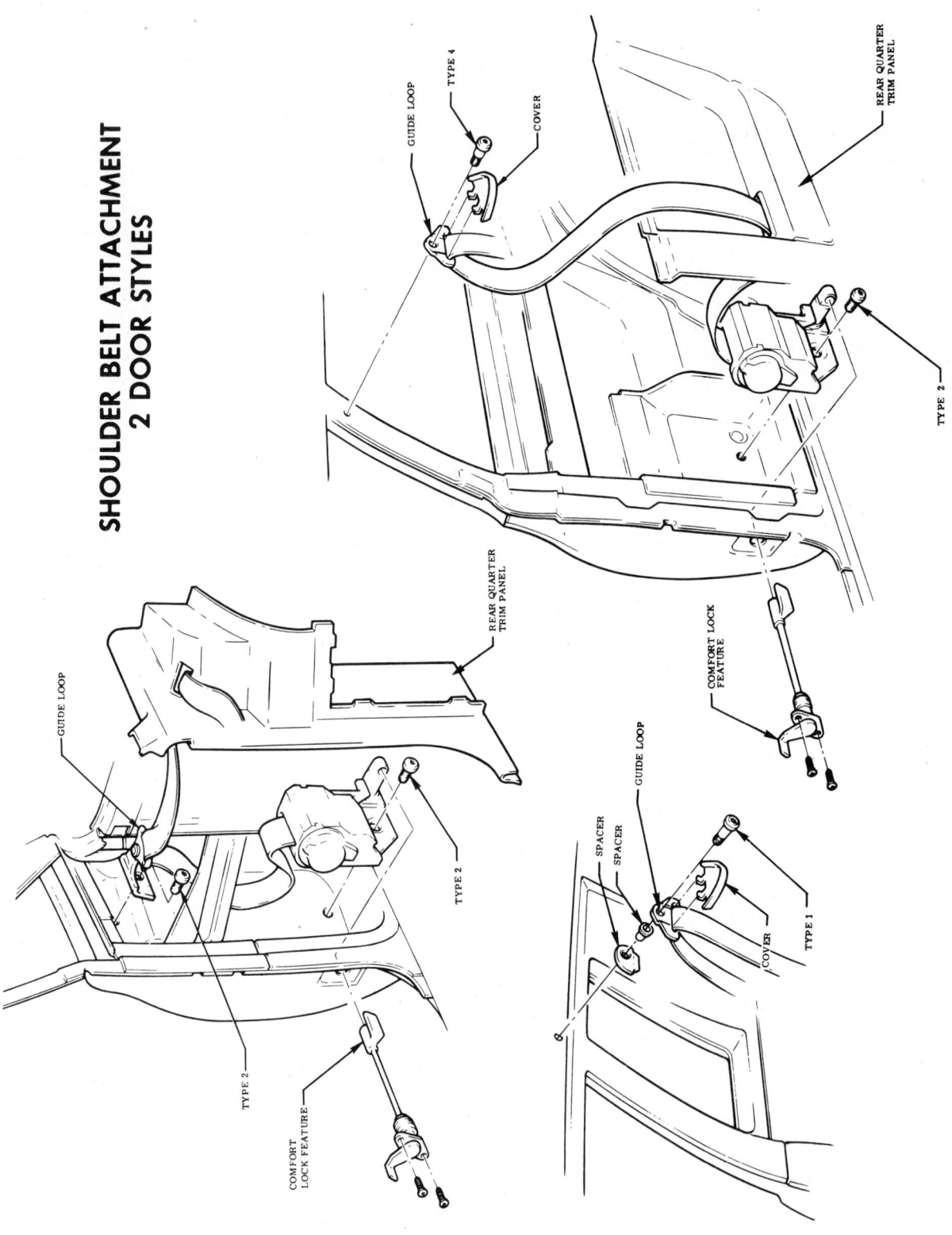

Fig. 52-8. Exploded view of front seat shoulder belt attachment on GM "A" body two door styles.

GM LAP AND SHOULDER BELTS

Front seat belts on GM cars incorporate a "timed" fasten seat belt reminder lamp and sound signal (buzzing). These warnings are designed to remind the driver and passengers to fasten lap and shoulder belts when the ignition key is turned to the ON position. If the driver's seat belt IS BUCKLED, the buzzer will not operate but the fasten seat belt reminder lamp will stay on for 4 to 8 seconds. If the driver's seat belt IS NOT BUCKLED, the reminder lamp and sound signal will automatically shut off after the 4 to 8 second interval.

When servicing seat belts, note that retractor portions of front seat lap belts can be serviced. Also serviceable is the buckle portion of the front seat lap belt for the driver and outboard passenger. Other belts are serviced in complete sets.

Lap belt-to-floor pan and shoulder belt-to-roof panel fasteners are especially important. Failure of these attaching parts could affect the performance of vital components and systems, and/or could result in major repair expenses. Fasteners must be replaced with a replacement part of the same part number or its equivalent.

Do not attempt to remove the seat belt retractor cover. The cover and long rivet securing the cover to the retractor are not available as service parts.

CADILLAC'S AUTOMATIC SEAT BELTS

Automatic lap/shoulder belts were introduced on 1981 Cadillac Sedan de Villes equipped with the V-6 gasoline-powered engine. These belts are activated without any specific action on the driver's part. As the door is opened, shoulder and lap belts extend outward across the seat, permitting easy entrance or exit. When the door is closed, a retractor assembly housed in the center console spools in all belt slack.

The retractor assemblies are the inertial-locking type which, in the event of an accident, lock out automatically. An additional one-half inch of belt slack may be obtained for added comfort by depressing a "comfort release" button and pulling out the belt.

FORD SEAT BELTS

Ford has two distinct front outboard seat belt systems. One is the "three point system"; the other is the "continuous loop system."

The three point system has a fixed tongue on the front outboard lap/shoulder belt and two retractors. The continuous loop system has a movable tongue on the front outboard belt and only one retractor.

The seat belts and shoulder belts are factory installed in their proper locations. If seat belts or shoulder belts are removed for any reason, they should be reinstalled in the original position. Details of the installation of front seat belts on two door models of the Fairmont and Zephyr are shown in Fig. 52-9. The rear belt installation is illustrated in Fig. 52-10.

Certain servicing cautions are given by the manufacturer:
1. Seat belt assemblies must be replaced after they have been subjected to "loading" by occupants in a collision.

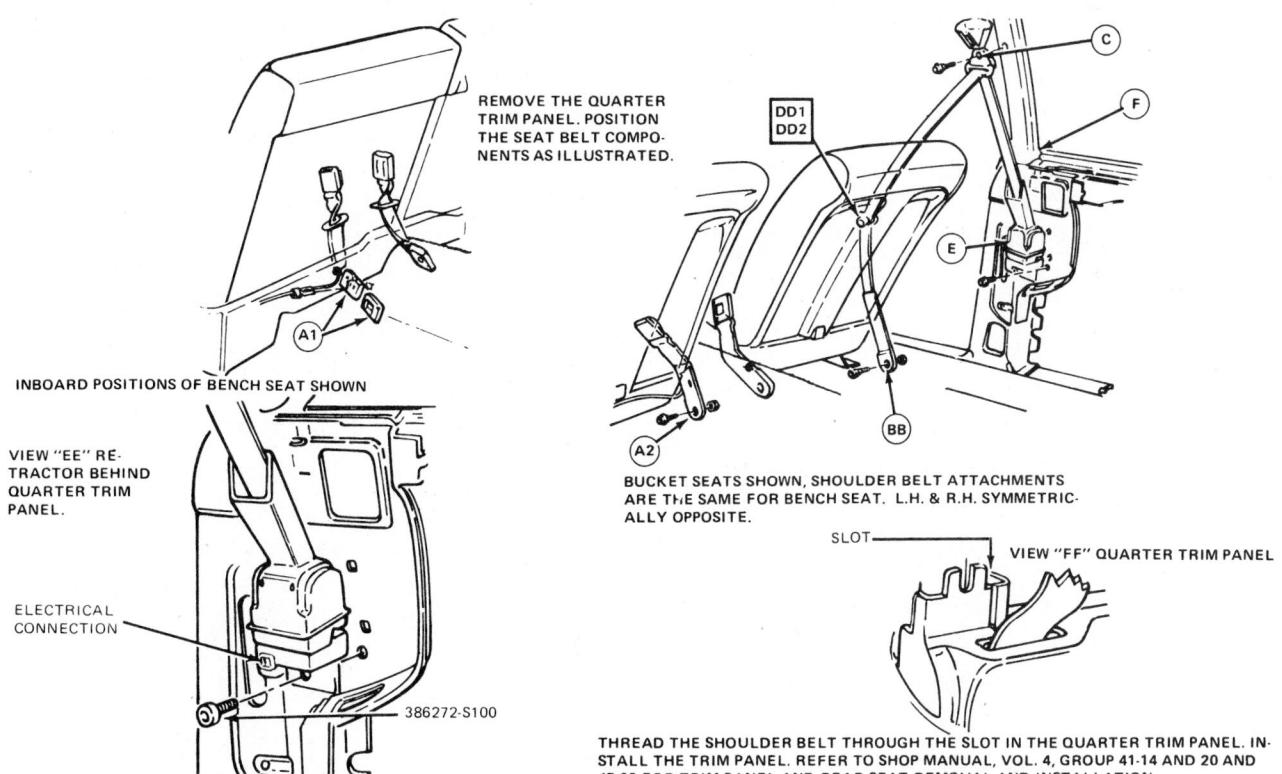

Fig. 52-9. Front seat belt assembly as installed on Fairmont and Zephyr two door models. (Ford Motor Co.)

REAR SEAT BELT INSTALLATION INSTRUCTIONS

REMOVE THE LOWER REAR SEAT CUSHION. POSITION ALL SEAT BELT COMPONENTS AS ILLUSTRATED
AND INSTALL ALL SEAT BELT ANCHOR BOLTS. TORQUE ALL ANCHOR BOLTS 22-32 FT-LBS (30-43 N·m).

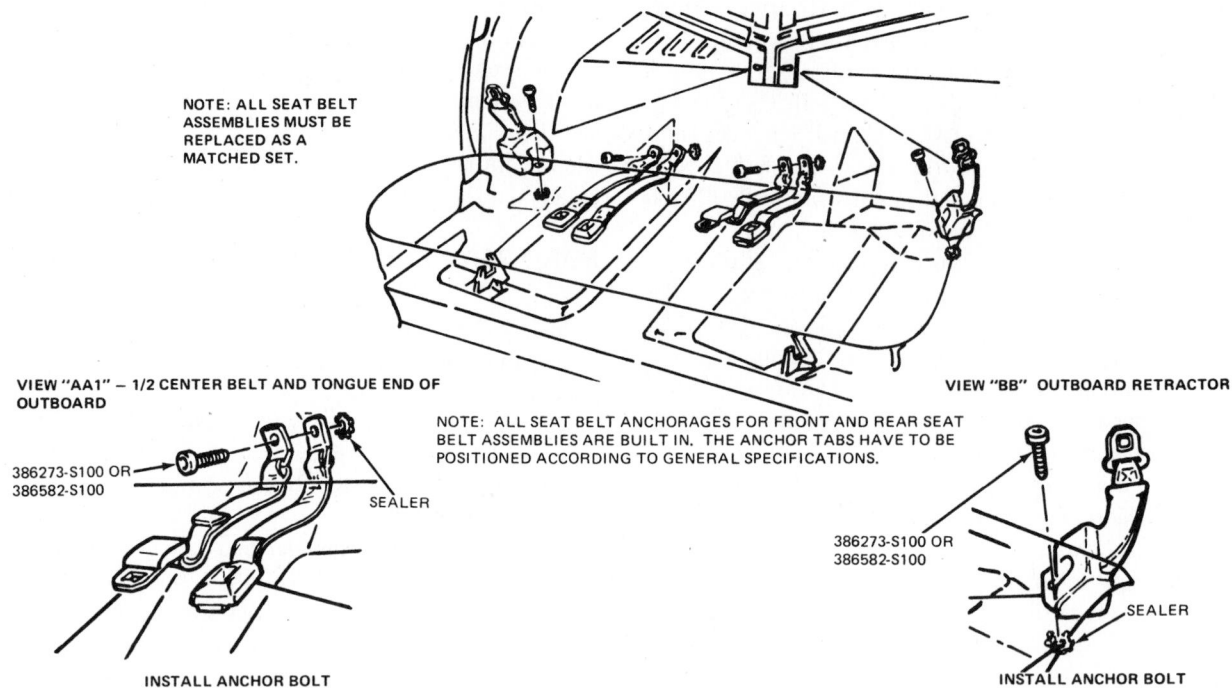

NOTE: ALL SEAT BELT
ASSEMBLIES MUST BE
REPLACED AS A
MATCHED SET.

VIEW "AA1" – 1/2 CENTER BELT AND TONGUE END OF
OUTBOARD

VIEW "BB" OUTBOARD RETRACTOR

386273-S100 OR
386582-S100

SEALER

NOTE: ALL SEAT BELT ANCHORAGES FOR FRONT AND REAR SEAT
BELT ASSEMBLIES ARE BUILT IN. THE ANCHOR TABS HAVE TO BE
POSITIONED ACCORDING TO GENERAL SPECIFICATIONS.

386273-S100 OR
386582-S100

SEALER

INSTALL ANCHOR BOLT

INSTALL ANCHOR BOLT

Fig. 52-10. Rear seat belt assembly of Fairmont and Zephyr. (Ford Motor Co.)

2. Belt assemblies must be installed in matched sets as received and must not be interchanged between vehicle models.

3. All seat belt anchor bolts in the floor pan should be correctly torqued, and sealer should be installed around the bolts.

The retractor of Ford's three point system is shown in Fig. 52-11. In this system, the webbing for the lap belt extends from a belt retractor that automatically locks when the belt is worn. This lock prevents the belt from being pulled out farther, but allows the belt to retract. In that way, it maintains a snug fit around the user. The lap belt retractor is located on or in the rocker panel, depending on the car line or model.

With the continuous loop system, the outboard lap/shoulder belt uses a common sliding tongue. To secure, insert the tongue into the inboard buckle. With this system, the webbing for the lap belt is anchored to the side of the sill without a retractor.

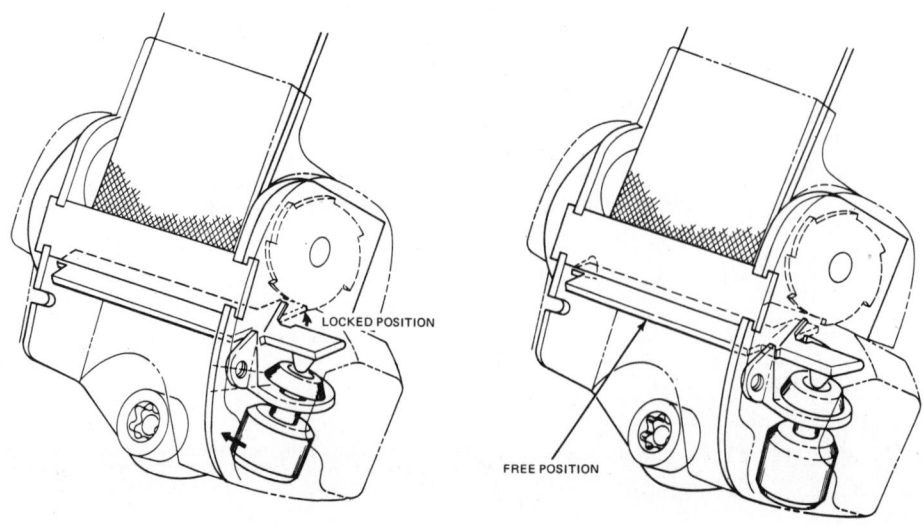

LOCKED POSITION

FREE POSITION

Fig. 52-11. Details of shoulder harness retractor as installed on some Ford models.

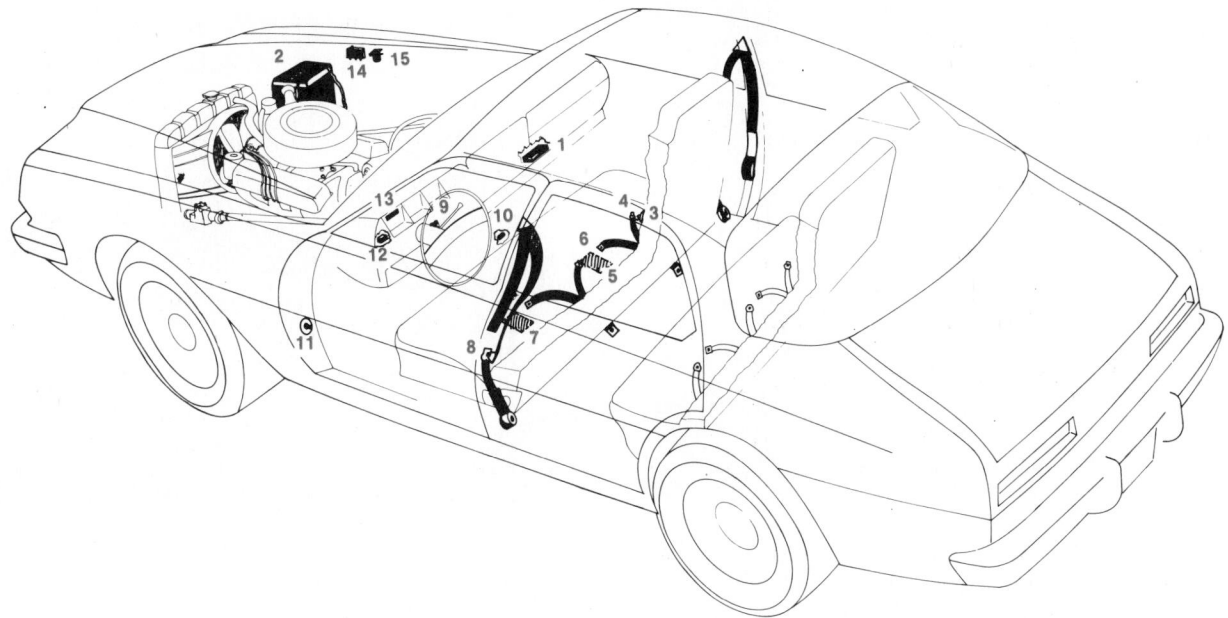

Fig. 52-12. Details of American Motors' seat belt interlock system: 1—Interlock logic module. 2—Battery. 3—Passenger seat sensor. 4—Passenger buckle switch. 5—Center seat sensor. 6—Center buckle switch. 7—Driver seat sensor. 8—Driver buckle switch. 9—Ignition switch. 10—Neutral safety switch. 11—LH door switch light. 12—Warning buzzer. 13—Warning light. 14—Starter relay. 15—Starter solenoid.

Federal regulations for one model year, 1974, called for the installation of seat belt interlock systems that were designed to keep the starting system de-energized until seat belts were fastened in both occupied front seat positions.

CHRYSLER'S RESTRAINT SYSTEM

A special type of passenger restraint system with starter interlock was installed on 1974 Chrysler Corporation cars. With this setup, front lap belt and shoulder belt are attached to a single tab. An inertia retractor automatically adjusts the shoulder belt to fit the driver or passenger. The Chrysler system also allows the user to lean forward normally, until a sudden stop occurs. Then, the inertia retractor locks the belt and restrains the user.

A starter interlock prevents the engine from starting until all front seat passengers are seated and belts are buckled.

AMC BELT/STARTER INTERLOCK SETUP

American Motors' Auto-Loc lap belt in 1974 models was combined with a vehicle-sensitive inertia reel shoulder harness and incorporated with a starter interlock system. With this arrangement, Fig. 52-12, front seat belts and harnesses must be fastened before the engine can be started.

All front seat belts are tied in with the vehicle interlock system. A logic module behind the instrument panel senses when seating positions are occupied and when belts have been fastened.

As with other car manufacturers' belt systems, the shoulder harness fits loosely across the body, permitting freedom of movement. When the car stops suddenly, the emergency-locking retractor locks the belt in place to hold the user firmly in position. Components of the AMC seat belt interlock system are shown in Fig. 52-12.

REVIEW QUESTIONS — BUILT-IN SAFETY SYSTEMS

1. What is an energy absorbing bumper?
2. GM's energy absorber works by hydraulic action and compressed gas reaction. Yes or No?
3. One of the earlier impact absorbing bumpers on Oldsmobiles works in conjunction with a hinged _____ that moves with the bumper on impact.
4. Chrysler Corporation's new bumper system uses hydraulic units similar in concept to suspension system shock absorbers. True or False?
5. Chrysler's hydraulic units on full size cars have a stroke of _____ in.
6. GM seat belt/shoulder belt fasteners must be replaced with _____.
7. Ford has two distinct front seat belt systems in current use. Name them.
8. Chrysler's Passenger Restraint System with Starter Interlock allows a person to lean forward normally while the shoulder belt is in place until a _____ _____ occurs. Then the belt locks and restrains the user.
9. American Motors' Seat Belt Interlock System features an interlock logic module, seat sensors and _____ _____.

Senior Research Engineer. This engineer in the Physics Department at General Motors Research Laboratories developed a laser-based instrument that measures minute diesel engine exhaust particles.

Parts Manager. Many car manufacturers' dealerships utilize computer systems to speed parts orders. Dealer shown here is entering an order for parts from closest parts depot.

Stylist. Styling studio of Ford Motor Company is the scene for this experiment with styling changes worked up on the drawing board and proposed by design engineers.

Assembly Line Inspector. Inspector "reads" bar codes on a build ticket with a special lightpen to assure that proper components are assembled on this particular engine.

CAREER OPPORTUNITIES

The automotive field offers unlimited career opportunities. Typical job classifications include testing, diagnosing, servicing, machining, estimating, selling, managing, transporting, engineering, styling, production planning and assembling.

There is a shortage of trained auto mechanics. The car manufacturers, both U.S. and foreign are expanding their training facilities and are attempting to attract career-minded high school graduates and individuals about to be discharged from the Armed Forces. Some dealers have worked out schedules whereby students spend mornings in school and afternoons in the dealer's shop working on cars.

Mechanically inclined students and recent graduates who have had some training in automotive service and repair work should consider these facts about automobiles and the nation's work force:

1. Over 100 million motor vehicles are registered and in use.
2. Over 13.5 million persons are employed in the manufacture, distribution, maintenance and commercial use of motor vehicles. About one out of every six workers is in an automotive-related occupation.
3. Over 800,000 automotive businesses are in operation, representing one out every six firms in the country.

The automotive field is so broad, persons attempting to choose a vocation may have a limited view of the total picture.

Job seekers may only investigate the role of the trainee or apprentice. This is a mistake, because the first job should be considered as a stepping stone toward a higher position and greater earnings.

The following brief job descriptions are designed to familiarize you with some of the many areas of opportunity that abound in the automotive field.

AUTO MECHANIC

Your first job in a retail automotive business is likely to be as an Apprentice Auto Mechanic, Fig. 53-1.

The days of the "greaseball" mechanic are over. Most shops today are clean, well lighted and properly ventilated. Modern shops are equipped with laborsaving tools and testing devices, which make the work easier and more interesting. The mechanics wear neat working clothes and are obliged to maintain their work area in reasonably clean condition.

Fig. 53-1. Auto Mechanic. Apprentice auto mechanics learn trade by studying principles of operation and by applying service techniques taught on the job.

An Auto Mechanic's job calls for a broad range of both light and heavy repair work. A general auto mechanic must know how to maintain all systems of automotive vehicles in good working order by applying recommended service procedures. This calls for the ability to diagnose and locate trouble, and to make the right adjustment or replacement. Good mechanics are well paid, and their work is always in demand.

TRUCK MECHANIC

A Truck Mechanic needs service know-how, plus special skills and strength in handling heavy parts and assemblies, both manually and with the aid of various jacks, cranes or chain hoists, wheel dollies and hydraulic presses. While tolerances, in general, are greater and "fits" are less critical, service techniques remain basically the same as with passenger car work. However, some areas require special training: double reduction axles, full floating axles, air brakes, etc. See Fig. 53-2.

Fig. 53-2. Truck Mechanic. Truck repair work involves a combination of skills in performing heavy-duty service operations. You must know what needs to be done and how to do it safely and efficiently.

SPECIALTY MECHANIC

A Specialty Mechanic, or Specialist, is a person who concentrates on a single phase of repair work. The modern trend in automotive service work favors this method of handling job assignments. Mechanics can choose a specialty they are especially well qualified to perform, then further improve efficiency and proficiency through daily involvement in jobs of a similar nature.

The specialty mechanic may choose to work in any one of these popular areas of automotive service:

1. Tune-up and emission control.
2. Diagnostic testing.
3. Electrical services.
4. Fuel supply and carburetion.
5. Air conditioning system service.
6. Engine repair.
7. Muffler and pipe replacement.
8. Radiator repair.
9. Brake work, Fig. 53-3.
10. Transmission and drive line.
11. Front end alignment and steering.
12. Tire sales and service, Fig. 53-4.
13. Body work.
14. Painting.
15. Trimming.
16. Glass installation.
17. Foreign car service.

Fig. 53-4. Tire Service Technician. Experienced tire sales and service representative chalks built-in tire wear indicator in tread of old tire to show car owner evidence of need for new tire.

CHIEF MECHANIC

The Chief Mechanic performs the duties of an auto mechanic, especially in helping to get work back on schedule in the shop by filling in for missing mechanics. The chief mechanic also authorizes repairs when unexpected defects are found, oversees the apprentice training program, and generally represents the dealership at the car manufacturer's service school.

SHOP SUPERVISOR

The Shop Supervisor is in charge of mechanics, directing routing and scheduling service and repair work. The supervisor helps hire, transfer, promote and discharge mechanics to meet the needs of the service department; supervises and instructs

Fig. 53-3. Brake Service Technician. Brake work offers a broad range of job assignments from on-car service and repair to a variety of machining operations.

the mechanics in work procedures; inspects finished repairs and is responsible for quality workmanship and satisfactory shop operation.

SERVICE MANAGER

The Service Manager is the department head in charge of planning, supervising and coordinating the activities of all shop employees. Primarily responsible for hiring, transferring, promoting and discharging workers, the service manager oversees scheduling of service and repair work, training of apprentices and familiarizing of auto mechanics in new vehicle service procedures. The service manager also reviews records of operation to plan cost control changes, improve shop practices and raise work standards; investigates complaints and assigns responsibility for service errors or adjusts bills or charges. In addition, the service manager must try to build business for the service department with advertising and sales promotion activities.

MOTOR VEHICLE SALES PERSON

Motor Vehicle Sales is the job for you if you have a special liking for selling. Experience in the service department gives you an excellent background for sales work. If you know the mechanics of a vehicle, you can do a much better job of

Fig. 53-5. Automotive Systems Technician. Technicians with automotive products manufacturers aid engineers in developing new and improved components and assemblies.

talking about the car or truck, demonstrating it and comparing it with competing makes.

SALES MANAGER

A Sales Manager has charge of the entire selling activity of a dealership, including service. This is one of the best positions in the retail automotive business. It usually is held by someone who has made a success of selling and who has managerial ability. The sales manager must work closely with the Service Manager, Parts Manager and Service Writer, who writes orders for repair by interpreting customers' descriptions of problems.

PARTS MANAGER

A Parts Manager for a car or truck dealer has an important job ordering, stocking and selling replacement parts and accessories. The parts manager supplies the shop in the dealership and sells parts and accessories at wholesale to the independent repair garages, service stations and specialty shops in the community. Training in service work and parts sales are valuable experience for this job.

JOBBER SALES PERSON

Jobber Sales is a job in the parts field that should appeal to a sales-minded young person with automotive service training. A jobber sales person, representing a wholesale house, travels over a certain territory selling the products of several manufacturers to automotive repair and supply shops.

EMPLOYMENT WITH MANUFACTURERS OF MOTOR VEHICLES

Employment with Manufacturers of Motor Vehicles often attracts workers with automotive mechanics training and other qualifications. This applies to positions such as: Factory District Manager, Factory Service Manager, Factory Service Representative, Factory Parts Manager, Factory Service Instructor and Research Laboratory Technician.

EMPLOYMENT IN AUTOMOTIVE FACTORIES

Employees in Automotive Factories make good use of training in automotive mechanics in jobs such as: Final Assembly Inspection, Final Assembly Repair, Dynamometer Testing, Experimental Driver, Driver Mechanic, Engineering Garage Mechanic and Technician, Fig. 53-5.

TECHNICAL TEACHER

Technical Teacher is an interesting career. If you obtain experience as an auto mechanic and have teaching ability, you might be employed by the factory to train service personnel in new developments, or you might teach automotive mechanics in a public or trade school or private industry, Fig. 53-6.

Fig. 53-6. Technical Teacher. Manufacturers often employ auto mechanics-turned-teacher to conduct clinics in product changes and related service techniques. (Bendix Corp.)

DRIVER OF A TRUCK OR BUS

Driver of a Truck or Bus is a job employing over 6 million men and women, second largest occupational group in the U.S. Many operators of large fleets of trucks or buses prefer that their drivers have automotive mechanics training. Driver-mechanics take better care of their vehicles and can make emergency repairs if necessary.

INSURANCE ADJUSTER AND CLAIM EXAMINER

Insurance Adjuster and Claim Examiner are jobs that insurance companies like to fill with young people who, in addition to other qualifications, have automotive service training. Knowledge of body work, painting and replacement parts pricing are vital.

REPRESENTATIVES

Sales and service representatives of many companies that supply parts and/or equipment to the automotive industry frequently are aggressive, high-caliber young people who began their careers with training in auto mechanics.

OWNERS OF SERVICE STATIONS OR SPECIALTY REPAIR SHOPS

Owners of Service Stations or Specialty Repair Shops certainly can use automotive service training to their advantage. If you have ambition to head up this kind of independent business operation, auto mechanics can help you achieve your goal.

AUTOMOTIVE DEALERS

Automotive Dealers, those who operate their own businesses and frequently are leaders in their communities, often started out as employees of the dealership.

CAREER IN AUTO MECHANICS

From these job descriptions, you can see that training in automotive mechanics could be your key to any one of a number of interesting careers. You can see that automotive service is a big, broad, many-sided business with enough opportunities to interest almost anyone who has the desire and determination to make good in a worthwhile job.

Remember, your most valuable asset is the ambition and determination to succeed. By alertness, application and perseverance, you can gain automotive knowledge and skill for which there is an expanding career market offering many rewards.

DICTIONARY OF AUTOMOTIVE TERMS

AAA: American Automobile Association.

ABRASION: Wearing or rubbing away.

A/C: Air conditioning.

AC: Alternating current.

ACCELERATOR: A pedal for regulating speed of an engine.

ACCELERATOR PUMP: Small pump in carburetor, operated by accelerator pedal linkage, which supplies additional fuel needed for acceleration of vehicle.

ACETYLENE OR OXY-ACETYLENE WELDING: Utilization of an acetylene flame to heat metal to fusion or melting point when uniting it.

ACKERMAN PRINCIPLE: Design having wheel spindles mounted on axle ends to permit spindles to be turned at an angle to axle for steering purposes.

ACRYLIC: A surface finish, made from synthetic polymers, which dries by solvent evaporation.

ACTIVE MATERIAL: In a storage battery, peroxide of lead (brown) in positive plates and metallic lead (gray) in negative plates upon which sulphuric acid acts.

ADAPTOR CARBURETOR: A device attached to a gasoline carburetor which permits an internal combustion engine to run either on gasoline or liquefied petroleum gas (LP-Gas).

ADDITIVE: In automotive oils, material added to oil to give it certain properties. Example: to lessen its tendency to thicken at low temperature.

ADS: Association of Diesel Specialists.

AEA: Automotive Electric Association.

AERA: Automotive Engine Rebuilders Association.

AIR: A gas containing approximately 4/5 nitrogen, 1/5 oxygen and some carbonic gas. Also, abbreviation for Air Injection Reactor.

AIR CLEANER: A device for filtering, cleaning and removing dust from intake air to an engine, air compressor, etc.

AIR-FUEL RATIO: Ratio by weight of fuel compared to air in carburetor mixture.

AIR GAP: Space between spark plug electrodes, starting motor and generator armatures, field shoes, etc.

AIR HORN: Air inlet of carburetor to which air cleaner is ordinarily attached.

AIR-LOCK: A bubble of air trapped in a fluid circuit which interferes with normal circulation of fluid.

AIR SPRING: An air-filled bag or device that is pressurized to provide spring action.

ALIGNMENT: An adjustment to bring related components into a line.

ALLEN WRENCH: A hexagonal wrench which fits into a recessed hexagonal hole.

ALLOY: A mixture of different metals. Example: solder is an alloy of lead and tin.

ALTERNATING CURRENT: An electric current alternating back and forth in direction of flow.

ALTERNATOR: Generator in which alternating current is changed to direct current by means of a rectifier.

ALUMINUM: A metal, noted for its lightness, often alloyed with small quantities of other metals.

AMA: See MVMA.

AMBIENT: Surrounding on all sides.

AMMETER: An instrument for measuring flow of electric current.

AMPERE: Unit of measurement for flow of electric current.

AMPERE-HOUR CAPACITY: A term used to indicate capacity of a storage battery. Example: delivery of a certain number of amperes for a certain number of hours.

ANNEALING: A process of softening metal. Example: heating and slow cooling of a piece of iron.

ANNULAR BALL BEARING: A ball bearing with a nonadjustable inner and outer race or races.

ANNULUS: In planetary gear system, an internal ring gear that operates in conjunction with a sun gear, pinion gears and pinion carrier. See RING GEAR.

ANODE: A positive pole of an electric current.

ANTIFREEZE: A material, such as ethylene glycol, added to water to lower its freezing point.

ANTIFRICTION BEARING: A bearing constructed with balls or rollers between journal and bearing surface to provide rolling instead of sliding friction.

ANTISMOG DEVICE: A special part or system designed to reduce or eliminate emission of noxious gases from exhaust of engine. See EXHAUST EMISSIONS.

APERTURE: An opening, hole or port.

API: American Petroleum Institute.

ARC WELDING: A method of utilizing an electric current jumping an air gap to provide heat for welding metal.

ARMATURE: Part of an electrical device which includes main, current-carrying winding. In a generator, it is usually core which rotates within pole shoes which are surrounded by field coils.

ARTICULATED MOUNTING: A term used where parts are connected by links and links are anchored to provide a double hinging action.

ASBESTOS: A natural fibrous mineral with a great heat resisting ability.

ASIA: Automotive Service Industry Association.

ASME: American Society of Mechanical Engineers.

ASPECT RATIO: Ratio of tire section height to section width.

ATA: American Trucking Association.

ATMOSPHERIC PRESSURE: Weight of air at sea level, about 14.7 psi.

ATOM: Smallest distinct chemical unit of a substance, composed of electrons, neutrons and protons.

AUTOMATIC STEERING EFFECT: Built-in tendency of an automobile to resume travel in a straight line when released from a turn.

AXLE: Shaft or shafts of a vehicle upon which wheels are mounted.

B & S GAUGE: Brown and Sharpe gauge, which is a standard measure of wire size. Smaller the number, larger the wire.

BACKFIRE: Ignition of mixture in intake manifold by flame from a cylinder.

BACKLASH: Clearance or "play" between two parts, such as meshed gears.

BACK PRESSURE: A resistance to free flow, such as a restriction in exhaust system.

BAFFLE OR BAFFLE PLATE: An obstruction for checking or deflecting flow of gases or sound.

BALK RING: A friction-regulated pawl or plunger used to facilitate engagement of gears.

BALL BEARING: An antifriction bearing consisting of a hardened inner and outer race with hardened steel balls interposed between two races.

BATTERY: Any number of complete electrical cells assembled in one housing or case.

BCI: Battery Council International.

BDC: Bottom dead center.

BEAD: Part of tire shaped to fit the rim.

BEARING: A part in which a journal, shaft or pivot turns or moves.

BELL HOUSING: Covering around flywheel and clutch or torque converter.

BELTED BIAS: Basic BIAS PLY structure, plus two or more tread plies, or belts, around circumference of tire under the tread.

BENDIX GEAR OR BENDIX DRIVE: A gear mounted on a screw shaft attached to starting motor armature, which automatically engages and disengages electric starting motor.

BENZOL: A by-product of manufacture of coke, sometimes used as an engine fuel.

BEZEL: A grooved ring or rim in which a transparent instrument cover is placed.

BHP: Brake horsepower is a measurement of power developed by an engine in actual operation.

BIAS PLY: Pneumatic tire structure in which ply cords extend diagonally from bead to bead, laid at alternate angles.

BLOW-BY: A leakage or loss of pressure, often used with reference to leakage of compression past piston ring between piston and cylinder.

BOILING POINT: Temperature at atmospheric pressure at which bubbles or vapors rise to surface and escape.

BONDED LINING: Brake lining cemented to shoes or bands which eliminates need for rivets.

BOOSTER: A mechanical or hydraulic device attached to brake or steering system to increase power or effectiveness.

BORE: Diameter of a hole, such as a cylinder. Also, to enlarge a hole as distinguished from making a hole with a drill.

BORING BAR: A stiff bar equipped with multiple cutting bits used to machine a series of bearing bores in proper alignment with each other.

BOSS: An extension or strengthened section, such as projections within a piston which support piston pin or piston pin bushings.

BOTTLED GAS: Liquefied petroleum gas compressed and contained in portable cylinders.

BOUNCE: Applied to engine valves, a condition where valve is not held tightly to its seat when cam is not lifting it. In ignition distributor, a condition where breaker points make and break contact when they should remain closed.

BRAKE: An energy conversion mechanism used to retard, stop or hold a vehicle.

BRAKE ANCHOR: Pivot pin on brake backing plate

against which shoe bears.

BRAKE BAND: A band, surrounding a brake drum, to which lining is attached.

BRAKE BLEEDING: Procedure for removing air from lines of a hydraulic system.

BRAKE CYLINDER: A cylinder in which a movable piston converts pressure to mechanical force to move brake shoes against braking surface of drum or rotor.

BRAKE DISC: Parallel-faced circular plate against which brake lining is forced to retard vehicle. Also ROTOR.

BRAKE DRUM: A metal cylinder attached to wheel and acted upon by friction material.

BRAKE "FADE": A condition where repeated severe applications of brakes cause expansion of brake drum or loss of frictional ability or both, which results in impaired braking efficiency.

BRAKE FLUID: A compounded liquid for use in hydraulic brake systems, which must meet exacting conditions (impervious to heat, freezing, thickening, bubbling, etc.).

BRAKE FLUSHING: A procedure for removing fluid from a brake system and washing out sediment.

BRAKE HORSEPOWER: Actual horsepower delivered by crankshaft, measured by means of a dynamometer or prony brake.

BRAKE HOSE: A flexible conductor for transmission of fluid pressure in brake system.

BRAKE LINING: A material having a suitable coefficient of friction, which is attached to brake shoe and which contacts brake drum to retard vehicle.

BRAKE SHOE: Carrier to which brake lining is attached, used to force lining in contact with brake drum or rotor.

BRAKE SHOE HEEL: Generally, end of brake shoe opposite anchor pin.

BRAKE SHOE TOE: Generally, end of brake shoe nearest anchor pin.

BRAZE: To join two pieces of metal with use of a comparatively high melting point material. Example: join two pieces of steel by using brass or bronze as a solder.

BREAKER ARM: Movable part of a pair of contact points in an ignition distributor or magneto.

BREAKER POINTS: Two separable points, usually faced with silver, platinum or tungsten, which interrupt primary circuit in distributor or magneto for purpose of inducing a high tension current in ignition system.

BREAK-IN: Process of wearing into a desirable fit between surfaces of two new or reconditioned parts.

BRINELL HARDNESS: A scale for designating degree of hardness possessed by a substance.

BROACH: To finish surface of metal by pushing or pulling a multiple edge cutting tool over or through it.

BRUSHES: Bars of carbon or other conducting material which contact commutator of an electric motor or generator.

BTU (British Thermal Unit): A measurement of amount of heat required to raise temperature of 1 lb. of water, 1 deg. F.

BUCKLED PLATES: Battery plates that have been bent or warped out of a flat plane.

BURNISH: To smooth or polish by use of a sliding tool under pressure.

BUSHING: A removable liner for a bearing.

BUTANE: A petroleum hydrocarbon compound which has a boiling point of about 32 deg. F, which is used as engine fuel. Loosely referred to as Liquefied Petroleum Gas and often combined with Propane.

BYPASS: An alternate path for a flowing substance.

CALIBRATE: To determine or adjust graduation or scale of any instrument giving quantitative measurements.

CALIBRATION: A precise factory setting, made to produce a given output or effect.

CALIPER: Non-rotational components of disc brake that straddles disc and contains hydraulic components.

CALIPERS: An adjustable tool for determining inside or outside diameter by contact and retaining dimension for measurement or comparison.

CALORIFIC VALUE: A measure of heating value of fuel.

CALORIMETER: An instrument to measure amount of heat given off by a substance when burned.

CALORY: Metric measurement of amount of heat required to raise 1 gram of water from zero deg. to 1 deg. Celsius.

CAM OR BREAKER CAM: Multi-lobed cam rotating in ignition distributor, which serves to interrupt primary circuit to induce a high tension spark for ignition.

CAM ANGLE: Number of degrees of rotation of distributor shaft during which contact points are closed.

CAMBER: In wheel alignment, it is outward or inward tilt of wheel at top.

CAM GROUND PISTON: A piston ground to a slightly oval shape which, under heat of operation, becomes round.

CAMSHAFT: Shaft containing lobes or cams which operate engine valves.

CANISTER: Reservoir of evaporative emission control system, usually containing activated charcoal granules for absorbing fuel vapors.

CAPE CHISEL: A metal cutting chisel shaped to cut or work in channels or grooves.

CARBON: A common, nonmetallic element that is an excellent conductor of electricity. It also forms in combustion chamber of an engine during burning of fuel and lubricating oil.

CARBON DIOXIDE: Compressed into solid form, this material is known as "dry ice" and remains at a temperature of -109 deg. F. It goes directly from a solid to a vapor state.

CARBON MONOXIDE: Gas formed by incomplete combustion. Colorless, odorless, poisonous.

CARBONIZE: Process of carbon formation within an engine. Examples: deposits on spark plugs and within combustion chamber.

CARBURETOR: A device for automatically mixing fuel in proper proportion with air to produce a combustible gas.

CARBURETOR "ICING": A term used to describe formation of ice on a carburetor throttle plate during certain atmospheric conditions.

CARCASS: Tire structure except for sidewall and tread.

CARDAN JOINT: A universal joint with corresponding yokes at a right angle with each other.

CAS: Cleaner Air System.

CASE-HARDEN: To harden surface of steel.

CASING HEAD GASOLINE: A term used to describe lighter parts of petroleum products, which were obtained as a natural gasoline by condensing natural gas from an oil well.

CASTELLATE: Formed to resemble a castle battlement. Example: a castellated nut.

CASTER: In wheel alignment, backward or forward tilt of steering axis.

CATALYTIC CONVERTER: Emission control device in exhaust stream that chemically treats exhaust gases after combustion to oxidize noxious emissions.

CATHODE: Negative pole of an electric current.

CCS: Controlled Combustion System.

CEC: Combination Emission Control.

CELL: Unit of a battery containing a group of positive and negative plates along with electrolyte.

CELL CONNECTOR: Lead bar or link connecting pole of one cell to pole of another.

CELSIUS: A scale of temperature measurement on which, under standard atmospheric pressure, water freezes at 0 deg. and boils at 100 deg.

CENTER OF GRAVITY: Point of a body from which it could be suspended, or on which it could be supported, and be in balance. Example: center of gravity of a wheel is center of wheel hub.

CENTIGRADE: See CELSIUS.

CENTRIFUGAL FORCE: A force which tends to move a body away from its center of rotation. Example: a whirling weight attached to a string.

CENTRIFUSE BRAKE DRUMS: To combine strength of steel with desirable friction characteristics of cast iron, a lining of cast iron is sprayed on inside of a steel drum. Both metals are handled while hot to encourage fusing of two metals.

CHAMFER: A bevel or taper at edge of a hole.

CHARGE (or Recharge): Passing an electrical current through a battery to restore it to activity. Also, filling and pressurizing an air conditioning system with refrigerant.

CHASE: To straighten up or repair damaged threads.

CHASSIS: A French word meaning framework of a vehicle without a body and fenders.

CHASSIS DYNAMOMETER: A machine for measuring amount of power delivered to drive wheels of a vehicle.

CHECK VALVE: A gate or valve which allows passage of gas or fluid in one direction only.

CHEMICAL COMPOUND: Combination of two or more chemical elements, which can be a gas, a liquid or a solid.

CHEMICAL ELEMENT: Gaseous, liquid or solid matter which cannot be divided into simpler form.

CHILLED IRON: Cast iron with hardened surface.

CHIP: To cut with a chisel.

CHOKE: A reduced passage. Example: valve in carburetor air inlet to cut down volume of air admitted.

CHROMIUM STEEL: An alloy of steel with a small amount of chromium to produce a metal which is highly resistant to oxidation and corrosion.

CIRCUIT: Path of electric current, fluids or gases. Examples: for electricity, a wire; for fluids and gases, a pipe.

CIRCUIT BREAKER: A device for interrupting an electrical circuit; often automatic and also known as contact breaker, interrupter, cut-out or relay.

CLEARANCE: Space allowed between two parts. Example: space between a journal and a bearing.

CLOCKWISE ROTATION: Rotation in same direction as hands of a clock.

CLUTCH: A device for connecting and disconnecting engine from transmission, or for a similar purpose in other units.

CO: Carbon monoxide.

COEFFICIENT OF FRICTION: Amount of friction developed between two surfaces pressed together and moved one on the other.

"COLD" MANIFOLD: An intake manifold not heated by exhaust gas.

COMBUSTION: Process of burning.

COMBUSTION CHAMBER: Volume of cylinder above piston with piston on top center.

COMMUTATOR: A ring of adjacent copper bars, insulated from each other, to which wires of armature or winding are attached.

COMPENSATING PORT: An opening in a brake master cylinder to permit fluid return to reservoir.

COMPOUND: A mixture of two or more ingredients.

COMPOUND WINDING: Two electric windings: one in series, other in shunt or parallel with other electric units or equipment. Applied to electric motors or generators: one winding is shunted across armature; other is in series with armature.

COMPRESSION: Reduction in volume of a gas. Also, condition when coil spring is squeezed together, or opposite of tension.

Dictionary of Terms

COMPRESSION RATIO: Volume of cylinder and combustion chamber with piston at bottom center as compared with volume of chamber at end of compression stroke.

COMPRESSOR: Engine-driven unit that circulates and pressurizes refrigerant in air conditioning system. Also, engine-driven unit that pressurizes air in truck air brake system.

CONCENTRIC: Two circles having same center but different diameters.

CONDENSATION: Process of a vapor becoming a liquid. Reverse of evaporation.

CONDENSER: Device for turning refrigerant vapor into liquid, causing heat to be discharged from refrigerant. Also, a device for temporarily collecting and storing a surge of electrical current for later discharge.

CONDUCTOR: A material along or through which electricity will flow with slight resistance. Silver, copper and carbon are good conductors.

CONNECTING ROD: Rod that connects piston to crankshaft.

CONSTANT MESH TRANSMISSION: An arrangement of gearing where gears remain in mesh instead of sliding in and out of engagement.

CONSTANT VELOCITY: Double universal joint that cancels out vibrations caused by driving power being transmitted through an angle.

CONTACT BREAKER: See CIRCUIT BREAKER.

CONTACT POINTS: See BREAKER POINTS.

CONTRACTION: A reduction in mass or dimension; opposite of expansion.

CONVECTION: A transfer of heat by circulating heated air.

CONVERTER: Applied to liquefied petroleum gas: a device which converts or changes LP-Gas from liquid to vapor for use in engine.

COOLANT: Liquid circulated through cooling system of a "water-cooled" engine, usually a mixture of about 50 percent ethylene glycol and 50 percent water.

CORD: Textile, steel wire strands, etc., forming plies of a tire.

CORE HOLE PLUG: See FREEZE PLUG.

CORRODE: To eat away gradually as if by gnawing, especially by rust.

COUNTERBORE: To enlarge a hole to a given depth.

COUNTERCLOCKWISE ROTATION: Rotating opposite direction of hands on a clock.

COUNTERSINK: To cut or form a depression to allow head of a screw to go below surface.

COUPLING: A connecting means for transferring movement from one part to another. May be mechanical, hydraulic or electrical.

COWL: Portion of body between engine compartment and driver, which ordinarily contains instruments used by operator.

CRANKCASE: Housing within which crankshaft operates.

CRANKCASE DILUTION: Under certain conditions of operation, unburned portions of fuel get past piston rings into crankcase where they "thin" engine lubricating oil.

CRANKSHAFT: Main shaft of an engine which, in conjunction with connecting rods, changes reciprocating motion of pistons into rotary motion.

CRANKSHAFT COUNTERBALANCE: Series of weights attached to or forged integrally with crankshaft and placed to offset reciprocating weight of each piston and rod assembly.

CRUDE OIL: Liquid oil as it comes from the ground.

CTO: Coolant Temperature Override.

CU. IN.: Cubic inch.

CURRENT: Flow of electricity.

CUT-OUT: A valve used to divert exhaust gases directly to atmosphere instead of through muffler. Also, see CIRCUIT BREAKER.

CYCLE: A series of events which are repeated.

Example: intake, compression, power and exhaust strokes of an internal combustion engine.

CYLINDER: A round hole having some depth bored to receive a piston. Also referred to as "bore."

CYLINDER BLOCK: Largest single part of an engine. Basic or main mass of metal in which cylinders are bored or placed.

CYLINDER HEAD: A detachable portion of an engine fastened securely to cylinder block which contains all or a portion of combustion chamber.

CYLINDER HEAD GASKET: Seal between engine block and cylinder head.

CYLINDER SLEEVE: A liner or tube interposed between piston and cylinder wall or cylinder block to provide a readily renewable wearing surface for cylinder.

DASH: Also known as fire wall. A partition between engine and operator.

DASHPOT: A device consisting of a piston and cylinder with a restricted opening used to slow down or delay operation of some moving part.

DC: Direct current.

DEAD CENTER: Extreme upper or lower position of crankshaft throw at which point piston is not moving in either direction.

DEAD REAR AXLE: A rear axle that does not turn. Example: rear axle of front wheel drive car.

DEBAR: English term for prevent.

DEGREE: Abbreviated deg. or indicated by a small ° placed alongside of a figure. May be used to designate temperature readings or angularity, one degree being 1/360 part of a circle.

DEMAGNETIZE: To remove magnetization of a pole which has previously been magnetized.

DEMOUNTABLE RIM: A rim for a tire that is readily removable from wheel.

DE-MISTER: English term for defroster.

DENATURED ALCOHOL: Ethyl alcohol to which a denaturant has been added.

DENSITY: Compactness: relative mass of matter in a given volume.

DEPOLARIZE: To remove polarity. Example: to demagnetize a permanent magnet.

DETERGENT: A compound of a soap-like nature used in engine oil to remove engine deposits and hold them in suspension in oil.

DETONATION: An engine sound that indicates a too rapid burning or explosion of air-fuel mixture in engine cylinders. It becomes audible through a vibration of combustion chamber walls.

DIAGNOSIS: Refers to use of instruments to determine cause of improper function of parts or systems of a vehicle.

DIAL GAUGE: A type of test instrument which indicates precise readings on a dial.

DIAPHRAGM: A flexible partition or wall separating two cavities.

DIE: One of a pair of hardened metal blocks for forming metal into a desired shape, or a device for cutting external threads.

DIE CASTING: An accurate and smooth casting made by pouring molten metal or composition into a metal mold or die under pressure.

DIESEL ENGINE: Named after its developer, Dr. Rudolph Diesel, engine ignites fuel in cylinder from heat generated by compression. Fuel is an oil rather than gasoline and no spark plug or carburetor is required.

DIESELING: Engine tends to keep running after ignition key is turned off.

DIFFERENTIAL: Gear system which permits one drive wheel to turn faster than other.

DILUTION: See CRANKCASE DILUTION.

DIODE: An electronic device that permits current to flow through it in one direction only.

DIRECT CURRENT: Electric current which flows continuously in one direction. Example: current from a storage battery.

DIRECT DRIVE: In automobile transmissions: refers to direct engagement between engine and drive shaft where engine crankshaft and drive shaft turn at same rpm.

DISC BRAKE: Brake system utilizing rotors to which frictional forces are applied to retard motion of vehicle.

DISCHARGE: Flow of electric current from a battery. Opposite of charge.

DISPLACEMENT: See ENGINE DISPLACEMENT.

DISTORTION: A warpage or change in form from original shape.

DISTRIBUTORS: A valve, often rotary in design, which conducts a vapor or fluid to a number of outlets. Example: diesel engine oil distributors. See IGNITION DISTRIBUTOR.

DOG CLUTCH: Mating collars, flanges or lugs which can be moved as desired to engage or disengage similar collars, flanges or lugs in order to transmit rotary motion.

DOUBLE REDUCTION AXLE: A drive axle construction in which two sets of reduction gears are used for extreme reduction of gear ratio.

DOWEL PIN: A pin inserted in matching holes in two parts to maintain those parts in fixed relation to each other.

DOWN-DRAFT: Carburetor in which mixture flows downward to engine.

DRAG LINK: Connecting rod or link between steering gear pitman arm and steering control linkage.

DRAW: To form by a stretching process, or to soften hard metal.

DRAW-FILING: A method of filing where file is drawn across work at right angles.

DRILL: A tool for making a hole, or to sink a hole with a pointed cutting tool rotated under pressure.

DRIVE-FIT: Term used when shaft is slightly larger than hole and must be forced in place.

DRIVE LINE: Universal joints, drive shaft and other parts connecting transmission with driving axles.

DROP FORGING: A piece of steel shaped between dies while hot.

DRY CHARGED BATTERIES: A complete battery unit which does not contain liquid electrolyte.

DUAL FUEL ENGINE: An engine equipped to operate on two different fuels such as gasoline and LP-Gas.

DUAL MASTER CYLINDER: Primary unit consisting of two sections for displacing fluid under pressure in a split hydraulic brake system.

DUAL REDUCTION AXLE: A drive axle construction with two sets of pinions and gears, either of which can be used.

DWELL PERIOD: See CAM ANGLE.

DYNAMO: A generator of electricity.

DYNAMOMETER: A machine for measuring power produced by an internal combustion engine.

ECCENTRIC: One circle within another circle not having same center.

ECONOMIZER: A device installed in a carburetor to control amount of fuel used under certain conditions.

EEC: Evaporative Emission Controls.

EGR: Exhaust Gas Recirculation.

ELECTRIC WELDING: Welding by using an electric current to melt both metal (work) and welding rod, or electrode.

ELECTRODE: Refers to insulated center rod and rod attached to shell of spark plug. Also, welding rod.

ELECTROLYTE: A mixture of sulphuric acid and distilled water used in storage batteries of wet type.

ELECTROMAGNET: A coil of insulated wire wound around an iron rod (or series of rods) will magnetize it when an electric current is passed through wire. Example: a solenoid magnet.

ELECTRON: That portion of an atom which carries a negative charge of electricity.

ELEMENT: One set of positive battery plates and one set of negative plates, complete with separators and assembled together.

ELLIOTT STEERING KNUCKLE: Type of axle in which ends of axle beam straddle spindle.

EMF: Electromotive force, or voltage.

EMULSION: A milk-like viscous mixture of two liquids.

ENAMEL: A combination of varnish and coloring pigment, sometimes heated during or after application to provide a hard surface.

EN-BLOC: Refers to cylinder block of an engine cast in one section.

ENERGY: Capacity for doing work.

ENGINE: Prime source of power generated to propel a vehicle.

ENGINE DISPLACEMENT: Sum of piston displacement of all engine cylinders. See PISTON DISPLACEMENT.

EPA: Environmental Protection Agency.

ETHYL GASOLINE: Gasoline to which a compound of tetraethyl lead, ethylene dibromide and ethylene dichloride has been added. Material slows down and controls rate of burning of fuel in cylinder to produce an expansive force rather than an explosive force to reduce detonation or "knocking" in an engine.

ETHYLENE GLYCOL: Liquid chemical mixed with water to form low-freezing-point coolant.

EVAPORATION: Process of changing from a liquid to a vapor. Example: boiling water to produce steam. Evaporation is opposite of condensation.

EVAPORATOR: Device for turning liquid refrigerant into vapor, causing heat in passenger compartment of vehicle to be absorbed by refrigerant.

EXHAUST EMISSIONS: Products of combustion that are discharged through exhaust system of vehicle.

EXHAUST GAS ANALYZER: An instrument for determining efficiency with which an engine is burning fuel. Also called combustion analyzer or emissions tester.

EXHAUST PIPE: Pipe connecting engine to muffler to conduct spent gases away from engine.

EXPANSION: An increase in size. Example: when a metal rod is heated, it increases in length and diameter. Expansion is opposite of contraction.

EXPANSION PLUG: See FREEZE PLUG.

EXTREME PRESSURE LUBRICANTS (E.P.): A lubricant to which an ingredient has been added to increase lubricant's ability to withstand high pressures between gear teeth, etc.

FAHRENHEIT (F): A scale of temperature measurement on which, under standard atmospheric pressure, water freezes at 32 deg. and boils at 212 deg.

FEELER GAUGE: A metal strip or blade, finished accurately with regard to thickness, used for measuring clearance between two parts. Blades are graduated in thickness by increments of .001 in.

FERROUS METAL: Metals which contain iron or steel, making them subject to rust.

F-HEAD ENGINE: An engine designed with one valve in cylinder block at side of piston and other valve in cylinder head above piston.

FIELD: Area in which magnetic flow occurs in a generator or starting motor.

FIELD COIL: A coil of insulated wire surrounding field pole.

FILE: To finish or trim with a hardened metal tool with cutting ridges.

FILLET: A rounded filling between two parts joined at an angle.

FILTER: A device designed to remove suspended impurities or particles of foreign matter from intake air, fuel system or lubricating system.

FIREWALL: Insulated partition between engine and vehicle occupants.

FIT: Satisfactory contact between two machined surfaces.

FLANGE: A projecting rim or collar on an object for keeping it in place.

FLASH POINT: Temperature at which an oil will flash and burn.

FLOAT: A hollow part which is lighter than fuel or fluid in which it rests, and ordinarily used to operate a valve controlling entrance of fuel or fluid.

FLOATING PISTON PIN: A piston pin which is free to turn or oscillate in both connecting rod and piston.

FLOAT LEVEL: Predetermined setting of float to control height of fuel in carburetor bowl, usually regulated by means of a suitable valve.

FLUID COUPLING: A hydraulic clutch used to transmit engine torque to transmission gears. See FLUID DRIVE.

FLUID DRIVE: A pair of vaned rotating elements held close to each other without touching. Rotation is imparted to driven member by driving member through resistance of a body of oil.

FLUTTER: See BOUNCE.

FLUX: Electric or magnetic lines of force passing or flowing in a magnetic field. Also, material used to cause joining metal to adhere to both parts to be joined.

FLYWHEEL: A heavy wheel in which energy is absorbed and stored by means of momentum.

FOOT POUND (or lb. ft.): A measure of amount of energy or work required to lift 1 lb. 1 ft.

FORCE-FIT: See DRIVE FIT.

FORGE: To shape metal while hot and plastic by hammering.

FOUR CYCLE ENGINE: Engine in which an explosion occurs every other revolution of crankshaft. A cycle, also known as Otto cycle, is considered 1/2 revolution of crankshaft. Strokes are: suction, compression, power, exhaust.

FREE-WHEELING: A mechanical device in which driving member imparts motion to a driven member in one direction but not other.

FREEZE PLUG: A disc or cup-shaped metal device inserted in a hole in a casting through which core was removed when casting was formed. Also known as a core hole plug or expansion plug.

FREEZING POINT: Temperature at which coolant starts to freeze, based on mixture percentages and pressure in system.

FRICTION DRIVE: A method of power transmission used on early automobiles where power is transmitted from a driving to a driven wheel by means of pressing one wheel against another at a right angle.

FUEL KNOCK: See DETONATION.

FULCRUM: A support, often wedge-shaped, on which a lever pivots when it lifts an object.

FULL-FLOATING AXLE: Drive axle construction where axle driving shaft does not carry vehicle weight.

FUSE: A piece of wire which will carry a limited amount of current only, then melt and open electrical circuit as a safety measure to avoid damage from excessive current flow.

GAL.: Gallon.

GALVANIZE: To coat with a molten alloy of lead and tin to prevent rusting.

GALVANOMETER: An instrument used for location, measurement and direction of an electric current.

GAS: A substance which can be changed in volume and shape according to temperature and pressure applied to it. Example: air can be compressed into smaller volume or expanded by application of heat.

GASSING: Bubbling of battery electrolyte which occurs during process of charging a battery.

GASKET: Anything used as a packing, such as a nonmetallic substance placed between two metal surfaces to act as a seal.

GEAR RATIO: Number of revolutions made by a driving gear as compared to number of revolutions made by a driven gear of different size. Example: if one gear makes three revolutions while other gear makes one revolution, gear ratio is 3 to 1.

GENERATOR: A device consisting of an armature, field coils and other parts which, when rotated, will generate electricity.

GLAZE: An extremely smooth or glossy engine cylinder surface polished over a long period of time by friction of piston rings.

GLAZE BREAKER: A tool for removing glossy surface finish in an engine cylinder.

GOVERNOR: A device to control and regulate speed. May be mechanical, hydraulic or electrical.

GRAM: A unit of measure of weight or mass equal to 0.03527 oz.

GRID: Metal framework of an individual battery plate in which active material is placed.

GRIND: To finish or polish a surface by means of an abrasive wheel.

GROOVE: Space between two adjacent tire tread ribs.

GROUND: Noninsulated terminal of battery. By connecting one terminal of each electrically operated unit to frame of vehicle, only one insulated wire is required to carry current to unit since frame serves as a return wire.

GROUP: A set of battery plates, either positive or negative, joined together but not assembled with separators.

GROWLER: An electrical device for testing electric motor or generator armatures.

GUDGEON PIN: See PISTON PIN.

GUM: Oxidized petroleum products that accumulate in fuel system, carburetor or engine parts.

HARD PEDAL: A loss in braking efficiency so that an excessive amount of pressure is needed to actuate brakes.

HARD SOLDER: Uniting two pieces of metal with a material having a melting point higher than "soft" solder. Example: silver soldering.

HARMONIC BALANCER: A device designed to reduce torsional or twisting vibration which occurs along length of crankshaft used in multiple cylinder engines.

HC: Hydrocarbons.

HEADER: Special exhaust pipes, used on high performance engines to reduce back pressure.

HEAT EXCHANGER: A device that utilizes exhaust system heat to aid in fuel vaporization.

HEAT RISER: Passage between exhaust and intake manifolds.

HEAT SINK: Metal bracket in end frame of alternator that contains and absorbs heat from diodes.

HEAT TREATMENT: A combination of heating and cooling operations timed and applied to a metal in a solid state in a way that will produce desired properties.

HEEL: Outside or larger half of gear tooth. Also, end of brake shoe not against anchor.

HEI: High Energy Ignition.

HELICAL: Shaped like a coil of wire or a screw thread.

HELICAL GEAR: A gear design where gear teeth are cut at an angle to shaft.

HEMI: Hemispherical or dome-shaped combustion chamber in some engines.

HERRINGBONE GEAR: A pair of helical gears designed to operate together in form of a V.

HIGH TENSION: Secondary or induced high voltage electrical current. Circuit includes wiring from ignition distributor cap to coil and to each spark plug.

HONE: An abrasive tool for correcting small irregularities or differences in diameter in an engine cylinder, brake cylinder, etc.

HORSEPOWER: Energy required to lift 550 lb. 1 ft. in 1 sec.

HOTCHKISS DRIVE: A driving axle design in which axle torque is absorbed by chassis springs or control arms.

HOT SPOT: Refers to a comparatively thin section of wall between intake and exhaust manifolds of an engine to allow hot exhaust gases to heat comparatively cool incoming mixture. Also, designates local areas of cooling system that have attained above average temperatures.

HP: Horsepower: energy required to lift 550 lb. 1 ft. in 1 second is 1 hp.

HYDRAULIC: Pertains to fluids in motion, such as hydraulically operated brakes, hydraulic torque converters, power steering, etc.

HYDRAULIC BRAKE SYSTEM: System in which brake operation and control utilizes hydraulic brake fluid.

HYDROCARBON: Any compound composed entirely of carbon and hydrogen.

HYDROCARBON ENGINE: An engine using petroleum products, such as gas, liquefied gas, gasoline, kerosene or fuel oil as a fuel.

HYDROMETER: An instrument for determining state of charge in a battery by measuring specific gravity of electrolyte.

HYDROSTATIC GAUGE: Used in referring to gauges, such as a gasoline tank gauge, where depth of gasoline in tank controls air in connecting line to instrument which registers depth on a scale or dial.

HYPOID GEARS: A design of pinion and ring gear where center line of pinion is offset from center line of ring gear.

ID: Inside diameter.

IDLE: Refers to engine operating at its slowest speed with a vehicle not in motion.

IGNITION DISTRIBUTOR: An electrical device usually containing circuit breaker for primary circuit and providing a means for conveying secondary or high tension current to spark plug wires as required.

IGNITION SYSTEM: Means for igniting fuel in cylinders. Includes spark plugs, wiring, ignition distributor, ignition coil and source of electrical current supply.

IHP: Indicated horsepower developed by an engine and a measure of pressure of explosion within cylinder expressed in pounds per square inch.

IMCO: Improved Combustion.

IN.: Inch.

INCLUDED ANGLE: Combined angles of camber and steering axis inclination.

INDEPENDENT SUSPENSION: A construction in which wheel on one side of vehicle may rise or fall independently of wheel on other side.

INDUCTION: Influence of magnetic fields of different strength not electrically connected to one another.

INDUCTION COIL: Essentially a transformer which, through induction, creates a high tension current by means of an increase in voltage.

INDUCTION HARDENING: Method of heating cast iron (valve seats, for example) to approximately 1700 deg. F, which hardens it to a depth of .05 to .08 in.

INERTIA: A physical law that tends to keep a motionless body at rest or keep a moving body in motion. Effort is required to start a mass moving or to retard it once it is in motion.

INHIBITOR: A material to restrain or hinder some unwanted action. Example: a rust inhibitor added to cooling systems to retard formation of rust.

INJECTOR: A pump which injects or inserts a fluid or gas, usually against pressure, into a cylinder or chamber.

INLET VALVE: See INTAKE VALVE.

INPUT SHAFT: Transmission shaft which receives power from engine and transmits it to transmission gears.

INSULATION: Any material, which does not conduct electricity, used to prevent leakage of current from a conductor. Also, a material which does not readily conduct heat.

INSULATOR: A nonconducting material or shield covering an electrical conductor.

INTAKE MANIFOLD OR INLET PIPE: Tube or housing used to conduct air-fuel mixture from carburetor to engine cylinders.

INTAKE VALVE: A valve which permits a fluid or gas to enter a chamber and seals against exit.

INTEGRAL: Formed as a unit with another part.

INTENSIFY: To increase or concentrate. Example: increase voltage of an electrical current.

INTERMEDIATE GEAR: Transmission gear or gears between low and high.

INTERMITTENT: Motion or action that occurs at intervals.

INTERNAL COMBUSTION: Burning of a fuel within an enclosed space.

INTERRUPTER: See CIRCUIT BREAKER.

JOURNAL: That part of a shaft or axle in actual contact with bearing.

JUMP SPARK: A high tension electrical current which jumps through the air from one terminal to another.

JUNK RING: A flexible ring used in cylinder head to provide a seal with inner sleeve of a sleeve valve engine.

KEY: A small block inserted between shaft and hub to prevent circumferential movement.

KEYWAY OR KEYSEAT: A groove or slot cut to permit insertion of a key.

KICK-DOWN SWITCH: An electrical switch used to cause a transmission to downshift from a higher to a lower gear ratio.

KILOMETER: A metric measurement of distance which is equivalent to approximately 5/8 of a mile.

KILOWATT: A measure of electrical energy consisting of 1000 watts or 1 1/3 horsepower.

KINGPIN: Shaft or journal around which steering spindle of a truck front wheel turns.

KINGPIN INCLINATION: Angle at which kingpin is inclined inward from true vertical center line.

KNURL: To indent or roughen a finished surface.

KNOCK: Term used to describe various noises in an engine made by loose or worn mechanical parts, preignition, detonation, etc.

LACQUER: In automotive painting, a solution of solids in solvents that evaporate with great rapidity.

LAMINATE: To build up or construct out of a number of thin sheets. Example: laminated core in an electric motor or generator.

LAPPING: Process of fitting one surface to another by rubbing them together with an abrasive material between two surfaces.

LATERAL RUNOUT: Amount of side movement of a rotating wheel, tire or rotor from the vertical.

LATHE: Machine on which a piece of solid material is spun on a horizontal axes and shaped by a fixed cutting or abrading tool.

LB.: Pound.

LEAD BURNING: Joining two pieces of lead by melting or fusing the metal.

L-HEAD ENGINE: An engine design in which both valves are located on one side of engine cylinder.

LIFT: Maximum distance valve head is raised off its seat.

LIMITER: Device placed on carburetor idle mixture adjustment screw so that richness of mixture can be made only within predetermined limits.

LINER: Usually a thin section placed between two parts. Example: a replaceable cylinder liner in an engine.

LINKAGE: Any series of rods, yokes and levers, etc.,

used to transmit motion from one unit to another.

LIQUID: Neither a gas nor a solid. Any substance which assumes shape of vessel in which it is placed without changing volume.

LIQUID WITHDRAWAL SYSTEM: A method of piping where liquid is taken from bottom of an LP-Gas tank and converted into gas by a vaporizer.

LITER: A measure of volume equal to 61.027 cu. in.

LIVE: Electrical parts connected to insulated side of electrical system. Example: an insulated wire connected to battery. Often referred to as a "hot" wire.

LIVE AXLE: Shaft through which power travels from drive axle gears to driving wheels.

LOAD RANGE: Tire designation, with a letter (A,B,C,etc.), used to identify a given size tire with its load and inflation limits. Replaces term PLY RATING.

LOCK WASHER: A form of washer designed to prevent attaching nut from working loose.

LOST MOTION: See BACKLASH.

LOUVER OR LOUVRE: Openings or vents in hood or body, usually intended for ventilation.

LOW PEDAL: A condition where excessive clearance at some point in braking system causes almost full pedal movement for application of brakes.

LOW SPEED: Gearing provided in an automobile which causes greatest number of revolutions of engine as compared to driving wheels.

LP-GAS, LIQUEFIED PETROLEUM GAS: Made usable as a fuel for internal combustion engines by compressing volatile petroleum gases to liquid form. LP-Gas must be kept under pressure or at low temperature in order to remain in liquid form.

LUG: Extension of battery plate grid for connecting plate to strap.

MAGNET (Permanent): A piece of hard steel often bent into a "U" shape to create and retain opposite poles when charged with magnetic power.

MAGNETIC FIELD: Flow of magnetic force or magnetism between opposite poles of a magnet.

MAGNETO: An electrical device which generates alternating current when rotated by an outside source of power. Device used to generate either low tension or high tension current.

MALLEABLE CASTING: A casting which has been toughened by annealing.

MANIFOLD: A pipe with multiple openings used to connect various cylinders to one inlet or outlet.

MANGANESE BRONZE: An alloy of copper, zinc and manganese.

MANOMETER: A device for measuring a vacuum, consisting of a "U" shaped tube partially filled with fluid. One end of tube is open to air, other is connected to chamber in which vacuum is to be measured. A column of mercury 30 in. high equals 14.7 psi, which is atmospheric pressure at sea level. Readings are given in inches of mercury (Hg).

MANUAL: Pertaining to or done with the hands. Also, requiring or using physical skill or energy.

MASTER CYLINDER: Single or dual primary unit for displacing hydraulic fluid under pressure in brake system.

MECHANICAL EFFICIENCY: Ratio between indicated horsepower and brake horsepower of an engine.

MELTING POINT: Temperature at which solid material becomes liquid.

MEMA: Motor and Equipment Manufacturers Association.

MERCURY COLUMN: A reference term used in connection with a manometer.

METER: A measure of length equal to 39.37 in.

METHANOL OR WOOD ALCOHOL: A poisonous alcohol made synthetically or from distillation of wood.

MEWA: Motor and Equipment Wholesalers Association.

MICRO FINISH: Degree of surface roughness, measured with a profilometer.

MICROMETER: A measuring instrument for either external or internal measurement in thousandths and sometimes tenths of thousandths of inches.

MILL: To cut or machine with rotating tooth cutters.

MILLIMETER (mm.): One millimeter is metric equivalent of .039370 of an inch. One inch is equivalent to 25.4 mm.

MISFIRING: Failure of an explosion to occur in one or more cylinders while engine is running. This may be a continuous or intermittent failure.

MODULATOR: A pressure regulating device used in automatic transmissions.

MONEL METAL: Corrosion resistant alloy of nickel, copper, iron and manganese.

MONO-BLOCK: All cylinders of an engine are contained in one casting. Same as en-bloc or in-block.

MOTOR: Principally, a machine which converts electrical energy to mechanical energy.

MPH: Miles per hour.

MUFFLER: A chamber attached to exhaust pipe which allows exhaust gases to expand and cool. It is usually fitted with baffles or porous plates and serves to reduce noise created by exhaust.

MULTIPLE DISC: A clutch having a number of driving and driven discs as compared to a single plate clutch.

MVMA: Motor Vehicle Manufacturers Association.

NADA: National Automobile Dealers Association.

NAPA: National Automotive Parts Association.

NEEDLE BEARING: An antifriction bearing using a great number of rollers of small diameter in relation to their length.

NEGATIVE POLE: Point from which an electrical current flows as it passes through circuit. Designated by a minus sign (-).

NET HORSEPOWER: Brake horsepower remaining at flywheel of engine after power required by engine accessories (fan, water pump, alternator, etc.).

NEUTRON: Portion of an atom which carries no electrical charge and, with protons, form central core of atom about which electrons rotate.

NIASE: National Institute for Automotive Service Excellence.

NICKEL STEEL: Nickel is alloyed with steel to form a heat and corrosion resistant metal.

NONFERROUS METALS: Metals which contain no iron or very little iron, and not subject to rusting.

NORTH POLE: Pole of a magnet from which lines of force start. Opposite of south pole.

NOx: Nitrogen oxides.

OCTANE NUMBER: A unit of measurement on a scale intended to indicate tendency of a fuel to detonate or knock.

OD: Outside diameter.

ODOMETER: A device for measuring and registering number of miles traveled.

OHM: A measurement of resistance to flow of an electrical current through a conductor.

OIL PUMPING: A term used to describe an engine which is using an excessive amount of lubricating oil.

ONE-WAY CLUTCH: See FREE-WHEELING.

OPEN CIRCUIT: A break or opening in an electrical circuit which stops passage of current.

ORIFICE: Small opening in a tube, pipe or valve.

OSAC: Orifice Spark Advance Control.

OSCILLATE: To swing back and forth like a pendulum.

OSCILLOSCOPE: An electrical testing device which shows a pattern wave form of spark ignition action on a viewing screen.

OSHA: Occupational Safety and Health Administration.

OTTO CYCLE: Four stroke cycle named after man who adopted principle of four stroke operation for each explosion in an engine cylinder. They are:

suction, compression, power and exhaust.

OUTPUT SHAFT: Shaft which receives power from transmission and transmits it to vehicle drive shaft.

OVERDRIVE: Any arrangement of gearing which produces more revolutions of driven shaft than driving shaft.

OVERHEAD VALVE OR VALVE-IN-HEAD ENGINE (OHV): An engine design having valves located in cylinder head directly above pistons.

OVERRUNNING CLUTCH OR COUPLING: See FREE-WHEELING.

OXIDIZE: To combine an element with oxygen or convert into its oxide. Examples: when carbon burns, it combines with oxygen to form carbon dioxide or carbon monoxide; iron combines with oxygen in air to form an oxide of iron, or rust.

PAD: Disc brake friction material generally molded to metal backing, or shoe.

PANCAKE ENGINE: A design where cylinders are laid horizontal to obtain a minimum of height.

PARKING BRAKE: Brake system used to hold one or more brakes continuously in applied position.

PARTICULATES: Minute solid particles emitted from vehicle's exhaust system.

PAWL: A pivoted bar adapted to engage with teeth of a ratchet to prevent or impart motion.

PCV: Positive crankcase ventilation.

PEEN: To stretch or clinch over by pounding with rounded end of a hammer.

PERIPHERY: Circumference of a circle. Example: tread of a tire.

PETCOCK: A small valve placed in a fluid circuit for draining purposes.

PETROLEUM: A group of liquid and gaseous compounds composed of carbon and hydrogen.

PHILLIPS SCREW OR SCREWDRIVER: A type of screwhead having a cross instead of a slot for a corresponding type of screwdriver.

PHOSPHOR-BRONZE: An alloy consisting of copper, tin and lead, sometimes used in heavy-duty bearings.

PILOT VALVE: A small valve used to control action of a larger valve.

PINION: A small gear which engages a larger gear.

PINION CARRIER: Mounting or bracket which retains bearings supporting a pinion shaft.

PISTON: A cylindrical part, closed at one end, which is connected to the crankshaft by a connecting rod. Force of explosion in cylinder is exerted against closed end of piston causing connecting rod to move crankshaft.

PISTON COLLAPSE: A condition describing a sudden reduction in diameter of piston skirt due to heat or stress.

PISTON DISPLACEMENT: Volume of air moved or displaced by moving piston from one end of its stroke to other.

PISTON HEAD: Part of piston above rings.

PISTON LANDS: Parts of piston between piston rings.

PISTON PIN: Journal for bearing in small end of an engine connecting rod which also passes through piston walls.

PISTON RING: An expanding ring placed in grooves of piston to provide a seal to prevent passage of fluid or gas past piston.

PISTON RING EXPANDER: A spring placed behind piston ring in groove to increase pressure of ring against cylinder wall.

PISTON RING GAP: Clearance between ends of piston ring.

PISTON RING GROOVE: Channel or slots in piston in which piston rings are placed.

PISTON SKIRT: Part of piston below rings.

PISTON SKIRT EXPANDER: A spring or other device inserted in piston skirt to compensate for collapse or decrease in diameter.

PITMAN ARM: Lever extending from steering gear to

which steering linkage is attached.

PITOT TUBE: An instrument for measuring fluid velocity by means of difference in pressure between tip and side openings.

PIVOT: A pin or short shaft upon which another part rests or turns, or about which another part rotates or oscillates.

PLANETARY GEARS: A system of gearing which is modeled after solar system. A pinion is surrounded by an internal ring gear with planet gears in mesh between ring gear and pinion.

PLANET CARRIER: Carrier or bracket in a planetary system which contains shafts upon which pinions or planet gears turn.

PLANET GEARS: Pinions or gears interposed between ring gear and sun gear and meshing with both in a planetary system.

PLATINUM: An expensive metal having an extremely high melting point and good electrical conductivity.

PLY: Layer of rubber-coated parallel cords forming tire body, or carcass.

PLY RATING: Index of tire strength. See LOAD RANGE.

PNEUMATIC: Pertaining to air. Example: a device operated by air pressure is a pneumatic device.

POLARITY: Refers to positive or negative terminal of a battery or an electric circuit; also north or south pole of a magnet.

POPPET VALVE: A valve structure consisting of a circular head with an elongated stem attached in center. It is designed to open and close a circular hole or port.

PORCELAIN: General term applied to material or element used for insulating center electrode of a spark plug.

PORT: Openings in cylinder block for valves, exhaust and inlet pipes, or water connections. In two cycle engines, openings for inlet and exhaust purposes.

PORTING: Enlarging, matching, streamlining and polishing of inside of manifolds and valve ports to reduce friction of flow of gases.

POSITIVE POLE: Point to which current returns after passing through a circuit. Designated by plus sign (+).

POST: Heavy, circular part to which a group of battery plates is attached, and which extends through cell cover to provide a means of attachment to adjacent cell or battery cable.

POTENTIAL: An indication of amount of energy available.

POTENTIAL DIFFERENCE: A difference of electrical pressure that sets up a flow of electric current.

POTENTIAL DROP: A loss of electrical pressure due to resistance or leakage.

POWER STEERING: Application of hydraulic or mechanical power in addition to manual power in steering of an automobile.

PPM: Parts Per Million.

PREHEATING: Application of heat as a preliminary step to some further thermal or mechanical treatment.

PREIGNITION: Ignition occurring earlier than intended. Example: explosive mixture being fired in a cylinder by a flake of incandescent carbon before electric spark occurs.

PRELOADING: To adjust a small amount of pressure on an antifriction bearing to eliminate any looseness.

PRESS-FIT: See DRIVE FIT.

PRIMARY BRAKE SHOE: Brake shoe in a set which initiates self-energizing action.

PRIMARY WINDING: A wire which conducts low tension current to be transformed by induction into high tension current in secondary winding of ignition coil or magneto armature.

PRIMARY WIRES: Wiring circuit used for conducting low tension or primary current to points where it is used.

PROTON: Portion of an atom which carries a positive charge of electricity.

PRONY BRAKE: A machine for testing power of an engine while running against a friction brake.

PROPANE: A petroleum hydrocarbon compound which has a boiling point about -44 deg. F. It is used as an engine fuel and is loosely referred to as LP-Gas. It is often combined with butane.

PROPELLER SHAFT: Drive shaft connecting transmission with rear axle.

PROPORTIONING VALVE: Device used to improve braking balance during heavy brake application.

PSI: Pounds per square inch; a measure of pressure.

PUSH ROD: A connecting link in an operating mechanism. Example: rod interposed between valve lifter and rocker arm on an overhead valve engine.

QUADRANT: Designates gear-shift or transmission control lever selective mounting.

QUENCHING: A process of rapid cooling of hot metal by contact with liquids, gases or solids.

RACE: A finished inner and outer surface in which or on which ball bearings or roller bearings operate.

RACE-CAM: A type of camshaft for race car engines which increases lift of valve, speed of valve opening and closing, length of time valve is held open, etc. Also known as Full, Three-quarter or Semi-race cams, depending upon design.

RADIAL PLY: Pneumatic tire structure in which ply cords extend from bead to bead, laid at right angles to center line of tire.

RADIAL RUNOUT: Variation in diameter of a wheel, tire or rotor from a specified amount.

RADIATION: Transfer of heat by rays. Example: heat from sun.

RADIUS RODS: Rods attached to axle and to frame to maintain correct horizontal position of axle, yet permit vertical motion.

RATIO: Relation or proportion that one number bears to another.

REAM: To finish a hole accurately with a rotating fluted tool.

RECAP: Used tire to which a top strip of synthetic or reclaimed rubber strip has been added.

RECIPROCATING: A back and forth movement. Example: action of a piston in a cylinder.

RECTIFIER: An electrical device for transforming or changing alternating current into direct current.

REFRIGERANT: A substance used in an air conditioning system which absorbs and gives up heat as it changes from a liquid to a gas to a liquid.

REGULATOR: An automatic pressure reducing valve.

RELAY: See CIRCUIT BREAKER.

RELIEF: Amount one surface is set below or above another surface.

RELIEVING: Removal of some metal from around racing engine valves and between cylinder and valves to facilitate flow of gases.

RESISTOR: A current-consuming piece of metal wire or carbon inserted into circuit to decrease flow of electricity.

RETARD: To cause spark to occur at a later time in cycle of engine operation. Opposite of spark advance.

RETREAD: Used tire with new rubber bonded to worn surface from shoulder to shoulder.

REVERSE ELLIOT STEERING KNUCKLE: Type of axle construction in which steering spindle straddles ends of axle beam.

RIM: Metal support for tire or tire and tube assembly on wheel.

RING GEAR: Outer gear within which other gears revolve in a planetary system. Term also refers to driven gear which mates with drive pinion in a differential assembly.

RIVET: To attach with rivets or to batter or upset end of a pin.

RMA: The Rubber Manufacturers Association.

ROCKER ARM: In engines, a lever located on a fulcrum or shaft; one end bearing on valve stem, other on push rod.

ROCKWELL HARDNESS: A scale for designating degrees of hardness possessed by a substance.

ROLLER BEARING: An inner and outer race upon which hardened steel rollers operate.

ROTARY ENGINE: Wankel type internal combustion engine causes cycle of intake, compression, expansion and exhaust by rotation of a triangular rotor in a housing shaped roughly like a figure 8. Air-fuel mixture enters and burned gases are ejected through ports covered and uncovered by movement of rotor. Ignition is by spark.

ROTARY VALVE: A valve construction in which ported holes come into and out of register with each other to allow entrance and exit of fluids or gases.

ROTOR: Parallel-faced circular plate against which brake lining is forced to retard vehicle. Also, a rotating part of an electrical or mechanical device.

ROTOR RUNOUT: Lateral movement of rotor friction surface as it rotates past a fixed point.

RPM: Revolutions per minute.

RUBBER: An elastic vibration absorbing material of either natural or synthetic origin.

RUN-ON: See DIESELING.

RUNNING-FIT: Where sufficient clearance has been allowed between shaft and journal to allow free running without overheating.

RUNOUT: Out-of-round condition of a rotating part.

SAE: Society of Automotive Engineers.

SAE STEELS: A numerical index system used to identify composition of SAE steel.

SAE THREAD: Refers to a table of threads set up by Society of Automotive Engineers and determines number of threads per inch. Example: a quarter inch diameter rod with an SAE thread would have 28 threads per inch.

SAFETY FACTOR: Degree of strength above normal requirements which serves as insurance against failure.

SAFETY RELIEF VALVE: A spring-loaded valve designed to open and relieve excessive pressure in a device when it exceeds a predetermined safe point.

SANDBLAST: To clean a surface by means of sand propelled by compressed air.

SAYBOLT TEST: A method of measuring viscosity of oil with use of a viscosimeter.

SCALE: A flaky deposit occurring on steel or iron. Ordinarily used to describe accumulation of minerals and metals accumulating in an automobile cooling system.

SCORE: A scratch, ridge or groove marring a finished surface.

SEALED BEAM LAMPS: Lamp construction with reflector, lens and filament hermetically sealed in one unit.

SEAT: A surface, usually machined, upon which another part rests or seats. Example: surface upon which a valve face rests.

SECONDARY BRAKE SHOE: Brake shoe in a set which is energized by primary shoe and increases servo, or self-energizing, action of brake.

SECONDARY WINDING: A wire in which a secondary or high tension current is created by induction due to interruption of current in adjacent primary winding of an ignition coil or magneto armature.

SECTION HEIGHT: Height of an inflated tire from bottom of bead to top of tread.

SECTION WIDTH: Width between exteriors of sidewalls of an inflated tire at its widest point.

SEDIMENT: Active material of battery plates that is gradually shed and accumulates in a space provided below plates.

SEIZE: When a surface moving upon another binds, then sticks, it is said to seize. For example: a piston seizes in a cylinder due to a lack of lubrication or

overexpansion due to excessive heat.

SELECTIVE TRANSMISSION: Arrangement of gearing and shifting device in which it is possible to go directly from neutral position into any desired pair of gears.

SELF-ENERGIZATION: Placing of brake shoes so that drum tends to drag lining along with it, resulting in a wedging action between anchor and drum.

SEMI-DIESEL: A semi-diesel engine operates on comparatively high compression and utilizes solid injection of fuel. However, it does use an electrical ignition system rather than depend solely upon heat generated by compression to furnish ignition.

SEMI-FLOATING AXLE: A drive axle construction in which axle shafts support weight of car.

SEPARATORS: Sheets of rubber or wood inserted between positive and negative battery plates of a cell to keep them out of contact with each other.

SERIES WINDING: An electric winding or coil of wire in series with other electrical equipment.

SERVO: Automatic transmission hydraulic piston and cylinder assembly used to control drum bands.

SERVO ACTION: A brake construction in which a primary shoe pushes a secondary shoe to generate self-energization.

SHACKLE BOLT: A link for connecting one end of a chassis spring to frame which allows spring end to oscillate laterally.

SHEAR: To cut between two blades.

SHIM: Thin sheets used as spacers between two parts. Example: alignment shims between control arm pivot shaft and frame serve to adjust caster and camber.

SHIMMY: In automobile steering, a wobbling or shaking of front wheels.

SHOCK ABSORBER: A device to provide mechanical or hydraulic friction to control excessive deflection of automobile springs.

SHORT CIRCUIT: To provide a shorter electrical path. Often used to indicate an accidental ground in an electrical device or conductor.

SHRINK FIT: An exceptionally tight fit. Example: if shaft or part is slightly larger than hole in which it is to be inserted, outer part is heated above its normal operating temperature or inner part chilled below its normal operating temperature, or both, and assembled in this condition. Upon cooling, a shrink fit is obtained.

SHUNT: To bypass around or turn aside. Also, an alternate path for current in electrical apparatus.

SHUNT WINDING: An electric winding or coil of wire which forms a bypass or alternate path for electric current. Example: in certain electric generators or motors, each end of field winding is connected to an armature brush.

SHUTTLE VALVE: A valve for diverting pressure from one channel to another.

SIDEWALL: Portion of tire between tread and bead.

SILENCER: See MUFFLERS.

SILICON: A nonmetallic element, often alloyed with steel.

SILICON STEEL: An alloy of silicon and chromium with steel, often used for exhaust valves of internal combustion engines.

SILICONE: Any of a group of semi-organic polymers, used in lubricants, adhesives and protective coverings.

SILVER SOLDERING: See HARD SOLDER.

SLEEVE VALVE: A reciprocating sleeve or sleeves with ported openings placed between piston and cylinders of an engine to serve as valves.

SLIDING FIT: Where sufficient clearance has been allowed between shaft and journal to allow free running without overheating.

SLIP-IN BEARING: A liner, made to extremely accurate measurements, which can be used for replacement purposes without additional fitting.

SLIP RINGS: Insulated metal rings mounted on alternator rotor shaft on which brushes make continuous sliding contact.

SLUDGE: A pasty composition of oxidized petroleum products along with an emulsion formed by a mixture of engine oil and water that clogs oil lines and passages.

SMOG: Unburned hydrocarbons combined with oxides of nitrogen and acted upon by sunlight.

SOLDER: An alloy of lead and tin used to unite two metal parts.

SOLDERING: To unite two pieces of metal with a material having a comparatively low melting point.

SOLENOID: An iron core, surrounded by a coil of wire, which moves due to magnetic attraction when electric current is fed to coil. Often used to actuate mechanisms by electrical means.

SOLID INJECTION: System used in full diesel and semi-diesel, where fuel in fluid state is injected into cylinder rather than a mixture of air and fuel drawn from a carburetor.

SOLID STATE: Electronic device or assembly with no moving parts.

SOLVENT: A solution which dissolves some other material. Example: water is a solvent for sugar.

SOUTH POLE: Pole of a magnet to which lines of force flow. Opposite of north pole.

SPACER, SPACER WASHER: A sheet of metal or other material placed between two surfaces to reduce clearance or to provide a better thrust surface for a fastener.

SPARK: An electric current possessing sufficient pressure to jump through air from one conductor to another.

SPARK ADVANCE: To cause spark to occur at an earlier time in cycle of engine operation. Opposite of retard.

SPARK GAP: Space between electrodes of a spark plug through which spark jumps. Also, a safety device in a magneto to provide an alternate path for current when it exceeds a safe value.

SPARK KNOCK: See PREIGNITION.

SPARK PLUG: A device, inserted into combustion chamber of an engine, containing an insulated center electrode for conducting high tension current from ignition distributor or magneto. This insulated electrode is spaced a predetermined distance from side electrode to control dimensions of gap for spark to jump across.

SPECIFIC GRAVITY: Relative weight of a substance compared to water. Example: if a cubic inch of acid weighs twice as much as a cubic inch of water, specific gravity of substance is 2.0.

SPEED CONTROL: Accessory system designed to maintain rate of speed of vehicle desired by driver.

SPEEDOMETER: A device for measuring and indicating speed of a vehicle in miles per hour.

SPIRAL BEVEL GEAR: A ring gear and pinion in which mating teeth are curved and placed at an angle with pinion shaft.

SPLAYED SPRING: A design in which leaf springs are placed at other than a 90 degree angle to axle.

SPLINE: A long keyway.

SPLINE JOINT: Two mating parts each with a series of splines around their circumference, one inner and one outer to provide a longitudinally movable joint without circumferential motion.

SPLIT HYDRAULIC BRAKE SYSTEM: Service brake system with two separate hydraulic circuits to provide braking action in one circuit if other one fails.

SPONGY BRAKE PEDAL: Air in hydraulic lines, distortion or stretching of connecting parts or swelling of hydraulic hose may allow pedal to be spongy or springy instead of solid.

SPOT WELD: To attach in spots by localized fusion of metal parts with aid of an electric current.

SPRUNG WEIGHT: A term used to describe all parts of an automobile that are supported by car springs. Example: frame, engine, body, etc.

SPUR GEAR: A gear in which teeth are cut parallel to shaft.

SPURT-HOLE: A hole drilled through a connecting rod and bearing that allows oil under pressure to be squirted out of bearing for additional lubrication of cylinder walls.

SQ. FT.: Square feet.

SQ. IN.: Square inch.

STANDARD THREAD: Refers to U.S.S. table of number of threads per inch. Example: a quarter inch diameter standard thread has 20 threads per inch.

STATIC ELECTRICITY: Atmospheric electricity as distinguished from electricity produced by a mechanical device.

STATOR: A wheel having curved blades interposed between torque converter pump and turbine elements. Also a metal frame of alternator with three stationary windings that give over-lapping pulses of alternating current.

STEEL CASTING: Cast iron to which varying amounts of scrap steel have been added.

STEERING AXIS INCLINATION: Angle formed by center line of suspension ball joints and true vertical center line.

STEERING GEAR: Gears in steering unit. Also, assembly of parts and units required to control angularity of wheels to body of a vehicle.

STEERING GEOMETRY: See TOE-OUT ON TURNS.

STEERING KNUCKLE: Part about which front wheel pivots when turning.

STEERING POST OR COLUMN: Shaft connecting steering gear unit with steering wheel.

STEERING SPINDLE: A journal or shaft upon which steerable wheels of a vehicle are mounted.

STELLITE: An alloy of cobalt, chrome and tungsten often used for exhaust valve seat inserts. It has a high melting point, good corrosion resistance and unusual hardness when hot.

STRAP: A lead section to which battery plates of a group are joined.

STRESS: Force or strain to which a material is subjected.

STROBOSCOPE: A term applied to an ignition timing light which, by being connected to distributor points, gives effect of making a mark on a rapidly rotating pulley or harmonic balancer which appears to stand still for observation.

STROKE: Distance traveled by a piston from BDC to TDC.

STROKING: Remachining crankshaft throws "off center" to alter stroke.

STUDS: A rod with threads cut on both ends. It screws into cylinder block on one end and has a nut placed on other end.

SUCTION: Suction exists in a vessel when pressure is lower than atmospheric pressure. See VACUUM.

SULPHATED: When a battery is improperly charged, or allowed to remain in a discharged condition for some length of time, plates will be coated with an abnormal amount of lead sulphate.

SUN GEAR: Central gear around which other gears revolve in a planetary gear system.

SUPERCHARGER: A blower or pump which forces air into cylinders at higher than atmospheric pressure, enabling more gasoline to be burned and more power to be produced.

SWEAT: To join metal pieces by clamping them together with solder in between, then applying heat.

SYNCHROMESH: A device used in transmission gearing to facilitate meshing of two gears by causing speed of both gears to coincide.

SYNCHRONIZE: To cause two events to occur in unison or at same time.

TAC: Thermostatically Controlled Air cleaner.

TACHOMETER: A device for measuring and indicating rotary speed of an engine.

TAP: To cut threads in a hole with a tapered, fluted, threaded tool.

TAPPET: Adjusting screw for varying clearance between valve stem and cam. May be built into valve lifter in L-head engine or may be installed in rocker arm on an overhead valve engine.

TCS: Transmission Controlled Spark.

TDC: Top dead center.

TEMPER: To change physical characteristics of metal by application of heat.

TENSION: Effort that is devoted towards elongation or "stretching" of a material.

TERMINAL: A junction point where electrical connections are made.

T-HEAD ENGINE: An engine design in which inlet valves are placed on one side of the cylinder and exhaust valves placed on other.

THERMACTOR: Ford air pump type exhaust emission control system.

THERMAL EFFICIENCY: A gallon of fuel contains potential energy in form of heat when burned in combustion chamber. Some heat is lost and some is converted into power. Thermal efficiency is ratio of work accomplished compared to total quantity of heat contained in fuel.

THERMAL REACTOR: Emission control device that accepts raw exhaust gases from engine and subjects them to extremely high temperatures to oxidize noxious emissions.

THERMOSTAT: A heat-controlled valve used in cooling system of engine to regulate flow of water between cylinder block and radiator. A thermostat is also used in modern air cleaners in which inlet air temperature is regulated.

THERMO-SYPHON: A method of cooling an engine which utilizes difference in specific gravity of hot and cold water. No pump is used, but water passages are larger than in pump circulation system.

THIRD BRUSH: In DC generators, an auxiliary brush placed on commutator to control current output of generator.

THROW: Distance from center of crankshaft main bearing to center of connecting rod journal.

TIE ROD: Metal rod connecting steering spindle arms on opposite sides of vehicle.

TIMER: Ignition distributor times and supplies spark to spark plugs at proper instant.

TIMING CHAIN: Chain used to drive camshaft and accessory shafts of an engine.

TIMING GEARS: Any group of gears driven from engine crankshaft to cause valves, ignition and other engine-driven apparatus to operate at desired time during engine cycle.

TIRE: A tubular corded carcass covered with rubber or synthetic rubber, mounted on a wheel and inflated to provide traction for moving and stopping the vehicle.

TOE: Inside or smaller half of a gear tooth. Also, end of brake shoe against anchor.

TOE-OUT ON TURNS: Related angles assumed by front wheels of vehicle when turning.

TOLERANCE: A permissible variation between two extremes of a specification of dimensions.

TORQUE: Effort devoted toward twisting or turning.

TORQUE CONVERTER: A turbine device utilizing a rotary pump, one or more reactors and a driven circular turbine. Power is transmitted from a driving to a driven member by hydraulic action.

TORQUE WRENCH: A special wrench with a built-in indicator to measure applied force.

TORSION BAR: Rod with built-in twist to provide spring action.

TORUS: An oil-filled member of a torque converter.

TRACTOR FUEL: A fuel, similar to kerosene or diesel oil, which is less volatile than gasoline.

Dictionary of Terms

TRAMP: An oscillating motion and heavy vibration when wheels are turning.

TRANSAXLE: Transmission and differential combined in one unit.

TRANSFORMER: An electrical device, such as a high tension coil, which transforms or changes characteristics of an electrical current.

TRANSISTOR: In electronics, a miniature amplifying device.

TRANSMISSION: A system of trading speed for power, or vice versa, through gearing or torque conversion. It includes various devices and combinations for changing ratio between engine revolutions and driving wheel revolutions.

TREAD: Portion of tire that comes in contact with road. Also, distance between center of tires at points where they contact road surface.

TROUBLESHOOTING: A process of diagnosing possible sources of trouble by observation and testing.

TUNE-UP: A process of accurate and careful adjustments and parts replacements to obtain utmost in engine performance.

TURBINE: A series of blades on a wheel, situated at an angle to the shaft, against which fluids or gases are impelled to impart rotary motion to shaft.

TURBOCHARGER: A device which utilizes pressure of exhaust gases to drive a supercharger which, in turn, forces more air into cylinders.

TURBULENCE: A disturbed, irregular motion of fluids or gases.

TURNING RADIUS: Diameter of a circle within which a vehicle can be turned around.

TVS: Thermostatic Vacuum Switch.

TWO CYCLE ENGINE: An engine design permitting a power stroke once for each revolution of the crankshaft.

UNDERCOATING: Spraying insulating material on exposed undersections of an automobile to retard corrosion and deaden noise.

UNIT POWER PLANT: An assembly in which engine, clutch and transmission are combined in one unit.

UNIVERSAL JOINT: A connection for transmitting power from a driving to a driven shaft through an angle.

UNLEADED GASOLINE: Motor fuel containing no tetraethyl lead additive.

UNSPRUNG WEIGHT: Weight that includes wheels, axles, etc., that are not supported by car springs.

UP-DRAFT: Used to describe a carburetor in which mixture flows upward to engine.

UPPER CYLINDER LUBRICATION: A method of introducing a lubricant into fuel or intake manifold in order to permit lubrication of upper cylinder, valve guides, etc.

UPSET: To compress at ends, causing an increase in diameter.

VACUUM: A pressure less than atmospheric pressure (14.7 psi at sea level).

VACUUM CONTROL: A diaphragm attached to ignition distributor spark advance which is controlled by changing of vacuum in intake manifold.

VACUUM GAUGE: An instrument designed to measure degree of vacuum existing in a chamber.

VALVE: A device for opening and sealing an aperture.

VALVE CLEARANCE: Air gap allowed between end of valve stem and valve lifter or rocker arm to compensate for expansion due to heat.

VALVE FACE: Part of a valve which mates with and rests upon a seating surface.

VALVE GRINDING: A process of mating valve seat and valve face.

VALVE HEAD: Portion of a valve upon which valve face is machined.

VALVE-IN-HEAD ENGINE (OHV): See OVERHEAD VALVE ENGINE.

VALVE KEY OR VALVE LOCK: Key, keeper, washer or other device which holds valve spring cup or washer in place on valve stem.

VALVE LIFTER: Solid part or hydraulic plunger placed between cam and valve on an engine.

VALVE MARGIN: Space or rim on a poppet valve between surface of head and surface of valve face.

VALVE OVERLAP: An interval expressed in degrees where both valves of an automobile engine cylinder are open at same time.

VALVE SEAT: Mating surface upon which valve face rests.

VALVE SPRING: A spring attached to a valve to return it to seat after lift is released.

VALVE STEM: Portion of a valve which rests within a guide.

VALVE STEM GUIDE: A bushing or hole for valve stem which allows lateral motion only.

VALVE TIMING: Indicates relative position of valve (open or closed) to piston in its travel, in crankshaft degrees.

VALVE TRAIN: Mechanism or linkage used to transmit motion of engine cam to valve stem, causing valve to open.

VANES: Any plate or blade attached to an axis and moved by or in air or a liquid.

VAPORIZER: A device for transforming or helping to transform a liquid into a vapor.

VAPOR LOCK: A condition in which fuel boils in fuel system, forming bubbles which retard or stop flow of fuel to carburetor.

VAPOR PRESSURE: Pressure developed over a liquid in a closed vessel, depending upon liquid and temperature.

VAPOR WITHDRAWAL: A system of piping and connections to operate an engine directly on vapor taken from top of an LP-Gas tank.

VENTURI: Two tapering streamlined tubes joined at their small ends to reduce internal diameter.

VIBRATION DAMPER: See HARMONIC BALANCER.

VISCOSIMETER: An instrument for determining viscosity of an oil by passing a certain quantity at a definite temperature through a standard size orifice or port. Time required for oil to pass through, expressed in seconds, gives viscosity.

VISCOSITY: Resistance to flow, or adhesiveness characteristics of an oil.

VOLATILITY: Tendency of fluid to evaporate rapidly. Example: Gasoline is more volatile than kerosene, since it evaporates at lower temperature.

VOLT: A unit of electrical force that will cause a current of one ampere to flow through a resistance of one ohm.

VOLTAGE REGULATOR: An electrical device for controlling or regulating voltage.

VOLTMETER: An instrument for measuring voltage in an electrical circuit.

VOLUME: Measure of space expressed as cubic inches, cubic centimeters, etc.

VOLUMETRIC EFFICIENCY: A combination between ideal and actual efficiency of an internal combustion engine. If engine completely filled each cylinder on each induction stroke, volumetric efficiency of engine would be 100 percent. In actual operation, however, volumetric efficiency is lowered by inertia of the gases, friction between gases and manifolds, temperature of gases and pressure of air entering carburetor. Volumetric efficiency is ordinarily increased by use of large valves, ports and manifolds and can be further increased with aid of a supercharger.

VORTEX: A whirling movement or mass of liquid or air.

WANDERING: A condition in which steering wheels of an automobile tend to turn slowly in first one direction, then the other, interfering with directional control or stability.

WATER COLUMN: A reference term used in connection with a manometer.

WATT: A measuring unit of electrical power. It is obtained by multiplying amperes by volts.

WEDGE BLOCK: Combustion chamber design in which top of piston and surface of block form an angle.

WEIGHT TRANSFER EFFECT: Since center of gravity of vehicle is located above centers of wheel rotation, a sudden stoppage of vehicle tends to cause center of gravity to move forward, thus throwing more weight on front wheels and less on rear wheels.

WELDING: To join two pieces of metal by heating them to fusion or melting point.

WHEEL CYLINDER: Unit for converting hydraulic fluid pressure to mechanical force for actuation of brake shoes and lining against brake drum.

WHEELBASE: Distance between center lines of front and rear axles.

WHITE METAL: An alloy of tin, lead and antimony having a low melting point and a low coefficient of friction.

WIRING DIAGRAM: A detailed drawing of all wiring, connections and units connected together in an electrical circuit.

WORM GEAR: A shaft having an extremely coarse thread which is designed to operate in engagement with a toothed wheel, as a pair of gears.

WRINGING-FIT: A fit with less clearance than for a running or sliding fit. Shaft will enter hole by means of twisting and pushing by hand.

WRIST PIN: Journal for bearing in small end of an engine connecting rod which also passes through piston walls. See PISTON PIN.

1965	Wheelbase	No. of Cylinders Bore and Stroke	Displacement (cu. in.)	Valve and Cylinder Arrangement	Compression Pressure (lbs.)	Maximum Brake Horsepower	Valve Tappet Clearance Intake	Exhaust	Cylinder Bolt Torque (ft.-lbs.)
Buick-Special, Skylark	115	V-6-3.75x3.40	225	VO	160	155@4400	HY	HY	80
LeSabre	123	8-3.75x3.40	300	VO	160	210@4600	HY	HY	80
Wildcat, Electra 225	126	8-4.1875x3.64	401	VO	175	325@4400	HY	HY	80
Riviera	117	8-4.3125x3.64	425	VO	175	340@4400	HY	HY	80
Cadillac	129.5[1]	8-4.13x4.0	429	VO	175	340@4600	HY	HY	60
Chevrolet, Chevelle, Chevy II	119[2]	6-3.875x3.25	230	IO	130	140@4400	HY	HY	100
Chevrolet, Chevelle, Chevy II	119[2]	8-3.875x3.0	283	VO	150	195@4800	HY	HY	70
Chevrolet	119	8-4.001x3.25	327	VO	160	250@4400	HY	HY	65
Chevrolet	119	8-4.313x3.5	409	VO	.150	340@5000	HY	HY	70
Chevy II-100	110	4-3.875x3.25	153	IO	130	90@4000	HY	HY	100
Chevy II, Chevelle	110[2]	6-3.563x3.25	194	IO	130	120@4400	HY	HY	100
Chevy II, Chevelle	110[2]	8-4.001x3.25	327	VO	160	300@5000	HY	HY	70
Corvair	108	6-3.438x2.94	164	HO	130	95@3600	HY	HY	38
Corvair Corsa	108	6-3.438x2.94	164	HO	130	140@5200	HY	HY	38
Corvette	98	8-4.0x3.25	327	VO	160	250@4400	HY	HY	70
Corvette	98	8-4.0x3.25	327	VO	160	300@5000	HY	HY	70
Chrysler-Newport	124	8-4.25x3.38	383	VO	155	270@4400	HY	HY	70
300	124	8-4.25x3.38	383	VO	165	315@4400	HY	HY	70
New Yorker	124	8-4.19x3.75	413	VO	165	340@4600	HY	HY	70
300L	124	8-4.19x3.75	413	VO	165	360@4800	HY	HY	70
Imperial	129	8-4.19x3.75	413	VO	165	340@4600	HY	HY	70
Dodge-Dart	111	6-3.40x3.125	170	IO	140	101@4400	.010H	.020H	65
Dart, Coronet	111[7]	6-3.40x4.125	225	IO	140	145@4000	.010H	.020H	65
Dart, Coronet	111[7]	8-3.63x3.31	273	VO	150	180@4200	.013H	.021H	85
Coronet	117	8-3.91x3.31	318	VO	155	230@4400	.013H	.021H	85
Coronet	117	8-4.12x3.38	361	VO	155	265@4400	HY	HY	85
Coronet	117	8-4.25x3.38	383	VO	165	330@4600	HY	HY	70
Polara, Custom 880	121.5	8-4.25x3.38	383	VO	155	270@4400	HY	HY	70
Polara, Custom 880, Monaco	121.5	8-4.19x3.75	413	VO	165	340@4600	HY	HY	70
Ford-Falcon	109.5	6-3.50x2.94	170	IO	175	105@4400	HY	HY	75
Falcon	109.5	6-3.68x3.13	200	IO	175	120@4400	HY	HY	75
Falcon	109.5	8-4.0x2.87	289	VO	150	200@4400	HY	HY	75
Fairlane, Mustang	116[9]	6-3.68x3.13	200	IO	175	120@4400	HY	HY	75
Fairlane, Mustang	116[9]	8-4.0x2.87	289	VO	150	200@4400	HY	HY	70
Fairlane, Mustang-Exc. Sta. Wag.	116[9]	8-4.0x2.87	289	VO	150	271@6000	.020H	.020H	70
Ford-Except XL and LTD	119	6-4.0x3.18	240	IO	175	150@4000	HY	HY	75
Ford XL, LTD	119	8-4.0x2.87	289	VO	150	200@4400	HY	HY	75
Ford	119	8-4.0x3.5	352	VO	180	250@4400	HY	HY	90
Ford Thunderbird	113.2	8-4.05x3.78	390	VO	190	300@4600	HY	HY	90
Ford-Except Station Wagons	119	8-4.24x3.79	427	VO	180	425@6000	.025H	.025H	110
Lincoln Continental	126	8-4.30x3.70	430	VO	180	320@4000	HY	HY	135
Mercury-Comet	114	6-3.68x3.13	200	IO	175	120@4400	HY	HY	75
Comet	114	8-4.0x2.87	289	VO	150	225@4800	HY	HY	70
Mercury-Except Park Lane	123	8-4.05x3.78	390	VO	180	250@4400	HY	HY	90
Mercury-Park Lane	123	8-4.05x3.78	390	VO	190	300@4600	HY	HY	90
Mercury	123	8-4.05x3.78	390	VO	190	330@5000	.025H	.025H	90
Mercury-Except Station Wagons	123	8-4.23x3.78	427	VO	180	425@6000	.025H	.025H	110
Oldsmobile-F-85	115	V-6-3.75x3.4	225	VO	125	155@4400	HY	HY	70
F-85, Jetstar 88	115[12]	8-3.9375x3.385	330	VO	125	250@4800	HY	HY	80
Dynamic 88, Delta	123	8-4.125x3.975	425	VO	125	310@4400	HY	HY	80
98	126	8-4.125x3.975	425	VO	125	360@4800	HY	HY	80
Jetstar 1, Starfire	123	8-4.125x3.975	425	VO	125	370@4800	HY	HY	80
Plymouth-Valiant, Barracuda	106	6-3.4x3.125	170	IO	140	101@4400	.010H	.020H	65
Valiant, Barracuda	106	6-3.4x4.125	225	IO	140	145@4000	.010H	.020H	65
Valiant, Barracuda	106	8-3.63x3.31	273	VO	165	235@5200	.013H	.021H	85
Belvedere, Satellite, Fury	116[14]	6-3.4x4.125	225	IO	140	145@4000	.010H	.020H	85
Belvedere, Satellite	116	8-3.63x3.31	273	VO	150	180@4200	.013H	.021H	85
Fury	119	8-3.91x3.31	318	VO	155	230@4400	.013H	.021H	85
Belvedere, Satellite	116	8-4.12x3.38	361	VO	155	265@4400	HY	HY	70
Fury	119	8-4.25x3.38	383	VO	165	330@4600	HY	HY	70
Belvedere, Satellite, Fury	116[14]	8-4.25x3.75	426	VO	165	365@4800	HY	HY	70
Pontiac-Tempest, LeMans	115	6-3.75x3.25	215	IO	145	140@4200	HY	HY	95
Tempest-Except GTO	115	8-3.72x3.75	326	VO	160	250@4600	HY	HY	55
GTO	115	8-4.06x3.75	389	VO	160	335@5000	HY	HY	95
Catalina, Star Chief	121[16]	8-4.06x3.75	389	VO	160	290@4600	HY	HY	95
Grand Prix, Bonneville	121[16]	8-4.06x3.75	389	VO	160	333@5000	HY	HY	95
Pontiac	121[16]	8-4.09x4.0	421	VO	160	376@5000	HY	HY	95
Rambler-American 220, 330	106	6-3.125x4.25	195	IL	130	90@3800	.016C	.018C	60
American 440, 440H	106	6-3.125x4.25	195	IO	145	125@4200	.012H	.016H	60
Classic 550	112	6-3.75x3.0	199	IO	145	128@4400	HY	HY	60
Classic, Ambassador	112[17]	6-3.75x3.5	232	IO	145	155@4300	HY	HY	60
Classic	112	8-3.75x3.25	287	VO	145	198@4700	HY	HY	60
Ambassador	116	8-4.0x3.25	327	VO	145	270@4700	HY	HY	65
Studebaker-Commander, Cruiser	109[18]	6-3.563x3.25	194	IO	130	120@4400	HY	HY	100
Daytona	109[18]	8-3.875x3.0	283	VO	150	195@4800	HY	HY	70

ABBREVIATIONS - FOOTNOTES
AC - AC spark plugs
BF - Autolite spark plugs
BTF - Autolite spark plugs
C - Cold engine
CC - Timing case cover
CH - Champion spark plugs
CP - Crankshaft pulley
H - Hot engine
HO - Horizontal opposed cylinders
HY - Hydraulic valve lifters
IL - In-line engine, L-head
IO - In-line engine, overhead valves
N - Negative
P - Positive
VD - Vibration damper
VO - V-type engine, overhead valves
WP - Water pump housing

Tuneup Specifications

Connecting Rod Bolt Torque (ft.-lbs.)	Main Bearing Bolt Torque (ft.-lbs.)	Firing Order	Timing Mark Location	Breaker Point Opens B.T.D.C.	Breaker Point Gap	Cam Angle	Spark Plugs Make	Spark Plugs Model	Gap	Caster Man. Steer. (deg.)	Camber Rt. Wheel (deg.)	Toe-In (inches)	Steering Axis Inclination (deg.)	Cooling System Capacity (qts.)	Crankcase Capacity (qts.)
40	120	165432	VD	5	.016	30	AC	44S	.035	1/2N	1/2P	3/16	8	10.7	4
40	120	18436572	VD	2.5	.016	30	AC	44S	.035	1P	1/4P	1/4	10-3/4	12.4	4
50	120	12784563	VD	2.5	.016	30	AC	44S	.035	1P	1/4P	1/4	10-3/4	17.7	4
50	120	12784563	VD	2.5	.016	30	AC	44S	.035	1P	1/2P	3/16	10	18.5	4
40	95	18726543	VD	5	.016	30	AC	44	.035	1N	1/4N	7/32	6	18.5	4
35	70	153624	VD	4	.019	32	AC	46N	.035	1/4P[3]	1/4P	3/16	7-1/2[4]	12	4
35	70	18436572	VD	4	.019	30	AC	45	.035	1/4P[3]	1/4P	3/16	7-1/2[4]	16	4
30	65	18436572	VD	8	.019	30	AC	44	.035	1/4P	1/4P	3/16	7-1/2	16	4
45	100	18436572	VD	6	.019	30	AC	43N	.035	1/4P	1/4P	3/16	7-1/2	22	4
35	70	1342	CP	4	.019	32	AC	46N	.035	1P	1/2P	1/4	7	9	3.5
35	70	153624	VD	8	.019	32	AC	46N	.035	1P[3]	1/2P	1/4	7[4]	11	4
35	70	18436572	VD	8	.019	30	AC	44	.035	1P[3]	1/2P	1/4	7[4]	17	4
26	55	145236	CP	6	.019	33	AC	46FF	.035	4P	1P	5/16[5]	6-1/2	---	4
26	55	145236	VD	18	.019	33	AC	44FF	.030	4P	1P	5/16[5]	6-1/2	---	4
35	70	18436572	VD	4	.019	30	AC	44	.035	1-1/2P	3/4P	9/32[6]	7	19	4
35	70	18436572	VD	8	.019	30	AC	44	.035	1-1/2P	3/4P	9/32[6]	7	19	4
45	85	18436572	WP	10	.016	30	CH	J-14Y	.035	1/2N	1/4P	1/8	9	17	4
45	85	18436572	WP	10	.016	30	CH	J-14Y	.035	1/2N	1/4P	1/8	9	17	4
45	85	18436572	WP	12.5	.016	30	CH	J-14Y	.035	1/2N	1/4P	1/8	9	17	4
45	85	18436572	WP	10	.016	30	CH	J-10Y	.035	1/2N	1/4P	1/8	9	17	4
45	85	18436572	WP	12.5	.016	30	CH	J-14Y	.035	1/2P	1/4P	1/8	6-1/2	17	4
45	85	153624	WP	2.5	.020	42	CH	N-14Y	.035	1/2N	1/4P	1/8	7-1/2	12	4
45	85	153624	CC	2.5	.020	42	CH	N-14Y	.035	1/2N	1/4P	1/8	7-1/2	13	4
45	85	18436572	WP	5	.016	30	CH	N-14Y	.035	1/2N	1/4P	1/8	7-1/2	18	4
45	85	18436572	WP	5	.016	30	CH	J-14Y	.035	1/2N	1/4P	1/8	7-1/2	21	4
45	85	18436572	WP	10	.016	30	CH	J-14Y	.035	1/2N	1/4P	1/8	7-1/2	17	4
45	85	18436572	WP	10	.016	28[8]	CH	J-10Y	.035	1/2N	1/4P	1/8	7-1/2	17	4
45	85	18436572	WP	10	.016	30	CH	J-14Y	.035	1/2N	1/4P	1/8	9	17	4
45	85	18436572	WP	12.5	.016	28[8]	CH	J-10Y	.035	1/2N	1/4P	1/8	9	17	4
24	70	153624	CC	6	.025	37	BF	82	.034	3/4P	1/2P	9/32	7-1/4	9.5	3.5
24	70	153624	CC	6	.025	37	BF	82	.034	3/4P	1/2P	9/32	7-1/4	9.5	3.5
24	70	15426378	CC	6	.015	27	BF	42	.035	1/4N	1/2P	9/32	7-1/4	14.5	4
24	70	153624	CC	6	.025	37	BF	82	.035	0[10]	1/4P	7/32	7-3/4[11]	9.5	3.5
24	70	15426378	CC	6	.015	27	BF	42	.035	0	1/4P	7/32	7-3/4[11]	15	4
45	70	15426378	CC	12	.020	33	BF	32	.035	0	1/4P	7/32	7-3/4[11]	15	4
45	70	153624	VD	6	.025	37	BTF	6	.035	1P	1/2P	5/32	7-1/4	15	4
45	70	15426378	VD	6	.015	27	BF	42	.035	1P	1/2P	5/32	7-1/4	20.5	4
45	105	15426378	VD	6	.015	27	BF	42	.035	1P	1/2P	5/32	7-1/4	20.5	5
45	105	15426378	CC	6	.015	27	BF	42	.035	1-1/2N	1/2P	5/32	7	20	5
58	105	15426378	VD	8	.020	34	BF	32	.035	1P	1/2P	5/32	7-1/4	20.5	5
45	105	15426378	VD	6	.015	27	BF	42	.035	1-1/2N	3/4P	5/32	7	25	5
24	70	153624	CC	6	.025	37	BF	82	.035	3/4P	1/2P	9/32	7-1/4	9.5	3.5
24	70	15426378	CC	6	.015	27	BF	42	.030	1/4N	1/2P	9/32	7-1/4	15	4
45	105	15426378	CC	6	.015	27	BF	42	.035	1P	1/2P	5/32	7-1/4	20.5	5
45	105	15426378	CC	4	.015	27	BF	42	.035	1P	1/2P	5/32	7-1/4	20.5	5
45	105	15426378	CC	4	.015	27	BF	42	.035	1P	1/2P	5/32	7-1/4	20.5	5
58	105	15426378	VD	8	.020	27	BF	32	.035	1P	1/2P	5/32	7-1/4	20.5	5
35	70	165432	VD	5	.016	30	AC	44S	.035	1-1/4N	1/4P	5/32	9	11	4
42	80[13]	18436572	VD	7.5	.016	30	AC	45S	.030	1-1/4N	1/4P	5/32	9	17	4
42	80[13]	18436572	VD	5	.016	30	AC	44S	.030	1N	1/4P	5/32	11	18	4
42	80[13]	18436572	VD	5	.016	30	AC	44S	.030	1N	1/4P	5/32	11	17.5	4
42	80[13]	18436572	VD	5	.016	30	AC	44S	.030	1N	1/4P	5/32	11	17.5	4
45	85	153624	WP	2.5	.020	42	CH	N-14Y	.035	1/2N	1/4P	1/8	6-1/2	12	4
45	85	153624	WP	2.5	.020	42	CH	N-14Y	.035	1/2N	1/4P	1/8	6-1/2	13	4
45	85	18436572	CC	10	.016	30[8]	CH	N-14Y	.035	1/2N	1/4P	1/8	6-1/2	18	4
45	85	153624	CC	2.5	.020	42	CH	N-14Y	.035	1/2N	1/4P	1/8	6-1/2[15]	13	4
45	85	18436572	WP	5	.016	30	CH	N-14Y	.035	1/2N	1/4P	1/8	9	18	4
45	85	18436572	WP	5	.016	30	CH	J-14Y	.035	1/2N	1/4P	1/8	6-1/2	21	4
45	85	18436572	WP	10	.016	30	CH	J-14Y	.035	1/2N	1/4P	1/8	9	17	4
45	85	18436572	WP	10	.016	30[8]	CH	J-14Y	.035	1/2N	1/4P	1/8	9	17	4
45	85	18436572	WP	10	.016	30[8]	CH	J-10Y	.035	1/2N	1/4P	1/8	6-1/2[15]	17	4
45	95	153624	CP	4	.016	32	AC	46N	.035	1-1/2N	1/4P	1/16	9	13.5	4
35	55	18436572	VD	6	.016	30	AC	45S	.035	1-1/2N	1/4P	1/16	9	20.5	5
45	95	18436572	VD	6	.016	30	AC	45S	.035	1-1/2N	1/4P	1/16	9	20.5	5
45	95	18436572	VD	6	.016	30	AC	45S	.035	1-1/2N	1/4P	1/16	8-1/2	20	5
45	95	18436572	VD	6	.016	30	AC	45S	.035	1-1/2N	1/4P	1/16	8-1/2	20	5
30	70	153624	VD	3	.019	32	CH	H-10	.035	1/4P	0	1/8	6-1/4	11	4
30	70	153624	VD	8	.019	32	CH	H-18Y	.035	1/4P	0	1/8	6-1/4	11	4
30	70	153624	VD	8	.019	32	CH	N-14Y	.035	1/4P	0	1/8	6-1/4	10.5	4
30	70	153624	VD	8	.019	32	CH	N-14Y	.035	1/4P	0	1/8	6-1/4	10.5	4
30	70	18436572	VD	5	.016	30	CH	H-14Y	.035	1/4P	0	1/8	6-1/4	19	4
50	85	18436572	VD	5	.016	30	CH	H-14Y	.035	1/4P	0	1/8	6-1/4	19	4
35	70	153624	VD	8	.019	32	AC	46N	.035	1/2N	1/2P	7/32	6	13.5	4
35	70	18436572	CP	4	.019	30	AC	45	.035	1/2N	1/2P	7/32	6	16	4

1 - Sixty Special 133 in., Seventy-Five 149.8 in.
2 - Chevy II 110 in., Chevelle 115 in.
3 - Chevy II 1P, Chevelle 1N
4 - Chevy II 7, Chevelle 8-1/4
5 - Rear 1/4 in.
6 - Rear 1/32 in.
7 - Coronet 117 in.
8 - Both sets 38 deg.
9 - Mustang 108 in.
10 - Mustang 1P
11 - Mustang 7-1/4
12 - Jetstar 88 123 in.
13 - #5 main 120 ft. lbs.
14 - Fury 119 in.
15 - Fury 9 deg.
16 - Star Chief, Bonneville 124 in.
17 - Ambassador 116 in.
18 - 4 dr. and station wagon 113 in.

1966

	Wheelbase	No. of Cylinders Bore and Stroke	Displacement (cu. in.)	Valve and Cylinder Arrangement	Compression Pressure (lbs.)	Maximum Brake Horsepower	Valve Tappet Clearance Intake	Valve Tappet Clearance Exhaust	Cylinder Bolt Torque (ft. lbs.)
Buick – Special, Skylark	115	V6-3.75x3.40	225	VO	160	160@4200	HY	HY	80
Special	115	8-3.75x3.40	300	VO	175	210@4600	HY	HY	80
Skylark, Sportwagon	115 [1]	8-3.75x3.85	340	VO	175	220@4000	HY	HY	80
Skylark, Sportwagon	115 [1]	8-3.75x3.85	340	VO	175	260@4000	HY	HY	80
Skylark Gran Sport	115	8-4.1875x3.64	400	VO	175	325@4400	HY	HY	80
LeSabre	123	8-3.75x3.85	340	VO	175	260@4000	HY	HY	80
Wildcat, Electra	126	8-4.1875x3.64	401	VO	175	325@4400	HY	HY	80
Riviera	119	8-4.3125x3.64	425	VO	175	340@4400	HY	HY	80
Wildcat, Electra, Riviera	126 [2]	8-4.3125x3.64	425	VO	175	360@4400	HY	HY	80
Cadillac	129.5 [3]	8-4.13x4.00	429	VO	175	340@4600	HY	HY	60
Chevrolet	119	6-3.875x3.53	250	IO	130	155@4200	HY	HY	95
Chevrolet, Chevelle	119 [4]	8-3.875x3.00	283	VO	150	195@4800	HY	HY	65
Chevrolet, Chevelle	119 [4]	8-3.875x3.00	283	VO	150	220@4800	HY	HY	65
Chevrolet, Chevelle	119 [4]	8-4.00x3.25	327	VO	160	300@5000	HY	HY	65
Chevrolet, Chevelle	119 [4]	8-4.00x3.25	327	VO	160	275@4800	HY	HY	65
Corvette	98	8-4.00x3.25	327	VO	150	350@5800	HY	HY	65
Chevrolet, Chevelle	119 [4]	8-4.094x3.76	396	VO	160	325@4800	HY	HY	80
Chevelle	115	8-4.094x3.76	396	VO	160	360@5200	HY	HY	80
Chevelle	115	8-4.094x3.76	396	VO	160	375@5600	HY	HY	80
Chevrolet, Corvette	119 [4]	8-4.25x3.76	427	VO	160	390@5200	HY	HY	80
Chevrolet, Corvette	119 [4]	8-4.25x3.76	427	VO	150	425@5600	.024	.028	80
Chevelle, Chevy II	115 [4]	6-3.563x3.25	194	IO	130	120@4400	HY	HY	95
Chevelle, Chevy II	115 [4]	6-3.875x3.25	230	IO	130	140@4400	HY	HY	95
Chevy II	110	4-3.875x3.25	153	IO	130	90@4400	HY	HY	95
Corvair, Monza	108	6-3.4375x2.94	164	HO	130	95@3600	HY	HY	38
Corvair, Monza	108	6-3.4375x2.94	164	HO	130	110@4400	HY	HY	38
Corvair, Monza, Corsa	108	6-3.4375x2.94	164	HO	130	140@5200	HY	HY	38
Corsa	108	6-3.4375x2.94	164	HO	130	180@4000	HY	HY	38
Chrysler – Newport	124	8-4.25x3.38	383	VO	140	270@4400	HY	HY	70
Newport, 300	124	8-4.25x3.38	383	VO	140	325@4800	HY	HY	70
New Yorker	124	8-4.32x3.75	440	VO	150	350@4400	HY	HY	70
New Yorker, Newport, 300	124	8-4.32x3.75	440	VO	150	365@4600	HY	HY	70
Imperial	129	8-4.32x3.75	440	VO	150	350@4400	HY	HY	70
Dodge – Dart	111	6-3.40x3.125	170	IO	125	101@4400	.010H	.020H	65
Coronet, Dart	117 [14]	6-3.40x4.125	225	IO	125	145@4000	.010H	.020H	65
Coronet, Dart GT	117 [14]	8-3.63x3.31	273	VO	135	180@4200	.013H	.021H	85
Dart GT	111	8-3.63x3.31	273	VO	135	235@5200	.013H	.021H	85
Polara	121	8-3.91x3.31	318	VO	140	230@4400	.013H	.021H	85
Coronet	117	8-4.12x3.38	361	VO	140	265@4400	HY	HY	70
Polara, Monaco	121	8-4.25x3.38	383	VO	140	270@4400	HY	HY	70
Polara, Monaco	121	8-4.25x3.38	383	VO	140	325@4800	HY	HY	70
Coronet, Charger	117	8-4.25x3.75	426	VO	150	425@5000	.028C	.032C	70
Polara, Monaco	121	8-4.32x3.75	440	VO	150	350@4400	HY	HY	70
Ford – Falcon, Futura	110.9	6-3.50x2.94	170	IO	195	105@4400	HY	HY	75
Futura, Fairlane	110.9 [18]	6-3.684x3.13	200	IO	195	120@4400	HY	HY	75
Mustang	108	6-3.684x3.13	200	IO	195	120@4400	HY	HY	75
Ford	119	6-4.00x3.18	240	IO	175	150@4000	HY	HY	75
Falcon, Fairlane	110.9 [18]	8-4.005x2.87	289	VO	150	200@4400	HY	HY	70
Mustang	108	8-4.005x2.87	289	VO	150	225@4800	HY	HY	70
Mustang	108	8-4.005x2.87	289	VO	150	271@6000	.020H	.020H	70
Ford	119	8-4.00x3.50	352	VO	180	250@4400	HY	HY	90
Ford, Fairlane	119 [18]	8-4.05x3.78	390	VO	180	265@4400	HY	HY	90
Thunderbird	113	8-4.05x3.78	390	VO	180	315@4600	HY	HY	90
Fairlane GT, GTA	116	8-4.05x3.78	390	VO	180	335@4800	HY	HY	90
Ford	119	8-4.05x3.78	390	VO	180	275@4400	HY	HY	90

ABBREVIATIONS – FOOTNOTES:

AC – AC Spark Plugs
ATC – After Top Center
BF – Autolite Spark Plugs
BTF – Autolite Spark Plugs
C – Cold Engine
CC – Timing Case Cover
CH – Champion Spark Plugs
CP – Crankshaft Pulley
H – Hot Engine

HO – Horizontal Opposed Cylinders
HY – Hydraulic Valve Lifters
IO – In-line Engine, Overhead Valves
IOC – In-line Engine, Overhead Cam
N – Negative
NA – Not Applicable
P – Positive
TDC – Top Dead Center
VD – Vibration Damper
VO – V-Type Engine, Overhead Valves
WP – Water Pump Housing

1 – Sportwagon – 120 in.
2 – Riviera – 119 in.
3 – 60, Brougham – 133 in.; 75 – 149.8 in.
4 – Chevelle – 115 in.; Chevy II – 110 in.; Corvette – 98 in.
5 – Chevelle – 1/2 N.
6 – Chevelle – 8-1/4 deg.
7 – 4-Bolt Cap – 115 ft. lbs.
8 – Corvette – 3/4 P.
9 – Corvette – 1/4 in.
10 – Corvette – 7 deg.

Tuneup Specifications

Connecting Rod Bolt Torque (ft.lbs.)	Main Bearing Bolt Torque (ft.lbs.)	Firing Order	Timing Mark Location	Breaker Point Opens BTDC	Breaker Point Gap	Cam Angle	Spark Plugs Make	Model	Gap	Caster Man. Steer. (deg.)	Camber Rt. Wheel (deg.)	Toe-in (in.)	Steering Axis Inclination (deg.)	Cooling System Capacity (qts.)	Crankcase Capacity (qts.)
40	120	165432	VD	5	.016	30	AC	44S	.035	1/2N	1/2P	3/16	8	10.7	4
40	120	18436572	VD	2.5	.016	30	AC	44S	.035	1/2N	1/2P	3/16	8	12.7	4
40	120	18436572	CP	2.5	.016	30	AC	44S	.035	1/2N	1/2P	3/16	8	12.7	4
40	120	18436572	CP	2.5	.016	30	AC	44S	.035	1/2N	1/2P	3/16	8	12.7	4
50	80	18436572	VD	2.5	.016	30	AC	44S	.035	1/2N	1/2P	3/16	8	12.7	4
40	120	18436572	VD	2.5	.016	30	AC	44TS	.035	1P	1/4P	1/4	10-1/2	14.5	4
50	80	12784563	VD	2.5	.016	30	AC	44S	.035	1P	1/4P	1/4	10-1/2	18	4
50	80	12784563	VD	2.5	.016	30	AC	44S	.035	1P	1/4P	1/4	10-1/2	18	4
50	80	12784563	VD	2.5	.016	30	AC	44S	.035	1P	1/4P	1/4	10-1/2	18	4
40	90	18726543	VD	5	.016	30	AC	44	.035	1/2N	1/4P	7/32	6	17.2	4
35	65	153624	VD	6	.019	32	AC	46N	.035	3/4P	1/4P	3/32	7-1/2	13	4
35	80	18436572	VD	4	.019	30	AC	45	.035	3/4P[5]	1/4P	3/32	7-1/2[6]	17	4
35	80	18436572	VD	4	.019	30	AC	45	.035	3/4P[5]	1/4P	3/32	7-1/2[6]	17	4
35	80	18436572	VD	6	.019	30	AC	44	.037	3/4P[5]	1/4P	3/32	7-1/2[6]	15	4
35	80	18436572	VD	8	.019	30	AC	44	.037	3/4P[5]	1/4P	3/32	7-1/2[6]	15	4
35	80	18436572	VD	10	.019	30	AC	44	.037	3/4P	3/4P	1/4	7	19	5
50	95[7]	18436572	VD	4	.019	30	AC	43N	.037	3/4P[5]	1/4P	3/32	7-1/2[6]	23	4
50	95[7]	18436572	VD	4	.019	30	AC	43N	.037	1/2N	1/4P	3/32	8-1/4	23	4
50	95[7]	18436572	VD	10	.019	30	AC	43N	.037	1/2N	1/4P	3/32	8-1/4	23	4
50	95[7]	18436572	VD	4	.019	30	AC	43N	.035	3/4P	1/4P[8]	3/32[9]	7-1/2[10]	22	4[11]
50	95[7]	18436572	VD	8	NA	NA	AC	43N	.035	3/4P	1/4P[8]	3/32[9]	7-1/2[10]	23	4[11]
35	65	153624	VD	8	.019	33	AC	46N	.035	1/2N[12]	1/4P	3/32	8-1/4[13]	12	4
35	65	153624	VD	4	.019	33	AC	46N	.035	1/2N[12]	1/4P	3/32	8-1/4[13]	12	4
35	65	1342	CP	4	.019	33	AC	46N	.035	1P	1/4P	5/32	7	9	4
26	55	145236	CP	6	.019	33	AC	46FF	.035	3P	1P	1/4	6-1/2	NA	4
26	55	145236	VD	14	.019	33	AC	44FF	.030	3P	1P	1/4	6-1/2	NA	4
26	55	145236	VD	18	.019	33	AC	44FF	.030	3P	1P	1/4	6-1/2	NA	4
26	55	145236	VD	24	.019	33	AC	44FF	.035	3P	1P	1/4	6-1/2	NA	4
45	85	18436572	WP	12.5	.016	30	CH	J-14Y	.035	1/2P	1/4P	1/8	9	17	4
45	85	18436572	WP	12.5	.016	30	CH	J-13Y	.035	1/2P	1/4P	1/8	9	17	4
45	70	18436572	WP	12.5	.016	30	CH	J-13Y	.035	1/2P	1/4P	1/8	9	17	4
45	70	18436572	WP	12.5	.016	30	CH	J-13Y	.035	1/2P	1/4P	1/8	9	17	4
45	70	18436572	WP	12.5	.016	30	CH	J-13Y	.035	3/4P	1/4P	1/8	6-1/2	18	5
45	85	153624	WP	5	.020	42	CH	N-14Y	.035	1/2N	1/4P	1/8	7-1/2	12	4
45	85	153624	WP	25	.020	42	CH	N-14Y	.035	1/2N	1/4P	1/8	7-1/2	13	4
45	85	18436572	CC	5[15]	.016	30	CH	N-14Y	.035	1/2N	1/4P	1/8	7-1/2	18	4
45	85	18436572	CC	10	.016	29[16]	CH	N-9Y	.035	1/2N	1/4P	1/8	7-1/2	18	4
45	85	18436572	WP	10	.016	30	CH	J-14Y	.035	1/2N	1/4P	1/8	9	21	4
45	85	18436572	WP	12.5	.016	30	CH	J-14Y	.035	1/2N	1/4P	1/8	9	17	4
45	85	18436572	WP	12.5	.016	30	CH	J-14Y	.035	1/2N	1/4P	1/8	9	17	4
45	85	18436572	WP	12.5	.016	30	CH	J-13Y	.035	1/2N	1/4P	1/8	9	17	4
45	85	18436572	WP	5A	.017	29[17]	CH	J-13Y	.035	1/2N	1/4P	1/8	7-1/2	17	5
45	85	18436572	WP	12.5	.016	30	CH	J-13Y	.035	1/2N	1/4P	1/8	9	17	4
24	70	153624	CC	6	.025	37	BF	82	.034	1/2P	1/4P	1/4	6-1/2	9.5	3.5
24	70	153624	CC	6	.025	37	BF	82	.034	1/2P	1/4P	1/4[19]	6-1/2[20]	9.5	3.5
24	70	153624	CC	6	.025	37	BF	82	.034	1/2P	1/2P	9/32	7	9.5	3.5
45	70	153624	VD	6	.025	37	BTF	6	.034	1P	1-1/2P	3/16	7	13	4
24	70	15426378	CC	6	.015	27	BF	42	.034	1/2P	1/4P	1/4[19]	6-1/2[20]	15	4
24	70	15426378	CC	6	.015	27	BF	42	.034	1/2N	1/2P	9/32	7	15	4
24	70	15426378	CC	12	.020	34	BF	32	.034	1/2N	1/2P	9/32	7	15	4
45	105	15426378	VD	6	.025	37	BTF	6	.034	1P	1-1/2P	3/16	7	17	4
45	105	15426378	VD	6	.015	26	BF	42	.034	1P[21]	1-1/2P[22]	3/16[19]	7	20.5	4
45	105	15426378	VD	10	.015	27	BF	42	.034	1-1/2N	1/2P	3/16	7-1/2	20.5	4
45	105	15426378	VD	10	.015	26	BF	32	.034	1/4P	1/4P	1/8	7	20.5	4
45	105	15426378	VD	10	.015	27	BF	42	.034	1P	1-1/2P	3/16	7-1/2	20.5	4

11 - Corvette - 5 qts.
12 - Chevy II - 1 P.
13 - Chevy II - 7 deg.
14 - Dart - 111 in.
15 - Auto. Trans. - 10 BTDC.
16 - Both Breakers - 36 to 40 deg.
17 - Both Breakers - 37 to 42 deg.
18 - Fairlane - 116 in.
19 - Fairlane - 1/8 in.
20 - Fairlane - 7 deg.
21 - Fairlane - 1/2 P

22 - Fairlane - 1/4 P.
23 - Comet - 116 in.
24 - Comet - 0 deg.
25 - Comet - 1/4 in.
26 - Jetstar 88 - 123 in.
27 - Rear Main - 120 ft. lbs.
28 - Jetstar 88 - 44 S.
29 - Jetstar 88 - 16.5 qts.
30 - Dynamic 88, Delta 88 - 123 in.
31 - 98 - 126 in.
32 - Satellite - 116 in.

33 - Satellite - 7-1/2 deg.
34 - Both Breakers - 37 to 42 deg.
35 - Star Chief - 124 in.
36 - Grand Prix - 121 in.
37 - Bonneville - 116 in.
38 - Premium Fuel - 13 deg. BTDC.
39 - Premium Fuel - 3 deg. BTDC.
40 - Premium Fuel - 8 deg. BTDC.
41 - Classic, Marlin - 112 in.
42 - 4-Door Models - 113 in.
43 - 2-Door Models - 109 in.

1966	Wheelbase	No. of Cylinders Bore and Stroke	Displacement (cu. in.)	Valve and Cylinder Arrangement	Compression Pressure (lbs.)	Maximum Brake Horsepower	Valve Tappet Clearance Intake	Exhaust	Cylinder Bolt Torque (ft.-lbs.)
Thunderbird	113	8-4.13x3.98	428	VO	190	345@4600	HY	HY	110
Ford	119	8-4.13x3.98	428	VO	190	360@5400	HY	HY	110
Ford	119	8-4.23x3.78	427	VO	190	410@5600	.028H	.025	110
Ford	119	8-4.23x3.78	427	VO	190	425@6000	.028H	.025	110
Lincoln Continental	126	8-4.38x3.83	462	VO	180	340@4600	HY	HY	145
Mercury - Comet	116	6-3.68x3.13	200	IO	195	120@4400	HY	HY	75
Comet	116	8-4.00x2.87	289	VO	150	200@4400	HY	HY	70
Monterey, Montclair, Comet	123 [23]	8-4.054x3.78	390	VO	180	265@4400	HY	HY	90
Monterey, Montclair	123	8-4.054x3.78	390	VO	180	275@4400	HY	HY	90
Comet, Cyclone, GT, GTA	116	8-4.054x3.78	390	VO	180	335@4800	HY	HY	90
Parklane	123	8-4.054x3.98	410	VO	190	330@4600	HY	HY	90
S-55	123	8-4.13x3.98	428	VO	190	345@4600	HY	HY	110
Oldsmobile - F-85	115	6-3.875x3.53	250	IO	160	155@4200	HY	HY	95
F-85, Jetstar 88	115 [26]	8-3.9375x3.385	330	VO	175	250@4800	HY	HY	80
Cutlass	115	8-3.9375x3.385	330	VO	175	310@5200	HY	HY	80
Cutlass, Jetstar 88	115 [26]	8-3.9375x3.385	330	VO	175	320@5200	HY	HY	80
Jetstar 88	123	8-3.9375x3.385	330	VO	175	260@4800	HY	HY	80
F-85, Cutlass, 4-4-2	115	8-4.00x3.975	400	VO	175	350@5000	HY	HY	80
Dynamic 88, Delta 88	123	8-4.125x3.975	425	VO	175	300@4400	HY	HY	80
Dynamic 88, Delta 88	123	8-4.125x3.975	425	VO	175	310@4400	HY	HY	80
98, Dynamic 88, Delta 88	126 [30]	8-4.125x3.975	425	VO	175	365@4800	HY	HY	80
Starfire, 98, Delta 88	123 [31]	8-4.125x3.975	425	VO	175	375@4800	HY	HY	80
Toronado	119	8-4.125x3.975	425	VO	175	385@4800	HY	HY	80
Plymouth - Valiant, Signet	106	6-3.40x3.125	170	IO	125	101@4400	.010H	.020H	65
Belvedere	116	6-3.40x4.125	225	IO	125	145@4000	.010H	.020H	65
Barracuda, Satellite	106 [32]	8-3.63x3.31	273	VO	135	180@4200	.013H	.021H	85
Barracuda	106	8-3.63x3.31	273	VO	135	235@5200	.013H	.021H	85
Fury, Satellite	119 [32]	8-3.91x3.31	318	VO	140	230@4400	.013H	.021H	85
Satellite	116	8-4.12x3.38	361	VO	140	265@4400	HY	HY	70
Sport Fury, VIP	119	8-4.25x3.38	383	VO	140	270@4400	HY	HY	70
Sport Fury VIP, Satellite	119 [32]	8-4.25x3.38	383	VO	140	325@4800	HY	HY	70
Belvedere, Satellite	116	8-4.25x3.75	426	VO	150	425@5000	.028C	.032C	70
Fury, Sport Fury, VIP	119	8-4.32x3.75	440	VO	150	365@4600	HY	HY	70
Pontiac - Tempest, LeMans	115	6-3.875x3.245	230	IOC	160	165@4700	HY	HY	93
Tempest, LeMans	115	6-3.875x3.245	230	IOC	195	207@5200	HY	HY	93
Tempest, LeMans	115	8-3.7187x3.746	326	VO	160	250@4600	HY	HY	95
Tempest, LeMans	115	8-3.7187x3.746	326	VO	160	285@5000	HY	HY	95
GTO	115	8-4.0625x3.746	389	VO	160	335@5000	HY	HY	95
Catalina, Star Chief	121 [35]	8-4.0625x3.746	389	VO	160	256@4600	HY	HY	95
Catalina, Star Chief	121 [35]	8-4.0625x3.746	389	VO	160	290@4600	HY	HY	95
Bonneville, Grand Prix	124 [36]	8-4.0625x3.746	389	VO	160	333@5000	HY	HY	95
GTO	115	8-4.0625x3.746	389	VO	160	360@5200	HY	HY	95
2 + 2	121	8-4.0937x3.996	421	VO	160	338@4600	HY	HY	95
2 + 2, Catalina, Star Chief	121 [35]	8-4.0937x3.996	421	VO	160	356@4800	HY	HY	95
2 + 2, Bonneville, Grand Prix	121 [37]	8-4.0937x3.996	421	VO	160	376@5000	HY	HY	95
Rambler - American	106	6-3.75x3.00	199	IO	145	128@4400	HY	HY	85
American (1966 1/2)	106	8-3.75x3.28	290	VO	145	200@4600	HY	HY	100
American (1966 1/2)	106	8-3.75x3.28	290	VO	145	225@4700	HY	HY	100
Classic, Marlin	112	6-3.75x3.50	232	IO	145	145@4300	HY	HY	85
Ambassador	116	6-3.75x3.50	232	IO	145	155@4300	HY	HY	85
Ambassador, Classic, Marlin	116 [41]	8-3.75x3.25	287	VO	145	198@4700	HY	HY	60
Ambassador, Classic, Marlin	116 [41]	8-4.00x3.25	327	VO	145	250@4700	HY	HY	60
Ambassador, Classic, Marlin	116 [41]	8-4.00x3.25	327	VO	145	270@4700	HY	HY	60
Studebaker - Daytona, Commander	109 [42]	6-3.563x3.25	194	IO	130	120@4400	HY	HY	95
Cruiser, Commander	113 [43]	6-3.875x3.25	230	IO	130	140@4400	HY	HY	95

ABBREVIATIONS - FOOTNOTES:

AC - AC Spark Plugs
ATC - After Top Center
BF - Autolite Spark Plugs
BTF - Autolite Spark Plugs
C - Cold Engine
CC - Timing Case Cover
CH - Champion Spark Plugs
CP - Crankshaft Pulley
H - Hot Engine

HO - Horizontal Opposed Cylinders
HY - Hydraulic Valve Lifters
IO - In-line Engine, Overhead Valves
IOC - In-line Engine, Overhead Cam
N - Negative
NA - Not Applicable
P - Positive
TDC - Top Dead Center
VD - Vibration Damper
VO - V-Type Engine, Overhead Valves
WP - Water Pump Housing

1 - Sportwagon - 120 in.
2 - Riviera - 119 in.
3 - 60, Brougham - 133 in.; 75 - 149.8 in.
4 - Chevelle - 115 in.; Chevy II - 110 in.; Corvette - 98 in.
5 - Chevelle - 1/2 N.
6 - Chevelle - 8-1/4 deg.
7 - 4-Bolt Cap - 115 ft. lbs.
8 - Corvette - 3/4 P.
9 - Corvette - 1/4 in.
10 - Corvette - 7 deg.

Tuneup Specifications

Connecting Rod Bolt Torque (ft.-lbs.)	Main Bearing Bolt Torque (ft.-lbs.)	Firing Order	Timing Mark Location	Breaker Point Opens B.T.D.C.	Breaker Point Gap	Cam Angle	Spark Plugs Make	Spark Plugs Model	Gap	Caster Man. Steer. (deg.)	Camber Rt. Wheel (deg.)	Toe-In (inches)	Steering Axis Inclination (deg.)	Cooling System Capacity (qts.)	Crankcase Capacity (qts.)
45	105	15426378	VD	10	.015	27	BF	42	.034	1-1/2N	1/2P	3/16	7-1/2	20.5	4
45	105	15426378	VD	12	.015	27	BF	42	.034	1P	1-1/2P	3/16	7	20.5	4
58	105	15426378	VD	8	.020	23	BF	32	.034	1P	1-1/2P	3/16	7	20.5	4
58	105	15426378	VD	8	.020	23	BF	32	.034	1P	1-1/2P	3/16	7	20.5	4
45	105	15426378	VD	10	.017	29	BTF	42	.034	1-1/2N	1/2P	1/8	7-3/4	23	5
24	70	153624	VD	6	.025	32	BF	82	.034	0	1/4P	1/4	7-1/2	9.5	3.4
24	70	15426378	VD	6	.015	27	BF	42	.034	0	1/4P	1/4	15	15	4
45	105	15426378	VD	10	.015	26	BF	42	.034	1P[24]	1/4P	3/16[25]	7-1/2	20.5	4
45	105	15426378	VD	10	.015	26	BF	42	.034	1P	1/4P	3/16	7-1/2	20.5	4
45	105	15426378	VD	10	.015	26	BF	42	.034	0	1/4P	1/4	7-1/2	20.5	4
45	105	15426378	VD	10	.015	27	BF	42	.034	1P	1/4P	3/16	7-1/2	20.5	4
45	105	15426378	VD	10	.015	27	BF	42	.034	1P	1/4P	3/16	7-1/2	20.5	4
35	65	153624	VD	6	.020	34	AC	46N	.035	1-1/4N	0	1/8	8	17	4
42	80[27]	18436572	CP	7.5	.016	30	AC	45S[28]	.030	1-1/4N	0	1/8	8	17[29]	4
42	80[27]	18436572	VD	7.5	.016	30	AC	44S	.030	1-1/4N	0	1/8	8	17	4
42	80[27]	18436572	VD	7.5	.016	30	AC	44S	.030	1-1/4N	0	1/8	8	17	4
42	80[27]	18436572	CP	7.5	.016	30	AC	44S	.030	1-1/4N	0	1/8	8	16.5	4
42	120	18436572	CP	7.5	.016	30	AC	44S	.030	1-1/4N	0	1/8	8	16.9	4
42	120	18436572	CP	5	.016	30	AC	44S	.030	1-1/4N	1/4P	3/16	10	17.5	4
42	120	18436572	CP	5	.016	30	AC	44S	.030	1-1/4N	1/4P	3/16	10	17.5	4
42	120	18436572	CP	7.5	.016	30	AC	44S	.030	1-1/4N	1/4P	3/16	10	17.5	4
42	120	18436572	CP	7.5	.016	30	AC	44S	.030	2N	1/4P	1/16	11	17.5	5
45	85	153624	WP	5	.020	42	CH	N-14Y	.035	1/2N	1/4P	1/8	7-1/2	12	4
45	85	153624	WP	2.5	.020	42	CH	N-14Y	.035	1/2N	1/4P	1/8	7-1/2	13	4
45	85	18436572	CC	5	.016	30	CH	N-14Y	.035	1/2N	1/4P	1/8	7-1/2	18	4
45	85	18436572	CC	5	.016	30	CH	N-14Y	.035	1/2N	1/4P	1/8	7-1/2	18	4
45	85	18436572	WP	10	.016	30	CH	J-14Y	.035	1/2N	1/4P	1/8	9[33]	21	4
45	85	18436572	CC	12.5	.016	30	CH	J-14Y	.035	1/2N	1/4P	1/8	7-1/2	17	4
45	85	18436572	CC	12.5	.016	30	CH	J-14Y	.035	1/2N	1/4P	1/8	9	17	4
45	85	18436572	CC	12.5	.016	30	CH	J-14Y	.035	1/2N	1/4P	1/8	9[33]	17	4
45	85	18436572	CC	5A	.017	30[34]	CH	N-9Y	.035	1/2N	1/4P	1/8	7-1/2	18	5
45	85	18436572	WP	12.5	.016	30	CH	J-13Y	.035	1/2N	1/4P	1/8	9	17	4
33	100	153624	VD	5	.016	33	AC	44S	.035	1-1/2N	1/4P	1/16	9	13.5	5
33	100	153624	VD	5	.016	33	AC	44S	.035	1-1/2N	1/4P	1/16	9	13.5	5
43	100[27]	18436572	CP	6	.016	30	AC	44S	.035	1-1/2N	1/4P	1/16	9	20	6
43	100[27]	18436572	CP	6	.016	30	AC	44S	.035	1-1/2N	1/4P	1/16	9	20	6
43	100[27]	18436572	CP	6	.016	30	AC	45S	.035	1-1/2N	1/4P	1/16	9	20	6
43	100[27]	18436572	CP	6	.016	30	AC	45S	.035	1-1/2N	1/4P	1/16	8-1/2	20	6
43	100[27]	18436572	CP	6	.016	30	AC	45S	.035	1-1/2N	1/4P	1/16	8-1/2	20	6
43	100[27]	18436572	CP	6	.016	30	AC	45S	.035	1-1/2N	1/4P	1/16	9	20	6
43	100[27]	18436572	CP	6	.016	30	AC	44S	.035	1-1/2N	1/4P	1/16	8-1/2	19.5	6
43	100[27]	18436572	CP	6	.016	30	AC	44S	.035	1-1/2N	1/4P	1/16	8-1/2	19.5	6
43	100[27]	18436572	CP	6	.016	30	AC	44S	.035	1-1/2N	1/4P	1/16	8-1/2	19.5	6
30	85	153624	VD	10[38]	.016	33	CH	N-14Y	.035	1/4P	0	1/8	6-1/2	10.5	4
30	100	18436572	VD	TDC[39]	.016	30	CH	N-14Y	.035	1/4P	0	1/8	6-1/2	14	4
30	100	18436572	VD	TDC	.016	30	CH	N-9Y	.035	1/4P	0	1/8	6-1/2	14	4
30	85	153624	VD	5[40]	.016	33	CH	N-14Y	.035	1/4P	0	1/8	6-1/4	10.5	4
30	85	153624	VD	5[40]	.016	33	CH	N-14Y	.035	1/4P	0	1/8	6-1/4	10.5	4
50	85	18436572	VD	5[40]	.016	30	CH	H-14Y	.035	1/4P	0	1/8	6-1/4	19	4
50	85	18436572	VD	5[40]	.016	30	CH	H-14Y	.035	1/4P	0	1/8	6-1/4	19	4
50	85	18436572	VD	5	.016	30	CH	H-14Y	.035	1/4P	0	1/8	6-1/4	19	4
35	65	153624	VD	8	.016	33	AC	46N	.035	0	1/2P	7/32	6	13.5	4
35	65	153624	VD	4	.016	33	AC	46N	.035	0	1/2P	7/32	6	13.5	4

11 – Corvette – 5 qts.
12 – Chevy II – 1 P.
13 – Chevy II – 7 deg.
14 – Dart – 111 in.
15 – Auto. Trans. – 10 BTDC.
16 – Both Breakers – 36 to 40 deg.
17 – Both Breakers – 37 to 42 deg.
18 – Fairlane – 116 in.
19 – Fairlane – 1/8 in.
20 – Fairlane – 7 deg.
21 – Fairlane – 1/2 P.

22 – Fairlane – 1/4 P.
23 – Comet – 116 in.
24 – Comet – 0 deg.
25 – Comet – 1/4 in.
26 – Jetstar 88 – 123 in.
27 – Rear Main – 120 ft. lbs.
28 – Jetstar 88 – 44 S.
29 – Jetstar 88 – 16.5 qts.
30 – Dynamic 88, Delta 88 – 123 in.
31 – 98 – 126 in.
32 – Satellite – 116 in.

33 – Satellite – 7-1/2 deg.
34 – Both Breakers – 37 to 42 deg.
35 – Star Chief – 124 in.
36 – Grand Prix – 121 in.
37 – Bonneville – 123 in.
38 – Premium Fuel – 13 deg. BTDC.
39 – Premium Fuel – 3 deg. BTDC.
40 – Premium Fuel – 8 deg. BTDC.
41 – Classic, Marlin – 112 in.
42 – 4-Door Models – 113 in.
43 – 2-Door Models – 109 in.

1967	Wheelbase	No. of Cylinders Bore and Stroke	Displacement (cu. in.)	Valve and Cylinder Arrangement	Compression Pressure (lbs.)	Maximum Brake Horsepower	Valve Tappet Clearance Intake	Valve Tappet Clearance Exhaust	Cylinder Bolt Torque (ft. lbs.)
Buick – Special, Skylark	115	6-3.75x3.40	225	VO	160	160@4200	HY	HY	80
Skylark, Sportwagon	115[1]	8-3.75x3.85	340	VO	175	220@4200	HY	HY	80
Special, Skylark	115	8-3.75x3.85	340	VO	175	260@4200	HY	HY	80
GS 400	115	8-4.04x3.90	400	VO	175	340@5000	HY	HY	120
LeSabre	123	8-3.75x3.85	340	VO	175	220@4200	HY	HY	80
LeSabre	123	8-3.75x3.85	340	VO	175	260@4200	HY	HY	80
Wildcat, Electra	126	8-4.1875x3.90	430	VO	175	360@5000	HY	HY	120
Riviera, Riviera "GS"	119	8-4.1875x3.90	430	VO	175	360@5000	HY	HY	120
Special, Skylark	115	8-3.75x3.40	300	VO	175	210@4400	HY	HY	80
Cadillac	129.5[2]	8-4.13x4.00	429	VO	175	340@4600	HY	HY	60
Eldorado	120	8-4.13x4.00	429	VO	175	340@4600	HY	HY	60
Chevrolet, Chevelle	119[3]	6-3.875x3.53	250	IO	130	155@4200	HY	HY	95
Chevrolet, Chevelle	119[3]	8-3.875x3.00	283	VO	150	195@4800	HY	HY	65
Camaro	108	8-4.00x3.25	327	VO	160	210@4600	HY	HY	65
Chevrolet, Chevelle	119[3]	8-4.00x3.25	327	VO	160	275@4800	HY	HY	65
Chevelle	115	8-4.00x3.25	327	VO	160	325@5600	HY	HY	65
Corvette	98	8-4.00x3.25	327	VO	150	350@5800	HY	HY	65
Camaro	108	8-4.00x3.48	350	VO	150	295@4800	HY	HY	65
Chevrolet, Chevelle	119[3]	8-4.094x3.76	396	VO	160	325@4800	HY	HY	80
Chevelle	115	8-4.094x3.76	396	VO	160	350@5200	HY	HY	80
Chevrolet	119	8-4.251x3.76	427	VO	160	385@5200	HY	HY	80
Corvette	98	8-4.251x3.76	427	VO	160	390@5400	HY	HY	80
Corvette	98	8-4.251x3.76	427	VO	150	400@5400	HY	HY	80
Corvette	98	8-4.251x3.76	427	VO	150	435@5800	.024	.028	80
Corvette	98	8-4.00x3.25	327	VO	160	300@5000	HY	HY	65
Chevy II	110	4-3.875x3.25	153	IO	130	90@4000	HY	HY	95
Chevy II	110	6-3.563x3.25	194	IO	130	120@4400	HY	HY	95
Chevelle, Camaro	115[8]	6-3.875x3.25	230	IO	130	140@4400	HY	HY	95
Corvair	108	6-3.4375x2.94	164	HO	130	95@3600	HY	HY	40
Corvair	108	6-3.4375x2.94	164	HO	130	110@4400	HY	HY	40
Chrysler – Newport	124	8-4.25x3.38	383	VO	140	270@4400	HY	HY	70
Newport	124	8-4.25x3.38	383	VO	140	325@4800	HY	HY	70
300, New Yorker	124	8-4.32x3.75	440	VO	150	350@4400	HY	HY	70
Newport, 300, New Yorker	124	8-4.32x3.75	440	VO	150	375@4600	HY	HY	70
Imperial	127	8-4.32x3.75	440	VO	150	350@4400	HY	HY	70
Dodge – Dart, Dart GT	111	6-3.40x3.125	170	IO	125	115@4400	.010H	.013H	65
Dart, Dart GT, Coronet	111[13]	6-3.40x4.125	225	IO	125	145@4000	.010H	.020H	65
Dart, Dart GT, Coronet	111[13]	8-3.63x3.31	273	VO	140	180@4200	.013H	.021H	85
Dart, Dart GT	111	8-3.63x3.31	273	VO	140	235@5200	.013H	.021H	85
Dart GT	111	8-4.25x3.38	383	VO	140	280@4200	HY	HY	70
Charger, Polara	117[15]	8-3.91x3.31	318	VO	140	230@4400	HY	HY	85
Coronet, Polara, Monaco	117[15]	8-4.25x3.38	383	VO	140	270@4400	HY	HY	70
Coronet, Monaco 500	117[15]	8-4.25x3.38	383	VO	140	325@4800	HY	HY	70
Coronet R/T	117	8-4.25x3.75	426	VO	180	425@5000	.028C	.032C	75
Charger, Polara, Monaco	117[15]	8-4.32x3.75	440	VO	150	350@4400	HY	HY	70
Coronet R/T, Polara, Monaco	117[15]	8-4.32x3.75	440	VO	150	375@4600	HY	HY	70
Ford – Falcon	111	6-3.50x2.94	170	IO	195	105@4400	HY	HY	75
Falcon, Futura, Fairlane	111[18]	6-3.684x3.13	200	IO	195	120@4400	HY	HY	75
Mustang	108	6-3.684x3.13	200	IO	195	120@4400	HY	HY	75
Ford	119	6-4.00x3.18	240	IO	175	150@4000	HY	HY	75
Falcon, Futura, Fairlane GT	111[18]	8-4.005x2.87	289	VO	150	200@4400	HY	HY	72
Ford	119	8-4.005x2.87	289	VO	150	200@4400	HY	HY	72
Mustang	108	8-4.005x2.87	289	VO	150	225@4800	HY	HY	72
Mustang	108	8-4.005x2.87	289	VO	150	271@6000	.022H	.024H	72
Fairlane, Fairlane GT	116	8-4.05x3.78	390	VO	180	270@4000	HY	HY	90
Ford	119	8-4.05x3.78	390	VO	180	270@4000	HY	HY	90
Thunderbird, Ford	115[20]	8-4.05x3.78	390	VO	190	315@4600	HY	HY	90

ABBREVIATIONS - FOOTNOTES

AC – AC Spark Plugs	HO – Horizontal Opposed Cylinders
ATC – After Top Center	HY – Hydraulic Valve Lifters
BF – Autolite Spark Plugs	IO – In-line Engine, Overhead Valves
BTF – Autolite Spark Plugs	IOC – In-line Engine, Overhead Cam
C – Cold Engine	N – Negative
CC – Timing Case Cover	NA – Not Applicable
CH – Champion Spark Plugs	P – Positive
CP – Crankshaft Pulley	TR – Transistorized
H – Hot Engine	VD – Vibration Damper
	VO – V-Type Engine, Overhead Valves
	WP – Water Pump Housing

1 – Sportwagon – 120 in.
2 – 60 – 133 in.; 75 – 149.8 in.
3 – Chevelle – 115 in.
4 – Chevelle – 1 N.
5 – Chevelle – 1/2 P.
6 – Chevelle – 8-1/4 deg.
7 – 4-Bolt Cap – 115 ft. lbs.
8 – Camaro – 108 in.
9 – Camaro – 1/2 P.
10 – Camaro – 1/4 P.
11 – Camaro – 8-3/4 deg.

Tuneup Specifications

Connecting Rod Bolt Torque (ft. lbs.)	Main Bearing Bolt Torque (ft. lbs.)	Firing Order	Timing Mark Location	Breaker Point Opens BTDC	Breaker Point Gap	Cam Angle	Spark Plugs Make	Spark Plugs Model	Spark Plugs Gap	Caster Man. Steer. (deg.)	Camber Rt. Wheel (deg.)	Toe-in (in.)	Steering Axis Inclination (deg.)	Cooling System Capacity (qts.)	Crankcase Capacity (qts.)
40	120	165432	VD	5	.016	30	AC	44S	.035	1/2N	1/2P	3/16	8	10.7	4
40	120	18436572	VD	5	.016	30	AC	44S	.033	1/2N	1/2P	3/16	8	11.2	4
40	120	18436572	VD	5	.016	30	AC	44S	.033	1/2N	1/2P	3/16	8	11.2	4
50	115	18436572	VD	2.5	.016	30	AC	44TS	.033	1/2N	1/2P	3/16	8	16.6	4
40	120	18436572	VD	2.5	.016	30	AC	44S	.033	1P	1/4P	1/4	10-3/4	12.7	4
40	120	18436572	VD	2.5	.016	30	AC	44S	.033	1P	1/4P	1/4	10-3/4	12.7	4
50	115	18436572	VD	2.5	.016	30	AC	44TS	.033	1P	1/4P	1/4	10-3/4	16.7	4
50	115	18436572	VD	2.5	.016	30	AC	44TS	.033	1P	1/4P	1/4	10-3/4	16.7	4
40	120	18436572	VD	5	.016	30	AC	44S	.033	1/2N	1/2P	1/4	8	11.2	4
40	95	18726543	VD	5	.016	30	AC	44	.035	1-1/2N	1/8N	1/4	6	18.2	4
40	95	18726543	VD	5	.016	30	AC	44	.035	2N	0	1/16	6	18.2	4
35	65	153624	VD	4	.019	33	AC	46N	.035	3/4P[4]	1/4P[5]	3/16	7-1/2[6]	12	4
35	80	18436572	VD	4	.019	30	AC	45	.035	3/4P[4]	1/4P[5]	3/16	7-1/2[6]	17	4
35	80	18436572	VD	8	.019	30	AC	44	.035	1/2P	1/4P	3/16	8-3/4	16	4
35	80	18436572	VD	8	.019	30	AC	44	.035	3/4P[4]	1/4P[5]	3/16	7-1/2[6]	15	4
35	80	18436572	VD	10	.019	30	AC	44	.038	1N	1/2P	3/16	8-1/4	16	4
35	80	18436572	VD	10	.019	30	AC	44	.035	1P	3/4P	1/4	7	16	4
35	80	18436572	VD	4	.019	30	AC	44	.035	1/2P	1/4P	3/16	8-3/4	16	4
50	95	18436572	VD	4	.019	30	AC	43N	.035	3/4P[4]	1/4P[5]	3/16	7-1/2[6]	22	4
50	95	18436572	VD	4	.019	30	AC	43N	.038	1N	1/2P	3/16	8-1/4	23	4
50	95[7]	18436572	VD	4	.019	30	AC	43N	.035	3/4P	1/4P	3/16	7-1/2	22	4
50	95[7]	18436572	VD	5	.019	30	AC	43N	.035	1P	3/4P	1/4	7	23	5
50	95[7]	18436572	VD	4	.019	30	AC	43N	.035	1P	3/4P	1/4	7	23	5
50	95[7]	18436572	VD	8	TR	TR	AC	43N	.035	1P	3/4P	1/4	7	23	5
35	80	18436572	VD	6	.019	30	AC	44	.035	1P	3/4P	1/4	7	16	3.5
35	65	1342	CP	4	.019	33	AC	46N	.035	1P	1/2P	5/16	7	9	3.5
35	65	153624	VD	4	.019	33	AC	45N	.035	1P	1/2P	5/16	7	11	4
35	65	153624	VD	4	.019	33	AC	45N	.035	1N[9]	1/2P[10]	3/16	8-1/4[11]	11	4
25	55	145236	CP	6[12]	.019	33	AC	46FF	.035	2-1/4P	1P	1/4	6-1/2	NA	4
25	55	145236	VD	14	.019	33	AC	44FF	.031	2-1/4P	1P	1/4	6-1/2	NA	4
45	80	18436572	CC	12.5	.016	30	CH	J-14Y	.035	1/2N	1/4P	1/8	9	17	4
45	80	18436572	CC	12.5	.016	30	CH	J-13Y	.035	1/2N	1/4P	1/8	9	17	4
45	80	18436572	CC	12.5	.016	30	CH	J-13Y	.035	1/2N	1/4P	1/8	9	18	4
45	80	18436572	CC	12.5	.016	30	CH	J-13Y	.035	3/4P	1/4P	1/8	9	18	4
45	85	153624	WP	5	.020	43	CH	N-14Y	.035	1/2N	1/2P	1/8	7-1/2	12	4
45	85	153624	WP	5	.020	43	CH	N-14Y	.035	1/2N	1/2P	1/8	7-1/2	13	4
45	85	18436572	CC	10	.016	30	CH	N-14Y	.035	1/2N	1/2P	1/8	7-1/2	19	4
45	85	18436572	CC	10	.016	29[14]	CH	N-10Y	.035	1/2N	1/2P	1/8	7-1/2	19	4
45	80	18436572	CC	12.5	.016	30	CH	J-13Y	.035	1/2N	1/2P	1/8	7-1/2	17	4
45	80	18436572	CC	5	.016	30	CH	N-14Y	.035	1/2N	1/2P	1/8	7-1/2[16]	17	4
45	80	18436572	CC	12.5	.016	30	CH	J-14Y	.035	1/2N	1/2P	1/8	7-1/2[16]	17	4
45	80	18436572	CC	12.5	.016	30	CH	J-13Y	.035	1/2N	1/2P	1/8	7-1/2[16]	17	4
45	100	18436572	CC	12.5	.016	30[17]	CH	N-10Y	.035	1/2N	1/2P	1/8	7-1/2	18	5
45	80	18436572	CC	12.5	.016	30	CH	J-11Y	.035	1/2N	1/2P	1/8	7-1/2[16]	18	4
45	80	18436572	CC	12.5	.016	30	CH	J-11Y	.035	1/2N	1/2P	1/8	7-1/2[16]	18	4
24	70	153624	VD	6	.025	37	BF	82	.034	1/2N	1/4P	1/4	7	9.6	3.5
24	70	153624	VD	6	.025	37	BF	82	.034	1/2N	1/4P	1/4	7	9.5	3.5
24	70	153624	VD	6	.025	37	BF	82	.034	1P	1P	3/16	6-3/4	9.5	3.5
45	70	153624	VD	6[19]	.025	37	BTF	42	.034	1P	1/2P	3/16	7-1/2	13	4
24	70	15426378	VD	6	.015	27	BF	42	.034	1P	1/4P	1/4	7	15	4
24	70	15426378	VD	6	.015	27	BF	42	.034	1P	1P	3/16	7-1/2	15	4
24	70	15426378	VD	9	.015	27	BF	42	.034	1P	1P	3/16	6-3/4	15	4
45	70	15426378	VD	12	.020	34	BF	32	.034	1P	1P	3/16	6-3/4	15	4
45	105	15426378	VD	10	.015	26	BF	42	.034	1/2N	1/4P	1/4	7	20.5	4
45	105	15426378	VD	10	.017	29	BF	42	.034	1P	1/2P	3/16	7-1/2	20.5	4
45	105	15426378	VD	10	.017	29	BF	42	.034	1P	1/2P	3/16	7[21]	20.5	4

12 – With Auto. Trans. – 14 deg.
13 – Coronet – 117 in.
14 – Both Breakers – 36 to 40 deg.
15 – Polara, Monaco – 122 in.
16 – Polara, Monaco – 9 deg.
17 – Both Breakers – 37 to 42 deg.
18 – With Auto. Trans. – 10 deg.
19 – Fairlane, GT – 116 in.
20 – Ford – 119 in.
21 – Ford – 7-1/2 deg.
22 – T-Bird 4-Door Landau – 117 in.

23 – Thunderbird – 7 deg.
24 – Cougar – 111 in.
25 – Cougar – 1/4 P.
26 – Cougar – 1 P.
27 – Cougar – 6-3/4 deg.
28 – Cougar – 6-3/4 deg.
29 – Both Breakers – 36 to 40 deg.
30 – Rear Main Bearing – 120 ft. lbs.
31 – Fury – 119 in.
32 – Fury – 9 deg.
33 – Both Breakers – 37 to 42 deg.

34 – Belvedere GTX – 116 in.
35 – Belvedere GTX – 7-1/2 deg.
36 – Executive – 124 in.
37 – Grand Prix – 121 in.
38 – Premium Fuel – 13 deg.
39 – Premium Fuel – 8 deg.
40 – Premium Fuel – 3 deg.
41 – Rebel, Marlin, Ambassador – 6-1/8 deg.
42 – Rebel – 114 in.; Marlin, Ambassador – 118 in.

1967

	Wheelbase	No. of Cylinders Bore and Stroke	Displacement (cu. in.)	Valve and Cylinder Arrangement	Compression Pressure (lbs.)	Maximum Brake Horsepower	Valve Tappet Clearance Intake	Valve Tappet Clearance Exhaust	Cylinder Bolt Torque (ft.-lbs.)
Fairlane, Fairlane GT	116	8-4.05x3.78	390	VO	190	320@4000	HY	HY	90
Mustang	108	8-4.05x3.78	390	VO	190	320@4000	HY	HY	90
Ford - Thunderbird	119[22]	8-4.13x3.98	428	VO	190	345@4600	HY	HY	110
Ford	119	8-4.13x3.98	428	VO	190	360@5400	HY	HY	110
Ford	119	8-4.23x3.78	427	VO	180	410@5600	.028	.025	110
Ford	119	8-4.23x3.78	427	VO	180	425@6000	.028	.025	110
Lincoln Continental	126	8-4.38x3.83	462	VO	180	340@4600	HY	HY	145
Mercury - Comet	116	6-3.684x3.13	200	IO	195	120@4400	HY	HY	75
Comet, Cyclone, Cougar	116[24]	8-4.00x2.87	289	VO	150	200@4400	HY	HY	72
Cougar	111	8-4.00x2.87	289	VO	150	225@4800	HY	HY	72
Comet, Cyclone	116	8-4.05x3.78	390	VO	150	270@4400	HY	HY	90
Cyclone GT, Cougar	116[24]	8-4.05x3.78	390	VO	190	320@4800	HY	HY	90
Monterey, Montclair	123	8-4.05x3.78	390	VO	180	270@4400	HY	HY	90
Park Lane, Brougham, Marquis	123	8-4.054x3.984	410	VO	190	330@4600	HY	HY	90
S-55	123	8-4.13x3.984	428	VO	190	345@4600	HY	HY	110
Oldsmobile - F-85	115	6-3.875x3.53	250	IO	160	155@4200	HY	HY	95
Cutlass	115	8-3.9375x3.385	330	VO	175	250@4800	HY	HY	80
Cutlass Supreme	115	8-3.9375x3.385	330	VO	175	320@5200	HY	HY	80
4-4-2	115	8-4.00x3.975	400	VO	175	350@5000	HY	HY	80
Delmont 88	123	8-3.9375x3.385	330	VO	175	250@4800	HY	HY	80
Delmont 88	123	8-4.125x3.975	425	VO	175	300@4400	HY	HY	80
Delta 88, Custom	123	8-4.125x3.975	425	VO	175	300@4400	HY	HY	80
98	126	8-4.125x3.975	425	VO	175	365@4800	HY	HY	80
Toronado	119	8-4.125x3.975	425	VO	175	385@4800	HY	HY	80
Plymouth - Valiant, Signet	108	6-3.40x3.125	170	IO	125	115@4400	.010H	.020H	65
Valiant, Signet, Barracuda	108	6-3.40x4.125	225	IO	125	145@4000	.010H	.020H	65
Valiant, Signet, Barracuda	108	8-3.63x3.31	273	VO	140	180@4200	.013H	.021H	85
Valiant, Signet, Barracuda	108	8-3.63x3.31	273	VO	140	235@5200	.013H	.021H	85
Barracuda	108	8-4.25x3.38	383	VO	140	280@4200	HY	HY	70
Belvedere, Fury	116[31]	6-3.40x4.125	225	IO	125	145@4000	.010H	.020H	65
Belvedere	116	8-3.63x3.31	273	VO	140	180@4200	.013H	.021H	85
Belvedere, Satellite, Fury	116[31]	8-3.91x3.31	318	VO	140	230@4400	HY	HY	85
Belvedere, Satellite, Fury	116[31]	8-4.25x3.38	383	VO	140	270@4400	HY	HY	70
Belvedere, Satellite, Fury	116[31]	8-4.25x3.38	383	VO	140	325@4800	HY	HY	70
Belvedere, Satellite	116	8-4.25x3.75	426	VO	180	425@5000	.028C	.032C	75
Fury	119	8-4.32x3.75	440	VO	150	350@4400	HY	HY	70
Fury, Belvedere GTX	119[34]	8-4.32x3.75	440	VO	150	375@4400	HY	HY	70
Pontiac - Tempest, LeMans	115	6-3.875x3.245	230	IOC	160	165@4700	HY	HY	95
Tempest, LeMans	115	6-3.875x3.245	230	IOC	195	215@5200	HY	HY	95
Tempest, LeMans	115	6-3.875x3.245	230	IOC	160	250@4600	HY	HY	95
Tempest, LeMans	115	8-3.7187x3.746	326	VO	160	285@5000	HY	HY	95
GTO	115	8-4.12x3.746	400	VO	160	335@5000	HY	HY	95
GTO Ram Air	115	8-4.12x3.746	400	VO	160	360@5400	HY	HY	95
Catalina, Executive	121[36]	8-4.12x3.746	400	VO	160	265@4600	HY	HY	95
Catalina, Executive	121[36]	8-4.12x3.746	400	VO	160	290@4600	HY	HY	95
Catalina, Executive	121[36]	8-4.12x3.746	400	VO	160	325@4800	HY	HY	95
Bonneville	124	8-4.12x3.746	400	VO	160	333@5000	HY	HY	95
Grand Prix	121	8-4.12x3.746	400	VO	160	350@5000	HY	HY	95
2 + 2, Catalina	121	8-4.12x3.996	428	VO	200	360@4600	HY	HY	95
Bonneville, Grand Prix	124[37]	8-4.12x3.996	428	VO	200	376@5100	HY	HY	95
Rambler - American	106	6-3.75x3.00	199	IO	145	128@4400	HY	HY	85
American, Marlin, Rebel	114[42]	6-3.75x3.50	232	IO	145	145@4300	HY	HY	85
American, Rebel, Ambassador	106[42]	6-3.75x3.50	232	IO	145	155@4400	HY	HY	85
American	106	8-3.75x3.28	290	VO	145	225@4700	HY	HY	100
Rebel, Ambassador	114[42]	8-3.75x3.28	290	VO	145	200@4600	HY	HY	100
Ambassador, Rebel	118[42]	8-4.08x3.28	343	VO	145	235@4400	HY	HY	100
Ambassador, Rebel	118[42]	8-4.08x3.28	343	VO	145	280@4800	HY	HY	100

ABBREVIATIONS - FOOTNOTES

AC - AC Spark Plugs
ATC - After Top Center
BF - Autolite Spark Plugs
BTF - Autolite Spark Plugs
C - Cold Engine
CC - Timing Case Cover
CH - Champion Spark Plugs
CP - Crankshaft Pulley
H - Hot Engine

HO - Horizontal Opposed Cylinders
HY - Hydraulic Valve Lifters
IO - In-line Engine, Overhead Valves
IOC - In-line Engine, Overhead Cam
N - Negative
NA - Not Applicable
P - Positive
TR - Transistorized
VD - Vibration Damper
VO - V-Type Engine, Overhead Valves
WP - Water Pump Housing

1 - Sportwagon - 120 in.
2 - 60 - 133 in.; 75 - 149.8 in.
3 - Chevelle - 115 in.
4 - Chevelle - 1 N.
5 - Chevelle - 1/2 P.
6 - Chevelle - 8-1/4 deg.
7 - 4-Bolt Cap - 115 ft. lbs.
8 - Camaro - 108 in.
9 - Camaro - 1/2 P.
10 - Camaro - 1/4 P.
11 - Camaro - 8-3/4 deg.

Connecting Rod Bolt Torque (ft.-lbs.)	Main Bearing Bolt Torque (ft.-lbs.)	Firing Order	Timing Mark Location	Breaker Point Opens B.T.D.C.	Breaker Point Gap	Cam Angle	Spark Plugs Make	Spark Plugs Model	Spark Plugs Gap	Caster Man. Steer. (deg.)	Camber Rt. Wheel (deg.)	Toe-In (inches)	Steering Axis Inclination (deg.)	Cooling System Capacity (qts.)	Crankcase Capacity (qts.)
45	105	15426378	VD	12	.015	26	BF	42	.034	1/2N	1/4P	1/4	7	20.5	4
45	105	15426378	VD	12	.015	27	BF	32	.034	1P	1P	3/16	6-3/4	20.5	4
45	105	15426378	VD	12	.020	32	BF	32	.030	1P	1/2P	3/16	7-1/2[23]	20.5	4
45	105	15426378	VD	12	.020	32	BF	32	.030	1P	1/2P	3/16	7-1/2	20.5	4
58	105	15426378	VD	8	.020	23	BF	32	.034	1P	1/2P	3/16	7-1/2	20.5	4
58	105	15426378	VD	8	.020	23	BF	32	.034	1P	1/2P	3/16	7-1/2	20.5	4
45	105	15426378	VD	10	.017	29	BTF	42	.034	1-1/2N	1/2P	1/8	7-3/4	23	5
24	70	153624	CC	6	.025	32	BF	82	.034	1/2N	1/4P	1/4	7-1/2	9.5	3.4
24	70	15426378	VD	6	.015	26	BF	42	.034	1/2N[25]	1/4P[26]	1/4[27]	7-1/2[28]	15	4
24	70	15426378	VD	6	.015	26	BF	42	.034	1/4P	1P	3/16	6-3/4	15	4
45	105	15426378	VD	10	.015	26	BF	42	.034	1/2N	1/4P	1/4	7-1/2	20.5	4
45	105	15426378	VD	12	.015	26	BF	42	.034	1/2N[25]	1/4P[26]	1/4[27]	7-1/2[28]	20.5	4
45	105	15426378	VD	10	.015	26	BF	42	.034	1P	1/4P	3/16	7-1/2	20.5	4
45	105	15426378	VD	10	.017	29	BF	42	.034	1P	1/4P	3/16	7-1/2	20.5	4
45	105	15426378	VD	10	.017	29	BF	42	.034	1P	1/4P	3/16	7-1/2	20.5	4
35	65	153624	VD	7.5	.016	34	AC	46N	.035	1-1/4N	0	1/8	8	12	4
42	80[30]	18436572	CP	7.5	.016	30	AC	45S	.030	1-1/4N	0	1/8	8	17	4
42	80[30]	18436572	VD	7.5	.016	30	AC	44S	.030	1-1/4N	0	1/8	8	17	4
42	120	18436572	CP	7.5	.016	30	AC	44S	.030	1-1/4N	0	1/8	8	17	4
42	80[30]	18436572	CP	7.5	.016	30	AC	44S	.030	1-1/4N	1/4P	3/16	10	16.5	4
42	120	18436572	CP	5	.016	30	AC	44S	.030	1-1/4N	1/4P	3/16	10	17.5	4
42	120	18436572	CP	5	.016	30	AC	44S	.030	1-1/4N	1/4P	3/16	10	17.5	4
42	120	18436572	CP	7.5	.016	30	AC	44S	.030	1-1/4N	1/4P	3/16	10	17.5	4
42	120	18436572	CP	7.5	.016	30	AC	44S	.030	2N	1/4P	1/16	11	17.5	4
45	85	153624	WP	5	.020	43	CH	N-14Y	.035	1/2N	1/4P	1/8	7-1/2	12	4
45	85	153624	WP	5	.020	43	CH	N-14Y	.035	1/2N	1/4P	1/8	7-1/2	13	4
45	85	18436572	CC	10	.016	30	CH	N-14Y	.035	1/2N	1/4P	1/8	7-1/2	19	4
45	85	18436572	CC	10	.016	29[29]	CH	N-10Y	.035	1/2N	1/4P	1/8	7-1/2	19	4
45	80	18436572	CC	12.5	.016	29	CH	N-13Y	.035	1/2N	1/4P	1/8	7-1/2	17	4
45	85	153624	WP	5	.019	43	CH	N-14Y	.035	1/2N	1/4P	1/8	7-1/2[32]	13	4
45	85	18436572	CC	10	.016	30	CH	N-14Y	.035	1/2N	1/4P	1/8	7-1/2	19	4
45	85	18436572	CC	10	.016	30	CH	N-14Y	.035	1/2N	1/4P	1/8	7-1/2[32]	19	4
45	80	18436572	CC	12.5	.016	30	CH	J-14Y	.035	1/2N	1/4P	1/8	7-1/2[32]	17	4
45	80	18436572	CC	12.5	.016	30	CH	J-11Y	.035	1/2N	1/4P	1/8	7-1/2[32]	17	4
45	100	18436572	CC	12.5	.016	30[33]	CH	N-10Y	.035	1/2N	1/4P	1/8	7-1/2	18	5
45	80	18436572	CC	12.5	.016	30	CH	J-11Y	.035	1/2N	1/4P	1/8	9	18	4
45	80	18436572	CC	12.5	.016	30	CH	J-11Y	.035	1/2N	1/4P	1/8	9[35]	18	4
33	100	153624	VD	5	.016	33	AC	44N	.035	1-1/2N	1/4P	1/16	9	12.1	5
33	100	153624	CP	5	.016	33	AC	44N	.035	1-1/2N	1/4P	1/16	9	12.1	5
43	100[30]	153624	CP	5	.016	33	AC	44N	.035	1-1/2N	1/4P	1/16	9	12.1	5
43	100[30]	18436572	CP	6	.016	30	AC	45S	.035	1-1/2N	1/4P	1/16	9	18.6	6
43	100[30]	18436572	CP	6	.016	30	AC	44S	.035	1-1/2N	1/4P	1/16	9	17.8	6
43	100[30]	18436572	CP	6	.016	30	AC	45S	.035	1-1/2N	1/4P	1/16	8-1/2	18	6
43	100[30]	18436572	CP	6	.016	30	AC	45S	.035	1-1/2N	1/4P	1/16	8-1/2	18	6
43	100[30]	18436572	CP	6	.016	30	AC	45S	.035	1-1/2N	1/4P	1/16	8-1/2	18	6
43	100[30]	18436572	CP	6	.016	30	AC	45S	.035	1-1/2N	1/4P	1/16	8-1/2	18.6	6
43	100[30]	18436572	CP	6	.016	30	AC	44S	.035	1-1/2N	1/4P	1/16	8-1/2	17.2	6
43	100[30]	18436572	CP	6	.016	30	AC	44S	.035	1-1/2N	1/4P	1/16	8-1/2	17.2	6
30	85	153624	VD	10[38]	.016	33	CH	N-14Y	.035	0	0	1/8	6-1/2	10.5	4
30	85	153624	VD	5[39]	.016	33	CH	N-14Y	.035	0	0	1/8	6-1/2[41]	10.5	4
30	85	153624	VD	5[39]	.016	33	CH	N-14Y	.035	0	0	1/8	6-1/2[41]	10.5	4
30	105	18436572	VD	TDC[40]	.016	30	CH	N-12Y	.035	0	0	1/8	6-1/2	13	4
30	105	18436572	VD	TDC[40]	.016	30	CH	N-12Y	.035	0	0	1/8	6-1/8	13	4
30	105	18436572	VD	TDC	.016	30	CH	N-12Y	.035	0	0	1/8	6-1/8	14	4
30	105	18436572	VD	TDC	.016	30	CH	N-12Y	.035	0	0	1/8	6-1/8	14	4

12 - With Auto. Trans. - 14 deg.
13 - Coronet - 117 in.
14 - Both Breakers - 36 to 40 deg.
15 - Polara, Monaco - 122 in.
16 - Polara, Monaco - 9 deg.
17 - Both Breakers - 37 to 42 deg.
18 - With Auto. Trans. - 10 deg.
19 - Fairlane, GT - 116 in.
20 - Ford - 119 in.
21 - Ford - 7-1/2 deg.
22 - T-Bird 4-Door Landau - 117 in.
23 - Thunderbird - 7 deg.
24 - Cougar - 111 in.
25 - Cougar - 1/4 P.
26 - Cougar - 1 P.
27 - Cougar - 6-3/4 deg.
28 - Cougar - 6-3/4 deg.
29 - Both Breakers - 36 to 40 deg.
30 - Rear Main Bearing - 120 ft. lbs.
31 - Fury - 119 in.
32 - Fury - 9 deg.
33 - Both Breakers - 37 to 42 deg.
34 - Belvedere GTX - 116 in.
35 - Belvedere GTX - 7-1/2 deg.
36 - Executive - 124 in.
37 - Grand Prix - 121 in.
38 - Premium Fuel - 13 deg.
39 - Premium Fuel - 8 deg.
40 - Premium Fuel - 3 deg.
41 - Rebel, Marlin, Ambassador - 6-1/8 deg.
42 - Rebel - 114 in.; Marlin, Ambassador - 118 in.

1968

	Wheelbase	No. of Cylinders Bore and Stroke	Displacement (cu. in.)	Valve and Cylinder Arrangement	Compression Pressure (lbs.)	Maximum Brake Horsepower	Valve Tappet Clearance Intake	Valve Tappet Clearance Exhaust	Cylinder Bolt Torque (ft. lbs.)
Buick - Special, Skylark	116	6-3.875x3.53	250	IO	165	155@4200	HY	HY	95
Special Deluxe, Skylark Custom	116	8-3.80x3.85	350	VO	175	230@4400	HY	HY	75
Sportwagon, GS "350"	121¹	8-3.80x3.85	350	VO	175	280@4600	HY	HY	75
GS "400"	112	8-4.04x3.90	400	VO	175	340@5000	HY	HY	100
LeSabre	123	8-3.80x3.85	350	VO	175	230@4400	HY	HY	75
LeSabre	123	8-3.80x3.85	350	VO	175	280@4600	HY	HY	75
Wildcat, Electra, Riviera	126⁴	8-4.1875x3.90	430	VO	195	360@5000	HY	HY	100
Cadillac	129⁵	8-4.30x4.06	472	VO	175	375@4400	HY	HY	115
Eldorado	120	8-4.30x4.06	472	VO	175	375@4400	HY	HY	115
Chevrolet, Chevelle	119⁷	6-3.875x3.53	250	IO	130	155@4200	HY	HY	95
Chevrolet, Chevelle	119⁷	8-3.875x3.25	307	VO	150	200@4600	HY	HY	65
Chevrolet, Chevelle	119⁷	8-4.001x3.25	327	VO	160	250@4800	HY	HY	65
Chevrolet, Chevelle	119⁷	8-4.001x3.25	327	VO	160	275@4800	HY	HY	65
Corvette	98	8-4.001x3.25	327	VO	160	300@5000	HY	HY	65
Chevelle	112⁷	8-4.001x3.25	327	VO	150	325@5600	HY	HY	65
Corvette	98	8-4.001x3.25	327	VO	150	350@5800	HY	HY	65
Chevrolet, SS 396	119⁷	8-4.094x3.76	396	VO	160	325@4800	HY	HY	80
SS 396	112	8-4.094x3.76	396	VO	160	350@5200	HY	HY	80
Chevrolet	119	8-4.251x3.76	427	VO	160	385@5200	HY	HY	80
Corvette	98	8-4.251x3.76	427	VO	160	390@5400	HY	HY	80
Corvette	98	8-4.251x3.76	427	VO	150	400@5400	HY	HY	80
Corvette	98	8-4.251x3.76	427	VO	150	435@5400	.024	.028	80
Chevy II	111	4-3.875x3.25	153	IO	130	90@4000	HY	HY	95
Chevy II, Camaro	111¹⁵	6-3.875x3.25	230	IO	130	140@4400	HY	HY	95
Chevy II, Camaro	111¹⁵	6-3.875x3.53	250	IO	130	155@4200	HY	HY	95
Chevy II	111	8-3.875x3.25	307	VO	150	200@4600	HY	HY	65
Camaro	108	8-4.001x3.25	327	VO	160	210@4600	HY	HY	65
Chevy II, Camaro	111¹⁵	8-4.001x3.25	327	VO	160	275@4800	HY	HY	65
Chevy II, Camaro	111¹⁵	8-4.00x3.48	350	VO	160	295@4800	HY	HY	65
Camaro	108	8-4.094x3.76	396	VO	150	325@4800	HY	HY	80
Corvair, Monza	108	6-3.4375x2.94	164	HO	130	95@3600	HY	HY	40
Corvair, Monza	108	6-3.4375x2.94	164	HO	130	110@4400	HY	HY	40
Corvair, Monza	108	6-3.4375x2.94	164	HO	130	140@5200	HY	HY	40
Chrysler - Newport	124	8-4.25x3.38	383	VO	140	290@4400	HY	HY	70
Newport	124	8-4.25x3.38	383	VO	140	330@5000	HY	HY	70
New Yorker, 300	124	8-4.32x3.75	440	VO	150	350@4400	HY	HY	70
New Yorker, 300, Newport	124	8-4.32x3.75	440	VO	150	375@4600	HY	HY	70
Imperial	127	8-4.32x3.75	440	VO	150	350@4400	HY	HY	70
Dodge - Dart, Dart GT	111	6-3.40x3.125	170	IO	125	115@4400	.010H	.020H	65
Dart, Dart GT, Coronet	111²¹	6-3.40x4.125	225	IO	125	145@4000	.010H	.020H	65
Dart, Dart GT, Coronet	111²¹	8-3.63x3.31	273	VO	135	190@4400	HY	HY	85
Dart, Dart GT	111	8-3.91x3.31	318	VO	135	230@4400	HY	HY	85
Dart GTS	111	8-4.04x3.31	340	VO	140	275@5000	HY	HY	95
Dart GTS	111	8-4.25x3.38	383	VO	140	300@4400	HY	HY	70
Coronet, Charger	117	8-3.91x3.31	318	VO	135	230@4400	HY	HY	85
Coronet, Charger	117	8-4.25x3.38	383	VO	140	290@4400	HY	HY	70
Coronet, Charger	117	8-4.25x3.38	383	VO	140	330@5000	HY	HY	70
Coronet R/T, Charger R/T	117	8-4.32x3.75	440	VO	150	375@4600	HY	HY	70
Coronet R/T, Charger R/T	117	8-4.25x3.75	426	VO	150	425@5000	.028C	.032C	75
Polara	122	8-3.91x3.31	318	VO	135	230@4400	HY	HY	85
Polara, Monaco	122	8-4.25x3.38	383	VO	140	290@4400	HY	HY	70
Polara, Monaco	122	8-4.25x3.38	383	VO	140	330@5000	HY	HY	70
Polara, Monaco	122	8-4.32x3.75	440	VO	150	375@4600	HY	HY	70
Ford - Falcon	110.9	6-3.50x2.94	170	IO	175	100@4000	HY	HY	75
Falcon Deluxe, Fairlane	110.9²⁵	6-3.68x3.13	200	IO	175	115@3800	HY	HY	75
Mustang	108	6-3.68x3.13	200	IO	175	115@3800	HY	HY	75
Ford	119	6-4.00x3.18	240	IO	175	150@4000	HY	HY	75
Mustang, Falcon, Deluxe	108²⁶	8-4.00x2.87	289	VO	150	195@4600	HY	HY	72
Ford LTD, Torino GT	119²⁵	8-4.00x3.00	302	VO	150	210@4600	HY	HY	72
Mustang GT, Falcon	108²⁶	8-4.00x3.00	302	VO	150	230@4800	HY	HY	90
Ford, Fairlane	119²⁵	8-4.05x3.78	390	VO	180	265@4400	HY	HY	90
Thunderbird, Ford	114.7³¹	8-4.05x3.78	390	VO	190	315@4600	HY	HY	90
Mustang GT	108	8-4.05x3.78	390	VO	190	325@4800	HY	HY	90
Torino GT	116	8-4.05x3.78	390	VO	190	335@4800	HY	HY	90
Ford	119	8-4.13x3.98	428	VO	190	340@4600	HY	HY	90

ABBREVIATIONS - FOOTNOTES

AC - AC Spark Plugs
ATC - After Top Center
BF - Autolite Spark Plugs
BTF - Autolite Spark Plugs
C - Cold Engine
CC - Timing Case Cover
CH - Champion Spark Plugs
CP - Crankshaft Pulley
H - Hot Engine
HO - Horizontal Opposed Cylinders
HY - Hydraulic Valve Lifters

IO - In-line Engine, Overhead Valves
IOC - In-line Engine, Overhead Cam
MP - Magnetic Pulse Ignition
N - Negative
NA - Not Applicable
P - Positive
VD - Vibration Damper
VO - V-Type Engine, Overhead Valves
WP - Water Pump Housing

1 - GS "350" - 112 in.
2 - GS "350" - CP
3 - GS "350" - 10 qts.

4 - Riviera - 119 in.
5 - 60 and Brougham - 133 in.; 75 - 149.8 in.
6 - 75 - 23.8 qts.
7 - Chevelle 4-Door Sedans - 116 in.;
    2-Door Sedans - 112 in.
8 - Auto. Trans. - 4 BTDC.
9 - Chevelle - 1 N.
10 - Chevelle - 1/2 P.
11 - Chevelle - 8-1/4 deg.
12 - Chevelle - 16 qts.
13 - 4-Bolt Cap - 105 ft. lbs.
14 - Chevelle SS 396 - 24 qts.
15 - Camaro - 108 in.

Tuneup Specifications

Connecting Rod Bolt Torque (ft. lbs.)	Main Bearing Bolt Torque (ft. lbs.)	Firing Order	Timing Mark Location	Breaker Point Opens BTDC	Breaker Point Gap	Cam Angle	Make	Spark Plugs Model	Gap	Caster Man. Steer. (deg.)	Camber Kr. Wheel (deg.)	Toe-in (in.)	Steering Axis Inclination (deg.)	Cooling System Capacity (qts.)	Crankcase Capacity (qts.)
35	65	153624	VD	0	.019	33	AC	46N	.035	1/2N	1/2P	3/16	8	11.3	4
35	110	18436572	VD	0	.016	30	AC	45TS	.030	1/2N	1/2P	3/16	8	13.5	4
35	110	18436572	VD[2]	0	.016	30	AC	45TS	.030	1/2N	1/2P	3/16	8	13.5[2]	4
45	110	18436572	VD	0	.016	30	AC	44TS	.030	1/2N	1/2P	3/16	8	15	4
35	110	18436572	VD	0	.016	30	AC	45TS	.030	1P	1/4P	1/4	10-3/4	13.2	4
35	110	18436572	VD	0	.016	30	AC	45TS	.030	1P	1/4P	1/4	10-3/4	13.2	4
45	110	18436572	VD	0	.016	30	AC	44TS	.030	1P	1/4P	1/4	10-3/4	13.2	4
40	90	15634278	CP	5	.016	30	AC	44N	.035	1P	1/4P	1/4	6	20.8[6]	4
40	90	15634278	CP	5	.016	30	AC	44N	.035	2N	0	1/16	6	20.8	4
35	65	153624	VD	TDC[8]	.019	33	AC	46N	.035	3/4P[9]	1/4P[10]	3/16	7-1/2[11]	12	4
50	80	18436572	VD	2	.019	30	AC	45S	.035	3/4P[9]	1/4P[10]	3/16	7-1/2[11]	17	4
50	80	18436572	VD	4	.019	30	AC	44S	.035	3/4P[9]	1/4P[10]	3/16	7-1/2[11]	15[12]	4
50	80	18436572	VD	TDC[8]	.019	30	AC	44	.035	3/4P[9]	1/4P[10]	3/16	7-1/2[11]	15[12]	4
50	80	18436572	VD	4	.019	30	AC	44	.035	1P	3/4P	1/4	7	15	4
50	80	18436572	VD	4	.019	30	AC	44	.035	1P	3/4P	1/4	7	17	4
50	80	18436572	VD	4	.019	30	AC	44	.035	1P	3/4P	1/4	7	15	4
50	95[13]	18436572	VD	4	.019	30	AC	43N	.035	3/4P[9]	1/4P[10]	3/16	7-1/2[11]	22[14]	4
50	95[13]	18436572	VD	TDC	.019	30	AC	43N	.035	1N	1/2P	3/16	8-1/2	24	4
50	95[13]	18436572	VD	4	.019	30	AC	43N	.035	3/4P	1/4P	3/16	7-1/2	22	4
50	95[13]	18436572	VD	4	.019	30	AC	43N	.035	1P	3/4P	1/4	7	22	5
50	95[13]	18436572	VD	4	.019	30	AC	43N	.035	1P	3/4P	1/4	7	22	5
50	95[13]	18436572	VD	4	MP	MP	AC	43N	.035	1P	3/4P	1/4	7	22	5
35	65	1342	VD	TDC[8]	.019	33	AC	46N	.035	1/2P	1/4P	3/16	8-3/4	9	4
35	65	153624	VD	TDC[8]	.019	33	AC	46N	.035	1/2P	1/4P	3/16	8-3/4	12	4
35	65	153624	VD	TDC[8]	.019	33	AC	46N	.035	1/2P	1/4P	3/16	8-3/4	12	4
50	80	18436572	VD	2	.019	30	AC	45S	.035	1/2P	1/4P	3/16	8-3/4	17	4
50	80	18436572	VD	2ATC[16]	.019	30	AC	44	.035	1/2P	1/4P	3/16	8-3/4	16	4
50	80	18436572	VD	TDC[8]	.019	30	AC	44	.035	1/2P	1/4P	3/16	8-3/4	16	4
50	80	18436572	VD	TDC[8]	.019	30	AC	44	.035	1/2P	1/4P	3/16	8-3/4	16	4
50	95[13]	18436572	VD	4	.019	30	AC	43N	.035	1/2P	1/4P	3/16	8-3/4	23	4
25	55	145236	CP	6[17]	.019	33	AC	46FF	.035	2-1/4P	1P	1/4	6-1/2	NA	4
25	55	145236	VD	4[18]	.019	33	AC	44FF	.031	2-1/4P	1P	1/4	6-1/2	NA	4
25	55	145236	VD	4	.019	33	AC	44FF	.031	2-1/4P	1P	1/4	6-1/2	NA	4
45	85	18436572	VD	TDC[19]	.016	30	CH	J-14Y	.035	1/2N	1/4P	1/8	9	17	4
45	85	18436572	VD	5	.016	30	CH	J-11Y	.035	1/2N	1/4P	1/8	9	17	4
45	85	18436572	VD	7.5	.016	30	CH	J-13Y	.035	1/2N	1/4P	1/8	9	18	4
45	85	18436572	VD	5	.016	30	CH	J-11Y	.035	1/2N	1/4P	1/8	9	18	4
45	85	18436572	VD	7.5	.016	30	CH	J-13Y	.035	3/4P	1/4P	1/8	9	17	5
45	85	153624	VD	5ATC[20]	.020	43	CH	N-14Y	.035	1/2N	1/4P	1/8	7-1/2	12	4
45	85	153624	VD	TDC	.020	43	CH	N-14Y	.035	1/2N	1/4P	1/8	7-1/2	13	4
45	85	18436572	VD	5ATC[20]	.016	31	CH	N-14Y	.035	1/2N	1/4P	1/8	7-1/2	19	4
45	85	18436572	VD	5ATC[20]	.016	31	CH	N-14Y	.035	1/2N	1/4P	1/8	7-1/2	18	4
45	85	18436572	VD	TDC[22]	.016	30[23]	CH	N-9Y	.035	1/2N	1/4P	1/8	7-1/2	17	4
45	85	18436572	VD	TDC[22]	.016	31	CH	J-11Y	.035	1/2N	1/4P	1/8	7-1/2	18	4
45	85	18436572	VD	5ATC[20]	.016	31	CH	N-14Y	.035	1/2N	1/4P	1/8	7-1/2	18	4
45	85	18436572	VD	TDC[19]	.016	31	CH	J-14Y	.035	1/2N	1/4P	1/8	7-1/2	17	4
45	85	18436572	VD	TDC[22]	.016	31	CH	J-11Y	.035	1/2N	1/4P	1/8	7-1/2	18	4
45	85	18436572	VD	TDC[22]	.016	30[24]	CH	J-11Y	.035	1/2N	1/4P	1/8	7-1/2	18	4
45	100	18436572	VD	TDC	.016	30[23]	CH	N-10Y	.035	1/2N	1/4P	1/8	7-1/2	18	5
45	85	18436572	VD	5ATC[20]	.016	31	CH	N-14Y	.035	1/2N	1/4P	1/8	9	18	4
45	85	18436572	VD	TDC[19]	.016	31	CH	J-14Y	.035	1/2N	1/4P	1/8	9	17	4
45	85	18436572	VD	TDC[22]	.016	31	CH	J-11Y	.035	1/2N	1/4P	1/8	9	17	4
45	85	18436572	VD	TDC[22]	.016	30[24]	CH	J-11Y	.035	1/2N	1/4P	1/8	9	17	4
24	70	153624	CC	6	.025	37	BF	82	.034	1/2P	1/4P	1/4	7	9.5	3.5
24	70	153624	VD	6	.025	37	BF	82	.034	1/2P	1/4P	1/4	7	9.5	3.5
24	70	153624	VD	6	.025	37	BF	82	.034	1/4P	1P	3/16	6-3/4	9.5	3.5
45	70	153624	CC	6	.025	37	BF	42	.034	1P	1P	3/16	7-3/4	13	4
24	70	15426378	VD	6	.017	27	BF	42	.034	1/4P[27]	1P[28]	3/16[29]	6-3/4[30]	15	4
24	70	15426378	VD	6	.017	29	BF	32	.034	1P[27]	1/2P[28]	3/16[29]	7-3/4[30]	15	4
24	70	15426378	VD	6	.017	29	BF	32	.034	1/4P[27]	1P[28]	3/16[29]	6-3/4[30]	15	4
45	105	15426378	VD	6	.017	29	BF	32	.034	1P[27]	1/2P[28]	3/16[29]	7-3/4[30]	20.5	4
45	105	15426378	VD	6	.017	29	BF	32	.034	1P	1/2P	3/16	7-3/4	20.5	4
45	105	15426378	VD	6	.020	29	BF	32	.034	1/4P	1P	3/16	6-3/4	20.5	4
45	105	15426378	VD	6	.015	27	BF	32	.034	1/2P	1/4P	1/4	7	20.5	4
45	105	15426378	VD	6	.017	29	BF	32	.034	1P	1/2P	3/16	7-3/4	20.5	4

16 - Auto. Trans. - 2 BTDC.
17 - Auto. Trans. - 14 BTDC.
18 - Auto. Trans. - 12 BTDC.
19 - Auto. Trans. - 7.5 BTDC.
20 - Auto. Trans. - 2.5 ATC.
21 - Coronet - 117 in.
22 - Auto. Trans. - 5 BTDC.
23 - Both Breakers - 37 to 42 deg.
24 - Man. Trans., Both Breakers - 37 to 42 deg.
25 - Fairlane, Torino - 116 in.
26 - Falcon - 110.9 in.
27 - Falcon, Fairlane - 1/2 P.
28 - Falcon, Fairlane - 1/4 P.

29 - Falcon, Fairlane - 1/4 in.
30 - Falcon, Fairlane - 7 deg.
31 - Ford - 119 in.
32 - Montego, Comet - 116 in.
33 - Montego, Comet - 1/2 P.
34 - Montego, Comet - 1/4 P.
35 - Montego, Comet - 1/4 in.
36 - Montego, Comet - 7 deg.
37 - Auto. Trans. - 6 BTDC.
38 - Rear Main - 120 ft. lbs.
39 - Auto. Trans. - 2.5 ATC.
40 - Belvedere - 116 in.
41 - Auto. Trans. - 5 BTDC.

42 - Fury - 119 in.
43 - Both Breakers - 37 to 42 deg.
44 - Fury - 9 deg.
45 - Man. Trans., Both Breakers - 37 to 42 deg.
46 - Firebird - 108.1 in.
47 - Firebird - 1/2 P.
48 - Firebird - 3/16 in.
49 - Firebird - 8-3/4 deg.
50 - Executive - 124 in.
51 - Grand Prix - 121 in.
52 - Javelin - 109 in.
53 - Ambassador - 118 in.

1968

	Wheelbase	No. of Cylinders Bore and Stroke	Displacement (cu. in.)	Valve and Cylinder Arrangement	Compression Pressure (lbs.)	Maximum Brake Horsepower	Valve Tappet Clearance		Cylinder Bolt Torque (ft.-lbs.)
							Intake	Exhaust	
Thunderbird	114.7	8-4.36x3.59	429	VO	190	360@4600	HY	HY	90
Mustang GT	108	8-4.23x3.78	427S	VO	180	390@5600	HY	HY	90
Ford	119	8-4.23x3.78	427S	VO	180	390@5600	HY	HY	90
Lincoln Continental	126	8-4.38x3.83	462	VO	180	340@4600	HY	HY	145
Mercury – Montego, Comet	116	6-3.68x3.13	200	IO	175	115@3800	HY	HY	75
Cougar, Montego, Comet	111[32]	8-4.00x3.00	302	VO	150	210@4600	HY	HY	72
Cougar, Montego, Comet	111[32]	8-4.00x3.00	302	VO	150	230@4800	HY	HY	72
Montego, Comet	116	8-4.05x3.78	390	VO	180	265@4400	HY	HY	90
Cougar	111	8-4.05x3.78	390	VO	180	280@4400	HY	HY	90
Cougar, Montego, Comet	111[32]	8-4.05x3.78	390	VO	190	325@4800	HY	HY	90
Cougar, Montego, Comet	111[32]	8-4.23x3.78	427	VO	180	390@5600	HY	HY	90
Monterey, Montclair	123	8-4.05x3.78	390	VO	180	265@4400	HY	HY	90
Monterey, Montclair	123	8-4.05x3.78	390	VO	180	280@4400	HY	HY	90
Park Lane, Brougham, Marquis	123	8-4.05x3.78	390	VO	190	315@4600	HY	HY	90
Park Lane, Brougham, Marquis	123	8-4.13x3.984	428	VO	190	340@4600	HY	HY	90
Oldsmobile – F-85, Cutlass	116	6-3.875x3.53	250	IO	160	155@4200	HY	HY	95
F-85, Cutlass, Supreme	116	8-4.057x3.385	350	VO	175	250@4400	HY	HY	80
F-85, Cutlass, Supreme	116	8-4.057x3.385	350	VO	175	310@4600	HY	HY	80
4-4-2	112	8-3.87x4.25	400	VO	175	325@4600	HY	HY	80
4-4-2	112	8-3.87x4.25	400	VO	175	350@4800	HY	HY	80
4-4-2	112	8-3.87x4.25	400	VO	175	360@5400	HY	HY	80
Delmont	123	8-4.057x3.385	350	VO	175	250@4400	HY	HY	80
Delmont	123	8-4.057x3.385	350	VO	175	310@4800	HY	HY	80
Delmont, Delta	123	8-4.125x4.25	455	VO	175	310@4200	HY	HY	80
98, Delmont, Delta	126	8-4.125x4.25	455	VO	175	365@4600	HY	HY	80
Toronado	119	8-4.125x4.25	455	VO	175	375@4600	HY	HY	80
Toronado	119	8-4.125x4.25	455	VO	175	400@4800	HY	HY	80
Plymouth – Valiant, Signet	108	6-3.40x3.125	170	IO	125	115@4400	.010H	.020H	65
Valiant, Signet, Barracuda	108	6-3.40x4.125	225	IO	125	145@4000	.010H	.020H	65
Valiant, Signet, Belvedere	108[40]	8-3.63x3.31	273	VO	135	190@4400	HY	HY	85
Valiant, Barracuda, Belvedere	108[40]	8-3.91x3.31	318	VO	135	230@4400	HY	HY	85
Barracuda Formula S	108	8-4.04x3.31	340	VO	140	275@5000	HY	HY	95
Barracuda Formula S	108	8-4.25x3.38	383	VO	140	300@4400	HY	HY	85
Belvedere, Satellite, Fury	116[42]	8-4.25x3.38	383	VO	140	290@4400	HY	HY	85
Belvedere Road Runner	116	8-4.25x3.38	383	VO	140	335@5200	HY	HY	85
GTX	116	8-4.32x3.75	440	VO	150	375@4600	HY	HY	85
Belvedere, Satellite, GTX	116	8-4.25x3.75	426	VO	150	425@5000	.028C	.032C	100
Belvedere, Satellite, Fury	116[42]	6-3.40x4.125	225	IO	125	145@4000	.010H	.020H	85
Fury, VIP	119	8-3.91x3.31	318	VO	135	230@4000	HY	HY	85
Fury, Sport Fury, VIP	119	8-4.25x3.38	383	VO	140	330@5000	HY	HY	85
Fury, Sport Fury, VIP	119	8-4.32x3.75	440	VO	150	375@4600	HY	HY	85
Pontiac – Tempest, Firebird	116[46]	6-3.875x3.525	250	IOC	160	175@4800	HY	HY	95
Tempest, LeMans, Firebird	116[46]	6-3.875x3.525	250	IOC	195	215@5200	HY	HY	95
Tempest, LeMans, Firebird	116[46]	8-3.875x3.746	350	VO	160	265@4600	HY	HY	95
Tempest, LeMans, Firebird	116[46]	8-3.875x3.746	350	VO	160	320@5100	HY	HY	95
GTO	112	8-4.120x3.746	400	VO	160	265@4600	HY	HY	95
GTO Ram Air	112	8-4.120x3.746	400	VO	160	360@5400	HY	HY	95
Firebird 350	108.1	8-3.875x3.746	350	VO	160	265@4600	HY	HY	95
Firebird 350	108.1	8-3.875x3.746	350	VO	160	320@5100	HY	HY	95
Firebird 400	108.1	8-4.120x3.746	400	VO	160	330@4800	HY	HY	95
Firebird 400 Ram Air	108.1	8-4.120x3.746	400	VO	160	335@5300	HY	HY	95
Catalina, Executive	121[50]	8-4.120x3.746	400	VO	160	265@4600	HY	HY	95
Catalina, Executive	121[50]	8-4.120x3.746	400	VO	160	290@4600	HY	HY	95
Bonneville	124	8-4.120x3.746	400	VO	160	340@4800	HY	HY	95
Grand Prix	121	8-4.120x3.746	400	VO	160	350@5000	HY	HY	95
Catalina, Executive	121[50]	8-4.120x3.996	428	VO	200	375@4800	HY	HY	95
Bonneville, Grand Prix	124[51]	8-4.120x3.996	428	VO	200	390@5200	HY	HY	95
Rambler American	106	6-3.75x3.00	199	IO	145	128@4400	HY	HY	85
Rogue	106	6-3.75x3.50	232	IO	145	145@4300	HY	HY	85
American, Rogue, Javelin	106[52]	8-3.75x3.28	290	VO	145	225@4700	HY	HY	100
Rebel, Ambassador	114[53]	6-3.75x3.50	232	IO	145	145@4300	HY	HY	85
Rebel, Ambassador	114[53]	6-3.75x3.50	232	IO	145	155@4400	HY	HY	85
Rebel SST, Ambassador SST	114[53]	8-3.75x3.28	290	VO	145	200@4600	HY	HY	100
Rebel, Ambassador	114[53]	8-4.08x3.28	343	VO	145	235@4400	HY	HY	100
AMX	97	8-4.165x3.574	390	VO	145	315@4600	HY	HY	100

ABBREVIATIONS - FOOTNOTES

AC – AC Spark Plugs
ATC – After Top Center
BF – Autolite Spark Plugs
BTF – Autolite Spark Plugs
C – Cold Engine
CC – Timing Case Cover
CH – Champion Spark Plugs
CP – Crankshaft Pulley
H – Hot Engine
HO – Horizontal Opposed Cylinders
HY – Hydraulic Valve Lifters

IO – In-line Engine, Overhead Valves
IOC – In-line Engine, Overhead Cam
MP – Magnetic Pulse Ignition
N – Negative
NA – Not Applicable
P – Positive
VD – Vibration Damper
VO – V-Type Engine, Overhead Valves
WP – Water Pump Housing

1 – GS "350" – 112 in.
2 – GS "350" – CP
3 – GS "350" – 10 qts.

4 – Riviera – 119 in.
5 – 60 and Brougham – 133 in.; 75 – 149.8 in.
6 – 75 – 23.8 qts.
7 – Chevelle 4-Door Sedans – 116 in.; 2-Door Sedans – 112 in.
8 – Auto. Trans. – 4 BTDC.
9 – Chevelle – 1 N.
10 – Chevelle – 1/2 P.
11 – Chevelle – 8-1/4 deg.
12 – Chevelle – 16 qts.
13 – 4-Bolt Cap – 105 ft. lbs.
14 – Chevelle SS 396 – 24 qts.
15 – Camaro – 108 in.

Tuneup Specifications

Connecting Rod Bolt Torque (ft.-lbs.)	Main Bearing Bolt Torque (ft.-lbs.)	Firing Order	Timing Mark Location	Breaker Point Opens B.T.D.C.	Breaker Point Gap	Cam Angle	Spark Plugs Make	Spark Plugs Model	Spark Plugs Gap	Caster Man. Steer. (deg.)	Camber Rt. Wheel (deg.)	Toe-In (inches)	Steering Axis Inclination (deg.)	Cooling System Capacity (qts.)	Crankcase Capacity (qts.)
45	105	15426378	VD	6	.015	27	BF	42	.034	1P	1/2P	3/16	7-3/4	20.5	4
45	105	15426378	VD	6	.017	29	BF	32	.034	1/4P	1P	3/16	6-3/4	20.5	4
45	105	15426378	VD	6	.017	29	BF	32	.034	1P	1/2P	3/16	7-3/4	20.5	4
45	105	15426378	VD	10	.017	29	BTF	42	.034	1-1/2N	1/2P	1/8	7-3/4	23	5
24	70	153624	VD	6	.025	37	BF	82	.034	1/2P	1/4P	1/4	7	9.5	3.5
24	70	15426378	VD	6	.021	27	BF	32	.034	1/4P[33]	1P[34]	3/16[35]	6-3/4[36]	15	4
24	70	15426378	VD	6	.021	27	BF	32	.034	1/4P[33]	1P[34]	3/16[35]	6-3/4[36]	15	4
45	105	15426378	VD	6	.021	27	BF	32	.034	1/2P	1P	1/4	7	20.5	4
45	105	15426378	VD	6	.021	·27	BF	32	.034	1/4P	1P	3/16	6-3/4	20.5	4
45	105	15426378	VD	6	.021	27	BF	32	.034	1/4P[33]	1P[34]	3/16[35]	6-3/4[36]	20.5	4
45	105	15426378	VD	6	.017	29	BF	32	.034	1P	1/4P	3/16	7-1/2	20.5	4
45	105	15426378	VD	6	.021	27	BF	32	.034	1P	1/4P	3/16	7-1/2	20.5	4
45	105	15426378	VD	6	.017	29	BF	32	.034	1P	1/4P	3/16	7-1/2	20.5	4
45	105	15426378	VD	6	.017	29	BF	32	.034	1P	1/4P	3/16	7-1/2	20.5	4
35	65	153624	VD	4[37]	.016	33	AC	46N	.035	1-1/4N	1/8P	3/16	9	12.2	4
42	80[38]	18436572	VD	5	.016	30	AC	45S	.030	1-1/4N	1/8P	3/16	9	15.2	4
42	80[38]	18436572	VD	7.5	.016	30	AC	44S	.030	1-1/4N	1/8P	3/16	9	15.2	4
42	120	18436572	VD	0	.016	30	AC	44S	.030	1-1/4N	1/8P	3/16	9	16.2	4
42	120	18436572	VD	0	.016	30	AC	44S	.030	1-1/4N	1/8P	3/16	9	16.2	4
42	120	18436572	VD	0	.016	30	AC	44S	.030	1-1/4N	1/8P	3/16	9	16.2	4
42	120	18436572	VD	5	.016	30	AC	45S	.030	1N	1/8P	1/8	11	17.5	4
42	120	18436572	VD	5	.016	30	AC	45S	.030	1N	1/8P	1/8	11	17.5	4
42	120	18436572	VD	10	.016	30	AC	45S	.030	1N	1/8P	1/8	11	17.5	4
42	120	18436572	VD	10	.016	30	AC	45S	.030	1N	1/8P	1/8	11	17.5	4
42	120	18436572	VD	7.5	.016	30	AC	44S	.030	2N	1/8P	1/32	11	18	5
42	120	18436572	VD	7.5	.016	30	AC	44S	.030	2N	1/8P	1/32	11	18	5
45	85	153624	VD	5ATC[39]	.020	43	CH	N-14Y	.035	1/2N	1/4P	1/8	7-1/2	12	4
45	85	153624	VD	TDC	.020	43	CH	N-14Y	.035	1/2N	1/4P	1/8	7-1/2	13	4
45	85	18436572	VD	5ATC[39]	.016	30	CH	N-14Y	.035	1/2N	1/4P	1/8	7-1/2	19	4
45	85	18436572	VD	5ATC[39]	.016	30	CH	N-14Y	.035	1/2N	1/4P	1/8	7-1/2	17	4
45	85	18436572	VD	TDC[41]	.016	30[43]	CH	N-9Y	.035	1/2N	1/4P	1/8	7-1/2	18	4
45	85	18436572	VD	TDC[41]	.016	30	CH	J-11Y	.035	1/2N	1/4P	1/8	7-1/2	17	4
45	85	18436572	VD	TDC[41]	.016	30	CH	J-14Y	.035	1/2N	1/4P	1/8	7-1/2[44]	17	4
45	85	18436572	VD	TDC[41]	.016	30	CH	J-11Y	.035	1/2N	1/4P	1/8	7-1/2	17	4
45	85	18436572	VD	TDC[41]	.016	30[45]	CH	J-11Y	.035	1/2N	1/4P	1/8	7-1/2	17	4
45	85	18436572	VD	TDC	.016	30[43]	CH	N-10Y	.035	1/2N	1/4P	1/8	7-1/2	18	5
45	100	153624	VD	TDC	.020	43	CH	N-14Y	.035	1/2N	1/4P	1/8	7-1/2[44]	13	4
45	85	18436572	VD	5ATC[39]	.016	30	CH	N-14Y	.035	1/2N	1/4P	1/8	9	18	4
45	85	18436572	VD	TDC[41]	.016	30	CH	J-11Y	.035	1/2N	1/4P	1/8	9	17	4
45	85	18436572	VD	TDC[41]	.016	30[45]	CH	J-11Y	.035	1/2N	1/4P	1/8	9	18	4
33	100	153624	VD	TDC	.016	33	AC	44N	.035	1-1/2N[47]	1/4P	1/16[48]	9[49]	12.1	5
33	100	153624	VD	5	.016	33	AC	44N	.035	1-1/2N[47]	1/4P	1/16[48]	9[49]	12.1	5
43	100[38]	18436572	CP	9	.016	30	AC	45S	.035	1-1/2N[47]	1/4P	1/16[48]	9[49]	18.6	5
43	100[38]	18436572	CP	9	.016	30	AC	45S	.035	1-1/2N	1/4P	1/16	9	17.8	5
43	100[38]	18436572	CP	9	.016	30	AC	44S	.035	1-1/2N	1/4P	1/16	9	17.8	5
43	100[38]	18436572	CP	9	.016	30	AC	45S	.035	1/2P	1/4P	3/16	8-3/4	18.6	5
43	100[38]	18436572	CP	9	.016	30	AC	45S	.035	1/2P	1/4P	3/16	8-3/4	18.6	5
43	100[38]	18436572	CP	9	.016	30	AC	44S	.035	1/2P	1/4P	3/16	8-3/4	17.8	5
43	100[38]	18436572	CP	9	.016	30	AC	45S	.034	1-1/2N	1/4P	1/16	8-1/2	18	5
43	100[38]	18436572	CP	9	.016	30	AC	45S	.034	1-1/2N	1/4P	1/16	8-1/2	18	5
43	100[38]	18436572	CP	9	.016	30	AC	45S	.034	1-1/2N	1/4P	1/16	8-1/2	18.6	5
43	100[38]	18436572	CP	9	.016	30	AC	44S	.034	1-1/2N	1/4P	1/16	8-1/2	17.2	5
43	100[38]	18436572	CP	9	.016	30	AC	44S	.034	1-1/2N	1/4P	1/16	8-1/2	17.2	5
30	85	153624	VD	TDC[41]	.016	33	CH	N-14Y	.035	0	0	1/8	6-1/2	10.5	4
30	85	153624	VD	TDC[41]	.016	33	CH	N-14Y	.035	0	0	1/8	6-1/2	10.5	4
30	105	18436572	VD	TDC	.016	30	CH	N-12Y	.035	0	0	1/8	6-1/2	13	4
30	85	153624	VD	TDC	.016	33	CH	N-14Y	.035	1/2N	0	1/8	6-1/2	10.5	4
30	85	153624	VD	TDC	.016	33	CH	N-14Y	.035	1/2N	0	1/8	6-1/2	10.5	4
30	105	18436572	VD	TDC	.016	30	CH	N-12Y	.035	1/2N	0	1/8	6-1/4	14	4
30	105	18436572	VD	TDC	.016	30	CH	N-12Y	.035	1/2N	0	1/8	6-1/4	13	4
30	105	18436572	VD	TDC	.016	30	CH	N-12Y	.035	0	0	1/8	6-1/2	13	4

16 – Auto. Trans. – 2 BTDC.
17 – Auto. Trans. – 14 BTDC.
18 – Auto. Trans. – 12 BTDC.
19 – Auto. Trans. – 7.5 BTDC.
20 – Auto. Trans. – 2.5 ATC.
21 – Coronet – 117 in.
22 – Auto. Trans. – 5 BTDC.
23 – Both Breakers – 37 to 42 deg.
24 – Man. Trans., Both Breakers – 37 to 42 deg.
25 – Fairlane, Torino – 116 in.
26 – Falcon – 110.9 in.
27 – Falcon, Fairlane – 1/2 P.
28 – Falcon, Fairlane – 1/4 P.

29 – Falcon, Fairlane – 1/4 in.
30 – Falcon, Fairlane – 7 deg.
31 – Ford – 119 in.
32 – Montego, Comet – 116 in.
33 – Montego, Comet – 1/2 P.
34 – Montego, Comet – 1/4 P.
35 – Montego, Comet – 1/4 in.
36 – Montego, Comet – 7 deg.
37 – Auto. Trans. – 6 BTDC.
38 – Rear Main – 120 ft. lbs.
39 – Auto. Trans. – 2.5 ATC.
40 – Belvedere – 116 in.
41 – Auto. Trans. – 5 BTDC.

42 – Fury – 119 in.
43 – Both Breakers – 37 to 42 deg.
44 – Fury – 9 deg.
45 – Man. Trans., Both Breakers – 37 to 42 deg.
46 – Firebird – 108.1 in.
47 – Firebird – 1/2 P.
48 – Firebird – 3/16 in.
49 – Firebird – 8-3/4 deg.
50 – Executive – 124 in.
51 – Grand Prix – 121 in.
52 – Javelin – 109 in.
53 – Ambassador – 118 in.

1969

	Wheelbase	No. of Cylinders Bore and Stroke	Displacement (cu. in.)	Valve and Cylinder Arrangement	Compression Pressure (lbs.)	Maximum Brake Horsepower	Valve Tappet Clearance Intake	Exhaust	Cylinder Bolt Torque (ft. lbs.)
Ford	121	8-4.0x3.5	351	VO	180	250@4600	HY	HY	105
Ford	121	8-4.052x3.784	390	VO	190	265@4400	HY	HY	90
Ford	121	8-4.362x3.59	429	VO	190	320@4400	HY	HY	90
Ford, Thunderbird	121[1]	8-4.362x3.59	429	VO	190	360@4600	HY	HY	90
Lincoln Continental	126[2]	8-4.362x3.85	460	VO	180	365@4600	HY	HY	140
Mercury - Comet, Montego, Cyclone	116	6-3.682x3.91	250	IO	175	155@4000	HY	HY	75
Comet, Montego, Cyclone	116	8-4.002x3.00	302	VO	150	220@4600	HY	HY	72
Comet, Montego, Cyclone	116	8-4.002x3.50	351	VO	180	250@4600[6]	HY	HY	105
Comet, Montego, Cyclone	116	8-4.052x3.784	390	VO	190	320@4600	HY	HY	90
Comet, Montego, Cyclone	116	8-4.132x3.984	428	VO	190	335@5200[7]	HY[8]	HY[8]	90
Cougar, Cougar GT	111	8-4.002x3.50	351	VO	180	250@4600[6]	HY	HY	105
Cougar, Cougar GT	111	8-4.052x3.784	390	VO	190	320@4600	HY	HY	90
Cougar, Cougar GT	111	8-4.132x3.984	428	VO	190	335@5200[7]	HY	HY	90
Mercury (Except Brougham)	124	8-4.052x3.784	390	VO	190	265@4400[10]	HY	HY	90
Mercury (All)	124	8-4.362x3.59	429	VO	190	320@4400[11]	HY	HY	90
Oldsmobile - F-85, Cutlass	116[12]	6-3.875x3.53	250	IO	160	155@4200	HY	HY	95
F-85, Cutlass	116[12]	8-4.057x3.385	350	VO	175	250@4400[13]	HY	HY	80
F-85, Cutlass	116[12]	8-4.057x3.385	350	VO	175	325@5400	HY	HY	80
4-4-2	112	8-3.87x4.25	400	VO	175	350@4800	HY	HY	80
4-4-2	112	8-3.87x4.25	400	VO	175	325@4600[18]	HY	HY	80
Delta 88	124	8-4.057x3.385	350	VO	175	250@4400	HY	HY	80
Delta 88	124	8-4.125x4.25	455	VO	175	310@4200	HY	HY	80
Delta 88	124	8-4.125x4.25	455	VO	175	365@4600[20]	HY	HY	80
Ninety Eight	127	8-4.125x4.25	455	VO	175	365@4600	HY	HY	80
Toronado	119	8-4.126x4.25	455	VO	175	375@4600[22]	HY	HY	80
Plymouth - Valiant, Signet	108	6-3.40x3.125	170	IO	125	115@4400	.010H	.020H	65
Valiant, Signet, Belvedere, Barracuda	108[23]	6-3.40x4.125	225	IO	125	145@4000	.010H	.020H	65
Valiant, Signet	108	8-3.63x3.31	273	VO	135	190@4400	HY	HY	85
Valiant, Signet, Belvedere, Barracuda	108[23]	8-3.91x3.31	318	VO	135	230@4400	HY	HY	85
Barracuda	108	8-4.04x3.31	340	VO	140	275@5000	HY	HY	95
Belvedere	116	8-4.25x3.38	383	VO	140	290@4400	HY	HY	70
Belvedere Road Runner	116	8-4.25x3.38	383	VO	140	335@5200	HY	HY	70
Belvedere, Barracuda	116[27]	8-4.25x3.38	383	VO	140	330@5000	HY	HY	70
Belvedere	116	8-4.25x3:75	426	VO	150	425@4000	.028C	.032C	75
Belvedere, Fury, VIP	116[29]	8-4.32x3.75	440	VO	150	375@4600	HY	HY	70
Fury I, II, III	120	6-3.40x4.125	225	IO	125	145@4000	.010H	.020H	65
Fury, Sport Fury, VIP	120	8-3.91x3.31	318	VO	135	230@4400	HY	HY	85
Fury, Sport Fury, VIP	120	8-4.25x3.38	383	VO	140	290@4400	HY	HY	70
Fury, Sport Fury, VIP	120	8-4.25x3.38	383	VO	140	330@5000	HY	HY	70
Pontiac - Tempest, LeMans	116[32]	6-3.875x3.525	250	IOC	160[34]	175@4800[33]	HY	HY	95
Tempest, LeMans	116[32]	8-3.875x3.746	350	VO	160	265@4600[35]	HY	HY	95
GTO	112	8-4.12x3.746	400	VO	160	265@4600	HY	HY	95
GTO	112	8-4.12x3.746	400	VO	160	350@5000	HY	HY	95
GTO	112	8-4.12x3.746	400	VO	160	366@5100[36]	HY	HY	95
Firebird	112	6-3.875x3.525	250	IOC	160	175@4800	HY	HY	95
Firebird	112	8-3.875x3.746	350	VO	160	325@5100	HY	HY	95
Firebird	112	8-4.12x3.746	400	VO	160	330@4800[37]	HY	HY	95
Firebird	112	8-4.12x3.746	400	VO	160	345@5400	HY	HY	95
Grand Prix	118	8-4.12x3.746	400	VO	160	265@4600	HY	HY	95
Grand Prix	118	8-4.12x3.746	400	VO	160	350@5000	HY	HY	95
Grand Prix	118	8-4.12x3.996	428	VO	200	370@4800[38]	HY	HY	95
Catalina, Executive, Bonneville	122[39]	8-4.12x3.746	400	VO	160	265@4600	HY	HY	95
Catalina, Executive, Bonneville	122[39]	8-4.12x3.746	400	VO	160	290@4600	HY	HY	95
Catalina, Executive	122[39]	8-4.12x3.746	400	VO	160	340@4800	HY	HY	95
Catalina, Executive, Bonneville	122[39]	8-4.12x3.996	428	VO	200	360@4600	HY	HY	95
Catalina, Executive, Bonneville	122[39]	8-4.12x3.996	428	VO	200	390@5200	HY	HY	95
Rambler	106	6-3.75x3.0	199	IO	145	128@4400	HY	HY	85
Rambler, Javelin, AMX	106[42]	6-3.75x3.50	232	IO	145	145@4300	HY	HY	85
Rambler, Javelin, AMX	106[42]	8-3.75x3.28	290	VO	145	200@4600	HY	HY	100
Rambler, Javelin, AMX	106[42]	8-3.75x3.28	290	VO	145	225@4700	HY	HY	100
Rebel, Ambassador	114[43]	6-3.75x3.50	232	IO	145	145@4300[44]	HY	HY	85
Rebel, Ambassador	114[43]	8-3.75x3.28	290	VO	145	200@4600	HY	HY	100
Rebel, Ambassador	114[43]	8-4.08x3.28	343	VO	145	235@4400[45]	HY	HY	100
Ambassador	122	8-4.165x3.574	390	VO	145	315@4600	HY	HY	100
Javelin, AMX	109[42]	8-4.165x3.574	390	VO	145	315@4600	HY	HY	100

ABBREVIATIONS - FOOTNOTES

AC - AC Spark Plugs
ATC - After Top Center
BF - Autolite Spark Plug
BTDC - Before Top Dead Center
C - Cold Engine
CC - Timing Case Cover
CH - Champion Spark Plugs
CP - Crankshaft Pulley
H - Hot Engine
HO - Horizontal Opposed

HY - Hydraulic Valve Lifters
IO - In-Line Engine, Overhead Valves
IOC - In-Line Engine, Overhead Cam
MP - Magnetic Pulse Ignition
N - Negative
NA - Not Applicable
P - Positive
TDC - Top Dead Center
VD - Vibration Damper
VO - V-Type Engine - Overhead Valves
1 - T-Bird - 2-Door, 114.7 in., 4-Door, 117.2 in.

2 - Continental Mark III - 117.2 in.
3 - Continental Mark III - 1P
4 - Continental Mark III - 3/16 in.
5 - Continental Mark III - 7-3/4 deg.
6 - Also 290@4800
7 - Also Ram Air
8 - X-70 - .025 in. H.
9 - 290 hp - BF32
10 - Also 280@4400
11 - Also 360@4600
12 - Coupe, Convertible - 112 in.
13 - Also 310@4800

Tuneup Specifications

Connecting Rod Bolt Torque (ft. lbs.)	Main Bearing Bolt Torque (ft. lbs.)	Firing Order	Timing Mark Location	Breaker Point Opens BTDC	Breaker Point Gap	Cam Angle	Spark Plugs Make	Spark Plugs Model	Spark Plugs Gap	Caster Man. Steer. (deg.)	Camber Rt. Wheel (deg.)	Toe-in (in.)	Steering Axis Inclination (deg.)	Cooling System Capacity (qts.)	Crankcase Capacity (qts.)
45	70	13726548	VD	6	.017	28	BF	42	.034	1P	1/2P	3/16	7-3/4	15.4	4
45	105	15426378	VD	6	.017	28	BF	42	.034	1P	1/2P	3/16	7-3/4	20.1	4
45	105	15426378	VD	6	.016	28	BF	42	.034	1P	1/2P	3/16	7-3/4	18.6	4
45	105	15426378	VD	6	.016	28	BF	42	.034	1P	1/2P	3/16	7-3/4	18.6	4
45	105	15426378	VD	10	.017	28	BF	42	.034	1-1/2N[3]	1/2P	1/8[4]	7[5]	19.5	4
26	70	153624	CC	6	.027	37	BF	82	.034	0	1/4P	1/4	7	9.9	4
24	70	15426378	VD	6	.021	28	BF	42	.034	0	1/4P	1/4	7	13.5	4
45	70	13726548	VD	6	.021	28	BF	42	.034	0	1/4P	1/4	7	14.6	4
45	105	15426378	VD	6	.017	28	BF	42	.034	0	1/4P	1/4	7	19.9	4
45	105	15426378	VD	6	.016	28	BF	32	.034	0	1/4P	1/4	7	19.6	4
45	70	13726548	VD	6	.017	28	BF	42[9]	.034	1/4P	1P	3/16	6-3/4	14.6	4
45	105	15426378	VD	6	.017	28	BF	42	.034	1/4P	1P	3/16	6-3/4	20.1	4
45	105	15426378	VD	6	.017	28	BF	32	.034	1/4P	1P	3/16	6-3/4	19.3	4
45	105	15426378	VD	6	.017	28	BF	42	.034	1P	1/4P	3/16	7-1/2	20.1	4
45	105	15426378	VD	6	.018	28	BF	42	.034	1P	1/4P	3/16	7-1/2	19.7	4
35	65	153624	VD	TDC[15]	.016	33	AC	R46N	.035	1-1/4N	1/8P	3/16	9	10.1	4
42	80[14]	18436572	VD	6[16]	.016	30	AC	R45S	.030	1-1/4N	1/8P	3/16	9	22	4
42	80[14]	18436572	VD	12	.016	30	AC	R44S	.030	1-1/4N	1/8P	3/16	9	22	4
42	120	18436572	VD	2[17]	.016	30	AC	R44S	.030	1-1/4N	1/8P	3/16	9	16.2	4
42	120	18436572	VD	8[19]	.016	30	AC	R44S	.030	1-1/4N	1/8P	3/16	9	16.2	4
42	120	18436572	VD	6	.016	30	AC	R45S	.030	1N	3/8N	3/16	11	17.5	4
42	120	18436572	VD	6	.016	30	AC	R45S	.030	1N	3/8N	3/16	11	17.5	4
42	120	18436572	VD	6[21]	.016	30	AC	R43S	.030	1N	3/8N	3/16	11	17.5	4
42	120	18436572	VD	8	.016	30	AC	R44S	.030	1N	1/8P	3/16	11	17.5	4
42	120	18436572	VD	8	.016	30	AC	R44S	.030	2N	1/8P	0	11	18	5
45	85	153624	VD	2.5ATC[24]	.020	45	CH	N14Y	.035	1/2N	1/4P	1/8	7-1/2	12	4
45	85	153624	VD	TDC	.020	45	CH	N14Y	.035	1/2N	1/4P	1/8	7-1/2	13[32]	4
45	85	18436572	VD	2.5ATC	.017	33	CH	N14Y	.035	1/2N	1/4P	1/8	7-1/2	17[33]	4
45	85	18436572	VD	TDC	.017	33	CH	N14Y	.035	1/2N	1/4P	1/8	7-1/2	17[33]	4
45	85	18436572	VD	TDC[25]	.020	30[26]	CH	N9Y	.035	1/2N	1/4P	1/8	7-1/2	16	4
45	85	18436572	VD	TDC[25]	.017	33	CH	J14Y	.035	1/2N	1/4P	1/8	7-1/2	16	4
45	85	18436572	VD	TDC[25]	.017	30[26]	CH	J11Y	.035	1/2N	1/4P	1/8	7-1/2	16	4
45	85	18436572	VD	TDC[25]	.017	30[26]	CH	J11Y	.035	1/2N	1/4P	1/8	7-1/2	16	4
45	100	18436572	VD	TDC	.017	30[26]	CH	N10Y	.035	1/2N	1/4P	1/8	7-1/2	18	5
45	85	18436572	VD	5	.017	30[28]	CH	J11Y	.035	1/2N	1/4P	1/8	7-1/2[31]	18	4
45	85	153624	VD	TDC	.020	45	CH	N14Y	.035	1/2N	1/4P	1/8	9	13	4
45	85	18436572	VD	TDC	.017	33	CH	N14Y	.035	1/2N	1/4P	1/8	9	16	4
45	85	18436572	VD	TDC[30]	.017	33	CH	J14Y	.035	1/2N	1/4P	1/8	9	16	4
45	85	18436572	VD	TDC[25]	.017	33	CH	J11Y	.035	1/2N	1/4P	1/8	9	16	4
33	100	153624	VD	TDC[40]	.016	33	AC	R44NS	.035	1-1/2N	1/4P	1/16	9	11.9	4.5
43	100[14]	18436572	CP	9	.016	30	AC	R45S	.035	1-1/2N	1/4P	1/16	9	19.9	5
43	100[14]	18436572	CP	9	.016	30	AC	R46S	.035	1-1/2N	1/4P	1/16	9	18.3	5
43	100[14]	18436572	CP	9	.016	30	AC	R45S	.035	1-1/2N	1/4P	1/16	9	18.3	5
43	100[14]	18436572	CP	15	.016	30	AC	R44S	.035	1-1/2N	1/4P	1/16	9	18.3	5
33	100	153624	VD	TDC[40]	.016	33	AC	R44NS	.035	1/2P	1/4P	3/16	8-3/4	11.8	4.5
43	100[14]	18436572	CP	9	.016	30	AC	R45S	.035	1/2P	1/4P	3/16	8-3/4	19.4	5
43	100[14]	18436572	CP	9	.016	30	AC	R44S	.035	1/2P	1/4P	3/16	8-3/4	18.6	5
43	100[14]	18436572	CP	15	.016	30	AC	R44S	.035	1/2P	1/4P	3/16	8-3/4	18.6	5
43	100[14]	18436572	CP	9	.016	30	AC	R46S	.035	1-1/2N	1/4P	1/16	9	18.7	5
43	100[14]	18436572	CP	9	.016	30	AC	R45S	.035	1-1/2N	1/4P	1/16	9	18.7	5
43	100[14]	18436572	CP	9	.016	30	AC	R44S	.035	1-1/2N	1/4P	1/16	9	17.5	5
43	100[14]	18436572	CP	9	.016	30	AC	R46S	.035	1-1/2N	1/4P	1/16	8-1/2	18[41]	5
43	100[14]	18436572	CP	9	.016	30	AC	R46S	.035	1-1/2N	1/4P	1/16	8-1/2	18[41]	5
43	100[14]	18436572	CP	9	.016	30	AC	R46S	.035	1-1/2N	1/4P	1/16	8-1/2	18	5
43	100[14]	18436572	CP	9	.016	30	AC	R45S	.035	1-1/2N	1/4P	1/16	8-1/2	18[41]	5
43	100[14]	18436572	CP	9	.016	30	AC	R44S	.035	1-1/2N	1/4P	1/16	8-1/2	18[41]	5
30	85	153624	VD	TDC[25]	.016	33	CH	N14Y	.035	0	0	1/8	6-1/2	10.5	4
30	85	153624	VD	TDC[25]	.016	33	CH	N14Y	.035	0	0	1/8	6-1/2	10.5	4
30	105	18436572	VD	TDC	.016	30	CH	N12Y	.035	0	0	1/8	6-1/2	14	4
30	105	18436572	VD	TDC	.016	30	CH	N12Y	.035	0	0	1/8	6-1/2	14	4
30	85	153624	VD	TDC	.016	33	CH	N14Y	.035	1/2N	0	1/8	6-1/4	10.5	4
30	105	18436572	VD	TDC	.016	30	CH	N12Y	.035	1/2N	0	1/8	6-1/4	14	4
30	105	18436572	VD	TDC	.016	30	CH	N12Y	.035	1/2N	0	1/8	6-1/4	13	4
30	105	18436572	VD	TDC	.016	30	CH	N12Y	.035	0	0	1/8	6-1/2	13	4

14 – Rear Main – 120 ft. lbs.
15 – Auto. Trans. – 4 deg. BTDC
16 – 310 hp – 8 deg. BTDC
17 – Auto. Trans. – 8 deg. BTDC
18 – Also 360@5400
19 – 360 hp, W-30 – 14 deg. BTDC
20 – Also GT – 390@5000
21 – 390 hp GT – 10 deg. BTDC
22 – Also W-34 – 400@4800
23 – Belvedere – 116 in.
24 – Auto. Trans. – TDC
25 – Auto. Trans. – 5 BTDC

26 – Both Breakers – 37 to 42 deg.
27 – Barracuda – 108 in.
28 – Both Breakers – 37 to 42 deg., Auto. Trans. – 30 to 35 deg.
29 – Fury, VIP – 120 in.
30 – Auto. Trans. – 7.5 deg.
31 – Fury, VIP – 9 deg.
32 – 2-Door – 112 in.
33 – Also 215@5200, 230@5400
34 – 215 and 230 hp – 195 ft. lbs.
35 – Also 330@5100
36 – Also 370@5500, Ram Air

37 – Also 335@5000
38 – Also 390@5200
39 – Executive, Bonneville – 125 in.
40 – 215 and 230 hp – 5 deg. BTDC
41 – Bonneville – 17.2 qts.
42 – Javelin – 109 in., AMX – 97 in.
43 – Ambassador – 122 in.
44 – Also 155@4400
45 – Also 280@4800

1970

	Wheelbase	No. of Cylinders Bore and Stroke	Displacement (cu. in.)	Valve and Cylinder Arrangement	Compression Pressure (lbs.)	Maximum Brake Horsepower	Valve Tappet Clearance Intake	Valve Tappet Clearance Exhaust	Cylinder Bolt Torque (ft. lbs.)
American Motors - Hornet	108	6-3.75x3.0	199	IO	145	128@4400	HY	HY	80
Hornet, Javelin, Rebel	108 [2]	6-3.75x3.50	232	IO	145	145@4300	HY	HY	80
Hornet, Rebel, Ambassador	108 [2]	6-3.75x3.50	232	IO	145	155@4400	HY	HY	80
Hornet, Javelin, Rebel, Ambassador	108 [2]	8-3.75x3.44	304	VO	145	210@4400	HY	HY	110
Javelin, Rebel, Ambassador	109 [2]	8-4.08x3.44	360	VO	145	245@4400	HY	HY	110
Javelin, Rebel, Ambassador	109 [2]	8-4.08x3.44	360	VO	145	290@4800	HY	HY	110
AMX	97	8-4.08x3.44	360	VO	145	290@4800	HY	HY	110
AMX, Javelin, Rebel, Ambassador	97 [2]	8-4.165x3.574	390	VO	145	325@5000	HY	HY	110
Rebel (Machine)	114	8-4.165x3.574	390	VO	145	340@5100	HY	HY	110
Buick - Skylark	112 [4]	6-3.875x3.53	250	IO	165	155@4200	HY	HY	95
Skylark, Custom, "350", Sportwagon	112 [4]	8-3.80x3.85	350	VO	175	260@4600 [5]	HY	HY	75
GS	112	8-3.80x3.85	350	VO	175	315@4800	HY	HY	75
GS "455"	112	8-4.3125x3.90	455	VO	175	350@4600 [7]	HY	HY	100
LeSabre	124	8-3.80x3.85	350	VO	175	260@4600 [5]	HY	HY	75
LeSabre "455", Wildcat Custom	124	8-4.3125x3.90	455	VO	175	370@4600	HY	HY	100
Electra "225"	127	8-4.3125x3.90	455	VO	175	370@4600	HY	HY	100
Riviera	119	8-4.3125x3.90	455	VO	175	370@4600	HY	HY	100
Cadillac	129.5 [9]	8-4.30x4.06	472	VO	175	375@4400	HY	HY	115
Eldorado	120	8-4.30x4.304	500 [12]	VO	175	400@4400	HY	HY	115
Chevrolet, Chevelle	119 [11]	6-3.875x3.53	250	IO	130	155@4200	HY	HY	95
Chevelle	112 [11]	8-3.875x3.25	307	VO	150	200@4600	HY	HY	65
Chevelle, Monte Carlo	112 [11]	8-4.0x3.48	350	VO	160	250@4800 [17]	HY	HY	65
Chevrolet	119	8-4.0x3.48	350	VO	160	250@4800 [17]	HY	HY	65
Chevrolet	119	8-4.125x3.75	400	VO	160	265@4400	HY	HY	65
Monte Carlo	116	8-4.125x3.75	400	VO	160	265@4400	HY	HY	65
Monte Carlo, Chevelle	116 [11]	8-4.126x3.76	402	VO	160	330@4800	HY	HY	80 [18]
Chevelle SS 396	112	8-4.126x3.76	402	VO	160	350@5200	HY	HY	80 [18]
Chevrolet	119	8-4.251x4.0	454	VO	160	345@4400	HY	HY	80 [18]
Monte Carlo	116	8-4.251x4.0	454	VO	160	360@4400	HY	HY	80 [18]
Chevrolet	119	8-4.251x4.0	454	VO	160	390@4800	HY	HY	80 [18]
Chevy Nova	111	4-3.875x3.25	153	IO	130	90@4000	HY	HY	95
Nova, Camaro	111 [19]	6-3.875x3.25	230	IO	130	140@4400	HY	HY	95
Nova, Camaro	111 [19]	6-3.875x3.53	250	IO	130	155@4200	HY	HY	95
Nova, Camaro	111 [19]	8-3.875x3.25	307	VO	150	200@4600	HY	HY	65
Nova, Camaro	111 [19]	8-4.0x3.48	350	VO	160	250@4800 [17]	HY	HY	65
Camaro SS	108	8-4.126x3.76	402	VO	160	325@4800	HY	HY	80 [18]
Corvette	98	8-4.0x3.48	350	VO	160	300@4800	HY	HY	65
Corvette	98	8-4.0x3.48	350	VO	160	350@5600	HY	HY	65
Corvette	98	8-4.251x3.76	427	VO	160	390@5400 [21]	HY	HY	80 [18]
Corvette	98	8-4.251x3.76	427	VO	150	435@5800	.024H	.028H	80 [18]
Chrysler - Newport, Custom	124	8-4.25x3.38	383	VO	140	290@4400 [22]	HY	HY	70
New Yorker, 300	124	8-4.32x3.75	440	VO	150	350@4400	HY	HY	70
Newport, Custom, New Yorker, 300	124	8-4.32x3.75	440	VO	150	375@4600	HY	HY	70
Dodge - Dart, Swinger	111	6-3.4x3.64	198	IO	125	125@4400	.010H	.020H	65
Dart, Swinger, Coronet, Charger	111 [27]	6-3.4x4.12	225	IO	125	145@4400	.010H	.020H	65
Dart, Swinger, Coronet, Charger	111 [27]	8-3.91x3.31	318	VO	140	230@4400	HY	HY	85
Swinger 340, Challenger	111 [28]	8-4.04x3.31	340	VO	150	275@5000	HY	HY	95
Coronet, Charger, Challenger	117 [28]	8-4.25x3.38	383	VO	140	290@4400	HY	HY	70
Coronet, Challenger	117 [28]	8-4.25x3.38	383	VO	150	330@5000	HY	HY	70
Coronet, Charger, Super Bee	117	8-4.25x3.38	383	VO	150	335@5200	HY	HY	70
Coronet R/T, Charger R/T, Super Bee	117	8-4.25x3.75	426	VO	150	425@5000	HY	HY	75
Coronet R/T, Charger R/T, Challenger R/T	117 [28]	8-4.32x3.75	440	VO	150	375@4600	HY	HY	70
Coronet R/T, Charger R/T, Super Bee	117	8-4.32x3.75	440	VO	150	290@4700	HY	HY	70
Polara	122	8-3.91x3.31	318	VO	140	230@4400	HY	HY	85
Polara, Monaco	122	8-4.25x3.38	383	VO	140	290@4400	HY	HY	70
Polara, Monaco	122	8-4.32x3.75	440	VO	150	350@4700	HY	HY	70
Challenger	110	6-3.4x4.12	225	IO	125	145@4000	.010H	.020H	65
Challenger	110	8-3.91x3.31	318	VO	140	230@4400	HY	HY	85
Challenger, Challenger R/T	110	8-4.25x3.38	383	VO	150	335@5200	HY	HY	70
Challenger R/T	110	8-4.25x3.75	426	VO	150	425@5000	HY	HY	75
Challenger R/T	110	8-4.32x3.75	440	VO	150	390@4700	HY	HY	70
Ford - Falcon, Futura	110.9	6-3.682x3.126	200	IO	175	120@4000	HY	HY	75
Falcon, Futura	110.9	8-4.002x3.0	302	VO	150	220@4600	HY	HY	72
Maverick	103	6-3.502x2.94	170	IO	175	105@4200	HY	HY	75
Maverick	103	6-3.682x3.126	200	IO	175	120@4000	HY	HY	75

ABBREVIATIONS - FOOTNOTES

AC - AC Spark Plugs	H - Hot Engine	1 - Power Steering - 1P
BF - Autolite Spark Plugs	HY - Hydraulic Lifters	2 - Javelin - 108 in., Rebel - 114 in., Ambassador - 122 in.
BTDC - Before Top Dead Center	IO - In-Line Engine - Overhead Valves	3 - Effective with Engine Code 209x26, 5 deg. BTDC on Earlier Engines
C - Cold Engine	MP - Magnetic Pulse Ignition	4 - Custom and 4-Door Sedans - 116 in.
CF - Crankshaft Flange	N - Negative	5 - Also 285 and 315 hp
CH - Champion Spark Plugs	P - Positive	6 - Auto. Trans. - 4 deg. BTDC
CP - Crankshaft Pulley	TDC - Top Dead Center	7 - Also 360 hp
	VD - Vibration Damper	
	VO - V-Type Engine - Overhead Valves	

Tuneup Specifications

Connecting Rod Bolt Torque (ft. lbs.)	Main Bearing Bolt Torque (ft. lbs.)	Firing Order	Timing Mark Location	Breaker Point Opens BTDC	Breaker Point Gap	Cam Angle	Spark Plugs Make	Spark Plugs Model	Spark Plugs Gap	Caster Man. Steer. (deg.)	Camber Rt. Wheel (deg.)	Toe-in (in.)	Steering Axis Inclination (deg.)	Cooling System Capacity (qts.)	Crankcase Capacity (qts.)
28	80	153624	VD	3	.016	33	CH	N14Y	.035	0[1]	1P	1/8	7-3/4	10.5	4
28	80	153624	VD	3	.016	33	CH	N14Y	.035	0[1]	1P	1/8	7-3/4	10.5	4
28	80	153624	VD	3	.016	33	CH	N12Y	.035	0[1]	1P	1/8	7-3/4	10.5	4
28	100	18436572	VD	5	.016	30	CH	N12Y	.035	0[1]	1P	1/8	7-3/4	14	4
28	100	18436572	VD	5	.016	30	CH	N12Y	.035	0[1]	1P	1/8	7-3/4	13	4
28	100	18436572	VD	5	.016	30	CH	N12Y	.035	0[1]	1P	1/8	7-3/4	13	4
28	100	18436572	VD	5	.016	30	CH	N12Y	.035	0[1]	1P	1/8	7-3/4	13	4
33	100	18436572	VD	TDC[3]	.016	30	CH	N12Y	.035	0[1]	1P	1/8	7-3/4	13	4
33	100	18436572	VD	TDC[3]	.016	30	CH	N10Y	.035	0[1]	1P	1/8	7-3/4	13	4
35	65	153624	VD	TDC[6]	.019	32	AC	R46N	.035	1/2N	1/2P	3/16	8	16	4
35	95	18436572	CF	6	.016	30	AC	R45TS	.030	1/2N	1/2P	3/16	8	16.5	4
35	95	18436572	VD	6	.016	30	AC	R45TS	.030	1/2N	1/2P	3/16	8	16.5	4
45	110	18436572	VD	6[8]	.016	30	AC	R44TS	.030	1/2N	1/2P	3/16	8	19	4
35	95	18436572	VD	6	.016	30	AC	R45TS	.030	3/4P	0	1/4	10-3/4	16	4
45	110	18436572	VD	6	.016	30	AC	R44TS	.030	3/4P	0	1/4	10-3/4	19.7	4
45	110	18436572	VD	6	.016	30	AC	R44TS	.030	3/4P	0	1/4	10-3/4	19.7	4
45	110	18436572	VD	6	.016	30	AC	R44TS	.030	1P	0	3/16	10-3/4	19.7	4
40	90	15634278	CP	7.5	.016	30	AC	R46N	.035	1N	0	3/16	6	21.3[10]	4
40	90	15634278	CP	7.5	.016	30	AC	R46N	.035	2N	0	1/16	11	21.3	5
35	65	153624	VD	TDC[6]	.019	33	AC	R46T	.035	3/4P[13]	1/4P[14]	3/16	7-1/2[15]	12	4
45	75[16]	18436572	VD	2	.019	30	AC	R45	.035	1N	1/2P	3/16	8	15	4
45	75[16]	18436572	VD	TDC	.019	30	AC	R44	.035	1N	1/2P	3/16	8	16	4
45	75[16]	18436572	VD	4	.019	30	AC	R44	.035	3/4P	1/4P	3/16	7-1/2	16	4
45	75[16]	18436572	VD	8	.019	30	AC	R44	.035	3/4P	1/4P	3/16	7-1/2	16	4
45	75[16]	18436572	VD	8	.019	30	AC	R44	.035	1N	1/2P	3/16	8	16	4
50	105	18436572	VD	4	.019	29	AC	R44T	.035	1N	1/2P	3/16	8	23	4
50	105	18436572	VD	TDC	.019	29	AC	R44T	.035	1N	1/2P	3/16	8	23	4
50	105	18436572	VD	6	.019	29	AC	R44T	.035	3/4P	1/4P	3/16	7-1/2	22	4
50	105	18436572	VD	4	.019	29	AC	R43T	.035	1N	1/2P	3/16	8	22	4
50	105	18436572	VD	6	.019	29	AC	R43T	.035	3/4P	1/4P	3/16	7-1/2	22	4
35	65	1342	VD	TDC	.019	33	AC	R46N	.035	1/2P	1/4P	3/16	8-3/4	9	3.5
35	65	153624	VD	TDC	.019	33	AC	R46N	.035	1/2P	1/4P	3/16	8-3/4	13	4
35	65	153624	VD	TDC	.019	33	AC	R46N	.035	1/2P	1/4P	3/16	8-3/4	13	4
45	75[16]	18436572	VD	2	.019	30	AC	R45S	.035	1/2P	1/4P	3/16	8-3/4	17	4
*45	75[16]	18436572	VD	TDC	.019	30	AC	R44S	.035	1/2P	1/4P	3/16	8-3/4	16	4
50	105	18436572	VD	4	.019	29	AC	R44N	.035	1/2P	1/4P	3/16	8-3/4	23	4
45	75[16]	18436572	VD	4	.019	30	AC	R44S	.035	1P[20]	3/4P	1/8	7	15	4
45	75[16]	18436572	VD	8	.019	30	AC	R44	.035	1P[20]	3/4P	1/8	7	15	4
50	105	18436572	VD	4	.019	30	AC	43N	.035	1P[20]	3/4P	1/8	7	22	5
50	105	18436572	VD	4	MP	MP	AC	43N	.035	1P[20]	3/4P	1/8	7	22	5
45	85	18436572	VD	2.5[23]	.019	30.5	CH	J14Y[24]	.035	1/2N	1/4P	1/8	9	14.5[25]	4
45	85	18436572	VD	5	.019	30.5	CH	J13Y	.035	1/2N	1/4P	1/8	9	15.5	4
45	85	18436572	VD	TDC	.019	30.5	CH	J11Y	.035	1/2N	1/4P	1/8	9	15.5	6
45	85	153624	VD	TDC	.020	44	CH	N14Y	.035	1/2N[26]	1/4P	1/8	7-1/2	13	4
45	85	153624	VD	TDC	.020	44	CH	N14Y	.035	1/2N[26]	1/4P	1/8	7-1/2	13	4
45	85	18436572	VD	TDC	.017	32	CH	N14Y	.035	1/2N[26]	1/4P	1/8	7-1/2	16	4
45	85	18436572	VD	5	.017	32	CH	N9Y	.035	1/2N[26]	1/4P	1/8	7-1/2	15	4
45	85	18436572	VD	TDC[29]	.019	30.5	CH	J14Y	.035	1/2N[26]	1/4P	1/8	7-1/2	14.5	4
45	85	18436572	VD	TDC[29]	.019	30.5	CH	J11Y	.035	1/2N[26]	1/4P	1/8	7-1/2	14.5	4
45	85	18436572	VD	TDC[29]	.019	30.5	CH	J11Y	.035	1/2N[26]	1/4P	1/8	7-1/2	14.5	4
75	100	18436572	VD	TDC[30]	.017	30[31]	CH	N10Y	.035	1/2N[26]	1/4P	1/8	7-1/2	17	5
45	85	18436572	VD	TDC[29]	.019	30.5	CH	J11Y	.035	1/2N[26]	1/4P	1/8	7-1/2	17	4
45	85	18436572	VD	5	.017	30.5	CH	J11Y	.035	1/2N[26]	1/4P	1/8	7-1/2	17	4
45	85	18436572	VD	TDC	.017	32	CH	N14Y	.035	1/2N	1/4P	1/8	9	17	4
45	85	18436572	VD	TDC[29]	.019	30.5	CH	J14Y	.035	1/2N	1/4P	1/8	9	14.5	4
45	85	18436572	VD	5	.019	30.5	CH	J13Y	.035	1/2N	1/4P	1/8	9	15.5	4
45	85	153624	VD	TDC	.020	44	CH	N14Y	.035	1/2N[26]	1/4P	1/8	7-1/2	13	4
45	85	18436572	VD	TDC	.017	32	CH	N14Y	.035	1/2N[26]	1/4P	1/8	7-1/2	16	4
45	85	18436572	VD	TDC[29]	.019	30.5	CH	J14Y	.035	1/2N[26]	1/4P	1/8	7-1/2	14.5	4
75	100	18436572	VD	TDC[30]	.017	30[31]	CH	N10Y	.035	1/2N[26]	1/4P	1/8	7-1/2	17	5
45	85	18436572	VD	5	.017	30[31]	CH	J11Y	.035	1/2N[26]	1/4P	1/8	7-1/2	17	4
24	70	153624	VD	6	.027	38	BF	82	.034	3/4N	1/4P	1/4	6-3/4	8.7	3.5
24	70	15426378	VD	6	.021	27	BF	42	.034	3/4N	1/4P	1/4	6-3/4	13.7	4
24	70	153624	VD	6	.027	38	BF	82	.034	1/4P	1/4P	3/16	6-3/4	8.9	3.5
24	70	153624	VD	6	.027	38	BF	82	.034	1/4P	1/4P	3/16	6-3/4	8.7	3.5

8 – 360 hp – 10 deg. BTDC
9 – 60 and Brougham – 133 in., 75 – 149.8 in.
10 – 75 – 24.8 qts.
11 – Chevelle 2-Door Sedans – 112 in., 4-Door – 116 in., Monte Carlo – 116 in.
12 – 8.2 Litre Engine
13 – Chevelle – 1N
14 – Chevelle – 1/2P
15 – Chevelle – 8 deg.

16 – Outer Bolts on 4-Bolt Cap – 65 ft. lbs.
17 – Also 300 hp @ 4800
18 – Alum. Head Short Bolts – 65 ft. lbs., Long Bolts – 75 ft. lbs.
19 – Camaro – 108 in.
20 – Power Steering – 2-1/4P
21 – Also 400 hp @ 5400
22 – Also 330 hp @ 5000
23 – Man. Trans. – TDC

24 – 330 hp – J11Y
25 – 330 hp – 15.5 qts.
26 – Power Steering 3/4P
27 – Coronet, Charger – 117 in.
28 – Challenger – 110 in.
29 – Auto. Trans. – 2.5 BTDC
30 – Auto. Trans. – 5 BTDC
31 – Both Breakers – 37 to 42 deg.

1970	Wheelbase	No. of Cylinders Bore and Stroke	Displacement (cu. in.)	Valve and Cylinder Arrangement	Compression Pressure (lbs.)	Maximum Brake Horsepower	Valve Tappet Clearance		Cylinder Bolt Torque (ft. lbs.)
							Intake	Exhaust	
Mustang, Deluxe, Grande	108	6-3.682x3.126	200	IO	175	120@4000	HY	HY	75
Mustang, Deluxe, Grande	108	6-3.682x3.910	250	IO	175	155@4000	HY	HY	75
Mustang, Deluxe, Grande	108	8-4.002x3.0	302	VO	150	220@4600	HY	HY	72
Mustang, Deluxe, Grande	108	8-4.002x3.50	351	VO	170	250@4600 [1]	HY	HY	100
Mustang, Deluxe, Grande	108	8-4.002x3.50	351	VO	170	300@5400 [1]	HY	HY	100
Mustang, Deluxe, Grande, Mach 1	108	8-4.132x3.984	428	VO	190	335@5200 [5]	HY	HY	90
Fairlane, Torino	117	6-3.682x3.91	250	IO	175	155@4000	HY	HY	75
Fairlane, Torino, GT	117	8-4.002x3.0	302	VO	150	220@4600	HY	HY	72
Fairlane, Torino, GT	117	8-4.002x3.50	351	VO	160	250@4600 [2]	HY	HY	100
Fairlane, Torino, GT, Cobra	117	8-4.362x3.59	429	VO	190	360@4600	HY	HY	140
Fairlane, Torino, GT, Cobra	117	8-4.362x3.59	429	VO	190	370@4700 [5]	HY	HY	140
Fairlane, Torino, GT, Cobra	117	8-4.362x3.59	429	VO	190	375@5600	.020H	.020H	140
Ford Custom, 500, Galaxie 500	121	6-4.0x3.18	240	IO	175	150@4000	HY	HY	75
Ford Custom, 500, Galaxie 500	121	8-4.0x3.0	302	VO	150	220@4600	HY	HY	72
Ford (All)	121	8-4.0x3.50	351	VO	160	250@4600	HY	HY	100
Ford (All)	121	8-4.052x3.784	390	VO	180	265@4400	HY	HY	90
Ford (All)	121	8-4.362x3.59	429	VO	190	320@4400	HY	HY	140
Ford (All), Thunderbird	121[8]	8-4.362x3.59	429	VO	190	360@4600	HY	HY	140
Imperial	127	8-4.32x3.75	440	VO	150	350@4400	HY	HY	70
Lincoln Continental	127[10]	8-4.362x3.85	460	VO	180	365@4600	HY	HY	140
Mercury - Cougar, XR-7	111.1	8-4.002x3.0	302	VO	150	220@4600	HY	HY	72
Cougar, XR-7	111.1	8-4.002x3.50	351	VO	170	250@4600 [2]	HY	HY	100
Cougar, XR-7, Eliminator	111.1	8-4.132x3.984	428	VO	190	335@5200 [5]	HY	HY	90
Montego, MX, MX Brougham	117	6-3.682x3.91	250	IO	175	155@4000 [13]	HY	HY	75
Montego, MX, MX Brougham	117	8-4.002x3.0	302	VO	150	220@4600 [13]	HY	HY	72
Montego, Cyclone GT	117	8-4.002x3.50	351	VO	160	250@4600 [14]	HY	HY	100
Montego, Cyclone, Spoiler, GT	117	8-4.362x3.590	429	VO	190	360@4600 [15]	HY	HY	140
Cyclone, Spoiler, GT	117	8-4.362x3.590	429	VO	190	375@3600	.020H	.020H	140
Mercury	124	8-4.052x3.784	390	VO	180	265@4400 [19]	HY	HY	90
Mercury (All)	124	8-4.362x3.59	429	VO	190	320@4400 [20]	HY	HY	140
Oldsmobile - F-85, Cutlass	116	6-3.875x3.53	250	IO	160	155@4200	HY	HY	95
F-85, Cutlass, Supreme	116	8-4.057x3.385	350	VO	175	250@4400 [22]	HY	HY	80
F-85, Cutlass, Supreme	116	8-4.057x3.385	350	VO	175	325@5400	HY	HY	80
Delta 88	124	8-4.057x3.385	350	VO	175	250@4400	HY	HY	80
Delta 88, Custom, Royale	124	8-4.125x4.250	455	VO	175	310@4200	HY	HY	80
Delta 88, Custom, Royale, 98	124[24]	8-4.125x4.250	455	VO	175	365@4600	HY	HY	80
4-4-2	112	8-4.125x4.250	455	IO	175	365@4600 [25]	HY	HY	80
Toronado	119	8-4.125x4.250	455	VO	175	375@4600	HY	HY	80
Toronado	119	8-4.125x4.250	455	VO	175	400@3200	HY	HY	80
Plymouth - Valiant, Duster	108	6-3.40x3.64	198	IO	125	125@4400	.010H	.020H	65
Valiant, Duster, Belvedere, Satellite	108[27]	6-3.40x4.12	225	IO	125	145@4000	.010H	.020H	65
Valiant, Duster, Belvedere, Satellite	108[27]	8-3.91x3.31	318	VO	140	230@4400	HY	HY	85
Valiant, Duster, 'Cuda	108	8-4.04x3.31	340	VO	150	275@5000	HY	HY	95
Belvedere, Satellite, Barracuda	116[28]	8-4.25x3.38	383	VO	140	290@4400	HY	HY	70
Belvedere, Satellite, Road Runner	116	8-4.25x3.38	383	VO	150	330@5000 [31]	HY	HY	70
Road Runner, GTX, 'Cuda	116[28]	8-4.25x3.75	426	VO	150	425@5000	HY	HY	75
GTX, 'Cuda, Fury I, II, III, Sport Fury	116[28]	8-4.32x3.75	440	VO	150	375@4600	HY	HY	70
Fury I, II, III, Sport Fury, Barracuda	120[28]	6-3.40x4.12	225	IO	125	145@4000	.010H	.020H	65
Fury I, II, III, Barracuda	120[28]	8-3.91x3.31	318	VO	140	230@4400	HY	HY	85
Fury I, II, III, Sport Fury, Barracuda	120[28]	8-4.25x3.38	383	VO	140	290@4400	HY	HY	70
Fury I, II, III, Sport Fury, Barracuda	120[28]	8-4.25x3.38	383	VO	150	330@5000 [31]	HY	HY	70
Road Runner, GTX, 'Cuda, Sport Fury GT	116[28]	8-4.32x3.75	440	VO	150	390@4700 [36]	HY	HY	70
Pontiac - Tempest, LeMans, LeMans Sport	112[39]	6-3.875x3.525	250	IO	160	155@4200	HY	HY	95
Tempest, LeMans, LeMans Sport	112[39]	8-3.875x3.746	350	VO	160	255@4600	HY	HY	95
Tempest, LeMans, LeMans Sport, Grand Prix	112[39]	8-4.12x3.746	400	VO	160	265@4600	HY	HY	95
Tempest, LeMans, LeMans Sport	112[39]	8-4.12x3.746	400	VO	160	330@4800	HY	HY	95
GTO, Grand Prix	112[39]	8-4.12x3.746	400	VO	160	350@5000	HY	HY	95
GTO	112	8-4.12x3.746	400	VO	160	366@5100 [40]	HY	HY	95
Catalina	122	8-3.875x3.746	350	VO	160	255@4600	HY	HY	95
Catalina, Executive, Bonneville	122[41]	8-4.12x3.746	400	VO	160	265@4600	HY	HY	95
Catalina, Executive	122[41]	8-4.12x3.746	400	VO	160	290@4600	HY	HY	95
Catalina, Executive	122[41]	8-4.12x3.746	400	VO	160	330@4800	HY	HY	95
GTO	112	8-4.151x4.206	455	VO	160	360@4300	HY	HY	95
Catalina, Executive, Bonneville	122[40]	8-4.151x4.206	455	VO	160	360@4300 [41]	HY	HY	95

ABBREVIATIONS - FOOTNOTES

AC	AC Spark Plugs
AF, BF	Autolite Spark Plugs
BA	Balancer Assembly
BTDC	Before Top Dead Center
C	Cold Engine
CH	Champion Spark Plugs
CP	Crankshaft Pulley
H	Hot Engine
HY	Hydraulic Lifters

IO - In-Line Engine - Overhead Valves
N - Negative
P - Positive
TDC - Top Dead Center
VD - Vibration Damper
VO - V-Type Engine - Overhead Valves
1 - Mach 1 Only - Ram Air
2 - Also 300 hp @ 5400
3 - Auto. Trans. - .017 in.
4 - 300 hp - AF - 32
5 - Also Ram Air

6 - Auto. Trans. - .020 in.
7 - Auto. Trans. - 28.5 deg.
8 - T-Bird 2-Door - 114.7 in., 4-Door - 117.1 in.
9 - T-Bird - 19.4 qts.
10 - Continental Mark III - 117.2 in.
11 - Continental Mark III - 1P
12 - Continental Mark III - 3/16 in.
13 - Except 2-Door Hardtops
14 - Also Eliminator - 300 hp @ 5400
15 - Also Cyclone - 370 hp @ 5400 and Ram Air

Tuneup Specifications

Connecting Rod Bolt Torque (ft. lbs.)	Main Bearing Bolt Torque (ft. lbs.)	Firing Order	Timing Mark Location	Breaker Point Opens BTDC	Breaker Point Gap	Cam Angle	Spark Plugs			Caster Man. Steer. (deg.)	Camber Rt. Wheel (deg.)	Toe-in (in.)	Steering Axis Inclination (deg.)	Cooling System Capacity (qts.)	Crankcase Capacity (qts.)
							Make	Model	Gap						
24	70	153624	VD	6	.027	38	BF	82	.034	0	1P	3/16	6-3/4	9	4
26	70	153624	VD	6	.027	38	BF	82	.034	0	1P	3/16	6-3/4	9.8	4
24	70	15426378	VD	6	.021	27	BF	42	.034	0	1P	3/16	6-3/4	13.5	4
45	70	13726548	VD	6	.021	27	AF	42	.034	0	1P	3/16	6-3/4	13.6	4
45	70	13726548	VD	6	.021	27	AF	32	.034	0	1P	3/16	6-3/4	13.6	4
58	105	15426378	VD	6	.021	27	BF	32	.034	0	1P	3/16	6-3/4	19.3	4
26	70	153624	VD	6	.027	38	BF	82	.034	3/4N	1/4P	1/4	7-3/4	11.4	4
24	70	15426378	VD	6	.021	27	BF	42	.034	3/4N	1/4P	1/4	7-3/4	15.2	4
45	105	13726548	VD	6	.021[3]	27	AF	42[4]	.034	3/4N	1/4P	1/4	7-3/4	15.4	4
45	105	15426378	VD	6	.021	27	BF	42	.034	3/4N	1/4P	1/4	7-3/4	19	4
45	105	15426378	VD	10	.021[6]	24.5[7]	AF	32	.034	3/4N	1/4P	1/4	7-3/4	19.6	6
45	105	15426378	VD	10	.021[6]	24.5[7]	AF	32	.034	3/4N	1/4P	1/4	7-3/4	19.6	6
45	70	153624	VD	6	.027	38	BF	42	.034	1P	1/2P	3/16	7-3/4	14.4	4
24	70	15426378	VD	6	.021	27	BF	42	.034	1P	1/2P	3/16	7-3/4	15.4	4
45	105	13726548	VD	6	.021	27	AF	42	.034	1P	1/2P	3/16	7-3/4	16.5	4
45	105	15426378	VD	6	.017	28	BF	42	.034	1P	1/2P	3/16	7-3/4	20.1	4
45	105	15426378	VD	6	.021	27	BF	42	.034	1P	1/2P	3/16	7-3/4	18.6	4
45	105	15426378	VD	6	.021	27	BF	42	.034	1P	1/2P	3/16	7-3/4	18.6[9]	4
45	85	18436572	VD	5	.019	30.5	CH	J13Y	.035	1/2N	1/4P	1/8	9	16.5	4
45	105	15426378	VD	10	.017	29	BF	42	.034	1-1/2P[11]	1/2P	0[12]	7-3/4	19.6	4
24	70	15426378	VD	6	.021	27	BF	42	.034	0	1P	3/16	6-3/4	13.5	4
45	70	13726548	VD	6	.021[3]	27	AF	42[4]	.034	0	1P	3/16	6-3/4	14.6	4
58	105	15426378	VD	6	.021[3]	27	BF	32	.034	0	1P	3/16	6-3/4	19.3	4
26	70	153624	VD	6	.027	38	BF	82	.034	3/4N	1/4P	1/4	7-3/4	11.4	4
24	70	15426378	VD	6	.021	27	BF	42	.034	3/4N	1/4P	1/4	7-3/4	15.2	4
45	105	13726548	VD	6	.021[3]	27	AF	42[4]	.034	3/4N	1/4P	1/4	7-3/4	15.4	4
45	105	15426378	VD	6[16]	.021[3]	27	BF	42	.034	3/4N	1/4P	1/4	7-3/4	19[17]	4[18]
45	105	15426378	VD	10	.021	27	AF	32	.034	3/4N	1/4P	1/4	7-3/4	19.6	6
45	105	15426378	VD	6	.021	27	BF	42	.034	1P	1/2P	3/16	7-1/2	20.1	4
45	105	15426378	VD	6	.021	27	BF	42	.034	1P	1/2P	3/16	7-1/2	18.6	4
35	65	153624	VD	TDC[21]	.016	33	AC	R46T	.035	1-1/4N	1/8P	3/16	9	12.2	4
42	80[23]	18436572	BA	10	.016	30	AC	R46S	.030	1-1/4N	1/8P	3/16	9	15.2	4
42	80[23]	18436572	BA	14	.016	30	AC	R43S	.030	1-1/4N	1/8P	3/16	9	15.2	4
42	80	18436572	BA	10	.016	30	AC	R46S	.030	1N	1/8P	3/16	11	17.5	4
42	120	18436572	BA	8	.016	30	AC	R46S	.030	1N	1/8P	3/16	11	17.5	4
42	120	18436572	BA	8	.016	30	AC	R45S	.030	1N	1/8P	3/16	11	17.5	4
42	120	18436572	BA	12	.016	30	AC	R44S	.030	1-1/4N	1/8P	3/16	9	16.2	4
42	120	18436572	BA	8	.016	30	AC	R45S	.030	2-1/4N	1/8P	0	11	18	5
42	120	18436572	BA	12	.016	30	AC	R44S	.030	2-1/4N	1/8P	0	11	18	5
45	85	153624	VD	TDC	.020	44	CH	N14Y	.035	1/2N[26]	1/4P	1/8	7-1/2	13	4
45	85	153624	VD	TDC	.020	44	CH	N14Y	.035	1/2N[26]	1/4P	1/8	7-1/2	13	4
45	85	18436572	VD	TDC	.017	32	CH	N14Y	.035	1/2N[26]	1/4P	1/8	7-1/2	16	4
45	85	18436572	VD	5	.017	30[29]	CH	N9Y	.035	1/2N[26]	1/4P	1/8	7-1/2	15	4
45	85	18436572	VD	2.5	.019	30.5	CH	N14Y	.035	1/2N[26]	1/4P	1/8	7-1/2	14.5[33]	4
45	85	18436572	VD	TDC[30]	.019	30.5	CH	J11Y	.035	1/2N[26]	1/4P	1/8	7-1/2	14.5	4
75	100	18436572	VD	TDC[32]	.017	30[29]	CH	N10Y	.035	1/2N[26]	1/4P	1/8	7-1/2	17[34]	6[36]
45	85	18436572	VD	TDC[30]	.019	30.5	CH	J11Y	.035	1/2N[26]	1/4P	1/8	7-1/2[38]	17[34]	4
45	85	153624	VD	TDC	.020	44	CH	N14Y	.035	1/2N[26]	1/4P	1/8	9	17[35]	4
45	85	18436572	VD	TDC	.017	32	CH	N14Y	.035	1/2N[26]	1/4P	1/8	9	16	4
45	85	18436572	VD	2.5	.019	30.5	CH	N14Y	.035	1/2N[26]	1/4P	1/8	9	16	4
45	85	18436572	VD	TDC[30]	.019	30.5	CH	J11Y	.035	1/2N[26]	1/4P	1/8	9	16	4
45	85	18436572	VD	5	.017	30[29]	CH	J11Y	.035	1/2N[26]	1/4P	1/8	7-1/2[38]	17[34]	6[37]
35	65	153624	VD	TDC[21]	.019	33	AC	R46T	.035	1-1/2N	1/4P	1/16	9	13	4
43	100[23]	18436572	CP	9	.016	30	AC	R45S	.035	1-1/2N	1/4P	1/16	9	19.9	5
43	100[23]	18436572	CP	9	.016	30	AC	R45S	.035	1-1/2N	1/4P	1/16	9	18.3	5
43	100[23]	18436572	CP	9	.016	30	AC	R45S	.035	1-1/2N	1/4P	1/16	9	18.3	5
43	100[23]	18436572	CP	15	.016	30	AC	R44S	.035	1-1/2N	1/4P	1/16	9	18.3	5
43	100[23]	18436572	CP	9	.016	30	AC	R46S	.035	1-1/2N	1/4P	1/16	9	19.6	5
43	100[23]	18436572	CP	9	.016	30	AC	R46S	.035	1-1/2N	1/4P	1/16	8-1/2	18[43]	5
43	100[23]	18436572	CP	9	.016	30	AC	R45S	.035	1-1/2N	1/4P	1/16	8-1/2	18	5
43	100[23]	18436572	CP	9	.016	30	AC	R45S	.035	1-1/2N	1/4P	1/16	8-1/2	18	5
43	100[23]	18436572	CP	9	.016	30	AC	R46S	.035	1-1/2N	1/4P	1/16	9	18.3	5
43	100[23]	18436572	CP	9	.016	30	AC	R44S	.035	1-1/2N	1/4P	1/16	8-1/2	18[43]	5

16 – 370 hp – 10 deg. BTDC
17 – 370 hp – 19.6 qts.
18 – 370 hp – 6 qts.
19 – All Except Brougham
20 – Also 360 hp @ 4600
21 – Auto. Trans. – 4 deg. BTDC
22 – Also 310 hp @ 4800
23 – Rear Main – 120 ft. lbs.
24 – Ninety Eight – 127 in.
25 – Also 370 hp @ 5200
26 – Power Steering – 3/4P

27 – Belvedere, Satellite – 116 in.
28 – Barracuda – 108 in., Fury – 120 in.
29 – Both Breakers – 37 to 42 deg.
30 – Auto. Trans. – 2.5 deg. BTDC
31 – Also 335 hp @ 5200
32 – Auto. Trans. – 5 deg. BTDC
33 – Barracuda – 16 qts.
34 – Barracuda – 15.5 qts.
35 – Barracuda – 13 qts.
36 – Also GT – 350 hp @ 4400
37 – Road Runner, GTX – 4 qts.

38 – Fury, Sport Fury – 9 deg.
39 – 2-Door – 112 in., 4-Door – 116 in., Grand Prix – 118 in.
40 – Ram Air – Also 370 hp @ 5500
41 – Executive, Bonneville – 125 in.
42 – Also 370 hp @ 4600 on Catalina, Executive, Bonneville and Grand Prix
43 – Bonneville – 17.2 qts.

1971

	Wheelbase (in.)	No. of Cylinders Bore and Stroke (in.)	Displacement (cu. in.)	Valve and Cylinder Arrangement	Compression Pressure (lbs.)	Maximum Brake Horsepower @ rpm	Valve Tappet Clearance Intake	Exhaust	Cylinder Bolt Torque (ft. lbs.)
American Motors – Gremlin, Hornet	96 [1]	6–3.75x3.50	232	IO	185	135@4000	HY	HY	85
Sportabout, Javelin, SST, Matador	108 [3]	6–3.75x3.50	232	IO	185	135@4000	HY	HY	85
Gremlin, Hornet, SST, Sportabout	96 [1]	6–3.75x3.90	258	IO	185	150@3800	HY	HY	85
Javelin, SST, Matador, Ambassador DPL	110 [3]	6–3.75x3.90	258	IO	185	150@3800	HY	HY	85
Hornet SST, Sportabout, Javelin, SST	108 [3]	8–3.75x3.44	304	VO	185	210@4400	HY	HY	110
Matador SST, Ambassador, SST, Brougham	118 [3]	8–3.75x3.44	304	VO	185	210@4400	HY	HY	110
Hornet SC/360, Javelin, SST, AMX	108 [3]	8–4.08x3.44	360	VO	185	245@4400 [6]	HY	HY	110
Matador SST, Ambassador SST, Brougham	118 [3]	8–4.08x3.44	360	VO	185	245@4400 [6]	HY	HY	110
Javelin, SST, AMX	110	8–4.165x3.68	401	VO	200	330@5000	HY	HY	110
Matador SST, Ambassador SST, Brougham	118 [3]	8–4.165x3.68	401	VO	200	330@5000	HY	HY	110
Buick – Skylark	112 [7]	6–3.874x3.53	250	IO	165 [8]		HY	HY	95
Skylark, Custom, Sportwagon	112 [7]	8–3.80x3.85	350	VO	175 [8]	230@4400 [9]	HY	HY	75
LeSabre, LeSabre Custom	124	8–3.80x3.85	350	VO	175 [8]	230@4400 [9]	HY	HY	75
LeSabre, Custom, Estate Wagon	124 [12]	8–4.125x3.90	455	VO	175 [8]	315@4400	HY	HY	100
GS	112	8–4.125x3.90	455	VO	175 [8]	315@4400 [15]	HY	HY	100
Centurion, Electra 225, Custom	124 [16]	8–4.125x3.90	455	VO	175 [8]	315@4400 [17]	HY	HY	100
Riviera	122	8–4.125x3.90	455	VO	175 [8]	315@4400 [18]	HY	HY	100
Cadillac – All Except Eldorado	130 [19]	8–4.30x4.06	472	VO	175	345@4400	HY	HY	115
Eldorado	126.3	8–4.30x4.304	500	VO	175	365@4400	HY	HY	115
Chevrolet – Vega 2300	97	4–3.501x3.625	140	IOC	140	90@4600	.015C [22]	.030C [22]	60
Vega 2300 (L11)	97	4–3.501x3.625	140	IOC	140	110@4800	.015C [22]	.030C [22]	60
Camaro	108	6–3.875x3.53	250	IO	130	145@4200	HY	HY	95
Nova	111	6–3.875x3.53	250	IO	130	145@4200	HY	HY	95
Chevelle	112 [7]	6–3.875x3.53	250	IO	130	145@4200	HY	HY	95
Chevrolet (All Except Caprice)	121.5	6–3.875x3.53	250	IO	130	145@4200	HY	HY	95
Camaro, Nova, Chevelle	108 [25]	8–3.875x3.25	307	VO	150	200@4600	HY	HY	65
Camaro, Nova, Chevelle, Monte Carlo	108 [25]	8–4.0x3.48	350	VO	160	245@4800	HY	HY	65
Chevrolet (All Except Caprice)	121.5	8–4.0x3.48	350	VO	160	245@4800	HY	HY	65
Chevrolet (All)	121.5	8–4.0x3.48	350	VO	160	270@4800	HY	HY	65
Corvette	98	8–4.0x3.48	350	VO	160	270@4800	HY	HY	65
Camaro, Nova, Chevelle, Monte Carlo	108 [25]	8–4.0x3.48	350	VO	160	270@4800	HY	HY	65
Camaro (Z28)	108	8–4.0x3.48	350	VO	150	330@5600	.020	.025	65
Corvette	98	8–4.0x3.48	350	VO	150	330@5600	.020	.025	65
Chevrolet (All)	121.5	8–4.125x3.75	400	VO	160	255@4400	HY	HY	80
Chevrolet (All)	121.5	8–4.126x3.76	402	VO	160	300@4800	HY	HY	65
Camaro, Chevelle, Monte Carlo	108 [25]	8–4.126x3.76	402	VO	160	300@4800	HY	HY	65
Chevelle, Monte Carlo	112 [25]	8–4.251x4.0	454	VO	160	365@4800 [33]	HY	HY	80
Chevrolet (All)	121.5	8–4.251x4.0	454	VO	160	365@4800	HY	HY	80
Corvette	98	8–4.251x4.0	454	VO	160	365@4800	HY	HY	80
Corvette	98	8–4.251x4.0	454	VO	160	425@5600	.024	.028	80
Chrysler – Newport Royal	124	8–4.0x3.58	360	VO	100	255@4000	HY	HY	95
Newport, Custom, Royal	124	8–4.25x3.38	383	VO	100	275@4400 [35]	HY	HY	70
300, New Yorker	124	8–4.32x3.75	440	VO	110	335@4400	HY	HY	70
Newport, Custom, Royal, 300, New Yorker	124	8–4.32x3.75	440	VO	110	370@4600	HY	HY	70
Imperial	127	8–4.32x3.75	440	VO	110	335@4400	HY	HY	70
Dodge – Dart, Dart Demon, Swinger Special	111 [37]	6–3.40x3.64	198	IO	100	125@4400	.010H	.020H	70
Challenger Coupe	111	6–3.40x3.84	198	IO	100	125@4400	.010H	.020H	70
Dart, Demon, Custom, Swinger Special	111 [37]	6–3.40x4.12	225	IO	100	145@4400	.010H	.020H	70
Challenger, Charger Coupe, Coronet, Custom	111 [38]	6–3.40x4.12	225	IO	100	145@4400	.010H	.020H	70
Polara	122	6–3.40x4.12	225	IO	100	145@4400	.010H	.020H	70
Dart, Demon, Custom, Swinger, Special	111 [37]	8–3.91x3.31	318	VO	100	230@4400	HY	HY	95
Challenger, Coupe, Charger, Coupe, 500, SE	111 [38]	8–3.91x3.31	318	VO	100	230@4400	HY	HY	95
Coronet, Custom, Brougham	118	8–3.91x3.31	318	VO	100	230@4400	HY	HY	95
Polara, Custom	122	8–3.91x3.31	318	VO	100	230@4400	HY	HY	95
Challenger, R/T, Demon 340	111 [37]	8–4.04x3.31	340	VO	110	275@5000	HY	HY	95
Charger, Super Bee	115	8–4.04x3.31	340	VO	110	275@5000	HY	HY	95
Polara, Custom	122	8–4.0x3.58	360	VO	100	255@4400	HY	HY	95
Challenger, Coupe, Charger, Coupe, 500, SE	111 [38]	8–4.25x3.38	383	VO	100	275@4400 [41]	HY	HY	70
Coronet, Custom, Brougham, Super Bee	118 [42]	8–4.25x3.38	383	VO	100	300@4800	HY	HY	70
Polara, Custom, Brougham, Monaco	122	8–4.25x3.38	383	VO	100	275@4400 [44]	HY	HY	70
Challenger R/T, Charger R/T, Super Bee	111 [38]	8–4.25x3.75	426	VO	110	425@5000	HY	HY	75
Charger R/T, Super Bee, SE	111 [38]	8–4.32x3.75	440	VO	110	370@4600	HY	HY	70
Challenger R/T, Charger R/T, Super Bee	111 [38]	8–4.32x3.75	440	VO	110	385@4700	HY	HY	70
Polara, Custom, Brougham, Monaco	122	8–4.32x3.75	440	VO	110	335@4400	HY	HY	70
Ford – Pinto	94	4–3.188x3.056	97.6	IO	70 [48]	75@5000	.010C	.017C	65
Pinto	94	4–3.575x3.029	122	IOC	80 [48]	100@5600	.008C	.010C	80
Maverick, GT	103 [50]	6–3.502x2.94	170	IO	175 [48]	100@4200	HY	HY	75
Maverick, GT	103 [50]	6–3.682x3.126	200	IO	175 [48]	115@4000	HY	HY	75
Ford Custom, 500, Galaxie 500	121	6–4.0x3.18	240	IO	175 [48]	140@4000	HY	HY	75
Maverick, GT, Mustang, Grande	103 [52]	6–3.682x3.91	250	IO	175 [48]	145@4000	HY	HY	75
Torino, 500, GT	117	6–3.682x3.91	250	IO	175 [48]	145@4000	HY	HY	75
Maverick, GT, Mustang, Grande, Mach 1	103 [52]	8–4.002x3.0	302	VO	150 [48]	210@4600	HY	HY	72
Torino, 500, GT, Brougham	117	8–4.002x3.0	302	VO	150 [48]	210@4600	HY	HY	72

ABBREVIATIONS – FOOTNOTES:

AC – AC Spark Plugs
AU – Autolite Spark Plugs
B – Before Top Dead Center
C – Cold Engine
CH – Champion Spark Plugs
CP – Crankshaft Pulley
EL – Electronic Ignition
H – Hot Engine
HY – Hydraulic Lifters
IO – In-Line Engine, Overhead Valves
IOC – In-Line Engine, Overhead Cam

N – Negative
P – Positive
TDC – Top Dead Center
VD – Vibration Damper
VO – V-Type Engine, Overhead Valves
1 – Hornet, Sportabout – 108
2 – Manual Trans. – 3B@700
3 – Javelin – 110, Matador – 118, Ambassador – 122
4 – Manual Trans. – 5B@700
5 – Manual Trans. – 2.5B@750
6 – Also 285@4800
7 – 4-Door – 116, Sportwagon – 116

8 – Lowest Cylinder Must Be At Least 70 Percent of Highest
9 – Also 260@4600, Incl. GS
10 – Manual Trans. – 6B@600
11 – Sportwagon – 1/2N
12 – Estate Wagon – 127
13 – Estate Wagon – 10-3/4
14 – Estate Wagon – 18.7
15 – Also GS Stage 1 – 345@5000
16 – Electra 225, Custom – 127
17 – Also Centurion – 330@4600
18 – Also Riviera GS – 330@4600
19 – Fleetwood Brougham – 133, 75 – 151.5

Firing Order	Timing Mark Location	Initial Ignition Timing @ rpm	Breaker Point Gap (in.)	Cam Angle (deg.)	Spark Plugs Make	Model	Gap (in.)	Caster Manual Steering (deg.)	Camber Right Wheel (deg.)	Toe-In (in.)	Steering Axis Inclination (deg.)	Cooling System Capacity (qts.)	Crankcase Capacity (qts.)
153624	VD	5B@600 [2]	.016	32	CH	N12Y	.035	1P	0	1/8	7-3/4	10.5	4
153624	VD	5B@600 [2]	.016	32	CH	N12Y	.035	1P	0	1/8	7-3/4	10.5	4
153624	VD	5B@600 [4]	.016	32	CH	N12Y	.035	1P	0	1/8	7-3/4	10.5	4
153624	VD	5B@600	.016	32	CH	N12Y	.035	1P	0	1/8	7-3/4	10.5	4
18436572	VD	2.5B@650 [5]	.016	30	CH	N12Y	.035	1P	0	1/8	7-3/4	14	4
18436572	VD	2.5B@650	.016	30	CH	N12Y	.035	1P	0	1/8	7-3/4	14	4
18436572	VD	2.5B@650 [5]	.016	30	CH	N12Y	.035	1P	0	1/8	7-3/4	13	4
18436572	VD	2.5B@650	.016	30	CH	N12Y	.035	1P	0	1/8	7-3/4	13	4
18436572	VD	2.5B@650 [5]	.016	30	CH	N12Y	.035	1P	0	1/8	7-3/4	13	4
18436572	VD	2.5B@650	.016	30	CH	N12Y	.035	1P	0	1/8	7-3/4	13	4
153624	VD	4B@600	.019	32	AC	R46T	.035	1/2P	1/2P	3/16	8	16	4
18436572	VD	10B@600 [10]	.016	30	AC	R45TS	.030	1/2P [11]	1/2P	3/16	8	16.45	4
18436572	VD	4B@600 [10]	.016	30	AC	R45TS	.030	1P	1/4P	3/16	9-5/8 [13]	16.45 [14]	4
18436572	VD	4B@600 [10]	.016	30	AC	R45TS	.030	1/2P	1/2P	3/16	8	16.45	4
18436572	VD	4B@600 [10]	.016	30	AC	R45TS	.030	1P	1/4P	3/16	9-5/8	18.7	4
18436572	VD	4B@600 [10]	.016	30	AC	R44TS	.030	1P	1/4P	3/16	9-5/8	18.7	4
18436572	VD	4B@600	.016	30	AC	R44T.S	.030	1P	1/4P	3/16	9-5/8	18.7	4
15634278	VD	8B@600	.016	30	AC	R46N	.035	1-1/2N [20]	0	3/16	6	21.3 [21]	4
15634278	VD	8B@600	.015	30	AC	R46N	.035	1N	0	0	11	21.8	5
1342	CP	6B@550 [23]	.019	32	AC	R42TS	.035	3/4N	1/4P	1/4	8-1/2	6.5	3
1342	CP	10B@550 [23]	.019	32	AC	R42TS	.035	3/4N	1/4P	1/4	8-1/2	6.5	3
153624	VD	4B@500 [24]	.019	32	AC	R46TS	.035	0	1P	3/16	9-1/2	12	4
153624	VD	4B@500 [24]	.019	32	AC	R46TS	.035	1/2P	1/2P	3/16	8-3/4	12	4
153624	VD	4B@500 [24]	.019	32	AC	R46TS	.035	1N	3/4P	3/16	8-1/4	12	4
153624	VD	4B@500 [24]	.019	32	AC	R46TS	.035	1N	1/2P	3/16	10	12	4
18436572	VD	8B@550 [26]	.019	30	AC	R45TS	.035	0 [27]	1P [28]	3/16	9-1/2 [29]	15	4
18436572	VD	6B@550 [30]	.019	30	AC	R45TS	.035	0 [27]	1P [28]	3/16	9-1/2 [29]	16	4
18436572	VD	6B@550 [30]	.019	30	AC	R45TS	.035	1N	1/2P	3/16	10	16	4
18436572	VD	8B@600	.019	30	AC	R44TS	.035	1N	1/2P	3/16	10	16	4
18436572	VD	8B@550 [31]	.019	30	AC	R44TS	.035	1P	3/4P	3/16	7	15	4
18436572	VD	8B@550 [26]	.019	30	AC	R44TS	.035	0 [27]	1P [28]	3/16	9-1/2 [29]	16	4
18436572	VD	12B@700 [32]	.019	30	AC	R43TS	.035	1N	3/4P	3/16	9-3/4	16	4
18436572	VD	8B@700	EL	EL	AC	R43TS	.035	1P	3/4P	3/16	7	18	4
18436572	VD	8B@550 [26]	.019	30	AC	R44TS	.035	1N	1/2P	3/16	10	16	4
18436572	VD	8B@600	.019	29	AC	R44TS	.035	1N	1/2P	3/16	10	23	4
18436572	VD	8B@600	.019	29	AC	R44TS	.035	0 [27]	1P [28]	3/16	9-1/2 [29]	24	4
18436572	VD	8B@600 [34]	.019	29	AC	R43TS	.035	1N	3/4P	3/16	8-1/4	22	4
18436572	VD	8B@600	.019	29	AC	R43TS	.035	1N	1/2P	3/16	10	22	4
18436572	VD	8B@600	.019	29	AC	R43TS	.035	1P	3/4P	1/4	7	22	5
18436572	VD	12B@600	EL	EL	AC	R44XL	.035	1P	3/4P	1/4	7	20	5
18436572	VD	2.5B@700 [5]	.016	32	CH	N10Y	.035	1/2N	1/4P	1/8	9	15.5	4
18436572	VD	12.5B@800 [36]	.018	30.5	CH	J14Y	.035	1/2N	1/4P	1/8	9	14.5	4
18436572	VD	12.5B@750	.018	30.5	CH	J13Y	.035	1/2N	1/4P	1/8	9	15.5	4
18436572	VD	12.5B@900	.018	30.5	CH	J11Y	.035	1/2N	1/4P	1/8	9	17.5	4
18436572	VD	5B@650	.018	30.5	CH	J13Y	.035	3/4P	1/4P	1/8	9	17.5	4
153624	VD	2.5B@800	.020	43	CH	N14Y	.035	1/2N	1/4P	1/8	7-1/2	13	4
153624	VD	2.5B@800	.020	43	CH	N14Y	.035	1/2N	1/4P	1/8	7-1/2	13	4
153624	VD	TDC@750	.020	43	CH	N14Y	.035	1/2N	1/4P	1/8	7-1/2	13	4
153624	VD	TDC@750	.020	43	CH	N14Y	.035	1/2N	1/4P	1/8	9	13	4
153624	VD	TDC@750	.020	43	CH	N14Y	.035	1/2N	1/4P	1/8	9	13	4
18436572	VD	TDC@700 [39]	.016	32	CH	N14Y	.035	1/2N	1/4P	1/8	7-1/2	16	4
18436572	VD	TDC@700 [39]	.016	32	CH	N14Y	.035	1/2N	1/4P	1/8	7-1/2	16	4
18436572	VD	TDC@700 [39]	.016	32	CH	N14Y	.035	1/2N	1/4P	1/8	9	16	4
18436572	VD	5B@900	.016	32	CH	N9Y	.035	1/2N	1/4P	1/8	7-1/2	15	4
18436572	VD	5B@700 [40]	.016	32	CH	N9Y	.035	1/2N	1/4P	1/8	7-1/2	15.5	4
18436572	VD	2.5B@700 [39]	.016	32	CH	N13Y	.035	1/2N	1/4P	1/8	9	14.5	4
18436572	VD	12.5B@700	.018	30.5	CH	J14Y	.035	1/2N	1/4P	1/8	9	14.5	4
18436572	VD	12.5B@800 [43]	.018	30.5	CH	J11Y	.035	1/2N	1/4P	1/8	9	14.5	4
18436572	VD	12.5B@700 [36]	.018	30.5	CH	J14Y	.035	1/2N	1/4P	1/8	7-1/2	17	4
18436572	VD	2.5B@900	.016	30	CH	N10Y	.035	1/2N	1/4P	1/8	7-1/2	15.5 [46]	6
18436572	VD	12.5B@800 [45]	.016	30.5	CH	J11Y	.035	1/2N	1/4P	1/8	7-1/2	15.5 [46]	6
18436572	VD	12.5B@900	.016	30 [47]	CH	J11Y	.035	1/2N	1/4P	1/8	9	15.5	4
18436572	VD	12.5B@750	.016	30.5	CH	J13Y	.035	1/2N	1/4P	1/8	9	15.5	4
1243	CP	12B@900	.025	40	AU	AGS22	.025	3/4P	3/4P	3/16	9	6.8	3
1342	CP	6B@650 [49]	.025	40	AU	BRF32	.034	1-1/2P	3/4P	3/16	9	7.5	4
153624	VD	6B@750	.027	35	AU	BRF82	.034	0	3/4P	3/16	6-3/4	9.2	4
153624	VD	6B@550 [49]	.027	35	AU	BRF82	.034	0	3/4P	3/16	6-3/4	14.1	4
153624	VD	6B@500 [51]	.027	35	AU	BRF42	.034	1P	1/2P	3/16	7-3/16	14.1	4
153624	VD	6B@600 [49]	.027	35	AU	BRF82	.034	0	3/4P	3/16	6-3/4	9.7 [53]	4
153624	VD	6B@600 [49]	.027	35	AU	BRF82	.034	3/4N	1/4P	1/4	7-3/4	11.2	4
15426378	VD	6B@575 [51]	.021	27	AU	BRF42	.034	0	3/4P	3/16	6-3/4	13.5 [54]	4
15426378	VD	6B@575 [51]	.017	28	AU	BRF42	.034	3/4N	1/4P	1/4	7-3/4	15.1	4

20 – Fleetwood Brougham - 1N, 75 - 2-1/2N
21 – 75 - 24.8
22 – Running - Intake .015, Exhaust .016
23 – Manual Trans. - 6B@700
24 – Manual Trans. - 4B@550
25 – Nova - 111, Chevelle - 112/116, Monte Carlo - 116
26 – Manual Trans. - 4B@600
27 – Chevelle - 1N, Nova - 1/2P
28 – Chevelle - 3/4P, Nova - 1/4P
29 – Nova - 8-3/4, Chevelle/Monte Carlo - 8-1/4
30 – Manual Trans. - 2B@600

31 – Manual Trans. - 8B@600
32 – Manual Trans. - 8B@700
33 – Also 425@5600
34 – Monte Carlo 425 - 12B@700, Manual Trans. - 8B@700
35 – Also 300@4800
36 – Manual Trans. - 10B@750
37 – Demon - 108, Swinger - 111
38 – Charger - 115, Coronet - 118
39 – Manual Trans. - TDC@750
40 – Manual Trans. - 5B@750
41 – Also Challenger R/T - 300@4800
42 – Super Bee - 115

43 – Manual Trans. - 10B@900
44 – Also 300@4800
45 – Manual Trans. - 10B@800
46 – Manual Trans. - 17
47 – Both Sets of Points - 39
48 – Lowest Cylinder Must Be At Least 75 Percent of Highest
49 – Manual Trans. - 6B@750
50 – 4-Door - 110
51 – Manual Trans. - 6B@800
52 – Mustang - 109
53 – Mustang - 11.2
54 – Mustang - 15.1

1971

	Wheelbase (in.)	No. of Cylinders Bore and Stroke (in.)	Displacement (cu. in.)	Valve and Cylinder Arrangement	Compression Pressure (lbs.)	Maximum Brake Horsepower @ rpm	Valve Tappet Clearance Intake	Valve Tappet Clearance Exhaust	Cylinder Bolt Torque (ft. lbs.)
Ford, Custom, 500, Galaxie 500	121	8-4.002x3.0	302	VO	150 [1]	210@4600	HY	HY	72
Ford LTD, Brougham	121	8-4.0x3.50	351W	VO	160 [1]	240@4600	HY	HY	112
Torino, 500, GT, Brougham	117	8-4.002x3.50	351C	VO	170 [1]	240@4600 [14]	HY	HY	100
Mustang, Grande, Mach 1	109	8-4.002x3.50	351C	VO	170 [1]	240@4600 [3]	HY	HY	100
Mustang, Grande, Mach 1	109	8-4.002x3.50	351C	VO	170 [1]	280@5800 [5]	HY	HY	100
Ford (All)	121	8-4.052x3.784	390	VO	180 [1]	255@4400	HY	HY	90
Ford (All)	121	8-4.0x4.0	400	VO	180 [1]	260@4400	HY	HY	100
Ford (All)	121	8-4.362x3.59	429	VO	190 [1]	320@4400 [7]	HY	HY	140
Thunderbird	114.7 [8]	8-4.362x3.59	429	VO	190 [1]	360@4600	HY	HY	140
Torino, 500, GT, Brougham	117	8-4.362x3.59	429	VO	190 [1]	370@5400	HY	HY	140
Mustang, Grande, Mach 1	109	8-4.362x3.59	429	VO	190 [1]	370@5400 [11]	HY	HY	140
Lincoln	127	8-4.362x3.85	460	VO	180 [1]	365@4600	HY	HY	140
Mark III	117.2	8-4.362x3.85	460	VO	180 [1]	365@4600	HY	HY	140
Mercury - Comet, GT	103 [12]	6-3.502x2.94	170	IO	175 [1]	100@4200	HY	HY	75
Comet, GT	103 [12]	6-3.682x3.126	200	IO	175 [1]	115@4000	HY	HY	75
Comet, GT	103 [12]	6-3.682x3.910	250	IO	175 [1]	145@4000	HY	HY	75
Montego, "MX", Brougham	117	6-3.682x3.910	250	IO	175 [1]	145@4000	HY	HY	75
Comet, GT	103 [12]	8-4.002x3.0	302	VO	150 [1]	210@4600	HY	HY	72
Montego, "MX", Brougham	117	8-4.002x3.0	302	VO	150 [1]	210@4600	HY	HY	72
Montego, "MX", Brougham, Cyclone GT	117	8-4.002x3.50	351C	VO	170 [1]	240@4600 [14]	HY	HY	100
Monterey, Custom	124	8-4.0x3.50	351W	VO	160 [1]	240@4600	HY	HY	112
Cougar, XR-7, GT	112.1	8-4.002x3.50	351C	VO	170 [1]	240@4600 [14]	HY	HY	100
Cougar, XR-7, GT	112.1	8-4.002x3.50	351C	VO	170 [1]	280@5800	HY	HY	100
Monterey, Custom	124	8-4.0x4.0	400	VO	180 [1]	260@4400	HY	HY	100
Monterey, Custom, Marquis, Brougham	124	8-4.362x3.59	429	VO	190 [1]	320@4400 [7]	HY	HY	140
Cyclone, GT, Spoiler	117	8-4.362x3.59	429	VO	190 [1]	370@5400	HY	HY	140
Cougar, XR-7, GT	112.1	8-4.362x3.59	429	VO	190 [1]	370@5400 [5]	HY	HY	140
Oldsmobile - F-85, Cutlass	112 [15]	6-3.875x3.53	250	IO	100 [16]	145@4200	HY	HY	85
F-85, Cutlass, Supreme	112 [15]	8-4.057x3.385	350	VO	100 [16]	240@4200 [18]	HY	HY	85
Delta 88	124	8-4.057x3.385	350	VO	100 [16]	240@4200	HY	HY	85
Delta 88, Custom, Royale	124	8-4.125x4.250	455	VO	100 [16]	280@4000	HY	HY	85
Delta 88, Custom, Royale, 98	124 [20]	8-4.125x4.250	455	VO	100 [16]	320@4400	HY	HY	85
Cutlass Supreme	112	8-4.125x4.250	455	VO	100 [16]	320@4400	HY	HY	85
4-4-2	112	8-4.125x4.250	455	VO	100 [16]	340@4600 [21]	HY	HY	85
Toronado	122.3	8-4.125x4.250	455	VO	100 [16]	350@4400	HY	HY	85
Plymouth - Valiant, Scamp	108 [22]	6-3.40x3.64	198	IO	100	125@4400	.010H	.020H	70
Barracuda, Coupe	108	6-3.40x3.64	198	IO	100	125@4400	.010H	.020H	70
Barracuda, Coupe	108	6-3.40x4.12	225	IO	100	145@4000	.010H	.020H	70
Valiant, Scamp	108 [22]	6-3.40x4.12	225	IO	100	145@4000	.010H	.020H	70
Satellite, Coupe, Custom, Sebring	115 [23]	6-3.40x4.12	225	IO	100	145@4000	.010H	.020H	70
Fury I, II, III	120	6-3.40x4.12	225	IO	100	145@4000	.010H	.020H	70
Valiant, Scamp, Barracuda, Coupe, Gran Coupe	108 [22]	8-3.91x3.31	318	VO	100	230@4400	HY	HY	95
Satellite, Coupe, Custom, Sebring, Road Runner	115 [23]	8-3.91x3.31	318	VO	100	230@4400	HY	HY	95
Fury I, II, III, Sport Fury	120	8-3.91x3.31	318	VO	110	230@4400	HY	HY	95
Duster 340, 'Cuda	108	8-4.04x3.31	340	VO	110	275@5000	HY	HY	95
Satellite Sebring, Road Runner	115	8-4.04x3.31	340	VO	110	275@5000	HY	HY	95
Fury I, II, III, Sport Fury	120	8-4.0x3.58	360	VO	100	255@4000	HY	HY	95
Barracuda, Coupe, Gran Coupe	108	8-4.25x3.38	383	VO	100	275@4400 [29]	HY	HY	70
Satellite, Coupe, Custom, Sebring, Brougham	115 [23]	8-4.25x3.38	383	VO	100	275@4400 [29]	HY	HY	70
Fury, I, II, III, Sport Fury	120	8-4.25x3.38	383	VO	100	275@4400 [29]	HY	HY	70
Road Runner, GTX, 'Cuda	115 [30]	8-4.25x3.75	426	VO	110	425@5000	HY	HY	75
Fury I, II, III, Sport Fury	120	8-4.32x3.75	440	VO	110	335@4400	HY	HY	70
Sport Fury GT	120	8-4.32x3.75	440	VO	110	370@4600	HY	HY	70
GTX	115	8-4.32x3.75	440	VO	110	370@4600	HY	HY	70
GTX, Road Runner, 'Cuda	115 [30]	8-4.32x3.75	440	VO	110	385@4700	HY	HY	70
Pontiac - Ventura II, Firebird	111 [33]	6-3.875x3.53	250	IO	130 [34]	145@4200	HY	HY	95
LeMans, T-37, Sport	112 [15]	6-3.875x3.53	250	IO	140 [34]	145@4200	HY	HY	95
Ventura II	111	8-3.875x3.25	307	VO	150 [34]	200@4400	HY	HY	65
Ventura II, Firebird, Esprit, Formula 350	111 [33]	8-3.875x3.75	350	VO	140 [34]	250@4400	HY	HY	95
LeMans, T-37, Sport	112 [15]	8-3.875x3.75	350	VO	140 [34]	250@4400	HY	HY	95
Catalina	123.5	8-3.875x3.75	350	VO	140 [34]	250@4400	HY	HY	95
Firebird Esprit	108	8-4.120x3.75	400	VO	140 [34]	265@4400 [40]	HY	HY	95
LeMans, T-37, Sport	112 [15]	8-4.120x3.75	400	VO	140 [34]	265@4400 [42]	HY	HY	95
Catalina, Brougham	123.5	8-4.120x3.75	400	VO	140 [34]	265@4400 [43]	HY	HY	95
Grand Prix	118	8-4.120x3.75	400	VO	140 [34]	300@4800	HY	HY	95
Grand Prix, Firebird Formula 455	118 [33]	8-4.152x4.21	455	VO	140 [34]	325@4400	HY	HY	95
Catalina, Brougham	123.5	8-4.152x4.21	455	VO	140 [34]	280@4400 [47]	HY	HY	95
Bonneville	126	8-4.152x4.21	455	VO	140 [34]	280@4400 [47]	HY	HY	95
Grand Ville	126	8-4.152x4.21	455	VO	140 [34]	325@4400	HY	HY	95
LeMans, T-37, Sport, GTO	112 [15]	8-4.152x4.21	455	VO	140 [34]	325@4400	HY	HY	95
LeMans, T-37, Sport, GTO	112	8-4.152x4.21	455	VO	140 [34]	335@4800	HY	HY	95
Firebird Formula 455, Trans AM	108	8-4.152x4.21	455	VO	140 [34]	335@4800	HY	HY	95

ABBREVIATIONS - FOOTNOTES:

AC - AC Spark Plugs
AU - Autolite Spark Plugs
B - Before Top Dead Center
CH - Champion Spark Plugs
H - Hot Engine
HY - Hydraulic Lifters
IO - In-Line Engine, Overhead Valves
N - Negative
P - Positive

TDC - Top Dead Center
VD - Vibration Damper
VO - V-Type Engine, Overhead Valves
1 - Lowest Cylinder Must Be At Least 75 Percent of Highest
2 - Manual Trans. - 6B@775
3 - Also Ram Air and 285@5400
4 - Manual Trans. - 6B@750
5 - Also Ram Air
6 - Manual Trans. - 10B@750
7 - Also 360@4600

8 - 4-Door - 117.2
9 - Manual Trans. - 10B@700
10 - Manual Trans. - Both Sets of Points - 33
11 - Also Ram Air and 375@5600
12 - 4-Door - 110
13 - Manual Trans. - 6B@800
14 - Also 285@5400
15 - 4-Door - 116
16 - Lowest Cylinder Must Be At Least 80 Percent of Highest

Firing Order	Timing Mark Location	Initial Ignition Timing @ rpm	Breaker Point Gap (in.)	Cam Angle (deg.)	Make	Model	Gap	Caster Manual Steering (deg.)	Camber Right Wheel (deg.)	Toe-In (in.)	Steering Axis Inclination (deg.)	Cooling System Capacity (qts.)	Crankcase Capacity (qts.)
15426378	VD	6B@575 [13]	.021	27	AU	BRF42	.034	1P	1/2P	3/16	7-3/16	15.2	4
13726548	VD	6B@575 [2]	.021	27	AU	BRF6	.034	1P	1/2P	3/16	7-3/16	16.3	4
13726548	VD	6B@625 [4]	.017	29	AU	ARF42	.034	3/4N	1/4	1/4	7-3/4	15.3	4
13726548	VD	6B@625 [4]	.017	29	AU	ARF42	.034	0	3/4P	3/16	6-3/4	15.7	4
13726548	VD	10B@600 [6]	.021	27	AU	ARF32	.034	0	3/4P	3/16	6-3/4	16.3	4
15426378	VD	6B@600	.021	27	AU	BRF6	.034	1P	1/2P	3/16	7-3/16	20.3	4
13726548	VD	6B@625	.017	29	AU	ARF42	.034	1P	1/2P	3/16	7-3/16	17.6	4
15426378	VD	4B@600	.021	27	AU	BRF42	.034	1P	1/2P	3/16	7-3/16	18.8	6
15426378	VD	4B@600	.017	29	AU	BRF42	.034	1P	1/2P	3/16	7-3/4	19.4	4
15426378	VD	10B@650 [9]	.020	28.5 [10]	AU	ARF32	.034	3/4N	1/4P	1/4	7-3/4	19.4	
15426378	VD	10B@650 [9]	.020	28.5 [10]	AU	ARF32	.034	3/4N	1/4P	1/4	7-3/4	19.4	6
15426378	VD	4B@590	.017	29	AU	BRF42	.034	1-1/2P	1/2P	1/8	7-7/8	19.6	4
15426378	VD	4B@600	.017	29	AU	BRF42	.034	1P	1/2P	3/16	7-3/4	19.4	4
153624	VD	6B@750	.027	35	AU	BRF82	.034	0	3/4P	3/16	6-3/4	9.2	4
153624	VD	6B@550 [4]	.027	35	AU	BRF82	.034	0	3/4P	3/16	6-3/4	9	4
153624	VD	6B@600	.027	35	AU	BRF82	.034	0	3/4P	3/16	6-3/4	9.7	4
153624	VD	6B@600	.027	35	AU	BRF82	.034	3/4N	1/4P	1/4	7-3/4	11.2	4
15426378	VD	6B@575 [13]	.021	27	AU	BRF42	.034	0	3/4P	1/4	6-3/4	13.5	4
15426378	VD	6B@575 [13]	.017	29	AU	BRF42	.034	3/4N	1/4P	1/4	7-3/4	15.1	4
13726548	VD	6B@625 [4]	.017	29	AU	BRF42	.034	3/4N	1/4P	1/4	7-3/4	15.3	4
13726548	VD	6B@575 [2]	.021	27	AU	BRF42	.034	1P	1/2P	3/16	7-3/4	16.3	4
13726548	VD	6B@625 [4]	.017	29	AU	ARF42	.034	0	3/4P	3/16	6-3/4	15.7	4
13726548	VD	10B@600 [6]	.021	27	AU	ARF32	.034	0	3/4P	3/16	6-3/4	15.7	4
13726548	VD	6B@625	.017	29	AU	ARF42	.034	1P	1/2P	3/16	7-3/4	17.6	4
15426378	VD	4B@600	.021	27	AU	BRF42	.034	1P	1/2P	3/16	7-3/4	18.8	6
15426378	VD	10B@650 [9]	.020	28.5 [10]	AU	ARF32	.034	3/4N	1/4P	1/4	7-3/4	19.4	6
15426378	VD	10B@650 [9]	.020	28.5 [10]	AU	ARF32	.034	0	3/4P	3/16	6-3/4	19.4	6
153624	VD	4B@500 [17]	.016	32	AC	R46TS	.035	1-1/4N	1/8P	1/8	8	12.2	4
18436572	VD	10B@1100 [19]	.016	30	AC	R46S	.040	1-1/4N	1/8P	1/8	8	15.2	4
18436572	VD	10B@1100	.016	30	AC	R46S	.040	1P	1/8P	1/8	10-1/2	17.5	4
18436572	VD	8B@1100	.016	30	AC	R46S	.040	1P	1/8P	1/8	10-1/2	17.5	4
18436572	VD	8B@1100	.016	30	AC	R46S	.040	1P	1/8P	1/8	10-1/2	17.5	4
18436572	VD	8B@1100	.016	30	AC	R46S	.040	1-1/4N	1/8P	1/8	8	17.5	4
18436572	VD	10B@1100	.016	30	AC	R45S	.040	1-1/4N	1/8P	1/8	8	16.2	4
18436572	VD	10B@1100	.016	30	AC	R46S	.040	2-1/4P	1/8P	1/16	11	18	5
153624	VD	2.5B@800	.020	43	CH	N14Y	.035	1/2N	1/4P	1/8	7-1/2	13	4
153624	VD	2.5B@800	.020	43	CH	N14Y	.035	1/2N	1/4P	1/8	7-1/2	13	4
153624	VD	TDC@750	.020	43	CH	N14Y	.035	1/2N	1/4P	1/8	7-1/2	13	4
153624	VD	TDC@750	.020	43	CH	N14Y	.035	1/2N	1/4P	1/8	7-1/2	13	4
153624	VD	TDC@750	.020	43	CH	N14Y	.035	1/2N	1/4P	1/8	9	13	4
18436572	VD	TDC@700 [24]	.016	32	CH	N14Y	.035	1/2N	1/4P	1/8	7-1/2	16	4
18436572	VD	TDC@700 [24]	.016	32	CH	N14Y	.035	1/2N	1/4P	1/8	7-1/2	16	4
18436572	VD	TDC@700 [24]	.016	32	CH	N14Y	.035	1/2N	1/4P	1/8	9	16	4
18436572	VD	5B@900	.016	32 [27]	CH	N9Y	.035	1/2N	1/4P	1/8	7-1/2	15 [25]	4
18436572	VD	5B@700 [26]	.016	32	CH	N9Y	.035	1/2N	1/4P	1/8	7-1/2	15	4
18436572	VD	2.5B@700 [28]	.016	32	CH	N13Y	.035	1/2N	1/4P	1/8	9	15.5	4
18436572	VD	12.5B@700	.018	30.5	CH	J14Y	.035	1/2N	1/4P	1/8	7-1/2	14.5	4
18436572	VD	12.5B@700	.018	30.5	CH	J14Y	.035	1/2N	1/4P	1/8	7-1/2	14.5	4
18436572	VD	12.5B@700 [6]	.018	30.5	CH	J14Y	.035	1/2N	1/4P	1/8	9	14.5	4
18436572	VD	2.5B@900	.016	29	CH	N10Y	.035	1/2N	1/4P	1/8	7-1/2	15.5	6
18436572	VD	12.5B@750	.018	30.5	CH	J13Y	.035	1/2N	1/4P	1/8	9	15.5	6
18436572	VD	12.5B@900	.018	30.5	CH	J11Y	.035	1/2N	1/4P	1/8	9	15.5	6
18436572	VD	12.5B@800 [31]	.018	30.5	CH	J11Y	.035	1/2N	1/4P	1/8	7-1/2	15.5	6
18436572	VD	12.5B@900	.016	29 [32]	CH	J11Y	.035	1/2N	1/4P	1/8	7-1/2	15.5	6
153624	VD	4B@550 [35]	.019	32	AC	R46T	.035	1/2P [36]	1/4P [37]	3/16	8-3/4	12.1	4
153624	VD	4B@550 [35]	.019	32	AC	R45T	.035	1-1/2N	1/4P	1/16	9	13	4
18436572	VD	8B@550 [38]	.019	30	AC	R45TS	.035	1/2P	1/4P	3/16	8-3/4	15	4
18436572	VD	9B@600 [39]	.016	30	AC	R47S	.035	1/2P [36]	1/4P [37]	3/16	8-3/4	19.4	5
18436572	VD	9B@600 [39]	.016	30	AC	R47S	.035	1/2P	1/4P	1/16	9	20.2	5
18436572	VD	9B@600 [39]	.016	30	AC	R46S	.035	1-1/2N	1/4P	1/16	8-1/2	20.2	5
18436572	VD	9B@700 [41]	.016	30	AC	R46S	.035	1N	3/4P	3/16	8-3/4	18.6	5
18436572	VD	9B@700 [41]	.016	30	AC	R46S	.035	1-1/2N	1/4P	1/16	9	18.6	5
18436572	VD	9B@700 [41]	.016	30	AC	R46S	.035	1-1/2N	1/4P	1/16	8-1/2	18.6	5
18436572	VD	9B@700 [41]	.016	30	AC	R46S	.035	1-1/2N	1/4P	1/16	9	18.7	5
18436572	VD	9B@700	.016	30	AC	R46S	.035	1-1/2N [36]	1/4P [37]	1/16 [44]	9 [45]	18.1 [46]	5
18436572	VD	9B@700 [41]	.016	30	AC	R46S	.035	1-1/2N	1/4P	1/16	8-1/2	17.9	5
18436572	VD	9B@700 [41]	.016	30	AC	R46S	.035	1-1/2N	1/4P	1/16	8-1/2	17.9	5
18436572	VD	9B@700	.016	30	AC	R46S	.035	1-1/2N	1/4P	1/16	9	17.9	5
18436572	VD	9B@700 [41]	.016	30	AC	R46S	.035	1-1/2N	1/4P	1/16	9	17.9	5
18436572	VD	9B@700 [41]	.016	30	AC	R46S	.035	1N	3/4P	3/16	8-3/4	17.9	5

17 – Manual Trans. – 4B@550
18 – Also 260@4600
19 – Manual Trans. – 260 hp – 10B@1100
20 – 98 – 127
21 – Also 350@4700
22 – Scamp – 111
23 – 4-Door – 117
24 – Manual Trans. – TDC@750
25 – 'Cuda – 15.5
26 – Manual Trans. – 5B@750
27 – Manual Trans. – Both Sets of Points – 33

28 – Manual Trans. – 2.5B@750
29 – Also 300@4800
30 – 'Cuda – 108
31 – Manual Trans. – 10B@900
32 – Both Sets of Points – 39
33 – Firebird – 108
34 – Lowest Cylinder Must Be More Than 80 Percent of Highest
35 – Manual Trans. – 5B@700
36 – Firebird – 1N
37 – Firebird – 3/4P

38 – Manual Trans. – 8B@700
39 – Manual Trans. – 9B@800
40 – Also Formula 400 – 300@4800
41 – Manual Trans. – 9B@600
42 – Also GTO – 300@4800
43 – Also 300@4800
44 – Firebird – 3/16
45 – Firebird – 8-3/4
46 – Firebird – 17.9
47 – Also 325@4400

1972

	Wheelbase (in.)	No. of Cylinders Bore and Stroke (in.)	Displacement (cu. in.)	Valve and Cylinder Arrangement	Compression Pressure (lbs.)	Net Brake Horsepower @ rpm	Valve Tappet Clearance Intake	Valve Tappet Clearance Exhaust	Cylinder Bolt Torque (ft. lbs.)
American Motors – Gremlin, Hornet SST	96 [1]	6–3.75x3.50	232	IO	185 [2]	100@3600	HY	HY	85
Sportabout, Javelin SST, Matador	108 [3]	6–3.75x3.50	232	IO	185 [2]	100@3600	HY	HY	85
Gremlin, Hornet SST, Sportabout	96 [1]	6–3.75x3.90	258	IO	185 [2]	110@3500	HY	HY	85
Javelin SST, Matador	110 [3]	6–3.75x3.90	258	IO	185 [2]	110@3500	HY	HY	85
Gremlin, Hornet SST, Sportabout	96 [1]	8–3.75x3.44	304	VO	185 [2]	150@4200	HY	HY	110
Javelin, Matador, Ambassador	110 [3]	8–3.75x3.44	304	VO	185 [2]	150@4200	HY	HY	110
Hornet SST, Sportabout, Javelin	108 [3]	8–4.08x3.44	360	VO	185 [2]	175@4000	HY	HY	110
Matador, Ambassador	118 [3]	8–4.08x3.44	360	VO	185 [2]	175@4000	HY	HY	110
Javelin, Matador, Ambassador	110 [3]	8–4.08x3.44	360	VO	185 [2]	195@4400	HY	HY	110
Javelin, Matador, Ambassador	110 [3]	8–4.165x3.68	401	VO	200 [2]	255@4600	HY	HY	110
Buick – Skylark, Skylark Custom, Sportwagon	112 [4]	8–3.80x3.85	350	VO	175 [5]	155@3800	HY	HY	75
LeSabre, LeSabre Custom	124	8–3.80x3.85	350	VO	175 [5]	155@3800	HY	HY	75
Skylark, Skylark Custom, GS, Sportwagon	112 [4]	8–3.80x3.85	350	VO	175 [5]	180@3800 [7]	HY	HY	75
LeSabre, LeSabre Custom, GS, Riviera	124 [8]	8–4.3125x3.90	455	VO	175 [5]	225@4000 [9]	HY	HY	100
Centurion, Electra 225, Electra 225 Custom	124 [14]	8–4.3125x3.90	455	VO	175 [5]	225@4000 [15]	HY	HY	100
Estate Wagon	127	8–4.3125x3.90	455	VO	175 [5]	225@4000	HY	HY	100
GS (Stage 1)	112	8–4.3125x3.90	455	VO	175 [5]	270@4400	HY	HY	100
Riviera, Centurion (GS Riviera Option)	122 [8]	8–4.3125x3.90	455	VO	175 [5]	260@4400	HY	HY	100
Cadillac – All Except Eldorado	130 [17]	8–4.30x4.06	472	VO	175	220@4000	HY	HY	115
Eldorado	126.3	8–4.30x4.304	500	VO	175	235@3800	HY	HY	115
Chevrolet – Vega 2300	97	4–3.501x3.625	140	IOC	140	80@4400	.015C [19]	.030C [19]	60
Vega 2300 (L11)	97	4–3.501x3.625	140	IOC	140	90@4800	.015C [19]	.030C [19]	60
Camaro	108	6–3.875x3.53	250	IO	130	110@3800	HY	HY	95
Nova	111	6–3.875x3.53	250	IO	130	110@3800	HY	HY	95
Chevelle	112 [21]	6–3.875x3.53	250	IO	130	110@3800	HY	HY	95
Chevrolet	121.5	6–3.875x3.53	250	IO	130	110@3800	HY	HY	95
Camaro, Nova, Chevelle	108 [22]	8–3.875x3.25	307	VO	150	130@4000	HY	HY	65
Camaro, Nova, Chevelle, Monte Carlo	108 [22]	8–4.0x3.48	350	VO	160	165@4000 [27]	HY	HY	65
Chevrolet	121.5	8–4.0x3.48	350	VO	160	165@4000	HY	HY	65
Camaro (Z27), Nova	108 [22]	8–4.0x3.48	350	VO	160	200@4400	HY	HY	65
Corvette	98	8–4.0x3.48	350	VO	160	200@4400	HY	HY	65
Camaro (Z28)	108	8–4.0x3.48	350	VO	150	255@5600	.020	.025	65
Corvette	98	8–4.0x3.48	350	VO	150	255@5600	.020	.025	65
Chevrolet	121.5	8–4.126x3.75	400	VO	160	170@3400	HY	HY	80
Chevrolet	121.5	8–4.126x3.76	402	VO	160	210@4400	HY	HY	65
Camaro, Chevelle, Monte Carlo	108 [22]	8–4.126x3.76	402	VO	160	240@4400	HY	HY	65
Chevelle, Monte Carlo	112 [21]	8–4.251x4.0	454	VO	160	270@4000	HY	HY	80
Chevrolet	121.5	8–4.251x4.0	454	VO	160	270@4000	HY	HY	80
Corvette	98	8–4.251x4.0	454	VO	160	270@4000	HY	HY	80
Chrysler – Newport Royal	124	8–4.0x3.58	360	VO	100	175@4000	HY	HY	95
Newport Royal, Custom	124	8–4.34x3.38	400	VO	100	190@4000	HY	HY	95
Newport Royal, Custom	124	8–4.32x3.75	440	VO	110	225@4400	HY	HY	70
New Yorker, Brougham	124	8–4.32x3.75	440	VO	110	225@4400	HY	HY	70
Imperial	127	8–4.32x3.75	440	VO	110	225@4400	HY	HY	70
Dodge – Dart, Dart Demon, Swinger Special	111 [30]	6–3.4x3.64	198	IO	100	100@4400	.010H	.020H	70
Dart Custom, Swinger	111	6–3.4x3.64	198	IO	100	100@4400	.010H	.020H	70
Dart, Demon, Custom, Swinger Special	111 [30]	6–3.4x4.12	225	IO	100	110@4000	.010H	.020H	70
Challenger, Charger, Coronet, Custom	110 [31]	6–3.4x4.12	225	IO	100	110@4000	.010H	.020H	70
Dart, Demon, Custom, Swinger Special	111 [30]	8–3.91x3.31	318	VO	100	150@4000	HY	HY	95
Challenger, Coronet, Charger, SE	110 [31]	8–3.91x3.31	318	VO	100	150@4000	HY	HY	95
Polara, Polara Custom	122	8–3.91x3.31	318	VO	100	150@4000	HY	HY	95
Dart Demon 340, Swinger	108 [30]	8–4.04x3.31	340	VO	100	240@4800	HY	HY	95
Challenger, Charger Coupe	110 [31]	8–4.04x3.31	340	VO	100	240@4800	HY	HY	95
Polara, Custom, Monaco	122	8–4.0x3.58	360	VO	100	175@4000	HY	HY	95
Charger, SE, Coronet, Custom	115 [31]	8–4.34x3.38	400	VO	100	190@4400	HY	HY	70
Charger, SE, Coronet, Custom	115 [31]	8–4.34x3.38	400	VO	100	255@4800	HY	HY	70
Polara, Custom, Monaco	122	8–4.34x3.38	400	VO	100	190@4000	HY	HY	70
Charger, SE, Coronet, Custom	115 [31]	8–4.32x3.75	440	VO	110	280@4800	HY	HY	70
Charger, SE, Coronet, Custom	115 [31]	8–4.32x3.75	440	VO	110	330@4800	HY	HY	70
Polara, Custom, Monaco	122	8–4.32x3.75	440	VO	110	225@4400	HY	HY	70
Ford – Pinto	94.2	4–3.188x3.056	97.6	IO	70 [2]	54@4600	.010H	.017H	70
Pinto	94.2	4–3.575x3.029	122	IOC	80 [2]	86@5400	.008C	.010C	80
Maverick	103 [34]	6–3.502x2.94	170	IO	175 [2]	82@4400	HY	HY	75
Maverick, GT	103 [34]	6–3.682x3.126	200	IO	175 [2]	91@4000	HY	HY	75
Ford Custom, 500, Galaxie 500	121	6–4.0x3.18	240	IO	175 [2]	103@3800	HY	HY	75
Maverick, GT, Mustang, Grande	103 [34]	6–3.682x3.91	250	IO	175 [2]	98@3600	HY	HY	75

ABBREVIATIONS – FOOTNOTES:

AC – AC Spark Plugs
AU – Autolite Spark Plugs
B – Before Top Dead Center
C – Cold Engine
CH – Champion Spark Plugs
CP – Crankshaft Pulley
EL – Electronic Ignition
H – Hot Engine
HY – Hydraulic Lifters

IO – In-Line Engine, Overhead Valves
IOC – In-Line Engine, Overhead Cam
N – Negative
P – Positive
TDC – Top Dead Center
VD – Vibration Damper
VO – V-Type Engine, Overhead Valves
1 – Hornet, Sportabout – 108
2 – Lowest Cylinder Must Be At Least 75 Percent of Highest

3 – Javelin – 110, Matador – 118, Ambassador – 122
4 – 4-Door and Sportwagon – 116
5 – Lowest Cylinder Must Be At Least 70 Percent of Highest
6 – Manual Trans. – 4B@800
7 – GS W/Dual Exh. – 195@4000
8 – GS – 112, Riviera – 122, Centurion – 124
9 – Riviera or Dual Exh., Except GS – 250@4000

Firing Order	Timing Mark Location	Initial Ignition Timing @ rpm	Breaker Point Gap (in.)	Cam Angle (deg.)	Spark Plugs Make	Model	Gap (in.)	Caster Manual Steering (deg.)	Camber Right Wheel (deg.)	Toe-In	Steering Axis Inclination (deg.)	Cooling System Capacity (qts.)	Crankcase Capacity (qts.)
153624	VD	5B@550	.016	32	CH	N12Y	.035	1P	1/8P	1/8	7-3/4	10.5	4
153624	VD	5B@550	.016	32	CH	N12Y	.035	1P	1/8P	1/8	7-3/4	10.5	4
153624	VD	3B@550	.016	32	CH	N12Y	.035	1P	1/8P	1/8	7-3/4	10.5	4
153624	VD	3B@550	.016	32	CH	N12Y	.035	1P	1/8P	1/8	7-3/4	10.5	4
18436572	VD	5B@650	.016	30	CH	N12Y	.035	1P	1/8P	1/8	7-3/4	14.0	4
18436572	VD	5B@650	.016	30	CH	N12Y	.035	1P	1/8P	1/8	7-3/4	14.0	4
18436572	VD	5B@700	.016	30	CH	N12Y	.035	1P	1/8P	1/8	7-3/4	13.0	4
18436572	VD	5B@700	.016	30	CH	N12Y	.035	1P	1/8P	1/8	7-3/4	13.0	4
18436572	VD	5B@650	.016	30	CH	N12Y	.035	1P	1/8P	1/8	7-3/4	13.0	4
18436572	VD	4B@650[6]	.016	30	AC	R45TS	.040	1/2P	1/2P	3/16[11]	8	16.45	4
18436572	VD	4B@650	.016	30	AC	R45TS	.040	1P	1/4P	3/16[11]	9-5/8	18.9	4
18436572	VD	4B@650[6]	.016	30	AC	R45TS	.040	1/2P	1/2P	3/16[11]	8	16.45	4
18436572	VD	4B@650[6]	.016	30	AC	R45TS	.040	1P[10]	1/4P[10]	3/16[11]	9-5/8[12]	18.9[13]	4
18436572	VD	4B@650	.016	30	AC	R45TS	.040	1P	1/4P	3/16[11]	9-5/8	18.7	4
18436572	VD	4B@650	.016	30	AC	R45TS	.040	1P	1/4P	3/16[11]	10-3/8	18.7	4
18436572	VD	10B@650[16]	.016	30	AC	R45TS	.040	1/2P	1/2P	3/16[11]	8	21.8	4
18436572	VD	4B@650	.016	30	AC	R45TS	.040	1P	1/4P	3/16[11]	9-5/8	18.7	4
15634278	VD	8B@600	.016	30	AC	R46N	.035	1N	0	3/16[11]	6	21.8[18]	4
15634278	VD	8B@600	.016	30	AC	R46N	.035	1N	0	0	11	21.3	5
1342	CP	6B@700	.019	32	AC	R42TS	.035	3/4N	1/4P	1/4	8-1/2	6.5	3
1342	VD	8B@700	.019	32	AC	R42TS	.035	3/4N	1/4P	1/4	8-1/2	6.5	3
153624	VD	4B@600[20]	.019	32	AC	R46T	.035	0	1P	3/16	9-1/2	12	4
153624	VD	4B@600[20]	.019	32	AC	R46T	.035	1/2P	1/4P	3/16	8-3/4	12	4
153624	VD	4B@600[20]	.019	32	AC	R46T	.035	1N	3/4P	3/16	8-1/4	12	4
153624	VD	4B@600[20]	.019	32	AC	R46T	.035	1N	1/2P	3/16	10	12	4
18436572	VD	8B@600[23]	.019	30	AC	R44T	.035	0[24]	1P[25]	3/16	9-1/2[26]	15	4
18436572	VD	6B@600[28]	.019	30	AC	R44T	.035	0[24]	1P[25]	3/16	9-1/2[26]	16	4
18436572	VD	6B@600	.019	30	AC	R44T	.035	1N	1/2P	3/16	10	16	4
18436572	VD	8B@600[28]	.019	30	AC	R44T	.035	0[24]	1P[25]	3/16	9-1/2[26]	16	4
18436572	VD	8B@600[29]	.019	30	AC	R44T	.035	1P	3/4P	1/4	7	15	4
18436572	VD	12B@700[6]	.019	30	AC	R44T	.035	0	1P	3/16	9-3/4	16	4
18436572	VD	4B@900	.019	30	AC	R44T	.035	1P	3/4P	1/4	7	18	4
18436572	VD	6B@600	.019	30	AC	R44T	.035	1N	1/2P	3/16	10	16	4
18436572	VD	6B@600	.019	29	AC	R44T	.035	1N	1/2P	3/16	10	23	4
18436572	VD	8B@600	.019	29	AC	R44T	.035	0	1P	3/16	9-1/2	24	4
18436572	VD	8B@600[29]	.019	29	AC	R44T	.035	1N	3/4P	3/16	8-1/4	22	4
18436572	VD	8B@600	.019	29	AC	R44T	.035	1N	1/2P	3/16	10	22	4
18436572	VD	8B@600[29]	.019	29	AC	R44T	.035	1P	3/4P	1/4	7	22	5
18436572	VD	TDC@750	.017	32	CH	N13Y	.035	5/8P	1/4P	1/8	9	15.5	4
18436572	VD	5B@700	.018	30.5	CH	J13Y	.035	5/8P	1/4P	1/8	9	14.5	4
18436572	VD	10B@750	.018	30.5	CH	J11Y	.035	5/8P	1/4P	1/8	9	15.5	4
18436572	VD	10B@750	.018	30.5	CH	J11Y	.035	5/8P	1/4P	1/8	9	15.5	4
18436572	VD	10B@750	EL	EL	CH	J11Y	.035	5/8P	1/4P	1/8	9	17.5	4
153624	VD	2.5B@800	.020	43	CH	N14Y	.035	5/8N	1/4P	1/8	7-1/2	13	4
153624	VD	2.5B@800	.020	43	CH	N14Y	.035	5/8N	1/4P	1/8	7-1/2	13	4
153624	VD	TDC@750	.020	43	CH	N14Y	.035	5/8N	1/4P	1/8	7-1/2	13	4
153624	VD	TDC@750	.020	43	CH	N14Y	.035	5/8N	1/4P	1/8	7-1/2	13	4
18436572	VD	TDC@750	.016	32	CH	N13Y	.035	5/8N	1/4P	1/8	7-1/2	16	4
18436572	VD	TDC@750	.016	32	CH	N13Y	.035	5/8P	1/4P	1/8	9	16	4
18436572	VD	2.5B@750[32]	EL	EL	CH	N9Y	.035	5/8N	1/4P	1/8	7-1/2	15	4
18436572	VD	2.5B@750[32]	EL	EL	CH	N9Y	.035	5/8N	1/4P	1/8	7-1/2	15	4
18436572	VD	TDC@750	.016	32	CH	N13Y	.035	5/8P	1/4P	1/8	9	15.5	4
18436572	VD	5B@700	.018	30.5	CH	J13Y	.035	5/8N	1/4P	1/8	7-1/2	14.5	4
18436572	VD	10B@750[32]	EL	EL	CH	J11Y	.035	5/8N	1/4P	1/8	7-1/2	14.5	4
18436572	VD	5B@750	.018	30.5	CH	J13Y	.035	5/8P	1/4P	1/8	9	14.5	4
18436572	VD	10B@900[32]	EL	EL	CH	J11Y	.035	5/8N	1/4P	1/8	7-1/2	15	4
18436572	VD	2.5B@900	EL	EL	CH	J11Y	.035	5/8N	1/4P	1/8	7-1/2	15	6
18436572	VD	10B@750	.018	30.5	CH	J11Y	.035	5/8P	1/4P	1/8	9	15.5	4
1243	CP	12B@900	.025	40	AU	AGR22	.030	1-1/2P	3/4P	3/16	9	7.8	3
1342	VD	6B@650[33]	.025	40	AU	BRF32	.034	1-1/2P	3/4P	3/16	9	8.5	4
153624	VD	6B@750	.027	35	AU	BRF82	.034	1/2N	1/4P	3/16	6-3/4	9.2	4
153624	VD	6B@550	.027	35	AU	BRF82	.034	1/2N	1/4P	3/16	6-3/4	9	4
153624	VD	6B@500	.027	37	AU	BRF42	.034	1P	1/2P	3/16	7-1/4	14.1	4
153624	VD	6B@600[33]	.027	35	AU	BRF82	.034	1/2N[35]	1/4P[36]	3/16	6-3/4	9.2[37]	4

10 – GS – 1/2P
11 – + or – 1/8 in.
12 – GS – 8
13 – GS – 16.2, Riviera – 18.7
14 – Electra 225, Custom – 127
15 – Dual Exhaust – 250@4000
16 – Manual Trans. – 8B@900
17 – Brougham – 133, 75 – 151.5
18 – 75 – 24.8
19 – Running – Intake .015, Exh. .016

20 – Manual Trans. – 4B@700
21 – Chevelle 4-Door, Monte Carlo – 116
22 – Nova – 111, Chevelle – 112/116, Monte Carlo – 116
23 – Manual Trans. – 4B@900
24 – Nova – 1/2P, Chevelle/Monte Carlo – 1N
25 – Nova – 1/4P, Chevelle/Monte Carlo – 3/4P
26 – Nova – 8-3/4, Chevelle/Monte Carlo – 8-1/4
27 – Chevelle/Monte Carlo – Also 175@4000
28 – Manual Trans. – 6B@900

29 – Manual Trans. – 8B@800
30 – Demon – 108, Swinger 111
31 – Charger – 115, Coronet 118
32 – Manual Trans. – 2.5B@900
33 – Manual Trans. – 6B@750
34 – 4-Door – 110, Mustang – 109
35 – Mustang – 0
36 – Mustang – 3/4P
37 – Mustang – 11.2

1972

	Wheelbase (in.)	No. of Cylinders Bore and Stroke (in.)	Displacement (cu. in.)	Valve and Cylinder Arrangement	Compression Pressure (lbs.)	Net Brake Horsepower @ rpm	Valve Tappet Clearance		Cylinder Bolt Torque (ft. lbs.)
							Intake	Exhaust	
Torino, Gran Torino, Sport	114 [1]	6-3.682x3.91	250	IO	175 [2]	95@3600	HY	HY	75
Maverick, GT, Mustang, Grande, Mach 1	103 [4]	8-4.002x3.0	302	VO	150 [2]	143@4200	HY	HY	72
Torino, Gran Torino, Sport	114 [1]	8-4.002x3.0	302	VO	150 [2]	140@4000	HY	HY	72
Ford Custom, 500	121	8-4.002x3.0	302	VO	150 [2]	140@4000	HY	HY	72
Ford LTD, Brougham	121	8-4.0x3.50	351W	VO	160 [2]	153@3800	HY	HY	112
Ford (All)	121	8-4.0x3.50	351C	VO	170 [2]	163@3800	HY	HY	100
Torino, Gran Torino, Sport	114 [1]	8-4.0x3.50	351C	VO	170 [2]	161@4000	HY	HY	100
Mustang, Grande, Mach 1	109	8-4.0x3.50	351C	VO	170 [2]	177@4000	HY	HY	100
Torino, Gran Torino, Sport	114 [1]	8-4.0x3.50	351C	VO	170 [2]	248@5400	HY	HY	100
Mustang, Grande, Mach 1	109	8-4.0x3.50	351C	VO	170 [2]	266@5400	HY	HY	100
Torino, Gran Torino, Sport	114 [1]	8-4.0x4.0	400	VO	180 [2]	168@4200	HY	HY	100
Ford (All)	121	8-4.0x4.0	400	VO	180 [2]	172@4000	HY	HY	100
Torino, Gran Torino, Sport	114 [1]	8-4.362x3.59	429	VO	190 [2]	205@4400	HY	HY	140
Ford (All)	121	8-4.362x3.59	429	VO	190 [2]	208@4400	HY	HY	140
Thunderbird	120.4	8-4.362x3.59	429	VO	190 [2]	212@4400	HY	HY	140
Thunderbird	120.4	8-4.362x3.85	460	VO	180 [2]	212@4400	HY	HY	140
Lincoln	127	8-4.362x3.85	460	VO	180 [2]	224@4400	HY	HY	140
Mark IV	120.4	8-4.362x3.85	460	VO	180 [2]	212@4400	HY	HY	140
Mercury – Comet (All)	103 [4]	6-3.502x2.94	170	IO	175 [2]	82@4400	HY	HY	75
Comet (All)	103 [4]	6-3.682x3.126	200	IO	175 [2]	91@4000	HY	HY	75
Comet (All)	103 [4]	6-3.682x3.91	250	IO	175 [2]	98@3600	HY	HY	75
Montego	114 [1]	6-3.682x3.91	250	IO	175 [2]	95@3600	HY	HY	75
Comet (All)	103 [4]	8-4.002x3.0	302	VO	150 [2]	143@4200	HY	HY	72
Montego	114 [1]	8-4.002x3.0	302	VO	150 [2]	140@4000	HY	HY	72
Montego, GT	114 [1]	8-4.0x3.0	351W	VO	160 [2]	161@4000	HY	HY	112
Cougar (All), Monterey	112.1 [11]	8-4.002x3.50	351C	VO	170 [2]	164@4000	HY	HY	100
Cougar (All)	112.1	8-4.002x3.50	351C	VO	170 [2]	262@5400 [14]	HY	HY	100
Montego, GT	112.1 [11]	8-4.002x3.50	351C	VO	170 [2]	248@5400	HY	HY	100
Montego, GT	112.1 [11]	8-4.0x4.0	400	VO	180 [2]	168@4200	HY	HY	100
Monterey, Custom	124	8-4.0x4.0	400	VO	180 [2]	172@4000	HY	HY	100
Monterey, Custom, Marquis, Brougham	124	8-4.362x3.59	429	VO	190 [2]	208@4400	HY	HY	140
Montego, GT	114	8-4.362x3.59	429	VO	190 [2]	205@4400	HY	HY	140
Monterey, Custom, Marquis, Brougham	124	8-4.362x3.85	460	VO	180 [2]	200@4400	HY	HY	140
Oldsmobile – F-85, Cutlass, Supreme	112 [17]	8-4.057x3.385	350	VO	160 [18]	160@4000 [19]	HY	HY	85
Delta 88, Royale	124	8-4.057x3.385	350	VO	160 [18]	160@4000	HY	HY	85
F-85, Cutlass, Supreme	112 [17]	8-4.057x3.385	350	VO	160 [18]	180@4000 [20]	HY	HY	85
Delta 88, Royale	124	8-4.057x3.385	350	VO	160 [18]	180@4000	HY	HY	85
Delta 88, Royale, 98	124 [22]	8-4.126x4.250	455	VO	160 [18]	225@3600 [23]	HY	HY	85
F-85, Cutlass, Supreme	112 [17]	8-4.126x4.250	455	VO	160 [18]	250@4200 [24]	HY	HY	85
Toronado	122	8-4.126x4.250	455	VO	160 [18]	265@4200	HY	HY	85
F-85, Cutlass, Supreme	112 [17]	8-4.126x4.250	455	VO	160 [18]	300@4700	HY	HY	85
Plymouth – Valiant, Duster, Scamp	108 [26]	6-3.40x3.64	198	IO	100	100@4400	.010H	.020H	70
Valiant, Duster, Scamp, Barracuda	108 [26]	6-3.40x4.12	225	IO	100	110@4000	.010H	.020H	70
Satellite, Custom, Sebring	115 [27]	6-3.40x4.12	225	IO	100	110@4000	.010H	.020H	70
Valiant, Duster, Scamp, Barracuda, 'Cuda	108 [26]	8-3.91x3.31	318	VO	100	150@4000	HY	HY	95
Satellite, Custom, Sebring, Sebring Plus	115 [27]	8-3.91x3.31	318	VO	100	150@4000	HY	HY	95
Fury I, II, III, Gran Coupe, Sedan	120	8-3.91x3.31	318	VO	100	150@4000	HY	HY	95
Duster 340, Barracuda, 'Cuda	108	8-4.04x3.31	340	VO	100	240@4800	HY	HY	95
Road Runner	115	8-4.04x3.31	340	VO	100	240@4800	HY	HY	95
Fury I, II, III, Gran Coupe, Sedan	120	8-4.0x3.58	360	VO	100	175@4000	HY	HY	95
Satellite, Custom, Sebring, Sebring Plus	115 [27]	8-4.34x3.38	400	VO	100	190@4400 [29]	HY	HY	70
Fury I, II, III, Gran Coupe, Sedan	120	8-4.34x3.38	400	VO	100	190@4400	HY	HY	70
Fury I, II, III, Gran Coupe, Sedan	120	8-4.32x3.75	440	VO	110	225@4400	HY	HY	70
Road Runner	115	8-4.32x3.75	440	VO	110	280@4800 [31]	HY	HY	70
Pontiac – Ventura II, Firebird	111 [32]	6-3.875x3.53	250	IO	140 [33]	110@3800	HY	HY	95
LeMans, Sport	112 [17]	6-3.875x3.53	250	IO	140 [33]	110@3800	HY	HY	95
Ventura II	111	8-3.875x3.25	307	VO	150 [33]	130@4400	HY	HY	65
Ventura II, Firebird, Esprit, Formula 350	111 [32]	8-3.875x3.75	350	VO	140 [33]	160@4400 [39]	HY	HY	95
LeMans, Sport, Luxury	112 [17]	8-3.875x3.75	350	VO	140 [33]	160@4400 [39]	HY	HY	95
LeMans, Sport, Luxury, GTO	112 [17]	8-4.120x3.75	400	VO	140 [33]	175@4000 [40]	HY	HY	95
Grand Prix, Firebird, Formula 400	118 [32]	8-4.120x3.75	400	VO	140 [33]	250@3600 [40]	HY	HY	95
Catalina, Brougham	123.5	8-4.120x3.75	400	VO	140 [33]	175@4000	HY	HY	95
Catalina, Brougham, Bonneville	123.5 [44]	8-4.152x4.21	455	VO	140 [33]	185@4000 [40]	HY	HY	95
Catalina, Brougham, Bonneville, Grand Ville	123.5 [44]	8-4.152x4.21	455	VO	140 [33]	220@3600 [45]	HY	HY	95
LeMans, Sport, Luxury, Grand Prix	112 [47]	8-4.152x4.21	455	VO	140 [33]	250@3600 [48]	HY	HY	95
LeMans, Sport, Firebird, Formula, Trans AM	112	8-4.152x4.21	455	VO	140 [33]	300@4000	HY	HY	95

ABBREVIATIONS - FOOTNOTES:

AC – AC Spark Plugs
AU – Autolite Spark Plugs
B – Before Top Dead Center
C – Cold Engine
CH – Champion Spark Plugs
EL – Electronic Ignition
H – Hot Engine
HY – Hydraulic Lifters
IO – In-Line Engine, Overhead Valves
N – Negative

P – Positive
TDC – Top Dead Center
VD – Vibration Damper
VO – V-Type Engine, Overhead Valves
1 – 4-Door – 118
2 – Lowest Cylinder Must Be At Least 75 Percent of Highest
3 – Manual Trans. – 6B@750
4 – 4-Door – 110, Mustang – 109
5 – Mustang – 6B@625, Manual Trans. – 6B@800
6 – Mustang – 0

7 – Mustang – 3/4P
8 – Mustang – 15.2
9 – Manual Trans. – 6B@850
10 – Manual Trans. – 10B@900
11 – Monterey – 124
12 – Monterey – 1P
13 – Monterey – 7-1/4
14 – Also CJ – 266@5400
15 – Manual Trans. – 6B@825
16 – CJ – 16.3
17 – 4-Door – 116

Firing Order	Timing Mark Location	Initial Ignition Timing @ rpm	Breaker Point Gap (in.)	Cam Angle (deg.)	Spark Plugs Make	Spark Plugs Model	Spark Plugs Gap (in.)	Caster Manual Steering (deg.)	Camber Right Wheel (deg.)	Toe-In (in.)	Steering Axis Inclination (deg.)	Cooling System Capacity (qts.)	Crankcase Capacity (qts.)
153624	VD	6B@600[3]	.027	37	AU	BRF82	.034	1-1/4P	3/4P	3/16	7-3/4	11.5	4
15426378	VD	6B@550[5]	.021	27	AU	BRF42	.034	1/2N[6]	1/4P[7]	3/16	6-3/4	13.4[8]	4
15426378	VD	6B@575[9]	.021	27	AU	BRF42	.034	1-1/4P	3/4P	3/16	7-3/4	15.2	4
15426378	VD	6B@600	.017	28	AU	BRF42	.034	1P	1/2P	3/16	7-1/4	15.8	4
13726548	VD	6B@600	.017	28	AU	BRF42	.034	1P	1/2P	3/16	7-1/4	15.8	4
13726548	VD	6B@600	.017	28	AU	ARF42	.034	1P	1/2P	3/16	7-3/4	16.3	4
13726548	VD	6B@625	.017	28	AU	ARF42	.034	1-1/4P	3/4P	3/16	7-3/4	15.5	4
13726548	VD	6B@625[3]	.021	27	AU	ARF42	.034	0	3/4P	3/16	6-3/4	15.8	4
13726548	VD	16B@700[10]	.017	28	AU	ARF42	.034	1-1/4P	3/4P	3/16	7-3/4	15.5	4
13726548	VD	16B@700[10]	.017	28	AU	ARF42	.034	0	3/4P	3/16	6-3/4	16.3	4
13726548	VD	6B@625	.017	28	AU	ARF42	.034	1-1/4P	3/4P	3/16	7-3/4	17.7	4
13726548	VD	6B@625	.017	28	AU	ARF42	.034	1P	1/2P	3/16	7-1/4	17.7	4
15426378	VD	10B@600	.017	28	AU	BRF42	.034	1-1/4P	3/4P	3/16	7-3/4	18.8	4
15426378	VD	10B@600	.017	28	AU	BRF42	.034	1P	1/2P	3/16	7-1/4	18.8	6
15426378	VD	10B@600	.020	28	AU	BRF42	.034	1-1/4P	3/4P	3/16	7-3/4	18.8	4
15426378	VD	10B@600	.020	28	AU	BRF42	.034	1-1/4P	3/4P	3/16	7-3/4	20	4
15425378	VD	10B@600	.017	28	AU	BRF42	.034	1-1/2P	1/2P	1/8	7-7/8	19.5	4
15426378	VD	10B@600	.017	28	AU	BRF42	.034	1-1/2P	3/4P	3/16	7-3/4	19.5	4
153624	VD	6B@750	.027	35	AU	BRF82	.034	1/2N	1/4P	3/16	6-3/4	9.2	4
153624	VD	6B@550[3]	.027	35	AU	BRF82	.034	1/2N	1/4P	3/16	6-3/4	9	4
153624	VD	6B@600	.027	35	AU	BRF82	.034	1/2N	1/4P	3/16	6-3/4	9.7	4
153624	VD	6B@625[3]	.027	37	AU	BRF82	.034	3/4P	3/4P	3/16	7-3/4	11.5	4
15426378	VD	6B@500[5]	.021	27	AU	BRF42	.034	1/2N	1/4P	3/16	6-3/4	13.4	4
15426378	VD	6B@625[9]	.021	27	AU	BRF42	.034	3/4P	3/4P	3/16	7-3/4	15.2	4
13726548	VD	6B@625	.017	28	AU	BRF42	.034	3/4P	3/4P	3/16	7-3/4	15.5	4
13726548	VD	6B@625[3]	.021	27	AU	ARF42	.034	0[12]	1/2P	3/16	6-3/4[13]	15.8	4
13726548	VD	6B@650[15]	.021	27	AU	ARF42	.034	0	1/2P	3/16	6-3/4	15.8[16]	4
13726548	VD	16B@700[10]	.017	28	AU	ARF42	.034	3/4P	3/4P	3/16	7-3/4	15.5	4
13726548	VD	6B@625	.017	28	AU	ARF42	.034	3/4P	3/4P	3/16	7-3/4	17.7	4
13726548	VD	6B@625	.017	28	AU	ARF42	.034	1P	1/2P	3/16	7-1/4	17.7	4
15426378	VD	10B@600	.017	28	AU	BRF42	.034	1P	1/2P	3/16	7-1/4	18.8	6
15426378	VD	10B@600	.017	28	AU	BRF42	.034	3/4P	3/4P	3/16	7-3/4	18.8	4
15426378	VD	10B@600	.017	28	AU	BRF42	.034	1P	1/2P	3/16	7-1/4	19.5	4
18436572	VD	8B@1100	.016	30	AC	R46S	.040	1-1/4N	1/4N	0	8	15.2	4
18436572	VD	8B@1100	.016	30	AC	R46S	.040	1P	1/4N	0	9-5/8	16.2	4
18436572	VD	12B@1100[21]	.016	30	AC	R46S	.040	1-1/4N	1/4N	0	8	15.2	4
18436572	VD	12B@1100	.016	30	AC	R46S	.040	1P	1/4N	0	9-5/8	16.2	4
18436572	VD	8B@1100	.016	30	AC	R46S	.040	1P	1/4N	0	9-5/8	17	4
18436572	VD	8B@1100[25]	.016	30	AC	R46S	.040	1-1/4N	1/4N	0	8	17	4
18436572	VD	8B@1100	.016	30	AC	R46S	.040	2N	1/4N	0	11	19.5	5
18436572	VD	10B@850[25]	.016	30	AC	R45S	.040	1-1/4N	1/4N	0	8	17	4
153624	VD	2.5B@800	.020	43	CH	N14Y	.035	5/8N	1/4P	1/8	7-1/2	13	4
153624	VD	TDC@750	.020	43	CH	N14Y	.035	5/8N	1/4P	1/8	7-1/2	13	4
153624	VD	TDC@750	.020	43	CH	N14Y	.035	5/8N	1/4P	1/8	7-1/2	13	4
18436572	VD	TDC@750	.016	32	CH	N13Y	.035	5/8N	1/4P	1/8	7-1/2	16	4
18436572	VD	TDC@750	.016	32	CH	N13Y	.035	5/8N	1/4P	1/8	7-1/2	16	4
18436572	VD	TDC@750	.016	32	CH	N13Y	.035	5/8P	1/4P	1/8	9	16	4
18436572	VD	2.5B@750[28]	EL	EL	CH	N9Y	.035	5/8N	1/4P	1/8	7-1/2	15	4
18436572	VD	2.5B@750[28]	EL	EL	CH	N9Y	.035	5/8N	1/4P	1/8	7-1/2	15	4
18436572	VD	TDC@750	.016	32	CH	N13Y	.035	5/8P	1/4P	1/8	9	15.5	4
18436572	VD	5B@700[30]	.018	30.5	CH	J13Y	.035	5/8N	1/4P	1/8	7-1/2	14.5	4
18436572	VD	5B@700	.018	30.5	CH	J13Y	.035	5/8P	1/4P	1/8	9	14.5	4
18436572	VD	10B@750	.018	30.5	CH	J11Y	.035	5/8P	1/4P	1/8	9	15.5	4
18436572	VD	10B@900	EL	EL	CH	J11Y	.035	5/8N	1/4P	1/8	7-1/4	15	4
153624	VD	4B@550[34]	.019	32	AC	R46TS	.035	1/2P[35]	1/4P[36]	3/16	8-3/4[37]	12	4
153624	VD	4B@550[34]	.019	32	AC	R46T	.035	1-1/2N	1/4P	1/16	9	13	4
18436572	VD	8B@550[38]	.019	30	AC	R45TS	.035	1/2P	1/4P	3/16	8-3/4	15	4
18436572	VD	10B@625	.016	30	AC	R46TS	.035	1/2P[35]	1/4P[36]	3/16	8-3/4[37]	19.4	5
18436572	VD	10B@550[38]	.016	30	AC	R46TS	.035	1-1/2N	1/4P	1/16	9	20.2	5
18436572	VD	10B@625[41]	.016	30	AC	R46TS	.035	1-1/2N	1/4P	1/16	9	18.6	5
18436572	VD	10B@500[42]	.016	30	AC	R45TS	.035	1-1/2N[35]	1/4P[36]	1/16[43]	9[37]	18.7	5
18436572	VD	10B@625	.016	30	AC	R45TS	.035	1-1/2N	1/4P	1/16	8-1/2	18.6	5
18436572	VD	10B@625	.016[46]	30[46]	AC	R45TS	.035	1-1/2N	1/4P	1/16	8-1/2	17.9	5
18436572	VD	10B@500	.016	30	AC	R45TS	.035	1-1/2N	1/4P	1/16	9	17.9	5
18436572	VD	10B@500	.016[46]	30[46]	AC	R45TS	.035	1-1/2N[35]	1/4P[36]	1/16[43]	9[37]	17.9	5

18 - Lowest Cylinder Must Be At Least 70 Percent of Highest
19 - Dual Exh. - 175@4000
20 - Dual Exh. - 200@4400
21 - Manual Trans. - 8B@1100
22 - 98-127
23 - Dual Exhaust - 250@4400
24 - Also 270@4400
25 - Manual Trans. - 10B@1100
26 - Scamp - 111
27 - 4-Door - 117
28 - Manual Trans. - 2.5B@900

29 - Also Road Runner - 255 and 265@4800
30 - 4 Bbl. with Auto. Trans. - 10B@750, Manual Trans. - 10B@900
31 - Also 290@4800
32 - Firebird - 108
33 - Lowest Cylinder Must Be At Least 80 Percent of Highest
34 - Manual Trans. - 4B@550
35 - Firebird - 1N
36 - Firebird - 3/4P
37 - Firebird - 8-1/2

38 - Manual Trans. - 8B@700
39 - Also Firebird, Esprit, LeMans - 175@4400
40 - Also 200@4000, GTO - 250@4400
41 - 4 Bbl. - 10B@500
42 - Manual Trans. - 8B@600
43 - Firebird - 3/16
44 - Bonneville, Grande Ville - 126
45 - Also 250@3600
46 - Grande Ville, HO, SJ - EL
47 - Grand Prix - 118
48 - Also 230@4400

1973

	Wheelbase (in.)	No. of Cylinders Bore and Stroke (in.)	Displacement (cu. in.)	Valve and Cylinder Arrangement	Compression Pressure (lbs.)	Net Brake Horsepower @ rpm	Valve Tappet Clearance Intake	Valve Tappet Clearance Exhaust	Cylinder Bolt Torque (ft. lbs.)
American Motors – Gremlin, Hornet, Javelin	96[1]	6-3.75x3.50	232	IO	185[2]	100@3600	HY	HY	85
Matador (W/EGR)	118	6-3.75x3.50	232	IO	185[2]	100@3600	HY	HY	85
Gremlin, Hornet, Javelin	96[1]	6-3.75x3.90	258	IO	185[2]	110@3500	HY	HY	85
Matador (W/EGR)	118	6-3.75x3.90	258	IO	185[2]	110@3500	HY	HY	85
Gremlin, Hornet, Javelin, AMX, Matador	96[1]	8-3.75x3.44	304	VO	185[2]	150@4200	HY	HY	55
Hornet, Javelin, AMX, Matador, Ambassador	108[1]	8-4.08x3.44	360	VO	185[2]	175@4000	HY	HY	55
Matador, Ambassador	118[1]	8-4.08x3.44	360	VO	185[2]	195@4400	HY	HY	55
Javelin, AMX, Matador, Ambassador	110[1]	8-4.08x3.44	360	VO	185[2]	220@4400	HY	HY	55
Javelin, AMX, Matador, Ambassador	110[1]	8-4.165x3.68	401	VO	200[2]	255@4600	HY	HY	55
Buick – Apollo	111	6-3.875x3.53	250	IO	130	100@3600	HY	HY	95
Apollo	111	8-3.80x3.85	350	VO	180	150@3800	HY	HY	80
Century, Luxus, Gran Sport, Regal	112[6]	8-3.80x3.85	350	VO	180	150@3800	HY	HY	80
LeSabre, Custom	124	8-3.80x3.85	350	VO	180	150@3800[7]	HY	HY	80
Gran Sport	112	8-3.80x3.85	350	VO	180	190@4000	HY	HY	80
LeSabre, Custom, Centurian	124	8-4.3125x3.90	455	VO	180	225@4000	HY	HY	100
Electra 225, Custom	127	8-4.3125x3.90	455	VO	180	225@4000	HY	HY	100
Century, Luxus, Gran Sport, Regal	112[6]	8-4.3125x3.90	455	VO	180	250@4000	HY	HY	100
LeSabre, Custom, Centurian	124	8-4.3125x3.90	455	VO	180	250@4000	HY	HY	100
Electra 225, Custom, Riviera	127[9]	8-4.3125x3.90	455	VO	180	250@4000	HY	HY	100
Riviera (Stage 1)	122	8-4.3125x3.90	455	VO	180	260@4400	HY	HY	100
Gran Sport (Stage 1)	112	8-4.3125x3.90	455	VO	180	270@4400	HY	HY	100
Cadillac – All Except Eldorado	130[10]	8-4.30x4.06	472	VO	175	220@4000	HY	HY	115
Eldorado	126.3	8-4.30x4.304	500	VO	175	235@3800	HY	HY	115
Chevrolet – Vega	97	4-3.501x3.625	140	IOC	140	72@4400	.015C[12]	.030C[12]	60
Vega (L11)	97	4-3.501x3.625	140	IOC	140	85@4800	.015C[12]	.030C[12]	60
Camaro	108	6-3.875x3.53	250	IO	130	100@3600	HY	HY	95
Nova	111	6-3.875x3.53	250	IO	130	100@3600	HY	HY	95
Chevelle	112[6]	6-3.875x3.53	250	IO	130	100@3600	HY	HY	95
Chevrolet	121.5	6-3.875x3.53	250	IO	130	100@3600	HY	HY	95
Camaro, Nova, Chevelle	108[13]	8-3.875x3.25	307	VO	150	115@3600	HY	HY	65
Camaro, Nova, Chevelle	108[13]	8-4.0x3.48	350	VO	160	145@4000	HY	HY	65
Chevrolet, Monte Carlo	121.5[20]	8-4.0x3.48	350	VO	160	145@4000	HY	HY	65
Camaro, Nova, Chevelle	108[13]	8-4.0x3.48	350	VO	160	175@4000	HY	HY	65
Chevrolet, Monte Carlo	121.5[20]	8-4.0x3.48	350	VO	160	175@4400	HY	HY	65
Corvette	98	8-4.0x3.48	350	VO	160	190@4400	HY	HY	65
Camaro (Z28)	108	8-4.0x3.48	350	VO	150	245@5200	HY	HY	65
Corvette	98	8-4.0x3.48	350	VO	150	250@5200	HY	HY	65
Chevrolet	121.5	8-4.126x3.75	400	VO	160	150@3200	HY	HY	80
Chevelle	112[6]	8-4.251x4.0	454	VO	160	245@4000	HY	HY	80
Chevrolet, Monte Carlo	121.5[20]	8-4.251x4.0	454	VO	160	245@4000	HY	HY	80
Corvette	98	8-4.251x4.0	454	VO	160	275@4400	HY	HY	80
Chrysler – Newport, Custom	124	8-4.34x3.38	400	VO	100[24]	185@3600	HY	HY	70
Newport, Custom, New Yorker, Brougham	124	8-4.32x3.75	440	VO	100[24]	215@3600	HY	HY	70
Imperial LeBaron	127	8-4.32x3.75	440	VO	100[24]	215@3600	HY	HY	70
Dodge – Dart, Swinger, Swinger Special	111[26]	6-3.40x3.64	198	IO	100[25]	95@4000	.010H	.020H	70
Dart Custom, Dart Sport	111	6-3.40x3.64	198	IO	100[25]	95@4000	.010H	.020H	70
Dart, Swinger, Special, Custom, Sport	111[26]	6-3.40x4.12	225	IO	100[25]	105@4000	.010H	.020H	70
Charger, Coronet, Custom	115	6-3.40x4.12	225	IO	100[25]	105@4000	.010H	.020H	70
Dart, Swinger, Special, Custom, Sport	111[26]	8-3.91x3.31	318	VO	100[24]	150@3600	HY	HY	95
Challenger, Charger, SE, Coronet	110[28]	8-3.91x3.31	318	VO	100[24]	150@3600	HY	HY	95
Polara, Custom	122	8-3.91x3.31	318	VO	100[24]	150@3600	HY	HY	95
Dart 340 Sport	108	8-4.04x3.31	340	VO	100[24]	240@4800	HY	HY	95
Challenger, Charger, Charger Coupe	110[28]	8-4.04x3.31	340	VO	100[24]	240@4800	HY	HY	95
Polara Custom, Monaco	110	8-4.00x3.58	360	VO	100[24]	170@4000	HY	HY	95
Charger, SE, Coronet	115	8-4.34x3.38	400	VO	100[24]	175@3600[30]	HY	HY	70
Polara, Custom, Monaco	122	8-4.34x3.38	400	VO	100[24]	185@3600	HY	HY	70
Polara, Custom, Monaco	122	8-4.32x3.75	440	VO	100[24]	220@3600	HY	HY	70
Charger	115	8-4.32x3.75	440	VO	100[24]	280@4800	HY	HY	70
Ford – Pinto (1600)	94.2	4-3.188x3.056	97.6	IO	70[2]	55.7@4600	.010H	.017H	70
Pinto (2000)	94.2	4-3.575x3.029	122	IOC	80[2]	84.9@5600	.008C	.010C	80
Maverick (All)	103[32]	6-3.683x3.126	200	IO	175[2]	84@3600	HY	HY	75
Torino	114[33]	6-3.682x3.91	250	IO	175[2]	92@3200	HY	HY	75
Maverick (All)	103[32]	6-3.682x3.91	250	IO	175[2]	93@3200[34]	HY	HY	75
Mustang	109	6-3.682x3.91	250[35]	IO	175[2]	95@3200	HY	HY	75
Torino	114[33]	8-4.002x3.0	302	VO	150[2]	137@4200	HY	HY	72
Maverick (All)	103[32]	8-4.002x3.0	302	VO	150[2]	138@4200	HY	HY	72
Mustang	109	8-4.002x3.0	302	VO	150[2]	141@4000	HY	HY	72
Torino	114[33]	8-4.002x3.50	351W[37]	VO	160[2]	156@3800	HY	HY	112
Ford	121	8-4.002x3.50	351W[37]	VO	160[2]	158@3800	HY	HY	112
Torino	114[33]	8-4.002x3.50	351C[38]	VO	170[2]	159@4000	HY	HY	105

ABBREVIATIONS – FOOTNOTES

AC – AC Spark Plugs
B – Before Top Dead Center
C – Cold Engine
CH – Champion Spark Plugs
CP – Crankshaft Pulley
EGR – Exhaust Gas Recirculation
EL – Electronic Ignition

H – Hot Engine
HY – Hydraulic Lifters
IO – In-Line Engine, Overhead Valves
IOC – In-Line Engine, Overhead Cam
M – Motorcraft Spark Plugs
N – Negative
P – Positive
TDC – Top Dead Center
VD – Vibration Damper
VO – V-Type Engine, Overhead Valves

1 – Hornet – 108, Javelin/AMX – 110
  Matador – 118, Ambassador – 122
2 – Lowest Cylinder Must Be At Least 75 Percent of Highest
3 – W/Manual Trans. – 700 rpm
4 – W/Manual Trans. – 600 rpm
5 – W/Manual Trans. – 750 rpm
6 – 4-Door – 116
7 – Also 175@3800, Including Centurian
8 – W/Manual Trans. – 800 rpm

Tuneup Specifications

Firing Order	Timing Mark Location	Initial Ignition Timing @ rpm	Breaker Point Gap (in.)	Cam Angle (deg.)	Spark Plugs Make	Spark Plugs Model	Spark Plugs Gap (in.)	Caster Manual Steering (deg.)	Camber Right Wheel (deg.)	Toe-In (in.)	Steering Axis Inclination (deg.)	Cooling System Capacity (qts.)	Crankcase Capacity (qts.)
153624	VD	5B@600[3]	.016	32	CH	N12Y	.035	1P	1/8P	1/8	7-3/4	10.5	4
153624	VD	5B@550[4]	.016	32	CH	N12Y	.035	1P	1/8P	1/8	7-3/4	10.5	4
153624	VD	3B@600[3]	.016	32	CH	N12Y	.035	1P	1/8P	1/8	7-3/4	10.5	4
153624	VD	3B@550[4]	.016	32	CH	N12Y	.035	1P	1/8P	1/8	7-3/4	10.5	4
18436572	VD	5B@700[5]	.016	30	CH	N12Y	.035	1P	1/8P	1/8	7-3/4	14	4
18436572	VD	5B@700[5]	.016	30	CH	N12Y	.035	1P	1/8P	1/8	7-3/4	13	4
18436572	VD	5B@700[5]	.016	30	CH	N12Y	.035	1P	1/8P	1/8	7-3/4	13	4
18436572	VD	5B@700[5]	.016	30	CH	N12Y	.035	1P	1/8P	1/8	7-3/4	13	4
18436572	VD	5B@700[5]	.016	30	CH	N12Y	.035	1P	1/8P	1/8	7-3/4	13	4
153624	VD	6B@600[3]	.019	32	AC	R46T	.035	1/2P	1/2P	3/16	8-3/4	14	4
18436572	VD	6B@650	.016	30	AC	R45TS	.040	1/2P	1/2P	3/16	8-3/4	13.9	4
18436572	VD	4B@650[8]	.016	30	AC	R45TS	.040	1/2P	1/2P	3/16	8	16.45	4
18436572	VD	4B@650	.016	30	AC	R45TS	.040	1P	1/4P	3/16	9-5/8	18.9	4
18436572	VD	4B@650[8]	.016	30	AC	R45TS	.040	1/2P	1/2P	3/16	8	16.45	4
18436572	VD	4B@650	.016	30	AC	R45TS	.040	1P	1/4P	3/16	9-5/8	18.9	4
18436572	VD	4B@650	.016	30	AC	R45TS	.040	1P	1/2P	3/16	9-5/8	18.7	4
18436572	VD	4B@650[8]	.016	30	AC	R45TS	.040	1/2P	1/2P	3/16	8	16.45	4
18436572	VD	4B@650	.016	30	AC	R45TS	.040	1P	1/4P	3/16	9-5/8	18.7	4
18436572	VD	4B@650	.016	30	AC	R45TS	.040	1P	1/4P	3/16	9-5/8	18.7	4
18436572	VD	4B@650[8]	.016	30	AC	R45TS	.040	1/2P	1/2P	3/16	8	16.45	4
15634278	VD	8B@600	.016	30	AC	R46N	.035	1N	1/4P	3/16	6	21.3[11]	4
15634278	VD	8B@600	.016	30	AC	R46N	.035	0	0	0	11	21.3	5
1342	CP	8B@750[3]	.019	32	AC	R42TS	.035	3/4N	1/4P	1/4	8-1/2	8.6	3
1342	CP	10B@750[3]	.019	32	AC	R42TS	.035	3/4N	1/4P	1/4	8-1/2	8.6	3
153624	VD	6B@600[3]	.019	32	AC	R46T	.035	0	1/4P	3/16	9	14	4
153624	VD	6B@600[3]	.019	32	AC	R46T	.035	1/2P	1/2P	1/16	9-5/8	14	4
153624	VD	6B@600[3]	.019	32	AC	R46T	.035	1-1/4N	1/2P	1/16	9-5/8	14	4
153624	VD	6B@700	.019	32	AC	R46T	.035	1/2P	1/2P	1/16	9-5/8	14	4
18436572	VD	8B@600[14]	.019	30	AC	R44T	.035	0[15]	1P[16]	3/16[17]	10-3/8[18]	17	4
18436572	VD	8B@600[19]	.019	30	AC	R44T	.035	0[15]	1P[16]	3/16[17]	10-3/8[18]	18	4
18436572	VD	8B@600	.019	30	AC	R44T	.035	1P[21]	1/2P	3/16	9-5/8	18	4
18436572	VD	12B@600[22]	.019	30	AC	R44T	.035	0[15]	1P[16]	3/16[17]	10-3/8[18]	18	4
18436572	VD	12B@600	.019	30	AC	R44T	.035	1P[21]	1/2P	1/16	9-5/8	18	4
18436572	VD	12B@600[23]	.019	30	AC	R44T	.035	1-1/2P	3/4P	1/16	7-5/8	19	4
18436572	VD	8B@700[22]	.019	30	AC	R44T	.035	0	1P	3/16	10-3/8	18	4
18436572	VD	8B@700[22]	.019	30	AC	R44T	.035	1/2P	3/4P	1/16	7-5/8	19	4
18436572	VD	8B@600	.019	30	AC	R44T	.035	1P	1/2P	1/16	9-5/8	18	4
18436572	VD	10B@600[5]	.019	29	AC	R44T	.035	1-1/4N	1/2P	1/16	9-5/8	25	4
18436572	VD	10B@600	.019	29	AC	R44T	.035	1P[21]	1/2P	1/16	9-5/8	24	4
18436572	VD	10B@600[19]	.019	29	AC	R44T	.035	1/2P	3/4P	1/16	7-5/8	24	5
18436572	VD	10B@700	EL	EL	CH	J13Y	.035	5/8P	1/4P	1/8	9	16	4
18436572	VD	10B@700	EL	EL	CH	J11Y	.035	5/8P	1/4P	1/8	9	15.5	4
18436572	VD	10B@700	EL	EL	CH	J11Y	.035	5/8P	1/4P	1/8	9	18	4
153624	VD	2.5B@750[8]	EL	EL	CH	N14Y	.035	5/8N	1/4P	1/8	7-1/2	13	4
153624	VD	2.5B@750[8]	EL	EL	CH	N14Y	.035	5/8N	1/4P	1/8	7-1/2	13	4
153624	VD	TDC@750	EL	EL	CH	N14Y	.035	5/8N	1/4P	1/8	7-1/2	13	4
153624	VD	TDC@750	EL	EL	CH	N14Y	.035	5/8N	1/4P	1/8	8	13	4
18436572	VD	TDC@700[27]	EL	EL	CH	N13Y	.035	5/8N	1/4P	1/8	7-1/2	16	4
18436572	VD	TDC@700[27]	EL	EL	CH	N13Y	.035	5/8N	1/4P	1/8	7-1/2	16	4
18436572	VD	TDC@700	EL	EL	CH	N13Y	.035	5/8P	1/4P	1/8	9	16	4
18436572	VD	2.5B@850	EL	EL	CH	N12Y	.035	5/8N	1/4P	1/8	7-1/2	15.5	4
18436572	VD	2.5B@850[29]	EL	EL	CH	N12Y	.035	5/8N	1/4P	1/8	7-1/2	15	4
18436572	VD	TDC@750	EL	EL	CH	N13Y	.035	5/8N	1/4P	1/8	9	15.5	4
18436572	VD	10B@700	EL	EL	CH	J13Y	.035	5/8N	1/4P	1/8	8	17	4
18436572	VD	10B@700	EL	EL	CH	J13Y	.035	5/8P	1/4P	1/8	9	16	4
18436572	VD	10B@700	EL	EL	CH	J11Y	.035	5/8P	1/4P	1/8	9	15.5	4
18436572	VD	10B@800	EL	EL	CH	J11Y	.035	5/8N	1/4P	1/8	8	16.5	4
1243	CP	12B@950	.025	39	M	AGR32	.034	1P	3/4P	1/8	8-7/8	7.8	3
1342	VD	9B@950[31]	.025	39	M	BRF42	.034	1P	3/4P	1/8	8-7/8	8.5	4
153624	VD	6B@550[5]	.027	37	M	BRF82	.034	3/4P	1/4P	3/16	6-3/4	9	4
153624	VD	6B@600[5]	.027	37	M	BRF82	.034	1-1/4P	3/4P	3/16	7-5/8	11.5	4
153624	VD	6B@600	.027	37	M	BRF82	.034	1/2N	1/4P	3/16	6-3/4	9.7	4
153624	VD	6B@600[5]	.027	37	M	BRF82	.034	0	3/4P	3/16	6-3/4	11.2	4
15426378	VD	6B@575[36]	.017	28	M	BRF42	.034	1-1/4P	3/4P	3/16	7-5/8	15.2	4
15426378	VD	6B@650[8]	.017	27	M	BRF42	.034	1/2N	1/4P	3/16	6-3/4	13.4	4
15426378	VD	6B@650[36]	.017	27	M	BRF42	.034	0	1/4P	3/16	6-3/4	15.2	4
13726548	VD	6B@600	.017	28	M	BRF42	.034	1-1/4P	3/4P	3/16	7-5/8	15.8	4
13726548	VD	6B@600	.017	27	M	BRF42	.034	1P	1/2P	3/16	7-1/4	16.5	4
13726548	VD	10B@625	.017	28	M	ARF42	.034	1-1/4P	3/4P	3/16	7-5/8	15.8	4

9 – Riviera – 122
10 – Brougham – 133, 75-151.5
11 – 75-26.8
12 – Running – Intake .015, Exh. .016
13 – Nova – III, Chevelle 2-Door – 112, 4-Door – 116
14 – W/Manual Trans. – 4B@900
15 – Nova – 1/2P, Chevelle 1-1/4N
16 – Nova – 1/4P, Chevelle 1/2P
17 – Chevelle – 1/16
18 – Nova – 9, Chevelle – 9-5/8
19 – W/Manual Trans. – 900 rpm
20 – Monte Carlo – 116
21 – Monte Carlo – 5N
22 – W/Manual Trans. – 8B@900
23 – W/Manual Trans. – 12B@900
24 – Minimum psi Allowable, Also 40 psi Maximum Variation
25 – Minimum psi Allowable, Also 25 psi Maximum Variation
26 – Sport – 108
27 – W/Manual Trans. – 2.5B@750
28 – Charger/SE – 115, Coronet – 115
29 – W/Manual Trans. – 5B@850
30 – Also 260@4800
31 – W/Manual Trans. – 6B@750
32 – 4-Door – 110
33 – 4-Door – 118
34 – W/Manual Trans. – 89@3200
35 – All Except Mach I
36 – W/Manual Trans. – 850 rpm
37 – Windsor Plant
38 – Cleveland Plant

1973

	Wheelbase (in.)	No. of Cylinders Bore and Stroke (in.)	Displacement (cu. in.)	Valve and Cylinder Arrangement	Compression Pressure (lbs.)	Net Brake Horsepower @ rpm	Valve Tappet Clearance Intake	Valve Tappet Clearance Exhaust	Cylinder Bolt Torque (ft. lbs.)
Ford	121	8–4.002x3.50	351C [1]	VO	170 [2]	161@4000	HY	HY	105
Mustang (All)	109	8–4.002x3.50	351C [1]	VO	170 [2]	173@4400	HY	HY	105
Torino	114 [3]	8–4.002x3.50	351CJ [1]	VO	170 [2]	246@5400	HY	HY	105
Mustang	109	8–4.002x3.50	351CJ [1]	VO	170 [2]	259@5600	HY	HY	105
Torino	114 [3]	8–4.00x4.00	400	VO	180 [2]	168@3800	HY	HY	105
Ford	121	8–4.00x4.00	400	VO	180 [2]	171@3600	HY	HY	105
Torino	114 [3]	8–4.362x3.59	429	VO	190 [2]	201@4400	HY	HY	140
Ford	121	8–4.362x3.59	429	VO	190 [2]	202@4400	HY	HY	140
Thunderbird	120.4	8–4.362x3.59	429	VO	190 [2]	208@4400	HY	HY	140
Thunderbird	120.4	8–4.362x3.85	460	VO	180 [2]	208@4400	HY	HY	140
Lincoln	127	8–4.362x3.85	460	VO	180 [2]	219@4400	HY	HY	140
Mark IV	120.4	8–4.362x3.85	460	VO	180 [2]	208@4400	HY	HY	140
Mercury – Comet (All)	103 [5]	6–3.683x3.126	200	IO	175 [2]	84@3600	HY	HY	75
Comet (All)	103 [5]	6–3.682x3.91	250	IO	175 [2]	89@3200	HY	HY	75
Montego	114 [3]	6–3.682x3.91	250	IO	175 [2]	92@3200	HY	HY	75
Montego	114 [3]	8–4.002x3.00	302	VO	150 [2]	137@4200	HY	HY	72
Comet (All)	103 [5]	8–4.002x3.00	302	VO	150 [2]	138@4200	HY	HY	72
Montego	114 [3]	8–4.002x3.50	351W [8]	VO	160 [2]	156@3800	HY	HY	112
Montego	114 [3]	8–4.002x3.50	351C [1]	VO	170 [2]	159@4000	HY	HY	105
Monterey, Custom, Marquis, Brougham	124	8–4.002x3.50	351C [1]	VO	170 [2]	161@4000	HY	HY	105
Cougar (All)	112.1	8–4.002x3.50	351C [1]	VO	170 [2]	173@4400	HY	HY	105
Montego	114 [3]	8–4.002x3.50	351CJ [1]	VO	170 [2]	246@5400	HY	HY	105
Cougar (All)	112.1	8–4.002x3.50	351CJ [1]	VO	170 [2]	253@5600	HY	HY	105
Montego	114 [3]	8–4.00x4.00	400	VO	180 [2]	168@3800	HY	HY	105
Monterey, Custom, Marquis, Brougham	124	8–4.00x4.00	400	VO	180 [2]	171@3600	HY	HY	105
Monterey, Custom, Marquis, Brougham	124	8–4.362x3.59	429	VO	190 [2]	198@4400	HY	HY	140
Montego	114 [3]	8–4.362x3.59	429	VO	190 [2]	201@4400	HY	HY	140
Monterey, Custom, Marquis, Brougham	124	8–4.362x3.59	460	VO	180 [2]	202@4400	HY	HY	140
Oldsmobile – Omega	111	6–3.87x3.53	250	IO	140 [10]	100@3600	HY	HY	95
Cutlass	112 [13]	8–4.057x3.385	350	VO	160 [10]	160@3800	HY	HY	85
Delta, Royale	124	8–4.057x3.385	350	VO	160 [10]	160@3800	HY	HY	85
Omega	111	8–4.057x3.385	350	VO	160 [10]	180@3800	HY	HY	85
Cutlass, Supreme	112 [13]	8–4.057x3.385	350	VO	160 [10]	180@3800	HY	HY	85
Delta, Royale, 98	124	8–4.126x4.250	455	VO	160 [10]	225@3600 [14]	HY	HY	85
Cutlass, Supreme	112 [13]	8–4.126x4.250	455	VO	160 [10]	250@4000 [15]	HY	HY	85
Toronado	122	8–4.126x4.250	455	VO	160 [10]	250@4000	HY	HY	85
Plymouth – Valiant, Duster, Scamp	108 [17]	6–3.40x3.64	198	IO	100 [14]	95@4000	.010H	.020H	70
Valiant, Duster, Scamp	108 [17]	6–3.40x4.12	225	IO	100 [14]	105@4000	.010H	.020H	70
Satellite, Custom, Sebring	115 [18]	6–3.40x4.12	225	IO	100 [14]	105@4000	.010H	.020H	70
Valiant, Duster, Scamp, Barracuda, 'Cuda	108 [17]	8–3.91x3.31	318	VO	100 [19]	150@3600	HY	HY	95
Satellite, Custom, Sebring, Sebring Plus	115 [18]	8–3.91x3.31	318	VO	100 [19]	150@3600	HY	HY	95
Fury I, II, III, Gran Coupe, Sedan	120	8–3.91x3.31	318	VO	100 [19]	150@3600	HY	HY	95
Road Runner	115	8–3.91x3.31	318	VO	100 [19]	170@4000	HY	HY	95
Duster 340, Barracuda, 'Cuda	108	8–4.04x3.31	340	VO	100 [19]	240@4800	HY	HY	95
Road Runner	115	8–4.04x3.31	340	VO	100 [19]	240@4800	HY	HY	95
Fury I, II, III, Gran Coupe, Sedan	120	8–4.00x3.58	360	VO	100 [19]	170@4000	HY	HY	95
Satellite, Custom, Sebring	115 [18]	8–4.34x3.38	400	VO	100 [19]	175@3600	HY	HY	70
Fury I, II, III, Gran Coupe, Sedan	120	8–4.34x3.38	400	VO	100 [19]	185@3600	HY	HY	70
Satellite, Custom, Sebring, Sebring Plus	115 [18]	8–4.34x3.38	400	VO	100 [19]	260@4800	HY	HY	70
Road Runner	115	8–4.34x3.38	400	VO	100 [19]	260@4800	HY	HY	70
Fury, I, II, III, Gran Coupe, Sedan	120	8–4.32x3.75	440	VO	100 [19]	220@3600	HY	HY	70
Road Runner	115	8–4.32x3.75	440	VO	100 [19]	280@4800	HY	HY	70
Pontiac – Ventura, Custom	111	6–3.875x3.53	250	IO	140	100@3600	HY	HY	95
Firebird	108	6–3.875x3.53	250	IO	140	100@3600	HY	HY	95
LeMans, GTO, Grand AM	112	6–3.875x3.53	250	IO	140	100@3600	HY	HY	95
Ventura, Custom	111	8–3.876x3.75	350	VO	140	150@4000 [24]	HY	HY	95
Firebird, Esprit, Formula 350	108	8–3.876x3.75	350	VO	140	150@4000 [24]	HY	HY	95
LeMans, Luxury LeMans, GTO	112	8–3.876x3.75	350	VO	140	150@4000 [24]	HY	HY	95
Catalina	124	8–3.876x3.75	350	VO	140	150@4000 [24]	HY	HY	95
LeMans, Luxury LeMans, Grand AM	112	8–4.121x3.75	400	VO	140	170@3600 [25]	HY	HY	95
Bonneville	124	8–4.121x3.75	400	VO	140	170@3600 [26]	HY	HY	95
Catalina	124	8–4.121x3.75	400	VO	140	185@4000 [26]	HY	HY	95
Firebird Esprit, Formula 400	108	8–4.121x3.75	400	VO	140	230@4400 [28]	HY	HY	95
LeMans, Luxury LeMans, GTO, Grand AM	112	8–4.121x3.75	400	VO	140	230@4400	HY	HY	95
Grand Prix	116	8–4.121x3.75	400	VO	140	230@4400	HY	HY	95
Grand Ville	124	8–4.152x4.21	455	VO	140	215@3600	HY	HY	95
Firebird, Trans AM, Formula 455	108	8–4.152x4.21	455	VO	140	250@4000 [30]	HY	HY	95
Grand Prix	116	8–4.152x4.21	455	VO	140	250@4000 [30]	HY	HY	95
LeMans, Luxury LeMans, GTO, Grand AM	112	8–4.152x4.21	455	VO	140	250@4000 [30]	HY	HY	95
Catalina, Bonneville	124	8–4.152x4.21	455	VO	140	250@4000	HY	HY	95

ABBREVIATIONS – FOOTNOTES

AC – AC Spark Plugs	H – Hot Engine	VO – V–Type Engine, Overhead Valves
B – Before Top Dead Center	HY – Hydraulic Lifters	1 – Cleveland Plant
C – Cold Engine	IO – In-Line Engine, Overhead Valves	2 – Lowest Cylinder Must Be At Least
CH – Champion Spark Plugs	IOC – In-Line Engine, Overhead Cam	75 Percent of Highest
CP – Crankshaft Pulley	M – Motorcraft Spark Plugs	3 – 4-Door – 118
EGR – Exhaust Gas Recirculation	N – Negative	4 – W/Manual Trans. – 16B@900
EL – Electronic Ignition	P – Positive	5 – 4-Door – 110
	TDC – Top Dead Center	6 – W/Manual Trans. – 800 rpm
	VD – Vibration Damper	7 – W/Manual Trans. – 850 rpm

Tuneup Specifications

Firing Order	Timing Mark Location	Initial Ignition Timing @ rpm	Breaker Point Gap (in.)	Cam Angle (deg.)	Spark Plugs Make	Model	Gap (in.)	Caster Manual Steering (deg.)	Camber Right Wheel (deg.)	Toe-In (in.)	Steering Axis Inclination (deg.)	Cooling System Capacity (qts.)	Crankcase Capacity (qts.)
13726548	VD	10B@625	.017	28	M	ARF42	.034	1P	1/2P	3/16	7-1/4	15.6	4
13726548	VD	6B@625	.017	28	M	ARF42	.034	0	3/4P	3/16	6-3/4	15.7	4
13726548	VD	18B@700[4]	.017	28	M	ARF42	.034	1-1/4P	3/4P	3/16	7-5/8	15.7	4
13726548	VD	18B@700[4]	.017	28	M	ARF42	.034	0	3/4P	3/16	6-3/4	15.7	4
13726548	VD	6B@625	.017	28	M	ARF42	.034	1-1/4P	3/4P	3/16	7-5/8	17.7	4
13726548	VD	6B@625	.017	28	M	ARF42	.034	1P	1/2P	3/16	7-1/4	18	4
15426378	VD	18B@650	.017	28	M	ARF42	.034	1-1/4P	3/4P	3/16	7-5/8	18.8	6
15426378	VD	10B@600	.017	28	M	ARF42	.034	1P	1/2P	3/16	7-1/4	19.4	4
15426378	VD	10B@600	.017	28	M	BRF42	.034	1-1/4P	3/4P	3/16	7-3/4	18.8	4
15426378	VD	14B@600	.017	28	M	BRF42	.034	1-1/4P	3/4P	3/16	7-3/4	19.5	4
15426378	VD	14B@600	.017	28	M	ARF42	.034	1-1/2P	1/2P	1/8	9-1/2	21.5	4
15426378	VD	14B@600	.017	28	M	BRF42	.034	1P	1/2P	3/16	7-3/4	20.5	4
153624	VD	6B@550[6]	.027	37	M	BRF82	.034	1/2N	1/4P	3/16	6-3/4	9	4
153624	VD	6B@600[6]	.027	37	M	BRF82	.034	1/2N	1/4P	3/16	6-3/4	9.7	4
153624	VD	6B@600[6]	.027	37	M	BRF82	.034	1-1/4P	3/4P	3/16	7-3/4	11.5	4
15426378	VD	6B@575[7]	.017	28	M	BRF42	.034	1-1/4P	3/4P	3/16	7-3/4	15.2	4
15426378	VD	6B@650[7]	.017	27	M	BRF42	.034	1/2N	1/4P	3/16	6-3/4	13.4	4
13726548	VD	6B@600	.017	28	M	BRF42	.034	1-1/4P	3/4P	3/16	7-3/4	16.3	4
13726548	VD	10B@625	.017	28	M	ARF42	.034	1-1/4P	3/4P	3/16	7-3/4	15.9	4
13726548	VD	10B@625	.017	28	M	ARF42	.034	1P	1/2P	3/16	7-1/4	15.6	4
13726548	VD	6B@625	.017[4]	28	M	ARF42	.034	0	3/4P	3/16	6-3/4	15.7	4
13726548	VD	18B@700[4]	.017	28	M	ARF42	.034	1-1/4P	3/4P	3/16	7-3/4	15.9	4
13726548	VD	16B@800[9]	.021	27	M	ARF42	.034	0	3/4P	3/16	6-3/4	15.7	4
13726548	VD	6B@625	.017	28	M	ARF42	.034	1-1/4P	3/4P	3/16	7-3/4	17.7	4
13726548	VD	6B@625	.017	28	M	ARF42	.034	1P	1/2P	3/16	7-1/4	18	4
15426378	VD	10B@600	.017	28	M	ARF42	.034	1P	1/2P	3/16	7-3/4	19.4	6
15426378	VD	18B@600	.017	28	M	ARF42	.034	1-1/4P	3/4P	3/16	7-3/4	17.7	6
15426378	VD	12B@600	.017	28	M	ARF42	.034	1P	1/2P	3/16	7-1/4	19.4	6
153624	VD	6B@600[11]	.019	32	AC	R46T	.035	1/2P	1/4P	3/16	9	12	4
18436572	VD	12B@1100[12]	.016	30	AC	R45S	.040	1-1/4N	1/2N	1/16	10-1/2	15.2	4
18436572	VD	12B@1100	.016	30	AC	R46S	.040	1P	1/4N	1/16	9-5/8	16.2	4
18436572	VD	10B@1100	.016	30	AC	R45S	.040	1/2P	1/4P	3/16	9	15.2	4
18436572	VD	12B@1100[12]	.016	30	AC	R45S	.040	1-1/4N	1/2N	1/16	10-1/2	15.2	4
18436572	VD	8B@1100	.016	30	AC	R46S	.040	1P	1/4N	1/16	9-5/8	17	4
18436572	VD	8B@1100	.016	30	AC	R45S	.040	1-1/4N	1/2N	1/16	10-1/2	15.2	4
18436572	VD	8B@1100	.016	30	AC	R46S	.040	2N	3/4P	1/16	11	19.5	5
153624	VD	2.5B@750[6]	EL	EL	CH	N14Y	.035	5/8N	1/4P	1/8	7-1/2	13	4
153624	VD	TDC@750	EL	EL	CH	N14Y	.035	5/8N	1/4P	1/8	7-1/2	13	4
153624	VD	TDC@750	EL	EL	CH	N14Y	.035	5/8N	1/4P	1/8	8	13	4
18436572	VD	TDC@700[20]	EL	EL	CH	N13Y	.035	5/8N	1/4P	1/8	7-1/2	16	4
18436572	VD	TDC@700[20]	EL	EL	CH	N13Y	.035	5/8N	1/4P	1/8	8	16	4
18436572	VD	TDC@700	EL	EL	CH	N13Y	.035	5/8P	1/4P	1/8	9	16	4
18436572	VD	TDC@700[20]	EL	EL	CH	N13Y	.035	5/8N	1/4P	1/8	8	16	4
18436572	VD	2.5B@850[21]	EL	EL	CH	N12Y	.035	5/8N	1/4P	1/8	8	15	4
18436572	VD	2.5B@850[21]	EL	EL	CH	N12Y	.035	5/8N	1/4P	1/8	8	15	4
18436572	VD	TDC@750	EL	EL	CH	N13Y	.035	5/8P	1/4P	1/8	9	15.5	4
18436572	VD	10B@700	EL	EL	CH	J13Y	.035	5/8N	1/4P	1/8	8	16	4
18436572	VD	10B@700	EL	EL	CH	J13Y	.035	5/8P	1/4P	1/8	9	16	4
18436572	VD	7.5B@850[22]	EL	EL	CH	J11Y	.035	5/8N	1/4P	1/8	8	17	4
18436572	VD	7.5B@850[22]	EL	EL	CH	J11Y	.035	5/8N	1/4P	1/8	8	17	4
18436572	VD	10B@700	EL	EL	CH	J11Y	.035	5/8P	1/4P	1/8	9	15.5	4
18436572	VD	10B@800	EL	EL	CH	J11Y	.035	5/8N	1/4P	1/8	8	16.5	4
153624	VD	6B@600[11]	.019	32	AC	R46T	.035	1/2P	1/4P	3/16	9	12.1	4
153624	VD	6B@600[11]	.019	32	AC	R46T	.035	0	1P	3/16	10-1/2	12.5	4
153624	VD	6B@600[11]	.019	32	AC	R46T	.035	1N	1/2P	1/16	10-1/2	13.3	4
18436572	VD	12B@650[23]	.016	30	AC	R46TS	.040	1/2P	1/4P	3/16	9	19.2	5
18436572	VD	12B@650[23]	.016	30	AC	R46TS	.040	0	1P	3/16	10-1/2	22.4	5
18436572	VD	12B@650[23]	.016	30	AC	R46TS	.040	1N	1/2P	1/16	10-1/2	22	5
18436572	VD	12B@650	.016	30	AC	R46TS	.040	1P	1/2P	1/16	10-1/2	21.9	5
18436572	VD	12B@650	.016	30	AC	R46TS	.040	1P	1/2P	1/16	10-1/2	22	5
18436572	VD	12B@650	.016	30	AC	R46TS[26]	.040	1P	1/2P	1/16	10-1/2	21.9	5
18436572	VD	12B@650	.016	30	AC	R46TS[26]	.040	1P	1/2P	1/16	10-1/2	21.9	5
18436572	VD	12B@650[29]	.016	30	AC	R45TS	.040	0	1P	3/16	10-1/2	22.4	5
18436572	VD	12B@650[29]	.016	30	AC	R45TS	.040	1N	1/2P	1/16	10-1/2	23	5
18436572	VD	10B@650	.016	30	AC	R45TS	.040	3P	1/2P	1/16	10-1/2	23.1	5
18436572	VD	12B@650	.016	30	AC	R45TS[31]	.040	1P	1/2P	1/16	10-1/2	21.2	5
18436572	VD	12B@650[29]	.016	30	AC	R45TS[31]	.040	0	1P	3/16	10-1/2	20.9	5
18436572	VD	12B@650	.016	30	AC	R45TS[31]	.040	3P	1/2P	1/16	10-1/2	21.3	5
18436572	VD	12B@650[29]	.016	30	AC	R45TS	.040	1N	1/2P	1/16	10-1/2	21.2	5
18436572	VD	12B@650	.016	30	AC	R45TS	.040	1P	1/2P	1/16	10-1/2	21.2	5

8 - Windsor Plant
9 - W/Manual Trans. - 1000 rpm
10 - Lowest Cylinder Must Be At Least 70 Percent of Highest
11 - W/Manual Trans. - 700 rpm
12 - W/Manual Trans. - 8B@1100
13 - 4-Door - 116
14 - Minimum psi Allowable, Also 25 psi Maximum Variation
15 - Also 250@4000
16 - Also 270@4000
17 - Scamp - III
18 - Satellite Custom - 117
19 - Minimum psi Allowable, Also 40 psi Maximum Variation
20 - W/Manual Trans. - 2.5B@750
21 - W/Manual Trans. - 5B@850
22 - W/Manual Trans. - 2.5B@900
23 - W/Manual Trans. - 10B@900
24 - Also 175@4400
25 - Also 185@4000
26 - Also 230@4400
27 - W/4 Bbl. Carburetor - R45TS
28 - Esprit - 170@3600
29 - W/Manual Trans. - 10B@600
30 - Also SD Engine - 310@4000
31 - SD Engine - R44TS

1974

Model	Wheelbase (in.)	No. of Cylinders Bore and Stroke (in.)	Displacement (cu. in.)	Valve and Cylinder Arrangement	Compression Pressure (lbs.)	Net Brake Horsepower @ rpm	Intake	Exhaust	Cylinder Bolt Torque (ft. lbs.)
American Motors – Gremlin, Hornet, Javelin	96[1]	6-3.75x3.50	232	IO	185[2]	100@3600	HY	HY	85
Matador (W/EGR)	118[5]	6-3.75x3.50	232	IO	185[2]	100@3600	HY	HY	85
Gremlin, Hornet, Javelin	96[1]	6-3.75x3.90	258	IO	185[2]	110@3500	HY	HY	85
Matador (W/EGR)	118[5]	6-3.75x3.90	258	IO	185[2]	110@3500	HY	HY	85
Gremlin, Hornet, Javelin, AMX, Matador	96[1]	8-3.75x3.44	304	VO	185[2]	150@4200	HY	HY	55
Hornet, Javelin, AMX, Matador, Ambassador	108[1]	8-4.08x3.44	360	VO	185[2]	175@4000	HY	HY	55
Matador, Ambassador	118[1]	8-4.08x3.44	360	VO	185[2]	195@4400	HY	HY	55
Javelin, AMX, Matador, Ambassador	110[1]	8-4.08x3.44	360	VO	185[2]	220@4400	HY	HY	55
Javelin, AMX, Matador, Ambassador	110[1]	8-4.165x3.68	401	VO	200[2]	235@4600	HY	HY	55
Buick – Apollo	111	6-3.87x3.53	250	IO	130	100@3600	HY	HY	95
Apollo	111	8-3.80x3.85	350	VO	180	150@3600[8]	HY	HY	80
Century, Luxus, Gran Sport, Regal	112[9]	8-3.80x3.85	350	VO	180	150@3600[8]	HY	HY	80
LeSabre, Luxus	124	8-3.80x3.85	350	VO	180	150@3600[8]	HY	HY	80
Century, Luxus, Gran Sport, Regal	112[9]	8-4.3125x3.90	455	VO	180	190@3600	HY	HY	100
LeSabre, Luxus	124	8-4.3125x3.90	455	VO	180	190@3600[10]	HY	HY	100
LeSabre, Luxus	124	8-4.3125x3.90	455	VO	180	210@3600[11]	HY	HY	100
Electra 225, Custom, Limited, Riviera	127[12]	8-4.3125x3.90	455	VO	180	230@3600[13]	HY	HY	100
Century, Luxus, Gran Sport, Regal	112[10]	8-4.3125x3.90	455	VO	180	230@3800[14]	HY	HY	100
LeSabre, Luxus (Stage 1)	124	8-4.3125x3.90	455	VO	180	245@4000	HY	HY	100
Electra 225, Custom, Limited, Riviera	127[12]	8-4.3125x3.90	455	VO	180	245@4000	HY	HY	100
Cadillac – All Except Eldorado	130[15]	8-4.30x4.06	472	VO	175	205@3600	HY	HY	115
Eldorado	126.3	8-4.30x4.304	500	VO	175	210@3600	HY	HY	115
Chevrolet – Vega	97	4-3.501x3.625	140	IOC	140	75@4400	.015C	.030C	60
Vega (L11)	97	4-3.501x3.625	140	IOC	140	85@4400	.015C	.030C	60
Camaro	108	6-3.875x3.53	250	IO	130	100@3600	HY	HY	95
Nova	111	6-3.875x3.53	250	IO	130	100@3600	HY	HY	95
Chevelle	112[9]	6-3.875x3.53	250	IO	130	100@3600	HY	HY	95
Camaro, Nova, Chevelle	108[19]	8-4.0x3.48	350	VO	160	145@3800	HY	HY	65
Chevrolet, Monte Carlo "S"	121.5[9]	8-4.0x3.48	350	VO	160	145@3800	HY	HY	65
Camaro, Nova, Chevelle	108[19]	8-4.0x3.48	350	VO	160	160@3800	HY	HY	65
Chevrolet, Monte Carlo "S"	121.5[9]	8-4.0x3.48	350	VO	160	160@3800	HY	HY	65
Camaro, Nova	108[19]	8-4.0x3.48	350	VO	160	185@4000	HY	HY	65
Corvette	98	8-4.0x3.48	350	VO	160	195@4400	HY	HY	65
Camaro (Z28)	108	8-4.0x3.48	350	VO	150	245@5200	HY	HY	65
Corvette	98	8-4.0x3.48	350	VO	160	250@5200	HY	HY	65
Chevelle	112[9]	8-4.126x3.75	400	VO	160	150@3200	HY	HY	80
Chevrolet, Monte Carlo "S"	121.5[9]	8-4.126x3.75	400	VO	160	150@3200	HY	HY	80
Chevelle	112[9]	8-4.251x4.0	454	VO	160	235@4000	HY	HY	80
Chevrolet, Monte Carlo "S"	121.5[9]	8-4.251x4.0	454	VO	160	235@4000	HY	HY	80
Corvette	98	8-4.251x4.0	454	VO	160	270@4400	HY	HY	80
Chrysler – Newport, Custom	124	8-4.32x3.375	400	VO	100[29]	205@4000	HY	HY	70
New Yorker, Brougham	124	8-4.32x3.75	440	VO	100[29]	230@4000	HY	HY	70
Imperial, LeBaron	124	8-4.32x3.75	440	VO	100[30]	230@4000	HY	HY	70
Dodge – Dart, Swinger, Swinger Special	111	6-3.40x3.64	198	IO	100[30]	95@4000	.010H	.020H	70
Dart Custom, Dart Sport	111[31]	6-3.40x3.64	198	IO	100[30]	95@4000	.010H	.020H	70
Dart, Swinger, Special, Custom, Sport	111[31]	6-3.40x4.12	225	IO	100[30]	105@3600	.010H	.020H	70
Charger, Coronet, Custom	115[32]	6-3.40x4.12	225	IO	100[30]	105@3600	.010H	.020H	70
Dart, Swinger, Special, Custom, Sport	111[31]	8-3.91x3.31	318	VO	100[29]	150@4000	HY	HY	95
Challenger, Charger, SE, Coronet, Custom	110[33]	8-3.91x3.31	318	VO	100[29]	150@4000	HY	HY	95
Monaco, Custom	122	8-4.0x3.58	360	VO	100[29]	180@4800	HY	HY	95
Charger, SE, Coronet, Custom	115[32]	8-4.0x3.58	360	VO	100[29]	200@4000	HY	HY	95
Dart 360 Sport	108	8-4.0x3.58	360	VO	100[29]	245@4800	HY	HY	95
Challenger, Charger, Coronet, Custom	110[33]	8-4.0x3.58	360	VO	100[29]	245@4800	HY	HY	95
Monaco, Brougham, Custom	122	8-4.34x3.38	400	VO	100[29]	205@4000[35]	HY	HY	70
Charger, SE, Coronet, Custom	115[32]	8-4.34x3.38	400	VO	100[29]	205@4000[36]	HY	HY	70
Monaco, Brougham, Custom	122	8-4.32x3.75	440	VO	100[29]	230@4000	HY	HY	70
Charger, SE, Coronet, Custom	115[32]	8-4.32x3.75	440	VO	100[29]	275@4400	HY	HY	70
Ford – Pinto (2000)	94.2	4-3.575x3.029	122	IOC	80[2]	80@5400	.008C	.010C	80
Pinto (2300)	94.2	4-3.781x3.126	140	IOC	80[2]	88@5000	HY	HY	90
Mustang II (2300)	96.2	4-3.781x3.126	140	IOC	80[2]	88@5000	HY	HY	90
Mustang II	96.2	6-3.66x2.70	170.8	VO	80[2]	105@4200	.014H	.016H	80
Maverick (All)	103[38]	6-3.683x3.126	200	IO	175[2]	84@3800	HY	HY	75
Maverick (All)	103[38]	6-3.682x3.91	250	IO	175[2]	91@3200	HY	HY	75
Torino	114[32]	6-3.682x3.91	250	IO	175[2]	91@3200	HY	HY	75
Maverick (All)	103[38]	8-4.002x3.0	302	VO	150[2]	140@3800	HY	HY	72
Torino	114[32]	8-4.002x3.0	302	VO	150[2]	140@3800	HY	HY	72
Torino	114[32]	8-4.002x3.50	351W[40]	VO	160[2]	163@4200	HY	HY	112
Ford	121	8-4.002x3.50	351W[40]	VO	160[2]	163@4200	HY	HY	112
Torino	114[32]	8-4.002x3.50	351C[41]	VO	170[2]	173@4200	HY	HY	105

ABBREVIATIONS – FOOTNOTES

AC – AC Spark Plugs
AU – Autolite Spark Plugs
B – Before Top Dead Center
C – Cold Engine
CH – Champion Spark Plugs
CP – Crankshaft Pulley
EGR – Exhaust Gas Recirculation
EL – Electronic Ignition
H – Hot Engine
HY – Hydraulic Lifters

IO – In-Line Engine, Overhead Valves
IOC – In-Line Engine, Overhead Cam
N – Negative
P – Positive
TDC – Top Dead Center
VD – Vibration Damper
VO – V-Type Engine, Overhead Valves
1 – Hornet – 108, Javelin/AMX – 110
   Matador – 114/118, Ambassador – 122
2 – Lowest Cylinder Must Be At Least
   75 Percent of Highest

3 – W/Manual Trans. – 700 rpm
4 – Javelin, Matador, Ambassador – 1P
5 – 2-Door – 114
6 – W/Manual Trans. – 600 rpm
7 – W/Manual Trans. – 750 rpm
8 – Also 175@3800
9 – 4-Door – 116, Monte Carlo – 116
10 – Also 175@3400
11 – Also 230@3800
12 – Riviera – 122
13 – Also 210@3600, Except Riviera

Tuneup Specifications

Firing Order	Timing Mark Location	Initial Ignition Timing @ rpm	Breaker Point Gap (in.)	Cam Angle (deg.)	Spark Plugs Make	Spark Plugs Model	Spark Plugs Gap (in.)	Caster Manual Steering (deg.)	Camber Right Wheel (deg.)	Toe-In (in.)	Steering Axis Inclination (deg.)	Cooling System Capacity (qts.)	Crankcase Capacity (qts.)
153624	VD	5B@600[3]	.016	32	CH	N12Y	.035	0[4]	1/8P	1/8	7-3/4	11	4
153624	VD	5B@550[6]	.016	32	CH	N12Y	.035	0[4]	1/8P	1/8	7-3/4	11	4
153624	VD	3B@600[3]	.016	32	CH	N12Y	.035	0[4]	1/8P	1/8	7-3/4	11	4
153624	VD	3B@550[6]	.016	32	CH	N12Y	.035	0[4]	1/8P	1/8	7-3/4	11	4
18436572	VD	5B@700[7]	.016	30	CH	N12Y	.035	0[4]	1/8P	1/8	7-3/4	16	4
18436572	VD	5B@750[3]	.016	30	CH	N12Y	.035	0[4]	1/8P	1/8	7-3/4	15	4
18436572	VD	5B@750[3]	.016	30	CH	N12Y	.035	0[4]	1/8P	1/8	7-3/4	15	4
18436572	VD	5B@750[3]	.016	30	CH	N12Y	.035	0[4]	1/8P	1/8	7-3/4	15	4
18436572	VD	5B@700[7]	.016	30	CH	N12Y	.035	0[4]	1/8P	1/8	7-3/4	15	4
153624	VD	6B@600[3]	.019	32	AC	R46T	.035	1/2P	1/4P	3/16	9	14	4
18436572	VD	4B@650	.016	30	AC	R45TS	.040	1/2P	1/2P	1/16	8	16.5	4
18436572	VD	4B@650	.016	30	AC	R45TS	.040	1P	1P	1/16	9-5/8	18.9	4
18436572	VD	4B@650	.016	30	AC	R45TS	.040	1/2P	1P	1/16	8	16.2	4
18436572	VD	4B@650	.016	30	AC	R45TS	.040	1P	1P	1/16	9-5/8	18.7	4
18436572	VD	4B@650	.016	30	AC	R45TS	.040	1P	1P	1/16	9-5/8	18.7	4
18436572	VD	4B@650	.016	30	AC	R45TS	.040	1/2P	1/2P	1/16	8	16.2	4
18436572	VD	4B@650	.016	30	AC	R45TS	.040	1P	1P	1/16	9-5/8	18.7	4
15634278	VD	10B@600	.016	30	AC	R45NS	.035	0	1/4N	1/8	6	21.3[16]	4
15634278	VD	10B@600	.016	30	AC	R45NS	.035	0	1/4N	0	11	21.3	5
1342	CP	12B@750[17]	.019	32	AC	R42TS	.035	3/4N	1/4P	1/4	8-1/2	8.6	3
1342	CP	12B@750[17]	.019	32	AC	R42TS	.035	3/4N	1/4P	1/4	8-1/2	8.6	3
153624	VD	8B@600[18]	.019	32	AC	R46T	.035	0	1P	3/16	10-3/8	14	4
153624	VD	8B@600[18]	.019	32	AC	R44T	.035	1/2P	1/4P	3/16	9	14	4
153624	VD	6B@600[18]	.019	33	AC	R46T	.035	1-1/4N	1/16	3/16	9	14	4
18436572	VD	8B@600[20]	.019	30	AC	R44T	.035	0[21]	1P[22]	3/16[23]	10-3/8[24]	18	4
18436572	VD	8B@600[25]	.019	30	AC	R44T	.035	1P[26]	1/2P	1/16	9-5/8	18	4
18436572	VD	8B@600[20]	.019	30	AC	R44T	.035	0[21]	1P[22]	3/16[23]	10-3/8[24]	18	4
18436572	VD	8B@600[25]	.019	30	AC	R44T	.035	1P[26]	1/2P	1/16	9-5/8	18	4
18436572	VD	8B@600[27]	.019	30	AC	R44T	.035	0[21]	1P[22]	3/16[23]	10-3/8[24]	18	4
18436572	VD	8B@600[27]	.019	30	AC	R44T	.035	1P	3/4P	1/8	7-5/8	19	4
18436572	VD	8B@700[27]	.019	30	AC	R44T	.035	0	1P	3/16	10-3/8	18	4
18436572	VD	8B@700[27]	.019	30	AC	R44T	.035	1P	3/4P	1/8	7-5/8	18	4
18436572	VD	8B@600	.019	30	AC	R44T	.035	1-1/4N	1/2P	1/16	9-5/8	18	4
18436572	VD	8B@600	.019	30	AC	R44T	.035	1P[26]	1/2P	1/16	9-5/8	18	4
18436572	VD	10B@600[28]	.019	30	AC	R44T	.035	1-1/4N	1/2P	1/16	9-5/8	24	4
18436572	VD	10B@600	.019	30	AC	R44T	.035	1P[26]	1/2P	1/16	9-5/8	24	4
18436572	VD	10B@600[28]	.019	30	AC	R44T	.035	1P	3/4P	1/8	7-5/8	24	5
18436572	VD	5B@750	EL	EL	CH	J13Y	.035	1/2N	1/4P	3/16	9	16.5	4
18436572	VD	10B@750	EL	EL	CH	J11Y	.035	1/2N	1/4P	3/16	9	16	4
18436572	VD	10B@750	EL	EL	CH	J11Y	.035	3/4P	1/4P	3/16	9	17	4
153624	VD	2.5B@750[28]	EL	EL	CH	N14Y	.035	5/8N	1/4P	5/32	7-1/2	13	4
153624	VD	2.5B@750[28]	EL	EL	CH	N14Y	.035	5/8N	1/4P	5/32	7-1/2	13	4
153624	VD	TDC@750[28]	EL	EL	CH	N14Y	.035	1/2N	1/4P	3/16	8	13	4
153624	VD	TDC@750[28]	EL	EL	CH	N14Y	.035	5/8N	1/4P	5/32	7-1/2	13	4
18436572	VD	TDC@750	EL	EL	CH	N13Y	.035	1/2N	1/4P	3/16	7-1/2[34]	16	4
18436572	VD	TDC@750	EL	EL	CH	N13Y	.035	5/8N	1/4P	3/16	9	16	4
18436572	VD	5B@750	EL	EL	CH	N12Y	.035	3/4P	1/4P	3/16	8-1/2	16.5	4
18436572	VD	5B@750	EL	EL	CH	N12Y	.035	1/2N	1/4P	3/16	9	16	4
18436572	VD	5B@850	EL	EL	CH	N12Y	.035	5/8N	1/4P	5/32	7-1/2	16	4
18436572	VD	5B@850	EL	EL	CH	N12Y	.035	1/2N	1/4P	3/16	7-1/2[34]	16	4
18436572	VD	5B@750	EL	EL	CH	J13Y	.035	3/4P	1/4P	3/16	9	16.5	4
18436572	VD	5B@900	EL	EL	CH	J13Y[37]	.035	1/2N	1/4P	3/16	8	16.5	4
18436572	VD	10B@750	EL	EL	CH	J11Y	.035	3/4P	1/4P	3/16	9	16	4
18436572	VD	10B@800	EL	EL	CH	J11Y	.035	1/2N	1/4P	3/16	8	16	4
1342	VD	6B@750	.025	39	AU	BRF42	.034	1-1/4P	3/4P	1/4	10	8.5	4
1342	CP	6B@650	.025	39	AU	AGRF52	.034	1-1/4P	3/4P	1/4	10	8.5	4
1342	CP	6B@750	.025	38	AU	AGRF52	.034	3/4P	1/2P	1/8	9-3/4	8.8	4
142536	VD	12B@650[7]	.025	38	AU	AGR42	.034	3/4P	1/2P	1/8	9-3/4	12.5	4
153624	VD	6B@550[7]	.027	37	AU	BRF82	.034	1/2N	1/4P	3/16	6-3/4	9	4
153624	VD	6B@600[7]	.027	37	AU	BRF82	.044	1/2N	1/4P	3/16	6-3/4	9.7	4
153624	VD	6B@600[7]	.027	37	AU	BRF82	.044	2P	1/8P	1/8	9	9.7	4
15426378	VD	6B@650[28]	.017	27	AU	BRF42	.044	1/2N	1/4P	3/16	6-3/4	13.4	4
15426378	VD	6B@500[39]	.017	28	AU	BRF42	.044	2P	1/8P	1/8	9	15.7	4
13726548	VD	6B@600	.017	27	AU	BRF42	.044	2P	1/8P	1/8	9	16.4	4
13726548	VD	6B@600	.014	28	AU	BRF42	.034	2P	1/8P	3/16	9-1/2	16.3	4
13726548	VD	14B@650	.017	27	AU	ARF42	.044	2P	1/8P	1/8	9	15.9	4

14 – Also Gran Sport – 255@4400
15 – Brougham – 133, 75-151.5
16 – Brougham – 26.8
17 – W/Manual Trans. – 10B@700
18 – W/Manual Trans. – @850
19 – Nova – 111, Chevelle 2-Door – 112, 4-Door – 116
20 – W/Manual Trans. – 4B@900
21 – Nova – 1/2P, Chevelle – 1-1/4N
22 – Nova – 1/4P, Chevelle – 1/2P
23 – Chevelle – 1/16

24 – Nova – 9, Chevelle – 9-5/8
25 – Monte Carlo "S" W/Manual Trans. – 0@900
26 – Monte Carlo "S" – 4-3/4P
27 – W/Manual Trans. – @900
28 – W/Manual Trans. – @800
29 – Minimum psi Allowable, Also 40 psi Maximum Variation
30 – Minimum psi Allowable, Also 25 psi Maximum Variation
31 – 2-Door Special – 108

32 – 4-Door – 118
33 – Charger/SE – 115, Coronet/Custom – 118
34 – Charger/SE, Coronet/Custom – 8
35 – Also Brougham – 185@4000
36 – Also 250@4800
37 – 250 hp – J11Y
38 – 4-Door – 110
39 – W/Manual Trans. 10B@500
40 – Windsor Plant
41 – Cleveland Plant

1974

	Wheelbase (in.)	No. of Cylinders Bore and Stroke (in.)	Displacement (cu. in.)	Valve and Cylinder Arrangement	Compression Pressure (lbs.)	Net Brake Horsepower @ rpm	Valve Tappet Clearance Intake	Valve Tappet Clearance Exhaust	Cylinder Bolt Torque (ft. lbs.)
Ford	121	8-4.00x3.50	351C[1]	VO	170[2]	173@4200	HY	HY	105
Torino	114[3]	8-4.00x4.00	400	VO	180[2]	170@3400	HY	HY	105
Ford	121	8-4.00x4.00	400	VO	180[2]	170@3400	HY	HY	105
Torino	114[3]	8-4.362x3.85	460	VO	180[2]	195@3800	HY	HY	140
Ford	121	8-4.362x3.85	460	VO	180[2]	195@3800	HY	HY	140
Thunderbird	120.4	8-4.362x3.85	460	VO	180[2]	220@4000	HY	HY	140
Lincoln	127.2	8-4.362x3.85	460	VO	180[2]	220@4000	HY	HY	140
Mark IV	120.4	8-4.362x3.85	460	VO	180[2]	220@4000	HY	HY	140
Mercury – Comet (All)	103[4]	6-3.683x3.126	200	IO	175[2]	84@3800	HY	HY	75
Comet (All)	103[4]	6-3.682x3.910	250	IO	175[2]	91@3200	HY	HY	75
Comet (All)	103[4]	8-4.002x3.00	302	VO	150[2]	140@3800	HY	HY	72
Montego (All)	114[3]	8-4.002x3.00	302	VO	150[2]	140@3800	HY	HY	72
Montego (All)	114[3]	8-4.002x3.50	351W[8]	VO	160[2]	163@4200	HY	HY	112
Cougar (All)	114	8-4.002x3.50	351W[8]	VO	160[2]	163@4200	HY	HY	112
Montego XR7 (All)	114[3]	8-4.002x3.50	351C[1]	VO	170[2]	163@4200	HY	HY	105
Cougar XR7 (All)	114	8-4.002x3.50	351C[1]	VO	170[2]	163@4200	HY	HY	105
Montego (2-Door' Only), Cougar XR7	114	8-4.002x3.50	351C[1]	VO	170[2]	240@5400	HY	HY	105
Montego, Cougar XR7 (All)	114	8-4.00x4.00	400	VO	180[2]	170@3400	HY	HY	105
Mercury (All)	124	8-4.00x4.00	400	VO	180[2]	170@3400	HY	HY	105
Montego (All)	114[3]	8-4.362x3.85	460	VO	180[2]	195@3400	HY	HY	140
Cougar XR7 (All)	114	8-4.362x3.85	460	VO	180[2]	220@4000	HY	HY	140
Mercury (All)	124	8-4.362x3.85	460	VO	180[2]	220@4000	HY	HY	140
Oldsmobile – Omega	111	6-3.87x3.53	250	IO	140	100@3600	HY	HY	95
Omega	111	8-4.057x3.385	350	VO	160[9]	180@3800	HY	HY	85
Cutlass, Supreme	112[11]	8-4.057x3.385	350	VO	160[9]	180@3800	HY	HY	85
Cutlass, Supreme	112[11]	8-4.057x3.385	350	VO	160[9]	200@4200	HY	HY	85
Delta 88, Royale	124	8-4.057x3.385	350	VO	160[9]	180@3800	HY	HY	85
Delta 88, Royale	124	8-4.057x3.385	350	VO	160[9]	200@4200	HY	HY	85
Cutlass, Supreme	112[11]	8-4.126x4.250	455	VO	160[9]	230@4000[12]	HY	HY	85
Delta 88, Royale, 98	124[13]	8-4.126x4.250	455	VO	160[9]	210@3600	HY	HY	85
Delta 88, Royale, 98	124[13]	8-4.126x4.250	455	VO	160[9]	230@4000	HY	HY	85
Toronado	122	8-4.126x4.250	455	VO	160[9]	230@3800	HY	HY	85
Plymouth – Valiant, Duster, Scamp	111[14]	6-3.40x3.64	198	IO	100[15]	95@4000	.010H	.020H	70
Valiant, Duster, Scamp	111[14]	6-3.40x4.12	225	IO	100[15]	105@3600	.010H	.020H	70
Satellite, Custom, Sebring	115[18]	6-3.40x4.12	225	IO	100[15]	105@3600	.010H	.020H	70
Valiant, Duster, Scamp, Barracuda, 'Cuda	111[14]	8-3.91x3.31	318	VO	100[19]	150@4000	HY	HY	95
Satellite, Custom, Sebring, Sebring Plus	115[18]	8-3.91x3.31	318	VO	100[19]	150@4000	HY	HY	95
Road Runner	115	8-3.91x3.31	318	VO	100[19]	170@4000	HY	HY	95
Fury I, II, III	122	8-4.00x3.58	360	VO	100[19]	180@4000	HY	HY	95
Satellite, Sebring, Custom	115[18]	8-4.00x3.58	360	VO	100[19]	200@4000[22]	HY	HY	95
Duster 360	108	8-4.00x3.58	360	VO	100[19]	245@4800	HY	HY	95
Barracuda, 'Cuda	108	8-4.00x3.58	360	VO	100[19]	245@4800	HY	HY	95
Road Runner	115	8-4.00x3.58	360	VO	100[19]	245@4800	HY	HY	95
Fury, Gran Coupe, Sedan	122	8-4.34x3.38	400	VO	100[19]	185@4000	HY	HY	70
Fury I, II, III, Gran Coupe, Sedan	122	8-4.34x3.38	400	VO	100[19]	205@4800	HY	HY	70
Satellite, Sebring, Custom	115[18]	8-4.34x3.38	400	VO	100[19]	205@4800	HY	HY	70
Satellite, Sebring, Custom, Road Runner	115[18]	8-4.34x3.38	400	VO	100[19]	250@4800	HY	HY	70
Fury I, II, III, Gran Coupe, Sedan	122	8-4.32x3.75	440	VO	100[19]	220@4000	HY	HY	70
Fury I, II, III, Gran Coupe, Sedan	122	8-4.32x3.75	440	VO	100[19]	230@4000	HY	HY	70
Road Runner	115	8-4.32x3.75	440	VO	100[19]	275@4400	HY	HY	70
Pontiac – Ventura, Custom	111	6-3.875x3.53	250	IO	140	100@3600	HY	HY	95
Firebird	108	6-3.875x3.53	250	IO	140	100@3600	HY	HY	95
LeMans, Sport Coupe	112[11]	6-3.875x3.53	250	IO	140	100@3600	HY	HY	95
Ventura, Custom	111	8-3.8762x3.75	350	VO	140	155@3600[25]	HY	HY	95
Firebird, Esprit	108	8-3.8762x3.75	350	VO	140	155@3600[25]	HY	HY	95
LeMans, Sport Coupe, Luxury LeMans	112[11]	8-3.8762x3.75	350	VO	140	155@3600[26]	HY	HY	95
Ventura, Custom, GTO	111	8-3.8762x3.75	350	VO	140	200@4400	HY	HY	95
LeMans, Sport Coupe, Luxury LeMans	112[11]	8-4.1212x3.75	400	VO	140	175@3600[28]	HY	HY	95
Catalina, Bonneville	124	8-4.1212x3.75	400	VO	140	175@3600[29]	HY	HY	95
Firebird Esprit, Formula	108	8-4.1212x3.75	400	VO	140	190@4000[30]	HY	HY	95
Firebird Formula, Trans AM	108	8-4.1212x3.75	400	VO	140	225@4000	HY	HY	95
Grand Prix	116	8-4.1212x3.75	400	VO	140	225@4000	HY	HY	95
LeMans, Sport Coupe, Luxury LeMans	112[11]	8-4.1212x3.75	400	VO	140	225@4000	HY	HY	95
Catalina, Bonneville, Grand Ville	124	8-4.1522x4.21	455	VO	140	215@3600	HY	HY	95
Catalina, Bonneville, Grand Ville	124	8-4.1522x4.21	455	VO	140	250@4000	HY	HY	95
Firebird Formula, Trans AM	108	8-4.1522x4.21	455	VO	140	250@4000	HY	HY	95
Grand Prix SJ	116	8-4.1522x4.21	455	VO	140	250@4000	HY	HY	95
LeMans, Sport Coupe, Luxury LeMans	112[11]	8-4.1522x4.21	455	VO	140	250@4000	HY	HY	95
Firebird Formula, Trans AM	108	8-4.1522x4.21	455	VO	140	290@4000	HY	HY	95

ABBREVIATIONS – FOOTNOTES

AC – AC Spark Plugs
AU – Autolite Spark Plugs
B – Before Top Dead Center
C – Cold Engine
CH – Champion Spark Plugs
CP – Crankshaft Pulley
EL – Electronic Ignition

H – Hot Engine
HY – Hydraulic Lifters
IO – In-Line Engine, Overhead Valves
M – Motorcraft Spark Plugs
N – Negative
P – Positive
TDC – Top Dead Center
VD – Vibration Damper
VO – V-Type Engine, Overhead Valves

1 – Cleveland Plant
2 – Lowest Cylinder Must Be At Least 75 Percent of Highest
3 – 4-Door – 118
4 – 4-Door – 109.9
5 – W/Manual Trans. – 6B@750
6 – W/Manual Trans. – 6B@800
7 – W/Manual Trans. – 10B@500
8 – Windsor Plant

Tuneup Specifications

Firing Order	Timing Mark Location	Initial Ignition Timing @ rpm	Breaker Point Gap (in.)	Cam Angle (deg.)	Make	Model	Gap (in.)	Caster Manual Steering (deg.)	Camber Right Wheel (deg.)	Toe-In (in.)	Steering Axis Inclination (deg.)	Cooling System Capacity (qts.)	Crankcase Capacity (qts.)
13726548	VD	6B@600	.014	28	M	ARF42	.034	2P	1/4P	3/16	9-1/2	16.3	4
13726548	VD	12B@625	.017	27	M	ARF42	.044	2P	1/8P	1/8	9	17.7	4
13726548	VD	12B@625	EL	EL	M	ARF42	.044	2P	1/4P	3/16	9-1/2	18	4
15426378	VD	14B@650	.017	27	M	ARF52	.054	2P	1/8P	1/8	9	18.9	6
15426378	VD	14B@650	EL	EL	M	ARF52	.044	2P	1/4P	3/16	9-1/2	19.4	4
15426378	VD	14B@650	EL	EL	AU	ARF52	.054	2P	3/4P	3/16	9	21.5	4
15426378	VD	14B@650	EL	EL	AU	ARF52	.054	1-1/2P	3/4P	1/4	9-1/2	21.5,	4
15426378	VD	14B@650	EL	EL	AU	ARF52	.044	2P	3/4P	5/16	9	20.5	4
153624	VD	6B@550[5]	.027	37	AU	BRF82	.034	1/2N	1/4P	3/16	6-3/4	9	4
153624	VD	6B@600[5]	.027	37	AU	ARF42	.044	1/2N	1/4P	3/16	6-3/4	9.7	4
15426378	VD	6B@650[6]	.017	27	AU	BRF42	.044	1/2N	1/4P	3/16	6-3/4	13.4	4
15426378	VD	6B@500[7]	.117	28	M	BRF42	.044	2P	1/8P	1/8	9	15.7	4
13726548	VD	6B@600	.017	27	M	BRF42	.044	2P	1/8P	1/8	9	16.4	4
13726548	VD	6B@600	.017	27	M	BRF42	.034	2P	1/8P	1/8	9	16.3	4
13726548	VD	14B@650	.017	28	M	BRF42	.044	2P	1/8P	1/8	9	15.9	4
13726548	VD	14B@650	.017	27	M	ARF42	.044	2P	1/8P	1/8	9	15.9	4
13726548	VD	20B@500	.017	28	M	ARF42	.044	2P	1/8P	1/8	9	15.9	4
13726548	VD	12B@625	.017	27	M	ARF42	.044	2P	1/8P	1/8	9	17.7	4
13726548	VD	12B@625	EL	EL	M	ARF42	.044	2P	1/4P	3/16	9-1/2	18	4
15426378	VD	14B@650	.017	27	M	ARF52	.054	2P	1/8P	1/8	9	18.9	6
15426378	VD	14B@650	EL	EL	M	ARF52	.054	2P	1/8P	1/8	9	18.8	6
15426378	VD	10B@600	EL	EL	M	ARF52	.044	2P	1/4P	3/16	9-1/2	19.4	4
153624	VD	8B@600[10]	.019	33	AC	R46TS	.035	1/2P	1/4P	3/16	9	15.5	4
18436572	VD	12B@1100	.016	30	AC	R46S	.040	1/2P	1/4P	3/16	9	20	4
18436572	VD	12B@1100	.016	30	AC	R46S	.040	1-1/4N	1P	1/16	10-1/2	20	4
18436572	VD	12B@1100	.016	30	AC	R46S	.040	1-1/4N	1P	1/16	10-1/2	20	4
18436572	VD	12B@1100	.016	30	AC	R46S	.040	1P	3/4P	1/16	9-1/2	21	4
18436572	VD	12B@1100	.016	30	AC	R46S	.040	1P	3/4P	1/16	9-1/2	21	4
18436572	VD	8B@1100	.016	30	AC	R45S	.040	1-1/4N	1P	1/16	10-1/2	21	4
18436572	VD	8B@1100	.016	30	AC	R45S	.040	1P	3/4P	1/16	9-1/2	21	4
18436572	VD	8B@1100	.016	30	AC	R45S	.040	1P	3/4P	1/16	9-1/2	21	4
18436572	VD	8B@1100	.016	30	AC	R46S	.040	2N	3/4P	0	11	21	5
153624	VD	2.5B@750[16]	EL	EL	CH	N14Y	.035	5/8N	1/4P	5/32	7-1/2	13	4
153624	VD	TDC@750[17]	EL	EL	CH	N14Y	.035	5/8N	1/4P	5/32	7-1/2	13	4
153624	VD	TDC@750[17]	EL	EL	CH	N14Y	.035	1/2N	1/4P	3/16	8	13	4
18436572	VD	TDC@750	EL	EL	CH	N13Y	.035	1/2N	1/4P	5/32[20]	8[21]	16	4
18436572	VD	TDC@750	EL	EL	CH	N13Y	.035	1/2N	1/4P	3/16	8	16	4
18436572	VD	TDC@750	EL	EL	CH	N13Y	.035	1/2N	1/4P	3/16	8	16	4
18436572	VD	5B@750	EL	EL	CH	N12Y	.035	3/4P	1/4P	3/16	9	16	4
18436572	VD	5B@750	EL	EL	CH	N12Y	.035	1/2N	1/4P	3/16	9	16.5	4
18436572	VD	5B@850	EL	EL	CH	N12Y	.035	1/2N	1/4P	5/32	8	16	4
18436572	VD	5B@850	EL	EL	CH	N12Y	.035	1/2N	1/4P	3/16	7-1/2	16	4
18436572	VD	5B@850	EL	EL	CH	N12Y	.035	1/2N	1/4P	3/16	8	16.5	4
18436572	VD	5B@750	EL	EL	CH	J13Y	.035	3/4P	1/4P	3/16	9	16.5	4
18436572	VD	5B@900	EL	EL	CH	J13Y	.035	3/4P	1/4P	3/16	9	16.5	4
18436572	VD	5B@900	EL	EL	CH	J11Y	.035	1/2N	1/4P	3/16	8	16.5	4
18436572	VD	5B@900	EL	EL	CH	J11Y	.035	1/2N	1/4P	3/16	8	16.5	4
18436572	VD	10B@750	EL	EL	CH	J11Y	.035	3/4P	1/4P	3/16	9	16	4
18436572	VD	10B@750	EL	EL	CH	J11Y	.035	3/4P	1/4P	3/16	9	16	4
18436572	VD	10B@800	EL	EL	CH	J11Y	.035	1/2N	1/4P	3/16	8	16	4
153624	VD	8B@600[23]	.019	33	AC	R46T	.035	1/2P	1/4P	3/16	9	12.1	4
153624	VD	8B@600[23]	.019	33	AC	R46T	.035	0	1P	3/16	10-1/2	12.5	4
153624	VD	8B@600[23]	.019	33	AC	R46T	.035	1N	1/2P	1/16	10-1/2	13.3	4
18436572	VD	12B@650[24]	.016	30	AC	R46TS	.040	1/2P	1/4P	3/16	9	19.2	5
18436572	VD	12B@650[24]	.016	30	AC	R46TS	.040	0	1P	1/16	10-1/2	22.4	5
18436572	VD	12B@650[24]	.016	30	AC	R46TS	.040	1N	1/2P	1/16	10-1/2	22	5
18436572	VD	12B@650[27]	.016	30	AC	R46TS	.040	1/2P	1/4P	3/16	9	19.2	5
18436572	VD	12B@650	.016	30	AC	R46TS	.040	1N	1/2P	1/16	10-1/2	22	5
18436572	VD	12B@650	.016	30	AC	R46TS	.040	1P	1/2P	1/16	10-1/2	21.9	5
18436572	VD	12B@650	.016	30	AC	R46TS	.040	0	1P	3/16	10-1/2	22.4	5
18436572	VD	12B@650[27]	.016	30	AC	R45TS	.040	0	1P	3/16	10-1/2	22.4	5
18436572	VD	12B@650	.016	30	AC	R45TS	.040	3P	1/2P	1/16	10-1/2	23.1	5
18436572	VD	12B@650	.016	30	AC	R45TS	.040	1N	1/2P	1/16	10-1/2	23.1	5
18436572	VD	12B@650	.016	30	AC	R45TS	.040	1P	1/2P	1/16	10-1/2	21.2	5
18436572	VD	12B@650	.016	30	AC	R45TS	.040	1P	1/2P	1/16	10-1/2	21.2	5
18436572	VD	12B@650	.016	30	AC	R45TS	.040	0	1P	3/16	10-1/2	20.9	5
18436572	VD	12B@650	.016	30	AC	R45TS	.040	3P	1/2P	1/16	10-1/2	21.3	5
18436572	VD	12B@650	.016	30	AC	R45TS	.040	1N	1/2P	1/16	10-1/2	21.2	5
18436572	VD	12B@750[27]	.016	30	AC	R44TS	.040	0	1P	3/16	10-1/2	20.9	5

9 – Lowest Cylinder Must Be At Least 75 Percent of Highest
10 – W/Manual Trans. – 8B@850
11 – 4-Door – 116
12 – Also Cutlass – 275@4200
13 – 98 – 127
14 – Duster, Barracuda, 'Cuda – 108
15 – Minimum psi Allowable, Also 25 psi Maximum Variation
16 – W/Manual Trans. – 2.5B@800
17 – W/Manual Trans. – TDC@800
18 – 4-Door – 117
19 – Minimum psi Allowable, Also 40 psi Maximum Variation
20 – Barracuda – 3/16
21 – Barracuda, 'Cuda – 7-1/2
22 – Also Fury I, II, III, Gran Coupe, Sedan
23 – W/Manual Trans. – 8B@850
24 – W/Manual Trans. – 10B@900
25 – Also 170@3600
26 – Also 170@3600 and 200@4400
27 – W/Manual Trans. – 10B@1000
28 – Also 190@4000
29 – Also 200@4000
30 – Also Esprit – 175@3600

1975

	Wheelbase (in.)	No. of Cylinders Bore and Stroke (in.)	Displacement (cu. in.)	Valve and Cylinder Arrangement	Compression Pressure (lbs.)	Net Brake Horsepower @ rpm	Valve Tappet Clearance Intake	Exhaust	Cylinder Bolt Torque (ft. lbs.)
American Motors – Gremlin, Hornet	96 [1]	6–3.75x3.50	232	IO	140	100@3600	HY	HY	105
Matador 10, 80	114	6–3.75x3.50	232	IO	140	100@3600	HY	HY	105
Gremlin, Hornet	96 [1]	6–3.75x3.90	258	IO	150	110@3500	HY	HY	105
Matador 10, 80	114 [3]	6–3.75x3.90	258	IO	150	110@3500	HY	HY	105
Gremlin, Hornet	96 [1]	8–3.75x3.44	304	VO	140	150@4200	HY	HY	110
Matador 10, 80	114 [3]	8–3.75x3.44	304	VO	140	150@4200	HY	HY	110
Matador 10, 80	114 [3]	8–4.08x3.44	360	VO	140	175@4000	HY	HY	110
Matador 10, 80	114 [3]	8–4.08x3.44	360	VO	140	195@4000	HY	HY	110
Buick – Skyhawk	97	6–3.80x3.40	231	VO	160	110@4000	HY	HY	95
Skylark, S/R	111	6–3.80x3.40	231	VO	160	110@4000	HY	HY	95
Century, Custom, Special, Regal	112 [8]	6–3.80x3.40	231	VO	160	110@4000	HY	HY	95
Apollo, S/R	111	6–3.875x3.53	250	IO	130	105@3800	HY	HY	95
Apollo, S/R, Skylark, S/R	111	8–3.50x3.385	260	VO	160	110@3400	HY	HY	95
Apollo, S/R, Skylark, S/R	111	8–3.80x3.85	350	VO	180	145@3200	HY	HY	80
Century, Custom, Special, Regal	112 [8]	8–3.80x3.85	350	VO	180	145@3200	HY	HY	80
Apollo, S/R, Skylark, S/R	111	8–3.80x3.85	350	VO	180	165@3800	HY	HY	80
Century, Custom, Special, Regal	112 [8]	8–3.80x3.85	350	VO	180	165@3800	HY	HY	80
LeSabre, Custom	123.5	8–3.80x3.85	350	VO	180	165@3800	HY	HY	80
LeSabre, Custom	123.5	8–4.3125x3.90	455	VO	180	205@3800	HY	HY	100
Electra 225, Limited, Riviera, GS	127 [10]	8–4.3125x3.90	455	VO	180	205@3800	HY	HY	100
Cadillac	130 [11]	8–4.30x4.304	500	VO	175	190@3600	HY	HY	115
Eldorado	126.3	8–4.30x4.304	500	VO	175	190@3600	HY	HY	115
Chevrolet – Vega (L13)	97	4–3.501x3.625	140	IOC	140	78@4200	.015C	.030C	60
Vega (L11), Monza 2+2	97	4–3.501x3.625	140	IOC	140	87@4400	.015C	.030C	60
Camaro	108	6–3.875x3.53	250	IO	130	105@3800	HY	HY	95
Nova, Custom	111	6–3.875x3.53	250	IO	130	105@3800	HY	HY	95
Chevelle Malibu, Classic	112 [8]	6–3.875x3.53	250	IO	130	105@3800	HY	HY	95
Monza 2+2	97	8–3.671x3.10	262	VO	160	110@3600	HY	HY	65
Nova, Custom	111	8–3.671x3.10	262	VO	160	110@3600	HY	HY	65
Nova, Custom, Camaro, LT	111 [19]	8–4.0x3.48	350	VO	160	145@3800	HY	HY	65
Chevelle (All), Monte Carlo "S"	112 [8]	8–4.0x3.48	350	VO	160	145@3800	HY	HY	65
Chevrolet Bel Air, Impala, Caprice	121.5	8–4.0x3.48	350	VO	160	145@3800	HY	HY	65
Corvette	98	8–4.0x3.48	350	VO	160	165@3800	HY	HY	65
Nova, Custom, Camaro, LT	111 [19]	8–4.0x3.48	350	VO	160	165@3800	HY	HY	65
Chevelle (All), Monte Carlo "S"	112 [8]	8–4.0x3.48	350	VO	160	165@3800	HY	HY	65
Chevrolet (All)	121.5	8–4.0x3.48	350	VO	160	165@3800	HY	HY	65
Corvette	98	8–4.0x3.48	350	VO	160	205@4800	HY	HY	65
Chevelle (All), Monte Carlo "S"	112 [8]	8–4.125x3.75	400	VO	160	175@3600	HY	HY	80
Chevrolet (All)	121.5	8–4.125x3.75	400	VO	160	175@3600	HY	HY	80
Chevelle, Malibu, Classic, Monte Carlo "S"	112 [8]	8–4.251x4.0	454	VO	160	215@4000	HY	HY	80
Chevrolet (All)	121.5	8–4.251x4.0	454	VO	160	215@4000	HY	HY	80
Chrysler – Cordoba	115	8–3.91x3.31	318	VO	100 [27]	150@4000	HY	HY	95
Newport, Custom, Cordoba	124 [28]	8–4.0x3.58	360	VO	100 [27]	180@4000 [29]	HY	HY	95
Cordoba	115	8–4.34x3.38	400	VO	100 [27]	185@4000 [32]	HY	HY	70
Newport, Custom, New Yorker Brougham	124	8–4.34x3.38	400	VO	100 [27]	185@4000 [34]	HY	HY	70
Newport, Custom, New Yorker, Imperial	124	8–4.32x3.75	440	VO	100 [27]	275@4400	HY	HY	70
Dodge – Dart (All except 360 Sport)	111 [36]	6–3.40x4.12	225	IO	100 [37]	105@3600	.010H	.020H	70
Coronet, Coupe, Custom	115 [38]	6–3.40x4.12	225	IO	100 [37]	105@3600	.010H	.020H	70
Dart (All except 360 Sport)	111 [36]	8–3.91x3.31	318	VO	100 [27]	150@4000	HY	HY	95
Coronet, Coupe, Custom, Brougham	115 [38]	8–3.91x3.31	318	VO	100 [27]	150@4000	HY	HY	95
Charger Special Edition	115	8–3.91x3.31	318	VO	100 [27]	150@4000	HY	HY	95
Monaco, Royal Monaco, Brougham	122	8–3.91x3.31	318	VO	100 [27]	150@4000	HY	HY	95
Coronet (All)	115 [38]	8–4.0x3.58	360	VO	100 [27]	180@4000	HY	HY	95
Charger Special Edition	115	8–4.0x3.58	360	VO	100 [27]	180@4000 [39]	HY	HY	95
Monaco (All)	122	8–4.0x3.58	360	VO	100 [27]	180@4000	HY	HY	95
Dart 360 Sport	108	8–4.0x3.58	360	VO	100 [27]	245@4800	HY	HY	95
Coronet (All)	115 [38]	8–4.0x3.58	360	VO	100 [27]	245@4800	HY	HY	95
Coronet (All)	115 [38]	8–4.34x3.38	400	VO	100 [27]	185@4000	HY	HY	70
Charger Special Edition	115	8–4.34x3.38	400	VO	100 [27]	185@4000	HY	HY	70
Monaco (All)	122	8–4.34x3.38	400	VO	100 [27]	185@4000	HY	HY	70
Coronet (All)	115 [38]	8–4.34x3.38	400	VO	100 [27]	205@4000 [40]	HY	HY	70
Charger Special Edition	115	8–4.34x3.38	400	VO	100 [27]	205@4000 [40]	HY	HY	70
Monaco (All)	122	8–4.32x3.75	440	VO	100 [27]	275@4400	HY	HY	70
Ford – Pinto (2300)	94.5	4–3.781x3.126	140	IOC	80 [41]	83@4800	HY	HY	90
Mustang II, Ghia (2300)	96.2	4–3.781x3.126	140	IOC	80 [41]	87@4600	HY	HY	90
Pinto (2800)	94.5	6–3.66x2.70	170.8	VO	80 [41]	97@4400	.014H	.016H	80
Mustang II, Ghia, Mach 1 (2800)	96.2	6–3.66x2.70	170.8	VO	80 [41]	97@4400	.014H	.016H	80
Maverick, Grabber, Granada, Ghia	109.9 [43]	6–3.683x3.126	200	IO	175 [41]	65@3600	HY	HY	75
Maverick, Grabber, Granada, Ghia	109.9 [43]	6–3.682x3.910	250	IO	175 [41]	72@2900	HY	HY	75
Mustang II, Ghia, Mach 1	96.2	8–4.00x3.0	302	VO	150 [41]	97@4400	HY	HY	72

Tuneup Specifications

Firing Order	Timing Mark Location	Initial Ignition Timing @ rpm	Breaker Point Gap (in.)	Cam Angle (deg.)	Spark Plugs Make	Model	Gap (in.)	Caster Manual Steering (deg.)	Camber Right Wheel (deg.)	Toe-In (in.)	Steering Axis Inclination (deg.)	Cooling System Capacity (qts.)	Crankcase Capacity (qts.)
153624	VD	5B@550[2]	EL	EL	CH	N12Y	.035	0	1/8P	1/8	7-3/4	11	4
153624	VD	5B@550[2]	EL	EL	CH	N12Y	.035	1P	1/8P	1/8	7-3/4	11	4
153624	VD	3B@700	EL	EL	CH	N12Y	.035	0	1/8P	1/8	7-3/4	11	4
153624	VD	3B@700[4]	EL	EL	CH	N12Y	.035	1P	1/8P	1/8	7-3/4	16	4
18436572	VD	5B@700[5]	EL	EL	CH	N12Y	.035	0	1/8P	1/8	7-3/4	16.5[6]	4
18436572	VD	5B@700[5]	EL	EL	CH	N12Y	.035	1P	1/8P	1/8	7-3/4	15.5[7]	4
18436572	VD	5B@700	EL	EL	CH	N12Y	.035	1P	1/8P	1/8	7-3/4	15.5[7]	4
18436572	VD	5B@700	EL	EL	CH	N12Y	.035	1P	1/8P	1/8	8-1/2	13.4	4
165432	VD	12B@600	EL	EL	AC	R44SX	.060	3/4N	1/4P	1/16	10	13.4	4
165432	VD	12B@600	EL	EL	AC	R44SX	.060	1N	3/4P	1/16	10	13.4	4
165432	VD	12B@600	EL	EL	AC	R44SX	.060	2P	1/2P	1/16	8	15.4	4
153624	VD	10B@600[9]	EL	EL	AC	R46TX	.060	1N	3/4P	1/16	10	17	4
18436572	VD	16B@1100	EL	EL	AC	R46SX	.060	1N	3/4P	1/16	10	19.5	4
18436572	VD	12B@600	EL	EL	AC	R45TSX	.060	2P	1/2P	1/16	10	18.9	4
18436572	VD	12B@600	EL	EL	AC	R45TSX	.060	1N	3/4P	1/16	10	16.9	4
18436572	VD	12B@600	EL	EL	AC	R45TSX	.060	2P	1/2P	1/16	8	18.9	4
18436572	VD	12B@600	EL	EL	AC	R45TSX	.060	1-1/2P	1P	1/16	9-5/8	16.9	4
18436572	VD	12B@600	EL	EL	AC	R45TSX	.060	1-1/2P	1P	1/16	9-5/8	19.6	4
18436572	VD	12B@600	EL	EL	AC	R45TSX	.060	1-1/2P	1P	1/16	9-5/8	19.6	4
15634278	VD	6B@600	EL	EL	AC	R45NSX	.060	0[12]	1/4N	1/8	6	23[13]	4
15634278	VD	6B@600	EL	EL	AC	R45NSX	.060	0	1/4N	0	11	23	5
1342	CP	12B@750[14]	EL	EL	AC	R43TSX	.035	3/4N	1/2P	1/4	8-1/2	8.6	3
1342	CP	12B@750[14]	EL	EL	AC	R43TSX	.035	3/4N	1/2P	1/4	8-1/2	8.6[15]	3
153624	VD	10B@600[16]	EL	EL	AC	R46TX	.060	0	1P	1/16	10-3/8	14	4
153624	VD	10B@600[16]	EL	EL	AC	R46TX	.060	1N	3/4P	1/16	10	14	4
153624	VD	10B@600[16]	EL	EL	AC	R46TX	.060	1P[17]	1/2P	1/4	8-1/2	18	4
18436572	VD	8B@600[18]	EL	EL	AC	R44TX	.060	3/4N	1/2P	1/4	8-1/2	18	4
18436572	VD	8B@600[18]	EL	EL	AC	R44TX	.060	1N	3/4P	1/16	10	17	4
18436572	VD	6B@600[20]	EL	EL	AC	R44TX	.060	1N[21]	3/4P[22]	1/16[24]	10[23]	18	4
18436572	VD	6B@600[20]	EL	EL	AC	R44TX	.060	1P[17]	1/2P	1/16	9-1/2	18	4
18436572	VD	6B@600	EL	EL	AC	R44TX	.060	1-1/2P	1/2P	1/16	9	18	4
18436572	VD	6B@600[20]	EL	EL	AC	R44TX	.060	1P	3/4P	1/8	7-5/8	19	4
18436572	VD	4B@600[20]	EL	EL	AC	R44TX	.060	1N[21]	3/4P[22]	1/16	10[23]	18	4
18436572	VD	4B@600[20]	EL	EL	AC	R44TX	.060	1P[17]	1/2P	1/16[24]	9-1/2	18	4
18436572	VD	6B@600	EL	EL	AC	R44TX	.060	1-1/2P	1/2P	1/16	9	18	4
18436572	VD	12B@700[25]	EL	EL	AC	R44T	.060	1P	3/4P	1/8	7-5/8	18	4
18436572	VD	8B@600	EL	EL	AC	R44TX	.060	1P[17]	1/2P	1/16[24]	9-1/2	18	4
18436572	VD	8B@600	EL	EL	AC	R44TX	.060	1-1/2P	1/2P	1/16	9	18	4
18436572	VD	16B@600[2]	EL	EL	AC	R44TX	.060	1P[17]	1/2P	1/16[24]	9-1/2	24	4
18436572	VD	16B@650	EL	EL	AC	R44TX	.060	1-1/2P	1/2P	1/16	9	24	4
18436572	VD	2B@750	EL	EL	CH	N13Y	.035	3/4P	1/4N	3/16	8	16.5	4
18436572	VD	6B@750	EL	EL	CH	N12Y	.035	3/4P	1/4P[30]	3/16	9[31]	16	4
18436572	VD	10B@750[33]	EL	EL	CH	J13Y	.035	3/4P	1/4N	3/16	8	16.5	4
18436572	VD	10B@750[33]	EL	EL	CH	J13Y	.035	3/4P	1/4P	3/16	9	16[35]	4
18436572	VD	8B@750	EL	EL	CH	RY87P	.040	3/4P	1/4P	5/32	7-1/2	13	4
153624	VD	TDC@750[16]	EL	EL	CH	BL13Y	.035	5/8N	1/4P	5/32	7-1/2	13	4
153624	VD	TDC@750[16]	EL	EL	CH	BL13Y	.035	1/2N	1/4P	5/32	7-1/2	16	4
18436572	VD	2B@750	EL	EL	CH	N13Y	.035	5/8N	1/4P	3/16	8	16.5	4
18436572	VD	2B@750	EL	EL	CH	N13Y	.035	1/2N	1/4N	3/16	8	16.5	4
18436572	VD	2B@750	EL	EL	CH	N13Y	.035	3/4P	1/4P	3/16	9	17.5	4
18436572	VD	6B@750	EL	EL	CH	N12Y	.035	1/2N	1/4P	3/16	8	16	4
18436572	VD	6B@750	EL	EL	CH	N12Y	.035	3/4P	1/4N	3/16	8	16	4
18436572	VD	6B@750	EL	EL	CH	N12Y	.035	3/4P	1/4P	3/16	9	16	4
18436572	VD	6B@750	EL	EL	CH	N12Y	.035	5/8N	1/4P	5/32	7-1/2	16	4
18436572	VD	6B@750	EL	EL	CH	N12Y	.035	1/2N	1/4P	3/16	8	16.5	4
18436572	VD	10B@750	EL	EL	CH	J13Y	.035	1/2N	1/4P	3/16	8	16.5	4
18436572	VD	10B@750	EL	EL	CH	J13Y	.035	3/4P	1/4N	3/16	8	16.5	4
18436572	VD	10B@750	EL	EL	CH	J13Y	.035	3/4P	1/4P	3/16	9	16.5	4
18436572	VD	8B@750	EL	EL	CH	J13Y	.035	1/2N	1/4P	3/16	8	16.5	4
18436572	VD	8B@750	EL	EL	CH	J13Y	.035	3/4P	1/4N	3/16	8	16	4
18436572	VD	8B@750	EL	EL	CH	RY87P	.040	3/4P	1/4P	3/16	9	8.7	4
1342	CP	6B@550	EL	EL	AU	AGR52	.034	1-1/4P	3/4P	1/4	10	8.7	4
1342	CP	6B@550	EL	EL	AU	AGRF52	.034	7/8P	1/2P	1/8	9-3/4	8.5	4
142536	VD	10B@700	EL	EL	AU	AGR52	.034	1-1/4P	3/4P	1/4	10	12.5	4.5
142536	VD	10B@700[42]	EL	EL	AU	AGR42	.034	7/8P	1/2P	1/8	9-3/4	12.3	4.5
153624	VD	6B@600[5]	EL	EL	AU	BRF82	.034	1/2N	1/4P	3/16	6-3/4	9	4
153624	VD	6B@600[16]	EL	EL	AU	BRF82	.044	1/2N	1/4P	3/16	6-3/4	9.7	4
15426378	VD	6B@650	EL	EL	AU	ARF42	.044	7/8P	1/2P	1/8	9-3/4	16.3	4

16 – W/Manual Trans. – 800 rpm
17 – Chevelle W/Radial Tires – 2P, Monte Carlo "S" – 4-3/4P
18 – W/Manual Trans. – 8B@800
19 – Camaro – 108
20 – W/Manual Trans. – 6B@800
21 – Camaro – 0
22 – Camaro – 1P
23 – Camaro – 10-3/8
24 – Monte Carlo "S" – 1/4
25 – W/Manual Trans. – 12B@900

26 – Monte Carlo "S" – 16B@650
27 – Minimum psi Allowable, Also 40 psi Maximum Variation
28 – Cordoba – 115
29 – Cordoba – Also 245@4800
30 – Cordoba – 1/4N
31 – Cordoba – 8
32 – Also 205@4000, 250@4800
33 – W/4 Bbl. Carb. – 8B@750
34 – Also 205@4000
35 – Imperial – 17

36 – 2-Door Special – 108
37 – Minimum psi Allowable, Also 25 psi Maximum Variation
38 – 4-Door – 117
39 – Also W/4 Bbl. Carb. – 245@4800
40 – Also 250@4800
41 – Lowest Cylinder Must Be At Least 75 Percent of Highest
42 – W/Manual Trans. – 6B@850
43 – 2-Door – 103

1975	Wheelbase (in.)	No. of Cylinders Bore and Stroke (in.)	Displacement (cu. in.)	Valve and Cylinder Arrangement	Compression Pressure (lbs.)	Net Brake Horsepower @ rpm	Valve Tappet Clearance		Cylinder Bolt Torque (ft. lbs.)
							Intake	Exhaust	
Maverick, Grabber, Granada, Ghia	109.9[1]	8–4.00x3.00	302	VO	150[2]	129@3800	HY	HY	72
Torino, Gran Torino (All)	114[4]	8–4.00x3.50	351W[5]	VO	160[2]	154@3800	HY	HY	112
Granada, Ghia	109.9	8–4.00x3.50	351W[5]	VO	160[2]	143@3600	HY	HY	112
Torino, Gran Torino (All)	114[4]	8–4.00x3.50	351M[6]	VO	170[2]	148@3800	HY	HY	105
Ford LTD, Brougham, Elite	121	8–4.00x3.50	351M[6]	VO	170[2]	148@3800	HY	HY	105
Torino, Gran Torino (All)	114[4]	8–4.00x4.00	400	VO	180[2]	158@3800	HY	HY	105
Ford LTD, Brougham, Elite	121	8–4.00x4.00	400	VO	180[2]	158@3800	HY	HY	105
Torino, Gran Torino (All)	114[4]	8–4.362x3.850	460	VO	180[2]	216@4000	HY	HY	140
Ford LTD, Brougham, Elite	121	8–4.362x3.850	460	VO	180[2]	218@4000	HY	HY	140
Thunderbird	120.4	8–4.362x3.850	460	VO	180[2]	224@4000[7]	HY	HY	140
Lincoln Continental	127.2	8–4.362x3.850	460	VO	180[2]	206@3800	HY	HY	140
Continental Mark IV	120.4	8–4.362x3.850	460	VO	180[2]	194@3800	HY	HY	140
Mercury – Comet, GT, Monarch	109.9[1]	6–3.680x3.130	200	IO	175[2]	65@3600	HY	HY	75
Comet, GT, Monarch, Ghia	109.9[1]	6–3.680x3.910	250	IO	175[2]	72@2900	HY	HY	75
Comet, GT, Monarch, Ghia	109.9[1]	8–4.00x3.00	302	VO	150[2]	122@3800	HY	HY	72
Monarch, Ghia	109.9	8–4.00x3.50	351M[6]	VO	170[2]	143@3600	HY	HY	105
Montego, MX, Brougham	114[4]	8–4.00x3.50	351M[6]	VO	170[2]	150@3800	HY	HY	105
Cougar XR7	114	8–4.00x3.50	351M[6]	VO	170[2]	148@3800	HY	HY	105
Cougar XR7	114	8–4.00x3.50	351W[5]	VO	160[2]	154@3800	HY	HY	112
Montego, MX, Brougham	114[4]	8–4.00x4.00	400	VO	180[2]	144@3600	HY	HY	105
Cougar XR7	114	8–4.00x4.00	400	VO	180[2]	158@3800	HY	HY	105
Marquis	124	8–4.00x4.00	400	VO	180[2]	158@3800	HY	HY	105
Montego, MX, Brougham	114[4]	8–4.362x3.850	460	VO	180[2]	217@4000	HY	HY	140
Cougar XR7	114	8–4.362x3.850	460	VO	180[2]	216@4000	HY	HY	140
Marquis, Brougham, Grand Marquis	124	8–4.362x3.850	460	VO	180[2]	218@4000	HY	HY	140
Oldsmobile – Starfire	97	6–3.80x3.40	231	VO	160[11]	110@4000	HY	HY	95
Omega, Salon	111	6–3.875x3.530	250	IO	140[11]	105@3800	HY	HY	95
Cutlass, Supreme	112[13]	6–3.875x3.530	250	IO	140[11]	105@3800	HY	HY	95
Omega, Salon	111	8–3.50x3.385	260	VO	160[11]	110@3400	HY	HY	95
Cutlass, Supreme	112[13]	8–3.50x3.385	260	VO	160[11]	110@3400	HY	HY	95
Omega, Salon	111	8–4.057x3.850	350	VO	160[11]	165@3800[14]	HY	HY	85
Cutlass, Supreme	112[13]	8–4.057x3.850	350	VO	160[11]	170@3800	HY	HY	85
Delta 88, Royale	124	8–4.057x3.850	350	VO	160[11]	170@3800	HY	HY	85
98 Luxury Coupe Sedan	127	8–4.1212x3.750	400	VO	160[11]	185@4600	HY	HY	85
Cutlass, Supreme	112[13]	8–4.126x4.250	455	VO	160[11]	190@3400	HY	HY	85
Delta 88, Royale, 98	124[15]	8–4.126x4.250	455	VO	160[11]	190@3400	HY	HY	85
Toronado	122	8–4.126x4.250	455	VO	160[11]	215@3600	HY	HY	85
Plymouth – Valiant, Custom	111[13]	6–3.40x4.12	225	IO	100[17]	105@3600	.010H	.020H	70
Duster, Scamp, Brougham	111[13]	6–3.40x4.12	225	IO	100[17]	105@3600	.010H	.020H	70
Fury, Custom	115[16]	6–3.40x4.12	225	IO	100[17]	105@3600	.010H	.020H	70
Valiant, Custom	111[13]	8–3.91x3.31	318	VO	100[19]	150@4000	HY	HY	95
Duster, Scamp, Brougham	111[13]	8–3.91x3.31	318	VO	100[19]	150@4000	HY	HY	95
Fury, Custom, Sport Fury	115[16]	8–3.91x3.31	318	VO	100[19]	150@4000[20]	HY	HY	95
Gran Fury, Custom, Brougham	122	8–3.91x3.31	318	VO	100[19]	150@4000	HY	HY	95
Fury, Custom, Sport Fury	115[16]	8–4.0x3.58	360	VO	100[19]	180@4000[21]	HY	HY	70
Duster 360	108	8–4.0x3.58	360	VO	100[19]	245@4800[22]	HY	HY	95
Gran Fury, Custom, Sport Fury	122	8–4.0x3.58	360	VO	100[19]	245@4800	HY	HY	95
Fury, Custom, Brougham	115[16]	8–4.34x3.38	400	VO	100[19]	185@4000	HY	HY	70
Gran Fury, Custom, Sport Fury	122	8–4.34x3.38	400	VO	100[19]	185@4000	HY	HY	70
Fury, Custom, Brougham	115[16]	8–4.34x3.38	400	VO	100[19]	205@4000	HY	HY	70
Gran Fury, Custom, Sport Fury	122	8–4.34x3.38	400	VO	100[19]	205@4000	HY	HY	70
Fury, Custom, Brougham	115[16]	8–4.34x3.38	400	VO	100[19]	250@4800	HY	HY	70
Gran Fury, Custom, Sport Fury	122	8–4.32x3.75	440	VO	100[19]	275@4400	HY	HY	70
Pontiac – Astre	97	4–3.501x3.625	140	IOC	140	78@4200	.015C	.030C	60
Astre, SJ	97	4–3.501x3.625	140	IOC	140	87@4400	.015C	.030C	60
Ventura, Custom, SJ	111	6–3.875x3.53	250	IO	140	105@3800	HY	HY	95
LeMans, Sport Coupe, Grand LeMans	112[13]	6–3.875x3.53	250	IO	140	105@3800	HY	HY	95
Firebird, Esprit	108	6–3.875x3.53	250	IO	140	105@3800	HY	HY	95
Ventura, Custom, SJ	111	8–3.50x3.385	260	VO	140	110@3400	HY	HY	95
Ventura, Custom, SJ	111	8–3.80x3.85	350	VO	140	145@3200[23]	HY	HY	95
LeMans, Sport Coupe, Grand LeMans	112[13]	8–3.876x3.75	350	VO	140	155@4000[24]	HY	HY	95
Firebird, Esprit	108	8–3.876x3.75	350	VO	140	155@4000[26]	HY	HY	95
Catalina, Bonneville, Grand Ville	123.4	8–4.1212x3.75	400	VO	140	170@4000	HY	HY	95
Catalina, Bonneville, Grand Ville	123.4	8–4.1212x3.75	400	VO	140	185@4000	HY	HY	95
LeMans, Sport Coupe, Grand LeMans	112[13]	8–4.1212x3.75	400	VO	140	185@3600[28]	HY	HY	95
Grand Am	112[13]	8–4.1212x3.75	400	VO	140	185@3600[28]	HY	HY	95
Firebird Formula, Trans Am	108	8–4.1212x3.75	400	VO	140	185@3600[28]	HY	HY	95
Grand Prix	116	8–4.1212x3.75	400	VO	140	185@3600	HY	HY	95
Grand Prix	116	8–4.1522x4.21	455	VO	140	200@3500	HY	HY	95
Grand Am	112[13]	8–4.1522x4.21	455	VO	140	200@3500	HY	HY	95
Catalina, Bonneville, Grand Ville	123.4	8–4.1522x4.21	455	VO	140	200@3500	HY	HY	95

ABBREVIATIONS - FOOTNOTES

AC – AC Spark Plugs
AU – Autolite Spark Plugs
B – Before Top Dead Center
C – Cold Engine
CH – Champion Spark Plugs
CP – Crankshaft Pulley

EL – Electronic Ignition
H – Hot Engine
HY – Hydraulic Lifters
IO – In-Line Engine, Overhead Valves
IOC – In-Line Engine, Overhead Camshaft
N – Negative
P – Positive
TDC – Top Dead Center
VD – Vibration Damper

VO – V-Type Engine, Overhead Valves
1 – Comet, Maverick 2-Door – 103
2 – Lowest Cylinder Must Be At Least 75 Percent of Highest
3 – W/Manual Trans. – 900
4 – 4-Door – 118
5 – Windsor-Built
6 – Cleveland-Built
7 – Also 194@4800

Tuneup Specifications

Firing Order	Timing Mark Location	Initial Ignition Timing @ rpm	Breaker Point Gap (in.)	Cam Angle (deg.)	Spark Plugs Make	Model	Gap (in.)	Caster Manual Steering (deg.)	Camber Right Wheel (deg.)	Toe-In (in.)	Steering Axis Inclination (deg.)	Cooling System Capacity (qts.)	Crankcase Capacity (qts.)
15426378	VD	6B@650[3]	EL	EL	AU	BRF42	.044	1/2N	1/4P	3/16	6-3/4	13.4	4
13726548	VD	6B@600	EL	EL	AU	BRF42	.044	2P	1/8P	1/8	9	15.9	4
13726548	VD	6B@625	EL	EL	AU	BRF42	.044	1/2N	1/4P	3/16	6-3/4	13.4	4
13726548	VD	14B@700	EL	EL	AU	ARF42	.044	2P	1/8P	1/8	9	17.1	4
13726548	VD	14B@650	EL	EL	AU	ARF42	.044	2P	1/4P	3/16	9-1/2	16.3	4
13726548	VD	12B@625	EL	EL	AU	ARF42	.044	2P	1/8P	1/8	9	17.1	4
13726548	VD	12B@625	EL	EL	AU	ARF42	.044	2P	1/4P	3/16	9-1/2	18.0	4
15426378	VD	14B@650	EL	EL	AU	ARF52	.044	2P	1/8P	1/8	9	19.2	4
15426378	VD	14B@650	EL	EL	AU	ARF52	.044	2P	1/4P	3/16	9-1/2	19.4	4
15426378	VD	14B@650	EL	EL	AU	ARF52	.054	4P	1/2P	3/16	9	19.3	4
15426378	VD	14B@650	EL	EL	AU	ARF52	.044	1-1/2P	1/2P	1/8	9-1/2	19.7	4
15426378	VD	14B@650	EL	EL	AU	ARF52	.044	3-3/4P	1/4P	5/16	9	19.3	4
153624	VD	6B@600[8]	EL	EL	AU	BRF82	.034	1/2N	1/4P	3/16	6-3/4	9	4
153624	VD	6B@600[8]	EL	EL	AU	BRF82	.034	1/2N	1/4P	3/16	6-3/4	9.7[9]	4
15426378	VD	6B@650[3]	EL	EL	AU	BRF42	.044	1/2N	1/4P	3/16	6-3/4	13.5[10]	4
13726548	VD	14B@625	EL	EL	AU	BRF42	.044	1/2N	1/4P	3/16	6-3/4	15.7	4
13726548	VD	14B@700	EL	EL	AU	BRF42	.044	2P	1/8P	1/8	9	15.9	4
13726548	VD	14B@700	EL	EL	AU	BRF42	.044	2P	1/8P	1/8	9	16.3	4
13726548	VD	6B@600	EL	EL	AU	BRF42	.044	2P	1/8P	1/8	9	16.4	4
13726548	VD	12B@625	EL	EL	AU	ARF42	.044	2P	1/8P	1/8	9	17.7	4
13726548	VD	12B@625	EL	EL	AU	ARF42	.044	2P	1/8P	1/8	9	17.7	4
13726548	VD	12B@625	EL	EL	AU	ARF42	.044	2P	1/4P	3/16	9-1/2	17.1	4
15426378	VD	14B@650	EL	EL	AU	ARF52	.044	2P	1/8P	1/8	9	18.9	6
15426378	VD	14B@650	EL	EL	AU	ARF52	.044	2P	1/8P	1/8	9	18.8	6
15426378	VD	14B@650	EL	EL	AU	ARF52	.044	2P	1/4P	3/16	9-1/2	18.5	4
165432	VD	12B@600	EL	EL	AC	R44SX	.060	3/4N	1/2P	1/4	9	13.4	4
153624	VD	10B@600[12]	EL	EL	AC	R46TX	.060	1N	3/4P	1/16	10-1/2	15.5	4
153624	VD	10B@600[12]	EL	EL	AC	R46TX	.060	2P	1/2P	1/16	10-1/2	15.2	4
18436572	VD	16B@1100	EL	EL	AC	R46SX	.060	1N	3/4P	1/16	10-1/2	23	4
18436572	VD	16B@1100	EL	EL	AC	R46SX	.060	2P	1/2P	1/16	10-1/2	23	4
18436572	VD	20B@1100	EL	EL	AC	R45TSX	.060	1N	3/4P	1/16	10-1/2	21.5	4
18436572	VD	20B@1100	EL	EL	AC	R46SX	.080	2P	1/2P	1/16	10-1/2	20	4
18436572	VD	20B@1100	EL	EL	AC	R46SX	.080	1-1/2P	1/2P	1/16	10-1/2	20	4
18436572	VD	16B@650	EL	EL	AC	R45TSX	.080	1-1/2P	1/2P	1/16	10-1/2	21.5	5
18436572	VD	16B@1100	EL	EL	AC	R46SX	.080	2P	1/2P	1/16	10-1/2	21	4
18436572	VD	16B@1100	EL	EL	AC	R46SX	.080	1-1/2P	1/2P	1/16	10-1/2	21	4
18436572	VD	12B@1100	EL	EL	AC	R46SX	.080	0	1/4N	0	11	21	5
153624	VD	TDC@750	EL	EL	CH	BL13Y	.035	5/8N	1/4P	5/32	7-1/2	13	4
153624	VD	TDC@750	EL	EL	CH	BL13Y	.035	5/8N	1/4P	5/32	7-1/2	13	4
153624	VD	TDC@750[18]	EL	EL	CH	BL13Y	.035	1/2N	1/4P	3/16	8	13	4
18436572	VD	2B@700	EL	EL	CH	N13Y	.035	5/8N	1/4P	5/32	7-1/2	16	4
18436572	VD	2B@700	EL	EL	CH	N13Y	.035	5/8N	1/4P	5/32	7-1/2	16	4
18436572	VD	2B@700	EL	EL	CH	N13Y	.035	1/2N	1/4P	3/16	8	16.5	4
18436572	VD	2B@750	EL	EL	CH	N13Y	.035	3/4P	1/4P	3/16	9	17.5	4
18436572	VD	6B@750	EL	EL	CH	N12Y	.035	1/2N	1/4P	3/16	8	16	4
18436572	VD	2B@750[21]	EL	EL	CH	N12Y	.035	5/8N	1/4P	5/32	7-1/2	16	4
18436572	VD	6B@750	EL	EL	CH	N12Y	.035	3/4P	1/4P	3/16	9	16	4
18436572	VD	10B@750	EL	EL	CH	J13Y	.035	1/2N	1/4P	3/16	8	16.5	4
18436572	VD	10B@750	EL	EL	CH	J13Y	.035	3/4P	1/4P	3/16	9	16.5	4
18436572	VD	8B@750	EL	EL	CH	J13Y	.035	1/2N	1/4P	3/16	8	16.5	4
18436572	VD	8B@750	EL	EL	CH	J13Y	.035	3/4P	1/4P	3/16	9	16.5	4
18436572	VD	8B@750	EL	EL	CH	J13Y	.035	1/2N	1/4P	3/16	8	16.5	4
18436572	VD	8B@750	EL	EL	CH	RY87P	.040	3/4P	1/4P	3/16	9	16	4
1342	CP	10B@750	EL	EL	AC	R43TSX	.060	3/4N	1/4P	1/4	8-1/2	7.6	3
1342	CP	12B@750	EL	EL	AC	R43TSX	.060	3/4N	1/4P	1/4	8-1/2	7.6	3
153624	VD	10B@600	EL	EL	AC	R46TX	.060	1/2P	1/4P	1/16	10-7/8	18.8	4
153624	VD	10B@600	EL	EL	AC	R46TX	.060	1P	1/2P	1/16	10-3/8	20.5	4
153624	VD	10B@600	EL	EL	AC	R46TX	.060	0	1P	3/16	10-3/8	20.4	4
18436572	VD	16B@1100	EL	EL	AC	R45TSX	.060	1/2P	1/4P	1/16	10-7/8	19.6	4
18436572	VD	12B@600	EL	EL	AC	R46TSX	.060	1P	1/2P	1/16	10-3/8	17.8	5
18436572	VD	16B@600[25]	EL	EL	AC	R46TSX	.060	1P	1/2P	1/16	10-3/8	21.3	5
18436572	VD	16B@600[27]	EL	EL	AC	R46TSX	.060	0	1P	3/16	10-3/8	21	5
18436572	VD	16B@650	EL	EL	AC	R46TSX	.060	1-1/2P	1/2P	1/16	10-3/8	21.6	5
18436572	VD	16B@650	EL	EL	AC	R45TSX	.060	1-1/2P	1/2P	1/16	10-3/8	21.6	5
18436572	VD	16B@650	EL	EL	AC	R45TSX[29]	.060	1P	1/2P	1/16	10-3/8	23.6	5
18436572	VD	16B@650	EL	EL	AC	R45TSX[29]	.060	1P	1/2P	1/16	10-3/8	23.6	5
18436572	VD	16B@650	EL	EL	AC	R45TSX	.060	0	1P	3/16	10-3/8	23.3	5
18436572	VD	16B@650	EL	EL	AC	R45TSX	.060	3P	1/2P	1/16	10-3/8	22.1	5
18436572	VD	16B@650	EL	EL	AC	R45TSX	.060	3P	1/2P	1/16	10-3/8	20.3	5
18436572	VD	16B@650	EL	EL	AC	R45TSX	.060	1P	1/2P	1/16	10-3/8	22.3	5
18436572	VD	16B@650	EL	EL	AC	R45TSX	.060	1-1/2P	1/2P	1/16	10-3/8	22.3	5

8 – W/Manual Trans. – 750
9 – Monarch – 10.5
10 – Monarch – 14.4
11 – Lowest Cylinder Must Be At Least 70 Percent of Highest
12 – W/Manual Trans. – 10B@800
13 – 4-Door – 116
14 – Also 145@3200
15 – 98 – 127
16 – 4-Door – 117
17 – Minimum psi Allowable Also 25 psi Maximum Variation
18 – W/Manual Trans. – 800
19 – Minimum psi Allowable Also 40 psi Maximum Variation
20 – Also Road Runner – 170@4000
21 – Also 245@4000
22 – Also 200@4000
23 – Also 165@3800
24 – Also 175@4000
25 – W/Manual Trans. – 16B@650
26 – Also 175@4000, Including Formula
27 – W/Manual Trans. and 4-Bbl. Carb. – 12B@650
28 – Also 170@4000
29 – W/2-Bbl. Carb – R46TSX

1976

	Wheelbase (in.)	No. of Cylinders Bore and Stroke (in.)	Displacement (cu. in.)	Valve and Cylinder Arrangement	Compression Pressure (lb.)	Net Brake Horsepower @ rpm	Intake	Exhaust	Cylinder Bolt Torque (ft. lb.)
American Motors — Pacer, Gremlin, Hornet	100[1]	6—3.75x3.50	232	IO	140	90@3050	HY	HY	105
Pacer, Gremlin, Hornet, Matador	100[1]	6—3.75x3.90	258[4]	IO	150	95@3050[5]	HY	HY	105
Gremlin, Hornet, Matador	96[1]	8—3.75x3.44	304	VO	140	120@3400	HY	HY	110
Matador	114[1]	8—4.08x3.44	360	VO	140	140@3200	HY	HY	110
Matador	114[1]	8—4.08x3.44	360	VO	140	180@3600	HY	HY	110
Buick — Skyhawk, Skyhawk "S"	97	6—3.80x3.40	231	VO	160[8]	105@3400	HY	HY	80
Skylark, Skylark "S"	111	6—3.80x3.40	231	VO	160[8]	105@3400	HY	HY	80
Century, Custom, Regal	112[9]	6—3.80x3.40	231	VO	160[8]	105@3400	HY	HY	80
LeSabre	124	6—3.80x3.40	231	VO	160[8]	105@3400	HY	HY	80
Skylark, Skylark "S"	111	8—3.50x3.385	260	VO	160[8]	110@3400	HY	HY	85
Skylark, Skylark "S"	111	8—3.80x3.385	350	VO	180[8]	140@3200[10]	HY	HY	80
Century, Custom, Regal	112[9]	8—3.80x3.385	350	VO	180[8]	140@3200[10]	HY	HY	80
LeSabre Custom	124	8—3.80x3.385	350	VO	180[8]	155@3400	HY	HY	80
LeSabre Custom	124	8—4.3125x3.90	455	VO	180[8]	205@3800	HY	HY	100
Electra, Electra Limited	127	8—4.3125x3.90	455	VO	180[8]	205@3800	HY	HY	100
Riviera	122	8—4.3125x3.90	455	VO	180[8]	205@3800	HY	HY	100
Cadillac (All)	130[11]	8—4.30x4.304	500	VO	155	190@3600[12]	HY	HY	115
Eldorado	126.3	8—4.30x4.304	500	VO	155	190@3600[12]	HY	HY	115
Chevrolet — Chevette, Scooter	94.3	4—3.228x2.606	85	IOC	140	52@5200	HY	HY	60
Chevette	94.3	4—3.228x2.98	97.6	IOC	140	60@4800	HY	HY	60
Cosworth Vega	97	4—3.501x3.160	122	IOC	140	110@5600	.014	.014	60
Vega, Monza Towne Coupe, 2+2, Spyder	97	4—3.501x3.625	140	IOC	140	70@4400	HY	HY	60
Vega, Monza Towne Coupe, 2+2	97	4—3.501x3.625	140	IOC	140	84@4400[21]	HY	HY	60
Camaro	108	6—3.875x3.53	250	IO	130	105@3800	HY	HY	95
Nova, Concours	111	6—3.875x3.53	250	IO	130	105@3800	HY	HY	95
Chevelle	112[9]	6—3.875x3.53	250	IO	130	105@3800	HY	HY	95
Monza Towne Coupe, 2+2, Spyder	97	8—3.671x3.10	262	VO	155	110@3600	HY	HY	65
Camaro, Type LT	108	8—3.736x3.48	305	VO	155	140@3800	HY	HY	65
Nova, Concours	111	8—3.736x3.48	305	VO	155	140@3800	HY	HY	65
Chevelle, Monte Carlo "S"	112[9]	8—3.736x3.48	305	VO	155	140@3800	HY	HY	65
Camaro, Type LT	108	8—4.00x3.48	350	VO	150	165@3800	HY	HY	65
Nova, Concours	111	8—4.00x3.48	350	VO	150	165@3800	HY	HY	65
Chevelle, Monte Carlo "S"	112[9]	8—4.00x3.48	350	VO	150	145@3800[27]	HY	HY	65
Chevrolet Impala, Caprice Classic	121.5	8—4.00x3.48	350	VO	150	145@3800[27]	HY	HY	65
Corvette	98	8—4.00x3.48	350	VO	150	180@4000[29]	HY	HY	65
Chevelle, Monte Carlo "S"	112[9]	8—4.125x3.75	400	VO	160	175@3600	HY	HY	65
Chevrolet Impala, Caprice Classic	121.5	8—4.125x3.75	400	VO	160	175@3600	HY	HY	65
Chevrolet Impala, Caprice Classic	121.5	8—4.251x4.00	454	VO	160	225@3800	HY	HY	80
Chrysler — Cordoba	115	8—3.91x3.31	318	VO	100[35]	150@4000	HY	HY	95
Cordoba, Newport, Custom	115[32]	8—4.00x3.58	360	VO	100[35]	170@4000	HY	HY	95
Cordoba, Newport, Custom, New Yorker	115[32]	8—4.34x3.38	400	VO	100[35]	175@4000[36]	HY	HY	70
Newport, Custom, New Yorker	124	8—4.34x3.38	400[37]	VO	100[35]	210@4400	HY	HY	70
Newport, Custom, New Yorker	124	8—4.32x3.75	440	VO	100[35]	205@3600	HY	HY	70
Dodge — Aspen, Custom, Special Edition	108.5[38]	6—3.40x4.12	225	IO	100[39]	100@3600	.012H	.022H	70
Dart, Sport, Swinger, Swinger Special	108[41]	6—3.40x4.12	225	IO	100[39]	100@3600	.012H	.022H	70
Coronet, Charger	115[42]	6—3.40x4.12	225	IO	100[39]	100@3600	.012H	.022H	70
Aspen, Custom, Special Edition	108.5[38]	8—3.91x3.31	318	VO	100[35]	150@4000	HY	HY	95
Dart, Sport, Swinger, Swinger Special	108[41]	8—3.91x3.31	318	VO	100[35]	150@4000	HY	HY	95
Coronet, Charger, Special Edition	115[42]	8—3.91x3.31	318	VO	100[35]	150@4000	HY	HY	95
Monaco	121.5	8—3.91x3.31	318	VO	100[35]	150@4000	HY	HY	95
Aspen, Custom, Special Edition	108.5[38]	8—4.00x3.58	360	VO	100[35]	170@4000[45]	HY	HY	95
Coronet, Charger, Special Edition	115[42]	8—4.00x3.58	360	VO	100[35]	170@4000	HY	HY	95
Royal Monaco, Brougham	121.5	8—4.00x3.58	360	VO	100[35]	170@4000	HY	HY	95
Coronet, Charger, Special Edition	115[42]	8—4.34x3.38	400	VO	100[35]	175@4000[46]	HY	HY	70
Monaco, Royal Monaco, Brougham	121.5	8—4.34x3.38	400	VO	100[35]	175@4000[49]	HY	HY	70
Monaco, Royal Monaco, Brougham	121.5	8—4.32x3.75	440	VO	100[35]	205@3600	HY	HY	70
Ford — Pinto	94.5	4—3.781x3.126	140	IOC	80[8]	92@5000	HY	HY	85
Mustang II (except Mach I)	96.2	4—3.781x3.126	140	IOC	80[8]	92@5000	HY	HY	85
Pinto	94.5	6—3.66x2.70	170.8	VO	80[8]	103@4400	HY	HY	75
Mustang II, Ghia, Mach I	96.2	6—3.66x2.70	170.8	VO	80[8]	103@4400	.014	.016	75
Maverick	103[52]	6—3.682x3.126	200	IO	175[8]	78@3300[53]	.014	.016	75
Granada (except Ghia)	109.9	6—3.682x3.126	200	IO	175[8]	81@3400	HY	HY	75
Maverick	103[52]	6—3.682x3.910	250	IO	175[8]	81@3000[54]	HY	HY	75
Granada, Ghia	109.9	6—3.682x3.910	250	IO	175[8]	78@3000[56]	HY	HY	75
Mustang II, Ghia, Mach I	96.2	8—4.00x3.00	302	VO	150[8]	134@3600	HY	HY	70
Maverick	103[52]	8—4.00x3.00	302	VO	150[8]	134@3600	HY	HY	70
Granada, Ghia	109.9	8—4.00x3.00	302	VO	150[8]	133@3600	HY	HY	70
Granada, Ghia	109.9	8—4.00x3.50	351W	VO	160[8]	143@3200	HY	HY	110
Torino, Gran Torino, Brougham	114[58]	8—4.00x3.50	351W	VO	160[8]	154@3400	HY	HY	110
Torino, Gran Torino, Brougham	114[58]	8—4.00x3.50	351M	VO	170[8]	152@3800	HY	HY	100
Ford LTD, Brougham, Landau	121	8—4.00x3.50	351M	VO	170[8]	152@3800	HY	HY	100

ABBREVIATIONS — FOOTNOTES

AC — AC Spark Plugs
AU — Autolite Spark Plugs
B — Before Top Dead Center
C — Cold Engine
CH — Champion Spark Plugs
CP — Crankshaft Pulley
H — Hot Engine
HY — Hydraulic Lifters
IO — In-Line Engine, Overhead Valves
IOC — In-Line Engine, Overhead Camshaft
N — Negative
NA — Not Available

P — Positive
VD — Vibration Damper
VO — V-Type Engine, Overhead Valves
1 — Gremlin — 96, Hornet — 108, Matador 2-Door — 114, 4-Door — 118
2 — Gremlin, Hornet — 0
3 — Gremlin, Hornet — 11, Matador — 13.5
4 — Matador — NA in California
5 — Pacer — Also 120@3400
6 — Matador 2-Door — 18.5, 4-Door — 16.5
7 — Matador 4-Door — 15.5
8 — Lowest Cylinder Must Be At Least 75 Percent of Highest
9 — 4-Door —116, Monte Carlo "S" — 116

10 — Also 155@3400
11 — Fleetwood Brougham — 133, Sedan/Limo 151.5
12 — W/Electronic Fuel Injection — 215@3600
13 — W/Electronic Fuel Injection — 12B@600
14 — Limo — 1N
15 — Fleetwood Sedan/Limo — 25.8
16 — Manual Trans. Only
17 — Monza — R43TS
18 — Monza — .045
19 — Monza — 12B@750
20 — Vega, Monza — 8B@750
21 — Monza Towne Coupe and 2+2
22 — Monza — 10B@700

Firing Order	Timing Mark Location	Initial Ignition Timing @ rpm (auto. trans.)	Ignition Timing (rpm — manual trans.)	Ignition Timing (California)	Make	Model	Gap (in.)	Caster, Power Steering (deg.)	Camber, Right Wheel (deg.)	Toe-In (in.)	Steering Axis Inclination (deg.)	Cooling System Capacity (qt.)	Crankcase Capacity (qt.)
153624	VD	8B@550	850	8B	CH	N12Y	.035	1P[2]	1/8P	1/8	7–3/4	14[3]	4
153624	VD	6B@550	850	6B	CH	N12Y	.035	1P[2]	1/8P	1/8	7–3/4	14[3]	4
18436572	VD	10B@700	750	5B	CH	N12Y	.035	1P[2]	1/8P	1/8	7–3/4	16[6]	4
18436572	VD	10B@700	NA	5B	CH	N12Y	.035	1P	1/8P	1/8	7–3/4	17.5[7]	4
18436572	VD	10B@700	NA	5B	CH	N12Y	.035	1P	1/8P	1/8	7–3/4	17.5[7]	4
165432	VD	12B@600	600	12B	AC	R44SX	.060	3/4N	1/4P	1/16	8–1/2	13.4	4
165432	VD	12B@600	650	12B	AC	R44SX	.060	1N	3/4P	1/16	10	17	4
165432	VD	12B@600	650	12B	AC	R44SX	.060	2P	1/2P	1/16	8	15.4	4
165432	VD	12B@600	NA	12B	AC	R44SX	065	1–1/2P	1/2P	1/16	9–5/8	15.3	4
18436572	VD	18B@1100	650	14B	AC	R46SX	.080	1N	3/4P	1/16	10	22.4	4
18436572	VD	12B@600	NA	NA	AC	R45TSX	.065	1N	3/4P	1/16	10	17.9	4
18436572	VD	12B@600	NA	NA	AC	R45TSX	.060	2P	1/2P	1/16	8	16.9	4
18436572	VD	12B@600	NA	12B	AC	R45TSX	.065	1–1/2P	1/2P	1/16	9–5/8	16.9	4
18436572	VD	12B@600	NA	12B	AC	R45TSX	.065	1–1/2P	1/2P	1/16	9–5/8	19.6	4
18436572	VD	12B@600	NA	12B	AC	R45TSX	.060	1–1/2P	1/2P	1/16	9–5/8	19.6	4
18436572	VD	12B@600	NA	12B	AC	R45TSX	.060	1–1/2P	1/2P	1/16	9–5/8	19.6	4
15634278	VD	6B@600[13]	NA	6B[13]	AC	R45NSX	.060	0[14]	1/4N	1/8	6	23[15]	4
15634278	VD	6B@600[13]	NA	6B[13]	AC	R45NSX	.060	0	1/4N	0	11	23	5
1342	VD	10B@800	800	10B	AC	R43TS	.035	4–1/2P	1/4P	1/16	7–1/2	8.5	4
1342	VD	10B@800	800	10B	AC	R43TS	.035	4–1/2P	1/4P	1/16	7–1/2	9.0	4
1342	CP	12B@1600[16]	1600	12B	AC	R43LTS	.035	3/4N	1/2P	1/4	8–1/2	6.8	3.5
1342	CP	10B@750[19]	750[20]	10B[19]	AC	R43TSX[17]	.035[18]	3/4N	1/2P	1/4	8–1/2	8.0	3.5
1342	CP	12B@750[22]	700[20]	12B[22]	AC	R43TSX[17]	.035[18]	3/4N	1/2P	1/4	8–1/2	8.0	3.5
153624	VD	10B@550	850[23]	10B	AC	R46TS	.035	1P	1P	1/16	10–1/2	14.6	4
153624	VD	10B@550	850[23]	10B	AC	R46TS	.035	1P	3/4P	1/16	10	14.6	4
153624	VD	10B@550	850[23]	10B	AC	R46TS	.035	2P	1/2P	1/16	9–1/2	14.6	4
18436572	VD	8B@600	800	4B	AC	R45TS	.045	3/4N	1/2P	1/4	8–1/2	18	4
18436572	VD	8B@600	800[24]	8B	AC	R45TS	.045	1P	1P	1/16	10–1/2	17.2	4
18436572	VD	8B@600	800[24]	8B	AC	R45TS	.045	1P	3/4P	1/16	10	17.2	4
18436572	VD	8B@600	NA	8B	AC	R45TS	.045	2P[25]	1/2P	1/16	9–1/2	17.2	4
18436572	VD	8B@800	800	6B[26]	AC	R45TS	.045	1P	1P	1/16	10–1/2	17.3	4
18436572	VD	8B@800	800	6B[26]	AC	R45TS	.045	1P	3/4P	1/16	10	17.3	4
18436572	VD	6B@600	NA	6B[26]	AC	R45TS	.045	2P[25]	1/2P	1/16	9–1/2	17.2	4
18436572	VD	6B@600[28]	NA	6B	AC	R45TS	.045	1–1/2P	1/2P	1/16	9–1/8	18	4
18436572	VD	8B@600[30]	800[31]	6B	AC	R45TS	.045	1P	3P	1/8	7–5/8	20.7	4
18436572	VD	8B@600	NA	8B	AC	R45TS	.045	2P[25]	1/2P	1/16	9–1/2	17.2	4
18436572	VD	8B@600	NA	6B[26]	AC	R45TS	.045	1–1/2P	1/2P	1/16	9–1/8	18	4
18436572	VD	12B@550	NA	NA	AC	R45TSX	.060	1–1/2P	1/2P	1/16	9–1/8	25.8	4
18436572	VD	2B@750	NA	2B	CH	RN12Y	.035	3/4P	1/4N	3/16	8	16.5	4
18436572	VD	6B@700	NA	6B	CH	RN12Y	.035	3/4P	1/4N[33]	3/16	8[34]	16	4
18436572	VD	10B@700	NA	10B	CH	RJ13Y	.035	3/4P	1/4N[33]	3/16	8[34]	16.5	4
18436572	VD	6B@700	NA	8B	CH	RJ86P	.035	3/4P	1/4P	3/16	9	16.5	4
18436572	VD	8B@750	NA	8B	CH	RJ87P	.035	3/4P	1/4P	3/16	9	16	4
153624	VD	2B@750	750[40]	2B	CH	RBL13Y	.035	3/4P	1/4P	3/16	8	13	4
153624	VD	2B@750	750[40]	2B	CH	RBL13Y	.035	3/4P	1/4P	3/16	7–1/2	13	4
153624	VD	2B@750	750[40]	2B	CH	RBL13Y	.035	3/4P	1/4P	3/16	8	13	4
18436572	VD	2B@750	750	2B	CH	RN12Y	.035	3/4P	1/4P	3/16	8	16	4
18436572	VD	2B@750	750	2B	CH	RN12Y	.035	3/4P	1/4P	3/16	7–1/2	16	4
18436572	VD	2B@750	750	2B	CH	RN12Y	.035	3/4P[43]	1/4P[44]	3/16	8	17.5	4
18436572	VD	2B@750	NA	2B	CH	RN12Y	.035	3/4P	1/4P	3/16	9	17.5	4
18436572	VD	6B@700	NA	NA	CH	RN12Y	.035	3/4P	1/4P	3/16	8	16	4
18436572	VD	6B@700	NA	6B	CH	RN12Y	.035	3/4P[43]	1/4P[44]	3/16	8	16	4
18436572	VD	6B@700	NA	6B	CH	RN12Y	.035	3/4P	1/4P	3/16	9	16	4
18436572	VD	10B@700[47]	NA	8B	CH	RJ13Y[48]	.035	3/4P[43]	1/4P[44]	3/16	8	16.5	4
18436572	VD	10B@700[47]	NA	8B	CH	RJ13Y	.035	3/4P	1/4P	3/16	9	16.5	4
18436572	VD	8B@750	NA	8B	CH	RJ87P	.035	3/4P	1/4P	3/16	9	16	4
1342	CP	20B@550	550[50]	20B[50]	AU	AGRF52	.034	1–1/4P	3/4P	1/4	10	8.7	4
1342	CP	20B@550	550[50]	20B[50]	AU	AGRF52	.034	7/8P	1/2P	1/16	9–3/4	8.5	4
142536	VD	6B@700	NA	6B	AU	AGR42	.034	1–1/4P	3/4P	1/4	10	12.5	4.5
142536	VD	12B@700	700[51]	6B	AU	AGR42	.034	7/8P	1/2P	1/16	9–3/4	12.3	4.5
153624	VD	10B@500	600	NA	AU	BRF82	.044	1/2N	1/4P	1/8	6–3/4	9	4
153624	VD	NA	600[51]	NA	AU	BRF82	.044	1/2N	1/4P	1/8	6–3/4	9.7	4
153624	VD	8B@750	750	14B[55]	AU	BRF82	.044	1/2N	1/4P	1/8	6–3/4	9.7	4
153624	VD	8B@750	750	14B[55]	AU	BRF82	.044	1/2N	1/4P	1/8	6–3/4	10.5	4
15426378	VD	6B@500	NA	8B	AU	ARF42	.044	7/8P	1/2P	1/16	9–3/4	16.3	4
15426378	VD	12B@500	500	12B	AU	ARF42	.044	1/2N	1/4P	1/8	6–3/4	13.5	4
15426378	VD	8B@650	500[57]	4B	AU	ARF42	.044	1/2N	1/4P	1/8	6–3/4	14.6	4
13726548	VD	6B@625	NA	10B	AU	ARF42	.044	1/2N	1/4P	1/8	6–3/4	15.7	4
13726548	VD	12B@650	NA	NA	AU	ARF42	.044	4P	1/4P	1/8	9[59]	15.9	4
13726548	VD	12B@800	NA	8B	AU	ARF52	.044	4P	1/4P	1/8	9[59]	17.1	4
13726548	VD	12B@800	NA	8B	AU	ARF52	.044	2P	1/4P	3/16	9–3/8	17.2	4

23 — 6B@850
24 — 6B@800
25 — Monte Carlo "S" — 5P
26 — 6B@600
27 — Also 165@3800
28 — 165 hp — 8B@600
29 — Also 210@5200
30 — 210 hp — 12B@700
31 — 8B
32 — Newport, Custom, New Yorker — 124
33 — Newport, Custom — 1/4P
34 — Newport, Custom — 9
35 — Minimum psi Allowable.

Also 40 psi Maximum Variation
36 — Cordoba — Also 240@4400
37 — Electronic Lean Burn System
38 — 4-Door — 112.5
39 — Minimum psi Allowable.
      Also 25 psi Maximum Variation
40 — 6B
41 — 4-Door — 111
42 — 4-Door — 117.5
43 — Special Edition — 3/4P
44 — Special Edition — 1/4N
45 — Dart (except Swinger) — 220@4400
46 — Also 240@4400

47 — 240 hp — 6B
48 — 240 hp — RJ87P
49 — Also 205@3600 (see 37)
50 — Manual Trans. — 6B@550
51 — 10B
52 — 4-Door — 109.9
53 — Manual Trans. — 81@3400
54 — Manual Trans. — 90@3000
55 — 14B@500
56 — 87@3000
57 — 12B
58 — Torino 4-Door — 118
59 — Elite — 9–5/8

1976

	Wheelbase (in.)	No. of Cylinders Bore and Stroke (in.)	Displacement (cu. in.)	Valve and Cylinder Arrangement	Compression Pressure (lb.)	Net Brake Horsepower @ rpm	Intake	Exhaust	Cylinder Bolt Torque (ft. lb.)
Torino, Gran Torino, Brougham	114[1]	8—4.00x4.00	400	VO	180[2]	180@3800	HY	HY	100
Ford LTD, Brougham, Landau	121	8—4.00x4.00	400	VO	180[2]	180@3800	HY	HY	100
Torino, Gran Torino, Brougham	114[1]	8—4.362x3.85	460	VO	180[2]	202@3800	HY	HY	135
Thunderbird	120.4	8—4.362x3.85	460	VO	180[2]	202@3800	HY	HY	135
Ford LTD, Brougham, Landau	121	8—4.362x3.85	460	VO	180[2]	202@3800	HY	HY	135
Lincoln	127.2	8—4.362x3.85	460	VO	180[2]	202@3800	HY	HY	135
Mark IV	120.4	8—4.362x3.85	460	VO	180[2]	202@3800	HY	HY	135
Mercury — Bobcat	94.5	4—3.781x3.126	140	IOC	80[2]	92@5000	HY	HY	85
Bobcat	94.5	6—3.66x2.70	170.8	IO	80[2]	100@4600	.014H	.016H	75
Comet	103[6]	6—3.682x3.126	200	IO	175[2]	78@3300[7]	HY	HY	75
Monarch	109.9	6—3.682x3.126	200	IO	175[2]	81@3400	HY	HY	75
Comet	103[6]	6—3.682x3.910	250	IO	175[2]	81@3000[9]	HY	HY	75
Monarch, Ghia	109.9	6—3.682x3.910	250	IO	175[2]	78@3000[12]	HY	HY	75
Comet	103.6[6]	8—4.00x3.00	302	VO	150[2]	137@3600[14]	HY	HY	70
Monarch, Ghia	109.9	8—4.00x3.00	302	VO	150[2]	133@3600[15]	HY	HY	70
Monarch, Ghia	109.9	8—4.00x3.50	351W	VO	160[2]	143@3200	HY	HY	110
Montego, Cougar XR7	114[1]	8—4.00x3.50	351W	VO	160[2]	154@3400	HY	HY	110
Montego, Cougar XR7	114[1]	8—4.00x3.50	351M	VO	170[2]	152@3800	HY	HY	100
Montego, Cougar XR7	114[1]	8—4.00x4.00	400	VO	180[2]	180@3800	HY	HY	100
Marquis, Brougham, Grand Marquis	124	8—4.00x4.00	400	VO	180[2]	180@3800	HY	HY	100
Montego, Cougar	114[1]	8—4.362x3.85	460	VO	180[2]	202@3800	HY	HY	135
Marquis, Brougham, Grand Marquis	124	8—4.362x3.85	460	VO	180[2]	202@3800	HY	HY	135
Oldsmobile — Starfire, SX	97	6—3.80x3.40	231	VO	160[23]	105@3400	HY	HY	80
Omega, Brougham	111	6—3.875x3.53	250	IO	140[23]	105@3800	HY	HY	95
Cutlass "S," Supreme, Brougham	112[24]	6—3.875x3.53	250	IO	140[23]	105@3800	HY	HY	95
Omega, Brougham	97	8—3.50x3.385	260	VO	160[23]	110@3400	HY	HY	95
Cutlass "S," Supreme, Brougham	112[24]	8—3.50x3.385	260	VO	160[23]	110@3400	HY	HY	95
Omega, Brougham	97	8—3.80x3.850	350	VO	160[23]	155@3400[28]	HY	HY	80
Cutlass "S," Supreme, Brougham	112[24]	8—4.057x3.385	350	VO	160[23]	170@3800	HY	HY	85
Delta "88," Royale	124	8—4.057x3.385	350	VO	160[23]	170@3800	HY	HY	85
Cutlass "S," Supreme, Brougham	112[24]	8—4.126x4.250	455	VO	160[23]	190@3400	HY	HY	85
Delta "88," Royale, "98"	124[29]	8—4.126x4.250	455	VO	160[23]	190@3400	HY	HY	85
Toronado	122	8—4.126x4.250	455	VO	160[23]	215@3600	HY	HY	85
Plymouth — Valiant, Scamp, Special, Duster	111[30]	6—3.40x4.12	225	IO	100[31]	100@3600	.012H	.022H	70
Fury, Salon, Sport	115[34]	6—3.40x4.12	225	IO	100[31]	100@3600	.012H	.022H	70
Valiant, Scamp, Special, Duster	111[30]	8—3.91x3.31	318	VO	100[33]	150@4000	HY	HY	95
Fury, Salon, Sport	115[34]	8—3.91x3.31	318	VO	100[33]	150@4000	HY	HY	95
Gran Fury	121.5	8—3.91x3.31	318	VO	100[33]	150@4000	HY	HY	95
Fury, Salon, Sport	115[34]	8—4.00x3.58	360	VO	100[33]	170@4000	HY	HY	95
Gran Fury, Custom, Brougham	121.5	8—4.00x3.58	360	VO	100[33]	170@4000	HY	HY	95
Valiant (except Scamp)	111[30]	8—4.00x3.58	360	VO	100[33]	220@4000	HY	HY	95
Fury, Salon, Sport	115[34]	8—4.34x3.38	400	VO	100[33]	175@4000[35]	HY	HY	70
Gran Fury, Custom, Brougham	121.5	8—4.34x3.38	400	VO	100[33]	175@4000	HY	HY	70
Gran Fury, Custom, Brougham	121.5	8—4.34x3.38	400[36]	VO	100[33]	210@4400	HY	HY	70
Gran Fury, Custom, Brougham	121.5	8—4.32x3.75	440	VO	100[33]	205@3600	HY	HY	70
Pontiac — Astre, Custom, Sunbird	97	4—3.501x3.625	140	IOC	140	70@4400[37]	.015	.030	60
Sunbird	97	4—3.501x3.625	140	IOC	140	87@4400[38]	.015	.030	60
Sunbird	97	6—3.80x3.40	231	VO	140[23]	105@3400	HY	HY	75
Ventura, "SJ"	111.1	6—3.875x3.53	250	IO	140	110@3600	HY	HY	95
LeMans, Sport, Grand LeMans	112[24]	6—3.875x3.53	250	IO	140	110@3600	HY	HY	95
Firebird, Esprit	108.1	6—3.875x3.53	250	IO	140	110@3600	HY	HY	95
Ventura, "SJ"	111.1	8—3.50x3.385	260	VO	100[39]	110@3400	HY	HY	85
LeMans, Sport, Grand LeMans	112[24]	8—3.50x3.385	260	VO	100[39]	110@3400	HY	HY	85
Ventura, "SJ"	111.1	8—3.80x3.385	350	VO	140	140@3200[40]	HY	HY	80
LeMans, Sport, Grand LeMans	112[24]	8—3.876x3.75	350	VO	100[39]	160@4000	HY	HY	95
Firebird, Esprit, Formula	108.1	8—3.876x3.75	350	VO	100[39]	160@4000	HY	HY	95
Grand Prix	116	8—3.876x3.75	350	VO	100[39]	160@4000	HY	HY	95
LeMans, Sport, Grand LeMans	112[24]	8—3.876x3.75	350	VO	100[39]	165@4000	HY	HY	95
Firebird, Esprit, Formula	108.1	8—3.876x3.75	350	VO	100[39]	165@4000	HY	HY	95
Grand Prix	116	8—3.876x3.75	350	VO	100[39]	165@4000	HY	HY	95
LeMans, Sport, Grand LeMans	112[24]	8—4.121x3.75	400	VO	100[39]	170@4000	HY	HY	95
Grand Prix, "SJ"	116	8—4.121x3.75	400	VO	100[39]	170@4000	HY	HY	95
Catalina, Bonneville, Brougham	123.4	8—4.121x3.75	400	VO	100[39]	170@4000	HY	HY	95
LeMans, Sport, Grand LeMans	112[24]	8—4.121x3.75	400	VO	100[39]	185@3600	HY	HY	95
Firebird, Esprit, Formula, Trans Am	108.1	8—4.121x3.75	400	VO	100[39]	185@3600	HY	HY	95
Grand Prix, "SJ"	116	8—4.121x3.75	400	VO	100[39]	185@3600	HY	HY	95
Catalina, Bonneville, Brougham	123.4	8—4.121x3.75	400	VO	100[39]	185@3600	HY	HY	95
LeMans, Sport, Grand LeMans	112[24]	8—4.152x4.21	455	VO	100[39]	200@3500	HY	HY	95
Firebird Trans Am	108.1	8—4.152x4.21	455	VO	100[39]	200@3500	HY	HY	95
Grand Prix, "SJ"	116	8—4.152x4.21	455	VO	100[39]	200@3500	HY	HY	95
Catalina, Bonneville, Brougham	123.4	8—4.152x4.21	455	VO	100[39]	200@3500	HY	HY	95

ABBREVIATIONS — FOOTNOTES

AC — AC Spark Plugs
AU — Autolite Spark Plugs
B — Before Top Dead Center
C — Cold Engine
CH — Champion Spark Plugs
CP — Crankshaft Pulley
H — Hot Engine
HY — Hydraulic Lifters
IO — In-Line Engine, Overhead Valves

IOC — In-Line Engine, Overhead Camshaft
N — Negative
NA — Not Available
P — Positive
VD — Vibration Damper
VO — V-Type Engine, Overhead Valves
1 — Torino/Montego 4-Door — 118
2 — Lowest Cylinder Must Be At Least 75 Percent of Highest
3 — Elite — 9–5/8
4 — Manual Trans. — 6B@550

5 — 6B@700
6 — 4-Door — 109.9
7 — Manual Trans. — 81@3400
8 — 10B@600
9 — Manual Trans. — 90@3000
10 — 6B@750
11 — 14B@500
12 — Manual Trans. — 87@3000
13 — 8B@750
14 — Manual Trans. — 138@3600
15 — Manual Trans. — 134@3600

Firing Order	Timing Mark Location	Initial Ignition Timing @ rpm (auto. trans.)	Ignition Timing (rpm - manual trans.)	Ignition Timing (California)	Make	Model	Gap (in.)	Caster, Power Steering (deg.)	Camber, Right Wheel (deg.)	Toe-In (in.)	Steering Axis Inclination (deg.)	Cooling System Capacity (qt.)	Crankcase Capacity (qt.)
13726548	VD	10B@650	NA	10B	AU	ARF52	.044	4P	1/4P	1/8	9^3	17.1	4
13726548	VD	10B@650	NA	10B	AU	ARF52	.044	2P	1/4P	3/16	9-3/8	17.2	4
15426378	VD	8B@650	NA	14B	AU	ARF52	.044	4P	1/4P	1/8	9^3	19.2	4
15426378	VD	8B@650	NA	14B	AU	ARF52	.044	4P	1/4P	3/16	9-1/2	19.3	4
15426378	VD	8B@650	NA	14B	AU	ARF52	.044	2P	1/4P	3/16	9-3/8	19.3	4
15426378	VD	8B@650	NA	14B	AU	ARF52	.044	2P	1/4P	1/8	9-1/2	19.4	4
15426378	VD	10B@650	NA	10B	AU	ARF52	.044	4P	1/4P	3/16	9-1/2	19.8	4
1342	CP	20B@550	550[4]	20B[4]	AU	AGRF52	.034	1-1/4P	3/4P	1/4	10	8.7	4
142536	VD	12B@700	NA	6B[5]	AU	AGR42	.034	1-1/4P	3/4P	1/4	10	12.5	4.5
153624	VD	10B@500	600	NA	AU	BRF82	.044	1/2N	1/4P	1/8	6-3/4	9	4
153624	VD	NA	600[8]	NA	AU	BRF82	.044	1/2N	1/4P	1/8	6-3/4	9.7	4
153624	VD	8B@750	750[10]	14B[11]	AU	BRF82	.044	1/2N	1/4P	1/8	6-3/4	9.7	4
153624	VD	14B@500	750[10]	8B[13]	AU	BRF82	.044	1/2N	1/4P	1/8	6-3/4	10.5	4
15426378	VD	12B@500	500	12B	AU	ARF42	.044	1/2N	1/4P	1/8	6-3/4	13.5	4
15426378	VD	8B@650	500[16]	4B[17]	AU	ARF42	.044	1/2N	1/4P	1/8	6-3/4	14.6	4
13726548	VD	6B@625	500[16]	4B[17]	AU	ARF42	.044	1/2N	1/4P	1/8	6-3/4	14.6	4
13726548	VD	12B@650	NA	NA	AU	ARF42	.044	1/2N[18]	1/4P	1/8	6-3/4[19]	15.9[20]	4
13726548	VD	12B@800	NA	8B[21]	AU	ARF52	.044	1/2N[18]	1/4P	1/8	6-3/4[19]	17.1	4
13726548	VD	10B@650	NA	10B	AU	ARF52	.044	1/2N[18]	1/4P	1/8	6-3/4[19]	17.1	4
13726548	VD	10B@625	NA	10B	AU	ARF52	.044	2P	1/4P	1/4	9-7/16	17.2	4
15426378	VD	8B@650	NA	14B[22]	AU	ARF52	.044	1/2N[18]	1/4P	1/4	6-3/4[19]	19.2	4
15426378	VD	8B@650	NA	14B[22]	AU	ARF52	.044	2P	1/4P	1/4	9-7/16	18.5	4
165432	VD	12B@600	600	12B	AC	R44SX	.060	3/4N	1/2P	1/4	8-1/2	13.4	4
153624	VD	10B@600	600[25]	10B	AC	R46TX	.060	1P	3/4P	1/16	10-1/2	15.5	4
153624	VD	10B@600	800[26]	10B	AC	R46TX	.060	2P	1/2P	1/16	10-1/2	15.2	4
18436572	VD	16B@1100	1100	16B	AC	R46SX	.080	1P	3/4P	1/16	10-1/2	23	4
18436572	VD	18B@1100	1100[27]	18B	AC	R46SX	.080	2P	1/2P	1/16	10-1/2	23	4
18436572	VD	12B@600	NA	12B	AC	R46TX	.060	1P	3/4P	1/16	10-1/2	21.5	4
18436572	VD	20B@1100	NA	20B	AC	R46SX	.080	2P	1/2P	1/16	10-1/2	20	4
18436572	VD	26B@1100	NA	26B	AC	R46SX	.080	1-1/2P	1/2P	1/16	10-1/2	20	4
18436572	VD	16B@1100	NA	16B	AC	R46SX	.080	2P	1/2P	1/16	10-1/2	21	4
18436572	VD	16B@1100	NA	16B	AC	R46SX	.080	1-1/2P	1/2P	1/16	10-1/2	21	4
18436572	VD	14B@1100	NA	12B	AC	R46SX	.080	0	1/4N	0	11	21	5
153624	VD	2B@750	750[32]	2B	CH	RBL13Y	.035	3/4P	1/4P	3/16	7-1/2	13	4
153624	VD	2B@750	750[32]	2B	CH	RBL13Y	.035	3/4P	1/4P	3/16	8	13	4
18436572	VD	2B@750	750	2B	CH	RN12Y	.035	3/4P	1/4P	3/16	7-1/2	16	4
18436572	VD	2B@750	750	2B	CH	RN12Y	.035	3/4P	1/4P	3/16	8	16.5	4
18436572	VD	2B@750	NA	2B	CH	RN12Y	.035	3/4P	1/4P	3/16	9	17.5	4
18436572	VD	6B@700	NA	6B	CH	RN12Y	.035	3/4P	1/4P	3/16	8	16	4
18436572	VD	6B@700	NA	6B	CH	RN12Y	.035	3/4P	1/4P	3/16	9	16	4
18436572	VD	2B@850	NA	2B	CH	RN12Y	.035	3/4P	1/4P	3/16	7-1/2	16	4
18436572	VD	10B@700	NA	10B	CH	RJ13Y	.035	3/4P	1/4P	3/16	8	16.5	4
18436572	VD	10B@700	NA	10B	CH	RJ13Y	.035	3/4P	1/4P	3/16	9	16.5	4
18436572	VD	6B@700	NA	8B	CH	RJ13Y	.035	3/4P	1/4P	3/16	9	16.5	4
18436572	VD	8B@750	NA	8B	CH	RJ87P	.035	3/4P	1/4P	3/16	9	16	4
1342	CP	10B@750	700	NA	AC	R43TSX	.060	3/4N	1/4P	1/16	8-1/2	7.6	3
1342	CP	12B@700	700	12B	AC	R43TSX	.060	3/4N	1/4P	1/16	8-1/2	7.6	3
165432	VD	12B@600	600	12B	AC	R44SX	.060	3/4N	1/4P	1/16	8-1/2	13.4	4
153624	VD	10B@550	850	10B[25]	AC	R46TX	.060	0	3/4P	1/16	10	18.8	4
153624	VD	10B@550	850	10B[25]	AC	R46TX	.060	1-3/4P	1/2P	1/16	10-3/8	15	4
153624	VD	10B@550	850	10B	AC	R46TX	.060	0	1P	3/16	10-3/8	14.6	4
18436572	VD	16B@1100	1100	16B	AC	R46SX	.080	0	3/4P	1/16	10	23	4
18436572	VD	16B@1100	1100	16B	AC	R46SX	.080	1-3/4P	1/2P	1/16	10-3/8	19.6	4
18436572	VD	12B@600	NA	NA	AC	R45TSX	.060	0	3/4P	1/16	10	17.8	4
18436572	VD	16B@550	NA	NA	AC	R46TSX	.060	1-3/4P	1/2P	1/16	10-3/8	21.3	5
18436572	VD	16B@550	NA	NA	AC	R46TSX	.060	0	1P	3/16	10-3/8	21.3	5
18436572	VD	16B@550	NA	NA	AC	R46TSX	.060	3P	1/2P	1/16	10-3/8	22.1	5
18436572	VD	16B@550	NA	12B	AC	R45TSX	.060	1-3/4P	1/2P	1/16	10-3/8	21.3	5
18436572	VD	16B@550	NA	12B	AC	R45TSX	.060	0	1P	3/16	10-3/8	21.3	5
18436572	VD	16B@550	NA	16B	AC	R45TSX	.060	3P	1/2P	1/16	10-3/8	22.1	5
18436572	VD	16B@550	NA	NA	AC	R46TSX	.060	1-3/4P	1/2P	1/16	10-3/8	21.3	5
18436572	VD	16B@550	NA	NA	AC	R46TSX	.060	3P	1/2P	1/16	10-3/8	22.1	5
18436572	VD	16B@550	NA	NA	AC	R46TSX	.060	1-1/2P	1/2P	1/16	10-1/2	21.6	5
18436572	VD	16B@575	NA	16B	AC	R45TSX	.060	1-3/4P	1/2P	1/16	10-3/8	21.3	5
18436572	VD	16B@575	575[41]	16B	AC	R45TSX	.060	0	1P	3/16	10-3/8	21.3	5
18436572	VD	16B@575	NA	16B	AC	R45TSX	.060	3P	1/2P	1/16	10-3/8	22.1	5
18436572	VD	16B@575	NA	16B	AC	R45TSX	.060	1-1/2P	1/2P	1/16	10-1/2	21.6	5
18436572	VD	16B@550	NA	12B	AC	R45TSX	.060	1-3/4P	1/2P	1/16	10-3/8	22.3	5
18436572	VD	NA	12B[42]	NA	AC	R45TSX	.060	0	1P	3/16	10-3/8	22.3	5
18436572	VD	16B@550	12B[42]	12B	AC	R45TSX	.060	3P	1/2P	1/16	10-3/8	20.3	5
18436572	VD	16B@550	NA	12B[42]	AC	R45TSX	.060	1-1/2P	1/2P	1/16	10-1/2	19.8	5

16 — Manual Trans. — 12B@500
17 — 4B@700
18 — Cougar — 4P
19 — Cougar — 9
20 — Cougar — 17.1
21 — 8B@650
22 — 14B@650
23 — Lowest Cylinder Must Be At Least 70 Percent of Highest
24 — 4-Door — 116
25 — 10B@600
26 — 10B@800
27 — 16B@1100
28 — Also 140@3200
29 — "98" — 127
30 — 2-Door Coupe — 108
31 — Minimum psi Allowable. Also 25 psi Maximum Variation
32 — 6B@750
33 — Minimum psi Allowable. Also 40 psi Maximum Variation
34 — 4-Door — 117.5
35 — Also 240@4400
36 — Electronic Lean Burn System
37 — Also 84@4400
38 — California Engines — 79@4400
39 — Minimum psi Allowable. Lowest Cylinder Must Be At Least 70 Percent of Highest
40 — Also 155@3400
41 — 12B — NA In California
42 — 12B@600

1977

	Wheelbase (in.)	No. of Cylinders Bore and Stroke (in.)	Displacement (cu. in.)	Valve and Cylinder Arrangement	Compression Pressure (lb.)	Net Brake Horsepower @ rpm	Valve Clearance Intake	Valve Clearance Exhaust	Cylinder Bolt Torque (ft. lb.)
AMC — Pacer, Gremlin, Hornet	100[1]	6—3.75x3.50	232	IO	140	88@3400	HY	HY	105
Pacer, Gremlin, Hornet, Matador	100[1]	6—3.75x3.895	258	IO	150	98@3200	HY	HY	105
Pacer, Gremlin, Hornet	100[1]	6—3.75x3.895	258	IO	150	114@3600	HY	HY	105
Hornet, Matador	108[1]	8—3.75x3.44	304	VO	140[8]	121@3450	HY	HY	110
Matador	114[1]	8—4.08x3.44	360	VO	140[8]	129@3700	HY	HY	110
Buick — Skyhawk, "S"	97	6—3.80x3.40	231	VO	160[12]	105@3200	HY	HY	80
Skylark, "S"	111	6—3.80x3.40	231	VO	160[12]	105@3200	HY	HY	80
Century, Custom, Regal	116[14]	6—3.80x3.40	231	VO	160[12]	105@3200	HY	HY	80
LeSabre	115.9	6—3.80x3.40	231	VO	160[12]	105@3200	HY	HY	80
Skylark, "S"	111	8—4.0x3.0	301	VO	140[12]	135@4000	HY	HY	90
LeSabre	115.9	8—4.0x3.0	301	VO	140[12]	135@4000	HY	HY	90
Century, Custom, Regal	116[14]	8—3.80x3.85	350	VO	180[12]	155@3400[15]	HY	HY	80
Electra 225, Limited, Riviera	118.9[17]	8—3.80x3.85	350	VO	180[12]	155@3400	HY	HY	80
Skylark, "S"	111	8—4.057x3.385	350	VO	180[12]	170@3800	HY	HY	80
Century, Custom, Regal	116[14]	8—4.057x3.385	350	VO	180[12]	170@3800	HY	HY	80
LeSabre, Custom	115.9	8—3.80x3.85	350	VO	180[12]	155@3400	HY	HY	80
Electra 225, Limited, Riviera	118.9[17]	8—4.057x3.385	350	VO	180[12]	170@3800	HY	HY	80
LeSabre, Custom	115.9	8—4.351x3.385	403	VO	140[12]	185@3600	HY	HY	85
Electra 225, Limited, Riviera	118.9[17]	8—4.351x3.385	403	VO	140[12]	185@3600	HY	HY	85
Cadillac — Seville	114.3	8—4.057x3.385	350	VO	160[12]	180@4400	HY	HY	85
All except Seville and Eldorado	121.5[19]	8—4.082x4.060	425	VO	160[12]	180@4000	HY	HY	85
Eldorado	126.3	8—4.082x4.060	425	VO	160[12]	180@4000	HY	HY	85
Chevrolet — Chevette, Scooter	94.3	4—3.228x2.606	85	IOC	140	57@5200	HY	HY	60
Chevette, Scooter	94.3	4—3.228x2.980	97.6	IOC	140	63@4800	HY	HY	60
Vega, Monza Towne Coupe, 2 + 2, Spyder	97	4—3.501x3.6	140	IOC	140	84@4400	HY	HY	60
Camaro, LT	108	6—3.875x3.53	250	IO	130	110@3800	HY	HY	95
Nova, Concours	111	6—3.875x3.53	250	IO	130	110@3800	HY	HY	95
Chevelle, Malibu Classic	116[14]	6—3.875x3.53	250	IO	130	110@3800	HY	HY	95
Impala, Caprice Classic	116	6—3.875x3.53	250	IO	130	110@3800	HY	HY	95
Monza Towne Coupe, 2 + 2, Spyder	97	8—3.736x3.48	305	VO	155	145@3800	HY	HY	65
Camaro, LT	108	8—3.736x3.48	305	VO	155	145@3800	HY	HY	65
Nova, Concours	111	8—3.736x3.48	305	VO	155	145@3800	HY	HY	65
Chevelle, Malibu Classic	116[14]	8—3.736x3.48	305	VO	155	145@3800	HY	HY	65
Monte Carlo "S"	116	8—3.736x3.48	305	VO	155	145@3800	HY	HY	65
Impala, Caprice Classic	116	8—3.736x3.48	305	VO	155	145@3800	HY	HY	65
Camaro, LT	108	8—4.00x3.48	350	VO	150	170@3800	HY	HY	65
Nova, Concours	111	8—4.00x3.48	350	VO	150	170@3800	HY	HY	65
Chevelle, Malibu Classic	116[14]	8—4.00x3.48	350	VO	150	170@3800	HY	HY	65
Monte Carlo "S"	116	8—4.00x3.48	350	VO	150	170@3800	HY	HY	65
Impala, Caprice Classic	116	8—4.00x3.48	350	VO	150	170@3800	HY	HY	65
Corvette	98	8—4.00x3.48	350	VO	150	180@4000[27]	HY	HY	65
Chrysler — Cordoba	115	8—3.91x3.31	318[29]	VO	100[30]	145@4000	HY	HY	70
Cordoba	115	8—4.00x3.58	360	VO	100[30]	170@4000	HY	HY	95
Newport	124	8—4.00x3.58	360	VO	100[30]	170@4000	HY	HY	95
Cordoba	115	8—4.34x3.38	400[33]	VO	100[30]	190@3600	HY	HY	70
Newport, New Yorker, Brougham	124	8—4.34x3.38	400[33]	VO	100[30]	190@3600	HY	HY	70
Newport, New Yorker, Brougham	124	8—4.32x3.75	440	VO	100[30]	195@3600	HY	HY	70
Dodge — Aspen, Custom, Special Edition	108.7[34]	6—3.40x4.12	225	IO	100[8]	100@3600[35]	.010H	.020H	70
Monaco	115[36]	6—3.40x4.12	225	IO	100[8]	110@3600	.010H	.020H	70
Aspen, Custom, Special Edition	108.7[34]	8—3.91x3.31	318[29]	VO	100[30]	145@4000	HY	HY	95
Charger Special Edition	115	8—3.91x3.31	318[29]	VO	100[30]	145@4000	HY	HY	95
Monaco, Brougham, Royal Monaco	115[36]	8—3.91x3.31	318[29]	VO	100[30]	145@4000	HY	HY	95
Aspen, Custom, Special Edition	108.7[34]	8—4.00x3.58	360	VO	100[30]	155@3600	HY	HY	95
Charger Special Edition	115	8—4.00x3.58	360	VO	100[30]	170@4000	HY	HY	95
Monaco, Brougham, Royal Monaco, Brougham	115[36]	8—4.00x3.58	360	VO	100[30]	155@3600	HY	HY	95
Charger Special Edition	115	8—4.34x3.38	400[33]	VO	100[30]	190@3600	HY	HY	70
Monaco, Brougham, Royal Monaco, Brougham	115[36]	8—4.34x3.38	400[33]	VO	100[30]	190@3600	HY	HY	70
Royal Monaco, Brougham	121.4	8—4.32x3.75	440[33]	VO	100[30]	195@3600	HY	HY	70
Ford — Pinto	94.5	4—3.781x3.126	140	IOC	80[12]	89@4800	HY	HY	85
Mustang II, Ghia	96.2	4—3.78x3.126	140	IOC	80[12]	89@4800	HY	HY	85
Pinto	94.2	6—3.66x2.70	170.8	VO	80[12]	93@4200[39]	.014C	.016C	75
Mustang II, Ghia, Mach I	96.2	6—3.66x2.70	170.8	VO	80[12]	93@4200[39]	.014C	.016C	75
Maverick, Granada	109.9[40]	6—3.682x3.126	200	IO	175[12]	97@4400	HY	HY	75
Maverick, Granada, Ghia	109.9[40]	6—3.682x3.91	250	IO	175[12]	98@3600[42]	HY	HY	75
Mustang II, Ghia, Mach I	96.2	8—4.0x3.0	302	VO	150[12]	130@3400	HY	HY	70
Maverick, Granada, Ghia	109.9[40]	8—4.0x3.0	302	VO	150[12]	137@3600[47]	HY	HY	70
LTD II, S, Brougham, Thunderbird	114	8—4.0x3.0	302	VO	150[12]	130@3400	HY	HY	70
Granada Ghia	109.9	8—4.0x3.50	351W	VO	160[12]	135@3200	HY	HY	110
LTD II, S, Brougham, Thunderbird	114[51]	8—4.0x3.50	351W	VO	160[12]	149@3200	HY	HY	110
LTD II, S, Brougham, Thunderbird	114[51]	8—4.0x3.50	351M	VO	170[12]	161@3600	HY	HY	100

ABBREVIATIONS — FOOTNOTES

AC — AC Spark Plugs
AU — Autolite Spark Plugs
B — Before Top Dead Center
C — Cold Engine
CH — Champion Spark Plugs
CP — Crankshaft Pulley
H — Hot Engine
HY — Hydraulic Lifters
IO — In-Line Engine, Overhead Valves
IOC — In-Line Engine, Overhead Camshaft
N — Negative

NA — Not Available
P — Positive
VD — Vibration Damper
VO — V-Type Engine, Overhead Valves
1 — Gremlin — 96, Hornet — 108
   Matador Coupe — 114, Sedan — 118
2 — 8B@600
3 — 10B@700
4 — Gremlin, Hornet — 0
5 — Gremlin, Hornet — 11, Matador — 11.5
6 — 6B@600
7 — Hornet Only, Not Available In California

8 — Minimum Pressure, Also 25 psi
   Maximum Variation
9 — Matador, California
10 — Matador Coupe — 18.5, Sedan — 16.5
11 — Sedan — 15.5
12 — Lowest Cylinder Must Be At Least
   75 Percent of Highest
13 — No Manual Trans. In California
14 — 2-Door — 112
15 — Also 140@3200, Except California
16 — 4 Bbl., 155 hp Only
17 — Riviera — 115.9

766

Tuneup Specifications

Firing Order	Timing Mark Location	Initial Ignition Timing @ rpm (auto. trans.)	Ignition Timing (rpm – manual trans.)	Ignition Timing (California)	Spark Plugs Make	Spark Plugs Model	Gap (in.)	Caster, Power Steering (deg.)	Camber, Right Wheel (deg.)	Toe-In (in.)	Steering Axis Inclination (deg.)	Cooling System Capacity (qt.)	Crankcase Capacity (qt.)
153624	VD	10B@550	600[2]	10B[3]	CH	N12Y	.035	1P[4]	1/8P	1/8	7-3/4	14[5]	4
153624	VD	8B@550	600[6]	8B[3]	CH	N12Y	.035	1P[4]	1/8P	1/8	7-3/4	14[5]	4
153624	VD	8B@600	600[6]	8B[3]	CH	N12Y	.035	1P[4]	1/8P	1/8	7-3/4	14[5]	4
18436572	VD	10B@600[7]	NA	5B[9]	CH	RN12Y	.035	1P[4]	1/8P	1/8	7-3/4	16[10]	4
18436572	VD	10B@600	NA	5B[3]	CH	RN12Y	.035	1P	1/8P	1/8	7-3/4	17.5[11]	4
165432	VD	12B@600	800	12B	AC	R46TS	.040	3/4N	1/4P	1/16	8-1/2	12	4
165432	VD	12B@600	800[13]	12B	AC	R46TS	.040	3/4N	1/4P	1/16	10	12.7	4
165432	VD	12B@600	800[13]	12B	AC	R46TS	.040	2P	1/2P	1/16	8	12.9	4
165432	VD	12B@600	NA	12B	AC	R46TS	.040	3P	3/4P	1/8	9-5/8	12.7	4
18436572	VD	12B@600	NA	NA	AC	R46TS	.060	3/4N	1/4P	1/16	10	21.8	4
18436572	VD	12B@600	NA	NA	AC	R46TS	.060	3P	3/4P	1/8	9-5/8	21.9	4
18436572	VD	12B@600	800	12B[16]	AC	R46TS	.040	2P	1/2P	1/16	8	14.9	4
18436572	VD	12B@600	NA	NA	AC	R45TSX	060	3P	3/4P	1/8	9-5/8	14.2	4
18436572	VD	12B@600	800	12B	AC	R46TS	.040	3/4N	1/4P	1/16	10	14.9	4
18436572	VD	12B@600	NA	12B	AC	R46TS	.040	2P	1/2P	1/16	8	14.9	4
18436572	VD	12B@600	NA	12B	AC	R46TS	.040	3P	3/4P	1/8	8	14.9	4
18436572	VD	12B@600	NA	12B	AC	R45TSX	.060	3P	3/4P	1/8	9-5/8	14.2	4
18436572	VD	12B@600	NA	12B	AC	R45TSX	.060	3P	3/4P	1/8	9-5/8	20.8	4
18436572	VD	12B@600	NA	12B	AC	R45TSX	.060	3P	3/4P	1/8	9-5/8	20.9	4
18436572	VD	10B@600	NA	8B[18]	AC	R47SX	.060	2P	0	1/16	10-1/2	17.2	4
15634278	VD	18B@1400	NA	18B	AC	R45NSX	.060	3P	1/2P	1/8	10-5/8	20.8[20]	4
15634278	VD	18B@1400	NA	18B	AC	R45NSX	060	0	0	0	11	20.8	4
1342	VD	12B@800	800	NA	AC	R43TS	.035	4-1/2P	1/4P	1/16	7-1/2	8.5	4
1342	VD	8B@600	800	8B[21]	AC	R43TS	.035	4-1/2P	1/4P	1/16	7-1/2	9	4
1342	CP	2B@650	700[22]	0[23]	AC	R43TS	.035	3/4N	1/2P	1/4	8-1/2	8	3.5
153624	VD	8B@550	850[24]	6B[6]	AC	R46TS	.035	1P	1P	1/16	10-1/2	14.6	4
153624	VD	8B@550	850[24]	6B[6]	AC	R46TS	.035	1P	3/4P	1/16	10	14.6	4
153624	VD	8B@600	850[24]	8B	AC	R46TS	.035	2P	1/2P	1/16	9-5/8	14.6	4
153624	VD	6B@550	NA	6B[25]	AC	R46TS	.035	3P	3/4P	1/8	9-3/4	14.6	4
18436572	CP	8B@500	600[24]	6B[25]	AC	R45TS	.045	3/4N	1/2P	1/4	8-1/2	18	4
18436572	VD	8B@500	600	6B[25]	AC	R45TS	.045	1P	1P	1/16	10-1/2	17.2	4
18436572	VD	8B@500	600	6B[25]	AC	R45TS	.045	1P	3/4P	1/16	10	17.2	4
18436572	VD	8B@500	NA	NA	AC	R45TS	.045	2P	1/2P	1/16	9-5/8	17.2	4
18436572	VD	8B@500	NA	NA	AC	R45TS	.045	5P	1/2P	1/16	9-5/8	17.4	4
18436572	VD	8B@500	NA	6B[25]	AC	R45TS	.045	3P	3/4P	1/8	9-3/4	17.2	4
18436572	VD	8B@500	700[26]	8B	AC	R45TS	.045	1P	1P	1/16	10-1/2	17.3	4
18436572	VD	8B@500	700[26]	8B	AC	R45TS	.045	1P	3/4P	1/16	10	17.3	4
18436572	VD	8B@500	NA	8B	AC	R45TS	.045	2P	1/2P	1/16	9-5/8	17.2	4
18436572	VD	8B@500	NA	8B	AC	R45TS	.045	5P	1/2P	1/16	9-5/8	17.4	4
18436572	VD	8B@500	500	8B	AC	R45TS	.045	3P	3/4P	1/8	9-3/4	17.2	4
18436572	VD	8B@500[28]	700[26]	8B	AC	R45TS	.045	2-3/8P	3/4P	0	7-5/8	20.7	4
18436572	VD	8B@700	NA	8B[31]	CH	RN12Y	.035	3/4P	1/4P	1/8	8	16.5	4
18436572	VD	10B@700	NA	10B[32]	CH	RN12Y	.035	3/4P	1/4P	1/8	8	16	4
18436572	VD	10B@700	NA	10B[32]	CH	RN12Y	.035	3/4P	1/4P	1/8	9	16	4
18436572	VD	10B@750	NA	10B[32]	CH	RJ13Y	.035	3/4P	1/4P	1/8	8	16.5	4
18436572	VD	10B@750	NA	10B[32]	CH	RJ13Y	.035	3/4P	1/4P	1/8	9	16.5	4
18436572	VD	8B@750	NA	8B	CH	RJ13Y	.035	3/4P	1/4P	1/8	9	16	4
153624	VD	12B@700	700	8B	CH	RBL15Y	.035	2-1/2P	1/4P	1/8	8	12	4
153624	VD	12B@700	700	NA	CH	RBL15Y	.035	3/4P	1/4P	1/8	8	16	4
18436572	VD	8B@700	700	8B[31]	CH	RN12Y	.035	2-1/2P	1/4P	1/8	8	16.5	4
18436572	VD	8B@700	NA	8B[31]	CH	RN12Y	.035	3/4P	1/4P	1/8	8	16.5	4
18436572	VD	8B@700	700	8B[31]	CH	RN12Y	.035	2-1/2P	1/4P	1/8	8[37]	16.5	4
18436572	VD	10B@700	700	10B[32]	CH	RN12Y	.035	2-1/2P	1/4P	1/8	8	16	4
18436572	VD	10B@700	NA	10B[32]	CH	RN12Y	.035	3/4P	1/4P	1/8	8[37]	16.5	4
18436572	VD	10B@750	NA	NA	CH	RJ13Y	.035	3/4P	1/4P	1/8	8[37]	16.5	4
18436572	VD	10B@750	NA	NA	CH	RJ13Y	.035	3/4P	1/4P	1/8	9	16	4
18436572	VD	8B@750	NA	8B	CH	RJ13Y	.035	3/4P	1/4P	1/8	9	16	4
1342	CP	20B@800	850[24]	20B[38]	AU	AGRF52	.034	1-1/4P	3/4P	1/4	10-3/16	8.7	4.5
1342	CP	20B@800	850[24]	20B[38]	AU	AGRF52	.034	7/8P	1/2P	1/8	9-3/4	8.5	4.5
142536	VD	12B@700	NA	6B	AU	AGR42	.034	1-1/4P	3/4P	1/4	10	8.5	4.5
142536	VD	12B@700	NA	6B	AU	AGR42	.034	7/8P	1/2P	1/8	9-3/4	8.8	4.5
153624	VD	6B@650	800	NA	AU	BRF82	.050	1/2N	1/4P	1/8	6-3/4	9[41]	4
153624	VD	6B@650	800[43]	8B	AU	BRF82	.050	1/2N	1/4P	1/8	6-3/4	9.7[44]	4
15426378	VD	8B@650	NA	NA	AU	ARF52[45]	.050[46]	7/8P	1/2P	1/8	9-3/4	16.3	4
15426378	VD	4B@650	NA	12B	AU	ARF52[45]	.050[46]	1/2N	1/4P	1/8	6-3/4	13.5[48]	4
15426378	VD	8B@650	NA	NA	AU	ARF52	.050	4P	1/4P	1/8[49]	9[50]	13.5	4
13726548	VD	4B@625	NA	NA	AU	ARF52	.050	1/2N	1/4P	1/8	6-3/4	15.7	4
13726548	VD	4B@650	NA	NA	AU	ARF52	.050	4P	1/4P	1/8[49]	9[50]	15.9	4
13726548	VD	9B@650	NA	8B	AU	ARF52[45]	.050[46]	4P	1/4P	1/8[49]	9[50]	17.1	4

18 — 8B@600
19 — Limousine, Formal Limousine — 144.5
20 — Limousine, Formal Limousine — 23.5
21 — 8B@800
22 — 0@700, California — 2B@800
23 — 0@650
24 — 6B@850
25 — 6B@550
26 — 8B@700
27 — Also 210@5200, Except California
28 — Also 12B@700
29 — Available W/Electronic Lean Burn System

30 — Minimum psi Allowable
    Also 40 psi Maximum Variation
31 — 8B@850
32 — 10B@750
33 — Equipped W/Electronic Lean Burn System
34 — 4-Door — 112.7
35 — Also 2 Bbl., 110—3600, Except California
36 — 4-Door — 117.4, Royal Monaco — 121.4
37 — Royal Monaco — 9
38 — 20B@850
39 — California Engine — 90@4000

40 — Maverick 2-Door — 103
41 — Granada — 9.7
42 — California Engine — 86@3000
43 — California Engine — 4B@850
44 — Granada — 10.5
45 — California Engine — ARF52—6
46 — California Engine — .060
47 — California Engine — 122@3400
48 — Granada — 14.6
49 — Thunderbird — 3/16
50 — Thunderbird — 9-1/2
51 — 4-Door — 118

1977	Wheelbase (in.)	No. of Cylinders Bore and Stroke (in.)	Displacement (cu. in.)	Valve and Cylinder Arrangement	Compression Pressure (lb.)	Net Brake Horsepower @ rpm	Valve Clearance Intake	Valve Clearance Exhaust	Cylinder Bolt Torque (ft. lb.)
Ford LTD, Landau	121	8–4.0x3.50	351M	VO	170[1]	161@3600	HY	HY	70
LTD II, S, Brougham, Thunderbird	114[2]	8–4.0x4.0	400	VO	180[1]	173@3800[3]	HY	HY	100
Ford LTD, Landau	121	8–4.0x4.0	400	VO	180[1]	173@3800[3]	HY	HY	100
Ford LTD, Landau	121	8–4.362x3.85	460	VO	180[1]	197@4000	HY	HY	135
Lincoln Continental	127.2	8–4.0x4.0	400	VO	180[1]	181@4000	HY	HY	100
Mark V	120.4	8–4.0x4.0	400	VO	180[1]	181@4000	HY	HY	100
Lincoln	127.2	8–4.36x3.85	460	VO	180[1]	208@4000	HY	HY	135
Mark V	120.4	8–4.36x3.85	460	VO	180[1]	208@4000	HY	HY	135
Mercury — Bobcat	94.5	4–3.781x3.126	140	IOC	80[1]	89@4800	HY	HY	85
Bobcat	94.5	6–3.66x2.70	170.8	VO	80[1]	93@4200[10]	.014C	.016C	75
Comet, Monarch, Ghia	109.9[12]	6–3.682x3.126	200	IO	175[1]	97@4400	HY	HY	75
Comet, Monarch, Ghia	109.9[12]	6–3.682x3.910	250	IO	175[1]	98@3600[13]	HY	HY	75
Comet, Monarch, Ghia	109.9[12]	8–4.0x3.0	302	VO	150[1]	137@3600[15]	HY	HY	70
Cougar, Brougham, XR7	114[2]	8–4.0x3.0	302	VO	150[1]	130@3400	HY	HY	70
Monarch Ghia	109.9	8–4.0x3.50	351W	VO	160[1]	135@3200	HY	HY	110
Cougar, Brougham, XR7	114[2]	8–4.0x3.50	351W	VO	160[1]	149@3200	HY	HY	110
Cougar, Brougham, XR7	114[2]	8–4.0x3.50	351M	VO	170[1]	161@3600	HY	HY	100
Cougar, Brougham, XR7	114[2]	8–4.0x4.0	400	VO	180[1]	173@3800[3]	HY	HY	100
Marquis	124	8–4.0x4.0	400	VO	180[1]	173@3800[3]	HY	HY	100
Cougar, Brougham, Grand Marquis	124	8–4.36x3.85	460	VO	180[1]	197@4000	HY	HY	135
Oldsmobile — Starfire, SX	97	4–3.501x3.625	140	IOC	140	84@4400	HY	HY	60
Starfire, SX	97	6–3.80x3.40	231	VO	160	105@3400	HY	HY	80
Omega, Brougham	111	6–3.80x3.40	231	VO	160	105@3400	HY	HY	80
Cutlass, S, Supreme, Brougham	116[17]	6–3.80x3.40	231	VO	160	105@3400	HY	HY	80
Delta 88, Royale	116	6–3.80x3.40	231	VO	160	105@3400	HY	HY	80
Omega, Brougham	111	8–3.50x3.385	260	VO	160	110@3400	HY	HY	95
Delta 88, Royale, Cutlass (all)	116	8–3.50x3.385	260	VO	160	110@3400	HY	HY	95
Omega, Brougham	111	8–3.736x3.48	305	VO	155	145@3800	HY	HY	65
Omega, Brougham	111	8–4.0x3.48	350	VO	160	170@3800	HY	HY	80
Delta 88, Royale	116	8–4.0x3.48	350	VO	160	170@3800	HY	HY	80
Omega, Brougham	111	8–4.057x3.385	350	VO	160	170@3800	HY	HY	85
Cutlass, S, Supreme, Brougham	116[17]	8–4.057x3.385	350	VO	160	170@3800	HY	HY	85
Delta 88, Royale, 98	116[19]	8–4.057x3.385	350	VO	160	170@3800	HY	HY	85
Cutlass, S, Supreme, Brougham	116[19]	8–4.351x3.385	403	VO	160	185@3600	HY	HY	85
Delta 88, Royale, 98	116[20]	8–4.351x3.385	403	VO	160	185@3600	HY	HY	85
Toronado XSR, Custom Brougham	122	8–4.351x3.385	403	VO	160	200@3600	HY	HY	85
Plymouth — Volare', Custom, Premier	108.7[21]	6–3.40x4.12	225	IO	100[22]	100@3600	.010H	.020H	70
Volare', Custom, Premier	108.7[21]	6–3.40x4.12	225	IO	100[22]	110@3600	.010H	.020H	70
Fury, Sport, Salon	115[25]	6–3.40x4.12	225	IO	100[22]	110@3600	.010H	.020H	70
Volare', Custom, Premier	108.7[21]	8–3.91x3.31	318[26]	VO	100[27]	145@4000	HY	HY	95
Fury, Sport, Salon	115[25]	8–3.91x3.31	318[26]	VO	100[27]	145@4000	HY	HY	95
Gran Fury	121.4	8–3.91x3.31	318	VO	100[27]	145@4000	HY	HY	95
Volare', Custom, Premier	108.7[21]	8–4.00x3.58	360	VO	100[27]	155@3600	HY	HY	95
Fury, Sport, Salon	115[25]	8–4.00x3.58	360	VO	100[27]	155@3600[29]	HY	HY	95
Gran Fury, Brougham	121.4	8–4.00x3.58	360	VO	100[27]	155@3600[29]	HY	HY	95
Fury, Sport, Salon	115[25]	8–4.34x3.38	400[30]	VO	100[27]	190@3600	HY	HY	70
Gran Fury, Brougham	121.4	8–4.34x3.38	400[30]	VO	100[27]	190@3600	HY	HY	70
Gran Fury, Brougham	121.4	8–4.34x3.38	440	VO	100[27]	195@3600	HY	HY	70
Pontiac — Astre, Sunbird	97	4–3.501x3.625	140	OHC	140	84@4400	015	.030	60
Astre, Sunbird	97	4–4.0x3.0	151	IO	140	88@4400	HY	HY	95
Ventura	111.1	4–4.0x3.0	151	IO	140	88@4400	HY	HY	95
Sunbird	97	6–3.80x3.40	231	VO	140[31]	105@3200	HY	HY	75
Ventura, SJ	111.1	6–3.80x3.40	231	VO	140[31]	105@3200	HY	HY	75
LeMans, Sport, Grand LeMans	116[17]	6–3.80x3.40	231	VO	140[31]	105@3200	HY	HY	75
Firebird, Esprit	108.1	6–3.80x3.40	231	VO	140[31]	105@3200	HY	HY	75
Catalina	115.9	6–3.80x3.40	231	VO	140[31]	105@3200	HY	HY	75
Ventura, SJ	111.1	8–4.0x3.0	301	VO	140	135@4000	HY	HY	90
LeMans, Sport, Grand LeMans, Grand Prix, LJ	116[17]	8–4.0x3.0	301	VO	140	135@4000	HY	HY	90
Firebird, Esprit, Formula	108.1	8–4.0x3.0	301	VO	140	135@4000	HY	HY	90
Catalina, Bonneville, Brougham	115.9	8–4.0x3.0	301	VO	140	135@4000	HY	HY	90
Ventura, SJ (L34)	111.1	8–4.057x3.385[37]	350[38]	VO	140	170@3800	HY	HY	85
LeMans (all), Grand Prix, LJ (L76)	116[17]	8–3.8762x3.750[41]	350	VO	140	170@4000[42]	HY	HY	85
Firebird, Esprit, Formula (L76)	108.1	8–3.8762x3.750[41]	350	VO	140	170@4000[42]	HY	HY	85
Catalina, Bonneville, Brougham (L76)	115.9	8–3.8762x3.750[41]	350	VO	140	170@4000[42]	HY	HY	85
LeMans, Sport, Grand LeMans	116[17]	8–4.1212x3.750	400	VO	140	180@3600	HY	HY	95
Firebird Formula, Trans Am	108.1	8–4.1212x3.750	400	VO	140	180@3600[48]	HY	HY	95
Grand Prix, LJ, SJ	116	8–4.1212x3.750	400	VO	140	180@3600	HY	HY	95
LeMans, Sport, Grand LeMans, Grand Prix, LJ, SJ	116[17]	8–4.351x3.385	403	VO	140	185@3600	HY	HY	85
Firebird Formula, Trans Am	108.1	8–4.351x3.385	403	VO	140	185@3600	HY	HY	85
Catalina, Bonneville, Brougham	115.9	8–351x3.385	403	VO	140	185@3600	HY	HY	85

ABBREVIATIONS — FOOTNOTES

AC — AC Spark Plugs
AU — Autolite Spark Plugs
B — Before Top Dead Center
C — Cold Engine
CH — Champion Spark Plugs
CP — Crankshaft Pulley
H — Hot Engine
HY — Hydraulic Lifters
IO — In-Line Engine, Overhead Valves
IOC — In-Line Engine, Overhead Camshaft

N — Negative
NA — Not Available
P — Positive
VD — Vibration Damper
VO — V-Type Engine, Overhead Valves
1 — Lowest Cylinder Must Be At Least 75 Percent of Highest
2 — 4-Door — 118
3 — California Engine — 168@3800
4 — California Engine — ARF52–6
5 — California Engine — .060
6 — California Engine — 8B@625

7 — 8B@625
8 — 6B@850
9 — 20B@750
10 — California Engine — 90@4000
11 — 6B@750
12 — Comet 2-Door — 103
13 — California Engine — 86@3000
14 — 4B@800
15 — California Engine — 122@3400
16 — 10B@700
17 — 2-Door — 112
18 — Cutlass — 2P

Tuneup Specifications

Firing Order	Timing Mark Location	Initial Ignition Timing @ rpm (auto. trans.)	Ignition Timing (rpm – manual trans.)	Ignition Timing (California)	Make	Model	Gap (in.)	Caster, Power Steering (deg.)	Camber, Right Wheel (deg.)	Toe-In (in.)	Steering Axis Inclination (deg.)	Cooling System Capacity (qt.)	Crankcase Capacity (qt.)
13726548	VD	9B@650	NA	8B	AU	ARF52	.050	2P	1/4P	1/8	9-7/16	17.1	4
13726548	VD	8B@650	NA	8B	AU	ARF52[4]	.050[5]	4P	1/4P	1/8	9	17.1	4
13726548	VD	8B@650	NA	NA[6]	AU	ARF52	.050	2P	1/4P	1/8	9-7/16	17.5	4
15426378	VD	16B@650	NA	NA	AU	ARF52-6	.060	2P	1/4P	1/8	9-7/16	19.7	4
13726548	VD	NA	NA	8B[7]	AU	ARF52	.050	2P	1/4P	1/8	9-1/2	17.2	4
13726548	VD	NA	NA	8B[7]	AU	ARF52	.050	4P	1/4P	3/16	9-1/2	17.2	4
15426378	VD	16B@650	NA	NA	AU	ARF52-6	.060	2P	1/4P	1/8	9-1/2	18.5	4
15426378	VD	16B@650	NA	NA	AU	ARF52-6	.060	4P	1/4P	3/16	9-1/2	18.5	4
1342	CP	20B@800	850[8]	20B[9]	AU	AWRF42	.034	3/4P	1/2P	1/8	10	8.7	4
142536	CP	12B@700	NA	6B[11]	AU	AWSF42	.034	3/4P	1/2P	1/8	10	8.5	4.5
153624	VD	6B@650	800	NA	AU	BRF82	.050	1/2N	1/4P	1/8	6-3/4	9	4
153624	VD	6B@650	800[14]	8B	AU	BRF82	.050	1/2N	1/4P	1/8	6-3/4	9.7	4
15426378	VD	4B@650	NA	12B	AU	ARF52[4]	.050[5]	1/2N	1/4P	1/8	6-3/4	13.5	4
15426378	VD	8B@650	NA	NA	AU	ARF52	.050	4P	1/4P	1/8	9	13.5	4
13726548	VD	4B@625	NA	NA	AU	ARF52	.050	1/2N	1/4P	1/8	6-3/4	15.7	4
13726548	VD	4B@650	NA	NA	AU	ARF52	.050	4P	1/4P	1/8	9	15.9	4
13726548	VD	9B@650	NA	8B	AU	ARF52[4]	.050[5]	4P	1/4P	1/8	9	17.1	4
13726548	VD	8B@650	NA	8B	AU	ARF52[4]	.050[5]	4P	1/4P	1/8	9	17.1	4
13726548	VD	8B@650	NA	NA[6]	AU	ARF52[4]	.050[5]	2P	1/2P	1/4	9-7/16	17.1	4
15426378	VD	16B@650	NA	NA	AU	ARF52	.050	2P	1/2P	1/4	9-7/16	19.2	4
1342	CP	12B@750	700[16]	12B	AC	R43TS	.035	3/4N	1/2P	1/4	8-1/2	8.1	3.5
165432	VD	12B@800	800	12B	AC	R46TSX	.060	3/4N	1/2P	1/4	8-1/2	11.8	4
165432	VD	12B@600	800	12B	AC	R46TSX	.040	1P	3/4P	1/16	10-1/2	12.8	4
165432	VD	12B@600	600	12B	AC	R46TSX	.060	2P	1/2P	1/16	10-1/2	12.8	4
165432	VD	12B@600	NA	12B	AC	R46TSX	.060	1P	3/4P	1/16	10-1/2	12.2	4
18436572	VD	18B@1100	NA	18B	AC	R46SZ	.080	1P	3/4P	1/16	10-1/2	16.9	4
18436572	VD	18B@1100	NA	18B	AC	R46SZ	.080	1P[18]	3/4P[19]	1/16	10-1/2	16.4	4
18436572	VD	8B@500	NA	8B	AC	R45TS	.045	1P	3/4P	1/16	10-1/2	15.8	4
18436572	VD	8B@500	NA	8B	AC	R45TS	.045	1P	3/4P	1/16	10-1/2	16.0	4
18436572	VD	8B@500	NA	8B	AC	R45TS	.045	1P	3/4P	1/16	10-1/2	16.4	4
18436572	VD	20B@1100	NA	20B	AC	R46SZ	.080	1P	3/4P	1/16	10-1/2	14.6	4
18436572	VD	20B@1100	NA	20B	AC	R46SZ	.080	2P	1/2P	1/16	10-1/2	14.6	4
18436572	VD	20B@1100	NA	20B	AC	R46SZ	.080	1P	3/4P	1/16	10-1/2	14.6	4
18436572	VD	24B@1100	NA	20B	AC	R46SZ	.080	2P	1/2P	1/16	10-1/2	15.7	4
18436572	VD	24B@1100	NA	20B	AC	R46SZ	.080	1P	3/4P	1/16	10-1/2	15.7	4
18436572	VD	24B@1100	NA	20B	AC	R46SZ	.080	1P	3/4P	1/16	10-1/2	17.2	4
153624	VD	12B@700	700	8B[23]	CH	RBL15Y[24]	.035	2-1/2P	1/4P	1/8	8	12	4
153624	VD	12B@700	700	NA	CH	RBL15Y[24]	.035	2-1/2P	1/4P	1/8	8	12	4
153624	VD	12B@700	NA	NA	CH	RBL15Y[24]	.035	3/4P	1/4P	1/8	8	13	4
18436572	VD	8B@700	700	8B[28]	CH	RN12Y	.035	2-1/2P	1/4P	1/8	8	16	4
18436572	VD	8B@700	700	8B[28]	CH	RN12Y	.035	3/4P	1/4P	1/8	8	16.5	4
18436572	VD	8B@700	NA	NA	CH	RN12Y	.035	3/4P	1/4P	1/8	9	17.5	4
18436572	VD	10B@700	NA	NA	CH	RN12Y	.035	2-1/2P	1/4P	1/8	8	16	4
18436572	VD	10B@700	NA	6B[11]	CH	RN12Y	.035	3/4P	1/4P	1/8	8	16	4
18436572	VD	10B@700	NA	6B[11]	CH	RN12Y	.035	3/4P	1/4P	1/8	9	16	4
18436572	VD	10B@750	NA	NA	CH	RJ13Y	.035	3/4P	1/4P	1/8	8	16.5	4
18436572	VD	10B@750	NA	NA	CH	RJ13Y	.035	3/4P	1/4P	1/8	9	16.5	4
18436572	VD	8B@750	NA	8B	CH	RJ13Y	.035	3/4P	1/4P	1/8	9	16	4
1342	CP	12B@750	700[16]	12B	AC	R43TS	.060	3/4N	1/4P	1/16	8-1/2	7	3.5
1342	CP	14B@1000	1000	14B	AC	R44TSX	.060	3/4N	1/4P	1/16	8-1/2	10.7	3
1342	CP	14B@1000	1000	NA	AC	R44TSX	.060	0	3/4P	1/16	10	12.3	3
165432	VD	12B@800	800	12B	AC	R46TSX[32]	.060	3/4N	1/4P	1/16	10	12	4
165432	VD	12B@600	800[33]	12B	AC	R46TSX[32]	.060	0	3/4P	1/16	10	13.7	4
165432	VD	12B@600	800[33]	12B	AC	R46TSX[32]	.060	1-3/4P	1/2P	1/16	10-3/8	13.9	4
165432	VD	12B@600	800[33]	12B	AC	R46TSX[32]	.060	0	1P	3/16	10-3/8	15.8	4
165432	VD	12B@600	800[33]	12B	AC	R46TSX[32]	.060	3P	3/4P	1/8	10-3/8	12.8	4
18436572	VD	12B@700	700[34]	NA	AC	R46TSX	.060	0	3/4P	1/16	10	21.8	5
18436572	VD	12B@700	NA	NA	AC	R46TSX	.060	1-3/4P[35]	1/2P	1/16	10-3/8	21.9[36]	5
18436572	VD	12B@700	700[34]	NA	AC	R46TSX	.060	1P		3/16	10-3/8	20.9	5
18436572	VD	12B@700	NA	NA	AC	R46TSX	.060	3P	3/4P	1/8	10-3/8	20.9	5
18436572	VD	NA	NA	20B[39]	AC	R46SZ	.080	0	3/4P	1/16	10-3/8	16[40]	4
18436572	VD	16B@575	NA	20B[43]	AC	R45TSX[44]	.060[45]	1-3/4P[35]	1/2P	1/16	10-3/8	21[46]	5[47]
18436572	VD	16B@575	NA	20B[43]	AC	R45TSX[44]	.060[45]	0	1P	3/16	10-3/8	20[46]	5[47]
18436572	VD	16B@575	NA	20B[43]	AC	R45TSX[44]	.060[45]	3P	3/4P	1/8	10-3/8	15.1	5[47]
18436572	VD	16B@575	NA	NA	AC	R45TSX	.060	1-3/4P	1/2P	1/16	10-3/8	19.4	5
18436572	VD	16B@575	NA	NA	AC	R45TSX	.060	0	1P	3/16	10-3/8	18.4	5
18436572	VD	16B@575	NA	NA	AC	R45TSX	.060	3P	1/2P	1/16	10-3/8	19.5	5
18436572	VD	20B@1000	NA	20B[39]	AC	R46SZ	.080	1-3/4P[35]	1/2P	1/16	10-3/8	17.2	4
18436572	VD	20B@1000	NA	20B[39]	AC	R46SZ	.080	0	1P	3/16	10-3/8	20.4	4
18436572	VD	20B@1000	NA	20B	AC	R46SX[38]	.080	3P	3/4P	1/8	10-3/8	16.3	4

19 — Cutlass — 1/2P
20 — 98—119
21 — 4-Door — 112.7
22 — Minimum psi Allowable, Also 25 psi Maximum Variation
23 — 8B@750
24 — California Engine — RBL13Y
25 — 4-Door — 117.4
26 — Available W/Electronic Lean Burn System
27 — Minimum psi Allowable, Also 40 psi Maximum Variation

28 — 8B@850
29 — California Engine — 170@4000
30 — Equipped W/Electronic Lean Burn System
31 — Lowest Cylinder Must Be At Least 70 Percent of Highest
32 — California Engine — R45TSX
33 — 12B@800
34 — 16B@700
35 — Grand Prix — 3P
36 — Grand Prix — 22
37 — Also LMI Engine — 4.0x3.48

38 — California Only Engine
39 — California Only — 20B@1100
40 — LMI Engine — 16.6
41 — Also L34 Engine — 4.057x3.385
42 — L34 Engine — 170@3800
43 — 20B@1100
44 — California Engine — R46SZ
45 — L34 Engine — .080
46 — L34 Engine — 16.1
47 — L34 Engine — 4
48 — Also 200@4000

1978

Model	Wheelbase (mm)	Wheelbase (in.)	No. of Cylinders Bore and Stroke (in.)	Displacement (litres)	Displacement (cu. in.)	Valve and Cylinder Arrangement	Net Brake Horsepower @ rpm	Net Power (kW)	Compression Pressure (psi)	Valve Clearance
AMC – Gremlin	2438	96	4–3.41x3.32	2.0	121	IOC	80@5000	59.4	140	H[1]
Gremlin, Pacer, Concord, AMX	2438	96[2]	6–3.75x3.50	3.8	232	IO	90@3400	66.9	140	HY
Gremlin, Pacer, Concord, AMX, Matador	2438	96[2]	6–3.75x3.90	4.2	258	IO	120@3600[6]	89.2[6]	150	HY
Concord, AMX, Pacer	2743	108[2]	8–3.75x3.44	5.0	304	VO	130@3200	96.6	140[7]	HY
Matador	2896	114[2]	8–4.08x3.44	5.9	360	VO	140@3350	104	140[7]	HY
Buick – Century, Custom, Regal	2745	108.1	6–3.50x3.40	3.2	196	VO	90@3600	66.9	140[8]	HY
Skyhawk, S, Skylark, S, S/R	2464	97	6–3.80x3.40	3.8	231	VO	105@3400	78	140[8]	HY
Century, Custom, Regal	2745	108.1	6–3.80x3.40	3.8	231	VO	105@3400[11]	78[11]	140[8]	HY
LeSabre, Custom	2943	115.9	6–3.80x3.40	3.8	231	VO	105@3400[11]	78[11]	140[8]	HY
LeSabre, Custom	2943	115.9	8–3.40x3.00	4.9	301	VO	140@3600	104	140[8]	HY
Skylark, S, S/R	2464	97	8–3.736x3.48	5.0	305	VO	145@3800	108	155	HY
Century, Custom, Regal	2745	108.1	8–3.736x3.48	5.0	305	VO	145@3800[14]	108[14]	155	HY
LeSabre, Custom	2943	115.9	8–3.736x3.48	5.0	305	VO	145@3800	108	155	HY
Skylark, S, S/R	2464	97	8–4.0x3.48	5.7	350	VO	160@3800[15]	119[15]	150	HY
LeSabre, Custom	2943	115.9	8–4.0x3.48	5.7	350	VO	155@3800[15]	116[15]	150	HY
Electra, Riviera	3020	118.9	8–3.80x3.85	5.7	350	VO	155@3800[15]	116[15]	150	HY
Electra, Riviera	3020	118.9[16]	8–4.351x3.385	6.6	403	VO	185@3600	137	155[8]	HY
LeSabre, Custom	2943	115.9	8–4.351x3.385	6.6	403	VO	185@3600	137	155[8]	HY
Cadillac – Seville	2903	114.3	8–4.057x3.385	5.7	350	VO	170@4200	126	160[18]	HY
Brougham, DeVille	3085	121.5	8–4.082x4.060	7.0	425	VO	180@4000	134	160[18]	HY
Fleetwood	3670	144.5	8–4.082x4.060	7.0	425	VO	180@4000	134	160[18]	HY
Eldorado	3208	126.3	8–4.082x4.060	7.0	425	VO	180@4000	134	160[18]	HY
Chevrolet – Chevette	2394	94.3[19]	4–3.23x2.98	1.6	98	IOC	63@4800[20]	47[20]	145	HY
Monza	2459	97	4–4.0x3.0	2.5	151	IO	85@4400	63	145	HY
Monza	2459	97	6–3.50x3.40	3.2	196	VO	90@3600	66.9	140	HY
Malibu, Classic	2745	108.1	6–3.50x3.48	3.3	200	VO	95@3800	71	130[8]	HY
Monza, Malibu, Classic, Monte Carlo	2459	97[21]	6–3.80x3.40	3.8	231	VO	105@3400	78	140[8]	HY
Camaro, Nova, Custom	2743	108[24]	6–3.875x3.53	4.1	250	IO	110@3800	81.7	130[8]	HY
Impala, Caprice Classic	2945	116	6–3.875x3.53	4.1	250	IO	110@3800	81.7	130[8]	HY
Monza, Malibu, Classic, Monte Carlo	2459	97[21]	8–3.736x3.48	5.0	305	VO	145@3800	108	155	HY
Camaro, Nova, Custom	2743	108[24]	8–3.736x3.48	5.0	305	VO	145@3800	108	155	HY
Impala, Caprice Classic	2945	116	8–3.736x3.48	5.0	305	VO	145@3800	108	155	HY
Camaro, Nova, Custom	2743	108[24]	8–4.0x3.48	5.7	350	VO	170@3800[29]	127[29]	150	HY
Impala, Caprice Classic	2945	116	8–4.0x3.48	5.7	350	VO	170@3800	127	150	HY
Corvette	2489	98	8–4.0x3.48	5.7	350	VO	185@4000[31]	137[31]	150	HY
Chrysler, LeBaron, Medallion	2863	112.7	6–3.40x4.12	3.7	225	IO	110@3600[33]	81.7[33]	100[34]	H[35]
LeBaron, Medallion	2863	112.7	8–3.91x3.31	5.2	318	VO	140@4000[36]	104[36]	100[34]	HY
Cordoba	2919	114.9	8–3.91x3.31	5.2	318	VO	140@4000[36]	104[36]	100[34]	HY
LeBaron, Medallion	2863	112.7	8–4.0x3.58	5.8	360	VO	155@3600[37]	116[37]	100[34]	HY
Cordoba	2919	114.9	8–4.0x3.58	5.8	360	VO	155@3600[37]	116[37]	100[34]	HY
Newport, New Yorker Brougham	3147	123.9	8–4.0x3.58	5.8	360	VO	155@3600[37]	116[37]	100[34]	HY
Cordoba	2919	114.9	8–4.34x3.38	6.6	400	VO	190@3600	141.2	100[34]	HY
Newport, New Yorker Brougham	3147	123.9	8–4.34x3.38	6.6	400	VO	190@3600	141.2	100[34]	HY
Newport, New Yorker Brougham	3147	123.9	8–4.31x3.75	7.2	440	VO	195@3600[38]	145[38]	100[34]	HY
Dodge – Omni	2520	99.2	4–3.13x3.40	1.7	104.7	IOC	75@5600[39]	55[39]	100[34]	H[40]
Aspen	2761	108.7[41]	6–3.40x4.12	3.7	225	IO	110@3600[33]	74.3[33]	100[34]	H[35]
Diplomat, Medallion	2863	112.7	6–3.40x4.12	3.7	225	IO	110@3600[33]	74.3[33]	100[34]	H[35]
Monaco, Brougham	2919	114.9[42]	6–3.40x4.12	3.7	225	IO	110@3600	74.3	100[34]	H[35]
Aspen	2761	108.7[41]	8–3.91x3.31	5.2	318	VO	140@4000[36]	104[36]	100[34]	HY
Diplomat, Medallion	2863	112.7	8–3.91x3.31	5.2	318	VO	140@4000[36]	104[36]	100[34]	HY
Charger Special Edition, Magnum XE	2919	114.9	8–3.91x3.31	5.2	318	VO	140@4000[36]	104[36]	100[34]	HY
Monaco, Brougham	2919	114.9[42]	8–3.91x3.31	5.2	318	VO	140@4000[36]	104[36]	100[34]	HY
Aspen	2761	108.7[41]	8–4.0x3.58	5.8	360	VO	155@3600	130	100[34]	HY
Diplomat, Medallion	2863	112.7	8–4.0x3.58	5.8	360	VO	155@3600[37]	130[37]	100[34]	HY
Charger Special Edition, Magnum XE	2919	114.9	8–4.0x3.58	5.8	360	VO	155@3600[37]	130[37]	100[34]	HY
Monaco, Brougham	2919	114.9[42]	8–4.0x3.58	5.8	360	VO	155@3600[37]	130[37]	100[34]	HY
Charger Special Edition, Magnum XE	2919	114.9	8–4.34x3.38	6.6	400	VO	190@3600	141.2	100[34]	HY
Monaco, Brougham	2919	114.9[42]	8–4.34x3.38	6.6	400	VO	190@3600	141.2	100[34]	HY
Ford – Pinto	2400	94.5	4–3.781x3.126	2.3	140	IOC	88@4800	65.4	80[18]	HY
Mustang II, Ghia	2443	96.2	4–3.781x3.126	2.3	140	IOC	88@4800	65.4	80[18]	HY
Fairmont	2680	105.5	4–3.781x3.126	2.3	140	IOC	88@4800	65.4	80[18]	HY
Pinto	2400	94.5	6–3.66x2.70	2.8	170.8	VO	90@4200	66.9	80[18]	C[45]
Mustang II, Ghia, Mach I	2443	96.2	6–3.66x2.70	2.8	170.8	VO	90@4200	66.9	80[18]	C[45]
Fairmont	2680	105.5	6–3.682x3.126	3.3	200	IO	85@3600	63	175[18]	HY
Granada, Ghia, ESS	2792	109.9	6–3.68x3.91	4.1	250	IO	97@3200	73.1	175[18]	HY
Mustang II, Ghia, Mach I	2443	96.2	8–4.00x3.00	5.0	302	VO	139@3600[49]	103.3[49]	150[18]	HY
Fairmont	2680	105.5	8–4.00x3.00	5.0	302	VO	139@3600[49]	103.3[49]	150[18]	HY
Granada, Ghia, ESS	2792	109.9	8–4.00x3.00	5.0	302	VO	139@3600[49]	103.3[49]	150[18]	HY
LTD II, S, Thunderbird	2896	114[51]	8–4.00x3.00	5.0	302	VO	134@3400	99.6	150[18]	HY

ABBREVIATIONS – FOOTNOTES

AC – AC Spark Plugs
AU – Autolite Spark Plugs
B – Before Top Dead Center
C – Cold Engine
CH – Champion Spark Plugs
CP – Crankshaft Pulley
H – Hot Engine
HY – Hydraulic Lifters
IO – In-Line Engine – Overhead Valves
IOC – In-Line Engine – Overhead Camshaft
MO – Motorcraft Spark Plugs

N – Negative
NA – Not Available/Not Applicable
P – Positive
VD – Vibration Damper
VO – V-Type Engine, Overhead Valves
1 – Intake – .008 in./0.20 mm
Exhaust – .018 in./0.46 mm
2 – Gremlin – 2438/96, Concord – AMX – 2743/108,
Matador Coupe – 2896/114, Sedan – 2997/118
3 – 8B
4 – @700
5 – Pacer – 13.2/14, Concord – AMX – 10.4/11,
Matador – 10.9/11.5

6 – Also 100@3400, except Matador
7 – Minimum Pressure
8 – Lowest Cylinder Must Be At Least
70 Percent of Highest
9 – Skylark – 1P/3/4P
10 – Skylark – 12.9/13.6
11 – Turbo – 150/111@3800
And 165/123@4000
12 – Turbo – R44TSX
13 – @600
14 – Also 165/122.6@4000
15 – Also 170/126@3800
16 – Riviera – 2943/115.9

Tuneup Specifications

Firing Order	Timing Mark Location	Initial Ignition Timing @ rpm (auto. trans.)	Ignition Timing (rpm-manual trans.)	Ignition Timing (California)	Spark Plugs Make	Spark Plugs Model	Gap (in.)	Caster, Power Steering (deg.)	Camber, Right Wheel (deg.)	Toe-In (in.)	Crankcase Capacity (L/qt.)	Cooling System Capacity (L)	Cooling System Capacity (qt.)
1342	VD	12B@700	700	8B	CH	N8L	.035	1P	1/8P	1/8	3.78/4	6.1	6.5
153624	VD	10B@550	600[3]	8B	CH	N13L	.035	1P	1/8P	1/8	3.78/4	10.4[5]	11[5]
153624	VD	10B@600	600[3]	10B[4]	CH	N13L	.035	1P	1/8P	1/8	3.78/4	10.4[5]	11[5]
18436572	VD	10B@600	NA	10B[4]	CH	N12Y	.035	1P	1/8P	1/8	3.78/4	17	18
18436572	VD	10B@600	NA	10B[4]	CH	N13L	.035	1P	1/8P	1/8	3.78/4	16.5	17.5
165432	VD	15B@600	800	15B	AC	R46TS	.040	3P	1/2P	1/8	3.78/4	12.5	13.1
165432	VD	15B@600	800	15B	AC	R46TS	.040	3/4N[9]	1/4P[9]	1/16	3.78/4	11.1[10]	11.8[10]
165432	VD	15B@600	800	15B	AC	R46TS[12]	.040	3P	1/2P	1/8	3.78/4	12.5	13.1
165432	VD	15B@600	NA	15B	AC	R46TS[12]	.040	3P	3/4P	1/8	3.78/4	12.2	12.9
18436572	VD	12B@600	NA	NA	AC	R46TS	.060	3P	3/4P	1/8	3.78/4	19.8	20.9
18436572	VD	4B@500	NA	6B[13]	AC	R45TS	.045	1P	3/4P	1/16	3.78/4	15	15.9
18436572	VD	4B@500	NA	6B[13]	AC	R45TS	.045	3P	1/2P	1/8	3.78/4	18.1	19.2
18436572	VD	4B@500	NA	6B[13]	AC	R45TS	.045	3P	3/4P	1/8	3.78/4	15.7	16.6
18436572	VD	6B@600	NA	8B	AC	R45TS	.045	1P	3/4P	1/16	3.78/4	15.2	16.1
18436572	VD	6B@600	NA	8B	AC	R45TS	.045	3P	3/4P	1/8	3.78/4	15.7	16.6
18436572	VD	15B@600	NA	15B	AC	R46TSX	.045	3P	3/4P	1/16[17]	3.78/4	13.5	14.2
18436572	VD	15B@600	NA	15B	AC	R46TSX	.060	3P	3/4P	1/16[17]	3.78/4	14.9	15.7
18436572	VD	15B@600	NA	15B	AC	R46TSX	.060	3P	3/4P	1/8	3.78/4	14.9	15.7
18436572	VD	10B@600	NA	8B	AC	R47SX	.060	2P	0	1/16	3.78/4	16.4	17.2
15634278	VD	21B@1600	NA	21B	AC	R45NSX	.060	3P	1/2P	1/8	3.78/4	19.7	20.8
15634278	VD	18B@1600	NA	18B	AC	R45NSX	.060	3P	1/2P	1/8	3.78/4	19.7	20.8
15634278	VD	22B@1600	NA	22B	AC	R45NSX	.060	0	0	0	4.73/5	24.4	25.8
1342	VD	8B@600	800	8B	AC	R43TS	.035	4-1/2P	1/4P	1/16	3.78/4	8.6	9
1342	CP	14B@650	1000	14B	AC	R43TSX	.060	3/4N	1/2P	1/4	2.84/3	10.2	10.8
165432	VD	15B@600	800	15B	AC	R46TSX	.060	3/4N	1/2P	1/4	3.78/4	11	11.6
165432	VD	8B@600	600	8B	AC	R45TS	.045	3P	1/2P	1/8	3.78/4	12.5	13.1
165432	VD	15B@600	800	15B	AC	R46TSX	.060	3/4N[22]	1/2P	1/4[23]	3.78/4	14.8	15.6
153624	VD	10B@550	850	6B	AC	R46TS	.035	1P[25]		1/16	3.78/4	13.8[26]	14.6[26]
153624	VD	10B@550	NA	6B	AC	R46TS	.035	3P	3/4P	1/8	3.78/4	13.4	14.2
18436572	VD	4B@500	600	6B	AC	R45TS	.045	3/4N[22]	1/2P	1/4[23]	3.78/4	15.3[27]	16.2[27]
18436572	VD	6B@500	600	6B	AC	R45TS	.045	1P[25]		1/16	3.78/4	16.4[28]	17.2[28]
18436572	VD	4B@500	NA	6B	AC	R45TS	.045	3P	3/4P	1/8	3.78/4	15.7	16.6
18436572	VD	6B@500	NA	8B	AC	R45TS	.045	1P[25]		1/16	3.78/4	16.4[30]	17.3[30]
18436572	VD	6B@500	NA	8B	AC	R45TS	.045	3P	3/4P	1/8	3.78/4	15.7	16.6
18436572	VD	6B@500[32]	700	8B[32]	AC	R45TS	.045	2-3/8P	3/4P	0	3.78/4	20.4	21.6
153624	VD	12B@700	700	8B	CH	RBL16Y	.035	2-1/2P	1/4P	1/8	3.78/4	11.4	12
18436572	VD	16B@700	700	16B	CH	RN12Y	.035	2-1/2P	1/4P	1/8	3.78/4	15.1	16
18436572	VD	16B@700	NA	16B	CH	RN12Y	.035	3/4P	1/4P	1/8	3.78/4	15.6	16.5
18436572	VD	20B@750	NA	6B	CH	RN12Y	.035	2-1/2P	1/4P	1/8	3.78/4	15.1	16
18436572	VD	20B@750	NA	6B	CH	RN12Y	.035	3/4P	1/4P	1/8	3.78/4	15.1	16
18436572	VD	20B@750	NA	NA	CH	RJ13Y	.035	3/4P	1/4P	1/8	3.78/4	15.6	16.5
18436572	VD	20B@750	NA	NA	CH	RJ13Y	.035	3/4P	1/4P	1/8	3.78/4	15.6	16.5
18436572	VD	12B@750	NA	12B	CH	RJ13Y	.035	3/4P	1/4P	1/8	3.78/4	15.1	16
1342	CP	15B@900	900	15B	CH	RN12Y	.035	NA	1/4P	1/8	3.78/4	7.6	8
153624	VD	12B@700	700	8B[32]	CH	RBL16Y	.035	2-1/2P	1/4P	1/8	3.78/4	11.4	12
153624	VD	12B@700	700	8B[32]	CH	RBL16Y	.035	2-1/2P	1/4P	1/8	3.78/4	11.4	12
153624	VD	12B@700	700	NA	CH	RBL16Y	.035	3/4P	1/4P	1/8	3.78/4	12.5	13
18436572	VD	16B@700	NA	16B	CH	RN12Y	.035	2-1/2P	1/4P	1/8	3.78/4	15.6	16.5
18436572	VD	16B@700	700	16B	CH	RN12Y	.035	2-1/2P	1/4P	1/8	3.78/4	15.1	16
18436572	VD	16B@700	NA	16B	CH	RN12Y	.035	3/4P	1/4P	1/8	3.78/4	15.6	16.5
18436572	VD	16B@700	NA	16B	CH	RN12Y	.035	3/4P	1/4P	1/8	3.78/4	15.6	16.5
18436572	VD	20B@750	NA	6B	CH	RN12Y	.035	2-1/2P	1/4P	1/8	3.78/4	15.1	16
18436572	VD	20B@750	NA	6B	CH	RN12Y	.035	3/4P	1/4P	1/8	3.78/4	15.1	16
18436572	VD	20B@750	NA	NA	CH	RJ13Y	.035	3/4P	1/4P	1/8	3.78/4	15.6	16.5
1342	CP	20B@800	850[43]	20B[44]	AU/MO	AWRF42	.034	1P	1/2P	1/8	3.78/4	8.1	8.6
1342	CP	20B@800	850[43]	20B[44]	AU/MO	AWRF42	.034	7/8P	1/2P	1/8	3.78/4	8.3	8.8
1342	CP	20B@800	850[43]	20B[44]	AU/MO	AWRF42	.034	7/8P	5/16P	5/16	3.78/4	8.1	8.6
142536	VD	12B@650	NA	6B[13]	AU/MO	AWSF42	.034	1P	1/2P	1/8	4.26/4.5	8.0	8.5
142536	VD	12B@650	700[46]	6B[13]	AU/MO	AWSF42	.034	7/8P	1/2P	1/8	4.26/4.5	8.1	8.6
153624	VD	10B@650	800	6B	AU/MO	BRF82	.050[47]	7/8P	5/16P	5/16	3.78/4	8.6	9
153624	VD	14B@600	800[48]	6B[13]	AU/MO	BRF82	.050	1/2N	1/4P	1/4	3.78/4	9.9	10.5
15426378	VD	4B@700	900	12B[13]	AU/MO	ARF52[50]	.050[50]	7/8P	1/2P	1/8	3.78/4	13.4	14.2
15426378	VD	6B@600	NA	12B[13]	AU/MO	ARF52[50]	.050[50]	7/8P	5/16P	5/16	3.78/4	13.1	13.9
15426378	VD	6B@600	NA	NA	AU/MO	ARF52[50]	.050[50]	1/2N	1/4P	1/4	3.78/4	13.4	14.2
15426378	VD	14B@650	NA	NA	AU/MO	ARF52	.050	4P	1/4P	1/8	3.78/4	13.5	14.3

17 — Riviera — 1/8
18 — Lowest Cylinder Must Be At Least 75 Percent of Highest
19 — 4-Door — 2471/97.3
20 — Also 68/51@5000
21 — Malibu/Monte Carlo 2745/108.1
22 — Malibu/Monte Carlo 3P
23 — Malibu/Monte Carlo 1/8
24 — Nova — 2819/111
25 — Nova — 3/4P
26 — Nova — 12.9/13.6
27 — Malibu/Monte Carlo — 18.1/19.2
28 — Nova — 15.1/16.0

29 — Also 185/137@4000, Nova — 160/119@3800
30 — Nova — 15.2/16.1
31 — Also 220/163.5@5200 Except Cal. and Certain Specified Areas
32 — Also 12B@700
33 — Cal. — 90/66.9@3600
34 — Minimum Pressure. Also 25 psi (4 and 6) or 40 psi (8) Maximum Variation
35 — Int. .010 in./0.25 mm, Exh. .020 in./0.50 mm
36 — Also 155/116@4000
37 — Cal. — 170/126@3600
38 — Cal. — 185/137@3600

39 — Cal. — 70/50@5600
40 — Cal. — Int. .008 in./0.20 mm, Exh. .012 in./0.30 mm
41 — 4-Door — 2863/112.7
42 — 4-Door — 2982/117.4
43 — 6B
44 — Man. Trans. — 6B@750
45 — Int. .014 in./0.35 mm, Exh. .016 in./0.40 mm
46 — 10B
47 — Cal. — .060 in.
48 — 4B
49 — Cal. — 133/98.8@3600
50 — Cal. — ARF52-6, .060 in.
51 — 4-Door — 2997/118

1978

	Wheelbase (mm)	Wheelbase (in.)	No. of Cylinders Bore and Stroke (in.)	Displacement (litres)	Displacement (cu. in.)	Valve and Cylinder Arrangement	Net Brake Horsepower @ rpm	Net Power (kW)	Compression Pressure (psi)	Valve Clearance
Ford LTD, Landau	3073	121	8—4.00x3.00	5.0	302	VO	134@3400	99.6	150[1]	HY
Ford LTD II, S, Thunderbird	2997	114[2]	8—4.0x350	5.8	351W	VO	144@3200	107	160[1]	HY
Ford LTD, Landau	3073	121	8—4.0x3.50	5.8	351W	VO	144@3200	107	160[1]	HY
Ford LTD II, S, Thunderbird	2997	114	8—4.0x3.50	5.8	351M	VO	152@3600	113	170[1]	HY
Ford LTD, Landau	3073	121	8—4.0x3.50	5.8	351M	VO	145@3400	108	170[1]	HY
Ford LTD II, S, Thunderbird	2997	114[2]	8—4.0x4.0	6.6	400	VO	166@3800	123.4	180[1]	HY
Ford LTD, Landau	3073	121	8—4.0x4.0	6.6	400	VO	160@3800	119	180[1]	HY
Ford LTD, Landau	3073	121	8—4.362x3.85	7.5	460	VO	202@4000	150.1	180[1]	HY
Lincoln — Versailles	2792	109.9	8—4.0x3.0	5.0	302	VO	133@3600	99.8	150[1]	HY
Mark V	3058	120.4	8—4.0x4.0	6.6	400	VO	166@3800	123.4	180[1]	HY
Lincoln	3231	127.2	8—4.0x4.0	6.6	400	VO	166@3800	123.4	180[1]	HY
Mark V	3058	120.4	8—4.362x3.85	7.5	460	VO	210@4200	156	180[1]	HY
Lincoln	3231	127.2	8—4.362x3.85	7.5	460	VO	210@4200	156	180[1]	HY
Mercury — Bobcat	2400	94.5	4—3.781x3.126	2.3	140	IOC	88@4800	65.4	80[1]	HY
Zephyr	2680	105.5	4—3.781x3.126	2.3	140	IOC	88@4800	65.4	80[1]	HY
Bobcat	2400	94.5	6—3.66x2.70	2.8	170.8	VO	90@4200	66.9	80[1]	C[10]
Zephyr	2680	105.5	6—3.682x3.126	3.3	200	IO	85@3600	63	175[1]	HY
Monarch, Ghia, ESS	2792	109.9	6—3.68x3.91	4.1	250	IO	97@3200	73.1	175[1]	HY
Zephyr	2680	105.5	8—4.00x3.00	5.0	302	VO	139@3600[12]	103.3[12]	150[1]	HY
Monarch, Ghia, ESS	2792	109.9	8—4.00x3.00	5.0	302	VO	139@3600[12]	103.3[12]	150[1]	HY
Cougar, XR7	2997	114[2]	8—4.00x3.00	5.0	302	VO	134@3400	99.6	150[1]	HY
Cougar, XR7	2997	114[2]	8—4.00x3.50	5.8	351W	VO	144@3200	107	160[1]	HY
Cougar, XR7	2997	114[2]	8—4.00x3.50	5.8	351M	VO	152@3600	113	170[1]	HY
Marquis, Brougham, Grand Marquis	3150	124	8—4.00x3.50	5.8	351M	VO	145@3400	108	170[1]	HY
Cougar, XR7	2997	114[2]	8—4.00x4.00	6.6	400	VO	166@3800	123.4	180[1]	HY
Marquis, Brougham, Grand Marquis	3150	124	8—4.00x4.00	6.6	400	VO	160@3800	119	180[1]	HY
Marquis, Brougham, Grand Marquis	3150	124	8—4.36x3.85	7.5	460	VO	202@4000	150.1	180[1]	HY
Oldsmobile — Starfire, SX	2464	97	4—4.0x3.0	2.5	151	IO	85@4400	63	145[13]	HY
Starfire, SX, Omega, Brougham	2464	97[14]	6—3.80x3.40	3.8	231	VO	105@3400	78	140[13]	HY
Cutlass (all)	2745	108.1	6—3.80x3.40	3.8	231	VO	105@3400	78	140[13]	HY
Delta 88, Royale	2945	116	6—3.80x3.40	3.8	231	VO	105@3400	78	140[13]	HY
Cutlass (all)	2745	108.1	8—3.50x3.385	4.3	260	VO	110@3400	82	150[13]	HY
Delta 88, Royale	2945	116	8—3.50x3.385	4.3	260	VO	110@3400	82	150[13]	HY
Starfire, SX, Omega, Brougham	2464	97[14]	8—3.736x3.48	5.0	305	VO	145@3800	108	155	HY
Cutlass (all)	2745	108.1	8—3.736x3.48	5.0	305	VO	145@3800[17]	108[17]	155	HY
Omega, Brougham	2819	111	8—4.0x3.48	5.7	350	VO	160@3800	119	150	HY
Delta 88, Royale, 98 (all)	2945	116[18]	8—4.057x3.385	5.7	350	VO	170@3800	127	150	HY
Delta 88, Royale, 98 (all)	2945	116[18]	8—4.057x3.385[20]	5.7	350[20]	VO	120@3600	89.2	275[13]	HY
Delta 88, Royale, 98 (all)	2945	116[18]	8—4.351x3.385	6.6	403	VO	185@3600	138	155[13]	HY
Toronado XSR, Custom Brougham	3099	122	8—4.351x3.385	6.6	403	VO	190@3600	141.2	155[13]	HY
Plymouth — Horizon	2520	99.2	4—3.13x3.40	1.7	104.7	IOC	75@5600[21]	55[21]	100[22]	H[23]
Volaré	2761	108.7[26]	6—3.40x4.12	3.7	225	IO	100@3600[27]	74.3[27]	100[22]	H[28]
Fury, Sport, Salon	2919	114.9[30]	6—3.40x4.12	3.7	225	IO	110@3600	82	100[22]	H[28]
Volaré	2761	108.7[26]	8—3.91x3.31	5.2	318	VO	140@4000	104	100[22]	HY
Fury, Sport, Salon	2919	114.9[30]	8—3.91x3.31	5.2	318	VO	140@4000[31]	104[31]	100[22]	HY
Volaré	2761	108.7[26]	8—4.0x3.58	5.8	360	VO	155@3600[33]	130[33]	100[22]	HY
Fury, Sport, Salon	2919	114.9[30]	8—4.0x3.58	5.8	360	VO	155@3600[35]	130[35]	100[22]	HY
Fury, Sport, Salon	2919	114.9[30]	8—4.34x3.38	6.6	400	VO	190@3600	141.2	100[22]	HY
Pontiac — Sunbird (LX6)	2459	97	4—4.0x3.0[36]	2.5	151	IO	85@4400	63	140	HY
Phoenix, LJ (LX6)	2822	111.1	4—4.0x3.0	2.5	151	IO	85@4400	63	140	HY
Sunbird (LD5)	2459	97	6—3.80x3.40	3.8	231	VO	105@3400	78	140[13]	HY
Phoenix, LJ (LD5)	2822	111.1	6—3.80x3.40	3.8	231	VO	105@3400	78	140[13]	HY
LeMans, Grand LeMans, Grand Prix (LD5)	2745	108.1	6—3.80x3.40	3.8	231	VO	105@3400	78	140[13]	HY
Firebird, Esprit (LD5)	2745	108.1	6—3.80x3.40	3.8	231	VO	105@3400	78	140[13]	HY
Catalina (LD5)	2945	115.9	6—3.80x3.40	3.8	231	VO	105@3200	78	140[13]	HY
Grand AM, Grand Prix, LJ (L27)	2745	108.1	8—4.0x3.0[42]	4.9	301	VO	140@3600[41]	104[41]	140	HY
Catalina, Bonneville, Brougham (L27)	2945	115.9	8—4.0x3.0[42]	4.9	301	VO	140@3600[41]	104[41]	140	HY
Sunbird (LG3)	2459	97	8—3.736x3.48	5.0	305	VO	145@3800	108	155	HY
Phoenix, LJ (LG3)	2822	111.1	8—3.736x3.48	5.0	305	VO	145@3800	108	155	HY
LeMans (all), Grand Prix LJ, SJ (LG3)	2745	108.1	8—3.736x3.48	5.0	305	VO	145@3800[43]	108[43]	155	HY
Firebird, Esprit, Formula (LG3)	2745	108.2	8—3.736x3.48	5.0	305	VO	145@3800[43]	108[43]	155	HY
Phoenix, LJ (LM1)	2822	111.1	8—4.0x3.48	5.7	350	VO	160@3800	119	150	HY
Firebird, Esprit, Formula (LM1)	2745	108.2	8—4.0x3.48	5.7	350	VO	170@3800	127	150	HY
Catalina, Bonneville, Brougham (L77)	2945	115.9	8—3.80x3.85	5.7	350	VO	155@3400	116	150	HY
Catalina, Bonneville, Brougham (L34)	2945	115.9	8—4.057x3.385	5.7	350	VO	170@3800	127	150	HY
Firebird Formula, Trans AM (L78)	2745	108.2	8—4.121x3.75	6.6	400	VO	220@4000[45]	163[45]	140[13]	HY
Catalina, Bonneville, Brougham (L78)	2945	115.9	8—4.121x3.75	6.6	400	VO	180@3600	134	140[13]	HY
Firebird Formula, Trans AM (L80)	2745	108.2	8—4.351x3.385	6.6	403	VO	185@3600	138	140[13]	HY
Catalina, Bonneville, Brougham (L80)	2945	115.9	8—4.351x3.385	6.6	403	VO	185@3600	138	140[13]	HY

ABBREVIATIONS — FOOTNOTES

AC — AC Spark Plugs
AU — Autolite Spark Plugs
B — Before Top Dead Center
C — Cold Engine
CH — Champion Spark Plugs
CP — Crankshaft Pulley
H — Hot Engine
HY — Hydraulic Lifters
IO — In-Line Engine — Overhead Valves
IOC — In-Line Engine — Overhead Camshaft

MO — Motorcraft Spark Plugs
N — Negative
NA — Not Available/Not Applicable
P — Positive
VD — Vibration Damper
VO — Type Engine, Overhead Valves
1 — Lowest Cylinder Must Be At Least 75 Percent of Highest
2 — 4-Door — 2997/118
3 — Cal. — ARF52—6
4 — Cal. — .060 in.
5 — Electronic Engine Control

6 — @600
7 — 6B
8 — @750
9 — Manual Trans. Only
10 — Int. .014 in./0.35 mm, Exh. .016 in./0.40 mm
11 — Cal. — Automatic Trans. Only
12 — Cal. — 133/98.8@3600
13 — Lowest Cylinder Must Be At Least 70 Percent of Highest
14 — Omega, Brougham 2819/111
15 — 18B

Firing Order	Timing Mark Location	Initial Ignition Timing @ rpm (auto. trans.)	Ignition Timing (rpm-manual trans.)	Ignition Timing (California)	Make	Spark Plugs Model	Gap (in.)	Caster, Power Steering (deg.)	Camber, Right Wheel (deg.)	Toe-In (in.)	Crankcase Capacity (L./qt.)	Cooling System Capacity (L)	Cooling System Capacity (qt.)
15426378	VD	14B@650	NA	NA	AU/MO	ARF52	.050	2P	1/2P	5/16	3.78/4	14.3	15.1
13726548	VD	4B@650	NA	NA	AU/MO	ARF52	.050	4P	1/4P	1/8	3.78/4	14.6	15.4
13726548	VD	4B@650	NA	NA	AU/MO	ARF52	.050	2P	1/2P	5/16	3.78/4	15.3	16.2
13726548	VD	9B@650	NA	9B	AU/MO	ARF52	.050	4P	1/4P	1/8	3.78/4	16	16.9
13726548	VD	9B@650	NA	NA	AU/MO	ARF52	.050	2P	1/2P	5/16	3.78/4	16	16.9
13726548	VD	13B@800	NA	16B	AU/MO	ARF52[3]	.050[4]	4P	1/4P	1/8	3.78/4	15.6	16.5
13726548	VD	13B@800	NA	16B	AU/MO	ARF52[3]	.050[4]	2P	1/2P	5/16	3.78/4	16	16.9
15426378	VD	10B@580	NA	NA	AU/MO	ARF52	.050	2P	1/2P	5/16	3.78/4	17.6	18.6
15426378	VD	EEC[5]	NA	EEC[5]	AU/MO	ARF52	.050	1/2N	1/4P	1/8	3.78/4	13.5	14.3
13726548	VD	13B@575	NA	16B[6]	AU/MO	ARF52	.050	4P	1/4P	1/8	3.78/4	16	16.9
13726548	VD	13B@575	NA	16B[6]	AU/MO	ARF52	.050	2P	1/4P	1/8	3.78/4	16	16.9
15426378	VD	10B@580	NA	NA	AU/MO	ARF52	.050	4P	1/4P	1/8	3.78/4	17.7	18.7
15426378	VD	10B@580	NA	NA	AU/MO	ARF52	.050	2P	1/4P	1/8	3.78/4	17.6	18.6
1342	CP	20B@800	850[7]	20B[8]	AU/MO	AWRF42	.034	1P	1/2P	1/8	3.78/4	8.1	8.6
1342	CP	20B@800	850[7]	20B[9]	AU/MO	AWRF42	.034	7/8P	5/16P	1/8	3.78/4	8.1	8.6
142536	VD	12B@650	NA	6B[6]	AU/MO	AWSF42	.034	1P	1/2P	1/8	3.78/4	8	8.5
153624	VD	10B@650	800	6B[11]	AU/MO	BRF82	.050[4]	7/8P	5/16P	5/16	3.78/4	8.6	9
153624	VD	14B@600	800	6B[11]	AU/MO	BRF82	.050	1/2N	1/4P	1/4	3.78/4	9.9	10.5
15426378	VD	6B@600	NA	12B	AU/MO	ARF52[3]	.050[4]	7/8P	5/16P	5/16	3.78/4	13.1	13.9
15426378	VD	6B@600	500	6B[11]	AU/MO	ARF52[3]	.050[4]	1/2N	1/4P	1/4	3.78/4	13.4	14.2
15426378	VD	14B@650	NA	NA	AU/MO	ARF52	.050	4P	1/4P	1/8	3.78/4	13.5	14.3
13726548	VD	4B@650	NA	NA	AU/MO	ARF52	.050	4P	1/4P	1/8	3.78/4	14.6	15.4
13726548	VD	9B@650	NA	16B	AU/MO	ARF52	.050	4P	1/4P	1/8	3.78/4	16	16.9
13726548	VD	9B@650	NA	NA	AU/MO	ARF52	.050	2P	1/2P	5/16	3.78/4	16	16.9
13726548	VD	13B@800	NA	16B	AU/MO	ARF52	.050[4]	4P	1/4P	1/8	3.78/4	15.6	16.5
13726548	VD	13B@800	NA	16B	AU/MO	ARF52	.050[4]	2P	1/2P	5/16	3.78/4	16	16.9
15426378	VD	10B@580	NA	NA	AU/MO	ARF52	.050	2P	1/2P	5/16	3.78/4	17.6	18.6
1342	CP	14B@1000	1000	12B	AC	R44TSX	.060	1P	3/4P	1/16	2.84/3	10.4	11
165432	VD	12B@800	1000	12B	AC	R46TSX	.040	1P	3/4P	1/16	3.78/4	11.2	11.8
165432	VD	15B@600	800	15B	AC	R46TSX	.060	3P	1/2P	3/16	3.78/4	11.3	11.9
165432	VD	12B@600	NA	12B	AC	R46TSX	.060	3P	3/4P	1/8	3.78/4	11.5	12.2
18436572	VD	20B@1100	1100[15]	18B	AC	R46SZ	.080	3P	1/2P	3/16	3.78/4	15.3	16.2
18436572	VD	18B@1100	NA	18B	AC	R46SZ	.080	3P	3/4P	1/8	3.78/4	15.5	16.4
18436572	VD	8B@500	600[6]	6B[16]	AC	R45TS	.045	1P	3/4P	1/16	3.78/4	15.3	16.2
18436572	VD	4B@500	600	6B[16]	AC	R45TS	.045	3P	1/2P	3/16	3.78/4	14.8	15.6
18436572	VD	8B@500	NA	8B[16]	AC	R45TS	.045	1P	3/4P	1/16	3.78/4	15.1	16
18436572	VD	20B@1100	NA	20B[19]	AC	R46SZ	.080	3P	3/4P	1/8	3.78/4	13.8	14.6
18436572	VD	NA	NA	NA	NA	NA	NA	3P	3/4P	1/8	7.1/7.5	17	18
18436572	VD	24B@1100	NA	20B[19]	AC	R46SZ	.080	3P	3/4P	1/8	3.78/4	14.9	15.7
18436572	VD	24B@1100	NA	20B[19]	AC	R46SZ	.080	0	3/16P	1/8	3.78/4	16.3	17.2
1342	CP	15B@900	900	15B[24]	CH	RN12Y	.035	NA	9/32	3/32[25]	3.78/4	7.6	8
153624	VD	12B@700	700[29]	8B[8]	CH	RBL16Y	.035	2-1/2P	1/4P	1/8	3.78/4	11.4	12
153624	VD	12B@700	700[29]	8B[8]	CH	RBL16Y	.035	3/4P	1/4P	1/8	3.78/4	12.5	13
18436572	VD	16B@700	700[32]	16B	CH	RN12Y	.035	2-1/2P	1/4P	1/8	3.78/4	15.1	16
18436572	VD	16B@700	NA	16B	CH	RN12Y	.035	3/4P	1/4P	1/8	3.78/4	15.6	16.5
18436572	VD	20B@750	NA	6B[8]	CH	RN12Y	.035	2-1/2P	1/4P	1/8	3.78/4	15.1	16
18436572	VD	20B@750	NA	8B[8]	CH	RN12Y	.035	3/4P	1/4P	1/8	3.78/4	15.1	16
18436572	VD	20B@750	NA	NA	CH	RJ13Y	.035	3/4P	1/4P	1/8	3.78/4	15.6	16.5
1342	CP	12B@1000	1000	12B	AC	R43TSX	.060	3/4N	1/4N	1/16[25]	2.84/3	10.1	10.7
1342	CP	14B@1000	1000	12B	AC	R43TSX	.060	0	3/4P	1/16	2.84/3	11.6	12.3
165432	VD	15B@600	800	15B[6]	AC	R46TSX[38]	.060	3/4N	1/4N	1/16[25]	3.78/4	11.4	12
165432	VD	15B@600	800	15B[11]	AC	R46TSX[38]	.060	0	3/4P	1/16	3.78/4	12.9	13.7
165432	VD	15B@600	800	15B[11]	AC	R46TSX[38]	.060	3P	1/2P	1/16[40]	3.78/4	12.8	13.6
165432	VD	15B@600	800	15B	AC	R46TSX[38]	.060	0	1P	3/16	3.78/4	15	15.8
165432	VD	15B@600	NA	15B[6]	AC	R46TSX	.060	3P	3/4P	1/8	3.78/4	12.1	12.8
18436572	VD	12B@550[42]	NA	NA	AC	R46TSX	.060	3P	1/2P	1/16[40]	4.7/5	20.6	21.8
18436572	VD	12B@550	NA	NA	AC	R46TSX	.060	3P	3/4P	1/8	4.7/5	19.8	20.9
18436572	VD	4B@600	700	6B[16]	AC	R45TS	.045	3/4N	1/4N	1/16	3.78/4	15.7	16.6
18436572	VD	4B@600	600	6B[11]	AC	R45TS	.045	0	3/4P	1/16	3.78/4	15.7	16.6
18436572	VD	4B@500	NA	6B[11]	AC	R46TSX	.060	3P	1/2P	1/16[40]	3.78/4	15.2	16.1
18436572	VD	4B@500	600[44]	6B[11]	AC	R46TSX	.060	0	1P	3/16	3.78/4	16.6	17.5
18436572	VD	8B@500[11]	NA	8B[11]	AC	R45TS	.045	0	3/4P	1/16	3.78/4	15.7	16.6
18436572	VD	8B@500	700[11]	8B[11]	AC	R45TS	.045	0	1P	3/16	3.78/4	16.5	17.5
18436572	VD	15B@600	NA	NA	AC	R46TSX	.060	3P	3/4P	1/8	3.78/4	14.3	15.1
18436572	VD	20B@1100[11]	NA	20B[11]	AC	R45SX	.060	3P	3/4P	1/8	3.78/4	15.2	16.1
18436572	VD	16B@675	NA	NA	AC	R45TSX	.060	0	1P	3/16	4.7/5	17.4	18.4
18436572	VD	16B@675	NA	NA	AC	R45TSX	.060	3P	3/4P	1/8	4.7/5	18.8	19.9
18436572	VD	20B@1100[11]	NA	20B[11]	AC	R46SZ	.080	0	1P	3/16	3.78/4	19.3	20.4
18436572	VD	20B@1100[11]	NA	20B[11]	AC	R46SZ	.080	3P	3/4P	1/8	3.78/4	15.4	16.3

16 — @500
17 — Also 160/119@4000
18 — 98 – 3023/119
19 — @1100
20 — Diesel Compression Ignition Engine
21 — Cal. 70/50@5600
22 — Minimum Pressure. Also 25 psi (4 and 6) or 40 psi (8) Maximum Variation
23 — Int. .008 in./0.20 mm, Exh. .012 in./0.30 mm
24 — @900
25 — Toe-Out

26 — 4-Door – 2863/112.7
27 — Also 110/81.7@3600, Cal. 90/66.9@3600
28 — Int. .010 in./0.25 mm Exh. .020 in./0.50 mm
29 — 12B
30 — 4-Door – 2982/117.4
31 — Cal. – 155/116@4000
32 — 16B
33 — Also 175/130@4000, Cal. 160/119@4000
34 — 175 hp – 16B

35 — Cal. – 170/127@4000, and 160/119@3600
36 — Cal. – LS6 Engine
37 — 14B
38 — Cal. – R45TSX
39 — L37 Engine – R45TSX
40 — Grand Prix – 1/8 in.
41 — Also L37 Engine – 151/112@3800
42 — L37 Engine – @750
43 — Cal. – 135/100@3800
44 — 4B
45 — Also 180/134@3600

1979

	Wheelbase (mm)	Wheelbase (in.)	No. of Cylinders Bore and Stroke (in.)	Displacement (litres)	Displacement (cu. in.)	Valve and Cylinder Arrangement	Net Brake Horsepower @ rpm	Net Power (kW)	Compression Pressure (psi)	Valve Clearance
AMC — Spirit, AMX, Concord	2438	96[1]	4-3.4055x3.228	2.0	121	IOC	80@5000	60	135	H[2]
Spirit, AMX, Concord	2438	96[1]	6-3.75x3.50	3.8	232	IO	90@3400	67.1	140	HY
Spirit, AMX, Concord	2438	96[1]	6-3.75x3.90	4.23	258	IO	110@3200	82	150	HY
Pacer	2540	100	6-3.75x3.90	4.23	258	IO	110@3200	82	150	HY
Spirit, AMX, Concord	2438	96[1]	6-3.75x3.90	4.23	258	IO	100@3400	74.6	150	HY
Pacer	2540	100	6-3.75x3.90	4.23	258	IO	100@3400	74.6	150	HY
Spirit AMX, Concord	2438	96[1]	8-3.75x3.44	5.0	304	VO	125@3200	93.2	140	HY
Pacer	2540	100	8-3.75x3.44	5.0	304	VO	125@3200	93.2	140	HY
Buick — Century Special, Custom, Regal	2745	108.1	6-3.50x3.40	3.2	196	VO	105@4000	78	140[7]	HY
Skyhawk, S	2464	97	6-3.80x3.40	3.8	231	VO	115@3800	85.4	140[7]	HY
Skylark, S, S/R	2819	111	6-3.80x3.40	3.8	231	VO	115@3800	85.4	140[7]	HY
Century Special, Custom, Regal	2745	108.1	6-3.80x3.40	3.8	231	VO	115@3800[9]	85.4[9]	140[7]	HY
LeSabre, Limited, Sport Coupe	2943	115.9	6-3.80x3.40	3.8	231	VO	115@3800[12]	85.4[12]	140[7]	HY
Riviera Sport Coupe	2895	114	6-3.80x3.40	3.8	231	VO	185@4200	137.5	140[7]	HY
Century Special, Custom, Regal	2745	108.1	8-4.0x3.0	4.9	301	VO	140@3600[13]	104[13]	140[7]	HY
LeSabre, Limited	2943	115.9	8-4.0x3.0	4.9	301	VO	140@3600	104	140[7]	HY
Skylark, S, S/R	2819	111	8-3.736x3.48	5.0	305	VO	130@3200	96.6	155	HY
Century Special, Custom, Regal	2745	108.1	8-3.736x3.48	5.0	305	VO	155@4000	115.2	155	HY
Skylark, S, S/R	2819	111	8-4.0x3.48	5.7	350	VO	160@3800	119	150	HY
LeSabre, Limited	2943	115.9	8-3.80x3.85	5.7	350	VO	155@3400	115.2	150	HY
LeSabre, Limited	2943	115.9	8-4.057x3.385	5.7	350	VO	160@3800	119	150	HY
Electra	3020	118.9	8-3.80x3.85	5.7	350	VO	155@3400	115.2	150	HY
Electra, Riviera	3020	118.9[15]	8-4.057x3.385	5.7	350	VO	160@3800	119	150	HY
Electra	3020	118.9	8-4.351x3.385	6.6	403	VO	175@3600	130	155[7]	HY
Cadillac — Eldorado, Seville	2895	113.9[16]	8-4.057x3.385	5.7	350	VO	170@4200	126	100[17]	HY
Eldorado, Seville	2895	113.9[16]	8-4.057x3.385[19]	5.7	350[19]	VO	125@3600	93	275[7]	HY
Brougham, Coupe/Sedan de Villes, Fleetwoods	3085	121.5[20]	8-4.082x4.060	7.0	425	VO	180@4000	134	155[7]	HY
Brougham, Coupe/Sedan deVilles	3085	121.5	8-4.082x4.060	7.0	425	VO	195@3800	145	155[7]	HY
Chevrolet — Chevette	2394	94.3[21]	4-3.23x2.98	1.6	98	IOC	70@5200[22]	52[22]	145	HY
Monza	2464	97	4-4.0x3.0	2.5	151	IO	90@4000	66.9	145[7]	HY
Monza	2464	97	4-4.0x3.0	2.5	151	IO	85@4400	63.2	145[7]	HY
Monza	2464	97	6-3.5x3.4	3.2	196	VO	105@4000	78	140[7]	HY
Malibu, Classic, Monte Carlo	2745	108.1	6-3.50x3.48	3.3	200	VO	94@4000	70	130[7]	HY
Monza	2464	97	6-3.80x3.40	3.8	231	VO	115@3800	85.4	140[7]	HY
Malibu, Classic, Monte Carlo	2745	108.1	6-3.80x3.40	3.8	231	VO	115@3800	85.4	140[7]	HY
Camaro, Berlinetta	2743	108	6-3.875x3.53	4.1	250	IO	115@3800[31]	85.4[31]	130	HY
Nova, Custom	2819	111	6-3.875x3.53	4.1	250	IO	115@3800[31]	85.4[31]	130	HY
Impala, Caprice Classic	2945	116	6-3.875x3.53	4.1	250	IO	115@3800[31]	85.4[31]	130	HY
Malibu, Classic, Monte Carlo	2745	108.1	8-3.50x3.48	4.4	267	VO	125@3800	93	150	HY
Monza	2464	97	8-3.736x3.48	5.0	305	VO	130@3200[32]	96.6[32]	155	HY
Camaro, Berlinetta, Nova, Custom	2743	108[33]	8-3.736x3.48	5.0	305	VO	130@3200[32]	96.6[32]	155	HY
Impala, Caprice Classic	2945	116	8-3.736x3.48	5.0	305	VO	130@3200[32]	96.6[32]	155	HY
Malibu, Classic, Monte Carlo	2745	108.1	8-3.736x3.48	5.0	305	VO	160@4000[35]	119[35]	155	HY
Camaro, Berlinetta, Nova, Custom	2743	108[33]	8-4.0x3.48	5.7	350	VO	170@3800[36]	126[36]	150	HY
Impala, Caprice Classic	2945	116	8-4.0x3.48	5.7	350	VO	170@3800[36]	126[36]	150	HY
Camaro, Berlinetta	2743	108	8-4.0x3.48	5.7	350	VO	175@4000[37]	130[37]	150	HY
Corvette	2489	98	8-4.0x3.48	5.7	350	VO	195@4000	144.9	150	HY
Corvette	2489	98	8-4.0x3.48	5.7	350	VO	225@5200	167.2	150	HY
Chrysler — LeBaron, Medallion	2863	112.7	6-3.40x4.12	3.7	225	IO	100@3600[38]	75[38]	100[39]	H[40]
LeBaron, Medallion	2863	112.7	6-3.40x4.12	3.7	225	IO	110@3600	80	100[39]	H[40]
Newport	3010	118.5	6-3.40x4.12	3.7	225	IO	110@3600	80	100[39]	H[40]
LeBaron, Medallion	2863	112.7	8-3.91x3.31	5.2	318	VO	135@4000[35]	100[35]	100[39]	HY
Cordoba	2919	114.9	8-3.91x3.31	5.2	318	VO	135@4000[35]	100[35]	100[39]	HY
Newport, New Yorker	3010	118.5	8-3.91x3.31	5.2	318	VO	135@4000[35]	100[35]	100[39]	HY
LeBaron, Medallion	2863	112.7	8-4.0x3.58	5.9	360	VO	150@3600[37]	110[37]	100[39]	HY
Cordoba	2919	114.9	8-4.0x3.58	5.9	360	VO	150@3600[37]	110[37]	100[39]	HY
Newport, New Yorker	3010	118.5	8-4.0x3.58	5.9	360	VO	150@3600	110	100[39]	HY
Cordoba "300"	2919	114.9	8-4.0x3.58	5.9	360	VO	195@4000[42]	145[42]	100[39]	HY
New Yorker	3010	118.9	8-4.0x3.58	5.9	360	VO	195@4000[42]	145[42]	100[39]	HY
Dodge — Omni	2456	96.7[43]	4-3.13x3.40	1.7	104.7	IOC	70@5200[44]	52[44]	100[39]	H[45]
Aspen, Diplomat, Medallion	2863	112.7[46]	6-3.40x4.12	3.7	225	IO	100@3600[38]	75[38]	100[39]	H[40]
Aspen, Diplomat, Medallion	2863	112.7[46]	6-3.40x4.12	3.7	225	IO	110@3600	80	100[39]	H[40]
St. Regis	3010	118.5	6-3.40x4.12	3.7	225	IO	110@3600	80	100[39]	H[40]
Aspen, Diplomat, Medallion	2863	112.7[46]	8-3.91x3.31	5.2	318	VO	135@4000[35]	100[35]	100[39]	HY
St. Regis, Magnum XE	3010	118.5[47]	8-3.91x3.31	5.2	318	VO	135@4000[35]	100[35]	100[39]	HY
Diplomat, Medallion	2863	112.7	8-4.0x3.58	5.9	360	VO	150@3600	110	100[39]	HY
St. Regis, Magnum XE	3010	118.5[47]	8-4.0x3.58	5.9	360	VO	150@3600[37]	110[37]	100[39]	HY
Aspen, Diplomat, Medallion	2863	112.7[46]	8-4.0x3.58	5.9	360	VO	195@4000[42]	145[42]	100[39]	HY
St. Regis, Magnum XE	3010	118.5[47]	8-4.0x3.58	5.9	360	VO	195@4000[42]	145[42]	100[39]	HY

ABBREVIATIONS — FOOTNOTES

AC — AC Spark Plugs
B — Before Top Dead Center
CH — Champion Spark Plugs
CP — Crankshaft Pulley
H — Hot Engine
HY — Hydraulic Lifters
IO — In-Line Engine — Overhead Valves
IOC — In-Line Engine — Overhead Camshaft
N — Negative

NA — Not Available/Not Applicable
P — Positive
VD — Vibration Damper
VO — V-Type Engine, Overhead Valves

1 — Concord — 2743/108, Pacer — 2540/100
2 — Int. — .008 in./0.20 mm
　　Exh. — .018 in./0.45 mm
3 — Automatic Trans. Only
4 — Equivalent Resistor Type, Some Engines
5 — 4B
6 — @600; Manual Trans. — 4B@700

7 — Lowest Cylinder Must Be At Least 70 Percent of Highest
8 — 5B
9 — Century Turbo — 175/130@4000
　　Regal Turbo — 170/126.3@4000
10 — Turbo — 15B@650
11 — Turbo — R44TSX
12 — Turbo — 170/126.3@4000
13 — Also 150/111.5@4000
14 — 150 hp Engine — R45TSX
15 — Riviera — 2895/114
16 — Seville — 2903/114.3

Tuneup Specifications

Firing Order	Timing Mark Location	Initial Ignition Timing @ rpm (auto. trans.)	Ignition Timing (rpm-manual trans.)	Ignition Timing (California)	Spark Plugs Make	Spark Plugs Model	Gap (in.)	Caster, Power Steering (deg.)	Camber, Right Wheel (deg.)	Toe-In (in.)	Crankcase Capacity (L/qt.)	Cooling System Capacity (L)	Cooling System Capacity (qt.)
1342	CP	12B@800	900	8B[3]	CH	N8L[4]	.035	1P	1/4P	1/8	3.3/3.5	6.15	6.5
153624	VD	10B@550	600	NA	CH	N13L[4]	.035	1P	1/4P	1/8	3.78/4	10.4	11
153624	VD	8B@600	700[5]	8B[6]	CH	N13L[4]	.035	1P	1/4P	1/8	3.78/4	10.4	11
153624	VD	8B@600	700[5]	8B[6]	CH	N13L[4]	.035	2P	1/4P	1/8	3.78/4	13.24	14
153624	VD	NA	NA	8B[6]	CH	N13L[4]	.035	1P	1/4P	1/8	3.78/4	13.24	14
153624	VD	NA	NA	8B[6]	CH	N13L[4]	.035	2P	1/4P	1/8	3.78/4	13.24	14
18436572	VD	8B@600	800[8]	NA	CH	N12Y[4]	.035	1P	1/4P	1/8	3.78/4	16.1	17
18436572	VD	8B@600	NA	NA	CH	N12Y[4]	.035	2P	1/4P	1/8	3.78/4	17	18
165432	VD	15B@600	600	NA	AC	R46TSX	.060	3P	1/2P	1/4	3.78/4	12.6	13.3
165432	VD	15B@600	600	15B	AC	R46TSX	.060	3/4N	1/4P	1/16	3.78/4	12.3	13
165432	VD	15B@600	600	NA	AC	R46TSX	.060	1P	3/4P	1/16	3.78/4	13.7	14.5
165432	VD	15B@600[10]	600	15B[3]	AC	R46TSX[11]	.060	3P	1/2P	1/4	3.78/4	12.6	13.3
165432	VD	15B@600[10]	NA	15B[3]	AC	R46TSX[11]	.060	3P	13/16P	1/8	3.78/4	12.6	13.3
165432	VD	15B@650	NA	15B[3]	AC	R44TSX	.060	3P	13/16P	1/8	3.78/4	13.8	14.6
18436572	VD	12B@500	NA	NA	AC	R46TSX[14]	.060	3P	1/2P	1/4	4.7/5	19.8	20.9
18436572	VD	12B@500	NA	NA	AC	R46TSX	.060	3P	13/16P	1/8	4.7/5	19.8	20.9
18436572	VD	4B@500	NA	NA	AC	R45TS	.045	1P	3/4P	1/16	3.78/4	15.1	16
18436572	VD	4B@500	NA	4B[3]	AC	R43TS	.045	3P	1/2P	1/4	3.78/4	18	19
18436572	VD	8B@500	NA	8B[3]	AC	R45TS	.045	1P	3/4P	1/16	3.78/4	15.1	16
18436572	VD	15B@600	NA	NA	AC	R46TSX	.060	3P	13/16P	1/8	3.78/4	13.8	14.6
18436572	VD	20B@1100	NA	20B[3]	AC	R46SZ	.080	3P	13/16P	1/8	3.78/4	13.8	14.6
18436572	VD	15B@600	NA	NA	AC	R46TSX	.060	3P	13/16P	1/8	3.78/4	13.8	14.6
18436572	VD	20B@1100	NA	20B[3]	AC	R46SZ	.080	3P	13/16P	1/8	3.78/4	13.8	14.6
18436572	VD	24B@1100	NA	20B[3]	AC	R46SZ	.080	3P	13/16P	1/8	3.78/4	14.9	15.7
18436572	VD	10B@600	NA	10B[3]	AC	R47SX	.060	2P[18]	0	1/16[18]	3.78/4	16.2	17.2
18436572	VD	NA	NA	NA	NA	NA	NA	2P[18]	0	1/16[18]	7.10/7.5	17.4	18.4
15634278	VD	23B@1600	NA	23B[3]	AC	R45NSX	.060	3P	1/2P	1/8	3.78/4	19.7	20.8
15634278	VD	18B@1400	NA	18B[3]	AC	R45NSX	.060	3P	1/2P	1/8	3.78/4	19.7	20.8
1342	VD	18B@1000	750[23]	12B[24]	AC	R42TS	.035	1/2P	1/4P	1/16		8.7	9.2
1342	CP	12B@750	1000	NA	AC	R43TSX	.060	3/4N	1/4P	1/16[25]	2.9/3	10.7	11.3
1342	CP	NA	NA	14B[26]	AC	R43TSX	.060	3/4N	1/4P	1/16[25]	2.9/3	10.7	11.3
165432	VD	15B@600	600	NA	AC	R46TSX	.060	3/4N	1/4P	1/16[25]	3.78/4	11	11.6
165432	VD	14B@600	600[27]	NA	AC	R45TS	.045	3P	1/2P	1/8P	3.78/4	17.8	18.8
165432	VD	NA	NA	15B[29]	AC	R46TSX	.060	3/4N	1/4P	1/16[25]	3.78/4	11	11.6
165432	VD	NA[28]	NA[28]	15B[29]	AC	R46TSX	.060	3P	1/2P	1/8	3.78/4	14.6	15.4
153624	VD	10B@550	850	6B[30]	AC	R46TS	.035	1P	1P	1/8	3.78/4	13.8	14.6
153624	VD	10B@550	850	6B[30]	AC	R46TS	.035	1P	13/16P	1/8	3.78/4	12.9	13.6
153624	VD	10B@550	NA	6B	AC	R46TS	.035	3P	13/16P	1/8	3.78/4	13.4	14.2
18436572	VD	10B@550	750[5]	NA	AC	R45TS	.045	3P	1/2P	1/8	3.78/4	20.2	21.4
18436572	VD	4B@500	600	4B[3]	AC	R45TS	.045	3/4N	1/4P	1/16[25]	3.78/4	15.4	16.3
18436572	VD	4B@500	600	4B[3]	AC	R45TS	.045	1P	1P[34]	1/8	3.78/4	16.4	17.3
18436572	VD	4B@500	600	4B[3]	AC	R45TS	.045	3P	13/16P	1/8	3.78/4	15.7	16.6
18436572	VD	4B@500	600	4B[3]	AC	R43TS	.045	3P	1/2P	1/8	3.78/4	18	19
18436572	VD	6B@600	700	8B[3]	AC	R45TS	.045	1P	1P[34]	1/8	3.78/4	16.4	17.4
18436572	VD	6B@600	NA	8B[3]	AC	R45TS	.045	3P	13/16P	1/8	3.78/4	15.7	16.6
18436572	VD	6B@600	700	8B[3]	AC	R45TS	.045	1P	1P	1/8	3.78/4	16.4	17.4
18436572	VD	6B@700	900	8B[3]	AC	R45TS	.045	2—1/4P	3/4P	1/4	3.78/4	19.6	20.7
18436572	VD	12B@700	900[23]	NA	AC	R45TS	.045	2—1/4P	3/4P	1/4	3.78/4	19.6	20.7
153624	VD	12B@700	700[23]	15B[41]	CH	RBL16Y	.035	2—1/2P	1/4P	1/8	3.78/4	10.9	11.5
153624	VD	12B@750	NA	NA	CH	RBL16Y	.035	2—1/2P	1/4P	1/8	3.78/4	11.8	12.5
153624	VD	12B@750	NA	NA	CH	RBL16Y	.035	3/4P	1/4P	1/8	3.78/4	10.9	11.5
18436572	VD	16B@750	NA	16B[3]	CH	RN12Y	.035	2—1/2P	1/4P	1/8	3.78/4	14.2	15
18436572	VD	16B@750	NA	16B[3]	CH	RN12Y	.035	3/4P	1/4P	1/8	3.78/4	14.2	15
18436572	VD	16B@750	NA	16B[3]	CH	RN12Y	.035	3/4P	1/4P	1/8	3.78/4	16.6	17.5
18436572	VD	16B@750	NA	16B[3]	CH	RN12Y	.035	2—1/2P	1/4P	1/8	3.78/4	14.2	15
18436572	VD	16B@750	NA	16B[3]	CH	RN12Y	.035	3/4P	1/4P	1/8	3.78/4	15.1	16
18436572	VD	16B@750	NA	16B[3]	CH	RN12Y	.035	3/4P	1/4P	1/8	3.78/4	15.1	16
18436572	VD	16B@750	NA	16B[3]	CH	RN12Y	.035	3/4P	1/4P	1/8	3.78/4	15.1	16
1342	CP	15B@900	900	15B	CH	RN12Y	.037	NA	5/16P	1/8[25]	3.78/4	5.7	6
153624	VD	12B@700	700	15B[41]	CH	RBL16Y	.035	2—1/2P	1/4P	1/8	3.78/4	10.9	11.5
153624	VD	12B@750	NA	12B[41]	CH	RBL16Y	.035	2—1/2P	1/4P	1/8	3.78/4	10.9	11.5
153624	VD	12B@750	NA	NA	CH	RBL16Y	.035	3/4P	1/4P	1/8	3.78/4	10.9	11.5
18436572	VD	16B@750	NA	16B[3]	CH	RN12Y	.035	2—1/2P	1/4P	1/8	3.78/4	14.2	15
18436572	VD	16B@750	NA	16B[3]	CH	RN12Y	.035	3/4P	1/4P	1/8	3.78/4	14.2	15
18436572	VD	16B@750	NA	16B[3]	CH	RN12Y	.035	2—1/2P	1/4P	1/8	3.78/4	14.2	15
18436572	VD	16B@750	NA	16B[3]	CH	RN12Y	.035	3/4P	1/4P	1/8	3.78/4	15.1	16
18436572	VD	16B@750	NA	16B[3]	CH	RN12Y	.035	2—1/2P	1/4P	1/8	3.78/4	14.2	15
18436572	VD	16B@750	NA	16B[3]	CH	RN12Y	.035	3/4P	1/4P	1/8	3.78/4	15.1	16

17 — Minimum psi
18 — Eldorado – 0
19 — Diesel Compression Ignition Engine
20 — Fleetwood Limos – 3670/144.5
21 — 4-Door – 2471/97.3
22 — High Output – 74/55@5200
23 — 12B
24 — Manual Transmission Only
25 — Toe-Out
26 — Auto. Trans. – 14B@1000
Manual Trans. – 12B@1000
27 — 8B

28 — Monte Carlo – Auto. Trans. – 14B@600
Manual Trans. – 8B@600
29 — @600; Manual Trans. – 15B@600
30 — @550
31 — Cal. – 90/67@3600
32 — Cal. – 125/93@3200
33 — Nova – 2819/111
34 — Nova –13/16P
35 — Cal. – 155/116@4000
36 — Cal. – 165/122.6@3800
37 — Cal. – 170/126@4000
38 — Cal. – 90/65@3600

39 — Minimum Pressure. Also 25 psi (4 and 6)
or 40 psi (8) Maximum Variation
40 — Int. – .010 in./0.25 mm
Exh. – .020 in./0.50 mm
41 — @750. Manual Trans. – 12B
42 — Cal. – 190/140@4000
43 — 4-Door – 2520/99.2
44 — Cal. – 65/48@5200
45 — Int. – .010 in./0.25 mm
Exh. – .018 in./ 0.45 mm
46 — Aspen – 2-Door – 2761/108.7
47 — Magnum XE – 2919/114.9

1979

	Wheelbase (mm)	Wheelbase (in.)	No. of Cylinders Bore and Stroke (in.)	Displacement (litres)	Displacement (cu. in.)	Valve and Cylinder Arrangement	Net Brake Horsepower @ rpm	Net Power (kW)	Compression Pressure (psi)	Valve Clearance
Ford — Pinto	2400	94.5	4—3.781x3.126	2.3	140	IOC	88@4800	66	80[1]	HY
Mustang, Ghia, Fairmont, Futura	2550	100.4[4]	4—3.781x3.126	2.3	140	IOC	88@4800	66	80[1]	HY
Mustang, Ghia[7]	2550	100.4	4—3.781x3.126	2.3	140[7]	IOC	NA	NA	80[1]	HY
Pinto	2400	94.5	6—3.66x2.70	2.8	170.8	VO	102@4400	75.8	80[1]	C[10]
Mustang, Ghia	2550	100.4	6—3.66x2.70	2.8	170.8	VO	109@4800	81	80[1]	C[10]
Fairmont, Futura	2550	100.4	6—3.682x3.126	3.3	200	IO	85@3600	63	175[1]	HY
Granada, Ghia, ESS	2791	109.9	6—3.68x3.91	4.1	250	IO	97@3200	72	175[1]	HY
Mustang, Ghia, Fairmont, Futura	2550	100.4[4]	8—4.0x3.0	5.0	302	VO	140@3600	104	150[1]	HY
Granada, Ghia, ESS	2791	109.9	8—4.0x3.0	5.0	302	VO	137@3600	102	150[1]	HY
LTD II, S	2893	113.9[18]	8—4.0x3.0	5.0	302	VO	133@3600	99	150[1]	HY
LTD, Landau	2906	114.4	8—4.0x3.0	5.0	302	VO	129@3600	96	150[1]	HY
Thunderbird	2893	113.9	8—4.0x3.0	5.0	302	VO	133@3400	99	150[1]	HY
LTD II, S	2893	113.9[18]	8—4.0x3.50	5.8	351M	VO	151@3600	113	170[1]	HY
Thunderbird	2893	113.9	8—4.0x3.50	5.8	351M	VO	151@3600	113	170[1]	HY
LTD, Landau	2906	114.4	8—4.0x3.50	5.8	351W	VO	142@3200	106	160[1]	HY
Thunderbird	2893	113.9	8—4.0x3.50	5.8	351W	VO	135@3200	101	160[1]	HY
Lincoln — Versailles	2791	109.9	8—4.0x3.0	5.0	302	VO	130@3600	97	150[1]	HY
Mark V	3056	120.3	8—4.0x4.0	6.6	400	VO	159@3400	119	180[1]	HY
Lincoln	3231	127.2	8—4.0x4.0	6.6	400	VO	159@3400	119	180[1]	HY
Mercury — Bobcat	2400	94.5	4—3.781x3.126	2.3	140	IOC	88@4800	66	80[1]	HY
Zephyr, Z-7	2680	105.5	4—3.781x3.126	2.3	140	IOC	88@4800	66	80[1]	HY
Capri, Ghia	2550	100.4	4—3.781x3.126	2.3	140	IOC	88@4800	66	80[1]	HY
Capri, Ghia[7]	2550	100.4	4—3.781x3.126	2.3	140[7]	IOC	NA	NA	80[1]	HY
Bobcat	2400	94.5	6—3.66x2.70	2.8	170.8	VO	102@4400	75.8	80[1]	C[10]
Capri, Ghia	2550	100.4	6—3.66x2.70	2.8	170.8	VO	109@4800	81	80[1]	C[10]
Zephyr, Z-7	2680	105.5	6—3.682x3.126	3.3	200	IO	85@3600	63	175[1]	HY
Monarch, Ghia, ESS	2791	109.9	6—3.68x3.91	4.1	250	IO	97@3200	72	175[1]	HY
Zephyr, Z-7	2680	105.5	8—4.0x3.0	5.0	302	VO	140@3600	104	150[1]	HY
Capri, Ghia	2550	100.4	8—4.0x3.0	5.0	302	VO	140@3600	104	150[1]	HY
Monarch, Ghia, ESS	2791	109.9	8—4.0x3.0	5.0	302	VO	137@3600	102	150[1]	HY
Cougar, XR7	2893	113.9[18]	8—4.0x3.0	5.0	302	VO	133@3400	99	150[1]	HY
Marquis, Brougham, Grand Marquis	2906	114.4	8—4.0x3.0	5.0	302	VO	129@3600	96	150[1]	HY
Cougar, XR7	2893	113.9[18]	8—4.0x3.50	5.8	351M	VO	151@3600	113	170[1]	HY
Marquis, Brougham, Grand Marquis	2906	114.4	8—4.0x3.50	5.8	351W	VO	138@3200	103	170[1]	HY
Cougar XR7	2893	113.9[18]	8—4.0x3.50	5.8	351W	VO	135@3200	101	170[1]	HY
Oldsmobile — Starfire, SX	2464	97	4—4.0x3.0	2.5	151	IO	85@4400	63	145[19]	HY
Omega, Brougham, Starfire, SX	2819	111[22]	6—3.80x3.40	3.8	231	VO	115@3600	85.4	140[19]	HY
Delta 88, Royale, Cutlass	2945	116[24]	6—3.80x3.40	3.8	231	VO	115@3600	85.4	140[19]	HY
Cutlass Salon, Supreme, Brougham[28]	2745	108.1	8—3.50x3.385	4.3	260[28]	VO	90@3600	67	275[19]	HY
Delta 88, Royale, Cutlass	2945	116[24]	8—3.50x3.385	4.3	260	VO	105@3600	78	150[19]	HY
Delta 88, Royale	2945	116	8—4.0x3.0	4.9	301	VO	135@3800	101	140[19]	HY
Cutlass, Omega, Starfire	2745	108.1[22]	8—3.736x3.48	5.0	305	VO	160@4000[32]	119[32]	155	HY
Delta 88, 98, Toronado[28]	2945	116[35]	8—4.057x3.385	5.7	350[28]	VO	125@3600[29]	93[29]	275[19]	HY
Cutlass, Omega	2745	108.1[22]	8—4.0x3.48	5.7	350	VO	160@3600	119	150	HY
Delta 88, 98, Toronado	2945	116[35]	8—4.057x3.385	5.7	350	VO	160@3600	119	150	HY
Luxury, Regency 98	2945	116	8—4.351x3.385	6.6	403	VO	175@3600	130	155[19]	HY
Plymouth — Horizon, TC3	2456	96.7[41]	4—3.13x3.40	1.7	104.7	IOC	70@5200[42]	52[42]	100[43]	H[44]
Volaré	2761	108.7[45]	6—3.40x4.12	3.7	225	IO	100@3600[46]	75[46]	100[43]	H[47]
Volaré	2761	108.7[45]	6—3.40x4.12	3.7	225	IO	110@3600	80	100[43]	H[47]
Volaré	2761	108.7[45]	8—3.91x3.31	5.2	318	VO	135@4000	100	100[43]	HY
Volaré	2761	108.7[45]	8—3.91x3.31	5.2	318	VO	155@4000	115	100[43]	HY
Volaré	2761	108.7	8—4.0x3.58	5.9	360[49]	VO	145@4000[50]	145[50]	100[43]	HY
Pontiac — Sunbird	2464	97	4—4.0x3.0	2.5	151	IO	90@4400[51]	66.9[51]	140[19]	HY
Sunbird	2464	97	6—3.80x3.40	3.8	231	VO	115@3800	85.4	140[19]	HY
Grand Prix, LJ, LeMans, Grand Am	2745	108.1	6—3.80x3.40	3.8	231	VO	115@3800	85.4	140[19]	HY
Firebird, Esprit, Phoenix, LJ	2748	108.2[53]	6—3.80x3.40	3.8	231	VO	115@3800	85.4	140[19]	HY
Catalina	2945	116	6—3.80x3.40	3.8	231	VO	135@3800	100.3	140[19]	HY
Catalina, Bonneville, Brougham	2945	116	8—4.0x3.0	4.9	301	VO	150@4000[54]	111.5[54]	140[19]	HY
Grand Prix, LJ, SJ, LeMans, Grand Am	2745	108.1	8—4.0x3.0	4.9	301	VO	150@4000[54]	111.5[54]	140[19]	HY
Firebird, Esprit, Formula, Trans Am	2748	108.2	8—4.0x3.0	4.9	301	VO	150@4000[54]	111.5[54]	140[19]	HY
Sunbird	2464	97	8—3.736x3.48	5.0	305	VO	125@3200[55]	93[55]	155	HY
Firebird, Esprit, Formula, Phoenix, LJ	2748	108.2[53]	8—3.736x3.48	5.0	305	VO	125@3200	93	155	HY
Grand Prix, LJ, SJ, LeMans, Grand LeMans	2745	108.1	8—3.736x3.48	5.0	305	VO	155@4000	116	155	HY
Catalina, Bonneville, Brougham	2945	116	8—4.057x3.385	5.7	350	VO	160@3600	119	150	HY
Catalina, Bonneville, Brougham	2945	116	8—3.80x3.85	5.7	350	VO	155@3400	116	150	HY
Firebird, Esprit, Formula, Phoenix, LJ	2748	108.2[53]	8—4.0x3.48	5.7	350	VO	165@3800	122.5	150	HY
Firebird Formula, Trans Am	2748	108.2	8—4.1212x3.75	6.5	400	VO	220@4000	162.7	140[19]	HY
Catalina, Bonneville, Brougham	2945	116	8—4.351x3.385	6.6	403	VO	175@3600	130	140[19]	HY
Firebird Formula, Trans Am	2748	108.2	8—4.351x3.385	6.6	403	VO	185@3600	137.5	140[19]	HY

ABBREVIATIONS — FOOTNOTES

AC — AC Spark Plugs
AU — Autolite Spark Plugs
B — Before Top Dead Center
C — Cold Engine
CH — Champion Spark Plugs
CP — Crankshaft Pulley
EEC — Electronic Engine Control
FI — Fuel Injection
H — Hot Engine
HY — Hydraulic Lifters
IO — In-Line Engine — Overhead Valves
IOC — In-Line Engine — Overhead Camshaft
MO — Motorcraft Spark Plugs

N — Negative
NA — Not Available/Not Applicable
P — Positive
VD — Vibration Damper
VO — V-Type Engine, Overhead Valves
1 — Lowest Cylinder Must Be At Least 75 Percent of Highest
2 — 6B
3 — Manual Trans. — 6B@750
4 — Fairmont, Futura — 2680/105.5
5 — Fairmont, Futura — 7/8P
6 — Fairmont, Futura — 3/8P
7 — Turbocharged
8 — 2B

9 — Manual Trans. Only
10 — Intake .014 in./0.36 mm Exhaust, .016 in./0.41 mm
11 — @600
12 — 8B
13 — Cal. Engine — .060
14 — 4B
15 — Automatic Trans.
16 — 12B
17 — Cal. Engine — ASF52-6/.060
18 — 4-Door — 2995/117.9
19 — Lowest Cylinder Must Be At Least 70 Percent Of Highest
20 — With Ignition Module Disconnected

Tuneup Specifications

Firing Order	Timing Mark Location	Initial Ignition Timing @ rpm (auto. trans.)	Ignition Timing (rpm-manual trans.)	Ignition Timing (California)	Make	Model	Gap (in.)	Caster, Power Steering (deg.)	Camber, Right Wheel (deg.)	Toe-In (in.)	Crankcase Capacity (L/qt.)	Cooling System Capacity (L)	Cooling System Capacity (qt.)
1342	CP	20B@800	850[2]	20B[3]	AU	AWSF42	.034	1/4P	1/2P	1/8	3.78/4	8.1	8.6
1342	CP	20B@800	850[2]	20B[3]	AU	AWSF42	.034	1P[5]	1/4P[6]	5/16	3.78/4	8.1	8.6
1342	CP	NA	900[8]	2B[9]	AU	AWSF32	.034	1P	1/4P	5/16	4.26/4.5	9.7	10.2
142536	VD	9B@650	NA	6B[11]	AU	AWSF42	.034	1P	1/4P	5/16	4.26/4.5	8.0	8.5
142536	VD	9B@650	NA	6B[11]	MO	AWSF42	.034	1P	1/4P	5/16	4.26/4.5	8.7	9.2
153624	VD	10B@650	800[12]	10B	MO	BRF82	.050[13]	7/8P	3/8P	5/16	3.78/4	8.5	9.0
153624	VD	10B@600	800[14]	6B[15]	AU	BSF82	.050	1/2N	1/4P	1/8	3.78/4	10.1	10.7
15426378	VD	8B@600	800[16]	12B[15]	AU	ASF52[17]	.050[17]	1P	1/4P	5/16	3.78/4	13.2	13.9
15426378	VD	8B@600	800[16]	12B[15]	AU	ASF52[17]	.050[17]	1/2N	1/4P	1/8	3.78/4	13.4	14.2
15426378	VD	8B@600	NA	NA	AU	ASF52	.050	4P	1/4P	1/4	3.78/4	14.3	15.1
15426378	VD	6B@550	NA	10B	AU	ASF52[17]	.050[17]	3P	1/2P	1/16	3.78/4	12.6	13.3
15426378	VD	8B@600	NA	NA	AU	ASF52	.050	4P	1/4P	1/4	3.78/4	14.3	15.1
13726548	VD	12B@600	NA	14B	AU	D7SE-BA	.050	4P	1/4P	1/4	3.78/4	16.5	17.4
13726548	VD	12B@600	NA	14B	AU	D7SE-BA	.050	4P	1/4P	1/4	3.78/4	15.6	16.5
13726548	VD	10B@550	NA	10B	AU	ASF52[17]	.050[17]	3P	1/2P	1/16	3.78/4	13.6	14.4
13726548	VD	15B@650	NA	NA	AU	D7SE-BA	.050	4P	1/4P	1/4	3.78/4	15.6	16.5
15426378	VD	EEC	NA	EEC	AU	ARF52	.050	1/2N	1/4P	1/8	3.78/4	13.6	14.3
13726548	VD	14B@575	NA	14B[11]	AU	ASF52	.050	4P	1/4P	1/8	3.78/4	16.4	17.4
13726548	VD	14B@575	NA	14B[11]	AU	ARF52	.050	2P	1/4P	1/8	3.78/4	16.4	17.3
1342	CP	20B@800	850[2]	20B[3]	AU	AWSF42	.034	1/4P	1/2P	1/8	3.78/4	8.1	8.6
1342	CP	20B@800	850[2]	20B[3]	MO	AWSF42	.034	7/8P	3/8P	5/16	3.78/4	8.1	8.6
1342	CP	20B@800	850[2]	20B[3]	AU	AWSF42	.034	1P	1/4P	5/16	3.78/4	8.1	8.6
1342	CP	NA	900[8]	2B[9]	AU	AWSF32	.034	1P	1/4P	5/16	4.26/4.5	9.7	10.2
142536	VD	9B@650	NA	6B[11]	AU	AWSF42	.034	1/4P	1/2P	1/8	4.26/4.5	8.0	8.5
142536	VD	9B@650	NA	6B[11]	MO	AWSF42	.034	1P	1/4P	5/16	4.26/4.5	8.7	9.2
153624	VD	10B@650	800[12]	10B	MO	BRF82	.050[13]	7/8P	3/8P	5/16	3.78/4	8.5	9.0
153624	VD	10B@600	800[14]	6B[15]	AU	BSF82	.050	1/2N	1/4P	1/8	3.78/4	10.1	10.7
15426378	VD	8B@600	800[16]	12B[15]	MO	ASF52[17]	.050[17]	7/8P	3/8P	5/16	3.78/4	13.2	13.9
15426378	VD	8B@600	800[16]	12B[15]	AU	ASF52[17]	.050[17]	1P	1/4P	5/16	3.78/4	13.2	13.9
15426378	VD	8B@600	800[16]	12B[15]	AU	ARF52[17]	.050[21]	1/2N	1/4P	1/8	3.78/4	13.4	14.2
15426378	VD	8B@600	NA	NA	AU	ASF52	.050	1/4P	1/4P	1/8	3.78/4	14.3	15.1
15426378	VD	6B@550	NA	10B	AU	ASF52[17]	.050[17]	3P	1/2P	1/16	3.78/4	12.6	13.3
13726548	VD	12B@600	NA	14B	AU	DYSE-BA	.050	1/4P	1/4P	1/8	3.78/4	15.4	16.5
13726548	VD	10B@550	NA	10B	AU	ASF52[17]	.050[17]	3P	1/2P	1/16	3.78/4	13.6	14.4
13726548	VD	15B@650	NA	NA	AU	DYSE-BA	.050	1/4P	1/4P	1/8	3.78/4	15.4	16.5
1342	CP	14B@1000	1000	12B[15]	AC	R44TSX	.060	3/4P	3/4P	1/16	2.84/3	10.4	11.0
165432	VD	15B@600	600	15B	AC	R46TSX	.040	1P	3/4P	1/16	3.78/4	12.1[23]	12.8[23]
165432	VD	12B@600[25]	800	12B[15]	AC	R46TSX	.060	3P[26]	13/16P[27]	1/8	3.78/4	12.8	13.3
18436572	VD	FI	FI	FI	NA	NA	NA	1P	1/2P	1/8	6.5/7	18.7	19.7
18436572	VD	18B@1100[30]	1100[31]	18B[15]	AC	R46SZ	.060	3P[26]	13/16P[27]	1/8	3.78/4	15.5	16.4
18436572	VD	12B@500	NA	12B[15]	AC	R46TSX	.060	3P	13/16P	1/8	4.7/5	19.8	20.9
18436572	VD	8B@500	700	B	AC	R45TS	.045	1P	1/2P[33]	1/8[34]	3.78/4	14.9	15.8
18436572	VD	NA	NA	NA	NA	NA	NA	3P[36]	13/16P[37]	1/8[37]	7.1/7.5	17[38]	18[38]
18436572	VD	8B@500	NA	8B[15]	AC	R46TS	.045	1P	1/2P[33]	1/8[34]	3.78/4	15.1	16.0
18436572	VD	20B@1100	NA	20B[15]	AC	R46SZ	.080	3P[36]	13/16P[37]	1/8[37]	3.78/4	13.8[40]	14.6[40]
18436572	VD	18B@1100	NA	18B[15]	AC	R46SZ	.080	3P	13/16P	1/8	3.78/4	14.9	15.7
1342	CP	15B@900	900	15B	CH	RN12Y	.037	NA	5/16P	1/8N	3.78/4	5.7	6
153624	VD	12B@700	700	15B[48]	CH	RBL16Y	.035	2—1/2P	1/4P	1/8	3.78/4	10.9	11.5
153624	VD	12B@750	NA	NA	CH	RBL16Y	.035	2—1/2P	1/4P	1/8	3.78/4	10.9	11.5
18436572	VD	16B@750	NA	NA	CH	RN12Y	.035	2—1/2P	1/4P	1/8	3.78/4	14.2	15.0
18436572	VD	NA	NA	16B[48]	CH	RN12Y	.035	2—1/2P	1/4P	1/8	3.78/4	14.2	15.0
18436572	VD	16B@750	NA	16B[15]	CH	RN12Y	.035	2—1/2P	1/4P	1/8	3.78/4	14.2	15.0
1342	CP	12B@650	900	12B	AC	R43TSX	.060	3/4N	1/4N	1/8N	2.9/3	10.1	10.7
165432	VD	15B@600	800	15B	AC	R46TSX[52]	.060	3/4N	1/4N	1/8N	3.78/4	12.6	13.3
165432	VD	15B@600	800	15B	AC	R46TSX[52]	.060	3P	1/2P	1/8	3.78/4	12.6	13.3
165432	VD	15B@600	600	15B	AC	R46TSX[52]	.060	1P	1P	1/8	3.78/4	12.6	13.3
165432	VD	15B@600	NA	NA	AC	R45TSX	.060	3P	13/16P	1/4	4.7/5	19.8	20.9
18436572	VD	12B@500	NA	NA	AC	R46TSX	.060	3P	13/16P	1/4	4.7/5	19.8	20.9
18436572	VD	12B@500	600	NA	AC	R46TSX	.060	1P	1P	1/8	4.7/5	19.8	20.9
18436572	VD	4B@600	600	4B	AC	R45TS	.045	3/4N	1/4N	1/8N	3.78/4	15.7	16.6
18436572	VD	4B@600	NA	4B[56]	AC	R45TS	.045	1P	1P	1/8	3.78/4	15.7	16.6
18436572	VD	8B@600[39]	NA	4B[57]	AC	R45TSX	.060	3P	1/2P	1/8	3.78/4	15.2	16.1
18436572	VD	20B@1100[39]	NA	20B[15]	AC	R45TSX	.060	3P	13/16P	1/4	3.78/4	16.6	17.5
18436572	VD	15B@600	NA	NA	AC	R46TSX	.060	3P	13/16P	1/4	3.78/4	15.4	16.3
18436572	VD	8B@500[39]	NA	8B[57]	AC	R45TS	.045	1P	1P	1/8	3.78/4	16.6[58]	17.5[58]
18436572	VD	NA	775[59]	NA	AC	R45TSX	.060	1P	1P	1/8	3.78/4	17.4	18.4
18436572	VD	NA	NA	20B[15]	AC	R46SZ	.080	3P	13/16P	1/4	3.78/4	15.4	16.3
18436572	VD	18B@1100	NA	18B[15]	AC	R46SZ	.080	1P	1P	1/8	3.78/4	19.3	20.4

21 – Cal. Engine – ARF52-6/.060
22 – Omega – 2819/111, Starfire – 2464/97
23 – Starfire – 11.2/11.8
24 – Cutlass – 2745/108.1
25 – Cutlass – 15B@600
26 – Cutlass – 1P
27 – Cutlass – 1/2P
28 – Diesel Option
29 – Toronado – 165/123@3600
30 – Cutlass – 20B
31 – Cutlass – 18B
32 – Omega, Starfire – 130/96.6@3200
33 – Omega, Starfire – 3/4P
34 – Omega, Starfire – 1/16

35 – Toronado – 2895/114
36 – Toronado – 2—1/2P
37 – Toronado – O
38 – Toronado – 17.4/18.4
39 – High Altitude Option
40 – Toronado – 14.1/14.9
41 – 4-Door – 2520/99.2
42 – Cal. Engine – 65/48@5200
43 – Minimum Pressure. Also 25 psi (4 and 6) or 40 psi (8) Maximum Variation
44 – Intake .010 in./0.25 mm Exhaust .018 in./0.45 mm
45 – 4-Door – 2863/112.7
46 – Cal. Engine – 90/65@3600

47 – Intake .010 in./0.25 mm Exhaust .020 in./0.51 mm
48 – @750
49 – 2-Door Coupe Only
50 – Cal. Engine – 170/125@4000
51 – Cal. Engine – 85/63.2@4400
52 – Cal. Engine – R45TSX
53 – Phoenix – 2822/111.1
54 – Also 135/100.3@3800
55 – Also 130/96.6@3200
56 – @500, Phoenix Only
57 – @500
58 – Phoenix – 15.7/16.6
59 – 18B

FOREIGN MAKE	Year	Model	Nationality	No. of Cylinders and Piston Displacement	Firing Order	Valve Tappet Clearance		Ignition				Spark Plugs		Gap (in.)
						Intake (in.)	Exhaust (in.)	Breaker Timing (deg.)	Breaker Gap (in.)	Dwell (deg.)	Timing Mark Location	Make	Model	
Audi	1972	S90	Ger.	4-107.4	1342	.008	.016	9A	.016	50	CP	BO	W200T30	.02_
Audi	1972	100L S	Ger.	4-114.2	1342	.008	.016	8B[1]	.016	50	CP	BO	W200T30	.024
Audi	1973-74	100L S	Ger.	4-114.35	1342	.008	.016	8A	.016	50	FW	BO	W200T30	.02_
Audi	1975	100L S	Ger.	4-114.5	1342	.007	.015	6A	.016	50	FW	BO	W225T2	.03_
Audi	1973-74	Fox	Ger.	4-89.7	1342	.009	.017	3A	.016	50	FW	BO	W175T30	.02_
Audi	1975	Fox	Ger.	4-97.0	1342	.009	.017	3A	.016	50	FW	BO	W215T30	.02_
Austin	1971	1100	Eng.	4-67.0	1342	.012C	.012C	3B[2]	.015	60	FW	CH	N9Y	.02_
Austin	1968-72	1300, GT	Eng.	4-78.0	1342	.012C	.012C	8B[3]	.015	60	FW	CH	N9Y	.02_
Austin	1970-72	Maxi 1500	Eng.	4-90.0	1342	.018H	.022H	12B	.015	60	FW	CH	N9Y	.02_
Austin	1971	Maxi 1750	Eng.	4-106.0	1342	.018H	.022H	12B	.015	60	FW	CH	N9Y	.02_
Austin	1969-72	1800	Eng.	4-109.6	1342	.015C	.015C	12B	.015	60	FW	CH	N9Y	.02_
Austin	1969-72	3-Litre	Eng.	6-177.7	153624	.012C	.012C	4B[4]	.015	35	CP	CH	N9Y	.02_
Austin	1973	Marina	Eng.	4-109.6	1342	.013H	.013H	6B[5]	.015	60	CP	CH	N9Y	.03_
Austin-Healey	1967-72	Sprite Mark IV	Eng.	4-78.0	1342	.012C	.012C	7B	.015	60	CP	CH	UN-12Y[6]	.02_
Bentley	1973-74	Bentley T	Eng.	8-412.0	15486372	HY	HY	15B[7]	.018	27	VD	CH	N14Y	.02_
Capri	1972	1600	Ger.	4-97.5	1243	.017H	.017H	12B	.025	38	CP	AU	AGR22	.03_
Capri	1972	2000	Ger.	4-122.0	1342	.008C	.010C	6B[8]	.025	38	VD	AU	BF32D	.034
Capri	1973	2000	Ger.	4-122.0	1342	.008C	.010C	6B[9]	.025	39	VD	AU	BF32	.03_
Capri	1974	2000	Ger.	4-122.0	1342	.008C	.010C	6B[9]	.025	38	VD	AU	BRF42	.034
Capri	1972-73	2600	Ger.	V6-158.5	142536	.014	.016	12B[10]	.025	37	VD	AU	AGR32[11]	.034
Capri	1974	2800	Ger.	V6-170	142536	.014	.016	12B	.025	38	VD	AU	AGR42	.034
Capri II	1975	2300	Ger.	4-140	1342	.008C	.010C	6B	.025	38	VD	AU	AGRF52	.034
Capri II	1975	2800	Ger.	V6-170	142536	.014C	.016C	12B	.025	37	VD	AU	AGR42	.034
Citroen	1971-72	DS-21	Fre.	4-132.7[12]	1342	.008H	.010H	10B[13]	.016	57	FW[14]	CH	L92Y	.02_
Citroen	1971-72	SM	Fre.	V6-162.9	162534	.013C	.021C	27B[15]	.016	88	FW	CH	N6Y	.02_
Citroen	1973-74	SM	Fre.	V6-180.9	162534	.013C	.021C	27B	.016	88	FW	CH	N11Y	.02_
Datsun	1973	LB110	Jap.	4-71.5	1342	.014	.014	5B	.020	52	CP	NGK	BP5ES	.034
Datsun	1973	PL510, PL620	Jap.	4-97.3	1342	.010	.012	12B[16]	.020	52	CP	NGK	BP6ES	.03_
Datsun	1974	HL710, PL620	Jap.	4-108	1342	.010	.012	12B	.020	53	CP	NGK	B6ES	.03_
Datsun	1974	260-Z	Jap.	6-156.2	153624	.010	.012	8B[17]	.014[18]	TI[19]	CP	NGK	BP6ES	.034
Datsun	1975	B210	Jap.	4-85.2	1342	.014	.014	10B	.020	53	CP	NGK	BP5ES	.03_
Datsun	1975	710	Jap.	4-119.1	1342	.010	.012	12B	.020	53	CP	NGK	BP6ES	.03_
Datsun	1975	610	Jap.	4-119.1	1342	.010	.012	12B	.020	53	CP	NGK	BP6ES	.03_
Datsun	1975	260-Z	Jap.	6-156.5	153624	.010	.012	8B	.008[18]	TI[19]	CP	NGK	BP6ES	
Dodge	1971-72	Colt	Jap.	4-97.5	1342	.006H	.010H	TDC	.020	52	CP	CH	N11Y	.030
Dodge	1973	Colt	Jap.	4-97.5	1342	.006H	.010H	TDC	.020	52	CP	CH	N9Y	.030
Dodge	1974	Colt, GT	Jap.	4-97.5	1342	.006H	.010H	TDC[20]	.020	52	CP	NGK	BP6ES	.030
Dodge	1974	Colt, GT	Jap.	4-127.1	1342	.006H	.010H	3B	.020	52	CP	NGK	BP6ES	.030
Fiat	1972	850 Sport Spider	Ita.	4-54.4	1342	.006C	.008C	TDC	.016	55	VD	CH	N7Y	.022
Fiat	1972-73	128 Sedan, SL	Ita.	4-68.0	1342	.012C	.016C	TDC	.016	55	VD	CH	N9Y	.022
Fiat	1971-73	124 Sport Coupe, Spider	Ita.	4-98.0	1342	.018C	.020C	TDC[21]	.016	55	VD	CH	N6Y	.022
Jaguar	1971	XJ-6	Eng.	6-258.2	153624	.014C	.014C	22B[22]	.015	35	VD	CH	N11Y	.02_
Jaguar	1971	Series II, "E" 4.2 Litre	Eng.	6-258.2	153624	.014C	.014C	10B	.015	35	VD	CH	N11Y	.025
Jaguar	1972-73	XJ-6	Eng.	6-258.43	153624	.013C	.013C	8B	.015	35	VD	CH	N11Y	.02_
Jaguar	1973	Series III, "E" Type	Eng.	V12-326	1A, 6B[23]	.015C	.015C	10B	.021	25	VD	CH	N10Y	.02_
Jaguar	1974	Series III, "E" Type, XJ-12	Eng.	V12-326	1A, 6B[23]	.013C	.013C	4A[24]	.021	25	VD	CH	N10Y	.02_
Jaguar	1974	XJ-6	Eng.	6-258.43	153624	.013C	.013C	TDC[24]	.015	38	VD	CH	N11Y	.02_
MG	1968-72	Midget	Eng.	4-78.0	1342	.012H	.012H	7B	.015	60	CP	CH	N9Y	.02_
MG	1969-72	1300 Mark II	Eng.	4-78.0	1342	.012H	.012H	5B	.015	60	CP	CH	N9Y	.02_
MG	1971-72	MGB, MGB-GT	Eng.	4-109.6	1342	.013H	.013H	15B[25]	.015	60	CP	CH	N9Y	.02_
MG	1973-74	Midget	Eng.	4-78.0	1342	.012H	.012H	9B	.015	60	CP	CH	N9Y	.02_
MG	1973-74	MGB; MGB-GT	Eng.	4-109.6	1342	.013H	.013H	11B	.015	60	CP	CH	N9Y	.02_
Mazda	1969-72	R-100	Jap.	2x30[26]	12	NA	NA	0[27]	.018	58	FP	CH	N80B	.03_
Mazda	1971-72	RX-2	Jap.	2x35[26]	12	NA	NA	0[27]	.018	58	FP	NGK	B7EM	.024
Mazda	1974	RX-2	Jap.	2x35[26]	12	NA	NA	5A[27]	.018	58	FP	NGK	B7EM	.024
Mazda	1973-75	RX-3	Jap.	2x35[26]	12	NA	NA	5A[27]	.018	58	FP	NGK	B7EM	.024
Mazda	1974-75	RX-4	Jap.	2x40[26]	12	NA	NA	5A[28]	.018	58	FP	NGK	B7EM	.024
Mazda	1973-75	808	Jap.	4-96.8	1342	.012H	.012H	5B[29]	.020	52	FP	NGK	BP6ES	.03_
Mercedes-Benz	1972	220/8	Ger.	4-134.0	1342	.003C	.008C	5A[30]	.018	50	VD	BO	W175T30	.024
Mercedes-Benz	1973	220	Ger.	4-134.0	1342	.003C	.008C	10B	NA	47	VD	BO	W175T30	.024
Mercedes-Benz	1974-75	230	Ger.	4-140.8	1342	.004C	.008C	10B	NA	47	VD	BO	W175T30	.024
Mercedes-Benz	1973-74	280, 280 C	Ger.	6-167.6	153624	.004C	.008C[31]	4A	NA	34	VD	BO	W175T30	.024
Mercedes-Benz	1975	280, 280 C, 280 S	Ger.	6-167.6	153624	.004C	.010C	7B	NA	34	VD	BO	W175T30	.024
Mercedes-Benz	1973-74	450 SE, SEL, SL and SLC	Ger.	8-275.8	15486372	.003C	.008C	5A	NA	30	VD	BO	W175T30	.024
Mercedes-Benz	1975	450 SE, SEL, SL and SLC	Ger.	8-275.8	15486372	.004C	.008C	TDC	NA	30	VD	BO	W175T30	.024

A - After Top Center
AC - AC Spark Plugs
AU - Autolite Spark Plugs
B - Before Top Center
BO - Bosch Spark Plugs
C - Cold Engine
CH - Champion Spark Plugs
CP - Crankshaft Pulley
FP - Fan Pulley

FW - Flywheel
H - Hot Engine
HY - Hydraulic Lifters
NA - Not Applicable
NGK - NGK Spark Plugs
NI - Nippondenso Spark Plugs
TDC - Top Dead Center
TI - Transistor Ignition
VD - Vibration Damper

1 - W/Auto. Trans. - 8A@950
2 - W/Auto. Trans. - 5B
3 - W/Auto. Trans. - GT-3B
4 - 1971-72 - 12B@600
5 - Static Method
6 - 1971-72 - N9Y
7 - @1500 rpm
8 - W/Auto. Trans. - 10B
9 - W/Auto. Trans. - 10B@600

10 - 1973 - W/Auto. Trans. - 8B
11 - W/Auto. Trans. - AGR31
12 - DV Model - 121.1
13 - DV Model - 12B@2000
14 - 1972 - FP
15 - @2000 rpm
16 - Secondary - 8B
17 - W/Auto. Trans. - Secondary - 15B
18 - Air Gap

FOREIGN MAKE	Year	Model	Nationality	No. of Cylinders and Piston Displacement	Firing Order	Intake (in.)	Exhaust (in.)	Breaker Timing (deg.)	Breaker Gap (in.)	Dwell (deg.)	Timing Mark Location	Make	Model	Gap (in.)
el	1968-70	Kadett	Ger.	4-66.0	1342	.006H	.010H	10A	.018	50	CP	AC	43FFS	.030
el	1969-70	Rallye, Kadett, GT	Ger.	4-66.0	1342	.006H	.010H	10A	.018	50	CP	AC	43FFS	.030
el	1969-70	GT 1.9	Ger.	4-115.8	1342	.012H	.012H	TDC	.018	50	FW	AC	42FS	.030
el	1971	1.1R US	Ger.	4-66.0	1342	HY	HY	TDC	.018	50	CP	AC	42FS	.030
el	1971-72	1.9 US, GT, 1900, Rallye	Ger.	4-115.8	1342	HY	HY	TDC	.018	50	FW	AC	42FS	.030
el	1973-74	1900, Manta, Rallye, Luxus	Ger.	4-115.8	1342	HY	HY	TDC	.016	50	FW	AC	42FS	.030
geot	1969-70	504	Fre.	4-110.0	1342	.006C	.010C	TDC	.020	57	FW	CH	N9Y	.025
geot	1971-72	304	Fre.	4-78.6	1342	.004C	.010C	5A	.016	60	CP	CH	N7Y	.024
geot	1971	504	Fre.	4-120.3	1342	.004C	.010C	TDC	.016	60	CP	CH	N7Y	.024
geot	1972	504	Fre.	4-120.3	1342	.004C	.010C	5A	.016	60	CP	CH	N7Y	.024
mouth	1971-72	Cricket	Eng.	4-91.4[32]	1342	.008	.016	30B[33]	.015	62	CP	CH	N9Y	.025
mouth	1971-72	Cricket	Eng.	4-97.5	1342	.006H	.010H	TDC	.020	52	CP	CH	N11Y	.030
mouth	1973	Cricket	Eng.	4-97.5	1342	.006H	.010H	TDC	.019	52	CP	CH	N9Y	.030
sche	1971	911T	Ger.	6-121.5	162435	.004C	.004C	TDC	.016	38	CP	BO	W230T30	.020
sche	1971	914	Ger.	4-102.5	1432	.004C	.004C	27B[34]	.016	50	CP	BO	W175T2	.028
sche	1972	911T-E-S	Ger.	6-142.8	162435	.004C	.004C	5A[35]	.014	38	CP	BO	W265P21[36]	.028
sche	1972	914	Ger.	4-102.5	1432	.004C	.004C	27B[34]	.016	48	CP	BO	W175T2	.028
sche	1973	914/1.7	Ger.	4-102.3	1432	.006C	.006C	27B[34]	.016	47	CP	BO	W175T2	.028
sche	1973-75	914/2.0	Ger.	4-120.3	1432	.006C	.008C	27B[34]	.016	47	CP	BO	W175T2	.028
sche	1973	911T-E-S	Ger.	6-142.8	162435	.004C	.004C	5A[35]	.014	40	CP	BO	W235P21	.022
sche	1974	914/1.8	Ger.	4-109.5	1432	.006C	.006C	7.5B[37]	.016	47	CP	BO	W175T2	.028
sche	1974	911	Ger.	6-163.97	162435	.004C	.004C	5A[35]	.014	38	CP	BO	W215P21	.024
sche	1974	911S/Carrera	Ger.	6-163.97	162435	.004C	.004C	5A[35]	.014	38	CP	BO	W235P21	.024
sche	1975	914/1.8	Ger.	4-109.5	1432	.006C	.006C	7.5B[37]	.016	47	CP	BO	W175M30	.028
sche	1974-75	914/2.0	Ger.	4-120.27	1432	.006C	.008C	27B[34]	.016	47	CP	BO	W175T2	.028
sche	1975	911S/Carrera	Ger.	6-163.97	162435	.004C	.004C	5A[35]	.016	38	CP	BO	W235P21	.022
ault	1973	R12, R15	Fre.	4-100.5	1342	.008H	.010H	5B[38]	.018	57	FW	CH	N5	.025
ault	1973-74	R17 Gordini	Fre.	4-95.5	1342	.010H	.012H	TDC	.018	55	FW	CH	N3	.025
ault	1974	R12, R15, R17TL	Fre.	4-100.5	1342	.008H	.010H	10B	.018	55	FW	CH	N5	.025
ault	1975	R12L,12TL,12S/W,15TL,17TL	Fre.	4-100.5	1342	.008H	.010H	7B[39]	.018	57	FW	CH	N5	.027
ault	1975	R17 Gordini	Fre.	4-100.5	1342	.010H	.012H	12B	.018	57	FW	CH	N7Y	.027
ls-Royce	1971-72	Silver Shadow	Eng.	8-412.0	15486372	HY	HY	TDC	.015	27	VD	CH	N14Y	.025
ls-Royce	1973-74	Silver Shadow, Corniche	Eng.	8-412.0	15486372	HY	HY	15B[7]	.015	27	VD	CH	N14Y	.025
b	1971-72	99, 99E	Swe.	4-113.1	1342	.009H	.017H	9B[40]	.018	40[41]	FW	BO	W175T30	.026
b	1973-74	99	Swe.	4-121.0	1342	.009H	.017H	8B[42]	.014	50	CP	NGK	BP6ES	.026
b	1973	95, 96, 97	Swe.	V4-104.0	1342	.014C	.016C	3B	.016	50	CP	NGK	BP6E	.026
b	1974	97	Swe.	V4-104.0	1342	.014C	.016C	3B	.016	50	CP	NGK	BP6E	.026
b	1975	99	Swe.	4-121	1342	.009H	.017H	14B	.016	50	FW	NGK	BPGES	.026
aru	1971-72	"G"	Jap.	4-77.3	1324	.011C	.013C	TDC[4]	.019	53	FW	NGK	BP6ES	.030
aru	1973-74	1400	Jap.	4-83.2	1324	.012C	.012C	6B	.020	52	FW	NGK	BP6ES	.032
aru	1975	GL, DL	Jap.	4-83.2	1324	.012C	.012C	8B	.020	52	FW	NGK	BP6ES	.030
ota	1973-74	Corolla TE	Jap.	4-96.9	1342	.008H	.013H	5B	.018	52	CP	NI	W20EP[44]	.030
ota	1972-74	Corona	Jap.	4-120.0	1342	.008H	.014H	7B	.018	52	CP	NI	W20EP[44]	.030
ota	1973-74	MX	Jap.	6-156.4	153624	.007H	.010H	5B	.018	41	CP	NI	W20EP[44]	.030
ota	1973-74	Land Cruiser	Jap.	6-236.7	153624	.008H	.014H	7B	.018	41	FW	NI	W20EP[45]	.030
ota	1975	Corolla 2T-C	Jap.	4-96.9	1342	.008H	.013H	10B	.018	52	CP	NI	W20EP	.030
ota	1975	Corona, 20R	Jap.	4-133.6	1342	.008H	.012H	8B	.018	52	CP	NI	W16EP	.030
ota	1975	Corona Mark II	Jap.	6-156.4	153624	.007H	.010H	10B	.018	41	CP	NI	W16EP	.030
ota	1975	2F	Jap.	6-257.9	153624	.008H	.014H	7B	.018	41	FW	NI	W14EX	.037
umph	1973-74	Spitfire 1500	Eng.	4-91.0	1342	.010C	.010C	2A[24]	.015	39	VD	CH	N12Y	.025
umph	1973	GT-6 III	Eng.	6-122.0	153624	.010C	.010C	4A[46]	.015	41	VD	CH	N12Y	.025
umph	1973-74	TR-6	Eng.	6-152.0	153624	.010C	.010C	4A[24]	.014	36	VD	CH	N9Y	.025
umph	1973	Stag	Eng.	8-182.9	12784563	.009C	.017C	4A[24]	.015	31	VD	CH	N11Y	.025
kswagen	1971-73	Squareback, Type 3	Ger.	4-96.9	1432	.004C	.004C	TDC	.016	50	CP	BO	W145T1	.028
kswagen	1971-74	Sedan 111, Super Beetle 113	Ger.	4-96.9	1432	.006C	.006C	5A[47]	.016	50	CP	BO	W145T1	.028
kswagen	1975	Sedan 111, Super Beetle 113	Ger.	4-96.9	1432	.006C	.006C	5A[48]	.016	50	CP	BO	W145M1	.028
kswagen	1973-74	412 Type 4	Ger.	4-102.5	1432	.006C	.006C	27B[49]	.016	50	FP	BO	W175T2	.024
kswagen	1974-75	Dasher	Ger.	4-89.7	1342	.009H	.017H	3A[50]	.016	47	CP	BO	W200T30	.028
kswagen	1975	Rabbit, Scirocco	Ger.	4-89.7	1342	.010H	.018H	3A[50]	.015	47	CP	BO	W200T30	.028
vo	1970-71	B20E	Swe.	4-121	1342	.017H	.017H	10B[51]	.016	62	CP	BO	W200T35	.030
vo	1972	B20F	Swe.	4-121.0	1342	.017H	.017H	10B[52]	.016	62	CP	BO	W200T35	.030
vo	1969-72	B30A	Swe.	6-181.6	153624	.021H	.021H	10B[52]	.016	40	CP	BO	W200T35	.030
vo	1972	B30F	Swe.	6-181.6	153624	.021H	.021H	10B[52]	.016	40	CP	BO	W200T35	.030
vo	1973-74	B20F	Swe.	4-121.0	1342	.017H	.017H	10B[52]	.016	60	CP	BO	W200T35	.030
vo	1973-74	B30F	Swe.	6-181.6	153624	.021H	.021H	10B[52]	.010	42	CP	BO	W200T35	.030

19 - Transistor Ignition
20 - W/Auto. Trans. - 8B
21 - 1971 - 5B
22 - @1700
23 - 1A, 6B, 5A, 2B, 3A, 4B, 6A, 1B, 2A, 5B, 4A, 3B. A-Right From Driver's Seat
24 - Static - 10B
25 - 1972 - 16B
26 - 2-Rotor Rotary Engine
27 - Trailing Distributor - 10A
28 - Trailing Distributor - 15A
29 - W/Auto. Trans. - 8B
30 - @500 rpm W/Vacuum Connected
31 - 1974 - .010
32 - 1498 Engine
33 - @3000
34 - @3500
35 - @950
36 - 911T - W235P21
37 - @900
38 - W/Auto. Trans. - 3B
39 - W/Auto. Trans. - 10B@650
40 - W/Fuel Injection - 5B@800
41 - W/Fuel Injection - 50
42 - 1974 - 4B
43 - 1972 - 8B@750
44 - 1974 - W16EP
45 - 1974 - W14EP
46 - Static - 6B
47 - @800-900
48 - W/Auto. Trans. - TDC
49 - 27B@3500
50 - @975 rpm
51 - @800 rpm
52 - @700 rpm

FOREIGN MAKE	Year	Model	Nationality	No. of Cylinders and Piston Displacement	Firing Order	Intake (in.)	Exhaust (in.)	Breaker Timing (deg.)	Breaker Gap (in.)	Dwell (deg.)	Timing Mark Location	Make	Model	Gap (in.)
Audi	1975	100LS	Ger.	4–114.5	1342	.007	.015	6A	.016	50	FW	BO	W225T2	.02
Audi	1975	Fox	Ger.	4–97.0	1342	.009	.017	3A	.016	50	FW	BO	W175T30	.02
Audi	1977	100LS	Ger.	4–114.2	1342	.008	.018	10A	CD	47	FW	BO	W225T30	.02
Audi	1976–78	Fox	Ger.	4–97.0	1342	.008	.018	0	.016	47	FW	BO	W225T30	.02
Audi	1978	5000	Ger.	5–130.8	12453	.008	.018	10A	BR	NA	FW	BO	W200T30	.02
Audi	1979	Fox GTI	Ger.	4–97.0	1342	.008	.018	0	.016	47	FW	BO	W225T30	.02
Audi	1979	5000 "S"	Ger.	5–130.8	12453	.008	.018	10A	BR	NA	FW	BO	W200T30	.02
BMW	1975	2002	Ger.	4–122.2	1342	.0079[1]	.0079[1]	25B	.015	61	FW	BO	W145T30	.02
BMW	1975	530i	Ger.	6–182.2	153624	.012[1]	.012[1]	22B	.015	38	FW	BO	W145T30	.02
BMW	1975	3.0 Si	Ger.	6–182.2	153624	.012[1]	.012[1]	22B	.015	38	FW	BO	W145T30	.02
BMW	1976	2002	Ger.	4–122.2	1342	.0079[1]	.0079[1]	25B[2]	.015	61	FW	BO	W145T30	.02
BMW	1976–77	530i, 3.0 Si	Ger.	6–182.2	153624	.012[1]	.012[1]	22B	.015	38	FW	BO	W145T30	.02
BMW	1977	320i	Ger.	4–121.4	1342	.0079[1]	.0079[1]	25B[2]	.015	61	FW	BO	W145T30	.02
BMW	1977	630 csi	Ger.	6–182.2	153624	.012[1]	.012[1]	22B	.015	38	FW	BO	W144T30	.02
BMW	1978–79	320i	Ger.	4–121.4	1342	.008[1]	.008[1]	25B	.015	63	FW	BO	W125T30	.02
BMW	1979	528i	Ger.	6–170.1	153624	.012[1]	.012[1]	22B	NA	NA	FW	BO	W125T30	.02
Buick-Opel	1975	1900	Ger.	4–115.8	1342	HY	HY	10B	.016	50	CP	AC	42FS	.03
Buick-Opel	1976–79	WTT77, WTY77, 4TY69, 4TW77	Jap.	4–111	1342	.006C	.010C	6B	.018	53	CP	AC	R44XLS	.03
Capri II	1976–77	2300	Ger.	4–140	1342	NA	NA	10B	BR	NA	CP	MO	AGRF52	.03
Capri II	1976–77	2800	Ger.	6–170.8	142536	.014C	.016C	8B	BR	NA	CP	MO	AGRF42	.03
Datsun	1976–77	B210	Jap.	4–85.2	1342	.014H	.014H	10B	.020[3]	NA	CP	NGK	BP5ES	.03
Datsun	1976–77	F10	Jap.	4–85.2	1342	.014H	.014H	10B	.020[3]	52[4]	CP	NGK	BP5ES	.03
Datsun	1976	710, 610	Jap.	4–119.1	1342	.010H	.012H	12B	.020[3]	52[4]	CP	NGK	BP5ES	.03
Datsun	1977	710	Jap.	4–119.1	1342	.010H	.012H	12B	.020[3]	52[4]	CP	NGK	BP6ES11	.04
Datsun	1976	280Z	Jap.	6–168	153624	.010H	.012H	13B	.014[3]	NA	CP	NGK	B6ES	.03
Datsun	1977	280Z	Jap.	6–168	153624	.010H	.012H	10B	.014[3]	NA	CP	NGK	B6ES11	.04
Datsun	1978	F10	Jap.	4–85.2	1342	.010C	.010C	8B	.012[3]	NA	CP	NGK	BP5ES	.04
Datsun	1978–79	200SX, 510VX, 510	Jap.	4–119.1	1342	.008C	.010C	12B[5]	.012[6]	NA	CP	NGK	BP6ES11	.04
Datsun	1978–79	810	Jap.	6–146	153624	.008C	.010C	10B	.012[6]	NA	CP	NGK	B6ES11	.04
Datsun	1978–79	280Z	Jap.	6–168	153624	.008C	.010C	10B	.012[6]	NA	CP	NGK	B6ES11	.04
Datsun	1979	YB, 210	Jap.	4–91	1342	.014H	.014H	10B[7]	NA	NA	CP	NGK	BP5ES11	.04
Dodge	1976–77	Colt, GT	Jap.	4–97.5	1342	.006H	.010H	5A[8]	.020	52	CP	CH	RN9Y	.03
Dodge	1976–77	Colt, GT	Jap.	4–121.7	1342	.006H	.010H	5A[8]	.020	52	CP	CH	RN9Y	.04
Dodge	1978–79	Colt, Colt FF	Jap.	4–97.5	1342	.006H	.010H	5B	NA	NA	CP	CH	RN9Y	.04
Dodge	1978–79	Challenger	Jap.	4–97.5	1342	.006H	.010H	5B	NA	NA	CP	CH	RN9Y	.04
Dodge	1978	Colt	Jap.	4–156	1342	.006H	.010H	7B	NA	NA	CP	CH	RN12Y	.04
Dodge	1978–79	Challenger	Jap.	4–156	1342	.006H	.010H	7B	NA	NA	CP	CH	RN12Y	.04
Dodge	1979	Colt FF	Jap.	4–86	1342	.006H	.010H	5B	NA	NA	CP	CH	RN9Y	.04
Fiat	1975	128 Sedan, 128 Sport L, X1/9	Ita.	4–78.70	1342	.012C	.016C	TDC	.016	55	FW	CH	N9Y[9]	.02
Fiat	1975	131 Sedan, 124 Sport Coupe, Spider	Ita.	4–107.13	1342	.018C	.020C	TDC	.016	55	CP	CH	N9Y[9]	.02
Fiat	1976–77	128 Sedan, 128 3P, X1/9	Ita.	4–78.70	1342	.012C	.016C	TDC[10]	.016	55	CP	CH	N9Y[9]	.02
Fiat	1976–77	131 Sedan, 124 Spider	Ita.	4–107.13	1342	.018C	.020C	TDC	.016	55	CP	CH	N9Y[11]	.02
Fiat	1978	128, X1/9	Ita.	4–78.7	1342	.012C	.016C	TDC	.016	55	CP	CH	RN9Y[12]	.03
Fiat	1978	131, 124, Super Brava	Ita.	4–107.13	1342	.018C	.020C	TDC[13]	.016	55	CP	CH	RN9Y[12]	.03
Fiat	1978	Lancia Beta	Ita.	4–107.13	1342	.018C	.020C	TDC[14]	.016	55	CP	CH	RN9Y[12]	.03
Fiat	1979	128	Ita.	4–78.7	1342	.012C	.016C	TDC	.016	55	CP	CH	RN9Y[15]	.03
Fiat	1979	X1/9	Ita.	4–91.44	1342	.012C	.016C	5B	BR	NA	CP	CH	RN9Y[15]	.03
Fiat	1979	124 Spider, Brava, Lancia Beta	Ita.	4–121.74	1342	.018C	.020C	10B	BR	NA	CP	CH	RN9Y[15]	.03
Ford	1978–79	Fiesta, Decor, Sport, Ghia	Ger.	4–97.3	1243	.010C	.021C	12B	BR	NA	CP	MO	AWRF32	.05
Honda	1975–76	Civic	Jap.	4–75.5	1432	.006C	.006C	7B	.020	52	CP	NGK	BP6ES	.03
Honda	1975	Civic CVCC	Jap.	4–90.8	1432	.006C[16]	.006C[16]	TDC[17]	.020	52	FW	NGK	B6ES	.03
Honda	1976	Civic CVCC	Jap.	4–90.8	1432	.006C[16]	.006C[16]	2B	.020	52	FW	NGK	B6ES	.03
Honda	1976	Accord	Jap.	4–97.63	1432	.006C[16]	.006C[16]	2B[18]	.020	52	FW	NGK	B6ES	.03
Honda	1977	Civic	Jap.	4–75.48	1432	.006C[16]	.006C[16]	TDC	.020	52	CP	NGK	BP6ES	.03
Honda	1977	Civic CVCC	Jap.	4–90.8	1432	.006C[16]	.006C[16]	6B[20]	.020	52	FW	NGK	B6EB	.03
Honda	1977	Accord	Jap.	4–97.63	1432	.006C[16]	.006C[16]	6B[20]	.020	52	FW	NGK	B6EB	.03
Honda	1978–79	Civic 1200	Jap.	4–75.5	1342	.004C	.006C	2B[18]	.020	52	CP	NGK	BP6ES[19]	.03
Honda	1978–79	Civic CVCC	Jap.	4–90.8	1342	.006C[16]	.008C	6B[20]	.020	52	FW	NGK	B6EB[21]	.03
Honda	1978	Accord	Jap.	4–97.63	1342	.006C[16]	.008C	6B[20]	.020	52	FW	NGK	B6EB[21]	.03
Honda	1979	Accord	Jap.	4–107	1342	.006C[16]	.011C	6B[22]	BR	NA	FW	NGK	B7EB[23]	.03
Jaguar	1975–78	XJ-6	Eng.	6–258	153624	.013C	.013C	8B[24]	.015[25]	NA	VD	CH	N11Y	.02
Jaguar	1976–78	XJ-12, XJS	Eng.	12–326	1A, 6B[27]	.013C	.013C	10B[28]	.021[25]	NA	VD	CH	N10Y	.03
MG	1976–78	Midget	Eng.	4–91	1342	.010C	.010C	10B[29]	.015[25]	NA	VD	CH	N12Y	.02
MG	1976–78	MGB	Eng.	4–110	1342	.013H	.013H	10B	.015[25]	NA	VD	CH	N9Y	.03

ABBREVIATIONS — FOOTNOTES

A — After Top Dead Center	FW — Flywheel	1 — 95 Deg. Coolant Temperature
AC — AC Spark Plugs	H — Hot Engine	2 — Disconnect Vacuum Hose
B — Before Top Dead Center	HY — Hydraulic Lifters	3 — .014 in. Air Gap
BO — Bosch Spark Plugs	MO — Motorcraft Spark Plugs	4 — Except Cal.
BR — Breakerless Ignition	NA — Not Available/Not Applicable	5 — Manual Trans. — 200SX 9B, 510 11B
C — Cold Engine	NGK — NGK Spark Plugs	6 — 1979 — NA
CD — Capacitive Discharge Ignition	NI — Nippon Denso Spark Plugs	7 — Automatic Trans. — 210 8B
CH — Champion Spark Plugs	TDC — Top Dead Center	8 — Cal. — TDC
CP — Crankshaft Pulley	VD — Vibration Damper	9 — Or AC 42XLS

10 — Late Production X1/9 — 10B
11 — Or AC 41-2 For 124 Spider
12 — Or AC R42XLS, BO W175TR30
13 — Automatic Trans. — 5B, or Manual Trans. and Catalytic Converter — 5B
14 — With Catalytic Converter — 10B
15 — Or AC R42XLS, BO WR7D
16 — Also Auxiliary
17 — 2-Speed Trans. — 3A

and Tuneup Specifications

FOREIGN MAKE	Year	Model	Nationality	No. of Cylinders and Piston Displacement	Firing Order	Intake (in.)	Exhaust (in.)	Breaker Timing (deg.)	Breaker Gap (in.)	Dwell (deg.)	Timing Mark Location	Make	Model	Gap (in.)
Mazda	1977–79	RX-35P, RX-7	Jap.	2 Rotors–35	12	NA	NA	0,4A[44]	.018	58	ESP[44]	NGK	B6ET	.041
Mazda	1977–78	RX-4, Cosmo	Jap.	2 Rotors–40	12	NA	NA	5A,4A[44]	.018	58	ESP[44]	NGK	B6ET	.041
Mazda	1977	Mizer	Jap.	4–77.6	1342	.010[30]	.012[30]	11B[31]	.014[32]	NA	CP	NGK	BP6ES	.031
Mazda	1977–78	GLC (1300)	Jap.	4–77.6	1342	.010[30]	.012[30]	11B[31]	.014[32]	NA	CP	NGK	BP6ES	.031
Mazda	1977	808	Jap.	4–96.8	1342	.012[33]	.012[33]	13B[34]	.020	52	CP	NGK	BP6ES	.031
Mazda	1977–78	B1800	Jap.	4–109.6	1342	.012[33]	.012[33]	8B	.020	52	CP	NGK	BP6ES	.031
Mazda	1979	GLC (1400)	Jap.	4–86.4	1342	.010[30]	.012[30]	7B	.012[25]	NA	CP	NGK	BP5ES	.031
Mazda	1979	B2000	Jap.	4–120.2	1342	.012[33]	.012[33]	8B	.012[25]	NA	CP	NGK	BPR5ES	.031
Mercedes-Benz	1978	230	Ger.	4–140.8	1342	.004C	.008C	10B	NA	53	VD	BO	W145T30	.032
Mercedes-Benz	1978	6.9	Ger.	8–417.1	15486372	HY	HY	TDC	BR	NA	VD	BO	W125T30	.032
Mercedes-Benz	1978–79	280 E, 280 CE, 280 SE	Ger.	6–167.6	153624	.004C	.010C	TDC	BR	NA	VD	BO	W125T30	.032
Mercedes-Benz	1978–79	450 SEL, 450 SL, 450 SLC	Ger.	8–275.8	15486372	HY	HY	TDC	BR	NA	VD	BO	W125T30	.032
Peugeot	1977–78	504	Fre.	4–120.3	1342	.004C	.010C	8B	.016	57	CP	CH	N9Y	.024
Peugeot	1977–78	604	Fre.	6–162.6	163524	.004C	.010C	10B	BR	NA	CP	CH	BN9Y	.024
Plymouth	1976	Arrow	Jap.	4–97.5	1342	.006H	.010H	5A	.020	53	CP	CH	RN9Y	.032
Plymouth	1976	Arrow	Jap.	4–121.8	1342	.006H	.010H	5A	.020	53	CP	CH	RN9Y	.032
Plymouth	1977	Arrow	Jap.	4–97.5	1342	.006H	.010H	5B[40]	.020	53	CP	CH	RN9Y	.032
Plymouth	1977–79	Arrow	Jap.	4–121.8	1342	.006H	.010H	5B[40]	.020	53	CP	CH	RN9Y	.032
Plymouth	1978	Arrow, Sapporo	Jap.	4–97.5	1342	.006H	.010H	5B	.020	53	CP	CH	RN9Y	.042
Plymouth	1978–79	Arrow, Sport, Sapporo	Jap.	4–156	1342	.006H	.010H	7B[41]	.020[42]	53[42]	CP	CH	RN12Y	.042
Plymouth	1979	Champ	Jap.	4–86	1342	.006H	.010H	5B	.020	53	CP	CH	RN9Y	.042
Plymouth	1979	Sapporo, Champ	Jap.	4–97.5	1342	.006H	.010H	5B	.020	53	CP	CH	RN9Y	.042
Porsche	1976–77	924	Ger.	4–121	1342	.004C	.016C	10A	BR	NA	FW	BO	W200T30	.028
Porsche	1976–77	911S	Ger.	6–164	162435	.004C	.004C	5A	BR	NA	CP	BO	W235/P21	.024
Porsche	1976–77	Turbo Carrera	Ger.	6–182.7	162435	.004C	.004C	7A	BR	NA	CP	BO	W280/P21	.024
Porsche	1978–79	924	Ger.	4–121	1342	.008H	.018H	3A	BR	NA	FW	BO	W200T30	.028
Porsche	1978–79	911 SC	Ger.	6–182.7	162435	.004C	.004C	5B	BR	NA	CP	BO	W145T30	.031
Porsche	1978–79	Turbo	Ger.	6–201.3	162435	.004C	.004C	10A[49]	BR	NA	CP	BO	W280/P21	.024
Porsche	1978–79	928	Ger.	8–273	13726548	HY	HY	31B	BR	NA	CP	BO	W145T30	.028
Renault	1976–77	5	Fre.	4–78.7	1342	.006C	.008C	TDC	.018	57	FW	CH	L92Y	.027
Renault	1976	17 Gordoni	Fre.	4–100.5	1342	.008C	.010C	12B	.018	57	FW	CH	N3	.027
Renault	1976	12, 15, 17TL	Fre.	4–100.5	1342	.008C	.010C	7B[37]	.018	57	FW	CH	N9Y[9]	.027
Renault	1977	12, 17TL	Fre.	4–100.5	1342	.008C	.010C	7B	.018	57	FW	CH	N9Y[9]	.027
Renault	1978–79	LeCar	Fre.	4–78.7	1342	.006C	.008C	TDC	.018	57	FW	CH	L87Y	.027
Renault	1977–79	17 Gordoni	Fre.	4–100.5	1342	.008C	.010C	12B[39]	.018	57	FW	CH	N3[38]	.027[38]
Rolls-Royce	1976–77	Silver Shadow, Corniche, Camargue	Eng.	8–412	A1, B1[43]	HY	HY	15B	NA	NA	VD	CH	RN14Y	.030
Rolls-Royce	1978	Silver Shadow, Wraith, Camargue	Eng.	8–412	A1, B1[43]	HY	HY	15B	NA	NA	VD	CH	RN14Y	.035
Saab	1976–77	99	Swe.	4–121.1	1342	.009C	.017C	14B[45]	.016	50	FW	NGK	BP6ES	.026
Saab	1978–79	99, 900, 900 Turbo	Swe.	4–121.1	1342	.009C	.017C[46]	BR	NA	NA	FW	NGK	BP6ES	.026
Subaru	1976	GL, DL, GF	Jap.	4–85.4	1324	.010C	.014C	8B[2]	.018	52	FW	NGK	BP6ES	.032
Subaru	1976–78	GL, DL, GF	Jap.	4–97	1324	.012C	.012C	8B	.018[42]	52[42]	FW	NGK	BP6ES	.032
Subaru	1979	All Models	Jap.	4–97	1324	.012C	.012C	8B	.014[25]	NA	FW	NGK	BP6ES	.032
Toyota	1976	Corona Mark II MX	Jap.	6–156.4	153624	.007H	.010H	10B[47]	.018	41	VD	NGK	BP5ESL	.031
Toyota	1976–77	Celica RA, Corona RT	Jap.	4–133.6	1342	.008H	.012H	8B	.018	52	FP	NGK	BP5ESL	.031
Toyota	1977–79	Corolla KE	Jap.	4–71.1	1342	.008H	.012H	8B	.018	52	FP	NGK	BP5ESL	.031
Toyota	1976–79	Corolla TE	Jap.	4–96.9	1342	.008H	.013H	10B	.018	52	FP	NGK	BP5ESL	.032
Toyota	1978–79	Corona RT	Jap.	4–133.6	1342	.008H	.012H	8B	.012[25]	NA	FP	NGK	BP5EAL	.031
Toyota	1978–79	Cressida MX	Jap.	6–156.4	153624	.011H	.014H	10B[48]	.012[25]	NA	FP	NGK	BP5EAL	.031
Triumph	1976	TR6	Eng.	6–152	153624	.010C	.010C	4A	.015	36	VD	CH	N9Y	.025
Triumph	1976–78	Spitfire	Eng.	4–91	1342	.010C	.010C	2A[50]	.015[25]	NA	VD	CH	N12Y	.025
Triumph	1976–78	TR7	Eng.	4–122	1342	.008C	.018C	2A[50]	.015[25]	NA	VD	CH	N12Y	.025
Volkswagen	1976–77	Beetle Sedan, Convertible	Ger.	4–96.6	1432	.006C	.006C	5A	.016	50	CP	CH	L288	.026
Volkswagen	1976–77	Dasher, Rabbit, Scirocco	Ger.	4–97	1342	.010H	.018H	3A	.016	47	CP	CH	N7Y	.026
Volkswagen	1978–79	Beetle Convertible	Ger.	4–96.6	1432	.006C	.006C	5A	.016	50	CP	CH	L288	.028
Volkswagen	1978	Rabbit, Scirocco	Ger.	4–88.9	1342	.006H	.018H	3A	.016	47	CP	CH	N8Y	.026
Volkswagen	1978	Dasher	Ger.	4–97	1342	.010H	.018H	3A	.016	47	CP	CH	N8Y	.028
Volkswagen	1979	Rabbit	Ger.	4–88.9	1342	.010H	.018H	3A	.016	47	CP	CH	N8Y	.028
Volkswagen	1979	Dasher, Scirocco	Ger.	4–97	1342	.010H	.018H	3A	.016	47	CP	CH	N8Y	.028
Volvo	1975	242, 244, 245	Swe.	4–121.4	1342	.017H	.017H	5B[2]	BR	NA	VD	BO	W200T35	.030
Volvo	1975	164	Swe.	6–181.7	153624	.021H	.021H	10B	BR	NA	VD	BO	W200T35	.030
Volvo	1976–77	242, 244, 245	Swe.	4–129.9	1342	.015H	.015H	15B	BR	NA	VD	BO	W175T30	.030
Volvo	1976–79	262, 264, 265	Swe.	6–162.2	163524	.005C	.011C	10B	BR	NA	VD	BO	WA200T30	.030[51]
Volvo	1978	242, GT, 244, 245	Swe.	4–130	1342	.015C	.015C	12B	BR	NA	VD	BO	W7DC	.030
Volvo	1979	242, GT, 244, 245	Swe.	4–130	1342	.015C	.015C	10B[52]	BR	NA	VD	BO	W7DC	.028

8 — On Red Mark (2nd Mark)
9 — Or Nippon Denso — W20EP
0 — On Yellow Mark. Cal. — 2B (Red Mark)
1 — Or Nippon Denso — W20ESL
2 — On Yellow Mark, Hondamatic — 4B (Blue Mark)
3 — Or Nippon Denso — W22ESL
4 — 1978 — 4B Dynamic
5 — Air Gap
6 — 1978 — .035

27 — 1A, 6B, 5A, 2B, 3A, 4B, 6A, 1B, 2A, 5B, 4A, 3B
28 — 1978 Cal. — 4A Dynamic
29 — 1976 Midget, 1978 Cal. — 2A
30 — Cam Side — Int. .007, Exh. .009
31 — Retard — 7B, Cal. — 11B
32 — Fed. — Air Gap, Cal. — .020 Breaker Gap
33 — Cam Side — Int .009, Exh. .009
34 — Retard — 5B, Cal. — 8B

35 — 1978 — BP5ES
36 — Cyl. 2, 3 — .004, Cyl. 1, 4 — .008
37 — Automatic Trans. — 10B
38 — 1977, 1978 Cal. — N7Y .024
39 — 1977 — TDC
40 — 1977 Cal. — 5A
41 — 1977 Cal. — 3A
42 — 1979 or Cal. — Transistorized
43 — A, B1, A4, B4, B2, A3, B3, A2

44 — Leading, Trailing/Eccentric Shaft Pulley
45 — Cal. 12B (Vacuum Disconnected)
46 — Turbo — .020
47 — Cal. — 5B
48 — Cal. — 8B
49 — Cal. — 5A
50 — 1977 — 10B
51 — 1978, 1979 — .028
52 — Lamda-sond Engine — 8B

ACKNOWLEDGMENTS

In preparing this text, all U.S. car manufacturers, most parts and equipment manufacturers, and many automotive industry associations were consulted. Without exception, they cooperated by supplying technical information, specifications and illustrations. As a result, we have compiled an encyclopedia of basic operating principles, construction details and service procedures.

The editors and publisher thank the automotive industry and the following companies for their valued assistance.

AC Spark Plug Div., GMC; AP Parts Corp., A Questor Co.; Abex Corp.; Airtex Automotive; Allen Testproducts, The Allen Group, Inc.; American Bosch-Ambac Industries, Inc.; American Hammered Div., Sealed Power Corp.; American Motors Corp.; American Petroleum Institute (API); American Society of Testing Materials (ASTM); AMMCO Tools, Inc.; The Anderson Co.; Auto-Test, Inc.; Autolite-Ford Parts Div., Ford Marketing Corp.; Automotive Electric Assoc. (AEA); Automotive Service Industry Assoc. (ASIA); Battery Council International (BCI); John Bean Div., FMC Corp.; Bear Mfg. Corp., Applied Power Inc.; Bee-Line Co.; Behr-Manning Corp.; Belden Corp.; The Bendix Corp.; Binks Mfg. Co.; Blackhawk Mfg. Co., Applied Power Inc.; Borg-Warner Corp.; Robert Bosch Corp.; Briggs and Stratton Corp.; Buick Motor Div., GMC; Cadillac Motor Car Div., GMC; Carborundum Co.; Carter Carburetor Div., ACF Industries, Inc.; Caterpillar Tractor Co.; Central Tool Co., Inc.; Champion Spark Plug Co.; Chevrolet Motor Div., GMC; Chicago Pneumatic Tool Co.; Chrysler-Plymouth Div., Chrysler Motors Corp.; Clayton Mfg. Co.; Columbus Parts, A Questor Co.; Cummins Engine Co.; Curtiss-Wright Corp.; Dana Corp.; Deere and Co.; Delco Moraine Div., GMC; Delco Products Div., GMC; Delco-Remy Div., GMC; Deluxe Products Div., Walker Mfg. Co.; Detroit Diesel Allison Div., GMC; Deutz Diesel Corp.; The DeVilbiss Co.; Ditzler Automotive Finishes, PPG Industries, Inc.; Dodge Div., Chrysler Motors Corp.; Dow Chemical U.S.A.; Draf Tool Co., Inc.; E. I. du Pont de Nemours and Co.; Duro Metal Products Co.; ESB Brands, Inc.; Eaton Corp.; E. Edelmann and Co.; Electric Autopulse Div., Walbro Corp.; Evinrude Motors; Federal-Mogul Corp.; Firestone Tire & Rubber Co.; Ford Customers Service Div., Ford Motor Co.; Fox Products Co.; Fram Corp.; Gabriel Div., Maremont Corp.; The Gates Rubber Co.; General Electric Co.; Gibson Products Div., Rolero, Inc.; Globe Hoist; The Goodyear Tire and Rubber Co.; Grant Div., Royal Industries; Grizzly Div., Maremont Corp.; Grey-Rock Div., Raybestos-Manhattan, Inc.; Gumout Div., Pennsylvania Refining Co.; Hall-Toledo Corp.; Harley Davidson; Hastings Mfg. Co.; Hein-Werner Corp.; Heli-Coil Corp.; Hercules Engine Div., White Motor Corp.; Holley Carburetor Div., Colt Industries; Hunter Engineering Co.; IMPCO Carburetion, Inc.; Imperial-Eastman Corp.; International Harvester Corp.; International Mobile Air Conditioning Assoc. (IMACA); Jet-Air Products; Johns-Manville Sales Corp.; Kelsey-Hayes Co.; King Electronics Co.; Kwik-Way; Leece-Neville Div., VLN Corp.; Lempco Industries Inc.; Lincoln Electric Co.; Lincoln St. Louis; Lincoln-Mercury Div., Ford Motor Co.; Linde Div., Union Carbide Corp.; Lisle Corp.; Lucas Electric Services, Inc.; Magnaflux Corp.; Mallory Electric Corp.; Maremont Corp., Automotive Group; Marquette Mfg. Co., Applied Power Inc.; Marvel-Schebler/Tillotson Div., Borg-Warner Corp.; McCord Replacement Products Div., McCord Corp.; McCulloch Motors Corp.; Milwaukee Electric Tool Corp.; Monroe Auto Equipment Co.; Moog Automotive, Inc.; Motorcraft Parts Div., Ford Motor Co.; Mystik Adhesive Products; National LP-Gas Assoc. (NLPGA); Nicholson File Co.; C. E. Niehoff and Co.; Norton Co.; Oldsmobile Div., GMC; Oliver Farm Equipment; OSHA, U.S. Dept. of Labor; Perfect Circle Div., Dana Corp.; Pontiac Motor Div., GMC; H. K. Porter Co., Inc.; PPG Industries, Inc.; Pratt and Whitney Aircraft; The Prestolite Co.; Purolator, Inc.; Ramsey Corp.; Raybestos Div., Raybestos-Manhattan, Inc.; Reo Motors Inc.; Rochester Products Div., GMC; Roosa-Master Div., Standard Screw Co.; Rubber Manufacturers Association (RMA); Seal Lock Co.; Sealed Power Corp.; Sherwin-Williams Co.; Sioux Tools; Skil Corp.; Snap-on Tools Corp.; Society of Automotive Engineers; L. S. Starrett Mfg. Co.; Stewart-Warner Corp.; Storm-Vulcan, Inc.; Sun Electric Corp.; Sun Oil Co.; Sunnen Products Co.; Tecumseh Products Co.; TRW Replacement Products Div., TRW Inc.; 3M Co.; Trico Products Corp.; Union Carbide Corp.; United Delco Div., GMC; Universal Oil Products Co.; Van Norman Machine Co.; Wagner Electric Corp.; Walker Mfg. Co.; Warner Electric Brake Mfg. Co.; Waukesha Motor Co.; Weaver Div., Dura Corp.; S. K. Wellman Corp.; Westinghouse Air Brake Co.; Westinghouse Electric Corp.; Whitaker Cable Corp.; Wilton Corp.; Winona Tool Mfg. Co., Inc.; Wix Corp.; Zenith Carburetor Div., Bendix Corp.

We also are indebted to those who represent manufacturers of imported cars for fine cooperation in furnishing technical information and specifications. We hope that their efforts and ours will help bring about a better understanding of their products in the U.S., with better service and improved customer satisfaction as a worthwhile result.

American Honda Motor Co., Inc.. The Associated Octel Co., LTD.; BMW of North America, Inc.; British Leyland Motors Inc.; Buick Motor Div., GMC.; Chrysler Corp.; Fiat Motors of North America, Inc.; Mazda Motors of America (Central), Inc.; Mercedes-Benz of North America, Inc.; Nissan Motor Corp. in U.S.A.; Peugeot, Inc.; Porsche-Audi Div., Volkswagen of America, Inc.; Renault U.S.A., Inc.; Rolls-Royce Motors Inc.; Saab-Scania of America, Inc.; Subaru of America, Inc.; Toyota Motor Sales, U.S.A., Inc.; Volkswagen of America, Inc.; Volvo of America Corp.

1980-1981 SUPPLEMENT

MECHANICAL CHANGES

New developments and mechanical changes in the design and construction of the 1980 and 1981 U.S. car models continue the recent engineering trends toward smaller, lighter cars, four and six cylinder engines, front wheel drive, Fig. S-1, and the ultimate goal of increased fuel economy. Moves in this direction by the car manufacturers are evidenced by the introduction of General Motors X-body models (Buick Skylark, Chevrolet Citation, Oldsmobile Omega and Pontiac Phoenix), Ford Escort and Mercury Lynx, Fig. S-2, and Chrysler's Plymouth Reliant and Dodge Aries.

Generally, design and manufacturing changes by the car makers to reduce vehicle weight and size, coupled with the use of smaller, more fuel efficient engines, were evident throughout most lines of U.S. passenger cars. The 1980 and 1981 models feature weight reductions up to 930 lb., wheelbases shortened by as much as 10.2 in., and wide ratio transmissions coupled with low ratio rear axles or transaxle final drives.

Specifically, the following new vehicles and mechanical changes are some of the major technological advances introduced or refined for the 1980 and 1981 model years:

1. General Motors X-body cars.
2. Ford Escort and Mercury Lynx.
3. Plymouth Reliant and Dodge Aries, Fig. S-3.
4. American Motors four wheel drive Eagle.
5. Ford's Compound Valve Hemispherical (CVH) engine.
6. Cadillac's Modulated Displacement (V-8-6-4) engine.
7. American Motors' lightweight new 4.2 litre (258 cu. in.) six cylinder engine.
8. More turbocharged engine applications.
9. More diesel engine applications.
10. More electronic engine control systems.
11. More closed loop, oxygen sensing, fuel feedback controls and three-way catalysts.
12. Electronically controlled throttle body fuel injection systems.
13. Ford's automatic (ATX) and manual (MTX) transaxles.
14. More manual overdrive and automatic overdrive transmissions.
15. Self-adjusting clutch mechanisms.

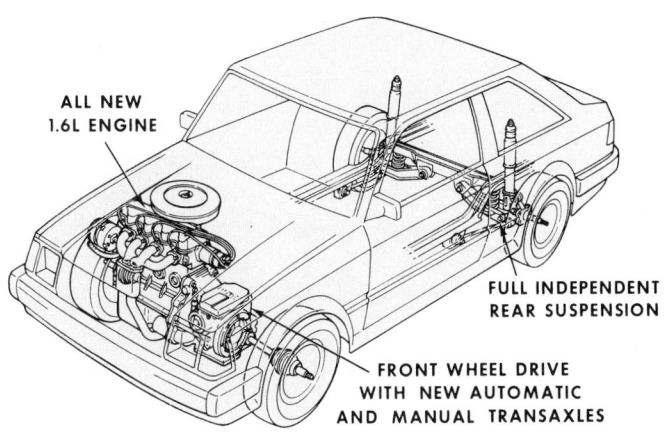

ALL NEW 1.6L ENGINE

FULL INDEPENDENT REAR SUSPENSION

FRONT WHEEL DRIVE WITH NEW AUTOMATIC AND MANUAL TRANSAXLES

Fig. S-2. Ford Escort follows current trend toward small, lightweight, front wheel drive cars. Body is unitized.

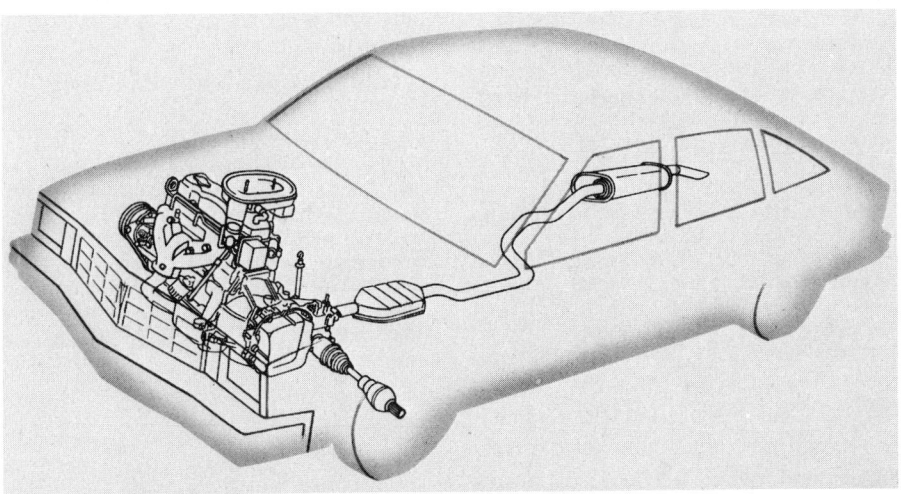

Fig. S-1. General Motors front wheel drive X-body cars are set on a 104.9 in. (2664 mm) wheelbase and are powered by a 151 cu. in. (2.5 L) in-line four cylinder engine.

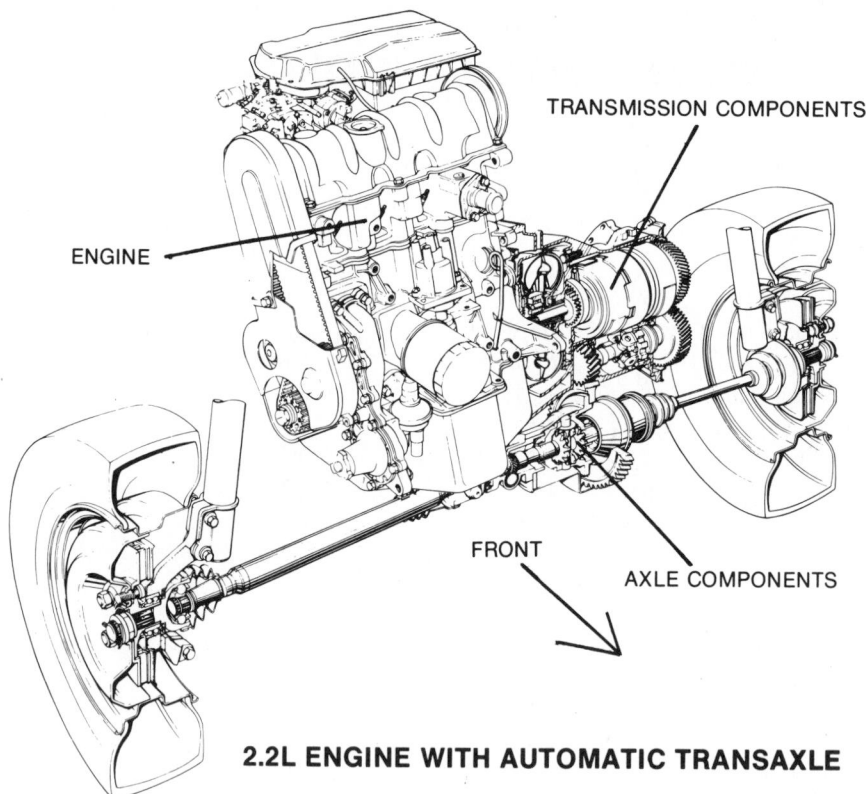

2.2L ENGINE WITH AUTOMATIC TRANSAXLE

ENGINE

TRANSMISSION COMPONENTS

FRONT

AXLE COMPONENTS

Fig. S-3. Plymouth Reliant and Dodge Aries models have a transverse-mounted, 125 cu. in. (2.2 L) four cylinder engine with overhead camshaft. Engine is canted backward toward driver at a 12 deg. angle. (Chrysler Corp.)

16. More lockup torque converters.
17. More MacPherson strut front suspension applications.
18. Four-wheel independent suspension.
19. More high pressure, P-metric radial ply tires.
20. Puncture sealing tires.
21. Semi-metallic brake lining.
22. Keyless entry system.
23. More halogen headlights.

NEW VEHICLES

Several all-new vehicles were introduced for 1980 and 1981. General Motors X-body cars were announced as 1980 models in the spring of 1979.

GM X-BODY CARS

The General Motors front wheel drive, front engine, X-body car, Fig. S-1, is powered by either a four cylinder 2.5 litre (151 cu. in.) engine, Fig. S-4, or a 2.8 litre (173 cu. in.) V-6 engine. See Fig. S-5. X-body cars are available from four different GM divisions.

Both the in-line four cylinder engine and the V-6 are overhead valve design and provided with hydraulic valve lifters. The "four" has a compression ratio of 8.3 to 1; the firing order is 1-3-4-2. Compression ratio of the V-6 is 8.6 to 1; firing order is 1-2-3-4-5-6. Staged, two barrel Varajet carburetors are

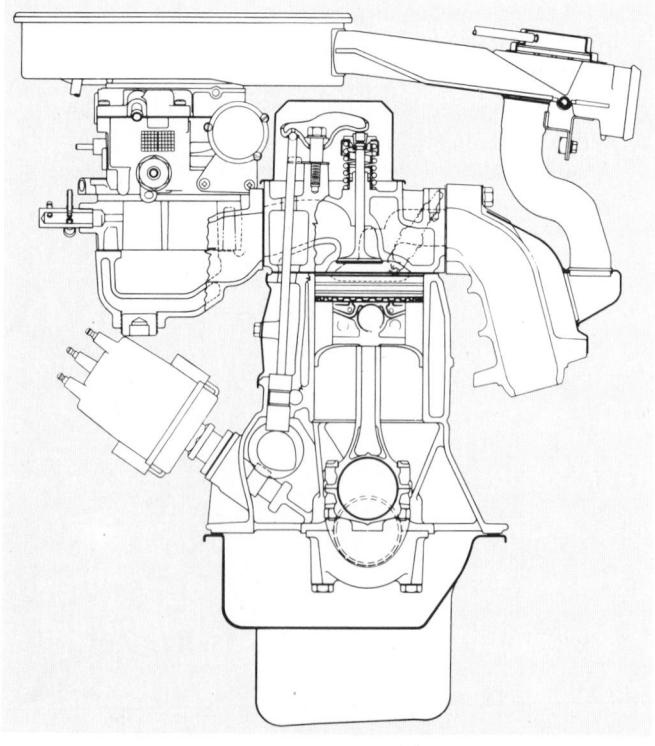

Fig. S-4. Sectional view shows construction details of four cylinder engine used in GM X-body cars. This cast iron engine is produced by the Pontiac Motor Division.

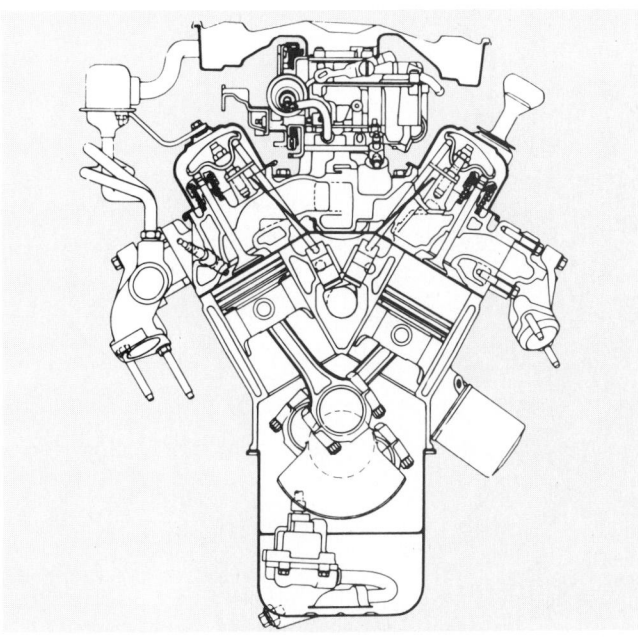

Fig. S-5. Chevrolet-built V-6 engine also available in GM X-body cars has a displacement of 173 cu. in. (2.8 L). Cylinder banks are set 60 deg. apart, rather than conventional 90 deg.

used on both engines available in GM X-body cars.

The engine, either the "four" or V-6, is installed transversely in the engine compartment aboard a framelike structure called a "cradle." The cradle itself is bolted to the car body, thereby helping to remove power train and suspension disturbances from the passenger compartment of the car. The cradle can be separated to give good access to engine and transaxle for service and repair.

In many repair operations, such as removing the front cover, oil pan or engine mounts, it is necessary to raise the engine a small amount. Special fixtures are available for supporting the engine assembly when this type of work is performed. These fixtures must be located in the center of the cowl, and all fasteners must be correctly torqued before putting the load on the fixture.

With regard to pistons, intermixing different size pistons has no effect on engine balance. All replacement pistons from standard size up to .030 in. (0.762 mm) oversize weigh exactly the same. Therefore, no attempt should be made to cut down oversize pistons to fit cylinder bores. Machining the piston would destroy the surface treatment. Also, cutting down oversize pistons would reduce weight which, in turn, would result in engine vibration due to unbalance.

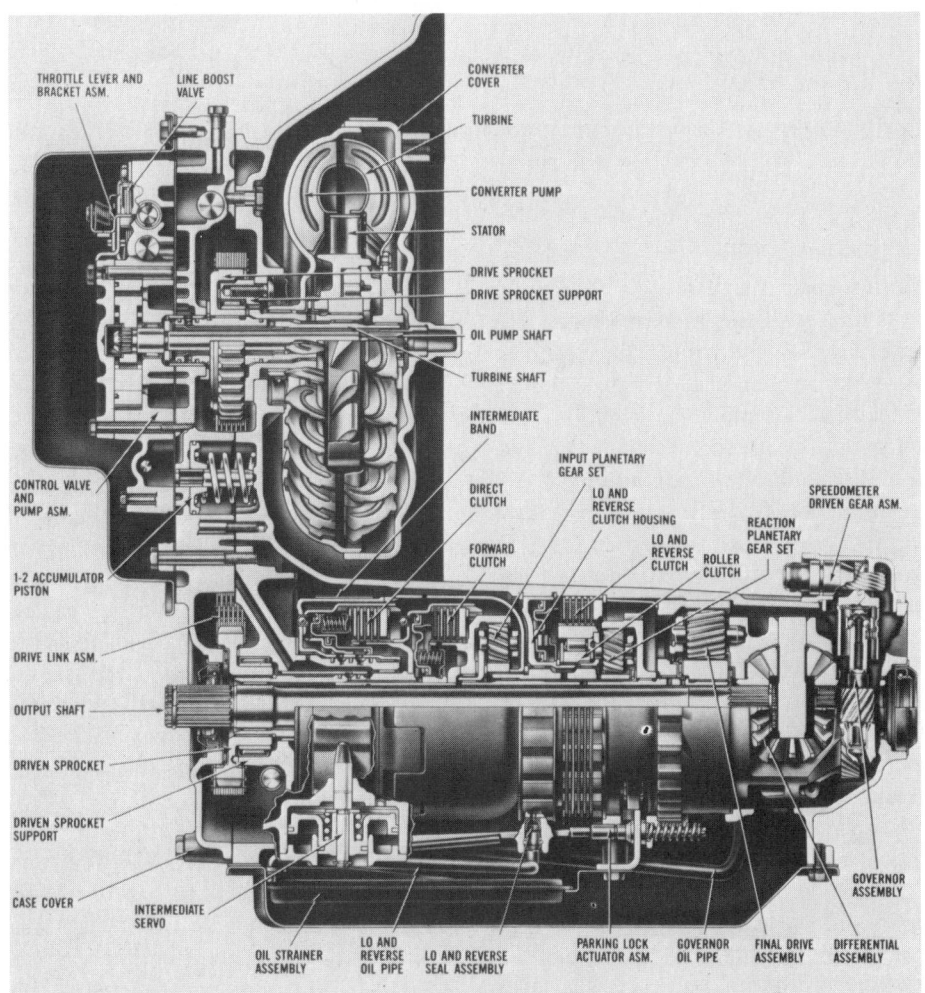

Fig. S-6. Automatic transaxle used in X-body cars. Note drive link assembly connecting torque converter to transmission.

Fig. S-7. Cutaway view of Chevrolet Citation front wheel drive train includes V-6 engine, manual transaxle and drive axle assemblies.

AUTOMATIC TRANSAXLE

Either a wide ratio automatic transaxle or a four-speed, manual shift transaxle is used with the X-body vehicle. The fully automatic transaxle, Fig. S-6, consists of a three element hydraulic torque converter, compound planetary gearset and a dual sprocket and drive link assembly. In addition, this "transaxle" (transmission and differential combined in one assembly) incorporates a differential and final gearset.

The three multiple disc clutches, a roller clutch and band provide the friction element to produce the desired function of the planetary gearset in the automatic transaxle. The hydraulic system, pressurized by a vane type pump, provides the working pressure required to operate the friction element.

Approximately 4 quarts (3.8 L) of transmission fluid are required to refill the transaxle after the pan has been drained. The total fluid capacity is 6 quarts (5.7 L). The transaxle operating temperature is the main consideration in establishing proper frequence of transaxle fluid change. Driving conditions have a major effect on operating temperature: if the car is driven in heavy traffic; when outside temperatures regularly reach 90 deg. F (32 C); in hilly or mountainous country; in frequent trailer pulling operations; in taxi or delivery service. Under any of these conditions, the transaxle fluid should be changed and a new strainer installed every 15,000 miles (24,000 km).

The oil cooler for the automatic transaxle is located in the side tank of the radiator. This is a sealed container. In case of a major transaxle failure, where metal particles are carried over to the cooler, the connecting lines and the cooler must be flushed out with clean oleum solvent or the equivalent.

MANUAL TRANSAXLE

The four speed manual transaxle used in X-body cars is combined with a differential unit, all assembled in a single transaxle case. All forward gears are of the constant mesh type. Synchronizers with blocker rings are used. The transaxle case is made of aluminum.

The manual transaxle uses two cable assemblies to control the clutch. The clutch pedal and control system include a constant "no lash" feature. There is a constant contact of the clutch release bearing with the fingers of the pressure plate, but very little (if any) effect on the pressure plate.

The four speed manual transaxle and front drive axles are shown in Fig. S-7.

FRONT WHEEL ALIGNMENT

To adjust camber on front wheel drive X-body cars, first loosen the locking nuts on the cam through bolts. Loosen enough to allow movement of the steering knuckle. Note that the top cam bolt nut must be loose whenever a camber adjustment is made. Then, rotate the eccentric cam bolt to move the knuckle and wheel in or out as required. Tighten locking nuts on cam bolts to 50 ft. lb. (70 N·m). Remove wheel and tighten locking nuts to 140 ft. lb. (190 N·m).

To adjust toe-in, loosen jam nuts on tie rod. Remove clamps on steering shaft boots. Square vehicle. Rotate tie rods to adjust toe-in to 3/32 in. (2.5 mm). Tighten jam nuts. Tighten steering shaft boot clamps.

IGNITION TUNE-UP

General Motors high energy ignition system is standard equipment on engines in X-body cars. Timing specifications are listed on the decal in the engine compartment. The hold-down clamp on the ignition distributor in V-6 engines is conventional. The distributor on the "four," however, has a slightly different construction. To remove the distributor, it is first necessary to loosen a fastening nut before sliding off the clamp. See Fig. S-8.

EMISSION CONTROL SYSTEMS

Emission control systems installed on GM X-body cars include: catalytic converter; early fuel evaporative system; exhaust gas recirculating system; closed positive crankcase ventilating system; Pulsair injection reactor system; thermostatic air cleaner; evaporative emission control (EEC) system. Also important and related are calibration of the carburetor and choke. In addition, engines in X-body cars sold in California are equipped with a computer controlled catalytic converter (C-4) system. The C-4 system controls exhaust emissions by close regulation of the carburetor air-fuel ratio and by use of a three-way catalytic converter.

FRONT DISC BRAKES

Front brakes on GM X-body cars are disc type; rear brakes are drum type. To remove caliper from front disc brake: First, remove about two thirds of brake fluid from master cylinder reservoir. Next, position a C-clamp as shown in Fig. S-9, then tighten clamp until piston bottoms in bore. Remove C-clamp. Next, remove bolt holding inlet fitting and remove fitting. Then, remove Allen head mounting bolts. Remove caliper from rotor. If only shoe and lining assembly are to be replaced, suspend caliper from chassis spring by means of a wire hook. Remove and replace shoe and lining assembly.

FORD ESCORT AND MERCURY LYNX

Escort and Lynx are all-new sub-compacts with new bodies, engines, transaxles and suspensions. Initially, two common design engines were offered in two sizes: 80 cu. in. (1.3 litre) and 98 cu. in. (1.6 litre). See Fig. S-10. Outstanding feature of new engines designed for use with these front wheel drive vehicles is the hemispherical combustion chamber. See Fig. S-11. This engine design is known as a "compound valve hemispherical engine (CVH)."

The smaller displacement engine develops 58 hp at 5700 rpm. The larger engine puts out 69 hp at 5000 rpm. This corresponds to .734 hp per cubic inch of displacement and .708 hp per cubic inch, respectively.

The CVH engine has a single, belt-driven overhead camshaft. The hemispherical combustion chamber is attained by canting the valves at an angle. See Fig. S-11. Hydraulic valve lifters are standard. The heads of the light alloy pistons are

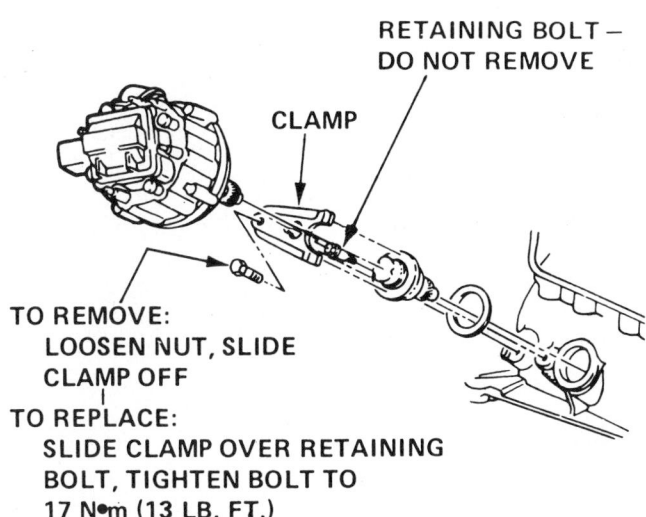

RETAINING BOLT —
DO NOT REMOVE

CLAMP

TO REMOVE:
LOOSEN NUT, SLIDE
CLAMP OFF
TO REPLACE:
SLIDE CLAMP OVER RETAINING
BOLT, TIGHTEN BOLT TO
17 N·m (13 LB. FT.)

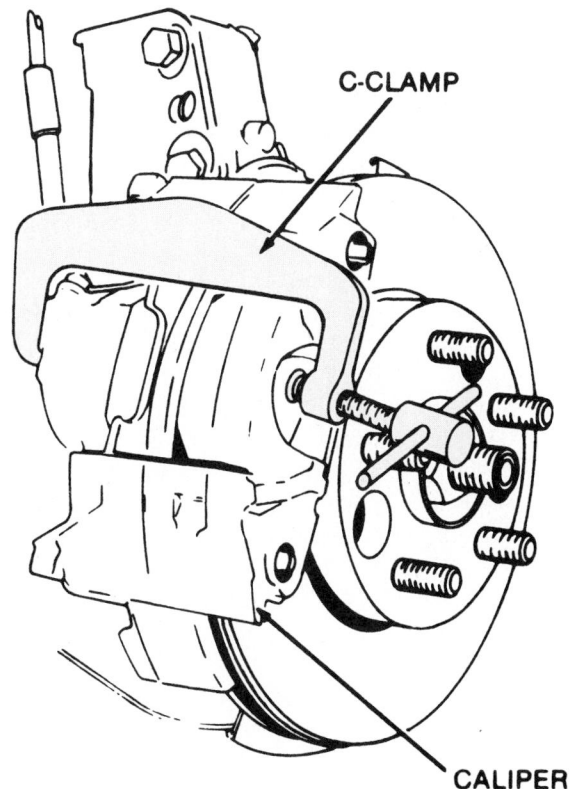

C-CLAMP

CALIPER

Fig. S-8. Drawing shows details of ignition distributor installation on 151 cu. in. (2.5 L) engine used in X-body cars.

Fig. S-9. When servicing front disc brakes on X-body cars, a C-clamp is used to force piston in caliper to bottom of bore.

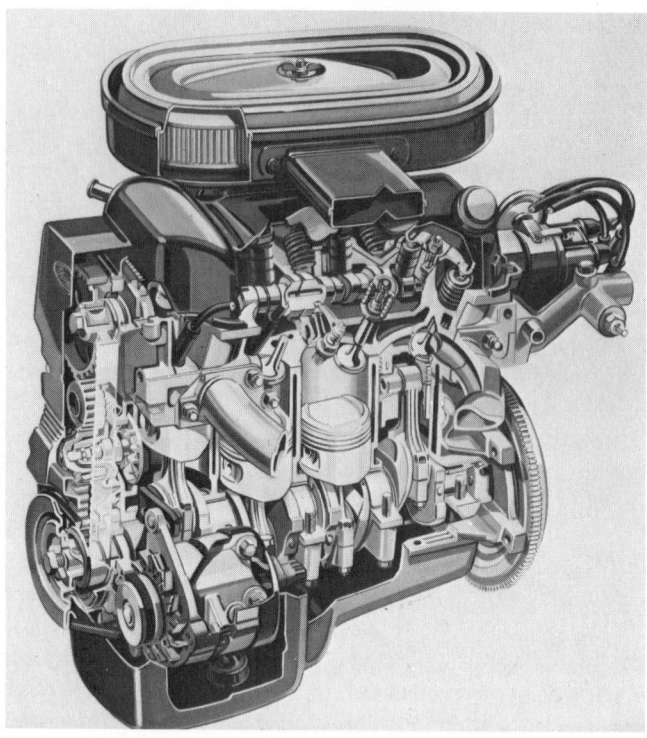

Fig. S-10. Ford Escort and Mercury Lynx cars are equipped with four cylinder, hemispherical combustion chamber engines. Note belt-driven overhead camshaft.

fully machined and provide a high degree of "squish." The cylinder head is aluminum, as is the intake manifold. The cylinder block is cast iron.

The CVH engine cruises on one barrel of the Holley-Weber carburetor. It utilizes the second venturi when additional power is required. The crossflow radiator has tanks molded from glass-filled nylon for reduced weight. Internal connec-

tions are sealed with gaskets instead of solder. The engine cooling fan is electrically operated and thermostatically controlled.

TRANSAXLE DESIGNS

Standard equipment for both the Escort and Lynx is a

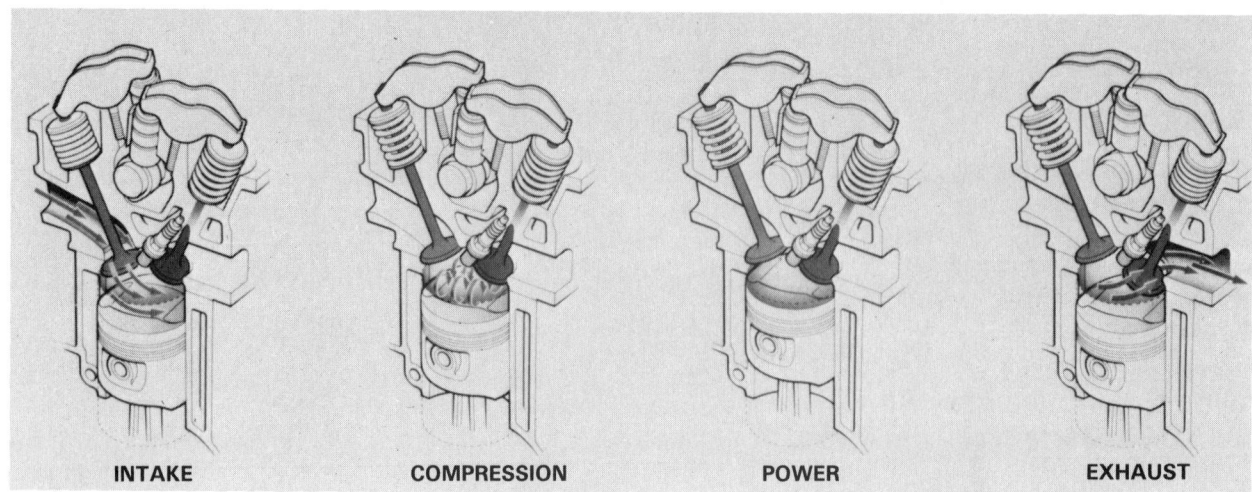

INTAKE   COMPRESSION   POWER   EXHAUST

Fig. S-11. Ford's compound valve hemispherical (CVH) engine is named for its fully machined combustion chambers and canted valve train. Note full flow characteristics of this design.

Fig. S-12. Ford's automatic transaxle is designed to split the torque in intermediate and driving ranges. Part of the torque is transmitted mechanically by direct connection between engine and transmission gears, while the rest is transmitted through the torque converter.

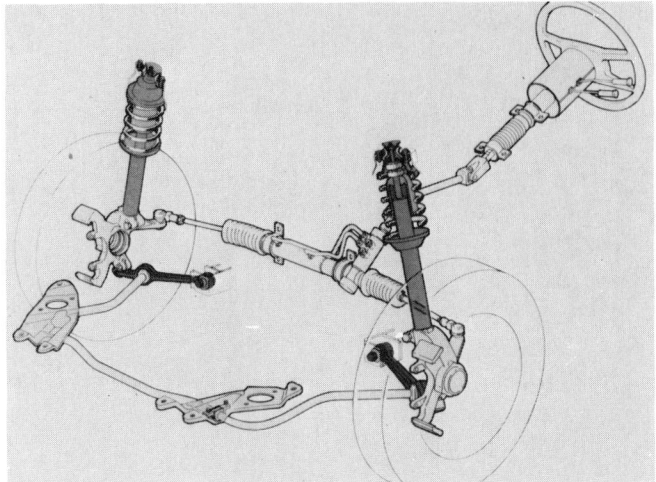

Fig. S-13. Ford Escort and Mercury Lynx cars feature MacPherson strut suspension in front, with unequal length steering arms.

four-speed, fully synchronized manual transaxle (MTX). It incorporates gear ratios of 3.6, 2.1, 1.2 and 0.8 to 1. The fourth gear overdrive of 0.8 to 1 permits engine speed to be reduced by 20 percent over the 1 to 1 ratio of conventional three and four-speed manual transmissions. The final drive ratio is 3.59 to 1. The clutch used with this transaxle is self adjusting.

The optional automatic transaxle, Fig. S-12, is a wide ratio, three-speed transaxle using an open torque converter in low and a split torque intermediate and drive range. The gearset splits the engine torque so that part is transmitted mechanically by direct connection between the engine and the transmission gears. The rest of the engine torque is transmitted hydrokinetically (by means of transmission fluid) through the torque converter. The splitter gearset ratios establish the quantity of torque flowing through the split paths.

The ATX transaxle holds 8.5 quarts of special Ford automatic transmission fluid. No fluid change is required in normal service.

SUSPENSION SETUPS

Four wheel fully independent suspension is featured on Escort and Lynx cars. Rear suspension utilizes a one-piece, forged wheel spindle on each side attached to a transverse arm. A fore-and-aft tie rod and MacPherson shock strut are also used. The transverse arm and tie rod provide lateral and longitudinal control. The shock strut counters braking forces and provides the necessary suspension damping. The coil spring is mounted on the lower control arm and acts as a metal-to-metal jounce stop.

Front suspension on Escort and Lynx cars uses full MacPherson strut assemblies, Fig. S-13, designed with a negative scrub radius. It uses unequal length steering arms: the left side is 0.35 in. (9 mm) longer. In addition, the camber specification is increased on the left side. The suspension is lubricated for life. Rack and pinion steering is used.

BRAKES AND BODY

The front disc brakes are a more compact version of the pin slider type introduced on the Fairmont. Rear brakes are drum type. Front wheel bearings are lubricated for life.

Escort and Lynx cars have a fully unitized body structure. There is no separate frame, and all structural loading is contained within the body structure.

Servicewise, it is interesting to note that the camshaft can be serviced without removing the cylinder head or disassembling the engine. The oil pan can be removed without raising the engine. Also: the transaxle can be taken from the car without first removing the engine; the bolt-on differential can be removed from the transaxle without removing the transaxle from the car.

CHRYSLER K-CARS

The all-new Chrysler K-cars (Plymouth Reliant and Dodge Aries) are powered by a 125 cu. in. (2.2 litre), four cylinder, overhead camshaft engine. See Fig. S-14. A 156 cu. in. Mitsubishi engine is optional.

The overhead camshaft on the 2.2 litre engine is driven by a link timing belt. Access to this belt is easy after removing the two-piece front cover. The valve train is activated by hydraulic lash adjusters, which serve the purpose of hydraulic lifters. Valve rotators are low friction type. Peak net horsepower is 84 at 4800 rpm. The compression ratio is 8.5 to 1.

Timing marks on the flywheel housing permit easy checking of valve timing and ignition timing. Firing order is 1-3-4-2. The

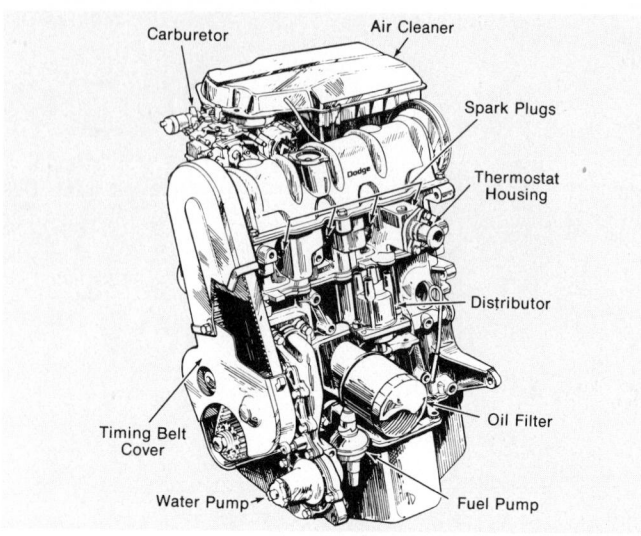

Fig. S-14. Chrysler K-cars have a new 2.2 litre, overhead camshaft, four cylinder engine with link timing belt.

coil springs and a flex arm beam with trailing links which result in low unsprung weight. Front brakes are disc type with drum brakes at the rear. The front calipers are floating type with rods instead of machined ways (guides) which tend to rust and stick.

NEW ENGINES

Several new engines made their debut in 1981 models. Newly introduced were the Ford 1.3/1.6 litre "fours"; the Cadillac V-8-6-4 engine; Chrysler's 2.2 litre "four"; and AMC's 4.2 litre "six."

FORD'S CVH ENGINE

Ford's compound valve hemispherical (CVH) engine is

ignition system is electronic; ignition timing is electronically controlled.

The carburetor on the 2.2 litre engine is two barrel type, mounted at the front of the engine. See Fig. S-14. The aluminum intake manifold includes a water jacket to supply heat for improved vaporization. A computer system is provided to enrich the carburetor air-fuel mixture as required by driving demands.

Power from this engine is transmitted to the front wheels by way of a transaxle. The standard four speed manual transmission has integral overdrive (fourth speed). A ratcheting device automatically adjusts the clutch.

The K-cars have unitized bodies. The front suspension system is described as "Iso" strut, a variation of the MacPherson strut design. Rear suspension, Fig. S-15, includes

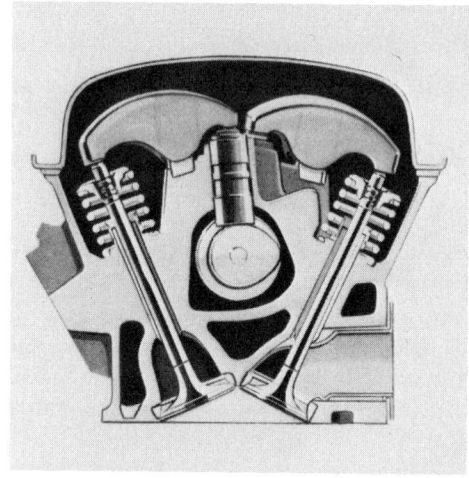

Fig. S-16. Hemispherical combustion chamber is key design feature of Ford's CVH four cylinder engine introduced in 1981.

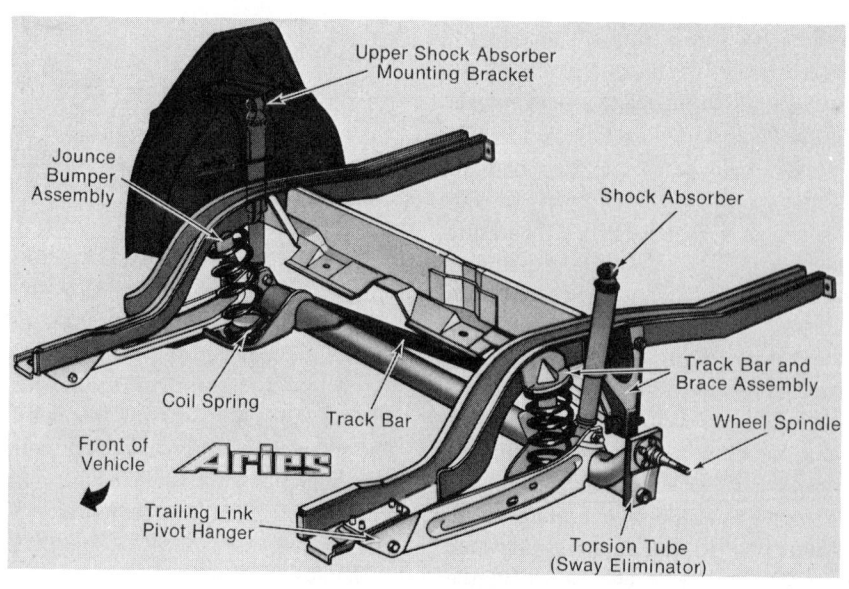

Fig. S-15. K-cars have flex arm beam rear suspension with trailing links.

shown and described on pages 797 and 798. The engine is named for its fully machined hemispherical combustion chamber design, Fig. S-16. The hemispherical shape was chosen over other designs because tests reportedly proved it superior in terms of fuel efficiency, power output, octane requirements, tolerance for low-grade fuels and spark advance characteristics.

engine operates as a 6.0 litre V-8, a 4.5 litre "six" or a 3.0 litre "four."

The operating principle of the valve selectors is to control the point of pivot of the rocker arm assembly. Doing this causes the rocker arm to open the valve or allow the valve to remain closed while the remainder of the valve gear operates through normal travel.

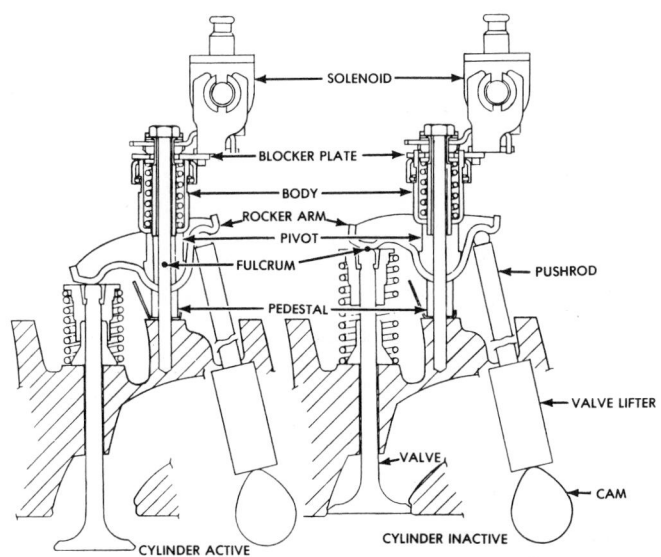

Fig. S-17. Cadillac's V-8-6-4 engine utilizes valve selectors mounted on valve assemblies of four cylinders to deactivate and activate selected cylinders. This permits engine to operate on eight, six or four cylinders to meet driving needs and conditions.

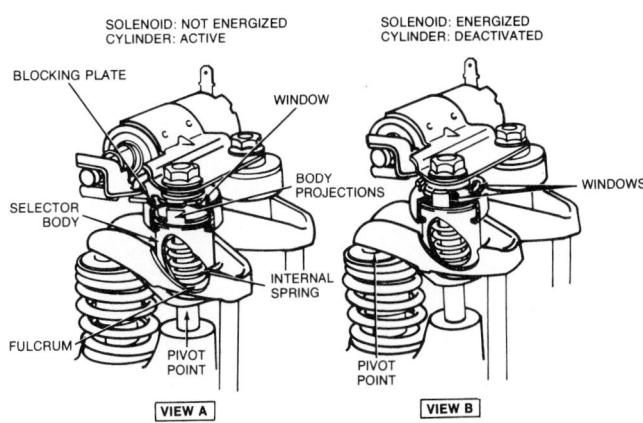

Fig. S-18. Details of valve selector of Cadillac's V-8-6-4 modulated displacement system. View A. Solenoid not energized; cylinder active. View B. Solenoid energized; cylinder deactivated.

CADILLAC'S V-8-6-4 ENGINE

Cadillac's modulated (variable) displacement engine will run on eight, six or four cylinders according to power demands. For this reason, the modulated displacement engine is also known as the "V-8-6-4" engine.

In operation, the V-8-6-4 engine deactivates the valves in selected cylinders in response to driving needs and conditions. This is accomplished by an electro-mechanical system controlled by a microprocessor. The engine also has an advanced digital fuel injection system that monitors a wide range of operating conditions.

Information related to engine speed, coolant temperature, throttle position and intake manifold absolute pressure or vacuum is sent to an electronic control module. Based on this input information, the control module energizes the electrical solenoids in the valve selectors. Each selector, Fig. S-17, controls both intake and exhaust valves of a single cylinder.

OPERATING PRINCIPLES. Using four valve selectors permits the selective operation of eight, six or four cylinders. The valve selectors are installed on cylinders one, four, six and seven. See Fig. S-17. When the engine is operating on six cylinders, cylinder numbers one and four are deactivated. When the engine is operating on four cylinders, cylinder numbers six and seven are also deactivated. In this way, the

During normal eight cylinder operation, the rocker arm pivots near the center, which is its fulcrum point. As the cam reaches its highest point, the valve is opened to allow the air-fuel mixture to enter the cylinder.

When the valve selector is activated for either six or four cylinder operation (cam again on high point), the valve will not open. There is no valve action because the selector will shift the rocker arm pivot point and allow the rocker arm to slide up and down its mounting stud. This, in effect, shifts the fulcrum point to the tip of this now stationary valve. Meanwhile, the valve spring holds the valve closed and the cylinder is deactivated.

CYLINDER SELECTION. The valve selectors are mounted on the intake and exhaust rocker arms above the rocker arm fulcrums. When the solenoid is not energized, view A in Fig. S-18, the selector body is restrained from moving upward by contact between the "body projections" and the "blocking plate" above it. The rocker arm pivots near its center, the valves operate normally and the cylinder is activated.

When the selector is energized to deactivate the valves, view B in Fig. S-18, the blocking plate is rotated by its solenoid to align the blocking plate "windows" with the body projections. As the rocker arm is lifted by the push rod, the rocker arm and body ride up the stud since the body is no longer restrained by the blocking plate. The rocker arm now pivots at the tip of the valve, the valve remains closed and the cylinder is deactivated. Spring tension in the body maintains zero valve lash.

DIGITAL FUEL INJECTION. The V-8-6-4 modulated displacement engine is monitored largely through a digital fuel

DIGITAL FUEL INJECTION/CLOSED LOOP

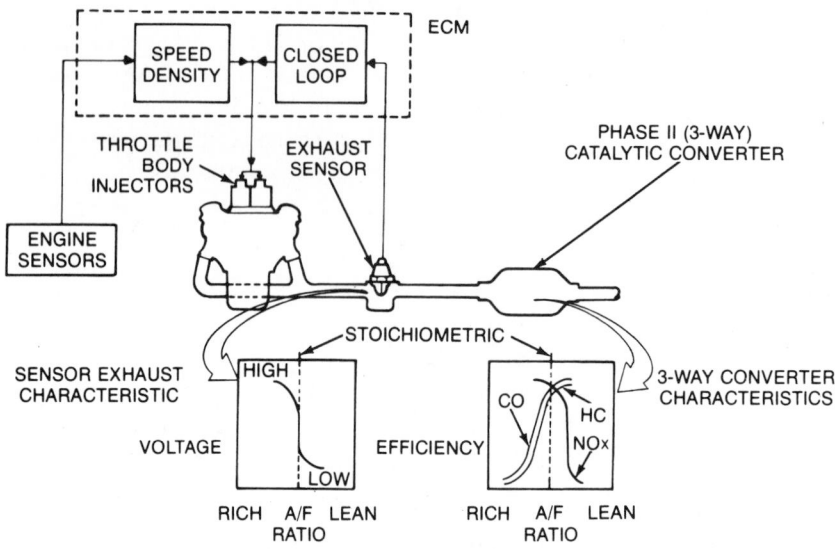

Fig. S-19. Cadillac's digital fuel injection system on V-8-6-4 engine uses various sensors, switches and an electronic control module to determine precise amount of fuel to inject into carburetor throttle body to obtain optimum air-fuel ratio.

injection system. See Fig. S-19. This "speed density" system is designed to accurately control the air-fuel mixture to achieve desired performance and exhaust emission control.

The manifold absolute pressure sensor, manifold air temperature sensor and the barometric pressure sensor are used to determine the amount (density) of air entering the engine. The high energy ignition distributor provides the engine speed information of revolutions per minute. See Fig. S-19. This information is fed to the electronic control module, which performs high speed digital computations to determine the exact amount of fuel necessary for the optimum air-fuel mixture. When this computation is completed, the electronic control module signals the fuel injectors to meter fuel into the throttle body.

When the combustion process has been completed, some hydrocarbons, carbon monoxide and oxides of nitrogen are formed. To clean these pollutants from the exhaust stream, an oxygen sensor is used to monitor the exhaust gases. The oxygen sensor sends this information to the electronic control module which makes any corrections that are required. This correction process is known as "closed loop" operation. See Fig. S-19.

Because the vehicle is operated under a wide range of conditions, additional sensors and switches are needed to determine what operating conditions exist so that the electronic control module can provide an acceptable level of driveability under all operating conditions.

CHRYSLER'S 2.2 LITRE FOUR

The new 2.2 litre four cylinder engine introduced in 1981 Plymouth Reliant and Dodge Aries cars is detailed on pages 799 and 800.

Servicewise, most engine components are easily accessible. Spark plugs, spark plug wires and ignition distributor are on the front side of the crosswise mounted engine. See Fig. S-14. The ignition coil is located on the passenger side inner fender. The electric fan relay, starter relay, anti-dieseling relay and voltage regulator are mounted on the driver's side suspension strut.

All belts except the air conditioning compressor belt can be adjusted from the top of the engine compartment. Working underneath the car, the compressor belt adjusts at an idler pulley. The air pump is at the transaxle end of the engine,

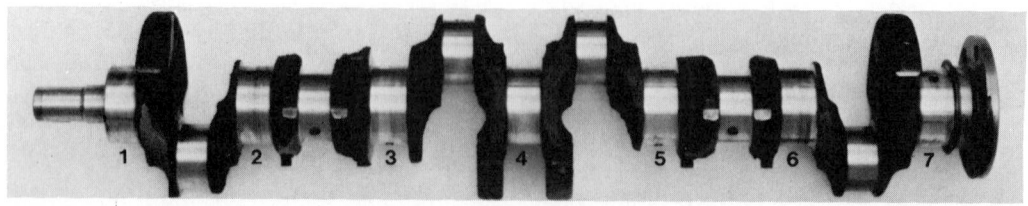

Fig. S-20. The crankshaft in AMC's new "258" engine is 20.5 lb. lighter than shaft in earlier "258." New shaft retains seven main bearing journals.

bolted to the cylinder head and driven off the back of the overhead camshaft. To change this belt, you have to pull the air pump.

Cooling system components are within easy reach: radiator hoses, draincock, thermostat housing and electric fan quick disconnect plugs. The engine oil pan can be dropped by simply removing the pan retaining screws. The pan uses RTV silicone, rather than a gasket, to seal it to the crankcase flange.

AMC'S 4.2 LITRE SIX

For 1981, AMC introduced a new 258 cu. in. (4.2 litre) six cylinder engine that is 90 lb. lighter than the previously used "258." To save weight, thickness of the block walls, webs and flanges was reduced. However, the seven main bearing construction was retained. See Fig. S-20. The cylinder head was redesigned with a reshaped rocker cover flange for improved sealing (RTV silicone).

The crankshaft of the new "258" was also redesigned, Fig. S-20. Eight of the twelve counterweights used previously were eliminated. The exhaust is separate from the intake manifold, and the exhaust manifold heat control valve was dropped. In its place, an electrically heated warmup device is located in the floor of the intake manifold below the carburetor. In addition, a water heating circuit is built into the intake manifold.

Improvements in emission control include an idle speed control system that consists of a mechanical/electrical servo and a programmed electronic module. The closed loop (fuel feedback) control system with dual bed catalyst is carried over to AMC's new "258" engine. All AMC engines for 1981 — four, six and V-8 — have tamperproof idle mixture adjustments and choke systems.

OTHER ENGINES

New and improved diesel, turbocharged, turbocharged diesel and turbo-compounded engines were produced for the 1980 and 1981 model years.

GM DIESEL. Applications of the Oldsmobile 350 cu. in. (5.7 litre) V-8 diesel were expanded to become optional equipment on full size Buick, Chevrolet and Pontiac cars. For 1981, the Oldsmobile diesel has roller hydraulic valve lifters and 5000-mile oil change and oil filter change intervals. Diesel powered GM cars also feature an across-the-board adoption of a water-in-fuel sensor and warning light on the dash.

The Oldsmobile diesel makes use of the CAV Microjector, a poppet valve type of fuel injector developed by Lucas CAV Limited. See Fig. S-21. It is smaller than previously used injectors and does not require fuel return piping.

In operation, fuel from the injection pump passes through the nozzle holder into the spring chamber. At that time, the nozzle valve is held against its seat by a combination of spring pressure and combustion pressure of the engine. The fuel flows through the spring chamber and two cross holes in the nozzle body below the upper valve guide, then passes through the helical grooves in the lower valve guide to the seat. When the fuel pressure overcomes the spring and compression forces, it will move the valve off its seat and outward fuel flow

continues past the large diameter pintle orifice into the combustion chamber.

If fuel pressure is high, the nozzle valve will move until the lift stop reaches the body. If fuel pressure is low, the valve will float in the pintle orifice. At the end of injection, spring pressure and combustion pressure will close the valve.

Lucas CAV Limited claims that the Microjector has made a significant contribution toward meeting emission standards.

DETROIT DIESEL ALLISON FUEL PINCHER. The 500 cu. in. (8.2 litre) "Fuel Pincher" diesel engine is designed for use in medium duty vehicles in the 10,000 to 50,000 GVW range. The naturally aspirated engine develops 165 hp (123 kW) at 3000 rpm. The turbocharged engine, Fig. S-22, is rated at 205 hp (153 kW).

The 8.2 litre diesel uses the GM unit injector system, Fig. 27-11. This system creates the high fuel pressure required for injection. It also meters and atomizes the exact amount of fuel needed for the existing load on the engine.

Metering of the fuel is accomplished by the upper and lower helix in the lower end of the injection plunger. See Fig. 27-12, which illustrates fuel metering from no-load to full-load.

The air intake system has helical shaped intake ports in the cylinder head designed to produce air swirl eddies in the combustion chamber. Pistons are made of aluminum alloy with a ni-Resist top ring groove. The combustion chamber is "open chamber" type located in the top of the piston.

The Fuel Pincher engine is designed so that the coolant completely surrounds the cylinder bore, thereby eliminating hot spots. In addition, this design is said to provide a reduction in weight and in noise of operation.

Exhaust valve seats are induction hardened. The exhaust ports are insulated with stainless steel heat shields to reduce

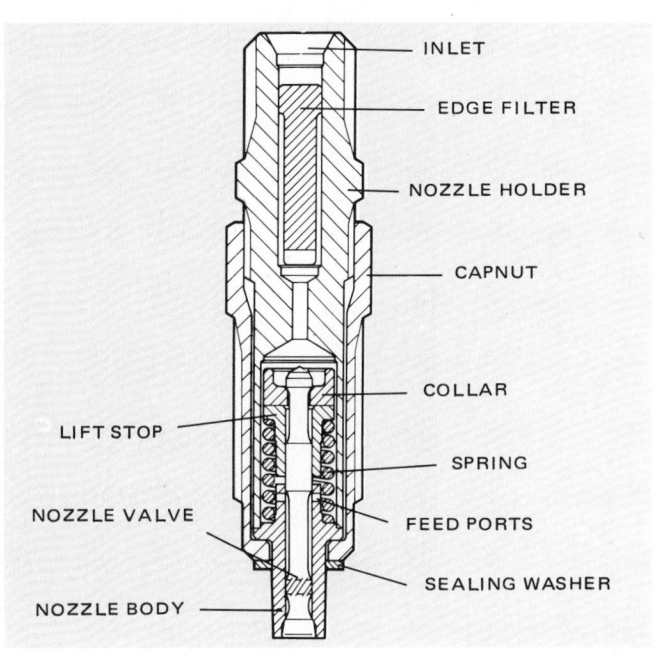

Fig. S-21. Sectional view of CAV Microjector used in Oldsmobile 5.7 L diesel V-8 engine. (Lucas CAV Limited)

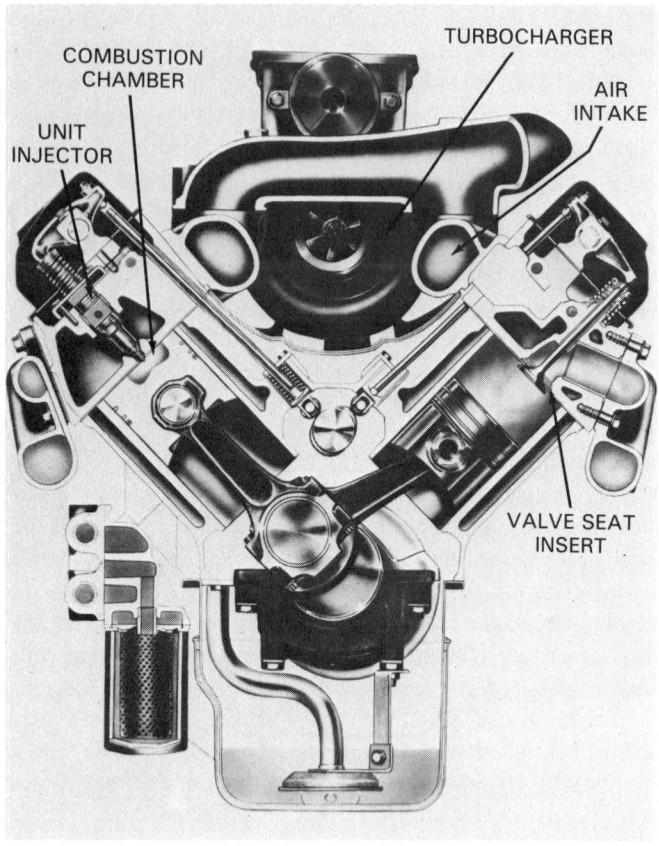

Fig. S-22. Air swirl eddies in "open" combustion chambers of Fuel Pincher diesel engine reportedly provide improved fuel economy and low exhaust emissions. (Detroit Diesel Allison Div., GM)

heat rejection to the coolant. In that way, more gas energy is available for operation of the turbocharger.

CUMMINS PT G-AFC FUEL PUMP. The PT G-AFC pump, Fig. S-23, largely supersedes the PT type R pump shown and described on pages 307 to 310. The PT G-AFC differs from the standard PT type G model by the addition of an air-fuel control section between the fuel pump throttle shaft and the shut-down valve.

The designation PT G-AFC stands for Pressure, Time, Governor, Air, Fuel Control. The system derives its name from the fact that fuel metered through an orifice into the injector depends on fuel pressure at the orifice. Pressure at the orifice is controlled by the fuel pump. The absolute time that the orifice is open is controlled by the cam injector plunger.

Typically, fuel is drawn from the fuel tank through a filter by a positive displacement gear pump and delivered through the fuel pump to the injectors. Fuel is circulated through the injectors for injection and to prime and cool the system. In addition, air is removed from the fuel, which is returned to the fuel supply tank by way of the fuel manifold. Since this pump is designed only to supply pressure, it does not time the injection as is the case with most other systems.

When the engine is running, fuel from the fuel passage enters into the injector through an adjustable orifice plug. When the plunger is retracted and the metering (feed) orifice is open, fuel pressure opens the check ball valve and fuel enters the cup. The amount entering depends on the fuel pressure and the time the metering orifice is open. The metering portion of the cycle is followed by injection, during which the plunger moves downward. The cam-actuated injector plunger

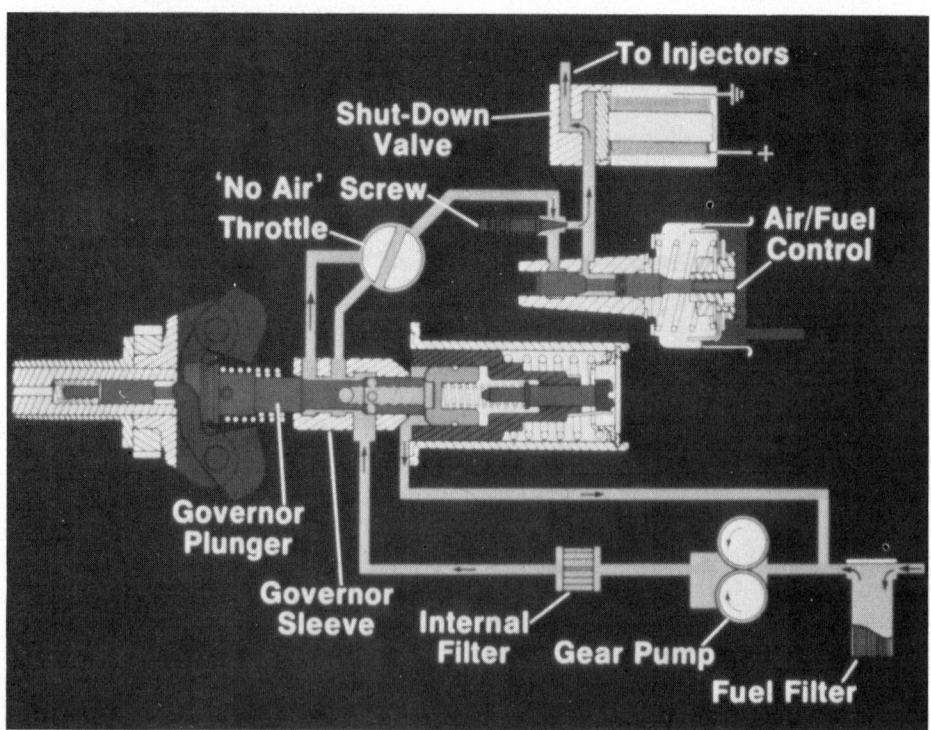

Fig. S-23. Simplified drawing of Cummins PT G-AFC fuel pump pressure regulating system. Fuel flow pattern is from positive displacement pump through porting and relief grooves to governor and plunger to fuel manifold and outlet to injectors. (Cummins Engine Co.)

then forces fuel through the spray holes into the combustion chamber.

The quantity of fuel delivered through the metering orifice is regulated by changing the fuel pressure at the entrance of the metering orifice. The fuel pump is calibrated to control and provide the correct pressure curve at all engine speeds.

The Cummins PT G-AFC fuel pump has a pressure regulating system in which governor weights control the fuel pressure as a function of engine speed. Basic parts of the pressure regulating system include:

1. A source of fuel flow and pressure produced by the positive displacement pump.
2. A governor and plunger with porting and relief grooves on the plunger that enables the fuel to flow through the governor when the port and the grooves are correctly aligned.
3. A throttle valve located in the pressure regulating system between the governor and fuel pump discharge is designed to reduce pressure to the fuel manifold, thereby providing part load control.
4. The fuel manifold to the injectors.
5. A fuel by-pass curcuit from the governor plunger fuel groove through an axial drilling, out the end of the plunger and back to the fuel supply pump inlet.

PONTIAC'S TURBOCHARGED 4.9 LITRE ENGINE. Pontiac has introduced a turbocharged 301 cu. in. (4.9 litre) four barrel V-8 engine on Formula and Trans Am models. See Fig. S-24. The turbo V-8 utilizes an electronic spark control system that helps sustain peak combustion pressures. The ESC system incorporates computerized combustion spark knock detection and control.

The turbocharging unit consists of compressor, a center rotating group (bearings and oil) and a turbine. A shaft connects the compressor and compressor wheel to the turbine wheel. Exhaust gases pass through the turbine, converting

Fig. S-24. Pontiac's 4.9 L turbocharged V-8 engine allows increased performance in a small displacement engine without a substantial decrease in fuel economy. (Pontiac Motor Div., GM)

thermal energy to mechanical energy to rotate the turbine wheel. Net horsepower of the Pontiac turbo V-8 is 210 at 4000 rpm.

PEUGEOT'S TURBOCHARGED DIESEL. Peugeot is offering an overhead valve, in-line four cylinder turbocharged diesel engine. The 140 cu. in. (2.3 litre) XD2S engine develops 88 hp (66 kW) at 4150 rpm. Peugeot claims an 18 percent increase in horsepower and 43 percent increase in torque for the turbocharged diesel over the normally aspirated XD2 diesel. Compression ratio is 21 to 1.

CUMMINS' TURBO-COMPOUNDED ENGINE. Cummins Engine Company is experimenting with a turbo-compounded engine. Turbo-compounding makes use of both supercharging and turbocharging to improve performance and economy. In this new system, the turbocharger exhaust is ducted to a low pressure turbine which is also coupled to the engine crankshaft by way of a speed reduction gear train.

In special runs from Florida to California, trucks equipped with turbo-compounded engines reportedly accumulated over 50,000 miles with an average combined weight of 72,000 lb. Average fuel consumption was 5.25 mpg, an estimated improvement of 4 percent over conventional 450 hp engines.

ENGINE ELECTRONIC CONTROL SYSTEMS

In order to meet the more stringent emission control standards proposed for 1981, most engines were equipped with electronic control systems which served to detect and correct too-rich and too lean carburetor air-fuel mixtures. The more sophisticated systems also control the air pump so that best efficiency of conversion of emissions in the catalytic converter is obtained. Also effected by some systems are engine spark advance, idle speed, transmission torque converter clutch operation and canister purge control to reduce evaporative emissions.

Goal of the systems is to reduce exhaust emissions (carbon dioxide, hydrocarbons and oxides of nitrogen) without penalizing fuel economy or engine performance.

CHEVROLET'S C-4 AND CCC SYSTEMS

A computer controlled catalytic converter (C-4) system was installed on some 1980 Chevrolet engines. C-4 is an electronically controlled exhaust emissions system that includes an exhaust gas oxygen sensor, electronic control module, controlled air-fuel ratio carburetor and a three-way catalytic converter.

The system also features a "check engine" warning lamp that will light if the system malfunctions. The lamp will stay ON as long as the engine runs and the malfunction remains uncorrected. This lamp — working in conjunction with the activated electronic control module diagnostic system — will flash a trouble code that will help pinpoint the cause of the trouble.

The C-4 oxygen sensor is a closed end sensor placed in the engine exhaust system. It generates a voltage that varies with the oxygen content in the exhaust stream. As oxygen content increases (lean mixture), voltage falls. As oxygen content decreases (rich mixture), the voltage rises.

The electronic control module monitors the voltage output of the oxygen sensor, along with information from input signals. The module generates a control signal to the carburetor solenoid, Fig. S-25. The control signal continually cycles the solenoid between ON (lean) and OFF (rich). When the solenoid is ON, it pulls down a metering rod in the carburetor that reduces fuel flow. When the solenoid is OFF, the spring-loaded metering rod returns to UP position, increasing fuel flow. The amount of ON time relative to OFF time is a function of the input voltage from the oxygen sensor.

To maintain good engine idle and driveability under all conditions, other input signals are used to modify the electronic control module output signal. On the 2.5 litre engine C-4 installation, the vacuum control switch monitors the vacuum signal, enabling the electronic control module to recognize closed throttle or open throttle operation. On the 2.8 litre V-6, the vacuum control switch monitors heated carburetor inlet air through the air cleaner and prevents the module from making the carburetor too lean for good driveability during cold operation.

The throttle position sensor on the V-6 engine — and the vacuum control switch on the four cylinder engine — supply throttle position information to the electronic control module. The module's "memory" stores an average of operating conditions with ideal air-fuel ratios for those conditions. When the module receives a signal that indicates throttle position change, it immediately shifts to the last "remembered" set of operating conditions that resulted in ideal air-fuel ratio control. During normal operation, the memory is continually being updated.

To assist in engine start-up (engine speeds under 200 rpm), the electronic control module does NOT send a signal to the carburetor mixture control solenoid.

The model E2SE carburetor used with the C-4 system is a controlled air-fuel ratio carburetor of two barrel, two-stage, downdraft design with the primary bore smaller than the secondary bore. Air-fuel ratio control is accomplished with a solenoid controlled ON-OFF fuel valve that supplements a preset flow of fuel supplying the idle and main metering systems.

GM'S COMPUTER COMMAND CONTROL SYSTEM. The Computer Command Control (CCC) system is utilized on engines throughout the 1981 GM car lines. It is a refinement of the earlier C-4 system, with further control of air-fuel mixture, air injection, spark timing, idle speed, catalytic convertor action and transmission torque converter clutch operation.

Heart of the CCC system is the electronic control module, Fig. S-26, which receives inputs from various sensors to command the electro-mechanical carburetor, Fig. S-27, electronic spark timing distributor, idle speed motor, torque converter clutch and other engine actuators to permit good fuel economy while reducing emissions.

CHRYSLER'S ELECTRONIC CONTROL SYSTEMS

Chrysler has expanded the use of its microprocessor spark control (digital microprocessor version of electronic spark control). See Fig. S-28. Also expanded in use is the closed loop feedback carburetor system. Newly introduced are the detonation suppressor system and a continuous flow, fully electronically controlled fuel injection system on certain models. Also related to engine control, a new high aspect ratio, platinum coated monolith catalytic converter system is installed on cars powered by six cylinder engines.

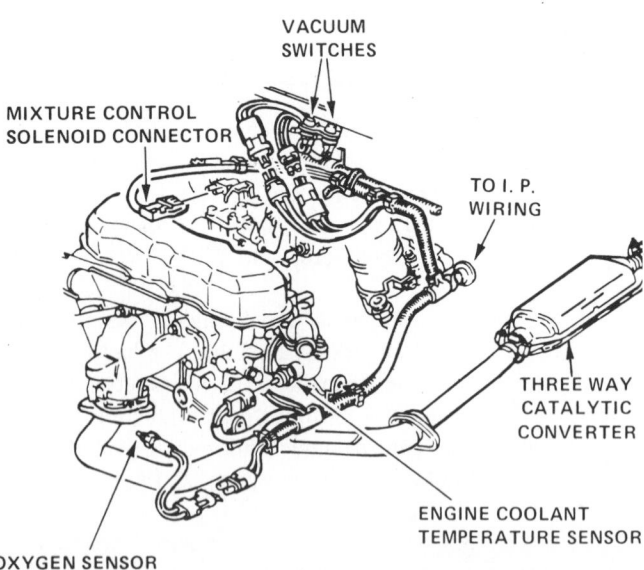

Fig. S-25. Major elements of Computer Controlled Catalytic Converter (C-4) system used on 1980 Chevrolet Citation 2.5 L "four." (Chevrolet Motor Div., GM)

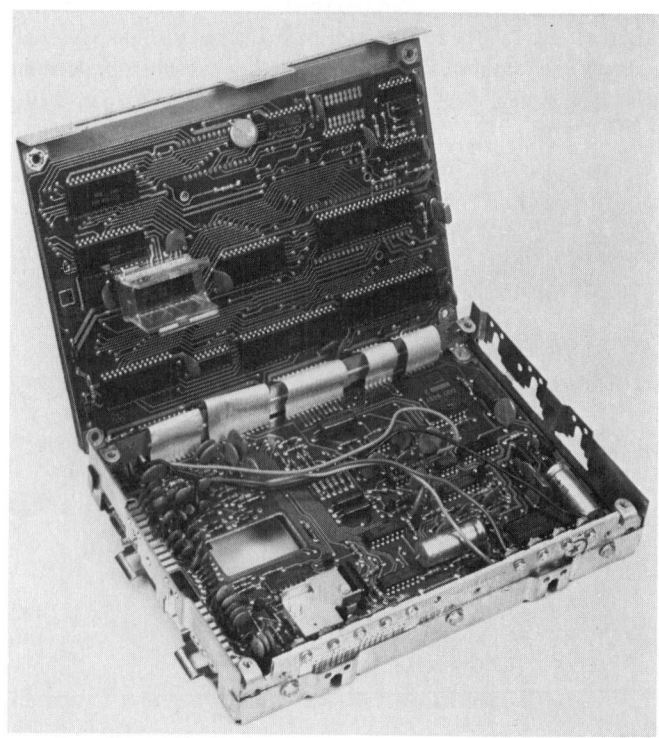

Fig. S-26. This electronic control module (ECM) is the "brain" of GM's computer command control (CCC) system. It receives signals from sensors and transmits commands to various engine controls.

FORD'S ELECTRONIC CONTROL SYSTEMS

Ford introduced a new version of electronic engine control called EEC-III, which uses an electronic control module with a changeable program. This permits standardization of various sensors and actuators and their use with different engine applications. The electronic control unit has been programmed to self-test to help pinpoint where problems may exist in the EEC-III system.

An electronically controlled throttle body fuel injection system is used on certain Lincoln engines, and the Mark VI models feature an electronic instrument cluster.

The Microprocessor Control Unit (MCU) with feedback carburetor and three-way catalyst appears on many Ford Motor company engines for 1981. In operation, the oxygen sensor, Fig. S-29, in the exhaust manifold measures any change in air-fuel ratio from normal, or the ideal ratio necessary for the most efficient functioning of the three-way catalyst. The MCU uses this signal to adjust the carburetor mixture control.

The three-way catalyst system has two divided monolithic catalysts sealed in a stainless steel converter. The front three-way catalyst reduces hydrocarbons (HC), carbon monoxide (CO) and oxides of nitrogen (NO_x). The second catalyst controls HC and CO with an assist of secondary air supplied by the thermactor air pump.

Turn to page 816, Figs. S-30, S-31, S-32, S-33 and S-34, for additional 1980 and 1981 mechanical features.

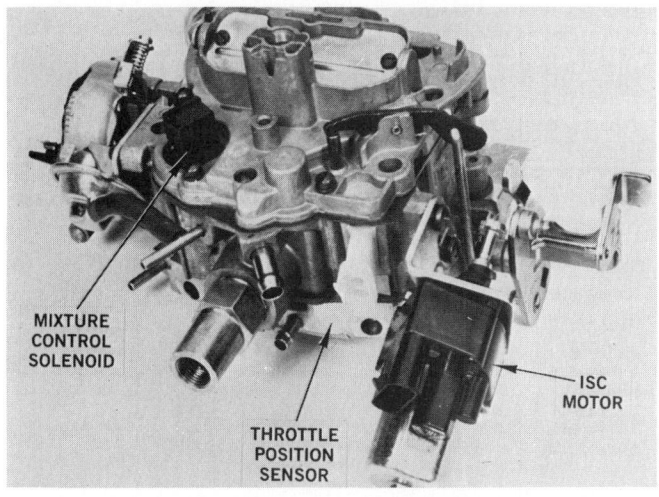

Fig. S-27. Electro-mechanical carburetors used on some 1981 GM engines provide automatic and precise air-fuel mixture ratios by means of metering rods (or bleed orifices) actuated on commands relayed by the electronic control module. (Pontiac Motor Div., GM)

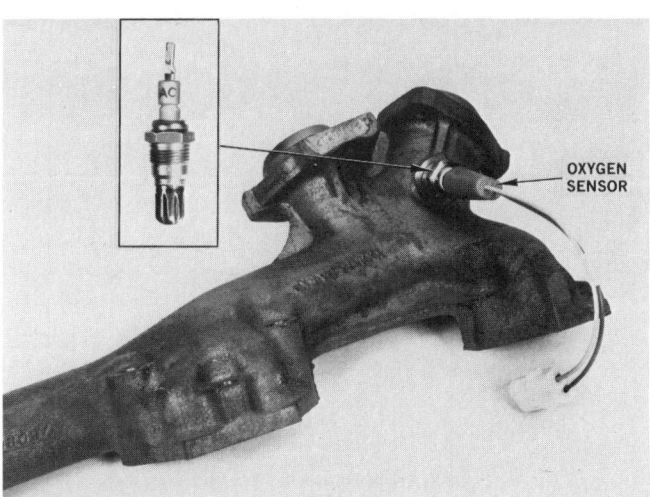

Fig. S-29. An oxygen sensor is a key element of Ford's Electronic Engine Control (EEC-III) system. This sensor monitors the oxygen in exhaust gases and signals the microprocessor unit which determines the optimum air-fuel ratio for operating conditions.

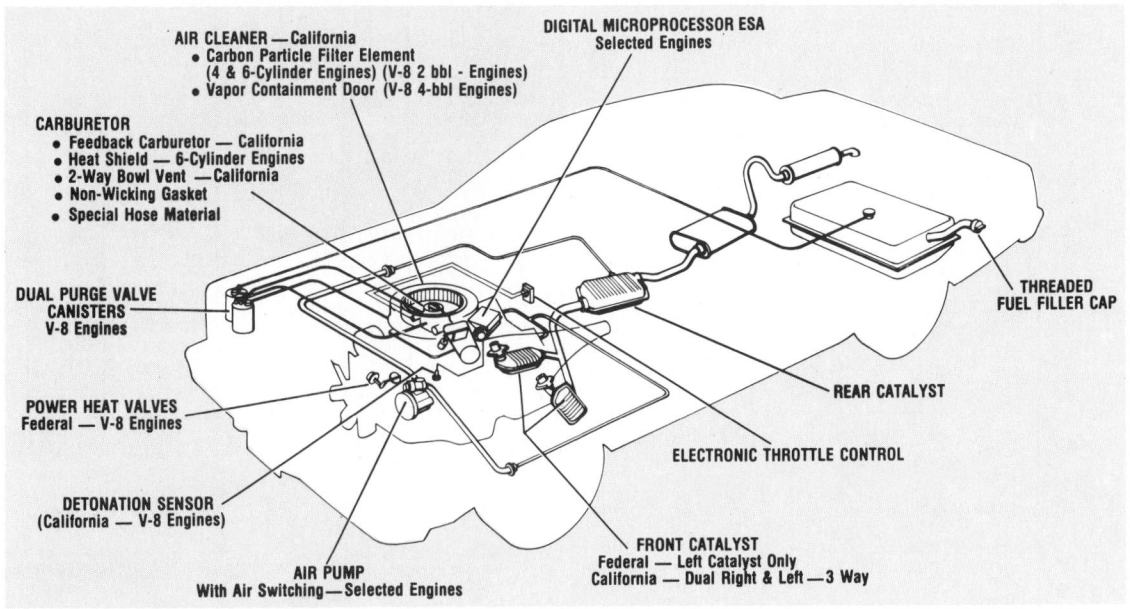

Fig. S-28. Chrysler's various electronic engine control system components are detailed. Each works individually or in concert to provide good fuel economy and fewer exhaust emissions.

1980

	Wheelbase (mm)	Wheelbase (in.)	No. of Cylinders Bore and Stroke (in.)	Displacement (litres)	Displacement (cu. in.)	Valve and Cylinder Arrangement	Net Brake Horsepower @ rpm	Net Power (kW)	Compression Pressure (psi)	Valve Clearance
AMC — Spirit, Concord	2438	96[1]	4—4.00x3.00	2.5	151	IO	82@5000	61.2	140	HY
Spirit, AMX, Concord	2438	96[1]	6—3.75x3.90	4.23	258	IO	108@3400[3]	80.6[3]	135	HY
Pacer	2540	100	6—3.75x3.90	4.23	258	IO	108@3400[3]	80.6[3]	135	HY
Eagle	2775	109.3	6—3.75x3.90	4.23	258	IO	108@3400[3]	80.6[3]	135	HY
Buick — Skylark	2664	104.9	4—4.0x3.0	2.5	151	IO	90@4000	67	140[5]	HY
Skylark	2664	104.9	6—3.50x3.0	2.8	173	VO	115@4800	85.4	140[5]	HY
Skyhawk, S	2466	97	6—3.80x3.40	3.8	231	VO	110@3800	80	140[5]	HY
Century, Regal	2745	108.1	6—3.80x3.40	3.8	231	VO	110@3800	80	140[5]	HY
LeSabre	2945	116	6—3.80x3.40	3.8	231	VO	110@3800	80	140[5]	HY
Riviera Sport Coupe	2895	114	6—3.80x3.40[9]	3.8	231	VO	170@4000	126	140[5]	HY
LeSabre, Electra	2945	116[10]	6—3.965x3.40	4.1	252	VO	125@4000	93.2	140[5]	HY
Century, Regal	2745	108.1	8—3.750x3.00	4.3	265	VO	120@3600	89.5	140[5]	HY
Century, Regal	2745	108.1	8—4.0x3.0	4.9	301	VO	140@4000	104	140[5]	HY
LeSabre	2945	116	8—4.0x3.0	4.9	301	VO	140@4000	104	140[5]	HY
Century, Regal	2745	108.1	8—3.736x3.48[12]	5.0	305	VO	155@4000	115.2	155	HY
LeSabre, Electra	2945	116[10]	8—3.80x3.850	5.7	350	VO	155@3400	115.2	150	HY
LeSabre	2945	116	8—4.057x3.385[12]	5.7	350	VO	160@3600	119	150	HY
Riviera, Electra	2895	114[10]	8—4.057x3.385[12]	5.7	350	VO	160@3600	119	150	HY
LeSabre, Wagon, Electra	2945	116[10]	8—4.057x3.385[18]	5.7	350	VO	105@3200	78.3	275[19]	HY
Cadillac — Eldorado, Seville	2895	114	8—4.057x3.385[12]	5.7	350	VO	160@4400	119	100[19]	HY
Eldorado, Seville	2895	114	8—4.057x3.385[18]	5.7	350	VO	105@3200	78	275[19]	HY
Brougham, DeVille	3085	121.4	8—4.057x3.385[18]	5.7	350	VO	105@3200	78	275[19]	HY
Eldorado, Seville	2895	114	8—3.80x4.060	6.0	368	VO	145@3600	108	155	HY
Brougham, DeVille	3085	121.4	8—3.80x4.060	6.0	368	VO	150@3800	112	155	HY
Fleetwoods	3670	144.5	8—3.80x4.060	6.0	368	VO	150@3800	112	155	HY
Chevrolet — Chevette	2394	94.3	4—3.230x2.980	1.6	98	IOC	70@5200	52	145	HY
Chevette	2394	94.3	4—3.230x2.980	1.6	98	IOC	74@5200	55	145	HY
Monza	2464	97	4—4.0x3.0	2.5	151	IO	90@4000	66.9	145[5]	HY
Citation	2664	104.9	4—4.0x3.0	2.5	151	IO	90@4000	67	140[5]	HY
Citation	2664	104.9	6—3.50x3.0	2.8	173	VO	115@4800	85.4	140[5]	HY
Camaro, Berlinetta	2743	108	6—3.736x3.480[24]	3.8	229	VO	115@3800	85.4	140[5]	HY
Monte Carlo, Malibu	2745	108.1	6—3.736x3.480	3.8	229	VO	115@3800	85.4	140[5]	HY
Chevrolet Impala, Caprice	2945	116	6—3.736x3.480	3.8	229	VO	115@3800	85.4	140[5]	HY
Monza	2464	97	6—3.80x3.40	3.8	231	VO	110@3800	82	140[5]	HY
Camaro, Berlinetta	2743	108	6—3.80x3.40[25]	3.8	231	VO	110@3800	82	140[5]	HY
Monte Carlo, Malibu	2745	108.1	6—3.80x3.40	3.8	231	VO	110@3800	82	140[5]	HY
Chevrolet Impala, Caprice	2945	116	6—3.80x3.40	3.8	231	VO	110@3800	82	140[5]	HY
Monte Carlo	2745	108.1	6—3.80x3.40[9]	3.8	231	VO	175@4000	130	140[5]	HY
Camaro, Berlinetta	2743	108	8—3.50x3.480[24]	4.4	267	VO	120@3600	89.2	150[5]	HY
Monte Carlo, Malibu	2745	108.1	8—3.50x3.480	4.4	267	VO	120@3600	89.2	150[5]	HY
Chevrolet Impala, Caprice	2945	116	8—3.50x3.480	4.4	267	VO	120@3600	89.2	150[5]	HY
Camaro, Berlinetta	2743	108	8—3.736x3.480[26]	5.0	305	VO	155@4000	115.2	155[5]	HY
Monte Carlo, Malibu	2745	108.1	8—3.736x3.480	5.0	305	VO	155@4000	115.2	155[5]	HY
Chevrolet Impala, Caprice	2945	116	8—3.736x3.480	5.0	305	VO	155@4000	115.2	155[5]	HY
Corvette	2489	98	8—3.736x3.480[12]	5.0	305	VO	165@4000	122.5	155[5]	HY
Camaro, Berlinette (Z28)	2743	108	8—4.0x3.480	5.7	350	VO	190@4000	122.5	150[5]	HY
Chevrolet Wagon	2945	116	8—4.057x3.385[18]	5.7	350	VO	125@3600	93	275[19]	HY
Corvette	2489	98	8—4.0x3.480	5.7	350	VO	190@4000	144.9	150[5]	HY
Corvette	2489	98	8—4.0x3.480	5.7	350	VO	230@5200	167.2	150[5]	HY
Chrysler — LeBaron	2761	108.7	6—3.40x4.120	3.7	225	IO	90@3600	67	100[28]	H[29]
Cordoba	2863	112.7	6—3.40x4.120	3.7	225	IO	90@3600	67	100[28]	H[29]
Newport	3010	118.5	6—3.40x4.120	3.7	225	IO	90@3600	67	100[28]	H[29]
LeBaron	2761	108.7	8—3.910x3.310	5.2	318	VO	120@3600[30]	89[30]	100[28]	HY
Cordoba	2863	112.7	8—3.910x3.310	5.2	318	VO	120@3600[30]	89[30]	100[28]	HY
Newport, New Yorker	3010	118.5	8—3.910x3.310	5.2	318	VO	120@3600[30]	89[30]	100[28]	HY
LeBaron	2761	108.7	8—3.910x3.310	5.2	318[31]	VO	155@4000	115	100[28]	HY
Cordoba	2863	112.7	8—3.910x3.310	5.2	318[31]	VO	155@4000	115	100[28]	HY
Newport, New Yorker	3010	118.5	8—3.910x3.310	5.2	318[31]	VO	155@4000	115	100[28]	HY
Newport, New Yorker	3010	118.5	8—4.0x3.580	5.9	360	VO	130@3200	97	100[28]	HY
Dodge — Omni, 024	2456	96.7[32]	4—3.130x3.40	1.7	104.7[31]	IOC	70@5200[33]	52[33]	100[28]	H[34]
Aspen, Diplomat	2761	108.7[35]	6—3.40x4.120	3.7	225	IOC	90@3600	67	100[28]	H[29]
St. Regis, Mirada	3010	118.5[36]	6—3.40x4.120	3.7	225	IOC	90@3600	67	100[28]	H[29]
Aspen, Diplomat	2761	108.7[35]	8—3.910x3.310	5.2	318	VO	120@3600	89	100[28]	HY
St. Regis, Mirada	3010	118.5[36]	8—3.910x3.310	5.2	318	VO	120@3600	89	100[28]	HY
Aspen, Diplomat	2761	108.7[35]	8—3.910x3.310	5.2	318[31]	VO	155@3600	115	100[28]	HY
St. Regis, Mirada	3010	118.5[36]	8—3.910x3.310	5.2	318[31]	VO	155@3600	115	100[28]	HY
St. Regis, Mirada CMX	3010	118.5[36]	8—4.0x3.580	5.9	360	VO	130@3200	97	100[28]	HY
Ford — Pinto	2400	94.5	4—3.781x3.126	2.3	140	IOC	88@4600	66	80[38]	HY
Fairmont, Mustang, Ghia	2679	105.5[39]	4—3.781x3.126	2.3	140	IOC	88@4600[40]	66	80[38]	HY

ABBREVIATIONS — FOOTNOTES

AC — AC Spark Plugs	M — MOPAR Spark Plugs	5 — Lowest Cylinder Must Be At Least 70 Percent Of Highest
B — Before Top Dead Center	MO — Motorcraft Spark Plugs	6 — Not Adjustable
CH — Champion Spark Plugs	N — Negative	7 — Degree Per Wheel
CP — Crankshaft Pulley	NA — Not Available/Not Applicable	8 — Toe-Out
F — Flywheel	P — Positive	9 — Turbocharged Engine—Installed In Riviera, Regal, LeSabre And Monte Carlo Sport Coupes
H — Hot Engine	VD — Vibration Damper	
HY — Hydraulic Lifters	VO — V-Type Engine—Overhead Valves	10 — Electra — 3020/118.9
IO — In-Line Engine—Overhead Valves	1 — Concord — 2743/108	11 — @550
IOC — In-Line Engine—Overhead Camshaft	2 — 10B	12 — Cal. Only
	3 — Also 115/85.4@3200	13 — @1100
	4 — 6B	

Tuneup Specifications

Firing Order	Timing Mark Location	Initial Ignition Timing @ rpm (auto. trans.)	Ignition Timing (rpm-manual trans.)	Ignition Timing (California)	Spark Plugs Make	Spark Plugs Model	Gap (in.)	Caster, Power Steering (deg.)	Camber, Right Wheel (deg.)	Toe-In (in.)	Crankcase Capacity (L/qt.)	Cooling System Capacity (L)	Cooling System Capacity (qt.)
1342	CP	12B@700	900[2]	12B	AC	R44TSX	.060	1P	1/4P	1/8	2.84/3	6.15	6.5
153624	VD	8B@600	700[4]	8B	CH	N−14LY	.035	1P	1/4P	1/8	3.78/4	10.4	11.0
153624	VD	8B@600	700[4]	8B	CH	N−14LY	.035	2P	1/4P	1/8	3.78/4	13.2	14.0
153624	VD	10B@600	NA	8B	CH	N−14LY	.035	4P	0	1/8	3.78/4	13.2	14.0
1342	CP	10B@650	1000	10B	AC	R43TSX	.060	0[6]	1/2P	.10[7]	2.84/3	7.9	8.4
123456	VD	8B@650	1000[4]	8B	AC	R44TS	.045	0[6]	1/2P	.10[7]	3.78/4	10.0	10.5
165432	VD	15B@600	600	15B	AC	R45TSX	.060	3/4N	1/4P	1/16[8]	3.78/4	12.3	13.0
165432	VD	15B@600	600	15B	AC	R45TSX	.060	3P	1/2P	1/8	3.78/4	12.3	13.0
165432	VD	15B@600	NA	15B	AC	R45TSX	.060	3P	3/4P	1/8	3.78/4	11.8	12.5
165432	VD	15B@800	NA	15B	AC	R46SZ	.080	2-1/2P	0	0	3.78/4	13.4	14.2
165432	VD	15B@600	NA	15B	AC	R45TSX	.060	3P	3/4P	1/8	3.78/4	11.8	12.5
18436572	VD	12B@525	NA	NA	AC	R45TSX	.060	3P	1/2P	1/8	3.78/4	19.8	20.9
18436572	VD	12B@500	NA	NA	AC	R45TSX	.060	3P	1/2P	1/8	3.78/4	19.8	20.9
18436572	VD	15B@600	NA	NA	AC	R45TSX	.060	3P	3/4P	1/8	3.78/4	19.8	20.9
18436572	VD	NA	NA	4B[11]	AC	R45TS	.045	3P	1/2P	1/8	3.78/4	15.5	16.4
18436572	VD	15B@550	NA	NA	AC	R45TSX	.060	3P	3/4P	1/8	3.78/4	13.5	14.3
18436572	VD	NA	NA	18B[13]	AC	R46SX	.080	3P	3/4P	1/8	3.78/4	13.7	14.5
18436572	VD	NA	NA	18B[13]	AC	R47SX	.080	2-1/2[14]	0[15]	0[16]	3.78/4	14.1[17]	14.9[17]
18436572	VD	7B@800	NA	7B	NA	NA	NA	3P	3/4P	1/8	6.0/6.5	17.0	18.0
18436572	VD	NA	NA	10B[20]	AC	R47SX	.060	2-1/2P	0	0	3.78/4	14.4	15.2
18436572	VD	NA	NA	NA	NA	NA	NA	2-1/2P	0	0	6.6/7	17.4	18.4
18436572	VD	NA	NA	NA	NA	NA	NA	3P	1/2P	1/8	6.6/7	22.4	23.7
15634278	VD	10B@800[21]	NA	NA	AC	R45NSX	.060	2-1/2P	0	0	4.7/5	21.2	22.4
15634278	VD	18B@1400	NA	10B	AC	R45NSX	.060	3P	1/2P	1/8	3.78/4	20.3	21.4
15634278	VD	18B@1400	NA	10B	AC	R45NSX	.060	3P	1/2P	1/8	3.78/4	20.3	21.4
1342	VD	18B@1000	750[22]	16B[23]	AC	R42TS	.035	1/2P	1/4P	1/16	3.78/4	8.7	9.1
1342	VD	18B@1000	750[22]	16B[23]	AC	R42TS	.035	1/2P	1/4P	1/16	3.78/4	8.7	9.1
1342	CP	12B@650	1000[23]	12B[23]	AC	R43TSX	.060	3/4N	1/4P	1/16[8]	2.84/3	11.5	11.9
1342	CP	10B@650	1000	10B	AC	R43TSX	.060	0[6]	1/2P	.10[7]	2.84/3	7.9	8.4
123456	VD	8B@650	1000[4]	8B	AC	R44TS	.045	0[6]	1/2P	.10[7]	3.78/4	10.0	10.5
165432	VD	10B@600	700[2]	NA	AC	R45TS	.045	1P	1P	1/8	3.78/4	14.2	15.0
165432	VD	10B@600	700[2]	NA	AC	R45TS	.045	3P	1/2P	1/8	3.78/4	17.7	18.7
165432	VD	12B@600	700[2]	NA	AC	R45TS	.045	3/4P	3P	1/8	3.78/4	13.4	14.2
165432	VD	15B@600[23]	800[23]	15B[23]	AC	R45TS	.045	3/4N	1/4P	1/16[8]	3.78/4	10.9	11.5
165432	VD	NA	NA	15B[23]	AC	R45TS	.045	1P	1P	1/8	3.78/4	14.2	15.0
165432	VD	NA	NA	15B[23]	AC	R45TS	.045	3P	1/2P	1/8	3.78/4	14.6	15.4
165432	VD	NA	NA	15B	AC	R45TS	.045	3P	3P	1/8	3.78/4	14.6	15.4
165432	VD	15B@600	NA	15B[23]	AC	R45TS	.045	3P	1/2P	1/8	3.78/4	14.6	15.4
18436572	VD	2B@500	NA	NA	AC	R45TS	.045	1P	1P	1/8	3.78/4	14.7	15.6
18436572	VD	4B@500	NA	NA	AC	R45TS	.045	3P	1/2P	1/8	3.78/4	20.7	21.9
18436572	VD	4B@500	NA	NA	AC	R45TS	.045	3/4P	3P	1/8	3.78/4	16.1	17.0
18436572	VD	4B@500	600	4B[23]	AC	R43TS	.045	1P	1P	1/8	3.78/4	14.8	15.7
18436572	VD	4B@500	600	4B[23]	AC	R43TS	.045	3P	1/2P	1/8	3.78/4	18.6	19.6
18436572	VD	4B@500	NA	4B	AC	R43TS	.045	3/4P	3P	1/8	3.78/4	14.7	15.5
18436572	VD	NA	NA	4B	AC	R43TS	.045	2-1/4P	3/4P	1/4	3.78/4	20.3	21.5
18436572	VD	6B@600	700[27]	NA	AC	R43TS	.045	1P	1P	1/8	3.78/4	15.5	16.4
18436572	VD	NA	NA	NA	NA	NA	NA	3/4P	3P	1/8	7.1/7.5	15.5	16.4
18436572	VD	12B@700	900	NA	AC	R43TS	.045	2-1/4P	3/4P	1/4	3.78/4	20.4	21.6
18436572	VD	6B@700	900[27]	NA	AC	R43TS	.045	2-1/4P	3/4P	1/4	3.78/4	20.4	21.6
153624	VD	12B@750	NA	NA	M	P−560PR	.035	3/4P	1/4P	1/8	3.78/4	10.9	11.5
153624	VD	12B@750	NA	NA	M	P−560PR	.035	3/4P	1/4P	1/8	3.78/4	10.9	11.5
153642	VD	12B@750	NA	NA	M	P−560PR	.035	3/4P	1/4P	1/8	3.78/4	10.9	11.5
18436572	VD	12B@750	NA	NA	M	P−65PR	.035	3/4P	1/4P	1/8	3.78/4	14.2	15.0
18436572	VD	12B@750	NA	NA	M	P−65PR	.035	3/4P	1/4P	1/8	3.78/4	14.2	15.0
18436572	VD	12B@750	NA	NA	M	P−65PR	.035	3/4P	1/4P	1/8	3.78/4	14.2	15.0
18436572	VD	12B@750	NA	16B	M	P−65PR	.035	3/4P	1/4P	1/8	3.78/4	14.2	15.0
18436572	VD	12B@750	NA	16B	M	P−65PR	.035	3/4P	1/4P	1/8	3.78/4	14.2	15.0
18436572	VD	12B@750	NA	16B	M	P−65PR	.035	3/4P	1/4P	1/8	3.78/4	14.2	15.0
18436572	VD	12B@750	NA	NA	M	P−65PR	.035	3/4P	1/4P	1/4	3.78/4	15.1	16.0
1342	CP	12B@900	900	10B	M	P−65PR	.037	0[6]	5/16	1/16[8]	2.84/3	5.5	6.0
153624	VD	12B@725	725	12B	M	P−560PR	.035	2-1/2P	1/4P	1/8	3.78/4	10.9	11.5
153624	VD	12B@725	725	NA	M	P−560PR	.035	3/4P	1/4P	1/8	3.78/4	10.9	11.5
18436572	VD	12B@700	NA	12B	M	P−65PR	.035	2-1/2P	1/4P	1/8	3.78/4	14.2	15.0
18436572	VD	12B@700	NA	NA	M	P−65PR	.035	3/4P	1/4P	1/8	3.78/4	14.2	15.0
18436572	VD	16B@700	NA	16B	M	P−65PR	.035	2-1/2P	1/4P	1/8	3.78/4	14.2	15.0
18436572	VD	16B@700	NA	16B	M	P−65PR	.035	3/4P	1/4P	1/8	3.78/4	14.2	15.0
18436572	VD	12B@700	NA	NA[37]	M	P−65PR	.035	3/4P	1/4P	1/8	3.78/4	15.1	16.0
1342	CP	20B@750	850[4]	12B	MO	AWSF−42	.034	1P	1/2P	1/8	3.78/4	8.1	8.6
1342	CP	20B@750	850[4]	12B	MO	AWSF−42	.034	1P	1/2P[41]	3/16	3.78/4	9.7	10.2

14 — Electra — 3P
15 — Electra — 3/4P
16 — Electra — 1/8
17 — Electra — 13.7/14.5
18 — Diesel Engine
19 — Minimum psi
20 — @600
21 — Maximum rpm
22 — 12B
23 — C4 Emission Control System
24 — In 49 States, All Models Available Except Z28

25 — Cal. Only, All Except Z28
26 — 49 States, All Except Z28; Cal. — Z28 Only
27 — 8B
28 — Minimum Pressure. Also 25 psi (4 and 6) Or 40 psi (8) Maximum Variation
29 — Int. − .010 in./0.25 mm Exh. − .020 in./0.50 mm
30 — Also 130/97@3200
31 — Combustion Computer With Feedback Carburetor Controller
32 — 4-Door — 2520/99.2

33 — Cal. — 65/48@5200
34 — Int. − .010 in./0.25 mm Exh. − .018 in./0.45 mm
35 — 4-Door — 2863/112.7
36 — Mirada — 2863/112.7
37 — Mirada CMX Only — 16B@700
38 — Lowest Cylinder Must Be At Least 75 Percent Of Highest
39 — Mustang — 2550/100.4
40 — Auto. Trans. — 90/67@4800
41 — Mustang — 1/4P

1980

	Wheelbase (mm)	Wheelbase (in.)	No. of Cylinders Bore and Stroke (in.)	Displacement (litres)	Displacement (cu. in.)	Valve and Cylinder Arrangement	Net Brake Horsepower @ rpm	Net Power (kW)	Compression Pressure (psi)	Valve Clearance
Ford — Fairmont, Futura	2679	105.5	4—3.781x3.126[1]	2.3	140	IOC	NA	NA	80[2]	HY
Mustang, Ghia	2550	100.4	4—3.781x3.126[1]	2.3	140	IOC	NA	NA	80[2]	HY
Fairmont, Futura, Mustang, Ghia	2679	105.5[5]	6—3.682x3.126	3.3	200	IO	94@9000[6]	68[6]	80[2]	HY
Granada, Ghia, ESS	2791	109.9	6—3.682x3.910	4.1	250	IO	90@3200	67	80[2]	HY
Fairmont, Futura, Mustang, Ghia	2679	105.5[5]	8—3.680x3.0	4.2	255	VO	119@3800[11]	89[11]	80[2]	HY
Granada, Ghia, ESS	2791	109.9	8—3.680x3.0	4.2	255	VO	117@3800	87	80[2]	HY
Thunderbird	2753	108.4	8—3.680x3.0	4.2	255	VO	115@3800[13]	86[13]	80[2]	HY
Granada, Ghia, ESS	2791	109.9	8—4.0x3.0	5.0	302	VO	134@3600	100	80[2]	HY
Thunderbird	2753	108.4	8—4.0x3.0	5.0	302	VO	131@3600[13]	98[13]	80[2]	HY
LTD, S, Crown Victoria	2904	114.3	8—4.0x3.0	5.0	302	VO	130@3600[11]	97[11]	80[2]	HY
LTD, S, Crown Victoria	2904	114.3	8—4.0x3.50	5.8	351W	VO	140@3400[11]	104.4[11]	80[2]	HY
Lincoln — Versailles	2791	109.9	8—4.0x3.0	5.0	302	VO	131@3600	98	80[2]	HY
Mark VI	2904	114.3[17]	8—4.0x3.0[18]	5.0	302	VO	129@3600	96.2	80[2]	HY
Lincoln	2980	117.3	8—4.0x3.0[18]	5.0	302	VO	129@3600	96.2	80[2]	HY
Mark VI	2904	114.3[17]	8—4.0x3.50	5.8	351W	VO	140@3400[13]	104.4[13]	80[2]	HY
Lincoln	2980	117.3	8—4.0x3.50	5.8	351W	VO	140@3400[13]	104.4[13]	80[2]	HY
Mercury — Bobcat	2400	94.5	4—3.781x3.126	2.3	140	IOC	88@4600	66	80[2]	HY
Zephyr, Capri, Ghia	2679	105.5[5]	4—3.781x3.126	2.3	140	IOC	88@4600[4]	66[4]	80[2]	HY
Zephyr, Z-7, Capri, Ghia	2679	105.5[5]	4—3.781x3.126[1]	2.3	140	IOC	NA	NA	80[2]	HY
Zephyr, Capri, Ghia	2679	105.5[5]	6—3.682x3.126	3.3	200	IO	94@4000[6]	68[6]	80[2]	HY
Monarch, Ghia, ESS	2791	109.9	6—3.680x3.910	4.1	250	IO	90@3200	67	80[2]	HY
Cougar X-R7	2753	108.4	8—3.680x3.0	4.2	255	VO	115@3800[13]	86[13]	80[2]	HY
Zephyr, Capri, Ghia	2679	105.5[5]	8—3.680x3.0	4.2	255	VO	119@3800[13]	89[13]	80[2]	HY
Monarch, Ghia, ESS	2791	109.9	8—3.680x3.0	4.2	255	VO	117@3800[13]	87[13]	80[2]	HY
Monarch, Ghia, ESS	2791	109.9	8—4.0x3.0	5.0	302	VO	131@3600[13]	98[13]	80[2]	HY
Cougar X-R7	2753	108.4	8—4.0x3.0	5.0	302	VO	131@3600[13]	98[13]	80[2]	HY
Marquis, Brougham, Grand Marquis	2904	114.3	8—4.0x3.0	5.0	302	VO	130@3600[11]	97[11]	80[2]	HY
Marquis, Brougham, Grand Marquis	2904	114.3	8—4.0x3.50	5.8	351W	VO	140@3400[11]	104.4[11]	80[2]	HY
Oldsmobile — Starfire, SX	2466	97	4—4.0x3.0	2.5	151	IO	86@4400	64	140[21]	HY
Omega, Brougham	2664	105	4—4.0x3.0	2.5	151	IO	90@4000	67	140[21]	HY
Omega, Brougham	2664	105	6—3.50x3.0	2.8	173	VO	115@4800	85.4	140[21]	HY
Starfire, SX	2466	97	6—3.80x3.40	3.8	231	VO	110@3800	80	140[21]	HY
Cutlass, Salon, Supreme, Brougham	2746	108.1	6—3.80x3.40	3.8	231	VO	110@3800	80	140[21]	HY
Delta, 88, Royale, Brougham	2945	116	6—3.80x3.40	3.8	231	VO	110@3800	80	140[21]	HY
Cutlass, Salon, Supreme, Brougham	2746	108.1	8—3.50x3.385	4.3	260	VO	NA	NA	140[21]	HY
Cutlass, Salon, Supreme, Brougham	2746	108.1	8—3.50x3.385[27]	4.3	260	IO	105@3200	78	275[28]	HY
Cutlass, Salon, Supreme, Brougham	2746	108.1	8—3.736x3.480	5.0	305	VO	155@4000	115.2	155[21]	HY
Delta, 88, Royale, Brougham, 98	2945	116[29]	8—3.80x3.385	5.0	307	VO	150@3800	112	155[21]	HY
Toronado	2895	114	8—3.80x3.385	5.0	307	VO	150@3800	112	155[21]	HY
Delta, 88, Royale, Brougham, 98	2945	116[29]	8—4.057x3.385	5.7	350	VO	160@3600	119	100[21]	HY
Toronado	2895	114	8—4.057x3.385	5.7	350	VO	160@3600	119	100[21]	HY
Cutlass, Salon, Supreme, Brougham	2746	108.1	8—4.057x3.385[27]	5.7	350	VO	105@3200	78	275[28]	HY
Delta, 88, Royale, Brougham, 98	2945	116[29]	8—4.057x3.385[27]	5.7	350	VO	105@3200	78	275[28]	HY
Toronado	2895	114	8—4.057x3.380[27]	5.7	350	VO	105@3200	78	275[28]	HY
Plymouth — Horizon, TC3	2456	96.7[30]	4—3.130x3.40	1.7	104.7[31]	IOC	65@5200	48	100[32]	H[33]
Volaré	2761	108.7[35]	6—3.40x4.120	3.7	225[31]	IO	90@3600	67	100[32]	H[36]
Gran Fury, Salon	3010	118.5	6—3.40x4.120	3.7	225	IO	90@3600	67	100[32]	H[36]
Volaré	2761	108.7[35]	8—3.910x3.310	5.2	318[31]	VO	120@3600[37]	89[37]	100[32]	HY
Gran Fury, Salon	3010	118.5	8—3.910x3.310	5.2	318[31]	VO	120@3600[37]	89[37]	100[32]	HY
Gran Fury, Salon	3010	118.5	8—4.0x3.580	5.9	360[38]	VO	130@3200	97	100[32]	HY
Pontiac — Sunbird	2464	97	4—4.0x3.0	2.5	151	IO	86@4000	64	140[21]	HY
Phoenix, LJ	2664	104.9	4—4.0x3.0	2.5	151	IO	90@4000	67	140[21]	HY
Phoenix, LJ	2664	104.9	6—3.50x3.0	2.8	173	VO	115@4800	85.4	140[21]	HY
Sunbird	2464	97	6—3.80x3.40	3.8	231	VO	115@3800	85.4	140[21]	HY
LeMans, Grand LeMans, Grand Prix, LJ	2745	108.1	6—3.80x3.40	3.8	231	VO	115@3800	85.4	140[21]	HY
Firebird, Esprit	2748	108.2	6—3.80x3.40	3.8	231	VO	120@3600	89.2	140[21]	HY
Catalina, Bonneville	2945	116	6—3.80x3.40	3.8	231	VO	115@3800	85.4	140[21]	HY
LeMans, Grand LeMans, Grand Prix, LJ	2745	108.1	8—3.75x3.0	4.3	265	VO	120@3600	89.2	140[21]	HY
Catalina, Bonneville, Brougham	2945	116	8—3.75x3.0	4.3	265	VO	120@3600	89.2	140[21]	HY
LeMans, Grand LeMans, Grand AM	2745	108.1	8—4.0x3.0	4.9	301	VO	140@4000[39]	104.4	140[21]	HY
Grand Prix, LJ, SJ	2745	108.1	8—4.0x3.0	4.9	301	VO	140@4000[39]	104.4	140[21]	HY
Firebird, Esprit, Formula, Trans AM	2748	108.2	8—4.0x3.0	4.9	301	VO	140@4000[40]	104.4	140[21]	HY
Formula, Trans AM	2748	108.2	8—4.0x3.0[1]	4.9	301	VO	210@4000	157	140[21]	HY
Catalina, Bonneville, Brougham	2945	116	8—4.0x3.0	4.9	301	VO	140@4000	104.4	140[21]	HY
LeMans, Grand LeMans, Grand AM	2745	108.1	8—3.736x3.480	5.0	305	VO	150@3800	112	140[21]	HY
Firebird, Esprit, Formula, Trans AM	2748	108.2	8—3.736x3.480	5.0	305	VO	150@3800	112	140[21]	HY
Formula, Trans AM	2748	108.2	8—3.736x3.480	5.7	350	VO	150@3800	112	140[21]	HY
Bonneville, Brougham	2945	116	8—4.057x3.385[27]	5.7	350	VO	125@3600	93.2	275[28]	HY
Catalina, Bonneville, Brougham	2945	116	8—4.057x3.385	5.7	350	VO	160@3600	119	100[28]	HY

ABBREVIATIONS — FOOTNOTES

AC — AC Spark Plugs
B — Before Top Dead Center
CH — Champion Spark Plugs
CP — Crankshaft Pulley
F — Flywheel
H — Hot Engine
HY — Hydraulic Lifters
IO — In-Line Engine — Overhead Valves
IOC — In-Line Engine — Overhead Camshaft

M — MOPAR Spark Plugs
MO — Motorcraft Spark Plugs
N — Negative
NA — Not Available/Not Applicable
P — Positive
VD — Vibration Damper
VO — V-Type Engine — Overhead Valves
1 — Turbocharged Engine
2 — Lowest Cylinder Must Be At Least
    75 Percent Of Highest
3 — @600

4 — Auto. Trans. — 90/67@4800
5 — Mustang, Capri — 2550/100.4
6 — Manual Trans. — 91/68@3800
7 — Mustang — 10B@550
8 — 10B
9 — Mustang — 1/4P
10 — 4B
11 — Variable Venturi Carburetor
12 — @550
13 — Variable Venturi — Cal. Only
14 — Cal. — ASF-52-6
15 — Cal. — .060

Tuneup Specifications

Firing Order	Timing Mark Location	Initial Ignition Timing (auto. trans.)	Ignition Timing (rpm-manual trans.)	Ignition Timing (California)	Spark Plugs Make	Spark Plugs Model	Gap (in.)	Caster, Power Steering (deg.)	Camber, Right Wheel (deg.)	Toe-In (in.)	Crankcase Capacity (L/qt.)	Cooling System Capacity (L)	Cooling System Capacity (qt.)
1342	CP	8B@800	NA	2B[3]	MO	AWSF—32	.034	1P	1/2P	3/16	4.3/4.5	9.7	10.2
1342	CP	10B@800	NA	2B[3]	MO	AWSF—42	.034	1P	1/4P	3/16	4.3/4.5	9.7	10.2
153624	VD	12B@550[7]	700[8]	12B[3]	MO	BRF—82	.050	1P	1/2P[9]	3/16	3.78/4	8.5	9.0
153624	VD	10B@550	700[10]	NA	MO	BSF—82	.050	1/2N	1/4P	1/4	3.78/4	9.9	10.5
15426378	VD	8B@550	NA	6B	MO	ASF—42	.050	1P	1/2P[9]	3/16	3.78/4	13.4	14.2
15426378	VD	NA	NA	6B[12]	MO	ASF—42	.050	1/2N	1/4P	1/4	3.78/4	13.4	14.2
15426378	VD	8B@550	NA	6B	MO	ASF—42	.050	1P	3/8P	1/4	3.78/4	13.4	14.2
15426378	VD	6B@500	NA	8B	MO	ASF—52	.050	1/2N	1/4P	1/4	3.78/4	13.4	14.2
15426378	VD	8B@550	NA	10B	MO	ASF—52[14]	.050	1P	3/8P	1/4	3.78/4	13.4	14.2
15426378	VD	6B@550	NA	10B	MO	ASF—52[14]	.050[15]	3P	1/2P	1/16	3.78/4	12.6	13.3
13726548	VD	10B@550	NA	10B	MO	ASF—52	.050	3P	1/2P	1/16	3.78/4	13.6	14.4
15426378	VD	8B@550	NA	6B	MO	ARF—52[16]	.050	1/2N	1/4P	1/8	3.78/4	13.6	14.4
15426378	VD	10B@550	NA	10B	MO	ASF—52	.050	3P	1/2P	1/16	3.78/4	12.6	13.3
15426378	VD	10B@550	NA	10B	MO	ASF—52	.050	3P	1/2P	1/16	3.78/4	12.6	13.3
13726548	VD	10B@550	NA	10B	MO	ASF—52	.050	3P	1/2P	1/16	3.78/4	13.6	14.4
13726548	VD	10B@550	NA	10B	MO	ASF—52	.050	3P	1/2P	1/16	3.78/4	13.6	14.4
1342	CP	20B@750	850	12B	MO	AWSF—42	.034	1P	1/2P	1/8	3.78/4	8.1	8.6
1342	CP	20B@750	850	12B	MO	AWSF—42	.034	1P	1/2P[19]	3/8	3.78/4	9.7	10.2
1342	CP	8B@800	NA	2B	MO	AWSF—32	.034	1P	1/2P[19]	3/8	4.3/4.5	9.7	10.2
153624	VD	12B@550	700[8]	12B[20]	MO	BRF—82	.050	1P	1/2P[19]	3/8	3.78/4	8.5	9.0
153624	VD	10B@550	700[10]	NA	MO	BSF—82	.050	1/2N	1/4P	1/4	3.78/4	9.9	10.5
15426378	VD	8B@550	NA	6B	MO	ASF—42	.050	1P	3/8P	1/4	3.78/4	13.4	14.2
15426378	VD	8B@550	NA	6B	MO	BRF—82	.050	1P	1/2P[19]	3/8	3.78/4	13.4	14.2
15426378	VD	NA	NA	6B[12]	MO	ASF—42	.050	1/2N	1/4P	1/4	3.78/4	13.4	14.2
15426378	VD	8B@550	NA	10B	MO	ASF—52[14]	.050	1/2N	1/4P	1/4	3.78/4	13.4	14.2
15426378	VD	8B@550	NA	10B	MO	ASF—52	.050	1P	3/8P	1/4	3.78/4	13.4	14.2
15426378	VD	16B@5500	NA	10B	MO	ASF—52[14]	.050[15]	3P	1/2P	1/16	3.78/4	12.6	13.3
13726548	VD	10B@550	NA	10B	MO	ASF—52	.050	3P	1/2P	1/16	3.78/4	13.6	14.4
1342	CP	12B@900	900	14B[22]	AC	R44TSX	.060	1P	3/4P	1/16	2.84/3	10.5	11.0
1342	CP	10B@650	1000	10B	AC	R43TSX	.060	0[23]	1/2P	.10[24]	2.84/3	7.9	8.4
123456	VD	8B@650	1000[25]	8B	AC	R44TS	.045	0[23]	1/2P	.10[24]	3.78/4	7.9	8.4
165432	VD	15B@600	600	15B	AC	R46TSX	.060	1P	3/4P	1/16	3.78/4	11.3	11.9
165432	VD	15B@600	600[26]	15B	AC	R46TSX	.060	1P	1/2P	1/8	3.78/4	11.3	11.9
165432	VD	15B@600	600	15B	AC	R46TSX	.060	3P	3/4P	1/8	3.78/4	12.3	13.0
18436572	VD	20B@500	NA	20B	AC	R46SX	.080	1P	1/2P	1/8	3.78/4	15.0	15.9
18436572	VD	NA	NA	NA	NA	NA	NA	1P	1/2P	1/8	6.0/6.5	18.5	19.6
18436572	VD	4B@500	NA	4B	AC	R45TS	.045	1P	1/2P	1/8	3.78/4	14.3	15.0
18436572	VD	20B@1100	NA	20B	AC	R46SX	.080	3P	3/4P	1/8	3.78/4	14.5	15.3
18436572	VD	20B@1100	NA	20B	AC	R46SX	.080	2-1/2P	0	0	3.78/4	15.5	16.4
18436572	VD	18B@1100	NA	18B	AC	R46SX	.080	3P	3/4P	1/8	3.78/4	13.7	14.5
18436572	VD	18B@1100	NA	18B	AC	R46SX	.080	2-1/2P	0	0	3.78/4	14.8	15.6
18436572	VD	NA	NA	NA	NA	NA	NA	1P	1/2P	1/8	6.0/6.5	16.5	17.4
18436572	VD	NA	NA	NA	NA	NA	NA	3P	3/4P	1/8	6.0/6.5	17.0	18.0
18436572	VD	NA	NA	NA	NA	NA	NA	2-1/2P	0	0	6.0/6.5	17.2	18.1
1342	CP	12B@900	900	10B	M	P—65PR	.037	0[23]	5/16P	1/16[34]	3.78/4	5.7	6.0
153624	CP	12B@725	725	12B	M	P—560PR	.035	2-1/2P	1/4P	1/8	3.78/4	10.9	11.5
153624	CP	12B@725	NA	NA	M	P—560PR	.035	3/4P	1/4P	1/8	3.78/4	10.9	11.5
18436572	VD	12B@725	NA	16B	M	P—65PR	.035	2-1/2P	1/4P	1/8	3.78/4	14.2	15.0
18436572	VD	12B@725	NA	16B	M	P—65PR	.035	3/4P	1/4P	1/8	3.78/4	14.2	15.0
18436572	VD	12B@725	NA	12B	M	P—65PR	.035	3/4P	1/4P	1/8	3.78/4	15.1	16.0
1342	VD	12B@650	1000	12B	AC	R44TSX	.060	3/4N	1/4N	1/8	2.84/3	8.0	8.5
1342	CP	10B@650	1000	10B	AC	R44TSX	.060	0[23]	1/2P	.10[24]	2.84/3	8.0	8.5
123456	VD	8B@650	1000[25]	8B	AC	R44TS	.045	0[23]	1/2P	.10[24]	3.78/4	7.9	8.4
165432	VD	15B@600	600	15B	AC	R45TSX	.060	3/4N	1/4N	1/16[34]	3.78/4	12.3	13.0
165432	VD	15B@600	600	15B	AC	R45TSX	.060	1P	1/2P	1/8	3.78/4	12.3	13.0
165432	VD	15B@600	600	15B	AC	R45TSX	.060	1P	1P	1/8	3.78/4	12.3	13.0
165432	VD	15B@600	NA	15B	AC	R46SZ	.080	3P	3/4P	5/16	3.78/4	11.8	12.5
18436572	VD	12B@525	NA	12B	AC	R45TSX	.060	1P	1/2P	1/8	3.78/4	19.8	20.9
18436572	VD	12B@525	NA	12B	AC	R45TSX	.060	3P	3/4P	5/16	3.78/4	19.8	20.9
18436572	VD	12B@525	NA	12B	AC	R45TSX	.060	1P	1/2P	1/8	3.78/4	19.8	20.9
18436572	VD	12B@525	NA	12B	AC	R45TSX	.060	1P	1P	1/8	3.78/4	19.8	20.9
18436572	VD	12B@500	NA	12B	AC	R45TSX	.060	1P	1/2P	1/8	3.78/4	19.8	20.9
18436572	VD	4B@500	NA	4B	AC	R45TS	.045	3P	3/4P	5/16	3.78/4	17.0	18.0
18436572	VD	4B@500	NA	4B	AC	R45TS	.045	1P	1/2P	1/8	3.78/4	17.0	18.0
18436572	VD	4B@500	NA	4B	AC	R45TS	.045	1P	1P	1/8	3.78/4	16.6	17.5
18436572	VD	4B@500	NA	4B	AC	R45TS	.045	1P	1P	1/8	3.78/4	16.6	17.5
18436572	VD	NA	NA	NA	NA	NA	NA	3P	3/4P	5/16	6.0/6.5	17.0	18.0
18436572	VD	18B@1100	NA	18B	AC	R46SX	.080	3P	3/4P	5/16	3.78/4	13.7	14.5

16 — Or ASF-52
17 — 4-Door — 2980/117.3
18 — Electronic Fuel Injection
19 — Capri — 1/4P
20 — Zephyr Only
21 — Lowest Cylinder Must Be At Least 70 Percent of Highest
22 — Cal. Auto. Trans. — @650, Manual Trans. — @1000
23 — Not Adjustable
24 — Degree Per Wheel
25 — 6B

26 — Not Supreme Nor Supreme Brougham
27 — Diesel Engine
28 — Minimum Pressure
29 — 98 — 3023/119
30 — 4-Door — 2520/99.2
31 — Cal. — Combustion Computer With Feedback Carburetor Controller
32 — Minimum Pressure. Also 25 psi (4 and 6) Or 40 psi (8) Maximum Variation
33 — Int. — .010 in./0.25 mm Exh. — .018 in./0.45 mm
34 — Toe-Out

35 — 4-Door — 2863/112.7
36 — Int. — .010 in./0.25 mm Exh. — .020 in./0.50 mm
37 — Cal. — 155/115.2@4000
38 — Electronic Spark Control System
39 — Grand AM, Grand Prix SJ — 155/115.2@4400
40 — Formula, Tran. AM — 155/115.2@4400

1981

	Wheelbase (mm)	Wheelbase (in.)	No. of Cylinders Bore and Stroke (in.)	Displacement (litres)	Displacement (cu. in.)	Valve and Cylinder Arrangement	Net Brake Horsepower @ rpm	Net Power (kW)	Compression Pressure (psi)	Valve Clearance
AMC — Spirit, Concord	2438	96[1]	4 — 4.00x3.00	2.5	151	IO	90@4000	67.1	140	HY
Eagle, SX4, Kammback	2775	109.3[4]	4 — 4.00x3.00	2.5	151	IO	90@4000	67.1	140	HY
Spirit, Concord	2438	96[1]	6 — 3.75x3.90	4.23	258	IO	NA	NA	140	HY
Eagle, SX4, Kammback	2775	109.3[4]	6 — 3.75x3.90	4.23	258	IO	NA	NA	140	HY
Buick — Skylark	2664	104.9	4 — 4.0x3.0	2.5	151	IO	90@4000	67.1	140[6]	HY
Skylark	2664	104.9	6 — 3.50x3.0	2.8	173	VO	115@4800	85.4	140[6]	HY
Century, Regal	2745	108.1	6 — 3.80x3.40	3.8	231	VO	110@3800	82	140[6]	HY
LeSabre	2945	115.9	6 — 3.80x3.40	3.8	231	VO	110@3800	82	140[6]	HY
Regal Sport Coupe	2745	108.1	6 — 3.80x3.40[10]	3.8	231	VO	170@4000	126	140[6]	HY
Riviera T Coupe	2894	114	6 — 3.80x3.40[10]	3.8	231	VO	180@4000	134	140[6]	HY
LeSabre, Electra	2945	115.9[11]	6 — 3.965x3.40	4.1	252	VO	125@4000	93	140[6]	HY
Riviera	2894	114	6 — 3.965x3.40	4.1	252	VO	125@4000	93	140[6]	HY
Century, Regal	2745	108.1	8 — 3.75x3.00	4.3	265	VO	119@4000	88.5	140[6]	HY
LeSabre	2945	115.9	8 — 3.736x3.48	5.0	305	VO	150@3600	111.5	155	HY
LeSabre, Electra	2945	115.9[11]	8 — 3.80x3.385	5.0	307	VO	150@3600	111.5	155	HY
Riviera	2894	114	8 — 3.80x3.385	5.0	307	VO	150@3600	111.5	155	HY
LeSabre, Electra	2945	115.9[11]	8 — 4.057x3.385[12]	5.7	350	VO	105@3200	78	275[13]	HY
Riviera	2894	114	8 — 4.057x3.385[12]	5.7	350	VO	105@3200	78	275[13]	HY
Cadillac — Seville, Eldorado	2895	114	6 — 3.965x3.40	4.1	252	VO	125@3800	93	140	HY
Brougham, DeVille	3085	121.4	6 — 3.965x3.40	4.1	252	VO	125@3800	93	140	HY
Seville, Eldorado	2895	114	8 — 4.057x3.385[12]	5.7	350	VO	105@3200	78	275[13]	HY
Brougham, DeVille	3085	121.4	8 — 4.057x3.385[12]	5.7	350	VO	105@3200	78	275[13]	HY
Seville, Eldorado	2895	114	8 — 3.80x4.060[14]	6.0	368	VO	140@3800	104	155	HY
Brougham, DeVille	3085	121.4	8 — 3.80x4.060[14]	6.0	368	VO	140@3800	104	155	HY
Fleetwood Limo	3670	144.5	8 — 3.80x4.060[14]	6.0	368	VO	140@3800	104	155	HY
Chevrolet — Chevette	2394	94.3[15]	4 — 3.23x2.98	1.6	98	IOC	70@5200	52	145	HY
Citation	2664	104.9	4 — 4.0x3.0	2.5	151	IO	84@4000	63	145[6]	HY
Citation	2664	104.9	6 — 3.50x2.99	2.8	173	VO	110@4800	82	140[6]	HY
Citation	2664	104.9	6 — 3.50x2.99	2.8	173	VO	135@5400	100	140[6]	HY
Camaro, Berlinetta	2743	108	6 — 3.736x3.48	3.8	229	VO	110@4200	82	140[6]	HY
Malibu, Classic, Monte Carlo	2745	108.1	6 — 3.736x3.48	3.8	229	VO	110@4200	82	140[6]	HY
Impala, Caprice Classic	2945	116	6 — 3.736x3.48	3.8	229	VO	110@4200	82	140[6]	HY
Camaro, Berlinetta	2743	108	6 — 3.80x3.40	3.8	231	VO	110@3800	82	140[6]	HY
Malibu, Classic, Monte Carlo	2745	108.1	6 — 3.80x3.40	3.8	231	VO	110@3800	82	140[6]	HY
Impala, Caprice Classic	2945	116	6 — 3.80x3.40	3.8	231	VO	110@3800	82	140[6]	HY
Monte Carlo	2745	108.1	6 — 3.80x3.40	3.8	231	VO	170@4000	127	140[6]	HY
Camaro, Berlinetta	2743	108	8 — 3.50x3.48	4.4	267	VO	115@4000	85.4	150[6]	HY
Malibu, Classic, Monte Carlo	2745	108.1	8 — 3.50x3.48	4.4	267	VO	115@4000	85.4	150[6]	HY
Impala, Caprice Classic	2945	116	8 — 3.50x3.48	4.4	267	VO	115@4000	85.4	150[6]	HY
Camaro, Berlinetta	2743	108	8 — 3.736x3.48	5.0	305	VO	150@3800[19]	110[19]	155[6]	HY
Malibu, Classic, Monte Carlo	2745	108.1	8 — 3.736x3.48	5.0	305	VO	150@3800	110	155[6]	HY
Impala, Caprice Classic	2945	116	8 — 3.736x3.48	5.0	305	VO	150@3800	110	155[6]	HY
Camaro, Berlinetta	2743	108	8 — 4.0x3.48	5.7	350	VO	175@4000[21]	130[21]	150[6]	HY
Corvette	2489	98	8 — 4.0x3.48	5.7	350	VO	190@4200	141.2	150[6]	HY
Impala, Caprice Classic	2945	116	8 — 4.057x3.385[12]	5.7	350	VO	105@3200	78	275[13]	HY
Chrysler — LeBaron	2761	108.7	6 — 3.40x4.12	3.7	225	IO	85@3600	63	100[22]	HY
Cordoba	2863	112.7	6 — 3.40x4.12	3.7	225	IO	85@3600	63	100[22]	HY
LeBaron	2761	108.7	8 — 3.91x3.31	5.2	318	VO	130@4000[24]	97[24]	100[22]	HY
Cordoba	2863	112.7	8 — 3.91x3.31	5.2	318	VO	130@4000[24]	97[24]	100[22]	HY
Newport	3010	118.5	8 — 3.91x3.31	5.2	318	VO	130@4000[24]	97[24]	100[22]	HY
New Yorker	3010	118.5	8 — 3.91x3.31	5.2	318	VO	130@4000[24]	97[24]	100[22]	HY
Imperial	2863	112.7	8 — 3.91x3.31[25]	5.2	318	VO	140@4000	104	100[22]	HY
Dodge — Omni, 024	2454	96.6[26]	4 — 3.13x3.40	1.7	104.7	IOC	65@5200[27]	48[27]	100[22]	H[28]
Omni, 024	2454	96.6[26]	4 — 3.44x3.62	2.2	135	IOC	84@4800	63	100[22]	HY
Aries Custom, SE	2530	99.6	4 — 3.44x3.62	2.2	135	IOC	84@4800	63	100[22]	HY
Aries Custom, SE	2530	99.6	4 — 3.59x3.86	2.6	155.9	IOC	92@5000	69	100[22]	H[32]
Diplomat, Salon, Medallion	2761	108.7[33]	6 — 3.40x4.12	3.7	225	IO	90@3600	67	100[22]	HY
Mirada, S	2863	112.7	6 — 3.40x4.12	3.7	225	IO	90@3600	67	100[22]	HY
St. Regis	3010	118.5	6 — 3.40x4.12	3.7	225	IO	90@3600	67	100[22]	HY
Diplomat, Salon, Medallion	2761	108.7[33]	8 — 3.91x3.31	5.2	318	VO	120@3600	89	100[22]	HY
Mirada, S	2863	112.7	8 — 3.91x3.31	5.2	318	VO	120@3600	89	100[22]	HY
St. Regis	3010	118.5	8 — 3.91x3.31	5.2	318	VO	120@3600	89	100[22]	HY
Diplomat, Salon, Medallion	2761	108.7[33]	8 — 3.91x3.31	5.2	318	VO	155@3600	115	100[22]	HY
Mirada, S	2863	112.7	8 — 3.91x3.31	5.2	318	VO	155@3600	115	100[22]	HY
St. Regis	3010	118.5[33]	8 — 3.91x3.31	5.2	318	VO	155@3600	115	100[22]	HY
Ford — Escort	2393	94.2	4 — 3.15x3.13	1.6	97.6	IOC	65@4500	48	80[34]	HY
Mustang, Ghia	2550	100.4	4 — 3.781x3.126	2.3	140	IOC	88@4600	66	80[34]	HY
Fairmont, Granada	2679	105.5	4 — 3.781x3.126	2.3	140	IOC	88@4600	66	80[34]	HY
Mustang, Ghia	2550	100.4	4 — 3.781x3.126[10]	2.3	140	IOC	NA	NA	80[34]	HY

ABBREVIATIONS — FOOTNOTES

AC — AC Spark Plugs	IOC — In-Line Engine—Overhead Camshaft	2 — 10B
B — Before Top Dead Center	M — MOPAR Spark Plugs	3 — Left 1/3P, Right 1/8P
CH — Champion Spark Plugs	MO — Motorcraft Spark Plugs	4 — SX4 And Kammback — 2469/97.2
CP — Crankshaft Pulley	N — Negative	5 — SX4 And Kammback Only
F — Flywheel	NA — Not Available/Not Applicable	6 — Lowest Cylinder Must Be At Least 70 Percent Of Highest
H — Hot Engine	P — Positive	7 — Not Adjustable
HY — Hydraulic Lifters	VD — Vibration Damper	8 — 6B
IO — In-Line Engine—Overhead Valves	VO — V-Type Engine—Overhead Valves	9 — Manual Trans. Not Available
	1 — Concord—2743/108	10 — Turbocharged Engine

Firing Order	Timing Mark Location	Initial Ignition Timing @ rpm (auto. trans.)	Ignition Timing (rpm-manual trans.)	Ignition Timing (California)	Spark Plugs Make	Spark Plugs Model	Gap (in.)	Caster, Power Steering (deg.)	Camber, Right Wheel (deg.)	Toe-In (in.)	Crankcase Capacity (L./qt.)	Cooling System Capacity (L)	Cooling System Capacity (qt.)
1342	CP	12B@700	900[2]	10B	AC	R44TSX	.060	1P	1/3P[3]	1/8	2.84/3	6.15	6.5
1342	CP	12B@700[5]	900[2]	10B	AC	R44TSX	.060	2-1/2P	1/3P	1/8	2.84/3	6.15	6.5
153624	VD	6B@500	600	6B	CH	RFN-14LY	.035	1P	1/3P[3]	1/8	3.78/4	10.4	11
153624	VD	6B@500	600	6B	CH	RFN-14LY	.035	2-1/2P	1/3P	1/8	3.78/4	13.2	14
1342	VD	4B@750	1000	4B	AC	R44TSX	.060	NA[7]	1/2P	1/8	2.84/3	8	8.5
123456	VD	10B@650	850[8]	10B	AC	R43TS	.045	NA[7]	1/2P	1/8	3.78/4	10.1	10.7
165432	VD	15B@600	NA	15B[9]	AC	R45TS8	.080	3P	1/2P	1/8	3.78/4	6.2	6.6
165432	VD	15B@600	NA	15B[9]	AC	R45TS4	.080	3P	3/4P	1/8	3.78/4	6.2	6.6
165432	VD	15B@800	NA	15B[9]	AC	R45TS8	.080	3P	1/2P	1/8	3.78/4	6.4	6.7
165432	VD	15B@600	NA	15B[9]	AC	R45TS	.080	2-1/2P	0	0	3.78/4	6.5	6.8
165432	VD	15B@600	NA	15B[9]	AC	R45TS8	.080	3P	3/4P	1/8	3.78/4	6.2	6.6
165432	VD	15B@600	NA	15B[9]	AC	R45TS8	.080	2-1/2P	0	0	3.78/4	6.2	6.6
18436572	VD	15B@600	NA	15B[9]	AC	R45TS8	.080	3P	1/2P	1/8	3.78/4	19.8	20.9
18436572	VD	15B@1100	NA	15B[9]	AC	R45TS8	.080	3P	3/4P	1/8	3.78/4	15.1	16
18436572	VD	15B@1100	NA	15B[9]	AC	R45TS8	.080	3P	3/4P	1/8	3.78/4	15.5	16.4
18436572	VD	15B@1100	NA	15B[9]	AC	R45TS8	.080	2-1/2P	0	0	3.78/4	15.5	16.4
18436572	VD	NA	NA	NA	NA	NA	NA	3P	3/4P	1/8	6.0/6.5	17.2	18.1
18436572	VD	NA	NA	NA	NA	NA	NA	2-1/2P	0	0	6.0/6.5	17.2	18.1
165432	VD	15B@1100	NA	15B[9]	AC	R45TSV	.060	2-1/2P	0	0	3.78/4	12.4	13.1
165432	VD	15B@550	NA	15B[9]	AC	R45TSX	.060	1P	3/4P	1/8	3.78/4	11.9	12.6
18436572	VD	NA	NA	NA	NA	NA	NA	2-1/2P	0	0	6.0/6.5	17.4	18.4
18436572	VD	NA	NA	NA	NA	NA	NA	1P	3/4P	1/8	6.0/6.5	22.4	23.7
18436572	VD	10B@450	NA	10B	AC	R45NSX	.060	2-1/2P	0	0	3.78/4	20.3	21.4
18436572	VD	10B@450	NA	10B	AC	R45NSX	.060	1P	3/4P	1/8	3.78/4	20.3	21.4
18436572	VD	10B@450	NA	10B	AC	R45NSX	.060	1P	3/4P	1/8	3.78/4	20.3	21.4
1342	VD	18B@700	800	18B	AC	R42TS	.035	1/2P	1/4P	1/16	3.78/4	8.7	9.2
1342	CP	4@675	1000	4B	AC	R44TSX	.060	0[7]	1/2P	.10[16]	2.8/3	8.3	8.7
123456	VD	10B@650	850[8]	10B	AC	R43TS	.045	0[7]	1/2P	.10[16]	3.78/4	10.1	10.7
123456	VD	10B@700	850	10B	AC	R42TS	.045	0[7]	1/2P	.10[16]	3.78/4	10.1	10.7
165432	VD	6B@600	700	NA	AC	R45TS	.045	1P	1P	1/8	3.78/4	14.3	15.1
165432	VD	6B@600	700	NA	AC	R45TS	.045	3P	1/2P	1/8	3.78/4	14.4	15.2
165432	VD	6B@600	NA	NA	AC	R45TS	.045	3/4P	3P	1/8	3.78/4	13.5	14.2
165432	VD	NA	NA	15B[17]	AC	R45TS8	.080	1P	1P	1/8	3.78/4	11.8	12.5
165432	VD	NA	NA	15B[17]	AC	R45TS8[18]	.080[18]	3P	1/2P	1/8	3.78/4	11.7	12.4
165432	VD	NA	NA	15B[17]	AC	R45TS8	.080	3/4P	3P	1/8	3.78/4	11.2	11.8
165432	VD	15B@650	NA	15B	AC	R45TS	.045	3P	1/2P	1/8	3.78/4	11.7	12.4
18436572	VD	6B@500	NA	NA	AC	R45TS	.045	1P	1P	1/8	3.78/4	16.4	17.4
18436572	VD	6B@500	NA	NA	AC	R45TS	.045	3P	1/2P	1/8	3.78/4	17.9	18.9
18436572	VD	6B@500	NA	NA	AC	R45TS	.045	3/4P	3P	1/8	3.78/4	16.1	17
18436572	VD	6B@500[20]	700	6B	AC	R45TS	.045	1P	1P	1/8	3.78/4	15	15.8
18436572	VD	6B@500	NA	NA	AC	R45TS	.045	3P	1/2P	1/8	3.78/4	15.7	16.6
18436572	VD	6B@500	NA	6B	AC	R45TS	.045	3/4P	3P	1/8	3.78/4	14.7	15.5
18436572	VD	6B@500	NA	6B	AC	R45TS	.045	1P	1P	1/8	3.78/4	15.7	16.6
18436572	VD	6B@500	700	6B	AC	R45TS	.045	2-1/4P	3/4P	1/4	3.78/4	20.4	21.6
18436572	VD	NA	NA	NA	NA	NA	NA	3/4P	3P	1/8	7.1/7.5	15.5	16.4
153624	VD	12B@750	NA	16B[23]	M	P-560PR4	.035	2-1/2P	1/2P	1/8	3.78/4	10.9	11.5
153624	VD	12B@750	NA	12B[23]	M	P-560PR4	.035	2-1/2P	1/2P	1/8	3.78/4	10.9	11.5
18436572	VD	16B@700[23]	NA	NA[24]	M	P-65PR4	.035	2-1/2P	1/2P	1/8	3.78/4	14.2	15
18436572	VD	16B@700[23]	NA	NA[24]	M	P-65PR4	.035	2-1/2P	1/2P	1/8	3.78/4	15.6	16.5
18436572	VD	16B@700[23]	NA	NA[24]	M	P-65PR4	.035	3/4P	1/4P	1/8	3.78/4	15.6	16.5
18436572	VD	16B@700[23]	NA	NA[24]	M	P-65PR4	.035	3/4P	1/4P	1/8	3.78/4	15.6	16.5
18436572	VD	12B@580	NA	12B	M	P-68ER	.048	2-1/2P	1/4P	1/8	3.78/4	14.7	15.5
1342	CP	10B@900	900[29]	NA	M	P-65PR4	.025	1-1/2P[30]	1/2N	1/16[31]	3.78/4	5.7	6
1342	F	10B@900[23]	900[29]	10B[23]	M	P-65PR4	.025	1-1/2P[30]	1/2N	1/16[31]	3.78/4	8.2	8.7
1342	F	10B@900[23]	900[29]	10B[23]	M	P-65PR4	.025	1-1/4P[7]	1/4P	1/16[31]	3.78/4	8.2	8.7
1342	CP	7B@800	NA	7B	M	P-65PR4	.025	1-1/4P[7]	1/4P	1/16[31]	3.78/4	8.2	8.7
153624	VD	12B@750	NA	16B[23]	M	P-560PR4	.035	2-1/2P	1/2P	1/8	3.78/4	10.9	11.5
153624	VD	12B@750	NA	12B[23]	M	P-560PR4	.035	2-1/2P	1/2P	1/8	3.78/4	10.9	11.5
153624	VD	12B@750	NA	NA	M	P-560PR4	.035	3/4P	1/4P	1/8	3.78/4	10.9	11.5
18436572	VD	16B@700[23]	NA	NA	M	P-65PR4	.035	2-1/2P	1/2P	1/8	3.78/4	14.2	15
18436572	VD	16B@700[23]	NA	NA	M	P-65PR4	.035	2-1/2P	1/2P	1/8	3.78/4	15.6	16.5
18436572	VD	16B@700[23]	NA	NA	M	P-65PR4	.035	3/4P	1/4P	1/8	3.78/4	15.6	16.5
18436572	VD	16B@700[23]	NA	16B[23]	M	P-65PR4	.035	2-1/2P	1/2P	1/8	3.78/4	14.2	15
18436572	VD	16B@700[23]	NA	16B[23]	M	P-65PR4	.035	2-1/2P	1/2P	1/8	3.78/4	15.6	16.5
18436572	VD	16B@700[23]	NA	16B[23]	M	P-65PR4	.035	2-1/2P	1/2P	1/8	3.78/4	15.6	16.5
1342	CP	10B@NA	NA[2]	8B[35]	MO	AGSP-32	.044	1-5/8P	1-1/4P	1/8[31]	2.9/3.06	6.15	6.5
1342	CP	20B@750	850	20B[36]	MO	AWSF-42	.034	1P	1/4P	3/16	3.78/4	9.7	10.2
1342	CP	20B@750	850	20B	MO	AWSF-42	.034	1P	3/8P	3/16	3.78/4	9.7	10.2
1342	CP	NA	800[2]	10B	MO	AWSF-32	.034	1P	1/4P	3/16	3.78/4	9.7	10.2

11 — Electra — 3020/118.9
12 — Diesel Engine
13 — Minimum psi
14 — Digital Fuel Injection (DFI)
15 — 4-Door — 2471/97.3
16 — Degree Per Wheel
17 — @500
18 — Monte Carlo — R45TS/.045
19 — With Z28 — 165/122.5@4000
20 — Not With Z28
21 — With Z28

22 — Minimum Pressure. Also 25 psi (4 and 6) Or 40 psi (V-8) Maximum Variation
23 — Combustion Computer With Feedback Carburetor Controller
24 — 4-Bbl. — 165/123@4000
25 — Electronic Fuel Injection (EFI)
26 — 4-Door — 2517/99.7
27 — Also 70/52@5200
28 — Int. — .010 in./0.25 mm H Exh. — .018 in./0.45 mm H
29 — 12B

30 — Not Adjustable — 4-Door 2P
31 — Toe-Out
32 — Int. — .006 in./0.15 mm H Exh. — .010 in./0.25 mm H
33 — 4-Door — 2863/112.7
34 — Lowest Cylinder Must Be At Least 75 Percent Of Highest
35 — Manual Trans. — 6B
36 — Manual Trans.

1981

	Wheelbase (mm)	Wheelbase (in.)	No. of Cylinders Bore and Stroke (in.)	Displacement (litres)	Displacement (cu. in.)	Valve and Cylinder Arrangement	Net Brake Horsepower @ rpm	Net Power (kW)	Compression Pressure (psi)	Valve Clearance
Ford — Mustang, Ghia	2550	100.4	6—3.682x3.126	3.3	200	IOC	94@4000	70	80[1]	HY
Fairmont, Granada	2679	105.5	6—3.682x3.126	3.3	200	IOC	88@3800	70	80[1]	HY
Thunderbird	2753	108.4	6—3.682x3.126	3.3	200	IOC	88@3800	66	80[1]	HY
Mustang, Ghia	2550	100.4	8—3.68x3.0	4.2	255	VO	115@3400[2]	86[2]	80[1]	HY
Fairmont, Granada	2679	105.5	8—3.68x3.0	4.2	255	VO	115@3400[2]	86[2]	80[1]	HY
Thunderbird	2753	108.4	8—3.68x3.0	4.2	255	VO	115@3400[2]	86[2]	80[1]	HY
LTD, S, Crown Victoria	2904	114.3	8—3.68x3.0	4.2	255	VO	120@3400[3]	90[3]	80[1]	HY
Thunderbird	2753	108.4	8—4.0x3.0	5.0	302	VO	130@3400[4]	97[4]	80[1]	HY
LTD, S, Crown Victoria	2904	114.3	8—4.0x3.0	5.0	302	VO	130@3400[3]	97[3]	80[1]	HY
LTD, S, Crown Victoria	2904	114.3	8—4.0x3.50	5.8	351	VO	145@3200[5]	108[5]	80[1]	HY
Lincoln — Mark VI	2904	114.3[6]	8—4.0x3.0[7]	5.0	302	VO	130@3400	97	80[1]	HY
Lincoln	2980	117.3	8—4.0x3.0[7]	5.0	302	VO	130@3400	97	80[1]	HY
Mercury — Lynx	2393	94.2	4—3.15x 3.13	1.6	97.6	IOC	65@5200	48	80[1]	HY
Capri, GS	2550	100.4	4—3.781x3.126	2.3	140	IOC	88@4600	66	80[1]	HY
Zephyr, Cougar	2679	105.5	4—3.781x3.126	2.3	140	IOC	88@4600	66	80[1]	HY
Capri, GS	2550	100.4	4—3.781x3.126[11]	2.3	140	IOC	NA	NA	80[1]	HY
Capri, GS	2550	100.4	6—3.682x3.126	3.3	200	IO	94@4000	70	80[1]	HY
Zephyr, Cougar	2679	105.5	6—3.682x3.126	3.3	200	IO	94@4000[15]	70[15]	80[1]	HY
Cougar XR-7	2753	108.4	6—3.682x3.126	3.3	200	IO	88@3800	66	80[1]	HY
Capri, GS	2550	100.4	8—3.68x3.0	4.2	255	VO	115@3400[2]	86[2]	80[1]	HY
Zephyr, Cougar	2679	105.5	8—3.68x3.0	4.2	255	VO	115@3400[2]	86[2]	80[1]	HY
Cougar XR-7	2753	108.4	8—3.68x3.0	4.2	255	VO	115@3400[16]	86[16]	80[1]	HY
Marquis, Brougham, Grand Marquis	2904	114.3	8—3.68x3.0	4.2	255	VO	120@3400[3]	90[3]	80[1]	HY
Cougar XR-7	2753	108.4	8—4.0x3.0	5.0	302	VO	130@3400[4]	97[4]	80[1]	HY
Marquis, Brougham, Grand Marquis	2904	114.3	8—4.0x3.0	5.0	302	VO	130@3400[4]	97[4]	80[1]	HY
Marquis, Brougham, Grand Marquis	2904	114.3	8—4.0x3.50	5.8	351	VO	145@3200[17]	97[17]	80[1]	HY
Oldsmobile — Omega, Brougham	2664	104.9	4—4.0x3.0	2.5	151	IO	90@4000	67.1	140[18]	HY
Omega, Brougham	2664	104.9	6—3.50x3.0	2.8	173	VO	115@4800	85.4	140[18]	HY
Cutlass, Calais, Supreme, Brougham	2745	108.1	6—3.80x3.40	3.8	231	VO	110@3800	82	140[18]	HY
Delta 88, Royale, Brougham	2945	116	6—3.80x3.40	3.8	231	VO	110@3800	82	140[18]	HY
Toronado	2895	114	6—3.965x3.40	4.1	252	VO	125@4000	93	140[18]	HY
98 Luxury, Regency	3020	119	6—3.965x3.40	4.1	252	VO	125@4000	93	140[18]	HY
Cutlass, Calais, Supreme, Brougham	2745	108.1	8—3.50x3.385	4.3	260	VO	NA	NA	140[18]	HY
Delta 88, Royale, Brougham	2945	116	8—3.50x3.385	4.3	260	VO	NA	NA	140[18]	HY
Toronado	2895	114	8—3.80x3.385	5.0	307	VO	150@3600	111.5	155[18]	HY
Delta, 88, Royale, Brougham	2945	116	8—3.80x3.385	5.0	307	VO	150@3600	111.5	155[18]	HY
98 Luxury, Regency	3020	119	8—3.80x3.385	5.0	307	VO	150@3600	111.5	155[18]	HY
Cutlass, Calais, Supreme, Brougham	2745	108.1	8—4.057x3.385	5.7	350	VO	105@3200	78	275[25]	HY
Toronado	2895	114	8—4.057x3.385[26]	5.7	350	VO	105@3200	78	275[25]	HY
Delta 88, Royale, Brougham	2945	116	8—4.057x3.385[26]	5.7	350	VO	105@3200	78	275[25]	HY
98 Luxury, Regency	3020	119	8—4.057x3.385[26]	5.7	350	VO	105@3200	78	275[25]	HY
Plymouth — Horizon, Miser, TC3	2454	96.6[27]	4—3.13x3.40	1.7	104.7	IOC	63@5200	47	100[28]	H[29]
Horizon, Miser, TC3	2454	96.6[27]	4—3.44x3.62	2.2	135	IOC	84@4800	63	100[28]	HY
Reliant, SE	2530	99.6	4—3.44x3.62	2.2	135	IOC	84@4800	63	100[28]	HY
Reliant, SE	2530	99.6	4—3.59x3.86	2.6	155.9	IOC	92@4500	69	100[28]	H[31]
Gran Fury, Salon	3010	118.5	6—3.40x4.12	3.7	225	IO	85@3600	63	100[28]	HY
Gran Fury, Salon	3010	118.5	8—3.91x3.31	5.2	318	VO	130@4000	97	100[28]	HY
Gran Fury, Salon	3010	118.5	8—3.91x3.31	5.2	318	VO	165@4000	123	100[28]	HY
Pontiac — Phoenix, LJ	2664	104.9	4—4.0x3.0	2.5	151	IO	84@4000	63	140[18]	HY
Phoenix, LJ	2664	104.9	6—3.50x2.99	2.8	173	VO	110@4800	82	140[18]	HY
LeMans, Grand LeMans	2745	108.1	6—3.80x3.40	3.8	231	VO	110@3800	82	140[18]	HY
Grand Prix, LJ, Brougham	2745	108.1	6—3.80x3.40	3.8	231	VO	110@3800	82	140[18]	HY
Firebird, Esprit	2748	108.2	6—3.80x3.40	3.8	231	VO	110@3800	82	140[18]	HY
Catalina, Bonneville, Brougham	2945	116	6—3.80x3.40	3.8	231	VO	110@3800	82	140[18]	HY
LeMans, Grand LeMans, Grand Prix	2745	108.1	8—3.75x3.0	4.3	265	VO	120@4000	89.2	140[18]	HY
Firebird, Esprit	2748	108.2	8—3.75x3.0	4.3	265	VO	120@4000	89.2	140[18]	HY
Formula	2748	108.2	8—3.75x3.0	4.3	265	VO	120@4000	89.2	140[18]	HY
Catalina, Bonneville, Brougham	2945	116	8—3.75x3.0	4.3	265	VO	120@4000	89.2	140[18]	HY
LeMans, Grand LeMans	2745	108.1	8—4.0x3.0	4.9	301	VO	135@3600	100	140[18]	HY
Formula	2745	108.1	8—4.0x3.0	4.9	301	VO	150@4000	111.5	140[18]	HY
Trans Am	2745	108.1	8—4.0x3.0	4.9	301	VO	150@4000	111.5	140[18]	HY
Formula	2745	108.1	8—4.0x3.0[11]	4.9	301	VO	200@4000	149.2	140[18]	HY
Trans Am	2745	108.1	8—4.0x3.0[11]	4.9	301	VO	200@4000	149.2	140[18]	HY
Formula	2745	108.1	8—3.736x3.48	5.0	305	VO	145@3800	97	140[18]	HY
Trans Am	2745	108.1	8—3.736x3.48	5.0	305	VO	145@3800	97	140[18]	HY
Catalina, Bonneville, Brougham	2945	116	8—3.8x3.385	5.0	307	VO	145@3800	97	140[18]	HY
LeMans, Grand LeMans	2745	108.1	8—4.057x3.385[26]	5.7	350	VO	105@3200	78	275[25]	HY
Grand Prix, LJ, Brougham	2745	108.1	8—4.057x3.385[26]	5.7	350	VO	105@3200	78	275[25]	HY
Catalina, Bonneville, Brougham	2945	116	8—4.057x3.385[26]	5.7	350	VO	105@3200	78	275[25]	HY

ABBREVIATIONS — FOOTNOTES

AC — AC Spark Plugs	M — MOPAR Spark Plugs	3 — Variable Venturi Carburetor
B — Before Top Dead Center	MO — Motorcraft Spark Plugs	4 — Cal. Only — Variable Venturi
CH — Champion Spark Plugs	N — Negative	5 — Also, Federal Only — 165/122.5@3600
CP — Crankshaft Pulley	NA — Not Available/Not Applicable	6 — 4-Door — 2980/117.3
F — Flywheel	P — Positive	7 — Electronic Fuel Injection
H — Hot Engine	VD — Vibration Damper	8 — Manual Trans. — 6B
HY — Hydraulic Lifters	VO — V-Type Engine — Overhead Valves	9 — Toe-Out
IO — In-Line Engine — Overhead Valves		10 — @600
IOC — In-Line Engine — Overhead Camshaft	1 — Lowest Cylinder Must Be At Least 75 Percent Of Highest	11 — Turbocharged Engine
	2 — Cal. — Variable Venturi, 120/90@3400	12 — 10B
		13 — Cal. — @600

804

Tuneup Specifications

Firing Order	Timing Mark Location	Initial Ignition Timing @ rpm (auto. trans.)	Ignition Timing (rpm-manual trans.)	Ignition Timing (California)	Make	Model	Gap (in.)	Caster, Power Steering (deg.)	Camber, Right Wheel (deg.)	Toe-In (in.)	Crankcase Capacity (L/qt.)	Cooling System Capacity (L)	Cooling System Capacity (qt.)
153624	VD	10B@550	700	10B	MO	BRF—82	.050	1P	1/4P	3/16	3.8/4	8.5	9
153624	VD	12B@700	NA	10B	MO	BSF—92	.050	1P	3/8P	3/16	3.8/4	7.9	8.4
153624	VD	12B@700	NA	10B	MO	BSF—92	.050	1P	3/8P	3/16	3.8/4	7.9	8.4
15426378	VD	8B@550	NA	6B	MO	ASF—42	.050	1P	1/4P	3/16	3.8/4	13.4	14.2
15426378	VD	8B@500	NA	6B	MO	ASF—52	.050	1P	3/8P	3/16	3.8/4	14	14.8
15426378	VD	8B@700	NA	6B	MO	ASF—52	.050	1P	3/8P	3/16	3.8/4	14.1	14.9
15426378	VD	8B@500	NA	6B	MO	ASF—52	.050	3P	1/2P	1/16	3.8/4	14	14.8
15426378	VD	8B@700	NA	10B	MO	ASF—52	.050	1P	3/8P	3/16	3.8/4	12.5	13.2
15426378	VD	6B@550	NA	10B	MO	ASF—52	.050	3P	1/2P	1/16	3.8/4	12.6	13.3
13726548	VD	10B@550	NA	10B	MO	ASF—52	.050	3P	1/2P	1/16	3.8/4	13.6	14.4
15426378	VD	10B@550	NA	10B	MO	ASF—52	.050	3P	1/2P	1/16	3.8/4	12.6	13.3
15426378	VD	10B@550	NA	10B	MO	ASF—52	.050	3P	1/2P	1/16	3.8/4	12.6	13.3
1342	CP	10B@NA	NA[8]	8B[8]	MO	AGSP—32	.044	1-5/8P	1-1/4P	1/8[9]	2.9/3.06	6.15	6.5
1342	CP	8B@750	850	2B[10]	MO	AWSF—42	.034	1P	1/4P	3/16	3.8/4	9.7	10.2
1342	CP	8B@750	850	2B[10]	MO	AWSF—42	.034	1P	3/8P	3/16	3.8/4	9.7	10.2
1342	CP	10B@800	800[12]	10B[13]	MO	AWSF—32	.034	1P	1/4P	3/16	3.8/4	9.7	10.2
153624	VD	10B@550	700	10B[14]	MO	BRF—82	.050	1P	1/4P	3/16	3.8/4	8.5	9
153624	VD	12B@700	NA	12B	MO	BSF—92	.050	1P	3/8P	3/16	3.8/4	7.9	8.4
153624	VD	12B@700	NA	12B	MO	BSF—92	.050	1P	3/8P	3/16	3.8/4	7.9	8.4
15426378	VD	8B@550	NA	6B	MO	ASF—42	.050	1P	1/4P	3/16	3.8/4	13.4	14.2
15426378	VD	8B@700	NA	6B	MO	ASF—52	.050	1P	3/8P	3/16	3.8/4	14	14.8
15426378	VD	8B@700	NA	6B	MO	ASF—52	.050	1P	3/8P	3/16	3.8/4	14.1	14.9
15426378	VD	8B@500	NA	6B	MO	ASF—52	.050	3P	1/2P	1/16	3.8/4	14	14.8
15426378	VD	8B@700	NA	10B	MO	ASF—52	.050	1P	3/8P	3/16	3.8/4	12.5	13.2
15426378	VD	8B@500	NA	10B	MO	ASF—52	.050	3P	1/2P	1/16	3.8/4	12.6	13.3
13726548	VD	10B@500	NA	10B	MO	ASF—52	.050	3P	1/2P	1/16	3.8/4	13.6	14.4
1342	CP	4B@750	1000	4B	AC	R44TSX	.060	0[19]	1P	.10[20]	2.84/3	7.9[21]	8.4[21]
123456	VD	10B@650	850	10B	AC	R44TS	.045	0[19]	1P	.10[20]	3.8/4	10.1[22]	10.7[22]
165432	VD	15B@600	600[23]	15B	AC	R45TS8	.080	1P	1/2P	.15[20]	3.8/4	6.2	6.6
165432	VD	15B@600	NA	15B	AC	R45TS8	.080	3P	3/4P	.15[20]	3.8/4	6.2	6.6
165432	VD	15B@600	NA	15B	AC	R45TSV	.060	2-1/2P	0	0	3.8/4	12.4	13.1
165432	VD	15B@600	NA	15B	AC	R45TSX	.060	3P	3/4P	.15[20]	3.8/4	11.9	12.6
18436572	VD	20B@1100[24]	NA	20B	AC	R46SX	.080	1P	1/2P	.15[20]	3.75/4	15	15.9
18436572	VD	18B@1100	NA	18B	AC	R46SX	.080	3P	3/4P	.15[20]	3.75/4	14.7	15.5
18436572	VD	15B@1100	NA	15B	AC	R46SX	.080	2-1/2P	0	0	3.75/4	15.5	16.4
18436572	VD	15B@1100	NA	15B	AC	R46SX	.080	3P	3/4P	.15[20]	3.75/4	14.8	15.6
18436572	VD	15B@1100	NA	15B	AC	R46SX	.080	3P	3/4P	.15[20]	3.75/4	14.8	15.6
18436572	VD	NA	NA	NA	NA	NA	NA	1P	1/2P	.15[20]	6.0/6.5	16.5	17.4
18436572	VD	NA	NA	NA	NA	NA	NA	2-1/2P	0	0	6.0/6.5	17.2	18.1
18436572	VD	NA	NA	NA	NA	NA	NA	3P	3/4P	.15[20]	6.0/6.5	17	18
18436572	VD	NA	NA	NA	NA	NA	NA	3P	3/4P	.15[20]	6.0/6.5	17	18
1342	CP	10B@900	900[30]	NA	M	P—65PR4	.048	1-1/2P[18]	1/2N	1/16	3.78/4	5.7	6
1342	F	10B@900	900	10B	M	P—65PR4	.035	1-1/2P[18]	1/2N	1/16[9]	3.78/4	8.2	8.7
1342	F	10B@900	900	10B	M	P—65PR4	.035	1-1/4P[18]	1/4P	1/16[9]	3.78/4	8.2	8.7
1342	CP	7B@800	NA	7B	M	P—65PR4	.035	1-1/4P[18]	1/4P	1/16[9]	3.78/4	8.2	8.7
153624	VD	12B@750	NA	NA	M	P—560PR4	.048	1P	1/2P	1/8	3.78/4	10.9	11.5
18436572	VD	16B@700	NA	NA	M	P—65PR4	.048	1P	1/2P	1/8	3.78/4	14.2	15
18436572	VD	16B@700	NA	16B	M	P—65PR4	.048	1P	1/2P	1/8	3.78/4	14.7	15.5
1342	CP	4B@750	1000	4B	AC	R44TSX	.060	0[18]	1P	.10[20]	2.84/3	8	8.5
123456	VD	10B@650	850[8]	10B[8]	AC	R43TS	.045	0[18]	1P	.10[20]	3.78/4	10.1	10.7
165432	VD	15B@500	NA	15B	AC	R45TS8	.080	1/4P	1/2P	.12[20]	3.78/4	6.2	6.6
165432	VD	15B@500	NA	15B	AC	R45TS8	.080	3P	1/2P	.12[20]	3.78/4	6.2	6.6
165432	VD	15B@500	700	15B	AC	R45TS8	.080	1P	1/2P	.06[20]	3.78/4	6.2	6.6
165432	VD	15B@500	NA	15B	AC	R45TS8	.080	3P	3/4P	.20[20]	3.78/4	6.2	6.6
18436572	VD	12B@600	NA	12B	AC	R45TSX	.060	1/4P[32]	1/2P	.12[20]	3.8/4	19.8	20.9
18436572	VD	12B@600	NA	12B	AC	R45TSX	.060	1P	1P	.06[20]	3.8/4	19.8	20.9
18436572	VD	12B@600	NA	12B	AC	R45TSX	.060	1P	1P	.06[20]	3.8/4	19.8	20.9
18436572	VD	12B@600	NA	12B	AC	R45TSX	.060	3P	3/4P	.20[20]	3.8/4	19.8	20.9
18436572	VD	12B@600	NA	12B	AC	R45TSX	.060	1/4P	1/2P	.12[20]	3.8/4	19.8	20.9
18436572	VD	12B@600	NA	12B	AC	R45TSX	.060	1P	1P	.06[20]	3.8/4	19.8	20.9
18436572	VD	12B@600	NA	12B	AC	R45TSX	.060	1P	1P	.06[20]	3.8/4	19.8	20.9
18436572	VD	12B@600	NA	12B	AC	R45TSX	.060	1P	1P	.06[20]	3.8/4	19.8	20.9
18436572	VD	NA[33]	700[8]	NA[33]	AC	R45TS	.045	1P	1P	.06[20]	3.8/4	15	15.8
18436572	VD	NA[33]	700[8]	NA[33]	AC	R45TS	.045	1P	1P	.06[20]	3.8/4	15	15.8
18436572	VD	15B@1100	NA	15B	AC	R46SX	.080	3P	3/4P	.20[20]	3.75/4	14.1	14.9
18436572	VD	NA	NA	NA	NA	NA	NA	1/4P	1/2P	.12[20]	6.0/6.5	14.1	14.9
18436572	VD	NA	NA	NA	NA	NA	NA	3P	1/2P	.12[20]	6.0/6.5	14.1	14.9
18436572	VD	NA	NA	NA	NA	NA	NA	3P	3/4P	.20[20]	6.0/6.5	14.1	14.9

14 — Cal. — @700
15 — Cougar — 88/66@3800
16 — Cal. — 120/90@3400
17 — Variable Venturi Carburetor
  Also, Federal — 165/122.5@3600
18 — Lowest Cylinder Must Be At Least
  70 Percent Of Highest
19 — Not Adjustable
20 — Degree Per Wheel

21 — Auto. Trans. — 7.8/8.3
22 — Auto. Trans. — 10/10.6
23 — Manual Trans. Only On Cutlass
24 — Sedans — 18B@1100
25 — Minimum Pressure
26 — Diesel Engine
27 — 4-Door — 2517/99.1
28 — Minimum Pressure. Also 25 psi (4 and 6)
  Or 40 psi (V-8) Maximum Variation

29 — Int. — .010 in./0.25 mm H
  Exh. — .018 in./0.45 mm H
30 — 12B
31 — Int. — .006 in./0.15 mm H
  Exh. — .010 in./0.25 mm H
32 — Grand Prix — 3P
33 — Auto. Trans. Not Available

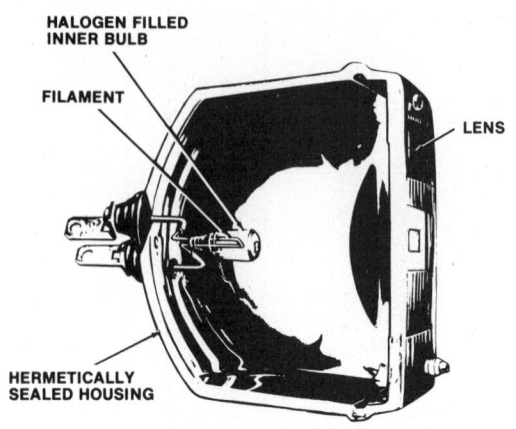

Fig. S-30. Halogen sealed beam headlamps were broadened in coverage in 1980 and 1981 models. Chrysler uses a halogen filled inner bulb with no increase in electrical power for a 25 percent increase in high beam lamp output. (Chrysler-Plymouth Div.)

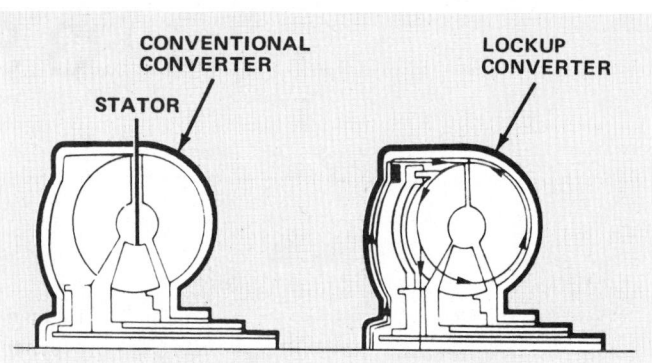

Fig. S-33. Lockup torque converters find wide application in 1980 and 1981 models. Lockup converter has an internal mechanism for locking the turbine and impeller in direct drive (third speed) to eliminate slippage. (American Motors)

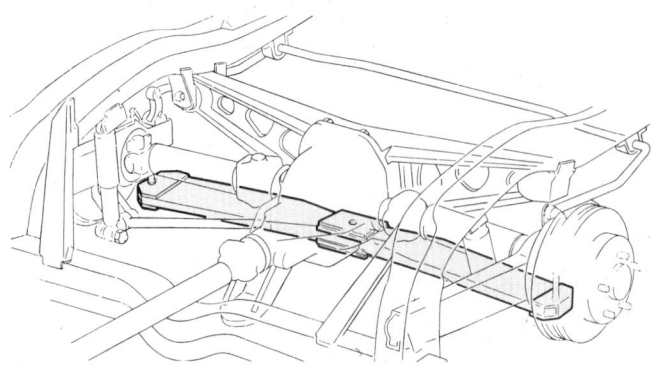

Fig. S-31. First fiber glass composite spring was introduced in 1981. It is an 8 lb., single leaf, filament-wound, glass/epoxy device which replaces a 41 lb., 10 leaf steel spring on Corvettes equipped with automatic transmission. (Chevrolet Motor Div., GM)

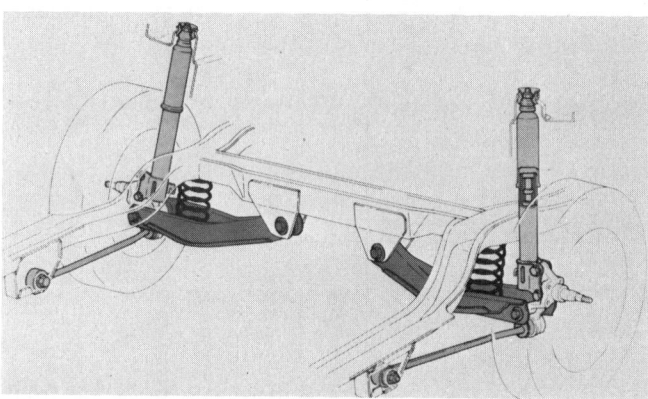

Fig. S-34. The 1981 Ford Escort and Mercury Lynx models have four wheel fully independent suspension. Rear suspension has coil springs, galvanized steel lower control arms, MacPherson shock struts, fore-and-aft tie rods and forged wheel spindles. (Ford Motor Co.)

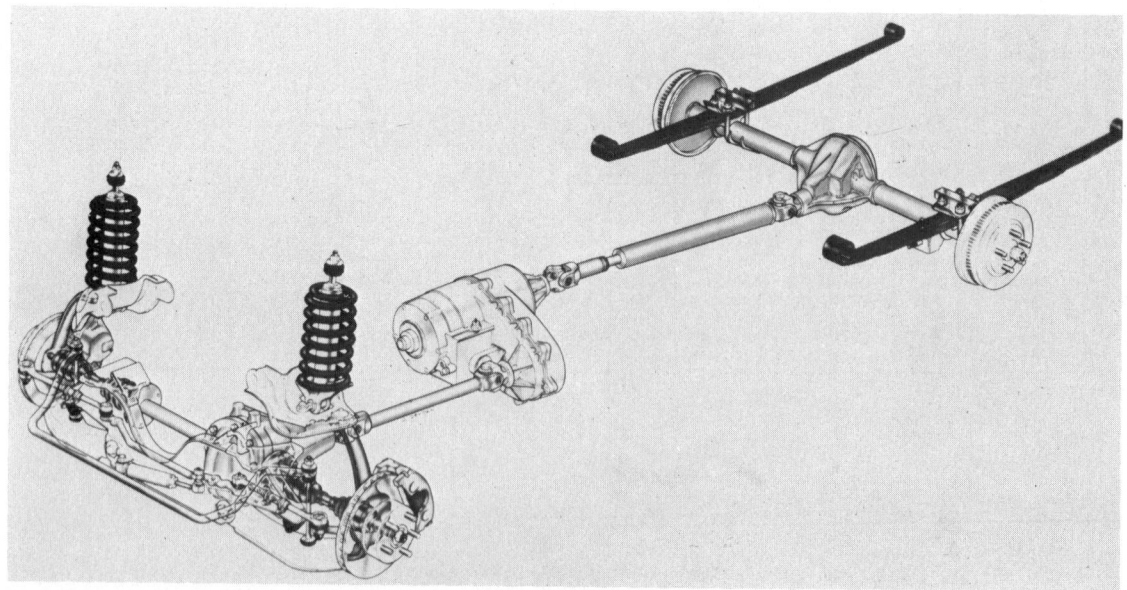

Fig. S-32. First U.S. automatic four wheel drive passenger car was made available in 1980. AMC Eagle couples three-speed automatic transmission with a transfer case that utilizes liquid silicone to provide limited slip action. (American Motors)

1982-1983 SUPPLEMENT

MECHANICAL CHANGES

Automotive industry trends are clearly indicated by engineering changes in the new models and by broadened application of other recent developments. The 1982 and 1983 models, for example, reflect the U.S. car manufacturers' commitment to downsizing vehicles, reducing weight, and improving fuel economy. They are producing more cars with smaller displacement engines, making greater use of front wheel drive, and expanding the use of electronics in several directions.

The "downsizing" of vehicles is evidenced by the introduction of many new small and midsized cars:

Alliance (AMC/Renault)
Skyhawk and Century (Buick)
Cimarron (Cadillac)
Cavalier and Celebrity (Chevrolet)
LeBaron and New Yorker (Chrysler)
400 (Dodge)
EXP and Tempo (Ford)
LN7 and Topaz (Mercury)
Firenza and Ciera (Oldsmobile)
1000, 2000, 6000 (Pontiac)

All of these models, except the Pontiac 1000, are front wheel drive design. See Fig. S-1.

New engines for 1982 and 1983 range from AMC/Renault's 1.4 L (85 cu. in.) electronic fuel injected (EFI) four cylinder gasoline-fueled engine to Cadillac's 4.1 L (250 cu. in.) "High Tech" V-8, Fig. S-2. Also new are Chevrolet's 1.8 L (111 cu. in.) four cylinder diesel-fueled engine and Oldsmobile's 4.3 L (262.5 cu. in.) V-6 diesel, Fig. S-3.

The engine manufacturers have concentrated on building small displacement engines with the expectation of greater fuel economy. For example, of the 20 new and upgraded engines made available for use in the 1982 and 1983 models, 16 have a displacement of 3.0 L (181 cu. in.) or less. See Fig. S-4. Details are provided under NEW ENGINES and in the OFFICIAL MECHANICAL AND TUNE-UP SPECIFICATIONS charts in this SUPPLEMENT.

Broader use of electronics is shown by:

1. Cadillac's across-the-board use of electronic fuel injection on 1983 models, Fig. S-2.
2. Ford's fourth generation Electronic Engine Control (EEC IV) system, Fig. S-5, on its 1.6 L (97.6 cu. in.) EFI four.
3. Pontiac's 2.5 L (151 cu. in.) EFI four with GM's Computer Command Control (CCC) and self-diagnostic capability.
4. Chrysler's Peugeot-sourced 1.6 L (97.1 cu. in.) EFI four with Combustion Computer Control (CCC), Fig. S-6.

Electronics, in fact, have spread throughout the vehicle, ignition, charging, fuel injection, instrumentation, etc.

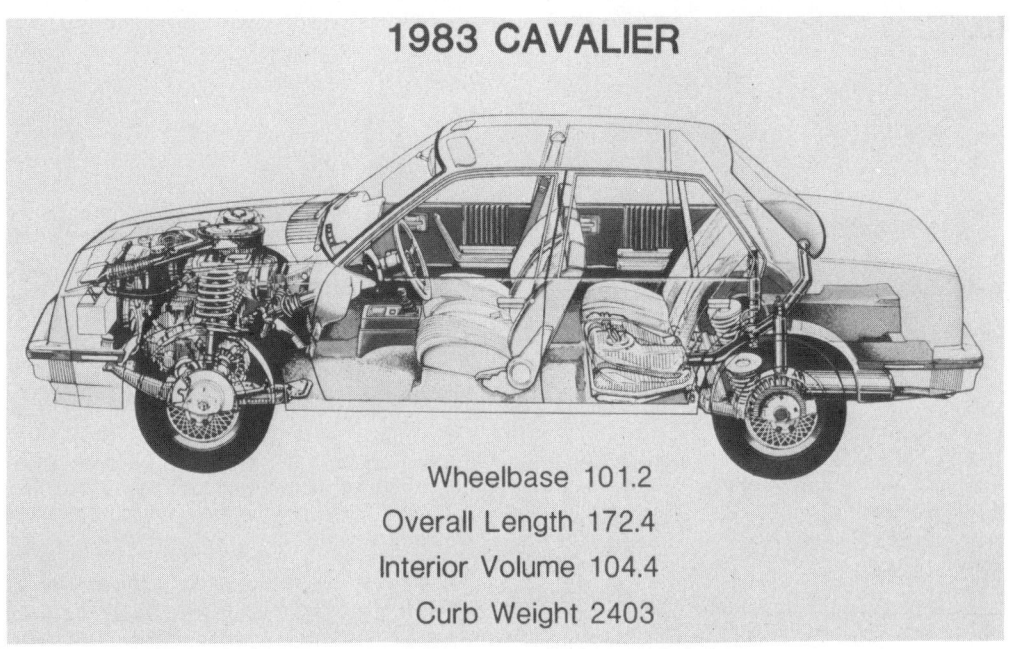

1983 CAVALIER

Wheelbase 101.2
Overall Length 172.4
Interior Volume 104.4
Curb Weight 2403

Fig. S-1. Note the size and construction features of this 1983 subcompact car. Powered by a fuel-injected four cylinder engine, the front wheel drive Chevrolet Cavalier typifies modern U.S. automotive engineering.

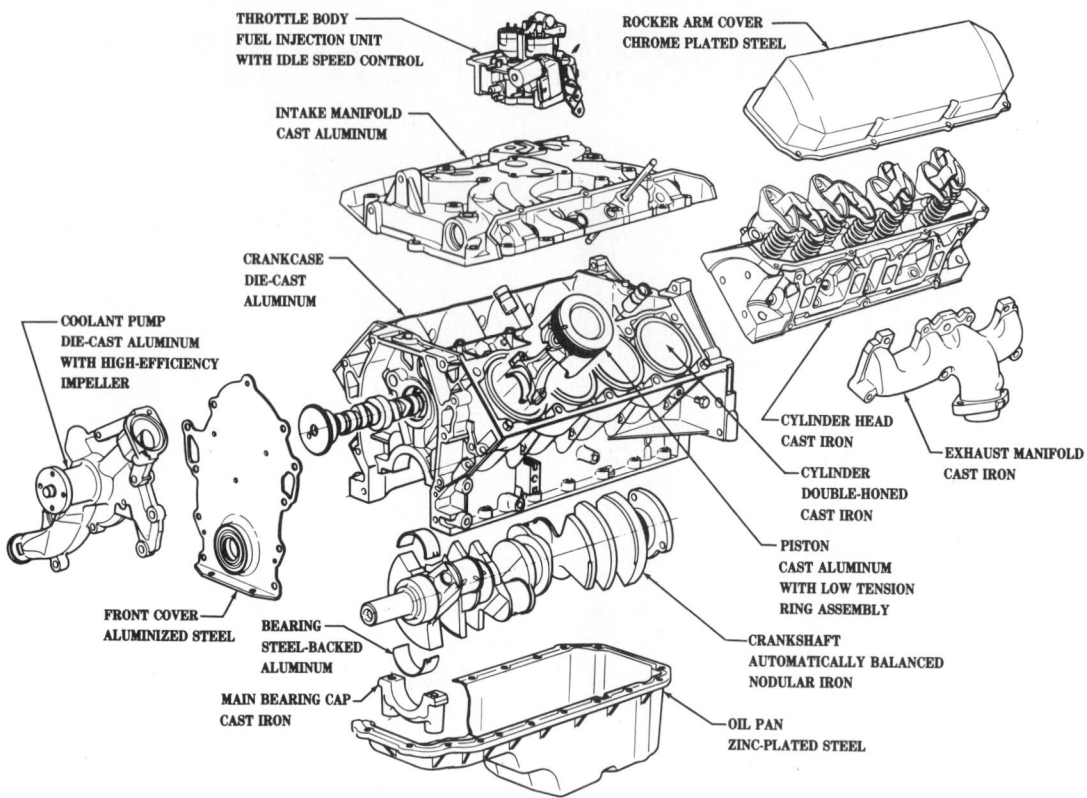

THROTTLE BODY
FUEL INJECTION UNIT
WITH IDLE SPEED CONTROL

ROCKER ARM COVER
CHROME PLATED STEEL

INTAKE MANIFOLD
CAST ALUMINUM

CRANKCASE
DIE-CAST
ALUMINUM

COOLANT PUMP
DIE-CAST ALUMINUM
WITH HIGH-EFFICIENCY
IMPELLER

CYLINDER HEAD
CAST IRON

EXHAUST MANIFOLD
CAST IRON

CYLINDER
DOUBLE-HONED
CAST IRON

PISTON
CAST ALUMINUM
WITH LOW TENSION
RING ASSEMBLY

FRONT COVER
ALUMINIZED STEEL

BEARING
STEEL-BACKED
ALUMINUM

CRANKSHAFT
AUTOMATICALLY BALANCED
NODULAR IRON

MAIN BEARING CAP
CAST IRON

OIL PAN
ZINC-PLATED STEEL

Fig. S-2. Cadillac's 4.1 L (250 cu. in.) V-8 engine uses an aluminum engine block, cast iron cylinder sleeves, and a separate aluminum valve lifter carrier. Reduced displacement (from 6.0 L in 1980) and use of aluminum results in a weight savings of over 200 lbs.

Fig. S-3. Oldsmobile's 4.3 L (262.5 cu. in.) V-8 diesel engine is used in both the front wheel drive Cutlass Ciera (shown) and in the rear wheel drive Cutlass Supreme.

Fig. S-4. Pontiac's 1.8 L (112 cu. in.) engine is characteristic of today's small displacement, overhead camshaft (OHC), four cylinder engines equipped with electronic fuel injection.

SERVICEABILITY

The serviceability of late model cars has come in for some welcome advances. Among the many designed-in serviceability features to be found on certain 1982 and 1983 models are:

1. Front disc brakes can be inspected for worn pads by removing only the wheel and tire assembly.
2. Front disc brake pads can be serviced without removing the wheel bearings and hub or bleeding the brake line.
3. Rear brake shoes can be visually inspected for wear by removing a rubber plug from inside the rear brake assembly.

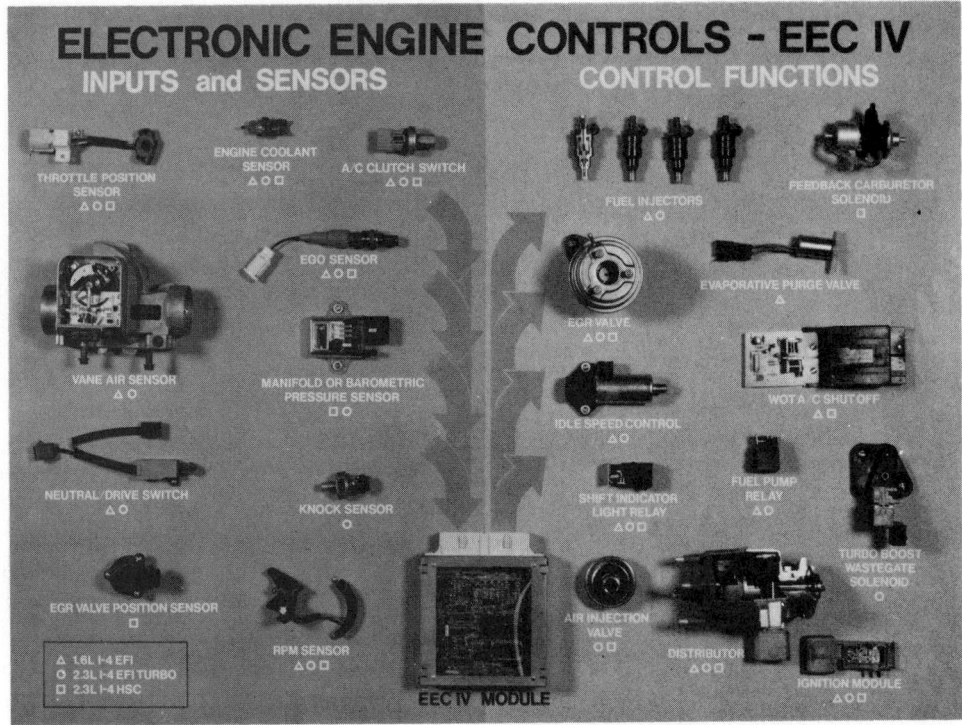

Fig. S-5. Ford's EEC IV Electronic Engine Control system includes many inputs, sensors, and controls. It provides accurate fuel metering control of fuel injection timing and duration.

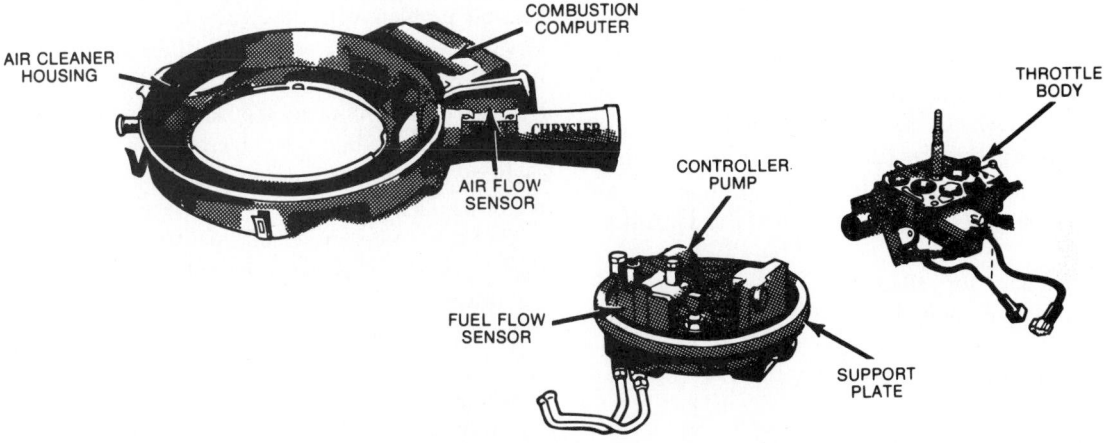

Fig. S-6. The major elements of Chrysler's Combustion Computer Control are identified in this diagram. Note the use of throttle body fuel injection and the location of the combustion computer.

4. Tailpipe and muffler are routed below the independent rear wheel suspension for easy replacement.

5. Struts for rear shock absorbers are mounted outside the springs so the struts can be replaced without compressing the springs.

6. Steering column-mounted switches can be serviced without removing the steering wheel or column.

7. Top of instrument panel lifts off or tilts for access to dash components.

8. Blower motor can be removed through the glove box.

9. Fuses, most exterior bulbs, and windshield wipers can be replaced without tools.

10. Windshield wiper motor is in the engine compartment.

11. Transaxle can be removed without removing the engine, Fig. S-7.

12. Engine "wiring" and "plumbing" have been rerouted for easy access.

13. Spark plugs are within easy reach, and the plug wires are numbered for quick identification.

14. Oil pan can be removed without removing the engine or other major components.

15. Camshaft can be serviced without removing the cylinder head or disassembling the engine.

16. Oil pump can be serviced without removing the oil pan.

Fig. S-7. Ford's five-speed manual transaxle can be removed from 1983 Escort or Lynx models without removing the engine from the vehicle. The transaxle housing and differential case are aluminum. Shift units are located within the transaxle housing.

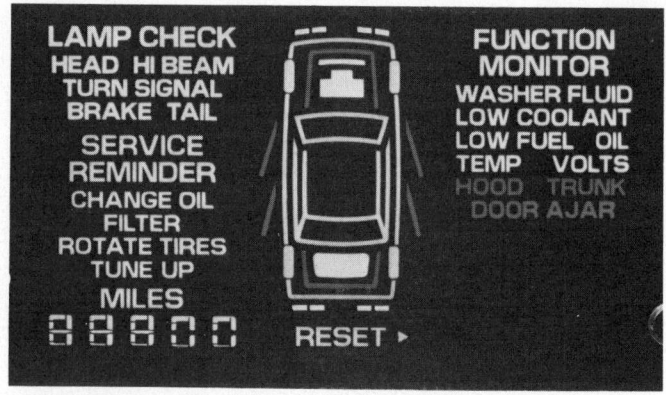

Fig. S-8. Pontiac's programmable driver information center utilizes a computer processor to monitor engine performance and to relay the status of the vehicle to an instrument panel display.

MAINTENANCE-FREE FEATURES

Recent advances in automotive engineering and manufacturing technology have greatly reduced the number of required maintenance operations. Ford Motor Company, for example, claims that "22 operations that were required for the maintenance of 1973 vehicles no longer are required for the 1983 models." Among these maintenance-free features are: battery, brakes (self-adjusting), clutch (self-adjusting), front end alignment, carburetor idle mixture, choke, and ignition timing.

Some Ford models for 1983 have wear-compensating materials that make it unnecessary to adjust automatic transmission bands. Some models have lubed-for-life front wheel bearings, suspension, and steering linkage.

DIAGNOSTIC CONNECTORS AND SELF-DIAGNOSIS

Some 1982 and 1983 vehicles have diagnostic connectors which permit electrical and electronic systems checks at a single location. Some vehicles also have "monitoring" systems that supply vital information to an instrument panel display. See Fig. S-8.

American Motors cars for 1983 and some Jeep vehicles have a built-in diagnostic connector. When the manufacturer's fuel feedback system tester is attached to this connector, it will diagnose vehicle malfunctions. The tester asks questions on a display screen. The mechanic answers by pressing a button on the tester. The tester then identifies (on the screen) the problem area or determines that the fuel feedback system does not need repair.

AMC/Renault have a self-diagnostic system on Alliance vehicles that electronically monitors all vital fluid levels within the car. A readout console mounted on the instrument panel warns the driver if any of the vehicle's fluids need attention. This system watches over engine oil, engine coolant, brake fluid, power steering fluid, windshield washer fluid, and transaxle fluid. It also checks front disc brake lining wear.

The GM Computer Command Control (CCC) system also has a self-diagnostic capability. When a "check engine" light on the instrument panel flashes, it warns that there is a possible problem with the electronic fuel injection system. The service technician performs a "diagnostic circuit check" through a ground lead in the assembly line communication link (ALCL). This will cause the "check engine" light to flash a trouble code. Using a troubleshooting chart, the technician analyzes the problem according to the code shown, then performs the necessary steps to correct the problem.

Chrysler offers an Electronic Voice Alert (EVA) system that "speaks" 11 messages through the radio system. It advises the driver about 11 separate mechanical or safety functions. The computer-programmed voice reacts to information received from sensors that monitor: key left in ignition; headlamps left on; door ajar; seat belts unfastened; low oil pressure; overheating engine; electrical system low voltage; parking brake on; washer fluid low; low fuel condition. If no problems are indicated at start-up, the voice advises, "All monitored systems are functioning."

Ford has an optional Voice Alert driver information and warning system for 1983 Thunderbird and Cougar cars. It, too, produces programmed warning messages along with warning chime sounds.

ENGINE CONSTRUCTION

Power plant construction for 1982 and 1983 heavily favors in-line four cylinder and V-6 designs. Even Cadillac (Cimarron) features a 2.0 L (121 cu. in.) four, and the Lincoln Continental is equipped with a 3.8 L (232 cu. in.) V-6. Overhead camshaft design has also gained in popularity, especially in Chrysler and Ford four cylinder engines, Fig. S-9.

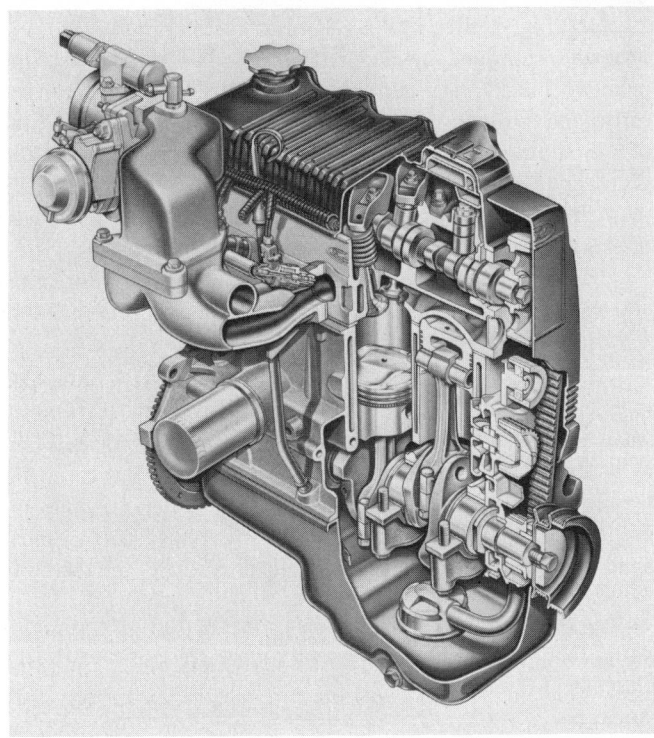

Fig. S-9. Ford's 1.6 L (97.6 cu. in.) fuel-injected CVH, (compound valve hemispherical) engine has an overhead camshaft, canted valves, and fully machined hemispherical combustion chambers.

FORD'S 1.6 L OHC FOUR. Ford is offering an optional 1.6 L electronic fuel injected four cylinder engine, Fig. S-9, on Escort/Lynx and EXP/LN7 models for 1983. The EFI system consists of a pressurized fuel supply system with multiple-port injection, an electronic engine control unit, and various sensors. The EEC-IV also governs exhaust gas recirculation (EGR) and ignition spark timing.

The 1.6 L EFI engine has a new "thick film" ignition module and a new ignition distributor. See Fig. S-10. Intake

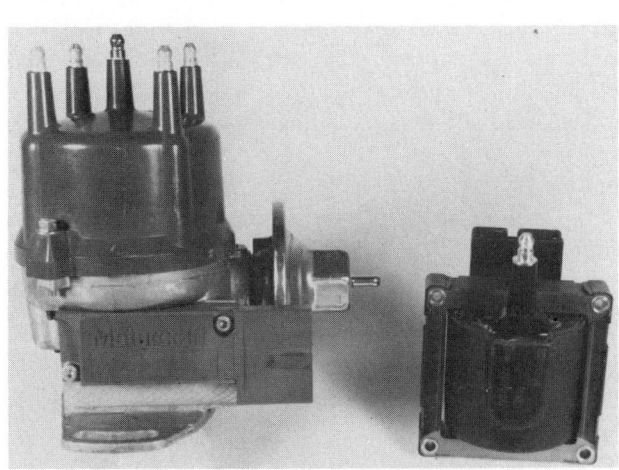

Fig. S-10. Ford's Thick Film Ignition (TFI) distributor includes a distributor-mounted electronic ignition module, along with a high-energy ignition coil. The module—controlled by the EEC IV micro-processor—provides precise spark timing under all engine operating conditions.

manifold passage lengths are "tuned" for improved engine performance. Exhaust manifolds are "tuned" to reduce back-pressure. An aluminum radiator with plastic end tanks is used on all 1.6 L engine applications.

CHRYSLER'S POWER TRAIN COMBINATIONS. For 1983, Chrysler Corporation cars have a new 1.6 L (97.1 cu. in.) engine and upgraded 2.2 L (135 cu. in.) and 2.6 L (156 cu. in.) four cylinder engines, all with new electronic engine controls.

The Peugeot-sourced 1.6 L engine has a cast-iron block and aluminum cylinder head with in-line valves, rocker arms, and push rods. See Fig. S-11. The rocker arms are screw-adjustable. A dual sprocket on the crankshaft drives the timing chains and acts as a vibration damper. Compression pressure is 8.8 to 1. Horsepower is rated at 62 hp (46 kW).

The 1.6 L engine has a bore of 3.17 in. (80.6 mm) and a stroke of 3.07 in. (78.0 mm). The cylinders are numbered from the flywheel side in reverse order from most other in-line engines. The combustion chambers are wedge-shaped. The cylinder head gasket is made of a composition material that does not require a sealer when installed.

Chrysler's 2.2 L engine, Fig. S-12, has increased power by way of a modified cylinder head, reshaped manifold to improve intake-exhaust air flow and the swirl and flow of the air-fuel mixture. A faster-opening throttle and retuned muffler reduce engine backpressure. The compression ratio is 9.0 to 1. Horsepower is up from 84 hp (63 kW) to 94 hp (70 kW). Early 1983 models are equipped with feedback carburetor, Fig. S-12. In mid-year, Chrysler's Throttle Body Injection (TBI) was introduced.

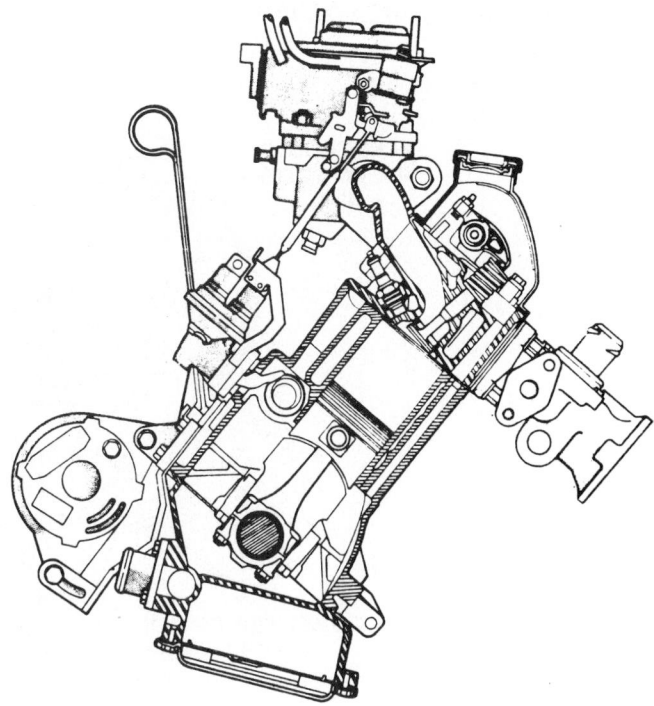

Fig. S-11. Chrysler's 1.6 L (97.1 cu. in.) four cylinder engine is supplied by Peugeot, but is equipped with Chrysler's electronic feedback carburetor system for best fuel economy and emissions control.

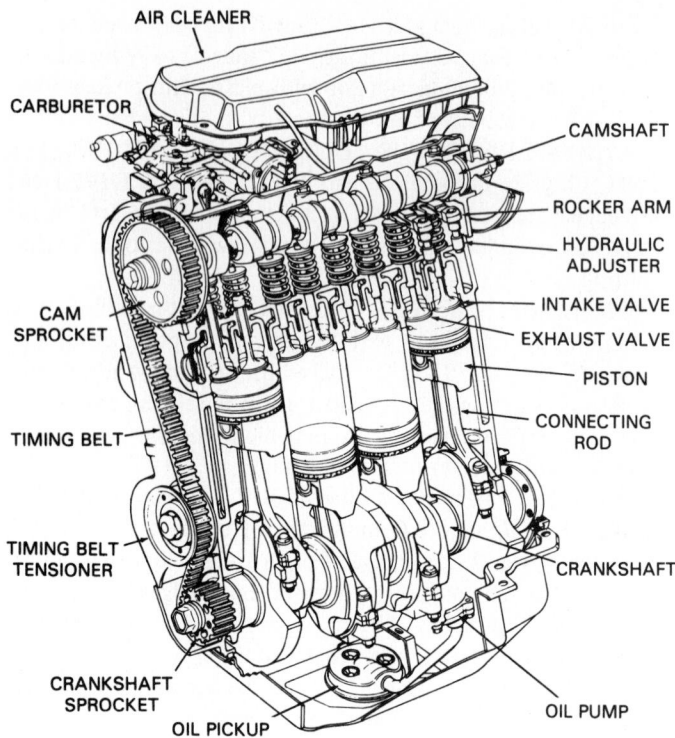

Fig. S-12. Cutaway view of Chrysler's 2.2 L (112 cu. in.) four reveals construction features. This is the first engine in corporation's history designed and developed to power a front wheel drive vehicle.

The 2.6 L engine supplied by Mitsubishi has quicker response on acceleration because of carburetor modifications, including jet recalibrations and advanced secondary throttle action. This engine is rated at 93 hp (69 kW).

PONTIAC'S 1.8 FOUR. Pontiac's 1.8 L (112 cu. in.) overhead cam-fuel injected engine, Fig. S-4, has a cast iron cylinder block, cast aluminum cylinder head with vertical valves and hydraulic lifters. The overhead camshaft is mounted in a separate aluminum housing for improved serviceability. A disc-shaped combustion chamber centrally locates the spark plug for faster combustion burn time. Hardened valve seat inserts are used for both intake and exhaust valves.

The 1.8 L engine has a cylinder bore of 3.30 in. (84.8 mm) and a stroke of 3.10 in. (79.5 mm). Compression ratio is 9.0 to 1. Horsepower rates at 84 hp (62.7 kW).

CHEVROLET'S 2.0 L TBI FOUR. High compression, high torque, and "cyclonic induction" are the key features of Chevrolet's 2.0 L (121 cu. in.) throttle body fuel injected four cylinder engine. The compression ratio is 9.3 to 1. Engine torque is 110 lb. ft. (81.1 N·m) at 2400 rpm. Cyclonic induction, Fig. S-13, makes use of a swirl inlet port cylinder head design to allow greater air-fuel mixture velocity and faster burn.

The 2.0 L four is rated at 90 hp (67.1 kW) at 5000 rpm. Engine bore is 3.50 cu. in. (89.0 mm). Stroke is 3.15 in. (80.0 mm). This engine uses a low-pressure electronic throttle body injection (TBI) system, similar to the one that will be described later for Pontiac's 2.5 L (151 cu. in.) engine.

PONTIAC'S 2.5 L EFI FOUR. Pontiac has incorporated electronic fuel injection in its 2.5 L four cylinder engine, Fig. S-14, for 1982 and 1983. This engine has a bore of 4.0 in. (101.6 mm) and a stroke of 3.0 in. (76.2 mm). Compression ratio is 8.2 to 1. The net horsepower rating is 90 hp (67.1 kW) at 4000 rpm. Heart of the EFI system is the throttle body injection assembly, pictured in Fig. S-15.

OLDSMOBILE'S 4.3 L DIESEL V-6. Oldsmobile's 4.3 L

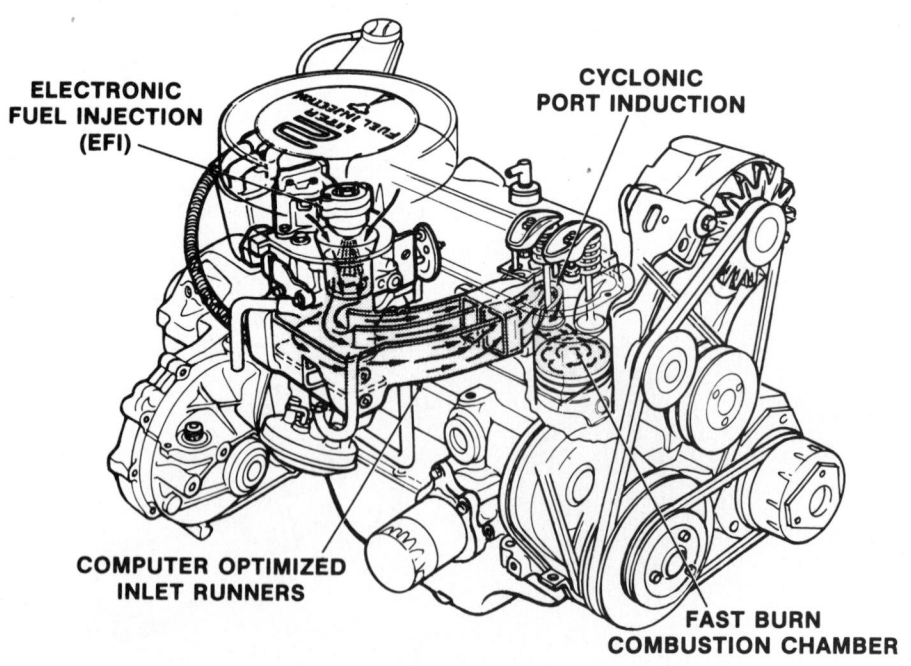

Fig. S-13. Chevrolet's high torque 2.0 L four cylinder engine has "cyclonic induction." Arrows show path of air-fuel mixture in swirl port cylinder head of this throttle body fuel injection engine.

Fig. S-14. Use of throttle body fuel injection on Pontiac's 2.5 L engine eliminates emission control "plumbing" such as the air pump, thermal control on exhaust gas recirculation (EGR) system, and early fuel evaporation (EFE) system.

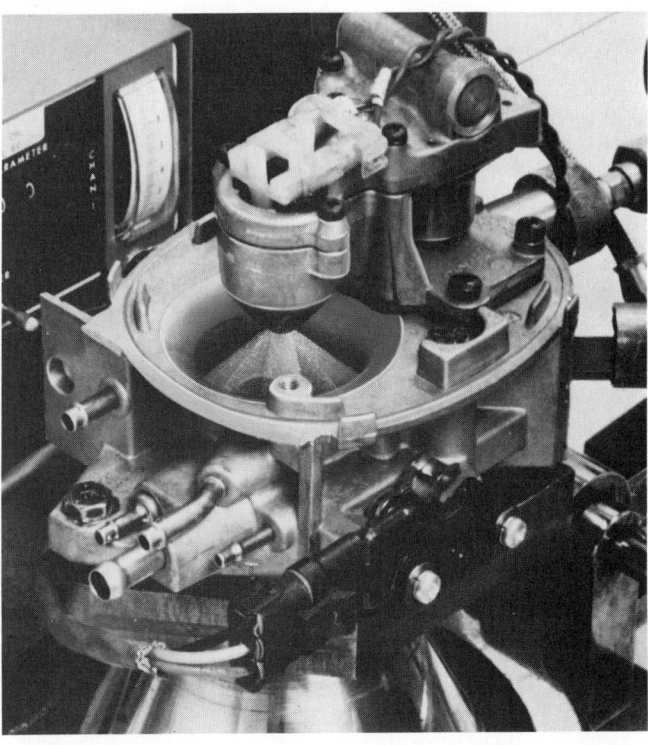

Fig. S-15. Pontiac's 2.5 L four cylinder engine has been upgraded with the use of a throttle body fuel injector assembly (TBIA). Electronic signals to the TBIA have replaced the mechanical carburetor choke, external linkage, and the need for usual carburetor adjustments.

diesel has a cylinder bore of 4.057 in. (103.05 mm) and a stroke of 3.385 in. (85.98 mm). All diesel-powered Cutlass models come equipped with a water separation system to signal if water is detected in the fuel tank, Fig. S-16.

Oldsmobile's 4.3 L diesel makes extensive use of aluminum, including the oil pump body, cylinder heads, water outlet, and intake manifold. This engine is of precombustion chamber design, Fig. S-17, and offers "fast glow" heating of the combustion chamber area for faster starts on cold days. Roller hydraulic valve lifters reduce friction between the lifters and

camshaft. A one-belt serpentine system (replaces accessory belts) features an automatic tensioner that eliminates periodic service adjustments.

The longitudinal engine has an engine-driven fan. Transverse

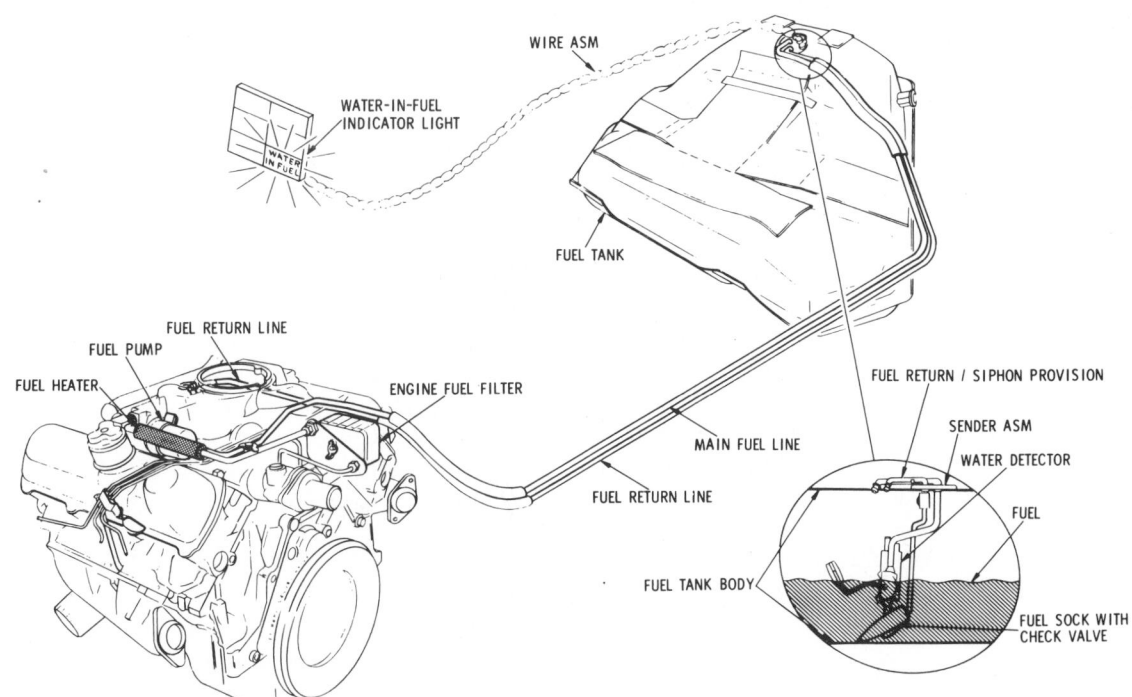

Fig. S-16. Main elements of the water separation system used on Oldsmobile's 4.3 L V-6 diesel engine are located in the fuel tank. A water-in-fuel indicator light is mounted on the instrument panel.

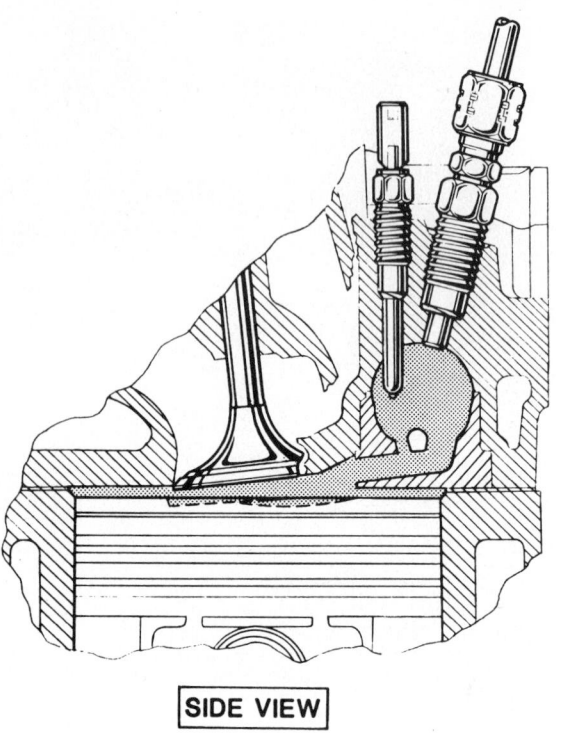

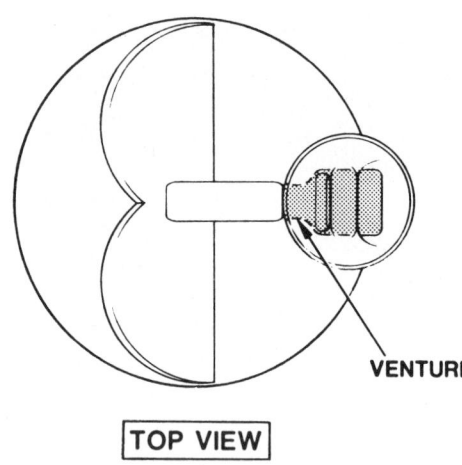

SIDE VIEW

TOP VIEW

VENTURI

Fig. S-17. Oldsmobile's 4.3 L V-6 diesel engine has a venturi-shaped precombustion chamber that swirls the flame of combustion into the main combustion chamber at great velocity.

engine-equipped cars use a cooling fan driven by a thermostatically controlled electric motor. Engine power pulses are absorbed by an "inertia weight" flywheel and a torque-pulse compensator that decouples the crankshaft from the drive pulley by driving the pulley through a rubber damper.

The 4.3 L V-6 diesel produces 85 hp (63 kW) at 3600 rpm. The compression ratio is 21.6 to 1. Oil capacity, including filter, is 6 qt. (5.7 L) with oil and oil filter changes recommended every 5000 miles.

CADILLAC'S 4.1 L (250 cu. in.) EFI V-8. Cadillac couples its 4.1 L V-8 with a tuned driveline and tuned suspension package and calls it "HT-4100 Power System." The engine has an aluminum block with free-standing cast iron cylinders and separate aluminum valve lifter carrier. RTV sealant is used on valve covers, cylinder heads, water pump, and oil pan. Only the intake manifold, water pump, and timing cover use gaskets.

The 4.1 L V-8 is an all-metric design engine. It reportedly can be field stripped using only 10 mm, 13 mm, 15 mm, 17 mm, and 19 mm sockets. All drive belts are adjustable by means of a tensioner bracket and bolt setup. A new power steering pump and remote fluid reservoir are part of the HT 4100 Power System. The reservoir is located on the fan shroud, providing easy access for servicing. A high-flow auxiliary air pump helps boost the reliability of the engine's vacuum-operated controls.

ELECTRONIC FUEL INJECTION

Fuel injection has replaced carburetion on most new and upgraded engines for several good reasons. Basically, fuel

injection provides more consistent and accurate fuel delivery. This results in more complete combustion, better fuel mileage, fewer exhaust emissions (and fewer emission controls needed), and improved driveability, especially during cold engine warm up and on acceleration.

CADILLAC'S DFI WITH ECM. Cadillac's 4.1 L V-8 engine uses closed loop digital fuel injection (DFI) induction. See Fig. S-2. It combines a throttle body injection assembly with two electronically pulsed fuel injectors that meter fuel to the engine. The DFI system incorporates an Electronic Control Module (ECM) that controls spark timing, fuel delivery rate, and idle speed. This "brain" of the system also compensates for variations in altitude, temperature, and accessory load.

In operation, the ECM receives input from sensors that monitor the following conditions:

1. Manifold absolute pressure.
2. Ambient barometric pressure.
3. Engine coolant temperature.
4. Air-fuel mixture temperature.
5. Engine speed.
6. Throttle position.
7. Exhaust gas oxygen.
8. Vehicle speed.

The ECM reacts to the input from these sensors to compute spark timing and fuel delivery rate to the two throttle body injectors. This rate is designed to maintain the desired air-fuel mixtures for given operating conditions. The two injectors, in turn, meter and direct the atomized fuel into the throttle body above the throttle blades.

Cadillac's ECM also includes provisions for monitoring emissions controls and driver assist systems (Fuel Data Panel, cruise control, and service diagnostics).

PONTIAC'S EFI WITH ECM. Pontiac's 2.5 L four cylinder engine also utilizes throttle body electronic fuel injection. The system includes a throttle body injection assembly (TBIA), Fig. S-18, a gasoline tank-mounted electric fuel pump, a single bed (three-way beaded) catalytic converter, ignition distributor with electronic spark timing, an electronic control module (ECM), and various emission control sensors.

This EFI system uses a single fuel injector and fuel pressure regulator, located in the TBIA. The fuel injector sprays fuel into the intake manifold above the throttle blade, Fig. S-18, and the air-fuel mixture is distributed to the cylinders by manifold runners. Fuel pressure is regulated to about 10 psi.

An idle air control motor controls engine idle speed by regulating air that bypasses the throttle blade. It regulates airflow by moving a pintle (on the motor shaft) in or out of an orifice, based on a signal received from the ECM. Minute adjustments are possible in pintle movement and, therefore, in air-fuel ratio. When the ignition is turned off, fuel shutoff is instantaneous. There is no "dieseling" effect with EFI.

For an overall look at the major elements of a typical General Motors' electronic fuel injection system, see Fig. S-19.

CHRYSLER'S EFI WITH CCC. Chrysler introduced its advanced engineering throttle body injection system in mid-1983. See Fig. S-20. This system is designed to accurately meter fuel under all operating conditions and to overcome inadequate air-fuel mixture during low air induction flow rates (starting and idling).

Chrysler's EFI system includes a pre-programmed computer known as a Logic Module, a Power Module, a throttle body assembly having a single injector, and a variety of sensors on which the Logic Module bases its commands.

Specific benefits of this EFI system are:

1. Automatic fuel-flow metering.
2. Automatic advance or retard of ignition timing.

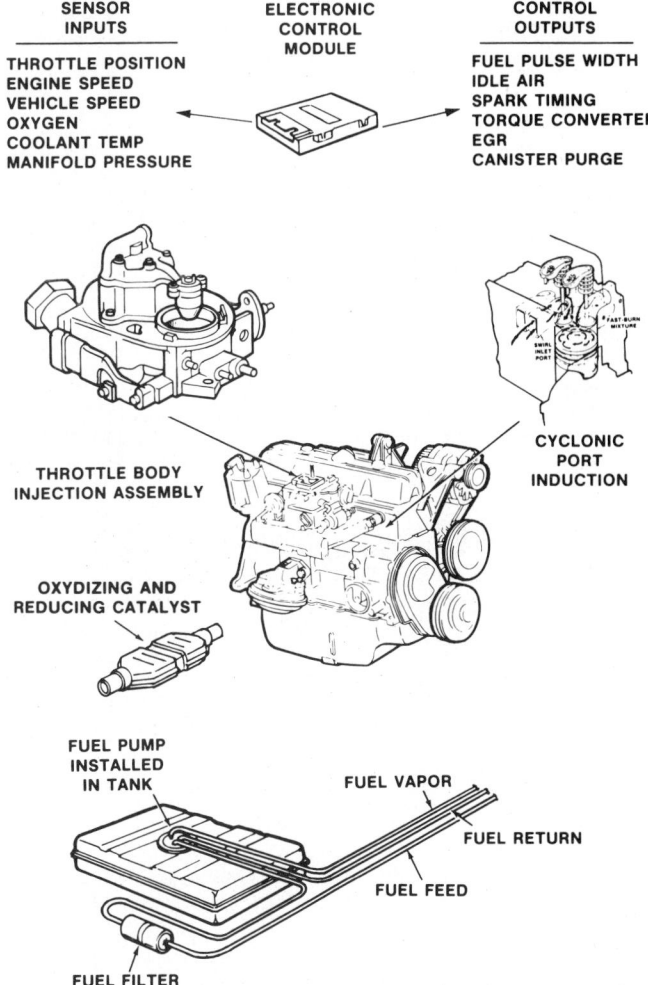

Fig. S-19. Basic elements of a typical low-pressure electronic fuel injection system are pictured. This particular throttle body injection system is used on Chevrolet's 2.0 L four cylinder engine.

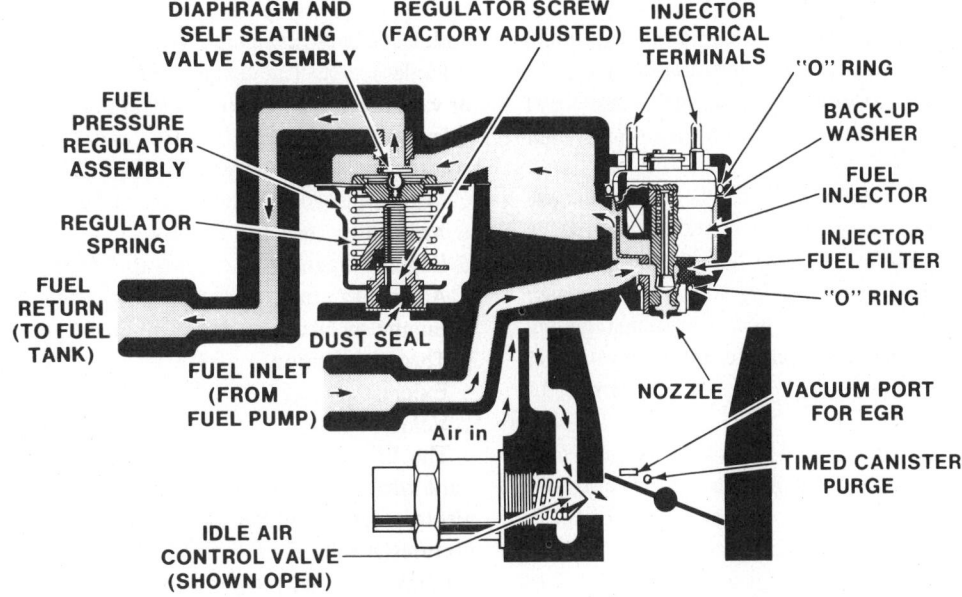

Fig. S-18. Diagram of Pontiac's throttle body injection assembly on the 2.5 L engine shows fuel flow to the injector. Airflow to the manifold and the fuel flow return route are also marked with arrows.

ELECTRONIC FUEL INJECTION COMPONENTS

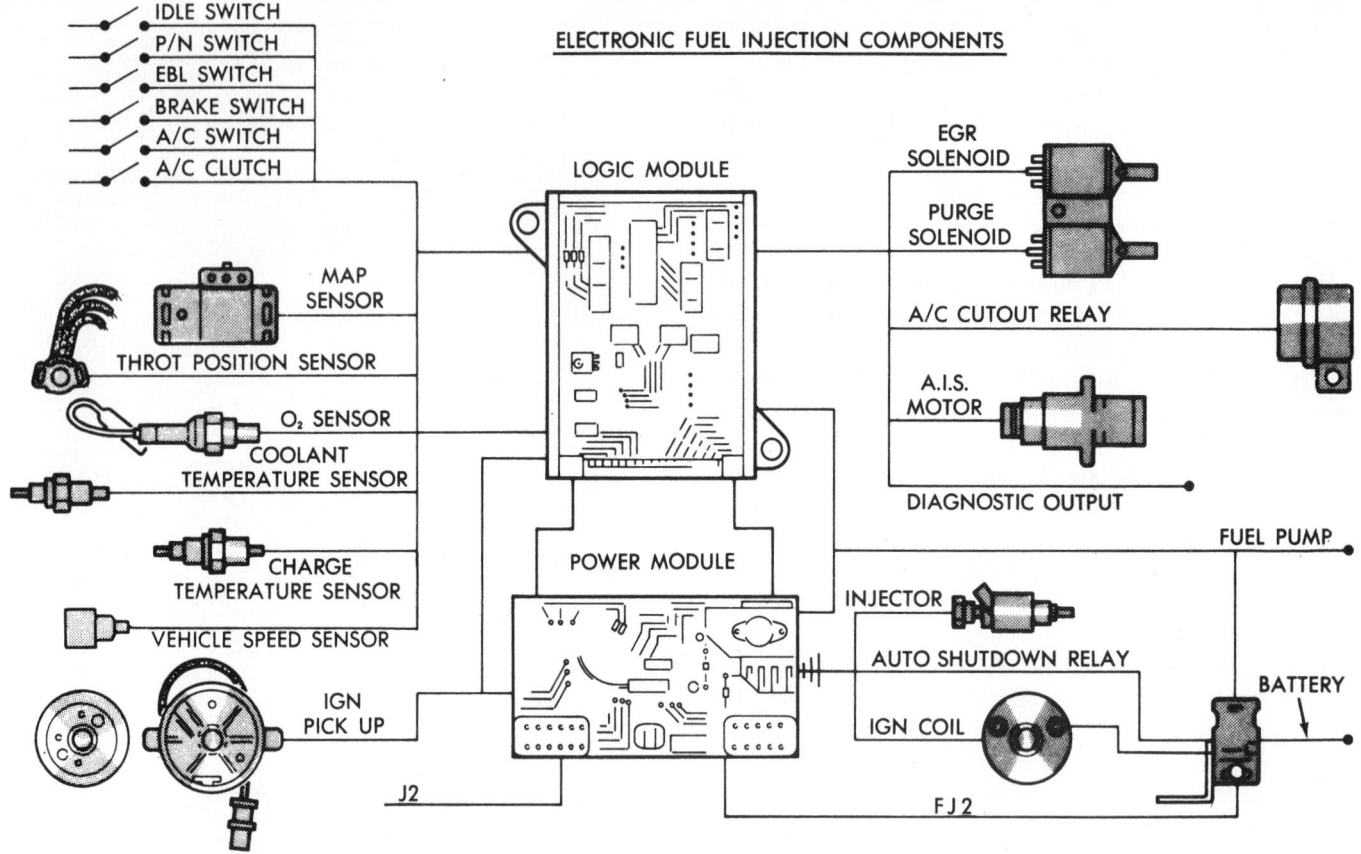

Fig. S-20. In Chrysler's electronic fuel injection system, the Logic Module regulates air-fuel ratio, ignition timing, idle speed, and emission controls. The Power Module powers the ignition coil and fuel injector.

3. Automatic idle adjustment when driver releases the accelerator.

4. Automatic fuel shutoff.

The shutoff system cuts the air-fuel mixture to very lean levels during deceleration. It maintains constant engine speed as the air conditioning system cycles. It prevents "dieseling."

Chrysler's throttle body assembly is wired to devices that regulate: air-fuel charge and coolant temperature, knock, oxygen feedback, various control solenoids and relays, automatic idle speed (AIS), throttle position, fuel pump, fuel injector, ignition coil, manifold absolute pressure sensor (MAP), and battery.

Many tests and service operations on Chrysler's EFI system can be done with an EFI tester. Before working on possible problems in this area, however, it is wise to check out all other engine systems for proper operation, including emission controls. As with other EFI systems, Chrysler's system involves pressurized fuel delivery. Therefore, system pressure should be relieved when components are to be removed for inspection or replacement.

FORD'S EFI WITH EEC IV. Some Ford 1.6 L four cylinder engines have a pressurized fuel supply system with multiple port injection, an electronic engine control (EEC IV) unit, and various sensing elements. In operation, an electric fuel pump supplies fuel at a maximum pressure of 40 psi to the inlet of each fuel injector. The pump operates only when the engine is turning. A pressure regulator maintains proper fuel pressure for existing conditions, varying the pressure with intake manifold vacuum. The amount of fuel being discharged by the injector is regulated by the length of time the injector valve remains open.

The fuel injectors at all four cylinders open and close simultaneously, providing two pulses of fuel for every intake stroke at each cylinder (each pulse delivers half the amount of fuel required). During cold starts, the injectors pulse twice each revolution, enriching the mixture.

A key sensing element is a vane type airflow meter measuring device installed in the path of air entering the intake manifold. A positive sensing element on the vane shaft transmits a signal to the EEC IV unit that reflects the amount of air entering the engine. Other sensors measure intake air temperature, coolant temperature, free oxygen remaining in the hot exhaust gas, crankshaft position, and engine speed. The EEC IV unit uses input from these sensors to open and close the electromagnetic valve in each fuel injector, metered for only the amount of fresh air drawn into the engine.

ELECTRONIC IGNITION ADVANCES

Advances in the area of electronic ignition have been ongoing for over a decade, and the progress continues yearly.

FORD'S EEC IV SYSTEM. Ford's fourth generation electronic engine control (EEC IV) system reportedly can process almost one million commands per second through the use of two microcircuits. The two circuits precisely control fuel metering and ignition spark timing. Input signals from six sensors are received by the microcomputer and processed into output signals to the fuel injectors and ignition distributor.

The distributor used with EEC IV is a self-contained system that includes a distributor-mounted "thick film" ignition module and high energy coil. See Fig. S-21. The new thick film technology reduces the size of the module and eliminates long wire leads.

In basic theory, the new distributor operates the same as Ford's earlier, vertically mounted, solid state distributors. The difference is in the Thick Film Integrated (TFI) ignition module. The rotating armature induces a signal in the stator assembly. This causes the TFI module to turn the ignition current on and off, generating the high voltage required to fire the spark plugs.

To remove the TFI ignition module:

1. Disconnect the vacuum advance lines.
2. Remove the distributor cap.
3. Remove the TFI harness connector.
4. Remove the rotor by unscrewing the two hold-down screws.
5. Remove the two distributor hold-down bolts. NOTE: Some engines are equipped with a security type hold-down bolt that requires a special tool for removal.
6. Remove the distributor from the engine.
7. Remove the two TFI attaching bolts.
8. Pull the right side of the module down the distributor mounting flange, then back up to disengage the module terminal from the connector.
9. Pull the module toward the flange and away from the distributor. NOTE: Follow this sequence or simply lifting the module from the mounting surface will break the pins at the distributor module connector.

GENERAL MOTORS' CCC SYSTEM. General Motors cars utilize a Computer Command Control (CCC) with a digital computer called an "electronic control module" (ECM). The CCC system is designed so that most failures will not result in stoppage of the engine. Therefore, when troubleshooting for poor engine performance, a drop in fuel economy, or a rise in exhaust emissions, check the ignition system first. Then, if necessary, inspect and service the CCC system.

In addition to the ECM, the CCC system includes many sensors and control devices. The sensors continuously monitor condition and send this information (in the form of varying voltage) to the ECM. See Fig. S-22.

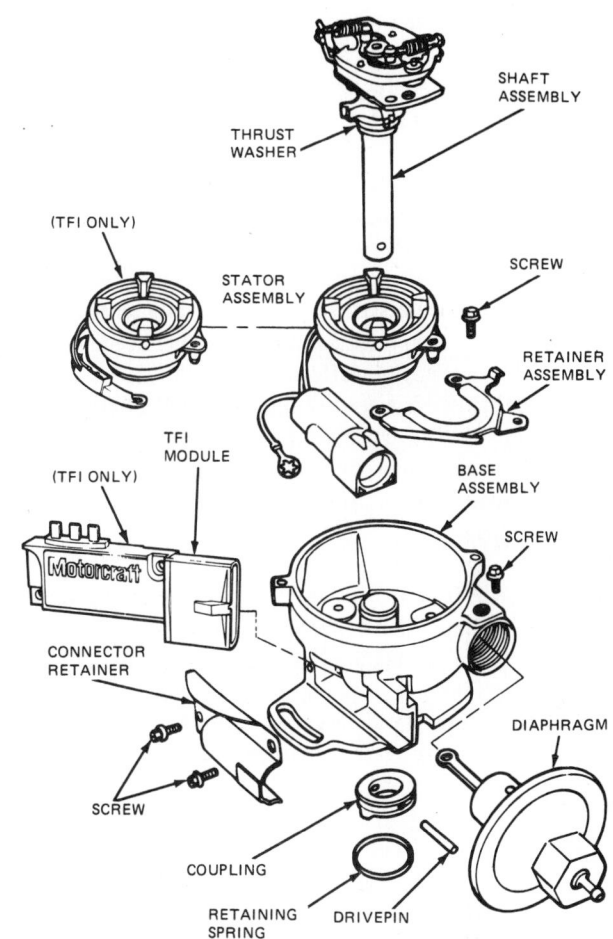

Fig. S-21. Exploded view of Ford's ignition distributor reveals the location of its Thick Film Ignition (TFI) module mounted at base of distributor housing. See text for removal cautions.

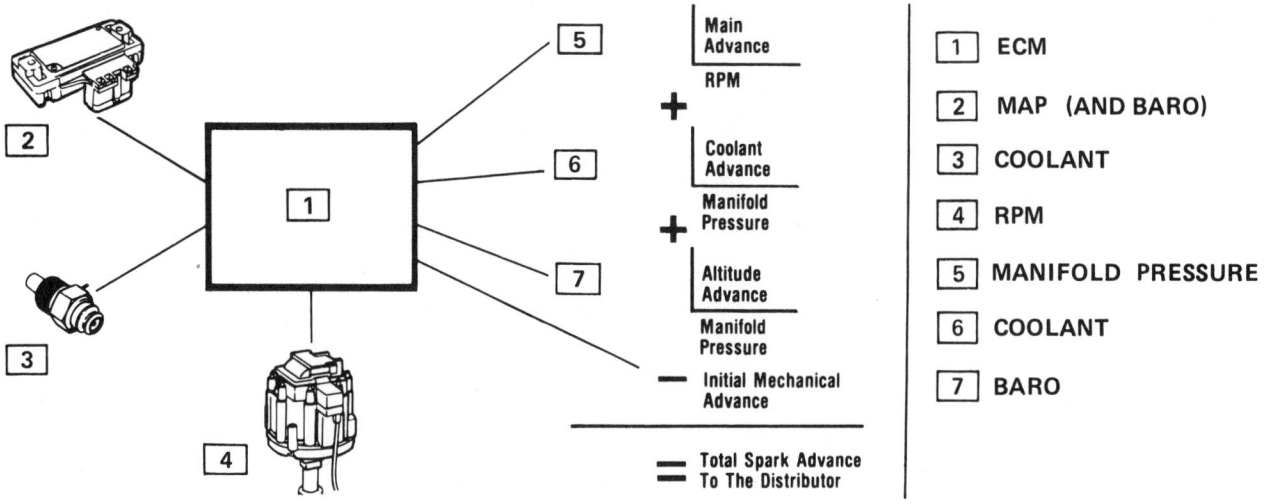

Fig. S-22. The heart of GM's engine control systems is an Electronic Control Module. The ECM is wired to various sensors, switches, and control devices.

The electronic spark timing (EST) distributor contains the ignition coil, amplifier, timing core, electronic switch, and pickup coil. Voltage is available to the EST distributor when the ignition switch is in run, bulb test, or start positions.

As the timing core turns, a magnetic circuit closes each time a spark plug is to fire. The magnetic circuit operates like an electric circuit, with the magnet acting like a battery and the pole pieces and shaft acting as wires. The pointed teeth on the pole piece and the timer core act like a switch. When the teeth come together, the switch closes and a magnetic pulse flows through the pickup.

As the timer core turns, the magnetic circuit rapidly opens and closes. Each magnetic pulse produces a low voltage pulse which is applied to the amplifier. The amplifier, in turn, increases the pulse voltage and sends a reference pulse to the ECM. The ECM processes these pulses and data received from the engine sensors, then selects the spark timing needed (retard or advance) for best engine performance.

The ECM then sends a control signal to an electronic switch in the EST distributor, closing the switch and connecting the ignition coil primary to ground. High voltage then builds up in the coil secondary, passes through the rotor, and is distributed to the spark plugs.

The ECM unit also detects the most common problems in the CCC system. It warns the driver of a problem by turning on the Check Engine light. The light also goes on for one to four seconds when the engine is started, then it goes out. This is the "bulb test."

The ECM records problems in its memory when the self-diagnostic system is activated. A set of calibration instructions

—Programmable Read Only Memory (PROM)—is furnished for each ECM. Each vehicle type has a specific PROM designed for its use. Should PROM replacement be necessary, care must be taken not to interchange or incorrectly install PROMs.

CHRYSLER'S CCC SYSTEM. Chrysler's Combustion Control Computer (CCC) system is controlled by an integrated and pre-programmed computer that commands ignition timing, air-fuel ratio (EFI system), and emission control devices. The CCC unit bases its commands on input from a variety of engine sensors for precise control of its output signals. The CCC also has the ability to update and revise its programming to better suit ambient and engine operating conditions.

The basic elements of an earlier (1982) CCC system are shown in Fig. S-5. A mid-year 1983 arrangement is illustrated in Fig. S-20.

STEERING/SUSPENSION SYSTEM DESIGN

The movement in engineering design from rear wheel drive to front wheel drive has quickened by the year as more and more sub-compact, compact, and midsized cars "get the treatment." With this switchover to FWD, there have been marked changes and multiple variations in steering and suspension system designs. Typical system designs are shown in Figs. S-23, S-24, and S-25.

Chevrolet's Celebrity model, for example, has rack and pinion standard power steering. The rack, Fig. S-26, is mounted to a rubber-isolated engine frame along with the front suspension lower control arms and transaxle. The engine frame is bolted to the body. The engine frame mounts are

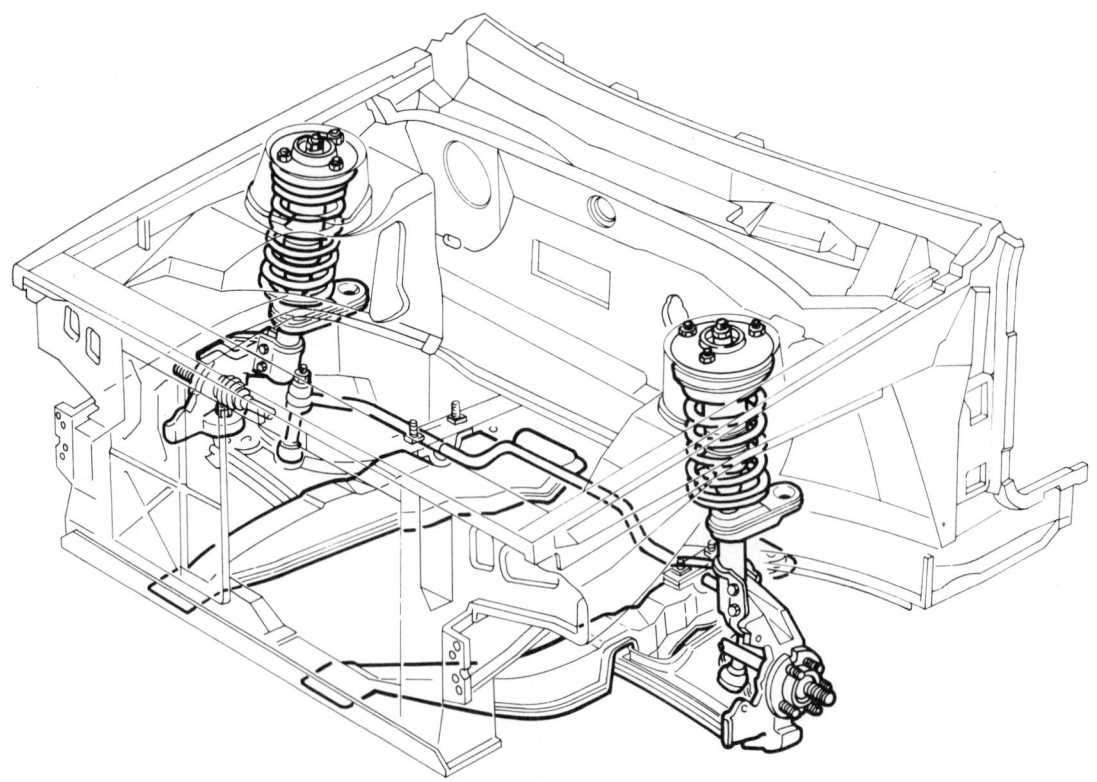

Fig. S-23. Most front wheel drive cars feature McPherson strut front suspension with a stabilizer bar. Note the frame rails in which the engine and transaxle are mounted.

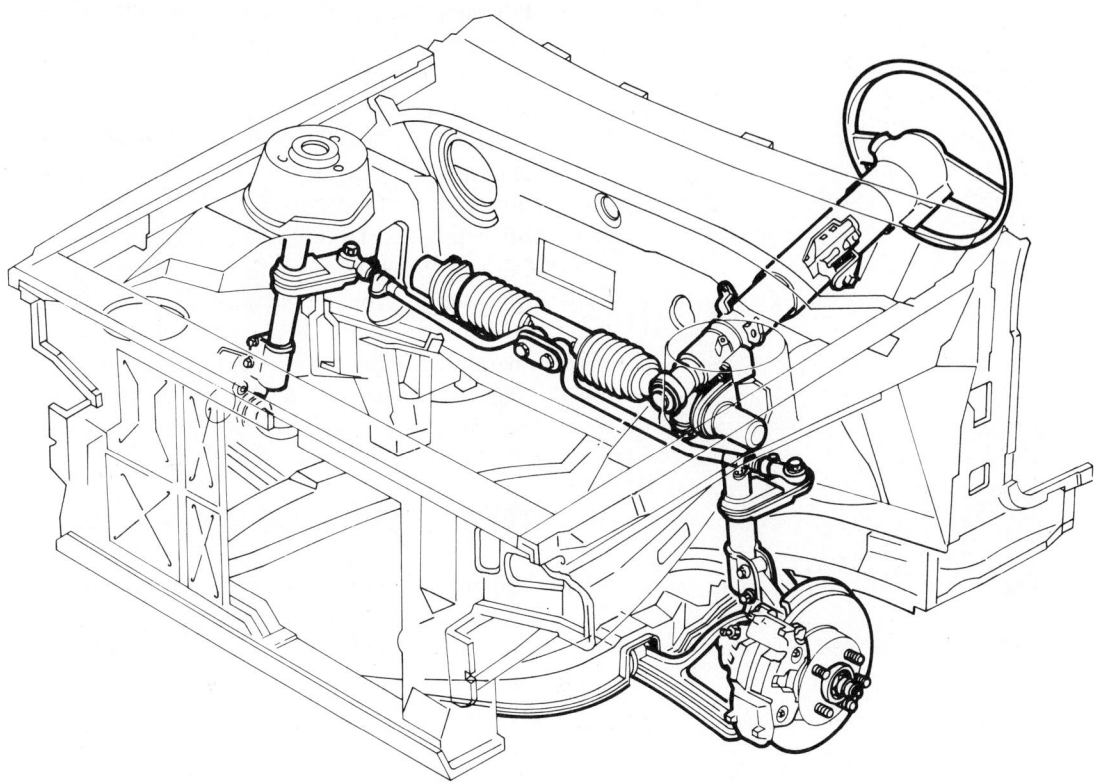

Fig. S-24. The rack and pinion steering system is usually installed on sub-compact and compact front wheel drive vehicles. Power steering is often standard equipment with this setup.

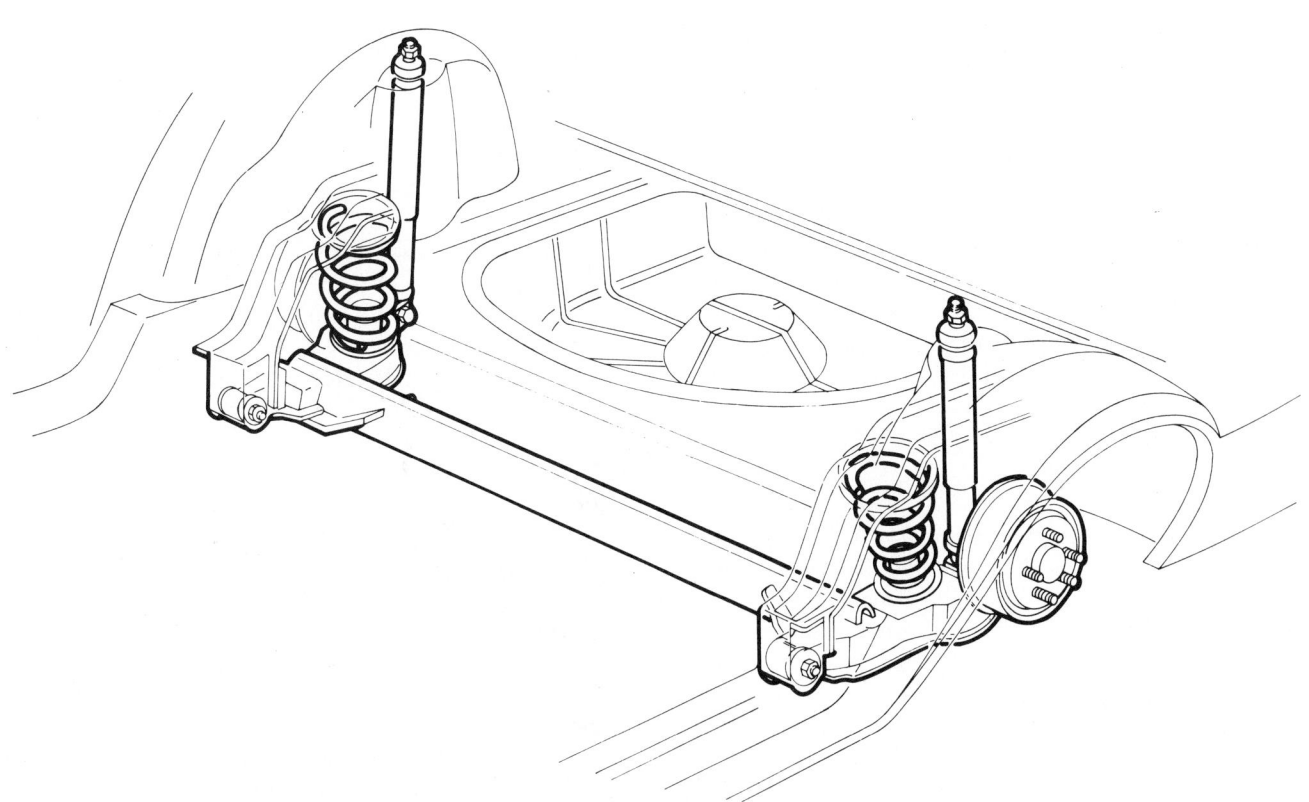

Fig. S-25. A typical rear suspension used on front wheel drive cars includes a trailing arm torsional beam system with coil springs and telescoping shock absorbers.

Fig. S-26. An unobstructed view of Chevrolet Cavalier's front wheel drive shows a four cylinder engine and transaxle mounted crosswise between the wheels. The horizontal tube in the upper foreground is the rack and pinion steering system.

"tuned," as are the lower control arm bushings, front and rear shock absorbers, and rear suspension track bar bushings.

Pontiac's front suspension on its 2000 model, Fig. S-27, uses McPherson struts with a strut-mounted spring, stabilizer bar, stamped lower control arm assembly, and cast steering knuckle. The design of the front suspension allows for replacement of the shock absorber portion or cartridge only, simplifying that service operation. The 2000 also features high-mounted rack and pinion steering.

BRAKE DEVELOPMENTS

Brake systems in front wheel drive vehicles reflect considerable changes from past disc brake systems. Chrysler engineers, for example, developed six new brake systems and four new actuation systems for the corporation's front wheel drive cars. Design changes include a single pin caliper in the power disc brakes, compared to a two-pin caliper used in the past. A larger phenolic piston is used instead of the steel piston and a smaller diameter master cylinder increases the power boost.

Other advances throughout the industry involve anti-squeak devices for disc brake calipers, dampened iron rotors for quieter operation, greater booster output, wider brake drums,

riveted brake shoes, brake pedal ratio changes to improve braking "feel," and improved parking brake capability.

TRANSMISSIONS/TRANSAXLES

With fuel economy in mind, the car manufacturers have reduced vehicle weight, lowered engine displacement, installed electronic fuel injection, improved body aerodynamics, and cut down on disc brake drag and tire rolling resistance. For 1983, they have turned to four and five-speed transmissions and transaxles to obtain higher fuel mileage ratings.

Ford's five-speed manual transaxle for Escort/Lynx and EXP/LN7 cars is shown in Fig. S-7. This transaxle has chrome alloy steel gears, assembled into matched sets and housed in an aluminum case to reduce weight. It uses a low viscosity transmission fluid with a friction modifier added to reduce lubricant drag. The five forward ratios are: 3.60 to 1; 2.12 to 1; 1.39 to 1; 1.02 to 1, and 0.75 to 1. The fifth gear provides overdrive (0.75 to 1).

Pontiac offers a five-speed manual transmission, Fig. S-28. The fifth gear overdrive and first gear ratio of 2.95 to 1 help improve fuel economy and acceleration. The overdrive ratio is 0.73 to 1 when used with V-8 or four cylinder engines; 0.78 to

1 when used with a V-6.

A four-speed automatic overdrive transmission is used in the Firebird. It utilizes a three-element torque converter with a lock-up converter clutch and a compound planetary gear set. The 3.06 to 1 first gear ratio provides improved acceleration. The 0.70 to 1 fourth gear overdrive ratio contributes to highway fuel economy.

Chrysler introduced a five-speed manual transaxle for 1983 front wheel drive domestic vehicles. The five-speed unit, Fig. S-29, comes with a 2.20 to 1 final gear ratio or 2.57 to 1 for performance. Fourth and fifth gears are "overdrive" in the Chrysler transaxle, allowing the engine to run slower than output.

Turn to page 830 for Fig. S-29.

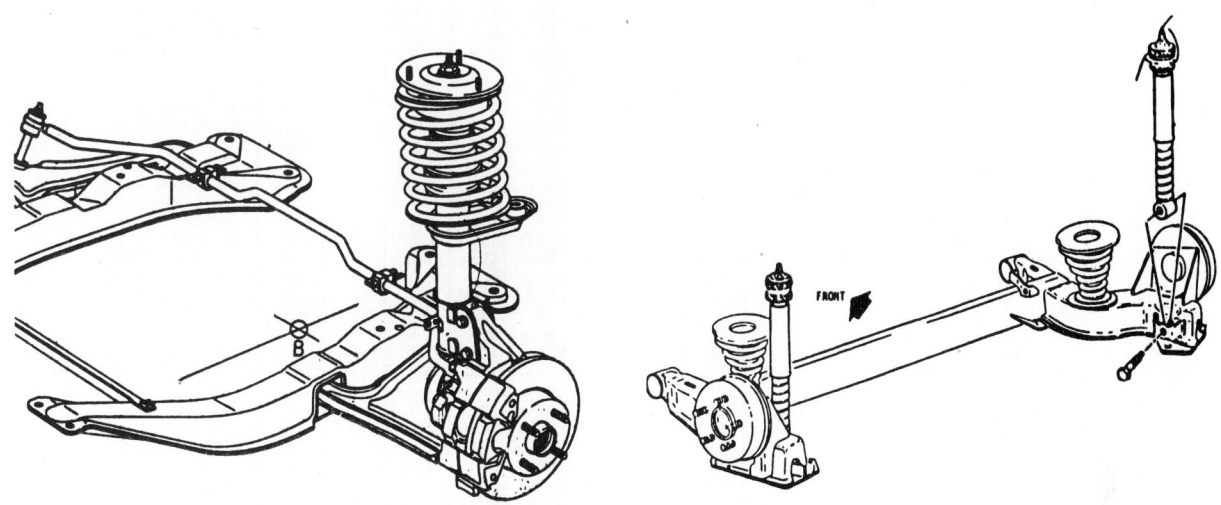

Fig. S-27. Pontiac's model 2000 utilizes independent front suspension and semi-independent rear suspension.

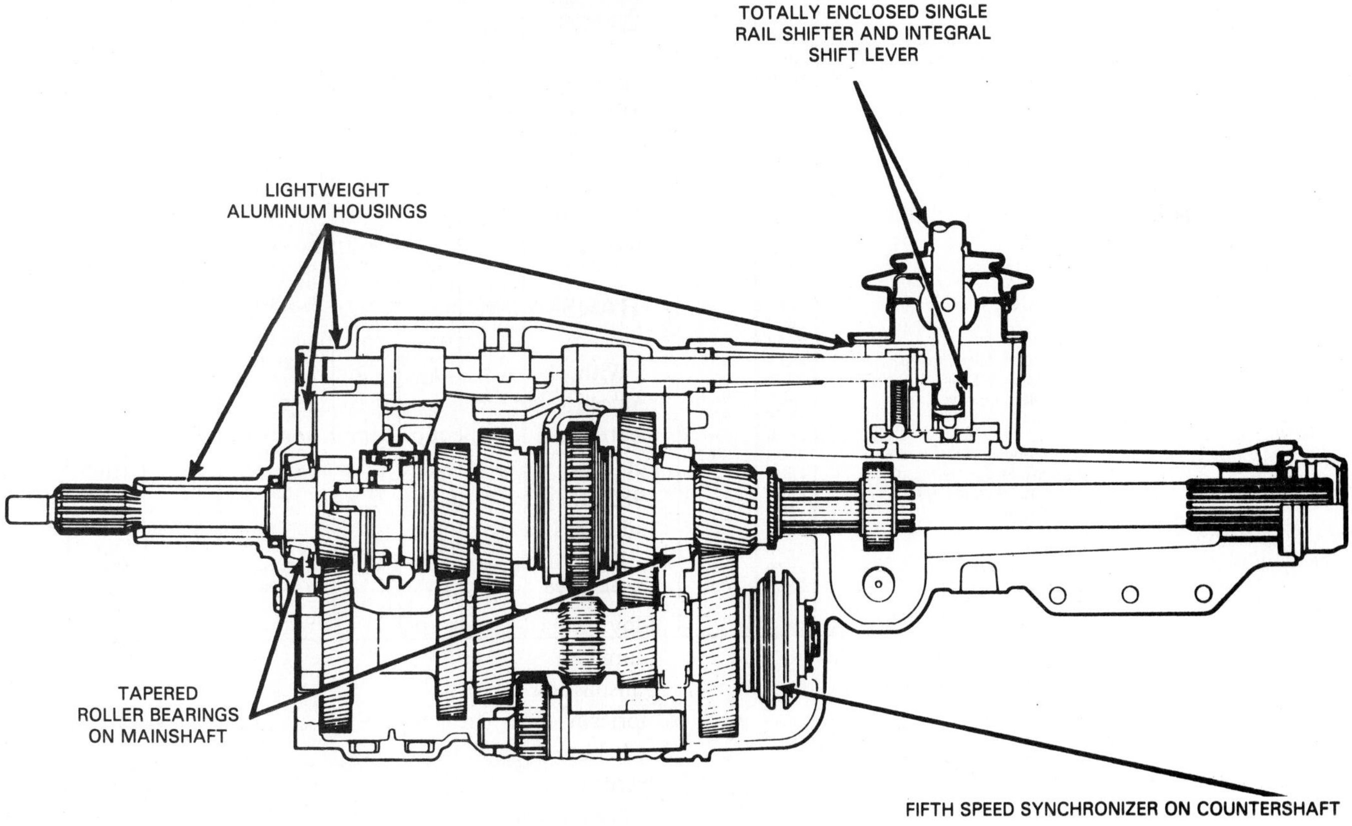

TOTALLY ENCLOSED SINGLE
RAIL SHIFTER AND INTEGRAL
SHIFT LEVER

LIGHTWEIGHT
ALUMINUM HOUSINGS

TAPERED
ROLLER BEARINGS
ON MAINSHAFT

FIFTH SPEED SYNCHRONIZER ON COUNTERSHAFT

Fig. S-28. Pontiac's five-speed manual transmission has aluminum housings, single rail enclosed shift mechanism, tapered roller bearings, live countershaft, and fifth gear overdrive.

1982

	Wheelbase (mm)	Wheelbase (in.)	No. of Cylinders Bore and Stroke (in.)	Displacement (litres)	Displacement (cu. in.)	Valve and Cylinder Arrangement	Net Brake Horsepower @ rpm	Net Power (kW)	Compression Pressure (psi)	Valve Clearance
AMC — Spirit, Concord	2438	96[1]	4-4.0x3.0	2.5	151	IO	86@4000	64.2	140[3]	HY
Eagle, SX/4, Kammback	2775	109.3[2]	4-4.0x3.0	2.5	151	IO	86@4000	64.2	140[3]	HY
Spirit, Concord	2438	96[1]	6-3.75x3.895	4.23	258	IO	110@3200	82	120[5]	HY
Eagle, SX/4, Kammback	2775	109.3[2]	6-3.75x3.895	4.23	258	IO	110@3200	82	120[5]	HY
Buick — Skyhawk	2570	101.2	4-3.50x2.91	1.8	112	IO	88@5100	65.6	100[6]	HY
Skyhawk	2570	101.2	4-3.56x2.96	1.8	112	IOC	84@5200	62.7	100[6]	HY
Skyhawk	2570	101.2	4-3.56x3.20	2.0	121	IO	90@5000	67.1	100[6]	HY
Skylark, Century	2664	104.9	4-4.0x3.0	2.5	151	IO	90@4000	67.1	140[3]	HY
Skylark	2664	104.9	6-3.50x2.99	2.8	173	VO	112@5100[9]	83.6[9]	100[6]	HY
Century	2664	104.9	6-3.80x2.66	3.0	181	VO	110@4800	82	100[6]	HY
Regal, Limited	2745	108.1	6-3.80x3.40	3.8	231	VO	110@3800[10]	82[10]	100[6]	HY
LeSabre, Custom, Limited	2945	115.9	6-3.80x3.40	3.8	231	VO	110@3800	82	100[6]	HY
Regal, Limited	2745	108.1	6-3.965x3.40	4.1	252	VO	125@4000	93	100[6]	HY
LeSabre, Electra	2945	115.9[12]	6-3.965x3.40	4.1	252	VO	125@4000	93	100[6]	HY
Riviera, T	2895	114	6-3.965x3.40	4.1	252	VO	125@4000	93	100[2]	HY
Century, Custom, Limited	2664	104.9	6-4.057x3.385[13]	4.3	262.5	VO	85@3600	63	275[6]	HY
Regal, Limited	2745	108.1	6-4.057x3.385[13]	4.3	262.5	VO	85@3600	63	275[6]	HY
LeSabre, Electra	2945	115.9[12]	8-3.80x3.385	5.0	307	VO	140@3600	104	120[6]	HY
Riviera, T	2895	114	8-3.80x3.385	5.0	307	VO	140@3600	104	120[6]	HY
LeSabre, Electra	2945	115.9[12]	8-4.057x3.385[13]	5.7	350	VO	105@3200	78	275[6]	HY
Riviera	2895	114	8-4.057x3.385[13]	5.7	350	VO	105@3200	78	275[6]	HY
Cadillac — Cimarron	2571	101.2	4-3.350x2.91	1.8	112	IO	88@5100	66	100[6]	HY
Eldorado, Seville	2895	114	8-3.465x3.307	4.1	250	VO	125@4200	94	120[6]	HY
Brougham, DeVille	3085	121.4	8-3.465x3.307	4.1	250	VO	125@4200	94	120[6]	HY
Eldorado, Seville	2895	114	6-3.965x3.40	4.1	252	VO	125@4000	94	100[6]	HY
Brougham, DeVille	3085	121.4	6-3.965x3.40	4.1	252	VO	125@4000	94	100[6]	HY
Eldorado, Seville	2895	114	8-4.057x3.385[13]	5.7	350	VO	105@3200	79	275[6]	HY
Brougham, DeVille	3085	121.4	8-4.057x3.385[13]	5.7	350	VO	105@3200	79	275[6]	HY
Fleetwood Limo	3670	144.5	8-3.80x4.060	6.0	368	VO	140@3800	105	120[6]	HY
Chevrolet — Chevette	2471	97.3[14]	4-3.23x2.98	1.6	98	IOC	70@5200	52	145[3]	HY
Chevette	2471	97.3[14]	4-3.31x3.23[13]	1.8	111	IOC	51@3200	38	370[6]	H[15]
Cavalier	2571	101.2	4-3.50x2.91	1.8	112	IO	88@5100	65.6	100[6]	HY
Cavalier	2571	101.2	4-3.50x3.15	2.0	121	IO	90@5000	67.1	100[6]	HY
Citation, Celebrity	2664	104.9	4-4.0x3.0	2.5	151	IO	90@4000	67.1	140[3]	HY
Camaro[17]	2566	101	4-4.0x3.0	2.5	151	IO	90@4000	67.1	140[3]	HY
Citation, Celebrity	2664	104.9	6-3.50x2.99	2.8	173	VO	112@5100[18]	83.6[18]	100[6]	HY
Camaro[17]	2566	101	6-3.50x2.99	2.8	173	VO	102@4800	76.1	100[6]	HY
Malibu Classic, Monte Carlo	2745	108.1	6-3.736x3.48	3.8	229	VO	110@4200	82	100[6]	HY
Impala, Caprice Classic	2945	116	6-3.736x3.48	3.8	229	VO	110@4200	82	100[6]	HY
Malibu Classic, Monte Carlo	2745	108.1	6-3.80x3.40	3.8	231	VO	110@3800	82	100[6]	HY
Impala, Caprice Classic	2945	116	6-3.80x3.40	3.8	231	VO	110@3800	82	100[6]	HY
Celebrity	2664	104.9	6-4.057x3.385[13]	4.3	260	VO	85@3600	63	275[6]	HY
Malibu Classic, Monte Carlo	2745	108.1	6-4.057x3.385[13]	4.3	262	VO	85@3600	63	275[6]	HY
Malibu Classic, Monte Carlo	2745	108.1	8-3.50x3.48	4.4	267	VO	115@4000	85.4	120[6]	HY
Impala, Caprice Classic	2945	116	8-3.50x3.48	4.4	267	VO	115@4000	85.4	120[6]	HY
Camaro[17]	2566	101	8-3.74x3.48	5.0	305	VO	145@4000	97	120[6]	HY
Impala, Caprice Classic	2945	116	8-3.74x3.48	5.0	305	VO	145@4000	97	120[6]	HY
Camaro[21]	2566	101	8-3.74x3.48	5.0	305	VO	165@4200	123	120[6]	HY
Malibu Classic, Monte Carlo	2745	108.1	8-4.057x3.385[13]	5.7	350	VO	105@3200	78	275[6]	HY
Impala, Caprice Classic	2945	116	8-4.057x3.385[13]	5.7	350	VO	105@3200	78	275[6]	HY
Corvette	2489	98	8-4.00x3.48	5.7	350	VO	200@4200	149.2	120[6]	HY
Chrysler — LeBaron	2538	99.9	4-3.44x3.62	2.2	135	IOC	84@4800	63	130[3]	HY
LeBaron	2538	99.9	4-3.59x3.86	2.6	156	IOC	92@4500	69	150[23]	H[24]
Cordoba, LS, New Yorker	2863	112.7	6-3.40x4.12	3.7	225	IO	90@3600	67	100[26]	HY
Cordoba, LS, New Yorker	2863	112.7	8-3.91x3.31	5.2	318[31]	VO	130@4000[28]	97[28]	100[26]	HY
Imperial	2863	112.7	8-3.91x3.31	5.2	318	VO	140@4000	104	100[26]	HY
Dodge — 024, Miser, Charger	2454	96.6	4-3.13x3.40	1.7	104.7[31]	IOC	63@4800	47	100[26]	H[27]
Omni, Miser, E-Type	2518	99.1	4-3.13x3.40	1.7	104.7	IOC	63@4800	47	100[26]	H[27]
024, Miser, Charger	2454	96.6	4-3.44x3.62	2.2	135	IOC	84@4800	63	130[3]	HY
Omni, Miser, E-Type	2518	99.1	4-3.44x3.62	2.2	135	IOC	84@4800	63	130[3]	HY
400, LS, Aries, Custom, S.E.	2538	99.9	4-3.44x3.62	2.2	135	IOC	84@4800	63	130[3]	HY
400, LS, Aries, Custom, S.E.	2538	99.9	4-3.59x3.86	2.6	156	IOC	92@4500	69	150[23]	H[24]
Diplomat, Medallion, Mirada	2863	112.7	6-3.40x4.12	3.7	225	IO	90@3600	67	100[26]	HY
Diplomat, Medallion, Mirada	2863	112.7	8-3.91x3.31	5.2	318	VO	130@4000[28]	97[28]	100[26]	HY
Ford — Escort	2393	94.2	4-3.15x3.13	1.6	97.6	IOC	70@4600	52	80[30]	HY
EXP	2393	94.2	4-3.15x3.13	1.6	97.6	IOC	70@4600	52	80[30]	HY
Mustang	2550	100.4	4-3.781x3.126	2.3	140	IOC	86@4600	64	80[30]	HY
Fairmont, Granada	2679	105.5	4-3.781x3.126	2.3	140	IOC	86@4600	64	80[30]	HY
Mustang	2550	100.4	6-3.682x3.126	3.3	200	IO	87@3800	65	80[30]	HY

ABBREVIATIONS — FOOTNOTES

AC — AC Spark Plugs
B — Before Top Dead Center
CH — Champion Spark Plugs
CP — Crankshaft Pulley
F — Flywheel
H — Hot Engine
HY — Hydraulic Lifters
IO — In-Line Engine — Overhead Valves
IOC — In-Line Engine — Overhead Camshaft

M — MOPAR Spark Plugs
MO — Motorcraft Spark Plugs
N — Negative
NA — Not Available/Not Applicable
P — Positive
VD — Vibration Damper
VO — V-Type Engine — Overhead Valves

1 — Concord — 2743/108
2 — SX/4 and Kammback — 2469/97.2

3 — Minimum Pressure — Maximum Variation Between Cylinders — 20 psi
4 — Toe-Out
5 — Minimum Pressure — Maximum Variation Between Cylinders — 30 psi
6 — Minimum Pressure — Maximum Variation Between Cylinders — 30 Percent
7 — Skylark — Auto. Trans. Only
8 — Not Adjustable

Tuneup Specifications

Firing Order	Timing Mark Location	Initial Ignition Timing @ rpm (auto. trans.)	Ignition Timing (rpm-manual trans.)	Ignition Timing (California)	Make	Model	Gap (in.)	Caster, Power Steering (deg.)	Camber, Right Wheel (deg.)	Toe-In (in.)	Crankcase Capacity (L qt.)	Cooling System Capacity (L)	Cooling System Capacity (qt.)
1342	CP	10B@700	900	8B	AC	R44TSX	.060	1P	1/8P	1/8	2.84/3	6.15	6.5
1342	CP	10B@700	900	8B	AC	R44TSX	.060	2-1/2P	1/3P	1/8[4]	2.84/3	6.15	6.5
153624	VD	19B@600	600	19B	CH	RFN-14LY	.035	1P	1/8P	1/8	3.78/4	13.3	14.0
153624	VD	21B@600	600	21B	CH	RFN-14LY	.035	2-1/2P	1/3P	1/8[4]	3.78/4	13.3	14.0
1342	VD	12B@700	750	12B	AC	R42TS	.045	1-3/4P	3/4P	1/8	3.30/4.5	8.8	9.3
1342	CP	8B@800	800	8B	AC	R42XLS6	.060	1-3/4P	3/4P	1/8	2.84/3	8.8	9.3
1342	CP	12B@700	750	12B	AC	R42TS	.045	1-3/4P	3/4P	1/8	3.30/4.5	8.8	9.3
1342	CP	8B@1050	1050[7]	8B	AC	R44TSX	.060	NA[8]	0	0	2.84/3	7.9	8.4
123456	CP	10B@600	850	10B	AC	R43TS	.045	NA[8]	0	0	3.78/4	9.2	9.7
165432	CP	15B@500	NA	15B	AC	R44TS8	.080	NA[8]	0	0	3.78/4	13.1	13.7
165432	CP	15B@500	NA	15B	AC	R45TS8	.080	3P	1/2P	1/8	3.78/4	11.7[11]	12.3[11]
165432	CP	15B@500	NA	15B	AC	R45TS8	.080	3P	3/4P	1/8	3.78/4	11.7	12.3
165432	CP	15B@500	NA	15B	AC	R45TS8	.080	3P	1/2P	1/8	3.78/4	11.7	12.3
165432	CP	15B@500	NA	15B	AC	R45TS8	.080	3P	3/4P	1/8	3.78/4	11.7	12.3
165432	CP	15B@500	NA	15B	AC	R45TS8	.080	2-1/2P	0	0	5.7/6	12.5	13.2
165432	CP	NA	NA	NA	NA	NA	NA	NA[8]	0	0	5.7/6	13.8	14.6
165432	CP	NA	NA	NA	NA	NA	NA	3P	1/2P	1/8	3.78/4	14.1	14.9
18436572	CP	20B@1100	NA	20B	AC	R45SX	.080	3P	3/4P	1/8	3.78/4	14.1	14.9
18436572	CP	20B@1100	NA	20B	AC	R45SX	.080	2-1/2P	0	0	6.0/6.5	16.5	17.5
18436572	VD	NA	NA	NA	NA	NA	NA	3P	3/4P	1/8	6.0/6.5	16.5	17.5
18436572	VD	NA	NA	NA	NA	NA	NA	2-1/2P	0	0	4.4/4.6	8.2	8.7
1342	CP	12B@700	750	12B	AC	R42TS	.045	NA[8]	NA[8]	1/8[4]	4.7/5	11.3	12.0
18436572	VD	10B@450	NA	10B	AC	R43NTS6	.060	2-1/2P	0	0	3.78/4	10.0	10.8
18436572	VD	8B@450	NA	10B	AC	R43NTS6	.060	1P	3/4P	1/8	3.78/4	11.8	12.5
165432	CP	15B@1100	NA	15B	AC	R45TSV	.060	2-1/2P	0	0	3.78/4	11.8	12.5
165432	CP	15B@1100	NA	15B	AC	R45TSX	.060	1P	3/4P	1/8	6.0/6.5	22.4	23.7
18436572	VD	NA	NA	NA	NA	NA	NA	2-1/2P	0	0	6.0/6.5	22.4	23.8
18436572	VD	NA	NA	NA	NA	NA	NA	1P	3/4P	1/8		20.3	21.4
15634278	CP	10B@450	NA	10B	AC	R45NAX	.060	3P	1/2P	1/8	3.78/4	8.7	9.2
1342	VD	18B@700	800	18B	AC	R42TS	.035	5P	1/4P	5/32	4.7/5	8.0	8.5
1342	VD	NA	NA	NA	NA	NA	NA	5P	1/4P	5/32	3.78/4	7.6	8.0
1342	CP	12B@700	750[2]	12B	AC	R42TS	.045	NA[8]	NA[8]	1/4	3.78/4	9.0	9.5
1342	CP	12B@700	750	12B	AC	R42TS	.045	NA[8]	NA[8]	1/4	3.78/4	9.0	9.5
1342	CP	8B@1050	1050[16]	8B	AC	R44TSX	.060	NA[8]	5/8P	1/8	2.84/3	12.4	13.1
1342	CP	8B@1050	1050	8B	AC	R44TSX	.060	3P	1P	1/8	3.78/4	10.1	10.7
123456	VD	10B@600	850[16]	10B	AC	R43TS[19]	.045	NA[8]	5/8P	1/8	3.78/4	10.1	10.7
123456	VD	10B@750	750	10B	AC	R43TS	.045	3P	1P	1/8	3.78/4	14.4	15.2
165432	VD	6B@600	NA	NA	AC	R45TS	.045	3P	1/2P	1/8	3.78/4	13.5	14.2
165432	VD	6B@600	NA	NA	AC	R45TS	.045	3P	1/2P	1/8	3.78/4	11.8	12.4
165432	VD	NA[20]	NA	15B	AC	R45TS8	.080	3P	1/2P	1/8	3.78/4	11.2	11.8
165432	VD	NA[20]	NA	15B	AC	R45TS8	.080	NA[8]	5/8P	1/8	4.7/5	12.3	12.9
165432	CP	NA	NA	NA	NA	NA	NA	3P	5/8P	1/8	6.0/6.5	14.1	14.9
165432	CP	NA	NA	NA	NA	NA	NA	3P	1/2P	1/8	3.78/4	17.9	18.9
18436572	VD	2B@500	NA	NA	AC	R45TS	.045	3P	1/2P	1/8	3.78/4	16.1	17.0
18436572	VD	2B@500	NA	NA	AC	R45TS	.045	1P	1/2P	1/8	3.78/4	14.2	15.0
18436572	VD	6B@500	700[22]	6B[22]	AC	R45TS	.045	3P	1/2P	1/8	3.78/4	14.6	15.5
18436572	VD	6B@500	700	6B	AC	R45TS	.045	3P	1/2P	1/8	3.78/4	14.2	15.0
18436572	VD	6B@500	700	6B	AC	R45TS	.045	3P	1/2P	1/8	6.0/6.5	17.5	18.5
18436572	VD	NA	NA	NA	NA	NA	NA	3P	1/2P	1/8	6.0/6.5	15.5	16.4
18436572	VD	6B@500	NA	6B	AC	R45TS	.045	2-1/4P	3/4P	1/4	3.78/4	20.4	21.6
1342	F	12B@900	850	12B	M	65PR	.035	1-1/4P	1/4P	1/4	4.8/5	8.2	8.7
1342	CP	7B@800	NA	7B	CH	RN-12Y	.040	1-1/4P[8]	1/4P	1/4	3.78/4	11.0	11.5
153624	VD	12B@625	NA	12B[25]	M	560PR	.035	2-1/2P	1/2P	1/8	3.78/4	14.2	15.0
18436572	VD	16B@600	NA	16B	M	65PR	.035	2-1/2P	1/2P	1/8	3.78/4	14.7	15.5
18436572	VD	12B@580	NA	12B	M	68ER	.048	2-1/2P	1/2P	1/16[4]	3.78/4	5.7	6.0
1342	F	NA	850	20B	M	65PR	.035	2P[8]	1/4P	1/16[4]	3.78/4	5.7	6.0
1342	F	NA	850	20B	M	65PR	.035	1-1/2P[8]	1/4P	1/16[4]	3.78/4	8.2	8.7
1342	F	12B@900	850	12B	M	65PR	.035	2P[7]	1/4P	1/16[4]	3.78/4	8.2	8.7
1342	F	12B@900	850	12B	M	65PR	.035	1-1/2P[8]	1/4P	1/16[4]	3.78/4	8.2	8.7
1342	F	12B@900	850	12B	M	65PR	.035	1P[7]	1/4P	1/16[4]	4.8/5	8.2	8.7
1342	CP	7B@800	NA	7B	CH	RN-12Y	.040	1P[7]	1/4P	1/8	3.78/4	11.0	11.5
153624	VD	12B@625	NA	12B[25]	M	560PR	.035	2-1/2P	1/2P	1/8	3.78/4	14.2	15.0
18436572	VD	16B@600	NA	16B	M	65PR	.035	2-1/2P	1/2P	1/8	3.78/4	14.7	15.5
1342	CP	10B@800	800	10B	MO	AGSP-32[29]	.044	1-1/4P	1-3/4P	1/8[4]	3.3/3.5	7.6	8.0
1342	CP	10B@800	800	10B	MO	AGSP-32[29]	.044	1-1/4P	1-3/4P	1/8[4]	3.3/3.5	8.0	8.0
1342	CP	12B@700	700[31]	12B[31]	MO	AWSF-42	.034	1-1/4P	1/4P	3/16	3.5/3.8	9.7	10.2
1342	CP	12B@700	700[31]	12B[31]	MO	AWSF-42	.034	1-1/8P[32]	7/16P	3/16	3.5/3.8	9.7	10.2
153624	VD	10B@900	NA	10B	MO	BSF-92	.050	1-1/4P	1/4P	3/16	3.78/4	7.9	8.4

9 — Optional — 135/100 @ 5400
10 — Turbo. (LC8) — Regal 170/126 @ 3800
     Riviera, T 180/134 @ 4000
11 — Turbo. — 12.2/12.7
12 — Electra — 3020/118.9
13 — Diesel Engine
14 — 2-Door — 2394/94.3
15 — Int. — .011 in./0.29 mm
     Exh. — .013 in./0.35 mm
16 — Celebrity — Auto. Trans. Only
17 — Not With Z28

18 — Also 2-Door Citation Coupe
     135/101@5400
19 — High Performance — R42TS
20 — California Only
21 — With Z28 Only
22 — Also Monte Carlo — California Only
23 — Minimum Pressure — Maximum
     Variation Between Cylinders — 15 psi
24 — Int. — .006 in./0.15 mm
     Exh. — .010 in./0.25 mm
25 — California — @725 rpm

26 — Minimum Pressure — Also 25 psi (4 and
     6) Or 40 psi (V-8) Maximum Variation
27 — Int. — .010 in./0.25 mm
     Exh. — .018 in./0.45 mm
28 — California — 165/123@4000
29 — Also AWSF-32. Check decal.
30 — Lowest Cylinder Must Be At Least
     75 Percent of Highest
31 — Manual Trans. — 6B
32 — Granada — 1P

1982	Wheelbase (mm)	Wheelbase (in.)	No. of Cylinders Bore and Stroke (in.)	Displacement (litres)	Displacement (cu. in.)	Valve and Cylinder Arrangement	Net Brake Horsepower @ rpm	Net Power (kW)	Compression Pressure (psi)	Valve Clearance
Ford — Fairmont, Granada	2679	105.5	6—3.682x3.126	3.3	200	IO	87@3800	65	80¹	HY
Thunderbird	2753	108.4	6—3.682x3.126	3.3	200	IO	87@3800	65	80¹	HY
Granada	2679	105.5	6—3.80x3.40	3.8	231	VO	112@4000³	84³	80¹	HY
Thunderbird	2753	108.4	6—3.80x3.40	3.8	231	VO	112@4000³	84³	80¹	HY
Mustang	2550	100.4	8—3.68x3.00	4.2	255	VO	111@3400	83	80¹	HY
Thunderbird	2753	108.4	8—3.68x3.00	4.2	255	VO	111@3400	83	80¹	HY
LTD, S, Crown Victoria	2904	114.3	8—3.68x3.00	4.2	255	VO	122@3400	91	80¹	HY
Mustang	2550	100.4	8—4.0x3.0	5.0	302	VO	157@4200	117	80¹	HY
LTD, S, Crown Victoria	2904	114.3	8—4.0x3.0	5.0	302	VO	132@3400	98	80¹	HY
LTD, S	2904	114.3	8—4.0x3.50	5.8	351	VO	165@3600	123	80¹	HY
Lincoln — Continental	2759	108.6	6—3.80x3.40	3.8	231	VO	112@4000³	84³	80¹	HY
Continental	2759	108.6	8—4.0x3.00	5.0	302	VO	131@3400	97	80¹	HY
Lincoln, Mark VI	2980	117.3⁶	8—4.0x3.00	5.0	302	VO	134@3400	100	80¹	HY
Mercury — Lynx	2393	94.2	4—3.15x3.13	1.6	97.6	IOC	70@4600	52	80¹	HY
LN7	2393	94.2	4—3.15x3.13	1.6	97.6	IOC	70@4600	52	80¹	HY
Capri	2550	100.4	4—3.781x3.126	2.3	140	IOC	86@4600	64	80¹	HY
Zephyr, Cougar	2679	105.5	4—3.781x3.126	2.3	140	IOC	86@4600	64	80¹	HY
Capri	2550	100.4	6—3.682x3.126	3.3	200	IO	87@3800	65	80¹	HY
Zephyr, Cougar	2679	105.5	6—3.682x3.126	3.3	200	IO	87@3800	65	80¹	HY
XR-7	2753	108.4	6—3.682x3.126	3.3	200	IO	87@3800	65	80¹	HY
Cougar	2679	105.5	6—3.80x3.40	3.8	231	VO	112@4000³	84³	80¹	HY
XR-7	2753	108.4	6—3.80x3.40	3.8	231	VO	112@4000³	84³	80¹	HY
Capri	2550	100.4	8—3.68x3.00	4.2	255	VO	111@3400	83	80¹	HY
XR-7	2753	108.4	8—3.68x3.00	4.2	255	VO	111@3400	83	80¹	HY
Marquis, Brougham, Grand Marquis	2904	114.3	8—3.68x3.00	4.2	255	VO	122@3400	91	80¹	HY
Capri	2550	100.4	8—4.0x3.0	5.0	302	VO	157@4200	117	80¹	HY
Marquis, Brougham, Grand Marquis	2904	114.3	8—4.0x3.0	5.0	302	VO	132@3400	98	80¹	HY
Marquis, Brougham	2904	114.3	8—4.0x3.50	5.8	351	VO	165@3600	123	80¹	HY
Oldsmobile — Firenza, S, SX, LX	2571	101.2	4—3.50x2.91	1.8	112	IO	88@5100	65.6	100⁹	HY
Omega, Brougham, Cutlass Ciera (all)	2664	104.9	4—4.0x3.0	2.5	151	IO	90@4000	67	140¹¹	HY
Omega, Brougham	2664	104.9	6—3.50x2.99	2.8	173	VO	112@5100	83.5	100⁹	HY
Cutlass Ciera, LS, Brougham	2664	104.9	6—3.80x2.66	3.0	181	VO	110@4800	82	100⁹	HY
Cutlass Supreme, Calais, Brougham	2745	108.1	6—3.80x3.40	3.8	231	VO	110@3800	82	100⁹	HY
Delta 88, Royale, Brougham	2945	116	6—3.80x3.40	3.8	231	VO	110@3800	82	100⁹	HY
98, Regency, Brougham	3020	119	6—3.965x3.40	4.1	252	VO	125@4000	93	100⁹	HY
Toronado	2895	114	6—3.965x3.40	4.1	252	VO	125@4000	93	100⁹	HY
Cutlass Supreme, Calais, Brougham	2745	108.1	8—3.50x3.385	4.3	260	VO	100@3600	75	120⁹	HY
Delta 88, Royale, Brougham	2945	116	8—3.50x3.385	4.3	260	VO	100@3600	75	120⁹	HY
Cutlass Ciera, LS, Brougham	2664	104.9	6—4.057x3.385¹⁴	4.3	262.5	VO	85@3600	63	275⁹	HY
Cutlass Supreme, Calais, Brougham	2745	108.1	6—4.057x3.385¹⁴	4.3	262.5	VO	85@3600	63	275⁹	HY
Delta 88 (all), 98 (all)	2945	116¹⁵	8—3.80x3.385	5.0	307	VO	140@3600	104	120⁹	HY
Toronado	2895	114	8—3.80x3.385	5.0	307	VO	140@3600	104	120⁹	HY
Cutlass Supreme, Calais, Brougham	2745	108.1	8—4.057x3.385¹⁴	5.7	350	VO	105@3200	79	275⁹	HY
Delta 88 (all), 98 (all)	2945	116¹⁵	8—4.057x3.385¹⁴	5.7	350	VO	105@3200	79	275⁹	HY
Toronado	2895	114	8—4.057x3.385¹⁴	5.7	350	VO	105@3200	79	275⁹	HY
Plymouth — Horizon, TC3 (all)	2518	99.1¹⁶	4—3.13x3.40	1.7	104.7	IOC	63@4800	47	100¹⁷	H¹⁸
Horizon, E-Type, TC3, Turismo	2518	99.1¹⁶	4—3.44x3.62	2.2	135	IOC	84@4800	63	130¹¹	HY
Reliant, Custom, S.E.	2538	99.9	4—3.44x3.62	2.2	135	IOC	84@4800	63	130¹¹	HY
Reliant, Custom, S.E.	2538	99.9	4—3.59x3.86	2.6	156	IOC	92@4500	69	150¹¹	H²¹
Gran Fury	2863	112.7	6—3.40x4.12	3.7	225	IO	90@3600	67	100¹⁷	HY
Gran Fury	2863	112.7	8—3.91x3.31	5.2	318	VO	130@4000²⁴	97²⁴	130¹⁷	HY
Pontiac — T1000	2466	97.2²⁵	4—3.23x2.98	1.6	98	IOC	62@5200	46	145²⁶	HY
J2000	2571	102.1	4—3.50x2.91	1.8	111	IOC	85@5100	63	100⁹	HY
J2000	2571	102.1	4—3.34x3.13	1.8	112	IOC	80@5200	60	100⁹	HY
Phoenix, LJ	2664	104.9	4—4.0x3.0	2.5	151	IO	90@4000	67.1	140¹¹	HY
A6000, LE	2664	104.9	4—4.0x3.0	2.5	151	IO	90@4000	67.1	140¹¹	HY
Firebird	2566	101	4—4.0x3.0	2.5	151	IO	90@4000	67.1	140¹¹	HY
Phoenix, LJ	2664	104.9	6—3.50x2.99	2.8	173	VO	102@5100	76.1	100⁹	HY
A6000, LE	2664	104.9	6—3.50x2.99	2.8	173	VO	108@5000	80.6	100⁹	HY
Phoenix, SJ	2664	104.9	6—3.50x3.0	2.8	173	VO	130@5400	97	100⁹	HY
Firebird, SE	2566	101	6—3.50x2.99	2.8	173	VO	105@4800	78	100⁹	HY
Grand Prix, LJ, Brougham	2745	108.1	6—3.80x3.40	3.8	231	VO	110@3800	82	100⁹	HY
Bonneville, G, Brougham	2745	108.1	6—3.965x3.40	3.8	231	VO	110@3800	82	100⁹	HY
Grand Prix, LJ, Brougham	2745	108.1	6—3.965x3.40	4.1	252	VO	125@4000	93	100⁹	HY
Bonneville, G, Brougham	2745	108.1	6—3.965x3.40	4.1	252	VO	125@4000	93	100⁹	HY
A6000, LE	2664	104.9	6—4.057x3.385¹⁴	4.3	262.5	VO	105@3200	78	275⁹	HY
Firebird TA, SE	2566	101	8—3.74x3.48	5.0	305	VO	150@4200	111.5	120⁹	HY
Grand Prix, LJ, Brougham	2745	108.1	8—4.057x3.385¹⁴	5.7	350	VO	105@3200	78	275⁹	HY
Bonneville, G, Brougham	2745	108.1	8—4.057x3.385¹⁴	5.7	350	VO	105@3200	78	275⁹	HY

ABBREVIATIONS — FOOTNOTES

AC — AC Spark Plugs
B — Before Top Dead Center
CH — Champion Spark Plugs
CP — Crankshaft Pulley
F — Flywheel
H — Hot Engine
HY — Hydraulic Lifters
IO — In-Line Engine—Overhead Valves
IOC — In-Line Engine—Overhead Camshaft

M — MOPAR Spark Plugs
MO — Motorcraft Spark Plugs
N — Negative
NA — Not Available/Not Applicable
P — Positive
VD — Vibration Damper
VO — V-Type Engine—Overhead Valves
1 — Lowest Cylinder Must Be At Least 75 Percent Of Highest

2 — Granada — 1P
3 — California -- 118/88@4000
4 — 12B@800
5 — Also AWSF-32. Check decal.
6 — 2-Door Mark VI — 2904/114.3
7 — Toe-Out
8 — Manual Trans. — 6B
9 — Minimum Pressure — Maximum Variation Between Cylinders — 30 Percent

Tuneup Specifications

Firing Order	Timing Mark Location	Initial Ignition Timing @ rpm (auto. trans.)	Ignition Timing (rpm-manual trans.)	Ignition Timing (California)	Spark Plugs Make	Spark Plugs Model	Gap (in.)	Caster, Power Steering (deg.)	Camber, Right Wheel (deg.)	Toe-In (in.)	Crankcase Capacity (L, qt.)	Cooling System Capacity (L)	Cooling System Capacity (qt.)
153624	VD	10B@900	NA	10B	MO	BSF-92	.050	1-1/8P[2]	7/16P	3/16	3.78/4	7.9	8.4
153624	VD	10B@900	NA	10B	MO	BSF-92	.050	1P	3/8P	3/16	3.78/4	7.9	8.4
142536	VD	10B@800	NA	12B	MO	AGSP-52	.044	1P	7/16P	3/16	3.78/4	7.8	8.3
142536	VD	10B@800	NA	12B	MO	AGSP-52	.044	1P	3/8P	3/16	3.78/4	7.8	8.3
15426378	VD	8B@800	NA	NA	MO	ASF-52	.050	1-1/4P	1/4P	3/16	3.78/4	13.9	14.7
15426378	VD	8B@800	NA	12B	MO	ASF-52	.050	1P	3/8P	3/16	3.78/4	14.1	14.9
15426378	VD	8B@800	NA	NA	MO	ASF-52	.050	3P	1/2P	1/16	3.78/4	14.0	14.8
15426378	VD	NA	800[4]	12B[4]	MO	ASF-42	.044	1-1/4P	1/4P	3/16	3.78/4	12.4	13.1
15426378	VD	8B@800	NA	12B	MO	ASF-52	.050	3P	1/2P	1/16	3.78/4	12.6	13.3
15426378	VD	8B@800	NA	8B	MO	ASF-42	.050	3P	1/2P	1/16	3.78/4	13.0	13.8
13726548	VD	8B@600	NA	8B	MO	ASF-42	.050	1-1/4P	3/16P	1/8	3.78/4	7.8	8.3
142536	VD	10B@800	NA	12B	MO	AGSP-52	.044	1-1/4P	3/16P	1/8	3.78/4	12.6	13.3
15426378	VD	8B@800	NA	8B	MO	ASF-52	.050	3P	1/2P	1/16	3.78/4	12.6	13.3
1342	CP	10B@800	800	10B	MO	AGSP-32[5]	.044	1-3/4P	1-1/4P	1/8[7]	3.3/3.5	7.6	8.0
1342	CP	10B@800	800	10B	MO	AGSP-32[5]	.044	1-1/4P	1-1/2P	1/8	3.3/3.5	7.6	8.0
1342	CP	12B@700	700[8]	12B[8]	MO	AWSF-42	.034	1P	1/4P	3/16	3.5/3.8	9.7	10.2
1342	CP	12B@700	700[8]	12B[8]	MO	AWSF-42	.034	1P	5/16P	3/16	3.5/3.8	9.7	10.2
153624	VD	10B@900	NA	10B	MO	BSF-92	.050	1P	1/4P	3/16	3.78/4	7.9	8.4
153624	VD	10B@900	NA	10B	MO	BSF-92	.050	1P	5/16P	3/16	3.78/4	7.9	8.4
153624	VD	10B@900	NA	10B	MO	BSF-92	.050	1P	5/16P	3/16	3.78/4	7.9	8.4
142536	VD	10B@800	NA	12B	MO	AGSP-52	.044	1P	5/16P	3/16	3.78/4	7.8	8.3
142536	VD	10B@800	NA	12B	MO	AGSP-52	.044	1P	5/16P	3/16	3.78/4	7.8	8.3
15426378	VD	8B@800	NA	NA	MO	ASF-52	.050	1P	1/4P	3/16	3.78/4	13.9	14.7
15426378	VD	8B@800	NA	12B	MO	ASF-52	.050	1P	5/16P	3/16	3.78/4	14.1	14.9
15426378	VD	8B@800	NA	NA	MO	ASF-52	.050	3P	1/2P	1/16	3.78/4	14.0	14.8
15426378	VD	NA	800[4]	12B[4]	MO	ASF-42	.044	1P	1/4P	3/16	3.78/4	12.4	13.1
15426378	VD	8B@800	NA	12B	MO	ASF-52	.050	3P	1/2P	1/16	3.78/4	12.6	13.3
13726548	VD	8B@600	NA	8B	MO	ASF-42	.050	3P	1/2P	1/16	3.78/4	13.0	13.8
1342	CP	12B@700	750	12B	AC	R42TS	.045	NA[10]	NA[10]	1/4[7]	3.78/4	7.6	8.0
1342	CP	8B@1050	1050[12]	8B	AC	R44TSX	.060	2P[10]	0	0	2.84/3	8.9	9.4
123456	VD	10B@600	850	10B	AC	R43TS	.045	2P[10]	0	0	3.78/4	13.1	13.7
165432	CP	15B@500	NA	15B	AC	R44TS8	.080	2P[10]	0	0	3.78/4	11.7	12.3
165432	VD	15B@500	NA	15B	AC	R45TS8	.080	1P	1/2P	.15[13]	3.78/4	11.7	12.3
165432	VD	15B@500	NA	15B	AC	R45TS8	.080	3P	3/4P	.15[13]	3.78/4	11.7	12.3
165432	CP	15B@500	NA	15B	AC	R45TS8	.080	3P	3/4P	.15[13]	3.78/4	11.7	12.3
165432	CP	15B@500	NA	15B	AC	R45TS8	.080	2-1/2P	0	0	3.78/4	11.7	12.3
18436572	CP	20B@1100	NA	20B	AC	R46SX	.080	1P	1/2P	.15[13]	3.78/4	15.0	15.9
18436572	CP	20B@1100	NA	20B	AC	R46SX	.080	3P	3/4P	.15[13]	3.78/4	15.6	16.5
165432	CP	NA	NA	NA	NA	NA	NA	2P[10]	0	0	5.7/6	12.5	13.2
165432	CP	NA	NA	NA	NA	NA	NA	1P	1/2P	.15[13]	5.7/6	13.8	14.6
18436572	CP	20B@1100	NA	20B	AC	R45SX	.080	3P	3/4P	.15[13]	3.78/4	14.8	15.6
18436572	CP	20B@1100	NA	20B	AC	R45SX	.080	2-1/2P	0	0	3.78/4	15.5	16.4
18436572	VD	NA	NA	NA	NA	NA	NA	1P	1/2P	.15[13]	5.7/6	16.5	17.4
18436572	VD	NA	NA	NA	NA	NA	NA	3P	3/4P	.15[13]	5.7/6	17.3	18.3
18436572	VD	NA	NA	NA	NA	NA	NA	2-1/2P	0	0	5.7/6	17.2	18.2
1342	F	12B@900	850[19]	12B[20]	M	65PR	.035	1-1/2P[22]	1/4P	1/16[7]	3.78/4	5.7	6.0
1342	F	12B@900	850	12B	M	65PR	.035	1-1/2P[22]	1/4P	1/16[7]	3.78/4	8.2	8.7
1342	F	12B@900	850	12B	M	65PR	.035	1-1/4P	1/4P	1/16[7]	3.78/4	8.2	8.7
1342	CP	7B@800	NA	7B	CH	RN-12Y	.040	1-1/4P	1/4P	1/16[7]	4.8/5	10.9	11.5
153624	VD	12B@625	NA	12B[23]	M	560PR	.035	2-1/2P	1/2P	1/8	3.78/4	15.6	16.5
18436572	VD	16B@600	NA	16B	M	65PR	.035	2-1/2P	1/2P	1/8	3.78/4	8.7	9.2
1342	VD	18B@700	800	18B	AC	R42TS	.035	5P	1/4P	5/32	3.78/4	7.6	8.0
1342	CP	12B@700	750	12B	AC	R42TS	.045	NA[10]	NA[10]	1/4	2.84/3	7.4	7.8
1342	CP	12B@700	750	12B	AC	R42TS	.045	NA[10]	NA[10]	1/4	2.84/3	9.3	9.8
1342	CP	8B@1050	1050	8B	AC	R44TSX	.060	0[10]	1P	.1[27]	2.84/3	9.2	9.7
1342	CP	8B@1050	1050	8B	AC	R44TSX	.060	0[10]	1P	.1[27]	2.84/3	12.4	13.1
1342	CP	8B@1050	750	8B	AC	R44TSX	.060	3P	1P	1/8	2.84/3	9.3	9.8
123456	VD	10B@750	750	10B	AC	R43TS	.045	0[10]	1P	.1[27]	3.78/4	10.1	10.7
123456	VD	10B@600	NA	10B	AC	R43TS	.045	0[10]	1P	.1[27]	3.78/4	9.2	9.7
123456	VD	10B@750	750	6B	AC	R43TS	.045	0[10]	1P	1/8	3.78/4	10.1	10.7
123456	VD	10B@600	850	10B	AC	R43TS	.045	3P	1P	.12[28]	3.78/4	11.7	12.3
165432	CP	15B@500	NA	15B	AC	R45TS8	.080	3P	1/2P	.12[28]	3.78/4	11.7	12.3
165432	CP	15B@500	NA	15B	AC	R45TS8	.080	3P	1/2P	.12[28]	3.78/4	11.7	12.3
165432	CP	15B@500	NA	15B	AC	R45TS8	.080	3P	1/2P	.12[28]	3.78/4	11.7	12.3
165432	CP	15B@500	NA	15B	AC	R45TS8	.080	3P	1/2P	.12[28]	5.7/6	13.8	14.6
165432	CP	NA	NA	NA	NA	NA	NA	0[10]	1P	1/8	3.78/4	14.2	15.0
18436572	VD	6B@500	700	6B	AC	R45TS	.045	3P	1P	1/8	6.0/6.5	17.5	18.5
18436572	VD	NA	NA	NA	NA	NA	NA	3P	1/2P	.12[28]	6.0/6.5	17.5	18.5
18436572	VD	NA	NA	NA	NA	NA	NA	3P	1/2P	.12[28]	6.0/6.5	17.5	18.5

10 — Not Adjustable	17 — Minimum Pressure — Also 25 psi (4 and 6) Or 40 psi (V-8) Maximum Variation	22 — TC3 — 2P
11 — Minimum Pressure — Maximum Variation Between Cylinders — 20 psi	18 — Int. — .010 in./0.25 mm Exh. — .018 in./0.45 mm	23 — California — @725 rpm
12 — Cutlass Ciera — Auto. Trans. Only	19 — Manual Trans. — 20B	24 — California — 165/123@4000
13 — Degree Per Wheel Or 5/32 in.	20 — Miser Only	25 — 2-Door — 2394/94.3
14 — Diesel Engine	21 — Int. — .006 in./0.15 mm Exh. — .010 in./0.25 mm	26 — Minimum Pressure — Maximum Variation Between Cylinders — 15 psi
15 — 98 — 3020/119		27 — Degree Per Wheel Or 3/32 in.
16 — TC3 — 2454/96.6		28 — Degree Per Wheel Or 1/8 in.

1983

	Wheelbase (mm)	Wheelbase (in.)	No. of Cylinders Bore and Stroke (in.)	Displacement (litres)	Displacement (cu. in.)	Valve and Cylinder Arrangement	Net Brake Horsepower @ rpm	Net Power (kW)	Compression Pressure (psi)	Valve Clearance
AMC — Alliance, L, DL, Limited	2484	97.8	4 – 2.994x3.034	1.4	85	IO	56@4200	42	110[1]	H[2]
Eagle, SX/4	2775	109.3[3]	4 – 4.0x3.0	2.5	151	IO	86@4000	64.2	140[1]	HY
Spirit, Concord	2438	96[5]	6 – 3.75x3.895	4.23	258	IO	112@3200	83.6	120[6]	HY
Eagle, SX/4	2775	109.3[3]	6 – 3.75x3.895	4.23	258	IO	112@3200	83.6	120[6]	HY
Buick — Skyhawk, T	2570	101.2	4 – 3.56x2.96	1.8	112	IOC	84@5200	62.7	100[7]	HY
Skyhawk	2570	101.2	4 – 3.56x3.20	2.0	121	IO	86@4900	64.2	100[7]	HY
Skylark, Century, Custom, Limited	2664	104.9	4 – 4.0x3.0	2.5	151	IO	90@4400	67	140[1]	HY
Skylark, Custom, Limited	2664	104.9	6 – 3.50x3.0	2.8	173	VO	112@5100	83.6	100[7]	HY
Skylark, Custom, Limited, T	2664	104.9	6 – 3.50x2.99	2.8	173	VO	135@5400	101	100[7]	HY
Century, Custom, Limited, T	2664	104.9	6 – 3.80x2.66	3.0	181	VO	110@4800	82	100[7]	HY
Regal, Limited	2745	108.1	6 – 3.80x3.40	3.8	231	VO	110@3800[9]	82	100[7]	HY
LeSabre, Custom, Limited	2945	115.9	6 – 3.80x3.40	3.8	231	VO	110@3800	82	100[7]	HY
Regal, Custom, Limited	2745	108.1	6 – 3.965x3.40	4.1	252	VO	125@4000	93	100[7]	HY
LeSabre, Electra	2945	115.9[12]	6 – 3.965x3.40	4.1	252	VO	125@4000	93	100[7]	HY
Riviera, Convertible	2895	114	6 – 3.965x3.40	4.1	252	VO	125@4000	93	100[7]	HY
Century, Custom, Limited	2664	104.9	6 – 4.057x3.385[13]	4.3	262.5	VO	85@3600	63	275[7]	HY
Regal, Limited	2745	108.1	6 – 4.057x3.385[13]	4.3	262.5	VO	85@3600	63	275[7]	HY
LeSabre, Electra	2945	115.9[12]	8 – 3.80x3.385	5.0	307	VO	140@3600	104	120[7]	HY
Riviera, Convertible	2895	114	8 – 3.80x3.385	5.0	307	VO	140@3600	104	120[7]	HY
Regal, Limited	2745	108.1	8 – 4.057x3.385[13]	5.7	350	VO	105@3200	78	275[7]	HY
LeSabre, Electra	2945	115.9[12]	8 – 4.057x3.385[13]	5.7	350	VO	105@3200	78	275[7]	HY
Riviera	2895	114	8 – 4.057x3.385[13]	5.7	350	VO	105@3200	78	275[7]	HY
Cadillac — Cimarron, D'ORO	2571	101.2	4 – 3.350x3.15	2.0	121	IO	88@4800	66	100[7]	HY
Eldorado, Seville	2895	114	8 – 3.465x3.307	4.1	250	VO	135@4400	101	140[7]	HY
Brougham, DeVille	3085	121.5	8 – 3.465x3.307	4.1	250	VO	135@4400	101	140[7]	HY
Eldorado, Seville	2895	114	8 – 4.057x3.385[13]	5.7	350	VO	105@3200	78	275[7]	HY
Brougham, DeVille	3085	121.5	8 – 4.057x3.385[13]	5.7	350	VO	105@3200	78	275[7]	HY
Fleetwood Limo	3670	144.5	8 – 3.80x4.060	6.0	368	VO	140@3800	105	140[7]	HY
Chevrolet — Chevette	2471	97.3[15]	4 – 3.23x2.98	1.6	98	IOC	65@5200	48.5	145[1]	H[16]
Chevette	2471	97.3[15]	4 – 3.31x3.23[13]	1.8	111	IOC	51@5000	38	370[7]	H[16]
Cavalier	2571	101.2	4 – 3.50x3.15	2.0	121	IO	88@4800	65.6	100[7]	HY
Citation, Celebrity	2664	104.9	4 – 4.0x3.0	2.5	151	IO	92@4000	68.6	140[1]	HY
Camaro[17]	2566	101	4 – 4.0x3.0	2.5	151	IO	92@4000	68.6	140[1]	HY
Citation, Celebrity	2664	104.9	6 – 3.50x2.99	2.8	173	VO	112@4800[19]	83.6	100[7]	HY
Camaro[17]	2566	101	6 – 3.50x2.99	2.8	173	VO	107@4800	79.8	100[7]	HY
Malibu, Monte Carlo	2745	108.1	6 – 3.736x3.48	3.8	229	VO	110@4000	82	100[7]	HY
Impala, Caprice Classic	2945	116	6 – 3.736x3.48	3.8	229	VO	110@4000	82	100[7]	HY
Malibu, Monte Carlo	2745	108.1	6 – 3.80x3.40	3.8	231	VO	110@3800	82	100[7]	HY
Impala, Caprice Classic	2945	116	6 – 3.80x3.40	3.8	231	VO	110@3800	82	100[7]	HY
Celebrity	2664	104.9	6 – 4.057x3.385[13]	4.3	260	VO	85@3600	63	275[7]	HY
Malibu, Monte Carlo	2745	108.1	6 – 4.057x3.385[13]	4.3	260	VO	85@3600	63	275[7]	HY
Camaro[17]	2566	101	8 – 3.736x3.48	5.0	305	VO	150@4000	111.9	120[7]	HY
Malibu, Monte Carlo, SS	2745	108.1	8 – 3.736x3.48	5.0	305	VO	150@4000[21]	111.9	120[7]	HY
Impala, Caprice Classic	2945	116	8 – 3.736x3.48	5.0	305	VO	150@4000	111.9	120[7]	HY
Camaro[22]	2566	101	8 – 3.736x3.48	5.0	305	VO	175@4200	123	120[7]	HY
Malibu, Monte Carlo	2745	108.1	8 – 4.057x3.385[13]	5.7	350	VO	105@3200	78	275[7]	HY
Impala, Caprice Classic	2945	116	8 – 4.057x3.385[13]	5.7	350	VO	105@3200	78	275[7]	HY
Corvette	2489	98	8 – 4.0x3.48	5.7	350	VO	200@4200	149.2	120[7]	HY
Chrysler — LeBaron	2542	100.1	4 – 3.44x3.62	2.2	135	IOC	94@5200	70	130[1]	HY
E Class Sedan	2618	103.1	4 – 3.44x3.62	2.2	135	IOC	94@5200	70	130[1]	HY
LeBaron	2542	100.1	4 – 3.59x3.86	2.6	156	IOC	93@4500	69	150[24]	H[25]
E Class Sedan	2618	103.1	4 – 3.59x3.86	2.6	156	IOC	93@4500	69	150[24]	H[25]
Cordoba, New Yorker, Fifth Ave. Edition	2863	112.7	6 – 3.40x4.12	3.7	225	IO	90@3600	67	100[26]	HY
Cordoba, New Yorker, Fifth Ave. Edition	2863	112.7	8 – 3.91x3.31	5.2	318	VO	130@4000	97	100[26]	HY
Imperial	2863	112.7	8 – 3.91x3.31	5.2	318	VO	140@4000	104	100[26]	HY
Dodge — 024	2454	96.6	4 – 3.17x3.07	1.6	97.1	IOC	62@4800	46	100[26]	H[27]
Omni, Custom	2518	99.1	4 – 3.17x3.07	1.6	97.1	IOC	62@4800	46	100[26]	H[27]
024, Omni, Custom	2454	96.6[29]	4 – 3.13x3.40	1.7	104.7	IOC	63@4800	47	100[26]	H[30]
024 Charger 2.2, Omni, Custom	2454	96.6[29]	4 – 3.44x3.62	2.2	135	IOC	94@5200	70	130[1]	HY
400, Aries	2543	100.1	4 – 3.44x3.62	2.2	135	IOC	94@5200	70	130[1]	HY
600, ES	2618	103.1	4 – 3.44x3.62	2.2	135	IOC	94@5200	70	130[1]	HY
400, Aries Special Edition	2543	100.1	4 – 3.59x3.86	2.6	156	IOC	93@4500	69	150[24]	H[25]
600, ES	2618	103.1	4 – 3.59x3.86	2.6	156	IOC	93@4500	69	150[24]	H[25]
Diplomat, Medallion, Mirada	2863	112.7	6 – 3.40x4.12	3.7	225	IO	90@3600	67	100[26]	HY
Diplomat, Medallion, Mirada	2863	112.7	8 – 3.91x3.31	5.2	318	VO	130@4000[32]	97	100[26]	HY
Ford — Escort	2393	94.2	4 – 3.15x3.13	1.6	97.6	IOC	72@5200	53.7	80[33]	HY
Escort, EXP	2393	94.2	4 – 3.15x3.13	1.6	97.6	IOC	80@5800	59.7	80[33]	HY
Escort, EXP	2393	94.2	4 – 3.15x3.13	1.6	97.6	IOC	88@5400	65.6	80[33]	HY
Tempo	2538	99.9	4 – 3.15x3.13	1.6	97.6	IOC	72@5200	53.7	80[33]	HY

ABBREVIATIONS — FOOTNOTES

AC — AC Spark Plugs
B — Before Top Dead Center
CH — Champion Spark Plugs
CP — Crankshaft Pulley
EC — Electronically Controlled
F — Flywheel
H — Hot Engine
HY — Hydraulic Lifters
IO — In-Line Engine—Overhead Valves
IOC — In-Line Engine—Overhead Camshaft

M — MOPAR Spark Plugs
MO — Motorcraft Spark Plugs
NA — Not Available/Not Applicable
P — Positive
VD — Vibration Damper
VO — V-Type Engine—Overhead Valves

1 — Minimum Pressure-Maximum Variation Between Cylinders — 20 psi
2 — Int. — .007 in./0.18 mm
Exh. — .009 in./0.25 mm

3 — 2-Door — 2469/97.2
4 — SX/4 Only
5 — Concord — 2743/108
6 — Minimum Pressure-Maximum Variation Between Cylinders — 30 psi
7 — Minimum Pressure-Maximum Variation Between Cylinders — 30 Percent
8 — Century — Auto. Trans. Only
9 — Turbo. (LC8)—Regal T 180/134@4000 Also Riviera T 180/134@4000
10 — Turbo. — 12.2/12.7

Tuneup Specifications

Firing Order	Timing Mark Location	Initial Ignition Timing (rpm) (auto. trans.)	Ignition Timing (rpm-manual trans.)	Ignition Timing (California)	Spark Plugs Make	Spark Plugs Model	Gap (in.)	Caster, Power Steering (deg.)	Camber, Right Wheel (deg.)	Toe-In (in.)	Crankcase Capacity (L qt.)	Cooling System Capacity (L)	Cooling System Capacity (qt.)
1342	F	8B@700	800	8B	CH	N-9Y	.024	NA	NA	NA	3.0/3.2	6.0	6.5
1342	VD	10B@700[4]	900	12B	AC	R44TSX	.060	2-3/4P	3/8P	1/8	2.84/3	6.15	6.6
153624	VD	6B@1600	1600	6B	CH	RFN-14LY	.035	1P	3/8P	1/8	3.78/4	13.3	14.0
153624	VD	6B@1600	1600	6B	CH	RFN-14LY	.035	2-3/4P	3/8P	1/8	3.78/4	13.3	14.0
1342	CP	NA	EC	8B	AC	R44XLS	.035	1-3/4P	3/4P	1/8	3.78/4	8.8	9.3
1342	CP	0@EC	EC	0	AC	R42CTS	.035	1-3/4P	3/4P	1/8	3.78/4	8.8	9.3
1342	CP	8B@EC	EC[8]	8B	AC	R44TSX	.060	2P	0	0	2.84/3	7.9	8.4
123456	VD	10B@600	775	10B	AC	R43TS	.045	2P	0	0	3.78/4	9.2	9.7
123456	VD	10B@600	850	10B	AC	R42TS	.045	2P	0	0	3.78/4	10.1	10.7
165432	CP	15B@EC	NA	15B	AC	R44TS8	.080	2P	0	0	3.78/4	13.1	13.7
165432	CP	15B@EC	NA	15B	AC	R45TS8	.080	3P	1/2P	1/8	3.78/4	11.7[10]	12.3[10]
165432	CP	15B@EC	NA	15B	AC	R45TS8	.080	3P	3/4P[11]	1/8	3.78/4	11.7	12.3
165432	CP	15B@EC	NA	15B	AC	R45TS8	.080	3P	1/2P	1/8	3.78/4	11.7	12.3
165432	CP	15B@EC	NA	15B	AC	R45TS8	.080	3P	3/4P[11]	1/8	3.78/4	11.7	12.3
165432	CP	15B@EC	NA	15B	AC	R45TS8	.080	2-1/2P	0[11]	0	5.7/6	12.5	13.2
165432	CP	NA	NA	NA	NA	NA	NA	2P	0	0	5.7/6	13.8	14.6
165432	CP	NA	NA	NA	NA	NA	NA	3P	1/2P	1/8	3.78/4	14.1	14.9
18436572	VD	20B@1100	NA	20B	AC	R45SX	.080	3P	3/4P	1/8	3.78/4	14.1	14.9
18436572	VD	20B@1100	NA	20B	AC	R45SX	.080	2-1/2P	0[11]	0	6.0/6.5	16.5	17.5
18436572	VD	NA	NA	NA	NA	NA	NA	3P	1/2P	1/8	6.0/6.5	16.5	17.5
18436572	VD	NA	NA	NA	NA	NA	NA	2-1/2P	0[11]	0	6.0/6.5	16.5	17.5
1342	CP	0@650	650	0	AC	R42CTS	.035	NA[11]	0[11]	1/4[14]	3.78/4	9.1	9.6
18436572	VD	10B@450	NA	10B	AC	R43NTS6	.060	2-1/2P	0[11]	0	3.78/4	10.0	10.8
18436572	VD	10B@450	NA	10B	AC	R43NTS6	.060	3P	1/2P	1/8	6.6/7	22.4	23.7
18436572	VD	NA	NA	NA	NA	NA	NA	2-1/2P	0[11]	0	6.6/7	22.4	23.7
18436572	VD	NA	NA	NA	NA	NA	NA	3P	1/2P	1/8	3.78/4	20.3	21.4
15634278	CP	10B@450	NA	10B	AC	R45NAX	.060	3P	1/2P	1/8	3.78/4	8.5	9.0
1342	CP	6B@700	800	6B	AC	R42TS	.035	5P	5/16P	1/16	4.7/5	8.5	9.0
1342	VD	NA	NA	NA	NA	NA	NA	5P	5/16P	1/16	3.78/4	9.0	9.5
1342	CP	0@EC	EC	0	AC	R42CTS	.035	NA	9/16P	1/8	2.84/3	8.5	8.9
1342	CP	8B@EC[18]	EC	8B	AC	R44TSX	.060	2P[11]	0	0	2.84/3	8.6	9.1
1342	CP	8B@EC	EC	8B	AC	R44TSX	.060	3P	1P	3/16	3.78/4	10.0	10.7
123456	VD	10B@600[18]	775	10B	AC	R43CTS[20]	.045	2P[11]	0	0	3.78/4	12.0	12.8
123456	VD	10B@725	800	10B	AC	R43CTS	.045	3P	1P	3/16	3.78/4	14.3	15.1
165432	VD	0@EC	NA	NA	AC	R45TS	.045	3P	3/4P	1/8	3.78/4	13.5	14.2
165432	VD	0@EC	NA	NA	AC	R45TS	.045	3P	1/2P	1/8	3.78/4	11.7	12.4
165432	CP	NA	NA	15B	AC	R45TS	.045	3P	3/4P	1/8	3.78/4	11.2	11.8
165432	CP	NA	NA	15B	AC	R45TS8	.080	3P	3/4P	1/8	4.7/5	12.3	12.9
165432	CP	NA	NA	NA	NA	NA	NA	2P[11]	0	0	6.0/6.5	13.8	14.6
165432	CP	NA	NA	NA	NA	NA	NA	3P	1/2P	1/8	4.5/5	14.4	15.2
18436572	VD	6B@500	NA	6B	AC	R45TS	.045	3P	1P	3/16	4.5/5	15.5	16.4
18436572	VD	6B@500	NA	6B	AC	R45TS	.045	3P	1/2P	1/8	4.5/5	14.6	15.5
18436572	VD	6B@500	NA	6B	AC	R45TS	.045	3P	3/4P	1/8	4.5/5	14.6	15.5
18436572	VD	6B@500	NA	6B	AC	R45TS	.045	3P	1P	3/16[23]	6.0/6.5	17.5	18.5
18436572	VD	NA	NA	NA	NA	NA	NA	3P	1/2P	1/8	6.0/6.5	15.5	16.4
18436572	VD	6B@500	NA	6B	AC	R45TS	.045	2-1/4P	3/4P	1/4	3.78/4	20.4	21.6
1342	F	10B@900	775	10B	M	65PR	.035	1-1/4P[11]	1/4P	3/32[14]	3.78/4	8.2	8.7
1342	F	10B@900	NA	10B	M	65PR	.035	1-1/4P[11]	1/4P	3/32[14]	4.8/5	8.2	8.7
1342	CP	7B@800	NA	7B	CH	RN-12Y	.040	1-1/4P[11]	1/4P	3/32[14]	4.8/5	8.2	8.7
1342	CP	7B@800	NA	7B	CH	RN-12Y	.040	2-1/2P	1/2P	1/8	3.78/4	10.9	11.5
153624	CP	16B@625	NA	16B	M	560PR	.035	2-1/2P	1/2P	1/8	3.78/4	15.6	16.5
18436572	VD	16B@625	NA	16B	M	65PR	.035	2-1/2P	1/2P	1/8	3.78/4	14.7	15.5
18436572	VD	12B@580	NA	12B	M	65PR	.035	2P[11]	3/8P	3/32[14]	3.3/3.5	6.6	7.0
1342	CP	NA	800[28]	12B	M	65PR	.035	1-3/8P[11]	3/8P	3/32[14]	3.3/3.5	6.6	7.0
1342	CP	NA	800[28]	12B	M	65PR	.035	2P[11]	3/8P	3/32[14]	3.78/4	5.7	6.0
1342	F	12B@900	850[31]	12B	M	65PR	.035	2P[11]	3/8P	3/32[14]	3.78/4	8.2	8.7
1342	F	10B@900	850	10B	M	65PR	.035	1-1/4P[11]	3/8P	3/32[14]	3.78/4	8.2	8.7
1342	F	10B@900	775	10B	M	65PR	.035	1-1/4P[11]	3/8P	3/32[14]	4.8/5	8.2	8.7
1342	CP	7B@800	NA	7B	CH	RN-11YC4	.040	1-1/4P[11]	3/8P	3/32[14]	4.8/5	8.2	8.7
1342	CP	7B@800	NA	7B	CH	RN-11YC4	.040	1-1/4P[11]	3/8P	3/32[14]	3.78/4	10.9	11.5
153624	CP	16B@725	NA	16B	M	560PR	.035	2-1/2P	1/2P	1/8	3.78/4	14.2	15.0
18436572	VD	16B@625	NA	16B	M	65PR	.035	2-1/2P	1/2P	1/8	3.3/3.5	7.6	8.0
1342	CP	NA	800[34]	NA	MO	AWSF-34	.044	1-1/4P	1-3/4P	1/8[14]	3.3/3.5	7.6	8.0
1342	CP	14B@800	800[35]	10B	MO	AWSF-34	.044	1-1/4P	1-3/4P	1/8[14]	3.3/3.5	7.6	8.0
1342	CP	10B@800	800	10B	MO	AWSF-34	.044	1-1/4P	1-3/4P	1/8[14]	3.3/3.5	7.6	8.0
1342	CP	10B@800	800	10B	MO	AWSF-34	.044	1-1/4P	1-3/4P	1/8[14]	3.3/3.5	7.6	8.0

11 — Not Adjustable
12 — Electra — 3020/118.9
13 — Diesel Engine
14 — Toe-Out
15 — 2-Door — 2394/94.3
16 — Int. — .011 in./0.29 mm
Exh. — .013 in./0.35 mm
17 — Not With Z28
18 — Celebrity — Auto. Trans. Only
19 — Citation — 135/101@5400
20 — High Performance — R42TCS

21 — Monte Carlo SS — 175/131@4200
22 — With Z28
23 — Z28 — 1/8
24 — Minimum Pressure-Maximum Variation Between Cylinders — 15 psi
25 — Int. — .006 in./0.15 mm
Exh. — .010 in./0.25 mm
26 — Minimum Pressure—Also 25 psi (4 and 6) Or 40 psi (V-8) Maximum Variation
27 — Int. — .006 in./0.15 mm
Exh. — .012 in./0.30 mm

28 — 12B
29 — Omni, Custom — 2518/99.1
30 — Int. — .010 in./0.25 mm
Exh. — .018 in./0.45 mm
31 — 20B
32 — Also — Diplomat 165/123@4000
33 — Lowest Cylinder Must Be At Least 75 Percent Of Highest
34 —
35 — 8B
Note — If timing differs on decal, use that setting!

1983

	Wheelbase (mm)	Wheelbase (in.)	No. of Cylinders Bore and Stroke (in.)	Displacement (litres)	Displacement (cu. in.)	Valve and Cylinder Arrangement	Net Brake Horsepower @ rpm	Net Power (kW)	Compression Pressure (psi)	Valve Clearance
Ford — LTD	2550	100.4	4—3.781x3.126[1]	2.3	140	IOC	93@4600	69	80[2]	HY
Mustang	2550	100.4	4—3.781x3.126	2.3	140	IOC	93@4600	69	80[2]	HY
Fairmont Futura	2679	105.5	4—3.781x3.126	2.3	140	IOC	93@4600	69	80[2]	HY
Thunderbird	2638	103.8	4—3.781x3.126[5]	2.3	140	IOC	NA	NA	80[2]	HY
LTD	2550	100.4	6—3.682x3.126	3.3	200	IO	87@3800	65	80[2]	HY
Fairmont Futura	2679	105.5	6—3.682x3.126	3.3	200	IO	87@3800	65	80[2]	HY
LTD	2550	100.4	6—3.80x3.40	3.8	232	VO	105@4000	78	80[2]	HY
Mustang	2550	100.4	6—3.80x3.40	3.8	232	VO	105@4000	78	80[2]	HY
Thunderbird	2638	103.8	6—3.80x3.40	3.8	232	VO	105@4000	78	80[2]	HY
Mustang	2550	100.4	8—4.0x3.0	5.0	302	VO	176@4200	131.3	80[2]	HY
LTD Crown Victoria	2904	114.3	8—4.0x3.0	5.0	302	VO	130@3200	97	80[2]	HY
Lincoln — Continental	2759	108.6	6—3.80x3.40	3.8	232	VO	105@4000	78	80[2]	HY
Continental	2759	108.6	8—4.0x3.0	5.0	302	VO	130@3200	97	80[2]	HY
Mark VI	2904	114.3	8—4.0x3.0	5.0	302	VO	130@3200	97	80[2]	HY
Lincoln	2980	117.3	8—4.0x3.0	5.0	302	VO	130@3200	97	80[2]	HY
Mercury — Lynx	2393	94.2	4—3.15x3.13	1.6	97.6	IOC	72@5200	53.7	80[2]	HY
Lynx, LN7	2393	94.2	4—3.15x3.13	1.6	97.6	IOC	80@5800	59.7	80[2]	HY
Lynx, LN7	2393	94.2	4—3.15x3.13	1.6	97.6	IOC	88@5400	65.6	80[2]	HY
Topaz	2538	99.9	4—3.15x3.13	1.6	97.6	IOC	72@5200	53.7	80[2]	HY
Capri	2550	100.4	4—3.781x3.126	2.3	140	IOC	93@4600	69	80[2]	HY
Zephyr, Z7, Marquis	2679	105.5	4—3.781x3.126[1]	2.3	140	IOC	93@4600	69	80[2]	HY
Zephyr, Z7, Marquis	2679	105.5	6—3.682x3.126	3.3	200	IO	87@3800	65	80[2]	HY
Marquis	2679	105.5	6—3.80x3.40	3.8	232	VO	105@4000	78	80[2]	HY
Capri	2550	100.4	6—3.80x3.40	3.8	232	VO	105@4000	78	80[2]	HY
Cougar	2638	103.8	6—3.80x3.40	3.8	232	VO	105@4000	78	80[2]	HY
Capri	2550	100.4	8—4.0x3.0	5.0	302	VO	176@4200	131.3	80[2]	HY
Grand Marquis	2904	114.3	8—4.0x3.0	5.0	302	VO	130@3200	97	80[2]	HY
Grand Marquis	2904	114.3	8—4.0x3.5	5.8	351	VO	165@3600	123	80[2]	HY
Oldsmobile — Firenza, S, LX	2571	101.2	4—3.34x3.13	1.8	112	IOC	82@5200	61	100[9]	HY
Firenza, S, LX	2571	101.2	4—3.50x3.15	2.0	122	IO	88@4800	65.6	100[9]	HY
Omega, Brougham	2664	104.9	4—4.0x3.0	2.5	151	IO	92@4000	68.6	140[11]	HY
Cutlass Ciera, LS, Brougham	2664	104.9	4—4.0x3.0	2.5	151	IO	92@4000	68.6	140[11]	HY
Omega, Brougham	2664	104.9	6—3.50x2.99	2.8	173	VO	112@4800	84	100[9]	HY
Omega, Brougham	2664	104.9	6—3.50x2.99	2.8	173	VO	130@5400	97	100[9]	HY
Cutlass Ciera, LS, Brougham	2664	104.9	6—3.80x2.66	3.0	181	VO	110@4800	82	100[9]	HY
Cutlass Supreme, Calais, Brougham	2745	108.1	6—3.80x3.40	3.8	231	VO	110@4000	82	100[9]	HY
Delta 88, Royale, Brougham	2945	115.9	6—3.80x3.40	3.8	231	VO	110@4000	82	100[9]	HY
Toronado Custom Brougham	2895	114	6—3.965x3.40	4.1	252	VO	125@4000	93	100[9]	HY
98 Regency, Brougham	3020	119	6—3.965x3.40	4.1	252	VO	125@4000	93	100[9]	HY
Cutlass Ciera, LS, Brougham	2664	104.9	6—4.057x3.385[14]	4.3	262.5	VO	85@3600	63	275[9]	HY
Cutlass Supreme, Calais, Brougham	2745	108.1	6—4.057x3.385[14]	4.3	262.5	VO	85@3600	63	275[9]	HY
Cutlass Supreme, Calais, Brougham	2745	108.1	8—3.80x3.385	5.0	307	VO	140@3600	104	120[9]	HY
Toronado Custom Brougham	2895	114	8—3.80x3.385	5.0	307	VO	140@3600	104	120[9]	HY
Delta 88 (all), 98 (all)	2945	115.9[15]	8—3.80x3.385	5.0	307	VO	140@3600	104	120[9]	HY
Cutlass Supreme, Calais, Brougham	2745	108.1	8—4.057x3.385[14]	5.7	350	VO	105@3200	78	275[9]	HY
Toronado Custom Brougham	2895	114	8—4.057x3.385[14]	5.7	350	VO	105@3200	78	275[9]	HY
Delta 88 (all), 98 (all)	2945	115.9[15]	8—4.057x3.385[14]	5.7	350	VO	105@3200	78	275[9]	HY
Plymouth — Horizon, Custom, TC3	2518	99.1[17]	4—3.17x3.07	1.6	97.1	IOC	62@4800	46	100[18]	H[19]
Horizon, Custom, TC3	2518	99.1[17]	4—3.13x3.40	1.7	104.7	IOC	63@4800	47	100[18]	H[22]
Horizon, Custom, TC3, Turismo	2518	99.1[17]	4—3.44x3.62	2.2	135	IOC	94@5200	70	130[11]	HY
Reliant	2543	100.1	4—3.44x3.62	2.2	135	IOC	94@5200	70	130[11]	HY
Reliant S.E.	2543	100.1	4—3.59x3.86	2.6	156	IOC	93@4800	69	150[24]	H[25]
Gran Fury Salon	2863	112.7	6—3.4x4.12	3.7	225	IO	90@3600	67	100[18]	HY
Gran Fury Salon	2863	112.7	8—3.91x3.31	5.2	318	VO	130@4000[27]	97[27]	100[18]	HY
Pontiac — 1000	2466	97.2[28]	4—3.23x2.98	1.6	98	IOC	65@5200	49	145[24]	HY
1000	2466	97.2[28]	4—3.31x3.23[14]	1.8	111	IOC	51@3200	38	370[9]	H[30]
2000, LE, S/E[29]	2571	102.1	4—3.34x3.13	1.8	112	IOC	84@5200	62	100[9]	HY
2000, LE, S/E	2571	102.1	4—3.50x3.15	2.0	121	IO	88@4800	63	100[9]	HY
Phoenix, LJ, 6000, LE	2664	104.9	4—4.0x3.0	2.5	151	IO	94@4000	70	140[11]	HY
Firebird	2566	101	4—4.0x3.0	2.5	151	IO	92@4000	68.6	140[11]	HY
Phoenix, LJ, 6000, LE	2664	104.9	6—3.5x2.99	2.8	173	VO	112@4800	84	100[9]	HY
Phoenix, SJ, 6000 STE	2664	104.9	6—3.5x2.99	2.8	173	VO	135@5400[34]	101[34]	100[9]	HY
Firebird, S/E	2566	101	6—3.5x2.99	2.8	173	VO	107@4800[35]	79.8[35]	100[9]	HY
Grand Prix (all), Bonneville (all)	2745	108.1	6—3.8x3.4	3.8	231	VO	110@3800	82	100[9]	HY
6000, LE, STE	2664	104.9	6—4.057x3.385[14]	4.3	262.5	VO	85@3600	63	275[9]	HY
Firebird, T/A, S/E	2566	101	8—3.736x3.48	5.0	305	VO	150@4000	112	120[9]	HY
Grand Prix (all), Bonneville (all)	2745	108.1	8—3.736x3.48	5.0	305	VO	150@4000	112	120[9]	HY
Firebird T/A	2566	101	8—3.736x3.48	5.0	305	VO	175@4200	123	120[9]	HY
Grand Prix (all), Bonneville (all)	2745	108.1	8—4.057x3.385[14]	5.7	350	VO	105@3200	78	275[9]	HY

ABBREVIATIONS — FOOTNOTES

AC — AC Spark Plugs
B — Before Top Dead Center
CH — Champion Spark Plugs
CP — Crankshaft Pulley
EC — Electronically Controlled
F — Flywheel
H — Hot Engine
HY — Hydraulic Lifters
IO — In-Line Engine — Overhead Valves
IOC — In-Line Engine — Overhead Camshaft

M — MOPAR Spark Plugs
MO — Motorcraft Spark Plugs
NA — Not Available/Not Applicable
P — Positive
VD — Vibration Damper
VO — V-Type Engine — Overhead Valves

1 — Also Propane Engine — LTD, Marquis
2 — Lowest Cylinder Must Be At Least 75 Percent of Highest
3 — Gasoline Engine Only

4 — Propane Engine — AWSF-34/.034
5 — Turbo. Engine
6 — 12B
7 — 8B
8 — Toe-Out
9 — Minimum Pressure-Maximum Variation Between Cylinders — 30 Percent
10 — Degree Per Wheel Or 3/32 in. Toe-Out
11 — Minimum Pressure-Maximum Variation Between Cylinders — 20 psi
12 — Cutlass Ciera — Auto. Trans. Only

Tuneup Specifications

Firing Order	Timing Mark Location	Initial Ignition Timing (auto. trans.)	Ignition Timing (rpm-manual trans.)	Ignition Timing (California)	Make	Model	Gap (in.)	Caster, Power Steering (deg.)	Camber, Right Wheel (deg.)	Toe-In (in.)	Crankcase Capacity (L 'qt.)	Cooling System Capacity (L)	Cooling System Capacity (qt.)
1342	CP	9B@700	700	9B[3]	MO	AWSF-44[4]	.044[4]	1-1/8P	7/16P	3/16	3.78/4	9.7	10.2
1342	CP	9B@700	700	9B	MO	AWSF-44	.044	1-1/4P	1/4P	3/16	3.78/4	9.7	10.2
1342	CP	9B@700	700	9B	MO	AWSF-44	.044	1-1/8P	3/8P	3/16	3.78/4	9.7	10.2
1342	CP	NA	NA	NA	MO	AWSF-32	.034	1P	3/8P	3/16	4.3/4.5	8.4	8.9
153624	CP	10B@900	NA	10B	MO	BSF-42	.050	1-1/8P	7/16P	3/16	4.3/4.75	7.5	8.4
153624	CP	10B@900	NA	10B	MO	BSF-92	.050	1-1/8P	3/8P	3/16	4.3/4.75	7.5	8.4
142536	VD	12B@800	NA	12B	MO	AWSF-52	.044	1-1/8P	7/16P	3/16	3.78/4	7.8	8.3
142536	VD	12B@800	NA	12B	MO	AWSF-52	.044	1-1/4P	1/4P	3/16	3.78/4	7.8	8.3
142536	VD	12B@800	NA	12B	MO	AWSF-52	.044	1P	3/8P	3/16	3.78/4	7.8	8.3
15426378	VD	NA	800	10B	MO	ASF-42	.044	1-1/4P	1/4P	3/16	3.78/4	12.4	13.1
15426378	VD	6B@800	NA	6B	MO	ASF-52	.050	3P	1/2P	1/16	3.78/4	12.6	13.3
142536	VD	12B@800	NA	NA	MO	ASF-52	.044	1-1/4P	3/8P	1/8	3.78/4	7.8	8.3
15426378	VD	6B@800	NA	6B	MO	ASF-52	.050	1-1/4P	1/2P	1/16	3.78/4	12.6	13.3
15426378	VD	6B@800	NA	6B	MO	ASF-52	.050	3P	1/2P	1/16	3.78/4	12.6	13.3
15426378	VD	6B@800	NA	6B	MO	ASF-52	.050	3P	1/2P	1/16	3.78/4	12.6	13.3
1342	CP	NA	800[6]	NA	MO	AWSF-34	.044	1-1/4P	1-3/4P	1/8[8]	3.3/3.5	7.6	8.0
1342	CP	14B@800	800[7]	10B	MO	AWSF-34	.044	1-1/4P	1-3/4P	1/8[8]	3.3/3.5	7.6	8.0
1342	CP	10B@800	800	10B	MO	AWSF-34	.044	1-1/4P	1-3/4P	1/8[8]	3.3/3.5	7.6	8.0
1342	CP	10B@800	800	10B	MO	AWSF-44	.044	1-1/4P	1/4P	3/16	3.78/4	9.7	10.2
1342	CP	9B@700	700	9B	MO	AWSF-44	.044	1-1/4P	1/4P	3/16	3.78/4	9.7	10.2
1342	CP	9B@700	700	9B[3]	MO	AWSF-44[4]	.044[4]	1-1/8P	7/16P	3/16	4.3/4.75	7.5	8.4
153624	CP	10B@900	NA	10B	MO	BSF-92	.050	1-1/8P	7/16P	3/16	3.78/4	7.8	8.3
142536	VD	12B@800	NA	12B	MO	AWSF-52	.044	1-1/4P	1/4P	3/16	3.78/4	7.8	8.3
142536	VD	12B@800	NA	12B	MO	AWSF-52	.044	1P	3/8P	3/16	3.78/4	7.8	8.3
15426378	VD	NA	800	10B	MO	ASF-42	.044	1-1/4P	1/4P	3/16	3.78/4	12.4	13.1
15426378	VD	6B@800	NA	6B	MO	ASF-52	.050	3P	1/2P	1/16	3.78/4	12.6	13.3
13726548	VD	8B@600	NA	8B	MO	ASF-52	.050	3P	1/2P	1/16	3.78/4	13.0	13.8
1342	CP	8B@EC	EC	8B	AC	R44XLS	.035	1-3/4P	3/4P	.10[10]	2.84/3	7.6	8.0
1342	CP	0@EC	EC	0	AC	R42CTS	.035	1-3/4P	3/4P	.10[10]	3.78/4	9.1	9.6
1342	CP	8B@EC	EC	8B	AC	R44TSX	.060	2P	0	0	2.84/3	9.0	9.5
1342	CP	8B@EC[12]	EC	8B	AC	R44TSX	.060	1P	0	0	2.84/3	8.6	9.1
123456	VD	10B@600	775	10B	AC	R43CTS	.045	2P	0	0	3.78/4	9.7	10.3
123456	VD	10B@725	800	10B	AC	R42CTS	.045	1P	0	0	3.78/4	10.1	10.7
165432	VD	15B@EC	NA	15B	AC	R44TS8	.080	3P	0	0	3.78/4	13.1	13.7
165432	CP	15B@EC	NA	15B	AC	R45TS8	.080	3P	1/2P	.15[13]	3.78/4	11.7	12.3
165432	CP	15B@EC	NA	15B	AC	R45TS8	.080	3P	3/4P	.15[13]	3.78/4	11.7	12.3
165432	CP	15B@EC	NA	15B	AC	R45TS8	.080	2-1/2P	0	0	3.78/4	11.7	12.3
165432	CP	15B@EC	NA	15B	AC	R45TS8	.080	3P	3/4P	.15[13]	5.7/6	11.7	12.3
165432	CP	NA	NA	NA	NA	NA	NA	1P	0	0	5.7/6	11.7	12.3
165432	CP	NA	NA	NA	NA	NA	NA	3P	1/2P	.15[13]	3.78/4	14.1	14.9
18436572	VD	20B@1100	NA	20B	AC	R46SX	.080	3P	1/2P	.15[13]	3.78/4	15.5	16.4
18436572	VD	20B@1100	NA	20B	AC	R46SX	.080	2-1/2P	0	0	3.78/4	14.8	15.6
18436572	VD	20B@1100	NA	20B	AC	R46SX	.080	3P	3/4P	.15[13]	6.6/7[16]	16.5	17.4
18436572	VD	NA	NA	NA	NA	NA	NA	2-1/2P	0	0	6.6/7[16]	17.2	18.2
18436572	VD	NA	NA	NA	NA	NA	NA	3P	3/4P	.15[13]	6.6/7[16]	17.3	18.3
1342	CP	NA	800	12B	CH	RN-12YC	.035	1-1/2P[20]	3/8N	1/16[8]	3.3/3.5	6.6	7.0
1342	F	12B@900	850[21]	12B	CH	RN-12YC	.035	1-1/2P[20]	3/8N	1/16[8]	3.78/4	8.2	8.7
1342	F	10B@900	775	10B	CH	RN-12YC	.035	1-1/2P[20]	3/8N	1/16[8]	3.78/4	8.2	8.7
1342	F	10B@900	775	10B	CH	RN-12YC	.035	1-3/16P[23]	1/4P	1/16[8]	4.8/5	8.2	8.7
1342	CP	NA	NA	7B[26]	CH	RN-11YC4	.040	1-3/16P[23]	1/4P	1/16[8]	3.78/4	10.9	11.5
153624	CP	16B@725	NA	16B	M	560PR	.035	2-1/2P	1/2P	1/8	3.78/4	14.2	15.0
18436572	VD	12B@580	NA	12B	M	65PR	.035	2-1/2P	1/2P	1/8	3.78/4	8.5	9.0
1342	CP	6B@700	800	6B	AC	R42TS	.035	5P	1/4P	5/32	4.7/5	8.4	8.9
1342	VD	NA	NA	NA	NA	NA	NA	5P	1/4P	5/32	2.84/3	7.4	7.8
1342	CP	8B@EC	EC	8B	AC	R44XLS	.035	NA[23]	5/8P	1/8[8]	3.8/4	9.0	9.5
1342	CP	NA	EC	0	AC	R42CTS	.035	NA[23]	5/8P	1/8[8]	2.8/3	9.3	9.8
1342	CP	8B@EC	EC[31]	8B	AC	R44TSX	.060	2P[23]	0	0	2.8/3	8.6	9.1
1342	CP	8B@EC	EC	8B	AC	R44TSX	.060	3P	1P	.2[32]	3.78/4	10.0[33]	10.6[33]
123456	VD	10B@600	775[31]	10B	AC	R43CTS	.045	2P[23]	0	0	3.78/4	10.0[33]	10.6[33]
123456	VD	10B@725	800[31]	10B	AC	R42CTS	.045	2P[23]	1P	.2[32]	3.78/4	12.0	12.8
123456	VD	10B@725	800	10B	AC	R43CTS[36]	.045	3P	1/2P	.15[13]	3.78/4	11.7	12.4
165432	VD	15B@EC	NA	15B	AC	R45TS	.045	3P	0	0	5.7/6	11.8	12.5
165432	CP	NA	NA	NA	NA	NA	NA	2P[23]	1P	.2[32]	4.5/5	14.4	15.2
18436572	VD	6B@500	700	6B	AC	R45TS	.045	3P	1/2P	.15[13]	4.5/5	15.5	16.4
18436572	VD	6B@500	NA	6B	AC	R45TS	.045	3P	1P	.2[32]	4.5/5	15.2	16.0
18436572	VD	6B@EC	NA	6B	AC	R45TS	.045	·3P	1/2P	.15[13]	6.0/6.5	17.5	18.4
18436572	VD	NA	NA	NA	NA	NA	NA						

13 — Degree Per Wheel Or 5/32 in.
14 — Diesel Engine
15 — 98 — 3020/119
16 — Service With Filter
17 — TC3 — 2454/96.6
18 — Minimum Pressure—Also 25 psi (4 and 6) Or 40 psi (V-8) Maximum Variation
19 — Int. — .006 in./0.15 mm Exh. — .012 in./0.30 mm
20 — Not Adjustable — TC3-2P
21 — 20B

22 — Int. — .010 in./0.25 mm Exh. — .018 in./0.45 mm
23 — Not Adjustable
24 — Minimum Pressure-Maximum Variation Between Cylinders — 15 psi
25 — Int. — .006 in./0.15 mm Exh. — .010 in./0.25 mm
26 — Cal. — Manual Trans. Only
27 — Also 165/123@4000
28 — 2-Door — 2394/94.3
29 — All Except Coupe

30 — Int. — .011 in./0.29 mm Exh. — .013 in./0.35 mm
31 — Phoenix Only
32 — Degree Per Wheel Or 1/4 in.
33 — 6000 STE — 11.8/12.5
34 — 6000 STE — 130/98@5400
35 — Also 125/93@5400 Except Cal.
36 — High Performance — R42TCS
Note 1 — If timing differs on decal, use that setting!
Note 2 — Ford's Tempo and Topaz have a 2.3 L (140 cu. in.) OHC four as standard equipment.

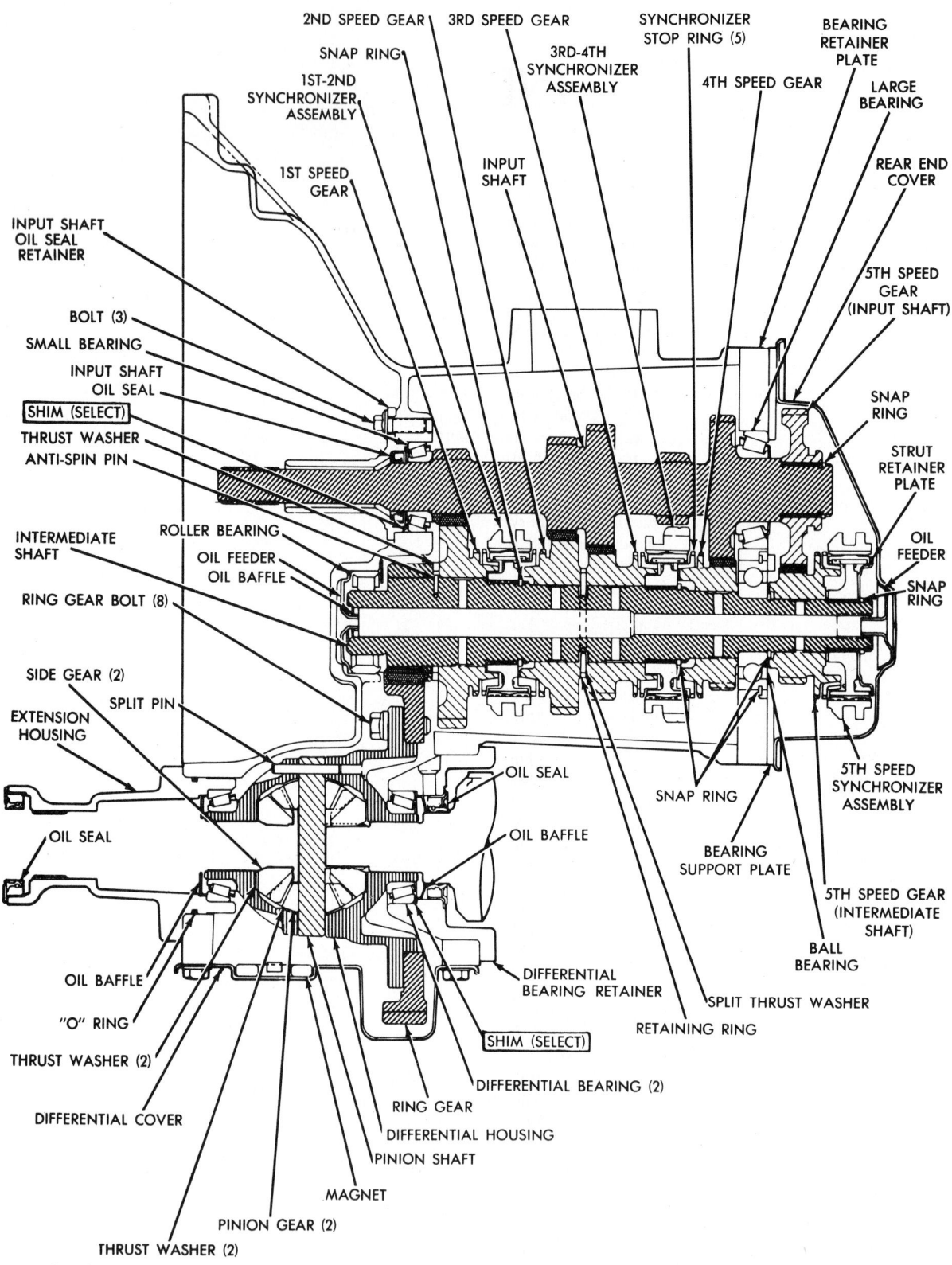

2ND SPEED GEAR

3RD SPEED GEAR

SNAP RING

1ST-2ND SYNCHRONIZER ASSEMBLY

3RD-4TH SYNCHRONIZER ASSEMBLY

SYNCHRONIZER STOP RING (5)

BEARING RETAINER PLATE

1ST SPEED GEAR

INPUT SHAFT

4TH SPEED GEAR

LARGE BEARING

REAR END COVER

INPUT SHAFT OIL SEAL RETAINER

5TH SPEED GEAR (INPUT SHAFT)

BOLT (3)

SMALL BEARING

INPUT SHAFT OIL SEAL

SHIM (SELECT)

THRUST WASHER

ANTI-SPIN PIN

SNAP RING

STRUT RETAINER PLATE

OIL FEEDER

INTERMEDIATE SHAFT

ROLLER BEARING

OIL FEEDER

OIL BAFFLE

SNAP RING

RING GEAR BOLT (8)

SIDE GEAR (2)

SPLIT PIN

EXTENSION HOUSING

OIL SEAL

OIL SEAL

OIL BAFFLE

5TH SPEED SYNCHRONIZER ASSEMBLY

SNAP RING

BEARING SUPPORT PLATE

5TH SPEED GEAR (INTERMEDIATE SHAFT)

BALL BEARING

DIFFERENTIAL BEARING RETAINER

SPLIT THRUST WASHER

RETAINING RING

OIL BAFFLE

"O" RING

THRUST WASHER (2)

DIFFERENTIAL COVER

SHIM (SELECT)

DIFFERENTIAL BEARING (2)

RING GEAR

DIFFERENTIAL HOUSING

PINION SHAFT

MAGNET

PINION GEAR (2)

THRUST WASHER (2)

Fig. S-29. Chrysler's five-speed manual transaxle is fully synchronized and provides overdrive in fourth and fifth gears for improved fuel economy over the corporation's four-speed unit.

830

INDEX

Index

Index

Index